O'CONNOR'S TEXAS RULES
CIVIL TRIALS

BY
MICHOL O'CONNOR

JONES MCCLURE PUBLISHING
HOUSTON, TEXAS

O'CONNOR'S TEXAS LITIGATION SERIES

Suggested cite form: *O'Connor's Texas Rules * Civil Trials* (2013)

JONES
McCLURE
PUBLISHING

Mailing address:
P.O. Box 3348
Houston, TX 77253-3348

Shipping address:
2160 Taylor St.
Houston, TX 77007

Phone: (713) 335-8200
(800) OCONNOR (626-6667)
Fax: (713) 335-8201

www.JonesMcClure.com

Copyright © 1991, 1992, 1994-2013 by McClure F.L.P.

Print date: December 21, 2012
Printed in the United States of America

ISBN 978-1-59839-158-9

✪

This year's edition of *O'Connor's Texas Rules * Civil Trials* has been updated to reflect 2012 rules changes and case law; see the sections below for summaries of many of these updates. We have also revised and reorganized parts of the commentaries to improve clarity and add further explanation. Here are some of the changes we made this year:

- We included a note titled "Proposed Rules Changes" in each section of the commentaries that will likely be affected by the recent proposed changes to the Texas Rules of Civil Procedure and Texas Rules of Evidence, as well as editor's notes in the rules, to indicate what may change based on the proposed amendments. We also included a placeholder subchapter, "Motion to Dismiss—Baseless Cause of Action," ch. 3-H, p. 256, which describes proposed Texas Rule of Civil Procedure 91a. Updates to the commentaries, rules, and a complete ch. 3-H will be available at www.JonesMcClure.com/TRCPamendments in a supplement to this book after the rules take effect. See "Proposed Rules Changes," below, for details about the proposed changes.

- We clarified language in "Objecting to Trial & Discovery Subpoenas," ch. 1-L, §4, p. 87, to more clearly explain how to challenge a subpoena.

- We expanded "Standing," ch. 2-B, §3.2.1, p. 96, to more fully discuss what an individual, association, or class-action plaintiff must show to establish standing.

- We added "Ruling," ch. 3-D, §3.7, p. 220, to cover the factors the trial court must consider when ruling on a code forum non conveniens motion, as well as the timing of the ruling.

- We revised and reorganized "Statutory jurisdictional requirements," ch. 3-F, §3.8, p. 242, to distinguish between when a plea to the jurisdiction is proper to challenge certain statutory claims in suits against governmental entities versus those against nongovernmental entities.

- We reorganized and expanded "Motion to compel arbitration under FAA," ch. 4-C, §5.2, p. 291, and "Motion to compel arbitration under TAA," ch. 4-C, §6.2, p. 293, to specify when a claim is not arbitrable and thus cannot be submitted to arbitration.

- We added a new subchapter "Motion for Additional Resources," ch. 5-H, p. 359, to discuss new Texas Rule of Judicial Administration 16, which implemented and elaborated on the legislatively mandated procedures for assigning additional judicial resources to a case.

- We revised and expanded "Waiver by contract," ch. 5-B, §7.4, p. 324, to clarify which party, depending on the circumstances surrounding the making of a contractual jury waiver, has the burden of proof on the issue of whether the waiver was knowingly and voluntarily made.

- We added "Motion to modify or withdraw temporary sealing order," ch. 5-L, §3.3, p. 396, to discuss the requirements for moving to modify or withdraw a temporary sealing order.

- We added "Search Techniques for Electronic Information," ch. 6-C, §6, p. 495, to include information on using keyword searches and predictive coding to locate relevant electronic information during discovery.

- We expanded "Resolving Electronic-Discovery Disputes," ch. 6-C, §9, p. 500, to more fully cover the procedures available to the parties when an electronic-discovery dispute arises.

RULES CHANGES

In 2012, the Texas Supreme Court amended Texas Rule of Civil Procedure 306 as well as several Texas Rules of Appellate Procedure. The Supreme Court also adopted Texas Rule of Judicial Administration 16 and amended Texas Rule of Judicial Administration 6. The orders for these new and amended rules can be found on the Texas Supreme Court's website at www.supreme.courts.state.tx.us.

⭐

TRCP

TRCP 306. TRCP 306 was amended to require a judgment in a suit for termination of the parent-child relationship or in a suit affecting the parent-child relationship filed by a governmental entity for managing conservatorship to state the specific grounds for termination or for appointment of the managing conservator. This change took effect March 1, 2012. For the amended text of the rule, see TRCP 306, p. 1017.

TRAPs

TRAP 20, 25, 28, 32, 35. TRAP 20.1, 25.1, 32.1, and 35.3 were amended and TRAP 28.4 was adopted. For a description of the changes to these rules, see *O'Connor's Texas Civil Appeals* (2012), "Introduction," pp. VI-VII. These changes took effect March 1, 2012. For the amended text of the rules, see the TRAPs in this book, beginning on p. 1159.

TRAP 9.4. TRAP 9.4 was amended to consolidate all length limits and to establish word limits for certain documents that are produced on a computer. Page limits remain in TRAP 9.4 for documents that are typewritten or otherwise not produced on a computer. TRAP 9.4 now also requires a larger font size for those computer-generated documents and a certificate of compliance from the attorney or unrepresented party stating the number of words in the document. By consolidating all length limits in TRAP 9.4, the Supreme Court correspondingly deleted TRAP 38.4, 49.10, 52.6, 53.6, 55.6, 64.6, and 68.5, and amended TRAP 70.3 and 71.3. These changes took effect December 1, 2012. For the amended text of the rules, see the TRAPs in this book, beginning on p. 1159.

Texas Rules of Judicial Administration (TRJAs)

TRJA 6. TRJA 6 was amended to conform with 2011 legislative amendments to Family Code §§107.013 and 263.405. The amendments added a section for appeals in certain cases involving the parent-child relationship, and renumbered the rest of the rule. *See* Tex.Sup.Ct. Order, Misc. Docket No. 12-9032 (eff. May 1, 2012). These changes took effect May 1, 2012. *Id.*

TRJA 16. TRJA 16 was adopted in response to a legislative mandate in Gov't Code §§74.251-74.257. The amendments describe the procedures for requesting additional judicial resources in large or complex civil cases. *See* Tex.Sup.Ct. Order, Misc. Docket No. 12-9033 (eff. May 1, 2012). The rule took effect May 1, 2012. *Id.* For a discussion of the new procedures for requesting additional resources, see "Motion for Additional Resources," ch. 5-H, p. 359.

PROPOSED RULES CHANGES

On November 13, 2012, the Supreme Court proposed two new rules of civil procedure in response to the 2011 legislative amendments to Gov't Code §22.004. As required by Gov't Code §22.004(g), the Supreme Court proposed TRCP 91a to allow a party to file a motion to dismiss a cause of action that has no basis in law or fact. *See* Tex.Sup.Ct. Order, Misc. Docket No. 12-9191 (eff. Mar. 1, 2013). As required by Gov't Code §22.004(h), the Supreme Court proposed TRCP 169 to establish a process for the prompt, efficient, and cost-effective resolution of civil actions (expedited actions). *See* Tex.Sup.Ct. Order, Misc. Docket No. 12-9191 (eff. Mar. 1, 2013). To conform with proposed TRCP 169, the Supreme Court proposed amendments to TRCP 47 and 190. *See* Tex.Sup.Ct. Order, Misc. Docket No. 12-9191 (eff. Mar. 1, 2013). The Supreme Court also proposed new TRE 902(10)(c). *See* Tex.Sup.Ct. Order, Misc. Docket No. 12-9191 (eff. Mar. 1, 2013). The public-comment period for the proposed rules ends on February 1, 2013, and the rules are to take effect March 1, 2013. *See id.* For the proposed version of the rules, see the appendix after this book's index. For the final version, go to the Supreme Court website at www.supreme.courts.state.tx.us. When the new rules take effect, a supplement to this book—with updated rules and commentaries that reflect the changes—will be available at www.JonesMcClure.com/TRCPamendments. The proposed amendments to the Texas Rules of Civil Procedure and Texas Rules of Evidence cover the following:

- **TRCP 91a.** This new rule would provide for a motion to dismiss a cause of action that has no basis in law or fact. The motion would generally have to be ruled on within 45 days after it is filed.

- **TRCP 169.** This new rule would establish a process for the prompt, efficient, and cost-effective resolution of civil actions (expedited actions) in which only monetary relief is sought and the amount in controversy is no more than $100,000.

✦

- **TRCP 47.** This amended rule would require a party, in an original pleading, to make a more specific statement of the relief sought; that is, the party would have to plead into or out of the expedited-actions process under TRCP 169.

- **TRCP 190.2, 190.5.** These amended rules would, among other things, (1) change the Level 1 discovery-control plan to apply to expedited actions under TRCP 169, (2) modify the length of the discovery period in Level 1 cases, and (3) limit the modification of a discovery-control plan when a suit is governed by TRCP 169.

- **TRE 902(10)(c).** This new rule would provide a self-authenticating form affidavit to prove medical expenses.

FORTHCOMING RULES

Small claims. In 2011, the Legislature abolished small-claims courts by repealing Gov't Code chapter 28. Under Gov't Code §27.060, justice courts must conduct proceedings in small-claims cases. These changes take effect May 1, 2013. Acts 2011, 82nd Leg., C.S., ch. 3, §5.09, eff. May 1, 2013. By May 1, the Supreme Court must adopt new rules of procedure that define small-claims cases and ensure their fair, expeditious, and inexpensive resolution. *See id.* §5.07. As of the publication of this book, the Supreme Court had not yet issued any proposed rules for small-claims cases. Check the Supreme Court website at www.supreme.courts.state.tx.us for any proposed and final rules.

E-filing. On December 11, 2012, the Supreme Court issued an order stating that, beginning January 1, 2014, the Court will implement mandatory e-filing in civil cases in district courts, statutory county courts, constitutional county courts, and statutory probate courts. *See* Tex.Sup.Ct. Order, Misc. Docket No. 12-9206. The Supreme Court has issued an implementation schedule based on a county's population size; implementation will begin January 1, 2014, for courts in counties with a population of at least 500,000, and will continue through July 1, 2016, for the rest of the courts. *Id.* The implementation schedule can be extended for good cause. *Id.* As part of the implementation schedule, the Supreme Court will adopt rules governing both e-filing and e-service. *Id.* Check the Supreme Court website at www.supreme.courts.state.tx.us for any proposed and final rules.

COMMON-LAW DEVELOPMENTS

In 2012, the Texas Supreme Court issued many significant opinions on civil procedure. Every trial attorney should become familiar with the following cases.

Pleadings

In *In re E.R.*, ___ S.W.3d ___ (Tex.2012) (No. 11-0282; 7-6-12), the Court stated that even though service by publication is a form of substituted service, it should be used as a last resort. The Court discussed the requirements for service by publication. See "Service by publication," ch. 2-H, §4.4, p. 162.

In *Andrade v. Venable*, 372 S.W.3d 134, 137 (Tex.2012), the Court held that when a taxpayer sues to enjoin the illegal expenditure of public funds, the plaintiff does not have to show that she suffered a particularized injury distinct from the general public, but instead must show (1) she is a taxpayer and (2) public funds are being expended on the allegedly illegal activity. See "Taxpayer standing," ch. 2-B, §3.2.1(1)(b)[2], p. 97.

In *Reddy Prtshp./5900 N. Freeway, L.P. v. Harris Cty. Appraisal Dist.*, 370 S.W.3d 373, 376-77 (Tex.2012), the Court held that if a plaintiff sues and serves the correct defendant but misnames itself, the error is misnomer. Courts generally allow parties to correct a misnomer as long as it is not misleading. See "Misnomer," ch. 2-B, §3.3.1(2)(a), p. 98.

In *Heckman v. Williamson Cty.*, 369 S.W.3d 137, 150-53 (Tex.2012), the Court discussed the requirements for both individual and class-action standing. See "Individual standing," ch. 2-B, §3.2.1(1), p. 97. For class-action suits, the Court held that (1) as long as an individual plaintiff has standing on *some* claim, she has standing to pursue class certification on that claim, (2) when multiple plaintiffs asserting multiple claims seek to represent a class, the trial

★

court must assess standing plaintiff by plaintiff and claim by claim, and (3) in limited situations, a class-action suit can survive even though the individual claims of the named plaintiffs become moot before the court decides whether to certify the class. See "Class-action standing," ch. 2-B, §3.2.1(3), p. 97, and annotation under TRCP 42, p. 871.

In *Mansions in the Forest, L.P. v. Montgomery Cty.*, 365 S.W.3d 314, 316-17 (Tex.2012), the Court held that an affidavit must contain a jurat or other evidence that it was sworn to before an authorized officer. See "Affidavits," ch. 1-B, §3.2.16, p. 11.

In *FDIC v. Lenk*, 361 S.W.3d 602, 609 (Tex.2012), the Court restated that the statute of repose is an affirmative defense. See "Statute of repose," ch. 3-E, §5.3.9, p. 234.

Plea to the Jurisdiction

In *Prairie View A&M Univ. v. Chatha*, ___ S.W.3d ___ (Tex.2012) (No. 10-0353; 8-31-12), the Court held that in a suit against a governmental entity, a plea to the jurisdiction is proper to challenge a statutory claim when the plaintiff did not comply with a statutory prerequisite to filing suit. The Court discussed the test for determining if something is a "statutory prerequisite." See "Statutory prerequisite," ch. 3-F, §3.8.2(1), p. 241.

In *Rusk State Hosp. v. Black*, ___ S.W.3d ___ (Tex.2012) (No. 10-0548; 8-31-12), the Court held that if the pleadings affirmatively negate jurisdiction, the suit should be dismissed. If the pleadings do not affirmatively negate jurisdiction, the court can dismiss only if the defendant has shown that the plaintiff—despite having had the opportunity to amend the petition—still cannot establish jurisdiction. See "Dismissal," ch. 3-F, §6.1.2, p. 245.

In *Mission Consol. ISD v. Garcia*, 372 S.W.3d 629, 635 (Tex.2012), the Court held that the trial court can allow the parties a reasonable opportunity for targeted discovery to prepare for a hearing on a plea to the jurisdiction. See "Necessary," ch. 3-F, §2.2.2, p. 240. The Court restated that when jurisdictional facts are disputed, the court cannot grant a plea to the jurisdiction, and the issue must be resolved by the fact-finder at trial; if the evidence is undisputed or if there is no fact question on the jurisdictional issue, the court will rule on the plea to the jurisdiction as a matter of law. See "Jurisdiction related to merits" ch. 3-F, §5.1.2, p. 244.

In *Heckman v. Williamson Cty.*, 369 S.W.3d 137, 150 (Tex.2012), the Court restated that the trial court must consider evidence on a plea to the jurisdiction when evidence is necessary to determine jurisdictional facts. See "Necessary," ch. 3-F, §2.2.2, p. 240. The Court also restated that a plea to the jurisdiction is generally proper to challenge a case that has become moot. See "Mootness," ch. 3-F, §3.4, p. 241.

Pretrial Motions

In *Freedom Comms. v. Coronado*, 372 S.W.3d 621, 623-24 (Tex.2012), the Court restated that parties cannot waive a constitutionally based ground for disqualifying a judge. See "Waiver," ch. 5-C, §4.1.3(3), p. 330. The Court also restated that all the orders and judgments of a trial judge who was constitutionally disqualified from sitting are void. See "Disqualification," ch. 5-C, §7.3.1, p. 335. The Court further restated the requirements for a court to take judicial notice of an adjudicative fact. See "Types of facts," ch. 5-M, §4.1.1, p. 404.

In *Paradigm Oil, Inc. v. Retamco Oper., Inc.*, 372 S.W.3d 177, 184 (Tex.2012), the Court restated that for a sanction to be just, it must be directly related to the offensive conduct and must not be excessive. See "Regular sanctions," ch. 5-K, §3.1, p. 378. The Court held that default judgment is an example of a death-penalty sanction. See "Death-penalty sanctions," ch. 5-K, §3.2, p. 378.

In *In re Frank Kent Motor Co.*, 361 S.W.3d 628, 632 (Tex.2012), the Court held that an at-will employer's threat to terminate an employee if she does not sign a jury-waiver agreement is not coercion that would invalidate the agreement. See "Burden on party opposing waiver," ch. 5-B, §7.4.2(1), p. 324.

Other Pretrial Matters

In *In re Lopez*, 372 S.W.3d 174, 175 (Tex.2012), the Court restated that after an arbitration hearing, a party must file an initial application for a proceeding arising from the arbitration in the county where the hearing was held. See "After hearing," ch. 2-G, §4.2.1(3)(c), p. 153.

---✦---

In *El Apple I, Ltd. v. Olivas*, 370 S.W.3d 757, 760-63 (Tex.2012), the Court discussed the process for calculating attorney fees under the "lodestar" method. See "Proving reasonableness," ch. 1-H, §10.3.3(1), p. 64. The Court held that to substantiate a claim for attorney fees, a party must provide sufficient details of the work performed through specific documentation. The Court stated that if an attorney expects to use the lodestar method to calculate a claim for attorney fees, the attorney should document her time with contemporaneous billing records or similar documentation recorded close to when her work was performed. See "Specific documentation," ch. 1-H, § 10.4.2, p. 66.

In *Ford Motor Co. v. Chacon*, 370 S.W.3d 359, 362 (Tex.2012), the Court restated that in determining the scope of a guardian ad litem's appointment, courts look to the context of the appointment and the duties assigned to the guardian ad litem. Specifically, a court may examine the timing of the appointment, the grounds in the motion for appointment, and the order granting the appointment. See "Determining scope," ch. 1-I, §6.1.3(2)(a)[1], p. 74.

In *Ford Motor Co. v. Garcia*, 363 S.W.3d 573, 577 (Tex.2012), the Court held that an improper designation in a trial court's order appointing a guardian ad litem does not control the nature of the appointment. See "Order," ch. 1-I, §3.3.2, p. 70. The Court also held that a guardian ad litem has the burden to ensure that her services do not exceed the scope of her appointment. See "Role of Guardian Ad Litem," ch. 1-I, §4, p. 70. The Court discussed the advantages of filing an application for compensation. See "Application for fees," ch. 1-I, §6.1, p. 73. The Court also held that a guardian ad litem may be compensated for services performed by a person other than the designated ad litem. See "For services of person other than guardian ad litem," ch. 1-I, §6.1.3(1)(b), p. 73.

Discovery

In *In re XL Specialty Ins.*, 373 S.W.3d 46, 50-52 (Tex.2012), the Court held that the privilege defined in Texas Rule of Evidence 503(b)(1)(C) is most accurately described as the "allied-litigant privilege," and stated the requirements to assert the privilege. See "Allied-litigant privilege," ch. 6-B, §3.5, p. 475. The Court clarified the differences between the joint-client privilege, the joint-defense privilege, and the common-interest privilege, and distinguished each from the allied-litigant privilege. See "Note," ch. 6-B, §3.5, p. 475.

Default Judgment

In *PNS Stores v. Rivera*, 379 S.W.3d 267, 275 & n.16 (Tex.2012), the Court restated that a petition for a bill of review must be filed after the trial court's plenary power expires, but within four years of the rendition of judgment, unless the defendant can show extrinsic fraud. The Court stated that although evidence of extrinsic fraud tolls the four-year statute of limitations, it does not do so indefinitely—the limitations period begins to run when the defendant-petitioner knew or should have known about the default judgment. See "Deadline," ch. 7-A, §7.1.3(1), p. 600. The Court also discussed when and how a defendant can collaterally attack a default judgment. See "Collateral attacks on default judgment," ch. 7-A, §7.2, p. 602.

In *Paradigm Oil, Inc. v. Retamco Oper., Inc.*, 372 S.W.3d 177, 183 (Tex.2012), the Court held that when a defendant does not file an answer, all allegations of facts in the plaintiff's petition are deemed admitted except for the amount of unliquidated damages. See "Effect of defendant's failure to answer," ch. 7-A, §3.1, p. 588. The Court also held that if the defendant appears at a hearing on unliquidated damages, it has the right to participate at the hearing. See "Unliquidated damages – hearing required," ch. 7-A, §3.13.2, p. 593.

In *Mabon Ltd. v. Afri-Carib Enters.*, 369 S.W.3d 809, 812 (Tex.2012), the Court restated that a defendant can attack a default judgment by a bill of review after it is too late either to appeal or to file a motion for new trial. See "Bill of review," ch. 7-A, §7.1.3, p. 600. The Court also discussed the standards for establishing sufficient cause for a bill of review depending on whether the defendant claims a due-process violation. See "Grounds," ch. 7-A, §7.1.3(2), p. 600.

Summary Judgment

In *Mansions in the Forest, L.P. v. Montgomery Cty.*, 365 S.W.3d 314, 316-17 (Tex.2012), the Court held that the minimum requirement for a summary-judgment affidavit is that it must be sworn; a jurat is not specifically required. See "Sworn," ch. 7-B, §9.4.1, p. 613. The Court also held that when a purported affidavit lacks a jurat and the offering party does not provide extrinsic evidence to show that it was sworn to before an authorized officer, the opposing party must object or else the objection is waived. See "Absence of jurat," ch. 7-B, §10.1.1(1)(c), p. 619.

★

Jury Charge

In *Texas Comm'n on Human Rights v. Morrison*, ___ S.W.3d ___ (Tex.2012) (No. 11-0644; 8-31-12), the Court restated that a broad-form submission is not always feasible when the governing law is unsettled or when there is doubt about the legal sufficiency of the evidence. See "Broad form not required," ch. 8-I, §2.1.2, p. 731. The Court also restated that an objection to the charge must clearly identify the error and explain the grounds for the complaint or else the objection is waived. See "Specific," ch. 8-I, §4.3.2, p. 737. The Court applied the presumed-harm analysis from *Crown Life Ins. v. Casteel*, 22 S.W.3d 378 (Tex.2000), to a broad-form question that allowed the jury to find liability based on a legal theory that was jurisdictionally barred. See "Valid & invalid theories – applicable," ch. 8-I, §9.1.2(1)(a), p. 746.

In *Thota v. Young*, 366 S.W.3d 678, 688 (Tex.2012), the Court restated that reversible error is presumed when a trial court submits a broad-form question with multiple theories of liability or elements of damages and one or more of those theories is invalid. The Court stated that this is often referred to as *Casteel* error, but held that a party does not have to specifically cite or reference *Casteel* to preserve an appellate court's right to apply the presumed-harm analysis, if applicable. The Court also held that defenses and inferential-rebuttal instructions are not theories of liability; thus, the *Casteel* presumed-harm analysis does not apply to cases involving a single theory of liability in which improper defenses or inferential-rebuttal instructions have also been submitted. See "Presumed harm," ch. 8-I, §9.1.2, p. 746.

In *Cruz v. Andrews Restoration, Inc.*, 364 S.W.3d 817, 830-31 (Tex.2012), the Court held that when a party submits a proposed charge in clusters of related requests, the party will not necessarily preserve error if the trial court does not submit all or part of the requests to the jury; the party must specifically object to the omission and obtain a ruling. See "Cluster of related requests," ch. 8-I, §2.3, p. 732. The Court restated that parties must make all objections and requests to amend the charge language before the court reads the charge to the jury. See "General rule," ch. 8-I, §4.2.1(1), p. 736.

In *Arvizu v. Estate of Puckett*, 364 S.W.3d 273, 275-76 (Tex.2012), the Court held that a party can argue on appeal that the jury's answers fatally conflict and thus the verdict should be reversed. The Court also stated what a court should consider in reviewing the jury's answers for fatal conflict. See "Fatal conflict in jury answers," ch. 8-K, §8.3, p. 755.

Motion for New Trial

In *In re E.R.*, ___ S.W.3d ___ (Tex.2012) (No. 11-0282; 7-6-12), the Court held that if a motion for new trial is based on invalid service by publication, the party does not have to show good cause. See "Sworn MNT," ch. 10-B, §10.2, p. 800. The Court also held that the deadline to file a motion for new trial for a defendant who was served by publication is two years after a judgment is rendered and signed. See "Deadline," ch. 10-B, §10.4, p. 800.

In *In re United Scaffolding, Inc.*, 377 S.W.3d 685, 689-90 (Tex.2012), the Court held that the trial court's order on a motion for new trial is reviewable by mandamus when the court's stated reasons for granting the new trial are not legally valid or reasonably specific. The Court restated that a broad statement like "in the interest of justice" is not a sufficiently specific reason for granting a new trial, and held that the court should not have used "and/or" in its order granting the new trial because, although the court had listed several reasons, the "and/or" left open the possibility that "in the interest of justice or fairness" was its sole reason. See "Reasons stated in order not valid or specific," ch. 10-B, §17.5.3, p. 810.

In *Sutherland v. Spencer*, 376 S.W.3d 752, 754-55 (Tex.2012), the Court restated that when reviewing an attack on a default judgment in a motion for new trial, a court should generally set aside the default judgment if the defendant did not appear because she never received the suit papers. If the defendant received the suit papers and had some other reason for not appearing, the default judgment should be set aside if the defendant proves the three elements of the test from *Craddock v. Sunshine Bus Lines, Inc.*, 133 S.W.2d 124 (Tex.1939). See "*Craddock* factors," ch. 10-B, §9.1.1(2), p. 795. The Court also restated that to establish the first *Craddock* factor—the failure to answer

---

or appear was not intentional or due to conscious indifference but was due to mistake or accident—even a bad excuse can be sufficient. The Court held that the defendant's failure to answer was accidental when the citation was left in a stack of papers on a desk and forgotten because the defendants spent little time at the office due to weather conditions. See "Not intentional, but accidental," ch. 10-B, §9.1.3(1), p. 796.

CONVENTIONS

In writing this book, we have tried to produce a plain-English reference guide that is easy for attorneys and judges to use. To this end, we should point out a few things about the book. First, the rules are in double columns so they can be instantly distinguished from the commentaries. Second, we supply page headers and side-tabs for quick reference. Third, when other sections of this and other books are relevant, we cross-reference them. Fourth, we include practice tips and caution notes that are separate from the main text so they can be easily spotted. Fifth, all rules changes are marked with ⓬ and proposed rules changes are marked with ⓭ to draw your attention to the change and alert you to check the effective date of the change. We have also underlined the new rule language. Sixth, in a history note under each Texas Rule of Civil Procedure, we include references to earlier versions of the rule located in the first pages of *South Western Reporter* volumes. Seventh, to save space we have eliminated the criminal appellate rules and the history notes to all but the most recently amended TRAPs. See *O'Connor's Texas Civil Appeals* for a complete set of the appellate rules. Finally, we include timetables for certain pretrial, trial, and post-trial procedures.

Throughout this book, we refer to forms in the companion volume *O'Connor's Texas Civil Forms* (2012) as *O'Connor's Texas Forms*. The forms are numbered to match the chapter in this book where each topic is discussed.

To reduce gender-specific language, we refer to trial judges as the "trial court" and to most parties as "it" as if the parties were corporations, which they often are. When gender-specific language cannot be avoided, we use the feminine pronoun. To save space, we abbreviate the name of the Texas Rules of Civil Procedure to TRCP, the Texas Rules of Evidence to TRE, the Texas Rules of Appellate Procedure to TRAP, the Texas Rules of Judicial Administration to TRJA, the Texas Civil Practice & Remedies Code to CPRC, and the Texas Revised Civil Statutes to TRCS. When you cite rules and statutes in a motion or brief, we suggest you use the more traditional citation forms. For the traditional rules for citations, see either *O'Connor's Texas Civil Appeals* (2012), "Simplified Citation Forms," p. 955, or *Texas Rules of Form* (i.e., the "Greenbook"), published by the Texas Law Review.

All websites cited or referenced in this book are current through December 7, 2012.

CAVEAT

This book provides citations to important opinions that interpret the Texas Rules of Civil Procedure and Texas Rules of Evidence through December 21, 2012. You may disagree with our explanations of the rules and cases cited in this book. You should therefore use this book only as a research guide. Read the rules and cases yourself and make your own evaluation of them.

YOUR SUGGESTIONS

We welcome your comments. If you think we should have included (or excluded) something, or if you see anything that needs to be corrected, please let us know. Send your comments to the mailing address or fax number shown on the copyright page, or by e-mail to Jessica Luna, Managing Legal Editor, at jessica@jonesmcclure.com.

SPECIAL THANKS

We wish to thank Brian Kilpatrick, Leonard Woods, Julia Mann, and David Curcio from Jackson Walker L.L.P. for reviewing the subchapters on motions for continuance, motions to exclude experts, securing discovery from experts, and the jury charge.

★

EDITORIAL & PRODUCTION STAFF

As always, the staff of Jones McClure worked hard to prepare this publication, both in its substance and in its layout. The people who worked on this edition of *O'Connor's Texas Rules * Civil Trials* are listed below.

EXECUTIVE EDITOR
Douglas Rosenzweig, J.D.

MANAGING LEGAL EDITOR
Jessica Ryan Luna, J.D.

DEVELOPMENT EDITOR
Jacalyn A. Hollabaugh, J.D.

LEGAL EDITORS
Anouchka Oppinger Bowne, J.D.
James K. Hancock, J.D.
Amanda Pattock, J.D.
Aditi Pemmaraju, J.D.

LEGAL EDITORIAL ASSISTANTS
Wade Allison
Eric T. Bean
Christy B. Bushnell, J.D.
Britney N. Cherry
Kacey M. Cox, J.D.
Sharon McCord Cozort, J.D.
Amyna Jenna Esmail, J.D.
Jessica Younger Field, J.D.
Paul T. Freeman
Rohan A. Hebbar, J.D.
Robert F. Holland, J.D.
Kacie E. Jaksa
Lindsay Kirton
Rebecca G. Shapiro
Lisa R. Stewart, J.D.
Caleb Ray Thornton
Nicole L. Washington, J.D.

PRODUCTION MANAGER
Beverly B. Bellot

PRODUCTION EDITOR
Sara Y. Rhodes

PRODUCTION STAFF
Danielle E. Boss
Nicole E. Hammond
Cassandra J. Pace
Sarah M. Rutledge
Daniel Spence
Jenny Sulak
Donna E. Vass
Annabelle M. Wilde

COPYEDITORS
Danielle E. Boss
Kathryn Hunter
Kathryn A. Ritcheske, J.D.
David W. Schultz, J.D.
Jenny Sulak

PROOFREADERS
Sarah M. Rutledge
Jenny Sulak

MICHOL O'CONNOR
HOUSTON, TEXAS

⭐

COMMENTARIES

TRCP

TRE

TRAP

TIMETABLES & INDEX

CONTENTS

★

★

⭐

★

1. GENERAL

A. INTRODUCTION TO THE TEXAS RULES

In 1939, the Texas Legislature gave the Supreme Court rulemaking power in civil actions. The Legislature placed two limits on the Court's authority over the rules: (1) the Court cannot enact rules that "abridge, enlarge, or modify the substantive rights of a litigant," and (2) the Legislature retains the power to disapprove of the Court's rules. Gov't Code §22.004(a), (b). The Court must file a copy of all rule changes with the Secretary of State and identify which statutes the rules repeal or modify. *Id.* §22.004(b), (c). On receipt of a written request from a member of the Legislature, the Secretary of State must provide the member with electronic notifications when the Supreme Court promulgates rules or amendments to the rules. *Id.* §22.004(b).

§1. TEXAS RULES OF CIVIL PROCEDURE (TRCP)

In 1941, the Supreme Court adopted the Texas Rules of Civil Procedure. *See* Gov't Code §22.004; TRCP 2, 814. The TRCPs have the same force and effect as statutes. *Missouri Pac. R.R. v. Cross*, 501 S.W.2d 868, 872 (Tex.1973). When a rule of procedure conflicts with a substantive statute or a statute passed after the rule, the statute prevails. *In re M.N.*, 262 S.W.3d 799, 802 (Tex.2008).

(13)

PROPOSED TRCP CHANGES

The Supreme Court has proposed two new rules of civil procedure in response to the 2011 legislative amendments to Gov't Code §22.004. As required by Gov't Code §22.004(g), the Supreme Court has proposed TRCP 91a to allow a party to file a motion to dismiss a cause of action that has no basis in law or fact. See Tex.Sup.Ct. Order, Misc. Docket No. 12-9191 (eff. Mar. 1, 2013). The motion to dismiss would have to be filed within 60 days after the first pleading that includes the baseless cause of action is served and would generally have to be ruled on within 45 days after the motion is filed. See id. As required by Gov't Code §22.004(h), the Supreme Court has proposed TRCP 169 to establish a process for the prompt, efficient, and cost-effective resolution of civil actions (expedited actions) in which only monetary relief is sought and the amount in controversy is no more than $100,000. See Tex.Sup.Ct. Order, Misc. Docket No. 12-9191 (eff. Mar. 1, 2013). The expedited-actions process would be mandatory—that is, any suit qualifying as an expedited action would have to follow the rule's provisions—but any party could seek to remove a suit from the expedited-actions process. See id. The public-comment period for the proposed rules ends on February 1, 2013, and the rules are to take effect March 1, 2013. For the proposed version of the rules, see the appendix after this book's index. For the final version, go to the Supreme Court website at www.supreme.courts.state.tx.us. When the new rules take effect, a supplement to this book—with updated rules and commentaries that reflect the changes—will be available at www.JonesMcClure.com/TRCPamendments.

§2. TEXAS RULES OF EVIDENCE (TRE)

In 1983, the Supreme Court adopted the Texas Rules of Evidence for civil cases. 641-642 S.W.2d (Tex.Cases) xxxv (1983). In 1988, it renamed them the "Texas Rules of Civil Evidence." 733-734 S.W.2d (Tex.Cases) lxxxv (1987). In 1998, the Supreme Court and the Court of Criminal Appeals merged the civil and criminal rules and renamed them the "Texas Rules of Evidence." 960 S.W.2d (Tex.Cases) xxxi (1998). See Brown & Rondon, *Texas Rules of Evidence Handbook* (2013), p. XII. The TREs govern civil and criminal proceedings in all Texas courts except small-claims courts. TRE 101(b).

§3. TEXAS RULES OF APPELLATE PROCEDURE (TRAP)

In 1986, the Supreme Court and the Court of Criminal Appeals adopted the Texas Rules of Appellate Procedure. 733-734 S.W.2d (Tex.Cases) xcviii (1986). As part of that process, the appellate rules in the TRCPs were repealed. In 1997, the Supreme Court and the Court of Criminal Appeals adopted a new set of TRAPs. 948-949 S.W.2d (Tex.Cases) lxi (1997).

✦

---

§4. LOCAL RULES

TRCP 3a permits the trial courts to establish local rules consistent with the TRCPs. Local rules cannot impose restrictions on or conflict with the TRCPs. *Jamar v. Patterson*, 868 S.W.2d 318, 318 n.2 (Tex.1993); *Approximately $14,980.00 v. State*, 261 S.W.3d 182, 188-89 (Tex.App.—Houston [14th Dist.] 2008, no pet.).

NOTE

Local rules are often available on county websites. For links to county websites, see www.county.org/about-texas-counties/county-websites/Pages/default.aspx.

---

§4.1 Notice of local rules. Litigants are charged with knowledge of local rules. *Mayad v. Rizk*, 554 S.W.2d 835, 839 (Tex.App.—Houston [14th Dist.] 1977, writ ref'd n.r.e.). *But see Kenley v. Quintana Pet. Corp.*, 931 S.W.2d 318, 321 (Tex.App.—San Antonio 1996, writ denied) (notice through imputed knowledge of local rules contradicts TRCP 165a). TRCP 3a requires the trial courts to file copies of their local rules with the Supreme Court for approval and to publish them at least 30 days before they become effective. TRCP 3a(3), (4).

§4.2 Effect of local rules. Litigants should pay particular attention to local rules. Some local rules provide that failure to file a response to a motion indicates acquiescence to the relief sought in the motion. *E.g.*, Harris Cty. Loc. R. 3.3.2 (district courts); *see Cire v. Cummings*, 134 S.W.3d 835, 844 (Tex.2004). Some local rules require a specific request for oral argument; without a proper request, no argument will be permitted. *E.g.*, Smith Cty. Loc. R. 2.3; *Rorie v. Goodwin*, 171 S.W.3d 579, 583 (Tex.App.—Tyler 2005, no pet.).

B. RULES OF PLEADING

§1. GENERAL

§1.1 Rules. TRCP 21, 21b, 22-24, 45-71, 74-98, 166(b).

§1.2 Purpose. The purpose of the pleadings is to define the issues for trial. *Murray v. O&A Express, Inc.*, 630 S.W.2d 633, 636 (Tex.1982).

§1.3 Forms. *O'Connor's Texas Civil Forms* (2012), FORMS 1B; *O'Connor's Texas Civil Appeals* (2012), FORM 1D:13.

§1.4 Other references. Brown & Rondon, *Texas Rules of Evidence Handbook* (2013) (referred to as Brown & Rondon, *Evidence Handbook*); *O'Connor's Texas Causes of Action* (2013) (*O'Connor's Texas COA*); *O'Connor's Texas Civil Appeals* (2012) (*O'Connor's Texas Appeals*).

§2. TYPES OF DOCUMENTS FILED WITH COURT

It is important to distinguish the different types of documents filed with the court and to understand their functions.

§2.1 Pleading. The Texas system of pleadings is composed of petitions and answers. *Elliott v. Elliott*, 797 S.W.2d 388, 391-92 (Tex.App.—Austin 1990, no writ). The pleadings define the suit, give notice of the facts and legal theories of the case, guide the trial court in admitting evidence and in charging the jury, restrict the trial court in rendering the judgment, and form the basis for appellate review. *See Erisman v. Thompson*, 167 S.W.2d 731, 733 (Tex.1943) (pleadings define lawsuit and determine issues for trial); *Crain v. San Jacinto Sav. Ass'n*, 781 S.W.2d 638, 639 (Tex.App.—Houston [14th Dist.] 1989, writ dism'd) (pleadings give notice of evidence to be introduced). The controversy described in the pleadings is resolved by a judgment. *Lindley v. Flores*, 672 S.W.2d 612, 614 (Tex. App.—Corpus Christi 1984, no writ).

§2.2 Motion. A motion is a request for an order from the court. *Durbin v. Culberson Cty.*, 132 S.W.3d 650, 656 (Tex.App.—El Paso 2004, no pet.); *Elliott v. Elliott*, 797 S.W.2d 388, 392 (Tex.App.—Austin 1990, no writ); *Lindley v. Flores*, 672 S.W.2d 612, 614 (Tex.App.—Corpus Christi 1984, no writ). Most motions are resolved by an order. When a motion requesting a judgment (e.g., a motion for summary judgment) is granted, the motion is resolved by a judgment; when it is denied, it is resolved by an order. See *O'Connor's Texas Forms*, FORMS 1B:1, 1G:1.

§2.3 Plea. "Plea" is an archaic term referring to certain defensive pleadings. *See **Bland ISD v. Blue**,* 34 S.W.3d 547, 554 (Tex.2000). In most instances, the TRCPs replaced the term "plea" with "motion." *See, e.g., **Toliver v. Dallas Fort Worth Hosp. Council**,* 198 S.W.3d 444, 447 (Tex.App.—Dallas 2006, no pet.) ("plea of privilege" is now motion to transfer venue). But some of the rules continue to refer to pleas. For example, TRCP 85 lists the pleas that may be included in the defendant's answer. In this book, most pleas are cast as motions (e.g., a motion to abate instead of a plea in abatement).

§2.4 Bill. A bill is a formal, written declaration, complaint, or statement of particular issues (e.g., a bill of review or a bill of exception).

§3. PLEADING PRACTICE

§3.1 Local requirements. In drafting and filing pleadings, the parties must comply with the requirements of local rules. Some local rules have specific requirements for the form and organization of the pleadings. For example, under Dallas County Civil Court Local Rule 2.04, a pleading must be prepunched at the top to accommodate the clerk's 2¾-inch center-to-center, flat-filing system; a pleading must include a footer at the bottom of each page with the document's caption and page number; and judgments and orders must be separate documents.

§3.2 Formal requirements.

1. In writing. All pleadings must be in writing and filed with the clerk, unless they are made in open court and transcribed by the court reporter. *See **Pennington v. Gurkoff**,* 899 S.W.2d 767, 771 (Tex.App.—Fort Worth 1995, writ denied). Written pleadings must be on 8½-by-11-inch paper. TRCP 45(d). TRCP 45(d) "strongly" encourages attorneys to use recycled paper.

2. Style. The style is the heading of the pleading. It contains the cause number, the names of the parties, the court, and the county of suit. See *O'Connor's Texas Forms*, FORM 1B:2.

(1) Cause number. The clerk assigns the cause number. TRCP 23. The parties should make sure all pleadings are filed with the correct cause number. However, filing a document with the wrong cause number generally should not be considered a jurisdictional defect. *See, e.g., **Curtis v. Gibbs**,* 511 S.W.2d 263, 268 (Tex.1974) (mistake in cause number of original petition was "irrelevant").

(2) List of parties. In the style of the petition and the answer, all the parties should be listed by their full names. In later pleadings, the list of parties in the style may be shortened by naming the first party and using the inclusive term "et al." *See, e.g., **Abramcik v. U.S. Home Corp.**,* 792 S.W.2d 822, 824 (Tex.App.—Houston [14th Dist.] 1990, writ denied) (generic reference to Ps using term "et al." in style of sixth amended petition was sufficient to maintain cause of action for individually named Ps in previous petition).

3. Caption. The caption is the title of the pleading.

NOTE

*Courts and practitioners are inconsistent in what they consider the "style" and "caption" of a case, and many use the terms interchangeably. This book uses "style" to refer to the entire heading and "caption" to refer only to the title. But see **Stewart v. USA Custom Paint & Body Shop, Inc.**, 870 S.W.2d 18, 20 (Tex.1994) (document was designated as "captionless" when missing cause number and names of parties).*

---

(1) Correct title. The title of a pleading should be useful to the court, the clerk, and the attorney's files. The title should include the version of the pleading, such as "Plaintiff's First Supplemental Petition." TRCP 78, 83; *see* TRCP 64.

───────────────────────────── ✦ ─────────────────────────────

(2) Incorrect title. If the party makes an error in the caption of the pleading, the court will treat the pleading as if it had been properly named. TRCP 71. The clerk will file a pleading using the caption the party provides, but the court may order the document redesignated. *Id.*

4. Party information.

(1) Name. Generally, the full names of all parties should be included in the body (not just the caption) of all petitions (amended and supplemental) and in any other documents that must be served with citation. Pleadings should not rely on "et al." to refer to the parties. *See* TRCP 79. In an amended petition, the omission of a party's name and the claims asserted against that party normally indicates an intent to nonsuit that party. *American Petrofina, Inc. v. Allen*, 887 S.W.2d 829, 831 (Tex.1994); *Woodruff v. Wright*, 51 S.W.3d 727, 731 (Tex.App.—Texarkana 2001, pet. denied). If the party was omitted from an amended pleading but renamed in a later pleading, the later pleading may relate back to the earlier pleading as long as the earlier omission was inadvertent, temporary, and not prejudicial to the other parties. *See American Petrofina*, 887 S.W.2d at 831; *Woodruff*, 51 S.W.3d at 733. But if a party's name was not included in the original petition and is mentioned for the first time in an amended or supplemental pleading, the amended or supplemental pleading does not relate back to the original pleading for limitations purposes. *Alexander v. Turtur & Assocs.*, 146 S.W.3d 113, 121 (Tex.2004). See *O'Connor's Texas COA*, "Amended or supplemental pleading," ch. 52, §4.3, p. 1499.

(2) Residence. Any pleading that must be served with citation must identify the residence of the party to be served, if it is known. TRCP 79; *see, e.g., Graham v. Huff*, 384 S.W.2d 904, 905 (Tex.App.—Dallas 1964, no writ) (petition did not include Ds' addresses or state that they were unknown). The parties' residences are important for purposes of service, personal jurisdiction, venue, and forum non conveniens. *See Kelly v. Demoss Owners Ass'n*, 71 S.W.3d 419, 424 (Tex.App.—Amarillo 2002, no pet.).

(3) ID number. The initial pleading filed in district court, county court, or statutory county court must include the last three digits of the filing party's driver's license number and the last three digits of her Social Security number. CPRC §30.014(a). A court may, on its own motion or on the motion of a party, order a party to amend a pleading to include this information. *Id.* §30.014(b). If the party does not amend the pleading as ordered, the court may find the party in contempt. *Id.*

5. Contents.
The pleadings must give fair notice of the claims, defenses, and relief sought. *Perez v. Briercroft Serv.*, 809 S.W.2d 216, 218 (Tex.1991); *Wortham v. Dow Chem. Co.*, 179 S.W.3d 189, 196 (Tex.App.—Houston [14th Dist.] 2005, no pet.); *see* TRCP 21 (pleadings must state grounds and relief sought), TRCP 45(b) (pleadings must state claims and defenses), TRCP 47(a) (pleading must contain statement sufficient to give fair notice of claim). See "Fair notice of claim," ch. 2-B, §6.2, p. 105.

6. Numbered paragraphs.
The paragraphs in pleadings must be numbered, and each paragraph should be limited to a single set of circumstances. TRCP 50. Arabic numerals (e.g., 1, 2, 3) should be used, and Roman numerals (e.g., I, II, III) should be avoided.

7. Separate counts or defenses.
The pleading should divide the allegations into counts or defenses. TRCP 48, 50; *see also* TRCP 47 (listing statements that must be included in original pleading). Headings and subheadings are useful in separating the sections of the pleading.

8. Alternative claims or defenses.
TRCP 48 permits parties to plead alternative or hypothetical theories, allege inconsistent claims or defenses, and allege claims or defenses based on legal grounds, equitable grounds, or both. TRCP 48; *see* TRCP 47 (party may plead for alternative relief); *Regency Advantage L.P. v. Bingo Idea-Watauga, Inc.*, 936 S.W.2d 275, 278 (Tex.1996) (same); *Zimmerman v. First Am. Title Ins.*, 790 S.W.2d 690, 698 (Tex.App.—Tyler 1990, writ denied) (party may plead and prove inconsistent claims). There must be a reasonable basis in fact or law for each alternative theory pleaded. *Low v. Henry*, 221 S.W.3d 609, 615 (Tex.2007). Generally, a pleading does not state a cause of action if it states inconsistent, contradictory facts that are material to the cause of action without alleging an alternative theory. *Vinklarek v. Vinklarek*, 596 S.W.2d 197, 199 (Tex.App.—Houston [1st Dist.] 1980, writ dism'd).

✯

9. Adopting by reference. TRCP 58 permits a party to adopt statements by reference from another pleading that has not been superseded by an amended pleading. *Chapman v. King Ranch, Inc.*, 41 S.W.3d 693, 700 (Tex. App.—Corpus Christi 2001), *rev'd on other grounds*, 118 S.W.3d 742 (Tex.2003); *see Texas Gas Utils. Co. v. Barrett*, 460 S.W.2d 409, 416 (Tex.1970). TRCP 59 permits a party to attach and adopt exhibits by reference or to copy them into the body of the pleading. A party should not adopt by reference from a superseded pleading, but if it does, the adopted material is not void and must be challenged by a special exception. *Hawkins v. Anderson*, 672 S.W.2d 293, 295 (Tex.App.—Dallas 1984, no writ).

10. Prayer. At the end of the pleading, under the heading "Prayer," the party should state exactly what relief it seeks. The prayer for relief should match the purpose of the pleading. See "Prayer," ch. 2-B, §14, p. 110.

11. Signature block.

(1) Who must sign. The pleading must be signed by the party's attorney or by the party if the party is not represented by an attorney. TRCP 45(d), 57. The lack of a signature does not alter the legal effect of the pleading. *W.C. Turnbow Pet. Co. v. Fulton*, 194 S.W.2d 256, 257 (Tex.1946); *Frank v. Corbett*, 682 S.W.2d 587, 588 (Tex. App.—Waco 1984, no writ). Pleadings that are e-filed must contain a digital signature. See "Signing documents," ch. 1-C, §4.4.1(2), p. 24.

(a) Attorney in charge. When a pleading is signed by an attorney, the pleading must identify the attorney by name, State Bar number, address, telephone number, and fax number (if any). TRCP 57; *see* TRCP 191.3(a)(1). When a pleading is e-filed, the signature block must include the attorney's e-mail address. *See* Loc. E-Filing Rules Template, rule 4.7, www.courts.state.tx.us/jcit/Efiling/EfilingHome.asp. The signature fixes responsibility for the allegations and identifies the party the attorney represents. CPRC §§9.011, 10.001; TRCP 13; *Ingram v. Card Co.*, 540 S.W.2d 803, 804 (Tex.App.—Corpus Christi 1976, no writ). The attorney whose signature first appears on the initial pleading for any party is the "attorney in charge," unless another attorney is specifically designated. TRCP 8. See "Attorney in charge," ch. 1-H, §3.1, p. 54. There is no requirement that the attorney in charge sign and file all pleadings. *See Sunbeam Env'tl Servs. v. Texas Workers' Comp. Ins. Facility*, 71 S.W.3d 846, 851 (Tex. App.—Austin 2002, no pet.).

(b) Pro se party. An unrepresented (pro se) party must sign a pleading. A pro se party's signature block must include its address, telephone number, and fax number (if any). TRCP 57; *see* TRCP 191.3(a)(2); *Kelly*, 71 S.W.3d at 424. When a pleading is e-filed, the signature block must contain the pro se party's e-mail address. *See* Loc. E-Filing Rules Template, rule 4.7.

(2) Certification by signature. A person who signs a pleading (or motion) represents that the pleading is not frivolous or groundless. TRCP 13. The court can impose sanctions on the signer of a frivolous or groundless pleading, a party represented by the signer, or both. See "Groundless or frivolous pleadings," §3.3, p. 14; "Groundless or frivolous pleadings, motions, or other papers," ch. 5-K, §5.2, p. 381.

(a) Under CPRC ch. 10. Under CPRC §10.001, signing a pleading (or motion) constitutes a certificate that to the signatory's best knowledge, information, and belief, formed after a reasonable inquiry, the following is true:

[1] The matters in the pleading are not presented for an improper purpose, including to harass or to cause unnecessary delay or needless increase in the cost of litigation. CPRC §10.001(1). A pleading is "presented" to a court when the person signs, files, submits, or later advocates it. *Cf.* FRCP 11(b) (representations to federal court).

[2] Each claim, defense, or other legal contention is warranted by existing law or by a non-frivolous argument for the extension, modification, or reversal of existing law or the establishment of new law. CPRC §10.001(2). Filing a general denial does not violate §10.001(2). CPRC §10.004(f).

[3] Each allegation or factual contention has evidentiary support or, for a specifically identified allegation or factual contention, is likely to have evidentiary support after a reasonable opportunity for further investigation or discovery. *Id.* §10.001(3).

✦

[4] Each denial of a factual contention is warranted by the evidence or, for a specifically identified denial, is reasonably based on a lack of information or belief. *Id.* §10.001(4).

(b) Under TRCP 13. Under TRCP 13, signing a pleading (or motion or other paper) constitutes a certificate that (1) the signatory has read the document and (2) to the signatory's best knowledge, information, and belief, formed after reasonable inquiry, the document is not groundless and is not brought in bad faith or for the purpose of harassment.

(c) Under CPRC ch. 9. Under CPRC §9.011, signing a pleading (or motion) constitutes a certificate that to the signatory's best knowledge, information, and belief, formed after reasonable inquiry, the pleading (1) is not groundless, (2) is not brought in bad faith or for the purpose of harassment, and (3) is not brought for any improper purpose, such as to cause unnecessary delay or expense. CPRC chapter 9 does not alter the TRCPs. CPRC §9.003.

(d) Under TRCP 191.3. The discovery rules impose obligations on the attorney (or pro se party) who signs the written discovery. See "Certification by signature," ch. 6-A, §4.1, p. 427.

12. Certificate of service. All pleadings required to be served under TRCP 21 (except those served with citation) must contain a certificate of service in the document itself. TRCP 21a. See *O'Connor's Texas Forms*, FORM 1B:11.

(1) Contents. The certificate must contain the recipient's address (or fax number), a statement that the document was served on opposing counsel (or opposing party, if the party is pro se) by a certain method (e.g., mail, delivery, or fax) on a certain date, and the signature of the attorney of record (or party, if pro se). *See generally* TRCP 21 & 21a (service of pleadings and motions). See "Note," ch. 1-H, §3.2, p. 54.

(2) Method of service. The certificate should identify the method of service (e.g., delivery, mail, fax, or e-service). *See Dunn v. Menassen*, 913 S.W.2d 621, 626 (Tex.App.—Corpus Christi 1995, writ denied). *But see Smith v. Mike Carlson Motor Co.*, 918 S.W.2d 669, 673 (Tex.App.—Fort Worth 1996, no writ) (nothing in TRCP 21a requires certificate of service to identify method of service). Including the method of service in the certificate of service is important for determining the deadline for the response. For example, when a document is served by mail or fax, the deadline is determined by adding three days to the date the document was mailed. TRCP 21a. See "Computing Response Deadlines," ch. 1-D, §6, p. 36. The certificate of service on appellate documents must describe the date and manner of service. TRAP 9.5(e)(1). See *O'Connor's Texas Appeals*, FORM 1D:13.

13. Exhibits. A pleading must identify and incorporate by reference the exhibits attached to it and those filed separately. TRCP 59. Simply attaching documents to a pleading does not make the documents admissible as evidence. *Ceramic Tile Int'l v. Balusek*, 137 S.W.3d 722, 724-25 (Tex.App.—San Antonio 2004, no pet.). If a pleading does not incorporate the exhibits by reference, the exhibits do not add anything to the pleading. *Street v. Cunningham*, 156 S.W.2d 541, 542 (Tex.App.—Fort Worth 1941, no writ). TRCP 59 lists the following exhibits that may be attached to a pleading, filed separately, or copied into the body of a pleading: notes, accounts, bonds, mortgages, records, and all other written instruments, in whole or in part, constituting the claim or defense. No other document may be attached as an exhibit to a pleading. TRCP 59; *see, e.g.*, *Texas Elec. Serv. v. Commercial Std. Ins.*, 592 S.W.2d 677, 684 (Tex.App.—Fort Worth 1979, writ ref'd n.r.e.) (improper to attach deposition as exhibit to pleading).

14. Unsworn declaration. When an affidavit, verification, written sworn declaration, certification, or oath—except for an oath of office or an oath before a specified official other than a notary public—is required, any person can instead make an unsworn declaration. CPRC §132.001(a), (b). See *O'Connor's Texas Forms*, FORMS 1B:8, 1B:10.

(1) Format – generally. The unsworn declaration must (1) be in writing, (2) be subscribed by the declarant as true and correct under penalty of perjury, and (3) include a jurat with the declarant's name, date of birth, and address. CPRC §132.001(c), (d). The jurat must substantially comply with the format in CPRC §132.001(d). These requirements apply only to declarations executed on or after September 1, 2011. Acts 2011, 82nd Leg., R.S., ch. 847,

---

★

---

§§3, 4, eff. Sept. 1, 2011. Before this date, an unsworn declaration could only be used as a substitute for an affidavit, verification, or other declaration if made by an inmate. *See id.* §1.

    (2) Format – inmate. If an inmate makes an unsworn declaration, the declaration must (1) be in writing, (2) be subscribed by the declarant as true and correct under penalty of perjury, and (3) include a jurat with the declarant's name, date of birth, inmate identification number, if any, and the name and address of the corrections unit. CPRC §132.001(c), (e). The jurat must substantially comply with the format in CPRC §132.001(e). These requirements apply to any unsworn declaration executed on or after September 1, 2011. Acts 2011, 82nd Leg., R.S., ch. 847, §§3, 4, eff. Sept. 1, 2011. If the inmate's unsworn declaration was executed before September 1, 2011, it is instead governed by former CPRC §132.001, as well as by CPRC §§132.002 and 132.003, which have been repealed. *See* Acts 2011, 82nd Leg., R.S., ch. 847, §§2-4, eff. Sept. 1, 2011.

    15. Verification. When a pleading contains facts outside the record, the party may be required to verify the pleading. A verification is a signed and notarized statement attached to a pleading by which a witness swears that the statements in the pleading are true and correct. See *O'Connor's Texas Forms*, FORM 1B:6. Some formal pleadings must be verified. See "Verified Pleas," ch. 3-E, §4, p. 228.

NOTE

Under CPRC §132.001, an unsworn declaration can be used instead of a verification. See "Unsworn declaration," §3.2.14, p. 10.

---

    16. Affidavits. When a pleading contains facts outside the record, the party may be required to verify the facts with an affidavit. An affidavit is a written, factual statement signed by the person making it, sworn to before an officer authorized to administer oaths, and officially certified by the officer under seal of office. Gov't Code §312.011(1); *Mansions in the Forest, L.P. v. Montgomery Cty.*, 365 S.W.3d 314, 316 (Tex.2012); *Ford Motor Co. v. Leggat*, 904 S.W.2d 643, 645-46 (Tex.1995). See *O'Connor's Texas Forms*, FORM 1B:7.

NOTE

Under CPRC §132.001, an unsworn declaration can be used instead of an affidavit. See "Unsworn declaration," §3.2.14, p. 10.

---

    (1) Form of affidavit.

    (a) Caption. The affidavit should contain a caption, such as "Affidavit of _____." *See Acme Brick v. Temple Assocs.*, 816 S.W.2d 440, 441 (Tex.App.—Waco 1991, writ denied).

    (b) Venue. The affidavit should state the county and state in which it was made. *See Acme Brick*, 816 S.W.2d at 441.

    (c) Body. The affidavit should contain the facts in the body of the instrument. *See Acme Brick*, 816 S.W.2d at 441.

    (d) Affiant's signature. The affidavit must contain the affiant's signature. Gov't Code §312.011(1). If the affidavit is not signed by the affiant, the affidavit provides no support for the motion and is fatally defective. *See Hawthorne v. Guenther*, 917 S.W.2d 924, 929 (Tex.App.—Beaumont 1996, writ denied).

    (e) Jurat. The affidavit must contain a jurat or other evidence that it was sworn to before an authorized officer. *Mansions in the Forest*, 365 S.W.3d at 316-17. A jurat is a certification under seal by an authorized officer (generally a notary public) stating that the writing was sworn to before the officer. *Id.* at 316. The jurat identifies the officer, the affiant, and the date the affidavit was made. *See Black's Law Dictionary* 926 (9th ed. 2009). See *O'Connor's Texas Forms*, FORM 1B:9. Gov't Code §312.011(1) requires that an affidavit be sworn to, but it does not specifically require a jurat. *Mansions in the Forest*, 365 S.W.3d at 316. Normally, an affiant includes a jurat to

———————————————— ★ ————————————————

prove that the written statement was made under oath before an authorized officer. *Id.* at 316-17. If the written statement does not include a jurat, there must be other evidence in the record to show that the written statement was sworn to before an authorized officer; otherwise, the statement is not an affidavit. *Id.* at 317.

(f) Officer's seal & signature. The affidavit must contain the authorized officer's seal and signature. *See* Gov't Code §312.011(1); ***Mansions in the Forest***, 365 S.W.3d at 316; ***Leggat***, 904 S.W.2d at 645-46; ***Griffin v. Baylor Coll. of Med.***, 945 S.W.2d 158, 159-60 (Tex.App.—Houston [1st Dist.] 1997, no pet.).

(2) Competency of witness. An affidavit must show that it was made by a person who is competent to testify. *See* TRE 601(a). The affiant must be over the age of 18 and of sound mind. *See id.* (children and insane persons are incompetent unless the court finds them competent after examination). Also, the affiant must be able to accurately perceive, recall, and recount. Brown & Rondon, *Evidence Handbook*, p. 537. Competency is determined by the trial court, which is not bound by the rules of evidence other than those relating to privilege. TRE 104(a); Brown & Rondon, *Evidence Handbook*, p. 538. Competency refers to the person's ability to be a witness—for example, is the witness too young, too old, or too mentally unstable to testify? Competency does not refer to the sufficiency of the specific testimony, which is an issue of personal knowledge. TRE 602; Brown & Rondon, *Evidence Handbook*, p. 538. Unfortunately, the courts sometimes treat the affiant's competency and personal knowledge as the same. *See, e.g.,* ***Laidlaw Waste Sys. v. City of Wilmer***, 904 S.W.2d 656, 661 (Tex.1995) (court concluded that witness was not competent to testify about property metes and bounds because he made only conclusory statements); ***First Nat'l Bank v. Lubbock Feeders, L.P.***, 183 S.W.3d 875, 881 (Tex.App.—Eastland 2006, pet. denied) (court concluded that affiant was competent to testify because affidavit established he had personal knowledge of the transactions).

(3) Factual statements.

(a) Personal knowledge. An affidavit must be based on the affiant's personal knowledge and must state that the facts in it are true. ***Kerlin v. Arias***, 274 S.W.3d 666, 668 (Tex.2008); ***Humphreys v. Caldwell***, 888 S.W.2d 469, 470 (Tex.1994); *see* TRE 602 (evidence must show witness has personal knowledge); *see, e.g.,* ***Radio Station KSCS v. Jennings***, 750 S.W.2d 760, 761-62 (Tex.1988) (affidavit did not show how witness became familiar with facts about operation of radio station). Personal knowledge is whether the witness knows enough about the subject to testify. *See* TRE 104(b), 602; Brown & Rondon, *Evidence Handbook*, p. 549. Any qualifying statement about the affiant's personal knowledge makes the affidavit legally invalid. *See, e.g.,* ***Ryland Grp. v. Hood***, 924 S.W.2d 120, 122 (Tex.1996) (affiant's statement about his "understanding" was conclusory and would not support summary judgment); ***Humphreys***, 888 S.W.2d at 470-71 (affiant's statement that information was based on personal knowledge acquired from inquiry made affidavit invalid). The affidavit must contain direct and unequivocal statements that, if false, would be grounds for perjury. ***Burke v. Satterfield***, 525 S.W.2d 950, 955 (Tex.1975); ***Hall v. Stephenson***, 919 S.W.2d 454, 466 (Tex.App.—Fort Worth 1996, writ denied). For a discussion of summary-judgment affidavits, see "Affidavits," ch. 7-B, §9.4, p. 613.

(b) Knowledge & belief. By statute or rule, some affidavits may be made on "knowledge and belief." *See, e.g.,* TRCP 18a(a)(4)(A) (motion to recuse or disqualify judge), TRCP 93(7), (8), (13), (15) (some verified denials). An affidavit cannot be based on "knowledge and belief" unless it is authorized by a special statute or rule. ***Burke***, 525 S.W.2d at 954-55; ***Slater v. Metro Nissan***, 801 S.W.2d 253, 254 (Tex.App.—Fort Worth 1990, writ denied); *see, e.g.,* ***Noriega v. Mireles***, 925 S.W.2d 261, 263-64 (Tex.App.—Corpus Christi 1996, writ denied) (expert's affidavit made on his "best knowledge and belief" was not fatally defective because TRE 702 and 703 contemplate that experts bring more to court than their personal knowledge of facts). TRCP 166a does not authorize an affidavit made on knowledge and belief. *See, e.g.,* ***Kerlin***, 274 S.W.3d at 668 (affiant's statement "to the best of my personal knowledge and belief" would not support summary judgment).

(4) Executed by party or agent. TRCP 14 provides that whenever an affidavit is required, it may be made by either the party or the party's agent or attorney. However, before assuming that an affidavit may be made by someone else, the party should check the statutes and rules. *E.g.,* TRCP 197.2(d) & cmt. 2 (certain interrogatories must be signed by party under oath).

━━━━━━━━━━ ✦ ━━━━━━━━━━

(5) Copy of affidavit. If a copy of an affidavit is admitted, the copy does not need to be authenticated unless (1) a question is raised about the authenticity of the original, or (2) the circumstances make it unfair to permit a copy instead of the original. TRE 1003; *see Leggat*, 904 S.W.2d at 646.

(6) Exhibits. If there are exhibits attached to an affidavit, the affidavit must show they are authentic and admissible. *See* TRE 901(a).

(a) Authentic. To authenticate the exhibit, the affidavit should state that the attached exhibit is a true and correct copy of the original or that it is self-proving. *See Kleven v. TDCJ-Inst. Div.*, 69 S.W.3d 341, 345 (Tex.App.—Texarkana 2002, no pet.). An exhibit attached to an affidavit is not competent summary-judgment evidence unless the exhibit is self-proving or the affidavit proves the exhibit is true. *See Republic Nat'l Leasing Corp. v. Schindler*, 717 S.W.2d 606, 607 (Tex.1986) (documents submitted as summary-judgment proof must be sworn or certified); *Norcross v. Conoco, Inc.*, 720 S.W.2d 627, 632 (Tex.App.—San Antonio 1986, no writ) (documents submitted as summary-judgment proof must be authenticated by affidavit). See "Authenticity," ch. 8-C, §8.4, p. 704.

(b) Admissible. To show the admissibility of the exhibit, the affidavit should overcome any objection to the exhibit's admissibility. For example, invoices attached as exhibits are not admissible without the statements required by TRE 803(6) and 902(10). *Norcross*, 720 S.W.2d at 632. See "Introducing Documents," ch. 8-C, §8, p. 703.

17. Notice of party's name & address. Each party's name and address must be provided in writing to the clerk when the party files its initial pleading or within seven days after the clerk requests the information, and whenever the party changes its address. CPRC §30.015(a), (c), (d). To comply with CPRC §30.015, an attorney—when filing the first pleading in the case—should file a one-page notice, titled "Notice of Current Address," that contains the caption of the case, the party's name and current address, and the attorney's signature. See *O'Connor's Texas Forms*, FORM 1B:14. Many counties require the party filing suit to complete a case cover sheet that includes this information.

18. Notice to Attorney General.

(1) Suits involving the State. If a party files suit in certain cases involving the State of Texas, the party must mail a copy of the petition to the Attorney General. *See* CPRC §30.004(a), (b). The party must mail a copy of the petition for suits in which (1) the State of Texas is named as a party, (2) an agency in the legislative or executive department is named as a party, or (3) the Attorney General may represent a party based on state liability for conduct of a public servant under CPRC chapter 104. *Id.* §30.004(a). The petition must be mailed to the Attorney General's office in Austin, Texas by certified mail, return receipt requested. *Id.* §30.004(b). Mailing the petition does not relieve the party from serving process on any named party in the case. *Id.* §30.004(c). See "Serving the Defendant with Suit," ch. 2-H, p. 157. If the required notice is not given, any default judgment in the case can be set aside without costs. CPRC §30.004(d). See "After notice to Attorney General," ch. 7-A, §3.9.1(4), p. 591.

(2) Suits involving constitutional question.

(a) Generally. If a party files a petition or other pleading (or motion) challenging the constitutionality of a Texas statute, the court must serve notice of the constitutional question and a copy of the petition or other pleading on the Attorney General, unless the Attorney General is a party to or counsel in the suit. Gov't Code §402.010(a). The notice must identify the statute in question, state the basis for the challenge, and specify the petition or other pleading challenging the statute. *Id.* Notice must be sent either by certified or registered mail or electronically to an e-mail address designated by the Attorney General. *Id.* Even if the required notice is not filed or served, the court retains jurisdiction over the case and any timely filed claim or defense based on the constitutional challenge is not forfeited. *Id.* §402.010(c). However, a court cannot enter a final judgment holding a Texas statute unconstitutional until 45 days after the date notice is served on the Attorney General. *Id.* §402.010(b).

─────────────── ✦ ───────────────

> **NOTE**
> *Although Gov't Code §402.010 requires the court to serve the Attorney General with notice, a party challenging the constitutionality of a Texas statute should clearly notify the court of its challenge. See* **O'Connor's Texas Forms,** *FORM 2B:25.*

(b) Declaratory action. If a party files an action for declaratory relief that challenges the constitutionality of a statute, an ordinance, or a franchise, the Attorney General must be served with a copy of the pleadings. CPRC §37.006(b); *see* **Scurlock Permian Corp. v. Brazos Cty.**, 869 S.W.2d 478, 483 (Tex.App.—Houston [1st Dist.] 1993, writ denied) (trial court has no jurisdiction if Attorney General is not notified of declaratory-judgment action based on constitutional challenge to statute, ordinance, or franchise). See "Declaratory Judgment," ch. 2-D, p. 125.

19. Case-information sheet. All original petitions and applications must include a civil-case-information sheet. TRCP 78a(a)(1). The case-information sheet is not a pleading or discovery request, is not admissible at trial, and does not affect any substantive right. *See* TRCP 78a(d) & cmt. It is merely used to collect data for statistical and administrative purposes. TRCP 78a(d) & cmt. When e-filing a petition or application, the case-information sheet cannot be the first document. *Instructions for Completing the Texas Civil Case Information Sheet*, www.courts.state.tx.us/tjc/pdf/CaseInformationSheetInstructions.pdf.

(1) When to use. A civil-case-information sheet must be included with the filing of (1) an original petition, (2) an original application, or (3) a postjudgment petition for modification or motion for enforcement in a case under the Family Code. TRCP 78a(a). The case-information sheet is not required for cases filed in justice or small-claims courts or for cases under Title 3 (Juvenile Justice Code) of the Family Code. TRCP 78a(e).

> **NOTE**
> *Although a civil-case-information sheet is now required, the clerk cannot reject a pleading that does not include the case-information sheet. TRCP 78a(c). The court and clerk will take appropriate measures, however, to enforce compliance with the new rule. Id.*

(2) Form. The civil-case-information sheet must be in the format provided by the Supreme Court. TRCP 78a(a). For the required case-information sheet, see TRCP 78a. For an electronic fill-in-the-blank version, see www.courts.state.tx.us/tjc/forms/CivilFamilyCoverSheet.pdf. For instructions on completing the case-information sheet, see www.courts.state.tx.us/tjc/pdf/CaseInformationSheetInstructions.pdf.

(3) Signature. The civil-case-information sheet must be signed by the attorney filing the pleading or by the party. TRCP 78a(b). If the case-information sheet is submitted electronically, the person completing the form can use a scanned image for the signature or "/s/" followed by the name of the attorney or party where the signature would otherwise appear. *Instructions for Completing the Texas Civil Case Information Sheet*, www.courts.state .tx.us/tjc/pdf/CaseInformationSheetInstructions.pdf.

§3.3 Groundless or frivolous pleadings. A party or attorney who files groundless or frivolous pleadings may be sanctioned under CPRC chapter 9 (frivolous pleadings), CPRC chapter 10 (frivolous pleadings), and TRCP 13 (groundless pleadings).

1. Purpose. The purpose of CPRC chapter 9, CPRC chapter 10, and TRCP 13 is to curb abuses in the pleading process so that when a pleading is filed, the litigant's position is factually well-grounded and legally tenable. *See* **Skepnek v. Mynatt**, 8 S.W.3d 377, 381-82 (Tex.App.—El Paso 1999, pet. denied) (CPRC ch. 10 and TRCP 13); **Falk & Mayfield L.L.P. v. Molzan**, 974 S.W.2d 821, 827 (Tex.App.—Houston [14th Dist.] 1998, pet. denied) (TRCP 13); **Herrmann & Andreas Ins. Agency, Inc. v. Appling**, 800 S.W.2d 312, 320 (Tex.App.—Corpus Christi 1990, no writ) (CPRC §9.012).

2. Sanctions. For the motion for sanctions for frivolous or groundless pleadings, see "Motion for Sanctions," ch. 5-K, p. 377.

✦

§3.4 Vexatious litigant. CPRC chapter 11 provides a procedure to restrict plaintiffs from filing vexatious litigation. The statute provides two different methods for restricting a plaintiff from filing vexatious litigation: (1) a motion requesting that the plaintiff be declared a vexatious litigant and be required to furnish security, and (2) a motion requesting that the plaintiff be prohibited from filing new litigation without the permission of the local administrative judge. CPRC §§11.051, 11.101.

1. Motion for security. A defendant can file a motion asking the court to determine that the plaintiff is a vexatious litigant and to require the plaintiff to furnish security. CPRC §11.051. See *O'Connor's Texas Forms*, FORM 1B:17.

(1) Deadline. The defendant must file the motion within 90 days after it files its original answer or makes its special appearance. CPRC §11.051; *Spiller v. Spiller*, 21 S.W.3d 451, 454 (Tex.App.—San Antonio 2000, no pet.).

(2) Grounds. First the defendant must show there is no reasonable probability that the plaintiff will prevail in the litigation. CPRC §11.054; *Douglas v. American Title Co.*, 196 S.W.3d 876, 880 (Tex.App.—Houston [1st Dist.] 2006, no pet.). Then the defendant must show one of the following:

(a) Multiple lawsuits. In the seven years before the motion, the plaintiff (while acting pro se) commenced, prosecuted, or maintained at least five lawsuits (excluding filings in small-claims courts) that were (1) decided against the plaintiff, (2) pending for at least two years without being brought to trial or hearing, or (3) determined by a trial or appellate court to be frivolous or groundless. CPRC §11.054(1).

(b) Relitigation. Another lawsuit between the parties was finally determined against the plaintiff, and the plaintiff (while acting pro se) has repeatedly relitigated or is attempting to relitigate the cause of action, claim, controversy, issues of fact, issues of law, or validity of the final judgment against the same defendant. CPRC §11.054(2).

(c) Declared vexatious litigant. The plaintiff has already been declared a vexatious litigant by a state or federal court in an action or proceeding based on the same or substantially similar facts, transactions, or occurrences. CPRC §11.054(3).

(3) Stay of litigation. A motion filed under CPRC §11.051 stays the litigation until the trial court rules on the motion. CPRC §11.052; *Douglas*, 196 S.W.3d at 880.

(4) Hearing. On receiving the motion, the court, after notice to all parties, must conduct a hearing on the motion. CPRC §11.053(a). The court can consider written or oral evidence and testimony presented by witnesses or by affidavits. *Id.* §11.053(b).

(5) Order. If the defendant meets its burden, the plaintiff will be declared a vexatious litigant. *See* CPRC §11.054. The court will then order the plaintiff to furnish security to cover reasonable expenses incurred by the defendant, including costs and attorney fees, that will be recoverable by the defendant if the litigation is dismissed on the merits. *See id.* §§11.055, 11.057. See *O'Connor's Texas Forms*, FORM 1B:19. If the plaintiff does not furnish security within the time period ordered by the court, the litigation will be dismissed. CPRC §11.056.

2. Motion for prefiling order prohibiting new litigation.

(1) Motion. Any party, or a court on its own initiative, can move to prohibit a person from filing new litigation in a Texas court as a pro se party. CPRC §11.101(a). The motion must show that (1) the person has been declared a vexatious litigant, and (2) the local administrative judge of the court in which the person wants to file new litigation has not granted the person permission under CPRC §11.102 to do so. *See id.* §11.101(a).

(2) Orders.

(a) Prefiling order – litigation prohibited. If, after notice and a hearing under CPRC §11.053, (1) the person has been declared a vexatious litigant, and (2) the local administrative judge of the court in which the person wants to file new litigation has not granted the person permission under CPRC §11.102 to do so, the court can issue a prefiling order prohibiting the person from filing new litigation as a pro se party. CPRC §11.101(a).

─────────────── ★ ───────────────

NOTE

The Office of Court Administration must post on its website a list of vexatious litigants subject to a prefiling order under CPRC §11.101(a). CPRC §11.104(b). If requested by the person designated as a vexatious litigant, the list must indicate whether an appeal of that designation has been filed. Id. See "Appeal," §3.4.2(3)(a), this page.

(b) Order permitting new litigation. Even if a prefiling order has been entered prohibiting a person from filing new litigation in a Texas court as a pro se party, the person may file new litigation if she obtains an order from the local administrative judge permitting her to do so. *See* CPRC §§11.101(a), 11.102(a). The local administrative judge must find that the litigation (1) has merit and (2) has not been filed to harass or to cause delay. *Id.* §11.102(a). The judge may permit the new litigation on the condition that the person furnish adequate security. *Id.* §11.102(b).

(3) Review.

(a) Appeal. A person may appeal an order under CPRC §11.101(a) designating her a vexatious litigant and prohibiting her from filing new litigation. CPRC §11.101(c). But a local administrative judge's decision under CPRC §11.102 to deny a person permission to file new litigation or to condition permission on furnishing security cannot be appealed. *Id.* §11.102(c).

(b) Mandamus. A person may file a writ of mandamus with the court of appeals to review a local administrative judge's decision under CPRC §11.102 to deny the person permission to file new litigation or to condition permission on furnishing security. CPRC §11.102(c). The writ of mandamus must be filed within 30 days after the local administrative judge's decision. *Id.* If the writ of mandamus is denied, the person cannot seek relief in the Supreme Court. *Id.*

§3.5 Defective pleadings.

1. Waiver of pleading defect. There are two types of pleading defects that the opponent must object to: (1) defects in form (e.g., failure to include a verification) and (2) defects in substance (e.g., failure to plead a cause of action or defense with sufficient specificity). *Aquila Sw. Pipeline, Inc. v. Harmony Expl., Inc.*, 48 S.W.3d 225, 233 (Tex.App.—San Antonio 2001, pet. denied). If the opponent does not object to these pleading defects by special exception before the charge to the jury, or in nonjury cases before the judgment is signed, the defects are waived. TRCP 90; *see Shoemake v. Fogel, Ltd.*, 826 S.W.2d 933, 937 (Tex.1992). For example, when a plaintiff claims that a defendant's action caused injury but does not use the term "negligence," the error is waived unless the defendant objects to the petition by special exception. *Roark v. Allen*, 633 S.W.2d 804, 810 (Tex.1982). See "Special Exceptions—Challenging the Pleadings," ch. 3-G, p. 248. If the pleadings are defective, the party should immediately move to amend. See "Amending or supplementing pleadings," §3.6, this page; "Options for plaintiff," ch. 3-G, §9.3, p. 253. An objection to a pleading defect is not necessary in a case resolved by a default judgment. TRCP 90; *Stoner v. Thompson*, 578 S.W.2d 679, 684-85 (Tex.1979).

2. Trial by consent. Generally, a party cannot obtain discovery, offer evidence, or submit jury questions on issues that were not pleaded. However, an issue that is not included in the pleadings is "tried by consent" when it is supported by evidence at trial and is submitted to the jury without objection. See "Issue tried by consent," ch. 8-F, §2.4.2(1), p. 723. If the opponent objects to evidence on the ground that the issue was not pleaded, or objects to the submission of the jury question for the same reason, the issue is not tried by consent. See "Issue not tried by consent," ch. 8-F, §2.4.2(2), p. 723.

§3.6 Amending or supplementing pleadings.

1. Two methods. The rules permit the parties to change, correct, revise, or explain a previously filed pleading by filing amended or supplemental pleadings. Unless the amended or supplemental pleading alleges a wholly new, distinct, or different transaction, the statute of limitations is tolled and the amended or supplemental pleading

★

relates back to the original pleading. CPRC §16.068; *Alexander v. Turtur & Assocs.*, 146 S.W.3d 113, 121 (Tex.2004). See *O'Connor's Texas COA*, "Amended or supplemental pleading," ch. 52, §4.3, p. 1499.

(1) Amended pleadings. An amended pleading adds or withdraws matters to correct or change the previous pleading. TRCP 62; *J.M. Huber Corp. v. Santa Fe Energy Res.*, 871 S.W.2d 842, 844 (Tex.App.—Houston [14th Dist.] 1994, writ denied); *see Retzlaff v. TDCJ*, 135 S.W.3d 731, 737 (Tex.App.—Houston [1st Dist.] 2003, no pet.) (amended pleading appropriate to add new cause of action or affirmative defense); *Tex-Hio Prtshp. v. Garner*, 106 S.W.3d 886, 890 (Tex.App.—Dallas 2003, no pet.) (amended pleading appropriate to bring new parties into suit). Filing an amended pleading that does not include a party or cause of action effectively nonsuits or voluntarily dismisses the omitted party or claim when the amended pleading is filed. *FKM Prtshp. v. Board of Regents of the Univ. of Houston Sys.*, 255 S.W.3d 619, 632 (Tex.2008); *Randolph v. Jackson Walker L.L.P.*, 29 S.W.3d 271, 274 (Tex.App.—Houston [14th Dist.] 2000, pet. denied). The amended pleading completely replaces and supersedes the previous pleading. TRCP 65; *Phifer v. Nacogdoches Cty. Cent. Appr. Dist.*, 45 S.W.3d 159, 172 (Tex.App.—Tyler 2000, pet. denied); *Hill v. Heritage Res.*, 964 S.W.2d 89, 142 (Tex.App.—El Paso 1997, pet. denied). Once an amended pleading is filed, the previous pleading is no longer part of the proceedings. TRCP 65; *Drake Ins. v. King*, 606 S.W.2d 812, 817 (Tex.1980). The last amended pleading filed is called the "live" pleading. The amended pleading must comply with the rules that applied to the original pleading (e.g., if the original pleading was verified, the amended pleading must also be verified). After an amendment, statements in the earlier pleadings are no longer judicial admissions. *Sosa v. Central Power & Light*, 909 S.W.2d 893, 895 (Tex.1995). See "Pleadings as judicial admissions," §3.7, p. 18.

(2) Supplemental pleadings. A supplemental or reply pleading is made in response to an adverse party's last pleading. TRCP 69; *Sixth RMA Partners v. Sibley*, 111 S.W.3d 46, 53 (Tex.2003); *J.M. Huber Corp.*, 871 S.W.2d at 844. It adds to, but does not supersede or replace, the previous pleading. The plaintiff's supplemental petition may contain the following matters in reply to what the defendant alleges: special exceptions, general denials, and the allegation of new matters not already alleged. TRCP 80. A supplemental pleading should restate only the matters from the previous pleading that are necessary to introduce the things being changed, added, or challenged. *See* TRCP 69; *Sibley*, 111 S.W.3d at 53. When a supplemental pleading contains matters outside the scope of TRCP 69, the adverse party must object or it waives the error. *See Sibley*, 111 S.W.3d at 54.

PRACTICE TIP

Avoid using supplemental pleadings. If you amend pleadings instead of supplementing them, the case file will contain fewer live pleadings and will be less confusing. See Alert Synteks, Inc. v. Jerry Spencer, L.P., 151 S.W.3d 246, 253 (Tex.App.—Tyler 2004, no pet.).

---

2. Procedure for amending pleadings. The procedure for amending pleadings at various stages of the trial is discussed in other sections of this book.

(1) Amending pleadings before trial. See "Motion to Amend Pleadings—Pretrial," ch. 5-F, p. 350.

(2) Amending pleadings in a summary-judgment case. See "Amending the Petition or Answer," ch. 7-B, §8, p. 610.

(3) Amending pleadings during trial and after verdict. See "Motion to Amend Pleadings—Trial & Post-trial," ch. 8-F, p. 721.

3. Appellate review of amended pleadings. On appeal, the court reviews the trial court's rulings on trial amendments under the abuse-of-discretion standard. *Hardin v. Hardin*, 597 S.W.2d 347, 349-50 (Tex.1980); *Dunnagan v. Watson*, 204 S.W.3d 30, 38 (Tex.App.—Fort Worth 2006, pet. denied). Whether an amendment is appropriate is a function of three factors: the nature of the amendment, the evidence introduced at trial, and the timeliness of the amendment.

(1) Nature of amendment.

(a) Amendment is procedural. If the amendment corrected a procedural defect in the pleadings, it was less likely to cause surprise and should have been permitted late in the trial. *See Stephenson v. LeBoeuf,*

───────────────────────── ✦ ─────────────────────────

16 S.W.3d 829, 839 (Tex.App.—Houston [14th Dist.] 2000, pet. denied) (trial court has no discretion to refuse amendment that is merely procedural); *see, e.g., Chapin & Chapin, Inc. v. Texas Sand & Gravel Co.*, 844 S.W.2d 664, 665 (Tex.1992) (trial court should have permitted D to add verified denial to its answer).

(b) Amendment is substantive. If the amendment made a substantive change and altered the nature of the trial itself, the trial court had the discretion to deny leave to amend. *Chapin & Chapin*, 844 S.W.2d at 665; *see, e.g., Hardin*, 597 S.W.2d at 350 (trial court had discretion to deny amendment, offered on day of trial, to add affirmative defenses). On appeal, an appellant who objected to the amendment must show that the amendment (1) caused surprise or prejudice or (2) asserted a new cause of action or defense and thus was prejudicial on its face. *State Bar v. Kilpatrick*, 874 S.W.2d 656, 658 (Tex.1994); *Chapin & Chapin*, 844 S.W.2d at 665; *Stephenson*, 16 S.W.3d at 839.

(2) Evidence introduced at trial. If the party offered an amendment that conforms the pleadings to the evidence, the trial court should have permitted the amendment. See "Grounds," ch. 8-F, §2.4, p. 722.

(3) Timeliness of amendment. If the party filed an amendment as soon as it realized an amendment was necessary, the trial court should have permitted the amendment because it was unlikely to have surprised or prejudiced the other party. See "Rules Regarding Amending Pleadings Before Trial," ch. 5-F, §3, p. 350; "Motion for Leave to Amend," ch. 8-F, §2, p. 721.

§3.7 Pleadings as judicial admissions.

1. Pleading assertions of fact. Assertions of fact in a party's live pleadings that are not pleaded in the alternative are regarded as formal judicial admissions. *Holy Cross Church of God in Christ v. Wolf*, 44 S.W.3d 562, 568 (Tex.2001); *Houston First Am. Sav. v. Musick*, 650 S.W.2d 764, 767 (Tex.1983). To be a judicial admission, a statement in a pleading must be deliberate, clear, and unequivocal. *Mapco, Inc. v. Carter*, 817 S.W.2d 686, 687 (Tex. 1991); *Charles Brown, L.L.P. v. Lanier Worldwide, Inc.*, 124 S.W.3d 883, 900 (Tex.App.—Houston [14th Dist.] 2004, no pet.); *see PPG Indus. v. JMB/Houston Ctrs. Partners*, 146 S.W.3d 79, 95 (Tex.2004). A party may plead alternative theories without judicially admitting them. *Dowling v. NADW Mktg., Inc.*, 631 S.W.2d 726, 729 (Tex.1982); *see* TRCP 48.

(1) Effect. A judicial admission is conclusive against the party making it, relieves the opposing party of the burden of proving the admitted fact, and bars the admitting party from disputing it when it is subject to an objection. *Mendoza v. Fidelity & Guar. Ins. Underwriters, Inc.*, 606 S.W.2d 692, 694 (Tex.1980); *Charles Brown, L.L.P.*, 124 S.W.3d at 900; *Frazer v. Texas Farm Bur. Mut. Ins.*, 4 S.W.3d 819, 825 (Tex.App.—Houston [1st Dist.] 1999, no pet.). Once a fact is conclusively established by judicial admission, no jury questions on the fact need to be submitted. *Horizon/CMS Healthcare Corp. v. Auld*, 34 S.W.3d 887, 905 (Tex.2000).

(2) Waiver of judicial admission. A party relying on an opponent's pleadings as judicial admissions of fact must protect the record by objecting both to the introduction of controverting evidence and to the submission of a jury question on the admitted fact. *Marshall v. Vise*, 767 S.W.2d 699, 700 (Tex.1989); *Musick*, 650 S.W.2d at 769; *e.g., Hurlbut v. Gulf Atl. Life Ins.*, 749 S.W.2d 762, 765 (Tex.1987) (admission waived because Ds did not object to submission of jury question). See "Making & Preserving Objections," ch. 1-F, p. 43.

(3) Not in superseded pleadings. Statements in superseded pleadings are not conclusive or indisputable judicial admissions. *Sosa v. Central Power & Light*, 909 S.W.2d 893, 895 (Tex.1995); *Drake Ins. v. King*, 606 S.W.2d 812, 817 (Tex.1980). Statements in superseded pleadings may, however, be admitted into evidence against the pleader. *See Bay Area Healthcare Grp. v. McShane*, 239 S.W.3d 231, 235 (Tex.2007). Because a superseded statement is not conclusive, the pleader may dispute it. *Quick v. Plastic Solutions*, 270 S.W.3d 173, 185 (Tex.App.—El Paso 2008, no pet.).

2. Compared to testimonial admissions. A party's testimonial declarations that are contrary to its position are quasi-admissions, but they are not conclusive. *Hennigan v. I.P. Pet. Co.*, 858 S.W.2d 371, 372 (Tex.1993); *Mendoza*, 606 S.W.2d at 694. Quasi-admissions are distinguishable from true judicial admissions, which are a formal waiver of proof usually found in pleadings or the parties' stipulations. *Mendoza*, 606 S.W.2d at 694. For a party's

★

testimonial quasi-admission to be treated as a conclusive judicial admission, the following must be true: (1) the relied-on declaration was made during a judicial proceeding, (2) the declaration is contrary to a fact that is essential to the testifying person's claim or defense, (3) the declaration was deliberate, clear, and unequivocal, (4) allowing the declaration to have conclusive effect would be consistent with public policy, and (5) the declaration is not destructive to the other party's claim. *Id.*; *Griffin v. Superior Ins.*, 338 S.W.2d 415, 419 (Tex.1960).

§4. MOTION PRACTICE

§4.1 Drafting motions.

1. In writing. Most motions can only be made in writing. *E.g.*, TRCP 86 (transfer venue); *McConnell v. Southside ISD*, 858 S.W.2d 337, 343 n.7 (Tex.1993) (special exceptions); *City of Houston v. Clear Creek Basin Auth.*, 589 S.W.2d 671, 677 (Tex.1979) (summary judgment).

2. Style. The style is the heading of the motion. It contains the cause number, the names of the parties, the court, and the county of suit. See *O'Connor's Texas Forms*, FORM 1B:2.

(1) Cause number. The clerk assigns the cause number. TRCP 23. The parties should make sure all documents are filed with the correct cause number. However, filing a document with the wrong cause number generally should not be considered a jurisdictional defect. *See, e.g.*, *Blankenship v. Robins*, 878 S.W.2d 138, 138-39 (Tex.1994) (motion for new trial with wrong cause number was effective because it was "bona fide attempt" to invoke appellate jurisdiction); *McRoberts v. Ryals*, 863 S.W.2d 450, 454-55 (Tex.1993) (motion for new trial with wrong cause number was effective); *City of San Antonio v. Rodriguez*, 828 S.W.2d 417, 418 (Tex.1992) (notice of appeal with wrong cause number was effective). *But see Philbrook v. Berry*, 683 S.W.2d 378, 379 (Tex.1985) (motion for new trial was ineffective because of wrong cause number). The *Philbrook* holding on this issue has been distinguished, explained, and questioned into irrelevance. *See Paselk v. Rabun*, 293 S.W.3d 600, 606 (Tex.App.—Texarkana 2009, pet. denied) (*Philbrook* has been all but expressly overruled); *Leal v. City of Rosenberg*, 17 S.W.3d 385, 386 (Tex.App.—Amarillo 2000, order) (same).

(2) List of parties. In motions, the list of parties in the style may be shortened by naming the first party and using the inclusive term "et al." *Cf. Abramcik v. U.S. Home Corp.*, 792 S.W.2d 822, 824 (Tex.App.—Houston [14th Dist.] 1990, writ denied) (term "et al." can be used in later pleadings). If a party misnames itself or another party in a motion, the error is misnomer and can be corrected by amendment. *E.g.*, *In re Greater Houston Orthopaedic Specialists, Inc.*, 295 S.W.3d 323, 325-26 (Tex.2009) (misnomer when P omitted part of its name from motion for nonsuit). See "Misnomer," ch. 2-B, §3.3.1(2)(a), p. 98.

3. Caption. The caption is the title of the motion. See "Caption," §3.2.3, p. 7.

(1) Correct title. The title of a motion should be useful to the court, the clerk, and the attorney's files. The title should identify the party who filed the motion and the type of motion (e.g., "Defendant's Motion to Extend Time to ..."). If there are multiple parties, the title should use an abbreviated name for the party (e.g., "Bank's Motion to ..."). The title should indicate if a motion is agreed (e.g., "Agreed Motion to ...") or has been made before (e.g., "Bank's Second Motion to ...").

(2) Incorrect title. If the party makes an error in the caption of the motion, the court will treat the motion as if it had been properly named. See TRCP 71; *Speer v. Stover*, 685 S.W.2d 22, 23 (Tex.1985). A misnomer of the motion does not make it ineffective. See *General Motors Acceptance Corp. v. Harris Cty. MUD*, 899 S.W.2d 821, 824 n.3 (Tex.App.—Houston [14th Dist.] 1995, no writ). The court will look to the substance of a motion to determine its nature. *E.g.*, *State Bar v. Heard*, 603 S.W.2d 829, 833 (Tex.1980) (motion for summary judgment was actually motion to suspend law license under special statute); *see, e.g.*, *Speer*, 685 S.W.2d at 23 (plea in abatement was actually plea to the jurisdiction); *In re Bokeloh*, 21 S.W.3d 784, 789-90 (Tex.App.—Houston [14th Dist.] 2000, orig. proceeding) (motion to retain was not motion to reinstate because it did not address reinstatement).

4. Contents. A motion should state the relief sought and the grounds for the relief. TRCP 21.

5. Numbered paragraphs. The paragraphs must be numbered, and each paragraph should be limited to a single set of circumstances. TRCP 50. Arabic numerals (e.g., 1, 2, 3) should be used, and Roman numerals (e.g., I, II, III) should be avoided.

★

6. Adopting by reference. Parties may adopt statements by reference from another motion. TRCP 58.

7. Prayer. At the end of the motion, under the heading "Prayer," the party should state exactly what relief it seeks. The prayer for relief should match the purpose of the motion. *See, e.g.*, *Finley v. J.C. Pace Ltd.*, 4 S.W.3d 319, 320 (Tex.App.—Houston [1st Dist.] 1999, order) (motion for rehearing was actually motion for new trial because prayer requested relitigation of issues); *Mercer v. Band*, 454 S.W.2d 833, 835-36 (Tex.App.—Houston [14th Dist.] 1970, no writ) (motion for new trial was actually motion for judgment because prayer asked for different judgment, not new trial). See "Prayer," ch. 2-B, §14, p. 110.

8. Signature block. The requirements for a signature block for motions are the same as for pleadings. See "Signature block," §3.2.11, p. 9.

9. Certificate of conference. All motions relating to discovery should contain a certificate that the party made a reasonable attempt to resolve the discovery dispute without court intervention but failed. TRCP 191.2. See "Certificate of conference," ch. 6-A, §4.2, p. 427; *O'Connor's Texas Forms*, FORM 1B:13. Some local rules require a certificate of conference on other motions as well. *E.g.*, Tarrant Cty. Loc. R. 3.06(b) (no motion will be set for hearing without a certificate of conference).

10. Certificate of service. All documents required to be served under TRCP 21 (except those served with citation) must contain a certificate of service in the document itself. TRCP 21a. See "Certificate of service," §3.2.12, p. 10; *O'Connor's Texas Forms*, FORM 1B:11.

(1) Pleadings. All pleadings, motions, responses, or applications to the court for an order, unless served with citation or presented during a hearing or trial, must contain a certificate of service. *See* TRCP 21.

(2) Orders & judgments. All proposed orders and judgments sent to the court separately from a motion or response must contain a certificate of service. See "Certificate of service," ch. 1-G, §4.1.9, p. 51.

11. Exhibits. Although no rule specifies the method for attaching exhibits to motions, parties should follow the rules for attaching exhibits to pleadings. A motion should identify and incorporate by reference the exhibits attached to it and those filed separately. *See* *Hooks v. Davis*, No. 03-03-00739-CV (Tex.App.—Austin 2004, pet. denied) (memo op.; 7-29-04). See "Exhibits," §3.2.13, p. 10.

12. Verification & affidavits. When a motion contains facts outside the record, the party may be required to verify the motion by attaching a verification or affidavit. *See* *In re General Agents Ins. Co.*, 254 S.W.3d 670, 676 (Tex.App.—Houston [14th Dist.] 2008, orig. proceeding); *Raymond v. Raymond*, 190 S.W.3d 77, 82 (Tex. App.—Houston [1st Dist.] 2005, no pet.). See "Verification," §3.2.15, p. 11; "Affidavits," §3.2.16, p. 11. For the procedure for using an unsworn declaration instead of a verification or an affidavit, see "Unsworn declaration," §3.2.14, p. 10.

13. Notice of challenge to constitutionality of statute. If a party files a motion (or petition or other pleading) challenging the constitutionality of a Texas statute, the court must serve notice of the constitutional question and a copy of the motion on the Attorney General, unless the Attorney General is a party to or counsel in the suit. Gov't Code §402.010(a). See "Generally," §3.2.18(2)(a), p. 13.

§4.2 Serving & filing motions. All written motions must be served on all parties. TRCP 21. See "Rules for Serving Documents," ch. 1-D, p. 34. All motions should generally be filed. See "Rules for Filing Documents," ch. 1-C, p. 21.

§4.3 Hearing on motions. The court will not always hold a hearing before ruling on a motion. See "Hearing on Motion," ch. 1-E, §4, p. 41.

★

C. RULES FOR FILING DOCUMENTS

§1. GENERAL

§1.1 Rules. TRCP 4, 5, 21, 21a, 21b, 23-27, 45(d), 74. See Gov't Code §311.014; TRAP 4.1, 5, 9.

§1.2 Purpose. Documents are filed to put them into the court's record of the lawsuit. Filing documents should not be confused with serving documents. Documents are *filed* with the clerk; they are *served* on the other parties in the lawsuit. The rules for filing and serving are different. *Compare* TRCP 21 (filing and serving of pleadings and motions) *with* TRCP 21a (methods of service). See "Rules for Serving Documents," ch. 1-D, p. 34.

§1.3 Forms. *O'Connor's Texas Civil Forms* (2012), FORMS 1C, 6A:1.

§2. WHAT TO FILE

File all pleadings, motions, and other documents unless a rule explicitly states otherwise. *E.g.*, TRCP 191.4(a) (list of discovery materials that must not be filed).

§2.1 Pleadings.

1. Originals. Generally, parties file the signed original of petitions and answers with the court.

2. Copies. If a party files a copy of a pleading, the original must be kept for inspection in case a question is raised about the authenticity of the copy. TRCP 45(d).

§2.2 Motions. The party should file the signed original of all motions and responses.

§2.3 Exhibits. The party can attach the original or a copy of an exhibit to the pleading filed with the court. TRCP 59. However, an original negotiable financial document should never be filed with the court; instead, a copy should be attached to the pleadings.

§3. WITH WHOM TO FILE

Documents are considered filed when they reach the court. *Jamar v. Patterson*, 868 S.W.2d 318, 319 (Tex.1993); *In re Smith*, 263 S.W.3d 93, 95 (Tex.App.—Houston [1st Dist.] 2006, orig. proceeding); *see Stokes v. Aberdeen Ins.*, 917 S.W.2d 267, 268 (Tex.1996) (mailing document to proper court address controls over naming correct court representative). Documents must be filed with the court clerk unless they are presented during a trial or hearing (TRCP 21) or given to the judge for filing (TRCP 74).

§3.1 Clerk. Generally, documents should be presented to the court clerk for filing. TRCP 21, 74. When the courthouse is closed, documents may be filed with the clerk wherever she can be located, generally at her residence. *See Miller Brewing Co. v. Villarreal*, 829 S.W.2d 770, 771 (Tex.1992).

§3.2 Judge. Documents may be filed with the trial judge during a trial or hearing. TRCP 21, 74. When the courthouse is closed, documents may be filed with the trial judge—with her permission—wherever she can be located, generally at her residence. *See* TRCP 74; *Miller Brewing Co. v. Villarreal*, 829 S.W.2d 770, 771 (Tex.1992). When the trial judge is unavailable, documents may be filed with another judge occupying the same type of bench in the same county. *See, e.g.*, *In re Cuban*, 24 S.W.3d 381, 383 (Tex.App.—Dallas 2000, orig. proceeding) (motion to recuse judge in County Court at Law No. 2 filed with judge of County Court at Law No. 3). The judge must note the date and time of filing on the document and forward it to the clerk's office. TRCP 74.

§4. HOW TO FILE

Local rules cannot impose additional restrictions on what constitutes a "filing" under the TRCPs (or the TRAPs). *Jamar v. Patterson*, 868 S.W.2d 318, 318 n.2 (Tex.1993).

★

NOTE

Beginning January 1, 2014, the Supreme Court will implement mandatory e-filing in civil cases in district courts, statutory county courts, constitutional county courts, and statutory probate courts. See Tex.Sup.Ct. Order, Misc. Docket No. 12-9206 (Dec. 11, 2012). The Supreme Court has issued an implementation schedule based on a county's population size; implementation will begin January 1, 2014, for courts in counties with a population of at least 500,000 and will continue through July 1, 2016, for the rest of the courts. Id. The implementation schedule can be extended for good cause. Id. E-filing will be required for any party represented by an attorney; unrepresented parties may e-file but will not be required to do so. Id. As part of the implementation schedule, the Supreme Court will adopt rules governing both e-filing and e-service. Id. Check the Supreme Court website at www.supreme.courts.state.tx.us for any proposed and final rules.

---

§4.1 Mail. A party may file a document by mailing it to the clerk on or before the date it is due. TRCP 5; *Ramos v. Richardson*, 228 S.W.3d 671, 673 (Tex.2007); *see, e.g., Beard v. Beard*, 49 S.W.3d 40, 54 (Tex.App.—Waco 2001, pet. denied) (motion for new trial deposited in mail on day it was due was timely). When a party files a document by mail, it invokes the "mailbox rule" in TRCP 5. A document mailed to the clerk is considered filed on the day it is deposited with the U.S. Postal Service (USPS). A document submitted by mail is considered timely filed on the day of mailing if it meets all the criteria listed below.

1. The document was properly stamped and sent by first-class U.S. mail. TRCP 5; *Ramos*, 228 S.W.3d at 673.

CAUTION

*When a document is sent by FedEx, UPS, or any other commercial delivery service, the mailbox rule in TRCP 5 does not apply. **Fountain Parkway, Ltd. v. Tarrant Appr. Dist.**, 920 S.W.2d 799, 802-03 (Tex.App.—Fort Worth 1996, writ denied). Thus, when a document sent by a commercial delivery service is received by the clerk after the due date, it is not timely filed. Id.; **Carpenter v. Town & Country Bank**, 806 S.W.2d 959, 960 (Tex.App.—Eastland 1991, writ denied).*

---

2. The document was sent with the correct postage. TRCP 5.

3. The document was addressed to the proper clerk or court and sent to the correct address. TRCP 5; *Ramos*, 228 S.W.3d at 673; *Stokes v. Aberdeen Ins.*, 917 S.W.2d 267, 268 (Tex.1996); *see, e.g., Desai v. Chambers Cty. Appr. Dist.*, 376 S.W.3d 295, 301-02 (Tex.App.—Houston [14th Dist.] 2012, no pet.) (mailing petitions to district clerk's physical address, rather than mailing address, was proper under TRCP 5). An incorrect or omitted zip code does not make the address improper. *Judkins v. Davenport*, 59 S.W.3d 689, 691 (Tex.App.—Amarillo 2000, no pet.).

4. The document was mailed on or before the due date. TRCP 5; *Ramos*, 228 S.W.3d at 673; *e.g., Milam v. Miller*, 891 S.W.2d 1, 2 (Tex.App.—Amarillo 1994, writ ref'd) (answer mailed at post office at 8:30 a.m. on due date, 90 minutes before deadline for answer, was timely filed). If the document was sent with stamps (not stamped by a private postage meter) and the envelope bears a legible USPS postmark, the envelope is prima facie evidence of the date of mailing. TRCP 5; *Landers v. State Farm Lloyds*, 257 S.W.3d 740, 745 (Tex.App.—Houston [1st Dist.] 2008, no pet.).

5. The document arrived at the court within ten days of the due date. TRCP 5. The document or a copy of the document must reach the court no later than ten days after it is due. *Ramos*, 228 S.W.3d at 673; *e.g., Stokes*, 917 S.W.2d at 268 (party mailed motion to judge and copy to clerk; clerk's copy was received within ten days and considered timely filed). If the document arrives on the 11th day, it is not considered timely filed unless the party files, and the trial court grants, a motion to extend the time for filing. TRCP 5. See "Motion to extend time," §9.1, p. 30.

———————————— ✩ ————————————

6. The envelope bears a legible USPS postmark, which is prima facie evidence of the date of mailing. TRCP 5; *see Carpenter*, 806 S.W.2d at 960 (document sent by UPS did not qualify). See "Proving date of filing," §10.1, p. 30.

PRACTICE TIP

To prove that a document was received within ten days of the due date, send it to the clerk by certified mail, return receipt requested. The USPS will give you a signed receipt ("Domestic Return Receipt") showing the date that the clerk received the document. USPS Form 3811 (the "green card"). You could also send it with a certificate of mailing, which costs less than certified mail. USPS Form 3817. However, a certificate of mailing proves only that the document was mailed, not that it was received. See "Proving Filing," §10, p. 30.

---

§4.2 Delivery. A party may file a document by delivering it to the clerk of the trial court. TRCP 21, 74. Anyone—the attorney, a member of the attorney's office staff, or a receipted commercial delivery service (e.g., FedEx or UPS)—may deliver a document, as long as it is delivered on or before the date it is due. *See, e.g.*, *Carpenter v. Town & Country Bank*, 806 S.W.2d 959, 960 (Tex.App.—Eastland 1991, writ denied) (under TRCP 5, motion for new trial sent by UPS was late when received by clerk six days after deadline; ten-day period under mailbox rule does not apply to UPS delivery). A party may also file a document with the judge; for example, while in court, an attorney may personally hand a document to the judge for filing. TRCP 74.

§4.3 Fax. A party may file a document with the clerk by fax if the Supreme Court has approved local rules for fax filing in that county. *See* Gov't Code §51.807. The Supreme Court has approved local rules for fax filing in most counties. Because the TRCPs do not address fax filing, the party should refer to a court's local rules to determine when a faxed document is considered filed. For example, in Bexar County, a document is considered filed on the day it is received if the transmission is completed before midnight on a business day. Bexar Cty. Loc. R. 4.15 (district court fax-filing rules). The fax machine used for the filing should be set to produce a transmission-verification report confirming the date and time the document was sent and received. The party should attach the transmission-verification report to the file copy of the document as proof of the date and time of filing. If a court does not accept documents by fax, a party can fax the document to someone located near the courthouse who can deliver a copy of the faxed document to the clerk. *See* TRCP 45(d) (party may file photocopies of pleadings).

§4.4 E-filing. E-filing allows a party to file a document with a court through an online computer transmission of an electronic form of the document. This process is referred to as "e-filing" rather than "electronic filing," which is often used to describe fax filing. A party may e-file a document in a district or county court if a county has adopted the standard set of local e-filing rules approved by the Supreme Court (Loc. E-Filing Rules Template). *See* TRCP 3a. A party may e-file a document in a justice-of-the-peace (JP) court if that court has adopted the Statewide Rules Concerning the Electronic Filing and Service of Documents in Participating Justice of the Peace Courts (JP E-Filing & E-Service Rules). For the standard local e-filing rules, see the county-court and district-court templates at www.courts.state.tx.us/jcit/Efiling/EfilingHome.asp. For the JP E-Filing & E-Service Rules, see Misc. Docket No. 07-9200 (eff. Jan. 1, 2008). While the mechanics of e-filing are the same for all counties, the Supreme Court has approved minor variations for some counties. *See, e.g.*, Harris Cty. Loc. R. 6.1(a) (district court electronic-document-filing rules; Harris County requires paper orders, although standard rules allow judges to issue electronic orders). For a list of participating counties that have adopted and implemented e-filing rules, see www.texas.gov/en/tx-efiling/Pages/counties .aspx. For a list of approved rules by county and district, see www.courts.state.tx.us/jcit/Efiling/EfilingRules.asp.

NOTE

There are separate e-filing rules templates for district and county courts, but they are almost identical. Because the rule numbers are the same for each, we cite only one "Loc. E-Filing Rules Template" throughout this subchapter. Any differences between the rules for district and county courts are noted in the text.

---- ✯ ----

1. How to e-file. E-filing is optional unless ordered by the court. Loc. E-Filing Rules Template, rule 1.3. If a party decides to e-file or is ordered to do so by the court, the party must select and register with a certified electronic-filing service provider (EFSP). Loc. E-Filing Rules Template, rule 4.1(b), (c); JP E-Filing & E-Service Rules, rule 4.1(b), (c). Once registered, the party receives a unique identifier, which must be used each time the party e-files a document. Loc. E-Filing Rules Template, rule 4.2(a). Registering with an EFSP automatically registers the party with Texas.gov eFiling for Courts. www.texas.gov/en/tx-efiling/Pages/faq.aspx. The party does not file documents directly with the district clerk or JP court; instead, the party submits the document to its EFSP, which sends the document through TexasOnline to the district clerk or JP court. Loc. E-Filing Rules Template, rule 4.1(c); JP E-Filing & E-Service Rules, rule 4.1(c). For a list of available EFSPs, see www.texas.gov/en/tx-efiling/Pages/getting-started.aspx.

(1) Filing formats.

(a) Most documents. Most e-filed documents can be submitted in Microsoft Word and Corel WordPerfect, the standard word-processing formats specified by TexasOnline. *See* Loc. E-Filing Rules Template, rules 4.1(d), 4.8(a); JP E-Filing & E-Service Rules, rules 4.1(d), 4.7. The e-filed documents must be formatted for printing on 8½-by-11-inch paper. Loc. E-Filing Rules Template, rule 4.8(a); JP E-Filing & E-Service Rules, rule 4.7. E-filed pleadings are deemed to comply with the requirements of TRCP 45. Loc. E-Filing Rules Template, rule 4.8(b).

(b) Sworn or verified documents. Any e-filed document or attachment to an e-filed document that must be verified, notarized, sworn to under oath, or signed by opposing parties (e.g., Rule 11 agreements) may be e-filed only as a scanned image. Loc. E-Filing Rules Template, rule 3.4(a)-(c); JP E-Filing & E-Service Rules, rule 3.2(a)-(c). The court may also require the party to file the original document with the district clerk by traditional means. Loc. E-Filing Rules Template, rule 3.4(d); JP E-Filing & E-Service Rules, rule 3.2(d), (e).

(c) Exhibits. If an e-filed document contains exhibits, they should be e-filed as scanned images. *See* Loc. E-Filing Rules Template, rule 3.4.

(2) Signing documents. All e-filed documents must be signed with a "digital signature," and the signature block must include the e-mail address of the party's attorney or of the party, if pro se. *See* Loc. E-Filing Rules Template, rules 4.2(a), 4.7; JP E-Filing & E-Service Rules, rules 4.2(a), 4.6. The unique identifier the party received when it registered with TexasOnline constitutes a "digital signature" for each document filed through the party's EFSP. Loc. E-Filing Rules Template, rule 4.2(a); JP E-Filing & E-Service Rules, rule 4.2(a). The digital signature satisfies the signature requirements of the TRCPs or of any other law. Loc. E-Filing Rules Template, rule 4.2(b); JP E-Filing & E-Service Rules, rule 4.2(b).

2. What to e-file. Most documents that can be filed by traditional means can also be e-filed. Loc. E-Filing Rules Template, rule 3.3(a); JP E-Filing & E-Service Rules, rule 3.1(a). The only documents that cannot be e-filed are (1) citations or writs bearing the seal of the court, (2) returns of citations, (3) bonds, (4) subpoenas and proof of service of subpoenas, (5) documents presented for an in camera hearing to obtain a ruling on their discoverability, (6) documents sealed under TRCP 76a, (7) documents to which access is otherwise restricted by law or court order (in district and county courts only), and (8) wills and codicils (in county court only). Loc. E-Filing Rules Template, rule 3.3(a); JP E-Filing & E-Service Rules, rule 3.1(a). Documents that require a physical signature or that exist only in paper format can be e-filed as scanned images. *See* Loc. E-Filing Rules Template, rule 3.4; JP E-Filing & E-Service Rules, rule 3.2.

3. Effect of e-filing on deadlines. E-filing does not change a party's filing deadlines. Loc. E-Filing Rules Template, rule 4.4; *see* JP E-Filing & E-Service Rules, rule 4.3. However, a party has until 11:59 p.m. on the day of the filing deadline to e-file a document. *See* Loc. E-Filing Rules Template, rule 4.3(b). When the e-filed document is submitted to the EFSP, the party is deemed to have delivered the document to the clerk, and the document is deemed filed. Loc. E-Filing Rules Template, rule 4.3(b); JP E-Filing & E-Service Rules, rule 4.3(b). However, documents submitted to the EFSP on a Sunday are deemed filed on the following Monday. Loc. E-Filing Rules Template, rule 4.3(h) (does not apply to injunction, attachment, garnishment, sequestration, or distress proceedings); JP E-Filing & E-Service Rules, rule 4.3(h) (same). As long as the clerk receives the transmission no later than ten days after the

☆

document is e-filed, the document will be deemed timely filed. Loc. E-Filing Rules Template, rule 4.3(b). A transmission report from the party to its EFSP is prima facie evidence of the date and time of filing. Loc. E-Filing Rules Template, rule 4.3(b); JP E-Filing & E-Service Rules, rule 4.3(b).

4. Accepting or rejecting e-filing. The clerk or JP court must determine whether to accept or reject the e-filed document within one business day after receiving it. Loc. E-Filing Rules Template, rule 4.3(e); JP E-Filing & E-Service Rules, rule 4.3(e). If the clerk or JP court does not act within one business day, the document is deemed accepted and filed. Loc. E-Filing Rules Template, rule 4.3(e); JP E-Filing & E-Service Rules, rule 4.3(e).

(1) Accept e-filing. The clerk or JP court must accept the filing unless the filing is misdirected or does not comply with the filing requirements. Loc. E-Filing Rules Template, rule 4.3(e); JP E-Filing & E-Service Rules, rule 4.3(e). If the filing is accepted, the clerk must mark the front page of the document with the date and time it was filed, which is the date and time the document was transmitted to the party's EFSP. Loc. E-Filing Rules Template, rule 4.3(f); JP E-Filing & E-Service Rules, rule 4.3(f). On the same day, the EFSP will send a confirmation containing an electronically file-marked copy of the front page of the document to the filing party. Loc. E-Filing Rules Template, rule 4.3(f); JP E-Filing & E-Service Rules, rule 4.3(f).

(2) Reject e-filing. If the clerk or JP court rejects the filing, the clerk or JP court will inform TexasOnline; on the same day, TexasOnline will send an alert to the EFSP stating that the document was rejected and why. Loc. E-Filing Rules Template, rule 4.3(g); JP E-Filing & E-Service Rules, rule 4.3(g). The EFSP will transmit the alert to the filing party. Loc. E-Filing Rules Template, rule 4.3(g); JP E-Filing & E-Service Rules, rule 4.3(g).

5. E-filing fees. A party who e-files a document in a district or county court must pay the court's regular filing fees. Loc. E-Filing Rules Template, rule 4.1(e). These fees are paid through the party's TexasOnline account. *See id.* The party must also pay the $4 transaction fee charged by TexasOnline and any additional convenience fees charged by the EFSP and the county or district clerk. *See id.*, rule 4.1(f)-(h).

§5. WHEN TO FILE

Documents must be filed by the deadlines provided in the statutes, TRCPs, local rules, pretrial docketing orders, or other orders of the court.

§5.1 By deadline. A document is timely filed if it is filed on or before the deadline. See "Computing Filing Deadlines," §7, p. 26.

§5.2 Premature. Occasionally, a document is filed before the filing period begins. A prematurely filed document is deemed filed on the date of, but after, the event that begins the filing period. *See* TRCP 306c (motion for new trial, request for findings of fact); TRAP 27.1 (notice of appeal); *Padilla v. LaFrance*, 907 S.W.2d 454, 458 (Tex.1995) (motion to modify judgment); *In re Estate of Ayala*, 19 S.W.3d 477, 479-80 (Tex.App.—Corpus Christi 2000, pet. denied) (creditor suit filed before claim was rejected by representative of estate); *Perez v. Texas Employers' Ins.*, 926 S.W.2d 425, 427 (Tex.App.—Austin 1996, order) (verified motion to reinstate).

§6. FILING FEES

§6.1 Due when filed. Some filing fees must be paid when a document is filed. A fee is required for filing a suit, a cross-claim, a counterclaim, an intervention, a motion for contempt, a motion for new trial, or a third-party petition, or for requesting issuance of a citation or other writ. Gov't Code §51.317(b).

§6.2 Filing complete when paid. If a document is filed without the payment of the required fee, it is considered "conditionally filed" on the date it was tendered to the clerk. *Tate v. E.I. DuPont de Nemours & Co.*, 934 S.W.2d 83, 84 (Tex.1996); *Jamar v. Patterson*, 868 S.W.2d 318, 319 (Tex.1993). When the filing fee is paid, the document is deemed filed on the date it was originally tendered. *Jamar*, 868 S.W.2d at 319.

★

NOTE

When the filing fee for a motion for new trial is paid after the trial court loses plenary power, the motion does not preserve error for those issues that must be preserved in a motion for new trial. See, e.g., **Garza v. Garcia**, *137 S.W.3d 36, 38 (Tex.2004) (trial court was not required to review factual-sufficiency complaint in motion for new trial because fee was never paid). See "Paid after loss of plenary power," ch. 10-B, §4.2.2(2), p. 791.*

---

§7. COMPUTING FILING DEADLINES

A document that is filed or served late is not effective. Thus, calculating the time limits is extremely important. There are two rules on computation of time: TRCP 4, "Computation of Time," and TRCP 5, "Enlargement of Time." Gov't Code §311.014 also discusses computation of time.

§7.1 Computing time limits – days. Most deadlines are based on days.

1. General rules.

(1) First day. Begin counting the day after the period begins. Gov't Code §311.014(a); TRCP 4. The day the time period begins (e.g., the date of filing, the date of service) is not counted. For example, if a plaintiff is served with interrogatories on Friday and has 30 days to answer, Friday is "day 0," Saturday is "day 1," and Sunday is "day 2."

(2) Counted days. Count every day after the first day—including Saturdays, Sundays, and legal holidays—until the last day. Gov't Code §311.014(a); TRCP 4.

(3) Last day. Count the last day unless it is a Saturday, Sunday, or legal holiday. *Lewis v. Blake*, 876 S.W.2d 314, 315-16 (Tex.1994). If the last day is a Saturday, Sunday, or legal holiday, the deadline is the next regular business day. Gov't Code §311.014(b); TRCP 4; *Melendez v. Exxon Corp.*, 998 S.W.2d 266, 275 (Tex.App.—Houston [14th Dist.] 1999, no pet.); *e.g.,* *Williams v. Flores*, 88 S.W.3d 631, 632 (Tex.2002) (motion for new trial was timely filed on 32nd day after judgment because 30th day was Sunday and 31st day was legal holiday). See "Legal Holidays," §8, p. 27.

NOTE

For certain time periods that are counted backward (e.g., a response to a summary-judgment motion must be filed at least seven days before the hearing), when the last day is a Saturday, Sunday, or legal holiday, the next regular business day—counting forward—is the deadline. See, e.g., **Hammonds v. Thomas**, *770 S.W.2d 1, 2 (Tex.App.—Texarkana 1989, no writ) (when summary-judgment hearing was set for July 11, court should have considered nonmovant's affidavits in response to motion filed on July 5 because seventh day before hearing was July 4, a national holiday); see also* **Lewis**, *876 S.W.2d at 316 (Supreme Court approved of conclusion in* **Hammonds** *and applied TRCP 4 to 21-day notice requirement in TRCP 166a(c)). TRCP 4 applies to any time period under the TRCPs, not just time periods running "after" a specific event.* **Hammonds**, *770 S.W.2d at 3; see* **Lewis**, *876 S.W.2d at 316.*

---

2. Exception. There is an exception to the general rules for computing deadlines—and to make matters more confusing, the exception has its own exception.

(1) Period to act is 5 days or less. If the period to act is five days or less, do not count the intervening Saturdays, Sundays, and legal holidays for any purpose. TRCP 4. That is, start counting the day after the period begins, skip any Saturday, Sunday, or legal holiday, and count until the last day that is not a Saturday, Sunday, or legal holiday.

— ★ —

CAUTION

*Unlike TRCP 4, Gov't Code §311.014 has no provision for calculating time periods of five days or less. When computing statutory deadlines involving five days or less, ignore TRCP 4—that is, start counting the day after the period begins, do not skip any Saturday, Sunday, or legal holiday, and file on or before the last day that is not a Saturday, Sunday, or legal holiday. See **Peacock v. Humble**, 933 S.W.2d 341, 342-43 (Tex.App.—Austin 1996, orig. proceeding).*

---

(2) **Exception to the exception.** The three-day extensions of time in TRCP 21 and 21a and the five-day periods for forcible-entry-and-detainer actions in TRCP 748, 749, 749a, 749b, and 749c are counted in the same way as under the general rules. That is, count Saturdays, Sundays, and legal holidays for purposes of these rules unless the last day is a Saturday, Sunday, or legal holiday. Gov't Code §311.014(b); TRCP 4.

§7.2 Computing time limits – months. Some deadlines are based on months, not days. *E.g.*, TRCP 190.3(b)(1)(B)(ii) (discovery period in Level 2 nonfamily cases). If a number of months is to be computed, the period ends on the same numerical day in the last month as the day the period began in the first month. Gov't Code §311.014(c). If this is impossible because there are fewer days in the last month, the period ends on the last day of that month. *Id.* Thus, if the discovery period in a Level 2 nonfamily case began on December 31, the period would end on September 30, the last day of the ninth and last month, regardless of the number of days in the period.

§7.3 Computing time limits – years. Statute-of-limitations deadlines are based on years. These deadlines are computed in the same way as deadlines based on months. *See **Salahat v. Kincaid**, 195 S.W.3d 342, 344 (Tex. App.—Fort Worth 2006, no pet.); **Medina v. Lopez-Roman**, 49 S.W.3d 393, 398 (Tex.App.—Austin 2000, pet. denied).*

§7.4 Problems in computing deadlines. Computing deadlines is confusing. The rules do not describe the deadlines with uniform phrasing, and some rules apply the deadline to both filing and service, some only to filing, and some only to service. For example, TRCP 166a(c) requires a party to file and serve a motion for summary judgment "at least" 21 days before the hearing; TRCP 197.2(a) requires a party to serve responses to interrogatories "within" 30 days after service; TRCP 93(13) requires a party to file a verified denial of an Industrial Accident Board award "not less than" 7 days before the case proceeds to trial.

§8. LEGAL HOLIDAYS

The issue of "legal holidays" in relation to filing deadlines is more confusing than most appellate opinions acknowledge because the appellate courts have interpreted TRCP 4 as adopting the list of legal holidays from Gov't Code §662.003. Section 662.003 was not enacted to explain the impact of legal holidays on filing deadlines; it was enacted to inform state-paid employees which days are paid holidays. Section 662.003 does not address legal holidays for county employees. Legal holidays are a budget issue decided at both the state and county levels. The holidays for state employees are determined by the Legislature and published in the Government Code every other year. The holidays for county employees, on the other hand, are determined by the counties every year and published in their annual budgets. Because legal holidays are different for state and county employees, they are different for the different types of courts—the appellate courts follow the holiday schedule set by the Legislature, while the county courts and district courts follow the counties' holiday schedules.

§8.1 Definition of legal holiday. A "legal holiday," as used in TRCP 4, includes all days the courthouse is officially closed. *See **Miller Brewing Co. v. Villarreal**, 829 S.W.2d 770, 772 (Tex.1992).* Whether a holiday is a legal holiday for purposes of TRCP 4 generally depends on the type and location of the court.

    1. **Legal holidays for trial courts.**

        (1) **County courts.** Because a county court's personnel (e.g., the judge, clerk, and bailiff) are paid by the county, their paid holidays are set by the county commissioners court. For county courts, the term "legal holidays" in TRCP 4 includes only those days designated by the commissioners court. *Miller Brewing*, 829 S.W.2d at 772; *see also **Walles v. McDonald**, 889 S.W.2d 236, 237 (Tex.1994) (when courthouse is closed for local holiday, time to

★

file under Election Code is extended). See the shaded parts of column E in "Legal Holidays for Filing," chart 1-1, this page. Most counties observe most of the holidays listed in Gov't Code §662.003(a). However, if a holiday listed in Gov't Code §662.003 is not designated as a holiday by the commissioners court, it is not a legal holiday for purposes of TRCP 4 in that county, and the courthouse will be open. *See, e.g., **Lowe v. Rivera**,* 60 S.W.3d 366, 370 n.3 (Tex.App.— Dallas 2001, no pet.) (Dallas County commissioners court did not designate Presidents' Day as a legal holiday).

PRACTICE TIP

*To determine whether a certain day is a legal holiday for a particular county, call the court clerk or go to the county's website and search for "holidays." Do not rely on assurances from courthouse personnel (other than those in the clerk's office) that a certain day is an official holiday. See, e.g., **Seismic & Digital Concepts, Inc. v. Digital Res.**, 583 S.W.2d 442, 442 (Tex.App.— Houston [1st Dist.] 1979, no writ) (mistake of courthouse telephone operator, who told attorney that courthouse would be closed, did not extend time for filing).*

---

(2) District courts. The judge of a district court is paid by the State, and the district court's other personnel (e.g., the clerk and bailiff) are paid by the county. However, the county-paid employees, not the judge, determine whether the courthouse will be open. A district judge cannot operate the courtroom without a clerk and bailiff. So the rule for district courts is the same as for county courts—the term "legal holidays" in TRCP 4 includes only the days designated as holidays by the commissioners court. See "County courts," §8.1.1(1), p. 27.

(a) Single-county districts. Generally, district courts located in metropolitan areas are contained within the borders of one county. For example, the 11th District Court has jurisdiction and sits solely in Harris County. That court will close for the same holidays as the county courts in Harris County.

(b) Multiple-county districts. District courts in other areas of the state often have jurisdiction and sit in a number of counties. For example, the 155th District Court serves Waller, Austin, and Fayette Counties. That court will be closed for holidays in each county according to that county's commissioners court.

	A. Name of holiday	B. Date of holiday	C. Gov't Code provision	D. Appellate courts	E. District & county courts
	1-1. LEGAL HOLIDAYS FOR FILING				
1	New Year's Day	January 1	§662.003(a)(1)	Closed	Closed
2	MLK Day	January, 3rd Monday	§662.003(a)(2)	Closed	Call clerk
3	Confederate Heroes Day	January 19	§662.003(b)(1)	Skeleton staff	Call clerk
4	Presidents' Day	February, 3rd Monday	§662.003(a)(3)	Closed	Call clerk
5	Texas Independence Day	March 2	§662.003(b)(2)	Skeleton staff	Call clerk
6	San Jacinto Day	April 21	§662.003(b)(3)	Skeleton staff	Call clerk
7	Memorial Day	May, last Monday	§662.003(a)(4)	Closed	Closed
8	Emancipation Day	June 19	§662.003(b)(4)	Skeleton staff	Call clerk
9	Independence Day	July 4	§662.003(a)(5)	Closed	Closed
10	LBJ Day	August 27	§662.003(b)(5)	Skeleton staff	Call clerk
11	Labor Day	September, 1st Monday	§662.003(a)(6)	Closed	Closed
12	Veterans Day	November 11	§662.003(a)(7)	Closed	Call clerk

⎯⎯⎯⎯⎯ ★ ⎯⎯⎯⎯⎯

1-1. LEGAL HOLIDAYS FOR FILING (CONTINUED)				
A. Name of holiday	B. Date of holiday	C. Gov't Code provision	D. Appellate courts	E. District & county courts
13 Thanksgiving	November, 4th Thursday	§662.003(a)(8)	Closed	Closed
14 Day after Thanksgiving	November, 4th Friday	§662.003(b)(6)	Closed	Call clerk
15 Christmas Eve	December 24	§662.003(b)(7)	Closed	Call clerk
16 Christmas Day	December 25	§662.003(a)(9)	Closed	Closed
17 Day after Christmas	December 26	§662.003(b)(8)	Closed	Call clerk

2. Legal holidays for appellate courts. For appellate courts, legal holidays in TRCP 4 include the "legal holidays" listed in Gov't Code §662.003(a) (national holidays) and (b)(1) through (b)(6) (specified state holidays). *See* Gov't Code §662.0021 (defining "legal holiday"). But because the employees of appellate courts (i.e., the Supreme Court and the courts of appeals) are paid by the State, they are entitled to paid holidays on the national holidays and all of the state holidays recognized by the Legislature, which include the days before and after Christmas. *See id.* §662.003(a), (b)(1)-(b)(8). Thus, the days when appellate-court employees are generally "off" includes two days in addition to those defined as legal holidays. *Compare id.* §662.0021 *with id.* §662.003. Not all holidays listed in §662.003 extend filing deadlines, however, because Gov't Code §662.004 requires skeleton staffing for some, but not all, state holidays. The cumulative effect of these statutes is as follows:

(1) Closed. Appellate courts are closed, and no employees are present to accept filings, on all the federal holidays listed in §662.003(a) and the three state holidays listed in §662.003(b)(6) through (b)(8). *See* Gov't Code §§662.004(b), 662.021. When a court is closed on a state holiday, that day is considered a legal holiday for purposes of TRCP 4, which extends the date for filing. See the shaded parts of column D in chart 1-1, above.

(2) Not closed. Appellate courts must leave a skeleton staff on duty to accept filings on the five state holidays listed in §662.003(b)(1) through (b)(5). *See* Gov't Code §662.004(a). When a skeleton staff is on duty, that day is not considered a legal holiday for purposes of TRCP 4 and does not extend the date for filing. See the unshaded parts of column D in chart 1-1, above.

3. Emergency. When a clerk's office is closed on a day not designated as a holiday (e.g., for a hurricane), that day is considered a legal holiday for purposes of TRCP 4 and extends the date for filing. *See Miller Brewing*, 829 S.W.2d at 772; *see also Boone v. St. Paul Fire & Mar. Ins.*, 968 S.W.2d 468, 470 (Tex.App.—Fort Worth 1998, pet. denied) (two-hour delay in opening county clerk's office because of inclement weather did not make entire day a legal holiday and did not extend filing deadline).

PRACTICE TIP
If the issue of whether a trial court was closed on a particular day is critical on appeal, the attorney can direct the appellate court to the county's website that lists the court's holidays or file an affidavit from the clerk of the trial court stating that the day was a legal holiday.

---

§8.2 After hours. If a party is facing a nonextendable deadline to file a document (e.g., a motion for new trial), and it is after 5:00 p.m., there are five ways to timely file the document.

1. E-filing. If a county accepts e-filing, a party may e-file a document until 11:59 p.m. on the day of the filing deadline. See "Effect of e-filing on deadlines," §4.4.3, p. 24.

2. U.S. mail. A party may file a document when the courthouse is closed by mailing it. *See Miller Brewing Co. v. Villarreal*, 829 S.W.2d 770, 771 (Tex.1992). A document is considered filed the day it is mailed if it is sent to the proper clerk at the correct address, is sent by first-class U.S. mail, and gets to the courthouse within ten days

★

after the day it was due. TRCP 5. A document is "mailed" when it is deposited into a U.S. Postal Service (USPS) mailbox (not a party's own mailbox), left in a receptacle for mail at the post office, or given to a USPS mail carrier. *See* TRCP 21a. The postmark date on the envelope will be prima facie evidence of the day it was mailed. TRCP 5. See "Mail," §10.1.2, p. 31. Even without a postmark, a party can prove the date of mailing by filing an affidavit of an attorney, the clerk, or some other person. See "Affidavit," §10.1.1, p. 31.

3. Court drop box. Some counties provide a drop box for filing after hours or on holidays. Most drop boxes are located inside the courthouse, and a party who wants to file a document must contact the guard for access. Some counties provide a date-stamp device so the party filing the document can date-stamp it before dropping it into the box.

4. Fax. Some counties allow after-hours fax filing until 11:59 p.m. on the day of the filing deadline. See "Fax," §4.3, p. 23.

5. Delivery to clerk or judge. An attorney may call the court clerk and take the document to the clerk's residence to file. See "Clerk," §3.1, p. 21. If the attorney cannot locate the clerk, the attorney can call the trial judge and, with permission, take the document to the judge's residence to file. If neither the clerk nor the trial judge is available, the attorney can file the document with another judge occupying the same type of bench in the same county. See "Judge," §3.2, p. 21.

§9. SECURING ADDITIONAL TIME

If a party needs more time to file a document or to prepare for a hearing, the party should ask for it in advance.

§9.1 Motion to extend time. A motion to extend time is a request to extend the time to do some act that the rules or the court require to be done within a specified time. See *O'Connor's Texas Forms*, FORM 1C:1. TRCP 5 governs motions to extend time for all matters except discovery, which is governed by TRCP 191.1. For motions to extend time in discovery matters, see "Extending Time to Respond to Discovery," ch. 6-A, §15, p. 438; *O'Connor's Texas Forms*, FORM 6A:2. A motion to extend time should be filed as soon as it becomes apparent that more time is necessary. The longer a party waits to ask for an extension, the harder it is to get one.

1. Before deadline. When the party asks for additional time before the deadline, TRCP 5 permits the court to grant an extension of time for "cause shown," with or without a motion or notice. The party is not required to show "good cause," a higher burden, if the party files the motion before the deadline. TRCP 5. *But cf.* TRCP 191.1 (all motions to extend discovery deadlines require good cause). Even though a motion is not required, the party should always file a motion or make the request in open court on the record.

2. After deadline. When the party asks for additional time after the deadline, TRCP 5 requires the party to file a motion and show good cause for not acting before the deadline. *Remington Arms Co. v. Canales*, 837 S.W.2d 624, 625 (Tex.1992).

§9.2 Agreement to extend time. To extend the time for responding to a motion, the party seeking an extension should secure a signed agreement from the other party. TRCP 11. See "Agreements Between Attorneys – Rule 11," ch. 1-H, §9, p. 61; "Modifying discovery by agreement," ch. 6-A, §6.1, p. 429; *O'Connor's Texas Forms*, FORMS 1H:12, 6A:3.

CAUTION
The deadline to file a motion for new trial cannot be extended by the court or by agreement. TRCP 5.

---

§9.3 Motion for continuance. A motion for continuance is a request to postpone or delay a trial or hearing. *See* TRCP 252. See "Motion for Continuance," ch. 5-D, p. 336.

§10. PROVING FILING

§10.1 Proving date of filing. The easiest way to prove the filing date of a document is with the file-stamped copy. When mailing or delivering a document, include an extra copy, a self-addressed stamped envelope, and a request that the clerk file-stamp and return the extra copy. When a dispute arises about the filing date of a docu-

★

ment, however, the date the document was tendered to the clerk controls, even over the file-stamp date on the document. *Coastal Banc SSB v. Helle*, 988 S.W.2d 214, 216 (Tex.1999); *Jamar v. Patterson*, 868 S.W.2d 318, 319 (Tex.1993).

1. Affidavit. To prove the date a document was filed by mail, delivery, or fax, the party can file an affidavit of an attorney or the court clerk. *See, e.g., Coastal Banc*, 988 S.W.2d at 216 (date of filing was established by uncontroverted affidavits of court clerk and attorney, even though file-stamp indicated that document was filed on different date); *Lofton v. Allstate Ins.*, 895 S.W.2d 693, 693-94 (Tex.1995) (date appeal bond was mailed was established by uncontroverted affidavit of attorney). When relying on office routine or custom to support the inference that a document was sent, the party must provide corroborating evidence that the practice was actually carried out. *Wembley Inv. v. Herrera*, 11 S.W.3d 924, 928 (Tex.1999).

2. Mail. When a document is mailed with the correct address and proper postage, there is a presumption that it was received. *Cf. Thomas v. Ray*, 889 S.W.2d 237, 238 (Tex.1994) (case involved service of document, not filing).

(1) U.S. postmark. To prove filing by mail, a party may introduce a copy of the envelope with the postmark affixed. The date of the postmark stamped on an envelope by the USPS is prima facie proof of filing. TRCP 5; *Alvarez v. Thomas*, 172 S.W.3d 298, 301 (Tex.App.—Texarkana 2005, no pet.).

PRACTICE TIP

The date marked by a private postage meter is not prima facie proof of the date a document was mailed. **Landers v. State Farm Lloyds**, *257 S.W.3d 740, 745 n.5 (Tex.App.—Houston [1st Dist.] 2008, no pet.). When you use a private postage meter, you must introduce some evidence besides the envelope to prove the date it was mailed. See* **Texas Beef Cattle Co. v. Green**, *862 S.W.2d 812, 813-14 (Tex.App.—Beaumont 1993, order); see, e.g.,* **Doyle v. Grady**, *543 S.W.2d 893, 894 (Tex.App.—Texarkana 1976, no writ) (party filed affidavit from post-office employee that envelope was processed on postage-meter date). But see* **Ector Cty. ISD v. Hopkins**, *518 S.W.2d 576, 583 n.1 (Tex.App.—El Paso 1974, no writ) (private postage meter is some evidence of date of mailing).*

---

(2) Green card. To prove filing by certified mail, return receipt requested, a party may introduce the "green card" returned from the post office, which shows the date the document was received by the clerk, and the bar-coded, white-and-green postal receipt bearing the USPS cancellation. USPS Forms 3800, 3811. See "Return receipt – green card," ch. 1-D, §7.1.2(1), p. 38.

(3) Return receipt after mailing. To prove filing when the green card is lost or not returned, a party may introduce a domestic-mail return receipt. USPS Form 3811-A ("Request for Delivery Information/Return Receipt After Mailing"). The receipt establishes the date of delivery and the recipient according to the post office's records. *Id.*

(4) White slip. To prove the document was mailed (not received), a party may introduce a USPS certificate of mailing, the "white slip." USPS Form 3817. See "Certificate of mailing – white slip," ch. 1-D, §7.1.2(3), p. 38.

3. Delivery. To prove filing by delivery, a party may introduce a copy of the pleading presented to the clerk when the original was filed, with the clerk's date-stamp on it, or a signed receipt from a commercial delivery service such as FedEx or UPS.

4. Fax. To prove filing by fax, a party may introduce the transmission-verification report confirming the date and time the document was sent and received. See "Fax," §4.3, p. 23. Evidence showing a fax to the recipient's current fax number raises a presumption that the document was received by the addressee. *American Paging v. El Paso Paging, Inc.*, 9 S.W.3d 237, 240 (Tex.App.—El Paso 1999, pet. denied) (notice served by fax).

★

5. E-filing. To prove an e-filing, a party may introduce the transmission report from the party to its EFSP. A transmission report is prima facie evidence of the date and time of filing. See "Effect of e-filing on deadlines," §4.4.3, p. 24.

§10.2 Proving untimely filing. The presumption of receipt in TRCP 21a disappears when verified evidence is introduced that the document was not received. *See, e.g.*, *Thomas v. Ray*, 889 S.W.2d 237, 238-39 (Tex.1994) (party claiming nonreceipt did not present verified evidence).

1. Testimony of clerk. To prove that a document was not filed, the party should present sworn testimony from the clerk that the document was not received. If the clerk's office has any procedure for logging documents as they are received, the log should be produced.

2. Affidavit by USPS claims clerk. To disprove a date on a green card, it is possible to get an affidavit from the USPS claims clerk. The USPS keeps a record of each certified-mail delivery by date and number. *See Ogunboyejo v. Prudential Prop. & Cas. Co.*, 844 S.W.2d 860, 862 (Tex.App.—Texarkana 1992, writ denied).

§11. FILED DOCUMENTS

§11.1 Clerk's endorsement. The clerk must endorse each document presented for filing with the file number, the date and time the document was presented, and the clerk's name. TRCP 24. If for any reason the clerk believes a document should not be filed, the clerk must still accept the document and note on it the date it was presented for filing. If a party files a document with the judge instead of the clerk, the judge must endorse it, sign it, and give it to the clerk. *See* TRCP 21, 24, 74.

§11.2 Deemed filed. A document is deemed filed when it is put in the clerk's custody and control. *Warner v. Glass*, 135 S.W.3d 681, 684 (Tex.2004); *Jamar v. Patterson*, 868 S.W.2d 318, 319 (Tex.1993); *Standard Fire Ins. v. LaCoke*, 585 S.W.2d 678, 680 (Tex.1979). If the clerk refuses to file a document or file-marks it late, the document is considered filed on the date it was presented for filing. *See Jamar*, 868 S.W.2d at 318-19; *Mr. Penguin Tuxedo Rental & Sales, Inc. v. NCR Corp.*, 787 S.W.2d 371, 372 (Tex.1990). A party that has satisfied its duty of putting a document in the clerk's custody and control should not be penalized for filing errors made by the clerk. *Warner*, 135 S.W.3d at 684. If the date of filing becomes an issue, the party relying on the document must prove the date the document was tendered to the clerk. *See Biffle v. Morton Rubber Indus.*, 785 S.W.2d 143, 144 (Tex.1990) (affidavit stating date document was delivered to clerk's office). If a document is mailed to the clerk and the party meets all the requirements of TRCP 5, the document is considered filed on the day it was mailed. *See* TRCP 5; *see also Warner*, 135 S.W.3d at 684 (pro se inmate's document placed in properly addressed and stamped envelope is deemed filed when prison authorities receive document to be mailed).

PRACTICE TIP

*When you present a document to the clerk for filing, the clerk cannot refuse to file it because of a procedural shortcoming. See **Jamar**, 868 S.W.2d at 318-19. The clerk must file whatever document you present as long as it is in writing and properly identifies the suit in which it should be filed. If a clerk refuses to file a document, insist that the clerk take the document, note on the document that it was presented for filing, note the date and the time it was presented, and sign it. Once the clerk notes on the document that it was presented for filing, address the issue of whether it should be filed with the judge, not the clerk. See **In re Bernard**, 993 S.W.2d 453, 455 (Tex.App.—Houston [1st Dist.] 1999, orig. proceeding) (O'Connor, J., concurring).*

---

§11.3 Withdrawing pleadings. The clerk will not permit a party to withdraw a pleading from the court's file without a court order. TRCP 75.

§11.4 Lost pleadings. If a pleading is lost or destroyed during the prosecution of the suit, the parties can replace it with a copy. TRCP 77; TRE 1004(a); *Coke v. Coke*, 802 S.W.2d 270, 275 (Tex.App.—Dallas 1990, writ denied). Replacing lost or destroyed papers or records requires notice, a sworn motion, and a hearing. TRCP 77; *see In re Taylor*, 113 S.W.3d 385, 391 (Tex.App.—Houston [1st Dist.] 2003, orig. proceeding). However, the court can order a document replaced even if one of the parties does not agree to the replacement. *See* TRCP 77(b) (lost papers or records

⎯⎯⎯⎯⎯⎯⎯⎯ ★ ⎯⎯⎯⎯⎯⎯⎯⎯

during suit); TRAP 34.5(e) (clerk's record lost or destroyed); *see also* **Hackney v. First State Bank**, 866 S.W.2d 59, 61-62 (Tex.App.—Texarkana 1993, no writ) (refusal of one party to agree to replace exhibits does not automatically require new trial). *But see* **Hidalgo, Chambers & Co. v. FDIC**, 790 S.W.2d 700, 703 (Tex.App.—Waco 1990, writ denied) (under former TRAP 50(e), when the record is lost on appeal and appellant refuses to agree to a substitute, court will order new trial).

§12. COURT'S DOCKETS

The TRCPs require the clerk to keep five dockets.

§12.1 **Clerk's file docket – TRCP 25.** The clerk's file docket must show the cause number of the suit, the attorneys' names, the parties' names, the nature of the suit, the officer's return on the process (in brief form), and all proceedings in the case with the dates of each proceeding. TRCP 25.

1. Order of cases. The clerk must place cases on the docket as they are filed. TRCP 27. A case is "docketed" when the clerk places the case on the list of cases pending in the court. **Bigham v. Dempster**, 901 S.W.2d 424, 431 (Tex.1995).

2. Order of pleadings. The clerk must note on the docket every pleading, plea, motion, or application to the court for an order, regardless of its form. TRCP 21. The clerk must docket pleadings according to the title designated by the parties (e.g., motion for new trial). TRCP 71. If the court orders a pleading to be redesignated, the clerk must modify the docket and all other records to reflect the redesignation. *Id.* See "Incorrect title," ch. 1-B, §3.2.3(2), p. 8; "Incorrect title," ch. 1-B, §4.1.3(2), p. 19.

§12.2 **Clerk's court docket – TRCP 26.** Each clerk must keep a court docket in a permanent record that includes the cause number of the case and the parties' names, the attorneys' names, the nature of the action, the pleas, the motions, and the court's rulings. TRCP 26. The clerk's docket entries of rulings are made only for the clerk's convenience and are not considered rulings of the court. **Miller v. Kendall**, 804 S.W.2d 933, 944 (Tex.App.—Houston [1st Dist.] 1990, no writ). Only in a few situations can the appellate courts consider docket entries to determine a trial court's ruling. *See, e.g.*, **Escobar v. Escobar**, 711 S.W.2d 230, 232 (Tex.1986) (to determine whether court had authority to correct judgment by nunc pro tunc); **Pruet v. Coastal States Trading, Inc.**, 715 S.W.2d 702, 705 (Tex. App.—Houston [1st Dist.] 1986, no writ) (to determine clerical error in nunc pro tunc proceeding); **Buffalo Bag Co. v. Joachim**, 704 S.W.2d 482, 484 (Tex.App.—Houston [14th Dist.] 1986, writ ref'd n.r.e.) (to determine whether motion for new trial that was lost by clerk had been filed).

§12.3 **Jury docket – TRCP 218.** The court clerk must keep a docket, titled "The Jury Docket," to list the cases in which jury fees were paid or affidavits were filed instead of fees. TRCP 218; **Higginbotham v. Collateral Prot., Inc.**, 859 S.W.2d 487, 488 n.1 (Tex.App.—Houston [1st Dist.] 1993, writ denied).

§12.4 **Nonjury docket – TRCP 249.** Cases not set on the jury docket are set on the nonjury docket. TRCP 249.

§12.5 **Dismissal docket – TRCP 165a(2).** Any case not disposed of within the time standards set by the Supreme Court under its Administrative Rules may be placed on a dismissal docket. TRCP 165a(2); *In re Seals*, 83 S.W.3d 870, 874 (Tex.App.—Texarkana 2002, no pet.).

§12.6 **Unofficial dockets.** A clerk cannot establish unofficial dockets outside the rules of procedure or base dismissals on information in those dockets. *See, e.g.*, **Osterloh v. Ohio Decorative Prods.**, 881 S.W.2d 580, 582 (Tex.App.—Houston [1st Dist.] 1994, no writ) (clerk could not establish "Register of Attorneys" for purposes of dismissal notices).

★

D. RULES FOR SERVING DOCUMENTS

§1. GENERAL

§1.1 Rules. TRCP 21, 21a.

§1.2 Purpose. The purpose of serving documents is to give the other party a copy of the documents filed with the court. Recall the distinction between filing and serving: documents are *filed* with the clerk and *served* on other parties. This subchapter discusses serving documents after the suit has been filed. It does not discuss service of citation. TRCP 21 and 21a, which govern service of all documents other than citation, provide less-formal service requirements than the rules for service of citation. *Texas Nat. Res. Conserv. Comm'n v. Sierra Club*, 70 S.W.3d 809, 813 (Tex.2002). For service of citation, see "Serving the Defendant with Suit," ch. 2-H, p. 157.

§1.3 Forms. *O'Connor's Texas Civil Forms* (2012), FORMS 1B:9-10.

§2. WHAT TO SERVE

An attorney should serve all parties with a copy of each document filed with the court and copies of all other communications with the court about the lawsuit. TRCP 21. Any communication with the court about the lawsuit that is not served on opposing counsel is an improper ex parte communication unless there is a specific exception. *See* Tex. Disciplinary R. Prof'l Conduct 3.05(b)(2).

§3. WHOM TO SERVE

§3.1 Party or attorney? If a party is represented by an attorney, all documents must be served on the attorney. *See* TRCP 8. The rules of ethics prohibit an attorney from communicating about a lawsuit with a party who is represented by counsel. Tex. Disciplinary R. Prof'l Conduct 4.02. Only when a party is not represented by counsel should an attorney serve documents on the party. Once a party secures an attorney, all communications must be sent to the attorney. *Lester v. Capital Indus.*, 153 S.W.3d 93, 96 (Tex.App.—San Antonio 2004, no pet.); *Morin v. Boecker*, 122 S.W.3d 911, 914 (Tex.App.—Corpus Christi 2003, no pet.). *But see Trevino v. Hidalgo Publ'g*, 805 S.W.2d 862, 863 (Tex.App.—Corpus Christi 1991, no writ) (service of documents on party was not improper even though party was represented by attorney); *Krchnak v. Fulton*, 759 S.W.2d 524, 528 (Tex.App.—Amarillo 1988, writ denied) (same), *disapproved on other grounds*, *Carpenter v. Cimarron Hydrocarbons Corp.*, 98 S.W.3d 682 (Tex.2002).

§3.2 Which attorney? If a party is represented by more than one attorney, all documents must be served on the attorney in charge, generally the attorney who signed the first pleading or who has been specifically designated as the attorney in charge. TRCP 8; *see* TRCP 21, 21a. Service on an attorney other than the attorney in charge is not considered service. *See* TRCP 8; *Reichhold Chems., Inc. v. Puremco Mfg.*, 854 S.W.2d 240, 245-46 (Tex.App.—Waco 1993, writ denied); *cf. Kenley v. Quintana Pet. Corp.*, 931 S.W.2d 318, 321 (Tex.App.—San Antonio 1996, writ denied) (clerk's notice of dismissal to local counsel did not comply with TRCP 8, which requires notice to attorney in charge). See "Attorney in charge," ch. 1-H, §3.1, p. 54.

§3.3 How many parties? A copy of each document filed with the trial court should be sent to the attorney in charge for each party, no matter how many parties there are. TRCP 21. If there are so many parties that serving them all is burdensome, a party can ask the court for relief under TRCP 166, the pretrial-conference rule. The court may then designate certain key parties to receive documents on behalf of other parties. *See* TRCP 166.

§4. HOW TO SERVE

§4.1 Who can serve. The following persons can serve documents: the attorney of record, the party, a sheriff, a constable, or any other person competent to testify. TRCP 21a; *State v. Bristol Hotel Asset Co.*, 65 S.W.3d 638, 642 (Tex.2001).

§4.2 Methods of service.

1. Mail. A party may serve documents by mail. TRCP 21a; TRAP 9.5(b). Service by mail is complete upon mailing. TRCP 21a; TRAP 9.5(c)(1). When a party serves a document by mail, it invokes the "mailbox rule" in TRCP 21a. A document is considered served on the day it is dropped in the mailbox as long as the following conditions are met:

─────────────────────────── ✪ ───────────────────────────

(1) The document was sent by certified or registered mail. CPRC §136.001(a); TRCP 21a. Delivery by regular U.S. mail is not sufficient; it must be certified or registered. *Dunn v. Menassen*, 913 S.W.2d 621, 626 (Tex.App.—Corpus Christi 1995, writ denied). Delivery by any service other than the U.S. Postal Service (e.g., FedEx or UPS) does not invoke the mailbox rule. See "Delivery," §4.2.2, this page.

(2) The document was properly addressed to the other party at the party's last known address. TRCP 21a. Under TRCP 21a, a document that is properly addressed and mailed with postage paid is presumed to have been received by the addressee. *Thomas v. Ray*, 889 S.W.2d 237, 238 (Tex.1994).

(3) The document was mailed on or before the due date. *See* TRCP 21a. If there is no postmark, an attorney's uncontroverted affidavit may establish the date of mailing. *See Thomas*, 889 S.W.2d at 238.

(4) The attorney of record or the party signed a certificate of service stating that the filed document was served in compliance with TRCP 21a. The certificate is prima facie evidence of the date of service. TRCP 21a; *State v. Bristol Hotel Asset Co.*, 65 S.W.3d 638, 642 (Tex.2001); *Mosser v. Plano Three Venture*, 893 S.W.2d 8, 11 (Tex.App.—Dallas 1994, no writ).

CAUTION

The mailbox rule for **filing** *with the clerk differs from the mailbox rule for* **serving** *a document on the other party. The most important difference is that the ten-day grace period for receipt in TRCP 5 does not apply to service of documents on parties.* **Salazar v. Canales***, 85 S.W.3d 859, 864 (Tex.App.—Corpus Christi 2002, no pet.). See "Mail," ch. 1-C, §4.1, p. 22. Thus, when a document is mailed to the other party on the date it is due, it is considered served on the other party on the date it was mailed, no matter when the other party receives it.*

---

2. Delivery. A party may serve documents by personal delivery or receipted delivery service. TRCP 21a. See *O'Connor's Texas Forms*, FORM 1B:11. Service by delivery may be accomplished by the party, the attorney, a member of the attorney's office staff, an agent for the attorney, or a receipted commercial delivery service (e.g., FedEx or UPS). *See* TRCP 21a. Service of documents by delivery (either by private person or by commercial delivery service) is complete when the documents are delivered to the person or office they are addressed to. *See id. But cf.* TRAP 9.5(c)(2) (for appeals, documents are served when placed in control of commercial delivery service).

3. Fax. A party may serve documents by fax. TRCP 21a. See *O'Connor's Texas Forms*, FORM 1B:11. Documents served by fax are considered served on the day the fax is sent, as long as they are received before 5:00 p.m. local time of the recipient. *See* TRCP 21a. *But cf.* TRAP 9.5(c)(3) (for appeals, service by fax is complete upon receipt). If the document is received after 5:00 p.m. local time of the recipient, it is considered served on the next day. TRCP 21a. The sender's fax machine should be set to produce a transmission-verification report confirming the date and time the document was sent and received. The report should be attached to the attorney's file copy of the document, in case it becomes necessary to prove the date and time of service.

4. E-service. Besides the methods of service under TRCP 21a, a party may electronically serve documents. Loc. E-Filing Rules Template, rule 5.1(a); JP E-Filing & E-Service Rules, rule 5.1(a). E-service can be permitted by agreement of the parties or required by court order. Loc. E-Filing Rules Template, rule 5.1(b); *see* JP E-Filing & E-Service Rules, rule 5.1(b) (by agreement only). A party cannot e-serve an original petition. Loc. E-Filing Rules Template, rule 5.1(a). A party that has e-filed a document in a county or district court does not have to serve the document electronically unless the court orders e-service. *Id.*, rule 5.1(d). A party may e-serve documents whether or not a document has been e-filed. *Id.*, rule 5.1(e); JP E-Filing & E-Service Rules, rule 5.1(e). Even a party that has not registered to e-file documents can ask to receive e-served documents by setting up a complimentary account through Texas.gov. *See* www.texas.gov/en/tx-efiling/Pages/faq.aspx (contains link to www.efilingforcourts.com for setting up complimentary account).

⎯⎯⎯⎯ ✪ ⎯⎯⎯⎯

NOTE

While the mechanics of e-service are the same for all counties, the Supreme Court has approved minor variations for some counties. For a list of approved local rules by county and district, see www.courts.state.tx.us/jcit/Efiling/EfilingRules.asp. In this section, §4.2.4, and in "E-service," §6.4, p. 37, we cite the standard local rules approved by the Supreme Court and the rules for e-service in participating justice-of-the-peace (JP) courts. For the standard local e-filing rules, see the county-court and district-court templates at www.courts.state.tx.us/jcit/Efiling /EfilingHome.asp. For the JP E-Filing & E-Service Rules, see Misc. Docket No. 07-9200 (eff. Jan. 1, 2008).

(1) Deadlines. E-service is complete when the document is sent to the recipient's e-mail address. Loc. E-Filing Rules Template, rule 5.2(a); *see* JP E-Filing & E-Service Rules, rules 5.1(a), 5.2(a). However, if the document is sent after 5:00 p.m. local time of the recipient, it is deemed served on the next day that is not a Saturday, Sunday, or legal holiday. Loc. E-Filing Rules Template, rule 5.2(c); JP E-Filing & E-Service Rules, rule 5.2(c). A document must be served before or at the same time the document is filed. Loc. E-Filing Rules Template, rule 5.4(a); JP E-Filing & E-Service Rules, rule 5.3(a).

(2) Certificate of service. A party who e-serves a document must make a written certificate of service to accompany the document when it is filed. Loc. E-Filing Rules Template, rule 5.4(b); JP E-Filing & E-Service Rules, rule 5.3(b). Besides meeting the requirements of TRCP 21a, the written certificate must contain (1) the serving party's e-mail address or fax number, (2) the recipient's e-mail address, (3) the date and time of e-service, and (4) a statement that the document was e-served and the electronic transmission was reported as complete. Loc. E-Filing Rules Template, rule 5.4(b); *see* JP E-Filing & E-Service Rules, rule 5.3(b) (JP courts require #1-3 and a statement that the document was e-served or is being e-served concurrently with the e-filing of the document).

5. According to order. A party may use some other type of service if it can prove to the court that another method is necessary and the court signs an order to that effect. *See* TRCP 21a.

§4.3 Certificate of service. Once the defendant has been served with process and is before the court, all other documents filed with the court and served on other parties or nonparties should contain a certificate of service, signed by the attorney of record or the party. *See* TRCP 21a; ***State v. Bristol Hotel Asset Co.***, 65 S.W.3d 638, 642 (Tex.2001). The certificate of service should identify the person on whom it was served and, although not required, the method of service used. *See* TRCP 21a; ***Approximately $14,980.00 v. State***, 261 S.W.3d 182, 187 (Tex.App.—Houston [14th Dist.] 2008, no pet.). For the proper contents of the certificate, see "Contents," ch. 1-B, §3.2.12(1), p. 10; *O'Connor's Texas Forms*, FORM 1B:11.

§5. WHEN TO SERVE

§5.1 By deadline. A party should serve a document before the deadline established by the TRCPs, statutes, or court order. See "Computing Response Deadlines," §6, this page.

§5.2 Before hearing on motion. Motions presented to the court for an order (unless presented during a hearing or trial) must be served on all other parties at least three days before the hearing. TRCP 21. In some situations (e.g., an application for a TRO) the court can shorten the three-day notice requirement. *See id.* Saturdays, Sundays, and legal holidays are counted for purposes of calculating the three-day notice of hearings in TRCP 21. TRCP 4. Some rules require more than three days' notice. *E.g.*, TRCP 12 (motion for attorney to show authority, ten days before hearing), TRCP 76a(4) (motion to seal court records, no less than 14 days after motion is filed and notice is posted), TRCP 166a(c) (motion for summary judgment, 21 days before hearing).

§6. COMPUTING RESPONSE DEADLINES

If a served document requires a response within a certain time period, the recipient calculates the date the response is due from the date of service. The date to respond depends on the type of service used. For the general rules for computing deadlines, see "Computing Filing Deadlines," ch. 1-C, §7, p. 26.

★

§6.1 Mail. For a document served by mail, the party is considered served on the date the document is mailed. TRCP 21a. To determine the date to respond, add three days to whatever time the party has to respond to the document, counting from the date of mailing. *Id.* For example, TRCP 21a extends the minimum notice for a hearing on a motion for summary judgment from 21 to 24 days when the motion is served by mail. *Lewis v. Blake*, 876 S.W.2d 314, 315-16 (Tex.1994); *see also Cherry v. North Am. Lloyds*, 770 S.W.2d 4, 5 (Tex.App.—Houston [1st Dist.] 1989, writ denied) (when party receives request for admissions by mail, TRCP 21a adds three days to 30 days permitted by TRCP 198.2(a) to serve answers). The three-day grace period presumes that the post office delivered the document within three days after it was mailed. If there is an unusual delay, the recipient should file a motion with the court before the response is due, stating that the recipient did not receive the document within three days and needs additional time to respond. *See* TRCP 5, 21a; *Cudd v. Hydrostatic Transmission, Inc.*, 867 S.W.2d 101, 103 (Tex. App.—Corpus Christi 1993, no writ).

§6.2 Delivery. For a document served by delivery, service is complete when the document is delivered. To determine the date to respond, count from the date the document was delivered. TRCP 21a.

§6.3 Fax. For a document served by fax, service is complete on the day it is received, if received before 5:00 p.m. local time of the recipient. TRCP 21a. When a fax is received after 5:00 p.m. local time of the recipient, the document is deemed served on the next day, even if it is a Saturday, Sunday, or legal holiday. *See* TRCP 4, 21a; *Amaya v. Enriquez*, 296 S.W.3d 781, 784 (Tex.App.—El Paso 2009, pet. denied). When a party is served by fax, TRCP 21a adds three days to the time to respond, just as if the document had been sent by mail. See "Mail," §6.1, this page. To determine the date to respond, add three days to whatever time the party has to respond to the document, counting from the date the document was served.

§6.4 E-service. For a document served electronically, service is complete when the document is sent to the recipient's e-mail address. Loc. E-Filing Rules Template, rule 5.2(a); *see* JP E-Filing & E-Service Rules, rules 5.1(a), 5.2(a). However, if the document is sent after 5:00 p.m. local time of the recipient, it is deemed served on the next day that is not a Saturday, Sunday, or legal holiday. Loc. E-Filing Rules Template, rule 5.2(c); JP E-Filing & E-Service Rules, rule 5.2(c). To determine the date to respond for suits filed in county or district courts, add three days to whatever time the party has to respond to the document, counting from the date the document was served. Loc. E-Filing Rules Template, rule 5.3. To determine the date to respond for suits filed in participating JP courts, count from the date the document was served. Do not add three days. *See* JP E-Filing & E-Service Rules, rule 5.2. See "E-service," §4.2.4, p. 35.

1-2. COMPUTING RESPONSE DEADLINES	
Document served by	**Deadline**
1	Mail	Date of mailing (generally, postmark date) + 3 days + number of days to respond
2	Delivery	Date of delivery + number of days to respond
3	Fax before 5 p.m.	Date of fax + 3 days + number of days to respond
4	Fax after 5 p.m.	Date of fax + 4 days + number of days to respond
5	E-service before 5 p.m. (district and county courts)	Date of e-service + 3 days + number of days to respond
6	E-service after 5 p.m. (district and county courts)	Date of e-service* + 4 days + number of days to respond
7	E-service before 5 p.m. (JP courts)	Date of e-service + number of days to respond
8	E-service after 5 p.m. (JP courts)	Date of e-service* + 1 day + number of days to respond
* When next day is Saturday, Sunday, or legal holiday, document is deemed served on next regular business day.	

★

§7. PROVING SERVICE

TRCP 21a creates a presumption that a properly sent document was received by the addressee. *In re E.A.*, 287 S.W.3d 1, 5 (Tex.2009); *Mathis v. Lockwood*, 166 S.W.3d 743, 745 (Tex.2005); *Thomas v. Ray*, 889 S.W.2d 237, 238 (Tex. 1994). The presumption disappears when opposing evidence is introduced. *In re E.A.*, 287 S.W.3d at 5; *Wembley Inv. v. Herrera*, 11 S.W.3d 924, 927 (Tex.1999).

§7.1 Proving receipt.

1. Proving all methods of service.

(1) Certificate of service. To prove the receipt of a document served by mail, delivery, or fax, a party should call the court's attention to the certificate of service attached to the served document, signed by the attorney of record or the party. *See* TRCP 21a; *State v. Bristol Hotel Asset Co.*, 65 S.W.3d 638, 642 (Tex.2001). The certificate of service on the document is prima facie evidence of service. TRCP 21a; *In re E.A.*, 287 S.W.3d 1, 5 (Tex.2009); *Limestone Constr., Inc. v. Summit Commercial Indus. Props., Inc.*, 143 S.W.3d 538, 544 (Tex.App.—Austin 2004, no pet.).

(2) Affidavit. To prove the receipt of a document served by mail, delivery, or fax, a party can file the affidavit of any person describing the type and date of service. TRCP 21a; *Bristol Hotel*, 65 S.W.3d at 642; *see Thomas v. Ray*, 889 S.W.2d 237, 238 (Tex.1994). When relying on office routine or custom to support an inference that the document was sent, the party must provide corroborating evidence that the practice was actually carried out. *Wembley Inv. v. Herrera*, 11 S.W.3d 924, 928 (Tex.1999); *Mocega v. Urquhart*, 79 S.W.3d 61, 65 (Tex.App.—Houston [14th Dist.] 2002, pet. denied).

2. Proving service by mail. When proving receipt of a document served by mail by relying on one of the cards or slips provided by the U.S. Postal Service (USPS), the party must verify the contents of the card or slip by either attaching it to an affidavit or presenting sworn proof at a hearing.

(1) Return receipt – green card. To prove the receipt of a document served by mail, a party can introduce a domestic-mail return receipt, the "green card," which establishes the date of delivery and the person who received the delivery. USPS Form 3811; *see, e.g., Ruiz v. Nicolas Trevino Forwarding Agency, Inc.*, 888 S.W.2d 86, 88 (Tex.App.—San Antonio 1994, no writ) (when green card was not produced and other party swore document was not received, presumption of service was rebutted); *cf.* TRAP 9.2(b)(2)(B) (appellate courts will accept USPS receipt for registered or certified mail as conclusive proof of date of mailing). To obtain return-receipt service, the party must send the document by certified mail, which provides the party with a certified-mail receipt. USPS Form 3800. Although certified mail can be placed in a post-office mail drop, a party should present the document to a USPS employee and have a round-date applied to the form to show the date the article was accepted by the USPS.

PRACTICE TIP
When using certified mail, an attorney should type the certified-mail identification number on the document so certified-mail receipts can easily be matched to the document. This prevents opposing counsel from claiming that the receipt was for some other communication.

---

(2) Return receipt after mailing. To prove the receipt of a document served by mail when the green card is lost or not returned, a party can introduce a domestic-mail return receipt. USPS Form 3811-A ("Request for Delivery Information/Return Receipt After Mailing"). The receipt establishes the date of delivery and the person who received the delivery according to the post office's records. *Id.*

(3) Certificate of mailing – white slip. To prove the receipt of a document served by mail, a party can introduce a USPS certificate of mailing. *See* TRCP 21a; *cf.* TRAP 9.2(b)(2)(C) (appellate courts will accept USPS certificate of mailing as conclusive proof of date of mailing). The certificate of mailing provides evidence that a document was presented to the USPS for mailing; it does not provide proof of delivery. USPS Form 3817.

★

3. Proving service by delivery. To prove the receipt of a document served by delivery, a party can introduce the signed, dated receipt.

4. Proving service by fax. To prove the receipt of a document served by fax, a party can introduce the transmission-verification report. *See American Paging v. El Paso Paging, Inc.*, 9 S.W.3d 237, 240 (Tex.App.—El Paso 1999, pet. denied) (evidence showing fax to recipient's current fax number raises presumption that document was received by addressee). See "Fax," §4.2.3, p. 35. The report must be attached to an affidavit.

5. Proving e-service. To prove e-service, a party can introduce the written certificate of service. See "Certificate of service," §4.2.4(2), p. 36.

6. Proving constructive service. To prove constructive service, a party can prove the other party refused to accept service. *Etheredge v. Hidden Valley Airpark Ass'n*, 169 S.W.3d 378, 382 (Tex.App.—Fort Worth 2005, pet. denied); *see, e.g., Roberts v. Roberts*, 133 S.W.3d 661, 663 (Tex.App.—Corpus Christi 2003, no pet.) (P had constructive notice of judgment because she had refused to accept certified mail).

PRACTICE TIP

An addressee cannot obstruct service by refusing to accept delivery of or refusing to retrieve certified mail after notice by the post office. **Gonzales v. Surplus Ins.***, 863 S.W.2d 96, 102 (Tex. App.—Beaumont 1993, writ denied), disapproved on other grounds,* **Carpenter v. Cimarron Hydrocarbons Corp.***, 98 S.W.3d 682 (Tex.2002); see* **Osborn v. Osborn***, 961 S.W.2d 408, 412-13 (Tex.App.—Houston [1st Dist.] 1997, pet. denied).*

---

§7.2 Proving nonreceipt. The presumption of receipt in TRCP 21a disappears when verified evidence is introduced that the document was not received. *E.g., Wembley Inv. v. Herrera*, 11 S.W.3d 924, 927 (Tex.1999) (attorneys provided affidavits stating they never received nonsuit motion or judgment); *Thomas v. Ray*, 889 S.W.2d 237, 238-39 (Tex.1994) (party claiming nonreceipt did not present any verified evidence); *Cliff v. Huggins*, 724 S.W.2d 778, 779-80 (Tex.1987) (party and attorney swore they did not receive notice of trial setting); *see also Mathis v. Lockwood*, 166 S.W.3d 743, 745 (Tex.2005) (presumption did not apply because record contained no certificate of service, no return receipt of certified or registered mail, and no affidavit certifying service).

1. Affidavit by USPS claims clerk. To disprove the date on a green card, a party can secure an affidavit from the USPS claims clerk. *E.g., Ogunboyejo v. Prudential Prop. & Cas. Co.*, 844 S.W.2d 860, 862 (Tex.App.—Texarkana 1992, writ denied) (after D introduced clerk's affidavit, court concluded that P's attorney had altered number on green card to reflect earlier mailing date). The USPS keeps a record of each certified-mail delivery by date and number.

2. Testimony of attorney & party. To prove that a document was not received, a party can present sworn testimony that neither the attorney nor the party received the document. *See Cliff*, 724 S.W.2d at 779; *see, e.g., Smith v. Holmes*, 53 S.W.3d 815, 817-18 (Tex.App.—Austin 2001, no pet.) (pro se inmate submitted declaration denying he had received document). The attorney in charge of the case at the time the document was sent should testify that the document was not received. *See* TRCP 8; *Wembley Inv.*, 11 S.W.3d at 927. The testimony of another attorney in the same firm will not rebut the presumption that the document was received. *Gonzalez v. Stevenson*, 791 S.W.2d 250, 252 (Tex.App.—Corpus Christi 1990, no writ).

§8. SANCTIONS FOR FAILURE TO SERVE

TRCP 21b authorizes sanctions under TRCP 215.2(b) for failure to serve copies of pleadings and motions. See "Failure to serve – TRCP 21b," ch. 5-K, §5.3, p. 383; *O'Connor's Texas Forms*, FORM 5J:3.

✦

E. TYPES OF HEARINGS

§1. GENERAL

§1.1 Rule. TRCP 21.

§1.2 Purpose. A hearing brings the parties before the court to argue and sometimes to present evidence.

§1.3 Forms. *O'Connor's Texas Civil Forms* (2012), FORMS 1E.

§1.4 Other references. *O'Connor's Texas Civil Appeals* (2012) (*O'Connor's Texas Appeals*).

§2. NOTICE OF HEARING

§2.1 First setting. The party scheduling a hearing on a motion for an order must serve notice of the hearing on all parties at least three days before the hearing, unless the rules provide otherwise or the court shortens the period. TRCP 21. See *O'Connor's Texas Forms*, FORM 1E:1.

CAUTION

TRCP 4 seems to say that Saturdays, Sundays, and legal holidays "shall be counted for purposes of the three-day periods in rules 21 and 21a...." If the courts interpret it that way, a party may give notice on a Friday for a hearing the next Monday. Note, however, the ambiguity created by the qualifying phrase in TRCP 4 after the reference to the three-day periods in TRCP 21 and 21a—"extending other periods by three days when service is made by registered or certified mail or by telephonic document transfer...."

---

§2.2 Resetting. When a hearing on a motion is reset, the three-day notice requirement in TRCP 21 does not apply. *Magnuson v. Mullen*, 65 S.W.3d 815, 824 (Tex.App.—Fort Worth 2002, pet. denied).

§3. DUTIES OF COURT REPORTER

The duties of the court reporter are prescribed by TRAP 13 and Gov't Code §52.046. For a detailed description of the court reporter's duties, see *O'Connor's Texas Appeals*, "Duties of Court Reporter & Court Recorder," ch. 6-C, §3, p. 224.

§3.1 Attend court & make record.

1. TRAP 13.1. Under TRAP 13.1, the court reporter must attend all sessions of the court and make a full record of the proceedings unless excused by agreement of the parties. TRAP 13.1(a); *Michiana Easy Livin' Country, Inc. v. Holten*, 168 S.W.3d 777, 783 (Tex.2005); *see Rittenhouse v. Sabine Valley Ctr. Found.*, 161 S.W.3d 157, 161 (Tex.App.—Texarkana 2005, no pet.); *Palmer v. Espey Huston & Assocs.*, 84 S.W.3d 345, 350-51 (Tex.App.—Corpus Christi 2002, pet. denied); *see also* Fam. Code §105.003(c) (court reporter must record all suits affecting the parent-child relationship unless parties waive record with court's consent). In a pretrial hearing, the court reporter must make a record only if evidence is introduced in open court. *Michiana*, 168 S.W.3d at 781-82.

2. Gov't Code §52.046. Under Gov't Code §52.046, the court reporter must, on request, attend all sessions of the court and take shorthand notes of oral testimony and, if requested by a party's attorney, closing arguments. Gov't Code §52.046(a)(1)-(a)(3).

CAUTION

*Although TRAP 13.1(a) requires a court reporter to attend all sessions of the court and make a full record of all proceedings unless excused by agreement of the parties, Gov't Code §52.046(a) requires a court reporter to attend and make a full record of the proceedings only if requested by a party. Thus, it is unclear whether a party who wants a record made must request that a court reporter attend and make a record. In **Michiana**, the Supreme Court followed TRAP 13.1(a) without addressing the apparent conflict between the rule and the statute. See **Michiana**, 168 S.W.3d at 783 & n.20. Some courts of appeals, however, have held that the statute controls. See,*

HEARINGS

★

e.g., ***Nicholson v. Fifth Third Bank****, 226 S.W.3d 581, 583 (Tex.App.—Houston [1st Dist.] 2007, no pet.) (party must request record; Gov't Code §52.046(a) controls); see also* ***Nabelek v. District Atty. of Harris Cty.****, 290 S.W.3d 222, 231-32 (Tex.App.—Houston [14th Dist.] 2005, pet. denied) (applying Gov't Code §52.046; error not preserved because P did not request that court reporter record hearing and did not object to reporter's failure to record hearing); cf.* ***Langford v. State****, 129 S.W.3d 138, 139 (Tex.App.—Dallas 2003, no pet.) (criminal case; Gov't Code §52.046(a) controls, so party must request record). Until this conflict is resolved, the best practice is to request that a court reporter attend and make a full record of the proceedings. See* O'Connor's Texas Forms*, FORM 1E:2. If a court reporter does not record a hearing or part of a trial, the party must object to preserve error. See* ***Nabelek****, 290 S.W.3d at 231-32.*

§3.2 Accept & file exhibits. The court reporter must accept and mark all exhibits offered as evidence during a hearing or trial and file them with the court clerk. TRAP 13.1(b), (c).

§3.3 Preserve notes. On request, a court reporter must preserve the notes from a hearing or trial for three years from the date they were taken. Gov't Code §52.046(a)(4). See *O'Connor's Texas Forms*, FORM 1E:2. After three years, even if the case is still pending, the court reporter can destroy stale notes if no party has requested that they be preserved or transcribed. ***Piotrowski v. Minns***, 873 S.W.2d 368, 371 (Tex.1993); ***Ganesan v. Vallabhaneni***, 96 S.W.3d 345, 349 (Tex.App.—Austin 2002, pet. denied). Once a lawsuit has been pending for three years, a party should either ask the court reporter to transcribe the record or file a motion with the court to require the court reporter to preserve all notes from hearings and the trial. See *O'Connor's Texas Forms*, FORM 1E:3.

§3.4 Prepare reporter's record. The court reporter must prepare the reporter's record for appeal when requested by a party. *See* TRAP 13.1(d); *see also* Gov't Code §52.046(a)(5) (if requested, court reporter must furnish transcript of reported evidence or other proceedings); TRAP 35.3(b) (responsibility for filing reporter's record).

§4. HEARING ON MOTION

The court will not always hold a hearing before ruling on a motion. The term "hearing" does not necessarily mean a personal appearance before the court or an oral presentation to the court. ***Martin v. Martin, Martin & Richards, Inc.***, 989 S.W.2d 357, 359 (Tex.1998). If the court conducts a hearing, it will not always permit the parties to introduce evidence. Some rules provide for a hearing or submission date as a way of creating a deadline for filing the response (e.g., motion for summary judgment).

§4.1 Hearing for argument only. If a rule prohibits oral testimony at the hearing, the hearing is for argument only. When the hearing is for argument only, the party can submit a motion for the court's decision without actually making an appearance to argue the motion in court. For example, the summary-judgment rule states: "No oral testimony shall be received...." TRCP 166a(c). Because no evidence is presented at a summary-judgment hearing, the court can decide the motion on the pleadings, without an appearance by the attorneys before the court. See "Hearing on submission," ch. 7-B, §11.2, p. 622. A hearing for argument only does not need to be recorded by a court reporter. See *O'Connor's Texas Appeals*, "Reporter's record not necessary," ch. 6-C, §4.2, p. 229.

§4.2 Hearing for evidence. When a hearing is for the receipt of evidence, it should be recorded.

1. Hearing required. A few rules require the trial court to hold a hearing to receive evidence before ruling. For example, TRCP 165a, which governs the procedure to reinstate a case after dismissal for want of prosecution, requires the court to conduct a hearing even if the party does not ask for one. See "Hearing," ch. 10-F, §7, p. 829.

2. Hearing requested. If a rule authorizes a hearing for the receipt of evidence and the party asks for a hearing, the court must conduct one. For example, when a party objects to a legislative continuance on due-process grounds, the trial court cannot refuse the party a hearing. ***Waites v. Sondock***, 561 S.W.2d 772, 776 (Tex.1977).

§4.3 Submitted on pleadings & proof. Courts tend not to hold full evidentiary hearings in open court for most pretrial matters. ***Michiana Easy Livin' Country, Inc. v. Holten***, 168 S.W.3d 777, 782 (Tex.2005). The Supreme Court encourages the submission of written proof when testimony and evidence can fairly resolve factual issues. *See id.* at

✦

782-83. The Rules of Judicial Administration approve the submission of motions on written pleadings instead of by a personal appearance for a hearing. *See* TRJA 7(a)(6)(b); ***Koslow's v. Mackie***, 796 S.W.2d 700, 703 (Tex.1990). Some motions requiring evidence may be submitted on a verified motion and affidavits, without oral testimony.

PRACTICE TIP

If in doubt whether a particular motion may be submitted on the pleadings, file a written agreement stating that the parties agree to submit the motion for a ruling based on the motion, the response, and the evidence attached to the motion and response. Make sure the agreement meets the requirements of TRCP 11. See "Agreements Between Attorneys – Rule 11," ch. 1-H, §9, p. 61.

---

§4.4 Telephone hearing. The Rules of Judicial Administration permit a telephone hearing on a motion instead of a personal appearance. TRJA 7(a)(6)(b); ***Gulf Coast Inv. v. NASA 1 Bus. Ctr.***, 754 S.W.2d 152, 153 (Tex. 1988). Some courts have adopted local rules permitting telephone hearings on motions that do not require evidence. *E.g.*, ***Xu v. Davis***, 884 S.W.2d 916, 918 n.2 (Tex.App.—Waco 1994, orig. proceeding) (Brazos County).

§5. EVIDENCE FOR MOTIONS

§5.1 Live testimony. When a motion requires live testimony at the hearing, the parties must present evidence with all the formalities of a trial—the witnesses must be sworn, and the documents must be identified on the record, authenticated, and admitted into evidence. Statements made by an attorney during the hearing are not evidence. See "Attorney's appearance before court," ch. 1-H, §5.2, p. 55.

§5.2 Affidavit & other sworn proof. Some motions that require evidence and are generally supported with live testimony (e.g., a motion to abate) can be submitted on a motion and sworn proof, without live testimony. Motions that do not permit live testimony must be submitted on pleadings and sworn proof (e.g., a motion for summary judgment or motion to transfer venue). See "Affidavits," ch. 1-B, §3.2.16, p. 11.

§6. WAIVER

§6.1 Type of hearing. If a party appears for what it assumes is a hearing for argument only but instead is a hearing to receive evidence, the party must object on the record to preserve the error for appeal. ***Lemons v. EMW Mfg.***, 747 S.W.2d 372, 373 (Tex.1988). Similarly, if a party appears for what it assumes is a hearing for evidence but instead is a hearing for argument only, the party must object on the record. *See, e.g.*, ***Union Carbide Corp. v. Moye***, 798 S.W.2d 792, 793 (Tex.1990) (D's attorney filed motion for continuance and asked for additional time to file affidavits when he discovered that no evidence would be received). The party should tell the trial court on the record that it expected to present argument (or evidence) and is not prepared to go forward. The party should file a handwritten, verified motion for continuance and describe the type of notice that was sent. *See **Lemons**, 747 S.W.2d at 373. See "Verification," ch. 1-B, §3.2.15, p. 11; "Making & Preserving Objections," ch. 1-F, p. 43; "Motion for Continuance," ch. 5-D, p. 336.

§6.2 Order signed without hearing. To preserve error when the trial court signs an order without holding a hearing, a party who is entitled to a hearing and has properly requested one must file a motion asking the court to set aside the order and hold a hearing. *See, e.g.*, ***State v. Owens***, 907 S.W.2d 484, 486 (Tex.1995) (party waived right to hearing to contest master's recommendations). See "Making & Preserving Objections," ch. 1-F, p. 43.

§6.3 Motion waived. If the movant does not present evidence when a rule permits it, in some cases the movant waives the motion. For example, when a party files a sworn motion to abate and attaches affidavits, the party must still ask for a hearing and present testimony. ***Atkinson v. Reid***, 625 S.W.2d 64, 67 (Tex.App.—San Antonio 1981, no writ). If the party does not ask for a hearing and present evidence, the court will overrule the motion.

§7. SECURING ATTENDANCE OF WITNESS

When a party plans to introduce evidence at a hearing on a motion, the party may subpoena a witness to attend the hearing. *See* TRCP 176.2. See "Subpoenas," ch. 1-L, p. 84.

─────────────── ★ ───────────────

§8. REVIEW

The presumption on appeal is that pretrial hearings are nonevidentiary. *Michiana Easy Livin' Country, Inc. v. Holten*, 168 S.W.3d 777, 783 (Tex.2005). This presumption controls unless there is a specific indication or assertion to the contrary. *Id.* The presumption does not apply when the appellate court determines there was an evidentiary hearing because of the type of proceeding below, the trial court's order, or a specific assertion showing that an evidentiary hearing took place. *Id.* When an evidentiary hearing took place, the appellant must present a record of the hearing to the appellate court to establish harmful error. *Id.*

F. MAKING & PRESERVING OBJECTIONS

§1. GENERAL

§1.1 Rules. TRE 103; TRAP 33.1, 44.

§1.2 Purpose. There are two reasons to make objections. The first and most important reason is to convince the trial court of the merits of the party's position. The second reason is to make a record of the objection so that the party will be able to argue the objection on appeal as a ground for error. *See generally* TRAP 33.1 (preservation of complaints).

§1.3 Forms. None.

§1.4 Other references. Yeates et al., *Preservation of Error*, Advanced Evidence & Discovery Course, State Bar of Texas CLE, ch. 20 (2012).

§2. GROUNDS FOR OBJECTION

Almost every rule of procedure can be a ground for an objection. When a rule requires action by a party or by the court, the beneficiary of the rule may object to nonperformance or inadequate performance of the required action.

§3. TYPES OF ERROR

The type of objection and the timing of the objection depend on the type of error. If the error is committed by the jury in evaluating the facts, the objection must be made in writing, in either a motion for new trial or a motion for judgment notwithstanding the verdict. *See* TRCP 300, 320. If the error is committed by the trial judge in applying the law, the party may complain by making an oral objection in open court or by filing a written motion. See "Error in applying law," §3.3.1, p. 44; "Preserving Error," §4, p. 45. Thus, the objecting party must first decide who made what type of error.

§3.1 Role of jury. The jury's task is simple: it listens to the evidence and answers the questions the trial court submits to it by returning a verdict. The jury is the fact-finder. *Chitsey v. National Lloyds Ins.*, 738 S.W.2d 641, 643 (Tex.1987). Thus, a mistake by the jury is a mistake in evaluating the evidence.

§3.2 Role of trial judge. The trial judge can make mistakes in applying the law or in evaluating the evidence.

1. In jury trial. The trial judge plays two roles in a jury trial. During the trial, the judge decides which facts are admissible into evidence. After the judge admits the evidence and the jury resolves the fact issues by the verdict, the judge renders the final judgment. With one exception, the judge does not have fact-finding power in either role. For the exception, see "Incomplete claim or defense submitted," ch. 8-I, §7.2, p. 743. The judge is authorized only to apply the appropriate law to the established facts and sign the appropriate judgment. The judge has no discretion when applying the law. *Walker v. Packer*, 827 S.W.2d 833, 840 (Tex.1992).

2. In nonjury trial. In a nonjury trial, the judge is the substitute for the jury and has the same fact-finding power as the jury. Thus, in a nonjury trial, the judge plays three roles: (1) the judge decides which facts are admissible into evidence, (2) relying on the admitted evidence, the judge resolves the fact issues, and (3) relying on the resolution of the fact issues, the judge applies the law and signs the appropriate judgment.

———————————————— ✦ ————————————————

§3.3 Appealable error. In broad terms, there are three kinds of error made during a trial: (1) error in applying the law, (2) error in weighing the evidence, and (3) abuse of discretion. The third type of error is the most difficult to reverse on appeal.

1. Error in applying law. The trial court errs in applying the law when it misinterprets the law, applies the wrong law, ignores the law, exercises power it does not have, or refuses to exercise power it is required to exercise. *See **Walker v. Packer**,* 827 S.W.2d 833, 840 (Tex.1992) (trial court has no discretion to decide what the law is or how to apply it to the facts). Because the trial court has no discretion in these matters, appellate courts review these rulings de novo, without deference to the trial court's legal determinations. See "Review of legal issues," ch. 1-G, §5.2.1, p. 51.

2. Error in weighing evidence.

(1) Evaluating evidence. The fact-finder—either the jury or, in a nonjury trial, the judge—errs when it incorrectly evaluates the evidence. This error is challenged on appeal by allegations that the evidence is legally and factually insufficient. See "Review of fact issues," ch. 1-G, §5.2.2, p. 51.

(2) Deciding if fact issue exists. The trial court errs when it does not recognize that there is a fact issue. A fact issue exists when a party has introduced some evidence on an issue but has not proved the issue conclusively as a matter of law. Deciding if there is a fact issue is one of the most difficult tasks for the trial court.

(a) Fact issue. When there is a fact issue, the trial court must submit the contested issue to the jury and cannot grant a motion for summary judgment, a motion for directed verdict, or a motion for judgment notwithstanding the verdict. *See **White v. Southwestern Bell Tel. Co.**,* 651 S.W.2d 260, 262 (Tex.1983).

(b) No fact issue. When the facts on an issue are uncontested, they are established conclusively. When there are no contested issues to submit to the jury, the trial court should grant a motion for summary judgment, a motion for directed verdict, or a motion for judgment notwithstanding the verdict. *See **Massey v. Houston Baptist Univ.**,* 902 S.W.2d 81, 83 (Tex.App.—Houston [1st Dist.] 1995, writ denied).

For example, assume fact A is important to the outcome of a case. Before the trial starts, there is no evidence of fact A. After the plaintiff begins presenting evidence on fact A, there is some evidence of it, perhaps somewhere between no evidence and a preponderance of the evidence. Once the plaintiff makes a solid case on fact A, the plaintiff crosses the line marking preponderance of the evidence and is headed toward the great weight of the evidence. If the plaintiff produces indisputable evidence of fact A, the fact has been proved as a matter of law. The evidence of fact A went from one absolute (no evidence) through all the sufficiency stages to the other absolute (proved as a matter of law). The graph of fact A's progress looks like this:

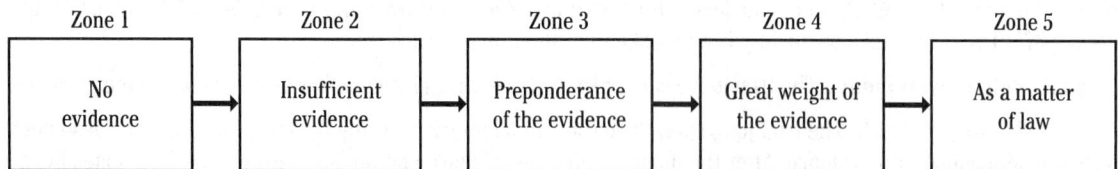

Zone 1	Zone 2	Zone 3	Zone 4	Zone 5
No evidence	Insufficient evidence	Preponderance of the evidence	Great weight of the evidence	As a matter of law

Think of the trial as a modified football game. A party scores in this game by taking the football, which represents the party's burden of proof on each one of its fact issues, beyond the 50-yard line, Zone 3. The party and its opponent face each other from opposite ends of the field, and both have the same objectives: (1) take the ball as far as possible past Zone 3 and (2) prevent the opponent from carrying the ball past Zone 3. The farther the party carries the ball down the field, the better the party proves its case. Each party wants to establish all the facts it needs by the strongest evidence it can produce, and it wants to prevent its opponent from crossing into Zone 3. If a party reaches its opponent's end zone, Zone 5, the party has proved an issue as a matter of law and there is no longer a fact issue.

─────────────── ★ ───────────────

The appellant should think of the trial as a football game that it lost. Its objective on appeal is to convince the appellate court of two things: (1) it carried the ball farther than the jury believed, far beyond Zone 3, and (2) its opponent never made it to Zone 3, as the jury thought it did. The appellant wants to demonstrate to the appellate court that the jury misunderstood the sufficiency of the evidence.

3. Abuse of discretion. The most nebulous type of error, and the most difficult to reverse on appeal, is the trial court's abuse of discretion. A trial court abuses its discretion when it (1) renders an arbitrary and unreasonable decision or (2) acts without reference to any guiding rules and principles. *Butnaru v. Ford Motor Co.*, 84 S.W.3d 198, 211 (Tex.2002); *Beaumont Bank v. Buller*, 806 S.W.2d 223, 226 (Tex.1991). A mere error in judgment is not an abuse of discretion. *Loftin v. Martin*, 776 S.W.2d 145, 146 (Tex.1989). Appellate courts will not reverse the trial court simply because they disagree with the trial court; they will reverse only if they find that the trial court acted in an unreasonable or arbitrary manner. See "Review of court's discretion," ch. 1-G, §5.2.3, p. 51.

§4. PRESERVING ERROR

Preserving error is governed by TRAP 33.1.

§4.1 Make proper objection. To make a proper objection, a party must do the following:

1. Assert valid complaint. The party must make a valid, timely, and specific request, motion, or objection. TRAP 33.1(a); TRE 103(a)(1); *In re Bates*, 555 S.W.2d 420, 432 (Tex.1977); *Till v. Thomas*, 10 S.W.3d 730, 734 (Tex.App.—Houston [1st Dist.] 1999, no pet.). Generally, if the party does not make an objection during trial, it cannot make the objection for the first time on appeal. *City of Fort Worth v. Zimlich*, 29 S.W.3d 62, 73 (Tex.2000); *e.g.*, *Mandell v. Mandell*, 214 S.W.3d 682, 691 (Tex.App.—Houston [14th Dist.] 2007, no pet.) (complaint against award of attorney fees could not be made for first time on appeal). However, in a nonjury case, a complaint about the legal or factual sufficiency of the evidence may be made for the first time on appeal. TRAP 33.1(d). Any complaint made must comply with the TREs, TRCPs, or TRAPs. TRAP 33.1(a)(1)(B).

2. Properly support it. When necessary, the party must support its objection or motion with evidence. Many motions and some objections require support in the form of affidavits or sworn testimony. *See, e.g.*, *Dillard Dept. Stores v. Hall*, 909 S.W.2d 491, 491-92 (Tex.1995) (when objecting to discovery request for all complaints filed within five-year period, Dillard filed affidavit that it had 227 stores).

3. Make it timely. The party must request relief within the time permitted by the rules and case law. *See* TRAP 33.1(a)(1); *see, e.g.*, *Zimlich*, 29 S.W.3d at 73 (city waived pleading error because it did not object before case was submitted to jury); *Vaughan v. Walther*, 875 S.W.2d 690, 690-91 (Tex.1994) (party waived disqualification of opposing counsel because she did not object as soon as conflict of interest became apparent); *Bushell v. Dean*, 803 S.W.2d 711, 712 (Tex.1991) (party waived objection to witness's testimony by objecting before witness testified instead of during testimony).

§4.2 Secure ruling on record. The party asking for relief must get the court to make a ruling and make a record of the ruling. TRAP 33.1(a)(2). See "Rulings of the Court," ch. 1-G, p. 47.

§4.3 Exception – fundamental error. It is not necessary to make a timely objection to preserve "fundamental error," which is an extremely rare form of error. Fundamental error occurs only when the record shows that the court lacked jurisdiction or that the public interest, as declared in the Texas Constitution or statutes, is directly and adversely affected. *Pirtle v. Gregory*, 629 S.W.2d 919, 920 (Tex.1982).

§5. SUMMARY CHART FOR MOTIONS

Chart 1-3, below, summarizes some of the requirements for various motions—when a motion must be in writing, when it must be verified, when affidavits should be attached, and what type of hearing should be requested. The last column indicates where in this book the motions are discussed.

★

1-3. SUMMARY CHART FOR MOTIONS					
Motion	File written motion	Verify motion	Attach affidavits	Hearing for evidence or argument	Cross-reference
1 Special appearance	Yes	Yes	Yes	Evidence	ch. 3-B, p. 189
2 Motion to transfer venue, generally	Yes	No	Yes	Argument	ch. 3-C, p. 203
3 Motion to change venue, local prejudice	Yes	No	Yes	Uncertain	ch. 3-C, §3, p. 211
4 Motion to transfer venue, Family Code	Yes	No	Yes	Evidence	ch. 3-C, §5.4.2, p. 215
5 Forum non conveniens	Yes	Yes	Yes	Argument	ch. 3-D, p. 216
6 Plea to the jurisdiction	Yes	No	Sometimes	Either	ch. 3-F, p. 239
7 Special exceptions	Yes	No	No	Argument	ch. 3-G, p. 248
8 Motion to abate	Yes	Yes	Yes	Evidence	ch. 3-I, p. 257
9 Motion for continuance	Yes	Yes	Yes	Evidence	ch. 5-D, p. 336
10 Motion in limine	Yes	No	No	Argument	ch. 5-E, p. 347
11 Motion for sanctions	Yes	Yes	Yes	Evidence	ch. 5-K, p. 377
12 Motion for no-answer default judgment	Not necessary	No	For damages	Evidence for unliquidated damages	ch. 7-A, §3, p. 588
13 Motion for summary judgment, TRCP 166a(a), (b)	Yes	No	Yes, in most cases	Argument	ch. 7-B, p. 603
14 No-evidence motion for summary judgment, TRCP 166a(i)	Yes	No	No	Argument	ch. 7-D, p. 640
15 Motion for nonsuit	Not necessary	No	No	Neither	ch. 7-F, p. 650
16 Motion for JNOV	Yes	No	No	Argument	ch. 9-B, p. 761
17 Unsworn motion for new trial	Yes	No	No	Argument	ch. 10-B, p. 789
18 Sworn motion for new trial	Yes	Yes	Yes	Evidence	ch. 10-B, p. 789
19 Motion to reinstate after DWOP	Yes	Yes	Yes	Evidence	ch. 10-F, p. 826

PRESERVING OBJECTIONS

—— ★ ——

G. RULINGS OF THE COURT

§1. GENERAL

§1.1 Rule. TRAP 33.1.

§1.2 Purpose. The purpose of a ruling is to announce the court's decision on a matter pending for resolution. The party seeking a ruling on a motion or objection must get the court to (1) make a ruling and (2) make a record of the ruling to preserve the issue for appeal. TRAP 33.1(a)(2); *see Volume Millwork, Inc. v. West Houston Airport Corp.*, 218 S.W.3d 722, 734 (Tex.App.—Houston [1st Dist.] 2006, pet. denied).

§1.3 Forms. *O'Connor's Texas Civil Forms* (2012), FORM 1G:1.

§1.4 Other references. *O'Connor's Texas Causes of Action* (2013) (*O'Connor's Texas COA*); *O'Connor's Texas Civil Appeals* (2012) (*O'Connor's Texas Appeals*).

§2. COURT'S RULING

§2.1 Judgment vs. order. A judgment is the documentation of the court's ruling that resolves the lawsuit. *See Lindley v. Flores*, 672 S.W.2d 612, 614 (Tex.App.—Corpus Christi 1984, no writ). In contrast, an order is the documentation of the court's ruling that resolves a motion or objection. *See id.* If an order resolves all the issues in a lawsuit, the order is a "judgment." *See Stewart v. USA Custom Paint & Body Shop, Inc.*, 870 S.W.2d 18, 20 (Tex.1994) (order of dismissal is a judgment). For a discussion of judgments, see "The Judgment," ch. 9-C, p. 764.

§2.2 Types of rulings. Under TRAP 33.1(a)(2), error is preserved by an express ruling, an implicit ruling, or a refusal to rule. TRAP 33.1 relaxed the requirement in former TRAP 52(a) for express rulings and codified case law recognizing implicit rulings. *Frazier v. Yu*, 987 S.W.2d 607, 610 (Tex.App.—Fort Worth 1999, pet. denied).

1. Express ruling. A party should attempt to secure an express ruling (i.e., a ruling on the record, either in open court or in writing, that specifically states the court's ruling) on each of its motions, objections, or offers of evidence. *See* TRAP 33.1(a)(2)(A). If an express ruling is ambiguous, the party should ask the court to clarify it. When a ruling is susceptible to two constructions, the appellate court will adopt the construction that correctly applies the law. *MacGregor v. Rich*, 941 S.W.2d 74, 75 (Tex.1997).

PRACTICE TIP
If, in response to an objection, the trial judge makes a statement that does not rule on the objection (e.g., "let's move on"), the polite way to secure a ruling is to say, "I am sorry, your Honor, did you sustain my objection?" The judge must then say yes or no.

---

2. Implicit ruling. If the court does not make an express ruling but takes other action that implicitly overrules the motion or objection, error is preserved. *See* TRAP 33.1(a)(2)(A); *In re Z.L.T.*, 124 S.W.3d 163, 165 (Tex. 2003); *see, e.g., Rosemond v. Al-Lahiq*, 331 S.W.3d 764, 767 (Tex.2011) (ruling on motion to dismiss for inadequate expert report implicitly overruled motion to dismiss for untimely service of report because court could rule on report's adequacy only if it was timely served); *Chilkewitz v. Hyson*, 22 S.W.3d 825, 828 (Tex.1999) (by rendering judgment on verdict, court "impliedly" overruled motion for JNOV); *Salinas v. Rafati*, 948 S.W.2d 286, 288 (Tex.1997) (ruling granting one party's motion, which was opposite of other party's motion, "automatically" denied other party's motion); *Woods v. Woods*, 193 S.W.3d 720, 723 (Tex.App.—Beaumont 2006, pet. denied) (objection to commissioner's report on division of property was implicitly overruled when court accepted the report); *Lopez v. Lopez*, 55 S.W.3d 194, 201 (Tex.App.—Corpus Christi 2001, no pet.) (ruling granting divorce implicitly overruled motion to reopen); *Amalgamated Acme Affiliates, Inc. v. Minton*, 33 S.W.3d 387, 392 n.2 (Tex.App.—Austin 2000, no pet.) (constitutional arguments in motion to dissolve injunction were implicitly overruled when court refused to consider motion). For the conflict between the courts of appeals on implicit rulings in summary-judgment cases, see "Secure ruling on objections," ch. 7-B, §10.2, p. 621.

─────────────────────── ★ ───────────────────────

3. Refusal to rule + objection. The trial court does not have the discretion to refuse to rule. *In re Shredder Co.*, 225 S.W.3d 676, 679 (Tex.App.—El Paso 2006, orig. proceeding); *Barnes v. State*, 832 S.W.2d 424, 426 (Tex. App.—Houston [1st Dist.] 1992, orig. proceeding). If the trial court refuses to rule, the party must (1) object to the court's refusal to rule and (2) make sure all of the following appear in the appellate record: the request for a ruling, the court's refusal to rule, and the objection to the court's refusal to rule. *See* TRAP 33.1(a)(2)(B), 33.2; *see, e.g.*, *In re Shredder Co.*, 225 S.W.3d at 679-80 (D attempted to secure ruling on motion to compel arbitration at five separate hearings, but court refused to rule); *Goodchild v. Bombardier-Rotax GMBH*, 979 S.W.2d 1, 6-7 (Tex.App.—Houston [14th Dist.] 1998, pet. denied) (error was waived because P did not object to court's refusal to rule); *O'Donnell v. Roger Bullivant, Inc.*, 940 S.W.2d 411, 416 (Tex.App.—Fort Worth 1997, writ denied) (error was preserved because P objected to court's refusal to rule), *overruled on other grounds*, *Perry Homes v. Alwattari*, 33 S.W.3d 376 (Tex.App.—Fort Worth 2000, pet. denied). See "Offer of Proof & Bill of Exception," ch. 8-E, p. 717.

───

PRACTICE TIP

Another way to secure a ruling from a judge who refuses to rule is to reurge the objection in a motion for new trial, along with an objection to the judge's refusal to rule. Even if the judge refuses to rule on the motion for new trial, the motion will be automatically overruled by operation of law. See TRCP 329b(c). See "Deadline to sign order on MNT," ch. 10-B, §8.4, p. 794.

───

4. Nonruling.

(1) Ruling deferred. If the trial court states that it will rule on the objection later or invites the party to reurge the objection later, the statement is not a ruling and does not preserve error. *See Bushell v. Dean*, 803 S.W.2d 711, 712 (Tex.1991); *Cain v. Rust Indus. Cleaning Servs.*, 969 S.W.2d 464, 466-67 (Tex.App.—Texarkana 1998, pet. denied).

(2) No ruling. If the trial court does not make either an express or an implicit ruling on a motion or objection, error is not preserved. *See, e.g.*, *Wal-Mart Stores v. Reece*, 32 S.W.3d 339, 347-48 (Tex.App.—Waco 2000) (D's objection to sidebar comments was not preserved because court's response asking parties to abide by motion in limine was too indefinite to constitute implicit ruling), *rev'd on other grounds*, 81 S.W.3d 812 (Tex.2002); *Martin v. Uvalde S&L Ass'n*, 773 S.W.2d 808, 814 (Tex.App.—San Antonio 1989, no writ) (because D did not secure ruling on motion to strike, error was waived).

§2.3 Timing of ruling. The trial court must consider and rule on a motion or objection within a reasonable time. *In re Kleven*, 100 S.W.3d 643, 644 (Tex.App.—Texarkana 2003, orig. proceeding). The trial court abuses its discretion if it refuses to rule on a pending motion. *Eli Lilly & Co. v. Marshall*, 829 S.W.2d 157, 158 (Tex.1992); *e.g.*, *In re Rodriguez*, 196 S.W.3d 454, 459 (Tex.App.—El Paso 2006, orig. proceeding) (trial judge did not abuse discretion by leaving on month-long vacation before ruling). When a motion is pending before a trial court, the act of giving it consideration and ruling on it is a ministerial act. *In re Kleven*, 100 S.W.3d at 644; *Safety-Kleen Corp. v. Garcia*, 945 S.W.2d 268, 269 (Tex.App.—San Antonio 1997, orig. proceeding). A party can seek a writ of mandamus from an appellate court if the trial court refuses to rule within a reasonable time. *In re Shredder Co.*, 225 S.W.3d 676, 679 (Tex.App.—El Paso 2006, orig. proceeding); *see, e.g.*, *Marshall*, 829 S.W.2d at 158 (appellate court conditionally issued mandamus to compel ruling on TRCP 76a motion).

───

PRACTICE TIP

*If you realize after the judgment is signed that the court did not make a record of some ruling, you can ask the court to reduce the ruling to writing before its plenary power expires. **Crocker v. Paulyne's Nursing Home, Inc.**, 95 S.W.3d 416, 421 (Tex.App.—Dallas 2002, no pet.).*

───

§3. RECORD OF RULING

To be effective, all orders and rulings must be made on the record, either in writing or in open court as transcribed by the court reporter. *See* TRAP 33.1(a)(2); *State Farm Ins. v. Pults*, 850 S.W.2d 691, 693 (Tex.App.—Corpus

———————— ✪ ————————

Christi 1993, no writ). The type of ruling required generally depends on the type of motion or objection. If the motion is in writing, the party should always ask the court to sign a written order. If the motion or objection is made orally during the trial, an oral ruling is usually sufficient.

§3.1 In writing.

1. Written order. The trial court should sign a written order that clearly reflects the ruling. *See, e.g.*, *McAdams v. Capitol Prods.*, 810 S.W.2d 290, 292 (Tex.App.—Fort Worth 1991, writ denied) (court's notations on motion that special exceptions were "or." or "sus." were not effective as rulings).

(1) Required by law. When the rules place a deadline on the court's jurisdiction to act on a matter, the court must make a written ruling; an oral ruling is not effective. *Walker v. Harrison*, 597 S.W.2d 913, 915 (Tex. 1980); *see, e.g.*, TRCP 165a(3) (order granting motion to reinstate must be in writing); TRCP 329b(c) (order granting new trial or modifying, correcting, or reforming judgment must be in writing); *Faulkner v. Culver*, 851 S.W.2d 187, 188 (Tex.1993) (oral order granting new trial was ineffective); *Emerald Oaks Hotel/Conf. Ctr., Inc. v. Zardenetta*, 776 S.W.2d 577, 578 (Tex.1989) (oral order reinstating case was ineffective).

(2) Not transcribed by reporter. When the trial court makes an oral ruling that the court reporter does not transcribe, the party must insist that the judge sign a written order. *Cf. In re Bledsoe*, 41 S.W.3d 807, 811 (Tex.App.—Fort Worth 2001, orig. proceeding) (when party files mandamus action without a signed written order, oral order will be considered only if it is clear, specific, enforceable, and shown by the record).

2. Signature. The trial judge should sign her name to her orders and judgments. However, the trial judge may direct a person under her immediate authority to affix the judge's signature using a rubber stamp. *In re Barber*, 982 S.W.2d 364, 366-67 (Tex.1998).

§3.2 In open court.
When the trial court makes an oral ruling in open court that is transcribed by the court reporter, the statement of the court's ruling in the reporter's record preserves the ruling for appeal. *Pride Pet. Servs. v. Criswell*, 924 S.W.2d 720, 721 (Tex.App.—El Paso 1996, writ denied) (construing former TRAP 52, now TRAP 33.1); *see* TRAP 33.2(b), (c); *State Farm Ins. v. Pults*, 850 S.W.2d 691, 693 (Tex.App.—Corpus Christi 1993, no writ).

§3.3 Docket entries.
A party should not rely on a docket entry as a ruling on a motion; a party should always get the trial court to sign an order. Docket entries are inherently unreliable. *Guyot v. Guyot*, 3 S.W.3d 243, 246 (Tex.App.—Fort Worth 1999, no pet.); *Energo Int'l v. Modern Indus. Heating*, 722 S.W.2d 149, 151 n.2 (Tex. App.—Dallas 1986, no writ). Most judges use their own shorthand for their rulings, and their docket notations are often unintelligible to others. In some cases, the court clerk makes the docket entries. *See State Farm Ins. v. Pults*, 850 S.W.2d 691, 693 (Tex.App.—Corpus Christi 1993, no writ). The docket sheet's function is limited to correcting clerical mistakes. *See Energo Int'l*, 722 S.W.2d at 151 n.2.

1. Not an order. A docket entry cannot contradict or take the place of a written order or judgment. *See, e.g.*, *Smith v. McCorkle*, 895 S.W.2d 692, 692 (Tex.1995) (docket entry indicating that affidavit of indigence was denied was not effective as order); *Faulkner v. Culver*, 851 S.W.2d 187, 188 (Tex.1993) (docket entry granting new trial was not effective); *Taack v. McFall*, 661 S.W.2d 923, 924 (Tex.1983) (docket entry and oral ruling granting motion for new trial were not effective); *N-S-W Corp. v. Snell*, 561 S.W.2d 798, 799 (Tex.1977) (docket entry granting motion to reinstate could not contradict order); *First Nat'l Bank v. Birnbaum*, 826 S.W.2d 189, 190 (Tex.App.—Austin 1992, no writ) (docket entry denying turnover relief was not order); *Grant v. American Nat'l Ins.*, 808 S.W.2d 181, 184 (Tex.App.—Houston [14th Dist.] 1991, no writ) (docket notation dismissing case was not appealable order); *Miller v. Kendall*, 804 S.W.2d 933, 943-44 (Tex.App.—Houston [1st Dist.] 1990, no writ) (docket entry denying motion was not order and did not preserve error).

2. Supplement to order. The trial court's notation on the docket sheet can sometimes be used as evidence to support the trial judge's testimony that judgment was orally rendered on a certain date. *See* Fam. Code §101.026 (rendition of judgment may be accomplished by docket notation for suits affecting parent-child relationship); *see, e.g.*, *Dearing v. Johnson*, 947 S.W.2d 641, 643 (Tex.App.—Texarkana 1997, no writ) (judge's affidavit that

---

✦

---

he orally rendered judgment and docket-sheet notation of "divorce granted" amounted to rendition of judgment); *Oak Creek Homes, Inc. v. Jones*, 758 S.W.2d 288, 290-91 (Tex.App.—Waco 1988, no writ) (judge's announcement that "I'll grant all the relief you've asked for" and docket notation of "default judgment," followed by judge's signature, amounted to rendition). See "Rendering, Signing & Entering Judgment," ch. 9-C, §3, p. 765, for the distinction between rendering a judgment and signing a written judgment.

§3.4 Letters. A letter from the trial court announcing the ruling generally is not the equivalent of a signed order or a rendition of judgment, except in the following circumstances:

1. Order. For a letter to be the equivalent of a signed order, the judge must have intended the letter to be a final, appealable order. *See Goff v. Tuchscherer*, 627 S.W.2d 397, 398 (Tex.1982). For example, a draft, directive, or subsequent order indicates that the judge did not intend the letter itself to be the order. *See Schaeffer Homes, Inc. v. Esterak*, 792 S.W.2d 567, 569 (Tex.App.—El Paso 1990, no writ); *see, e.g., Goff*, 627 S.W.2d at 398-99 (letter was not intended as appealable order because it directed attorney to submit draft of final order). Even if it appears that the judge intended the letter to be an order, the letter still must meet the requirements for a valid order. *See Schaeffer Homes*, 792 S.W.2d at 569. Specifically, the letter must (1) be filed with the clerk, (2) be written in the present tense (i.e., must not indicate an intent to be effectuated in the future), (3) be signed and dated and include the cause number and the parties' names, and (4) contain the command language that identifies an order. *See Gregory v. Foster*, 35 S.W.3d 255, 256-57 (Tex.App.—Texarkana 2000, no pet.); *Schaeffer Homes*, 792 S.W.2d at 569; *see, e.g., Barron v. Vanier*, 190 S.W.3d 841, 846 (Tex.App.—Fort Worth 2006, no pet.) (although letter used "present language," included cause number and parties' names, and was signed and dated, it did not constitute appealable order because it was not filed with clerk); *In re Fuentes*, 960 S.W.2d 261, 264-65 (Tex.App.—Corpus Christi 1997, orig. proceeding) (letter granting new trial was not valid because it required future action and was not filed with clerk).

2. Rendition of judgment. For a letter to be the equivalent of a rendition of judgment, the letter must qualify as a written memorandum and be filed with the clerk. *See Abarca v. Roadstar Corp.*, 647 S.W.2d 327, 327-28 (Tex.App.—Corpus Christi 1982, no writ); *see, e.g., Greene v. State*, 324 S.W.3d 276, 282-83 (Tex.App.—Austin 2010, no pet.) (letter qualified as memorandum because it was filed with clerk and written in present tense, stating "judgment is rendered for the plaintiffs on all claims"); *Ex parte Gnesoulis*, 525 S.W.2d 205, 209 (Tex.App.—Houston [14th Dist.] 1975, orig. proceeding) (letter outlining terms of divorce was not rendition of judgment because it was not filed with clerk and was intended as guideline for proposed judgments). See "Rendition," ch. 9-C, §3.1, p. 765; "Form of Judgment," ch. 9-C, §4, p. 767. A letter to the parties that describes the court's findings and asks the parties to prepare a judgment—although insufficient to serve as an appealable order—can serve as a rendition of judgment if it is filed with the clerk. *Greene*, 324 S.W.3d at 282; *see, e.g., Abarca*, 647 S.W.2d at 327-28 (summary judgment). Although a letter can serve as a rendition, it is not a final judgment for purposes of appeal. *See Greene*, 324 S.W.3d at 281-82. The judgment is not final, and appellate deadlines do not begin, until the judgment is signed. *See* TRCP 306a(1); *In re Bennett*, 960 S.W.2d 35, 38 (Tex.1997); *see also Greene*, 324 S.W.3d at 282 (judge who retired after rendering judgment in letter, but before signing final judgment, retained judicial capacity to sign judgment because doing so was ministerial act that merely recorded rendition). See "Signing," ch. 9-C, §3.2, p. 766.

§4. ORDER

§4.1 Form of order. See *O'Connor's Texas Forms*, FORM 1G:1. When a party submits an order to the trial court, the order should contain the following items:

1. Party names. The order should contain the full names of the parties. *Cf.* TRCP 306 (judgment must contain full names of parties).

2. Identification of motion. The order should identify the motion, the party that made the motion, whether the court held a hearing, and whether the hearing was for the receipt of evidence or for argument only.

3. Ruling. The order should resolve the issues presented in the motion.

★

---

4. Findings. Some rules require findings to be included in the order. *E.g.*, TRCP 13 (order must contain findings of good cause for sanctions). Other rules prohibit findings from being included in the order or judgment. *E.g.*, TRCP 299a (findings of fact cannot be included in the judgment).

5. Costs. Some rules permit the trial court to award costs as part of the relief granted on a motion. See *O'Connor's Texas COA*, "Court Costs," ch. 44, p. 1341.

6. Date. The order should include a line that reads, "Signed on _____, 201__," which appears immediately above the signature line for the trial judge. The Supreme Court has asked authors of legal form books to tell attorneys to draft orders and judgments that say "signed" on a certain date, not rendered or entered. *Burrell v. Cornelius*, 570 S.W.2d 382, 384 (Tex.1978).

7. Signature line for judge. The order must contain a signature line for the trial judge.

8. Signature line for attorneys. Most orders do not contain signature lines for the attorneys to approve the form of the order. Some judges, however, may require the attorneys to approve the form of the order. Approving the form of the order does not waive complaints about the ruling in the order. See "Signature line for attorneys," ch. 9-C, §4.13, p. 770.

9. Certificate of service. If the order is sent to a party or the court separately from a motion or response, the order must contain a certificate of service; however, if the order is served on the other party with a motion or response, the order does not need to have a separate certificate of service. *See* TRCP 21. The certificate of service on the motion or response must list the order as one of the documents served on the other party. See "Certificate of service," ch. 1-B, §4.1.10, p. 20.

§4.2 Changing the order. For the time limits for changing orders, see "Power to Change Judgment," ch. 9-C, §7, p. 778; "Deadline to change order on MNT," ch. 10-B, §8.5, p. 795.

§5. REVIEW

§5.1 Challenging ruling. There are three ways to challenge a ruling of the trial court.

1. Appeal after final judgment. Most rulings are challenged after the trial court renders a final judgment. See *O'Connor's Texas Appeals*, "Appeals from final judgments or orders," ch. 1-B, §2.1, p. 5.

2. Interlocutory appeal. An interlocutory (i.e., nonfinal) order can generally be appealed before final judgment if the appeal is authorized by statute or rule. See *O'Connor's Texas Appeals*, "Appeals from interlocutory orders," ch. 1-B, §2.3, p. 9. The majority of interlocutory appeals are authorized by CPRC §51.014. See *O'Connor's Texas Appeals*, "Motion for Interlocutory Appeal & Stay Pending Appeal," ch. 3-P, p. 148.

3. Mandamus. Any ruling that cannot be reviewed by either an appeal after final judgment or an interlocutory appeal can be challenged by mandamus. See *O'Connor's Texas Appeals*, "Writ of Mandamus," ch. 10-B, p. 343.

§5.2 Standards of review.

1. Review of legal issues. Legal issues are reviewed de novo, without deference to the trial court's decision. *Interstate Northborough Prtshp. v. State*, 66 S.W.3d 213, 220 (Tex.2001); *State v. Heal*, 917 S.W.2d 6, 9 (Tex.1996). The trial court has no discretion to decide what the law is or how to apply it to the facts. *Walker v. Packer*, 827 S.W.2d 833, 840 (Tex.1992). See *O'Connor's Texas Appeals*, "De novo," ch. 1-G, §6.1, p. 51.

2. Review of fact issues. Appellate courts will defer to the trial court's discretionary rulings when reviewing issues of fact. *See Walker*, 827 S.W.2d at 839-40; *Williams v. Chisolm*, 111 S.W.3d 811, 815 (Tex.App.—Houston [1st Dist.] 2003, no pet.). The appellate court cannot substitute its judgment for that of the trial court. *Walker*, 827 S.W.2d at 839. See *O'Connor's Texas Appeals*, "Legal & factual sufficiency," ch. 1-G, §6.3, p. 51.

3. Review of court's discretion. When the ruling was within the trial court's discretion, the inquiry on appeal is (1) did the trial court have sufficient information to exercise its discretion, and if it did, (2) did the trial court err in its application of discretion? *Heritage Res. v. Hill*, 104 S.W.3d 612, 618 (Tex.App.—El Paso 2003, no pet.).

★

Appellate courts will not reverse the trial court simply because they disagree with the trial court; they will reverse only if they find the trial court acted in an unreasonable or arbitrary manner. *Butnaru v. Ford Motor Co.*, 84 S.W.3d 198, 211 (Tex.2002); *Beaumont Bank v. Buller*, 806 S.W.2d 223, 226 (Tex.1991). See *O'Connor's Texas Appeals*, "Abuse of discretion," ch. 1-G, §6.2, p. 51.

H. THE ATTORNEY

§1. GENERAL

§1.1 Rules. TRCP 7-14. See Gov't Code §81.102 (requirement of state-bar membership).

§1.2 Purpose. A party has the right to be represented by the counsel of its choice. *Spinks v. Brown*, 103 S.W.3d 452, 459 (Tex.App.—San Antonio 2002, pet. denied); *see* TRCP 7. Unless there is a compelling reason, courts should not deprive litigants of this right. *Keller Indus. v. Blanton*, 804 S.W.2d 182, 185 (Tex.App.—Houston [14th Dist.] 1991, orig. proceeding).

§1.3 Forms. *O'Connor's Texas Civil Forms* (2012), FORMS 1H; *O'Connor's Texas Causes of Action Pleadings* (2012), FORMS 49 (*O'Connor's COA Pleadings*).

§1.4 Other references. Hinson & Anderson, *Attorney Disqualification*, 72 Tex.B.J. 828 (Nov.2009); *O'Connor's CPRC Plus* (2012-13) (*O'Connor's CPRC*); *O'Connor's Texas Causes of Action* (2013) (*O'Connor's Texas COA*); *O'Connor's Texas Civil Appeals* (2012) (*O'Connor's Texas Appeals*).

§2. APPEARING BEFORE TEXAS COURTS

§2.1 Requirements. To practice law in Texas state courts, an attorney must be a member of the State Bar of Texas, which is governed by the State Bar Act and is administratively controlled by the Texas Supreme Court. Gov't Code §81.102; *Daves v. State Bar*, 691 S.W.2d 784, 786 (Tex.App.—Amarillo 1985, writ ref'd n.r.e.). The Board of Law Examiners, appointed by the Supreme Court, is empowered to investigate the fitness and moral character of each license applicant. Gov't Code §82.028(a); *see id.* §82.001; *Board of Law Exam'rs v. Stevens*, 868 S.W.2d 773, 776 (Tex. 1994).

§2.2 Limited practice of law. The Supreme Court has the authority to make rules prescribing the procedure for limited practice of law by attorneys (including military attorneys) licensed in another jurisdiction, law students, unlicensed law-school graduates who are attending or have attended a law school approved by the Supreme Court, and foreign legal consultants. Gov't Code §81.102(b) (attorneys licensed in other jurisdiction, students, and unlicensed graduates), §82.036 (foreign attorneys); *e.g.*, Tex. R. Govern. Bar Adm'n XIV (foreign legal consultants), XXII (military attorneys).

1. Nonresident attorneys.

(1) Definition. A nonresident attorney is a person who resides in and is licensed to practice law in a state other than Texas and is not a member of the State Bar of Texas. Gov't Code §82.0361(a).

(2) Appearance in Texas court. A nonresident attorney may apply for permission to appear in a Texas state court by a sworn motion requesting admission to the court "pro hac vice," which means "for this one particular occasion." *See Keller Indus. v. Blanton*, 804 S.W.2d 182, 184 (Tex.App.—Houston [14th Dist.] 1991, orig. proceeding); *Commercial Credit & Control Data Corp. v. Wheeler*, 756 S.W.2d 769, 770-71 (Tex.App.—Corpus Christi 1988, writ denied). The procedure is governed by the Rules Governing Admission to the Bar of Texas, Rule XIX, "Requirements for Participation in Texas Proceedings by a Non-Resident Attorney," which can be found on the Texas Board of Law Examiners website at www.ble.state.tx.us, by selecting "Rulebook" from the main menu. The nonresident attorney must file two motions. See *O'Connor's Texas Forms*, FORMS 1H:2, 3.

(a) Motion by nonresident attorney. The nonresident attorney must file a sworn motion containing (1) her office address, telephone number, and, if available, fax number, (2) the name and State Bar card number of an attorney licensed in Texas with whom she will be associated in the trial, and that attorney's office address,

✦

telephone number, and, if available, fax number, (3) a list of all Texas cases, including cause numbers and captions, in which she has appeared or sought leave to appear or participate within the past two years, (4) a list of jurisdictions in which she is licensed, and a statement whether she is an active member in good standing in each of those jurisdictions, (5) a statement whether she has been the subject of disciplinary action during the last five years by the bar or courts of any jurisdiction in which she is licensed, and a description of any such actions, (6) a statement that she has not been denied admission to the courts of any state or to any federal court during the last five years, and (7) a statement that she is familiar with the rules of the State Bar of Texas governing the conduct of its members and will comply with those rules as long as the trial or hearing is pending. Tex. R. Govern. Bar Adm'n XIX(a); *see Keller Indus.*, 804 S.W.2d at 184 (requirements 2, 5-7).

(b) Motion by Texas attorney. The nonresident attorney must also attach a sworn motion from the Texas attorney with whom she will be associated in the trial. Tex. R. Govern. Bar Adm'n XIX(b). The motion must state that the Texas attorney (1) is associated with the nonresident attorney on the case, is employed as an attorney on the case, and will personally participate in the hearings and trial, (2) is a practicing attorney and a member in good standing of the State Bar of Texas, and (3) finds the nonresident attorney to be a reputable attorney and recommends that the nonresident attorney be permitted to practice in this proceeding before the court. *See id.*

(3) Fees. A nonresident attorney requesting permission to appear in a Texas state court must pay a $250 fee for each case in which the attorney wants to participate. Gov't Code §82.0361(b). The nonresident attorney must pay the fee to the Board of Law Examiners before filing the pro hac vice motion and must provide proof of payment to the court in which the attorney wants to participate. *Id.* §82.0361(b), (f). The fee may be waived or reduced for a nonresident attorney who represents an indigent. *Id.* §82.0361(e).

2. Nonresident military attorneys. Under Rule XXII of the Texas Rules Governing Admission to the Bar, military attorneys who are full-time, active-duty military officers stationed in Texas but licensed in another jurisdiction can represent military servicemembers or their dependents in limited civil proceedings. This rule does not prevent a military attorney from applying for permission to appear pro hac vice. Tex. R. Govern. Bar Adm'n XXII, §1. See "Motion by nonresident attorney," §2.2.1(2)(a), p. 52.

3. Law students & law-school graduates. Under Gov't Code §81.102(b) and the Rules & Regulations Governing the Participation of Qualified Law Students & Qualified Unlicensed Law School Graduates, law students and unlicensed law-school graduates have a limited ability to participate in the practice of law. See *O'Connor's Texas Forms*, FORM 1H:5.

4. Foreign legal consultants. Under Rule XIV of the Texas Rules Governing Admission to the Bar, foreign attorneys have a limited ability to participate in the practice of law as foreign legal consultants.

§2.3 Pro se representation.

1. Individual. An individual litigant has the right to represent herself without an attorney. TRCP 7; *Ayres v. Canales*, 790 S.W.2d 554, 557 (Tex.1990); *Thomas v. Anderson*, 861 S.W.2d 58, 61 n.1 (Tex.App.—El Paso 1993, no writ); *Nichols v. Martin*, 776 S.W.2d 621, 623 (Tex.App.—Tyler 1989, no writ). A court cannot deny a party the right to self-representation, nor can it order a party to be represented by an attorney unless the lack of an attorney is used to abuse the continuance privilege. *Ex parte Shaffer*, 649 S.W.2d 300, 302 (Tex.1983). A party acting pro se must comply with substantive law and procedural rules. *Martinez v. Leeds*, 218 S.W.3d 845, 848 (Tex.App.—El Paso 2007, no pet.). A party represented by an attorney cannot also proceed pro se. *Posner v. Dallas Cty. Child Welfare Unit*, 784 S.W.2d 585, 588 (Tex.App.—Eastland 1990, writ denied). A person not licensed as an attorney cannot represent another person as a "next friend" under TRCP 44. *Jimison v. Mann*, 957 S.W.2d 860, 861 (Tex.App.—Amarillo 1997, no writ).

2. Corporation. A corporation cannot be represented pro se by an officer who is not an attorney. *Dell Dev. Corp. v. Best Indus. Uniform Sup.*, 743 S.W.2d 302, 303 (Tex.App.—Houston [14th Dist.] 1987, writ denied); *see Kunstoplast v. Formosa Plastics Corp.*, 937 S.W.2d 455, 456 (Tex.1996) (although corporation must generally

THE ATTORNEY

━━━━━━━━━━━━━━━━━━━━━━━━ ✦ ━━━━━━━━━━━━━━━━━━━━━━━━

be represented by attorney, nonattorney may perform specific ministerial tasks, like depositing cash with clerk in lieu of cost bond). A corporation must appear and be represented by an attorney. *Electronic Data Sys. v. Tyson*, 862 S.W.2d 728, 737 (Tex.App.—Dallas 1993, orig. proceeding). The one exception is that a corporation may appear pro se in a small-claims court. Gov't Code §28.003(e).

3. Unincorporated business. A business entity that is not incorporated (e.g., a sole proprietorship or partnership) can be represented pro se by an owner who is not an attorney. *See Holberg & Co. v. Citizens Nat'l Assur. Co.*, 856 S.W.2d 515, 518 (Tex.App.—Houston [1st Dist.] 1993, no writ) (unincorporated sole proprietorship does not exist apart from its owner).

§3. DESIGNATION OF ATTORNEYS

§3.1 Attorney in charge. The attorney whose signature appears first on a party's first pleading is the "attorney in charge," unless another attorney is specifically designated. TRCP 8; *In re K.L.R.*, 162 S.W.3d 291, 299 (Tex. App.—Tyler 2005, no pet.); *Joyner v. Commission for Lawyer Discipline*, 102 S.W.3d 344, 347 (Tex.App.—Dallas 2003, no pet.). The attorney in charge, also called lead counsel, is responsible for the lawsuit. TRCP 8, 21; *Palmer v. Cantrell*, 747 S.W.2d 39, 41 (Tex.App.—Houston [1st Dist.] 1988, no writ). All communications from the court or other attorneys must be sent to the attorney in charge. TRCP 8; *City of Tyler v. Beck*, 196 S.W.3d 784, 787 (Tex.2006); *see, e.g.*, *Reichhold Chems., Inc. v. Puremco Mfg.*, 854 S.W.2d 240, 246 (Tex.App.—Waco 1993, writ denied) (service on cocounsel to attorney in charge was not effective). However, another attorney may file a motion or take other action on behalf of the party. *E.g.*, *City of Tyler*, 196 S.W.3d at 787 (motions filed by attorney not designated as attorney in charge were not void).

§3.2 Attorneys of record. The attorneys of record are all the attorneys who have made an appearance in the case or whose names appear in the pleadings, including the attorney in charge. Thirteen rules of procedure refer to the attorney of record: TRCP 21a, 44, 57, 119a, 130, 165a, 176.5, 306a, 315, 572, 655, 749a, and 791.

NOTE
There is a difference between "attorney in charge" and "attorney of record." While there can be only one attorney in charge for each party, a party may be represented by many attorneys of record. See TRCP 21a.

§4. AUTHORITY OF ATTORNEY

§4.1 Representing an individual. A party must authorize an attorney to bring suit. *See* TRCP 12; *Vela v. Vela*, 763 S.W.2d 601, 602 (Tex.App.—San Antonio 1988, writ denied).

§4.2 Representing a corporation. A corporation's board of directors must authorize the hiring of an attorney. *Square 67 Dev. Corp. v. Red Oak State Bank*, 559 S.W.2d 136, 138 (Tex.App.—Waco 1977, writ ref'd n.r.e.). Unless permitted by the bylaws or a directors' resolution, the president of the corporation has no authority to conduct litigation for the corporation. *Kaspar v. Thorne*, 755 S.W.2d 151, 154 (Tex.App.—Dallas 1988, no writ); *Valley Int'l Props. v. Brownsville S&L Ass'n*, 581 S.W.2d 222, 227 (Tex.App.—Corpus Christi 1979, no writ); *see* Bus. Orgs. Code §§3.101, 3.103, 21.401.

§4.3 Representing other entities. The authority to represent other business entities (e.g., joint ventures) depends largely on the agreements that formed the entity. *See, e.g.*, *Miller v. Stout*, 706 S.W.2d 785, 787 (Tex. App.—San Antonio 1986, no writ) (joint-venture agreement did not require all members to approve filing of suit).

§4.4 Challenging authority. To challenge an attorney's authority to represent the other party, see "Disqualification," §8, p. 57.

§5. COMMUNICATIONS WITH COURT

§5.1 No ex parte communications. Ex parte communications with the judge involve fewer than all the parties. *In re Thoma*, 873 S.W.2d 477, 496 (Tex.Rev.Trib.1994, no appeal). Except in limited circumstances, a judge cannot directly or indirectly initiate, permit, or consider ex parte or other private communications about the merits of a pending or upcoming judicial proceeding. Tex. Code Jud. Conduct, Canon 3(B)(8); *U.S. Gov't v. Marks*, 949 S.W.2d 320,

---

★

---

325 (Tex.1997); *Barnes v. Whittington*, 751 S.W.2d 493, 495 n.1 (Tex.1988); *In re Thoma*, 873 S.W.2d at 496. A judge cannot conduct private proceedings involving the adjudication of causes. *In re Thoma*, 873 S.W.2d at 496. The prohibition on communications with the court about the merits of the case extends to communications with the court's staff. *See, e.g., In re J.B.K.*, 931 S.W.2d 581, 583-84 (Tex.App.—El Paso 1996, order) (attorney should not have asked staff person what the chances were and if he should settle case).

§5.2 Attorney's appearance before court. An attorney's unsworn statements are not evidence. *U.S. Gov't v. Marks*, 949 S.W.2d 320, 326-27 (Tex.1997). However, an attorney's unsworn statement can be considered as evidence on appeal if the other side did not object at trial. *Banda v. Garcia*, 955 S.W.2d 270, 272 (Tex.1997). Texas Disciplinary Rule of Professional Conduct 3.03 forbids an attorney from making false statements of material fact or law to a tribunal.

1. To argue. The attorney does not need to be sworn when she is merely arguing the facts or the law. *See Las Palmas Med. Ctr. v. Moore*, 349 S.W.3d 57, 67 (Tex.App.—El Paso 2010, pet. denied).

2. To present evidence. An attorney's statement of fact must be under oath to be considered as evidence. *Banda*, 955 S.W.2d at 272; *see, e.g., Casino Magic Corp. v. King*, 43 S.W.3d 14, 20 (Tex.App.—Dallas 2001, pet. denied) (in garnishment action, attorney's unsworn statement that D was ex-husband's employer and thus liable for failing to withhold child support was not evidence).

(1) Objection to lack of oath. When an attorney who is not under oath presents facts as evidence to the court, the other party should object and ask that the attorney be sworn and subjected to cross-examination. *See Banda*, 955 S.W.2d at 272.

(2) Waiver of oath. When the other party is aware the attorney is testifying and does not object, the administration of the oath is waived. *Banda*, 955 S.W.2d at 272; *Knie v. Piskun*, 23 S.W.3d 455, 463 (Tex.App.—Amarillo 2000, pet. denied); *see, e.g., Fullenwider v. American Guar. & Liab. Ins.*, 821 S.W.2d 658, 662 (Tex.App.—San Antonio 1991, writ denied) (when issue was timely supplementation of interrogatory answers, attorney's statements were clearly regarded as evidence). However, if the other party is not in a position to object (e.g., in a default-judgment case), the administration of the oath is not waived. *See De La Garza v. Salazar*, 851 S.W.2d 380, 383 (Tex.App.—San Antonio 1993, no writ).

§6. COMMUNICATIONS FROM COURT

§6.1 Service of notice.

1. Most notices. Notices must be given by one of the following methods: (1) by delivery to the person, (2) by courier with receipted delivery, (3) by certified or registered mail, (4) by fax, or (5) as directed by court order. TRCP 21a; *see, e.g., P. Bosco & Sons Contracting Co. v. Conley, Lott, Nichols Mach. Co.*, 629 S.W.2d 142, 143 (Tex.App.—Dallas 1982, writ ref'd n.r.e.) (notification of trial setting sent by postcard, without direction from judge to do so, did not meet requirements of TRCP 21a).

2. Exceptions. Some rules permit notices to be sent by first-class mail. *E.g.*, TRCP 165a(1) (clerk must mail notice of intent to dismiss and must send notice of dismissal according to TRCP 306a(3)), TRCP 239a (clerk must mail notice of default judgment), TRCP 306a(3) (clerk must use first-class mail to send notice of judgment).

§6.2 Sent to attorney or party.

1. Attorney. When a party is represented by an attorney, notices must be sent to the attorney. *See* TRCP 21a. If the party is represented by more than one attorney, notices must be sent to the attorney in charge. *See* TRCP 8 (all communications must be sent to attorney in charge), TRCP 21 (copy of pleadings must be sent to attorney in charge); *Loffland Bros. v. Downey*, 822 S.W.2d 249, 251 (Tex.App.—Houston [1st Dist.] 1991, orig. proceeding) (all communications must be sent to attorney in charge). Two rules require notices to be sent to all attorneys of record, not just the attorney in charge: TRCP 165a (notice of dismissal) and TRCP 306a (notice of signing of a final judgment or an appealable order). *Cannon v. ICO Tubular Servs.*, 905 S.W.2d 380, 388 (Tex.App.—Houston [1st Dist.] 1995, no writ).

⭐

---

2. Party. When a party is pro se, notices must be sent to the party. *See* TRCP 21a; *General Elec. Co. v. Falcon Ridge Apts., Jt.V.*, 811 S.W.2d 942, 943 (Tex.1991) (notice to dismiss).

§6.3 Address. The attorney's address (or the party's, if pro se) must be included in the signature block to all pleadings and discovery. See "Signature block," ch. 1-B, §3.2.11, p. 9. The rules do not state how the clerk or other parties are to determine the attorney's or party's current address. *See* TRCP 21, 21a. Four courts have interpreted TRCP 165a(1) as requiring that notices of intent to dismiss be sent to the attorney's address shown on the docket or the papers on file with the court. *E.g.*, *Perdue v. Patten Corp.*, 142 S.W.3d 596, 605 (Tex.App.—Austin 2004, no pet.); *Ewton v. Gayken*, 130 S.W.3d 382, 384 (Tex.App.—Beaumont 2004, pet. denied); *Osterloh v. Ohio Decorative Prods.*, 881 S.W.2d 580, 582 (Tex.App.—Houston [1st Dist.] 1994, no writ); *see Dickerson v. Sonat Expl. Co.*, 975 S.W.2d 339, 341-42 (Tex.App.—Tyler 1998, pet. denied) (when notices are returned as undeliverable, the court should reexamine the file to determine whether there is evidence of a more recent address). Notices to pro se parties must be sent to their "last known address." TRCP 21a. Under CPRC §30.015, a party's current address must be provided to the court. See "Notice of party's name & address," ch. 1-B, §3.2.17, p. 13.

§7. WITHDRAWAL

The parties must give the trial court specific and unambiguous notice when an attorney withdraws or is substituted. *Palkovic v. Cox*, 792 S.W.2d 743, 745 (Tex.App.—Houston [14th Dist.] 1990, writ denied) (signing amended petition is not a substitution of counsel).

§7.1 Termination by client. A client may discharge its attorney at any time, even without cause. *Rogers v. Clinton*, 794 S.W.2d 9, 10 n.1 (Tex.1990). Once an attorney is discharged, she must withdraw from the case and cannot continue to appear or file motions for the party. *See, e.g.*, *Bloom v. Graham*, 825 S.W.2d 244, 248 (Tex.App.—Fort Worth 1992, writ denied) (attorney was sanctioned under TRCP 13 for filing groundless pleadings because he filed motions after discharge).

§7.2 Withdrawal by attorney. An attorney cannot withdraw from a case without satisfying the requirements of TRCP 10. *Rogers v. Clinton*, 794 S.W.2d 9, 10 n.1 (Tex.1990); *Moss v. Malone*, 880 S.W.2d 45, 49-50 (Tex.App.—Tyler 1994, writ denied).

1. Motion. To withdraw, the attorney must file a written motion showing good cause. TRCP 10; *e.g.*, *In re Daniels*, 138 S.W.3d 31, 32-33 (Tex.App.—San Antonio 2004, orig. proceeding) (withdrawal was justified because client did not fulfill obligations under agreement, including payment of attorney fees, and continued representation would have been financially burdensome to attorney). See *O'Connor's Texas Forms*, FORM 1H:6. Depending on whether an attorney is to be substituted, the motion must also state the following:

(1) Substitute attorney. If another attorney is to be substituted, the motion must state (1) the new attorney's name, address, telephone and fax numbers, and State Bar of Texas number, (2) that the client approves of the substitution, and (3) that the withdrawal is not for delay only. TRCP 10; *see Spinks v. Brown*, 103 S.W.3d 452, 459-60 (Tex.App.—San Antonio 2002, pet. denied).

(2) No substitute attorney. If no attorney is to be substituted, the motion must state (1) that a copy of the motion was delivered to the client, (2) that the client was notified in writing of its right to object to the motion, (3) whether the client consents to the motion, (4) the client's last known address, and (5) all pending settings and deadlines. TRCP 10; *Moss*, 880 S.W.2d at 49. *But see Williams v. Bank One*, 15 S.W.3d 110, 113-14 (Tex.App.—Waco 1999, no pet.) (attorney's failure to inform client of right to object was harmless when court gave party additional 42 days to hire new counsel).

2. Ruling. If the court denies the motion to withdraw, the attorney must continue her representation in the case. *See* TRCP 10. If the court grants the motion to withdraw, the attorney must immediately notify the party in writing of any additional settings or deadlines that the attorney has knowledge of at the time of withdrawal and that the attorney has not already notified the party about. *Id.* The court can impose further conditions if it grants the motion. *Id.*

★

§8. DISQUALIFICATION

Because disqualification of a party's attorney is a severe remedy, the courts must follow exacting standards when considering motions to disqualify. *In re Nitla S.A. de C.V.*, 92 S.W.3d 419, 422 (Tex.2002); *Spears v. Fourth Ct. of Appeals*, 797 S.W.2d 654, 656 (Tex.1990).

§8.1 Timely filed motion. A motion to disqualify an attorney must be timely filed. *In re George*, 28 S.W.3d 511, 513 (Tex.2000); *see, e.g., In re American Home Prods.*, 985 S.W.2d 68, 73 (Tex.1998) (two-month delay did not constitute waiver); *Vaughan v. Walther*, 875 S.W.2d 690, 691 (Tex.1994) (six-month delay was too long and constituted waiver). See *O'Connor's Texas Forms*, FORM 1H:11.

§8.2 Grounds for disqualification. To disqualify an attorney, the movant must show that (1) the attorney violated the Texas Disciplinary Rules of Professional Conduct (the "Rules") or (2) other circumstances justify the attorney's disqualification.

1. Violation of disciplinary rules. An attorney can be disqualified from representing a client if she violates the Texas Disciplinary Rules of Professional Conduct. *See In re Users Sys. Servs.*, 22 S.W.3d 331, 334 (Tex. 1999); *In re Epic Holdings, Inc.*, 985 S.W.2d 41, 48 (Tex.1998); *In re Brittingham*, 319 S.W.3d 95, 98 (Tex. App.—San Antonio 2010, orig. proceeding). The violation must be established with specificity; mere allegations of unethical conduct or evidence showing a remote possibility of a violation is not enough to support disqualification. *In re Sanders*, 153 S.W.3d 54, 57 (Tex.2004); *Spears v. Fourth Ct. of Appeals*, 797 S.W.2d 654, 656 (Tex.1990).

(1) Rule 1.09 – attorney conflict of interest.

(a) Attorney. An attorney must be disqualified from representing a client if (1) she personally represented a former client, (2) she currently represents another client in a matter adverse to the former client, (3) she does not have the former client's consent to represent the other client, and (4) the representation results in a conflict of interest under the Texas Disciplinary Rule of Professional Conduct 1.09. *See* Tex. Disciplinary R. Prof'l Conduct 1.09(a).

[1] Personally represented former client. An attorney personally represents a client under Rule 1.09(a) if she is exposed to the client's case and confidential information; she does not need to have personally and substantially participated in the case. *See Henderson v. Floyd*, 891 S.W.2d 252, 253-54 (Tex.1995).

[2] Current matter adverse to former client. A current matter is adverse to a former client under Rule 1.09(a) if the attorney's representation could harm the former client; it is not necessary that the former client be an opposing party in the matter. *See Cimarron Agric., Ltd. v. Guitar Holding Co.*, 209 S.W.3d 197, 201-02 (Tex.App.—El Paso 2006, no pet.) (court should focus on effect attorney's representation may have on former client's interests, not solely on former client's relationship with pending litigation); *see, e.g., National Med. Enters. v. Godbey*, 924 S.W.2d 123, 132-33 (Tex.1996) (representation was adverse even though former client was not party to suit); *In re Roseland Oil & Gas, Inc.*, 68 S.W.3d 784, 787 (Tex.App.—Eastland 2001, orig. proceeding) (adversity has nothing to do with sides of suit; representation was adverse even though parties were both Ds). To determine if the attorney should be disqualified based on adversity, the court should consider the likelihood that harm will occur and the seriousness of the harm. *National Med.*, 924 S.W.2d at 132. If the possible harm is severe, an attorney should be disqualified even if the likelihood of the harm is small. *E.g., id.* at 132-33 (threat of criminal prosecution is serious enough to require disqualification even if risk of prosecution is small).

[3] No consent. A former client waives a conflict of interest under Rule 1.09(a) only if the client gives informed consent to the representation. *See* Tex. Disciplinary R. Prof'l Conduct 1.09 cmt. 10; *see, e.g., In re Cerberus Capital Mgmt.*, 164 S.W.3d 379, 382-83 (Tex.2005) (disqualification improper when attorneys for former client sought and obtained valid written waiver of conflict). An attorney should not ask a former client to waive the conflict if a disinterested attorney would conclude that the former client should not agree to the conflicting representation. *See* Tex. Disciplinary R. Prof'l Conduct 1.06 cmt. 7, 1.09 cmt. 10.

✯

[a] Degree of disclosure. Consent is valid only if the attorney has fully disclosed the relevant circumstances, including her past or intended role on behalf of the former and current clients. Tex. Disciplinary R. Prof'l Conduct 1.09 cmt. 10. The degree of disclosure necessary for informed consent will vary depending on the client's level of sophistication. *See* Tex. Disciplinary R. Prof'l Conduct 1.06 cmt. 8.

[b] Form of consent. Although consent can be given orally, it is not advisable to obtain oral consent. *In re Cerberus Capital*, 164 S.W.3d at 383; *see* Tex. Disciplinary R. Prof'l Conduct 1.06 cmt. 8. In most cases, the attorney should obtain a written, signed conflict-of-interest waiver that discloses the following: (1) the proposed representation, (2) the subject matter of the work performed for the former client, (3) the time period involved, (4) the attorney involved, (5) the nature of discussions with the former client, and (6) how the earlier representation concluded. *See In re Cerberus Capital*, 164 S.W.3d at 382-83.

[4] Conflict of interest. An attorney's representation of a new client creates a conflict of interest with a former client under Rule 1.09(a) when the representation (1) may cause the current client to question the validity of the attorney's work for the former client, (2) will, in reasonable probability, require the attorney to reveal or use the former client's confidential information, or (3) involves a matter that is the same as or substantially related to the subject of the earlier representation. Tex. Disciplinary R. Prof'l Conduct 1.09(a).

[a] Questions validity of prior work. An attorney must be disqualified if her current client questions the validity of her services or work product—or those of her firm while she was employed there—for a former client. *See* Tex. Disciplinary R. Prof'l Conduct 1.09(a)(1); *In re Basco*, 221 S.W.3d 637, 638-39 (Tex.2007).

[b] Reveals or uses confidential information. An attorney must be disqualified if there is a reasonable probability the representation will involve a violation of Rule 1.05, which governs an attorney's duty to preserve a client's confidential information. Tex. Disciplinary R. Prof'l Conduct 1.09(a)(2); *see, e.g., In re Hoar Constr., L.L.C.*, 256 S.W.3d 790, 803-04 (Tex.App.—Houston [14th Dist.] 2008, orig. proceeding) (firm disqualified when former client's confidential information would be useful in current client's case).

[c] Involves substantially related matter. An attorney must be disqualified if she represents her current client in a matter that is the same as or substantially related to the subject of her representation of the former client. Tex. Disciplinary R. Prof'l Conduct 1.09(a)(3); *Metropolitan Life Ins. v. Syntek Fin. Corp.*, 881 S.W.2d 319, 320 (Tex.1994); *NCNB Tex. Nat'l Bank v. Coker*, 765 S.W.2d 398, 399-400 (Tex.1989). To satisfy the substantial-relationship test, the movant must show that the facts of the previous representation are so related to those in the pending litigation that there is a genuine threat the confidences revealed to the former counsel will be divulged to a present adversary. *Metropolitan Life*, 881 S.W.2d at 320-21; *Coker*, 765 S.W.2d at 400; *see* Tex. Disciplinary R. Prof'l Conduct 1.09 cmt. 4A.

NOTE

*Although there is some overlap between Rule 1.09(a)(2) and Rule 1.09(a)(3) because each involves the threatened revelation of a former client's confidences, the two are distinct and alternative grounds for disqualification. See **In re Butler**, 987 S.W.2d 221, 226 n.3 (Tex.App.—Houston [14th Dist.] 1999, orig. proceeding).*

(b) Attorney's current firm. An attorney's current firm can be disqualified from representing a client when any of the members or associates of the firm, if practicing alone, would be disqualified from representing that client under Rule 1.09. Tex. Disciplinary R. Prof'l Conduct 1.09(b); *In re Basco*, 221 S.W.3d at 638-39. See "Attorney," §8.2.1(1)(a), p. 57.

(c) Attorney's former firm. The partners and associates of an attorney's former firm who were associated with the attorney at the time she left can be disqualified from representing a client if the attorney would be disqualified from representing that client under Rule 1.09(a)(1) or (a)(2). Tex. Disciplinary R. Prof'l

⭐

Conduct 1.09(c) & cmt. 6 & 7; *In re Basco*, 221 S.W.3d at 638-39. See "Questions validity of prior work," §8.2.1(1)(a)[4][a], p. 58; "Reveals or uses confidential information," §8.2.1(1)(a)[4][b], p. 58.

NOTE

Disqualification based on previous government employment is governed by the Texas Disciplinary Rule of Professional Conduct 1.10.

---

(2) Rule 5.03 – work performed by nonattorney employee. An attorney and her firm can be disqualified from representing a client in a current matter if a nonattorney employee of the firm worked on the same matter for a different firm and her supervising attorney did not take steps to prevent the employee from sharing confidences and working on the matter at the new firm. *In re Guaranty Ins. Servs.*, 343 S.W.3d 130, 134-35 (Tex.2011); *In re Columbia Valley Healthcare Sys.*, 320 S.W.3d 819, 827 (Tex.2010); *Phoenix Founders, Inc. v. Marshall*, 887 S.W.2d 831, 834 (Tex.1994); *see* Tex. Disciplinary R. Prof'l Conduct 5.03(b). Disqualification is proper because the nonattorney employee is presumed to have both obtained confidences during her earlier employment and shared those confidences with her current firm. *In re Guaranty Ins.*, 343 S.W.3d at 134; *In re American Home Prods.*, 985 S.W.2d 68, 75 (Tex.1998); *Phoenix Founders*, 887 S.W.2d at 834. The first presumption is conclusive, but the second presumption is rebuttable. *In re Guaranty Ins.*, 343 S.W.3d at 134.

(a) Rebutting presumption of shared confidences. To rebut the presumption of shared confidences and avoid being disqualified, the attorney or firm should show (1) the nonattorney employee was instructed not to work on the matter, and (2) formal, institutionalized screening measures were put in place to limit the possibility of the employee having contact with the suit. *In re Guaranty Ins.*, 343 S.W.3d at 134; *Phoenix Founders*, 887 S.W.2d at 835. Effective screening measures can include removing the file from the employee's access, giving the employee a written policy about conflicts, and having the employee sign a confidentiality agreement. *See In re Guaranty Ins.*, 343 S.W.3d at 136-37; *In re Columbia Valley Healthcare*, 320 S.W.3d at 826. The court can consider the following factors to determine whether the screening was effective: (1) the substantiality of the relationship between the former and current matters, (2) the time elapsing between the matters, (3) the size of the firm, (4) the number of individuals presumed to have confidential information, (5) the nature of their involvement in the former matter, and (6) the timing and features of any measures taken to reduce the danger of disclosure. *In re Guaranty Ins.*, 343 S.W.3d at 134-35; *Phoenix Founders*, 887 S.W.2d at 836.

(b) Reestablishing presumption of shared confidences. To reestablish the presumption of shared confidences, the party seeking disqualification should show (1) information relating to the party's earlier representation was in fact disclosed to opposing counsel, (2) opposing counsel's screening is or would be ineffective, (3) opposing counsel necessarily will need the nonattorney employee to work on the current matter, or (4) the employee actually performed work, including clerical work, on the current matter at opposing counsel's directive and opposing counsel reasonably should have known about the conflict of interest. *In re Columbia Valley Healthcare*, 320 S.W.3d at 828; *e.g.*, *In re Guaranty Ins.*, 343 S.W.3d at 135 (firm was not disqualified even though assistant actually worked on matter because firm had effective screening measures, had no reason to know of conflict, and ordered assistant to stop working on matter once conflict was known).

(3) Rule 3.08 – attorney as witness. An attorney can be disqualified if (1) she is or may be a witness necessary to establish a disputed, essential fact for her client (other than attorney fees) or (2) she will or may be called to give testimony that is substantially adverse to her client without the client's consent. *Spears*, 797 S.W.2d at 657-58; *see* Tex. Disciplinary R. Prof'l Conduct 3.08(a), (b); *In re Sanders*, 153 S.W.3d at 56-57. The party requesting disqualification must show that the attorney's dual role as advocate-witness will cause the party actual prejudice. *Ayres v. Canales*, 790 S.W.2d 554, 558 (Tex.1990); *In re Guidry*, 316 S.W.3d 729, 738 (Tex.App.—Houston [14th Dist.] 2010, orig. proceeding); *e.g.*, *In re Sanders*, 153 S.W.3d at 57 (no actual prejudice when party could use evidentiary sources other than attorney testimony); *see, e.g.*, *In re Bahn*, 13 S.W.3d 865, 874 (Tex.App.—Fort Worth 2000, orig. proceeding) (testimony from trial counsel could cause jury confusion). An attorney who will be a witness

---

★

---

at trial can still participate in out-of-court matters such as preparing and signing pleadings, planning strategy, and negotiating settlement. ***Anderson Prod'g Inc. v. Koch Oil Co.***, 929 S.W.2d 416, 422 (Tex.1996); ***In re Guidry***, 316 S.W.3d at 738; *see* Tex. Disciplinary R. Prof'l Conduct 3.08 cmt. 8. Another attorney in the testifying attorney's firm may act as trial counsel if the client gives informed consent. ***Anderson Prod'g***, 929 S.W.2d at 424; *see* Tex. Disciplinary R. Prof'l Conduct 3.08(c).

CAUTION

An attorney should not testify as an expert in a case in which she is legal counsel. Everything an expert reviews is subject to discovery. See "Securing Discovery from Experts," ch. 6-D, p. 502. The attorney-client privilege will probably shield some of the information the expert-attorney reviews, but other information may need to be turned over to the opposing party.

---

2. Other circumstances.

(1) Attorney assumed duty to preserve nonclient's confidences. An attorney can be disqualified from a suit if she has assumed a duty to preserve the confidential information of a nonclient. *E.g.*, ***National Med.***, 924 S.W.2d at 130-31 (attorney was disqualified when suit was substantially related to earlier suit in which attorney was part of joint-defense agreement); ***In re Mitcham***, 133 S.W.3d 274, 276-77 (Tex.2004) (attorney was disqualified when he had entered into conflicts-of-interest agreement in which he agreed not to share any information regarding nonclient's use of asbestos). This duty arises most often in the context of providing a joint defense in a multiparty case because the attorney either expressly agrees in writing to maintain a nonclient's confidences or impliedly agrees by participating in a joint defense, which creates a joint-defense privilege. *See* ***In re Skiles***, 102 S.W.3d 323, 327 (Tex.App.—Beaumont 2003, orig. proceeding); *see also* TRE 503(b)(1)(C) (joint-defense privilege). To disqualify an attorney based on a joint-defense privilege, the party seeking disqualification must show (1) confidential information has been shared and (2) the matter in which the information was shared is substantially related to the matter in which disqualification is sought. ***In re Skiles***, 102 S.W.3d at 327; ***Rio Hondo Implement Co. v. Euresti***, 903 S.W.2d 128, 132 (Tex.App.—Corpus Christi 1995, orig. proceeding). For example, if an attorney represents a defendant, D1, in a suit with other defendants, D2 and D3, and the defendants shared information about their defense, the attorney cannot later represent a plaintiff against D2 or D3 in a suit substantially related to the earlier suit. *See* ***National Med.***, 924 S.W.2d at 129-30. This disqualification extends to the attorney's firm, even if the attorney does not work on the later suit. *Id.* at 131-32.

(2) Attorney received privileged materials. When an attorney receives an opponent's privileged materials, the attorney can be disqualified from continuing to represent the client. ***In re Nitla S.A. de C.V.***, 92 S.W.3d 419, 422-23 (Tex.2002); ***In re Meador***, 968 S.W.2d 346, 351 (Tex.1998).

(a) Outside discovery process. When an attorney receives privileged materials outside the normal discovery process, the attorney may be disqualified based on the following factors: (1) whether the attorney knew or should have known the materials were privileged, (2) the promptness with which the attorney notified opposing counsel, (3) the extent to which the attorney reviewed and digested the information, (4) the significance of the privileged information, (5) the extent to which the movant may be at fault for the disclosure, and (6) the extent to which the nonmovant will suffer prejudice from the disqualification. ***In re Meador***, 968 S.W.2d at 351-52.

(b) Through discovery process. When an attorney receives privileged materials through the normal discovery process (e.g., from the trial court after in camera review), the movant seeking to disqualify the attorney must show the following: (1) the attorney's review of the privileged materials caused the movant actual harm, and (2) the attorney's disqualification is necessary because there are no lesser means to remedy the harm. ***In re Nitla***, 92 S.W.3d at 423.

(3) Attorney not authorized. If a party believes that a suit is being prosecuted or defended without the other party's authority, the party should challenge the authority of the attorney under TRCP 12. The rules require the challenging party to file a sworn motion, before the parties announce ready for trial, alleging that the suit

★

is being prosecuted or defended without the other party's authority. TRCP 12. See *O'Connor's Texas Forms*, FORM 1H:8. However, if a new attorney is substituted after the parties announce ready, a Rule 12 motion may be brought to challenge that attorney. *See Air Park-Dallas Zoning Cmte. v. Crow-Billingsley Airpark, Ltd.*, 109 S.W.3d 900, 905-06 (Tex.App.—Dallas 2003, no pet.) (Rule 12 motion can be brought when new attorney appears after trial is over and files motion for new trial). The challenged attorney is entitled to ten days' notice before the hearing. TRCP 12. At the hearing, the challenged attorney has the burden to show sufficient authority to prosecute or defend the suit on the party's behalf. *Id.*; *Boudreau v. Federal Trust Bank*, 115 S.W.3d 740, 741 (Tex.App.—Dallas 2003, pet. denied); *City of San Antonio v. Aguilar*, 670 S.W.2d 681, 684 (Tex.App.—San Antonio 1984, writ dism'd). The challenged attorney's testimony is sufficient to support a ruling that the attorney has the authority to represent the party. *See Boudreau*, 115 S.W.3d at 742. If the challenged attorney does not show authority, the court cannot allow the attorney to appear and must strike the pleadings if no other authorized person appears. TRCP 12; *Boudreau*, 115 S.W.3d at 741.

§8.3 Disqualified attorney's file. When an attorney is disqualified, the successor attorney will want access to two types of information in the file.

1. Public materials. The successor attorney can have access to and use of the pleadings, discovery, correspondence, and other public materials from the disqualified attorney's file. *In re George*, 28 S.W.3d 511, 514 (Tex. 2000).

2. Work product. A successor attorney's access to the disqualified attorney's work product is restricted or denied "to the extent that such a remedy furthers the purposes underlying the disqualification." *In re George*, 28 S.W.3d at 512. When an attorney has been disqualified for representing an opposing party in an earlier suit, the presumption that the disqualified attorney's work product contains confidential information arises once the former client establishes that the two representations are substantially related. *Id.* at 518. The burden then shifts to the current client to rebut the presumption by demonstrating there is not a substantial likelihood that the work product contains confidential information. *Id.* Once the successor attorney moves for access to the work product or the former client moves to restrict access, the court should order the disqualified attorney to produce an inventory of the work product describing (1) the type of work, (2) the subject matter of the items, (3) the claims they relate to, and (4) any other relevant factors. *Id.* The court may also conduct an in camera inspection. *Id.* at 519.

§9. AGREEMENTS BETWEEN ATTORNEYS – RULE 11

The purpose of TRCP 11 is to avoid disputes over the terms of oral agreements made between attorneys in a pending lawsuit. *See Padilla v. LaFrance*, 907 S.W.2d 454, 461 (Tex.1995); *Kennedy v. Hyde*, 682 S.W.2d 525, 529-30 (Tex. 1984). See *O'Connor's Texas Forms*, FORM 1H:13.

§9.1 Agreements in pending suits. To be enforceable, an agreement about any matter in a pending lawsuit must meet the requirements of TRCP 11. *Knapp Med. Ctr. v. De La Garza*, 238 S.W.3d 767, 768 (Tex.2007); *London Mkt. Cos. v. Schattman*, 811 S.W.2d 550, 552 (Tex.1991); *Meza v. Hooker Contracting Co.*, 104 S.W.3d 111, 114-15 (Tex.App.—San Antonio 2003, no pet.). The agreement may be written or oral.

1. Written agreement. To be enforceable, a written agreement about a pending lawsuit must be in writing, signed, and filed with the court. TRCP 11; *Padilla v. LaFrance*, 907 S.W.2d 454, 460 (Tex.1995) (written settlement agreement); *e.g.*, *Knapp Med. Ctr.*, 238 S.W.3d at 768-69 (oral settlement agreement was unenforceable); *London Mkt.*, 811 S.W.2d at 552 (oral agreement to extend time for discovery was unenforceable); *Meza*, 104 S.W.3d at 115 (oral agreement to delay service was unenforceable). The "in writing" requirement may be satisfied by a series of documents as long as the agreement can be ascertained from the documents without resorting to oral testimony. *Padilla*, 907 S.W.2d at 460; *see Staley v. Herblin*, 188 S.W.3d 334, 336 (Tex.App.—Dallas 2006, pet. denied). The "filed with the court" requirement may be satisfied by filing the agreement with the court anytime before it is to be enforced. *Padilla*, 907 S.W.2d at 461; *see, e.g.*, *Southwestern Bell Tel. Co. v. Perez*, 904 S.W.2d 817, 822 (Tex.App.—San Antonio 1995, orig. proceeding) (letter agreement extending deadlines that was filed as an exhibit to party's motion to compel met filing requirement of TRCP 11).

★

2. Oral agreement in court. To be enforceable, an oral agreement about a pending lawsuit must be made in open court and entered into the record. TRCP 11; *Sitaram v. Aetna U.S. Healthcare*, 152 S.W.3d 817, 824 (Tex. App.—Texarkana 2004, no pet.) (parties must dictate all material terms into the record); *e.g.*, *Ronin v. Lerner*, 7 S.W.3d 883, 886 (Tex.App.—Houston [1st Dist.] 1999, no pet.) (oral settlement agreement met requirements of TRCP 11); *see Kennedy v. Hyde*, 682 S.W.2d 525, 529-30 (Tex.1984).

3. Agreement recorded in deposition. An agreement between attorneys about a pending lawsuit that is made part of the record of a deposition is enforceable to the extent that it affects the oral deposition. TRCP 191.1. Other agreements recorded in a deposition and filed with the court may be enforceable as TRCP 11 agreements. The courts disagree on the enforceability of agreements made during a deposition about matters not related to the deposition. *Compare Tindall v. Bishop, Peterson & Sharp, P.C.*, 961 S.W.2d 248, 251 (Tex.App.—Houston [1st Dist.] 1997, no writ) (settlement agreement dictated during deposition was not enforceable under TRCP 11, but was enforceable as exception to statute of frauds), *with Kosowska v. Khan*, 929 S.W.2d 505, 508 (Tex.App.—San Antonio 1996, writ denied) (settlement agreement dictated during deposition, not signed by parties or attorneys, was enforceable under TRCP 11).

§9.2 Exceptions to Rule 11. There are exceptions to the strict requirements of TRCP 11. *Kennedy v. Hyde*, 682 S.W.2d 525, 529 (Tex.1984). For example, a nonconforming Rule 11 agreement may be given effect if the terms are undisputed. *Id.*; *e.g.*, *Anderson v. Cocheu*, 176 S.W.3d 685, 689 (Tex.App.—Dallas 2005, pet. denied) (oral settlement agreement was enforced because it was not disputed). A nonconforming Rule 11 agreement may also be enforced for equitable reasons. *Kennedy*, 682 S.W.2d at 529; *e.g.*, *Massey v. Galvan*, 822 S.W.2d 309, 317-18 (Tex. App.—Houston [14th Dist.] 1992, writ denied) (nonconforming agreement to arbitrate was enforced because party's conduct indicated existence of agreement and because agreement to arbitrate was not challenged until after unfavorable result was rendered); *see Williams v. Huling*, 43 Tex. 113, 120 (1875). A conforming Rule 11 agreement can be challenged on grounds of fraud or mistake. *Kennedy*, 682 S.W.2d at 529; *see Burnaman v. Heaton*, 240 S.W.2d 288, 291 (Tex.1951).

§9.3 Agreements before suit filed. An agreement about a potential lawsuit does not need to be in writing. TRCP 11 applies only to agreements about pending suits. *E.g.*, *Estate of Pollack v. McMurrey*, 858 S.W.2d 388, 393 (Tex.1993) (oral presuit agreement to settle was enforceable as contract but not under TRCP 11). *But see Belleza-Gonzalez v. Villa*, 57 S.W.3d 8, 12 (Tex.App.—Houston [14th Dist.] 2001, no pet.) (presuit agreement to postpone service was not enforceable because it should have been reduced to writing once suit was filed). See "Presuit settlement agreement," ch. 7-I, §4.1.1, p. 673.

§10. ATTORNEY FEES FROM ADVERSE PARTY

A party cannot recover attorney fees from an adverse party unless permitted by a statute or a rule of procedure, by a contract between the parties, or under equity. *See* TRCP 215.2(b)(8) (attorney fees as sanctions); *1/2 Price Checks Cashed v. United Auto. Ins.*, 344 S.W.3d 378, 382 (Tex.2011) (recovery of attorney fees is allowed if permitted by statute or contract between parties); *Tony Gullo Motors I, L.P. v. Chapa*, 212 S.W.3d 299, 310-11 (Tex.2006) (same); *Travelers Indem. Co. v. Mayfield*, 923 S.W.2d 590, 593 (Tex.1996) (same); *Knebel v. Capital Nat'l Bank*, 518 S.W.2d 795, 799 (Tex.1974) (attorney fees can be awarded under equity). See *O'Connor's Texas Forms*, FORM 1H:14. For a more detailed discussion of recovering attorney fees from an adverse party, see *O'Connor's Texas COA*, "Attorney Fees," ch. 45, p. 1349. For a list of statutes authorizing attorney fees, see *O'Connor's CPRC*, "Statutory Attorney Fees Chart—Private Litigants," p. 910; "Statutory Attorney Fees Chart—Attorney General," p. 922.

§10.1 Pleadings required. Unless attorney fees are mandated by statute, a party must plead for attorney fees to be entitled to them. *Swate v. Medina Cmty. Hosp.*, 966 S.W.2d 693, 701 (Tex.App.—San Antonio 1998, pet. denied); *R. Conrad Moore & Assocs. v. Lerma*, 946 S.W.2d 90, 96 (Tex.App.—El Paso 1997, writ denied). The party should identify the authority for attorney fees in its pleadings, but if it does not, the party is still entitled to them if it pleads facts supporting attorney fees. *See O'Connell v. Hitt*, 730 S.W.2d 16, 18 (Tex.App.—Corpus Christi 1987, no writ). See *O'Connor's COA Pleadings*, FORMS 49B:2, 49C:1, 49D:1.

———————————————————— ★ ————————————————————

§10.2 Attorney fees under CPRC.

1. Requirements under §38.001. To be entitled to attorney fees under CPRC §38.001, a party must show the following:

(1) The party pleaded for attorney fees. See *O'Connor's Texas COA*, "Plaintiff pleaded for attorney fees," ch. 45-B, §2.1, p. 1368.

(2) The underlying claim is a CPRC §38.001 claim. *See 1/2 Price Checks Cashed v. United Auto. Ins.*, 344 S.W.3d 378, 383 (Tex.2011); *Coward v. Gateway Nat'l Bank*, 525 S.W.2d 857, 858-59 (Tex.1975) (citing former TRCS art. 2226); *London v. London*, 94 S.W.3d 139, 147-48 (Tex.App.—Houston [14th Dist.] 2002, no pet.). Section 38.001 lists the following claims that qualify for attorney fees: (1) rendered services, (2) performed labor, (3) furnished material, (4) freight or express overcharges, (5) lost or damaged freight or express, (6) killed or injured stock, (7) a sworn account, or (8) an oral or written contract. See *O'Connor's Texas COA*, "Suit involved §38.001 claim," ch. 45-B, §2.2, p. 1368.

(3) The party was represented by an attorney. CPRC §38.002(1); *1/2 Price Checks*, 344 S.W.3d at 383; *Great Am. Ins. v. North Austin MUD*, 908 S.W.2d 415, 427 n.10 (Tex.1995). Generally, a pro se litigant is not entitled to attorney fees. However, both a corporation represented by in-house counsel and an attorney appearing pro se are entitled to attorney fees. See *O'Connor's Texas COA*, "Plaintiff represented by attorney," ch. 45-A, §2.3, p. 1351.

(4) The party against whom attorney fees are to be assessed is an individual or a corporation. CPRC §38.001; *e.g.*, *Harris Cty. MUD v. Mitchell*, 915 S.W.2d 859, 865-66 (Tex.App.—Houston [1st Dist.] 1995, writ denied) (municipal utility district is not corporation or individual and thus is not liable for attorney fees under CPRC §38.001); *Base-Seal, Inc. v. Jefferson Cty.*, 901 S.W.2d 783, 786-87 (Tex.App.—Beaumont 1995, writ denied) (same, for a county). See *O'Connor's Texas COA*, "Defendant was individual or corporation," ch. 45-B, §2.4, p. 1370.

(5) The §38.001 claim was presented to the opposing party or its agent. CPRC §38.002(2); *1/2 Price Checks*, 344 S.W.3d at 383; *Great Am. Ins.*, 908 S.W.2d at 427 n.10. The demand should include (1) the assertion of a debt or a claim and (2) a request for compliance. *Jones v. Kelley*, 614 S.W.2d 95, 100 (Tex.1981). The demand may be made orally or in writing. *Id.*; *Honeycutt v. Billingsley*, 992 S.W.2d 570, 581 (Tex.App.—Houston [1st Dist.] 1999, pet. denied). See *O'Connor's Texas COA*, "Plaintiff presented claim to defendant," ch. 45-B, §2.5, p. 1371.

(6) The opposing party did not tender payment within 30 days after the claim was presented. CPRC §38.002(3); *1/2 Price Checks*, 344 S.W.3d at 383; *Great Am. Ins.*, 908 S.W.2d at 427 n.10. See *O'Connor's Texas COA*, "Defendant did not tender payment," ch. 45-B, §2.6, p. 1372.

(7) The party prevailed (and recovered damages) on a cause of action for which attorney fees are recoverable. *E.g.*, *Green Int'l v. Solis*, 951 S.W.2d 384, 390 (Tex.1997) (prevailing party was not entitled to attorney fees because it was not awarded damages); *State Farm Life Ins. v. Beaston*, 907 S.W.2d 430, 437 (Tex.1995) (same); *Stevens v. Anatolian Shepherd Dog Club*, 231 S.W.3d 71, 77-78 (Tex.App.—Houston [14th Dist.] 2007, pet. denied) (party was not entitled to attorney fees because she did not prevail on undecided claim); *see Ashford Partners v. ECO Res.*, ___ S.W.3d ___ (Tex.2012) (No. 10-0615; 4-20-12). A net recovery is not required. See *O'Connor's Texas COA*, "Plaintiff prevailed," ch. 45-B, §2.7, p. 1372.

(8) The party requesting attorney fees established the elements of proof for the recovery of attorney fees, either by judicial notice or by evidence. See *O'Connor's Texas COA*, "Plaintiff incurred reasonable attorney fees," ch. 45-B, §2.8, p. 1373.

2. Judicial notice. Judicial notice of attorney fees can be taken only when (1) the claim is a CPRC §38.001 claim and (2) the claim is tried on the merits. The trial court, without receiving evidence, can take judicial notice of (1) the usual and customary attorney fees and (2) the content of the file. CPRC §38.004. Under CPRC §38.003, the usual and customary fees are presumed reasonable.

(1) **Section 38.001 claim.** The claim must be a CPRC §38.001 claim. *Charette v. Fitzgerald*, 213 S.W.3d 505, 514 (Tex.App.—Houston [14th Dist.] 2006, no pet.); *see* CPRC §38.004; *Coward*, 525 S.W.2d at 859 (ana-

★

lyzing predecessor statute). If the claim is not included in CPRC §38.001, the court cannot take judicial notice of the fees. *E.g.*, *Dilston House Condo. Ass'n v. White*, 230 S.W.3d 714, 719 (Tex.App.—Houston [14th Dist.] 2007, no pet.) (no judicial notice for violation of Property Code); *Pheng Invs. v. Rodriquez*, 196 S.W.3d 322, 333 (Tex.App.—Fort Worth 2006, no pet.) (no judicial notice for fraudulent misrepresentation); *Gorman v. Gorman*, 966 S.W.2d 858, 866-67 (Tex.App.—Houston [1st Dist.] 1998, pet. denied) (no judicial notice in declaratory-judgment case); *Richards v. Mena*, 907 S.W.2d 566, 573-74 (Tex.App.—Corpus Christi 1995, writ dism'd) (no judicial notice in redistricting and voting-rights case); *Smith v. Smith*, 757 S.W.2d 422, 425 (Tex.App.—Dallas 1988, writ denied) (no judicial notice in DTPA case). *But see Matelski v. Matelski*, 840 S.W.2d 124, 130 (Tex.App.—Fort Worth 1992, no writ) (court took judicial notice of attorney fees in family-law case).

(2) Section 38.004 hearings. The hearing must be either (1) a proceeding before the court or (2) a jury case in which the amount of attorney fees is submitted to the court by agreement. CPRC §38.004. The term "proceeding before the court" is not defined in CPRC §38.004. The Supreme Court has said the trial judge may take judicial notice of attorney fees only "in his role of trier of fact in the conventional trial of a nonjury case but not in passing on a motion for summary judgment." *Coward*, 525 S.W.2d at 859; *see Garcia v. Martinez*, 894 S.W.2d 806, 807 (Tex.App.—Corpus Christi 1994, no writ) (dicta; trial court cannot adjudicate attorney fees based on judicial notice without hearing evidence); *General Elec. Sup. v. Gulf Electroquip, Inc.*, 857 S.W.2d 591, 601 (Tex.App.—Houston [1st Dist.] 1993, writ denied) (in summary-judgment case, fact issue about attorney fees cannot be resolved by judicial notice). *But see Purvis Oil Corp. v. Hillin*, 890 S.W.2d 931, 939 (Tex.App.—El Paso 1994, no writ) (in summary-judgment case, fact issue about attorney fees can be resolved by judicial notice).

§10.3 Elements of proof for attorney fees. To support a claim for attorney fees from the adverse party, the party must offer the following proof:

1. Fees were incurred. The record must show that attorney fees were incurred. See *O'Connor's Texas COA*, "Plaintiff incurred attorney fees," ch. 45-A, §2.6, p. 1354.

2. Fees were necessary. Under some statutes, the party must prove that the attorney fees were necessary. *See, e.g.*, *Arthur Andersen & Co. v. Perry Equip. Corp.*, 945 S.W.2d 812, 818-19 (Tex.1997) (DTPA). See *O'Connor's Texas COA*, "Requirement of necessity," ch. 45-A, §2.7.1, p. 1355.

3. Fees were reasonable. In most cases, the party claiming attorney fees must prove the attorney fees were reasonable. *Arthur Andersen*, 945 S.W.2d at 818; *see Smith v. Smith*, 757 S.W.2d 422, 424 (Tex.App.—Dallas 1988, writ denied) (reasonableness must be supported by evidence except when it may be presumed). See *O'Connor's Texas COA*, "Statutory presumption," ch. 45-A, §2.7.2(1), p. 1355. For a CPRC §38.001 claim, the court can take judicial notice of attorney fees. See "Judicial notice," §10.2.2, p. 63.

(1) Proving reasonableness.

(a) Base amount. The base amount (also called the "lodestar") is determined by multiplying the number of hours reasonably spent on the case by the reasonable hourly rate for such work. *El Apple I, Ltd. v. Olivas*, 370 S.W.3d 757, 760 (Tex.2012). A party should generally follow the *Arthur Andersen* factors to demonstrate the reasonableness of attorney fees; however, the *Arthur Andersen* factors are not exclusive. See *O'Connor's Texas COA*, "Factors to determine reasonableness," ch. 45-A, §2.7.2(3), p. 1356.

[1] The time and labor required, the novelty and difficulty of the questions involved, and the skill required to perform the legal service properly. Tex. Disciplinary R. Prof'l Conduct 1.04(b)(1); *Arthur Andersen*, 945 S.W.2d at 818; *see Ragsdale v. Progressive Voters League*, 801 S.W.2d 880, 881 (Tex.1990).

[2] The likelihood that the acceptance of the particular employment prevented other employment by the attorney. Tex. Disciplinary R. Prof'l Conduct 1.04(b)(2); *Arthur Andersen*, 945 S.W.2d at 818. *But see Stuart v. Bayless*, 964 S.W.2d 920, 921-22 (Tex.1998) (lost contingent fees from other cases are not reasonably foreseeable).

───────────────────────── ✦ ─────────────────────────

[3]   The fee customarily charged in the locality for similar legal services. Tex. Disciplinary R. Prof'l Conduct 1.04(b)(3); *Arthur Andersen*, 945 S.W.2d at 818.

[4]   The amount involved and the results obtained. Tex. Disciplinary R. Prof'l Conduct 1.04(b)(4); *Smith v. Patrick W.Y. Tam Trust*, 296 S.W.3d 545, 548 (Tex.2009); *Arthur Andersen*, 945 S.W.2d at 818.

[5]   The time limitations imposed by the client or by the circumstances. Tex. Disciplinary R. Prof'l Conduct 1.04(b)(5); *Arthur Andersen*, 945 S.W.2d at 818.

[6]   The nature and length of the professional relationship with the client. Tex. Disciplinary R. Prof'l Conduct 1.04(b)(6); *Arthur Andersen*, 945 S.W.2d at 818.

[7]   The experience, reputation, and ability of the attorney performing the services. Tex. Disciplinary R. Prof'l Conduct 1.04(b)(7); *Arthur Andersen*, 945 S.W.2d at 818.

[8]   Whether the fee is fixed or contingent on results obtained or uncertainty of collection before the legal services have been rendered. Tex. Disciplinary R. Prof'l Conduct 1.04(b)(8); *Arthur Andersen*, 945 S.W.2d at 818; *Miller v. Kennedy & Minshew, P.C.*, 142 S.W.3d 325, 337 (Tex.App.—Fort Worth 2003, pet. denied).

(b)   **Adjustment of base amount.**   Once the base amount is determined, the court may adjust the amount up or down depending on other factors used to determine the reasonableness of the fee. *El Apple*, 370 S.W.3d at 760. Because the base amount is presumptively reasonable, an adjustment for a fee award should be made only in rare or exceptional circumstances. *See Perdue v. Kenny A.*, ___ U.S. ___, 130 S.Ct. 1662, 1673 (2010); *El Apple*, 370 S.W.3d at 765. See *O'Connor's Texas COA*, "Step 2 – Adjust lodestar figure," ch. 45-A, §4.1.3(1)(d)[2], p. 1361.

(2)   **Attorney fees by contract.**

(a)   **Hourly fee.**   When the contract between the plaintiff and its attorney states the fee in terms of an hourly rate, attorney fees can be recovered from the defendant based on that rate if the rate was reasonable. See *O'Connor's Texas COA*, "Hourly fee," ch. 45-A, §2.7.2(2)(a), p. 1355.

(b)   **Contingent fee.**   When the contract between the plaintiff and its attorney provides for a contingent award of attorney fees (i.e., attorney fees based on a percentage of the plaintiff's recovery), attorney fees cannot be recovered from the defendant based solely on evidence of the fee agreement. *Arthur Andersen*, 945 S.W.2d at 818. Before attorney fees can be awarded based on a contingent-fee contract, the court must consider the factors outlined in *Arthur Andersen*. See "Base amount," §10.3.3(1)(a), p. 64; *O'Connor's Texas COA*, "Contingent fee," ch. 45-A, §2.7.2(2)(b), p. 1356.

(c)   **Fixed fee.**   When the contract between the plaintiff and the defendant states that, in the event of litigation, the prevailing party is to be awarded a certain amount of attorney fees, attorney fees can be awarded based on the contract. See *O'Connor's Texas COA*, "Fixed fee," ch. 45-A, §2.7.2(2)(c), p. 1356.

4.   Fees were segregated.   When a party is entitled to attorney fees from the adverse party on one cause of action but not another, the party claiming attorney fees must segregate the recoverable fees from the nonrecoverable fees. *Tony Gullo Motors I, L.P. v. Chapa*, 212 S.W.3d 299, 313 (Tex.2006); *K-2, Inc. v. Fresh Coat, Inc.*, 253 S.W.3d 386, 397 (Tex.App.—Beaumont 2008), *rev'd in part on other grounds*, 318 S.W.3d 893 (Tex.2010). Segregation is not necessary if the legal services advanced all the claims in the suit. *Tony Gullo Motors*, 212 S.W.3d at 313-14. Even if the underlying facts are the same for different claims, attorney fees are not necessarily recoverable for all the claims. *Id.* The test is no longer whether the claims were based on the same facts and were intertwined; the focus is on which legal services were necessary for each claim. *Id.*; *see Varner v. Cardenas*, 218 S.W.3d 68, 69 (Tex. 2007). The attorney can provide proof of segregation by estimating the percentage of time spent on nonrecoverable tasks. *See Tony Gullo Motors*, 212 S.W.3d at 314. If the trial court awards attorney fees based on unsegregated fees

★

without objection by the adverse party, the issue of segregation is waived on appeal. *Green Int'l v. Solis*, 951 S.W.2d 384, 389 (Tex.1997); *K-2, Inc.*, 253 S.W.3d at 398. If the trial court overrules an objection and awards attorney fees based on unsegregated fees, the appellate court must remand the issue of attorney fees to the trial court for a new hearing. *Stewart Title Guar. Co. v. Sterling*, 822 S.W.2d 1, 11-12 (Tex.1991), *modified on other grounds*, *Tony Gullo Motors I, L.P. v. Chapa*, 212 S.W.3d 299 (Tex.2006); *see Tony Gullo Motors*, 212 S.W.3d at 314. See *O'Connor's Texas COA*, "Proof of segregated fees," ch. 45-A, §4.1.3(1)(b), p. 1360.

§10.4   Proof of attorney fees. In most cases, a party must prove attorney fees by offering evidence through an attorney who testifies as an expert. In some cases, however, the plaintiff can rely on judicial notice to establish proof of attorney fees. See "Judicial notice," §10.2.2, p. 63. For a detailed discussion of proving attorney fees, see *O'Connor's Texas COA*, "Proving Attorney Fees," ch. 45-A, §4, p. 1359.

1.   Types of testimony. The party can prove attorney fees through the following methods.

(1)   Affidavits. The court can award attorney fees based on affidavit testimony. *Texas Commerce Bank v. New*, 3 S.W.3d 515, 517-18 (Tex.1999); *see Save Our Springs Alliance, Inc. v. City of Dripping Springs*, 304 S.W.3d 871, 892-93 (Tex.App.—Austin 2010, pet. denied).

(2)   Other evidence. Attorney fees are often proved by the deposition or in-court testimony of the attorney in the case. Generally, the testimony of an interested witness raises a fact issue, even when it is not contradicted. *Ragsdale v. Progressive Voters League*, 801 S.W.2d 880, 882 (Tex.1990). However, testimony by an interested witness may establish attorney fees as a matter of law if (1) the testimony is uncontroverted, (2) it is clear, direct, and positive, and (3) there are no circumstances tending to discredit or impeach it. *Garcia v. Gomez*, 319 S.W.3d 638, 642 (Tex.2010).

2.   Specific documentation. The party must provide sufficient details of the work performed to substantiate the claim for attorney fees. *El Apple I, Ltd. v. Olivas*, 370 S.W.3d 757, 762 (Tex.2012). The party should use specific documentation (e.g., billing records, time records) to prove the following basic facts underlying the lodestar calculation: (1) the nature of the work performed, (2) who performed the work and the hourly rate for that work, (3) when the work was performed, and (4) the total hours worked. *Id.* at 763. Without specific documentation of the work performed, a party will likely be unable to provide the court with sufficient proof of reasonable attorney fees. *See, e.g., id.* at 763-64 (attorney fees award reversed when attorneys' affidavits based proof of hours spent on amount of discovery, number of pleadings filed, number of witnesses questioned, and length of trial, rather than on time records or other specific documentary evidence).

PRACTICE TIP
In all but the simplest cases, an attorney testifying about attorney fees will have to refer to some record to provide facts to support an award. Thus, if a party's attorney expects to use the "lodestar" method to calculate a claim for attorney fees, the attorney should be sure to document her time with contemporaneous billing records or similar documentation recorded close to when her work was performed, just as an attorney would when billing her own clients. El Apple, 370 S.W.3d at 763.

---

§11.   REVIEW

§11.1   Disqualification.

1.   Standard of review. The standard of review for a disqualification motion is abuse of discretion. *See In re Meador*, 968 S.W.2d 346, 351 (Tex.1998) (mandamus); *Metropolitan Life Ins. v. Syntek Fin. Corp.*, 881 S.W.2d 319, 321 (Tex.1994) (appeal).

★

2. Appeal. Disqualification issues are subject to review on appeal. *See Metropolitan Life*, 881 S.W.2d at 320-21; *see also Hall v. Birchfield*, 718 S.W.2d 313, 322 n.1 (Tex.App.—Texarkana 1986) (mandamus would be better procedure than awaiting outcome of main trial), *rev'd on other grounds sub nom. Birchfield v. Texarkana Mem'l Hosp.*, 747 S.W.2d 361 (Tex.1987).

3. Mandamus. Mandamus is often appropriate when a trial judge erroneously grants or denies a motion to disqualify an attorney or law firm. See *O'Connor's Texas Appeals*, "Disqualification of attorney," ch. 10-B, §4.3.6, p. 348.

§11.2 Attorney fees. A party can preserve error by complaining for the first time in a motion for judgment notwithstanding the verdict that the opposing party is not entitled to attorney fees. *See Holland v. Wal-Mart Stores*, 1 S.W.3d 91, 94 (Tex.1999) (statute did not permit attorney fees).

I. GUARDIAN AD LITEM UNDER TRCP 173

§1. GENERAL

§1.1 Rules. TRCP 44, 173.

§1.2 Purpose. The purpose of appointing a guardian ad litem under TRCP 173 is to protect the interest of an incapacitated party—generally a minor or other person incapable of self-representation—when that party's next friend or guardian has an adverse interest in the division of settlement proceeds. *Jocson v. Crabb*, 196 S.W.3d 302, 305-06 (Tex.App.—Houston [1st Dist.] 2006, no pet.); TRCP 173 cmt. 3; *see Land Rover U.K., Ltd. v. Hinojosa*, 210 S.W.3d 604, 607 (Tex.2006) (guardian ad litem is appointed to assist court in protecting child's interest); *Goodyear Dunlop Tires v. Gamez*, 151 S.W.3d 574, 584 (Tex.App.—San Antonio 2004, no pet.) (guardian ad litem has duty to evaluate settlement offer from minor's perspective). The term "ad litem" means "for the suit." *Brownsville-Valley Reg'l Med. Ctr., Inc. v. Gamez*, 894 S.W.2d 753, 756 (Tex.1995); *Black's Law Dictionary* 49 (9th ed. 2009). TRCP 173 does not apply to an appointment of a guardian ad litem governed by statutes, such as the Family Code or the Probate Code, or by other rules, such as the Parental Notification Rules. TRCP 173.1 & cmt. 2.

NOTE

In this subchapter, we use "incapacitated party" to refer to a person who needs a guardian ad litem.

---

§1.3 Forms. *O'Connor's Texas Civil Forms* (2012), FORMS 1I.

§1.4 Other references. Anton, Comment, *The Ambiguous Role & Responsibilities of a Guardian Ad Litem in Texas in Personal Injury Litigation*, 51 SMU L.Rev. 161 (1997) (referred to as Anton, *Role of Guardian Ad Litem*); Wood, *The Duties of Guardians & Attorneys Ad Litem*, State Bar of Texas CLE, The New Guardianship Laws in Texas, at F (1994) (referred to as Wood, *Duties of Ad Litem*); *O'Connor's Texas Causes of Action* (2013) (*O'Connor's Texas COA*); *O'Connor's Texas Family Law Handbook* (2013) (*O'Connor's Fam. Law Handbook*).

§2. COMPARISON OF GUARDIAN AD LITEM & ATTORNEY AD LITEM

The term "guardian ad litem" is often confused with the term "attorney ad litem" because both are used in the TRCPs, the Probate Code, the Family Code, and other statutes. *See, e.g., International Dairy Queen, Inc. v. Matthews*, 126 S.W.3d 629, 630 (Tex.App.—Beaumont 2004, no pet.) (parties used terms interchangeably); *Brownsville-Valley Reg'l Med. Ctr., Inc. v. Gamez*, 871 S.W.2d 781, 784 (Tex.App.—Corpus Christi 1994) (court referred to guardian ad litem as attorney ad litem), *rev'd on other grounds*, 894 S.W.2d 753 (Tex.1995). Because the roles of a guardian ad litem and an attorney ad litem are different, attorneys should understand the differences and insist on correct references in all court documents.

§2.1 Guardian ad litem. A guardian ad litem is an officer appointed by the court to assist in protecting the settlement interest of an incapacitated party who is represented by a next friend or guardian, and the next friend or

★

guardian appears to have an adverse interest to the incapacitated party. *Ford Motor Co. v. Chacon*, 370 S.W.3d 359, 361 (Tex.2012); *Ford Motor Co. v. Garcia*, 363 S.W.3d 573, 577 (Tex.2012); *see* TRCP 173.2(a)(1) (court must appoint guardian ad litem for incapacitated party if represented by next friend or guardian who appears to have adverse interest), TRCP 173.4(a) (guardian ad litem acts as officer of and adviser to court); TRCP 173 cmt. 3 (guardian ad litem will be appointed when incapacitated party's next friend or guardian appears to have adverse interest to incapacitated party because of division of settlement proceeds). Although a guardian ad litem may be a licensed attorney, she is the personal representative of the incapacitated party, not an attorney for the incapacitated party. *Land Rover U.K., Ltd. v. Hinojosa*, 210 S.W.3d 604, 607 (Tex.2006); *American Gen. Fire & Cas. Co. v. Vandewater*, 907 S.W.2d 491, 493 n.2 (Tex.1995); *see Ford Motor Co. v. Garcia*, 363 S.W.3d 573, 577 (Tex.2012) (duty of guardian ad litem is different from duty of incapacitated party's attorney); *see also* TRCP 173.4(d)(3) (guardian ad litem cannot participate in litigation except by court order). See *O'Connor's Fam. Law Handbook*, "Guardian Ad Litem," ch. 4-C, §4, p. 368.

NOTE

*A guardian ad litem appointed under TRCP 173, acting as an adviser to and officer of the court, has derived judicial immunity—that is, she has a common-law defense to being sued in her individual capacity for performing judicial acts. See TRCP 173 cmt. 5. See generally **Dallas Cty. v. Halsey**, 87 S.W.3d 552, 554-57 (Tex.2002) (discussing applicability of derived judicial immunity to court reporters). See **O'Connor's Texas COA**, "Judicial Immunity," ch. 46-C, p. 1411. But the guardian ad litem can be sanctioned for violating TRCP 173. TRCP 173 cmt. 8.*

---

§2.2 Attorney ad litem. An attorney ad litem performs the same services as any attorney—giving legal advice, doing research, and conducting litigation—for an incapacitated party. *City of Houston v. Woods*, 138 S.W.3d 574, 582 (Tex.App.—Houston [14th Dist.] 2004, no pet.); *Coleson v. Bethan*, 931 S.W.2d 706, 713 (Tex.App.—Fort Worth 1996, no writ); *see* Fam. Code §107.003 (duties of attorney ad litem for child in family-law cases include investigation, reviewing medical and psychological records, interviewing parties, and participating in litigation). See *O'Connor's Fam. Law Handbook*, "Attorney Ad Litem," ch. 4-C, §2, p. 350.

Chart 1-4, below, shows when a guardian ad litem or an attorney ad litem should be appointed.

	Guardian ad litem	Attorney ad litem
	1-4. COMPARISON OF AD LITEMS	
	TRCP	
1	In civil litigation, guardian ad litem must be appointed to represent person whose guardian or next friend has adverse interest. TRCP 173.2(a).	In default-judgment proceedings against D who was served by publication but did not answer or appear, attorney ad litem must be appointed to represent D. TRCP 244.
	Probate Code	
2		In any probate proceeding, attorney ad litem may be appointed to represent person with legal disability, nonresident, unborn or unascertained person, or unknown heir. Prob. Code §34A.
3	In heirship proceedings, guardian ad litem may be appointed to represent minor, incompetent person, or known heir whose name or whereabouts is unknown, if the appointment is necessary to protect that person's interest. Prob. Code §53(b).	In heirship proceedings, attorney ad litem may be appointed to represent minor, incompetent person, or known heir whose name or whereabouts is unknown, if the appointment is necessary to protect that person's interest. Prob. Code §53(b).
4		In heirship proceedings, attorney ad litem must be appointed to represent the interest of unknown heir. Prob. Code §53(c).

GUARDIAN AD LITEM

1-4. COMPARISON OF AD LITEMS (CONTINUED)

Guardian ad litem	Attorney ad litem
Probate Code (continued)	
5 — In guardianship proceedings, guardian ad litem may be appointed to represent best interest of incapacitated person. Prob. Code §§601(12), 645(a).	In guardianship proceedings, attorney ad litem may be appointed to represent: • Proposed ward. Prob. Code §601(1). • Incapacitated person. *Id.* • Unborn person. *Id.* • Ward when settling guardianship. *Id.* §§745(d), 755.
6	In guardianship proceedings, attorney ad litem must be appointed to represent ward when: • Appointing guardian. Prob. Code §646(a). • Modifying guardianship. *Id.* §649C. • Restoring ward's capacity. *Id.* • Guardian wants to buy ward's property. *Id.* §831(c). • Removing community administrator. *Id.* §833D(a) (incapacitated spouse).
Family Code	
7 — In suit seeking termination of parent-child relationship or appointment as a conservator in which the best interest of a child is at issue, guardian ad litem may be appointed. Fam. Code §107.021(a)(3). If the suit is brought by governmental unit, guardian ad litem must be appointed. Fam. Code §107.011. For other suits under the Family Code in which a guardian ad litem may be necessary, see generally *O'Connor's Fam. Law Handbook*.	In suit seeking termination of parent-child relationship or appointment as a conservator in which the best interest of a child is at issue, attorney ad litem may be appointed. Fam. Code §107.021(a)(2). If the suit is brought by governmental unit, attorney ad litem must be appointed. Fam. Code §107.012. For other suits under the Family Code in which an attorney ad litem may be necessary, see generally *O'Connor's Fam. Law Handbook*.

§3. APPOINTING A GUARDIAN AD LITEM UNDER TRCP 173

§3.1 Appointment of guardian ad litem.

1. When required.

(1) **Adverse interest.** The court must appoint a guardian ad litem for an incapacitated party represented by a next friend or guardian when the next friend or guardian appears to the court to have an interest adverse to the incapacitated party. TRCP 173.2(a)(1); *see Brownsville-Valley Reg'l Med. Ctr., Inc. v. Gamez*, 894 S.W.2d 753, 755 (Tex.1995) (court can appoint guardian ad litem only when there is conflict between minor and next friend). The Texas Supreme Court has not defined "adverse interest" under TRCP 173. *In re KC Greenhouse Patio Apts., LP*, ___ S.W.3d ___ (Tex.App.—Houston [1st Dist.] 2012, orig. proceeding) (No. 01-12-00226-CV; 8-16-12). Courts usually apply TRCP 173 to adverse interests relating to the division of settlement proceeds. *Id.*; *see* TRCP 173 cmt. 3. But courts have applied the rule to other conflicts of interest. *In re KC Greenhouse Patio Apts.*, ___ S.W.3d at ___. For example, when a parent appears as next friend for a child who has sustained serious injuries requiring medical treatment, an adverse interest may arise because the claim for the child's medical expenses belongs to the parent, while the claim for personal injuries belongs to the child. *Id.*; *see In re Richardson*, No. 09-10-00032-CV (Tex.App.—Beaumont 2010, orig. proceeding) (memo op.; 3-11-10). A parent or guardian may also have a conflict of interest in handling a minor's settlement fund, in receiving compensation for services as managing conservator, or in a minor's inheritance if the minor predeceases the parent or guardian. *In re KC Greenhouse Patio Apts.*, ___ S.W.3d at ___; *see McGough v. First Ct. of Appeals*, 842 S.W.2d 637, 640 (Tex.1992).

(2) **Agreement of parties.** The court must appoint a guardian ad litem for an incapacitated party represented by a next friend or guardian if the parties agree to the appointment. TRCP 173.2(a)(2).

★

2. Same ad litem for similarly situated parties. The court must appoint the same guardian ad litem for similarly situated parties unless the court finds that the appointment of different guardians ad litem is necessary. TRCP 173.2(b). For example, when a settlement is to be divided between parents and their two children, the court must appoint the same guardian ad litem for both children.

§3.2 Qualifications. TRCP 173 does not provide a list of qualifications for a guardian ad litem. Although Probate Code §681 does not apply to a guardian ad litem appointed under TRCP 173, the statute gives broad guidelines for determining when a person is not qualified. *Cf. Gallegos v. Clegg*, 417 S.W.2d 347, 352 (Tex.App.—Corpus Christi 1967, writ ref'd n.r.e.) (former Prob. Code §110, now §681, was applied to decide if next friend was disqualified). Because the guardian ad litem's main function is to evaluate the division of settlement proceeds, the court should appoint a person who has the experience to properly evaluate the incapacitated party's case. When deciding whether a person is qualified to act as a guardian ad litem in a personal-injury suit, the court should consider, among other things, whether that person has experience in personal-injury litigation. Anton, *Role of Guardian Ad Litem*, 51 SMU L.Rev. at 170.

PRACTICE TIP

Some courts might require an attorney to have certain training or certification to qualify for an appointment as a guardian ad litem. Thus, an attorney should check with the local or state bar association about available seminars or CLEs that would qualify her for appointment as a guardian ad litem.

---

§3.3 Procedure to appoint.

1. Motion. Any party who believes a guardian ad litem is necessary may file a motion for the court to appoint one. TRCP 173.3(a). The court may also appoint a guardian ad litem on its own initiative. *Id.*

2. Order. The appointment must be made by written order. TRCP 173.3(b); *e.g.*, *Ford Motor Co. v. Chacon*, 370 S.W.3d 359, 362 (Tex.2012) (order for appointment of guardian ad litem specifically limited guardian ad litem's appointment to representing minor's interest as to settlement with D1; no order in record appointing guardian ad litem to represent minor's interest in settlement with D2). An improper designation in the trial court's order does not control the nature of the appointment. *E.g.*, *Ford Motor Co. v. Garcia*, 363 S.W.3d 573, 577-78 (Tex.2012) (although motion used "attorney ad litem" in one sentence and order stated ad litem was appointed "to serve as Attorney Ad Litem," his appointment was requested only after division of settlement with D created a conflict; appointment was as guardian ad litem).

§3.4 Objections to appointment. Any party may object to the appointment of a guardian ad litem. TRCP 173.3(c). Objections to the appointment could include the following:

1. Necessity. The appointment of a guardian ad litem is not necessary because there is no conflict between the incapacitated party and the guardian or next friend. *See* TRCP 173.2(a)(1).

2. Unqualified. The person appointed as guardian ad litem is not qualified to serve in that capacity. See "Qualifications," §3.2, this page.

3. Dual appointment. The court should not appoint more than one guardian ad litem for similarly situated incapacitated parties. *See* TRCP 173.2(b).

§4. ROLE OF GUARDIAN AD LITEM

Once appointed, the guardian ad litem displaces the next friend or guardian—to the limited extent of protecting the incapacitated party's interest that appears to be adverse to the next friend's or guardian's interest—and becomes the personal representative of the incapacitated party. *City of Houston v. Woods*, 138 S.W.3d 574, 579 (Tex.App.—Houston [14th Dist.] 2004, no pet.); *see In re KC Greenhouse Patio Apts., LP*, ___ S.W.3d ___ (Tex.App.—Houston [1st Dist.] 2012, orig. proceeding) (No. 01-12-00226-CV; 8-16-12). The guardian ad litem is not an attorney

★

for the incapacitated party but an officer appointed by the court to assist in protecting the incapacitated party's interest. See "Guardian ad litem," §2.1, p. 67. The guardian ad litem has the burden to ensure that her services do not exceed the scope of her appointed role. *Ford Motor Co. v. Chacon*, 370 S.W.3d 359, 362 (Tex.2012); *Ford Motor Co. v. Garcia*, 363 S.W.3d 573, 577 (Tex.2012).

PRACTICE TIP

A guardian ad litem who is an attorney may choose to become involved in litigation beyond her role as a guardian ad litem (e.g., review the file or attend proceedings when it is unnecessary), but she will not be compensated for these expenses or services. TRCP 173 cmt. 3. See "Outside scope of duties," §6.1.3(2)(a), p. 74.

---

§4.1 Role during trial.

1. Settlement proceedings.

(1) Advise on settlement offer. The guardian ad litem's primary, and in most cases only, role is to advise the court on a settlement offer. When an offer has been made to settle the claim of an incapacitated party represented by a next friend or guardian, a guardian ad litem has the limited duty to determine whether the settlement is in the incapacitated party's best interest and make a recommendation to the trial court. TRCP 173.4(c); *see Jocson v. Crabb*, 196 S.W.3d 302, 308 (Tex.App.—Houston [1st Dist.] 2006, no pet.). When a settlement is proposed, the guardian ad litem must do the following:

(a) Evaluate settlement offer. The guardian ad litem must determine whether the settlement offer is fair and reasonable to the incapacitated party. *See Jocson*, 196 S.W.3d at 308; *Byrd v. Woodruff*, 891 S.W.2d 689, 707 (Tex.App.—Dallas 1994, writ dism'd). To determine the adequacy of a settlement agreement, the guardian ad litem should evaluate (1) the damages suffered by the incapacitated party, (2) the proposed apportionment of the settlement proceeds among the parties, (3) the proposed manner of disbursing the settlement proceeds, and (4) the amount of attorney fees charged by the incapacitated party's attorney. *Jocson*, 196 S.W.3d at 308; *Goodyear Dunlop Tires v. Gamez*, 151 S.W.3d 574, 584 (Tex.App.—San Antonio 2004, no pet.); *Byrd v. Woodruff*, 891 S.W.2d 689, 707 (Tex.App.—Dallas 1994, writ dism'd).

(b) Attend settlement hearing. The guardian ad litem must participate in any proceeding before the court that is intended to determine whether a settlement of the incapacitated party's claim is in the party's best interest. TRCP 173.4(d)(2).

(c) Make recommendation. The guardian ad litem must make a recommendation to the trial court on the incapacitated party's behalf. *Goodyear*, 151 S.W.3d at 584; *Byrd*, 891 S.W.2d at 707.

(d) Review final judgment. The guardian ad litem should review the final settlement documents and judgment submitted to the court. Wood, *Duties of Ad Litem*, at F-19.

(2) Participate in mediation proceeding. The guardian ad litem may, but is not required to, participate in mediation or similar proceedings to attempt to reach a settlement. TRCP 173.4(d)(1). Unless the guardian ad litem's presence is required at the mediation proceeding, there is some question whether she can claim compensation for attending. *See* TRCP 173 cmt. 7.

2. Other trial proceedings. Only in exceptional cases should a guardian ad litem become involved in anything other than settlement issues. TRCP 173 cmt. 4. In these situations, the role is limited to determining whether an incapacitated party's next friend or guardian has an interest adverse to the party that should be considered by the court under TRCP 44. TRCP 173 cmt. 4. A guardian ad litem may never supervise or supplant the next friend or undertake to represent the incapacitated party while serving as guardian ad litem. *Id.*

(1) Adverse-interest proceeding. A guardian ad litem must participate in any proceeding before the court that is intended to determine whether an incapacitated party's next friend or guardian has an interest adverse to the incapacitated party. TRCP 173.4(d)(2); *see, e.g., Stewart, Cox & Hatcher, P.C. v. Ford Motor Co.*, 350

★

S.W.3d 369, 378-79 (Tex.App.—Beaumont 2011, pet. filed 12-15-11) (next friend challenged appointment of guardian ad litem, alleging no conflict between next friend and her daughter; participation in court proceedings to defend against this type of challenge is within scope of guardian ad litem's duties and is compensable). The guardian ad litem must advise the court whether the incapacitated party's next friend or guardian has an interest adverse to the incapacitated party. TRCP 173.4(b).

   (2) Discovery & trial proceeding. Generally, the guardian ad litem must not participate in discovery, trial, or any other part of the litigation. TRCP 173.4(d)(3); *see, e.g., Jocson v. Crabb*, 133 S.W.3d 268, 270-71 (Tex.2004) (court remanded award to guardian ad litem to permit Ds to challenge compensation for attending 50 depositions and for other work). The guardian ad litem can participate in discovery, trial, or any other part of the litigation only if the participation (1) is necessary to protect the incapacitated party's interest that is adverse to the next friend's or guardian's and (2) is directed by the court in a written order stating sufficient reasons. TRCP 173.4(d)(3).

PRACTICE TIP
A guardian ad litem appointed under TRCP 173 should not take any action that requires a bar card. If she does, the other parties should object. A guardian ad litem cannot be paid for work performed outside the scope of that role unless the court signs an order under TRCP 173.4(d)(3). When the guardian ad litem believes that an incapacitated party needs an attorney ad litem, the guardian ad litem should petition the court to appoint one. See "Attorney ad litem," §2.2, p. 68.

---

§4.2 Role after trial. A guardian ad litem is appointed only for the duration of the case. After the judgment is signed, the guardian ad litem usually has no further responsibilities. *See Brownsville-Valley Reg'l Med. Ctr., Inc. v. Gamez*, 894 S.W.2d 753, 755 (Tex.1995). Once the conflict ends, the guardian ad litem should be removed. *Id.* However, at the conclusion of the case, the guardian ad litem should be expected to do the following:

   1. The guardian ad litem should provide her address and telephone number to the incapacitated party and the next friend or guardian in case the incapacitated party needs help in the future. Anton, *Role of Guardian Ad Litem*, 51 SMU L.Rev. at 193.

   2. The guardian ad litem should retain the incapacitated party's file. *Id.*

   3. The guardian ad litem should expect, on a no-fee basis, to assist the incapacitated party in securing funds from the court registry when the incapacity is lifted (e.g., when the minor becomes an adult). Wood, *Duties of Ad Litem*, at F-20; *see Brownsville-Valley Reg'l*, 894 S.W.2d at 756-57 (guardian ad litem cannot recover fees for services rendered after resolution of conflict for which she was appointed).

§5. GUARDIAN AD LITEM COMMUNICATIONS

   §5.1 With parties. Communications between the guardian ad litem and the incapacitated party, the next friend, the guardian, or their attorneys are privileged just as if the guardian ad litem were the attorney for the incapacitated party. TRCP 173.5.

   §5.2 With court. A guardian ad litem cannot have ex parte communications with the court, even though she is an adviser to the court. TRCP 173 cmt. 6; *see* Tex. Code Jud. Conduct, Canon 3(B)(8).

§6. COMPENSATION

A guardian ad litem may be reimbursed for reasonable and necessary expenses incurred and may receive a reasonable hourly fee for her services. TRCP 173.6(a). See "For services of guardian ad litem," §6.1.3(1)(a), p. 73. A guardian ad litem has a limited role in the litigation and thus may be compensated only for limited types of activities. *Ford Motor Co. v. Garcia*, 363 S.W.3d 573, 579 (Tex.2012); *see* TRCP 173 cmt. 7. A guardian ad litem cannot receive, directly or indirectly, anything of value in consideration of the appointment other than as provided by TRCP 173. TRCP 173.6(d).

★

§6.1 Application for fees. If the guardian ad litem intends to request reimbursement for expenses and compensation for service, she may file an application for compensation at the conclusion of the appointment. TRCP 173.6(b).

NOTE
Filing an application (1) allows other parties to see the exact compensation requested and the reasons the compensation is appropriate and (2) gives the parties a better opportunity to agree to a fee and avoid a hearing. **Ford Motor Co. v. Garcia**, *363 S.W.3d 573, 575 n.1 (Tex.2012). See "Agreed application," §6.1.2, this page; "Hearing on application," §6.3, p. 75. At a minimum, filing an application will provide specifics of the fee request and allow the parties and the court to better prepare for the hearing.* **Garcia**, *363 S.W.3d at 575 n.1.*

---

1. **Verified.** The application must be verified. TRCP 173.6(b).

2. **Agreed application.** The guardian ad litem should ask the parties to agree to the application. If the parties agree, the court can render judgment on the application. *See* TRCP 173.6(b).

3. **Fees.** The application must describe in detail the basis for the compensation requested. TRCP 173.6(b).

   (1) **Fees permitted.**

   (a) **For services of guardian ad litem.** Generally, only the person appointed as a guardian ad litem can be compensated for services under TRCP 173. *Garcia*, 363 S.W.3d at 580. The guardian ad litem may (1) be reimbursed for reasonable and necessary expenses incurred and (2) receive a reasonable hourly fee for necessary services performed. TRCP 173.6(a); *Ford Motor Co. v. Chacon*, 370 S.W.3d 359, 362 (Tex.2012). For the guardian ad litem's necessary services, see "Role of Guardian Ad Litem," §4, p. 70.

   [1] **Expenses.** The guardian ad litem should list the reasonable and necessary expenses incurred. TRCP 173.6(b).

   [2] **Hourly fees.** The guardian ad litem should identify a reasonable hourly fee for services performed, the services performed as a guardian ad litem by date and amount of time spent on each task, why each task was necessary, and the total amount claimed. *See* TRCP 173.6. A reasonable fee for a guardian ad litem is a reasonable hourly rate multiplied by the number of hours spent performing services within the guardian ad litem's role. *Garcia*, 363 S.W.3d at 580; *Land Rover U.K., Ltd. v. Hinojosa*, 210 S.W.3d 604, 608 (Tex.2006).

   (b) **For services of person other than guardian ad litem.** A guardian ad litem may be compensated for services performed by a person other than the designated guardian ad litem. *Garcia*, 363 S.W.3d at 580. If claiming compensation for time spent by another person, the guardian ad litem should identify the particular person and prove (1) unusual circumstances required the services of the particular person to fulfill the guardian ad litem's duties, (2) the specific services that were performed, (3) when the services were performed, (4) the amount of time spent on each task, (5) why each task was necessary in light of the guardian ad litem's appointment, (6) a reasonable hourly rate for the person, and (7) the total amount claimed. *See id.* The following are examples of when unusual circumstances may occur: • A paralegal supervised by the guardian ad litem could perform tasks necessary to fulfilling the guardian ad litem's appointed role, but at a lower hourly rate. *Id.* • An emergency arises that requires an attorney familiar with the matter, rather than the guardian ad litem, to make an appearance at a hearing. *Id.* • An actuary or accountant is necessary to evaluate the finances of a structured settlement. *Id.* at 580 n.5.

PRACTICE TIP
Although nothing in TRCP 173 precludes awarding compensation based on services performed by a person other than a guardian ad litem, the guardian ad litem should, if possible, get the trial court's authorization for using those services before any expenses are actually incurred. **Garcia**, *363 S.W.3d at 580 & n.5.*

──────────────────────── ★ ────────────────────────

(2) Fees not permitted.

(a) Outside scope of duties. A guardian ad litem cannot be paid for work performed outside the scope of her duties as a guardian ad litem. *Garcia*, 363 S.W.3d at 580; *Land Rover*, 210 S.W.3d at 607.

[1] **Determining scope.** In determining the scope of the guardian ad litem's appointment, courts look to the context of the appointment and the duties assigned to the guardian ad litem. *Chacon*, 370 S.W.3d at 362; *Garcia*, 363 S.W.3d at 577. Specifically, a court may examine the timing of the appointment, the grounds in the motion for appointment, and the order granting the appointment. *E.g., Chacon*, 370 S.W.3d at 362-63 (motion and order for appointment of guardian ad litem specifically limited guardian ad litem's appointment to representing minor's interest as to settlement with D1; guardian ad litem's work on settlement with D2 was beyond scope of his appointment and was not compensable).

[2] **Examples.** The following are examples of services performed outside the scope of the guardian ad litem's duties: • Reviewing the litigation file or attending trial proceedings, unless those services are necessary to protect the incapacitated party's interest. *See* TRCP 173 cmt. 3; *see, e.g., Garcia*, 363 S.W.3d at 582 (no compensation for reviewing motions to transfer venue, various discovery requests and responses, correspondence about postponed hearings, and pleadings on already-settled claims). See "Other trial proceedings," §4.1.2, p. 71. • Consulting daily with plaintiff's attorney about trial strategy. *Land Rover*, 210 S.W.3d at 609. • Conducting independent legal research or similar services more appropriate for the incapacitated party's attorney. *See, e.g., Youngstown Area Jewish Fed'n v. Dunleavy*, 223 S.W.3d 604, 609-10 (Tex.App.—Dallas 2007, no pet.) (no compensation for legal research, review of case law, and telephone calls and letters to obtain medical records).

(b) After conflict is resolved. A guardian ad litem cannot be awarded fees for services to be performed after the conflict of interest that necessitated her appointment has been resolved. *Frank A. Smith Sales, Inc. v. Flores*, 907 S.W.2d 487, 488 (Tex.1995); *Brownsville-Valley Reg'l Med. Ctr., Inc. v. Gamez*, 894 S.W.2d 753, 757 (Tex.1995).

(c) For guardian ad litem's own interest. A guardian ad litem cannot be awarded fees for representing her own interest. *Holt Tex., Ltd. v. Hale*, 144 S.W.3d 592, 598 (Tex.App.—San Antonio 2004, no pet.). Courts disagree, however, on whether a guardian ad litem can be awarded fees for defending a fee dispute. *Compare id.* at 597-98 (abuse of discretion to award guardian ad litem fees for time spent in fee dispute), *with DeSai v. Islas*, 884 S.W.2d 204, 206 (Tex.App.—Eastland 1994, writ denied) (court affirmed contingent fee awarded if guardian ad litem had to defend original fee on appeal).

§6.2 Objection to fees. To complain about the guardian ad litem fees on appeal, a party must make its objection known to the trial court either orally (on the record during the litigation or at the hearing on guardian ad litem fees) or in writing (in a motion or response filed with the court). *See, e.g., Jocson v. Crabb*, 133 S.W.3d 268, 269-70 (Tex.2004) (Ds preserved issue by objecting at final fee hearing); *Goodyear Dunlop Tires v. Gamez*, 151 S.W.3d 574, 582 (Tex.App.—San Antonio 2004, no pet.) (same); *see also Samco Props., Inc. v. Cheatham*, 977 S.W.2d 469, 478-79 (Tex.App.—Houston [14th Dist.] 1998, pet. denied) (D could challenge excessiveness of guardian ad litem fees even though it did not raise issue in motion for new trial because fees are taxed as costs). Objections to the award could include the following:

1. Amount. The amount of the award sought by the guardian ad litem is excessive. *See Jocson*, 133 S.W.3d at 270.

2. Scope. The guardian ad litem should not be compensated for work performed outside the scope of her duties as a guardian ad litem. See "Outside scope of duties," §6.1.3(2)(a), this page.

3. Overbilling. The guardian ad litem should not be compensated for overbilling her expenses and services. *See, e.g., Jocson*, 133 S.W.3d at 270 (guardian ad litem submitted bill for, among other things, $5,250 for reviewing deposition notices, $35,900 for attending depositions, and $19,000 for reviewing letters); *Goodyear*, 151 S.W.3d at 588-89 (six guardians ad litem submitted bill for just under $400,000, including charges for time spent sleeping, for summarizing depositions, for associate's work, and for more than 24 hours in a day for more than one attorney).

★

4. Hourly rate. The guardian ad litem should not be compensated at the hourly rate requested because it is an unreasonable hourly rate. *See, e.g.*, *Goodyear*, 151 S.W.3d at 590-91 (court of appeals found hourly rate of $400 to $500 excessive).

5. Percent of recovery. The guardian ad litem is not entitled to a percentage of the judgment or settlement. TRCP 173.6(b).

6. Lost opportunity. Unless there are exceptional circumstances, the guardian ad litem is not entitled to be compensated for lost opportunity for other employment. *See Land Rover U.K., Ltd. v. Hinojosa*, 210 S.W.3d 604, 608-09 (Tex.2006).

7. Appellate fees. The guardian ad litem should not be awarded appellate attorney fees. *Goodyear*, 151 S.W.3d at 592.

§6.3 Hearing on application. If the parties do not agree to the guardian ad litem's application for fees, the court must conduct an evidentiary hearing to determine the total amount of reasonable and necessary fees and expenses. TRCP 173.6(b). The hearing is for the receipt of evidence to determine the amount of the guardian ad litem's fees. *See Jocson v. Crabb*, 133 S.W.3d 268, 270 (Tex.2004); *Garcia v. Martinez*, 988 S.W.2d 219, 221-22 (Tex. 1999); *DaimlerChrysler Corp. v. Brannon*, 67 S.W.3d 294, 299 (Tex.App.—Texarkana 2001, no pet.). The determination of guardian ad litem fees is within the sound discretion of the trial court. *Ford Motor Co. v. Chacon*, 370 S.W.3d 359, 362 (Tex.2012); *Ford Motor Co. v. Garcia*, 363 S.W.3d 573, 578 (Tex.2012); *Land Rover U.K., Ltd. v. Hinojosa*, 210 S.W.3d 604, 607 (Tex.2006). The court cannot base its award to the guardian ad litem on a percentage of the judgment or settlement. TRCP 173.6(b).

§6.4 Taxed as costs. The court may tax a guardian ad litem's compensation as court costs. TRCP 173.6(c); *Ford Motor Co. v. Garcia*, 363 S.W.3d 573, 577 (Tex.2012); *City of Houston v. Woods*, 138 S.W.3d 574, 581 (Tex. App.—Houston [14th Dist.] 2004, no pet.).

1. Unsuccessful party. The guardian ad litem fees should be taxed as costs against the unsuccessful party in the suit. *See* TRCP 131; *Woods*, 138 S.W.3d at 581; *Borden, Inc. v. Martinez*, 19 S.W.3d 469, 471 (Tex. App.—San Antonio 2000, no pet.).

2. Prevailing party. As a rule, the guardian ad litem fees should not be taxed against the prevailing party. *See* TRCP 131. The court can tax costs against the prevailing party only when the court finds good cause and states it on the record. TRCP 141; *e.g.*, *Rogers v. Walmart Stores*, 686 S.W.2d 599, 601 (Tex.1985) (good cause to assess part of guardian ad litem fees against prevailing party for prolonging trial); *Price Constr., Inc. v. Castillo*, 147 S.W.3d 431, 443 (Tex.App.—San Antonio 2004) (remanded case to determine whether there was good cause to assess guardian ad litem fees against prevailing party based on unsuccessful parties' inability to pay), *pet. denied*, 209 S.W.3d 90 (Tex.2005); *Davis v. Henley*, 471 S.W.2d 883, 884-85 (Tex.App.—Houston [1st Dist.] 1971, writ ref'd n.r.e.) (good cause to assess guardian ad litem fees against prevailing parties because unsuccessful parties had no assets or income to pay the fee). Without evidence of good cause, the court abuses its discretion by taxing the guardian ad litem fees against the prevailing party. *See, e.g.*, *Suiter v. Woodard*, 635 S.W.2d 639, 641 (Tex.App.—Waco 1982, writ ref'd n.r.e.) (court could not tax costs against P, who was neither adverse to nor on the same side as minor Ps).

3. Both parties. Without a finding of good cause, the court cannot split the guardian ad litem fees between the parties. *See Roberts v. Williamson*, 111 S.W.3d 113, 124 (Tex.2003).

§6.5 Separate order. The order awarding a fee to the guardian ad litem should be recorded in a written order, separate from the judgment. Tex.Sup.Ct. Order, Misc. Docket No. 94-9143, §2, 890-891 S.W.2d (Tex.Cases) xlvii (1994). The district and county court clerks must report to the Supreme Court all fees of $500 or more paid to any person appointed by each court by listing the amount of the fees and the names of the persons receiving them. *Id.* §5, at xlviii.

§7. REVIEW

§7.1 Record on appeal. If any party plans to challenge the appointment of the guardian ad litem or the fees awarded to the guardian ad litem, that party must ensure that a record is made of the hearing at which those issues

✦

are heard and resolved. *See City of Houston v. Woods*, 138 S.W.3d 574, 580 (Tex.App.—Houston [14th Dist.] 2004, no pet.). Without a record, the appellate court will assume the evidence was sufficient to support the trial court's ruling. *Id.*

§7.2 Right of appeal. Any party may seek mandamus review of an order appointing a guardian ad litem or directing a guardian ad litem's participation in the litigation. TRCP 173.7(a). Any party or the guardian ad litem may appeal an order awarding fees to the guardian ad litem. *Id.*

§7.3 Severance. If the order awarding fees to a guardian ad litem is included in the judgment, on the motion of the guardian ad litem or any party, the court must sever it to create a final, appealable order. TRCP 173.7(b).

§7.4 Finality not affected. Appellate proceedings to review an order pertaining to a guardian ad litem do not affect the finality of a settlement or judgment. TRCP 173.7(c).

J. ASSOCIATE JUDGE

§1. GENERAL

In 2011, the Legislature enacted Government Code chapter 54A to reclassify subordinate judicial officers (e.g., special judges, magistrates) as associate judges and create uniform standards for their authority and powers. *See* Senate Cmte. on Jurisprudence, Bill Analysis, Tex. H.B. 79, 82nd Leg., C.S. (2011). Chapter 54A enables counties to create positions for associate judges who can preside over civil matters. *See* Gov't Code §§54A.101, 54A.102(a). Once the positions are created by the county commissioners court, district and statutory county court judges can appoint associate judges to handle various matters, including trials, referred to them. *See id.* §54A.102(a). These uniform standards went into effect on January 1, 2012. Acts 2011, 82nd Leg., C.S., ch. 3, §16.02, eff. Jan. 1, 2012.

NOTE

This subchapter covers the standards for associate judges who preside over civil matters. It does not cover the standards for associate judges who preside over criminal, juvenile, family, or probate matters.

---

§1.1 Rules. Gov't Code §§54A.101-54A.118.

§1.2 Purpose. Under Gov't Code §54A.101 et seq., a district or statutory county court judge can refer some or all of a civil case, including a trial, to an associate judge for resolution as long as an associate-judge position has been authorized by the county commissioners court and filled by appointment.

§1.3 Forms. *O'Connor's Texas Civil Forms* (2012), FORMS 1J.

§2. CREATING & APPOINTING

§2.1 Creating associate-judge positions. Before a matter can be referred to an associate judge, the county commissioners court must authorize the creation of an associate-judge position for a district or statutory county court. Gov't Code §54A.102(a); *see id.* §54A.101.

    1. District court has jurisdiction in more than one county. For district courts that have jurisdiction in more than one county, the commissioners courts for those counties must designate each county where the associate judge may serve. *See* Gov't Code §54A.102(b).

    2. County has more than one court. For counties with more than one district court, statutory county court, or both, the county commissioners court may either create an associate-judge position for each court or authorize one or more associate judges to serve the courts. Gov't Code §54A.102(c).

§2.2 Appointing associate judges. Once an associate-judge position is created, a district or statutory county court judge can appoint an associate judge to perform the duties granted under Gov't Code §54A.101 et seq. *See* Gov't Code §54A.102(a). If the associate judge serves more than one court, however, the judge's appointment must be made as established by local rule, and requires at least a vote of two-thirds of the judges under whom the associate judge serves. *Id.* §54A.102(d).

⭐

§3. REFERRING CASES

§3.1 Scope of referral. A district or statutory county court judge can refer any civil case or part of a civil case to an associate judge for resolution. Gov't Code §54A.106(a).

§3.2 Order of referral. A case can be referred to an associate judge by an order of referral in a specific case or by an omnibus order. Gov't Code §54A.107(a). Unless otherwise specified, the associate judge can do any of the following under the order of referral:

1. Conduct hearings. *Id.* §54A.108(a)(1).

2. Regulate proceedings in a hearing. *Id.* §54A.108(a)(12).

3. Conduct trials. *Id.* §54A.106(b). See "Objection to referral," §3.3, this page.

4. Hear evidence. Gov't Code §54A.108(a)(2).

5. Compel production of relevant evidence. *Id.* §54A.108(a)(3).

6. Rule on the admissibility of evidence. *Id.* §54A.108(a)(4).

7. Issue summonses for the appearance of witnesses, examine witnesses, and swear witnesses for hearings. *Id.* §54A.108(a)(5)-(a)(7).

8. Order the attachment of a witness or party who fails to obey a subpoena. *Id.* §54A.108(a)(13). See "Enforcing Subpoenas," ch. 1-L, §5, p. 88.

9. Make findings of fact on evidence. Gov't Code §54A.108(a)(8).

10. Formulate conclusions of law. *Id.* §54A.108(a)(9).

11. Rule on pretrial motions. *Id.* §54A.108(a)(10).

12. Recommend the rulings, orders, or judgment to be made in a case. *Id.* §54A.108(a)(11).

13. Take action as necessary and proper for the efficient performance of the duties required by the order of referral. *Id.* §54A.108(a)(14).

§3.3 Objection to referral. A party can file an objection to an associate judge hearing a trial on the merits or presiding at a jury trial. Gov't Code §54A.106(c). The party must file the objection no later than ten days after the party receives notice that the associate judge will hear the trial. *Id.* If an objection is filed, the referring court must hear the trial on the merits or preside at the jury trial. *Id.*

§3.4 Referral back. An associate judge can, in the interest of justice, refer a case back to the referring court regardless of whether a party has made a timely objection to the associate judge hearing the trial on the merits or presiding at a jury trial. Gov't Code §54A.108(b).

§4. PROCEEDINGS

§4.1 Hearing. Hearings before an associate judge are performed in the same manner as hearings before the referring court.

1. Waiving de novo review. Before the hearing begins, a party can waive its right to de novo review of the associate judge's decision by the referring court either in writing or on the record. Gov't Code §54A.112(c). See "To referring court – de novo hearing," §9.1, p. 79.

2. Preserving the record. A court reporter can be provided—whether by a party, the associate judge, the referring court, or otherwise—during a hearing held by an associate judge. Gov't Code §54A.110(a), (b). If there is no court reporter, or if the parties agree, the record may be preserved by any means approved by the associate judge. *Id.* §54A.110(c). If other means are used, the referring court or associate judge can assess the expense of preserving the record as costs. *Id.* §54A.110(d).

★

CAUTION

If the record is not taken by a court reporter, the referring court will not be able to consider the record on appeal from the associate judge's decision. See Gov't Code §§54A.110(e), 54A.115(f).

---

§4.2 Trial. Trials before an associate judge are performed in the same manner as trials before the referring court. A "trial on the merits" is any final adjudication from which an appeal can be taken to a court of appeals. Gov't Code §54A.106(b). Unlike with hearings before an associate judge, a court reporter must be provided when the associate judge presides over a jury trial. *Id.* §54A.110(a).

§4.3 Witnesses. Witnesses who appear before an associate judge are subject to the same penalties of perjury as other witnesses in civil matters. Gov't Code §54A.109(a). The referring court—not the associate judge—can fine or imprison a witness if the witness does not appear after being summoned or improperly refuses to answer questions and the refusal has been certified by the associate judge. *Id.* §54A.109(b).

§5. NOTICE OF RIGHT TO DE NOVO HEARING

The referring court or the associate judge must give all parties notice of the right to a de novo hearing before the referring court. *See* Gov't Code §54A.112(a). The notice can be given (1) by oral statement in open court, (2) by posting inside or outside the courtroom of the referring court, or (3) as otherwise directed by the referring court. *Id.* §54A.112(b).

§6. DECISION

An associate judge can take actions, render decisions, and propose orders or judgments in civil matters referred to her. An associate judge's decision has the same force and effect as an order of the referring court, unless a party appeals the decision. Gov't Code §54A.111(a). See "Effect of request on order or judgment only," §9.1.2, p. 79. If the decision is not rendered in open court after hearing the matter, the associate judge must notify each attorney participating in the hearing of the decision. *See* Gov't Code §54A.111(a).

§6.1 Temporary restraining orders. A temporary restraining order issued by an associate judge is effective immediately and expires 15 days later unless, after a hearing, the order is modified or extended by the associate judge or referring judge. Gov't Code §54A.111(c).

§6.2 Temporary injunctions. A temporary injunction issued by an associate judge is effective immediately and continues during the trial unless, after a hearing, the order is modified by the referring judge. Gov't Code §54A.111(d).

§6.3 Orders for detention or incarceration. An order for the temporary detention or incarceration of a witness or party issued by an associate judge must be presented to the referring court on the day the witness or party is detained or incarcerated. Gov't Code §54A.113(c). The referring court, without prejudice to the right to a de novo hearing, can approve the temporary detention or incarceration or can order the release of the witness or party, with or without bond, pending a de novo hearing. *Id.* If the referring court is not immediately available, the associate judge can order the release of the witness or party, with or without bond, pending a de novo hearing or can continue the detention or incarceration for up to 72 hours. *Id.* See "To referring court – de novo hearing," §9.1, p. 79.

§7. CONSIDERATION OF DECISION

The referring court can take certain actions on the associate judge's decision, but those actions will depend on whether the decision was in the nature of an "action taken" or a proposed order or judgment.

§7.1 Action taken. If the associate judge has taken an action in the matter, the referring court has 30 days after the action was taken to modify, correct, reject, reverse, or recommit for further information the action taken. Gov't Code §54A.117(a). If the referring court does not do so, the associate judge's action becomes the decree of the court. *Id.* §54A.117(b).

✦

§7.2 Proposed order or judgment. If the associate judge has proposed an order or judgment and no party has filed a written request for a de novo hearing (or the parties have waived the right to a de novo hearing), the referring court can (1) adopt, modify, or reject the associate judge's proposed order or judgment, (2) hear additional evidence, or (3) recommit the matter to the associate judge for further proceedings. Gov't Code §54A.114; *see id.* §54A.113(b). When the referring court signs the proposed order or judgment, it becomes the order or judgment of the referring court. *Id.* §54A.113(b).

§8. RECONSIDERATION OF ORDER OR JUDGMENT – POSTJUDGMENT MOTIONS

A party can file a motion for new trial, a motion for judgment notwithstanding the verdict, or other postjudgment motions after the referring court signs the associate judge's proposed order or judgment. *See* Gov't Code §§54A.113(b), 54A.115(g). See "Postjudgment Motions," ch. 10, p. 787.

§9. APPEAL

A party can appeal the associate judge's decision to either the referring court or an appellate court. *See* Gov't Code §§54A.111(b), 54A.116(a). A party does not lose the right to appeal to or request other relief from a court of appeals or the Texas Supreme Court if it does not request or otherwise waives its right to a de novo hearing before the referring court. *Id.* §54A.116(a).

§9.1 To referring court – de novo hearing. When an appeal is made to the referring court, the referring court holds a de novo hearing. Gov't Code §54A.111(e). A de novo hearing is a new hearing without deference to the associate judge's decision. *See id.* §54A.115; *Black's Law Dictionary* 789 (9th ed. 2009).

1. Request hearing.

(1) Deadline. A party must file an appeal in the referring court within seven working days after the date the party receives notice of the associate judge's decision unless the request is for a hearing to modify a temporary restraining order (TRO) or temporary injunction, which can be made anytime before the TRO or injunction expires. *See* Gov't Code §54A.111(b). If a request for a de novo hearing is timely made, any other party can file its own request for a de novo hearing before the referring court and must do so within seven working days after the date the initial request was filed. *Id.* §54A.115(d). See "Temporary restraining orders," §6.1, p. 78; "Temporary injunctions," §6.2, p. 78; "Orders for detention or incarceration," §6.3, p. 78.

(2) Where to file. The party should file a request for a de novo hearing with the clerk of the referring court. Gov't Code §54A.115(a).

(3) What to file. The request must be in writing and must specify the issues that will be presented to the referring court. Gov't Code §54A.115(a), (b). The de novo hearing is limited to the specified issues. *Id.* §54A.115(b).

NOTE

If a party requests a de novo hearing to review the associate judge's proposed order or judgment after a jury trial, the party cannot demand a second jury to review that order or judgment. Gov't Code §54A.115(h).

---

(4) Notice. Notice of a request for a de novo hearing before the referring court must be given to the opposing attorney in the manner provided by TRCP 21a. Gov't Code §54A.115(c). See "How to Serve," ch. 1-D, §4, p. 34.

2. Effect of request on order or judgment only. A proposed order issued or a judgment rendered by an associate judge, except for an order providing for the appointment of a receiver, remains in full force and effect and is enforceable as an order or judgment of the referring court while the de novo hearing is pending. Gov't Code §54A.113(a).

MASTER IN CHANCERY

★

3. Hearing.

(1) Deadline. The referring court, after notice to the parties, must hold a de novo hearing no later than 30 days after the initial request for a de novo hearing was filed. Gov't Code §54A.115(e).

(2) Scope. The de novo hearing is limited to only those matters specified in the appeal. Gov't Code §54A.111(e). Except on leave of court, a party cannot submit any additional evidence or pleadings. *Id.*

(3) Evidence. The parties can present witnesses on the issues specified in the request for hearing. Gov't Code §54A.115(f). If a record of the hearing before the associate judge was taken by a court reporter, the referring court can consider it, including the charge to and verdict returned by a jury. *Id.*

4. Order. The referring court should issue a written order on its ruling. *See **Klentzman v. Brady**,* 312 S.W.3d 886, 908 (Tex.App.—Houston [1st Dist.] 2009, no pet.). This order can be appealed to the appellate court. *See id.* at 908 & n.21.

5. Reconsideration of order or judgment – postjudgment motions. A party can file a motion for new trial, a motion for judgment notwithstanding the verdict, or other postjudgment motions if the referring court denies relief after a de novo hearing and signs the associate judge's proposed order or judgment. *See* Gov't Code §54A.115(g); *see also id.* §54A.116(b) (date order or judgment was signed by referring court is controlling date for purposes of appeal). See "Postjudgment Motions," ch. 10, p. 787.

§9.2 To appellate court. The procedure and deadline for appealing to the court of appeals or the Texas Supreme Court is the same as with other judgments or orders. See "Calculating appellate deadlines," ch. 9-C, §9.1, p. 778. Generally, the date an order or judgment is signed by the referring court is the controlling date for appellate deadlines. Gov't Code §54A.116(b). If the order is an agreed order or a default order, the date the order is signed by an associate judge is the controlling date for appellate deadlines. *Id.* §54A.116(c).

K. MASTER IN CHANCERY

§1. GENERAL

§1.1 Rule. TRCP 171.

§1.2 Purpose. A master in chancery is a person designated by a judicial officer to hear certain matters. ***Simpson v. Canales**,* 806 S.W.2d 802, 806 (Tex.1991) (master appointed for discovery). The theory underlying the use of masters is that, by delegating certain matters to them, the trial judge is free to devote more time to trials and substantive decisions, thus expediting the trial docket. *Id.* at 809 n.9. For a discussion of the historical development of the office of masters and an explanation of the courts' inherent distrust of them, read ***Simpson***.

§1.3 Forms. *O'Connor's Texas Civil Forms* (2012), FORMS 1K.

§1.4 Other references. Furgeson et al., *E-Discovery & the Use of Special Masters*, Litigation Update Institute, State Bar of Texas CLE, ch. 3 (2011); Moore, *The Use of Masters in Chancery in Texas Courts*, 53 Tex.B.J. 442 (May 1990); *O'Connor's Texas Civil Appeals* (2012) (*O'Connor's Texas Appeals*).

§2. AUTHORITY FOR REFERRAL TO MASTER

There are three sources of authority for a master: TRCP 171, statutes, and the consent of the parties.

§2.1 TRCP 171. Every referral to a master must comply with TRCP 171 unless authorized by statute or consented to by the parties. ***Simpson v. Canales**,* 806 S.W.2d 802, 810 (Tex.1991); ***Hansen v. Sullivan**,* 886 S.W.2d 467, 469 (Tex.App.—Houston [1st Dist.] 1994, orig. proceeding).

§2.2 Statutes. The Legislature has created certain types of masters, limited to specific subjects and counties. For example, the following matters may be referred to a master: family-law matters—Family Code §§201.101-201.113; juvenile matters in certain counties—e.g., Gov't Code §§54.801-54.820 (Harris County); and criminal matters in certain counties—e.g., Gov't Code §§54.301-54.313 (Dallas County). These provisions for the appointment of masters contain their own procedures for appointing and compensating masters and for appealing their decisions.

───────────────────── ★ ─────────────────────

§2.3 Consent. The parties may consent to the referral of a case to a master, even when there is no authority under TRCP 171 or any statute. *Simpson v. Canales*, 806 S.W.2d 802, 810-11 (Tex.1991); *In re Polybutylene Plumbing Litig.*, 23 S.W.3d 428, 439 (Tex.App.—Houston [1st Dist.] 2000, pet. dism'd). Consent to the referral of a matter to a master demonstrates a party's intent to be bound on the matters referred. *In re Sheets*, 971 S.W.2d 745, 747 (Tex.App.—Dallas 1998, orig. proceeding).

§3. MOTION FOR REFERRAL TO MASTER UNDER TRCP 171

§3.1 Written. A motion for referral to a master should be in writing. See *O'Connor's Texas Forms*, FORM 1K:1.

§3.2 Grounds. A motion for referral to a master under TRCP 171 should include the following allegations:

1. Specific, pending matter. The motion should identify a specific, pending matter that the party requests be referred to a master. The motion should not ask the trial court to refer all present and future issues of a particular type to a master. *See Academy of Model Aeronautics, Inc. v. Packer*, 860 S.W.2d 419, 419 (Tex.1993).

2. Exceptional matter. The matter should be referred to a master because it is exceptional. TRCP 171; *Simpson v. Canales*, 806 S.W.2d 802, 811 (Tex.1991). For example, the court may appoint a master with technical knowledge to conduct a comprehensive analysis of highly technical data. *E.g.*, *In re Harris*, 315 S.W.3d 685, 705-06 (Tex.App.—Houston [1st Dist.] 2010, orig. proceeding) (court abused discretion by referring electronic-discovery matter to special master when case was not of a highly technical nature); *TransAmerican Nat. Gas Corp. v. Mancias*, 877 S.W.2d 840, 843 (Tex.App.—Corpus Christi 1994, orig. proceeding) (geologist appointed to assist in review of documents); *see also Chapa v. Garcia*, 848 S.W.2d 667, 668 (Tex.1992) (Supreme Court suggested that trial court appoint a master with special expertise to assist in review of documents). Referral to a master is not justified just because a case is complicated or time-consuming or because the court is busy. *Simpson*, 806 S.W.2d at 811; *In re Sheets*, 971 S.W.2d 745, 747 (Tex.App.—Dallas 1998, orig. proceeding); *see Owens-Corning Fiberglas Corp. v. Caldwell*, 830 S.W.2d 622, 626 (Tex.App.—Houston [1st Dist.] 1991, orig. proceeding).

3. Good cause. The court has good cause to refer the matter to a master. TRCP 171; *Simpson*, 806 S.W.2d at 811; *Owens-Corning*, 830 S.W.2d at 626; *see In re Harris*, 315 S.W.3d at 705-06 (presence of electronic discovery alone is not good cause for appointing special master). The "good cause" requirement has not been precisely defined. *See generally Simpson*, 806 S.W.2d at 811-12 (discussing difficulty in defining "good cause" requirement of TRCP 171).

§4. ORDER OF REFERRAL TO MASTER

The decision to appoint a master is within the trial court's discretion. *Simpson v. Canales*, 806 S.W.2d 802, 811 (Tex.1991); *Tollett v. Carmona*, 915 S.W.2d 562, 564 (Tex.App.—Houston [14th Dist.] 1995, orig. proceeding). See *O'Connor's Texas Forms*, FORM 1K:3.

§4.1 Findings. To refer a case to a master without the parties' consent, the trial court must find that (1) the case is an exceptional one and (2) there is good cause for the appointment. TRCP 171; *Simpson v. Canales*, 806 S.W.2d 802, 811 (Tex.1991); *In re Sheets*, 971 S.W.2d 745, 747 (Tex.App.—Dallas 1998, orig. proceeding).

§4.2 Scope of referral. The order referring a matter to a master should identify the scope and limits of the master's authority. TRCP 171. The order should specify the master's powers and direct the master to report only on particular matters, perform only particular acts, or receive and report evidence only. *Id.*

§4.3 No blanket referral. The court cannot make a blanket referral of all discovery matters to a master. *See Academy of Model Aeronautics, Inc. v. Packer*, 860 S.W.2d 419, 419 (Tex.1993) (trial court could not refer all present and future discovery disputes to master); *Simpson v. Canales*, 806 S.W.2d 802, 811-12 (Tex.1991) (even in exceptional case, court would be reluctant to refer all discovery matters to master); *Owens-Corning Fiberglas Corp. v. Caldwell*, 830 S.W.2d 622, 626 (Tex.App.—Houston [1st Dist.] 1991, orig. proceeding) (same).

§4.4 Appointee. The master must be a citizen of Texas and cannot be related to or be an attorney for any of the parties. TRCP 171.

━━━━━━━━━━━━━━━━━━━━━ ☆ ━━━━━━━━━━━━━━━━━━━━━

§4.5 Time & place. The order of referral may set the time and place for the hearings and the time for the filing of the master's report. TRCP 171.

§5. OBJECTION TO MASTER'S APPOINTMENT

§5.1 Types of objections. A party must make its objections when the court refers a matter to a master, or it waives them. *See Tollett v. Carmona*, 915 S.W.2d 562, 564-65 (Tex.App.—Houston [14th Dist.] 1995, orig. proceeding) (party must object to appointment either before participating in any proceedings in front of master, or before parties, master, and trial court have relied on appointment); *Owens-Corning Fiberglas Corp. v. Caldwell*, 830 S.W.2d 622, 625 (Tex.App.—Houston [1st Dist.] 1991, orig. proceeding) (same). See "Making & Preserving Objections," ch. 1-F, p. 43; *O'Connor's Texas Forms*, FORM 1K:2. Objections include the following:

1.   This is not the type of matter that should be referred to a master because it is not exceptional, and the referral is without good cause. TRCP 171; *Simpson v. Canales*, 806 S.W.2d 802, 811 (Tex.1991); *see AIU Ins. v. Mehaffy*, 942 S.W.2d 796, 802-03 (Tex.App.—Beaumont 1997, orig. proceeding) (trial court was not authorized to appoint master to go to New York to investigate discovery abuse). See "Grounds," §3.2, p. 81.

2.   The scope of the appointment and the master's duties are not clearly defined in the order of referral. TRCP 171.

3.   The referral is a blanket referral, in violation of TRCP 171. *Academy of Model Aeronautics, Inc. v. Packer*, 860 S.W.2d 419, 419 (Tex.1993); *Simpson*, 806 S.W.2d at 812; *Owens-Corning*, 830 S.W.2d at 626.

4.   The person appointed to serve as a master is objectionable.

(1)   The appointee is not qualified to serve because she is not a citizen of Texas, is related to one of the parties, or is an attorney for one of the parties. TRCP 171.

(2)   The parties already objected to the same person serving as a visiting judge in the case. *See Tollett*, 915 S.W.2d at 563.

§5.2 Deadline to object. TRCP 171 does not specify the deadline for a party to object to the appointment of a master. A party must object to the appointment either before participating in any proceedings in front of the master or before the parties, master, and trial court act in reliance on the appointment. *Tollett v. Carmona*, 915 S.W.2d 562, 564-65 (Tex.App.—Houston [14th Dist.] 1995, orig. proceeding); *see Owens-Corning Fiberglas Corp. v. Caldwell*, 830 S.W.2d 622, 624-25 (Tex.App.—Houston [1st Dist.] 1991, orig. proceeding).

§6. HEARING BEFORE MASTER

§6.1 Record of hearing. When requested, the master must make a record of the evidence just as if the case were tried before the court. TRCP 171. When a party wants the proceeding recorded, the party should file a written request as soon as the appointment is made. See *O'Connor's Texas Forms*, FORM 1K:4. If a court reporter is not present, any party who wants the hearing recorded should object in writing.

§6.2 Attendance of witnesses. The parties may procure the attendance of witnesses by the issuance and service of process as provided by the same rules as for a trial before a judge. TRCP 171. See "Subpoenas," ch. 1-L, p. 84.

§6.3 Scope of hearing. The scope of the hearing is determined by the trial court's order referring the matter to the master. See "Scope of referral," §4.2, p. 81.

§6.4 Authority of master. Subject to the limitations stated in the order, the master may regulate the hearing and take all measures necessary or proper for the efficient performance of the duties specified in the order. The master may require the production of evidence, including books, papers, vouchers, documents, and other writings; may rule on the admissibility of evidence; and may place parties and witnesses under oath and examine them. TRCP 171.

§7. MASTER'S REPORT

§7.1 Report. The master's report should conform to the instructions in the order of referral. If the order instructed the master to receive evidence and settle factual disputes, the master should file findings of fact just as if the case were tried to a court without a jury. The master does not have the authority to render judgment. *Hansen v. Sullivan*, 886 S.W.2d 467, 469 (Tex.App.—Houston [1st Dist.] 1994, orig. proceeding).

———————————————————— ✦ ————————————————————

§7.2 Notice. Once the master files the report with the trial court, the parties are entitled to notice and an opportunity to object.

§8. OBJECTION TO MASTER'S REPORT

§8.1 No objection. When issues are referred to a master under TRCP 171, the master's report is conclusive on all issues to which the parties do not object. *Lesikar v. Moon*, 237 S.W.3d 361, 371 (Tex.App.—Houston [14th Dist.] 2007, pet. denied); *Young v. Young*, 854 S.W.2d 698, 701 (Tex.App.—Dallas 1993, writ denied).

§8.2 Objection. To the extent that a party objects to the master's report, the report is not binding. *Lesikar v. Moon*, 237 S.W.3d 361, 371 (Tex.App.—Houston [14th Dist.] 2007, pet. denied); *Young v. Young*, 854 S.W.2d 698, 701 (Tex.App.—Dallas 1993, writ denied). See *O'Connor's Texas Forms*, FORM 1K:5.

1. Timely. A party must object to the master's report before the trial court adopts it. *Robles v. Robles*, 965 S.W.2d 605, 612 (Tex.App.—Houston [1st Dist.] 1998, pet. denied). However, if the trial court adopts the report before a party has notice of the report, the party does not waive its objections. *Republic Ins. v. Davis*, 856 S.W.2d 158, 160 (Tex.1993).

2. Specific. An objection to the report must be specific. *Lesikar*, 237 S.W.3d at 371; *see, e.g.*, *Young*, 854 S.W.2d at 700-01 (wife objected to finding that she executed agreement voluntarily). A party does not need to support its objection with evidence; only a formal objection is necessary. *See Young*, 854 S.W.2d at 703. See "Making & Preserving Objections," ch. 1-F, p. 43.

3. Effect of objection. An objection to the master's findings raises a fact issue. *Young*, 854 S.W.2d at 701.

§9. TRIAL COURT'S REVIEW OF MASTER'S REPORT

§9.1 Court review of report. The court may confirm, modify, correct, reject, reverse, or recommit the report after it is filed. TRCP 171. If the court makes a finding without specifically rejecting a master's finding on the same issue, the court's finding supersedes the master's. *Hyundai Motor Am. v. O'Neill*, 839 S.W.2d 474, 481 (Tex.App.—Dallas 1992, orig. proceeding). *But see In re Polybutylene Plumbing Litig.*, 23 S.W.3d 428, 439-42 (Tex.App.—Houston [1st Dist.] 2000, pet. dism'd) (trial court had no jurisdiction to modify terms of fully performed attorney-fee agreement when master was appointed solely to implement parties' agreement and to determine whether parties' proposed formula accomplished that agreement).

§9.2 Trial de novo. The fact issues raised by the objections are tried de novo. *Hyundai Motor Am. v. O'Neill*, 839 S.W.2d 474, 480 (Tex.App.—Dallas 1992, orig. proceeding). That is, each party has the right to present evidence on the issues specified in the objections and have the court or jury decide those issues based on the evidence presented in court. *Young v. Young*, 854 S.W.2d 698, 701 (Tex.App.—Dallas 1993, writ denied).

§9.3 Jury or nonjury trial? If one of the parties properly requested a jury, the court must conduct a jury trial on the fact issues raised by the objections to the master's report. *Young v. Young*, 854 S.W.2d 698, 701 (Tex.App.—Dallas 1993, writ denied); *Minnich v. Jones*, 799 S.W.2d 327, 328-29 (Tex.App.—Texarkana 1990, orig. proceeding); *see also Mann v. Mann*, 607 S.W.2d 243, 246 (Tex.1980) (request for jury trial in divorce proceeding does not prevent appointment of master). If no jury was requested, the court will conduct a nonjury trial on those issues.

§10. PAYMENT OF MASTER

§10.1 Reasonable compensation. The trial court will award the master reasonable compensation, which will be taxed as a cost of the suit. TRCP 171; *TransAmerican Nat. Gas Corp. v. Mancias*, 877 S.W.2d 840, 844 (Tex. App.—Corpus Christi 1994, orig. proceeding). Fees for masters are not necessarily determined by the stringent requirements of proof for attorney fees. *Frost v. Frost*, 695 S.W.2d 279, 282 (Tex.App.—San Antonio 1985, no writ). A fee awarded to the master will be reversed only on a showing of a clear abuse of discretion. *Mann v. Mann*, 607 S.W.2d 243, 246 (Tex.1980); *Texas Bank & Trust Co. v. Moore*, 595 S.W.2d 502, 511 (Tex.1980).

⬦

§10.2 Not in advance. The trial court cannot require the parties to deposit funds into the court's registry to cover the master's fee. *TransAmerican Nat. Gas Corp. v. Mancias*, 877 S.W.2d 840, 844 (Tex.App.—Corpus Christi 1994, orig. proceeding). The Supreme Court has not addressed this issue. *Simpson v. Canales*, 806 S.W.2d 802, 812 n.14 (Tex.1991).

§11. REVIEW

§11.1 Appeal.

1. Master's appointment. Generally, when the trial court grants a motion to appoint a master, the order cannot be appealed until after a final judgment is rendered in the case. *See Moyer v. Moyer*, 183 S.W.3d 48, 58 (Tex.App.—Austin 2005, no pet.).

2. Master's report. If the court overrules an objection to the master's report, the party may appeal and challenge the ruling after a final judgment is rendered.

§11.2 Mandamus. If the court improperly overrules a party's objection to the order of referral to a master, the party can file a petition for writ of mandamus. *See Simpson v. Canales*, 806 S.W.2d 802, 812 (Tex.1991); *Tollett v. Carmona*, 915 S.W.2d 562, 564 (Tex.App.—Houston [14th Dist.] 1995, orig. proceeding). Appointment of a master will be reversed only on a showing of a clear abuse of discretion. *Simpson*, 806 S.W.2d at 811; *In re Harris*, 315 S.W.3d 685, 704 (Tex.App.—Houston [1st Dist.] 2010, orig. proceeding).

L. SUBPOENAS

§1. GENERAL

§1.1 Rules. TRCP 176, 199.3, 205. See CPRC §§22.001, 22.002.

§1.2 Purpose. A subpoena is a process or writ that commands a person either to appear and give testimony or to produce or permit inspection and copying of documents or other tangible things. TRCP 176.2; *see* TRCP 199.3, 205.3; *In re Z.A.T.*, 193 S.W.3d 197, 207 (Tex.App.—Waco 2006, pet. denied).

§1.3 Forms. *O'Connor's Texas Civil Forms* (2012), FORMS 1L, 6A:13-14.

§1.4 Other references. Griesel, *The "New" Texas Discovery Rules: Three Years Later*, Advanced Evidence & Discovery Course, State Bar of Texas CLE, ch. 2, §IV, p. 3 (2002); *Texas Trial Handbook* §8:15 (3d ed. 2012-13).

§2. TYPES OF SUBPOENAS

Subpoenas may be issued to command a person (1) to attend and give testimony, (2) to produce and permit inspection of books, papers, documents, or tangible things designated in the subpoena, or (3) to do both. TRCP 176.2.

§2.1 Discovery subpoena. A discovery subpoena is a writ by which a court, at the request of a party, commands a person to appear or produce documents or other things for discovery. TRCP 176.2. A person commanded to produce documents or other things does not need to appear in person unless the subpoena commands the person to attend and give testimony. TRCP 176.6(c). A subpoena cannot be used for discovery in a manner or time other than as provided by the rules of discovery. TRCP 176.3(b); *see Prestige Ford Co. v. Gilmore*, 56 S.W.3d 73, 80 (Tex.App.—Houston [14th Dist.] 2001, pet. denied). In most cases, a discovery subpoena is issued to compel a nonparty to attend a deposition and produce documents. See "Securing Things from a Nonparty," ch. 6-I, §5, p. 569.

§2.2 Trial subpoena. A subpoena for a hearing or trial commands a witness to attend and give testimony or to produce documents or things at a hearing or trial, and to remain there from day to day until discharged by either the court or the party issuing the subpoena. TRCP 176.2(a), 176.6(a), (f). Attorneys may issue their own trial subpoenas. TRCP 176.4(b). See "Who may issue subpoenas," §3.3, p. 86. A party cannot secure a trial subpoena by making an oral request to the court. *Holleman v. West End Cab Co.*, No. 07-99-0232-CV (Tex.App.—Amarillo 2000, pet. denied) (no pub.; 7-6-00).

★

PRACTICE TIP

If the witness to be subpoenaed can be characterized as "friendly," the attorney may include in the trial subpoena a request that the witness call the attorney to set up a date and time for the witness to appear at trial.

---

1. Time for issuance. TRCP 176 does not state how much advance notice should be allowed for issuing a subpoena for a hearing or trial. The only rule is that the party who issued the subpoena should be "diligent" in procuring the witness's testimony. *See, e.g.,* ***Hatteberg v. Hatteberg***, 933 S.W.2d 522, 526 (Tex.App.—Houston [1st Dist.] 1994, no writ) (continuance denied; attempted service of subpoena nine days before trial was not diligent); ***Victor M. Solis Underground Util. & Paving Co. v. City of Laredo***, 751 S.W.2d 532, 537 (Tex.App.—San Antonio 1988, writ denied) (continuance denied; subpoena issued for out-of-town witness only three days before trial was not diligent); ***Dairyland Cty. Mut. Ins. v. Keys***, 568 S.W.2d 457, 460 (Tex.App.—Tyler 1978, writ ref'd n.r.e.) (continuance denied; party waited to have subpoena issued on day of trial rather than two weeks earlier at time of docket call).

2. Discharging the witness. The court or the summoning party may discharge a witness summoned for a hearing or trial. TRCP 176.6(a). A discharged witness may be subpoenaed again to appear and give testimony. ***Burttschell v. Sheppard***, 69 S.W.2d 402, 404 (Tex.1934).

§3. FORMAL REQUIREMENTS FOR SUBPOENAS

The subpoena must meet the formal requirements of TRCP 176.1 and any additional requirements imposed by local district or county rules that apply where the case is pending.

§3.1 Form of subpoena. The subpoena must (1) be issued in the name of "The State of Texas," (2) include the style and cause number of the suit, (3) identify the court where the suit is pending, (4) state the date the subpoena is issued, (5) identify the person to whom the subpoena is directed, (6) state the time, place, and nature of the action required of the person being subpoenaed, (7) identify the party who secured the subpoena, (8) include the text of TRCP 176.8(a) regarding contempt, (9) be signed by the person issuing the subpoena, and (10) command a person (a) to attend and give testimony, (b) to produce and permit inspection of the books, papers, documents, or tangible things designated in the subpoena, or (c) to do both. TRCP 176.1, 176.2. See *O'Connor's Texas Forms*, FORM 1L:1.

§3.2 Range of subpoena. Both TRCP 176.3 and CPRC §22.002 limit the geographic reach of subpoenas to 150 miles, but the range of a subpoena is broader under TRCP 176.3 than under CPRC §22.002. Other statutes, however, may modify the 150-mile range in TRCP 176.3 and CPRC §22.002.

1. TRCP 176.3. A witness may be required by subpoena to appear or produce documents in any county within 150 miles of the place where the witness resides or was served. TRCP 176.3(a). To determine the range of a subpoena under TRCP 176.3, trace a circle with a radius of 150 miles from the place where the witness resides or was served. The witness may be required to appear or produce documents at any place in any county that is even partially in that circle. TRCP 176.3 does not restrict the places for deposition listed in TRCP 199.2(b)(2) for parties and other witnesses who can be compelled to appear by notice alone.

2. CPRC §22.002. A witness may be required by subpoena to appear for a trial or hearing in the county of suit if the witness resides or was served within 150 miles of that county. CPRC §22.002. To determine the range under CPRC §22.002, trace a circle around the county of suit with a radius of 150 miles out from the county line. If the witness resides or was served within that circle, the witness can be compelled to attend.

PRACTICE TIP

An attorney may be able to use online tools to determine whether a subpoenaed person is located within the 150-mile radius required by TRCP 176.3 and CPRC §22.002. See, e.g., Radius Around Point Tool, www.freemaptools.com/radius-around-point.htm.

★

1-5. DISTANCE NONPARTY CAN BE COMPELLED TO TRAVEL		
Authority	Residence	Where served
1 TRCP 176.3	To any county, if part of county is within radius of 150 miles from witness's residence	To any county, if part of county is within radius of 150 miles from place served
2 CPRC §22.002	To county of suit, if witness's residence is within 150 miles of that county	To county of suit, if witness was served within 150 miles of that county

3. Other statutes. Other statutes may modify the 150-mile subpoena range in TRCP 176.3 and CPRC §22.002 for particular suits. For example, in a suit to prohibit restraint on trade, a witness located anywhere in the state may be required by subpoena to appear for a trial or hearing. Bus. & Com. Code §15.11; *see also id.* §17.57 (in DTPA suits, witness residing or served within 100 miles of courthouse, or, for suits pending in Travis County, within 100 miles of courthouse of county where suit could have been brought, can be subpoenaed to appear or produce documents).

§3.3 Who may issue subpoenas. Subpoenas may be issued by the court clerk, an attorney, or a deposition officer. TRCP 176.4. For the definition of "deposition officer," see "Deposition Officer," ch. 6-F, §3, p. 525. When a subpoena is issued by the clerk, the clerk must provide the party requesting the subpoena with an original and a copy (both to be completed by the party) for each witness. TRCP 176.4(a).

§3.4 Who may serve subpoenas. Subpoenas may be served by the sheriff, constable, or any other person who is not a party and is at least 18 years old. TRCP 176.5(a). Generally, when a witness is subpoenaed for a deposition, the court reporter serves the subpoena with the notice of deposition. *See* TRCP 176.4(c). For detailed information about who may serve subpoenas, see "Who May Serve Process," ch. 2-H, §3, p. 160.

§3.5 Who may be subpoenaed. Subpoenas may require the attendance of parties and nonparties (e.g., witnesses, custodians of records). TRCP 176.2, 199.3, 205.1; *see St. Luke's Episcopal Hosp. v. Garcia*, 928 S.W.2d 307, 311 (Tex.App.—Houston [14th Dist.] 1996, orig. proceeding) (a subpoena is the instrument that compels nonparties to respond to a deposition); *Cheatham v. Rogers*, 824 S.W.2d 231, 234 (Tex.App.—Tyler 1992, orig. proceeding) (nonparty witness can be subpoenaed to attend deposition). When securing documents from a custodian of records, the subpoena does not need to name the person; the subpoena can be addressed to the "custodian of records" of the business entity. When securing documents from a party, it is not necessary to serve a subpoena. See "Securing Things from a Party," ch. 6-I, §3, p. 565.

§3.6 Notice to other parties. A party is not required to give other parties notice of its trial subpoenas, but it must give other parties notice of its discovery subpoenas. *See* TRCP 191.5. A party cannot secure discovery by using a trial subpoena to avoid the notice requirements of TRCP 191.5. *See* TRCP 176.3(b) (prohibiting use of subpoena to circumvent discovery rules); *Prestige Ford Co. v. Gilmore*, 56 S.W.3d 73, 80 (Tex.App.—Houston [14th Dist.] 2001, pet. denied) (same).

§3.7 Manner of service. A subpoena is served by delivering a copy of the subpoena, with the subpoena fee, to the witness. TRCP 176.5(a). If the witness is a party and is represented by an attorney, the subpoena and fee may be served on the witness's attorney of record. *Id.* When a discovery subpoena requires the witness to attend a deposition, the notice of deposition may be served with the subpoena. TRCP 176.4(c).

§3.8 Subpoena fee. The subpoena fee is $10 for each day the witness is required to attend trial or discovery. CPRC §22.001(a); Tex. Att'y Gen. Op. No. DM-342 (1995). When a person is subpoenaed to attend, the person is entitled to receive payment of one day's witness fee at the time the subpoena is served. CPRC §22.001 ($10 per day, first day payable at service). Subpoena fees are recoverable as court costs. CPRC §22.001(c); *see Shenandoah Assocs. v. J&K Props., Inc.*, 741 S.W.2d 470, 487 (Tex.App.—Dallas 1987, writ denied).

§3.9 Proof of service. Proof of service must be made by filing with the court (1) the witness's signed written memorandum or (2) a statement by the person who served the subpoena stating the date, time, and manner of service and the name of the person served. TRCP 176.5(b).

SUBPOENAS

———————————————— ★ ————————————————

§4. OBJECTING TO TRIAL & DISCOVERY SUBPOENAS

§4.1 Who can challenge. The subpoena can be challenged by the person being subpoenaed, the parties, or any other person affected by the subpoena. *See* TRCP 176.6(d)-(f).

1. Person subject to subpoena. A subpoenaed person may challenge the subpoena by filing (1) a motion for protective order or (2) an objection to the subpoena. *See* TRCP 176.6(d), (e), 192.6; *In re Diversicare Gen. Partner*, 41 S.W.3d 788, 794 (Tex.App.—Corpus Christi 2001, orig. proceeding), *overruled on other grounds*, *In re Arriola*, 159 S.W.3d 670 (Tex.App.—Corpus Christi 2004, orig. proceeding). See "Filing motion for protective order or objection," §4.3.1, this page. A subpoenaed person may also withhold material or information claimed to be privileged. See "Asserting privileges," §4.3.2, p. 88.

2. Party or other person. A party or any other person affected by the subpoena may challenge the subpoena by filing a motion for protective order. *See* TRCP 176.6(e), 192.6. See "Motion for protective order," §4.3.1(1), this page.

§4.2 Deadline to challenge.

1. Trial subpoena. If possible, a person challenging a trial subpoena should make the challenge before the time specified for appearing in court. TRCP 176.6(d), (e). However, the person may wait to challenge the subpoena until the witness appears in court. TRCP 176.6(f).

2. Discovery subpoena. A person challenging a discovery subpoena must make the challenge before the time specified for compliance in the subpoena, or the challenge will be waived. TRCP 176.6(d), (e); *In re University of Tex. Health Ctr.*, 198 S.W.3d 392, 395 (Tex.App.—Texarkana 2006, orig. proceeding).

§4.3 Types of challenges.

1. Filing motion for protective order or objection. The subpoena may be challenged by filing a motion for protective order or an objection to the subpoena.

NOTE

*Under TRCP 176.6(d)-(f), a person can challenge a subpoena by filing a motion for protective order or an objection to the subpoena; nothing in the rule provides for filing a motion to quash the subpoena. See **In re K.L.&J. L.P.**, 336 S.W.3d 286, 293 n.3 (Tex.App.—San Antonio 2010, orig. proceeding). However, some parties still file—and courts may review—a motion to quash the subpoena issued under TRCP 176. See, e.g., **In re Rabb**, 293 S.W.3d 865, 866 (Tex.App.— Dallas 2009, orig. proceeding) (persons subject to trial subpoena filed motion to quash); see also TRCP 177a (repealed 1999) (motion to quash subpoena allowed if it is unreasonable and oppressive).*

---

(1) Motion for protective order.

(a) To challenge procedural defect. If a subpoena is procedurally defective, the person challenging the subpoena should file a motion for protective order. *See* TRCP 176.6(e), 192.6. See "Motion for Protective Order," ch. 6-A, §20, p. 449; *O'Connor's Texas Forms*, FORM 6A:13 (motion for protection from discovery subpoena). The following are examples of challenges a person can make to a subpoena that is procedurally defective: • The subpoena was not dated and signed by a person authorized under TRCP 176.4 to issue subpoenas. TRCP 176.1(h). • The subpoena was not served by a sheriff, constable, or other person authorized by law. TRCP 176.5(a). • There was no witness fee attached to the subpoena. CPRC §22.001; TRCP 176.8(b); *Kieffer v. Miller*, 560 S.W.2d 431, 432 (Tex. App.—Beaumont 1977, writ ref'd n.r.e.). • Only one subpoena was issued for two or more witnesses, including the subpoenaed person. TRCP 176.1(d).

(b) To challenge discovery request. If a subpoena requests information that is unduly burdensome or expensive, harassing, annoying, or invasive of a protected right, the person challenging the subpoena should file a motion for protective order. *See* TRCP 176.7, 192.6. See "Grounds to limit scope of discovery," ch. 6-A, §20.1, p. 449.

★

(2) **Objection.** If the person challenging the subpoena is the person being subpoenaed, the person can file an objection to the subpoena rather than a motion for protective order. TRCP 176.6(d).

2. **Asserting privileges.** A subpoenaed person may withhold any material or information claimed to be privileged, but that person must comply with TRCP 193.3. TRCP 176.6(c). When an assertion of privilege is appropriate, a person should not seek a protective order; however, a motion for protective order will not waive the privilege. TRCP 192.6(a). See "Motion for Protective Order," ch. 6-A, §20, p. 449. The privilege claim must be asserted before the deadline for complying with the subpoena. See "Asserting privileges," ch. 6-A, §18.2, p. 443; "When necessary," ch. 6-A, §18.7.1, p. 446.

§5. ENFORCING SUBPOENAS

The court may impose a fine or confine the subpoenaed person for contempt of court for not complying with a subpoena. TRCP 176.8(a). If a subpoenaed witness does not appear for trial, the trial court may issue a writ of attachment to compel her attendance. *In re Z.A.T.*, 193 S.W.3d 197, 207 (Tex.App.—Waco 2006, pet. denied). The court cannot impose a fine or issue a writ of attachment in a civil suit until the summoning party provides an affidavit stating that all lawful fees were paid or tendered to the witness. TRCP 176.8(b); *Kieffer v. Miller*, 560 S.W.2d 431, 432 (Tex.App.—Beaumont 1977, writ ref'd n.r.e.); Tex. Att'y Gen. Op. No. DM-342 (1995). The trial court has no authority to issue a writ of attachment for a witness discharged by the summoning party. *Alcocer v. Travelers Ins.*, 446 S.W.2d 927, 928-29 (Tex.App.—Houston [14th Dist.] 1969, no writ).

⭐

★

CHAPTER 2

★

─────────────────── ✦ ───────────────────

2. PLAINTIFF'S LAWSUIT

A. PREFILING CONSIDERATIONS

§1. GENERAL

§1.1 Rule. TRCP 54.

§1.2 Purpose. Before filing suit, the plaintiff should check appropriate statutes and any document on which the suit is based to determine whether there are any prerequisites to filing suit.

§1.3 Forms. *O'Connor's Texas Civil Forms* (2012), FORMS 2A.

§1.4 Other references. Guiberteau & Motheral, *The Changing Role of Guardian & Attorney Ad Litems*, 58 Tex.B.J. 955 (1995); *O'Connor's Federal Rules * Civil Trials* (2013) (*O'Connor's Federal Rules*); *O'Connor's Texas Causes of Action* (2013) (*O'Connor's Texas COA*).

§2. NOTICES & DEMANDS

The plaintiff should consider whether it must give the defendant notice or make a pretrial demand before filing suit.

§2.1 Statutory notice. Before plaintiffs can file certain types of suits against certain defendants, they must give written notice. *See, e.g.*, CPRC §74.051(a) (before filing suit against health-care provider, P must give 60 days' written notice of claim); CPRC §101.101(a) (under Texas Tort Claims Act, P should give written notice to state entity within six months after date of incident giving rise to claim). See *O'Connor's Texas COA*, "Notice," ch. 20-A, §7.1, p. 625; "Presuit written notice," ch. 25-A, §2.7.1(1), p. 881. The time limits for most statutory notices are substantially shorter than limitations periods. In some cases, the suit is barred if the plaintiff does not give the required statutory notice. *See, e.g.*, *Cathey v. Booth*, 900 S.W.2d 339, 340 (Tex.1995) (suit barred because Ps did not give written notice and governmental unit did not have actual notice). In other cases, the plaintiff's failure to give notice is merely a reason to abate, not dismiss. *See, e.g.*, Bus. & Com. Code §17.505(c)-(e) (DTPA claim); *De Checa v. Diagnostic Ctr. Hosp., Inc.*, 852 S.W.2d 935, 939 (Tex.1993) (health-care liability claim). See *O'Connor's Texas Forms*, FORMS 2A.

§2.2 Statutory demand. Under some statutes, before filing suit, a plaintiff must make a written demand stating the extent of the plaintiff's damages, attorney fees, and costs. *E.g.*, Bus. & Com. Code §17.505(a) (60 days before filing DTPA suit); Ins. Code §541.154 (60 days before filing suit for deceptive acts). See *O'Connor's Texas Forms*, FORMS 2A.

§2.3 Conditions precedent in contracts. Many contracts contain provisions that are conditions precedent to filing suit. Typically, the provisions require the plaintiff to give notice of the claim and notice of its intent to sue. See "Conditions Precedent," ch. 2-B, §11, p. 109; *O'Connor's Texas Forms*, FORM 2B:2.

§2.4 Preservation letter for electronic discovery. To ensure that all parties to a potential suit are aware of electronic-discovery intentions, a letter should be sent to each of them outlining the type of information to be preserved. See "Preservation letter," ch. 6-C, §4.2.2(1), p. 491.

§2.5 Consent to sue. In some situations, a party must obtain consent to sue. *E.g.*, *Federal Sign v. Texas S. Univ.*, 951 S.W.2d 401, 404-05 (Tex.1997) (party who contracts with State must secure consent to sue State); *State Farm Mut. Auto. Ins. v. Azima*, 896 S.W.2d 177, 177-78 (Tex.1995) (some insurance contracts require consent from insurer before suit can be filed against uninsured motorist).

§3. FILING CONSIDERATIONS

Before filing suit, the plaintiff should determine where it may file suit, whether it must first seek an administrative remedy, and whether the suit is subject to alternative dispute resolution.

─────────────── ✦ ───────────────

§3.1 State vs. federal court. Some cases must be filed in federal court (e.g., patent and copyright), some may be filed only in state court (e.g., suits with no federal question or diversity), and others may be filed in either state or federal court. In the last situation, the plaintiff should decide where it has an advantage and file in that jurisdiction. If the plaintiff wants to avoid removal to federal court, it should include a local defendant if possible. For information about federal jurisdiction and removal to federal court, see *O'Connor's Federal Rules*, "Choosing the Court—Jurisdiction," ch. 2-F, p. 112; "Defendant's Notice of Removal," ch. 4-A, p. 241.

§3.2 Administrative procedure. Before filing a claim against a governmental unit, the plaintiff should determine whether it must first submit the dispute to an administrative procedure. *See Texas DOT v. Jones Bros. Dirt & Paving Contractors, Inc.*, 92 S.W.3d 477, 484 (Tex.2002); *General Servs. Comm'n v. Little-Tex Insulation Co.*, 39 S.W.3d 591, 597 (Tex.2001). When an agency has exclusive jurisdiction (not just primary jurisdiction) over a dispute, a party must exhaust all administrative remedies before seeking judicial review of the agency's action. *Subaru, Inc. v. David McDavid Nissan, Inc.*, 84 S.W.3d 212, 221 (Tex.2002); *Cash Am. Int'l v. Bennett*, 35 S.W.3d 12, 15 (Tex.2000). See "Administrative agency has exclusive jurisdiction," ch. 3-F, §3.6, p. 241; *O'Connor's Texas COA*, "Administrative remedies," ch. 24-A, §2.8, p. 836.

§3.3 ADR. Sometimes the plaintiff is required by either statute or contract to submit a dispute to some form of dispute resolution. See "The ADR System," ch. 4-A, p. 277.

§4. MISCELLANEOUS

Before filing suit, the plaintiff should consider other miscellaneous matters.

§4.1 Internet research. Information about a defendant can be found on the Internet. For example, to find information about a corporation (registered agent, officers, directors, etc.), go to the website of the Texas Comptroller of Public Accounts, ourcpa.cpa.state.tx.us/coa/Index.html. Information about property appraisal can be found on county appraisal district websites. *See, e.g.*, www.hcad.org (Harris County). To find a person's address and telephone number, go to www.anywho.com. Other Internet companies can, for a fee, provide comprehensive information about individuals, including location, family members, nearest neighbors with listed telephone numbers, judgments, and bankruptcies. *See, e.g.*, www.ussearch.com.

§4.2 Presuit discovery. A plaintiff may secure discovery before filing suit. A plaintiff can file a verified motion and obtain an order authorizing the taking of depositions before suit. TRCP 202.1, 202.2. Presuit discovery is useful to preserve evidence when a critical witness is elderly, infirm, or about to leave the jurisdiction. It can also be used to investigate a case before filing suit to avoid penalties under TRCP 13 and CPRC §§9.012 and 10.004 for groundless and frivolous lawsuits. See "Deposition Before Suit," ch. 6-F, §16, p. 543; *O'Connor's Texas Forms*, FORMS 6F:9-12.

§4.3 Appointment of legal representative. When a party is incompetent to represent herself in court (e.g., a minor, an incapacitated person), the attorney should determine whether the party has a legal representative with the capacity to file or defend the suit. See "Minor as P," ch. 2-B, §3.4.2, p. 101; "Minor as D," ch. 2-B, §3.5.4, p. 102.

§4.4 Lis pendens notice. In cases involving a direct interest in real property, the plaintiff may file a lis pendens notice. *See* Prop. Code §§12.007, 13.004; *In re Collins*, 172 S.W.3d 287, 292-93 (Tex.App.—Fort Worth 2005, orig. proceeding). For there to be a direct interest in real property, the action must involve (1) title to the property, (2) the establishment of an interest in the property, or (3) the enforcement of an interest in the property. *See* Prop. Code §12.007(a); *In re Collins*, 172 S.W.3d at 292-93. The filing of a lis pendens notice puts the public on notice that the property is involved in litigation. *In re Collins*, 172 S.W.3d at 292; *Prappas v. Meyerland Cmty. Imprv. Ass'n*, 795 S.W.2d 794, 795 (Tex.App.—Houston [14th Dist.] 1990, writ denied). The notice warns a prospective buyer that any interest the buyer may acquire in the property is subject to the outcome of the litigation. *Gene Hill Equip. Co. v. Merryman*, 771 S.W.2d 207, 209 (Tex.App.—Austin 1989, no writ); *see Cherokee Water Co. v. Advance Oil & Gas Co.*, 843 S.W.2d 132, 135 (Tex.App.—Texarkana 1992, writ denied). The notice is effective regardless of whether the parties to the proceedings were served. Prop. Code §13.004; *In re Collins*, 172 S.W.3d at 293. The notice does not prevent transfer of the property during the litigation. *Cherokee*, 843 S.W.2d at 135.

★

B. PLAINTIFF'S ORIGINAL PETITION

§1. GENERAL

§1.1 Rules. TRCP 45-61, 78-82, 190.

§1.2 Purpose. The plaintiff's petition defines the issues for trial. *Murray v. O&A Express, Inc.*, 630 S.W.2d 633, 636 (Tex.1982). The petition should give fair notice of the facts relied on, enabling the defendant to prepare a defense. *Horizon/CMS Healthcare Corp. v. Auld*, 34 S.W.3d 887, 897 (Tex.2000); *Garvey v. Vawter*, 795 S.W.2d 741, 742 (Tex.1990); *Roark v. Allen*, 633 S.W.2d 804, 810 (Tex.1982); *see* TRCP 45(b).

§1.3 Forms. *O'Connor's Texas Civil Forms* (2012), FORMS 2B; *O'Connor's Texas Causes of Action Pleadings* (2012) (*O'Connor's Texas COA Pleadings*).

§1.4 Other references. Reese, *Misnomer & Misidentification: Suing the Wrong Defendant*, 60 Tex.B.J. 548 (1997); *O'Connor's CPRC Plus* (2012-13) (*O'Connor's CPRC*); *O'Connor's Federal Rules * Civil Trials* (2013) (*O'Connor's Federal Rules*); *O'Connor's Texas Causes of Action* (2013) (*O'Connor's Texas COA*).

§2. DISCOVERY-CONTROL PLANS

In the first numbered paragraph of its petition, the plaintiff must allege whether discovery is intended to be conducted under Level 1, 2, or 3 of TRCP 190. TRCP 190.1. See "Discovery-Control Plans," ch. 6-A, §7, p. 430. The level designated for the discovery-control plan must relate to the type of suit and the amount of damages. See "Damages," §8, p. 107. The plaintiff must also include the statement about the discovery level in any amended pleading. If the plaintiff does not plead a discovery level as required by TRCP 190.1, the defendant may file special exceptions. *See* TRCP 190 cmt. 1. See "Special Exceptions—Challenging the Pleadings," ch. 3-G, p. 248.

(13)

PROPOSED TRCP CHANGES

In response to Gov't Code §22.004(h), the Supreme Court has proposed TRCP 169 to establish a process for the prompt, efficient, and cost-effective resolution of civil actions (expedited actions) in which only monetary relief is sought and the amount in controversy is no more than $100,000. See Tex.Sup.Ct. Order, Misc. Docket No. 12-9191 (eff. Mar. 1, 2013). The Supreme Court has proposed corresponding amendments to TRCP 190.2 that would change the Level 1 discovery-control plan to apply to these expedited actions under TRCP 169. See Tex.Sup.Ct. Order, Misc. Docket No. 12-9191 (eff. Mar. 1, 2013). The public-comment period for the proposed amendments ends on February 1, 2013, and the rules are to take effect March 1, 2013. For the proposed version of the rules, see the appendix after this book's index. For the final version, go to the Supreme Court website at www.supreme.courts.state.tx.us. When the new and amended rules take effect, a supplement to this book—with updated rules and commentaries that reflect the changes—will be available at www.JonesMcClure.com/TRCPamendments.

§2.1 Level 1. If the plaintiff intends discovery to be conducted under Level 1, its petition should allege one of the following:

1. Suits for monetary damages. "Plaintiff intends that discovery be conducted under Level 1 and affirmatively pleads that it seeks only monetary relief aggregating $50,000 or less, excluding costs, prejudgment interest, and attorney fees." TRCP 190.2(a)(1); *see* TRCP 190 cmt. 2.

2. Suits for divorce. "Plaintiff intends that discovery be conducted under Level 1 and affirmatively pleads this is a suit for divorce in which there are no children and the value of the marital estate is more than zero but less than $50,000." TRCP 190.2(a)(2); *see* TRCP 190 cmt. 2.

─────────────────────── ★ ───────────────────────

§2.2 Level 2. If the plaintiff intends discovery to be conducted under Level 2, its petition should allege one of the following:

1. Suits for monetary damages. "Plaintiff intends that discovery be conducted under Level 2 and affirmatively pleads that it seeks monetary relief aggregating more than $50,000." *See* TRCP 190.2(a)(1), 190.3(a) & cmt. 2.

2. Suits for divorce.

(1) Children. "Plaintiff intends that discovery be conducted under Level 2 and affirmatively pleads this is a suit for divorce in which there are children." Discovery for a divorce involving children cannot be conducted under Level 1. *See* TRCP 190.2(a)(2), 190.3(a) & cmt. 2.

(2) Estate over $50,000. "Plaintiff intends that discovery be conducted under Level 2 and affirmatively pleads this is a suit for divorce in which the value of the marital estate is more than $50,000." *See* TRCP 190.2(a)(2), 190.3(a).

3. Suits for injunctive relief. "Plaintiff intends that discovery be conducted under Level 2 and affirmatively pleads that it seeks injunctive relief." *See* TRCP 190 cmt. 2.

§2.3 Level 3. If the plaintiff intends that discovery be conducted under Level 3, its petition should allege the following: "Plaintiff intends that discovery be conducted under Level 3." *See* TRCP 190.4(a). A plaintiff should plead Level 3 when a discovery-control plan must be tailored to the circumstances of the specific suit. *Id.* A plaintiff's allegation that the case is to be governed by Level 3 does not make Level 3 applicable; a case can be conducted under Level 3 only by court order. TRCP 190 cmt. 1.

§3. PARTIES

§3.1 General rule.

1. Named party. A person or entity is not a party to a lawsuit unless named as a party. *See* TRCP 79; *Mapco, Inc. v. Carter*, 817 S.W.2d 686, 687 (Tex.1991). See "Parties & Claims," ch. 2-E, p. 129; *O'Connor's Texas Forms*, FORMS 2B:9-19. A suit may be maintained only by and against parties who have an actual or legal existence. *Bailey v. Vanscot Concrete Co.*, 894 S.W.2d 757, 759 (Tex.1995), *disapproved on other grounds*, *Chilkewitz v. Hyson*, 22 S.W.3d 825 (Tex.1999).

2. Virtual party. Under the virtual-representation doctrine, persons who are not joined by name as parties may still be parties in substance and legal effect. *New Boston Gen. Hosp., Inc. v. Texas Workforce Comm'n*, 47 S.W.3d 34, 39 (Tex.App.—Texarkana 2001, no pet.). To claim virtual representation, an unnamed party must show the following: (1) it is bound by the judgment, (2) its privity of estate, title, or interest is apparent from the record, and (3) there is a common interest between the named and unnamed parties. *In re Lumbermens Mut. Cas. Co.*, 184 S.W.3d 718, 722 (Tex.2006); *City of San Benito v. Rio Grande Valley Gas Co.*, 109 S.W.3d 750, 755 (Tex.2003); *Motor Vehicle Bd. of Tex. DOT v. El Paso Indep. Auto. Dealers Ass'n*, 1 S.W.3d 108, 110 (Tex.1999). The unnamed party must take some timely action to attain named-party status. *In re Lumbermens*, 184 S.W.3d at 722. An unnamed party cannot appeal unless it is virtually represented. *E.g.*, *City of San Benito*, 109 S.W.3d at 754-55 (unnamed class members who would be bound by judgment approving settlement were "parties" for purposes of appeal); *see Motor Vehicle Bd.*, 1 S.W.3d at 110 (generally, appeal is available only to parties of record).

§3.2 Standing & capacity. Before filing suit, the plaintiff should ensure that (1) it has standing and capacity to file the suit and (2) the correct defendant is sued in the correct capacity.

1. Standing. Standing is a constitutional prerequisite to filing suit. *Heckman v. Williamson Cty.*, 369 S.W.3d 137, 150 (Tex.2012); *City of Houston v. Williams*, 353 S.W.3d 128, 145 (Tex.2011). A court does not have jurisdiction over a claim made by a plaintiff who does not have standing to assert it. *Heckman*, 369 S.W.3d at 150. See "No standing," ch. 3-F, §3.2, p. 240. Because standing is a component of subject-matter jurisdiction, it cannot be

★

waived and can be raised for the first time on appeal. *West Orange-Cove Consol. ISD v. Alanis*, 107 S.W.3d 558, 583 (Tex.2003); *Texas Ass'n of Bus. v. Texas Air Control Bd.*, 852 S.W.2d 440, 445 (Tex.1993).

(1) Individual standing.

(a) Generally. Generally, for a plaintiff to have standing, there must be a concrete injury to the plaintiff and a real controversy between the parties that will be resolved by the court. *Heckman*, 369 S.W.3d at 154.

[1] Injury. The plaintiff must show that she is suffering or has suffered an actual or threatened injury. *Heckman*, 369 S.W.3d at 155. The injury must be concrete, particularized, and actual or imminent; it cannot be hypothetical. *Id.*; *DaimlerChrysler Corp. v. Inman*, 252 S.W.3d 299, 304-05 (Tex.2008). The injury must be personal to the plaintiff, rather than to a third party or the public at large. *Heckman*, 369 S.W.3d at 155; *see DaimlerChrysler Corp.*, 252 S.W.3d at 304-05; *Brown v. Todd*, 53 S.W.3d 297, 302 (Tex.2001).

[2] Traceability. The plaintiff must show the injury can fairly be traced to the defendant's conduct and is not the result of an independent action of a third party. *Heckman*, 369 S.W.3d at 155.

[3] Redressability. The plaintiff must show there is a substantial likelihood that the requested relief will remedy the alleged injury. *Heckman*, 369 S.W.3d at 155. The plaintiff must establish this element for each form of relief sought. *Id.* If, for example, a party requests injunctive relief as well as damages, but the injunctive relief could not possibly remedy her injury, she lacks standing to bring the claim for injunctive relief. *Id.*

(b) Exceptions.

[1] Statutory standing. When standing is conferred by statute, the plaintiff does not have to show she suffered a particularized injury distinct from the general public. *Andrade v. Venable*, 372 S.W.3d 134, 137 (Tex.2012); *see SCI Tex. Funeral Servs. v. Hijar*, 214 S.W.3d 148, 154 (Tex.App.—El Paso 2007, pet. denied) (legislature may by statute exempt Ps from proving "special injury" required for common-law standing); *Everett v. TK-Taito, L.L.C.*, 178 S.W.3d 844, 850 (Tex.App.—Fort Worth 2005, no pet.) (same). Instead, the plaintiff must establish how she has been injured within the parameters of the statutory language. *OAIC Commercial Assets, L.L.C. v. Stonegate Village, L.P.*, 234 S.W.3d 726, 736 (Tex.App.—Dallas 2007, pet. denied); *SCI Tex. Funeral*, 214 S.W.3d at 154; *Everett*, 178 S.W.3d at 851.

[2] Taxpayer standing. When a taxpayer sues to enjoin the illegal expenditure of public funds, she does not have to show she suffered a particularized injury. *Andrade*, 372 S.W.3d at 137; *Williams v. Lara*, 52 S.W.3d 171, 179 (Tex.2001). Instead, to establish standing, the plaintiff must show that (1) she is a taxpayer and (2) public funds are expended on the allegedly illegal activity. *Andrade*, 372 S.W.3d at 137; *Williams*, 52 S.W.3d at 179; *see, e.g.*, *South Tex. Water Auth. v. Lomas*, 223 S.W.3d 304, 308 (Tex.2007) (taxpayer lacked standing under taxpayer exception because funds used did not derive from taxes). The taxpayer must demonstrate that the expenditure is illegal, rather than just unwise or indiscreet. *Lomas*, 223 S.W.3d at 308; *see Williams*, 52 S.W.3d at 180. Further, the taxpayer must plead facts showing that the government is actually spending money on the alleged illegal activity, not on a related activity. *Andrade*, 372 S.W.3d at 138; *Williams*, 52 S.W.3d at 181. The prospective expenditure must be significant and measurable, and it must be an added expenditure, not one that would have been made in spite of the alleged illegal activity. *Andrade*, 372 S.W.3d at 138.

(2) Associational standing.
An association has standing to sue on behalf of its members when (1) its members would otherwise have standing to sue on their own, (2) the interests the association seeks to protect are germane to its purpose, and (3) neither the nature of the claim nor the relief sought requires the participation of the individual members in the suit. *Texas Ass'n of Bus.*, 852 S.W.2d at 447; *see Lomas*, 223 S.W.3d at 308.

(3) Class-action standing.
A named plaintiff in a class action must have individual standing to assert the claim at the time suit is filed. *Heckman*, 369 S.W.3d at 151. See "Generally," §3.2.1(1)(a), this page. When multiple plaintiffs asserting multiple claims seek to represent a class, the court must assess standing plaintiff by plaintiff and claim by claim. *Heckman*, 369 S.W.3d at 153. To have standing, a plaintiff need not have standing on each of the class's claims; as long as she has standing as an individual plaintiff on some claim, she has standing to pursue

★

class certification on that claim. *Id.* at 154. Standing is a threshold inquiry that must be determined before the court can consider whether (1) the named plaintiff is a proper class representative and (2) it can certify the putative class. *See id.* at 151; *M.D. Anderson Cancer Ctr. v. Novak*, 52 S.W.3d 704, 710 (Tex.2001).

2. Capacity. A party has capacity to file or defend a suit if it has the legal authority to act, regardless of whether it has a justiciable interest. *Austin Nursing Ctr., Inc. v. Lovato*, 171 S.W.3d 845, 848-49 (Tex.2005); *Coastal Liquids Transp. v. Harris Cty. Appr. Dist.*, 46 S.W.3d 880, 884 (Tex.2001); *Nootsie, Ltd. v. Williamson Cty. Appr. Dist.*, 925 S.W.2d 659, 661 (Tex.1996); *see, e.g.*, *Christi Bay Temple v. GuideOne Specialty Mut. Ins.*, 330 S.W.3d 251, 253 (Tex.2010) (church that had always operated as unincorporated religious association had capacity to bring suit). A court can render judgment for or against a party only in the capacity in which the party sued or was sued. *See, e.g.*, *Werner v. Colwell*, 909 S.W.2d 866, 870 (Tex.1995) (because D was sued only in individual capacity, judgment could not be rendered against her as trustee); *Gracia v. RC Cola-7-Up Bottling Co.*, 667 S.W.2d 517, 519-20 (Tex.1984) (because P brought suit only as next friend, judgment mistakenly rendered for her individually was not res judicata to second suit by her individually). Unlike standing, an objection to a party's capacity to file or defend a suit can be waived. *Nootsie, Ltd.*, 925 S.W.2d at 662; *see Austin Nursing*, 171 S.W.3d at 849.

3. Distinction between standing & capacity. It is sometimes difficult to distinguish between a party's standing to sue and its capacity to sue. *See Austin Nursing*, 171 S.W.3d at 848. A person has standing if she is personally aggrieved, regardless of whether she has legal authority to act; a person has capacity if she has the authority to file suit, regardless of whether she has a justiciable interest in the suit. *Id.* at 848-49; *Nootsie, Ltd.*, 925 S.W.2d at 661. One way of looking at the distinction between standing and capacity is this: when a party to a suit has an interest in the suit but needs a surrogate to bring or defend the suit, the party does not have capacity. For example, capacity is a problem for a minor who attempts to file suit. *See Austin Nursing*, 171 S.W.3d at 849; *Byrd v. Woodruff*, 891 S.W.2d 689, 704 (Tex.App.—Dallas 1994, writ dism'd). Even though the minor has an interest in the litigation, the suit must be filed by a surrogate.

§3.3 Party identification.

1. Full name. The petition should state the full names of the parties and allege the suing party's capacity in one of the early paragraphs under a section titled "Parties." *See* TRCP 79.

(1) Misspelled name. Under the rule of *idem sonans* (Latin for "sounding the same"), a misspelled name is sufficient identification if it sounds practically identical to the correct name. *E.g.*, *Mantis v. Resz*, 5 S.W.3d 388, 391 & n.5 (Tex.App.—Fort Worth 1999, pet. denied) ("Mantis" sounds like "Mantas"), *overruled on other grounds*, *Sheldon v. Emergency Med. Consultants, I.P.A.*, 43 S.W.3d 701 (Tex.App.—Fort Worth 2001, no pet.); *Chumney v. Craig*, 805 S.W.2d 864, 866 (Tex.App.—Waco 1991, writ denied) ("Damond" sufficiently similar to "Damon").

(2) Misnomer vs. misidentification.

(a) Misnomer. A misnomer occurs when a plaintiff misnames itself or another party but the correct parties are involved. *Reddy Prtshp./5900 N. Freeway, L.P. v. Harris Cty. Appr. Dist.*, 370 S.W.3d 373, 376 (Tex.2012); *In re Greater Houston Orthopaedic Specialists, Inc.*, 295 S.W.3d 323, 325 (Tex.2009). A misnomer can be corrected by amendment even after the statute of limitations expires. *In re Greater Houston*, 295 S.W.3d at 326; *Enserch Corp. v. Parker*, 794 S.W.2d 2, 4-5 (Tex.1990); *see Pierson v. SMS Fin. II, L.L.C.*, 959 S.W.2d 343, 347 (Tex.App.—Texarkana 1998, no pet.). The amendment containing the correct name relates back to the original filing date. *In re Greater Houston*, 295 S.W.3d at 326; *Pierson*, 959 S.W.2d at 347; *see Reddy Prtshp.*, 370 S.W.3d at 377. Courts generally allow parties to correct a misnomer as long as it is not misleading. *Reddy Prtshp.*, 370 S.W.3d at 377.

[1] Misnaming D. If a plaintiff sues and serves the correct defendant but misnames the defendant, the error is misnomer. *Chilkewitz v. Hyson*, 22 S.W.3d 825, 828 (Tex.1999); *Charles Brown, L.L.P. v. Lanier Worldwide, Inc.*, 124 S.W.3d 883, 894 (Tex.App.—Houston [14th Dist.] 2004, no pet.); *see, e.g.*, *Barth v. Bank*

———————————— ★ ————————————

of Am., 351 S.W.3d 875, 876-77 (Tex.2011) (misnomer when P sued Bank of America Corporation instead of Bank of America, N.A.; Bank of America, N.A. answered, agreed it had not been misled, and had representative testify that it was the entity involved in the dispute). "John Doe" is not a misnomer for a person or entity. *Riston v. Doe*, 161 S.W.3d 525, 528 (Tex.App.—Houston [14th Dist.] 2004, pet. denied). When the error is misnomer, service is proper on the correct defendant, and the defendant then has the burden of pleading misnomer and seeking an abatement. *Charles Brown, L.L.P.*, 124 S.W.3d at 894. See "Name," ch. 2-H, §2.5.1(1), p. 158.

[2] **Misnaming P.** If a plaintiff sues and serves the correct defendant but misnames itself, the error is misnomer. *E.g.*, *Reddy Prtshp.*, 370 S.W.3d at 376-77 (misnomer when P misnamed itself as "Reddy Partnership, ETAL," rather than as "Reddy Partnership/5900 North Freeway, L.P."); *Pierson*, 959 S.W.2d at 347 (misnomer when P mistakenly named a related corporate entity rather than itself as P); *cf. In re Greater Houston*, 295 S.W.3d at 325 (misnomer when P omitted part of its name in motion for nonsuit).

(b) **Misidentification.** If the plaintiff sues and serves a party that does not have an interest in the suit, the error is misidentification. *See Diamond v. Eighth Ave. 92, L.C.*, 105 S.W.3d 691, 695 (Tex.App.—Fort Worth 2003, no pet.); *Fleener v. Williams*, 62 S.W.3d 284, 286 (Tex.App.—Houston [1st Dist.] 2001, no pet.). Misidentification occurs when there are two separate individuals or legal entities with similar names, and the plaintiff sues the wrong one. *Reddy Prtshp.*, 370 S.W.3d at 376; *Chilkewitz*, 22 S.W.3d at 828; *see, e.g.*, *Continental S. Lines, Inc. v. Hilland*, 528 S.W.2d 828, 829-30 (Tex.1975) (P sued Continental Trailways, Inc., instead of Continental Southern Lines, Inc., which did business as "Continental Trailways"); *Cortinas v. Wilson*, 851 S.W.2d 324, 327 (Tex. App.—Dallas 1993, no writ) (P sued and served mother of intended D). A suit mistakenly filed against the wrong defendant imposes no duty on the correct defendant to intervene and point out the plaintiff's error. *Matthews Trucking Co. v. Smith*, 682 S.W.2d 237, 239 (Tex.1984). Misidentification generally does not toll limitations. *Enserch Corp.*, 794 S.W.2d at 5. However, limitations can be tolled in a misidentification case if (1) there were two separate but related entities (not individuals) using a similar name, (2) the correct entity had notice of the suit, and (3) the correct entity was not misled or disadvantaged (prejudiced) by the mistake. *Flour Bluff ISD v. Bass*, 133 S.W.3d 272, 274 (Tex.2004); *Chilkewitz*, 22 S.W.3d at 830; *see Diamond*, 105 S.W.3d at 695; *McCord v. Dodds*, 69 S.W.3d 230, 234 (Tex.App.—Corpus Christi 2001, pet. denied); *see also* TRCP 28 (permits suits against entities under their trade names). As soon as the plaintiff discovers a misidentification, it should serve the correct defendant with citation, even if the entities are related. *Wilkins v. Methodist Health Care Sys.*, 108 S.W.3d 565, 570 (Tex.App.—Houston [14th Dist.] 2003) (court noted that filing amended petition without citation or final service was sufficient in previous S.Ct. misidentification cases), *rev'd on other grounds*, 160 S.W.3d 559 (Tex.2005); *see* TRCP 124.

PRACTICE TIP
Always file an answer for your client, even when you believe the client is misidentified. First, you could be wrong and the defendant could have been properly identified, which could subject you to a malpractice case. Second, if a default judgment is rendered and execution of judgment is attempted, your client will incur substantial costs in setting aside the judgment. Third, it is easier to dispose of a case by filing an answer and a motion for summary judgment than by challenging a final judgment.

---

2. Estate. Because the estate of a decedent is not a legal entity, a suit by or against an estate must be brought in the name of its personal representative. *Embrey v. Royal Ins.*, 22 S.W.3d 414, 415 n.2 (Tex.2000); *Price v. Estate of Anderson*, 522 S.W.2d 690, 691 (Tex.1975); *see Austin Nursing Ctr., Inc. v. Lovato*, 171 S.W.3d 845, 849 (Tex.2005); *Henson v. Estate of Crow*, 734 S.W.2d 648, 649 (Tex.1987). The personal representative is the plaintiff or defendant. If a suit names the estate rather than the personal representative, the trial court may still have jurisdiction if the personal representative is served with citation and participates in the suit. *Miller v. Estate of Self*, 113 S.W.3d 554, 557 (Tex.App.—Texarkana 2003, no pet.); *see Embrey*, 22 S.W.3d at 415 n.2 (if unnamed personal representative participated in case, judgment involving estate may be valid).

★

---

(1) Personal representative qualified in Texas. A personal representative of an estate must be qualified by a Texas court to bring or defend a suit relating to the estate in a Texas court. *Minga v. Perales*, 603 S.W.2d 240, 242 (Tex.App.—Corpus Christi 1980, no writ); *see, e.g., McAdams v. Capitol Prods.*, 810 S.W.2d 290, 293 (Tex. App.—Fort Worth 1991, writ denied) (administrator appointed by Arkansas court was not qualified to bring suit in Texas until she was appointed by Texas court); *see also* Prob. Code §105 (qualification of foreign executor).

(2) Death of plaintiff during suit. When a plaintiff dies after suit is filed, the personal representative of the estate—or the heirs, if there is no personal representative—should file a "suggestion of death" with the court, stating that the person has died and naming the personal representative or heirs of the person's estate. TRCP 151. If the cause of action survives the plaintiff's death, the personal representative or heirs may then enter an appearance and prosecute the suit in their own names. TRCP 150, 151; *see Kenseth v. Dallas Cty.*, 126 S.W.3d 584, 596 (Tex.App.—Dallas 2004, pet. denied). If, within a reasonable time, the personal representative or heirs do not file a suggestion of death and appear to prosecute the suit, the defendant should file a suggestion of death and ask the court clerk to issue and serve a writ of scire facias—similar to a citation—on the personal representative or heirs. TRCP 151; *Gracey v. West*, 422 S.W.2d 913, 917 (Tex.1968); *see also* TRCP 154 (requisites of scire facias). If the personal representative or heirs do not appear and prosecute the suit by 10:00 a.m. on the first Monday after the expiration of 20 days from the date the scire facias is served, the defendant can ask the court to dismiss the suit for want of prosecution. *See* TRCP 99(b), 151, 154; *Gracey*, 422 S.W.2d at 917 (D cannot ask for dismissal until scire facias is issued and personal representative does not appear).

(3) Death of defendant during suit. When a defendant dies after suit is filed, if the cause of action survives the defendant's death, the plaintiff must amend the suit to name the estate's personal representative or, if the representative is unavailable, the estate's heirs. TRCP 152; *Rooke v. Jenson*, 838 S.W.2d 229, 230 (Tex. 1992); *see Price*, 522 S.W.2d at 691. Once the plaintiff has amended the petition, or if a suggestion of death is filed, the court clerk must issue a writ of scire facias, requiring the personal representative or heirs to appear and defend the suit. TRCP 152. On the return of service, the plaintiff may proceed with the suit against the personal representative or heirs. *Id.*

(4) Death or replacement of personal representative. If a personal representative dies, resigns, or is removed while party to a suit, the suit then proceeds in the name of the successor personal representative (or the heirs, if there is no successor). TRCP 153. The procedure for substituting the successor personal representative or heirs into the suit is similar to that for the death of a plaintiff or defendant. *Id.*

(5) Real property. In a suit against an estate of a decedent that involves title to real property, the executor or administrator of the estate, if any, and the heirs to the estate must be made party-defendants. CPRC §17.002.

3. Trust. Because a trust is not a legal entity, a suit by or against a trust must be brought in the name of the trustee. *Ray Malooly Trust v. Juhl*, 186 S.W.3d 568, 570 (Tex.2006); *see Huie v. DeShazo*, 922 S.W.2d 920, 926 (Tex.1996). The Legislature has created an exception to this rule: a real-estate investment trust may sue or be sued in its own name. TRCS art. 6138A, §6.10(A)(2).

4. Corporation. A corporation may sue or be sued as a corporate entity. Except for derivative actions, a stockholder cannot file suit individually for damages owed to the corporation because the stockholder lacks both standing (stockholder was not personally aggrieved) and capacity (stockholder is not the right surrogate) to bring suit for damages to the corporation. *See Emmett Props., Inc. v. Halliburton Energy Servs.*, 167 S.W.3d 365, 371 (Tex. App.—Houston [14th Dist.] 2005, pet. denied); *see also* Bus. Orgs. Code §21.055 et seq. (derivative actions). If the corporation is the defendant, individual liability may be imposed only if the plaintiff is able to show that the corporate form was abused. See *O'Connor's Texas COA*, "Piercing the Corporate Veil," ch. 38-F, p. 1213.

5. Assumed name. A person or business entity (partnership, unincorporated association, or private corporation) doing business under an assumed name may sue or be sued in its assumed or common name. TRCP 28; *Chilkewitz*, 22 S.W.3d at 828-29; *see Christi Bay Temple v. GuideOne Specialty Mut. Ins.*, 330 S.W.3d 251, 253

★

(Tex.2010). A person or business entity doing business under an assumed name must file an assumed-name certificate. Bus. & Com. Code §§36.10, 36.11; *Sixth RMA Partners v. Sibley*, 111 S.W.3d 46, 55 (Tex.2003). The court may abate an action until the certificate is filed. *Sibley*, 111 S.W.3d at 55. Before judgment is rendered, the person or entity's correct legal name must be substituted for its assumed name. *Id.* at 53; *see* TRCP 28. The correct name may be substituted by motion of a party or the court, by an amended pleading, or, if there is no objection, by a supplemental pleading. *See* TRCP 28; *Sibley*, 111 S.W.3d at 53. When a person is doing business under an assumed name, a judgment rendered against the unincorporated association is binding on that person. *Holberg & Co. v. Citizens Nat'l Assur. Co.*, 856 S.W.2d 515, 517 (Tex.App.—Houston [1st Dist.] 1993, no writ).

(1) Unincorporated for-profit association. Members of an unincorporated for-profit association are individually liable for the act of an agent or employee of the association if the act is committed within the scope of the agent's or employee's authority. *Hutchins v. Grace Tabernacle United Pentecostal Ch.*, 804 S.W.2d 598, 599 (Tex.App.—Houston [1st Dist.] 1991, no writ).

(2) Unincorporated nonprofit association. Unincorporated nonprofit associations (e.g., churches, property owners' groups) are legal entities liable for their contracts and torts. *See* Bus. Orgs. Code §252.006(a). The members of an unincorporated nonprofit association are relieved from individual responsibility. *Id.* §252.006(b).

6. County or city. A suit by or against a county or incorporated city must be in the entity's corporate name. TRCP 33.

§3.4 Plaintiff.

1. P's residence. The petition must state the residence of each party, if it is known. TRCP 79. The plaintiff should include its county of residence in the petition; a street address is not necessary. *See Isaacson v. Anderson*, 982 S.W.2d 39, 40 (Tex.App.—Houston [1st Dist.] 1998, no pet.).

2. Minor as P. In Texas, a minor is an unmarried person under age 18. CPRC §129.001; *see* Prob. Code §3(t). A minor does not have the legal capacity to employ an attorney or anyone else to watch over her interests. *Byrd v. Woodruff*, 891 S.W.2d 689, 704 (Tex.App.—Dallas 1994, writ dism'd). A minor cannot bring a cause of action on her own behalf unless her disability has been removed. *Sax v. Votteler*, 648 S.W.2d 661, 666 (Tex.1983); *see* CPRC §16.001(b) (tolling limitations period while person is under legal disability). However, a lawsuit may be filed on behalf of a minor by (1) the guardian of the minor, (2) the guardian of the estate of the minor, or (3) if the minor has no guardian, by a next friend or by a representative appointed by the court. *See* Fam. Code §102.003(a)(2) (representative authorized by court), §102.003(a)(4) (guardian of person or estate); Prob. Code §773 (guardian of estate); TRCP 44 (next friend). A parent is a proper next friend, although any competent adult may act as a next friend. *See* Fam. Code §102.003(a)(1) (parent may file suit for child).

3. Death actions. The proper plaintiff in a survival action is the legal representative of the decedent's estate. *See* CPRC §71.021. See *O'Connor's Texas COA*, "Survival," ch. 7-A, p. 178. The proper plaintiffs in a wrongful-death case are the decedent's spouse, children, and parents. CPRC §71.004(b). See *O'Connor's Texas COA*, "Wrongful Death," ch. 7-B, p. 187.

§3.5 Defendant.
The petition (and the citation) should designate as the defendant the person or entity against whom the plaintiff can collect the judgment. See *O'Connor's Texas Forms*, FORMS 2B:10-19. This can be confusing when the defendant must be sued through a representative. For example, because an estate is not a legal entity, the petition, citation, and judgment should name the representative of the estate as the defendant on behalf of the estate, not the decedent. See "Estate," §3.3.2, p. 99. A judgment is void if the trial court did not have personal jurisdiction over the defendant. *American Gen. Fire & Cas. Co. v. Vandewater*, 907 S.W.2d 491, 492 (Tex.1995).

1. D's address for service. For purposes of service, the petition must identify the address, if known, of the defendant or the defendant's agent. *See* TRCP 79. See "Address for service," ch. 2-H, §2.5.1(3), p. 159.

2. D's agent for service. When the defendant is a corporation or another entity served through an agent, the petition must identify the defendant's agent for service and its address. *See Harmon & Reid v. Quin*, 258 S.W.2d

★

441, 442 (Tex.App.—San Antonio 1953, orig. proceeding); *see also Interaction, Inc. v. State*, 17 S.W.3d 775, 779-80 (Tex.App.—Austin 2000, pet. denied) (corporation doing business in Texas must maintain current name and address of its registered agent on file with Secretary of State).

3. Agency. If a principal is liable for the acts of its agent, the plaintiff should sue the principal and allege the agency relationship. *See Southern Cty. Mut. Ins. v. First Bank & Trust*, 750 S.W.2d 170, 172 (Tex.1988).

4. Minor as D. Generally, a minor who is sued must be personally served with process. *Wright v. Jones*, 52 S.W.2d 247, 251 (Tex.Comm'n App.1932, holding approved); *In re Estate of Bean*, 120 S.W.3d 914, 920 (Tex. App.—Texarkana 2003, pet. denied). This is because the minor lacks the capacity to waive service of process, and no one can waive it for the minor. *Wheeler v. Ahrenbeak*, 54 Tex. 535, 539 (Tex.1881); *Wright*, 52 S.W.2d at 251; *In re M.W.*, 523 S.W.2d 513, 515 (Tex.App.—El Paso 1975, no writ). Once the minor has been served, the court has personal jurisdiction over the minor and can appoint a guardian ad litem to represent the minor's interests. *Sprague v. Haines*, 4 S.W. 371, 373 (Tex.1887); *Wright*, 52 S.W.2d at 251; *see also* TRCP 173 (guardian ad litem rule). See "Guardian Ad Litem Under TRCP 173," ch. 1-I, p. 67. There are two exceptions to the rule that a minor must be served directly:

(1) Guardian of estate. If, before suit is filed, the minor has a guardian of the estate appointed under the Probate Code, the plaintiff should sue and serve the guardian as defendant instead of the minor ward. *See* Prob. Code §768; *Peek v. DeBerry*, 819 S.W.2d 217, 218 (Tex.App.—San Antonio 1991, writ denied).

(2) Minor as claimant. If the minor, even though named as a defendant, is actually a claimant through a parent-next friend, the plaintiff can sue and serve the minor's parent as the minor's next friend. *See, e.g., Vandewater*, 907 S.W.2d at 492 (settlement of minor's personal-injury claim was followed by declaratory-judgment action to determine insurance-policy limits); *Orange Grove ISD v. Rivera*, 679 S.W.2d 482, 483 (Tex.1984) (workers' compensation award to minor was followed by appeal of award to district court).

NOTE

Neither the rules of civil procedure nor case law specifies a different method of serving process on minors from the method for serving it on adults. Some methods of service, however, may be inappropriate for use with minors, especially infants and young children. See "Methods of Service," ch. 2-H, §4, p. 161. Rather than attempting a "crib drop" to serve an infant by personal delivery, a plaintiff should consider serving the minor by another method, such as by mail, and if necessary petitioning the court to permit service on a minor through a parent or guardian. See "Service by court order," ch. 2-H, §4.3, p. 162.

---

5. Partnership. A petition against a partnership should allege that there is a partnership, state the name of the partnership, list all the partners, and state that the partners are sued as members of the partnership. *See, e.g., Ben Fitzgerald Rlty. Co. v. Muller*, 846 S.W.2d 110, 115 (Tex.App.—Tyler 1993, writ denied) (petition did not allege partnership or that Ds were partners). If the petition names and individually serves all the partners, a judgment may be entered against the partnership and each partner. CPRC §31.003; *see also* Bus. Orgs. Code §152.304(a) (all partners are jointly and severally liable for all obligations of partnership unless otherwise agreed by claimant or provided by law). If the petition names only the partnership, a judgment may be entered only against the partnership. CPRC §§17.022, 31.003; *Kao Holdings, L.P. v. Young*, 261 S.W.3d 60, 64 (Tex.2008). See *O'Connor's Texas COA*, "Partnership," ch. 39-A, p. 1223.

6. Corporation.

(1) Privileges forfeited. In a suit against a corporation whose right to sue was forfeited for nonpayment of taxes, the plaintiff should name the corporation and all the stockholders. *See Humble Oil & Ref. Co. v. Blankenburg*, 235 S.W.2d 891, 894 (Tex.1951). If a domestic or foreign corporation does not pay its assessed franchise tax within 45 days after notice of forfeiture is mailed, the comptroller will forfeit its corporate privileges. Tax

⭐

Code §171.251(2). Upon forfeiture of corporate privileges, the corporation is denied the right to sue or defend in a Texas court. *Id.* §171.252(1); *G. Richard Goins Constr. Co. v. S.B. McLaughlin Assocs.*, 930 S.W.2d 124, 127-28 (Tex.App.—Tyler 1996, writ denied); *see also Humble Oil*, 235 S.W.2d at 894 (when corporation's charter is forfeited, stockholders may defend actions to protect their property rights); *M&M Constr. Co. v. Great Am. Ins.*, 747 S.W.2d 552, 555 (Tex.App.—Corpus Christi 1988, no writ) (same). For the difference between forfeiture of privilege to sue and forfeiture of corporate charter, see "Stages of Corporate Decay" in *El T. Mexican Rests., Inc. v. Bacon*, 921 S.W.2d 247, 252-53 (Tex.App.—Houston [1st Dist.] 1995, writ denied).

(2) Corporate merger. In a suit against a corporation that was merged with another corporation, the plaintiff should name the surviving corporation and, to be safe, the merged corporation. When a merger takes effect, the separate existence of the corporations ceases, except for any surviving or new domestic corporation. Bus. Orgs. Code §10.008(a)(1); *Bailey v. Vanscot Concrete Co.*, 894 S.W.2d 757, 759 (Tex.1995), *disapproved on other grounds*, *Chilkewitz v. Hyson*, 22 S.W.3d 825 (Tex.1999). In a merger, the privileges, powers, rights, and duties of the corporation are transferred to the surviving corporation. *Bailey*, 894 S.W.2d at 759.

7. Governmental unit. For the substantive law on suits against the State of Texas or other governmental units, see *O'Connor's Texas COA*, "The Doctrines of Sovereign & Governmental Immunity," ch. 24-A, p. 810.

§3.6 Necessary parties. The plaintiff should sue all defendants for all claims necessary to avoid the preclusive effects of res judicata. See "Multiple Defendants," ch. 2-E, §4, p. 130; "Res Judicata & Collateral Estoppel," ch. 9-D, p. 780.

§4. JURISDICTION

Unlike the federal rules, the Texas rules of pleading do not require a plaintiff to allege the court has jurisdiction over the case. However, the plaintiff must plead enough facts to affirmatively demonstrate the trial court has jurisdiction over the suit. *TDCJ v. Miller*, 51 S.W.3d 583, 587 (Tex.2001); *Texas Ass'n of Bus. v. Texas Air Control Bd.*, 852 S.W.2d 440, 446 (Tex.1993). See *O'Connor's Texas Forms*, FORM 2B:20. To render a binding judgment, the trial court must have (1) jurisdiction over the parties or property, (2) jurisdiction over the subject matter of the suit, (3) jurisdiction to enter the particular judgment, and (4) capacity to act as a court. *State Bar v. Gomez*, 891 S.W.2d 243, 245 (Tex.1994); *see State v. Owens*, 907 S.W.2d 484, 485 (Tex.1995). See "Personal jurisdiction," §4.1, this page; "Subject-matter jurisdiction," §4.2, p. 104; "Choosing the Court—Jurisdiction," ch. 2-F, p. 135; "Plea to the Jurisdiction—Challenging the Court," ch. 3-F, p. 239. Before filing suit, the plaintiff should examine its petition to determine whether it has made sufficient jurisdictional allegations to satisfy due-process requirements under the U.S. Constitution and to require the defendant to answer. *See Paramount Pipe & Sup. Co. v. Muhr*, 749 S.W.2d 491, 496 (Tex. 1988). Unless the pleadings demonstrate the absence of jurisdiction, the court will assume it has jurisdiction over the case. *Peek v. Equipment Serv.*, 779 S.W.2d 802, 804 (Tex.1989); *Beacon Nat'l Ins. v. Montemayor*, 86 S.W.3d 260, 266 (Tex.App.—Austin 2002, no pet.).

§4.1 Personal jurisdiction. Jurisdiction over the defendant concerns whether the defendant is properly before the court, as authorized by procedural statutes and rules, within the limits of due process. *Perry v. Ponder*, 604 S.W.2d 306, 322 (Tex.App.—Dallas 1980, no writ); *see* CPRC ch. 17. The plaintiff should draft its petition to support a default judgment in case the defendant does not file an answer. See *O'Connor's Texas Forms*, FORM 2B:1.

1. Over resident. When the petition states the defendant is a resident of Texas and provides an address in Texas where the defendant can be served, it satisfies the threshold requirement for jurisdiction over a resident defendant.

2. Over nonresident. When a plaintiff files suit against a nonresident defendant, the plaintiff should allege facts that, if true, would make the nonresident defendant subject to the in personam jurisdiction of a Texas court. *See Paramount Pipe & Sup. Co. v. Muhr*, 749 S.W.2d 491, 496 (Tex.1988); *see, e.g., Frank A. Smith Sales, Inc. v. Atlantic Aero, Inc.*, 31 S.W.3d 742, 746 (Tex.App.—Corpus Christi 2000, no pet.) (P did not allege facts showing actions in Texas); *Biotrace Int'l v. Wilwerding*, 937 S.W.2d 146, 147 (Tex.App.—Houston [1st Dist.] 1997, no

★

writ) (default judgment reversed because P did not allege any activity in Texas). *But see* **Temperature Sys. v. Bill Pepper, Inc.**, 854 S.W.2d 669, 673 (Tex.App.—Dallas 1993, writ dism'd) (judgment affirmed even though P did not allege facts to support general jurisdiction because issue was tried by consent). The plaintiff should allege facts showing that the defendant "purposefully availed" itself of the privilege of conducting activities in Texas. *See* **Kelly v. General Interior Constr., Inc.**, 301 S.W.3d 653, 660-61 (Tex.2010); **Guardian Royal Exch. Assur., Ltd. v. English China Clays, P.L.C.**, 815 S.W.2d 223, 226 (Tex.1991). The petition should state how, when, and where each nonresident defendant made itself subject to the jurisdiction of Texas courts. When the facts for personal jurisdiction fall within one of the provisions of the Texas long-arm statute, the plaintiff should track the language of the section that confers personal jurisdiction; the list in CPRC chapter 17, however, is not exclusive. **BMC Software Belgium, N.V. v. Marchand**, 83 S.W.3d 789, 795 (Tex.2002); *see* CPRC ch. 17 (long-arm statute). See "Long-arm service," ch. 2-H, §5.3, p. 164; "Special Appearance—Challenging Personal Jurisdiction," ch. 3-B, p. 189.

§4.2 Subject-matter jurisdiction. Subject-matter jurisdiction concerns the kinds of controversies a court has the authority to resolve. **Davis v. Zoning Bd.**, 865 S.W.2d 941, 942 (Tex.1993). Subject-matter jurisdiction requires that the party bringing suit have standing, that there be a live controversy between the parties, and that the case be justiciable. **State Bar v. Gomez**, 891 S.W.2d 243, 245 (Tex.1994). See "Standing," §3.2.1, p. 96. Subject-matter jurisdiction cannot be granted by consent and cannot be waived. *See* **Carroll v. Carroll**, 304 S.W.3d 366, 367 (Tex.2010). See "Purpose," ch. 3-F, §1.2, p. 239.

1. Common-law claims. In most civil cases, a trial court's jurisdiction is based on the allegations in the petition about the amount in controversy. **Continental Coffee Prods. v. Cazarez**, 937 S.W.2d 444, 449 (Tex.1996). If jurisdiction depends on the amount in controversy, the plaintiff's petition must allege facts showing the court has jurisdiction. *See* **Richardson v. First Nat'l Life Ins.**, 419 S.W.2d 836, 839 (Tex.1967). This is often accomplished by the statement that the plaintiff pleads for damages within the court's jurisdiction. Many of the trial courts have overlapping monetary jurisdiction. For example, a suit for $500 can be brought in any trial court. See "Monetary jurisdiction," ch. 2-F, §2.3, p. 135.

2. Statutory claims.

(1) Not dependent on amount in controversy. If a statute that creates a cause of action identifies the court in which the suit must be brought, the suit must be brought in that court. *See, e.g.*, Gov't Code §25.1032(c) (condemnation claims in Harris County must be brought in a county court at law in Harris County); *In re Burlington N. & Santa Fe Ry.*, 12 S.W.3d 891, 899 (Tex.App.—Houston [14th Dist.] 2000, orig. proceeding) (statute conferred jurisdiction on Fort Bend County court at law for eminent-domain cases). When a statute that creates a claim specifies the court in which the claim must be brought, a plaintiff is not required to allege an amount in controversy. *In re Burlington*, 12 S.W.3d at 899. In such a case, the plaintiff should plead the statute.

(2) Dependent on amount in controversy. If a statute that creates a cause of action does not identify the court in which the suit must be brought, the court's jurisdiction depends on the amount in controversy. *See In re Burlington*, 12 S.W.3d at 899. In such a case, the plaintiff should plead both the statute and that the amount in controversy is within the court's jurisdiction. For example, Gov't Code §§501.007-501.008, which authorize a suit by an inmate for lost or damaged property, do not specify the court in which the suit must be filed; thus, the suit may be filed in district, county, justice-of-the-peace, or small-claims court, depending on the amount in controversy.

§4.3 Nonremovable claim. If, by statute, a case filed in state court is not removable to federal court (e.g., FELA or Jones Act case), the plaintiff should expressly plead that the suit is not removable. If a defendant attempts to remove to federal court a case that is not removable, and the plaintiff's pleadings state that the case is not removable, the defendant could face sanctions in federal court under FRCP 11 or in state court under TRCP 13 and CPRC §§9.012 and 10.004. To prevent a suit from being removed to federal court when filing suit against a non-Texas corporation doing business in Texas, the plaintiff should consider suing one of the corporation's employees who resides in Texas.

§5. VENUE

The Texas rules of pleading do not require a plaintiff to plead the basis for venue in the county of suit. **Electronic Data Sys. v. Pioneer Elecs. (USA) Inc.**, 68 S.W.3d 254, 260 (Tex.App.—Fort Worth 2002, no pet.) (dicta). However,

---

★

---

the plaintiff's original petition should state enough facts about the cause of action to establish venue in the county where the suit is filed. Pleading specific venue facts in the petition and citing the venue statute may prevent a defendant from pursuing a fruitless motion to transfer venue. *See* CPRC ch. 15; TRCP 86, 87. If a particular venue statute is cited in the petition, it does not limit the plaintiff to that ground. *Electronic Data*, 68 S.W.3d at 260. See "Choosing the Court—Venue," ch. 2-G, p. 150; "Motion to Transfer—Challenging Venue," ch. 3-C, p. 203; *O'Connor's Texas Forms*, FORM 2B:21.

§6. PLEADING A CAUSE OF ACTION

A cause of action consists of a plaintiff's primary right and the defendant's act or omission that violated that right. *Jones v. Ray*, 886 S.W.2d 817, 821 (Tex.App.—Houston [1st Dist.] 1994, orig. proceeding). For a cause of action to be adequately pleaded, the trial court must be able to determine with reasonable certainty the elements of the cause of action and the relief sought. *Stoner v. Thompson*, 578 S.W.2d 679, 683 (Tex.1979). For a list of the elements of many causes of action, see *O'Connor's Texas COA*.

§6.1 Essential allegations. At a minimum, the pleaded facts must show (1) the plaintiff's right and the defendant's duty, (2) the defendant's breach of its duty, and (3) the plaintiff's injury as a result of the defendant's breach. *See, e.g.*, *Greater Houston Transp. v. Phillips*, 801 S.W.2d 523, 525 (Tex.1990) (elements of common-law negligence).

§6.2 Fair notice of claim. The pleadings must give a short statement of the cause of action sufficient to give the defendant fair and adequate notice of the claim involved and to enable it to prepare a defense. TRCP 45(b), 47(a); *Garvey v. Vawter*, 795 S.W.2d 741, 742 (Tex.1990); *Roark v. Allen*, 633 S.W.2d 804, 810 (Tex.1982); *see SmithKline Beecham Corp. v. Doe*, 903 S.W.2d 347, 354 (Tex.1995). Texas follows the "fair-notice" standard for pleading, which determines whether the opposing party can ascertain from the pleading the nature and basic issues of the controversy and what type of evidence might be relevant. *Low v. Henry*, 221 S.W.3d 609, 612 (Tex.2007); *Horizon/CMS Healthcare Corp. v. Auld*, 34 S.W.3d 887, 896 (Tex.2000). The "fair-notice" requirement does not require the pleader to plead evidentiary matters with meticulous particularity. *State Fid. Mortg. Co. v. Varner*, 740 S.W.2d 477, 480 (Tex.App.—Houston [1st Dist.] 1987, writ denied); *see Low*, 221 S.W.3d at 612 (fair-notice standard is relatively liberal).

1. **Alleging facts.** The petition must state enough facts to inform the defendant of the nature of the claim. The petition does not need to include the evidence the plaintiff intends to rely on. *Paramount Pipe & Sup. Co. v. Muhr*, 749 S.W.2d 491, 494-95 (Tex.1988). The petition is sufficient if it alleges facts generally. *See* TRCP 45(b), 47(a); *Willock v. Bui*, 734 S.W.2d 390, 392 (Tex.App.—Houston [1st Dist.] 1987, no writ). The plaintiff should evaluate its petition to determine whether it would support a default judgment in the event the defendant does not answer. See "Sufficiency of plaintiff's petition," ch. 7-A, §3.2, p. 588.

PRACTICE TIP

If you are unsure of the exact date when something happened, you should allege that the event occurred "on or about" the date. See Winfield v. Renfro, 821 S.W.2d 640, 646-47 (Tex.App.— Houston [1st Dist.] 1991, writ denied); Fortner v. Merrill Lynch, Pierce, Fenner & Smith, Inc., 687 S.W.2d 8, 11 (Tex.App.—Dallas 1984, writ ref'd n.r.e.). The courts have upheld as much as a three-month variance in dates between a plaintiff's allegation of when an event occurred and the proof of when it occurred. Winfield, 821 S.W.2d at 647.

---

2. **Alleging legal theories.** The plaintiff must identify the legal basis for the defendant's liability for the injury. A plaintiff has no right to recover against a defendant if the defendant did not breach a legal duty it owed to the plaintiff. *See, e.g.*, *El Chico Corp. v. Poole*, 732 S.W.2d 306, 311 (Tex.1987) (duty in negligence suit). A duty represents a legally enforceable obligation to conform to a particular standard of conduct. *Prosser & Keeton on Torts* §53, at 356 (5th ed. 1984).

━━━━━━━━━━━━━━━━━━━━━━━━ ★ ━━━━━━━━━━━━━━━━━━━━━━━━

3. Inferring legal theories from facts. A court may infer a legal theory from the facts presented, but the facts must be expressly stated. *See, e.g.*, *Troutman v. Traeco Bldg. Sys.*, 724 S.W.2d 385, 387 (Tex.1987) (P cited section of DTPA and alleged facts that made obvious its theory that D made a false representation). A court cannot infer facts from legal theories. *See, e.g.*, *White v. Jackson*, 358 S.W.2d 174, 178 (Tex.App.—Waco 1962, writ ref'd n.r.e.) (court would not infer facts to support bare allegation that D was negligent).

§6.3 General vs. specific allegations. A petition may allege a cause of action generally or specifically. Often, plaintiffs will plead a cause of action generally and follow it with specific allegations. A specific allegation controls over a general allegation. *Monsanto Co. v. Milam*, 494 S.W.2d 534, 536 (Tex.1973); *see also Chuck Wagon Feeding Co. v. Davis*, 768 S.W.2d 360, 364 (Tex.App.—El Paso 1989, writ denied) (specific pleadings of contract precluded proof on collateral note). If a petition contains specific causes of action, the court will not infer another cause of action unless the petition gives fair notice of that cause of action. *See Boyles v. Kerr*, 855 S.W.2d 593, 601 (Tex.1993).

━━━

PRACTICE TIP
As a plaintiff, always describe your cause of action with general allegations. If you plead specific acts of breach of duty, you will be limited to proving those specific acts at trial. **Mobil Chem. Co. v. Bell**, *517 S.W.2d 245, 254 (Tex.1974). As a defendant, consider filing special exceptions to limit the plaintiff's proof at trial. See "Special Exceptions—Challenging the Pleadings," ch. 3-G, p. 248.*

━━━

1. Tort cases. Certain theories of tort law must be specifically pleaded.

(1) Negligence per se. Negligence per se is a common-law doctrine in which a duty is imposed based on a standard of conduct created by a penal statute rather than on the "reasonably prudent person" standard used in ordinary-negligence claims. *Smith v. Merritt*, 940 S.W.2d 602, 607 (Tex.1997). See *O'Connor's Texas COA*, "Negligence Per Se," ch. 21-B, p. 696; *O'Connor's Texas COA Pleadings*, FORMS 21B. Under the doctrine of negligence per se, the unexcused violation of a statute setting the standard of care constitutes negligence as a matter of law if the statute was designed to prevent injuries to a class of persons that the plaintiff belongs to. *El Chico Corp. v. Poole*, 732 S.W.2d 306, 312 (Tex.1987). A plaintiff relying on negligence per se must specifically plead it and should identify the specific statute. *Daugherty v. Southern Pac. Transp.*, 772 S.W.2d 81, 83 (Tex.1989). If the plaintiff does not specifically plead negligence per se and makes only a general allegation of negligence, the defendant should challenge the pleading by a special exception. *See Murray v. O&A Express, Inc.*, 630 S.W.2d 633, 636-37 (Tex.1982).

(2) Res ipsa loquitur. Res ipsa loquitur is a rule of evidence that allows the jury to infer negligence. *Haddock v. Arnspiger*, 793 S.W.2d 948, 950 (Tex.1990). A general allegation of negligence includes an allegation of res ipsa loquitur. *See Farm Servs. v. Gonzales*, 756 S.W.2d 747, 751 (Tex.App.—Corpus Christi 1988, writ denied). If a petition alleges specific acts of negligence, it excludes res ipsa loquitur unless the petition (1) gives fair notice it is not relying solely on specific acts or (2) alleges res ipsa loquitur in the alternative. *See Mobil Chem.*, 517 S.W.2d at 254. The doctrine of res ipsa loquitur is applicable only when (1) the character of the injury is such that it would not have occurred without negligence and (2) the instrumentality that caused the injury is shown to have been under the sole management and control of the defendant. *Gaulding v. Celotex Corp.*, 772 S.W.2d 66, 68 (Tex.1989). See *O'Connor's Texas COA*, "Res ipsa loquitur," ch. 21-A, §6.4, p. 690.

2. Contract cases. Certain types of relief must be specifically pleaded in a contract case. See *O'Connor's Texas COA*, "Contract Actions," ch. 5, p. 55.

(1) Rescission. Rescission must be specifically pleaded, or the trial court cannot grant it. *Burnett v. James*, 564 S.W.2d 407, 409 (Tex.App.—Dallas 1978, writ dism'd). *But see Perez v. Briercroft Serv.*, 809 S.W.2d 216, 218 (Tex.1991) (because D raised rescission as defense, it was not necessary for P to plead it). See *O'Connor's Texas COA*, "Rescission," ch. 5-B, §3.5.2, p. 85.

———————— ⭐ ————————

(2) Modification. New consideration to support modification of a contract must be pleaded. *Barnhill v. Moore*, 630 S.W.2d 817, 820 (Tex.App.—Corpus Christi 1982, no writ). See *O'Connor's Texas COA*, "New consideration for modification," ch. 5-A, §2.5.2, p. 64.

(3) Quantum meruit. Quantum meruit is an equitable theory of recovery based on an implied agreement to pay for benefits received. *Heldenfels Bros. v. City of Corpus Christi*, 832 S.W.2d 39, 41 (Tex.1992). Quantum meruit must be specifically pleaded and is often pleaded in the alternative to a contract claim. *See Centex Corp. v. Dalton*, 840 S.W.2d 952, 955 & n.7 (Tex.1992). See *O'Connor's Texas COA*, "Quantum Meruit," ch. 5-C, p. 109.

§6.4 Notice allegation. Some causes of action require the plaintiff to plead and prove notice. See *O'Connor's Texas Forms*, FORMS 2A. For example, a DTPA plaintiff must plead that it gave the defendant notice before filing suit. *Hines v. Hash*, 843 S.W.2d 464, 467 (Tex.1992). See "Statutory notice," ch. 2-A, §2.1, p. 93.

§6.5 Alternative claims. The plaintiff may plead alternative theories of recovery, even if they are inconsistent. TRCP 48; *see* TRCP 47. See "Alternative claims or defenses," ch. 1-B, §3.2.8, p. 8.

§6.6 Joinder of multiple claims. See "Parties & Claims," ch. 2-E, p. 129.

§7. ANTICIPATING DEFENSES

Before filing the original petition, the plaintiff should check the affirmative defenses listed in TRCP 94 to see whether any defenses should be pleaded to support its cause of action. See "Affirmative Defenses," ch. 3-E, §5, p. 230. TRCP 94 applies to plaintiffs as well as to defendants. *Simmons v. Compania Financiera Libano, S.A.*, 830 S.W.2d 789, 792 (Tex.App.—Houston [1st Dist.] 1992, writ denied). For example, if the plaintiff must rely on estoppel to establish its cause of action, the plaintiff must plead it. *Nicholson v. Memorial Hosp. Sys.*, 722 S.W.2d 746, 749 (Tex. App.—Houston [14th Dist.] 1986, writ ref'd n.r.e.). If the plaintiff knows the defendant will challenge the suit based on limitations, it should plead the discovery rule in its original petition. *Woods v. William M. Mercer, Inc.*, 769 S.W.2d 515, 518 (Tex.1988). See *O'Connor's Texas COA*, "Discovery rule," ch. 52, §2.4.1, p. 1486.

§8. DAMAGES

The damages alleged in the petition must be within the level designated for the discovery-control plan. See "Discovery-Control Plans," §2, p. 95. A party's pleadings limit the damages the party may recover; the party cannot recover damages it did not request in its pleadings. *See, e.g.*, *Fubar, Inc. v. Turner*, 944 S.W.2d 64, 66 (Tex.App.—Texarkana 1997, no writ) (P, who pleaded for net revenues, waived recovery for gross revenues). However, if it alleges sufficient facts to state a cause of action from which the court can determine the proper measure of damages, the plaintiff is not required to allege the measure of damages sought. *Bowen v. Robinson*, 227 S.W.3d 86, 95 (Tex.App.—Houston [1st Dist.] 2006, pet. denied); *Hedley Feedlot, Inc. v. Weatherly Trust*, 855 S.W.2d 826, 834 (Tex.App.—Amarillo 1993, writ denied).

§8.1 Definition. Damages are defined as compensation in money imposed by law for loss or injury. *Geters v. Eagle Ins.*, 834 S.W.2d 49, 50 (Tex.1992). Damages are also defined as "legal injuries," which are invasions of the plaintiff's legally protected interests. *American Med. Elecs., Inc. v. Korn*, 819 S.W.2d 573, 577 n.3 (Tex.App.—Dallas 1991, writ denied). If a plaintiff pleads a cause of action but does not plead damages, the omission is a pleading defect that the defendant may challenge by a special exception. *Peek v. Equipment Serv.*, 779 S.W.2d 802, 805 (Tex.1989). See "Special Exceptions—Challenging the Pleadings," ch. 3-G, p. 248.

§8.2 Unliquidated damages. "Unliquidated damages" are damages that cannot be accurately calculated from either the factual allegations in the petition or the attached instruments. *Atwood v. B&R Sup. & Equip. Co.*, 52 S.W.3d 265, 268 (Tex.App.—Corpus Christi 2001, no pet.). The plaintiff should not state a specific amount of unliquidated damages it seeks in its original petition. *Capitol Brick, Inc. v. Fleming Mfg. Co.*, 722 S.W.2d 399, 401 (Tex. 1986); *see* TRCP 47(b); *see also* CPRC §74.053 (same as TRCP 47(b) in medical-malpractice cases). Instead, the plaintiff should allege that the unliquidated damages are within the jurisdictional limits of the court. TRCP 47(b); *In re United Servs. Auto. Ass'n*, 307 S.W.3d 299, 312 (Tex.2010); *see Sears, Roebuck & Co. v. Big Bend Motor Inn, Inc.*,

PLAINTIFF'S PETITION

★

818 S.W.2d 542, 546 & n.5 (Tex.App.—Fort Worth 1991, writ denied). The defendant should file special exceptions to require the plaintiff to specify the maximum amount claimed. TRCP 47; *see Cruz v. Morris*, 877 S.W.2d 45, 47 (Tex. App.—Houston [14th Dist.] 1994, no writ) (specificity of damages not required without proper special exception); *see also* CPRC §74.053 (same as TRCP 47 in medical-malpractice cases).

⑬

PROPOSED TRCP CHANGES

In response to Gov't Code §22.004(h), the Supreme Court has proposed TRCP 169 to establish a process for the prompt, efficient, and cost-effective resolution of civil actions (expedited actions) in which only monetary relief is sought and the amount in controversy is no more than $100,000. See Tex.Sup.Ct. Order, Misc. Docket No. 12-9191 (eff. Mar. 1, 2013). The Supreme Court has proposed corresponding amendments to TRCP 47 that would require a party, in an original pleading, to make a more specific statement of the relief sought; that is, the party would have to plead into or out of the expedited-actions process under TRCP 169. See Tex.Sup.Ct. Order, Misc. Docket No. 12-9191 (eff. Mar. 1, 2013). The public-comment period for the proposed amendments ends on February 1, 2013, and the rules are to take effect March 1, 2013. For the proposed version of the rules, see the appendix after this book's index. For the final version, go to the Supreme Court website at www.supreme.courts.state.tx.us. When the new and amended rules take effect, a supplement to this book—with updated rules and commentaries that reflect the changes—will be available at www.JonesMcClure.com/TRCPamendments.

§8.3 Types of damages. For a detailed discussion of damages, see *O'Connor's Texas COA*, "Damages," ch. 41, p. 1241.

1. Actual damages. Actual damages are damages recoverable under common law. *Arthur Andersen & Co. v. Perry Equip. Corp.*, 945 S.W.2d 812, 816 (Tex.1997). Actual damages are classified as either direct (general damages) or consequential (special damages). *Id.* The distinction is important because general damages do not need to be specifically pleaded, but special damages must be pleaded. TRCP 56. *See generally* Cagle et al., *The Classification of General & Special Damages for Pleading Purposes in Texas*, 51 Baylor L.Rev. 629 (1999).

PRACTICE TIP

Rule 56 does not define which damages are special. Because the courts do not always agree on which damages are special (and must be specifically pleaded), the plaintiff should plead all damages, general and special.

(1) General damages. General damages are damages that naturally and necessarily flow from a wrongful act and would normally compensate for the loss, damage, or injury that is presumed to have been foreseen or contemplated by the party as a consequence of its wrongful act. *Arthur Andersen*, 945 S.W.2d at 816. The plaintiff does not have to specifically plead general damages. *Green v. Allied Interests, Inc.*, 963 S.W.2d 205, 208 (Tex. App.—Austin 1998, pet. denied). The following are examples of general damages: • In a personal-injury suit, damages for pretrial pain and suffering. *Pecos & N.T. Ry. v. Huskey*, 166 S.W. 493, 494 (Tex.App.—Amarillo 1914, writ ref'd). • In a negligent-misrepresentation case, damages for benefit of the bargain and out-of-pocket expenses. *Airborne Freight Corp. v. C.R. Lee Enters.*, 847 S.W.2d 289, 296 (Tex.App.—El Paso 1992, writ denied). • In a breach-of-contract case, the difference between the cost of a substitute product from another company and the original contract price. *Hess Die Mold, Inc. v. American Plasti-Plate Corp.*, 653 S.W.2d 927, 929 (Tex.App.—Tyler 1983, no writ).

(2) Special damages. Special damages are foreseeable damages that are directly traceable to and result from the defendant's wrongful act. *Arthur Andersen*, 945 S.W.2d at 816; *see Stuart v. Bayless*, 964 S.W.2d 920, 921 (Tex.1998); *Haynes & Boone v. Bowser Bouldin, Ltd.*, 896 S.W.2d 179, 182 (Tex.1995). Because special damages vary from person to person, a party must specifically plead for them. TRCP 56; *see Harkins v. Crews*, 907 S.W.2d

★

51, 61 (Tex.App.—San Antonio 1995, writ denied). See *O'Connor's Texas COA*, "Damages that Must Be Specifically Pleaded," chart 41-1, p. 1244. The following are examples of special damages: • Loss of investment. *Haynes & Boone*, 896 S.W.2d at 182. • Loss of family companionship. *See Reagan v. Vaughn*, 804 S.W.2d 463, 466 (Tex.1990) (loss of parental companionship); *Sanchez v. Schindler*, 651 S.W.2d 249, 252-53 (Tex.1983) (loss of companionship of child). • Loss of credit reputation. *Mead v. Johnson Grp.*, 615 S.W.2d 685, 688 (Tex.1981); *Boat Superstore, Inc. v. Haner*, 877 S.W.2d 376, 379 (Tex.App.—Houston [1st Dist.] 1994, no writ). • Cost of repairs. *Kissman v. Bendix Home Sys.*, 587 S.W.2d 675, 677 (Tex.1979). • Loss of earning capacity. *Peshak v. Greer*, 13 S.W.3d 421, 427 (Tex.App.—Corpus Christi 2000, no pet.); *Weingartens, Inc. v. Price*, 461 S.W.2d 260, 264 (Tex.App.—Houston [14th Dist.] 1970, writ ref'd n.r.e.). • Lost profits. *Naegeli Transp. v. Gulf Electroquip, Inc.*, 853 S.W.2d 737, 739 (Tex.App.—Houston [14th Dist.] 1993, writ denied).

2. Exemplary damages. Exemplary (or punitive) damages are designed to penalize and deter conduct that is outrageous, malicious, or morally culpable. *Owens-Corning Fiberglas Corp. v. Malone*, 972 S.W.2d 35, 40 (Tex.1998); *see* CPRC §41.001(5); *Transportation Ins. v. Moriel*, 879 S.W.2d 10, 16 (Tex.1994). Exemplary damages are not compensatory. CPRC §41.001(5); *Owens-Corning*, 972 S.W.2d at 39-40. Exemplary damages, like special damages, must be specifically pleaded. *See K-Mart Apparel Fashions Corp. v. Ramsey*, 695 S.W.2d 243, 247 (Tex.App.—Houston [1st Dist.] 1985, writ ref'd n.r.e.). For a detailed discussion of exemplary damages, see *O'Connor's Texas COA*, "Exemplary Damages," ch. 42, p. 1311.

§8.4 Damages not permitted. Some claims do not entitle the plaintiff to damages, only to equitable relief. *See, e.g., City of Beaumont v. Bouillion*, 896 S.W.2d 143, 149 (Tex.1995) (no monetary damages for violation of Texas Constitution). See "Injunctive Relief," ch. 2-C, p. 111.

§9. COURT COSTS & INTEREST

The plaintiff should always plead for court costs and prejudgment and postjudgment interest, even though pleading for them is not always necessary. See "Prejudgment interest," ch. 9-C, §4.5, p. 768; "Postjudgment interest," ch. 9-C, §4.6, p. 769; *O'Connor's Texas COA*, "Interest," ch. 43, p. 1335; *O'Connor's Texas COA Pleadings*, FORMS 47, 48.

§10. ATTORNEY FEES

See "Attorney Fees from Adverse Party," ch. 1-H, §10, p. 62. For a list of statutes that authorize attorney fees, see *O'Connor's CPRC*, "Statutory Attorney Fees Chart—Private Litigants," p. 910; "Statutory Attorney Fees Chart— Attorney General," p. 922. For a detailed discussion of attorney fees, see *O'Connor's Texas COA*, "Attorney Fees," ch. 45, p. 1349.

§11. CONDITIONS PRECEDENT

In its petition, the plaintiff should always allege that "all conditions precedent have been performed or have occurred." TRCP 54. A condition precedent is an event that must occur or be performed before a plaintiff can sue to enforce an obligation. *Solar Applications Eng'g v. T.A. Oper. Corp.*, 327 S.W.3d 104, 108 (Tex.2010); *Centex Corp. v. Dalton*, 840 S.W.2d 952, 956 (Tex.1992). A plaintiff who makes the TRCP 54 allegation is not required to prove that it complied with any conditions precedent unless the defendant specifically denies them. TRCP 54; *Community Bank & Trust v. Fleck*, 107 S.W.3d 541, 542 (Tex.2002); *Associated Indem. Corp. v. CAT Contracting, Inc.*, 964 S.W.2d 276, 283 n.6 (Tex.1998); *see Greathouse v. Charter Nat'l Bank*, 851 S.W.2d 173, 176-77 (Tex.1992) (TRCP 54 allegation prevails against general denial); *see, e.g., Knupp v. Miller*, 858 S.W.2d 945, 955 (Tex.App.—Beaumont 1993, writ denied) (in suit that provided for statutory attorney fees, unchallenged TRCP 54 allegation was sufficient to support attorney fees). See "Denial of conditions precedent," ch. 3-E, §6.1, p. 234. The TRCP 54 allegation shifts the burden of pleading (not of proof) to the defendant to specifically deny those conditions precedent that have not occurred. *Trevino v. Allstate Ins.*, 651 S.W.2d 8, 11 (Tex.App.—Dallas 1983, writ ref'd n.r.e.). If a plaintiff does not include the TRCP 54 allegation in its petition and the defendant makes a general denial, the plaintiff will need to prove the performance of all conditions precedent. *See Grimm v. Grimm*, 864 S.W.2d 160, 162 (Tex.App.—Houston [14th Dist.] 1993, no writ).

★

PRACTICE TIP

The TRCP 54 allegation should be pleaded generally and should not identify any specific claim. When pleaded specifically for a claim, the allegation is limited to that claim. **Cook Composites, Inc. v. Westlake Styrene Corp.**, *15 S.W.3d 124, 138 (Tex.App.—Houston [14th Dist.] 2000, pet. dism'd).*

---

§12. JURY DEMAND

If the plaintiff wants a jury trial, it should include a request for a jury in its petition. For the request to be effective, the plaintiff must pay the appropriate jury fees. See "Request for Jury Trial," ch. 5-B, p. 320.

§13. REQUEST FOR DISCLOSURE

The plaintiff should consider including a request for disclosure in its original petition. The only statement necessary for a request for disclosure is the following: "Pursuant to Rule 194, you are requested to disclose, within 50 days of the service of this request, the information or material described in Rule [*identify rule, e.g., 194.2; 194.2(a), (c), and (f); 194.2(d)-(g)*]." TRCP 194.1; *see* TRCP 194.3(a). See "Requests for Disclosure," ch. 6-E, p. 515. If the plaintiff includes the request in the petition, it should change the title of the pleading to "Plaintiff's Original Petition and Request for Disclosure."

§14. PRAYER

The plaintiff's petition should include a demand for judgment for all the relief sought. TRCP 47(c).

§14.1 General prayer. A general prayer for relief requests "all other relief to which plaintiff is entitled." A general prayer authorizes a judgment for any relief within the court's jurisdiction, justified by the proof and consistent with the claims asserted in the petition. *See* **Kissman v. Bendix Home Sys.**, 587 S.W.2d 675, 677 (Tex.1979); **Stoner v. Thompson**, 578 S.W.2d 679, 683-84 (Tex.1979); **Daniels v. Allen**, 811 S.W.2d 278, 280 (Tex.App.—Tyler 1991, no writ). A general prayer for relief for "other sums as shall be found due" does not enlarge a specific allegation of damages. *See* **Richardson v. First Nat'l Life Ins.**, 419 S.W.2d 836, 837, 839 (Tex.1967).

§14.2 Special prayer. If a party wants relief other than damages, the party must specifically plead for it in the prayer (e.g., injunctive relief, rescission of a contract, attorney fees, costs of court, appointment of a receiver).

§15. SIGNATURE

The attorney (or party if pro se) must sign the pleading, which must contain an address and telephone number and, if available, a fax number. TRCP 45(d), 57. See "Signature block," ch. 1-B, §3.2.11, p. 9.

§16. EXHIBITS

If exhibits are attached to the petition, the petition must identify them and incorporate them by reference. TRCP 59. TRCP 59 lists the types of documents that may be properly attached as exhibits to pleadings. See "Exhibits," ch. 1-B, §3.2.13, p. 10.

§17. VERIFICATION & AFFIDAVITS

Some pleadings must be verified, and some require affidavits. Verification may be necessary to assert certain defenses when the issue is not apparent on the face of the plaintiff's pleadings. If a plaintiff does not verify a pleading that requires it, the trial court should permit an amendment to add the verification. *See, e.g.,* **Chapin & Chapin, Inc. v. Texas Sand & Gravel Co.**, 844 S.W.2d 664, 665 (Tex.1992) (D permitted to amend to add verification). See "Verification," ch. 1-B, §3.2.15, p. 11; "Affidavits," ch. 1-B, §3.2.16, p. 11; "Verified Pleas," ch. 3-E, §4, p. 228; *O'Connor's Texas Forms*, FORMS 1B:5, 1B:7. For the requirements for using an unsworn declaration in place of a verification or an affidavit, see "Unsworn declaration," ch. 1-B, §3.2.14, p. 10.

⬥

§18. CASE-INFORMATION SHEET

All original petitions and applications must include a civil-case-information sheet. TRCP 78a(a)(1). See "Case-information sheet," ch. 1-B, §3.2.19, p. 14.

§19. RESPONDING TO DEFENDANT'S PLEADINGS

Once the defendant files its answer, the plaintiff should review the answer to determine whether it needs to file any additional pleadings.

§19.1 Defense to defense. The plaintiff should determine whether it needs to plead a defense to the defendant's defense. For example, to avoid the defendant's defense of statute of limitations, a plaintiff must plead the discovery rule. *Woods v. William M. Mercer, Inc.*, 769 S.W.2d 515, 518 (Tex.1988). The plaintiff is not required to plead affirmative defenses when a defendant files only a general denial. *See Berry v. Berry*, 786 S.W.2d 672, 673 n.3 (Tex. 1990).

§19.2 Response to counterclaim. The plaintiff is not required to file a general denial in response to a counterclaim. *See* TRCP 92. But the plaintiff should file an answer in some situations. First, if the plaintiff intends to assert an affirmative defense (TRCP 94) or a defensive theory that must be verified (TRCP 93), it must file an answer. *Greater Fort Worth & Tarrant Cty. Cmty. Action Agency v. Mims*, 627 S.W.2d 149, 152 (Tex.1982); *$191,452 v. State*, 827 S.W.2d 430, 432 (Tex.App.—Corpus Christi 1992, writ denied). See "Verified Pleas," ch. 3-E, §4, p. 228; "Affirmative Defenses," ch. 3-E, §5, p. 230. Second, the plaintiff must assert all of its compulsory counterclaims to the defendant's counterclaim, or they will be barred in a later suit. The compulsory-counterclaim rule applies to a party against whom a counterclaim has been filed. See "Compulsory Joinder of Claims," ch. 2-E, §6, p. 131.

§19.3 Special exceptions. The plaintiff must obey the same rules for special exceptions in objecting to pleading defects in the defendant's answer that the defendant follows in objecting to the plaintiff's petition. *See, e.g., Shoemake v. Fogel, Ltd.*, 826 S.W.2d 933, 937 (Tex.1992) (counter-P failed to specially except to affirmative defense that counter-D was not liable "as a matter of law," and thus waived objection to defense of parental immunity). See "Special Exceptions—Challenging the Pleadings," ch. 3-G, p. 248.

C. INJUNCTIVE RELIEF

§1. GENERAL

§1.1 Rules. TRCP 680-693a. See CPRC ch. 65.

§1.2 Purpose. There are two general types of injunctive relief: prohibitory and mandatory. *RP&R, Inc. v. Territo*, 32 S.W.3d 396, 400 (Tex.App.—Houston [14th Dist.] 2000, no pet.). Most injunctions are prohibitory—that is, they prohibit a party from continuing certain conduct. Shannon et al., *Temporary Restraining Orders & Temporary Injunctions in Texas—A Ten Year Survey, 1975-1985*, 17 St. Mary's L.J. 689, 736 (1986). In some cases, a party may need a mandatory injunction—that is, one requiring another party to act affirmatively rather than merely to refrain from certain conduct. *Id.; e.g., Territo*, 32 S.W.3d at 400 (injunction required P to give weekly paychecks to D). There are three types of injunctive orders: temporary restraining orders, temporary injunctions, and permanent injunctions.

1. Temporary restraining order (TRO). The purpose of a TRO is to preserve the status quo of the subject matter of the litigation until a preliminary hearing can be held on an application for a temporary injunction. *See Cannan v. Green Oaks Apts., Ltd.*, 758 S.W.2d 753, 755 (Tex.1988); Moore, *The Ingenious Use of Injunctive Remedies in Texas*, 18 S.Tex.L.J. 87, 88 (1977). The status quo is the last actual, peaceable, noncontested status that preceded the controversy. *In re Newton*, 146 S.W.3d 648, 651 (Tex.2004); *Big Three Indus. v. Railroad Comm'n*, 618 S.W.2d 543, 548 (Tex.1981); *State v. Southwestern Bell Tel. Co.*, 526 S.W.2d 526, 528 (Tex.1975).

2. Temporary injunction. The purpose of a temporary injunction is to preserve the status quo of the subject matter of the litigation until a final hearing can be held on the merits of the case. *Butnaru v. Ford Motor Co.*, 84 S.W.3d 198, 204 (Tex.2002); *see Walling v. Metcalfe*, 863 S.W.2d 56, 58 (Tex.1993).

────────────────────────────── ✦ ──────────────────────────────

3. Permanent injunction. The purpose of a permanent injunction is to grant the injunctive relief the applicant is entitled to as part of the final judgment after a trial on the merits. *NMTC Corp. v. Conarroe*, 99 S.W.3d 865, 868 (Tex.App.—Beaumont 2003, no pet.); *see Elizondo v. Williams*, 643 S.W.2d 765, 767 (Tex.App.—San Antonio 1982, orig. proceeding).

§1.3 Forms. *O'Connor's Texas Civil Forms* (2012), FORMS 2C.

§1.4 Other references. Moore, *The Ingenious Use of Injunctive Remedies in Texas*, 18 S.Tex.L.J. 87 (1977); Thomas et al., *TRO's & TI's: Still Extraordinary?*, Advanced Civil Trial Course, State Bar of Texas CLE (2010); Walker et al., *Extraordinary Remedies: Some Remedies Every Trial Lawyer Should Know, or, Overcoming Newton's Law of Inertia*, part II, www.brownmccarroll.com/public/documents/Extraordinary_Remedies_-_Litigation_-_Walker _Mark.pdf (2009); *O'Connor's Texas Civil Appeals* (2012) (*O'Connor's Texas Appeals*); *O'Connor's Texas Causes of Action* (2013) (*O'Connor's Texas COA*).

§2. OVERVIEW OF INJUNCTION PROCESS

Before getting into the pleading requirements for the three types of injunctions, it is necessary to have a general idea of the procedure for obtaining an injunctive order. Because injunction procedures vary somewhat from county to county, the following is not intended to be representative of every county but is merely a general guide to the process of obtaining injunctive relief—from the ex parte TRO to the permanent injunction.

§2.1 Prepare petition & application. The plaintiff should prepare the petition for suit and include with it an application for the type or types of injunction order requested—TRO, temporary injunction, or permanent injunction. See "Application," §5.1, p. 116 (TRO); "Application," §6.2, p. 119 (temporary injunction); "Application," §7.1, p. 120 (permanent injunction). The application for injunctive relief can be filed as a separate instrument. If the plaintiff seeks an ex parte TRO, the application must state why a TRO is necessary. See "Ex parte allegations," §5.1.4, p. 116. Many local rules require the plaintiff to certify, as part of the application for TRO, one of the following: (1) to the best of its knowledge, the defendant is unrepresented, (2) the defendant is represented but does not want to be heard or could not be reached, or (3) notifying the defendant or its counsel would cause irreparable harm to the plaintiff. Bexar Cty. Loc. R. 6(C) (district courts); *see* Dallas Cty. Loc. R. 2.02; Tarrant Cty. Loc. R. 3.30(c).

§2.2 Prepare for bond. Before filing the petition and application, the plaintiff should call the court clerk to ask what type of bond and surety the court might require. See "Bond," §5.4, p. 118.

§2.3 File petition & application. In some counties, the plaintiff must file the application for a TRO with the clerk, who will assign the case to a court and forward the papers to the presiding judge of that court. *E.g.*, Collin Cty. Loc. R. 2.2(a) (unless courthouse is closed, petition and application must first be filed and assigned to a court); Dallas Cty. Loc. R. 2.01(a) (same); El Paso Cty. Loc. R. 1.05(A) (same); Tarrant Cty. Loc. R. 3.30(a) (unless impossible, application must be filed with clerk and assigned to a court before it can be presented to judge). In other counties, the plaintiff can take the application for TRO directly to the judge designated to hear TROs without filing it with the clerk. *E.g.*, Bexar Cty. Loc. R. 6(C) (district courts). In Harris County, the plaintiff must present the petition and application to an ancillary court that is designated for hearing TRO applications. *See* Harris Cty. Loc. R. 3.5.1 (district courts).

§2.4 Notify defendant. Unless the application seeks an ex parte TRO, the plaintiff should notify the defendant of its intent to ask for a TRO and the time and place for the hearing.

§2.5 TRO hearing. The plaintiff must present the petition and application to the trial court. If both sides are present, the court will hear arguments. Generally, the court reviews the application and issues a ruling immediately. If the court grants the TRO, the court will set the amount of the bond and set the hearing on the temporary injunction at the earliest possible date, but no later than 14 days after the TRO is signed. *See* TRCP 680. See "Bond," §5.4, p. 118.

§2.6 Service on defendant. If the court grants the TRO, the court's clerk will deliver the original petition, TRO application, and signed TRO to the district or county clerk's office for preparation of the service of process, precept (notice of TRO injunction), and writ. Once the plaintiff posts the bond with the clerk, the clerk will issue a citation for the original petition, the notice of TRO injunction, and the writ of injunction. See "Serving the TRO," §5.3.3, p. 117. The defendant must be given an opportunity to present evidence, raise defenses, and be heard at the temporary-injunction hearing. See "Notice," §6.3, p. 119.

§2.7 Temporary-injunction hearing. At the temporary-injunction hearing, the court will hear arguments and receive evidence. See "Hearing," §6.4, p. 119. If the court grants the injunction, the court will set an amount for a bond for the temporary injunction (or, if the court authorizes it, the bond can be a continuation of the bond set for the TRO). See "Bond," §5.4, p. 118. Unless the petitioner needs to post a new bond, the clerk will issue the writ of injunction when it receives the temporary-injunction order. The temporary-injunction order must specify a date for trial. TRCP 683. See "Order," §6.5, p. 120.

§2.8 Trial on merits. If the plaintiff asked for permanent injunctive relief, the court may grant the relief after the trial on the merits. See "Application," §7.1, p. 120. If the court grants permanent injunctive relief, a bond is no longer required, and the applicant may request the return of its bond. See "Bond," §7.4, p. 121. Although a writ of permanent injunction is not necessary, the petitioner can ask the court to instruct the clerk to issue one. *See* TRCP 688 (permanent injunction not listed as requiring a writ).

§3. WHERE TO FILE

§3.1 Jurisdiction. The district and county courts have jurisdiction to hear applications for injunctions. *See* Tex. Const. art. 5, §8 (district court), art. 5, §16 (county court); CPRC §65.021(a) (district and county courts); Gov't Code §24.007 (district courts), §25.0026 (statutory probate courts), §26.051 (county courts). See "Choosing the Court—Jurisdiction," ch. 2-F, p. 135. An application for injunctive relief invokes a court's equity jurisdiction. *In re Gamble*, 71 S.W.3d 313, 317 (Tex.2002).

§3.2 Venue. The venue of the suit depends on whether the request for injunctive relief is ancillary to the lawsuit or is the primary reason for it. *Brown v. Gulf TV Co.*, 306 S.W.2d 706, 708 (Tex.1957). See "Choosing the Court—Venue," ch. 2-G, p. 150.

1. Ancillary relief. When injunctive relief is ancillary to the lawsuit, venue is determined by the lawsuit, not by the request for injunction. *O'Quinn v. Hall*, 77 S.W.3d 452, 456 (Tex.App.—Corpus Christi 2002, orig. proceeding); *Hogg v. Professional Pathology Assocs.*, 598 S.W.2d 328, 330 (Tex.App.—Houston [14th Dist.] 1980, writ dism'd).

2. Primary relief. When injunctive relief is the primary relief requested in the petition, CPRC §65.023 determines venue. *In re Continental Airlines, Inc.*, 988 S.W.2d 733, 736 (Tex.1998); *e.g.*, *Karagounis v. Bexar Cty. Hosp. Dist.*, 70 S.W.3d 145, 147 (Tex.App.—San Antonio 2001, pet. denied) (because primary relief was specific performance of contract, not injunctive relief, venue not governed by §65.023); *Billings v. Concordia Heritage Ass'n*, 960 S.W.2d 688, 693 (Tex.App.—El Paso 1997, pet. denied) (because primary relief was to prevent Ds from exhuming body of John Wesley Hardin, a famous outlaw, venue was governed by §65.023). Generally, a suit for injunctive relief against a resident of Texas must be tried in the county of the defendant's domicile. CPRC §65.023(a). If the writ is to stay either a proceeding in a suit or the execution of a judgment, it must be tried in the court where the suit is pending or the judgment was rendered. CPRC §§15.012, 15.013, 65.023(b).

§4. GROUNDS FOR INJUNCTIVE RELIEF

To determine whether a party is entitled to injunctive relief, two questions must be answered. First, what are the grounds for the injunctive relief sought? Second, has the party made the appropriate showing of each prerequisite for obtaining injunctive relief?

§4.1 Grounds for injunctive relief. Several statutes authorize injunctive relief.

1. CPRC §65.011. The most common statutory grounds for injunctive relief are found in CPRC §65.011, the general injunction statute, which authorizes injunctive relief in the following situations:

★

---

(1)   When the applicant is entitled to the relief demanded, and all or part of the relief requires the restraint of some act prejudicial to the applicant. CPRC §65.011(1); *see Coastal Mar. Serv. v. City of Port Neches*, 11 S.W.3d 509, 515 (Tex.App.—Beaumont 2000, no pet.); *see, e.g., Dallas Cty. v. Sweitzer*, 881 S.W.2d 757, 769 (Tex. App.—Dallas 1994, writ denied) (P sought injunction to prevent enforcement of unconstitutional fee-collection statute). Although earlier cases suggested CPRC §65.011(1) does not require a showing of lack of an adequate legal remedy, the Supreme Court held it does. *Town of Palm Valley v. Johnson*, 87 S.W.3d 110, 111 (Tex.2001).

(2)   When a party performs or is about to perform, or is procuring or allowing the performance of, an act relating to the subject of pending litigation, in violation of the applicant's rights, and the act would tend to render the judgment in that litigation ineffectual. CPRC §65.011(2). Types of injunctions under CPRC §65.011(2) include the following:

(a)   An injunction to preserve the subject matter of the suit until the suit is resolved by a judgment. *See City of Dallas v. Wright*, 36 S.W.2d 973, 975 (Tex.1931); *see, e.g., PILF Invs. v. Arlitt*, 940 S.W.2d 255, 258-59 (Tex.App.—San Antonio 1997, no writ) (to prevent forced sale of property); *Vannerson v. Vannerson*, 857 S.W.2d 659, 674 (Tex.App.—Houston [1st Dist.] 1993, writ denied) (to safeguard property during divorce).

(b)   An anti-suit injunction to (1) address a threat to the court's jurisdiction, (2) prevent the evasion of important public policy, (3) prevent a multiplicity of suits, or (4) protect a party from vexatious or harassing litigation. *Frost Nat'l Bank v. Fernandez*, 315 S.W.3d 494, 512 (Tex.2010); *Golden Rule Ins. v. Harper*, 925 S.W.2d 649, 651 (Tex.1996); *AVCO Corp. v. Interstate Sw., Ltd.*, 145 S.W.3d 257, 262 (Tex.App.—Houston [14th Dist.] 2004, no pet.). The courts of appeals are split on whether the *Golden Rule* test applies only during the trial court's plenary power or whether it also applies after the trial court loses plenary power. *Compare Panda Energy Corp. v. Allstate Ins.*, 91 S.W.3d 29, 35 (Tex.App.—Dallas 2002, pet. granted, judgm't vacated w.r.m.) (applies only while court has plenary jurisdiction), *with Bridas Corp. v. Unocal Corp.*, 16 S.W.3d 887, 890 (Tex.App.—Houston [14th Dist.] 2000, pet. dism'd) (applies while case is on appeal).

(3)   When the applicant is entitled to a writ of injunction under the principles of equity and the laws of Texas relating to injunctions. CPRC §65.011(3); *see Butnaru v. Ford Motor Co.*, 84 S.W.3d 198, 210 (Tex.2002).

(4)   When a cloud would be placed on the title to real property being sold under an execution, against a party having no interest in the real property, irrespective of any remedy at law. CPRC §65.011(4); *Citizens State Bank v. Caney Invs.*, 733 S.W.2d 581, 585 (Tex.App.—Houston [1st Dist.] 1987), *rev'd on other grounds*, 746 S.W.2d 477 (Tex.1988).

(5)   When irreparable injury to real or personal property is threatened, irrespective of any remedy at law. CPRC §65.011(5).

2. Other statutory grounds. Other statutes that authorize injunctive relief include the following: Business & Commerce Code §15.51(a) (injunction to enforce covenant not to compete), §24.008(a)(3)(A) (injunction to prevent further disposition of assets in suit for fraudulent transfer); and Property Code §21.064(a) (injunctive relief in eminent-domain suits).

§4.2 Prerequisites for injunctive relief. Unless excepted by statute, the following prerequisites must be pleaded and proved before a party can obtain injunctive relief:

1. Permanent relief. The applicant must plead for some form of permanent relief—either a cause of action (e.g., suit for damages) or, if injunctive relief is the only relief sought, a permanent injunction. *See Butnaru v. Ford Motor Co.*, 84 S.W.3d 198, 204 (Tex.2002); *Walling v. Metcalfe*, 863 S.W.2d 56, 57 (Tex.1993); *Jordan v. Rash*, 745 S.W.2d 549, 554-55 (Tex.App.—Waco 1998, no pet.). For the elements of various causes of action, see *O'Connor's Texas COA*. If the applicant pleads a cause of action that is not recognized in Texas, the trial court cannot grant an injunction. *See, e.g., Valenzuela v. Aquino*, 853 S.W.2d 512, 513 (Tex.1993) (because Texas has no cause of action for negligent infliction of emotional distress, trial court could not enjoin picketers).

2. Probable right to relief. The applicant must show it has a probable right to the relief it seeks on final hearing. *Butnaru*, 84 S.W.3d at 204; *Walling*, 863 S.W.2d at 58; *Sun Oil Co. v. Whitaker*, 424 S.W.2d 216, 218

⭐

(Tex.1968). That is, the applicant must prove it is likely to succeed on the merits of its lawsuit. *DeSantis v. Wackenhut Corp.*, 793 S.W.2d 670, 686 (Tex.1990); *Southwestern Bell Tel. Co. v. Public Util. Comm'n*, 571 S.W.2d 503, 506 (Tex.1978). It is not necessary for the applicant to prove it will ultimately prevail. *Walling*, 863 S.W.2d at 58; *Sun Oil*, 424 S.W.2d at 218.

3. Probable injury. The applicant must plead it will suffer a probable injury. *Butnaru*, 84 S.W.3d at 204; *Universal Health Servs. v. Thompson*, 24 S.W.3d 570, 577 (Tex.App.—Austin 2000, no pet.). Probable injury requires a showing that the harm is imminent, the injury would be irreparable, and the applicant has no other adequate legal remedy. *Harbor Perfusion, Inc. v. Floyd*, 45 S.W.3d 713, 716 (Tex.App.—Corpus Christi 2001, no pet.); *Henderson v. KRTS, Inc.*, 822 S.W.2d 769, 773 (Tex.App.—Houston [1st Dist.] 1992, no writ).

(1) Imminent harm. The applicant must plead the harm is imminent. *See Operation Rescue–Nat'l v. Planned Parenthood*, 975 S.W.2d 546, 554 (Tex.1998) (permanent injunction); *Bell v. Texas Workers Comp. Comm'n*, 102 S.W.3d 299, 302 (Tex.App.—Austin 2003, no pet.) (temporary injunction); *see also Surko Enters. v. Borg-Warner Acceptance Corp.*, 782 S.W.2d 223, 225 (Tex.App.—Houston [1st Dist.] 1989, no writ) (in suit over collateral, P showed imminent harm because D was insolvent and transferring property to another). An injunction will not be issued unless it is shown that the respondent will otherwise engage in the activity enjoined. *State v. Morales*, 869 S.W.2d 941, 946-47 (Tex.1994). An applicant's fear or apprehension of the possibility of injury is not sufficient; the applicant must prove the respondent has attempted or intends to harm the applicant. *Jones v. Jefferson Cty.*, 15 S.W.3d 206, 213 (Tex.App.—Texarkana 2000, pet. denied); *see Matrix Network, Inc. v. Ginn*, 211 S.W.3d 944, 947-48 (Tex.App.—Dallas 2007, no pet.); *EMSL Analytical, Inc. v. Younker*, 154 S.W.3d 693, 697 (Tex.App.—Houston [14th Dist.] 2004, no pet.).

(2) Irreparable injury. The applicant must plead that, if the injunction is not issued, the harm that will occur is irreparable. *Town of Palm Valley v. Johnson*, 87 S.W.3d 110, 111 (Tex.2001) (permanent injunction); *Butnaru*, 84 S.W.3d at 204 (temporary injunction). An injury is irreparable if the injured party cannot be adequately compensated in damages or if the damages cannot be measured by any certain pecuniary standard. *Butnaru*, 84 S.W.3d at 204; *e.g.*, *Wright v. Sport Sup.*, 137 S.W.3d 289, 294 (Tex.App.—Beaumont 2004, no pet.) (irreparable injury because P's damages were not presently ascertainable or easily calculated); *Haq v. America's Favorite Chicken Co.*, 921 S.W.2d 728, 730 (Tex.App.—Corpus Christi 1996, writ dism'd) (no irreparable injury because P did not prove damages it might suffer pending trial were different from damages recoverable for breach of contract); *see also Liberty Mut. Ins. v. Mustang Tractor & Equip. Co.*, 812 S.W.2d 663, 666 (Tex.App.—Houston [14th Dist.] 1991, no writ) (disruption of business can be irreparable harm). The courts are split on whether cost and delay are sufficient injuries to be considered irreparable. *Compare In re Estate of Dilasky*, 972 S.W.2d 763, 767 (Tex.App.—Corpus Christi 1998, no pet.) (costs and delay can be factors in irreparable harm), *with Reynolds, Shannon, Miller, Blinn, White & Cook v. Flanary*, 872 S.W.2d 248, 252 (Tex.App.—Dallas 1993, no writ) (costs and delay alone were not sufficient injuries). The following are some exceptions to the irreparable-injury requirement:

(a) Restrictive covenant. An applicant seeking an injunction to enforce a restrictive covenant is not required to prove irreparable injury. *Jim Rutherford Invs. v. Terramar Beach Cmty. Ass'n*, 25 S.W.3d 845, 849 (Tex.App.—Houston [14th Dist.] 2000, pet. denied); *Munson v. Milton*, 948 S.W.2d 813, 815 (Tex.App.—San Antonio 1997, pet. denied). An applicant needs to show only that the nonmovant intends to do an act that would breach the covenant. *Marcus v. Whispering Springs Homeowners Ass'n*, 153 S.W.3d 702, 707 (Tex.App.—Dallas 2005, no pet.); *Munson*, 948 S.W.2d at 815.

(b) Zoning violation. A city seeking to enjoin the violation of a zoning ordinance is not required to prove the violation would cause injury to it or its residents. *San Miguel v. City of Windcrest*, 40 S.W.3d 104, 108 (Tex.App.—San Antonio 2000, no pet.).

(c) Covenant not to compete. An applicant seeking a permanent injunction to enforce a covenant not to compete is not required to prove an irreparable injury. *Butler v. Arrow Mirror & Glass, Inc.*, 51 S.W.3d 787, 795 (Tex.App.—Houston [1st Dist.] 2001, no pet.); *see also Wright*, 137 S.W.3d at 294 (employee's breach of covenant not to compete creates rebuttable presumption of irreparable injury). But an applicant seeking a temporary injunction to enforce a covenant not to compete must prove an irreparable injury. *Reach Grp. v. Angelina Grp.*, 173 S.W.3d 834, 837 (Tex.App.—Houston [14th Dist.] 2005, no pet.). See *O'Connor's Texas COA*, "Injunctive relief," ch. 5-I, §3.3.1, p. 156.

(3) Inadequate remedy. The applicant must plead there is no adequate remedy at law. *Synergy Ctr., Ltd. v. Lone Star Franchising Inc.*, 63 S.W.3d 561, 567 (Tex.App.—Austin 2001, no pet.); *Fasken v. Darby*, 901 S.W.2d 591, 592 (Tex.App.—El Paso 1995, no writ). A court will not issue a temporary injunction when there is a plain and adequate remedy at law. *McGlothlin v. Kliebert*, 672 S.W.2d 231, 232 (Tex.1984). For a legal remedy to be adequate, it must give the applicant complete, final, and equal relief. *Henderson*, 822 S.W.2d at 773; *see Universal Health*, 24 S.W.3d at 577. For purposes of injunctive relief, there is no adequate remedy at law if (1) damages cannot be calculated or (2) the defendant will be unable to pay damages. *Texas Indus. Gas v. Phoenix Metallurgical Corp.*, 828 S.W.2d 529, 533 (Tex.App.—Houston [1st Dist.] 1992, no writ); *see Surko Enters.*, 782 S.W.2d at 225 (no adequate remedy at law if D is insolvent); *cf. Butnaru*, 84 S.W.3d at 204 (irreparable injury if damages cannot be measured by any certain pecuniary standard). The following are some exceptions to the requirement of no adequate remedy at law.

(a) Statutory right. An applicant who has a statutory right to an injunction is not required to prove it has no adequate remedy at law. *Butnaru*, 84 S.W.3d at 210.

(b) City ordinance. An applicant seeking to enjoin the violation of a city ordinance is not required to prove it has no adequate remedy at law. *San Miguel*, 40 S.W.3d at 108.

(c) Cloud on title. An applicant seeking to prevent a cloud from being cast on the title to real property does not have to prove there is no adequate remedy at law. CPRC §65.011(4).

(d) Irreparable injury to property. An applicant seeking to prevent irreparable injury to real or personal property does not have to prove there is no adequate remedy at law. CPRC §65.011(5).

§5. REQUEST FOR TEMPORARY RESTRAINING ORDER (TRO)

§5.1 Application.

1. Grounds. The application for a TRO must identify one or more of the grounds for injunction. See "Grounds for injunctive relief," §4.1, p. 113.

2. Prerequisites. The application for a TRO must plead the prerequisites for injunctive relief. See "Prerequisites for injunctive relief," §4.2, p. 114. The applicant must plead all of the necessary facts supporting the issuance of injunctive relief; legal conclusions are not sufficient. *Texas State Bd. of Medical Exam'rs v. McKinney*, 315 S.W.2d 387, 390 (Tex.App.—Waco 1958, no writ).

3. Request for injunction. The application for a TRO must include a request for a temporary injunction. *See* TRCP 680; Urquhart, *The Most Extraordinary Remedy: The Injunction*, 45 Tex.B.J. at 359. See "Request for Temporary Injunction," §6, p. 118.

4. Ex parte allegations. If an applicant is seeking a TRO without notice to the other party, the application must identify specific facts showing why the order should be entered ex parte. TRCP 680. The application must show (1) the applicant will suffer irreparable injury, loss, or damage if the TRO is not granted, and (2) there is not enough time to serve notice on the respondent and hold a hearing. *See id.* Some local rules may require an additional written certificate.

5. Bond. The application for a TRO must state the applicant's willingness to post bond. *See* TRCP 684.

6. Relief. The application for a TRO must identify the relief sought. A trial court can grant only the injunctive relief an applicant specifically requests. *Fairfield v. Stonehenge Ass'n*, 678 S.W.2d 608, 611 (Tex.App.—Houston [14th Dist.] 1984, no writ); *see* TRCP 682. A general prayer for relief does not allow injunctive relief beyond what is specifically requested. *Fairfield*, 678 S.W.2d at 611; *Colorado River Valley Co. v. Schiavone*, 476 S.W.2d 368, 370 (Tex.App.—Austin 1972, writ ref'd n.r.e.).

★

7. Verified. The application for a TRO must be verified or supported with affidavits. TRCP 680, 682. Affidavits must be based on the personal knowledge of the affiant. *See Williams v. Bagley*, 875 S.W.2d 808, 810 (Tex. App.—Beaumont 1994, no writ).

§5.2 Hearing. The court should conduct a hearing on the TRO, but the TRO can be granted ex parte, without a hearing. *See* TRCP 680.

§5.3 TRO.

1. Form. A TRO must be in writing. *See* TRCP 680, 683 (both rules assume, but do not state, that order must be in writing); *Ex parte Lesikar*, 899 S.W.2d 654, 654 (Tex.1995) (TRO extension order must be in writing). Until the TRO is signed by the judge, it is not enforceable by contempt. *Ex parte Price*, 741 S.W.2d 366, 367 (Tex. 1987). The order must make certain specific statements. *See* TRCP 680, 683. See "Order," §6.5, p. 120. In its order, the court must do the following:

(1) Identify the person or entity to be restrained. *See* TRCP 683.

(2) State why the TRO was granted without notice if it is granted ex parte. TRCP 680.

(3) State the reasons for the issuance of the TRO by defining the injury and describing why it is irreparable. TRCP 680, 683.

(4) Define, in reasonable detail, the act to be restrained. TRCP 683. The act to be restrained cannot be described by reference to the pleadings or other documents. *Id.*

(5) State the date and hour of issuance if it was granted ex parte. TRCP 680. The trial court cannot hold a party in contempt for an act that occurred before the date and time of issuance. *See Ex parte Guetersloh*, 935 S.W.2d 110, 111 (Tex.1996) (appeal of temporary injunction).

(6) State the date the order expires. TRCP 680. The court can grant a TRO for only 14 days. *Id.* The 14-day time limit does not consist of 14 24-hour periods that begin running at the time the TRO is signed; the TRO expires at midnight 14 calendar days after it is signed. *In re Walkup*, 122 S.W.3d 215, 217-18 (Tex.App.—Houston [1st Dist.] 2003, orig. proceeding) (TRO granted on 1-30-03 at 2:30 p.m. expired at midnight, not at 2:30 p.m., on 2-13-03).

(7) State the date for the hearing on the temporary injunction. TRCP 680. The injunction hearing must be set at the earliest possible time. *Id.* The hearing on the temporary injunction takes precedence over other matters. *Id.*

(8) Fix the amount of the TRO bond. TRCP 684. See "Bond," §5.4, p. 118.

2. Extending the TRO. An order extending a TRO must be in writing. An oral order extending a TRO is not effective. *Ex parte Lesikar*, 899 S.W.2d at 654.

(1) On motion & order. The applicant may ask the trial court to extend the TRO by filing a motion, before the TRO expires, showing good cause. TRCP 680; *In re Texas Nat. Res. Conserv. Comm'n*, 85 S.W.3d 201, 203 (Tex.2002). The court can grant one extension of the TRO for an additional 14 days. TRCP 680; *In re Texas Nat. Res.*, 85 S.W.3d at 203.

(2) By agreement. If the respondent agrees, the TRO may be extended for more than 14 days. TRCP 680.

3. Serving the TRO. Once the clerk has received the original petition and application for TRO, and the bond has been filed into the registry of the court, the clerk will issue a precept for the TRO and a notice of the hearing on the temporary injunction. The precept will be served with the citation and writ of injunction. All the documents are served on the defendant by the sheriff or constable or by a private process server as authorized by court order. *See* TRCP 686, 688. See "Who May Serve Process," ch. 2-H, §3, p. 160.

— ★ —

§5.4 Bond. The order for temporary injunctive relief must set the amount for the bond. TRCP 684. If the order does not set the bond, the order is void and not enforceable. *Qwest Comms. v. AT&T Corp.*, 24 S.W.3d 334, 337 (Tex. 2000) (temporary injunction); *Ex parte Jordan*, 787 S.W.2d 367, 368 (Tex.1990) (TRO). The bond protects the respondent from any harm it may sustain as a result of the TRO. *See DeSantis v. Wackenhut Corp.*, 793 S.W.2d 670, 686 (Tex.1990).

1. Setting the bond.

(1) Bond required. To protect the respondent, the amount of the bond must have some relation to the potential damages in the lawsuit. *See, e.g., Franklin Sav. Ass'n v. Reese*, 756 S.W.2d 14, 16 (Tex.App.—Austin 1988, no writ) ($10,000 bond was not adequate for debt of $34 million); *El Paso Dev. Co. v. Berryman*, 729 S.W.2d 883, 888-89 (Tex.App.—Corpus Christi 1987, no writ) ($15,000 was adequate for debt of over $7 million because there was sufficient collateral). A bond for a TRO does not continue on and act as security for a temporary injunction unless expressly authorized by the court. *Bay Fin. Sav. Bank v. Brown*, 142 S.W.3d 586, 591 (Tex.App.—Texarkana 2004, no pet.).

(2) Bond amount discretionary. If the suit is against the State or its agency or subdivision, or against a city in its governmental capacity, and the governmental unit has no pecuniary interest in the suit and no monetary damages can be shown, the court may set the amount in its discretion. TRCP 684.

(3) Bond not required. The court may not require an indigent party to post a bond for a TRO or an injunction if (1) the applicant submits an affidavit that meets the requirements of CPRC §65.043, and (2) the court finds the order is intended to restrain the adverse party from foreclosing on the applicant's residence. CPRC §§65.041, 65.042(a).

2. Posting bond.
The applicant must post the bond before the clerk issues the writ. *See Goodwin v. Goodwin*, 456 S.W.2d 885, 885 (Tex.1970) (temporary injunction); *Williams v. Bagley*, 875 S.W.2d 808, 810 (Tex. App.—Beaumont 1994, no writ) (TRO).

3. Challenging bond.
The party restrained by the injunction may challenge the adequacy of the bond by filing a motion to increase the bond. *See Maples v. Muscletech, Inc.*, 74 S.W.3d 429, 430 (Tex.App.—Amarillo 2002, no pet.). The party must make a "clear showing" that its potential losses are greater than the amount of the bond. *See id.* at 432.

§5.5 Writ.

1. Form.
The court clerk will prepare the writ of injunction for issuance. *See* TRCP 688. The clerk is responsible for ensuring the form of the writ complies with TRCP 687.

2. Service.
The writ of injunction must be served on the respondent by a sheriff or constable of the county of the respondent's residence or by a person authorized by court order. *See* TRCP 103, 688, 689. See "Who May Serve Process," ch. 2-H, §3, p. 160. The applicant should ensure that copies of the writ are also served on any other persons acting in concert with the respondent or the respondent's officers, agents, servants, employees, or attorneys. *See* TRCP 683.

3. Return of service.
The officer or authorized person serving the writ of injunction must complete and file a return of service for the writ that meets the requirements of TRCP 107. TRCP 689.

4. Copy in court's file.
The clerk must keep a copy of the TRO (or temporary injunction) in the court's file. TRCP 688.

§6. REQUEST FOR TEMPORARY INJUNCTION

§6.1 Parties. Before the court can grant temporary injunctive relief, the applicant must join all indispensable parties under TRCP 39. See "Parties to be joined," ch. 2-E, §6.2, p. 133. The following parties have been held to be indispensable to an injunction proceeding:

⭐

1. Those whose rights will be directly affected by the writ. *See Ladner v. Reliance Corp.*, 293 S.W.2d 758, 764-65 (Tex.1956); *Scott v. Graham*, 292 S.W.2d 324, 327 (Tex.1956).

2. All parties to a contract if the applicant is seeking to restrain enforcement of the contract. *McCharen v. Bailey*, 87 S.W.2d 284, 285 (Tex.App.—Eastland 1935, no writ).

3. Any state, county, or city if the applicant is seeking to restrain a public official acting on behalf of the state, county, or city. *See Davis v. Wildenthal*, 241 S.W.2d 620, 622 (Tex.App.—El Paso 1951, writ ref'd n.r.e.).

§6.2 Application. When the applicant's original petition includes a request for a TRO, its request for a temporary injunction is merely an additional paragraph asking the court to set a hearing for a temporary injunction. When the applicant seeks a temporary injunction without a TRO, its petition must meet all the pleading requirements for a TRO except the request for ex parte relief. That is, the petition for a temporary injunction must be verified and must allege the following: (1) a cause of action, (2) a probable right to relief, (3) a probable injury in the interim (which includes proof of imminent and irreparable injury and no adequate remedy at law), and (4) a willingness to post bond. *See* TRCP 682 (verified petition), TRCP 684 (bond). See "Prerequisites for injunctive relief," §4.2, p. 114.

§6.3 Notice. The party to be enjoined is entitled to notice and an opportunity to be heard. TRCP 681; *PILF Invs. v. Arlitt*, 940 S.W.2d 255, 259-60 (Tex.App.—San Antonio 1997, no writ); *City of Houston v. Houston Lighting & Power Co.*, 530 S.W.2d 866, 869 (Tex.App.—Houston [14th Dist.] 1975, writ ref'd n.r.e.). When a request for injunction is ancillary to a pending suit, notice through service by citation is not necessary; when a request is independent of a pending suit, the defendant must be served by citation. *See In re Poe*, 996 S.W.2d 281, 282-83 (Tex.App.—Amarillo 1999, orig. proceeding). The party must be given three days' notice of the temporary-injunction hearing. *See* TRCP 21.

§6.4 Hearing.

1. Scope of proceeding. The only issue presented at the temporary-injunction hearing is the need for immediate relief pending the trial on the merits. *Transport Co. v. Robertson Transps.*, 261 S.W.2d 549, 552 (Tex. 1953); *Coastal Mar. Serv. v. City of Port Neches*, 11 S.W.3d 509, 515 (Tex.App.—Beaumont 2000, no pet.).

2. Appearance.

(1) Applicant does not appear. If the applicant does not appear for the hearing on the temporary injunction, any TRO granted earlier will be dissolved, and the injunction will be denied.

(2) Respondent does not appear. If the respondent does not appear for the hearing on the temporary injunction, the petitioner is not entitled to a default judgment; a full evidentiary hearing is still required. *See Millwrights Local Un. v. Rust Eng'g*, 433 S.W.2d 683, 686-87 (Tex.1968).

3. Evidence.

(1) Applicant's burden. At the hearing, the applicant must introduce competent evidence to support a probable right to recovery and a probable injury. *Letson v. Barnes*, 979 S.W.2d 414, 417 (Tex.App.—Amarillo 1998, pet. denied); *see Bay Fin. Sav. Bank v. Brown*, 142 S.W.3d 586, 589-90 (Tex.App.—Texarkana 2004, no pet.). See "Prerequisites for injunctive relief," §4.2, p. 114. An injunction cannot be upheld without evidence. *Atkinson v. Arnold*, 893 S.W.2d 294, 297 (Tex.App.—Texarkana 1995, no writ); *see Millwrights Local Un.*, 433 S.W.2d at 687 (conduct of hearing under TRCP 680 implies evidence will be offered). The court cannot consider the affidavits attached to the application for temporary injunction unless the parties agree or no one objects. *Millwrights Local Un.*, 433 S.W.2d at 686 (no agreement); *Ahmed v. Shimi Ventures, L.P.*, 99 S.W.3d 682, 684 n.2 (Tex.App.—Houston [1st Dist.] 2003, no pet.) (no objection).

(2) Limitation on evidence. The trial court can impose reasonable limits on the parties' presentation of evidence in a temporary-injunction hearing. *Reading & Bates Constr. Co. v. O'Donnell*, 627 S.W.2d 239, 244 (Tex.App.—Corpus Christi 1982, writ ref'd n.r.e.); *City of Houston v. Houston Lighting & Power Co.*, 530 S.W.2d 866, 869 (Tex.App.—Houston [14th Dist.] 1975, writ ref'd n.r.e.); *see, e.g., Birds Constr., Inc. v. Gonzalez*,

─────────────────────────── ✦ ───────────────────────────

595 S.W.2d 926, 928-29 (Tex.App.—Corpus Christi 1981, no writ) (court did not abuse discretion in granting temporary injunction based on stipulated facts, argument, and summary of other expected evidence from both parties). The court's limitations, however, cannot deprive the parties of their right to be heard. *E.g.,* ***Houston Lighting & Power***, 530 S.W.2d at 869 (court's ruling deprived D of right to offer any evidence at hearing); ***Oertel v. Gulf States Abrasive Mfg.***, 429 S.W.2d 623, 623 (Tex.App.—Houston [1st Dist.] 1968, no writ) (court refused to allow D to call any witnesses).

§6.5 Order. To be valid, an injunction order must be in writing, signed by the judge, and entered into the minutes of the court. *See* ***Ex parte Price***, 741 S.W.2d 366, 367-68 (Tex.1987) (permanent injunction). The order must make certain specific statements. TRCP 683. The requirements of TRCP 683 are mandatory and must be strictly followed. ***Qwest Comms. v. AT&T Corp.***, 24 S.W.3d 334, 337 (Tex.2000). An injunction order that does not comply with TRCP 683 is subject to being declared void and dissolved. ***Qwest Comms.***, 24 S.W.3d at 337. In its order, the court must do the following:

1. State the reasons for the issuance of the injunction by defining the injury and describing why it is irreparable. TRCP 683; ***State v. Cook United, Inc.***, 464 S.W.2d 105, 106 (Tex.1971). TRCP 683 requires the injunction order to state the reasons an injury will be suffered if the interlocutory relief is not granted. ***Cook United***, 464 S.W.2d at 106; ***Kotz v. Imperial Capital Bank***, 319 S.W.3d 54, 56 (Tex.App.—San Antonio 2010, no pet.); ***International Bhd. of Elec. Workers Local Un. v. Becon Constr. Co.***, 104 S.W.3d 239, 243 (Tex.App.—Beaumont 2003, no pet.); ***Fasken v. Darby***, 901 S.W.2d 591, 593 (Tex.App.—El Paso 1995, no writ); ***Moreno v. Baker Tools, Inc.***, 808 S.W.2d 208, 210 (Tex.App.—Houston [1st Dist.] 1991, no writ). *Contra* ***Pinebrook Props., Ltd. v. Brookhaven Lake Prop. Owners Ass'n***, 77 S.W.3d 487, 504 (Tex.App.—Texarkana 2002, pet. denied) (TRCP 683 does not require court to state reasons injury would be suffered). The reasons must be stated because the appellate court cannot infer them from the evidence, the pleadings, or the court's oral pronouncement at the hearing. ***Moreno***, 808 S.W.2d at 211.

2. Define, in reasonable detail, the act to be restrained. TRCP 683. The act to be restrained cannot be described by reference to the pleadings or to other documents. *Id.*; *see, e.g.,* ***Maloy v. City of Lewisville***, 848 S.W.2d 380, 385 (Tex.App.—Fort Worth 1993, no writ) (when order described acts to be enjoined in reasonable detail, it was not error to refer to a city ordinance), *disapproved on other grounds,* ***Schleuter v. City of Fort Worth***, 947 S.W.2d 920 (Tex.App.—Fort Worth 1997, pet. denied). When an injunction is granted to protect confidential information and trade secrets, the order can refer to sealed exhibits as long as the activity to be enjoined is described in reasonable detail. ***Rugen v. Interactive Bus. Sys.***, 864 S.W.2d 548, 553 (Tex.App.—Dallas 1993, no writ).

3. Include an order setting the case for a trial on the merits. TRCP 683; ***Qwest Comms.***, 24 S.W.3d at 337; ***InterFirst Bank San Felipe v. Paz Constr. Co.***, 715 S.W.2d 640, 641 (Tex.1986). If the injunction does not set the case for a trial on the merits, it is void. ***Qwest Comms.***, 24 S.W.3d at 337; ***InterFirst Bank***, 715 S.W.2d at 641; ***City of Sherman v. Eiras***, 157 S.W.3d 931, 931 (Tex.App.—Dallas 2005, no pet.); ***EOG Res. v. Gutierrez***, 75 S.W.3d 50, 52-53 (Tex.App.—San Antonio 2002, no pet.).

4. Fix the amount of the bond. TRCP 684; ***Qwest Comms.***, 24 S.W.3d at 337. See "Bond," §5.4, p. 118.

§6.6 Writ. See "Writ," §5.5, p. 118.

§7. REQUEST FOR PERMANENT INJUNCTION

§7.1 Application. When the applicant's original petition includes pleadings for other injunctive relief (a TRO or temporary injunction), its request for a permanent injunction is merely an additional paragraph asking the court to grant a permanent injunction after the trial on the merits. When the applicant seeks a permanent injunction without other injunctive relief, its petition must meet all the requirements for a TRO except (1) a request for ex parte relief, (2) a statement of willingness to post bond, and (3) verification or affidavits. *See* ***Town of Palm Valley v. Johnson***, 17 S.W.3d 281, 288 (Tex.App.—Corpus Christi 2000) (verification not necessary), *pet. denied,* 87 S.W.3d 110 (Tex.2001). That is, the petition for a permanent injunction must allege the following: (1) a cause of action, (2) a

★

probable right to the relief, and (3) a probable injury (which includes imminent and irreparable injury and no adequate remedy at law). See "Prerequisites for injunctive relief," §4.2, p. 114.

§7.2 Hearing. The hearing on the permanent injunction is a full trial of the issues in the applicant's petition. The applicant is entitled to a jury at the hearing. *Citizens State Bank v. Caney Invs.*, 746 S.W.2d 477, 478 (Tex. 1988).

§7.3 Judgment. A judgment for a permanent injunction must describe in reasonable detail the acts to be restrained, but the judgment should not be so broad as to preclude a party from lawful activities that are a proper exercise of its rights. *Computek Computer & Office Sups. v. Walton*, 156 S.W.3d 217, 220-21 (Tex.App.—Dallas 2005, no pet.); *see San Antonio Bar Ass'n v. Guardian Abstract & Title Co.*, 291 S.W.2d 697, 702 (Tex.1956); *Adust Video v. Nueces Cty.*, 996 S.W.2d 245, 249-50 (Tex.App.—Corpus Christi 1999, no pet.). The judgment does not need to describe in detail the reasons for its issuance. *Adust Video*, 996 S.W.2d at 249-50. The requirement in TRCP 683—that the order contain detailed explanations of the reasons for the issuance of the injunction—does not apply to a permanent injunction when the injunction is the only relief sought by the action. *Shields v. State*, 27 S.W.3d 267, 273 (Tex.App.—Austin 2000, no pet.); *Adust Video*, 996 S.W.2d at 249; *see Qaddura v. Indo-European Foods, Inc.*, 141 S.W.3d 882, 891-92 (Tex.App.—Dallas 2004, pet. denied); *City of Houston v. Morgan Guar. Int'l Bank*, 666 S.W.2d 524, 536 (Tex.App.—Houston [1st Dist.] 1983, writ ref'd n.r.e.).

§7.4 Bond. A bond is not required for a permanent injunction. *Citizens State Bank v. Caney Invs.*, 733 S.W.2d 581, 585 (Tex.App.—Houston [1st Dist.] 1987), *rev'd on other grounds*, 746 S.W.2d 477 (Tex.1988); *see Canteen Corp. v. Republic of Tex. Props., Inc.*, 773 S.W.2d 398, 400 (Tex.App.—Dallas 1989, no writ).

§7.5 Writ. A writ of injunction is not issued after a permanent injunction. *See* TRCP 688 (refers only to writs for TROs and temporary injunctions).

§8. RESPONSE

§8.1 Defenses to request for injunction. Defenses to injunctive relief include the following: (1) the applicant has an adequate remedy at law, (2) a temporary injunction will accomplish the whole object of the suit, (3) a temporary injunction will destroy, rather than preserve, the status quo, (4) the applicant is not entitled to equitable relief because it is guilty of inequitable conduct (e.g., laches, unclean hands), and (5) the applicant's verification is insufficient. *McGlothlin v. Kliebert*, 672 S.W.2d 231, 232 (Tex.1984) (#1); *Texas Foundries, Inc. v. International Moulders & Foundry Workers' Un.*, 248 S.W.2d 460, 464 (Tex.1952) (#2); *Friona ISD v. King*, 15 S.W.3d 653, 659 (Tex.App.—Amarillo 2000, no pet.) (#2); *Crystal Media, Inc. v. HCI Acquisition Corp.*, 773 S.W.2d 732, 734 (Tex. App.—San Antonio 1989, no writ) (#5); *Ballenger v. Ballenger*, 668 S.W.2d 467, 469-70 (Tex.App.—Corpus Christi 1984, writ dism'd) (#3); *Landry's Seafood Inn & Oyster Bar-Kemah, Inc. v. Wiggins*, 919 S.W.2d 924, 927 (Tex. App.—Houston [14th Dist.] 1996, no writ) (#4).

§8.2 Motion to modify or dissolve.

1. Ex parte TRO. The respondent can move to modify or dissolve an ex parte TRO. The respondent must give the applicant two days' notice (unless the notice period is shortened by court order) of the hearing on the motion. TRCP 680; *see, e.g., Forestier v. San Antonio Sav. Ass'n*, 564 S.W.2d 160, 163-64 (Tex.App.—El Paso 1978, writ ref'd n.r.e.) (hearing on motion to dissolve held same day TRO was issued).

2. TRO & temporary injunction.

(1) Modify. The respondent can move to modify a temporary injunction on the following grounds: • The injunction is overbroad. *Harbor Perfusion, Inc. v. Floyd*, 45 S.W.3d 713, 718 (Tex.App.—Corpus Christi 2001, no pet.). • The injunction granted more relief than requested. *Easton v. Brasch*, 277 S.W.3d 558, 560 (Tex.App.— Houston [1st Dist.] 2009, no pet.). • The claimed injury is speculative. *Fox v. Tropical Warehouses Inc.*, 121 S.W.3d 853, 861 (Tex.App.—Fort Worth 2003, no pet.). • An injunction would be an unconstitutional prior restraint on speech. *Texas Mut. Ins. v. Surety Bank*, 156 S.W.3d 125, 131 (Tex.App.—Fort Worth 2005, no pet.).

———————————————————— ✪ ————————————————————

(2) Dissolve. The respondent can move to dissolve a temporary injunction on the grounds that the injunction order is void. A TRO or temporary injunction is void if it does not comply with the requirements of TRCP 683 and 684. *Qwest Comms. v. AT&T Corp.*, 24 S.W.3d 334, 337 (Tex.2000); *e.g.*, *InterFirst Bank San Felipe v. Paz Constr. Co.*, 715 S.W.2d 640, 641 (Tex.1986) (injunction order void because it did not set case for trial on merits); *Goodwin v. Goodwin*, 456 S.W.2d 885, 885 (Tex.1970) (injunction order void because bond was not filed before injunction issued); *Beckham v. Beckham*, 672 S.W.2d 41, 43 (Tex.App.—Houston [14th Dist.] 1984, no writ) (injunction order void because it did not set out reasons for issuance); *see In re Office of the Atty. Gen.*, 257 S.W.3d 695, 697 (Tex.2008) (injunction order void if it does not comply with TRCPs 680 and 684). Most courts have held that a party cannot waive an objection to a temporary injunction that does not comply with TRCP 683 because the rule's requirements are mandatory and must be strictly followed. *E.g.*, *International Bhd. of Elec. Workers Local Un. v. Becon Constr. Co.*, 104 S.W.3d 239, 243 (Tex.App.—Beaumont 2003, no pet.); *Evans v. C. Woods, Inc.*, 34 S.W.3d 581, 582-83 (Tex.App.—Tyler 1999, no pet.); *Big D Props., Inc. v. Foster*, 2 S.W.3d 21, 23 (Tex.App.—Fort Worth 1999, no pet.); *360 Degree Comm. v. Grundman*, 937 S.W.2d 574, 575 (Tex.App.—Texarkana 1996, no writ). *But see Texas Tech Univ. Health Sci. Ctr. v. Rao*, 105 S.W.3d 763, 768 (Tex.App.—Amarillo 2003, pet. dism'd) (error waived); *Emerson v. Fires Out, Inc.*, 735 S.W.2d 492, 493-94 (Tex.App.—Austin 1987, no writ) (same).

3. Temporary & permanent injunction. The respondent can move to modify or dissolve a temporary or permanent injunction on the grounds of either changed circumstances or fundamental error. *Universal Health Servs. v. Thompson*, 24 S.W.3d 570, 580 (Tex.App.—Austin 2000, no pet.); *see City of San Antonio v. Singleton*, 858 S.W.2d 411, 412 (Tex.1993) (changed circumstances for permanent injunction); *Smith v. O'Neill*, 813 S.W.2d 501, 502 (Tex.1991) (same); *Murphy v. McDaniel*, 20 S.W.3d 873, 877 (Tex.App.—Dallas 2000, no pet.) (changed circumstances for temporary injunction). The respondent must present new evidence showing changed circumstances or fundamental error. *Universal Health*, 24 S.W.3d at 580. The respondent cannot use the motion to modify or dissolve to relitigate the basis for the injunction when that basis has not changed. *Chase Manhattan Bank v. Bowles*, 52 S.W.3d 871, 879 (Tex.App.—Waco 2001, no pet.).

(1) Changed circumstances. Changed circumstances are conditions that either alter the status quo after the issuance of the injunction or make the injunction unnecessary or improper. *Bowles*, 52 S.W.3d at 879; *Henke v. Peoples State Bank*, 6 S.W.3d 717, 721 (Tex.App.—Corpus Christi 1999, pet. dism'd). Changed circumstances can include changes in the law, newly revealed facts, or an agreement of the parties. *Murphy*, 20 S.W.3d at 878; *see Kubala Pub. Adjusters, Inc. v. Unauthorized Practice of Law Cmte.*, 133 S.W.3d 790, 794-95 (Tex. App.—Texarkana 2004, no pet.) (changes in law or facts); *Bowles*, 52 S.W.3d at 878-79 (changes in law).

(2) Fundamental error. Fundamental error, which is rare, occurs when the record shows either the trial court did not have jurisdiction or the error directly and adversely affects the public interest as that interest is declared in a statute or the Texas Constitution. *In re C.O.S.*, 988 S.W.2d 760, 765 (Tex.1999); *Universal Health*, 24 S.W.3d at 580.

§8.3 Answer to the lawsuit.

1. Special appearance & venue. If the temporary-injunction hearing was held before the respondent's deadline under TRCP 99 to answer the suit, the respondent does not waive any objection to personal jurisdiction or venue by participating at the hearing or by filing an answer to the application for temporary injunction or a motion for continuance of the hearing. *See, e.g.*, *Valsangiacomo v. Americana Juice Imp., Inc.*, 35 S.W.3d 201, 204 n.3 (Tex.App.—Corpus Christi 2000, no pet.) (participation in temporary-injunction hearing did not waive special appearance); *Gentry v. Tucker*, 891 S.W.2d 766, 768 (Tex.App.—Texarkana 1995, no writ) (filing motion for continuance did not waive venue challenge); *Perkola v. Koelling & Assocs.*, 601 S.W.2d 110, 111-12 (Tex.App.—Dallas 1980, writ dism'd) (appearance at temporary-injunction hearing did not waive venue challenge); *Gibson v. State*, 288 S.W.2d 577, 578 (Tex.App.—Waco 1956, writ dism'd) (answer to application for temporary injunction did not waive venue challenge).

─────────────── ★ ───────────────

2. Answer. The respondent should remember to file an answer to the underlying suit. Once the deadline to file an answer has expired, the petitioner can take a default judgment against a nonanswering respondent, even if the respondent appeared at the injunction hearing. *See Borrego v. del Palacio*, 445 S.W.2d 620, 621 (Tex. App.—El Paso 1969, no writ).

§9. ENFORCING THE INJUNCTION

An injunction is binding on (1) the parties, (2) the parties' officers, agents, servants, employees, and attorneys, and (3) any other person who acts in concert with the parties or their agents and who receives actual notice of the order. TRCP 683.

§9.1 Motion for contempt. The trial court may enforce an injunction by holding the enjoined party in contempt for violating the injunction order. TRCP 692; *Ex parte Blasingame*, 748 S.W.2d 444, 447 (Tex.1988); *see also State v. Credit Bureau of Laredo, Inc.*, 530 S.W.2d 288, 290-91 (Tex.1975) (distinguishing between proceedings for contempt and civil penalty). The trial court may punish the contemnor for violating an injunction by imposing a fine or imprisonment. *Ex parte Blasingame*, 748 S.W.2d at 447; *Southwest Prof'l Indem. Corp. v. Texas Dept. of Ins.*, 914 S.W.2d 256, 265 (Tex.App.—Austin 1996, writ denied). A fine for contempt cannot exceed $500. Gov't Code §21.002(b); *Ex parte Hudson*, 917 S.W.2d 24, 26 (Tex.1996). The order cannot punish the contemnor for actions taken before the court signed its order. *Ex parte Guetersloh*, 935 S.W.2d 110, 111 (Tex.1996).

§9.2 Suit to enforce penalty in injunction. The party who obtained the injunction may enforce it by filing a suit to enforce a penalty within the injunctive order. *Transcontinental Gas Pipe Line Corp. v. American Nat'l Pet. Co.*, 763 S.W.2d 809, 824 (Tex.App.—Texarkana 1988), *rev'd on other grounds*, 798 S.W.2d 274 (Tex.1990); *see also State v. Credit Bureau of Laredo, Inc.*, 530 S.W.2d 288, 290-91 (Tex.1975) (distinguishing between proceedings for contempt and civil penalty).

§9.3 Other means of enforcement. It is unclear whether the party who obtained the injunction may sue the enjoined party, even if there is a cause of action for damages because of the violation of the injunction. *See Cannan v. Green Oaks Apts., Ltd.*, 758 S.W.2d 753, 755 (Tex.1988).

§10. RELIEF FROM WRONGFUL INJUNCTION

A person who wrongfully obtained a TRO or temporary injunction is liable for damages caused by the injunction. *DeSantis v. Wackenhut Corp.*, 793 S.W.2d 670, 686 (Tex.1990). There are two types of actions for wrongful injunction.

§10.1 Suit on bond. To prevail on a cause of action on a bond, the claimant must prove the injunction was issued or perpetuated when it should not have been and that it was later dissolved. *DeSantis v. Wackenhut Corp.*, 793 S.W.2d 670, 685-86 (Tex.1990). The damages are limited to the amount of the bond. *Id.*

§10.2 Malicious prosecution. To prevail on a cause of action for malicious prosecution of an injunction, the claimant must prove that the injunction suit was (1) prosecuted maliciously, (2) prosecuted without probable cause, and (3) terminated in the claimant's favor. *DeSantis v. Wackenhut Corp.*, 793 S.W.2d 670, 686 (Tex.1990); *Sweezy Constr., Inc. v. Murray*, 915 S.W.2d 527, 531 (Tex.App.—Corpus Christi 1995, orig. proceeding). The suit should be brought as a counterclaim in the same lawsuit. *Sweezy Constr.*, 915 S.W.2d at 531-32. The claimant is entitled to all actual damages. *DeSantis*, 793 S.W.2d at 686. See *O'Connor's Texas COA*, "Malicious Civil Prosecution," ch. 19-B, p. 566.

§11. REVIEW

§11.1 TRO. A TRO cannot be appealed. *In re Texas Nat. Res. Conserv. Comm'n*, 85 S.W.3d 201, 205 (Tex. 2002); *Ex parte Tucci*, 859 S.W.2d 1, 2 n.4 (Tex.1993); *Henke v. Peoples State Bank*, 6 S.W.3d 717, 720 (Tex. App.—Corpus Christi 1999, pet. dism'd); *see* TRCP 680 (TRO "shall expire by its terms").

§11.2 Temporary injunction. An order that grants or denies a temporary injunction, or grants or overrules a motion to dissolve a temporary injunction as provided by CPRC chapter 65, is an appealable interlocutory order. CPRC §51.014(a)(4); *see In re Texas Nat. Res. Conserv. Comm'n*, 85 S.W.3d 201, 205 (Tex.2002); *Qwest Comms. v. AT&T*

★

Corp., 24 S.W.3d 334, 338 (Tex.2000); *Wyatt v. Cowley*, 74 S.W.3d 576, 577 (Tex.App.—Corpus Christi 2002, pet. dism'd); *Cellular Mktg., Inc. v. Houston Cellular Tel. Co.*, 784 S.W.2d 734, 735 (Tex.App.—Houston [14th Dist.] 1990, no writ). If the trial court modifies the temporary-injunction order during the appeal of the original order, the appellate court has jurisdiction to review the modified order if it concerns the same subject matter as the original order. TRAP 29.6(a)(1); *Ahmed v. Shimi Ventures, L.P.*, 99 S.W.3d 682, 689 (Tex.App.—Houston [1st Dist.] 2003, no pet.). The interlocutory appeal of any order under CPRC §51.014(a)(4) does not stay the commencement of the trial. CPRC §51.014(b). Appellate review of a temporary injunction cannot be used to secure an advance ruling on the merits. *Iranian Muslim Org. v. City of San Antonio*, 615 S.W.2d 202, 208 (Tex.1981).

1. Accelerated appeal. Appeals of interlocutory orders are accelerated appeals. TRAP 28.1(a); *In re Gorman*, 1 S.W.3d 894, 895 (Tex.App.—Fort Worth 1999, orig. proceeding). The deadlines for perfecting the appeal (20 days), filing the record (10 days after filing the notice of appeal), and filing the briefs (20 days after filing the record) are much shorter than for regular appeals. *See* TRAP 26.1(b), 35.1(b), 38.6(a). The deadlines in TRAP 26.1(b) are mandatory and jurisdictional. *State v. Gibson's Distrib. Co.*, 436 S.W.2d 122, 123 (Tex.1968) (discussing former TRCP 385). See *O'Connor's Texas Appeals*, "Motion to Accelerate Appeal or to Give Appeal Precedence," ch. 3-C, p. 89.

2. Motion for new trial. A party may file a motion for new trial after an interlocutory order. *See* TRAP 28.1(b). The motion does not extend the time to file the notice of appeal, which is only 20 days. *See* TRAP 26.1(b), 28.1(b).

3. Necessity of brief. Although TRAP 28.1(e) permits the appellate court to proceed without a brief, the courts are reluctant to do so. *See Lagrone v. John Robert Powers Sch., Inc.*, 841 S.W.2d 34, 36 (Tex.App.—Dallas 1992, no writ) (under former TRAP 42(c), now TRAP 28.1(e)).

4. Standard of review. Appellate review of the temporary injunction is limited to deciding whether the trial court clearly abused its discretion. *Butnaru v. Ford Motor Co.*, 84 S.W.3d 198, 204 (Tex.2002); *Davis v. Huey*, 571 S.W.2d 859, 861-62 (Tex.1978). The trial court abuses its discretion when it misapplies the law to established facts or when it concludes the applicant has a probable right of recovery and the conclusion is not reasonably supported by the evidence. *State v. Southwestern Bell Tel. Co.*, 526 S.W.2d 526, 528 (Tex.1975). The trial court does not abuse its discretion when it bases its decision on conflicting evidence presented by the parties. *Davis*, 571 S.W.2d at 862. The appellate court should not substitute its judgment for the trial court's unless the court's action was so arbitrary that it exceeded the bounds of reasonable discretion. *Butnaru*, 84 S.W.3d at 204.

5. Mootness. The appellate courts cannot review a temporary injunction that is moot; such a review constitutes an impermissible advisory opinion. *National Collegiate Athletic Ass'n v. Jones*, 1 S.W.3d 83, 86 (Tex. 1999); *Camarena v. Texas Empl. Comm'n*, 754 S.W.2d 149, 151 (Tex.1988). A temporary injunction becomes moot when a change in the status of the parties or the passage of time makes the injunction inoperative or when the objective of the injunction is accomplished. *See Jones*, 1 S.W.3d at 86; *see, e.g.*, *Reagan Nat'l Adver. v. Vanderhoof Fam. Trust*, 82 S.W.3d 366, 371 (Tex.App.—Austin 2002, no pet.) (threat to P of loss of property was no longer an issue). If the trial court renders a final judgment during the pendency of the appeal of the temporary injunction, the case becomes moot on appeal. *Isuani v. Manske-Sheffield Radiology Grp.*, 802 S.W.2d 235, 236 (Tex.1991); *Jordan v. Landry's Seafood Rest., Inc.*, 89 S.W.3d 737, 741 (Tex.App.—Houston [1st Dist.] 2002, pet. denied). When a case becomes moot on appeal, the appellate court must set aside all orders pertaining to the temporary injunction and dismiss the case. *Isuani*, 802 S.W.2d at 236.

6. Review by Supreme Court. As a general rule, the courts of appeals' decisions on injunctions are final. *See* Gov't Code §22.225(b)(4) (no appeal to Supreme Court from court of appeals' decision on temporary injunctions); *Butnaru*, 84 S.W.3d at 202 (jurisdiction over order granting or denying temporary injunction typically is final in court of appeals). See *O'Connor's Texas Appeals*, "Review by Supreme Court," ch. 3-P, §4, p. 155.

§11.3 Permanent injunction.

1. Correct standard of review. In the appeal of a permanent injunction, the appellate court reviews all the evidence to determine whether the trial court's ruling was correct. *Brown v. Carroll*, 683 S.W.2d 61, 62 (Tex.

———————————— ✦ ————————————

App.—Tyler 1984, no writ); *Texas Commerce Bank-Irving v. McCreary*, 677 S.W.2d 643, 644 (Tex.App.—Dallas 1984, no writ); *Diesel Injection Sales & Servs. v. Renfro*, 656 S.W.2d 568, 571 (Tex.App.—Corpus Christi 1983, writ ref'd n.r.e.). By comparison, in the appeal of a temporary injunction, the appellate court reviews the trial court's decision for an abuse of discretion. *See Texas Foundries, Inc. v. International Moulders & Foundry Workers' Un.*, 248 S.W.2d 460, 462 (Tex.1952). The different standards result from the different purposes of the two injunctions—a temporary injunction is issued to preserve the status quo or to prevent irreparable injury pending final determination of the case on the merits; a permanent injunction is the final determination on the merits.

    2. Incorrect standard of review. Many courts, however, apply the abuse-of-discretion standard when reviewing permanent injunctions. *E.g.*, *Operation Rescue–Nat'l v. Planned Parenthood*, 975 S.W.2d 546, 560 (Tex. 1998); *Indian Beach Prop. Owners' Ass'n v. Linden*, 222 S.W.3d 682, 690 (Tex.App.—Houston [1st Dist.] 2007, no pet.); *Capital Senior Mgmt. 1, Inc. v. Texas Dept. of Human Servs.*, 132 S.W.3d 71, 74 (Tex.App.—Austin 2004, pet. denied); *Triantaphyllis v. Gamble*, 93 S.W.3d 398, 402 (Tex.App.—Houston [14th Dist.] 2002, pet. denied); *Jamestown Partners v. City of Fort Worth*, 83 S.W.3d 376, 384 (Tex.App.—Fort Worth 2002, pet. denied).

D. DECLARATORY JUDGMENT

§1. GENERAL

    §1.1 Rules. No rule of procedure deals directly with declaratory judgments; only a few rules even mention them. See TRCP 42(b)(2), 166a(a), 166a(b). The authority for declaratory actions is found in the Declaratory Judgments Act (DJ Act), which is located in CPRC chapter 37.

    §1.2 Purpose. The purpose of a declaratory action is to establish existing rights, status, or other legal relationships. *City of El Paso v. Heinrich*, 284 S.W.3d 366, 370 (Tex.2009); *City of Garland v. Dallas Morning News*, 22 S.W.3d 351, 357 (Tex.2000) (plurality op.); *Bonham State Bank v. Beadle*, 907 S.W.2d 465, 467 (Tex.1995); *Republic Ins. v. Davis*, 856 S.W.2d 158, 164 (Tex.1993). A declaratory action is an additional and cumulative remedy and does not supplant any existing remedy. *Creative Thinking Sources, Inc. v. Creative Thinking, Inc.*, 74 S.W.3d 504, 513 (Tex.App.—Corpus Christi 2002, no pet.) (presence of another adequate remedy does not bar declaratory action). A declaratory action cannot be used as an affirmative ground of recovery to alter rights, status, or relationships. *Republic Ins.*, 856 S.W.2d at 164. The DJ Act is "remedial" only. CPRC §37.002(b); *Texas Nat. Res. Conserv. Comm'n v. IT-Davy*, 74 S.W.3d 849, 855 (Tex.2002) (plurality op.); *Bonham State Bank*, 907 S.W.2d at 467. The DJ Act is a procedural device for deciding cases that are already within the trial court's jurisdiction and cannot independently establish jurisdiction. *City of Dallas v. Albert*, 354 S.W.3d 368, 378 (Tex.2011); *Chenault v. Phillips*, 914 S.W.2d 140, 141 (Tex.1996); *State v. Morales*, 869 S.W.2d 941, 947 (Tex.1994).

    §1.3 Forms. *O'Connor's Texas Civil Forms* (2012), FORMS 2D:1, 3E:9.

    §1.4 Other references. *O'Connor's Texas Causes of Action* (2013) (*O'Connor's Texas COA*).

§2. AVAILABILITY OF DECLARATORY JUDGMENT

An action for declaratory judgment is neither legal nor equitable but is sui generis—that is, of its own kind. *Texas Liquor Control Bd. v. Canyon Creek Land Corp.*, 456 S.W.2d 891, 895 (Tex.1970).

    §2.1 When available. A declaratory judgment is appropriate only when there is a justiciable controversy about the rights and status of the parties, and the declaration would resolve the controversy. *Bonham State Bank v. Beadle*, 907 S.W.2d 465, 467 (Tex.1995); *see Etan Indus. v. Lehmann*, 359 S.W.3d 620, 624 (Tex.2011). The controversy must be real and substantial, involving a genuine conflict of tangible interests and not merely a theoretical dispute. *Bonham State Bank*, 907 S.W.2d at 467; *see City of Dallas v. VSC, LLC*, 347 S.W.3d 231, 240 (Tex.2011); *see, e.g.*, *Farmers Tex. Cty. Mut. Ins. v. Griffin*, 955 S.W.2d 81, 84 (Tex.1997) (whether insurance carrier had duty to defend when pedestrian was shot by occupant of insured vehicle); *Holmes v. Morales*, 924 S.W.2d 920, 922 (Tex. 1996) (whether DA was required to turn over "closed" criminal-litigation files under Open Records Act); *Davis v. Shanks*, 898 S.W.2d 285, 286 (Tex.1995) (whether word "contents" in will was ambiguous); *R Comm. v. Sharp*, 875

———————————————— ✦ ————————————————

S.W.2d 314, 317-18 (Tex.1994) (whether assessed taxes were owed). The controversy does not need to be fully ripe, but it must indicate that immediate litigation is unavoidable. *Unauthorized Practice of Law Cmte. v. Nationwide Mut. Ins.*, 155 S.W.3d 590, 595 (Tex.App.—San Antonio 2004, pet. denied); *Texas DPS v. Moore*, 985 S.W.2d 149, 153-54 (Tex.App.—Austin 1998, no pet.).

1. Under CPRC ch. 37. CPRC chapter 37 lists suits that are appropriate for declaratory relief; however, the list is not exhaustive. CPRC §37.003(c). Examples of when a party can seek declaratory relief under CPRC chapter 37 include the following:

(1) Construction or validity of written instrument. A person interested under a deed, will, written contract, or other writings constituting a contract can seek a declaratory judgment to determine any question of construction or validity arising under the instrument and obtain a declaration of rights, status, or other legal relationships. CPRC §37.004(a).

(2) Construction or validity of statute, ordinance, contract, or franchise. A person whose rights, status, or other legal relationships are affected by a statute, municipal ordinance, contract, or franchise can seek a declaratory judgment to determine any question of construction or validity arising under the statute, ordinance, contract, or franchise and obtain a declaration of rights, status, or other legal relationships. CPRC §37.004(a).

(3) Rights relating to trust or estate. A person interested as or through an executor or administrator, including an independent executor or administrator, a trustee, guardian, other fiduciary, creditor, devisee, legatee, heir, next of kin, or cestui que trust (i.e., beneficiary) in the administration of a trust or estate of a decedent, infant, mentally incapacitated person, or insolvent can seek a declaratory judgment for the trust or estate to do any of the following:

(a) To ascertain any class of creditors, devisees, legatees, heirs, next of kin, or others. CPRC §37.005(1).

(b) To direct the executors, administrators, or trustees to do or abstain from doing a particular act in their fiduciary capacity. *Id.* §37.005(2).

(c) To determine any question arising in the trust's or estate's administration, including questions of construction of wills and other writings. *Id.* §37.005(3).

(d) To determine rights or legal relationships of an independent executor or independent administrator about fiduciary fees and the settling of accounts. *Id.* §37.005(4).

2. Counterclaims. When a counterclaim for declaratory relief will have greater ramifications than the original suit, declaratory relief is appropriate. *BHP Pet. Co. v. Millard*, 800 S.W.2d 838, 842 (Tex.1990); *Georgiades v. Di Ferrante*, 871 S.W.2d 878, 880 (Tex.App.—Houston [14th Dist.] 1994, writ denied); *e.g.*, *Winslow v. Acker*, 781 S.W.2d 322, 328 (Tex.App.—San Antonio 1989, writ denied) (in Ps' suit for recovery of royalty interests assigned to Ds, Ds' counterclaim for declaratory relief was appropriate because it would settle all future royalty disputes).

§2.2 When not available. A declaratory judgment is not available in the following instances:

1. No justiciable conflict. A declaratory judgment is not available when there is no justiciable conflict. *Bonham State Bank v. Beadle*, 907 S.W.2d 465, 467 (Tex.1995); *e.g.*, *Di Portanova v. Monroe*, 229 S.W.3d 324, 329 (Tex.App.—Houston [1st Dist.] 2006, pet. denied) (beneficiary could not bring DJ action to resolve dispute over how trustee should exercise discretion given to trustee in trust instrument); *Paulsen v. Texas Equal Access to Justice Found.*, 23 S.W.3d 42, 44-45 (Tex.App.—Austin 1999, pet. denied) (parties agreed on constitutionality of challenged statute and desired the same result); *Barcroft v. State*, 900 S.W.2d 370, 372 (Tex.App.—Texarkana 1995, no writ) (P could not bring suit to be declared "Private State Citizen of Texas").

2. Potential tort liability. Generally, a defendant cannot use a declaratory-judgment action to determine potential tort liability. *E.g.*, *Abor v. Black*, 695 S.W.2d 564, 566 (Tex.1985) (personal injury); *Trantham v. Isaacks*, 218 S.W.3d 750, 756 (Tex.App.—Fort Worth 2007, pet. denied) (defamation); *Stein v. First Nat'l Bank*, 950 S.W.2d

──────────────── ✦ ────────────────

172, 174 (Tex.App.—Austin 1997, no writ) (fraud and conspiracy arising from a note); *see also Texas State Bank v. Amaro*, 87 S.W.3d 538, 545 (Tex.2002) (trustee tort liability).

    3. Future controversy. A declaratory judgment is not available to resolve issues that are not yet mature and are subject to change. *See, e.g., City of Garland v. Louton*, 691 S.W.2d 603, 605 (Tex.1985) (parties not entitled to DJ on constitutionality of referendum statute before election); *California Prods. v. Puretex Lemon Juice, Inc.*, 334 S.W.2d 780, 783 (Tex.1960) (P not entitled to advisory opinion on whether bottle design would violate injunction); *Paulsen*, 23 S.W.3d at 47 (parties not entitled to advisory opinion on how broadly a U.S. Supreme Court opinion could be read); *Lane v. Baxter Healthcare Corp.*, 905 S.W.2d 39, 41-42 (Tex.App.—Houston [1st Dist.] 1995, no writ) (P not entitled to resolve issue of ownership of trade secrets before any dispute). The DJ Act does not permit litigants to "fish in judicial ponds for legal advice." *California Prods.*, 334 S.W.2d at 781.

    4. In another court. Generally, a declaratory judgment is not available to resolve an issue that will be adjudicated by a separate proceeding involving the same parties. *Texas Liquor Control Bd. v. Canyon Creek Land Corp.*, 456 S.W.2d 891, 895 (Tex.1970); *Creative Thinking Sources, Inc. v. Creative Thinking, Inc.*, 74 S.W.3d 504, 513 (Tex.App.—Corpus Christi 2002, no pet.).

    5. In same suit. Generally, a declaratory judgment is not available to resolve issues already pending in the same suit before the court. *See BHP Pet. Co. v. Millard*, 800 S.W.2d 838, 841 (Tex.1990); *Hageman/Fritz, Byrne, Head & Harrison, L.L.P. v. Luth*, 150 S.W.3d 617, 627 (Tex.App.—Austin 2004, no pet.); *Universal Printing Co. v. Premier Victorian Homes, Inc.*, 73 S.W.3d 283, 296 (Tex.App.—Houston [1st Dist.] 2001, pet. denied); *see, e.g., Boatman v. Lites*, 970 S.W.2d 41, 43 (Tex.App.—Tyler 1998, no pet.) (DJ action to determine rights under Water Code §11.086 requested no greater or different relief from that requested in pending suit); *Staff Indus. v. Hallmark Contracting, Inc.*, 846 S.W.2d 542, 547-48 (Tex.App.—Corpus Christi 1993, no writ) (counterclaim for declaratory relief concerning amount due under purchase order presented no issues beyond those in underlying suit).

    6. No jurisdiction over underlying dispute. A declaratory judgment is not available if the court does not have jurisdiction over the underlying cause of action. *Chenault v. Phillips*, 914 S.W.2d 140, 141 (Tex.1996); *Southwest Airlines Co. v. Texas High-Speed Rail Auth.*, 863 S.W.2d 123, 125-26 (Tex.App.—Austin 1993, writ denied); *see, e.g., State Bar v. Gomez*, 891 S.W.2d 243, 246 (Tex.1994) (district court had no jurisdiction over suit to compel mandatory pro bono).

    7. Earlier judgment. A declaratory judgment is not available to seek a judicial interpretation of an earlier judgment. *Samedan Oil Corp. v. Louis Dreyfus Nat. Gas Corp.*, 52 S.W.3d 788, 792 (Tex.App.—Eastland 2001, pet. denied) (dicta); *Martin v. Dosohs I, Ltd.*, 2 S.W.3d 350, 353 (Tex.App.—San Antonio 1999, pet. denied); *Cohen v. Cohen*, 632 S.W.2d 172, 173 (Tex.App.—Waco 1982, no writ).

    8. Criminal issue. A declaratory judgment is not available to determine the rights, status, or other legal relationships arising under a penal statute. *E.g., State v. Morales*, 869 S.W.2d 941, 947 (Tex.1994) (court could not decide constitutionality of sodomy law).

    9. Suit against the government. Generally, a declaratory judgment is not available to (1) circumvent a government's sovereign immunity by having a suit for monetary damages characterized as a suit to determine rights or (2) determine the rights of the parties under a contract when a contractual dispute with the government must be submitted to an administrative procedure. *See City of Dallas v. Albert*, 354 S.W.3d 368, 378 (Tex.2011) (#1); *City of El Paso v. Heinrich*, 284 S.W.3d 366, 371 (Tex.2009) (#1); *Texas DOT v. Jones Bros. Dirt & Paving Contractors, Inc.*, 92 S.W.3d 477, 484-85 (Tex.2002) (#2). See *O'Connor's Texas COA*, "Other Issues," ch. 24-B, §6, p. 853.

§3. PROCEDURE

    §3.1 Court. Only a court of record that has jurisdiction may hear an action for declaratory relief. CPRC §37.003(a); *Wilson v. Wilson*, 378 S.W.2d 156, 160 (Tex.App.—Tyler 1964, no writ).

    §3.2 Parties. The petition should name as parties all persons or entities who have a claim or interest that would be affected by the declaration. CPRC §37.006(a); *Musgrave v. Owen*, 67 S.W.3d 513, 521 (Tex.App.—Texarkana 2002, no pet.); *Dahl v. Hartman*, 14 S.W.3d 434, 436 (Tex.App.—Houston [14th Dist.] 2000, pet. denied); *see Brooks*

———————————————— ✦ ————————————————

v. Northglen Ass'n, 141 S.W.3d 158, 162 (Tex.2004). The court does not have jurisdiction to issue a declaratory judgment for parties who are not before the court. *See Brooks*, 141 S.W.3d at 162-63. When a suit challenges the validity of a municipal ordinance or franchise, the municipality must be made a party. CPRC §37.006(b). When a suit challenges the constitutionality of a statute, an ordinance, or a franchise, the Attorney General must be served. *Id.*

§3.3 Jurisdiction. The DJ Act does not enlarge the existing jurisdiction of the court or create new jurisdiction. *Texas Nat. Res. Conserv. Comm'n v. IT-Davy*, 74 S.W.3d 849, 855 (Tex.2002) (plurality op.); *State v. Morales*, 869 S.W.2d 941, 947 (Tex.1994); *Kadish v. Pennington Assocs.*, 948 S.W.2d 301, 304 (Tex.App.—Houston [1st Dist.] 1995, no writ). The DJ Act is not a grant of jurisdiction, but merely a procedural device for deciding cases already within the court's jurisdiction. *Chenault v. Phillips*, 914 S.W.2d 140, 141 (Tex.1996); *see Frasier v. Yanes*, 9 S.W.3d 422, 427 (Tex.App.—Austin 1999, no pet.).

§3.4 Venue. Venue for a declaratory-judgment action is governed by the rules relating to civil actions generally. *Bonham State Bank v. Beadle*, 907 S.W.2d 465, 471 (Tex.1995); *Stiba v. Bowers*, 756 S.W.2d 835, 837 (Tex.App.—Corpus Christi 1988, no writ). Thus, to determine venue for a suit requesting a declaratory judgment, a party must look to the facts of the underlying cause of action. See "Choosing the Court—Venue," ch. 2-G, p. 150.

§3.5 Relief. The petition may ask for affirmative or negative relief. CPRC §37.003(b). The declaratory action may ask for relief in questions of construction or validity arising under a deed, will, written contract, or other instrument, or arising under another relation affected by a statute, municipal ordinance, contract, or franchise. *Id.* §37.004(a). The declaratory action may also ask for relief regarding a trust or estate. *Id.* §37.005. The lists in §§37.004 and 37.005 do not limit the power of the court to grant declaratory relief. *Id.* §37.003(c).

§3.6 Jury trial. The parties are entitled to a jury trial, as in other civil cases. CPRC §37.007.

§3.7 Judgment. The declaration has the force and effect of a final judgment or decree. CPRC §37.003(b); *see Brooks v. Northglen Ass'n*, 141 S.W.3d 158, 162 (Tex.2004).

§3.8 Costs & attorney fees. The trial court has the discretion to award costs and attorney fees as part of a declaratory judgment. CPRC §37.009; *John G. & Marie Stella Kenedy Mem'l Found. v. Dewhurst*, 90 S.W.3d 268, 289 (Tex.2002); *Bocquet v. Herring*, 972 S.W.2d 19, 20 (Tex.1998); *Barshop v. Medina Cty. Underground Water Conserv. Dist.*, 925 S.W.2d 618, 637 (Tex.1996). Attorney fees under the DJ Act can be awarded to any party, not just the prevailing party. *See Barshop*, 925 S.W.2d at 637; *SAVA gumarska v. Advanced Polymer Sci., Inc.*, 128 S.W.3d 304, 323-24 (Tex.App.—Dallas 2004, no pet.); *Templeton v. Dreiss*, 961 S.W.2d 645, 671 (Tex.App.—San Antonio 1998, pet. denied).

   1. Requirements. There are four requirements for an award of attorney fees under the DJ Act—the fees must be reasonable, necessary, equitable, and just. CPRC §37.009; *GuideOne Elite Ins. v. Fielder Rd. Baptist Ch.*, 197 S.W.3d 305, 311 (Tex.2006); *Bocquet*, 972 S.W.2d at 21. The issue of the amount of attorney fees (reasonable and necessary) is an issue for the trier of fact; the issue of whether to award attorney fees (equitable and just) is within the trial court's discretion. *GuideOne Elite*, 197 S.W.3d at 311; *Ridge Oil Co. v. Guinn Invs.*, 148 S.W.3d 143, 162 (Tex.2004); *Bocquet*, 972 S.W.2d at 21. However, CPRC §37.009's "equitable and just" language authorizes the court to award attorney fees in an amount less than what was determined by the jury to be reasonable and necessary. *Ridge Oil Co.*, 148 S.W.3d at 162. See *O'Connor's Texas COA*, "Attorney fees reasonable & necessary," ch. 45-A, §2.7, p. 1355.

   2. Not available.

      (1) Attorney fees otherwise impermissible. A party cannot recover attorney fees under the DJ Act when they are otherwise impermissible. *MBM Fin. Corp. v. Woodlands Oper. Co.*, 292 S.W.3d 660, 669 (Tex. 2009); *see In re Allcat Claims Serv., L.P.*, 356 S.W.3d 455, 472 (Tex.2011); *Jackson v. State Office of Admin. Hearings*, 351 S.W.3d 290, 301 (Tex.2011); *Martin v. Amerman*, 133 S.W.3d 262, 267 (Tex.2004). If attorney fees would not be permitted under the specific common-law or statutory claims involved, they are unavailable under the DJ Act as well. *See Etan Indus. v. Lehmann*, 359 S.W.3d 620, 624 (Tex.2011); *MBM Fin.*, 292 S.W.3d at 669-70; *see, e.g.,*

★

Sharyland Water Sup. v. City of Alton, 354 S.W.3d 407, 424 (Tex.2011) (because party could not recover attorney fees under Local Gov't Code §271.153 for breach-of-contract claim, it could not recover them under DJ Act when claim for declaratory relief was subset of breach-of-contract claim).

(2) Incidental claim for declaratory relief. A party cannot recover attorney fees under the DJ Act if the claim for declaratory relief is merely incidental to other claims for relief. *E.g.*, *Jackson*, 351 S.W.3d at 301 (claims for attorney fees were incidental to central claim for relief under the Texas Public Information Act); *see Dewhurst*, 90 S.W.3d at 289.

§3.9 Motion to enforce judgment. The DJ Act empowers the trial court to make supplemental rulings to aid in the enforcement of a declaratory judgment. CPRC §37.011; *In re Crow-Billingsley Air Park, Ltd.*, 98 S.W.3d 178, 179 (Tex.2003). While on appeal, the trial court may hear a motion to enforce its final judgment if the judgment was not superseded. *In re Crow-Billingsley*, 98 S.W.3d at 179.

§3.10 Answer. To file an answer to a declaratory-judgment action, a party must follow the same steps it would for filing any other answer. See "The Answer—Denying Liability," ch. 3-E, p. 227; *O'Connor's Texas Forms*, FORM 3E:9.

§4. REVIEW

§4.1 Standard of review. Declaratory judgments are reviewed under the same standards as other judgments and decrees. *Roberts v. Squyres*, 4 S.W.3d 485, 488 (Tex.App.—Beaumont 1999, pet. denied); *FDIC v. Projects Am. Corp.*, 828 S.W.2d 771, 772 (Tex.App.—Texarkana 1992, writ denied). Thus, if the declaratory judgment was granted on a motion for summary judgment, the review is governed by the rules for summary judgment; if the declaratory judgment was granted on an agreed statement of facts under TRCP 263, review is governed by the rules for agreed statement of facts. *See, e.g.*, *Roberts*, 4 S.W.3d at 488 (case submitted on agreed statement); *Unauthorized Practice of Law Cmte. v. Jansen*, 816 S.W.2d 813, 814-15 (Tex.App.—Houston [14th Dist.] 1991, writ denied) (case submitted on agreed statement and on summary judgment).

§4.2 Appeal. The trial court's decision, which is a conclusion of law, will be upheld on appeal if it can be sustained on any legal theory supported by the evidence. *Alma Invs. v. Bahia Mar Co-Owners Ass'n*, 999 S.W.2d 820, 823 (Tex.App.—Corpus Christi 1999, pet. denied); *FDIC v. Projects Am. Corp.*, 828 S.W.2d 771, 772 (Tex.App.—Texarkana 1992, writ denied). If reversal is warranted, the appellate court can render the judgment the trial court should have rendered, unless a remand for further proceedings is necessary. *FDIC*, 828 S.W.2d at 772.

E. PARTIES & CLAIMS

§1. GENERAL

§1.1 Rules. TRCP 28-44, 51, 174. See CPRC ch. 33 (proportionate responsibility).

§1.2 Purpose. For the sake of judicial economy, the rules encourage parties to combine multiple claims and parties into a single lawsuit. There are, however, limits to what claims and parties can be joined.

§1.3 Forms. *O'Connor's Texas Civil Forms* (2012), FORMS 2B:9-19, 3E:1, 3E:12-17, 5G, 5H, 5I.

§1.4 Other references. *O'Connor's Texas Causes of Action* (2013) (*O'Connor's Texas COA*).

§2. JOINING PARTIES & CLAIMS

Parties and claims are brought into a lawsuit by any of the following methods:

§2.1 Petition. The plaintiff initially decides who the parties are and what the claims are. *See* TRCP 22. See "Plaintiff's Original Petition," ch. 2-B, p. 95.

§2.2 Cross-actions. The term "cross-action" is used only once in the TRCPs, in TRCP 85.

1. Counterclaim. A counterclaim is an affirmative claim for relief filed against an opposing party. TRCP 97. A counterclaim is most often raised by the defendant, although it may be raised by a plaintiff in response to a defendant's or other party's pleading. Counterclaims are either compulsory or permissive. TRCP 97(a), (b). For the difference between them, see "Compulsory Joinder of Claims," §6, p. 131; "Permissive Joinder of Claims," §7, p. 134.

⭐

2. Cross-claim. A cross-claim is an affirmative claim for relief filed by one party against its coparty. TRCP 97(e). For example, if a counterclaim is brought against a plaintiff, the plaintiff may file a cross-claim against another plaintiff. See "Cross-claims," ch. 3-E, §7.2, p. 235.

§2.3 Third-party practice. Third-party practice, also called impleader, is the procedure by which a defendant can bring an additional party into the suit who may be liable for all or part of the plaintiff's claim. TRCP 38. See "Third-party petitions," ch. 3-E, §7.3, p. 235. A plaintiff may implead an additional party in response to a counterclaim by the defendant. TRCP 38(b).

§2.4 Responsible third party. Under CPRC §33.004, the defendant can designate a person as a responsible third party who is alleged to have caused or contributed to causing the harm for which recovery of damages is sought. See "RTP," ch. 3-E, §7.4, p. 235.

§2.5 Intervention. A plea in intervention is the procedure for a person to join a lawsuit already in progress. TRCP 60, 61. See "Petition in Intervention," ch. 5-J, §2, p. 371.

§2.6 Interpleader. A bill of interpleader is the procedure for a person in possession of property claimed by others to transfer the property and the dispute to the court. *See* TRCP 43. See "Interpleader Suit," ch. 5-J, §3, p. 373.

§2.7 Consolidation. A motion to consolidate asks the court to consolidate two or more suits with a common question of law or fact. TRCP 174(a). The consolidated suit will have one cause number and be resolved by a single judgment. See "Motion to Consolidate," ch. 5-J, §4, p. 376.

§2.8 Joint trial. A motion for joint trial asks the court to hold one trial for two or more suits. *See* TRCP 174(a). The cases are joined for trial only, are tried at the same time but under separate cause numbers, and are resolved by separate judgments.

§3. GENERAL RULES FOR JOINDER OF CLAIMS

§3.1 Single plaintiff & single defendant. There can be no misjoinder of claims when there is only one plaintiff and one defendant. *See* TRCP 51(a); *see, e.g.*, *Twyman v. Twyman*, 855 S.W.2d 619, 625 (Tex.1993) (tort claims could be joined with divorce). The plaintiff can bring as many claims as it may have against the defendant, and the defendant can bring as many claims as it may have against the plaintiff. The claims do not need to arise from the same transaction or occurrence and may be entirely unrelated. *See* TRCP 51(a).

§3.2 Multiple parties. When there are multiple parties in the suit, the parties can bring as many claims as they may have against each other as long as the claims arise from the same transaction, occurrence, or series of transactions or occurrences and have a common question of law or fact. *See* TRCP 39(a), 40(a), 43, 51(a). In joining other plaintiffs in a pending suit, the plaintiff should consider the effect of the venue provisions that require each plaintiff to justify venue in the county. *See* CPRC §15.003.

§4. MULTIPLE DEFENDANTS

Multiple defendants may be joined in a suit when (1) a right to relief relating to or arising from the same transaction or occurrence is asserted against them jointly, severally, or in the alternative, and (2) any questions of law or fact common to all of them will arise in the action. TRCP 40(a); *In re Caballero*, 53 S.W.3d 391, 397 (Tex.App.—Amarillo 2001, pet. denied).

§4.1 Joint liability. Joint liability is when a defendant is liable with others for damages to the plaintiff.

§4.2 Several liability. Several liability is when a defendant is liable separately and distinctly from another defendant. *Black's Law Dictionary* 998 (9th ed. 2009). The term "several" implies that each defendant is liable alone.

§4.3 Joint & several liability. Joint and several liability refers to a defendant who is liable both jointly with other defendants and separately. When the acts of two or more wrongdoers join to produce an indivisible injury, all the wrongdoers are jointly and severally liable for the entire amount of damages. *Amstadt v. U.S. Brass Corp.*, 919 S.W.2d 644, 654 (Tex.1996); *Landers v. East Tex. Salt Water Disposal Co.*, 248 S.W.2d 731, 734 (Tex.1952). The

✯

plaintiff has the option to sue all the defendants responsible for an indivisible injury in one suit, or any one defendant separately. *Morgan v. Compugraphic Corp.*, 675 S.W.2d 729, 733 (Tex.1984). *But see Jones v. Ray*, 886 S.W.2d 817, 822 (Tex.App.—Houston [1st Dist.] 1994, orig. proceeding) (severing P's claims against jointly and severally liable Ds was inequitable because suits were intertwined). There can be only one recovery for one injury. *Stewart Title Guar. Co. v. Sterling*, 822 S.W.2d 1, 8 (Tex.1991), *modified on other grounds*, *Tony Gullo Motors I, L.P. v. Chapa*, 212 S.W.3d 299 (Tex.2006); *see Crown Life Ins. v. Casteel*, 22 S.W.3d 378, 390 (Tex.2000). This rule applies even though more than one defendant may have caused the injury or there may be more than one theory of liability. *Crown Life*, 22 S.W.3d at 390; *Stewart Title*, 822 S.W.2d at 8. See *O'Connor's Texas COA*, "Defendant jointly & severally liable," ch. 51, §6.2, p. 1475.

§5. PROPORTIONATE RESPONSIBILITY FOR DAMAGES

For a more detailed discussion of proportionate responsibility, see *O'Connor's Texas COA*, "Proportionate Responsibility & Contribution," ch. 51, p. 1461.

§5.1 Plaintiff's bar. The claimant (usually the plaintiff) is barred from recovering damages if its responsibility is found to be greater than 50% in any cause of action based on tort. CPRC §§32.001(a), 33.001.

§5.2 Among defendants.

1. Most cases. In most cases, a defendant will be held jointly and severally liable when its responsibility with respect to the cause of action is found to be greater than 50%. CPRC §33.013(b)(1).

2. Intentional criminal acts. If the jury finds the defendant engaged in intentional conduct constituting any of the Penal Code offenses listed in CPRC §33.013(b)(2), the defendant will be held jointly and severally liable. CPRC §33.013(b)(2).

§5.3 Third-party responsibility. The defendant can designate a person as a responsible third party who is alleged to have caused or contributed to causing the harm for which recovery of damages is sought. See "RTP," ch. 3-E, §7.4, p. 235.

§6. COMPULSORY JOINDER OF CLAIMS

The parties should join to the suit all claims that are compulsory. A claim is compulsory only if it meets all the criteria in TRCP 97(a) and (d). *Ingersoll-Rand Co. v. Valero Energy Corp.*, 997 S.W.2d 203, 207 (Tex.1999); *Wyatt v. Shaw Plumbing Co.*, 760 S.W.2d 245, 247 (Tex.1988). See "Criteria," §6.1.1, this page. If a compulsory claim is not brought in the suit, the party with the claim is barred from asserting it in a later suit. *Wyatt*, 760 S.W.2d at 247; *Tindle v. Jackson Nat'l Life Ins.*, 837 S.W.2d 795, 800 (Tex.App.—Dallas 1992, no writ); *see* TRCP 97(a).

§6.1 Compulsory-counterclaim rule. The compulsory-counterclaim rule is designed to avoid piecemeal or duplicative litigation. *Bard v. Charles R. Myers Ins. Agency, Inc.*, 839 S.W.2d 791, 796 (Tex.1992). The sole compelling interest underlying the rule is judicial economy (i.e., to prevent multiple suits arising from the same transaction or occurrence). *Id.*

NOTE

Although this rule is called the "compulsory-counterclaim rule," it is not limited to defendants. The rule also applies to plaintiffs, cross-claim defendants, and third-party defendants. Although the plaintiff may initially choose the claims it wants to bring against the defendant, if the defendant asserts claims against the plaintiff, the plaintiff must then assert all of its compulsory counterclaims, or they will be barred in a later suit.

---

1. Criteria.

(1) Within jurisdiction. The claim must be within the court's subject-matter jurisdiction. TRCP 97(a); *Ingersoll-Rand Co. v. Valero Energy Corp.*, 997 S.W.2d 203, 207 (Tex.1999); *Wyatt v. Shaw Plumbing Co.*,

★

760 S.W.2d 245, 247 (Tex.1988); *Compass Expl., Inc. v. B–E Drilling Co.*, 60 S.W.3d 273, 277 (Tex.App.—Waco 2001, no pet.). A court can reach below its minimum jurisdictional limits if the claim arises from the same transaction or occurrence as the plaintiff's claim. If the damages are above the court's maximum jurisdictional limits, the claim is permissive, not compulsory. *See* TRCP 97(a); *Pinckard v. Associated Popcorn Distribs., Inc.*, 611 S.W.2d 491, 492 (Tex.App.—Dallas 1981, no writ). See "Permissive Joinder of Claims," §7, p. 134. The counterclaims of multiple defendants are not aggregated when determining whether the amount in controversy exceeds the court's maximum statutory jurisdictional limit and divests the court of jurisdiction. *Smith v. Clary Corp.*, 917 S.W.2d 796, 798 (Tex. 1996). See "Multiple parties," ch. 2-F, §2.3.1(2), p. 136; "Counterclaims," ch. 2-F, §2.3.1(3), p. 136.

(2) **Not filed elsewhere.** The claim must not be pending as a suit in another court. TRCP 97(a); *Ingersoll-Rand*, 997 S.W.2d at 207; *Wyatt*, 760 S.W.2d at 247; *Compass Expl.*, 60 S.W.3d at 277.

CAUTION

TRCP 97(a) states that the claim must not be the subject of a pending suit "at the time of filing the pleading," while the Supreme Court has stated that the claim must not be the subject of a pending suit "at the time of filing the answer." See TRCP 97(a); Ingersoll-Rand, 997 S.W.2d at 207; Wyatt, 760 S.W.2d at 247. One court of appeals has held that the language of TRCP 97(a) should apply to prevent a party from strategically circumventing the application of the compulsory-counterclaim rule. Commint Tech. Servs. v. Quickel, 314 S.W.3d 646, 652 (Tex. App.—Houston [14th Dist.] 2010, no pet.). If the claim cannot be the subject of a pending suit "at the time of filing the answer," as stated by the Supreme Court, a party could avoid the compulsory-counterclaim rule by filing suit against the opposing party immediately after being served with notice of suit and before the answer is due in the original suit. Id.

---

(3) **Mature.** The claim must be mature and owned by the pleader when it files its answer. TRCP 97(d); *Ingersoll-Rand*, 997 S.W.2d at 207; *Wyatt*, 760 S.W.2d at 247; *Compass Expl.*, 60 S.W.3d at 277. Claims that are speculative and premature at the time the answer is filed are not considered compulsory counterclaims. *See, e.g.*, *Ingersoll-Rand*, 997 S.W.2d at 208 (claim for indemnity did not mature until date of judgment). Claims for attorney fees, however, are compulsory even though they are contingent on the outcome of the suit. *Fidelity Mut. Life Ins. v. Kaminsky*, 820 S.W.2d 878, 882 (Tex.App.—Texarkana 1991, writ denied).

(4) **Same transaction or occurrence.** The claim must arise from the same transaction or occurrence as the opposing party's claim. TRCP 97(a); *Ingersoll-Rand*, 997 S.W.2d at 207; *Wyatt*, 760 S.W.2d at 247; *Compass Expl.*, 60 S.W.3d at 277-78. Texas applies the "logical-relationship" test to determine whether claims arise from the same transaction or occurrence. *Commint Tech. Servs.*, 314 S.W.3d at 653; *Community State Bank v. NSW Invs.*, 38 S.W.3d 256, 258 (Tex.App.—Texarkana 2001, pet. dism'd); *Jack H. Brown & Co. v. Northwest Sign Co.*, 718 S.W.2d 397, 399-400 (Tex.App.—Dallas 1986, writ ref'd n.r.e.). Under this test, a transaction is flexible and may be a series of many occurrences logically related to one another. *Community State Bank*, 38 S.W.3d at 258; *Tindle v. Jackson Nat'l Life Ins.*, 837 S.W.2d 795, 798 (Tex.App.—Dallas 1992, no writ). For the claims to arise from the same transaction, at least some of the facts must be relevant to both claims. *Community State Bank*, 38 S.W.3d at 258; *Tindle*, 837 S.W.2d at 798. The Supreme Court has drawn a parallel between the transactional approach embodied in the compulsory-counterclaim rule and the transactional approach to res judicata. *Barr v. Resolution Trust Corp.*, 837 S.W.2d 627, 628-30 (Tex.1992); *Weiman v. Addicks-Fairbanks Rd. Sand Co.*, 846 S.W.2d 414, 419 (Tex. App.—Houston [14th Dist.] 1992, writ denied). Under *Barr*, factors to consider in determining whether events constitute the same transaction include (1) whether they are related in time, space, origin, or motivation, (2) whether, taken together, they form a convenient unit for trial purposes, and (3) whether their treatment as a trial unit conforms to the parties' expectations or business understanding or usage. *Barr*, 837 S.W.2d at 631; *see Getty Oil Co. v. Insurance Co. of N. Am.*, 845 S.W.2d 794, 798-99 (Tex.1992); *see also* Restatement (2d) of Judgments §24 cmt. b (1982) ("transaction" connotes natural grouping or common nucleus of operative facts).

———————————————— ✦ ————————————————

(5) In same capacity. The claim must be against the opposing party in the same capacity in which that party filed its claim. *Ingersoll-Rand*, 997 S.W.2d at 207; *Wyatt*, 760 S.W.2d at 247; *Compass Expl.*, 60 S.W.3d at 277-78; *see* TRCP 97(a). For example, when the plaintiff files suit in only a representative capacity, any claim against the plaintiff in its individual capacity is not compulsory. For a discussion of capacity, see "Capacity," ch. 2-B, §3.2.2, p. 98.

(6) All parties available. The claim must not require the presence of additional parties over whom the court cannot acquire personal jurisdiction. TRCP 97(a); *Ingersoll-Rand*, 997 S.W.2d at 207; *Wyatt*, 760 S.W.2d at 247; *Compass Expl.*, 60 S.W.3d at 277-78.

CAUTION
*A default judgment bars any claim the defendant could have asserted as a compulsory counter-claim if the defendant had answered. **Jack H. Brown & Co.**, 718 S.W.2d at 400.*

---

2. Cross-claim. When parties are coparties rather than opposing parties, the compulsory-counterclaim rule acts as a bar to a coparty's claim in a later suit only if the coparties had "issues drawn between them" in the first suit. *State & Cty. Mut. Fire Ins. v. Miller*, 52 S.W.3d 693, 696 (Tex.2001); *Getty Oil*, 845 S.W.2d at 800. For purposes of res judicata, coparties have issues drawn between them and become adverse when one coparty files a cross-claim against another coparty. *Miller*, 52 S.W.3d at 696.

§6.2 Parties to be joined. The parties should join all persons and entities needed for the just adjudication of the claims. TRCP 39(a).

1. Feasible parties. The parties should join all feasible parties. TRCP 39(a). Before the 1971 amendment to TRCP 39, the courts used the phrase "necessary parties"; now the preferred phrase is "persons to be joined if feasible." *Wyatt v. Shaw Plumbing Co.*, 760 S.W.2d 245, 248 & n.2 (Tex.1988).

(1) Primary parties. A party subject to service of process should be joined if either one of the following applies:

(a) Without the absent party, complete relief cannot be given to those who are already parties. TRCP 39(a); *Wilchester W. Concerned Homeowners LDEF, Inc. v. Wilchester W. Fund, Inc.*, 177 S.W.3d 552, 559 (Tex.App.—Houston [1st Dist.] 2005, pet. denied); *see Brooks v. Northglen Ass'n*, 141 S.W.3d 158, 162 (Tex.2004).

(b) The absent party claims an interest in the subject matter of the action and its absence from the suit may either (1) prevent it from protecting this interest or (2) leave the parties already joined subject to a substantial risk of multiple liability or inconsistent obligations to the absent party. TRCP 39(a); *Brooks*, 141 S.W.3d at 162-63; *Wilchester W.*, 177 S.W.3d at 559; *see also Cooper v. Texas Gulf Indus.*, 513 S.W.2d 200, 204 (Tex.1974) (no precise standard for determining whether a person falls within provisions of TRCP 39(a)).

(2) Secondary parties.

(a) Sureties. A plaintiff can sue a surety without suing the principal only if judgment has already been taken against the principal or a statute (such as the CPRC or the UCC) authorizes the suit. TRCP 31; *see* CPRC §17.001.

(b) Contracts with several obligors. A judgment can be rendered against a person who is not primarily liable on a contract only if judgment is also rendered against the principal obligor. CPRC §17.001(a). There are four exceptions. An assignor, endorser, guarantor, or surety on a contract may be sued individually if the principal obligor (1) is a nonresident or resides where she cannot be reached by the ordinary process of law, (2) resides in an unknown place that cannot be ascertained by reasonable diligence, (3) is dead, or (4) is actually or notoriously insolvent. *Id.* §17.001(b).

(c) Under UCC. Assignors, endorsers, and other parties not primarily liable on commercial paper may be sued with the principal obligor or sued alone when permitted by statute. TRCP 30; *see* Bus. & Com. Code ch. 3.

2. Indispensable parties. If a feasible party cannot be joined (see "Feasible parties," §6.2.1, this page), the court must decide whether the absent person is an indispensable party and the case should be dismissed. TRCP

★

39(b). To determine whether a person is an indispensable party, the court must consider the following factors: (1) the extent to which a judgment rendered in the person's absence might be prejudicial to it or to those already parties, (2) the extent to which the prejudice can be lessened or avoided by protective provisions in the judgment, by the shaping of relief, or by other measures, (3) whether a judgment rendered in the person's absence will be adequate, and (4) whether the plaintiff will have an adequate remedy if the action is dismissed for nonjoinder. *Id.*

    (1) Indispensable. If a party is truly indispensable, it is fundamental error for the court to proceed without that party. *Vondy v. Commissioners Ct.*, 620 S.W.2d 104, 106 (Tex.1981). Instead, the court should dismiss the case. *See, e.g., Gilmer ISD v. Dorfman*, 156 S.W.3d 586, 588-89 (Tex.App.—Tyler 2003, no pet.) (trial court granted plea to jurisdiction in suit contesting constitutionality of Educ. Code because Commissioner of Education is indispensable party).

    (2) Not indispensable. Seldom is a person's presence in a suit so indispensable that the person's absence will deprive the court of jurisdiction to adjudicate the dispute between the parties already joined. *Cooper*, 513 S.W.2d at 204; *see, e.g., Allison v. National Un. Fire Ins.*, 703 S.W.2d 637, 638 (Tex.1986) (failure of P-attorneys to join their clients in declaratory-judgment action against insurance companies that insured clients was not fundamental error); *Cox v. Johnson*, 638 S.W.2d 867, 868 (Tex.1982) (failure to join joint payee in suit on a note was not fundamental error).

§7. PERMISSIVE JOINDER OF CLAIMS

    §7.1 General. Any claim that involves some or all of the same parties to an ongoing suit and has common issues of fact and law, but does not satisfy the compulsory-counterclaim test, is a permissive claim in that suit. *See* TRCP 40, 174(a); *see, e.g., Valley Forge Ins. v. Ryan*, 824 S.W.2d 236, 239 (Tex.App.—Fort Worth 1992, no writ) (because claim between same parties was not compulsory, it was permissive); *see also Getty Oil Co. v. Insurance Co. of N. Am.*, 845 S.W.2d 794, 800 (Tex.1992) (cross-claim under TRCP 97(e) against coparty is permissive). The compulsory-counterclaim rule does not bar the assertion of a permissive counterclaim in a later lawsuit. *See, e.g., Brown Lex Real Estate Dev. Corp. v. American Nat'l Bank*, 736 S.W.2d 205, 206-07 (Tex.App.—Corpus Christi 1987, writ ref'd n.r.e.) (because D admitted counterclaim was permissive, he conceded that denial of leave to file it was not error).

    §7.2 Joining & separating permissive claims. There are four rules of procedure to consider in determining whether permissive claims should be tried together or separately: TRCP 40 (permissive joinder of parties), TRCP 41 (misjoinder and nonjoinder of parties), TRCP 51 (joinder of claims and remedies), and TRCP 174 (consolidation and separate trials). The relevant inquiry is whether a joint (or separate) trial of the claims will prevent manifest injustice and will not prejudice the rights of the parties. *Womack v. Berry*, 291 S.W.2d 677, 683 (Tex.1956); *see* TRCP 40(b) (prevent embarrassment, delay, or additional expense), TRCP 174(b) (further convenience and avoid prejudice); *see also Jones v. Ray*, 886 S.W.2d 817, 822 (Tex.App.—Houston [1st Dist.] 1994, orig. proceeding) (separate trials would permit Ds to make "empty chair" argument); *Dal-Briar Corp. v. Baskette*, 833 S.W.2d 612, 616-17 (Tex.App.—El Paso 1992, orig. proceeding) (joint trial would create unacceptable probability of unfair result). The judicial economy and convenience that may be gained by consolidation must be weighed against the likelihood that consolidation may result in delay, prejudice, or jury confusion. *Dal-Briar Corp.*, 833 S.W.2d at 616-17.

§8. REMEDIES

    §8.1 For misjoinder. If there is misjoinder of claims or parties (e.g., in a multiparty action, claims are added that are not part of the same transaction or occurrence), the court should drop or add parties, consolidate separate actions, sever actions improperly joined, or order separate trials within the same case. TRCP 41; *see* TRCP 40(b), 174. The court cannot dismiss all or part of the suit. TRCP 41.

    1. Drop or add parties. A court may order that parties be added or dropped from the suit. TRCP 41.

    2. Consolidate actions. A court may order consolidation of two or more suits with common questions of law or fact. TRCP 174(a). The consolidated suit will have one cause number and be resolved by a single judgment. See "Motion to Consolidate," ch. 5-J, §4, p. 376.

———————————— ★ ————————————

3. Sever claims. A court may order severance of claims into two or more suits from what was originally one suit. *See* TRCP 41. Each suit will be given its own cause number and be resolved by a separate judgment. See "Motion for Severance," ch. 5-I, §3, p. 364.

4. Separate trials. A court may order separate trials of issues in one case for reasons of convenience or to avoid prejudice or embarrassment. TRCP 40(b), 174(b). The claims remain part of the same suit and are resolved by a single judgment. See "Motion for Separate (Bifurcated) Trial," ch. 5-I, §4, p. 367.

§8.2 For absent party. If a party that should be joined is absent, the complaining party should file a motion to abate. See "Motion to Abate—Challenging the Suit," ch. 3-I, p. 257.

F. CHOOSING THE COURT—JURISDICTION

§1. GENERAL

§1.1 Rules. None. See Tex. Const. art. 5; CPRC chs. 51, 61-64; Gov't Code ch. 24-28; Prob. Code §§4A-5B, 605-608; Prop. Code §115.001.

§1.2 Purpose. Before filing suit, the plaintiff must decide in which of the Texas trial courts the lawsuit should be filed. That decision is made by choosing the court with both jurisdiction over the dispute and proper venue. For venue, see "Choosing the Court—Venue," ch. 2-G, p. 150. To challenge the subject-matter jurisdiction of the court, see "Plea to the Jurisdiction—Challenging the Court," ch. 3-F, p. 239.

§1.3 Forms. *O'Connor's Texas Civil Forms* (2012), FORM 2B:20.

§1.4 Other references. Office of Court Administration, *Texas Judicial System: Subject-Matter Jurisdiction of the Courts*, www.courts.state.tx.us/oca/judinfo.asp (select "Subject Matter Jurisdiction of the Courts, Index to Subject Matter Jurisdiction"); Pargaman, *Probate, Guardianship, and Trust Law*, 72 Tex.B.J. 674 (2009).

§2. JURISDICTION OF TEXAS TRIAL COURTS

The jurisdiction of Texas courts is conferred solely by the Texas Constitution and state statutes. *Chenault v. Phillips*, 914 S.W.2d 140, 141 (Tex.1996).

§2.1 Types of trial courts. In Texas, there are district, county, justice-of-the-peace, and various other courts established by legislative enactment. Each type of court has jurisdiction over specific types of cases and amounts in controversy. *See In re United Servs. Auto. Ass'n*, 307 S.W.3d 299, 303 (Tex.2010). Although all courts can render a judgment for damages, not all courts can render a judgment for other types of relief (e.g., injunctive relief).

§2.2 Nonmonetary jurisdiction. Some claims do not depend on the amount of damages sought to establish jurisdiction (e.g., divorce suits, defamation suits, forcible-entry-and-detainer suits).

§2.3 Monetary jurisdiction. Most claims depend on the amount of damages sought to establish jurisdiction (e.g., breach-of-contract suits, personal-injury suits). See "Damages," ch. 2-B, §8, p. 107.

1. Computing amount in controversy. The amount in controversy is determined by the plaintiff's good-faith pleadings. *Peek v. Equipment Serv.*, 779 S.W.2d 802, 804 (Tex.1989); *Smith Detective Agency & Nightwatch Serv. v. Stanley Smith Sec., Inc.*, 938 S.W.2d 743, 747 (Tex.App.—Dallas 1996, writ denied); *see also Tune v. Texas DPS*, 23 S.W.3d 358, 362 (Tex.2000) (amount in controversy determined by subjective value of rights asserted by P, if asserted in good faith).

(1) Single plaintiff vs. single defendant. When one plaintiff asserts multiple claims against a single defendant, jurisdiction is determined by adding the amounts together. *Texas City Tire Shop, Inc. v. Alexander*, 333 S.W.2d 690, 693 (Tex.App.—Houston 1960, no writ); *see also Tejas Toyota, Inc. v. Griffin*, 587 S.W.2d 775, 776 (Tex.App.—Waco 1979, writ ref'd n.r.e.) (cross-actions are treated as separate suits; sum of damages in

★

cross-action exceeded jurisdiction of trial court). When a plaintiff asserts claims based on alternative theories, jurisdiction is determined according to the theory that would yield the highest award. *Lucey v. Southeast Tex. Emerg. Physicians Assocs.*, 802 S.W.2d 300, 302 (Tex.App.—El Paso 1990, writ denied).

(2) Multiple parties.

(a) By multiple plaintiffs. When multiple plaintiffs assert claims against a defendant, their claims are aggregated to determine the amount in controversy. Gov't Code §24.009; *Dubai Pet. Co. v. Kazi*, 12 S.W.3d 71, 75 n.4 (Tex.2000). Thus, a class action with 100 plaintiffs each suing for $10 would have $1,000 in controversy and could be filed in district court.

(b) Against multiple defendants. When a plaintiff asserts separate, independent, and distinct claims against multiple defendants, jurisdiction is determined by looking at the claims separately, and the amounts are not aggregated. *Borrego v. del Palacio*, 445 S.W.2d 620, 622 (Tex.App.—El Paso 1969, no writ). Thus, one plaintiff suing 100 defendants for $10 each would have only $10 in controversy and would file the suit in justice court.

(3) Counterclaims. Counterclaims, whether permissive or compulsory, are judged on their own merits and must be within the court's jurisdiction. *Color Tile, Inc. v. Ramsey*, 905 S.W.2d 620, 623 (Tex.App.—Houston [14th Dist.] 1995, no writ); *see* TRCP 97; *Smith v. Clary Corp.*, 917 S.W.2d 796, 798 (Tex.1996). A permissive or compulsory counterclaim can be for an amount within or below the court's minimum jurisdiction, but it cannot be for an amount above the court's maximum jurisdiction. *See, e.g., Dykes v. Crausbay*, 214 S.W.3d 200, 202 (Tex. App.—Amarillo 2007, no pet.) (claim above jurisdictional limit not a compulsory counterclaim); *Kitchen Designs, Inc. v. Wood*, 584 S.W.2d 305, 307 (Tex.App.—Texarkana 1979, writ ref'd n.r.e.) (same); *Watkins v. Cossaboom*, 204 S.W.2d 56, 57-58 (Tex.App.—Galveston 1947, writ dism'd) (compulsory counterclaim below jurisdictional limit). If a counterclaim is above the jurisdictional limit of the court, the trial court should dismiss the counterclaim. *Kitchen Designs*, 584 S.W.2d at 307. Counterclaims of multiple defendants are not aggregated under the aggregating statute. *Smith*, 917 S.W.2d at 798; *see* Gov't Code §24.009.

(4) Actions other than for damages. When the action is to recover or foreclose on personal property, the amount in controversy is either the fair market value of the property or the amount of the underlying debt, whichever is higher. If the suit is for injunctive relief, and there is no amount in controversy, jurisdiction is in the district court based on residual jurisdiction. *Super X Drugs v. State*, 505 S.W.2d 333, 336 (Tex.App.—Houston [14th Dist.] 1974, no writ); *see Martin v. Victoria ISD*, 972 S.W.2d 815, 818 (Tex.App.—Corpus Christi 1998, pet. denied) (county court cannot hold injunction hearing unless amount in controversy is alleged). See "General jurisdiction," §3.1, p. 137.

(5) Other related claims. A court can assert jurisdiction over claims that are below its minimum jurisdictional limits if those claims arise from the same transaction or occurrence as a claim that the court has jurisdiction over. *Watkins*, 204 S.W.2d at 57. A court cannot assert jurisdiction over a claim that is above its maximum jurisdictional limits. *Hawkins v. Anderson*, 672 S.W.2d 293, 296 (Tex.App.—Dallas 1984, no writ).

(6) Amendments in excess of jurisdictional limits. Generally, once jurisdiction is properly acquired, no later fact or event can defeat the court's jurisdiction. *Continental Coffee Prods. v. Cazarez*, 937 S.W.2d 444, 449 (Tex.1996); *Dallas ISD v. Porter*, 709 S.W.2d 642, 643 (Tex.1986); *Weidner v. Sanchez*, 14 S.W.3d 353, 360-61 (Tex.App.—Houston [14th Dist.] 2000, no pet.). If the plaintiff's original petition was properly brought in a particular court, but an amendment increases the amount in controversy above the court's jurisdictional limits, the court will continue to have jurisdiction if the additional damages accrued as a result of the passage of time. *Continental Coffee*, 937 S.W.2d at 449; *Mr. W. Fireworks, Inc. v. Mitchell*, 622 S.W.2d 576, 577 (Tex.1981). If an amendment adds a claim for damages that existed at the time the suit was filed but was not included in the original petition, and if the additional claim is outside the court's jurisdiction, the additional claim should be dismissed on a plea to the jurisdiction. *Hawkins*, 672 S.W.2d at 296.

(7) Interest. Interest is seldom included in the amount in controversy. The courts distinguish between interest eo nomine (interest as interest), which is excluded, and interest as damages, which is included.

★

Weidner, 14 S.W.3d at 362; *see also* Gov't Code §25.0003(c)(1) (specifically excludes interest eo nomine in determining the amount in controversy in suits filed in county courts at law); *Smith*, 917 S.W.2d at 798 (same). Interest eo nomine is interest as provided for by agreement or by statute; it is part of the debt. Interest as damages is interest that is added to the debt for not paying a sum certain at the time the debt was due. For example, prejudgment interest is usually considered interest as damages, but if it is provided for by contract or statute it is interest eo nomine. *Weidner*, 14 S.W.3d at 362; *see Barnes v. U.S. Fid. & Guar. Co.*, 279 S.W.2d 919, 921 (Tex.App.—Waco 1955, no writ).

(8) **Attorney fees & exemplary damages.** Attorney fees are generally included in the amount in controversy. *Johnson v. Universal Life & Acc. Ins.*, 94 S.W.2d 1145, 1146 (Tex.1936); *Long v. Fox*, 625 S.W.2d 376, 378 (Tex.App.—San Antonio 1981, writ ref'd n.r.e.). *But see* Gov't Code §25.0003(c)(1) (specifically excludes attorney fees, penalties, and statutory or punitive damages from the amount in controversy in suits filed in county courts at law); *Smith*, 917 S.W.2d at 798 (same).

(9) **Costs.** Court costs are not included in the amount in controversy.

2. **Amending to correct amount in controversy.** If a pleading makes a claim for nonseverable liquidated damages that are outside the trial court's jurisdiction (either above or below), the party cannot amend its damages to state an amount within the court's jurisdiction. *Smith Detective Agency*, 938 S.W.2d at 747. If the claim is for unliquidated damages, however, a party may amend its damages to state an amount within the court's jurisdiction if the party pleads in good faith. *Id.*

§3. DISTRICT COURTS

§3.1 General jurisdiction. The district courts are the primary trial courts of Texas. *Dubai Pet. Co. v. Kazi*, 12 S.W.3d 71, 75 (Tex.2000). District courts are courts of general jurisdiction. *See* Gov't Code §24.008. That is, the Constitution gives district courts exclusive, appellate, and original jurisdiction over all actions, proceedings, and remedies, except in cases in which jurisdiction is conferred by the Texas Constitution or other law on another court, tribunal, or administrative body. Tex. Const. art. 5, §8; *Dubai Pet.*, 12 S.W.3d at 75; *see* Gov't Code §§24.007(a), 24.008, 24.011. District courts have jurisdiction over all types of claims over which justice and county courts do not. *See* Tex. Const. art. 5, §8; Gov't Code §24.008. District courts have concurrent jurisdiction with each other over the same cases in the same county. *See* Gov't Code §24.003(b); *Pinnacle Gas Treating, Inc. v. Read*, 160 S.W.3d 564, 566 (Tex. 2005).

§3.2 Specialized jurisdiction. The Constitution gives the Legislature the power to "establish such other courts as it may deem necessary," to prescribe the jurisdiction of those legislative courts, and to "conform the jurisdiction of the district and other inferior courts thereto." Tex. Const. art. 5, §1. Examples of the most common types of courts with specialized jurisdiction are the following:

1. **Family district courts.** The Legislature created family district courts with jurisdiction equal to that of constitutional district courts but with primary responsibility for family-law matters such as divorce, annulment, child conservatorship, and child support. The family district courts have the same jurisdiction as other district courts in the county in which they are located. Gov't Code §24.601(a); *Beach v. Beach*, 912 S.W.2d 345, 347 n.3 (Tex. App.—Houston [14th Dist.] 1995, no writ).

2. **Juvenile-court designation.** A district court is one of the courts that may be designated as a juvenile court. *See* Gov't Code §23.001 (other courts that may be designated are a county court or a statutory county court that is exercising jurisdiction of district or county court); Fam. Code §51.04(b) (other courts that may be designated are a criminal district court, domestic-relations court, juvenile court, county court, or county court at law). The designation as a juvenile court is made by the county's juvenile board. Fam. Code §51.04(b). Juvenile courts have original, exclusive jurisdiction over proceedings under the Juvenile Justice Code, except that in counties with a population of less than 100,000, juvenile courts have concurrent jurisdiction with justice and municipal courts for conduct by a child that violates Educ. Code §25.094 (failure to attend school). Fam. Code §51.04(a), (h).

─────────────── ★ ───────────────

§3.3 Amount in controversy. District courts have original jurisdiction in civil cases in which the amount in controversy exceeds $500, excluding interest. Gov't Code §24.007(b). There is no upper limit to their amount-in-controversy jurisdiction. *See generally* Tex. Const. art. 5, §8 (jurisdiction of district court); Gov't Code §§24.007 & 24.008 (same). See "Overlapping Monetary Jurisdiction of Trial Courts," chart 2-1, p. 148.

§3.4 Relief available. A district court can grant all types of relief, including writs of injunction, mandamus, sequestration, attachment, garnishment, certiorari, and supersedeas, and all other writs necessary to enforce its jurisdiction. *See* Tex. Const. art. 5, §8; Gov't Code §§24.008, 24.011.

§3.5 Transfer of cases & exchange of benches. District judges may transfer cases to or exchange benches with another district court in the same county. Tex. Const. art. 5, §11; Gov't Code §24.003(b); TRCP 330(e). A formal order of transfer is not required. ***Pinnacle Gas Treating, Inc. v. Read***, 160 S.W.3d 564, 566 (Tex.2005). The rules for transferring cases and exchanging benches apply to counties with two or more district courts. Gov't Code §24.003(a); TRCP 330(e).

───────────────────────────────

NOTE

When a case is transferred from one district court to another, all processes, writs, bonds, and other obligations that are issued by the transferring court can be returned to the court to which the case is being transferred as if that court had originally issued the obligation. Gov't Code §24.023.

───────────────────────────────

1. Judge's power to transfer & exchange. Unless local rules of administration provide otherwise, a district judge in a county with two or more district courts can do the following:

(1) Transfer any civil case or proceeding on the court's docket to the docket of another district court in the county. Gov't Code §24.003(b)(1); *see* TRCP 330(e).

(2) Hear and determine any case or proceeding, or any part or question of a case or proceeding, pending in another district court in the county without having the case transferred. Gov't Code §24.003(b)(2), (d); *see* TRCP 330(e) (district judge may, in her own courtroom, try and determine case or proceeding pending in another district court).

(3) Sit for another district court in the county and hear and determine any case or proceeding pending in that court. Gov't Code §24.003(b)(3); TRCP 330(e).

(4) Temporarily exchange benches with the judge of another district court in the county. Gov't Code §24.003(b)(4); *see* TRCP 330(e).

(5) Try different cases in the same court at the same time. Gov't Code §24.003(b)(5); TRCP 330(e).

(6) Occupy the judge's own courtroom or the courtroom of another district court in the county. Gov't Code §24.003(b)(6); TRCP 330(e).

2. Absent judge. If a district judge in the county is sick or otherwise absent, another district judge in the county can hold court for that judge. Gov't Code §24.003(c).

3. Matters to be heard & determined. Under Gov't Code §24.003, a district judge can hear and determine the following matters in a case or proceeding pending in another court without transferring the case or proceeding:

(1) Motions, including motions for new trial. Gov't Code §24.003(d).

(2) Petitions for injunctive relief. *Id.*

(3) Applications for the appointment of a receiver. *Id.*

(4) Petitions in intervention. *Id.*

★

(5)   Pleas in abatement or other dilatory pleas. *Id.*

(6)   All preliminary matters, questions, and proceedings. *Id.*

4.   Judgment or order.

(1)   Restraining order or injunction. A district judge can issue a restraining order or an injunction that is returnable to any other district court. Gov't Code §24.003(d); TRCP 330(e).

(2)   Rendition of judgment. A district judge who hears and determines certain matters in a case or proceeding pending in another district court can render judgment in the case or proceeding. *See* Gov't Code §24.003(d); TRCP 330(e). See "Judge's power to transfer & exchange," §3.5.1(3), p. 138. The district judge in whose court a matter is pending can also hear, complete, and determine the matter, or all or any part of another matter, and render a final judgment. Gov't Code §24.003(d). If a district judge hears and determines any part or question of a pending case or proceeding, any other district judge can then complete the hearing and render judgment. *Id.*

(3)   Entry of judgment or order. A district judge who hears and determines a matter can enter a judgment or an order on that matter without transferring the case or proceeding. Gov't Code §24.003(d). Any judgment or order must be entered in the minutes of the court where the case is pending. *Id.* §24.003(e); TRCP 330(e); *see* Gov't Code §24.003(d).

5.   No limitation of powers.
Gov't Code §24.003 does not limit a district judge's powers when that judge is acting for another judge because of the transfer of a case or proceeding, the exchange of benches, or any other reason under Gov't Code §24.003. *See* Gov't Code §24.003(f).

§4.   COUNTY COURTS

There are various types of county courts with different types of jurisdiction. The most complicated aspect of county-court jurisdiction is probate jurisdiction. As the Supreme Court noted, "Texas probate jurisdiction is, to say the least, somewhat complex." ***Palmer v. Coble Wall Trust Co.***, 851 S.W.2d 178, 180 n.3 (Tex.1992).

NOTE
*The revisions to the Probate Code amending §§4D, 4H, 605, and 608 and enacting §§6B, 606A, and 607A-607E, discussed in the sections below, apply only to actions filed or proceedings commenced on or after September 1, 2011. See Acts 2011, 82nd Leg., R.S., ch. 1085, §§43(b), 44, eff. Sept. 1, 2011 (§§605, 606A, 607A-607E, 608); Acts 2011, 82nd Leg., R.S., ch. 1338, §§1.43(a), 3.02, eff. Sept. 1, 2011 (§§4D, 4H, 6B). Most prominently, the changes (1) deleted the "appertaining or incident to" language for guardianship proceedings and substituted the "related to" language as used in probate proceedings and (2) made the assignment and transfer of probate and guardianship proceedings substantially more similar. For the law applicable to an action that was filed or a proceeding that was commenced before September 1, 2011, see O'Connor's Texas Rules * Civil Trials (2011), "County Courts," ch. 2-F, §4, p. 124. Many sections of the Probate Code have simultaneously been transferred to and redesignated under the new Estates Code, which will replace the Probate Code effective January 1, 2014.*

---

§4.1   Constitutional county courts. Every county has a constitutional county court, which is the office of the chief administrator of the county. *See* Tex. Const. art. 5, §§15, 16. In some counties the constitutional county judge exercises probate jurisdiction, and in others the judge acts only as the county's administrator and takes no action as a trial judge. The Texas Constitution states that the jurisdiction of the constitutional county court is "as provided by law." Tex. Const. art. 5, §16. Its jurisdiction, therefore, is governed by statutes. *See* CPRC §§51.001, 51.002, 61.021; Gov't Code §§26.041-26.044, 26.048, 26.050, 26.051.

1.   Amount in controversy. The constitutional county courts have concurrent jurisdiction with (1) the justice courts in civil cases in which the amount in controversy is $200.01 through $10,000, excluding interest, and (2) the district courts in civil cases in which the amount in controversy is $500.01 through $5,000, excluding interest.

⭐

Gov't Code §26.042(a), (d). The amount in controversy does not limit the court's probate jurisdiction. *Womble v. Atkins*, 331 S.W.2d 294, 299 (Tex.1960). See "Overlapping Monetary Jurisdiction of Trial Courts," chart 2-1, p. 148.

2. Probate & guardianship matters.

(1) Original jurisdiction. Except in the counties where probate jurisdiction rests exclusively in other courts, constitutional county courts have original jurisdiction over probate and guardianship proceedings. *See* Prob. Code §4C(a) (probate), §607A(a) (guardianship).

(2) Matters related to probate proceeding. Constitutional county courts with original probate jurisdiction also have jurisdiction over certain matters "related to" probate proceedings. *See* Prob. Code §4A(a).

(a) County without county court at law. If the constitutional county court is located in a county that does not have a county court at law, the court has jurisdiction over the following matters related to a probate proceeding:

[1] An action against a personal representative or former personal representative arising from the representative's performance of the duties of a personal representative. Prob. Code §§4A(a), 4B(a)(1).

[2] An action against a surety of a personal representative or former personal representative. *Id.* §§4A(a), 4B(a)(2).

[3] A claim brought by a personal representative on behalf of the estate. *Id.* §§4A(a), 4B(a)(3).

[4] An action brought against a personal representative in the representative's capacity as personal representative. *Id.* §§4A(a), 4B(a)(4).

[5] An action for trial of title to real property that is estate property, including the enforcement of a lien against the property. *Id.* §§4A(a), 4B(a)(5).

[6] An action for trial of the right of property that is estate property. *Id.* §§4A(a), 4B(a)(6).

(b) County with county court at law. If the constitutional county court is located in a county that also has a county court at law, the constitutional county court has jurisdiction over the following matters related to a probate proceeding:

[1] An action against a personal representative or former personal representative arising from the representative's performance of the duties of a personal representative. Prob. Code §§4A(a), 4B(a)(1), (b)(1).

[2] An action against a surety of a personal representative or former personal representative. *Id.* §§4A(a), 4B(a)(2), (b)(1).

[3] A claim brought by a personal representative on behalf of the estate. *Id.* §§4A(a), 4B(a)(3), (b)(1).

[4] An action brought against a personal representative in the representative's capacity as personal representative. *Id.* §§4A(a), 4B(a)(4), (b)(1).

[5] An action for trial of title to real property that is estate property, including the enforcement of a lien against the property. *Id.* §§4A(a), 4B(a)(5), (b)(1).

[6] An action for trial of the right of property that is estate property. *Id.* §§4A(a), 4B(a)(6), (b)(1).

[7] The interpretation and administration of a testamentary trust if the will creating the trust has been admitted to probate in the court. *Id.* §§4A(a), 4B(b)(2).

[8] The interpretation and administration of an inter vivos trust created by a decedent whose will has been admitted to probate in the court. *Id.* §§4A(a), 4B(b)(3).

★

(3) Pendent & ancillary jurisdiction for probate estate. A constitutional county court with original jurisdiction over probate proceedings may exercise pendent and ancillary jurisdiction as necessary to promote judicial efficiency and economy. *See* Prob. Code §4A(b) ("probate court" may exercise pendent and ancillary jurisdiction); *see also id.* §3(e) ("probate court" is any court exercising original probate jurisdiction).

(4) Matters related to guardianship proceeding. Constitutional county courts have jurisdiction over matters that are "related to" a guardianship proceeding. Prob. Code §§605(a), 606A(a), 607A(a). Specifically, these matters include:

(a) The granting of letters of guardianship. *Id.* §606A(a)(1).

(b) The settling of a guardian's account and all other matters relating to the settlement, partition, or distribution of a ward's estate. *Id.* §606A(a)(2).

(c) A claim by or against a guardianship estate. *Id.* §606A(a)(3).

(d) An action for trial of title to land that is guardianship-estate property, including the enforcement of a lien against the property. *Id.* §606A(a)(4).

(e) An action for trial of the right of property that is guardianship-estate property. *Id.* §606A(a)(5).

(f) After a guardianship of a ward's estate is required to be settled under Probate Code §745:

[1] An action by or on behalf of the former ward against a former guardian of the ward for alleged misconduct arising from the performance of the person's duties as guardian. *Id.* §606A(a)(6)(A).

[2] An action calling on the surety of a guardian or former guardian to perform in place of the guardian or former guardian, which may include the award of a judgment against the guardian or former guardian in favor of the surety. *Id.* §606A(a)(6)(B).

[3] An action against a former guardian of the former ward that is brought by a surety called on to perform in place of the former guardian. *Id.* §606A(a)(6)(C).

[4] A claim for the payment of compensation, expenses, and court costs, and any other matter authorized under Probate Code §§665-670. *Id.* §606A(a)(6)(D).

[5] A matter related to an authorization made or duty performed by a guardian under Probate Code §§745-758. *Id.* §606A(a)(6)(E).

(g) The appointment of a trustee for a trust created under Probate Code §867, the settling of an account of the trustee, and all other matters related to the trust. *Id.* §606A(a)(7).

3. Juvenile matters. A constitutional county court may be designated as a juvenile court. Gov't Code §23.001; Fam. Code §51.04(b); *see* Gov't Code §26.042(b) (county court has juvenile jurisdiction as provided by §23.001). See "Juvenile-court designation," §3.2.2, p. 137. If a county court is designated as a juvenile court, at least one other court must also be designated as a juvenile court. Fam. Code §51.04(c). If the judge of the county court is not a licensed attorney, an alternate court must be designated. *Id.* §51.04(d).

4. Appellate jurisdiction. Constitutional county courts have appellate jurisdiction over cases originating in the justice or small-claims courts when the amount in controversy or the judgment exceeds $250, not including costs. CPRC §51.001(a); Gov't Code §26.042(e); *see Weeks v. Hobson*, 877 S.W.2d 478, 480 n.1 (Tex.App.— Houston [1st Dist.] 1994, orig. proceeding) (appellate jurisdiction includes forcible-entry-and-detainer suits). Review is by trial de novo. Gov't Code §28.053(b); *Oropeza v. Valdez*, 147 S.W.3d 480, 482 (Tex.App.—San Antonio 2004, no pet.).

5. Additional jurisdiction. The Legislature has given some constitutional county courts limited jurisdiction over other matters. *See, e.g.*, Gov't Code §26.134 (Cass County constitutional county court has the power to receive and enter guilty pleas in misdemeanor cases).

★

6. Relief available. A constitutional county court can grant all types of relief, including writs of injunction, mandamus, sequestration, attachment, garnishment, certiorari, and supersedeas, and all other writs necessary to enforce its jurisdiction. *See* Tex. Const. art. 5, §16; Gov't Code §§26.044, 26.051; *Martin v. Victoria ISD*, 972 S.W.2d 815, 817 (Tex.App.—Corpus Christi 1998, pet. denied).

7. Cases excluded. Constitutional county courts do not have jurisdiction over suits for (1) recovery of damages for defamation, (2) enforcement of liens on land, (3) escheat on behalf of the State, (4) divorce, (5) forfeiture of a corporate charter, (6) the trial of the right to property valued at $500 or more and levied under a writ of execution, sequestration, or attachment, (7) eminent domain, or (8) recovery of land. Gov't Code §26.043.

§4.2 County courts at law. Every county court at law (also called a statutory county court) has the same jurisdiction as the constitutional county court in that county, unless modified by (1) the statute that created the county court at law or (2) a statute that applies to all county courts at law. Gov't Code §§25.0003(a), 25.0004(c); *see id.* §25.0001(a); *see also* Tex. Const. art. 5, §1 (Legislature may establish other courts as it deems necessary).

PRACTICE TIP
To determine the jurisdiction of a particular county court at law, consult the specific Government Code provision for that county's courts at law and the general code provisions that apply to more than one legislative court. See Gov't Code ch. 25.

---

1. Amount in controversy. The county courts at law have concurrent jurisdiction with the district courts for cases in which the amount in controversy exceeds $500 but does not exceed $200,000, excluding mandatory damages and penalties, attorney fees, interest, and court costs. Gov't Code §25.0003(c)(1). The amount in controversy includes all damages the plaintiff seeks to recover, not the amount of damages the plaintiff is likely to recover. *United Servs. Auto. Ass'n v. Brite*, 215 S.W.3d 400, 402-03 (Tex.2007). Because county courts at law have the same jurisdiction as constitutional county courts, the actual dollar range of the amount in controversy for county courts at law starts as low as $200.01 and goes as high as $200,000, depending on which statute governs that court's jurisdiction. *See* Gov't Code §§25.0003(a), 26.042(a). Although some county courts at law have very limited jurisdiction, others have about the same jurisdiction as the district courts. *E.g., id.* §25.0592(a) (Dallas County), §25.0732(a) (El Paso County), §25.0862(a) (Galveston County); *see, e.g., Weinberger v. Longer*, 222 S.W.3d 557, 560-61 (Tex.App.— Houston [1st Dist.] 2007, pet. denied) (because Galveston County court at law had concurrent jurisdiction with district court regardless of amount in controversy, county court had jurisdiction over counterclaim exceeding $100,000; decided under former Gov't Code §25.003(c)(1) with amount-in-controversy ceiling of $100,000); *Schuld v. Dembrinski*, 12 S.W.3d 485, 489 (Tex.App.—Dallas 2000, no pet.) (because Dallas County court at law had concurrent jurisdiction with district court in civil cases regardless of amount in controversy, county court had jurisdiction over partition suit). See "Overlapping Monetary Jurisdiction of Trial Courts," chart 2-1, p. 148. A county court may have exclusive jurisdiction over certain claims regardless of the amount in controversy. *E.g., AIC Mgmt. v. Crews*, 246 S.W.3d 640, 644 (Tex.2008) (Harris County court at law had exclusive jurisdiction over eminent-domain proceedings regardless of amount in controversy).

2. Probate & guardianship matters.

(1) Original jurisdiction. Gov't Code §25.0003(d) authorizes county courts at law to exercise original probate jurisdiction, unless there is a statutory probate court in the same county. *See* Gov't Code §25.0003(e); *see also* Prob. Code §4C(b) (probate), §607A(b) (guardianship). However, a county court at law does not have the same jurisdiction granted to statutory probate courts under the Probate Code. Gov't Code §25.0003(f); *Carroll v. Carroll*, 304 S.W.3d 366, 368 (Tex.2010); *see In re G.C.*, 66 S.W.3d 517, 522 (Tex.App.—Fort Worth 2002, no pet.) (county court at law does not become statutory probate court merely by exercising its probate jurisdiction). Instead, a county court at law has the general probate jurisdiction of a constitutional county court over probate and guardianship proceedings. *See* Gov't Code §25.0003(d); Prob. Code §4C(b) (probate), §607A(b) (guardianship).

★

(2) Matters related to probate proceeding. A county court at law has jurisdiction over the same matters "related to" probate proceedings as do the constitutional county courts located in the same county. *See* Prob. Code §§4B(b), 4C(b). See "County with county court at law," §4.1.2(2)(b), p. 140.

(3) Pendent & ancillary jurisdiction for probate estate. A county court at law with original jurisdiction over probate proceedings may exercise pendent and ancillary jurisdiction as necessary to promote judicial efficiency and economy. *See* Prob. Code §4A(b) ("probate court" may exercise pendent and ancillary jurisdiction); *see also id.* §3(e) ("probate court" is any court exercising original probate jurisdiction).

(4) Matters related to guardianship proceeding. A county court at law has jurisdiction over the same matters "related to" guardianship proceedings as do the constitutional county courts. *See* Prob. Code §§605(a), 606A(a), 607A(b). See "Matters related to guardianship proceeding," §4.1.2(4), p. 141.

3. Civil & criminal. County courts at law have jurisdiction over all civil and criminal causes prescribed by law for constitutional county courts. Gov't Code §25.0003(a); *Weeks v. Hobson*, 877 S.W.2d 478, 480 n.1 (Tex. App.—Houston [1st Dist.] 1994, orig. proceeding).

4. Relief available. A county court at law can grant all types of relief, including writs of injunction, mandamus, sequestration, attachment, garnishment, certiorari, and supersedeas, and other writs necessary to enforce its jurisdiction. *See* Gov't Code §25.0004(a), (c); *In re Burlington N. & Santa Fe Ry.*, 12 S.W.3d 891, 896 (Tex. App.—Houston [14th Dist.] 2000, orig. proceeding); *Martin v. Victoria ISD*, 972 S.W.2d 815, 817 (Tex.App.— Corpus Christi 1998, pet. denied).

5. Juvenile matters. A county court at law may be designated as a juvenile court. Gov't Code §23.001; Fam. Code §51.04(b). See "Juvenile-court designation," §3.2.2, p. 137.

6. Matters excluded. A county court at law does not have jurisdiction over county business of the commissioners court or over matters excluded from the jurisdiction of the constitutional county court. *See* Gov't Code §25.0003(b) (county-business exclusion), §26.043 (exclusions for constitutional county courts); *see, e.g., Matherne v. Carre*, 7 S.W.3d 903, 906 (Tex.App.—Beaumont 1999, pet. denied) (county court at law does not have jurisdiction over suit for enforcement of lien on land); *Loville v. Loville*, 944 S.W.2d 818, 819 (Tex.App.—Beaumont 1997, writ denied) (like constitutional county court, statutory county court does not have jurisdiction in suit to recover land). *But see* Gov't Code §25.1032(c)(1) (Harris County civil court at law has jurisdiction over issue of title to real property).

§4.3 Statutory probate courts. Certain courts are designated as "statutory probate courts" under Gov't Code chapter 25. Gov't Code §21.009(4); Prob. Code §3(ii).

1. Original jurisdiction. In a county with a statutory probate court, all probate and guardianship matters must be heard in the statutory probate court, whether contested or not. Prob. Code §4F(a) (probate), §607D(a) (guardianship); *see id.* §607A(c) (guardianship). Statutory probate courts have general probate jurisdiction under the Probate Code. *See* Gov't Code §25.0021(b)(1); *Schuld v. Dembrinski*, 12 S.W.3d 485, 487 (Tex.App.—Dallas 2000, no pet.); *Green v. Watson*, 860 S.W.2d 238, 242 (Tex.App.—Austin 1993, no writ). Gov't Code §25.0021(a) does, however, limit the jurisdiction of statutory probate courts to matters in probate, guardianship, mental health, and eminent domain, superseding any other Government Code provisions that give additional jurisdiction to statutory probate courts in specific counties.

2. Matters related to probate proceeding. Unless a statutory probate court's jurisdiction is concurrent with that of the district court, all matters "related to" a probate proceeding must be brought in the statutory probate court. Prob. Code §4F(a). The statutory probate court has jurisdiction over the same matters related to probate proceedings as do county courts at law and constitutional county courts located in a county with a county court at law. *See id.* §4B(c)(1). See "County with county court at law," §4.1.2(2)(b), p. 140; "Matters related to probate proceeding," §4.2.2(2), this page. If any estate is pending in a statutory probate court, the court also has jurisdiction over any action in which the personal representative of that estate is a party in her capacity as personal representative. Prob. Code §4B(c)(2).

———————————————— ✦ ————————————————

3. Matters related to guardianship proceeding. Unless a statutory probate court's jurisdiction is concurrent with that of the district court, all matters "related to" a guardianship proceeding must be brought in the statutory probate court. Prob. Code §607D(b). The statutory probate court has jurisdiction over the same matters related to guardianship proceedings as do constitutional county courts and county courts at law. *See id.* §606A(b)(1). See "Matters related to guardianship proceeding," §4.1.2(4), p. 141; "Matters related to guardianship proceeding," §4.2.2(4), p. 143. The statutory probate court also has jurisdiction over (1) a suit, action, or application filed against or on behalf of a guardianship or a trustee of a trust created under Probate Code §867 and (2) a cause of action in which a guardian in a guardianship pending in the statutory probate court is a party. Prob. Code §606A(b)(2), (b)(3).

4. Trust matters. Statutory probate courts have concurrent jurisdiction with district courts in actions involving inter vivos, testamentary, and charitable trusts, and in actions brought by or against a trustee. Prob. Code §§4G(1), (2), 4H(2), (3). Constitutional county courts and county courts at law do not have jurisdiction over trusts. *In re Estate of Alexander*, 188 S.W.3d 327, 331 (Tex.App.—Waco 2006, no pet.); *see* Prop. Code §115.001(a) (district court has exclusive jurisdiction over trusts); *Carroll v. Carroll*, 304 S.W.3d 366, 368 (Tex.2010) (same).

5. Actions by, against, or involving personal representative or guardian. Statutory probate courts have concurrent jurisdiction with district courts in (1) all personal-injury, survival, or wrongful-death actions by or against a person in her capacity as a personal representative or a guardian and (2) all actions involving a personal representative of an estate or a guardian in which no other party aligned with the personal representative or guardian is an interested person in that estate or guardianship. Prob. Code §4H(1) & (4) (probate), §607E (guardianship).

6. Power-of-attorney matters. Statutory probate courts have concurrent jurisdiction with district courts in actions (1) against an agent or former agent under a power of attorney arising from the agent's performance of its duties, (2) to determine the validity of a power of attorney, or (3) to determine an agent's rights, powers, or duties under a power of attorney. Prob. Code §§4G(3), (4), 4H(5), (6).

7. Pendent & ancillary jurisdiction. Statutory probate courts may exercise pendent and ancillary jurisdiction necessary to promote judicial efficiency and economy. Prob. Code §4A(b) (probate), §605(b) (guardianship). Generally, probate courts exercise pendent or ancillary jurisdiction when there is a close relationship between the nonprobate claims and the claims against the estate. *Shell Cortez Pipeline Co. v. Shores*, 127 S.W.3d 286, 294 (Tex.App.—Fort Worth 2004, no pet.). Other courts exercising probate jurisdiction do not have pendent and ancillary jurisdiction.

§4.4 Contested matters – assignment or transfer from constitutional county court. If the constitutional county court retains probate jurisdiction in a particular county and a party contests any matter in a probate (Probate Code §§4D, 4E) or guardianship (Probate Code §§607B, 607C) case before that court, the contested matter or the entire proceeding may be assigned or transferred.

1. Assignment to statutory probate judge. In a county that does not have a statutory probate court or a county court at law exercising original probate jurisdiction, either the contested matter or the entire proceeding can be assigned to a statutory probate judge. *See* Prob. Code §607B.

(1) Assignment of contested matter.

(a) On party's motion or court's own initiative. If any party moves for a statutory probate judge to be assigned to hear the contested matter, the constitutional county court must grant the motion. Prob. Code §§4D(a)(1), 607B(a)(1); *see id.* §4D(b). The motion can be made at any time before or after the matter is contested. *Id.* §§4D(c), 607B(d). Even if no party moves to assign the contested matter to a statutory probate judge, the constitutional county court may assign the contested matter on its own initiative. *Id.* §§4D(a), 607B(a). After the court grants the motion or assigns the matter on its own initiative, the presiding statutory probate judge will then assign a current or former statutory probate judge to hear the contested matter. *See* Gov't Code §25.0022(h).

(b) Later-filed contested matter. After a contested matter has been assigned to a statutory probate judge, any other contested matter that is later filed in the proceeding must also be assigned to that judge. Prob. Code §§4D(h), 607B(i).

———————————— ★ ————————————

(c) Statutory probate judge's power. The statutory probate judge has all the jurisdictional tools of a statutory probate court available when hearing the contested matter, including the power to transfer other pending matters under Probate Code §§5B and 608. *See* Gov't Code §25.0022(i); Prob. Code §§4D(e), 607B(f). Unless a party objects, the statutory probate judge can hear ancillary motions in that judge's home county, but the trial on the merits must be conducted in the county where the probate proceeding is pending. Gov't Code §25.0022(n).

(d) Constitutional county court's jurisdiction. The constitutional county court retains jurisdiction over the estate or guardianship, except for the contested matter. Prob. Code §§4D(g), 607B(h). Once the statutory probate judge resolves the contested matter, including any appeals, the matter is transferred back to the constitutional county court for further proceedings. *Id.* §§4D(e), 607B(f).

(2) Assignment of entire proceeding. If any party, or the judge of the constitutional county court on her own initiative, moves for a statutory probate judge to be assigned to hear the contested matter, the judge may request, on her own initiative or on a party's motion, that the statutory probate judge be assigned to the entire proceeding. Prob. Code §§4D(b-1), 607B(c). The statutory probate judge has all the jurisdictional tools of a statutory probate court available when hearing the entire proceeding, including the power to transfer other pending matters under Probate Code §§5B and 608. *See* Gov't Code §25.0022(i); Prob. Code §§4D(e), 607B(f). Once the statutory probate judge resolves the contested matter, including any appeals, the entire proceeding is transferred back to the constitutional county court for further proceedings. Prob. Code §§4D(e), 607B(f).

2. Transfer to district court. In a county that does not have a statutory probate court or a county court at law exercising original probate jurisdiction, the contested matter and any matter related to the proceeding can be transferred to the district court. Prob. Code §§4D(a)(2), (g), 607B(a)(2), (h).

(1) Transfer of contested matter.

(a) On party's motion or court's own initiative. If any party moves to transfer a contested matter to the district court, the constitutional county court must grant the motion. Prob. Code §§4D(a)(2), 607B(a)(2). Even if no party moves to transfer a contested matter to the district court, the constitutional county court may transfer the contested matter on its own initiative. *Id.* §§4D(a)(2), 607B(a)(2). After the court grants the motion or transfers the matter on its own initiative, the district court can then hear the contested matter as if it had originally been filed there. *Id.* §§4D(a)(2), 607B(a)(2).

(b) Motion to assign controls. A motion to assign a statutory probate judge to the contested matter controls over a motion to transfer the matter to the district court. *See* Prob. Code §§4D(b), 607B(b). Thus, a motion to assign a statutory probate judge must be granted, unless the motion is withdrawn or the constitutional county court has already transferred the contested matter to a district court. *See id.* §§4D(b), 607B(b).

(c) Later-filed contested matter. Once a contested matter has been transferred to the district court, any other contested matter that is later filed in the proceeding must also be transferred to that court. Prob. Code §§4D(h), 607B(i).

(d) District court's power. The district court has all the jurisdictional tools of a statutory probate court available when hearing the contested matter, including the power to transfer other pending matters under Probate Code §§5B and 608. *See* Gov't Code §25.0022(i); Prob. Code §§4D(f), 607B(g).

(e) Constitutional county court's jurisdiction. The constitutional county court retains jurisdiction over the estate or guardianship, except for the contested matter. Prob. Code §§4D(g), 607B(h). Once the district court resolves the contested matter, including any appeals, the matter is transferred back to the constitutional county court for further proceedings. *Id.* §§4D(f), 607B(g).

(2) Transfer of related matter. Any matter related to a probate or guardianship proceeding in which a contested matter is transferred to a district court may be brought in the district court. Prob. Code §§4D(g), 607B(h). The district court may, on its own initiative or on any party's motion, find that the related matter is not a contested matter and transfer the matter to the constitutional county court with jurisdiction over the management of the estate or guardianship. *Id.* §§4D(g), 607B(h).

★

3. Transfer to county court at law. In a county that does not have a statutory probate court but does have a county court at law exercising original probate jurisdiction, either the contested matter or the entire proceeding can be transferred to the county court at law. Prob. Code §§4E(a), 607C(a).

(1) Transfer of contested matter. If any party moves to transfer the contested matter to the county court at law, the constitutional county court must grant the motion. Prob. Code §§4E(a), 607C(a). The county court at law then hears the contested matter as if it had originally been filed there. *Id.* §§4E(b), 607C(b). Even if no party moves to transfer a contested matter to the county court at law, the constitutional county court may transfer the contested matter on its own initiative. *Id.* §§4E(a), 607C(a). Once the county court at law resolves the contested matter, including any appeals, the matter is transferred back to the constitutional county court for further proceedings. *Id.* §§4E(b), 607C(b).

(2) Transfer of entire proceeding. If any party moves to transfer the entire proceeding to the county court at law, the constitutional county court may grant the motion. Prob. Code §§4E(a), 607C(a). The county court at law then hears the proceeding as if it had originally been filed there. *Id.* §§4E(b), 607C(b). Even if no party moves to transfer the proceeding to the county court at law, the constitutional county court may transfer it on its own initiative. *Id.* §§4E(a), 607C(a).

§4.5 Transfer to statutory probate court.

1. Matter related to probate proceeding. On the motion of a party or person interested in an estate, a statutory probate court may transfer to itself from a district court, constitutional county court, or county court at law a cause of action (1) related to a probate proceeding pending in the statutory probate court or (2) in which the personal representative of an estate pending in the statutory probate court is a party. Prob. Code §5B(a); *see also id.* §4B (identifying matters related to probate proceedings). See "Matters related to probate proceeding," §4.3.2, p. 143. The court can consolidate the transferred cause of action with any other proceedings related to the estate. Prob. Code §5B(a).

2. Matter related to guardianship proceeding. On the motion of a party or person interested in a guardianship, a statutory probate court may transfer to itself from a district court, constitutional county court, or county court at law a cause of action related to a guardianship proceeding pending in the statutory probate court, including one in which a guardian, ward, or proposed ward in the pending guardianship proceeding is a party. Prob. Code §608(a)(1); *see also id.* §606A (identifying matters related to guardianship proceedings). See "Matters related to guardianship proceeding," §4.3.3, p. 144. The court can consolidate the transferred cause of action with the related guardianship proceeding and any other proceedings related to the guardianship proceeding. Prob. Code §608(a)(2).

3. Venue. For an action by or against a personal representative or a guardian, ward, or proposed ward for personal injury, death, or property damage, venue is determined under CPRC §15.007. Prob. Code §5B(b) (personal representative), §6B (same), §608(b) (guardian, ward, or proposed ward); *see* CPRC §15.007 (in suits for personal injury, death, or property damage brought by or against executor, administrator, or guardian, venue under CPRC overrides Prob. Code venue provisions). When a party timely objects, a statutory probate court cannot transfer a suit for personal injury, death, or property damage to itself if venue for the suit under CPRC chapter 15 is not proper in the county where the probate court is located. *Gonzalez v. Reliant Energy, Inc.*, 159 S.W.3d 615, 621 (Tex.2005); *see* CPRC §15.007. Thus, a statutory probate court's authority to transfer cases is limited by the venue provisions in CPRC chapter 15 for claims for personal injury, death, and property damage. *Gonzalez*, 159 S.W.3d at 621.

§5. JUSTICE COURTS

The justice courts were created by the Texas Constitution. *See* Tex. Const. art. 5, §19. Jury trials are available in justice courts. Gov't Code §28.035.

§5.1 Amount in controversy. Justice courts have jurisdiction over cases in which the amount in controversy is not more than $10,000, excluding interest. Gov't Code §27.031(a)(1). The amount in controversy should include

★

punitive damages and attorney fees. *Garza v. Chavarria*, 155 S.W.3d 252, 256 (Tex.App.—El Paso 2004, no pet.). The justice courts have original exclusive jurisdiction over civil cases in which the amount in controversy is $200 or less. Tex. Const. art. 5, §19. Their original jurisdiction is concurrent with the district and county courts in civil cases in which the amount in controversy exceeds $200 but does not exceed $10,000. *See* Gov't Code §27.031(a)(1). Their jurisdiction is also concurrent with small-claims courts in actions for the recovery of an amount that does not exceed $10,000. *Id.* §28.003(a). See "Overlapping Monetary Jurisdiction of Trial Courts," chart 2-1, p. 148.

§5.2 Special cases.

1. FED. Justice courts in the precinct where the real property is located generally have original, exclusive jurisdiction over suits for forcible entry and detainer (FED). Prop. Code §24.004; *see* Gov't Code §27.031(a)(2). The only issue tried and determined in an FED suit is the right to possession. TRCP 746; *Aguilar v. Weber*, 72 S.W.3d 729, 732 (Tex.App.—Waco 2002, no pet.); *Carlson's Hill Country Beverage, L.C. v. Westinghouse Rd. Jt.V.*, 957 S.W.2d 951, 954 (Tex.App.—Austin 1997, no pet.). A claim for unpaid rent or other damages is not part of the FED case and therefore cannot be heard by the justice court unless the amount is within the jurisdictional limits and the claim is joined in the suit. TRCP 738; *Haginas v. Malbis Mem'l Found.*, 354 S.W.2d 368, 371 (Tex.1962). An FED suit cannot be used to determine title to real property. *Geldard v. Watson*, 214 S.W.3d 202, 206 (Tex.App.—Texarkana 2007, no pet.); *Aguilar*, 72 S.W.3d at 732; *Martinez v. Daccarett*, 865 S.W.2d 161, 163 (Tex.App.—Corpus Christi 1993, no writ).

2. PTSES. Justice courts have original, exclusive jurisdiction over suits arising under the Photographic Traffic Signal Enforcement System (PTSES) statute, as long as the case is outside a municipality's territorial limits. Gov't Code §27.031(a)(4); *see* Transp. Code ch. 707. The PTSES is a camera system and vehicle sensor that can produce recorded images of a motor vehicle's license plate when the operator of the vehicle has violated the instructions of the traffic-control signal (e.g., running a red light). Transp. Code §707.001(3). The PTSES statute authorizes "local authorities" (i.e., counties, municipalities, and other local entities authorized to enact traffic laws) to impose a civil penalty, not to exceed $75, on the owner of any motor vehicle that is shown by the PTSES to have violated such a traffic law. *Id.* §§707.002, 707.007(1); *see also id.* §541.002(3) (defining "local authority"), §707.001(1) (same). A vehicle owner can contest the penalty by requesting an administrative adjudication hearing. *Id.* §707.014(a). If the owner is found liable by the hearing officer, she can appeal the decision in the justice court of the county in which the local authority is located, unless the local authority is a municipality. *Id.* §707.016(a).

§5.3 Relief available. Justice courts have jurisdiction to (1) foreclose mortgages and enforce liens on personal property when the amount in controversy is within their jurisdictional limits, (2) issue writs of attachment, garnishment, and sequestration in cases within their jurisdiction, and (3) enforce deed restrictions that do not involve a structural change to a dwelling. When a statute provides that the jurisdiction of the justice court is concurrent with that of a superior court, the justice court has all the authority of the superior court. Gov't Code §27.031(a)(3) (#1), §27.032 (#2), §27.034(a) (#3); *see, e.g., Malmgren v. Inverness Forest Residents Civic Club, Inc.*, 981 S.W.2d 875, 879 (Tex.App.—Houston [1st Dist.] 1998, no pet.) (because Gov't Code §27.034 states justice court's jurisdiction is concurrent with jurisdiction of district court, justice court can issue injunctions).

§5.4 Cases excluded. Justice courts do not have jurisdiction over the following suits: (1) on behalf of the State to recover penalties, forfeitures, and escheats, (2) for divorce, (3) for slander or defamation, (4) for title to land, and (5) to enforce liens on land. Gov't Code §27.031(b). Unless expressly permitted by the Legislature, justice courts cannot issue writs of mandamus or injunction. *See Bowles v. Angelo*, 188 S.W.2d 691, 693 (Tex.App.—Galveston 1945, no writ).

§5.5 Right to appeal. If the amount in controversy exceeds $250, a party may appeal from a justice court to a county court. Gov't Code §26.042(e); *see Kendziorski v. Saunders*, 191 S.W.3d 395, 409 (Tex.App.—Austin 2006, no pet.). The standard of review in the county court is de novo. *Kendziorski*, 191 S.W.3d at 409. The county court's

★

appellate jurisdiction is restricted to the jurisdictional limits of the justice court. *Id.* A county court cannot award damages that exceed the jurisdictional limits of the justice court unless additional damages have been incurred because of the passage of time (e.g., attorney fees). *E.g., id.* at 409-10 (portion of county court's award that exceeded justice court's jurisdictional limit was void because additional amount was not result of passage of time).

§6. SMALL-CLAIMS COURTS

Jury trials are available in small-claims courts. Gov't Code §28.035(a). The parties (even corporations) may represent themselves or may choose to be represented by attorneys. *Id.* §28.003(c), (e). Small-claims courts use a less-formal procedure than justice courts.

CAUTION

In 2011, the Legislature abolished small-claims courts by repealing Gov't Code chapter 28. Under newly enacted Gov't Code §27.060, justice courts must conduct proceedings in small-claims cases. These changes take effect May 1, 2013. Acts 2011, 82nd Leg., C.S., ch. 3, §5.09, eff. May 1, 2013. The Supreme Court, no later than May 1, 2013, must adopt new rules of procedure that define small-claims cases and ensure their fair, expeditious, and inexpensive resolution. See id. §5.07. As of the publication of this book, the Supreme Court had not proposed these new rules for small-claims cases. Check the Supreme Court website at www.supreme.courts.state.tx.us/ for the proposed and final rules.

---

§6.1 Presiding judge. A justice of the peace is the judge of the small-claims court. Gov't Code §28.002.

§6.2 Amount in controversy. Small-claims courts have concurrent jurisdiction with the justice courts in actions by any person for the recovery of money in which the amount involved does not exceed $10,000, excluding costs. Gov't Code §28.003(a). Thus, small-claims courts have jurisdiction over claims from $.01 to $10,000. See "Overlapping Monetary Jurisdiction of Trial Courts," chart 2-1, this page.

§6.3 Matters excluded. An action cannot be brought by (1) an assignee of the claim or other person seeking to bring an action on an assigned claim, (2) a person primarily engaged in the business of lending money at interest, or (3) a collection agency or collection agent. Gov't Code §28.003(b).

§6.4 Right to appeal. If the amount in controversy exceeds $250, a party may appeal from a small-claims-court judgment to the constitutional county court or county court at law. Gov't Code §28.052(a); *Sultan v. Mathew*, 178 S.W.3d 747, 748 (Tex.2005). The party may further appeal the judgment of the county court or county court at law to the court of appeals. Gov't Code §28.053(d).

§7. SUMMARY CHART OF AMOUNT IN CONTROVERSY

Chart 2-1, below, shows the overlapping monetary jurisdiction of the trial courts.

2-1. OVERLAPPING MONETARY JURISDICTION OF TRIAL COURTS					
$200,000.01 +	**District courts**				
$200,000			**County courts at law**		
$10,000		**Constitutional county courts**		**Justice courts**	**Small-claims courts**
$500.01 +	See §3.3, p. 138				
$200.01 +		See §4.1.1, p. 139	See §4.2.1, p. 142		
$.01 +				See §5.1, p. 146	See §6.2, this page

★

§8. SUMMARY CHART OF JURISDICTION

Chart 2-2, below, shows the various levels of civil courts in Texas and their jurisdiction. This chart is derived from the Office of Court Administration, *Court Structure of Texas*, at www.courts.state.tx.us.

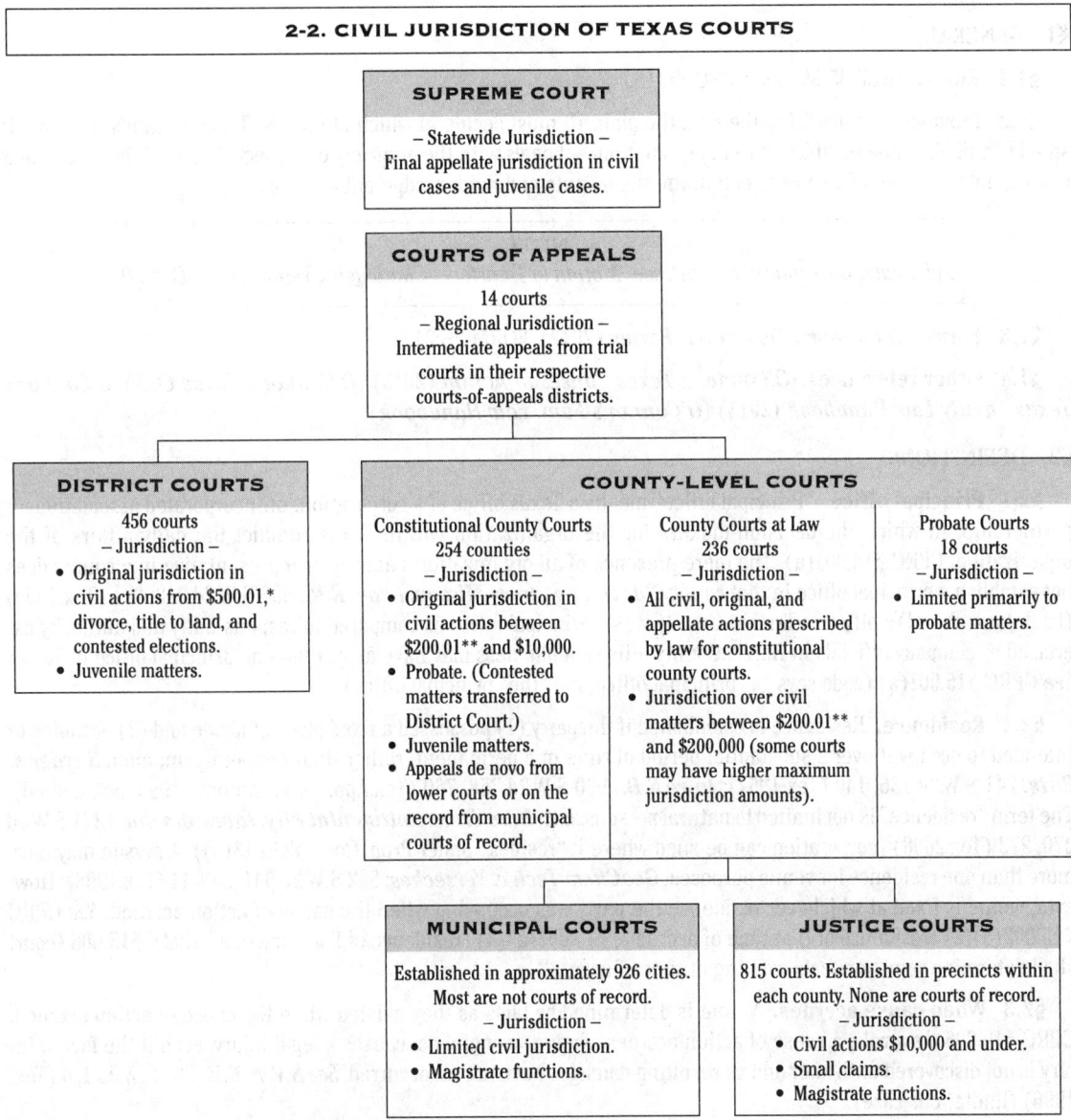

2-2. CIVIL JURISDICTION OF TEXAS COURTS

SUPREME COURT

– Statewide Jurisdiction –
Final appellate jurisdiction in civil cases and juvenile cases.

COURTS OF APPEALS

14 courts
– Regional Jurisdiction –
Intermediate appeals from trial courts in their respective courts-of-appeals districts.

DISTRICT COURTS

456 courts
– Jurisdiction –
• Original jurisdiction in civil actions from $500.01,* divorce, title to land, and contested elections.
• Juvenile matters.

COUNTY-LEVEL COURTS

Constitutional County Courts
254 counties
– Jurisdiction –
• Original jurisdiction in civil actions between $200.01** and $10,000.
• Probate. (Contested matters transferred to District Court.)
• Juvenile matters.
• Appeals de novo from lower courts or on the record from municipal courts of record.

County Courts at Law
236 courts
– Jurisdiction –
• All civil, original, and appellate actions prescribed by law for constitutional county courts.
• Jurisdiction over civil matters between $200.01** and $200,000 (some courts may have higher maximum jurisdiction amounts).

Probate Courts
18 courts
– Jurisdiction –
• Limited primarily to probate matters.

MUNICIPAL COURTS

Established in approximately 926 cities. Most are not courts of record.
– Jurisdiction –
• Limited civil jurisdiction.
• Magistrate functions.

JUSTICE COURTS

815 courts. Established in precincts within each county. None are courts of record.
– Jurisdiction –
• Civil actions $10,000 and under.
• Small claims.
• Magistrate functions.

* Based on Gov't Code §24.007(b) (eff. 1-1-12). See "Amount in controversy," §3.3, p. 138.
** Amount in controversy must exceed $200. See "Amount in controversy," §4.1.1, p. 139; "Amount in controversy," §4.2.1, p. 142.

VENUE

————————————————————————— ★ —————————————————————————

G. CHOOSING THE COURT—VENUE

In 1995, the Legislature reversed the bias in the venue scheme from one that favored the plaintiff's choice of venue to one that favored the defendant's choice. When researching the issue of venue, avoid venue cases that predate the 1995 revisions.

§1. GENERAL

§1.1 Rules. TRCP 85-89. See CPRC ch. 15.

§1.2 Purpose. Before filing the suit, the plaintiff must decide in which of the 254 Texas counties the lawsuit should be filed. Venue is different from jurisdiction—it deals with the propriety of prosecuting a suit in a particular county, not the power of a court to determine the dispute and render judgment.

NOTE

To challenge the venue of the suit, see "Motion to Transfer—Challenging Venue," ch. 3-C, p. 203.

---

§1.3 Forms. *O'Connor's Texas Civil Forms* (2012), FORM 2B:21.

§1.4 Other references. *O'Connor's Texas Causes of Action* (2013) (*O'Connor's Texas COA*); *O'Connor's Texas Family Law Handbook* (2013) (*O'Connor's Fam. Law Handbook*).

§2. DEFINITIONS

§2.1 Principal office. "Principal office" means a Texas office of a corporation, unincorporated association, or partnership, in which the decision-makers for the organization within Texas conduct the daily affairs of the organization. CPRC §15.001(a). The mere presence of an organization's agency or representative in a county does not establish a principal office in that county. *Id.*; *see, e.g.*, *In re Missouri Pac. R.R.*, 998 S.W.2d 212, 221 (Tex.1999) (Ps did not show D's office in Tarrant County was a principal office as compared to responsibility and authority exercised by company officials in Harris County office). A business may have more than one principal office in Texas. *See* CPRC §15.001(a) (code says "a" principal office, not "the" principal office).

§2.2 Residence. Residence is established if the party (1) possessed a fixed place of abode and (2) occupied or intended to occupy it over a substantial period of time in a permanent, rather than temporary, manner. *Snyder v. Pitts*, 241 S.W.2d 136, 140 (Tex.1951); *In re S.D.*, 980 S.W.2d 758, 760 (Tex.App.—San Antonio 1998, pet. denied). The term "residence" is not limited to natural persons. *E.g.*, *In re Transcontinental Rlty. Investors, Inc.*, 271 S.W.3d 270, 272 (Tex.2008) (corporation can be sued where it "resides" under Prop. Code §21.013(a)). A person may have more than one residence for venue purposes. *GeoChem Tech v. Verseckes*, 962 S.W.2d 541, 543-44 (Tex.1998). However, venue is fixed at whichever residence the party was occupying when the cause of action accrued. *See* CPRC §15.002(a)(2) (residence of D at time of accrual), §15.002(a)(4) (residence of P at time of accrual), §15.006 (court shall determine venue on facts existing at time of accrual).

§2.3 When cause accrues. Venue is determined by facts as they existed when the cause of action accrued. CPRC §15.006. As a rule, a cause of action accrues when a wrongful act causes a legal injury, even if the fact of injury is not discovered until later and all resulting damages have not yet occurred. *See S.V. v. R.V.*, 933 S.W.2d 1, 4 (Tex. 1996) (limitations case).

§2.4 Where cause accrues. A cause of action accrues in a county in which all or a substantial part of the events or omissions that give rise to the claim occurred. CPRC §15.002(a)(1); *see, e.g.*, *KW Constr. v. Stephens & Sons Concrete Contractors, Inc.*, 165 S.W.3d 874, 882-83 (Tex.App.—Texarkana 2005, pet. denied) (events that occurred in Lamar County pertaining to 2 of 4 elements of P's breach-of-contract claim qualified as substantial part of cause of action). A substantial part of the act or omission may occur in more than one county. *Velasco v. Texas Kenworth Co.*, 144 S.W.3d 632, 635 (Tex.App.—Dallas 2004, pet. denied); *Southern Cty. Mut. Ins. v. Ochoa*, 19 S.W.3d 452, 458-59 (Tex.App.—Corpus Christi 2000, no pet.). The phrase "a substantial part" restricts venue choices to fewer

✦

counties than other venue provisions. *Compare* CPRC §15.002(a)(1) ("in the county in which all or a substantial part of the events or omissions giving rise to the claim occurred") *with* §101.102(a) ("in the county in which the cause of action or a part of the cause of action arises"). In cases predating CPRC §15.002, the Supreme Court interpreted "occurred" to mean where the negligent act—not the results of the occurrence—took place. *E.g.*, *Leonard v. Abbott*, 366 S.W.2d 925, 927 (Tex.1963) (in suit for damage to crops from aerial spraying, venue was in county where aerial spraying occurred, not in county where crops were damaged). The parties may stipulate that all or a substantial part of the cause of action accrued in a particular county. *See In re Omni Hotel Mgmt.*, 159 S.W.3d 627, 628-29 (Tex.2005).

§3. COUNTY OF PROPER VENUE

The venue scheme describes "proper venue" in hierarchical terms. CPRC §15.001(b). All lawsuits must be brought according to the following venue scheme:

§3.1 Mandatory-venue provisions. A suit must be filed in the county of mandatory venue, as required by CPRC chapter 15, subchapter B, or other statutes prescribing mandatory venue. *See generally* CPRC §§15.011-15.020 (mandatory-venue provisions). See "Mandatory-Venue Provisions," §4, this page.

§3.2 General venue rule. If there is no mandatory venue, the general venue rule applies. See "General Venue Rule," §5, p. 155.

§3.3 Permissive-venue provisions. The permissive-venue provisions come into play if no mandatory provision applies. CPRC §15.001(b)(2). The permissive-venue provisions provide alternatives to the general venue rule. See "Permissive-Venue Provisions," §6, p. 155.

NOTE

If a plaintiff files suit in a county of proper venue either under the general rule or under a permissive exception, the defendant cannot transfer the case unless (1) a mandatory-venue provision controls or (2) the court transfers the case for convenience and in the interest of justice. See "Other considerations," §5.2, p. 155.

---

§4. MANDATORY-VENUE PROVISIONS

Mandatory venue is compulsory only if a defendant properly objects to the plaintiff's choice of venue. Most of the mandatory-venue provisions are listed in CPRC chapter 15, subchapter B. *See In re Sosa*, 370 S.W.3d 79, 81 (Tex. App.—Houston [14th Dist.] 2012, orig. proceeding). An action governed by any other statute prescribing mandatory venue outside of CPRC chapter 15 must be brought in the county required by that statute. CPRC §15.016; *In re Sosa*, 370 S.W.3d at 81.

§4.1 Mandatory venue in CPRC ch. 15.

1. Land dispute. A suit involving a land dispute must be filed in the county where all or part of the land is located. CPRC §15.011; *In re Applied Chem. Magnesias Corp.*, 206 S.W.3d 114, 117 (Tex.2006). Suits involving land disputes include suits to (1) recover real property, (2) recover an estate or interest in real property, (3) partition real property, (4) remove encumbrances on title to real property, (5) recover damages to real property, and (6) quiet title to real property. CPRC §15.011. Two venue facts must be established to invoke the mandatory-venue provision for land: (1) all or part of the land is located in the county of suit, and (2) the nature of the claim is enumerated in CPRC §15.011. *In re Stroud Oil Props., Inc.*, 110 S.W.3d 18, 24 (Tex.App.—Waco 2002, orig. proceeding); *see, e.g.*, *In re Applied Chem.*, 206 S.W.3d at 117-18 (suit to determine whether D had right to mine marble on P's land based on agreement was suit for recovery of land); *Kilgore v. Black Stone Oil Co.*, 15 S.W.3d 666, 670 (Tex. App.—Beaumont 2000, pet. denied) (suit for conversion of oil & gas and title to minerals was suit for recovery of land). The dominant purpose of the suit determines which venue provision controls. *Stiba v. Bowers*, 756 S.W.2d 835, 839 (Tex.App.—Corpus Christi 1988, no writ).

───────────────────── ✦ ─────────────────────

2. Landlord-tenant. A suit between a landlord and a tenant arising under a lease must be brought in the county where all or part of the real property is located. CPRC §15.0115(a). If another provision prescribes mandatory venue, that provision controls over the landlord-tenant provision in CPRC §15.0115(a). The term "lease" includes any written or oral agreement between the landlord and tenant that establishes or modifies the terms, conditions, or other provisions relating to the use and occupancy of the real property. *Id.* §15.0115(b). See *O'Connor's Texas COA*, "Landlord-Tenant Actions," ch. 16, p. 413.

3. Injunction against suit. An action to stay a proceeding in a suit must be filed in the county where the suit is pending. CPRC §15.012; *O'Quinn v. Hall*, 77 S.W.3d 452, 455 (Tex.App.—Corpus Christi 2002, orig. proceeding); *see also* CPRC §65.023(b) (writ of injunction to stay proceedings must be tried in the court in which suit is pending or judgment was rendered).

4. Injunction against execution of judgment. An action to restrain the execution of a judgment based on the invalidity of the judgment or writ of execution must be filed in the county where the judgment was rendered. CPRC §15.013; *see also id.* §65.023(b) (execution on judgment must be tried in the court in which suit is pending or judgment was rendered).

5. Mandamus against State. A petition for a writ of mandamus against the head of a department of the State of Texas must be filed in Travis County. CPRC §15.014.

6. Suit against county. A suit against a county must be filed in that county. CPRC §15.015; *Wichita Cty. v. Hart*, 917 S.W.2d 779, 781 (Tex.1996); *see also In re Fort Bend Cty.*, 278 S.W.3d 842, 844-45 (Tex.App.—Houston [14th Dist.] 2009, orig. proceeding) (in suit under TTCA, CPRC §15.015 controlled over CPRC §101.102(a)). A suit against a county official only in that person's individual capacity is not a suit against the county for purposes of CPRC §15.015. *See McIntosh v. Copeland*, 894 S.W.2d 60, 63-64 (Tex.App.—Austin 1995, writ denied).

7. Suit against political subdivisions. A suit filed against a political subdivision that is located in a county with a population of 100,000 or less must be brought in the county where the political subdivision is located. CPRC §15.0151(a).

8. Defamation or invasion of privacy. A suit for libel, slander, or invasion of privacy must be filed in one of the following: (1) the county where the plaintiff resided when the action accrued, (2) the county where the defendant resided when the suit was filed, (3) the county where any of the defendants reside, or (4) the domicile of any corporate defendant. CPRC §15.017; *Rodriguez v. Printone Color Corp.*, 982 S.W.2d 69, 71 (Tex.App.—Houston [1st Dist.] 1998, pet. denied); *Acker v. Denton Publ'g*, 937 S.W.2d 111, 114 (Tex.App.—Fort Worth 1996, no writ). See *O'Connor's Texas COA*, "Defamation," ch. 18-A, p. 507.

9. FELA & Jones Act. A suit brought under the Federal Employers' Liability Act (FELA) (45 U.S.C. §51) or the Jones Act (46 U.S.C. §688) must be brought in one of the following counties: (1) the county where all or a substantial part of the events or omissions giving rise to the claim occurred, (2) the county where the defendant's principal office in Texas is located, or (3) the county where the plaintiff resided when the cause of action accrued. CPRC §15.018(b) (FELA), §15.0181(c) (Jones Act); *In re Missouri Pac. R.R.*, 998 S.W.2d 212, 214 (Tex.1999). However, under the Jones Act, if a substantial part of the event or omission giving rise to the claim occurred on inland waters, ashore in Texas or a Gulf Coast state, or during an erosion-response project in Texas or a Gulf Coast state, suit may need to be brought in a different county. CPRC §15.0181(d), (e); *see also id.* §15.0181(a)(4), (a)(5) (defining "Gulf Coast state" and "inland waters").

10. Inmate litigation. A suit brought by an inmate for an action that accrued while the inmate was in a Texas prison operated by the Texas Department of Criminal Justice must be filed in the county where the facility is located. CPRC §15.019(a).

11. Contractual agreement for venue. Under CPRC §15.020, parties may agree to venue in writing in a "major transaction." That is, the suit must be filed in a certain county determined according to a written agreement signed before suit. *See* CPRC §15.020(a)-(c); *In re Texas Ass'n of Sch. Bds.*, 169 S.W.2d 653, 657 (Tex.2005).

✫

A major transaction is one in which the consideration has an aggregate value of at least $1 million. CPRC §15.020(a); *e.g.*, *In re Texas Ass'n*, 169 S.W.3d at 657 (insurance-premium payment of $41,973, not coverage amount of $17 million, was aggregate value of consideration for insurance-coverage agreement; no major transaction). By definition, it does not include a transaction for personal, family, or household purposes or for settlement of a personal-injury or wrongful-death suit. CPRC §15.020(a). Except for major transactions, the parties cannot contractually agree before suit to a venue contrary to a mandatory-venue provision or a specific venue statute. *See, e.g.*, *Leonard v. Paxson*, 654 S.W.2d 440, 441-42 (Tex.1983) (settlement agreement could not override venue in Fam. Code); *Fidelity Un. Life Ins. v. Evans*, 477 S.W.2d 535, 537 (Tex.1972) (contract agreement on venue could not override venue provision in injunction statute).

§4.2 Other mandatory-venue provisions.

1. CPRC.

(1) TTCA. The Texas Tort Claims Act (TTCA) provides that a suit under the TTCA "shall" be brought in the county where "the cause of action or a part of the cause of action arises." CPRC §101.102(a); *e.g.*, *In re Texas DOT*, 218 S.W.3d 74, 76 (Tex.2007) (suit should have been transferred from county where negligence was alleged to county of accident because Ps did not properly plead negligence claim); *Wilson v. Texas Parks & Wildlife Dept.*, 886 S.W.2d 259, 262 (Tex.1994) (suit should not have been transferred from county where negligence was alleged to county of accident).

(2) Injunction suit against Texas resident. CPRC §65.023(a) provides that, except as mandated by subsection (b), injunction suits against a resident party must be tried in a district or county court in the county where the party is domiciled. CPRC §65.023(a); *In re Continental Airlines, Inc.*, 988 S.W.2d 733, 736 (Tex.1998). For venue under CPRC §65.023(b), see "Injunction against suit," §4.1.3, p. 152; "Injunction against execution of judgment," §4.1.4, p. 152.

(3) Arbitration. Where to file an initial application in an arbitration proceeding depends on whether the arbitration agreement specifies the county of venue, whether the arbitration hearing has already taken place, and whether a suit involving an issue referable to arbitration is already pending in the court.

(a) Generally. A party generally must file an initial application in the county in which an adverse party resides or has a place of business, or, if an adverse party does not have a residence or place of business in Texas, in any county. CPRC §171.096(a).

(b) By contract. If the agreement to arbitrate specifies that an arbitration hearing be held in a particular Texas county, a party must file the initial application in that county. CPRC §171.096(b).

(c) After hearing. If an arbitration hearing has been held, a party must file an initial application for a proceeding arising from the arbitration in the county in which the hearing was held. CPRC §171.096(c); *e.g.*, *In re Lopez*, 372 S.W.3d 174, 175 (Tex.2012) (although arbitration agreement specified venue in Victoria County, parties disregarded agreement and arbitrated in Travis County; thus, under mandatory-venue provision in CPRC §171.096(c), proper venue for application to vacate arbitration award was Travis County).

(d) Pending proceeding. If there is a proceeding pending in a court that involves an issue that is referable to arbitration, a party must file an initial application in that court. CPRC §§171.024(a), 171.096(d).

2. Other statutes.

(1) Attorney disciplinary action. In a suit against an attorney for disciplinary action, venue is in the district court (1) in the county of the attorney's principal place of practice, (2) in the county of the attorney's residence, or (3) in the county where the misconduct occurred in whole or in part. Tex. R. Disciplinary P. 3.03; *see State Bar v. McGee*, 972 S.W.2d 770, 774 (Tex.App.—Corpus Christi 1998, no pet.). In all other instances, venue is in Travis County. Tex. R. Disciplinary P. 3.03.

(2) Condemnation. In a condemnation proceeding, if the owner resides in a county where part of the property is located, venue is in the county where the owner resides. Prop. Code §21.013(a). Otherwise, venue is in any county where at least part of the property is located. *Id.*

─────────────────────────── ✦ ───────────────────────────

(3) Probate & guardianship. Probate Code §§6, 8, and 610 establish venue for the probate of wills, letters testamentary or letters of administration, and appointments of guardians. Prob. Code §§6, 8, 610; *see also id.* §6A (any cause of action related to probate proceeding pending in statutory probate court), §6C (proceeding to determine heirship), §6D (breach of fiduciary duty by charitable entity), §433(a) (recovery of funds paid to State). However, in suits brought by or against a personal representative or a guardian, ward, or proposed ward for personal injury, death, or property damage, proper venue is determined under CPRC §15.007. Prob. Code §5B(b) (personal representative), §6B (same), §608(b) (guardian, ward, or proposed ward). See "Venue," ch. 2-F, §4.5.3, p. 146. Venue for probate depends largely on where the applicant resides, where the decedent was domiciled, or where the majority of the estate is located. In general, the court with venue over probate matters has venue over all similar matters if two or more courts have jurisdiction. Venue for guardianship of a minor depends largely on where the parents reside. Prob. Code §610.

───

NOTE

The 2011 legislative revisions to the Probate Code amending §§6 and 608 and enacting §§6A-6D apply only to actions filed or proceedings commenced on or after September 1, 2011. See Acts 2011, 82nd Leg., R.S., ch. 1085, §§43(b), 44, eff. Sept. 1, 2011 (§608); Acts 2011, 82nd Leg., R.S., ch. 1338, §§1.43(a), 3.02, eff. Sept. 1, 2011 (§§6, 6A-6D). Under the former law in Probate Code §607(e) for venue in guardianship proceedings, venue was properly determined under CPRC §15.007 only in suits by or against the personal representative for personal injury, death, or property damage.

───

(4) Trust. For suits involving a trust, venue is in any county where, during the four-year period before the suit was filed, the trustee resided or the trust was administered. Prop. Code §115.002(b), (c). An action against a corporate trustee may also be brought in the county of the trustee's principal office. *Id.* §115.002(c). If the settlor is deceased and an administration of the settlor's estate is pending in Texas, an action for the interpretation and administration of an inter vivos trust created by the settlor or a testamentary trust created by the settlor's will may be brought in a county in which (1) venue is generally proper for suits involving a trust under Property Code §115.002(b) or (c) or (2) the administration of the settlor's estate is pending. *Id.* §115.002(c-1); *see* Acts 2011, 82nd Leg., R.S., ch. 657, §§9(c), 10, eff. Sept. 1, 2011 (venue under §115.002(c-1) applies only to an action that began on or after Sept. 1, 2011). Venue may be transferred to another county for the convenience of the parties and witnesses, or if all parties agree. Prop. Code §115.002(d), (e).

(5) Family law. The Family Code has its own rules and procedures governing mandatory venue. For example, in an original suit affecting the parent-child relationship (SAPCR), venue is in the county where the child resides, unless an exception applies. Fam. Code §103.001. See *O'Connor's Fam. Law Handbook*, "Where to File SAPCR," ch. 4-A, §3, p. 326.

(6) Insurance contract. In a suit against an insurance company regarding coverage, Insurance Code §1952.110 provides two mandatory venues: (1) in the county where the policyholder or beneficiary who instituted the suit resided at the time of the accident or (2) in the county where the accident involving the uninsured or underinsured motorist's vehicle occurred. Ins. Code §1952.110. For the types of insurance suits to which permissive venue applies, see "Insurance contract," §6.1.4, p. 156.

§4.3 Miscellaneous rules governing mandatory venue.

1. Two counties of mandatory venue. Courts disagree on the proper method for determining venue when there are two counties of mandatory venue. *Compare* **In re Adan Volpe Props., Ltd.**, 306 S.W.3d 369, 375 (Tex.App.—Corpus Christi 2010, orig. proceeding) (P can choose between two conflicting mandatory-venue provisions), *and* **Marshall v. Mahaffey**, 974 S.W.2d 942, 947 (Tex.App.—Beaumont 1998, pet. denied) (same), *with* **In re Sosa**, 370 S.W.3d 79, 81 (Tex.App.—Houston [14th Dist.] 2012, orig. proceeding) (no venue statute gives P the right to choose between two conflicting mandatory-venue provisions; court must resolve conflict by statutory-construction analysis).

✦

2. Permissive & mandatory counties. When there is a county of mandatory venue and a county of permissive venue, the suit should be brought in—and on motion must be transferred to—the county of mandatory venue. *See* CPRC §15.004; TRCP 86(3)(b); *see, e.g.*, **Wichita Cty. v. Hart**, 917 S.W.2d 779, 781 (Tex.1996) (whistleblower suit against county was governed by mandatory provision, not by permissive-venue provision).

3. Multiple claims. If any claim in a suit is controlled by a mandatory-venue provision, all properly joined claims arising from the same transaction, occurrence, or series of transactions or occurrences are controlled by the same provision. CPRC §15.004; **Madera Prod. v. Atlantic Richfield Co.**, 107 S.W.3d 652, 658 (Tex.App.—Texarkana 2003, pet. denied). See "Multiple Parties & Claims," §7, p. 157.

§5. GENERAL VENUE RULE

§5.1 Selecting venue if no mandatory venue. If no mandatory-venue provision applies, the plaintiff must decide where to file the suit according to the general venue rule. Under the general venue rule, a suit must be brought in one of the following counties:

1. In the county where all or a substantial part of the events giving rise to the claim occurred. CPRC §15.002(a)(1).

2. In the county of the defendant's residence when the cause of action accrued, if the defendant is a natural person. *Id.* §15.002(a)(2).

3. In the county of the defendant's principal office in Texas, if the defendant is not a natural person (i.e., if defendant is a corporation). *Id.* §15.002(a)(3).

4. In the county where the plaintiff resided when the action accrued, if none of the other provisions applies. *Id.* §15.002(a)(4). The purpose of CPRC §15.002(a)(4) is to provide venue for a plaintiff's suit against a nonresident defendant when the cause of action arises outside Texas.

§5.2 Other considerations. The present venue system does not favor the plaintiff's choice of venue. Thus, in choosing the county for suit, the plaintiff should consider the counties to which the trial court may transfer the case "for convenience" and "in the interest of justice." CPRC §15.002(b). When the defendant makes a timely motion to transfer venue based on CPRC §15.002(b), the court may transfer a suit from a county of proper venue to any other county of proper venue if the court finds all of the following:

1. Maintenance in the county of suit will work an economic and personal hardship on the defendant. CPRC §15.002(b)(1).

2. The balance of interests of all the parties favors the action being brought in the other county. *Id.* §15.002(b)(2).

3. The transfer will not work an injustice on any other party. *Id.* §15.002(b)(3).

NOTE

The court's decision on a convenience transfer is not appealable and is not reversible error. CPRC §15.002(c). See "No appeal of convenience transfer," ch. 3-C, §5.1, p. 213.

---

§6. PERMISSIVE-VENUE PROVISIONS

The permissive-venue provisions provide venue alternatives to the general venue rule. Most of the permissive-venue provisions are listed in CPRC chapter 15, subchapter C.

§6.1 Permissive venue in CPRC ch. 15.

1. Executor, administrator, or guardian. CPRC §15.031 is a permissive-venue provision that governs suits against an executor, administrator, or guardian. The provisions in CPRC §15.031 control over any conflicting venue provisions in the Probate Code in a suit against an executor, administrator, or guardian for personal injury, death, or property damage. CPRC §15.007.

★

(1) Negligent act. In a suit against an executor, administrator, or guardian for a negligent act or omission of the person whose estate is being represented, venue is permissive in the county where the negligent act or omission occurred. CPRC §15.031.

(2) Debt of estate. In a suit for a debt of an estate, venue is permissive in the county where the estate is being administered. CPRC §15.031.

2. Breach of warranty. In a suit against a manufacturer of consumer goods for breach of warranty, venue is permissive in any of the following counties: (1) the county where all or a substantial part of the events or omissions giving rise to the claim occurred, (2) the county where the manufacturer has its principal office in Texas, or (3) the county where the plaintiff resided when the cause of action accrued. CPRC §15.033.

3. Written contract.

(1) County of performance. In a suit on a written contract that states the contract is to be performed in a certain county or a definite place in that county, venue is permissive either in the specified county or in the county of the defendant's domicile. CPRC §15.035(a); *see also Midland Nat'l Life Ins. v. Bridges*, 889 S.W.2d 17, 19 (Tex.App.—Eastland 1994, writ denied) (promissory note); *Trafalgar House Oil & Gas, Inc. v. De Hinojosa*, 773 S.W.2d 797, 798 (Tex.App.—San Antonio 1989, no writ) (oil lease). For an exception to CPRC §15.035(a), see "Contract in consumer transaction," §6.1.3(2), this page.

(2) Contract in consumer transaction. In a suit by a creditor involving a consumer transaction, venue is permissive in the county where the defendant signed the contract or where the defendant resided when the suit was filed. CPRC §15.035(b). Subsection (b) of CPRC §15.035 controls over subsection (a) and cannot be waived. *See id.* §15.035(b). Thus, if a consumer contract identifies the creditor's home county as the place of payment, the creditor cannot sue there unless it is also the county where the defendant signed the contract or the county of the defendant's residence.

NOTE

It is a false, misleading, or deceptive act under the DTPA to file suit based on a consumer transaction involving a written contract signed by the defendant-consumer in any county other than the county (1) where the defendant-consumer resides at the time the suit is brought or (2) where the defendant-consumer signed the contract. Bus. & Com. Code §17.46(b)(23).

---

4. Insurance contract. CPRC §15.032 provides two permissive venues for suits on insurance policies: (1) in a suit against a fire, marine, or inland insurance company, venue is permissive in the county where the insured property is located, or (2) in a suit against any life, accident, or health-insurance company, venue is permissive in the county where the insurance company's principal office is located, in the county where the loss occurred, or in the county where the policyholder or beneficiary resided when the cause of action accrued. CPRC §15.032. Suits against an insurance company regarding coverage are governed by mandatory-venue provisions in the Insurance Code. See "Insurance contract," §4.2.2(6), p. 154.

§6.2 Other permissive-venue statutes. An action governed by any other statute prescribing permissive venue may be brought in the county allowed by that statute. CPRC §15.038. The following are some permissive-venue provisions in other codes.

1. DTPA. A suit under the DTPA may be filed only in a county (1) where venue is proper under CPRC chapter 15 (except in a suit against an insurer relating to uninsured-motorist coverage) or (2) where the defendant or its authorized agent solicited the transaction that forms the basis of the suit. Bus. & Com. Code §17.56.

2. Whistleblower. A whistleblower suit brought by a state employee may be filed either in the county where the cause of action arose or in Travis County. Gov't Code §554.007(a). The venue provision in a whistleblower suit is permissive. *City of Fort Worth v. Zimlich*, 29 S.W.3d 62, 72 (Tex.2000); *Wichita Cty. v. Hart*, 917 S.W.2d 779, 782 (Tex.1996). For whistleblower suits filed by local-government employees, see Gov't Code §554.007(b).

———————————— ★ ————————————

§7. MULTIPLE PARTIES & CLAIMS

§7.1 Multiple plaintiffs. In a suit with multiple plaintiffs, a plaintiff or intervenor may remain in the suit only if it is able to establish one of the following:

1. Proper venue. Venue in the county of suit is proper for that plaintiff, independent of every other plaintiff. CPRC §15.003(a); *Surgitek, Bristol-Myers Corp. v. Abel*, 997 S.W.2d 598, 602 (Tex.1999); *Shell Oil Co. v. Baran*, 258 S.W.3d 719, 721 (Tex.App.—Beaumont 2008, pet. abated 1-30-09); *O'Quinn v. Hall*, 77 S.W.3d 438, 448 (Tex.App.—Corpus Christi 2002, no pet.).

2. Proper joinder. Venue in the county of suit meets the requirements for proper joinder of multiple plaintiffs under CPRC §15.003(a)(1)-(a)(4). *Surgitek*, 997 S.W.2d at 602; *Shell Oil*, 258 S.W.3d at 721; *O'Quinn*, 77 S.W.3d at 448. See "Joinder proper under CPRC §15.003(a)," ch. 3-C, §2.6.4(2), p. 206.

§7.2 Multiple claims. If a plaintiff properly joins two or more claims arising from the same transaction, occurrence, or series of transactions or occurrences, and one of the claims is governed by a mandatory-venue provision in CPRC chapter 15, subchapter B, the mandatory-venue provision controls venue for the suit. CPRC §15.004; *In re Stroud Oil Props., Inc.*, 110 S.W.3d 18, 23 (Tex.App.—Waco 2002, orig. proceeding). CPRC chapter 15 venue provisions trump conflicting venue provisions in the Probate Code. See "Probate & guardianship," §4.2.2(3), p. 154; "Executor, administrator, or guardian," §6.1.1, p. 155.

§7.3 Multiple defendants.

1. Venue against all. In a suit with multiple defendants, if the plaintiff establishes proper venue against one defendant, then venue is proper for all defendants as long as the claims arise from the same transaction, occurrence, or series of transactions or occurrences. CPRC §15.005; *American Home Prods. v. Clark*, 38 S.W.3d 92, 94 (Tex.2000).

2. No waiver. A waiver of venue by one defendant does not prevent another defendant from appropriately challenging venue. CPRC §15.0641; *WTFO, Inc. v. Braithwaite*, 899 S.W.2d 709, 718 (Tex.App.—Dallas 1995, no writ); *see, e.g., Pearson v. Jones Co.*, 898 S.W.2d 329, 331-32 (Tex.App.—Eastland 1994, no writ) (two Ds' waiver of venue by filing answers does not waive third D's venue objection).

§7.4 Counterclaim, cross-claim, or third-party claim. Venue for the main action establishes venue for a defendant's counterclaim or cross-claim or for a third-party claim if the claim is properly joined under the TRCPs or any applicable statute. CPRC §15.062(a). When the original defendant joins a third-party defendant, venue for the main action establishes venue for any claim by the plaintiff against that third-party defendant arising from the same transaction, occurrence, or series of transactions or occurrences. *Id.* §15.062(b).

H. SERVING THE DEFENDANT WITH SUIT

§1. GENERAL

§1.1 Rules. TRCP 15-17, 99, 103, 105-109a, 118-124, 237. See CPRC ch. 17; Bus. Orgs. Code §§5.201, 5.251-5.257.

§1.2 Purpose.

1. Generally. "Service of citation" is a term that describes the formal process by which a plaintiff gives a defendant notice that it has been sued. *Texas Nat. Res. Conserv. Comm'n v. Sierra Club*, 70 S.W.3d 809, 813 (Tex. 2002). The purpose of the citation is to give the court jurisdiction over the defendant, to satisfy due-process requirements, and to give the defendant the opportunity to appear and defend. *Cockrell v. Estevez*, 737 S.W.2d 138, 140 (Tex.App.—San Antonio 1987, no writ). The citation and a copy of the plaintiff's petition, which is attached, are collectively referred to as the "process." Service of process is accomplished when the citation and a copy of the petition are delivered to the defendant, or the defendant is given notice of the suit through some other authorized means. *See* TRCP 99(a). The plaintiff, not the process server, is responsible for ensuring that service is properly accomplished.

✦

Id.; *Primate Constr., Inc. v. Silver*, 884 S.W.2d 151, 153 (Tex.1994); *see, e.g.*, *In re Buggs*, 166 S.W.3d 506, 508 (Tex. App.—Texarkana 2005, orig. proceeding) (P's duty, not clerk's, to locate newspaper and pay for service by publication).

2. Default judgment. The rules for the issuance of citation, the service of process, and the return of process are especially important when the court renders a default judgment. A judgment cannot be rendered against a defendant unless the defendant was served with process, accepted or waived service, or made an appearance. TRCP 124; *Werner v. Colwell*, 909 S.W.2d 866, 869-70 (Tex.1995); *Mapco, Inc. v. Carter*, 817 S.W.2d 686, 687 (Tex.1991). Because the ordinary presumptions of valid service do not apply in an appeal of a no-answer default judgment, the judgment will be reversed unless there is strict compliance with the rules. *Primate Constr.*, 884 S.W.2d at 152. See "Sufficiency of service," ch. 7-A, §3.4, p. 589.

§1.3 Timetables & forms. Timetable, Pretrial Motions, p. 1216; Timetable, No-Answer Default Judgment, p. 1225; *O'Connor's Texas Civil Forms* (2012), FORMS 2B:10-19, 2H.

§1.4 Other references. Anderson, *Transnational Litigation Involving Mexican Parties*, 25 St. Mary's L.J. 1059 (1994); Jones, *International Judicial Assistance: Procedural Chaos & a Program for Reform*, 62 Yale L.J. 515 (1953) (referred to as Jones, *International Judicial Assistance*); Miller, *Misnomers: Default Judgments & Strict Compliance with Service of Process Rules*, 46 Baylor L.Rev. 633 (1994); *O'Connor's Federal Rules * Civil Trials* (2013) (*O'Connor's Federal Rules*).

§2. REQUIREMENTS FOR THE CITATION

The citation, which is issued by the court clerk after payment of a fee, must comply with TRCP 15 and 99. The clerk must keep a copy of the citation in the court's file. TRCP 99(a).

§2.1 Style of process. The style of the process must be "The State of Texas." TRCP 15, 99(b)(1). The process must be directed to any sheriff or constable in the State of Texas. TRCP 15.

§2.2 Information about suit. The citation must identify the suit by showing the cause number. TRCP 99(b)(6) (called "file" number). If the citation omits the cause number or contains the wrong number, the citation is fatally defective. *Martinez v. Wilber*, 810 S.W.2d 461, 463 (Tex.App.—San Antonio 1991, writ denied). Service of process with one cause number will not support a suit with a different cause number. *See, e.g.*, *Finlay v. Jones*, 435 S.W.2d 136, 137 (Tex.1968) (D was served under cause number 144,608 instead of 144,607).

§2.3 Information about court. The citation must contain the following information about the court:

1. Identification of court. The citation must contain the name and location of the court and the address of the clerk who issued the citation. TRCP 99(b)(3), (b)(11).

2. Signature & seal. The citation must be signed by the clerk and issued under the seal of the court. TRCP 15, 99(b)(2); *Verlander Enters. v. Graham*, 932 S.W.2d 259, 262 (Tex.App.—El Paso 1996, no writ).

§2.4 Information about P. The citation must contain the following information about the plaintiff:

1. Identification of P. The citation must contain the name of the plaintiff. TRCP 99(b)(7).

2. P's attorney. The citation must contain the name and address of the plaintiff's attorney. TRCP 99(b)(9). If the plaintiff is pro se, the citation must contain the plaintiff's address. *Id.*

§2.5 Information about D.

1. Identification of D.

(1) Name. The citation must contain the defendant's correct name. TRCP 99(b)(7); *see Amato v. Hernandez*, 981 S.W.2d 947, 949 (Tex.App.—Houston [1st Dist.] 1998, pet. denied). If the correct defendant was incorrectly named in the petition, the error is a misnomer, and a default judgment against that defendant will be affirmed if (1) the correct defendant was actually served and (2) the petition describes the facts in such a way that

---

★

---

the correct defendant knows it is the intended defendant. *Union Pac. Corp. v. Legg*, 49 S.W.3d 72, 78 (Tex.App.—Austin 2001, no pet.). If the wrong defendant was named in the petition, the error is a misidentification, and a default judgment must be reversed. *See, e.g., id.* (P named and served Union Pacific Railroad, not Union Pacific Corp.). See "Misnomer vs. misidentification," ch. 2-B, §3.3.1(2), p. 98.

(2) Capacity. When the defendant is sued in a representative capacity, the defendant must be identified in the petition by that capacity (e.g., trustee, executor). *See, e.g., Werner v. Colwell*, 909 S.W.2d 866, 870 (Tex. 1995) (judgment could not be rendered against D as trustee when she was sued only as individual). See "Capacity," ch. 2-B, §3.2.2, p. 98.

(3) Address for service. The citation should include the defendant's address for service of process. *See* TRCP 99(b), 106.

(a) Defendant is resident. In most cases, the citation should contain a statement identifying the address as either the defendant's residence or its usual place of business. When service is by order under TRCP 106, the order is considered part of the record; if the order identifies the address as the defendant's residence or usual place of business, the citation does not need to contain the same statement. *Brown v. Magnetic Media, Inc.*, 795 S.W.2d 41, 43 (Tex.App.—Houston [1st Dist.] 1990, no writ).

(b) Defendant is nonresident. When the defendant is a nonresident, the petition should use the exact language from the long-arm statute, TRCP 108, or other applicable statute to describe the place for service. The general long-arm statute requires that the petition and citation to be served on the Secretary of State include a statement of the nonresident's name and home or home-office address where the process is to be served. CPRC §17.045(a). See "Service on Secretary of State," §5, p. 163.

2. Citation directed to D. The citation must "be directed to the defendant." TRCP 99(b)(8); *see, e.g., Plains Chevrolet, Inc. v. Thorne*, 656 S.W.2d 631, 633 (Tex.App.—Waco 1983, no writ) (service void because citation directed to G.M. Corporation, not Plains Chevrolet). TRCP 15, however, also requires the process to "be directed to any sheriff or any constable within the State of Texas." Two courts of appeals have harmonized these rules and determined that the citation must be expressly directed to the defendant under TRCP 99 and may also be addressed to the sheriff or constable under TRCP 15. *Williams v. Williams*, 150 S.W.3d 436, 445 (Tex.App.—Austin 2004, pet. denied); *see, e.g., Barker CATV Constr., Inc. v. Ampro, Inc.*, 989 S.W.2d 789, 792-93 (Tex.App.—Houston [1st Dist.] 1999, no pet.) (overruling other First Court of Appeals cases that held citation defective because it was directed to sheriff as well as D). The omission of directions to the sheriff or constable on the form of the citation will not render it void. *Williams*, 150 S.W.3d at 445.

§2.6 Identification of D's agent for service. The citation must name the agent for service and state the address for service on the agent if the defendant is to be served through an agent. Even though an agent is to be served for the defendant, the citation must be directed to the defendant and not to the agent. *See Barker CATV Constr., Inc. v. Ampro, Inc.*, 989 S.W.2d 789, 792 (Tex.App.—Houston [1st Dist.] 1999, no pet.). If the citation is directed to the agent, it does not confer jurisdiction over the defendant. *Dan Edge Motors, Inc. v. Scott*, 657 S.W.2d 822, 823 (Tex.App.—Texarkana 1983, no writ); *see, e.g., Verlander Enters. v. Graham*, 932 S.W.2d 259, 261 (Tex.App.—El Paso 1996, no writ) (citation was directed to a vice president instead of the corporation). When the citation names one person as agent for service, but the return of the citation shows it was served on another person, the trial court does not acquire jurisdiction over the defendant. *Pharmakinetics Labs. v. Katz*, 717 S.W.2d 704, 706 (Tex. App.—San Antonio 1986, no writ).

1. Corporation. When the defendant is a corporation, the citation should be directed to the corporation and name as agent for service the president, any vice president, or the registered agent. *Dan Edge Motors*, 657 S.W.2d at 823.

2. Partnership. When the defendant is a partnership, the citation should be directed to the defendant-partnership and name the individual partners for service. *See* CPRC §17.022; *Shawell v. Pend Oreille Oil & Gas*

★

Co., 823 S.W.2d 336, 337-38 (Tex.App.—Texarkana 1991, writ denied); *Fincher v. B&D Air Conditioning & Heating Co.*, 816 S.W.2d 509, 513 (Tex.App.—Houston [1st Dist.] 1991, writ denied). If a claim is also brought against a partner in her individual capacity, the citation must be directed to the individual partner. *See Kao Holdings, L.P. v. Young*, 261 S.W.3d 60, 64 (Tex.2008).

§2.7 Critical dates. The citation must contain the following dates:

1. Date petition filed. The citation must state the date the plaintiff filed the petition. TRCP 99(b)(4). If the petition's filing date is omitted, the defect is fatal. *See Hance v. Cogswell*, 307 S.W.2d 277, 278-79 (Tex.App.—Austin 1957, no writ). If the citation states an impossible date for filing, the defect is fatal. *E.g.*, *McGraw-Hill, Inc. v. Futrell*, 823 S.W.2d 414, 417 (Tex.App.—Houston [1st Dist.] 1992, writ denied) (date of service was 17 days before suit filed); *George v. Elledge*, 261 S.W.2d 201, 201 (Tex.App.—San Antonio 1953, no writ) (date of service was seven months before suit filed).

2. Date citation issued. The citation must state the date it was issued. TRCP 15, 99(b)(5); *London v. Chandler*, 406 S.W.2d 203, 204 (Tex.1966). The date the citation is issued may be different from the date the clerk signs and seals the citation. *London*, 406 S.W.2d at 204. The citation is issued when the clerk authorizes delivery and gives the citation to an officer or other authorized person for service. *Id.* If the date the citation was issued is omitted, the citation is not invalid and may be amended. *Id.; see* TRCP 118.

3. Time to answer. The citation for district and county courts must state that the defendant is required to file a written answer by 10:00 a.m. on the first Monday after the expiration of 20 days from the date of service. TRCP 15, 99(b), (c). This requirement must be stated in the exact language of TRCP 99(c). If the 20th day falls on a Monday, the answer must be filed by the next Monday. The citation for justice courts must make the same statement as the citation for district and county courts, but it has a shorter deadline—10 days. TRCP 534(b).

§2.8 Warning of default. The citation must notify the defendant that if it does not file an answer, judgment by default may be rendered for the relief demanded in the petition. TRCP 99(b)(12). This requirement must be stated in the exact language of TRCP 99(c).

§2.9 Attachment of petition. The plaintiff's original petition must be attached to the citation. TRCP 106(a)(1); *see* TRCP 99(a). If the plaintiff amends the petition before service by adding parties, claims, or damages, the amended petition must be attached to the citation. *See, e.g.*, *Primate Constr., Inc. v. Silver*, 884 S.W.2d 151, 152-53 (Tex.1994) (default J reversed because D served with original petition, which did not name it as D, instead of amended petition); *Seeley v. KCI USA, Inc.*, 100 S.W.3d 276, 277-78 (Tex.App.—San Antonio 2002, no pet.) (same). See "Description of documents," §9.4.3, p. 169; "Amending the petition," §10.1, p. 171.

§2.10 Endorsement on process. The officer or other authorized person serving process must endorse on it the day and hour when she received it. TRCP 16, 105; *In re Z.J.W.*, 185 S.W.3d 905, 907 (Tex.App.—Tyler 2006, no pet.); *see, e.g.*, *Melendez v. John R. Schatzman, Inc.*, 685 S.W.2d 137, 138 (Tex.App.—El Paso 1985, no writ) (officer did not endorse day and hour he received process). See "Who May Serve Process," §3, this page. When process is served, the officer or other authorized person must also endorse on the process the manner in which she issued it and the time and place it was served. TRCP 16. See "Methods of Service," §4, p. 161.

§3. WHO MAY SERVE PROCESS

The plaintiff should make sure that service is accomplished by a person who is authorized by rule, statute, or court order to serve process. *See* TRCP 103. Service of process by a person who is not authorized is invalid and will not support a default judgment. Process includes citation and other notices, writs, orders, and papers issued by the court. *Id.*

§3.1 Court clerk. The court clerk is authorized to serve process by registered or certified mail and to serve citation by publication. TRCP 103.

§3.2 Officers. A sheriff, constable, or other person authorized by law may serve process in Texas. TRCP 103; *see* Local Gov't Code §85.021(a) (sheriff), §86.021(c) (constable). Sheriffs may serve process anywhere in Texas; nothing in Local Gov't Code §85.021 limits sheriffs to serving process only in their own counties. Constables, however, may serve process only in their own and contiguous counties. Local Gov't Code §86.021(c), (d). Only a sheriff

⭐

or constable can serve the following types of process without a court order: for an action for forcible entry and detainer; for a writ that requires taking actual possession of a person, property, or thing; and for an enforcement action that must be physically performed by the person delivering process. TRCP 103 & cmt.

§3.3 Authorized by court order. TRCP 103 permits service of process by persons authorized by court order.

1. Trial-court order. A person may serve process if she has no interest in the lawsuit, is at least 18 years old, and is authorized by law or a written court order. TRCP 103; *see Mayfield v. Dean Witter Fin. Servs.*, 894 S.W.2d 502, 505 (Tex.App.—Austin 1995, writ denied); *cf.* Ins. Code §804.201(b) (service on insurance company). See "Not interested person," §3.4, this page. The process must include a copy of the court order that authorized the person to serve process; without it, the person cannot effectuate service. *See, e.g., HB & WM, Inc. v. Smith*, 802 S.W.2d 279, 281 (Tex.App.—San Antonio 1990, no writ) (no order authorizing commercial process server).

2. Supreme Court order. A person who is certified by order of the Supreme Court may serve process. TRCP 103. The Supreme Court issued guidelines for a person to be certified to serve process under TRCP 103 (district and county courts) and TRCP 536(a) (justice courts). The person must file an application with the Texas Process Server Review Board and must complete a course on civil process service. *See* Tex.Sup.Ct. Order, Misc. Docket No. 06-9142, 209 S.W.3d (Tex.Cases) xvii (eff. Oct. 27, 2006).

§3.4 Not interested person. No person who is a party or who is interested in the outcome of the suit may serve process. TRCP 103. A person who is "interested in the outcome of a suit" includes the party, the party's attorney, and their agents and employees. *See, e.g., Palomin v. Zarsky Lumber Co.*, 26 S.W.3d 690, 695 (Tex.App.—Corpus Christi 2000, pet. denied) (bookkeeper for P's attorney was not interested person because she was off duty when she served D and she received additional pay for service); *Jackson v. U.S.*, 138 F.R.D. 83, 87-88 (S.D.Tex.1991) (secretary who served process was interested person because she was employee of P's attorney).

§4. METHODS OF SERVICE

Process may be served on the defendant according to several different methods. If the citation restricts service to a particular method, service must be made according to the citation's terms. *See, e.g., Smith v. Commercial Equip. Leasing Co.*, 678 S.W.2d 917, 917-18 (Tex.1984) (service invalid because citation was restricted to personal service and process was served by certified mail).

NOTE

A citation cannot be served on Sunday, except in cases of injunction, attachment, garnishment, sequestration, or distress proceedings. TRCP 6; Nichols v. Nichols, 857 S.W.2d 657, 659 (Tex. App.—Houston [1st Dist.] 1993, no writ).

---

§4.1 Service by U.S. mail. Service by certified mail, return receipt requested, is the most popular method of service. It is much less expensive and time-consuming than any other method of service. Service by certified mail may be made by (1) the court clerk, (2) the sheriff or constable or any other person authorized by law, (3) any person 18 years of age or older, authorized by law or by order of court, or (4) any person certified by order of the Supreme Court. TRCP 103, 106(a)(2); *see P&H Transp. v. Robinson*, 930 S.W.2d 857, 859 (Tex.App.—Houston [1st Dist.] 1996, writ denied) (authorized private process server can serve by mail); *cf.* Gov't Code §28.013(c) (service in small-claims courts). CPRC §17.026(a) authorizes the court clerk or a party or its representative to serve the Secretary of State with process by certified mail, return receipt requested.

§4.2 Service by personal delivery. Any person who has the authority to serve process (by law or court order) may serve the defendant by delivering the process to the defendant personally. TRCP 106(a)(1); *see Woodall v. Lansford*, 254 S.W.2d 540, 541 (Tex.App.—Fort Worth 1953, no writ). When the authorized person hands the citation to the defendant, the defendant must be made to understand that it is a lawsuit and that the defendant is being served. *See Texas Indus. v. Sanchez*, 521 S.W.2d 133, 135-36 (Tex.App.—Dallas 1975), *writ ref'd n.r.e.*, 525 S.W.2d 870 (Tex.1975).

✮

§4.3 Service by court order. If personal service or service by mail was attempted but was unsuccessful, the court may authorize another method of service. TRCP 106(b); *Hubicki v. Festina*, 226 S.W.3d 405, 408 (Tex.2007); *State Farm Fire & Cas. Co. v. Costley*, 868 S.W.2d 298, 299 (Tex.1993). When a court orders substituted service under TRCP 106, the only authority for the service is the order itself. *Dolly v. Aethos Comms. Sys.*, 10 S.W.3d 384, 388 (Tex.App.—Dallas 2000, no pet.). The order must contain specific instructions for the process server to follow or it is defective. *Steinke v. Mann*, 276 S.W.3d 608, 610 (Tex.App.—Waco 2008, no pet.); *see* TRCP 107(f) (when service authorized under TRCP 106, proof of service must be made in the manner ordered by the court).

1. Motion & affidavit. The plaintiff must file a motion for substituted service supported by an affidavit describing the unsuccessful attempts at service under TRCP 106(a)(1) or (a)(2), and stating a place where the defendant can probably be found (e.g., usual place of residence or business). TRCP 106(b); *Costley*, 868 S.W.2d at 299; *In re Sloan*, 214 S.W.3d 217, 222 (Tex.App.—Eastland 2007, orig. proceeding); *see Hubicki*, 226 S.W.3d at 408. The party should make multiple attempts at service before moving for substituted service; one attempt is insufficient. *See, e.g., Hubicki*, 226 S.W.3d at 408 (single attempt at service by certified mail; substituted service ineffective); *Costley*, 868 S.W.2d at 298-99 (ten failed attempts at personal service; substituted service effective). If the plaintiff does not file an affidavit verifying the unsuccessful efforts to serve the defendant, the trial court cannot order substitute service. *Wilson v. Dunn*, 800 S.W.2d 833, 836 (Tex.1990). A party needs to show only that attempts failed under either TRCP 106(a)(1) or (a)(2). *Costley*, 868 S.W.2d at 299 n.2.

2. Types of service. Under TRCP 106(b), the following types of service are permissible:

(1) Delivery of process to any authorized person over 16 years of age at the location of the defendant's usual place of residence or business, or any other place where the defendant may be found, as stated in the affidavit. TRCP 106(b)(1); *Walker v. Brodhead*, 828 S.W.2d 278, 280 (Tex.App.—Austin 1992, writ denied); *see Olympia Marble & Granite v. Mayes*, 17 S.W.3d 437, 444-45 (Tex.App.—Houston [1st Dist.] 2000, no pet.).

(2) Service of process in any other manner that the affidavit or other evidence shows will be reasonably effective to give the defendant notice of the suit. TRCP 106(b)(2); *e.g., Costley*, 868 S.W.2d at 299 (first-class mail service); *see, e.g., Dolly*, 10 S.W.3d at 388-89 (posting copy on D's front door).

§4.4 Service by publication. Service by publication is a form of substituted service in which a small notice is published in the classified section of a local newspaper. *In re E.R.*, ___ S.W.3d ___ (Tex.2012) (No. 11-0282; 7-6-12). The intent of the notice is to inform a defendant that her rights are at stake. *Id.* Service by publication is a poor substitute for actual service and should be used as a last resort. *Id.; see Mullane v. Central Hanover Bank & Trust Co.*, 339 U.S. 306, 315 (1950).

1. Requirements.

(1) **Unknown defendant.** Service by publication is authorized for use in actions against a defendant whose residence is unknown (TRCP 109), against unknown heirs or stockholders of defunct corporations (TRCP 111), against unknown owners or claimants of an interest in land (TRCP 112), or for delinquent ad valorem taxes (TRCP 117a). Service by publication also may be authorized by order of the court under TRCP 106(b)(2). However, if a defendant's identity is known, service by publication is generally inadequate. *In re E.R.*, ___ S.W.3d at ___.

(2) **Diligent search.** The party serving citation must conduct a diligent search for the defendant before resorting to service by publication. *In re E.R.*, ___ S.W.3d at ___. A diligent search must include inquiries that someone who really wants to find the defendant would make, and should be measured by the quality, rather than the quantity of the search. *Id.* A lack of diligence makes service by publication ineffective. *Id.*

2. Form. The form of citation and technicalities of service are set out in TRCP 114-117. *See, e.g., Wiebusch v. Wiebusch*, 636 S.W.2d 540, 542 (Tex.App.—San Antonio 1982, no writ) (notice of nature of suit is necessary for service by publication); *see also Wood v. Brown*, 819 S.W.2d 799, 800 (Tex.1991) (attorney's affidavit did not satisfy TRCP 109).

3. Representation. A defendant served by publication who does not answer or appear must be represented by an attorney appointed by the court. TRCP 244. See "Trial," ch. 10-B, §10.1, p. 800.

★

4. Challenging. A defendant served by publication can file a motion for new trial up to two years after the judgment. TRCP 329(a). See "MNT After Service by Publication," ch. 10-B, §10, p. 799.

§5. SERVICE ON SECRETARY OF STATE

Several statutory provisions designate the Secretary of State as an agent for service of process. For the list of the statutes, see www.sos.state.tx.us/statdoc/statutes-service-of-process.shtml. The two most important of these involve service on a nonresident and service on a corporation. See "Long-arm service," §5.3, p. 164; "Service on corporation," §5.4, p. 164. The other statutes include CPRC §17.091 (nonresident in a delinquent-tax case), §101.102(c) (Tort Claims Act); Insurance Code §§541.255(b)(3) & 804.301 (insurance company); and Probate Code §105A(b) (foreign corporate fiduciary). For information about serving the Secretary of State, call the Citations Unit at (512) 463-5560.

§5.1 General rules. When serving the Secretary of State with process, the plaintiff should consult the specific statutes and observe the following general rules:

1. Service on Secretary. The plaintiff may accomplish service on the Secretary of State by certified mail, by delivery by a qualified officer or a private process server, or by any other means permitted by rule or statute. CPRC §17.026(a) (certified mail is sent by clerk or party). Personal service on the Secretary of State is not necessary. *See Capitol Brick, Inc. v. Fleming Mfg. Co.*, 722 S.W.2d 399, 401 (Tex.1986) (service under long-arm statute). Two copies of the process must be served on the Secretary of State. 1 Tex. Admin. Code §71.21(a). When process is served by a sheriff or constable, the plaintiff must include an additional copy of the process for the return. When process is served by a private process server, the plaintiff must include copies of the order appointing the process server. When process is served by mail, the citation should be sent to the Secretary of State's post-office address; when process is served by delivery, it should be sent to the street address of the Citations Unit.

2. Necessary information. The citation must contain the following information: (1) the defendant's name, (2) the defendant's address for service, and (3) when specified in the statute, the proper identification of the address. *See* CPRC §17.045(a); 1 Tex. Admin. Code §71.21(a). The citation should also identify the statute authorizing service. If the statute authorizing service identifies the address by name, the plaintiff should use the same language. For example, for service on a nonresident under CPRC §17.045(a), the plaintiff should identify the address as that of the nonresident's "home" or "home office." *World Distribs., Inc. v. Knox*, 968 S.W.2d 474, 477-78 (Tex. App.—El Paso 1998, no pet.); *see Wachovia Bank v. Gilliam*, 215 S.W.3d 848, 849-50 (Tex.2007). If the plaintiff does not state that the address is the nonresident's home or home office and the face of the record does not show that it is, service is invalid. *Wachovia Bank*, 215 S.W.3d at 849-50; *World Distribs.*, 968 S.W.2d at 477-78.

Chart 2-3, below, lists some of the statutory identifications of the addresses for service on defendants through the Secretary of State.

2-3. SERVICE THROUGH SECRETARY OF STATE	
Statute	**Identify address as the**
1	Bus. Orgs. Code §5.253(b)(1)	Most recent address of entity on file
2	Bus. Orgs. Code §9.011(b)(6)	Address of foreign entity
3	Long-Arm Statute—CPRC §17.045(a)	Home or home office
4	Ins. Code §804.302	Last known home office or principal place of business

3. Fees. The fee payable to the Secretary of State is $40 for each defendant for maintaining a record of service of process and $15 for the issuance of a certificate of service. Gov't Code §405.031(a)(1), (a)(4).

4. Secretary forwards process. Once served, the Secretary of State will mail a copy of the citation and petition to the defendant by registered or certified mail, return receipt requested. *See* CPRC §17.045(b)-(d) (notice to nonresident). Service is complete on the defendant when the Secretary of State is served, not when the defendant receives notice. *Bonewitz v. Bonewitz*, 726 S.W.2d 227, 230 (Tex.App.—Austin 1987, writ ref'd n.r.e.); *see also*

⭐

Whitney v. L&L Rlty. Corp., 500 S.W.2d 94, 96 (Tex.1973) (service under long-arm statute). In other words, the Secretary is the agent for receiving process on the defendant's behalf, not for serving process. *Campus Invs. v. Cullever*, 144 S.W.3d 464, 466 (Tex.2004).

§5.2 Proof of service. Proof the citation was served on the Secretary of State is not enough to support jurisdiction over the defendant; the plaintiff must prove the Secretary of State forwarded the process to the defendant. *Whitney v. L&L Rlty. Corp.*, 500 S.W.2d 94, 96 (Tex.1973). To prove the Secretary forwarded the process, the plaintiff should secure a certificate (sometimes referred to as a "Whitney certificate") from the Secretary of State. *Capitol Brick, Inc. v. Fleming Mfg. Co.*, 722 S.W.2d 399, 401 (Tex.1986). The certificate showing the Secretary forwarded process to the defendant is conclusive proof that process was served. *Campus Invs. v. Cullever*, 144 S.W.3d 464, 466 (Tex.2004); *see Wachovia Bank v. Gilliam*, 215 S.W.3d 848, 850 (Tex.2007); *Capitol Brick*, 722 S.W.2d at 401. Once the Secretary of State forwards process to the defendant, the defendant is considered served even if the process is returned to the Secretary of State. *See, e.g.*, *Campus Invs.*, 144 S.W.3d at 465 (process returned marked "Attempted—Not Known"); *Zuyus v. No'Mis Comm.*, 930 S.W.2d 743, 746 (Tex.App.—Corpus Christi 1996, no writ) (process returned with notation "unclaimed"); *BLS Limousine Serv. v. Buslease, Inc.*, 680 S.W.2d 543, 546 (Tex.App.—Dallas 1984, writ ref'd n.r.e.) (process returned with notation "refused"); *see also Mahon v. Caldwell, Haddad, Skaggs, Inc.*, 783 S.W.2d 769, 772 (Tex.App.—Fort Worth 1990, no writ) (D's agent, not D, signed return receipt). *But see GMR Gymnastics Sales, Inc. v. Walz*, 117 S.W.3d 57, 59 (Tex.App.—Fort Worth 2003, pet. denied) (return labeled "not deliverable as addressed, unable to forward" was prima facie evidence that address P provided to Secretary of State was incorrect; thus D not served). If the Secretary of State forwards the process to the wrong address because of a typographical error, the service is invalid. *E.g.*, *Royal Surplus Lines Ins. v. Samaria Baptist Ch.*, 840 S.W.2d 382, 383 (Tex.1992) (citation mailed to 1201 Bassie, instead of 1201 Bessie, was invalid).

PRACTICE TIP

Before taking a default judgment, the plaintiff should contact the Secretary of State's Citations Unit at (512) 463-5560 and request a certificate of service. The certificate will show the date the Secretary of State's office received the process, the date it forwarded the process to the defendant, and the date it received the return receipt.

---

§5.3 Long-arm service.

1. Minimum contacts. The test for service on a nonresident is whether Texas has provisions for service on a defendant under the facts presented and, if so, whether service on the defendant violates the Due Process Clause of the U.S. Constitution. See "Grounds," ch. 3-B, §2.3, p. 189.

2. Long-arm allegations in petition. When serving a nonresident defendant by service on the Secretary of State, the face of the plaintiff's petition must support long-arm service. *McKanna v. Edgar*, 388 S.W.2d 927, 929 (Tex.1965). Thus, the petition must allege (1) the Secretary of State is the agent for service on the nonresident, (2) the nonresident engaged in business in Texas, (3) the nonresident does not maintain a regular place of business in Texas, (4) the nonresident does not have a designated agent for service of process, and (5) the lawsuit arises from the nonresident's business in Texas. CPRC §17.044(b); *Lozano v. Hayes Wheel Int'l*, 933 S.W.2d 245, 247-48 (Tex.App.—Corpus Christi 1996, no writ); *South Mill Mushrooms Sales, Inc. v. Weenick*, 851 S.W.2d 346, 350 (Tex.App.—Dallas 1993, writ denied). For other allegations regarding service on a nonresident, see CPRC §17.044(a), (c), (d). See *O'Connor's Texas Forms*, FORMS 2B:14-18.

§5.4 Service on corporation. Domestic and foreign corporations that do business in Texas must designate and maintain registered agents for service in Texas. Bus. Orgs. Code §5.201(a), (b); *Ingram Indus. v. U.S. Bolt Mfg.*, 121 S.W.3d 31, 34 (Tex.App.—Houston [1st Dist.] 2003, no pet.); *see Interaction, Inc. v. State*, 17 S.W.3d 775, 779 (Tex.App.—Austin 2000, pet. denied); *see also* Bus. Orgs. Code §9.004(b) (registration procedure for registered agents).

★

NOTE

A registered agent may be an individual or an organization. Bus. Orgs. Code §5.201(b)(2). If the registered agent is an organization, the organization must have an employee available at the registered office during normal business hours to receive service of process. Id. §5.201(d). Any employee may receive service. Id.

---

1. Diligence. The record must show on its face that the plaintiff used reasonable diligence to serve the corporation's president, vice president, or registered agent at its registered office. *See* Bus. Orgs. Code §§5.251(1)(B), 5.255(1); *Wright Bros. Energy, Inc. v. Krough*, 67 S.W.3d 271, 274 (Tex.App.—Houston [1st Dist.] 2001, no pet.); *National Multiple Sclerosis Soc'y v. Rice*, 29 S.W.3d 174, 176 (Tex.App.—Eastland 2000, no pet.); *Maddison Dual Fuels, Inc. v. Southern Un. Co.*, 944 S.W.2d 735, 738 (Tex.App.—Corpus Christi 1997, no writ); *see, e.g., Marrot Comms. v. Town & Country Prtshp.*, 227 S.W.3d 372, 378 (Tex.App.—Houston [1st Dist.] 2007, pet. denied) (record did not show reasonable diligence because affidavit describing attempted service was not made part of record until after trial court signed default J). To establish reasonable diligence, the record must reflect more than just some problem with the address. *Wright Bros.*, 67 S.W.3d at 275 (return citation must explain why service was not accepted); *see, e.g., Ingram Indus.*, 121 S.W.3d at 34 (return stated that registered agent was not at registered address and that location had been occupied by another person for the past ten years; one attempt at service constituted reasonable diligence). If the corporation's president, vice president, or registered agent cannot be found through reasonable diligence, the plaintiff can serve the Secretary of State. *Interaction, Inc.*, 17 S.W.3d at 779.

2. Secretary forwards process. Once served, the Secretary of State will immediately mail a copy of the citation and petition to the defendant by registered mail or certified mail, return receipt requested. Bus. Orgs. Code §5.253. If the Secretary of State forwards the process to the wrong address because the corporation did not notify the Secretary of State of a change of address of its registered office, the service is still valid. *Tankard-Smith, Inc. Gen. Contractors v. Thursby*, 663 S.W.2d 473, 475-76 (Tex.App.—Houston [14th Dist.] 1983, writ ref'd n.r.e.).

§6. WHO MAY BE SERVED

There are two issues regarding the proper person to serve. First, when the defendant is not an individual, who is the person that is authorized to receive service of process for the defendant? Second, when service on the defendant is not possible, who can be served as a substitute for the defendant? See chart 2-4, below.

2-4. PROPER PERSON TO SERVE		
If defendant is	**Actual service is made on**	**Constructive service may be made on**
1	Authorized foreign corporation	President, vice president, or registered agent. Bus. Orgs. Code §§5.201(a), (b), 5.255(1).	Sec'y of State. CPRC §17.044; Bus. Orgs. Code §5.251.
2	Corporation	President, vice president, or registered agent. Bus. Orgs. Code §§5.201(a), (b), 5.255(1).	Sec'y of State. CPRC §17.044; Bus. Orgs. Code §5.251.
3	County	County judge. CPRC §17.024(a).	
4	Credit union	Registered agent. CPRC §17.028(c).	President or vice president. CPRC §17.028(c).
5	Estate	Executor or administrator. *See* Prob. Code §33(e). If suit involves title to land, executor or administrator and heirs must be served. CPRC §17.002.	Sec'y of State (only for estate of nonresident defendant). CPRC §17.044(c).
6	Financial institution	A registered agent. CPRC §17.028(b).	President or branch manager at any office located in the state. CPRC §17.028(b).
7	Foreign country	Depends on U.S. treaties and laws of foreign country.	

SERVING DEFENDANT

★

	If defendant is	Actual service is made on	Constructive service may be made on
	**2-4. PROPER PERSON TO SERVE (CONTINUED)**		
8	Foreign insurance company	Agent for service. Ins. Code §804.103(b).	Commissioner of Insurance. Ins. Code §804.103(c); *see id.* §883.103(a)(3).
9	Foreign railway	The defendant. *See* TRCP 108.	Some train conductors, CPRC §17.093(1); agent in Texas who arranges transport on railway, *id.* §17.093(2); person in charge of Texas office, *id.* §17.043; Sec'y of State, *id.* §17.044.
10	Incorporated city, town, or village	Mayor, clerk, secretary, or treasurer. CPRC §17.024(b).	
11	Individual	The defendant. TRCP 106(a).	Various persons by court order, TRCP 106(b), 109a; by publication, TRCP 109; agent or clerk at defendant's office, CPRC §17.021; TRCP 106(b); Sec'y of State, CPRC §17.044.
12	Inmate	Agent for service, who is a designated employee at the facility where defendant is confined. CPRC §17.029(c).	
13	Insurance company	President, active vice president, secretary, or attorney-in-fact at home office or principal place of business, or by leaving copy of process at home office or principal place of business during business hours. Ins. Code §804.101(b).	Commissioner of Insurance. Ins. Code §804.102(c).
14	Minor	Minor or guardian of minor's estate if one has been appointed. *In re Estate of Bean*, 120 S.W.3d 914, 920 (Texark. 2003, denied); *see* Prob. Code §768.	Same as permitted on an individual. See Individual, above.
15	Nonprofit corporation	President, vice president, registered agent, or members of executive committee. Bus. Orgs. Code §§5.201(a), (b), 5.255(1), (5).	Sec'y of State. Bus. Orgs. Code §5.251.
16	Nonresident or out-of-state defendant	The defendant. TRCP 108.	Person in charge of Texas office, CPRC §17.043; Sec'y of State, *id.* §17.044.
17	Out-of-state defendant driver	The defendant. CPRC §17.065(a); *see* TRCP 108.	Chair of the Texas Transportation Commission. CPRC §17.062.
18	Out-of-U.S. defendant	The defendant. TRCP 108a.	Person in charge of Texas office, CPRC §17.043; Sec'y of State, *id.* §17.044. Service in foreign country depends on Hague Convention, U.S. treaties, and laws of foreign country. *See* TRCP 108a.
19	Partnership	Partners. CPRC §§17.022, 31.003.	Agent or clerk at partnership office, CPRC §17.021(a); Sec'y of State, *id.* §17.044.
20	School district	President of school board or superintendent. CPRC §17.024(c).	
21	State of Texas	Sec'y of State. CPRC §101.102(c).	
22	Trust	Trustee. *See* Prop. Code §§114.083, 114.084. If charitable trust, also serve Att'y Gen. *Id.* §115.011(c).	Sec'y of State (only for nonresident trustee). *Cf.* CPRC §17.044(c) (constructive service on Sec'y of State for nonresident executor, administrator, or heir of nonresident decedent).

───────────── ★ ─────────────

2-4. PROPER PERSON TO SERVE (CONTINUED)		
If defendant is	Actual service is made on	Constructive service may be made on
23 Unincorporated business association	President, secretary, treasurer, or general agent. TRCS art. 6134.	Agent or clerk at association's office, CPRC §17.021(a); Sec'y of State, *id.* §17.044.
24 United States	U.S. Att'y Gen., D.C. and Assistant U.S. Attorney (AUSA) for district where suit is brought, or designated AUSA or clerk.	

§7. DEADLINE FOR SERVICE

§7.1 Within limitations. The process should be served on the defendant within the limitations period.

§7.2 Outside limitations. Service outside the limitations period is valid only if both of the following conditions are met:

1. Petition filed. The petition was filed within the limitations period. *Gant v. DeLeon*, 786 S.W.2d 259, 260 (Tex.1990).

2. Diligence in service. The plaintiff exercised diligence in procuring service of process on the defendant. *Ashley v. Hawkins*, 293 S.W.3d 175, 179 (Tex.2009); *Gant*, 786 S.W.2d at 260; *Harrell v. Alvarez*, 46 S.W.3d 483, 485 (Tex.App.—El Paso 2001, no pet.); *Roberts v. Padre Island Brewing Co.*, 28 S.W.3d 618, 621 (Tex.App.—Corpus Christi 2000, pet. denied). When a plaintiff serves the defendant after limitations, the date of service relates back to the date of filing the suit if the plaintiff exercised diligence in effecting service. *Proulx v. Wells*, 235 S.W.3d 213, 215 (Tex.2007); *Gant*, 786 S.W.2d at 260. The test for diligence is whether the plaintiff (1) acted as an ordinary, prudent person would act under the same circumstances and (2) was diligent up until the time the defendant was served. *Ashley*, 293 S.W.3d at 179; *Proulx*, 235 S.W.3d at 216; *see, e.g.*, *Tarrant Cty. v. Vandigriff*, 71 S.W.3d 921, 925 (Tex.App.—Fort Worth 2002, pet. denied) (delay of service for over two years showed no due diligence as a matter of law). Repeated ineffective attempts at service do not constitute due diligence if easily available and more effective alternatives are ignored. *Carter v. MacFadyen*, 93 S.W.3d 307, 314-15 (Tex.App.—Houston [14th Dist.] 2002, pet. denied). If the plaintiff learns, or through the exercise of due diligence should have learned, that the clerk has not fulfilled her duty to issue citation in compliance with TRCP 99, the plaintiff must ensure that the defendant is served. *Allen v. Rushing*, 129 S.W.3d 226, 230-31 (Tex.App.—Texarkana 2004, no pet.); *e.g.*, *Tarrant Cty.*, 71 S.W.3d at 926 (although error in clerk's office was reason for 28-month delay in serving D, P should have discovered through diligence that D was not properly served); *Boyattia v. Hinojosa*, 18 S.W.3d 729, 734 (Tex.App.—Dallas 2000, pet. denied) (after three months, clerk's duty to serve citation was replaced by P's duty to ensure that service was actually completed).

───────────────────────────

PRACTICE TIP

*To prove diligence, the plaintiff should keep a log of its attempts to serve the defendant. The log must show constant and continual attempts at service. Any period in which there are no attempts to serve the defendant may negate diligence. **Ashley**, 293 S.W.3d at 179; **Proulx**, 235 S.W.3d at 216; see, e.g., **Webster v. Thomas**, 5 S.W.3d 287, 291 (Tex.App.—Houston [14th Dist.] 1999, no pet.) (four-month delay, when efforts to procure service were careless and not persistent, negated diligence); **Butler v. Ross**, 836 S.W.2d 833, 835-36 (Tex.App.—Houston [1st Dist.] 1992, no writ) (no activity for over five months after return of unserved original citation); **Hansler v. Mainka**, 807 S.W.2d 3, 5 (Tex.App.—Corpus Christi 1991, no writ) (no request for process for five months after suit filed). If there was a gap between service attempts, the plaintiff should explain the reason for the gap. **Ashley**, 293 S.W.3d at 179.*

★

§8. WAIVER OF SERVICE

§8.1 Voluntary appearance. A defendant who is legally competent may appear in open court and waive service of process in person, by an attorney, or by an authorized agent. TRCP 120; *Gonzalez v. Phoenix Frozen Foods, Inc.*, 884 S.W.2d 587, 589 (Tex.App.—Corpus Christi 1994, no writ); *see also Shamrock Oil Co. v. Gulf Coast Nat. Gas, Inc.*, 68 S.W.3d 737, 739 (Tex.App.—Houston [14th Dist.] 2001, pet. denied) (appearance by corporate attorney did not waive service on corporate officers). Once a defendant makes a voluntary appearance, the court must note the appearance on the docket and enter it in the minutes. TRCP 120.

§8.2 Written waiver. A defendant who is legally competent may waive service of process in writing. TRCP 119. To be effective, the waiver must (1) expressly state that the defendant waives service, (2) acknowledge that the defendant received a copy of the plaintiff's petition, (3) be in writing, (4) be signed by the defendant or its authorized agent or attorney, (5) be verified before someone other than an attorney in the case, (6) be dated after the suit was filed, and (7) be filed among the papers of the case. TRCP 119; *see, e.g., Deen v. Kirk*, 508 S.W.2d 70, 71 (Tex.1974) (waiver ineffective because it was signed before suit filed); *Dunn v. Wilson*, 752 S.W.2d 15, 17 (Tex.App.—Fort Worth 1988) (document ineffective because it did not state D waived service), *aff'd*, 800 S.W.2d 833 (Tex.1990). In a divorce action, the waiver must include the defendant's mailing address. TRCP 119; *Travieso v. Travieso*, 649 S.W.2d 818, 820 (Tex.App.—San Antonio 1983, no writ) (default judgment). *But see Spivey v. Holloway*, 902 S.W.2d 46, 48 (Tex.App.—Houston [1st Dist.] 1995, no writ) (address can be waived by consent judgment).

§8.3 Presuit waiver. There is one statutorily created exception that permits a presuit waiver of service. A waiver of service in an affidavit to relinquish parental rights, signed before suit is filed, effectively waives service of process. *See* Fam. Code §§102.009(a)(7), 161.103(c), 161.106(a); *Brown v. McLennan Cty. C.P.S.*, 627 S.W.2d 390, 393 (Tex. 1982).

§9. PROOF OF SERVICE – THE RETURN

The officer or other authorized person issuing the citation must complete a return of service. TRCP 107(a). The return of service is not a trivial, formulaic document. *Primate Constr., Inc. v. Silver*, 884 S.W.2d 151, 152 (Tex.1994); *Rivers v. Viskozki*, 967 S.W.2d 868, 870 (Tex.App.—Eastland 1998, no pet.). Unless the plaintiff strictly complies with the rules relating to proper service, the service is invalid. *Primate Constr.*, 884 S.W.2d at 152; *Union Pac. Corp. v. Legg*, 49 S.W.3d 72, 77 (Tex.App.—Austin 2001, no pet.). Strict compliance is determined by whether the exact procedural requirements have been met, not whether the intended party received notice of the lawsuit. *Union Pac.*, 49 S.W.3d at 78; *see In re Z.J.W.*, 185 S.W.3d 905, 908 (Tex.App.—Tyler 2006, no pet.) (strict compliance means literal compliance with the rules). However, strict compliance does not require "obeisance to the minutest detail." *Williams v. Williams*, 150 S.W.3d 436, 443-44 (Tex.App.—Austin 2004, pet. denied); *Westcliffe, Inc. v. Bear Creek Constr., Ltd.*, 105 S.W.3d 286, 290 (Tex.App.—Dallas 2003, no pet.); *Herbert v. Greater Gulf Coast Enters.*, 915 S.W.2d 866, 871 (Tex.App.—Houston [1st Dist.] 1995, no writ).

§9.1 Endorsed or attached. The return may be, but does not have to be, endorsed on or attached to the citation. TRCP 107(a); *see* CPRC §17.030(b)(1)(A).

§9.2 Verification. The return generally does not have to be verified. *See* CPRC §17.030(c). The return must be verified, however, if it is signed by an authorized person other than a sheriff, constable, or court clerk and it is not signed under penalty of perjury. TRCP 107(e). See "Other authorized person," §9.6.2, p. 171.

§9.3 Filing return. The return and any document to which it is attached must be filed and may be filed electronically or by fax, if those methods of filing are available. TRCP 107(g); *see* CPRC §17.030(b)(1)(B).

§9.4 Recitation of due service. The plaintiff must make sure the court's record of the case reflects that the defendant was properly served. *Primate Constr., Inc. v. Silver*, 884 S.W.2d 151, 153 (Tex.1994). That responsibility involves checking the statements on the return, including the preprinted statements on the form used by the sheriff's or constable's office. *Id.* The return and any document to which it is attached must include the following information. *See* TRCP 107(b).

—— ★ ——

1. Case information. The return must identify the case name, the cause number, and the court where the case is filed. TRCP 107(b)(1), (b)(2).

2. Date of receipt of process by server. The return must show the date and time the officer or other authorized person received the process for service. TRCP 107(b)(4).

3. Description of documents. The return must include a description of what was served. TRCP 107(b)(3). That is, the return must state that a copy of the citation and a copy of the petition were served on the defendant. *See* TRCP 106(a)(1). The return must correctly identify the petition served on the defendant. *See, e.g.*, *Primate Constr.*, 884 S.W.2d at 152 (recitation that original petition was served, instead of second petition, was fatal); *Shamrock Oil Co. v. Gulf Coast Nat. Gas, Inc.*, 68 S.W.2d 737, 738-39 (Tex.App.—Houston [14th Dist.] 2001, pet. denied) (recitation that "[blank] petition" was served was fatal); *Ortiz v. Avante Villa at Corpus Christi, Inc.*, 926 S.W.2d 608, 612 (Tex.App.—Corpus Christi 1996, writ denied) (recitation that "petition attached" was served was sufficient); *Herbert v. Greater Gulf Coast Enters.*, 915 S.W.2d 866, 871 (Tex.App.—Houston [1st Dist.] 1995, no writ) (recitation that "complaint" was served was sufficient); *Woodall v. Lansford*, 254 S.W.2d 540, 542 (Tex. App.—Fort Worth 1953, no writ) (recitation that "copy of the citation" was served instead of petition was fatal). The return must show that the defendant was named as a defendant in the petition. *See, e.g.*, *Primate Constr.*, 884 S.W.2d at 152-53 (default J reversed because return showed D served with original petition but not named as D until amended petition); *Seeley v. KCI USA, Inc.*, 100 S.W.3d 276, 277-78 (Tex.App.—San Antonio 2002, no pet.) (same).

4. Person or entity served. The return must identify the person or entity served. TRCP 107(b)(5).

(1) Fatal errors. The following mistakes in the name on the return made the return invalid: • The return did not include "Jr." *Uvalde Country Club v. Martin Linen Sup. Co.*, 690 S.W.2d 884, 885 (Tex.1985). • The citation named one person as agent for service on the defendant, but the return showed service on another person. *All Commercial Floors, Inc. v. Barton & Rasor*, 97 S.W.3d 723, 726-27 (Tex.App.—Fort Worth 2003, no pet.). • The return did not identify the defendant-corporation as the entity served. *Benefit Planners, L.L.P. v. Rencare, Ltd.*, 81 S.W.3d 855, 861 (Tex.App.—San Antonio 2002, pet. denied); *see, e.g.*, *Barker CATV Constr., Inc. v. Ampro, Inc.*, 989 S.W.2d 789, 793 (Tex.App.—Houston [1st Dist.] 1999, no pet.) (return defective because name of "James Barker" alone on return did not establish he was D's agent for service or that D-corporation was actually served). • The return did not give the complete and correct name of the defendant. *Hercules Concrete Pumping Serv. v. Bencon Mgmt. & Gen. Contracting Corp.*, 62 S.W.3d 308, 310-11 (Tex.App.—Houston [1st Dist.] 2001, pet. denied); *see, e.g.*, *North Carolina Mut. Life Ins. v. Whitworth*, 124 S.W.3d 714, 720 (Tex.App.—Austin 2003, pet. denied) (return omitted "Life" from North Carolina Mutual Life Insurance Company). • The return contained only the surname. *Exposition Apts. Co. v. Barba*, 630 S.W.2d 462, 465 (Tex.App.—Austin 1982, no writ) ("Mr. Thompson"). • The return did not include the correct middle initial. *Zaragoza v. Morales*, 616 S.W.2d 295, 296 (Tex.App.—Eastland 1981, writ ref'd n.r.e.). • The return did not identify the defendant as a corporation, as it was identified in the petition and citation. *Brown-McKee, Inc. v. J.F. Bryan & Assocs.*, 522 S.W.2d 958, 959 (Tex.App.—Texarkana 1975, no writ).

(2) Nonfatal errors. The following mistakes in the name on the return did not make the return invalid: • The return omitted "Group, L.L.C." *Myan Mgmt. Grp. v. Adam Sparks Family Revocable Trust*, 292 S.W.3d 750, 753-54 (Tex.App.—Dallas 2009, no pet.). • The return omitted an accent mark and the word "Inc." and substituted the symbol "@" for the word "at." *Ortiz*, 926 S.W.2d at 613. • The return omitted "Ltd." after "Co." *Stephenson v. Corporate Servs.*, 650 S.W.2d 181, 183-84 (Tex.App.—Tyler 1983, writ ref'd n.r.e.).

5. Service address. The return must show the address of service. TRCP 107(b)(6); *see Jacksboro Nat'l Bank v. Signal Oil & Gas Co.*, 482 S.W.2d 339, 341-42 (Tex.App.—Tyler 1972, no writ).

6. Manner of service or attempted service. The return must identify the manner of delivery of service or attempted service. TRCP 107(b)(8); *see Wohler v. La Buena Vida in W. Hills, Inc.*, 855 S.W.2d 891, 892 (Tex.App.—Fort Worth 1993, no writ). The return should also show that the citation was served on a person capable of accepting service. *Faggett v. Hargrove*, 921 S.W.2d 274, 277 (Tex.App.—Houston [1st Dist.] 1995, no writ), *overruled on other grounds*, *Barker CATV Constr., Inc. v. Ampro, Inc.*, 989 S.W.2d 789 (Tex.App.—Houston [1st Dist.]

———————————— ✦ ————————————

1999, no pet.); *see, e.g.*, ***Reed Elsevier, Inc. v. Carrollton-Farmers Branch ISD***, 180 S.W.3d 903, 905-06 (Tex. App.—Dallas 2005, pet. denied) (return did not show person served was authorized to accept service); ***Curry Motor Freight, Inc. v. Ralston Purina Co.***, 565 S.W.2d 105, 106-07 (Tex.App.—Amarillo 1978, no writ) (return merely said service was accomplished by "serving" a person); *see also* ***Dolly v. Aethos Comms. Sys.***, 10 S.W.3d 384, 388 (Tex. App.—Dallas 2000, no pet.) (return that stated D was served "in person," but also noted that process was "posted to front door," was inherently inconsistent).

7. Name of server. The return must identify the name of the person who served or attempted to serve the defendant. TRCP 107(b)(9).

(1) Sheriffs & constables. When public officials such as sheriffs and constables are authorized to effect service, they may personally serve process, or they may serve process through their deputies. ***Pratt v. Moore***, 746 S.W.2d 486, 487 (Tex.App.—Dallas 1988, no writ). When citation is served by a deputy, the deputy must indicate who employed him as a deputy. ***Houston Pipe Coating Co. v. Houston Freightways, Inc.***, 679 S.W.2d 42, 45 (Tex.App.—Houston [14th Dist.] 1984, writ ref'd n.r.e.). See "Officers," §3.2, p. 160.

(2) Person authorized by trial court. If the trial court appointed a disinterested person to serve process, the return must show service by that person, and the name of the person in the order must match the name of the person who served process. *See, e.g.*, ***Cates v. Pon***, 663 S.W.2d 99, 102 (Tex.App.—Houston [14th Dist.] 1983, writ ref'd n.r.e.) (invalid service because order appointed disinterested adult to serve process and return was signed by deputy constable); ***Mega v. Anglo Iron & Metal Co.***, 601 S.W.2d 501, 504 (Tex.App.—Corpus Christi 1980, no writ) (invalid service because order appointed "A.R. 'Tony' Martinez" to serve process and the return was signed by "A.R. Martinez, Jr."). See "Trial-court order," §3.3.1, p. 161.

(3) Process server certified by Supreme Court. If the Supreme Court, by order, has certified a person to serve process, the return must show her identification number and the expiration date of her certification. TRCP 107(b)(10). See "Supreme Court order," §3.3.2, p. 161.

8. Date of service or attempted service. The return must show the date of service or attempted service and should also show the time of service or attempted service. *See* TRCP 16, 107(b)(7); ***Conseco Fin. Servicing Corp. v. Klein ISD***, 78 S.W.3d 666, 672 (Tex.App.—Houston [14th Dist.] 2002, no pet.); *see, e.g.*, ***TAC Americas, Inc. v. Boothe***, 94 S.W.3d 315, 320-22 (Tex.App.—Austin 2002, no pet.) (service was invalid when return indicated process server delivered documents before receiving them). When service is made by certified mail, the postmark is sufficient to show the latest date of delivery. ***Nelson v. Remmert***, 726 S.W.2d 171, 172 (Tex.App.—Houston [14th Dist.] 1987, writ ref'd n.r.e.).

9. Filing date. The return must state the date on which it was filed; if it does not, the record cannot establish that the return was on file for ten days, which is necessary before a default judgment may be granted. *See* TRCP 107(h); ***HB & WM, Inc. v. Smith***, 802 S.W.2d 279, 281-82 (Tex.App.—San Antonio 1990, no writ); *see, e.g.*, ***Melendez v. John R. Schatzman, Inc.***, 685 S.W.2d 137, 138 (Tex.App.—El Paso 1985, no writ) (because clerk did not include date and file mark on citation, it was impossible to determine how long return had been on file). See "Filing return," §9.3, p. 168; "In most cases," ch. 7-A, §3.9.1(1), p. 590.

10. Diligence of attempted service. When service has not been accomplished, the return must show the following:

(1) The diligence used by the officer or other authorized person in attempting to serve process. TRCP 107(d).

(2) The reason service was not accomplished. *Id.*

(3) The defendant's location, if it is known. *Id.*

11. Other information. The return must include any other information that is required by rule or by law. TRCP 107(b)(11).

★

§9.5 Addressee's signature. When the process is served by registered or certified mail, the return must contain the return receipt with the addressee's signature. TRCP 107(c); *Hubicki v. Festina*, 226 S.W.3d 405, 408 (Tex. 2007); *Ramirez v. Consolidated HGM Corp.*, 124 S.W.3d 914, 916 (Tex.App.—Amarillo 2004, no pet.); *All Commercial Floors, Inc. v. Barton & Rasor*, 97 S.W.3d 723, 726 (Tex.App.—Fort Worth 2003, no pet.); *Fowler v. Quinlan ISD*, 963 S.W.2d 941, 943 (Tex.App.—Texarkana 1998, no pet.); *e.g.*, *Union Pac. Corp. v. Legg*, 49 S.W.3d 72, 79 (Tex.App.—Austin 2001, no pet.) (return invalid because it was stamped with signature and no proof was offered to show signature was authorized). If the defendant is a corporation, the return receipt must be signed by the corporation's president, vice president, or registered agent. *See* Bus. Orgs. Code §§5.201(a), (b), 5.255(1); *Cox Mktg. v. Adams*, 688 S.W.2d 215, 217 (Tex.App.—El Paso 1985, no writ); *see also Harmon Truck Lines, Inc. v. Steele*, 836 S.W.2d 262, 264 (Tex.App.—Texarkana 1992, writ dism'd) (when signature was not plainly the agent's, service was not adequate). When a return recites that the person served is a corporation's registered agent, it is prima facie evidence of that person's status. *Primate Constr., Inc. v. Silver*, 884 S.W.2d 151, 152 n.1 (Tex.1994). *Primate* overruled those cases that held the record must affirmatively show that the person served was in fact the registered agent.

§9.6 Signature of server. The signature of the server must appear on the return. CPRC §17.030(c); TRCP 107(e); *Hot Shot Messenger Serv. v. State*, 818 S.W.2d 905, 907 (Tex.App.—Austin 1991, no writ); *American Bankers Ins. v. State*, 749 S.W.2d 195, 197 (Tex.App.—Houston [14th Dist.] 1988, no writ).

    1. Sheriff, constable, or court clerk. If the return is signed by a sheriff, constable, or court clerk, a stamped or printed signature is sufficient. *See, e.g.*, *Payne & Keller Co. v. Word*, 732 S.W.2d 38, 40 (Tex.App.—Houston [14th Dist.] 1987, writ ref'd n.r.e.) (constable).

    2. Other authorized person. If the return is signed by an authorized person other than a sheriff, constable, or court clerk, the return must be verified or signed under penalty of perjury. TRCP 107(e); *see* CPRC §17.030(c). If the return is signed under penalty of perjury, it must (1) contain a statement that includes the server's name, date of birth, and address, and (2) substantially comply with the form in TRCP 107(e). TRCP 107(e). For the complete statement that must be signed under penalty of perjury, see TRCP 107(e).

§9.7 Falsifying return. A person who knowingly or intentionally falsifies a return of service may be prosecuted under Penal Code chapter 37 for tampering with a governmental record. CPRC §17.030(d).

§10. AMENDING THE SERVICE DOCUMENTS

§10.1 Amending the petition. When the plaintiff amends the petition after service but before the defendant files an answer and the amended petition asks for a more onerous judgment, the defendant must be served with citation and the amended petition. See "Service of amended pleadings," ch. 5-F, §3.3, p. 352; "Adding claims or damages – service required," ch. 7-A, §3.2.1(1), p. 588.

§10.2 Amending citation & return. The trial court may allow the process or proof of service to be amended at any time in the court's discretion and on such notice and terms as it deems just. TRCP 118. No other person has the authority to amend the citation or the return. *See, e.g.*, *Barker CATV Constr., Inc. v. Ampro, Inc.*, 989 S.W.2d 789, 793-94 (Tex.App.—Houston [1st Dist.] 1999, no pet.) (no proof trial court authorized amended return; amended return disallowed); *Plains Chevrolet, Inc. v. Thorne*, 656 S.W.2d 631, 633 (Tex.App.—Waco 1983, no writ) (serving officer cannot correct D's name in citation; amended citation disallowed). If the court signs an order permitting amendment of the citation or the return, the plaintiff does not need to re-serve the defendant with process.

    1. Amending the citation. The court may permit the citation to be amended. TRCP 118; *London v. Chandler*, 406 S.W.2d 203, 204 (Tex.1966).

    2. Amending the return. The court, at any time during its plenary power, may permit proof of service to be amended to reflect the actual service on the defendant. *See* TRCP 118; *Higginbotham v. General Life & Acc. Ins.*, 796 S.W.2d 695, 696 (Tex.1990); *Dawson v. Briggs*, 107 S.W.3d 739, 747 (Tex.App.—Fort Worth 2003, no pet.); *see, e.g.*, *Walker v. Brodhead*, 828 S.W.2d 278, 282 (Tex.App.—Austin 1992, writ denied) (verification of return added; amendment permitted); *Bavarian Autohaus, Inc. v. Holland*, 570 S.W.2d 110, 113 (Tex.App.—Houston [1st Dist.]

⎯⎯⎯⎯⎯⎯⎯⎯⎯⎯ ★ ⎯⎯⎯⎯⎯⎯⎯⎯⎯⎯

1978, no writ) (return amended and filed before judgment to reflect service on corporation by delivery to vice president; amendment permitted). The return cannot be amended without court approval. *Barker CATV*, 989 S.W.2d at 793-94. The amended return must be attached to a valid citation. *Verlander Enters. v. Graham*, 932 S.W.2d 259, 262 (Tex.App.—El Paso 1996, no writ). A properly amended return relates back to and is considered filed on the date the original return was filed. *Brodhead*, 828 S.W.2d at 282; *Bavarian Autohaus*, 570 S.W.2d at 113.

§11. SERVICE OUTSIDE THE UNITED STATES

Service of process in a foreign country must give the defendant actual notice of the proceeding in time to answer and defend. TRCP 108a; *Hubicki v. Festina*, 226 S.W.3d 405, 407 (Tex.2007).

§11.1 Comity. Comity is the extent to which the laws of one nation are allowed to operate within the territory of another nation. *Hilton v. Guyot*, 159 U.S. 113, 163 (1895). No nation can demand that its laws have effect beyond the limits of its sovereignty. *Id.* Some countries consider service of judicial documents as requiring the performance of a judicial or "sovereign" act, and thus view service of judicial documents from another country within their borders as offensive to their sovereignty. *See* Jones, *International Judicial Assistance*, 62 Yale L.J. at 537.

§11.2 Methods of service permitted. A person outside the United States may be served by any method permitted by TRCP 108a. *Hubicki v. Festina*, 226 S.W.3d 405, 407 (Tex.2007). A nonresident defendant may be served with process outside the United States as provided by (1) foreign law, (2) foreign authority in response to a letter rogatory, (3) TRCP 106, (4) a treaty, (5) the U.S. Department of State, or (6) any other means directed by the court that is not prohibited by law in the country where service is to be made. TRCP 108a(1); *Commission of Contracts v. Arriba, Ltd.*, 882 S.W.2d 576, 584 & n.6 (Tex.App.—Houston [1st Dist.] 1994, no writ).

CAUTION

Unless a plaintiff uses the appropriate method of service in a foreign country as required by a treaty with that country, a judgment rendered for the plaintiff may not be enforceable in that country. See Kreimerman v. Casa Veerkamp, S.A. de C.V., 22 F.3d 634, 643-44 (5th Cir.1994).

---

§11.3 Preference for service according to international agreements. The preferred method of serving a defendant in another country is under the Hague Convention on the Service Abroad of Judicial & Extrajudicial Documents (Hague Convention), or under any other applicable treaty. *O'Connor's Federal Rules*, 1993 Notes of Adv. Cmte. to FRCP 4, ¶41, p. 1142; *Volkswagenwerk A.G. v. Schlunk*, 486 U.S. 694, 706 (1988) (voluntary use of conventional procedures may be desirable even when service could constitutionally be made in another manner). Service abroad must be made under a treaty if (1) there is a treaty and (2) the treaty requires service to be made according to its terms. FRCP 4(f)(1); *O'Connor's Federal Rules*, 1993 Notes of Adv. Cmte. to FRCP 4, ¶41, p. 1142. A convention or treaty does not necessarily preempt all other methods of service on a defendant who resides in a signatory country; preemption depends on the language, history, and purpose of the treaty. *Kreimerman v. Casa Veerkamp, S.A. de C.V.*, 22 F.3d 634, 638, 642 (5th Cir.1994). The Hague Convention preempts inconsistent methods of service prescribed by state law in all cases to which it applies. *Volkswagenwerk A.G.*, 486 U.S. at 699; *see Ackermann v. Levine*, 788 F.2d 830, 840 (2d Cir.1986). By contrast, the Inter-American Convention on Letters Rogatory does not preempt other methods of service. *Kreimerman*, 22 F.3d at 647. For the procedure for service under the Hague Convention, see *O'Connor's Federal Rules*, "Serving an individual abroad," ch. 2-H, §6.3, p. 157.

PRACTICE TIP

To determine whether a particular country is presently a signatory to the Hague Convention or any other treaty affecting service, contact the Treaty Affairs Section, Department of State, Washington, D.C., at (202) 647-1345, www.state.gov/s/l/treaty, or refer to the Hague Conference website, hcch.net.

———————— ★ ————————

I. SUIT BY INDIGENT

§1. GENERAL

§1.1 Rules. TRCP 145, 217; in suits for forcible entry and detainer, see TRCP 749a, 749b; TRAP 20. See CPRC chs. 13, 14.

§1.2 Purpose. The Texas Constitution and the rules of procedure recognize that courts must be open to all persons with legitimate disputes, not just those who can afford to pay the court fees. *Griffin Indus. v. Thirteenth Ct. of Appeals*, 934 S.W.2d 349, 353 (Tex.1996); *see* Tex. Const. art. 1, §13; TRCP 145, 217; TRAP 20.1; *In re C.H.C.*, 331 S.W.3d 426, 429 (Tex.2011). TRCP 145 gives an indigent access to the courthouse without the payment of costs. *Spellmon v. Sweeney*, 819 S.W.2d 206, 208 (Tex.App.—Waco 1991, no writ). TRCP 217 gives an indigent the right to a jury trial without the payment of the jury fee. Although a litigant is not entitled to appointed counsel in a civil case, under exceptional circumstances, when public and private interests are at stake, the court may appoint an attorney to represent an indigent civil litigant. *Gibson v. Tolbert*, 102 S.W.3d 710, 712 (Tex.2003) (Gov't Code §24.016); *see* Fam. Code §107.013(a)(1) (in suit by government to terminate parent-child relationship, court must appoint attorney ad litem to represent indigent parent who opposes termination).

§1.3 Timetable & forms. *O'Connor's Texas Civil Appeals* (2012), Timetable, Appeal by Indigent to Court of Appeals, p. 1118; *O'Connor's Texas Civil Forms* (2012), FORMS 1B:8, 2I.

§1.4 Other references. Hewitt & Warton, *Dismissing Pauper Suits in Texas Courts*, 26 Tex. Tech L.Rev. 123 (1995); *O'Connor's Texas Civil Appeals* (2012) (*O'Connor's Texas Appeals*).

§2. WHO IS INDIGENT?

An indigent is a person who has no ability to pay the costs for the suit. TRCP 145(a). Generally, an individual receiving a governmental entitlement or public assistance may proceed as an indigent. *See id.*; *Griffin Indus. v. Thirteenth Ct. of Appeals*, 934 S.W.2d 349, 351 (Tex.1996); *Baughman v. Baughman*, 65 S.W.3d 309, 315 (Tex.App.—Waco 2001, pet. denied).

§2.1 Parties who are indigent. The following parties are considered indigent: • A personal-injury plaintiff who has a contingent-fee contract with an attorney who cannot or will not advance the costs. *Griffin Indus. v. Thirteenth Ct. of Appeals*, 934 S.W.2d 349, 354 (Tex.1996). • A prisoner at the Texas Department of Criminal Justice (TDCJ) who has no money or property. *Allred v. Lowry*, 597 S.W.2d 353, 355 (Tex.1980). • A person who has been depending on welfare, has not been regularly employed, and has not been able to obtain loans to pay for court costs. *Goffney v. Lowry*, 554 S.W.2d 157, 159-60 (Tex.1977). • A corporation in bankruptcy. *See Modern Living, Inc. v. Alworth*, 730 S.W.2d 444, 445-46 (Tex.App.—Beaumont 1987, orig. proceeding).

§2.2 Parties who are not indigent. The following parties are not considered indigent: • A person who remains voluntarily unemployed and lives on the generosity of relatives. *Keller v. Walker*, 652 S.W.2d 542, 544 (Tex.App.—Dallas 1983, orig. proceeding). • An inmate who has funds in his trust account. *See* CPRC §14.006(b)(1) (prisoner must pay costs from trust account according to specific formula).

§3. AFFIDAVIT OF INDIGENCE

An affidavit of indigence does not need to strictly comply with the requirements of the rules of procedure; substantial compliance is sufficient. *Walker v. Blue Water Garden Apts.*, 776 S.W.2d 578, 580-81 (Tex.1989). See *O'Connor's Texas Forms*, FORM 2I:1.

§3.1 Contents of affidavit. The affidavit must contain complete information about the party and her financial status: the party's identity, the nature and amount of income (governmental entitlement, employment, interest, dividends, and any other income), spouse's income if available to the party, property owned (other than homestead),

⭐

cash or checking account, dependents, debts, and monthly expenses. TRCP 145(b). In addition, the affidavit must state the following:

1. The indigent desires to prosecute the lawsuit without paying costs. *See* TRCP 145(a).

2. The indigent is unable to pay the costs required by the rules. The indigent must make the statement, "I am unable to pay the court costs. I verify that the statements made in this affidavit are true and correct." TRCP 145(b). The indigent must state facts supporting the statement of inability to pay costs. For example, plaintiff is on welfare; plaintiff is unemployed and looking for work; plaintiff's expenses exceed income (itemizing both); plaintiff has no other available sources of money (e.g., cannot get a loan, no income available from spouse); plaintiff owns no real property; plaintiff's only personal property consists of his clothes and other personal items; plaintiff's only asset is a truck, and if it were sold, plaintiff could not keep a job and support a family. *Cf.* TRAP 20.1(b) (affidavit of indigence for appeal). For a comprehensive list of facts to cover in an affidavit of indigence, see *O'Connor's Texas Appeals*, "Indigent's affidavit," ch. 2-A, §3.2, p. 64.

3. If the indigent is an inmate, the inmate must file a separate affidavit or unsworn declaration that provides specific information about other actions, including any appeal or original proceeding, previously brought by the inmate and attach to it a certified copy of the inmate's trust account statement. *See* CPRC §§14.002(a), 14.004; *Obadele v. Johnson*, 60 S.W.3d 345, 348 (Tex.App.—Houston [14th Dist.] 2001, no pet.); *see also Thomas v. Wichita Gen. Hosp.*, 952 S.W.2d 936, 939-40 (Tex.App.—Fort Worth 1997, pet. denied) (CPRC §14.004 is not unconstitutional). See "Declaration relating to previous filings," §4.2, p. 175.

NOTE

The revisions amending CPRC §§14.002(a) and 14.004 apply only to an action brought on or after January 1, 2012. See Acts 2011, 82nd Leg., C.S., ch. 3, §§12.04, 16.02, eff. Jan. 1, 2012. Under the law governing actions brought before January 1, 2012, the inmate's affidavit or unsworn declaration had to provide information only about other suits; the statute did not specifically require information about appeals or original proceedings.

---

§3.2 Verification.

1. **Affidavit of indigence.** The affidavit of indigence must be sworn before a notary public or other officer authorized to administer oaths. TRCP 145(b).

2. **Unsworn declaration.** An unsworn declaration must be in writing and subscribed as true under penalty of perjury. CPRC §132.001(c). See "Unsworn declaration," ch. 1-B, §3.2.14, p. 10; *O'Connor's Texas Forms*, FORM 1B:8.

CAUTION

CPRC §132.001 allows anyone to file an unsworn declaration instead of a written sworn declaration, verification, certification, oath, or affidavit. However, TRCP 145 still requires an affidavit; thus, parties should be wary of filing unsworn declarations and, at a minimum, should make sure to include all the information required by TRCP 145 in the declaration.

---

§3.3 Time to file. The affidavit should be filed along with the original petition and served on the defendant along with the citation. *See* TRCP 145(a); *Baughman v. Baughman*, 65 S.W.3d 309, 312 (Tex.App.—Waco 2001, pet. denied). If the affidavit is not filed with the original petition, it must be served on the other parties under TRCP 21a.

§3.4 Amending the affidavit. A party may amend a defective affidavit of indigence. *In re J.W.*, 52 S.W.3d 730, 732 (Tex.2001); *American Comm. Telecomm. v. Commerce N. Bank*, 660 S.W.2d 570, 571 (Tex.App.—San Antonio 1983, order).

———————————— ★ ————————————

§3.5 Attorney's statement. An attorney who represents an indigent on a contingent-fee basis because of indigency may file a statement to that effect to help the court understand the indigent's financial condition. TRCP 145(b). See *O'Connor's Texas Forms*, FORM 21:2.

§3.6 IOLTA certificate. If an attorney is providing free legal services to an indigent without contingency, either directly or by referral from a program funded by the Interest on Lawyers Trust Accounts (IOLTA), the attorney may file an IOLTA certificate to confirm that the indigent was screened by the IOLTA-funded program for income eligibility under the IOLTA income guidelines. TRCP 145(c). See *O'Connor's Texas Forms*, FORM 21:3.

§4. SUIT BY INDIGENT INMATE

§4.1 Declaration of indigence. An indigent inmate must file the affidavit of indigence required by TRCP 145. See "Affidavit of Indigence," §3, p. 173.

§4.2 Declaration relating to previous filings. An indigent inmate must file the declaration required by CPRC §14.004. See *O'Connor's Texas Forms*, FORM 21:4. In the declaration, the inmate must provide the following:

1. A list of all actions (including any appeal or original proceeding but excluding actions under the Family Code) brought by the inmate in which the inmate was not represented by an attorney. *See* CPRC §§14.002(a), 14.004(a)(1); *see also Light v. Womack*, 113 S.W.3d 872, 874 (Tex.App.—Beaumont 2003, no pet.) (must disclose all pro se suits, not just suits filed as indigent). See "Note," §3.1.3, p. 174. The inmate must include the following information: (1) the operative facts for which relief was sought, (2) the case name, cause number, and court in which the action was brought, (3) the identity of each party named in the action, (4) the results of the action, including whether the action or a claim that was the basis for the action was dismissed as frivolous or malicious, and (5) if a previous action or claim was dismissed as frivolous or malicious, the date of the final order affirming the dismissal. CPRC §14.004(a)(2), (b). If an inmate files a declaration that does not provide this required information, the court may assume the action is substantially similar to one previously filed and dismiss the case as frivolous. *Williams v. TDCJ-Inst. Div.*, 176 S.W.3d 590, 594 (Tex.App.—Tyler 2005, pet. denied); *Bell v. TDCJ-Inst. Div.*, 962 S.W.2d 156, 158 (Tex.App.—Houston [14th Dist.] 1998, pet. denied); *e.g., Clark v. Unit*, 23 S.W.3d 420, 421-22 (Tex.App.—Houston [1st Dist.] 2000, pet. denied) (inmate did not include operative facts in affidavit; dismissal affirmed).

2. A certified copy of the inmate's trust account statement. CPRC §14.006(f); *Bonds v. TDCJ*, 953 S.W.2d 233, 233 (Tex.1997) (if statement not certified, court must request that inmate file certified copy before ordering inmate to pay full amount of court fees and costs).

3. When a claim is subject to the grievance system established under Gov't Code §501.008, the inmate must file (1) an affidavit or unsworn declaration stating the date the grievance was filed and the date the written decision was received by the inmate and (2) a copy of the written decision. CPRC §14.005(a); *Bishop v. Lawson*, 131 S.W.3d 571, 574 (Tex.App.—Fort Worth 2004, pet. denied); *Draughon v. Cockrell*, 112 S.W.3d 775, 776 (Tex.App.—Beaumont 2003, no pet.); *see also Garrett v. Borden*, 283 S.W.3d 852, 853 (Tex.2009) ("copy" is not limited to photocopies; hand-typed, verbatim reproduction of decision is sufficient). The inmate must file the claim within 31 days after receiving the written decision. CPRC §14.005(b).

§4.3 Other information. For additional information about the hearing, the costs, the submission of evidence, and the order of dismissal, see CPRC §§14.006-14.014.

§5. SUMMARY DISMISSAL ON COURT'S MOTION

Under CPRC §13.001(c) (indigents) and CPRC §14.003(a) (indigent inmates), the trial court has the authority to dismiss an indigent's suit even before process is served. *Pedraza v. Tibbs*, 826 S.W.2d 695, 698 (Tex.App.—Houston [1st Dist.] 1992, writ dism'd). This action spares the prospective defendant the inconvenience and expense of answering a frivolous complaint.

§5.1 Hearing. The trial court may dismiss a lawsuit without a hearing on factual issues only when there is no arguable basis in law for the suit. *Denson v. TDCJ-Inst. Div.*, 63 S.W.3d 454, 459 (Tex.App.—Tyler 1999, pet. denied); *Leon Springs Gas Co. v. Restaurant Equip. Leasing Co.*, 961 S.W.2d 574, 579 (Tex.App.—San Antonio 1997,

———————————————— ✦ ————————————————

no pet.); *Hector v. Thaler*, 862 S.W.2d 176, 178 (Tex.App.—Houston [1st Dist.] 1993, no writ). Before a court can dismiss a suit for having no arguable basis in fact, it must hold a hearing. *Harrison v. TDCJ-Inst. Div.*, 164 S.W.3d 871, 875 (Tex.App.—Corpus Christi 2005, no pet.); *Hector*, 862 S.W.2d at 178. *But see Timmons v. Luce*, 840 S.W.2d 582, 586 (Tex.App.—Tyler 1992, no writ) (court is not required to hold hearing if action is frivolous).

§5.2 No amendment. The trial court is not required to give the indigent an opportunity to amend the petition before dismissing under CPRC §13.001 or §14.003. *See Kendrick v. Lynaugh*, 804 S.W.2d 153, 156 (Tex.App.—Houston [14th Dist.] 1990, no writ) (case involved §13.001). However, if the court gives an indigent the opportunity to amend her pleadings and the indigent does not amend, the trial court can dismiss the indigent's suit with prejudice. *Lentworth v. Trahan*, 981 S.W.2d 720, 722-23 (Tex.App.—Houston [1st Dist.] 1998, no pet.); *see Hughes v. Massey*, 65 S.W.3d 743, 746 (Tex.App.—Beaumont 2001, no pet.) (if indigent not given opportunity to amend, dismissal should be "without prejudice").

§5.3 No notice. Neither CPRC §13.001 nor §14.003 requires the trial court to give the indigent notice that it intends to dismiss the suit for "no arguable basis in law." *See Timmons v. Luce*, 840 S.W.2d 582, 586 (Tex.App.—Tyler 1992, no writ) (CPRC §13.001). If there is a hearing, however, the indigent must be given notice.

§5.4 Grounds for dismissal. The trial court has the authority to dismiss a suit filed by an indigent if the trial court finds any of the following:

    1. Not indigent. The allegation of poverty in the affidavit is false. CPRC §§13.001(a)(1), 14.003(a)(1).

    2. No arguable basis. The action or claim is frivolous or malicious. CPRC §13.001(a)(2) (uses term "action"), §14.003(a)(2) (uses term "claim"); *Johnson v. Lynaugh*, 796 S.W.2d 705, 706 (Tex.1990); *McDonald v. Houston Dairy*, 813 S.W.2d 238, 238 (Tex.App.—Houston [1st Dist.] 1991, no writ). To determine whether an action is frivolous or malicious, the court is limited to the standard under CPRC §13.001(b)(2), which permits the court to dismiss if the claim has no arguable basis in law or in fact. *Johnson*, 796 S.W.2d at 706 (dismissal under CPRC §13.001(b)(3) not appropriate); *Pedraza v. Tibbs*, 826 S.W.2d 695, 698 (Tex.App.—Houston [1st Dist.] 1992, writ dism'd) (dismissal under CPRC §13.001(b)(1) & (3) is discouraged). A claim that has no arguable basis in law or in fact does not constitute a cause of action. *Pedraza*, 826 S.W.2d at 698; *Spellmon v. Sweeney*, 819 S.W.2d 206, 210 (Tex.App.—Waco 1991, no writ).

    3. Inmate – false filing. The indigent inmate filed an affidavit or unsworn declaration required by CPRC chapter 14 that the inmate knew was false. CPRC §14.003(a)(3); *see id.* §14.004 (affidavit regarding previous filings).

    4. Inmate – substantially similar claim. The indigent inmate filed a claim that was substantially similar to a previous claim and was based on the same operative facts. CPRC §14.003(a)(2), (b)(4); *Vacca v. Farrington*, 85 S.W.3d 438, 440 (Tex.App.—Texarkana 2002, no pet.).

    5. Inmate – untimely claim. The indigent inmate filed a claim more than 30 days after the inmate received a written decision from the grievance system. CPRC §14.005(b); *Warner v. Glass*, 135 S.W.3d 681, 683 (Tex. 2004). An indigent inmate's claim is deemed filed when the prison authorities receive the document to be mailed. *Warner*, 135 S.W.3d at 684.

§5.5 Order on summary dismissal. The court's order summarily dismissing the indigent's suit must state the reasons for the dismissal. *Dillon v. Ousley*, 890 S.W.2d 500, 502 (Tex.App.—Corpus Christi 1994, no writ). The trial court's order dismissing an inmate's suit should be based on CPRC chapter 14, not CPRC chapter 13. *E.g., Thompson v. Henderson*, 927 S.W.2d 323, 324 (Tex.App.—Houston [1st Dist.] 1996, no writ) (remanded for trial court to consider provisions of CPRC ch. 14).

§6. DUTIES OF THE CLERK

§6.1 Issue citation. Once the indigent files an affidavit under TRCP 145, the clerk must docket the action, issue a citation, and provide other customary services as are provided to any other party. TRCP 145(a). The clerk must issue a citation even though the court has not yet ruled on the affidavit of indigence. *McDonald v. Houston Dairy*, 813 S.W.2d 238, 238 (Tex.App.—Houston [1st Dist.] 1991, no writ).

✦

---

§6.2 Give notice. The clerk will give the defendant notice of the filing of the affidavit along with the service of the citation. *See* TRCP 145(a). There is no requirement for the indigent plaintiff to give the defendant notice of the suit and the affidavit.

§7. CONTESTING THE AFFIDAVIT

§7.1 Contest. The defendant or the clerk may contest an affidavit of indigence by filing a written contest with notice to all the parties. TRCP 145(d). If the suit is an appeal from a small-claims court, the defendant or clerk must give notice to both the small-claims court and the county clerk. TRCP 145(d); *see* Gov't Code §28.052(c). The defendant's contest cannot delay a temporary hearing. TRCP 145(d).

§7.2 Limits of contest.

1. IOLTA certificate. If the indigent's affidavit is accompanied by an attorney's IOLTA certificate, the affidavit cannot be contested. TRCP 145(c) & cmt.

2. No IOLTA certificate. If the indigent's affidavit is not accompanied by an IOLTA certificate, the affidavit can be contested. TRCP 145(d).

3. Government entitlement. If the indigent's affidavit does not include an IOLTA certificate but attests that the indigent receives a government entitlement based on indigence, only the truth of that attestation can be contested. TRCP 145(d).

§7.3 Waiver. If no contest is filed, the uncontested affidavit is conclusive as a matter of law. *Equitable Gen. Ins. v. Yates*, 684 S.W.2d 669, 671 (Tex.1984).

§8. HEARING ON THE CONTEST

§8.1 Notice of hearing. The indigent must be given notice of the hearing or submission of the contest to the affidavit of indigence. *Aguilar v. Stone*, 68 S.W.3d 1, 2 (Tex.App.—Houston [1st Dist.] 1997, orig. proceeding).

§8.2 Hearing for indigents. The court should conduct a hearing on the contest to the affidavit at the first regular hearing in the suit. *See* TRCP 145(d). At that hearing, the indigent should provide proof of indigence. The proper consideration is the present ability to pay costs rather than a future, more speculative ability. *Brown v. Clapp*, 613 S.W.2d 78, 80 (Tex.App.—Tyler 1981, orig. proceeding).

NOTE

*Nothing in TRCP 145 states who has the burden of proof at the contest hearing. See TRCP 145. The burden is probably on the indigent to prove indigent status. See former TRCP 145, 661-662 S.W.2d (Tex.Cases) xliii (1984) (under former rule, burden of proof in contest of affidavit of indigence for trial was on indigent); **Griffin Indus. v. Thirteenth Ct. of Appeals**, 934 S.W.2d 349, 351 (Tex.1996) (interpreting earlier versions of trial and appellate rules, both of which stated burden was on indigent).*

---

§8.3 Hearing for indigent inmates. A court may hold a hearing by video communications for an indigent inmate at a jail facility. CPRC §14.008(a). A court may also consider the case on submission, by requiring that written statements be submitted and copies be provided to the inmate. *Id.* §14.009.

§9. ORDER ON THE CONTEST

§9.1 Indigent. If the court finds the plaintiff is indigent, the suit will proceed, and the plaintiff will not be liable for costs. *See* TRCP 145(d). If the court finds that another party to the suit can pay the costs of the action, the court will order the other party to do so. *Id.* If the plaintiff recovers a monetary judgment from the defendant, the court may order the indigent to pay costs from the award. *Id.*

───────────────────── ✫ ─────────────────────

§9.2 Not indigent. If the court finds the plaintiff is not indigent, the court must state the reasons in the order. TRCP 145(d); *Varkonyi v. Troche*, 802 S.W.2d 63, 65 (Tex.App.—El Paso 1990, orig. proceeding).

1. Valid grounds. A court may dismiss if it finds the allegations of poverty are false or the action is frivolous or malicious. *Creel v. District Atty.*, 818 S.W.2d 45, 46 n.2 (Tex.1991).

2. No further action. If the court signs an order sustaining the contest, the indigent may take no further action in the suit, except with leave of court, until the indigent makes payment. TRCP 145(d).

§10. ATTORNEY FEES & COSTS

Nothing in TRCP 145 prohibits the indigent party from recovering attorney fees, expenses, or costs from any other party. TRCP 145(e).

§11. REVIEW

§11.1 To file suit as indigent. If the trial court dismisses the indigent's suit because the allegations of poverty are false or the claim is frivolous or malicious, the indigent can challenge the order by filing a notice of appeal. *See In re Arroyo*, 988 S.W.2d 737, 738 (Tex.1998) (appeal, not mandamus, is the proper vehicle to challenge order sustaining contest to affidavit of indigence).

§11.2 To appeal as indigent. To challenge the order of dismissal on appeal, the indigent who claimed indigence for purposes of the trial must claim indigence for the appeal and file another affidavit of indigence. See *O'Connor's Texas Appeals*, "Affidavit of Indigence," ch. 2-A, p. 61, and FORM 2A:1. Indigence provisions are liberally construed in favor of the right to appeal. *Jones v. Stayman*, 747 S.W.2d 369, 370 (Tex.1987).

★

CHAPTER 3

───────────────────── ★ ─────────────────────

─────────────────────── ★ ───────────────────────

───────────────────────────── ✦ ─────────────────────────────

3. DEFENDANT'S RESPONSE & PLEADINGS

A. DEFENDANT'S PLEADINGS

§1. GENERAL

§1.1 Rules. TRCP 83-98.

§1.2 Purpose. Initially, the most important function of the defendant's pleadings in response to the suit is to avoid a default judgment. After that, the defendant's pleadings challenge the plaintiff's petition and answer its allegations.

§1.3 Timetables & forms. Timetable, Special Appearance, p. 1210; Timetable, Motion to Transfer Venue—Wrong or Inconvenient County, p. 1211; Timetable, Motion to Dismiss—Code Forum Non Conveniens, p. 1213; Timetable, Motion to Abate, p. 1215; Timetable, Pretrial Motions, p. 1216; *O'Connor's Texas Civil Forms* (2012), FORMS 1, 3.

§1.4 Other references. *O'Connor's Federal Rules * Civil Trials* (2013) (*O'Connor's Federal Rules*).

§2. PREFILING CONSIDERATIONS

§2.1 Notice to carrier. If the claim is covered by insurance, the defendant should read its policy and give its insurance carrier all required notices. *See Harwell v. State Farm Mut. Auto. Ins.*, 896 S.W.2d 170, 173-74 (Tex. 1995) (D must notify carrier; notice of claim sent to carrier by P's attorney was not sufficient); *Struna v. Concord Ins. Servs.*, 11 S.W.3d 355, 359 (Tex.App.—Houston [1st Dist.] 2000, no pet.) (D must notify carrier whenever claim is made and must forward relevant documents).

§2.2 Offer to settle.

    1. Presuit offer. If a potential defendant receives a demand notice before suit is filed, it should consider making a reasonable offer to settle. *See* Bus. & Com. Code §17.5052(a); Ins. Code §541.156(a); Prop. Code §27.004(b).

    2. Offer after suit filed.

        (1) Limit damages. A defendant's offer to settle can limit the amount of damages. *See, e.g.*, CPRC §38.002(3) (tendering payment bars recovery of attorney fees); Fin. Code §304.105 (settlement offer in wrongful-death, personal-injury, and property-damage cases may prevent accrual of prejudgment interest during period that offer may be accepted).

        (2) Recover litigation costs. A defendant can recover litigation costs under CPRC chapter 42 and TRCP 167 if the other party rejected an offer to settle a claim for monetary damages that was significantly more favorable than the judgment. See "Offer of Settlement," ch. 7-H, p. 664.

§2.3 State vs. federal court. Once the defendant is served with the suit, it should consider whether it would prefer to try the case in federal court and, if so, whether the case is removable. For a discussion about removing a case to federal court, see *O'Connor's Federal Rules*, "Removal & Remand," ch. 4, p. 239.

§2.4 ADR. If the parties are required by statute or contract to submit a dispute to a form of alternative dispute resolution (ADR), the defendant should file a motion to abate and a motion to compel ADR after filing its answer. See "The ADR System," ch. 4-A, p. 277.

§3. DUE ORDER OF PLEADING

§3.1 Order of filing. Under the due-order-of-pleading rule, a defendant must file certain pleadings or motions in a specific order. *See Exito Elecs. Co. v. Trejo*, 142 S.W.3d 302, 305 (Tex.2004). If the defendant files a pleading or motion out of order, it waives that pleading or motion. *See, e.g., Allianz Risk Transfer Ltd. v. S.J. Camp & Co.*, 117

★

S.W.3d 92, 97 (Tex.App.—Tyler 2003, no pet.) (D filed motion to transfer venue and original answer one minute before filing special appearance; special appearance waived). The defendant must file pleadings and motions in the following order:

1. **Special appearance.** When challenging personal jurisdiction, the defendant must file a special appearance before any other pleading or motion. TRCP 120a(1); *see* TRCP 86(1). See "Due order of pleading," ch. 3-B, §2.2, p. 189.

2. **Motion to transfer venue.** When challenging venue, the defendant must file a motion to transfer venue after a special appearance (if any) and before or along with any other pleading or motion. TRCP 86(1), 120a(1); *see Massey v. Columbus State Bank*, 35 S.W.3d 697, 700 (Tex.App.—Houston [1st Dist.] 2000, pet. denied); *Antonio v. Rico Marino, S.A.*, 910 S.W.2d 624, 630 (Tex.App.—Houston [14th Dist.] 1995, no writ). See "Due order of pleading," ch. 3-C, §2.2.2, p. 203.

3. **All other pleadings or motions.** After a special appearance (if any) or a motion to transfer venue (if any) is filed, the defendant can file any other pleading or motion without violating the due-order-of-pleading rule. *See* TRCP 86(1), 120a(1); *Exito Elecs.*, 142 S.W.3d at 305.

§3.2 Exceptions to due-order-of-pleading rule. There are a few exceptions to the rules on the order of filing. A defendant can take the following actions without waiving the special appearance or the motion to transfer venue.

---

⑬   **PROPOSED TRCP CHANGES**

In response to Gov't Code §22.004(g), the Supreme Court has proposed TRCP 91a to allow a defendant to file a motion to dismiss a cause of action that has no basis in law or fact. See Tex.Sup.Ct. Order, Misc. Docket No. 12-9191 (eff. Mar. 1, 2013). The proposed rule would allow a defendant to file a motion to dismiss without waiving the special appearance or the motion to transfer venue. Id. The public-comment period for the proposed rule ends on February 1, 2013, and the rule is to take effect March 1, 2013. For the proposed version of the rule, see the appendix after this book's index. For the final version, go to the Supreme Court website at www.supreme.courts.state.tx.us. When the new rule takes effect, a supplement to this book—with updated rules and commentaries that reflect the changes—will be available at www.JonesMcClure.com/TRCPamendments.

---

1. **Removal to federal court.** The defendant can file a notice of removal to federal court before the special appearance without waiving the special appearance or the motion to transfer venue. *Antonio v. Rico Marino, S.A.*, 910 S.W.2d 624, 629 (Tex.App.—Houston [14th Dist.] 1995, no writ).

2. **Other pleadings.** The defendant can file motions that are not related to the merits of the suit and do not invoke the court's general jurisdiction before the special appearance without waiving the special appearance or the motion to transfer venue. *See, e.g., Gentry v. Tucker*, 891 S.W.2d 766, 768 (Tex.App.—Texarkana 1995, no writ) (D did not waive venue by filing motion to continue temporary-injunction hearing before answer date); *Perkola v. Koelling & Assocs.*, 601 S.W.2d 110, 112 (Tex.App.—Dallas 1980, writ dism'd) (D did not waive venue by contesting temporary injunction).

3. **Correspondence with court.** Under certain circumstances, the defendant can correspond with the court without waiving the special appearance or the motion to transfer venue. *See, e.g., Gales v. Denis*, 260 S.W.3d 22, 30 (Tex.App.—Houston [1st Dist.] 2008, no pet.) (pro se D's letter to court was answer, which waived special appearance because letter did not challenge jurisdiction); *N803RA, Inc. v. Hammer*, 11 S.W.3d 363, 367 (Tex.App.—Houston [1st Dist.] 2000, no pet.) (pro se D's letter to court was answer, but special appearance was not waived because letter also challenged jurisdiction); *Moore v. Elektro-Mobil Technik GmbH*, 874 S.W.2d 324, 327 (Tex.App.—El Paso 1994, writ denied) (German company did not waive special appearance when it wrote to court stating service was improper, requesting case be dismissed, and making objections to interrogatories).

★

4. Rule 11 agreement. The defendant can file a Rule 11 agreement without waiving the special appearance or the motion to transfer venue. *See Exito Elecs. Co. v. Trejo*, 142 S.W.3d 302, 305 (Tex.2004). See "Rule 11 agreement," ch. 3-B, §3.4.1(3), p. 197; *O'Connor's Texas Forms*, FORM 1H:13.

§3.3 Ruling order.

1. General rule – due order of pleading. The defendant should ask the court to rule first on the special appearance, then on venue, and then on other motions. *See* CPRC §15.063; TRCP 86(1), 120a(2); *see, e.g.*, *Landry v. Daigrepont*, 35 S.W.3d 265, 267 (Tex.App.—Corpus Christi 2000, no pet.) (special appearance waived because D asked for ruling on motion for new trial first).

2. Exceptions. The defendant can secure a ruling on the following without violating the due-order-of-pleading rule:

(1) Motion for continuance. The defendant can secure a ruling on (1) a motion for continuance of the hearing on a special appearance, venue, or FNC, or (2) a motion to continue some preliminary motion filed by the plaintiff. *See* TRCP 120a(3) (rule permits continuance in special appearance); *Gentry v. Tucker*, 891 S.W.2d 766, 768 (Tex.App.—Texarkana 1995, no writ) (D's motion for continuance of temporary-injunction hearing did not waive right to transfer venue).

(2) Plaintiff's motions. The defendant can ask the court to rule on the plaintiff's preliminary motions or on pleadings filed by the defendant in response to those motions. *See Gentry*, 891 S.W.2d at 768; *Perkola v. Koelling & Assocs.*, 601 S.W.2d 110, 112 (Tex.App.—Dallas 1980, writ dism'd).

§4. CONSTRUCTING THE ORIGINAL ANSWER

§4.1 Options. A defendant has three options for filing its answer and other pleas and motions: (1) file the answer and all other initial pleas and motions in one document, (2) file the answer and each of the other pleas and motions separately, or (3) file the answer and some of the pleas and motions in one document, and file the other pleas and motions separately. When filed separately, the documents must be filed in the appropriate order; when included in one document, they should be listed in the appropriate order.

§4.2 Inclusive answer + some motions. The best practice is to file an original answer containing some of the defendant's pleas and motions, and to file other pleas and motions separately.

1. Original answer. The defendant should consider the following when preparing the original answer:

• Is the defendant a nonresident of Texas claiming it has not done business in Texas? If so, the first part of the answer must be a special appearance. See "Special Appearance—Challenging Personal Jurisdiction," ch. 3-B, p. 189.

• Is there another county in Texas where the defendant contends the suit should or could have been filed? If so, the next part of the answer must be a motion to transfer venue. See "Motion to Transfer—Challenging Venue," ch. 3-C, p. 203.

• Is there a court in another jurisdiction outside Texas that the defendant contends has jurisdiction over the lawsuit and is a more appropriate forum? If so, the defendant must file a motion for FNC. See "Forum Non Conveniens—Challenging the Texas Forum," ch. 3-D, p. 216.

• The next part of the answer is the general denial. See "General Denial," ch. 3-E, §3, p. 228.

• Does the defendant want to assert any of the pleas listed in TRCP 93? If so, the defendant must specifically plead them and verify the answer. See "Verified Pleas," ch. 3-E, §4, p. 228.

• Does the defendant want to plead defenses establishing an independent reason why the plaintiff cannot prevail? If so, the defendant must affirmatively plead the defenses. See "Affirmative Defenses," ch. 3-E, §5, p. 230.

★

- Did the plaintiff plead that "all conditions precedent have been performed or have occurred" according to TRCP 54? If so, the defendant must specifically deny the statement, identify the specific conditions the plaintiff did not comply with, and verify the denial. See "Denial of conditions precedent," ch. 3-E, §6.1, p. 234.

- Does the defendant have claims against the plaintiff or other persons? If so, the next part of the answer should identify the defendant's counterclaims, cross-claims, or third-party claims. TRCP 38, 97. See "Cross-actions," ch. 2-E, §2.2, p. 129.

- The next part of the answer is the request for disclosure. See "Request for Disclosure," ch. 3-E, §8, p. 239.

- The last part of the answer is the conclusion, prayer, signature block, and if necessary, verification and affidavits.

2. Separate motions. The defendant should consider the following when deciding whether to file additional motions:

13

PROPOSED TRCP CHANGES

In response to Gov't Code §22.004(g), the Supreme Court has proposed TRCP 91a to allow a defendant to file a motion to dismiss a cause of action that has no basis in law or fact. See Tex.Sup.Ct. Order, Misc. Docket No. 12-9191 (eff. Mar. 1, 2013). The motion to dismiss would have to be filed within 60 days after the first pleading that includes the baseless cause of action is served and would generally have to be ruled on within 45 days after the motion is filed. See id. The public-comment period for the proposed rule ends on February 1, 2013, and the rule is to take effect March 1, 2013. For the proposed version of the rule, see the appendix after this book's index. For the final version, go to the Supreme Court website at www.supreme .courts.state.tx.us. When the new rule takes effect, a supplement to this book—with updated rules and commentaries that reflect the changes—will be available at www .JonesMcClure.com/TRCPamendments.

- *Motion 1:* Are there responsible third parties (RTPs), as defined in CPRC §33.011(6), that the defendant should designate? If so, the defendant should file a motion for leave to designate a person as an RTP. The motion must be filed at least 60 days before trial. See "RTP," ch. 3-E, §7.4, p. 235.

- *Motion 2:* Are there defects in the court's subject-matter jurisdiction that prevent this particular court from hearing the case? If so, the defendant should file a plea to the jurisdiction. See "Plea to the Jurisdiction—Challenging the Court," ch. 3-F, p. 239.

- *Motion 3:* Are there defects in the plaintiff's lawsuit that are apparent from the face of the plaintiff's petition? If so, the defendant should file special exceptions to object to the pleading defects and, if necessary, a motion for summary judgment. See "Special Exceptions—Challenging the Pleadings," ch. 3-G, p. 248.

- *Motion 4:* Are there defects in the plaintiff's lawsuit that are not apparent from the face of the petition? That is, must the defendant inform the court of facts not in the petition to illustrate the defect? If so, the defendant should file a verified motion to abate. Many of the matters the defendant files as part of a verified answer should also be the subject of a motion to abate. See "Motion to Abate—Challenging the Suit," ch. 3-I, p. 257.

- *Motion 5:* Is the plaintiff's lawsuit based on, related to, or in response to the defendant's exercise of the right of free speech, the right to petition, or the right of association? If so, the defendant should file a motion to dismiss under CPRC chapter 27. The motion must be filed within 60 days after service of the lawsuit. See "Motion to Dismiss—Anti-SLAPP Motion," ch. 3-K, p. 266.

✦

---

§5. DEADLINE TO FILE DEFENDANT'S ANSWER & MOTIONS

See the appropriate subchapter of this chapter for deadlines to file. For example, for the deadline to file an answer, see "Deadline to Answer," ch. 3-E, §2, p. 227.

§6. SUMMARY OF DEFENDANT'S PLEADINGS

Chart 3-1, below, matches the challenges defendants can make with the proper procedural steps.

3-1. SUMMARY OF DEFENDANT'S PLEADINGS		
To urge this		**File this**
Challenging jurisdiction		
1	The defendant, a nonresident, has never conducted business in Texas, and Texas courts do not have jurisdiction over the defendant or its property.	A special appearance with a prayer to dismiss.
2	The court does not have jurisdiction over the subject matter of this suit.	A plea to the jurisdiction with a prayer to dismiss.
Challenging the court where the suit was filed		
3	The case should be tried in another county because this county is not a county of proper venue.	A motion to transfer venue.
4	The case should be tried in another county that is more convenient.	A motion to transfer venue.
5	The case should be tried in another county because of local prejudice.	A motion to change venue.
6	Another court outside Texas has jurisdiction and is more appropriate.	A motion to stay or dismiss for FNC with a prayer to stay or dismiss.
7	The same dispute between the same parties is pending in another court.	A verified denial and a motion to abate. If nothing is left to litigate in this suit after the other suit is litigated, file a motion to dismiss.
Challenging the pleadings		
8	The plaintiff did not plead notice or proof of the claim, as required by statute.	Special exceptions.
9	The plaintiff should amend to delete an unspecified claim for damages and plead damages specifically.	Special exceptions.
10	The plaintiff did not verify its petition.	Special exceptions.
11	The pleadings do not state a cause of action (e.g., fraud) because they do not include the element of injury.	Special exceptions.
12	The pleadings do not state a viable cause of action (e.g., pleadings state cause of action for death of unborn child).	Special exceptions, a motion to dismiss, and if necessary, a motion for summary judgment.
Challenging the suit		
13	The government is immune from suit.	A plea to the jurisdiction and a motion to dismiss.
14	The government is immune from liability.	An affirmative defense and a motion for summary judgment.
15	The suit is barred by a statute of limitations.	An affirmative defense and a motion for summary judgment.
16	The suit is barred by laches.	An affirmative defense and a motion for summary judgment.
17	The same dispute was litigated and resolved by final judgment.	An affirmative defense and a motion for summary judgment.
18	The dispute is subject to arbitration.	A motion to abate and to compel arbitration.

COMMENTARIES
CHAPTER 3. DEFENDANT'S RESPONSE & PLEADINGS
A. DEFENDANT'S PLEADINGS

★

3-1. SUMMARY OF DEFENDANT'S PLEADINGS (CONTINUED)	
To urge this	**File this**
Challenging the suit (continued)	
19 The plaintiff's TRCP 54 conditions precedent were not met.	A verified denial listing conditions the plaintiff did not comply with.
20 The plaintiff's lawsuit is based on, related to, or in response to the defendant's exercise of the right of free speech, the right to petition, or the right of association.	A motion to dismiss under CPRC chapter 27.
Challenging the parties	
21 The plaintiff (or defendant) cannot sue (or be sued) in that capacity.	A verified denial and a motion to abate. If the matter cannot be cured by an amendment, file a motion for summary judgment.
22 The plaintiff lacks standing to bring suit.	A plea to the jurisdiction.
23 Another entity is a necessary party to this suit.	A verified denial and a motion to abate.
24 The defendant is secondarily liable, and the plaintiff has not sued the principal.	A verified denial and a motion to abate.
25 The plaintiff is a foreign corporation doing business in Texas, has not registered with the Secretary of State, and cannot bring a suit for relief.	A verified denial and a motion to dismiss.
26 The plaintiff did not file an assumed-name certificate.	A verified denial and a motion to abate.
27 The death of a party requires the substitution of a representative.	A motion to abate. If a representative is not substituted, the defendant must get a scire facias before moving to dismiss.
28 The plaintiff (or defendant) is not a corporation (or partnership), as pleaded.	A verified denial and a motion to abate. If the matter cannot be cured by amendment, file a motion for summary judgment.
29 The death of a party extinguished the cause of action.	A verified plea to the jurisdiction with a prayer to dismiss.
30 The defendant is a debtor in bankruptcy.	A notice of bankruptcy with a copy of the bankruptcy petition. The bankruptcy order acts as an automatic stay.
31 Misnomer of the defendant.	A motion to abate alleging the defendant was sued in the wrong name.
32 The plaintiff sued the wrong defendant.	A verified denial and a motion for summary judgment.
Challenging liability	
33 The defendant is not responsible for the plaintiff's injury.	A general denial and a motion for summary judgment.
34 Other persons are responsible for some or all of the plaintiff's injury.	A motion for leave to designate an RTP.
35 The defendant did not execute the contract as the plaintiff alleges.	A verified denial and a motion for summary judgment.
36 The endorsement on the note was not genuine.	A verified denial and a motion for summary judgment.
37 There was no consideration for the contract subject to the suit or the contract is usurious.	A verified denial and a motion for summary judgment.
38 A contingency in the contract precludes liability, the contract was modified, there was a failure of consideration, or there was a mutual mistake.	An affirmative defense and a motion for summary judgment.
39 The defendant's debts were discharged in bankruptcy.	An affirmative defense and a motion for summary judgment.

★

3-1. SUMMARY OF DEFENDANT'S PLEADINGS (CONTINUED)	
To urge this	**File this**
Challenging liability (continued)	
40 Duress, estoppel, illegality, license, payment, or waiver.	An affirmative defense and a motion for summary judgment.
41 The loss was within a specific exclusion in an insurance contract.	An affirmative defense and a motion for summary judgment.
42 Any other matter constituting avoidance.	An affirmative defense and a motion for summary judgment.

B. SPECIAL APPEARANCE—CHALLENGING PERSONAL JURISDICTION

§1. GENERAL

§1.1 Rule. TRCP 120a. See CPRC ch. 17.

§1.2 Purpose. A special appearance allows a nonresident defendant to challenge the court's personal jurisdiction over the defendant without becoming subject to the jurisdiction of Texas courts. TRCP 120a; *Kawasaki Steel Corp. v. Middleton*, 699 S.W.2d 199, 201 (Tex.1985). The Due Process Clause of the U.S. Constitution guarantees that a party cannot be bound by the judgment of a forum with which the party has established no meaningful contacts, ties, or relations. *National Indus. Sand Ass'n v. Gibson*, 897 S.W.2d 769, 772 (Tex.1995). The only question addressed in the special appearance is whether a Texas court can constitutionally exercise jurisdiction over the defendant. *Kawasaki*, 699 S.W.2d at 202.

§1.3 Timetables & forms. Timetable, Special Appearance, p. 1210; Timetable, Pretrial Motions, p. 1216; *O'Connor's Texas Civil Forms* (2012), FORMS 3B.

§1.4 Other references. Lensing, *Personal Jurisdiction Doctrine in Texas*, 72 Tex.B.J. 348 (May 2009); Rhodes, *The Predictability Principle in Personal Jurisdiction Doctrine: A Case Study on the Effects of a "Generally" Too Broad, but "Specifically" Too Narrow Approach to Minimum Contacts*, 57 Baylor L.Rev. 135 (2005); *O'Connor's Texas Causes of Action* (2013) (*O'Connor's Texas COA*); *O'Connor's Texas Civil Appeals* (2012) (*O'Connor's Texas Appeals*).

§2. SPECIAL APPEARANCE

§2.1 Deadline to file. The special appearance must be filed before the deadline for filing the answer. For the deadlines for filing the answer, see "Deadline to Answer," ch. 3-E, §2, p. 227.

§2.2 Due order of pleading. The special appearance must be the first pleading the defendant files. See "Due Order of Pleading," ch. 3-A, §3, p. 183. Every other pleading or motion is presumed to be subject to the court's ruling on the special appearance. *Dawson-Austin v. Austin*, 968 S.W.2d 319, 322 (Tex.1998). See "No waiver," §3.4, p. 197.

§2.3 Grounds. The defendant must negate all grounds for personal jurisdiction alleged in the plaintiff's petition. *Kelly v. General Interior Constr., Inc.*, 301 S.W.3d 653, 658 (Tex.2010); *BMC Software Belgium, N.V. v. Marchand*, 83 S.W.3d 789, 793 (Tex.2002); *CSR Ltd. v. Link*, 925 S.W.2d 591, 596 (Tex.1996). The defendant should plead and prove (1) it is not a Texas resident, (2) it did not have minimum contacts with Texas, and (3) even if it had some contacts with Texas, the exercise of jurisdiction would offend the traditional notions of fair play and substantial justice. *BMC Software*, 83 S.W.3d at 795; *Guardian Royal Exch. Assur., Ltd. v. English China Clays, P.L.C.*, 815 S.W.2d 223, 226 (Tex.1991). If the defendant produces sufficient evidence negating jurisdiction, the burden shifts to

★

the plaintiff to show that the court has jurisdiction over the defendant. *M.G.M. Grand Hotel, Inc. v. Castro*, 8 S.W.3d 403, 408 (Tex.App.—Corpus Christi 1999, no pet.).

1. Not Texas resident. The defendant should state that it is not a Texas resident. If the plaintiff did not allege a basis for personal jurisdiction over the defendant (i.e., that the defendant committed or conspired to commit an act in Texas, or that the defendant's acts outside Texas had reasonably foreseeable consequences in Texas), then the defendant needs to prove only that it is a nonresident. *See Kelly*, 301 S.W.3d at 658-59; *Siskind v. Villa Found. for Educ., Inc.*, 642 S.W.2d 434, 438 & n.5 (Tex.1982); *Perna v. Hogan*, 162 S.W.3d 648, 653 (Tex.App.—Houston [14th Dist.] 2005, no pet.); *Frank A. Smith Sales, Inc. v. Atlantic Aero, Inc.*, 31 S.W.3d 742, 746 (Tex.App.—Corpus Christi 2000, no pet.). See *O'Connor's Texas Forms*, FORM 3B:2.

PRACTICE TIP

To determine whether a defect in the petition regarding personal jurisdiction should be challenged by a special appearance or by a motion to quash, consider whether the defect is curable. If the defect is incurable (the defendant is a nonresident and not subject to the jurisdiction of Texas courts), challenge it with a special appearance; if the defect is curable and the defendant admits that Texas courts have personal jurisdiction (e.g., the defendant contracted with the plaintiff in Texas but was not properly served with suit), challenge it with a motion to quash. Kawasaki Steel Corp. v. Middleton, 699 S.W.2d 199, 202-03 (Tex.1985). See "Motion to Quash—Challenging the Service," ch. 3-J, p. 264.

---

2. No minimum contacts. The defendant should plead that it did not have sufficient minimum contacts with Texas to confer jurisdiction on Texas courts. *CSR*, 925 S.W.2d at 594-95; *Guardian Royal*, 815 S.W.2d at 226-27; *Schlobohm v. Schapiro*, 784 S.W.2d 355, 358 (Tex.1990). To negate minimum contacts for personal jurisdiction, the defendant must allege and prove a negative—that is, it did not have any (or enough) contacts with Texas to justify a Texas court's claim of personal jurisdiction over it or over the property subject to the suit. *See BMC Software*, 83 S.W.3d at 795; *Siskind*, 642 S.W.2d at 438. To prove it had no minimum contacts with Texas, the defendant must show that (1) it did not purposefully avail itself of the privilege of conducting activities within Texas and (2) any contacts it may have had with Texas do not give rise to specific or general jurisdiction. *See Moki Mac River Expeditions v. Drugg*, 221 S.W.3d 569, 575-76 (Tex.2007); *Commonwealth Gen. Corp. v. York*, 177 S.W.3d 923, 925 (Tex.2005); *BMC Software*, 83 S.W.3d at 795; *Guardian Royal*, 815 S.W.2d at 227-28; *Schlobohm*, 784 S.W.2d at 358. See *O'Connor's Texas Forms*, FORM 3B:2.

(1) No purposeful availment. In the "purposeful-availment" analysis, (1) only the defendant's contacts with Texas are considered, (2) the defendant's acts must have been purposeful rather than random, fortuitous, or attenuated, and (3) the defendant must have sought some benefit, advantage, or profit by availing itself of the jurisdiction. *IRA Res. v. Griego*, 221 S.W.3d 592, 596 (Tex.2007); *Michiana Easy Livin' Country, Inc. v. Holten*, 168 S.W.3d 777, 784-85 (Tex.2005); *e.g., Retamco Oper., Inc. v. Republic Drilling Co.*, 278 S.W.3d 333, 338-39 (Tex.2009) (D who purchased Texas real property purposefully availed itself of Texas forum); *Riverside Exps., Inc. v. B.R. Crane & Equip., LLC*, 362 S.W.3d 649, 652-53 (Tex.App.—Houston [14th Dist.] 2011, pet. denied) (P, a Texas resident, bought equipment from nonresident D and then sued D in Texas for DTPA violations and breach of contract; D's e-mail correspondence and return of deposit to Texas were not sufficient to show purposeful availment); *see American Type Culture Collection, Inc. v. Coleman*, 83 S.W.3d 801, 808 (Tex.2002) (nonresident D can avoid state's jurisdiction by purposefully structuring transactions to avoid benefits and protections of state's laws).

(a) Analyzing contacts – generally. When analyzing the defendant's contacts, the court should consider the quality and nature of the contacts, not the number of contacts or whether the contacts themselves were tortious. *See Retamco Oper.*, 278 S.W.3d at 339; *Michiana*, 168 S.W.3d at 791-92.

★

(b) Analyzing contacts – stream of commerce. A defendant purposefully avails itself of the Texas forum if it does the following:

[1] Puts products in the stream of commerce knowing that some of them will reach Texas. *Spir Star AG v. Kimich*, 310 S.W.3d 868, 873 (Tex.2010); *Moki Mac*, 221 S.W.3d at 576-77; *see Michiana*, 168 S.W.3d at 786; *see also Zinc Nacional, S.A. v. Bouché Trucking, Inc.*, 308 S.W.3d 395, 397-98 (Tex.2010) (knowledge that goods will end up in forum state is not sufficient; D must actually direct sales to forum state, not through it).

[2] Engages in additional conduct that indicates an intent to serve the Texas market. *Spir Star*, 310 S.W.3d at 873; *Moki Mac*, 221 S.W.3d at 577; *Michiana*, 168 S.W.3d at 786. Additional conduct can include:

[a] Designing the product for the Texas market. *Spir Star*, 310 S.W.3d at 873; *Moki Mac*, 221 S.W.3d at 577.

[b] Advertising in Texas. *Spir Star*, 310 S.W.3d at 873; *Moki Mac*, 221 S.W.3d at 577.

[c] Establishing channels of regular communication with Texas customers. *Spir Star*, 310 S.W.3d at 873; *Moki Mac*, 221 S.W.3d at 577.

[d] Marketing the product through a distributor who will sell the product in Texas. *Spir Star*, 310 S.W.3d at 873; *see Moki Mac*, 221 S.W.3d at 577. When sales of a product in Texas are conducted through a distributor, the actions of the nonresident-manufacturer defendant, not the distributor or affiliate, are analyzed to determine purposeful availment. *See Spir Star*, 310 S.W.3d at 874. Usually, when a nonresident manufacturer specifically targets Texas as a market for its products by using a distributor as an in-state sales agent, the manufacturer is subject to a products-liability suit in Texas based on a product sold in the state. *Id.* But there may be situations when the use of a Texas distributor will not support a finding that the nonresident manufacturer intended to serve the Texas market—for example, the manufacturer may have chosen to use the Texas distributorship to increase the manufacturer's bottom line through gained efficiencies and economies of scale rather than to serve the Texas market. *Id.* at 875.

(c) Analyzing contacts – Internet activity. To determine whether contacts arising from Internet activity are sufficient to establish personal jurisdiction, courts consider three categories of Internet activity: (1) websites used for transacting business, (2) passive websites used only for advertising, and (3) interactive websites that allow for the exchange of information. *All Star Enter. v. Buchanan*, 298 S.W.3d 404, 426-27 (Tex.App.— Houston [14th Dist.] 2009, no pet.); *Schexnayder v. Daniels*, 187 S.W.3d 238, 248 (Tex.App.—Texarkana 2006, pet. dism'd); *Reiff v. Roy*, 115 S.W.3d 700, 705-06 (Tex.App.—Dallas 2003, pet. denied); *Michel v. Rocket Eng'g*, 45 S.W.3d 658, 677 (Tex.App.—Fort Worth 2001, no pet.); *Daimler-Benz A.G. v. Olson*, 21 S.W.3d 707, 725 (Tex.App.—Austin 2000, pet. dism'd). The nature and quality of these Internet contacts are evaluated on a sliding scale. *Experimental Aircraft Ass'n v. Doctor*, 76 S.W.3d 496, 506 (Tex.App.—Houston [14th Dist.] 2002, no pet.). If the website is clearly used for business transactions, such as entering into contracts or repeatedly transmitting information, it will generally be sufficient to establish minimum contacts. *Schexnayder*, 187 S.W.3d at 248; *Exito Elecs. Co. v. Trejo*, 166 S.W.3d 839, 857-58 (Tex.App.—Corpus Christi 2005, no pet.); *Reiff*, 115 S.W.3d at 705; *Daimler-Benz*, 21 S.W.3d at 725. If the website is passive (i.e., used only to provide contact information or to advertise), it is insufficient to establish minimum contacts, even if the website is accessible to residents of Texas. *Riverside Exps.*, 362 S.W.3d at 655; *Schexnayder*, 187 S.W.3d at 248; *Exito Elecs.*, 166 S.W.3d at 858; *Reiff*, 115 S.W.3d at 705-06; *see Waterman S.S. Corp. v. Ruiz*, 355 S.W.3d 387, 412 (Tex.App.—Houston [1st Dist.] 2011, pet. denied). If the website is interactive, allowing for the exchange of information between the potential customer and the person or company hosting the website, personal jurisdiction is determined by the degree of interaction. *Schexnayder*, 187 S.W.3d at 248; *Exito Elecs.*, 166 S.W.3d at 858 n.16; *Reiff*, 115 S.W.3d at 706; *Daimler-Benz*, 21 S.W.3d at 725. The court will evaluate this middle ground based on the level of interaction and the commercial nature of the information exchanged. *Experimental Aircraft*, 76 S.W.3d at 507. An interactive website alone may not be sufficient to establish personal jurisdiction, but courts will consider it along with a defendant's other contacts. *See Daimler-Benz*, 21 S.W.3d at 725. Whether

SPECIAL APPEARANCE

Internet contacts are sufficient to establish personal jurisdiction is determined on a case-by-case basis. See chart 3-2, below, for examples.

3-2. INTERNET CONTACTS		
	Facts	Case
Sufficient contacts		
1	D's products were available to Texas residents on its website, and D paid search engines to direct users to website to place orders.	*I & JC*, 164 S.W.3d 877, 889 (E.P. 2005, denied).
2	Interactive website had online shop with e-mail purchasing capabilities, encouraged people to become members online, and heavily promoted membership benefits, including insurance plans and discounted prices.	*Experimental Aircraft*, 76 S.W.3d 496, 507 (Hous. [14th] 2002, no pet.) (commercial nature of exchange of information was significant factor supporting personal jurisdiction).
3	Interactive website allowed customers to submit comments and questions to D's representatives and to receive e-mails from D.	*Daimler-Benz*, 21 S.W.3d 707, 725 (Aus. 2000, dism'd).
Insufficient contacts		
4	Passive website provided contact information, but customers could not book cargo or enter into contracts through website and D could not respond to customer inquiries through website.	*Waterman S.S.*, 355 S.W.3d 387, 412 (Hous. [1st] 2011, denied).
5	Passive website posted D's telephone number, e-mail address, and a contact form.	*Jackson*, 312 S.W.3d 146, 155 (Hous. [14th] 2010, no pet.).
6	Website allowed visitors to submit online employment application but instructed them to contact Utah office for more information.	*All Star Enter.*, 298 S.W.3d 404, 427(Hous. [14th] 2009, no pet.).
7	Website displayed D-doctor's biography, credentials, and job description, but did not allow doctors to interact about patient care online.	*Schexnayder*, 187 S.W.3d 238, 249 (Texark. 2006, dism'd).
8	Passive website identified catalogue items and provided contact information for potentially interested customers.	*Exito Elecs.*, 166 S.W.3d 839, 858 (C.C. 2005, no pet.); *see Townsend*, 83 S.W.3d 913, 922 (Texark. 2002, denied).
9	Website did not allow D to directly respond over Internet to information provided by potential customers; sales representative followed up personally.	*Michel*, 45 S.W.3d 658, 678 (F.W. 2001, no pet.).
10	Website allowed customers to make room reservations with D-hotel/casino but did not allow customers to obtain line of credit.	*Riviera Oper.*, 29 S.W.3d 905, 910-11 (Beau. 2000, denied).

(d) Analyzing contacts – attributed actions.

[1] Agents. An agent's contacts can be attributed to its principal. *Olympia Capital Assocs. v. Jackson*, 247 S.W.3d 399, 412 (Tex.App.—Dallas 2008, no pet.); *Walker Ins. v. Bottle Rock Power Corp.*, 108 S.W.3d 538, 549 & n.4 (Tex.App.—Houston [14th Dist.] 2003, no pet.). The plaintiff must show (1) that the principal had the right to control both the means and the details of the agent's work, (2) evidence of actual or apparent authority, or (3) that the principal later ratified the agent's conduct. *See Greenfield Energy, Inc. v. Duprey*, 252 S.W.3d 721, 734 (Tex.App.—Houston [14th Dist.] 2008, no pet.); *Coleman v. Klöckner & Co.*, 180 S.W.3d 577, 588 (Tex.App.—Houston [14th Dist.] 2005, no pet.). See *O'Connor's Texas COA*, "Principal-Agent Liability," ch. 38, p. 1183.

[2] Corporate subsidiaries. A parent corporation's contacts can be attributed to its subsidiary if the parent corporation and the subsidiary can be "fused" for jurisdictional purposes (i.e., jurisdictional veil-piercing). *See PHC-Minden, L.P. v. Kimberly-Clark Corp.*, 235 S.W.3d 163, 175 (Tex.2007). To fuse the parent corporation and its subsidiary, the plaintiff must prove that the parent controls the internal business operations and

---

☆

---

affairs of the subsidiary. *Id.*; *BMC Software*, 83 S.W.3d at 799. The degree of control must be greater than is normally associated with common ownership and directorship; the evidence must show that the two entities are no longer separate and distinct and that the corporate identities should be fused to prevent fraud or injustice. *PHC-Minden*, 235 S.W.3d at 175; *BMC Software*, 83 S.W.3d at 799.

[3] **Corporate officers & employees.** A corporation's contacts usually cannot be attributed to its employees. *Nichols v. Tseng Hsiang Lin*, 282 S.W.3d 743, 750 (Tex.App.—Dallas 2009, no pet.). Under the fiduciary-shield doctrine, a court cannot exercise general jurisdiction over a nonresident corporate officer or employee if the only continuing and systematic contacts with Texas are those the defendant made on behalf of her employer. *Nichols*, 282 S.W.3d at 750; *see Siskind*, 642 S.W.2d at 438; *Garner v. Furmanite Australia Pty., Ltd.*, 966 S.W.2d 798, 803 (Tex.App.—Houston [1st Dist.] 1998, pet. denied). The corporation's contacts can be considered if the plaintiff shows (1) the defendant was using the corporate entity as a sham or (2) the corporation is the defendant's alter ego. *Wolf v. Summers-Wood, L.P.*, 214 S.W.3d 783, 790 (Tex.App.—Dallas 2007, no pet.); *J&J Marine, Inc. v. Le*, 982 S.W.2d 918, 927 (Tex.App.—Corpus Christi 1998, no pet.); *see Nichols*, 282 S.W.3d at 750 (alter ego).

(2) **Insufficient Texas contacts.**

(a) **Specific jurisdiction.** To negate specific jurisdiction, the defendant should plead and prove that the plaintiff's cause of action did not arise from or relate to the defendant's contacts with Texas. *See Kelly*, 301 S.W.3d at 659; *Moki Mac*, 221 S.W.3d at 579; *BMC Software*, 83 S.W.3d at 796; *Guardian Royal*, 815 S.W.2d at 227; *Schlobohm*, 784 S.W.2d at 358. The "arise from or relate to" requirement means the defendant's contacts must be substantially connected to the operative facts of the litigation. *Spir Star*, 310 S.W.3d at 874; *Retamco Oper.*, 278 S.W.3d at 340; *see Guardian Royal*, 815 S.W.2d at 228 (focus is on relationship among D, forum, and litigation); *see, e.g.*, *Moki Mac*, 221 S.W.3d at 585 (although nonresident D purposefully availed itself of Texas forum by advertising and soliciting customers for out-of-state rafting trips, contacts did not substantially relate to P's suit, which was for negligence based on personal injury in Arizona). Whether contacts are sufficient to establish specific jurisdiction is determined on a case-by-case basis. See chart 3-3, below, for examples.

3-3. SPECIFIC JURISDICTION	
Facts	**Case**
Sufficient contacts	
1	D marketed products to Texas customers and sold them through its Texas distributor.	*Spir Star AG*, 310 S.W.3d 868, 874 (Tex.2010).
2	D received transfer of Texas oil and gas interests that were already subject of suit between two Texas companies.	*Retamco Oper.*, 278 S.W.3d 333, 341 (Tex.2009).
3	Joint venture between Florida and Texas companies, in which both shared control, contracted for elevators to be delivered to Texas.	*Zac Smith & Co.*, 734 S.W.2d 662, 664-65 (Tex.1987).
4	D had sales office in Texas and annual sales of $40-48 million worth of steel that reached Texas.	*Kawasaki Steel*, 699 S.W.2d 199, 201 (Tex.1985).
5	D purchased puppy located in Texas and traveled to Texas twice for training, observation, and receipt of puppy.	*Fleischer*, 270 S.W.3d 334, 338 (Dal. 2008, no pet.).
6	D solicited P's business by calling P's Texas offices three times to renew agreement and offered to perform contract in Texas.	*Holk*, 149 S.W.3d 769, 776 (Aus. 2004, no pet.).
7	D purchased promissory notes executed by Texas residents, with knowledge that notes were subject of Texas litigation.	*Kelly Inv.*, 85 S.W.3d 371, 373-74 (Dal. 2002, no pet.).

COMMENTARIES
CHAPTER 3. DEFENDANT'S RESPONSE & PLEADINGS
B. SPECIAL APPEARANCE—CHALLENGING PERSONAL JURISDICTION

SPECIAL APPEARANCE

★

3-3. SPECIFIC JURISDICTION (CONTINUED)	
Facts	**Case**
Sufficient contacts (continued)	
8 Over five-year period, D audited Texas firm managed entirely in San Antonio, which later was subject of securities-fraud class action.	*Gutierrez*, 100 S.W.3d 261, 272-73 (S.A. 2002, dism'd).
9 D-sales agent contracted with Texas corporation, sent orders to Texas, received payments from Texas, and cashed checks drawn on Texas bank.	*Billingsley Parts*, 881 S.W.2d 165, 169-70 (Hous. [1st] 1994, denied).
Insufficient contacts	
10 D used third-party trucking service to transport goods through Texas to out-of-state customer.	*Zinc Nacional*, 308 S.W.3d 395, 397-98 (Tex.2010).
11 P bought RV from D-factory outlet located in Indiana; RV was constructed, equipped, and paid for outside Texas and was shipped by D to Texas at P's request and expense.	*Michiana*, 168 S.W.3d 777, 787-88 (Tex.2005).
12 D sent employees to Texas to attend corporate meetings during its purchase of insurance company headquartered in Texas.	*Commonwealth Gen.*, 177 S.W.3d 923, 925 (Tex.2005).
13 Officers of wholly-owned Belgian subsidiary of Texas company had conversation in Texas about whether to offer employment and stock options to P, who was not present.	*BMC Software*, 83 S.W.3d 789, 796-97 (Tex.2002).
14 Foreign manufacturer knew product would be shipped to Texas but did not design product for use in Texas or market it there.	*CMMC*, 929 S.W.2d 435, 439 (Tex.1996).
15 P alleged conspiracy between D-Maryland organization and Texas corporation.	*National Indus.*, 897 S.W.2d 769, 774-76 (Tex.1995).
16 D-foreign reinsurer contracted with foreign primary insurer to pay primary insurer for claims paid to its insureds, some of whom lived in Texas.	*Malaysia British Assur.*, 830 S.W.2d 919, 921 (Tex.1992).
17 D-doctor performed surgery on P in Michigan and prescribed follow-up care to take place at health-care facility in Texas.	*Brocail*, 132 S.W.3d 552, 562-63 & n.5 (Hous. [14th] 2004, denied).
18 D initiated and entered into contract with Texas corporation; contract was to be performed entirely outside Texas, and payments were forwarded to Texas.	*Blair Comm.*, 80 S.W.3d 723, 730 (Hous. [1st] 2002, no pet.).
19 One of Ps traveled to Texas for reasons unrelated to suit and made one telephone call to Ds' agent to confirm transaction.	*Al-Turki*, 958 S.W.2d 258, 262 (East. 1997, denied).

    (b) General jurisdiction. To negate general jurisdiction, the defendant should plead and prove it did not have continuous or systematic contacts with Texas. See *BMC Software*, 83 S.W.3d at 796; *Guardian Royal*, 815 S.W.2d at 228; *Schlobohm*, 784 S.W.2d at 358. General jurisdiction requires a showing of substantial contact with the forum, a more demanding minimum-contacts analysis than for specific jurisdiction. *BMC Software*, 83 S.W.3d at 797; *see Spir Star*, 310 S.W.3d at 873; *PHC-Minden*, 235 S.W.3d at 168. Unlike a specific-jurisdiction analysis, which focuses on the contacts that substantially relate to the litigation, a general-jurisdiction analysis requires that all of the defendant's contacts with Texas be carefully investigated, compiled, sorted, and analyzed for proof of a pattern of continuing and systematic activity. *American Type Culture*, 83 S.W.3d at 809; *IRA Res. v. Griego*, 235 S.W.3d 263, 266 (Tex.App.—Corpus Christi 2007, no pet.); *see PHC-Minden*, 235 S.W.3d at 168 (general jurisdiction is "dispute-blind," i.e., court's jurisdiction is determined without regard to the nature of the claim presented). Thus, the general-jurisdiction analysis should focus on the defendant's contacts with Texas, rather than on the incident that is the basis of the suit. *PHC-Minden*, 235 S.W.3d at 169. The court can consider all of the defendant's contacts with Texas up to the date suit is filed. *Id.* Whether contacts are sufficient to establish general jurisdiction is determined on a case-by-case basis. See chart 3-4, below, for examples.

★

3-4. GENERAL JURISDICTION	
Facts	**Case**
Sufficient contacts	
1	D frequently traveled to Texas to visit his children and conducted job search while visiting.	*In re S.A.V.*, 837 S.W.2d 80, 86 (Tex.1992).
2	D, who loaned money to Texas corporation in exchange for stock, became corporation's sole director and conducted corporation's first meeting, which took place in Dallas.	*Schlobohm*, 784 S.W.2d 355, 356 (Tex.1990).
3	D had bank account in Texas used to exchange currency, invest money, deposit loans, and provide profits to subsidiary corporations.	*El Puerto*, 82 S.W.3d 622, 633 (C.C. 2002, dism'd).
4	D-company continuously used its trademarks and service marks in Texas to identify its cars and related parts and services.	*Daimler-Benz*, 21 S.W.3d 707, 720 (Aus. 2000, dism'd).
5	D conducted business from permanent office in Texas.	*James*, 965 S.W.2d 594, 598-99 (Hous. [1st] 1998, no pet.).
6	D-attorney in Colorado was licensed to practice in Texas and handled Texas cases.	*Nikolai*, 922 S.W.2d 229, 239 (F.W. 1996, denied).
7	D owned real estate in Texas that was involved in lawsuit.	*Potkovick*, 904 S.W.2d 846, 850 (East. 1995, no writ).
8	D, who lived in California, was director of two Texas corporations.	*Thorpe*, 882 S.W.2d 592, 597 (Hous. [1st] 1994, no writ).
9	D signed contract with Texas company and made routine sales to Texas companies.	*General Elec.*, 804 S.W.2d 527, 531 (Hous. [1st] 1990, denied).
Insufficient contacts	
10	D purchased helicopters, negotiated contracts, and trained its pilots in Texas.	*Helicopteros Nacionales*, 466 U.S. 408, 416 (1984).
11	D's employees attended seminars in Texas, and D made purchases from Texas vendors and had three contracts with Texas entities.	*PHC-Minden*, 235 S.W.3d 163, 170-71 (Tex.2007).
12	Nonprofit organization sold products to Texans mostly through orders received in Maryland, purchased supplies from Texas vendors, and set up exhibit booths and distributed corporate publications at conferences in Texas.	*American Type Culture*, 83 S.W.3d 801, 807-08 (Tex.2002).
13	D purchased products from wholly-owned subsidiary in Texas to distribute in Europe.	*BMC Software*, 83 S.W.3d 789, 797 (Tex.2002).
14	Maryland organization mailed letters and publications to its members, some of whom lived in Texas.	*National Indus.*, 897 S.W.2d 769, 774 (Tex.1995).
15	Mexican company transported cargo through Mexico to U.S. border; cargo was delivered to another company in "border zone" that extended into Texas and was then sent to its final destination.	*Grupo TMM*, 327 S.W.3d 357, 362-63 (Hous. [14th] 2010, denied).
16	Nevada corporation owned loans secured by real-estate liens on properties in Texas.	*Bryant*, 153 S.W.3d 626, 631 (Amar. 2004, no pet.).
17	Chinese corporation shipped goods to Texas at the direction of third party it had contracted with.	*Hitachi Shin Din Cable*, 106 S.W.3d 776, 784-85 (Texark. 2003, no pet.).
18	German corporation owned indirect interests in six companies doing business in Texas.	*Preussag*, 16 S.W.3d 110, 123 (Hous. [1st] 2000, dism'd).

3. Exercise of jurisdiction unfair. The defendant should state that the court's exercise of jurisdiction over the defendant and its property will offend traditional notions of fair play and substantial justice and will be inconsistent with the constitutional requirements of due process. *International Shoe Co. v. Washington*, 326 U.S.

———————————————— ☆ ————————————————

310, 316 (1945); *Guardian Royal*, 815 S.W.2d at 231-33; *see Spir Star*, 310 S.W.3d at 878-79. The exercise of jurisdiction will rarely be deemed unfair when the defendant has established minimum contacts with the state. *Spir Star*, 310 S.W.3d at 878; *Guardian Royal*, 815 S.W.2d at 231; *Minucci v. Sogevalor, S.A.*, 14 S.W.3d 790, 798-99 (Tex. App.—Houston [1st Dist.] 2000, no pet.).

(1) U.S. defendant. If the defendant is a resident of the United States, the defendant should allege that the exercise of jurisdiction by the Texas court over the defendant would be unfair, considering the following factors:

(a) The burden on the defendant. *Guardian Royal*, 815 S.W.2d at 231; *Schexnayder*, 187 S.W.3d at 246; *e.g.*, *Small v. Small*, 216 S.W.3d 872, 879-80 (Tex.App.—Beaumont 2007, pet. denied) (D's status as graduate student at university in Virginia was insufficient to establish undue burden).

(b) The interest of Texas in adjudicating the dispute. *Guardian Royal*, 815 S.W.2d at 231; *Schexnayder*, 187 S.W.3d at 246.

(c) The plaintiff's interest in obtaining convenient and effective relief. *Guardian Royal*, 815 S.W.2d at 231; *Schexnayder*, 187 S.W.3d at 246.

(d) The interstate judicial system's interest in obtaining the most efficient resolution of controversies. *Guardian Royal*, 815 S.W.2d at 231; *Schexnayder*, 187 S.W.3d at 246.

(e) The shared interest of the states in furthering fundamental and substantive social policies. *Guardian Royal*, 815 S.W.2d at 231; *Schexnayder*, 187 S.W.3d at 246.

(2) Foreign defendant. If the defendant is a resident of a foreign country, the defendant should allege that the exercise of jurisdiction by the Texas court over the defendant would be unfair, considering the following factors:

(a) The burden on the defendant. *Spir Star*, 310 S.W.3d at 878; *Guardian Royal*, 815 S.W.2d at 232.

(b) The interest of Texas in adjudicating the dispute. *Spir Star*, 310 S.W.3d at 878; *Guardian Royal*, 815 S.W.2d at 232.

(c) The plaintiff's interest in obtaining convenient and effective relief. *Spir Star*, 310 S.W.3d at 878; *Guardian Royal*, 815 S.W.2d at 232.

(d) The international interest in obtaining the most efficient resolution of controversies. *Spir Star*, 310 S.W.3d at 878 & n.3; *see Guardian Royal*, 815 S.W.2d at 232 & n.17.

(e) The shared interest of the nations in furthering fundamental and substantive social policies. *Spir Star*, 310 S.W.3d at 878.

§2.4 Verification. The special appearance must be verified—that is, made by sworn motion. TRCP 120a(1); *Exito Elecs. Co. v. Trejo*, 142 S.W.3d 302, 307 (Tex.2004); *Siemens AG v. Houston Cas. Co.*, 127 S.W.3d 436, 439 (Tex.App.—Dallas 2004, pet. dism'd); *International Turbine Serv. v. Lovitt*, 881 S.W.2d 805, 808 (Tex.App.—Fort Worth 1994, writ denied). The motion cannot be verified based on information and belief. *See International Turbine*, 881 S.W.2d at 808. An unverified special appearance may be amended to cure the defect, even after the trial court has ruled on the special appearance, as long as the amendment is filed before the defendant enters a general appearance. *Dawson-Austin v. Austin*, 968 S.W.2d 319, 322 (Tex.1998); *see Exito Elecs.*, 142 S.W.3d at 307 (unverified special appearance does not concede jurisdiction). See "Amending special appearance," §2.7, p. 197. If the plaintiff does not object to an unverified special appearance, and sworn proof is presented at the hearing, the issue is tried by consent. *General Refractories Co. v. Martin*, 8 S.W.3d 818, 820 n.1 (Tex.App.—Beaumont 2000, pet. denied). If the special-appearance motion is not verified, and no sworn proof attests to the truth of the statements in the motion (either by affidavit or at the hearing), the court should deny the motion. *See Casino Magic Corp. v. King*, 43 S.W.3d 14, 18 (Tex.App.—Dallas 2001, pet. denied).

─────────────────────────────── ★ ───────────────────────────────

§2.5 Evidence. A defendant should file affidavits with the special appearance that provide evidentiary support for the factual allegations. See "Evidence," §8.3, p. 200.

§2.6 Requesting hearing. A defendant must ask for and secure a hearing. *Milacron Inc. v. Performance Rail Tie, L.P.*, 262 S.W.3d 872, 876 (Tex.App.—Texarkana 2008, no pet.); *Bruneio v. Bruneio*, 890 S.W.2d 150, 154 (Tex.App.—Corpus Christi 1994, no writ). If a defendant does not secure a hearing, it waives the special appearance and effectively makes a general appearance. *See Bruneio*, 890 S.W.2d at 154. See "Making general appearance," §3.3, this page.

§2.7 Amending special appearance. A defendant may amend a special appearance. TRCP 120a(1); *e.g.*, *Dawson-Austin v. Austin*, 968 S.W.2d 319, 322 (Tex.1998) (amendment to add verification permitted after hearing but before entering a general appearance); *Zamarron v. Shinko Wire Co.*, 125 S.W.3d 132, 139 (Tex.App.—Houston [14th Dist.] 2003, pet. denied) (D did not waive special appearance by submitting amended affidavit).

§3. WAIVER OF SPECIAL APPEARANCE

§3.1 Consenting to jurisdiction. A defendant expressly consents to and waives its objection to personal jurisdiction if it executes a contract with a forum-selection clause selecting Texas as the forum. *See Abacan Tech. Servs. v. Global Mar. Int'l Servs.*, 994 S.W.2d 839, 843 (Tex.App.—Houston [1st Dist.] 1999, no pet.).

§3.2 Not observing due order of pleading. A defendant waives its objection to personal jurisdiction if it files any other pleading before its special appearance. See "Due Order of Pleading," ch. 3-A, §3, p. 183.

§3.3 Making general appearance. A defendant waives its objection to personal jurisdiction if it makes a general appearance. *Von Briesen, Purtell & Roper v. French*, 78 S.W.3d 570, 575 (Tex.App.—Amarillo 2002, pet. dism'd). Every appearance before judgment that does not comply with TRCP 120a is a general appearance. TRCP 120a(1); *Exito Elecs. Co. v. Trejo*, 142 S.W.3d 302, 304 (Tex.2004). A party makes a general appearance when it (1) invokes the trial court's judgment on any question other than the court's jurisdiction, (2) recognizes by its acts that an action is properly pending, or (3) seeks affirmative action from the court. *Exito Elecs.*, 142 S.W.3d at 304; *Dawson-Austin v. Austin*, 968 S.W.2d 319, 322 (Tex.1998); *Moore v. Elektro-Mobil Technik GmbH*, 874 S.W.2d 324, 327 (Tex.App.—El Paso 1994, writ denied).

§3.4 No waiver.

1. Actions before filing special appearance. The defendant does not make a general appearance (and thus does not waive its objection to personal jurisdiction) if it takes the following actions before filing the special appearance.

(1) Notice of removal. The defendant may file a notice of removal to federal court before the special appearance without waiving the special appearance. *Antonio v. Rico Marino, S.A.*, 910 S.W.2d 624, 629 (Tex. App.—Houston [14th Dist.] 1995, no writ).

(2) Correspondence with court. Under certain circumstances, the defendant can correspond with the court without waiving the special appearance. See "Correspondence with court," ch. 3-A, §3.2.3, p. 184.

(3) Rule 11 agreement. A Rule 11 agreement that extends the time for the defendant to file its initial pleading in response to the plaintiff's petition is not a general appearance, even if the agreement is not expressly made subject to the ruling on the special appearance. *Exito Elecs. Co. v. Trejo*, 142 S.W.3d 302, 306 (Tex.2004); *see, e.g.*, *Crystalix Grp. Int'l v. Vitro Laser Grp. USA, Inc.*, 127 S.W.3d 425, 428 (Tex.App.—Dallas 2004, pet. denied) (Rule 11 agreement to extend TRO did not alter material components of TRO and was not general appearance); *Angelou v. African Overseas Un.*, 33 S.W.3d 269, 275-76 (Tex.App.—Houston [14th Dist.] 2000, no pet.) (Rule 11 agreement to extend answer date filed before special appearance was not general appearance because agreement did not seek affirmative action from court or recognize action as properly pending). A Rule 11 agreement is not by itself a request for enforcement or for any other affirmative action by the court. *Exito Elecs.*, 142 S.W.3d at 305.

★

---

2. Actions after filing special appearance. A defendant does not make a general appearance (and thus does not waive its objection to personal jurisdiction) if it asks for intermediate relief by filing other pleadings and motions after the special appearance, as long as the documents do not acknowledge the trial court's jurisdiction or seek court action other than a dismissal for lack of jurisdiction. *See **Dawson-Austin v. Austin**,* 968 S.W.2d 319, 322-23 (Tex.1998) (statement that pleading is "subject to the ruling on the special appearance" is not required to avoid waiver); *see, e.g., **GFTA Trendanalysen v. Varme**,* 991 S.W.2d 785, 786-87 (Tex.1999) (D did not consent to personal jurisdiction by challenging service in its special appearance); ***Yuen v. Fisher**,* 227 S.W.3d 193, 199 (Tex. App.—Houston [1st Dist.] 2007, no pet.) (motion to set aside default judgment, in which D asked for sanctions subject to court's ruling on special appearance, did not waive special appearance). TRCP 120a(1) provides that any pleading or motion may be filed after the special appearance without waiving the special appearance. ***Dawson-Austin**,* 968 S.W.2d at 322-23.

(1) Motion for continuance. The defendant does not waive its special appearance by filing a motion for continuance. *See **Dawson-Austin**,* 968 S.W.2d at 323. See "Defendant," §7.2, p. 200.

(2) Discovery. The defendant does not waive its special appearance by engaging in discovery related to the special appearance. TRCP 120a(1). See "Discovery," §6, p. 199.

(3) Motion for new trial after default judgment. The defendant does not waive its special appearance by filing a motion for new trial with or after a special appearance. See "Special Appearance After Default Judgment," §4, this page.

§4. SPECIAL APPEARANCE AFTER DEFAULT JUDGMENT

If a nonresident defendant discovers that a default judgment was rendered against it before the deadline for filing a motion for new trial, the nonresident defendant can preserve the due order of pleading while challenging the default judgment by filing the documents in the following order: (1) a special appearance, (2) a motion for new trial, and (3) an answer. *See* TRCP 120a(1) (special appearance must be filed before any other pleading or motion); *see, e.g., **Lang v. Capital Res.**,* 102 S.W.3d 861, 864 (Tex.App.—Dallas 2003, no pet.) (D filed special appearance and, subject to that, motion for new trial); ***Puri v. Mansukhani**,* 973 S.W.2d 701, 706-07 (Tex.App.—Houston [14th Dist.] 1998, no pet.) (same); ***Koch Graphics, Inc. v. Avantech, Inc.**,* 803 S.W.2d 432, 433 (Tex.App.—Dallas 1991, no writ) (D filed special appearance and, subject to that, motion to quash, motion for new trial, and answer). The defendant must request a ruling on the special appearance before a ruling on any other motion. *E.g., **Landry v. Daigrepont**,* 35 S.W.3d 265, 267-68 (Tex.App.—Corpus Christi 2000, no pet.) (D waived special appearance by arguing motion for new trial first). A motion for new trial and a motion to quash service, filed with or after a special appearance, do not waive the special appearance; matters in the same or a later instrument are subject to the special appearance. TRCP 120a(1); *Dawson-Austin v. Austin,* 968 S.W.2d 319, 322 (Tex.1998). The defendant may include language in the motion for new trial that it is ready to proceed to trial without waiving the special appearance as long as the motion does not acknowledge jurisdiction or ask for some action other than dismissal for lack of jurisdiction. *See **Lang**,* 102 S.W.3d at 864; *Puri,* 973 S.W.2d at 707.

§5. RESPONSE

The plaintiff may file a response challenging the defendant's allegations of lack of personal jurisdiction. See ***O'Connor's Texas Forms**,* FORM 3B:3. The response should be verified and supported with affidavits. The plaintiff may respond to the defendant's special appearance in the following ways.

§5.1 Amend petition. If the defendant filed a bare-bones response and affidavit, alleging simply that it is a nonresident, the plaintiff should review its petition. See "Not Texas resident," §2.3.1, p. 190. If the plaintiff finds it did not allege any actions in Texas by the defendant, it should amend its pleading to include them. ***Kelly v. General Interior Constr., Inc.**,* 301 S.W.3d 653, 659 & n.6 (Tex.2010). See "Over nonresident," ch. 2-B, §4.1.2, p. 103.

§5.2 Object to procedural errors. The plaintiff should object to any procedural errors in the defendant's special appearance. If the plaintiff does not object, it waives the error. *See, e.g., **International Turbine Serv. v. Lovitt**,* 881 S.W.2d 805, 808 (Tex.App.—Fort Worth 1994, writ denied) (P waived error in inadequate affidavit).

---------------------- ✯ ----------------------

§5.3 Allege waiver by defendant. The plaintiff should watch for any action the defendant takes that is inconsistent with a special appearance and that could be construed as a general appearance. In the response, the plaintiff should allege the defendant waived its special appearance because (as is appropriate to the case) the defendant did not observe the due order of pleading, the defendant made a general appearance, or the defendant did not limit the special appearance to the issue of personal jurisdiction.

§5.4 Challenge defendant's allegations. The plaintiff should challenge the defendant's factual grounds for denying jurisdiction and the defendant's legal interpretation of the factors that constitute jurisdiction over a nonresident.

1. Minimum contacts. The plaintiff should state that the court has jurisdiction over the defendant because the defendant purposefully established minimum contacts with Texas. *Schlobohm v. Schapiro*, 784 S.W.2d 355, 358 (Tex.1990); *see Guardian Royal Exch. Assur., Ltd. v. English China Clays, P.L.C.*, 815 S.W.2d 223, 232 (Tex.1991). In certain situations, the court can analyze the contacts of the defendant's parent corporation, agents, or corporate officers and employees. See "Analyzing contacts – attributed actions," §2.3.2(1)(d), p. 192.

(1) Specific jurisdiction. To establish specific jurisdiction, the plaintiff should plead and prove that its cause of action arose from and relates to the nonresident defendant's contacts with Texas. *Schlobohm*, 784 S.W.2d at 358. See "Specific Jurisdiction," chart 3-3, p. 193.

(2) General jurisdiction. To establish general jurisdiction, the plaintiff should plead and prove that the nonresident defendant had continuous and systematic contacts with Texas. See "General Jurisdiction," chart 3-4, p. 195.

2. No issue of fair play. The plaintiff should plead and prove that the court's exercise of jurisdiction over the defendant and its property will not offend traditional notions of fair play and substantial justice and is consistent with the constitutional requirements of due process. *See Schlobohm*, 784 S.W.2d at 359.

§6. DISCOVERY

The parties may engage in discovery before the hearing on the special appearance. *See* TRCP 120a(1). A defendant does not waive its special appearance by engaging in discovery related to the special appearance. *Exito Elecs. Co. v. Trejo*, 142 S.W.3d 302, 306-07 (Tex.2004). The defendant's participation in the court's resolution of discovery matters related to the special appearance is not a request for affirmative relief or a recognition that the suit is properly pending. *Id.* at 306-07 & n.27. Discovery conducted before the special appearance is resolved should be limited to issues related to the special appearance. *See Dawson-Austin v. Austin*, 968 S.W.2d 319, 323-24 (Tex.1998) (dicta). Some courts of appeals have held, however, that a defendant does not waive its special appearance by engaging in discovery unrelated to the special appearance, even if the discovery involves the merits of the case. *E.g.*, *Case v. Grammar*, 31 S.W.3d 304, 311 (Tex.App.—San Antonio 2000, no pet.) (nothing in TRCP 120a(1) limits discovery only to matters related to special appearance), *disapproved on other grounds*, *BMC Software Belgium, N.V. v. Marchand*, 83 S.W.3d 789 (Tex.2002); *Minucci v. Sogevalor, S.A.*, 14 S.W.3d 790, 801 (Tex.App.—Houston [1st Dist.] 2000, no pet.) (same); *see, e.g.*, *Silbaugh v. Ramirez*, 126 S.W.3d 88, 93 (Tex.App.—Houston [1st Dist.] 2002, no pet.) (filing motions opposing discovery and serving nonjurisdictional discovery on P did not waive special appearance); *Gutierrez v. Deloitte & Touche*, 100 S.W.3d 261, 267-68 (Tex.App.—San Antonio 2002, pet. dism'd) (filing mandamus to challenge discovery order compelling production of allegedly privileged materials did not waive special appearance).

§7. CONTINUANCE

§7.1 Plaintiff. TRCP 120a authorizes the court to grant a plaintiff's sworn motion for continuance if the plaintiff cannot present facts by affidavit to respond to the special appearance and needs time to secure affidavits, take depositions, or engage in other discovery. TRCP 120a(3). See *O'Connor's Texas Forms*, FORM 3B:5.

1. Grounds. The plaintiff should show that (1) the information sought is material to establishing jurisdiction and (2) it acted diligently in trying to obtain the information sought. *Barron v. Vanier*, 190 S.W.3d 841, 847 (Tex.App.—Fort Worth 2006, no pet.); *see Lamar v. Poncon*, 305 S.W.3d 130, 139-40 (Tex.App.—Houston [1st Dist.] 2009, pet. denied).

⎯⎯⎯⎯⎯⎯⎯⎯⎯⎯ ✫ ⎯⎯⎯⎯⎯⎯⎯⎯⎯⎯

2. Limited discovery – jurisdictional facts. When the court grants a continuance for the plaintiff to conduct additional discovery, the discovery is limited to the jurisdictional facts necessary to justify the plaintiff's opposition to the special appearance. *In re Stern*, 321 S.W.3d 828, 839 (Tex.App.—Houston [1st Dist.] 2010, orig. proceeding). Discovery irrelevant to the jurisdictional facts is not allowed; that type of discovery is limited to when the court considers whether a defendant waives a special appearance by engaging in discovery. *Id.* at 840. See "Discovery," §6, p. 199.

§7.2 Defendant. A defendant may file a motion for continuance. *See, e.g., Dawson-Austin v. Austin*, 968 S.W.2d 319, 323 (Tex.1998) (when P requested hearing on special appearance, D filed motion for continuance on day of hearing on grounds that she had been given inadequate notice, her counsel had just been hired and was in trial, and discovery was necessary).

1. Grounds. Although TRCP 120a does not identify the contents of a motion for continuance for a hearing on a special appearance, the defendant should probably follow the outline for a continuance based on the need for additional evidence. See "Continuance for Additional Discovery," ch. 5-D, §8, p. 338; *O'Connor's Texas Forms*, FORM 5D:1.

2. Discovery. When the court grants a continuance for the defendant, discovery should be limited to issues related to the special appearance. See "Discovery," §6, p. 199.

§8. HEARING

§8.1 Type of hearing.

1. Evidentiary. The trial court must resolve a special appearance based on the evidence. *See* TRCP 120a(3). The evidence can be received in open court or by written submission. *Michiana Easy Livin' Country, Inc. v. Holten*, 168 S.W.3d 777, 782 (Tex.2005). See "Evidence," §8.3, this page.

2. Nonjury. When the trial court holds a hearing in open court on a special appearance, the hearing is not before a jury. *See Roquemore v. Roquemore*, 431 S.W.2d 595, 601 (Tex.App.—Corpus Christi 1968, no writ).

§8.2 Defendant's burden. At the hearing on a special appearance, the nonresident defendant must disprove jurisdiction by negating all alleged grounds for personal jurisdiction. *BMC Software Belgium, N.V. v. Marchand*, 83 S.W.3d 789, 793 (Tex.2002); *Kawasaki Steel Corp. v. Middleton*, 699 S.W.2d 199, 203 (Tex.1985). If the defendant does not provide sufficient evidence in support of its special appearance, the court should deny the motion. *See Exito Elecs. Co. v. Trejo*, 142 S.W.3d 302, 307-08 (Tex.2004). See "Evidence," §8.3, this page. A defect in the defendant's proof does not waive the special appearance. *Exito Elecs.*, 142 S.W.3d at 308 (issue of defective verification and affidavit relates to merits of appeal of ruling on special appearance; defect in proof is not waiver of issue).

§8.3 Evidence. TRCP 120a(3) lists the types of proof that are allowed at the hearing on a special appearance.

1. Stipulations. Stipulations must meet the requirements of TRCP 11—that is, they must be in writing and signed by the attorneys or parties and filed with the court, or made in open court and entered in the record. See "Agreements Between Attorneys – Rule 11," ch. 1-H, §9, p. 61.

2. Discovery. Discovery submitted to the court at the special-appearance hearing may include requests for disclosure, interrogatories, depositions, requests for admissions, and documents produced through discovery. See "Forms of Discovery," ch. 6-A, §5, p. 428.

3. Oral testimony. The trial court can consider live testimony from witnesses at the hearing. TRCP 120a(3).

4. Affidavits. Affidavits and attachments must meet certain requirements. They must be filed and served at least seven days before the hearing on the special appearance. TRCP 120a(3); *Potkovick v. Regional Ventures, Inc.*, 904 S.W.2d 846, 850 (Tex.App.—Eastland 1995, no writ). They must be made on personal knowledge, set forth specific facts that would be admissible as evidence, and affirmatively show that the affiant is competent to testify.

★

TRCP 120a(3); *see SPA Giacomini v. Lamping*, 42 S.W.3d 265, 270 (Tex.App.—Corpus Christi 2001, no pet.); *International Turbine Serv. v. Lovitt*, 881 S.W.2d 805, 808 (Tex.App.—Fort Worth 1994, writ denied). See "Affidavits," ch. 1-B, §3.2.16, p. 11.

PRACTICE TIP

If you intend to object to any of the statements in an affidavit, you should object on the ground that you will not have an opportunity to cross-examine the witness at the hearing. The court may require you to take a deposition of the witness. By objecting before the hearing, you will give the court and the other party notice that you intend to assert your right to cross-examine the witness.

---

§9. RULING

After the court rules on a special appearance, it should sign the appropriate order. TRCP 120a(4). See *O'Connor's Texas Forms*, FORM 3B:4. Without a ruling on the special appearance, the party cannot preserve error for review. *Wilson v. Chemco Chem. Co.*, 711 S.W.2d 265, 266 (Tex.App.—Dallas 1986, no writ).

§9.1 Sustains motion. If the court sustains the special appearance, it will sign an order of dismissal, which is a final and appealable judgment. *See* CPRC §51.014; TRCP 120a(4). When sustaining the special appearance, the trial court should not rule on the merits of the claims. *E.g.*, *Nguyen v. Desai*, 132 S.W.3d 115, 117 (Tex.App.—Houston [14th Dist.] 2004, no pet.) (in sustaining special appearance, court erred by ordering that Ps take nothing and by dismissing suit with prejudice). If the court hears other motions and sustains them at the same time it sustains the special appearance, the order should state that the other rulings are made in the alternative. *See, e.g.*, *Antonio v. Rico Marino, S.A.*, 910 S.W.2d 624, 626 (Tex.App.—Houston [14th Dist.] 1995, no writ) (court ordered dismissal based on special appearance and forum non conveniens and sustained D's venue challenge). If the order sustains the special appearance and dismisses the suit first, with the other rulings as alternative reasons to dismiss or transfer, the plaintiff is forced to challenge each ruling separately on appeal.

§9.2 Overrules motion. If the court overrules the special appearance, it will sign an order overruling the motion and continue with the trial of the case. Once the court overrules the defendant's special appearance, the defendant's participation in the trial does not waive its objection to jurisdiction. TRCP 120a(4); *Equitable Prod. v. Canales-Treviño*, 136 S.W.3d 235, 238 (Tex.App.—San Antonio 2004, pet. denied); *N.H. Helicopters, Inc. v. Brown*, 841 S.W.2d 424, 425 (Tex.App.—Dallas 1992, orig. proceeding).

§9.3 Sanctions. The court may impose sanctions for affidavits that violate TRCP 13 and CPRC chapter 10. *See* TRCP 120a(3); *see, e.g.*, *Skepnek v. Mynatt*, 8 S.W.3d 377, 381-82 (Tex.App.—El Paso 1999, pet. denied) (attorney fined $30,000 for filing special appearance that was groundless, presented for improper purposes, and based on false affidavit of president of corporation).

§10. FINDINGS OF FACT

The party who receives an adverse ruling on the special appearance should request findings of fact. *Goodenbour v. Goodenbour*, 64 S.W.3d 69, 75 (Tex.App.—Austin 2001, pet. denied); *see* TRCP 296; *see also* TRAP 28.1(c) (trial court may file findings of fact within 30 days after signing interlocutory order). But the court is not required to file findings of fact on the special appearance. *Niehaus v. Cedar Bridge, Inc.*, 208 S.W.3d 575, 579 n.5 (Tex.App.—Austin 2006, no pet.). See "Jurisdictional challenge," ch. 10-E, §2.2.2(2), p. 818. When no findings of fact are filed, all facts necessary to support the judgment and supported by the evidence are implied. *BMC Software Belgium, N.V. v. Marchand*, 83 S.W.3d 789, 795 (Tex.2002); *see American Type Culture Collection, Inc. v. Coleman*, 83 S.W.3d 801, 806 (Tex.2002).

§11. REVIEW

§11.1 Record. If the trial court received evidence in open court, the reporter's record is necessary on appeal. *Michiana Easy Livin' Country, Inc. v. Holten*, 168 S.W.3d 777, 782 (Tex.2005). If nothing indicates the trial court

✶

received evidence in open court, the reporter's record is not necessary. *Id.* On appeal, there is a presumption that no evidence was received in open court at a pretrial hearing. See "Review," ch. 1-E, §8, p. 43.

§11.2 Standard of review. The issue on appeal is whether the nonresident defendant negated all alleged grounds for personal jurisdiction. *Kawasaki Steel Corp. v. Middleton*, 699 S.W.2d 199, 203 (Tex.1985); *Minucci v. Sogevalor, S.A.*, 14 S.W.3d 790, 794 (Tex.App.—Houston [1st Dist.] 2000, no pet.). Whether the court can exercise personal jurisdiction over a nonresident defendant is a question of law that is reviewed de novo. *Zinc Nacional, S.A. v. Bouché Trucking, Inc.*, 308 S.W.3d 395, 397 (Tex.2010); *Kelly v. General Interior Constr., Inc.*, 301 S.W.3d 653, 657 (Tex.2010); *Moki Mac River Expeditions v. Drugg*, 221 S.W.3d 569, 574 (Tex.2007). If the trial court issues findings of fact and conclusions of law, the court of appeals should review the trial court's factual findings for legal and factual sufficiency and review the trial court's legal conclusions de novo. *American Type Culture Collection, Inc. v. Coleman*, 83 S.W.3d 801, 806 (Tex.2002); *BMC Software Belgium, N.V. v. Marchand*, 83 S.W.3d 789, 794 (Tex.2002).

§11.3 Interlocutory appeal.

1. Appeal. An order granting or denying a special appearance may be appealed immediately (except in a suit brought under the Family Code). CPRC §51.014(a)(7); *see In re E.I. du Pont de Nemours & Co.*, 92 S.W.3d 517, 521 & n.8 (Tex.2002). In an interlocutory appeal, the appellant must file a notice of appeal within 20 days after the trial court signs the order. TRAP 26.1(b). See *O'Connor's Texas Appeals*, "Special appearance," ch. 1-B, §2.3.1(6), p. 14.

2. Stay of trial. The interlocutory appeal of an order granting a special appearance automatically stays the commencement of trial during the appeal. *See* CPRC §51.014(b). The interlocutory appeal of an order denying a special appearance, however, does not automatically stay the commencement of trial during the appeal. *Id.* §51.014(c). For a discussion of when the defendant may be entitled to a stay after the denial of a special appearance, see *O'Connor's Texas Appeals*, "Orders resulting in automatic stay after motion denied & deadlines met," ch. 3-P, §3.1.2, p. 154.

§11.4 Mandamus.

1. Family Code cases. Mandamus is the appropriate method for challenging the trial court's ruling on a special appearance in cases involving child-custody and child-support disputes because of the special interests involved and the unavailability of interlocutory appeal from these orders. *In re Barnes*, 127 S.W.3d 843, 846 (Tex. App.—San Antonio 2003, orig. proceeding) (child-custody suit); *In re Cannon*, 993 S.W.2d 354, 355 (Tex.App.—San Antonio 1999, orig. proceeding) (proceeding to enforce child support); *see also* CPRC §51.014(a)(7) (order granting or denying special appearance is appealable except in suit brought under Family Code); *cf. Proffer v. Yates*, 734 S.W.2d 671, 672 (Tex.1987) (mandamus appropriate to review mandatory venue transfer in Family Code case).

2. Other cases. Mandamus is not an appropriate method for challenging orders granting or denying a special appearance in most other cases because those orders can be appealed immediately. CPRC §51.014(a)(7). See "Interlocutory appeal," §11.3, this page.

—————————— ✦ ——————————

C. MOTION TO TRANSFER—CHALLENGING VENUE

§1. GENERAL

§1.1 Rules. TRCP 85-89, 255, 257-259, 261. See Tex. Const. art. 3, §45; CPRC ch. 15.

§1.2 Purpose. A motion to transfer venue is the procedure for transferring a case to another county in Texas. There are three types of motions to transfer: (1) improper county and convenience of the parties and witnesses, (2) local prejudice, and (3) consent of the parties. Only the defendant can file the first type; either the plaintiff or the defendant can file the second and third types. *See **Tenneco, Inc. v. Salyer**,* 739 S.W.2d 448, 449 (Tex.App.—Corpus Christi 1987, orig. proceeding).

§1.3 Timetables & forms. Timetable, Motion to Transfer Venue—Wrong or Inconvenient County, p. 1211; Timetable, Motion to Change Venue—Local Prejudice, p. 1212; *O'Connor's Texas Civil Forms* (2012), FORMS 3C.

§1.4 Other references. Hazel, *Texas Venue: The Legislature and Court Battle for Toughness,* 68 Tex.B.J. 216 (Mar.2005); *O'Connor's Texas Civil Appeals* (2012) (*O'Connor's Texas Appeals*); *O'Connor's Texas Family Law Handbook* (2013) (*O'Connor's Fam. Law Handbook*).

NOTE

For the rules governing venue selection, see "Choosing the Court—Venue," ch. 2-G, p. 150.

---

§2. IMPROPER COUNTY & CONVENIENCE

Venue selection assumes the parties to the lawsuit have choices and preferences about where the case will be tried. ***Wilson v. Texas Parks & Wildlife Dept.***, 886 S.W.2d 259, 260 (Tex.1994). "Proper venue" means venue under the mandatory-venue provisions or, if none apply, under the general venue rule or the permissive-venue provisions. CPRC §15.001(b); *O'Quinn v. Hall*, 77 S.W.2d 438, 448-49 (Tex.App.—Corpus Christi 2002, no pet.).

§2.1 Plaintiff's choice of venue. The plaintiff chooses the venue by filing the suit in a proper county. ***In re Team Rocket, L.P.***, 256 S.W.3d 257, 259 (Tex.2008); ***In re Masonite Corp.***, 997 S.W.2d 194, 197 (Tex.1999).

§2.2 Defendant's motion to transfer venue. A defendant raises the question of proper venue by challenging the plaintiff's choice through a motion to transfer venue. ***Wichita Cty. v. Hart***, 917 S.W.2d 779, 781 (Tex.1996); *see* TRCP 86(1). Without a motion, the court cannot transfer venue, even to a county of proper venue. ***In re Masonite Corp.***, 997 S.W.2d 194, 198 (Tex.1999).

1. Deadline to file. A motion to transfer for improper venue is waived if it is made after any written motion (other than a special appearance) is filed. TRCP 86(1). The motion to transfer may be filed concurrently with the answer. *Id.*; *see* CPRC §15.063. For the deadlines for filing an answer, see "Deadline to Answer," ch. 3-E, §2, p. 227.

	Grounds	Deadlines	Authority	Cross-reference
	3-5. DEADLINES FOR MOTIONS TO TRANSFER VENUE			
1	Improper county and convenience	Before or with filing of D's answer	CPRC §15.063(1); TRCP 86(1)	§2.2.1, this page
2	Local prejudice	None	Common law	§3.4, p. 212
3	Consent	None	CPRC §15.063(3); TRCP 86(1)	§4.1, p. 213

2. Due order of pleading.

(1) Consent or improper county & convenience. The defendant must file a motion to transfer venue based on consent or improper county and convenience before or along with all other pleadings or motions except the special appearance, which must be filed first. TRCP 86(1). See "Due Order of Pleading," ch. 3-A, §3, p. 183.

★

The defendant waives its objection to improper venue if it files a motion to transfer after it files an answer. *See* TRCP 86(1); *Kshatrya v. Texas Workforce Comm'n*, 97 S.W.3d 825, 832 (Tex.App.—Dallas 2003, no pet.).

(2) Local prejudice. The due-order-of-pleading rule does not apply to a motion to transfer based on local prejudice under TRCP 257-259. See "Local Prejudice," §3, p. 211.

3. Form. The motion to transfer venue must be in writing and may be made either as part of the defendant's first responsive pleading or as a separate document. TRCP 86(1), (2). See *O'Connor's Texas Forms*, FORMS 3C:1-3.

4. No affidavits necessary. The defendant may, but is not required to, support the motion with affidavits when it is filed. TRCP 86(3) (last paragraph); *GeoChem Tech v. Verseckes*, 962 S.W.2d 541, 543 (Tex.1998). The question of proper venue is raised by simply objecting to a plaintiff's venue choice through a motion to transfer venue. *Billings v. Concordia Heritage Ass'n*, 960 S.W.2d 688, 692 (Tex.App.—El Paso 1997, pet. denied). But once the plaintiff responds to the motion and denies the defendant's venue facts, the defendant must provide proof as required by TRCP 87(3). *See* TRCP 87(2).

5. Request hearing. The defendant must request a hearing, give the plaintiff notice of the hearing, and secure a setting for the hearing. *See* TRCP 87(1); *see, e.g., Carlile v. RLS Legal Solutions, Inc.*, 138 S.W.3d 403, 408 (Tex.App.—Houston [14th Dist.] 2004, no pet.) (14-month delay between filing motion to transfer and obtaining hearing showed lack of diligence in securing hearing); *Bristol v. Placid Oil Co.*, 74 S.W.3d 156, 159 (Tex.App.—Amarillo 2002, no pet.) (32-month delay between motion to transfer and ruling not attributable to D because D's motion asked court to set hearing); *Grozier v. L-B Sprinkler & Plumbing Repair*, 744 S.W.2d 306, 311 (Tex.App.—Fort Worth 1988, writ denied) (although D asked for hearing, he did not ask for setting). See "Procedure for hearing," §2.11, p. 209.

6. No codefendant waiver. Although a defendant can waive its own venue rights, it cannot waive the venue rights of a codefendant. No act or omission constituting waiver by one defendant impairs the right of any other defendant to challenge venue. CPRC §15.0641; *WTFO, Inc. v. Braithwaite*, 899 S.W.2d 709, 718 (Tex.App.—Dallas 1995, no writ); *e.g., Pearson v. Jones Co.*, 898 S.W.2d 329, 331-32 (Tex.App.—Eastland 1994, no writ) (waiver of venue when D1 and D2 filed answers did not waive D3's venue objection).

§2.3 Defendant's grounds. A defendant should allege that the court should transfer the suit to another county for one of the following reasons:

1. Mandatory venue. The defendant should allege that venue is not proper in the county of suit because a mandatory-venue provision requires transfer to another county. *See* CPRC §15.001(b)(1). The defendant must identify the mandatory-venue provision that requires transfer to a specific county. See "Mandatory-Venue Provisions," ch. 2-G, §4, p. 151.

2. General venue rule. The defendant should allege that venue is not proper in the county of suit because the general venue rule requires transfer to another county. *See* CPRC §15.002. The defendant must identify the specific part of the statute that was violated when the plaintiff filed suit and the specific county where the suit should be transferred. See "General Venue Rule," ch. 2-G, §5, p. 155.

3. Permissive venue. The defendant should allege that venue is not proper in the county of suit, no mandatory provision applies, and venue is permissive in another county. The defendant must state why the plaintiff's choice of venue is not proper and identify the permissive-venue provision that permits transfer to a specific county. See "Permissive-Venue Provisions," ch. 2-G, §6, p. 155.

4. Improper venue for some plaintiffs. The defendant should allege that venue is improper for one plaintiff but not for the others, and that specific plaintiff cannot establish venue under a mandatory-venue provision, the general venue rule, or a permissive-venue provision. *See* CPRC §15.003. See "Multiple plaintiffs," ch. 2-G, §7.1, p. 157.

———————————— ★ ————————————

5. Venue convenient elsewhere. The defendant should allege that, although suit was filed in a county of proper venue, the court should transfer the suit to another county of proper venue in the interest of justice and for the convenience of the parties and witnesses. CPRC §15.002(b). See *O'Connor's Texas Forms*, FORMS 3C. A defendant may file a motion to transfer venue to another county of proper venue based on convenience whenever venue is not controlled by a mandatory-venue provision. *See* CPRC §15.002(b). A defendant should include a request for a convenience transfer in every motion because a ruling granting a convenience transfer is not subject to review. *Id.* §15.002(c).

(1) Allegations. The defendant should show that the parties and witnesses will be inconvenienced by maintaining the suit in the county where suit was filed because of all of the following:

(a) Hardship on defendant. Maintaining the suit in the original county will impose an economic and personal hardship on the defendant. CPRC §15.002(b)(1). The defendant should state why litigation in the other county will not impose an economic or personal hardship.

(b) Balance of interests. The balance of all the parties' interests weighs in favor of the suit being brought in the other county. CPRC §15.002(b)(2). The defendant should list the factors that favor the other county.

(c) No hardship on plaintiff. The transfer will not impose a hardship or injustice on any other party. CPRC §15.002(b)(3). The defendant should state why the move would not impose a hardship or injustice on the plaintiff or any other party.

(d) Proper county. The original county is not a county of mandatory venue, and the other county is a county of proper venue. *See* CPRC §15.002(b).

(2) Affidavits. The defendant should support all of its factual allegations with affidavits or other sworn proof. The general rule is that a defendant is not required to support a motion to transfer with affidavits when it is filed. See "No affidavits necessary," §2.2.4, p. 204. But because a motion to transfer for convenience is based on facts outside the plaintiff's petition, the defendant is probably required to file sworn proof with its motion.

§2.4 Defendant's other allegations.

1. Deny plaintiff's venue facts. The defendant must specifically deny the venue facts in the plaintiff's petition; if it does not, they are accepted as true. TRCP 87(3)(a). A specific denial requires more than just the words "we specifically deny." See "Denial of venue facts," §2.11.4(1), p. 209.

2. Allege specific county. The motion to transfer venue must ask the court to transfer the case to a specific county and provide facts showing why venue is proper in that county. *See* TRCP 86(3). See "Prima facie proof," §2.11.4(2), p. 210. Nothing in the venue rule or the CPRC prevents a defendant from alleging that two or more counties are counties of proper venue. *See GeoChem Tech v. Verseckes*, 962 S.W.2d 541, 543-44 (Tex.1998); *Rosales v. H.E. Butt Grocery Co.*, 905 S.W.2d 745, 748 (Tex.App.—San Antonio 1995, writ denied). The defendant does not admit the plaintiff has a valid claim by filing a motion to transfer to the county where the cause of action accrued. TRCP 87(2)(b).

3. File motion to sever & transfer.

(1) Multiple plaintiffs. In a suit with multiple plaintiffs, a defendant may file a motion to sever and transfer a claim asserted against it if the claim was brought by a plaintiff who has not established proper venue. *See* CPRC §15.003(a). See *O'Connor's Texas Forms*, FORM 3C:2. When there are multiple plaintiffs, each plaintiff must, independently of every other plaintiff, establish proper venue or proper joinder. See "Improper venue for some plaintiffs," §2.3.4, p. 204; "Venue or joinder proper for all plaintiffs," §2.6.4, p. 206.

(2) Multiple defendants. In a suit with multiple defendants, a defendant may file a motion to sever and transfer a claim asserted against it if severance is proper. *See* TRCP 89; *see, e.g., Jones v. Ray*, 886 S.W.2d 817, 823 (Tex.App.—Houston [1st Dist.] 1994, orig. proceeding) (because severance order for multiple Ds was improper,

————————————————— ✪ —————————————————

order transferring venue was also improper). Severance is proper if (1) the controversy involves more than one cause of action, (2) the severed cause is one that would be the proper subject of a lawsuit if independently asserted, and (3) the severed and remaining causes are not so intertwined as to involve the same facts and issues. *Guaranty Fed. Sav. Bank v. Horseshoe Oper. Co.*, 793 S.W.2d 652, 658 (Tex.1990); *Jones*, 886 S.W.2d at 820. See "Motion for Severance," ch. 5-I, §3, p. 364.

PRACTICE TIP
If a defendant in a suit with multiple defendants wants to sever and transfer the claims against it, the defendant should use a general motion to sever along with an appropriate motion to transfer. See **O'Connor's Texas Forms**, *FORMS 3C:1-4, 5H:1.*

---

§2.5 Plaintiff's procedure. The plaintiff is not required to file a response to a motion to transfer unless proof is necessary. TRCP 86(4). But as a general rule, the plaintiff should file a response and address the grounds asserted in the defendant's motion. See "Plaintiff's proof," §2.7, p. 207.

1. Deadline to file. The deadline to file a response to the motion to transfer is 30 days before the venue hearing unless the plaintiff secures permission to file it later. TRCP 87(1); *Moriarty v. Williams*, 752 S.W.2d 610, 611 (Tex.App.—El Paso 1988, writ denied). See "Continuance," §2.10.3, p. 209.

2. Form. The response to the motion to transfer venue must be in writing. *See* TRCP 86(1). See *O'Connor's Texas Forms*, FORMS 3C:5-7.

3. Affidavits & attachments. The plaintiff must file affidavits and any necessary discovery products to establish prima facie proof of its venue facts once the defendant has specifically denied those facts. The discovery products should be attached to affidavits verifying their authenticity. See "Procedure for securing evidence," §2.10, p. 208.

§2.6 Plaintiff's response to defendant's grounds.

1. Venue not mandatory elsewhere. If the defendant alleged that a mandatory-venue provision requires transfer to another county, the plaintiff should argue that the defendant's county of choice is not a mandatory county for venue. *See* CPRC §15.001(b)(1). *See generally* CPRC §§15.011-15.020 (mandatory-venue provisions).

2. Venue proper under general rule. If the defendant alleged that the general venue rule requires a transfer, the plaintiff should argue that its county of choice complies with the general venue rule because (1) a substantial part of the events or omissions occurred in the county, (2) the defendant, a natural person, resides in the county, (3) the defendant, a corporation or other organization, has its principal office in Texas in the county, or (4) if no other provision in CPRC §15.002(a) applies, the suit is proper in the county because the plaintiff resided there when the cause of action accrued. CPRC §15.002(a); *see, e.g.*, *In re Missouri Pac. R.R.*, 998 S.W.2d 212, 221 (Tex. 1999) (Ps did not show D's office in county of suit was a principal office as compared to responsibility and authority exercised by company officials in another Texas county).

3. Venue not permissive elsewhere. If the defendant alleged that venue is not proper in the county of suit and is permissive in another county, the plaintiff should argue that (1) venue is proper and (2) the defendant's county of choice is not a permissive county for venue.

4. Venue or joinder proper for all plaintiffs. If the defendant alleged that venue was improper for one of the plaintiffs, that plaintiff has the following two options:

(1) Venue proper. The plaintiff can establish proper venue under the general venue rule, a mandatory-venue provision, or a permissive-venue provision. *O'Quinn v. Hall*, 77 S.W.3d 438, 448-49 (Tex.App.—Corpus Christi 2002, no pet.); *see* CPRC §§15.001(b), 15.003.

(2) Joinder proper under CPRC §15.003(a). If the plaintiff cannot establish proper venue, that plaintiff's claims and causes of action must be transferred to a county of proper venue or be dismissed, whichever is appropriate, unless that plaintiff establishes—independently of every other plaintiff—all of the following:

———————————— ★ ————————————

(a) Joinder of that plaintiff or intervention by that plaintiff is proper under the TRCPs. CPRC §15.003(a)(1); *see also* TRCP 40 (permissive joinder), TRCP 43 (interpleader), TRCP 60 & 61 (intervention), TRCP 174(a) (consolidation).

(b) Maintaining venue for that plaintiff in the county of suit does not unfairly prejudice another party to the suit. CPRC §15.003(a)(2).

(c) There is an essential need to have that plaintiff's claim tried in the county where the suit is pending. *Id.* §15.003(a)(3). The "essential need" requirement means that each plaintiff must demonstrate it is "indispensably necessary" to try its claims in that county; "essential" means that it is "necessary, such that one cannot do without it." *Surgitek, Bristol-Myers Corp. v. Abel*, 997 S.W.2d 598, 604 (Tex.1999); *see O'Quinn*, 77 S.W.3d at 451; *American Home Prods. v. Burrough*, 998 S.W.2d 696, 699-700 (Tex.App.—Eastland 1999, no pet.).

(d) The county where the suit is pending is a fair and convenient venue for the plaintiff seeking to join in or maintain venue and for all persons against whom the suit is brought. CPRC §15.003(a)(4).

5. Venue not convenient elsewhere. If the defendant alleged that venue is more convenient in another county, the plaintiff should argue that in the interest of justice and for the convenience of the parties and witnesses, the suit should be maintained in the county where suit was originally filed. CPRC §15.002(b). The plaintiff should show how the parties and witnesses will be inconvenienced by the move and should identify the witnesses who will probably testify by deposition and thus will not be inconvenienced by maintaining the suit in the original county. In its response, the plaintiff should argue the following:

(1) No hardship on defendant. Maintaining the suit in the original county will not impose an economic or personal hardship on the defendant. CPRC §15.002(b)(1). The plaintiff should include reasons why the suit will be no more inconvenient for the defendant in the original county than in the defendant's county of choice.

(2) Balance of interests. The balance of all the parties' interests weighs in favor of the suit remaining in the original county. CPRC §15.002(b)(2). The plaintiff should list the factors that favor the original county.

(3) Hardship on plaintiff. The transfer to the other county will impose a hardship or injustice on the plaintiff or another party. CPRC §15.002(b)(3). The plaintiff should include specific examples of the hardship or injustice.

(4) Improper county for transfer. The other county is not a county of proper venue. CPRC §15.002(b).

6. Deny defendant's venue facts. When appropriate, the plaintiff should specifically deny the venue facts pleaded by the defendant. Unless the plaintiff specifically denies them, the defendant's venue facts will be accepted as true. TRCP 87(3)(a). See "Denial of venue facts," §2.11.4(1), p. 209.

7. Allege waiver. When appropriate, the plaintiff should allege the defendant waived a change of venue (e.g., the defendant waived venue by filing its motion to transfer after filing its answer). See "Due order of pleading," §2.2.2, p. 203.

§2.7 Plaintiff's proof. The plaintiff should support all factual allegations in its response with affidavits or other sworn proof.

1. Proof of denied venue facts. If the defendant specifically denied the plaintiff's venue facts, the plaintiff must make a prima facie case of the facts through sworn proof. TRCP 87(3)(a); *In re Missouri Pac. R.R.*, 998 S.W.2d 212, 216 (Tex.1999); *GeoChem Tech v. Verseckes*, 962 S.W.2d 541, 543 (Tex.1998); *Rosales v. H.E. Butt Grocery Co.*, 905 S.W.2d 745, 748-49 (Tex.App.—San Antonio 1995, writ denied); *see, e.g., Maranatha Temple, Inc. v. Enterprise Prods.*, 833 S.W.2d 736, 740 (Tex.App.—Houston [1st Dist.] 1992, writ denied) (because Ds did not specifically deny venue facts, P was not required to offer prima facie proof).

2. Proof of joinder elements. The plaintiff is required to offer prima facie proof of each of the four joinder elements of CPRC §15.003(a). *Surgitek, Bristol-Myers Corp. v. Abel*, 997 S.W.2d 598, 602 (Tex.1999). See "Joinder proper under CPRC §15.003(a)," §2.6.4(2), p. 206.

★

3. Proof of convenience issues. The plaintiff should support its allegations about the convenience of the forum with sworn proof. See "Venue not convenient elsewhere," §2.6.5, p. 207.

4. No proof of cause of action. The plaintiff is not required to prove the existence of a cause of action. TRCP 87(2)(b), (3)(a). By its pleading, the plaintiff establishes all the elements of its cause of action, which the defendant cannot controvert for venue purposes.

§2.8 Plaintiff's other options.

1. Amend petition. The plaintiff may add or drop claims from its original petition to establish proper venue. The plaintiff must file an amended petition at least seven days before the hearing on the motion to transfer. TRCP 63. If the plaintiff timely amends its petition, the court must consider the amended petition at the hearing. *See, e.g.*, *Watson v. City of Odessa*, 893 S.W.2d 197, 199-200 (Tex.App.—El Paso 1995, writ denied) (P amended petition to drop claim on which motion to transfer was based); *Moriarty v. Williams*, 752 S.W.2d 610, 611 (Tex. App.—El Paso 1988, writ denied) (P amended petition to add claims not addressed by D's motion to transfer).

2. Take nonsuit. In some circumstances, the plaintiff may be able to avoid an unfavorable venue ruling by taking a nonsuit of the entire case and refiling the case in another county. *See GeoChem Tech v. Verseckes*, 962 S.W.2d 541, 543 (Tex.1998). If the plaintiff nonsuits a case after the defendant files a motion to transfer and before the court rules on the motion, the dismissal does not fix venue in the county designated in the defendant's motion. *See id.* at 544. On refiling, the plaintiff still has the right to choose between two counties where mandatory venue is proper even though it filed its first suit in a county where venue was improper. *Id.* After the nonsuit, the court where the case is pending must sign the order of nonsuit; that court cannot transfer the suit to the defendant's county of choice. *Zimmerman v. Ottis*, 941 S.W.2d 259, 263 (Tex.App.—Corpus Christi 1996, orig. proceeding). See "Effect on venue," ch. 7-F, §6.4, p. 654.

§2.9 Procedure for defendant's reply. The defendant is not required to file a reply to the plaintiff's response. TRCP 87(1).

1. Deadline to file. The deadline to file a reply to the plaintiff's response is seven days before the venue hearing unless the defendant secures permission to file it later. TRCP 87(1).

2. Affidavits & attachments. If the plaintiff specifically denied the defendant's venue facts, the defendant must file affidavits and any necessary discovery products establishing prima facie proof of the facts. TRCP 87(3)(a).

§2.10 Procedure for securing evidence.

1. Affidavits. The parties may support their factual allegations with affidavits and sworn proof attached to the affidavits. Affidavits must be made on personal knowledge, set forth specific facts that would be admissible as evidence, and affirmatively show that the affiant is competent to testify. TRCP 87(3)(a). For the requirements for the affidavit, see "Affidavits," ch. 1-B, §3.2.16, p. 11. For the requirements for using an unsworn declaration in place of an affidavit, see "Unsworn declaration," ch. 1-B, §3.2.14, p. 10.

2. Discovery. The parties may engage in discovery for the motion to transfer venue and for the case-in-chief without waiving the issue of venue. TRCP 88. Reasonable discovery is permitted to support or oppose the motion. TRCP 88, 258; *Beard v. Gonzalez*, 924 S.W.2d 763, 765 (Tex.App.—El Paso 1996, orig. proceeding) (motion under TRCP 257); *City of La Grange v. McBee*, 923 S.W.2d 89, 91 (Tex.App.—Houston [1st Dist.] 1996, writ denied) (same). The parties must be given reasonable time to conduct discovery before the venue hearing. *Union Carbide Corp. v. Moye*, 798 S.W.2d 792, 793 (Tex.1990) (motion under TRCP 257); *see, e.g.*, *Bridgestone/Firestone, Inc. v. Thirteenth Ct. of Appeals*, 929 S.W.2d 440, 442 (Tex.1996) (five months and one continuance of hearing was reasonable time). To be considered at the hearing on the motion to transfer, the discovery must be attached to or incorporated by reference in an affidavit of a party, witness, or attorney who has knowledge of the discovery. TRCP 88. For the requirements for these affidavits, see "Affidavits," ch. 1-B, §3.2.16, p. 11.

★

NOTE

Although TRCP 88 requires the discovery to be attached to or incorporated by reference in an affidavit, CPRC §132.001 allows for the use of an unsworn declaration instead of an affidavit. See CPRC §132.001(a). For the requirements for using an unsworn declaration, see "Unsworn declaration," ch. 1-B, §3.2.14, p. 10.

---

3. Continuance. If one of the parties needs additional time to collect affidavits and conduct discovery solely on the issue of venue, it should file a motion for continuance. *Beard*, 924 S.W.2d at 765 (motion under TRCP 257); *see McBee*, 923 S.W.2d at 91 (same). See "Continuance for Additional Discovery," ch. 5-D, §8, p. 338.

§2.11 Procedure for hearing. The court cannot rule on the motion without a hearing. *Henderson v. O'Neill*, 797 S.W.2d 905, 905 (Tex.1990). The hearing must be held promptly and within a reasonable time before the beginning of the trial on the merits. TRCP 87(1).

1. Burden to ask for hearing. A defendant must request a hearing on its motion within a reasonable time. TRCP 87(1); *e.g.*, *Whitworth v. Kuhn*, 734 S.W.2d 108, 111 (Tex.App.—Austin 1987, no writ) (one-year delay between filing motion to transfer and requesting hearing showed lack of diligence); *see, e.g.*, *Accent Energy Corp. v. Gillman*, 824 S.W.2d 274, 276-77 (Tex.App.—Amarillo 1992, writ denied) (three-year delay reasonable because P asked for continuance and filed amended pleadings after motion was set for hearing).

2. Notice of hearing. Each party is entitled to at least 45 days' notice of the hearing on the motion. TRCP 87(1); *HCA Health Servs. v. Salinas*, 838 S.W.2d 246, 247-48 (Tex.1992); *Henderson*, 797 S.W.2d at 905; *Bench Co. v. Nations Rent, L.P.*, 133 S.W.3d 907, 908 (Tex.App.—Dallas 2004, no pet.); *cf. Beard v. Gonzalez*, 924 S.W.2d 763, 765 (Tex.App.—El Paso 1996, orig. proceeding) (45 days' notice required for motion under TRCP 257); *City of La Grange v. McBee*, 923 S.W.2d 89, 91 (Tex.App.—Houston [1st Dist.] 1996, writ denied) (same). To preserve an objection to lack of sufficient notice, the party must file a written objection and a motion for continuance. *Bench Co.*, 133 S.W.3d at 908; *Beard*, 924 S.W.2d at 765; *Gonzalez v. Nielson*, 770 S.W.2d 99, 101 (Tex.App.—Corpus Christi 1989, writ denied).

3. Hearing. The motion may be submitted for an oral hearing before the court or may be submitted on written documents. *See* TRCP 87(1); *Orion Enters. v. Pope*, 927 S.W.2d 654, 657 (Tex.App.—San Antonio 1996, orig. proceeding). The hearing is not before a jury. TRCP 87(4); *Eddins v. Parker*, 63 S.W.3d 15, 18 (Tex.App.—El Paso 2001, pet. denied).

(1) Most cases. Generally, the hearing on a motion to transfer venue is for argument only, and no evidence may be received. *See* CPRC §15.064(a); *Jack B. Anglin Co. v. Tipps*, 842 S.W.2d 266, 269 n.4 (Tex.1992); *Eddins*, 63 S.W.3d at 18.

(2) Joinder cases. In cases under CPRC §15.003(a) dealing with joinder determination, the trial court may limit the scope of evidence to pleadings and affidavits, but it has discretion to consider a broad range of evidence, including live testimony. *Surgitek, Bristol-Myers Corp. v. Abel*, 997 S.W.2d 598, 602 (Tex.1999).

4. Burden of proof.

(1) Denial of venue facts. The court must accept as true any pleaded venue facts that are not specifically denied by the other party. TRCP 87(3)(a); *GeoChem Tech v. Verseckes*, 962 S.W.2d 541, 543 (Tex.1998); *Sanes v. Clark*, 25 S.W.3d 800, 803 (Tex.App.—Waco 2000, pet. denied). A global denial (e.g., "I specifically deny the venue facts") is not a specific denial. *Bleeker v. Villarreal*, 941 S.W.2d 163, 176 (Tex.App.—Corpus Christi 1996, writ dism'd) (denying "the fact that venue is proper" is not specific denial); *Maranatha Temple, Inc. v. Enterprise Prods.*, 833 S.W.2d 736, 740 (Tex.App.—Houston [1st Dist.] 1992, writ denied) (specific denial requires more than just the words "we specifically deny"). When a party's venue facts are not specifically denied, there is no burden on the party to submit proof of the facts. *Bleeker*, 941 S.W.2d at 175. Undenied venue facts will not conclusively establish proper venue, however, if the facts would not support venue even if true. *See, e.g.*, *In re Fort Bend Cty.*, 278 S.W.3d 842, 845 (Tex.App.—Houston [14th Dist.] 2009, orig. proceeding) (D did not need to challenge Ps' venue facts because facts, even if true, did not establish proper venue).

⭐

(2) Prima facie proof. Once a venue fact has been specifically denied, the party pleading the venue fact has the burden to make prima facie proof of that fact. *GeoChem Tech*, 962 S.W.2d at 543; *KW Constr. v. Stephens & Sons Concrete Contractors, Inc.*, 165 S.W.3d 874, 879 (Tex.App.—Texarkana 2005, pet. denied). Prima facie proof is made when the venue facts are properly pleaded and are supported by proper affidavit proof. TRCP 87(3)(a); *see O'Quinn v. Hall*, 77 S.W.3d 438, 449 (Tex.App.—Corpus Christi 2002, no pet.).

(a) No rebuttal – most cases. Generally, prima facie proof is not subject to rebuttal, cross-examination, impeachment, or disproof. *Ruiz v. Conoco, Inc.*, 868 S.W.2d 752, 757 (Tex.1993). The trial court should not weigh the credibility of the affiants when it evaluates the venue proof. *Humphrey v. May*, 804 S.W.2d 328, 329 (Tex.App.—Austin 1991, writ denied).

(b) Rebuttal – joinder cases. Because the four joinder elements a plaintiff must establish under CPRC §15.003(a)—proper joinder under the TRCPs, unfair prejudice, essential need, and fairness and convenience—do not lend themselves to the prima facie standard applied in venue hearings, the defendant must be given the opportunity to rebut the plaintiff's prima facie proof. *Surgitek*, 997 S.W.2d at 603; *American Home Prods. v. Bernal*, 5 S.W.3d 344, 346-47 (Tex.App.—Corpus Christi 1999, no pet.). To the extent that a defendant's joinder evidence rebuts the plaintiff's prima facie proof on any of the joinder elements, the court has discretion to consider all available evidence to resolve any disputes that the parties' proof creates. *Surgitek*, 997 S.W.2d at 603.

§2.12 Order. The court will decide venue based on the pleadings, motion, response, affidavits, and discovery filed in support of both the defendant's motion to transfer and the plaintiff's response. CPRC §15.064(a); TRCP 87(3)(b), 87(4), 88. The defendant has the burden to secure a ruling; if it does not, it will waive its venue challenge. *See Marathon Corp. v. Pitzner*, 55 S.W.3d 114, 138 (Tex.App.—Corpus Christi 2001), *rev'd on other grounds*, 106 S.W.3d 724 (Tex.2003).

1. Transfer denied. If the court denies the motion to transfer, the case should proceed to trial.

2. Transfer granted. If the court sustains the motion to transfer, the clerk will begin the process of transferring the case to the other county; the case will not be dismissed. TRCP 89.

NOTE

*If the court grants a motion to transfer venue that includes a request to transfer for convenience, the order does not need to state that the case was or was not transferred for the convenience of the parties under CPRC §15.002(b). See **Garza v. Garcia**, 137 S.W.3d 36, 39 (Tex.2004). The convenience-transfer order is not subject to appeal. See "No appeal of convenience transfer," §5.1, p. 213.*

---

§2.13 Rehearing & later motions. A timely motion to transfer venue may be amended to cure defects if the amended motion is filed before the court rules on the original motion. *In re Pepsico, Inc.*, 87 S.W.3d 787, 794 (Tex. App.—Texarkana 2002, orig. proceeding) (amended motion relates back to and supersedes original motion). Once the court rules on the motion to transfer, it cannot consider any later motion to transfer, regardless of whether the movant was a party when the original motion was heard. TRCP 87(5); *see Marathon Corp. v. Pitzner*, 55 S.W.3d 114, 137 n.6 (Tex.App.—Corpus Christi 2001), *rev'd on other grounds*, 106 S.W.3d 724 (Tex.2003). This rule does not bar a later-added defendant's motion based on grounds of either mandatory venue, if the earlier defendants could not have filed such a motion, or impartial trial under TRCP 257-259. TRCP 87(5). See "Local Prejudice," §3, p. 211.

1. Rehearing of initial motion. The court may reconsider its ruling granting the motion to transfer before the case is transferred to another county and while it still has plenary power. *See U.S. Res. v. Placke*, 682 S.W.2d 403, 405 (Tex.App.—Austin 1984, orig. proceeding). The court retains plenary power over the order transferring the case to another county for 30 days after it signs the order of transfer. *In re Southwestern Bell Tel. Co.*, 35 S.W.3d 602, 605 (Tex.2000); *HCA Health Servs. v. Salinas*, 838 S.W.2d 246, 248 (Tex.1992). After those 30 days, the order is final as to the transferring court, even though it is interlocutory as to the parties. *In re Team Rocket, L.P.*, 256 S.W.3d 257, 260 (Tex.2008); *In re Southwestern Bell*, 35 S.W.3d at 605.

★

2. Motion by new defendant. A new defendant is limited to motions to transfer based on (1) local prejudice or (2) a ground of mandatory venue not available to the other defendants. TRCP 87(5). However, under CPRC §15.0641, no act or omission by one defendant impairs the rights of another defendant. Thus, it is uncertain whether a defendant is limited in its venue objections when it is brought into the suit after the court ruled on another defendant's motion to transfer venue.

3. Motion by third-party defendant. Venue for the main action establishes venue for a defendant's third-party claim as long as the claim is properly joined under the TRCPs or other applicable statutes. CPRC §15.062(a). When an original defendant joins a third-party defendant, venue for the main action establishes venue for any claim by the plaintiff against that third-party defendant arising from the same transaction, occurrence, or series of transactions or occurrences. *Id.* §15.062(b). The third-party defendant can object that the claim was not properly joined and, on that ground, move to transfer to another county.

4. Motion by substituted defendant. A substituted defendant is bound by the actions of its predecessor and cannot change the venue status of the case. *First Heights Bank v. Gutierrez*, 852 S.W.2d 596, 618 (Tex. App.—Corpus Christi 1993, writ denied); *see* TRCP 87(5).

5. Motion by intervening defendant. An intervening defendant has the status of a plaintiff and is in no better position to contest venue than the plaintiff. *First Heights*, 852 S.W.2d at 618.

§3. LOCAL PREJUDICE

A motion to change venue because of local prejudice is different from a motion to transfer under the CPRC. A motion to change venue because of local prejudice is governed by TRCP 257-259, which were not altered by the 1983 codification of the venue statute or the 1995 revisions to the CPRC.

§3.1 Purpose. The motion to change venue because of local prejudice allows the court to transfer a case from a county if trial in that county would be unfair to one or both parties. The allegation that a party cannot get a fair trial implicates the Due Process Clause of the 14th Amendment to the U.S. Constitution and the "due course of law" provision of Texas Constitution article 1, §19. Most motions to change venue made under TRCP 257-259 involve prejudice generated by extensive pretrial publicity.

§3.2 Motion. Either party may make a motion to change venue because of local prejudice, even though the plaintiff chose the venue. TRCP 257; *e.g.*, *Carrasco v. Goatcher*, 623 S.W.2d 769, 771 (Tex.App.—El Paso 1981, no writ) (P filed motion). See *O'Connor's Texas Forms*, FORM 3C:4.

NOTE

The due-order-of-pleading rule on filing venue motions before most other pleadings does not apply to a motion to change venue based on local prejudice for two reasons: (1) the local prejudice might arise or become known after the answer is due and (2) either party may file this type of motion.

---

§3.3 Grounds. The grounds for change of venue because of local prejudice include the following:

1. Prejudice. The prejudice against the party in the county of suit is so great that the party cannot get a fair trial. TRCP 257(a).

2. Combination. There is a "combination" against the party instigated by influential persons in the county of suit that would prevent a fair trial. TRCP 257(b).

3. No impartial trial. An impartial trial cannot be had in the county of suit. TRCP 257(c); *In re East Tex. Med. Ctr. Athens*, 154 S.W.3d 933, 935 (Tex.App.—Tyler 2005, orig. proceeding). The movant should also allege that local prejudice will deprive the movant of its due-process rights to a fair trial under both the U.S. and Texas Constitutions.

★

---

4. Other reasons. The party may assert any other relevant reasons to support the motion. *See* TRCP 257(d).

§3.4 Deadline to file. The motion to change venue should be filed as soon as the local prejudice becomes known. *See, e.g.*, *City of Abilene v. Downs*, 367 S.W.2d 153, 155-56 (Tex.1963) (motion to change venue filed after case reset for trial); *Lone Star Steel Co. v. Scott*, 759 S.W.2d 144, 146 (Tex.App.—Texarkana 1988, writ denied) (motion to change venue filed after D announced ready for trial). Although CPRC §15.063 includes the motion to transfer venue on grounds of local prejudice among those that must be filed before or with the defendant's answer, its inclusion is generally acknowledged as an error. *See Union Carbide Corp. v. Moye*, 798 S.W.2d 792, 797 & n.5 (Tex.1990) (Gonzalez, J., concurring) (CPRC §15.063 does not establish exclusive circumstances for transfer based on local prejudice).

§3.5 Affidavits. The movant must file its own affidavit and the affidavits of at least three credible residents of the county where the suit is pending to support the grounds for change of venue because of local prejudice. TRCP 257; *In re East Tex. Med. Ctr. Athens*, 154 S.W.3d 933, 935 (Tex.App.—Tyler 2005, orig. proceeding); *Acker v. Denton Publ'g*, 937 S.W.2d 111, 118 (Tex.App.—Fort Worth 1996, no writ).

§3.6 Discovery & continuance. Discovery is permitted to support or oppose the motion. A continuance may be needed to obtain the necessary discovery. See "Procedure for securing evidence," §2.10, p. 208.

§3.7 Response. By filing the affidavit of a credible person, the nonmovant may challenge the credibility of the movant's affiants and their means of knowing the truth of the facts stated in the motion. TRCP 258. If the party needs additional time to respond, it must file a motion for continuance. See "Continuance for Additional Discovery," ch. 5-D, §8, p. 338.

§3.8 Waiver. If the nonmovant does not file affidavits controverting the claim of local prejudice, the court must transfer the case. *City of Abilene v. Downs*, 367 S.W.2d 153, 155 (Tex.1963); *Lone Star Steel Co. v. Scott*, 759 S.W.2d 144, 146 (Tex.App.—Texarkana 1988, writ denied). If the movant waits too long to ask for a hearing, the motion can be waived. *See, e.g.*, *Whitworth v. Kuhn*, 734 S.W.2d 108, 111 (Tex.App.—Austin 1987, no writ) (one-year delay in asking for hearing is inconsistent with purpose of TRCP 87(1)).

§3.9 Notice of hearing. Each party is entitled to at least 45 days' notice of the hearing. See "Notice of hearing," §2.11.2, p. 209.

§3.10 Hearing. If the credibility of the movant's affiants is attacked, the issue of local prejudice must be tried by the court. TRCP 258. It is not clear whether the court must hear live testimony. *Union Carbide Corp. v. Moye*, 798 S.W.2d 792, 793 n.1 (Tex.1990); *see* CPRC §15.064(a) (court must determine venue on pleadings and affidavits). The Supreme Court did not address the issue when presented with the opportunity in *Moye*, and the concurring opinions reached different conclusions. *Compare Moye*, 798 S.W.2d at 794 (Hecht, J., concurring) (trial court may hear live testimony or may decide motion on affidavits), *with id.* at 795 (Gonzales, J., concurring) (trial court must hear live testimony).

PRACTICE TIP

Until the Texas Supreme Court resolves the issue of whether a hearing under TRCP 258 is for the receipt of live testimony or merely for argument, support a motion to transfer for local prejudice with affidavits and discovery products and ask for a hearing to present evidence. If the trial court refuses to give you a hearing, make an offer of proof to create the record you would have made if the court had given you the opportunity to present evidence. See "Offer of Proof & Bill of Exception," ch. 8-E, p. 717.

---

§3.11 Ruling. If the court grants a motion to change venue under TRCP 257, it should transfer the suit according to the following rules. First, if the transfer is from a district court, the court should transfer to any county of proper venue in the same or an adjoining district. TRCP 259(a). Second, if the transfer is from a county court, the court

———————————————— ★ ————————————————

should transfer to any adjoining county of proper venue. TRCP 259(b). Third, if neither TRCP 259(a) nor (b) applies, the court should transfer to any county of proper venue. TRCP 259(c). Fourth, when there is no county of proper venue other than the county where suit was originally filed, the court should transfer according to the following guidelines: (1) when the transfer is from a district court, the court should transfer to any county in the same or an adjoining district or to any district where an impartial trial can be had, (2) when the transfer is from a county court, the court should transfer to any adjoining county or to any district where an impartial trial can be had, or (3) when the parties agree to some other county, the court should transfer to that county. TRCP 259(d).

§4. CONSENT OF THE PARTIES

The parties can agree to transfer the case to another county of proper venue. CPRC §15.063(3); TRCP 255.

§4.1 Deadline to file. There is no deadline to file written consent to transfer venue. CPRC §15.063(3); TRCP 86(1); *see Farris v. Ray*, 895 S.W.2d 351, 352 (Tex.1995).

§4.2 Filing. The agreement must be filed with the clerk of the court in which the case is pending. *See* TRCP 86(1); *Farris v. Ray*, 895 S.W.2d 351, 352 (Tex.1995).

§5. REVIEW

§5.1 No appeal of convenience transfer. The court's decision to grant or deny a motion to transfer based on convenience is not subject to review by appeal or mandamus, and if appealed, the decision is not reversible error. CPRC §15.002(c); *Garza v. Garcia*, 137 S.W.3d 36, 39 (Tex.2004); *see In re Continental Airlines, Inc.*, 988 S.W.2d 733, 735 (Tex.1998); *Lopez v. Texas Workers' Comp. Ins. Fund*, 11 S.W.3d 490, 494 (Tex.App.—Austin 2000, pet. denied). The appellate court cannot review the order on a motion to transfer for convenience or the evidence to support the order. *Garza*, 137 S.W.3d at 39. When the trial court grants a motion to transfer based on convenience and another venue ground without stating in the order the basis for its decision, the appellate court cannot review either ground. *Id.* When the trial court overrules a motion to transfer based on convenience and another venue ground, the appellate court can review only the other ground. *Id.*

§5.2 Interlocutory appeal. For the rules on interlocutory appeal, see *O'Connor's Texas Appeals*, "Motion for Interlocutory Appeal & Stay Pending Appeal," ch. 3-P, p. 148.

1. Most cases. Generally, there is no interlocutory appeal from trial-court rulings on venue motions. CPRC §15.064(a); TRCP 87(6); *In re Team Rocket, L.P.*, 256 S.W.3d 257, 259 (Tex.2008); *Electronic Data Sys. v. Pioneer Elecs. (USA) Inc.*, 68 S.W.3d 254, 257 (Tex.App.—Fort Worth 2002, no pet.).

2. Joinder. In joinder cases, CPRC §15.003 allows an interlocutory appeal to contest the trial court's decision that (1) a plaintiff did or did not independently establish proper venue or (2) a plaintiff who did not independently establish proper venue did or did not establish the elements of CPRC §15.003(a)(1)-(a)(4). CPRC §15.003(b); *Ramirez v. Collier, Shannon, Scott, PLLC*, 123 S.W.3d 43, 47 (Tex.App.—Houston [1st Dist.] 2003, pet. denied). See "Joinder proper under CPRC §15.003(a)," §2.6.4(2), p. 206. CPRC §15.003(c) suggests that any affected party may take an interlocutory appeal from an order granting or denying intervention or joinder. CPRC §15.003(c); *see Surgitek, Bristol-Myers Corp. v. Abel*, 997 S.W.2d 598, 601 (Tex.1999); *Electronic Data*, 68 S.W.3d at 257. The court of appeals will make an independent determination—without any deference to the trial court's decision—of whether the trial court's order was proper. *See* CPRC §15.003(c)(1). An interlocutory appeal under CPRC §15.003(b) stays the commencement of trial until the appeal has been resolved. CPRC §15.003(d).

§5.3 Appeal after trial on merits. Most venue rulings must be appealed after a judgment is rendered on the merits. *See Mauro v. Banales*, 858 S.W.2d 651, 652-53 (Tex.App.—Corpus Christi 1993, orig. proceeding). For exceptions, see "Mandamus," §5.4, p. 214.

1. Record.

(1) Entire reporter's record. To appeal the venue ruling, the appellant must bring forward the entire reporter's record from the trial and from the venue hearing. See "Scope of review," §5.3.2, p. 214.

---✭---

(2) Limited reporter's record. One court of appeals has approved the appeal of a venue ruling with a limited reporter's record under TRAP 34.6(c). *Steger & Bizzell, Inc. v. VandeWater Constr., Inc.*, 811 S.W.2d 687, 689 (Tex.App.—Austin 1991, writ denied) (analysis under former TRAP 53(d)). Under this procedure, the appellant serves the court reporter and the appellee with a request for the preparation of part of the record along with a statement of points or issues to be presented on appeal. TRAP 34.6(c)(1). The appellee can designate any additions from the testimony to be incorporated into the reporter's record. TRAP 34.6(c)(2). If the appellant complies with the procedure, there is a presumption that nothing omitted from the reporter's record is relevant to the appeal. TRAP 34.6(c)(4). In *Steger & Bizzell*, the court noted that the trial on the merits lasted 22 days, so the limited record for venue was an appropriate use of the former TRAP 53(d) procedure. *Steger & Bizzell*, 811 S.W.2d at 689 & n.2. For a description of the procedure for limited appeals, see *O'Connor's Texas Appeals*, "Requesting a Partial Record Under TRAP 34.6(c)," ch. 6-C, §8, p. 234.

2. Scope of review. When the trial court's venue ruling is challenged on appeal after a trial on the merits, the appellate court conducts an independent review of the entire record to determine whether the evidence introduced during the trial on the merits supports the venue ruling. CPRC §15.064(b); *Wilson v. Texas Parks & Wildlife Dept.*, 886 S.W.2d 259, 261 (Tex.1994); *Ruiz v. Conoco, Inc.*, 868 S.W.2d 752, 758 (Tex.1993); *see Ford Motor Co. v. Miles*, 967 S.W.2d 377, 380 (Tex.1998). The appellate court may reverse a decision that was correct when it was made at the venue hearing but was erroneous in light of the evidence introduced at the trial on the merits. *Bleeker v. Villarreal*, 941 S.W.2d 163, 167 (Tex.App.—Corpus Christi 1996, writ dism'd). The requirement that the appellate court review the entire record was designed to prevent fraud in pleading venue facts that might not be discoverable until after the trial on the merits. *Humphrey v. May*, 804 S.W.2d 328, 330 (Tex.App.—Austin 1991, writ denied).

3. Appellate court order.

(1) Other error. If the defendant presents arguments on appeal that entitle it to rendition of judgment—not just remand—the appellate court should consider those points first and, if it sustains them, reverse and render judgment for the defendant without reaching the venue issue. *Bradleys' Elec., Inc. v. Cigna Lloyds Ins.*, 995 S.W.2d 675, 677 (Tex.1999); *see CMH Homes, Inc. v. Daenen*, 15 S.W.3d 97, 99 (Tex.2000).

(2) Venue error.

(a) Uphold venue. If the record contains any probative evidence that venue was proper, even if the preponderance of the evidence is to the contrary, the appellate court must uphold the trial court's venue determination. *Bonham State Bank v. Beadle*, 907 S.W.2d 465, 471 (Tex.1995); *Ruiz*, 868 S.W.2d at 758; *see* CPRC §15.064(b).

(b) Reverse venue. If the record contains no probative evidence that venue was proper, the appellate court must reverse the trial court's venue determination. *Ruiz*, 868 S.W.2d at 758; *see* CPRC §15.064(b); *Bonham State Bank*, 907 S.W.2d at 471. When the appellate court reverses, it must determine whether to remand for trial in another county or for a new venue hearing.

[1] **Remand for trial.** If there is any probative evidence that venue is proper in the county where the defendant sought to transfer the case, the appellate court must instruct the trial court to transfer the case to that county. *Ruiz*, 868 S.W.2d at 758.

[2] **Remand for hearing.** If there is no probative evidence that venue is proper in the county of suit or the county to which transfer was sought, the appellate court must remand the case for further proceedings on the venue issue. *Ruiz*, 868 S.W.2d at 758.

§5.4 Mandamus. Most venue determinations are correctable on appeal and cannot be challenged by mandamus. *Montalvo v. Fourth Ct. of Appeals*, 917 S.W.2d 1, 2 (Tex.1995). But mandamus is appropriate in the following instances:

1. Mandatory venue in CPRC. A party may file a writ of mandamus to enforce a mandatory-venue provision in CPRC chapter 15. CPRC §15.0642; *In re Missouri Pac. R.R.*, 998 S.W.2d 212, 215 (Tex.1999); *In re Continental Airlines, Inc.*, 988 S.W.2d 733, 735 (Tex.1998). Under CPRC §15.0642, the relator is not required to show it

★

lacks an adequate remedy on appeal. *In re Missouri Pac.*, 998 S.W.2d at 216; *KJ Eastwood Invs. v. Enlow*, 923 S.W.2d 255, 258 (Tex.App.—Fort Worth 1996, orig. proceeding). The application for writ of mandamus must be filed before the later of the following dates: (1) the 90th day before the trial starts or (2) the 10th day after the party receives notice of the trial setting. CPRC §15.0642.

2. **Mandatory venue in Family Code.** When a court has a mandatory duty to transfer a case under the Family Code, a party may seek mandamus relief to enforce the transfer. See *Proffer v. Yates*, 734 S.W.2d 671, 673 (Tex.1987) (under former Fam. Code §11.06(b), now §155.201); *In re Knotts*, 62 S.W.3d 922, 923 n.1 (Tex.App.—Texarkana 2001, orig. proceeding) (under Fam. Code §155.201); *In re Kramer*, 9 S.W.3d 449, 450 (Tex.App.—San Antonio 1999, orig. proceeding) (same). See *O'Connor's Fam. Law Handbook*, "Challenging Venue," ch. 4-B, §3, p. 334.

3. **Exceptional circumstances.** Occasionally, a party may be entitled to mandamus relief from a venue order when "exceptional circumstances" make appeal an inadequate remedy. *In re Masonite Corp.*, 997 S.W.2d 194, 197 (Tex.1999); *see, e.g.*, *HCA Health Servs. v. Salinas*, 838 S.W.2d 246, 247-48 (Tex.1992) (order transferring venue signed by mistake); *Union Carbide Corp. v. Moye*, 798 S.W.2d 792, 793 (Tex.1990) (trial court misled party about acceptable form of venue proof); *Henderson v. O'Neill*, 797 S.W.2d 905, 905 (Tex.1990) (no notice of hearing); *Dorchester Master L.P. v. Anthony*, 734 S.W.2d 151, 152 (Tex.App.—Houston [1st Dist.] 1987, orig. proceeding) (order granting second motion was void); *see also In re City of Irving*, 45 S.W.3d 777, 779 (Tex.App.—Texarkana 2001, orig. proceeding) (trial court's erroneous venue order that was eventually reversed on appeal was not exceptional circumstance warranting mandamus).

§5.5 Standard of review. The standard of review for venue rulings depends on the type of venue ruling being challenged.

1. **Most venue rulings.**

(1) **Venue proper.** If the record contains any probative evidence that venue was proper—even if the preponderance of the evidence is to the contrary—the appellate court must uphold the trial court's venue determination. *Bonham State Bank v. Beadle*, 907 S.W.2d 465, 471 (Tex.1995); *Ruiz v. Conoco, Inc.*, 868 S.W.2d 752, 758 (Tex.1993); *see* CPRC §15.064(b).

(2) **Venue improper.** If the record contains no evidence that venue was proper, the appellate court must reverse the trial court's venue ruling and remand the case for a new trial without conducting the usual harm analysis under TRAP 44.1(a). *Wichita Cty. v. Hart*, 917 S.W.2d 779, 781 (Tex.1996); *Bleeker v. Villarreal*, 941 S.W.2d 163, 167 (Tex.App.—Corpus Christi 1996, writ dism'd); *see* CPRC §15.064(b). Thus, venue is one of the rare situations where the harmless-error rule does not apply. If the trial court makes an erroneous venue ruling, the case must be reversed even if the appellant cannot show harm. *Wilson v. Texas Parks & Wildlife Dept.*, 886 S.W.2d 259, 261 (Tex.1994); *Maranatha Temple, Inc. v. Enterprise Prods.*, 833 S.W.2d 736, 740-41 (Tex.App.—Houston [1st Dist.] 1992, writ denied). The Legislature intended venue rulings to be exempt from the harmless-error rule to discourage the prosecution of meritless venue claims. *Maranatha Temple*, 833 S.W.2d at 741.

2. **Mandamus under CPRC §15.0642.** The standard of review for mandatory venue under CPRC §15.0642 is abuse of discretion. *In re Missouri Pac. R.R.*, 998 S.W.2d 212, 215 (Tex.1999); *In re Continental Airlines, Inc.*, 988 S.W.2d 733, 735 (Tex.1998).

3. **Joinder under CPRC §15.003.** The standard of review for the trial court's order under CPRC §15.003 is de novo. *See* CPRC §15.003(c)(1); *Surgitek, Bristol-Myers Corp. v. Abel*, 997 S.W.2d 598, 603 (Tex.1999). If a party contends that it was improperly denied the opportunity to present proof, the standard of review for that complaint is abuse of discretion. *Surgitek*, 997 S.W.2d at 603.

4. **Local prejudice.** The standard of review for local prejudice is abuse of discretion. *See, e.g.*, *Union Carbide Corp. v. Moye*, 798 S.W.2d 792, 793 (Tex.1990) (court did not allow reasonable opportunity to supplement venue record); *Beard v. Gonzalez*, 924 S.W.2d 763, 764 (Tex.App.—El Paso 1996, orig. proceeding) (court did not allow reasonable discovery); *City of La Grange v. McBee*, 923 S.W.2d 89, 90 (Tex.App.—Houston [1st Dist.] 1996, writ denied) (same).

———————————————— ★ ————————————————

D. FORUM NON CONVENIENS—CHALLENGING THE TEXAS FORUM

§1. GENERAL

§1.1 Rule. None. See CPRC §71.051.

§1.2 Purpose. A forum non conveniens (FNC) motion asks the court to dismiss or stay a suit because a court outside Texas that has jurisdiction over the dispute is a more appropriate forum. *A.P. Keller Dev., Inc. v. One Jackson Place, Ltd.*, 890 S.W.2d 502, 505 (Tex.App.—El Paso 1994, no writ). The FNC doctrine presumes at least two forums have jurisdiction over the dispute. *Yoroshii Invs. (Mauritius) Pte. Ltd. v. BP Int'l*, 179 S.W.3d 639, 643 (Tex. App.—El Paso 2005, pet. denied); *see In re ENSCO Offshore Int'l*, 311 S.W.3d 921, 925 (Tex.2010). FNC is an equitable doctrine that courts exercise to avoid imposing an inconvenient jurisdiction on a litigant, even if jurisdiction is supported by the long-arm statute and would not violate due process. *Tullis v. Georgia-Pac. Corp.*, 45 S.W.3d 118, 122 (Tex.App.—Fort Worth 2000, no pet.). A motion to stay or dismiss on grounds of FNC is appropriate only when the defendant wants to defend the suit in another state or country.

§1.3 Timetables & forms. Timetable, Motion to Dismiss—Code Forum Non Conveniens, p. 1213; Timetable, Motion to Dismiss—Common-Law Forum Non Conveniens, p. 1214; *O'Connor's Texas Civil Forms* (2012), FORMS 3D.

§1.4 Other references. Restatement (2d) of Conflict of Laws §84 & cmts. (a)-(f) (1971); Scherz, Comment, *Section 71.051 of the Texas Civil Practice & Remedies Code—The Texas Legislature's Answer to Alfaro*, 46 Baylor L.Rev. 99 (1994); *O'Connor's Texas Causes of Action* (2013) (*O'Connor's Texas COA*).

§2. TYPES OF MOTIONS

There are generally two types of motions for FNC in Texas courts: (1) a motion to stay or dismiss under the CPRC when a foreign plaintiff asserts a claim for personal injury or death and (2) a motion to dismiss for common-law FNC when the plaintiff asserts almost any other cause of action. A party can also file a motion to enforce a forum-selection clause in a contract, which is related to an FNC motion. FNC for cases under the CPRC will be referred to as "Code FNC." FNC for all other cases will be referred to as "common-law FNC."

§3. CODE FNC MOTION

NOTE

The Texas Legislature has made significant changes to CPRC §71.051 since it enacted the statute in 1993. When researching Code FNC motions, avoid cases that predate the most recent amendments to the statute, made in 2005.

---

§3.1 Motion. If the plaintiff is not a legal resident of Texas and has asserted a claim for personal injury or death, the defendant may file a motion to stay or dismiss under CPRC §71.051(b).

    1. In writing. A Code FNC motion must be made in writing. CPRC §71.051(b). See *O'Connor's Texas Forms*, FORM 3D:1.

    2. Deadline to file. The deadline to file a Code FNC motion is 180 days after the last date for filing a motion to transfer venue. CPRC §71.051(d). Because the deadline to file a motion to transfer venue is the same as the deadline to file an answer, the deadline to file a Code FNC motion is approximately 200 days after the lawsuit is served (180 days plus 20+ days). See "Motion to extend time," §3.4, p. 220; "Deadline to Answer," ch. 3-E, §2, p. 227.

    3. Grounds. To be entitled to a stay or dismissal, the defendant must address the following grounds in the Code FNC motion:

        (1) Plaintiff is not legal resident. The defendant must show the plaintiff is not a legal resident. *See* CPRC §71.051(e).

        (a) Who is a plaintiff? A plaintiff is a party seeking to recover damages for personal injury or wrongful death. CPRC §71.051(h)(2). The term includes both the person who was injured and the party seeking recovery, but does not include a counterclaimant, a cross-claimant, a third-party plaintiff, a person who is assigned a

★

cause of action for personal injury, or a person appointed as a personal representative in a wrongful-death action who accepts the appointment in bad faith for the purpose of affecting the application of CPRC §71.051. *Id.* §71.051(h)(2).

(b) Who is a legal resident? A legal resident is an individual who (1) intends a specified political subdivision to be her permanent residence and intends to return to that political subdivision despite temporary residence elsewhere or temporary absences, and (2) has not adopted a residence in Texas in bad faith to avoid the application of CPRC §71.051. CPRC §71.051(h)(1). The individual's country of citizenship or national origin is irrelevant. *Id.*

[1] Single plaintiff. If the suit involves a single plaintiff, the defendant can allege the plaintiff is not a legal resident of Texas. *See* CPRC §71.051(e); *see also* ***Tullis v. Georgia-Pac. Corp.***, 45 S.W.3d 118, 124 (Tex.App.—Fort Worth 2000, no pet.) (D did not allege P was nonresident in its pleading, and P did not object; P waived error).

[2] Multiple plaintiffs. If the suit involves multiple plaintiffs who are not all Texas residents, the defendant can do any of the following:

[a] Show by a preponderance of the evidence that the plaintiffs who are legal residents of Texas were joined solely for the purpose of obtaining or maintaining jurisdiction in Texas and that the claims of the plaintiffs would be more properly heard in a forum outside Texas. *See* CPRC §71.051(e).

[b] Show that the occurrence that gave rise to the claims of the plaintiffs who are legal residents of Texas was not the same occurrence that gave rise to the claims of the nonresidents. *See id.*

(2) Action should be heard in alternate forum. The defendant must allege that the plaintiff's claim or action would be more properly heard in a forum outside Texas based on the interest of justice and for the convenience of the parties. CPRC §71.051(b); *see* ***In re ENSCO Offshore Int'l***, 311 S.W.3d 921, 924 (Tex.2010); ***In re General Elec. Co.***, 271 S.W.3d 681, 686-87 (Tex.2008). "Interest of justice" and "convenience of the parties" are essentially defined by the factors in CPRC §71.051(b). *In re General Elec.*, 271 S.W.3d at 686. To support its request to stay or dismiss, the defendant should address in its motion all of the factors under CPRC §71.051(b).

NOTE

The defendant is not required to prove or present evidence on each factor under CPRC §71.051(b); the statute simply requires the trial court to consider the factors to the extent they apply. **In re General Elec.**, *271 S.W.3d at 687. See "Burden of proof," §3.6.4, p. 220; "Review of §71.051 factors," §3.7.1, p. 220. At the very least, however, a defendant should argue that another forum is both available and adequate. See* **Piper Aircraft Co. v. Reyno**, *454 U.S. 235, 254 n.22 (1981) (requiring both factors before dismissing case for FNC; wrongful-death claim brought before enactment of CPRC §71.051).*

(a) Alternate forum available. The defendant must identify an alternate forum where the claim may be tried. CPRC §71.051(b)(1). An alternate forum is available if the defendant would be amenable to service of process there. *In re ENSCO*, 311 S.W.3d at 924.

(b) Alternate forum adequate. The defendant must show that the alternate forum provides an adequate remedy. CPRC §71.051(b)(2). An inadequate forum is one in which the remedies the forum offers are so unsatisfactory they are the equivalent of no remedy at all. *In re ENSCO*, 311 S.W.3d at 924; *In re General Elec.*, 271 S.W.3d at 688. If there is a question about the adequacy of the alternate forum's remedy, the defendant may have to compare the rights, remedies, and procedures available in each of the forums, but such comparative analysis is usually unnecessary. *See* ***In re ENSCO***, 311 S.W.3d at 924-25; ***In re General Elec.***, 271 S.W.3d at 688; *see, e.g.,* ***In re BPZ Res.***, 359 S.W.3d 866, 875 (Tex.App.—Houston [14th Dist.] 2012, orig. proceeding) (because there was no evidence that Peru's courts are so corrupt as to provide inadequate remedy, no comparative analysis between Texas and

✦

Peru was necessary). If there is more than one alternate forum, the defendant is not required to pick one, but may show how any or all of them are adequate. *See In re ENSCO*, 311 S.W.3d at 925.

(c) Substantial injustice imposed. The defendant must show how maintaining the action in Texas would impose a substantial injustice on the defendant. CPRC §71.051(b)(3); *e.g.*, *In re ENSCO*, 311 S.W.3d at 925 (maintaining action in Texas would be substantially unjust when majority of witnesses could not be subpoenaed to appear in Texas and related suit for contractual indemnity against foreign party was already pending in Australia).

(d) Alternate forum can exercise jurisdiction. The defendant must show the alternate forum, as a result of the parties' submission or otherwise, can exercise jurisdiction over all the defendants properly joined to the plaintiff's claim. CPRC §71.051(b)(4); *e.g.*, *In re ENSCO*, 311 S.W.3d at 925-26 (all Ds agreed to submit to jurisdiction in either of the alternate forums).

(e) Statutory factors favor alternate forum. The defendant must show that the balance of the parties' private interests and the state's public interests favors the alternate forum. CPRC §71.051(b)(5); *In re ENSCO*, 311 S.W.3d at 926; *Tullis*, 45 S.W.3d at 132. Most of the private and public interests generally referred to in CPRC §71.051(b)(5) originated in *Gulf Oil Corp. v. Gilbert*, 330 U.S. 501, 508-09 (1947), and are called the *Gulf Oil* factors.

[1] Private interests. To support the request to stay or dismiss, the defendant should establish that the private interests of the parties will be better served in the alternate forum.

[a] The defendant should address whether access to sources of proof will be easier in the alternate forum than in Texas. *See Gulf Oil*, 330 U.S. at 508.

[b] The defendant should address whether compulsory process for the attendance of unwilling witnesses is available in the alternate forum. *See id.*; *see, e.g.*, *In re ENSCO*, 311 S.W.3d at 926 (lack of compulsory process in Texas to secure production of witnesses and other documents weighed in favor of alternate forums).

[c] The defendant should address whether the costs of securing the presence of willing witnesses will be lower in the alternate forum than in Texas. *See Gulf Oil*, 330 U.S. at 508.

[d] The defendant should address whether viewing the relevant premises is necessary to the suit and whether the possibility of viewing the premises is better in the alternate forum than in Texas. *See id.*

[e] The defendant should address whether the enforceability of the judgment in the alternate forum is as good as or better than in Texas. *See id.*

[f] The defendant should address all other practical problems that make trial easy, expeditious, and inexpensive. *See id.*; *In re ENSCO*, 311 S.W.3d at 926; *see also In re BPZ*, 359 S.W.3d at 879 (allegations of political unrest in alternate forum generally will not suffice to outweigh other factors favoring dismissal). For example, an alternate forum would be preferable if the cost, time, and scheduling difficulties necessary to obtain evidence and present witness testimony would be far greater in Texas than in the alternate forum. *See In re ENSCO*, 311 S.W.3d at 926.

[2] Public interests. To support the request to stay or dismiss, the defendant should establish that the public interests will be better served in the alternate forum.

[a] The defendant should address whether the administrative burden (e.g., congested docket, jury duty of citizens) on the alternate-forum court is less than the burden on the Texas court. *See Gulf Oil*, 330 U.S. at 508-09.

[b] The defendant should address the extent to which the interest in deciding the case in the alternate forum is greater than that in Texas. *See id.* at 509; *see, e.g.*, *In re ENSCO*, 311 S.W.3d at 927 (Texas had no significant relationship to case involving injury occurring in Singapore's territorial waters on Liberian-flagged vessel to Australian citizen employed by Australian company).

—⭐—

[c] The defendant should address whether the law of the alternate forum will control the disposition of the case. *See Gulf Oil*, 330 U.S. at 509; *see, e.g.*, *In re BPZ*, 359 S.W.3d at 878 (Peruvian law applied and events giving rise to claim were more substantially connected with Peru than with Texas).

[d] The defendant should address whether the law of the alternate forum must be applied to the facts of the case and, if so, whether that law is so dissimilar to Texas law that its enforcement in Texas will be difficult or impossible. *Gurvich v. Tyree*, 694 S.W.2d 39, 46 (Tex.App.—Corpus Christi 1985, no writ).

[3] No act or omission in Texas. To support the request to stay or dismiss, the defendant must show that the plaintiff's personal injury or death did not result from acts or omissions that occurred in Texas. CPRC §71.051(b)(5); *see In re ENSCO*, 311 S.W.3d at 926.

(f) No duplication or proliferation of litigation. The defendant must show that the stay or dismissal will not result in unreasonable duplication or proliferation of litigation. CPRC §71.051(b)(6); *In re ENSCO*, 311 S.W.3d at 928; *see, e.g.*, *In re General Elec.*, 271 S.W.3d at 692-93 (D asked for dismissal of entire case, but even if court dismissed only part of the case, fragmentation of litigation would not be unreasonable).

4. Verified. Because most of the defendant's factual allegations are outside the record, the defendant should probably verify the motion, even though nothing in CPRC §71.051 requires verification.

5. Request hearing. The defendant must request a hearing on the motion. CPRC §71.051(d). See "Hearing," §3.6, p. 220.

§3.2 Response.

1. Form.

(1) Written. The plaintiff should file a written response to challenge the allegations in the defendant's motion. See *O'Connor's Texas Forms*, FORM 3D:3.

(2) No verification required. The plaintiff is not required to provide verified evidence to support its response. *See* CPRC §71.051(b). The plaintiff should, however, verify the response if it relies on facts outside the record. See "Verification & affidavits," ch. 1-B, §4.1.12, p. 20.

(3) Deadline to file. There is no deadline in CPRC §71.051 for filing the plaintiff's response.

2. Grounds. The plaintiff should negate the defendant's allegations and identify any exceptions to the application of CPRC §71.051.

(1) Plaintiff is Texas resident.

(a) Single plaintiff. If the action involves a single plaintiff, the plaintiff can allege that, contrary to the defendant's allegation, the plaintiff is a Texas resident. *See* CPRC §71.051(e); *see also Tullis v. Georgia-Pac. Corp.*, 45 S.W.3d 118, 124 (Tex.App.—Fort Worth 2000, no pet.) (D did not allege P was nonresident in its motion and P did not object; P waived error).

(b) Multiple plaintiffs. If the action involves multiple plaintiffs who are not all Texas residents, the plaintiff can allege that the plaintiffs who are Texas residents are properly joined in the action and that the action arose from a single occurrence. CPRC §71.051(e).

(2) No forum outside Texas. The plaintiff can allege that the claim or action would not be more properly heard in a forum outside Texas.

(a) No alternate forum. The plaintiff can allege that the defendant did not identify an alternate forum or, if it did, that the defendant is not amenable to service of process in that forum. *See* CPRC §71.051(b)(1).

(b) No adequate remedy. The plaintiff can allege that the alternate forum does not provide an adequate remedy. *See* CPRC §71.051(b)(2).

─────────────────────────── ✬ ───────────────────────────

(c) No substantial injustice. The plaintiff can allege that maintaining the suit in Texas would not impose a substantial injustice on the defendant. *See* CPRC §71.051(b)(3).

(d) No jurisdiction. The plaintiff can allege that the alternate forum does not have jurisdiction over the claim. *See* CPRC §71.051(b)(4). The plaintiff can argue that the defendant has not submitted itself to the jurisdiction of the alternate forum and that the alternate forum has no other means of exercising personal jurisdiction over the defendant. *See id.*

(e) Balance of interests. The plaintiff can allege that the balance of private and public interests favors the Texas forum. *See* CPRC §71.051(b)(5).

[1] *Gulf Oil* factors. The plaintiff should construct its argument around the *Gulf Oil* factors. See "*Gulf Oil* factors," §4.1.3(2)(a), p. 222.

[2] Act or omission occurred in Texas. The plaintiff can allege that her claim for personal injury or wrongful death was the result of the defendant's act or omission that occurred in Texas. *See* CPRC §71.051(b)(5).

(f) Duplication or proliferation. The plaintiff can allege that the alternate forum's stay or dismissal would result in unreasonable duplication or proliferation of litigation. *See* CPRC §71.051(b)(6).

(3) Improper notice of hearing. If the defendant did not give proper notice, the plaintiff must challenge the notice, or it waives the issue. The plaintiff can object if the defendant set the hearing within 30 days of trial or did not give the plaintiff 21 days' notice of the hearing. *See* CPRC §71.051(d). See "Hearing," §3.6, this page.

(4) Waiver. If the defendant filed its Code FNC motion after the deadline, the plaintiff should allege that the defendant waived the motion. See "Deadline to file," §3.1.2, p. 216.

§3.3 Defendant's reply. If the plaintiff provides evidence to negate the defendant's allegations, the defendant should respond by supplying verified evidence to support its motion. See "No verification required," §3.2.1(2), p. 219.

§3.4 Motion to extend time. The court may extend any time limit established under CPRC §71.051 at the request of any party for good cause. CPRC §71.051(g). If a party needs additional time to file a response or reply, it should file a motion for continuance. See "Motion for Continuance," ch. 5-D, p. 336.

§3.5 Discovery. The court must give the parties "ample opportunity" for discovery of information relevant to the FNC motion before the hearing on the motion. CPRC §71.051(d). See "Discovery," ch. 6, p. 419. If a party needs additional time for discovery, it should file a motion for continuance. See "Motion for Continuance," ch. 5-D, p. 336.

§3.6 Hearing. The court must hold a hearing before ruling on a Code FNC motion. CPRC §71.051(d).

1. Notice. The court cannot rule on a motion unless the parties have at least 21 days' notice of the hearing. CPRC §71.051(d).

2. Deadline. The hearing must be held a reasonable time before trial—at least 30 days. CPRC §71.051(d).

3. Evidence. The parties should produce affidavits, deposition testimony, discovery responses, or other verified evidence. CPRC §71.051 does not explicitly prohibit oral testimony at the hearing.

4. Burden of proof. CPRC §71.051 does not place the burden of proof on either the plaintiff or the defendant to show whether the court should exercise jurisdiction. *In re ENSCO Offshore Int'l*, 311 S.W.3d 921, 927 (Tex.2010); *In re General Elec. Co.*, 271 S.W.3d 681, 687 (Tex.2008). The statute does not require that a party prove each of the §71.051(b) factors or that the factors "strongly" favor granting the FNC motion. *See In re ENSCO*, 311 S.W.3d at 929; *In re General Elec.*, 271 S.W.3d at 687.

§3.7 Ruling.

1. Review of §71.051 factors. In ruling on the FNC motion, the trial court must consider the CPRC §71.051(b) factors to the extent they apply. *In re General Elec. Co.*, 271 S.W.3d 681, 687 (Tex.2008). If the statutory factors weigh in favor of the claim being heard in an alternate forum, the trial court must grant the FNC motion. *Id.*

at 686. When evidence is necessary to support a party's position, the court will base its decision on the greater weight of the evidence. *In re ENSCO Offshore Int'l*, 311 S.W.3d 921, 927 (Tex.2010); *In re General Elec.*, 271 S.W.3d at 687.

2. Timing.

(1) Generally – after resolving jurisdictional challenges. Generally, a court must determine whether it has jurisdiction over a defendant before ruling on an FNC motion. *Cf. Exxon Corp. v. Choo*, 881 S.W.2d 301, 302 n.2 (Tex.1994) (suit filed before effective date of §71.051). See "Due Order of Pleading," ch. 3-A, §3, p. 183; "Special Appearance—Challenging Personal Jurisdiction," ch. 3-B, p. 189.

(2) Exception – jurisdictional challenges difficult to resolve. A court may take the less-burdensome approach and resolve an FNC motion before a jurisdictional challenge if the jurisdictional challenge would be more difficult to resolve and the FNC considerations weigh heavily in favor of dismissal. *Sinochem Int'l Co. v. Malaysia Int'l Shipping Corp.*, 549 U.S. 422, 436 (2007); *see, e.g.*, *Schippers v. Mazak Props., Inc.*, 350 S.W.3d 294, 296 (Tex.App.—San Antonio 2011, pet. denied) (because FNC is a determination of whether merits of claim should be decided elsewhere rather than a determination of substantive law, court addressed FNC motion before special appearance); *cf. Vinmar Trade Fin., Ltd. v. Utility Trailers de Mex., S.A. de C.V.*, 336 S.W.3d 664, 671-72 (Tex.App.—Houston [1st Dist.] 2010, no pet.) (common-law FNC; court addressed FNC motion before special appearance because it enabled court to address issues against both parties while special appearance involved only one party).

§4. COMMON-LAW FNC MOTION

In cases other than personal injury or death, the court can decline to exercise its jurisdiction over the action to avoid imposing an inconvenient forum on a litigant and witnesses. *See Sarieddine v. Moussa*, 820 S.W.2d 837, 839-41 (Tex.App.—Dallas 1991, writ denied). A common-law FNC motion to dismiss asks the court to decline jurisdiction because a court outside Texas has jurisdiction over the dispute and defendants and is a more appropriate forum. *See Van Winkle-Hooker Co. v. Rice*, 448 S.W.2d 824, 826 (Tex.App.—Dallas 1969, no writ).

§4.1 Motion.

1. In writing. A common-law FNC motion should be made in writing. *See RSR Corp. v. Siegmund*, 309 S.W.3d 686, 710 (Tex.App.—Dallas 2010, no pet.) (D bears burden of invoking doctrine of FNC in motion to dismiss); *see also Seung Ok Lee v. Ki Pong Na*, 198 S.W.3d 492, 495 (Tex.App.—Dallas 2006, no pet.) (there must be some evidence in record that allows trial court to balance FNC factors and determine whether they weigh in favor of trying case in another forum). See *O'Connor's Texas Forms*, FORM 3D:2.

2. Deadline to file. Generally, there is no deadline for filing a motion for common-law FNC; however, the motion should be brought before trial. *See Flaiz v. Moore*, 359 S.W.2d 872, 875 (Tex.1962); *Direct Color Servs. v. Eastman Kodak Co.*, 929 S.W.2d 558, 567 (Tex.App.—Tyler 1996, writ denied).

3. Grounds. To be entitled to a dismissal, the defendant must address the following grounds in the common-law FNC motion:

(1) Alternate forum available. The defendant must show there is another available forum. *Vinmar Trade Fin., Ltd. v. Utility Trailers de Mex., S.A. de C.V.*, 336 S.W.3d 664, 674 (Tex.App.—Houston [1st Dist.] 2010, no pet.); *Yoroshii Invs. (Mauritius) Pte. Ltd. v. BP Int'l*, 179 S.W.3d 639, 643 (Tex.App.—El Paso 2005, pet. denied); *Sarieddine v. Moussa*, 820 S.W.2d 837, 841 (Tex.App.—Dallas 1991, writ denied). Another forum is "available" when the entire case and all the defendants can come within the jurisdiction of the forum. *See Vinmar Trade*, 336 S.W.3d at 674; *Yoroshii Invs.*, 179 S.W.3d at 643; *Direct Color*, 929 S.W.2d at 564; *Sarieddine*, 820 S.W.2d at 841. This requirement is satisfied if the defendant establishes that it is amenable to process in the alternate forum. *Direct Color*, 929 S.W.2d at 564. A defendant is amenable to process when either it has minimum contacts sufficient for a court to exercise jurisdiction over it or it agrees to submit to the court's jurisdiction. *Id.*; *see, e.g.*, *Seguros Comercial Am., S.A. de C.V. v. American President Lines, Ltd.*, 966 S.W.2d 652, 656 (Tex.App.—San Antonio 1998, no

———————————————————— ✦ ————————————————————

pet.) (Mexico was available forum because D was willing to submit to jurisdiction of Mexican court); *Sarieddine*, 820 S.W.2d at 842 (Abu Dhabi was available forum because Ds consented to jurisdiction there).

(2) *Gulf Oil* **factors favor alternate forum.** The defendant must show that the balance of the parties' private interests and the state's public interests favors the alternate forum. *Quixtar Inc. v. Signature Mgmt. Team, LLC*, 315 S.W.3d 28, 33-34 (Tex.2010); *RSR Corp.*, 309 S.W.3d at 710; *Yoroshii Invs.*, 179 S.W.3d at 643.

(a) *Gulf Oil* **factors.** The private- and public-interest factors originated in *Gulf Oil Corp. v. Gilbert*, 330 U.S. 501, 508 (1947), and are called the *Gulf Oil* factors.

[1] Private interests. To support the motion to dismiss, the defendant should establish that the private interests of the parties will be better served in the alternate forum.

[a] The defendant should address whether access to sources of proof will be easier in the alternate forum than in Texas. *Quixtar*, 315 S.W.3d at 33; *RSR Corp.*, 309 S.W.3d at 710; *Yoroshii Invs.*, 179 S.W.3d at 643.

[b] The defendant should address whether compulsory process for the attendance of unwilling witnesses is available in the alternate forum. *Quixtar*, 315 S.W.3d at 33; *RSR Corp.*, 309 S.W.3d at 710; *Yoroshii Invs.*, 179 S.W.3d at 643.

[c] The defendant should address whether the costs of securing the presence of willing witnesses will be lower in the alternate forum than in Texas. *Quixtar*, 315 S.W.3d at 33; *RSR Corp.*, 309 S.W.3d at 710.

[d] The defendant should address whether viewing the relevant premises is necessary to the suit and whether the possibility of viewing the premises is better in the alternate forum than in Texas. *Quixtar*, 315 S.W.3d at 33.

[e] The defendant should address whether the enforceability of the judgment in the alternate forum is as good as or better than in Texas. *Id.*; *RSR Corp.*, 309 S.W.3d at 710; *Yoroshii Invs.*, 179 S.W.3d at 643.

[f] The defendant should address all other practical problems that make the trial of a case easy, expeditious, and inexpensive. *Quixtar*, 315 S.W.3d at 33; *RSR Corp.*, 309 S.W.3d at 710.

[2] Public interests. To support the motion to dismiss, the defendant should establish that the public interests will be better served in the alternate forum.

[a] The defendant should address whether the burden of jury duty is more appropriately placed on the alternate forum's citizens rather than on Texas citizens. *Quixtar*, 315 S.W.3d at 34; *see RSR Corp.*, 309 S.W.3d at 710; *Yoroshii Invs.*, 179 S.W.3d at 643.

[b] The defendant should address whether the administrative burden (e.g., congested docket) on the alternate-forum court is less than the burden on the Texas court. *Quixtar*, 315 S.W.3d at 33-34; *see RSR Corp.*, 309 S.W.3d at 710; *Yoroshii Invs.*, 179 S.W.3d at 643.

[c] The defendant should address the extent to which the interest in deciding the case in the alternate forum is greater than that in Texas. *Quixtar*, 315 S.W.3d at 34; *see RSR Corp.*, 309 S.W.3d at 710; *Yoroshii Invs.*, 179 S.W.3d at 643.

[d] The defendant should address whether the law of the alternate forum will control the disposition of the case. *See Quixtar*, 315 S.W.3d at 34; *RSR Corp.*, 309 S.W.3d at 710; *Yoroshii Invs.*, 179 S.W.3d at 643.

(b) D's burden of persuasion & proof.

[1] Persuasion. To support the motion to dismiss, the defendant must provide the court with enough information to enable the court to determine that the *Gulf Oil* factors support dismissal. *Quixtar*, 315 S.W.3d at 34. This burden of persuasion does not require, however, that the defendant make an "extensive investigation" to produce evidence for the dismissal hearing. *Id.*

─────────────── ★ ───────────────

[2] Proof. The defendant's burden of proof on the balance of the *Gulf Oil* factors depends on the plaintiff's status as a Texas resident.

[a] P is resident. If the plaintiff (either an individual or a corporation) is a Texas resident, the defendant must show the balance of factors "strongly favors" dismissal. *See Vinmar Trade*, 336 S.W.3d at 678; *Sarieddine*, 820 S.W.2d at 842; *see also Quixtar*, 315 S.W.3d at 33 n.2 (disapproving of "strongly favors" standard as applied to nonresidents). But if the plaintiff is a Texas corporation that does extensive foreign business, the defendant must show the balance of factors simply "favors" dismissal. *See Vinmar Trade*, 336 S.W.3d at 678 (choice of forum for Texas corporation doing extensive foreign business is given less deference).

[b] P is nonresident. If the plaintiff is a nonresident, the defendant must show the balance of factors simply "favors" dismissal. *See Quixtar*, 315 S.W.3d at 33 (nonresident's choice of forum is entitled to less deference, and thus D's burden of proof is less stringent than if P were a resident).

§4.2 Response.

1. In writing. The plaintiff should file a written response challenging the allegations in the defendant's motion.

2. Deadline to file. Although there is no deadline for filing the response, the plaintiff should file (and serve) it far enough in advance of the hearing for the court to consider the argument and evidence.

3. Grounds. The plaintiff should challenge the defendant's allegations raised in the motion. See *O'Connor's Texas Forms*, FORM 3D:4.

(1) Forum is not adequate. If the defendant establishes that an alternate forum is "available," the plaintiff must show that the forum is not adequate. *RSR Corp. v. Siegmund*, 309 S.W.3d 686, 710 (Tex.App.—Dallas 2010, no pet.); *see Vinmar Trade Fin., Ltd. v. Utility Trailers de Mex., S.A. de C.V.*, 336 S.W.3d 664, 674 (Tex. App.—Houston [1st Dist.] 2010, no pet.) (alternate forum's laws presumed adequate unless P makes contrary showing). An alternate forum is adequate when the parties will not be deprived of all remedies or treated unfairly. *RSR Corp.*, 309 S.W.3d at 710.

(2) *Gulf Oil* factors favor Texas forum. The plaintiff should address the *Gulf Oil* factors and demonstrate how the balance of those factors favors the Texas forum. See "*Gulf Oil* factors," §4.1.3(2)(a), p. 222.

§4.3 Hearing. The court must hold a hearing and allow for evidence to be presented before it can rule on a common-law FNC motion. *See Seung Ok Lee v. Ki Pong Na*, 198 S.W.3d 492, 495 (Tex.App.—Dallas 2006, no pet.); *Garden City Boxing Club, Inc. v. 3425 Club, Inc.*, No. 05-08-00571-CV (Tex.App.—Dallas 2009, no pet.) (memo op.; 4-8-09).

§4.4 Ruling. If the alternate forum is available and adequate and the balance of private- and public-interest factors either strongly favors or simply favors the alternate forum (depending on the plaintiff's status as a Texas resident), the trial court must grant the common-law FNC motion to dismiss. *See Quixtar Inc. v. Signature Mgmt. Team, LLC*, 315 S.W.3d 28, 33-35 (Tex.2010). See "Proof," §4.1.3(2)(b)[2], this page. For a discussion of whether the ruling on the motion can be made before a ruling on any jurisdictional challenges, see "Timing," §3.7.2, p. 221.

§5. ORDER

The court must sign a written order sustaining or overruling the motion.

§5.1 Dismissal or stay under Code. When the court sustains a motion for Code FNC, it can grant either a dismissal or a stay. The court must issue specific findings of fact and conclusions of law. CPRC §71.051(f). The court may set terms and conditions for dismissing or staying a claim, as the interest of justice requires. *Id.* §71.051(c). If a defendant violates the terms or conditions of the order of dismissal or stay, the court must withdraw the order and proceed as if the order had never been issued, despite any other law on jurisdiction. *Id.*

——————————————— ✦ ———————————————

NOTE

A Texas court does not have the power to transfer a case to another state's court. See **Accelerated Christian Educ., Inc. v. Oracle Corp.**, *925 S.W.2d 66, 70 (Tex.App.—Dallas 1996, no writ); Restatement (2d) of Conflict of Laws §84 cmt. e (1971). Thus, a Texas court can only dismiss or stay the suit.*

§5.2 Dismissal under common law. When the court sustains a motion for common-law FNC, it will usually dismiss the case. *See* **Sarieddine v. Moussa**, 820 S.W.2d 837, 839 (Tex.App.—Dallas 1991, writ denied). The court may, however, consider granting a stay instead. If the court grants a dismissal under common law, it cannot later withdraw the order of dismissal as it can under CPRC §71.051(c). By granting a stay, the court retains the case on its docket in the event the defendant does not comply with its agreement to be sued in the alternate forum.

§6. FORUM SELECTION BY CONTRACT

Contractual forum-selection clauses are presumed to be valid and enforceable in Texas. *In re Laibe Corp.*, 307 S.W.3d 314, 316 (Tex.2010); *In re International Profit Assocs.*, 274 S.W.3d 672, 675 (Tex.2009); *In re Lyon Fin. Servs.*, 257 S.W.3d 228, 232 (Tex.2008).

§6.1 Enforcement.

1. Within scope. For a trial court to enforce a forum-selection clause, a plaintiff's claims must fall within the scope of the clause. *See* **In re Lisa Laser USA, Inc.**, 310 S.W.3d 880, 884-85 (Tex.2010); **Stokes Interest, G.P. v. Santo-Pietro**, 343 S.W.3d 441, 445 (Tex.App.—El Paso 2010, no pet.); *see also* **In re International Profit Assocs.**, 274 S.W.3d 672, 677 (Tex.2009) (court should use "common sense" approach in determining whether forum-selection clause covers P's claims). A forum-selection clause may be in a contract that consists of only one document or a contract that consists of multiple documents. *See* **In re Lisa Laser**, 310 S.W.3d at 885; **In re Laibe Corp.**, 307 S.W.3d 314, 317 (Tex.2010). If those documents relate to the same transaction, reference each other, and are substantially incomplete without each other, they can be construed together to determine whether the claims are within the scope of the forum-selection clause. *E.g.*, **In re Lisa Laser**, 310 S.W.3d at 885 (agreement comprised of multiple exhibits, one of which contained forum-selection clause applicable to sales between P and D-distributor, was read as multiple documents describing one transaction; forum-selection clause applied to all of P's claims under agreement).

2. No exception or waiver. If the plaintiff's claims fall within the scope of the forum-selection clause, the trial court must enforce the clause unless the party opposing it can show an exception to enforcement or a waiver by the other party.

(1) Exceptions. The party opposing the forum-selection clause has a heavy burden of proof. *In re Laibe Corp.*, 307 S.W.3d at 316; *In re International Profit*, 274 S.W.3d at 675. The party must clearly show that (1) enforcement of the clause would be unreasonable and unjust, (2) the clause is invalid because of fraud or overreaching, (3) enforcement would contravene a strong Texas public policy, or (4) the selected forum is seriously inconvenient for trial. *In re Laibe Corp.*, 307 S.W.3d at 316; *In re ADM Investor Servs.*, 304 S.W.3d 371, 375 (Tex.2010); *In re Lyon Fin. Servs.*, 257 S.W.3d 228, 231-32 (Tex.2008). See *O'Connor's Texas Forms*, FORM 3D:8.

(a) Unreasonable & unjust. The party opposing the forum-selection clause may claim that enforcement of the clause would be unreasonable and unjust. *In re Laibe Corp.*, 307 S.W.3d at 316; *In re ADM Investor*, 304 S.W.3d at 375; *In re International Profit*, 274 S.W.3d at 675; *In re AutoNation, Inc.*, 228 S.W.3d 663, 668 (Tex.2007); *In re AIU Ins.*, 148 S.W.3d 109, 112 (Tex.2004). Enforcement will be unreasonable and unjust only in extreme or exceptional circumstances. *See In re ADM Investor*, 304 S.W.3d at 376.

(b) Fraud or overreaching. The party opposing the forum-selection clause may claim that the clause is invalid because it is the result of fraud or overreaching. *In re Laibe Corp.*, 307 S.W.3d at 316; *In re ADM Investor*, 304 S.W.3d at 375; *In re Lyon Fin.*, 257 S.W.3d at 231-32; *In re AutoNation*, 228 S.W.3d at 668; *see, e.g., In*

★

re International Profit Assocs., 286 S.W.3d 921, 923-24 (Tex.2009) (P claimed D did not show page of contract containing forum-selection clause to P's representative; no evidence of fraud or overreaching without some misrepresentation or fraudulent concealment of part of contract). Fraud in a forum-selection clause is shown by proving the usual elements of fraud. *See In re International Profit*, 274 S.W.3d at 678. See *O'Connor's Texas COA*, "Fraud," ch. 12, p. 279. The claim of fraud must relate to the forum-selection clause itself, not to the contract as a whole. *See In re Lyon Fin.*, 257 S.W.3d at 232. The courts analyze claims of overreaching by determining whether the forum-selection clause results in unfair surprise or oppression to the party opposing it. *In re International Profit*, 274 S.W.3d at 678; *see In re Lyon Fin.*, 257 S.W.3d at 232-33.

(c) **Against public policy.** The party opposing the forum-selection clause may claim that enforcement of the clause would contravene a strong Texas public policy. *In re Laibe Corp.*, 307 S.W.3d at 316; *In re ADM Investor*, 304 S.W.3d at 375; *In re International Profit*, 274 S.W.3d at 675; *In re Lyon Fin.*, 257 S.W.3d at 231-32. A Texas statute that simply specifies the application of Texas law, but does not require that suit be brought in Texas, does not establish a public policy that would prevent enforcement of a forum-selection clause. *E.g.*, *In re Lyon Fin.*, 257 S.W.3d at 234 (P's inability to assert usury claim in Pennsylvania did not create public-policy reason to deny enforcement of forum-selection clause); *see In re AutoNation*, 228 S.W.3d at 669.

(d) **Inconvenience.** The party opposing the forum-selection clause may claim that the selected forum would be seriously inconvenient such that enforcement of the clause would deprive the party of its day in court. *In re Laibe Corp.*, 307 S.W.3d at 316-17; *In re ADM Investor*, 304 S.W.3d at 375; *In re International Profit*, 274 S.W.3d at 675; *e.g.*, *In re Lyon Fin.*, 257 S.W.3d at 233-34 (Pennsylvania was not such an inconvenient forum that enforcing forum-selection clause would produce an "unjust result"). The party should show that special and unusual circumstances have developed that would make litigation in the selected forum extremely difficult and inconvenient. *E.g.*, *In re International Profit*, 274 S.W.3d at 680 (witnesses' residences in location other than where suit was brought was not special or unusual circumstance). Conclusory statements are insufficient to establish serious inconvenience. *In re Laibe Corp.*, 307 S.W.3d at 318; *e.g.*, *In re ADM Investor*, 304 S.W.3d at 375 (P's conclusory statements about her health problems were insufficient to establish inconvenience); *see In re Lyon Fin.*, 257 S.W.3d at 234 (party must do more than just state that change in financial or "logistical" conditions will preclude litigation in another state).

NOTE

*The Court in **In re ADM Investor** did not decide whether health problems would, in a different case, be sufficient grounds to establish inconvenience or what proof would be necessary to do so. **In re ADM Investor**, 304 S.W.3d at 376 n.1. In the concurring opinion, one justice did suggest that, at a minimum, testimony from a medical provider is necessary, and the provider should state that the patient's condition makes travel to the agreed forum not only seriously inconvenient, but also medically prohibited. Id. at 377 (Willett, J., concurring).*

---

(2) **Waiver.** The party opposing the forum-selection clause may claim that the other party waived its right to rely on the clause. *See In re AIU Ins.*, 148 S.W.3d at 121; *In re Boehme*, 256 S.W.3d 878, 884 (Tex.App.—Houston [14th Dist.] 2008, no pet.). To determine whether the forum-selection clause is waived, the court should apply the test for waiver of an arbitration clause—that is, whether a party substantially invoked the judicial process causing prejudice to the other party. *In re Boehme*, 256 S.W.3d at 884; *e.g.*, *In re ADM Investor*, 304 S.W.3d at 374 (filing answer and motion to transfer venue at same time as motion to dismiss based on forum-selection clause did not substantially invoke judicial process to P's detriment); *see In re AIU Ins.*, 148 S.W.3d at 115 (arbitration agreement is type of forum-selection clause). See "Waiver," ch. 4-C, §7.5, p. 297.

§6.2 **Effect of court's ruling.** Dismissal is the appropriate remedy after granting a motion based on a forum-selection clause that identifies another state as the proper forum. *Accelerated Christian Educ., Inc. v. Oracle Corp.*, 925 S.W.2d 66, 70 (Tex.App.—Dallas 1996, no writ); *see Stokes Interest, G.P. v. Santo-Pietro*, 343 S.W.3d

—————————————————— ✦ ——————————————————

441, 444 (Tex.App.—El Paso 2010, no pet.); *Greenwood v. Tillamook Country Smoker, Inc.*, 857 S.W.2d 654, 657 (Tex.App.—Houston [1st Dist.] 1993, no writ). The denial of a motion based on a valid, enforceable forum-selection clause that specifies another state as the chosen forum is reversible error. *In re AIU Ins.*, 148 S.W.3d 109, 118 (Tex. 2004).

§7. REVIEW

§7.1 Appealability.

1. Motion granted. A trial court's ruling granting a motion to dismiss for FNC or to enforce a forum-selection clause can be appealed. *See, e.g.*, *Quixtar Inc. v. Signature Mgmt. Team, LLC*, 315 S.W.3d 28, 31 (Tex. 2010) (common-law FNC); *Stokes Interest, G.P. v. Santo-Pietro*, 343 S.W.3d 441, 444 (Tex.App.—El Paso 2010, no pet.) (forum-selection clause); *Vinson v. American Bur. of Shipping*, 318 S.W.3d 34, 41 (Tex.App.—Houston [1st Dist.] 2010, pet. denied) (Code FNC). *But see Martinez v. Bell Helicopter Textron, Inc.*, 49 S.W.3d 890, 891 (Tex. App.—Fort Worth 2001, pet. denied) (Code FNC order that dismissed suit pending resolution in foreign country was not appealable).

2. Motion denied.

(1) Interlocutory appeal. A trial court's denial of a motion to stay or dismiss for FNC or to enforce a forum-selection clause cannot be appealed. *See* CPRC §51.014(a) (Code FNC); *In re ENSCO Offshore Int'l*, 311 S.W.3d 921, 923 (Tex.2010) (Code FNC); *In re AIU Ins.*, 148 S.W.3d 109, 115-16 (Tex.2004) (forum-selection clause).

(2) Mandamus. A defendant can challenge the denial of a motion to stay or dismiss for FNC or to enforce a forum-selection clause by filing a petition for writ of mandamus. *In re ENSCO*, 311 S.W.3d at 923 (Code FNC); *In re ADM Investor Servs.*, 304 S.W.3d 371, 374 (Tex.2010) (forum-selection clause); *In re Pirelli Tire, L.L.C.*, 247 S.W.3d 670, 676 (Tex.2007) (Code FNC).

§7.2 Standard of review.

1. FNC. A trial court's ruling on an FNC motion is reviewed for abuse of discretion. *Quixtar Inc. v. Signature Mgmt. Team, LLC*, 315 S.W.3d 28, 31 (Tex.2010); *In re ENSCO Offshore Int'l*, 311 S.W.3d 921, 923 (Tex. 2010); *In re General Elec. Co.*, 271 S.W.3d 681, 685 (Tex.2008). To determine whether the trial court abused its discretion, the appellate court must decide whether the trial court acted without reference to any guiding rules or principles—that is, whether the act was arbitrary or unreasonable. *In re Pirelli Tire, L.L.C.*, 247 S.W.3d 670, 676 (Tex.2007).

2. Forum-selection clause. A trial court's ruling on a motion to enforce a forum-selection clause is reviewed for abuse of discretion. *In re Lisa Laser USA, Inc.*, 310 S.W.3d 880, 883 (Tex.2010); *In re ADM Investor Servs.*, 304 S.W.3d 371, 374 (Tex.2010); *In re AIU Ins.*, 148 S.W.3d 109, 114-15 (Tex.2004). When reviewing a trial court's ruling on whether a claim comes within the scope of a forum-selection clause, the court of appeals will apply a de novo standard. *Stokes Interest, G.P. v. Santo-Pietro*, 343 S.W.3d 441, 444 (Tex.App.—El Paso 2010, no pet.).

§7.3 Filing suit in another jurisdiction.
After a dismissal based on an FNC order, the plaintiff can file the suit in another jurisdiction while pursuing an appeal in Texas. *See VE Corp. v. Ernst & Young*, 860 S.W.2d 83, 84 (Tex.1993).

───────────────────── ★ ─────────────────────

E. THE ANSWER—DENYING LIABILITY

§1. GENERAL

§1.1 Rules. TRCP 38, 83-85, 90-95, 97, 98.

§1.2 Purpose. With its answer, the defendant enters an appearance, denies the allegations in the plaintiff's petition, identifies its defenses, and avoids a default judgment. Once the defendant files an answer, it is entitled to notice of all proceedings in the case.

§1.3 Timetable & forms. Timetable, Pretrial Motions, p. 1216; *O'Connor's Texas Civil Forms* (2012), FORMS 3E.

§1.4 Other references. 2 McDonald & Carlson, *Texas Civil Practice* §7:17 (2d ed. 2002 & Supp.2011-12); *O'Connor's Texas Causes of Action* (2013) (*O'Connor's Texas COA*); *O'Connor's CPRC Plus* (2012-13) (*O'Connor's CPRC*).

§2. DEADLINE TO ANSWER

§2.1 Most cases. In district and county courts, the defendant must file its answer by 10:00 a.m. on the first Monday after the expiration of 20 days from the date the defendant was served with the citation. TRCP 99(b); *Solis v. Garcia*, 702 S.W.2d 668, 671 (Tex.App.—Houston [14th Dist.] 1985, no writ). An answer is timely if the defendant puts it in the custody of the U.S. Postal Service before 10:00 a.m. on the day it is due, as long as the clerk receives it no later than ten days after the due date. *Milam v. Miller*, 891 S.W.2d 1, 2 (Tex.App.—Amarillo 1994, writ ref'd). If the 20th day after service falls on a Monday, the answer is due on the next Monday. *Proctor v. Green*, 673 S.W.2d 390, 392 (Tex.App.—Houston [1st Dist.] 1984, no writ). If the first Monday after 20 days is a legal holiday, the answer is due on Tuesday. *See* TRCP 4; *Conaway v. Lopez*, 880 S.W.2d 448, 450 (Tex.App.—Austin 1994, writ ref'd); *Solis*, 702 S.W.2d at 671; *Proctor*, 673 S.W.2d at 392. In that situation, the defendant has until the end of the next day that is not a legal holiday to file the answer, not just until 10:00 a.m. *E.g.*, *Conaway*, 880 S.W.2d at 450 (default judgment granted on Tuesday afternoon was reversed).

NOTE

*Although the Supreme Court has not addressed whether a motion to transfer venue affects the deadline for filing an answer, there is some authority stating that the deadline is delayed until after the court rules on the motion. **Glover v. Moser**, 930 S.W.2d 940, 943-44 (Tex.App.— Beaumont 1996, writ denied); 2 McDonald & Carlson, Texas Civil Practice, §7:17.*

---

§2.2 Service through Secretary of State. When a defendant is served through the Secretary of State, service of process on the Secretary is constructive service on the defendant and triggers the defendant's answer date. *Bonewitz v. Bonewitz*, 726 S.W.2d 227, 230 (Tex.App.—Austin 1987, writ ref'd n.r.e.). Thus, if the Secretary is served with process on May 8 and forwards it to the defendant on May 12, and the defendant receives it on May 16, the defendant starts counting from the day the Secretary received the process—May 8 is "day 0," May 9 is "day 1," May 10 is "day 2," and so on. See "Computing time limits – days," ch. 1-C, §7.1, p. 26; "Service on Secretary of State," ch. 2-H, §5, p. 163.

§2.3 Service by publication. In district and county courts, the defendant must file its answer by 10:00 a.m. on the first Monday after the expiration of 42 days from the date the citation was issued. TRCP 114. In justice-of-the-peace courts, the defendant must file its answer on or before the first day of the first term of court that convenes after the expiration of 42 days from the date the citation was issued. *Id.* For other rules on service by publication, see "Service by publication," ch. 2-H, §4.4, p. 162.

§2.4 After bankruptcy. When a case is in bankruptcy, the automatic stay tolls the time for a bankruptcy defendant to answer. The time for a bankruptcy defendant to answer in state court resumes running 30 days after the bankruptcy court lifts the stay, dismisses the case, or closes the case. 11 U.S.C. §108(c); *see HBA E., Ltd. v. JEA Boxing Co.*, 796 S.W.2d 534, 536 (Tex.App.—Houston [1st Dist.] 1990, writ denied).

★

---

§2.5 After remand. Once a case has been remanded to state court after removal to federal court, TRCP 237a gives the defendant 15 days to file its answer, counting from the date the defendant receives notice of the federal court's remand. *See HBA E., Ltd. v. JEA Boxing Co.*, 796 S.W.2d 534, 538 (Tex.App.—Houston [1st Dist.] 1990, writ denied). TRCP 237a places the burden on the plaintiff to file a copy of the remand order with the clerk of the state court and to give the defendant written notice of the remand. *HBA*, 796 S.W.2d at 538; *see Gonzalez v. Guilbot*, 315 S.W.3d 533, 538 (Tex.2010). Actual notice of the remand is irrelevant. *HBA*, 796 S.W.2d at 537. Until the plaintiff gives the defendant notice of the remand, the defendant's deadline to answer does not begin to run. *Id.* at 538. If the defendant filed an answer in federal court during removal, that answer will suffice in state court once the case is remanded. *See* TRCP 237a.

§3. GENERAL DENIAL

Every answer should contain a general denial.

§3.1 Definition. A general denial is a statement that the defendant "generally denies all the allegations in the plaintiff's petition." By comparison, a special denial is a denial that must be specifically pleaded (i.e., when a general denial is insufficient). *See, e.g.*, TRCP 52 (denial of corporate status), TRCP 93 (verified pleas), TRCP 94 (affirmative defenses).

§3.2 Effects. The effects of filing a general denial include the following:

1. Puts plaintiff's allegations at issue. A general denial puts at issue everything in the plaintiff's petition that is not required to be denied under oath or specially denied. TRCP 92; *Shell Chem. Co. v. Lamb*, 493 S.W.2d 742, 744 (Tex.1973); *Cadle Co. v. Castle*, 913 S.W.2d 627, 631 (Tex.App.—Dallas 1995, writ denied).

2. Prevents default. A general denial prevents the plaintiff from taking a default judgment, even if the answer is defective. See "Filing constituted answer," ch. 7-A, §3.7.1, p. 590.

3. No jury questions. A general denial does not permit the defendant to submit any questions to the jury. *Luther Transfer & Storage, Inc. v. Walton*, 296 S.W.2d 750, 754 (Tex.1956); *see also* TRCP 278 (court must submit questions raised by written pleadings and evidence). If the defendant intends to submit a jury question (e.g., on an affirmative defense), the defendant must plead it in the answer. See "Affirmative Defenses," §5, p. 230.

§4. VERIFIED PLEAS

A general denial may not put all the plaintiff's allegations at issue because some matters must be specifically pleaded and verified by affidavit based on personal knowledge. *See Roark v. Stallworth Oil & Gas, Inc.*, 813 S.W.2d 492, 494 (Tex.1991). If the defendant does not verify a denial that must be verified under the rules, the plaintiff must object to the defect, or it waives the error. *See Werner v. Colwell*, 909 S.W.2d 866, 870 (Tex.1995); *Southern Cty. Mut. Ins. v. Ochoa*, 19 S.W.3d 452, 461 (Tex.App.—Corpus Christi 2000, no pet.). A pleading may usually be amended to include a verification, even during trial. *E.g.*, *Chapin & Chapin, Inc. v. Texas Sand & Gravel Co.*, 844 S.W.2d 664, 664-65 (Tex.1992) (trial court should have permitted amendment on day of trial).

PRACTICE TIP

If you need to file a verified plea under TRCP 93, you may also need to file a motion to abate on the same ground to avoid waiving the error. See "Motion to Abate—Challenging the Suit," ch. 3-I, p. 257.

---

§4.1 Verified pleas in TRCP 93. TRCP 93 contains a list of defenses, pleas, and other matters that must be verified "unless the truth of such matters appear[s] of record." *Apresa v. Montfort Ins.*, 932 S.W.2d 246, 248 n.2 (Tex.App.—El Paso 1996, no writ). Verification is thus necessary to assert certain defenses when the issue is not apparent on the face of the plaintiff's pleadings. *See Pledger v. Schoellkopf*, 762 S.W.2d 145, 146 (Tex.1988). If there is any doubt, the defendant should verify its answer. As a rule, the following pleas must be verified:

★

1. An attack on the legal capacity of either the plaintiff to sue or the defendant to be sued. TRCP 93(1); *Austin Nursing Ctr., Inc. v. Lovato*, 171 S.W.3d 845, 849 (Tex.2005); *Sixth RMA Partners v. Sibley*, 111 S.W.3d 46, 56 (Tex.2003); *Nootsie, Ltd. v. Williamson Cty. Appr. Dist.*, 925 S.W.2d 659, 662 (Tex.1996). See "Capacity," ch. 2-B, §3.2.2, p. 98; "Defects in parties," ch. 3-I, §3.1.1, p. 258.

2. An allegation that the plaintiff is not entitled to recover in the capacity in which it sues or that the defendant is not liable in the capacity in which it is sued. TRCP 93(2); *Pledger*, 762 S.W.2d at 146; *W.O.S. Constr. Co. v. Hanyard*, 684 S.W.2d 675, 676 (Tex.1985). Even though the failure to file a verified plea waives any complaint about a judgment rendered against a party in the capacity in which it was sued, the failure does not authorize a court to render a judgment against the party in any capacity in which it was not sued. *Werner v. Colwell*, 909 S.W.2d 866, 870 (Tex.1995). See "Defects in parties," ch. 3-I, §3.1.1, p. 258.

3. An allegation that another suit is pending in Texas between the same parties involving the same claim. TRCP 93(3); *Southern Cty. Mut. Ins. v. Ochoa*, 19 S.W.3d 452, 461 (Tex.App.—Corpus Christi 2000, no pet.). See "Abate – same dispute in another Texas court," ch. 3-I, §3.2, p. 259.

4. An allegation of any other defect of the parties. TRCP 93(4); *Cantu v. Holiday Inns, Inc.*, 910 S.W.2d 113, 115 (Tex.App.—Corpus Christi 1995, writ denied). Any defect of the parties not covered by some other section of TRCP 93 must be denied under oath under TRCP 93(4). *See, e.g., Allison v. National Un. Fire Ins.*, 703 S.W.2d 637, 638 (Tex.1986) (D should have filed verified denial that necessary parties were not joined); *Beacon Nat'l Ins. v. Reynolds*, 799 S.W.2d 390, 395 (Tex.App.—Fort Worth 1990, writ denied) (D should have filed verified denial that it was not the correct insurance company); *see also CHCA E. Houston, L.P. v. Henderson*, 99 S.W.3d 630, 633 (Tex. App.—Houston [14th Dist.] 2003, no pet.) (misidentification must be raised by verified pleading).

5. A denial of a partnership alleged in a pleading for any party to the suit. TRCP 93(5); *Cadle Co. v. Bankston & Lobingier*, 868 S.W.2d 918, 922-23 (Tex.App.—Fort Worth 1994), *writ denied*, 893 S.W.2d 949 (Tex.1994); *e.g., Champion v. Wright*, 740 S.W.2d 848, 851 (Tex.App.—San Antonio 1987, writ denied) (D did not file verified denial that P did not have authority to recover damages to partnership). The failure to deny partnership status is an admission of the partnership that cannot be controverted at trial. *Washburn v. Krenek*, 684 S.W.2d 187, 191 (Tex.App.—Houston [14th Dist.] 1984, writ ref'd n.r.e.).

6. A denial that a party is incorporated as alleged. TRCP 93(6); *see Panama Ref. Co. v. Crouch*, 124 S.W.2d 988, 989 (Tex.1939); *see also* TRCP 52 (alleging a corporation).

7. A denial that the defendant or a person under the defendant's authority executed a written instrument that is the subject of the suit. TRCP 93(7); *Methodist Hosps. v. Corporate Communicators, Inc.*, 806 S.W.2d 879, 882 (Tex.App.—Dallas 1991, writ denied). To deny the execution of a document alleged to have been executed by a person now deceased, a party may state that it "has reason to believe and does believe that such instrument was not executed by the decedent or by his authority." TRCP 93(7). Without a verified denial, the document is fully proved. *Id.; e.g., Boyd v. Diversified Fin. Sys.*, 1 S.W.3d 888, 891 (Tex.App.—Dallas 1999, no pet.) (documents were admissible regardless of their hearsay status because no verified denial was filed).

8. A denial of the genuineness of an indorsement or assignment of a written instrument that is the subject of the suit. TRCP 93(8). The denial may be made based on information and belief. *Id.* If no verified denial is filed, the indorsement is fully proved. *Id.; see also Overall v. Southwestern Bell Yellow Pages, Inc.*, 869 S.W.2d 629, 632 (Tex.App.—Houston [14th Dist.] 1994, no writ) (evidence contesting genuineness of contract was excluded because no verified denial was filed).

9. An allegation that a written instrument that is the subject of the suit is without consideration or that the consideration for the instrument failed in whole or in part. TRCP 93(9), 94; *Brown v. Aztec Rig Equip., Inc.*, 921 S.W.2d 835, 845 (Tex.App.—Houston [14th Dist.] 1996, writ denied); *Champion*, 740 S.W.2d at 851-52. If no verified plea is filed, the plaintiff is not required to prove consideration. See *O'Connor's Texas COA*, "Consideration defenses," ch. 5-B, §5.1.9, p. 94.

———————————————— ✦ ————————————————

10. A denial of an account, supported by an affidavit. TRCP 93(10), 185; *Panditi v. Apostle*, 180 S.W.3d 924, 927 (Tex.App.—Dallas 2006, no pet.); *Powers v. Adams*, 2 S.W.3d 496, 498 (Tex.App.—Houston [14th Dist.] 1999, no pet.); *Cooper v. Scott Irrigation Constr., Inc.*, 838 S.W.2d 743, 745 (Tex.App.—El Paso 1992, no writ). A general denial, even if it is verified, does not comply with the requirements of TRCP 93(10) and 185. *Andrews v. East Tex. Med. Ctr.-Athens*, 885 S.W.2d 264, 268 (Tex.App.—Tyler 1994, no writ). If no verified denial is filed, the plaintiff is not required to introduce additional evidence. *Northeast Wholesale Lumber, Inc. v. Leader Lumber, Inc.*, 785 S.W.2d 402, 407 (Tex.App.—Dallas 1989, no writ); *see* TRCP 185. See *O'Connor's Texas COA*, "Suit on Sworn Account," ch. 5-E, p. 121.

11. An allegation that the contract is usurious. TRCP 93(11); *Powers*, 2 S.W.3d at 498. See *O'Connor's Texas COA*, "Usury," ch. 31, p. 1011.

12. An allegation that notice and proof of the loss or claim were not given as alleged. TRCP 93(12); *see also* TRCP 54 (conditions precedent). The denial must be made with specificity. If a verified denial is not filed, notice and proof are presumed, and no evidence to the contrary may be admitted. TRCP 93(12); *Sanchez v. Jary*, 768 S.W.2d 933, 936 (Tex.App.—San Antonio 1989, no writ).

13. A denial of specific matters in an appeal from the Industrial Accident Board. TRCP 93(13). TRCP 93(13) lists the allegations that must be denied. A defendant may make a denial based on information and belief under TRCP 93(13)(a) (notice of injury) and (13)(g) (plaintiff did not have good cause for filing the claim outside the one-year deadline). TRCP 93(13) (second-to-last paragraph); *National Un. Fire Ins. v. Reyna*, 897 S.W.2d 777, 779 (Tex. 1995).

14. A denial that a party is doing business under an assumed or trade name. TRCP 93(14); *Hyson v. Chilkewitz*, 971 S.W.2d 563, 569 (Tex.App.—Dallas 1998), *rev'd on other grounds*, 22 S.W.3d 825 (Tex.1999).

15. A denial of the occurrence or performance of a condition precedent in a suit by an insured against an auto insurer. TRCP 93(15). The denial may be made based on information and belief. *Id.*

16. An allegation of any other matter required by statute to be pleaded under oath. TRCP 93(16).

§4.2 Verified pleas in other rules. Other matters that must be verified include the following: a special appearance (TRCP 120a(1)), a confession of judgment (TRCP 314), a writ of certiorari to a county court (TRCP 577), a garnishee's answer (TRCP 665), a complaint seeking an injunction (TRCP 680, 682), a request to dissolve an injunction before a final hearing (TRCP 690), a claimant's oath by a third party to reclaim personal property that has been levied (TRCP 717), and a claim of right of property (TRCP 717).

§5. AFFIRMATIVE DEFENSES

A general denial does not include affirmative defenses. If a defendant wants to rely on an affirmative defense, it must specifically plead it. TRCP 94. An affirmative defense is an independent reason why the plaintiff should not recover. *Texas Beef Cattle Co. v. Green*, 921 S.W.2d 203, 212 (Tex.1996); *Gorman v. Life Ins. Co. of N. Am.*, 811 S.W.2d 542, 546 (Tex.1991). An affirmative defense allows the defendant to avoid liability even if the allegations in the plaintiff's petition are true.

NOTE

The defendant does not waive an affirmative defense by not pleading it if the plaintiff anticipated the defense in its pleading and the defense is established at trial as a matter of law. Shoemake v. Fogel, Ltd., 826 S.W.2d 933, 937 (Tex.1992) (parental immunity); Phillips v. Phillips, 820 S.W.2d 785, 789 (Tex.1991) (illegality).

---

§5.1 Affirmative defense vs. counterclaim. Some claims (e.g., fraud) can be raised as either an affirmative defense or a counterclaim. *See Kuehnhoefer v. Welch*, 893 S.W.2d 689, 692 (Tex.App.—Texarkana 1995, writ denied); *Adams v. Tri-Continental Leasing Corp.*, 713 S.W.2d 152, 153 (Tex.App.—Dallas 1986, no writ). See "Counterclaims," §7.1, p. 235. The test to determine if a claim should be raised as an affirmative defense or a counterclaim

⎯⎯⎯⎯⎯ ★ ⎯⎯⎯⎯⎯

is whether the defendant asks for affirmative relief. If the defendant asks for affirmative relief, it is a counterclaim; if the defendant does not ask for affirmative relief, it is an affirmative defense. *See My-Tech, Inc. v. University of N. Tex. Health Sci. Ctr.*, 166 S.W.3d 880, 884 (Tex.App.—Dallas 2005, pet. denied). For example, if a defendant alleges fraud and asks for damages, fraud is a counterclaim. *Kuehnhoefer*, 893 S.W.2d at 692. If a defendant does not ask for damages, fraud is an affirmative defense.

§5.2 Affirmative defenses in TRCP 94. Many, but not all, of the affirmative defenses are listed in TRCP 94. The following are the affirmative defenses listed in that rule:

1. Accord and satisfaction. *Hunt, Hopkins & Mitchell, Inc. v. Facility Ins.*, 78 S.W.3d 564, 568 (Tex. App.—Austin 2002, pet. denied).

2. Arbitration and award. *Transwestern Pipeline Co. v. Horizon Oil & Gas Co.*, 809 S.W.2d 589, 593 (Tex.App.—Dallas 1991, writ dism'd).

3. Assumption of the risk. The Supreme Court abolished the affirmative defense of assumption of the risk in negligence actions. *Farley v. M M Cattle Co.*, 529 S.W.2d 751, 758 (Tex.1975). In products-liability cases, assumption of the risk is included under the defense of contributory negligence. *Duncan v. Cessna Aircraft Co.*, 665 S.W.2d 414, 428 (Tex.1984). Assumption of the risk retains limited viability in the following instances:

(1) When the plaintiff was injured while committing a felony or attempting suicide. CPRC §93.001(a)(1), (a)(2).

(2) When the plaintiff knowingly and expressly consented (orally or in writing) to the dangerous activity or condition. *Farley*, 529 S.W.2d at 758; *see, e.g.*, *Newman v. Tropical Visions, Inc.*, 891 S.W.2d 713, 718-19 (Tex.App.—San Antonio 1994, writ denied) (by written agreement, P assumed risk of scuba diving). For example, participants in certain sports activities are deemed to accept the risk of being injured. See *O'Connor's Texas COA*, "Competitive-sports doctrine," ch. 21-A, §5.5.1(2), p. 683.

4. Contributory negligence. See *O'Connor's Texas COA*, "Proportionate Responsibility & Contribution," ch. 51, p. 1461.

5. Discharge in bankruptcy. *Burnam v. Patterson*, 119 S.W.3d 12, 15 (Tex.App.—Amarillo 2003, pet. denied). An allegation that the defendant filed for bankruptcy is not sufficient; the defendant must plead that it was discharged in bankruptcy. *Seiffert v. Bowden*, 556 S.W.2d 406, 409 (Tex.App.—Corpus Christi 1977, no writ).

6. Duress. *Gooch v. American Sling Co.*, 902 S.W.2d 181, 186 (Tex.App.—Fort Worth 1995, no writ). See *O'Connor's Texas COA*, "Duress," ch. 5-B, §5.1.10, p. 94.

7. Estoppel. *Phillips v. Flying J Inc.*, 375 S.W.3d 367, 369 (Tex.App.—Amarillo 2012, no pet.) (judicial estoppel); *Hennessey v. Vanguard Ins.*, 895 S.W.2d 794, 798 (Tex.App.—Amarillo 1995, writ denied) (equitable estoppel); *Huddleston v. Texas Commerce Bank*, 756 S.W.2d 343, 346-47 (Tex.App.—Dallas 1988, writ denied) (estoppel by deed). See *O'Connor's Texas COA*, "Estoppel Defenses," ch. 49, p. 1433.

8. Failure of consideration. *Murphy v. Canion*, 797 S.W.2d 944, 949 (Tex.App.—Houston [14th Dist.] 1990, no writ); *see also* TRCP 93(9) (verified plea). See *O'Connor's Texas COA*, "Consideration defenses," ch. 5-B, §5.1.9, p. 94.

9. Fraud. *Texas Farmers Ins. v. Murphy*, 996 S.W.2d 873, 879-80 (Tex.1999). See *O'Connor's Texas COA*, "Fraud as affirmative defense," ch. 12-A, §6.1, p. 293.

10. Illegality. *Phillips v. Phillips*, 820 S.W.2d 785, 789 (Tex.1991). The defendant does not need to plead illegality as a defense if (1) illegality is apparent on the face of the plaintiff's pleadings because the plaintiff anticipated the defense and (2) the defense is proved as a matter of law at trial. *Id.*; *Lewkowicz v. El Paso Apparel Corp.*, 625 S.W.2d 301, 303 (Tex.1981). See *O'Connor's Texas COA*, "Illegality," ch. 5-B, §5.1.6, p. 92.

11. Injury by a fellow servant. *City of San Antonio v. Mendoza*, 532 S.W.2d 353, 360 (Tex.App.—San Antonio 1975, writ ref'd n.r.e.).

─────────────────────────────── ✦ ───────────────────────────────

12. Laches. ***Exxon Mobil Chem. Co. v. Ford***, 187 S.W.3d 154, 160 n.7 (Tex.App.—Beaumont 2006), *rev'd in part on other grounds*, 235 S.W.3d 615 (Tex.2007); ***Murray v. Murray***, 611 S.W.2d 172, 173 (Tex.App.—El Paso 1981, no writ). See *O'Connor's Texas COA*, "Laches," ch. 52, §3.2, p. 1497.

13. License. *See* ***Moore v. Sedig***, 791 S.W.2d 556, 561 (Tex.App.—Dallas 1990, no writ) (absence of license is affirmative defense).

14. Loss within an exception to general liability. *See* ***Venture Encoding Serv. v. Atlantic Mut. Ins.***, 107 S.W.3d 729, 733 (Tex.App.—Fort Worth 2003, pet. denied). When a plaintiff sues to collect on a general-hazards insurance policy that has provisions limiting general liability, the insurer-defendant must specifically allege that the loss was within a particular exception to general liability. *Id.* If the carrier pleads an exclusion under the policy, the plaintiff must then prove that the loss was not within the exclusion. ***Southern Ins. v. Progressive Cty. Mut. Ins.***, 708 S.W.2d 549, 551 (Tex.App.—Houston [1st Dist.] 1986, writ ref'd n.r.e.).

15. Payment. ***Southwestern Fire & Cas. Co. v. Larue***, 367 S.W.2d 162, 163 (Tex.1963); ***Equitable Trust Co. v. Roland***, 644 S.W.2d 46, 53 (Tex.App.—San Antonio 1982, no writ); *see also* TRCP 93(10) (verified denial), TRCP 95 (plea of payment). When a defendant claims it paid the sums sued for, it should either (1) file with its answer an account that distinctly states the details of payment or (2) describe the payment in the answer so plainly and particularly as to give the plaintiff full notice of the character of the payment. TRCP 95. If the defendant does not do either, it will not be allowed to prove the payment at trial. *See* ***Jack Parker Indus. v. FDIC***, 769 S.W.2d 700, 702 (Tex.App.—El Paso 1989, no writ).

16. Release. ***Dresser Indus. v. Page Pet., Inc.***, 853 S.W.2d 505, 508 (Tex.1993) (preinjury); ***Williams v. Glash***, 789 S.W.2d 261, 264 (Tex.1990) (postinjury). See "Release," ch. 7-I, §3.1, p. 670.

17. Res judicata. ***Texas Beef Cattle Co. v. Green***, 921 S.W.2d 203, 206-07 (Tex.1996); ***Dardari v. Texas Commerce Bank***, 961 S.W.2d 466, 470 (Tex.App.—Houston [1st Dist.] 1997, no pet.). See "Res Judicata & Collateral Estoppel," ch. 9-D, p. 780.

18. Statute of frauds. ***First Nat'l Bank v. Zimmerman***, 442 S.W.2d 674, 675-76 (Tex.1969); ***Adams v. H&H Meat Prods.***, 41 S.W.3d 762, 776 (Tex.App.—Corpus Christi 2001, no pet.). See *O'Connor's Texas COA*, "Statute of Frauds," ch. 50, p. 1447.

19. Statute of limitations. ***In re United Servs. Auto. Ass'n***, 307 S.W.3d 299, 308 (Tex.2010); ***Woods v. William M. Mercer, Inc.***, 769 S.W.2d 515, 517 (Tex.1988). See *O'Connor's CPRC*, "Statutes of Limitations Chart," p. 896; *O'Connor's Texas COA*, "Limitations," ch. 52, p. 1481.

20. Waiver. ***Tenneco Inc. v. Enterprise Prods.***, 925 S.W.2d 640, 643 (Tex.1996); *see, e.g.*, ***T.O. Stanley Boot Co. v. Bank of El Paso***, 847 S.W.2d 218, 223 (Tex.1992) (by not pleading waiver, P waived affirmative defense of waiver).

§5.3 Other affirmative defenses. Any other matter constituting an "avoidance" may be pleaded as an affirmative defense. TRCP 94. The following are some other affirmative defenses:

1. Contract-related actions.

   (1) Ambiguity. See *O'Connor's Texas COA*, "Ambiguity," ch. 5-B, §6.1.2(3), p. 105.

   (2) Justification. See *O'Connor's Texas COA*, "Justification," ch. 5-G, §5.4.2, p. 142.

   (3) Mistake. See *O'Connor's Texas COA*, "Mistake," ch. 5-B, §5.1.11, p. 96.

   (4) Penalty. See *O'Connor's Texas COA*, "Penalty," ch. 5-B, §5.1.23, p. 103.

   (5) Ratification. See *O'Connor's Texas COA*, "Ratification," ch. 5-B, §5.1.19, p. 102.

2. Criminal acts.

   (1) By plaintiff. If the plaintiff was injured while committing an offense for which she was convicted, neither she nor those with derivative claims are entitled to recover for her injuries. CPRC §§86.001-86.003; *see also*

✯

CPRC §93.001(a) (P cannot recover if injured while attempting to commit felony or suicide). See *O'Connor's Texas COA*, "Felony or suicide," ch. 21-A, §5.5.2, p. 684. The defense in CPRC chapter 86 does not apply to injuries arising from traffic offenses and certain conduct involving criminal trespass. *See* CPRC §§86.005, 86.007.

(2) By third person. As a general rule, a person has no duty to protect another from the criminal acts of a third person. *See Walker v. Harris*, 924 S.W.2d 375, 377 (Tex.1996). If the defendant is negligent but the plaintiff is injured as the result of a criminal act by a third person, the criminal conduct is a superseding cause that relieves the defendant of liability unless the criminal act was a foreseeable result of the defendant's negligence. *El Chico Corp. v. Poole*, 732 S.W.2d 306, 313-14 (Tex.1987); *Wilson v. Brister*, 982 S.W.2d 42, 44-45 (Tex.App.—Houston [1st Dist.] 1998, pet. denied).

3. DTPA. See *O'Connor's Texas COA*, "Defenses," ch. 8, §5, p. 232.

4. Disclaimer. See *O'Connor's Texas COA*, "Disclaimers of Warranty," ch. 32-A, §4, p. 1036.

5. ERISA. The claim is preempted by the Employee Retirement Income Security Act of 1974, 29 U.S.C. §1001 et seq. *Gorman v. Life Ins. Co. of N. Am.*, 811 S.W.2d 542, 546 (Tex.1991).

6. Failure to mitigate. The defendant may assert that the plaintiff did not make reasonable efforts to mitigate its damages. *E.g.*, *Gunn Infiniti, Inc. v. O'Byrne*, 996 S.W.2d 854, 856-57 (Tex.1999) (DTPA claimant's duty to mitigate); *Austin Hill Country Rlty., Inc. v. Palisades Plaza, Inc.*, 948 S.W.2d 293, 296-97 (Tex.1997) (landlord's duty to mitigate); *Gulf Consol. Int'l v. Murphy*, 658 S.W.2d 565, 566 (Tex.1983) (discharged employee's duty to mitigate). When the defendant offers evidence showing the plaintiff actually mitigated its damages, the evidence of the plaintiff's mitigation rebuts the plaintiff's evidence of damages and is admissible under a general denial. *Austin Hill*, 948 S.W.2d at 300. See *O'Connor's Texas COA*, "Mitigation of damages," ch. 5-B, §5.1.21, p. 103.

7. First Amendment. When a plaintiff's suit implicates a defendant's free exercise of rights, the defendant may assert the First Amendment as an affirmative defense. See *O'Connor's Texas COA*, "First Amendment," ch. 21-E, §5.5, p. 725.

8. Immunity.

(1) Charitable. CPRC ch. 84 provides limited immunity for the acts of volunteers, employees, and charities, including the officers of charitable organizations and health-care providers.

(2) Governmental. The defendant may be immune from liability because it is a governmental unit. *Kinnear v. Texas Comm'n on Human Rights*, 14 S.W.3d 299, 300 (Tex.2000). See *O'Connor's CPRC*, "Waivers of Governmental Immunity Chart," p. 942; *O'Connor's Texas COA*, "Suits Against the Government," ch. 24, p. 809. If the defendant is immune from suit, it should file a plea to the jurisdiction. See "Governmental immunity from suit," ch. 3-F, §3.7, p. 241.

(3) Judicial. See *O'Connor's Texas COA*, "Judicial Immunity," ch. 46-C, p. 1411.

(4) Legislative. See *O'Connor's Texas COA*, "Legislative Immunity," ch. 46-B, p. 1402.

(5) Official. The common-law defense of official immunity protects individual officials from personal liability when they perform discretionary duties in good faith within the scope of their authority. See *O'Connor's Texas COA*, "Official Immunity," ch. 46-A, p. 1389.

(6) Parental. See *O'Connor's Texas COA*, "Parental Immunity," ch. 48, p. 1429.

(7) Professional employee of school district or charter school. A professional employee of a school district or charter school is immune from liability for any discretionary act committed within the scope of her duties. Educ. Code §22.0511(a) (school district), §22.1056 (charter school); *see Downing v. Brown*, 935 S.W.2d 112, 114 (Tex.1996); *LTTS Charter Sch., Inc. v. C2 Constr., Inc.*, 358 S.W.3d 725, 734 (Tex.App.—Dallas 2011, pet. filed 6-15-12). See *O'Connor's Texas COA*, "Employee immunity," ch. 47, §2.1, p. 1426.

—————————————— ✦ ——————————————

9. **Statute of repose.** The statute of repose is an affirmative defense. *FDIC v. Lenk*, 361 S.W.3d 602, 609 (Tex.2012). See *O'Connor's Texas COA*, "Statute of repose," ch. 52, §2.7, p. 1495.

10. **Suicide.** It is an affirmative defense to a suit for personal injury or death that the plaintiff's suicide or attempted suicide was the sole cause of the injury. CPRC §93.001(a)(2); *Kassen v. Hatley*, 887 S.W.2d 4, 12 (Tex. 1994). See *O'Connor's Texas COA*, "Felony or suicide," ch. 21-A, §5.5.2, p. 684.

11. **Truth.** In defamation suits brought by private individuals, truth is an affirmative defense. See *O'Connor's Texas COA*, "Substantial truth," ch. 18-A, §5.4, p. 535.

§6. OTHER DEFENSIVE MATTERS

§6.1 Denial of conditions precedent. If the plaintiff alleges that "all conditions precedent have been performed or have occurred," the defendant must specifically deny any conditions that were not performed or have not occurred. TRCP 54; *Greathouse v. Charter Nat'l Bank*, 851 S.W.2d 173, 174 (Tex.1992); *see also* TRCP 93(12) (requires specific denial for notice and proof of loss or claim for damages). The defendant cannot simply deny that some conditions precedent have occurred. *Hill v. Thompson & Knight*, 756 S.W.2d 824, 826 (Tex.App.—Dallas 1988, no writ). By specifically denying the plaintiff's TRCP 54 allegations, the defendant forces the plaintiff to prove the conditions that were specifically denied. *Betty Leavell Rlty. Co. v. Raggio*, 669 S.W.2d 102, 104 (Tex.1984); *Phifer v. Nacogdoches Cty. Cent. Appr. Dist.*, 45 S.W.3d 159, 174 (Tex.App.—Tyler 2000, pet. denied); *Love of God Holiness Temple Ch. v. Union Std. Ins.*, 860 S.W.2d 179, 180 (Tex.App.—Texarkana 1993, writ denied). If the defendant does not identify the specific conditions the plaintiff did not comply with, it admits that all conditions precedent occurred. *See Greathouse*, 851 S.W.2d at 177. A specific denial under TRCP 54 should be verified, just like specific pleas under TRCP 93.

§6.2 Inferential rebuttals. An inferential rebuttal is a defensive theory used in negligence cases that rebuts one of the elements of the plaintiff's claim by proving certain other facts. *Dillard v. Texas Elec. Coop.*, 157 S.W.3d 429, 430 (Tex.2005); *Buls v. Fuselier*, 55 S.W.3d 204, 211 (Tex.App.—Texarkana 2001, no pet.). An inferential rebuttal is not an affirmative defense because it does not admit the truth of the plaintiff's claims, as an affirmative defense does. *See Buls*, 55 S.W.3d at 211. Inferential-rebuttal theories include act of God, unavoidable accident, and new and independent cause. For a discussion of these and other inferential rebuttals, see *O'Connor's Texas COA*, "Inferential rebuttals," ch. 21-A, §5.10, p. 686.

1. **Pleading.** It is not necessary for the defendant to plead an inferential rebuttal in its answer. The defendant may introduce evidence of an inferential rebuttal under a general denial because the evidence rebuts the plaintiff's cause of action. *Buls*, 55 S.W.3d at 211; *see Reinhart v. Young*, 906 S.W.2d 471, 475 (Tex.1995) (Hecht & Owen, JJ., concurring).

2. **Jury charge.** If the defendant introduces evidence that raises an inferential rebuttal, the inferential-rebuttal issue is submitted to the jury as an instruction, not as a question. See "Inferential-rebuttal instructions," ch. 8-I, §6.2.2(1), p. 742.

§7. DEFENDANT'S CLAIMS

A defendant may make claims under several different authorities. TRCP 97 permits parties to file counterclaims and cross-claims, TRCP 38 permits parties to bring in third parties who may be liable for all or part of the claims involved in the suit, and CPRC §33.004 permits a defendant to designate a person as a responsible third party (RTP).

PRACTICE TIP

If a defendant asserts a counterclaim or cross-claim that changes the discovery level, the defendant should probably allege a new discovery level in the first paragraph of its pleading, even though TRCP 190 does not mention defendants. See "Discovery-Control Plans," ch. 6-A, §7, p. 430.

✦

§7.1 Counterclaims. A defendant may file a claim against the plaintiff through a counterclaim. TRCP 97(a), (b). A counterclaim is an affirmative claim for relief filed against an opposing party. Generally, the term "counterclaim" denotes a defendant's claim against a plaintiff that will, in some way, defeat or reduce a judgment for the plaintiff. *Doyer v. Pitney Bowes, Inc.*, 80 S.W.3d 215, 218 (Tex.App.—Austin 2002, pet. denied).

1. Types of counterclaims. A counterclaim can be either compulsory or permissive.

(1) Compulsory. For the test for a compulsory counterclaim, see "Compulsory Joinder of Claims," ch. 2-E, §6, p. 131.

(2) Permissive. Any counterclaim that does not satisfy the compulsory-counterclaim test is a permissive counterclaim. For a test for permissive claims, see "Permissive Joinder of Claims," ch. 2-E, §7, p. 134.

2. Service of process not necessary. Service of process is not necessary when a counterclaim is filed against a party who has already made an appearance in the case; service under TRCP 21a is sufficient. TRCP 124; *In re A.L.H.C.*, 49 S.W.3d 911, 916-17 (Tex.App.—Dallas 2001, pet. denied); *see Houston Crushed Concrete, Inc. v. Concrete Recycling Corp.*, 879 S.W.2d 258, 261 (Tex.App.—Houston [14th Dist.] 1994, no writ) (counterplaintiff—the original defendant—may serve counterclaim on counterdefendant—the original plaintiff—through service of process or under TRCP 21a).

§7.2 Cross-claims. A cross-claim is an affirmative claim for relief filed against a coparty. A defendant may file a cross-claim against a codefendant if the claim arises from the same transaction or occurrence as the original action or any counterclaim. TRCP 97(e). The cross-defendant must assert its compulsory claims against the cross-claimant, or its claims will be barred. *See Getty Oil Co. v. Insurance Co. of N. Am.*, 845 S.W.2d 794, 800 (Tex.1992). In such a case, the parties are no longer merely coparties but are opposing parties, and the compulsory-counterclaim rule applies. For example, if A sues B and C, and B files a cross-claim against C, C must file its compulsory counterclaims against A and B, or the claims will be barred in a later suit. Service of process is not necessary when a cross-claim is filed against a party who has already made an appearance in the case; service under TRCP 21a is sufficient. TRCP 124; *Mays v. Perkins*, 927 S.W.2d 222, 227 (Tex.App.—Houston [1st Dist.] 1996, no writ); *see Von Briesen, Purtell & Roper v. French*, 78 S.W.3d 570, 575 (Tex.App.—Amarillo 2002, pet. dism'd). If the party has not made an appearance, service of process is necessary.

§7.3 Third-party petitions. A third-party petition is the procedure used by a defendant to bring into the suit a third party who is or may be liable to the defendant or the plaintiff for all or part of the plaintiff's claim. TRCP 38(a); *Omega Contracting, Inc. v. Torres*, 191 S.W.3d 828, 837 (Tex.App.—Fort Worth 2006, no pet.); *Goose Creek Consol. ISD v. Jarrar's Plumbing, Inc.*, 74 S.W.3d 486, 492 (Tex.App.—Texarkana 2002, pet. denied). See *O'Connor's Texas Forms*, FORM 3E:12. The third-party petition is limited to contribution and indemnification claims, making it more restrictive than the "same transaction or occurrence" test used for counterclaims and cross-claims.

1. Leave of court. The defendant may file a third-party action without leave of court within 30 days after filing its answer; after 30 days, leave of court is required. TRCP 38(a); *Bilek & Purcell Indus. v. Paderwerk Gebr. Benteler GmbH*, 694 S.W.2d 225, 227 (Tex.App.—Houston [1st Dist.] 1985, no writ).

2. Service of citation. The defendant, as a third-party plaintiff, must serve the third-party defendant with citation and petition. TRCP 38(a).

§7.4 RTP. A defendant can designate a person who bears some responsibility for the plaintiff's injuries as an RTP in the suit. *See* CPRC §§33.004(a), 33.011(6).

1. Identifying an RTP.

(1) Who is an RTP. An RTP is any person who is alleged to have caused or contributed to the harm for which recovery of damages is sought, whether by (1) a negligent act or omission, (2) any defective or unreasonably dangerous product, or (3) other conduct or activity that violates an applicable legal standard. CPRC §33.011(6); *see also* Gov't Code §311.005(2) ("person" includes corporation, organization, or other legal entity). The following persons can be designated as an RTP:

★

    (a) A person who is immune from liability to the plaintiff. *In re Unitec Elevator Servs.*, 178 S.W.3d 53, 58 n.5 (Tex.App.—Houston [1st Dist.] 2005, orig. proceeding).

    (b) A person who is not subject to the court's jurisdiction. *Id.*

    (c) An unknown person. *See* CPRC §33.004(j). See "RTP – unknown criminal," §7.4.2(1), this page.

(2) Who is not an RTP. A seller eligible for indemnity in a products-liability action under CPRC §82.002 cannot be designated as an RTP. CPRC §33.011(6).

  2. Designating an RTP. The defendant may designate a person as an RTP by filing a motion for leave to designate that person as an RTP. CPRC §33.004(a). See "Motion for leave to designate," §7.4.2(2), this page. If the RTP is an unknown criminal, the defendant must first file an amended answer before seeking leave to designate. See "RTP – unknown criminal," §7.4.2(1), this page. A defendant that has entered into a settlement agreement with the plaintiff can still seek to designate a person as an RTP as long as the plaintiff has not filed a nonsuit against the defendant. *Flack v. Hanke*, 334 S.W.3d 251, 258 (Tex.App.—San Antonio 2010, pet. denied).

NOTE

*The filing or granting of a motion for leave to designate a person as an RTP or the finding of fault against a person does not by itself impose liability on the RTP in the current suit or in any other proceeding. CPRC §33.004(i). The designation simply allows the jury to consider the third party's percentage of responsibility. Id. §33.003(a). By designating an RTP who shares the blame for the injury, the defendant can reduce its own percentage of responsibility. If the RTP is joined by the plaintiff, the RTP becomes a defendant and can be liable to the plaintiff. See **Flack**, 334 S.W.3d at 256. See "Plaintiff's joinder," §7.4.2(6), p. 238.*

---

  (1) RTP – unknown criminal. If the RTP is an unknown person alleged to have committed a criminal act, the defendant must file an amended answer before filing a motion for leave to designate the person as an RTP. *See* CPRC §33.004(j). The amended answer must be filed no later than 60 days after the defendant filed its original answer. *Id.*; *In re Unitec Elevator*, 178 S.W.3d at 61. In the amended answer, the defendant must do the following:

    (a) Allege that an unknown person committed a criminal act that caused the loss or injury that is the subject of the suit. CPRC §33.004(j).

    (b) Plead facts sufficient to show a reasonable probability that the person's act was criminal. *Id.* §33.004(j)(1).

    (c) Plead all identifying characteristics of the person that are known at the time the amended answer is filed. *Id.* §33.004(j)(2).

    (d) Plead facts about the person's responsibility sufficient to satisfy the pleading requirements of the TRCPs. CPRC §33.004(j)(3).

    (e) Refer to the person as "Jane Doe" or "John Doe" until the person's identity is known. *Id.* §33.004(k).

  (2) Motion for leave to designate. The defendant may file a motion for leave to designate a person as an RTP. CPRC §33.004(a). See *O'Connor's Texas Forms*, FORM 3E:14.

  (a) Deadline to file.

    [1] Case filed before 9-1-11. The defendant must file a motion for leave to designate an RTP at least 60 days before the trial date. CPRC §33.004(a). If the trial date is reset, the deadline to file the motion remains 60 days before the original trial date unless the court or the parties agree to extend it. *See American*

———————————— ★ ————————————

Title Co. v. Bomac Mortg. Holdings, L.P., 196 S.W.3d 903, 908-09 (Tex.App.—Dallas 2006, pet. granted, judgm't vacated w.r.m.). On a finding of good cause, the court may allow the motion for leave to designate an RTP to be filed at a later date. CPRC §33.004(a).

[2] **Case filed on or after 9-1-11.** The deadline for filing a motion for leave to designate an RTP may depend on whether the statute of limitations for the underlying cause of action against the RTP has expired.

[a] **Limitations has expired.** If the limitations period against the RTP has expired when the motion for leave to designate is to be filed, the defendant cannot file the motion if the defendant knew but did not timely disclose that the person might be designated as an RTP (e.g., during discovery). CPRC §33.004(d). If the defendant timely disclosed her intent to designate the RTP, the deadline for filing the motion is the same as if the case were filed before September 1, 2011. *See id.* §33.004(a), (d).

[b] **Limitations has not expired.** If the limitations period against the RTP has not expired when the motion for leave to designate is to be filed, the deadline for filing the motion is the same as if the case were filed before September 1, 2011. *See* CPRC §33.004(a), (d).

(b) **Grounds.** The defendant must plead sufficient facts about the RTP's alleged responsibility to satisfy the pleading requirements of the TRCPs. *See* CPRC §33.004(g)(1).

(c) **Amended answer – unknown criminal.** If the RTP is an unknown criminal, the defendant should attach a copy of the amended answer to the motion. *See* CPRC §33.004(j).

(3) **Objection.** Any party can file an objection to the motion for leave to designate an RTP. *See* CPRC §33.004(f); *Flack*, 334 S.W.3d at 262. See *O'Connor's Texas Forms*, FORM 3E:15.

(a) **Deadline.** A party must file the objection within 15 days after the motion is served. CPRC §33.004(f).

(b) **Grounds.** To defeat the motion for leave to designate, the objecting party must assert certain grounds in the following objections:

[1] **Initial objection.** The objecting party must establish that the defendant did not plead sufficient facts about the RTP's alleged responsibility to satisfy the pleading requirements of the TRCPs. CPRC §33.004(g)(1).

[2] **Second objection.** If the trial court sustains the initial objection, it must give the defendant an opportunity to replead. *See* CPRC §33.004(g)(2); *In re Oncor Elec. Delivery Co.*, 355 S.W.3d 304, 306 (Tex.App.—Dallas 2011, orig. proceeding). See "Insufficient facts pleaded," §7.4.2(4)(b)[1], p. 238. After the defendant has had an opportunity to replead, the objecting party must establish that the defendant still did not satisfy the pleading requirements of the TRCPs. *See* CPRC §33.004(g)(2).

(4) **Ruling on motion.**

(a) **Grant.** If the court grants the motion for leave to designate, the person named in the motion is designated as an RTP without any further action by the court or any party. CPRC §33.004(h). The court must grant the motion for either of the following reasons:

[1] **No objection.** The court must grant the motion for leave to designate if a party does not object to it. CPRC §33.004(f); *e.g.*, *In re Brokers Logistics, Ltd.*, 320 S.W.3d 402, 406 (Tex.App.—El Paso 2010, orig. proceeding) (court granted motion because P filed objection after 15-day deadline); *see also Valverde v. Biela's Glass & Aluminum Prods.*, 293 S.W.3d 751, 755 (Tex.App.—San Antonio 2009, pet. denied) (even if no objection is filed, designation is not effective until court grants motion).

[2] **Sufficient facts pleaded.** The court must grant the motion for leave to designate if the defendant pleaded sufficient facts about the RTP's alleged responsibility to satisfy the pleading requirements of the TRCPs. *See* CPRC §33.004(g).

─────────────────────────────── ✦ ───────────────────────────────

(b) Deny. The court must deny the motion for either of the following reasons:

[1] Insufficient facts pleaded. The court must deny the motion for leave to designate if the objecting party establishes that the defendant did not plead sufficient facts about the RTP's alleged responsibility to satisfy the pleading requirements of the TRCPs. *See* CPRC §33.004(g). Before the court can deny the motion for leave to designate, it must give the defendant an opportunity to replead after an initial objection is filed. *See* CPRC §33.004(g)(2); *In re Oncor Elec.*, 355 S.W.3d at 306. If the defendant still has not satisfied the pleading requirements of the TRCPs after having had an opportunity to replead, only then can the court deny the motion. *See* CPRC §33.004(g)(2); *In re Oncor Elec.*, 355 S.W.3d at 306. See "Grounds," §7.4.2(3)(b), p. 237.

[2] Motion or amended answer not timely. The court must deny the motion for leave to designate if the motion or amended answer was not timely filed. See "RTP – unknown criminal," §7.4.2(1), p. 236; "Deadline to file," §7.4.2(2)(a), p. 236.

(5) Motion to strike designation. After an adequate time for discovery, a party may move to strike the designation of an RTP if there is no evidence the designated person was responsible for any part of the plaintiff's injury or damages. CPRC §33.004(*l*). See *O'Connor's Texas Forms*, FORM 3E:17. The court must grant the motion to strike unless the defendant presents sufficient evidence to raise a fact issue about the designated person's responsibility for the plaintiff's injury or damages. CPRC §33.004(*l*).

(6) Plaintiff's joinder. Generally, a plaintiff may join a person as a defendant if that person has been designated as an RTP. See *O'Connor's Texas Forms*, FORM 3E:16. The plaintiff must file an amended petition adding the RTP as a defendant. See "Motion to Amend Pleadings—Pretrial," ch. 5-F, p. 350.

───

NOTE

Even if the plaintiff does not join the RTP as a defendant, a jury charge on the responsibility for the injury among the plaintiff, the defendant, the designated RTP, and any settling person will be submitted to the jury. See CPRC §33.003(a). A question about the conduct of any person cannot be submitted to the jury without sufficient evidence to support the submission. Id. §33.003(b). The defendant is liable for the percentage of responsibility attributed to it by the trier of fact, as well as for the amounts it is jointly and severally liable for. Id. §33.013(a), (b). See O'Connor's Texas COA, "Determining What Each Defendant Owes," ch. 51, §6, p. 1475.

───

(a) Deadline for case filed before 9-1-11.

[1] Limitations has expired. Generally, if the limitations period for the underlying cause of action against the RTP has expired, the plaintiff may join the RTP as a defendant no later than 60 days after the person is designated as an RTP. CPRC §33.004(e) (repealed 2011); *see, e.g., Flack*, 334 S.W.3d at 258 (P and D entered into settlement agreement requiring D to designate certain RTPs; even though limitations period had expired for P's claims against RTPs, P could join them as Ds under CPRC §33.004(e)). In certain circumstances, however, a plaintiff cannot join an RTP after the limitations period has expired. *See, e.g., Molinet v. Kimbrell*, 356 S.W.3d 407, 409 (Tex.2011) (P cannot join RTP in medical-malpractice claim after limitations has expired).

[2] Limitations has not expired. If the limitations period for the underlying cause of action against the RTP has not expired, the plaintiff may join the RTP as a defendant anytime before the deadline for joinder set by the trial court. *See* TRCP 40(a), 41. See "Pleading deadlines," ch. 5-A, §3.4, p. 316.

(b) Deadline for case filed on or after 9-1-11.

[1] Limitations has expired. If the limitations period for the underlying cause of action against the RTP has expired, the plaintiff cannot join the RTP as a defendant. *See* Acts 2011, 82nd Leg., R.S., ch. 203, §5.02, eff. Sept. 1, 2011 (repeal of CPRC §33.004(e), which allowed for joinder after limitations expired).

[2] Limitations has not expired. If the limitations period for the underlying cause of action against the RTP has not expired, the plaintiff may join the RTP as a defendant anytime before the deadline for joinder set by the trial court. *See* TRCP 40(a), 41. See "Pleading deadlines," ch. 5-A, §3.4, p. 316.

★

(c) **Effect of joinder.** When the RTP is joined, it becomes a party to the suit and is no longer an RTP, even if the claim against the designating defendant is later dismissed. *See Flack*, 334 S.W.3d at 262.

§8. REQUEST FOR DISCLOSURE

The defendant should consider including a request for disclosure in its original answer. The only statement necessary for a request for disclosure is the following: "Pursuant to Rule 194, you are requested to disclose, within 30 days of the service of this request, the information or material described in Rule [*identify rule, e.g., 194.2; 194.2(a), (c), and (f); 194.2(d)-(g)*]." TRCP 194.1. See "Requests for Disclosure," ch. 6-E, p. 515. If the defendant includes the request in the answer, the defendant must change the title of the instrument to "Defendant's Original Answer and Request for Disclosure."

§9. DRAFTING THE ANSWER

For a series of considerations that will help the defendant construct its original answer, see "Constructing the Original Answer," ch. 3-A, §4, p. 185.

F. PLEA TO THE JURISDICTION—CHALLENGING THE COURT

§1. GENERAL

§1.1 Rule. TRCP 85. See CPRC §16.064.

§1.2 Purpose. The purpose of a plea to the jurisdiction is to dismiss a cause of action without regard to whether the claim has merit. *Mission Consol. ISD v. Garcia*, 372 S.W.3d 629, 635 (Tex.2012); *Bland ISD v. Blue*, 34 S.W.3d 547, 554 (Tex.2000). The plea challenges the court's power to adjudicate the subject matter of the controversy. *Heckman v. Williamson Cty.*, 369 S.W.3d 137, 149 (Tex.2012); *Texas DOT v. Arzate*, 159 S.W.3d 188, 190 (Tex.App.—El Paso 2004, no pet.); *Axtell v. University of Tex.*, 69 S.W.3d 261, 263 (Tex.App.—Austin 2002, no pet.). Subject-matter jurisdiction is essential to the authority of a court to decide a case. *Bland ISD*, 34 S.W.3d at 553-54; *Texas Ass'n of Bus. v. Texas Air Control Bd.*, 852 S.W.2d 440, 443 (Tex.1993). Whether a court has subject-matter jurisdiction is a question of law. *Hearts Bluff Game Ranch, Inc. v. State*, ___ S.W.3d ___ (Tex.2012) (No. 10-0491; 8-31-12); *City of Dallas v. Carbajal*, 324 S.W.3d 537, 538 (Tex.2010); *Texas Dept. of Parks & Wildlife v. Miranda*, 133 S.W.3d 217, 226 (Tex.2004). Without subject-matter jurisdiction, a court cannot render a valid judgment. *Dubai Pet. Co. v. Kazi*, 12 S.W.3d 71, 74-75 (Tex.2000). Subject-matter jurisdiction cannot be given or taken away by consent and cannot be waived. *Carroll v. Carroll*, 304 S.W.3d 366, 367 (Tex.2010); *see University of Houston v. Barth*, 313 S.W.3d 817, 818 (Tex.2010); *Continental Coffee Prods. v. Cazarez*, 937 S.W.2d 444, 449 n.2 (Tex.1996). Lack of subject-matter jurisdiction makes a judgment void, not just voidable. *In re United Servs. Auto. Ass'n*, 307 S.W.3d 299, 309 (Tex.2010); *Mapco, Inc. v. Forrest*, 795 S.W.2d 700, 703 (Tex.1990).

NOTE

If the jurisdictional defect is a pleading defect that can be cured by amendment, it should be challenged by special exceptions. See "Curable defects in jurisdiction," ch. 3-G, §2.2.4, p. 249.

---

§1.3 Timetable & forms. Timetable, Pretrial Motions, p. 1216; *O'Connor's Texas Civil Forms* (2012), FORMS 3F; *O'Connor's Texas Causes of Action Pleadings* (2012) (*O'Connor's COA Pleadings*).

§1.4 Other references. Simmons & Patton, *Plea to the Jurisdiction: Defining the Undefined*, 40 St. Mary's L.J. 627 (2009); *O'Connor's Texas Causes of Action* (2013) (*O'Connor's Texas COA*); *O'Connor's Texas Civil Appeals* (2012) (*O'Connor's Texas Appeals*).

§2. PLEA TO THE JURISDICTION

§2.1 Form. A plea to the jurisdiction may be included in the general answer or filed as a separate motion. TRCP 85. If filed as a motion, it should be captioned as a motion to dismiss for lack of jurisdiction. See *O'Connor's Texas Forms*, FORM 3F:1.

———————————— ✦ ————————————

§2.2 Evidence. The trial court may consider evidence in ruling on a plea to the jurisdiction and must consider evidence when necessary to resolve the jurisdictional issues raised. *Bland ISD v. Blue*, 34 S.W.3d 547, 555 (Tex. 2000). Thus, when necessary, a defendant should attach affidavits, discovery, or other evidence to the plea.

1. Not necessary. Evidence is not necessary to resolve a plea to the jurisdiction when the plaintiff's petition (1) affirmatively demonstrates the court's jurisdiction, (2) affirmatively negates the court's jurisdiction, or (3) is insufficient to determine jurisdiction but does not affirmatively demonstrate incurable defects (and thus may be amended). *Texas Dept. of Parks & Wildlife v. Miranda*, 133 S.W.3d 217, 226-27 (Tex.2004).

2. Necessary. The trial court must consider evidence on a plea to the jurisdiction when evidence is necessary to determine jurisdictional facts. *Heckman v. Williamson Cty.*, 369 S.W.3d 137, 150 (Tex.2012); *Miranda*, 133 S.W.3d at 227; *Bland ISD*, 34 S.W.3d at 555. See "Evidence to determine jurisdictional facts," §5.1, p. 244. The trial court can allow the parties a reasonable opportunity for targeted discovery and time to gather evidence and prepare for a hearing. *Mission Consol. ISD v. Garcia*, 372 S.W.3d 629, 642-43 (Tex.2012); *see Miranda*, 133 S.W.3d at 229; *see, e.g., Hearts Bluff Game Ranch, Inc. v. State*, ___ S.W.3d ___ (Tex.2012) (No. 10-0491; 8-31-12) (court allowed limited discovery through which P served requests for production and obtained documents, but P did not take depositions and did not answer D's discovery requests until ordered by court; P's opportunity for discovery was sufficient); *Diocese of Galveston-Houston v. Stone*, 892 S.W.2d 169, 176-77 (Tex.App.—Houston [14th Dist.] 1994, orig. proceeding) (in suit against church by employee, discovery permitted to determine whether church could assert ecclesiastical privilege). See "Hearing," §5, p. 244.

§2.3 No verification. No rule or statute requires that the plea to the jurisdiction be verified. *Ab-Tex Bev. Co. v. Angelo State Univ.*, 96 S.W.3d 683, 688 (Tex.App.—Austin 2003, no pet.); *see Pakdimounivong v. City of Arlington*, 219 S.W.3d 401, 413-14 (Tex.App.—Fort Worth 2006, pet. denied) (because pleas to the jurisdiction are not listed in TRCP 93, they do not need to be verified). See "Verified pleas in TRCP 93," ch. 3-E, §4.1, p. 228. If jurisdictional evidence is necessary, affidavits and other sworn proof should be attached to the plea.

§2.4 No deadline. There is no deadline for the plea to the jurisdiction. Lack of subject-matter jurisdiction is fundamental error and can be raised at any time. *Sivley v. Sivley*, 972 S.W.2d 850, 855 (Tex.App.—Tyler 1998, no pet.). The challenge can be raised for the first time on appeal. *Waco ISD v. Gibson*, 22 S.W.3d 849, 851 (Tex.2000); *Tullos v. Eaton Corp.*, 695 S.W.2d 568, 568 (Tex.1985); *see Rusk State Hosp. v. Black*, ___ S.W.3d ___ (Tex.2012) (No. 10-0548; 8-31-12) (defense of governmental immunity implicates subject-matter jurisdiction and can be raised for first time on appeal). A court can inquire into its jurisdiction on its own initiative without a motion at any time. *See Texas Workers' Comp. Comm'n v. Garcia*, 893 S.W.2d 504, 517 n.15 (Tex.1995).

§3. GROUNDS

§3.1 No justiciable issue. A plea to the jurisdiction is proper to challenge the lack of a justiciable issue. To present a justiciable issue, a lawsuit must involve a real controversy that will be resolved by the judicial relief sought. *E.g., State Bar v. Gomez*, 891 S.W.2d 243, 245-46 (Tex.1994) (district court did not have authority to compel State Bar or Supreme Court to implement mandatory pro bono); *see, e.g., In re Nolo Press*, 991 S.W.2d 768, 778 (Tex.1999) (district court did not have authority to modify Supreme Court order).

§3.2 No standing. A plea to the jurisdiction is proper to challenge a party's lack of standing. *See M.D. Anderson Cancer Ctr. v. Novak*, 52 S.W.3d 704, 710-11 (Tex.2001); *Waco ISD v. Gibson*, 22 S.W.3d 849, 850 (Tex.2000). Standing focuses on who is the correct party to bring the suit. *Patterson v. Planned Parenthood*, 971 S.W.2d 439, 442 (Tex.1998). See "Standing," ch. 2-B, §3.2.1, p. 96.

§3.3 Not ripe. A plea to the jurisdiction is proper to challenge the lack of "ripeness." *See Waco ISD v. Gibson*, 22 S.W.3d 849, 851-52 (Tex.2000). Ripeness focuses on when an action may be brought. *Patterson v. Planned Parenthood*, 971 S.W.2d 439, 442 (Tex.1998); *American Nat'l Ins. v. Cannon*, 86 S.W.3d 801, 806 (Tex.App.—Beaumont 2002, no pet.); *Texas Dept. of Banking v. Mount Olivet Cemetery Ass'n*, 27 S.W.3d 276, 282 (Tex. App.—Austin 2000, pet. denied). See *O'Connor's Texas COA*, "Ripeness," ch. 52, §3.4, p. 1498.

⭐

§3.4 Mootness.

1. Generally. A plea to the jurisdiction is generally proper to challenge a case that has become moot. *See Heckman v. Williamson Cty.*, 369 S.W.3d 137, 162 (Tex.2012) (when case is moot, court normally dismisses for lack of jurisdiction); *Hansen v. JP Morgan Chase Bank*, 346 S.W.3d 769, 773 (Tex.App.—Dallas 2011, no pet.) (mootness implicates subject-matter jurisdiction); *Pantera Energy Co. v. Railroad Comm'n of Tex.*, 150 S.W.3d 466, 471 (Tex.App.—Austin 2004, no pet.) (same). A case becomes moot if (1) a party seeks a judgment based on a controversy that no longer exists (i.e., the controversy is not "live") or (2) the parties have no legally cognizable interest in the outcome. *Heckman*, 369 S.W.3d at 162; *Allstate Ins. v. Hallman*, 159 S.W.3d 640, 642 (Tex.2005); *Hansen*, 346 S.W.3d at 772; *Pantera Energy*, 150 S.W.3d at 471; *see also Speer v. Presbyterian Children's Home & Serv. Agency*, 847 S.W.2d 227, 229 (Tex.1993) (courts have no jurisdiction to issue advisory opinions). A dismissal for mootness is not a ruling on the merits. *Speer*, 847 S.W.2d at 229.

2. Exceptions. A court may have jurisdiction to decide the merits of a case, even if it is moot, based on certain exceptions. *See Heckman*, 369 S.W.3d at 163-64; *FDIC v. Nueces Cty.*, 886 S.W.2d 766, 767 (Tex.1994); *General Land Office v. OXY U.S.A., Inc.*, 789 S.W.2d 569, 571 (Tex.1990). For the specific exceptions, see *O'Connor's Texas Appeals*, "Exceptions," ch. 3-E, §3.1.4(1)(b), p. 100.

§3.5 Another court has exclusive jurisdiction.

A plea to the jurisdiction is proper to challenge a suit brought in one court when another court has continuing, exclusive jurisdiction. *Jansen v. Fitzpatrick*, 14 S.W.3d 426, 430-31 (Tex.App.—Houston [14th Dist.] 2000, no pet.); *see also Speer v. Stover*, 685 S.W.2d 22, 23 (Tex.1985) (district court did not have jurisdiction over case pending in probate court); *Howe State Bank v. Crookham*, 873 S.W.2d 745, 747-48 (Tex.App.—Dallas 1994, no writ) (same); *cf. Geary v. Peavy*, 878 S.W.2d 602, 604-05 (Tex.1994) (Minnesota court had exclusive jurisdiction over child-custody case). By comparison, when two courts have concurrent jurisdiction, the issue of dominant jurisdiction should be challenged by a plea in abatement. *E.g.*, *In re Puig*, 351 S.W.3d 301, 305 (Tex.2011) (county court at law exercising probate jurisdiction had concurrent jurisdiction with district court; plea to jurisdiction was improper method for contesting dominant jurisdiction). See "Abate – same dispute in another Texas court," ch. 3-I, §3.2, p. 259.

NOTE

For the rules governing the plaintiff's selection of a court, see "Choosing the Court—Jurisdiction," ch. 2-F, p. 135.

---

§3.6 Administrative agency has exclusive jurisdiction.

A plea to the jurisdiction is proper to allege that an administrative agency has exclusive jurisdiction over the dispute. *See Subaru, Inc. v. David McDavid Nissan, Inc.*, 84 S.W.3d 212, 221 (Tex.2002). When an agency's jurisdiction is exclusive, a party must exhaust all administrative remedies before seeking judicial review of a decision; until the party exhausts those remedies, a court lacks subject-matter jurisdiction, and dismissal is mandatory. *Thomas v. Long*, 207 S.W.3d 334, 340 (Tex.2006); *In re Entergy Corp.*, 142 S.W.3d 316, 321-22 (Tex.2004); *Subaru*, 84 S.W.3d at 221. But when an agency's jurisdiction is primary, abatement is appropriate. See "Abate – administrative agency has primary jurisdiction," ch. 3-I, §3.4, p. 260.

§3.7 Governmental immunity from suit.

A plea to the jurisdiction is proper to challenge a suit filed against a governmental unit when the governmental unit is immune from suit. *State v. Lueck*, 290 S.W.3d 876, 880 (Tex. 2009); *Harris Cty. v. Sykes*, 136 S.W.3d 635, 639 (Tex.2004); *see Rusk State Hosp. v. Black*, ___ S.W.3d ___ (Tex. 2012) (No. 10-0548; 8-31-12); *see, e.g., Federal Sign v. Texas S. Univ.*, 951 S.W.2d 401, 404 (Tex.1997) (without State's consent, TSU was immune from suit). When filing suit for damages against the government, the plaintiff must affirmatively demonstrate the court's jurisdiction to hear the lawsuit under the Texas Tort Claims Act or another statute that waives the government's immunity from suit. *TDCJ v. Miller*, 51 S.W.3d 583, 587 (Tex.2001); *see University of*

———————————— ✦ ————————————

Tex. v. Hayes, 327 S.W.3d 113, 115 (Tex.2010). For the elements of a suit against a governmental unit, see *O'Connor's Texas COA*, chs. 24-26; for the allegations to include in the petition, see *O'Connor's COA Pleadings*, FORMS 24-26. If the government has immunity from suit but the plaintiff can cure the defect (e.g., obtain legislative consent to sue), the case should be abated until the defect is remedied. *See Texas A&M Univ. Sys. v. Koseoglu*, 233 S.W.3d 835, 839-40 (Tex.2007); *Federal Sign*, 951 S.W.2d at 403-04.

§3.8 Statutory jurisdictional requirements.

1. Suits generally. A plea to the jurisdiction is proper to challenge a statutory claim when the plaintiff did not comply with a statutory jurisdictional requirement. When a plaintiff does not comply with a jurisdictional requirement, it deprives the court of subject-matter jurisdiction. *See City of DeSoto v. White*, 288 S.W.3d 389, 393 (Tex. 2009). Not all statutory requirements for filing suit are jurisdictional. *See id.*; *Dubai Pet. Co. v. Kazi*, 12 S.W.3d 71, 76-77 (Tex.2000). When a statutory requirement is not jurisdictional, failure to comply with it is a defensive matter that should be raised in a different pleading. *See, e.g.*, Tex. Bus. & Com. Code §17.505(c) (when statutory notice not received, D may file plea in abatement).

(1) Unambiguous. If a statute identifies a requirement as jurisdictional, the failure to comply with the requirement should be challenged by a plea to the jurisdiction. *See, e.g.*, *Sierra Club v. Texas Nat. Res. Conserv. Comm'n*, 26 S.W.3d 684, 688 (Tex.App.—Austin 2000) (requirements in §2001.174 of Administrative Procedure Act are jurisdictional because they restrict the kind of case a court may decide and the kind of relief a court may grant), *aff'd*, 70 S.W.3d 809 (Tex.2002). When a statute unambiguously identifies a requirement as jurisdictional, the statute's plain language controls unless that interpretation would lead to absurd results. *See TDPRS v. Mega Child Care, Inc.*, 145 S.W.3d 170, 177 (Tex.2004).

(2) Ambiguous. If a statute does not clearly identify a requirement as jurisdictional, the presumption is that it is not jurisdictional. *City of DeSoto*, 288 S.W.3d at 394; *see In re United Servs. Auto. Ass'n*, 307 S.W.3d 299, 307 (Tex.2010). This presumption can be overcome only by clear legislative intent to the contrary. *In re United Servs. Auto. Ass'n*, 307 S.W.3d at 307; *City of DeSoto*, 288 S.W.3d at 394. To determine legislative intent, the court begins with an analysis of the statute's text. *City of DeSoto*, 288 S.W.3d at 395. The court may also consider one or more of the following: (1) the object sought to be obtained, (2) the statute's legislative history, (3) the presence or absence of specific consequences for noncompliance with the statute, and (4) the consequences of each possible interpretation of the statute. *See* Gov't Code §311.023; *City of DeSoto*, 288 S.W.3d at 396.

(a) Intended as jurisdictional. If the courts determine the Legislature intended the statutory requirement to be jurisdictional, failure to comply with the requirement should be challenged by a plea to the jurisdiction. *See, e.g.*, *Subaru, Inc. v. David McDavid Nissan, Inc.*, 84 S.W.3d 212, 220-21 (Tex.2002) (failure to exhaust administrative remedies before filing suit is jurisdictional if administrative body has exclusive jurisdiction over dispute).

(b) Intended as defensive. If the courts determine the Legislature intended the statutory requirement to be defensive and not jurisdictional, failure to comply with the requirement cannot be challenged by a plea to the jurisdiction. *See, e.g.*, *City of DeSoto*, 288 S.W.3d at 398 (notice provision in Fire Fighter & Police Officer Civil Service Act is not jurisdictional); *Hubenak v. San Jacinto Gas Transmission Co.*, 141 S.W.3d 172, 182-83 (Tex. 2004) ("unable-to-agree" requirement in Prop. Code §20.012 is not jurisdictional); *Subaru*, 84 S.W.3d at 221 (failure to exhaust administrative remedies before filing suit is not jurisdictional if administrative body has only primary jurisdiction over dispute); *Dubai Pet.*, 12 S.W.3d at 76-77 (in wrongful-death case, statute's "equal-treaty-rights" provision is not jurisdictional).

2. Suits against governmental entity. In a suit against a governmental entity, a plea to the jurisdiction is proper to challenge certain statutory claims.

—————————— ✯ ——————————

NOTE

Although a governmental entity's jurisdictional challenge can be asserted in a plea to the juris-diction, another procedural vehicle, such as a motion for summary judgment, would also be proper. State v. Lueck, 290 S.W.3d 876, 884 (Tex.2009); see TDCJ v. Simons, 140 S.W.3d 338, 349 (Tex.2004) (interlocutory appeal under Gov't Code §51.014(a)(8) can be taken from re-fusal to dismiss for want of jurisdiction whether jurisdictional argument is made in plea to ju-risdiction or some other instrument).

(1) Statutory prerequisites. In a suit against a governmental entity, a plea to the jurisdiction is proper to challenge a statutory claim when the plaintiff did not comply with a statutory prerequisite to filing suit. *See* Gov't Code §311.034; *Prairie View A&M Univ. v. Chatha*, ___ S.W.3d ___ (Tex.2012) (No. 10-0353; 8-31-12). To be a statutory prerequisite, the prerequisite must (1) appear in the statutory language, (2) be mandatory, and (3) be accomplished before suit is filed. *Prairie View A&M*, ___ S.W.3d at ___. In all suits against a governmental entity, a statutory prerequisite—whether administrative (e.g., filing a charge of discrimination) or procedural (e.g., timely filing suit)—is a jurisdictional requirement. *See* Gov't Code §311.034; *see, e.g., Prairie View A&M*, ___ S.W.3d at ___ (administrative filing requirement for employment-discrimination claim under Texas Commission on Human Rights Act is statutory prerequisite to suit under Gov't Code §311.034 and is jurisdictional).

(2) Statutory elements of a cause of action. In a suit against a governmental entity, a plea to the jurisdiction is proper to challenge a statutory claim when the statutory elements of a cause of action are juris-dictional and the plaintiff did not comply with those elements. *See, e.g., Mission Consol. ISD v. Garcia*, 372 S.W.3d 629, 637 (Tex.2012) (plea to jurisdiction was proper to challenge whether P pleaded prima facie elements for age-discrimination claim under Texas Commission on Human Rights Act); *Lueck*, 290 S.W.3d at 883-84 (elements un-der Gov't Code §554.002(a) that whistleblower-P must be public employee and must state good-faith report of viola-tion of Whistleblower Act were jurisdictional; plea to jurisdiction was proper). In such cases, the statutory elements can be considered to determine both jurisdiction and liability. *Lueck*, 290 S.W.3d at 883; *see Mission Consol.*, 372 S.W.3d at 636-37.

§3.9 Federal preemption. A plea to the jurisdiction is proper to challenge a suit preempted by a federal law requiring that the claim be tried in a federal court. *See Southland Life Ins. v. Estate of Small*, 806 S.W.2d 800, 801 (Tex.1991) (ERISA). But if federal law does not require that the claim be tried in federal court, preemption is merely an affirmative defense and does not deprive a state court of jurisdiction. *Mills v. Warner Lambert Co.*, 157 S.W.3d 424, 427 (Tex.2005).

§3.10 Death. A plea to the jurisdiction is proper to challenge the continuation of a suit when the cause is ex-tinguished by a party's death. A suit for a claim such as divorce or usury should be dismissed if either party dies be-fore the trial court renders judgment on the merits. *E.g., Whatley v. Bacon*, 649 S.W.2d 297, 299 (Tex.1983) (di-vorce); *Turner v. Ward*, 910 S.W.2d 500, 503 (Tex.App.—El Paso 1994, no writ) (divorce); *Orr v. International Bank of Commerce*, 649 S.W.2d 769, 772 (Tex.App.—San Antonio 1983, no writ) (usury). If the claim survives the party's death, dismissal is not appropriate, and the suit should proceed to judgment. *See* TRCP 150. For example, a suit for wrongful acquisition of property by fraud survives the death of either party. *Pace v. McEwen*, 574 S.W.2d 792, 800 (Tex.App.—El Paso 1978, writ ref'd n.r.e.). Once a judgment is rendered, the death of one of the parties does not ex-tinguish the claim. *See* TRAP 7.1(a)(1) (when party dies after trial court renders judgment, case may be appealed). See "Rendition," ch. 9-C, §3.1, p. 765.

§3.11 Fabricated jurisdiction. A plea to the jurisdiction is proper to challenge fraudulent allegations of an amount in controversy. *See Texas Dept. of Parks & Wildlife v. Miranda*, 133 S.W.3d 217, 224 & n.4 (Tex.2004); *see, e.g., Delk v. City of Dallas*, 560 S.W.2d 519, 520 (Tex.App.—Texarkana 1977, no writ) (in suit to foreclose lien, D argued that P made fraudulent allegation of property value). The defendant must plead and prove that the allega-tions of the amount in controversy in the plaintiff's pleadings are false and were made fraudulently for the purpose of conferring jurisdiction. *Delk*, 560 S.W.2d at 520.

★

§3.12   Religious matters. A plea to the jurisdiction is proper when the dispute clearly involves ecclesiastical matters over which the courts have no jurisdiction. *See Westbrook v. Penley*, 231 S.W.3d 389, 394-95 (Tex.2007); *Hawkins v. Friendship Missionary Baptist Ch.*, 69 S.W.3d 756, 758-59 (Tex.App.—Houston [14th Dist.] 2002, no pet.); *Green v. United Pentecostal Ch. Int'l*, 899 S.W.2d 28, 30 (Tex.App.—Austin 1995, writ denied); *see also Williams v. Gleason*, 26 S.W.3d 54, 55-56 (Tex.App.—Houston [14th Dist.] 2000, pet. denied) (resolved issue by motion for summary judgment). Secular courts cannot constitutionally determine the truth or falsity of religious matters. *Tilton v. Marshall*, 925 S.W.2d 672, 678-79 (Tex.1996); *see also Serbian E. Orthodox Diocese v. Milivojevich*, 426 U.S. 696, 723 (1976) (religious controversies are not proper subject of civil-court inquiry).

§3.13   Estate as defendant. A plea to the jurisdiction is proper when the plaintiff names an estate as the defendant without any reference to the personal representative. *See Henson v. Estate of Crow*, 734 S.W.2d 648, 649 (Tex.1987); *Miller v. Estate of Self*, 113 S.W.3d 554, 556 (Tex.App.—Texarkana 2003, no pet.); *Estate of C.M. v. S.G.*, 937 S.W.2d 8, 10 (Tex.App.—Houston [14th Dist.] 1996, no writ). *But see Estate of Crawford v. Town of Flower Mound*, 933 S.W.2d 727, 731 (Tex.App.—Fort Worth 1996, writ denied) (claim that estate lacks legal capacity to be sued must be raised in verified pleading). See "Estate," ch. 2-B, §3.3.2, p. 99.

§4. RESPONSE

If the plea to the jurisdiction is not valid, the plaintiff should file a response and contest the factual allegations in the plea. See *O'Connor's Texas Forms*, FORM 3F:2. The response should follow the format of the plea. For example, if the plea includes evidence and is verified, the response should also include evidence and be verified. If the defendant's plea to the jurisdiction is valid and the plaintiff filed suit in the wrong court, the plaintiff should admit the validity of the plea and do whatever is necessary to get the lawsuit into a proper court that has jurisdiction. If the limitations period has run, the plaintiff must be careful to avoid losing the tolling benefits of CPRC §16.064. See "Dismissal & limitations," §6.2, p. 246.

§5. HEARING

The trial court can rule on a plea to the jurisdiction by submission or after a hearing. *See F/R Cattle Co. v. State*, 866 S.W.2d 200, 201-02 (Tex.1993).

§5.1   Evidence to determine jurisdictional facts. The trial court must consider evidence on a plea to the jurisdiction when evidence is necessary to determine jurisdictional facts. *Heckman v. Williamson Cty.*, 369 S.W.3d 137, 150 (Tex.2012); *Texas Dept. of Parks & Wildlife v. Miranda*, 133 S.W.3d 217, 227 (Tex.2004); *Bland ISD v. Blue*, 34 S.W.3d 547, 555 (Tex.2000). For a discussion of situations when evidence is not necessary to resolve a plea to the jurisdiction, see "Not necessary," §2.2.1, p. 240.

1.   Jurisdiction unrelated to merits. In most pleas to the jurisdiction, the court should limit the evidence to only what is relevant to the jurisdictional issue and avoid considering evidence that goes to the merits of the case. *Bland ISD*, 34 S.W.3d at 555; *Harris Cty. v. Progressive Nat'l Bank*, 93 S.W.3d 381, 384 (Tex.App.—Houston [14th Dist.] 2002, pet. denied); *see Miranda*, 133 S.W.3d at 223.

2.   Jurisdiction related to merits. In some cases, jurisdiction involves the merits of the case. For example, to prove jurisdiction against the State under the Recreational Use Statute, the plaintiff must prove the State was grossly negligent. See *O'Connor's Texas COA*, "Injury While Engaged in Recreation," ch. 26-F, p. 945. When jurisdiction involves the merits of the case, the trial court must review the evidence to determine whether there is a fact issue. *Miranda*, 133 S.W.3d at 227; *see Mission Consol. ISD v. Garcia*, 372 S.W.3d 629, 635 (Tex.2012); *City of Elsa v. Gonzalez*, 325 S.W.3d 622, 625 (Tex.2010). This standard mirrors summary-judgment procedure under TRCP 166a(c). *Mission Consol.*, 372 S.W.3d at 635; *Miranda*, 133 S.W.3d at 228. That is, the defendant must first present evidence to show that the court lacks subject-matter jurisdiction; if the defendant does so, the plaintiff must then show there is a disputed material fact on the jurisdictional issue. *Mission Consol.*, 372 S.W.3d at 635; *Miranda*, 133

———————————————————— ✦ ————————————————————

S.W.3d at 228. If the facts are disputed, the court cannot grant the plea to the jurisdiction, and the issue must be resolved by the fact-finder at trial; however, if the evidence is undisputed or if there is no fact question on the jurisdictional issue, the trial court will rule on the plea to the jurisdiction as a matter of law. *Mission Consol.*, 372 S.W.3d at 635; *University of Tex. v. Hayes*, 327 S.W.3d 113, 116 (Tex.2010); *Miranda*, 133 S.W.3d at 227-28. See "Ruling," §6, this page.

§5.2 Form of evidence received. When a trial court holds an evidentiary hearing, it may receive evidence in the form of oral testimony, discovery, and exhibits. *See, e.g.*, *TDCJ v. Miller*, 51 S.W.3d 583, 586 (Tex.2001) (in TTCA suit, court considered deposition testimony); *Bland ISD v. Blue*, 34 S.W.3d 547, 550 (Tex.2000) (trial court conducted evidentiary hearing and received oral testimony); *State v. Sledge*, 36 S.W.3d 152, 155 (Tex.App.—Houston [1st Dist.] 2000, pet. denied) (trial court conducted hearing and received oral testimony, affidavits, exhibits, and stipulations).

§6. RULING

§6.1 Order. If a claim is not within a court's jurisdiction and the impediment to jurisdiction cannot be removed, the claim must be dismissed; in contrast, if the impediment to jurisdiction can be removed, the court should abate the proceedings to allow the plaintiff a reasonable opportunity to cure the jurisdictional problem. *American Motorists Ins. v. Fodge*, 63 S.W.3d 801, 805 (Tex.2001); *see Thomas v. Long*, 207 S.W.3d 334, 338 (Tex.2006). A petition containing multiple claims should not be dismissed just because the court lacks jurisdiction over one of the claims. *See Thomas*, 207 S.W.3d at 338-39. The court may dismiss or abate the claims over which it does not have subject-matter jurisdiction and retain the claims over which it does have jurisdiction. *Id.*

1. Opportunity to amend. If the jurisdictional defect can be cured by an amendment, the court must allow the plaintiff to amend. *Westbrook v. Penley*, 231 S.W.3d 389, 395 (Tex.2007); *Texas Dept. of Parks & Wildlife v. Miranda*, 133 S.W.3d 217, 226-27 (Tex.2004); *County of Cameron v. Brown*, 80 S.W.3d 549, 555 (Tex.2002); *Peek v. Equipment Serv.*, 779 S.W.2d 802, 805 (Tex.1989). A plaintiff is not entitled to amend if its petition affirmatively negates jurisdiction. *Miranda*, 133 S.W.3d at 227; *County of Cameron*, 80 S.W.3d at 555.

2. Dismissal. If the pleadings affirmatively negate jurisdiction, the suit should be dismissed. *Rusk State Hosp. v. Black*, ___ S.W.3d ___ (Tex.2012) (No. 10-0548; 8-31-12); *see Heckman v. Williamson Cty.*, 369 S.W.3d 137, 150 (Tex.2012); *Miranda*, 133 S.W.3d at 227. If the pleadings do not affirmatively negate jurisdiction, the court can dismiss only if the defendant has shown that the plaintiff—despite having had the opportunity to amend the petition—still cannot establish jurisdiction. *Rusk State Hosp.*, ___ S.W.3d at ___; *see TDCJ–Cmty. Justice Assistance Div. v. Campos*, ___ S.W.3d ___ (Tex.2012) (No. 11-0728; 10-26-12); *Miranda*, 133 S.W.3d at 226-27.

(1) Without prejudice – most pleas. Generally, if the court does not have jurisdiction over the subject matter of the suit, it must dismiss the suit for lack of jurisdiction without rendering a judgment on the merits. *Black v. Jackson*, 82 S.W.3d 44, 56 (Tex.App.—Tyler 2002, no pet.); *see Jansen v. Fitzpatrick*, 14 S.W.3d 426, 431 (Tex.App.—Houston [14th Dist.] 2000, no pet.). The dismissal must be without prejudice because a dismissal with prejudice is a final decision on the merits. *See Black v. Jackson*, 82 S.W.3d 44, 56 (Tex.App.—Tyler 2002, no pet.); *Jansen v. Fitzpatrick*, 14 S.W.3d 426, 431 (Tex.App.—Houston [14th Dist.] 2000, no pet.).

(2) With prejudice – governmental immunity. If a plaintiff in a suit against a governmental entity has been given a reasonable opportunity to amend and the plaintiff's amended pleading still does not allege facts that would constitute a waiver of immunity, the trial court should dismiss the plaintiff's action with prejudice. *Harris Cty. v. Sykes*, 136 S.W.3d 635, 639 (Tex.2004); *City of Carrollton v. Harlan*, 180 S.W.3d 894, 898 (Tex.App.—Dallas 2005, pet. denied); *see also Texas A&M Univ. Sys. v. Koseoglu*, 233 S.W.3d 835, 839-40 (Tex.2007) (P is not required to amend its pleading until after court rules on plea to the jurisdiction). The dismissal is with prejudice because a plaintiff should not be permitted to relitigate jurisdiction once a court has determined there is no waiver of governmental immunity. *See Harris Cty.*, 136 S.W.3d at 639; *City of Carrollton*, 180 S.W.3d at 898.

3. No transfer. If the court lacks subject-matter jurisdiction, it does not have the power to transfer the case to the appropriate court. *State v. Benavides*, 772 S.W.2d 271, 273 (Tex.App.—Corpus Christi 1989, writ denied). After the case is dismissed, the plaintiff may refile it in the proper court.

—————————————— ✯ ——————————————

§6.2 Dismissal & limitations.

1. Refiling suit & tolling limitations. If the statute of limitations expired after the suit was filed in the first court and before the case was dismissed, the plaintiff may refile the suit in the proper court within 60 days after the dismissal of the first suit becomes final. CPRC §16.064(a). CPRC §16.064(a) tolls the statute of limitations for the period between the date the plaintiff filed the suit in the first court and the date the plaintiff refiles the suit in the correct court. To defeat the plaintiff's use of CPRC §16.064(a), a defendant must show that either (1) the first suit was not dismissed for want of jurisdiction or (2) the causes of action are not the same for purposes of the tolling provision. *Turner v. Texas Dept. of MHMR*, 920 S.W.2d 415, 418 (Tex.App.—Austin 1996, writ denied); *see, e.g.*, *Malmgren v. Inverness Forest Residents Civic Club, Inc.*, 981 S.W.2d 875, 879 (Tex.App.—Houston [1st Dist.] 1998, no pet.) (because P voluntarily dismissed suit, CPRC §16.064 did not apply).

2. No tolling – intentional disregard. If the plaintiff filed the suit in the first court with intentional disregard for proper jurisdiction, CPRC §16.064(a) does not toll limitations. CPRC §16.064(b); *e.g.*, *In re United Servs. Auto. Ass'n*, 307 S.W.3d 299, 313 (Tex.2010) (even though P anticipated verdict within jurisdictional limits, he strategically decided to seek damages outside the county court at law's jurisdiction; limitations not tolled). The intent standard under §16.064(b) is similar to the *Craddock* requirement for setting aside a default judgment; a mistake of law may be a sufficient excuse. *In re United Servs. Auto. Ass'n*, 307 S.W.3d at 313. See "Not intentional, but accidental," ch. 10-B, §9.1.3(1), p. 796. Once the defendant moves for relief under §16.064(b), the plaintiff has the burden of showing she did not intentionally disregard proper jurisdiction when filing the case. *In re United Servs. Auto. Ass'n*, 307 S.W.3d at 312.

§6.3 Findings.
Findings of fact are not necessary when the trial court rules on a motion to dismiss based on the face of the pleadings. *Awde v. Dabeit*, 938 S.W.2d 31, 32 (Tex.1997). But findings of fact are helpful on appeal when the trial court considers evidence (e.g., in a plea based on fabricated jurisdiction). See "Jurisdictional challenge," ch. 10-E, §2.2.2(2), p. 818.

§7. REVIEW

§7.1 Record.
A reporter's record is not necessary to appeal the trial court's ruling on subject-matter jurisdiction unless the trial court held an evidentiary hearing.

§7.2 Standard of review.
The appellate court's standard of review for a trial court's ruling on a plea to the jurisdiction is de novo. *Houston Mun. Empls. Pension Sys. v. Ferrell*, 248 S.W.3d 151, 156 (Tex.2007); *State v. Holland*, 221 S.W.3d 639, 642 (Tex.2007); *Texas Dept. of Parks & Wildlife v. Miranda*, 133 S.W.3d 217, 228 (Tex.2004); *Mayhew v. Town of Sunnyvale*, 964 S.W.2d 922, 928 (Tex.1998).

1. Jurisdictional facts. In the appeal of a case dismissed for want of jurisdiction based on facts that were primarily jurisdictional, the appellate court reviews both the plaintiff's petition and the evidence introduced at trial. *Bland ISD v. Blue*, 34 S.W.3d 547, 554-55 (Tex.2000).

2. Jurisdictional allegations. In the appeal of a case dismissed for want of jurisdiction based on the plaintiff's petition, the appellate court must accept as true all the factual allegations in the plaintiff's petition. *Axtell v. University of Tex.*, 69 S.W.3d 261, 264 (Tex.App.—Austin 2002, no pet.); *Jansen v. Fitzpatrick*, 14 S.W.3d 426, 431 (Tex.App.—Houston [14th Dist.] 2000, no pet.). The court examines the pleader's intent and construes the pleadings in the plaintiff's favor. *County of Cameron v. Brown*, 80 S.W.3d 549, 555 (Tex.2002); *Texas Ass'n of Bus. v. Texas Air Control Bd.*, 852 S.W.2d 440, 446 (Tex.1993).

§7.3 Interlocutory appeal.

1. Appeal.

(1) Plea to the jurisdiction by governmental unit. A party may appeal an interlocutory order granting or denying a plea to the jurisdiction filed by a governmental unit. CPRC §51.014(a)(8); *City of Houston v. Estate of Jones*, ___ S.W.3d ___ (Tex.2012) (No. 10-0755; 12-21-12). See *O'Connor's Texas Appeals*, "Government's plea to the jurisdiction," ch. 1-B, §2.3.1(7), p. 14.

──────────────── ✦ ────────────────

(2) Plea to the jurisdiction by other party.

(a) Generally prohibited. Generally, no order on a plea to the jurisdiction filed by a party other than a governmental unit may be appealed before final judgment. *See* CPRC §51.014(a)(8).

(b) Exception.

[1] Before 9-1-11. For an action commenced before September 1, 2011, a trial court can allow an interlocutory appeal from an order that is not otherwise appealable only if the parties agree to the order granting an interlocutory appeal and the following conditions are met: (1) the order to be appealed involves a controlling question of law about which there is a substantial ground for difference of opinion and (2) an immediate appeal from the order may materially advance the ultimate termination of the litigation. See *O'Connor's Texas Appeals*, "Interlocutory appeal by agreement – before 9-1-11," ch. 3-P, §2.2, p. 152.

[2] On or after 9-1-11. For an action commenced on or after September 1, 2011, a trial court, on its own initiative or on a party's motion, can allow an appeal from an order that is not otherwise appealable if the following conditions are met: (1) the order to be appealed involves a controlling question of law about which there is a substantial ground for difference of opinion and (2) an immediate appeal from the order may materially advance the ultimate termination of the litigation. CPRC §51.014(d); TRCP 168. Permission must be stated in the order being appealed rather than in a separate order. TRCP 168 & cmt. Although the trial court can grant permission to appeal, the court of appeals has discretion to accept or refuse to hear the appeal. *See* CPRC §51.014(f). See *O'Connor's Texas Appeals*, "Interlocutory appeal by permission – on or after 9-1-11," ch. 3-P, §2.1, p. 149.

2. Stay of trial & other proceedings.

(1) For governmental unit. The interlocutory appeal of an order granting a plea to the jurisdiction by a governmental unit automatically stays the commencement of trial during the appeal. *See* CPRC §51.014(b). An interlocutory appeal under CPRC §51.014(a)(8) also stays all other proceedings in the trial court pending resolution of the appeal. *Id.* §51.014(b). The interlocutory appeal of an order denying a plea to the jurisdiction by a governmental unit does not automatically stay the commencement of trial during the appeal. *Id.* §51.014(c). For a discussion of when the defendant may be entitled to a stay after the denial of a plea to the jurisdiction by a governmental unit, see *O'Connor's Texas Appeals*, "Orders resulting in automatic stay after motion denied & deadlines met," ch. 3-P, §3.1.2, p. 154.

(2) Under CPRC §51.014(d).

(a) Before 9-1-11. For an action commenced before September 1, 2011, the interlocutory appeal of an order under CPRC §51.014(d) stays proceedings in the trial court only if (1) the parties agree to a stay and (2) the trial court, the court of appeals, or a judge of the court of appeals orders a stay. See *O'Connor's Texas Appeals*, "Interlocutory appeal by agreement – before 9-1-11," ch. 3-P, §3.2.2, p. 155.

(b) On or after 9-1-11. For an action commenced on or after September 1, 2011, the interlocutory appeal of an order under CPRC §51.014(d) stays proceedings in the trial court if (1) the parties agree to a stay or (2) the trial or appellate court orders a stay pending the appeal. CPRC §51.014(e). See *O'Connor's Texas Appeals*, "Interlocutory appeal by permission – on or after 9-1-11," ch. 3-P, §3.2.1, p. 155.

§7.4 Mandamus.

1. Mandamus not available. In most cases, a party cannot challenge the trial court's lack of subject-matter jurisdiction by mandamus. *Bell Helicopter Textron, Inc. v. Walker*, 787 S.W.2d 954, 955 (Tex.1990); *In re Liberty Mut. Ins.*, 24 S.W.3d 637, 639 (Tex.App.—Texarkana 2000, orig. proceeding); *Brown v. Herman*, 852 S.W.2d 91, 92 (Tex.App.—Austin 1993, orig. proceeding). Typically, remedy by appeal is adequate.

2. Mandamus available.

(1) Child custody. A party is entitled to challenge the trial court's ruling on a plea to the jurisdiction by mandamus when two trial courts issue conflicting child-custody orders. *Geary v. Peavy*, 878 S.W.2d 602, 603-05 (Tex.1994).

✦

(2) Constitutional challenges to suit. If a constitutional issue is not resolved by the trial court, mandamus may be available to resolve the issue before a trial on the merits. *See, e.g.*, *Tilton v. Marshall*, 925 S.W.2d 672, 676 & n.4 (Tex.1996) (D challenged trial court's refusal to dismiss and refusal to bar discovery on grounds of free exercise of religion).

(3) Agency has exclusive jurisdiction. A party is entitled to challenge the trial court's denial of a plea to the jurisdiction if an agency has exclusive jurisdiction over the suit. *In re Southwestern Bell Tel. Co.*, 235 S.W.3d 619, 623-24 (Tex.2007); *In re Entergy Corp.*, 142 S.W.3d 316, 321 (Tex.2004).

(4) Court lacks authority. If the court erroneously concludes that it has subject-matter jurisdiction, its order is void and the party may challenge the order by mandamus. *Miller v. Woods*, 872 S.W.2d 343, 346 (Tex.App.—Beaumont 1994, orig. proceeding); *Qwest Microwave, Inc. v. Bedard*, 756 S.W.2d 426, 434 (Tex. App.—Dallas 1988, orig. proceeding). *Contra Herman*, 852 S.W.2d at 93.

G. SPECIAL EXCEPTIONS—CHALLENGING THE PLEADINGS

§1. GENERAL

§1.1 Rules. TRCP 90, 91.

§1.2 Purpose. The purpose of special exceptions is to inform the opposing party of defects in its pleadings so it can cure them, if possible, by amendment. *Horizon/CMS Healthcare Corp. v. Auld*, 34 S.W.3d 887, 897 (Tex. 2000). By filing special exceptions, the opposing party identifies defects that should be remedied before a substantive response is required. *O'Neal v. Sherck Equip. Co.*, 751 S.W.2d 559, 562 (Tex.App.—Texarkana 1988, no writ). Unless a party challenges pleading defects by special exceptions, the defects are waived. See "Waiver," §6, p. 251.

NOTE

Special exceptions may be filed by either party. See "Grounds," §5, p. 250; O'Connor's Texas Forms, FORM 3G:1. Because most special exceptions are filed by the defendant, this subchapter uses "defendant" as the objecting party and "plaintiff" as the party with the challenged pleading.

---

§1.3 Timetable & forms. Timetable, Pretrial Motions, p. 1216; *O'Connor's Texas Civil Forms* (2012), FORMS 3G.

§1.4 Other references. *O'Connor's Texas Causes of Action* (2013) (*O'Connor's Texas COA*).

§2. TYPES OF PLEADINGS TO CHALLENGE BY SPECIAL EXCEPTIONS

There are two types of pleading defects that a defendant must object to before trial: defects in form and defects in substance. *Aquila Sw. Pipeline, Inc. v. Harmony Expl., Inc.*, 48 S.W.3d 225, 233 (Tex.App.—San Antonio 2001, pet. denied).

§2.1 Defects in form.

1. Lack of verification. If the plaintiff did not verify its petition when necessary, the defendant may file special exceptions to require the plaintiff to correct the defect. *Huddleston v. Western Nat'l Bank*, 577 S.W.2d 778, 781 (Tex.App.—Amarillo 1979, writ ref'd n.r.e.).

2. Failure to plead discovery level. If the plaintiff did not plead the discovery level in its original petition as required by TRCP 190.1, the defendant may file special exceptions to require the plaintiff to do so. *See* TRCP 190 cmt. 1.

§2.2 Defects in substance.

1. General allegations. If the plaintiff pleaded a cause of action in general terms, the defendant may file special exceptions to require the plaintiff to plead specifically. *Subia v. Texas Dept. of Human Servs.*, 750 S.W.2d

─────────────────── ★ ───────────────────

827, 829 (Tex.App.—El Paso 1988, no writ). Texas follows the "fair notice" standard for pleading, which looks at whether the opposing party can ascertain from the pleading the nature and basic issues of the controversy and what testimony will be relevant. *Horizon/CMS Healthcare Corp. v. Auld*, 34 S.W.3d 887, 896 (Tex.2000); *see also* TRCP 45(b) (action must be stated in plain and concise language), TRCP 47(a) (action must be sufficient to give fair notice of claim). TRCP 45 does not require the plaintiff to describe the evidence in detail in its petition. *Paramount Pipe & Sup. Co. v. Muhr*, 749 S.W.2d 491, 494-95 (Tex.1988). If the plaintiff's petition does not give fair notice of the facts, the trial court can either require the plaintiff to amend its petition or require the defendant to obtain additional facts through discovery.

    2. Inadequate allegations. If the plaintiff did not plead all the elements of its cause of action, the defendant may file special exceptions to require the plaintiff to plead specifically. *See Mowbray v. Avery*, 76 S.W.3d 663, 677 (Tex.App.—Corpus Christi 2002, pet. denied). The defendant must specifically identify the missing elements. *See Spencer v. City of Seagoville*, 700 S.W.2d 953, 957 (Tex.App.—Dallas 1985, no writ). The plaintiff's omission of an element of the cause of action does not deprive the court of jurisdiction; it is merely a defect in pleading subject to special exceptions and amendment. *E.g.*, *Peek v. Equipment Serv.*, 779 S.W.2d 802, 805 (Tex.1989) (P did not allege amount of damages). For the elements of various causes of action, see *O'Connor's Texas COA*.

    3. No viable cause of action. If the plaintiff's suit is not permitted by law, the defendant may file special exceptions and a motion to dismiss. *Wayne Duddlesten, Inc. v. Highland Ins.*, 110 S.W.3d 85, 96-97 (Tex. App.—Houston [1st Dist.] 2003, pet. denied); *see, e.g.*, *Trevino v. Ortega*, 969 S.W.2d 950, 951 (Tex.1998) (no cause of action for spoliation of evidence); *Friesenhahn v. Ryan*, 960 S.W.2d 656, 658 (Tex.1998) (no cause of action for social-host liability); *Krishnan v. Sepulveda*, 916 S.W.2d 478, 479 (Tex.1995) (no cause of action for negligence to fetus, but mother may have had action for mental anguish). Another option is to file special exceptions and a motion for summary judgment. See "Move for summary judgment," §9.4.1(3), p. 254.

    4. Curable defects in jurisdiction. If a jurisdictional defect is a pleading defect that can be cured by amendment, it should be challenged by special exceptions, not by a plea to the jurisdiction or a motion for summary judgment. *Texas Dept. of Corr. v. Herring*, 513 S.W.2d 6, 9-10 (Tex.1974); *see Texas DOT v. Beckner*, 74 S.W.3d 98, 104 (Tex.App.—Waco 2002, no pet.); *Washington v. Fort Bend ISD*, 892 S.W.2d 156, 159 (Tex.App.—Houston [14th Dist.] 1994, writ denied). For example, when a plaintiff's allegation of unliquidated damages is above or below the trial court's limits of jurisdiction, it may be amended. *Smith Detective Agency & Nightwatch Serv. v. Stanley Smith Sec., Inc.*, 938 S.W.2d 743, 747 (Tex.App.—Dallas 1996, writ denied).

    5. Unliquidated damages. If the plaintiff pleaded for unliquidated damages as required by TRCP 47(b) (i.e., "the damages sought are within the jurisdictional limits of the court"), the defendant may specially except and require the plaintiff to state the maximum amount of its damages. Pleading for damages that are "at least" a certain amount is the same as pleading for unliquidated damages, and unless the defendant specially excepts, the plaintiff can recover more than its "at least" pleadings. *See, e.g.*, *City of Wichita Falls v. Dye*, 517 S.W.2d 680, 682 (Tex. App.—Fort Worth 1974, writ ref'd n.r.e.) (P did not specially except to Ds' cross-action that sought relief for sum of "at least $900.00"; trial court's award of $1,007.50 was proper).

─────────────────────────────

⑬   ***PROPOSED TRCP CHANGES***

In response to Gov't Code §22.004(h), the Supreme Court has proposed TRCP 169 to establish a process for the prompt, efficient, and cost-effective resolution of civil actions (expedited actions) in which only monetary relief is sought and the amount in controversy is no more than $100,000. See Tex.Sup.Ct. Order, Misc. Docket No. 12-9191 (eff. Mar. 1, 2013). The Supreme Court has proposed corresponding amendments to TRCP 47 that would require a party, in an original pleading, to make a more specific statement of the relief sought; that is, the party would have to plead into or out of the expedited-actions process under TRCP 169. See Tex.Sup.Ct. Order, Misc.

★

Docket No. 12-9191 (eff. Mar. 1, 2013). The public-comment period for the proposed amendments ends on February 1, 2013, and the rules are to take effect March 1, 2013. For the proposed version of the rules, see the appendix after this book's index. For the final version, go to the Supreme Court website at www.supreme.courts.state.tx.us. When the new and amended rules take effect, a supplement to this book—with updated rules and commentaries that reflect the changes—will be available at www.JonesMcClure.com/TRCPamendments.

---

§3. FORM

§3.1 Written. Special exceptions must be in writing. TRCP 90. An oral objection to pleadings does not comply with the TRCPs. *Nassar v. Hughes*, 882 S.W.2d 36, 38 (Tex.App.—Houston [1st Dist.] 1994, writ denied); *Hawkins v. Anderson*, 672 S.W.2d 293, 295 (Tex.App.—Dallas 1984, no writ).

§3.2 Specific. When drafting special exceptions, the defendant must identify the particular part of the plaintiff's pleading it challenges and point out the particular defect, omission, obscurity, duplicity, generality, or other insufficiency. TRCP 91; *Muecke v. Hallstead*, 25 S.W.3d 221, 224 (Tex.App.—San Antonio 2000, no pet.); *Gutierrez v. Karl Perry Enters.*, 874 S.W.2d 103, 105 (Tex.App.—El Paso 1994, no writ). The defendant should identify the defective paragraph by number, state why it is defective, and explain how it can be corrected. General allegations that the petition is vague, is indefinite, or does not state a cause of action are not sufficient to identify the defect. *Spillman v. Simkins*, 757 S.W.2d 166, 168 (Tex.App.—San Antonio 1988, writ dism'd); *Farrar v. Farrar*, 620 S.W.2d 801, 802 (Tex.App.—Houston [14th Dist.] 1981, no writ). If the special exception is not specific, it is a prohibited general demurrer and should be overruled. *See* TRCP 90; *Fuentes v. McFadden*, 825 S.W.2d 772, 778 (Tex.App.—El Paso 1992, no writ); *Spillman*, 757 S.W.2d at 168.

§3.3 Limited to pleadings. When drafting special exceptions, the defendant cannot challenge pleading defects by relying on facts outside the plaintiff's petition. *O'Neal v. Sherck Equip. Co.*, 751 S.W.2d 559, 562 (Tex.App.—Texarkana 1988, no writ) (referred to as a "speaking demurrer"); *Augustine v. Nusom*, 671 S.W.2d 112, 114 (Tex.App.—Houston [14th Dist.] 1984, writ ref'd n.r.e.) (same). If a defendant must rely on facts that are not in the petition to demonstrate the defect, the defendant should file some other type of pleading (e.g., a motion to abate or a motion for summary judgment). *Bader v. Cox*, 701 S.W.2d 677, 686-87 (Tex.App.—Dallas 1985, writ ref'd n.r.e.); *Augustine*, 671 S.W.2d at 114.

§3.4 Not verified. Special exceptions should not be verified. *See* TRCP 90, 91.

§3.5 Request hearing. The party challenging the pleadings must secure a hearing on the special exceptions, or the exceptions are waived. *Brooks v. Housing Auth.*, 926 S.W.2d 316, 322 (Tex.App.—El Paso 1996, no writ).

§4. DEADLINE

As a general rule, special exceptions should be filed by the defendant either with its answer or shortly thereafter, and by the plaintiff shortly after the defendant files its answer. Special exceptions may also be raised during trial. In a jury trial, a party urging special exceptions must bring them to the trial court's attention before the charge is read to the jury; in a nonjury trial, they must be brought before the judgment is signed. TRCP 90; *see, e.g.*, *Hudspeth v. Hudspeth*, 756 S.W.2d 29, 34 (Tex.App.—San Antonio 1988, writ denied) (party waived error in pleadings by objecting only after trial court signed judgment).

§5. GROUNDS

§5.1 Proper objections to pleadings. For examples of special exceptions that are valid objections to the pleadings, see *O'Connor's Texas Forms*, FORM 3G:1.

§5.2 Improper objections to pleadings. The following are examples of special exceptions that are not valid objections to the pleadings:

★

1. The pleadings do not set out enough factual details. *See, e.g.*, *Roark v. Allen*, 633 S.W.2d 804, 810 (Tex. 1982) (P was not required to plead exactly how doctor used forceps; general allegation of negligent delivery was sufficient).

2. The pleadings do not state a cause of action. *Martin v. Hunter*, 233 S.W.2d 354, 355 (Tex.App.—San Antonio 1950, writ ref'd n.r.e.). The complaint that the pleadings do not state a cause of action is a general demurrer, which is prohibited by TRCP 90. *See Texas Dept. of Corr. v. Herring*, 513 S.W.2d 6, 10 (Tex.1974); *Martin*, 233 S.W.2d at 355-56.

3. The pleadings do not allege all the elements necessary to support a cause of action. *See Spencer v. City of Seagoville*, 700 S.W.2d 953, 957 (Tex.App.—Dallas 1985, no writ). When a defendant objects that the plaintiff did not plead a complete cause of action, the defendant must list the specific elements the plaintiff omitted.

4. The plaintiff's pleadings allege matters that are immaterial, prejudicial, and inflammatory. *Pargas of Canton, Inc. v. Clower*, 434 S.W.2d 192, 196 (Tex.App.—Tyler 1968, no writ). These objections are too general.

5. The plaintiff did not attach a copy of the relevant contract to its pleadings. *Randolph Junior Coll. v. Isaacks*, 113 S.W.2d 628, 629 (Tex.App.—Eastland 1938, no writ). The plaintiff is not required to attach documents to its petition. *See id.*

6. The damages allegations do not specify the dollar value for each element of special damages. *See Phillips v. Vinson Sup.*, 581 S.W.2d 789, 791 (Tex.App.—Houston [14th Dist.] 1979, no writ). TRCP 47 requires the plaintiff to designate only the maximum amount claimed, not how much money is attributable to each element of damages. *Phillips*, 581 S.W.2d at 791.

(13)

PROPOSED TRCP CHANGES

In response to Gov't Code §22.004(h), the Supreme Court has proposed TRCP 169 to establish a process for the prompt, efficient, and cost-effective resolution of civil actions (expedited actions) in which only monetary relief is sought and the amount in controversy is no more than $100,000. See Tex.Sup.Ct. Order, Misc. Docket No. 12-9191 (eff. Mar. 1, 2013). The Supreme Court has proposed corresponding amendments to TRCP 47 that would require a party, in an original pleading, to make a more specific statement of the relief sought; that is, the party would have to plead into or out of the expedited-actions process under TRCP 169. See Tex.Sup.Ct. Order, Misc. Docket No. 12-9191 (eff. Mar. 1, 2013). The public-comment period for the proposed amendments ends on February 1, 2013, and the rules are to take effect March 1, 2013. For the proposed version of the rules, see the appendix after this book's index. For the final version, go to the Supreme Court website at www.supreme.courts.state.tx.us. When the new and amended rules take effect, a supplement to this book—with updated rules and commentaries that reflect the changes—will be available at www.JonesMcClure.com/TRCPamendments.

§6. WAIVER

§6.1 Unchallenged pleadings. When pleadings are not challenged by special exceptions, the court will construe them liberally in favor of the pleader. *Horizon/CMS Healthcare Corp. v. Auld*, 34 S.W.3d 887, 897 (Tex.2000); *Boyles v. Kerr*, 855 S.W.2d 593, 601 (Tex.1993). The court will look to the pleader's intent and will supply every fact "that can reasonably be inferred from what is specifically stated." *Roark v. Allen*, 633 S.W.2d 804, 809 (Tex.1982). Without special exceptions, the court will uphold the pleading even if an element of a cause of action is omitted. *Id.*

§6.2 Waiver on appeal. Every defect not specifically pointed out by special exception before the jury is charged (or in a nonjury case, before the judgment is signed) is waived by the party seeking reversal. TRCP 90.

1. Appellant. The party seeking reversal (the appellant) cannot urge any defects in the appellee's pleadings as a ground for reversal unless the appellant specially excepted to that defect. For example, if the plaintiff did not object to defects in the defendant's pleading of exclusions in an insurance policy, the plaintiff-appellant cannot

★

complain about them for the first time on appeal. *Sherman v. Provident Am. Ins.*, 421 S.W.2d 652, 654 (Tex.1967); *see also Sixth RMA Partners v. Sibley*, 111 S.W.3d 46, 54-55 (Tex.2003) (P-appellant waived error by not objecting when D-appellee filed amended answer instead of supplemental answer); *Troutman v. Traeco Bldg. Sys.*, 724 S.W.2d 385, 387 (Tex.1987) (D-appellant waived error by not objecting when P-appellee did not properly plead DTPA violation); *Tullis v. Georgia-Pac. Corp.*, 45 S.W.3d 118, 124 (Tex.App.—Fort Worth 2000, no pet.) (P-appellant waived error by not objecting when D-appellee did not allege that P was nonresident in forum non conveniens motion).

2. Appellee. The party seeking affirmance (the appellee) can argue on appeal that defects in the appellant's pleadings are reasons to affirm, even if it did not specially except to them. TRCP 90 does not require the party seeking affirmance to have objected to a defect that is a basis for its argument on appeal. *See Ward v. Clark*, 435 S.W.2d 621, 624 (Tex.App.—Tyler 1968, no writ). For example, if the plaintiff pleads "all conditions precedent have occurred" under TRCP 54, and the defendant responds with a general (instead of specific) statement that the plaintiff did not meet all conditions precedent, the plaintiff-appellee can argue on appeal that the defendant's failure to make a specific denial is grounds for affirmance. *See, e.g., Dairyland Cty. Mut. Ins. v. Roman*, 498 S.W.2d 154, 158-59 (Tex.1973) (P did not waive defects in D's general response to TRCP 54 allegation because P was urging affirmance).

§7. RESPONSE

If the plaintiff agrees the exceptions are valid, it should amend its pleadings without contesting the exceptions. If the plaintiff does not agree the exceptions are valid, it should file a response stating why the exceptions should be denied.

§8. HEARING

§8.1 Argument only. The hearing on special exceptions is for argument only. No evidence may be presented.

§8.2 Standard. When ruling on special exceptions, the court must accept as true all material factual allegations and all factual statements reasonably inferred from the allegations in the challenged pleadings. *Sorokolit v. Rhodes*, 889 S.W.2d 239, 240 (Tex.1994) (appellate court); *City of Austin v. Houston Lighting & Power Co.*, 844 S.W.2d 773, 783 (Tex.App.—Dallas 1992, writ denied) (trial court). The trial court has wide discretion in ruling on special exceptions. *LaRue v. GeneScreen, Inc.*, 957 S.W.2d 958, 961 (Tex.App.—Beaumont 1997, pet. denied); *City of Austin*, 844 S.W.2d at 783.

§9. RULING

§9.1 Written order. The defendant must get a written ruling on its special exceptions, or the exceptions are waived. *See* TRCP 90; *Smith v. Grace*, 919 S.W.2d 673, 678 (Tex.App.—Dallas 1996, writ denied); *In re Marriage of Moore*, 890 S.W.2d 821, 826-27 (Tex.App.—Amarillo 1994, no writ). When making its ruling, the court should not merely make margin notations on the special exceptions. *E.g., McAdams v. Capitol Prods.*, 810 S.W.2d 290, 292 (Tex.App.—Fort Worth 1991, writ denied) (unclear whether notations "OR," "Sus.," or "withdrawn" constituted court's ruling on special exceptions). The defendant should insist that the judge sign a written order. *See id.* See *O'Connor's Texas Forms*, FORM 3G:2.

§9.2 Options for court.

1. Court overrules special exceptions. When the court overrules the special exceptions, it will proceed with other matters. When exceptions are overruled, error regarding the defective pleadings is preserved. *See, e.g., Johnson v. Willis*, 596 S.W.2d 256, 260 (Tex.App.—Waco 1980) (court held special exceptions were improperly overruled because pleading did not provide proper notice under DTPA), *writ ref'd n.r.e.*, 603 S.W.2d 828 (Tex.1980).

2. Court sustains special exceptions.

(1) Curable defect. When the court sustains the special exceptions, it must give the plaintiff a chance to amend its pleadings by ordering it to replead. *Parker v. Barefield*, 206 S.W.3d 119, 120 (Tex.2006); *Friesenhahn v. Ryan*, 960 S.W.2d 656, 658-59 (Tex.1998); *Texas Dept. of Corr. v. Herring*, 513 S.W.2d 6, 10 (Tex.1974); *Mowbray v. Avery*, 76 S.W.3d 663, 677 (Tex.App.—Corpus Christi 2002, pet. denied). The court cannot dismiss the

—————————————————— ✦ ——————————————————

case at the same time it sustains the special exceptions. *See Texas Dept. of Corr.*, 513 S.W.2d at 10; *Mowbray*, 76 S.W.3d at 678. To dismiss without giving the plaintiff the opportunity to amend is the functional equivalent of a general demurrer, which is prohibited by TRCP 90. *Hunter v. Johnson*, 25 S.W.3d 247, 249 (Tex.App.—El Paso 2000, no pet.).

(2) Incurable defect. The court is not required to give the plaintiff an opportunity to amend if the pleading defect is one that cannot be cured by amendment (e.g., a pleading that asserts an unrecognized cause of action). *Mowbray*, 76 S.W.3d at 678. See "No viable cause of action," §2.2.3, p. 249.

§9.3 Options for plaintiff. When special exceptions are sustained, the plaintiff may do any of the following:

1. Amend. The plaintiff may amend its pleadings to correct the defect. *Mowbray v. Avery*, 76 S.W.3d 663, 677 (Tex.App.—Corpus Christi 2002, pet. denied); *Butler Weldments Corp. v. Liberty Mut. Ins.*, 3 S.W.3d 654, 658 (Tex.App.—Austin 1999, no pet.); *Cameron v. University of Houston*, 598 S.W.2d 344, 345 (Tex.App.—Houston [14th Dist.] 1980, writ ref'd n.r.e.). In the amended pleading, the plaintiff may include new allegations.

2. Refuse to amend. The plaintiff may challenge the trial court's ruling by refusing to amend. *Mowbray*, 76 S.W.3d at 677; *Muecke v. Hallstead*, 25 S.W.3d 221, 223-24 (Tex.App.—San Antonio 2000, no pet.); *Butler Weldments*, 3 S.W.3d at 658. When the plaintiff believes it is entitled to the claim, the plaintiff should ask the trial court to sign an order striking the defective paragraphs; the plaintiff should not voluntarily amend its pleadings to delete the allegations. By refusing to amend, the plaintiff can test the validity of the trial court's ruling on appeal. *Mowbray*, 76 S.W.3d at 677; *Muecke*, 25 S.W.3d at 223-24; *Butler Weldments*, 3 S.W.3d at 658. If the plaintiff amends its pleadings to delete the allegations, it waives the issue on appeal. *Long v. Tascosa Nat'l Bank*, 678 S.W.2d 699, 703 (Tex.App.—Amarillo 1984, no writ).

3. Partially comply. If the trial court sustains a number of special exceptions, the plaintiff may agree to make some changes but refuse to make others. For example, assume the trial court sustained two special exceptions: the first, to a bad-faith claim, and the second, that the plaintiff did not plead all the elements of fraud. If the plaintiff believes it has a cause of action for bad faith, it should amend the defective allegations of fraud but refuse to delete the bad-faith allegation. By reasserting the bad-faith allegation in the amended petition and having the court strike that part of the petition, the plaintiff preserves for appeal the issue of whether it has such a cause of action. *Fuentes v. Texas Employers' Ins.*, 757 S.W.2d 31, 33 (Tex.App.—San Antonio 1988, no writ).

4. Request time to amend & obtain ruling. If the trial court sustained the special exceptions but did not give the plaintiff an opportunity to replead, the plaintiff must ask the court for time to amend and obtain a ruling on the record denying the requested opportunity to amend, or the error is waived. *E.g.*, *Parker v. Barefield*, 206 S.W.3d 119, 120-21 (Tex.2006) (error preserved because record showed that Ps requested leave to amend and filed amended pleadings; trial court effectively denied request when it sustained special exceptions); *Inglish v. Prudential Ins.*, 928 S.W.2d 702, 705 (Tex.App.—Houston [1st Dist.] 1996, writ denied) (error waived because record did not reflect that Ps ever sought to amend their pleadings); *see* TRAP 33.1(a). If the court's ruling denying the plaintiff the opportunity to amend is not reflected in the record, the plaintiff should file a motion for new trial to preserve the error for appeal. *Inglish*, 928 S.W.2d at 705.

§9.4 Options for defendant.

1. If defect not cured. When special exceptions were sustained and the plaintiff was given an opportunity to amend but failed or refused to do so, the defendant may do any of the following:

(1) Move to dismiss. If the entire pleading was subject to a special exception, the defendant may file a motion to dismiss based on the plaintiff's failure to cure the defect. *See Baca v. Sanchez*, 172 S.W.3d 93, 96 (Tex.App.—El Paso 2005, no pet.). If the request for a dismissal was included in the special exceptions, the defendant may need to set a hearing on only the request to dismiss.

(2) Move to strike. If only part of the pleading was subject to a special exception, the defendant may file a motion to strike that part of the petition, not a motion to dismiss the entire suit.

———————————————————— ✯ ————————————————————

(3) Move for summary judgment. The defendant may file a motion for a partial or full summary judgment. *See Friesenhahn v. Ryan*, 960 S.W.2d 656, 658 (Tex.1998). A summary judgment is preferable to a dismissal without prejudice because it is a resolution on the merits and invokes res judicata. See "Special Exceptions & Summary Judgments," §10, p. 255.

2. If original defect cured but others created. When the plaintiff files an amended petition in response to special exceptions, the defendant should review the new allegations to determine whether it should file additional special exceptions to the new allegations. *See Humphreys v. Meadows*, 938 S.W.2d 750, 753-54 (Tex. App.—Fort Worth 1996, writ denied).

§9.5 Options for court after plaintiff given opportunity to replead.

1. Plaintiff amended & cured defect. If the plaintiff amended the pleadings and cured the defect, the trial court should allow the suit to go forward. If the plaintiff added other allegations that are objectionable, the defendant must file special exceptions to the new allegations, and the court must again give the plaintiff the opportunity to amend. *See Geochem Labs. v. Brown & Ruth Labs.*, 689 S.W.2d 288, 290 (Tex.App.—Houston [1st Dist.] 1985, writ ref'd n.r.e.).

2. Plaintiff amended but did not cure defect.

(1) Good-faith attempt to cure. If the plaintiff made a good-faith attempt to cure the defect in an amended petition, the court cannot strike the objectionable allegations. *Humphreys v. Meadows*, 938 S.W.2d 750, 753 (Tex.App.—Fort Worth 1996, writ denied). Instead, the defendant must file new special exceptions, the court must sustain them, and the plaintiff must be given another opportunity to amend before the court can dismiss. *Id.*; *see Baca v. Sanchez*, 172 S.W.3d 93, 95-96 (Tex.App.—El Paso 2005, no pet.). But a plaintiff's right to amend is not unlimited. *Ford v. Performance Aircraft Servs.*, 178 S.W.3d 330, 336 (Tex.App.—Fort Worth 2005, pet. denied); *Mowbray v. Avery*, 76 S.W.3d 663, 678 (Tex.App.—Corpus Christi 2002, pet. denied). The court may deny leave to amend if there is no reasonable probability that further amendment would state facts legally sufficient to sustain the cause of action. *Mowbray*, 76 S.W.3d at 678.

(2) Lack of good faith. If the plaintiff amended the pleadings but did not cure the objectionable allegations or make a good-faith attempt to do so, the court can strike the objectionable allegations. *Cf. Cruz v. Morris*, 877 S.W.2d 45, 47 (Tex.App.—Houston [14th Dist.] 1994, no writ) (if P refuses to amend, court can strike objectionable allegations). If the plaintiff added new allegations that are objectionable, the following must occur before the court can strike the new allegations: (1) the defendant must file special exceptions, (2) the court must order the plaintiff to replead, and (3) the plaintiff must be given the opportunity to amend. *See Geochem Labs.*, 689 S.W.2d at 290.

3. Plaintiff refused to amend. If the plaintiff refused to amend, the trial court should strike the objectionable allegations. *E.g., Cruz*, 877 S.W.2d at 47 (court struck damages allegations after P refused to replead).

(1) Proceed on remainder of petition. The plaintiff may proceed to trial based on the rest of its pleadings.

(2) No cause of action remains. If no cause of action is stated in the remainder of the petition, the trial court will dismiss the suit. *Ford*, 178 S.W.3d at 336; *Mowbray*, 76 S.W.3d at 678. The issue then is whether the court should dismiss with or without prejudice.

(a) Without prejudice. In most cases, the dismissal after a refusal to amend is without prejudice. *Kutch v. Del Mar Coll.*, 831 S.W.2d 506, 508 (Tex.App.—Corpus Christi 1992, no writ). If the defect can be cured by amendment, dismissal should be without prejudice. *Hajdik v. Wingate*, 753 S.W.2d 199, 202 (Tex. App.—Houston [1st Dist.] 1988), *aff'd*, 795 S.W.2d 717 (Tex.1990); *Atkinson v. Reid*, 625 S.W.2d 64, 66 (Tex. App.—San Antonio 1981, no writ).

(b) With prejudice. If the defect cannot be cured by amendment, dismissal may be with prejudice. *See, e.g., Joseph E. Seagram & Sons, Inc. v. McGuire*, 814 S.W.2d 385, 386 (Tex.1991) (with prejudice;

———————— ✦ ————————

no cause of action because no duty to warn of alcoholism); *Hickman v. Myers*, 632 S.W.2d 869, 869-70 (Tex.App.—Fort Worth 1982, writ ref'd n.r.e.) (with prejudice; no cause of action because no recovery for healthy but unplanned child).

§9.6 Amendments after pleadings struck. After the court strikes a claim or defense in the pleadings, if the plaintiff needs to amend its pleadings for some reason unrelated to the special exceptions, the plaintiff should not include the struck paragraphs in its amended pleading. Once the court strikes allegations in the pleadings, a party is not required to violate the court's order and include them in its amended pleadings. *Melendez v. Exxon Corp.*, 998 S.W.2d 266, 272 & n.1 (Tex.App.—Houston [14th Dist.] 1999, no pet.). In fact, there is some risk in repleading struck allegations. In *Duncan v. Cessna Aircraft Co.*, 665 S.W.2d 414, 433 (Tex.1984), after the trial court struck allegations in the defendant's pleadings, the defendant repleaded them in an amended pleading. On appeal, the court said the defendant waived the issues because it had not introduced evidence to support them. *Duncan*, 665 S.W.2d at 433.

§10. SPECIAL EXCEPTIONS & SUMMARY JUDGMENTS

§10.1 No viable cause of action. If the plaintiff has no viable cause of action and refuses to amend after special exceptions are sustained, the defendant has two options. First, it may ask the court to dismiss the case with prejudice. See "With prejudice," §9.5.3(2)(b), p. 254. Second, it may move for summary judgment on the pleadings. *Friesenhahn v. Ryan*, 960 S.W.2d 656, 658 (Tex.1998); *Pietila v. Crites*, 851 S.W.2d 185, 186 n.2 (Tex.1993); *Massey v. Armco Steel Co.*, 652 S.W.2d 932, 934 (Tex.1983); *see, e.g.*, *Castleberry v. Goolsby Bldg. Corp.*, 617 S.W.2d 665, 666 (Tex.1981) (affirmed summary judgment on pleadings when P's pleadings showed that suit was barred by statute). See "Special Exceptions in Summary-Judgment Procedure," ch. 7-B, §5, p. 604. A motion for summary judgment is more favorable to the defendant because it is a ruling on the merits; a dismissal is not, unless it is with prejudice. For causes of action that can be challenged as not viable, see *O'Connor's Texas COA*, "Causes of Action Not Recognized in Texas," ch. 35, p. 1153.

§10.2 Defective pleading. When the plaintiff has a viable cause of action but pleaded it defectively, the defendant should file special exceptions, not a motion for summary judgment. *Friesenhahn v. Ryan*, 960 S.W.2d 656, 659 (Tex.1998); *Pietila v. Crites*, 851 S.W.2d 185, 186 n.2 (Tex.1993); *see Natividad v. Alexsis, Inc.*, 875 S.W.2d 695, 699 (Tex.1994). Because the summary-judgment procedure does not provide an opportunity to replead, it cannot be used to terminate a suit based on pleading defects. *Sixth RMA Partners v. Sibley*, 111 S.W.3d 46, 54-55 (Tex.2003); *Saenz v. Southern Un. Gas Co.*, 916 S.W.2d 703, 705 (Tex.App.—El Paso 1996, writ denied); *see, e.g.*, *Friesenhahn*, 960 S.W.2d at 658-59 (summary judgment reversed when Ps were not given opportunity to amend their claims for wrongful death of minor); *Peek v. Equipment Serv.*, 779 S.W.2d 802, 804-05 (Tex.1989) (failure to plead for damages in the jurisdictional amount should have been challenged by special exception, not summary judgment); *Texas Dept. of Corr. v. Herring*, 513 S.W.2d 6, 9-10 (Tex.1974) (summary judgment reversed when P did not correctly plead TTCA requirements).

§10.3 Viability of claim uncertain. If the defendant is uncertain whether the plaintiff has a viable cause of action or merely pleaded a cause of action defectively, the defendant should first file special exceptions and then, if the plaintiff is not able to plead a viable cause of action, file a motion for summary judgment. *Friesenhahn v. Ryan*, 960 S.W.2d 656, 658 (Tex.1998); *Pietila v. Crites*, 851 S.W.2d 185, 186 n.2 (Tex.1993). Summary judgment based on a pleading deficiency is proper if a plaintiff had an opportunity to amend after a special exception and refused to do so. *Natividad v. Alexsis, Inc.*, 875 S.W.2d 695, 699 (Tex.1994); *see Friesenhahn*, 960 S.W.2d at 658; *Pietila*, 851 S.W.2d at 186 & n.2.

§10.4 Waiver. If the defendant files a motion for summary judgment when it should have first filed special exceptions, the plaintiff must object to the defendant's motion for summary judgment on the ground that it is an attempt to circumvent the special-exception practice. *Vawter v. Garvey*, 786 S.W.2d 263, 264 (Tex.1990); *San Jacinto River Auth. v. Duke*, 783 S.W.2d 209, 209 (Tex.1990); *Dickey v. Jansen*, 731 S.W.2d 581, 583 (Tex.App.—Houston [1st Dist.] 1987, writ ref'd n.r.e.). If the plaintiff does not object, the issue is waived. *Duke*, 783 S.W.2d at 209-10.

★

§11. SPECIAL EXCEPTIONS & DEFAULT JUDGMENTS

Special exceptions are not required to preserve pleading errors in default-judgment cases. TRCP 90; *Stoner v. Thompson*, 578 S.W.2d 679, 684-85 (Tex.1979); *Rose v. Burton*, 614 S.W.2d 651, 652 (Tex.App.—Texarkana 1981, writ ref'd n.r.e.).

§12. REVIEW

§12.1 Appeal. The trial court's ruling on special exceptions can be appealed. *Low v. King*, 867 S.W.2d 141, 142 (Tex.App.—Beaumont 1993, orig. proceeding); *Hill v. Lopez*, 858 S.W.2d 563, 565 (Tex.App.—Amarillo 1993, orig. proceeding).

1. Complaint on appeal. An appellant who complains of the dismissal of a cause of action following special exceptions must attack both the trial court's decision to sustain the special exceptions and the decision to dismiss the cause of action. *Perry v. Cohen*, 272 S.W.3d 585, 588 (Tex.2008); *Mowbray v. Avery*, 76 S.W.3d 663, 678 (Tex.App.—Corpus Christi 2002, pet. denied); *Cole v. Hall*, 864 S.W.2d 563, 566 (Tex.App.—Dallas 1993, writ dism'd). The appellant must challenge both rulings, or it waives the unchallenged issue. *Mowbray*, 76 S.W.3d at 678.

2. Standard of review. The appellate court reviews the trial court's ruling on special exceptions for abuse of discretion. *Muecke v. Hallstead*, 25 S.W.3d 221, 224 (Tex.App.—San Antonio 2000, no pet.); *LaRue v. Gene-Screen, Inc.*, 957 S.W.2d 958, 961 (Tex.App.—Beaumont 1997, pet. denied). The appellate court must construe the pleadings liberally and accept as true all factual allegations in the pleadings. *See Sorokolit v. Rhodes*, 889 S.W.2d 239, 240 (Tex.1994). The appellate court must ignore any factual propositions outside the petition that tend to contradict the petition. *Hur v. City of Mesquite*, 893 S.W.2d 227, 233 (Tex.App.—Amarillo 1995, writ denied).

3. Record. To appeal a dismissal based on refusal to amend pleadings after special exceptions, the appellant must request the clerk's record and file it with the court of appeals. The reporter's record is not necessary because the dismissal will be judged on the pleadings, not on the evidence. *See Holt v. Reproductive Servs.*, 946 S.W.2d 602, 604 (Tex.App.—Corpus Christi 1997, writ denied); *Cole*, 864 S.W.2d at 566.

§12.2 No mandamus. The trial court's ruling on special exceptions cannot be reviewed by mandamus. *Hill v. Lopez*, 858 S.W.2d 563, 566 (Tex.App.—Amarillo 1993, orig. proceeding).

H. MOTION TO DISMISS—BASELESS CAUSE OF ACTION

⑬ §1. PROPOSED TRCP CHANGES

In 2011, the Legislature enacted Gov't Code §22.004(g) requiring the Supreme Court to adopt rules for the dismissal of a cause of action that has no basis in law or fact. In response to the legislative mandate, the Supreme Court has proposed TRCP 91a. *See* Tex.Sup.Ct. Order, Misc. Docket No. 12-9191 (eff. Mar. 1, 2013). The dismissal procedure under TRCP 91a would allow the court to dispose of a cause of action as a matter of law and without considering any evidence. *See* Tex.Sup.Ct. Order, Misc. Docket No. 12-9191 (eff. Mar. 1, 2013). Specifically, a motion to dismiss would have to be filed within 60 days after the first pleading that includes the baseless cause of action is served and would generally have to be ruled on within 45 days after the motion is filed. *See id.* By filing a motion to dismiss, a defendant would not waive a special appearance or a motion to transfer venue. *Id.* The public-comment period for the proposed rule ends on February 1, 2013, and the rule is to take effect March 1, 2013. For the proposed version of the rule, see the appendix after this book's index. For the final version, go to the Supreme Court website at www.supreme.courts.state.tx.us. When the new rule takes effect, a supplement to this book—with a complete subchapter that reflects the changes—will be available at www.JonesMcClure.com/TRCPamendments.

★

I. MOTION TO ABATE—CHALLENGING THE SUIT

§1. GENERAL

§1.1 Rules. TRCP 85, 150-160, 175.

§1.2 Purpose. A defendant uses a motion to abate, also called a plea in abatement, to challenge the plaintiff's pleadings by alleging facts outside the pleadings that prove the suit cannot go forward in its present condition. *Martin v. Dosohs I, Ltd.*, 2 S.W.3d 350, 354 (Tex.App.—San Antonio 1999, pet. denied). A motion to abate cannot be used to determine the merits of an action. *KSNG Architects, Inc. v. Beasley*, 109 S.W.3d 894, 898 (Tex.App.—Dallas 2003, no pet.). In a motion to abate, the defendant identifies some impediment to the continuation of the suit, identifies an effective cure, and asks the court to suspend the suit until the plaintiff cures the defect. *Martin*, 2 S.W.3d at 354; *see American Motorists Ins. v. Fodge*, 63 S.W.3d 801, 805 (Tex.2001). By granting the motion to abate, the court gives the plaintiff an opportunity to cure the defect. *Speer v. Stover*, 685 S.W.2d 22, 23 (Tex.1985). If the plaintiff cures the defect, the court will permit the suit to continue; if not, the court will dismiss the suit. *See Garcia-Marroquin v. Nueces Cty. Bail Bond Bd.*, 1 S.W.3d 366, 374 (Tex.App.—Corpus Christi 1999, no pet.).

§1.3 Timetable & forms. Timetable, Motion to Abate, p. 1215; *O'Connor's Texas Civil Forms* (2012), FORMS 3H.

§1.4 Other references. *O'Connor's Texas Causes of Action* (2013) (*O'Connor's Texas COA*).

§2. MOTION

§2.1 Separate instrument. A defendant should ask for an abatement in a separate instrument from the answer. If a motion to abate is included in the answer, it is called a plea in abatement. *See* TRCP 85; *Southwestern Life Ins. v. Sanguinet*, 231 S.W.2d 727, 730 (Tex.App.—Fort Worth 1950, no writ).

§2.2 Specific allegations. A motion to abate must specify the improper grounds on which a suit is brought and show how the suit should have been brought. *Bryce v. Corpus Christi Area Convention & Tourist Bur.*, 569 S.W.2d 496, 499 (Tex.App.—Corpus Christi 1978, writ ref'd n.r.e.). The motion must inform the court and the other party exactly what is wrong and how to cure it. *M&M Constr. Co. v. Great Am. Ins.*, 747 S.W.2d 552, 554 (Tex. App.—Corpus Christi 1988, no writ).

§2.3 Verified. The motion to abate must be verified. *Sparks v. Bolton*, 335 S.W.2d 780, 785 (Tex.App.—Dallas 1960, no writ); *see* TRCP 93. *But see Southern Cty. Mut. Ins. v. Ochoa*, 19 S.W.3d 452, 461-62 (Tex.App.—Corpus Christi 2000, no pet.) (verification requirement excused when D filed verified answer and verified motion to transfer venue with plea in abatement). The movant may also file affidavits if necessary to support the allegations in the motion.

§2.4 Deadline to file. A motion to abate must be made in a timely manner, or else it is waived. *Wyatt v. Shaw Plumbing Co.*, 760 S.W.2d 245, 248 (Tex.1988); *Lopez v. Texas Workers' Comp. Ins. Fund*, 11 S.W.3d 490, 493 (Tex.App.—Austin 2000, pet. denied). The motion must be made while the purpose of the motion remains viable. *See Hines v. Hash*, 843 S.W.2d 464, 469 (Tex.1992) (when objecting to lack of notice, D must request abatement with filing of answer or soon thereafter); *Garcia-Marroquin v. Nueces Cty. Bail Bond Bd.*, 1 S.W.3d 366, 374 (Tex. App.—Corpus Christi 1999, no pet.) (same); *see, e.g., Bluebonnet Farms, Inc. v. Gibraltar Sav. Ass'n*, 618 S.W.2d 81, 83-84 (Tex.App.—Houston [1st Dist.] 1980, writ ref'd n.r.e.) (motion to abate filed four years after suit filed and after limitations ran was too late).

PRACTICE TIP

In deciding whether to file a motion to abate, a defendant should look at the verified denials in its original answer. Many of the matters that a party is required to deny under oath, listed in TRCP 93, are also matters that should be made the subject of a verified motion to abate. See "Verified pleas in TRCP 93," ch. 3-E, §4.1, p. 228.

★

§3. TYPES OF MOTIONS TO ABATE

§3.1 Abate – defect in pleadings. A defendant should file a motion to abate when there is a defect in the pleadings that must be supported by extrinsic evidence. See *O'Connor's Texas Forms*, FORM 3H:1. If the defect is apparent from the face of the pleadings, it can be challenged by special exceptions. See "Limited to pleadings," ch. 3-G, §3.3, p. 250. There are two types of pleading defects that can be challenged by a motion to abate: defects in parties and defects in allegations.

1. Defects in parties.

(1) Minor or incapacitated person. A motion to abate is appropriate to challenge a minor or incapacitated person who files suit in her own name, instead of the next friend or guardian's name. *Sax v. Votteler*, 648 S.W.2d 661, 666 (Tex.1983). See "Minor as P," ch. 2-B, §3.4.2, p. 101.

(2) Estate of decedent. A motion to abate is appropriate to challenge the following defects when the estate of a decedent is a party: • To challenge a suit brought on behalf of an estate by an individual, instead of by the estate's representative. *Coakley v. Reising*, 436 S.W.2d 315, 317 (Tex.1968). • To contest the authority of an administrator to represent the estate, who must then file proof of authority (the bond and oath). *Shiffers v. Estate of Ward*, 762 S.W.2d 753, 755 (Tex.App.—Fort Worth 1988, writ denied). See "Estate," ch. 2-B, §3.3.2, p. 99.

(3) Death-action beneficiary. A motion to abate is appropriate to challenge the plaintiff in its representative capacity under the Texas Survival Statute and the Texas Wrongful Death Act. *See Ford Motor Co. v. Aguiniga*, 9 S.W.3d 252, 259 (Tex.App.—San Antonio 1999, pet. denied). See *O'Connor's Texas COA*, "Legal representative of estate," ch. 7-A, §2.1.2, p. 179; "Statutory beneficiaries," ch. 7-B, §2.1.2, p. 188.

(4) Wrong representative of corporation. A motion to abate is appropriate to challenge whether a stockholder suing for damages to a corporation has standing and capacity to bring suit. A stockholder lacks both standing (because the stockholder was not personally aggrieved) and capacity (because the stockholder is not the right surrogate) to bring suit for damages to a corporation. *See White v. Independence Bank*, 794 S.W.2d 895, 898 n.3 (Tex.App.—Houston [1st Dist.] 1990, writ denied). See "Corporation," ch. 2-B, §3.3.4, p. 100.

(5) Not corporation or partnership. A motion to abate is appropriate to challenge whether the plaintiff is a corporation or partnership, as it alleges. TRCP 52, 93(5), (6); *see Lighthouse Ch. v. Texas Bank*, 889 S.W.2d 595, 600 (Tex.App.—Houston [14th Dist.] 1994, writ denied).

(6) Unauthorized foreign corporation. A motion to abate is appropriate to challenge whether a foreign corporation is registered with the Secretary of State and may maintain an action for affirmative relief. *See Jay-Lor Textiles, Inc. v. Pacific Compress Whs. Co.*, 547 S.W.2d 738, 740 (Tex.App.—Corpus Christi 1977, writ ref'd n.r.e.).

(7) No assumed-name certificate. A motion to abate is appropriate to challenge the lack of an assumed-name certificate. *Sixth RMA Partners v. Sibley*, 111 S.W.3d 46, 55 (Tex.2003); *see* Bus. & Com. Code §36.25 (party is prohibited from prosecuting suit until it files assumed-name certificate).

(8) Necessary party absent. A motion to abate is appropriate to challenge the absence of a necessary party and force the plaintiff to add the missing party. *See, e.g.*, *Allison v. National Un. Fire Ins.*, 703 S.W.2d 637, 638 (Tex.1986) (challenging absence of necessary parties from contract dispute); *Dahl v. Hartman*, 14 S.W.3d 434, 435-36 (Tex.App.—Houston [14th Dist.] 2000, pet. denied) (challenging absence of necessary parties in declaratory-judgment action); *Wolfe v. Schuster*, 591 S.W.2d 926, 931 (Tex.App.—Dallas 1979, no writ) (challenging P's failure to sue principal when D is surety and P has not already taken judgment against principal); *see also* TRCP 31 (surety), TRCP 32 (same).

(9) Misnomer of defendant. A motion to abate is appropriate to challenge the name under which the defendant was sued. *See Matthews Trucking Co. v. Smith*, 682 S.W.2d 237, 238-39 (Tex.1984) (if correct D sued in wrong name, D should file motion to abate); *Charles Brown, L.L.P. v. Lanier Worldwide, Inc.*, 124 S.W.3d 883, 894 (Tex.App.—Houston [14th Dist.] 2004, no pet.) (same).

★

2. Defects in allegations.

(1) Lack of notice. A motion to abate is generally appropriate to challenge the lack of notice or the allegation that the plaintiff gave proper presuit notice. In some cases, however, lack of notice subjects the suit to dismissal, not abatement. *See, e.g.*, *Reese v. Texas State Dept. of Highways & Pub. Transp.*, 831 S.W.2d 529, 530-31 (Tex.App.—Tyler 1992, writ denied) (lack of notice under TTCA was not subject to abatement; suit was perpetually barred). A motion to abate is appropriate in the following instances:

(a) To challenge notice of suit against a professional employee of a school district. Educ. Code §22.0513(c).

(b) To challenge notice of a DTPA claim. *See Hines v. Hash*, 843 S.W.2d 464, 469 (Tex.1992). Under the DTPA, a defendant must move to abate for lack of notice within 30 days after filing its answer. Bus. & Com. Code §17.505(c); *America Online, Inc. v. Williams*, 958 S.W.2d 268, 277 (Tex.App.—Houston [14th Dist.] 1997, no pet.). The abatement is automatic when a verified plea in abatement is filed and lack of presuit notice is not controverted within 11 days after the plea was filed. Bus. & Com. Code §17.505(d); *America Online*, 958 S.W.2d at 273. See *O'Connor's Texas COA*, "Presuit notice of claim," ch. 8, §6.1, p. 236.

(c) To challenge notice of a health-care-liability claim. *See* CPRC §§74.051(a), 74.052(a). If a medical-authorization form is not attached to the notice, all proceedings against a physician or health-care provider must be abated until 60 days after the physician or health-care provider receives the authorization. *Id.* §74.052(a). See *O'Connor's Texas COA*, "Authorization form," ch. 20-A, §7.1.5, p. 625.

(2) Lack of residency. A motion to abate is appropriate to challenge the lack of residency when there is a residency requirement for filing suit. *Cook v. Mayfield*, 886 S.W.2d 840, 841 (Tex.App.—Waco 1994, orig. proceeding); *see, e.g.*, Fam. Code §6.301(2) (one of the parties to a divorce must have been resident of county for 90 days); *Reynolds v. Reynolds*, 86 S.W.3d 272, 277 (Tex.App.—Austin 2002, no pet.) (divorce petition did not properly allege residency requirements under Fam. Code §6.301).

§3.2 Abate – same dispute in another Texas court. When two lawsuits involving the same subject matter are filed in courts of concurrent jurisdiction, a party may file a motion to abate in one court, claiming the other court has dominant jurisdiction. *See In re Puig*, 351 S.W.3d 301, 305 (Tex.2011); *Wyatt v. Shaw Plumbing Co.*, 760 S.W.2d 245, 248 (Tex.1988); *In re Sims*, 88 S.W.3d 297, 302 (Tex.App.—San Antonio 2002, orig. proceeding); *cf. Miles v. Ford Motor Co.*, 914 S.W.2d 135, 139 (Tex.1995) (appeals filed by different parties in different courts of appeals). See *O'Connor's Texas Forms*, FORM 3H:2. By comparison, if a suit is brought in one court when another court has continuing, exclusive jurisdiction, a party should challenge the issue of exclusive jurisdiction by a plea to the jurisdiction. See "Another court has exclusive jurisdiction," ch. 3-F, §3.5, p. 241. If the movant can prove the grounds for abatement as set out below, the court should abate the suit because the other court has dominant jurisdiction. *See Curtis v. Gibbs*, 511 S.W.2d 263, 267 (Tex.1974); *Hartley v. Coker*, 843 S.W.2d 743, 746 (Tex.App.—Corpus Christi 1992, no writ).

1. Dominant jurisdiction. To be entitled to an abatement based on dominant jurisdiction, the movant must file a motion to abate in the court where the other suit (the "second suit") was filed and must allege and prove the following:

(1) Commenced. The movant's suit (the "first suit") was commenced first. *See In re Sims*, 88 S.W.3d at 303. A suit is "commenced" when the petition is served on the defendant. The mere filing of a petition does not fulfill the commencement requirement for purposes of abatement, even though TRCP 22 states that a civil suit is commenced by filing a petition with the clerk. *See Russell v. Taylor*, 49 S.W.2d 733, 737 (Tex.Comm'n App.1932, judgm't adopted); *Grimes v. Harris*, 695 S.W.2d 648, 651 (Tex.App.—Dallas 1985, orig. proceeding). The movant must show citation in that suit was timely served. See "Lack of intent to prosecute," §3.2.2(2), p. 260.

(2) Venue proper. The first suit was filed in a county of proper venue. The court where the first suit was filed generally has exclusive jurisdiction if venue is proper in that county. *Gonzalez v. Reliant Energy, Inc.*, 159 S.W.3d 615, 622 (Tex.2005); *Wyatt*, 760 S.W.2d at 248; *Gordon v. Jones*, 196 S.W.3d 376, 383 (Tex.App.—Houston [1st Dist.] 2006, no pet.).

———————————————— ✦ ————————————————

(3) **Pending.** The first suit is still pending in the other court. *In re Sims*, 88 S.W.3d at 303; *Southern Cty. Mut. Ins. v. Ochoa*, 19 S.W.3d 452, 468 (Tex.App.—Corpus Christi 2000, no pet.).

(4) **Same parties & dispute.** The two suits involve the same parties and the same dispute. *In re Sims*, 88 S.W.3d at 303; *see Wyatt*, 760 S.W.2d at 248; *Southern Cty.*, 19 S.W.3d at 468. The exact issues and all the parties do not need to be included in the first suit as long as the petition in the first suit can be amended to bring in all necessary parties and issues. *Wyatt*, 760 S.W.2d at 247; *In re Sims*, 88 S.W.3d at 303.

2. Exceptions to dominant jurisdiction. There are three exceptions to the dominant jurisdiction of the first court. *Wyatt*, 760 S.W.2d at 248; *Mission Res. v. Garza Energy Trust*, 166 S.W.3d 301, 328 (Tex.App.—Corpus Christi 2005), *rev'd in part on other grounds sub nom. Coastal Oil & Gas Corp. v. Garza Energy Trust*, 268 S.W.3d 1 (Tex.2008).

(1) **Estoppel.** A party can be estopped from asserting the dominant jurisdiction of the first court. *Wyatt*, 760 S.W.2d at 248; *Mission Res.*, 166 S.W.3d at 328. For example, a party can be estopped by representing to a second court that it has jurisdiction, by not requesting abatement in a timely fashion, and by not acting while different courts issue conflicting orders. *Sweezy Constr., Inc. v. Murray*, 915 S.W.2d 527, 532 (Tex.App.—Corpus Christi 1995, orig. proceeding); *see, e.g., Gordon*, 196 S.W.3d at 385 (party was estopped from asserting dominant jurisdiction when he allowed first suit to end and then delayed in asserting dominant jurisdiction of first court). A party can be estopped from asserting dominant jurisdiction if it files a claim, by either an original or an amended pleading, that is not ripe. *Perry v. Del Rio*, 66 S.W.3d 239, 252-53 (Tex.2001).

(2) **Lack of intent to prosecute.** A party's lack of intent to prosecute a suit deprives the first court of dominant jurisdiction. *Wyatt*, 760 S.W.2d at 248; *Mission Res.*, 166 S.W.3d at 328. The first suit does not confer dominant jurisdiction if the plaintiff delayed service of process. *See Russell*, 49 S.W.2d at 737 (suit is not commenced if P directs clerk not to issue service of citation); *see, e.g., Curtis*, 511 S.W.2d at 268 (delay of service for 26 days was not unreasonable; abatement of second suit should have been sustained); *Reed v. Reed*, 311 S.W.2d 628, 631 (Tex. 1958) (delay of service for almost 15 months was unreasonable; second suit should not have been abated); *Southern Cty.*, 19 S.W.3d at 468 (delay of service for four months was unreasonable; denial of abatement of second suit affirmed).

(3) **Lack of necessary parties.** A lack of necessary parties deprives the first court of dominant jurisdiction. *Wyatt*, 760 S.W.2d at 248; *Mission Res.*, 166 S.W.3d at 328.

3. Strategy. When two suits involving the same parties and the same dispute are on file in two counties, each party will want to abate the other party's suit. A party must make a strategic decision—whether to file a motion to abate the suit in which it is a defendant or to move the other suit forward and force the defendant in that suit to file a motion to abate.

§3.3 Abate – same dispute is subject to arbitration. A defendant may file a motion to abate requesting a suspension of the suit when the dispute should have been submitted to arbitration. See "Arbitration," ch. 4-C, p. 286.

§3.4 Abate – administrative agency has primary jurisdiction. A defendant may file a motion to abate requesting a suspension of the suit when an administrative agency has primary jurisdiction over the dispute. *In re Southwestern Bell Tel. Co.*, 226 S.W.3d 400, 403 (Tex.2007); *Subaru, Inc. v. David McDavid Nissan, Inc.*, 84 S.W.3d 212, 221 (Tex.2002); *see O'Neal v. Ector Cty. ISD*, 251 S.W.3d 50, 52 (Tex.2008) (if agency has exclusive jurisdiction over some claims but no jurisdiction over others, court can abate case until administrative proceedings are concluded). When an agency shares jurisdiction over a dispute with the courts, courts defer to the agency for policy reasons. *See In re Southwestern Bell*, 226 S.W.3d at 403 (agency is staffed with experts trained to handle complex issues presented and is better able to uniformly interpret its laws and regulations than the courts); *Subaru*, 84 S.W.3d at 221 (same). But when an administrative agency has exclusive jurisdiction, dismissal is mandatory. See "Administrative agency has exclusive jurisdiction," ch. 3-F, §3.6, p. 241.

⋆

§4. TYPES OF MOTIONS TO STAY

§4.1 Motion to stay vs. motion to abate. A motion to stay is included in this subchapter, even though it is different in some respects from a motion to abate, because it is used instead of a motion to abate when the same suit is filed in a Texas court and in a court of another jurisdiction.

1. Comity. When a suit filed in a Texas court was first filed in a federal court or in another state's court, the defendant should file a motion to stay—not a motion to abate—in the Texas suit, requesting that the court suspend the Texas suit. A motion to abate contends that one court has dominant jurisdiction over the other court; a motion to stay recognizes that sister courts are foreign to each other, and the concept of dominant jurisdiction does not apply. *Crown Leasing Corp. v. Sims*, 92 S.W.3d 924, 927 (Tex.App.—Texarkana 2002, no pet.). As a matter of comity, it is customary for the second court to stay its proceedings for a reasonable time or until the first suit is resolved. *Id.* Many parties and even the appellate courts make the mistake of referring to a motion to stay as a motion to abate. *See, e.g.*, *VE Corp. v. Ernst & Young*, 860 S.W.2d 83, 84 (Tex.1993) (court's mistake); *Crown Leasing*, 92 S.W.3d at 926-27 (party's mistake).

2. Discretion. When a party makes a motion to stay in a Texas court because the same suit was first filed in a federal court or in another state's court, the court's ruling is within its discretion. The difference between the rulings on a motion to abate and a motion to stay is that the court must grant a proper motion to abate but can deny a proper motion to stay. *Williamson v. Tucker*, 615 S.W.2d 881, 886 (Tex.App.—Dallas 1981, writ ref'd n.r.e.). The court's ruling on a motion to stay will be reversed only if the court abuses its discretion by its ruling. *Id.*; *see In re State Farm Mut. Auto. Ins.*, 192 S.W.3d 897, 903 (Tex.App.—Tyler 2006, orig. proceeding) (trial court's ruling on motion to stay reversed for abuse of discretion). Because the granting of a motion to stay is within the trial court's discretion, the trial court can consider a number of factors before ruling on a motion to stay. *See In re State Farm*, 192 S.W.3d at 901.

(1) First suit. Which suit was filed first? *In re State Farm*, 192 S.W.3d at 901.

(2) Same parties. Are the parties the same in both suits? *In re State Farm*, 192 S.W.3d at 901; *see, e.g.*, *Williamson*, 615 S.W.2d at 886 (no abuse of discretion to deny motion because first suit involved more parties than second suit).

(3) Same suit. Do the suits involve the same cause of action, concern the same subject matter, involve the same issues, and seek the same relief? *In re State Farm*, 192 S.W.3d at 901.

(4) Effect of judgment. What will be the effect of a judgment in the second suit on any order or judgment in the first suit? *In re State Farm*, 192 S.W.3d at 901.

§4.2 Stay – same dispute in another state's court. A defendant may file a motion to stay in a Texas court requesting that the court suspend the case because the same case was first filed in another state's court. *See In re State Farm Mut. Auto. Ins.*, 192 S.W.3d 897, 899 (Tex.App.—Tyler 2006, orig. proceeding) (first suit filed in Louisiana; D in first suit entitled to stay of Texas suit); *Crown Leasing Corp. v. Sims*, 92 S.W.3d 924, 927 (Tex.App.—Texarkana 2002, no pet.) (first suit filed in Florida; P in first suit entitled to stay of Texas suit). See *O'Connor's Texas Forms*, FORM 3H:2.

§4.3 Stay – same dispute in federal court. A defendant may file a motion to stay in a Texas court requesting that the court suspend the case because the same case was first filed in a federal court. *See, e.g.*, *Space Master Int'l v. Porta-Kamp Mfg.*, 794 S.W.2d 944, 946 (Tex.App.—Houston [1st Dist.] 1990, no writ) (first suit removed to federal court in Massachusetts; P in first suit entitled to stay of Texas suit); *Alpine Gulf, Inc. v. Valentino*, 563 S.W.2d 358, 359 (Tex.App.—Houston [14th Dist.] 1978, writ ref'd n.r.e.) (first suit filed in federal court in New York; D in first suit entitled to stay of Texas suit). See *O'Connor's Texas Forms*, FORM 3H:2.

§5. RESPONSE

§5.1 Cure. The plaintiff may agree with the motion to abate and cure the defect. For example, when a motion to abate is filed in the second court on the ground that the first court has dominant jurisdiction, there is no longer a reason to abate if the plaintiff dismisses the first suit. *See Pleasants v. Emmons*, 871 S.W.2d 296, 298 (Tex.App.—Eastland 1994, no writ).

★

§5.2 Object. The plaintiff may file a response that challenges the factual matters alleged by the defendant. See *O'Connor's Texas Forms*, FORM 3H:3. The response should follow the format of the motion to abate. It should be verified and, if necessary, include affidavits.

§6. HEARING

§6.1 Evidence. The hearing on a motion to abate is for the receipt of evidence, not just for argument. *See Upchurch v. Albear*, 5 S.W.3d 274, 277 & n.4 (Tex.App.—Amarillo 1999, pet. denied); *Kriegel v. Scott*, 439 S.W.2d 445, 447 (Tex.App.—Houston [14th Dist.] 1969, writ ref'd n.r.e.). The defendant must introduce evidence at the hearing. *Bernal v. Garrison*, 818 S.W.2d 79, 82 (Tex.App.—Corpus Christi 1991, writ denied). When a defendant does not introduce evidence to support its motion to abate, the court must overrule it, unless the matters alleged in the motion appear on the face of the plaintiff's pleadings. *See id.* at 83; *see also Brazos Elec. Power Coop. v. Weatherford ISD*, 453 S.W.2d 185, 189 (Tex.App.—Fort Worth 1970, writ ref'd n.r.e.) (reversible error for abatement to be sustained without any evidence).

§6.2 No jury. The hearing is before the court, not a jury. *Union Pac. Fuels, Inc. v. Johnson*, 909 S.W.2d 130, 135 (Tex.App.—Houston [14th Dist.] 1995, orig. proceeding); *Miller v. Stout*, 706 S.W.2d 785, 787 (Tex.App.—San Antonio 1986, no writ).

§6.3 Waiver. A motion to abate is waived if it is not set for a hearing before the trial. *Shiffers v. Estate of Ward*, 762 S.W.2d 753, 755 (Tex.App.—Fort Worth 1988, writ denied).

§6.4 Burden of proof. The defendant has the burden of proof on the allegations in its motion to abate. *Flowers v. Steelcraft Corp.*, 406 S.W.2d 199, 199 (Tex.1966); *Southern Cty. Mut. Ins. v. Ochoa*, 19 S.W.3d 452, 469 (Tex.App.—Corpus Christi 2000, no pet.); *Lopez v. Texas Workers' Comp. Ins. Fund*, 11 S.W.3d 490, 493 (Tex.App.—Austin 2000, pet. denied). The defendant must prove the relevant facts by a preponderance of the evidence. *Lopez*, 11 S.W.3d at 493; *Bernal v. Garrison*, 818 S.W.2d 79, 82 (Tex.App.—Corpus Christi 1991, writ denied); *Brazos Elec. Power Coop. v. Weatherford ISD*, 453 S.W.2d 185, 188 (Tex.App.—Fort Worth 1970, writ ref'd n.r.e.). If the defendant does not disprove the facts in the plaintiff's petition, the court must accept the facts as true. *Bernal*, 818 S.W.2d at 82; *Seth v. Meyer*, 730 S.W.2d 884, 885 (Tex.App.—Fort Worth 1987, no writ).

§7. ORDER

§7.1 Motion overruled. The first court to overrule a motion to abate becomes vested with dominant jurisdiction; the case will proceed to trial in that court. *4M Linen & Unif. Sup. v. W.P. Ballard & Co.*, 793 S.W.2d 320, 322 (Tex.App.—Houston [1st Dist.] 1990, writ denied). The other court cannot enjoin the court that overruled the motion to abate from proceeding to trial. *Johnson v. Avery*, 414 S.W.2d 441, 442-43 (Tex.1966). If the other court continues to issue conflicting orders in the case, that court is subject to mandamus. *Hall v. Lawlis*, 907 S.W.2d 493, 494 (Tex.1995). See "Mandamus," §8.3, p. 263.

§7.2 Motion sustained. If the motion to abate is sustained, the case is abated until the obstacle to its prosecution is removed. *Texas Highway Dept. v. Jarrell*, 418 S.W.2d 486, 488 (Tex.1967). A court must set the terms for the abatement; a case cannot be abated indefinitely. *Gebhardt v. Gallardo*, 891 S.W.2d 327, 332 (Tex.App.—San Antonio 1995, orig. proceeding).

1. Suspending suit. The order sustaining a motion to abate suspends all action in the suit until the cause of the abatement is cured. *See America Online, Inc. v. Williams*, 958 S.W.2d 268, 272 (Tex.App.—Houston [14th Dist.] 1997, no pet.); *Permanente Med. Ass'n v. Johnson*, 917 S.W.2d 515, 517 (Tex.App.—Waco 1996, orig. proceeding). The parties should not attempt to engage in discovery while an abatement is in effect; discovery requests filed during abatement are invalid and are not revived when the suit is revived. *Lumbermens Mut. Cas. Co. v. Garza*, 777 S.W.2d 198, 198-99 (Tex.App.—Corpus Christi 1989, orig. proceeding). The abatement prevents both the court and the parties from taking any action in the case. *In re Kimball Hill Homes*, 969 S.W.2d 522, 527 (Tex.App.—Houston [14th Dist.] 1998, orig. proceeding). But the abatement does not prevent the plaintiff from dismissing claims or taking a nonsuit. *United Oil & Minerals, Inc. v. Costilla Energy, Inc.*, 1 S.W.3d 840, 846 (Tex.App.—Corpus Christi 1999, pet. dism'd).

★

PRACTICE TIP

If you want to continue with discovery, ask that the trial court's order state that discovery is exempt from the abatement. In other words, ask for a partial abatement.

---

2. Reviving suit. When the cause for the abatement is cured, the suit may be revived if anything remains to be litigated. *Texas Employers' Ins. v. Baeza*, 584 S.W.2d 317, 321 (Tex.App.—Amarillo 1979, no writ).

3. Dismissing suit. If the trial court grants a motion to abate and the plaintiff refuses to cure the defect, the trial court may dismiss the suit. The dismissal should be without prejudice. *See Gordon v. Jones*, 196 S.W.3d 376, 386 (Tex.App.—Houston [1st Dist.] 2006, no pet.); *M&M Constr. Co. v. Great Am. Ins.*, 747 S.W.2d 552, 555 (Tex.App.—Corpus Christi 1988, no writ). The trial court cannot dismiss a lawsuit immediately after granting the motion to abate; it must give the party whose pleadings were attacked the opportunity to amend to cure the defect. *Martin v. Dosohs I, Ltd.*, 2 S.W.3d 350, 354 (Tex.App.—San Antonio 1999, pet. denied); *Lighthouse Ch. v. Texas Bank*, 889 S.W.2d 595, 600 (Tex.App.—Houston [14th Dist.] 1994, writ denied); *Polk v. Braddock*, 864 S.W.2d 78, 80 (Tex.App.—Dallas 1992, no writ).

§8. REVIEW

§8.1 Interlocutory appeal.

1. Most orders. Generally, there is no interlocutory appeal from rulings on a motion to abate. *See* CPRC §51.014(a); *Serrano v. Union Planter's Bank*, 155 S.W.3d 381, 382 (Tex.App.—El Paso 2004, no pet.).

2. Order denying arbitration. An order denying a motion to abate for arbitration in a suit that is subject to the Texas Arbitration Act can be appealed before final judgment. See "Order denying motion," ch. 4-C, §8.3.1(1)(a), p. 299.

§8.2 Appeal after final judgment.
In most cases, the order on a motion to abate is reviewable on appeal only after the case is terminated by a final judgment. *Johnson v. Avery*, 414 S.W.2d 441, 443 (Tex.1966); *see also Wyatt v. Shaw Plumbing Co.*, 760 S.W.2d 245, 248 (Tex.1988) (Supreme Court reversed judgment from Nueces County court, which denied D's plea in abatement, with instructions to abate until after suit was completed in Duval County).

1. Standard of review. On appeal, the standard of review on a motion to abate is for abuse of discretion. *Dolenz v. Continental Nat'l Bank*, 620 S.W.2d 572, 575 (Tex.1981); *Dahl v. Hartman*, 14 S.W.3d 434, 436 (Tex. App.—Houston [14th Dist.] 2000, pet. denied).

2. Record. To properly present an allegation that the trial court erred in its ruling on a motion to abate, the complaining party must give the court of appeals a record of the hearing on the motion. *4M Linen & Unif. Sup. v. W.P. Ballard & Co.*, 793 S.W.2d 320, 322-23 (Tex.App.—Houston [1st Dist.] 1990, writ denied). The reporter's record must contain the evidence from the hearing on the motion to abate and from the trial. *See Hartley v. Coker*, 843 S.W.2d 743, 748 (Tex.App.—Corpus Christi 1992, no writ).

§8.3 Mandamus.
The appellate courts have granted mandamus to review abatement orders in the following situations: • The trial court abated the case indefinitely. *Gebhardt v. Gallardo*, 891 S.W.2d 327, 333 (Tex. App.—San Antonio 1995, orig. proceeding). • The trial court refused to acknowledge another court's ruling on an abatement and interfered with that court's jurisdiction. *Hall v. Lawlis*, 907 S.W.2d 493, 494 (Tex.1995); *Abor v. Black*, 695 S.W.2d 564, 567 (Tex.1985); *Curtis v. Gibbs*, 511 S.W.2d 263, 267 (Tex.1974); *see In re Mendoza*, 83 S.W.3d 233, 236 (Tex.App.—Corpus Christi 2002, orig. proceeding). • The trial court sustained a plea in abatement that suspended the suit, but no other court was willing to go forward. *Trapnell v. Hunter*, 785 S.W.2d 426, 429 (Tex.App.—Corpus Christi 1990, orig. proceeding); *see In re Sims*, 88 S.W.3d 297, 306 (Tex.App.—San Antonio 2002, orig. proceeding) (by granting plea in abatement, court effectively refused to proceed to trial). • The plaintiff did not give notice of the claim before suit was filed as required by statute. *Hines v. Hash*, 843 S.W.2d 464, 469 (Tex.1992) (DTPA); *In re Kimball Hill Homes*, 969 S.W.2d 522, 526-27 (Tex.App.—Houston [14th Dist.] 1998, orig. proceeding) (Residential Construction Liability Act); *Permanente Med. Ass'n v. Johnson*, 917 S.W.2d 515, 517 (Tex.App.—Waco 1996, orig. proceeding) (medical malpractice).

⋆

J. MOTION TO QUASH—CHALLENGING THE SERVICE

§1. GENERAL

PRACTICE TIP

A defendant should avoid filing a motion to quash service. The benefit of a motion to quash (the delayed date for answering) is greatly outweighed by the risk of filing a late answer and having a default judgment rendered.

---

§1.1 Rule. TRCP 122.

§1.2 Purpose. A motion to quash is used to challenge defects in the citation or the service of process. *Kawasaki Steel Corp. v. Middleton*, 699 S.W.2d 199, 203 (Tex.1985); *Texas DPS v. Kreipe*, 29 S.W.3d 334, 336 (Tex.App.—Houston [14th Dist.] 2000, pet. denied). A successful motion to quash service merely delays the date when the defendant must answer the plaintiff's suit. *Kawasaki*, 699 S.W.2d at 202; *Kreipe*, 29 S.W.3d at 336; *see* TRCP 122. The motion to quash service is like the motion to abate in that it delays but does not end the suit. But a motion to quash cannot be used to challenge the court's jurisdiction over the defendant. *See Wheat v. Toone*, 700 S.W.2d 915, 915 (Tex.1985); *Kawasaki*, 699 S.W.2d at 202-03. In fact, because a party makes a general appearance when it files a motion to quash, the motion actually confers jurisdiction. *Onda Enters. v. Pierce*, 750 S.W.2d 812, 814 (Tex.App.—Tyler 1988, orig. proceeding).

CAUTION

The Corpus Christi Court of Appeals, relying on **Kawasaki***, said in dicta that a defendant should challenge inadequate allegations of personal jurisdiction by a motion to quash.* **Exito Elecs. Co. v. Trejo***, 99 S.W.3d 360, 367 (Tex.App.—Corpus Christi 2003), rev'd in part on other grounds, 142 S.W.3d 302 (Tex.2004). Until the Supreme Court clarifies the issue, a party should not challenge inadequate allegations of personal jurisdiction by a motion to quash. By doing so, the defendant subjects itself to the court's jurisdiction. See TRCP 122.* **Kawasaki** *does not support the dicta in* **Exito***. The only jurisdictional defect discussed in* **Kawasaki** *was the failure to bring a suit under the correct statute. See* **Kawasaki***, 699 S.W.2d at 202 ("an attempt to bring the defendant before the court under the wrong statute does not authorize the use of the special appearance" (quoting Thode, In Personam Jurisdiction, 42 Tex.L.Rev. 279, 312 (1964))).*

---

§1.3 Forms. None.

§2. MOTION TO QUASH

A defendant may challenge defective service of citation with a motion to quash or a motion for new trial, depending on whether a no-answer default judgment was rendered.

§2.1 Motion to quash – no default judgment.

1. Resident defendant. If, before filing an answer, a defendant discovers that service of process was defective, the defendant may file a motion to quash service. *See Onda Enters. v. Pierce*, 750 S.W.2d 812, 814 (Tex.App.—Tyler 1988, orig. proceeding). The effect of the motion to quash is to make an appearance before the court and, when the motion is granted, to delay the filing of the answer. *Alcala v. Williams*, 908 S.W.2d 54, 56 (Tex.App.—San Antonio 1995, no writ); *see Allright, Inc. v. Roper*, 478 S.W.2d 245, 247-48 (Tex.App.—Houston [14th Dist.] 1972, writ dism'd).

2. Nonresident defendant. A nonresident defendant who intends to challenge personal jurisdiction should not file a motion to quash. *See, e.g., Onda Enters.*, 750 S.W.2d at 814 (D should have filed special appearance, not motion to quash). A special appearance is the correct motion to challenge personal jurisdiction. If the defendant alternatively contends that service of process was technically defective, it should file a motion to quash after it files the special appearance. See "Ruling," ch. 3-B, §9, p. 201.

★

§2.2 Motion for new trial after default judgment. Once a no-answer default judgment is rendered, any challenge to service can be made in a motion for new trial, with affidavits attached proving defective service. See "MNT After Default Judgment," ch. 10-B, §9, p. 795. A motion for new trial must be filed within 30 days after the date of the default judgment. TRCP 329b(a). If the court grants the motion for new trial, the defendant will have additional time to answer, counting from the date of the ruling on the motion for new trial. See "Time to answer," §4.2.1, this page. If the court denies the motion for new trial, the defendant should perfect its appeal.

    1. Resident defendant. If a resident defendant discovers that the service of process was defective after a no-answer default judgment was rendered but before the deadline to file a motion for new trial has expired, the defendant should file a motion for new trial to challenge service. See "Improper service + no-answer default," ch. 10-B, §9.1.1, p. 795.

    2. Nonresident defendant. If a nonresident defendant discovers that the service of process was defective after a no-answer default judgment was rendered but before the deadline to file a motion for new trial has expired, the defendant should first file a special appearance (alleging no personal jurisdiction) and then a motion for new trial (alleging defective service). See TRCP 120a(1); *see, e.g.*, **Puri v. Mansukhani**, 973 S.W.2d 701, 707 (Tex. App.—Houston [14th Dist.] 1998, no pet.) (D filed motion for new trial subject to special appearance); *see also* **Koch Graphics, Inc. v. Avantech, Inc.**, 803 S.W.2d 432, 433 (Tex.App.—Dallas 1991, no writ) (D filed special appearance and then filed motion to quash, motion for new trial, and answer, all subject to special appearance). The defendant must request a ruling on the special appearance before a ruling on the motion for new trial. **Landry v. Daigrepont**, 35 S.W.3d 265, 267 (Tex.App.—Corpus Christi 2000, no pet.). See "Due order of pleading," ch. 3-B, §2.2, p. 189.

§3. RESPONSE

In most cases, the plaintiff should not contest the defendant's motion to quash service and should encourage the trial court to grant the motion and see if the defendant files an answer as required. If the defendant does not file an answer by the new answer date, the plaintiff may take a default judgment. TRCP 122; **Kawasaki Steel Corp. v. Middleton**, 699 S.W.2d 199, 202 (Tex.1985).

§4. ORDER

§4.1 Court denies motion. If the court denies the motion to quash, the time for the defendant to file its answer is not extended.

§4.2 Court grants motion.

    1. Time to answer. If the court grants the defendant's motion to quash or a motion for new trial challenging service, the defendant must file an answer on the first Monday after the expiration of 20 days from the date of the order. TRCP 122; *see* **Kawasaki Steel Corp. v. Middleton**, 699 S.W.2d 199, 202 (Tex.1985) (remedy for defective service is additional time to answer). The plaintiff is not required to re-serve the defendant. **Boreham v. Hartsell**, 826 S.W.2d 193, 197 (Tex.App.—Dallas 1992, no writ); *see* **Allright, Inc. v. Roper**, 478 S.W.2d 245, 248 (Tex. App.—Houston [14th Dist.] 1972, writ dism'd). The defendant is deemed served when the trial court quashes the service or citation. TRCP 122.

    2. No dismissal. The court will not grant a motion to dismiss after granting a motion to quash. **Texas DPS v. Kreipe**, 29 S.W.3d 334, 336 (Tex.App.—Houston [14th Dist.] 2000, pet. denied); *see* TRCP 122; **Kawasaki**, 699 S.W.2d at 202.

§5. REVIEW

If the trial court denies the motion to quash, the defendant can appeal that order after a final judgment. If the appellate court decides the trial court erred in denying the motion to quash, the appellate court will reverse the judgment and remand the case to the trial court, which will give the defendant additional time to answer the suit. **Boreham v. Hartsell**, 826 S.W.2d 193, 197 (Tex.App.—Dallas 1992, no writ). On remand, the plaintiff does not need to reissue service. *Id.*

★

K. MOTION TO DISMISS—ANTI-SLAPP MOTION

§1. GENERAL

§1.1 Rules. CPRC ch. 27.

§1.2 Purpose. A motion to dismiss under CPRC chapter 27 is used (1) to encourage and safeguard the constitutional rights of a person to petition, speak and associate freely, and otherwise participate in government as permitted by law and (2) to protect the rights of a person to file a meritorious lawsuit for a demonstrable injury. CPRC §27.002. A cause of action that attempts to infringe on a person's right to petition or to speak or associate freely is referred to as a "SLAPP" action (strategic lawsuit against public participation). Senate Cmte. on State Affairs, Bill Analysis, Tex. H.B. 2973, 82nd Leg., R.S. (2011). The motion to dismiss such an action—generally referred to as an "anti-SLAPP" motion—was created by the Legislature through the Citizen Participation Act and is designed to protect defendants by allowing them to have cases dismissed sooner than they previously could. *Id.* CPRC chapter 27 does not abrogate or lessen any other defense, remedy, immunity, or privilege available under other constitutional, statutory, case, common-law, or rule provisions. CPRC §27.011(a).

NOTE

Texas joins the District of Columbia and 27 other states, including California, in adopting an anti-SLAPP law. Senate Cmte. on State Affairs, Bill Analysis, Tex. H.B. 2973, 82nd Leg., R.S. (2011); see **Jennings v. Wallbuilder Presentations, Inc.,** *___ S.W.3d ___ n.1 (Tex.App.—Fort Worth 2012, no pet.) (No. 02-12-00047-CV; 8-16-12). See* **O'Connor's California Practice * Civil Pretrial** *(2012), "Special Motion to Strike—Anti-SLAPP Motion," ch. 4-K, p. 421. CPRC chapter 27 is effective for legal actions filed on or after June 17, 2011; legal actions filed before June 17, 2011, are governed by the law in effect before that date. See Acts 2011, 82nd Leg., R.S., ch. 341, §§3, 4, eff. June 17, 2011. For the definition of a "legal action," see "Legal action," §2.1, p. 267.*

---

§1.3 Forms. See *O'Connor's Texas Civil Forms* (2012), FORMS 3J.

§1.4 Other references. Walker & Mirazo, *The Texas Anti-SLAPP Statute: Issues for Business Tort Litigation*, State Bar of Texas Webcast (May 22, 2012); *O'Connor's California Practice * Civil Pretrial* (2012) (*O'Connor's Cal. Civil Pretrial*); *O'Connor's Texas Causes of Action* (2013) (*O'Connor's Texas COA*); *O'Connor's Texas Civil Appeals* (2012) (*O'Connor's Texas Appeals*).

§2. DEFENDANT'S BURDEN

To prevail on an anti-SLAPP motion, the defendant must show by a preponderance of the evidence that the plaintiff's legal action is based on, related to, or in response to the defendant's exercise of (1) the right of free speech, (2) the right to petition, or (3) the right of association. CPRC §27.005(b). See "Protected acts," §2.3, p. 267; "Contents," §3.4, p. 269. Once the defendant has made the required showing, the burden shifts to the plaintiff to establish by clear and specific evidence a prima facie case for each essential element of its claim. CPRC §27.005(c). See "Response," §4, p. 269.

NOTE

Generally, a defendant files an anti-SLAPP motion in response to a plaintiff's legal action. See CPRC §27.003(a); Senate Cmte. on State Affairs, Bill Analysis, Tex. H.B. 2973, 82nd Leg., R.S. (2011). But because a legal action can be a cross-claim or counterclaim from the defendant, the original plaintiff could also file an anti-SLAPP motion. See "Legal action," §2.1, p. 267. In this subchapter, we use "defendant" to refer to the party who files an anti-SLAPP motion and "plaintiff" to refer to the party who files the legal action.

━━━━━━━━━━━━━━━━━━ ✦ ━━━━━━━━━━━━━━━━━━

§2.1 Legal action. To meet its burden under the anti-SLAPP statute, the defendant must show it is seeking to dismiss a legal action. *See* CPRC §27.003(a).

1. What is included. A "legal action" includes any of the following: (1) a lawsuit, (2) a cause of action, (3) a petition, (4) a complaint, (5) a cross-claim, (6) a counterclaim, or (7) any other judicial pleading or filing that requests legal or equitable relief. CPRC §27.001(6).

2. What is excluded. A "legal action" does not include any of the following:

(1) Enforcement action. An enforcement action brought in the name of the State of Texas or a political subdivision of the State by the Attorney General, a district attorney, a criminal district attorney, or a county attorney. CPRC §27.010(a).

(2) Commercial-speech action. A legal action involving commercial speech if the following are true:

(a) D engaged in business. The action is against a defendant primarily engaged in the business of selling or leasing goods or services. CPRC §27.010(b).

(b) Statement or conduct. The action is based on, related to, or in response to the defendant's statement or conduct that (1) arises from the sale or lease of goods, services, or an insurance product or from a commercial transaction and (2) is intended to reach an actual or potential buyer or customer. CPRC §27.010(b).

(3) Action to recover for bodily injury, wrongful death, or survival. A legal action seeking recovery for bodily injury, wrongful death, or survival. CPRC §27.010(c). Similarly, statements about a legal action seeking recovery for bodily injury, wrongful death, or survival are not protected under the statute. *Id.*

§2.2 Legal action based on, related to, or in response to protected act. To meet its burden under the anti-SLAPP statute, the defendant must show the legal action is based on, related to, or in response to the defendant's exercise of its right of free speech, right to petition, or right of association. CPRC §27.003(a); *see id.* §27.005(b).

§2.3 Protected acts. To meet its burden under the anti-SLAPP statute, the defendant must show that the plaintiff's legal action alleges acts that were protected by the defendant's constitutional right of free speech, right to petition, or right of association. CPRC §27.005(b); *see id.* §27.003(a).

1. Right of free speech. A communication made in connection with a matter of public concern is an act protected by the right of free speech. CPRC §27.001(3).

(1) Communication. A communication is the making or submission of a statement or document in any form or medium, including oral, visual, written, audiovisual, or electronic. CPRC §27.001(1).

(2) Public concern. A matter of public concern includes an issue related to (1) health or safety, (2) environmental, economic, or community well-being, (3) the government, (4) a public official or figure, or (5) a good, product, or service in the marketplace. CPRC §27.001(7).

2. Right to petition. The following types of communication are acts protected by the right to petition. For the definition of a "communication," see "Communication," §2.3.1(1), this page.

(1) A communication in or about one of the following:

(a) A judicial proceeding. CPRC §27.001(4)(A)(i).

(b) An official proceeding, other than a judicial proceeding, to administer the law. *Id.* §27.001(4)(A)(ii). An official proceeding is any type of administrative, executive, legislative, or judicial proceeding that may be conducted before a public servant. *Id.* §27.001(8). A public servant is a person elected, selected, appointed, employed, or otherwise designated as one of the following, even if the person has not yet qualified for office or assumed her duties: (1) an officer, employee, or agent of government, (2) a juror, (3) an arbitrator, referee, or other

━━━━━━━━━━━━━━━ ✦ ━━━━━━━━━━━━━━━

person who is authorized by law or private written agreement to hear or determine a cause or controversy, (4) an attorney or notary public when participating in the performance of a governmental function, or (5) a person who is performing a governmental function under a claim of right but is not legally qualified to do so. *Id.* §27.001(9).

(c)　An executive or other proceeding before a department or subdivision of the state or federal government. *Id.* §27.001(4)(A)(iii).

(d)　A legislative proceeding, including a proceeding of a legislative committee. *Id.* §27.001(4)(A)(iv).

(e)　A proceeding before an entity that requires by rule that public notice be given before its proceedings. *Id.* §27.001(4)(A)(v).

(f)　A proceeding in or before a managing board of an educational or nonprofit institution supported directly or indirectly by public revenue. *Id.* §27.001(4)(A)(vi).

(g)　A proceeding of the governing body of any political subdivision of the State. *Id.* §27.001(4)(A)(vii).

(h)　A report of or debate and statements made in (1) an executive or other proceeding before a department or subdivision of the state or federal government, (2) a legislative proceeding, including a proceeding of a legislative committee, (3) a proceeding before an entity that requires by rule that public notice be given before its proceedings, (4) a proceeding in or before a managing board of an educational or nonprofit institution supported directly or indirectly by public revenue, or (5) a proceeding of the governing body of any political subdivision of the State. *Id.* §27.001(4)(A)(viii).

(i)　A public meeting dealing with a public purpose, including statements and discussions at the meeting or other matters of public concern occurring at the meeting. *Id.* §27.001(4)(A)(ix). For the definition of "matters of public concern," see "Public concern," §2.3.1(2), p. 267.

(2)　A communication in connection with an issue under consideration or review by a legislative, executive, judicial, or other governmental body or in another governmental or official proceeding. CPRC §27.001(4)(B). A governmental proceeding is a proceeding, other than a judicial proceeding, by (1) an officer, official, or body of the State of Texas or a political subdivision of the State, including a board or commission, or (2) an officer, official, or body of the federal government. *Id.* §27.001(5). For the definition of an "official proceeding," see "Right to petition," §2.3.2(1)(b), p. 267.

(3)　A communication reasonably likely to encourage consideration or review of an issue by a legislative, executive, judicial, or other governmental body or in another governmental or official proceeding. CPRC §27.001(4)(C). For the definition of an "official proceeding," see "Right to petition," §2.3.2(1)(b), p. 267; for the definition of a "governmental proceeding," see "Right to petition," §2.3.2(2), this page.

(4)　A communication reasonably likely to secure public participation in an attempt to effect consideration of an issue by a legislative, executive, judicial, or other governmental body or in another governmental or official proceeding. CPRC §27.001(4)(D). For the definition of an "official proceeding," see "Right to petition," §2.3.2(1)(b), p. 267; for the definition of a "governmental proceeding," see "Right to petition," §2.3.2(2), this page.

(5)　Any other communication that falls within the protection of the right to petition government under the U.S. or Texas Constitution. CPRC §27.001(4)(E).

3. Right of association. A communication between individuals who join together to collectively express, promote, pursue, or defend common interests is an act protected by the right of association. CPRC §27.001(2). For the definition of a "communication," see "Communication," §2.3.1(1), p. 267.

§3. MOTION

§3.1　Who can file. Any person against whom a legal action was filed—if the action was based on, related to, or in response to the person's exercise of its right of free speech, right to petition, or right of association—can file an anti-SLAPP motion. CPRC §27.003(a); *see also* Gov't Code §311.005(2) ("person" can include legal entity). See *O'Connor's Texas Forms*, FORM 3J:1.

★

---

§3.2 Deadline to file & serve.

1. Deadline to file. The anti-SLAPP motion must be filed within 60 days after service of the legal action. CPRC §27.003(b). See "Computing Filing Deadlines," ch. 1-C, §7, p. 26. The court may extend the deadline if the defendant shows good cause. CPRC §27.003(b). See "Motion to extend time," ch. 1-C, §9.1, p. 30.

2. Deadline to serve. CPRC chapter 27 does not specify when to serve the anti-SLAPP motion. Thus, a defendant should serve the motion before the deadline established by TRCP 21, which is at least three days before the hearing, or before the deadline established by a court order. See "When to Serve," ch. 1-D, §5, p. 36.

§3.3 Deadline for hearing.
The hearing on the anti-SLAPP motion must be set within 30 days after service of the motion unless the court's docket conditions require a later hearing. CPRC §27.004. See "Hearing on Motion," ch. 1-E, §4, p. 41.

§3.4 Contents.

1. Grounds. The defendant must show by a preponderance of the evidence that the legal action is based on, related to, or in response to the defendant's exercise of its right of free speech, right to petition, or right of association. CPRC §27.005(b). See "Defendant's Burden," §2, p. 266.

2. Supporting evidence. The motion should be supported by admissible evidence in the form of pleadings and affidavits stating the facts on which the defense is based. CPRC §27.006(a). See "Verification & affidavits," ch. 1-B, §4.1.12, p. 20.

3. Request for attorney fees & costs. The defendant can request attorney fees and costs for bringing the anti-SLAPP motion. CPRC §27.009(a)(1). See "Proof of attorney fees," ch. 1-H, §10.4, p. 66; *O'Connor's Texas COA*, "General Concepts," ch. 45-A, p. 1349.

4. Request for sanctions. The defendant can request sanctions against the plaintiff to deter the plaintiff from bringing similar actions. CPRC §27.009(a)(2). See "Motion for Sanctions," ch. 5-K, p. 377.

§3.5 Effect of motion on discovery.
The filing of an anti-SLAPP motion stays all discovery proceedings. CPRC §27.003(c). The discovery stay remains in effect until the court has granted or denied the anti-SLAPP motion. *Id.* The court, on its own initiative or on a party's motion and for good cause shown, can order that specified and limited discovery relevant to the anti-SLAPP motion be conducted during the stay. *Id.* §27.006(b). See "Motion to conduct discovery," §4.1, this page.

§4. RESPONSE

§4.1 Motion to conduct discovery.
The plaintiff can respond to the anti-SLAPP motion by filing a motion asking the court to allow it to conduct discovery if discovery is necessary to oppose the anti-SLAPP motion. *See* CPRC §27.006(b). See *O'Connor's Texas Forms*, FORM 3J:2.

NOTE

If discovery cannot be completed before the hearing on the anti-SLAPP motion, the plaintiff may file a motion to continue the hearing. See "Continuance for Additional Discovery," ch. 5-D, §8, p. 338. There is no authority, however, in CPRC chapter 27 for filing a motion for continuance. Because a motion for continuance may contravene the purpose of filing an anti-SLAPP motion—that is, to have cases dismissed sooner and in a more cost-effective manner than they typically would be—a motion for continuance is unlikely to be granted. See "Purpose," §1.2, p. 266.

---

1. Deadline to file & serve. CPRC chapter 27 does not specify when to file and serve the motion to conduct discovery. Because the hearing on the anti-SLAPP motion must be set within 30 days after service of the motion, the plaintiff should file and serve the motion to conduct discovery as soon as possible after the anti-SLAPP motion is served, unless local rules or a court order specify otherwise. *See* CPRC §27.004. See "When to File," ch. 1-C, §5, p. 25; "When to Serve," ch. 1-D, §5, p. 36.

2. Grounds. The plaintiff must show good cause to conduct discovery. CPRC §27.006(b).

★

§4.2 Response to anti-SLAPP motion. The plaintiff can oppose an anti-SLAPP motion by filing a response. *See* CPRC §27.005(c). See *O'Connor's Texas Forms*, FORM 3J:3.

1. Deadline to file & serve. CPRC chapter 27 does not specify when to file and serve the response. Because the hearing on the anti-SLAPP motion must be set within 30 days after service of the motion, the plaintiff should file and serve the response as soon as possible after the anti-SLAPP motion is served, unless local rules or a court order specify otherwise. *See* CPRC §27.004. See "When to File," ch. 1-C, §5, p. 25; "When to Serve," ch. 1-D, §5, p. 36.

2. Contents.

(1) Grounds.

NOTE

The plaintiff may be able to oppose the anti-SLAPP motion on the ground that the defendant waived its right to anti-SLAPP protection. For example, a defendant may waive its right by contractually agreeing not to speak or petition on an issue.

(a) Procedural defect. The plaintiff can oppose the anti-SLAPP motion on the ground that the motion was not timely filed and served. *See* CPRC §27.003(b).

(b) Evidentiary objection. The plaintiff can oppose the anti-SLAPP motion on the ground that some or all of the evidence submitted in support of the motion was inadmissible. *See* CPRC §27.006(a). See "Objecting to Evidence," ch. 8-D, p. 708.

(c) Legal action is exempt. The plaintiff can oppose the anti-SLAPP motion on the ground that the challenged legal action is exempt from the anti-SLAPP statute. *See* CPRC §27.010. See "What is excluded," §2.1.2, p. 267.

(d) No preponderance of evidence. The plaintiff can oppose the anti-SLAPP motion on the ground that the defendant did not meet the required burden of a preponderance of the evidence. *See* CPRC §27.005(b).

[1] D's act not protected. The plaintiff can argue that the defendant has not shown that its act is protected under the anti-SLAPP statute because the act did not involve the defendant's exercise of its right of free speech, right to petition, or right of association. *See* CPRC §27.005(b). See "Protected acts," §2.3, p. 267.

[2] P's legal action not based on, related to, or in response to protected act. The plaintiff can argue that the defendant has not shown that the challenged legal action is based on, related to, or in response to a protected act. *See* CPRC §27.003(a). See "Legal action based on, related to, or in response to protected act," §2.2, p. 267.

(e) Prima facie showing. The plaintiff can oppose the anti-SLAPP motion, even if the defendant met its initial burden, on the ground that the plaintiff can establish by clear and specific evidence a prima facie case for each essential element of the challenged claim. CPRC §27.005(b), (c) Prima facie evidence is evidence that, until its effect is overcome by contrary evidence, will suffice as proof of a fact in issue. ***Dodson v. Watson***, 220 S.W. 771, 772 (Tex.1920); ***Duncan v. Butterowe, Inc.***, 474 S.W.2d 619, 621 (Tex.App.—Houston [14th Dist.] 1971, no writ).

(2) Supporting evidence. The response should be supported by admissible evidence in the form of pleadings and affidavits stating the facts on which the defendant's liability is based. CPRC §27.006(a). See "Verification & affidavits," ch. 1-B, §4.1.12, p. 20.

NOTE

Although CPRC §27.005(c) only requires the plaintiff to make a prima facie showing that its challenged claim has merit to defeat a motion to dismiss, CPRC §27.006(a) also requires the court to consider any defenses to the legal action in determining whether to dismiss the claim. See "Pleadings & affidavits," §5.2.1, p. 271. Thus, the plaintiff should also provide supporting evidence to negate those defenses raised by the defendant.

⭐

(3) Request for costs & reasonable attorney fees. The plaintiff can argue that the anti-SLAPP motion is frivolous or solely intended to cause unnecessary delay and request that the plaintiff be awarded costs and reasonable attorney fees. CPRC §27.009(b). The plaintiff should support its request with sufficient evidence establishing the amount of attorney fees and costs incurred in making the response. See "Proof of attorney fees," ch. 1-H, §10.4, p. 66; *O'Connor's Texas COA*, "General Concepts," ch. 45-A, p. 1349.

§4.3 Amended petition. Although not explicitly provided for in CPRC chapter 27, a plaintiff may be able to respond to an anti-SLAPP motion by filing an amended petition. *Cf. Verizon Del., Inc. v. Covad Comms.*, 377 F.3d 1081, 1091 (9th Cir.2004) (granting anti-SLAPP motion without allowing P leave to amend would directly conflict with FRCP 15(a)). See "Motion to Amend Pleadings—Pretrial," ch. 5-F, p. 350.

NOTE

In California, filing an amended complaint before the hearing does not make the anti-SLAPP motion moot; the court can still award attorney fees and costs to the defendant based on the allegations in the original complaint. See O'Connor's Cal. Civil Pretrial, "Amending complaint," ch. 4-K, §4.2, p. 433.

---

§4.4 Voluntary dismissal. A plaintiff may be able to respond to an anti-SLAPP motion by filing a voluntary dismissal. See "Voluntary Dismissal—Nonsuit," ch. 7-F, p. 650. But the plaintiff may still be liable for attorney fees and costs and may be subject to sanctions. See "Contents," §3.4, p. 269; "Effect on sanctions," ch. 7-F, §6.7, p. 656. To avoid liability on an anti-SLAPP motion after a voluntary dismissal in California, the plaintiff must obtain a voluntary waiver of fees and costs from the defendant. See *O'Connor's Cal. Civil Pretrial*, "Voluntary dismissal," ch. 4-K, §4.3, p. 434.

§5. HEARING

§5.1 Deadline. The hearing on the anti-SLAPP motion must be set within 30 days after service of the motion unless the court's docket conditions require a later hearing. CPRC §27.004. See "Hearing on Motion," ch. 1-E, §4, p. 41.

§5.2 Evidence.

1. Pleadings & affidavits. The court must consider admissible evidence in the form of pleadings and supporting affidavits stating the facts on which the liability or defense is based. CPRC §27.006(a).

2. Limited discovery. The court must consider any limited discovery relevant to the anti-SLAPP motion that the court allowed. CPRC §27.006(b). See "Effect of motion on discovery," §3.5, p. 269.

§6. RULING

In ruling on an anti-SLAPP motion, the court must construe CPRC chapter 27 liberally to fully effectuate its purpose and intent. CPRC §27.011(b).

§6.1 Deadline. The court must rule on an anti-SLAPP motion within 30 days after the hearing. CPRC §27.005(a); *see Jennings v. Wallbuilder Presentations, Inc.*, ___ S.W.3d ___ (Tex.App.—Fort Worth 2012, no pet.) (No. 02-12-00047-CV; 8-16-12). If the court does not rule within 30 days, the motion is considered denied by operation of law and the defendant may appeal. CPRC §27.008(a). See "Appellate Review," §9, p. 272.

§6.2 Court's determination. In ruling on an anti-SLAPP motion, the court applies a two-step analysis. *See* CPRC §27.005(b), (c).

1. Determine if D has met its burden. The court first determines if the defendant has shown by a preponderance of the evidence that the plaintiff's legal action is based on, related to, or in response to the defendant's exercise of its right of free speech, right to petition, or right of association. CPRC §27.005(b). See "Defendant's Burden," §2, p. 266. If the defendant has not met its burden, the court must deny the motion; if the defendant has met its burden, the court must then determine if the plaintiff has met its burden. *See* CPRC §27.005(b), (c).

2. Determine if P has met its burden. If the defendant has met its burden, the court must determine whether the plaintiff has established by clear and specific evidence a prima facie case for each essential element of its claim. CPRC §27.005(c). If the plaintiff has not met its burden, the court must grant the motion; if the plaintiff has met its burden, the court must deny the motion. *See id.* §27.005(b), (c).

§7. ORDER

§7.1 Motion denied. If the court denies the motion to dismiss, the discovery stay is lifted and the legal action will continue. *See* CPRC §27.003(c). See "Effect of motion on discovery," §3.5, p. 269. The court can award court costs and reasonable attorney fees to the plaintiff if the court finds that the motion to dismiss was frivolous or solely intended to delay. CPRC §27.009(b). See "Request for costs & reasonable attorney fees," §4.2.2(3), p. 271.

§7.2 Motion granted. If the court grants the motion, the legal action will be dismissed with prejudice. *See* CPRC §27.005(b). See "Effect of dismissal," ch. 7-G, §6.3, p. 662. When the legal action is dismissed, the court must (1) award the defendant court costs, reasonable attorney fees, and other expenses incurred in defending the legal action and (2) sanction the plaintiff sufficiently to deter it from bringing similar actions. CPRC §27.009(a). See "Contents," §3.4, p. 269.

PRACTICE TIP
*The defendant should draft the order to dismiss only the legal action and nothing else. See "Language of dismissal," ch. 7-G, §6.1, p. 661. See **O'Connor's Texas Forms**, FORM 3J:4.*

---

§8. ADDITIONAL FINDINGS

§8.1 Request. The defendant can request that the court issue findings that the legal action was brought to deter or prevent the defendant from exercising its constitutional rights and was brought for an improper purpose, including to harass, cause unnecessary delay, or increase the cost of litigation. CPRC §27.007(a).

§8.2 Deadline.

1. For defendant to make request. CPRC §27.007 does not specify a deadline for requesting additional findings. For the general deadline for requesting findings of fact, see "Requesting Findings of Fact," ch. 10-E, §3, p. 820.

2. For court to issue findings. The court must issue findings within 30 days after the request. CPRC §27.007(b).

§9. APPELLATE REVIEW

§9.1 Method of review. The method for appellate review of an order on an anti-SLAPP motion depends on whether the motion was granted or denied.

1. Granted – appeal after final judgment. If a court grants the anti-SLAPP motion, the order dismissing the case may be appealable as a final order that has disposed of all parties and claims. *Jennings v. Wallbuilder Presentations, Inc.*, ___ S.W.3d ___ (Tex.App.—Fort Worth 2012, no pet.) (No. 02-12-00047-CV; 8-16-12).

2. Denied by operation of law – interlocutory appeal. If the court does not timely rule on the anti-SLAPP motion and the motion is thus considered denied by operation of law, the defendant may file an interlocutory appeal. *Jennings*, ___ S.W.3d at ___; *see* CPRC §27.008(a). See "Deadline," §6.1, p. 271.

3. Denied.

(1) No interlocutory appeal. If the court denies the anti-SLAPP motion within 30 days after a timely hearing, the order denying the motion cannot be reviewed by interlocutory appeal. *Jennings*, ___ S.W.3d at ___.

★

NOTE

*The Fort Worth Court of Appeals recently held that based on the plain language of CPRC §27.008, an interlocutory appeal is permissible only in a limited situation—when an anti-SLAPP motion is denied by operation of law. See **Jennings**, ___ S.W.3d at ___. The court explained that relying on the plain language of the statute would not lead to absurd results for two reasons. Id. First, the statutory deadlines imposed indicated a legislative intent to avoid delays that an interlocutory appeal would create, except for cases in which the limited exception would apply. Id. Second, when a court denies an anti-SLAPP motion, the defendant may still be able to file a no-evidence summary-judgment motion based on the free-speech or free-press clause of the First Amendment to the U.S. Constitution, Texas Constitution article 1, §8, or CPRC chapter 73 (libel); if that motion is denied, the denial may be subject to an interlocutory appeal. See CPRC §51.014(a)(6); **Jennings**, ___ S.W.3d at ___. See **O'Connor's Texas Appeals**, "Denial of free-speech summary judgment," ch. 1-B, §2.3.1(5), p. 13.*

---

(2) Mandamus. If the court denies the anti-SLAPP motion but the plaintiff did not make a prima facie showing for each essential element of its claim, the order denying the motion may be reviewed on mandamus. *Jennings*, ___ S.W.3d at ___. See "Court's determination," §6.2, p. 271.

§9.2 Deadline. An appeal or other writ must be filed within 60 days after the court signs its order or, if the court does not rule, within 90 days after the date of the hearing. *See* CPRC §§27.005, 27.008(c).

§9.3 Expedited. An appeal or other writ, whether interlocutory or not, must be expedited by the appellate court. CPRC §27.008(b). The appeal or writ is expedited whether the trial court issues an order on a motion to dismiss or the motion is denied by operation of law. *Id.* See "Method of review," §9.1, p. 272.

CHAPTER 4

✦

---

4. ALTERNATIVE DISPUTE RESOLUTION

A. THE ADR SYSTEM

The alternative-dispute-resolution (ADR) system is a method of privatizing justice. The parties are taken out of the public justice system by agreement or by court order and are sent to resolve their dispute before a private tribunal.

§1. GENERAL

§1.1 Rules. None. See CPRC ch. 154.

§1.2 Purpose. The purpose of ADR is to encourage the peaceable resolution of civil disputes and the early settlement of litigation through voluntary settlement procedures. CPRC §154.002; *Keene Corp. v. Gardner*, 837 S.W.2d 224, 232 (Tex.App.—Dallas 1992, writ denied); *Downey v. Gregory*, 757 S.W.2d 524, 525 (Tex.App.—Houston [1st Dist.] 1988, orig. proceeding).

§1.3 Forms. *O'Connor's Texas Civil Forms* (2012), FORMS 4A-D.

§1.4 Other references. Evans & Wettman, *Managed Dispute Resolution: Designing a Dispute Resolution Process for Efficiency & Affordability*, Alternative Dispute Resolution Course, State Bar of Texas CLE, ch. 2.2 (2010); Levy & Prather, *Texas Practice Guide: ADR* (2011); Lopez, *Alternative Dispute Resolution*, 71 Tex.B.J. 36 (Jan.2008); Said, Comment, *The Mediator's Dilemma: The Legal Requirements Exception to Confidentiality Under the Texas ADR Statute*, 36 S.Tex.L.Rev. 579 (1995) (referred to as Said, *The Mediator's Dilemma*); Skinner, *Alternative Dispute Resolution Expands into Pre-Trial Practice: An Introduction to the Role of E-Neutrals*, 13 Cardozo J. Conflict Resolution 113 (2011); State Bar of Texas, *Alternative Dispute Resolution Handbook* (3d ed. 2003); Trachte-Huber & Huber, *Alternative Dispute Resolution: Strategies for Law & Business* (1996); *O'Connor's Family Law Handbook* (2013) (*O'Connor's Fam. Law Handbook*).

§2. TYPES OF ADR

§2.1 By agreement, motion, or order. The following types of ADR are available by agreement of the parties, by motion of one of the parties, or by order of the court.

   1. Mediation. Most cases referred to ADR are referred to mediation. Mediation is a nonbinding procedure in which an impartial person (the mediator) facilitates communication between the parties to promote reconciliation, settlement, or understanding. CPRC §154.023(a); *see Black's Law Dictionary* 1070 (9th ed. 2009). See "Mediation," ch. 4-B, p. 284; *O'Connor's Texas Forms*, FORMS 4B.

   2. Moderated settlement conference. A moderated settlement conference is a nonbinding procedure in which the case is submitted to a panel of impartial third parties for an evaluation of the case intended to lead to realistic settlement negotiations. CPRC §154.025(a), (b), (d). This procedure requires each party and its attorney to present the party's position before a panel of impartial third parties (often three attorneys). *Id.* §154.025(b). The parties may be asked to give the panel a written memorandum of the issues before the proceeding begins. The typical conference starts with an introduction from the panel and a presentation from each party. The panel will ask questions, and each party will get an opportunity to summarize its case. After the panel deliberates, it will issue a nonbinding advisory opinion on liability, damages, or both. *Id.* §154.025(c), (d). The opinion often takes the form of ranges based on the panel's experience with similar suits. See *O'Connor's Texas Forms*, FORMS 4A:1, 4A:5.

   3. Early neutral evaluation. Early neutral evaluation is a nonbinding procedure in which the case is submitted to an evaluator with expertise in the subject matter. *See* Lopez, *Alternative Dispute Resolution*, 71 Tex.B.J., at 36-37. The parties present summaries of their positions and evidence, possibly including witness testimony, to the evaluator while all parties are present. *Id.* The evaluator provides a written evaluation after questioning the parties. *Id.* at 36. The parties can have the evaluator present the evaluation to them, or they can engage in further settlement negotiations with the evaluator's assistance. *Id.* at 37. Any agreement the parties reach can be finalized

─────────────────────────── ✯ ───────────────────────────

in writing. *Id.* If the parties do not reach an agreement, the evaluator can help develop a plan for how to move forward in the case, including specifying the issues, identifying witnesses, and exchanging documentary evidence. *Id.*

4. Summary jury trial. A summary jury trial is a nonbinding procedure in which the case is submitted to a panel of jurors drawn from the county's jury pool. *See* Judge Brown, *The Summary Jury Trial: Perspectives of Bench and Bar*, Parts I & II, 38 Houston Lawyer 5, p. 32 (Mar.-Apr. 2001) and 38 Houston Lawyer 6, p. 16 (May-June 2001). The jury is not told that it is not providing a binding verdict. This procedure requires each party and its attorney to present the party's position before a panel of six jurors (unless the parties agree to a different number). CPRC §154.026(b), (c). After deliberations, the jury will issue a nonbinding advisory opinion on liability, damages, or both. *Id.* §154.026(d), (e). A summary jury trial uses a format similar to a regular jury trial, but the rules of procedure and evidence are relaxed. The supervising court will establish guidelines for voir dire, opening statements, summary of admissible evidence, closing arguments, jury deliberations, verdict, and final discussion. The final discussion takes place between the jurors and the parties outside the presence of the judge. See *O'Connor's Texas Forms*, FORMS 4A:1, 4A:6.

5. Arbitration. In arbitration, each party and its attorney present the party's position to an impartial third party or panel, who renders a specific award. *See* CPRC §154.027. See *O'Connor's Texas Forms*, FORMS 4A:1, 4A:7.

(1) Binding arbitration. There are three types of binding arbitration: (1) agreed, in which the parties agree to settle a particular dispute by binding arbitration, (2) contractual, in which the parties agree as part of a contract to refer all disputes to arbitration, and (3) statutory, in which a statute requires the parties to arbitrate their disputes instead of litigating them. *See* CPRC §154.027(b). See "Arbitration," ch. 4-C, p. 286; *O'Connor's Texas Forms*, FORMS 4C.

(2) Nonbinding arbitration. If the parties do not agree in advance that the award will be binding, the award will be nonbinding. CPRC §154.027(b). A nonbinding arbitration award is advisory only and provides the basis for further settlement negotiations between the parties. *Id.*

§2.2 By agreement only. The court can order the following types of ADR only when all parties agree to participate.

1. Minitrial. A minitrial is a nonbinding settlement procedure that uses several dispute-resolution processes. In a minitrial, each party and its attorney present the party's position to an impartial third party or to selected representatives of the parties. CPRC §154.024(b). The impartial third party may issue a nonbinding advisory opinion on the merits of the case. *Id.* §154.024(c), (d). The advisory opinion becomes binding if the parties agree and enter into a written settlement agreement. *Id.* §154.024(d). In most cases, the procedure for a minitrial is as follows: (1) each party makes an opening statement summarizing the facts and legal arguments, (2) each party has an opportunity to respond to the other parties' opening statements, (3) the parties are questioned by the impartial third party or the parties' selected representatives, (4) the parties negotiate, and, if necessary, (5) an advisory opinion is issued. See *O'Connor's Texas Forms*, FORMS 4A:8-9.

2. Special-judge trial. In a trial by a special judge, the parties try their case before a retired or former judge who is selected by the parties to hear the case. The procedure is described in CPRC chapter 151. See "Special Judge," ch. 4-D, p. 306; *O'Connor's Texas Forms*, FORMS 4D.

3. Expert panel. Many cases hinge on issues involving highly technical, scientific, medical, or other specialized concepts or theories that cannot be established without expert testimony. An expert panel provides an ADR forum in which one expert or a group of experts serves as a neutral third-party decision-maker to review and evaluate the merits of a case and make a determination based on the facts and evidence presented. *See* Kovach, *Mediation: Principles & Practice*, at 10. The expert determination may be either binding or advisory. *See id.* If the parties decide to be bound by the expert panel's opinions, the parties must agree in advance that the expert panel's evaluation of the issues presented is conclusive. *Id.* If the expert panel's opinion is merely advisory, the parties can agree that a trial court or subsequent decision-maker is free to reach new, independent conclusions about the evidence and that the expert panel's decision is not controlling. *See id.*

✦

4. Jury-determined settlement. Jury-determined settlement (JDS) combines the ADR procedures of a summary jury trial and arbitration into one proceeding. Kovach, *Mediation: Principles & Practice*, at 18. Under a JDS approach, a jury is impaneled and the trial moves forward like a summary jury trial. *Id.* The JDS participants retain some control over the outcome of the process by setting exposure limits through a high-low settlement agreement. *See id.* Once the JDS proceeding is completed, the jury does not render a verdict; instead, it issues a settlement decision that is binding on the JDS participants. *Id.*

5. Collaborative-law procedure. In suits for dissolution of marriage or suits affecting the parent-child relationship, the parties may agree to enter into a collaborative-law agreement. Collaborative-law agreements signed before September 1, 2011, are governed by Family Code §§6.603 and 153.0072. Acts 2011, 82nd Leg., R.S., ch. 1048, §§2-4, eff. Sept. 1, 2011. Collaborative-law agreements signed on or after September 1, 2011, are governed by Family Code chapter 15, which is the newly enacted Collaborative Family Law Act. Acts 2011, 82nd Leg., R.S., ch. 1048, §§1, 3, 4, eff. Sept. 1, 2011. For a detailed discussion of the Collaborative Family Law Act, see *O'Connor's Fam. Law Handbook*, "Collaborative law," ch. 3-A, §13.1.2, p. 235.

§3. REFERRAL PROCEDURES FOR ADR

§3.1 Procedure for proposing ADR.

1. By agreement. The parties may agree to submit a dispute to ADR.

(1) Presuit agreements. The parties may agree by contract to submit a dispute to ADR.

(2) Pretrial agreements. Once the parties are in litigation, they may agree to take all or part of the dispute out of litigation and submit it to another form of dispute resolution. *See Massey v. Galvan*, 822 S.W.2d 309, 318 (Tex.App.—Houston [14th Dist.] 1992, writ denied); *see, e.g.*, Fam. Code §153.0071(a) (parties can execute binding agreement to submit suit affecting parent-child relationship to arbitration or mediation). The ADR agreement should (1) be signed by the parties and their attorneys, (2) identify which part of the lawsuit is subject to the agreement, (3) state whether the ADR result is binding or nonbinding, and (4) be filed with the court.

2. On party's motion. A party may ask the court to refer the suit to ADR at any time during the trial or appellate process. *Downey v. Gregory*, 757 S.W.2d 524, 525 (Tex.App.—Houston [1st Dist.] 1988, orig. proceeding); *see* CPRC §154.021(a).

3. On court's motion. The court may, on its own initiative, refer a suit to ADR. CPRC §154.021(a); *Texas Parks & Wildlife Dept. v. Davis*, 988 S.W.2d 370, 375 (Tex.App.—Austin 1999, no pet.); *Decker v. Lindsay*, 824 S.W.2d 247, 250 (Tex.App.—Houston [1st Dist.] 1992, orig. proceeding); *see In re Acceptance Ins.*, 33 S.W.3d 443, 451 (Tex.App.—Fort Worth 2000, orig. proceeding). The court may refer a case to ADR at any time during the trial. *Downey*, 757 S.W.2d at 525. Even an appellate court can refer a case to ADR. *See, e.g.*, *In re Cassey D.*, 783 S.W.2d 592, 598 (Tex.App.—Houston [1st Dist.] 1990, no writ) (court of appeals referred case to ADR after reversing trial court's denial of visitation privileges to parent).

§3.2 Pre-referral issues for the court.

1. Considerations for referral. The court may consider several factors in deciding whether to refer a case to ADR, including (1) the nature of the dispute, (2) the complexity of the issues, (3) the number of parties, (4) the extent of past settlement discussions, (5) the positions of the parties, and (6) whether there has been sufficient discovery to permit an accurate evaluation of the case. *Walton v. Canon, Short & Gaston, P.C.*, 23 S.W.3d 143, 150 (Tex.App.—El Paso 2000, no pet.); *Downey v. Gregory*, 757 S.W.2d 524, 525 (Tex.App.—Houston [1st Dist.] 1988, orig. proceeding).

2. Consultation with parties. The court must "confer" with the parties to determine the most appropriate ADR procedure. CPRC §154.021(b). This does not mean the court must give the parties an oral hearing. *See Downey*, 757 S.W.2d at 525 (trial court may, but is not required to, hold a hearing before making a decision about referral to ADR). The court cannot order mediation in an action that is subject to the Federal Arbitration Act (FAA) unless the parties agree. CPRC §154.021(c).

———————————— ✦ ————————————

3. Notice of intent to refer. When the court decides that a case should go to ADR, it must notify the parties that it intends to send the case to ADR. CPRC §154.022(a). The trial court cannot require ADR without giving at least ten days' notice. *E.g.*, *Keene Corp. v. Gardner*, 837 S.W.2d 224, 232 (Tex.App.—Dallas 1992, writ denied) (24 hours' notice to mediate violated the statute); *see* CPRC §154.022(b).

§4. OBJECTING TO ADR

§4.1 Written. An objection to ADR must be in writing. CPRC §154.022(b). See *O'Connor's Texas Forms*, FORMS 4A:2, 4A:3. The objection should be verified if it includes any statement of facts outside the record.

§4.2 Deadline. To object to ADR, a party must file its objections within ten days after the referral. CPRC §154.022(b); *Keene Corp. v. Gardner*, 837 S.W.2d 224, 232 (Tex.App.—Dallas 1992, writ denied).

§4.3 Grounds. To avoid ADR, the objections must state a "reasonable basis." CPRC §154.022(c). Nothing in the ADR statute provides guidance for making objections that have a "reasonable basis." The following are some possible objections to a referral to ADR:

1. Too broad. A party should challenge the court's referral if the court's order is too broad and goes beyond the statute. *See In re Acceptance Ins.*, 33 S.W.3d 443, 451 (Tex.App.—Fort Worth 2000, orig. proceeding). For example, while a court may compel the parties to participate in mediation, it cannot compel them to negotiate in good faith or to settle their dispute. *Avary v. Bank of Am.*, 72 S.W.3d 779, 797 (Tex.App.—Dallas 2002, pet. denied); *In re Acceptance Ins.*, 33 S.W.3d at 451-52; *Texas Parks & Wildlife Dept. v. Davis*, 988 S.W.2d 370, 375 (Tex.App.—Austin 1999, no pet.); *see Decker v. Lindsay*, 824 S.W.2d 247, 251-52 (Tex.App.—Houston [1st Dist.] 1992, orig. proceeding).

2. No conference with parties. A party may challenge the court's referral if the court did not "confer" with the parties to determine the most appropriate ADR procedure, as required by CPRC §154.021(b). *See, e.g.*, *Decker*, 824 S.W.2d at 248-49 (parties did not object to lack of conference).

3. Less than 10 days' notice. A party may challenge the court's referral if the court did not give the parties at least ten days' notice of the referral. *Keene Corp. v. Gardner*, 837 S.W.2d 224, 232 (Tex.App.—Dallas 1992, writ denied).

4. Case not appropriate. A party may challenge the court's referral if the case is not appropriate for ADR. So far, challenges of this nature have not been successful. *See Decker*, 824 S.W.2d at 249-50 (not reasonable to object on grounds that mediation will not resolve lawsuit).

5. Other ADR procedure. After the court refers the case to ADR, a party may file a written proposal suggesting a more appropriate ADR procedure. *Paul v. Paul*, 870 S.W.2d 349, 350 (Tex.App.—Waco 1994, no writ).

6. Mediation order in FAA case. A party may challenge the court's referral if a case is subject to the FAA and the court ordered mediation without the parties' agreement. *See* CPRC §154.021(c).

7. Multiple referrals in same case. A party may challenge the court's referral if the case has already been submitted to ADR. Some trial courts repeatedly send the same case to ADR.

§5. ORDER FOR ADR

§5.1 Ruling on objection. If the trial court finds there is a reasonable basis for an objection, the court cannot refer the dispute to ADR. CPRC §154.022(c).

§5.2 Order. The court may require the parties to attend ADR; however, the court cannot compel the parties to negotiate in good faith because doing so violates the "open-courts" provision of the Texas Constitution. *Hansen v. Sullivan*, 886 S.W.2d 467, 469 (Tex.App.—Houston [1st Dist.] 1994, orig. proceeding). An order requiring good-faith negotiations is void. *In re Acceptance Ins.*, 33 S.W.3d 443, 452 (Tex.App.—Fort Worth 2000, orig. proceeding).

★

§5.3 ADR providers. Under CPRC §154.021(a), a court is authorized to refer a case to any of the following ADR providers:

1. County-sponsored ADR system. A county-sponsored ADR system established under CPRC chapter 152. CPRC §§152.002, 154.021(a)(1). An ADR system is an informal forum using mediation, conciliation, or non-binding arbitration to resolve disputes among individuals, entities, or governmental units. *Id.* §152.001. To establish and maintain an ADR system, each county has the authority to collect money, which may be taxed as a cost of suit (up to $15 per case). *Id.* §152.004(a). A county may contract with a private nonprofit corporation, a political subdivision, a public corporation, or any combination of these entities to establish a dispute-resolution center (DRC). *Id.* §152.002(b)(1). If the DRC is located in a county that borders the Gulf of Mexico with a population of 250,000 or more but less than 300,000, it may collect a reasonable fee from the person receiving the services in an amount set by the commissioners court. *Id.* §152.006. Management of the ADR system may be vested in a committee selected by the county bar association. *Id.* §152.002(b)(3). For example, in Harris County, the Harris County DRC is sponsored by the Houston Bar Association, www.co.harris.tx.us/drc/. For a list of DRCs in Texas and their contact information, see www.utexas.edu/law/centers/cppdr/resources/adr_drcs.php.

2. Dispute-resolution organization. A dispute-resolution organization, which is a private for-profit or nonprofit corporation, political subdivision, or public corporation that offers ADR services to the public. CPRC §§154.001(2), 154.021(a)(2).

3. Impartial third party. A nonjudicial and informally conducted forum for the voluntary settlement of citizens' disputes through the intervention of an impartial third party. CPRC §154.021(a)(3). See "Appointment of Impartial Third Party," §6, this page.

4. Other ADR providers. Any other ADR provider the court deems appropriate. *See* CPRC §154.021(a) (uses the term "including" before list of ADR providers).

§6. APPOINTMENT OF IMPARTIAL THIRD PARTY

If the court refers a dispute to ADR, the court may appoint one or more impartial third parties agreed on by the parties to facilitate the ADR. CPRC §154.051.

§6.1 Qualifications.

1. Generally. To qualify for appointment as an impartial third party, the person must have completed 40 classroom hours of training provided by an ADR system or other organization approved by the court. CPRC §154.052(a).

2. For parent-child disputes. To qualify for appointment in a dispute relating to the parent-child relationship, a person must have 24 hours of training in family dynamics, child development, and family law along with the 40 classroom hours of general ADR training. CPRC §154.052(b).

3. Exceptions. A court has the discretion to appoint a person who does not otherwise qualify, as long as the court bases its appointment on the person's legal or other professional training or experience. CPRC §154.052(c). For example, the court could appoint a former judge who has not satisfied the training requirement.

§6.2 Standards & duties. A person appointed as an impartial third party must encourage and assist the parties in reaching a settlement but cannot compel or coerce the parties to settle. CPRC §154.053(a). The third party's role is to facilitate communication between the parties, to encourage reconciliation, settlement, and understanding, and to avoid further litigation. *In re Marriage of Ames*, 860 S.W.2d 590, 592 (Tex.App.—Amarillo 1993, no writ). Impartial third parties cannot alter the agreement between the parties or interject their own terms into the agreement. *See In re Marriage of McIntosh*, 918 S.W.2d 87, 89 (Tex.App.—Amarillo 1996, no writ).

§6.3 Fees. The court may set a reasonable fee for the services of an impartial third party appointed to facilitate an ADR procedure. CPRC §154.054(a); *Decker v. Lindsay*, 824 S.W.2d 247, 249-50 (Tex.App.—Houston [1st Dist.] 1992, orig. proceeding). Unless otherwise agreed by the parties, the court must tax the fee as a cost of the suit. CPRC §154.054(b); *Paul v. Paul*, 870 S.W.2d 349, 350 (Tex.App.—Waco 1994, no writ).

✦

---

§7. CONFIDENTIALITY

Any communication about the subject matter of a dispute made by a participant in an ADR procedure is confidential, is not subject to disclosure, and cannot be used as evidence against the participant in any judicial or administrative proceeding. CPRC §154.073(a); *In re M.S.*, 115 S.W.3d 534, 543 (Tex.2003); *In re Cartwright*, 104 S.W.3d 706, 713-14 (Tex.App.—Houston [1st Dist.] 2003, orig. proceeding); *see* TRE 408 (evidence of statements in compromise negotiations is not admissible); *see, e.g.*, *Rabe v. Dillard's, Inc.*, 214 S.W.3d 767, 769 (Tex.App.—Dallas 2007, no pet.) (statement made by attorney during mediation was not competent summary-judgment evidence).

§7.1 No disclosure by impartial third party. The impartial third party cannot disclose the following:

1. To any party, the information given in confidence by the other party, unless authorized by the disclosing party. CPRC §154.053(b).

2. To any person, including the court, any matter relating to the settlement process, including the conduct and demeanor of the parties and their attorneys, unless the parties agree otherwise. CPRC §154.053(c); *see also In re Cartwright*, 104 S.W.3d 706, 714 (Tex.App.—Houston [1st Dist.] 2003, orig. proceeding) (improper for mediator to later serve as arbitrator of same or related dispute between same parties). Mediators generally cannot testify about the bargaining sessions they attend. *In re Anonymous*, 283 F.3d 627, 639-40 (4th Cir.2002); *NLRB v. Joseph Macaluso, Inc.*, 618 F.2d 51, 53 (9th Cir.1980). The complete exclusion of mediator testimony is necessary to preserve an effective system of mediation. *NLRB*, 618 F.2d at 56; *see also Wilson v. Attaway*, 757 F.2d 1227, 1245 (11th Cir.1985) (trial court did not abuse its discretion by refusing to admit report of community mediator who witnessed a riot).

§7.2 Confidential record. Any record made at an ADR procedure is confidential; the participants and the impartial third party cannot be required to testify in any proceeding relating to or arising from the matter in dispute and cannot be subject to process requiring disclosure of confidential information or data relating to or arising from the matter in dispute. CPRC §154.073(b).

§7.3 Exceptions. There are several exceptions to the general rule of confidentiality for communications made in an ADR procedure.

1. **Independently discoverable.** A communication made in an ADR procedure is discoverable and admissible if the same information is discoverable independently of the ADR procedure. CPRC §154.073(c); *In re Learjet Inc.*, 59 S.W.3d 842, 845 (Tex.App.—Texarkana 2001, orig. proceeding).

2. **Legal requirements for disclosure.** If CPRC §154.073 conflicts with other legal requirements for disclosure of communications or materials, the confidential information may be presented to the court for an in camera determination of whether it is discoverable. CPRC §154.073(e); *Avary v. Bank of Am.*, 72 S.W.3d 779, 796 (Tex. App.—Dallas 2002, pet. denied); *In re Acceptance Ins.*, 33 S.W.3d 443, 453 (Tex.App.—Fort Worth 2000, orig. proceeding); *see* Said, *The Mediator's Dilemma*, 36 S.Tex.L.Rev. at 586-87; *see also* TRE 408 (permits in-court disclosure of evidence of settlement if evidence is offered for another purpose listed in TRE 408).

3. **Report of abuse.** CPRC §154.073 does not affect the requirements for reporting abuse under Family Code chapter 261 or Human Resources Code chapter 48. CPRC §154.073(f).

4. **Unrelated to dispute.** When a communication does not relate to or arise from the subject matter of a dispute, it may not be confidential under CPRC §154.073(a) and (b). *Avary*, 72 S.W.3d at 794; *see, e.g.*, *In re Daley*, 29 S.W.3d 915, 918 (Tex.App.—Beaumont 2000, orig. proceeding) (deposition questions about whether participant attended mediation and whether he had permission to leave did not relate to subject matter of underlying suit and thus were not confidential).

§8. SANCTIONS

§8.1 Sanctions. The trial court may impose sanctions for refusal to participate in court-ordered ADR. *See, e.g.*, *In re K.A.R.*, 171 S.W.3d 705, 715 (Tex.App.—Houston [14th Dist.] 2005, no pet.) (sanctions appropriate against party who canceled court-ordered mediation); *Roberts v. Rose*, 37 S.W.3d 31, 34-35 (Tex.App.—San Antonio 2000, no pet.)

(attorney who misinformed client about need to appear at ADR was sanctioned, but client was not); *Texas DOT v. Pirtle*, 977 S.W.2d 657, 658 (Tex.App.—Fort Worth 1998, pet. denied) (sanctions appropriate against prevailing party for not filing written objections to ADR and for refusing to participate); *Luxenberg v. Marshall*, 835 S.W.2d 136, 141 (Tex.App.—Dallas 1992, orig. proceeding) (trial court struck D's pleadings because D did not comply with numerous pretrial orders, including an order to mediate). The court cannot dismiss a case or render a default judgment for failure to observe court-imposed ADR deadlines unless it first applies the test for death-penalty sanctions. *See Wal-Mart Stores v. Butler*, 41 S.W.3d 816, 817-18 (Tex.App.—Dallas 2001, no pet.). See "Death-penalty sanctions," ch. 5-K, §3.2, p. 378.

§8.2 No sanctions. The trial court cannot impose sanctions for refusal to settle a case in court-ordered ADR. *See Hansen v. Sullivan*, 886 S.W.2d 467, 469 (Tex.App.—Houston [1st Dist.] 1994, orig. proceeding). The court also cannot compel a party to negotiate in good faith. *Avary v. Bank of Am.*, 72 S.W.3d 779, 797 (Tex.App.—Dallas 2002, pet. denied); *Texas Parks & Wildlife Dept. v. Davis*, 988 S.W.2d 370, 375 (Tex.App.—Austin 1999, no pet.); *Gleason v. Lawson*, 850 S.W.2d 714, 717 (Tex.App.—Corpus Christi 1993, no writ). Once the case is settled, the trial court cannot impose sanctions for failure to pay the settlement agreement. *E.g.*, *Island Entm't, Inc. v. Castaneda*, 882 S.W.2d 2, 5 (Tex.App.—Houston [1st Dist.] 1994, writ denied) (written settlement agreement after mediation).

§9. SETTLEMENT WEEKS

In every county with a population of at least 150,000, the ADR statute requires two weeks—law week and judicial-conference week—to be set aside each year for the courts to facilitate the voluntary settlement of pending cases. CPRC §155.001. Any licensed attorney may serve as a mediator during settlement weeks under the terms, conditions, and training required by the administrative judge of the judicial district. *Id.* §155.003.

§10. SETTLEMENT AGREEMENT

§10.1 Agreement reached. If the parties execute a written agreement disposing of the dispute through ADR, the agreement is enforceable like any other written contract. CPRC §154.071(a); *Mantas v. Fifth Ct. of Appeals*, 925 S.W.2d 656, 658 (Tex.1996); *Castano v. San Felipe Agric., Mfg., & Irrigation Co.*, 147 S.W.3d 444, 448 (Tex. App.—San Antonio 2004, no pet.); *Davis v. Wickham*, 917 S.W.2d 414, 416 (Tex.App.—Houston [14th Dist.] 1996, no writ). If the agreement complies with TRCP 11 or contract law, one of the parties can enforce it without the other parties' consent. *Davis*, 917 S.W.2d at 416; *Stevens v. Snyder*, 874 S.W.2d 241, 243 (Tex.App.—Dallas 1994, writ denied). As with any enforceable contract, a party who signs a settlement agreement disposing of a dispute through ADR cannot unilaterally repudiate the agreement. *In re Marriage of Banks*, 887 S.W.2d 160, 163 (Tex.App.—Texarkana 1994, no writ); *In re Marriage of Ames*, 860 S.W.2d 590, 591 (Tex.App.—Amarillo 1993, no writ). See "Settlement of the Suit," ch. 7-I, p. 669.

§10.2 Action to enforce. The court cannot take action on a settlement agreement without a request to do so, such as a motion for summary judgment based on the agreement or an amended pleading that requests relief or proposes a defense based on the agreement. *Pickell v. Guaranty Nat'l Life Ins.*, 917 S.W.2d 439, 441-42 (Tex.App.—Houston [14th Dist.] 1996, no writ). The court may incorporate the terms of the agreement into the final decree disposing of the case. CPRC §154.071(b). The terms of the settlement agreement can be enforced as contract rights regardless of whether they were incorporated into the judgment. *McFarland v. Bridges*, 104 S.W.3d 906, 910 (Tex. App.—El Paso 2003, no pet.). The court cannot modify the agreement reached in ADR without the consent of all parties. See "Enforcing settlement agreement," ch. 7-I, §4.2, p. 673.

§10.3 Family-law cases.

1. Mediated settlement agreement. If the parties reach a settlement, they can dispose of their dispute by executing a written mediated settlement agreement (MSA). *See* CPRC §154.071. In certain family-law suits, the parties can make the MSA binding at the time of its execution if the agreement (1) includes a prominently displayed statement, in boldfaced type or in capital letters or underlined, that the agreement is not subject to revocation, (2) is signed by each party to the agreement, and (3) is signed by the party's attorney, if any, who is present

---

✦

---

when the agreement is signed. Fam. Code §6.602(b) (divorce cases), §153.0071(d) (suits affecting parent-child relationship); *Milner v. Milner*, 361 S.W.3d 615, 618 (Tex.2012) (divorce case); *Beyers v. Roberts*, 199 S.W.3d 354, 358 (Tex.App.—Houston [1st Dist.] 2006, pet. denied) (suit affecting parent-child relationship); *In re Calderon*, 96 S.W.3d 711, 717 (Tex.App.—Tyler 2003, orig. proceeding) (same). If the parties entered into a binding MSA that is not illegal or procured by dishonest means, a party to the MSA is entitled to judgment on the agreement even if the other party withdraws her consent. *See In re Calderon*, 96 S.W.3d at 718; *Boyd v. Boyd*, 67 S.W.3d 398, 402-03 (Tex.App.—Fort Worth 2002, no pet.). See *O'Connor's Fam. Law Handbook*, "Binding agreement," ch. 3-A, §13.1.1(6)(b)[1], p. 234; "Illegality, public policy & fraud," ch. 4-D, §10.1.1(6)(a)[1], p. 402. In suits affecting the parent-child relationship, a court may decline to enter a judgment on the MSA if the court finds that (1) a party to the agreement was a victim of family violence, (2) the circumstance of being a victim of family violence impaired the party's ability to make decisions, and (3) the agreement is not in the child's best interest. Fam. Code §153.0071(e-1). See *O'Connor's Fam. Law Handbook*, "Family violence," ch. 4-D, §10.1.1(6)(a)[2], p. 402.

    2. Collaborative-law agreement. Parties in certain family-law suits can resolve their dispute through the collaborative-law process. *See* Fam. Code §§15.001-15.116. A collaborative-law agreement is enforceable in the same manner as a written settlement agreement under CPRC §154.071. Fam. Code §15.105(a). For a complete discussion of the collaborative-law process, see *O'Connor's Fam. Law Handbook*, "Collaborative law," ch. 3-A, §13.1.2, p. 235.

B. MEDIATION

§1. GENERAL

    §1.1 Rules. None. See CPRC §154.023.

    §1.2 Purpose. The purpose of mediation is to provide a forum in which an impartial person—the mediator—facilitates communication among the parties to promote reconciliation, settlement, or understanding. CPRC §154.023(a); *see In re Jones*, 55 S.W.3d 243, 247 (Tex.Spec.Ct.Rev.2000) (CPRC contemplates mediation only in family or civil context).

    §1.3 Forms. *O'Connor's Texas Civil Forms* (2012), FORMS 4A, 4B.

    §1.4 Other references. Bayer & VanBuren, *Mediation*, Advanced Personal Injury Course, State Bar of Texas CLE, ch. 8 (2011); Galton, *Representing Clients in Mediation* (1994); Kovach, *Ethical Considerations in the Practice of Mediation*, Alternative Dispute Resolution Course, State Bar of Texas CLE, ch. 1.1 (2012); Kovach, *Mediation: Principles & Practice* (3d ed. 2004); Lowry & Robinson, *Advanced Mediation Skills for the Negotiation & Closing Stages*, Advanced Mediation: Skills & Techniques Course, State Bar of Texas CLE, ch. 1 (2009); *O'Connor's Texas Causes of Action* (2013) (*O'Connor's Texas COA*).

§2. AGREEMENTS TO MEDIATE

See "By agreement," ch. 4-A, §3.1.1, p. 279.

§3. COMPULSORY MEDIATION

    §3.1 DTPA claims. A party can compel mediation by filing a motion to compel mediation within 90 days after service of a pleading requesting relief under the DTPA. Bus. & Com. Code §17.5051(a). A claim for damages less than $15,000 cannot be forced into mediation unless the party moving for mediation (1) files a motion to compel within 90 days of service and (2) agrees to pay the costs of the mediation. *Id.* §17.5051(a), (f). Section 17.5051 does not apply to a suit for a restraining order brought by the Texas Attorney General. *Id.* §17.5051(h).

    1. Order. The court has 30 days after the motion is filed to sign an order setting the time and place of the mediation. Bus. & Com. Code §17.5051(b). The mediation must be held within 30 days after the date the order is signed, unless the parties agree otherwise or the court determines that additional time, not to exceed an additional 30 days, is warranted. *Id.* §17.5051(d).

———————————————————— ✦ ————————————————————

2. Fees. Unless the parties agree otherwise, the parties share the mediation fees. Bus. & Com. Code §17.5051(e).

§3.2 By local rule. Some courts require mediation by local rule. For example, the Harris County family courts require all disputed custody or visitation matters that are set for a temporary hearing to be submitted for mediation to Family Court Services or another private mediator, as agreed by the parties and their attorneys. Harris Cty. Fam. Ct. Loc. R. 7.1; *see also* Travis Cty. Loc. R. 2.2 (provides for automatic referral of civil cases to pretrial mediation).

§4. MEDIATOR

§4.1 Appointment. Most of the rules governing mediation are contained in the general ADR statutes. *See* CPRC §§154.001-154.073. For rules on the appointment, qualifications, standards, duties, and compensation of the mediator, see "Appointment of Impartial Third Party," ch. 4-A, §6, p. 281.

§4.2 Resolution. The mediator cannot substitute her own judgment on the issues for that of the parties. CPRC §154.023(b); *Decker v. Lindsay*, 824 S.W.2d 247, 251 (Tex.App.—Houston [1st Dist.] 1992, orig. proceeding). The mediator cannot alter any resulting agreement or interject her own terms into the agreement. *In re Marriage of McIntosh*, 918 S.W.2d 87, 89 (Tex.App.—Amarillo 1996, no writ).

§5. PREPARING FOR MEDIATION

§5.1 Have authority to settle. Mediation can be successful only if a party or its representative with settlement authority attends the mediation. *See, e.g.*, *Suarez v. Jordan*, 35 S.W.3d 268, 273 (Tex.App.—Houston [14th Dist.] 2000, no pet.) (mediated settlement agreement signed by son did not bind father because son did not have settlement authority). The ADR statute is silent on the issue of who must attend, but there are cases addressing this issue. *See, e.g.*, *Nueces Cty. v. De Pena*, 953 S.W.2d 835, 836-37 (Tex.App.—Corpus Christi 1997, orig. proceeding) (county judge could not be ordered to attend mediation because he had no authority to settle the case without agreement of commissioners court); *Hur v. City of Mesquite*, 893 S.W.2d 227, 232-34 (Tex.App.—Amarillo 1995, writ denied) (city agreed during mediation to settle for specific amount but later claimed agreement was subject to city council's approval; court held that P could sue city for breach of oral agreement to settle); *In re Stone*, 986 F.2d 898, 904-05 (5th Cir.1993) (court recommended "practical approach" to settlement-authority requirements imposed on government bodies, such as allowing official with ultimate authority to be fully prepared and available by telephone at time of conference).

§5.2 Send documents to mediator. Most mediations begin when the parties send the mediator copies of the pleadings and other important documents and copies of any legal authority necessary to resolve the issues. In some cases, the parties also send the mediator a short position paper explaining their version of the issues.

§5.3 Send documents to other parties. Each party should send the other parties copies of all the materials it sent to the mediator, except for confidential materials.

§5.4 Review file. The attorneys should review their files thoroughly and be prepared to argue the facts, the issues, and the law.

§5.5 Prepare the party. The attorneys should explain the mediation process to the parties and explain their roles. *See* Galton, *Representing Clients in Mediation*, at 69-72. The attorneys should review all the documents the parties sent to the mediator and make each party aware of the other parties' positions. *See id.*

§5.6 Take documents to mediation. If possible, the attorney should take the entire file to mediation. The documents a party will most likely need will be those sent to the mediator, but a party may want to refer to additional documents and discovery during mediation. As the parties review their positions in the mediation, it is sometimes necessary to refer to the documents and discovery to verify the accuracy of a party's memory of events and discovery concessions.

§6. MEDIATION SESSION

§6.1 Mediator's opening statement. The mediator will begin the session by explaining the procedure for mediation. In most cases, the mediator will require the parties to sign an acknowledgment that the mediation procedure is confidential.

★

§6.2 Parties' opening statements. Each party is given an opportunity to make an opening statement explaining its position on the issues. The attorneys, as well as the parties, may make an opening statement. An attorney should determine whether allowing the party to make the opening statement will enhance the presentation of the case. A party who is articulate and who will make a good witness should probably be allowed to participate in the opening statement. A party's opening statement allows the opposition to assess that party's understanding of the lawsuit and its determination to proceed with settlement or trial, and it helps the attorneys evaluate the party as a witness in case mediation fails.

§7. CAUCUSING

After the joint session, the parties normally separate into different rooms, and "shuttle diplomacy" begins. The mediator spends time with each party, learning about the case and conveying settlement ideas back and forth without disclosing confidential information. *See* CPRC §§154.053(b), (c), 154.073. Some mediators ask each party to submit a written "wish list" and a list of nonnegotiable matters. From that point, the mediator tries to move the parties toward settlement.

§8. DURATION

Most mediations are set for one day. Mediation rarely ends at 5:00 p.m., and it can go on into the night. It is often late in the afternoon before the parties start making serious efforts to settle the case. In cases involving child custody and visitation, several shorter sessions are probably more appropriate than a single extended one. The parties in these cases should not be pushed to exhaustion because financial issues are not the most important issues to be resolved.

§9. SANCTIONS

See "Sanctions," ch. 4-A, §8, p. 282.

§10. SETTLEMENT AGREEMENT

See "Settlement Agreement," ch. 4-A, §10, p. 283.

C. ARBITRATION

§1. GENERAL

§1.1 Rules. None. See the Federal Arbitration Act, U.S.C. title 9 (FAA); the Texas Arbitration Act (TAA), CPRC ch. 171; and the Alternative Dispute Resolution Code, CPRC title 7 (ADR Act).

§1.2 Purpose. Arbitration is a method of settling a dispute outside the courtroom. One purpose behind arbitration is to avoid large litigation expenses, particularly the costs for longer proceedings, complicated appeals, discovery, investigations, fees, and expert witnesses. *In re Olshan Found. Repair Co.*, 328 S.W.3d 883, 894 (Tex.2010). Federal and state laws strongly favor arbitration. *In re FirstMerit Bank*, 52 S.W.3d 749, 753 (Tex.2001); *EZ Pawn Corp. v. Mancias*, 934 S.W.2d 87, 90 (Tex.1996); *Cantella & Co. v. Goodwin*, 924 S.W.2d 943, 944 (Tex.1996). There are three kinds of arbitration: ADR arbitration, statutory arbitration, and contractual arbitration under the FAA or TAA.

§1.3 Forms. *O'Connor's Texas Civil Forms* (2012), FORMS 4C.

§1.4 Other references. Bayer & VanBuren, *Evidence & Discovery in Arbitration, Advanced Evidence & Discovery Course*, State Bar of Texas CLE, ch. 18 (2010); Bland et al., *Consumer Arbitration Agreements: Enforceability and Other Topics* (6th ed. 2011); Hecht, *Arbitration & the Vanishing Jury Trial*, 69 Tex.B.J. 852 (Oct.2006); Ho, Comment, *Discovery in Commercial Arbitration Proceedings*, 34 Hous.L.Rev. 199 (1997); Levinson, *Lawyering Skills, Principles & Methods Offer Insight as to Best Practices for Arbitration*, 60 Baylor L.Rev. 1 (2008); Stilwell, *Correcting Errors: Imperfect Awards in Texas Arbitration*, 58 Baylor L.Rev. 467 (2006); *O'Connor's Federal Rules * Civil Trials*

———————————— ✪ ————————————

(2013) (*O'Connor's Federal Rules*); *O'Connor's Texas Causes of Action* (2013) (*O'Connor's Texas COA*); *O'Connor's Texas Civil Appeals* (2012) (*O'Connor's Texas Appeals*).

§2. MOTION TO COMPEL ADR ARBITRATION

§2.1 Types of ADR arbitration.

1. Nonbinding. A party may file a motion to refer its case to nonbinding arbitration as part of an ADR procedure. *See* CPRC §§152.003, 154.021, 154.027(a). For the procedure the parties should follow, see "Referral Procedures for ADR," ch. 4-A, §3, p. 279.

2. Binding. If the parties stipulate in advance that court-ordered arbitration will be binding, the award is binding and enforceable like any contract obligation. CPRC §154.027(b); *In re Cartwright*, 104 S.W.3d 706, 711 (Tex.App.—Houston [1st Dist.] 2003, orig. proceeding).

§2.2 Procedure for ADR arbitration. See "The ADR System," ch. 4-A, p. 277.

§3. MOTION TO COMPEL STATUTORY ARBITRATION

§3.1 Statutes requiring arbitration. A number of statutes require parties to arbitrate disputes instead of litigating them. *See, e.g.*, Agric. Code ch. 64 (seed-performance disputes); Alco. Bev. Code §102.77 (intra-industry disputes); Local Gov't Code §143.057 (matters affecting firefighters and police officers), §212.902 (school-district land-development standards); Tax Code §42.225 (property owner's appeal of appraisal-review-board order). *But see City of League City v. Blevins*, 821 S.W.2d 212, 215 (Tex.App.—Houston [14th Dist.] 1991, no writ) (arbitration under Local Gov't Code §143.001 is not really arbitration, even though that is what it is called).

§3.2 Procedure for statutory arbitration. When a case is referred to arbitration under a specific code provision, the attorney should check the provisions in that code for the procedures to follow.

§4. MOTION TO COMPEL CONTRACTUAL ARBITRATION—FAA OR TAA?

Parties that agree to arbitrate can be compelled to arbitrate under the Federal Arbitration Act (FAA), the Texas Arbitration Act (TAA), or both, depending on the terms of the agreement and the nature of the claim. When both acts apply, the FAA preempts the TAA to the extent that they conflict. See "FAA preemption of TAA," §4.5, p. 288. Many of the same substantive principles apply regardless of whether cases are governed by the FAA or the TAA, and courts rely on FAA and TAA cases interchangeably. *Forest Oil Corp. v. McAllen*, 268 S.W.3d 51, 56 n.10 (Tex.2008).

NOTE

Both the FAA and the TAA refer to an "application" to compel contractual arbitration, but the phrases "application to compel" and "motion to compel" seem to be used interchangeably by the courts. We use "motion to compel" throughout this subchapter.

---

§4.1 Agreement specifies FAA. If an agreement requires arbitration under the FAA, a party can be compelled to arbitrate under the FAA regardless of whether the transaction involved or affected interstate commerce. *Teel v. Beldon Roofing & Remodeling Co.*, 281 S.W.3d 446, 449 (Tex.App.—San Antonio 2007, pet. denied); *In re Kellogg Brown & Root*, 80 S.W.3d 611, 617 (Tex.App.—Houston [1st Dist.] 2002, orig. proceeding); *see In re Rubiola*, 334 S.W.3d 220, 223 (Tex.2011). Texas courts have the power to compel arbitration under the FAA. *USX Corp. v. West*, 781 S.W.2d 453, 454 (Tex.App.—Houston [1st Dist.] 1989, orig. proceeding).

§4.2 Agreement specifies TAA. If an agreement requires arbitration under the TAA, a party can be compelled to arbitrate under the TAA regardless of whether the transaction involved or affected interstate commerce. *See In re Olshan Found. Repair Co.*, 328 S.W.3d 883, 890-91 (Tex.2010); *In re L&L Kempwood Assocs.*, 9 S.W.3d 125, 127-28 (Tex.1999). An arbitration clause specifically invoking the TAA designates the TAA to govern all aspects of the arbitration agreement. *See In re Olshan Found.*, 328 S.W.3d at 890-91. The FAA is not part of the TAA and is thus excluded when the TAA is specifically invoked. *Id.* at 891; *see In re L&L Kempwood*, 9 S.W.3d at 127-28. The FAA, however, is part of "the arbitration laws in your state." See "Law of the place," §4.4.2, p. 288. The parties' choice should be the focus when determining whether the TAA or FAA applies. *In re Olshan Found.*, 328 S.W.3d at 891.

—————————— ★ ——————————

§4.3 Agreement specifies FAA & TAA. If the agreement provides for arbitration under both the FAA and the TAA or if the agreement can be interpreted as invoking both acts, both the FAA and the TAA may apply. *See In re D. Wilson Constr. Co.*, 196 S.W.3d 774, 778-79 (Tex.2006). When both acts apply, preemption becomes an issue. See "FAA preemption of TAA," §4.5, this page.

§4.4 Agreement does not specify either FAA or TAA.

1. Interstate commerce. If an agreement requires arbitration and involves interstate commerce but does not specify either the FAA or the TAA, both acts may apply. *See In re D. Wilson Constr. Co.*, 196 S.W.3d 774, 778-79 (Tex.2006); *see, e.g.*, *Sporran Kbusco, Inc. v. Cerda*, 227 S.W.3d 288, 291 (Tex.App.—San Antonio 2007, pet. denied) (agreement did not specify FAA or TAA; both applied because contract involved interstate commerce and TAA was not preempted). When both the FAA and the TAA apply, preemption becomes an issue. See "FAA preemption of TAA," §4.5, this page.

2. Law of the place. If an agreement requires arbitration and does not specify either the FAA or the TAA but states that arbitration is under "the arbitration laws in your state" or that it "shall be governed by the law of the place where the Project is located" or uses similar language, both the FAA and the TAA may apply. *In re Olshan Found. Repair Co.*, 328 S.W.3d 883, 890 (Tex.2010); *see In re D. Wilson Constr.*, 196 S.W.3d at 778-79; *In re L&L Kempwood Assocs.*, 9 S.W.3d 125, 127-28 (Tex.1999). The Texas Supreme Court has interpreted a law-of-the-place provision to include both federal and state laws. *In re L&L Kempwood*, 9 S.W.3d at 127-28; *see In re Olshan Found.*, 328 S.W.3d at 890 (FAA is part of "arbitration laws of Texas"). Thus, if the contract has a law-of-the-place provision, it is not necessary to show the contract involved interstate commerce to invoke the FAA. To apply only the TAA, a law-of-the-place provision must contain language that specifically excludes application of the FAA. *In re Olshan Found.*, 328 S.W.3d at 890.

3. No interstate commerce or law-of-the-place provision. If an agreement requires arbitration and (1) does not specify either the FAA or the TAA, (2) does not involve interstate commerce, and (3) does not contain a law-of-the-place provision, only the TAA applies. See "Motion to compel arbitration under TAA," §6.2, p. 293.

§4.5 FAA preemption of TAA. If an agreement refers to both the FAA and the TAA, or if it does not refer to either act, both acts may apply, raising the issue of preemption. *See In re D. Wilson Constr. Co.*, 196 S.W.3d 774, 778-79 (Tex.2006).

1. When FAA preempts. When both acts apply, courts use the four-part test set out in *In re Nexion Health*, 173 S.W.3d 67, 69 (Tex.2005), to determine whether the TAA thwarts the goals and policies of the FAA and is thus preempted. For the FAA to preempt the TAA, the following must be true:

(1) In writing. The agreement is in writing. *Nafta Traders, Inc. v. Quinn*, 339 S.W.3d 84, 98 (Tex. 2011); *In re D. Wilson Constr.*, 196 S.W.3d at 780; *In re Nexion Health*, 173 S.W.3d at 69.

(2) Interstate commerce. The agreement involves interstate commerce. *Nafta Traders*, 339 S.W.3d at 98; *In re Olshan Found. Repair Co.*, 328 S.W.3d 883, 888 (Tex.2010); *In re D. Wilson Constr.*, 196 S.W.3d at 780; *In re Nexion Health*, 173 S.W.3d at 69; *see* 9 U.S.C. §2. Under the FAA, "commerce" is read broadly, and almost anything can bring a dispute under the FAA. *See, e.g.*, *In re Nexion Health*, 173 S.W.3d at 69 (Medicare payments made to health-care center on D's behalf established interstate commerce); *In re L&L Kempwood Assocs.*, 9 S.W.3d 125, 127 (Tex.1999) (contract involved interstate commerce because parties resided in different states); *In re Nasr*, 50 S.W.3d 23, 25-26 & n.1 (Tex.App.—Beaumont 2001, orig. proceeding) (contract to build Texas residence listing Wal-Mart as subcontractor involved interstate commerce); *Palm Harbor Homes, Inc. v. McCoy*, 944 S.W.2d 716, 720 (Tex.App.—Fort Worth 1997, orig. proceeding) (purchase of mobile home manufactured in Texas that included components purchased or manufactured in other states involved interstate commerce). The FAA does not require a substantial effect on interstate commerce; it requires only that commerce be involved or affected. *In re L&L Kempwood*, 9 S.W.3d at 126-27; *Royce Homes, L.P. v. Bates*, 315 S.W.3d 77, 85 (Tex.App.—Houston [1st Dist.] 2010, no pet.); *In re Big 8 Food Stores*, 166 S.W.3d 869, 879 (Tex.App.—El Paso 2005, orig. proceeding); *see also Service Corp.*

─────────────────── ★ ───────────────────

v. Lopez, 162 S.W.3d 801, 807 (Tex.App.—Corpus Christi 2005, no pet.) (whether party anticipated substantial effect on interstate commerce is irrelevant). For example, interstate commerce can be involved or affected by (1) location of headquarters in another state, (2) transportation of materials across state lines, (3) manufacture of parts in another state, (4) preparation of invoices in another state, or (5) interstate mail and phone calls supporting a contract. *In re Big 8*, 166 S.W.3d at 879; *Service Corp.*, 162 S.W.3d at 807; *see Royce Homes*, 315 S.W.3d at 85. However, the mere fact that the contract involves interstate commerce does not preclude enforcement under the TAA as well as the FAA. *Nafta Traders*, 339 S.W.3d at 98; *In re D. Wilson Constr.*, 196 S.W.3d at 780.

      (3) Contract defenses. The agreement can withstand scrutiny under traditional state-law contract defenses. *Nafta Traders*, 339 S.W.3d at 98; *In re D. Wilson Constr.*, 196 S.W.3d at 780; *In re Nexion Health*, 173 S.W.3d at 69.

      (4) Contrary Texas law. Texas law adversely affects the enforceability of the agreement. *See Nafta Traders*, 339 S.W.3d at 98; *In re Olshan Found.*, 328 S.W.3d at 891; *In re D. Wilson Constr.*, 196 S.W.3d at 780; *In re Nexion Health*, 173 S.W.3d at 69. For the FAA to preempt the TAA, an FAA-enforceable agreement must be unenforceable under Texas law because the Texas law (1) expressly exempts the agreement from coverage or (2) imposes a requirement for enforceability not found in the FAA. *Nafta Traders*, 339 S.W.3d at 98; *In re D. Wilson Constr.*, 196 S.W.3d at 780; *see Ellis v. Schlimmer*, 337 S.W.3d 860, 862 (Tex.2011); *see, e.g., In re Olshan Found.*, 328 S.W.3d at 891 (TAA affected enforceability by adding signature requirement to arbitration agreements in service contracts of $50,000 or less); *In re Nexion Health*, 173 S.W.3d at 69 (TAA affected enforceability by adding signature requirement to arbitration agreements in personal-injury cases); *Cleveland Constr., Inc. v. Levco Constr., Inc.*, 359 S.W.3d 843, 855-56 (Tex.App.—Houston [1st Dist.] 2012, pet. dism'd) (Tex. Bus. & Com. Code §272.001 affected enforceablity because it voided choice of venue in arbitration agreement).

      2. What FAA preempts. When both acts apply, the FAA preempts the TAA only to the extent that the TAA would thwart the goals and policies of the FAA. *See In re D. Wilson Constr.*, 196 S.W.3d at 779; *Royce Homes*, 315 S.W.3d at 85. The FAA and the TAA are not mutually exclusive; the FAA preempts only contrary state law, not consonant state law. *In re D. Wilson Constr.*, 196 S.W.3d at 779. The FAA does not, however, preempt state law that allows parties to agree to a greater review of arbitration awards. *Nafta Traders*, 339 S.W.3d at 101. When the FAA preempts the TAA, the agreement does not necessarily have to be arbitrated exclusively under the FAA. *See In re D. Wilson Constr.*, 196 S.W.3d at 780. The agreement can still be arbitrated under the TAA, but TAA provisions inconsistent with the FAA are not enforceable. *See id.*

§5. MOTION TO COMPEL CONTRACTUAL ARBITRATION UNDER FAA

The substantive law created under the FAA applies in both federal and state courts. *Nitro-Lift Techs. v. Howard*, ___ U.S. ___ (2012) (No. 11-1377; 11-26-12) (FAA).

§5.1 Who may compel or be compelled under FAA.

      1. Signatory. Either party to a contract that contains an arbitration provision can compel the other party to participate in arbitration. The party may initiate the arbitration proceedings either before or after suit is filed. An assignee of a contract is in the same position as the original party to the contract. *See In re FirstMerit Bank*, 52 S.W.3d 749, 755-56 (Tex.2001) (FAA). A party's name change after signing a contract does not convert the party into a nonsignatory. *In re H&R Block Fin. Advisors, Inc.*, 235 S.W.3d 177, 178 (Tex.2007) (FAA).

      2. Nonsignatory. A nonsignatory to an arbitration agreement can sometimes compel arbitration or be compelled to arbitrate. *See In re Labatt Food Serv.*, 279 S.W.3d 640, 643 (Tex.2009) (FAA); *In re Weekley Homes, L.P.*, 180 S.W.3d 127, 131 (Tex.2005) (FAA); *see, e.g., In re Rubiola*, 334 S.W.3d 220, 224-25 (Tex.2011) (FAA; because arbitration agreement expressly provided that certain nonsignatories were considered parties, nonsignatories could compel arbitration). Whether a nonsignatory can compel arbitration or be compelled to arbitrate is a matter for the courts, not the arbitrators, to decide, unless the parties clearly provide otherwise, because that determination goes to the validity of the arbitration clause. *See In re Rubiola*, 334 S.W.3d at 224 (FAA; whether nonsignatory can compel); *In re Labatt Food*, 279 S.W.3d at 643 (FAA; whether nonsignatory can be compelled); *In re Weekley Homes*,

✭

180 S.W.3d at 130 (same). See "Valid," §5.2.1(1)(b), p. 291; "Agreement not valid," §7.2, p. 295. When making this determination, courts apply Texas procedural rules. *In re Labatt Food*, 279 S.W.3d at 643; *In re Weekley Homes*, 180 S.W.3d at 130. Courts have recognized several theories under which a nonsignatory may enforce or be bound by an arbitration agreement. See *O'Connor's Federal Rules*, "Exception – party is not signatory," ch. 7-E, §2.1.3(1)(a)[2], p. 651.

NOTE

The FAA does not specify whether state or federal substantive law applies to the determination of whether a nonsignatory can compel arbitration or be compelled to arbitrate. In **Labatt**, *the Texas Supreme Court stated that until the U.S. Supreme Court addresses this issue, it will apply state substantive law and attempt to keep it consistent with federal law.* **In re Labatt Food**, *279 S.W.3d at 643.*

---

(1) Incorporation by reference. A nonsignatory can be compelled to arbitrate if the arbitration clause was incorporated by reference into the agreement that relates to the dispute. *See In re Kellogg Brown & Root, Inc.*, 166 S.W.3d 732, 739 (Tex.2005) (FAA); *Kirby Highland Lakes Surgery Ctr., L.L.P. v. Kirby*, 183 S.W.3d 891, 902-03 (Tex.App.—Austin 2006, orig. proceeding) (FAA).

(2) Assumption. A nonsignatory can be compelled to arbitrate under the theory of assumption. *In re Kellogg Brown & Root*, 166 S.W.3d at 739 (FAA).

(3) Agency. A nonsignatory can compel arbitration or be compelled to arbitrate under the theory of agency. *In re Kaplan Higher Educ. Corp.*, 235 S.W.3d 206, 209 (Tex.2007) (FAA; can compel); *In re Kellogg Brown & Root*, 166 S.W.3d at 739 (FAA; can be compelled); *see In re Vesta Ins. Grp.*, 192 S.W.3d 759, 762-63 (Tex.2006) (FAA; can compel).

(4) Alter ego. A nonsignatory can be compelled to arbitrate under the theory of alter ego. *In re Kellogg Brown & Root*, 166 S.W.3d at 739 (FAA). Generally, a corporate relationship alone will not bind a nonsignatory to an arbitration agreement. *In re Merrill Lynch Trust Co.*, 235 S.W.3d 185, 191 (Tex.2007) (FAA).

(5) Third-party beneficiary. Under Texas law, a nonsignatory who is a third-party beneficiary of the contract can compel arbitration or be compelled to arbitrate. *In re NEXT Fin. Grp.*, 271 S.W.3d 263, 267 (Tex. 2008) (FAA); *In re Kellogg Brown & Root*, 166 S.W.3d at 739 (FAA); *e.g.*, *In re Labatt Food*, 279 S.W.3d at 645-46 (FAA; beneficiary bringing wrongful-death action was bound by arbitration agreement made by decedent because wrongful-death actions are derivative in nature under Texas law); *see In re Rangel*, 45 S.W.3d 783, 787 (Tex.App.— Waco 2001, orig. proceeding) (FAA).

(6) Equitable estoppel. A nonsignatory can be compelled to arbitrate under the theory of equitable estoppel. *In re Kellogg Brown & Root*, 166 S.W.3d at 739 (FAA). There are two equitable-estoppel theories that support the enforcement of an arbitration clause against a nonsignatory:

(a) Direct-benefits estoppel. Under direct-benefits estoppel, a nonsignatory plaintiff is estopped from claiming benefits under a contract while seeking to avoid an arbitration agreement that is included in the contract. *See In re Kellogg Brown & Root*, 166 S.W.3d at 739 (FAA). Direct-benefits estoppel applies if the nonsignatory either pursues a claim "on the contract" or seeks and obtains substantial benefits from the contract. *See In re Weekley Homes*, 180 S.W.3d at 132-33 (FAA); *In re Kellogg Brown & Root*, 166 S.W.3d at 740 (FAA). However, a nonsignatory will not be compelled to arbitrate under a claim on the contract simply because its claim relates to the contract. *In re Kellogg Brown & Root*, 166 S.W.3d at 741 (FAA). Arbitration will be compelled only if the nonsignatory seeks, through its claim, to derive a direct benefit from the contract containing the arbitration agreement. *Id.*

(b) Concerted-misconduct estoppel. Under concerted-misconduct estoppel, a nonsignatory can be compelled to arbitrate when one signatory to the contract alleges that the nonsignatory and one or more of the other signatories engaged in substantially interdependent and concerted misconduct. *See In re Merrill Lynch*

———————————————— ✦ ————————————————

Trust, 235 S.W.3d at 191 (FAA). However, neither the U.S. Supreme Court nor the Texas Supreme Court has compelled arbitration based solely on the theory of concerted-misconduct estoppel. *See id.* at 191-92. Although concerted-misconduct estoppel has been recognized by the Fifth Circuit, the issue of whether it is a viable theory for compelling arbitration is not well settled in federal courts. *Id.* at 192. See *O'Connor's Federal Rules*, "Equitable estoppel," ch. 7-E, §2.1.3(1)(a)[2][a], p. 652.

§5.2 Motion to compel arbitration under FAA. For the court to compel arbitration under the FAA, the party seeking to compel arbitration must show that the claim is subject to a valid arbitration agreement and falls within the scope of that agreement. *In re Dillard Dept. Stores*, 186 S.W.3d 514, 515 (Tex.2006). The claim must also be arbitrable under federal law. *See In re American Homestar*, 50 S.W.3d 480, 485 (Tex.2001).

1. Valid agreement & claim within scope.

(1) Valid arbitration agreement. The party moving for arbitration must show that the claim is subject to a valid arbitration agreement. *In re Odyssey Healthcare, Inc.*, 310 S.W.3d 419, 422 (Tex.2010). Courts must resolve any doubts about an agreement to arbitrate in favor of arbitration. *Cantella & Co. v. Goodwin*, 924 S.W.2d 943, 944 (Tex.1996). Generally, state law governs whether a party agreed to arbitrate. *In re Labatt Food Serv.*, 279 S.W.3d 640, 643 (Tex.2009); *In re Weekley Homes, L.P.*, 180 S.W.3d 127, 130 (Tex.2005).

(a) Written. The terms of the arbitration agreement must be in writing. *See* 9 U.S.C. §4; *Dean Witter Reynolds, Inc. v. Byrd*, 470 U.S. 213, 218 (1985).

(b) Valid. There must be a valid arbitration agreement for the court to compel arbitration. *In re 24R, Inc.*, 324 S.W.3d 564, 566 (Tex.2010) (FAA); *In re Odyssey Healthcare*, 310 S.W.3d at 422 (FAA); *In re D. Wilson Constr. Co.*, 196 S.W.3d 774, 781 (Tex.2006) (FAA); *J.M. Davidson, Inc. v. Webster*, 128 S.W.3d 223, 227 (Tex.2003) (TAA). An agreement to arbitrate is valid if it meets the requirements of the general contract law of the state. *In re Rubiola*, 334 S.W.3d 220, 224 (Tex.2011) (FAA); *In re Poly-America, L.P.*, 262 S.W.3d 337, 347 (Tex.2008) (FAA); *In re Dillard Dept. Stores*, 186 S.W.3d at 515 (FAA); *see* 9 U.S.C. §2 (FAA; written agreement to arbitrate is considered valid unless it can be revoked under contract law). Thus, the arbitration agreement must be based on valid consideration. *In re Palm Harbor Homes, Inc.*, 195 S.W.3d 672, 676 (Tex.2006) (FAA); *see, e.g., In re 24R*, 324 S.W.3d at 566-67 (FAA; mutual agreement to arbitrate in an at-will employment situation provided sufficient consideration to support arbitration agreement). If one party to the agreement can avoid its promise to arbitrate by amending the provision or terminating it altogether, the agreement is illusory and not enforceable. *In re 24R*, 324 S.W.3d at 567 (FAA). See "Illusory agreement," §7.2.4, p. 296; *O'Connor's Texas COA*, "Proving an Enforceable Contract," ch. 5-A, §2, p. 57.

(c) Signature not required. The FAA does not require that an agreement to arbitrate be signed by the parties. *In re Polymerica*, 296 S.W.3d 74, 76 (Tex.2009); *In re Macy's Tex., Inc.*, 291 S.W.3d 418, 419 (Tex. 2009); *In re AdvancePCS Health L.P.*, 172 S.W.3d 603, 606 (Tex.2005).

[1] Signed. If the parties signed an arbitration agreement, they are bound by its terms unless there is fraud, misrepresentation, or deceit. *In re McKinney*, 167 S.W.3d 833, 835 (Tex.2005). This is true even if the parties did not read the agreement before they signed it or thought the agreement stated different terms. *Id.*; *see In re Merrill Lynch Trust Co.*, 235 S.W.3d 185, 190 (Tex.2007).

[2] Unsigned. If the parties did not sign the agreement, the party seeking to enforce arbitration must establish that the parties agreed to arbitrate the dispute. *In re Big 8 Food Stores*, 166 S.W.3d 869, 876 (Tex.App.—El Paso 2005, orig. proceeding).

(2) Claim within scope. The party moving for arbitration must show that the claim falls within the scope of the arbitration agreement. *In re Rubiola*, 334 S.W.3d at 223 (FAA); *In re Dallas Peterbilt, Ltd.*, 196 S.W.3d 161, 163 (Tex.2006) (FAA); *J.M. Davidson, Inc.*, 128 S.W.3d at 227 (TAA); *In re Dillard Dept. Stores*, 186 S.W.3d at 515 (FAA); *Prudential Secs. Inc. v. Marshall*, 909 S.W.2d 896, 900 (Tex.1995) (FAA). To determine whether the claim is within the scope of the arbitration agreement, the court examines the terms of the agreement and the factual allegations of the plaintiff's claim. *See In re Rubiola*, 334 S.W.3d at 225 (FAA). Generally, federal law governs the scope of the arbitration agreement. *In re Labatt Food*, 279 S.W.3d at 643; *In re Weekley Homes*, 180 S.W.3d at 130.

✫

(a) Terms of agreement. Many arbitration agreements provide that "any controversy or claim arising from or relating to" the contract is subject to arbitration. *E.g.*, *In re Kaplan Higher Educ. Corp.*, 235 S.W.3d 206, 208 & n.1 (Tex.2007) (FAA); *In re Bank One*, 216 S.W.3d 825, 826 (Tex.2007) (FAA). Under a broad arbitration clause, arbitration can be compelled even though the particular dispute is not specifically covered. *See In re D. Wilson Constr.*, 196 S.W.3d at 783 (FAA). Such an arbitration clause may encompass different causes of action and claims for different types of damages. For example, an agreement to arbitrate all disputes arising from a contract may encompass some tort claims. *Merrill Lynch, Pierce, Fenner & Smith, Inc. v. Wilson*, 805 S.W.2d 38, 39 (Tex. App.—El Paso 1991, no writ) (FAA). An arbitration agreement includes a tort claim if the tort is so interwoven with the contract that it could not stand alone. *Id.*

(b) Factual allegations. If the facts alleged in support of the claim have a "significant relationship" to or are "factually intertwined" with the contract that is subject to the arbitration agreement, the claim is within the scope of the agreement and is arbitrable. *Dennis v. College Station Hosp., L.P.*, 169 S.W.3d 282, 285 (Tex.App.—Waco 2005, pet. denied) (TAA); *Pennzoil Co. v. Arnold Oil Co.*, 30 S.W.3d 494, 498 (Tex.App.—San Antonio 2000, orig. proceeding) (FAA); *see, e.g.*, *In re Dallas Peterbilt, Ltd.*, 196 S.W.3d at 163 (FAA; arbitration clause in employment contract covered race-discrimination claim); *In re Dillard Dept. Stores*, 186 S.W.3d at 515 (FAA; arbitration clause in employment contract covered defamation claim). However, if the facts alleged stand alone and are completely independent of the contract, the claim is not subject to arbitration. *Pennzoil Co.*, 30 S.W.3d at 498 (FAA).

2. Arbitrable claim. For the court to compel arbitration under the FAA, the claim must be arbitrable and there must be no other legal constraint, such as a federal statute, that renders the claim nonarbitrable. *See In re American Homestar*, 50 S.W.3d at 485; *see, e.g.*, *In re FirstMerit Bank*, 52 S.W.3d 749, 755 (Tex.2001) (loan agreement's broad arbitration language covered all claims relating to purchase of home and bank's right to repossess).

(1) Conflicting federal statute. If a federal statute shows clear congressional intent to preclude application of the FAA, a claim cannot be submitted to arbitration. *In re American Homestar*, 50 S.W.3d at 485. To determine whether a federal statute overrides the FAA, courts look to (1) the statute's text, (2) the statute's legislative history, and (3) whether there is an inherent conflict between arbitration and the statute's underlying purpose. *Shearson/American Express, Inc. v. McMahon*, 482 U.S. 220, 226-27 (1987); *In re American Homestar*, 50 S.W.3d at 485; *In re David's Supermkts., Inc.*, 43 S.W.3d 94, 98 (Tex.App.—Waco 2001, orig. proceeding). See *O'Connor's Federal Rules*, "Dispute is arbitrable," ch. 7-E, §2.1.3(2), p. 652.

(2) Conflicting state statute. If a state statute precludes application of the FAA, the FAA controls over the conflicting state statute as long as the claim is subject to a valid arbitration clause. *See, e.g.*, *Nitro-Lift Techs. v. Howard*, ___ U.S. ___ (2012) (No. 11-1377; 11-26-12) (parties entered into noncompetition agreement that contained valid arbitration clause; FAA controlled over state statute that limited enforceability of noncompetition agreements).

NOTE

If the court has determined that an arbitration agreement is valid and enforceable, questions about the validity of the remainder of the contract are for the arbitrator to decide. **Nitro-Lift Techs**, *___ U.S. at ___. See "Questions of arbitrability," §8.2.2, p. 298.*

---

§6. MOTION TO COMPEL CONTRACTUAL ARBITRATION UNDER TAA

The procedure to compel contractual arbitration under the Texas Arbitration Act (TAA) is outlined in CPRC §§171.021-171.026 and 171.096(d).

§6.1 Who may compel or be compelled under TAA.

1. Signatory. Either party to a contract that contains an arbitration provision may compel the other party to participate in arbitration. See "Signatory," §5.1.1, p. 289.

✦

2. Nonsignatory. A nonsignatory to an arbitration agreement can sometimes compel arbitration or be compelled to arbitrate. *See Meyer v. WMCO-GP, LLC*, 211 S.W.3d 302, 305-06 (Tex.2006). The courts rely on the same legal theories to bind nonsignatories to arbitration agreements under the TAA as under the FAA. See "Nonsignatory," §5.1.2, p. 289.

§6.2 Motion to compel arbitration under TAA. For the court to compel arbitration under the TAA, the party seeking arbitration must establish that the claim is subject to a valid arbitration agreement and falls within the scope of that agreement. *Phillips v. ACS Mun. Brokers, Inc.*, 888 S.W.2d 872, 875 (Tex.App.—Dallas 1994, no writ); *Merrill Lynch, Pierce, Fenner & Smith v. Eddings*, 838 S.W.2d 874, 878 (Tex.App.—Waco 1992, writ denied). The claim must also be arbitrable. *See* CPRC §171.002. Once these matters are proved, the court must order the parties to arbitrate, even if the opposing party does not want to arbitrate. *Kilroy v. Kilroy*, 137 S.W.3d 780, 787 (Tex.App.—Houston [1st Dist.] 2004, orig. proceeding); *Phillips*, 888 S.W.2d at 875; *see* CPRC §171.021(a).

1. Valid agreement & claim within scope.

(1) Valid arbitration agreement. The party moving for arbitration must show that the claim is subject to a valid arbitration agreement.

(a) Written. The TAA requires that the terms of the arbitration agreement be in writing. *Burlington N. R.R. v. Akpan*, 943 S.W.2d 48, 52 (Tex.App.—Fort Worth 1996, no writ); *see* CPRC §171.001(a). The language of the arbitration agreement must clearly indicate the intent to arbitrate; however, the language does not have to take any particular form. *Bates v. MTH Homes-Tex., L.P.*, 177 S.W.3d 419, 422 (Tex.App.—Houston [1st Dist.] 2005, orig. proceeding).

(b) Valid. There must be a valid arbitration agreement for the court to compel arbitration. See "Valid," §5.2.1(1)(b), p. 291.

(c) Signature.

[1] Generally – not required. The TAA generally does not require that the agreement be signed by either party. *In re AdvancePCS Health L.P.*, 172 S.W.3d 603, 606 (Tex.2005); *Akpan*, 943 S.W.2d at 52; *see* CPRC §171.001.

[2] Required by statute. An agreement to arbitrate must be signed when required by statute. However, the FAA preempts state contractual requirements that apply only to arbitration clauses. *In re Weekley Homes, L.P.*, 180 S.W.3d 127, 130 n.4 (Tex.2005). The following statutes require that the arbitration agreement be signed:

[a] The CPRC requires that an arbitration agreement be signed by the parties and their attorneys in two situations: (1) for contracts of $50,000 or less and (2) for personal-injury claims. CPRC §171.002(a)(2), (a)(3), (b)(2), (c)(2).

[b] The Government Code requires that an arbitration clause in a contingent-fee agreement be signed by the attorney and the client. Gov't Code §82.065(a); *In re Godt*, 28 S.W.3d 732, 738 (Tex. App.—Corpus Christi 2000, orig. proceeding). If the contingent-fee agreement involves a personal-injury claim, the agreement must also be signed by the other parties and their attorneys, as required by CPRC §171.002(a)(3), (c). *In re Godt*, 28 S.W.3d at 738-39. A contingent-fee agreement that does not meet the statutory requirements is voidable by the client. *Tillery & Tillery v. Zurich Ins.*, 54 S.W.3d 356, 360 (Tex.App.—Dallas 2001, pet. denied).

NOTE

The courts disagree on whether a mandatory arbitration clause in an attorney-client agreement is enforceable in a legal-malpractice case if the agreement is not (1) signed by each party on the advice of counsel and (2) signed by each party's attorney, as required by CPRC §171.002(c). See **O'Connor's Texas COA**, *"Mandatory arbitration," ch. 17, §6.4, p. 499.*

ARBITRATION

✯

(d) Type of arbitration.

[1] Binding. Arbitration is binding if the arbitration clause states that it is binding or that any controversy or claim arising from or relating to the contract or a breach of the contract will be settled by arbitration and that any court having jurisdiction over the case may enter a judgment on the award. *See Porter & Clements, L.L.P. v. Stone*, 935 S.W.2d 217, 220-21 (Tex.App.—Houston [1st Dist.] 1996, no writ); *Belmont Constructors, Inc. v. Lyondell Pet. Co.*, 896 S.W.2d 352, 358 n.2 (Tex.App.—Houston [1st Dist.] 1995, no writ). Unless the contract to arbitrate specifically forecloses certain relief, the relief can be granted. *See, e.g., Mastrobuono v. Shearson Lehman Hutton, Inc.*, 514 U.S. 52, 59-61 & n.7 (1995) (punitive damages allowed because arbitration clause made no express reference to them); *J.J. Gregory Gourmet Servs. v. Antone's Import Co.*, 927 S.W.2d 31, 35-36 (Tex.App.—Houston [1st Dist.] 1995, no writ) (injunctive relief allowed because arbitration clause did not specifically prohibit it).

[2] Nonbinding. Arbitration is not binding if the arbitration clause specifically states that the arbitration is nonbinding. *See Porter & Clements*, 935 S.W.2d at 221-22. When a contract does not state whether arbitration is binding or nonbinding, the courts assume it is binding. *See id.*

(2) Claim within scope. The party moving for arbitration must show that the claim falls within the scope of the arbitration agreement. See "Claim within scope," §5.2.1(2), p. 291.

2. Arbitrable claim. For the court to compel arbitration under the TAA, the claim must be arbitrable and there must be no other legal constraint, such as a statutory restriction, that renders the claim nonarbitrable. *See* CPRC §171.002. Although most disputes are arbitrable, a claim cannot be submitted to arbitration if a statute shows clear legislative intent to preclude application of the TAA. Under the TAA, the following matters cannot be submitted to arbitration:

(1) A contract subject to arbitration that is unconscionable when it is made. CPRC §171.022.

(2) A collective-bargaining agreement between an employer and a labor union. *Id.* §171.002(a)(1).

(3) A contract for acquisition by an individual (not a corporation or other business entity) of property, services, money, or credit when the total consideration is $50,000 or less, unless the agreement is in writing and signed by both parties and their attorneys. *Id.* §171.002(a)(2).

(4) A claim for personal injury, unless each party, on the advice of counsel, agrees in writing to arbitrate and the agreement is signed by each party and its attorney. *Id.* §171.002(a)(3).

(5) A claim for workers' compensation benefits. *Id.* §171.002(a)(4).

(6) An agreement made before January 1, 1966. *Id.* §171.002(a)(5).

§7. OBJECTIONS TO ARBITRATION

Once a party seeking arbitration establishes the existence of a valid arbitration agreement, the burden shifts to the party opposing arbitration to raise an affirmative defense to the agreement's enforcement. *Ellis v. Schlimmer*, 337 S.W.3d 860, 861-62 (Tex.2011); *J.M. Davidson, Inc. v. Webster*, 128 S.W.3d 223, 227 (Tex.2003). For a comprehensive discussion of objections used to defeat arbitration, see Bland et al., *Consumer Arbitration Agreements* (6th ed. 2011).

§7.1 No agreement. The party opposing arbitration may claim that there was never an agreement to arbitrate. The parties' agreement to arbitrate must be clear. *Bates v. MTH Homes-Tex., L.P.*, 177 S.W.3d 419, 422 (Tex.App.—Houston [1st Dist.] 2005, orig. proceeding). Whether there is an agreement to arbitrate is a threshold inquiry for the court. *In re Morgan Stanley & Co.*, 293 S.W.3d 182, 187 (Tex.2009) (FAA). The party opposing arbitration has the burden to prove there is no agreement to arbitrate. *Cantella & Co. v. Goodwin*, 924 S.W.2d 943, 944 (Tex.1996) (FAA). To do so, the party can raise a contract-formation defense. *See, e.g., In re Morgan Stanley & Co.*, 293 S.W.3d at 187 (FAA; lack of mental capacity is contract-formation defense). A contract-formation defense raises the issue of whether there was ever an agreement to arbitrate and thus must be decided by the court. *Id.* at 189 (FAA). When a

———————————— ✦ ————————————

party files a response denying that there is an agreement to arbitrate, the court must summarily resolve that issue. CPRC §171.021(b) (TAA); *Jack B. Anglin Co. v. Tipps*, 842 S.W.2d 266, 268-69 (Tex.1992) (FAA and TAA). For the requirements for the formation of an FAA agreement, see "Valid arbitration agreement," §5.2.1(1), p. 291. For the requirements for the formation of a TAA agreement, see "Valid arbitration agreement," §6.2.1(1), p. 293.

§7.2 Agreement not valid. The party opposing arbitration may claim that the agreement to arbitrate is not valid. Validity defenses to arbitration that relate to the arbitration agreement itself, not to the contract as a whole, are determined by the court. *Nitro-Lift Techs. v. Howard*, ___ U.S. ___ (2012) (No. 11-1377; 11-26-12) (FAA); *Perry Homes v. Cull*, 258 S.W.3d 580, 589 (Tex.2008) (FAA); *see In re Olshan Found. Repair Co.*, 328 S.W.3d 883, 891-92 (Tex.2010) (FAA and TAA); *In re Morgan Stanley & Co.*, 293 S.W.3d 182, 185 (Tex.2009) (FAA); *In re First-Merit Bank*, 52 S.W.3d 749, 756 (Tex.2001) (FAA). *But see IHS Acquisition No. 131, Inc. v. Iturralde*, ___ S.W.3d ___ (Tex.App.—El Paso 2012, no pet.) (No. 08-11-00091-CV; 4-25-12) (validity defenses to arbitration agreement are determined by arbitrator if agreement clearly and unmistakably provides that issues of validity or enforceability are subject to arbitration). A defensive claim relates to the arbitration agreement if it singles out the arbitration clause from other contractual provisions. *See In re RLS Legal Solutions, L.L.C.*, 221 S.W.3d 629, 630 (Tex.2007) (FAA). If the defensive claim relates to the validity of the contract as a whole, it must be decided by the arbitrator, not the court. *Nitro-Lift Techs.*, ___ U.S. at ___ (FAA); *e.g., In re Labatt Food Serv.*, 279 S.W.3d 640, 648 (Tex.2009) (FAA; claim that one of contract's provisions was illegal related to entire contract and was question for arbitrator); *see, e.g., In re Kaplan Higher Educ. Corp.*, 235 S.W.3d 206, 208-09 (Tex.2007) (FAA; fraudulent-inducement claim was dispute involving entire contract and was question for arbitrator); *In re Merrill Lynch Trust Co.*, 235 S.W.3d 185, 190 (Tex. 2007) (FAA; claim that arbitration agreement was illusory related to entire contract and was question for arbitrator); *see also In re Olshan Found.*, 328 S.W.3d at 900 (Hecht & Medina, JJ., concurring) (FAA and TAA; if arbitrator determines contract is void, court can sanction party for filing groundless motion to compel arbitration). The following are some defenses the party can raise to prove the arbitration agreement is not valid:

1. Fraud. The party opposing arbitration may claim that the arbitration agreement was induced or procured by fraud. *Forest Oil Corp. v. McAllen*, 268 S.W.3d 51, 56 (Tex.2008) (TAA); *In re FirstMerit*, 52 S.W.3d at 756 (FAA); *see, e.g., In re U.S. Home Corp.*, 236 S.W.3d 761, 764 (Tex.2007) (FAA; evidence that Ps did not read arbitration clause because it was on the back of a single-sheet contract was insufficient to show fraud); *In re Oakwood Mobile Homes, Inc.*, 987 S.W.2d 571, 573-74 (Tex.1999) (FAA; no fraud because P did not assert that D-seller made any false representations); *Henry v. Gonzalez*, 18 S.W.3d 684, 691 (Tex.App.—San Antonio 2000, pet. dism'd) (TAA; evidence that P did not know contract included arbitration agreement was insufficient to show fraud). See *O'Connor's Texas COA*, "Fraud," ch. 12, p. 279.

2. Unconscionability. The party opposing arbitration may claim that the arbitration agreement was unconscionable at the time it was made. CPRC §171.022 (TAA); *In re FirstMerit*, 52 S.W.3d at 756 (FAA); *American Employers' Ins. v. Aiken*, 942 S.W.2d 156, 160 (Tex.App.—Fort Worth 1997, no writ) (TAA); *see In re Odyssey Healthcare, Inc.*, 310 S.W.3d 419, 422-23 (Tex.2010) (FAA). An agreement will generally be considered unconscionable if it is grossly one-sided. *In re Poly-America, L.P.*, 262 S.W.3d 337, 348 (Tex.2008) (FAA); *see In re Olshan Found.*, 328 S.W.3d at 892 (FAA and TAA). A party's claim of unconscionability can include procedural unconscionability or substantive unconscionability. *See In re Olshan Found.*, 328 S.W.3d at 892. See *O'Connor's Texas COA*, "Unconscionability," ch. 5-B, §5.1.17, p. 100.

(1) Procedural unconscionability. Procedural unconscionability refers to the circumstances surrounding the actual making of the arbitration agreement. *In re Palm Harbor Homes, Inc.*, 195 S.W.3d 672, 677 (Tex. 2006) (FAA). A gross disparity in bargaining power between the parties does not amount to procedural unconscionability. *See In re AdvancePCS Health L.P.*, 172 S.W.3d 603, 608 (Tex.2005) (FAA); *In re Halliburton Co.*, 80 S.W.3d 566, 572 (Tex.2002) (FAA). For example, the disparity in bargaining power between an employer and an at-will employee is not unconscionable. *In re Halliburton Co.*, 80 S.W.3d at 572 (FAA). Adhesion contracts are not automatically unconscionable. *In re U.S. Home*, 236 S.W.3d at 764 (FAA); *In re Palm Harbor Homes*, 195 S.W.3d at 678 (FAA); *In re AdvancePCS*, 172 S.W.3d at 608 (FAA). See *O'Connor's Texas COA*, "Procedural unconscionability," ch. 5-B, §5.1.17(1), p. 100.

———————————————— ✦ ————————————————

(2) Substantive unconscionability. Substantive unconscionability refers to the fairness of the terms and conditions of the arbitration agreement itself. *In re Palm Harbor Homes*, 195 S.W.3d at 677 (FAA); *In re Halliburton Co.*, 80 S.W.3d at 571 (FAA); *see In re Odyssey Healthcare*, 310 S.W.3d at 422 (FAA; substantive unconscionability refers to whether arbitration agreement preserves party's substantive rights and remedies).

(a) Test. The test for substantive unconscionability is whether, given the parties' backgrounds, the arbitration agreement is so one-sided that it is unconscionable under the circumstances at the time the parties signed the contract. *In re Olshan Found.*, 328 S.W.3d at 892 (FAA and TAA); *e.g.*, *In re Poly-America*, 262 S.W.3d at 348-49 (FAA; arbitration provision that eliminated key remedies under Workers' Compensation Act's antiretaliation provisions was unconscionable); *In re Fleetwood Homes*, 257 S.W.3d 692, 695 (Tex.2008) (FAA; allowing prevailing party to recover attorney fees and limiting discovery for both parties was not unconscionable); *In re Palm Harbor Homes*, 195 S.W.3d at 678 (FAA; binding only one party to arbitration was not unconscionable).

(b) Excessive costs. Although arbitration is intended to be a less expensive and more efficient alternative to litigation, when the costs imposed by an arbitration agreement are excessive and effectively prevent a party from asserting her rights in an arbitration proceeding, the arbitration agreement may be substantively unconscionable. *In re Olshan Found.*, 328 S.W.3d at 893 (FAA and TAA).

[1] Burden to prove excessive costs. The party opposing arbitration has the burden to show that the costs of arbitration would be prohibitively expensive such that the arbitration agreement is unconscionable. *In re Olshan Found.*, 328 S.W.3d at 893 (FAA and TAA); *see In re Odyssey Healthcare*, 310 S.W.3d at 422 (FAA). The party opposing arbitration must submit specific evidence showing the likelihood of incurring excessive costs for her particular arbitration. *In re Olshan Found.*, 328 S.W.3d at 895 & n.5 (FAA and TAA); *see, e.g.*, *In re Odyssey Healthcare*, 310 S.W.3d at 422-23 (FAA; even if being forced to arbitrate in different city from where P lived would have caused her substantial expense, P did not prove that incurred costs would be likely). The party can submit invoices, expert testimony, cost estimates, or other comparable evidence. *In re Olshan Found.*, 328 S.W.3d at 895 (FAA and TAA). Evidence that other parties in similar cases have incurred excessive costs is not sufficient to show excessive costs for the party's particular arbitration. *Id.* Once the party has met her burden, the other party must show contradictory evidence that arbitration costs will not be excessive. *See id.*

[2] Factors that determine excessive costs. In determining whether costs are excessive, a court will generally use a case-by-case analysis that should focus on the following: (1) the party's ability to pay the arbitration fees and costs, (2) the actual amount of the fees compared to the amount of the underlying claim, (3) the expected cost differential between arbitration and litigation, and (4) whether that cost differential is so substantial that it would deter a party from bringing a claim. *In re Olshan Found.*, 328 S.W.3d at 893-94 (FAA and TAA); *see, e.g.*, *Olshan Found. Repair Co. v. Ayala*, 180 S.W.3d 212, 215-16 (Tex.App.—San Antonio 2005, pet. denied) (cost of arbitration was more than three times the amount of underlying claim; agreement was unconscionable). The key inquiry is what the total cost is to the party pursuing the claim, not where the cost goes. *In re Olshan Found.*, 328 S.W.3d at 893 (FAA and TAA).

3. Duress. The party opposing arbitration may claim that it agreed to the arbitration clause under duress. *In re RLS Legal Solutions*, 221 S.W.3d at 630 (FAA). See *O'Connor's Texas COA*, "Duress," ch. 5-B, §5.1.10, p. 94. However, proof that the party was under duress to execute the contract containing the arbitration clause is not sufficient; the party must prove it was under duress to agree to the arbitration clause apart from the other provisions in the contract. *In re RLS Legal Solutions*, 221 S.W.3d at 630 (FAA); *see, e.g.*, *In re FirstMerit*, 52 S.W.3d at 758 (FAA; no duress when sellers refused to sell home unless buyers signed arbitration addendum).

4. Illusory agreement. The party opposing arbitration may claim that the arbitration clause is illusory because one party has the unilateral and unrestricted right to amend or terminate the arbitration agreement and avoid its promise to arbitrate. *In re 24R, Inc.*, 324 S.W.3d 564, 567 (Tex.2010) (FAA); *J.M. Davidson, Inc. v. Webster*, 128 S.W.3d 223, 230 n.2 (Tex.2003) (TAA); *see In re Halliburton Co.*, 80 S.W.3d at 569-70 (FAA); *see, e.g.*, *In re Odyssey Healthcare*, 310 S.W.3d at 424 (FAA; arbitration agreement was enforceable because both parties mutually promised to submit all employment disputes to arbitration and limitations were placed on D's right to amend or terminate agreement).

———————————————————— ✦ ————————————————————

§7.3 Claim outside scope of agreement. The party opposing arbitration may argue that the claim is outside the scope of the arbitration agreement. *See In re Poly-America, L.P.*, 262 S.W.3d 337, 348 (Tex.2008) (FAA); *In re FirstMerit Bank*, 52 S.W.3d 749, 754-55 (Tex.2001) (FAA). See "Claim within scope," §5.2.1(2), p. 291. Any doubts about whether the claim falls within the scope of an arbitration agreement are resolved in favor of arbitration. *In re Bank One*, 216 S.W.3d 825, 826 (Tex.2007) (FAA); *see In re Poly-America*, 262 S.W.3d at 348 (FAA).

§7.4 Claim not arbitrable. The party opposing arbitration may argue that the claim is not arbitrable by law. *See In re American Homestar*, 50 S.W.3d 480, 485 (Tex.2001) (FAA; party opposing arbitration must show clear congressional intent to preclude application of FAA). See "Arbitrable claim," §5.2.2, p. 292 (FAA); "Arbitrable claim," §6.2.2, p. 294 (TAA).

§7.5 Waiver. The party opposing arbitration may claim that the party seeking arbitration waived its right to arbitrate. There is a strong presumption against the waiver of a contractual right to arbitrate. *Perry Homes v. Cull*, 258 S.W.3d 580, 584 (Tex.2008) (FAA); *In re Bank One*, 216 S.W.3d 825, 827 (Tex.2007) (FAA); *EZ Pawn Corp. v. Mancias*, 934 S.W.2d 87, 89 (Tex.1996) (FAA and TAA).

1. Express waiver. A party may waive its right to arbitrate by expressly indicating that it wants to resolve the case in a judicial forum. *Interconex, Inc. v. Ugarov*, 224 S.W.3d 523, 533 (Tex.App.—Houston [1st Dist.] 2007, no pet.).

2. Implied waiver. A party may impliedly waive its right to arbitrate. To establish implied waiver of the right to arbitrate, the party opposing arbitration must show that (1) the other party substantially invoked the litigation process and (2) this action was prejudicial to the party opposing arbitration.

(1) Substantially invoked judicial process. The party opposing arbitration must show that the other party substantially invoked the judicial process. *Perry Homes*, 258 S.W.3d at 589-90 (FAA); *In re Fleetwood Homes*, 257 S.W.3d 692, 694 (Tex.2008) (FAA); *In re Bank One*, 216 S.W.3d at 827 (FAA); *EZ Pawn*, 934 S.W.2d at 89 (FAA). The court will apply a totality-of-the-circumstances test to determine whether the litigation conduct was substantial. *Perry Homes*, 258 S.W.3d at 592-93 (FAA); *In re Fleetwood Homes*, 257 S.W.3d at 694 (FAA).

(a) Waiver. The presumption against waiver is so strong that the Texas Supreme Court has held only one time that a party waived arbitration by substantially invoking the judicial process. *Perry Homes*, 258 S.W.3d at 589-90 (FAA; P objected to arbitration, conducted extensive discovery, and then moved to compel arbitration just before trial); *see also CropMark Direct, LLC v. Urbanczyk*, ___ S.W.3d ___ (Tex.App.—Amarillo 2012, pet. filed 10-30-12) (No. 07-11-0426-CV; 6-7-12) (P waived arbitration when it engaged in discovery, demanded a jury trial, and failed to comply with arbitration deadlines); *Adams v. StaxxRing, Inc.*, 344 S.W.3d 641, 648-50 (Tex.App.—Dallas 2011, pet. denied) (P waived arbitration when he engaged in extensive discovery during 13 months of aggressive litigation, sought injunctive relief, and brought in third parties). Courts have also suggested that a party may substantially invoke the judicial process by moving for summary judgment. *Interconex, Inc.*, 224 S.W.3d at 534; *Williams Indus. v. Earth Dev. Sys.*, 110 S.W.3d 131, 135 (Tex.App.—Houston [1st Dist.] 2003, no pet.).

(b) No waiver. A party does not substantially invoke the judicial process by doing any of the following: • Moving between federal courts before filing an answer and a motion to compel in state court. *In re Citigroup Global Mkts., Inc.*, 258 S.W.3d 623, 625 (Tex.2008) (FAA). • Filing a motion to set aside a default judgment. *In re Bank One*, 216 S.W.3d at 827 (FAA). • Filing an answer and conducting discovery. *In re Bruce Terminix Co.*, 988 S.W.2d 702, 704 (Tex.1998) (FAA). • Attempting to settle the claim. *Texas Residential Mortg., L.P. v. Portman*, 152 S.W.3d 861, 863-64 (Tex.App.—Dallas 2005, no pet.).

(2) Prejudicial. The party opposing arbitration must show that it suffered actual prejudice as a result of the other party's inconsistent action. *See Perry Homes*, 258 S.W.3d at 595 (FAA); *In re Fleetwood Homes*, 257 S.W.3d at 694 (FAA); *In re Bruce Terminix*, 988 S.W.2d at 704 (FAA). "Prejudice" refers to the inherent unfairness, in terms of delay, expense, or damage to a party's legal position, that occurs when a party forces litigation of an issue and then seeks to compel arbitration of the same issue. *Perry Homes*, 258 S.W.3d at 597 (FAA). Mere delay

———————————— ✪ ————————————

in seeking arbitration does not demonstrate prejudice. *In re Vesta Ins. Grp.*, 192 S.W.3d 759, 763 (Tex.2006) (FAA); *EZ Pawn*, 934 S.W.2d at 89-90 (FAA); *Prudential Secs. Inc. v. Marshall*, 909 S.W.2d 896, 898-99 (Tex.1995) (FAA).

§8. TRIAL COURT'S ORDER COMPELLING OR DENYING ARBITRATION

§8.1 Hearing. Texas courts follow Texas's procedural rules when applying both the FAA and the TAA. *See Jack B. Anglin Co. v. Tipps*, 842 S.W.2d 266, 268 (Tex.1992). If material facts are uncontroverted, the trial court may decide whether to compel arbitration based on the affidavits, pleadings, discovery, and stipulations. *See id.* at 269. If material facts are controverted by admissible evidence, the trial court must conduct an evidentiary hearing to resolve the disputed facts. *See id.* Although pre-arbitration discovery is authorized under the TAA when the trial court cannot make a proper decision on the motion to compel because it lacks information, the court cannot order discovery on the merits of the underlying controversy. *In re Houston Pipe Line Co.*, 311 S.W.3d 449, 451 (Tex.2009). The court also cannot defer ruling on a motion to compel arbitration until all discovery is complete. *In re MHI Prtshp.*, 7 S.W.3d 918, 923 (Tex.App.—Houston [1st Dist.] 1999, orig. proceeding). However, parties can modify an arbitration agreement (e.g., through a Rule 11 agreement) to allow for certain discovery to take place before the hearing on the motion to compel. *See In re F.C. Holdings*, 349 S.W.3d 811, 815 (Tex.App.—Tyler 2011, orig. proceeding). When the court holds a hearing to resolve fact questions, the parties should introduce evidence with all the formalities of a nonjury trial (i.e., with witnesses and a court reporter).

§8.2 Ruling.

1. Arbitration agreements favored. Public policy strongly favors resolving disputes through arbitration. *Jack B. Anglin Co. v. Tipps*, 842 S.W.2d 266, 268 (Tex.1992) (FAA and TAA); *see Nitro-Lift Techs. v. Howard*, ___ U.S. ___ (2012) (No. 11-1377; 11-26-12) (FAA); *Howsam v. Dean Witter Reynolds, Inc.*, 537 U.S. 79, 83 (2002) (FAA). The court should resolve any doubts about whether a claim falls within the scope of an agreement to arbitrate in favor of arbitration. *In re Rubiola*, 334 S.W.3d 220, 225 (Tex.2011) (FAA); *In re Kellogg Brown & Root, Inc.*, 166 S.W.3d 732, 737 (Tex.2005) (FAA); *Prudential Secs. Inc. v. Marshall*, 909 S.W.2d 896, 899 (Tex.1995) (FAA).

2. Questions of arbitrability. In ruling on a motion to compel arbitration, courts decide questions of arbitrability—that is, questions relating to whether the parties to a dispute have agreed to submit the dispute to arbitration. *Howsam*, 537 U.S. at 83 (FAA). Generally, a court, not an arbitrator, will decide questions of arbitrability, but the parties can agree to submit such questions to an arbitrator as long as the evidence is "clear and unmistakable" that they agreed to do so. *Id.* (FAA); *Saxa Inc. v. DFD Architecture Inc.*, 312 S.W.3d 224, 229 (Tex.App.—Dallas 2010, pet. denied) (TAA); *see Nitro-Lift Techs.*, ___ U.S. at ___ (FAA). Questions of arbitrability include those relating to the validity of the arbitration agreement itself; however, questions relating to the validity of the contract as a whole must be decided by the arbitrator, not the court. *See Nitro-Lift Techs.*, ___ U.S. at ___ (FAA). See "Agreement not valid," §7.2, p. 295.

3. Order.

(1) Granting motion. If the court grants the motion to compel arbitration, the court must do the following:

(a) Order arbitration. Order the parties to proceed to arbitration if (1) no objection is filed to the motion to compel arbitration or (2) an objection is filed but the court overrules the objection. *See* CPRC §171.021 (TAA).

(b) Stay proceedings. Sign an order that stays the proceedings during the arbitration. CPRC §§171.021(c), 171.025(a) (TAA); *In re Merrill Lynch Trust Co.*, 235 S.W.3d 185, 195 (Tex.2007) (FAA); *see Cash Am. Int'l v. Exchange Servs.*, 83 S.W.3d 183, 186-87 (Tex.App.—Amarillo 2002, no pet.) (TAA); *see also In re Merrill Lynch & Co.*, 315 S.W.3d 888, 891-92 (Tex.2010) (FAA) (litigation can be stayed even when arbitration is potentially pending). Arbitration should be given priority over litigation if it will likely resolve material issues in the suit. *In re Merrill Lynch & Co.*, 315 S.W.3d at 891; *In re Merrill Lynch Trust*, 235 S.W.3d at 195-96. Litigation involving claims related to both signatories and nonsignatories should be stayed. *See In re Merrill Lynch & Co.*, 315 S.W.3d

★

at 891; *In re Merrill Lynch Trust*, 235 S.W.3d at 195-96. If the matter referred to arbitration is severable from the rest of the proceeding, the order must stay only the matter referred to arbitration. CPRC §171.025(b) (TAA); *Cash Am. Int'l*, 83 S.W.3d at 186-87 (TAA).

(2) Denying motion. If the court sustains an objection to arbitration, the court must deny the motion to compel arbitration. CPRC §171.021(b) (TAA). For a discussion of the review of the trial court's denial of a motion to compel, see "Order denying motion," §8.3.1(1)(a), this page (TAA); "Order denying arbitration," §8.3.1(2)(a), p. 300 (FAA).

§8.3 Appellate court's review of order.

1. Review after interlocutory order. Generally, interlocutory orders are not appealable unless made appealable by statute. The CPRC permits appeal of certain interlocutory orders regarding arbitration. *See* CPRC §51.016 (FAA), §171.098 (TAA).

(1) TAA. Whether the party can file an interlocutory appeal or must seek relief by filing a petition for mandamus generally depends on whether the court granted or denied the motion to compel arbitration.

(a) Order denying motion. If the court denies a motion to compel arbitration made under CPRC §171.021, the party seeking arbitration may file an interlocutory appeal. CPRC §171.098(a)(1); *Chambers v. O'Quinn*, 242 S.W.3d 30, 31 (Tex.2007); *Certain Underwriters at Lloyd's v. Celebrity, Inc.*, 988 S.W.2d 731, 732 (Tex.1998).

(b) Order granting motion. If the court grants a motion to compel arbitration, the party objecting to arbitration is not entitled to an interlocutory appeal of the order. *Elm Creek Villas Homeowner Ass'n v. Beldon Roofing & Remodeling Co.*, 940 S.W.2d 150, 153 (Tex.App.—San Antonio 1996, no writ). The party may be able to seek review of the order by petition for writ of mandamus. *In re Wolff*, 231 S.W.3d 466, 467 (Tex.App.—Dallas 2007, orig. proceeding). Mandamus relief is generally unavailable, however, because an order compelling arbitration is appealable from a final judgment, and therefore the party seeking mandamus will rarely be able to meet the requirement of no adequate remedy by appeal. *Cf. In re Gulf Expl., LLC*, 289 S.W.3d 836, 842 (Tex.2009) (FAA; any balancing of benefits and detriments of delaying arbitration in determining adequacy of appeal must "tilt strongly against mandamus review" because FAA and TAA both exclude immediate review of orders compelling arbitration).

(c) Other orders. Mandamus relief may be available for an interlocutory order that is not subject to immediate appeal if the order defers ruling on the motion to compel arbitration. *See, e.g., In re MHI Prtshp.*, 7 S.W.3d 918, 920-21 (Tex.App.—Houston [1st Dist.] 1999, orig. proceeding) (court had no discretion to defer ruling on arbitration motion until after completion of discovery).

(2) FAA. CPRC §51.016 allows an interlocutory appeal of an FAA order that would be appealable in federal court under 9 U.S.C. §16. *E.g., CMH Homes v. Perez*, 340 S.W.3d 444, 451-52 (Tex.2011) (appeal of order appointing arbitrator was not permitted under 9 U.S.C. §16). See *O'Connor's Federal Rules*, "Appealable order," ch. 7-E, §5.1, p. 666. If an interlocutory appeal is unavailable, a party may be entitled to mandamus relief in limited circumstances. *See CMH Homes*, 340 S.W.3d at 452.

PRACTICE TIP

If you are unsure whether the order is covered under 9 U.S.C. §16 and is immediately appealable under CPRC §51.016, you should file both an appeal and a petition for writ of mandamus or, at a minimum, ask in the alternative that the appellate court consider the appeal as a petition for mandamus. See CMH Homes, 340 S.W.3d at 453-54; Texas La Fiesta Auto Sales, LLC v. Belk, 349 S.W.3d 872, 877-78 (Tex.App.—Houston [14th Dist.] 2011, no pet.). If your appeal is dismissed for lack of jurisdiction, mandamus relief is then potentially available. See CMH Homes, 340 S.W.3d at 454; Texas La Fiesta, 349 S.W.3d at 879.

ARBITRATION

─────────────── ★ ───────────────

(a) Order denying arbitration. If the court denies a motion to compel arbitration in a suit subject to the FAA, the party may file an interlocutory appeal. *See* CPRC §51.016; 9 U.S.C. §16(a)(1)(B).

CAUTION

*Until September 1, 2009, there was no Texas statute allowing for interlocutory appeals of orders denying arbitration under the FAA; mandamus was the only avenue for reviewing these orders. See **In re NEXT Fin. Grp.**, 271 S.W.3d 263, 266 (Tex.2008); **Jack B. Anglin Co. v. Tipps**, 842 S.W.2d 266, 272 (Tex.1992). However, the Texas Legislature enacted CPRC §51.016, effective September 1, 2009, to allow for interlocutory appeals of FAA orders that would be appealable in a federal district court under 9 U.S.C. §16(a). See Acts 2009, 81st Leg., R.S., ch. 820, §§2, 3, eff. Sept. 1, 2009. Because TAA and FAA provisions are similar but not identical, parties seeking review of an order under both acts should make sure an interlocutory appeal is authorized. See **O'Connor's Texas Appeals**, "Arbitration orders," ch. 1-B, §2.3.3(1), p. 16; "Other orders," ch. 10-B, §4.3.11(2)(b), p. 350.*

(b) Order granting arbitration. The FAA does not allow immediate appellate review of an interlocutory order compelling arbitration. 9 U.S.C. §16(b)(2), (b)(3); *see also **In re Gulf Expl., LLC**,* 289 S.W.3d at 839-40 (order compelling arbitration and staying underlying litigation is not immediately appealable, but order compelling arbitration and dismissing underlying litigation is appealable as final judgment). Mandamus relief is usually not available in such cases either, because an order compelling arbitration is appealable from a final judgment, and therefore the party seeking mandamus will rarely be able to meet the requirement of no adequate remedy by appeal. *In re Gulf Expl., LLC*, 289 S.W.3d at 842. See "Review after final judgment," §8.3.2, this page. In rare situations, however, mandamus relief may be available. For example, when there are conflicting statutory mandates, mandamus may be necessary to preserve important substantive and procedural rights. *In re Gulf Expl., LLC*, 289 S.W.3d at 843; *see **In re Poly-America, L.P.**,* 262 S.W.3d 337, 352 (Tex.2008); *In re Prudential Ins.*, 148 S.W.3d 124, 136 (Tex.2004).

(c) Other orders.

[1] Order denying contracted-for arbitration rights. Mandamus relief may be available for an interlocutory order that is not subject to immediate appeal if the order denies a party its contracted-for arbitration rights. *See **CMH Homes**,* 340 S.W.3d at 452; *see, e.g., **In re Serv. Corp.**,* 355 S.W.3d 655, 658 (Tex.2011) (mandamus relief was available because court abused its discretion by denying party's right to choose its own arbitrator; party had no adequate remedy by appeal because FAA does not provide for review of this type of order in state court); *In re Louisiana Pac. Corp.*, 972 S.W.2d 63, 65 (Tex.1998) (same).

[2] Order deferring ruling on motion to compel. Mandamus relief may be available for an interlocutory order that is not subject to immediate appeal if the order defers ruling on the motion to compel arbitration. *See, e.g., **In re Heritage Bldg. Sys.**,* 185 S.W.3d 539, 542 (Tex.App.—Beaumont 2006, orig. proceeding) (court had no discretion to delay ruling on motion to compel arbitration until after court-ordered mediation); *In re Champion Techs.*, 173 S.W.3d 595, 599 (Tex.App.—Eastland 2005, orig. proceeding) (court had no discretion to defer ruling on arbitration motion until after completion of discovery).

2. Review after final judgment. After final judgment, a party may appeal an order denying or compelling arbitration. *See* CPRC §51.016 (FAA; appeal from judgment may be taken in same manner as permitted under 9 U.S.C. §16); *Green Tree Fin. Corp. v. Randolph*, 531 U.S. 79, 89 (2000) (FAA; order compelling arbitration); *Perry Homes v. Cull*, 258 S.W.3d 580, 587 (Tex.2008) (same); *Chambers*, 242 S.W.3d at 32 (TAA; order compelling arbitration); *see also* 9 U.S.C. §16(a)(3) (appeal can be taken from final decision on arbitration). See *O'Connor's Federal Rules*, "Final order," ch. 7-E, §5.1.1, p. 667.

3. Standard of review.

(1) Abuse of discretion. Generally, orders granting or denying arbitration under either the TAA or the FAA are reviewed under the abuse-of-discretion standard. *See **In re Labatt Food Serv.**,* 279 S.W.3d 640, 642-43

✦

(Tex.2009) (FAA; order denying); *Perry Homes*, 258 S.W.3d at 598 (FAA; order granting); *Cleveland Constr., Inc. v. Levco Constr., Inc.*, 359 S.W.3d 843, 851 (Tex.App.—Houston [1st Dist.] 2012, pet. dism'd) (FAA; order denying); *Chambers v. O'Quinn*, 305 S.W.3d 141, 146 (Tex.App.—Houston [1st Dist.] 2009, pet. denied) (TAA; order granting); *Stanford Dev. Corp. v. Stanford Condo. Owners Ass'n*, 285 S.W.3d 45, 48 (Tex.App.—Houston [1st Dist.] 2009, no pet.) (TAA; order denying); *Teel v. Beldon Roofing & Remodeling Co.*, 281 S.W.3d 446, 448 (Tex. App.—San Antonio 2007, pet. denied) (FAA; order granting). Under this standard, the appellate court defers to the trial court's factual findings if they are supported by evidence, but reviews the trial court's legal determinations de novo. *In re Labatt Food*, 279 S.W.3d at 643; *Perry Homes*, 258 S.W.3d at 598; *Stanford Dev.*, 285 S.W.3d at 48. The following are examples of legal issues that are reviewed de novo. • Whether the arbitration agreement is valid. *In re D. Wilson Constr. Co.*, 196 S.W.3d 774, 781 (Tex.2006); *J.M. Davidson, Inc. v. Webster*, 128 S.W.3d 223, 227 (Tex. 2003). • Whether an arbitration agreement is enforceable. *In re Labatt Food*, 279 S.W.3d at 643. • Whether the claim falls within the scope of the agreement. *In re Stanford Grp.*, 273 S.W.3d 807, 813 (Tex.App.—Houston [14th Dist.] 2008, orig. proceeding). • Whether a party waived its right to arbitrate. *Perry Homes*, 258 S.W.3d at 598; *Citizens Nat'l Bank v. Bryce*, 271 S.W.3d 347, 354 (Tex.App.—Tyler 2008, no pet.).

    (2) No evidence. When only the trial court's factual findings are at issue, some appellate courts review those findings under the no-evidence standard. *See Certain Underwriters at Lloyd's v. Celebrity, Inc.*, 950 S.W.2d 375, 377 (Tex.App.—Tyler 1996) (TAA; order denying), *writ dism'd*, 988 S.W.2d 731 (Tex.1998); *Phillips v. ACS Mun. Brokers, Inc.*, 888 S.W.2d 872, 874 (Tex.App.—Dallas 1994, no writ) (same); *Hearthshire Braeswood Plaza L.P. v. Bill Kelly Co.*, 849 S.W.2d 380, 384 (Tex.App.—Houston [14th Dist.] 1993, writ denied) (same). Under this standard, the appellate court reviews only the evidence that supports the factual findings and disregards all contrary evidence. *Certain Underwriters*, 950 S.W.2d at 377; *Phillips*, 888 S.W.2d at 874; *Hearthshire Braeswood*, 849 S.W.2d at 384.

§9. ARBITRATOR'S AWARD

    §9.1 Written. The arbitrator's award must be in writing and signed by the arbitrators. CPRC §171.053(a) (TAA).

    §9.2 Attorney fees. An attorney representing a party in an arbitration proceeding may be entitled to attorney fees as part of the arbitration award. CPRC §171.048(a), (c) (TAA). Attorney fees must be awarded if the fees are provided for in the arbitration agreement or by law. *Id.* §171.048(c); *see Cooper v. Bushong*, 10 S.W.3d 20, 26 (Tex. App.—Austin 1999, pet. denied) (TAA); *see, e.g., Monday v. Cox*, 881 S.W.2d 381, 384 (Tex.App.—San Antonio 1994, writ denied) (TAA; attorney fees awarded under DTPA, which provides for attorney fees for groundless suit).

    §9.3 Arbitrator's review of award. The parties may file an application asking the arbitrator to clarify, modify, or correct its award. CPRC §171.054(a), (b) (TAA); *see, e.g., Sydow v. Verner, Liipfert, Bernhard, McPherson & Hand*, 218 S.W.3d 162, 170 (Tex.App.—Houston [14th Dist.] 2007, no pet.) (TAA; arbitrator could correct award because he intended to include prejudgment interest on attorney fees but forgot to do so).

    1. Deadline. The deadline to file an application with the arbitrator to modify, correct, or clarify an award is 20 days after the award is delivered to the party. CPRC §171.054(a), (c) (TAA).

    2. Notice. The applicant must give prompt written notice of the application. CPRC §171.054(d) (TAA). The notice should instruct the opposing party to serve any objection within ten days of the notice. *Id.*

    3. Grounds. To ask the arbitrator to modify or correct an award, the party must have proper grounds. *See* CPRC §§171.054(a), 171.091(a) (TAA); *Sydow*, 218 S.W.3d at 167 (TAA); *Barsness v. Scott*, 126 S.W.3d 232, 240-41 (Tex.App.—San Antonio 2003, pet. denied) (TAA). See "Grounds," §9.4.2(2), p. 302.

    §9.4 Trial court's review of award.

    1. Motion to confirm award. A party may file a motion with the court to confirm the arbitrator's award. CPRC §171.087 (TAA); 9 U.S.C. §9 (FAA). The court must confirm the award unless the other party offers grounds for modifying, correcting, or vacating the award. CPRC §171.087 (TAA); 9 U.S.C. §9 (FAA); *Callahan & Assocs. v. Orangefield ISD*, 92 S.W.3d 841, 844 (Tex.2002) (TAA).

★

PRACTICE TIP

*A party may file a motion for summary judgment to confirm the award, but it is not recommended. By filing a motion for summary judgment, the party assumes the additional burdens and procedural requirements of summary-judgment practice. **Baker Hughes Oilfield Opers., Inc. v. Hennig Prod.**, 164 S.W.3d 438, 442-43 (Tex.App.—Houston [14th Dist.] 2005, no pet.) (TAA); see, e.g., **Mariner Fin. Grp. v. Bossley**, 79 S.W.3d 30, 35 (Tex.2002) (under National Association of Securities Dealers Code of Arbitration; although Ps had ultimate burden of proving arbitrator's partiality, Ds who moved for traditional summary judgment did not carry summary-judgment burden of establishing that there was no fact issue on arbitrator's partiality).*

---

2. Motion to modify or correct award.

(1) Deadlines.

(a) **Under FAA.** Under the FAA, the deadline to serve notice of a motion to modify or correct the award is three months after the arbitration award is filed or delivered. 9 U.S.C. §12.

(b) **Under TAA.** Under the TAA, the deadline to file a motion with the trial court to modify or correct the arbitrator's award is 90 days after the award is delivered to the party. CPRC §171.091(b).

(2) Grounds.

(a) **Under FAA.** The exclusive grounds for modifying an arbitration award under the FAA are those listed in 9 U.S.C. §11. *Hall St. Assocs. v. Mattel, Inc.*, 552 U.S. 576, 584 (2008). A party may file a motion with the court to modify or correct the award on any of the following grounds:

[1] **Evident miscalculation.** The arbitrator's award contains an evident miscalculation of numbers or a mistake in the description of any person, thing, or property referred to in the award. 9 U.S.C. §11(a). "Miscalculation" implies inadvertence or an error caused by an oversight. *Cf. Crossmark, Inc. v. Hazar*, 124 S.W.3d 422, 436 (Tex.App.—Dallas 2004, pet. denied) (TAA).

[2] **Unsubmitted issue.** The arbitrator's award resolves a matter that was not submitted to arbitration, unless the unsubmitted matter does not affect the merits of the decision on the matter that was submitted. 9 U.S.C. §11(b).

[3] **Error in form.** The arbitrator's award contains an error in the form of the award, on a matter not affecting the merits of the controversy. 9 U.S.C. §11(c).

(b) **Under TAA.** Under the TAA, a party may file a motion with the court to modify or correct an award on any of the following grounds:

[1] **Evident miscalculation.** The arbitrator's award contains an evident miscalculation of numbers or a mistake in the description of any person, thing, or property referred to in the award. CPRC §171.091(a)(1). "Miscalculation" implies inadvertence or an error caused by an oversight. *Crossmark, Inc. v. Hazar*, 124 S.W.3d 422, 436 (Tex.App.—Dallas 2004, pet. denied). By comparison, an arbitrator's "evident mistake" in failing to award damages is not a ground for modifying or correcting an award. *Callahan & Assocs.*, 92 S.W.3d at 844.

[2] **Unsubmitted issue.** The arbitrator's award resolves a matter that was not submitted to arbitration, and the award can be corrected without affecting any decision made on issues that were submitted. CPRC §171.091(a)(2). The arbitrator is limited to deciding matters submitted to arbitration. *Sydow v. Verner, Liipfert, Bernhard, McPherson & Hand*, 218 S.W.3d 162, 168 (Tex.App.—Houston [14th Dist.] 2007, no pet.); *Baker Hughes*, 164 S.W.3d at 443.

[3] **Error in form.** The arbitrator's award contains an error in the form of the award, on a matter not affecting the merits of the controversy. CPRC §171.091(a)(3).

★

3. Motion to vacate award.

(1) Deadlines.

(a) Under the FAA. Under the FAA, the deadline to serve notice of a motion to vacate the award is three months after the arbitration award is filed or delivered. 9 U.S.C. §12; *Eurocapital Grp. v. Goldman Sachs & Co.*, 17 S.W.3d 426, 430 (Tex.App.—Houston [1st Dist.] 2000, no pet.).

(b) Under the TAA. Under the TAA, the deadline to file a motion to vacate the arbitrator's award is 90 days after the party receives a copy of the award. CPRC §171.088(b); *Sydow*, 218 S.W.3d at 170-71. If the ground for the motion to vacate is corruption of the process (see "Corruption of the process," §9.4.3(2)(b)[1][a], p. 304), the deadline is 90 days after the party learned or should have learned of the ground. CPRC §171.088(b); *Louisiana Nat. Gas Pipeline, Inc. v. Bludworth Bond Shipyard, Inc.*, 875 S.W.2d 458, 462 (Tex.App.—Houston [1st Dist.] 1994, writ denied); *see Hou-Scape, Inc. v. Lloyd*, 945 S.W.2d 202, 204 (Tex.App.—Houston [1st Dist.] 1997, orig. proceeding). A motion to vacate is waived if it is filed after the statutory deadline. *Teleometrics Int'l v. Hall*, 922 S.W.2d 189, 192 (Tex.App.—Houston [1st Dist.] 1995, writ denied).

CAUTION

*The challenging party may not have a full 90 days to file a motion to vacate. **Hamm v. Millennium Income Fund, L.L.C.**, 178 S.W.3d 256, 264 (Tex.App.—Houston [1st Dist.] 2005, pet. denied) (FAA and TAA). If the other party moves to confirm the award, the challenging party should immediately move to vacate. Id.*

---

(2) Grounds.

(a) Under FAA. The exclusive grounds for vacating an arbitration award under the FAA are those listed in 9 U.S.C. §10(a). *Hall St.*, 552 U.S. at 584; *see Nafta Traders, Inc. v. Quinn*, 339 S.W.3d 84, 87 (Tex. 2011). A party may file a motion with the court to vacate an arbitration award on any of the following grounds:

[1] Corruption of the process. The award was procured by corruption, fraud, or other undue means. 9 U.S.C. §10(a)(1); *Perry Homes v. Cull*, 173 S.W.3d 565, 570 (Tex.App.—Fort Worth 2005), *rev'd on other grounds*, 258 S.W.3d 580 (Tex.2008).

[2] Arbitrator's evident partiality or corruption. There was "evident partiality" or corruption of the arbitrator who was appointed as a neutral arbitrator. 9 U.S.C. §10(a)(2). A neutral arbitrator has a duty to disclose dealings she is aware of that might create an impression of possible bias. *Mariner Fin.*, 79 S.W.3d at 35; *see Perry Homes*, 173 S.W.3d at 571 (familial relationships or other close social ties should be disclosed, but trivial relationships do not need to be). A party establishes a neutral arbitrator's evident partiality by proving that the arbitrator did not disclose facts that might have created a reasonable impression of the arbitrator's partiality to an objective observer. *E.g.*, *Henry v. Halliburton Energy Servs.*, 100 S.W.3d 505, 509 (Tex.App.—Dallas 2003, pet. denied) (no evident partiality when arbitrator did not disclose his move to law firm that had represented D more than six years before arbitration began); *Thomas James Assocs. v. Owens*, 1 S.W.3d 315, 320-21 (Tex.App.—Dallas 1999, no pet.) (no evident partiality when arbitrator did not disclose involvement in earlier, unrelated arbitration for which he was later sued).

[3] Procedural misconduct. The arbitrator refused to postpone the hearing after a sufficient showing of cause for the postponement, refused to hear pertinent and material evidence, or otherwise conducted the hearing in a way that prejudiced the rights of the party. 9 U.S.C. §10(a)(3); *Perry Homes*, 173 S.W.3d at 570.

[4] Arbitrator exceeded powers. The arbitrator exceeded her powers, or so imperfectly executed them that a mutual, final, and definite award on the subject matter submitted was not made. 9 U.S.C. §10(a)(4); *Perry Homes*, 173 S.W.3d at 570-71.

★

NOTE

*The Supreme Court has determined that "manifest disregard of the law" is not an independent ground for vacating an arbitration award under the FAA. **Hall St.**, 552 U.S. at 583-85. After **Hall Street**, courts have disagreed on what role that phrase continues to play in FAA cases. Compare **Frazier v. CitiFinancial Corp.**, 604 F.3d 1313, 1323-24 (11th Cir.2010) (manifest disregard is not independent ground to vacate; arbitration awards under the FAA can be vacated only for reasons in 9 U.S.C. §10), and **Citigroup Global Mkts., Inc. v. Bacon**, 562 F.3d 349, 353 (5th Cir. 2009) (same), with **Wachovia Secs., LLC v. Brand**, 671 F.3d 472, 483 (4th Cir.2012) (manifest disregard continues either as independent ground for review or as "judicial gloss" on 9 U.S.C. §10), and **Comedy Club, Inc. v. Improv W. Assocs.**, 553 F.3d 1277, 1290 (9th Cir.2009) (manifest disregard remains valid ground to vacate because it is part of, or shorthand for, 9 U.S.C. §10(a)(4)). In 2010, the Supreme Court refused to rule on this disagreement. See **Stolt-Nielsen S.A. v. AnimalFeeds Int'l**, ___ U.S. ___, 130 S.Ct. 1758, 1768 n.3 (2010).*

(b) Under TAA. To vacate an arbitration award under the TAA, a party generally must allege a statutory or common-law ground. **Pheng Invs. v. Rodriquez**, 196 S.W.3d 322, 328-29 (Tex.App.—Fort Worth 2006, no pet.); **Koch v. Koch**, 27 S.W.3d 93, 96 (Tex.App.—San Antonio 2000, no pet.); **Anzilotti v. Gene D. Liggin, Inc.**, 899 S.W.2d 264, 266 (Tex.App.—Houston [14th Dist.] 1995, no writ).

[1] Statutory grounds. A party may file a motion with the court to vacate an arbitration award on any of the following statutory grounds:

[a] Corruption of the process. The award was procured by corruption, fraud, or other undue means. CPRC §171.088(a)(1); **Pheng Invs.**, 196 S.W.3d at 329.

[b] Evident partiality. The party's rights were prejudiced by the "evident partiality" of the arbitrator who was appointed as a neutral arbitrator. CPRC §171.088(a)(2)(A); **Burlington N. R.R. v. TUCO Inc.**, 960 S.W.2d 629, 636 (Tex.1997). The party cannot file suit against the individual arbitrator on the ground of evident partiality; a motion to vacate is the exclusive remedy to challenge the arbitrator's evident partiality. **Blue Cross Blue Shield v. Juneau**, 114 S.W.3d 126, 135-36 (Tex.App.—Austin 2003, no pet.). A party establishes a neutral arbitrator's evident partiality by proving that the arbitrator did not disclose facts that might have created a reasonable impression of the arbitrator's partiality to an objective observer. *E.g.*, **TUCO**, 960 S.W.2d at 636-37 (nondisclosure of arbitrator's referral to represent co-arbitrator's law firm in federal lawsuit was evident partiality); **Karlseng v. Cooke**, 346 S.W.3d 85, 94 (Tex.App.—Dallas 2011, no pet.) (nondisclosure of arbitrator's direct, personal, professional, social, and business relationship with P's attorney was evident partiality); **J.D. Edwards World Solutions Co. v. Estes, Inc.**, 91 S.W.3d 836, 840 (Tex.App.—Fort Worth 2002, pet. denied) (nondisclosure of arbitrator's ongoing representation of D was evident partiality). The potential arbitrator should disclose all information that might reasonably affect her impartiality, including a familial or close social relationship. **TUCO**, 960 S.W.2d at 637; *see also* **Ponderosa Pine Energy, LLC v. Tenaska Energy, Inc.**, 376 S.W.3d 358, 370 (Tex.App.—Dallas 2012, n.p.h.) (parties can make intelligent choice when selecting neutral arbitrator only if they have access to all information that could reasonably affect arbitrator's partiality, but arbitrator cannot be expected to provide parties with all the minute details of every relationship); **Karlseng**, 346 S.W.3d at 97 (arbitrator must make reasonable effort to determine if she has any interests, contacts, or relationships that are required to be disclosed). Evident partiality is exhibited by the nondisclosure itself, regardless of whether the undisclosed information establishes actual bias. **TUCO**, 960 S.W.2d at 636; **Karlseng**, 346 S.W.3d at 95.

★

NOTE

*A party seeking to vacate an arbitration award on evident-partiality grounds waives the objection if the party did not object to known facts showing the arbitrator's partiality before the arbitrator made the award. TUCO, 960 S.W.2d at 637 n.9; **Ponderosa Pine Energy**, 376 S.W.3d at 370-71; e.g., **Kendall Builders, Inc. v. Chesson**, 149 S.W.3d 796, 806 (Tex.App.—Austin 2004, pet. denied) (trial court erred in vacating arbitration award because P knew of arbitrator's partiality and waited to object until after unfavorable arbitration award was issued). The complaining party is presumed to have known of the arbitrator's partiality if the undisclosed relationship was open, obvious, or easy to discover. See **Mariner Fin.**, 79 S.W.3d at 33-34.*

---

[c] Arbitrator's corruption or misconduct. The party's rights were prejudiced by the arbitrator's corruption, misconduct, or willful misbehavior. CPRC §171.088(a)(2)(B), (a)(2)(C).

[d] Arbitrator exceeded powers. The arbitrator exceeded her powers. CPRC §171.088(a)(3)(A). An arbitrator's authority derives from the arbitration agreement and is limited to a decision on the matters specified in the agreement, either expressly or by necessary implication. *City of Pasadena v. Smith*, 292 S.W.3d 14, 20 & n.41 (Tex.2009); *see **Barton v. Fashion Glass & Mirror, Ltd.***, 321 S.W.3d 641, 646-47 (Tex. App.—Houston [14th Dist.] 2010, no pet.). An arbitrator exceeds her authority if she decides a matter that the parties did not agree to submit to arbitration; she does not exceed her authority by making a mistake of fact or law in applying substantive law. *See **Pheng Invs.**, 196 S.W.3d at 329. However, parties can contractually agree in their arbitration agreement to limit an arbitrator's power to that of a judge, thereby allowing for judicial review of an arbitration award for reversible error. **Nafta Traders**, 339 S.W.3d at 95. If the parties contractually limit the scope of the arbitrator's power and the arbitrator exceeds those powers, the parties have contractually provided a means for vacating the award under CPRC §171.088(a)(3)(A). See **Nafta Traders**, 339 S.W.3d at 96. The FAA does not preempt state law permitting such expanded judicial review. See "FAA preemption of TAA," §4.5, p. 288.

PRACTICE TIP

*The expanded scope of judicial review under the TAA differs from the scope of review under the FAA, in which 9 U.S.C. §16 provides the exclusive grounds for vacating an arbitration award. See **Nafta Traders**, 339 S.W.3d at 87. Thus, when drafting an arbitration agreement, parties should (1) specify whether the TAA would apply and (2) add language to the agreement that limits the arbitrator's powers to allow for expanded judicial review of the arbitration award. See id. at 101. By doing so, parties can get the benefits of arbitration while also retaining the right to have an adverse award reviewed by the courts. If the parties contractually agree to expanded judicial review of the arbitration award, however, the arbitration should be conducted more like a trial, which may result in a loss of some of the potential time or money savings of arbitration. Id. at 101-02. For example, a record of the proceedings must be kept, and all complaints must be preserved. Id. at 101.*

---

[e] Procedural misconduct. The arbitrator refused to postpone the hearing after a showing of sufficient cause for the postponement, refused to hear material evidence, or otherwise conducted the hearing in a way that substantially prejudiced the rights of the party. CPRC §171.088(a)(3)(B)-(a)(3)(D); *see, e.g.*, *Kosty v. South Shore Harbour Cmty. Ass'n*, 226 S.W.3d 459, 463-64 (Tex.App.—Houston [1st Dist.] 2006, pet. denied) (arbitrator did not err in excluding evidence that was immaterial to the arbitration).

[f] No arbitration agreement. There was no arbitration agreement, the issue was not adversely determined in proceedings to compel arbitration, and the party did not participate in the arbitration hearing without raising the objection. CPRC §171.088(a)(4); *see **Pheng Invs.***, 196 S.W.3d at 329.

─────────────────── ✦ ───────────────────

[2] Common-law grounds. A party may file a motion to vacate an arbitration award on any of the following grounds:

[a] Public-policy violation. The award violates public policy or the law. *CVN Grp. v. Delgado*, 95 S.W.3d 234, 239 (Tex.2002).

[b] Fraud or misconduct. The award appears to be tainted with fraud or misconduct. *See Pheng Invs.*, 196 S.W.3d at 329; *see, e.g.*, *IPCO-G.&C. Jt.V. v. A.B. Chance Co.*, 65 S.W.3d 252, 258 (Tex.App.—Houston [1st Dist.] 2001, pet. denied) (ex parte telephone call by arbitrator to P's attorney did not deprive P of right to fair hearing).

[c] Arbitrator's gross mistake. The arbitrator makes a "gross mistake" of such magnitude that it clearly implies bad faith and a lack of honest judgment. *Baker Hughes*, 164 S.W.3d at 446; *Nuno v. Pulido*, 946 S.W.2d 448, 452 (Tex.App.—Corpus Christi 1997, no writ). A mere mistake of fact or law in applying substantive law is insufficient to vacate an arbitration award. *Pheng Invs.*, 196 S.W.3d at 329; *see Riha v. Smulcer*, 843 S.W.2d 289, 294 (Tex.App.—Houston [14th Dist.] 1992, writ denied).

§9.5 Appellate court's review of trial court's order. Certain orders from the trial court's review of an arbitration award (e.g., order confirming an award) are immediately appealable. For lists of those orders under either the FAA or the TAA that can be appealed, see *O'Connor's Texas Appeals*, "Arbitration orders," ch. 1-B, §2.3.3(1), p. 16.

1. Procedure to challenge arbitration orders. Arbitration orders under the TAA may be appealed in the same manner and to the same extent as an order or judgment in any other civil action. CPRC §171.098(b).

2. Standards of review for arbitration orders. The trial court's arbitration orders are subject to the following standards of review on appeal:

(1) Confirmation of award – de novo. The trial court's confirmation of the arbitration award is reviewed de novo. *Providian Bancorp Servs. v. Thomas*, 255 S.W.3d 411, 414 (Tex.App.—El Paso 2008, no pet.) (TAA); *American Rlty. Trust, Inc. v. JDN Real Estate–McKinney, L.P.*, 74 S.W.3d 527, 531 (Tex.App.—Dallas 2002, pet. denied) (FAA). The review of arbitration awards is narrow, and the court must indulge every reasonable presumption in favor of the arbitration award. *Providian Bancorp*, 255 S.W.3d at 415 (TAA); *International Bank of Commerce v. International Energy Dev. Corp.*, 981 S.W.2d 38, 42-43 (Tex.App.—Corpus Christi 1998, pet. denied) (FAA); *see East Tex. Salt Water Disposal Co. v. Werline*, 307 S.W.3d 267, 271 (Tex.2010).

(2) SAPCR order – child's best interest. In a suit affecting the parent-child relationship (SAPCR), the standard of review to challenge a SAPCR order is whether the award is in the best interest of the child. *See* Fam. Code §153.0071(b); *Cooper v. Bushong*, 10 S.W.3d 20, 25-26 (Tex.App.—Austin 1999, pet. denied) (TAA).

D. SPECIAL JUDGE

§1. GENERAL

§1.1 Rules. None. See CPRC ch. 151.

§1.2 Purpose. A trial by a special judge is a procedure by which the parties try all or part of their case to a retired or former judge (not a sitting judge) who is selected by the parties to hear the case. This type of ADR is sometimes called "rent a former judge" ADR or "private trial," and is functionally the same as a trial before the court. Compared to a trial by a sitting judge, a special-judge procedure is more predictable (no multiple trial settings), more economical for both attorneys and parties, and more effective for complex trials or trials involving secret or private matters (e.g., noncompete agreements, trade-secret cases, divorces). *See* Marshall, *Tex. Civ. Prac. & Rem. Code ch. 151 – Special Judges: Special Judge and Special Setting*, Chapter 151: Real Trial and Real Appeal, State Bar of Texas CLE 1, 3 (2008). The special-judge procedure also provides several advantages over arbitration: (1) the matter is heard

★

by a former judge, rather than by an arbitrator who may not be an attorney, (2) the special judge's decision can be appealed, which is not possible with an arbitration decision, and (3) a trial by special judge is likely to be less expensive than arbitration. See "Arbitration," ch. 4-C, p. 286.

§1.3 Forms. *O'Connor's Texas Civil Forms* (2012), FORMS 4D.

§1.4 Other references. State Bar of Texas, *Chapter 151: Real Trial & Real Appeal*, Online CLE (2008), www.texasbarcle.com/CLE/OLSearch.asp (referred to as *Chapter 151: Real Trial & Real Appeal* Online CLE); Marshall, *Tex. Civ. Prac. & Rem. Code ch. 151 – Special Judges: Special Judge and Special Setting*, Chapter 151: Real Trial and Real Appeal, State Bar of Texas CLE (2008) (referred to as Marshall, *Tex. Civ. Prac. & Rem. Code ch. 151 – Special Judges*); *O'Connor's Texas Civil Appeals* (2012) (*O'Connor's Texas Appeals*).

§2. TYPES OF CASES FOR REFERRAL TO SPECIAL JUDGE

Any civil or family-law matter pending in a district court, a statutory probate court, or a statutory county court can be referred to a special judge by agreement of the parties. CPRC §151.001. See *O'Connor's Texas Forms*, FORM 4D:1.

§3. SPECIAL JUDGE'S QUALIFICATIONS & POWERS

§3.1 Qualifications. The special judge must be a retired or former judge who (1) served as a judge for at least four years in a district court, statutory county court, or appellate court, (2) developed substantial experience in her area of specialty, (3) was not removed from office and did not resign while under investigation for discipline or removal, and (4) annually completes at least five days (i.e., 30 hours) of continuing legal education in courses approved by the state bar or the Texas Supreme Court. CPRC §151.003. In effect, the special judge must maintain a level of professional competence beyond that required of sitting judges.

§3.2 Powers. While trying the case, the special judge has the same powers as the referring judge, except the special judge cannot hold a person in contempt of court unless the person is a witness before the special judge. CPRC §151.006(b); *e.g.*, *NCF, Inc. v. Harless*, 846 S.W.2d 79, 82-83 (Tex.App.—Dallas 1992, orig. proceeding) (special judge could not enforce turnover order by contempt).

§4. AGREED MOTION FOR TRIAL BY SPECIAL JUDGE

§4.1 Referral request. The motion must request a referral to a special judge. CPRC §151.002(1). The case must be a "pending matter," which can include arbitration; a referral cannot be requested before a suit is filed. *See id.* §151.001. The parties may, however, be able to provide by contract that they agree to a referral to a special judge in the event of a lawsuit. *See* Marshall, *Tex. Civ. Prac. & Rem. Code ch. 151 – Special Judges*, at 5.

§4.2 Jury waiver. The motion must waive the parties' right to a jury trial. CPRC §151.002(2).

§4.3 Issues to be referred. The motion must identify the issues to be referred to the special judge. CPRC §151.002(3).

    1. Trial issues. The motion can ask that the special judge hear any or all of the issues in the case, whether they are issues of law or fact. CPRC §151.001. For example, the motion could ask for the special judge to resolve all discovery disputes or a motion for summary judgment. *See* Marshall, *Tex. Civ. Prac. & Rem. Code ch. 151 – Special Judges*, at 5-6.

    2. Post-trial issues. The motion can ask that the special judge hear all postjudgment issues, including remand from the appellate court, collection of judgment, writ of attachment, and turnover orders. *See Chapter 151: Real Trial & Real Appeal* Online CLE.

§4.4 Place for trial. The motion must identify the time and place for the agreed trial. CPRC §151.002(4). Chapter 151 places no restrictions on venue; thus, the trial can be held at the place most convenient for the parties and witnesses. See "Place for trial," §6.3, p. 308.

─────────────────── ★ ───────────────────

§4.5 Special judge. The motion must identify the name of the special judge, state that the special judge has agreed to hear the case, and identify the fee the parties have agreed to pay the judge. CPRC §151.002(5).

───

PRACTICE TIP

One simple way to locate a special judge is to search the Internet for "private trials." Chapter 151: Real Trial & Real Appeal Online CLE. Then verify with the Texas Center for the Judiciary that the judge has fulfilled the CLE requirements for the calendar year. Id.

───

§5. ORDER OF REFERRAL

§5.1 Discretionary. Whether to refer a case to a special judge is within the discretion of the referring judge. CPRC §151.001 (judge "may" order referral). Some judges are reluctant to refer a case to a special judge.

§5.2 Contents of order. The order of referral must identify the issues referred and the name of the special judge. CPRC §151.004. The order may designate the time and place for trial and the time for filing the special judge's report. *Id.* The court clerk will send the special judge a copy of the order. *Id.* See *O'Connor's Texas Forms*, FORM 4D:2.

§5.3 Effect of referral. The referral will stay all proceedings until after the conclusion of the special trial. CPRC §151.001. The stay prevents conflicting rulings if the special judge hears only part of the case and then returns it to the referring judge.

§6. TRIAL PROCEDURE

§6.1 Rules for special trial. The case will be conducted in the same manner as a nonjury trial under the TRCPs and the TREs. CPRC §§151.005, 151.006(a). The parties have the right to be represented by an attorney. *Id.* §151.007.

§6.2 Court reporter. A court reporter is required for the trial. CPRC §151.008. The court reporter must have the same qualifications required for a reporter in the referring judge's court. *Id.* The court reporter cannot be a public employee if the trial is held during regular work hours, unless the referring judge orders otherwise. *Id.* §151.010. Although the CPRC states "the special judge shall provide a court reporter," the attorneys should probably arrange for the court reporter. *See id.* §151.008.

───

PRACTICE TIP

In a relatively simple matter (e.g., proving up a divorce, the hearing for a summary judgment), the parties can ask the referring judge to allow the hearing before the special judge to be recorded by audio or video recording, to reduce the cost of the procedure.

───

§6.3 Place for trial.

1. Private location. The parties must agree on a place for the trial. *See* CPRC §151.002(4) (motion must state place agreed on by parties). Typically, they agree to hold the trial in one of the attorneys' conference rooms or to rent a conference room at a local hotel. The privacy of the special-judge proceeding is one of the reasons for its popularity, especially in family-law matters. *See* Marshall, *Tex. Civ. Prac. & Rem. Code ch. 151 – Special Judges*, at 3.

2. Not public courtroom. The trial cannot be held in a public courtroom, unless otherwise ordered by the referring judge. CPRC §151.010.

§6.4 Special judge's file. The file of the case remains with the referring judge's clerk. The special judge can obtain copies of relevant documents from the referring judge's file, or the attorneys can provide the special judge with the copies. *Chapter 151: Real Trial & Real Appeal* Online CLE. Any additional pleadings filed with the special judge become part of the special judge's file.

★

§6.5 Costs & fees. The parties must pay "in equal shares" for the costs related to the trial—that is, the special judge's fee, the court reporter's fee, and other administrative costs. CPRC §151.009(a). In multiparty cases, the costs are divided between the parties, not between the sides of the litigation. *See id.* ("the parties" shall pay the costs). Each party must pay the costs of its own witnesses and any other costs related only to its case. *Id.* §151.009(b). Neither the state nor the local government may pay any costs related to a trial by a special judge. *Id.* §151.009(c).

§6.6 Special judge's verdict. The verdict of the special judge must comply with the requirements for a verdict by the court in which the action was filed. CPRC §151.011. The verdict will stand as a verdict of the referring judge's court. *Id.* The special judge must submit the verdict to the referring judge within 60 days after the date the trial adjourns, unless the order of referral specifies a different date. *Id.*

§6.7 Return of special judge's file. At the conclusion of the proceedings (i.e., verdict is signed and post-trial motions are resolved), the special judge must send all documents in the file to the referring court's clerk. *See Chapter 151: Real Trial & Real Appeal* Online CLE.

§7. POST-TRIAL MOTIONS

§7.1 Motion for verdict. At the conclusion of the hearing, the parties can make a motion for the special judge to sign a verdict. *See* CPRC §151.011.

§7.2 Motion to seal records. If the issues that were submitted to the special judge involved private or confidential matters, the parties should consider asking the special judge to seal the record. See "Motion to Seal Court Records," ch. 5-L, p. 394. The special judge's verdict, however, cannot be sealed. TRCP 76a(1). If one of the parties files an appeal, the record is automatically unsealed.

   1. Agreed motion. The parties can make an agreed motion to seal the record. Whether an agreed motion to seal can bypass the requirements of TRCP 76a is an open question. The agreed motion should include a request that the sealing order permit unsealing only when both parties consent to unsealing or when an appeal is filed. *See Chapter 151: Real Trial & Real Appeal* Online CLE.

   2. Opposed motion. A party can make a motion under TRCP 76a to seal the record. Before the special judge can sign an order sealing the record, the motion to seal must be posted for the public to read and the judge must hold a public hearing. See "Public Notice," ch. 5-L, §4, p. 397; "Hearing on Motion to Seal," ch. 5-L, §5, p. 397.

NOTE
Documents filed in family-law cases, unfiled discovery in trade-secret cases, and some settlement agreements are not "court records" as defined by TRCP 76a; thus, they may be sealed only if permitted by another rule or statute. See "Documents that are not court records," ch. 5-L, §2.3, p. 395.

---

§7.3 Motion for new trial.

   1. Filed with referring judge. If the special judge does not file a verdict within the time specified by CPRC §151.011, the referring court may grant a new trial on a party's motion after notice and a hearing. CPRC §151.012. See *O'Connor's Texas Forms*, FORM 4D:3. If the parties still want a special trial, the referring court can refer the case to a new special judge.

   2. Filed with special judge. If one of the parties disagrees with the verdict, that party can file a motion for new trial with the special judge.

§8. REVIEW

§8.1 Judgment. If the verdict results in a final judgment or an appealable order, the date the special judge signs the verdict begins the deadlines for the appeal. See *O'Connor's Texas Appeals*, "Appellate Deadlines," ch. 1-C, p. 22.

SPECIAL JUDGE

★

§8.2 Right to appeal. The parties have a right to appeal. CPRC §151.013. The case is appealed to the appellate courts, not to the referring court. *Id.* The right to appeal cannot be invoked until (1) the special judge submits a verdict to the trial court, (2) all claims are resolved, and (3) the trial court signs an order memorializing the finality of the case. *Baroid Equip., Inc. v. Odeco Drilling, Inc.*, 64 S.W.3d 504, 505 (Tex.App.—Houston [1st Dist.] 2001, pet. denied).

§8.3 Record on appeal. If the case is appealed, the record will consist of the following: (1) the relevant pleadings filed in the referring judge's court and those filed with the special judge and (2) the transcript of the testimony and the exhibits received by the special judge. See *O'Connor's Texas Appeals*, "Record on Appeal," ch. 6, p. 209.

CHAPTER 5

★

★

CHAPTER 5

⭐

---

5. PRETRIAL MOTIONS

A. PRETRIAL CONFERENCE

§1. GENERAL

§1.1 Rule. TRCP 166. See Gov't Code §21.001(a) (courts have power to enforce their orders); TRJA 7(a)(6) (courts must "utilize methods to expedite the disposition of cases on the docket").

§1.2 Purpose. TRCP 166 gives trial judges the power to control pretrial matters and to assist in settling cases. *See Lindley v. Johnson*, 936 S.W.2d 53, 55 (Tex.App.—Tyler 1996, writ denied). The purpose of a pretrial conference is to narrow the issues and to dispose of other matters, thus aiding final disposition of the case. *Walden v. Affiliated Computer Servs.*, 97 S.W.3d 303, 322 (Tex.App.—Houston [14th Dist.] 2003, pet. denied); *Griffin v. Wolfe*, 626 S.W.2d 895, 897 (Tex.App.—Fort Worth 1981, no writ).

§1.3 Timetables & forms. Timetable, Pretrial Motions, p. 1216; Timetable, Discovery Schedule for Level 1, p. 1219; Timetable, Discovery Schedule for Level 2, p. 1222; *O'Connor's Texas Civil Forms* (2012), FORM 5A:1.

§2. PROCEDURE

§2.1 Automatic pretrial calendar. The court may establish a pretrial calendar "by rule." TRCP 166. Attorneys should always check the local rules to see if the rules create automatic deadlines for discovery, pleadings, motions, or any other matters.

§2.2 Initiating pretrial conference. The court can schedule a pretrial conference either on its own initiative or on the motion of a party. To request a pretrial conference, a party should file a motion stating the reasons for the conference. Whether the trial court conducts a pretrial conference is a matter within its discretion; a party cannot force the trial court to conduct one. *Taiwan Shrimp Farm Vill. Ass'n v. U.S.A. Shrimp Farm Dev., Inc.*, 915 S.W.2d 61, 69 (Tex.App.—Corpus Christi 1996, writ denied); *Ryland Grp. v. White*, 723 S.W.2d 160, 163 (Tex. App.—Houston [1st Dist.] 1986, orig. proceeding). Parties should move for a pretrial conference during the early stages of litigation if electronic information will likely be sought in discovery. See "Differences Between Electronic & Conventional Discovery," ch. 6-C, §3, p. 488.

§3. SCOPE OF PRETRIAL CONFERENCE

§3.1 Outside scope of conference. A court cannot resolve contested issues of fact at a pretrial conference. *Provident Life & Acc. Ins. v. Hazlitt*, 216 S.W.2d 805, 807 (Tex.1949); *McCreight v. City of Cleburne*, 940 S.W.2d 285, 288 (Tex.App.—Waco 1997, writ denied); *see Caldwell v. Barnes*, 154 S.W.3d 93, 97 (Tex.2004); *see also Walden v. Affiliated Computer Servs.*, 97 S.W.3d 303, 323 (Tex.App.—Houston [14th Dist.] 2003, pet. denied) (court may receive evidence and hear expert testimony to identify and rule on only legal issues). It is a violation of due process for a court to convert a pretrial conference into a trial on the merits without notice to the defendant. *Murphree v. Ziegelmair*, 937 S.W.2d 493, 495 (Tex.App.—Houston [1st Dist.] 1995, no writ); *see, e.g., Ulloa v. Davila*, 860 S.W.2d 202, 204 (Tex.App.—San Antonio 1993, no writ) (at settlement conference, court could not dismiss counterclaim on its own motion).

§3.2 Matters that aid disposition. TRCP 166 contains a catch-all provision that allows the court to consider any matter that "may aid in the disposition of the action." TRCP 166(p); *see Williams v. Akzo Nobel Chems., Inc.*, 999 S.W.2d 836, 842 (Tex.App.—Tyler 1999, no pet.).

§3.3 Trial setting. Although not specifically listed in TRCP 166, setting the date for trial is commonly done by pretrial order. *See, e.g., Loffland Bros. v. Downey*, 822 S.W.2d 249, 250-51 (Tex.App.—Houston [1st Dist.] 1991, orig. proceeding) (docket-control order set trial date and deadlines for discovery and amending pleadings). The trial court must give the parties 45 days' notice of the first trial setting. TRCP 245; *Smith v. Lippmann*, 826 S.W.2d 137,

─────────────────── ✦ ───────────────────

138 n.1 (Tex.1992). See "Deadline begins – notice of trial," ch. 5-B, §4.1.1, p. 321. However, if the case has been previously set for trial and the parties received 45 days' notice of the original trial setting, the court may reset the trial to a later date on any reasonable notice. TRCP 245; *Arkla, Inc. v. Harris*, 846 S.W.2d 623, 628 (Tex.App.—Houston [14th Dist.] 1993, orig. proceeding).

§3.4 Pleading deadlines. By a pretrial order, the court can set deadlines for amendments to pleadings that supersede the deadlines in TRCP 63. TRCP 166; *see Wilson v. Korthauer*, 21 S.W.3d 573, 577-78 (Tex.App.—Houston [14th Dist.] 2000, pet. denied); *Texas Commerce Bank Reagan v. Lebco Constructors, Inc.*, 865 S.W.2d 68, 79 (Tex.App.—Corpus Christi 1993, writ denied). After those deadlines have passed, parties must secure leave of court to amend their pleadings. *Texas Commerce Bank*, 865 S.W.2d at 79. See "After deadline in pretrial order," ch. 5-F, §3.2.1, p. 351; "Motion for Leave to Amend," ch. 8-F, §2, p. 721.

§3.5 Discovery deadlines. The pretrial conference is most often used to determine what discovery has been completed and what discovery has not yet begun. *See* TRCP 166(c) (court can consider discovery schedule at pretrial conference). Every case must be governed by a discovery-control plan, which sets the deadlines for discovery. TRCP 190.1. See "Discovery-Control Plans," ch. 6-A, §7, p. 430; "Discovery Periods," ch. 6-A, §8, p. 433. The court can change the deadlines set by the discovery rules only for good cause. TRCP 191.1.

§3.6 Pending motions. At the pretrial conference, the trial court may require the parties to argue pending motions—dilatory pleas, motions, and exceptions. TRCP 166(a). A dilatory plea, most commonly a plea in abatement, asks the court to abate or dismiss the proceeding because of a fundamental defect in how the action was brought. The court can set an abbreviated discovery schedule to resolve pretrial motions. *See Montalvo v. Fourth Ct. of Appeals*, 917 S.W.2d 1, 2 (Tex.1995).

§3.7 Joint pretrial status report. The trial court has the authority to require the parties to confer and file a joint pretrial status report. *See Koslow's v. Mackie*, 796 S.W.2d 700, 703 (Tex.1990).

§3.8 Contentions & admissions of parties. The court may require the parties to confer and narrow the factual and legal issues of the trial. TRCP 166(d)-(g), (j); *Koslow's v. Mackie*, 796 S.W.2d 700, 703 (Tex.1990).

1. Facts. The court may require the parties to submit written statements of their contentions, to consider the contested issues of fact and simplification of the issues, and to discuss possible stipulations of fact. TRCP 166(d)-(f).

2. Law. The court may require the parties to identify the legal issues for the court and to agree to the application of the law and the contested issues of law. TRCP 166(g), (j).

§3.9 Trial witnesses & exhibits.

1. Identification of experts. The court may require the parties to appear for a pretrial conference to exchange information about experts—names, addresses, telephone numbers, and the subject of each expert's testimony. TRCP 166(i). The schedule for designating experts is determined with reference to the end of the discovery period and according to whether the party is seeking affirmative relief. TRCP 195.2. When a court signs an order setting the deadline for the parties to identify experts, the order controls over the deadlines in TRCP 195.2(a) and (b). TRCP 195.2; *see State Farm Fire & Cas. Co. v. Price*, 845 S.W.2d 427, 434 (Tex.App.—Amarillo 1992, writ dism'd). The court cannot set an unreasonable deadline. *See, e.g., Loffland Bros. v. Downey*, 822 S.W.2d 249, 252 (Tex.App.—Houston [1st Dist.] 1991, orig. proceeding) (eight months before trial was unreasonable). If the court does not sign an order setting the deadline for disclosure of experts, the parties must designate experts according to the schedule in TRCP 195.2. See "Deadlines for Securing Discovery from Experts," ch. 6-D, §6, p. 512. When the court signs a pretrial order on the discovery of experts, it cannot disregard its own order at trial. *See, e.g., Dennis v. Haden*, 867 S.W.2d 48, 51 (Tex.App.—Texarkana 1993, writ denied) (court should not have admitted testimony of expert whose report had not been provided).

2. Witness list. The court may require the parties to exchange information about the fact witnesses who will be called to testify at trial and the rebuttal and impeachment witnesses whose testimony can reasonably be anticipated before trial—names, addresses, telephone numbers, and the subject of each witness's testimony. TRCP

✦

166(h). A party may also obtain discovery of the names, addresses, and telephone numbers of the other party's trial witnesses through interrogatories. *See* TRCP 192.3(d). See "Trial witnesses," ch. 6-B, §2.9, p. 462.

 3. Exhibits. The court may require the parties to mark and exchange exhibits, stipulate to the exhibits' authenticity and admissibility, and make written objections. TRCP 166(*l*) & (m); *see, e.g.*, ***Owens-Corning Fiberglas Corp. v. Malone***, 916 S.W.2d 551, 556-57 (Tex.App.—Houston [1st Dist.] 1996) (court ordered D to file list of objections to P's exhibits), *aff'd*, 972 S.W.2d 35 (Tex.1998); ***British Am. Ins. v. Howarton***, 877 S.W.2d 347, 350 (Tex.App.—Houston [1st Dist.] 1994, writ dism'd) (videotape not listed as exhibit was excluded at trial); *see also* TRCP 192.5(c)(2) (trial exhibits disclosed under TRCP 166 are not "work product").

PRACTICE TIP

There are two reasons to request a pretrial exchange of trial exhibits. First, if a privileged document has been inadvertently produced, the producing party may use the snap-back provisions of TRCP 193.3(d) to assert a privilege. See TRCP 193 cmt. 4. See "Use snap-back provision," ch. 6-A, §18.2.4, p. 444. Second, if a party produces a document in response to discovery, the producing party may prevent the self-authentication of the document by objecting to its authenticity. TRCP 193.7 & cmt. 7; see TRCP 176.6(c) (production by nonparties). See "Authenticity," ch. 8-C, §8.4, p. 704.

---

§3.10   Jury questions. The court may require the parties to prepare proposed jury questions, instructions, and definitions or, for a nonjury trial, proposed findings of fact and conclusions of law. TRCP 166(k).

§3.11   Master or auditor. The court may consider the advisability of referring issues to a master or auditor for findings to be used as evidence in a jury trial. TRCP 166(n), 171. See "Master in Chancery," ch. 1-K, p. 80.

§3.12   Settlement. The court may encourage the parties to settle the case. TRCP 166(o). See "Alternative Dispute Resolution," ch. 4, p. 275.

§4.   HEARING ON PRETRIAL CONFERENCE

§4.1   Type of hearing. The pretrial conference may be held by telephone, by mail, in the judge's chambers, or in the courtroom. *See* TRJA 7(a)(6)(b); *see, e.g.*, ***Koslow's v. Mackie***, 796 S.W.2d 700, 703 (Tex.1990) (court required written status report to be mailed).

§4.2   Attendance. The court can require the parties' attorneys, the parties themselves, or the parties' authorized agents to attend the pretrial conference. TRCP 166; *see, e.g.*, ***Koslow's v. Mackie***, 796 S.W.2d 700, 703 (Tex. 1990) (pleadings were struck after Ds did not submit status report or appear at hearing).

§4.3   Evidence. If a pending motion is one that must be supported by evidence (e.g., a motion to abate), the parties should be prepared to present evidence at the pretrial conference.

§4.4   Objections. Generally, objections at the pretrial conference about rulings that must be made at trial are premature and do not preserve error. *See* ***Clark v. Trailways, Inc.***, 774 S.W.2d 644, 647 n.2 (Tex.1989) (dicta); *see, e.g.*, ***Texas Commerce Bank Reagan v. Lebco Constructors, Inc.***, 865 S.W.2d 68, 78 (Tex.App.—Corpus Christi 1993, writ denied) (objection at pretrial conference to allocation of peremptory challenges did not preserve error); *see also* ***Reveal v. West***, 764 S.W.2d 8, 10 (Tex.App.—Houston [1st Dist.] 1988, orig. proceeding) (pretrial ruling that document was privileged was merely a ruling similar to motion in limine). But under TRCP 166(m), the trial court has the authority to rule on objections to exhibits at a pretrial conference, and one court has held that those rulings will preserve error. ***Owens-Corning Fiberglas Corp. v. Malone***, 916 S.W.2d 551, 557 (Tex.App.—Houston [1st Dist.] 1996), *aff'd*, 972 S.W.2d 35 (Tex.1998); *see also* ***Huckaby v. A.G. Perry & Son, Inc.***, 20 S.W.3d 194, 203-04 (Tex.App.—Texarkana 2000, pet. denied) (court can make pretrial ruling on admissibility of evidence; relying on ***Owens-Corning***).

✭

CAUTION

Do not rely on an objection made at a pretrial conference to preserve error. If the matter is one that will arise at trial (e.g., the introduction of evidence), make sure to object on the record during the trial.

---

§5. ORDER ON PRETRIAL CONFERENCE

§5.1 In writing. The pretrial order must be in writing. *Palacios v. Winters*, 26 S.W.3d 734, 735 (Tex.App.—Corpus Christi 2000, no pet.); *FDIC v. Finlay*, 832 S.W.2d 158, 160 (Tex.App.—Houston [1st Dist.] 1992, writ denied).

§5.2 Contents. The pretrial order must specify the actions taken and rulings made at the pretrial conference. TRCP 166; *FDIC v. Finlay*, 832 S.W.2d 158, 160 (Tex.App.—Houston [1st Dist.] 1992, writ denied). The pretrial order will control the suit unless it is modified at trial to prevent manifest injustice. In most cases, the pretrial order includes the following: (1) the actions taken at the pretrial conference, (2) the pleadings that can be amended and the deadline to amend, (3) any agreements made by the parties, (4) the court's rulings on any pleas or motions, and (5) whether the case will be tried to the court or to a jury. *See* TRCP 166.

§5.3 Notice. The parties are entitled to notice of pretrial or docket-control orders. *See Loffland Bros. v. Downey*, 822 S.W.2d 249, 251 (Tex.App.—Houston [1st Dist.] 1991, orig. proceeding). The court must send the pretrial order to each party's attorney in charge. TRCP 8; *Loffland Bros.*, 822 S.W.2d at 251.

§5.4 Discretion to modify order. Under TRCP 166, the court can modify its pretrial order to prevent "manifest injustice." *Treviño v. Treviño*, 64 S.W.3d 166, 170 (Tex.App.—San Antonio 2001, no pet.); *see, e.g., Griffin v. Wolfe*, 626 S.W.2d 895, 897 (Tex.App.—Fort Worth 1981, no writ) (court's refusal to permit amendment was not abuse of discretion). The modification does not have to be in writing; the court can implicitly overrule its pretrial order. *See In re Estate of Henry*, 250 S.W.3d 518, 527 (Tex.App.—Dallas 2008, no pet.); *Treviño*, 64 S.W.3d at 170; *Schoen v. Redwood Constr., Inc.*, No. 01-09-00371-CV (Tex.App.—Houston [1st Dist.] 2011, no pet.) (memo op.; 1-31-11). *But see Susanoil, Inc. v. Continental Oil Co.*, 516 S.W.2d 260, 264 (Tex.App.—San Antonio 1973, no writ) (written order or oral statement on the record required to modify pretrial order).

§6. BINDING EFFECT OF PRETRIAL ORDER

§6.1 On procedure for trial. A pretrial order controls the procedure for the case. If the order changes the deadlines in the rules of procedure, the order prevails. *Lindley v. Johnson*, 936 S.W.2d 53, 55 (Tex.App.—Tyler 1996, writ denied); *see, e.g., ForScan Corp. v. Dresser Indus.*, 789 S.W.2d 389, 393 (Tex.App.—Houston [14th Dist.] 1990, writ denied) (deadline for amending pleadings in pretrial order prevailed over deadline in TRCP 63).

§6.2 On procedure for SJ. A pretrial order controls the procedure for the case in a summary-judgment proceeding. For example, if a pretrial order requires the parties to designate experts by a certain date, a party generally cannot rely on the affidavit of an undesignated expert in a summary-judgment proceeding. *Fort Brown Villas III Condo. Ass'n v. Gillenwater*, 285 S.W.3d 879, 882 (Tex.2009); *Total Clean, LLC v. Cox Smith Matthews Inc.*, 330 S.W.3d 657, 663-64 (Tex.App.—San Antonio 2010, pet. denied); *see* TRCP 193.6(a). See "Timely," ch. 6-A, §16.3, p. 439.

§6.3 On trial judge. The trial court cannot disregard its own pretrial order. *Mercedes-Benz Credit Corp. v. Rhyne*, 925 S.W.2d 664, 666 (Tex.1996). For example, if the trial court signed an order setting the case on the jury docket, the court cannot ignore that order on the eve of trial, even if no jury fee was paid. *Id.* The parties are entitled to rely on the trial court's pretrial order. *Dennis v. Haden*, 867 S.W.2d 48, 51 (Tex.App.—Texarkana 1993, writ denied). But this does not mean that the trial court is prohibited from modifying its pretrial order. *See, e.g., Treviño v. Treviño*, 64 S.W.3d 166, 170 (Tex.App.—San Antonio 2001, no pet.) (court implicitly modified docket-control order by overruling Ps' motion to strike and by setting Ds' motion for summary judgment for submission). See "Discretion to modify order," §5.4, this page.

★

§6.4 On parties. The parties must comply with the pretrial order. *See, e.g., **British Am. Ins. v. Howarton**, 877 S.W.2d 347, 350-51 (Tex.App.—Houston [1st Dist.] 1994, writ dism'd) (party could not introduce videotape because it was not listed as exhibit as required by pretrial order); **Dennis v. Haden**, 867 S.W.2d 48, 51 (Tex.App.—Texarkana 1993, writ denied) (party could not call expert to testify because expert's report was not produced as required by pretrial order); **ForScan Corp. v. Dresser Indus.**, 789 S.W.2d 389, 393 (Tex.App.—Houston [14th Dist.] 1990, writ denied) (party could not amend pleadings after deadline set in pretrial order).

§6.5 On rescheduled trial. A pretrial or docket-control order setting discovery deadlines applies unless the trial is rescheduled for a date more than three months after the discovery period ends. *See* TRCP 190.5(b).

---

⑬

PROPOSED TRCP CHANGES

In response to Gov't Code §22.004(h), the Supreme Court has proposed TRCP 169 to establish a process for the prompt, efficient, and cost-effective resolution of civil actions (expedited actions) in which only monetary relief is sought and the amount in controversy is no more than $100,000. See Tex.Sup.Ct. Order, Misc. Docket No. 12-9191 (eff. Mar. 1, 2013). The Supreme Court has proposed corresponding amendments to TRCP 190.2 and 190.5 that would (1) change the Level 1 discovery-control plan to apply to these expedited actions under TRCP 169 and (2) limit the modification of a discovery-control plan when a suit is governed by TRCP 169. See Tex.Sup.Ct. Order, Misc. Docket No. 12-9191 (eff. Mar. 1, 2013). The public-comment period for the proposed amendments ends on February 1, 2013, and the rules are to take effect March 1, 2013. For the proposed version of the rules, see the appendix after this book's index. For the final version, go to the Supreme Court website at www.supreme.courts.state.tx.us. When the new and amended rules take effect, a supplement to this book—with updated rules and commentaries that reflect the changes—will be available at www.JonesMcClure.com/TRCPamendments.

---

§6.6 Not on retrial. The discovery deadlines in a pretrial order do not apply after a new trial is granted. *See, e.g., **State Dept. of Hwys. & Pub. Transp. v. Ross**, 718 S.W.2d 5, 11 (Tex.App.—Tyler 1986, orig. proceeding) (order closing discovery did not remain in effect after mistrial). After a new trial is ordered, a suit stands on the docket as if it had never been tried. *Id.*

§7. SANCTIONS

The trial court has the power to enforce its orders with sanctions. *In re Patton*, 47 S.W.3d 825, 827 (Tex.App.—Fort Worth 2001, orig. proceeding); *see* Gov't Code §21.001(a) (court has all powers necessary to enforce its orders); *Woodall v. Clark*, 802 S.W.2d 415, 418 (Tex.App.—Beaumont 1991, no writ) (Gov't Code §21.001(a) gives court power to dismiss suit for repeated refusal to comply with pretrial order). Courts may impose the sanctions listed in TRCP 215 for violations of pretrial orders. *See **Koslow's v. Mackie**, 796 S.W.2d 700, 703-04 & n.1 (Tex.1990) (sanctions for not appearing at pretrial conference). Any sanctions imposed for violation of a pretrial order must be just and appropriate. *Id.* at 703 n.1; *In re Bledsoe*, 41 S.W.3d 807, 812 (Tex.App.—Fort Worth 2001, orig. proceeding); *see, e.g., **Roberts v. Golden Crest Waters, Inc.**, 1 S.W.3d 291, 292-93 (Tex.App.—Corpus Christi 1999, no pet.) (court abused its discretion by imposing death-penalty sanctions for failure to file pretrial statement). See "Motion for Sanctions," ch. 5-K, p. 377.

§8. REVIEW

§8.1 Standard of review. In most cases, the standard of review for a pretrial order is abuse of discretion. *E.g., **TransAmerican Nat. Gas Corp. v. Powell**, 811 S.W.2d 913, 916-17 (Tex.1991) (pretrial discovery order). However, if the trial court summarily disposes of a party's claim or defense, the court will review the pretrial order the same as it would an appeal of a partial summary judgment. *McCreight v. City of Cleburne*, 940 S.W.2d 285, 287 (Tex. App.—Waco 1997, writ denied). See "Both parties move for SJ," ch. 7-B, §14.4.1, p. 626.

---

§8.2 Appeal. A pretrial order may be appealed after a final judgment is entered. *See FDIC v. Finlay*, 832 S.W.2d 158, 161 (Tex.App.—Houston [1st Dist.] 1992, writ denied).

§8.3 Mandamus. A pretrial order can be the subject of a petition for writ of mandamus if an appeal would not provide effective relief. *See, e.g., Loffland Bros. v. Downey*, 822 S.W.2d 249, 251-52 (Tex.App.—Houston [1st Dist.] 1991, orig. proceeding) (party missed deadline for naming experts because it did not receive docket-control order).

B. REQUEST FOR JURY TRIAL

§1. GENERAL

§1.1 Rules. TRCP 216-220, 245. See U.S. Const. amend. 7; Tex. Const. art. 1, §15, art. 5, §10; Gov't Code §51.604 (jury fee); Fam. Code §6.703 (right to jury in divorce action); Prob. Code §21 (contested issues tried by jury).

§1.2 Purpose. A request for a jury trial invokes the party's right to a jury trial.

§1.3 Forms. *O'Connor's Texas Civil Forms* (2012), FORMS 5B.

§2. RIGHT TO A JURY TRIAL

The U.S. and Texas Constitutions guarantee the right to a jury trial. U.S. Const. amend. 7; Tex. Const. art. 1, §15. In civil matters, a party has the right to a jury trial for any action that is the same as or analogous to those actions that could have been submitted to a jury in 1876, the year the Texas Constitution was adopted. *Barshop v. Medina Cty. Underground Water Conserv. Dist.*, 925 S.W.2d 618, 636 (Tex.1996). To receive a jury trial, a party must have a right to a jury trial and must properly request a jury under TRCP 216(a). *Huddle v. Huddle*, 696 S.W.2d 895, 895 (Tex. 1985); *In re J.N.F.*, 116 S.W.3d 426, 431 (Tex.App.—Houston [14th Dist.] 2003, no pet.). A summary judgment does not violate a party's constitutional right to a jury trial. *Willms v. Americas Tire Co.*, 190 S.W.3d 796, 810 (Tex. App.—Dallas 2006, pet. denied); *see also Ramirez v. Consolidated HGM Corp.*, 124 S.W.3d 914, 916 (Tex.App.—Amarillo 2004, no pet.) (party is not entitled to jury trial on fact issues arising from preliminary motions and pleas that do not involve merits or ultimate disposition of case).

§3. REQUIREMENTS

To make a proper request for a jury trial, a party must do two things at least 30 days before the date the case is set for trial: (1) make a written request for a jury trial and (2) pay the jury fee or file an affidavit of inability to pay. TRCP 216 (request and jury fee), TRCP 217 (affidavit of inability); *see Huddle v. Huddle*, 696 S.W.2d 895, 895 (Tex.1985); *Universal Printing Co. v. Premier Victorian Homes, Inc.*, 73 S.W.3d 283, 289 (Tex.App.—Houston [1st Dist.] 2001, pet. denied). When one party requests a jury and pays a fee, all other parties in the suit acquire the right to a jury trial. *White Motor Co. v. Loden*, 373 S.W.2d 863, 865 (Tex.App.—Dallas 1963, no writ); *see Mercedes-Benz Credit Corp. v. Rhyne*, 925 S.W.2d 664, 666 (Tex.1996). Thus, any party in the suit can rely on any other party's proper jury request. *See Mercedes-Benz*, 925 S.W.2d at 666; *White Motor*, 373 S.W.2d at 865.

§3.1 Request.

1. In writing. The request for a jury trial (also called a jury demand) must be in writing and must be filed with the clerk. TRCP 216(a); *In re T.H.*, 131 S.W.3d 598, 601 (Tex.App.—Texarkana 2004, pet. denied). The request may be included in the plaintiff's petition or the defendant's answer, or it can be filed as a separate document. A party should not rely on a request for a jury trial in a cover letter to the clerk. *ForScan Corp. v. Dresser Indus.*, 789 S.W.2d 389, 392 (Tex.App.—Houston [14th Dist.] 1990, writ denied). One court has held that the request for a setting on the jury docket was a sufficient request for a jury trial under TRCP 216. *Sheth v. White*, 722 S.W.2d 805, 805 (Tex. App.—Houston [14th Dist.] 1987, orig. proceeding).

2. Allegations.

(1) For timely request. In the request, the party should state that it wants a jury trial and that it is tendering the jury fee to the clerk. *See* TRCP 216. See *O'Connor's Texas Forms*, FORM 5B:1.

⋆

(2) For untimely request. If the case is set for trial on the nonjury docket, the party should file a request for a jury trial and a motion to strike the nonjury setting. See *O'Connor's Texas Forms*, FORMS 5B:1-2. In the motion to strike the nonjury setting, the party should allege the following under oath (and attach affidavits if necessary):

(a) A jury is available. The attorney should contact the clerk to determine whether a jury is available. If a jury is not available, the party should file a motion for continuance so the case can be reset on the jury docket. *See McCrann v. Tandy Computer Leasing*, 737 S.W.2d 10, 11 (Tex.App.—Corpus Christi 1987, no writ).

(b) A jury trial can be had without any (1) additional delay, (2) interference with the trial court's docket, or (3) injury to the opposing party. *General Motors Corp. v. Gayle*, 951 S.W.2d 469, 476 (Tex.1997); *Monroe v. Alternatives in Motion*, 234 S.W.3d 56, 70 (Tex.App.—Houston [1st Dist.] 2007, no pet.).

(c) There is a disputed fact in the case, and an instructed verdict would not be proper. *Halsell v. Dehoyos*, 810 S.W.2d 371, 372 (Tex.1991); *In re V.R.W.*, 41 S.W.3d 183, 194 (Tex.App.—Houston [14th Dist.] 2001, no pet.), *disapproved on other grounds, In re J.F.C.*, 96 S.W.3d 256 (Tex.2002).

(d) The reason the jury request was not made earlier.

(e) The Texas Constitution guarantees a jury trial in this type of case. Tex. Const. art. 1, §15.

§3.2 Jury fee. To make a proper request for a jury trial, the party must not only file a request for a jury but also pay the jury fee or file an affidavit of inability to pay. *In re J.N.F.*, 116 S.W.3d 426, 431 (Tex.App.—Houston [14th Dist.] 2003, no pet.); *see Huddle v. Huddle*, 696 S.W.2d 895, 895 (Tex.1985); *Walton v. Canon, Short & Gaston, P.C.*, 23 S.W.3d 143, 149 (Tex.App.—El Paso 2000, no pet.).

1. Amount. The jury fee is $30 in district court and $22 in county court. Gov't Code §51.604(a). This fee includes the amount required under TRCP 216. Gov't Code §51.604(c); *see* TRCP 216(b) (jury fee in district court is $10; jury fee in county court is $5).

PRACTICE TIP

*When paying the filing fees and the jury fee, give the clerk separate checks. If you give the clerk one check and it is not enough to cover both fees, the clerk will apply it to the filing fees and you will not have paid the jury fee. See, e.g., **Universal Printing Co. v. Premier Victorian Homes, Inc.**, 73 S.W.3d 283, 289-90 (Tex.App.—Houston [1st Dist.] 2001, pet. denied) ($105 paid by Ds did not cover jury fee after filing costs were deducted).*

---

2. Indigent. An indigent is not required to pay a jury fee. TRCP 217. Instead, the indigent must file a jury request before the deadline in TRCP 217 and file an affidavit of inability to pay before the deadline for paying the fee. See "Deadline to pay jury fee," §4.2, p. 322. In the affidavit, the indigent must swear that she cannot obtain the money necessary for the fee, by pledge of property or otherwise. TRCP 217. See "Suit by Indigent," ch. 2-I, p. 173.

§4. DEADLINES

§4.1 Deadline to file jury request.

1. Deadline begins – notice of trial. A party's notice from the trial court that the case is set for trial triggers the party's deadline to request a jury trial. TRCP 245 requires the trial court to give the parties 45 days' notice of the first trial setting so that a party can make a timely request for a jury trial. *See In re J.C.*, 108 S.W.3d 914, 916-17 (Tex.App.—Texarkana 2003, no pet.); *Hardin v. Hardin*, 932 S.W.2d 566, 567 (Tex.App.—Tyler 1995, no writ). If the trial court notifies the parties that a case is set on the nonjury docket without giving the parties enough time to request a jury trial, the appellate court will consider a late request to have been timely. *In re J.C.*, 108 S.W.3d at 916-17; *In re V.R.W.*, 41 S.W.3d 183, 195 (Tex.App.—Houston [14th Dist.] 2001, no pet.), *disapproved on other grounds, In re J.F.C.*, 96 S.W.3d 256 (Tex.2002); *see, e.g., Simpson v. Stem*, 822 S.W.2d 323, 324 (Tex.App.—Waco 1992, orig. proceeding) (court gave less than 30 days' notice of trial setting; party's request for jury trial was deemed

★

timely); *see also Martin v. Black*, 909 S.W.2d 192, 197-98 (Tex.App.—Houston [14th Dist.] 1995, writ denied) (because case was not set for trial, request made as soon as P thought fact issue would be tried was timely).

2. Reasonable time before trial. The request for a jury trial should be made a "reasonable time before" the date the case is set for trial on the nonjury docket, but at least 30 days in advance. TRCP 216(a); *Mercedes-Benz Credit Corp. v. Rhyne*, 925 S.W.2d 664, 666 (Tex.1996); *Halsell v. Dehoyos*, 810 S.W.2d 371, 371 (Tex.1991); *e.g.*, *In re T.H.*, 131 S.W.3d 598, 601-02 (Tex.App.—Texarkana 2004, pet. denied) (oral request for jury trial after trial began was not acceptable).

(1) 30 days – presumed reasonable. A request for a jury trial made at least 30 days before trial is presumed to have been made a reasonable time before the trial. *Halsell*, 810 S.W.2d at 371; *Southern Farm Bur. Cas. Ins. v. Penland*, 923 S.W.2d 758, 760 (Tex.App.—Corpus Christi 1996, no writ).

(2) Less than 30 days – no presumption. If the request is made less than 30 days before trial, there is no presumption the request is reasonable. In such a case, the decision to permit a jury trial is strictly within the trial court's discretion.

3. Reschedule trial after late request. If the case is reset, the 30-day deadline is based on the final trial date. *Halsell*, 810 S.W.2d at 371; *Whiteford v. Baugher*, 818 S.W.2d 423, 425 (Tex.App.—Houston [1st Dist.] 1991, writ denied). Thus, when a case is reset for trial, an untimely request can become timely. *Halsell*, 810 S.W.2d at 371; *see also Ricardo N., Inc. v. Turcios de Argueta*, 907 S.W.2d 423, 429 (Tex.1995) (untimely request for 1987 trial was timely for 1991 trial after remand from federal court).

4. Retrial after waiver. If a party waived a jury on the first trial but the case is reversed and remanded for another trial, the party may request a jury trial for the retrial. *Gordon v. Gordon*, 704 S.W.2d 490, 492 (Tex. App.—Corpus Christi 1986, writ dism'd).

§4.2 Deadline to pay jury fee.

1. Deadline in TRCP 216. Under TRCP 216, the deadlines for paying the jury fee and filing the written jury request are the same—30 days before the date the case is set for trial. TRCP 216(a), (b); *Mercedes-Benz Credit Corp. v. Rhyne*, 925 S.W.2d 664, 666 (Tex.1996). Even if a jury fee is not timely paid, the trial court has discretion to permit a jury trial if it will not interfere with the court's docket, delay the trial, or prejudice the opposing party. *General Motors Corp. v. Gayle*, 951 S.W.2d 469, 476 (Tex.1997); *In re D.R.*, 177 S.W.3d 574, 579-80 (Tex.App.—Houston [1st Dist.] 2005, pet. denied). See "Reasonable time before trial," §4.1.2, this page.

2. Deadline in Gov't Code §51.604. Under Gov't Code §51.604, the deadline to pay the jury fee is "not later than the 10th day before the jury trial is scheduled to begin." Gov't Code §51.604(b); *Universal Printing Co. v. Premier Victorian Homes, Inc.*, 73 S.W.3d 283, 292 (Tex.App.—Houston [1st Dist.] 2001, pet. denied).

CAUTION

The jury fee paid under Gov't Code §51.604 includes the fee paid under TRCP 216. Gov't Code §51.604(c). Thus, the portion of the jury fee due under Rule 216—$10 in district court or $5 in county court—must be paid 30 days before trial, and the remainder of the jury fee due under §51.604—$20 in district court or $17 in county court—must be paid 10 days before trial. See In re I.M.B., 148 S.W.3d 653, 656 (Tex.App.—Beaumont 2004, no pet.); Universal Printing, 73 S.W.3d at 292; Askew v. State, No. 03-03-00661-CV (Tex.App.—Austin 2005, no pet.) (memo op.; 1-21-05). See "Amount," §3.2.1, p. 321. To be safe, pay both fees at the same time you make your request, at least 30 days before the date the case is set for trial. See "Deadline in TRCP 216," §4.2.1, this page.

⭐

§5. RESPONSE

§5.1 Request timely. The trial court may deny a timely request for a jury trial only if the party opposing it can rebut the presumption that the request is reasonable. *Halsell v. Dehoyos*, 810 S.W.2d 371, 371 (Tex.1991); *Southern Farm Bur. Cas. Ins. v. Penland*, 923 S.W.2d 758, 760 (Tex.App.—Corpus Christi 1996, no writ). To oppose a timely request for a jury trial, the party should file a response showing that a jury trial will (1) injure the party, (2) disrupt the court's docket, or (3) interfere with the ordinary handling of the court's business. *See Halsell*, 810 S.W.2d at 371; *see, e.g., In re Lesikar*, 285 S.W.3d 577, 581 (Tex.App.—Houston [14th Dist.] 2009, orig. proceeding) (P moved to strike remanded case from jury docket); *Crittenden v. Crittenden*, 52 S.W.3d 768, 770 (Tex.App.—San Antonio 2001, pet. denied) (wife's timely request for jury was denied because husband's objection showed that wife had earlier agreed to settlement, no jury was available for six months, and she had engaged in tactics to delay divorce). Because the right to a jury trial is guaranteed by the Texas Constitution, a court should seldom deny a party a jury trial if the request for a jury was timely. *See* Tex. Const. art. 1, §15.

§5.2 Request untimely. To oppose a request for a jury trial and a motion to strike the nonjury setting made after the deadline, a party should allege the following:

1. The request was made too late. *See Monroe v. Alternatives in Motion*, 234 S.W.3d 56, 69 (Tex.App.—Houston [1st Dist.] 2007, no pet.) (denying untimely jury request is within trial court's discretion).

2. Granting the request would (1) delay the trial, (2) interfere with the court's docket, or (3) injure the opposing party. *General Motors Corp. v. Gayle*, 951 S.W.2d 469, 476 (Tex.1997); *Monroe*, 234 S.W.3d at 70.

§6. ORDER

§6.1 Clerk's duty. Generally the court does not sign an order on a request for a jury trial. *Mercedes-Benz Credit Corp. v. Rhyne*, 925 S.W.2d 664, 666 (Tex.1996). The court clerk simply notes on the court's docket sheet that the jury fee was paid. Gov't Code §51.604(a); TRCP 216(b). When the court actually signs an order setting the case for a jury trial, it cannot disregard the order and withdraw the case from the jury docket just before trial, even if no jury fee was paid. *Mercedes-Benz*, 925 S.W.2d at 666.

§6.2 Request contested. The court will make a ruling on the request for a jury trial only if the request is contested.

PRACTICE TIP
If the trial court denies you a jury trial, immediately file a verified motion for continuance, even if handwritten, asking that the case be continued so it may be reset on the jury docket. See "Motion for Continuance," ch. 5-D, p. 336.

---

§6.3 Withdrawing request for jury. A party may withdraw its request for a jury trial so the case may be heard by the court. If the party who requested the jury trial withdraws its request, the other party may prevent the withdrawal by either making a timely objection or filing its own request for a jury. *Lambert v. Coachmen Indus.*, 761 S.W.2d 82, 85 (Tex.App.—Houston [14th Dist.] 1988, writ denied). The trial court cannot withdraw a case from the jury docket over a party's objection, even if the objecting party did not request a jury or pay the fee. *See* TRCP 220; *In re J.N.F.*, 116 S.W.3d 426, 434 (Tex.App.—Houston [14th Dist.] 2003, no pet.). If the court permits withdrawal of the jury request, the party may also be able to withdraw the jury fee deposit. TRCP 220.

§6.4 No sua sponte withdrawal. A trial court cannot withdraw a case from the jury docket on its own initiative. *Bank of Houston v. White*, 737 S.W.2d 387, 388 (Tex.App.—Houston [14th Dist.] 1987, orig. proceeding). If the court signed an order setting the case for a jury trial—even if the order was signed by mistake—the court cannot disregard its own order and force the parties to try the case without a jury. *Mercedes-Benz Credit Corp. v. Rhyne*, 925 S.W.2d 664, 666 (Tex.1996); *Texas Valley Ins. Agency v. Sweezy Constr., Inc.*, 105 S.W.3d 217, 221 (Tex.App.—Corpus Christi 2003, no pet.).

★

§7. WAIVER OF JURY

§7.1 Failure to appear at trial. A party will waive its request for a jury trial if it does not appear for a scheduled trial. TRCP 220; *Bradley Motors, Inc. v. Mackey*, 878 S.W.2d 140, 141 (Tex.1994); *see In re W.B.W.*, 2 S.W.3d 421, 422-23 (Tex.App.—San Antonio 1999, no pet.) (party, even if not personally present, appears for trial when attorney is present).

§7.2 Failure to object to nonjury trial. A party will waive its request for a jury trial if it does not object when the trial court begins a nonjury trial. *In re D.R.*, 177 S.W.3d 574, 580 (Tex.App.—Houston [1st Dist.] 2005, pet. denied); *Sunwest Reliance Acquisitions Grp. v. Provident Nat'l Assur. Co.*, 875 S.W.2d 385, 387 (Tex.App.—Dallas 1993, no writ).

§7.3 Failure to object to discharge of jury. A party will waive its request for a jury trial if it does not object when the trial court dismisses the jury, resolves the case by summary disposition, and signs a judgment. *Rodriguez v. Texas Dept. of MHMR*, 942 S.W.2d 53, 55-56 (Tex.App.—Corpus Christi 1997, no writ).

§7.4 Waiver by contract. Parties may contractually agree to waive their right to a jury trial. *In re Prudential Ins.*, 148 S.W.3d 124, 132 (Tex.2004); *see In re Bank of Am.*, 278 S.W.3d 342, 344 (Tex.2009) (clarifying that *In re Prudential* does not impose a presumption against contractual jury waiver).

1. Conspicuous. A jury-waiver provision should be conspicuous. *See In re Bank of Am.*, 278 S.W.3d at 345. To be conspicuous, the jury-waiver provision should be in capital letters, bolded, and captioned as a waiver provision. *See, e.g., id.* (waiver provision was captioned "Waiver of Trial by Jury," was bolded, and had words "waiver" and "trial by jury" underlined); *In re General Elec. Capital Corp.*, 203 S.W.3d 314, 316 (Tex.2006) (waiver provision was in capital letters and bolded); *see also* Bus. & Com. Code §1.201(b)(10) (conspicuous term is one that is written or displayed in a manner that a reasonable person against whom the term would operate should have noticed it).

2. Knowingly & voluntarily made. A jury waiver must be knowingly and voluntarily made. *In re Prudential Ins.*, 148 S.W.3d 124, 132 (Tex.2004); *see In re Bank of Am.*, 278 S.W.3d at 344-45. Which party has the burden of proof on this issue depends on whether the jury-waiver provision is conspicuous and whether fraud or imposition is alleged.

(1) Burden on party opposing waiver. If a jury-waiver provision is conspicuous, it is presumed to have been knowingly and voluntarily made unless one of the parties alleges fraud or imposition connected to the execution of the waiver provision. *In re Bank of Am.*, 278 S.W.3d at 345; *see In re Frank Kent Motor Co.*, 361 S.W.3d 628, 632 (Tex.2012) (employer's threat to terminate at-will employee if jury-waiver agreement is not signed does not constitute coercion that would invalidate agreement). Thus, if the jury-waiver provision is conspicuous and no fraud or imposition is alleged, the party opposing the waiver has the burden to rebut the presumption that the waiver was knowingly and voluntarily made. *See In re Bank of Am.*, 278 S.W.3d at 345.

(2) Burden on party seeking to enforce waiver.

(a) Fraud or imposition. If one of the parties alleges fraud or imposition connected to the execution of the jury-waiver provision, the party seeking to enforce the waiver provision—even if it is conspicuous—must prove that it was knowingly and voluntarily made. *See In re Bank of Am.*, 278 S.W.3d at 345.

(b) Inconspicuous provision. If a jury-waiver provision is not conspicuous, the party seeking to enforce the waiver provision must prove that it was knowingly and voluntarily made. *E.g., In re Key Equip. Fin. Inc.*, 371 S.W.3d 296, 302-03 (Tex.App.—Houston [1st Dist.] 2012, orig. proceeding) (although not conspicuous, jury-waiver provision enforced because provision was reasonably placed and in same typeface as other provisions, parties had history of signing similar agreements, and P's in-house counsel reviewed the agreement).

3. Timely. A party should timely assert a contractual jury waiver or the waiver can be lost. *See, e.g., In re General Elec.*, 203 S.W.3d at 314-15 (P retained right to assert contractual jury waiver, despite ten-month delay in filing motion to quash D's jury demand, because P never received notice of demand); *Rivercenter Assocs. v. Rivera*, 858 S.W.2d 366, 367 (Tex.1993) (P lost right to assert contractual jury waiver because it did not file motion to quash D's jury demand until more than four months after receiving notice of demand).

4. Nonsignatories. A nonsignatory agent can assert a valid jury waiver when it acts on behalf of a signatory. *In re Credit Suisse First Boston Mortg. Capital, L.L.C.*, 273 S.W.3d 843, 847 (Tex.App.—Houston [14th Dist.] 2008, orig. proceeding).

§8. REVIEW

When the trial court erroneously refuses to grant a jury trial, the error is always harmful, unless there are no material issues of fact and the court could have granted an instructed verdict. *Halsell v. Dehoyos*, 810 S.W.2d 371, 372 (Tex.1991); *see Caldwell v. Barnes*, 154 S.W.3d 93, 98 (Tex.2004). If the party was entitled to a jury trial and there were material fact issues in the case, the appellate court will reverse for a retrial. *See Caldwell*, 154 S.W.3d at 98; *Halsell*, 810 S.W.2d at 372.

C. MOTION TO CHALLENGE THE JUDGE

§1. GENERAL

A judge may be removed from a case for one of three reasons: (1) she is subject to a statutory strike as an assigned judge, (2) she is constitutionally disqualified, or (3) she is subject to disqualification or recusal under rules promulgated by the Supreme Court. Tex. Const. art. 5, §11 (constitutional disqualifications); Gov't Code §74.053(d) (statutory strike); TRCP 18a & 18b (disqualification and recusal rules promulgated by Court); *In re Union Pac. Res.*, 969 S.W.2d 427, 428 (Tex.1998).

§1.1 Rules. TRCP 18a, 18b. See Tex. Const. art. 5, §11 (disqualification); CPRC §30.016 (tertiary motion to disqualify or recuse in district and statutory county courts); Gov't Code §24.002 (assignment of judge or transfer of case on recusal), §25.00255 (motion to disqualify or recuse statutory probate judge), §25.00256 (tertiary motion to disqualify or recuse in statutory probate courts), §74.053 (objection to assigned judge); TRAP 16.2, 16.3 (recusal of appellate justice).

§1.2 Purpose. A motion to challenge the trial judge seeks to remove the judge from the case so another judge can be assigned to preside over the case.

§1.3 Forms. *O'Connor's Texas Civil Forms* (2012), FORMS 5C.

§1.4 Other references. *O'Connor's Texas Civil Appeals* (2012) (*O'Connor's Texas Appeals*).

§2. TYPES OF MOTIONS

There are four types of challenges to the trial judge.

§2.1 Objection to assigned judges. An objection to an assigned judge is a peremptory challenge that, if timely made, results in the automatic removal of the assigned judge. Gov't Code §74.053(b); *In re Perritt*, 992 S.W.2d 444, 446 (Tex.1999). Various code provisions refer to a judge assigned to serve as an "assigned" or a "visiting" judge. *See* Gov't Code §§74.053-74.054 (uses "assigned judge"), §74.060(b) (uses "visiting judge"). See "Objection to Assigned Judge," §3, p. 326.

§2.2 Motion to disqualify or recuse. A motion to disqualify seeks to prevent a judge from hearing a case for a constitutional reason or a reason under TRCP 18b(a), which is based on constitutional grounds. *See Tesco Am., Inc. v. Strong Indus.*, 221 S.W.3d 550, 553 (Tex.2006); *In re Union Pac. Res.*, 969 S.W.2d 427, 428 (Tex.1998). A motion to recuse seeks to prevent a judge from hearing a case for a nonconstitutional reason under TRCP 18b(b). See "Motion to Disqualify or Recuse," §4, p. 329.

§2.3 Tertiary motion to disqualify or recuse. The third (or later) motion to disqualify or recuse a judge in the same case by the same party is called a "tertiary" motion. CPRC §30.016; Gov't Code §25.00256. Although the substantive law is the same as for motions to disqualify or recuse, separate rules govern the procedure for tertiary motions. See "Tertiary Motion to Disqualify or Recuse," §5, p. 334.

───────────────── ★ ─────────────────

5-1. COMPARISON OF DISQUALIFICATION, RECUSAL & OBJECTION TO ASSIGNED JUDGE			
	Disqualification	**Recusal**	**Objection to assigned judge**
1 Source of challenge	Constitution, statutes, and rules	Statutes and rules	Statute
2 Discretionary or mandatory	Mandatory	Mandatory, unless waived	Mandatory, if timely
3 Waivable	No	Yes	Yes
4 Parties may consent to judge	No	Yes	Yes
5 Effect if judge serves after valid challenge	Judgment void	Reversible error	Judgment void
6 Requires written motion	No	Yes	Yes
7 Judgment subject to collateral attack	Yes	No	No

§3. OBJECTION TO ASSIGNED JUDGE

§3.1 Who may make assignment. Most assignments of judges are made by the presiding judge of the administrative region, who has the authority to assign judges residing within the region. Gov't Code §74.056(c); *Chandler v. Chandler*, 991 S.W.2d 367, 379 (Tex.App.—El Paso 1999, pet. denied). However, assignments of judges can be made by the Chief Justice of the Texas Supreme Court when (1) the assigned judge does not reside within the administrative region to which she is assigned, or (2) the presiding judge of the administrative region is incapacitated, dies, resigns, or is disqualified in the matter. Gov't Code §74.049 (situation 2), §74.057(a) (situation 1); *State v. Preslar*, 751 S.W.2d 477, 479 (Tex.1988) (situations 1 and 2).

§3.2 Who may be assigned. An assigned judge is assigned under Gov't Code chapter 74 to sit temporarily for the regular judge of the court. *See* Gov't Code §74.052 (assignment of judges generally), §74.053 (objection to assigned judges), §74.054 (judges who may be assigned). Judges assigned to hear a TRCP 18a motion (disqualification or recusal) are appointed under Gov't Code chapter 74—not under TRCP 18a—and are subject to challenge as an assigned judge. *In re Perritt*, 992 S.W.2d 444, 447 (Tex.1999). There are four types of judges who may be assigned as visiting judges, and the assignment order must state which type of judge is being assigned. Gov't Code §74.053(a)(1).

  1. **Active judge.** An "active judge" is a current judicial officeholder. Gov't Code §74.041(4). The term includes the following judges: a district judge, a constitutional or statutory county-court judge, or an active appellate justice (Supreme Court, Court of Criminal Appeals, or court of appeals) who has had trial-court experience. *Id.* §74.054(a)(1), (a)(5); *see, e.g., O.C.S., Inc. v. Pi Energy Corp.*, 24 S.W.3d 548, 551 (Tex.App.—Houston [1st Dist.] 2000, no pet.) (district judge was assigned to hear motion to recuse in another court).

  2. **Retired judge.** A "retired judge" (1) is a retiree or (2) served as an active judge for at least eight years in a district, statutory probate, statutory county, or appellate court and was vested under the Texas County and District Retirement System when she left office. Gov't Code §§74.041(6), 74.055(c)(1); *see id.* §74.054(a)(3), (a)(4); *Mitchell Energy Corp. v. Ashworth*, 943 S.W.2d 436, 440-41 (Tex.1997); *Chandler v. Chandler*, 991 S.W.2d 367, 380 (Tex.App.—El Paso 1999, pet. denied). To be eligible for assignment, a retired judge must meet the qualifications listed in Gov't Code §74.055(c).

  3. **Former judge.** A "former judge" served for at least eight years as an active judge in a district, statutory probate, statutory county, or appellate court but is not a retired judge. Gov't Code §§74.041(5), 74.055(c)(1); *see id.* §74.054(a)(3), (a)(4). To be eligible for assignment, a former judge must meet the qualifications listed in Gov't Code §74.055(c). A judge's status as a former judge is fixed when she leaves office. *Mitchell Energy*, 943 S.W.2d at 437.

✦

4. Senior judge. A "senior judge" is a retired judge who has chosen to be a judicial officer. Gov't Code §74.041(7); *see id.* §§74.054(a)(2), 75.001.

§3.3 Notice of assignment. If time permits, and if it is practical, the presiding judge of the administrative region must give the parties notice of the assignment of a visiting judge. Gov't Code §74.053(a)(2); *In re Canales*, 52 S.W.3d 698, 701 (Tex.2001); *Tivoli Corp. v. Jewelers Mut. Ins.*, 932 S.W.2d 704, 709 (Tex.App.—San Antonio 1996, writ denied). Notice of assignment may be given by e-mail. Gov't Code §74.053(f).

§3.4 Deadline to object. An objection to an assigned judge must be filed before the date of the first hearing (including pretrial hearings) or trial over which the assigned judge is to preside, or within seven days after receiving actual notice of the assignment, whichever is earlier. Gov't Code §74.053(c); *In re Approximately $17,239.00*, 129 S.W.3d 167, 168 (Tex.App.—Houston [14th Dist.] 2003, orig. proceeding). The presiding judge may extend the deadline for good cause on a party's written motion. Gov't Code §74.053(c). If an assigned judge who heard part of the case is reassigned to hear an additional part of the case by a new order of assignment, the reassignment does not give the parties a new opportunity to object. *In re Canales*, 52 S.W.3d 698, 704 (Tex.2001). The requirement in TRCP 18a(b)(1)(B) that the motion to recuse be filed at least ten days before the hearing or trial does not apply to objections to assigned judges. *See* Gov't Code §74.053(c); TRCP 18a(b)(1)(B). See "Motion to recuse," §4.1.6(2), p. 331.

CAUTION

*The objection must be the first matter presented to the assigned judge for a ruling. **Chandler v. Chandler**, 991 S.W.2d 367, 383 (Tex.App.—El Paso 1999, pet. denied); see **In re Approximately $17,239.00**, 129 S.W.3d at 168-69. The objection is too late if it is filed after the assigned judge makes a ruling, even on a pretrial motion submitted without a hearing. **Perkins v. Groff**, 936 S.W.2d 661, 666-67 (Tex.App.—Dallas 1996, writ denied); **Tivoli Corp. v. Jewelers Mut. Ins.**, 932 S.W.2d 704, 709 (Tex.App.—San Antonio 1996, writ denied). An objection after ordinary docket call is timely. **Lee v. Bachus**, 900 S.W.2d 390, 392 (Tex.App.—Texarkana 1995, orig. proceeding).*

---

§3.5 Challenges.

1. Active judge – no challenge. A party cannot challenge an active judge. An active judge assigned under Gov't Code chapter 74 is not subject to a §74.053 objection. Gov't Code §74.053(e).

PRACTICE TIP

*If the presiding judge discusses possible appointments for an assigned judge and the parties voice an objection to one of the judges mentioned, the oral objection does not count as a formal objection to an assigned judge. **Kellogg v. Martin**, 810 S.W.2d 302, 304-05 (Tex.App.—Texarkana 1991, orig. proceeding).*

---

2. Retired, former, or senior judge.

(1) Single challenge. Each party is entitled to make one challenge in a case to an assigned judge who is a retired, former, or senior judge appointed under Gov't Code §74.054. *See* Gov't Code §74.053(b); *see, e.g.*, *In re Perritt*, 992 S.W.2d 444, 446 n.2 (Tex.1999) (former judge); *Flores v. Banner*, 932 S.W.2d 500, 501 (Tex.1996) (retired judge). For definitions of retired, former, and senior judges, see "Who may be assigned," §3.2, p. 326. Under Gov't Code §74.053, "party" includes multiple parties aligned in a case as determined by the presiding judge. Gov't Code §74.053(g).

(2) Multiple challenges. Each party has unlimited challenges to an assigned judge who was defeated in the last primary or general election in which she was seeking reelection. *See* Gov't Code §74.053(b), (d).

★

§3.6 Automatic removal. A proper and timely objection to an assigned judge is a peremptory objection; the removal is mandatory and automatic. Gov't Code §74.053(b); *In re Canales*, 52 S.W.3d 698, 701 (Tex.2001); *Flores v. Banner*, 932 S.W.2d 500, 501 (Tex.1996).

§3.7 How to object to assigned judge.

1. In writing. The objection must be in writing and must be filed with the court. *Morris v. Short*, 902 S.W.2d 566, 569 (Tex.App.—Houston [1st Dist.] 1995, writ denied); *see Wolfe v. Wolfe*, 918 S.W.2d 533, 540-41 (Tex.App.—El Paso 1996, writ denied). See *O'Connor's Texas Forms*, FORM 5C:1. Gov't Code §74.053(b) does not state that an objection must be in writing, but the use of the word "files" presupposes that it will be. *Morris*, 902 S.W.2d at 569; *Kellogg v. Martin*, 810 S.W.2d 302, 305 (Tex.App.—Texarkana 1991, orig. proceeding). The objection may be handwritten. *Morris*, 902 S.W.2d at 569. The objection may also be filed by e-mail. Gov't Code §74.053(f). If a party learns at docket call that a visiting judge was assigned to the case, the objection must still be in writing—an oral objection at the hearing is not enough. *Morris*, 902 S.W.2d at 569; *see Money v. Jones*, 766 S.W.2d 307, 308 (Tex.App.—Dallas 1989, writ denied).

2. Identify challenged judge. The objection should identify the assigned judge by name. *See, e.g., Texas Empl. Comm'n v. Alvarez*, 915 S.W.2d 161, 164 (Tex.App.—Corpus Christi 1996, orig. proceeding) (because party did not name judge in objection and did not reurge objection when case was reset, judge was unaware of objection). However, if the challenged judge's identity can be determined from the objection, the lack of a name is not critical. *See, e.g., Flores v. Banner*, 932 S.W.2d 500, 501-02 (Tex.1996) (because movant did not know name of judge to be assigned, she filed objection to "any" assigned judge; objection was effective).

3. Grounds.

(1) Standard objection. An objection under Gov't Code §74.053 to an assigned judge should state that the party objects to the judge's assignment. Because a §74.053 objection depends on the judge's status, the judge's status should be identified in the objection. A party does not need to provide a reason for the objection. *In re Perritt*, 992 S.W.2d 444, 446 (Tex.1999).

(2) Objections to procedural errors in assignment. A party must object to any procedural errors in the assignment or waive the error. *See, e.g., In re General Elec. Capital Corp.*, 63 S.W.2d 568, 572 (Tex.App.—El Paso 2001, orig. proceeding) (waived objection that assigned judge did not take required oath); *cf. Lopez v. State*, 57 S.W.3d 625, 629 (Tex.App.—Corpus Christi 2001, pet. ref'd) (criminal case; waived objection that record did not contain copy of order of assignment).

(3) Disqualification or recusal challenges. When a party has exhausted its objections to assigned judges, the party can assert any available disqualification or recusal challenges. See "Motion to Disqualify or Recuse," §4, p. 329.

4. Identify number of challenges. Although not required by statute, the party should state the number of objections to other assigned judges, if any, that it has made in the same case. *See Amateur Athletic Found. v. Hoffman*, 893 S.W.2d 602, 604 (Tex.App.—Dallas 1994, orig. proceeding) (Whittington, J., dissenting).

5. Verification.

(1) Standard objection. There is no statutory requirement that a standard objection to an assigned judge be verified. *O'Connor v. Lykos*, 960 S.W.2d 96, 99 (Tex.App.—Houston [1st Dist.] 1997, orig. proceeding). The standard objection does not need to be verified because a party does not need to assert any facts in an objection to an assigned judge. *Id.* However, one court of appeals has held that the objection must be verified. *See Hawkins v. Estate of Volkmann*, 898 S.W.2d 334, 343-44 (Tex.App.—San Antonio 1994, writ denied) (court overruled unverified challenge to assigned judge). Until the issue is resolved by the Supreme Court, parties should verify objections to assigned judges.

(2) Other challenges. If facts are necessary to support other challenges to the assigned judge (see "Objections to procedural errors in assignment," §3.7.3(2), this page), the motion should be verified. See "Verified," §4.1.2, p. 329.

————————————— ✮ —————————————

§3.8 No hearing. When a party files a timely objection to an assigned judge under Gov't Code §74.053(b), no hearing is necessary because the removal is automatic. The only fact issue that could arise is whether the objection was timely, and for that reason, the judge and the parties should make a record. If the assigned judge is challenged for other reasons (see "Objections to procedural errors in assignment," §3.7.3(2), p. 328), a hearing is necessary. See "Hearing after referral," §4.6, p. 333.

§3.9 Termination of assignment. The term for an assignment depends on the language in the order of assignment. *In re Republic Parking Sys.*, 60 S.W.3d 877, 879 (Tex.App.—Houston [14th Dist.] 2001, orig. proceeding). Generally, judges are assigned either for a period of time or for a particular case. *Id.* Typical orders of assignment contain the language that the assignment is to continue until the assigned judge completes the trial of any case begun during the period of assignment, passes on motions for new trial, and completes all other matters arising from any cause heard by the assigned judge. *See Davis v. Crist Indus.*, 98 S.W.3d 338, 341 (Tex.App.—Fort Worth 2003, pet. denied). The following is a representative sample of cases determining when an assignment ends: • Power expires on the date set in the order, if the judge does not begin the trial by that date. *In re Republic Parking Sys.*, 60 S.W.3d at 880. • Power expires when the court loses plenary power over the case. *Ex parte Eastland*, 811 S.W.2d 571, 572 (Tex.1991). • Power expires when the appeal is perfected. *Starnes v. Chapman*, 793 S.W.2d 104, 106 (Tex.App.—Dallas 1990, orig. proceeding). • Power expires when the assigned judge grants a new trial. *O'Connor v. Lykos*, 960 S.W.2d 96, 98 (Tex.App.—Houston [1st Dist.] 1997, orig. proceeding). • Power extends to post-judgment discovery after the trial court loses plenary power, unless limited by language in the assignment. *O'Connor v. Smith*, 815 S.W.2d 338, 346 (Tex.App.—Houston [1st Dist.] 1991, orig. proceeding).

§4. MOTION TO DISQUALIFY OR RECUSE

A motion to disqualify seeks to prevent a judge from hearing a case for a constitutional reason or a reason under TRCP 18b(a). *See In re Union Pac. Res.*, 969 S.W.2d 427, 428 (Tex.1998). TRCP 18b(a) incorporates the grounds for disqualification from the Texas Constitution. *See* Tex. Const. art. 5, §11; *Tesco Am., Inc. v. Strong Indus.*, 221 S.W.3d 550, 553 (Tex.2006). A motion to recuse, on the other hand, seeks to prevent a judge from hearing a case for a non-constitutional reason. *See* TRCP 18b(b).

NOTE

In this section, we use the phrase "regional presiding judge" to refer to the presiding judge of the administrative judicial region in which the court considering the motion to disqualify or recuse is located. See TRCP 18a(e)(1).

---

§4.1 Motion. A party in a case can file a motion to disqualify or recuse a judge sitting in the case in any trial court, except a statutory probate court (which is governed by Gov't Code chapter 25), justice court (which is governed by TRCP 528), or municipal court (which is governed by Gov't Code chapter 29). *See* TRCP 18a(a) & cmt. See *O'Connor's Texas Appeals*, "Motion to disqualify or recuse," ch. 3-I, §5.1, p. 126.

1. Written.

(1) Motion to disqualify. A motion to disqualify should be in writing. *See* TRCP 18a(a) (party may seek to disqualify by "filing" motion). Because disqualification can be raised at any time, even on appeal or in a collateral attack on the judgment, an oral motion to disqualify may be permissible. *See Zarate v. Sun Oper. Ltd.*, 40 S.W.3d 617, 621 (Tex.App.—San Antonio 2001, pet. denied). See "Disqualification," §7.3.1, p. 335.

(2) Motion to recuse. A motion to recuse should be in writing. *See* TRCP 18a(a); *see, e.g., Barron v. State*, 108 S.W.3d 379, 383 (Tex.App.—Tyler 2003, no pet.) (oral motion to recuse improper). TRCP 18a(a) does not state that a motion to recuse must be in writing, but its use of the word "filing" presupposes that it will be.

2. Verified. Any motion to remove a judge from hearing the case must be verified. TRCP 18a(a)(1); *see Johnson v. Sepulveda*, 178 S.W.3d 117, 118-19 (Tex.App.—Houston [14th Dist.] 2005, no pet.) (unverified motion to recuse was ineffective).

─────────────── ✦ ───────────────

3. Grounds. To conserve space in this book, a complete discussion of the grounds for disqualification and recusal is included in a companion book, *O'Connor's Texas Appeals*. For the forms for disqualification and recusal, see *O'Connor's Texas Forms*, FORMS 5C:3-4.

(1) Identify specific grounds. A motion to disqualify or recuse must identify the specific legal grounds for disqualification or recusal. TRCP 18a(a)(2).

(a) Disqualification. A trial judge may be disqualified under Texas Constitution art. 5, §11, or under TRCP 18b(a), which is based on constitutional grounds. *See Tesco Am., Inc. v. Strong Indus.*, 221 S.W.3d 550, 553 (Tex.2006).

[1] Texas Constitution. Under the Texas Constitution, a judge must be disqualified from hearing a case if (1) the judge served as an attorney in the case, (2) the judge "may be interested" in the outcome of the case, or (3) one of the parties is related to the judge. Tex. Const. art. 5, §11. See *O'Connor's Texas Appeals*, "Disqualification under Texas Constitution," ch. 3-I, §3.1, p. 119.

[2] TRCP 18b(a). Under TRCP 18b(a), a judge must be disqualified from hearing a case under any of the following circumstances:

[a] The judge served as an attorney in the case. TRCP 18b(a)(1); *In re O'Connor*, 92 S.W.3d 446, 448 (Tex.2002).

[b] An attorney with whom the judge previously practiced law served on the case while associated with the judge. TRCP 18b(a)(1); *In re O'Connor*, 92 S.W.3d at 448-49.

[c] The judge knows that she has an interest in the suit, either individually or as a fiduciary. TRCP 18b(a)(2). A disqualifying interest is generally either financial or personal. See *O'Connor's Texas Appeals*, "Disqualifying interests," ch. 3-I, §3.1.2, p. 120.

[d] The judge is related to a party by affinity or consanguinity within the third degree. TRCP 18b(a)(3). Government Code §§573.021-573.025 define the relationships that fall within and trigger this prohibition. See *O'Connor's Texas Appeals*, "Related to party," ch. 3-I, §3.1.3, p. 121.

(b) Recusal. A trial judge may be subject to recusal under TRCP 18b(b) or a statute that supports grounds for recusal. See *O'Connor's Texas Appeals*, "Grounds for Recusal," ch. 3-I, §4, p. 123.

(2) Not based on judge's rulings. The motion must not be based only on the judge's rulings in the case. TRCP 18a(a)(3) & cmt. See "Challenged judge's rulings," §4.6.3(2), p. 333.

(3) Waiver. The parties may waive a ground for recusal after it is fully disclosed on the record. TRCP 18b(e). Parties cannot waive a constitutionally based ground for disqualification. *See* TRCP 18a(b)(2), (g)(3)(B); *Freedom Comms. v. Coronado*, 372 S.W.3d 621, 624 (Tex.2012); *Buckholts ISD v. Glaser*, 632 S.W.2d 146, 148 (Tex. 1982); *Jennings v. Garner*, 721 S.W.2d 445, 446 (Tex.App.—Tyler 1986, no writ).

4. Facts. A motion to disqualify or recuse must state facts with particularity that would be admissible in evidence and support the challenge. *See* TRCP 18a(a)(4). Facts should be based on personal knowledge but may be stated on information and belief if the grounds supporting the belief are specifically stated. TRCP 18a(a)(4)(A).

5. Defects in motion.

(1) Motion to disqualify. A challenged judge cannot deny a motion to disqualify because of procedural defects; instead, she must either order the disqualification or refer the motion to the regional presiding judge. TRCP 18a(f)(1). See "Response by challenged judge," §4.3, p. 332. The regional presiding judge cannot deny a motion to disqualify because it was not filed or served in compliance with TRCP 18a. TRCP 18a(g)(3)(B).

(2) Motion to recuse. A challenged judge cannot deny a motion to recuse because of procedural defects; instead, she must either order the recusal or refer the motion to the regional presiding judge. TRCP 18a(f)(1). See "Response by challenged judge," §4.3, p. 332. If the motion is referred, the regional presiding judge may then

⭐

deny the motion to recuse if it does not comply with TRCP 18a. TRCP 18a(g)(3)(A). The regional presiding judge can deny the motion without an oral hearing, but the order must describe how the motion does not comply. *Id.* Even if the motion is amended to correct the procedural defect, the motion will count in determining whether a tertiary motion to recuse has been filed. *Id.* See "Tertiary Motion to Disqualify or Recuse," §5, p. 334.

6. Deadline to file.

(1) Motion to disqualify. A motion to disqualify should be filed as soon as practicable after the party learns of the reason for disqualification. TRCP 18a(b)(2). Disqualification cannot be waived, however, and thus can be raised at any time, even on appeal or in a collateral attack on the judgment. See "Waiver," §4.1.3(3), p. 330; "Disqualification," §7.3.1, p. 335.

(2) Motion to recuse. A motion to recuse must be filed (1) as soon as practicable after the party learns of the reason for recusal and (2) at least ten days before the date set for the trial or other hearing. TRCP 18a(b)(1). A motion to recuse may be filed after the ten-day deadline if the party did not know and should not have reasonably known (1) that the judge it seeks to recuse would preside at the trial or hearing or (2) of the reason for recusal until after that deadline. TRCP 18a(b)(1)(B). A party who does not comply with the filing requirements of TRCP 18a waives any complaint on appeal of a judge's refusal to recuse. *See Barron*, 108 S.W.3d at 382 & n.4; *Spigener v. Wallis*, 80 S.W.3d 174, 180 (Tex.App.—Waco 2002, no pet.).

NOTE

*When a case is reversed for retrial, a party can file a motion to recuse after remand. See **Winfield v. Daggett**, 846 S.W.2d 920, 922 (Tex.App.—Houston [1st Dist.] 1993, orig. proceeding) (under former TRCP 18a(a), now TRCP 18a(b)(1)(B); when new trial is granted, case stands on docket as if it had not been tried).*

---

7. Notice to other parties. The party filing the motion must serve all other parties copies of the motion by the same method that was used for filing, if possible. TRCP 18a(d). TRCP 18a does not specify when to serve a motion to disqualify or recuse. Because the challenged judge must either grant the motion or refer it within three business days after it is filed, a party should serve the motion at the same time it is filed. See "When to Serve," ch. 1-D, §5, p. 36; "Response by challenged judge," §4.3, p. 332.

8. Delivery by clerk. Once the motion to disqualify or recuse is filed, the clerk must immediately deliver a copy of the motion to the challenged judge and the regional presiding judge. TRCP 18a(e)(1).

§4.2 Response by other party. Any other party in the case can file a response to the motion. TRCP 18a(c)(1).

1. Grounds.

(1) Refute grounds in motion. The party should refute the allegations made in the motion to disqualify or recuse. See "Motion," §4.1, p. 329.

(2) Request sanctions. If the motion to disqualify or recuse was (1) groundless and filed in bad faith or to harass or (2) brought solely for the purpose of delay and without sufficient cause, the party responding to the motion may ask for sanctions. TRCP 18a(h). See "Sanctions," §4.7.4, p. 334; *O'Connor's Texas Forms*, FORM 5C:6.

2. Deadline to file. A response must be filed before the motion is heard. TRCP 18a(c)(1).

3. Notice to other parties. The party filing the response must serve all other parties copies of the response by the same method that was used for filing, if possible. TRCP 18a(d). TRCP 18a does not specify when to serve a response to a motion to disqualify or recuse. Thus, a party should serve the response at the same time it is filed. See "When to Serve," ch. 1-D, §5, p. 36.

4. Delivery by clerk. Once the response to the motion is filed, the clerk must immediately deliver a copy of the response to the challenged judge and the regional presiding judge. TRCP 18a(e)(1).

✦

---

§4.3 Response by challenged judge.

1. Judge's options. The challenged judge should not file a response to a motion to disqualify or recuse. TRCP 18a(c)(2). The judge has two options—either (1) grant the motion to disqualify or recuse or (2) refer the motion for a hearing before another judge. *See* TRCP 18a(f)(1).

NOTE

*A challenged judge cannot overrule or refuse to rule on a motion that is procedurally or substantively defective; the judge must grant the motion or refer it. Then another judge will determine the procedural adequacy and merits of the motion. See **In re Norman**, 191 S.W.3d 858, 861 (Tex.App.—Houston [14th Dist.] 2006, orig. proceeding) (under former TRCP 18a(c), now TRCP 18a(f)(1)). See "Defects in motion," §4.1.5, p. 330; "Hearing after referral," §4.6, p. 333.*

---

(1) Judge grants motion. When a challenged judge grants a motion to disqualify or recuse, she must sign and file an order to that effect and request that the regional presiding judge assign another judge to the case. *See* TRCP 18a(f)(1)(A); *see also* Gov't Code §24.002 (voluntary recusal).

(2) Judge refers motion. When a challenged judge declines to disqualify or recuse herself, she must sign and file an order referring the motion to the regional presiding judge. TRCP 18a(f)(1)(B); *see* Gov't Code §74.059(c)(3). The challenged judge cannot deny the motion; she must refer the motion to the presiding judge for a hearing. *See* TRCP 18a(f)(1)(B); *In re Perritt*, 992 S.W.2d 444, 447 (Tex.1999) (under former TRCP 18a(d), now TRCP 18a(f)(1)(B)).

2. Deadline to grant motion or refer. The challenged judge must either grant the motion to disqualify or recuse or refer the motion within three business days after the motion is filed. TRCP 18a(f)(1).

3. Delivery of order. The clerk must immediately deliver a copy of the order of disqualification, recusal, or referral to the regional presiding judge. TRCP 18a(e)(2).

4. Prohibited actions.

(1) Ignore or overrule. The challenged judge cannot ignore the motion or overrule it and proceed to trial. *See* TRCP 18a(f)(1); *Johnson v. Pumjani*, 56 S.W.3d 670, 672 (Tex.App.—Houston [14th Dist.] 2001, no pet.) (under former TRCP 18a(c), now TRCP 18a(f)(1)).

(2) Take any further action.

(a) Motion filed before evidence offered at trial. When a motion to disqualify or recuse has been filed before evidence has been offered at trial, the challenged judge cannot take any further action in the case until the motion to disqualify or recuse is resolved. TRCP 18a(f)(2)(A). Any order signed by the challenged judge while the motion is pending is void. *In re Rio Grande Valley Gas Co.*, 987 S.W.2d 167, 179 (Tex.App.—Corpus Christi 1999, orig. proceeding); *see Brosseau v. Ranzau*, 911 S.W.2d 890, 893 (Tex.App.—Beaumont 1995, no writ). There is one exception—a judge may sign an order while the motion is pending if "good cause" is identified in the order or on the record. *See* TRCP 18a(f)(2)(A). The judge cannot just state that there is good cause to take further action in the case; she must include the basis for finding good cause. *See In re Stearman*, 252 S.W.3d 113, 116-17 (Tex.App.—Waco 2008, orig. proceeding) (under former TRCP 18a(d), now TRCP 18a(f)(2)(A)).

(b) Motion filed after evidence offered at trial. When a motion to disqualify or recuse is filed after evidence has been offered at trial, the challenged judge can proceed with the trial unless the regional presiding judge issues a stay. TRCP 18a(f)(2)(B).

5. Noncompliance. If the challenged judge does not comply with a duty under TRCP 18a, the movant can notify the regional presiding judge. TRCP 18a(f)(3).

§4.4 Duties of regional presiding judge & assigned judge.

1. After challenged judge's response.

(1) Order of disqualification or recusal. Once the challenged judge orders herself disqualified or recused, the regional presiding judge must assign another judge to the case. *See* Gov't Code §74.059(c)(3).

———————————— ✦ ————————————

(2) **Order of referral.** Once the challenged judge refers the motion, the regional presiding judge must rule on the motion or assign a judge to rule on it. TRCP 18a(g)(1). If a party moves to disqualify or recuse the regional presiding judge, the judge can do either of the following:

(a) Assign a judge to rule on the original referred motion. TRCP 18a(g)(1).

(b) Sign and file with the clerk an order referring the motion that challenges the regional presiding judge to the Chief Justice. *Id.* The Chief Justice has authority to assign judges and issue orders as allowed under TRCP 18a or by statute. TRCP 18a(i).

NOTE

Either party may file an objection to the assigned judge. See Gov't Code §74.053(b). For the procedure for objecting to an assigned judge, see "Objection to Assigned Judge," §3, p. 326.

---

2. Interim orders in pending case. The regional presiding judge or assigned judge may issue interim or ancillary orders in the pending case as justice may require. TRCP 18a(g)(4).

§4.5 Discovery. Discovery requests and subpoenas cannot be issued to the challenged judge unless ordered by the regional presiding judge or assigned judge. TRCP 18a(g)(5).

§4.6 Hearing after referral. The party that filed the motion to disqualify or recuse is entitled to a hearing on the motion. *See* TRCP 18a(g)(6). The motion must be heard by the regional presiding judge or assigned judge as soon as practicable and may be heard immediately after the motion is referred. TRCP 18a(g)(6)(A). The hearing gives the movant an opportunity to develop a record to support its motion. *In re Rio Grande Valley Gas Co.*, 987 S.W.2d 167, 179 (Tex.App.—Corpus Christi 1999, orig. proceeding) (under former TRCP 18a(d), now TRCP 18a(g)(6)).

1. Notice of hearing. All parties must receive notice of the hearing on a motion to disqualify or recuse. TRCP 18a(g)(6)(B).

2. By telephone. The hearing on a motion to disqualify or recuse can be conducted by telephone on the record. TRCP 18a(g)(6)(C). Evidence submitted by fax or e-mail may be considered as long as it is admissible under the TREs. *Id.*

3. Burden of proof. The party who filed the motion to disqualify or recuse has the burden of proof at the hearing on the motion. *See Sparkman v. Peoples Nat'l Bank*, 553 S.W.2d 680, 681 (Tex.App.—Waco 1977, writ ref'd n.r.e.) (judge is presumed to be qualified until contrary evidence is shown).

(1) **Evidence – generally.** The movant must provide sworn evidence to support the allegations in its motion. *See* TRCP 18a(a)(4)(C); *Urdiales v. Concord Techs. Del., Inc.*, 120 S.W.3d 400, 403-04 (Tex.App.—Houston [14th Dist.] 2003, pet. denied).

(2) **Challenged judge's rulings.** Although a challenged judge's rulings cannot be the sole basis for a motion to disqualify or recuse, the judge hearing the motion can consider evidence of the challenged judge's rulings when one or more sufficient other grounds are raised. TRCP 18a cmt. Rulings do not include the judge's statements or remarks about a case. *Id.*

4. No participation by challenged judge. The challenged judge should not voluntarily participate in the recusal hearing or in a mandamus proceeding regarding the recusal. *Blanchard v. Krueger*, 916 S.W.2d 15, 19 n.9 (Tex.App.—Houston [1st Dist.] 1995, orig. proceeding). Active participation in the recusal proceedings, such as hiring an attorney or filing a response, can lead to the judge's recusal. *Id.*

§4.7 Order on motion to disqualify or recuse.

1. Written. The ruling must be by a written order. TRCP 18a(g)(2).

2. Granting the motion.

(1) **Motion to disqualify or recuse – generally.** If the motion to disqualify or recuse is granted, the regional presiding judge must transfer the case to another court or assign another judge to hear the case. TRCP

───────────────────────────── ✯ ─────────────────────────────

18a(g)(7). The phrase "another judge" does not exclude the judge assigned to hear the motion to disqualify or recuse. *District Judges of Collin Cty. v. Commissioner's Ct. of Collin Cty.*, 677 S.W.2d 743, 745 (Tex.App.—Dallas 1984, writ ref'd n.r.e.) (under former TRCP 18a(f), now TRCP 18a(g)(7)).

(2) Motion to disqualify – constitutional grounds. If a district-court judge is disqualified on constitutional grounds, the parties may, by consent, appoint a proper person to try the case. Tex. Const. art. 5, §11. If they are unable to do so, a competent person may be appointed to try the case in the same county where it is pending. *Id.*

3. Denying the motion. If the motion to disqualify or recuse is denied, the case will be returned to the challenged judge for a trial on the merits. *See* TRCP 18a(f)(2).

4. Sanctions. If a motion to disqualify or recuse was (1) groundless and filed in bad faith or to harass or (2) brought solely for the purpose of delay and without sufficient cause, the judge who heard the motion, after notice and a hearing, may order the party who filed the motion, her attorney, or both to pay the attorney fees and expenses of the other parties. TRCP 18a(h).

§5. TERTIARY MOTION TO DISQUALIFY OR RECUSE

§5.1 Definition. A tertiary motion to disqualify or recuse is a party's third (or later) motion filed in the same case to disqualify or recuse a judge in a district court or statutory county court. CPRC §30.016(a) (district and statutory county courts); Gov't Code §25.00256(a) (statutory probate courts). Under either CPRC §30.016(a) or Gov't Code §25.00256(a), a tertiary motion may be filed against a different judge than the judge against whom the previous motions for disqualification or recusal were filed. *See Gonzalez v. Guilbot*, 315 S.W.3d 533, 539-40 (Tex.2010).

§5.2 Differences in procedure. Except for the differences noted below, the procedure for a tertiary motion to disqualify or recuse a judge is the same as for other motions to disqualify or recuse. CPRC §30.016(b).

1. Judge declines to recuse. When a judge declines to recuse herself after a tertiary motion, the judge must continue to (1) preside over the case, (2) sign orders in the case, and (3) move the case to final disposition as though a motion had not been filed. CPRC §30.016(b); Gov't Code §25.00256(b); *Gonzalez v. Guilbot*, 315 S.W.3d 533, 539 (Tex.2010).

2. Attorney fees & costs. If the judge hearing the tertiary motion denies it, attorney fees and costs must be awarded to the party opposing the motion. CPRC §30.016(c); Gov't Code §25.00256(c). The party making the motion and its attorney are jointly and severally liable for the attorney fees and costs. CPRC §30.016(c); Gov't Code §25.00256(c). The fees and costs must be paid within 30 days after the order is rendered, unless the order is superseded. CPRC §30.016(c); Gov't Code §25.00256(c).

3. Review. The denial of a tertiary disqualification or recusal motion is reviewable only on appeal from a final judgment. CPRC §30.016(d); Gov't Code §25.00256(d).

4. If denial reversed. If a tertiary motion is ultimately sustained, the new judge for the case must vacate all orders signed by the sitting judge while the motion was pending. CPRC §30.016(e); Gov't Code §25.00256(e).

§6. VOLUNTARY DISQUALIFICATION OR RECUSAL

Even if a party has not filed a motion, a judge, on her own motion, should voluntarily disqualify or recuse herself in any proceeding in which one of the grounds listed in TRCP 18b is present (e.g., the judge's impartiality might reasonably be questioned). *See* Gov't Code §24.002; TRCP 18b; *Dunn v. County of Dallas*, 794 S.W.2d 560, 562 (Tex. App.—Dallas 1990, no writ); *see also Sao Paulo State v. American Tobacco Co.*, 535 U.S. 229, 230 (2002) (interpreting 28 U.S.C. §455(a)). The judge must sign an order of disqualification or recusal. *See, e.g., Carmody v. State Farm Lloyds*, 184 S.W.3d 419, 423 (Tex.App.—Dallas 2006, no pet.) (notation on docket sheet satisfied requirement of order of recusal). Once the judge enters the order, the judge must (1) request that the regional presiding judge

★

assign another judge to hear the case and (2) take no further action in the case unless there is good cause. Gov't Code §24.002. The judge should generally follow the same procedures as if a party had filed a motion to disqualify or recuse. See "Motion to Disqualify or Recuse," §4, p. 329.

§7. REVIEW

§7.1 Appeal.

1. Record. For a proper review of the trial court's decision, the party must present the appellate court with a record of the motion and proceedings. *See Ceballos v. El Paso Health Care Sys.*, 881 S.W.2d 439, 445 (Tex. App.—El Paso 1994, writ denied).

2. Motion to disqualify. A party can appeal an order granting or denying a motion to disqualify as allowed by other law. TRCP 18a(j)(2).

3. Motion to recuse.

(1) **Denying motion.** A party can challenge an order denying a motion to recuse by appeal from the final judgment. TRCP 18a(j)(1)(A). The standard of review for an order denying a motion to recuse is abuse of discretion. *Id.*

(2) **Granting motion.** A party cannot challenge an order granting a motion to recuse by appeal; the order cannot be reviewed by appeal, mandamus, or any other means. TRCP 18a(j)(1)(B).

§7.2 Mandamus.

1. Motion to disqualify. An order denying or granting a motion to disqualify can be reviewed by mandamus. TRCP 18a(j)(2).

2. Motion to recuse. An order denying or granting a motion to recuse cannot be reviewed by mandamus. *See* TRCP 18a(j)(1).

3. Objection to assigned judge. An order denying an objection to an assigned judge can be reviewed by mandamus. *See In re Canales*, 52 S.W.3d 698, 701 (Tex.2001); *Flores v. Banner*, 932 S.W.2d 500, 501 (Tex.1996).

§7.3 Effect of erroneous denial. The erroneous denial of a motion to disqualify, a motion to recuse, or an objection to an assigned judge may affect any rulings made by the challenged judge.

1. Disqualification. All the orders or judgments of a trial judge who was constitutionally disqualified from sitting are void. *Tesco Am., Inc. v. Strong Indus.*, 221 S.W.3d 550, 555 (Tex.2006); *In re Union Pac. Res.*, 969 S.W.2d 427, 428 (Tex.1998); *see, e.g., Freedom Comms. v. Coronado*, 372 S.W.3d 621, 624 (Tex.2012) (trial judge who took bribe was disqualified, and his order denying D's summary-judgment motion was void; appellate court had no jurisdiction to consider D's appeal from voided order). An order or judgment that is void because of the judge's disqualification is subject to collateral attack. *Gulf Maritime Whs. Co. v. Towers*, 858 S.W.2d 556, 559 (Tex.App.—Beaumont 1993, writ denied).

2. Recusal. The orders of a judge who should have recused herself as a result of a valid motion to recuse are not void. *In re Union Pac. Res.*, 969 S.W.2d at 428. Even though a judgment rendered by a judge subject to a valid motion for recusal may be reversed on appeal, it is not fundamental error. *Id.*

3. Objection to assigned judge. The orders of an assigned judge who should have been removed after an objection under Gov't Code §74.053 are void. *In re Canales*, 52 S.W.3d 698, 701 (Tex.2001); *Dunn v. Street*, 938 S.W.2d 33, 34-35 (Tex.1997); *Flores v. Banner*, 932 S.W.2d 500, 501 (Tex.1996).

✭

D. MOTION FOR CONTINUANCE

§1. GENERAL

§1.1 Rules. TRCP 247, 251-254, 330(d).

§1.2 Purpose. A motion for continuance is a request to postpone or delay a case that has been set for a hearing or trial. By comparison, a motion to extend is a request for more time to file a document. *See* TRCP 5. See "Motion to extend time," ch. 1-C, §9.1, p. 30.

§1.3 Forms. *O'Connor's Texas Civil Forms* (2012), FORMS 5D, 7B:2, 7B:4.

§2. MOTION

If a motion for continuance does not comply with the rules, the appellate court will presume the trial court did not abuse its discretion in denying the motion. *Villegas v. Carter*, 711 S.W.2d 624, 626 (Tex.1986); *see* TRCP 251-254.

PRACTICE TIP
Parties should consult the court's local rules for additional requirements for a motion for continuance. See, e.g., Dallas Cty. Loc. R. 3.01(b) (client must personally approve motion for continuance in writing when case is more than one year old).

---

§2.1 Written. A motion for continuance must be in writing. *See Green v. TDPRS*, 25 S.W.3d 213, 218 (Tex. App.—El Paso 2000, no pet.); *Favaloro v. Commission for Lawyer Discipline*, 13 S.W.3d 831, 838 (Tex.App.—Dallas 2000, no pet.). An oral request for a continuance does not preserve error. *See Phifer v. Nacogdoches Cty. Cent. Appr. Dist.*, 45 S.W.3d 159, 173 (Tex.App.—Tyler 2000, pet. denied). In an emergency, a handwritten motion is sufficient. *See Higginbotham v. Collateral Prot., Inc.*, 859 S.W.2d 487, 489 (Tex.App.—Houston [1st Dist.] 1993, writ denied).

PRACTICE TIP
If a party made only an oral motion for continuance during trial, on appeal, the party should attempt to circumvent the requirement for a written and verified motion by arguing that the attorney's unsworn statement should be considered as sworn evidence because the other party did not object. See Banda v. Garcia, 955 S.W.2d 270, 272 (Tex.1997) (opponent of attorney's unsworn testimony can waive oath requirement by not objecting when she knows or should know objection is necessary). See "Verification & affidavits," §2.3, this page.

---

§2.2 Specific. The motion must state the specific facts that support it. *See Blake v. Lewis*, 886 S.W.2d 404, 409 (Tex.App.—Houston [1st Dist.] 1994, no writ). General allegations (e.g., the attorney is busy with personal matters or other cases, or the attorney has not had time to prepare for the trial or hearing) are not enough to support a motion. *Id.*

§2.3 Verification & affidavits. The facts in the motion must be verified or supported by affidavits. TRCP 251, 252; *Taherzadeh v. Ghaleh-Assadi*, 108 S.W.3d 927, 928 (Tex.App.—Dallas 2003, pet. denied); *Hawthorne v. Guenther*, 917 S.W.2d 924, 929 (Tex.App.—Beaumont 1996, writ denied). *But see Villegas v. Carter*, 711 S.W.2d 624, 626 (Tex.1986) (unreasonable to require lay litigant, whose attorney withdrew two days before trial, to file sworn proof). If the motion is not verified or supported by affidavits, the appellate courts presume the trial court did not abuse its discretion in denying the motion. *Serrano v. Ryan's Crossing Apts.*, 241 S.W.3d 560, 564 (Tex.App.—El Paso 2007, pet. denied); *Daugherty v. Jacobs*, 187 S.W.2d 607, 619 (Tex.App.—Houston [14th Dist.] 2006, no pet.). See "Verification & affidavits," ch. 1-B, §4.1.12, p. 20; *O'Connor's Texas Forms*, FORM 5D:4.

★

NOTE

Although TRCP 251 requires the motion to be verified or supported by an affidavit, CPRC §132.001 allows for the use of an unsworn declaration instead of a verification or an affidavit. See CPRC §132.001(a). For the requirements for using an unsworn declaration, see "Unsworn declaration," ch. 1-B, §3.2.14, p. 10.

§2.4 Request hearing. A hearing is generally not required on a motion for continuance. Most motions for continuance—whether verified or supported by affidavits—are decided on written submission. See "Verification & affidavits," §2.3, p. 336. However, a movant may want to request a hearing to bring live witnesses to support the allegations in the motion.

§3. DEADLINE

A motion for continuance may be filed at any time after the defendant files an answer. TRCP 251.

§3.1 Before announcement of ready. A party should file a continuance before making an unconditional announcement of ready for trial. *Reyna v. Reyna*, 738 S.W.2d 772, 775 (Tex.App.—Austin 1987, no writ); *see E.C. v. Graydon*, 28 S.W.3d 825, 828 (Tex.App.—Corpus Christi 2000, no pet.) (announcement of ready waived motion for continuance).

§3.2 During trial. A party may file a written motion for continuance during trial if an unforeseeable emergency arises through no fault of that party. *See Butcher v. Tinkle*, 183 S.W.2d 227, 230 (Tex.App.—Beaumont 1944, writ ref'd w.o.m.). A continuance sought during trial will rarely be granted, and the trial court's denial of the motion is difficult to reverse on appeal.

§4. RESPONSE

If the nonmovant disagrees with the request for continuance, it should file a response, and when necessary, attach affidavits to controvert the allegations in the motion for continuance. See *O'Connor's Texas Forms*, FORM 5D:3. Uncontroverted statements in a sworn motion for continuance must be accepted as true. See "Uncontested motion," §5.3, this page.

§5. RULING

§5.1 Obtain a ruling. To preserve error when the trial court refuses to grant a motion for continuance, the party should ask the trial court to make a ruling, either on the record in open court or by a written order. *Direkly v. ARA Devcon, Inc.*, 866 S.W.2d 652, 656 (Tex.App.—Houston [1st Dist.] 1993, writ dism'd). See "Record of Ruling," ch. 1-G, §3, p. 48. When a motion for continuance is presented in open court, an oral ruling on the record is sufficient to preserve error. See "Express ruling," ch. 1-G, §2.2.1, p. 47. If the record does not contain an express ruling on the motion but shows some other action by the court that implicitly overruled the motion, error is preserved. *See* TRAP 33.1(a)(2)(A). See "Implicit ruling," ch. 1-G, §2.2.2, p. 47.

§5.2 Court's discretion. The trial court may grant a motion for continuance if the motion is supported by an affidavit and states sufficient cause. TRCP 247, 251, 252. The trial court's ruling on most motions for continuance is within its discretion. *State v. Wood Oil Distrib.*, 751 S.W.2d 863, 865 (Tex.1988); *Villegas v. Carter*, 711 S.W.2d 624, 626 (Tex.1986). But the court's ruling on some motions for continuance for legislators is mandatory. See "Ruling," §12.4, p. 345.

§5.3 Uncontested motion. If a motion for continuance is in substantial compliance with the rule, is properly verified, and is not controverted, the trial court must accept the statements in the motion as true. *Verkin v. Southwest Ctr. One, Ltd.*, 784 S.W.2d 92, 94 (Tex.App.—Houston [1st Dist.] 1989, writ denied); *Garza v. Serrato*, 699 S.W.2d 275, 281 (Tex.App.—San Antonio 1985, writ ref'd n.r.e.). The trial court has no discretion to reject uncontroverted facts in a sworn motion for continuance. *Verkin*, 784 S.W.2d at 94.

⭐

§6. CONTINUANCE ON AGREED MOTION

The court should respect agreements to postpone or continue a case unless the delay would unreasonably interfere with other business of the court. TRCP 330(d). The parties should prepare a written agreement to pass or continue a case, have the attorneys for all parties sign it, and file it with the court on or before docket call. TRCP 11, 247, 251. See "Agreements Between Attorneys – Rule 11," ch. 1-H, §9, p. 61. A party may orally announce the agreement to pass a case at docket call, but it should also file a written agreement. An agreement to pass, postpone, or continue a case pending in a district court is not binding on the court when the case has reached trial on two or more occasions. TRCP 330(d).

§7. CONTINUANCE BASED ON INSUFFICIENT NOTICE OF TRIAL

§7.1 Notice of trial. The trial court must give the parties reasonable notice of the first trial setting of "not less than 45 days." TRCP 245; *Smith v. Lippmann*, 826 S.W.2d 137, 138 n.1 (Tex.1992). The trial court violates due process if it does not give the party reasonable notice of a trial setting. *Hardin v. Hardin*, 932 S.W.2d 566, 567 (Tex. App.—Tyler 1995, no writ). The language of TRCP 245 is mandatory. *Hardin*, 932 S.W.2d at 567.

§7.2 Motion. When a party seeks a continuance because of insufficient notice of trial, the motion must state that (1) the party received less than 45 days' notice of trial, (2) the notice given was not reasonable, (3) the notice was not adequate to permit the party to prepare for trial, (4) the lack of reasonable notice violated the party's right of due process, and (5) the lack of 45 days' notice violated TRCP 245. *See Hardin v. Hardin*, 932 S.W.2d 566, 567 (Tex.App.—Tyler 1995, no writ). The allegations must be supported by sworn proof. TRCP 251. See "Verification & affidavits," §2.3, p. 336.

§8. CONTINUANCE FOR ADDITIONAL DISCOVERY

A party requesting additional time for discovery, whether to obtain evidence or testimony, must fulfill the requirements of TRCP 252 under oath. *Verkin v. Southwest Ctr. One, Ltd.*, 784 S.W.2d 92, 94 (Tex.App.—Houston [1st Dist.] 1989, writ denied). See *O'Connor's Texas Forms*, FORM 5D:1.

PRACTICE TIP

Every case has a discovery-control plan that sets limits for the discovery period, interrogatories, and depositions. See "Discovery-Control Plans," ch. 6-A, §7, p. 430. TRCP 190 permits the court to extend the time for discovery. TRCP 190.5. See "Modification of discovery periods," ch. 6-A, §8.2, p. 434. Thus, before you file a motion for continuance for additional discovery, check whether you also need to file a motion to modify the discovery-control plan. See "Modifying Discovery Procedures," ch. 6-A, §6, p. 429.

---

§8.1 Contents of motion.

1. Description of discovery. The motion must describe the specific discovery sought. *Wal-Mart Stores Tex., LP v. Crosby*, 295 S.W.3d 346, 356 (Tex.App.—Dallas 2009, pet. denied); *see, e.g.*, *Martinez v. Flores*, 865 S.W.2d 194, 197-98 (Tex.App.—Corpus Christi 1993, writ denied) (request for more time "to complete discovery" was not sufficient).

(1) Procedure for discovery. The motion should describe the procedure the party intends to use to obtain the discovery and the person from whom the discovery will be sought. *See, e.g.*, *State v. Wood Oil Distrib.*, 751 S.W.2d 863, 865 (Tex.1988) (depositions); *Tri-Steel Structures, Inc. v. Baptist Found.*, 166 S.W.3d 443, 447 (Tex.App.—Fort Worth 2005, pet. denied) (same); *Verkin v. Southwest Ctr. One, Ltd.*, 784 S.W.2d 92, 94 (Tex. App.—Houston [1st Dist.] 1989, writ denied) (requests for production and interrogatories). If a continuance is sought to depose a witness, the motion must include the witness's name and address (street, county, and state of residence). TRCP 252.

⭐

(2) Substance of discovery. The motion should describe the evidence or testimony needed. *See* TRCP 252; *Wal-Mart Stores*, 295 S.W.3d at 356. If a continuance is sought to depose a witness, the motion must state what the party expects to prove from the witness's testimony. TRCP 252.

(3) Discovery period. The motion should state whether the discovery period has expired.

2. Materiality. The motion must state that the discovery sought is material and show why it is material. TRCP 252; *J.E.M. v. Fidelity & Cas. Co.*, 928 S.W.2d 668, 676 (Tex.App.—Houston [1st Dist.] 1996, no writ); *see, e.g.*, *Celotex Corp. v. Gracy Meadow Owners Ass'n*, 847 S.W.2d 384, 388 (Tex.App.—Austin 1993, writ denied) (appellate court decided deposition testimony was immaterial).

3. Diligence. The motion must show that the party used due diligence to obtain the discovery. TRCP 252; *Risner v. McDonald's Corp.*, 18 S.W.3d 903, 909 (Tex.App.—Beaumont 2000, pet. denied); *Rhima v. White*, 829 S.W.2d 909, 912 (Tex.App.—Fort Worth 1992, writ denied). The motion must describe the party's previous attempts to obtain the discovery. *See* TRCP 252 (party must state "such diligence"); *see, e.g.*, *J.E.M.*, 928 S.W.2d at 676 (diligence shown when Ps stated they noticed witness's deposition soon after need for deposition arose but D refused to produce witness); *see also Barron v. Vanier*, 190 S.W.3d 841, 851 (Tex.App.—Fort Worth 2006, no pet.) (failure to file motion to compel or to otherwise attempt to obtain objected-to items may indicate lack of diligence). Conclusory statements about diligence do not satisfy the requirements of TRCP 252. *Gregg v. Cecil*, 844 S.W.2d 851, 853 (Tex. App.—Beaumont 1992, no writ); *e.g.*, *Rocha v. Faltys*, 69 S.W.3d 315, 319 (Tex.App.—Austin 2002, no pet.) (no showing of diligence when affidavit did not describe particular efforts made to locate witness for deposition). If a party does not diligently use the discovery procedures, it can seldom claim reversible error when the trial court refuses the continuance. *Wood Oil Distrib.*, 751 S.W.2d at 865; *e.g.*, *Hatteberg v. Hatteberg*, 933 S.W.2d 522, 526-27 (Tex. App.—Houston [1st Dist.] 1994, no writ) (party did not diligently use discovery procedures when she waited until nine days before trial to attempt to serve witnesses).

4. Not obtainable earlier. The motion must explain why the party was unable to obtain the discovery earlier. *See* TRCP 252 (party must state "cause of failure, if known"); *see, e.g.*, *Risner*, 18 S.W.3d at 909 (party did not explain why affidavits could not have been timely obtained during 18 months between filing of suit and summary-judgment hearing).

5. Not for delay. The motion must include the statement, "The continuance is not sought for delay only, but so that justice may be done." TRCP 252.

6. Not otherwise available. In a second (or later) motion for continuance, the motion must state that the evidence or testimony sought cannot be obtained from any other source. *See* TRCP 252; *Verkin*, 784 S.W.2d at 95. This statement is not necessary in the first motion for continuance based on the need for additional discovery. TRCP 252; *Verkin*, 784 S.W.2d at 95.

§8.2 Attachments.

1. Affidavits. The party must attach affidavits to support all factual allegations. TRCP 251; *see, e.g.*, *Rhima v. White*, 829 S.W.2d 909, 912 (Tex.App.—Fort Worth 1992, writ denied) (party did not file affidavit describing diligence). See "Note," §2.3, p. 337. The person with knowledge of the facts stated in the motion (either the party or the attorney) should make an affidavit stating the facts supporting the motion. See "Affidavits," ch. 1-B, §3.2.16, p. 11; *O'Connor's Texas Forms*, FORM 5D:4.

PRACTICE TIP

An attorney should sign an affidavit only for facts exclusively within her personal knowledge (e.g., the continuance is being sought because of her scheduling conflicts). An attorney should avoid signing an affidavit in support of a client's request for a continuance when the purported basis for the request is outside the attorney's personal knowledge; in such a case, the client should sign the affidavit.

———————————— ✦ ————————————

2. Exhibits. Although not required, the party should attach outstanding discovery requests as exhibits to the motion. *See Verkin v. Southwest Ctr. One, Ltd.*, 784 S.W.2d 92, 96 (Tex.App.—Houston [1st Dist.] 1989, writ denied) (parties are not required to attach copies of discovery requests). All attachments to the motion should be verified by affidavit. See "Exhibits," ch. 1-B, §4.1.11, p. 20.

§9. CONTINUANCE IN SUMMARY-JUDGMENT CASE

A party who needs additional time to respond to a motion for summary judgment must ask for it. *Tenneco Inc. v. Enterprise Prods.*, 925 S.W.2d 640, 647 (Tex.1996).

§9.1 Continuance by agreement. The parties may change the summary-judgment deadlines by agreement. See "Continuance on Agreed Motion," §6, p. 338; "By agreement," ch. 7-B, §6.2, p. 606.

§9.2 Motion to reset SJ hearing for lack of 21 days' notice. When requesting a resetting of the hearing on a motion for summary judgment because the movant did not provide the nonmovant with the required 21 days' notice, the motion should rely on TRCP 166a(c). See "Summary-Judgment Deadlines," ch. 7-B, §6, p. 605. The 21-day notice requirement is waived if the nonmovant does not object in writing. *Nguyen v. Short, How, Frels & Heitz, P.C.*, 108 S.W.3d 558, 560 (Tex.App.—Dallas 2003, pet. denied); *Veal v. Veterans Life Ins.*, 767 S.W.2d 892, 895 (Tex. App.—Texarkana 1989, no writ). The objection that the movant did not provide the full 21 days' notice should be made before the hearing, but can be made as late as a motion for new trial. *See Nickerson v. E.I.L. Instrs., Inc.*, 817 S.W.2d 834, 835-36 (Tex.App.—Houston [1st Dist.] 1991, no writ) (objection in motion for new trial). The nonmovant should object to the lack of the 21 days' notice, file a motion to reset or delay the hearing, present sworn proof, and make a record. *See Nguyen*, 108 S.W.3d at 560; *see, e.g.*, *Roob v. Von Beregshasy*, 866 S.W.2d 765, 766 (Tex.App.—Houston [1st Dist.] 1993, writ denied) (appellant should have made and filed a reporter's record in appellate court).

Some cases hold that a nonmovant must comply with the requirements of TRCP 166a(g) when the movant does not give 21 days' notice. *See, e.g.*, *Pankow v. Colonial Life Ins.*, 932 S.W.2d 271, 275 (Tex.App.—Amarillo 1996, writ denied) (court required motion for continuance to explain need for additional evidence even though nonmovant did not get the required 21 days' notice). However, a nonmovant should file a request for continuance under TRCP 166a(g) only when it needs more than 21 days to prepare for the hearing, not when it seeks the 21 days it is entitled to under TRCP 166a(c). To preserve error when the nonmovant does not get the required 21 days' notice, the nonmovant only needs to make an objection and offer proof that the nonmovant did not get proper notice. *See, e.g.*, *Guinn v. Zarsky*, 893 S.W.2d 13, 17 (Tex.App.—Corpus Christi 1994, no writ) (because nonmovant received less than 21 days' notice, court reversed SJ without requiring nonmovant to show need for time to obtain affidavits or discovery). See *O'Connor's Texas Forms*, FORM 7B:2.

PRACTICE TIP

A nonmovant should not file a motion for continuance under TRCP 166a(g) when it objects that it did not get the notice required by TRCP 166a(c) because the trial court has the discretion to deny a motion for continuance under TRCP 166a(g). However, the court does not have the discretion to refuse a request to reset the hearing when the nonmovant received less than the 21 days' notice required by TRCP 166a(c). When the trial court improperly overrules an objection to inadequate notice, it commits an error of law, not an abuse of discretion.

---

§9.3 Motion to continue SJ hearing. A motion requesting a continuance for additional time to secure affidavits or discovery for a summary-judgment hearing should satisfy all the requirements of both TRCP 166a(g) and TRCP 252. *Tenneco Inc. v. Enterprise Prods.*, 925 S.W.2d 640, 647 (Tex.1996); *see, e.g.*, *Kahanek v. Rogers*, 900 S.W.2d 131, 134 (Tex.App.—San Antonio 1995, no writ) (court noted the motion complied with both TRCP 166a(g) and 251). See *O'Connor's Texas Forms*, FORM 7B:5.

1. Grounds. The party should allege that it cannot present by affidavits the facts essential to justify its opposition to the motion for summary judgment and that it needs additional time to secure affidavits or conduct discovery. TRCP 166a(g); *Joe v. Two Thirty Nine Jt.V.*, 145 S.W.3d 150, 161 (Tex.2004); *see Ford Motor Co. v. Castillo*, 279 S.W.3d 656, 662 (Tex.2009).

✦

2. Factors to cover in motion. The request for additional time should cover the following:

(1) Discovery period. The motion should identify the end of the discovery period.

(a) Motion during discovery period. When a motion for summary judgment is filed during the discovery period, the motion for continuance should (1) state that the discovery period has not expired, (2) identify the date it expires, and (3) argue that the motion for summary judgment addresses complex fact issues that require full discovery. When a case is complex and the motion for summary judgment challenges the merits of the case, full discovery is probably necessary. *See McClure v. Attebury*, 20 S.W.3d 722, 729 (Tex.App.—Amarillo 1999, no pet.) (when threshold issue is question of law, discovery requirements are minimal).

(b) Motion after discovery period. When a motion for summary judgment is filed after the discovery period, the party seeking a continuance must also ask the court to enlarge the discovery period. *See* TRCP 190.5(a), 191.1. See "Modification of discovery periods," ch. 6-A, §8.2, p. 434.

(2) Description of specific discovery or affidavits. See "Description of discovery," §8.1.1, p. 338.

(3) Materiality. See "Materiality," §8.1.2, p. 339.

(4) Diligence. See "Diligence," §8.1.3, p. 339.

(5) Length of time suit has been on file. The motion for continuance should state how long the case has been on file.

(a) Fact issues. When a motion for summary judgment based on facts is filed shortly after the lawsuit is commenced, the trial court should grant a motion for continuance. *See, e.g., Levinthal v. Kelsey-Seybold Clinic, P.A.*, 902 S.W.2d 508, 512 (Tex.App.—Houston [1st Dist.] 1994, no writ) (P's motion for continuance should have been granted because D filed for SJ three months after P filed lawsuit and before D responded to discovery); *Verkin v. Southwest Ctr. One, Ltd.*, 784 S.W.2d 92, 96 (Tex.App.—Houston [1st Dist.] 1989, writ denied) (D's motion for continuance should have been granted because P filed for SJ 50 days after filing lawsuit and before D responded to discovery). *But see Joe*, 145 S.W.3d at 162 (even though D filed for SJ two months after P filed lawsuit, P's motion for continuance was denied because discovery sought was not material and would not raise fact issue justifying P's opposition to D's SJ motion).

(b) Legal issues. When a motion for summary judgment is based on a legal issue and facts are unnecessary, the court can overrule a motion for continuance even if the motion for summary judgment was filed shortly after the suit was commenced. *See, e.g., White v. Mellon Mortg. Co.*, 995 S.W.2d 795, 804 (Tex.App.—Tyler 1999, no pet.) (even though D filed for SJ three months after suit was filed, P's motion for continuance was denied because discovery was unnecessary and irrelevant to determination of legal issues); *see also National Un. Fire Ins. v. CBI Indus.*, 907 S.W.2d 517, 521-22 (Tex.1995) (additional time for discovery was unnecessary because contract was unambiguous); *J.E.M. v. Fidelity & Cas. Co.*, 928 S.W.2d 668, 676-77 (Tex.App.—Houston [1st Dist.] 1996, no writ) (no discovery was necessary on issue of duty to defend, which was controlled by contract); *Mayhew v. Town of Sunnyvale*, 774 S.W.2d 284, 298 (Tex.App.—Dallas 1989, writ denied) (no discovery was necessary to review legislation).

(6) Abuse of discovery. If the movant for summary judgment abused the discovery process by withholding key evidence, the nonmovant is entitled to a continuance to complete the discovery before the court considers the motion for summary judgment. *See TemPay, Inc. v. TNT Concrete & Constr., Inc.*, 37 S.W.3d 517, 522-23 (Tex.App.—Austin 2001, pet. denied).

(7) Not for delay. See "Not for delay," §8.1.5, p. 339.

3. Affidavits. The grounds for the continuance must be supported by affidavit. TRCP 166a(g); *see Ford Motor*, 279 S.W.3d at 662. See "Affidavits," ch. 7-B, §9.4, p. 613. The affidavit must be specific. The affidavit must show why the continuance is necessary; conclusory statements are not sufficient. *Lee v. Haynes & Boone, L.L.P.*,

⭐

129 S.W.3d 192, 198 (Tex.App.—Dallas 2004, pet. denied); *Carter v. MacFadyen*, 93 S.W.3d 307, 310 (Tex.App.—Houston [14th Dist.] 2002, pet. denied). See "Not legal conclusions," ch. 7-B, §9.4.5, p. 614; "Not factual conclusions," ch. 7-B, §9.4.6, p. 614.

4. Response to motion. The movant for summary judgment may either agree or disagree with the non-movant's request for a continuance. By agreeing with the request for a continuance, the movant prevents the non-movant from arguing on appeal that, if it had had more time, it would have been able to secure evidence to prove a fact issue. If the movant disagrees with the request for a continuance, it should attempt to negate the grounds in the request.

5. Order on motion. The court may grant the party additional time to secure affidavits or discovery, deny the motion for summary judgment, or "make such other order as is just." TRCP 166a(g). To preserve error, the party requesting a continuance must get a ruling on the record. See "Obtain a ruling," §5.1, p. 337.

§10. CONTINUANCE – PARTY OR WITNESS UNAVAILABLE FOR TRIAL

If a party or witness is unavailable for trial and the party cannot proceed to trial without that person, the party should move for a continuance. *See Hawthorne v. Guenther*, 917 S.W.2d 924, 929 (Tex.App.—Beaumont 1996, writ denied) (same rules apply when continuance sought for unavailability of party or witness). A trial court is not required to grant a motion for continuance just because a party is unable to be present at trial. *Briscoe v. Goodmark Corp.*, 130 S.W.3d 160, 169 (Tex.App.—El Paso 2003, no pet.); *Humphrey v. Ahlschlager*, 778 S.W.2d 480, 483 (Tex.App.—Dallas 1989, no writ). The motion for continuance must include the following information. See *O'Connor's Texas Forms*, FORM 5D:2, ¶¶9-18.

§10.1 Name & address of witness. The movant must provide the unavailable party's or witness's name and residential address (street, county, and state), not her office address. *See* TRCP 252; *see, e.g.*, *Hatteberg v. Hatteberg*, 933 S.W.2d 522, 526 (Tex.App.—Houston [1st Dist.] 1994, no writ) (motion did not identify home address, only office); *Gabaldon v. General Motors Corp.*, 876 S.W.2d 367, 370 (Tex.App.—El Paso 1993, no writ) (motion did not identify witnesses to be deposed).

§10.2 Unavailable. The movant should explain why the unavailable party or witness is not available to testify at trial. Conflicting business plans of the party or witness usually do not constitute sufficient grounds for continuance. *See Echols v. Brewer*, 524 S.W.2d 731, 734 (Tex.App.—Houston [14th Dist.] 1975, no writ).

§10.3 Description of testimony. The movant must describe the unavailable party's or witness's testimony and what the testimony is expected to prove. *E.g.*, *Richards v. Schion*, 969 S.W.2d 131, 133 (Tex.App.—Houston [1st Dist.] 1998, no pet.) (motion did not describe testimony of party who could not attend trial); *Lynd v. Wesley*, 705 S.W.2d 759, 764 (Tex.App.—Houston [14th Dist.] 1986, no writ) (motion did not describe testimony of witness); *see* TRCP 252.

§10.4 Materiality. The movant must state that the unavailable party's or witness's testimony is material and show how it is material. TRCP 252; *Aguilar v. Alvarado*, 39 S.W.3d 244, 249 (Tex.App.—Waco 1999, pet. denied); *see Richards v. Schion*, 969 S.W.2d 131, 132-33 (Tex.App.—Houston [1st Dist.] 1998, no pet.). The party must show that proceeding without the party or witness will prejudice the party's case. *Richards*, 969 S.W.2d at 133.

§10.5 Diligence. The movant must describe its diligence in attempting to obtain the required testimony of the unavailable party or witness. TRCP 252; *Aguilar v. Alvarado*, 39 S.W.3d 244, 249 (Tex.App.—Waco 1999, pet. denied); *Humphrey v. Ahlschlager*, 778 S.W.2d 480, 483 (Tex.App.—Dallas 1989, no writ). Without this diligence, the inability of a material witness to attend trial is not a sufficient ground for a continuance. *City of Gatesville v. Truelove*, 546 S.W.2d 79, 83 (Tex.App.—Waco 1976, no writ).

1. Witness within 100-mile range.

(1) Deposition not necessary to show diligence. If the witness lives within 100 miles of the courthouse where the suit is pending, the movant can prove diligence for a continuance based on that witness's absence by showing that the movant subpoenaed the witness to attend trial but the witness did not appear. *See* TRCP 252. See "Subpoenas," ch. 1-L, p. 84. The movant does not need to have taken the witness's deposition. TRCP 252. A last-minute attempt at service of a subpoena does not constitute diligence. *E.g.*, *Hatteberg v. Hatteberg*, 933 S.W.2d 522, 526 (Tex.App.—Houston [1st Dist.] 1994, no writ) (attempted service nine days before trial did not show diligence).

(2) **Deposition necessary to show diligence.** The movant's failure to depose a witness who lives within 100 miles of the courthouse where the suit is pending shows a lack of diligence if (1) the movant could have anticipated the witness would not be able to attend the trial because of age, infirmity, sickness, or official duty, or (2) the witness is about to leave or has left the state or county of suit and will not be present for the trial. TRCP 252.

2. Witness lives outside 100-mile range. If the witness lives more than 100 miles from the courthouse where the suit is pending, the movant should take the witness's deposition and not rely on a promise to attend the trial. If the witness lives more than 100 miles from the courthouse, the witness's absence is not a ground for a continuance. *See* TRCP 252.

§10.6 Medical-excuse affidavit. If a party or witness is unavailable because of illness, the movant must attach to the motion the affidavit of a doctor for the party or witness. *Hawthorne v. Guenther*, 917 S.W.2d 924, 930 (Tex.App.—Beaumont 1996, writ denied); *see, e.g.*, *Burke v. Scott*, 410 S.W.2d 826, 827 (Tex.App.—Austin 1967, writ ref'd n.r.e.) (court should have granted continuance because two doctors' affidavits confirmed D and critical witness were too ill to attend trial). The doctor's affidavit should state the nature and severity of the illness, that the party or witness is too ill to attend the trial, that the party's or witness's health will be jeopardized if the party or witness is forced to attend the trial, and the prognosis for recovery. *See Olivares v. State*, 693 S.W.2d 486, 490 (Tex.App.—San Antonio 1985, writ dism'd); *see, e.g.*, *Humphrey v. Ahlschlager*, 778 S.W.2d 480, 484 (Tex.App.—Dallas 1989, no writ) (court denied fourth motion for continuance based on witness's health problems because movant did not attempt to depose witness and motion did not contain any prognosis of witness's recovery or ability to testify); *see also American Trendex Corp. v. Ultradyne Corp.*, 490 S.W.2d 205, 207 (Tex.App.—Austin 1973, writ ref'd n.r.e.) (court denied third motion for continuance when one of several parties was ill because motion did not state that deposition could not be taken).

§10.7 Not for delay. See "Not for delay," §8.1.5, p. 339.

§10.8 Verified. See "Verification & affidavits," §2.3, p. 336.

§10.9 Testimony not available. In a second (or later) motion for continuance, the movant must state that the unavailable party's or witness's testimony cannot be procured from any other source. TRCP 252.

§11. CONTINUANCE – ATTORNEY UNAVAILABLE

§11.1 Attorney-vacation letter. When a local rule mandates that the lead attorney is entitled to a continuance when a case is set for trial within the period designated by the attorney in a vacation letter, the court must grant the continuance. *In re North Am. Refractories Co.*, 71 S.W.3d 391, 394 (Tex.App.—Beaumont 2001, orig. proceeding). The trial court has a ministerial duty to grant the continuance in compliance with the local rules of procedure, unless the other party proves a due-process exception. *Id.*

§11.2 Attorney not available. Absence of counsel is not a ground for a continuance except at the discretion of the trial court. TRCP 253; *Rehabilitation Facility v. Cooper*, 962 S.W.2d 151, 155 (Tex.App.—Austin 1998, no pet.); *Rabe v. Guaranty Nat'l Ins.*, 787 S.W.2d 575, 578 (Tex.App.—Houston [1st Dist.] 1990, writ denied). When an attorney is unavailable for trial, the record must show good cause or that the judge had knowledge of good cause for the continuance. *Rabe*, 787 S.W.2d at 578. The motion for continuance should include the information described below. See *O'Connor's Texas Forms*, FORM 5D:2, ¶¶22-25.

1. Attorney is necessary. The motion should state that the attorney's presence is necessary for the proper representation of the case and give the reasons. *See* TRCP 253; *see, e.g.*, *Rabe*, 787 S.W.2d at 579 (continuance was denied because motion contained no explanation of what P's attorney could have accomplished at hearing after P did not file response to motion for summary judgment).

⭐

2. Reason attorney unavailable. The motion should state why the attorney is not available for trial. If the attorney is in trial in another case, the motion should state why that case has priority. *See, e.g.*, *Smith v. Babcock & Wilcox Constr. Co.*, 913 S.W.2d 467, 468 (Tex.1995) (attorney was in trial in another county); *Dancy v. Daggett*, 815 S.W.2d 548, 549 & n.1 (Tex.1991) (attorney had hearing on criminal case in federal court, and under local rules, criminal case had priority). The motion must show some attempt to avoid the conflict in settings. *See Smock v. Fischel*, 207 S.W.2d 891, 892 (Tex.1948).

3. No substitute possible. The motion should state why another attorney in the firm could not handle the case. For a trial, the motion should state that no other attorney could try the case; for a hearing, it should state that the hearing is important and involves difficult questions of law as applied to the facts of the case. If two attorneys signed the pleadings, the trial court can presume that either attorney can represent the party. *See, e.g.*, *Rehabilitation Facility*, 962 S.W.2d at 155-56 (continuance was denied because motion contained no explanation why attorney who signed pleadings could not conduct trial); *Rabe*, 787 S.W.2d at 579 (continuance was denied because motion contained no explanation why another attorney at firm could not represent P at summary-judgment hearing); *Echols v. Brewer*, 524 S.W.2d 731, 734 (Tex.App.—Houston [14th Dist.] 1975, no writ) (continuance was denied because another attorney's name appeared on pleadings). If the attorney has no associates, the motion should state this.

4. Not for delay. See "Not for delay," §8.1.5, p. 339.

§11.3 Party not represented. When a party discovers shortly before trial that it does not have an attorney, through no fault or negligence of its own, the trial court should grant a motion for continuance. *State v. Crank*, 666 S.W.2d 91, 94 (Tex.1984); *see, e.g.*, *St. Gelais v. Jackson*, 769 S.W.2d 249, 254 (Tex.App.—Houston [14th Dist.] 1988, no writ) (court granted attorney's motion to withdraw one month before trial; denial of continuance was not abuse of discretion because withdrawal was party's fault). The court should allow the party time to get another attorney. *Villegas v. Carter*, 711 S.W.2d 624, 626 (Tex.1986); *Kahanek v. Rogers*, 900 S.W.2d 131, 133-34 (Tex.App.—San Antonio 1995, no writ).

§11.4 Verified. See "Verification & affidavits," §2.3, p. 336.

§12. CONTINUANCE FOR LEGISLATOR

A party is entitled to a legislative continuance while the Legislature is in session if either the party or the attorney is unavailable because the party or attorney is a member or member-elect of the Legislature. CPRC §30.003(b); TRCP 254. When properly requested, a legislative continuance is mandatory, unless the continuance violates the other party's due-process rights. *In re Ford Motor Co.*, 165 S.W.3d 315, 319 (Tex.2005); *Waites v. Sondock*, 561 S.W.2d 772, 776 (Tex.1977); *In re Starr Produce Co.*, 988 S.W.2d 808, 811 (Tex.App.—San Antonio 1999, orig. proceeding); *First Interstate Bank v. Burns*, 951 S.W.2d 237, 240 (Tex.App.—Austin 1997, no writ). See *O'Connor's Texas Forms*, FORM 5D:2, ¶¶26-31.

§12.1 Motion. To obtain a legislative continuance, the party must file a sworn motion for continuance supported by an affidavit. CPRC §30.003(d); TRCP 251, 254. The motion must be filed during the legislative session or within 30 days of the date the Legislature is to be in session. CPRC §30.003(b).

1. Grounds.

(1) Status of attorney. The motion and affidavit must state that the party or its attorney is a member or member-elect of the Legislature and is or will be in actual attendance at the legislative session. CPRC §30.003(b); TRCP 254; *In re Ford Motor Co.*, 165 S.W.3d 315, 319 (Tex.2005).

(2) Legislator statements. If the continuance is based on the attorney's participation in the Legislature, the motion and affidavit must also make these statements:

(a) The attorney intends to actively participate in the preparation or presentation of the case. CPRC §30.003(e); TRCP 254; *In re Ford Motor Co.*, 165 S.W.3d at 319; *In re I.E.F.*, 345 S.W.3d 637, 638-39 (Tex. App.—San Antonio 2011, orig. proceeding).

✦

(b) The attorney did not take the case for the purpose of getting a continuance. CPRC §30.003(e); *In re Ford Motor Co.*, 165 S.W.3d at 319; *In re I.E.F.*, 345 S.W.3d at 638-39.

(3) Trial date. The motion should identify the date the case is set for trial; the timing of the attorney's employment in relation to the trial date determines whether the court has discretion to deny the motion. See "Ruling," §12.4, this page. The motion should state whether, based on the date, the court's ruling is mandatory or discretionary.

(a) Mandatory. If the attorney was employed more than 30 days before the trial date, the motion should state that it is a mandatory motion and the court must grant the continuance. CPRC §30.003(c).

(b) Discretionary. If the attorney was employed within 30 days of the trial date, the motion should state that it is a discretionary motion and the court may grant the continuance. CPRC §30.003(c).

(4) No TRO. The motion should state that the case is not set for a temporary restraining order (TRO). *See* CPRC §30.003(a); TRCP 254.

2. File with Ethics Commission. If the attorney for a party seeking a continuance is a member or member-elect of the Legislature, the attorney must file a copy of the motion for continuance with the Texas Ethics Commission. CPRC §30.003(g). The copy must be sent to the Commission within three business days after the date the motion is filed. *Id.*

§12.2 Response. To contest a legislative continuance, a party should file a sworn response supported by affidavits that challenge the allegations in the motion. See *O'Connor's Texas Forms*, FORM 5D:3, ¶¶39-46. The response must state the following:

1. The movant's attorney was employed within 30 days of the trial and the court has the discretion to deny the motion for continuance. CPRC §30.003(c); *see In re CNA Holdings, Inc.*, 102 S.W.3d 280, 281 (Tex.App.—Beaumont 2003, orig. proceeding) (applying ten-day rule in former version of CPRC §30.003(c)).

2. The movant's attorney was employed for the purpose of getting a continuance.

3. The movant's attorney has no intention of participating in the preparation or presentation of the case.

4. Irreparable injury and harm will occur if the continuance is granted. This is the due-process exception (or "*Waites* exception") to a legislative continuance. The open-courts provision of the Texas Constitution prohibits a continuance when a party can show irreparable harm by the delay. *See Waites v. Sondock*, 561 S.W.2d 772, 776 (Tex.1977); *see also* Tex. Const. art. 1, §13 (remedy by due course of law).

§12.3 Hearing. The party opposing the continuance should move for a hearing. When a party claims that a legislative continuance will result in the loss of a substantial existing right, the trial court must hold a hearing. *In re Ford Motor Co.*, 165 S.W.3d 315, 319 (Tex.2005); *Waites v. Sondock*, 561 S.W.2d 772, 776 (Tex.1977). At the hearing, the party opposing the continuance must present evidence. *See Amoco Prod. v. Salyer*, 814 S.W.2d 211, 213 (Tex.App.—Corpus Christi 1991, orig. proceeding).

§12.4 Ruling. Some rulings on a legislative continuance are mandatory, and some are discretionary.

1. Mandatory rulings. The trial court has a mandatory duty to grant or deny a motion in the following instances:

(1) Mandatory grant – more than 30 days. The trial court must grant a properly requested motion for a legislative continuance if the attorney was employed more than 30 days before the date the case is set for trial. CPRC §30.003(c); *In re Ford Motor Co.*, 165 S.W.3d 315, 318 (Tex.2005); *see In re CNA Holdings, Inc.*, 102 S.W.3d 280, 281 (Tex.App.—Beaumont 2003, orig. proceeding) (applying ten-day rule in former version of CPRC §30.003(c)). If the trial court grants the motion for a legislative continuance, the court must continue the case until 30 days after the Legislature adjourns. CPRC §30.003(b); TRCP 254.

★

NOTE

TRCP 254 provides that the continuance is mandatory if the attorney was employed more than 10 days before trial; however, the Legislature's 2003 amendment of CPRC §30.003(c) overrides the rule. See Gov't Code §22.004(b) (rules adopted by Supreme Court remain in effect until disapproved by Legislature).

(2) Mandatory denial. The trial court must overrule the motion in the following instances:

(a) TRO hearing. If a party makes a motion to continue a hearing on a TRO on legislative-continuance grounds, the court has no discretion and must overrule it. CPRC §30.003(a); TRCP 254.

(b) Due process. If the *Waites* exception to the mandatory-legislative-continuance rule applies, the court must overrule the motion and deny the continuance. *E.g.*, *Waites v. Sondock*, 561 S.W.2d 772, 776 (Tex.1977) (mother filed contempt motion for enforcement of child support, claiming to be unable to feed her children). The *Waites* exception applies only if the party opposing the motion proves it has a substantial existing right that will be irreparably harmed by the continuance. *See id.; see, e.g.*, *In re Ford Motor Co.*, 165 S.W.3d at 319 (party did not have substantial existing right); *Amoco Prod. v. Salyer*, 814 S.W.2d 211, 212-13 (Tex.App.—Corpus Christi 1991, orig. proceeding) (party did not prove irreparable harm); *Condovest Corp. v. John St. Builders, Inc.*, 662 S.W.2d 138, 141 (Tex.App.—Austin 1983, no writ) (party proved substantial existing right).

(c) Purpose of hiring legislator. If the attorney took the case for the purpose of getting a continuance or does not intend to participate in the case, the court must overrule the motion for continuance. *See* CPRC §30.003(e); TRCP 254.

2. Discretionary rulings – less than 30 days. The trial court has the discretion to overrule the motion for a legislative continuance if the attorney was employed within 30 days of the date the case is set for trial. CPRC §30.003(c); *see In re CNA Holdings*, 102 S.W.3d at 281 (applying ten-day rule in former version of CPRC §30.003(c)).

§13. CONTINUANCE FOR RELIGIOUS HOLY DAY

§13.1 Motion. A party or attorney who wants a continuance for a religious holy day must file an affidavit stating (1) the grounds for continuance and (2) that the party or attorney holds religious beliefs that prohibit her from taking part in court proceedings on the day she is required to appear in court. CPRC §30.005(c). See *O'Connor's Texas Forms*, FORM 5D:2, ¶¶32-36.

§13.2 Verified. See "Verification & affidavits," §2.3, p. 336.

§14. REVIEW

§14.1 Standard of review. The ruling on a motion for continuance is reviewed for abuse of discretion. *Villegas v. Carter*, 711 S.W.2d 624, 626 (Tex.1986); *State v. Crank*, 666 S.W.2d 91, 94 (Tex.1984).

§14.2 Record. If the trial court conducted a hearing on the motion for continuance, the appellate record consists of the reporter's record of the hearing and the clerk's record with the motion, affidavits, response, and order. *See Roob v. Von Beregshasy*, 866 S.W.2d 765, 766 (Tex.App.—Houston [1st Dist.] 1993, writ denied). If no hearing was held, the reporter's record is not required.

§14.3 Appeal. Generally, the trial court's ruling on a motion for continuance can be reviewed only after the case is tried and appealed.

1. First motion. The trial court does not have the discretion to reject uncontroverted facts established in a party's first motion for continuance. *Roob v. Von Beregshasy*, 866 S.W.2d 765, 766 (Tex.App.—Houston [1st Dist.] 1993, writ denied); *Garza v. Serrato*, 699 S.W.2d 275, 281 (Tex.App.—San Antonio 1985, writ ref'd n.r.e.).

2. Second motion. Appellate courts rarely reverse a trial court for overruling a second (or later) motion for continuance seeking additional time for discovery. *See Eckman v. Centennial Sav. Bank*, 757 S.W.2d 392, 395 (Tex.App.—Dallas 1988, writ denied); *Employers Mut. Cas. Co. v. Gifford*, 723 S.W.2d 811, 812-13 (Tex.App.—

✦

Fort Worth 1987, no writ). If a party states sufficient good cause, however, the trial court should grant a second motion for continuance. *See, e.g.*, *Garza*, 699 S.W.2d at 281 (D should have been given more time to find rebuttal evidence after P produced last-minute medical evidence different from earlier evidence).

§14.4 Mandamus. When a continuance is within the discretion of the trial court, mandamus is not generally available to review the trial court's ruling. *See General Motors Corp. v. Gayle*, 924 S.W.2d 222, 227 (Tex.App.—Houston [14th Dist.] 1996, orig. proceeding). When the trial court has no discretion, mandamus may be available. *See, e.g.*, *Amoco Prod. v. Salyer*, 814 S.W.2d 211, 213 (Tex.App.—Corpus Christi 1991, orig. proceeding) (legislative continuance).

E. MOTION IN LIMINE

§1. GENERAL

§1.1 Rule. None. See TRE 103, 104.

§1.2 Purpose. A motion in limine is a procedural device that permits a party to identify, before trial, certain evidentiary rulings that the court may be asked to make. *Greenberg Traurig of New York, P.C. v. Moody*, 161 S.W.3d 56, 91 (Tex.App.—Houston [14th Dist.] 2004, no pet.); *Lohmann v. Lohmann*, 62 S.W.3d 875, 881 (Tex.App.—El Paso 2001, no pet.). The purpose of this procedure is to prevent the jury from being exposed to potentially prejudicial information before a ruling on admissibility can be obtained. *Hartford Acc. & Indem. Co. v. McCardell*, 369 S.W.2d 331, 335 (Tex.1963); *Greenberg Traurig*, 161 S.W.3d at 91. It avoids the injection of irrelevant, inadmissible, and prejudicial information into the trial. *Wilkins v. Royal Indem. Co.*, 592 S.W.2d 64, 66 (Tex.App.—Tyler 1979, no writ). A motion in limine is optional; it is not a required procedural step for objections to evidence and does not preserve error for appeal. *See Bridges v. City of Richardson*, 354 S.W.2d 366, 367-68 (Tex.1962).

PRACTICE TIP

Do not file a motion in limine when you want a pretrial ruling that excludes evidence. Instead, file a motion to exclude evidence. For an example, see "Motion to Exclude Expert," ch. 5-N, p. 410.

---

§1.3 Forms. *O'Connor's Texas Civil Forms* (2012), FORMS 5E.

§2. MOTION

Because no rule or statute provides for a motion in limine, the procedures for such motions have developed through case law.

§2.1 Procedure. A motion in limine must be in writing, and copies must be served on all parties. *See* TRCP 21. The motion should state (1) exactly what evidence the party anticipates its opponent will attempt to introduce or the question the opponent will ask in front of the jury, and (2) why the evidence or question is inadmissible.

§2.2 Deadline. A motion in limine should be filed and presented for a ruling before voir dire. *See City of Houston v. Watson*, 376 S.W.2d 23, 33 (Tex.App.—Houston 1964, writ ref'd n.r.e.) (after parties announce ready). However, because error can be based only on a ruling on evidence during trial and not on the motion itself, the timing of the motion is not critical.

§2.3 Grounds. Before drafting a motion in limine, the attorney should review the rules of evidence that govern the exclusion of evidence: TRE 401-610. A motion in limine can address any evidence the rules classify as inadmissible. For a collection of grounds for motions in limine, see *O'Connor's Texas Forms*, FORM 5E:1.

§3. RESPONSE

It is not generally necessary to file a response to a motion in limine, although the party may file a response to address the issue of the admissibility of the evidence.

★

§4. HEARING

If the court holds a hearing on a motion in limine, it is solely for argument of counsel, not for presentation of evidence. If the court schedules a pretrial conference, the party may ask the court to consider the motion at that time. *See* TRCP 166(g).

§5. RULING ON THE MOTION

§5.1 Written order. The party should present a written order for the trial court's signature and file it with the court. *See* TRE 103(a)(1); TRAP 33.1(a)(1); *Wilkins v. Royal Indem. Co.*, 592 S.W.2d 64, 67 (Tex.App.—Tyler 1979, no writ). See *O'Connor's Texas Forms*, FORM 5E:2.

§5.2 Function of order. The trial court's ruling on a motion in limine is not a ruling that excludes or admits evidence. *Fort Worth Hotel L.P. v. Ensearch Corp.*, 977 S.W.2d 746, 757 (Tex.App.—Fort Worth 1998, no pet.). It is merely a tentative ruling that prohibits a party from asking a certain question or offering certain evidence in front of the jury without first approaching the bench for a ruling. *Id.*; *Chavis v. Director, State Workers' Comp. Div.*, 924 S.W.2d 439, 446 (Tex.App.—Beaumont 1996, no writ). A limine order may also prevent parties from referring to matters during voir dire or the opening statement without first approaching the bench for a ruling. *See, e.g., Babcock v. Northwest Mem'l Hosp.*, 767 S.W.2d 705, 708-09 (Tex.1989) (P could mention the "lawsuit crisis" or "liability-insurance crisis" in voir dire).

§6. OFFER & OBJECTION AT TRIAL

§6.1 When motion denied. When a trial court denies a motion in limine, the court has refused to require the person who intends to offer the evidence to approach the bench before offering it.

    1. Offer. At trial, the party seeking to introduce the evidence must offer the evidence. The denial of the motion in limine does not admit the evidence.

    2. Objection. If the evidence is offered at trial, the party that wants to exclude it must object when the evidence is offered. *Hartford Acc. & Indem. Co. v. McCardell*, 369 S.W.2d 331, 335 (Tex.1963); *Sims v. State*, 816 S.W.2d 502, 504 (Tex.App.—Houston [1st Dist.] 1991, writ denied). The denial of the motion in limine does not preserve error.

§6.2 When motion granted. When a trial court grants a motion in limine, the person offering the evidence must approach the bench for a ruling on the admissibility of the evidence before offering it in front of the jury.

    1. Offer. When a motion in limine is granted, the party that wants to introduce the evidence must (1) approach the bench and ask for a ruling, (2) formally offer the evidence, and (3) obtain a ruling on the offer. *See Johnson v. Garza*, 884 S.W.2d 831, 834 (Tex.App.—Austin 1994, writ denied); *Tempo Tamers, Inc. v. Crow-Houston Four, Ltd.*, 715 S.W.2d 658, 662-63 (Tex.App.—Dallas 1986, writ ref'd n.r.e.). The court's ruling granting the motion in limine does not exclude the evidence. *See Johnson*, 884 S.W.2d at 834. If necessary, the party offering the evidence should ask the court to remove the jury for a hearing on the admissibility of the evidence. Whether the offer takes place at a bench conference or in a hearing outside the presence of the jury, the party should make sure the court reporter records the offer and the ruling.

    2. Objection. If a party introduces evidence in violation of the ruling on the motion in limine (i.e., without first asking for a bench conference), the party that made the motion in limine must object. *Pool v. Ford Motor Co.*, 715 S.W.2d 629, 637 (Tex.1986). If the party does not object, the jury will consider the evidence, and the error in its admission is waived. *Id.* The court's ruling granting the motion in limine does not preserve error. *Id.*

    3. Bill of exception. If the trial court rules the evidence is not admissible, the party seeking to introduce the evidence must preserve it in a bill of exception (or offer of proof). *Johnson*, 884 S.W.2d at 834. See "Offer of Proof & Bill of Exception," ch. 8-E, p. 717.

★

§7. RULING ON THE OFFER

Once the party offers the evidence and the opposing party makes an objection, both parties should ensure the court makes a ruling on the record to either admit or exclude the evidence. See "Court's Ruling," ch. 1-G, §2, p. 47.

§8. WHEN LIMINE ORDER VIOLATED

§8.1 Pursue adverse ruling. If an order on a motion in limine is violated and prejudicial information is revealed to the jury, the party that wanted the evidence excluded must object immediately after the information is revealed or else it waives the error. *Weidner v. Sanchez*, 14 S.W.3d 353, 364-65 (Tex.App.—Houston [14th Dist.] 2000, no pet.). The party must make a series of objections, called "pursuing an adverse ruling." See "When jury hears inadmissible evidence," ch. 8-D, §6.6, p. 713. By making the appropriate objections, the party preserves the issue for appeal. *See, e.g.*, *Kendrix v. Southern Pac. Transp.*, 907 S.W.2d 111, 112-13 (Tex.App.—Beaumont 1995, writ denied) (party objected and made motion for mistrial); *Dove v. Director, State Empls. Workers' Comp. Div.*, 857 S.W.2d 577, 579 & n.2 (Tex.App.—Houston [1st Dist.] 1993, writ denied) (same); *Cody v. Mustang Oil Tool Co.*, 595 S.W.2d 214, 216 (Tex.App.—Eastland 1980, writ ref'd n.r.e.) (party moved for mistrial).

§8.2 Sanction. A court may strike pleadings as a sanction for a violation of a motion in limine if the circumstances warrant harsh sanctions. *E.g.*, *Lassiter v. Shavor*, 824 S.W.2d 667, 669-70 (Tex.App.—Dallas 1992, no writ) (sanction was abuse of discretion because there was no evidence of direct relationship between sanctions and offensive conduct). A court may impose a fine or hold a party or witness in contempt of court for violating an order on a motion in limine. *See Onstad v. Wright*, 54 S.W.3d 799, 802 (Tex.App.—Texarkana 2001, pet. denied) (attorney was fined $32,198); *Kidd v. Lance*, 794 S.W.2d 586, 588 (Tex.App.—Austin 1990, orig. proceeding) (attorney and party were held in contempt; fine limited to $500 by statute).

§9. REVIEW

§9.1 Court's ruling on motion. The trial court's ruling on a motion in limine is never reversible error. *Hartford Acc. & Indem. Co. v. McCardell*, 369 S.W.2d 331, 335 (Tex.1963); *see also State v. Wood Oil Distrib.*, 751 S.W.2d 863, 866 (Tex.1988) (appellate complaint of ruling on motion in limine presents nothing for review). Even if the trial court makes an erroneous ruling on a motion in limine, there is no reversible error unless the court, during the trial, erroneously admits or excludes evidence over a proper objection. *Acord v. General Motors Corp.*, 669 S.W.2d 111, 116 (Tex.1984). The right to appeal an erroneous ruling on the admission or exclusion of evidence does not depend on a motion in limine. *Hartford Acc. & Indem.*, 369 S.W.2d at 335.

§9.2 Violation of order. The violation of an order on the motion in limine is reversible if the harm resulting from the violation is incurable. *See Lohmann v. Lohmann*, 62 S.W.3d 875, 881 (Tex.App.—El Paso 2001, no pet.); *Weidner v. Sanchez*, 14 S.W.3d 353, 363 (Tex.App.—Houston [14th Dist.] 2000, no pet.); *see, e.g.*, *National Un. Fire Ins. v. Kwiatkowski*, 915 S.W.2d 662, 664-65 (Tex.App.—Houston [14th Dist.] 1996, no writ) (reversed because jury argument violated motion in limine, even though appellant made no objection to some comments); *Kendrix v. Southern Pac. Transp.*, 907 S.W.2d 111, 112-14 (Tex.App.—Beaumont 1995, writ denied) (reversed because no instructions could cure improper impression the statement left in minds of jurors); *Dove v. Director, State Empls. Workers' Comp. Div.*, 857 S.W.2d 577, 580 (Tex.App.—Houston [1st Dist.] 1993, writ denied) (reversed because repeated violations of order to first approach the bench permitted jury to hear prejudicial matters not curable by instruction to disregard).

★

F. MOTION TO AMEND PLEADINGS—PRETRIAL

§1. GENERAL

§1.1 Rules. TRCP 63-65. See TRCP 66-67 (trial amendments).

§1.2 Purpose. A party amends its pleadings to correct errors and defects in the pleadings.

§1.3 Forms. *O'Connor's Texas Civil Forms* (2012), FORMS 5F.

§2. GENERAL RULES FOR AMENDING PLEADINGS

Three sections in this book discuss amending pleadings: see "Amending or supplementing pleadings," ch. 1-B, §3.6, p. 16; this subchapter, "Motion to Amend Pleadings—Pretrial"; and "Motion to Amend Pleadings—Trial & Post-trial," ch. 8-F, p. 721.

§3. RULES REGARDING AMENDING PLEADINGS BEFORE TRIAL

TRCP 63 does not allow a party the unlimited right to amend its pleadings before trial. *Stevenson v. Koutzarov*, 795 S.W.2d 313, 321 (Tex.App.—Houston [1st Dist.] 1990, writ denied).

§3.1 No leave to amend required. A party is not required to secure leave of court to amend its pleadings in the following instances:

1. Before deadline in pretrial order. When a pretrial order establishes deadlines to amend, a party must file amendments according to those deadlines. *Mackey v. U.P. Enters.*, 935 S.W.2d 446, 461 (Tex.App.—Tyler 1996, no writ); *ForScan Corp. v. Dresser Indus.*, 789 S.W.2d 389, 393 (Tex.App.—Houston [14th Dist.] 1990, writ denied). TRCP 166, the rule governing pretrial orders, prevails over TRCP 63, the rule governing pretrial amendments. *G.R.A.V.I.T.Y. Enters. v. Reece Sup.*, 177 S.W.3d 537, 542-43 (Tex.App.—Dallas 2005, no pet.); *ForScan Corp.*, 789 S.W.2d at 393.

2. At least seven days before trial. When no pretrial order establishes deadlines to amend, the following rules govern amendments made at least seven days before trial:

(1) No surprise. A party has the right to amend pleadings at least seven days before trial, as long as the amendment does not operate as a surprise to the opposing party. TRCP 63; *Sosa v. Central Power & Light*, 909 S.W.2d 893, 895 (Tex.1995). The seven days are counted from the original trial date; that is, the date the case is set for trial, not the date the trial actually begins. *Taiwan Shrimp Farm Vill. Ass'n v. U.S.A. Shrimp Farm Dev., Inc.*, 915 S.W.2d 61, 69 (Tex.App.—Corpus Christi 1996, writ denied); *AmSav Grp. v. American S&L Ass'n*, 796 S.W.2d 482, 490 (Tex.App.—Houston [14th Dist.] 1990, writ denied). If the case actually goes to trial at a later date, the new setting does not enlarge the time to amend pleadings. *See Taiwan Shrimp*, 915 S.W.2d at 69-70; *AmSav Grp.*, 796 S.W.2d at 490.

(2) Surprise. The court has the discretion to strike an amendment filed seven days or more before trial if the party opposing the amendment shows the amendment was a surprise. *See, e.g., Flo Trend Sys. v. Allwaste, Inc.*, 948 S.W.2d 4, 7 (Tex.App.—Houston [14th Dist.] 1997, no writ) (no abuse of discretion in striking amendment filed seven days before trial because it added new theory of liability); *Favor v. Hochheim Prairie Farm Mut. Ins.*, 939 S.W.2d 180, 181-82 (Tex.App.—San Antonio 1996, writ denied) (same); *Stevenson v. Koutzarov*, 795 S.W.2d 313, 321 (Tex.App.—Houston [1st Dist.] 1990, writ denied) (court abused discretion in refusing to strike amendment filed eight days before trial because it was a wholesale revision of lawsuit). See "Surprise," §5.2.1, p. 353.

3. At least 45 days before trial. A party may amend its pleadings to change from a Level 1 discovery-control plan to a Level 2 or 3 plan without filing a motion for leave to file if the amendment is filed at least 45 days before trial. TRCP 190.2(b) (last paragraph).

★

---

⑬

PROPOSED TRCP CHANGES

In response to Gov't Code §22.004(h), the Supreme Court has proposed TRCP 169 to establish a process for the prompt, efficient, and cost-effective resolution of civil actions (expedited actions) in which only monetary relief is sought and the amount in controversy is no more than $100,000. See Tex.Sup.Ct. Order, Misc. Docket No. 12-9191 (eff. Mar. 1, 2013). The Supreme Court has proposed corresponding amendments to TRCP 190.2 that, along with the adoption of Rule 169, would change the deadline requirements for filing an amended pleading without leave of court. See Tex.Sup.Ct. Order, Misc. Docket No. 12-9191 (eff. Mar. 1, 2013). The public-comment period for the proposed amendments ends on February 1, 2013, and the rules are to take effect March 1, 2013. For the proposed version of the rules, see the appendix after this book's index. For the final version, go to the Supreme Court website at www.supreme.courts.state.tx.us. When the new and amended rules take effect, a supplement to this book—with updated rules and commentaries that reflect the changes—will be available at www.JonesMcClure.com/ TRCPamendments.

---

§3.2 Leave to amend required. A party must secure leave of court to amend pleadings in the following instances:

1. After deadline in pretrial order. To amend its pleadings after the deadline in a pretrial order, the party must secure leave of court. *Hart v. Moore*, 952 S.W.2d 90, 95 (Tex.App.—Amarillo 1997, pet. denied); *Texas Commerce Bank Reagan v. Lebco Constructors, Inc.*, 865 S.W.2d 68, 78-79 (Tex.App.—Corpus Christi 1993, writ denied); *see, e.g., Roskey v. Continental Cas. Co.*, 190 S.W.3d 875, 881 (Tex.App.—Dallas 2006, pet. denied) (court did not abuse discretion in refusing amendment six days after deadline in pretrial order because party could have amended pleading during 17 months that case was pending). The rules that govern late amendments, addressed in §3.2.2, below, also control late amendments filed after the deadline in a pretrial order. *Texas Commerce Bank*, 865 S.W.2d at 79; *see, e.g., Brown v. State*, 984 S.W.2d 348, 350 (Tex.App.—Fort Worth 1999, pet. denied) (court abused its discretion in permitting amendment that changed nature of case 18 days after deadline in pretrial order).

2. Less than seven days before trial. All pleadings, responses, or pleas offered for filing less than seven days from the date of trial can be filed only with leave of court, which the court must grant unless the party resisting the amendment objects and shows surprise. TRCP 63; *Chapin & Chapin, Inc. v. Texas Sand & Gravel Co.*, 844 S.W.2d 664, 665 (Tex.1992); *see Burrow v. Arce*, 997 S.W.2d 229, 246 (Tex.1999); *see, e.g., Guereque v. Thompson*, 953 S.W.2d 458, 463-64 (Tex.App.—El Paso 1997, pet. denied) (because party did not file motion for leave, pleading was not "filed"); *see also Nichols v. Bridges*, 163 S.W.3d 776, 782 (Tex.App.—Texarkana 2005, no pet.) (TRCP 63 applies to special-appearance and summary-judgment proceedings because they are considered "trials").

(1) Procedural change. If a change to the pleading is merely procedural and does not change any substantive issues in the trial, the court must permit the amendment unless there is a showing of surprise or prejudice. *See* TRCP 63; *Chapin & Chapin*, 844 S.W.2d at 665. For example, adding a verified denial to an answer is a procedural change. *Chapin & Chapin*, 844 S.W.2d at 665.

(2) Substantive change. If a change to the pleading is substantive and changes the nature of the trial, the trial judge has discretion to deny leave to amend. *Chapin & Chapin*, 844 S.W.2d at 665; *see, e.g., Hardin v. Hardin*, 597 S.W.2d 347, 349-50 (Tex.1980) (court had discretion to deny amendment offered on day of trial to add affirmative defenses); *Bekins Moving & Storage Co. v. Williams*, 947 S.W.2d 568, 574 (Tex.App.—Texarkana 1997, no writ) (same). When a party offers an amendment that makes a substantive change, the burden is on the party opposing the amendment to object and show surprise. TRCP 63; *Burrow*, 997 S.W.2d at 246; *Chapin & Chapin*, 844 S.W.2d at 665.

3. Less than 45 days before trial. If an amendment changes a case from a Level 1 discovery-control plan to a Level 2 or 3 plan and is filed less than 45 days before trial, the party must file a motion for leave to amend, showing that good cause to file the pleading outweighs any prejudice to the other party. TRCP 190.2(b) (last

✦

paragraph). A late amendment that changes the discovery level upward has the following effects: (1) it reopens the discovery period, (2) any person previously deposed may be redeposed, and (3) the trial date should be reset if necessary to permit completion of discovery. TRCP 190.2(d).

⑬

PROPOSED TRCP CHANGES

In response to Gov't Code §22.004(h), the Supreme Court has proposed TRCP 169 to establish a process for the prompt, efficient, and cost-effective resolution of civil actions (expedited actions) in which only monetary relief is sought and the amount in controversy is no more than $100,000. See Tex.Sup.Ct. Order, Misc. Docket No. 12-9191 (eff. Mar. 1, 2013). The Supreme Court has proposed corresponding amendments to TRCP 190.2 that, along with the adoption of Rule 169, would change the deadline requirements for filing an amended pleading without leave of court. See Tex.Sup.Ct. Order, Misc. Docket No. 12-9191 (eff. Mar. 1, 2013). The public-comment period for the proposed amendments ends on February 1, 2013, and the rules are to take effect March 1, 2013. For the proposed version of the rules, see the appendix after this book's index. For the final version, go to the Supreme Court website at www.supreme.courts.state.tx.us. When the new and amended rules take effect, a supplement to this book—with updated rules and commentaries that reflect the changes—will be available at www.JonesMcClure.com/ TRCPamendments.

---

§3.3 Service of amended pleadings. Amended pleadings do not need to be served on parties who have filed petitions or answers in the case; service of the amended pleading needs only to comply with the requirements of TRCP 21 and 21a. *See **Burrow v. Arce**, 997 S.W.2d 229, 246 (Tex.1999).* However, service of an amended petition on a non-answering defendant must be by service of process if the petition includes more claims or more damages. See "Amending the petition," ch. 7-A, §3.2.1, p. 588.

§4. MOTION FOR LEAVE TO AMEND PLEADINGS BEFORE TRIAL

§4.1 Written motion for leave. When a motion for leave is required (see "Leave to amend required," §3.2, p. 351), the motion should be in writing, unless it is made in open court and dictated into the record. ***Pennington v. Gurkoff***, 899 S.W.2d 767, 771 (Tex.App.—Fort Worth 1995, writ denied); *see* TRCP 45(d). The better practice is to file a written motion, even when an oral motion was made on the record. In the motion for leave to amend, the party should state why the amendment is appropriate and necessary. See *O'Connor's Texas Forms*, FORM 5F:1.

§4.2 Amended pleading. The amended pleading must be in writing and signed by the attorney or the party. ***Pennington v. Gurkoff***, 899 S.W.2d 767, 771 (Tex.App.—Fort Worth 1995, writ denied); *see* TRCP 45(d), 63; *see, e.g.*, ***First Nat'l Indem. Co. v. First Bank & Trust***, 753 S.W.2d 405, 407 (Tex.App.—Beaumont 1988, no writ) (error was not preserved when amendment to pleadings was not reduced to writing). The amended pleading should be filed along with (but not attached to) the motion for leave to amend.

§5. RESPONSE TO MOTION FOR PRETRIAL AMENDMENT

§5.1 Motion to strike vs. response. To object to an amended pleading that is already on file, the party should file a motion to strike; to object to a motion for leave to file an amended pleading, the party should file a response with objections. See *O'Connor's Texas Forms*, FORM 5F:2 (response), FORM 5F:3 (motion to strike).

§5.2 Objections. A motion to strike or a response should object to the amendment by alleging surprise and prejudice.

✦

PRACTICE TIP

*Although TRCP 63 does not require a showing of lack of diligence by the party offering the amendment, some courts of appeals require it. See, e.g., **Taiwan Shrimp Farm Vill. Ass'n v. U.S.A. Shrimp Farm Dev., Inc.**, 915 S.W.2d 61, 70 (Tex.App.—Corpus Christi 1996, writ denied) (no error to refuse pretrial amendment filed three days before trial because defense was known earlier); **AmSav Grp. v. American S&L Ass'n**, 796 S.W.2d 482, 490 (Tex.App.—Houston [14th Dist.] 1990, writ denied) (same; 11 days after deadline). The Supreme Court, however, has never recognized lack of diligence as a factor in pretrial amendments, and one court of appeals has specifically held that it is not a proper factor. **Zavala v. Trujillo**, 883 S.W.2d 242, 249 (Tex.App.—El Paso 1994, writ denied) (only factors are surprise or prejudice). When a case is in an appellate district where diligence has been recognized as a factor, the party opposing the amendment should show the offering party's lack of diligence.*

---

1. Surprise. The party opposing the amendment must show surprise. Unless the party opposing the amendment shows surprise, the court must permit the amended pleading. TRCP 63; **Hardin v. Hardin**, 597 S.W.2d 347, 349 (Tex.1980). Courts must construe TRCP 63 liberally. **Goswami v. Metropolitan S&L Ass'n**, 751 S.W.2d 487, 490 (Tex.1988). Courts may consider the following factors:

(1) How long the suit had been on file before the amendment was filed. **Dunnagan v. Watson**, 204 S.W.3d 30, 38 (Tex.App.—Fort Worth 2006, pet. denied).

(2) How close to trial the amendment was filed. *Id.*

(3) Whether the amendment presents a new claim. *Id.*

(4) If the amendment presents a new claim, whether it is based on recently discovered matters. *Id.*

(5) Whether the opposing party alleged surprise and that it was not prepared to try the new claim. *Id.*

2. Prejudice. Although TRCP 63 does not require a showing of prejudice, the Supreme Court has discussed it as a factor in evaluating pretrial amendments. *See* **Hardin**, 597 S.W.2d at 349 (amended answer filed after filing deadline). Thus, the party opposing a pretrial amendment should attempt to convince the trial court that the amendment will prejudice its claim or defense on the merits. *See* **Halmos v. Bombardier Aerospace Corp.**, 314 S.W.3d 606, 622 & n.3 (Tex.App.—Dallas 2010, no pet.); *cf.* TRCP 66 (prejudice for trial amendment). The party can prove prejudice or show prejudice on the face of the amendment. See "Show prejudice on its face," ch. 8-F, §3.2.2, p. 724.

§6. RULINGS ON PRETRIAL AMENDMENTS

§6.1 Amendment denied. If the trial court denies the amendment and makes a record of its ruling, the party who wanted to amend has preserved error on the issue for appeal.

§6.2 Amendment permitted.

1. Express ruling. If the trial court permits the amendment and makes a record of its ruling, both parties have preserved error on the issue for appeal.

2. Presumed ruling. If the trial court does not make a ruling on whether the amendment is permitted (or if the trial court denies the amendment but the ruling does not appear in the record), the trial court is presumed to have granted leave to file the amended pleading. *E.g.*, **Lee v. Key W. Towers, Inc.**, 783 S.W.2d 586, 588 (Tex.1989) (trial court was presumed to have considered verified denial filed three days before trial); **Goswami v. Metropolitan S&L Ass'n**, 751 S.W.2d 487, 490 (Tex.1988) (trial court was presumed to have considered amendment filed four days before summary-judgment hearing). The presumption results from the liberal construction of TRCP 63 in favor of amendments. **Lee**, 783 S.W.2d at 588; **Goswami**, 751 S.W.2d at 490. The party opposing the amendment should ensure that the court makes a ruling on the record denying the filing of the amendment.

★

3. Motion for continuance. If the trial court permits a late amendment and the party opposing the amendment needs additional time to prepare for trial (e.g., time for additional discovery), that party can request a continuance. *Fletcher v. Edwards*, 26 S.W.3d 66, 74 (Tex.App.—Waco 2000, pet. denied); *Louisiana & Ark. Ry. v. Blakely*, 773 S.W.2d 595, 597 (Tex.App.—Texarkana 1989, writ denied). *But see Stevenson v. Koutzarov*, 795 S.W.2d 313, 321 (Tex.App.—Houston [1st Dist.] 1990, writ denied) (party opposing amendment was not required to move for continuance because amendments filed ten and eight days before trial were wholesale revision of lawsuit). See "Motion for Continuance," ch. 5-D, p. 336.

(1) Cost of continuance. The court may order the party filing a late amendment that causes surprise to the other party to pay the cost of the continuance, including attorney fees. TRCP 70.

(2) Refusal of continuance = waiver. If the party opposing an amendment refuses the trial court's offer of continuance, that party waives its right to complain of the late amendment on appeal. *Kaufman Nw., Inc. v. Bi-Stone Fuel Co.*, 529 S.W.2d 281, 288 (Tex.App.—Tyler 1975, writ ref'd n.r.e.).

4. Motion to reopen discovery period. If the trial court permits a late amendment and (1) the party opposing the amendment needs additional discovery or (2) the late amendment makes a Level 1 discovery-control plan inapplicable and discovery cannot be completed before the deadline under a Level 2 or 3 discovery-control plan, that party can file a motion to reopen the discovery period. *See* TRCP 190.2(d), 190.5. See "Period reopens," ch. 6-A, §8.1.1(2), p. 434; "Modification of discovery periods," ch. 6-A, §8.2, p. 434.

(13)   **PROPOSED TRCP CHANGES**

In response to Gov't Code §22.004(h), the Supreme Court has proposed TRCP 169 to provide a process for the prompt, efficient, and cost-effective resolution of civil actions (expedited actions) in which only monetary relief is sought and the amount in controversy is no more than $100,000. See Tex.Sup.Ct. Order, Misc. Docket No. 12-9191 (eff. Mar. 1, 2013). The Supreme Court has proposed corresponding amendments to TRCP 190.2 and TRCP 190.5 that would change the requirements for reopening the discovery period when a suit is governed by TRCP 169. See Tex.Sup.Ct. Order, Misc. Docket No. 12-9191 (eff. Mar. 1, 2013). The public-comment period for the proposed amendments ends on February 1, 2013, and the rules are to take effect March 1, 2013. For the proposed version of the rules, see the appendix after this book's index. For the final version, go to the Supreme Court website at www.supreme.courts.state.tx.us. When the new and amended rules take effect, a supplement to this book—with updated rules and commentaries that reflect the changes—will be available at www.JonesMcClure.com/TRCPamendments.

§6.3 Sample rulings.

1. Amendments permitted. The following pretrial amendments were permitted: • In personal-injury suit, amendment of petition seven days before summary-judgment hearing to delete factual allegations on which motion for summary judgment was based and to add lack of discovery of injury. *Sosa v. Central Power & Light*, 909 S.W.2d 893, 894-95 (Tex.1995). • In suit on sworn account, amendment to add a verified denial of allegations of open account six days before trial. *Chapin & Chapin, Inc. v. Texas Sand & Gravel Co.*, 844 S.W.2d 664, 664-65 (Tex. 1992).

2. Amendments denied. The following pretrial amendments were denied: • In suit for promissory note, amendment to add claims for duress, failure of consideration, fraud, illegality, and unjust enrichment on day of trial. *Hardin v. Hardin*, 597 S.W.2d 347, 348, 350 (Tex.1980). • In suit to recover delinquent taxes, amended answer raising new defense less than seven days before trial. *Phifer v. Nacogdoches Cty. Cent. Appr. Dist.*, 45 S.W.3d 159, 171 (Tex.App.—Tyler 2000, pet. denied). • In suit for damages arising from divorce action, amendments received seven days before trial that completely revised lawsuit. *Stevenson v. Koutzarov*, 795 S.W.2d 313, 321 (Tex.App.—Houston [1st Dist.] 1990, writ denied).

✯

---

§7. COSTS

If the trial court allows a party to file a late-amended or supplemental pleading that causes surprise to the other party, the trial court may charge the cost of a continuance to the filing party. TRCP 70.

§8. REVIEW

See "Appellate review of amended pleadings," ch. 1-B, §3.6.3, p. 17.

G. MOTION TO TRANSFER TO MULTIDISTRICT LITIGATION PRETRIAL COURT

§1. GENERAL

Under Texas Rule of Judicial Administration (TRJA) 13, cases pending in different counties that involve the same material questions of fact may be consolidated for pretrial purposes, including summary judgment, and transferred to a multidistrict litigation (MDL) pretrial court. *See* Gov't Code §74.162; TRJA 13.3(a)(1), 13.6(b). TRJA 13 applies to civil actions involving one or more common questions of fact, including civil actions involving claims for asbestos-related or silica-related injuries, that are filed on or after September 1, 2003; to the extent permitted by CPRC chapter 90, the rule also applies to civil actions involving claims for asbestos-related or silica-related injuries that were filed before September 1, 2003. TRJA 13.1(b); *see* Gov't Code §74.162; TRJA 13.11(a); *see also* CPRC §90.010 (MDL rules for asbestos and silica claims). For all other cases, TRJA 11 applies. TRJA 13.1(c). See *O'Connor's Texas Rules * Civil Trials* (2003), "Motion for Pretrial Consolidation Between Counties," ch. 5-G, p. 256.

§1.1 **Rules.** Gov't Code §§74.161-74.164; TRJA 11.7, 13.

§1.2 **Purpose.** Under TRJA 13, consolidation of related cases in a single pretrial court allows for more efficient resolution of recurring or related legal issues and more consistent rulings in those cases. *In re GlobalSantaFe Corp.*, 275 S.W.3d 477, 483 (Tex.2008) (consolidation of asbestos and silica cases); *see In re Champion Indus. Sales, LLC*, ___ S.W.3d ___ (Tex.App.—Corpus Christi 2012, orig. proceeding) (No. 13-12-00505-CV; 10-29-12) (goal of TRJA 13 is to eliminate duplicative discovery, limit demands on witnesses, prevent inconsistent decisions on common issues, and lessen unecessary travel).

§1.3 **Forms.** *O'Connor's Texas Civil Forms* (2012), FORMS 5G.

§2. JUDICIAL PANEL ON MULTIDISTRICT LITIGATION

§2.1 **MDL panel.** The MDL procedure is governed by a judicial panel (MDL Panel) consisting of five members, who must be active court of appeals justices or administrative judges, designated by the Supreme Court chief justice. Gov't Code §74.161(a). The MDL Panel includes temporary members designated by the Supreme Court chief justice when regular members are unable to sit. TRJA 13.2(a). Any action taken by the panel must have a concurrence of three panel members. Gov't Code §74.161(b). The panel may prescribe any rules for conducting its business, as long as they are not inconsistent with the law or the rules adopted by the Supreme Court. *Id.* §74.163(b).

§2.2 **MDL clerk.** The MDL Panel Clerk is the clerk of the Supreme Court. TRJA 13.2(c). The motion to transfer, the response, and any reply are filed with the MDL Panel Clerk, and the clerk is responsible for filing notice of a request for transfer filed by a judge. See "Notice," §3.4, p. 356; "Filing & Service," §5, p. 356.

§3. MOTION TO TRANSFER TO PRETRIAL COURT

§3.1 **Who may file.**

1. **Party.** A party in the case may file a motion to transfer the case and related cases to a pretrial court. TRJA 13.3(a).

2. **Judge.** A trial court judge or a presiding judge of an administrative judicial region may file a written request listing related cases to be transferred. TRJA 13.3(b).

★

§3.2 Motion.

1. In writing. The motion must be in writing and must conform to TRAP 9.4. TRJA 13.3(a), (e). Unless leave of the MDL Panel is requested, the portions of the motion required by TRJA 13.3(a)(1) and (a)(2) must not exceed 20 pages. TRJA 13.3(e).

2. Common issues. The motion must identify the common questions of fact involved in the cases. TRJA 13.3(a)(1).

3. Reasons to transfer. The motion must state why the transfer would be convenient for the parties and witnesses and would promote the just and efficient conduct of the action. TRJA 13.3(a)(2); *see* Gov't Code §74.163(a)(2); *In re GlobalSantaFe Corp.*, 275 S.W.3d 477, 483 (Tex.2008).

4. Agreement of parties. The motion must state whether all parties agree to the motion. TRJA 13.3(a)(3).

5. Appendix. The motion must contain an appendix that lists the following:

(1) **Related cases.** The cause number, style, and trial court of each related case for which transfer is sought. TRJA 13.3(a)(4)(A).

(2) **Parties.** A list of all parties in those cases, along with their attorneys' names, addresses, telephone and fax numbers, and e-mail addresses. TRJA 13.3(a)(4)(B).

§3.3 Brief.
The MDL Panel may request additional briefing from any party. TRJA 13.3(e).

§3.4 Notice.
A party must file a notice with the trial court that a motion for transfer has been filed. TRJA 13.3(i). If a judge files a request for transfer, the MDL Panel Clerk must file the notice with the trial court. *Id.*

§3.5 Stay.
Filing a motion to transfer does not automatically limit the trial court's jurisdiction or suspend proceedings or orders in that court. TRJA 13.4(a). However, the trial court or MDL Panel may stay all or a part of any proceedings until the MDL Panel makes a ruling. TRJA 13.4(b).

§3.6 Retransfer.
On a party's motion, at the request of the pretrial court, or on its own initiative, the MDL Panel may transfer cases from one pretrial court to another when the pretrial judge has died, resigned, been replaced, or been disqualified, or in any other situation when retransfer would promote the just and efficient conduct of the cases. TRJA 13.3(o).

§3.7 Show-cause order.
The MDL Panel may, on its own initiative, issue an order to show cause why related cases should not be transferred to a pretrial court. TRJA 13.3(c).

§4. RESPONSE

§4.1 Who may respond.
Any other party in the cases to be transferred may file the following:

1. A response to a motion or request for transfer within 20 days after service of the motion or request. TRJA 13.3(d)(1).

2. A response to an MDL Panel show-cause order within the time provided in the order. TRJA 13.3(d)(2). See "Show-cause order," §3.7, this page.

3. A reply to a response within ten days after service of the response. TRJA 13.3(d)(3).

§4.2 Form of response.
The response or reply must be in writing and must conform with TRAP 9.4. TRJA 13.3(e). Unless leave of the MDL Panel is requested, the response or reply must not exceed 20 pages. TRJA 13.3(e).

§4.3 Brief.
The MDL Panel may request additional briefing from any party. TRJA 13.3(e).

§5. FILING & SERVICE

§5.1 Filing.
A motion, request, response, or reply must be electronically filed with the MDL Panel Clerk. www.supreme.courts.state.tx.us/mdl/mdlhome.asp; *see* TRJA 13.3(f). In addition, a paper copy must be mailed to the MDL Panel clerk, as well as to each member of the MDL Panel. www.supreme.courts.state.tx.us/mdl/mdlhome.asp; *see* TRJA 13.3(f).

──────────────────────────── ✦ ────────────────────────────

NOTE

Although TRJA 13.3(f) does not specify whether a document must be electronically filed, all documents must be electronically filed with the MDL Panel Clerk using the electronic-filing system through Texas.gov. See www.supreme.courts.state.tx.us/mdl/mdlhome.asp. For the procedure to electronically file a document, see **O'Connor's Texas Appeals**, *"How to file," ch. 1-E, §5.3.2(1), p. 36, or go to the Supreme Court website.*

---

§5.2 Service. All papers filed under TRJA 13.3 must be served on all parties to the cases to be transferred in accordance with TRAP 9.5. TRJA 13.3(h). The MDL Panel Clerk may designate a party to serve a request on all other parties. *Id.*

§5.3 Filing fees. The MDL Panel Clerk may set reasonable fees approved by the Supreme Court for filing and other services. TRJA 13.3(g). For the current fees for filing a motion under TRJA 13.3, see Tex.Sup.Ct. Order, Misc. Docket No. 07-9138 (eff. Sept. 1, 2007).

§6. HEARING

§6.1 Hearing. The MDL Panel is not required to hold a hearing; it may decide the matter on the written submission. TRJA 13.3(k). The panel may hold an oral hearing at a time and place of its choosing, and the MDL Panel Clerk must give notice of the date of submission or the time and place of the hearing to all parties. TRJA 13.3(k), (n). The clerk may determine the manner in which notice is given, including whether notice should be given by e-mail or fax. TRJA 13.3(n).

§6.2 Evidence. A party may file evidence only with leave of the MDL Panel. TRJA 13.3(j). The panel will accept as true the facts stated in a motion, response, or reply, unless another party contradicts them. *Id.* If the panel decides to accept evidence, it may order the parties to submit affidavits or deposition evidence and to file documents, discovery, or stipulations from the related cases. *Id.*

§7. ORDER

The MDL Panel must issue a written order to transfer the case. TRJA 13.3(*l*). The written order must have a concurrence of at least three members of the panel and contain a finding that (1) the related cases involve one or more common questions of fact, and (2) the transfer will be for the convenience of the parties and will promote the just and efficient conduct of the related cases. *Id.* The order must be signed by either the MDL Panel chair or the clerk and must identify the members who concurred in the ruling. TRJA 13.3(m). If the panel refuses to rule, the movant may file an original mandamus proceeding in the Supreme Court. See "MDL Panel order," §10.1, p. 359.

§8. TRANSFER

§8.1 When effective. A case is deemed transferred when the transfer notice is filed with the trial and pretrial courts. TRJA 13.5(a); *In re Fluor Enters.*, 186 S.W.3d 639, 646 (Tex.App.—Austin 2006, orig. proceeding). After the notice is filed, the trial court cannot take any further action in the case except for good cause stated in the order and after conferring with the pretrial court. TRJA 13.5(b). Any service of process issued by the trial court may be completed and the return filed in the pretrial court. *Id.*

§8.2 Contents of notice. The transfer notice must include the following:

1. A list of all parties who have appeared and remain in the case, along with the names, addresses, telephone and bar numbers of their attorneys, or if a party is pro se, the party's name, address, and telephone number. TRJA 13.5(a)(1).

2. A list of the parties who have not yet appeared in the case. TRJA 13.5(a)(2).

3. A copy of the MDL transfer order. TRJA 13.5(a)(3). See "Order," §7, this page.

⎯⎯⎯⎯⎯⎯⎯⎯⎯⎯ ✦ ⎯⎯⎯⎯⎯⎯⎯⎯⎯⎯

§8.3 Transfer of files. If the trial and pretrial courts are in different counties, the trial-court clerk must transmit the case file to the pretrial-court clerk. TRJA 13.5(c). If the trial and pretrial courts are in the same county, the trial court must transfer the case file to the pretrial court according to the local rules of the courts of that county. *Id.* The pretrial court may direct the manner in which the pretrial documents are filed, including electronic filing. *Id.*

§8.4 Fees. The party moving for transfer must pay the costs of refiling the transferred cases in the pretrial court, including filing fees and other reasonable costs, unless the MDL Panel decides otherwise. TRJA 13.5(d).

§8.5 Tag-along cases. A tag-along case is one that is related to the transferred cases but is not subject to the transfer order. TRJA 13.2(g). Tag-along cases are deemed transferred when the transfer notice is filed in both the trial and pretrial courts. TRJA 13.5(e). Within 30 days after the transfer notice is served, a party to the tag-along case or any of the related cases may move for the pretrial court to remand on the ground that the case is not a tag-along case. *Id.* If the motion to remand is granted, the case must be returned to the trial court, and the pretrial court may assess costs, including attorney fees, in the remand order. *Id.* The remand order may be appealed to the MDL Panel by filing a motion for rehearing with the MDL Panel Clerk. *Id.*

NOTE

TRJA 13 does not state whether a pretrial court can allow a late-filed motion for remand on the ground that the case is not a tag-along case. One court, however, has assumed—without deciding—that the pretrial court has such discretion. **In re Champion Indus. Sales, LLC,** ___ *S.W.3d ___ (Tex.App.—Corpus Christi 2012, orig. proceeding) (No. 13-12-00505-CV; 10-29-12).*

---

§9. PRETRIAL PROCEEDINGS

§9.1 Assignment of pretrial judge. The MDL Panel may assign as the pretrial judge any active district judge or any former or retired district or appellate judge approved by the Supreme Court Chief Justice. TRJA 13.6(a); *see* Gov't Code §74.164. For definitions of active, former, and retired judges, see "Who may be assigned," ch. 5-C, §3.2, p. 326. The assigned judge has exclusive jurisdiction over each related case that is transferred unless a case (1) is retransferred by the MDL panel, (2) is finally resolved, or (3) is remanded to the trial court for trial. TRJA 13.6(a). A pretrial judge appointed under TRJA 13 is not subject to an objection to an assigned judge under Gov't Code §74.053. TRJA 13.6(a); *see* **In re Perritt**, 992 S.W.2d 444, 447 n.4 (Tex.1999) (TRJA 11).

§9.2 Authority of pretrial court. The pretrial court has the authority to decide all pretrial matters (e.g., jurisdiction, joinder, venue) in the related cases transferred to the court. TRJA 13.6(b). This includes disposition by means other than a trial on the merits (e.g., default judgment, summary judgment, settlement). *Id.; see* Gov't Code §§74.162, 74.163(a)(3). The pretrial court may set aside or modify any pretrial ruling made by the trial court before transfer over which the trial court would not have lost plenary power. TRJA 13.6(b). After transfer, the pretrial court should, at the earliest practical date, conduct a hearing and enter a case-management order. TRJA 13.6(c). The case-management order should address all matters pertinent to the conduct of the litigation. *Id.* For a list of these matters, see TRJA 13.6(c).

§9.3 Trial settings. The pretrial court must confer, or order the parties to confer, with the trial court regarding trial settings or matters regarding remand. TRJA 13.6(d). The pretrial court must defer appropriately to the trial court's docket. *Id.* The trial court must not continue or postpone a trial setting without the pretrial court's concurrence. *Id.*

§9.4 Remand. The pretrial court may order remand of cases or separable triable portions of cases when pretrial proceedings are sufficiently completed. TRJA 13.7(b). However, remand is required for a trial on the merits. Gov't Code §74.163(a)(3). The pretrial court will not remand a case in which it has rendered a final and appealable judgment. TRJA 13.7(a).

§9.5 Orders after remand.

    1. Concurrence required. The trial court cannot, over an objection, vacate, set aside, or modify pretrial-court orders without the written concurrence of the pretrial court. TRJA 13.8(b). If the pretrial court is unavailable for any reason, the concurrence of the MDL Panel Chair must be obtained. TRJA 13.8(d).

⭐

2. Exception. The trial court does not need a written concurrence to vacate, set aside, or modify pretrial-court orders regarding the admissibility of evidence at trial (other than expert evidence) when the ruling is necessary because of changed circumstances, to correct an error of law, or to prevent manifest injustice. TRJA 13.8(c). The trial court must support its action with specific findings and conclusions in a written order or stated on the record. *Id.*

§10. REVIEW

§10.1 MDL Panel order. An order of the MDL Panel, including an order granting or denying a motion for transfer, may be reviewed only by the Supreme Court in an original mandamus proceeding. TRJA 13.9(a); *see* Gov't Code §74.163(a)(4).

§10.2 Pretrial or trial-court order. An order or judgment of the pretrial or trial court may be reviewed by the appellate court that normally reviews orders of the court in which the case is pending, whether or not that court issued the order or judgment to be reviewed. TRJA 13.9(b); *In re Fluor Enters.*, 186 S.W.3d 639, 642 (Tex.App.—Austin 2006, orig. proceeding). A case under such a review cannot be transferred for docket equalization among the appellate courts. TRJA 13.9(b). The appellate court must expedite the review of an order or judgment in a case pending in a pretrial court regardless of whether review is sought by appeal, accelerated appeal, or mandamus. TRJA 13.9(c) & cmt.

H. MOTION FOR ADDITIONAL RESOURCES

§1. GENERAL

In 2011, the Legislature enacted Gov't Code §§74.251-74.257 to provide for the allocation of additional judicial resources to large or complex civil cases. *See* House Cmte. on Judiciary & Civil Jurisprudence, Bill Analysis, Tex. H.B. 79, 82nd Leg., C.S. (2011). Gov't Code §74.252(a) directed the Supreme Court to adopt rules implementing these new provisions. In response, the Supreme Court adopted Texas Rule of Judicial Administration (TRJA) 16, which implemented and elaborated on the procedures for assigning judicial resources to a case. *See* TRJA 16.1(a) & cmt. The new procedures for additional resources took effect on May 1, 2012. H.B. 79, §7.06, 82nd Leg., C.S., eff. May 1, 2012; Tex.Sup.Ct. Order, Misc. Docket No. 12-9033 (eff. May 1, 2012).

§1.1 Rules. Gov't Code §§74.251-74.257; TRJA 16.

§1.2 Purpose. A motion for additional resources is designed to give courts the ability to get a variety of additional resources for cases that require special attention. *See* House Cmte. on Judiciary & Civil Jurisprudence, Bill Analysis, Tex. H.B. 79, 82nd Leg., C.S. (2011); TRJA 16 cmt.

§1.3 Forms. None.

§2. JUDICIAL COMMITTEE FOR ADDITIONAL RESOURCES

The Legislature established the Judicial Committee for Additional Resources (JCAR) to oversee the process of assigning additional resources to a case. *See* Gov't Code §74.254; TRJA 16.2(a).

§2.1 Members of JCAR. The JCAR consists of the chief justice of the Texas Supreme Court and the nine presiding judges of the administrative judicial regions, with the chief justice serving as the presiding officer. Gov't Code §74.254(a), (b); TRJA 16.2(a), (c).

NOTE

In this subchapter, "presiding judge" means the presiding judge of the administrative judicial region in which the case is filed.

---

§2.2 JCAR clerk. The Administrative Director of the Office of Court Administration (OCA) serves as the JCAR clerk. TRJA 16.2(b).

─────────────── ★ ───────────────

§2.3 OCA. The OCA, which operates under the direction and supervision of the Texas Supreme Court and the chief justice, must help the JCAR fulfill its duties. *See* Gov't Code §§72.011(a), 72.026; TRJA 16.3(a). See "Review of request by JCAR," §5.3, p. 362.

§3. SCOPE OF RULE

§3.1 When applicable. The procedures for allocating additional resources to a case apply only to civil actions in a constitutional county court, county court at law, probate court, or district court. TRJA 16.1(b).

§3.2 When not applicable. The procedures for allocating additional resources to a case do not apply to the following:

1. Criminal matters. Gov't Code §74.251(1); TRJA 16.1(c)(1).

2. Grants for local court improvement under Gov't Code §72.029. TRJA 16.1(c)(2).

3. Cases in which judicial review of a state-agency decision in a contested case is sought under Gov't Code §§2001.171-2001.178. *See* Gov't Code §74.251(2); TRJA 16.1(c)(3).

4. Cases that have been transferred by the judicial panel on multidistrict litigation to a district court for consolidated pretrial proceedings under Gov't Code §§74.161-74.164. Gov't Code §74.251(3); TRJA 16.1(c)(4). See "Motion to Transfer to Multidistrict Litigation Pretrial Court," ch. 5-G, p. 355.

§4. MOTION FOR ADDITIONAL RESOURCES

§4.1 By party. Any party to a case can file a motion for additional resources. Gov't Code §74.253(a); TRJA 16.6(a).

    1. In writing. A party's motion for additional resources must be in writing. TRJA 16.6(a).

    2. Grounds. The motion for additional resources must state the following:

        (1) How the case involves or is likely to involve considerations that justify additional resources. TRJA 16.6(a)(1). See "Factors to consider," §5.1.1, p. 361.

        (2) What additional resources will promote the just and efficient conduct of the case. TRJA 16.6(a)(2). For the additional resources available, see "Available resources," §4.3, this page.

        (3) When the requested resources are needed. TRJA 16.6(a)(3).

        (4) Whether all the parties to the case agree to the motion. TRJA 16.6(a)(4).

    3. Deadline. TRJA 16.6(a) does not provide a deadline for filing a motion for additional resources. A party should, however, file the motion as soon as possible after learning that the case involves or is likely to involve considerations that justify additional resources. See "Factors to consider," §5.1.1, p. 361.

§4.2 On court's initiative. The trial court, on its own initiative, can determine whether a case requires additional resources. Gov't Code §74.253(a); TRJA 16.6(b); *see also* TRJA 16.2(d) ("trial court" means the judge of the court in which a case is filed or assigned). See "Trial-court action," §5.1, p. 361. For the additional resources available, see "Available resources," §4.3, this page.

§4.3 Available resources. The additional resources that can be made available are the following:

1. The assignment of an active or retired judge, subject to the consent of the trial court. Gov't Code §74.254(d)(1); TRJA 16.5(a).

NOTE

Because the TRJA 16 procedures are not exclusive, judges can still be assigned under the general provisions of Gov't Code §§74.052-74.062. TRJA 16 cmt. However, a judge who was defeated in the last primary or general election in which she was seeking reelection cannot be assigned to a case under Gov't Code §74.254(d). See Gov't Code §74.254(e) (judge to whom Gov't Code §74.053(d) applies cannot be assigned); see also id. §74.053(d) (judge or justice defeated in last primary or general election in which she was seeking reelection cannot sit in case if either party objects). See "Objection to Assigned Judge," ch. 5-C, §3, p. 326.

⭐

2. Legal, administrative, or clerical personnel. Gov't Code §74.254(d)(2); TRJA 16.5(b).

3. Information and communication technology, including case-management software, video teleconferencing, and specially designed hardware or software to facilitate showing evidence to the judge or jury. Gov't Code §74.254(d)(3); TRJA 16.5(c).

4. Specialized continuing legal education. Gov't Code §74.254(d)(4); TRJA 16.5(d).

5. An associate judge. Gov't Code §74.254(d)(5); TRJA 16.5(e). See "Associate Judge," ch. 1-J, p. 76.

6. Special accommodations or furnishings for the parties. Gov't Code §74.254(d)(6); TRJA 16.5(f).

7. Other services or items necessary to try the case. Gov't Code §74.254(d)(7); TRJA 16.5(g).

8. Any other appropriate resources. Gov't Code §74.254(d)(8); TRJA 16.5(h).

§5. DETERMINING WHETHER ADDITIONAL RESOURCES ARE NECESSARY

§5.1 Trial-court action. The trial court, on a party's motion or its own initiative, must determine whether a case requires additional resources. Gov't Code §74.253(a); TRJA 16.6(b).

1. Factors to consider. In determining whether a case requires additional resources, the trial court may consider whether the case involves or is likely to involve any of the following:

(1) A large number of parties separately represented by counsel. Gov't Code §74.252(b)(1); TRJA 16.4(a).

(2) Coordination with related actions pending in one or more courts in other Texas counties or in one or more U.S. district courts. Gov't Code §74.252(b)(2); TRJA 16.4(b).

(3) Numerous pretrial motions that present difficult or novel legal issues that will be time-consuming to resolve. Gov't Code §74.252(b)(3); TRJA 16.4(c).

(4) A large number of witnesses or substantial documentary evidence. Gov't Code §74.252(b)(4); TRJA 16.4(d).

(5) Substantial postjudgment supervision. Gov't Code §74.252(b)(5); TRJA 16.4(e).

(6) A trial that will last more than four weeks. Gov't Code §74.252(b)(6); TRJA 16.4(f).

(7) A substantial additional burden on the trial court's docket and the resources available to hear the case. Gov't Code §74.252(b)(7); TRJA 16.4(g).

2. Optional hearing. The trial court has discretion whether to conduct an evidentiary hearing to determine if additional resources are required. Gov't Code §74.253(a). The court may direct the parties to attend a conference to provide information to help the court make the determination. *Id.*

3. Request for additional resources. If the trial court determines that additional resources are needed, it must do the following:

(1) **Prepare request.** The trial court must prepare a written request describing the case, what additional resources are needed, and why the resources are needed. TRJA 16.6(c)(1); *see* Gov't Code §74.253(b)(2). For the additional resources available, see "Available resources," §4.3, p. 360.

(2) **Submit request.** The trial court must submit the request to the presiding judge. TRJA 16.6(c)(2); *see* Gov't Code §74.253(b)(1).

(3) **Notify JCAR clerk.** The trial court must mail or e-mail a copy of the request to the JCAR clerk. TRJA 16.6(c)(3); *see* TRJA 16.2(b). On receiving the request, the JCAR clerk must send a copy to the JCAR. TRJA 16.6(d); *see also* TRJA 16.3(b) (JCAR clerk must file any requests for additional resources).

★

§5.2 Review of request by presiding judge. On receipt of the trial court's request for additional resources, the presiding judge must review the request. TRJA 16.7(a). In reviewing the request, the presiding judge can consider the same factors that the trial court considered in determining that additional resources were necessary. *See* TRJA 16.4. See "Factors to consider," §5.1.1, p. 361. The presiding judge's options depend on whether she agrees with the trial court's determination.

1. Agrees with trial court. If the presiding judge agrees with the trial court that additional resources are necessary, she must do one of the following:

(1) Use existing resources. The presiding judge can use resources previously allotted to the presiding judge, if the resources are permitted for the requested purpose. TRJA 16.7(a)(1); *see* Gov't Code §74.253(c)(1).

(2) Submit request to JCAR. If there are not enough existing resources at the presiding judge's disposal or the previously allotted resources are not permitted to be used for the requested purpose, the presiding judge can submit a request to the JCAR for additional resources. *See* Gov't Code §74.253(c)(2); TRJA 16.7(a)(2); *see also* TRJA 16.3(b) (JCAR clerk must file any requests for additional resources). See "Review of request by JCAR," §5.3, this page.

2. Does not agree with trial court. If the presiding judge does not agree with the trial court that additional resources are necessary, she can deny the request for additional resources. *See* Gov't Code §74.253(c); TRJA 16.7(a), (c).

§5.3 Review of request by JCAR. If the JCAR receives a request for additional resources from the presiding judge, it must determine whether the case requires additional resources. Gov't Code §74.254(c); TRJA 16.7(b). The OCA must provide the JCAR with staff, meeting facilities, or technology if necessary to help the JCAR determine whether additional resources are required. TRJA 16.3(a)(1); *see* Gov't Code §74.254(b). In reviewing the request, the JCAR can consider the same factors that the trial court and the presiding judge considered in determining that additional resources were necessary. *See* TRJA 16.4. See "Factors to consider," §5.1.1, p. 361. The JCAR's options depend on whether it agrees with the presiding judge's determination.

1. Agrees with presiding judge. If the JCAR agrees with the presiding judge that additional resources are necessary, it can make available whatever resources it deems necessary or appropriate. Gov't Code §74.254(c); TRJA 16.7(b).

(1) Additional resources. For the additional resources available, see "Available resources," §4.3, p. 360.

(2) Cost limitations. The JCAR cannot provide additional resources in an amount that exceeds the amount appropriated for that purpose. Gov't Code §74.254(f). Additional resources are subject to the availability of (1) appropriations made by the Legislature or through budget execution authority or other budget adjustment methods or (2) funds provided by grants or donations. TRJA 16.11(b); *see* Gov't Code §74.254(c). The OCA must request appropriations from the Legislature if necessary to help the JCAR provide additional resources. TRJA 16.3(a)(2).

2. Does not agree with presiding judge. If the JCAR does not agree with the presiding judge that additional resources are necessary, it can deny the request for additional resources. *See* Gov't Code §74.254(c); TRJA 16.7(b), (c).

§6. NOTICE OF ACTION TAKEN ON REQUEST FOR ADDITIONAL RESOURCES

§6.1 To trial court within 15 days after receiving request. Within 15 days after the presiding judge and the JCAR clerk receive the copy of the trial court's request for additional resources under TRJA 16.6(c), either the presiding judge or the JCAR clerk must notify the trial court of any action on the request, including the inability to take action. TRJA 16.6(d). See "Request for additional resources," §5.1.3, p. 361. That is, within 15 days after the presiding judge and the JCAR clerk receive the copy of the trial court's request, the trial court must receive notice of one of the following: (1) the presiding judge has approved or denied the request, (2) the presiding judge submitted

─────────────────────────────── ★ ───────────────────────────────

the request to the JCAR and it has approved or denied the request, (3) the presiding judge is still reviewing the request, (4) the presiding judge submitted the request to the JCAR and it is still reviewing the request, or (5) the presiding judge or the JCAR has been unable to take any action on the request. *See* TRJA 16.6(d), 16.7(a), (b).

§6.2 To JCAR clerk after approval or denial of request.

1. By presiding judge. The presiding judge must notify the JCAR clerk in writing once she approves or denies the request for additional resources under TRJA 16.7(a)(1). TRJA 16.7(c).

2. By JCAR. The JCAR must notify the JCAR clerk in writing once it approves or denies the request for additional resources under TRJA 16.7(a)(2). TRJA 16.7(c).

§6.3 To trial court after approval or denial of request.
After receiving notice from the presiding judge or the JCAR approving or denying the request for additional resources, the JCAR clerk must transmit a copy to the affected trial court. TRJA 16.7(c).

NOTE

The 15-day notice required under TRJA 16.6(d) and the notice required under TRJA 16.7(c) may overlap if the presiding judge or the JCAR makes a final decision before the 15-day deadline expires. That is, if the presiding judge or the JCAR has approved or denied the trial court's request within 15 days after receiving the request, the notice given to the trial court under TRJA 16.7(c) will likely satisfy the 15-day notice requirement under TRJA 16.6(d). But if the presiding judge or the JCAR takes longer than 15 days to reach a decision, the trial court must receive notice of both (1) the status of the request within 15 days under TRJA 16.6(d) and (2) the final decision under TRJA 16.7(c). Regardless of when a final decision is reached, within 15 days after the presiding judge and the JCAR clerk receive the copy of the trial court's request, the trial court must receive notice of the status of the request. See "To trial court within 15 days after receiving request," §6.1, p. 362.

---

§7. IMPLEMENTING DECISION ON REQUEST FOR ADDITIONAL RESOURCES

§7.1 Filing approval or denial of request.
The JCAR clerk must file any written determination by the presiding judge or the JCAR on the request for additional resources. TRJA 16.3(b).

§7.2 Filing cost report.
If additional resources are allocated under TRJA 16.7, the OCA must prepare and file with the JCAR clerk a report stating the additional resources and their cost. TRJA 16.3(c).

NOTE

The costs for additional resources will be paid by the State and cannot be taxed against any party or against the county where the case is pending. Gov't Code §74.255; TRJA 16.11(a).

---

§7.3 Providing resources to trial court.

1. Determination by presiding judge. If the presiding judge determines that a case requires additional resources and the judge can use resources previously allotted to her, she must provide those approved additional resources to the trial court. *See* TRJA 16.7(a)(1).

2. Determination by JCAR. If the JCAR determines that a case requires additional resources, the presiding judge and the OCA must cooperate with the trial court or its designee in providing the approved additional resources. TRJA 16.8; *see* TRJA 16.3(a)(3) (OCA must help JCAR by providing additional resources approved by JCAR to trial court).

§8. EFFECT OF MOTION FOR ADDITIONAL RESOURCES

§8.1 Jurisdiction.
Filing a motion for additional resources does not deprive the trial court of jurisdiction or suspend any proceedings or orders of the court. TRJA 16.9(a).

★

§8.2 No stay or continuance. Filing a motion for additional resources is not grounds for a stay or continuance of the proceedings while the motion or request is being considered by the trial court, the presiding judge, or the JCAR. Gov't Code §74.256; *see* TRJA 16.9(b).

§9. REVIEW

A determination made by a trial court, a presiding judge, or the JCAR of a motion or request for additional resources is not appealable or subject to review by mandamus. Gov't Code §74.257; TRJA 16.10.

I. MOTIONS FOR SEVERANCE & SEPARATE TRIALS

§1. GENERAL

§1.1 Rules. TRCP 41 (severance), TRCP 174(b) (separate trials). See CPRC §41.009 (bifurcated trial for exemplary damages).

§1.2 Purpose. The rules permit a court to divide a lawsuit into separate lawsuits or separate parts.

§1.3 Forms. *O'Connor's Texas Civil Forms* (2012), FORMS 5H.

§1.4 Other references. Cunningham & Hutchinson, *Bifurcated Trials: Creative Uses of the Moriel Decision*, 46 Baylor L.Rev. 807 (1994); *O'Connor's Texas Causes of Action* (2013) (*O'Connor's Texas COA*); *O'Connor's Texas Civil Appeals* (2012) (*O'Connor's Texas Appeals*).

§2. DISTINCTION BETWEEN MOTIONS FOR SEVERANCE & FOR SEPARATE TRIALS

§2.1 Severance. When a court grants a motion for severance, it divides a lawsuit into two or more independent lawsuits, each of which will terminate with a separate, final, enforceable, and appealable judgment. See "Motion for Severance," §3, this page.

§2.2 Separate trials – bifurcation. When the court orders separate trials under TRCP 174, the court divides the case into two or more parts, which are tried separately to the same jury and resolved by one final judgment. An order for a separate trial leaves the lawsuit intact but enables the court to determine some issues separately from others. See "Motion for Separate (Bifurcated) Trial," §4, p. 367. For a separate trial for exemplary damages under CPRC chapter 41, see "Motion to Bifurcate Exemplary Damages," §5, p. 369.

NOTE

For the rules that govern joining and separating permissive claims, see "Permissive Joinder of Claims," ch. 2-E, §7, p. 134.

---

§3. MOTION FOR SEVERANCE

A motion to sever asks the court to divide a lawsuit into independent suits that may be resolved separately. A severance splits a single suit into two or more independent lawsuits, with each resulting in a separate judgment. *Van Dyke v. Boswell, O'Toole, Davis & Pickering*, 697 S.W.2d 381, 383 (Tex.1985). Courts sever cases primarily to avoid prejudice, promote justice, and increase convenience. *In re State*, 355 S.W.3d 611, 613 (Tex.2011); *F.F.P. Oper. Partners v. Duenez*, 237 S.W.3d 680, 693 (Tex.2007); *Guaranty Fed. Sav. Bank v. Horseshoe Oper. Co.*, 793 S.W.2d 652, 658 (Tex.1990). See *O'Connor's Texas Forms*, FORM 5H:1.

PRACTICE TIP

*In a motion to sever, you can ask the trial court, as an alternative, to grant a separate trial for the claim or issue that you want severed. TRCP 174(b). A severable cause of action can be tried separately under TRCP 174(b). **Kansas Univ. Endowment Ass'n v. King**, 350 S.W.2d 11, 19 (Tex.1961). See "Motion for Separate (Bifurcated) Trial," §4, p. 367.*

★

§3.1 Motion. For allegations supporting severance, the movant should review *Liberty Nat'l Fire Ins. v. Akin*, 927 S.W.2d 627, 629 (Tex.1996), and *Guaranty Fed. Sav. Bank v. Horseshoe Oper. Co.*, 793 S.W.2d 652, 658 (Tex. 1990). The motion should allege the following:

1. More than one cause. The controversy involves more than one cause of action. *In re State*, 355 S.W.3d 611, 614 (Tex.2011); *F.F.P. Oper. Partners v. Duenez*, 237 S.W.3d 680, 693 (Tex.2007); *Liberty Nat'l*, 927 S.W.2d at 629; *Guaranty Fed.*, 793 S.W.2d at 658; *e.g.*, *McGuire v. Commercial Un. Ins.*, 431 S.W.2d 347, 351 (Tex. 1968) (one P's wrongful-death suit and other P's personal-injury suit); *Black v. Smith*, 956 S.W.2d 72, 75 (Tex. App.—Houston [14th Dist.] 1997, orig. proceeding) (personal-injury claims and claims against D's insurer for invasion of privacy); *U.S. Fire Ins. v. Millard*, 847 S.W.2d 668, 672 (Tex.App.—Houston [1st Dist.] 1993, orig. proceeding) (claims for uninsured-motorist benefits and bad-faith insurance claims).

2. Independent claim. The severed claim could be independently asserted in a separate lawsuit. *In re State*, 355 S.W.3d at 614; *Duenez*, 237 S.W.3d at 693; *Liberty Nat'l*, 927 S.W.2d at 629; *Guaranty Fed.*, 793 S.W.2d at 658. To be severable, the causes must be capable of being brought as separate suits with separate, final judgments. *Martinez v. Humble Sand & Gravel, Inc.*, 875 S.W.2d 311, 312 (Tex.1994); *e.g.*, *H.E. Butt Grocery Co. v. Currier*, 885 S.W.2d 175, 177 (Tex.App.—Corpus Christi 1994, no writ) (discovery order could not be severed because it was not a claim).

3. Not interwoven. The severed cause is not so interwoven with the remaining action that it involves the same facts and issues. *In re State*, 355 S.W.3d at 614; *Duenez*, 237 S.W.3d at 693; *Liberty Nat'l*, 927 S.W.2d at 629; *Guaranty Fed.*, 793 S.W.2d at 658; *e.g.*, *Pilgrim Enters. v. Maryland Cas. Co.*, 24 S.W.3d 488, 491-92 (Tex. App.—Houston [1st Dist.] 2000, no pet.) (severance of P's claims was proper because insurer's duties to defend and to indemnify are not inextricably interwoven).

§3.2 Objection. To object to a motion to sever, the party must make a specific and timely objection. TRAP 33.1(a)(1); *Shank, Irwin, Conant & Williamson v. Durant, Mankoff, Davis, Wolens & Francis*, 748 S.W.2d 494, 501 (Tex.App.—Dallas 1988, no writ).

§3.3 Hearing & evidence. It is unclear whether the trial court should receive and consider evidence in ruling on a severance. In *Jones v. Ray*, 886 S.W.2d 817, 820 (Tex.App.—Houston [1st Dist.] 1994, orig. proceeding), the court held that the trial court should look exclusively to the live pleadings on file and should not consider evidence. Other courts have made statements indicating that evidence should be considered. *See, e.g.*, *Allstate Ins. v. Hunter*, 865 S.W.2d 189, 194 (Tex.App.—Corpus Christi 1993, orig. proceeding) (D did not carry its burden of proof on motion to sever); *Progressive Cty. Mut. Ins. v. Parks*, 856 S.W.2d 776, 780 (Tex.App.—El Paso 1993, orig. proceeding) (pleadings alone are insufficient to require severance); *Geophysical Data Processing Ctr., Inc. v. Cruz*, 576 S.W.2d 666, 667 (Tex.App.—Beaumont 1978, no writ) (propriety of severance does not always depend on pleadings).

§3.4 Order on motion to sever. Under TRCP 41, the trial court has broad discretion to sever a lawsuit into separate suits. *Liberty Nat'l Fire Ins. v. Akin*, 927 S.W.2d 627, 629 (Tex.1996); *Guaranty Fed. Sav. Bank v. Horseshoe Oper. Co.*, 793 S.W.2d 652, 658 (Tex.1990). However, the trial court's discretion is not unlimited. *Womack v. Berry*, 291 S.W.2d 677, 683 (Tex.1956); *see, e.g.*, *In re Union Carbide Corp.*, 273 S.W.3d 152, 156 (Tex.2008) (court should not order severance before ruling on motion to strike intervention). The court must exercise "a sound and legal discretion within limits created by the circumstances of the particular case." *Cf. Womack*, 291 S.W.2d at 683 (separate trials under TRCP 174(b)).

1. Immediately effective. The order severing part of a lawsuit is effective when it is signed. *McRoberts v. Ryals*, 863 S.W.2d 450, 452-53 (Tex.1993). When a lawsuit is severed, the clerk assigns the severed cause a new cause number. If the clerk delays in assigning a cause number, it does not delay the effectiveness of the severance, but it can sometimes cause problems for the parties. *See id.* at 453 n.3. The trial court should assign a cause number to the severed action at the same time it signs the order of severance. *Id.* As an alternative, the trial court can condition the severance order's effectiveness on the clerk's assignment of a cause number and the party's payment of fees for the severance. *Id.*

─────────────────────── ✦ ───────────────────────

2. Separate file. The clerk does not need to create a separate physical file for a severed cause of action. *McRoberts*, 863 S.W.2d at 453 n.4; *see Darden v. Kitz Corp.*, 997 S.W.2d 388, 392 (Tex.App.—Beaumont 1999, pet. denied).

§3.5 Deadline for motion to sever. The trial court cannot sever a case after the case has been submitted to the trier of fact. TRCP 41; *State Dept. of Hwys. & Pub. Transp. v. Cotner*, 845 S.W.2d 818, 819 (Tex.1993) (jury trial); *In re El Paso Cty. Hosp. Dist.*, 979 S.W.2d 10, 12 (Tex.App.—El Paso 1998, orig. proceeding) (nonjury trial on stipulated facts). Despite the prohibition in TRCP 41 against postsubmission severances, the trial court may order a partial new trial. *See* TRCP 320. TRCP 320 is an exception to TRCP 41. *Cotner*, 845 S.W.2d at 819. See "Partial new trial," ch. 10-B, §8.3, p. 794.

§3.6 Severance proper but not required.

1. Interlocutory summary judgment. The trial court may sever from the rest of the lawsuit a partial summary judgment granted on a claim or defense or granted to one of multiple parties, thus allowing the summary judgment to be appealed. *See, e.g., Cherokee Water Co. v. Forderhause*, 641 S.W.2d 522, 525 (Tex.1982) (SJ on suit to declare rights under a deed could be severed from suit to reform deed); *Pilgrim Enters. v. Maryland Cas. Co.*, 24 S.W.3d 488, 491-92 (Tex.App.—Houston [1st Dist.] 2000, no pet.) (SJ on duty-to-defend claims severed from remaining claims); *Guidry v. National Freight, Inc.*, 944 S.W.2d 807, 812 (Tex.App.—Austin 1997, no writ) (SJ in favor of one D severed from claims against other Ds). The trial court cannot be forced to sever an interlocutory summary judgment. *Marshall v. Harris*, 764 S.W.2d 34, 35 (Tex.App.—Houston [1st Dist.] 1989, orig. proceeding).

PRACTICE TIP
*If you discover on appeal that what you thought was a final summary judgment is really a partial judgment, you may be able to convert it to a final summary judgment under the authority of TRAP 27.2 while the appeal is abated. For the procedure, see **Iacono v. Lyons**, 6 S.W.3d 715, 717 (Tex.App.—Houston [1st Dist.] 1999, no pet.).*

---

2. Attorney fees. The trial court should not sever a claim for attorney fees without distinguishing between a claim for attorney fees that is an independent lawsuit (e.g., an attorney's suit against the client for not paying fees) and a claim that is dependent on another claim (e.g., claim for attorney fees as part of a suit on a note). If the claim for attorney fees is an independent cause of action, it may be severed and resolved by a separate judgment. If the claim is dependent on another claim, it should not be severed because it cannot be resolved by a separate judgment. Trial courts, however, rarely make this distinction. Though it cannot be severed, a dependent claim for attorney fees can be bifurcated for a separate trial and all issues resolved by one judgment. See "Motion for Separate (Bifurcated) Trial," §4, p. 367.

3. Third-party action. The court may sever a third party's claims from the rest of the suit. *See, e.g., Guaranty Fed. Sav. Bank v. Horseshoe Oper. Co.*, 793 S.W.2d 652, 658 (Tex.1990) (fraud severed from wrongful dishonor of check).

4. Permissive counterclaim. The trial court may sever a permissive counterclaim. *See* TRCP 41 (any claim may be severed); *see, e.g., Straughan v. Houston Citizens Bank & Trust Co.*, 580 S.W.2d 29, 33 (Tex.App.—Houston [1st Dist.] 1979, no writ) (trial court did not abuse discretion in severing permissive counterclaim). For the rules governing permissive counterclaims, see "Permissive Joinder of Claims," ch. 2-E, §7, p. 134.

5. Separate cause of action. The trial court may, and in some cases must, sever a lawsuit involving two or more separate and distinct causes of action.

§3.7 Severance required. If the joint trial of multiple claims will prejudice one of the claims, the trial court must either sever the lawsuit into separate trials or bifurcate the trial (see "Motion for Separate (Bifurcated) Trial," §4, p. 367). This type of prejudice occurs when evidence is admissible on one claim but is prejudicial to the other claim. *Liberty Nat'l Fire Ins. v. Akin*, 927 S.W.2d 627, 630 (Tex.1996). For example, when a plaintiff sues an insurer

★

for breach of contract and for bad faith, evidence of a settlement offer could prejudice the insurer's defense of the coverage dispute. *Id.*; *U.S. Fire Ins. v. Millard*, 847 S.W.2d 668, 672-73 (Tex.App.—Houston [1st Dist.] 1993, orig. proceeding); *State Farm Mut. Auto. Ins. v. Wilborn*, 835 S.W.2d 260, 261-62 (Tex.App.—Houston [14th Dist.] 1992, orig. proceeding). *But see Allstate Ins. v. Evins*, 894 S.W.2d 847, 850 (Tex.App.—Corpus Christi 1995, orig. proceeding) (decision whether to sever contract and bad-faith claims against insurer when evidence of settlement offer could prejudice insurer's defense should be left to trial court's discretion).

§3.8 **Severance not permitted.** When a party makes a proper objection, severance is not permitted in the following instances:

1. **Indivisible injury.** The court cannot sever claims against several defendants when the injury is indivisible. *Landers v. East Tex. Salt Water Disposal Co.*, 248 S.W.2d 731, 734 (Tex.1952). *But see Morgan v. Compugraphic Corp.*, 675 S.W.2d 729, 733-34 (Tex.1984) (court did not abuse its discretion when it severed case involving indivisible injury; any error in severing would have been harmless). When the torts of two or more parties cause an indivisible injury, the claims should be tried together. If not, each tortfeasor could make the "empty-chair" argument. *Jones v. Ray*, 886 S.W.2d 817, 821-22 (Tex.App.—Houston [1st Dist.] 1994, orig. proceeding).

2. **Dividing a cause of action.** The court cannot sever a single cause of action into multiple claims. *E.g.*, *Pierce v. Reynolds*, 329 S.W.2d 76, 78 & n.1 (Tex.1959) (court should not have divided one claim into two lawsuits based on dates the damages accrued); *Duncan v. Calhoun Cty. Nav. Dist.*, 28 S.W.3d 707, 711 (Tex.App.—Corpus Christi 2000, pet. denied) (in condemnation suit, issues of right-to-take and just compensation are components of one claim); *Ryland Grp. v. White*, 723 S.W.2d 160, 162 (Tex.App.—Houston [1st Dist.] 1986, orig. proceeding) (in personal-injury suit, negligence cannot be severed from contribution); *Garrison v. Texas Commerce Bank*, 560 S.W.2d 451, 453 (Tex.App.—Houston [1st Dist.] 1977, writ ref'd n.r.e.) (in divorce suit, property issues cannot be severed from divorce). However, an erroneous severance is waived if the party does not object. *See Pierce*, 329 S.W.2d at 78.

3. **Compulsory counterclaim.** The court cannot sever a compulsory counterclaim that arises from the same transaction or occurrence as the issue in the main suit. *E.g.*, *Rucker v. Bank One Tex.*, 36 S.W.3d 649, 651-52 (Tex.App.—Waco 2000, pet. denied) (counterclaim for fraudulent inducement was intertwined with suit for breach of contract); *Fuentes v. McFadden*, 825 S.W.2d 772, 779-80 (Tex.App.—El Paso 1992, no writ) (same); *Mathis v. Bill De La Garza & Assocs.*, 778 S.W.2d 105, 106 (Tex.App.—Texarkana 1989, no writ) (suit for payment on a contract was intertwined with counterclaim for breach of contract). *But see In re Occidental Permian Ltd.*, ___ S.W.3d ___ (Tex.App.—Amarillo 2003, orig. proceeding) (No. 07-03-0016-CV; 4-7-03) (undesignated op.) (as long as court complies with TRCP 41, it is not error to sever and proceed with counterclaim). For the rules governing compulsory counterclaims, see "Compulsory-counterclaim rule," ch. 2-E, §6.1, p. 131.

4. **Same liability.** The court cannot sever a cause of action against one defendant from a cause of action against another defendant when the defendants are alleged to have the same liability. *See, e.g.*, *McRoberts v. Tesoro S&L Ass'n*, 781 S.W.2d 705, 706 (Tex.App.—San Antonio 1989, writ denied) (court cannot sever cause of action against maker of note—the partnership—from cause of action against guarantors—the individual partners).

5. **Prejudice.** The court cannot sever a case if separate trials of the claims would prejudice one of the parties. *See, e.g.*, *In re State*, 355 S.W.3d 611, 614 (Tex.2011) (in suit for condemnation of tract of land, Ds split property into eight parcels; suit could not be severed into eight cases without causing great inconvenience and prejudice to P).

§4. MOTION FOR SEPARATE (BIFURCATED) TRIAL

The purpose of a motion for separate trials on issues or between the parties is to avoid prejudice, promote justice, and further convenience of the parties and the court. *In re Ethyl Corp.*, 975 S.W.2d 606, 610 (Tex.1998); *Womack v. Berry*, 291 S.W.2d 677, 683 (Tex.1956). A separate trial on issues leaves the lawsuit intact but bifurcates the case into two or more parts that are tried separately to the same jury. *See, e.g.*, *Transportation Ins. v. Moriel*, 879 S.W.2d

⎯⎯⎯⎯⎯⎯⎯⎯⎯⎯ ✯ ⎯⎯⎯⎯⎯⎯⎯⎯⎯⎯

10, 30 (Tex.1994) (liability and damages should have been tried separately). See *O'Connor's Texas Forms*, FORM 5H:4. Although TRCP 174(b) gives the trial court the power to conduct bifurcated trials, the courts generally should not try cases piecemeal. *Moriel*, 879 S.W.2d at 30 n.29.

§4.1 Motion. TRCP 174(b) permits the trial court to bifurcate the trial of any claim, cross-claim, counterclaim, third-party claim, or separate issue.

1. Grounds in most cases. The trial court may bifurcate the case for convenience or to avoid prejudice. TRCP 174(b); *Tarrant Reg'l Water Dist. v. Gragg*, 151 S.W.3d 546, 556 (Tex.2004). The following are some examples of when bifurcation is proper: • In a suit against insurance company in which there was a settlement offer, bifurcated trial on contractual and bad-faith claims. *See Liberty Nat'l Fire Ins. v. Akin*, 927 S.W.2d 627, 630 (Tex.1996). • Bifurcated exemplary damages from the issues of liability and actual damages. *Transportation Ins. v. Moriel*, 879 S.W.2d 10, 30 (Tex.1994); *see* CPRC §41.009. See "Motion to Bifurcate Exemplary Damages," §5, p. 369. • Bifurcated trials on the issues of marriage and divorce. *See Winfield v. Renfro*, 821 S.W.2d 640, 652 (Tex.App.—Houston [1st Dist.] 1991, writ denied). • In a suit for recovery under uninsured-motorist provision of contract, bifurcated trial on issue of whether the plaintiff released the insurance company. *Johnson v. State Farm Mut. Auto. Ins.*, 762 S.W.2d 267, 268-69 (Tex.App.—San Antonio 1988, writ denied). • Bifurcated trial on defendant's issue of limitations from plaintiff's personal-injury suit. *Phipps v. Miller*, 597 S.W.2d 458, 460 (Tex.App.—Dallas 1980, writ ref'd n.r.e.).

NOTE

In a personal-injury case, the trial court cannot bifurcate the trial on liability from the issue of actual damages. Iley v. Hughes, 311 S.W.2d 648, 651 (Tex.1958).

---

2. Grounds in mass torts. For mass-tort litigation (e.g., asbestos litigation), the Supreme Court expanded on the TRCP 174(b) grounds (convenience and prejudice) by adopting the "Maryland factors." *See In re Ethyl Corp.*, 975 S.W.2d 606, 610-11 (Tex.1998) (Maryland factors useful in determining whether to consolidate or order separate trials).

§4.2 Response. If any party objects to a motion to bifurcate, the party must make a specific and timely objection or it waives error. *See* TRAP 33.1(a)(1); *Winkle v. Tullos*, 917 S.W.2d 304, 312-13 (Tex.App.—Houston [14th Dist.] 1995, writ denied). The party opposing a motion to bifurcate should file a response stating its objections. See *O'Connor's Texas Forms*, FORM 5H:5. Some of the objections a party may assert are the following:

1. Bifurcating the trial will not be convenient. *See Kaiser Found. Health Plan v. Bridewell*, 946 S.W.2d 642, 645 (Tex.App.—Waco 1997, orig. proceeding).

2. Bifurcating the trial will not avoid prejudice. *See id.* at 645-46; *Greater Houston Transp. v. Zrubeck*, 850 S.W.2d 579, 587 (Tex.App.—Corpus Christi 1993, writ denied).

3. The court should not try the case piecemeal. *Transportation Ins. v. Moriel*, 879 S.W.2d 10, 30 n.29 (Tex.1994).

4. Liability and damages are elements of an indivisible cause of action and cannot be tried separately. *Iley v. Hughes*, 311 S.W.2d 648, 651 (Tex.1958); *Waples-Platter Co. v. Commercial Std. Ins.*, 294 S.W.2d 375, 377 (Tex. 1956).

§4.3 Hearing to bifurcate. Unless there is a reason to present evidence, a hearing for the receipt of evidence is not necessary. The motion can be resolved either by submission or at a hearing for argument only.

§4.4 One judgment. After one part of a bifurcated case is tried, any order the court signs is interlocutory and not appealable; the court cannot sign a final, appealable judgment until all parts of the case have been tried. *Hall v. City of Austin*, 450 S.W.2d 836, 838 (Tex.1970).

★

§5. MOTION TO BIFURCATE EXEMPLARY DAMAGES

§5.1 Defendant's motion. Only the defendant may move to bifurcate the issue of exemplary damages from the suit. CPRC §41.009(a). When there are multiple defendants, any one of them may make the motion. *Id.* §41.009(b). See *O'Connor's Texas Forms*, FORM 5H:6.

1. Deadline. The defendant must make a motion to bifurcate the trial before the voir dire examination of the jury or the time specified in a pretrial order. CPRC §41.009(a).

2. Grounds. The motion should state that the defendant requests a bifurcated trial on exemplary damages, as provided by CPRC §41.009(c)(1).

§5.2 Plaintiff's response. If the defendant makes a timely request under CPRC §41.009, the trial court must grant the motion. The only ground for objecting is that the defendant's motion is untimely. *See* CPRC §41.009(a).

§5.3 Trial procedure. For more information about the jury questions and the burdens of proof for the issues in an exemplary-damages case, see *O'Connor's Texas COA*, "Bifurcated Trial on Exemplary Damages," ch. 42-B, §9, p. 1332.

1. Phase 1. In Phase 1, the jury will resolve the issues of liability for actual damages, the amount of actual damages, and liability for exemplary damages. CPRC §41.009(c); *Transportation Ins. v. Moriel*, 879 S.W.2d 10, 30 (Tex.1994). The jury is presented with evidence and jury questions on all the issues except the amount of exemplary damages. *Moriel*, 879 S.W.2d at 30. Evidence that is relevant only to the amount of exemplary damages is not admissible during the first phase of a bifurcated trial. CPRC §41.011(b).

2. Phase 2. If the jury found the defendant was liable for actual damages, awarded actual damages, and was unanimous in finding liability for exemplary damages, the jury will determine the amount of exemplary damages in Phase 2. *See* CPRC §§41.003(d), 41.009(d). The jury is given questions to determine the proper amount of exemplary damages, considering the evidence presented during both parts of the trial. *Moriel*, 879 S.W.2d at 30. In determining the amount of exemplary damages, the jury must consider evidence relating to the following issues: (1) the nature of the wrong, (2) the character of the conduct involved, (3) the degree of culpability of the wrongdoer, (4) the situation and sensibilities of the parties concerned, (5) the extent to which the conduct offends a public sense of justice and propriety, and (6) the net worth of the defendant. CPRC §41.011(a). Some courts have allowed other factors, not mentioned in CPRC §41.004(a), to be submitted to the jury, including (1) the frequency of the wrongs committed, (2) the plaintiff's attorney fees and other damages, and (3) the size of the award needed to deter similar wrongs in the future. See *O'Connor's Texas COA*, "Proving Aggravated Conduct," ch. 42-B, §6, p. 1324. A claimant who elects to have her recovery multiplied under another statute cannot be awarded exemplary damages. CPRC §41.004(b).

§5.4 Plaintiff's burden.

1. Preponderance of the evidence. The Phase 1 issues of liability for and the amount of actual damages must be decided by a preponderance of the evidence. See *O'Connor's Texas COA*, "Issues on actual damages," ch. 42-B, §9.2.1(1), p. 1332. "Preponderance of the evidence" means the greater weight and degree of credible evidence. *Upjohn Co. v. Freeman*, 847 S.W.2d 589, 591 (Tex.App.—Dallas 1992, no writ).

2. Clear & convincing evidence. The Phase 1 issue of liability for exemplary damages and the Phase 2 issue of the amount of exemplary damages must be decided by clear and convincing evidence. To decide liability, the plaintiff must prove in Phase 1 that the harm for which it seeks recovery of exemplary damages resulted from fraud, malice, or gross negligence. CPRC §41.003(a); *Dillard Dept. Stores v. Silva*, 148 S.W.3d 370, 372-73 (Tex. 2004); *see also* Tex. Const. art. 16, §26 (liability for exemplary damages when D causes death by willful act or omission or gross neglect). "Clear and convincing evidence" means the degree of proof that will produce in the fact-finder's mind a firm belief or conviction about the truth of the allegations. *State v. Addington*, 588 S.W.2d 569, 570 (Tex. 1979). The burden of proof cannot be shifted to the defendant or be satisfied by evidence of ordinary negligence, bad faith, or deceptive trade practice. CPRC §41.003(b).

✦

§5.5 Actual, not nominal, damages. As a rule, the plaintiff must recover actual damages; nominal damages are not sufficient to support an award of exemplary damages. CPRC §41.004(a). See *O'Connor's Texas COA*, "Actual damages required," ch. 42-B, §4.1, p. 1321. However, an award of actual damages is not required to recover exemplary damages in a wrongful-death suit brought under Labor Code §408.001 by an employee's surviving spouse or heirs for the death of the employee caused by the intentional act or omission or the gross negligence of the employer. See *Wright v. Gifford-Hill & Co.*, 725 S.W.2d 712, 714 (Tex.1987).

§5.6 Unanimous jury. The jury must render a unanimous verdict on liability for and the amount of exemplary damages. CPRC §41.003(d); TRCP 292(b). See "Exemplary-damages cases," ch. 8-K, §4.2, p. 754. The jury may render a less-than-unanimous verdict on the issues of liability for and the amount of actual damages. See "Most trials," ch. 8-K, §4.1, p. 754.

§5.7 One judgment. After a bifurcated trial under CPRC chapter 41, the trial court will enter one judgment that resolves all the issues.

§6. REVIEW

§6.1 Motion to sever.

1. No interlocutory appeal. When the trial court grants or denies a motion for severance, the order cannot be appealed until after a final judgment is rendered in the case. See *Finder v. E.L. Cheeney Co.*, 368 S.W.2d 62, 64 (Tex.App.—Beaumont 1963, no writ).

2. Regular appeal. The appellate court will not reverse an order granting a severance unless the trial court abused its discretion. *Guaranty Fed. Sav. Bank v. Horseshoe Oper. Co.*, 793 S.W.2d 652, 658 (Tex.1990). If the trial court abused its discretion, the appellate court will reverse and remand. *Nicor Expl. Co. v. Florida Gas Transmission Co.*, 911 S.W.2d 479, 482-83 (Tex.App.—Corpus Christi 1995, writ denied).

3. Mandamus. When the trial court has a duty to either grant or deny severance, it has no discretion, and its order can be reviewed by mandamus. *See, e.g.*, *Lusk v. Puryear*, 896 S.W.2d 377, 380-81 (Tex.App.—Amarillo 1995, orig. proceeding) (trial court improperly granted severance); *F.A. Richard & Assocs. v. Millard*, 856 S.W.2d 765, 767 (Tex.App.—Houston [1st Dist.] 1993, orig. proceeding) (trial court improperly denied severance). Mandamus is appropriate to review the issue of severance only when there is no adequate remedy by appeal. *E.g.*, *In re State*, 355 S.W.3d 611, 614-15 (Tex.2011) (mandamus conditionally granted); *Liberty Nat'l Fire Ins. v. Akin*, 927 S.W.2d 627, 629 (Tex.1996) (mandamus denied); *McLain v. Smith*, 899 S.W.2d 412, 414 (Tex.App.—Amarillo 1995, orig. proceeding) (same). See *O'Connor's Texas Appeals*, "Motion to sever," ch. 10-B, §4.3.15, p. 351.

4. Severance on appeal. The rules that prohibit severance by the trial court of part of a cause of action do not apply to appellate courts. Under TRCP 320 and TRAP 44.1(b), an appellate court can grant a new trial on points that affect only a part of the case if that part is clearly separable without unfairness to the parties; however, an appellate court cannot grant a new trial on damages if liability was contested. A partial new trial may be ordered despite the prohibition in TRCP 41 against postsubmission severance. *State Dept. of Hwys. & Pub. Transp. v. Cotner*, 845 S.W.2d 818, 819 (Tex.1993). An appellate court may affirm part of a case and sever part for remand, even though the trial court could not have. See TRAP 43.2(a), (d); *see, e.g.*, *Collins v. Collins*, 904 S.W.2d 792, 795 (Tex. App.—Houston [1st Dist.] 1995) (appellate court can affirm divorce and remand property issues), *writ denied*, 923 S.W.2d 569 (Tex.1996). Appellate courts regularly sever and remand the issue of attorney fees from the rest of the case, even when the attorney fees are dependent on another claim. *See, e.g.*, *Woods Expl. & Prod'g Co. v. Arkla Equip. Co.*, 528 S.W.2d 568, 571 (Tex.1975) (claim for attorney fees for suit on a note was severed on appeal); *Permian Report v. Lacy*, 817 S.W.2d 175, 178 (Tex.App.—El Paso 1991, writ denied) (claim for attorney fees for declaratory-judgment action was severed on appeal).

§6.2 Motion to bifurcate. The trial court's decision on bifurcation is reviewed for abuse of discretion. *Johnson v. State Farm Mut. Auto. Ins.*, 762 S.W.2d 267, 269 (Tex.App.—San Antonio 1988, writ denied).

★

J. JOINING PARTIES OR CLAIMS

§1. GENERAL

§1.1 Rules. TRCP 43 (interpleader), TRCP 60-61 (intervention), TRCP 174 (consolidation).

§1.2 Purpose. The rules of joinder permit additional parties and claims to be brought into a lawsuit. Joinder may be accomplished through intervention, interpleader, or consolidation.

§1.3 Forms. *O'Connor's Texas Civil Forms* (2012), FORMS 5I.

§1.4 Other references. 1 McDonald & Carlson, *Texas Civil Practice* §5.82 (2d ed. 2004 & Supp.2011-12).

§2. PETITION IN INTERVENTION

The purpose of a petition in intervention is to join a lawsuit that is already in progress. The sufficiency of the petition in intervention is tested by the allegations of fact on which the right to intervene depends. *Serna v. Webster*, 908 S.W.2d 487, 492 (Tex.App.—San Antonio 1995, no writ); *H. Tebbs, Inc. v. Silver Eagle Distribs.*, 797 S.W.2d 80, 84 (Tex.App.—Austin 1990, no writ).

§2.1 Filing the petition. The rules of pleading apply to intervenors just as they do to other parties. TRCP 61.

1. In writing. To intervene, a party must file a written pleading. *Diaz v. Attorney Gen.*, 827 S.W.2d 19, 22 (Tex.App.—Corpus Christi 1992, no writ). See *O'Connor's Texas Forms*, FORMS 5I.

2. No motion for leave. An intervenor is not required to get the court's permission to intervene. TRCP 60; *In re Union Carbide Corp.*, 273 S.W.3d 152, 154-55 (Tex.2008); *Guaranty Fed. Sav. Bank v. Horseshoe Oper. Co.*, 793 S.W.2d 652, 657 (Tex.1990); *Morgan v. City of Alvin*, 175 S.W.3d 408, 416 n.6 (Tex.App.—Houston [1st Dist.] 2004, no pet.). A nonparty may intervene in a suit as a plaintiff or a defendant without leave of court. *See* TRCP 60.

3. Interest of intervenor.

(1) Legal or equitable. The interest the intervenor asserts in the lawsuit may be legal or equitable. *Guaranty Fed.*, 793 S.W.2d at 657; *Zeifman v. Michels*, 229 S.W.3d 460, 464 (Tex.App.—Austin 2007, no pet.); *Gracida v. Tagle*, 946 S.W.2d 504, 506 (Tex.App.—Corpus Christi 1997, orig. proceeding).

(2) Not contingent or remote. The interest must be more than a mere contingent or remote interest. *Zeifman*, 229 S.W.3d at 464; *Intermarque Auto. Prods. v. Feldman*, 21 S.W.3d 544, 549 (Tex.App.—Texarkana 2000, no pet.).

(3) Justiciable interest. The intervenor must have a justiciable interest in the suit. *In re Union Carbide*, 273 S.W.3d at 154-55; *Henderson Edwards Wilson, L.L.P. v. Toledo*, 244 S.W.3d 851, 853 (Tex.App.—Dallas 2008, no pet.). A party has a justiciable interest in the suit when its interests will be affected by the litigation. *Law Offices of Windle Turley, P.C. v. Ghiasinejad*, 109 S.W.3d 68, 70 (Tex.App.—Fort Worth 2003, no pet.); *see In re Union Carbide*, 273 S.W.3d at 155. That is, a party can intervene if it (1) could have brought all or part of the same suit in its own name or (2) would have been able to defeat all or part of the recovery if the suit had been filed against it. *Guaranty Fed.*, 793 S.W.2d at 657; *e.g.*, *Jenkins v. Entergy Corp.*, 187 S.W.3d 785, 796-97 (Tex.App.—Corpus Christi 2006, pet. denied) (subsidiary corporation accused of conspiring with parent corporation had justiciable interest in P's suit against parent corporation); *Feldman*, 21 S.W.3d at 549 (corporate policy owner could not intervene to claim right to defense costs paid by insurer to additional insured); *see, e.g.*, *Ghiasinejad*, 109 S.W.3d at 70-71 (attorney with contingent-fee contract had justiciable interest in P's suit); *Live Oak Resort, Inc. v. Texas Alcoholic Bev. Comm'n*, 920 S.W.2d 795, 798 (Tex.App.—Houston [1st Dist.] 1996, no writ) (protesters could not intervene in suit involving denial of TABC license because Alco. Bev. Code §11.67 provides that in such a suit TABC is the only D); *Beutel v. Dallas Cty. Flood Control Dist.*, 916 S.W.2d 685, 691-92 (Tex.App.—Waco 1996, writ denied) (lienholder who did not have interest in property at time of taking could not intervene in condemnation).

✦

4. Proper venue or joinder. Each intervening plaintiff must, independently of every other plaintiff, establish proper venue or proper joinder. CPRC §15.003(a). See "Venue or joinder proper for all plaintiffs," ch. 3-C, §2.6.4, p. 206.

5. For all purposes. Once a party intervenes, the intervenor becomes a party to the suit for all purposes.

§2.2 Deadline to file.

1. Before judgment. Generally, a petition in intervention must be filed before judgment is rendered. *See Texas Mut. Ins. v. Ledbetter*, 251 S.W.3d 31, 36 (Tex.2008); *First Alief Bank v. White*, 682 S.W.2d 251, 252 (Tex. 1984). Although the petition can be filed anytime before judgment is rendered, the petition must still be timely filed. *See Texas Mut. Ins.*, 251 S.W.3d at 36-37; *see, e.g.*, *Armstrong v. Tidelands Life Ins.*, 466 S.W.2d 407, 412 (Tex. App.—Corpus Christi 1971, no writ) (petition in intervention untimely when intervenors filed it after suit had been on file for almost four years and after D filed motion for summary judgment).

NOTE

*A petition in intervention is not subject to the seven-day requirement in TRCP 63 concerning amendments and responses to pleadings. **In re Estate of York**, 951 S.W.2d 122, 124-25 (Tex. App.—Corpus Christi 1997, no writ).*

---

2. After judgment.

(1) Generally. A petition in intervention is generally too late if it is filed after judgment is rendered. *Texas Mut. Ins.*, 251 S.W.3d at 36; *First Alief Bank*, 682 S.W.2d at 252; *Gore v. Peck*, 191 S.W.3d 927, 928 (Tex. App.—Dallas 2006, no pet.); *see, e.g.*, *Keim v. Anderson*, 943 S.W.2d 938, 943 (Tex.App.—El Paso 1997, no writ) (intervention filed after oral rendition of judgment was too late). Unless an exception applies, an intervention filed after rendition of judgment may be considered only if the trial court sets aside the judgment. *First Alief Bank*, 682 S.W.2d at 252; *State & Cty. Mut. Fire Ins. v. Kelly*, 915 S.W.2d 224, 227 (Tex.App.—Austin 1996, orig. proceeding).

(2) Exceptions. A petition in intervention filed after judgment is not too late if (1) the intervenor does not attack the existing judgment but instead seeks protection of property interests under CPRC §31.002, or (2) the intervenor is a subrogee whose interest was at first adequately represented by someone else, but was later abandoned. *Texas Mut. Ins.*, 251 S.W.3d at 36 (exception #2; exception only applies if intervention will not cause unnecessary delay or prejudice to existing parties); *Breazeale v. Casteel*, 4 S.W.3d 434, 436 (Tex.App.—Austin 1999, pet. denied) (exception #1).

§2.3 Notice of petition.

1. Citation not necessary. An intervenor may serve a petition in intervention on the parties in the suit under TRCP 21 and 21a. *See Baker v. Monsanto Co.*, 111 S.W.3d 158, 160 (Tex.2003); TRCP 60 cmt. 785-786 S.W.2d (Tex.Cases) xlii (1990). The intervenor does not need to serve process on the parties that are before the court or on a defendant who makes a general appearance before the limitations period runs. *Baker*, 111 S.W.3d at 160; *see McWilliams v. Snap-Pac Corp.*, 476 S.W.2d 941, 949-50 (Tex.App.—Houston [1st Dist.] 1971, writ ref'd n.r.e.); 1 McDonald & Carlson, *Texas Civil Practice*, §5:82. An intervenor's claim against a defendant served under TRCP 21 and 21a is barred if the limitations period runs before the defendant makes a general appearance. *See Baker*, 111 S.W.3d at 160-61.

2. Citation necessary. An intervenor must serve citation on (1) any defendant that has not made a general appearance and from whom the intervenor seeks affirmative relief, and (2) any third party brought into the lawsuit by the intervenor. *Baker*, 111 S.W.3d at 160; 1 McDonald & Carlson, *Texas Civil Practice*, §5:82.

§2.4 Motion to strike.
If any party in the suit opposes the intervention, that party must challenge it by filing a motion to strike the petition in intervention. TRCP 60; *In re Union Carbide Corp.*, 273 S.W.3d 152, 154-55 (Tex. 2008); *Guaranty Fed. Sav. Bank v. Horseshoe Oper. Co.*, 793 S.W.2d 652, 657 (Tex.1990); *Intermarque Auto.*

⭐

Prods. v. Feldman, 21 S.W.3d 544, 549 (Tex.App.—Texarkana 2000, no pet.). See *O'Connor's Texas Forms*, FORM 5I:2. A court cannot strike an intervention on its own initiative. *See Guaranty Fed.*, 793 S.W.2d at 657; *Flores v. Melo-Palacios*, 921 S.W.2d 399, 404 (Tex.App.—Corpus Christi 1996, writ denied). If the party opposing the intervention does not move to strike, that party waives any right to object. *Ghidoni v. Stone Oak, Inc.*, 966 S.W.2d 573, 587 (Tex.App.—San Antonio 1998, pet. denied) (motions to abate or sever are not substitutes for motion to strike). The motion to strike should allege the following:

1. The intervenor does not have a justiciable interest in the suit—that is, the intervenor (1) could not have brought all or part of the same suit in its own name or (2) would not have been able to defeat all or part of the recovery if the suit had been filed against it. *See Guaranty Fed.*, 793 S.W.2d at 657; *Law Offices of Windle Turley, P.C. v. Ghiasinejad*, 109 S.W.3d 68, 70 (Tex.App.—Fort Worth 2003, no pet.).

2. The intervention will complicate the case by an excessive multiplication of the issues. *See Guaranty Fed.*, 793 S.W.2d at 657; *Ghiasinejad*, 109 S.W.3d at 70.

3. The intervention is not essential to protect the intervenor's interest. *See Guaranty Fed.*, 793 S.W.2d at 657; *Ghiasinejad*, 109 S.W.3d at 70.

§2.5 Hearing on motion to strike.

1. **Make a record.** If the trial court conducts a hearing to receive evidence on the motion to strike, the parties should request a court reporter. Without a reporter's record of the hearing, an appellant cannot challenge the ruling on appeal. *See Saldana v. Saldana*, 791 S.W.2d 316, 320 (Tex.App.—Corpus Christi 1990, no writ).

2. **Burden on intervenor.** At the hearing, the burden is on the intervenor to show it has a justiciable interest in the lawsuit. *Intermarque Auto. Prods. v. Feldman*, 21 S.W.3d 544, 549 (Tex.App.—Texarkana 2000, no pet.). The intervenor should be given the opportunity to respond to the motion, but the issue of whether it has a justiciable interest may be resolved by reference to the petition in intervention. *Potash Corp. v. Mancias*, 942 S.W.2d 61, 64 (Tex.App.—Corpus Christi 1997, orig. proceeding). To establish the right to intervene as a plaintiff, the intervenor must show that it could have brought all or part of the same action in its own name; to establish the right to intervene as a defendant, the intervenor must show it would be able to defeat all or part of the suit if the suit had been brought against it. *Guaranty Fed. Sav. Bank v. Horseshoe Oper. Co.*, 793 S.W.2d 652, 657 (Tex.1990); *Feldman*, 21 S.W.3d at 549.

§2.6 Order on motion to strike.

1. **Trial-court standard.** The trial court has broad discretion to rule on the motion to strike the petition in intervention. *Guaranty Fed. Sav. Bank v. Horseshoe Oper. Co.*, 793 S.W.2d 652, 657 (Tex.1990). The trial court may strike a petition in intervention if (1) the intervenor does not meet the test for intervention (see "Petition in Intervention," §2, p. 371), (2) the intervention will complicate the case by an excessive multiplication of the issues, or (3) the intervention is not essential to protect the intervenor's interest. *See Guaranty Fed.*, 793 S.W.2d at 657; *see, e.g., Law Offices of Windle Turley, P.C. v. Ghiasinejad*, 109 S.W.3d 68, 71 (Tex.App.—Fort Worth 2003, no pet.) (intervention was struck because it would have injected new issues into already complicated case). To determine whether an intervention is appropriate, the trial court can consider the allegations of fact in both the plea in intervention and the motion to strike. *Intermarque Auto. Prods. v. Feldman*, 21 S.W.3d 544, 548 n.7 (Tex.App.—Texarkana 2000, no pet.).

2. **Options.** The trial court has a number of options regarding a petition in intervention. It may (1) try the intervention claim, (2) sever the intervention claim, (3) order a separate trial on the intervention claim, or (4) strike the petition in intervention for good cause. *Saldana v. Saldana*, 791 S.W.2d 316, 320 (Tex.App.—Corpus Christi 1990, no writ). However, the court must rule on the motion to strike before considering other matters. *E.g., In re Union Carbide Corp.*, 273 S.W.3d 152, 156 (Tex.2008) (court must rule on motion to strike before considering severance).

§3. INTERPLEADER SUIT

By filing an interpleader, a party may protect itself from multiple liability by interpleading the property that is subject to conflicting claims. TRCP 43; *Clayton v. MONY Life Ins.*, 284 S.W.3d 398, 401 (Tex.App.—Beaumont 2009, no

───────────────────────── ✦ ─────────────────────────

pet.); *see Davis v. East Tex. S&L Ass'n*, 354 S.W.2d 926, 930 (Tex.1962); *Tri-State Pipe & Equip., Inc. v. Southern Cty. Mut. Ins.*, 8 S.W.3d 394, 402 (Tex.App.—Texarkana 1999, no pet.). This procedure is useful when two or more persons claim insurance proceeds, escrow accounts, or trust funds that are in the hands of a disinterested party. *See, e.g., Great Am. Reserve Ins. v. Sanders*, 525 S.W.2d 956, 958 (Tex.1975) (insurance proceeds claimed by widow and former wife). A suit filed as an interpleader is a suit in equity. *Northshore Bank v. Commercial Credit Corp.*, 668 S.W.2d 787, 790 (Tex.App.—Houston [14th Dist.] 1984, writ ref'd n.r.e.). See *O'Connor's Texas Forms*, FORMS 5I:4-6.

§3.1 Interpleader-party.

1. Plaintiff-stakeholder. A party that is subject to multiple liability because several claims have been or may be asserted against the same property may file a petition in interpleader, joining the competing claimants to the lawsuit as defendants. TRCP 43.

2. Defendant-stakeholder. A defendant already in a suit may file an interpleader as a cross-claim or counterclaim. TRCP 43. When multiple claims are made for the same property, TRCP 43 authorizes a defendant to join all claimants in the lawsuit and tender the disputed property into the registry of the court. *Clayton v. MONY Life Ins.*, 284 S.W.3d 398, 402 (Tex.App.—Beaumont 2009, no pet.); *Olmos v. Pecan Grove MUD*, 857 S.W.2d 734, 741 (Tex.App.—Houston [14th Dist.] 1993, no writ).

3. Garnishee. A garnishee subject to conflicting claims may file an interpleader. *Northshore Bank v. Commercial Credit Corp.*, 668 S.W.2d 787, 789 (Tex.App.—Houston [14th Dist.] 1984, writ ref'd n.r.e.).

§3.2 Petition.

1. Deadline to file. The TRCPs do not provide a deadline for filing the petition in interpleader. *See* TRCP 43.

───────────────────────────────

NOTE

*Some courts of appeals have applied a timeliness requirement to interpleader suits. See **Clements v. Minnesota Life Ins.**, 176 S.W.2d 258, 263 (Tex.App.—Houston [1st Dist.] 2004, no pet.); **Serna v. Webster**, 908 S.W.2d 487, 491 (Tex.App.—San Antonio 1995, no writ); **Olmos v. Pecan Grove MUD**, 857 S.W.2d 734, 741 (Tex.App.—Houston [14th Dist.] 1993, no writ). Thus, if the stakeholder unreasonably delayed in filing the action for interpleader, the action was barred. The Supreme Court, however, has clarified that the only requirement for bringing an action in interpleader under the TRCPs is conflicting claims; thus, unreasonable delay does not make interpleader improper. **State Farm Life Ins. v. Martinez**, 216 S.W.3d 799, 807 (Tex. 2007). See "Rival claims," §3.2.2, this page. But unreasonable delay may bar the stakeholder from recovering attorney fees or may subject the stakeholder to any applicable statutory penalties. **Martinez**, 216 S.W.3d at 807. See "Attorney fees," §3.2.5, p. 375.*

───────────────────────────────

2. Rival claims. The stakeholder must show it is subject to (or has reasonable grounds to anticipate) rival claims to the same fund or property and there is a reasonable doubt in law or fact as to which claim is valid. *Tri-State Pipe & Equip., Inc. v. Southern Cty. Mut. Ins.*, 8 S.W.3d 394, 402 (Tex.App.—Texarkana 1999, no pet.); *see Martinez*, 216 S.W.3d at 807 (only requirement for interpleader is conflicting claims); *Davis v. East Tex. S&L Ass'n*, 354 S.W.2d 926, 930 (Tex.1962) (claims must place stakeholder in some real doubt or hazard); *Clayton v. MONY Life Ins.*, 284 S.W.3d 398, 402 (Tex.App.—Beaumont 2009, no pet.) (stakeholder must face rival claims).

3. Unconditional tender. The stakeholder must show it unconditionally tendered the disputed money or property into the court's registry. *Rapp v. Mandell & Wright, P.C.*, 127 S.W.3d 888, 895 (Tex.App.—Corpus Christi 2004, pet. denied); *Tri-State Pipe & Equip.*, 8 S.W.3d at 402; *Serna*, 908 S.W.2d at 491. Only an unconditional tender is required, not an actual deposit of the funds into the court's registry. *Clayton*, 284 S.W.3d at 404; *Heggy v.*

★

American Trading Empl. Ret. Account Plan, 123 S.W.3d 770, 776 (Tex.App.—Houston [14th Dist.] 2003, pet. denied); *see also Young v. Gumfory*, 322 S.W.3d 731, 741 (Tex.App.—Dallas 2010, no pet.) (tender is unconditional offer by debtor to pay full amount of debt or obligation). The stakeholder must tender the money or property so the court can allocate it among the parties as part of the judgment.

4. Discharge. The stakeholder should ask the court to sign an order of discharge.

5. Attorney fees. A stakeholder is entitled to recover attorney fees from the tendered funds unless there were no rival claimants or the stakeholder unreasonably delayed in filing the action for interpleader. *Martinez*, 216 S.W.3d at 803; *see U.S. v. Ray Thomas Gravel Co.*, 380 S.W.2d 576, 580 (Tex.1964) (stakeholder is entitled to attorney fees if it had reasonable doubts about which party was entitled to funds and it interpleaded the claimants in good faith). However, the stakeholder is not entitled to attorney fees if it was responsible for the conflicting claims to the funds. *Olmos*, 857 S.W.2d at 742; *e.g.*, *Brown v. Getty Reserve Oil, Inc.*, 626 S.W.2d 810, 815 (Tex.App.—Amarillo 1981, writ dism'd) (stakeholder improperly created fund that became subject of conflicting claims). The party must segregate claims for which attorney fees are recoverable (e.g., interpleader) from claims for which they are not. *Tony Gullo Motors I, L.P. v. Chapa*, 212 S.W.3d 299, 311 (Tex.2006). See "Fees were segregated," ch. 1-H, §10.3.4, p. 65.

§3.3 Response. The following are some of the allegations a party opposing the interpleader may assert:

1. No rival claims. The stakeholder is not subject to and has no reasonable grounds to anticipate rival claims to the same property. *See Davis v. East Tex. S&L Ass'n*, 354 S.W.2d 926, 930 (Tex.1962); *Olmos v. Pecan Grove MUD*, 857 S.W.2d 734, 741 (Tex.App.—Houston [14th Dist.] 1993, no writ).

2. No unconditional tender. The stakeholder has not unconditionally tendered the fund or property into the court's registry. *Tri-State Pipe & Equip., Inc. v. Southern Cty. Mut. Ins.*, 8 S.W.3d 394, 402-03 (Tex.App.—Texarkana 1999, no pet.); *e.g.*, *Rapp v. Mandell & Wright, P.C.*, 127 S.W.3d 888, 895-96 (Tex.App.—Corpus Christi 2004, pet. denied) (deposit was not unconditional because it was made without waiver of rights and there was no disinterested person to qualify as stakeholder).

3. Unreasonable delay. The stakeholder has unreasonably delayed filing the action for interpleader and is not entitled to recover attorney fees. *See State Farm Life Ins. v. Martinez*, 216 S.W.3d 799, 807 (Tex.2007).

4. Interested stakeholder. The stakeholder is an interested stakeholder, is responsible for the conflicting claims, and thus should not recover costs and attorney fees. *Brown v. Getty Reserve Oil, Inc.*, 626 S.W.2d 810, 815 (Tex.App.—Amarillo 1981, writ dism'd).

§3.4 Hearing on interpleader. The court must conduct a hearing on the initial issue of whether interpleader is appropriate. *See Taliaferro v. Texas Commerce Bank*, 669 S.W.2d 172, 174 (Tex.App.—Fort Worth 1984, no writ). The stakeholder must introduce evidence to support the petition in interpleader and, if appropriate, attorney fees. *Id.*

§3.5 Order on interpleader.

1. Interpleader appropriate. If the court determines the suit is properly an interpleader action, it may do the following: (1) require the stakeholder to deposit the funds or property into the court's registry (if not already on deposit), (2) discharge the stakeholder from the suit, (3) grant costs and attorney fees to the stakeholder, and (4) continue the suit on the merits between the rival claimants to determine their respective rights to the money or property.

2. Interpleader not appropriate. If the suit is not properly brought as an interpleader action, the court will dismiss it.

§3.6 Trial on the merits. During the trial on the merits, each claimant has the burden to prove its own claim to the funds; a claimant cannot merely disprove the other's right. *McBryde v. Curry*, 914 S.W.2d 616, 620 (Tex. App.—Texarkana 1995, writ denied); *Northshore Bank v. Commercial Credit Corp.*, 668 S.W.2d 787, 789 (Tex. App.—Houston [14th Dist.] 1984, writ ref'd n.r.e.).

★

---

§4. MOTION TO CONSOLIDATE

The same legal principles apply in ordering consolidation under TRCP 174(a) as in ordering separate trials under TRCP 174(b). *Dal-Briar Corp. v. Baskette*, 833 S.W.2d 612, 615 (Tex.App.—El Paso 1992, orig. proceeding). See "Motion for Separate (Bifurcated) Trial," ch. 5-I, §4, p. 367.

§4.1 Motion. TRCP 174(a) gives the trial court broad discretion to consolidate cases with common issues of law or fact. *Owens-Corning Fiberglas Corp. v. Martin*, 942 S.W.2d 712, 716 (Tex.App.—Dallas 1997, no writ). See *O'Connor's Texas Forms*, FORM 5I:7.

    1. Standards to apply. Suits to be consolidated should relate to substantially the same subject matter, and the same evidence should be material, relevant, and admissible in both suits. *Owens-Corning*, 942 S.W.2d at 716; *Lone Star Ford, Inc. v. McCormick*, 838 S.W.2d 734, 737 (Tex.App.—Houston [1st Dist.] 1992, writ denied).

    2. Pending before the court. A court may consolidate lawsuits pending in different district courts within the same county. *Starnes v. Holloway*, 779 S.W.2d 86, 96 (Tex.App.—Dallas 1989, writ denied). A court in one county cannot order a matter pending in another county to be transferred out of that county and into its court unless there is some specific statutory authority. *Flores v. Peschel*, 927 S.W.2d 209, 213 (Tex.App.—Corpus Christi 1996, orig. proceeding). See "Motion to Transfer to Multidistrict Litigation Pretrial Court," ch. 5-G, p. 355.

    3. Filing of motion – local rules. Some local rules require that the motion to consolidate be filed in the court in which the first-filed case is pending. *E.g.*, *Starnes*, 779 S.W.2d at 96 (Dallas County Local Rule 1.1(e), now 1.04); *see also* *Santa Fe Drilling Co. v. O'Neill*, 774 S.W.2d 423, 424 (Tex.App.—Houston [14th Dist.] 1989, orig. proceeding) (Harris County District Court Local Rule 3.2.3 requires that motion to consolidate be heard in court where first-filed case is pending). However, a consolidation order based on a motion filed in the court of the later-filed case is not void. *Starnes*, 779 S.W.2d at 96.

§4.2 Objection. A party that objects to a motion to consolidate must make a specific and timely objection. TRAP 33.1(a)(1).

§4.3 Order. In deciding whether to consolidate, the trial court must weigh the judicial economy and convenience that may be gained by the consolidation against the risk of an unfair trial because of prejudice or jury confusion. *In re Ethyl Corp.*, 975 S.W.2d 606, 610 (Tex.1998); *Owens-Corning Fiberglas Corp. v. Martin*, 942 S.W.2d 712, 716 (Tex.App.—Dallas 1997, no writ). If consolidation would result in an unfair trial, the cases should not be joined. *In re Van Waters & Rogers, Inc.*, 145 S.W.3d 203, 207 (Tex.2004); *see In re Ethyl Corp.*, 975 S.W.2d at 610.

§5. REVIEW

§5.1 Intervention.

    1. Interlocutory appeal. When the trial court strikes the petition in intervention, the order generally cannot be appealed until after the court renders a final judgment in the case. *Metromedia Long Distance, Inc. v. Hughes*, 810 S.W.2d 494, 499 (Tex.App.—San Antonio 1991, writ denied). But if venue is at issue, CPRC §15.003(b) allows an interlocutory appeal of an intervention decision. See "Joinder," ch. 3-C, §5.2.2, p. 213.

    2. Standard. The appellate court will review the trial court's ruling for abuse of discretion. *In re Lumbermens Mut. Cas. Co.*, 184 S.W.3d 718, 722 (Tex.2006); *Guaranty Fed. Sav. Bank v. Horseshoe Oper. Co.*, 793 S.W.2d 652, 657 (Tex.1990). The trial court abuses its discretion in denying an intervention if (1) the intervenor could have brought all or part of the same action in its own name, or if the action had been brought against it, the intervenor could have defeated all or part of the recovery, (2) the intervention would not complicate the case by an excessive multiplication of issues, and (3) the intervention was essential (or almost essential) to protect the intervenor's interest. *Guaranty Fed.*, 793 S.W.2d at 657; *Zeifman v. Michels*, 229 S.W.3d 460, 466 (Tex.App.—Austin 2007, no pet.) (list is not exclusive); *Jenkins v. Entergy Corp.*, 187 S.W.3d 785, 796-97 (Tex.App.—Corpus Christi 2006, pet. denied). If the appellate court finds the trial court's ruling was wrong, the court applies the harmless-error rule in TRAP 44.1 and 61.1.

⸻ ★ ⸻

§5.2 Interpleader. If the order granting interpleader disposes of all issues involving the interpleader, it is a final, appealable order. *K&S Interests, Inc. v. Texas Am. Bank/Dallas*, 749 S.W.2d 887, 889-90 (Tex.App.—Dallas 1988, writ denied); *Taliaferro v. Texas Commerce Bank*, 660 S.W.2d 151, 154-55 (Tex.App.—Fort Worth 1983, no writ). If the order is final, any party that wants to appeal must perfect its appeal from the date the court signs the order granting the interpleader.

§5.3 Consolidation.

1. No interlocutory appeal. When the trial court grants a motion to consolidate separate lawsuits, the order generally cannot be appealed until after a final judgment is rendered in the case. *Carter v. Sun City Towing & Recovery, L.P.*, 225 S.W.3d 161, 162 (Tex.App.—El Paso 2005, no pet.).

2. Regular appeal. The same standard of review that controls separation of issues controls the consolidation of issues (i.e., abuse of discretion). See "Motion to bifurcate," ch. 5-I, §6.2, p. 370.

K. MOTION FOR SANCTIONS

§1. GENERAL

§1.1 Rules. CPRC §§9.011-9.014 (groundless pleadings), CPRC §§10.001-10.006 (frivolous pleadings); TRCP 13 (groundless pleadings), TRCP 21b (failure to serve copies), TRCP 215 (discovery abuse). See Gov't Code §21.002 (officer of court can be held in contempt), Gov't Code §82.061 (attorney can be fined or imprisoned for misbehavior or contempt); TRCP 166a(h) (party can be ordered to pay reasonable expenses for filing affidavit in bad faith).

§1.2 Purpose. The purpose of sanctions is to secure the parties' compliance with the rules, punish those that violate the rules, and deter other litigants from violating the rules. *Chrysler Corp. v. Blackmon*, 841 S.W.2d 844, 849 (Tex.1992); *Bodnow Corp. v. City of Hondo*, 721 S.W.2d 839, 840 (Tex.1986); *Tidrow v. Roth*, 189 S.W.3d 408, 412 (Tex.App.—Dallas 2006, no pet.); *see Falk & Mayfield L.L.P. v. Molzan*, 974 S.W.2d 821, 827 (Tex.App.—Houston [14th Dist.] 1998, pet. denied) (purpose of sanctions for groundless pleadings under TRCP 13 is to prevent abuses in the pleading process). In most cases, the imposition of sanctions should not prevent a decision on the merits of the case. *Chrysler Corp.*, 841 S.W.2d at 850; *TransAmerican Nat. Gas Corp. v. Powell*, 811 S.W.2d 913, 918 (Tex.1991).

§1.3 Forms. *O'Connor's Texas Civil Forms* (2012), FORMS 5J.

§1.4 Other references. *O'Connor's Texas Civil Appeals* (2012) (*O'Connor's Texas Appeals*).

§2. AUTHORITY FOR SANCTIONS

§2.1 Rule or statute. Most sanctions are imposed under the authority of a specific statute or rule that permits the court to order sanctions. See CPRC §§9.012, 10.002, 10.004; TRCP 13, 166a(h), 215.

§2.2 Inherent power. Sanctions may also be imposed under the court's inherent power. A trial court has inherent power to impose sanctions for abuses of the judicial process not covered by rule or statute. *Ezeoke v. Tracy*, 349 S.W.3d 679, 685 (Tex.App.—Houston [14th Dist.] 2011, no pet.); *Kutch v. Del Mar Coll.*, 831 S.W.2d 506, 510 (Tex.App.—Corpus Christi 1992, no writ). For the court to exercise this inherent power, the conduct complained about must significantly interfere with the court's legitimate exercise of one of its core functions (e.g., hearing evidence, deciding issues of fact or questions of law). *Ezeoke*, 349 S.W.3d at 685; *Kutch*, 831 S.W.2d at 510; *e.g.*, *Kennedy v. Kennedy*, 125 S.W.3d 14, 19 (Tex.App.—Austin 2002, pet. denied) (court could not punish spouse under inherent power by granting interlocutory divorce).

§3. STANDARDS FOR IMPOSING SANCTIONS

Sanctions must be "just." TRCP 215.2(b); *Paradigm Oil, Inc. v. Retamco Oper., Inc.*, 372 S.W.3d 177, 184 (Tex. 2012); *Spohn Hosp. v. Mayer*, 104 S.W.3d 878, 882 (Tex.2003); *Chrysler Corp. v. Blackmon*, 841 S.W.2d 844, 849

———————————————————— ✯ ————————————————————

(Tex.1992); *TransAmerican Nat. Gas Corp. v. Powell*, 811 S.W.2d 913, 917 (Tex.1991). In other words, the punishment should fit the crime. *Paradigm Oil*, 372 S.W.3d at 187; *TransAmerican*, 811 S.W.2d at 917.

§3.1 Regular sanctions. Courts use a two-part test to determine whether sanctions are just:

1. Direct relationship. The sanction must be directly related to the offensive conduct. *Paradigm Oil, Inc. v. Retamco Oper., Inc.*, 372 S.W.3d 177, 184 (Tex.2012); *American Flood Research, Inc. v. Jones*, 192 S.W.3d 581, 583 (Tex.2006); *TransAmerican Nat. Gas Corp. v. Powell*, 811 S.W.2d 913, 917 (Tex.1991); *e.g.*, *Remington Arms Co. v. Caldwell*, 850 S.W.2d 167, 171 (Tex.1993) (striking pleadings is not appropriate sanction for failure to designate witness; proper sanction is to exclude witness); *In re J.D.N.*, 183 S.W.3d 128, 131-32 (Tex.App.—Dallas 2006, no pet.) (direct relationship between D's conduct and striking his answer because D refused to provide information about finances necessary for child-support determination); *Magnuson v. Mullen*, 65 S.W.3d 815, 826 (Tex. App.—Fort Worth 2002, pet. denied) (direct relationship between P's conduct and dismissal because P frustrated all attempts to define the cause of action and investigate defenses); *see Spohn Hosp. v. Mayer*, 104 S.W.3d 878, 882 (Tex.2003) ("direct nexus among the offensive conduct, the offender, and the sanction imposed"). A just sanction must be directed against the abuse and toward remedying the prejudice caused to the innocent party. *American Flood*, 192 S.W.3d at 583; *Spohn Hosp.*, 104 S.W.3d at 882; *TransAmerican*, 811 S.W.2d at 917.

2. Necessary severity. The sanction must not be excessive; it should be no more severe than necessary to promote full compliance. *Paradigm Oil*, 372 S.W.3d at 187; *Spohn Hosp.*, 104 S.W.3d at 882; *Chrysler Corp. v. Blackmon*, 841 S.W.2d 844, 849 (Tex.1992); *TransAmerican*, 811 S.W.2d at 917; *e.g.*, *Jones v. American Flood Research, Inc.*, 218 S.W.3d 929, 932-33 (Tex.App.—Dallas 2007, no pet.) ($15,000 sanction against attorney for failure of his clients to appear for deposition was excessive); *see, e.g.*, *Zappe v. Zappe*, 871 S.W.2d 910, 913 (Tex.App.—Corpus Christi 1994, no writ) (incomplete answers to discovery did not justify striking party's pleadings and other sanctions in child-custody suit). Discovery sanctions severe enough to inhibit presentation of the merits of a case should be reserved for a party's flagrant bad faith or an attorney's callous disregard for the discovery rules. *Spohn Hosp.*, 104 S.W.3d at 883; *TransAmerican*, 811 S.W.2d at 918; *see, e.g.*, *Paradigm Oil*, 372 S.W.3d at 186-87 (court properly struck Ds' answer and rendered default judgment, but sanction barring Ds from participating in post-default damages trial for unliquidated damages was excessive; sanction precluding Ds from damages trial more likely justified if discovery abuse involved spoliation). See "Sanctions for discovery abuse," §7.1, p. 384. The courts should consider the least-stringent sanction necessary to promote compliance. *American Flood*, 192 S.W.3d at 583; *Spohn Hosp.*, 104 S.W.3d at 882.

§3.2 Death-penalty sanctions. A death-penalty sanction is one that has the effect of adjudicating the dispute without regard to the merits. *TransAmerican Nat. Gas Corp. v. Powell*, 811 S.W.2d 913, 918 (Tex.1991). Death-penalty sanctions should be imposed only in exceptional cases when they are clearly justified and it is apparent that no lesser sanctions would promote compliance with the rules. *Cire v. Cummings*, 134 S.W.3d 835, 840-41 (Tex.2004); *Spohn Hosp. v. Mayer*, 104 S.W.3d 878, 882 (Tex.2003); *GTE Comms. Sys. v. Tanner*, 856 S.W.2d 725, 729 (Tex. 1993). Death-penalty sanctions include dismissal, default judgment, excluding evidence, and jury instructions resolving fact issues in favor of one party. *See, e.g.*, *Paradigm Oil, Inc. v. Retamco Oper., Inc.*, 372 S.W.3d 177, 181 (Tex.2012) (default judgment); *Spohn Hosp.*, 104 S.W.3d at 883 (jury instructions); *Hernandez v. Mid-Loop, Inc.*, 170 S.W.3d 138, 144 (Tex.App.—San Antonio 2005, no pet.) (dismissal); *Adkins Servs. v. Tisdale Co.*, 56 S.W.3d 842, 845 (Tex.App.—Texarkana 2001, no pet.) (order excluding evidence). Courts use a four-part test to determine whether death-penalty sanctions are appropriate.

1. Direct relationship. See "Direct relationship," §3.1.1, this page.

2. Necessary severity. See "Necessary severity," §3.1.2, this page.

3. Lesser sanction first.

(1) Typical misconduct. Generally, the trial court must use a lesser sanction first to determine whether it is adequate to secure compliance, deterrence, and punishment of the offender. *Chrysler Corp. v. Blackmon*, 841 S.W.2d 844, 849 (Tex.1992); *see Cire*, 134 S.W.3d at 840-41. The trial court is not required to order every lesser sanction that could possibly be imposed before imposing death-penalty sanctions. *Cire*, 134 S.W.3d at 842. An order compelling discovery, by itself, is not a lesser sanction. *Paradigm Oil, Inc. v. Retamco Oper., Inc.*, 161 S.W.3d 531, 539 (Tex.App.—San Antonio 2004, pet. denied); *In re Western Star Trucks US, Inc.*, 112 S.W.3d 756, 766 (Tex.App.—Eastland 2003, orig. proceeding); *Andras v. Memorial Hosp. Sys.*, 888 S.W.2d 567, 572 (Tex.App.—Houston [1st Dist.] 1994, writ denied). The courts of appeals are split on whether an order to compel, joined with a statement that noncompliance will result in sanctions, constitutes a lesser sanction. *Compare In re Polaris Indus.*, 65 S.W.3d 746, 753 (Tex.App.—Beaumont 2001, orig. proceeding) (neither threat nor intent to sanction constitute sanctions), *and Williams v. Akzo Nobel Chems., Inc.*, 999 S.W.2d 836, 844 (Tex.App.—Tyler 1999, no pet.) (threat of dismissal for noncompliance is not lesser sanction), *with Paradigm Oil*, 161 S.W.3d at 539 (order to compel under threat of dismissal met requirement of "lesser" sanction), *and Andras*, 888 S.W.2d at 572 (same).

(2) **Egregious misconduct.** In a case of egregious misconduct (e.g., violation of earlier court orders, blatant disregard for discovery process), the court is not required to use a lesser sanction before imposing death-penalty sanctions as long as the record reflects that the court considered lesser sanctions and the party's conduct justifies the presumption that its claims or defenses lack merit. *Cire*, 134 S.W.3d at 842. See "No merit," §3.2.4, this page. The court must give a reasoned explanation why lesser sanctions would have been ineffective and why the sanction imposed was appropriate. *See Cire*, 134 S.W.3d at 842; *GTE*, 856 S.W.2d at 729-30. The order cannot just say the court "considered" a lesser sanction before imposing death-penalty sanctions. *See In re Adkins*, 70 S.W.3d 384, 391 (Tex.App.—Fort Worth 2002, orig. proceeding); *see also In re N.R.C.*, 94 S.W.3d 799, 812 (Tex.App.—Houston [14th Dist.] 2002, pet. denied) (silent record does not support conclusion that court considered lesser sanctions).

4. No merit. For death-penalty sanctions to be appropriate, the party's conduct must justify the presumption that its claims or defenses lack merit. *Paradigm Oil*, 372 S.W.3d at 184; *Hamill v. Level*, 917 S.W.2d 15, 16 (Tex. 1996); *TransAmerican*, 811 S.W.2d at 918; *e.g., Cire*, 134 S.W.3d at 839 (death-penalty sanctions were justified when P deliberately destroyed audiotapes she refused to produce because they were unfavorable to her claims); *see, e.g., Andras*, 888 S.W.2d at 573 (lawsuit against hospital for overcharging was properly dismissed because P's attorney refused to produce canceled checks).

§4. PERSONS WHO MAY BE SANCTIONED

The trial court should impose the sanctions against the offender. *Spohn Hosp. v. Mayer*, 104 S.W.3d 878, 882 (Tex. 2003); *TransAmerican Nat. Gas Corp. v. Powell*, 811 S.W.2d 913, 917 (Tex.1991). Before imposing sanctions that severely inhibit the presentation of a party's claim, the court should make a record identifying who was responsible for the sanctionable conduct—the party, the attorney, or both. *See Spohn Hosp.*, 104 S.W.3d at 882; *Paradigm Oil, Inc. v. Retamco Oper., Inc.*, 161 S.W.3d 531, 537 (Tex.App.—San Antonio 2004, pet. denied).

§4.1 Party. The court may impose sanctions on the party. *E.g.*, CPRC §§9.012(c), 10.004(a); TRCP 13, 215.1(d), 215.2(b), 215.3; *see TransAmerican Nat. Gas Corp. v. Powell*, 811 S.W.2d 913, 917 (Tex.1991). A party must bear some responsibility for its counsel's sanctionable conduct when the party is or should be aware of counsel's conduct and any violation of the discovery rules. *TransAmerican*, 811 S.W.2d at 917; *Paradigm Oil, Inc. v. Retamco Oper., Inc.*, 161 S.W.3d 531, 537 (Tex.App.—San Antonio 2004, pet. denied); *see, e.g., Nath v. Texas Children's Hosp.*, 375 S.W.3d 403, 410-11 (Tex.App.—Houston [14th Dist.] 2012, pet. filed 10-10-12) (trial court did not abuse discretion in sanctioning represented party for filing groundless pleadings; P was actively involved in litigation and assisted in planning of claims and tactics). A party should not be punished for discovery abuse for which it is not responsible. *TransAmerican*, 811 S.W.2d at 917; *e.g., Paradigm Oil*, 161 S.W.3d at 537 (sanctions on party were proper because party was responsible for discovery abuse); *In re Harvest Cmty.*, 88 S.W.3d 343, 348 (Tex.App.—San Antonio 2002, orig. proceeding) (no evidence party was guilty of anything but hiring offensive attorney); *Smith v. Nguyen*, 855 S.W.2d 263, 266-67 (Tex.App.—Houston [14th Dist.] 1993, writ denied) (nothing in record implicated party in late designation of witnesses). The trial court cannot impose a sanction that adversely affects parties who were not implicated in the abuse. *Arkla, Inc. v. Harris*, 846 S.W.2d 623, 628-29 (Tex.App.—Houston [14th Dist.] 1993, orig. proceeding).

★

---

§4.2 Attorney. If the attorney was responsible for the sanctionable conduct and the party was unaware of it, the court should sanction the attorney, not the party. *See* CPRC §§9.012(c), 10.004(a); TRCP 13, 215.1(d), 215.2(b)(8); *American Flood Research, Inc. v. Jones*, 192 S.W.3d 581, 584 (Tex.2006); *TransAmerican Nat. Gas Corp. v. Powell*, 811 S.W.2d 913, 917 (Tex.1991); *In re Barnes*, 956 S.W.2d 746, 748 (Tex.App.—Corpus Christi 1997, orig. proceeding); *see, e.g., Jones v. Andrews*, 873 S.W.2d 102, 106 (Tex.App.—Dallas 1994, no writ) (party should not be punished by death-penalty sanctions because attorney did not timely ask for extension). When multiple attorneys are involved in the sanctionable conduct, they can be held jointly and severally liable. *See, e.g., Kugle v. DaimlerChrysler Corp.*, 88 S.W.3d 355, 364-65 (Tex.App.—San Antonio 2002, pet. denied) (three attorneys were jointly and severally liable for fraud in personal-injury suit). There is disagreement, however, on whether law firms are sanctionable. *Compare Yuen v. Gerson*, 342 S.W.3d 824, 828-29 (Tex.App.—Houston [14th Dist.] 2011, pet. denied) (law firms cannot be sanctioned), *with Finlay v. Olive*, 77 S.W.3d 520, 527 (Tex.App.—Houston [1st Dist.] 2002, no pet.) (law firm can be sanctioned for groundless pleadings filed on its behalf by attorney employed at firm).

§4.3 Both party & attorney. When both the party and the attorney are implicated in sanctionable conduct, the court may sanction both of them. *E.g.*, CPRC §§9.012(c), 10.004(a); TRCP 13, 215.1(d); *see, e.g., Kugle v. DaimlerChrysler Corp.*, 88 S.W.3d 355, 365-66 (Tex.App.—San Antonio 2002, pet. denied) (attorneys were liable for monetary sanctions and suit was dismissed); *In re Zenergy, Inc.*, 968 S.W.2d 1, 11 (Tex.App.—Corpus Christi 1997, orig. proceeding) (party and attorney were jointly and severally liable for monetary sanctions).

§4.4 Nonparty.

1. Discovery abuse. When a nonparty refuses to comply with a subpoena (to produce documents or to appear) or a court order (e.g., to appear for a deposition, to permit inspection of land), the court can treat the non-compliance as contempt. *See* TRCP 176.8(a), 196.7, 205.3(a), 215.2(a), (c); *City of Houston v. Chambers*, 899 S.W.2d 306, 309 (Tex.App.—Houston [14th Dist.] 1995, orig. proceeding) (addressed former TRCP 215(2)(a)). Neither TRCP 215.2(b) nor TRCP 215.3 authorizes other sanctions against a nonparty. *Pope v. Davidson*, 849 S.W.2d 916, 920 (Tex.App.—Houston [14th Dist.] 1993, orig. proceeding); *see, e.g., Chambers*, 899 S.W.2d at 309 (because nonparty had not violated order in resisting discovery, court could not impose monetary sanctions); *Texas Att'y Gen. Office v. Adams*, 793 S.W.2d 771, 775 (Tex.App.—Fort Worth 1990, no writ) (court could not sanction nonparty by ordering it to pay attorney fees of $9,628 for refusing to comply with subpoena). When a person is found guilty of contempt, the court is limited to a monetary fine ($500 limit) or incarceration. Gov't Code §21.002(b); *In re Acceptance Ins.*, 33 S.W.3d 443, 450 (Tex.App.—Fort Worth 2000, orig. proceeding); *see, e.g., Pope*, 849 S.W.2d at 920 (court could not require nonparty to perform community service).

2. Pleading abuse. A nonparty cannot be sanctioned for pleading abuse under TRCP 13. *Chambers*, 899 S.W.2d at 309; *see also* CPRC §9.012 (addresses pleading abuse by party). TRCP 13 applies only to parties and their attorneys. *Chambers*, 899 S.W.2d at 309; *see, e.g., Jimenez v. Transwestern Prop. Co.*, 999 S.W.2d 125, 130 (Tex.App.—Houston [14th Dist.] 1999, no pet.) (paralegal could not be sanctioned under TRCP 13); *Adams*, 793 S.W.2d at 775 (nonparty's groundless claims of privilege could not be punished under TRCP 13).

§5. CONDUCT THAT JUSTIFIES SANCTIONS

§5.1 Discovery abuse.

1. No designation of witness. The court can impose sanctions on a corporation or other entity that does not designate a witness under TRCP 199.2(b)(1) or TRCP 200.1(b). TRCP 215.1(b)(1). See "When organization deposed," ch. 6-F, §4.6.3, p. 531.

2. Oral discovery. The court can impose sanctions on a party, other deponent, or person designated to testify on behalf of a party or other deponent. See "Grounds for sanctions," ch. 6-F, §10.1, p. 537.

3. Written discovery. The court can impose sanctions on a party for any of the following:

(1) Not serving answers or objections to interrogatories submitted under TRCP 197. TRCP 215.1(b)(3)(A); *see Swain v. Southwestern Bell Yellow Pages, Inc.*, 998 S.W.2d 731, 732-33 (Tex.App.—Fort Worth 1999, no pet.).

✦

---

(2)   Not answering an interrogatory submitted under TRCP 197. TRCP 215.1(b)(3)(B).

(3)   Not serving a written response to a properly served request for inspection submitted under TRCP 196. TRCP 215.1(b)(3)(C).

(4)   Not responding that discovery will be permitted as requested or not permitting discovery in response to a request for inspection submitted under TRCP 196. TRCP 215.1(b)(3)(D).

(5)   Not responding to a request for disclosures. *Magnuson v. Mullen*, 65 S.W.3d 815, 828 (Tex. App.—Fort Worth 2002, pet. denied).

4. Evasive or incomplete answer. For purposes of sanctions, an evasive or incomplete answer is treated as a failure to answer. TRCP 215.1(c).

5. Frivolous objections. The court can impose sanctions when an attorney files frivolous objections to discovery. *See, e.g., Childs v. Argenbright*, 927 S.W.2d 647, 649 (Tex.App.—Tyler 1996, no writ) (attorney filed nine pages of objections to interrogatories without answering any of them).

6. False discovery certification. The court can impose sanctions available under CPRC chapter 10 on an attorney who signed a discovery disclosure, request, notice, response, or objection in violation of TRCP 191.3(b) or (c). TRCP 191.3(e). For the representations certified by the signer of discovery under TRCP 191.3, see "Certification by signature," ch. 6-A, §4.1, p. 427. The sanction can be imposed on the person who made the certification, the party on whose behalf it was made, or both. TRCP 191.3(e). See "Sanctions under CPRC §10.004," §7.2, p. 386.

7. False testimony. The court can impose sanctions when a party gives false testimony. *See In re Reece*, 341 S.W.3d 360, 368 (Tex.2011) (if party-deponent lies during deposition, court can impose sanctions that range from payment of attorney fees to default judgment); *see, e.g., Schaver v. British Am. Ins.*, 795 S.W.2d 875, 877-78 (Tex. App.—Beaumont 1990, no writ) (because P did not disclose postinjury work history and falsified employment status, causing extra depositions of doctors, court imposed monetary sanctions; when P did not pay, court dismissed suit).

8. Improper discovery methods. The court can impose sanctions when an attorney engages in improper discovery procedures. *See, e.g., Sanchez v. Brownsville Sports Ctr., Inc.*, 51 S.W.3d 643, 659 (Tex.App.—Corpus Christi 2001, pet. granted, judgm't vacated w.r.m.) (attorney went to D's store and pretended to be interested in buying vehicle).

9. Spoliation of evidence. The court can impose sanctions when a party deliberately destroys evidence it had a duty to preserve. *See Cire v. Cummings*, 134 S.W.3d 835, 841 (Tex.2004); *Vela v. Wagner & Brown, Ltd.*, 203 S.W.3d 37, 58-59 (Tex.App.—San Antonio 2006, no pet.); *In re Dynamic Health, Inc.*, 32 S.W.3d 876, 885 (Tex. App.—Texarkana 2000, orig. proceeding).

10. Pattern of abuse. The court can consider a pattern of discovery abuse to justify sanctions. *See Downer v. Aquamarine Operators, Inc.*, 701 S.W.2d 238, 242-43 (Tex.1985); *see, e.g., Chasewood Oaks Condos. Homeowners Ass'n v. Amatek Holdings, Inc.*, 977 S.W.2d 840, 844-45 (Tex.App.—Fort Worth 1998, pet. denied) (P actively frustrated D's legitimate attempts to investigate potential defenses).

§5.2 Groundless or frivolous pleadings, motions, or other papers. When seeking sanctions for the signing of groundless or frivolous pleadings, motions, or other papers, the party can choose between CPRC §9.012 (pleadings and motions), CPRC §10.004 (same), and TRCP 13 (pleadings, motions, and other papers). Of the three, CPRC §10.004 is usually the best choice. First, CPRC §9.012 does not apply in any proceeding to which either CPRC §10.004 or TRCP 13 applies. CPRC §9.012(h). Second, TRCP 13 is narrower in scope than CPRC §10.004 and imposes a greater burden of proof on the party seeking sanctions. TRCP 13 requires a showing that a pleading, motion, or other paper was both groundless and brought in bad faith or for the purpose of harassment. *Skepnek v. Mynatt*, 8 S.W.3d 377, 382 (Tex.App.—El Paso 1999, pet. denied). By comparison, CPRC §10.004 allows sanctions when pleadings or motions are brought for an improper purpose, including harassment, delay, or increasing the cost of litigation, even if

———————————————— ✦ ————————————————

they are not groundless or frivolous. *See* CPRC §§10.001, 10.004; *Save Our Springs Alliance, Inc. v. Lazy Nine MUD*, 198 S.W.3d 300, 321 (Tex.App.—Texarkana 2006, pet. denied); *Alpert v. Crain, Caton & James, P.C.*, 178 S.W.3d 398, 411-12 (Tex.App.—Houston [1st Dist.] 2005, pet. denied). CPRC §10.004 also allows sanctions for groundless pleadings or motions that are brought negligently or as a result of poor judgment. *See* CPRC §10.001(2)-(4); *Low v. Henry*, 221 S.W.3d 609, 617 (Tex.2007). The advantage of TRCP 13, however, is that it permits death-penalty sanctions. See "Sanctions under TRCP 13," §7.3, p. 386. When in doubt, a party should seek sanctions under both CPRC §10.004 and TRCP 13. *See Alexander v. Alexander*, 956 S.W.2d 712, 713 (Tex.App.—Houston [14th Dist.] 1997, pet. denied).

1. CPRC ch. 10. The court can impose sanctions on the attorney (or pro se party) who signed the pleading or motion, the party represented by the attorney, or both if the pleading or motion was signed in violation of CPRC §10.001. CPRC §10.004(a); *see Low*, 221 S.W.3d at 617. See "Order under CPRC ch. 10," §11.2, p. 391; *O'Connor's Texas Forms*, FORM 5J:1, §B. For the representations certified by the signer of the pleading or motion under CPRC §10.001, see "Under CPRC ch. 10," ch. 1-B, §3.2.11(2)(a), p. 9.

2. TRCP 13. The court can impose sanctions on the attorney (or pro se party) who signed the pleading, motion, or other paper, the party represented by the attorney, or both if the pleading, motion, or other paper was signed in violation of TRCP 13. TRCP 13. See "Order under TRCP 13," §11.3, p. 391; *O'Connor's Texas Forms*, FORM 5J:1, §A. For the representations certified by the signer of the pleading, motion, or other paper under TRCP 13, see "Under TRCP 13," ch. 1-B, §3.2.11(2)(b), p. 10.

(1) Objective test – groundless. A groundless pleading, motion, or other paper is one that has no basis in law or fact and is not warranted by a good-faith argument for the extension, modification, or reversal of existing law. TRCP 13; *GTE Comms. Sys. v. Tanner*, 856 S.W.2d 725, 730 (Tex.1993). The standard is objective: Did the party and attorney make a "reasonable inquiry" into the legal and factual basis of the claim? *Lake Travis ISD v. Lovelace*, 243 S.W.3d 244, 254 (Tex.App.—Austin 2007, no pet.). To decide whether the investigation was reasonable, the court looks to the facts available to the litigant and the circumstances at the time the party filed the pleading, motion, or other paper. *Tarrant Cty. v. Chancey*, 942 S.W.2d 151, 155 (Tex.App.—Fort Worth 1997, no writ). In some cases, the court must also determine whether, at the time the pleading, motion, or other paper was filed, the legal arguments asserted in it were warranted by a good-faith argument for the extension of existing law. *Compare Lake Travis ISD*, 243 S.W.3d at 254-55 (sanction reversed; P offered arguable legal basis for extension of law); *McIntyre v. Wilson*, 50 S.W.3d 674, 687 (Tex.App.—Dallas 2001, pet. denied) (same), *with Bradt v. Sebek*, 14 S.W.3d 756, 765-66 (Tex.App.—Houston [1st Dist.] 2000, pet. denied) (sanctions affirmed; P offered no arguable legal basis for extension of law), *and Stites v. Gillum*, 872 S.W.2d 786, 792 (Tex.App.—Fort Worth 1994, writ denied) (same).

(2) Subjective test – bad faith, harassment. A groundless pleading, motion, or other paper is not sanctionable unless it was brought in bad faith or for the purpose of harassment. *GTE*, 856 S.W.2d at 731. Bad faith is more than mere bad judgment or negligence; it is motivated by dishonest, discriminatory, or malicious purposes. *Parker v. Walton*, 233 S.W.3d 535, 540 (Tex.App.—Houston [14th Dist.] 2007, no pet.); *In re Estate of Davis v. Cook*, 9 S.W.3d 288, 298 (Tex.App.—San Antonio 1999, no pet.). Thus, the party seeking sanctions must prove the pleading party's subjective state of mind.

3. CPRC ch. 9. The court can impose sanctions on the attorney (or pro se party) who signed the pleading or motion, the party represented by the attorney, or both if the pleading or motion was signed in violation of CPRC §9.011. CPRC §9.012(c). See *O'Connor's Texas Forms*, FORM 5J:1, §C. For the representations certified by the signer of the pleading or motion under CPRC §9.011, see "Under CPRC ch. 9," ch. 1-B, §3.2.11(2)(c), p. 10. Sanctions under CPRC §9.012 are not available in any proceeding in which sanctions are available under CPRC §10.004 or TRCP 13. CPRC §9.012(h). Under CPRC §9.011, the court may sanction a party for filing pleadings or motions that are (1) groundless and (2) brought in bad faith, to harass, or for any improper purpose (e.g., to cause delay or needless increase in cost of litigation). *Elkins v. Stotts-Brown*, 103 S.W.3d 664, 668 (Tex.App.—Dallas 2003, no pet.); *Herrmann & Andreas Ins. Agency, Inc. v. Appling*, 800 S.W.2d 312, 320 (Tex.App.—Corpus Christi 1990, no writ). CPRC §9.012(d) gives the party a 90-day grace period to withdraw, amend, or move to dismiss the offending pleading or motion.

———————————————— ✦ ————————————————

§5.3 Failure to serve – TRCP 21b. The court can impose sanctions on a party (or attorney advising it) that does not serve on or deliver to other parties copies of pleadings, motions, or other papers as required by TRCP 21 and TRCP 21a. TRCP 21b; *Union City Body Co. v. Ramirez*, 911 S.W.2d 196, 200 (Tex.App.—San Antonio 1995, orig. proceeding); *see* TRCP 215.2(b). See *O'Connor's Texas Forms*, FORM 5J:3.

§5.4 Contempt under Government Code. Under Gov't Code §21.002, a court can punish an attorney or other person for contempt of court; under Gov't Code §82.061, a court can punish an attorney for misbehavior or contempt of court. See "Sanctions under Government Code," §7.5, p. 386.

§5.5 Affidavits made in bad faith – TRCP 166a(h). In a summary-judgment proceeding, if a party relies on an affidavit made in bad faith or for the purpose of delay, the court must order the party to pay the other party reasonable expenses caused by the affidavit, including reasonable attorney fees. TRCP 166a(h). See "Sanctions under TRCP 166a(h)," §7.6, p. 387.

§5.6 Violation of limine order. The court may strike pleadings as a sanction for a violation of a motion in limine. See "Sanction," ch. 5-E, §8.2, p. 349.

5-2. SUMMARY OF SANCTIONS			
Sanctionable conduct	**Authority**	**Who can be sanctioned**	**Available relief**
1	Frivolous pleadings	CPRC ch. 10	Attorney and party	Reasonable expenses (including attorney fees), penalty to be paid into court, and directive to perform or refrain from performing act.
2	Groundless pleadings	CPRC §§9.011-9.014	Attorney and party	Striking of pleadings, dismissal of party and order to pay reasonable expenses (including attorney fees) incurred because of filing of pleadings.
3	Groundless pleadings brought in bad faith or for harassment	TRCP 13	Attorney and party	Sanctions under TRCP 215.2(b)—for list of sanctions under TRCP 215, see §7.1, p. 384.
4	Failure to serve or deliver pleadings and motions	TRCP 21b	Attorney and party	Sanctions under TRCP 215.2(b)—for list of sanctions under TRCP 215, see §7.1, p. 384.
5	Bad-faith affidavits in summary-judgment proceedings	TRCP 166a(h)	Attorney and party	Reasonable expenses, including attorney fees.
6	Discovery abuses	TRCP 191.3, 199.5(d), 215	Attorney and party	See §7.1, p. 384.
7	Contempt of court	Gov't Code §21.002	Attorney and party	Justice or municipal court: confinement up to 3 days or fine up to $100, or both. Other courts: confinement up to 6 months or fine up to $500, or both.
8	Contempt of court or related misbehavior	Gov't Code §82.061	Attorney	Imprisonment or fine.
9	Any improper conduct related to trial	Inherent power	Attorney and party	Sanction necessary to deter, alleviate, and counteract abuse.

§6. CONDUCT THAT DOES NOT JUSTIFY SANCTIONS

The rules do not permit sanctions in the following circumstances: • A court cannot impose a sanction when there has been no conduct justifying sanctions in the matter before the court. *See, e.g., Thompson v. Davis*, 901 S.W.2d 939, 940 (Tex.1995) (court could not extend sanction from earlier motion to modify child support to later motion to modify custody). • A court cannot sanction a party for filing a motion for summary judgment claiming there is no fact issue about a disputed issue, unless the motion is groundless. *GTE Comms. Sys. v. Tanner*, 856 S.W.2d 725, 730 (Tex.1993). • A court cannot sanction a party or attorney for a groundless affidavit filed by the party but signed by a witness. *Id.* • A court cannot impose sanctions under TRCP 13 for a plaintiff's failure to give the defendant the required notice of intention to file suit; the appropriate remedy is abatement, not dismissal. *Trimble v. Itz*, 898 S.W.2d 370, 374 (Tex.App.—San Antonio 1995), *writ denied*, 906 S.W.2d 481 (Tex.1995). • A court cannot impose sanctions under TRCP 13 on a plaintiff for lacking sufficient proof of its claim. *Trimble*, 898 S.W.2d at 374. • A court cannot strike all of a party's pleadings because the party filed an amended petition after the deadline in the pretrial order. *Granado v. Madsen*, 729 S.W.2d 866, 871 (Tex.App.—Houston [14th Dist.] 1987, writ ref'd n.r.e.). • A court cannot impose sanctions under TRCP 13 for the continuation of a suit after it is shown to be baseless. *Karagounis v. Property Co. of Am.*, 970 S.W.2d 761, 765 (Tex.App.—Amarillo 1998, pet. denied).

§7. TYPES OF SANCTIONS

The choice of sanctions is within the discretion of the court. *Bodnow Corp. v. City of Hondo*, 721 S.W.2d 839, 840 (Tex.1986).

NOTE

*The ultimate sanctions of dismissal or default are limited by constitutional considerations. When a trial court imposes the ultimate sanction, it is adjudicating the party's claims without regard to the merits. **TransAmerican Nat. Gas Corp. v. Powell**, 811 S.W.2d 913, 918 (Tex.1991). A court may dismiss or default a party only when a party's actions justify the presumption that its claims or defenses lack merit. Id.*

---

§7.1 Sanctions for discovery abuse.

1. Disallow discovery. The court may disallow further discovery of any kind or of a particular kind by the disobedient party. TRCP 215.2(b)(1).

2. Award costs & expenses. The court may charge all or part of the expenses of discovery, taxable court costs, or both, against the disobedient party or the party's attorney. TRCP 215.2(b)(2); *see Chrysler Corp. v. Blackmon*, 841 S.W.2d 844, 849 (Tex.1992); *see also Onstad v. Wright*, 54 S.W.3d 799, 804-05 (Tex.App.—Texarkana 2001, pet. denied) (P's attorney fined $32,198 to compensate D for mistrial due to violation of limine order). If the disobedient party is not able to pay, the trial court cannot enforce the sanctions by jailing the party until it pays. *Ex parte Dolenz*, 893 S.W.2d 677, 680-81 (Tex.App.—Dallas 1995, orig. proceeding).

3. Establish facts. The court may order that the discovery matters the disobedient party did not produce will be deemed in favor of the other party. TRCP 215.2(b)(3); *Spohn Hosp. v. Mayer*, 104 S.W.3d 878, 881 n.2 (Tex. 2003).

4. Limit or exclude evidence. The court may refuse to allow the disobedient party to support or oppose designated claims or defenses, or the court may prohibit the party from introducing designated matters into evidence. TRCP 215.2(b)(4); *see also* TRCP 193.6(a) (party who does not timely respond to discovery request cannot introduce material into evidence unless there is good cause or no unfair surprise or prejudice to other parties). Whether the court should limit or exclude evidence that the disobedient party refused to produce or attempted to conceal depends on whether the evidence is beneficial or detrimental to the disobedient party's case. *CRSS, Inc. v. Montanari*, 902 S.W.2d 601, 610 (Tex.App.—Houston [1st Dist.] 1995, writ denied).

(1) Undisclosed evidence beneficial. When the evidence that the disobedient party did not disclose is beneficial to the disobedient party, the court may (1) prohibit the party from introducing it, (2) establish those facts against the party, and (3) prohibit the party from supporting or opposing designated claims or defenses. *See* TRCP 215.2(b)(3), (b)(4); *see, e.g., Adkins Servs. v. Tisdale Co.*, 56 S.W.3d 842, 843 (Tex.App.—Texarkana 2001, no pet.) (court excluded P's evidence because P did not answer interrogatories and requests for admissions); *CRSS*,

---

★

---

902 S.W.2d at 610 (court should have prevented disobedient party from offering witnesses and prohibited it from cross-examining opposing party's witnesses). See "Objecting to Unidentified Witness," ch. 6-E, §10, p. 522.

(2) Undisclosed evidence detrimental. When the evidence that the disobedient party did not disclose is detrimental to the disobedient party, the court should permit the other party to introduce the evidence. As a sanction on the disobedient party, the court may prohibit it from supporting or opposing designated claims or defenses and may establish the facts in the concealed evidence against that party. *See* TRCP 215.2(b)(3), (b)(4); *City of San Antonio v. Fulcher*, 749 S.W.2d 217, 220 (Tex.App.—San Antonio 1988, writ denied) (disobedient party should not be permitted to offer evidence that contradicts nondisclosed evidence). See "Establish facts," §7.1.3, p. 384.

5. Strike pleadings. The court may (1) strike all or part of the disobedient party's pleadings, (2) dismiss (with or without prejudice) all or part of the disobedient party's suit or proceedings, or (3) render a default judgment against the disobedient party. TRCP 215.2(b)(5). See "Death-penalty sanctions," §3.2, p. 378.

6. Stay proceedings. The court may stay further proceedings until the order is obeyed. TRCP 215.2(b)(5).

7. Hold in contempt. Along with any of the sanctions in TRCP 215.2(b)(1)-(b)(5), the court may treat a party's refusal to obey an order as contempt of court. TRCP 215.2(b)(6). However, the court cannot hold a party or person in contempt for refusing to submit to a physical or mental examination under TRCP 204. TRCP 215.2(b)(6).

8. Sanctions for refusal to comply with TRCP 204. When a party refuses to comply with an order under TRCP 204 requiring the party to appear or to produce another person for a physical or mental examination, the court may impose the sanctions listed in TRCP 215.2(b)(1)-(b)(5) (see §7.1.1 through §7.1.6, above), unless the party shows that it was unable to appear or to produce the person for examination. TRCP 215.2(b)(7).

9. Attorney fees & reasonable expenses. Along with any of the sanctions in TRCP 215.2(b)(1)-(b)(7), the court may require the offending party, the attorney advising the party, or both to pay reasonable expenses, including attorney fees, incurred because of the discovery abuse. TRCP 215.2(b)(8); *see also Scott Bader, Inc. v. Sandstone Prods.*, 248 S.W.3d 802, 817 (Tex.App.—Houston [1st Dist.] 2008, no pet.) (when attorney fees are imposed as sanctions, party does not have to prove necessity or reasonableness of those fees). The court should not impose sanctions under subsection (b)(8) if the court finds the noncompliance was substantially justified or if other circumstances make an award of expenses unjust. TRCP 215.2(b)(8).

10. Loss of privilege. When a party refuses to comply with discovery, the trial court may permit privileged information (noncore work product) to be produced as a sanction. *Occidental Chem. Corp. v. Banales*, 907 S.W.2d 488, 490 (Tex.1995).

11. Any sanctions under TRCP 215.2(b). If the court finds a party is abusing the discovery process in seeking, making, or resisting discovery, or if the court finds that any interrogatory or request for inspection or production is unreasonably frivolous, oppressive, or harassing or that a response or answer is unreasonably frivolous or made for the purpose of delay, then the court may, after notice and a hearing, impose any appropriate sanction authorized by TRCP 215.2(b)(1)-(b)(5) and (b)(8). TRCP 215.3; *see, e.g., Aguilar v. Trujillo*, 162 S.W.3d 839, 848 (Tex.App.—El Paso 2005, pet. denied) (sanctions striking Ps' experts were upheld because one P violated Disciplinary Rule 4.02(b) by contacting D's consulting expert without consent and by hiring him to be Ps' expert witness).

12. Deem admissions. For sanctions for failure to comply with a request for admissions, see "Challenging the Response," ch. 6-H, §5, p. 560.

13. Strike expert testimony. The trial court may strike the testimony of a disobedient party's expert witness. *See State Farm Fire & Cas. Co. v. Rodriguez*, 88 S.W.3d 313, 325-26 (Tex.App.—San Antonio 2002, pet. denied). As long as the exclusion of testimony impairs only the presentation of a party's case and does not prevent a trial on the merits, striking the testimony is within the court's discretion and is not a death-penalty sanction. *Id.* at 326.

★

14. Other sanctions that are "just." The trial court is not limited to the sanctions listed in TRCP 215.2(b). For example, even though TRCP 215.2(b) does not mention community service, the trial court can impose it as a sanction under the rule. *E.g.*, *Cap Rock Elec. Coop. v. Texas Utils. Elec. Co.*, 874 S.W.2d 92, 98 (Tex. App.—El Paso 1994, no writ) (court ordered corporate officers and directors who attempted to hide documents to perform 200 hours of community service); *Braden v. South Main Bank*, 837 S.W.2d 733, 742 (Tex.App.—Houston [14th Dist.] 1992, writ denied) (court ordered attorney who filed frivolous objections to interrogatories to perform ten hours of community service); *see Braden v. Downey*, 811 S.W.2d 922, 930 (Tex.1991) (order to perform community service must be deferred until it can be challenged on appeal); *see, e.g.*, *Hill & Griffith Co. v. Bryant*, 139 S.W.3d 688, 694 (Tex.App.—Tyler 2004, pet. denied) (court ordered attorney who attempted to hide documents to perform 50 hours of community service).

§7.2 Sanctions under CPRC §10.004. The following sanctions are available under CPRC §10.004: (1) ordering the party to perform or refrain from performing an act, (2) ordering a monetary penalty paid to the court, and (3) ordering the party to pay the other party the amount of reasonable expenses it incurred because of the filing of the frivolous pleading, including attorney fees. CPRC §10.004(c).

§7.3 Sanctions under TRCP 13. Under TRCP 13, the court can impose any appropriate sanction in TRCP 215.2(b). *Bradt v. Sebek*, 14 S.W.3d 756, 762 (Tex.App.—Houston [1st Dist.] 2000, pet. denied). The rules leave the choice of sanctions to the trial court. See "Sanctions for discovery abuse," §7.1, p. 384.

§7.4 Sanctions under CPRC §9.012. The following sanctions are available under CPRC §9.012: (1) striking the pleadings or the offending part of the pleadings, (2) dismissing the party, or (3) ordering the party to pay the other party the amount of reasonable expenses it incurred because of the filing of the pleading, including costs, reasonable attorney fees, witness fees, fees of experts, and deposition expenses. CPRC §9.012(e).

§7.5 Sanctions under Government Code. A court may impose fines and confinement or imprisonment as sanctions for a person held in contempt of court under Gov't Code §21.002 or §82.061. Contempt can be either civil or criminal; however, the distinction does not depend on whether the underlying case is civil or criminal but on the nature and purpose of the court's punishment. *See Ex parte Werblud*, 536 S.W.2d 542, 545-46 (Tex.1976) (civil contempt is to coerce person to obey court order; criminal contempt is to punish person for some act); *Cadle Co. v. Lobingier*, 50 S.W.3d 662, 667 (Tex.App.—Fort Worth 2001, pet. denied) (same). See *O'Connor's Texas Appeals*, "Types of contempt," ch. 10-E, §2.1, p. 359.

1. Section 21.002.

(1) Civil contempt. The court can fine a person or require a person to be confined in jail for civil contempt. See *O'Connor's Texas Appeals*, "Civil contempt," ch. 10-E, §2.3.1, p. 362.

(a) Fine. Gov't Code §21.002 does not limit the maximum fine a court can impose for civil contempt. *In re Reece*, 341 S.W.3d 360, 366 n.9 (Tex.2011); *Galtex Prop. Investors, Inc. v. City of Galveston*, 113 S.W.3d 922, 927 (Tex.App.—Houston [14th Dist.] 2003, no pet.); *Cadle Co.*, 50 S.W.3d at 667-68.

(b) Confinement. The court can require a person to be confined in jail for civil contempt until she complies with the court's order. Gov't Code §21.002(e). The maximum time a person can be confined for civil contempt is 18 months. *Id.* §21.002(h)(2). The 18-month limit does not apply to contempt under Family Code chapter 157, when a person disobeys a court order to make child-support payments. Gov't Code §21.002(f).

(2) Criminal contempt. If the offensive conduct takes place in a county or district court, the court can impose a fine of up to $500 or order confinement for up to six months, or both. Gov't Code §21.002(b); *In re Long*, 984 S.W.2d 623, 625 (Tex.1999); *Cadle Co.*, 50 S.W.3d at 667-68; *see also* Gov't Code §21.002(c) (for contemptuous conduct in justice or municipal courts, the limit is $100 and three days' confinement). The maximum time a person can be confined for criminal contempt is 18 months, including three or more periods of confinement for contempt arising from the same matter that equal a total of 18 months. Gov't Code §21.002(h)(1). See *O'Connor's Texas Appeals*, "Criminal contempt," ch. 10-E, §2.3.2, p. 362.

———————————————— ✦ ————————————————

2. Section 82.061. Gov't Code §82.061 does not provide limits for monetary fines or imprisonment for contempt. However, under Gov't Code §21.002, an attorney cannot be confined for contempt for longer than 18 months. *See* Gov't Code §21.002(h) ("notwithstanding any other law," person cannot be confined for contempt for more than 18 months).

§7.6 Sanctions under TRCP 166a(h). In a summary-judgment proceeding, the court can impose sanctions requiring a party to pay the other party's reasonable expenses, including reasonable attorney fees, caused by an affidavit made in bad faith or for the purpose of delay. TRCP 166a(h); *Ramirez v. Encore Wire Corp.*, 196 S.W.3d 469, 476 (Tex.App.—Dallas 2006, no pet.). The court can also find any offending party or attorney guilty of contempt. TRCP 166a(h); *Ramirez*, 196 S.W.3d at 476.

§7.7 Improper sanctions. There are limits to the types of sanctions a trial court may impose, even when the conduct justifies sanctions.

1. Prohibit access to court. A trial court cannot sanction a party by prohibiting it from filing pleadings. *Glass v. Glass*, 826 S.W.2d 683, 687 (Tex.App.—Texarkana 1992, writ denied); *Kahn v. Garcia*, 816 S.W.2d 131, 133-34 (Tex.App.—Houston [1st Dist.] 1991, orig. proceeding); *see also* Tex. Const. art. 1, §13 (open-courts provision). *But cf.* CPRC §11.101(a) (court may prohibit pro se litigant from filing suit without permission of local administrative judge if court determines, after notice and hearing, that the person is a vexatious litigant). Such a prohibition denies the party the means to communicate with the trial court. *Kahn*, 816 S.W.2d at 133.

2. Prevent review. A trial court cannot sanction a party by striking post-trial motions, thus foreclosing the appeal. *Lehtonen v. Clarke*, 784 S.W.2d 945, 946-47 (Tex.App.—Houston [14th Dist.] 1990, writ denied). TRAP 42.3 does not authorize an appellate court to dismiss a party's appeal as punishment. *See O'Connor v. Sam Houston Med. Hosp., Inc.*, 807 S.W.2d 574, 576 (Tex.1991) (applying former TRAP 60(a)).

3. Dismiss separate lawsuit. A trial court cannot dismiss a separate lawsuit as a discovery sanction. *McKellar Dev. Grp. v. Fairbank*, 827 S.W.2d 579, 581 (Tex.App.—San Antonio 1992, no writ).

4. Sanctions after special exceptions. A trial court cannot impose a monetary sanction for refusal to amend pleadings after special exceptions are sustained. *D.A. Buckner Constr., Inc. v. Hobson*, 793 S.W.2d 74, 75-76 (Tex.App.—Houston [14th Dist.] 1990, orig. proceeding). When special exceptions are sustained, the party can either amend the pleadings or refuse to amend and test the validity of the court's ruling. *Id.* at 75. See "Special Exceptions—Challenging the Pleadings," ch. 3-G, p. 248.

5. Security for costs. A trial court cannot require a party to post a specific amount of a bond as security for the suit as a sanction. *Johnson v. Smith*, 857 S.W.2d 612, 615-16 (Tex.App.—Houston [1st Dist.] 1993, orig. proceeding).

6. Charity work by nonparty. A trial court cannot require a nonparty to perform indigent medical care as a sanction. *Pope v. Davidson*, 849 S.W.2d 916, 920 (Tex.App.—Houston [14th Dist.] 1993, orig. proceeding). Contempt is the only sanction that a court may impose on a nonparty. See "Nonparty," §4.4, p. 380.

7. Arbitrary fine under TRCP 215.3. Under TRCP 215.3, a trial court cannot impose an arbitrary monetary fine on a party for discovery abuse. *E.g., Ford Motor Co. v. Tyson*, 943 S.W.2d 527, 532-33 (Tex.App.—Dallas 1997, orig. proceeding) (fine of $10 million set aside); *Owens-Corning Fiberglas Corp. v. Caldwell*, 807 S.W.2d 413, 415-16 (Tex.App.—Houston [1st Dist.] 1991, orig. proceeding) (fine of $2.3 million set aside). A sanction under TRCP 215.3 must be compensatory or remedial; an arbitrary fine cannot be imposed solely for punishment. *Ford Motor*, 943 S.W.2d at 533. Monetary sanctions under TRCP 215.3 must be related to the expenses caused by the abuse. *Clone Component Distribs. v. State*, 819 S.W.2d 593, 597 (Tex.App.—Dallas 1991, no writ) (reversed $50,000 fine). A fine for discovery abuse is arbitrary if it is unrestrained by law or statute and unrelated to any damages or expenses incurred by the injured party. *Ford Motor*, 943 S.W.2d at 534. Arbitrariness is a characteristic of a substantive due-process violation. *Id.*

8. Arbitrary amount for expenses. When a court awards expenses under TRCP 215.2(b)(2) or awards expenses and attorney fees under TRCP 215.2(b)(8), the amount awarded cannot be arbitrary; the amount must be related to the harm suffered by the other party. *Hanley v. Hanley*, 813 S.W.2d 511, 522 (Tex.App.—Dallas 1991, no

⭐

writ); *see, e.g.*, *Kugle v. DaimlerChrysler Corp.*, 88 S.W.3d 355, 364-65 (Tex.App.—San Antonio 2002, pet. denied) (monetary sanction of $865,000 assessed against P's attorneys was upheld as cost for defense of fraudulent PI suit).

9. Discovery of attorney notes. The privilege for core work product, which relates to an attorney's thought processes, is absolute, and the trial court cannot order production of core work product as a sanction. *Occidental Chem. Corp. v. Banales*, 907 S.W.2d 488, 490 (Tex.1995). The court can order noncore work product to be produced as a sanction. *See id.*

10. Trial setting. An early trial setting is not an appropriate sanction for discovery abuse. *Arkla, Inc. v. Harris*, 846 S.W.2d 623, 629 (Tex.App.—Houston [14th Dist.] 1993, orig. proceeding).

11. Penalty paid to litigant. When a statute authorizes a monetary penalty as a sanction, the trial court cannot require a party to pay the penalty into the court registry for the other party's benefit. *Sterling v. Alexander*, 99 S.W.3d 793, 799-800 (Tex.App.—Houston [14th Dist.] 2003, pet. denied).

12. Death-penalty sanctions. Sanctions that terminate the lawsuit are proper only under certain conditions. See "Death-penalty sanctions," §3.2, p. 378.

§8. MOTION FOR SANCTIONS

§8.1 On court's initiative. A court may impose sanctions under CPRC chapter 10, TRCP 13, or TRCP 191.3 on its own initiative without a motion. *See* CPRC §10.002(b); TRCP 13, 191.3(e); *Koslow's v. Mackie*, 796 S.W.2d 700, 704 (Tex.1990). The sanctioned party is entitled to notice and a hearing. *Aldine ISD v. Baty*, 946 S.W.2d 851, 852 (Tex.App.—Houston [14th Dist.] 1997, no writ) (sanctions under TRCP 13); *see* CPRC §10.002(b) (person to be sanctioned under §10.001 must receive show-cause hearing), §10.003 (court must provide notice and reasonable opportunity to respond). The trial court cannot impose monetary sanctions on its own initiative after a voluntary dismissal or settlement unless the court issued the show-cause order before the dismissal or settlement. CPRC §10.004(e); *In re Bennett*, 960 S.W.2d 35, 40 n.5 (Tex.1997); *Scott & White Mem'l Hosp. v. Schexnider*, 940 S.W.2d 594, 596 n.1 (Tex.1996).

§8.2 By party.

1. Identify sanctionable conduct. The motion for sanctions must identify the specific conduct that deserves sanction. Because the trial court may consider other matters that have occurred in the litigation, the motion for sanctions may include other, earlier conduct that warrants sanctions. *See Downer v. Aquamarine Operators, Inc.*, 701 S.W.2d 238, 241 (Tex.1985); *Medical Prot. Co. v. Glanz*, 721 S.W.2d 382, 388 (Tex.App.—Corpus Christi 1986, writ ref'd).

2. Identify authority for sanction. The motion for sanctions must identify the specific statute, rule, or order the party violated. A court cannot grant sanctions under a statute or rule that is not identified in the motion. *E.g.*, *Ball v. Rao*, 48 S.W.3d 332, 338 (Tex.App.—Fort Worth 2001, pet. denied) (court could not grant sanctions under CPRC §9.011 because statute was not included as ground for sanctions in motion).

3. Request sanction. The movant should identify the sanction it wants the court to impose (e.g., monetary sanctions, default, dismissal) and argue that the sanction (1) has a direct relationship to the offensive conduct and (2) is not excessive. A party should not ask for a death-penalty sanction in its first motion for sanctions unless it is apparent that a lesser sanction will not promote compliance. *GTE Comms. Sys. v. Tanner*, 856 S.W.2d 725, 729 (Tex.1993); *Sanchez v. Brownsville Sports Ctr., Inc.*, 51 S.W.3d 643, 659 (Tex.App.—Corpus Christi 2001, pet. granted, judgm't vacated w.r.m.). See "Standards for Imposing Sanctions," §3, p. 377.

4. Be verified. If the motion for sanctions contains evidence that does not appear in the court's record, the motion should be verified and affidavits attached as necessary.

5. Deadline to file.

(1) Pretrial conduct. To be entitled to sanctions based on pretrial conduct, the party must secure a pretrial hearing and ruling on that conduct, or it waives any claim for sanctions based on that conduct. *Remington*

✯

Arms Co. v. Caldwell, 850 S.W.2d 167, 170 (Tex.1993); *Finlay v. Olive*, 77 S.W.3d 520, 526 (Tex.App.—Houston [1st Dist.] 2002, no pet.). However, if the grounds for pretrial sanctions are not known until after the trial has begun, the claim for sanctions is not waived. *Remington Arms*, 850 S.W.2d at 170.

(2) **Trial conduct.** To be entitled to sanctions based on trial conduct, the party must file a motion for sanctions before the court loses plenary power over its judgment. *Scott & White Mem'l Hosp. v. Schexnider*, 940 S.W.2d 594, 596 (Tex.1996); *see Unifund CCR Partners v. Villa*, 299 S.W.3d 92, 95-96 (Tex.2009); *Crites v. Collins*, 284 S.W.3d 839, 843 (Tex.2009). See "Postjudgment motions & finality," ch. 9-C, §6.5.1, p. 775. Neither the filing of a nonsuit nor the removal of a case to federal court deprives the trial court of jurisdiction to impose sanctions for conduct before the nonsuit or removal. *In re Bennett*, 960 S.W.2d 35, 38-40 (Tex.1997); *see Crites*, 284 S.W.3d at 843 (court has power to impose sanctions after a nonsuit as long as motion is filed before court loses plenary power). But when sanctions are imposed after removal to federal court, the sanctions cannot affect the merits of the litigation pending in federal court. *See In re Bennett*, 960 S.W.2d at 39-40.

§8.3 Proper court. Ordinarily, a motion for sanctions should be filed in the court where the action is pending. *Mantri v. Bergman*, 153 S.W.3d 715, 718 (Tex.App.—Dallas 2005, pet. denied) (sanctions under CPRC ch. 10). When sanctions are sought against a nonparty who refuses to answer questions at a deposition, the motion should be filed in the court in the district where the deposition is being taken. TRCP 215.1(a); *Latham v. Thornton*, 806 S.W.2d 347, 349-50 (Tex.App.—Fort Worth 1991, orig. proceeding).

§9. RESPONSE

When a party is notified that a motion for sanctions is pending against it, the party should take the following steps.

§9.1 File response. The party charged with sanctionable conduct should file a response to the motion for sanctions and inform the trial court, under oath, why sanctions should not be imposed. The response should make the following arguments, as appropriate: (1) no sanctionable conduct occurred, (2) there is no relationship between the offensive conduct and the sanction requested, (3) the sanction requested is excessive and, if death-penalty sanctions are requested, the court did not impose a lesser sanction first, and (4) the party's claims or defenses in the underlying suit are meritorious. See "Standards for Imposing Sanctions," §3, p. 377; *O'Connor's Texas Forms*, FORMS 5J:2, 5J:4. The party should attach as many affidavits as necessary.

§9.2 Ask for hearing. The party charged with sanctionable conduct should follow the procedure in the local rules for securing a hearing to present evidence.

§10. HEARING

§10.1 Necessity of hearing. CPRC §§9.012(c), 10.003, TRCP 13, 21b, 215.2(b), 215.3, and due process require the court to hold a hearing before imposing sanctions. *See R.M. Dudley Constr. Co. v. Dawson*, 258 S.W.3d 694, 709-10 (Tex.App.—Waco 2008, pet. denied) (sanctions under CPRC ch. 10). A court cannot strike a party's pleadings, render a default judgment, or impose monetary sanctions without giving the party an opportunity to be heard. *See Sears, Roebuck & Co. v. Hollingsworth*, 293 S.W.2d 639, 642 (Tex.1956) (sanctions for disregarding subpoena were reversed because there was no notice or hearing); *Tidrow v. Roth*, 189 S.W.3d 408, 413 (Tex.App.—Dallas 2006, no pet.) (sanctions for discovery abuse were reversed because there was no notice or hearing).

1. **Oral hearing.** In most cases, the court should conduct an oral hearing to receive evidence on the allegation that sanctions are warranted. *See Bedding Component Manufactors, Ltd. v. Royal Sleep Prods.*, 108 S.W.3d 563, 564 (Tex.App.—Dallas 2003, no pet.) (sanctions under TRCP 13 were reversed because there was no hearing to present evidence); *Bisby v. Dow Chem. Co.*, 931 S.W.2d 18, 21 (Tex.App.—Houston [1st Dist.] 1996, no writ) (same). At an oral hearing, the trial court must permit the party to introduce evidence before imposing sanctions. *Davila v. World Car Five Star*, 75 S.W.3d 537, 544 (Tex.App.—San Antonio 2002, no pet.).

2. **Hearing by submission.** The court is not required to hold an oral hearing; sanctions can be resolved by a hearing on submission. *See, e.g., Cire v. Cummings*, 134 S.W.3d 835, 843-44 (Tex.2004) (nothing in TRCP 215.3 requires an oral hearing).

★

§10.2   Necessity of adequate notice. Due process and various provisions in the CPRC and TRCPs require the court to give the party notice of the hearing on sanctions. *See* CPRC §§9.012(c), 10.003; TRCP 13, 21b, 215.2(b), 215.3; *Low v. Henry*, 221 S.W.3d 609, 618 (Tex.2007); *Cire v. Cummings*, 134 S.W.3d 835, 843 (Tex.2004). The notice of the hearing on sanctions must be adequate. *Plano S&L Ass'n v. Slavin*, 721 S.W.2d 282, 284 (Tex.1986). Oral notice is not adequate; the party must be given written notice of the hearing. *In re Acceptance Ins.*, 33 S.W.3d 443, 451 (Tex.App.—Fort Worth 2000, orig. proceeding). One day's notice of the hearing is not adequate. *Plano S&L*, 721 S.W.2d at 284.

§10.3   Make a record. The party charged with sanctionable conduct should treat the hearing on sanctions as a hearing for evidence, not just for argument. The party should make sure the court reporter is present and transcribes the entire hearing, including arguments. Once the hearing starts, the attorneys and parties should be sworn and should formally offer evidence on the issue of sanctions. One court has said that the party, not the attorney, should testify at the hearing on sanctions. *Walsh v. Mullane*, 725 S.W.2d 263, 264 (Tex.App.—Houston [1st Dist.] 1986, writ ref'd n.r.e.). But the attorney should testify if the attorney knows about the failure to comply with discovery (when the fault lies with the attorney).

§10.4   Burden.

1.   On court's initiative. When the court sets a matter for sanctions on its own initiative, the party seeking to avoid sanctions must prove that sanctions should not be imposed. *See* CPRC §10.002(b) (show-cause hearing).

2.   On party's motion. At a hearing on sanctions, the party that filed the motion for sanctions must first prove the allegations in its motion. *GTE Comms. Sys. v. Tanner*, 856 S.W.2d 725, 729 (Tex.1993). Once the movant proves that the other party's conduct justifies sanctions, the other party must produce evidence demonstrating why sanctions should not be imposed.

3.   Burden on party to be sanctioned. To avoid sanctions, the party or attorney charged with sanctionable conduct should prove the allegations in its response. See "File response," §9.1, p. 389.

NOTE

*Under TRCP 13, the trial court begins with the presumption that all pleadings are filed in good faith. GTE, 856 S.W.2d at 731; **Trimble v. Itz**, 898 S.W.2d 370, 374 (Tex.App.—San Antonio 1995), writ denied, 906 S.W.2d 481 (Tex.1995). CPRC §10.001 does not have the same presumption, but courts have extended the good faith presumption found in TRCP 13 to §10.001 sanctions claims. E.g., **Low v. Henry**, 221 S.W.3d 609, 614 (Tex.2007); **Thottumkal v. McDougal**, 251 S.W.3d 715, 718 (Tex.App.—Houston [14th Dist.] 2008, pet. denied); **Save Our Springs Alliance, Inc. v. Lazy Nine MUD**, 198 S.W.3d 300, 321 (Tex.App.—Texarkana 2006, pet. denied).*

---

§10.5   Entire case. In imposing sanctions, the trial court may consider all matters that have occurred in the litigation; the court is not limited to considering the specific violation. *Downer v. Aquamarine Operators, Inc.*, 701 S.W.2d 238, 241 (Tex.1985); *Medical Prot. Co. v. Glanz*, 721 S.W.2d 382, 388 (Tex.App.—Corpus Christi 1986, writ ref'd).

§10.6   Violations by both parties. The trial court is justified in refusing to impose sanctions if both sides are equally guilty. *See Larson v. H.E. Butt Grocery Co.*, 769 S.W.2d 694, 695-96 (Tex.App.—Corpus Christi 1989, writ denied) (record showed lack of candor and attempts at gamesmanship on both sides).

§11. ORDER FOR SANCTIONS

The court may impose sanctions on a person who abused the discovery process or signed a pleading in violation of CPRC §9.011, CPRC §10.001, or TRCP 13. The court's discretion is limited by a requirement that the sanction be "just." TRCP 215.2(b); *Spohn Hosp. v. Mayer*, 104 S.W.3d 878, 882 (Tex.2003); *TransAmerican Nat. Gas Corp. v. Powell*, 811 S.W.2d 913, 917 (Tex.1991). See *O'Connor's Texas Forms*, FORM 5J:5.

★

§11.1 Order for discovery sanctions.

1. Sanctions. The court may impose sanctions on the party, the attorney, both the party and the attorney, or a nonparty. See "Persons Who May Be Sanctioned," §4, p. 379.

2. Attorney fees & costs. The court may award attorney fees and costs to the prevailing party. See "Attorney fees & reasonable expenses," §7.1.9, p. 385.

3. Explanation. The court must explain the reason for imposing sanctions by stating the following: (1) a description of the sanctionable conduct, (2) the relationship between the conduct and the sanctions, and (3) the necessity for the severity of the sanctions. *See Spohn Hosp. v. Mayer*, 104 S.W.3d 878, 882 (Tex.2003). If death-penalty sanctions are imposed, the court must also (1) state that a lesser sanction was imposed without effect, or provide a reasoned explanation why a lesser sanction was not imposed and why the death-penalty sanction was appropriate, and (2) state that the party's conduct justifies the presumption that its claims or defenses lack merit. *See Cire v. Cummings*, 134 S.W.3d 835, 842 (Tex.2004); *GTE Comms. Sys. v. Tanner*, 856 S.W.2d 725, 729-30 (Tex.1993). See "Standards for Imposing Sanctions," §3, p. 377. The court is not required to list each possible lesser sanction in its order and explain why each would be ineffective. *Cire*, 134 S.W.3d at 842.

4. Separate findings. When judgment is rendered as a sanction for discovery abuse, the court should file separate findings of fact. See "After hearing on sanctions under TRCP 215," ch. 10-E, §2.2.1, p. 818.

§11.2 Order under CPRC ch. 10.

1. Sanctions. The court may impose sanctions on the attorney, the party, or both. CPRC §10.004(a). The sanction is limited to an amount sufficient to deter repetition of the conduct by others. *Id.* §10.004(b); *University of Tex. v. Bishop*, 997 S.W.2d 350, 357 (Tex.App.—Fort Worth 1999, pet. denied). When a party is represented by an attorney, the court cannot impose monetary sanctions on the party for violating CPRC §10.001(2) (pleadings not supported by existing law or argument to extend existing law). CPRC §10.004(d); *Bishop*, 997 S.W.2d at 357. If a party appears pro se, the court may impose sanctions on the party for violating CPRC §10.001(2). *See* CPRC §10.004(d).

2. Attorney fees & costs. The court may award the prevailing party attorney fees and costs for inconvenience, harassment, and out-of-pocket expenses incurred by the party or caused by the litigation. CPRC §§10.002(c), 10.004(c)(3).

3. Explanation. When the court imposes sanctions, it must include in the order a description of the conduct that violated CPRC §10.001 and an explanation of the basis for the sanctions imposed. CPRC §10.005; *Bishop*, 997 S.W.2d at 355. When imposing a monetary penalty, the court should explain how it determined the amount of sanctions, particularly when those sanctions are severe. *Low v. Henry*, 221 S.W.3d 609, 620-21 (Tex.2007).

4. Not separate findings. The court should not file separate findings of fact to support sanctions under CPRC chapter 10. See "Groundless pleadings," ch. 10-E, §2.2.2(3), p. 818.

§11.3 Order under TRCP 13.

1. Sanctions. The court may impose sanctions on the attorney, the party, or both. TRCP 13. The trial court has the discretion to determine the severity of the sanctions, but the rule requires the court to impose punishment for a violation. *See id.*

2. Attorney fees & costs. The court may award attorney fees and costs to the prevailing party. See "Attorney fees & reasonable expenses," §7.1.9, p. 385.

3. Explanation.

(1) Identify sanctionable conduct. The order must identify the specific acts or omissions on which the court based the sanctions. *Jimenez v. Transwestern Prop. Co.*, 999 S.W.2d 125, 130 (Tex.App.—Houston [14th Dist.] 1999, no pet.); *Luxenberg v. Marshall*, 835 S.W.2d 136, 140-41 (Tex.App.—Dallas 1992, orig. proceeding); *e.g.*, *Tarrant Cty. v. Chancey*, 942 S.W.2d 151, 155 (Tex.App.—Fort Worth 1997, no writ) (statement that pleading

★

was filed to harass and cause unnecessary delays was too general). When imposing death-penalty sanctions, the court should explain why it imposed the sanction on the party and not just the attorney. See *TransAmerican Nat. Gas Corp. v. Powell*, 811 S.W.2d 913, 917 (Tex.1991).

(2) State good cause. Sanctions can be imposed only for good cause. TRCP 13; *Daniel v. Webb*, 110 S.W.3d 708, 711-12 (Tex.App.—Amarillo 2003, no pet.); *Murphy v. Friendswood Dev. Co.*, 965 S.W.2d 708, 709 (Tex.App.—Houston [1st Dist.] 1998, no pet.). Thus, the court must include a statement of good cause in the order to support the imposition of sanctions. TRCP 13; *Tarrant Restoration v. TX Arlington Oaks Apts., Ltd.*, 225 S.W.3d 721, 733 (Tex.App.—Dallas 2007, pet. dism'd); *Chancey*, 942 S.W.2d at 155; *Kahn v. Garcia*, 816 S.W.2d 131, 133 (Tex.App.—Houston [1st Dist.] 1991, orig. proceeding).

PRACTICE TIP

Make an objection on the record if the order does not identify the sanctionable conduct or does not make a statement of good cause. See **Jimenez***, 999 S.W.2d at 130-31. If no objection is made, the error is waived.* **Appleton v. Appleton***, 76 S.W.3d 78, 87 (Tex.App.—Houston [14th Dist.] 2002, no pet.);* **Texas-Ohio Gas, Inc. v. Mecom***, 28 S.W.3d 129, 135-36 (Tex.App.—Texarkana 2000, no pet.). The objection can be preserved in a motion for new trial, if not made earlier.* **Thomas v. Thomas***, 917 S.W.2d 425, 433 (Tex.App.—Waco 1996, no writ).*

---

4. Not separate findings. The court should not file separate findings of fact to support sanctions under TRCP 13. See "Groundless pleadings," ch. 10-E, §2.2.2(3), p. 818.

§11.4   Order under CPRC ch. 9.

1. Withdraw or amend. Before imposing sanctions, the court must give the attorney or party 90 days to withdraw or amend the offending pleadings. CPRC §9.012(c), (d); *Elkins v. Stotts-Brown*, 103 S.W.3d 664, 668 (Tex.App.—Dallas 2003, no pet.).

2. Sanctions. The court may impose sanctions on the attorney, the party, or both. CPRC §9.012(c). The court may strike the pleadings or dismiss the offending party. *Id.* §9.012(e)(1), (e)(2).

3. Attorney fees & costs. The court may award the objecting party reasonable expenses incurred because of the filing, including attorney fees, witness fees, expert fees, and deposition expenses. CPRC §9.012(e)(3). If the objecting party has been sanctioned in the same matter, that party cannot be awarded costs and fees. *Id.* §9.012(f).

§12. REVIEW

§12.1   Standard of review.
Sanctions orders are reviewed for abuse of discretion. *Unifund CCR Partners v. Villa*, 299 S.W.3d 92, 97 (Tex.2009); *American Flood Research, Inc. v. Jones*, 192 S.W.3d 581, 583 (Tex.2006); *Chrysler Corp. v. Blackmon*, 841 S.W.2d 844, 852 (Tex.1992); *see also Falk & Mayfield L.L.P. v. Molzan*, 974 S.W.2d 821, 827 (Tex.App.—Houston [14th Dist.] 1998, pet. denied) (degree of discretion for trial court is greater when sanctions are imposed for groundless pleadings rather than for discovery abuse). If the trial court made findings of fact to support the sanctions order, the appellate court should not treat the findings as findings of fact made under TRCP 296, which are reviewable under legal-sufficiency and factual-sufficiency standards. *IKB Indus. v. Pro-Line Corp.*, 938 S.W.2d 440, 442 (Tex.1997); *Chrysler Corp.*, 841 S.W.2d at 852. The findings filed by the trial court after sanctions are merely to assist the appellate court in deciding whether the trial court abused its discretion. *Chrysler Corp.*, 841 S.W.2d at 852. The appellate court should not limit its review to the findings of fact; it must make an independent review of the entire record to determine whether the trial court abused its discretion. *American Flood*, 192 S.W.3d at 583.

§12.2   Method of review.

1. By appeal. A party is entitled to challenge the sanctions on appeal after a final judgment is rendered in the case. TRCP 215.1(d), 215.2(b)(8), 215.3. When a sanction can be appealed, mandamus is not appropriate. *See, e.g.*, *Street v. Second Ct. of Appeals*, 715 S.W.2d 638, 639 (Tex.1986) (sanction of attorney fees should be challenged

✯

on appeal); *Keller Indus. v. Blanton*, 804 S.W.2d 182, 186 (Tex.App.—Houston [14th Dist.] 1991, orig. proceeding) (sanctions for costs of out-of-state depositions should be challenged on appeal). Even when a case is settled or dismissed by a nonsuit, sanctions can be reviewed on appeal. *See Felderhoff v. Knauf*, 819 S.W.2d 110, 111 (Tex.1991) (appeal after nonsuit); *Braden v. South Main Bank*, 837 S.W.2d 733, 741 (Tex.App.—Houston [14th Dist.] 1992, writ denied) (appeal after settlement).

2. By mandamus. Ordinarily, sanctions are not reviewable by mandamus because the party has an adequate remedy by appeal. *See Street*, 715 S.W.2d at 639. However, mandamus is appropriate in some cases.

(1) Sanction terminates litigation. When the trial court imposes severe sanctions that effectively preclude a decision on the merits of a party's claims, appellate review may be inadequate and mandamus review is appropriate. *TransAmerican Nat. Gas Corp. v. Powell*, 811 S.W.2d 913, 920 (Tex.1991); *In re Carnival Corp.*, 193 S.W.3d 229, 233 (Tex.App.—Houston [1st Dist.] 2006, orig. proceeding).

(2) Monetary sanction threatens litigation. When the trial court imposes monetary sanctions that threaten a party's ability or willingness to continue with the litigation so that an eventual appeal would not provide an adequate remedy, mandamus review is appropriate. *See Braden v. Downey*, 811 S.W.2d 922, 929 (Tex.1991); *see also In re Ford Motor Co.*, 988 S.W.2d 714, 723 (Tex.1998) (appeal is not adequate remedy when court imposes monetary penalty on a party's exercise of its legal rights). In most situations, however, the trial court can prevent this by either (1) providing that the sanction is payable only at a date that coincides with or follows the rendition of a final order terminating the litigation, or (2) making express written findings after a hearing on why the monetary sanctions do not have a preclusive effect. *Downey*, 811 S.W.2d at 929; *Prime Grp. v. O'Neill*, 848 S.W.2d 376, 379 (Tex.App.—Houston [14th Dist.] 1993, orig. proceeding); *Susman Godfrey, L.L.P. v. Marshall*, 832 S.W.2d 105, 108 (Tex.App.—Dallas 1992, orig. proceeding). *But see Onstad v. Wright*, 54 S.W.3d 799, 802-03 (Tex.App.—Texarkana 2001, pet. denied) (attorney fined $32,198 was required to place it into registry of court until appeal).

(3) Community service before judgment. When the trial court orders a party or attorney to perform community service that must be completed before final judgment, mandamus review is appropriate. *Downey*, 811 S.W.2d at 930.

§12.3 Record. The record should include the order imposing sanctions, the motion for sanctions, the response, the findings of fact and conclusions of law (if filed), and a transcript of the hearing on the motion. If the trial court does not hear evidence and states that it bases its opinion on the papers on file and argument of counsel, the parties are not required to produce a reporter's record. *Otis Elevator Co. v. Parmelee*, 850 S.W.2d 179, 180-81 (Tex. 1993).

§12.4 Abate appeal for good-cause statement. If the sanctioned party objected to the lack of particularized findings as required by TRCP 13, on appeal, the court may abate the appeal and order the trial court to state properly the particulars of good cause. *Campos v. Ysleta Gen. Hosp., Inc.*, 879 S.W.2d 67, 70-71 (Tex.App.—El Paso 1994, writ denied). *But see Murphy v. Friendswood Dev. Co.*, 965 S.W.2d 708, 710 (Tex.App.—Houston [1st Dist.] 1998, no pet.) (abatement was not feasible because new judge was elected; case was remanded for new hearing).

L. MOTION TO SEAL COURT RECORDS

§1. GENERAL

§1.1 Rule. TRCP 76a.

§1.2 Purpose. In response to a legislative directive, the Supreme Court adopted TRCP 76a to establish a system to control the sealing of court records. Gov't Code §22.010 (legislative directive); *General Tire, Inc. v. Kepple*, 970 S.W.2d 520, 523 & n.8 (Tex.1998); *Boardman v. Elm Block Dev. L.P.*, 872 S.W.2d 297, 298-99 (Tex.App.—Eastland 1994, no writ). Because TRCP 76a recognizes the public's right to have access to judicial records, the rule provides strict requirements for securing an order to seal court records. *See Boardman*, 872 S.W.2d at 299.

§1.3 Forms. *O'Connor's Texas Civil Forms* (2012), FORMS 5K, 6A:10.

§1.4 Other references. Doggett & Mucchetti, *Public Access to Public Courts: Discouraging Secrecy in the Public Interest*, 69 Tex.L.Rev. 643 (1991) (referred to as Doggett & Mucchetti, *Public Access*).

§2. WHAT DOCUMENTS ARE "COURT RECORDS"

§2.1 Presumption of openness. All court records are presumed to be open to the general public and can be sealed only after all the requirements set out in TRCP 76a are satisfied. *General Tire, Inc. v. Kepple*, 970 S.W.2d 520, 523 (Tex.1998); *Burlington N. R.R. v. Southwestern Elec. Power Co.*, 905 S.W.2d 683, 684 (Tex.App.—Texarkana 1995, no writ).

§2.2 Documents that are court records. All documents that relate to the lawsuit, with few exceptions, are considered court records.

1. Court orders. Court orders are court records and cannot be sealed under any circumstances. TRCP 76a(1); *Fox v. Anonymous*, 869 S.W.2d 499, 503 (Tex.App.—San Antonio 1993, writ denied).

2. Filed documents. Generally, all documents filed with the court in connection with any civil matter are court records. TRCP 76a(2)(a); *e.g., Cortez v. Johnston*, ___ S.W.3d ___ (Tex.App.—Texarkana 2012, n.p.h.) (No. 06-11-00089-CV; 9-4-12) (motion to compel and for sanctions, which had attached as exhibits P's deposition and D's complaint with Judicial Conduct Commission, was court record); *McAfee, Inc. v. Weiss*, 336 S.W.3d 840, 843-44 (Tex.App.—Dallas 2011, pet. denied) (arbitration award was court record). The exceptions are listed in "Documents that are not court records," §2.3, p. 395.

3. Filed settlement agreements. Settlement agreements filed with the court are considered court records. TRCP 76a(2)(a). Unfiled settlement agreements are court records only if they seek to restrict disclosure of information concerning matters that have a probable adverse effect on the general public health or safety, the administration of public office, or the operation of government. TRCP 76a(2)(b). The financial portions of all settlement agreements, however, may be redacted. *See Anonymous*, 869 S.W.2d at 507.

4. Discovery products.

(1) Filed discovery. Filed discovery products are court records. TRCP 76a(2)(a).

(2) Unfiled discovery. TRCP 76a does not presume that unfiled discovery products are court records. *Eli Lilly & Co. v. Biffle*, 868 S.W.2d 806, 808 (Tex.App.—Dallas 1993, no writ). Unfiled discovery products are court records only if they concern matters that have a probable adverse effect on the general public health or safety, the administration of public office, or the operation of government. TRCP 76a(2)(c); *General Tire, Inc. v. Kepple*, 970 S.W.2d 520, 523 (Tex.1998); *e.g., Cortez*, ___ S.W.3d at ___ (trial court did not abuse discretion in determining that documents, including responses to requests for disclosure, were court records; documents contained allegations that could affect reputations of four judges and questioned operations of certain district courts). If a court attempts to limit the disclosure or distribution of unfiled discovery (e.g., by a protective order), it must comply with TRCP 76a. *See Chandler v. Hyundai Motor Co.*, 829 S.W.2d 774, 774-75 (Tex.1992).

✭

---

§2.3 Documents that are not court records. TRCP 76a does not apply to documents that are not court records, as defined in TRCP 76a(2). *See General Tire, Inc. v. Kepple*, 970 S.W.2d 520, 523 (Tex.1998); *Wood v. James R. Moriarty, P.C.*, 940 S.W.2d 359, 361 (Tex.App.—Dallas 1997, no writ). Documents that are not court records under TRCP 76a may be sealed only if another rule or statute permits. See "Protecting Documents that Are Not Court Records," §8, p. 399.

1. In camera discovery. Documents filed for in camera inspection, solely for the purpose of getting a ruling on their discoverability, are not court records. TRCP 76a(2)(a)(1); *Texans United Educ. Fund v. Texaco, Inc.*, 858 S.W.2d 38, 40 (Tex.App.—Houston [14th Dist.] 1993, writ denied); *see also U.S. Gov't v. Marks*, 949 S.W.2d 320, 324 (Tex.1997) (transcript of certain statements about grand-jury investigation made by federal prosecutor during ex parte hearing was not court record under TRCP 76a(2)(a)(2)).

2. Restricted by other law. Documents to which another law restricts access (e.g., certain employment records, financial information, medical records) are not court records. TRCP 76a(2)(a)(2); Doggett & Mucchetti, *Public Access*, 69 Tex.L.Rev. at 658-59.

3. Family Code cases. Documents filed in a suit that originally arose under the Family Code (e.g., divorce, adoption, termination of parental rights, paternity, juvenile-delinquency cases) are not court records. TRCP 76a(2)(a)(3); *P.I.A., Inc. v. Sullivan*, 837 S.W.2d 844, 845-46 (Tex.App.—Fort Worth 1992, orig. proceeding).

4. Unfiled discovery.

(1) Trade-secret suit. Unfiled discovery products in a case initiated to preserve bona fide trade secrets or other intangible property rights are not court records. TRCP 76a(2)(c); *Eli Lilly & Co. v. Marshall*, 829 S.W.2d 157, 158 (Tex.1992) (trade-secret interest can justify restricting access to documents). A trade secret is a formula, pattern, device, or compilation of information that is used in one's business and presents an opportunity to obtain an advantage over competitors. *Computer Assocs. Int'l v. Altai, Inc.*, 918 S.W.2d 453, 455 (Tex.1996).

(2) No adverse effect on public. Unfiled discovery products are not court records if they do not have a probable adverse effect on the general public health or safety, the administration of public office, or the operation of government. TRCP 76a(2)(c). There is no presumption in TRCP 76a that unfiled discovery products are court records. *BP Prods. v. Houston Chronicle Publ'g*, 263 S.W.3d 31, 34 (Tex.App.—Houston [1st Dist.] 2006, no pet.); *Eli Lilly & Co. v. Biffle*, 868 S.W.2d 806, 808 (Tex.App.—Dallas 1993, no writ); *see Kepple*, 970 S.W.2d at 523. For the procedure to limit the dissemination of unfiled discovery, see "Protecting Documents that Are Not Court Records," §8, p. 399.

5. Settlement agreement + no adverse effect on public. Unfiled settlement agreements are not court records if they do not seek to restrict disclosure of information concerning matters that have a probable adverse effect on the general public health or safety, the administration of public office, or the operation of government. TRCP 76a(2)(b).

PRACTICE TIP
*If a party wants to limit dissemination of documents it believes are not court records, the party should file a motion for protective order under TRCP 192.6, not a motion to seal under TRCP 76a. See **Kepple**, 970 S.W.2d at 525 (analyzing former TRCP 166b(5)(c), now TRCP 192.6(b)(5)); **Roberts v. West**, 123 S.W.3d 436, 440 (Tex.App.—San Antonio 2003, pet. denied). See "Protecting Documents that Are Not Court Records," §8, p. 399.*

---

§3. SEALING COURT RECORDS

§3.1 Motion to seal records under TRCP 76a.

1. In writing. The party or intervenor who wants court records sealed must file a written motion to seal. TRCP 76a(3); *see* TRCP 76a(7) (any person can intervene anytime before or after judgment to seal records). See *O'Connor's Texas Forms*, FORM 5K:1. The motion itself must be open to public inspection. TRCP 76a(3).

★

2. Grounds. A party or an intervenor seeking to have documents protected from disclosure under TRCP 76a should allege the following:

(1) There is a serious, specific, and substantial interest in sealing the records that outweighs the presumption of openness and any probable adverse effect on the general public health or safety. TRCP 76a(1)(a); *e.g.*, *Fox v. Doe*, 869 S.W.2d 507, 512 (Tex.App.—San Antonio 1993, writ denied) (public health and safety would not be adversely affected by nondisclosure of names in settlement agreement of minor's sexual-assault claim against employee of corporation).

(2) There are no other, less-restrictive means that will adequately protect the specific interest asserted. TRCP 76a(1)(b); *e.g.*, *BP Prods. v. Houston Chronicle Publ'g*, 263 S.W.3d 31, 35 (Tex.App.—Houston [1st Dist.] 2006, no pet.) (by producing redacted witness statements, D conceded less-restrictive means to sealing witness statements was available); *Compaq Computer Corp. v. Lapray*, 75 S.W.3d 669, 674 (Tex.App.—Beaumont 2002, no pet.) (fact that documents contained trade secrets was insufficient to establish element of no other, less-restrictive means).

3. Notice. The party or intervenor seeking to seal court records must post a public notice. TRCP 76a(3). See "Public Notice," §4, p. 397; *O'Connor's Texas Forms*, FORM 5K:2.

4. Request to close courtroom. In addition to the request to seal court records, a party or an intervenor may request that the courtroom be closed to the public when the records are later presented in court. *See Volvo Car Corp. v. Marroquin*, No. 13-06-00070-CV (Tex.App.—Corpus Christi 2009, pet. denied) (memo op.; 11-5-09). A trial court may close its courtroom to protect the dissemination of certain sensitive information to the public. *See In re Samsung Telecomms.*, No. 05-99-01960-CV (Tex.App.—Dallas 1999, orig. proceeding) (no pub.; 12-2-99) (civil courtroom can be closed to protect trade secrets).

§3.2 Motion for temporary sealing order. A party or an intervenor can ask the court to immediately enter a temporary order sealing court records. TRCP 76a(5); *see* TRCP 76a(7) (any person can intervene anytime before or after judgment to seal records). See *O'Connor's Texas Forms*, FORM 5K:1.

1. Grounds. The party or intervenor must show a compelling need for a temporary sealing order. TRCP 76a(5). Specifically, the party or intervenor must show that she will suffer an immediate and irreparable injury to a specific interest of hers before public notice can be posted and a hearing held. *Id.* See "Public Notice," §4, p. 397; "Hearing on Motion to Seal," §5, p. 397.

2. By affidavit or verification. The party or intervenor must show a compelling need for a temporary sealing order through specific facts presented in an affidavit or verification. TRCP 76a(5).

3. Request final sealing order. If the court grants a temporary sealing order, it must set a time for the hearing, as required under TRCP 76a(4). TRCP 76a(5). See "Hearing on Motion to Seal," §5, p. 397; "Contents," §6.1.2, p. 398. At the hearing, the party or intervenor has the same burden of proof for sealing court records as if a temporary sealing order had not been requested. *See* TRCP 76a(5). Thus, in the motion for a temporary sealing order, the party or intervenor should request a final sealing order and show the required grounds. See "Grounds," §3.1.2, this page.

4. Notice. The party or intervenor must give notice of the motion for a temporary sealing order under TRCP 21 and 21a to all parties that have filed an answer. TRCP 76a(5).

§3.3 Motion to modify or withdraw temporary sealing order. If a temporary sealing order is entered, any party or intervenor can file a motion to modify or withdraw the order. TRCP 76a(5). See "Temporary order," §6.1, p. 398; *O'Connor's Texas Forms*, FORM 5K:7. The party or intervenor can file a motion to withdraw the entire sealing order or to modify it by having certain documents removed from the order.

1. Grounds.

(1) **Not court records.** The party or intervenor can show that all or some of the documents under the temporary sealing order are not court records. *See* TRCP 76a(2). See "Documents that are not court records," §2.3, p. 395.

—————————————— ★ ——————————————

(2) No compelling need. The party or intervenor can show that the adverse party did not show a compelling need to have all or some of the documents sealed under the temporary sealing order—that is, the adverse party did not show that she will suffer an immediate and irreparable injury to a specific interest of hers before public notice can be posted and a hearing held. *See* TRCP 76a(5).

2. Notice. The movant must give notice of the motion to all parties. *See* TRCP 76a(5).

3. Hearing. A hearing must be held on the motion as soon as practicable. TRCP 76a(5).

§3.4 Agreement not to disclose under TRCP 11. A TRCP 11 agreement not to disclose unfiled discovery cannot protect court documents from disclosure without the additional procedural requirements of a motion under TRCP 76a. *Cf. General Tire, Inc. v. Kepple*, 970 S.W.2d 520, 524 (Tex.1998) (before court can protect discovery from dissemination under TRCP 166b(5)(c), now TRCP 192.6(b)(5), it must observe the requirements of TRCP 76a). The Supreme Court obliquely addressed the issue of TRCP 11 agreements limiting disclosure of documents in *In re Dallas Morning News, Inc.*, 10 S.W.3d 298, 299 (Tex.1999), which dealt with appellate jurisdiction over a TRCP 11 order protecting documents from disclosure. In that case, the court reversed the mandamus granted by the court of appeals, presumably because an appeal was an adequate remedy to challenge the decision to hold a hearing on the TRCP 11 agreement long after the trial court's plenary power had expired. *See In re Dallas Morning News*, 10 S.W.3d at 299. If the TRCP 11 agreement had prevented disclosure of documents, appeal would not have been an adequate remedy and the Supreme Court could have decided the issue by mandamus.

§4. PUBLIC NOTICE

Court records may be sealed only after public notice and a hearing. TRCP 76a(3), (4).

§4.1 Public notice. The party or intervenor seeking to seal court records must post a public notice wherever meetings of county governmental bodies are required to be posted. TRCP 76a(3); *General Tire, Inc. v. Kepple*, 970 S.W.2d 520, 523 (Tex.1998). The notice must state the following:

1. The hearing will be in open court. TRCP 76a(3). See "Hearing on Motion to Seal," §5, this page.

2. Any person may intervene and be heard. TRCP 76a(3).

3. The specific time and place of the hearing. *Id.*

4. The style and number of the case. *Id.*

5. A brief description of the nature of the case and the records sought to be sealed. *Id.*; *e.g.*, *Fox v. Doe*, 869 S.W.2d 507, 510-11 (Tex.App.—San Antonio 1993, writ denied) (guardian ad litem's description of suit as one involving minor's claim of sexual abuse against employee of corporation was sufficient).

6. The identity of the movant. TRCP 76a(3); *e.g.*, *Fox v. Anonymous*, 869 S.W.2d 499, 510-11 (Tex. App.—San Antonio 1993, writ denied) (guardian ad litem's description of P as anonymous was sufficient).

§4.2 Filed with two clerks. Immediately after posting the notice, the movant must file a verified copy of the notice with the clerk of the trial court and the clerk of the Supreme Court. TRCP 76a(3).

§5. HEARING ON MOTION TO SEAL

Court records may be sealed only after a public hearing. TRCP 76a(4); *Chandler v. Hyundai Motor Co.*, 844 S.W.2d 882, 884-85 (Tex.App.—Houston [1st Dist.] 1992, no writ).

§5.1 Open court. A hearing to seal court records must be open to the public. TRCP 76a(4). At the hearing, the court may inspect documents in camera when necessary. *Id.*

§5.2 Deadline. A public hearing must be held as soon as practical, but not less than 14 days after a motion to seal is filed and public notice is posted. TRCP 76a(4).

§5.3 Participants. Both parties and any nonparty intervenor may participate in the hearing on a motion to seal court records. TRCP 76a(4).

★

§5.4 Burden. The burden of proof is on the movant seeking to seal the records to establish the standards by a preponderance of the evidence. ***Wood v. James R. Moriarty, P.C.***, 940 S.W.2d 359, 361 (Tex.App.—Dallas 1997, no writ); *see* TRCP 76a(1); ***Roberts v. West***, 123 S.W.3d 436, 440 (Tex.App.—San Antonio 2003, pet. denied). The party with the burden of proof must show (1) there is a specific, serious, and substantial interest that clearly outweighs both the presumption of openness and any probable adverse effect that sealing would have on the general public health or safety, and (2) there are no other, less-restrictive means that will adequately protect the specific interest asserted. See "Grounds," §3.1.2, p. 396.

§5.5 Procedure. TRCP 76a(4) provides that the same procedure as in TRCP 120a (special appearance) applies to motions to seal or unseal cases. ***Fox v. Doe***, 869 S.W.2d 507, 512 (Tex.App.—San Antonio 1993, writ denied). TRCP 120a allows proof by way of pleadings, stipulations, discovery, affidavits, and oral testimony. TRCP 120a(3). See "Hearing," ch. 3-B, §8, p. 200.

§6. ORDERS ON MOTION TO SEAL

§6.1 Temporary order. The trial court may enter a temporary sealing order after the motion is filed and notice is given to the parties. TRCP 76a(5). See "Motion for temporary sealing order," §3.2, p. 396.

    1. **Written.** The order must be in writing. TRCP 76a(6).

    2. **Contents.** The temporary sealing order must identify the specific court records to be temporarily sealed, state the time for a hearing, and direct the movant to post the necessary public notice. *See* TRCP 76a(5). See *O'Connor's Texas Forms*, FORM 5K:6.

§6.2 Sealing order.

    1. **Written.** The order sealing court records must be in writing, separate from any other order and from the judgment in the case. TRCP 76a(6). A trial court cannot evade the requirements of TRCP 76a by closing the record with an unwritten order. ***Davenport v. Garcia***, 834 S.W.2d 4, 24 (Tex.1992).

    2. **Contents.** The sealing order must include (1) the style and number of the case, (2) the specific reasons for the court's findings and conclusions, (3) the specific portions of the records to be sealed, and (4) the time period for which the records are to be sealed. TRCP 76a(6). See *O'Connor's Texas Forms*, FORM 5K:5.

§7. CONTINUING JURISDICTION

An order sealing court records is subject to challenge by any person at any time, even after the trial court loses plenary power over the case. The order is always subject to challenge by nonparty intervenors, even after the court has held a hearing to order the records sealed. TRCP 76a(7). There is no finality to the order, no res judicata, no law of the case, and no judicial estoppel. *See id.*

§7.1 Intervenors. Any person has the right to intervene anytime before or after an order is entered to seal or unseal court records. TRCP 76a(7); ***General Tire, Inc. v. Kepple***, 970 S.W.2d 520, 523 (Tex.1998); ***Roberts v. West***, 123 S.W.3d 436, 443 (Tex.App.—San Antonio 2003, pet. denied).

§7.2 Jurisdiction. The trial court that issued the sealing order will maintain continuing jurisdiction to enforce, alter, or vacate the order sealing or unsealing court records. TRCP 76a(7); *see* ***Boyles v. Kerr***, 815 S.W.2d 545, 545 (Tex.1991).

§7.3 Rehearing. No party or intervenor who had actual notice of the hearing preceding the sealing or unsealing order may ask the court to reconsider the order without first showing a change in circumstances that materially affects the order. TRCP 76a(7); *see also* ***Public Citizen v. Insurance Servs. Office, Inc.***, 824 S.W.2d 811, 813 (Tex. App.—Austin 1992, no writ) (nonparty represented at TRCP 76a hearing is "a party with actual notice"). The changed circumstances do not need to relate to the case. TRCP 76a(7).

§7.4 Burden. The burden of proof under TRCP 76a(1) is always on the party seeking to seal records, even after an order sealing the records is signed. TRCP 76a(7).

———————————— ✯ ————————————

§8. PROTECTING DOCUMENTS THAT ARE NOT COURT RECORDS

§8.1 Motion for protective order. A party who wants to restrict the dissemination of unfiled discovery documents or other documents that are not court records should file a motion for a protective order under TRCP 192.6(a). *General Tire, Inc. v. Kepple*, 970 S.W.2d 520, 524-25 (Tex.1998) (analyzing former TRCP 166b(5)(c), now TRCP 192.6(b)(5)); *Roberts v. West*, 123 S.W.3d 436, 440 (Tex.App.—San Antonio 2003, pet. denied). See "Motion for Protective Order," ch. 6-A, §20, p. 449; *O'Connor's Texas Forms*, FORM 6A:10. The party should not cite TRCP 76a in such a motion. If no person (another party, intervenor, or the court) claims that the unfiled discovery documents are court records, TRCP 76a does not apply. *Kepple*, 970 S.W.2d at 525.

§8.2 Response to motion for protective order. In response to the motion for protective order under TRCP 192.6(a), anyone who wants the documents to be accessible (the other party, an intervenor, or even the judge) must show that the documents are court records. *General Tire, Inc. v. Kepple*, 970 S.W.2d 520, 525 (Tex.1998) (analyzing former TRCP 166b(5)(c), now TRCP 192.6(b)(5)). The burden is on the person attempting to benefit from the presumption of openness in TRCP 76a to prove that the documents are court records. *Upjohn Co. v. Freeman*, 906 S.W.2d 92, 96 (Tex.App.—Dallas 1995, no writ).

§8.3 Decision on court-records allegations. Before the court addresses the issue of whether TRCP 76a prevents sealing, the court must decide whether the documents are court records. *General Tire, Inc. v. Kepple*, 970 S.W.2d 520, 525 (Tex.1998); *see Compaq Computer Corp. v. Lapray*, 75 S.W.3d 669, 673-74 (Tex.App.—Beaumont 2002, no pet.) (called a "*Kepple* inquiry"). For purposes of that decision, the trial court is not required to post a notice or hold a hearing. *Kepple*, 970 S.W.2d at 525. The court should not give an intervenor access to the records before deciding whether the records are court records. *Id.* at 524-25.

1. Not court records. If the court determines that the documents are not court records, dissemination can be restricted under TRCP 192.6(a) without reference to TRCP 76a. *Kepple*, 970 S.W.2d at 525 (analyzing former TRCP 166b(5)(c), now TRCP 192.6(b)(5)).

2. Court records. If the court determines that the documents are court records, the party seeking to restrict dissemination must comply with the requirements of TRCP 76a. *Kepple*, 970 S.W.2d at 525. For a discussion of these requirements, see "Sealing Court Records," §3, p. 395; "Public Notice," §4, p. 397; and "Hearing on Motion to Seal," §5, p. 397.

§9. GAG ORDER

§9.1 Constitutional limitations. Any restraint on speech is presumptively unconstitutional, even if imposed by court order. *E.g.*, *Davenport v. Garcia*, 834 S.W.2d 4, 10 (Tex.1992) (trial court could not prevent guardian ad litem, who had been dismissed from case, from discussing case); *Low v. King*, 867 S.W.2d 141, 142 (Tex.App.—Beaumont 1993, orig. proceeding) (trial court could not prevent party from placing ad in newspaper seeking witnesses); *see also Star-Telegram, Inc. v. Walker*, 834 S.W.2d 54, 56-58 (Tex.1992) (trial court could not prevent newspaper from using rape victim's name, even though it had been expunged from court records). A gag order in a civil proceeding is valid only when (1) an imminent and irreparable harm to the judicial process will deprive litigants of a just resolution of their dispute, and (2) the judicial action represents the least-restrictive means to prevent that harm. *Grigsby v. Coker*, 904 S.W.2d 619, 620 (Tex.1995); *Davenport*, 834 S.W.2d at 10; *cf. In re Houston Chronicle Publ'g*, 64 S.W.3d 103, 107-08 (Tex.App.—Houston [14th Dist.] 2001, orig. proceeding) (gag order in Yates criminal trial, which restricted parties and attorneys from making statements to press, did not violate constitutional rights of publisher).

§9.2 Motion. The party moving for a gag order should file a motion stating the specific reasons a gag order should be imposed and the limits of the gag order. *See Grigsby v. Coker*, 904 S.W.2d 619, 620-21 (Tex.1995). See *O'Connor's Texas Forms*, FORM 5K:9.

§9.3 Notice & hearing. The court must hold a hearing to receive evidence. *Grigsby v. Coker*, 904 S.W.2d 619, 620-21 (Tex.1995).

★

§9.4 Findings. The court must make written findings supported by the evidence. *Grigsby v. Coker*, 904 S.W.2d 619, 620 (Tex.1995). The findings must state both of the following: (1) an imminent and irreparable harm to the judicial process will deprive litigants of a just resolution of their dispute, and (2) the judicial action represents the least-restrictive means to prevent that harm. *Davenport v. Garcia*, 834 S.W.2d 4, 10 (Tex.1992). See *O'Connor's Texas Forms*, FORM 5K:11.

§10. REVIEW

§10.1 Record. For the appellate court to review an error in a sealing order or gag order, the appellant must file a reporter's record from the hearing. *See Wood v. James R. Moriarty, P.C.*, 940 S.W.2d 359, 362 (Tex.App.—Dallas 1997, no writ). Without the reporter's record, the appellate court must presume that sufficient evidence was produced at the trial-court level to support the order. *Id.* at 363.

§10.2 Motion to seal.

1. Standard of review. TRCP 76a decisions are reviewed for abuse of discretion. *General Tire, Inc. v. Kepple*, 970 S.W.2d 520, 526 (Tex.1998).

2. Sufficiency of evidence. The appellate courts review the trial court's order restricting access to documents for factual and legal sufficiency of the evidence. *Chandler v. Hyundai Motor Co.*, 829 S.W.2d 774, 775 (Tex. 1992).

3. Appeal. Any party or intervenor who participated in the hearing preceding the order may seek review by appeal. TRCP 76a(8); *Eli Lilly & Co. v. Marshall*, 829 S.W.2d 157, 158 (Tex.1992); *see Wood v. James R. Moriarty, P.C.*, 940 S.W.2d 359, 360-61 (Tex.App.—Dallas 1997, no writ).

(1) Severed. Any order sealing or unsealing court records is deemed to be severed from the case and is a final judgment that may be appealed. TRCP 76a(8).

(2) Expedited. The appellate court may expedite the appeal of a TRCP 76a order. *Dallas Morning News, Inc. v. Fifth Ct. of Appeals*, 842 S.W.2d 655, 657 n.2 (Tex.1992).

(3) Abatement. The appellate court may abate the appeal and order the trial court to give further notice or to hold additional hearings. TRCP 76a(8); *Chandler*, 829 S.W.2d at 775 n.1.

(4) Other orders. During the appeal of a TRCP 76a order sealing records, the court may limit access to the records subject to the order. *Dallas Morning News*, 842 S.W.2d at 657-58.

4. Mandamus not necessary. Mandamus is not necessary to challenge a TRCP 76a order because TRCP 76a(8) deems such an order severed and final. *See* TRCP 76a(8); *Chandler*, 829 S.W.2d at 775; *Marshall*, 829 S.W.2d at 158. Mandamus may be appropriate to challenge an interim order that causes harm that cannot be remedied by appeal. *In re Dallas Morning News, Inc.*, 10 S.W.3d 298, 306 (Tex.1999) (Gonzales, J., concurring).

§10.3 Gag order. A party may challenge a gag order by mandamus. *Grigsby v. Coker*, 904 S.W.2d 619, 621 (Tex. 1995). The test on review is (1) whether an imminent and irreparable harm to the judicial process will deprive litigants of a just resolution of their dispute, and (2) whether the judicial action represents the least-restrictive means to prevent that harm. *Id.* at 620.

———————————————————— ✦ ————————————————————

M. MOTION FOR JUDICIAL NOTICE

This subchapter discusses judicial notice under TRE 201-204. For a discussion of a court's ability to take judicial notice of the reasonableness of attorney fees under CPRC chapter 38, see "Judicial notice," ch. 1-H, §10.2.2, p. 63.

§1. GENERAL

§1.1 Rules. TRE 201-204.

§1.2 Purpose. Judicial notice promotes judicial efficiency by avoiding the expenditure of time and effort involved in producing unnecessary evidence. Brown & Rondon, *Texas Rules of Evidence Handbook* (2013), p. 95. It dispenses with formal proof of a fact that is either known throughout the jurisdiction or easily determined from reliable sources. *See id.*

§1.3 Forms. *O'Connor's Texas Civil Forms* (2012), FORMS 5L.

§1.4 Other references. Brown & Rondon, *Texas Rules of Evidence Handbook* (2013) (referred to as Brown & Rondon, *Evidence Handbook*); Hardberger, *Texas Courtroom Evidence*, ch. 29 (5th ed. 2011); Wellborn, *Judicial Notice Under Article II of the Texas Rules of Evidence*, 19 St. Mary's L.J. 1 (1987).

§2. TYPES OF JUDICIAL NOTICE

Matters that can be judicially noticed are often divided into four categories: adjudicative facts, law, legislative facts, and reasoning facts. *See* Brown & Rondon, *Evidence Handbook*, pp. 96-97. Different rules of proof and procedure apply to each.

§2.1 Adjudicative facts. A court can take judicial notice of certain adjudicative facts. *See* TRE 201(b). Adjudicative facts are those facts that go to the jury and are proved by the introduction of evidence. Brown & Rondon, *Evidence Handbook*, p. 98. They relate to the parties, their activities, their properties, and their businesses. *Id.* When an adjudicative fact is not subject to reasonable dispute, the fact can be judicially noticed under the procedural requirements of TRE 201. See "Adjudicative facts," §4.1, p. 404.

§2.2 Law. A court can take judicial notice of the law of the forum and the law of the United States, sister states, and foreign countries. *See* Brown & Rondon, *Evidence Handbook*, p. 101.

1. Texas law. Generally, a Texas court is required to take judicial notice of Texas public statutes and case law. *See Kish v. Van Note*, 692 S.W.2d 463, 467 (Tex.1985); *Watts v. State*, 99 S.W.3d 604, 610 (Tex.Crim.App.2003). Judicial notice of such law is not governed by the TREs, and is mandatory without the need for any formal motion or request. *See Kish*, 692 S.W.2d at 467; *Watts*, 99 S.W.3d at 610. When a statute is ambiguous, however, a party (1) may request that the court take judicial notice of pertinent legislative facts to support a particular construction of the statute and (2) must provide appropriate information and materials. Brown & Rondon, *Evidence Handbook*, p. 99. See "Legislative facts," §2.3, this page; "Texas statutes," §4.2, p. 406; *O'Connor's Texas Forms*, FORM 5L:1. Judicial notice of the existence and content of Texas local laws and ordinances, as well as the contents of the Texas Register and Administrative Code, is governed by the requirements and procedures under TRE 204. See "Texas city & county ordinances," §4.3, p. 406; "Texas Register & Administrative Code," §4.4, p. 406.

2. Foreign law. Judicial notice of federal law, a sister state's law, or a foreign country's law is governed by the requirements and procedures under TRE 202 and 203. See "Laws of sister state," §4.5, p. 406; "Federal laws," §4.6, p. 407; "Foreign laws," §4.7, p. 407; *O'Connor's Texas Forms*, FORMS 5L:2, 3. Although the TREs require the court to take judicial notice of foreign law if properly requested, the court will not necessarily apply the law to the case. *Pittsburgh Corning Corp. v. Walters*, 1 S.W.3d 759, 769 (Tex.App.—Corpus Christi 1999, pet. denied). The court's power to take judicial notice of foreign law is distinct from a choice-of-law determination. *Id.* Thus, to have foreign law applied to a case, a party must file a preliminary motion requesting application of foreign law in addition to the request to take judicial notice. *Id.*

§2.3 Legislative facts. A court can take judicial notice of legislative facts. See Brown & Rondon, *Evidence Handbook*, pp. 98-99.

★

1. Defined. Unlike adjudicative facts, legislative facts do not just concern the parties; they are general facts that help the court determine the content of law and policy and exercise its judgment or discretion in determining what judicial course of action to take. Brown & Rondon, *Evidence Handbook*, p. 98. Legislative facts typically include information on the impact of earlier and proposed law, legislative history of a statute, and the basis for the exercise of legislative power. *Id.* at 99; *see, e.g.*, *In re Sigmar*, 270 S.W.3d 289, 302 (Tex.App.—Waco 2008, orig. proceeding) (legal practices and procedures of foreign country are legislative facts). Legislative facts are not limited, however, to materials developed by or for legislatures. Brown & Rondon, *Evidence Handbook*, p. 99. Legislative facts have been broadly defined by the courts to include established truths, facts, or pronouncements that do not change from case to case. *Cf. U.S. v. Bowers*, 660 F.2d 527, 530-31 (5th Cir.1981) (interpreting FRE 201). For example, courts have judicially noticed the validity of certain well-established scientific principles and techniques as legislative facts. *E.g.*, *Emerson v. State*, 880 S.W.2d 759, 764 (Tex.Crim.App.1994) (HGN testing for sobriety); *see* Brown & Rondon, *Evidence Handbook*, p. 100.

2. Not governed by TREs. Because legislative facts are not adjudicative facts, they are not governed by the requirements or procedures under TRE 201. *In re Sigmar*, 270 S.W.3d at 301-02; Brown & Rondon, *Evidence Handbook*, p. 100. Thus, a party's right to be heard, the requirement of indisputability, and the court's duty to instruct the jury do not apply to legislative facts. *See In re Graves*, 217 S.W.3d 744, 751 n.6 (Tex.App.—Waco 2007, orig. proceeding); *Perkins v. Delaney*, 170 S.W.3d 136, 137 (Tex.App.—Eastland 2005, no pet.). See "Types of facts," §4.1.1, p. 404; "Response," §5, p. 408; "Jury instruction," §7.3, p. 409.

3. Discretionary. Whether legislative facts will be judicially noticed is within the court's discretion; a formal motion will not make judicial notice mandatory. *See In re Graves*, 217 S.W.3d at 751 n.6; Brown & Rondon, *Evidence Handbook*, p. 100.

§2.4 Reasoning facts. A court can take judicial notice of reasoning facts (also referred to as "nonadjudicative" or "nonevidence" facts). See Brown & Rondon, *Evidence Handbook*, pp. 102-03.

1. Defined. Reasoning facts are not adjudicative facts, but are facts of general knowledge that an average fact-finder has about humankind, human affairs, and the environment. Brown & Rondon, *Evidence Handbook*, p. 102; *see, e.g.*, *El Chico Corp. v. Poole*, 732 S.W.2d 306, 311 (Tex.1987) (common knowledge that alcohol distorts perception, slows reaction, and impairs motor skills); *City of Austin v. Selter*, 415 S.W.2d 489, 501 (Tex.App.—Austin 1967, writ ref'd n.r.e.) (common knowledge that death by drowning is painful). Reasoning facts are used to draw inferences, evaluate evidence, judge the credibility of witnesses, and interpret what is seen and heard from the witness stand. Brown & Rondon, *Evidence Handbook*, p. 102.

2. Not governed by TREs. Because reasoning facts are not adjudicative facts, they are not governed by the requirements or procedures under TRE 201. *See* Brown & Rondon, *Evidence Handbook*, p. 102. Thus, a party's right to be heard, the requirement of indisputability, and the court's duty to instruct the jury do not apply to reasoning facts. *See id.* at 97. See "Types of facts," §4.1.1, p. 404; "Response," §5, p. 408; "Jury instruction," §7.3, p. 409.

3. Formalized notice unnecessary. Because reasoning facts are universally known and of such a fundamental nature, they are not introduced into evidence or appropriate subjects for formalized judicial notice. *See* Brown & Rondon, *Evidence Handbook*, p. 102.

§3. MOTION FOR JUDICIAL NOTICE

§3.1 Court's motion. A court may take judicial notice on its own motion, without a request from the parties, under TRE 201(c) (adjudicative facts), TRE 202 (laws of other states), and TRE 204 (city and county ordinances, contents of Texas Register, and published agency rules). *See, e.g.*, *In re Houston Chronicle Publ'g*, 64 S.W.3d 103, 105 (Tex.App.—Houston [14th Dist.] 2001, orig. proceeding) (on its own, trial court in Yates criminal trial judicially noticed that parties were discussing case with media and issued gag order); *International Ass'n of Firefighters v. City of San Antonio*, 822 S.W.2d 122, 127 (Tex.App.—San Antonio 1991, writ denied) (on its own, appellate court judicially noticed city charter even though trial court was not asked to do so). It is unclear whether the court can inquire into the law of a foreign jurisdiction on its own initiative. Brown & Rondon, *Evidence Handbook*, p. 132.

★

§3.2 Party's motion.

1. In writing. In most cases, when a formal request for judicial notice is required, the request should be in writing, although there is no such requirement in the TREs. During trial, a motion may be oral. *See, e.g.*, ***Cutler v. Cutler***, 543 S.W.2d 1, 2 (Tex.App.—Dallas 1976, writ ref'd n.r.e.) (oral motion made on the record during trial); ***Utica Mut. Ins. v. Bennett***, 492 S.W.2d 659, 663-64 (Tex.App.—Houston [1st Dist.] 1973, writ dism'd) (oral motion requesting notice of Mississippi law, along with copies of cases, was sufficient).

PRACTICE TIP
When it is apparent that foreign law applies at the outset of a case, it is common to request judicial notice of the law in a pleading and not in a motion. See TRE 203. But the failure to plead foreign law does not prevent the court from judicially noticing the law in a later motion. ***Daugherty v. Southern Pac. Transp.***, *772 S.W.2d 81, 83 (Tex.1989).*

---

2. Type of information. The type of information required depends on the type of judicial notice requested. *See, e.g.*, TRE 201(d) (for adjudicative facts, "necessary information"), TRE 202 (for laws of U.S. and sister states, "sufficient information"), TRE 204 (for ordinances, "sufficient information"). The parties should attach to the motion copies of the information that supports the request for judicial notice. The trial court has discretion to determine whether the party has complied with this requirement. ***Daugherty***, 772 S.W.2d at 83. For adjudicative facts, see "Necessary information for 'verifiable' adjudicative facts," §4.1.2, p. 405. For city or county ordinances, see "Texas city & county ordinances," §4.3, p. 406. For Texas Register or codified rules of the agencies published in the Administrative Code, see "Texas Register & Administrative Code," §4.4, p. 406. For laws of sister states, see "Laws of sister state," §4.5, p. 406. For federal laws, see "Federal laws," §4.6, p. 407.

3. Verification. Whenever the party furnishes the court with factual information outside the record and the information is not universally known, the information must be supported by an affidavit. For example, the movant should verify the laws of foreign jurisdictions and statements of experts on those laws. *See, e.g.*, ***Holden v. Capri Lighting, Inc.***, 960 S.W.2d 831, 833 (Tex.App.—Amarillo 1997, no pet.) (copy of California case without affidavit from California attorney was insufficient). Although TRE 204 does not require it, some appellate courts require municipal ordinances to be verified. See "Texas city & county ordinances," §4.3, p. 406.

§3.3 Notice.
A party is entitled to notice of the request to take judicial notice. If the court takes judicial notice on its own initiative without notice to the parties, either party may request an opportunity to be heard after judicial notice has been taken. TRE 201(e) (adjudicative facts), TRE 202 (laws of sister states), TRE 204 (city and county ordinances).

§3.4 Deadlines.
A court may take judicial notice of most matters at any stage of the proceeding. TRE 201(f) (adjudicative facts), TRE 202 (laws of sister states); *see, e.g.*, ***City of Dallas v. Moreau***, 718 S.W.2d 776, 781 (Tex. App.—Corpus Christi 1986, writ ref'd n.r.e.) (request for judicial notice of city charter at JNOV hearing was timely); *see also* ***Office of Pub. Util. Counsel v. Public Util. Comm'n***, 878 S.W.2d 598, 600 (Tex.1994) (court may take judicial notice for first time during appeal). Judicial notice of a foreign country's law, however, must be made far enough in advance of trial to comply with the deadlines in TRE 203 and 1009. See "Foreign laws," §4.7, p. 407.

CAUTION
Although TRE 202 and 203 give the court wide latitude in taking judicial notice of foreign law during a proceeding, this does not mean that choice-of-law issues can be raised at any point. ***Pittsburgh Corning Corp. v. Walters***, *1 S.W.3d 759, 769 (Tex.App.—Corpus Christi 1999, pet. denied). If a party is also requesting the application of foreign law, the party must make that request in a preliminary motion, preferably at the same time the request for judicial notice is made. Id.*

★

---

§4. GROUNDS FOR JUDICIAL NOTICE

§4.1 Adjudicative facts.

1. Types of facts. For a court to take judicial notice of an adjudicative fact, the fact must not be subject to reasonable dispute because either (1) it is generally known within the territorial jurisdiction of the trial court (a notorious fact) or (2) it is capable of accurate and ready determination by resort to sources whose accuracy cannot reasonably be questioned (a verifiable fact). TRE 201(b); *Freedom Comms. v. Coronado*, 372 S.W.3d 621, 623 (Tex. 2012); *In re J.L.*, 163 S.W.3d 79, 84 (Tex.2005). See "Adjudicative facts," §2.1, p. 401.

(1) Notorious fact. If a fact is generally known within the court's territorial jurisdiction, it is a notorious fact. *See* TRE 201(b); Brown & Rondon, *Evidence Handbook*, p. 105. Notorious facts are facts that everyone of average intelligence and knowledge within the court's territorial jurisdiction can be presumed to know. *See City of Garland v. Louton*, 683 S.W.2d 725, 726 (Tex. App.—Dallas 1984), *rev'd on other grounds*, 691 S.W.2d 603 (Tex.1985); *see, e.g., Choice Auto Brokers, Inc. v. Dawson*, 274 S.W.3d 172, 174 n.1 (Tex.App.—Houston [1st Dist.] 2008, no pet.) (judicial notice of eBay auction process). One of the most common types of notorious facts is geographic facts, such as the location of cities and counties, boundaries, dimensions, and distances. *See Barber v. Intercoast Jobbers & Brokers*, 417 S.W.2d 154, 157-58 (Tex.1967); *see, e.g., Harper v. Killion*, 348 S.W.2d 521, 523 (Tex.1961) (Jacksonville is in Cherokee County); *Apostolic Ch. v. American Honda Motor Co.*, 833 S.W.2d 553, 555-56 (Tex.App.—Tyler 1992, writ denied) (Highway 96 is known as Tenaha Highway and is in Shelby County). A fact can be commonly known even though it has to be processed with commonly possessed mental skills. *Drake v. Holstead*, 757 S.W.2d 909, 910 (Tex.App.—Beaumont 1988, no writ). Because notorious facts are commonly known, it is not necessary to provide the court with any extrinsic documentation to support them. *Tranter v. Duemling*, 129 S.W.2d 257, 262 (Tex.App.—El Paso 2004, no pet.); *Drake*, 757 S.W.2d at 911. Facts known personally by the trial judge or known only to a specially informed group of people are not notorious. Brown & Rondon, *Evidence Handbook*, p. 106. See "Fact not generally known," §5.2.1, p. 408.

(2) Verifiable fact. If a fact is capable of easy and accurate determination from a reliable source, it is a verifiable fact. TRE 201(b); *see, e.g., Concord Oil Co. v. Pennzoil Expl. & Prod.*, 966 S.W.2d 451, 459 (Tex.1998) (standard royalty in oil and gas leases around 1937); *City of Houston v. Todd*, 41 S.W.3d 289, 301 (Tex.App.—Houston [1st Dist.] 2001, pet. denied) (railroads supplied transportation to all developed sections of Texas by 1900, determined by consulting history sources); *Texas DPS v. Ackerman*, 31 S.W.3d 672, 676 (Tex.App.—Waco 2000, pet. denied) (population, determined by consulting federal census). See Brown & Rondon, *Evidence Handbook*, pp. 106-13. Some common types of verifiable facts that courts have taken judicial notice of include the following:

(a) Court's records. A court can take judicial notice of its own records (e.g., pleadings, affidavits, orders, judgments) in a case involving the same subject matter and between the same, or practically the same, parties. *See, e.g., In re Shell E&P, Inc.*, 179 S.W.3d 125, 130 (Tex.App.—San Antonio 2005, orig. proceeding) (trial judge could take judicial notice of his own order from related case between substantially same parties); *see also Texas Real Estate Comm'n v. Nagle*, 767 S.W.2d 691, 694 (Tex.1989) (use to which judicial notice of court's own files may be put is limited by doctrines of res judicata and collateral estoppel). Unlike other verifiable facts, because the court has access to its own records, it is not necessary to supply the court with a copy of the records to be judicially noticed. *See Estate of York*, 934 S.W.2d 848, 851 (Tex.App.—Corpus Christi 1996, no writ) (for purposes of judicial economy, party need not offer proof of what is contained in court's own file).

[1] Generally. In general, the facts that the court can take judicial notice of are whether a particular document has been filed with the court, the date on which the document was filed, and whether the document was before the court at the time of a hearing or trial. *In re C.S.*, 208 S.W.3d 77, 81 (Tex. App.—Fort Worth 2006, pet. denied). The court cannot take judicial notice of the truth of the factual statements and allegations in the pleadings, affidavits, or other documents in the court's file. *E.g., Guyton v. Monteau*, 332 S.W.3d 687, 693 (Tex.App.—Houston [14th Dist.] 2011, no pet.) (court cannot take judicial notice of testimony from earlier hearing or trial; for earlier testimony to be considered, it must be authenticated and entered into evidence).

⎯⎯⎯⎯⎯⎯⎯⎯⎯⎯⎯⎯⎯⎯ ✯ ⎯⎯⎯⎯⎯⎯⎯⎯⎯⎯⎯⎯⎯⎯

[2] Orders & judgments. For a court's own orders and judgments, the court can take judicial notice of the truth of the results reached. *See, e.g.*, *In re H.M.P.*, No. 13-08-00643-CV (Tex.App.—Corpus Christi 2010, no pet.) (memo op.; 1-7-10) (in determining whether party violated earlier court order, court took judicial notice of order's requirements); *Longhurst v. Clark*, No. 01-07-00226-CV (Tex.App.—Houston [1st Dist.] 2008, no pet.) (memo op.; 8-21-08) (in calculating amount of overdue child-support payments, court took judicial notice of amount awarded and interest charged in earlier order).

(b) Records of another court. A court can take judicial notice of another court's records if a party provides proof of the records. *Freedom Comms.*, 372 S.W.3d at 623; *see Brown v. Brown*, 145 S.W.3d 745, 750 (Tex.App.—Dallas 2004, pet. denied). See "Necessary information for 'verifiable' adjudicative facts," §4.1.2, this page. Proof can be shown by a verified copy of the record or a reference to where the record can be found if it has been made public. *See, e.g.*, *Freedom Comms.*, 372 S.W.3d at 624 (D provided copy of federal-court plea agreement; court took judicial notice); *MCI Sales & Serv. v. Hinton*, 329 S.W.3d 475, 497 n.21 (Tex.2010) (P provided copy of amicus brief filed in U.S. Supreme Court; court took judicial notice); *Ramey v. Bank of N.Y.*, No. 14-06-00824-CV (Tex. App.—Houston [14th Dist.] 2010, no pet.) (memo op.; 7-22-10) (P provided court with URL where published bankruptcy order could be found; court took judicial notice).

(c) Matters of public record. A court can take judicial notice of matters that are verified by a public record. *Besing v. Smith*, 843 S.W.2d 20, 21 (Tex.1992); *Langdale v. Villamil*, 813 S.W.2d 187, 190 (Tex. App.—Houston [14th Dist.] 1991, no writ); *see, e.g.*, *Office of Pub. Util. Counsel v. Public Util. Comm'n*, 878 S.W.2d 598, 600 (Tex.1994) (court erred in not taking judicial notice of order from Public Utility Commission (PUC); movant provided court with citation to volume and page number where published order could be located in PUC bulletin); *In re Caraway*, No. 02-05-00359-CV (Tex.App.—Fort Worth 2007, no pet.) (memo op.; 6-28-07) (court took judicial notice that judge's oath or anti-bribery affidavit was not filed with Secretary of State or the appropriate judicial administrative region).

(d) Weather. A court can take judicial notice of the weather on a particular day when verified. *See J. Weingarten, Inc. v. Tripplett*, 530 S.W.2d 653, 656 (Tex.App.—Beaumont 1975, writ ref'd n.r.e.) (court may consult weather-bureau records to judicially notice weather for particular day).

(e) Dates & holidays. A court can take judicial notice of dates and holidays when verified. *See, e.g.*, *Higginbotham v. General Life & Acc. Ins.*, 796 S.W.2d 695, 696 (Tex.1990) (court could take judicial notice that 12:01 p.m. on March 18, 1986, was an early afternoon on Tuesday and not a statutory holiday); *Garcia v. Vera*, No. 01-05-01161-CV (Tex.App.—Houston [1st Dist.] 2006, no pet.) (memo op.; 10-5-06) (date courthouse was closed was verified by district clerk's office).

(f) Definitions. A court can take judicial notice of definitions of terms and phrases when verified. *See, e.g.*, *Burger v. Burger*, No. 02-05-00170-CV (Tex.App.—Fort Worth 2006, no pet.) (memo op.; 3-2-06) (footnote 24; court took judicial notice of dictionary definition of "Jocasta").

2. Necessary information for "verifiable" adjudicative facts. For judicial notice of "verifiable" adjudicative facts, a party is required to furnish the court with "necessary information." TRE 201(d); *see Freedom Comms.*, 372 S.W.3d at 623. Necessary information includes documentation that qualifies as a source whose accuracy cannot reasonably be questioned. *Public Util. Comm'n*, 878 S.W.2d at 600 (published PUC order); *see, e.g.*, *Magee v. Ulery*, 993 S.W.2d 332, 338-39 (Tex.App.—Houston [14th Dist.] 1999, no pet.) (court supplied with information from Medical Examiners Board should have taken judicial notice of physician's age and practice status); *Drake*, 757 S.W.2d at 911 (court supplied with computation should have taken judicial notice of the distance a car would travel at a given speed); *Wagner & Brown v. E.W. Moran Drilling Co.*, 702 S.W.2d 760, 772-73 (Tex.App.—Fort Worth 1986, no writ) (court supplied with appropriate Federal Reserve bulletins took judicial notice of the discount rate on 90-day commercial paper in effect at a Federal Reserve bank); *see also* Brown & Rondon, *Evidence Handbook*, p. 116 (industry source routinely used and relied on by those in same industry qualifies as necessary information). A movant should attach verified copies of the information to the motion. Once the court has been given the motion and necessary information, judicial notice of the adjudicative fact is mandatory. TRE 201(d); *Drake*, 757 S.W.2d at 910-11.

⭐

§4.2 Texas statutes. A party is not required to provide the court with information about Texas laws. Texas courts are required to take judicial notice of the public statutes of this state. *Kish v. Van Note*, 692 S.W.2d 463, 467 (Tex.1985).

1. Unambiguous statute. If a statute is clear and unambiguous, a party should not provide the court with legislative facts to explain its meaning. Instead, the court should give the statute its common meaning. *St. Luke's Episcopal Hosp. v. Agbor*, 952 S.W.2d 503, 505 (Tex.1997).

2. Ambiguous statute. When a statute is ambiguous, the party should provide the court with information about the following: (1) the object sought to be attained, (2) the circumstances under which the statute was enacted, (3) the legislative history, (4) the common law or former statutory provisions, (5) the consequences of a particular construction, (6) the administrative construction of the statute, and (7) the effect of the title (caption), preamble, and emergency provisions. Gov't Code §311.023. The court may take judicial notice of these sources. *See, e.g., Bally Total Fitness Corp. v. Jackson*, 53 S.W.3d 352, 365 (Tex.2001) (Owen, Hecht, Abbott, JJ., dissenting) (court considered object sought to be attained and consequences of particular construction). The party should argue that it seeks an interpretation (1) to obtain a just and reasonable result, as intended by the Legislature, (2) to make execution of the statute reasonably feasible, as intended by the Legislature, and (3) that favors the public interest over any private interest. *See* Gov't Code §311.021.

§4.3 Texas city & county ordinances. For judicial notice of Texas municipal and county ordinances, the party must furnish the court with "sufficient information" to enable it to comply with the request. TRE 204. The movant must attach copies of the ordinance, which probably should be certified or verified even though TRE 204 does not specifically impose such a requirement. *See, e.g., City of Houston v. Southwest Concrete Constr., Inc.*, 835 S.W.2d 728, 733 n.5 (Tex.App.—Houston [14th Dist.] 1992, writ denied) (refused to take judicial notice because ordinance was not verified); *Hollingsworth v. King*, 810 S.W.2d 772, 774 (Tex.App.—Amarillo 1991) (refused to take judicial notice of unauthenticated municipal ordinances), *writ denied*, 816 S.W.2d 340 (Tex.1991).

§4.4 Texas Register & Administrative Code. The provisions of TRE 204 that refer to taking judicial notice of the contents of the Texas Register and the Texas Administrative Code duplicate provisions in the Administrative Procedure and Texas Register Acts. *Metro Fuels, Inc. v. City of Austin*, 827 S.W.2d 531, 532 n.3 (Tex.App.—Austin 1992, no writ); *see* Gov't Code §2002.022(a) (contents of Texas Register are to be judicially noticed), §2002.054(1) (state-agency rules published in Administrative Code are to be judicially noticed). Because Gov't Code §2002.022(a) and §2002.054(1) require the court to take judicial notice, it is probably not necessary for the party to file a written motion or supply sufficient information, as stated in TRE 204. However, for the convenience of a court that does not regularly deal with matters in the Texas Register or the Texas Administrative Code, the party should file a motion and provide copies of the information it wants the court to take notice of. As a source of law, agency regulations are like statutes or the decisions of a higher court to which a lower court owes obedience under the doctrine of stare decisis. *Eckmann v. Des Rosiers*, 940 S.W.2d 394, 399 (Tex.App.—Austin 1997, no writ).

§4.5 Laws of sister state. For judicial notice of the constitutions, public statutes, rules, regulations, ordinances, court decisions, and common law of other states, territories, or any jurisdiction of the United States, a party must furnish the court with "sufficient information" before the court is required to take judicial notice. TRE 202; *Pittsburgh Corning Corp. v. Walters*, 1 S.W.3d 759, 769 (Tex.App.—Corpus Christi 1999, pet. denied).

1. Sufficient information. The party requesting notice should attach sufficient information to its motion so the court can determine the applicability of another state's law to the case. *Daugherty v. Southern Pac. Transp.*, 772 S.W.2d 81, 83 (Tex.1989); *see Knops v. Knops*, 763 S.W.2d 864, 867 (Tex.App.—San Antonio 1988, no writ) (broad request without any information is not sufficient); *see also Wickware v. Session*, 538 S.W.2d 466, 469 (Tex.App.—Tyler 1976, writ ref'd n.r.e.) (photocopy of statute and oral motion requesting notice of California probate code were sufficient). The movant should attach copies of the law to be judicially noticed and include citations to the law in its motion and notice. *See, e.g., Burns v. Resolution Trust Corp.*, 880 S.W.2d 149, 151 (Tex.App.—Houston [14th Dist.] 1994, no writ) (copies of relevant Colorado statutes were attached to request); *Cal Growers,*

⎯⎯⎯⎯⎯ ✦ ⎯⎯⎯⎯⎯

Inc. v. Palmer Whs. & Transfer Co., 687 S.W.2d 384, 386 (Tex.App.—Houston [14th Dist.] 1985, no writ) (even though copy of California statute was not provided, court could take judicial notice because motion cited statute). In some instances, it might be helpful to supply the court with deposition testimony or an affidavit from a practicing attorney in the sister state to prove that the documentary evidence—such as a copy of the statute or case law—is still controlling law in that jurisdiction. Brown & Rondon, *Evidence Handbook*, pp. 128-29.

2. No request. If no one makes a request for judicial notice of the laws of another state, or if no one submits proper proof, a Texas court can presume that the laws of that state are the same as the laws of Texas. *Coca-Cola Co. v. Harmar Bottling Co.*, 218 S.W.3d 671, 684-85 (Tex.2006). However, the court cannot make this presumption if it is contrary to a policy directive in a Texas statute. *See id.* at 685. For example, the policy of the Texas Antitrust Act to promote competition in trade "within the state of Texas" is contrary to the presumption that antitrust statutes of Arkansas, Louisiana, and Oklahoma are the same as that of Texas. *Id.* The dissent in *Harmar* makes a compelling argument that the reasoning behind the exception is flawed. *See id.* at 695-96 (Brister, J., Jefferson, C.J., O'Neill, Medina, JJ., dissenting). See Brown & Rondon, *Evidence Handbook*, p. 127 n.209.

§4.6 Federal laws. For judicial notice of federal laws, a party should attach sufficient information to its motion so the court can determine the law's applicability to the case. On a party's motion supported by sufficient information, a court must take judicial notice of federal laws. TRE 202; *e.g.*, *Daugherty v. Southern Pac. Transp.*, 772 S.W.2d 81, 83 (Tex.1989) (OSHA regulation). TRE 202 does not permit judicial notice of private orders. *Centex Corp. v. Dalton*, 810 S.W.2d 812, 824 (Tex.App.—San Antonio 1991), *rev'd on other grounds*, 840 S.W.2d 952 (Tex.1992).

§4.7 Foreign laws. The procedure for judicial notice of foreign laws is more complicated than that for other types of laws. TRE 203 is considered a "hybrid rule"; the presentation of the law to the court resembles the presentment of evidence, but it is ultimately decided as a question of law. *Long Distance Int'l v. Telefonos de Mexico, S.A. de C.V.*, 49 S.W.3d 347, 351 (Tex.2001); *Pennwell Corp. v. Ken Assocs.*, 123 S.W.3d 756, 760 (Tex.App.—Houston [14th Dist.] 2003, pet. denied). For more detailed information about proving laws of foreign countries, see Brown & Rondon, *Evidence Handbook*, pp. 130-33.

1. Pleading. To raise an issue about the laws of a foreign country, a party must plead the law in its petition, its answer, or a written motion. TRE 203.

2. Proof of foreign law – 30 days before trial. The party must provide the proof of foreign law at least 30 days before the date of trial. TRE 203.

(1) Copies of law. The movant must provide copies of the foreign law on which it intends to rely. TRE 203.

(2) Expert opinion. TRE 203 permits the movant to provide proof from an expert in the form of affidavits or deposition testimony explaining the foreign law. *See, e.g.*, *Reading & Bates Constr. Co. v. Baker Energy Res.*, 976 S.W.2d 702, 707 (Tex.App.—Houston [1st Dist.] 1998, pet. denied) (parties provided affidavits of law professors explaining Canadian law); *Trailways, Inc. v. Clark*, 794 S.W.2d 479, 484 (Tex.App.—Corpus Christi 1990, writ denied) (P provided letter explaining Mexican law with copies of law).

3. Translation of foreign law – 45 days. If the foreign laws, the expert's opinion explaining the laws, or other sources of information are in a language other than English, the movant must provide the following information to the court and other parties at least 45 days before trial: (1) a copy of the foreign-language text, (2) a copy of the English translation, and (3) an affidavit from a qualified translator that sets forth the translator's qualifications and certifies that the translation is fair and accurate. *See* TRE 203, 1009(a); *In re Estates of Garcia-Chapa*, 33 S.W.3d 859, 862 (Tex.App.—Corpus Christi 2000, no pet.); *see, e.g.*, *Trailways*, 794 S.W.2d at 484 (P provided certified translation). The 45-day deadline can be enlarged or shortened on a motion showing good cause. TRE 1009(f).

4. Challenging translation – 15 days before trial.

(1) Objection. To challenge the accuracy of the translation of a foreign law, a party must serve objections to the translation at least 15 days before trial. TRE 1009(b). The 15-day period can be enlarged or shortened on a motion showing good cause. TRE 1009(f). The objection must identify specific inaccuracies of the translation and state with specificity a fair and accurate translation. TRE 1009(b). See *O'Connor's Texas Forms*, FORM 5L:7.

(2) Effect of objection. The trial court must determine whether there is a genuine issue, to be resolved by the trier of fact, about the accuracy of a material part of the translation. TRE 1009(d). If necessary, the trial court may appoint a qualified translator to translate the foreign law. TRE 1009(g). The reasonable value of the translator's services is taxed as court costs. *Id.*

(3) When no objection made. When no objection or conflicting translation is timely served, the trial court must admit a translation if it complies with TRE 1009(a) and the underlying foreign-language documents are otherwise admissible under the TREs. TRE 1009(c). A party who does not serve a conflicting translation or objections cannot attack the translation or offer evidence contradicting its accuracy at trial. *Id.*

5. Court's sources of proof. If the court considers sources other than those submitted by a party, the court must give all parties notice and a reasonable opportunity to comment on the sources and to submit further materials to the court. *Lawrenson v. Global Mar., Inc.*, 869 S.W.2d 519, 525 (Tex.App.—Texarkana 1993, writ denied); *see also Ossorio v. Leon*, 705 S.W.2d 219, 221-22 (Tex.App.—San Antonio 1985, no writ) (after introduction of foreign law in motion for summary judgment, court granted postponement to comply with requirements in TRE 203).

6. Court's ruling. The court, not the jury, determines the laws of foreign countries. TRE 203. The court's determination is reviewed on appeal as a question of law. *Id.*

§5. RESPONSE

If timely requested, a party is entitled to an opportunity to be heard on the propriety of taking judicial notice and the nature of the matter noticed. TRE 201(e) (adjudicative facts), TRE 202 (laws of sister states), TRE 204 (city and county ordinances).

§5.1 Form. If the motion for judicial notice was in writing, the response should be in writing. See *O'Connor's Texas Forms*, FORMS 5L:4-6.

§5.2 Objections. Some of the objections a party can file in response to a motion for judicial notice include the following:

1. Fact not generally known. The adjudicative fact to be judicially noticed is not indisputable because it is not generally known within the court's territorial jurisdiction. *See* TRE 201(b). Some arguments that can be made to support this response include the following:

(1) Fact only personally known. The adjudicative fact to be judicially noticed is based on the personal knowledge of the other party or the trial judge, but it is disputed. *E.g.*, *Eagle Trucking Co. v. Texas Bitulithic Co.*, 612 S.W.2d 503, 506 (Tex.1981) (court could not take judicial notice that certain land was outside residential or business district); *1.70 Acres v. State*, 935 S.W.2d 480, 489 (Tex.App.—Beaumont 1996, no writ) (court could not take judicial notice of time to drive a certain 9.2 miles).

(2) Fact known by special class. The adjudicative fact to be judicially noticed is commonly known by only a specially informed class of persons. *See, e.g.*, *Soto v. Texas Indus.*, 820 S.W.2d 217, 220 (Tex.App.—Fort Worth 1991, no writ) (fact that concrete walls do not fall in the absence of negligence was not within general knowledge).

2. Fact not verifiable. The adjudicative fact to be judicially noticed is not indisputable because it is not capable of easy and accurate determination from a reliable source. *See* TRE 201(b).

3. Lack of sufficient information. The movant did not present sufficient information for the court to take judicial notice. *See, e.g.*, *Pittsburgh Corning Corp. v. Walters*, 1 S.W.3d 759, 769-70 (Tex.App.—Corpus Christi 1999, pet. denied) (D's motion did not contain significant recitation of California law or note where such law could be located).

───────────────── ✭ ─────────────────

4. Foreign law. Some objections to a motion to take judicial notice of foreign laws include the following: (1) the movant did not provide a copy of the foreign-language text and an English translation at least 45 days before trial, as required by TRE 203 and 1009(a), (2) the movant did not provide the proof at least 30 days before trial, as required by TRE 203, or (3) the movant's expert did not properly interpret the law of the foreign jurisdiction. When objecting to the interpretation, the nonmovant must provide its own expert testimony to counter the movant's expert's interpretation. *See* TRE 1009(c).

§6. HEARING

Most motions for judicial notice can be resolved without a formal hearing to receive evidence.

§7. RULING

§7.1 Order. The court should determine whether the matter requested is to be judicially noticed. To preserve error, the party should make sure the court signs a written order. See *O'Connor's Texas Forms*, FORMS 5L:8-9.

1. When mandatory.

(1) Adjudicative facts.

(a) Notorious facts. Judicial notice of notorious facts is mandatory when properly requested by a party. *See* TRE 201(d). Notorious facts do not require extrinsic support. *Tranter v. Duemling*, 129 S.W.3d 257, 262 (Tex.App.—El Paso 2004, no pet.).

(b) Verifiable facts. Judicial notice of verifiable facts is mandatory when properly requested by a party and the court has been supplied with the necessary information. TRE 201(d); *Office of Pub. Util. Counsel v. Public Util. Comm'n*, 878 S.W.2d 598, 600 (Tex.1994).

(2) Law. Under TRE 202 and 204, judicial notice of Texas and sister-state law is mandatory when properly requested by a party and the court has been supplied with the necessary information. TRE 202 (law of sister state), TRE 204 (Texas city and county ordinances). No similar mandate exists for judicial notice of a foreign country's law under TRE 203.

2. When discretionary. Judicial notice of adjudicative facts and law is discretionary when the court exercises its right to judicially notice facts and law on its own motion. TRE 201(c), 202, 204; *see Daugherty v. Southern Pac. Transp.*, 772 S.W.2d 81, 83 (Tex.1989).

§7.2 Established fact. Once the court has judicially noticed a fact, that fact is established as a matter of law. *Langdale v. Villamil*, 813 S.W.2d 187, 190 (Tex.App.—Houston [14th Dist.] 1991, no writ).

§7.3 Jury instruction. Once the court has judicially noticed an adjudicative fact, it must instruct the jury in a civil case to accept that fact as conclusive. TRE 201(g); *see, e.g.*, *Hoechst Celanese Corp. v. Arthur Bros.*, 882 S.W.2d 917, 930 (Tex.App.—Corpus Christi 1994, writ denied) (dicta; trial court took judicial notice of and instructed jury on D's net worth); *Allied Gen. Agency, Inc. v. Moody*, 788 S.W.2d 601, 607 (Tex.App.—Dallas 1990, writ denied) (court took judicial notice of and instructed jury on definition of "promotion" from three dictionaries); *see also O'Connell v. State*, 17 S.W.3d 746, 749 (Tex.App.—Austin 2000, no pet.) (error for court to instruct jury on legislative fact, rather than adjudicative fact).

§8. REVIEW

§8.1 Record. The appellate record must contain (1) the motion for judicial notice, (2) all supporting information, and (3) the court's ruling. *See Metro Fuels, Inc. v. City of Austin*, 827 S.W.2d 531, 532 (Tex.App.—Austin 1992, no writ) (court of appeals refused to take judicial notice of ordinance because it was not included in record).

§8.2 Standard of review. Generally, a court's decision to take or refuse to take judicial notice will be reviewed for an abuse of discretion. *See In re A.R.*, 236 S.W.3d 460, 477 (Tex.App.—Dallas 2007, no pet.); *In re Graves*, 217 S.W.3d 744, 752 (Tex.App.—Waco 2007, orig. proceeding). A court's decision to judicially notice a foreign country's law, however, will be reviewed de novo. *See* TRE 203 (question of law). When a court erroneously takes or refuses to

★

take judicial notice of a matter, the error is reversible only if it probably caused the rendition of an improper judgment. TRAP 44.1(a)(1); *Daugherty v. Southern Pac. Transp.*, 772 S.W.2d 81, 83 (Tex.1989); *Magee v. Ulery*, 993 S.W.2d 332, 339 (Tex.App.—Houston [14th Dist.] 1999, no pet.).

N. MOTION TO EXCLUDE EXPERT

§1. GENERAL

§1.1 Rules. TRE 104, 401-403, 702-705.

§1.2 Purpose. Under TRE 702, the trial court must act as a "gatekeeper" to determine an expert's qualifications and whether the expert's opinion is admissible. *E.I. du Pont de Nemours & Co. v. Robinson*, 923 S.W.2d 549, 556 (Tex.1995).

§1.3 Forms. *O'Connor's Texas Civil Forms* (2012), FORMS 5M.

§1.4 Other references. Brown, *Eight Gates for Expert Witnesses*, 36 Hous.L.Rev. 743 (1999); Brown & Love, *Tips on Expert Witness Practice*, 33 The Advocate: State Bar Litigation Section Report 34 (Winter 2005); Brown & Rondon, *Texas Rules of Evidence Handbook* (2013) (referred to as Brown & Rondon, *Evidence Handbook*); Johnson, *Appellate Issues Regarding the Admission or Exclusion of Expert Testimony in Texas*, 52 S.Tex.L.Rev. 153 (2010-2011) (referred to as Johnson, *Appellate Issues Regarding Expert Testimony*); Temple & Hollabaugh, *Expert Witness Issues on Appeal in State & Federal Court: Securing the Record from Adverse Robinson/Havner Rulings & the Standards of Review*, 33 The Advocate: State Bar Litigation Section Report 28 (Winter 2005); *O'Connor's Texas Causes of Action* (2013) (*O'Connor's Texas COA*).

§2. *DAUBERT-ROBINSON* TEST FOR EXPERT TESTIMONY

The language of TRE 702 and 705(c) suggests four distinct but interrelated tests for the admissibility of expert testimony: qualifications, knowledge, helpfulness, and foundation data. See *Whirlpool Corp. v. Camacho*, 298 S.W.3d 631, 637 (Tex.2009).

§2.1 Qualifications test. The witness must be qualified to give an expert opinion "by knowledge, skill, experience, training, or education." TRE 702. See Brown & Rondon, *Evidence Handbook*, p. 680. In deciding if a witness is qualified as an expert, trial courts must ensure that those who purport to be experts have expertise in the actual subject they are offering an opinion about. *Cooper Tire & Rubber Co. v. Mendez*, 204 S.W.3d 797, 800 (Tex. 2006); *Roberts v. Williamson*, 111 S.W.3d 113, 121 (Tex.2003); *Broders v. Heise*, 924 S.W.2d 148, 153 (Tex.1996). When a subject is substantially developed in more than one field, testimony can come from a qualified expert in any of those fields. *Broders*, 924 S.W.2d at 154.

1. **Education or training.** The first inquiry is whether the witness is qualified by education or training to give an expert opinion.

(1) **Qualified.** The following witnesses were qualified: • Pediatrician, who was not a neurologist but was certified in pediatric advanced life support and studied and advised parents of the effects of pediatric neurological injuries, was qualified to testify about a newborn child's neurological injuries. *Roberts*, 111 S.W.3d at 121-22. • Police officer with training and experience in investigating accidents was qualified to testify that the driver's inattention caused the accident. *Ter-Vartanyan v. R&R Freight, Inc.*, 111 S.W.3d 779, 781 (Tex.App.—Dallas 2003, pet. denied). • Otolaryngologist was qualified to testify about facial plastic surgery. *Keo v. Vu*, 76 S.W.3d 725, 732-33 (Tex.App.—Houston [1st Dist.] 2002, pet. denied). • Neurologist was qualified to testify on standard of care and treatment of strokes even though he admitted no knowledge of the standard of care applied to cardiologists. *Blan v. Ali*, 7 S.W.3d 741, 746 (Tex.App.—Houston [14th Dist.] 1999, no pet.). • Nonphysician with doctorate in neuroscience, who conducted research on the causes of neurological injuries and taught doctors how the brain works, could testify about the cause of brain damage. *Ponder v. Texarkana Mem'l Hosp., Inc.*, 840 S.W.2d 476, 477-78 (Tex.App.—Houston [14th Dist.] 1991, writ denied).

★

(2) Not qualified. The following witnesses were not qualified: • Witness with chemistry and engineering degrees was not qualified to testify about wax migration and contamination in tires and its effect on tire failure because he had no training or experience relating specifically to tire chemistry or design. *Cooper Tire*, 204 S.W.3d at 806-07. • Witness with bacteriology and public-health degrees was not qualified to testify about transmission of AIDS virus through blood transfusion because he had no medical training or experience relating to blood transfusions. *United Blood Servs. v. Longoria*, 938 S.W.2d 29, 30-31 (Tex.1997). • Emergency-room doctor was not qualified to testify in death case about cause of brain injury. *Broders*, 924 S.W.2d at 153. • Psychiatrist was not qualified to give opinion about postoperative care following neurosurgery. *Tomasi v. Liao*, 63 S.W.3d 62, 66 (Tex. App.—San Antonio 2001, no pet.).

2. Specialized knowledge, skill & experience. If a witness is not qualified by education or training to give an expert opinion, the second inquiry is whether the witness is qualified by specialized knowledge, skill, or experience. *See Guadalupe-Blanco River Auth. v. Kraft*, 77 S.W.3d 805, 807 (Tex.2002) (appraisal expertise is a form of specialized knowledge).

(1) Qualified. The following witnesses were qualified: • Witness with 35 years of experience in construction damage and repair of residential and commercial property who was a licensed master plumber and property inspector and who consulted treatises and other works by engineers and people involved in construction was qualified to testify about damage to residences caused by construction-equipment vibrations even though he was not an engineer. *C.C. Carlton Indus. v. Blanchard*, 311 S.W.3d 654, 658 (Tex.App.—Austin 2010, no pet.). • Witness with experience in conducting grain-performance trials was qualified to testify about suitability of a particular seed to dry-land farming even though he was not a plant pathologist. *Helena Chem. Co. v. Wilkins*, 47 S.W.3d 486, 500 (Tex.2001). • Surgeon with 11 years of surgical practice was qualified to testify that foreign object he removed from patient was a surgical sponge. *Mitchell v. Baylor Univ. Med. Ctr.*, 109 S.W.3d 838, 842 (Tex.App.—Dallas 2003, no pet.). • Trooper with 16 years of experience in accident investigation was qualified to testify about highway design. *Huckaby v. A.G. Perry & Son, Inc.*, 20 S.W.3d 194, 208 (Tex.App.—Texarkana 2000, pet. denied). • Appraiser with 20 years of experience was qualified to testify that ranch could not be partitioned. *Egan v. Egan*, 8 S.W.3d 1, 4 (Tex. App.—San Antonio 1999, pet. denied).

(2) Not qualified. The following witnesses were not qualified: • Engineer who had experience in designing and testing fighter planes, but had no experience regarding cars, could not testify about design defects in cars. *Gammill v. Jack Williams Chevrolet, Inc.*, 972 S.W.2d 713, 719 (Tex.1998). • Coworker was not qualified to testify that lift belt would have prevented back injury. *Leitch v. Hornsby*, 935 S.W.2d 114, 119 (Tex.1996). • Railroad engineer was not qualified to testify about braking defects because nothing connected engineer's experience and training with the matter at issue. *Houghton v. Port Terminal R.R.*, 999 S.W.2d 39, 48-49 (Tex.App.—Houston [14th Dist.] 1999, no pet.).

3. License. The courts disagree whether an expert may testify about the standard of care in a particular profession without a license in the same profession. *Compare Harnett v. State*, 38 S.W.3d 650, 659 (Tex.App.—Austin 2000, pet. ref'd) (license unnecessary), *State v. Northborough Ctr., Inc.*, 987 S.W.2d 187, 194 (Tex.App.—Houston [14th Dist.] 1999, pet. denied) (same), *and Southland Lloyd's Ins. v. Tomberlain*, 919 S.W.2d 822, 827 (Tex.App.—Texarkana 1996, writ denied) (same), *with Prellwitz v. Cromwell, Truemper, Levy, Parker & Woodsmale, Inc.*, 802 S.W.2d 316, 317 (Tex.App.—Dallas 1990, no writ) (license necessary). Before an expert can testify about the standard of care in a medical-malpractice suit, the expert must meet the requirements of CPRC §§74.401-74.403. See *O'Connor's Texas COA*, "Expert's qualifications," ch. 20-A, §8.3, p. 635.

§2.2 Knowledge test. The subject of the testimony must be "scientific, technical, or other specialized knowledge." TRE 702; *Helena Chem. Co. v. Wilkins*, 47 S.W.3d 486, 499 (Tex.2001). An expert cannot offer an opinion based on a discipline that itself lacks reliability (e.g., astrology). *Kumho Tire Co. v. Carmichael*, 526 U.S. 137, 151 (1999). Valid knowledge consists of facts, as well as conclusions or ideas inferred from facts "on good grounds." *Daubert v. Merrell Dow Pharms.*, 509 U.S. 579, 590 (1993); *e.g.*, *GTE Sw., Inc. v. Bruce*, 998 S.W.2d 605, 619-20 (Tex.1999) (in suit for emotional distress, expert could not testify that certain conduct was extreme and outrageous;

✦

issue did not involve specialized knowledge); *Warren v. Hartnett*, 561 S.W.2d 860, 863 (Tex.App.—Dallas 1977, writ ref'd n.r.e.) (in probate case, expert could not testify based on handwriting sample that testatrix lacked testamentary capacity).

§2.3 Helpfulness test. The knowledge must "assist the trier of fact to understand the evidence or to determine a fact in issue." TRE 702; *e.g.*, *K-Mart Corp. v. Honeycutt*, 24 S.W.3d 357, 360-61 (Tex.2000) (human-factors expert was excluded as not helpful to the jury; opinions were within the average juror's common knowledge). Under TRE 702, it is the court's duty to determine whether the expert's testimony is sufficiently reliable and relevant to assist a jury. *Gammill v. Jack Williams Chevrolet, Inc.*, 972 S.W.2d 713, 725 (Tex.1998). See Brown & Rondon, *Evidence Handbook*, p. 694. Thus, there are two parts of the helpfulness test.

 1. Reliability of opinion. Each material part of an expert's opinion must be reliable. *Whirlpool Corp. v. Camacho*, 298 S.W.3d 631, 637 (Tex.2009); *see E.I. du Pont de Nemours & Co. v. Robinson*, 923 S.W.2d 549, 557 (Tex.1995). All expert testimony—not just scientific expert testimony—must be shown to be reliable before it is admitted. *Kumho Tire Co. v. Carmichael*, 526 U.S. 137, 147 (1999); *Gammill*, 972 S.W.2d at 726. To determine whether an expert's testimony is reliable, the court should consider (1) the factors set out in *Daubert-Robinson* and (2) the "analytical gap" analysis expressed in *Gammill*. *See Transcontinental Ins. v. Crump*, 330 S.W.3d 211, 219 (Tex.2010); *see also Whirlpool*, 298 S.W.3d at 638 (in few cases will evidence be such that reliability determination can be based only on factors in *Robinson* to the exclusion of qualified expert's experience, and vice versa).

 (1) *Daubert-Robinson* factors. In the area of hard science, experts are qualified to give an opinion according to the rules of scientific discipline as provided in *Daubert-Robinson*. *Gammill*, 972 S.W.2d at 725-26; *e.g.*, *Helm v. Swan*, 61 S.W.3d 493, 497 (Tex.App.—San Antonio 2001, pet. denied) (experts' medical opinions on causation did not meet *Daubert-Robinson* criteria for scientific reliability). An expert's opinion is not admissible if it is based on flawed methodology and reasoning. *Merrell Dow Pharms. v. Havner*, 953 S.W.2d 706, 714 (Tex.1997); *Austin v. Kerr-McGee Ref. Corp.*, 25 S.W.3d 280, 288 (Tex.App.—Texarkana 2000, no pet.). Some of the relevant factors that can be considered when assessing the reliability of expert testimony are the following:

 (a) The extent to which the theory has been or can be tested. *Daubert v. Merrell Dow Pharms.*, 509 U.S. 579, 593 (1993); *Cooper Tire & Rubber Co. v. Mendez*, 204 S.W.3d 797, 801 (Tex.2006); *Robinson*, 923 S.W.2d at 557; *e.g.*, *Texas Workers' Comp. Ins. Fund v. Lopez*, 21 S.W.3d 358, 364-65 (Tex.App.—San Antonio 2000, pet. denied) (P's expert introduced articles demonstrating that his theory had been subjected to reliable testing); *America W. Airlines, Inc. v. Tope*, 935 S.W.2d 908, 918-19 (Tex.App.—El Paso 1996, writ dism'd) (mental-health worker's opinion could not be tested).

 (b) The extent to which the technique relies on the expert's subjective interpretation. *Robinson*, 923 S.W.2d at 557; *e.g.*, *Cooper Tire*, 204 S.W.3d at 802 (expert conducted no quantitative analysis of his theory); *Lopez*, 21 S.W.3d at 364-65 (expert's causation testimony was based on objective criteria); *America W. Airlines*, 935 S.W.2d at 918-19 (mental-health worker's opinion was entirely subjective).

 (c) Whether the theory has been or could be subjected to peer review or publication. *Daubert*, 509 U.S. at 593; *Robinson*, 923 S.W.2d at 557; *e.g.*, *Cooper Tire*, 204 S.W.3d at 802 (expert's theory was never subjected to peer review, and the only publication supporting theory was his own); *America W. Airlines*, 935 S.W.2d at 918-19 (peer review of mental-health worker's opinion was limited, and she offered no examples of publication of her work). Publication and other peer review are significant indicators of the reliability of scientific evidence when the expert's testimony is in an area in which peer review or publication would not be uncommon. *Havner*, 953 S.W.2d at 726. Publication in reputable, established scientific journals and other forms of peer review increase the likelihood that substantive flaws in methodology will be detected. *Id.* at 726-27. Publication is not a prerequisite for scientific reliability in every case. *Id.* at 727.

★

(d) The technique's potential rate of error. *Daubert*, 509 U.S. at 594; *Robinson*, 923 S.W.2d at 557; *e.g.*, *Cooper Tire*, 204 S.W.3d at 802 (rate of error was unknown because there was no testing of expert's theory); *Lopez*, 21 S.W.3d at 364-65 (confidence level in studies cited by P was 95%, within the acceptable range required under *Havner*); *America W. Airlines*, 935 S.W.2d at 918-19 (potential rate of error in mental-health worker's opinion was "wholly unexplored").

(e) Whether the underlying theory or technique has been generally accepted as valid by the relevant scientific community. *Daubert*, 509 U.S. at 594; *Robinson*, 923 S.W.2d at 557; *see, e.g.*, *Neal v. Dow Agrosciences, LLC*, 74 S.W.3d 468, 473-74 (Tex.App.—Dallas 2002, no pet.) (court struck causation testimony; scientific literature relied on by expert did not support expert's conclusion).

(f) The nonjudicial uses of the theory or technique. *Robinson*, 923 S.W.2d at 557; *e.g.*, *Lopez*, 21 S.W.3d at 364-66 (expert's theory had been used to develop better clothing to protect workers from lung disease); *Waring v. Wommack*, 945 S.W.2d 889, 892 (Tex.App.—Austin 1997, no writ) (test performed by accident-reconstruction engineer had nonjudicial uses).

(2) *Gammill* "analytical gap" analysis. The *Daubert-Robinson* rules of scientific discipline do not always help evaluate the reliability of opinions in areas not considered "hard science," such as fields based primarily on experience and training. *Gammill*, 972 S.W.2d at 726; *see* *Kumho Tire*, 526 U.S. at 150-51 (*Daubert-Robinson* factors can be helpful but are not definitive); *Mack Trucks, Inc. v. Tamez*, 206 S.W.3d 572, 579 (Tex.2006) (courts can apply *Daubert-Robinson* factors to determine reliability of nonscientific expert's opinion if doing so would be helpful). In the area of so-called "soft sciences," experts are qualified to give an opinion as long as the analytical gap between the expert's methodology and the opinion offered is not too great. *See* *Transcontinental Ins.*, 330 S.W.3d at 219; *Gammill*, 972 S.W.2d at 727. In assessing the gap, the court should consider the following:

(a) Is the expert's field of expertise legitimate? *Coastal Tankships, U.S.A., Inc. v. Anderson*, 87 S.W.3d 591, 601 (Tex.App.—Houston [1st Dist.] 2002, pet. denied); *e.g.*, *In re A.J.L.*, 136 S.W.3d 293, 298-99 (Tex.App.—Fort Worth 2004, no pet.) (play therapy is a legitimate field of expertise).

(b) Is the subject matter of the expert's testimony within the scope of that field? *Coastal Tankships*, 87 S.W.3d at 601; *see, e.g.*, *Gammill*, 972 S.W.2d at 726 (beekeeper could testify that bees take off into the wind based on beekeeper's own observations); *JCPenney Life Ins. v. Baker*, 33 S.W.3d 417, 428 (Tex.App.—Fort Worth 2000, no pet.) (internist's opinion about cause of death, based on his experience and observation, was reliable even though he was not a pathologist).

(c) Does the expert's testimony properly rely on the principles involved in the expert's field of study? *Coastal Tankships*, 87 S.W.3d at 601; *see, e.g.*, *Transcontinental Ins.*, 330 S.W.3d at 220 (treating physician's opinion on cause of P's death based on differential diagnosis was reliable).

(d) Did the expert show a connection between the data relied upon and the opinion offered? *Volkswagen v. Ramirez*, 159 S.W.3d 897, 906 (Tex.2004). If the "analytical gap" between the expert's data and the expert's offered testimony is too great, the testimony is unreliable. *Kerr-McGee Corp. v. Helton*, 133 S.W.3d 245, 254 (Tex.2004); *Exxon Pipeline Co. v. Zwahr*, 88 S.W.3d 623, 629 (Tex.2002); *Gammill*, 972 S.W.2d at 727; *e.g.*, *Gross v. Burt*, 149 S.W.3d 213, 240-41 (Tex.App.—Fort Worth 2004, pet. denied) (expert's experience and review of scientific literature did not support opinion and was therefore "no evidence" that D's medical negligence was proximate cause of Ps' harm); *Wiggs v. All Saints Health Sys.*, 124 S.W.3d 407, 414 (Tex.App.—Fort Worth 2003, pet. denied) (medical literature and experts' experience did not form reliable bases for opinions, creating analytical gap); *see, e.g.*, *Halim v. Ramchandani*, 203 S.W.3d 482, 492 (Tex.App.—Houston [14th Dist.] 2006, no pet.) (expert's testimony based on experience and knowledge of relevant literature was reliable; analytical connection was sufficient).

2. Relevance of opinion. The expert's opinion must be relevant. *Daubert*, 509 U.S. at 597; *Robinson*, 923 S.W.2d at 555; *see* TRE 702; *see also* TRE 401 (definition of relevant evidence), TRE 402 (admissibility of relevant evidence). To be relevant, the testimony must be so "sufficiently tied to the facts of the case that it will aid the jury

✯

in resolving a factual dispute." *Robinson*, 923 S.W.2d at 556. Evidence that has no relationship to any of the issues in the case is irrelevant and does not satisfy TRE 702's requirement that the testimony assist the jury. *Robinson*, 923 S.W.2d at 556; *see U.S. Rest. Props. Oper. L.P. v. Motel Enters.*, 104 S.W.3d 284, 292 (Tex.App.—Beaumont 2003, pet. denied). Thus, the testimony is inadmissible under TRE 702 as well as under TRE 401 and 402. *Robinson*, 923 S.W.2d at 556.

NOTE

An expert witness may offer an opinion on a mixed question of law and fact as long as the opinion is confined to the relevant issues and is based on proper legal concepts. **Birchfield v. Texarkana Mem'l Hosp.**, *747 S.W.2d 361, 365 (Tex.1987). An expert cannot testify about an opinion on a pure question of law.* **Greenberg Traurig of New York, P.C. v. Moody**, *161 S.W.3d 56, 94 (Tex.App.—Houston [14th Dist.] 2004, no pet.);* **Upjohn Co. v. Rylander**, *38 S.W.3d 600, 611 (Tex.App.—Austin 2000, pet. denied).*

---

§2.4 Foundation test. The expert's opinion must be based on sufficient "underlying facts or data" under TRE 702 (testimony by experts) and TRE 703 (bases of opinion testimony by experts). TRE 705(c). An expert's opinion is not admissible if it is based on unreliable foundation evidence. *Merrell Dow Pharms. v. Havner*, 953 S.W.2d 706, 714 (Tex.1997); *see, e.g.*, *Marathon Corp. v. Pitzner*, 106 S.W.3d 724, 729 (Tex.2003) (expert opinion was speculation not based on evidence). For example, an expert's opinion may be excluded for lack of a proper foundation when the expert does not rule out alternative causes of an incident. *See, e.g.*, *Wal-Mart Stores v. Merrell*, 313 S.W.3d 837, 839-40 (Tex.2010) (expert's testimony was conclusory because he did not adequately explain how he excluded other possible cause of fire); *E.I. du Pont de Nemours & Co. v. Robinson*, 923 S.W.2d 549, 558-59 (Tex.1995) (expert's testimony was not based on reliable foundation because he did not conduct test to exclude other possible causes); *Martinez v. City of San Antonio*, 40 S.W.3d 587, 594-95 (Tex.App.—San Antonio 2001, pet. denied) (expert's testimony was properly excluded; expert did not rule out other plausible causes of contamination).

§3. GATEKEEPER HEARING ON QUALIFICATIONS & OPINIONS OF EXPERTS

If specialized knowledge will assist the fact-finder to understand the evidence or decide a fact issue, a witness who qualifies as an expert may testify in the form of an opinion "or otherwise." TRE 702; *see Louder v. De Leon*, 754 S.W.2d 148, 149 (Tex.1988); *see, e.g.*, *GTE Sw., Inc. v. Bruce*, 998 S.W.2d 605, 620 (Tex.1999) (in suit for intentional infliction of emotional distress, expert could not testify that certain conduct was extreme and outrageous; issue involved only general knowledge and experience rather than expertise).

§3.1 Deadline to object to expert. Issues about the admissibility of the expert's opinion should be resolved as early as possible, preferably before trial. *Maritime Overseas Corp. v. Ellis*, 971 S.W.2d 402, 412-13 (Tex.1998) (Gonzalez, J., concurring). However, a deficiency in the expert's opinion may not emerge until after the trial begins. *E.g.*, *General Motors Corp. v. Iracheta*, 161 S.W.3d 462, 471 (Tex.2005) (objection after cross-examination of expert was not too late because unreliability of expert's testimony was not fully apparent until cross-examination); *see also North Dallas Diagnostic Ctr. v. Dewberry*, 900 S.W.2d 90, 96 (Tex.App.—Dallas 1995, writ denied) (expert was challenged on voir dire). For a discussion of when an objection is required to preserve error, see "Preserving error," §6.2, p. 418.

PRACTICE TIP

To avoid surprises at trial, the parties can consider including a specific date in the scheduling order for objections to be made and heard. See "Scope of Pretrial Conference," ch. 5-A, §3, p. 315.

---

§3.2 Objection to expert. To object to an expert, the party should make a written pretrial objection to the admissibility of the expert's opinion under TRE 104(c). See the procedures used in *Merrell Dow Pharms. v. Havner*, 953 S.W.2d 706, 709 (Tex.1997), and *E.I. du Pont de Nemours & Co. v. Robinson*, 923 S.W.2d 549, 552 (Tex.1995). For more details on the procedures for making the motion, see *O'Connor's Texas Forms*, FORMS 5M:1, 5M:3.

✦

PRACTICE TIP

Do not include an objection to an expert in a motion in limine. A ruling on a motion in limine does not preserve error for either party. See "Preserving error," §3.7, p. 416.

---

1. Allegations. The party must specifically identify each expert and each expert's opinion and conclusion that the party seeks to exclude. The motion should challenge the expert on some or all of the following grounds:

(1)   The expert is not qualified to give the opinion. See "Qualifications test," §2.1, p. 410.

(2)   The subject of the testimony is not specialized knowledge. See "Knowledge test," §2.2, p. 411.

(3)   The expert's opinion is not reliable. See "Reliability of opinion," §2.3.1, p. 412.

(4)   The expert's opinion is not relevant. See "Relevance of opinion," §2.3.2, p. 413.

(5)   The underlying facts of the expert's opinion do not provide a sufficient basis for the opinion. See "Foundation test," §2.4, p. 414. An objection to an expert's qualifications does not preserve error regarding the foundation for the expert's opinion. *City of Paris v. McDowell*, 79 S.W.3d 601, 605 (Tex.App.—Texarkana 2002, no pet.).

(6)   The probative value of the opinion is substantially outweighed by the danger of unfair prejudice, confusion, or delay. TRE 403; *Robinson*, 923 S.W.2d at 557; *State v. Malone Serv.*, 829 S.W.2d 763, 767 (Tex.1992); *North Dallas Diagnostic Ctr. v. Dewberry*, 900 S.W.2d 90, 95-96 (Tex.App.—Dallas 1995, writ denied). Once the court finds that the expert's opinion is admissible, the court has the additional duty to weigh the expert's testimony against the danger of unfair prejudice, confusion of the issues, the possibility of misleading the jury, or undue delay. TRE 403; *see Texas Workers' Comp. Ins. Fund v. Lopez*, 21 S.W.3d 358, 364 (Tex.App.—San Antonio 2000, pet. denied).

2. Challenger's evidence. Because the party challenging the expert initially bears no burden to undermine the expert or the expert's opinion, that party is not required to provide evidence to support its challenges.

3. Hearing. The party objecting to the expert should ask the court to set the objections for a hearing. Johnson, *Appellate Issues Regarding Expert Testimony*, 52 S.Tex.L.Rev. at 185-86. See "TRE 104 hearing," §3.5, p. 416.

§3.3   Sponsor's response to objection. Once a party objects to the expert's testimony, the party sponsoring the expert bears the burden of responding to each objection and showing that the testimony is admissible by a preponderance of the evidence. *See E.I. du Pont de Nemours & Co. v. Robinson*, 923 S.W.2d 549, 557 (Tex.1995); *Texas Mut. Ins. v. Lerma*, 143 S.W.3d 172, 175 (Tex.App.—San Antonio 2004, pet. denied); *Frias v. Atlantic Richfield Co.*, 104 S.W.3d 925, 927 (Tex.App.—Houston [14th Dist.] 2003, no pet.); *Purina Mills, Inc. v. Odell*, 948 S.W.2d 927, 933 (Tex.App.—Texarkana 1997, pet. denied); *see also Weiss v. Mechanical Associated Servs.*, 989 S.W.2d 120, 124 n.6 (Tex.App.—San Antonio 1999, pet. denied) (in no-evidence summary-judgment proceeding, nonmovant had burden to bring forward competent evidence supporting admissibility of expert opinion). See *O'Connor's Texas Forms*, FORMS 5M:2, 4.

1. Allegations. If the party challenging the expert made specific complaints about the expert's qualifications or the relevance or reliability of the opinion, the sponsor of the expert should respond only to those complaints. If, however, the movant made only a general complaint under *Robinson*, the sponsor of the expert should assume the full burden and allege the following:

(1)   The expert is qualified. The party sponsoring the expert must show that the expert's knowledge, experience, skill, training, or education qualifies the expert to give an opinion on the specific issue before the court. See "Qualifications test," §2.1, p. 410.

(2)   The subject of the testimony is specialized knowledge that is appropriate for an expert's opinion. See "Knowledge test," §2.2, p. 411.

(3)   The expert's opinion is reliable. See "Reliability of opinion," §2.3.1, p. 412.

★

(4)   The expert's opinion is relevant. See "Relevance of opinion," §2.3.2, p. 413.

(5)   The underlying facts of the expert's opinion provide a sufficient basis for the expert's opinion. See "Foundation test," §2.4, p. 414.

(6)   The probative value of the opinion is not substantially outweighed by the danger of unfair prejudice, confusion, or delay. TRE 403; *Robinson*, 923 S.W.2d at 557. See "Allegations," §3.2.1, p. 415.

2.   Sponsor's evidence. To meet its burden of showing that the opinion is admissible, the party sponsoring the expert should attach verified proof to the response, either by affidavit or by deposition testimony. The evidence should show the expert is qualified, the expert's opinion is relevant, and the expert's opinion is reliable. See "Allegations," §3.3.1, p. 415. To bolster the expert's testimony, the party may also submit other evidence, including the affidavit or deposition of another expert and the published works of the challenged expert or other experts. *See Pink v. Goodyear Tire & Rubber Co.*, 324 S.W.3d 290, 301 & n.5 (Tex.App.—Beaumont 2010, pet. dism'd).

§3.4   Reply by party challenging expert. If the response of the expert's sponsor seems to meet its burden of showing that its expert's opinion is admissible, the party challenging the expert should probably file a reply with verified proof showing that (1) the expert is not qualified, (2) the expert's opinion is not relevant, or (3) the expert's opinion is not reliable. By filing evidence with its reply, the party will preserve its evidence in the event the trial court resolves the issue without a hearing.

§3.5   TRE 104 hearing. In making the determination of admissibility, the court is not bound by the rules of evidence except those that deal with privileges. TRE 104(a). In most cases, the court should conduct a pretrial hearing to determine the admissibility of the expert's opinion. The court has discretion, however, to decide whether to even conduct an evidentiary hearing. *State v. Petropoulos*, 346 S.W.3d 525, 529 n.1 (Tex.2011); *see, e.g., Piro v. Sarofim*, 80 S.W.3d 717, 720 (Tex.App.—Houston [1st Dist.] 2002, no pet.) (court's refusal to hold live gatekeeper hearing was not abuse of discretion). If a live hearing is held, it should be conducted with all the formalities of trial and should be recorded by the court reporter. Without a record from the hearing, the appellant will not be able to show harm. See "Record," §6.1, p. 417.

1.   Sponsor. To meet its burden of showing that the opinion is admissible, the expert's sponsor should offer the testimony of the challenged expert, either live or by deposition. To bolster the expert's testimony, qualifications, relevance, and reliability, the sponsor may offer other evidence, including the testimony of another expert and the published works of the challenged expert or other experts. *See Pink v. Goodyear Tire & Rubber Co.*, 324 S.W.3d 290, 301 & n.5 (Tex.App.—Beaumont 2010, pet. dism'd).

2.   Challenger. If the sponsor meets its burden of showing that the opinion is admissible, the party challenging the expert should attempt to undermine the expert by providing the testimony of its own expert that challenges (1) the qualifications of the sponsor's expert and (2) the scientific validity of the challenger's expert. The challenger's expert should show why the sponsor's expert's opinion fails the *Daubert-Robinson* test.

§3.6   Ruling. After receiving evidence, the trial court must rule on each objection raised by the motion. If the sponsoring party does not meet its burden of proof, the trial court should exclude the expert. To exclude the expert witness, the order should state unequivocally that the expert and the expert's evidence are excluded.

PRACTICE TIP
If the trial court excludes the expert testimony, the sponsoring party should make a separate offer of proof for every excluded opinion. See "Offer of Proof & Bill of Exception," ch. 8-E, p. 717.

---

§3.7   Preserving error. To preserve a complaint that an expert's testimony is unreliable and thus no evidence, a party must object to the testimony before trial or when the testimony is offered. See "Preserving error," §6.2, p. 418. The court's order after a gatekeeper hearing should be considered a pretrial ruling on the admissibility of the expert's opinion, not a ruling on a motion in limine. A ruling on a motion in limine does not preserve error. See "Function of order," ch. 5-E, §5.2, p. 348. Whether the ruling after the gatekeeper hearing preserves error depends on the

★

wording of the order. If the order unequivocally states that the expert's testimony will or will not be admitted at trial, the ruling is a pretrial ruling on the admissibility of the evidence and preserves error. *See* TRE 103(a)(2); *Huckaby v. A.G. Perry & Son, Inc.*, 20 S.W.3d 194, 205-06 (Tex.App.—Texarkana 2000, pet. denied). If the ruling is tentative and requires the parties to approach the bench or to reurge their objections at trial, the ruling is a motion-in-limine ruling and does not preserve error. See "Offer & Objection at Trial," ch. 5-E, §6, p. 348.

§4. MOTION TO DISQUALIFY EXPERT

The only Texas court to consider the issue of disqualifying a nonattorney expert because the expert switched sides is the Corpus Christi Court of Appeals in *Formosa Plastics Corp. v. Kajima Int'l*, 216 S.W.3d 436, 447 (Tex.App.—Corpus Christi 2006, pet. denied). In doing so, the court applied the *Koch* test. *Id.* at 448; *see Koch Ref. Co. v. Jennifer L. Boudreaux MV*, 85 F.3d 1178, 1181 (5th Cir.1996).

§4.1 **Burden of proof.** The party moving for disqualification has the burden to establish that disqualification is necessary. *Formosa Plastics Corp. v. Kajima Int'l*, 216 S.W.3d 436, 449 (Tex.App.—Corpus Christi 2006, pet. denied); *Koch Ref. Co. v. Jennifer L. Boudreaux MV*, 85 F.3d 1178, 1181 (5th Cir.1996). To disqualify an expert who switched sides, the first party to hire the expert must establish the two *Koch* factors and (perhaps) additional factors:

1. ***Koch* factor #1 – confidential relationship.** It was objectively reasonable for the first party who claims to have retained the expert to conclude that it had a confidential relationship with the expert. *Formosa Plastics*, 216 S.W.3d at 449; *Koch Ref.*, 85 F.3d at 1181. In evaluating whether there was a confidential relationship, the *Formosa* court listed 11 factors to consider. *Formosa Plastics*, 216 S.W.3d at 449. A confidential relationship with one expert in a firm of experts is not imputed to the entire firm, as it is with the disqualification of attorneys. *Id.* at 451.

2. ***Koch* factor #2 – confidential information.** The party who first retained the expert disclosed confidential or privileged information to the expert. *Formosa Plastics*, 216 S.W.3d at 448; *Koch Ref.*, 85 F.3d at 1181. Confidential information is information that either (1) is of particular significance or (2) can be identified as either attorney work product or within the scope of the attorney-client privilege. *Formosa Plastics*, 216 S.W.3d at 449. It can include the following: discussions of litigation strategy, the kinds of experts the party will employ, the role of each expert, the party's evaluation of the strengths and weaknesses of each side, and anticipated defenses. *Id.* at 450.

3. **Additional factors.** The *Formosa* court suggested—but did not apply—other factors: (1) whether the disqualification would be prejudicial, (2) whether the disqualification would promote the integrity of the judicial process, and (3) whether the disqualification would affect the public interest. *Formosa Plastics*, 216 S.W.3d at 448 (dicta); *see also Koch Ref.*, 85 F.3d at 1181 (dicta; factor #3).

§4.2 **Trial-court order.** The trial court has the inherent power to disqualify an expert who switched sides, which is derived from the necessity to protect privileges and to preserve public confidence in the judicial proceedings. *Formosa Plastics Corp. v. Kajima Int'l*, 216 S.W.3d 436, 488 (Tex.App.—Corpus Christi 2006, pet. denied) (Yañez, J., dissenting); *see Koch Ref. Co. v. Jennifer L. Boudreaux MV*, 85 F.3d 1178, 1181 (5th Cir.1996).

§5. EXPERTS IN MEDICAL-MALPRACTICE SUITS

Information about experts in medical-malpractice suits is covered in detail in *O'Connor's Texas COA*, "Expert Testimony," ch. 20-A, §8, p. 634.

§6. REVIEW

§6.1 **Record.** When appealing from a final judgment rendered in a trial in which the trial court ruled on a motion to exclude an expert at an evidentiary hearing, the appellant should include the record of the hearing in the appellate record. *Exxon Corp. v. Makofski*, 116 S.W.3d 176, 196 (Tex.App.—Houston [14th Dist.] 2003, pet. denied) (Seymore, J., dissenting). *But see id.* at 180 (majority op.) (D did not waive error by not submitting record of pretrial hearing because P waived complaint on appeal). For example, if the trial court excluded an expert in a gatekeeper

⭐

hearing and later rendered a summary judgment, the appellant should request the reporter's record from the gate-keeper hearing and the clerk's record from the trial, which includes all the pleadings necessary to challenge the summary judgment and the court's ruling on the expert.

§6.2 Preserving error. A party should always object to deficiencies in the other party's expert evidence (e.g., the underlying methodology, technique, or foundation evidence used). However, when a party's expert evidence is deficient on its face, an objection may not be necessary.

    1. Underlying methodology. An objection is required to challenge the underlying methodology, technique, or foundation evidence used by the expert. *City of San Antonio v. Pollock*, 284 S.W.3d 809, 817 (Tex.2009); *Coastal Transp. Co. v. Crown Cent. Pet. Corp.*, 136 S.W.3d 227, 233 (Tex.2004); *In re Commitment of Barbee*, 192 S.W.3d 835, 843 (Tex.App.—Beaumont 2006, no pet.). To preserve a complaint that scientific evidence is unreliable, a party must object to the evidence before trial or when the evidence is offered. *Borg-Warner Corp. v. Flores*, 232 S.W.3d 765, 769 n.11 (Tex.2007); *Guadalupe-Blanco River Auth. v. Kraft*, 77 S.W.3d 805, 807 (Tex.2002); *Maritime Overseas Corp. v. Ellis*, 971 S.W.2d 402, 409 (Tex.1998); *e.g.*, *Kerr-McGee Corp. v. Helton*, 133 S.W.3d 245, 251-52 (Tex.2004) (complaint was preserved when D objected to testimony immediately after cross-examination). The objecting party cannot argue for the first time on appeal that the scientific evidence is unreliable and should be ignored. *See Maritime Overseas*, 971 S.W.2d at 409. Without a timely objection, the offering party would not have a chance to cure the defect in the evidence and would be subject to trial and appeal by ambush. *City of San Antonio*, 284 S.W.3d at 817; *Kerr-McGee*, 133 S.W.3d at 252; *Maritime Overseas*, 971 S.W.2d at 409.

    2. Conclusory evidence. An objection is not required to challenge the face of the record—for example, when expert testimony is speculative or conclusory on its face. *City of San Antonio*, 284 S.W.3d at 818; *Coastal Transp.*, 136 S.W.3d at 233; *In re S.A.P.*, 169 S.W.3d 685, 691 n.3 (Tex.App.—Waco 2005, no pet.); *see Wal-Mart Stores v. Merrell*, 313 S.W.3d 837, 839 (Tex.2010); *Volkswagen v. Ramirez*, 159 S.W.3d 897, 910 (Tex.2004). In such a case, the party may challenge the legal sufficiency of the evidence on appeal even when no objection was made to its admissibility. *Coastal Transp.*, 136 S.W.3d at 233; *In re S.A.P.*, 169 S.W.3d at 691 n.3. For ways to preserve a legal-sufficiency challenge, see "Preserving legal-sufficiency point," ch. 10-B, §13.1.3, p. 803.

PRACTICE TIP
Because it can be difficult to distinguish between "underlying methodology" and "conclusory evidence" during trial, a party should always object to deficiencies in the other party's expert evidence.

---

§6.3 Standard of review. The trial court's decision to admit expert testimony is reviewed for abuse of discretion. *Whirlpool Corp. v. Camacho*, 298 S.W.3d 631, 638 (Tex.2009); *Cooper Tire & Rubber Co. v. Mendez*, 204 S.W.3d 797, 800 (Tex.2006); *Guadalupe-Blanco River Auth. v. Kraft*, 77 S.W.3d 805, 807 (Tex.2002); *Gammill v. Jack Williams Chevrolet, Inc.*, 972 S.W.2d 713, 727 (Tex.1998). When a party claims that the evidence or expert testimony is unreliable and thus legally insufficient to support a verdict, the appellate court will use a no-evidence review and consider whether the testimony would allow reasonable and fair-minded jurors to reach the verdict. *Whirlpool*, 298 S.W.3d at 638.

⭐

✪

— ★ —

CHAPTER 6

★

★

────────── ✦ ──────────

6. DISCOVERY

A. GENERAL RULES FOR DISCOVERY

§1. GENERAL

§1.1 Rules. TRCP 176, 190-205, 215.

§1.2 Purpose. The purpose of discovery is to allow the parties to obtain full knowledge of the issues and facts of the lawsuit before trial. *West v. Solito*, 563 S.W.2d 240, 243 (Tex.1978). The objective of the Texas discovery rules is to prevent trial by ambush. *Gutierrez v. Dallas ISD*, 729 S.W.2d 691, 693 (Tex.1987).

§1.3 Timetables & forms. Timetable, Discovery Schedule for Level 1, p. 1219; Timetable, Discovery Schedule for Level 2, p. 1222; *O'Connor's Texas Civil Forms* (2012), FORMS 1B:13, 1H:13, 6A.

§1.4 Other references. Brown & Rondon, *Texas Rules of Evidence Handbook* (2013) (referred to as Brown & Rondon, *Evidence Handbook*); Downing et al., *"Be Careful What You Ask For, You May Get It": Common Sense Discovery Requests & Responses*, Advanced Family Law Course, State Bar of Texas CLE, ch. 15 (2006); Griesel, *The "New" Texas Discovery Rules: Three Years Later*, Advanced Evidence & Discovery Course, State Bar of Texas CLE, ch. 2 (2002) (referred to as Griesel, *The "New" Texas Discovery Rules*); *O'Connor's Texas Civil Appeals* (2012) (*O'Connor's Texas Appeals*).

PRACTICE TIP

Before engaging in discovery, prepare a draft of the jury charge based on all the pleadings. Only when you know what questions the jury will be asked can you design an intelligent discovery plan.

---

§2. TERMS & DEFINITIONS

The following are definitions of several key terms used throughout this chapter.

§2.1 Discovery periods. Discovery periods determine the length of time the parties have to conduct discovery. See "Discovery Periods," §8, p. 433.

§2.2 Documents & tangible things. The phrase "documents and tangible things" includes papers, books, accounts, drawings, graphs, charts, photographs, electronic or videotape recordings, data, and data compilations. TRCP 192.3(b).

§2.3 Nonparty witness. The term "nonparty witness," in the context of discovery rules, means a witness who is not a party and is not retained by, employed by, or otherwise subject to the control of a party. *See* TRCP 199.3, 205.1; *see, e.g., In re Carnival Corp.*, 193 S.W.3d 229, 235 (Tex.App.—Houston [1st Dist.] 2006, orig. proceeding) (D's independent contractor not subject to D's control).

§2.4 Party witness. The term "party witness," in the context of discovery rules, includes the party and witnesses who are retained by, employed by, or otherwise subject to the control of the party. TRCP 199.3.

§2.5 Possession. The phrase "possession, custody, or control" of an item means that the person either has physical possession of the item or has a right to possession that is equal or superior to that of the person who has physical possession. TRCP 192.7(b); *In re Kuntz*, 124 S.W.3d 179, 181 (Tex.2003); *GTE Comms. Sys. v. Tanner*, 856 S.W.2d 725, 729 (Tex.1993). Mere access to documents is not "physical possession" of the documents under TRCP 192.7(b). *In re Kuntz*, 124 S.W.3d at 184. The right to obtain possession is a legal right based on the relationship between the party responding to discovery and the person or entity that has actual possession. *GTE*, 856 S.W.2d at 729; *see, e.g., State v. Lowry*, 802 S.W.2d 669, 673-74 (Tex.1991) (request to Attorney General was sufficient to require production of documents held by all divisions of office). A party is required to produce only those documents or tangible things in its possession, custody, or control. TRCP 192.3(b); *GTE*, 856 S.W.2d at 728-29; *see also In re*

─────────────── ✦ ───────────────

U-Haul Int'l, 87 S.W.3d 653, 656-57 (Tex.App.—San Antonio 2002, orig. proceeding) (P did not meet burden of proving that D had right to obtain possession of documents from D's related subsidiary).

§2.6 Privilege & confidentiality. Although the terms "privilege" and "confidentiality" are used interchangeably in many rules and statutes limiting the scope of discovery, they represent different legal concepts. An evidentiary privilege is part of a body of evidence law that addresses what evidence is or is not discoverable for purposes of litigation (e.g., communications and records between a dentist and patient are privileged under Occupations Code §258.102). By comparison, confidentiality is part of a body of law that defines the ethical responsibilities of a certain person or entity to certain other persons (e.g., HIV-test results are confidential under Health & Safety Code §81.103).

§2.7 Side. The term "side" refers to all the litigants with generally common interests in the litigation. TRCP 190.3(b)(2). The concept of "side" in TRCP 190.3(b)(2) was borrowed from TRCP 233, which governs the allocation of peremptory strikes, and from FRCP 30(a)(2). TRCP 190 cmt. 6. In most cases there are only two sides—plaintiffs and defendants. *Id.* In complex cases, however, there may be more than two sides, such as when defendants have sued third parties not named by the plaintiffs or when defendants have sued each other. *Id.*

§2.8 Withholding statement. The term "withholding statement" means a statement in a response to discovery in which a party claims that information responsive to written discovery is privileged. TRCP 193.3(a). A withholding statement may be included in the response or filed separately. *Id.* The withholding statement must (1) state that information responsive to the written-discovery request is being withheld, (2) identify the request to which the information or material relates, and (3) identify the privilege asserted. *Id.*; *In re Monsanto Co.*, 998 S.W.2d 917, 924 (Tex.App.—Waco 1999, orig. proceeding); Griesel, *The "New" Texas Discovery Rules*, §VII(A)(2), at 13.

§2.9 Work product. The term "work product" includes (1) material prepared or mental impressions developed in anticipation of litigation or for trial, by or for a party or its representatives, including the party's attorneys, consultants, sureties, indemnitors, insurers, employees, or agents, or (2) communications made in anticipation of litigation or for trial between a party and its representatives or among a party's representatives, including the party's attorneys, consultants, sureties, indemnitors, insurers, employees, or agents. TRCP 192.5(a). The work-product discovery exemption replaced the "attorney work product" and "party communication" exemptions in former TRCP 166b. TRCP 192 cmt. 8.

   1. Core work product. Core work product is the work product of an attorney or an attorney's representative containing that person's mental impressions, opinions, conclusions, or legal theories. TRCP 192.5(b)(1).

   2. Noncore work product. Noncore work product, which is not specifically defined in the TRCPs, is all work product except the work product of an attorney or an attorney's representative containing that person's mental impressions, opinions, conclusions, or legal theories. *See* TRCP 192.5(b)(1). Noncore work product includes party communications. *See* TRCP 192.5(a)(2).

§2.10 Written discovery. The term "written discovery" includes (1) requests for disclosure, (2) requests for production and inspection of documents and tangible things, (3) requests for entry on property, (4) interrogatories, and (5) requests for admission. TRCP 192.7(a). It does not include depositions on written questions. *See id.*

§3. PRESERVATION OF EVIDENCE

A party may have a common-law, statutory, regulatory, or ethical duty to preserve evidence. *Clements v. Conard*, 21 S.W.3d 514, 523 (Tex.App.—Amarillo 2000, pet. denied); *Trevino v. Ortega*, 969 S.W.2d 950, 955 (Tex.1998) (Baker, J., concurring).

§3.1 Common-law duty.

   1. When duty arises. A party has a common-law duty to preserve evidence when it knows or reasonably should know that (1) there is a substantial chance that a claim will be filed and (2) evidence in its possession or control will be material and relevant to that claim. *Wal-Mart Stores v. Johnson*, 106 S.W.3d 718, 722 (Tex.2003); *Walker v. Thomasson Lumber Co.*, 203 S.W.3d 470, 477 (Tex.App.—Houston [14th Dist.] 2006, no pet.). See "Possession," §2.5, p. 425.

★

2. Scope of duty. The common-law duty to preserve evidence does not require a party to keep every document or item in its possession. *Adobe Land Corp. v. Griffin, L.L.C.*, 236 S.W.3d 351, 357 (Tex.App.—Fort Worth 2007, pet. denied). A party must, however, preserve evidence that it knows or reasonably should know is relevant to the action, is likely to be requested in discovery, or is the subject of a discovery order. *Id.* at 357-58; *Trevino v. Ortega*, 969 S.W.2d 950, 957 (Tex.1998) (Baker, J., concurring). Although a party does not have to take extraordinary measures, it must exercise reasonable care in preserving potentially relevant evidence. *Adobe Land*, 236 S.W.3d at 359; *Trevino*, 969 S.W.2d at 957 (Baker, J., concurring).

§3.2 Statutory, regulatory & ethical duties. A number of statutes, regulations, and canons of ethics require the preservation of records for certain periods of time. *See Trevino v. Ortega*, 969 S.W.2d 950, 955 (Tex.1998) (Baker, J., concurring); *see, e.g.*, Bus. & Com. Code §35.48(b) (three-year retention of business records required to be kept by state law unless another law provides otherwise); 29 C.F.R. §1602.40 (two-year retention of school-personnel or employment records); 17 C.F.R. §240.17a-4 (six-year retention of certain brokerage-firm records); Council on Ethical & Judicial Affairs, American Med. Ass'n, *Code of Medical Ethics*, §7.05 (1994) (doctors must keep medical records that may reasonably be of value to patient).

§4. DISCOVERY CERTIFICATES

§4.1 Certification by signature. All written discovery—including disclosures, discovery requests, notices, objections, and responses—must be signed. TRCP 191.3(a). The signature must be the attorney's, unless the party is pro se. *Id.* TRCP 191.3(a) applies to documents used to satisfy a discovery request, response, or objection (e.g., a withholding statement). TRCP 191 cmt. 3. See "Who must sign," ch. 1-B, §3.2.11(1), p. 9.

1. Effect of signature on disclosure. The signature of an attorney (or pro se party) on a disclosure made under TRCP 194 constitutes a certification that, to the best of the signer's knowledge, information, and belief, formed after a reasonable inquiry, the disclosure is complete and correct at the time it is made. TRCP 191.3(b).

2. Effect of signature on other discovery. The signature of an attorney (or pro se party) on a discovery request, notice, response, or objection constitutes a certification that, to the best of the signer's knowledge, information, and belief, formed after a reasonable inquiry, the discovery (1) is consistent with the TRCPs or presents a good-faith argument for the extension, change, or reversal of existing law, (2) has a good-faith factual basis, (3) is not made for an improper purpose such as delay, harassment, or expense, and (4) is not unreasonable or unduly burdensome or expensive, given the needs of the case. TRCP 191.3(c); *see also* CPRC §9.011 (signing of pleadings), §10.001 (signing of pleadings and motions).

3. Effect of no signature. If a discovery request, notice, response, or objection is not signed, it must be struck. TRCP 191.3(d). The omission of a signature can be remedied by providing one as soon as the omission is called to the party's attention. *Id.* A party who receives an unsigned request or notice is not required to take any action in response to it. *Id.*

4. Effect of false signature. The court can impose sanctions under CPRC chapter 10 on a person who signs a false certification on a discovery disclosure, request, notice, response, or objection. TRCP 191.3(e).

§4.2 Certificate of conference.

1. Under TRCP 191. Parties and their attorneys are expected to cooperate in discovery and to make any agreements that are reasonably necessary to efficiently dispose of the case. TRCP 191.2 & cmt. 2; *In re Alford Chevrolet-Geo*, 997 S.W.2d 173, 184 (Tex.1999). All discovery motions or requests for hearings relating to discovery must contain a certificate by the party filing the document stating that a reasonable effort was made to resolve the dispute without the need for court intervention and that the effort failed. TRCP 191.2; *United Servs. Auto. Ass'n v. Thomas*, 893 S.W.2d 628, 629 (Tex.App.—Corpus Christi 1994, writ denied). See *O'Connor's Texas Forms*, FORM 1B:13. Because TRCP 191.2 is for the benefit of the trial court, the failure to include a certificate is not grounds for mandamus. *Groves v. Gabriel*, 874 S.W.2d 660, 661 n.3 (Tex.1994).

✮

---

2. **Under local rules.** In some counties (e.g., Harris, Dallas, Tarrant), courts require a more detailed certificate. See the local rules for each county. See *O'Connor's Texas Forms*, FORM 1B:13.

§4.3 Certificate of written discovery. Some local rules require parties to file a certificate of written discovery with the court when serving discovery requests or responses. See *O'Connor's Texas Forms*, FORM 6A:5. TRCP 191.4 contains no such requirement, so a certificate is necessary only if required by a local rule.

§5. FORMS OF DISCOVERY

The discovery rules provide the only permissible forms of discovery. *See* TRCP 192.1. However, a court may order, or the parties may agree to, discovery methods other than those provided in the discovery rules. TRCP 191 cmt. 1. The written forms of discovery may be combined in the same document and may be taken in any sequence. TRCP 192.2.

§5.1 Request for disclosure. A request for disclosure allows a party to obtain the basic discoverable information listed in TRCP 194.2. Generally, a party must respond to a request for disclosure and cannot object or assert privileges. *See* TRCP 194 & cmt. 1. See "Requests for Disclosure," ch. 6-E, p. 515.

§5.2 Deposition on oral examination. A deposition on oral examination allows a party to question a witness under oath before trial. Depositions can be used to acquire information from both parties and nonparties. TRCP 199-203, 205. Because they are expensive and time-consuming, depositions should be used only after a party knows something about the case. See "Depositions," ch. 6-F, p. 525.

§5.3 Deposition on written questions. A deposition on written questions allows a party to submit written questions to a witness who answers them orally under oath. TRCP 200. Depositions on written questions can be used to acquire information from both parties and nonparties. Although they sound like depositions on oral examination, they are actually similar to interrogatories because they are written and are relatively inexpensive. Depositions on written questions are most often used to obtain records from a nonparty (e.g., a hospital) and, at the same time, to ask the custodian of records the necessary questions to "prove up" the records. See "Deposition on Written Questions," ch. 6-F, §15, p. 541.

§5.4 Interrogatories. Interrogatories are written questions used to acquire information from another party. TRCP 197. Most interrogatory answers are signed by the party under oath. See "Signed & verified by party," ch. 6-G, §4.1.1(4), p. 551. Interrogatories are a relatively inexpensive method of discovery, but they are slower than depositions. They should be used to narrow the issues and to identify the legal theories and factual bases of the parties' claims or defenses. The rule on discovery limitations specifies the number of interrogatories a party may submit. TRCP 190. See "Interrogatories," ch. 6-G, p. 548.

§5.5 Request for admissions. A request for admissions is used to force another party to admit or deny specific facts, thus narrowing the fact issues for trial. TRCP 198. Responses to requests for admissions are signed by the attorney. The rule on requests for admissions does not limit the number of requests. *See id.* See "Requests for Admissions," ch. 6-H, p. 557.

§5.6 Request for production & inspection. A request for production is used to obtain documents, records, and other tangible things in a party's possession. TRCP 196. To obtain or inspect documents or tangible things from a nonparty, a party must file a notice of production and a subpoena, not a request. TRCP 176, 205.3. See "Securing Documents & Tangible Things," ch. 6-I, p. 565.

§5.7 Request for medical records. A party may obtain the medical records of another party or of a nonparty by a request for disclosure or by a medical authorization. TRCP 194.2(j), (k), 196.1(c). See "Medical Records," ch. 6-J, p. 576.

§5.8 Motion for physical or mental examination. A motion for physical or mental examination may be used to obtain an examination of a party, someone in the party's custody, or someone under the party's legal control. TRCP 204.1. See "Motion to Examine the Person," ch. 6-J, §5, p. 577.

★

---

§5.9 Request for entry on land. A request to enter land may be used to gain entry on land owned by a party to inspect the land or anything on it. TRCP 196.7. To gain entry on the land of a nonparty, the party must file a motion (not a request), ask for a hearing, and get a court order. TRCP 196.7(a)(2), (b). See "Entry on Land," ch. 6-K, p. 580.

§5.10 Subpoena. A subpoena may be used to secure documents from a party or nonparty. TRCP 176, 205. In most cases, a subpoena is issued to compel a nonparty to attend a deposition and to produce documents. See "Securing Things from a Nonparty," ch. 6-I, §5, p. 569.

§5.11 Expert's report. An expert's report includes the discoverable factual observations, tests, supporting data, calculations, photographs, and opinions of the expert. *See* TRCP 195.5. If a retained testifying expert has not reduced her report to tangible form, the court may order the expert to reduce it to tangible form and to produce it. *Id.* See "Expert's Report," ch. 6-D, §7, p. 513; *O'Connor's Texas Forms*, FORM 6D:1.

§6. MODIFYING DISCOVERY PROCEDURES

§6.1 Modifying discovery by agreement. The discovery rules permit the parties to modify most discovery procedures. For example, the parties can agree to use a form of discovery not provided for in the TRCPs. TRCP 191 cmt. 1. However, agreements to modify discovery are subject to the following rules.

1. Rule 11. To be enforceable, the parties' agreement to modify a discovery rule must comply with TRCP 11 or, if it affects an oral deposition, be made part of the record of the deposition. TRCP 191.1; *In re BP Prods. N. Am., Inc.*, 244 S.W.3d 840, 845-46 (Tex.2008); *see Remington Arms Co. v. Canales*, 837 S.W.2d 624, 625 (Tex.1992) (written agreement must comply with TRCP 11). An agreement that does not comply with TRCP 11 is not enforceable. *E.g.*, *London Mkt. Cos. v. Schattman*, 811 S.W.2d 550, 552 (Tex.1991) (oral agreement to extend time to respond to discovery was not enforceable because it did not meet requirements of TRCP 11). See "Agreements Between Attorneys – Rule 11," ch. 1-H, §9, p. 61; *O'Connor's Texas Forms*, FORM 1H:13 (Rule 11 agreement), FORM 6A:3 (agreement to extend time to respond to discovery).

2. Restrictions. The parties may modify a discovery rule unless the modification is specifically prohibited. TRCP 191.1; *In re BP Prods.*, 244 S.W.3d at 845. For example, the discovery rules prohibit parties from agreeing to increase the time for oral depositions in a Level 1 case to more than ten hours. TRCP 190.2(c)(2). The court may set aside the parties' enforceable agreement, but it should give effect to the agreement whenever possible. *In re BP Prods.*, 244 S.W.3d at 846. Generally, the court should not ignore the parties' agreement without a showing of specific misrepresentation or good cause.

§6.2 Modifying discovery by court order. Certain discovery rules permit a court to modify discovery procedures in specific instances. *See, e.g.*, TRCP 190.4(a) (court may set its own discovery-control plan "tailored to the circumstances of the specific suit"), TRCP 190.5 (court may modify discovery-control plan "at any time"). Other discovery rules may be modified by the court only under the following conditions.

1. Good cause. The court may modify a discovery rule if there is "good cause." TRCP 191.1; *In re BP Prods. N. Am., Inc.*, 244 S.W.3d 840, 846 (Tex.2008); *see, e.g.*, *Alvarado v. Farah Mfg.*, 830 S.W.2d 911, 914 (Tex. 1992) (courts should not excuse parties from their failure to timely respond to discovery without a strict showing of good cause). Inadvertence of counsel (i.e., an attorney's inadvertent noncompliance with discovery rules) is not sufficient to establish good cause. *Alvarado*, 830 S.W.2d at 915. See *O'Connor's Texas Forms*, FORM 6A:2 (motion to extend time to respond to discovery).

2. Restrictions. The court may modify a discovery rule if the modification is not specifically prohibited. TRCP 191.1. For example, the court cannot simply "opt out" of the discovery rules by form orders or approve a discovery-control plan that does not contain the matters specified in TRCP 190.4. TRCP 191.1 cmt. 1. A court also cannot abate discovery and thus prevent a party from obtaining basic information that goes to the heart of the litigation. *See In re Van Waters & Rogers, Inc.*, 62 S.W.3d 197, 200 (Tex.2001); *In re Colonial Pipeline Co.*, 968 S.W.2d 938, 941-42 (Tex.1998).

★

---

§6.3 Chart summary. Chart 6-1, below, summarizes the various types of enforceable agreements on discovery.

	Type of agreement	Can agree under TRCP 11?	Can agree during deposition?	Need court order?	TRCP
	6-1. ENFORCEABLE AGREEMENTS ON DISCOVERY				
1	To modify any court order	No	No	Yes	191 cmt. 1
2	To extend discovery deadlines	Yes	Yes*	No	191 cmt. 1
3	To extend time to supplement	Yes	Yes*	No	191.1, 193.5(b)
4	To modify deposition procedure	Yes	Yes*	No	191 cmt. 1
5	To modify time to designate experts	Yes	No	No	191.1, 195.2
6	To adopt new method of discovery	Yes	Yes*	No	191 cmt. 1
7	To serve request less than 30 days before end of discovery period	Yes	No	No	190 cmt. 4
8	To modify any discovery procedure not prohibited by TRCPs	Yes	Yes*	No	191.1
9	To produce documents or tangible things at a different time and place than stated in the request for discovery	Yes	Yes*	No	194.4, 196.3(a), 197.2(c)
10	To take deposition outside discovery period	Yes	Yes*	No	199.2(a), 200.1(a)
11	To be controlled by Level 3	No	No	Yes	190 cmt. 1
12	In Level 1 – To extend time for depositions to 10 hours	Yes	Yes*	No	190.2(c)(2)
13	In Level 1 – To extend time for depositions to more than 10 hours	No	No	Yes	190.2(c)(2)
14	In Level 1 – To agree to be controlled by Level 2	Yes	No	No	190.2(b)(1)**
15	In Level 3 – To modify discovery	No	No	Yes	190.4(a)

* Attorneys can make an enforceable agreement on the record during a deposition only as it affects the deposition. TRCP 191.1.

** The Supreme Court has proposed amendments to TRCP 190.2 that would no longer allow parties to agree to be controlled by a Level 2 discovery-control plan. *See* Tex.Sup.Ct. Order, Misc. Docket No. 12-9191 (eff. Mar. 1, 2013). The amendments correspond with the Supreme Court's proposal of TRCP 169. For further discussion of the proposed new rule, see §7.2, p. 431.

§7. DISCOVERY-CONTROL PLANS

The purpose of discovery-control plans is to promote the efficient resolution of cases by assigning each case to one of three levels, depending on the amount in controversy and the issues involved in the case.

§7.1 Discovery-control plan required. Every case filed after January 1, 1999, must be governed by a discovery-control plan. TRCP 190.1. A plaintiff must allege in the first numbered paragraph of the original petition whether discovery is intended to be conducted under Level 1, 2, or 3 of TRCP 190. TRCP 190.1. See "Discovery-Control Plans," ch. 2-B, §2, p. 95.

§7.2 Level 1. Level 1 discovery is designed as a "safe haven," enabling plaintiffs with small cases to avoid being overtaxed by the defendant's discovery. Griesel, *The "New" Texas Discovery Rules*, §V(A), at 4.

DISCOVERY

★

---

⑬

PROPOSED TRCP CHANGES
In response to Gov't Code §22.004(h), the Supreme Court has proposed TRCP 169 to establish a process for the prompt, efficient, and cost-effective resolution of civil actions (expedited actions) in which only monetary relief is sought and the amount in controversy is no more than $100,000. See Tex.Sup.Ct. Order, Misc. Docket No. 12-9191 (eff. Mar. 1, 2013). The Supreme Court has proposed corresponding amendments to TRCP 190.2 that would, among other things, (1) change the Level 1 discovery-control plan to apply to these expedited actions under TRCP 169 and (2) change the discovery limitations under TRCP 190.2. See Tex.Sup.Ct. Order, Misc. Docket No. 12-9191 (eff. Mar. 1, 2013). The public-comment period for the proposed amendments ends on February 1, 2013, and the rules are to take effect March 1, 2013. For the proposed version of the rules, see the appendix after this book's index. For the final version, go to the Supreme Court website at www.supreme.courts.state.tx.us. When the new and amended rules take effect, a supplement to this book—with updated rules and commentaries that reflect the changes—will be available at www.JonesMcClure.com/TRCPamendments.

---

1. Application. The Level 1 discovery-control plan governs cases in which the amount in controversy is no more than $50,000. TRCP 190.2(a). TRCP 190.2 does not conflict with TRCP 47(b) (which limits the plaintiff's statement of damages to "within the jurisdictional limits of the court") because the purpose of TRCP 190.2 is to bind the pleader to a maximum claim. TRCP 190 cmt. 2.

(1) $50,000 or less. A suit in which all plaintiffs plead that they seek only monetary relief totaling $50,000 or less (excluding costs, prejudgment interest, and attorney fees) will be governed by the Level 1 discovery-control plan. TRCP 190.2(a)(1).

PRACTICE TIP
The plaintiff should not choose Level 1 unless it wants to limit its damages to $50,000. In a Level 1 case, the court cannot award more than $50,000 in damages (excluding costs, prejudgment interest, and attorney fees) even if the jury returns a verdict for more than that amount. See TRCP 190 cmt. 2.

---

(2) Divorce suits. A suit for divorce not involving children in which a party pleads that the value of the marital estate is not more than $50,000 will be governed by the Level 1 discovery-control plan. TRCP 190.2(a)(2).

2. Exceptions. The Level 1 discovery-control plan does not apply in the following instances:

(1) Suit for injunctive relief or divorce involving children. When a party files a petition for injunctive relief or for a divorce involving children. TRCP 190 cmt. 2.

(2) Parties agree. When the parties agree to be governed by the Level 2 discovery-control plan. TRCP 190.2(b)(1).

(3) Court order. When the trial court orders a Level 3 discovery-control plan. TRCP 190.2(b)(2).

(4) Supplemental pleading. If a party files an amended or supplemental pleading seeking more than $50,000 in damages. TRCP 190.2(b)(3). A pleading that makes a Level 1 plan inapplicable must be filed at least 45 days before trial, unless the party secures leave of court by showing that good cause for filing the pleading outweighs any prejudice to the other party. *Id.* See "Period reopens," §8.1.1(2), p. 434.

3. Discovery limitations. In Level 1 cases, discovery is subject to the following limitations:

(1) Discovery period. See "Discovery period for Level 1," §8.1.1, p. 434.

(2) Oral depositions. Each party may take no more than six hours to examine and cross-examine all witnesses in oral depositions. TRCP 190.2(c)(2). The parties may agree to extend this time, but they cannot ex-

DISCOVERY

✦

tend it beyond ten hours without a court order. *Id.* The court may modify the deposition hours so that no party is given an unfair advantage. *Id.*

(3) Interrogatories. A party may serve no more than 25 interrogatories on any other party. TRCP 190.2(c)(3). Each discrete subpart of an interrogatory is considered a separate interrogatory. *Id.* However, not every separate factual inquiry is a discrete subpart. TRCP 190 cmt. 3. The limit of 25 does not include interrogatories that ask a party to identify or authenticate specific documents. TRCP 190.2(c)(3). See "Interrogatories," ch. 6-G, p. 548.

(4) Other written discovery. TRCP 190 does not limit other written discovery. However, depositions on written questions cannot be used to avoid the limits on interrogatories. TRCP 190 cmt. 5.

§7.3 Level 2. Level 2 discovery is the default discovery track that applies in most cases. Griesel, *The "New" Texas Discovery Rules*, at 4. If the plaintiff does not plead a discovery level in its original petition, the case is automatically a Level 2 case. TRCP 190 cmt. 1.

1. Application. Unless a suit is governed by Level 1 under TRCP 190.2 or Level 3 under TRCP 190.4, discovery will be governed by Level 2 under TRCP 190.3. TRCP 190.3(a). Most lawsuits will be conducted under a Level 2 discovery-control plan.

2. Discovery limitations. In Level 2 cases, discovery is subject to the following limitations:

(1) Discovery period. See "Discovery period for Level 2," §8.1.2, p. 434.

(2) Oral depositions. Each side is limited to 50 hours of oral depositions to examine and cross-examine parties on the opposing side, experts designated by those parties, and persons subject to those parties' control. TRCP 190.3(b)(2). See "Side," §2.7, p. 426. TRCP 190.3(b)(2) does not limit the time for deposing witnesses who are not subject to either party's control (e.g., an eyewitness to an accident). In addition, each side is limited to six hours when examining or cross-examining an individual witness. TRCP 199.5(c). See "Time Limits on Oral Depositions," ch. 6-F, §6, p. 532.

(a) If one side designates more than two experts, the opposing side may have an additional six hours of total deposition time for each additional expert designated. TRCP 190.3(b)(2). The rule does not state whether the additional six hours must be used for the expert's deposition. In most cases, the additional six hours would likely be used for additional expert testimony, but a party could make a compelling argument that additional testimony from nonexperts is necessary to counter an expert's testimony.

(b) The court has discretion to modify the deposition hours and must do so when one side or party would otherwise have an unfair advantage. TRCP 190.3(b)(2).

(3) Interrogatories. A party may serve no more than 25 interrogatories on any other party. TRCP 190.3(b)(3). Each discrete subpart of an interrogatory is considered a separate interrogatory. *Id.* However, not every separate factual inquiry is a discrete subpart. TRCP 190 cmt. 3. The limit of 25 does not include interrogatories that ask a party to identify or authenticate specific documents. TRCP 190.3(b)(3). See "Interrogatories," ch. 6-G, p. 548.

(4) Other written discovery. See "Other written discovery," §7.2.3(4), this page.

§7.4 Level 3. Level 3 discovery is court-managed discovery, similar to federal-court practice. Griesel, *The "New" Texas Discovery Rules*, at 4. Level 3 is designed for more complex cases that will not easily fit into the framework of Level 1 or 2. *Id.* Once a suit is designated as Level 3, all changes to the default provisions must be made by court order. *See* TRCP 191 cmt. 1; *see also* Griesel, *The "New" Texas Discovery Rules*, at 6 (court may modify any discovery procedure or limitation by order for good cause). Level 3 discovery cannot be changed by agreement of the parties without a court order.

1. Application. The court must on a party's motion, and may on its own initiative, order that discovery be conducted as a Level 3 case with a discovery-control plan tailored to the specific suit. TRCP 190.4(a). The court

✮

should act on a party's motion or agreed order as soon as reasonably possible. *Id.* See *O'Connor's Texas Forms*, FORMS 6A:5-6.

2. Discovery limitations. In Level 3 cases, discovery is subject to the following limitations:

(1) By court order. When the court signs an order instituting a discovery-control plan for a Level 3 suit, that plan will control. The court-ordered discovery-control plan may address any issue related to discovery or the matters listed in TRCP 166, and it may change any limitations on the time for or amount of discovery set forth in TRCP 190. TRCP 190.4(b); *see In re Alford Chevrolet-Geo*, 997 S.W.2d 173, 181 (Tex.1999) (trial court may limit discovery pending resolution of threshold issues like venue, jurisdiction, forum non conveniens, and official immunity). The plan must include the following information: (1) a date for trial or for a conference to determine a trial date, (2) a discovery period during which, for the entire case or an appropriate phase of it, all discovery must be conducted or all discovery requests must be sent, (3) appropriate limits on the amount of discovery, and (4) deadlines for joining additional parties, amending or supplementing pleadings, and designating expert witnesses. TRCP 190.4(b).

(2) Default discovery limitations. When the court does not sign an order adopting a discovery plan for a Level 3 case, the default discovery limitations are as follows:

(a) Amount of discovery. The amount of discovery is controlled by the provisions for Level 1 or 2, depending on the amount of damages sought and the issues involved. TRCP 190.4(b). See "Level 1," §7.2, p. 430; "Level 2," §7.3, p. 432.

(b) Discovery period. The length of the discovery is controlled by the provisions for Level 1 or 2, depending on the amount of damages sought and the issues involved. TRCP 190.4(b). See "Discovery period for Level 1," §8.1.1, p. 434; "Discovery period for Level 2," §8.1.2, p. 434.

§8. DISCOVERY PERIODS

The purpose of discovery periods is to speed the resolution of trials. Parties should begin discovery as soon as they file their original pleadings. Any delay in beginning discovery can show a lack of diligence. *E.g.*, *Broom v. Arvidson*, No. 04-00-00214-CV (Tex.App.—San Antonio 2001, no pet.) (no pub.; 3-7-01) (continuance denied; P waited three months before initiating discovery).

---

⑬   *PROPOSED TRCP CHANGES*

In response to Gov't Code §22.004(h), the Supreme Court has proposed TRCP 169 to establish a process for the prompt, efficient, and cost-effective resolution of civil actions (expedited actions) in which only monetary relief is sought and the amount in controversy is no more than $100,000. See Tex.Sup.Ct. Order, Misc. Docket No. 12-9191 (eff. Mar. 1, 2013). The Supreme Court has proposed corresponding amendments to TRCP 190.2 and 190.5 that would (1) change the Level 1 discovery-control plan to apply to these expedited actions under TRCP 169, (2) modify the length of the discovery period in Level 1 cases, and (3) limit the modification of a discovery-control plan when a suit is governed by TRCP 169. See Tex.Sup.Ct. Order, Misc. Docket No. 12-9191 (eff. Mar. 1, 2013). The public-comment period for the proposed amendments ends on February 1, 2013, and the rules are to take effect March 1, 2013. For the proposed version of the rules, see the appendix after this book's index. For the final version, go to the Supreme Court website at www.supreme.courts.state.tx.us. When the new and amended rules take effect, a supplement to this book—with updated rules and commentaries that reflect the changes—will be available at www.JonesMcClure.com/TRCPamendments.

★

§8.1 Discovery periods. The party seeking discovery must serve requests for discovery early enough to allow the responding party to serve its response within the discovery period. TRCP 190 cmt. 4; *Pape v. Guadalupe-Blanco River Auth.*, 48 S.W.3d 908, 913 (Tex.App.—Austin 2001, pet. denied). For purposes of defining discovery periods, "trial" does not include summary judgment. TRCP 190 cmt. 8. The trial court may change a deadline for sending discovery requests. TRCP 190 cmt. 4. Every case must be assigned to one of three levels, depending on the amount in controversy and the issues involved. See "Discovery-Control Plans," §7, p. 430.

1. Discovery period for Level 1.

(1) Original period. The discovery period in a Level 1 case begins when the suit is filed and continues until 30 days before the date set for trial. TRCP 190.2(c)(1).

(2) Period reopens. The discovery period in a Level 1 case reopens if, within 45 days of the trial date, a party files a pleading that turns the case into a Level 2 or 3 case, making TRCP 190.2 inapplicable. TRCP 190.2(b)(3), (d). See *O'Connor's Texas Forms*, FORM 6A:8. Discovery must then be completed within the limitations of TRCP 190.3 (Level 2) or TRCP 190.4 (Level 3), whichever applies. TRCP 190.2(d). Any person already deposed may be redeposed if there is still time in the six-hour limit for that person's deposition. *See* TRCP 190.2(c)(2), (d). The court should continue the trial date if necessary to permit the completion of discovery. TRCP 190.2(c)(2), (d).

2. Discovery period for Level 2.

(1) Most cases. Discovery in a Level 2 case begins when the suit is filed and continues until the earliest of the following: (1) 30 days before trial, (2) nine months after the date of the first oral deposition, or (3) nine months after the due date of the first response to written discovery. TRCP 190.3(b)(1)(B); *Ersek v. Davis & Davis, P.C.*, 69 S.W.3d 268, 273 (Tex.App.—Austin 2002, pet. denied); *Pape*, 48 S.W.3d at 913.

(2) Family Code cases. In Family Code cases, discovery begins when the suit is filed and continues until 30 days before the date set for trial. TRCP 190.3(b)(1)(A).

3. Discovery period for Level 3. Discovery in a Level 3 case must be conducted during the discovery period for Level 1 or Level 2, whichever applies, unless the court orders a different period. TRCP 190.4(b).

§8.2 Modification of discovery periods. The court may modify a discovery period at any time; it must do so when justice requires it. TRCP 190.5. See *O'Connor's Texas Forms*, FORM 6A:8.

1. Amended or supplemental pleadings. When pleadings are amended or supplemented, or when new information is disclosed in a discovery response, the court must allow additional related discovery if the movant shows both of the following:

(1) After deadline. The pleadings or responses were made after the discovery deadline or so close to the deadline that the movant did not have an adequate opportunity to conduct discovery related to the new matters. TRCP 190.5(a)(1).

(2) Unfair prejudice. The movant would be unfairly prejudiced without the additional discovery. TRCP 190.5(a)(2).

2. Material changes. The court must allow additional discovery on matters that have materially changed after the discovery deadline when there is more than a three-month gap between the end of the discovery period and the trial date. TRCP 190.5(b).

§8.3 Certain discovery excepted. The limits on discovery under TRCP 190 do not apply to discovery conducted under TRCP 202 ("Depositions Before Suit or to Investigate Claims") or TRCP 621a ("Discovery and Enforcement of Judgment"). TRCP 190.6. However, TRCP 202 cannot be used to avoid the limitations of TRCP 190. TRCP 190.6.

⭐

§9. SECURING DISCOVERY

Chart 6-2, below, summarizes the rules for the various types of discovery.

	6-2. SECURING & RESPONDING TO DISCOVERY				
		Need motion & order?	Response signed by	Response verified?	Cross-reference
	A. Party discovery				
1	Disclosures	No	Attorney	No	ch. 6-E, p. 515
2	Deposition (oral or written questions)	No	Party	Yes	ch. 6-F, p. 525
3	Interrogatories about fact and trial witnesses or legal contentions	No	Attorney	No	ch. 6-G, §4.1.1(4), (5), p. 551
4	Interrogatories about other matters	No	Attorney and party	Yes, by party	ch. 6-G, §4.1.1(4), (5), p. 551
5	Request for admissions	No	Attorney	No	ch. 6-H, p. 557
6	Request to produce documents	No	Attorney	No	ch. 6-I, p. 565
7	Authorization for medical records	No	Party	No	ch. 6-J, p. 576
8	Physical or mental examination	Yes	Attorney	No	ch. 6-J, §5, p. 577
9	Request to inspect land	No	Attorney	No	ch. 6-K, p. 580
	B. Nonparty discovery				
10	Deposition (oral or written questions)	No, just notice and subpoena	Nonparty	Yes	ch. 6-F, p. 525
11	Notice to produce documents	No, just notice and subpoena	Nonparty	No	ch. 6-I, §5, p. 569
12	Deposition before suit	Yes	Nonparty	Yes	ch. 6-F, §16, p. 543
13	Medical records	Yes	Nonparty	No	ch. 6-J, §4, p. 577
14	Motion to inspect land	Yes	Nonparty	No	ch. 6-K, §4, p. 581

§9.1 Securing discovery from parties.

1. By discovery procedures. All forms of discovery can be used to secure discovery from parties. See "Forms of Discovery," §5, p. 428.

2. By agreement. Parties are expected to cooperate in discovery. TRCP 191.2; *see In re Alford Chevrolet-Geo*, 997 S.W.2d 173, 184 (Tex.1999). To this end, parties may make any agreements that are reasonably necessary to efficiently dispose of the case. TRCP 191.2. See "Modifying discovery by agreement," §6.1, p. 429.

§9.2 Securing discovery from nonparties.

A party can use only the discovery procedures outlined in TRCP 205.1 to secure discovery from a nonparty. *In re Guzman*, 19 S.W.3d 522, 524 (Tex.App.—Corpus Christi 2000, orig. proceeding). See "Securing & Responding to Discovery," chart 6-2, this page.

1. Court order. A party can obtain a court order for (1) entry on land under TRCP 196.7, (2) taking a deposition before suit under TRCP 202, or (3) a physical or mental examination under TRCP 204. TRCP 205.1.

2. Subpoena. A party can serve a subpoena on a nonparty to compel (1) an oral deposition, (2) a deposition on written questions, (3) the production of documents or tangible things, served with a notice of deposition on oral examination under TRCP 199.2(b)(5) or written questions under TRCP 200.1(b), or (4) the production of documents and tangible things under TRCP 205. TRCP 205.1(a)-(d).

★

---

§10. PRETRIAL CONFERENCE

Generally, the trial court uses the pretrial conference to oversee discovery—to determine what discovery has been completed and what discovery remains to be done. See "Pretrial Conference," ch. 5-A, p. 315.

§11. SPECIAL MASTER FOR DISCOVERY

A special master may be appointed only for good cause and only in exceptional cases involving discovery questions that require examination of highly technical and complex matters. *In re Harris*, 315 S.W.3d 685, 705 (Tex.App.—Houston [1st Dist.] 2010, orig. proceeding); *see* TRCP 171. See "Master in Chancery," ch. 1-K, p. 80.

§12. FILING & RETAINING DISCOVERY

§12.1 Filing discovery. Most discovery is not filed until it is needed. This rule was adopted to resolve storage problems encountered by the court clerks. Griesel, *The "New" Texas Discovery Rules*, at 6.

1. Discovery materials to be filed. TRCP 191.4(b) lists the discovery documents that must be filed.

(1) Discovery requests, deposition notices, and subpoenas required to be served on nonparties. TRCP 191.4(b)(1). For rules on filing deposition materials, see "Filing Deposition Documents," chart 6-8, p. 526.

(2) Motions and responses to motions relating to discovery matters. TRCP 191.4(b)(2).

(3) Agreements relating to discovery matters, to the extent necessary to comply with TRCP 11. TRCP 191.4(b)(3).

2. Discovery materials not to be filed. TRCP 191.4(a) lists the discovery documents that must not be filed.

(1) Discovery requests, deposition notices, and subpoenas required to be served only on parties. TRCP 191.4(a)(1).

(2) Responses and objections to discovery requests and deposition notices from parties or nonparties. TRCP 191.4(a)(2).

(3) Documents and tangible things produced in discovery. TRCP 191.4(a)(3).

(4) Withholding statements prepared in compliance with TRCP 193.3(b), (d). TRCP 191.4(a)(4).

3. Exceptions. TRCP 191.4(c) lists the exceptions to the do-not-file rule:

(1) The court may order that discovery materials be filed. TRCP 191.4(c)(1). This provision is an additional safeguard against destruction of discovery in cases in which it should be preserved, such as cases involving TRCP 76a. Griesel, *The "New" Texas Discovery Rules*, §VI(A)(4), at 6.

(2) A person may file discovery materials in support of or in opposition to a motion or for other use in a court proceeding. TRCP 191.4(c)(2).

(3) A person may file discovery materials necessary for a proceeding in an appellate court. TRCP 191.4(c)(3).

§12.2 Retaining discovery during trial. When a person (whether a party or a nonparty) serves discovery materials that must not be filed under TRCP 191.4, that person must retain the original or a copy of the materials during the pendency of the case, including any appeals begun within six months after the judgment is signed. TRCP 191.4(d); *National Family Care Life Ins. v. Fletcher*, 57 S.W.3d 662, 667 n.6 (Tex.App.—Beaumont 2001, pet. denied). The court may modify this requirement. TRCP 191.4(d).

§12.3 Retaining depositions after trial. Beginning one year after a case is finally resolved (either by a final judgment that is not appealed or by an appellate-court mandate), a party has 30 days to withdraw any depositions (transcripts or depositions on written questions) that it offered. Tex.Sup.Ct. Order, Misc. Docket No. 05-9025 (eff.

✦

June 1, 2005); *see also* TRCP 191.4(e) (trial-court clerk must retain and dispose of depositions as directed by Supreme Court). After the 30-day deadline, the trial-court clerk may dispose of the depositions unless otherwise directed by the court. Tex.Sup.Ct. Order, Misc. Docket No. 05-9025 (eff. June 1, 2005).

§13. SERVICE OF DISCOVERY MATERIALS

§13.1 Service on all parties. When a party serves discovery materials (disclosures, discovery requests, notices, responses, objections), it must serve a copy of those materials on all other parties of record. TRCP 191.5.

§13.2 Serving discovery with original pleadings. Plaintiffs and defendants may serve discovery requests with their original pleadings.

PRACTICE TIP

Many plaintiffs include a request for disclosure as part of their original petition, changing the name of the petition to "Plaintiff's Original Petition & Request for Disclosures," and noting the full name of the document on the citation. If the plaintiff serves discovery with the petition but in a separate document, the citation must identify the discovery as one of the documents being served on the defendant. **Sosa v. Williams**, *936 S.W.2d 708, 710 (Tex.App.—Waco 1996, writ denied).*

---

§14. DEADLINE TO RESPOND TO DISCOVERY

For the general rules for computing deadlines, see "Computing Response Deadlines," ch. 1-D, §6, p. 36.

§14.1 Deadline to serve response. The party responding to the discovery must serve its response (answers, objections, and assertions of privilege) on the other party before the deadline for discovery.

1. Standard time to respond – 30 days. When a party is served with a request for written discovery, the request must provide at least 30 days to respond. TRCP 194.3 (request for disclosure), TRCP 196.2(a) (request for production), TRCP 196.7(c)(1) (request for entry on land), TRCP 197.2(a) (interrogatories), TRCP 198.2(a) (request for admissions). A discovery request can provide more than 30 days to answer, but it cannot provide less than 30 days. Depending on the type of service (mail, fax, or e-service), the party may have an additional three or four days to respond. TRCP 21a. See "Computing Response Deadlines," ch. 1-D, §6, p. 36; "Deadlines to Respond to Discovery," chart 6-3, this page.

2. Served before answer date – 50 days. When a defendant is served with requests for written discovery before its answer is due, the defendant must serve its response within 50 days after the discovery request was served. TRCP 194.3(a) (request for disclosure), TRCP 196.2(a) (request for production), TRCP 196.7(c)(1) (request for entry on land), TRCP 197.2(a) (interrogatories), TRCP 198.2(a) (request for admissions). This is true regardless of when the defendant actually files its answer. For example, if a request for written discovery is filed with the petition, the defendant has 50 days to respond even if it files its answer before the date it is due. Depending on the type of service (mail, fax, or e-service), the defendant may have an additional three or four days to respond. TRCP 21a. See "Computing Response Deadlines," ch. 1-D, §6, p. 36; chart 6-3, below.

6-3. DEADLINES TO RESPOND TO DISCOVERY	
Method of service	**Computing deadline**
1	Service by U.S. mail	Date of mailing (generally, the postmark) + 3 days + 30 days = 33 days
2	Service by delivery	Date of delivery + 30 days = 30 days
3	Service by fax before 5 p.m.	Date of fax + 3 days + 30 days = 33 days
4	Service by fax after 5 p.m.	Date of fax + 4 days + 30 days = 34 days

★

6-3. DEADLINES TO RESPOND TO DISCOVERY (CONTINUED)	
Method of service	**Computing deadline**
5	E-service before 5 p.m. (district and county courts)	Date of e-service + 3 days + 30 days = 33 days
6	E-service after 5 p.m. (district and county courts)	Date of e-service* + 4 days + 30 days = 34 days
7	E-service before 5 p.m. (JP courts)	Date of e-service + 30 days = 30 days
8	E-service after 5 p.m. (JP courts)	Date of e-service* + 1 day + 30 days = 31 days
9	Service on defendant before answer date—request for disclosure, request for entry, interrogatories, request for admissions, request for production	Date of service + 50 days = 50 to 54 days, depending on type of service. See rows 1-8, above.
* When next day is Saturday, Sunday, or legal holiday, document is deemed served on next regular business day.	

3. Discovery deadline in pretrial orders. If the court signs a pretrial order governing discovery, the parties must comply with its terms. *Werner v. Miller*, 579 S.W.2d 455, 456 (Tex.1979). However, the trial court cannot arbitrarily shorten discovery deadlines by pretrial order. *General Elec. Co. v. Salinas*, 861 S.W.2d 20, 23 (Tex. App.—Corpus Christi 1993, orig. proceeding). See "Discovery deadlines," ch. 5-A, §3.5, p. 316.

4. Discovery deadline when trial reset. When the date for trial is reset, the original discovery deadlines set in the docket-control order are generally not extended. *See In re Kings Ridge Homeowners Ass'n*, 303 S.W.3d 773, 779 n.6 (Tex.App.—Fort Worth 2009, orig. proceeding); *see also Fort Brown Villas III Condo. Ass'n v. Gillenwater*, 285 S.W.3d 879, 882 (Tex.2009) (pre-1999 discovery rules had fluid deadline for discovery disclosure; post-1999 discovery rules have specific date to complete discovery that depends on discovery-control plan, not trial date); *cf. Eaton Metal Prods. v. U.S. Denro Steels, Inc.*, No. 14-09-00757-CV (Tex.App.—Houston [14th Dist.] 2010, no pet.) (memo op.; 9-30-10) (resetting of trial did not extend discovery deadlines established in Rule 11 agreement). The "hard deadline" established by the discovery rules requires a party to comply with the discovery deadlines; otherwise, the evidence not timely disclosed may be excluded under TRCP 193.6. *See Fort Brown Villas*, 285 S.W.3d at 882. See "Timely," §16.3, p. 439. To extend the discovery deadlines, the party should move to modify the discovery-control plan under TRCP 190.5, or the parties should file a Rule 11 agreement. *See In re Kings Ridge*, 303 S.W.3d at 782. See "Modifying Discovery Procedures," §6, p. 429.

§14.2 Deadlines regarding experts. See "Deadlines for Securing Discovery from Experts," ch. 6-D, §6, p. 512.

§15. EXTENDING TIME TO RESPOND TO DISCOVERY

To extend the time to respond to discovery, a party must secure either an agreement or a court order. Without an extension, all untimely objections to the discovery request are waived. *See Hobson v. Moore*, 734 S.W.2d 340, 341 (Tex. 1987).

§15.1 Agreement to extend. See "Modifying discovery by agreement," §6.1, p. 429; *O'Connor's Texas Forms*, FORM 6A:3.

§15.2 Court order to extend. To secure additional time to respond to discovery, the party must file a motion to extend time showing good cause for the late response. TRCP 191.1. See *O'Connor's Texas Forms*, FORM 6A:2. Because TRCP 191.1 states that the court can modify discovery procedures (including the deadlines to respond) only on "good cause," the rule seems to conflict with TRCP 5. TRCP 5 requires only "cause shown" for a motion to extend that is filed before the deadline sought to be extended. See "Motion to extend time," ch. 1-C, §9.1, p. 30. Until the courts clarify this apparent conflict, all motions to extend time in discovery matters—even if filed before the deadline to respond—should include a showing of good cause. See "Modifying discovery by court order," §6.2, p. 429.

★

§16. PRODUCING WRITTEN DISCOVERY

§16.1 Form of response.

1. In writing. The party must provide written responses to discovery requests. TRCP 193.1, 196.2(a) (request for production), TRCP 197.2(a) (interrogatories), TRCP 198.2(a) (request for admissions). A party cannot answer written-discovery requests orally. *See* TRCP 193.1; *see, e.g., **Sharp v. Broadway Nat'l Bank**,* 784 S.W.2d 669, 671 (Tex.1990) (oral identification of witness not proper). The responding party's answers, objections, and other responses must be preceded by the corresponding request. TRCP 193.1. See *O'Connor's Texas Forms*, FORMS 6G:3, 6H:3, 6I:3.

2. Signed. The responses to written discovery must be signed by the attorney (or pro se party). TRCP 191.3(a). See "Certification by signature," §4.1, p. 427; "Securing & Responding to Discovery," chart 6-2, p. 435.

3. Verified. The only written responses to discovery that must be verified are answers to interrogatories. See "Securing & Responding to Discovery," chart 6-2, p. 435. For a discussion of interrogatory answers, see "Signed & verified by party," ch. 6-G, §4.1.1(4), p. 551.

§16.2 Service on attorney in charge.
Discovery responses must be served on the attorney in charge. *See* TRCP 8 (all communications about lawsuit must be sent to attorney in charge); *see, e.g., **Reichhold Chems., Inc. v. Puremco Mfg.**,* 854 S.W.2d 240, 246 (Tex.App.—Waco 1993, writ denied) (response to discovery served on cocounsel, instead of attorney in charge, was not timely). See "Attorney in charge," ch. 1-H, §3.1, p. 54.

§16.3 Timely.
A party must timely respond to discovery requests. TRCP 193.1. Discovery responses must be served within the time permitted by the rules, ordered by the court, or agreed to by the parties. See "Deadline to serve response," §14.1, p. 437. When a party does not produce discovery, or ignores the request, the evidence that was not timely disclosed will be excluded at trial unless there was good cause for not producing the discovery or unless the other parties will not be unfairly surprised or prejudiced. TRCP 193.6(a); *see **Fort Brown Villas III Condo. Ass'n v. Gillenwater**,* 285 S.W.3d 879, 881 (Tex.2009); ***F&H Invs. v. State**,* 55 S.W.3d 663, 670-71 (Tex.App.—Waco 2001, no pet.). The exclusion of evidence under TRCP 193.6 applies equally to trial proceedings and summary-judgment proceedings. ***Fort Brown Villas**,* 285 S.W.3d at 882. See "Objecting to Unidentified Witness," ch. 6-E, §10, p. 522.

§16.4 When production required.

1. Information requested. A party is required to produce all information requested, unless the party serves timely objections or assertions of privilege. TRCP 193.2, 193.3. See "Burden to partially comply," §18.10, p. 447.

2. Information in possession. A party is required to produce all documents or things requested that are in its possession, custody, or control. TRCP 196.3(a). See "Possession," §2.5, p. 425.

§16.5 When production not required.
A party who makes a proper and timely objection or assertion of privilege is not required to produce the following:

1. Evidence subject to objection or privilege. A party is not required to produce evidence that is subject to an objection or an assertion of privilege. See "Burden to partially comply," §18.10, p. 447.

2. Information not reasonably available. A party is not required to produce information that is not reasonably available to the party or its attorney when the response is made. *See* TRCP 193.1.

3. Impeachment or rebuttal evidence. A party is not required to produce impeachment or rebuttal evidence in anticipation of the other party's case. *See* TRCP 192.3(d) (parties may obtain discovery of trial witnesses but not of rebuttal or impeachment witnesses if the need for their testimony cannot reasonably be anticipated before trial).

§16.6 Organization of discovery materials.
The responding party must either (1) produce the discovery materials as they are kept in the usual course of business or (2) organize and label them to correspond with the categories of the request. TRCP 196.3(c).

§16.7 Authenticity of produced documents.
See "Offering documents," ch. 6-I, §8.1, p. 574.

✦

§17. SUPPLEMENTING DISCOVERY RESPONSES

§17.1 When supplementation required. The burden to supplement discovery responses is on the party responding to written discovery; the party requesting discovery has no burden to request supplementation. TRCP 193.5(a). A party should always supplement (even when unsure whether it is necessary) because the court may exclude the information if it is not properly supplemented. *See* TRCP 193.6(a); *Alvarado v. Farah Mfg.*, 830 S.W.2d 911, 913-14 (Tex.1992); *Boothe v. Hausler*, 766 S.W.2d 788, 789 (Tex.1989). See *O'Connor's Texas Forms*, FORMS 6A:27-28. A party must supplement a discovery response in the following instances:

1. Discovery response incomplete when made. A party must supplement a discovery response when the party obtains information revealing that its response was incomplete or incorrect when made. TRCP 193.5(a).

2. Discovery response no longer complete. A party must supplement a discovery response when the party discovers that its response, though complete and correct when made, is no longer complete and correct. TRCP 193.5(a); *see Boothe*, 766 S.W.2d at 789; *see, e.g., Alvarado*, 830 S.W.2d at 917 (P should have supplemented discovery response to include unlisted witness).

3. For summary-judgment witnesses. A party must timely supplement responses to written discovery requesting the designation of witnesses before submitting evidence in a summary-judgment procedure. *See Fort Brown Villas III Condo. Ass'n v. Gillenwater*, 285 S.W.3d 879, 882 (Tex.2009) (exclusion of witnesses not timely identified under TRCP 193.6 applies equally to trial and SJ proceedings); *F.W. Indus. v. McKeehan*, 198 S.W.3d 217, 221 (Tex.App.—Eastland 2005, no pet.) (timeliness of expert discovery is determined by discovery deadline in TRCP 195.2, even in SJ proceedings); *Cunningham v. Columbia/St. David's Healthcare Sys.*, 185 S.W.3d 7, 13 (Tex. App.—Austin 2005, no pet.) (nondesignated expert's affidavit cannot be considered as SJ evidence unless party shows good cause or lack of unfair surprise or prejudice).

§17.2 Extent of supplementation.

1. Written discovery.

(1) Identity of witnesses. A discovery request for the identification of persons with knowledge of relevant facts, trial witnesses, or expert witnesses must be supplemented in writing. TRCP 193.5(a)(1); *see, e.g., Sharp v. Broadway Nat'l Bank*, 784 S.W.2d 669, 671 (Tex.1990) (although expert witness was deposed, he was not identified in written supplement to request for disclosure; witness should have been excluded); *Yeldell v. Holiday Hills Ret. & Nursing Ctr., Inc.*, 701 S.W.2d 243, 246-47 (Tex.1985) (party did not supplement identity of fact witness after learning she had knowledge of relevant facts; witness was properly excluded).

(2) Other information. A discovery request for information other than the identification of witnesses must be supplemented in writing unless the information was made known in writing, on the record at a deposition, or through other discovery responses. TRCP 193.5(a)(2).

2. Discovery from retained testifying expert. When a party's retained testifying expert changes or modifies her opinion, the party must supplement the expert's deposition testimony or written report with the expert's mental impressions or opinions and the basis for them. TRCP 195.6; *VingCard A.S. v. Merrimac Hospitality Sys.*, 59 S.W.3d 847, 856 (Tex.App.—Fort Worth 2001, pet. denied); *see, e.g., Aluminum Co. of Am. v. Bullock*, 870 S.W.2d 2, 4 (Tex.1994) (Ps should have supplemented interrogatory answers to show material change in their expert's testimony; in deposition, expert stated that D was not consciously indifferent, but at trial, expert testified that D was grossly negligent). See "Supplementing discovery of retained testifying expert," ch. 6-D, §5.1, p. 511.

3. Order or agreement. Supplementation of discovery responses is required when the court orders it or the parties agree to it. *See* TRCP 191.1; *see, e.g., Cole v. Huntsville Mem'l Hosp.*, 920 S.W.2d 364, 376 (Tex. App.—Houston [1st Dist.] 1996, writ denied) (failure to supplement as required by order contributed to imposition of death-penalty sanctions).

§17.3 When supplementation not required.

1. Deposition testimony of fact witness. A party is not required to supplement the deposition testimony of fact witnesses. See "Deposition of fact witnesses," ch. 6-F, §11.1, p. 538.

—— ✦ ——

2. Information provided by other means. A party is not required to supplement responses to written-discovery requests for most discovery matters if the additional or corrective information was made known to the other party (1) in writing, (2) on the record at a deposition, or (3) through other discovery responses. TRCP 193.5(a)(2); *City of Paris v. McDowell*, 79 S.W.3d 601, 606 (Tex.App.—Texarkana 2002, no pet.). Supplementation by other means, as defined in TRCP 193.5(a)(2), applies only to "other information" and does not apply to supplementation of witness information listed in TRCP 193.5(a)(1).

3. Lapse of request. A party is not required to supplement discovery if the requesting party does not maintain a valid request for information. *E.g., Kawasaki Motors v. Thompson*, 872 S.W.2d 221, 224 (Tex.1994) (parties' agreement inadvertently eliminated question about experts).

§17.4 Deadline to supplement responses.

1. Under TRCPs.

(1) After discovering need to supplement. A party must supplement or amend its responses to written discovery "reasonably promptly" after the party discovers the need to do so. TRCP 193.5(b); *Wigfall v. TDCJ*, 137 S.W.3d 268, 273 (Tex.App.—Houston [1st Dist.] 2004, no pet.); *Snider v. Stanley*, 44 S.W.3d 713, 716 (Tex. App.—Beaumont 2001, pet. denied); *e.g., Hooper v. Chittaluru*, 222 S.W.3d 103, 110 (Tex.App.—Houston [14th Dist.] 2006, pet. denied) (P's supplemental expert designation one day after deposition of D's expert was reasonably prompt because P could not have cross-designated D's expert until learning of his opinions at deposition). Although there is a presumption that a supplemented discovery response made less than 30 days before trial is not reasonably prompt (see "Less than 30 days before trial," §17.4.1(3), this page), the converse is not true—a supplemented discovery response made more than 30 days before trial is not necessarily reasonably prompt. *Snider*, 44 S.W.3d at 715. The following supplementations were not reasonably prompt: • Disclosure of witness statements 41 days before trial, on last day for discovery, nine months after discovery request. *Matagorda Cty. Hosp. Dist. v. Burwell*, 94 S.W.3d 75, 81 (Tex.App.—Corpus Christi 2002), *rev'd on other grounds*, 189 S.W.3d 738 (Tex.2006). • Plaintiff's designation of expert eight months after request, after defendant filed motion for summary judgment. *Ersek v. Davis & Davis, P.C.*, 69 S.W.3d 268, 271 n.2 (Tex.App.—Austin 2002, pet. denied). • Defendants' designation of expert 30 days before trial. *Snider*, 44 S.W.3d at 715.

CAUTION

The Austin Court of Appeals has held that if a party responded to a request for disclosure of experts with "no experts at this time," the party cannot designate an expert for the first time after the deadline in TRCP 195.2 (90 days before end of discovery period for plaintiff, 60 days for defendant). Ersek, 69 S.W.3d at 270-71.

---

(2) At least 30 days before trial. A party may supplement its discovery responses as late as 30 days before trial. TRCP 193.5(b); *see Aluminum Co. of Am. v. Bullock*, 870 S.W.2d 2, 3-4 (Tex.1994) (experts under former TRCP 166b(6)(b)). If a case is set for trial "for the week of" instead of on a certain date, the 30 days run from the actual date of trial, not the Monday of that week. *See* TRCP 193.5(b) (specifies "before trial," not "before the week set for trial").

(3) Less than 30 days before trial. To supplement discovery responses less than 30 days before trial, a party must show good cause for the late supplementation or show that it will not unfairly surprise or prejudice the other parties. TRCP 193.6(a), (b); *Rutledge v. Staner*, 9 S.W.3d 469, 472 (Tex.App.—Tyler 1999, pet. denied); *see, e.g., Forman v. Fina Oil & Chem. Co.*, 858 S.W.2d 373, 374 (Tex.1993) (good cause for late designation of expert because P designated same doctor as D three days after receiving D's designation). There is a presumption that a supplemental or amended response made less than 30 days before trial is not made "reasonably promptly." TRCP 193.5(b). If the party does not carry its burden, the court may exclude the evidence or grant a continuance to allow the other parties to conduct discovery on new information disclosed in the supplementation. TRCP 193.6(a), (c).

★

2. By court order or agreement. A party must supplement its responses to written discovery according to the modified deadlines in any court order or agreement between the parties. *See* TRCP 191.1 (discovery procedures can be modified by court order or agreement); *see, e.g., **Mack v. Suzuki Motor Corp.**, 6 S.W.3d 732, 733-34 (Tex.App.—Houston [1st Dist.] 1999, no pet.) (expert report struck because P served it after deadline in agreed scheduling order).

§17.5 Not filed. Most supplemental or amended responses to written discovery are not filed with the court. See "Filing discovery," §12.1, p. 436.

§17.6 Form of supplemental discovery. Supplemental or amended responses to written discovery should be made in the same form as the original responses. TRCP 193.5(b); ***State Farm Fire & Cas. Co. v. Morua***, 979 S.W.2d 616, 618 (Tex.1998); *see, e.g., **Varner v. Howe***, 860 S.W.2d 458, 462-63 (Tex.App.—El Paso 1993, no writ) (witness identified by letter should have been excluded). See *O'Connor's Texas Forms*, FORMS 6A:27-28.

1. In writing. The party should provide the supplemental or amended response in writing. *See* TRCP 193.5(b). For exceptions, see "Information provided by other means," §17.3.2, p. 441.

2. Verified. A supplemental or amended response must be verified by the party if the original response was required to be verified by the party. TRCP 193.5(b); *see **Morua***, 979 S.W.2d at 618 (former TRCP 166b required verification of responses if original answer was required to be verified). For a list of written discovery that must be verified, see "Securing & Responding to Discovery," chart 6-2, p. 435.

3. Objections to form of response. A supplemental or amended response that is not in the correct form or that is not verified when required is not deemed untimely unless the party making the response refuses to correct the defect within a reasonable time after it is pointed out. TRCP 193.5(b).

§17.7 Review. If a party supplements discovery less than 30 days before trial and the trial court admits the untimely disclosed evidence over the opposing party's objection, the objecting party—to obtain a reversal on appeal—must show that the trial court's error probably caused the rendition of an improper judgment. TRAP 44.1(a)(1); ***Bott v. Bott***, 962 S.W.2d 626, 628 (Tex.App.—Houston [14th Dist.] 1997, no pet.).

§18. RESISTING DISCOVERY

6-4. BURDENS IN DISCOVERY PROCEDURE			
Burden		**Discovery from party**	**Discovery from nonparty***
		Burden is on—	
1	To plead objection	Party resisting discovery, §18.1, p. 443	
2	To assert privilege	Party resisting discovery, §18.2, p. 443	
3	To request privilege log	Party seeking discovery, §18.2.2, p. 444	
4	To secure hearing	Party seeking discovery, §18.6.1, p. 446	Party resisting discovery, §18.4.1, p. 445
5	To produce evidence at hearing	Party resisting discovery, §18.7, p. 446	
6	To ask for in camera inspection	Party resisting discovery, §18.8.1, p. 447	
7	To secure ruling	Party seeking discovery, §18.6.1, p. 446	Party resisting discovery, §18.4.1, p. 445
* Assumes that the nonparty does not object to producing discovery but one of the parties does.			

The discovery rules provide two procedures for resisting discovery: (1) the procedure for making most discovery objections, and (2) the procedure for asserting claims of privilege.

★

> ### NOTE
>
> *Even though TRCP 196.2(b) seems to say that a party responding to discovery must make its objections and assert its privileges at the same time, the discovery rules permit a party to file its objections first and wait until after the court rules on the objections to file its assertions of privilege if an objection and a privilege apply to the same information.* **In re Lincoln Elec. Co.,** *91 S.W.3d 432, 437 (Tex.App.—Beaumont 2002, orig. proceeding).*

§18.1 Making objections. The party resisting discovery has the burden to plead its objection to discovery. *State v. Lowry,* 802 S.W.2d 669, 671 (Tex.1991). No matter how improper the discovery request, the party to whom it is addressed must timely object, or else it waives its objections. *See* TRCP 193.2(a) (party must make "any" objection to written discovery in writing); *Young v. Ray,* 916 S.W.2d 1, 3 (Tex.App.—Houston [1st Dist.] 1995, orig. proceeding) (party must timely object or objection is waived). The only discovery request a party is not required to respond or object to is one that is not signed. See "Effect of no signature," §4.1.3, p. 427.

1. Timely objection. The party resisting discovery must object at or before the time to respond to discovery. TRCP 193.2(e); *see Remington Arms Co. v. Canales,* 837 S.W.2d 624, 625 (Tex.1992); *Hobson v. Moore,* 734 S.W.2d 340, 341 (Tex.1987). If not, the objection is waived unless the party (1) obtained an extension of time by agreement or by court order or (2) can show good cause for not timely objecting. TRCP 193.2(e); *see Remington Arms,* 837 S.W.2d at 625; *Hobson,* 734 S.W.2d at 341. After the deadline to respond, a party can only amend its objection or response to include a ground that was initially inapplicable or was unknown after reasonable inquiry. *See* TRCP 193.2(d), (e).

2. Specific objection. The party resisting discovery must make a specific objection for each item it wants to exclude from discovery. TRCP 193.2(a); *see, e.g., In re Alford Chevrolet-Geo,* 997 S.W.2d 173, 181 (Tex.1999) (party's conclusory objections alleging undue burden and harassment were unsuccessful); *see also National Un. Fire Ins. v. Hoffman,* 746 S.W.2d 305, 307 & n.3 (Tex.App.—Dallas 1988, orig. proceeding) (party made general objections by merely reciting particular privileges). Valid objections obscured by unfounded objections are automatically waived unless the party shows good cause. TRCP 193.2(e).

§18.2 Asserting privileges. To protect privileged information from written discovery, a party must timely "assert" a privilege under TRCP 193.3. *In re Shipmon,* 68 S.W.3d 815, 822 (Tex.App.—Amarillo 2001, orig. proceeding); *In re Monsanto Co.,* 998 S.W.2d 917, 924 (Tex.App.—Waco 1999, orig. proceeding); *see also* TRCP 176.6(c) (nonparty objecting to subpoena requesting documents must follow provisions of TRCP 193.3). A party should not "object" to discovery that asks for privileged information. TRCP 193.2(f); *In re Christus Health Se. Tex.,* 167 S.W.3d 596, 599 (Tex.App.—Beaumont 2005, orig. proceeding); *In re Anderson,* 163 S.W.3d 136, 140 (Tex.App.—San Antonio 2005, orig. proceeding); *In re Shipmon,* 68 S.W.3d at 822. If a party mistakenly objects to a request for privileged information instead of asserting a privilege, the privilege is not waived, but the party must comply with TRCP 193.3 when the error is pointed out. TRCP 193.2(f); *In re University of Tex. Health Ctr.,* 33 S.W.3d 822, 826 (Tex. 2000).

1. Claiming privilege. A privilege against written discovery must be asserted as follows:

(1) Withhold information. The party must withhold the privileged information from the discovery it produces. TRCP 193.3(a). The party can withhold only the information sought to be protected; it cannot withhold other information requested in the same discovery request. See "Burden to partially comply," §18.10, p. 447.

(2) Withholding statement. The party must serve a withholding statement. TRCP 193.3(a). See "Withholding statement," §2.8, p. 426; *O'Connor's Texas Forms,* FORM 6A:19.

(3) Exemption for litigation materials. A party is not required to assert a privilege in the withholding statement for materials created by or for attorneys for the litigation. TRCP 193.3(c). These materials will presumably be withheld on the grounds of attorney-client privilege or core work product. TRCP 193 cmt. 3. A party

─────────────────── ✦ ───────────────────

may withhold a privileged communication to or from an attorney or attorney's representative or a privileged document of an attorney or attorney's representative if (1) the communication was created when the party consulted an attorney to obtain professional legal services from the attorney in the prosecution or defense of a specific claim in the litigation in which discovery is requested, and (2) the communication was about the litigation in which the discovery is requested. TRCP 193.3(c).

NOTE

TRCP 193.3(c) does not prohibit a party from specifically requesting information that may be subject to an attorney-client privilege or core-work-product exemption if the party has a good-faith basis for asserting that the information is discoverable. TRCP 193 cmt. 3. For example, a party can request information described by TRE 503(d)(1), the crime-fraud exception.

---

2. Request privilege log. After receiving a withholding statement, the party seeking discovery may request in writing that the withholding party identify the information or material withheld. TRCP 193.3(b); *In re Christus Health*, 167 S.W.3d at 599; *In re Anderson*, 163 S.W.3d at 140; *In re Monsanto Co.*, 998 S.W.2d at 924. The document listing the information withheld from discovery is called a privilege log. See *O'Connor's Texas Forms*, FORM 6A:20.

3. Serve privilege log. Within 15 days after service of the request for the privilege log, the withholding party must serve a response. TRCP 193.3(b); *In re Anderson*, 163 S.W.3d at 140; *Spohn Hosp. v. Mayer*, 72 S.W.3d 52, 62 (Tex.App.—Corpus Christi 2001), *rev'd on other grounds*, 104 S.W.3d 878 (Tex.2003). See *O'Connor's Texas Forms*, FORM 6A:21. The response must include the following information:

(1) Assert privilege. The party must assert a specific privilege for each item or group of items withheld. TRCP 193.3(b)(2); *In re Christus Health*, 167 S.W.3d at 599; *In re Anderson*, 163 S.W.3d at 140; *In re Monsanto Co.*, 998 S.W.2d at 924.

(2) Describe information or material withheld. The party must specify the nature of the information or material withheld without revealing the privileged information itself. TRCP 193.3(b)(1); *In re Christus Health*, 167 S.W.3d at 599; *In re Anderson*, 163 S.W.3d at 140; *Spohn Hosp.*, 72 S.W.3d at 62. The withheld information or material must be described in a way that allows the party seeking discovery to assess the applicability of the privilege. TRCP 193.3(b)(1); *In re Christus Health*, 167 S.W.3d at 599; *In re Anderson*, 163 S.W.3d at 140-41; *In re Monsanto Co.*, 998 S.W.2d at 924. A description of a document should include the document number ("Bates number"), author or source, recipient, persons receiving copies, date, document title, document type, number of pages, and any other relevant information. *See In re Monsanto Co.*, 998 S.W.2d at 925.

4. Use snap-back provision. An inadvertent production of privileged information is considered involuntary. TRCP 193.3(d); *see In re Living Ctrs.*, 175 S.W.3d 253, 260 (Tex.2005); *In re Certain Underwriters*, 294 S.W.3d 891, 906 (Tex.App.—Beaumont 2009, orig. proceeding); *In re Monsanto Co.*, 998 S.W.2d at 921 n.2. Parties and nonparties may rely on TRCP 193.3(d) to assert a claim of privilege after inadvertent production of their own privileged documents. *In re Certain Underwriters*, 294 S.W.3d at 905.

(1) Purpose. The purpose of the snap-back provision in TRCP 193.3(d) is to reduce costs and risks in large document productions. TRCP 193 cmt. 4. The provision focuses on the intent to waive the privilege, not on the intent to produce the information or material. *In re Christus Spohn Hosp. Kleberg*, 222 S.W.3d 434, 439 (Tex. 2007); *Warrantech Corp. v. Computer Adapters Servs.*, 134 S.W.3d 516, 524-25 (Tex.App.—Fort Worth 2004, no pet.); TRCP 193 cmt. 4. A party who does not diligently screen documents before producing them does not waive a claim of privilege. *In re Christus Spohn Hosp. Kleberg*, 222 S.W.3d at 439; *Warrantech Corp.*, 134 S.W.3d at 525; *In re AEP Tex. Central Co.*, 128 S.W.3d 687, 693 (Tex.App.—San Antonio 2003, no pet.); TRCP 193 cmt. 4.

(2) Procedure. A party may claim a privilege on information inadvertently produced to the opposing party by following the snap-back provision of TRCP 193.3(d). *See* TRCP 193 cmt. 4 (snap-back provision in TRCP

★

193.3 overrules *Granada Corp. v. First Ct. of Appeals*, 844 S.W.2d 223 (Tex.1992), on inadvertent production). In limited circumstances, a party who inadvertently produced privileged information to its own testifying expert (making the information discoverable to the opposing party) may be able to use the snap-back provision. See "Invoke snap-back provision," ch. 6-D, §4.1.1(6)(b)[1], p. 508.

(a) **Amend withholding statement.** The party must serve on the other parties an amended withholding statement that (1) identifies the information produced, (2) identifies the privilege asserted for that information, and (3) requests that all copies of the privileged information be returned. TRCP 193.3(d). See *O'Connor's Texas Forms*, FORM 6A:22.

(b) **Deadline.** The party must amend its withholding statement within ten days after discovering the accidental production, unless the time is shortened by the court. TRCP 193.3(d). The ten-day period runs from the party's first awareness of the mistake, not from the production of the information. TRCP 193 cmt. 4.

(c) **Return materials.** Once the party has complied with the snap-back provision, the party who received the materials or information must promptly return them and all copies. TRCP 193.3(d).

PRACTICE TIP
To avoid complications at trial about inadvertently disclosed documents, ask the court to require all parties to make pretrial identification of documents that they intend to offer. TRCP 193 cmt. 4. This will trigger the obligation to assert any overlooked privileges under TRCP 193.3. TRCP 193 cmt. 4.

---

§18.3 Objecting to amended discovery requests. When a party receives an amended discovery request, the party is not required to restate its objections and reassert its privileges to the parts of the request that are the same as the original. *See, e.g.*, *In re University of Tex. Health Ctr.*, 33 S.W.3d 822, 826 (Tex.2000) (hospital was not required to reassert privileges when deposition was reset).

§18.4 Objections regarding discovery & nonparties.

1. Party information from nonparty. When discovery about a party is sought from a nonparty, the party should file a motion for protective order to prevent disclosure of the information. Only a protective order—not an objection—will prevent the nonparty from producing the discovery. *See* TRCP 192.6(b). When both the party and the nonparty object to the discovery, the party and the nonparty can coordinate their efforts, and the nonparty will withhold the requested information. When only the party objects and the nonparty is willing to produce the information, the party must quickly file a motion for protective order, set the motion for a hearing, and get a ruling before the nonparty produces the information requested. *See* TRCP 176.6(e) (party affected by subpoena may move for protective order before time to respond), TRCP 192.6(a) (party affected by discovery request may file motion for protective order within time to respond). However, when the nonparty produces the information, the party may recover any privileged information. *See* TRCP 193.3(d). See "Use snap-back provision," §18.2.4, p. 444.

2. Nonparty information from party. The discovery rules do not require notice to a nonparty when a party seeks information about it from another party. *See In re CI Host, Inc.*, 92 S.W.3d 514, 517 (Tex.2002). The party from whom the discovery is sought should inform the court when the information sought is the privileged information of a nonparty. The court should give serious consideration to the interest of a nonparty whose information is sought in discovery. *See id.*

§18.5 Burden to challenge objections. The party seeking discovery can put the other party's objections and claims of privilege at issue by a global challenge. *See In re E.I. DuPont de Nemours & Co.*, 136 S.W.3d 218, 226-27 (Tex.2004). At the hearing, the court may ask the party seeking discovery to specifically challenge the other party's objections and claims of privilege. *Id.* at 227 & n.5.

§18.6 Burden to secure hearing & ruling. Either party may ask for a hearing on objections, claims of privilege, motions for protective orders, motions to quash, or motions to compel. *See* TRCP 176.6(d), (e), 192.6, 193.4.

─────────────── ✦ ───────────────

1. Most discovery. If neither party asks for a hearing, the party who sent the request for discovery waives the requested discovery. *Roberts v. Whitfill*, 191 S.W.3d 348, 361 n.3 (Tex.App.—Waco 2006, no pet.); *cf. Remington Arms Co. v. Caldwell*, 850 S.W.2d 167, 170 (Tex.1993) (party who does not get pretrial ruling on discovery dispute waives sanctions claim for that issue). Thus, once objections or claims of privilege have been served, the party seeking discovery has the burden to secure a hearing to resolve the discovery dispute. *See* TRCP 193.4(a); *McKinney v. National Un. Fire Ins.*, 772 S.W.2d 72, 75 (Tex.1989).

2. Discovery involving nonparty. To block a nonparty from producing information about a party in response to a discovery request, the party should secure a hearing and a ruling before the nonparty produces the information. See "Party information from nonparty," §18.4.1, p. 445.

§18.7   Burden to provide evidence. Once a hearing is set, the person resisting discovery must produce any evidence necessary to support a claim of privilege or an objection to discovery.

1. When necessary. Generally, when a party makes an objection or asserts a claim of privilege, that party has the burden to produce evidence to support its objection or claim of privilege. TRCP 193.4(a), 199.6; *In re E.I. DuPont de Nemours & Co.*, 136 S.W.3d 218, 227 (Tex.2004); *e.g.*, *In re CI Host, Inc.*, 92 S.W.3d 514, 516-17 (Tex. 2002) (evidence necessary to support objection that information on computer tapes was protected); *Huie v. DeShazo*, 922 S.W.2d 920, 926 (Tex.1996) (evidence necessary to support privilege); *General Motors Corp. v. Tanner*, 892 S.W.2d 862, 863-64 (Tex.1995) (evidence necessary to support objection that testing would destroy evidence); *Axelson, Inc. v. McIlhany*, 798 S.W.2d 550, 553 n.6 (Tex.1990) (documents necessary for in camera inspection to support relevance objection). Merely listing a specific privilege or exemption from discovery in a privilege log is insufficient. *In re Crestcare Nursing & Rehab. Ctr.*, 222 S.W.3d 68, 73 (Tex.App.—Tyler 2006, orig. proceeding). When evidence is necessary, it must be produced at or before the hearing. TRCP 193.4(a). Evidence at the hearing can include the following:

(1)   Affidavits. When a party relies on affidavits, the affidavits must be served at least seven days before the hearing. TRCP 193.4(a), 199.6; *In re Monsanto Co.*, 998 S.W.2d 917, 924 (Tex.App.—Waco 1999, orig. proceeding). An affidavit must be based on the affiant's personal knowledge and must show that the facts in it are true. See "Personal knowledge," ch. 1-B, §3.2.16(3)(a), p. 12. The affidavit must contain something more than global allegations that the documents are privileged or a mere recitation of facts ascertainable from the documents themselves. *Barnes v. Whittington*, 751 S.W.2d 493, 495 (Tex.1988). An affidavit that addresses groups of documents rather than each document individually may be sufficient to make a prima facie showing of a privilege. *See In re E.I. DuPont de Nemours*, 136 S.W.3d at 223; *see, e.g.*, *In re Monsanto Co.*, 998 S.W.2d at 927-28 (corporate attorney's affidavit that log of 117 documents involved confidential communications among counsel and work papers reflecting attorneys' mental processes was prima facie proof of attorney-client privilege). The affidavits should be offered into evidence at the hearing. *See In re Monsanto Co.*, 998 S.W.2d at 926 (even though not offered, record showed that court considered affidavits).

(2)   Live testimony. If a party intends to rely on live testimony at the hearing, it should proceed with all the formalities of trial—make sure a court reporter is present, have the witnesses sworn, introduce exhibits, and make objections to the other party's evidence. *See* TRCP 193.4(a), 199.6. The witness should explain why specific documents are exempt from discovery. *See, e.g.*, *Conrad v. Wilson*, 873 S.W.2d 467, 469-70 (Tex.App.—Beaumont 1994, orig. proceeding) (testimony of hospital's general counsel that "some of the things asked for are protected" was not specific).

(3)   Documents for inspection. When a party is resisting discovery on the grounds of privilege or relevance, the documents themselves may be the only adequate evidence to support the claim. *In re E.I. DuPont de Nemours*, 136 S.W.3d at 223; *see Humphreys v. Caldwell*, 888 S.W.2d 469, 470-71 (Tex.1994) (work-product privilege); *State v. Lowry*, 802 S.W.2d 669, 673 (Tex.1991) (investigative privilege); *Axelson, Inc.*, 798 S.W.2d at 553 (relevance objection). A representative sample of documents, rather than each and every document, may be appropriate to establish the privilege. *See In re Living Ctrs.*, 175 S.W.3d 253, 261 (Tex.2005). See "In camera inspection," §18.8, p. 447.

───────────────────── ☆ ─────────────────────

2. When not necessary. In some cases, an objection or claim of privilege does not need to be supported by evidence. *See, e.g.*, *In re Union Pac. Res.*, 22 S.W.3d 338, 341 (Tex.1999) (evidence not necessary to support relevance objection); *Loftin v. Martin*, 776 S.W.2d 145, 148 (Tex.1989) (request was so vague and overbroad that party did not know how to respond); *Garner, Lovell & Stein, P.C. v. Burnett*, 911 S.W.2d 108, 112-13 (Tex.App.—Amarillo 1995, orig. proceeding) (request for documents created after lawsuit filed was clearly not proper discovery); *Texas Tech Univ. Health Sci. Ctr. v. Schild*, 828 S.W.2d 502, 504 (Tex.App.—El Paso 1992, orig. proceeding) (request obviously asked for attorney's thought processes). When in doubt, a party should file an affidavit that explains the reasons for the objection or claim of privilege.

§18.8 In camera inspection. The court must decide whether an in camera inspection is necessary. TRCP 193.4(a), 199.6; *In re CI Host, Inc.*, 92 S.W.3d 514, 516 (Tex.2002). When an inspection is critical for evaluating a privilege claim, the trial court must examine the documents before ruling on the claim. *In re E.I. DuPont de Nemours & Co.*, 136 S.W.3d 218, 223 (Tex.2004); *State v. Lowry*, 802 S.W.2d 669, 673 (Tex.1991).

1. Make prima facie case. The party resisting discovery must first establish a prima facie case for its claims of privilege by producing evidence (affidavits or live testimony). *In re Living Ctrs.*, 175 S.W.3d 253, 261 (Tex. 2005); *In re Monsanto Co.*, 998 S.W.2d 917, 924-25 (Tex.App.—Waco 1999, orig. proceeding); *see, e.g.*, *In re Crestcare Nursing & Rehab. Ctr.*, 222 S.W.3d 68, 74 (Tex.App.—Tyler 2006, orig. proceeding) (conclusory affidavit stating that personnel files were "confidential" was insufficient for prima facie showing). See "Affidavits," §18.7.1(1), p. 446; "Live testimony," §18.7.1(2), p. 446. The prima facie standard requires only the minimum amount of evidence necessary to support a rational inference that the fact allegation is true. *In re Crestcare Nursing*, 222 S.W.3d at 73.

2. Identify documents to be inspected. Once a party makes a prima facie case for its claims of privilege, the party seeking discovery should, based on the privilege log, identify the documents or groups of documents it believes the court should inspect in camera. *In re Monsanto Co.*, 998 S.W.2d at 925.

3. Produce documents for inspection. The party resisting discovery should mark each document with the appropriate privilege claimed for that document and file them in a sealed wrapper with the court for an in camera inspection. TRCP 193.4(a), 199.6; *Axelson, Inc. v. McIlhany*, 798 S.W.2d 550, 553 n.6 (Tex.1990).

4. Conduct inspection. Once the party makes a prima facie showing of privilege and tenders documents to the trial court, the court must conduct an in camera inspection before deciding whether to compel production. *In re E.I. DuPont de Nemours*, 136 S.W.3d at 223.

§18.9 Nonparty objections to discovery. Parties must follow the applicable rules of procedure for obtaining nonparty records. A nonparty (e.g., a witness subpoenaed for a deposition who is not subject to the control of a party) who objects to discovery must follow the same procedures as a party. TRCP 176.6(c)-(e); *In re Diversicare Gen. Partner*, 41 S.W.3d 788, 794 (Tex.App.—Corpus Christi 2001, orig. proceeding), *overruled on other grounds*, *In re Arriola*, 159 S.W.3d 670 (Tex.App.—Corpus Christi 2004, orig. proceeding); *see, e.g.*, *State v. Walker*, 873 S.W.2d 379, 380 (Tex.1994) (DA's office, a nonparty, filed motion to quash and for protective order); *Olinger v. Curry*, 926 S.W.2d 832, 835 (Tex.App.—Fort Worth 1996, orig. proceeding) (nonparty objected at deposition). See "Objecting to Trial & Discovery Subpoenas," ch. 1-L, §4, p. 87; "Challenging nonparty discovery subpoena," ch. 6-I, §5.5, p. 571.

§18.10 Burden to partially comply.

1. Partial compliance necessary. A party is required to comply with written discovery to the extent that it does not object. TRCP 192.6 (motion for protective order), TRCP 193.2(b) & cmt. 2 (objections to written discovery), TRCP 193.3(a) (assertions of privilege). For example, when a party objects to producing documents from a remote time period, it must produce documents from a more recent period. TRCP 193 cmt. 2.

2. No compliance necessary. A party is not required to partially comply if (1) complying before getting a ruling is unreasonable, (2) the production would be burdensome and duplicative if the objection were overruled, or (3) the request is overbroad and not in compliance with the rule requiring specific requests for documents (e.g., request for "all documents relevant to the lawsuit"). *See* TRCP 192.6, 193.2(b) & cmt. 2. See "Undue burden," §20.1.1, p. 449; "Overbroad," §20.1.3, p. 450.

★

§19. TYPES OF OBJECTIONS TO DISCOVERY

§19.1 Valid objections to discovery requests. See *O'Connor's Texas Forms*, FORM 6A:9. A party may object to a discovery request for the following reasons:

1. Not within scope of discovery. A party may object to a discovery request that asks for information outside the scope of discovery. A discovery request is outside the scope of discovery when it asks for information that (1) is not relevant and (2) will not lead to admissible evidence. TRCP 192.3(a); *see In re CSX Corp.*, 124 S.W.3d 149, 152 (Tex.2003); *Axelson, Inc. v. McIlhany*, 798 S.W.2d 550, 553 (Tex.1990).

(1) Is not relevant. For example, the amount paid by the defendant to settle other suits is not relevant to the subject matter of the suit and cannot be discovered for use in settlement discussions. *Ford Motor Co. v. Leggat*, 904 S.W.2d 643, 649 (Tex.1995); *see also Martin v. Khoury*, 843 S.W.2d 163, 165-67 (Tex.App.—Texarkana 1992, orig. proceeding) (membership list of nonparty organization for use in voir dire was not discoverable). For the form of objections based on relevance, see the charts produced by Ford in *Ford Motor Co. v. Ross*, 888 S.W.2d 879, 900-02 (Tex.App.—Tyler 1994, orig. proceeding).

(2) Will not lead to admissible evidence. For example, when a suit does not include a claim for exemplary damages, a defendant may object to a request for information about its net worth on the grounds that the information is not within the scope of discovery because it is not calculated to lead to admissible evidence. *Al Parker Buick Co. v. Touchy*, 788 S.W.2d 129, 130-31 (Tex.App.—Houston [1st Dist.] 1990, orig. proceeding).

2. Not permissible form of discovery. A party may object when a discovery request asks for a type of discovery that is not permitted by the rules of discovery. *See, e.g.*, TRCP 195.1 & 197.1 (party is prohibited from learning identity of other party's testifying expert witness through interrogatories); *In re Guzman*, 19 S.W.3d 522, 524-25 (Tex.App.—Corpus Christi 2000, orig. proceeding) (court cannot require party to execute authorization for nonparty to produce information; nonparty discovery must comply with TRCP 205.1). *But see* TRCP 191 cmt. 1 (court may order, or parties may agree to, use of discovery methods other than those prescribed in the rules).

3. Not reasonably available. A party is not required to produce information that is not reasonably available to the party or its attorney when the response is made. TRCP 193.1. When information is not available to answer a request for admissions, see "Lack of information," ch. 6-H, §4.2.4, p. 559.

4. Request lacks specificity. A party may object when a request lacks specificity or is so vague and unclear that the party cannot identify the information requested. *See Davis v. Pate*, 915 S.W.2d 76, 79 n.2 (Tex.App.—Corpus Christi 1996, orig. proceeding) (distinguishing requests that are overbroad from those that lack specificity).

5. Improper procedure. When a party makes an improper request for discovery, the other party may file either an objection or a motion for protective order, whichever is appropriate, before the response is due, stating why the request is improper. TRCP 192.6, 193.2. For example, a party may object when the other party serves more than 25 written interrogatories in Level 1 or 2 discovery. *See* TRCP 190.2(c)(3), 190.3(b)(3). The responding party should answer 25 interrogatories and object to the others. TRCP 193.2(b) & cmt. 2.

⑬   **PROPOSED TRCP CHANGES**

In response to Gov't Code §22.004(h), the Supreme Court has proposed TRCP 169 to establish a process for the prompt, efficient, and cost-effective resolution of civil actions (expedited actions) in which only monetary relief is sought and the amount in controversy is no more than $100,000. See Tex.Sup.Ct. Order, Misc. Docket No. 12-9191 (eff. Mar. 1, 2013). The Supreme Court has proposed corresponding amendments to TRCP 190.2 that would (1) change the Level 1 discovery-control plan to apply to these expedited actions under TRCP 169 and (2) change the limits on the number of interrogatories that can be served in Level 1 discovery. See Tex.Sup.Ct. Order, Misc. Docket No. 12-9191 (eff. Mar. 1, 2013). The public-comment period for the proposed

★

---

amendments ends on February 1, 2013, and the rules are to take effect March 1, 2013. For the proposed version of the rules, see the appendix after this book's index. For the final version, go to the Supreme Court website at www.supreme.courts.state.tx.us. When the new and amended rules take effect, a supplement to this book—with updated rules and commentaries that reflect the changes—will be available at www.JonesMcClure.com/TRCPamendments.

---

6. Same information already provided. A party may object if the information has already been provided in response to other discovery in another form. *See, e.g.*, *Sears, Roebuck & Co. v. Ramirez*, 824 S.W.2d 558, 559 (Tex.1992) (D not required to produce tax returns to prove net worth because it had produced audited, certified annual report).

7. Burdensome, harassing, or overbroad. A party may object when a discovery request is unduly burdensome, harassing, or overbroad. See "Grounds to limit scope of discovery," §20.1, this page.

§19.2   Invalid objections to discovery requests. The following are some invalid objections to discovery requests: • The information requested is privileged. A party must follow the procedure for asserting a privilege under TRCP 193.3. See "Asserting privileges," §18.2, p. 443. • The evidence will not be admissible at trial. As long as information appears reasonably calculated to lead to the discovery of admissible evidence, it is discoverable. TRCP 192.3(a). • The other party combined two forms of discovery. Different forms of discovery may be combined in the same document and may be taken in any order or sequence. TRCP 192.2.

§20. MOTION FOR PROTECTIVE ORDER

A party or nonparty resisting discovery may file a motion for protective order in response to a discovery request or a motion to compel. TRCP 192.6(a); *see In re Alford Chevrolet-Geo*, 997 S.W.2d 173, 180-81 (Tex.1999). See *O'Connor's Texas Forms*, FORMS 6A:9-10. If a party moves for a protective order, the party seeking the discovery should file a motion to compel rather than a response to the motion for protective order. *See Pace v. Jordan*, 999 S.W.2d 615, 622 (Tex.App.—Houston [1st Dist.] 1999, pet. denied). See "After objection to discovery," §22.1.7, p. 452; *O'Connor's Texas Forms*, FORM 6A:23. A person should not seek a protective order when an objection or a claim of privilege is more appropriate. TRCP 192.6(a).

§20.1   Grounds to limit scope of discovery. Under TRCP 192.4, the trial court has the authority to limit the scope of discovery. TRCP 192 cmt. 7. A person may file a motion for protective order for the following reasons:

1. Undue burden. A person may ask for protection from a discovery request that is unduly burdensome, annoying to produce, or unnecessarily expensive. TRCP 176.7 (undue burden of subpoena), TRCP 192.4(a) & (b) (limitations on scope of discovery), TRCP 192.6(b) (order to protect movant from undue burden, expense, or annoyance); *In re Alford Chevrolet-Geo*, 997 S.W.2d 173, 181 (Tex.1999) (same). The person resisting discovery has the burden to plead and prove that the request will impose an undue burden. *ISK Biotech Corp. v. Lindsay*, 933 S.W.2d 565, 568-69 (Tex.App.—Houston [1st Dist.] 1996, orig. proceeding); *Tjernagel v. Roberts*, 928 S.W.2d 297, 302 (Tex.App.—Amarillo 1996, orig. proceeding). To prove undue burden, the person resisting discovery must do more than make conclusory allegations that the requested discovery is unduly burdensome. *In re Alford Chevrolet-Geo*, 997 S.W.2d at 181; *see, e.g.*, *In re Amaya*, 34 S.W.3d 354, 358 (Tex.App.—Waco 2001, orig. proceeding) (no evidence produced to show burden). The person cannot rely on problems in retrieving documents caused by the way she filed them in her own records. *ISK Biotech*, 933 S.W.2d at 569. Once the person resisting discovery proves that the request for discovery is unduly burdensome, the person requesting discovery must show that it is not. *Forward v. Housing Auth.*, 864 S.W.2d 167, 169 (Tex.App.—Tyler 1993, no writ); *see also* TRCP 191.3(c)(4) (signature on discovery request is certification that request is not unduly burdensome). Undue burden occurs when discovery is any of the following:

(1) Duplicative. The discovery is unreasonably cumulative or duplicative. TRCP 192.4(a); *see Walker v. Packer*, 827 S.W.2d 833, 843 (Tex.1992) (discovery that compels production of patently irrelevant or duplicative documents can constitute undue burden).

───────────────────────── ✦ ─────────────────────────

(2) Obtainable from alternate source. The discovery can be obtained from some other source that is more convenient, less burdensome, or less expensive. TRCP 192.4(a); *Brewer & Pritchard, P.C. v. Johnson*, 167 S.W.3d 460, 466 (Tex.App.—Houston [14th Dist.] 2005, pet. denied); *e.g.*, *In re Arras*, 24 S.W.3d 862, 864 (Tex. App.—El Paso 2000, orig. proceeding) (deposition of nonparty for addresses of other parties was inconvenient and burdensome).

(3) Unduly expensive. The burden or expense of the proposed discovery outweighs its likely benefit, taking into account the needs of the case, the amount in controversy, the parties' resources, the importance of the issues at stake in the litigation, and the importance of the proposed discovery in resolving the issues. TRCP 192.4(b); *In re Alford Chevrolet-Geo*, 997 S.W.2d at 181; *see also* TRCP 176.7 (subpoena).

2. Harassing. A person may ask for protection from a discovery request that is harassing. *See* TRCP 192.6. By signing discovery requests, attorneys certify that the discovery is not sought for the purpose of harassment. TRCP 191.3(c)(3); *see also* TRCP 199.5(h) (attorney cannot ask deposition questions solely to harass or mislead the witness), TRCP 215.3 (harassing discovery is grounds for sanctions).

3. Overbroad. A person may ask for protection from a discovery request that is overbroad. Generally, an overbroad request for documents is merely a fishing expedition into the other party's files, which is prohibited. *In re American Optical Corp.*, 988 S.W.2d 711, 713 (Tex.1998); *Dillard Dept. Stores v. Hall*, 909 S.W.2d 491, 492 (Tex. 1995); *Loftin v. Martin*, 776 S.W.2d 145, 148 (Tex.1989). A trial court cannot permit a party to search through the other party's records to make sure the other party produced all the documents requested. *Texaco, Inc. v. Dominguez*, 812 S.W.2d 451, 455-56 (Tex.App.—San Antonio 1991, orig. proceeding).

(1) Overbroad request. The following are examples of overbroad requests: • Request for all documents without limitation on time, place, or subject matter. *Texaco, Inc. v. Sanderson*, 898 S.W.2d 813, 815 (Tex. 1995). • Request for approximately 20,000 pages of documents relating to defects in products that were not at issue in the case. *In re Graco Children's Prods.*, 210 S.W.3d 598, 600-01 (Tex.2006). • Request to identify all of the defendant's safety employees over a 30-year period. *In re CSX Corp.*, 124 S.W.3d 149, 153 (Tex.2003). • Request for almost every document related to asbestos products that the defendant produced over a 50-year period. *In re American Optical*, 988 S.W.2d at 713. • Request for all information about criminal conduct at a location for seven years. *K Mart Corp. v. Sanderson*, 937 S.W.2d 429, 431 (Tex.1996). • Request for all similar claims from every store. *Dillard Dept. Stores*, 909 S.W.2d at 492. When a request asks for "all documents," the party may object to the request as overbroad and refuse to comply with it entirely, or the party may file a motion for protective order. *See* TRCP 192.6(a) (protective order), TRCP 193 cmt. 2 (object and refuse to comply). When an overbroad request asks for irrelevant information, a party is not required to detail its objections to the request; an overbroad request for irrelevant information is improper whether it is burdensome or not. *In re Allstate Cty. Mut. Ins.*, 227 S.W.3d 667, 670 (Tex.2007).

(2) Limited request. A request for "any and all" documents is not overbroad if it is limited by time, location, or scope, or if it is restricted to a type or class of documents. *See In re Allstate*, 227 S.W.3d at 669; *In re Patel*, 218 S.W.3d 911, 915 (Tex.App.—Corpus Christi 2007, orig. proceeding). A request should be tailored to documents related to the litigated dispute. *See In re Allstate*, 227 S.W.3d at 670.

4. Invades protected rights. A person may ask for protection from a discovery request that is an invasion of personal, constitutional, or property rights. TRCP 192.6(b); *see Hoffman v. Fifth Ct. of Appeals*, 756 S.W.2d 723, 723 (Tex.1988).

5. Temporary protection. A person may ask for temporary protection from discovery pending the resolution of threshold issues like venue, jurisdiction, forum non conveniens, and official immunity. *In re Alford Chevrolet-Geo*, 997 S.W.2d at 181.

§20.2 Procedure for motion.

1. File timely. A motion for protective order should be filed as soon as the person realizes a protective order is necessary and before the deadline to produce the requested discovery. *See* TRCP 192.6(a); *see, e.g., Bohmfalk v. Linwood*, 742 S.W.2d 518, 520 (Tex.App.—Dallas 1987, no writ) (party waived inadequate notice of deposition because party did not file motion for protective order to reschedule it). See "Timely objection," §18.1.1, p. 443.

———————————————— ✦ ————————————————

2. Withhold information. The person must withhold the information subject to the motion for protective order. In most cases, a party must partially comply with a written-discovery request. See "Burden to partially comply," §18.10, p. 447.

3. Attach evidence. To support the motion, the person should attach affidavits, discovery pleadings, or other necessary documents. *See* TRCP 193.4(a), 199.6. See "Burden to provide evidence," §18.7, p. 446; "In camera inspection," §18.8, p. 447. The person "must show particular, specific and demonstrable injury by facts sufficient to justify a protective order." *Masinga v. Whittington*, 792 S.W.2d 940, 940 (Tex.1990); *In re Amaya*, 34 S.W.3d 354, 356-57 (Tex.App.—Waco 2001, orig. proceeding); *see also In re Collins*, 286 S.W.3d 911, 919 (Tex.2009) (health-care-liability claimants seeking protective order for information released under CPRC §74.052(c) have same burden as parties seeking protective order for ordinary discovery).

§20.3 Order. Generally, the person seeking discovery should secure a hearing and a ruling on an objection to discovery. However, there are exceptions. See "Burden to secure hearing & ruling," §18.6, p. 445. The trial court has broad discretion to protect a person with a protective order. *See* TRCP 192.6(b); *Axelson, Inc. v. McIlhany*, 798 S.W.2d 550, 553 (Tex.1990). The court may protect the person by ordering any of the relief listed in TRCP 192.6(b), but it is not limited by that list.

1. Limit scope of discovery. The protective order may provide that the requested discovery not be sought in whole or in part, or may limit the extent or subject matter of discovery. TRCP 192.6(b)(1), (b)(2). For example, the trial court can strike certain subject areas from a notice of deposition if it determines that they are not relevant. *Lindsey v. O'Neill*, 689 S.W.2d 400, 403 (Tex.1985). The court can also redact privileged or sensitive information from documents to be produced. *R.K. v. Ramirez*, 887 S.W.2d 836, 843 (Tex.1994); *M.A.W. v. Hall*, 921 S.W.2d 911, 916 (Tex.App.—Houston [14th Dist.] 1996, orig. proceeding).

2. Specify procedure for discovery. The protective order may provide that the discovery not be undertaken at the time or place specified. TRCP 192.6(b)(3). The protective order may specify the terms, conditions, methods, and time and place of the discovery. TRCP 192.6(b)(4).

3. Seal or limit distribution of discovery. The protective order may seal or limit the distribution of discovery to the parties. TRCP 192.6(b)(5); *see, e.g., In re Ford Motor Co.*, 211 S.W.3d 295, 300-01 (Tex.2006) (protective order provided that certain documents would not be disclosed or distributed).

4. Limits of protective order.

(1) **Sealing court records.** A trial court cannot use a protective order to bypass the requirements of TRCP 76a. TRCP 192.6(b)(5). An order sealing or limiting the distribution of documents must be made on a showing of good cause and in accordance with the provisions of TRCP 76a. *See* TRCP 192.6(b)(5); *Chandler v. Hyundai Motor Co.*, 829 S.W.2d 774, 774-75 (Tex.1992); *see also Stroud v. VBFSB Holding*, 917 S.W.2d 75, 83 (Tex. App.—San Antonio 1996, writ denied) (stipulation and protective order did not constitute sealing order). The person requesting the order to seal or limit distribution has the burden of proving the elements of TRCP 76a(1). *BP Prods. v. Houston Chronicle Publ'g*, 263 S.W.3d 31, 35 (Tex.App.—Houston [1st Dist.] 2006, no pet.). See "Motion to Seal Court Records," ch. 5-L, p. 394.

(2) **Preventing shared discovery.** A trial court cannot render a protective order so broad that it prevents the sharing of discovery products with other litigants in other lawsuits. *Garcia v. Peeples*, 734 S.W.2d 343, 348-49 (Tex.1987). Under the doctrine of shared discovery, the products of discovery may be disseminated to other litigants and potential litigants. *Eli Lilly & Co. v. Marshall*, 850 S.W.2d 155, 160 (Tex.1993).

§21. MOTION TO QUASH OR MODIFY SUBPOENA

See "Objecting to Trial & Discovery Subpoenas," ch. 1-L, §4, p. 87; "Challenging nonparty discovery subpoena," ch. 6-I, §5.5, p. 571; *O'Connor's Texas Forms*, FORM 6A:13.

§22. MOTION TO COMPEL DISCOVERY

A party is entitled to secure discovery from another party without court intervention. When a party refuses to comply with proper discovery requests, the party seeking discovery may file a motion to compel the other party to respond. TRCP 215.1(b). See *O'Connor's Texas Forms*, FORM 6A:23.

★

§22.1 Grounds. A party may file a motion to compel discovery and request a hearing in the following instances:

1. Inadequate responses to request for disclosure. See "Objecting to Responses," ch. 6-E, §7, p. 522.

2. Refusal to answer or appear at deposition. See "To compel attendance," ch. 6-F, §7.6, p. 534; "Motion to compel answer," ch. 6-F, §9.4, p. 536.

3. Inadequate answers to interrogatories. See "Objecting to Answers," ch. 6-G, §8, p. 555.

4. Inadequate responses to request for admissions. See "Challenging the Response," ch. 6-H, §5, p. 560.

5. Inadequate responses to request for production. See "Compelling Production & Sanctions," ch. 6-I, §6, p. 572.

6. Refusal to follow agreed schedule. When a party does not comply with a TRCP 11 agreement setting deadlines for discovery, the other party should file a motion to compel compliance. *See Sullivan v. Bickel & Brewer*, 943 S.W.2d 477, 484 (Tex.App.—Dallas 1995, writ denied).

7. After objection to discovery. When a party serves objections or claims of privilege to a discovery request, or files a motion to quash or a motion for protective order, the party seeking discovery can either move for a hearing on the objections or file a motion to compel production, or both. TRCP 193.4(a), 215.1(b); *McKinney v. National Un. Fire Ins.*, 772 S.W.2d 72, 75 (Tex.1989); *see, e.g., Pace v. Jordan*, 999 S.W.2d 615, 622 (Tex.App.—Houston [1st Dist.] 1999, pet. denied) (Ps waived deposition because they did not get ruling on Ds' motion for protective order and did not file motion to compel).

PRACTICE TIP

The advantage of filing a motion to compel, instead of merely requesting a hearing on the other party's objections, is that a motion to compel can include requests for expenses and attorney fees. See TRCP 215.1(d).

---

§22.2 Request for sanctions. The trial court can impose sanctions against a party for refusing to comply with proper discovery requests, regardless of whether the party has disobeyed an order compelling discovery. *See* TRCP 215.1(b). Thus, the party seeking discovery can include a motion for sanctions in its first motion to compel discovery. *Lewis v. Illinois Employers Ins.*, 590 S.W.2d 119, 120 (Tex.1979). A party may pursue sanctions instead of filing a motion to compel. *See* TRCP 215.1(b)(3)(D); *Adkins Servs. v. Tisdale Co.*, 56 S.W.3d 842, 845 (Tex.App.—Texarkana 2001, no pet.).

§22.3 Request for expenses. After ruling on a motion to compel, the court may award attorney fees and other expenses to the party or person who prevails. TRCP 215.1(d). If the court grants the motion in part and denies it in part, the court may allocate the expenses. *Id.* If the court finds the conduct was substantially justified or finds other reasons that make the award of expenses unjust, the court is not required to award them. *Id.*

§22.4 Response to motion to compel. The party against whom the motion to compel was filed should always file a response. Under some local rules, failure to file a response permits the trial court to conclude that there is no opposition to the relief sought in the motion. *Cire v. Cummings*, 134 S.W.3d 835, 844 (Tex.2004); *e.g.*, Harris Cty. Loc. R. 3.3.2 (district courts).

§23. SPOLIATION

Spoliation is the improper destruction of relevant evidence. *Walker v. Thomasson Lumber Co.*, 203 S.W.3d 470, 477 (Tex.App.—Houston [14th Dist.] 2006, no pet.); *Cresthaven Nursing Residence v. Freeman*, 134 S.W.3d 214, 225 (Tex.App.—Amarillo 2003, no pet.); *Kang v. Hyundai Corp. (U.S.A.)*, 992 S.W.2d 499, 502 (Tex.App.—Dallas 1999, no pet.). If the producing party has spoliated evidence, the requesting party may be entitled to a "spoliation

⭐

presumption"—that is, an evidentiary presumption that supports the requesting party's assertions and serves as some evidence of the particular issues that the destroyed evidence might have supported. *Trevino v. Ortega*, 969 S.W.2d 950, 960 (Tex.1998) (Baker, J., concurring).

§23.1 Establishing presumption.

1. Requesting party's burden. To establish a spoliation presumption, the requesting party must show that (1) the producing party had a duty to preserve evidence, (2) the producing party breached its duty and did not preserve the evidence, and (3) the spoliation prejudiced the requesting party. *Clark v. Randalls Food*, 317 S.W.3d 351, 356 (Tex.App.—Houston [1st Dist.] 2010, pet. denied); *Adobe Land Corp. v. Griffin, L.L.C.*, 236 S.W.3d 351, 357 (Tex.App.—Fort Worth 2007, pet. denied); *Lively v. Blackwell*, 51 S.W.3d 637, 643 n.4 (Tex.App.—Tyler 2001, pet. denied); *see Trevino v. Ortega*, 969 S.W.2d 950, 954-55 (Tex.1998) (Baker, J., concurring).

(1) Duty to preserve. The requesting party must show that the producing party had a duty to preserve evidence. *Wal-Mart Stores v. Johnson*, 106 S.W.3d 718, 722 (Tex.2003); *Walker v. Thomasson Lumber Co.*, 203 S.W.3d 470, 477 (Tex.App.—Houston [14th Dist.] 2006, no pet.); *Texas Elec. Coop. v. Dillard*, 171 S.W.3d 201, 209 (Tex.App.—Tyler 2005, no pet.). The duty to preserve arises when a party knows or reasonably should know that (1) there is a substantial chance a claim will be filed and (2) evidence in its possession or control will be material and relevant to the claim. *Johnson*, 106 S.W.3d at 722; *MRT, Inc. v. Vounckx*, 299 S.W.3d 500, 510 (Tex.App.—Dallas 2009, no pet.); *see Clark*, 317 S.W.3d at 356-57. See "Preservation of Evidence," §3, p. 426.

(2) Breach of duty. The requesting party must show that the producing party breached the duty to preserve by destroying evidence. *Adobe Land*, 236 S.W.3d at 359; *Hight v. Dublin Vet. Clinic*, 22 S.W.3d 614, 619 (Tex.App.—Eastland 2000, pet. denied). Courts do not agree whether the presumption applies only to the intentional destruction of evidence or also to unintentional loss or destruction. *Compare Adobe Land*, 236 S.W.3d at 359 (presumption applies to negligent or intentional spoliation), *and Offshore Pipelines, Inc. v. Schooley*, 984 S.W.2d 654, 666 (Tex.App.—Houston [1st Dist.] 1998, no pet.) (same), *with Cresthaven Nursing Residence v. Freeman*, 134 S.W.3d 214, 227 (Tex.App.—Amarillo 2003, no pet.) (presumption does not apply when documents are unintentionally lost). The Supreme Court has not addressed what state of mind is necessary to establish spoliation. *See Johnson*, 106 S.W.3d at 721-22.

(3) Prejudice. The requesting party must show that the spoliation prejudiced its ability to present its case or defense. *Adobe Land*, 236 S.W.3d at 360; *Offshore Pipelines*, 984 S.W.2d at 666. To establish prejudice, the requesting party should show the following: (1) it requested the missing evidence and pursued a court order to compel its production, (2) the missing evidence is relevant, (3) there is no other evidence available to replace the missing evidence, and (4) the missing evidence supports key issues in the case. *See Roberts v. Whitfill*, 191 S.W.3d 348, 361 & n.3 (Tex.App.—Waco 2006, no pet.); *Offshore Pipelines*, 984 S.W.2d at 666; *Trevino*, 969 S.W.2d at 958 (Baker, J., concurring).

2. Producing party's rebuttal. To rebut the spoliation presumption, the producing party should do the following:

(1) Challenge request. The producing party should make any challenges to the requesting party's discovery request (e.g., the requesting party did not establish that evidence was destroyed or that prejudice occurred). See "Requesting party's burden," §23.1.1, this page.

(2) Provide reasonable explanation. The producing party should provide a reasonable explanation for the destruction of the evidence. *Buckeye Ret. Co. v. Bank of Am.*, 239 S.W.3d 394, 401 (Tex.App.—Dallas 2007, no pet.); *Cresthaven Nursing Residence*, 134 S.W.3d at 227; *Crescendo Invs. v. Brice*, 61 S.W.3d 465, 479 (Tex.App.—San Antonio 2001, pet. denied); *Trevino*, 969 S.W.2d at 957 (Baker, J., concurring). For example, the producing party can show the following:

(a) Destruction beyond its control. The producing party can show that the destruction of the evidence was beyond its control. *Trevino*, 969 S.W.2d at 957 (Baker, J., concurring); *e.g.*, *Walker*, 203 S.W.3d at 477 (nonparty had possession and control of allegedly defective utility pole and destroyed it in ordinary course of business).

─────────────────────── ✦ ───────────────────────

(b) Destruction in ordinary course of business. The producing party can show that it destroyed or discarded the evidence in the ordinary course of business, such as in compliance with a corporate retention policy. *E.g.*, *Brumfield v. Exxon Corp.*, 63 S.W.3d 912, 920 (Tex.App.—Houston [14th Dist.] 2002, pet. denied) (videotapes were routinely taped over after 30 days); *Aguirre v. South Tex. Blood & Tissue Ctr.*, 2 S.W.3d 454, 457-58 (Tex.App.—San Antonio 1999, pet. denied) (D destroyed records in regular course of business); *Ordonez v. M.W. McCurdy & Co.*, 984 S.W.2d 264, 273-74 (Tex.App.—Houston [1st Dist.] 1998, no pet.) (log books were thrown away under D's normal business practice, not to conceal them from P). However, when a party's duty to preserve evidence arises before it destroys evidence, the fact that it followed a corporate retention policy will not justify the destruction. *E.g.*, *Adobe Land*, 236 S.W.3d at 360 (D's duty to preserve evidence arose before it destroyed herbicide sample).

§23.2 Requesting relief. Once the spoliation presumption is established, it can be applied to (1) prevent the granting of a no-evidence summary judgment, (2) support a request for sanctions, or (3) support a request for a spoliation jury instruction. *See Trevino v. Ortega*, 969 S.W.2d 950, 953 (Tex.1998) (sanctions or instruction); *Aguirre v. South Tex. Blood & Tissue Ctr.*, 2 S.W.3d 454, 457 (Tex.App.—San Antonio 1999, pet. denied) (no-evidence SJ).

───

NOTE

*In most cases, a party will request sanctions or, in the alternative, a spoliation instruction. The court will usually conduct a preliminary hearing to determine the appropriate remedy. See **Offshore Pipelines, Inc. v. Schooley**, 984 S.W.2d 654, 667 (Tex.App.—Houston [1st Dist.] 1998, no pet.). See "Motion for Sanctions," ch. 5-K, p. 377.*

───

1. Prevent no-evidence SJ. When the spoliation presumption is established, the court cannot grant a no-evidence summary judgment. *Adobe Land Corp. v. Griffin, L.L.C.*, 236 S.W.3d 351, 360 & n.11 (Tex.App.—Fort Worth 2007, pet. denied); *Aguirre*, 2 S.W.3d at 457; *see Clark v. Randalls Food*, 317 S.W.3d 351, 356 (Tex.App.—Houston [1st Dist.] 2010, pet. denied).

2. Sanctions. When the spoliation presumption is established, the court can grant sanctions. *Trevino*, 969 S.W.2d at 959 (Baker, J., concurring). The court should consider the degree of the producing party's culpability and the prejudice to the requesting party when determining whether sanctions are appropriate. *Id.*; *see Offshore Pipelines*, 984 S.W.2d at 666-67. The court can grant the following sanctions for spoliation: (1) exclusion of evidence or testimony, and (2) death-penalty sanctions. *See Trevino*, 969 S.W.2d at 959 (Baker, J., concurring). See "Motion for Sanctions," ch. 5-K, p. 377.

(1) Exclusion of evidence. The court can exclude evidence only when the producing party attempts to admit evidence or testimony related to the destroyed evidence. *See Trevino*, 969 S.W.2d at 960 (Baker, J., concurring). The exclusion of evidence relieves the requesting party from having to defend against allegations without being able to inspect the evidence. *See id.*

(2) Death-penalty sanctions. The court can strike the producing party's pleadings and impose death-penalty sanctions in extraordinary cases. *Trevino*, 969 S.W.2d at 959 (Baker, J., concurring); *e.g.*, *Cire v. Cummings*, 134 S.W.3d 835, 843 (Tex.2004) (P's pleadings struck because she deliberately destroyed evidence after court ordered production); *Daniel v. Kelley Oil Corp.*, 981 S.W.2d 230, 235 (Tex.App.—Houston [1st Dist.] 1998, pet. denied) (P's pleadings struck because she fabricated false evidence by altering audiotapes). Courts can dismiss a case when the spoliator's conduct was egregious, the prejudice to the other party was great, and lesser sanctions would not cure the prejudice. *Trevino*, 969 S.W.2d at 959 (Baker, J., concurring); *see Cire*, 134 S.W.3d at 841. See "Death-penalty sanctions," ch. 5-K, §3.2, p. 378.

3. Jury instruction. When the spoliation presumption is established, the court can give a spoliation instruction to the jury. *Wal-Mart Stores v. Johnson*, 106 S.W.3d 718, 721 (Tex.2003); *Offshore Pipelines*, 984 S.W.2d at 666. A spoliation instruction compensates for the absence of evidence that a party had a duty to preserve. *Johnson*, 106 S.W.3d at 724. The court can give one of two types of spoliation instructions depending on whether a party (1) does

—— ✩ ——

not produce relevant evidence or explain its nonproduction or (2) deliberately destroys relevant evidence. *Id.* at 721; *Anderson v. Taylor Publ'g*, 13 S.W.3d 56, 61 (Tex.App.—Dallas 2000, pet. denied). The court should consider the severity of the prejudice caused by the nonproduction of evidence when determining which type of spoliation instruction to deliver. *Trevino*, 969 S.W.2d at 960 (Baker, J., concurring).

(1) Instruction for nonproduction. When the requesting party introduces evidence that is harmful to the producing party, and the producing party does not rebut the harmful evidence with evidence within its control, the court can give an "adverse presumption" instruction. *Felix v. Gonzalez*, 87 S.W.3d 574, 580 & n.3 (Tex. App.—San Antonio 2002, pet. denied); *Watson v. Brazos Elec. Power Coop.*, 918 S.W.2d 639, 643 (Tex.App.—Waco 1996, writ denied). An adverse-presumption instruction allows the jury to consider that the unproduced evidence would have been unfavorable to the producing party. *Wal-Mart Stores v. Middleton*, 982 S.W.2d 468, 470 (Tex. App.—San Antonio 1998, pet. denied). The presumption does not relieve the requesting party of its burden to establish each element of its case, but the presumption has probative value and may support the requesting party's evidence. *Trevino*, 969 S.W.2d at 960-61 (Baker, J., concurring).

EXAMPLE

*You are instructed that if there is evidence pertinent to the issues in this case that was in the exclusive possession and control of {party} and that cannot be produced, and its disappearance or nonproduction has not been satisfactorily explained, then you may consider that the evidence contained information adverse to the position taken by {party}. See **Texas Elec. Coop. v. Dillard**, 171 S.W.3d 201, 208 (Tex.App.—Tyler 2005, no pet.).*

---

(2) Instruction for deliberate destruction. When the producing party deliberately destroyed evidence, and the requesting party cannot prove one or more elements of its case without that evidence, the court can give a more severe spoliation instruction. *See Trevino*, 969 S.W.2d at 960 (Baker, J., concurring). A deliberate-destruction instruction (1) informs the jury that the producing party deliberately destroyed relevant evidence, (2) allows the jury to presume the destroyed evidence was unfavorable to the producing party on the fact or issue the evidence would support, and (3) informs the jury that the producing party has the burden to disprove the presumed fact or issue. *Id.*; *see Johnson*, 106 S.W.3d at 721.

EXAMPLE

*You are instructed that {party} destroyed {identify evidence} that {explain nature of evidence} after that evidence had been requested from {opposing party} and after {party} had a duty to preserve that evidence and not destroy it. You may presume that the destroyed evidence was unfavorable to {party}. {Party} has the burden to rebut the presumption that the destroyed evidence was unfavorable to {party}. See **Bic Pen Corp. v. Carter**, 346 S.W.3d 569, 576 (Tex.App.—Corpus Christi 2008) (memo op.), rev'd on other grounds, 346 S.W.3d 533 (Tex.2011).*

---

§24. MOTION FOR DISCOVERY SANCTIONS

Sanctions for discovery abuse are imposed to (1) secure compliance with the discovery rules, (2) deter other litigants from violating the discovery rules, (3) punish parties that violate the discovery rules, and (4) promote settlements. *Schein v. American Rest. Grp.*, 852 S.W.2d 496, 497 (Tex.1993); *Chrysler Corp. v. Blackmon*, 841 S.W.2d 844, 849 (Tex.1992). See "Motion for Sanctions," ch. 5-K, p. 377; *O'Connor's Texas Forms*, FORM 6A:26.

§24.1 Standard for sanctions. See "Standards for Imposing Sanctions," ch. 5-K, §3, p. 377.

§24.2 Motion.

1. Grounds. See "Discovery abuse," ch. 5-K, §5.1, p. 380.

2. Persons against whom discovery sanctions may be imposed. See "Persons Who May Be Sanctioned," ch. 5-K, §4, p. 379.

─────────────────────────── ★ ───────────────────────────

3. **Permissible discovery sanctions.** See "Sanctions for discovery abuse," ch. 5-K, §7.1, p. 384.

4. **Impermissible sanctions.** See "Improper sanctions," ch. 5-K, §7.7, p. 387.

§24.3 Response. See *O'Connor's Texas Forms*, FORM 6A:27.

§24.4 Hearing. A party must be given notice and an opportunity to be heard before sanctions are imposed. The hearing on sanctions may be before the court or by submission. See "Hearing," ch. 5-K, §10, p. 389.

§24.5 Order for sanctions. See "Order for discovery sanctions," ch. 5-K, §11.1, p. 391; *O'Connor's Texas Forms*, FORM 6A:28.

§25. WAIVER OF SANCTIONS, DISCOVERY & OBJECTIONS

§25.1 Waiver of sanctions. If a party does not get a pretrial ruling on known discovery misconduct that occurred before the trial, the party waives any claim for sanctions based on that misconduct. *Meyer v. Cathey*, 167 S.W.3d 327, 333 (Tex.2005); *Remington Arms Co. v. Caldwell*, 850 S.W.2d 167, 170 (Tex.1993). However, if the misconduct involves failure to disclose information requested in discovery, the trial court can impose suitable trial sanctions, such as excluding the testimony of an undisclosed witness. *See Remington Arms*, 850 S.W.2d at 170-71.

§25.2 Waiver of discovery.

1. Discovery proponent. If a party seeking discovery does not ask for a hearing on the other party's objections or motion for protective order or on its own motion to compel, it waives its right to the requested discovery. *See, e.g.*, *Pace v. Jordan*, 999 S.W.2d 615, 622 (Tex.App.—Houston [1st Dist.] 1999, pet. denied) (party did not get ruling on other party's objections and did not file motion to compel).

2. Discovery opponent. A party resisting discovery is not required to request a ruling to preserve its own objections or assertions of privilege. TRCP 193.4(b). However, a party cannot use information it withheld from discovery under a claim of privilege at a hearing or trial without first amending or supplementing its discovery responses. TRCP 193.4(c). By contrast, if a party refuses to respond to discovery pending the resolution of its objections to a discovery request, nothing prohibits it from relying on the withheld discovery.

§25.3 Waiver of objections & privileges.

1. Failure to comply with procedures. If a party does not comply with the procedures for resisting discovery, the party waives its objections to the discovery and its claims of privilege, and the trial court should compel production. TRCP 193.2(e); *see, e.g.*, *Hobson v. Moore*, 734 S.W.2d 340, 341 (Tex.1987) (D waived law-enforcement privilege because he filed late objections to interrogatories); *Villarreal v. Dominguez*, 745 S.W.2d 570, 572 (Tex. App.—Corpus Christi 1988, orig. proceeding) (D waived its privileges from discovery by not objecting); *Dunn Equip. v. Gayle*, 725 S.W.2d 372, 374-75 (Tex.App.—Houston [14th Dist.] 1987, orig. proceeding) (P, objecting to discovery of its insurance company's file, waived privilege because it did not prove elements of privilege). However, a party does not waive a privilege if it mistakenly objects to a request for privileged information instead of complying with TRCP 193.3. See "Asserting privileges," §18.2, p. 443.

2. Failure to object to inadequate responses. If a party does not object before trial to the other party's discovery responses that it knows are inadequate, it waives the objection. *E.g.*, *Interceramic, Inc. v. South Orient R.R.*, 999 S.W.2d 920, 930 (Tex.App.—Texarkana 1999, pet. denied) (inadequate supplemental responses to discovery).

3. Failure to respond to motion to compel. Under some local rules, if a party does not file a response to the motion to compel, the trial court can conclude that the party does not oppose the relief sought in the motion. *Cire v. Cummings*, 134 S.W.3d 835, 844 (Tex.2004); *e.g.*, Harris Cty. Loc. R. 3.3.2 (district courts).

4. Sanctions. If a party abuses discovery, the court may find that the party waived its discovery privileges and objections. *Occidental Chem. Corp. v. Banales*, 907 S.W.2d 488, 490 (Tex.1995); *e.g.*, *In re Lavernia Nursing Facility, Inc.*, 12 S.W.3d 566, 571 (Tex.App.—San Antonio 1999, orig. proceeding) (court found that D concealed records).

—————————————— ✦ ——————————————

5. No ruling. If the party seeking discovery does not secure a ruling on the objections or assertions of privilege, the party waives the discovery. *See* TRCP 193.4(b), 199.6. The party resisting discovery does not waive its objections if they are not resolved before trial. TRCP 199.6.

6. Obscured objections. If a party obscures valid objections with unfounded objections, the party waives its valid objections unless it can show good cause. TRCP 193.2(e).

7. Deliberate disclosure. If a party voluntarily and deliberately discloses "any significant part" of the privileged matter, it waives the privilege. TRE 511(1); Brown & Rondon, *Evidence Handbook*, p. 515. In determining waiver by disclosure, the issue is whether the producing party intended to waive the particular privilege, not whether it intended to produce the information. TRCP 193.3(d) & cmt. 4. The disclosure of privileged material does not waive the privilege in the following circumstances:

(1) Inadvertent disclosure. The inadvertent disclosure of privileged material does not automatically waive a claim of privilege. TRCP 193.3(d) & cmt. 4; *In re Living Ctrs.*, 175 S.W.3d 253, 260 (Tex.2005); *see, e.g.*, *In re Ford Motor Co.*, 211 S.W.3d 295, 301-02 (Tex.2006) (court clerk's mistaken release of documents did not waive confidentiality of protective order). By using the snap-back provision, a party can preserve the privilege for documents inadvertently disclosed to the other party. See "Use snap-back provision," §18.2.4, p. 444.

(2) In camera disclosure. The disclosure of privileged material for an in camera inspection does not waive a claim of privilege. *M.A.W. v. Hall*, 921 S.W.2d 911, 916 (Tex.App.—Houston [14th Dist.] 1996, orig. proceeding); *Johnson v. Casseb*, 722 S.W.2d 253, 256 (Tex.App.—San Antonio 1986, orig. proceeding).

8. Disclosure to testifying expert. If a party discloses privileged materials, either deliberately or inadvertently, to its own testifying expert, it waives the privilege. *In re Christus Spohn Hosp. Kleberg*, 222 S.W.3d 434, 440-41 (Tex.2007). If the disclosure was inadvertent, the party must generally choose between waiving the privilege or replacing its testifying expert. See "Inadvertent disclosure," ch. 6-D, §4.1.1(6)(b), p. 508. In very limited circumstances, the party may be able to use the snap-back provision to retrieve the material. See "Invoke snap-back provision," ch. 6-D, §4.1.1(6)(b)[1], p. 508.

9. Use of document to refresh recollection. If a party uses documents to refresh the recollection of a witness, the documents are discoverable under certain circumstances.

(1) Before testifying. If the witness uses a document before testifying, the court has discretion to require that the document be produced. TRE 612(2); *Goode v. Shoukfeh*, 943 S.W.2d 441, 449 (Tex.1997); *Portland S&L Ass'n v. Bernstein*, 716 S.W.2d 532, 541 (Tex.App.—Corpus Christi 1985, writ ref'd n.r.e.), *overruled on other grounds*, *Dawson-Austin v. Austin*, 968 S.W.2d 319 (Tex.1998). The waiver applies to the parts of the document that relate to the witness's testimony. TRE 612. See Brown & Rondon, *Evidence Handbook*, p. 623.

(2) While testifying. If the witness uses a document while testifying, the adverse party has a right to see it. TRE 612(1); *see Goode*, 943 S.W.2d at 449; *City of Denison v. Grisham*, 716 S.W.2d 121, 123 (Tex.App.—Dallas 1986, orig. proceeding). See Brown & Rondon, *Evidence Handbook*, p. 624.

10. Waiver by offensive use. Under the doctrine of waiver by offensive use, a party cannot "use one hand to seek affirmative relief and with the other lower an iron curtain of silence" around the facts of the case. *E.g.*, *Ginsberg v. Fifth Ct. of Appeals*, 686 S.W.2d 105, 108 (Tex.1985) (P could not claim psychotherapist-patient privilege to exclude information that would assist D).

(1) Offensive-use doctrine. The Supreme Court set out the test for the application of the offensive-use doctrine in *Republic Ins. v. Davis*, 856 S.W.2d 158, 163 (Tex.1993) (attorney-client privilege), and restated it in *Texas DPS Officers Ass'n v. Denton*, 897 S.W.2d 757, 761 (Tex.1995) (5th Amendment privilege). Before a party waives a privilege by offensive use, the court must determine that (1) the party is seeking affirmative relief, (2) the evidence the party refuses to produce is outcome-determinative, and (3) there is no alternative source for the evidence. *E.g.*, *Denton*, 897 S.W.2d at 761 (privilege waived because party seeking evidence met all three elements); *TransAmerican Nat. Gas Corp. v. Flores*, 870 S.W.2d 10, 11-12 (Tex.1994) (trial court should not have found waiver

✦

because party seeking evidence met only first element); *Republic Ins.*, 856 S.W.2d at 164 (privilege not waived because party seeking evidence did not meet first element because declaratory-judgment action is not request for affirmative relief). If the party seeking evidence proves all three elements, the party asserting the privilege must decide whether to continue to assert the privilege or to abandon it and produce the evidence. *See Denton*, 897 S.W.2d at 761.

(2) Remedial action. If the party continues to assert the privilege even after the party seeking the evidence proves all three elements of the test, the court must take some remedial action. For example, the court may limit the discovery inquiry, restrict the evidence the party asserting the privilege introduces on the subject, delay the trial (when the Fifth Amendment privilege is asserted), and ultimately, if the party asserting the privilege is the plaintiff, dismiss the suit. *Denton*, 897 S.W.2d at 763. The court must consider a number of factors before forcing the party resisting discovery to choose between its privilege and the lawsuit. *Id.* For a list of factors affecting the choice of remedies, see *Denton*, 897 S.W.2d at 763.

11. Failure to timely respond.

(1) Waiver. When a party does not timely respond to a discovery request, the party waives its objections to the request and must produce the discovery. *See* TRCP 193.1, 193.2(e).

(2) Exceptions. There are four exceptions to the rule of mandatory waiver for not timely responding to a discovery request.

(a) The parties agree to an extension, and the agreement meets the requirements of TRCP 11. TRCP 191.1; *Remington Arms Co. v. Canales*, 837 S.W.2d 624, 625 (Tex.1992); *Young v. Ray*, 916 S.W.2d 1, 3 (Tex. App.—Houston [1st Dist.] 1995, orig. proceeding).

(b) The parties agree to an extension that affects an oral deposition, and the agreement is made part of the record of the deposition. TRCP 191.1.

(c) The court signs an order extending the time to respond to discovery. *Id.*; *Remington Arms*, 837 S.W.2d at 625; *Young*, 916 S.W.2d at 3.

(d) The party proves that it had good cause for not timely objecting. TRCP 193.2(e); *Remington Arms*, 837 S.W.2d at 625; *Young*, 916 S.W.2d at 3.

§26. REVIEW OF DISCOVERY ORDERS

For the rules and forms for prosecuting or responding to an appeal or original proceeding, see *O'Connor's Texas Appeals*.

§26.1 Review by appeal. Most orders relating to discovery disputes are reviewed on appeal after final judgment. *Walker v. Packer*, 827 S.W.2d 833, 842 (Tex.1992); *see, e.g., Vega v. Davila*, 31 S.W.3d 376, 378 (Tex. App.—Corpus Christi 2000, no pet.) (court had jurisdiction to hear appeal from order overruling motion to quash subpoena for deposition). The standard for review of a discovery order is abuse of discretion. *Ford Motor Co. v. Castillo*, 279 S.W.3d 656, 661 (Tex.2009); *TransAmerican Nat. Gas Corp. v. Powell*, 811 S.W.2d 913, 917 (Tex. 1991). A trial court abuses its discretion when it reaches a result so arbitrary and unreasonable that it amounts to a clear and prejudicial error of law. *Ford Motor*, 279 S.W.3d at 661; *Walker*, 827 S.W.2d at 839.

§26.2 Review by mandamus. Most orders relating to discovery disputes cannot be reviewed by mandamus. The appellate courts will grant a petition for writ of mandamus only if the following conditions are met:

1. Abuse of discretion. The trial court clearly abused its discretion in making a discretionary ruling. *In re Prudential Ins.*, 148 S.W.3d 124, 135 (Tex.2004). The party seeking mandamus must show that the trial court's discovery ruling was "so arbitrary and unreasonable as to amount to a clear and prejudicial error of law." *Walker v. Packer*, 827 S.W.2d 833, 839 (Tex.1992). That is, the party must show the appellate court that the trial court acted without reference to any guiding rules and principles. *In re Colonial Pipeline Co.*, 968 S.W.2d 938, 941 (Tex.1998).

———————————————— ⭐ ————————————————

2. No adequate remedy by appeal. There is no adequate remedy by appeal. *In re Dana Corp.*, 138 S.W.3d 298, 301 (Tex.2004); *Walker*, 827 S.W.2d at 842; *e.g.*, *In re Deere & Co.*, 299 S.W.3d 819, 820 (Tex.2009) (mandamus was proper because discovery order requiring D to produce documents from an indefinite time period was overbroad); *see, e.g.*, *In re Weekley Homes, L.P.*, 295 S.W.3d 309, 322-23 (Tex.2009) (harm from ordering access to party's computer hard drive cannot be remedied on appeal); *see also In re Bay Area Citizens Against Lawsuit Abuse*, 982 S.W.2d 371, 375 (Tex.1998) (no adequate remedy by appeal because discovery order violated 1st Amendment rights). An appellate remedy is adequate when the detriments of mandamus review outweigh the benefits. *In re Prudential*, 148 S.W.3d at 136. Whether an appellate remedy is adequate depends on the circumstances. *Id.* at 137. In *Walker*, the Supreme Court identified three discovery situations in which a party does not have an adequate appellate remedy for an erroneous ruling by the trial court. *Walker*, 827 S.W.2d at 843-44.

(1) When the appellate court cannot cure the trial court's discovery error. *Walker*, 827 S.W.2d at 843. This happens when the trial court erroneously orders the disclosure of privileged information that will materially affect the rights of the aggrieved party, such as attorney-client privileged information. *Id.*; *see also In re Perry*, 60 S.W.3d 857, 858 (Tex.2001) (mandamus appropriate to prevent disclosure of information protected by legislative immunity). This also happens when the discovery order imposes a burden on the producing party far out of proportion to any benefit to the requesting party. *In re Weekley Homes*, 295 S.W.3d at 322; *Walker*, 827 S.W.2d at 843.

(2) When the party's ability to present a viable claim or defense at trial is severely compromised by the trial court's discovery error. *In re Allied Chem. Corp.*, 227 S.W.3d 652, 658 (Tex.2007); *Montalvo v. Fourth Ct. of Appeals*, 917 S.W.2d 1, 2 (Tex.1995); *Walker*, 827 S.W.2d at 843. The party seeking mandamus must show harm to prove lack of adequate remedy by appeal. *Montalvo*, 917 S.W.2d at 2. The delay, inconvenience, or expense of an appeal is not sufficient harm. *Walker*, 827 S.W.2d at 843. Denial of discovery that goes to the heart of the party's case may be sufficient harm. *In re Allied Chem.*, 227 S.W.3d at 658; *Walker*, 827 S.W.2d at 843; *see, e.g.*, *Peters v. Moore*, 835 S.W.2d 764, 767 (Tex.App.—Houston [14th Dist.] 1992, orig. proceeding) (mandamus available when court refused to permit experts to testify).

(3) When the trial court disallows discovery, the missing discovery cannot be made part of the appellate record, and the reviewing court is unable to evaluate the effect of the trial court's error. *Walker*, 827 S.W.2d at 843-44. If the procedures of TRCP 193.4 are followed, however, this situation should seldom arise. *Walker*, 827 S.W.2d at 843-44 (discussing former TRCP 166b(4)).

§26.3 Record. If evidence was received at the hearing on discovery, the party challenging the trial court's order must provide the appellate court with a reporter's record from the hearing. *See* TRAP 34.6, 52.7(a)(2). For the record in an appeal, see *O'Connor's Texas Appeals*, "Record on Appeal," ch. 6, p. 209; for the record in a mandamus proceeding, see *O'Connor's Texas Appeals*, "Record for Petition for Original Writ," ch. 10-A, §6, p. 338. A reporter's record is not necessary if the trial court clearly based its order on the papers on file and the arguments of counsel. *Otis Elevator Co. v. Parmelee*, 850 S.W.2d 179, 181 (Tex.1993). When a reporter's record is not necessary, the petitioner may file with the petition an affidavit attesting that no evidence was heard. See *O'Connor's Texas Appeals*, "Statement," ch. 10-A, §6.1.2(2), p. 339.

§26.4 Findings of fact. Findings of fact are helpful, but not required, when challenging the trial court's findings on discovery sanctions. See "Findings of fact are helpful," ch. 10-E, §2.2, p. 818.

★

B. SCOPE OF DISCOVERY

§1. GENERAL

§1.1 Rule. TRCP 192.3.

§1.2 Purpose. The scope of discovery controls what information can and cannot be discovered. This subchapter discusses what is discoverable and what is not discoverable.

§1.3 Forms. *O'Connor's Texas Civil Forms* (2012), FORM 6B:1.

§1.4 Other references. Brown & Rondon, *Texas Rules of Evidence Handbook* (2013) (referred to as Brown & Rondon, *Evidence Handbook*); Browning, *Digging for the Digital Dirt: Discovery & Use of Evidence from Social Media Sites*, 14 SMU Sci. & Tech.L.Rev. 465 (2011) (referred to as Browning, *Digging for the Digital Dirt*); Bruce, *Social Media 101 for Lawyers*, 73 Tex.B.J. 186 (Mar.2010) (referred to as Bruce, *Social Media 101*); Downing et al., *"Be Careful What You Ask For, You May Get It": Common Sense Discovery Requests & Responses*, Advanced Family Law Course, State Bar of Texas CLE, ch. 15 (2006); Gold, *"I'd Rather Be Fishing": Scope of Discovery in Texas 2011*, Advanced Evidence & Discovery Course, State Bar of Texas CLE, ch. 6 (2011); Watler, *The Texas Journalist Shield Law*, 72 Tex.B.J. 686 (Sept.2009); *O'Connor's Texas Causes of Action* (2013) (*O'Connor's Texas COA*); *O'Connor's Texas Family Law Handbook* (2013) (*O'Connor's Fam. Law Handbook*).

§2. WHAT IS DISCOVERABLE?

TRCP 192.3 is the principal rule identifying information that is discoverable.

§2.1 General rule. A party can seek discovery of unprivileged information that is relevant to the subject of the lawsuit, including inadmissible evidence, as long as the request is reasonably calculated to lead to the discovery of admissible evidence. TRCP 192.3(a); *In re CSX Corp.*, 124 S.W.3d 149, 152 (Tex.2003); *In re American Optical Corp.*, 988 S.W.2d 711, 713 (Tex.1998); *Eli Lilly & Co. v. Marshall*, 850 S.W.2d 155, 160 (Tex.1993); *see* TRE 501; *Ford Motor Co. v. Castillo*, 279 S.W.3d 656, 664 (Tex.2009). While the scope of discovery is quite broad, it is confined by the subject matter of the case and the reasonable expectation of obtaining information that will help resolve the dispute. TRCP 192 cmt. 1; *In re CSX Corp.*, 124 S.W.3d at 152; *see In re American Optical*, 988 S.W.2d at 713 (court must impose reasonable discovery limits); *K Mart Corp. v. Sanderson*, 937 S.W.2d 429, 431 (Tex.1996) (discovery cannot be used to "fish" for evidence). There are five principal questions relating to the scope of discovery.

1. *Is the information relevant to the suit?* Discovery is limited to matters that are relevant to the case. TRCP 192.3(a); *Texaco, Inc. v. Sanderson*, 898 S.W.2d 813, 814 (Tex.1995). A party must preserve evidence when it knows or reasonably should know the evidence is relevant to litigation. *Vela v. Wagner & Brown, Ltd.*, 203 S.W.3d 37, 58 (Tex.App.—San Antonio 2006, no pet.).

2. *Will the information lead to the discovery of admissible evidence?* A party cannot object to discovery on the ground that the information sought is not admissible at trial. TRCP 192.3(a); *Axelson, Inc. v. McIlhany*, 798 S.W.2d 550, 553 (Tex.1990). If the information is reasonably calculated to lead to the discovery of admissible evidence, it is discoverable.

3. *Is there an exemption from discovery that prevents the discovery of the information?* If the information is subject to a discovery exemption, it is not discoverable. See "What Is Not Discoverable?," §3, p. 471.

4. *Do the discovery rules permit the type of discovery procedure necessary to secure the information?* If no discovery rule permits the type of discovery procedure involved, the information is not discoverable unless the court orders or the parties agree to the discovery procedure. *See* TRCP 191 & cmt. 1 (trial court may order or parties may agree to use discovery methods other than those prescribed in the rules). See "General Rules for Discovery," ch. 6-A, p. 425.

5. *Should the court limit discovery because it is cumulative, too expensive, or too burdensome?* The court's power to limit discovery based on the needs and circumstances of the case is expressly stated in TRCP 192.4. TRCP 192 cmt. 7. Courts should limit discovery under this rule only to prevent unwarranted delay and expense as stated in the rule. *Id.* See "Grounds to limit scope of discovery," ch. 6-A, §20.1, p. 449.

———————————————————— ✯ ————————————————————

§2.2 Potential parties. The names, addresses, and telephone numbers of potential parties to the suit are discoverable. TRCP 192.3(i) (scope of discovery), TRCP 192.5(c)(3) (exception to work-product privilege), TRCP 194.2(b) (request for disclosure); *Helfand v. Coane*, 12 S.W.3d 152, 157 n.3 (Tex.App.—Houston [1st Dist.] 2000, pet. denied).

§2.3 Party contentions. An opinion or contention relating to a fact or the application of the law to a fact is discoverable. TRCP 192.3(j), 194.2(c), 197.1. A party may request by disclosure or interrogatory the opinions or contentions of the other party. See "Contentions," ch. 6-E, §3.2.1(3), p. 517; "Party contentions," ch. 6-G, §3.2.5, p. 550.

§2.4 Party admissions. A party's statement of opinion, of fact, of the application of law to fact, or of the genuineness of a document described in the request (and attached or made available for inspection and copying) is discoverable through a request for admissions. TRCP 198.1. See "Requests for Admissions," ch. 6-H, p. 557.

§2.5 Party's statements. Some party statements are discoverable. TRCP 192.3(h). These statements, even if made or prepared in anticipation of litigation, are not protected by the work-product privilege. TRCP 192.5(c)(1).

   1. Party as witness. A party's statements as a witness are discoverable. See "Witness statements," §2.6, this page.

   2. Party's statements from another suit. A party's statements contained in noncore work product in one suit may be discoverable in another suit. *Republic Ins. v. Davis*, 856 S.W.2d 158, 164-65 (Tex.1993). To be privileged, work product must be made in the same suit. *Id.*; *see* TRCP 192.5(a)(2) (communication made in anticipation of litigation or trial).

§2.6 Witness statements. A witness statement is (1) a written statement signed, adopted, or approved in writing by the person making it, or (2) a stenographic, mechanical, electrical, or other type of recording of a witness's oral statement, or any substantially verbatim transcription of such a recording. TRCP 192.3(h). Notes taken by another person during a conversation or interview with a witness are not considered a witness statement. *Id.*

   1. Discoverable. Witness statements, regardless of when they are made, are not protected from discovery by the work-product privilege. TRCP 192.5(c)(1); *see Spohn Hosp. v. Mayer*, 72 S.W.3d 52, 62 (Tex.App.—Corpus Christi 2001), *rev'd on other grounds*, 104 S.W.3d 878 (Tex.2003); *In re Team Transp.*, 996 S.W.2d 256, 259 (Tex.App.—Houston [14th Dist.] 1999, orig. proceeding). For example, a letter to a party's insurance carrier describing an accident, prepared by an employee who witnessed the accident, is discoverable. *In re Team Transp.*, 996 S.W.2d at 259; *see also In re Learjet Inc.*, 59 S.W.3d 842, 846 (Tex.App.—Texarkana 2001, orig. proceeding) (edited and unedited versions of videotaped witness statements, which were used in mediation, were discoverable). Most insurance companies call witnesses immediately after an accident and record their statements over the telephone. Those statements are discoverable. *See, e.g., In re Jimenez*, 4 S.W.3d 894, 896 (Tex.App.—Houston [1st Dist.] 1999, orig. proceeding) (D's statement to carrier was discoverable); *In re W&G Trucking*, 990 S.W.2d 473, 475 (Tex. App.—Beaumont 1999, orig. proceeding) (same); *see also In re Ford Motor Co.*, 988 S.W.2d 714, 719 (Tex.1998) (in case predating 1999 discovery rules, P's statement to carrier was not protected from discovery because there was no attorney-client relationship between them). An insurance company cannot avoid producing these statements by hiring an attorney to conduct postaccident interviews. The work-product privilege does not permit an attorney to hide from discovery facts that were acquired by the attorney. *Owens-Corning Fiberglas Corp. v. Caldwell*, 818 S.W.2d 749, 750 n.2 (Tex.1991); *see also In re Texas Farmers Ins. Exch.*, 990 S.W.2d 337, 340 (Tex.App.—Texarkana 1999, orig. proceeding) (carrier was required to produce report of attorney hired to investigate claim). The purpose of the work-product privilege is to shelter the mental processes of the attorney, not the facts about the case. *Owens-Corning*, 818 S.W.2d at 750.

PRACTICE TIP

When an attorney sends an investigator to talk to a witness, the attorney should instruct the investigator not to take a statement (recorded or signed) if the information is not favorable. When the information is not favorable, the investigator can simply prepare a memo stating the substance of the interview. That memo is not discoverable as a witness statement. TRCP 192.3(h).

─────────────────────── ✭ ───────────────────────

2. Not discoverable. Witness statements are protected from discovery if they are shielded by some other objection or privilege (e.g., the attorney-client privilege). *See* TRCP 192 cmt. 9; *In re Fontenot*, 13 S.W.3d 111, 113 (Tex.App.—Fort Worth 2000, orig. proceeding). For example, a party's statement provided to its attorney is not discoverable because it is protected under TRE 503. *See, e.g., In re Fontenot*, 13 S.W.3d at 114 (P's written narrative and confidential claim questionnaire, given by P to his attorneys, were not discoverable).

§2.7 Person's own statements. If a person (whether a party or a witness) made a statement about the subject matter of the litigation, that person is entitled to receive a copy of the statement from any party who has possession of it. TRCP 192.3(h). The person must make a written request for the copy. *Id.* See *O'Connor's Texas Forms*, FORM 6B:1.

§2.8 Fact witnesses. A party may obtain discovery of the names, addresses, and telephone numbers of people with knowledge of relevant facts. TRCP 192.3(c); *see Smith v. Southwest Feed Yards*, 835 S.W.2d 89, 90 (Tex.1992). The reason for requiring the disclosure of the names, addresses, and telephone numbers is to allow the opposing party to locate, interview, and depose the witnesses. *$23,900 v. State*, 899 S.W.2d 314, 316-17 (Tex.App.—Houston [14th Dist.] 1995, no writ). The plain language of TRCP 192.3(c) and 192.5(c)(3) clearly indicates that information about the identity and location of people with knowledge of relevant facts can never be protected from discovery. *Giffin v. Smith*, 688 S.W.2d 112, 113 (Tex.1985) (under former TRCP 166b).

1. Who is a fact witness. A person has knowledge of relevant facts when that person has or may have knowledge of discoverable matters. TRCP 192.3(c); *Jamail v. Anchor Mortg. Servs.*, 809 S.W.2d 221, 223 (Tex. 1991). The person does not need to have admissible information. TRCP 192.3(c); *see In re Team Transp.*, 996 S.W.2d 256, 259 (Tex.App.—Houston [14th Dist.] 1999, orig. proceeding). Personal knowledge is not required. TRCP 192.3(c); *In re Team Transp.*, 996 S.W.2d at 259. Fact witnesses include expert witnesses who have discoverable factual information. See "Types of Experts," ch. 6-D, §2, p. 502.

2. What is discoverable about fact witnesses. Information about fact witnesses is discoverable. TRCP 192.3(c) (scope of discovery), TRCP 192.5(c)(1) (exception to work-product privilege), TRCP 194.2(e) (request for disclosure).

(1) Identity. A party is entitled to the name, address, and telephone number of any person with knowledge of relevant facts. TRCP 192.3(c), 194.2(e); *see, e.g., $23,900*, 899 S.W.2d at 316-17 (address of police headquarters was sufficient for officer, even though interrogatory also asked for residential address). See "Identify witness," ch. 6-E, §4.2.5(1), p. 519.

(2) Connection with case. A party is entitled to a brief description of the person's connection with the suit. TRCP 192.3(c), 194.2(e). See "Identify connection with case," ch. 6-E, §4.2.5(2), p. 520.

(3) Witness statements. A party is entitled to any witness statements made by a fact witness. TRCP 192.3(h). See "Witness statements," §2.6, p. 461.

(4) Matters not privileged. A party is entitled to any information in the possession of the witness that is not privileged and is relevant to the subject matter of the pending action, whether it relates to the claim or defense of the party seeking discovery or to the claim or defense of any other party. TRCP 192.3(a).

§2.9 Trial witnesses. The discovery rules permit a party to obtain discovery of the name, address, and telephone number of any person who is expected to be called to testify at trial. TRCP 192.3(d), 192.5(c)(1) (exception to work product). A party is not entitled to secure information about rebuttal or impeaching witnesses unless the need for the testimony can reasonably be anticipated before trial. TRCP 192.3(d). Because TRCP 194, which governs requests for disclosure, does not mention trial witnesses, information about trial witnesses cannot be discovered through such a request. Therefore, parties should seek this information through interrogatories. See "Trial witnesses," ch. 6-G, §3.2.3, p. 550.

★

PRACTICE TIP

In interrogatories, a party should always ask specifically for (1) trial witnesses and (2) rebuttal and impeachment witnesses whose testimony can reasonably be anticipated before trial. See TRCP 192.3(d).

---

§2.10 Experts. See "Information Discoverable from Experts," ch. 6-D, §4, p. 506.

§2.11 Documents & tangible things. A party can discover the existence, description, nature, custody, condition, location, and contents of documents and tangible things that constitute or contain relevant information and are in the possession, custody, or control of the other party. TRCP 192.3(b); *see* TRCP 196 (request for production). See "Documents & tangible things," ch. 6-A, §2.2, p. 425; "Possession," ch. 6-A, §2.5, p. 425. To be discoverable, the document or thing must already exist. *Smith v. O'Neal*, 850 S.W.2d 797, 799 (Tex.App.—Houston [14th Dist.] 1993, no writ). A request for production does not require a party to create a document to satisfy the request. *Id.* See "Securing Documents & Tangible Things," ch. 6-I, p. 565. The following types of documents are discoverable:

1. Income-tax returns. Income-tax returns are discoverable if they are relevant and material. *Hall v. Lawlis*, 907 S.W.2d 493, 494-95 (Tex.1995). If part, but not all, of an income-tax return is discoverable, discovery must be limited to the relevant and material parts. *See Maresca v. Marks*, 362 S.W.2d 299, 301 (Tex.1962). Unlike other discovery requests, when a party objects to a request for income-tax returns, the requesting party has the burden to show that all or part of the return is relevant and material to the case. *In re Williams*, 328 S.W.3d 103, 116 (Tex. App.—Corpus Christi 2010, orig. proceeding); *In re Brewer Leasing, Inc.*, 255 S.W.3d 708, 713-14 (Tex.App.—Houston [1st Dist.] 2008, orig. proceeding). The requesting party must also show that the relevant information cannot be obtained from another source. *In re Williams*, 328 S.W.3d at 116; *El Centro del Barrio, Inc. v. Barlow*, 894 S.W.2d 775, 780 (Tex.App.—San Antonio 1994, orig. proceeding); *see Wal-Mart Stores v. Alexander*, 868 S.W.2d 322, 331 (Tex.1993) (Gonzalez, J., concurring) (trial courts should not allow discovery of tax returns if there are other adequate methods to determine net worth); *see, e.g., Sears, Roebuck & Co. v. Ramirez*, 824 S.W.2d 558, 559 (Tex. 1992) (trial court should not have ordered production of tax return because D had already produced audited, certified annual report containing D's net worth and the tax return was duplicative).

2. Financial statements. Financial statements reflecting the defendant's net worth are discoverable when a plaintiff sues for exemplary damages. *Lunsford v. Morris*, 746 S.W.2d 471, 473 (Tex.1988) (P not required to make prima facie case), *disapproved on other grounds*, *Walker v. Packer*, 827 S.W.2d 833 (Tex.1992). If the pleadings do not request exemplary damages, the defendant's net worth is outside the scope of discovery. *Al Parker Buick Co. v. Touchy*, 788 S.W.2d 129, 131 (Tex.App.—Houston [1st Dist.] 1990, orig. proceeding).

3. Photographs. "Photographs" are defined in the TREs to include still photographs, X-ray films, videotapes, and motion pictures. TRE 1001(b). *But see County of Dallas v. Harrison*, 759 S.W.2d 530, 531 (Tex.App.—Dallas 1988, no writ) (request for production of all "photographs" did not require production of videotapes). Photographs and other electronic images are discoverable. TRCP 192.3(b). Photographs are not "communications" exempt from discovery under TRCP 192.5(a) (work product). TRCP 192.5(c)(4); *see Terry v. Lawrence*, 700 S.W.2d 912, 913 (Tex.1985) (investigative privilege does not protect photos from discovery).

4. Insurance & indemnity agreements. Insurance policies and indemnity agreements are generally discoverable. TRCP 192.3(f). By permitting the discovery of insurance and indemnity agreements, the plaintiff can determine the settlement value of the case. *Carroll Cable Co. v. Miller*, 501 S.W.2d 299, 299 (Tex.1973). Even though an insurance policy or indemnity agreement may be discoverable, it is not automatically admissible as evidence at trial. TRCP 192.3(f). TRCP 192.3(f) does not preclude other discovery on insurance issues as long as the information is otherwise discoverable under TRCP 192.3(a). *In re Dana Corp.*, 138 S.W.3d 298, 302-03 (Tex.2004). See "General rule," §2.1, p. 460.

5. Settlement agreements. The existence and contents of relevant portions of a settlement agreement are discoverable. TRCP 192.3(g). A settlement agreement made in another dispute may be discoverable if it is relevant to the pending litigation. *Ford Motor Co. v. Leggat*, 904 S.W.2d 643, 649 (Tex.1995); *In re Frank A. Smith*

———————————————— ✦ ————————————————

Sales, 32 S.W.3d 871, 874 (Tex.App.—Corpus Christi 2000, orig. proceeding). In most cases, the dollar amount of the parties' settlement is not relevant. *See, e.g.*, *Leggat*, 904 S.W.2d at 649 (settlement amounts not relevant to determine D's net worth or motives); *Palo Duro Pipeline Co. v. Cochran*, 785 S.W.2d 455, 457 (Tex.App.—Houston [14th Dist.] 1990, orig. proceeding) (settlement amounts not relevant to issue of conspiracy). Even though a settlement agreement may be discoverable, it is not automatically admissible as evidence at trial. TRCP 192.3(g); *see also* TRE 408 (settlement agreements not admissible to prove or disprove liability); *Leggat*, 904 S.W.2d at 649 (settlement agreements not admissible to prove liability).

6. Claim files.

(1) Claim file in same suit. The claim file of a party's insurance company is generally discoverable in the same suit. *See, e.g.*, *In re Ford Motor Co.*, 988 S.W.2d 714, 719 (Tex.1998) (D entitled to claim file from P's carrier); *Dunn Equip. v. Gayle*, 725 S.W.2d 372, 374-75 (Tex.App.—Houston [14th Dist.] 1987, orig. proceeding) (P entitled to claim file from D's carrier). However, if the claim file is exempt from discovery under one cause of action (e.g., contract), the party cannot get it for another cause of action (e.g., bad faith) in the same suit. *Maryland Am. Gen. Ins. v. Blackmon*, 639 S.W.2d 455, 457-58 (Tex.1982).

(2) Claim file in separate suit. The claim file of an insurance company is sometimes discoverable in another suit. *Compare Turbodyne Corp. v. Heard*, 720 S.W.2d 802, 804 (Tex.1986) (documents from claim file in main suit were discoverable in subrogation action), *Lewis v. Wittig*, 877 S.W.2d 52, 58 (Tex.App.—Houston [14th Dist.] 1994, orig. proceeding) (claim files of client companies were discoverable in malpractice suit against attorneys), *and Eddington v. Touchy*, 793 S.W.2d 335, 337 (Tex.App.—Houston [1st Dist.] 1990, orig. proceeding) (documents from claim file were discoverable by attorney who sued insurance company for settling with attorney's client without attorney's permission), *with Humphreys v. Caldwell*, 888 S.W.2d 469, 471 (Tex.1994) (after first suit, D in that suit sued P's carrier; claim file in first suit was not discoverable).

7. Investigative reports. Investigative reports are discoverable when they are not prepared in anticipation of litigation. *See, e.g.*, *Axelson, Inc. v. McIlhany*, 798 S.W.2d 550, 552-53 (Tex.1990) (internal kickback investigation, unrelated to the matter that gave rise to litigation, was discoverable); *In re Weeks Mar., Inc.*, 31 S.W.3d 389, 391 (Tex.App.—San Antonio 2000, orig. proceeding) (D's investigative report made after P hired attorney was not discoverable). See "Work-product privilege," §3.3, p. 472.

8. Electronic information. Much information stored or available electronically, either on a computer database or on some form of social media, is discoverable.

(1) Computer database. If discoverable information is contained in a party's computer databases or files, it is discoverable upon a specific request. *See* TRCP 192.3(b) (any data compilations), TRCP 196.4 (electronic or magnetic data). Computer data can be requested in hard copy (printed version) or in electronic files. TRCP 196.4. See "Electronic Discovery," ch. 6-C, p. 485.

(2) Social media. "Social media" refers to social interaction using technology (e.g., the Internet, cellular telephones) with any combination of words, pictures, video, or audio. Bruce, *Social Media 101*, at 186. Information about these social interactions is discoverable and is most effectively obtained through (1) specific requests to the party or (2) by having the party execute a consent form or authorization that allows the discovering party to request the information directly from the social networking site. *See* Browning, *Digging for Digital Dirt*, at 473.

9. Personnel files. When relevant, a party may discover the documents in the personnel file of a party or witness. *See In re Crestcare Nursing & Rehab. Ctr.*, 222 S.W.3d 68, 74 (Tex.App.—Tyler 2006, orig. proceeding); *In re Lavernia Nursing Facility, Inc.*, 12 S.W.3d 566, 570 (Tex.App.—San Antonio 1999, orig. proceeding). A personnel file includes all matters about the employee, even if filed separately under a different name. *E.g.*, *In re Lavernia Nursing*, 12 S.W.3d at 570 (personnel file included disciplinary actions filed separately).

10. Ongoing studies. Status reports of ongoing clinical studies and the identities of clinical research organizations are discoverable. *In re American Home Prods.*, 980 S.W.2d 506, 510 (Tex.App.—Waco 1998, orig. proceeding).

★

§2.12 Entry on land. A party has a right of entry on land when it is relevant to the lawsuit. The purpose of the entry must be to inspect, measure, survey, photograph, conduct nondestructive tests, or sample the land or a designated object or operation on the land. TRCP 196.7(a). See "Entry on Land," ch. 6-K, p. 580.

§2.13 Certain work product. For the definition of work product, see "Work product," ch. 6-A, §2.9, p. 426. Most work product is not discoverable. See "Work-product privilege," §3.3, p. 472. However, some work product is discoverable.

1. Facts. Most facts about the case are discoverable. The work-product privilege does not permit the attorney to hide from discovery facts that were acquired by the attorney and are relevant and not exempt from discovery by some other privilege. *Owens-Corning Fiberglas Corp. v. Caldwell*, 818 S.W.2d 749, 750 n.2 (Tex.1991); *see In re Ford Motor Co.*, 988 S.W.2d 714, 719 (Tex.1998); *see also Hickman v. Taylor*, 329 U.S. 495, 511 (1947) (relevant and nonexempt information in attorney's file may be discovered); *Leede Oil & Gas, Inc. v. McCorkle*, 789 S.W.2d 686, 687 (Tex.App.—Houston [1st Dist.] 1990, orig. proceeding) (neutral facts about case in attorney's file were discoverable because attorney obtained information from fact witness who died after interview). An attorney cannot classify a document as work product simply by including it in a litigation file. *National Un. Fire Ins. v. Valdez*, 863 S.W.2d 458, 460 (Tex.1993); *Lewis v. Wittig*, 877 S.W.2d 52, 57-58 (Tex.App.—Houston [14th Dist.] 1994, orig. proceeding).

2. Need & hardship exception. A party may secure noncore work product under the need-and-hardship exception in TRCP 192.5(b)(2). *In re Maher*, 143 S.W.3d 907, 912 (Tex.App.—Fort Worth 2004, orig. proceeding); *In re Monsanto Co.*, 998 S.W.2d 917, 930 (Tex.App.—Waco 1999, orig. proceeding). If the court permits discovery of noncore work product under this exception, it must prevent the disclosure of mental impressions, opinions, conclusions, or legal theories, which are not discoverable. TRCP 192.5(b)(4). To meet the need-and-hardship exception, the party seeking discovery must show the following:

(1) Noncore work product. The information is not core work product. *See* TRCP 192.5(b)(1); *In re Team Transp.*, 996 S.W.2d 256, 259 (Tex.App.—Houston [14th Dist.] 1999, orig. proceeding) (need-and-hardship exception applies only to "other work product"). For a definition, see "Noncore work product," ch. 6-A, §2.9.2, p. 426.

(2) Substantial need. The party has a substantial need for the information to prepare its case. TRCP 192.5(b)(2); *In re Bexar Cty. Crim. Dist. Atty's Office*, 224 S.W.3d 182, 188 (Tex.2007); *Flores v. Fourth Ct. of Appeals*, 777 S.W.2d 38, 42 (Tex.1989), *modified on other grounds*, *National Tank Co. v. Brotherton*, 851 S.W.2d 193 (Tex.1993); *see, e.g., State v. Lowry*, 802 S.W.2d 669, 673 (Tex.1991) (Ds had substantial need because State collected information during investigation that led to lawsuit and could provide evidence for defense); *Dillard Dept. Stores v. Sanderson*, 928 S.W.2d 319, 321-22 (Tex.App.—Beaumont 1996, orig. proceeding) (issues of witness credibility and witness's failing memory were sufficient to show substantial need).

(3) Undue hardship. The party is unable, without undue hardship, to obtain the substantial equivalent of the information by other means. TRCP 192.5(b)(2); *In re Bexar Cty.*, 224 S.W.3d at 188; *Flores*, 777 S.W.2d at 42; *e.g., Lowry*, 802 S.W.2d at 673 (Ds showed undue hardship because it would have been extremely difficult and costly to duplicate material that State had gathered).

3. Exceptions in TRCP 192.5(c). The following information is discoverable even if it was collected or prepared in anticipation of litigation:

(1) Witness information. Information discoverable under TRCP 192.3 (scope of discovery) concerning experts, trial witnesses, witness statements, and contentions. TRCP 192.5(c)(1). See "Witness statements," §2.6, p. 461.

(2) Trial exhibits. Trial exhibits required to be disclosed by court order under TRCP 166 (pretrial order) or by TRCP 190.4 (Level 3 discovery-control plan). TRCP 192.5(c)(2).

(3) Party & fact witnesses. The name, address, and telephone number of any potential party or any person with knowledge of relevant facts. TRCP 192.5(c)(3).

⭐

(4) Photographs. Photographs and other electronic images that contain images of underlying facts (e.g., a photograph of the accident scene) or that the party intends to offer into evidence. TRCP 192.5(c)(4); *see also* TRCP 192.3(b) (scope of discovery). See "Photographs," §2.11.3, p. 463.

(5) TRE 503(d) exceptions. Any work product created under circumstances within an exception to the attorney-client privilege in TRE 503(d) (crime-fraud and other exceptions). TRCP 192.5(c)(5); ***Goode v. Shoukfeh***, 943 S.W.2d 441, 448 (Tex.1997). The same exceptions that apply to attorney-client communications apply to work product. TRCP 192.5(c)(5). See "TRE 503(d) exceptions," §2.14.1, this page.

4. Waiver by offensive use. Information classified as noncore work product may be discoverable under the offensive-use doctrine. *See Occidental Chem. Corp. v. Banales*, 907 S.W.2d 488, 490 (Tex.1995) (dicta; case involved sanctions). See "Waiver by offensive use," ch. 6-A, §25.3.10, p. 457.

§2.14 Certain attorney-client communications. For a definition of the attorney-client privilege, see "Attorney-client privilege," §3.4, p. 473. The following communications between an attorney and a client are not privileged and are discoverable:

1. TRE 503(d) exceptions. If the communication falls within one of the five exceptions listed in TRE 503(d), it is discoverable.

(1) Crime or fraud. Communications made in furtherance of a crime or fraud are discoverable. TRE 503(d)(1); TRCP 192.5(c)(5); *see Granada Corp. v. First Ct. of Appeals*, 844 S.W.2d 223, 227 (Tex.1992), *overruled on other grounds*, TRCP 193.3 & cmt. 4 (TRCP 193.3(d) overrules *Granada* to the extent that they conflict). The crime-fraud exception applies only if (1) the party seeking the information makes a prima facie case of contemplated crime or fraud, and (2) the information sought is related to the prima facie proof. *Granada*, 844 S.W.2d at 227; *In re General Agents Ins. Co.*, 224 S.W.3d 806, 819 (Tex.App.—Houston [14th Dist.] 2007, orig. proceeding); *In re JDN Real Estate-McKinney L.P.*, 211 S.W.3d 907, 924 (Tex.App.—Dallas 2006, orig. proceeding). The prima facie proof must show a violation serious enough to defeat the privilege. *In re Monsanto Co.*, 998 S.W.2d 917, 934 (Tex.App.—Waco 1999, orig. proceeding).

(2) Claimants through same deceased client. Communications that are relevant to an issue between parties who assert claims through the same deceased client are discoverable. TRE 503(d)(2); TRCP 192.5(c)(5); *In re Texas A&M–Corpus Christi Found.*, 84 S.W.3d 358, 361 (Tex.App.—Corpus Christi 2002, orig. proceeding). Other than this narrow exception, communications between an attorney and client survive the client's death. *See* TRE 503(c); *Swidler & Berlin v. U.S.*, 524 U.S. 399, 410 (1998).

(3) Breach of duty. Communications relevant to the breach of a duty either by an attorney to the client or by a client to the attorney are discoverable. TRE 503(d)(3); TRCP 192.5(c)(5); *Scrivner v. Hobson*, 854 S.W.2d 148, 152 (Tex.App.—Houston [1st Dist.] 1993, orig. proceeding).

(4) Attestation by attorney. Communications relevant to an issue about a document to which the attorney was an attesting witness are discoverable. TRE 503(d)(4); TRCP 192.5(c)(5).

(5) Joint clients. In a suit between clients who jointly consulted or retained an attorney, communications with the attorney that are common to the interests of both clients and are relevant to the dispute are discoverable. TRE 503(d)(5); TRCP 192.5(c)(5); *see Scrivner*, 854 S.W.2d at 152.

2. Preexisting document. Documents that preexisted the attorney-client relationship, delivered to the attorney by the client, are discoverable. *MortgageAmerica Corp. v. American Nat'l Bank*, 651 S.W.2d 851, 858 (Tex.App.—Austin 1983, writ ref'd n.r.e.).

3. Conditions of employment. Nonconfidential matters of employment, such as the terms, conditions, and purpose of the attorney's employment, are discoverable. *Allstate Tex. Lloyds v. Johnson*, 784 S.W.2d 100, 105 (Tex.App.—Waco 1989, orig. proceeding); *Borden, Inc. v. Valdez*, 773 S.W.2d 718, 720-21 (Tex.App.—Corpus Christi 1989, orig. proceeding).

✦

4. Discussions with employee. Communications with the client's employees are discoverable unless the discussion falls within the provisions of TRE 503(a) (definition of client and representative) and TRE 503(b) (attorney-client privilege). See "Who is included," §3.4.1, p. 474.

5. Identity of witnesses. The names and locations of the people with knowledge of relevant facts are discoverable. See "Fact witnesses," §2.8, p. 462.

6. Offensive use. Information covered by the attorney-client privilege may be discoverable under the offensive-use doctrine. *E.g.*, *In re Tjia*, 50 S.W.3d 614, 617 (Tex.App.—Amarillo 2001, orig. proceeding) (in breach-of-contract suit, attorney's letter to P, his client, was discoverable by D when P said it relied on advice of counsel in making decision not to sublease). See "Waiver by offensive use," ch. 6-A, §25.3.10, p. 457.

§2.15 Certain accountant-client communications. Information transferred between an accountant and a client is usually not discoverable. See "Accountant-client privilege," §3.7, p. 475. Accountant-client information is discoverable in the following instances:

1. When the client or its representative gives permission to disclose the information. Occ. Code §901.457(a).

2. When required by the professional standards for reporting on the examination of a financial statement. *Id.* §901.457(b)(1).

3. To respond to a summons under the provisions of the Internal Revenue Code, the 1933 Securities Act, the 1934 Securities Exchange Act, or a court order if the summons or order meets the requirements of Occupations Code §901.457(b)(2)(A)-(b)(2)(C). Occ. Code §901.457(b)(2).

4. In an investigation conducted by the Texas State Board of Public Accountancy. *Id.* §901.457(b)(3).

5. In an ethical investigation conducted by a professional organization of CPAs. *Id.* §901.457(b)(4).

6. In the course of a peer-review proceeding under Occupations Code §901.159. *Id.* §901.457(b)(5).

§2.16 Certain husband-wife communications. Most communications between spouses are not discoverable. *See* TRE 504. See "Husband-wife-communication privilege," §3.9, p. 476. The husband-wife privilege does not protect the following information from disclosure:

1. Nonconfidential communications. There is no husband-wife-communication privilege for communications made in the presence of a third person. *Fasken v. Fasken*, 260 S.W. 701, 702 (Tex.1924). These communications are not privileged and are discoverable. *See id.*; *Wiggins v. Tiller*, 230 S.W. 253, 254 (Tex.App.—San Antonio 1921, no writ); *cf. Bear v. State*, 612 S.W.2d 931, 931-32 (Tex.Crim.App.1981) (criminal case interpreting former Code of Crim. Proc. art. 38.11). If one spouse discusses the other spouse with a third person, that conversation is not privileged. *Cf. Gibbons v. State*, 794 S.W.2d 887, 892 (Tex.App.—Tyler 1990, no pet.) (interpreting former TRCrE 504).

2. Nonverbal communications. There is no husband-wife-communication privilege for nonverbal communications. *See Pereira v. U.S.*, 347 U.S. 1, 6 (1954) (actions are not communications and thus are not privileged); *cf. Freeman v. State*, 786 S.W.2d 56, 59 (Tex.App.—Houston [1st Dist.] 1990, no pet.) (criminal case interpreting former TRCrE 504(2)(a)).

3. Crime or fraud. There is no husband-wife-communication privilege for communications made in furtherance of a crime or fraud. TRE 504(a)(4)(A). See "Crime or fraud," §2.14.1(1), p. 466.

4. Suits between spouses. There is no husband-wife-communication privilege in a civil suit between spouses or in a proceeding between a surviving spouse and a person who makes a claim through the deceased spouse. TRE 504(a)(4)(B); *see, e.g.*, *Earthman's, Inc. v. Earthman*, 526 S.W.2d 192, 206 (Tex.App.—Houston [1st Dist.] 1975, no writ) (discussions between spouses were admissible in lawsuit between them).

✦

---

5. Crime against spouse or minor child. There is no husband-wife-communication privilege in a proceeding in which the party is accused of a criminal act against the spouse, any minor child, or any member of either spouse's household. TRE 504(a)(4)(C).

6. Commitment proceedings. There is no husband-wife-communication privilege at a proceeding to commit either spouse or to place the property of one spouse under the control of the other because of a mental or physical condition. TRE 504(a)(4)(D).

7. Competence hearings. There is no husband-wife-communication privilege in a hearing brought by or on behalf of either spouse to establish competence. TRE 504(a)(4)(E).

8. Communications made before marriage. There is no husband-wife-communication privilege for communications made before marriage. *See* TRE 504(a)(1) (communication is confidential if made to "person's spouse").

§2.17 Parent-child communications. There is no privilege for communications between parent and child. *Cf. Port v. Heard*, 764 F.2d 423, 428-30 (5th Cir.1985) (in criminal case, parent spent six months in jail for refusing to divulge communications by child accused of murder); *Diehl v. State*, 698 S.W.2d 712, 712-14 (Tex.App.—Houston [1st Dist.] 1985, pet. ref'd) (search warrant based on affidavit of D's 11-year-old child).

§2.18 Certain physician-patient information. Medical information about a patient is usually not discoverable. See "Physician-patient privilege," §3.10, p. 476. There are seven exceptions to the physician-patient privilege. TRE 509(e).

1. Patient vs. physician. Medical information is discoverable if (1) the patient sues the physician or the patient is the complainant in a license-revocation proceeding, and (2) disclosure is relevant to the claims against or defenses of the physician. TRE 509(e)(1); *Mutter v. Wood*, 744 S.W.2d 600, 600-01 (Tex.1988); *see In re Collins*, 286 S.W.3d 911, 916 (Tex.2009).

2. Written consent. Medical information is discoverable if the patient or an agent consents in writing, as provided in TRE 509(f), to release privileged information. TRE 509(e)(2); *In re Collins*, 286 S.W.3d at 916; *Mutter*, 744 S.W.2d at 600-01. A patient's authorization for doctors to release information to an insurance company does not authorize the insurance company to release the information in a lawsuit in which the patient is not a party. *Alpha Life Ins. v. Gayle*, 796 S.W.2d 834, 836 (Tex.App.—Houston [14th Dist.] 1990, orig. proceeding); *see* TRE 509(f)(3).

3. Suit for debt. Medical information is discoverable in a suit to substantiate and collect on a claim for medical services rendered to the patient. TRE 509(e)(3).

4. Relevant to claim or defense. Medical information is discoverable if the communication or record is relevant to an issue of the physical, mental, or emotional condition of a patient in a proceeding in which any party relies on the condition as part of its claim or defense, even when the patient is not a party to the litigation. TRE 509(e)(4); *In re Collins*, 286 S.W.3d at 916; *Mutter*, 744 S.W.2d at 600-01; *see, e.g.*, *In re Whiteley*, 79 S.W.3d 729, 733-34 (Tex.App.—Corpus Christi 2002, orig. proceeding) (other patients' redacted medical records were discoverable because D relied on defense that the same surgical procedure was successful on the other patients); *Rios v. Texas Dept. of MHMR*, 58 S.W.3d 167, 169 (Tex.App.—San Antonio 2001, no pet.) (in personal-injury suit, D could depose doctor that P consulted for second opinion). For discoverable mental-health information relevant to suit, see "Relevant to claim or defense," §2.19.5, p. 469.

5. Disciplinary investigation. Medical information is discoverable in the disciplinary investigation of a physician under the Medical Practice Act, Occupations Code §159.003(a)(5), or of a registered nurse under Occupations Code chapter 301. *See* TRE 509(e)(5).

6. Involuntary commitment. Medical information is discoverable in an involuntary-commitment proceeding, a proceeding for court-ordered treatment, or a probable-cause hearing under various statutes. TRE 509(e)(6).

★

7. Institutional abuse or neglect. Medical information is discoverable in a suit for abuse or neglect of a resident in an "institution," as defined by Health & Safety Code §242.002(10). TRE 509(e)(7); *see, e.g., In re Arriola*, 159 S.W.3d 670, 677 (Tex.App.—Corpus Christi 2004, orig. proceeding) (medical information about P who was resident of nursing home was discoverable).

§2.19 Certain mental-health information. Mental-health information about a patient is usually not discoverable. TRE 510(b). See "Mental-health-information privilege," §3.11, p. 477. There are six exceptions to the mental-health-information privilege that make mental-health information discoverable. TRE 510(d).

1. Patient vs. professional. Mental-health information is discoverable if (1) the patient sues the professional for malpractice or if the patient is the complainant in a license-revocation proceeding, and (2) disclosure is relevant to the claims against or defenses of the professional. TRE 510(d)(1).

2. Written waiver. Mental-health information is discoverable if a patient waives the right to the privilege in writing. TRE 510(d)(2).

3. Suit for debt. Mental-health information is discoverable if the professional sues to collect on a claim for mental-health or emotional-health services rendered to the patient. TRE 510(d)(3).

4. Communication made without privilege. Mental-health information is discoverable if the patient made the disclosure in the course of a court-ordered examination, and the judge makes a finding that the patient was told the communication would not be privileged. TRE 510(d)(4); *Subia v. Texas Dept. of Human Servs.*, 750 S.W.2d 827, 830 (Tex.App.—El Paso 1988, no writ); *Dudley v. State*, 730 S.W.2d 51, 54 (Tex.App.—Houston [14th Dist.] 1987, no writ).

5. Relevant to claim or defense. Mental-health information is discoverable when any party relies on the patient's physical, mental, or emotional condition as part of its claim or defense, even when the patient is not a party to the litigation. TRE 510(d)(5); *e.g., R.K. v. Ramirez*, 887 S.W.2d 836, 842-44 (Tex.1994) (P claimed hospital was negligent because its doctor was physically and emotionally impaired); *Groves v. Gabriel*, 874 S.W.2d 660, 661 (Tex.1994) (P's allegation of severe emotional distress waived her privilege relating to her mental-health records); *M.A.W. v. Hall*, 921 S.W.2d 911, 913-14 (Tex.App.—Houston [14th Dist.] 1996, orig. proceeding) (Ps claimed doctor was impaired by drugs); *Easter v. McDonald*, 903 S.W.2d 887, 890-91 (Tex.App.—Waco 1995, orig. proceeding) (P claimed mental-health counselor was negligent). The patient's condition becomes part of a claim or defense if the pleadings indicate that the jury must make a factual determination about the condition itself. *R.K.*, 887 S.W.2d at 843. Whether the patient's condition is part of a claim or defense is determined from the face of the pleadings. *Id.* at 843 n.7; *see Easter*, 903 S.W.2d at 891 n.1. See Brown & Rondon, *Evidence Handbook*, p. 507.

6. Institutional abuse or neglect. Mental-health information is discoverable in a suit for abuse or neglect of a resident in an "institution," as defined by Health & Safety Code §242.002(10). TRE 510(d)(6).

§2.20 Certain medical matters under TRCP 204. If the mental or physical condition of a party or a person under the party's control is in controversy, the person may be compelled on a motion showing good cause to submit to an examination. TRCP 204.1; *see Coates v. Whittington*, 758 S.W.2d 749, 750-51 (Tex.1988) (mental exam); *In re Caballero*, 36 S.W.3d 143, 144 (Tex.App.—Corpus Christi 2000, orig. proceeding) (physical exam). For more details on TRCP 204, see "Motion to Examine the Person," ch. 6-J, §5, p. 577.

§2.21 Certain medical requests under Family Code. In a suit affecting the parent-child relationship under Family Code title 2 or 5, the court, on a party's motion or on its own initiative, may appoint (1) a psychiatrist or psychologist to examine a child who is the subject of a lawsuit, or (2) a nonphysician expert qualified to take blood and other samples to conduct a paternity test. TRCP 204.4(a), (b); *see* Fam. Code §§160.501-160.511 (genetic testing). See *O'Connor's Fam. Law Handbook*, "Experts," ch. 4-D, §12.3.5, p. 413.

───────────────────── ✦ ─────────────────────

§2.22 Certain medical records under HIPAA. Nonparty medical records are discoverable under the Health Information Portability & Accountability Act (HIPAA) in the following situations:

    1. Court order. In response to a court order. 45 C.F.R. §164.512(e)(1)(i).

    2. Subpoena. In response to a subpoena, if the covered entity (i.e., the health-care entity providing the records) receives assurance that (1) the nonparty patient whose records are sought has received notice of the request, or (2) a protective order has been obtained. 45 C.F.R. §164.512(e)(1)(ii).

§2.23 Certain health-care information from hospital. Most health-care information in a hospital's possession is not discoverable. However, a hospital and its agents or employees may release health-care information about a patient if (1) the patient or the patient's legally authorized representative makes the request, (2) a person presents a written authorization signed by the patient that meets the requirements of Health & Safety Code §241.152(b), or (3) the disclosure is authorized by Health & Safety Code §241.153. Health & Safety Code §241.152.

§2.24 Certain trade secrets. Generally, a person has a qualified privilege to refuse to disclose a trade secret. See "Trade-secret privilege," §3.14, p. 480. But in certain situations, trade secrets may be discoverable. A party's opinion that the information is a trade secret or a party's desire to avoid disclosing the information to others does not protect the information under the trade-secret privilege. *See In re Lowe's Cos.*, 134 S.W.3d 876, 878-79 (Tex.App.—Houston [14th Dist.] 2004, orig. proceeding). If the court requires disclosure, it must do so subject to an appropriate protective order. *In re Continental Gen. Tire, Inc.*, 979 S.W.2d 609, 613 (Tex.1998); *In re Leviton Mfg. Co.*, 1 S.W.3d 898, 902 (Tex.App.—Waco 1999, orig. proceeding); *see* TRE 507.

    1. What is a trade secret? A trade secret is a formula, pattern, device, or compilation of information that is used in the holder's business and gives the holder an advantage over competitors. *In re Bass*, 113 S.W.3d 735, 739 (Tex.2003); *Computer Assocs. Int'l v. Altai, Inc.*, 918 S.W.2d 453, 455 (Tex.1996); *see also* Pen. Code §31.05(a)(4) (definition of "trade secret"). For a more detailed discussion of the definition of a trade secret, see *O'Connor's Texas COA*, "Plaintiff owned trade secret," ch. 28, §2.1, p. 966.

    2. When is a trade secret discoverable?

        (1) Necessary for fair adjudication. Information protected by the trade-secret privilege may be disclosed if the information is necessary for fair adjudication of a claim or defense and unavailable from any other source. *In re Continental Gen. Tire, Inc.*, 979 S.W.2d at 615; *see In re Bridgestone/Firestone, Inc.*, 106 S.W.3d 730, 732 (Tex.2003) (court determines whether information is necessary for fair adjudication by weighing requesting party's need for information against potential harm to resisting party); *In re Rockafellow*, ___ S.W.3d ___ (Tex.App.—Amarillo 2011, orig. proceeding) (No. 07-11-00066-CV; 7-19-11) (for a trade-secret production to be material to a claim or defense, there must first be a claim or defense; thus, requesting party cannot use TRCP 202 to discover trade-secret information to determine if it has a claim). The requesting party must show that the presentation of the case on the merits will suffer without the information, likely leading to an unjust result. *In re Union Pac. R.R.*, 294 S.W.3d 589, 592 (Tex.2009); *In re Bridgestone/Firestone*, 106 S.W.3d at 732-33.

        (2) Fraud or injustice. A party cannot assert the trade-secret privilege if doing so will tend to conceal fraud or cause an injustice. TRE 507; *In re Bass*, 113 S.W.3d at 737; *In re Leviton Mfg. Co.*, 1 S.W.3d at 902.

§2.25 Certain information about informant. The United States, Texas, and political subdivisions of Texas have a privilege to not disclose the identity of a person who has furnished information about an investigation of a possible violation of the law. TRE 508(a); *Roviaro v. U.S.*, 353 U.S. 53, 59-60 (1957). However, information about an informant is discoverable in the following situations:

    1. The informant's identity or interest in the subject matter of the communication was disclosed to those who would have cause to resent the communication, by the holder of the privilege or by the informant's own action. TRE 508(c)(1).

    2. The informant appears as a witness for the public entity. *Id.*

───────────────────────────── ★ ─────────────────────────────

3. The informant can testify about a material issue on the merits of a civil case. TRE 508(c)(2). The court must permit the entity with the privilege to present the matter for an in camera hearing, generally by affidavit, to determine whether the informant can supply the testimony. *Id.*

4. The information from an informant is relied on to establish the legality of the means by which evidence was obtained, and the court does not believe that the evidence is reliable or credible. TRE 508(c)(3); Harris, *Informers in Civil Cases*, 31 Houston Lawyer at 32.

§2.26 Shared discovery. The doctrine of shared discovery allows litigants access to discovery in other lawsuits for use in their own suits. ***Eli Lilly & Co. v. Marshall***, 850 S.W.2d 155, 160 (Tex.1993); *see* TRCP 192.3(a) ("any matter that is not privileged").

§2.27 Certain information in journalist's possession. Information obtained or prepared while acting as a journalist is usually not discoverable. *See* CPRC §22.023. See "Journalist's privilege," §3.18, p. 481. But in certain situations, any information, document, or item, or the source of any such information, document, or item, obtained or prepared while acting as a journalist may be discoverable. CPRC §22.024.

1. When information is discoverable. The journalist's privilege does not apply when, after notice and a hearing, a party makes a clear and specific showing of the following:

(1) The party exhausted all reasonable efforts to get the information from other sources. CPRC §22.024(1).

(2) The subpoena compelling the information is not overbroad, unreasonable, or oppressive and, when appropriate, is limited to verifying published information and any circumstances about the accuracy of the published information. *Id.* §22.024(2).

(3) The party gave reasonable and timely notice of the demand for the information. *Id.* §22.024(3).

(4) The interest of the requesting party outweighs the public interest in gathering and disseminating the news. *Id.* §22.024(4).

(5) The subpoena is not being used to obtain peripheral, nonessential, or speculative information. *Id.* §22.024(5).

(6) The information is relevant and material to the proceeding for which the information is sought and is essential for the requesting party's maintenance of a claim or defense. *Id.* §22.024(6).

2. Who may be compelled to disclose. A journalist, the journalist's employer, or an independent contractor of the journalist may be compelled to testify about the information or to produce or disclose it. CPRC §22.024. For the definition of a journalist, see "Journalist," §3.18.1(1), p. 481.

§2.28 Any matter subject to waiver. A party is entitled to discover anything it requested if the other party has waived its objections or claims of privilege. See "Waiver of Sanctions, Discovery & Objections," ch. 6-A, §25, p. 456.

§3. WHAT IS NOT DISCOVERABLE?

To determine what is not discoverable, read TRCP 192, which outlines the scope of discovery and, by implication, the matters outside the scope of discovery. Also read TRE 501-513, which lists the privileges from discovery.

§3.1 Outside scope of discovery. Information is not discoverable if it is not relevant to the subject matter of the pending action or if it will not lead to the discovery of admissible evidence. TRCP 192.3(a); *see* TRE 501. The scope of discovery is confined by the subject matter of the case and reasonable expectations of obtaining information that will help resolve the dispute. TRCP 192 cmt. 1.

§3.2 Limitation on scope of discovery. TRCP 192.4 gives the court power to limit discovery if it determines that (1) the discovery is cumulative or duplicative, (2) the discovery can be obtained from a more convenient source, or (3) the burden or expense of the discovery outweighs its benefits. TRCP 192.4; *see **In re Colonial Pipeline Co.***, 968 S.W.2d 938, 941-42 (Tex.1998) (scope of discovery is largely within trial court's discretion). See "Grounds to limit scope of discovery," ch. 6-A, §20.1, p. 449.

★

§3.3 Work-product privilege. For the definition of work product, see "Work product," ch. 6-A, §2.9, p. 426. The work product of a party or its representatives—including the party's attorneys, consultants, sureties, indemnitors, insurers, employees, or agents—is exempt from discovery. TRCP 192.5(a), (b); *Goode v. Shoukfeh*, 943 S.W.2d 441, 448 (Tex.1997); *National Tank Co. v. Brotherton*, 851 S.W.2d 193, 201 (Tex.1993). The work-product discovery exemption replaced the "attorney work product" and "party communication" exemptions from former TRCP 166b. TRCP 192 cmt. 8. The term "work product" applies only to materials prepared, mental impressions developed, or communications made in anticipation of litigation or for trial. TRCP 192.5(a); *Huie v. DeShazo*, 922 S.W.2d 920, 927 (Tex. 1996); *National Tank*, 851 S.W.2d at 200. The primary purpose of the work-product privilege is to protect the mental processes, conclusions, and legal theories of the attorney and provide a privileged area so the attorney can analyze and prepare the case for trial. *In re Bexar Cty. Crim. Dist. Atty's Office*, 224 S.W.3d 182, 186 (Tex.2007); *Owens-Corning Fiberglas Corp. v. Caldwell*, 818 S.W.2d 749, 750 (Tex.1991); *see* TRCP 192.5(b)(1) (defining "core work product"); *see also National Tank*, 851 S.W.2d at 202-03 n.11 (explanation of work-product privilege under former TRCP 166b(3)(a)). The work-product privilege is essential to the attorney-client relationship. *Occidental Chem. Corp. v. Banales*, 907 S.W.2d 488, 490 (Tex.1995). The work-product privilege promotes the adversary system by safeguarding the fruits of an attorney's trial preparations from the other party. *Wiley v. Williams*, 769 S.W.2d 715, 717 (Tex.App.—Austin 1989, orig. proceeding).

NOTE

*The work-product privilege and the attorney-client privilege are often confused. They cover much of the same material, but with some important differences. The work-product privilege covers work relating to the preparation of the client's lawsuit; the attorney-client privilege covers communications with the client. See **National Tank**, 851 S.W.2d at 200; **Owens-Corning**, 818 S.W.2d at 750. The work-product privilege depends on proof that the materials were prepared in anticipation of litigation or for trial; the attorney-client privilege does not. **National Tank**, 851 S.W.2d at 202; **Boring & Tunneling Co. v. Salazar**, 782 S.W.2d 284, 288 (Tex. App.—Houston [1st Dist.] 1989, orig. proceeding). See "Attorney-client privilege," §3.4, p. 473.*

---

1. Date of occurrence. To qualify as work product, material must have been prepared or mental impressions developed in anticipation of litigation or for trial—that is, after the occurrence or transaction on which the suit is based. *See* TRCP 192.5(a). In most cases, the date of the occurrence is easy to determine—it is the date of the injury. Sometimes, however, it is more difficult. *See, e.g., Jackson v. Downey*, 817 S.W.2d 858, 860 (Tex.App.—Houston [1st Dist.] 1991, orig. proceeding) (in suit against insurance company for refusal to pay medical claim, occurrence was date insurance company denied coverage, not date of surgery); *National Sur. Corp. v. Dominguez*, 715 S.W.2d 67, 68-69 (Tex.App.—Corpus Christi 1986, orig. proceeding) (in suit to recover on surety bond, occurrence was date surety denied coverage).

2. Anticipation of litigation. The materials must have been prepared or the mental impressions developed in anticipation of litigation or for trial. TRCP 192.5(a); *National Tank*, 851 S.W.2d at 202-03. The test to determine whether the party asserting the privilege had good cause to anticipate litigation has two parts:

(1) Objective test. First, the court must determine whether a reasonable person, based on the circumstances at the time of the investigation, would have anticipated litigation. *National Tank*, 851 S.W.2d at 203. "Imminence" of litigation is not a factor. *Id.* at 204. This objective part of the test is satisfied when a reasonable person would conclude from the severity of the accident and other circumstances surrounding it that there is a substantial chance that litigation will follow. *Id.* at 203-04.

(2) Subjective test. Second, the court must make a subjective determination whether the party resisting discovery believed in good faith that there was a substantial chance that litigation would follow and conducted the investigation for the purpose of preparing for the litigation. *National Tank*, 851 S.W.2d at 204. This subjective part of the test examines the defendant-to-be's reaction to circumstances surrounding the occurrence.

✦

> ### NOTE
> *Reports prepared in the ordinary course of business may be exempt from discovery under the anticipation-of-litigation exception. There is no specific rule that makes ordinary-course-of-business documents discoverable. **National Tank**, 851 S.W.2d at 206. The courts must consider the reasons that gave rise to the defendant's ordinary business practice. Id. This does not mean, however, that all the claim files of an insurance company are privileged. Id. at 206 n.13.*

3. Prepared by or for party. To qualify as work product, the materials assembled for litigation must have been prepared by or for a party or a party's representatives, including the party's attorneys, consultants, sureties, indemnitors, insurers, employees, or agents. TRCP 192.5(a)(1); *see **Humphreys v. Caldwell**,* 888 S.W.2d 469, 471 (Tex. 1994); *see, e.g., **Marshall v. Hall**,* 943 S.W.2d 180, 183 (Tex.App.—Houston [1st Dist.] 1997, orig. proceeding) (interview notes prepared by attorney's employee were protected); ***Bearden v. Boone**,* 693 S.W.2d 25, 28 (Tex.App.—Amarillo 1985, orig. proceeding) (investigator's work conducted for attorney was protected). In a criminal prosecution, the work-product privilege extends only to a litigation file that is still active. See "Law-enforcement privilege," §3.22, p. 483.

4. Work product exempt from discovery.

(1) Core work product. Core work product—work product that contains the attorney's (or her representative's) mental impressions, opinions, conclusions, or legal theories—is not discoverable. TRCP 192.5(b)(1); *In re Bexar Cty.,* 224 S.W.3d at 187. The protection for the attorney's thought processes is absolute. *Occidental Chem.,* 907 S.W.2d at 490. The privilege protects the following: • The attorney's litigation file. *National Un. Fire Ins. v. Valdez,* 863 S.W.2d 458, 460 (Tex.1993). • Indexes, notes, and memos prepared by an attorney. *Garcia v. Peeples,* 734 S.W.2d 343, 348 (Tex.1987). • The attorney's notes and correspondence prepared in connection with the lawsuit. *Occidental Chem.,* 907 S.W.2d at 490; *Humphreys,* 888 S.W.2d at 471. • The attorney's notes made during trial. *Goode,* 943 S.W.2d at 449. Core work product is not subject to the need-and-hardship exception in TRCP 192.5(b)(2).

(2) Noncore work product. Noncore work product—work product that does not reflect the attorney's thought processes—is exempt from discovery. However, if the party seeking discovery proves the need-and-hardship exception, noncore work product is discoverable. TRCP 192.5(b)(2). See "Need & hardship exception," §2.13.2, p. 465.

5. Duration. The work-product privilege is perpetual. *Occidental Chem.,* 907 S.W.2d at 490; *Owens-Corning,* 818 S.W.2d at 751-52. This means the attorney's mental impressions and opinions from one suit are not discoverable in another suit. *Humphreys,* 888 S.W.2d at 471; *Owens-Corning,* 818 S.W.2d at 751-52; *Cigna Corp. v. Spears,* 838 S.W.2d 561, 564 (Tex.App.—San Antonio 1992, orig. proceeding); *see In re Bexar Cty.,* 224 S.W.3d at 186 (privilege continues indefinitely beyond suit for which materials were originally prepared).

§3.4 Attorney-client privilege. The purpose of the attorney-client privilege is to foster the client's confidence in the attorney and to encourage free communication between them. *Maryland Am. Gen. Ins. v. Blackmon,* 639 S.W.2d 455, 458 (Tex.1982); *West v. Solito,* 563 S.W.2d 240, 245 (Tex.1978). The attorney-client privilege, a creation of common law now codified in TRE 503(b), ensures that confidential communications between the attorney and the client made for the purpose of rendering legal services will not be disclosed. *In re Ford Motor Co.,* 988 S.W.2d 714, 718 (Tex.1998); *Huie v. DeShazo,* 922 S.W.2d 920, 922 (Tex.1996); *Republic Ins. v. Davis,* 856 S.W.2d 158, 160 (Tex.1993). The attorney-client privilege is the oldest of the privileges for confidential communications known to the common law. *In re XL Specialty Ins.,* 373 S.W.3d 46, 49 (Tex.2012); *In re City of Georgetown,* 53 S.W.3d 328, 332 (Tex.2001). For attorney-client information that is discoverable, see "Certain attorney-client communications," §2.14, p. 466.

———————————————————— ✯ ————————————————————

1. Who is included. The attorney-client privilege covers attorney-client communications between the following persons:

(1) Attorney. Under TRE 503(a)(1), there must be a professional relationship between the attorney and the client. *E.g.*, *Huie*, 922 S.W.2d at 925 (no attorney-client relationship between trustee's attorney and beneficiary); *see also Joe v. Two Thirty Nine Jt.V.*, 145 S.W.3d 150, 164 (Tex.2004) (conducting legal research for city-council vote did not create attorney-client relationship between D and city); *Parker v. Carnahan*, 772 S.W.2d 151, 156 (Tex.App.—Texarkana 1989, writ denied) (signing tax return in attorney's office did not create attorney-client relationship).

(2) Attorney's representative. A representative of the attorney includes a person "employed by the attorney to assist the attorney in the rendition of professional legal services." TRE 503(a)(4)(A); *National Tank Co. v. Brotherton*, 851 S.W.2d 193, 197 (Tex.1993). Secretaries, paralegals, accountants, and investigators are included in this definition. *Bearden v. Boone*, 693 S.W.2d 25, 27-28 (Tex.App.—Amarillo 1985, orig. proceeding).

(3) Client. A "client" is a person, public officer, corporation, association, or other organization or entity, either public or private. TRE 503(a)(1); *see, e.g.*, *Markowski v. City of Marlin*, 940 S.W.2d 720, 726-27 (Tex. App.—Waco 1997, writ denied) (city council's consultation with its attorney in closed session was protected by privilege).

(4) Client's representative. A client's representative includes (1) a person with the authority to obtain legal services or to act on legal advice rendered on the client's behalf, and (2) any other person who, for the purpose of effectuating legal representation for the client, makes or receives a confidential communication while acting in the scope of employment for the client. TRE 503(a)(2); *In re Monsanto Co.*, 998 S.W.2d 917, 922 (Tex. App.—Waco 1999, orig. proceeding) (element 2). TRE 503(a)(2) was amended in 1998, by adding (a)(2)(B), to adopt the subject-matter test. *See* TRE 503 cmt.; *In re Monsanto Co.*, 998 S.W.2d at 922. The subject-matter test covers more types of communications by more people at different levels within a corporation than the old control-group test did. *Ford Motor Co. v. Leggat*, 904 S.W.2d 643, 646 (Tex.1995). For an in-depth discussion of these tests, see Brown & Rondon, *Evidence Handbook*, pp. 391-97.

2. Who may assert. The attorney-client privilege belongs to the client, not the attorney. *West*, 563 S.W.2d at 244 n.2. The attorney-client privilege may be asserted by the client, the client's guardian, the personal representative of a deceased client, or the successor, trustee, or similar representative of the client. TRE 503(c). The attorney is presumed to have the authority to assert the privilege on the client's behalf. *Id.*; *e.g.*, *Cole v. Gabriel*, 822 S.W.2d 296, 296 (Tex.App.—Fort Worth 1991, orig. proceeding) (attorney had no standing to assert attorney-client privilege in his individual capacity).

3. Duration. The attorney-client privilege continues for as long as the client asserts it. *Bearden*, 693 S.W.2d at 27-28; *see Maryland Am.*, 639 S.W.2d at 458. It does not terminate at the conclusion of the employment or the end of the dispute for which the client hired the attorney. *Bearden*, 693 S.W.2d at 27-28. The privilege survives the client's death. *Swidler & Berlin v. U.S.*, 524 U.S. 399, 410 (1998); *see* TRE 503(c).

4. What is protected. The attorney-client privilege will protect information when the communication meets the following criteria:

(1) Attorney-client communication. There must be a communication between the attorney and the client. *See* TRE 503(b). See "Who is included," §3.4.1, this page. The attorney-client privilege applies to the complete communication, including legal advice, opinions, mental analysis, and the specific facts they are based on. *See Pittsburgh Corning Corp. v. Caldwell*, 861 S.W.2d 423, 425 (Tex.App.—Houston [14th Dist.] 1993, orig. proceeding) (attorney-client privilege covers whole document, not just parts relating to legal advice). Not all statements and communications made between a client and an attorney are privileged. *Borden, Inc. v. Valdez*, 773 S.W.2d 718, 720-21 (Tex.App.—Corpus Christi 1989, orig. proceeding) (client's attorney can be deposed but cannot be questioned about privileged matters). A communication made to an attorney after a person was told that no attorney-client relationship would be accepted is not a privileged communication. *McGrede v. Rembert Nat'l Bank*, 147 S.W.2d 580, 584 (Tex.App.—Texarkana 1941, writ dism'd).

───────────────────────────── ✦ ─────────────────────────────

(2) Confidential communication. The communication must be confidential. TRE 503(b)(1). A communication is confidential if it is not intended to be disclosed to third persons. TRE 503(a)(5); *see, e.g., Huie*, 922 S.W.2d at 925 (trustee had expectation that communication to attorney would be confidential). If the communication between the client and the attorney is made in the presence of a third person who is not an agent or representative of the attorney, it is not privileged. *Ledisco Fin. Servs. v. Viracola*, 533 S.W.2d 951, 959 (Tex.App.—Texarkana 1976, no writ).

(3) For legal assistance. The communication must be made to facilitate the rendition of professional legal services. TRE 503(b)(1); *Huie*, 922 S.W.2d at 923. The attorney-client privilege does not apply if the attorney is acting in a capacity other than that of an attorney. *In re Texas Farmers Ins. Exch.*, 990 S.W.2d 337, 340 (Tex.App.—Texarkana 1999, orig. proceeding); *see, e.g., Clayton v. Canida*, 223 S.W.2d 264, 266 (Tex.App.—Texarkana 1949, no writ) (no privilege because attorney was acting as accountant). A person cannot cloak a material fact with the privilege merely by communicating it to an attorney. *Huie*, 922 S.W.2d at 923.

§3.5 Allied-litigant privilege. The allied-litigant privilege is an exception to the rule that disclosure of privileged information to third parties waives the privilege. *In re XL Specialty Ins.*, 373 S.W.3d 46, 50 (Tex.2012). To assert the allied-litigant privilege, the parties must be represented by different attorneys, be parties to a pending litigation, and share a common legal interest. *Id.* at 51-53. However, the privilege only protects communications between a party, its attorney, or a representative of either, to another party's attorney or its attorney's representative about a matter of common interest; it does not protect communications made to the other party. *See* TRE 503(b)(1)(C); *In re XL Specialty*, 373 S.W.3d at 52-53. See Brown & Rondon, *Evidence Handbook*, pp. 376-77.

─────────────────────────────────────

NOTE

*In **In re XL Specialty**, 373 S.W.3d at 50, 52, the Supreme Court stated that although the privilege defined in TRE 503(b)(1)(C) has been called many things by the courts—the "joint-client" privilege, the "joint-defense" privilege, and the "common-interest" privilege—it is most accurately described as the "allied-litigant privilege." These privileges are distinct doctrines that serve different purposes, but only the allied-litigant privilege serves the purpose intended by TRE 503(b)(1)(C). **In re XL Specialty**, 373 S.W.3d at 50, 52. The joint-client privilege can be asserted by parties who are represented by the same attorney in the same matter, while TRE 503(b)(1)(C) requires the parties to have different attorneys. **In re XL Specialty**, 373 S.W.3d at 50, 53. The joint-defense privilege can be asserted only by defendants in pending litigation, but the TRE 503(b)(1)(C) privilege applies to both plaintiffs and defendants. **In re XL Specialty**, 373 S.W.3d at 51-52. The common-interest privilege can be asserted by both litigants and nonlitigants, but the TRE 503(b)(1)(C) privilege applies only to parties to pending litigation. **In re XL Specialty**, 373 S.W.3d at 51-52.*

─────────────────────────────────────

§3.6 Confidential client information. A client's confidential information is protected from discovery because an attorney is prohibited from disclosing it. *See* Tex. Disciplinary R. Prof'l Conduct 1.05(b); *Perez v. Kirk & Carrigan*, 822 S.W.2d 261, 265 (Tex.App.—Corpus Christi 1991, writ denied). Confidential information includes both privileged and unprivileged information. Tex. Disciplinary R. Prof'l Conduct 1.05(a). Rule 1.05 expands privilege from discovery in TRE 503 to include unprivileged information. An attorney may reveal confidential client information only as permitted under Rule 1.05(b), (c), (d), and other rules. *Duncan v. Board of Disciplinary Appeals*, 898 S.W.2d 759, 761 (Tex.1995).

§3.7 Accountant-client privilege. Generally, a communication made by a client to an accountant or to a partner, member, officer, shareholder, or employee of the accountant or the accountant's firm in connection with services provided to the client is confidential and not discoverable. Occ. Code §901.457(a). For information that is discoverable, see "Certain accountant-client communications," §2.15, p. 467. No accountant-client privilege is recognized under federal law. *U.S. v. Arthur Young & Co.*, 465 U.S. 805, 817 (1984).

★

§3.8 Nondiscoverable consulting expert. Consulting experts are protected from discovery as part of the work-product privilege. *See* TRCP 195 cmt. 1. See "Consulting-only expert," ch. 6-D, §2.2.1, p. 503.

§3.9 Husband-wife-communication privilege. The purpose of the husband-wife-communication privilege is to preserve the integrity of the marital relationship. Generally, communications between spouses are privileged and are not subject to discovery. TRE 504. See Brown & Rondon, *Evidence Handbook*, p. 418. For a list of discoverable matters between spouses, see "Certain husband-wife communications," §2.16, p. 467.

1. **Existence of marriage.** The person claiming the husband-wife privilege must prove a marriage. *Cf. Lara v. State*, 740 S.W.2d 823, 837 (Tex.App.—Houston [1st Dist.] 1987, pet. ref'd) (applying former TRCrE 504; held no common-law marriage).

2. **Who may assert.** The husband-wife-communication privilege may be asserted by the person who made the statement, her guardian or representative, or her spouse on her behalf. TRE 504(a)(3). There is a presumption that one spouse has the authority to assert the privilege on the other spouse's behalf. *Id.*

3. **Duration.** The husband-wife-communication privilege survives a divorce or the death of one of the spouses. *Wiggins v. Tiller*, 230 S.W. 253, 254 (Tex.App.—San Antonio 1921, no writ).

4. **What is protected.** The privilege exempts from discovery any husband-wife communication made privately and not intended for disclosure. TRE 504(a)(1).

§3.10 Physician-patient privilege. Generally, a confidential communication between a physician and a patient about the professional services rendered by the physician is privileged and not discoverable. Occ. Code §159.002(a); TRE 509(c); *Mutter v. Wood*, 744 S.W.2d 600, 600 (Tex.1988); *Kavanaugh v. Perkins*, 838 S.W.2d 616, 621 (Tex.App.—Dallas 1992, orig. proceeding); *see also* Health & Safety Code §241.152 (hospital must have written authorization to disclose patient's health-care information). For information that is discoverable, see "Certain physician-patient information," §2.18, p. 468. There are two rationales for the physician-patient privilege: (1) to encourage the full communication necessary for effective treatment, and (2) to prevent the unnecessary disclosure of a patient's highly personal information. *In re Collins*, 286 S.W.3d 911, 916 (Tex.2009); *R.K. v. Ramirez*, 887 S.W.2d 836, 840 (Tex.1994).

1. **Physician.** A physician is a person licensed to practice medicine in any state or nation, or a person the patient reasonably believes to be licensed. TRE 509(a)(2).

2. **Patient.** A patient is any person who consults or is seen by a physician to receive medical care. TRE 509(a)(1); *see, e.g., Tarrant Cty. Hosp. Dist. v. Hughes*, 734 S.W.2d 675, 677 (Tex.App.—Fort Worth 1987, orig. proceeding) (because blood donors were not patients, their identities were not protected by physician-patient privilege). Generally, the physician-patient relationship is voluntary and wholly contractual, created by an express or implied agreement. *E.g., Garay v. County of Bexar*, 810 S.W.2d 760, 764 (Tex.App.—San Antonio 1991, writ denied) (even though person was unconscious, physician-patient relationship was established). However, a physician may agree in advance to the creation of a physician-patient relationship, such as when a physician's agreement with a hospital requires the physician to treat all the hospital's patients. *Lection v. Dyll*, 65 S.W.3d 696, 704 (Tex.App.—Dallas 2001, pet. denied); *see Hand v. Tavera*, 864 S.W.2d 678, 680 (Tex.App.—San Antonio 1993, no writ) (when patient enrolled in prepaid medical plan goes to hospital emergency room and plan's designated doctor is consulted, there is physician-patient relationship).

3. **Who may assert.** The physician-patient privilege may be asserted by the patient, a representative of the patient, or the physician on the patient's behalf. TRE 509(d); *Bristol-Myers Squibb Co. v. Hancock*, 921 S.W.2d 917, 920 (Tex.App.—Houston [14th Dist.] 1996, orig. proceeding). There is a presumption that the doctor has the authority to assert the privilege on the patient's behalf. TRE 509(d)(2).

4. **What is protected.** The privilege protects from discovery confidential communications that are made by the patient and records of the patient's identity, diagnosis, evaluation, or treatment that are created or maintained by a physician in connection with professional services rendered by the physician to the patient. TRE 509(c); *see,*

✦

---

e.g., *In re Columbia Valley Reg'l Med. Ctr.*, 41 S.W.3d 797, 801 (Tex.App.—Corpus Christi 2001, orig. proceeding) (information about nurse's charting customs was privileged because it related to treatment of patient, and redaction of privileged portions of nonparty's medical records did not defeat privilege).

§3.11 Mental-health-information privilege. Generally, a confidential communication made to a mental-health professional is privileged and not discoverable. TRE 510(b)(1); *R.K. v. Ramirez*, 887 S.W.2d 836, 839-40 (Tex. 1994). For information that is discoverable, see "Certain mental-health information," §2.19, p. 469. There are two rationales for the mental-health-information privilege: (1) to encourage the full communication necessary for effective treatment, and (2) to prevent the unnecessary disclosure of a patient's highly personal information. *R.K.*, 887 S.W.2d at 840.

 1. Professional. A mental-health professional is (1) a person authorized to practice medicine in any state or nation, (2) a person licensed or certified by Texas in the diagnosis, evaluation, or treatment of mental or emotional disorders, (3) a person involved in the treatment or examination of drug abusers, or (4) a person the patient reasonably believes is in one of the above categories. TRE 510(a)(1). The definition includes clinical psychologists.

 2. Patient. A patient is any person who consults or is seen by a professional to receive diagnosis, evaluation, or treatment of any mental or emotional condition, including alcoholism and drug addiction, or who is being treated voluntarily for drug abuse. TRE 510(a)(2).

 3. Who may assert. The mental-health-information privilege may be asserted by the patient, a representative of the patient, or the professional on the patient's behalf. TRE 510(c). There is a presumption that the professional has the authority to assert the privilege on the patient's behalf. TRE 510(c)(2).

 4. Duration. The mental-health-information privilege applies regardless of when the professional's services were received. Brown & Rondon, *Evidence Handbook*, p. 492. Confidentiality attaches and continues even if the professional therapeutic relationship predates the existence of the rule, the relationship has ended, or the patient has died. *Id.*

 5. What is protected. The privilege protects from discovery communications by the patient and records of the patient's identity, diagnosis, evaluation, and treatment. TRE 510(b).

§3.12 Other medical privileges. A number of other statutes protect a patient's medical records.

 1. Chiropractor records. The communications and records of a chiropractor's patient are confidential and privileged. Occ. Code §201.402.

 2. Podiatrist records. The communications and records of a podiatrist's patient are confidential and privileged. Occ. Code §202.402.

 3. Dentist records. The communications and records of a dentist's patient are privileged. Occ. Code §258.102.

 4. Results of HIV test. The results of a person's HIV test are confidential and not subject to discovery. *J.K. & Susie L. Wadley Research Inst. & Blood Bank v. Whittington*, 843 S.W.2d 77, 85-86 (Tex.App.—Dallas 1992, orig. proceeding); *see* Health & Safety Code §81.103(a).

 5. Blood-bank records. The medical and donor records of a blood bank are confidential and cannot be disclosed except as permitted under Health & Safety Code chapter 162. Health & Safety Code §162.003; *see, e.g.*, *Tarrant Cty. Hosp. Dist. v. Curry*, 907 S.W.2d 445, 445-46 (Tex.1995) (donor's birth date is confidential).

 6. EMS-patient communications & records. The communications and records of a patient treated by emergency-medical-services personnel or by a physician providing medical supervision are confidential and privileged. Health & Safety Code §773.091.

 7. Hospital patient's privilege. A hospital and its agents or employees may not disclose health-care information about a patient except as provided in Health & Safety Code §§241.152 and 241.153. For the categories of information that are discoverable from a hospital, see "Certain health-care information from hospital," §2.23, p. 470.

✬

§3.13 Peer-review & medical-committee privileges. Occupations Code §160.007(e) (for peer review) and Health & Safety Code §161.032 (for medical committee) limit the discovery of documents from medical institutions. In analyzing these two statutory exemptions from discovery, attorneys should read these four Supreme Court cases: *In re University of Tex. Health Ctr.*, 33 S.W.3d 822, 824-27 (Tex.2000) (discovery requested by third party); *Brownwood Reg'l Hosp. v. Eleventh Ct. of Appeals*, 927 S.W.2d 24, 26-27 (Tex.1996) (same); *Irving Healthcare Sys. v. Brooks*, 927 S.W.2d 12, 16-17 (Tex.1996) (discovery requested by doctor); *Memorial Hosp. v. McCown*, 927 S.W.2d 1, 12 (Tex.1996) (discovery requested by third party).

1. Information exempt from discovery.

(1) Peer-review committee. Peer-review proceedings are confidential, and communications to a peer-review committee are privileged. Occ. Code §160.007(a). The peer-review privilege in the Occupations Code applies to professional-review actions or medical peer review conducted by a professional-review body or medical-peer-review committee. *Id.* §160.001.

(a) Protected entities. The term "medical-peer-review committee" or "professional-review body" means a committee of a health-care entity, of the governing board of a health-care entity, or of the medical staff of a health-care entity, that (1) operates under written bylaws approved by the policy-making body or the governing board of the health-care entity, and (2) is authorized to evaluate the quality of medical and health-care services or the competence of physicians, including evaluation of the performance of the functions specified by Health & Safety Code §85.204. Occ. Code §151.002(a)(8); *see Martinez v. Abbott Labs. & Abbott Labs.*, 146 S.W.3d 260, 265-66 (Tex.App.—Fort Worth 2004, pet. denied). For a list of people and entities included in the medical-peer-review committee, see Occupations Code §151.002(a)(8).

(b) The privilege. The peer-review privilege provides that medical-peer-review records (1) are not subject to subpoena or discovery, and (2) are not admissible as evidence in any civil, judicial, or administrative proceeding without a written waiver of the privilege of confidentiality, "unless disclosure is required or authorized by law." Occ. Code §160.007(e); *In re University of Tex. Health Ctr.*, 33 S.W.3d at 827; *Memorial Hosp.*, 927 S.W.2d at 4; *see Irving Healthcare*, 927 S.W.2d at 16-17. Records, reports, evaluations, and recommendations received, maintained, or developed by a peer-review committee are privileged from discovery. Occ. Code §160.007(e); *e.g.*, *Brownwood Reg'l*, 927 S.W.2d at 27 (peer-review documents were privileged even though patient sued hospital for malpractice); *Irving Healthcare*, 927 S.W.2d at 16-17 (peer-review documents were privileged even though doctor sued other doctor for maliciously providing false information to peer-review committee); *Memorial Hosp.*, 927 S.W.2d at 4 (peer-review documents were privileged even though media-D in libel case sought peer-review documents to defend itself); *see In re Living Ctrs.*, 175 S.W.3d 253, 258 & n.4 (Tex.2005) (peer-review privilege protects the evaluative process, including discussions about future committee operating procedures).

(c) Waiver of privilege. The privilege may be waived in writing by the chair, vice chair, or secretary of the peer-review committee. Occ. Code §160.007(e), (g); *see In re University of Tex. Health Ctr.*, 33 S.W.3d at 827; *Irving Healthcare*, 927 S.W.2d at 16-17.

(2) Medical committee.

(a) Protected entities. The term "medical committee" means any committee of a hospital, medical organization, university medical school or health-science center, HMO, extended-care facility, hospital district, or hospital authority, including ad hoc and joint committees. Health & Safety Code §161.031(a), (b).

(b) The privilege. The medical-committee privilege provides that records and proceedings of medical committees are confidential and are not subject to court subpoena. Health & Safety Code §161.032(a); *In re University of Tex. Health Ctr.*, 33 S.W.3d at 827; *Memorial Hosp.*, 927 S.W.2d at 8.

2. What is not exempt. Not all information reviewed by the committee is exempt from discovery.

(1) Disclosure required by law. Medical-peer-review records are discoverable and admissible into evidence when their "disclosure is required or authorized by law." Occ. Code §160.007(e); *In re University of Tex.*

⎯⎯⎯⎯⎯⎯⎯⎯⎯ ✦ ⎯⎯⎯⎯⎯⎯⎯⎯⎯

Health Ctr., 33 S.W.3d at 827; *Memorial Hosp.*, 927 S.W.2d at 4; *see Irving Healthcare*, 927 S.W.2d at 16-17. When disclosure is required by law and that disclosure is itself privileged, the privilege is not waived by the disclosure. Occ. Code §160.007(d)-(g); *see In re University of Tex. Health Ctr.*, 33 S.W.3d at 827. When a protected entity responds to discovery with privileged information, that limited waiver does not extend to other privileged information. *See In re University of Tex. Health Ctr.*, 33 S.W.3d at 827 (voluntary production of information about committee recommendations does not waive privilege protecting committee documents themselves). For a list of disclosures authorized by law, see Occupations Code §§160.002 and 160.007.

(2) Business records & other documents. The business records of a hospital, HMO, medical organization, university medical center or health-science center, hospital district, hospital authority, or extended-care facility are discoverable. Health & Safety Code §161.032(f); *Irving Healthcare*, 927 S.W.2d at 18; *see Memorial Hosp.*, 927 S.W.2d at 10-11 (business records must be treated the same under Health & Safety Code §161.032 and Occupations Code §160.007); *see, e.g., In re Osteopathic Med. Ctr.*, 16 S.W.3d 881, 886 (Tex.App.—Fort Worth 2000, orig. proceeding) (incident report on slip-and-fall submitted to peer-review committee was discoverable). For other exceptions, see chart 6-5, below.

3. Application of exemption. The extent of the exemption from discovery depends on whether the party seeking discovery from the committee is the doctor who was investigated by the committee or a third party, generally the plaintiff in a medical-malpractice suit. See chart 6-5, below.

	6-5. MEDICAL-COMMITTEE PRIVILEGES		
	Information sought in discovery	**Is information discoverable by—**	
		Doctor who was investigated?	**Party who sued doctor?**
1	Committee's final decision to censure, revoke, etc., membership or privileges in health-care entity	Yes. Occ. §160.007(d); *Irving Healthcare*, 927 S.W.2d 12, 18 (Tex.1996).	No. *See* Occ. §160.007(d), (e); *Irving Healthcare*, 927 S.W.2d at 18.
2	Committee documents relating to peer review, other than those in row 1, above	No. *See* Occ. §160.007(a); H&S §161.032(a); *Irving Healthcare*, 927 S.W.2d at 18.	No. *See* Occ. §160.007(a); H&S §161.032(a); *Irving Healthcare*, 927 S.W.2d at 18.
3	Committee's initial credentialing of doctor	No. *Brownwood Reg'l*, 927 S.W.2d 24, 26-27 (Tex.1996); *Memorial Hosp.*, 927 S.W.2d 1, 11 (Tex.1996); *see* H&S §161.032(a).	No. *Brownwood Reg'l*, 927 S.W.2d at 26-27; *Memorial Hosp.*, 927 S.W.2d at 11; *see* H&S §161.032(a).
4	Committee's minutes of meetings	No. *Brownwood Reg'l*, 927 S.W.2d at 27; *Memorial Hosp.*, 927 S.W.2d at 10; *see* H&S §161.032(a).	No. *Brownwood Reg'l*, 927 S.W.2d at 27; *Memorial Hosp.*, 927 S.W.2d at 10; *see* H&S §161.032(a).
5	Documents created by or at request of committee to evaluate medical care	No. *In re UT Health*, 33 S.W.3d 822, 825 (Tex.2000); *see Brownwood Reg'l*, 927 S.W.2d at 27.	No. *In re UT Health*, 33 S.W.3d at 825; *see Brownwood Reg'l*, 927 S.W.2d at 27.
6	Documents provided by doctor to committee, including application	Yes. *Irving Healthcare*, 927 S.W.2d at 21.	No. *Irving Healthcare*, 927 S.W.2d at 21.
7	Doctor- or hospital-generated patient medical records, in possession of committee	Yes. ❶ *Irving Healthcare*, 927 S.W.2d at 18; *see* H&S §161.032(c); *Memorial Hosp.*, 927 S.W.2d at 9-10.	Yes. ❶ *Irving Healthcare*, 927 S.W.2d at 18; *see* H&S §161.032(c); *Memorial Hosp.*, 927 S.W.2d at 9-10.
8	Health-care facility's business records in possession of committee	Yes. ❷ H&S §161.032(c); *Irving Healthcare*, 927 S.W.2d at 18; *Memorial Hosp.*, 927 S.W.2d at 9.	Yes. ❷ H&S §161.032(c); *Irving Healthcare*, 927 S.W.2d at 18; *Memorial Hosp.*, 927 S.W.2d at 9.
9	Documents in public domain reviewed by committee	Yes. *Irving Healthcare*, 927 S.W.2d at 18.	Yes. *Irving Healthcare*, 927 S.W.2d at 18.

─────────────── ✦ ───────────────

	Information sought in discovery	Is information discoverable by—	
		Doctor who was investigated?	**Party who sued doctor?**
		6-5. MEDICAL-COMMITTEE PRIVILEGES (CONTINUED)	
10	Committee's documents when doctor waives privilege	No. *See* Occ. §160.007(e); *Irving Healthcare*, 927 S.W.2d at 16-17.	No. *See* Occ. §160.007(e); *Irving Healthcare*, 927 S.W.2d at 16-17.
11	Committee's documents when committee waives privilege in writing	Yes. Occ. §160.007(e); *Irving Healthcare*, 927 S.W.2d at 16-17.	Yes. Occ. §160.007(e); *Irving Healthcare*, 927 S.W.2d at 16-17.
12	Documents provided to committee shared with persons not covered by privilege	Yes. ❷ *Irving Healthcare*, 927 S.W.2d at 18.	Yes. ❷ *Irving Healthcare*, 927 S.W.2d at 18.
13	Committee's documents sought in anticompetitive actions or in civil-rights suits brought under 42 U.S.C. §1983	Yes. Occ. §160.007(b); *Irving Healthcare*, 927 S.W.2d at 16.	Yes. Occ. §160.007(b); *Irving Healthcare*, 927 S.W.2d at 16.
14	Bylaws, rules, and regulations of hospital's medical staff or board of trustees	Yes. *Brownwood Reg'l*, 927 S.W.2d at 27.	Yes. *Brownwood Reg'l*, 927 S.W.2d at 27.
15	Deposition of committee member about committee deliberations	No. *Irving Healthcare*, 927 S.W.2d at 18.	No. *Irving Healthcare*, 927 S.W.2d at 18.

❶ The information is discoverable unless subject to some other privilege (e.g., physician-patient) but must be obtained from some source other than the committee.

❷ The information is discoverable but must be obtained from some source other than the committee.

4. Other peer-review committees. There are a number of other peer-review discovery exemptions that protect records created by peer-review committees of nonphysicians. *E.g.*, Occ. Code §202.454 (podiatric peer review), §261.051 (dental peer review), §303.006 (nursing peer review).

§3.14   Trade-secret privilege. Generally, a person has a qualified privilege to refuse to disclose and to prevent other persons from disclosing a trade secret that the person owns. TRE 507; *In re Continental Gen. Tire, Inc.*, 979 S.W.2d 609, 613 (Tex.1998); *see also* TRCP 76a(2)(c) (court records open to public do not include discovery in cases initiated to preserve bona fide trade secrets). See Brown & Rondon, *Evidence Handbook*, p. 449. Discoverable documents cannot, however, be shielded from discovery by placing them in a file with trade secrets. *See Chapa v. Garcia*, 848 S.W.2d 667, 668 (Tex.1992). For the definition of a trade secret, and a discussion of when a trade secret is discoverable, see "Certain trade secrets," §2.24, p. 470.

§3.15   Privilege against self-incrimination. A person cannot be compelled to give self-incriminating evidence in a criminal proceeding. U.S. Const. amend. 5; Tex. Const. art. 1, §10. A witness (whether a party or a nonparty) has the right to assert the Fifth Amendment privilege to avoid civil discovery if the witness has a reasonable fear that the answers might be incriminating. *Texas DPS Officers Ass'n v. Denton*, 897 S.W.2d 757, 760 (Tex.1995); *Gebhardt v. Gallardo*, 891 S.W.2d 327, 330 (Tex.App.—San Antonio 1995, orig. proceeding). The Fifth Amendment privilege against self-incrimination also applies to document production, as long as the incriminating documents are personally connected to the witness. *In re Speer*, 965 S.W.2d 41, 47 (Tex.App.—Fort Worth 1998, orig. proceeding). That is, the documents must have been written by the witness or under the witness's immediate supervision. *Id.* The person asserting the Fifth Amendment privilege must raise it in response to each specific inquiry, or the privilege is waived.

1. Remedial steps & sanctions. If a party refuses on Fifth Amendment grounds to comply with a discovery order, the court should consider remedial steps short of sanctions; if they are not effective, the court can impose graduated levels of sanctions, up to and including death-penalty sanctions. *Denton*, 897 S.W.2d at 759.

2. Adverse impact. There are a number of adverse consequences to invoking the Fifth Amendment in discovery. First, the deposition of a witness in which she invoked the Fifth Amendment can be read into evidence.

✦

Smith v. Smith, 720 S.W.2d 586, 594-95 (Tex.App.—Houston [1st Dist.] 1986, no writ). Second, in a civil trial, a party can be forced to invoke the Fifth Amendment in front of a jury. Brown & Rondon, *Evidence Handbook*, p. 531. Third, the jury can be asked to draw an inference against the party who invoked the Fifth Amendment. TRE 513(c); *see Baxter v. Palmigiano*, 425 U.S. 308, 318 (1976); *Wilz v. Flournoy*, 228 S.W.3d 674, 677 (Tex.2007); *In re Edge Capital Grp.*, 161 S.W.3d 764, 769 (Tex.App.—Beaumont 2005, orig. proceeding). Fourth, the party's invocation of the Fifth Amendment may be the subject of comment by the other party. TRE 513(c).

§3.16 Clergy privilege. Confidential communications are privileged if they are made to a member of the clergy "in the member's professional character as spiritual advisor." TRE 505(b). See Brown & Rondon, *Evidence Handbook*, p. 442.

1. Member of clergy. The term "member of the clergy" includes a minister, priest, rabbi, accredited Christian Science Practitioner, or other similar functionary of a religious organization, or an individual that a communicant reasonably believes is a member of the clergy. TRE 505(a)(1).

2. Who may assert. The communicant, her guardian or conservator, or her personal representative (if she is deceased) may assert the clergy privilege. TRE 505(c). The clergy member to whom the communication was made is presumed to have authority to assert the privilege on the communicant's behalf. *Id.*

3. What is protected. The privilege protects confidential communications made privately and not intended for further disclosure except to other people present in furtherance of the purpose of the communication. TRE 505(a)(2); *see, e.g., Nicholson v. Wittig*, 832 S.W.2d 681, 685 (Tex.App.—Houston [1st Dist.] 1992, orig. proceeding) (clergy privilege includes all conversations with hospital chaplain, even secular ones conducted when other people are present). The clergy privilege may protect the identity of the communicant. *Simpson v. Tennant*, 871 S.W.2d 301, 306 (Tex.App.—Houston [14th Dist.] 1994, orig. proceeding).

§3.17 ADR privilege. Generally, any communication about the subject matter of a dispute made by any participant in an alternative-dispute-resolution procedure is confidential and not subject to disclosure. See "Confidentiality," ch. 4-A, §7, p. 282.

§3.18 Journalist's privilege. Generally, information obtained by a journalist is privileged and not discoverable. *See* CPRC §22.023. The rationale for the journalist's privilege is to (1) increase the free flow of information, (2) preserve a free and active press, and (3) protect the public's right to effective law enforcement and the fair administration of justice. *Id.* §22.022. For a discussion of when information from a journalist is discoverable, see "Certain information in journalist's possession," §2.27, p. 471.

1. Who is protected.

(1) Journalist. A journalist is protected from being compelled to disclose information. *See* CPRC §22.023(a). The term "journalist" is defined as the following:

(a) A person or a parent, subsidiary, division, or affiliate of a person who "gathers, compiles, prepares, collects, photographs, records, writes, edits, reports, investigates, processes, or publishes" information that is disseminated by a news medium (see "News medium," §3.18.1(2)(a), p. 482) or communication-service provider (see "Communication-service provider," §3.18.1(2)(b), p. 482) for a substantial portion of her livelihood or for substantial financial gain. CPRC §22.021(2).

(b) A person who supervises or assists in gathering, preparing, and disseminating information. *Id.*

(c) A journalist, scholar, or researcher employed by an institution of higher education at the time she obtained or prepared the information. *Id.*

(d) A person who at the time she obtained or prepared the information (1) earned a significant portion of her livelihood by obtaining or preparing information for dissemination by a news medium or communication-service provider or (2) was an agent, assistant, employee, or supervisor of a news medium or communication-service provider. *Id.*

★

(2) News medium or communication-service provider. A parent, subsidiary, division, or affiliate of a news medium or communication-service provider is protected from being compelled to disclose information. CPRC §22.023(b).

(a) News medium. A news medium is an entity that disseminates news or information to the public through print, television, radio, or photographic, mechanical, electronic, or other means that are accessible to the public. CPRC §22.021(3). A news medium includes the following: (1) a newspaper, magazine, or periodical, (2) a book publisher, (3) a news agency, (4) a wire service, (5) a radio or television station or network, (6) a cable, satellite, or other transmission system, carrier, or channel, (7) a channel or programming service for a station, network, system, or carrier, (8) an audio or audiovisual production company, (9) an Internet company or provider, or (10) a parent, subsidiary, division, or affiliate of such an entity. *Id.*

(b) Communication-service provider. A communication-service provider is a person or a parent, subsidiary, division, or affiliate of a person who transmits information chosen by a customer through electronic means. CPRC §22.021(1). A communication-service provider includes the following: (1) a telecommunications carrier, (2) an information-service provider, (3) an interactive-computer-service provider, and (4) an information-content provider. *Id.*; *see also* 47 U.S.C. §153 (defining telecommunications carrier and information-service provider), §230 (defining interactive-computer-service provider and information-content provider).

2. What is protected. The privilege protects (1) any information, document, or item—regardless of its confidentiality—obtained or prepared while acting as a journalist, and (2) the source of any such information, document, or item. CPRC §22.023.

3. When privilege applies. The privilege applies during an official proceeding before a public servant. *See* CPRC §§22.021(4), 22.023(a).

(1) Official proceeding. An official proceeding means any administrative, executive, legislative, or judicial proceeding, including presuit depositions and arbitrations. *See* CPRC §22.021(4), (5)(C); Watler, *The Texas Journalist Shield Law*, 72 Tex.B.J. at 687.

(2) Public servant. A public servant is a person elected, selected, appointed, employed, or designated as one of the following, even if the person has not qualified for office or begun her duties: (1) a government officer, employee, or agent, (2) a juror, (3) an arbitrator, referee, or other person authorized by law or a written agreement to hear or decide a controversy, (4) an attorney or notary public performing a governmental function, or (5) a person performing a governmental function under a claim of right, although not legally qualified to do so. CPRC §22.021(5).

4. No waiver. Publication or dissemination of the privileged information by a news medium or communication-service provider does not waive the journalist's privilege. CPRC §22.026.

§3.19 Political vote. No person can be forced to disclose her vote in a political election conducted by secret ballot, unless the vote was cast illegally. TRE 506. A person who casts an illegal vote does not have a privilege to refuse to disclose the vote; an illegal voter is not considered a "voter" for any purpose. *Oliphint v. Christy*, 299 S.W.2d 933, 939 (Tex.1957); *Simmons v. Jones*, 838 S.W.2d 298, 300 (Tex.App.—El Paso 1992, no writ).

§3.20 Reports required by law. Any person or entity required by law to make a report has a privilege to refuse to disclose the contents of the report if the law requiring the report permits the person to refuse to disclose it. TRE 502. The purpose of this privilege is to enhance the government's ability to obtain self-reporting information. The rule protects reports "required by law to be made" if the law requiring the report to be made makes such a report privileged. *See Star-Telegram, Inc. v. Schattman*, 784 S.W.2d 109, 111 (Tex.App.—Fort Worth 1990, orig. proceeding) (EEOC sexual-harassment guidelines in 29 C.F.R. §1604.11 do not require a report, and thus an internal investigation was not exempt from discovery under TRE 502).

§3.21 Social Security information. The Social Security Act provides that information obtained by the Secretary of Health and Human Services or the Secretary of Labor or any employee of either must not be disclosed, except as provided by regulation. 42 U.S.C. §1306(a). The statute does not say who can assert the privilege or how it is waived. *Texas Employers' Ins. v. Jackson*, 719 S.W.2d 245, 247 (Tex.App.—El Paso 1986, writ ref'd n.r.e.).

———————————— ★ ————————————

§3.22 Law-enforcement privilege.

NOTE

In 2007, the Legislature enacted CPRC §30.006, which is similar to Gov't Code §552.108. The bill analysis for CPRC §30.006 does not mention the Government Code section or indicate which section should apply when the sections overlap. Senate Research Center, Bill Analysis, Tex. H.B. 1572, 80th Leg., R.S. (2007).

---

1. Under Government Code.

(1) Information about crime. Information about detection, investigation, or prosecution of a crime and records or notations maintained for internal use in matters relating to law enforcement or prosecution are not discoverable if the law-enforcement agency or prosecutor can show one of the following:

(a) The release of information would interfere with the detection, investigation, or prosecution of a crime, or the release of internal records or notations would interfere with law enforcement or prosecution. Gov't Code §552.108(a)(1) (release of information), §552.108(b)(1) (release of internal records or notations).

(b) The information relates only to an investigation that did not result in conviction or deferred adjudication. *Id.* §552.108(a)(2), (b)(2).

(c) The information relates to a threat against a peace officer or detention officer that was collected or distributed under Gov't Code §411.048. *Id.* §552.108(a)(3).

(d) The information was prepared by an attorney for the State in anticipation of or in the course of preparing for criminal litigation. *Id.* §552.108(a)(4)(A), (b)(3)(A). In a criminal prosecution, the work-product privilege extends only to a litigation file that is still active. *See, e.g.*, **State v. Walker**, 873 S.W.2d 379, 380-81 (Tex. 1994) (case still active when Ds received deferred adjudication and probation).

(e) The information reflects the mental impressions or legal reasoning of an attorney representing the State. Gov't Code §552.108(a)(4)(B), (b)(3)(B). See "Work-product privilege," §3.3, p. 472.

(2) Exception. Basic information about an arrested person, an arrest, or a crime is considered public information and is discoverable. Gov't Code §552.108(c). Although "basic information" is not defined in the Government Code, the courts have held that it includes the arrestee's name, alias, Social Security number, race, sex, age, occupation, physical condition, name of arresting officer, and the charge, as well as a detailed description of the offense. **Thomas v. Cornyn**, 71 S.W.3d 473, 479 (Tex.App.—Austin 2002, no pet.).

2. Under CPRC.

(1) Information regarding crime. Information, records, documents, evidentiary materials, and tangible things from a nonparty law-enforcement agency are not discoverable if the following are shown:

(a) The information, records, documents, evidentiary materials, or tangible things deal with (1) the detection, investigation, or prosecution of a crime, or (2) an investigation by the nonparty law-enforcement agency that does not result in conviction or deferred adjudication. CPRC §30.006(c)(1).

(b) The release of the information, records, documents, evidentiary materials, or tangible things would interfere with the detection, investigation, or prosecution of criminal acts. *Id.* §30.006(c)(2).

(2) Exceptions.

(a) By motion. On a party's motion, a court can order discovery of information, records, documents, evidentiary materials, or tangible things from a nonparty law-enforcement agency if the court determines, after an in camera inspection, that (1) the discovery sought is relevant and (2) there is a specific need for the discovery. CPRC §30.006(d).

★

(b) By law. CPRC §30.006 does not apply to (1) actions in which a law-enforcement agency is a party, (2) a report of an accident under Transportation Code ch. 550, or (3) photographs, field measurements, scene drawings, and accident reconstruction done in conjunction with the investigation of the underlying accident. CPRC §30.006(b), (e).

§3.23 Identity of informant. The United States, Texas, and political subdivisions of Texas have the privilege to refuse to disclose the identity of a person who has furnished information about an investigation of a possible violation of the law. TRE 508(a); *Roviaro v. U.S.*, 353 U.S. 53, 59-60 (1957); *see also State v. Lowry*, 802 S.W.2d 669, 673 (Tex.1991) (discussing informant and investigative privileges). For discoverable information about an informant, see "Certain information about informant," §2.25, p. 470.

§3.24 Disclosure of membership list. The First Amendment protects the right of association, which in turn protects from discovery the membership list of an organization engaged in the advocacy of particular beliefs. *NAACP v. Alabama*, 357 U.S. 449, 462-63 (1958); *Ex parte Lowe*, 887 S.W.2d 1, 2 (Tex.1994). Before a court may order disclosure of the membership list of an organization engaged in the advocacy of particular beliefs, the party seeking the list must show a compelling state interest. *Ex parte Lowe*, 887 S.W.2d at 3; *Tilton v. Moye*, 869 S.W.2d 955, 956 (Tex.1994); *Martin v. Khoury*, 843 S.W.2d 163, 167 (Tex.App.—Texarkana 1992, orig. proceeding).

§3.25 Environmental-audit privilege. The Texas Environmental, Health, & Safety Audit Privilege Act creates a documentary privilege for environmental audits and assessments conducted at real-property operations and facilities in Texas. *See* TRCS art. 4447cc, §5. The privilege may be waived only by the owner or operator of the land. *Id.* §6(a). See the EPA's policy statement on audit privileges, "Voluntary Environmental Self-Policing & Self-Disclosure Interim Policy Statement," 60 Fed. Reg. 16875 (4-3-95).

§3.26 Public Information Act. If documents or other information are privileged or confidential under the TRCPs or the TREs, they are confidential under the Public Information Act (formerly known as the Open Records Act). *Texas DPS v. Cox Tex. Newspapers, L.P.*, 343 S.W.3d 112, 114 & n.4 (Tex.2011); *see* Gov't Code §§552.022, 552.101; *In re City of Georgetown*, 53 S.W.3d 328, 331-32 (Tex.2001); *see also City of Dallas v. Abbott*, 304 S.W.3d 380, 381 (Tex.2010) (city's request to Attorney General claiming exception to public-disclosure requirement was timely under Gov't Code §552.301; attorney-client privilege protected documents from public disclosure).

§3.27 Legislative privilege. People acting in a legislative capacity generally cannot be compelled to testify about their legislative activities. *In re Perry*, 60 S.W.3d 857, 860 (Tex.2001).

§3.28 Privileges of foreign jurisdictions. When the laws of a foreign jurisdiction protect relevant information from discovery, the court must balance the interest of the Texas court with that of the foreign nation. *Volkswagen, A.G. v. Valdez*, 909 S.W.2d 900, 902 (Tex.1995). The court must weigh the following factors: (1) the importance of the discovery request to the investigation or litigation, (2) the degree of specificity of the request, (3) whether the information originated in the United States, (4) the availability of alternative means of securing the information, and (5) the extent to which noncompliance with the request would undermine important interests of the United States, or the extent to which compliance would undermine important interests of the foreign jurisdiction where the information is located. *Id.*; *see* Restatement (3d) of Foreign Relations Law §442(1)(c) (1987).

✮

C. ELECTRONIC DISCOVERY

§1. GENERAL

§1.1 Rules. TRCP 192.3(b), 196.4.

§1.2 Purpose. Electronic discovery (or e-discovery) involves the process of collecting, preparing, reviewing, and producing discoverable information that is stored in electronic, magnetic, or digital form. *See Sedona Conference Glossary: E-Discovery & Digital Information Management (Third Edition)*, at 18 (Sedona Conference Working Group Series, 2010), www.thesedonaconference.org/publications; *Sedona Principles Addressing Electronic Document Production, Second Edition*, at 1 (Sedona Conference Working Group Series, 2007), www.thesedonaconference.org /publications; Van Duizend, *Electronic Discovery: Questions & Answers*, at 1, 3 Civil Action 2 (2004), www.ncsconline .org/Projects_Initiatives/Images/CivilActionSummer04.pdf. Electronic discovery requires, at the very least, an understanding of (1) the systems for creating, storing, and reading electronic data, (2) the methods for preserving electronic data, (3) the methods for searching, identifying, and producing relevant electronic data, and (4) the traditional discovery methods for obtaining and producing electronic data and the evidentiary implications of those methods. Unfortunately, the TRCPs and the CPRC do not provide a comprehensive scheme for electronic discovery. Although the 1999 amendments to TRCP 196.4 provided some guidelines on discovering and producing "electronic or magnetic data," the TRCPs remain silent on many (and often costly) issues involving electronic discovery and the means for resolving electronic-discovery disputes. Thus, the process for electronic discovery in Texas is a collection of informal guidelines with few statutory or decisional rules.

NOTE

The TRCPs were amended in 1999 and the FRCPs were amended in 2006 to include specific rules on electronic discovery. Federal cases construing the FRCPs provide some guidance on electronic-discovery issues, but the TRCPs and FRCPs differ in several substantive ways. For a discussion of federal electronic-discovery rules, see **O'Connor's Federal Rules * Civil Trials** *(2013), "Electronic Discovery," ch. 6-C, p. 481. Although few reported Texas cases address electronic discovery, in 2009 the Texas Supreme Court issued* **In re Weekley Homes, L.P.**, *295 S.W.3d 309 (Tex. 2009), detailing an extensive procedure for requesting production of electronic information. See "Requests for production," §8.1.5, p. 498.*

---

§1.3 Forms. *O'Connor's Texas Civil Forms* (2012), FORMS 2A:1 (preservation letter), 6A:1 (rule 11 agreed preservation plan), 6A:10 (motion for protective order), 6A:23 (motion to compel); *O'Connor's Federal Civil Forms* (2012), 6A:3 (stipulated preservation plan and order), 6A:4 (stipulated discovery plan and order) (*O'Connor's Federal Forms*).

§1.4 Other references.

1. **Sedona Conference.**

• *Sedona Conference Cooperation Proclamation: Resources for the Judiciary* (Sedona Conference Working Group Series, 2011), www.thesedonaconference.org/publications.

• *Sedona Conference "Jumpstart Outline": Questions to Ask Your Client and Your Adversary to Prepare for Preservation, Rule 26 Obligations, Court Conferences and Requests for Production* (Sedona Conference Working Group Series, 2011), www.thesedonaconference.org/publications (referred to as *Sedona Conference "Jumpstart Outline"*).

• *Sedona Conference Cooperation Guidance for Litigators & In-House Counsel* (Sedona Conference Working Group Series, 2011), www.thesedonaconference.org/publications.

• *Sedona Conference Glossary: E-Discovery & Digital Information Management (Third Edition)* (Sedona Conference Working Group Series, 2010), www.thesedonaconference.org/publications (referred to as *Sedona Conference Glossary*).

———————————————— ✦ ————————————————

- *Sedona Conference Cooperation Proclamation* (Sedona Conference Working Group Series, 2008), www.thesedonaconference.org/publications.

- *Sedona Principles Addressing Electronic Document Production, Second Edition* (Sedona Conference Working Group Series, 2007) (referred to as *Sedona Principles, Second Edition*), www.thesedonaconference.org /publications.

- *Navigating the Vendor Proposal Process: Best Practices for the Selection of Electronic Discovery Vendors (Second Edition)* (Sedona Conference Working Group Series, 2007), www.thesedonaconference.org/ publications (referred to as *Navigating the Vendor Proposal Process*).

2. Standards & guidelines.

- Conference of Chief Justices, *Guidelines for State Trial Courts Regarding Discovery of Electronically-Stored Information* (2006), www.ncsconline.org/images/EDiscCCJGuidelinesFinal.pdf (referred to as Conference of Chief Justices, *Guidelines for State Trial Courts*).

- National Conference of Commissioners on Uniform State Laws, *Uniform Rules Relating to the Discovery of Electronically Stored Information* (2007), www.uniformlaws.org/shared/docs/discovery%20of% 20electronically%20stored%20information/urrdoesi_final_07.pdf (referred to as NCCUSL, *Uniform Rules*).

- Rothstein et al., *Managing Discovery of Electronic Information: A Pocket Guide for Judges*, Federal Judicial Center (2d ed. 2012), www.fjc.gov (referred to as Rothstein, *Managing Discovery of Electronic Information*).

3. White papers.

- Feldman, *Collecting and Preserving Electronic Media*, www.forensicfocus.com/collecting-preserving-electronic-media.

- Isom, *Electronic Discovery Primer for Judges* (2005), Federal Courts Law Review, www.fclr.org/fclr /articles/html/2005/fedctslrev1.pdf.

- Scheindlin, *The Ten Most FAQ's in the Post-December 1, 2006 World of E-Discovery* (2006), In Camera (Fed. Judges Ass'n), www.fjc.gov/public/pdf.nsf/lookup/FAQEDisc.pdf/$file/FAQEDisc.pdf (referred to as Scheindlin, *Ten Most FAQ's*).

4. Additional references.

- Ball, *E-Discovery: A Special Master's Perspective*, 51 The Advocate: State Bar Litigation Section Report 42 (Summer 2010) (referred to as Ball, *A Special Master's Perspective*).

- Chaumette, *Electronic Discovery: Legal Issues & Practical Challenges*, Advanced Evidence & Discovery Course, State Bar of Texas CLE, ch. 3 (2012) (referred to as Chaumette, *Legal Issues & Practical Challenges*).

- Hecht, *Taking Point on E-Discovery: Texas Rule of Civil Procedure 196.4*, 51 The Advocate: State Bar Litigation Section Report 18 (Summer 2010) (referred to as Hecht, *Taking Point on E-Discovery*).

- Hedges, *Discovery of Electronically Stored Information: Surveying the Legal Landscape* (BNA Books, 2007) (referred to as Hedges, *Discovery of Electronically Stored Information*).

- Henderson, *The Duty to Preserve Electronic Data*, 66 Tex.B.J. 24 (Jan.2003) (referred to as Henderson, *Duty to Preserve*).

- Peck, *Search, Forward: Will manual document review & keyword searches be replaced by computer-assisted coding?*, Law Technology News (2011), www.law.com/jsp/lawtechnologynews/index.jsp (referred to as Peck, *Search, Forward*)

- Pooley & Shaw, *Finding Out What's There: Technical & Legal Aspects of Discovery*, 4 Tex.Intell.Prop.L.J. 57 (1995) (referred to as Pooley & Shaw, *Finding Out What's There*).

—★—

- Raymond, *Tackling E-Discovery on a Budget*, 51 The Advocate: State Bar Litigation Section Report 50 (Summer 2010).

- Shah, *Use of "Predictive Coding" to Limit Cost & Improve Efficiency in Healthcare E-discovery: The Light Is Green, But Proceed With Caution*, AHLA (2012), www.ebglaw.com/articles.aspx (referred to as Shah, *Use of "Predictive Coding" to Limit Cost & Improve Efficiency*).

- Van Duizend, *Electronic Discovery: Questions & Answers*, 3 Civil Action 2 (2004), www.ncsconline .org/Projects_Initiatives/Images/CivilActionSummer04.pdf (referred to as Van Duizend, *Questions & Answers*).

- Van Oostenrijk, *Paper or Plastic?: Electronic Discovery & Spoliation in the Digital Age*, 42 Hous.L.Rev. 1163 (2005) (referred to as Van Oostenrijk, *Electronic Discovery & Spoliation*).

- Withers & Latin, *Living Daily with Weekley Homes*, 51 The Advocate: State Bar Litigation Section Report 23 (Summer 2010).

5. *O'Connor's* books. *O'Connor's Federal Rules * Civil Trials* (2013), "Electronic Discovery," ch. 6-C, p. 481 (*O'Connor's Federal Rules*).

§2. ELECTRONIC INFORMATION

Electronic information is any type of information that is created, stored, or retrieved and processed in electronic, magnetic, or digital form. *See Sedona Principles, Second Edition*, at 1; Conference of Chief Justices, *Guidelines for State Trial Courts*, at 1; Isom, *Electronic Discovery Primer for Judges*, 2005 Fed.Cts.L.Rev. at 2 n.1. It is distinct from information stored only on paper, film, or other nonelectronic media. NCCUSL, *Uniform Rules*, Rule 1 cmt.; *see Sedona Principles, Second Edition*, at 1; Isom, *Electronic Discovery Primer for Judges*, 2005 Fed.Cts.L.Rev. at 2 n.1. Electronic information is subject to discovery just like conventional documents and tangible things. *See* TRCP 192 cmt. 2 (things relevant to the subject matter of the suit are within the scope of discovery regardless of their form); *see also* TRCP 196.4 (to discover information that is in electronic or magnetic form, party must specifically request production of electronic or magnetic data and specify form of production).

NOTE

The TRCPs use the term "electronic or magnetic data." TRCP 196.4. The FRCPs use the term "electronically stored information," often referred to as "ESI." See, e.g., FRCP 26(b)(2)(B). There is no substantive difference between the terms. In this subchapter, the terms "electronic data," "electronic information," and "electronically stored information" are used interchangeably.

---

§2.1 Types of information. Electronic information includes the following: (1) databases, (2) data files, (3) program files, (4) image files (e.g., JPEG, TIFF), (5) e-mail messages and files, (6) voice-mail messages and files, (7) text messages, (8) temporary files, (9) system-history files, (10) deleted files, programs, or e-mails, (11) backup files and archival tapes, (12) website files, (13) website information stored in textual, graphical, or audio format, (14) cache files, and (15) cookies. ***Super Film v. UCB Films, Inc.***, 219 F.R.D. 649, 657 (D.Kan.2004); ***Thompson v. U.S. Dept. of Hous. & Urban Dev.***, 219 F.R.D. 93, 96 (D.Md.2003); *see **In re Weekley Homes, L.P.***, 295 S.W.3d 309, 314 (Tex.2009) (e-mails and deleted e-mails stored in electronic or magnetic form are electronic information). See *O'Connor's Federal Rules*, "What Is ESI?," ch. 6-C, §2, p. 482.

§2.2 Sources of information. Electronic information can be located in many places, including the following: (1) mainframe computers, (2) network servers, (3) Internet ("web") servers, (4) desktop and laptop computers, (5) hard drives, (6) flash drives, which include "thumb" drives, secure digital cards, and other flash memory cards, (7) e-mail servers, (8) handheld devices like personal digital assistants (PDAs) and personal media players (PMPs), (9) cell phones and smart phones (e.g., iPhones, BlackBerrys, Windows Mobile devices), (10) event recorders in cars, trucks, and trains, (11) medical devices, and (12) global positioning system (GPS) devices. *See **In re Seroquel Prods. Liab. Litig.***, 244 F.R.D. 650, 654 (M.D.Fla.2007); Conference of Chief Justices, *Guidelines for State Trial Courts*, at v; Isom, *Electronic Discovery Primer for Judges*, 2005 Fed.Cts.L.Rev. at 15-16.

─────────── ✦ ───────────

§3. DIFFERENCES BETWEEN ELECTRONIC & CONVENTIONAL DISCOVERY

Although electronic discovery and conventional discovery involve the same procedural methods (e.g., requests for production), the process of electronic discovery is much more complicated. For example, in conventional discovery, an attorney does not have to worry about what type of filing system the other party uses (e.g., a filing cabinet), but in electronic discovery, she does. Significant differences between electronic and conventional information affect how discovery is conducted, but the general discovery rules in the TRCPs apply to electronic information when not otherwise specified.

§3.1 Volume. Most information today is stored in some sort of digital or electronic format. The volume of electronic information is almost always much greater than paper-based information. Rothstein, *Managing Discovery of Electronic Information*, at 2; *Sedona Principles, Second Edition*, at 2. For example, the employees of even a medium-sized company of about 100 employees send and receive more than two million e-mails a year. Rothstein, *Managing Discovery of Electronic Information*, at 2.

§3.2 Locations. Electronic information can be stored in many different locations. See "Sources of information," §2.2, p. 487.

§3.3 Format. The format in which electronic information is created, stored, and produced differs from that of conventional information in the following ways:

1. Some digital transactions create no permanent documents in any form and are stored in databases that do not allow for any corresponding hard-copy materials. *See* Conference of Chief Justices, *Guidelines for State Trial Courts*, at vi; Rothstein, *Managing Discovery of Electronic Information*, at 3.

2. Some electronic information depends on the system that created it and is incomprehensible and unusable when separated from the system. *Sedona Principles, Second Edition*, at 4; Rothstein, *Managing Discovery of Electronic Information*, at 3.

3. Electronic information can be produced for discovery in a variety of forms and formats, including the following:

(1) Hard-copy printouts. *See Sedona Conference Glossary*, at 41.

(2) Static format (i.e., a TIFF or PDF file—essentially a photograph of a document). Rothstein, *Managing Discovery of Electronic Information*, at 22; *see Sedona Conference Glossary*, at 39, 50. See "Static format," §4.1.14, p. 490.

(3) Native format—the form in which it was created and used in the normal course of business. *Sedona Conference Glossary*, at 35; Rothstein, *Managing Discovery of Electronic Information*, at 22.

§3.4 Complexity. Electronic information is complex in the way it is created, maintained, and stored. Withers, *Living Daily with Weekley Homes*, at 24. Because of the complex relationships between the equipment, operating systems, and software used for creating and storing electronic information, a party may have difficulty knowing what to ask for in a request for production or how to respond to that request. *Id.*

§3.5 Indestructibility. Deletion of electronic information does not necessarily get rid of the information (as shredding a paper document does). Rothstein, *Managing Discovery of Electronic Information*, at 4. See "Deleted file," §4.1.5, p. 489.

§3.6 Dynamic nature. Information stored in a static medium like paper does not change. Electronic data, however, is dynamic; it changes every time a user saves a file, loads new software, turns off a computer, or performs other everyday functions. *See Sedona Principles, Second Edition*, at 3; Pooley & Shaw, *Finding Out What's There*, 4 Tex.Intell.Prop.L.J. at 62. Thus, as part of ordinary computer operations, electronic information is routinely altered, overwritten, or erased. *Sedona Principles, Second Edition*, at 28. As a result, normal computer use creates a risk that a party may unintentionally lose potentially discoverable information.

———————————————— ✯ ————————————————

§3.7 Costs. The cost to a responding party of locating, reviewing, and preparing electronic information for production is generally much greater than it is for conventional discovery. Conference of Chief Justices, *Guidelines for State Trial Courts*, at vi; *see* Raymond, *Tackling E-Discovery on a Budget*, at 50 (explaining how to lower the high costs of e-discovery). The cost of restoring backup tapes, for example, is much higher than the cost of making documents available for the requesting party to review. Conference of Chief Justices, *Guidelines for State Trial Courts*, at vi. Recovery or retrieval of electronic information may also require the added cost of outside experts or forensic examiners. *Id.* See "Costs," §4.5, p. 492.

§3.8 Preservation. Because electronic information is easily altered or destroyed in ways that conventional information is not, electronic information presents unique problems when there is a duty to preserve evidence. See "Preservation," §4.2, p. 490.

§4. PRELITIGATION PLANNING

§4.1 Technical terminology. In preparing for electronic discovery, an attorney should learn some of the technical terminology related to electronic information. Learning this terminology will help the attorney become more precise in her discovery requests and more effective in her communications with the court, particularly if the judge is not well versed in technology. The following are some of the most common terms used in electronic discovery. For a more comprehensive list, see the *Sedona Conference Glossary*.

    1. Active data. "Active data" refers to information that is currently being created, received, or processed, or that needs to be accessed frequently and quickly. Rothstein, *Managing Discovery of Electronic Information*, at 14. It includes information located in a computer system's memory or in storage media attached to the system (e.g., disk drives). *Sedona Conference Glossary*, at 2. Active data is immediately accessible and does not have to be restored or reconstructed. *Id.*

    2. Archival data. "Archival data" refers to information that is maintained by an organization for long-term storage and record-keeping purposes. *Sedona Conference Glossary*, at 4. Archival data is not immediately accessible. *Id.*

    3. Backup data. "Backup data" refers to an exact copy of electronic data that serves as a source of recovery of that data if a system problem or disaster occurs. *Sedona Conference Glossary*, at 5. Backup data is often stored on magnetic backup tapes. *See id.*

    4. Backup tape recycling. "Backup tape recycling" refers to the process by which an organization's backup tapes are overwritten with new data, usually on a fixed schedule. *Sedona Conference Glossary*, at 5.

    5. Deleted file. "Deleted file" refers to data that has been deleted by the user or by the computer system. *Sedona Conference Glossary*, at 14. Generally, deleting a file does not actually erase the data from the computer storage system. ***Zubulake v. UBS Warburg LLC***, 217 F.R.D. 309, 313 n.19 (S.D.N.Y.2003). It merely designates the space as available for reuse. *Sedona Conference Glossary*, at 14. The deleted file remains on the computer until it is overwritten. *Id.*

    6. Form of production. "Form of production" refers to the manner in which requested electronic information is produced. *Sedona Conference Glossary*, at 23. Electronic information can be produced in a variety of forms and formats. Rothstein, *Managing Discovery of Electronic Information*, at 22. See "Format," §3.3, p. 488. The form of production determines whether the information can be electronically searched, whether relevant information is obscured, and whether confidential or privileged information is disclosed, and how the information can be used in later stages of the litigation. Rothstein, *Managing Discovery of Electronic Information*, at 22.

    7. Hard drive. "Hard drive" refers to a computer's primary storage unit that has components on which data can be written and erased magnetically. *Sedona Conference Glossary*, at 25.

    8. Legacy data. "Legacy data" refers to electronic data that was created on a computer system or with software that has become obsolete. Rothstein, *Managing Discovery of Electronic Information*, at 14-15. Legacy data may be expensive to produce. *See Sedona Conference Glossary*, at 31.

⭐

9. Metadata. "Metadata" refers to information describing the history, tracking, or management of an electronic file. *In re Weekley Homes, L.P.*, 295 S.W.3d 309, 320 n.9 (Tex.2009); *In re Honza*, 242 S.W.3d 578, 580 n.4 (Tex.App.—Waco 2008, orig. proceeding). It can describe how, when, and by whom the electronic information was created and modified. *Sedona Conference Glossary*, at 34. Some metadata can be seen by users, while other metadata is hidden or embedded and not visible to users. *Id.* Metadata is generally not reproduced in paper copies or electronic images of the electronic information. *Id.*

10. Mirror image. "Mirror imaging," also called forensic imaging or forensic duplication, refers to the creation of an exact copy of a computer hard drive or other physical storage media. *Sedona Conference Glossary*, at 23, 34.

11. Native format. "Native format" refers to the form in which electronic information was created and is used in the normal course of business. Rothstein, *Managing Discovery of Electronic Information*, at 22.

12. Near-line data. "Near-line data" refers to electronic information stored in a system that is not a direct part of a network in daily use but that can be accessed automatically through the network. *Sedona Conference Glossary*, at 36.

13. Offline storage. "Offline storage" refers to removable-disk or magnetic-tape media that can be labeled and stored on a shelf. *Zubulake*, 217 F.R.D. at 319. Offline storage is generally used to make disaster-recovery copies of electronic records. *Id.* Access to offline storage requires manual action and takes longer than active or near-line data. *Id.*

14. Static format. "Static format," also called "imaged format," refers to a format used to retain an image of an electronic document as it would appear in its original program or application. *Sedona Conference Glossary*, at 35 ("native format" entry). The document's metadata cannot be seen, and the document information cannot be manipulated. *Id.* Common static formats are Adobe PDF and TIFF. *See id.*

15. Storage device. "Storage device" refers to a device that can store electronic information. *Sedona Conference Glossary*, at 49. The device is generally a mass storage device, such as a disc or tape drive. *Id.*

16. Systems data. "Systems data" refers to computer records about a computer's use, such as when users logged on or off a computer or network, what passwords they used, what websites they visited, and what documents they printed or faxed. Conference of Chief Justices, *Guidelines for State Trial Courts*, at vi; *see* Rothstein, *Managing Discovery of Electronic Information*, at 14. Systems data may be more remote and more costly to produce than active data. Rothstein, *Managing Discovery of Electronic Information*, at 14.

§4.2 Preservation. In preparing for electronic discovery, an attorney should give potential parties notice to keep them from altering or destroying relevant evidence. Preservation of electronically stored evidence is particularly challenging because information stored on computer systems is by its nature so dynamic. See "Dynamic nature," §3.6, p. 488. Further complicating the preservation issue is that many organizations have document-retention policies that require their data to be stored only for a predetermined amount of time, after which it is automatically permanently deleted. Van Oostenrijk, *Electronic Discovery & Spoliation*, 42 Hous.L.Rev. at 1185. Thus, to ensure that electronically stored evidence is preserved, the party seeking the information should take appropriate steps.

1. Determining source of duty to preserve. The party's duty to preserve electronic evidence is similar to that for traditional paper-based evidence. Namely, parties have a duty to preserve information they know is relevant to potential or ongoing litigation. *See Wal-Mart Stores v. Johnson*, 106 S.W.3d 718, 722 (Tex.2003); *Adobe Land Corp. v. Griffin, L.L.C.*, 236 S.W.3d 351, 357-58 (Tex.App.—Fort Worth 2007, pet. denied). See "Common-law duty," ch. 6-A, §3.1, p. 426. Besides this common-law duty, parties may also have a statutory, regulatory, or ethical duty to preserve evidence. See "Statutory, regulatory & ethical duties," ch. 6-A, §3.2, p. 427. The source of an opposing party's duty to preserve evidence should be cited in any request to preserve that evidence.

2. Securing preservation. At the first sign of a potential lawsuit, all parties must be given notice if they will be asked to produce electronically stored information. *See Zubulake v. UBS Warburg LLC*, 220 F.R.D. 212, 216 (S.D.N.Y.2003); *Sedona Principles, Second Edition*, at 32. Without some form of notice, the trial court is unlikely to

---

★

---

be sympathetic to a party's complaint about the destruction of evidence by its adversary. *See, e.g.*, ***Chidichimo v. University of Chi. Press***, 681 N.E.2d 107, 110 (Ill.App.Ct.1997) (because P did not take reasonable steps to give notice of suit and ensure preservation and protection against routine destruction of data, court found no duty to preserve relevant computer records; reasonable person in D's position would not have foreseen that data would be material to potential suit).

(1) Preservation letter. To ensure that all parties to the potential suit are aware of electronic-discovery intentions, a letter should be sent to each of them outlining the type of information to be preserved. *See* ***Cache La Poudre Feeds, LLC v. Land O'Lakes, Inc.***, 244 F.R.D. 614, 623 (D.Colo.2007) (because of dynamic nature of electronic information, attorneys should address preservation issues in demand letters sent to potential adverse parties); Henderson, *Duty to Preserve*, 66 Tex.B.J. at 24 (attorney should send letter asking opposing party to preserve electronic information that might be deleted in ordinary course of business). A preservation letter usually (1) describes the potential litigation and the parties involved, (2) asks the recipient to suspend any document-destruction policy, (3) reminds the recipient of the duty to preserve all information relevant to the suit, (4) identifies the specific documents, electronic information, and tangible things that should be preserved, and (5) provides instructions on how to preserve those items. *See Sedona Principles, Second Edition*, at 32. See ***O'Connor's Texas Forms***, FORM 2A:1. This initial preservation letter is vital, not only to protect relevant data but also to enable the court to impose sanctions on parties who destroy or modify electronic information after receiving notice of its relevance. See "Spoliation," ch. 6-A, §23, p. 452; ***O'Connor's Federal Rules***, "Sanctions for Lost ESI," ch. 6-C, §12, p. 513.

PRACTICE TIP

When requesting that an opposing party preserve electronic information, follow up on the preservation letter by having opposing counsel agree to the preservation in writing. See "Agreements & stipulations," §5.2.2, p. 494; ***O'Connor's Texas Forms***, *FORM 6A:1.*

---

(2) Litigation hold. Once a duty to preserve evidence arises, a party should suspend its document-retention policy and put a "litigation hold" in place to ensure that relevant electronic information is preserved. ***Zubulake***, 220 F.R.D. at 218; *see* Rothstein, *Managing Discovery of Electronic Information*, at 3 (dynamic nature of electronically stored information makes it vital that litigant or potential litigant institute litigation hold whenever litigation is reasonably anticipated). A litigation hold suspends the normal disposition or processing of records. *Sedona Conference Glossary*, at 31 ("legal hold"). An effective litigation hold requires a party to (1) identify and preserve relevant electronic information, (2) give written notice of the hold to the employees most likely to have relevant information, clearly identifying the information that must be preserved and specifying how it must be kept, and (3) monitor compliance. Scheindlin, *Ten Most FAQ's*, at 2. A party should consider making a mirror image of its computer system at the time the duty to preserve arises. ***Zubulake***, 220 F.R.D. at 218.

CAUTION

In an influential opinion, a federal court imposed specific responsibilities on attorneys representing parties who are under a duty to preserve electronic information. ***Zubulake v. UBS Warburg LLC***, *229 F.R.D. 422, 433-34 (S.D.N.Y.2004). Under* ***Zubulake***, *an attorney should (1) understand the client's document-retention policies and related computer systems, (2) issue a litigation hold and reissue it periodically, (3) monitor compliance with the litigation hold, (4) speak directly to "key players" about the preservation duty, (5) tell all employees to produce electronic copies of their relevant active electronic files, and (6) identify all backup media that must be preserved and make sure it is safely stored. Id. at 432-34. See* ***O'Connor's Federal Rules***, *"Zubulake steps," ch. 6-C, §4.2.3(1), p. 488. Six years after* ***Zubulake***, *the same court held that (1) the failure to either issue a written litigation hold or collect records from key players constitutes gross negligence per se, and (2) the failure to collect records from all employees*

★

---

constitutes negligence. ***Pension Cmte. of the Univ. of Montreal Pension Plan v. Banc of Am. Secs., LLC***, *685 F.Supp.2d 456, 465 (S.D.N.Y.2010). But see **Surowiec v. Capital Title Agency, Inc.**, 790 F.Supp.2d 997, 1007 (D.Ariz.2011) (failure to issue litigation hold does not constitute negligence per se). No Texas court has specifically addressed the duties of parties or attorneys to preserve electronic information.*

---

§4.3 Electronic-discovery vendor. In preparing for electronic discovery, an attorney should evaluate the need for an electronic-discovery vendor. *See Sedona Principles, Second Edition*, at 40; *see also* Hedges, *Discovery of Electronically Stored Information*, at 143 (party should hire expert when electronic-discovery issues become complicated). An electronic-discovery vendor may be helpful or even necessary because of the vendor's experience in sampling and testing different electronic-information systems and knowledge about the accuracy and sufficiency of different search and retrieval methods. *See Sedona Principles, Second Edition*, at 40. There are three general types of electronic-discovery vendors: (1) vendors that process data (i.e., data collection, storage, and review), (2) vendors that provide electronic solutions (i.e., document-management providers, providers of search-and-retrieval tools), and (3) vendors that consult (i.e., discovery strategy, risk management). *Navigating the Vendor Proposal Process*, at 22. For a detailed discussion of finding an appropriate electronic-discovery vendor, see *Navigating the Vendor Proposal Process*. Generally, a party should take the following actions:

1. Collect information. The party should collect information on prospective vendors by requesting technical literature, case studies, and mission statements, by attending seminars, or by researching on the Internet. *Navigating the Vendor Proposal Process*, at 5.

2. Detail concerns. When requesting information from a vendor, the party should give enough detail about the service being requested and any technical concerns the party has to allow the vendor to anticipate potential problems and to realistically address any limitations in the vendor's service. *Navigating the Vendor Proposal Process*, at 8-9.

3. Evaluate background. The party should evaluate background information about the potential vendor, its personnel, and the service it is providing. *Navigating the Vendor Proposal Process*, at 6. This step is critical because the party, not the vendor, is ultimately responsible for ensuring that the electronic information is preserved. *Sedona Principles, Second Edition*, at 40. Thus, a party's evaluation of a vendor's software and services should include the defensibility of the vendor's process in the litigation context, the costs, and the vendor's experience and expertise. *Id.*

4. Ask about security measures. The party should ask the potential vendor about security measures taken to protect both the physical nature and the confidentiality of the electronic information. *Navigating the Vendor Proposal Process*, at 14-15.

5. Draft proposal. The party should draft a "request for proposal" for the vendor to complete that is specifically tailored to the party's needs. *Navigating the Vendor Proposal Process*, at 25-26.

§4.4 Inadvertent disclosure of privileged information. Because of the volume of information that may be subject to a discovery request and the time necessary to screen it, discovery of electronic information carries an increased risk of inadvertent disclosure of privileged information. NCCUSL, *Uniform Rules*, Rule 9 cmt. However, there is a general presumption against waiver. *See* TRCP 193.3(d). A party who produces information without intending to waive a claim of privilege does not waive that claim if, within ten days (or a shorter time ordered by the court) after learning of the inadvertent production, the party amends its response, identifying the information produced and stating the privilege asserted. *Id.* See "Use snap-back provision," ch. 6-A, §18.2.4, p. 444.

§4.5 Costs. Electronic data is voluminous and can be stored in many locations, some of which are difficult to access. The cost of locating requested electronic information, screening it, and preparing it for production can thus be much higher than the cost of conventional discovery. Rothstein, *Managing Discovery of Electronic Information*, at 17; Van Duizend, *Questions & Answers*, 3 Civil Action at 1. See "Costs," ch. 6-I, §3.3.4, p. 567.

⭐

1. Responding party's burden. Generally, the responding party bears the cost of producing electronic discovery. TRCP 196.6. If the trial court orders the responding party to comply with a request over the party's objection that it cannot, through reasonable efforts, retrieve or produce the information requested, the court must order the requesting party to pay the reasonable expenses of any extraordinary steps required to retrieve and produce the information. TRCP 196.4; *see In re Weekley Homes, L.P.*, 295 S.W.3d 309, 316 (Tex.2009). See "Response," §8.1.5(2), p. 499.

2. Requesting party's burden. The requesting party must bear the cost of inspecting, sampling, testing, photographing, or copying electronic data. TRCP 196.6.

§5. LITIGATION PLANNING

Once suit has been filed, the attorney must plan for how electronic information will be discovered and produced.

§5.1 Learn about parties' systems. In preparing for electronic discovery, an attorney should learn about the types of systems the parties use to create, store, and retrieve electronic information. Conference of Chief Justices, *Guidelines for State Trial Courts*, at 1; *see In re Weekley Homes, L.P.*, 295 S.W.3d 309, 321-22 (Tex.2009). The attorney must be familiar with how the parties regularly use computers and must understand what information is available, how routine computer operations may change it, and what is involved in producing it. This knowledge will allow the attorney to instruct the client about specific preservation and production responsibilities and to properly structure discovery requests tailored to the opposing party's electronic systems. *Sedona Conference "Jumpstart Outline,"* at 1. The attorney should consider gathering information on the following when preparing for electronic discovery:

1. Any document-retention policies. *Id.*; *see* Ball, *A Special Master's Perspective*, at 44.

2. Any people with potentially relevant information about the client's computer or e-mail system. *Sedona Conference "Jumpstart Outline,"* at 1. The attorney must identify the people who know the most about the client's computer system and meet with them well before the pretrial conference. Rothstein, *Managing Discovery of Electronic Information*, at 9. Those people should probably be present at the conference. *Id.*

3. Any current or former databases, e-mail systems, and file servers on the parties' networks that store or have stored electronic information, as well as any information stored outside the parties' own networks (e.g., web-based e-mail). *See* Ball, *A Special Master's Perspective*, at 43-44; *Sedona Conference "Jumpstart Outline,"* at 2-5. The attorney should focus on whether (1) the system backs up information and allows for selective restoration of files, (2) content is regularly overwritten, reformatted, or otherwise destroyed, and (3) there is a company-wide intranet that may store potentially relevant information. *Sedona Conference "Jumpstart Outline,"* at 2-3; *see* Ball, *A Special Master's Perspective*, at 44.

4. Any hard drives in current and former employees' desktop or laptop computers. *Sedona Conference "Jumpstart Outline,"* at 5-6. The attorney should focus on the parties' policies for (1) backing up the hard drives, (2) erasing or reformatting the hard drives, and (3) saving files and e-mails to the hard drives. *Id.*

§5.2 Schedule pretrial meeting or conference. If an attorney anticipates that electronic discovery will be an issue in the case, she should consider requesting a Rule 11 agreement or a pretrial conference to discuss the issues and develop an electronic-discovery plan. *See* TRCP 11 (agreements between attorneys), TRCP 166 (at pretrial conference, court can consider any matter that will aid in disposition of suit); *In re Weekley Homes, L.P.*, 295 S.W.3d 309, 321 (Tex.2009) (before requesting electronic information, parties should share information and try to agree on protocols for electronic discovery); *Sedona Principles, Second Edition*, at 21 (parties should confer early in discovery about preservation and production of electronic information); Rothstein, *Managing Discovery of Electronic Information*, at 6 (parties should meet and confer in earliest stages of suit and try to agree on electronic-discovery issues); *see, e.g., MRT, Inc. v. Vounckx*, 299 S.W.3d 500, 508 (Tex.App.—Dallas 2009, no pet.) (parties did not discuss their electronic-information systems and had different expectations about what the discovery requests meant, resulting in multiple discovery motions); *see also* Raymond, *Tackling E-Discovery on a Budget*, at 50 (cost-effective tips for

✭

agreements regarding electronic discovery); Withers, *Living Daily with Weekley Homes*, at 33 (the Sedona Conference "Jumpstart Outline" is a useful guide for attorneys unaccustomed to discussing electronic discovery); *cf.* FRCP 26(f)(3)(C) (parties must meet early in litigation process, confer on issues about disclosure or discovery of electronically stored information, and develop a discovery plan). See "Agreements Between Attorneys – Rule 11," ch. 1-H, §9, p. 61; "Initiating pretrial conference," ch. 5-A, §2.2, p. 315.

PRACTICE TIP

Although there is no requirement under Texas law that parties meet to discuss electronic-discovery matters, the parties should still meet informally to formulate a specific request for electronic information. See Hecht, Taking Point on E-Discovery, at 19. If further information is needed after the informal meeting, a party should obtain it through discovery or a pretrial conference with the court. Id. A party should not wait until a hearing on a motion to compel to make a specific request. Id.

---

    1. Issues to discuss. The parties should consider discussing the following issues:

    (1) The types of electronic information that are discoverable. *See Sedona Principles, Second Edition*, at 21; Conference of Chief Justices, *Guidelines for State Trial Courts*, at 2; Rothstein, *Managing Discovery of Electronic Information*, at 7. See "Types of information," §2.1, p. 487.

    (2) The sources and locations of electronic information. *See Sedona Principles, Second Edition*, at 21; Conference of Chief Justices, *Guidelines for State Trial Courts*, at 2-3; Rothstein, *Managing Discovery of Electronic Information*, at 7. See "Sources of information," §2.2, p. 487. The parties should also consider how to conduct searches for relevant electronic information in those sources. See "Search Techniques for Electronic Information," §6, p. 495.

    (3) The identification of people who know about the parties' computer systems and custodians of electronic information. *See Sedona Principles, Second Edition*, at 21; Conference of Chief Justices, *Guidelines for State Trial Courts*, at 2; Rothstein, *Managing Discovery of Electronic Information*, at 7. See "Disclosures," §8.1.1, p. 498.

    (4) The availability of electronic information. *See* Conference of Chief Justices, *Guidelines for State Trial Courts*, at 2-3; Rothstein, *Managing Discovery of Electronic Information*, at 8. See "Scope of Electronic Discovery," §7, p. 497.

    (5) The preservation of electronic information. *See Sedona Principles, Second Edition*, at 21; Conference of Chief Justices, *Guidelines for State Trial Courts*, at 3; Rothstein, *Managing Discovery of Electronic Information*, at 7. See "Preservation," §4.2, p. 490.

    (6) The forms of production of electronic information and the associated costs. *See Sedona Principles, Second Edition*, at 21; Conference of Chief Justices, *Guidelines for State Trial Courts*, at 3; Rothstein, *Managing Discovery of Electronic Information*, at 8. See "Costs," §4.5, p. 492; "Discovering & Producing Electronic Information," §8, p. 498.

    (7) The procedures for asserting privileges and objections. *See Sedona Principles, Second Edition*, at 21; Conference of Chief Justices, *Guidelines for State Trial Courts*, at 4; Rothstein, *Managing Discovery of Electronic Information*, at 8. See "Inadvertent disclosure of privileged information," §4.4, p. 492; "Resolving Electronic-Discovery Disputes," §9, p. 500.

    2. Agreements & stipulations. Parties and their attorneys are expected to cooperate in discovery and to make any agreements that are reasonably necessary for the efficient disposition of the case. TRCP 191.2; *In re Weekley Homes*, 295 S.W.3d at 321; *In re BP Prods. N. Am., Inc.*, 244 S.W.3d 840, 847-48 (Tex.2008). An agreement of the parties is enforceable if it complies with TRCP 11. TRCP 191.1; *In re BP Prods.*, 244 S.W.3d at 845. If the parties meet informally, they should incorporate their discovery plan into a Rule 11 agreement. See "Agreements Between Attorneys – Rule 11," ch. 1-H, §9, p. 61; "Rule 11," ch. 6-A, §6.1.1, p. 429; *O'Connor's Federal Forms*, FORM 6A:4.

—— ✪ ——

§6. SEARCH TECHNIQUES FOR ELECTRONIC INFORMATION

The parties must consider how to conduct searches to locate electronic information within sources identified as likely to contain relevant material (e.g., an e-mail database). Aside from traditional, manual review of electronic information, the parties can consider the following search techniques.

PRACTICE TIP

If the parties intend to use a new or complex search technique, they should consider having a representative from the electronic-discovery vendor that will perform the searches attend any conferences or hearings that address the search technique. See, e.g., **Da Silva Moore v. Publicis Groupe**, *No. 11 Civ. 1279 (ALC) (AJP) (S.D.N.Y.2012) (slip op.; 2-24-12) (court stated that it was "very helpful" when vendors were present and spoke at hearing about protocol involving predictive coding), aff'd, No. 11 Civ. 1279 (ALC) (AJP) (S.D.N.Y.2012) (slip op.; 4-25-12).*

---

§6.1 Keyword searches. The parties can consider keyword searches to locate relevant electronic information. A keyword search involves a specified word or combination of words. *Sedona Conference Glossary*, at 30. Keyword searches are currently the most common search technique used to cull an entire set of electronic information. *See* **Da Silva Moore v. Publicis Groupe**, No. 11 Civ. 1279 (ALC) (AJP) (S.D.N.Y.2012) (slip op.; 2-24-12), *aff'd*, No. 11 Civ. 1279 (ALC) (AJP) (S.D.N.Y.2012) (slip op.; 4-25-12).

1. Process. The process of using keyword searches usually includes the following steps: (1) attorneys develop a list of keywords, (2) the list of keywords is applied to all of the electronic information, and (3) the parties manually review only the electronic information that contains the keywords. *See* **Da Silva Moore**, No. 11 Civ. 1279 (ALC) (AJP) (slip op.). Especially in cases involving a high volume of electronic information, keyword searches may be necessary to narrow the amount of electronic information because traditional manual review of all of the electronic information is virtually impossible. *See id.* To improve the effectiveness of keyword searches, the parties can consider seeking expert assistance to create an effective list of keywords. See "Electronic-discovery vendor," §4.3, p. 492. To enhance keyword searches, the parties can use more advanced search techniques such as Boolean connectors, elimination of duplicate documents, grouping of "near duplicates," and threading e-mail chains. Peck, *Search, Forward.*

2. Limitations. Keyword searches are limited because the people who originally created the electronic information may describe the same concept using different words, may misspell words, or may use abbreviations and acronyms for certain terms. *See* Peck, *Search, Forward.* Without cooperation from all the parties, the attorneys who develop the list of keywords are essentially guessing what words will produce relevant information; thus, the list of keywords is often overinclusive, resulting in a high return of irrelevant information. *See* **Da Silva Moore**, No. 11 Civ. 1279 (ALC) (AJP) (slip op.); Peck, *Search, Forward.*

§6.2 Predictive coding. The parties can consider predictive coding to locate relevant electronic information. *See* **Da Silva Moore v. Publicis Groupe**, No. 11 Civ. 1279 (ALC) (AJP) (S.D.N.Y.2012) (slip op.; 2-24-12), *aff'd*, No. 11 Civ. 1279 (ALC) (AJP) (S.D.N.Y.2012) (slip op.; 4-25-12). Predictive coding, also referred to as computer-assisted review, is an emerging search tool that requires a person (usually a senior attorney or team of attorneys) to review a small amount of electronic information to "train" the predictive-coding software to identify relevant electronic information; the software then applies what it learns from the human review to predict the relevancy of the remaining electronic information. *See id.*; Shah, *Use of "Predictive Coding" to Limit Cost & Improve Efficiency*, at 9. To determine whether predictive coding is an appropriate search technique, courts may consider the following factors: (1) the parties' agreement, (2) the amount of electronic information, (3) the reasonableness of predictive coding compared to other available search techniques, (4) the need for cost-effectiveness, and (5) the transparency of the discovery process. *See* **Da Silva Moore**, No. 11 Civ. 1279 (ALC) (AJP) (slip op.).

ELECTRONIC DISCOVERY

✪

CAUTION

*Predictive coding is a relatively new technology, and only a handful of cases have addressed whether it is an appropriate way to conduct discovery. See **Da Silva Moore**, No. 11 Civ. 1279 (ALC) (AJP) (slip op.) (court approved use of predictive coding when parties agreed to its use). Also, because of its relative newness, it is unclear to what extent predictive coding can handle privilege determinations. See Shah, Use of "Predictive Coding" to Limit Cost & Improve Efficiency, at 10. At a minimum, if a party seeks to use predictive coding, it should address the topic early in the litigation, usually at an informal pretrial meeting or a pretrial conference. See "Schedule pretrial meeting or conference," §5.2, p. 493.*

---

1. Process. Although the specific process for predictive coding may differ depending on the software used, the process usually includes the following steps:

(1) Attorneys code "seed" set. Attorneys review and code a small amount of the electronic information—known as a "seed" set—to train the predictive-coding software. *See **Da Silva Moore**, No. 11 Civ. 1279 (ALC) (AJP) (slip op.) (attorneys typically need to review only a few thousand documents).*

(2) Software predicts. The software applies the principles it learned from the seed set to predict how the attorneys would code electronic information outside of the seed set. ***Da Silva Moore***, No. 11 Civ. 1279 (ALC) (AJP) (slip op.).

(3) Software codes all electronic information. The coding and predicting continues until the software is able to accurately predict how the attorneys would code the electronic information, at which point the software codes all of the electronic information. ***Da Silva Moore***, No. 11 Civ. 1279 (ALC) (AJP) (slip op.).

(4) Random sample selected. When the software completes the coding, it selects a random sample of the coded electronic information for quality control. Shah, *Use of "Predictive Coding" to Limit Cost & Improve Efficiency*, at 9.

(5) Attorneys review sample. Attorneys assess the sample of coded electronic information for both the percentage of relevant electronic information identified (called "completeness" or "recall") and the percentage of the identified electronic information that is actually relevant (called "accuracy" or "precision"). Shah, *Use of "Predictive Coding" to Limit Cost & Improve Efficiency*, at 9; *see **Da Silva Moore***, No. 11 Civ. 1279 (ALC) (AJP) (slip op.).

(6) Additional seed set may be chosen. If the attorneys find errors, an additional seed set is chosen, reviewed, and coded until the software reaches acceptable levels of completeness and accuracy. Shah, *Use of "Predictive Coding" to Limit Cost & Improve Efficiency*, at 9.

2. Benefits. The benefits of predictive coding include the following:

(1) Minimal human review. Predictive coding requires minimal input from human reviewers. *See* Peck, *Search, Forward*; Shah, *Use of "Predictive Coding" to Limit Cost & Improve Efficiency*, at 9.

(2) Lower costs. Predictive coding potentially lowers costs. *See* Peck, *Search, Forward*. Predictive coding may offer the potential for lower costs because it requires fewer attorneys and fewer review hours. *See* Shah, *Use of "Predictive Coding" to Limit Cost & Improve Efficiency*, at 10.

(3) Greater accuracy. Predictive coding may provide greater accuracy. *See* Peck, *Search, Forward*; *see also **Da Silva Moore***, No. 11 Civ. 1279 (ALC) (AJP) (slip op.) (statistics have shown that predictive coding is at least as accurate as traditional manual review, which has been considered "gold standard" in document review). Predictive coding provides greater accuracy than keyword searches because it does not rely on attorneys to develop the list of keywords and it is not based on particular keywords or Boolean operators. *See **Da Silva Moore***, No. 11 Civ. 1279 (ALC) (AJP) (slip op.); Peck, *Search, Forward*. See "Limitations," §6.1.2, p. 495.

⭐

§6.3 Testing & sampling. The parties can consider testing or sampling to locate relevant electronic information contained in sources identified as not reasonably available. *See* Rothstein, *Managing Discovery of Electronic Information*, at 15. See "Information not reasonably available," §7.2, this page. Sampling can help refine the search parameters and determine the benefits and burdens of a more complete search. Rothstein, *Managing Discovery of Electronic Information*, at 16. See "Testing or sampling," §8.1.5(1)(b), p. 499.

§6.4 Other restrictions. The parties can consider other restrictions on searches for electronic information, such as limiting the time period for discovery or the amount of hours the producing party must spend searching, compiling, and reviewing electronic information.

§7. SCOPE OF ELECTRONIC DISCOVERY

A party may secure the production of electronic information that is not privileged and that is relevant or reasonably calculated to lead to the discovery of relevant evidence. *See* TRCP 192.3(a), 196.4. The responding party must produce electronic information that is reasonably available to it in the ordinary course of business. TRCP 196.4; *In re Weekley Homes, L.P.*, 295 S.W.3d 309, 315 (Tex.2009). The responding party may also need to produce electronic information that is not reasonably available if ordered to do so by the court. TRCP 196 cmt. 3; *In re Weekley Homes*, 295 S.W.3d at 315. Courts should determine on a case-by-case basis whether electronic information is reasonably available. *In re Weekley Homes*, 295 S.W.3d at 315. Focused discovery (e.g., sampling of electronic information systems, depositions of persons knowledgeable about electronic information systems) may be necessary to determine the scope of production. *Id.* at 315-16. See "Discovery from parties," §8.1, p. 498.

NOTE

*Because TRCP 196.4 does not provide express guidelines for how to produce electronic information that is not reasonably available, the Texas Supreme Court has referred to federal rules and case law for guidance. See **In re Weekley Homes**, 295 S.W.3d at 316-19.*

---

§7.1 Information reasonably available.

1. Generally. Electronic information is reasonably available if it is stored in a readily usable format. *Zubulake v. UBS Warburg LLC*, 217 F.R.D. 309, 320 (S.D.N.Y.2003). Reasonably available data may include (1) active data that is available to the responding party in the ordinary course of business, (2) near-line data, and (3) off-line storage. *See id.* at 318-19; Rothstein, *Managing Discovery of Electronic Information*, at 14; *Sedona Principles, Second Edition*, at 18 (reasonably available data includes files available on or from a computer user's desktop or on a company's network used in the ordinary course of business). See "Technical terminology," §4.1, p. 489. Most discovery needs can be satisfied from the production of reasonably available information. *See* TRCP 196 cmt. 3.

2. Limits on production. A party should determine whether any factors that generally limit the scope of discovery (e.g., discovery is unreasonably cumulative, discovery is obtainable from another source, burden and expense of discovery outweigh its likely benefit) support not producing the reasonably available electronic information. *See* TRCP 192.4. See "Grounds to limit scope of discovery," ch. 6-A, §20.1, p. 449.

§7.2 Information not reasonably available. Electronic information is not reasonably available if the producing party must take extraordinary steps to retrieve and produce it. *See* TRCP 196.4. See "Extraordinary steps," §8.1.5(1)(c), p. 499. Information that is not reasonably available may include (1) backup tapes, (2) erased, fragmented, or damaged data, and (3) legacy data. *See Zubulake v. UBS Warburg LLC*, 217 F.R.D. 309, 319-20 (S.D.N.Y. 2003); Rothstein, *Managing Discovery of Electronic Information*, at 15-16. See "Technical terminology," §4.1, p. 489. Systems data, which includes such information as when people logged on or off a computer or network, what applications and passwords they used, and what websites they visited, may be more remote than active data and more costly to produce. Rothstein, *Managing Discovery of Electronic Information*, at 14. These types of data are even more removed from the ordinary course of business and may involve substantial costs, time, and active intervention of computer specialists to produce. *Id.*

★

---

§8. DISCOVERING & PRODUCING ELECTRONIC INFORMATION

§8.1 Discovery from parties.

1. Disclosures. A party should disclose the identities of people who have knowledge of the party's electronic information systems and each person's connection with the case. *See* TRCP 194.2(e). The party should also disclose certain information about any expert it plans to call as a witness. *See* TRCP 194.2(f). See "Select forensic expert," §9.1.2(4), p. 501; "Testifying experts," ch. 6-E, §4.2.6, p. 520.

2. Depositions. A party seeking information about an organization's sources of electronic information should consider deposing an information-technology employee or other person who knows about the organization's electronic-information system. *See* TRCP 195.1, 199.2(b)(1); *In re Weekley Homes, L.P.*, 295 S.W.3d 309, 315 (Tex. 2009). See "Unknown corporate witness," ch. 6-F, §4.5.1(2)(c), p. 527; "When organization deposed," ch. 6-F, §4.6.3, p. 531.

3. Interrogatories. A party may use interrogatories to request information about the opposing party's electronic information. *See* TRCP 197.1. Interrogatories can be useful in determining the extent of the opposing party's discoverable electronic information (e.g., ask for identity of opposing party's computer-network specialist, ask about document-retention or destruction policies) or the opposing party's compliance with its preservation duty (e.g., ask for dates and actions taken to preserve electronic information, ask about recipients of any litigation holds). See "Interrogatories," ch. 6-G, p. 548.

4. Requests for admissions. A party may request that the opposing party admit the truth of matters relating to electronic information. *See* TRCP 198.1. A party may respond by admitting, denying, or stating why it cannot truthfully admit or deny each matter. TRCP 198.2(b). See "Requests for Admissions," ch. 6-H, p. 557.

5. Requests for production.

(1) Request. To obtain electronic information, a party must specifically request it. TRCP 196.4 & cmt. 3; *In re Weekley Homes*, 295 S.W.3d at 314; *see MRT, Inc. v. Vounckx*, 299 S.W.3d 500, 508-09 (Tex.App.—Dallas 2009, no pet.). A request for "all documents" does not include electronic information. *See, e.g., In re Lowe's Cos.*, 134 S.W.3d 876, 880 n.7 (Tex.App.—Houston [14th Dist.] 2004, orig. proceeding) (dicta; although Ps claimed that database was within request for all documents concerning claims against D, Ps did not specifically request electronic information); *cf. County of Dallas v. Harrison*, 759 S.W.2d 530, 531 (Tex.App.—Dallas 1988, no writ) (because "photographs" and "videotape recordings" are two different categories of documents under former TRCP 166b(2)(b), now TRCP 192.3(b), D's request for photographs did not apply to videotapes). If the party does not make a specific request for electronic information, the responding party generally cannot be compelled to produce it and cannot be sanctioned for not producing it. *See In re Harris*, 315 S.W.3d 685, 700-02 (Tex.App.—Houston [1st Dist.] 2010, orig. proceeding); *MRT, Inc.*, 299 S.W.3d at 508-09; *In re Lowe's Cos.*, 134 S.W.3d at 880 n.7 (dicta). But if the responding party understands the scope of the discovery sought before the court intervenes, the request will be considered reasonably specific. *See, e.g., In re Weekley Homes*, 295 S.W.3d at 314-15 (although P should have specifically requested production of deleted e-mails, purpose of TRCP 196.4 was met because request was made clear during course of discovery and before hearing on motion to compel); *In re Clark*, 345 S.W.3d 209, 212 (Tex.App.—Beaumont 2011, orig. proceeding) (P did not specifically request production of deleted e-mails, but response to motion to compel showed that respondent knew P was requesting e-mails that respondent had recently deleted).

PRACTICE TIP
To properly draft a request for electronic information, first familiarize yourself with how the opposing party's computer system operates, including how information is stored and retrieved. See "Learn about parties' systems," §5.1, p. 493.

★

(a) Form of production. A party's request for production must specify the form in which it wants the electronic information to be produced. TRCP 196.4 & cmt. 3.

(b) Testing or sampling. A party's request for production may ask for an opportunity to test or sample sources of electronic information to see if there is any relevant evidence. *See* TRCP 196.1(b); *In re Weekley Homes*, 295 S.W.3d at 315. See "Items to be tested," ch. 6-I, §3.2.2, p. 566. Such a request may allow the requesting party direct access to the producing party's electronic-information systems; however, direct access should not routinely be given because of confidentiality and privacy issues. *See Sedona Principles, Second Edition*, at 52. To prevent the release of any confidential or personal electronic information, the responding party should ensure that a protective order is in place. *Id.* See "Motion for protective order," §9.2, p. 502.

(c) Extraordinary steps. A party's request for production must specify any extraordinary steps the producing party must take to retrieve, translate, and produce the electronic information. TRCP 196.4 cmt. 3. See "Information not reasonably available," §7.2, p. 497.

NOTE

No Texas appellate court has addressed the meaning of "extraordinary steps." The requesting party should consider whether the burden or expense of the proposed discovery outweighs its likely benefits when evaluating any extraordinary steps necessary to produce the requested information. See TRCP 192.4(b); In re Weekley Homes, 295 S.W.3d at 315. See "Object," §8.1.5(2)(b), this page.

(d) Access to hard drive. A party may request access to an opposing party's computer hard drive or other electronic storage device. *See In re Honza*, 242 S.W.3d 578, 581-82 (Tex.App.—Waco 2008, orig. proceeding). The request must demonstrate (1) the particular characteristics of the electronic storage devices involved, (2) the familiarity of the requesting party's experts with those characteristics, and (3) a reasonable likelihood that the proposed search methodology will yield the information sought. *See In re Weekley Homes*, 295 S.W.3d at 320; *In re Jordan*, 364 S.W.3d 425, 426 (Tex.App.—Dallas 2012, orig. proceeding). If the responding party does not adequately produce the requested data, the requesting party can file a motion to compel. See "Accessing hard drive," §9.1.2, p. 500.

(2) Response.

(a) Produce. The responding party must produce electronic information that is responsive to the request, reasonably available to the responding party in the ordinary course of business, and in a reasonably usable form. TRCP 196.4 & cmt. 3; *In re Weekley Homes*, 295 S.W.3d at 322. See "Scope of Electronic Discovery," §7, p. 497.

(b) Object. If the responding party cannot, through reasonable efforts, retrieve the requested electronic information or produce it in the form requested, that party must object. TRCP 193.2, 196.4; *In re Weekley Homes*, 295 S.W.3d at 322. See "Contents of response," ch. 6-I, §3.4, p. 568. If the responding party is able to produce some but not all of the requested electronic information, it must object to the information it cannot retrieve or produce. *See* Hecht, *Taking Point on E-Discovery*, at 20; *see* TRCP 193.2(b). The responding party must state specifically the reason for the objection. TRCP 193.2(a). The responding party has the burden to produce evidence to support its objection. *E.g., In re CI Host, Inc.*, 92 S.W.3d 514, 516-17 (Tex.2002) (evidence was necessary to support objection that information on computer tapes was protected); *see* TRCP 193.4.

(3) Hearing. Either party may request a hearing on the responding party's objection. TRCP 193.4(a); *In re Weekley Homes*, 295 S.W.3d at 322.

(a) Responding party's burden. The responding party must show that the requested information is not reasonably available because of undue burden or expense. TRCP 192.4(b); *In re Weekley Homes*, 295 S.W.3d at 322. See "Undue burden," ch. 6-A, §20.1.1, p. 449.

───────────────────── ✦ ─────────────────────

PRACTICE TIP

*A responding party should inform the court if production of requested electronic information affects the privacy rights of nonparties. E.g., **In re CI Host**, 92 S.W.3d at 517 (requested backup tapes contained some nonparty information protected from disclosure under federal law). See "Nonparty information," ch. 6-I, §4.1, p. 569. The responding party should also consider notifying the nonparty about the request so that the nonparty can raise its own objections to the production of the information.*

(b) **Requesting party's response.** If the court determines the information is not reasonably available, the requesting party should show that (1) the benefits of production outweigh any burden or expense incurred by the responding party and (2) the information is not cumulative or obtainable from a less burdensome source. *See* TRCP 192.4; *In re Weekley Homes*, 295 S.W.3d at 322. See "Undue burden," ch. 6-A, §20.1.1, p. 449.

(c) **Order.** If the requesting party has shown that the benefits of production outweigh the burden and expense incurred, the court may then overrule the objection and order the responding party to comply with the request for production. *In re Weekley Homes*, 295 S.W.3d at 322; *see* TRCP 196.4.

[1] **Protect sensitive information.** The court should attempt to protect sensitive information and choose the least-intrusive means of retrieval. *In re Weekley Homes*, 295 S.W.3d at 322; *e.g.*, *In re Clark*, 345 S.W.3d at 212-13 (order requiring that surnames of party's attorneys, as well as the words "attorney" and "lawyer," be excluded from hard-drive search was not sufficient attempt to protect sensitive information). To protect sensitive information, the court can do the following: (1) limit the forensic expert's search or her access to the electronic storage device, (2) require the expert to provide copies of the information retrieved for the responding party's review, and (3) subject the expert to a protective order prohibiting her from disclosing confidential information outside of that allowed by the discovery order. *See In re Honza*, 242 S.W.3d at 582-83. See "Select forensic expert," §9.1.2(4), p. 501.

[2] **Payment of reasonable expenses.** If the court orders production over the responding party's objection, it must also order the requesting party to pay the reasonable expenses of any extraordinary steps required to retrieve and produce the information. TRCP 196.4; *In re Weekley Homes*, 295 S.W.3d at 322.

§8.2 Discovery from nonparties. A party may request production of electronic information from a nonparty. *See* TRCP 196 cmt. 6, 205.3(a). Because of the considerable costs involved with nonparty discovery of electronic information, requests to nonparties should be narrowly focused to avoid any undue burden or expense. See "Securing Things from a Nonparty," ch. 6-I, §5, p. 569.

§9. RESOLVING ELECTRONIC-DISCOVERY DISPUTES

When an electronic-discovery dispute arises, the requesting party can file a motion to compel. If the party has incurred fees or other costs associated with the request, it can also request sanctions. See *O'Connor's Federal Rules*, "Sanctions for Lost ESI," ch. 6-C, §12, p. 513. If the responding party disputes the request for electronically stored information, the party can file a motion for protective order.

§9.1 Motion to compel.

1. Generally. If the responding party does not produce the requested electronic information, the requesting party can file a motion to compel. *See* TRCP 215.1 (motion for order compelling discovery). See "Motion to Compel Discovery," ch. 6-A, §22, p. 451. For a discussion of specific grounds for compelling discovery of electronic information, see *O'Connor's Federal Rules*, "Motion to compel," ch. 6-C, §11.2, p. 510.

2. Accessing hard drive. If a party requested access to an opposing party's computer hard drive and the opposing party did not adequately produce the requested data, the requesting party can file a motion to compel. *See In re Weekley Homes, L.P.*, 295 S.W.3d 309, 312 (Tex.2009); *In re Clark*, 345 S.W.3d 209, 212 (Tex.App.—

───────────────── ✪ ─────────────────

Beaumont 2011, orig. proceeding). Access to a party's computer hard drive will normally be granted only if that party's conduct suggests that it may be withholding, concealing, or destroying discoverable electronic information. *See In re Weekley Homes*, 295 S.W.3d at 317 (examination of computer hard drive is generally discouraged). See *O'Connor's Federal Rules*, "ESI withheld, concealed, or destroyed," ch. 6-C, §11.2.2(2)(a)[3], p. 511. In its motion to compel, the requesting party should do the following:

(1) **Show inadequate production.** The requesting party should show that the responding party has not adequately produced the requested data and that a search of that party's computer hard drive may recover deleted material. *In re Weekley Homes*, 295 S.W.3d at 317; *see In re Clark*, 345 S.W.3d at 212. A conclusory statement that deleted material "must exist" is not sufficient. *See In re Weekley Homes*, 295 S.W.3d at 320; *In re Harris*, 315 S.W.3d 685, 700 (Tex.App.—Houston [1st Dist.] 2010, orig. proceeding).

(2) **Show that retrieval of data is feasible.** The requesting party should show that retrieval of the requested data is feasible. *In re Weekley Homes*, 295 S.W.3d at 318; *e.g.*, *In re Stern*, 321 S.W.3d 828, 846 (Tex. App.—Houston [1st Dist.] 2010, orig. proceeding) (D stated that e-mail was stored on web-based Internet service and could not be found on hard drive; P did not show that e-mails were saved to hard drive, so hard drive should not be produced). The requesting party should show that the particular electronic storage device will allow retrieval of deleted or overwritten material and what that retrieval will involve. *In re Weekley Homes*, 295 S.W.3d at 320. Thus, to show feasibility, the requesting party must have some knowledge of the responding party's electronic storage devices. *Id.* at 318. See "Learn about parties' systems," §5.1, p. 493.

(3) **Show relationship between hard drive & claim.** The requesting party should show that there is some direct relationship between the computer hard drive and the claim itself. *In re Weekley Homes*, 295 S.W.3d at 319; *In re Harris*, 315 S.W.3d at 701.

(4) **Select forensic expert.** The requesting party should select a forensic expert to make a mirror image of the computer hard drive. *In re Honza*, 242 S.W.3d 578, 582 (Tex.App.—Waco 2008, orig. proceeding); *see In re Weekley Homes*, 295 S.W.3d at 319. See "Mirror image," §4.1.10, p. 490. A forensic expert is a computer expert who creates forensic images of a particular electronic storage device and then searches the images for specified documents using a predetermined list of terms. *In re Harris*, 315 S.W.3d at 704; *see In re Weekley Homes*, 295 S.W.3d at 321.

(a) **Qualifications.** The party should show (1) how the expert is qualified to perform the search, (2) that the expert is familiar with the particularities of the hard drive at issue, and (3) any methodologies used by the expert to allow for retrieval of deleted data. *See In re Weekley Homes*, 295 S.W.3d at 321.

(b) **Limited access.** The expert should be given limited access to the documents on the electronic storage device; unrestricted authorization to search the electronic storage device would be an impermissible "fishing expedition." *In re Weekley Homes*, 295 S.W.3d at 318; *see, e.g.*, *In re Stern*, 321 S.W.3d at 845-46 (court abused discretion by allowing expert to have unrestricted access to all documents on D's hard drive and freedom to use or modify search terms); *In re Honza*, 242 S.W.3d at 582-83 (discovery order not overbroad when expert was limited to searching for two specific documents).

(c) **Copies to opposing party.** After creating the mirror image and analyzing it for relevant documents, the expert must compile the documents obtained and provide copies to the opposing party. *In re Honza*, 242 S.W.3d at 582. The opposing party must be allowed to review the documents, produce documents responsive to the request for production, and create a privilege log for any withheld documents. *Id.*

(d) **Protective order.** The expert must be subject to a protective order that prohibits her from disclosing confidential or privileged information other than what is allowed by the discovery order. *E.g.*, *In re Honza*, 242 S.W.3d at 582-83 (expert was prohibited from disclosing confidential information observed during imaging process, and expert and P's representatives were subject to contempt for violating order); *see Sedona Principles, Second Edition*, at 52.

★

    (5) **Request in camera review.** The requesting party should ask the trial court to conduct an in camera review if there are any disputes over the privilege log. *In re Honza*, 242 S.W.3d at 582.

§9.2 Motion for protective order. A responding party who resists discovery may file a motion for protective order in response to a discovery request or to a motion to compel. TRCP 192.6(a). See "Motion for Protective Order," ch. 6-A, §20, p. 449. For a discussion of specific grounds for protecting the disclosure of electronic information, see *O'Connor's Federal Rules*, "Motion for protective order," ch. 6-C, §11.1, p. 505.

D. SECURING DISCOVERY FROM EXPERTS

§1. GENERAL

§1.1 Rules. TRCP 192.3, 192.7, 194.2(f), 195; see TRCP 197.1 (interrogatories cannot be used to secure information covered by TRCP 195).

§1.2 Purpose. This section discusses discovery about and from expert witnesses.

§1.3 Forms. *O'Connor's Texas Civil Forms* (2012), FORMS 6D.

§1.4 Other references. Brown & Rondon, *Texas Rules of Evidence Handbook* (2013) (referred to as Brown & Rondon, *Evidence Handbook*); Gold, *"Questioning God": Issues & Tactics When a Party Is Designated as a Testifying Expert*, Spring Training: Litigation Strategies Course, State Bar of Texas CLE, ch. 2 (2011); Gold, *"So, Who Died & Made You King?": How & When to Ask the Right Questions About Experts Under Texas' New Discovery Rules*, Advanced Medical Malpractice Course, State Bar of Texas CLE, Tab K (2000) (referred to as Gold, *How & When to Ask the Right Questions About Experts*); Griesel, *The "New" Texas Discovery Rules: Three Years Later*, Advanced Evidence & Discovery Course, State Bar of Texas CLE, ch. 2, §IX, p. 22 (2002) (referred to as Griesel, *The "New" Texas Discovery Rules*); *O'Connor's Texas Causes of Action* (2013) (*O'Connor's Texas COA*).

§2. TYPES OF EXPERTS

For purposes of litigation, an expert witness is a person with specialized knowledge who is consulted in anticipation of litigation or in preparation for trial and who renders opinions concerning the matters at issue. *See* TRCP 192.3(e); TRE 702-704. TRCP 192.3(e) recognizes two categories of experts: (1) testifying experts, which can be subdivided into retained and nonretained, and (2) consulting experts, which can be subdivided into consulting-only experts, consulting experts whose work was reviewed by a testifying expert, and consulting experts who obtain factual knowledge about the case.

§2.1 Testifying experts. A testifying expert is an expert who may be called to testify as an expert witness at trial. TRCP 192.7(c). Testifying experts are either retained or nonretained. Different discovery rules apply depending on whether the expert is retained.

    1. Retained testifying expert. A retained testifying expert is an expert who is retained by, employed by, or otherwise subject to the control of the party. *See* TRCP 194.2(f)(4), 195.3. Examples include a doctor employed to give an opinion in a breast-implant case and an accident reconstructionist retained in a car-accident case. Retained testifying experts are discoverable. See "Discovery about retained expert," §3.1.1, p. 504.

PRACTICE TIP

In medical-malpractice cases, plaintiff and defense attorneys are sure to argue about the phrase "retained by, employed by" in TRCP 194.2(f)(4). Does it include an emergency-room physician that the plaintiff did not choose and perhaps did not even pay? Probably not. Whether it includes treating physicians, who are seldom under a party's control and are often hostile to being called as witnesses, is an open question. Until this phrase is clarified by the courts, retained experts should probably be limited to physicians employed for litigation or subject to a party's control.

---------------------------------- ★ ----------------------------------

2. Nonretained testifying expert. A nonretained expert is an expert who is not retained by, employed by, or otherwise subject to the party's control. *See* TRCP 194.2(f)(3). Examples include an emergency-room doctor, an accident investigator for the DPS, and the other party's expert whom the party intends to call to testify. Nonretained testifying experts are discoverable. See "Discovery about nonretained expert," §3.1.2, p. 504.

§2.2 Consulting experts. A consulting expert is an expert who has been consulted, retained, or specially employed by a party in anticipation of litigation or in preparation for trial, but who is not a testifying expert. TRCP 192.7(d).

1. Consulting-only expert. A consulting-only expert is an expert (1) who is hired as a trial consultant only, (2) who is not expected to testify, (3) who has no firsthand factual knowledge about the case and no secondhand factual knowledge except for knowledge acquired through the consultation, and (4) whose work product, opinions, or mental impressions are not reviewed by the testifying expert. TRCP 192.3(e), 192.7(d); *see* TRCP 192.3(c); *In re Ford Motor Co.*, 988 S.W.2d 714, 719 (Tex.1998); *Lindsey v. O'Neill*, 689 S.W.2d 400, 402 (Tex.1985). The consulting-only expert privilege grants the party and its attorney a sphere of protection and privacy in which to develop their case. *General Motors Corp. v. Gayle*, 951 S.W.2d 469, 474 (Tex.1997). A party's employee can be a consulting-only expert if she was not employed in the area that is the subject of litigation, has no firsthand knowledge of facts, and was reassigned to that area specifically to assist her employer in anticipation of litigation or in preparation for trial. *Axelson, Inc. v. McIlhany*, 798 S.W.2d 550, 555 (Tex.1990); *see* TRCP 192.7(d). Information about consulting-only experts is not discoverable. *See Axelson, Inc.*, 798 S.W.2d at 554 & n.8; *see, e.g., Castellanos v. Littlejohn*, 945 S.W.2d 236, 239 (Tex.App.—San Antonio 1997, orig. proceeding) (because P's attorney hired doctor to examine P, not to treat P or to testify, doctor was not discoverable). See "No discovery about consulting-only expert," §3.2.1, p. 506.

PRACTICE TIP

Initially treating an expert as a consulting-only expert and assuring that the expert does not obtain factual knowledge of the case may allow the attorney to explore the consulting expert's opinions before designating her as a testifying expert and exposing those opinions to discovery in the case. To protect an expert's status as just a consulting-only expert, do not let the consulting expert view the site of the accident or examine or test the physical evidence in the case; do not let the consulting expert's work be reviewed by the testifying expert; and do not let the consulting expert interact with the testifying expert. Keep separate, segregated files for each expert, and keep a log of all documents reviewed by each expert.

---

2. Consulting expert + work reviewed = testifying expert. A consulting expert whose mental impressions and opinions were reviewed by a testifying expert is considered to be, and is treated just like, a testifying expert. TRCP 192.3(e); *In re Ford Motor Co.*, 988 S.W.2d at 719; *Martin v. Boles*, 843 S.W.2d 90, 92 (Tex.App.—Texarkana 1992, orig. proceeding). A consulting expert whose work was reviewed by the testifying expert is discoverable to the same extent as a testifying expert. *Beam v. A.H. Chaney, Inc.*, 56 S.W.3d 920, 925 (Tex.App.—Fort Worth 2001, pet. denied). Because employees of the testifying expert are not considered consulting experts if they did not form an opinion reviewed by the testifying expert, their disclosure is not required. *See, e.g., id.* at 925-26 (testifying expert's employee who did not form opinions or mental impressions in case and simply functioned as assistant was not consulting expert). See "Discovery about consulting expert + work reviewed," §3.2.2, p. 506.

3. Consulting expert + obtained facts = dual-capacity witness. A consulting expert who obtained knowledge about the case either firsthand or in some way other than in consultation about the case is considered a "dual-capacity witness" and is discoverable as a fact witness. TRCP 192.3(c). For example, when a consulting expert visits the accident site to measure skid marks, the expert acquires firsthand information about the case; thus, the expert's identity and factual knowledge must be disclosed, just as with other fact witnesses. *See, e.g., Axelson, Inc.*, 798 S.W.2d at 555 (consultants hired after accident to examine wellhead equipment were discoverable as fact witnesses; employee could not be a consulting-only expert because he was employed in area that became subject of

─────────────────────── ✦ ───────────────────────

litigation). By comparison, when a consulting expert examines a photograph of the accident site, the expert does not become discoverable as a fact witness. See "Discovery about consulting expert + obtained facts," §3.2.3, p. 506.

§3. AVAILABLE DISCOVERY PROCEDURES

		Testifying expert who is—		Consulting expert—	
6-6. PROCEDURES FOR SECURING DISCOVERY ABOUT & FROM EXPERTS					
Type of discovery		**Retained**	**Nonretained**	**Whose work was reviewed**	**With facts**
1	Request for disclosure. TRCP 192.1(a), 194.	Yes. TRCP 194.2(f), 195.1.	Yes. TRCP 194.2(f).	No.	Yes. TRCP 194.2(e).
2	Oral deposition. TRCP 192.1(f), 199.	Yes. TRCP 195.4.	Yes. TRCP 205.1(a).	Yes. TRCP 205.1(a).	Yes. TRCP 205.1(a).
3	Court-ordered expert report. TRCP 195.5.	Yes.	No.	No.	No.
4	Request for documents, separate from deposition. TRCP 176, 192.1(b).	No.	Yes. TRCP 195 cmt. 2.	Yes.	Yes.
5	Deposition on written questions. TRCP 192.1(f), 200, 205.1(b).	No.	Yes.	Yes.	Yes.
6	Interrogatories. TRCP 192.1(d), 197.1.	No.	No.	Yes.	Yes.
7	Request for admissions. TRCP 192.1(e), 198.1.	No.	No.	Yes.	Yes.

§3.1 Testifying experts. TRCP 195 is the main rule governing discovery from testifying experts.

1. Discovery about retained expert. There are four discovery procedures that can be used to secure information about or from a retained testifying expert: (1) a request for disclosure, (2) an expert report, (3) an oral deposition, and (4) a request for production with oral deposition. TRCP 194.2(f), 195.1, 195.4, 195.5. A party may not seek information about a retained testifying expert through depositions on written questions, interrogatories, or other forms of discovery not listed in TRCP 195.1. For the types of discoverable information about retained testifying experts, see "Information about retained testifying experts," §4.1.1, p. 506; for the types of discoverable information about retained nontestifying experts, see "Consulting experts," §4.2, p. 510.

2. Discovery about nonretained expert. There are four discovery procedures that can be used to secure information about or from a nonretained testifying expert: (1) a request for disclosure, (2) an oral deposition, (3) a deposition on written questions, and (4) a subpoena. TRCP 176, 194.2(f)(1)-(f)(3), 205.1. For example, a DPS officer who investigated an accident can be deposed on written questions or subpoenaed to attend an oral deposition, and information about the officer can be secured from a party by a request for disclosures (see "Nonretained testifying experts," ch. 6-E, §3.2.1(7), p. 517). Although TRCP 195.1 lists the permissible discovery tools for testifying experts, Comment 2 states that TRCP 195 does not address depositions of nonretained testifying experts nor the production from them of the materials listed in TRCP 192.3(e)(5) (witness bias) and TRCP 192.3(e)(6) (documents provided to or reviewed by the expert). TRCP 195 cmt. 2. For the scope of discovery from nonretained experts, see "Information about nonretained experts," §4.1.2, p. 509.

(1) Discovery from party. To secure information from the party about a designated, nonretained testifying expert, the other party should first secure the basic information available through a request for disclosure and then use the other discovery procedures (e.g., oral depositions of the party) to obtain more specific information.

(2) Discovery from nonretained expert. To secure information from a nonretained testifying expert, a party can use a subpoena and deposition (oral or written) to secure the following: (1) detailed information

✦

about those matters listed in TRCP 194.2(f)(2) and (f)(3) (the subject of testimony and substance of opinion), (2) information outlined in TRCP 194.2(f)(4) and 192.3 (things used or prepared by the expert in anticipation of testimony, and the expert's résumé and bibliography), and (3) any other discoverable information outlined in TRCP 192.3(e)(1)-(e)(6) (scope of discovery). For example, to secure information about a nonretained testifying expert's bias, the party may depose the expert or subpoena records from her.

(3) Discovery from treating doctors. Medical information is protected from disclosure by a number of federal and state rules and statutes. See "Physician-patient privilege," ch. 6-B, §3.10, p. 476; "Mental-health-information privilege," ch. 6-B, §3.11, p. 477; "Other medical privileges," ch. 6-B, §3.12, p. 477.

(a) Ex parte communications not prohibited. Ex parte communications between an attorney and the treating doctor of a party-patient are not specifically prohibited by any rule or statute. *Durst v. Hill Country Mem'l Hosp.*, 70 S.W.3d 233, 237-38 (Tex.App.—San Antonio 2001, no pet.); *see, e.g., Hogue v. Kroger Store*, 875 S.W.2d 477, 480-81 (Tex.App.—Houston [1st Dist.] 1994, writ denied) (court implicitly agreed that ex parte communications are not improper; court refused to permit P to cross-examine P's treating doctor about propriety of ex parte communications with D's attorney). But ex parte communications are limited by the physician-patient privilege, which generally prohibits the disclosure of confidential communications between a physician and patient. *See In re Collins*, 286 S.W.3d 911, 916 (Tex.2009). See "Physician-patient privilege," ch. 6-B, §3.10, p. 476. For exceptions to the physician-patient privilege, see "Certain physician-patient information," ch. 6-B, §2.18, p. 468. In most cases, a treating doctor will not speak to an attorney ex parte without a signed medical authorization. See "Disclosure from other health-care provider or entity," ch. 6-J, §3.2.2, p. 577. The Supreme Court has suggested that the statutory authorization forms given in medical-malpractice suits under CPRC §74.052 actually authorize ex parte communications. *See In re Collins*, 286 S.W.3d at 916-18 (CPRC §74.052 contemplates that ex parte communications are necessary to allow Ds to evaluate claims and settle those with merit early in litigation). For a discussion of the CPRC §74.052 authorization form for release of protected health-care information, see *O'Connor's Texas COA*, "Authorization form," ch. 20-A, §7.1.5, p. 625.

NOTE

In In re Collins, 286 S.W.3d 911 (Tex.2009), the Supreme Court clarified its opinion in Mutter v. Wood, 744 S.W.2d 600, 601 (Tex.1988), which held that the trial court abused its discretion by requiring the plaintiff to sign an authorization form allowing the defendant's attorney to discuss the plaintiff's medical information with treating physicians. See In re Collins, 286 S.W.3d at 918. In Collins, the Supreme Court made clear that the Mutter holding was not because the authorization form allowed for ex parte communications, but because it allowed access to information that was not relevant to the underlying suit, which was a clear violation of the physician-patient privilege. Id.

(b) Preventing ex parte communications. To prevent ex parte communications with a treating doctor, the attorney should take the following steps:

[1] Notify the treating doctor in writing that the doctor's patient (the attorney's client) does not authorize the doctor to discuss the patient's treatment or condition outside the presence of the patient's attorney, and that divulging any confidential information is a violation of the physician-patient privilege.

[2] Draft the medical authorization to expressly prohibit any ex parte communications. See "No ex parte discovery," ch. 6-J, §3.2.3, p. 577.

[3] Move for a protective order at the outset of the case to prevent ex parte communications with any of the patient's doctors. *See In re Collins*, 286 S.W.3d at 914; *In re Trostel*, No. 05-00-02059-CV (Tex. App.—Dallas 2001, orig. proceeding) (no pub.; 6-15-01). The motion should include the following arguments: (1) the patient's treating doctor has information that is not relevant to the suit, (2) the nonrelevant information is privileged, and (3) prohibiting ex parte communications with the doctor is necessary to protect the patient's privileged information. *See In re Collins*, 286 S.W.3d at 914. See "Motion for Protective Order," ch. 6-A, §20, p. 449.

⭐

§3.2 Consulting experts.

1. No discovery about consulting-only expert. Consulting-only experts are protected from discovery as part of the work-product privilege. *See* TRCP 195 cmt. 1. Because no information about a consulting-only expert is discoverable, there are no discovery tools that can be used to secure information about them or from them.

2. Discovery about consulting expert + work reviewed. A party cannot use TRCP 194.2(f) (request for disclosures about testifying experts) or TRCP 195 (discovery from testifying experts) to secure information about a consulting expert whose work was reviewed by the testifying expert. See "Procedures for Securing Discovery About & from Experts," chart 6-6, p. 504. However, a party may use any other discovery rule to secure this information. *See* TRCP 195 cmt. 1 (methods of securing discovery about consulting expert whose work was reviewed by testifying expert are not limited by TRCP 195). Thus, a party may use interrogatories, requests for admissions, requests for production, and any other type of discovery.

3. Discovery about consulting expert + obtained facts. The discovery procedures available to secure information about a consulting expert who has firsthand knowledge about the facts or secondhand knowledge gained outside the consultation are the same as those for securing information about fact witnesses. *See* TRCP 192.3(c). Thus, to secure information about these consulting experts, a party may use requests for disclosures in TRCP 194.2(e) (for fact witnesses), interrogatories, requests for admissions, and any other type of discovery.

§4. INFORMATION DISCOVERABLE FROM EXPERTS

6-7. SCOPE OF DISCOVERY FROM EXPERTS				
	Testifying expert who is—		**Consulting expert—**	
Information to be discovered	**Retained**	**Nonretained**	**Whose work was reviewed**	**With facts**
1 Identity of expert. TRCP 192.3(e)(1).	Yes	Yes	Yes	Yes
2 Subject matter of testimony. TRCP 192.3(e)(2).	Yes	Yes	Yes	N/A
3 Facts learned through consultation. TRCP 192.3(e)(3).	Yes	Yes	Yes	No
4 Firsthand facts acquired directly from evidence. TRCP 192.3(e)(3).	Yes	Yes	Yes	Yes
5 Secondhand facts learned outside of consultation. TRCP 192.3(e)(3).	Yes	Yes	Yes	Yes
6 Mental impressions, opinions and methods used to derive opinions. TRCP 192.3(e)(4).	Yes	Yes	Yes	No
7 Bias of witness. TRCP 192.3(e)(5).	Yes	Yes	Yes	Maybe ❶
8 Materials and documents created or used by expert. TRCP 192.3(e)(6).	Yes	Yes	Yes	No
9 Written report. TRCP 192.3(e)(6).	Yes	Maybe ❷	Yes	N/A
10 Résumé and bibliography. TRCP 192.3(e)(7).	Yes	Yes	Yes	No

❶ When a party is entitled to bias information about a consulting expert with facts, it cannot obtain that information under TRCP 192.3(e), which outlines the scope of discovery for consulting and testifying experts.

❷ If the nonretained expert did not create a written report, a party cannot force the expert to prepare one.

§4.1 Testifying experts.

1. Information about retained testifying experts. Parties are entitled to full discovery of each other's retained testifying experts. TRCP 192.3(e), 192.5(c)(1), 194.2(f); *Aluminum Co. of Am. v. Bullock*, 870 S.W.2d

2, 4 (Tex.1994); *Collins v. Collins*, 904 S.W.2d 792, 800 (Tex.App.—Houston [1st Dist.] 1995), *writ denied*, 923 S.W.2d 569 (Tex.1996). The following is a list of the discoverable information about retained testifying experts:

(1) Identity. A party is entitled to the names, addresses, and telephone numbers of the retained testifying expert witnesses. TRCP 192.3(e)(1); *see Morrow v. H.E.B., Inc.*, 714 S.W.2d 297, 297 (Tex.1986) (duty to supplement if witness acquires new address). This information can be secured through a request for disclosure. TRCP 194.2(f)(1).

(2) Subject of testimony. A party is entitled to discover the subject matter on which the retained testifying expert will testify. TRCP 192.3(e)(2); *see Aluminum Co.*, 870 S.W.2d at 4. A brief form of this information can be obtained from the other party through a request for disclosure. TRCP 194.2(f)(2). More detailed information can be secured through an oral deposition or an expert's report. *See* TRCP 195.1, 195.4, 195.5.

(3) Facts. A party is entitled to discover the facts known by the retained testifying expert that relate to or form the basis of the expert's mental impressions and opinions formed or made in connection with the case, regardless of when and how the factual information was acquired. TRCP 192.3(e)(3). A brief form of this information can be obtained from the other party through a request for disclosure. TRCP 194.2(f)(3). More detailed information can be secured through an oral deposition or an expert's report. *See* TRCP 195.1, 195.4, 195.5.

(4) Opinions. A party is entitled to discover the mental impressions and opinions of the retained testifying expert and any methods used to derive them. TRCP 192.3(e)(4); *Yarborough v. Tarrant Appr. Dist.*, 846 S.W.2d 552, 553 (Tex.App.—Fort Worth 1993, no writ). Any information about the testifying expert's mental impressions or opinions is discoverable. TRCP 192.3(e)(4); *see, e.g., In re Family Hospice, Ltd.*, 62 S.W.3d 313, 316 (Tex. App.—El Paso 2001, orig. proceeding) (expert's notes made while reviewing interrogatories were discoverable). The general substance of the retained testifying expert's mental impressions and opinions and a brief summary of the basis for them can be obtained from the other party through a request for disclosure. TRCP 194.2(f)(3). More detailed information can be secured through an oral deposition or an expert's report. *See* TRCP 195.1, 195.4, 195.5.

PRACTICE TIP
*TRCP 192.3(e)(4) permits discovery of, among other things, the expert's method in arriving at an opinion. However, TRCP 194.2(f) does not include this among the matters that must be disclosed in response to a request for disclosure. A responding party should include the expert's methodology, even though it is not required by TRCP 194.2(f), because that party will have the burden to show the expert's methodology is sound if the expert's opinion is challenged as inadmissible under TRE 702. See **Merrell Dow Pharms. v. Havner**, 953 S.W.2d 706, 714 (Tex.1997) (expert's opinion is not admissible if it is based on flawed methodology). See "Motion to Exclude Expert," ch. 5-N, p. 410.*

---

(5) Evidence of bias. A party is entitled to discover information about the retained testifying expert's potential bias. TRCP 192.3(e)(5); *In re Doctors' Hosp.*, 2 S.W.3d 504, 507 (Tex.App.—San Antonio 1999, orig. proceeding); *see also* TRE 613(b) (evidence of witness's bias is considered relevant and admissible). See Brown & Rondon, *Evidence Handbook*, p. 636. When discoverable, bias information from a retained testifying expert can be secured through questions during an oral deposition, a request for production of documents sent with a notice of an oral deposition, and as part of the expert's report. *See* TRCP 195.4, 195.5.

(a) List of expert's other cases. A party should always ask the expert to produce a list of all other cases in which she submitted an expert report within the last four years, and the amount of money paid for any appearance at a deposition or trial. *Cf.* FRCP 26(a)(2)(B) (in federal cases, the rule requires, as part of expert's written report, a list of all other cases in which she testified as expert at trial or by deposition within the last four years). This information can be secured through a targeted request for disclosure asking for the information as part of the expert's résumé, by deposition, or as part of a court-ordered report.

───────────────────────────── ✦ ─────────────────────────────

(b) Personal records to impeach. Personal financial records and appointment books are generally not discoverable to demonstrate bias of a nonparty witness. *See Russell v. Young*, 452 S.W.2d 434, 435 (Tex. 1970); *In re Makris*, 217 S.W.3d 521, 524 (Tex.App.—San Antonio 2006, orig. proceeding). Whether a party can obtain a nonparty expert's personal records (i.e., records not directly related to the suit) to impeach depends on whether the expert's credibility is at issue.

[1] Credibility not at issue. If the expert's credibility is not at issue, the party must show the possibility that the expert is biased before it is entitled to discovery of the expert's personal records to impeach. *See, e.g.*, *Walker v. Packer*, 827 S.W.2d 833, 838-39 (Tex.1992) (P proved expert possibly biased); *In re Wharton*, 226 S.W.3d 452, 457-58 (Tex.App.—Waco 2005, orig. proceeding) (P did not prove expert possibly biased); *In re Makris*, 217 S.W.3d at 524-25 (same).

[2] Credibility at issue. If the party can show that the expert's credibility is at issue, the party is entitled to the expert's personal records in order to impeach. *See, e.g.*, *Walker*, 827 S.W.2d at 838 (expert's credibility at issue when contradicted by colleague).

(6) Materials used by expert.

(a) General. A party is entitled to all documents, tangible things, physical models, reports, compilations of data, or other material provided to, reviewed by, or prepared by or for the retained testifying expert in anticipation of the expert's testimony. TRCP 192.3(e)(6), 194.2(f)(4)(A); *see In re Christus Spohn Hosp. Kleberg*, 222 S.W.3d 434, 437-38 (Tex.2007); *Vela v. Wagner & Brown, Ltd.*, 203 S.W.3d 37, 58 (Tex.App.—San Antonio 2006, no pet.). These materials are discoverable if they are provided to a testifying expert, regardless of whether they were actually read by or prepared for the expert. TRCP 192.5(c)(1); *see In re Christus Spohn Hosp. Kleberg*, 222 S.W.3d at 444-45. Everything provided to, reviewed by, or prepared by or for the retained testifying expert in preparation of the expert's testimony is discoverable, including the expert's file, communications with the parties and their attorneys, and drafts of reports prepared by the expert. TRCP 194.2(f)(4)(A). This information can be secured from the party through either a request for disclosure or an oral deposition with a request for documents. TRCP 194.2(f)(4)(A), 195.4.

───

PRACTICE TIP

Do not rely on cases that apply old TRCP 166b to decide what documents used by retained testifying experts are discoverable. TRCP 192.3(e)(6), which was adopted in 1999 to replace TRCP 166b, expanded the list of the discoverable documents used by an expert to form an opinion. TRCP 192.3(e)(6) includes documents that were "provided to [or] reviewed by" an expert. In re Christus Spohn Hosp. Kleberg, 222 S.W.3d at 438. The change was made to avoid disputes about what documents the expert may have relied on to reach an opinion. Id.

───

(b) Inadvertent disclosure. When a party inadvertently discloses privileged materials to its own testifying expert, those materials become discoverable and generally cannot be retrieved by the party under the snap-back rule. *In re Christus Spohn Hosp. Kleberg*, 222 S.W.3d at 441. The policy concerns underlying the expert-disclosure rule mandate that the rules requiring discovery of the materials provided to an expert, TRCP 192.3(e)(6) and TRCP 192.5(c)(1), prevail over the snap-back provision in TRCP 193.3(d). Once privileged materials are inadvertently disclosed, the party has two options to avoid waiving the privilege.

───

PRACTICE TIP

One way to avoid inadvertent disclosure of privileged information to a testifying expert is to keep a detailed log of all documents provided and to make sure all documents provided contain an identifying "Bates number."

───

[1] Invoke snap-back provision. Although the snap-back provision generally does not apply to privileged documents inadvertently disclosed to an expert, the party may be able to make a persuasive argument that the disclosed materials could not, by their nature, have influenced the expert's opinion. *In re Christus*

⎯⎯⎯⎯⎯⎯⎯⎯⎯⎯⎯⎯ ✯ ⎯⎯⎯⎯⎯⎯⎯⎯⎯⎯⎯⎯

Spohn Hosp. Kleberg, 222 S.W.3d at 441. See "Use snap-back provision," ch. 6-A, §18.2.4, p. 444. The party seeking snap-back under this argument bears a heavy burden, considering the underlying purpose of the expert-disclosure rule. *In re Christus Spohn Hosp. Kleberg*, 222 S.W.3d at 441.

[2] **Request replacement expert.** As an alternative to snap-back, the party can withdraw the expert's designation and name a new expert. *In re Christus Spohn Hosp. Kleberg*, 222 S.W.3d at 445. If the deadline for designating experts has passed, the party should file a motion for leave to designate a replacement. *Id.* The trial court should carefully weigh a request for leave to designate a replacement expert against the possibility of imposing what may amount to death-penalty sanctions against the party. *Id.*

(7) Expert's report. A party is entitled to copies of reports prepared by or for the retained testifying expert in anticipation of the expert's testimony. TRCP 192.3(e)(6), 194.2(f)(4)(A). A report prepared by a retained testifying expert can be secured as part of a request for disclosure. TRCP 194.2(f)(4)(A). When the retained testifying expert has not prepared a written report, the trial court may order that a report be put in writing or other tangible form and produced. TRCP 195.5; *Loftin v. Martin*, 776 S.W.2d 145, 147 (Tex.1989); *see, e.g.*, *Dennis v. Haden*, 867 S.W.2d 48, 51-52 (Tex.App.—Texarkana 1993, writ denied) (because party did not provide expert's report as required by pretrial order, expert should have been excluded). See "Expert's Report," §7, p. 513; *O'Connor's Texas Forms*, FORM 6D:1.

(8) Résumé & bibliography. A party is entitled to the current résumé and bibliography of retained testifying experts. TRCP 192.3(e)(7), 194.2(f)(4)(B). The résumé and bibliography can be secured through a request for disclosure. TRCP 194.2(f)(4)(B). If the facts on the résumé change before trial, the party has a duty to supplement. *See, e.g.*, *City of Paris v. McDowell*, 79 S.W.3d 601, 606 (Tex.App.—Texarkana 2002, no pet.) (expert earned a master's degree between initial disclosure and trial, which was not reflected on résumé).

2. Information about nonretained experts. The following is a list of the information discoverable about and from nonretained testifying experts:

(1) Identity. A party is entitled to the name, address, and telephone number of the nonretained testifying expert witnesses. TRCP 192.3(e)(1).

(2) Subject of testimony. A party is entitled to discover the subject matter of the nonretained testifying expert's testimony. TRCP 192.3(e)(2). A brief form of this information may be obtained from the other party through a request for disclosure. TRCP 194.2(f)(2). A more detailed form of the information may be obtained from the nonretained expert through an oral deposition, a deposition on written questions, or a subpoena. TRCP 176, 205; TRCP 195 cmt. 2.

(3) Facts. A party is entitled to discover the facts known by the nonretained testifying expert that relate to or form the basis of the expert's mental impressions and opinions. TRCP 192.3(e)(3). A brief form of this information may be obtained from the other party through a request for disclosure. TRCP 194.2(f)(3). A more detailed form of this information may be obtained from the nonretained expert through an oral deposition, a deposition on written questions, or a subpoena. TRCP 176, 205; TRCP 195 cmt. 2.

(4) Opinions. A party is entitled to discover the general substance of the nonretained testifying expert's mental impressions and opinions and the basis for them. TRCP 192.3(e)(4). A brief form of this information or documents that reflect this information may be obtained from the other party through a request for disclosure. TRCP 194.2(f)(3). A more detailed form of this information may be obtained from the nonretained expert through an oral deposition, a deposition on written questions, or a subpoena. TRCP 176, 205; TRCP 195 cmt. 2.

(5) Evidence of bias. A party is entitled to discover information about the nonretained testifying expert's potential bias. TRCP 192.3(e)(5). This information can be secured from the nonretained expert through an oral deposition, a deposition on written questions, or a subpoena for documents. TRCP 176, 205; TRCP 195 cmt. 2. Bias evidence about a nonretained testifying expert cannot be secured through TRCP 194 (request for disclosure) or TRCP 195 (discovery about testifying expert). TRCP 195 cmt. 2.

✦

(6) Materials used by expert. A party is entitled to all documents, tangible things, physical models, reports, compilations of data, or other materials provided to, reviewed by, or prepared by or for the nonretained testifying expert in anticipation of the expert's testimony. TRCP 192.3(e)(6). This information can be secured from the nonretained expert through an oral deposition, a deposition on written questions, or a subpoena for documents. TRCP 176, 205; TRCP 195 cmt. 2. Materials used by a nontestifying expert cannot be secured through TRCP 194 (request for disclosure) or TRCP 195 (discovery about testifying expert). TRCP 195 cmt. 2.

(7) Expert's report. A report prepared by the nonretained testifying expert may be secured from the expert through TRCP 176 or TRCP 205. A nonretained expert's report cannot be secured through TRCP 194 or TRCP 195. TRCP 195 cmt. 2. See "Expert's Report," §7, p. 513.

(8) Résumé & bibliography. A party is entitled to the current résumé and bibliography of the nonretained testifying expert. TRCP 192.3(e)(7). The nonretained expert's résumé and bibliography can be secured from the nonretained expert through an oral deposition, a deposition on written questions, or a subpoena. TRCP 176, 205; TRCP 195 cmt. 2.

§4.2 Consulting experts.

1. Consulting-only expert – no discovery. Consulting-only experts are protected from discovery as part of the work-product privilege. *See* TRCP 195 cmt. 1. No information about a consulting-only expert is discoverable—not the expert's identity, mental impressions, opinions, or work product. TRCP 192.3(e); *In re City of Georgetown*, 53 S.W.3d 328, 334 (Tex.2001); *In re Ford Motor Co.*, 988 S.W.2d 714, 719 (Tex.1998); *see also Aguilar v. Trujillo*, 162 S.W.3d 839, 848 (Tex.App.—El Paso 2005, pet. denied) (P abused discovery process when he contacted D's consulting expert without D's consent and hired him to be Ps' expert witness). Tests conducted by a consulting expert are protected from discovery as long as the tests are not conducted on the physical evidence in the case and the results are not reviewed by a testifying expert. *See* TRCP 192.3(e); *see, e.g.,* ***General Motors Corp. v. Gayle***, 951 S.W.2d 469, 474-75 (Tex.1997) (consulting experts could conduct crash tests). Materials protected by the privilege for the nondiscoverable consulting-only expert cannot be discovered, and the privilege is not subject to the "need-and-hardship" exception stated in TRCP 192.5(b)(2). *See* TRCP 192.3(e); TRCP 195 cmt. 1.

2. Information about consulting expert + work reviewed. A party is entitled to obtain the same information about a consulting expert whose work was reviewed by a testifying expert as it can obtain about the testifying expert. TRCP 192.3(e); *Vela v. Wagner & Brown, Ltd.*, 203 S.W.3d 37, 58 (Tex.App.—San Antonio 2006, no pet.). See "Information about retained testifying experts," §4.1.1, p. 506.

PRACTICE TIP
Although TRCP 195 limits the procedures for securing discovery about testifying experts, it does not limit the procedures for securing discovery about discoverable consulting experts. TRCP 195 cmt. 1. Discovery about discoverable consulting experts can be obtained through any means permitted by the TRCPs (interrogatories, requests for production, depositions, etc.).

---

3. Information about consulting expert + obtained facts. A consulting expert with facts about the case is discoverable as a fact witness. See "Consulting expert + obtained facts = dual-capacity witness," §2.2.3, p. 503. A party can obtain the same information about a consulting expert who has knowledge of facts as it can obtain about a fact witness. TRCP 192.3(c) (scope of discovery), TRCP 192.5(c)(1) (exception to work product), TRCP 194.2(e) (request for disclosure). A party may obtain this discovery through TRCP 194.2(e) and any other discovery rule except TRCP 195. The information discoverable about a consulting expert with facts includes the following:

(1) Identity. A party is entitled to the name, address, and telephone number of an expert who has firsthand knowledge of facts or secondhand knowledge of facts obtained outside of the consultation. TRCP 192.3(c) (scope of discovery), TRCP 194.2(e) (request for disclosure of fact witnesses).

✦

(2) Connection with case. A party is entitled to obtain a brief description of the consulting expert's connection with the case. TRCP 192.3(c), 194.2(e). This does not mean the party must provide a narrative statement of the facts the expert knows. TRCP 192 cmt. 3. For example, the description could be "examined wellhead after accident." *Id.*

(3) Facts known by consultant. A party is entitled to obtain the following information known by the consultant:

(a) Firsthand facts. The consultant's firsthand knowledge about information in the case. TRCP 192.3(c).

(b) Secondhand facts. The consultant's secondhand knowledge (i.e., hearsay) about facts in the case learned in some way other than in consultation about the case (i.e., not in anticipation of litigation or in preparation for trial). TRCP 192.3(c).

(4) Witness statements. A party is entitled to obtain a witness statement given by a consulting expert who has knowledge of the facts. TRCP 192.3(h).

§5. SUPPLEMENTING EXPERT DISCOVERY

A party has a duty to amend and supplement discovery about its testifying experts. TRCP 195.6. See *O'Connor's Texas Forms*, FORMS 6D:2-3.

§5.1 Supplementing discovery of retained testifying expert. An expert cannot give an opinion at trial that was not provided in response to discovery, unless there is good cause to permit it or the opinion would not unfairly surprise or prejudice the other parties. TRCP 193.6(a); *Moore v. Memorial Hermann Hosp. Sys.*, 140 S.W.3d 870, 874 (Tex.App.—Houston [14th Dist.] 2004, no pet.); *see, e.g., VingCard A.S. v. Merrimac Hospitality Sys.*, 59 S.W.3d 847, 856-57 (Tex.App.—Fort Worth 2001, pet. denied) (court did not find good cause but found admission of expert's opinion harmless error); *see also Ersek v. Davis & Davis, P.C.*, 69 S.W.3d 268, 271 (Tex.App.—Austin 2002, pet. denied) (court did not find good cause for designating expert after deadline, more than a year after filing suit).

1. Written discovery responses. A party's duty to amend and supplement written discovery about a retained testifying expert is governed by TRCP 193.5. TRCP 195.6; *VingCard A.S.*, 59 S.W.3d at 855. See "Supplementing Discovery Responses," ch. 6-A, §17, p. 440.

2. Deposition testimony.

(1) Supplementation required. To the extent a party's retained testifying expert changes or modifies her opinion, the party must amend and supplement the expert's deposition testimony regarding the expert's mental impressions or opinions and the basis for them. TRCP 195.6; *see Collins v. Collins*, 923 S.W.2d 569, 569 (Tex. 1996); *see, e.g., Farm Servs. v. Gonzales*, 756 S.W.2d 747, 750 (Tex.App.—Corpus Christi 1988, writ denied) (testimony of expert who changed her opinion after deposition should have been excluded); *see also Titus Cty. Hosp. Dist. v. Lucas*, 988 S.W.2d 740, 740 (Tex.1998) (acknowledging a narrow duty to supplement certain expert testimony); *Collins v. Collins*, 904 S.W.2d 792, 801 (Tex.App.—Houston [1st Dist.] 1995) (in divorce proceeding, husband could not testify about value of business because he did not identify himself as expert and said in deposition that he would not testify as expert), *writ denied*, 923 S.W.2d 569 (Tex.1996).

(2) Supplementation not required. An expert can modify her testimony based on refinements in her calculations made shortly before trial without invoking the need to supplement. *Exxon Corp. v. West Tex. Gathering Co.*, 868 S.W.2d 299, 304 (Tex.1993); *see, e.g., Koko Motel, Inc. v. Mayo*, 91 S.W.3d 41, 51 (Tex.App.—Amarillo 2002, pet. denied) (change in opinion was merely a refinement because data and formula were already in record). An expert can also modify her testimony without supplementation if the opinion expands on a subject that has already been disclosed. *Norfolk S. Ry. v. Bailey*, 92 S.W.3d 577, 581 (Tex.App.—Austin 2002, no pet.); *see Navistar Int'l Transp. v. Crim Truck & Tractor Co.*, 883 S.W.2d 687, 691 (Tex.App.—Texarkana 1994, writ denied).

✦

The testimony of an expert should not be barred because a change in some minor detail of the person's work was not disclosed a month before trial. *Exxon Corp.*, 868 S.W.2d at 304.

3. Expert's report. A party has a duty to amend and supplement the report of the retained testifying expert on the expert's mental impressions or opinions and the basis for them. TRCP 195.6.

§5.2 Supplementing discovery of nonretained testifying expert. A party has a duty to amend and supplement discovery about a nonretained testifying expert as set out in TRCP 193.5. Under that rule, a party has a duty to supplement its written responses to discovery relating to a nonretained expert. See "When supplementation required," ch. 6-A, §17.1, p. 440. A party has no burden to supplement the deposition testimony of a nonretained testifying expert. *See* TRCP 193.5(a) (duty to supplement written discovery, not oral discovery). The nonretained testifying expert has no burden to supplement her own responses to discovery. *See* TRCP 205 (discovery from nonparties).

PRACTICE TIP
Instruct your experts to promptly inform you of any change in their responses (oral or written) so you can timely supplement or amend your discovery responses. Whether or not you think the change is material, supplement or amend your discovery responses to ensure the expert's changed testimony is not excluded.

---

§6. DEADLINES FOR SECURING DISCOVERY FROM EXPERTS

The deadline for securing discovery from experts depends on the designation of the experts.

§6.1 Deadlines to designate testifying experts. The designation of testifying experts is accomplished by furnishing the information about the experts requested under TRCP 194.2(f). TRCP 195.2.

1. Making designation. TRCP 195.2 establishes a schedule for responding to requests for disclosure about testifying experts. The schedule may be modified by court order (for good cause) or by agreement of the parties. TRCP 191.1, 195.2. A party must designate its testifying experts and supply the information required by TRCP 194.2(f) within the following time periods:

(1) Plaintiff's expert. A party seeking affirmative relief (generally the plaintiff) must identify its testifying experts within 30 days after service of the request for disclosures or 90 days before the end of the discovery period, whichever is later. TRCP 195.2(a); *Ersek v. Davis & Davis, P.C.*, 69 S.W.3d 268, 270 (Tex.App.—Austin 2002, pet. denied); *Snider v. Stanley*, 44 S.W.3d 713, 715 (Tex.App.—Beaumont 2001, pet. denied).

(2) Defendant's expert. A party who is not seeking affirmative relief (generally the defendant) must identify its testifying experts within 30 days after service of the request for disclosures or 60 days before the end of the discovery period, whichever is later. *See* TRCP 195.2(b); *Wigfall v. TDCJ*, 137 S.W.3d 268, 272 (Tex.App.—Houston [1st Dist.] 2004, no pet.).

NOTE
Even though TRCP 195.2 and 195.3 require the plaintiff to designate and present its experts for deposition first, the trial court may alter this schedule under TRCP 191. TRCP 195 cmt. 3; Griesel, The "New" Texas Discovery Rules, at 22. For example, the court could modify the schedule if a contested issue on which expert testimony is required is raised by an affirmative defense rather than by the primary liability claim. Griesel, The "New" Texas Discovery Rules, at 22.

---

2. Changing designation. Once an expert is designated as a testifying expert, the expert can be redesignated as a consulting expert as long as there is no bargain between adversaries to suppress testimony or other improper purpose behind the redesignation. *In re Doctors' Hosp.*, 2 S.W.3d 504, 506 (Tex.App.—San Antonio 1999, orig. proceeding); *see, e.g., Tom L. Scott, Inc. v. McIlhany*, 798 S.W.2d 556, 560 (Tex.1990) (redesignation was improper because it was part of bargain between adversaries to suppress testimony); *Lopez v. Martin*, 10 S.W.3d 790,

———————————————————— ✯ ————————————————————

794 (Tex.App.—Corpus Christi 2000, pet. denied) (nothing in record indicated redesignation was made for improper purpose); *Castellanos v. Littlejohn*, 945 S.W.2d 236, 239 (Tex.App.—San Antonio 1997, orig. proceeding) (party who accidentally listed consulting expert as testifying expert could redesignate); *see also Harnischfeger Corp. v. Stone*, 814 S.W.2d 263, 265 (Tex.App.—Houston [14th Dist.] 1991, orig. proceeding) (D could not designate same expert as testifying expert in one case and nontestifying expert in companion case).

§6.2 Deadlines to depose testifying experts.

1. Deposing retained testifying experts. TRCP 195.3 establishes a schedule for deposing testifying experts retained by, employed by, or otherwise subject to the control of a party.

(1) Plaintiff did not furnish report. If the party seeking affirmative relief (generally, the plaintiff) did not furnish a report when it designated its retained testifying expert, it must tender the expert for deposition reasonably promptly after designation and before the other party is required to designate its experts. TRCP 195.3(a)(1) & cmt. 3; *Vaughn v. Ford Motor Co.*, 91 S.W.3d 387, 392 (Tex.App.—Eastland 2002, pet. denied). When, because of the actions of the plaintiff, the deposition cannot be concluded more than 15 days before the deadline for designating other experts, the deadline must be extended for other experts testifying on the same subject. TRCP 195.3(a)(1); *see also* Gold, *How & When to Ask the Right Questions About Experts* §IV(D), at 10 (under TRCP 195.3, deadline should not be extended if P attempted in good faith to schedule expert's deposition before deadline expired).

(2) Plaintiff furnished report. If the party seeking affirmative relief (generally the plaintiff) produced a report when it designated its retained testifying expert, the burden shifts to the other party to designate its experts testifying on the same subject before the plaintiff is required to tender its expert for deposition. TRCP 195.3(a)(2) & cmt. 3. This provision is a compromise designed to allow defendants to obtain sufficient information from plaintiffs to enable them to obtain appropriate experts, yet prevent plaintiffs from being unfairly surprised or "sandbagged." Griesel, *The "New" Texas Discovery Rules*, at 22.

(3) Defendant's experts. A party not seeking affirmative relief (generally the defendant) must tender its expert for deposition "reasonably promptly" after it designates its expert and after the plaintiff's experts have been deposed on the same subject. TRCP 195.3(b).

2. Deposing nonretained testifying experts. A party is not required to "tender" a nonretained testifying expert for a deposition. TRCP 195 cmt. 2 (TRCP 195 does not address depositions of nonretained testifying experts). The deposition of a nonretained testifying expert may be taken according to the same rules as for deposing nonparties. *See* TRCP 199 (oral depositions), TRCP 205 (discovery from nonparties). See "Procedure for Standard Oral Deposition," ch. 6-F, §4, p. 526.

§6.3 Deadlines to supplement. See "Deadline to supplement responses," ch. 6-A, §17.4, p. 441.

§6.4 Discovery deadline after trial reset. See "Discovery deadline when trial reset," ch. 6-A, §14.1.4, p. 438.

§7. EXPERT'S REPORT

There is no requirement that parties automatically produce expert reports.

§7.1 Contents of expert's report. An expert's report includes the discoverable factual observations, tests, supporting data, calculations, photographs, and opinions of the expert. TRCP 195.5. The report must provide the expert's opinion and the basis for it. *See Mauzey v. Sutliff*, 125 S.W.3d 71, 84 (Tex.App.—Austin 2003, pet. denied) (trial courts must ensure that expert report fully discloses substance of and basis for expert's mental impressions). For example, a report in a medical-malpractice suit might contain a medical history, diagnosis, prognosis, opinions, impressions, and causation. *Tibbetts v. Gagliardi*, 2 S.W.3d 659, 663 n.1 (Tex.App.—Houston [14th Dist.] 1999, pet. denied); *see* CPRC §74.351(j), (r)(6). The expert's report can be secured through a request for disclosure or by court order.

§7.2 Securing report from retained testifying expert.

1. By request for disclosure.

(1) Request. A party can ask for a report from the other party's retained testifying expert in a request for disclosure. TRCP 194.2(f)(4)(A).

★

(2) Response. The party responding to a request for disclosure under TRCP 194.2(f)(4)(A) has two choices:

(a) Produce report. The party may ask its retained expert to produce a report to be provided to the requesting party. TRCP 195 cmt. 3. The production of the report will trigger the designation of the other party's expert. *Id.*

(b) Tender expert. A party that does not want to incur the expense of creating a report may simply tender its retained expert for deposition. TRCP 195 cmt. 3.

2. By court order. A party can file a motion asking for a court order requiring the other party to produce an expert report from its retained testifying experts. TRCP 195.5. See *O'Connor's Texas Forms*, FORM 6D:1. The court can order that the report of a retained expert be reduced to a tangible form and produced. TRCP 195.5. The court can order a report from a testifying expert as well as a deposition. *Id.*

§7.3 Securing report from nonretained expert. A nonretained expert's report cannot be secured through TRCP 194 (request for disclosures) or TRCP 195.5 (court-ordered report). *See* TRCP 195 cmt. 2.

1. From nonretained expert.

(1) By deposition & subpoena. If the nonretained expert prepared a report, a copy can be secured from the expert through a discovery subpoena to appear and produce at a deposition or simply to produce. *See* TRCP 176, 205. See "Securing Things from a Nonparty," ch. 6-I, §5, p. 569.

(2) By request for medical records. In a suit alleging physical or mental injury, a party may request that the injured party produce medical records or furnish an authorization permitting disclosure of medical records. TRCP 194.2(j). See "Request for Party's Medical Records or Authorization," ch. 6-J, §3, p. 576.

(3) By payment. A party may offer to pay a nonretained expert to prepare a report. However, if the nonretained expert had a privileged relationship with the other party (e.g., doctor-patient), a party cannot offer to pay the nonretained expert to prepare a report without the patient's consent.

2. From other party.

(1) By request for disclosure. If the nonretained expert's report was provided to, reviewed by, or prepared for the retained testifying expert, the party can secure it as part of the request for information about the retained expert. TRCP 194.2(f)(4)(A).

(2) By request for production. If a party has a copy of a nontestifying expert's report that was not provided to its retained testifying expert, other parties can secure a copy of it by a request for production. *See* TRCP 196.1(a).

(3) By witness-statement request. If a party has a copy of a witness statement made by the nonretained testifying expert, other parties are entitled to obtain a copy of it. TRCP 192.3(h).

3. Under Public Information Act. If the nonretained expert is a police officer or other public official, a party may be able to secure a copy of the officer's report under the Public Information Act. *See* Gov't Code §§552.021, 552.022.

§8. PAYING THE EXPERT

§8.1 Expert fees for most discovery. As a rule, a party pays the fees charged by its expert. The amount of the fees is established by the contract between the party and the expert.

§8.2 Expert fees for depositions.

1. Retained expert of opposing party. When a party takes the oral deposition of an expert witness retained by the opposing party, all reasonable fees charged by the expert for time spent in preparing for, giving, reviewing, and correcting the deposition must be paid by the party who retained the expert. TRCP 195.7. If the party who

★

retained the expert suspects the other side is purposefully running up the costs and abusing TRCP 195.7, that party can seek relief under TRCP 191.1 (trial court has the power to modify discovery procedures and limitations) and TRCP 192.6 (the party can seek protective order). TRCP 191.1 permits a trial court, for good cause, to modify the allocation of fees and expenses. *See* TRCP 191.1 & cmt. 1. See "Modifying discovery by court order," ch. 6-A, §6.2, p. 429.

2. Nonretained expert. The TRCPs do not address the issue of who pays for the deposition of a nonretained expert. The nonretained expert's fees for the deposition should probably be paid by the party who notices the deposition. For example, if the defendant notices the deposition of an emergency-room doctor who treated the plaintiff after the accident, the defendant should pay for the expert's fees, not the plaintiff.

E. REQUESTS FOR DISCLOSURE

§1. GENERAL

§1.1 Rule. TRCP 194.

§1.2 Purpose. A request for disclosure is a written request for information designed to produce basic discovery of specific categories of information. TRCP 194 cmt. 1. This procedure is borrowed from the federal discovery rules. Griesel, *The "New" Texas Discovery Rules: Three Years Later*, Advanced Evidence & Discovery Course, State Bar of Texas CLE, ch. 2, p. 19 (2002). Unlike interrogatories, disclosure responses are not verified, and no objections are permitted. TRCP 194.5. Requests for disclosure will likely be the first form of discovery in a lawsuit.

§1.3 Forms. See *O'Connor's Texas Civil Forms* (2012), FORMS 6E.

§1.4 Other references. Griesel, *The "New" Texas Discovery Rules: Three Years Later*, Advanced Evidence & Discovery Course, State Bar of Texas CLE, ch. 2, §VIII, p. 19 (referred to as Griesel, *The "New" Texas Discovery Rules*); Pemberton, *The First Year Under the New Discovery Rules: The Big Issues Thus Far* (2000), www.supreme.courts .state.tx.us/rules/tdr/disc1yr.pdf (referred to as Pemberton, *The First Year*).

§2. SCOPE

The scope of discovery for disclosures is governed by TRCP 192 as limited by TRCP 194. See "Content of request," §3.2, p. 516.

(13)

PROPOSED TRCP CHANGES

In response to Gov't Code §22.004(h), the Supreme Court has proposed TRCP 169 to establish a process for the prompt, efficient, and cost-effective resolution of civil actions (expedited actions) in which only monetary relief is sought and the amount in controversy is no more than $100,000. See Tex.Sup.Ct. Order, Misc. Docket No. 12-9191 (eff. Mar. 1, 2013). The Supreme Court has proposed corresponding amendments to TRCP 190.2 that would (1) change the Level 1 discovery-control plan to apply to these expedited actions under TRCP 169 and (2) allow for additional requests for disclosures in Level 1 discovery. See Tex.Sup.Ct. Order, Misc. Docket No. 12-9191 (eff. Mar. 1, 2013). The public-comment period for the proposed amendments ends on February 1, 2013, and the rules are to take effect March 1, 2013. For the proposed version of the rules, see the appendix after this book's index. For the final version, go to the Supreme Court website at www.supreme.courts.state.tx.us. When the new and amended rules take effect, a supplement to this book—with updated rules and commentaries that reflect the changes—will be available at www.JonesMcClure.com/TRCPamendments.

§3. MAKING REQUESTS FOR DISCLOSURE

§3.1 Procedure.

1. Format. The request for disclosure should be typed on letter-size paper. Some attorneys include the request in their first pleading—either the original petition or the original answer. See "Request for Disclosure," ch. 2-B, §13, p. 110.

⎯⎯⎯⎯⎯⎯⎯⎯⎯⎯⎯⎯ ✪ ⎯⎯⎯⎯⎯⎯⎯⎯⎯⎯⎯⎯

2. Served on party. A request for disclosure can be served only on another party. TRCP 194.1. It cannot be served on a nonparty.

3. Time to serve request for disclosure.

(1) How early. A request for disclosure may be served anytime after suit is filed. TRCP 190.2(c)(1), 190.3(b)(1). The rules provide that a plaintiff may serve the initial set of discovery with its original petition.

(a) With or as part of P's original petition. The plaintiff should consider serving the request for disclosure along with or as part of the original petition. If the plaintiff includes the request in the petition, the plaintiff should change the title of the instrument to "Plaintiff's Original Petition and Request for Disclosure." If the plaintiff serves a request for disclosure as a separate document but with the original petition, the plaintiff must list the request as one of the documents served in both the citation and the return for the citation.

(b) Along with D's answer. Generally a defendant who wants to serve a request for disclosure early will serve it with the answer, even though a defendant may serve its request anytime after suit is filed.

(2) How late. The deadline to serve the request is 30 days before the end of the discovery period. TRCP 194.1. See "Discovery Periods," ch. 6-A, §8, p. 433. When served by mail or fax, the request should be served at least 34 days before the end of the discovery period. See "Deadline to Respond to Discovery," ch. 6-A, §14, p. 437.

4. Specify time to answer. The person serving the request for disclosure should specify when the answers are due, but must allow at least 30 days after service of the request. TRCP 194.1, 194.3.

(1) Most cases. In most cases, a party will ask the other party to answer a request for disclosure within the shortest time permitted by TRCP 194.1—that is, "within 30 days of service."

(2) Disclosures served before answer date. When the plaintiff serves a request for disclosure on the defendant before the defendant's answer is due, the defendant has 50 days after the date of service of the request to respond. TRCP 194.3(a). See "Deadline to Respond to Discovery," ch. 6-A, §14, p. 437.

(3) Disclosure of testifying experts. The time to respond to a request asking for disclosure of the other party's testifying experts is governed by TRCP 195.2. See "Deadlines to designate testifying experts," ch. 6-D, §6.1, p. 512.

(4) By agreement or court order. The parties may vary the deadlines in TRCP 194.3 by agreement or with a court order. TRCP 191.1. See "Modifying Discovery Procedures," ch. 6-A, §6, p. 429.

§3.2 Content of request.

1. Standard requests. A party may make the request in the language suggested by TRCP 194.1 by stating the following: "Pursuant to Rule 194, you are requested to disclose, within [*30 or 50*] days of the service of this request, the information or material described in Rule [*identify rule, e.g., 194.2; 194.2(a), (c), and (f); 194.2(d)-(g)*]." See *O'Connor's Texas Forms*, FORM 6E:1. Or, a party may make requests for the individual items in the subparts of TRCP 194.2.

⎯⎯⎯⎯⎯⎯⎯⎯⎯⎯⎯⎯⎯⎯⎯⎯⎯⎯⎯⎯⎯⎯⎯⎯

PRACTICE TIP

The problem with the request provided in TRCP 194.1 and the more specific requests below is that the party receiving the request might not be aware that a consulting expert with knowledge of facts is discoverable as a fact witness. Thus, you should use targeted requests to ask for experts. See "Targeted request," §3.2.2, p. 518.

⎯⎯⎯⎯⎯⎯⎯⎯⎯⎯⎯⎯⎯⎯⎯⎯⎯⎯⎯⎯⎯⎯⎯⎯

TRCP 194.2 permits a party to ask for the following information:

(1) Correct party names. A party may ask for the correct names of the parties to the lawsuit. TRCP 194.2(a).

—————————————— ✦ ——————————————

(2) Potential parties. A party may ask for the name, address, and telephone number of any potential party. TRCP 194.2(b). Potential parties can be a good source of information, just like fact witnesses.

(3) Contentions. A party may ask for the legal theories and, in general, the factual bases of the responding party's claims or defenses. TRCP 192.3(j), 194.2(c). These requests are similar to so-called "contention interrogatories" and may be used for the same purpose. TRCP 194 cmt. 2.

(4) Damages. A party may ask for the amount and any method of calculating economic damages. TRCP 194.2(d).

(5) Fact witnesses. A party may ask for the name, address, and telephone number of any person with knowledge of relevant facts, and a brief statement of each identified person's connection with the case. TRCP 194.2(e). See "Fact witnesses," ch. 6-B, §2.8, p. 462.

(6) Retained testifying experts. See "Information about retained testifying experts," ch. 6-D, §4.1.1, p. 506. A party may ask for the following information about a retained testifying expert:

(a) The expert's name, address, and telephone number. TRCP 194.2(f)(1).

(b) The subject matter on which the expert will testify. TRCP 194.2(f)(2).

(c) The general substance of the expert's mental impressions and opinions and a brief summary of the basis for them. TRCP 194.2(f)(3).

(d) All documents, tangible things, reports, models, or data compilations that have been provided to, reviewed by, or prepared by or for the expert in anticipation of the expert's testimony. TRCP 194.2(f)(4)(A); *VingCard A.S. v. Merrimac Hospitality Sys.*, 59 S.W.3d 847, 855 (Tex.App.—Fort Worth 2001, pet. denied).

(e) The expert's current résumé and bibliography. TRCP 194.2(f)(4)(B). The request should ask that the expert produce, as part of her résumé, a list of all other cases in which she has testified as an expert at trial or by deposition within the past four years. See "List of expert's other cases," ch. 6-D, §4.1.1(5)(a), p. 507.

(7) Nonretained testifying experts. See "Information about nonretained experts," ch. 6-D, §4.1.2, p. 509. A party may ask for the following information about a nonretained testifying expert:

(a) The expert's name, address, and telephone number. TRCP 194.2(f)(1).

(b) The subject matter on which the expert will testify. TRCP 194.2(f)(2).

(c) Either (1) the general substance of the expert's mental impressions and opinions and a brief summary of the basis for them or (2) documents reflecting this information. TRCP 194.2(f)(3).

(8) Documents. A party may ask for the following documents: (1) discoverable indemnity and insuring agreements, (2) discoverable settlement agreements, and (3) discoverable witness statements. TRCP 194.2(g)-(i).

(9) Medical records. See "Medical Records," ch. 6-J, p. 576. In a suit alleging physical or mental injury and damages from the occurrence that is the subject of the suit, a party may ask for medical records as follows:

(a) From the party who alleges injury, (1) all medical records and bills that are reasonably related to the injuries or damages asserted, or (2) as an alternative, an authorization permitting the disclosure of those medical records and bills. TRCP 194.2(j); *In re Shipmon*, 68 S.W.3d 815, 820 (Tex.App.—Amarillo 2001, orig. proceeding).

(b) From the party who obtained the injured party's medical records with an authorization furnished by the injured party, a copy of all the records it obtained. TRCP 194.2(k).

(10) Responsible third party. A party may ask for the name, address, and telephone number of any person who may be designated as a responsible third party. TRCP 194.2(*l*).

★

2. Targeted request. To secure specific information, the party should consider using a "targeted" request that identifies, in a separate sentence, the discoverable information sought under TRCP 194.2. For example, if a party wants a business entity to name others who may be potential parties because of their ownership interest in the entity, the request could state, "You are requested to disclose the information or material described in Rule 194.2(b). Please answer to the full extent authorized by the rules, which should include the names of all individuals and entities with an ownership interest in the business." For other targeted requests, see *O'Connor's Texas Forms*, FORM 6E:2. Although nothing prevents a party from focusing its request by targeting an issue, a party may not expand the scope of its request beyond TRCP 194.2.

NOTE

Some attorneys believe that TRCP 194.2 requires that a request for disclosure be stated in the language quoted in TRCP 194.1, without any elaboration. See Pemberton, The First Year, II.I.1, p. 19 (S.Ct. intended requests for disclosure to "precisely track" the language of TRCP 194.1). That certainly was the intent of the Supreme Court Advisory Committee (SCAC), which drafted Rule 9 (the SCAC's predecessor to TRCP 194.2) in 1995 to include the directive that the request for disclosure "shall state." See Appendix G, SCAC Report, Handbook on Texas Discovery Practice, p. 673, 685 (2005). However, the Supreme Court did not include "shall state" in the final version of TRCP 194.2.

---

§4. RESPONDING TO REQUESTS FOR DISCLOSURE

§4.1 Procedure.

1. Time to respond. Generally, a party has 30 days after the date of service to respond to a request for disclosure, depending on the type of service. TRCP 21, 21a, 194.3. See "Deadline to Respond to Discovery," ch. 6-A, §14, p. 437. There are two exceptions.

(1) Served before answer is due. When a request for disclosure is served on a defendant before the defendant's answer is due, the defendant has 50 days after service of the request to respond. TRCP 194.3(a). See "Served before answer date – 50 days," ch. 6-A, §14.1.2, p. 437. To extend the time, see "Extending Time to Respond to Discovery," ch. 6-A, §15, p. 438.

(2) Testifying experts. TRCP 195.2 establishes the schedule for furnishing information about testifying experts. TRCP 195.2; *see also* TRCP 194.2(f) (information party may request), TRCP 194.3(b) (response to 194.2(f) request controlled by TRCP 195). See "Deadlines for Securing Discovery from Experts," ch. 6-D, §6, p. 512.

2. Not filed. The responding party's disclosures are not filed with the court. TRCP 191.4(a)(2); *National Family Care Life Ins. v. Fletcher*, 57 S.W.3d 662, 667 n.6 (Tex.App.—Beaumont 2001, pet. denied). For exceptions, see "Exceptions," ch. 6-A, §12.1.3, p. 436.

3. Form of responses. To properly respond to requests for disclosure, the answers, objections, and other responses must be made in the form required by the rules. *O'Connor's Texas Forms*, FORM 6E:3.

(1) In writing. The response must be in writing. TRCP 193.1, 194.3; *VingCard A.S. v. Merrimac Hospitality Sys.*, 59 S.W.3d 847, 855 (Tex.App.—Fort Worth 2001, pet. denied). Each answer must follow the question it responds to. TRCP 193.1.

(2) Signed. The response must be signed by an attorney (or a pro se party). TRCP 191.3(a).

(3) Not verified. The response should not be verified.

(4) Separate answers. The response must provide separate answers for each request.

(5) Separate set of answers. In most cases, each set of requests for disclosure should be answered separately. In a multiparty case, a party responding to the same disclosures from different opposing parties may file

★

one response that is sufficient to answer all sets. *See, e.g.*, **Ward v. O'Connor**, 816 S.W.2d 446, 446 (Tex.App.—San Antonio 1991, no writ) (Ps filed one list of fact and expert witnesses in response to interrogatories from two Ds). *But see* **Clark Equip. Co. v. Pitner**, 923 S.W.2d 117, 121-22 (Tex.App.—Houston [14th Dist.] 1996, writ denied) (answer to one party's interrogatory on subject matter of expert's testimony could not serve as answer to another party's interrogatory on substance of expert's testimony).

(6) Produce documents. The responding party must serve copies of documents and other tangible items with the response, unless the responsive items are voluminous, in which case the response must state a reasonable time and place for the production of documents. TRCP 194.4. The responding party must produce the documents at the time and place stated in the request, unless otherwise agreed by the parties or ordered by the court. *Id.* The requesting party must have a reasonable opportunity to inspect the documents or other items. *Id.*

§4.2 Content of response. A party must provide a complete response, based on all information reasonably available to the responding party or its attorney at the time the response is made. TRCP 193.1. When asked, a party must produce the following information:

1. Correct party name. A party must provide its correct name. TRCP 194.2(a); *see* **Bailey v. Vanscot Concrete Co.**, 894 S.W.2d 757, 761 n.3 (Tex.1995), *disapproved on other grounds*, **Chilkewitz v. Hyson**, 22 S.W.3d 825 (Tex.1999).

2. Potential parties. A party must identify any potential parties and provide their names, addresses, and telephone numbers. TRCP 194.2(b); *see* **Helfand v. Coane**, 12 S.W.3d 152, 157 n.3 (Tex.App.—Houston [1st Dist.] 2000, pet. denied).

3. Contentions. A party must disclose its legal theories and, in general, the factual bases of its claims or defenses. TRCP 194.2(c). The party is not required to marshal all evidence that may be offered at trial or to brief legal issues. TRCP 194.2(c) & cmt. 2. For example, a plaintiff would be required to disclose that it claimed damages suffered in a car accident caused by the defendant's negligence in speeding but would not be required to state the speed at which the defendant was driving; a defendant in the same suit would be required to disclose its denial of the speeding allegation. TRCP 194 cmt. 2. TRCP 194.2(c) is intended to require disclosure of a party's basic assertions made in prosecution or defense of claims. TRCP 194 cmt. 2. A defendant cannot respond to a request for contentions by reurging its general denial. Pemberton, *The First Year*, II.I.2, at 20.

PRACTICE TIP

When responding to a contention request, the parties should review their pleadings and include all of their legal theories and the factual bases for them. If a legal theory or factual basis is omitted, the court may limit the subject matter on which the party can present evidence. See, e.g., **National Family Care Life Ins. v. Fletcher**, *57 S.W.3d 662, 668 (Tex.App.—Beaumont 2001, pet. denied) (in limiting evidence, trial court was too restrictive in interpreting D's response).*

---

4. Damages. A party must disclose the amount of economic damages and any method of calculating them. TRCP 194.2(d). For example, a plaintiff would be required to state how loss of past earnings and future earning capacity was calculated, and a defendant in the same suit would be required to disclose any grounds for contesting the damages calculations. TRCP 194 cmt. 2. If a plaintiff cannot demonstrate its method of calculation, the court may limit the damages the plaintiff can recover. *See* **Butan Valley, N.V. v. Smith**, 921 S.W.2d 822, 832 (Tex.App.—Houston [14th Dist.] 1996, no writ). A party is not required to state a method of calculating noneconomic damages, such as for mental anguish. TRCP 194 cmt. 2.

5. Fact witnesses. A party must identify persons who have knowledge of relevant facts and provide a brief statement of each person's connection with the case. TRCP 194.2(e). See "Fact witnesses," ch. 6-B, §2.8, p. 462.

(1) Identify witness. A party must identify all persons (other than herself) who have knowledge of relevant facts by name, address, and telephone number. TRCP 194.2(e); *see, e.g.,* **Apresa v. Montfort Ins.**, 932 S.W.2d

★

246, 248 (Tex.App.—El Paso 1996, no writ) (witnesses excluded at trial because answers did not provide addresses and telephone numbers). Even when a party answering the request for disclosure has little or no use for a witness's testimony, the party must still identify the witness as a source of relevant facts. *See Walsh v. Mullane*, 725 S.W.2d 263, 265 (Tex.App.—Houston [1st Dist.] 1986, writ ref'd n.r.e.). The other party may have an important use for that witness's testimony. *Stevenson v. Koutzarov*, 795 S.W.2d 313, 318 (Tex.App.—Houston [1st Dist.] 1990, writ denied). Fact witnesses typically include eyewitnesses; parties and their spouses, employers, and co-workers; treating doctors; other medical personnel; attorneys (for attorney fees); nonretained experts (e.g., police officers); and experts who have firsthand knowledge of the facts of the case or secondhand knowledge obtained outside the consultation. See "Consulting expert + obtained facts = dual-capacity witness," ch. 6-D, §2.2.3, p. 503.

(2) Identify connection with case. A party must provide a brief description of the person's connection with the suit. TRCP 192.3(c), 194.2(e); *Beam v. A.H. Chaney, Inc.*, 56 S.W.3d 920, 922 (Tex.App.—Fort Worth 2001, pet. denied). This does not mean the party must provide a narrative statement of the facts the person knows. TRCP 192 cmt. 3. The description could be "treating physician," "eyewitness," "chief financial officer," or "plaintiff's mother and eyewitness to accident." *Id.*

6. Testifying experts. A party must provide information about the experts it plans to call as witnesses. *See* TRCP 194.2(f). The requirement to identify experts does not depend on whether the expert is compensated for her time as a witness. *Baylor Med. Plaza Servs. v. Kidd*, 834 S.W.2d 69, 73 (Tex.App.—Texarkana 1992, writ denied).

(1) Retained testifying experts. For retained testifying experts, a party must provide (1) the identity and location, including the name, address, and telephone number, of its expert witness, (2) the subject matter of the expert's testimony, (3) the expert's mental impressions and opinions, including facts known by the expert that relate to or form the basis of those mental impressions and opinions, (4) all documents, reports, or compilations provided to, reviewed by, or prepared by or for the expert in anticipation of the expert's testimony, and (5) the expert's current résumé and bibliography. TRCP 194.2(f); *see Mares v. Ford Motor Co.*, 53 S.W.3d 416, 418-19 (Tex. App.—San Antonio 2001, no pet.). A list of specific facts known by the expert is not required; a general description of the categories of facts known is sufficient. *See J.G. v. Murray*, 915 S.W.2d 548, 550-51 (Tex.App.—Corpus Christi 1995, orig. proceeding). For the definition of retained experts, see "Retained testifying expert," ch. 6-D, §2.1.1, p. 502.

(a) Name of retained experts. A party should list the names of all experts it has retained to testify on its behalf and the experts subject to the party's control. For example, the party should list a doctor who was hired to give an opinion in a medical-malpractice case or an accident reconstructionist who was hired to give an opinion in a car-accident case.

(b) Parties. A party should always list the name of any party who might testify as an expert witness. *See, e.g.*, *Collins v. Collins*, 904 S.W.2d 792, 799-800 (Tex.App.—Houston [1st Dist.] 1995) (in divorce suit, husband could not testify about value of business because he was not identified as expert witness), *writ denied*, 923 S.W.2d 569 (Tex.1996); *Tinkle v. Henderson*, 777 S.W.2d 537, 539 (Tex.App.—Tyler 1989, writ denied) (because D-doctors did not list themselves as experts, they could not testify as expert witnesses).

(c) Attorney. If there is a claim for attorney fees, the party should list the attorney as an expert to testify about attorney fees. *See, e.g.*, *E.F. Hutton & Co. v. Youngblood*, 741 S.W.2d 363, 364 (Tex.1987) (because attorney was not listed, he could not testify about attorney fees); *Campos v. State Farm Gen. Ins.*, 943 S.W.2d 52, 54-55 (Tex.App.—San Antonio 1997, writ denied) (same); *see also Northwestern Nat'l Cty. Mut. Ins. v. Rodriguez*, 18 S.W.3d 718, 721-22 (Tex.App.—San Antonio 2000, pet. denied) (good cause permitted undesignated attorney to testify about fees because he was identified as fact witness on damages). The answer should state that the attorney will testify about attorney fees for trial and appeal.

(2) Nonretained testifying experts. For nonretained testifying experts, a party must provide (1) the identity and location, including the name, address, and telephone number of its expert, (2) the subject matter of the expert's testimony, and (3) either (a) the general substance of the expert's mental impressions and opinions, including facts known by the expert that relate to or form the basis of those mental impressions and opinions,

★

or (b) documents reflecting this information. TRCP 194.2(f). A list of specific facts known by the expert is not required; a general description of the categories of facts known is sufficient. For the definition of nonretained experts, see "Nonretained testifying expert," ch. 6-D, §2.1.2, p. 503. The list of nonretained testifying experts could include the following:

(a) **Treating doctor.** A party should list the treating doctor as a nonretained testifying expert if the party intends to call the doctor to testify and the doctor is not retained by, employed by, or otherwise subject to the control of the party. For example, if the party was treated by an emergency-room doctor, the doctor is a nonretained expert as long as the doctor is not paid for her expert opinion and is not otherwise subject to the party's control. Not all treating doctors are nonretained. For example, if the attorney referred the party to a doctor for purposes of treatment and litigation, the doctor would be a retained doctor.

(b) **Accident investigator.** A party should list an accident investigator who is employed by a local police department or some state agency (e.g., the DPS) as a nonretained testifying expert if the party intends to call the person to testify as an expert.

7. Documents. A party must produce the following documents in response to a request for disclosure: (1) discoverable indemnity and insuring agreements, (2) discoverable settlement agreements, and (3) discoverable witness statements. TRCP 194.2(g)-(i).

8. Medical records. In a suit alleging physical or mental injury, the parties must produce the following medical records:

(1) The party alleging injury must produce medical records and bills reasonably related to the injuries or damages asserted, or an authorization permitting disclosure of those medical records and bills. TRCP 194.2(j). For medical authorization under Health & Safety Code §241.152, see "Medical authorization," ch. 6-J, §3.2, p. 576.

(2) The other party must produce medical records and bills that it obtained through an authorization furnished by the party alleging injury. TRCP 194.2(k).

9. Responsible third party. A party must provide the name, address, and telephone number of any person who may be designated as a responsible third party. TRCP 194.2(*l*).

§5. OBJECTING TO REQUESTS

A party abuses the discovery process if it does not respond fully to a request for disclosure. TRCP 194 cmt. 1.

§5.1 No objections. No objections are permitted to requests for disclosure. TRCP 194.5. The procedure for requests for disclosure is designed to afford parties basic discovery without objection. TRCP 194 cmt. 1; *see* TRCP 194.5.

§5.2 Asserting privileges.

1. Most privileges. A party may assert privileges to protect information sought in a request for disclosure (other than work product). TRCP 194 cmt. 1. See "Asserting privileges," ch. 6-A, §18.2, p. 443.

2. Work product. A party cannot assert work-product privilege in response to a request for disclosure. TRCP 194.5 & cmt. 1; *see, e.g., In re Jimenez*, 4 S.W.3d 894, 896 (Tex.App.—Houston [1st Dist.] 1999, orig. proceeding) (D's statement to his insurer was not protected as work product).

§5.3 Moving for protection. Only in rare cases will a party be able to protect information requested in disclosures. For example, a party could file a motion for protective order to prevent disclosure of a person's residential address if the disclosure might result in harm to that person. TRCP 194 cmt. 1. See "Motion for Protective Order," ch. 6-A, §20, p. 449; *O'Connor's Texas Forms*, FORM 6A:10.

§6. SUPPLEMENTING OR AMENDING DISCLOSURES

§6.1 Deadline to supplement answers. See "Deadline to supplement responses," ch. 6-A, §17.4, p. 441.

§6.2 Deadlines to designate experts. See "Deadlines to designate testifying experts," ch. 6-D, §6.1, p. 512.

§6.3 Substance of supplemental response. For the substance of what additional information must be provided, see "Extent of supplementation," ch. 6-A, §17.2, p. 440.

§7. OBJECTING TO RESPONSES

§7.1 Technical errors. If a party makes a technical error in responding to requests for disclosure (e.g., the response is not signed), the requesting party must raise the issue as soon as possible. *See* TRCP 191.3(d) (unsigned discovery response will be struck unless signed after party is made aware of omission); *State Farm Fire & Cas. Co. v. Morua*, 979 S.W.2d 616, 617 (Tex.1998) (verification of interrogatories under former TRCP 168); *Kramer v. Lewisville Mem'l Hosp.*, 858 S.W.2d 397, 407 (Tex.1993) (same). A party waives any technical defect it does not raise before trial. *Morua*, 979 S.W.2d at 619.

§7.2 Procedure. The procedure for objecting to answers filed in response to requests for disclosure is similar to that for objecting to answers to interrogatories. See "Objecting to Answers," ch. 6-G, §8, p. 555.

§8. USING DISCLOSURES AS EVIDENCE

§8.1 Similar to interrogatories. The procedures for using disclosures as evidence is similar to that for using answers to interrogatories. See "Using Interrogatories as Evidence," ch. 6-G, §9, p. 555.

§8.2 Superseded responses. A response to a request for disclosure under TRCP 194.2(c) (legal theories) or TRCP 194.2(d) (damages) that has been changed by an amended or supplemental response is not admissible and cannot be used for impeachment. TRCP 194.6. The purpose of this provision is to encourage parties to disclose and discuss their basic legal and factual assertions early in the case. Griesel, *The "New" Texas Discovery Rules*, at 19.

§9. OBJECTING TO LATE OR PARTIAL DISCLOSURES

§9.1 Late disclosure. When a party's response to the requests is late, the trial court can exclude the information or testimony that was not timely disclosed. TRCP 193.6(a); *see, e.g.*, *Ersek v. Davis & Davis, P.C.*, 69 S.W.3d 268, 273 (Tex.App.—Austin 2002, pet. denied) (expert witness's testimony was excluded because expert was not timely designated). If a party serves a late response to the requests, the trial court can also look to TRCP 215.3 for sanctions—that is, postpone the trial and impose appropriate sanctions to compensate the nonoffending party for any wasted expenses in preparing for trial. *See* TRCP 215.3; *see also* TRCP 193.6(c) (court may grant a continuance). At a hearing on a motion for sanctions, the party objecting to the untimely designated expert witness has the burden to produce evidence showing that the designation was not timely. *See Mentis v. Barnard*, 870 S.W.2d 14, 16 (Tex. 1994); *Sims v. Brackett*, 885 S.W.2d 450, 454 (Tex.App.—Corpus Christi 1994, writ denied).

§9.2 Partial disclosure. When a party's response to the requests does not furnish all the information required by TRCP 194, the trial court must exclude the testimony on the omitted information unless there is a showing of good cause, lack of surprise, or lack of prejudice. *See, e.g.*, *VingCard A.S. v. Merrimac Hospitality Sys.*, 59 S.W.3d 847, 855-56 (Tex.App.—Fort Worth 2001, pet. denied) (although P identified its expert, it did not provide mental impressions and opinions; thus, court should have excluded expert's opinion).

§10. OBJECTING TO UNIDENTIFIED WITNESS

To exclude the testimony of a witness not identified in disclosures, a party must make a timely objection. The objection should be made either in a pretrial motion to exclude or when the witness is offered at trial. *Clark v. Trailways, Inc.*, 774 S.W.2d 644, 647 (Tex.1989). Once an objection is made, the exclusion is automatic unless the other party proves good cause or lack of unfair surprise or prejudice.

§10.1 Form of objection. The party should object that the witness should not be permitted to testify because the witness was not disclosed in response to a request asking for the identity of fact or expert witnesses.

§10.2 Exclude witness. On objection, the court must exclude a witness (other than a named party) from testifying if the witness was not listed in response to the requests, unless the court finds (1) there was good cause for the failure to timely respond, or (2) the failure to timely respond will not unfairly surprise or prejudice the other

⭐

parties. TRCP 193.6(a); *Fort Brown Villas III Condo. Ass'n v. Gillenwater*, 285 S.W.3d 879, 881 (Tex.2009); *Snider v. Stanley*, 44 S.W.3d 713, 715 (Tex.App.—Beaumont 2001, pet. denied); *see Alvarado v. Farah Mfg.*, 830 S.W.2d 911, 914 (Tex.1992). The purpose of the exclusion rule is to require complete responses to discovery, promote responsible assessment of settlement, and prevent trial by ambush. *Alvarado*, 830 S.W.2d at 914.

§10.3 Continuance. If the party offering the witness cannot prove good cause, lack of unfair surprise, or lack of unfair prejudice, the party should ask for a continuance. The court may grant a continuance to allow the party to make, amend, or supplement the response and to allow discovery on any new information presented. TRCP 193.6(c); *see Henderson v. Wellmann*, 43 S.W.3d 591, 598 (Tex.App.—Houston [1st Dist.] 2001, no pet.).

§10.4 Appropriate sanctions. See "Sanctions for discovery abuse," ch. 5-K, §7.1, p. 384.

§10.5 Preserving error when witness excluded.

1. Hearing on exclusion. If an objection is made to an unidentified witness, the party offering the witness should ask the court to conduct a hearing on its failure to identify the witness. The burden is on the party offering an unidentified witness to prove good cause, lack of unfair surprise, or lack of unfair prejudice. TRCP 193.6(b); *see Sharp v. Broadway Nat'l Bank*, 784 S.W.2d 669, 671 (Tex.1990); *Morrow v. H.E.B., Inc.*, 714 S.W.2d 297, 298 (Tex.1986). The court should permit the witness to testify if the party offering the witness can show either (1) good cause for not timely listing the witness or (2) no unfair surprise or prejudice to the other party. TRCP 193.6(a), (b); *see Gee v. Liberty Mut. Fire Ins.*, 765 S.W.2d 394, 395-96 (Tex.1989) (court found no good cause under former TRCP 215(5)); *Northwestern Nat'l Cty. Mut. Ins. v. Rodriguez*, 18 S.W.3d 718, 722-23 & n.1 (Tex.App.—San Antonio 2000, pet. denied) (court found no unfair surprise under TRCP 193.6(a)). The trial court has discretion to determine whether there is good cause to permit the witness to testify or whether there is no surprise or prejudice. *See Morrow*, 714 S.W.2d at 298. The trial court's findings must be supported by the record. TRCP 193.6(b); *Northwestern Nat'l*, 18 S.W.3d at 722 n.1. The hearing must be conducted outside the presence of the jury.

(1) Unidentified witness permitted to testify. The following are examples of when an unidentified witness was or should have been permitted to testify: • D's experts permitted to give same opinions given in earlier trial, even though D did not disclose the experts' opinions in response to request for disclosure. *Mares v. Ford Motor Co.*, 53 S.W.3d 416, 419 (Tex.App.—San Antonio 2001, no pet.). • P's unidentified witness should have been permitted to testify because she was P's employee and was a substitute for another of P's employees who had been identified as witness but had left P's employment. *Best Indus. Unif. Sup. Co. v. Gulf Coast Alloy Welding, Inc.*, 41 S.W.3d 145, 148-49 (Tex.App.—Amarillo 2000, pet. denied).

NOTE

Under the discovery rules, a named party cannot be excluded as a fact witness because the party was not listed as a fact witness in response to a request for disclosure. See TRCP 193.6(a) (party cannot offer the testimony of a witness "other than a named party" who was not listed). Even though an unlisted party may testify as a fact witness, nothing in the rules or case law permits a party not designated as a testifying expert to testify as an expert. Collins v. Collins, 904 S.W.2d 792, 801 (Tex.App.—Houston [1st Dist.] 1995), writ denied, 923 S.W.2d 569 (Tex.1996).

---

(2) Unidentified witness excluded. The following are examples of when the unidentified witness was not or should not have been permitted to testify: • P's expert's affidavit should have been excluded when P disclosed expert in response to no-evidence motion for summary judgment five months after expert-designation deadline. *Fort Brown Villas III Condo. Ass'n v. Gillenwater*, 285 S.W.3d 879, 882 (Tex.2009). • P's expert should have been excluded, even though deposed, because he was not identified in response to interrogatories. *Sharp*, 784 S.W.2d at 670-72. • P's expert should have been excluded because he was not identified in response to interrogatories, and counsel's inadvertence was not good cause. *Id.*; *E.F. Hutton & Co. v. Youngblood*, 741 S.W.2d 363, 364 (Tex.1987). • P's witnesses should have been excluded even though D's attorney already had the special knowledge

★

necessary to cross-examine the witnesses at trial. *E.F. Hutton*, 741 S.W.2d at 364. • D's expert should have been excluded because D did not provide the expert's opinions, but the error was harmless. *VingCard A.S. v. Merrimac Hospitality Sys.*, 59 S.W.3d 847, 856-57 (Tex.App.—Fort Worth 2001, pet. denied). • State's witnesses should have been excluded because State did not file a response to the request for disclosures and did not prove good cause. *F&H Invs. v. State*, 55 S.W.3d 663, 669-70 (Tex.App.—Waco 2001, no pet.). • Witness who had been a party to the suit but had settled before trial and who had identified himself as expert witness could not testify as expert for another party who had not identified him as expert. *Codner v. Arellano*, 40 S.W.3d 666, 675 (Tex.App.—Austin 2001, no pet.). • Witness should have been excluded because party's expectation that case would settle was not good cause for not identifying witness. *Rainbo Baking Co. v. Stafford*, 787 S.W.2d 41, 41 (Tex.1990); *Cruz v. Furniture Technicians*, 949 S.W.2d 34, 36 (Tex.App.—San Antonio 1997, pet. denied). • Designated fact witness should have been excluded as expert witness. *Collins*, 904 S.W.2d at 802 (party); *Baylor Med. Plaza Servs. v. Kidd*, 834 S.W.2d 69, 73 (Tex.App.—Texarkana 1992, writ denied) (witness).

    2. Present evidence. A party offering an unidentified witness must present sworn testimony to explain why the witness was not listed. The court reporter should transcribe the proceeding. To prove good cause or lack of unfair surprise or prejudice for not listing the unidentified witness, the party should establish the following:

    (1) The party made a good-faith effort to locate the witness. *See Clark v. Trailways, Inc.*, 774 S.W.2d 644, 647 (Tex.1989) (inability to locate witness despite good-faith efforts might support finding of good cause).

    (2) The party did not know of the existence of the witness or did not know the witness had knowledge about the case. To prove this, both the attorney and the party should testify at the hearing that they did not know of the witness. If either the party or the attorney had the information, it should have been disclosed. *Yeldell v. Holiday Hills Ret. & Nursing Ctr., Inc.*, 701 S.W.2d 243, 246 (Tex.1985) (attorney knew of witness); *Williams v. Union Carbide Corp.*, 734 S.W.2d 699, 701 (Tex.App.—Houston [1st Dist.] 1987, writ ref'd n.r.e.) (party knew of witness).

    (3) The other parties were aware of the unidentified witness and her testimony. To prove this, the party should demonstrate that the identity of the witness was certain and her personal knowledge of relevant facts was communicated to all other parties through a timely response to other written discovery or deposition. TRCP 193.5(a)(2); *see Northwestern Nat'l*, 18 S.W.3d at 722-23.

    3. Get ruling on record. The party attempting to overcome the automatic exclusion of the witness should ask the court to (1) state on the record whether good cause, lack of unfair surprise, or lack of unfair prejudice was proved, and (2) identify the particulars of its ruling.

    4. Make offer of proof. If the court excludes any evidence, the party must make an offer of proof to preserve the testimony of the witness so the appellate courts can determine whether the erroneous exclusion was harmful. TRE 103(a)(2). If a party presents the witness's testimony as part of the hearing on exclusion, and the court reporter transcribes it, the court reporter's record will include the evidence. If the witness's testimony is not presented at the hearing, the party should ask the court for permission to make an offer of proof during the trial. If for some reason the court does not permit the party to make an offer of proof, the evidence may be preserved in a formal bill of exception. TRE 103; TRAP 33.2. See "Offer of Proof & Bill of Exception," ch. 8-E, p. 717; *O'Connor's Texas Forms*, FORMS 8E.

    §10.6 Offering witness for impeachment or rebuttal. A party may ask the trial court for permission to offer an undesignated witness for impeachment or rebuttal. See "Impeachment & rebuttal evidence not produced in discovery," ch. 8-C, §5.3, p. 700.

§11. REVIEW

For the rules and forms for prosecuting or responding to an appeal or original proceeding, see *O'Connor's Texas Civil Appeals* (2012).

    §11.1 Appeal or mandamus? See "Review of Discovery Orders," ch. 6-A, §26, p. 458.

    §11.2 Undisclosed witness. On appeal, the party objecting to the exclusion or admission of the testimony of an unidentified witness must show that the court abused its discretion. *Mentis v. Barnard*, 870 S.W.2d 14, 16 (Tex. 1994) (objection to exclusion under former TRCP 166b); *Henry S. Miller Co. v. Bynum*, 836 S.W.2d 160, 162 (Tex.

★

1992) (objection to admission). Obtaining a reversal on the admission or exclusion of an undisclosed witness is a two-step process: the party must show (1) it proved good cause or lack of unfair surprise or prejudice (or the other party did not prove good cause or lack of unfair surprise or prejudice), and (2) the trial court's erroneous ruling was harmful. *See Mentis*, 870 S.W.2d at 16 (testimony excluded at trial); *Alvarado v. Farah Mfg.*, 830 S.W.2d 911, 916-17 (Tex.1992) (testimony admitted at trial). Once error in the trial court's ruling is demonstrated, the appellate court must review the entire record to determine the harm. To determine whether the erroneous admission or exclusion of the testimony of an undisclosed witness was harmful, the appellate court must determine whether the error probably caused the rendition of an improper judgment. TRAP 44.1(a)(1).

1. Undisclosed witness permitted to testify. If the court admitted the testimony of an undisclosed witness, to challenge that ruling on appeal, the appellant must show that the admitted testimony (1) disputed a material allegation in the case and (2) was not cumulative. *Boothe v. Hausler*, 766 S.W.2d 788, 789 (Tex.1989). If the testimony of the undisclosed witness was cumulative of other evidence, the courts will hold that it was harmless error to admit it. *Id.*; *Beam v. A.H. Chaney, Inc.*, 56 S.W.3d 920, 924 (Tex.App.—Fort Worth 2001, pet. denied). The test of whether the evidence was cumulative is whether other similar evidence was offered at trial, not whether other similar evidence was available in discovery. *Jamail v. Anchor Mortg. Servs.*, 809 S.W.2d 221, 223 (Tex.1991).

2. Undisclosed witness excluded. If the court excluded the testimony of an undisclosed witness, to challenge that ruling on appeal, the appellant must show that the excluded testimony (1) was preserved by an offer of proof or a formal bill of exception, (2) was controlling on a material issue in the case, and (3) was not cumulative. *Williams Distrib. Co. v. Franklin*, 898 S.W.2d 816, 817 (Tex.1995) (element 2); *Mentis*, 870 S.W.2d at 16 (elements 2 and 3); *McInnes v. Yamaha Motor Corp.*, 673 S.W.2d 185, 187 (Tex.1984) (element 1). To prove the "controlling" element, it is not necessary for the party to show that no other controlling evidence could have been introduced through another witness. *Williams Distrib.*, 898 S.W.2d at 817.

F. DEPOSITIONS

§1. GENERAL

§1.1 Rules. TRCP 176, 199-203, 205, 215.5. See CPRC §7.011 (attorney's liability for costs), §§20.001 & 20.002 (persons who may take depositions); Gov't Code §52.021 (certification of court reporter), §52.059 (charges for depositions).

§1.2 Purpose. The purpose of depositions is to elicit and preserve sworn testimony for use in trial.

§1.3 Forms. See *O'Connor's Texas Civil Forms* (2012), FORMS 6F.

§1.4 Other references. Bishop, *International Litigation in Texas*, 19 Hous.L.Rev. 361 (1982); Brown & Rondon, *Texas Rules of Evidence Handbook* (2013) (referred to as Brown & Rondon, *Evidence Handbook*); Fineberg & Shore, *Discovery Update*, Advanced Civil Trial Course, State Bar of Texas CLE, ch. 1 (2001); Graham, *Depositions: Procedure*, Advanced Evidence & Discovery Course, State Bar of Texas CLE, ch. 7 (2011); Hoffman, *Depositions*, Spring Training: Winning Before Trial, State Bar of Texas CLE, ch. 5 (2010); Pemberton, *The First Year Under the New Discovery Rules: The Big Issues Thus Far* (2000), www.supreme.courts.state.tx.us/rules/tdr/disc1yr.pdf (referred to as Pemberton, *The First Year*); Court Reporters Certification Board, *Uniform Format Manual for Texas Reporters' Records* (2010), §§3.4 cmt., 3.7 cmt., www.crcb.state.tx.us/ufm.asp (referred to as *Uniform Format Manual*).

§2. SCOPE

The scope of discovery for depositions is governed by TRCP 192. See "Scope of Discovery," ch. 6-B, p. 460.

§3. DEPOSITION OFFICER

The deposition officer is a person who is authorized by law to administer an oath and who is in charge of the stenographic or nonstenographic recording of the deposition. *See* TRCP 199.1. The deposition officer is responsible for the amount of time each party or side uses during the deposition. For the definition of "side," see "Side," ch. 6-A, §2.7, p. 426.

———————— ✦ ————————

§3.1 Stenographic depositions. Stenographic oral depositions taken in Texas must be recorded by a certified shorthand reporter. Gov't Code §52.021(b), (f).

§3.2 Nonstenographic depositions. Audio or video depositions may be recorded by any person who is qualified to administer an oath. TRCP 199.1(c); *see also* Gov't Code §602.002 (list of persons who are qualified to administer oath, including notaries public). A court reporter or any person authorized to administer oaths may act as the deposition officer at a nonstenographic deposition. See "Alternative means for conducting deposition," §4.5.4, p. 529.

§3.3 Deposition on written questions. Depositions on written questions may be taken by (1) a clerk of the district court, (2) a judge or clerk of the county court, (3) a court reporter, or (4) a notary public. CPRC §20.001(a) (persons 1, 2, and 4).

§4. PROCEDURE FOR STANDARD ORAL DEPOSITION

The most common type of deposition is the oral deposition recorded stenographically by a court reporter or by a mechanical recording device operated by a notary public. The deposition consists of a series of questions by one attorney, answers by the deponent, and objections and cross-examination by the other attorneys.

§4.1 Agreements for scheduling deposition. Most depositions are taken by agreement. TRCP 191.1 permits the parties to modify the deposition procedure by agreement and to take the deposition before any person, at any time or place and on any notice. If the parties make an agreement about the taking of the deposition, it should be recorded in the deposition transcript. TRCP 191.1. To be enforceable when not recorded in the transcript, the agreement must comply with TRCP 11. TRCP 191.1. See "Agreement recorded in deposition," ch. 1-H, §9.1.3, p. 62; "Modifying discovery by agreement," ch. 6-A, §6.1, p. 429; *O'Connor's Texas Forms*, FORM 6F:1.

§4.2 Scheduling expert's deposition. TRCP 195.3 establishes a schedule for depositions of testifying experts retained by, employed by, or otherwise subject to the control of a party. See "Deadlines to depose testifying experts," ch. 6-D, §6.2, p. 513. Depositions of experts who are not retained by a party are controlled by TRCP 176, 205, and the deposition rules. TRCP 195 cmt. 2.

§4.3 Deadline to take deposition. An oral deposition must be taken during the discovery period unless the parties agree otherwise or a party obtains leave of court. TRCP 199.2(a). See "Discovery Periods," ch. 6-A, §8, p. 433; *O'Connor's Texas Forms*, FORM 6F:7. For expert depositions, see "Deadlines to depose testifying experts," ch. 6-D, §6.2, p. 513.

§4.4 Filing deposition documents. Chart 6-8, below, summarizes the filing requirements for deposition documents.

	6-8. FILING DEPOSITION DOCUMENTS		
	Document	**File?**	**TRCP**
1	Notice of deposition and subpoena required to be served only on a party	No	191.4(a)(1)
2	Notice of deposition and subpoena required to be served on a nonparty	Yes	191.4(b)(1)
3	Motions for protection and to quash	Yes	191.4(b)(2)
4	Agreements about depositions	Yes	11, 191.4(b)(3)
5	The deposition	No	191.4(a)(3)
6	The responses and objections to deposition notices	No	191.4(a)(2)
7	Any document the trial court orders to be filed	Yes	191.4(c)(1)
8	Any document necessary to support or oppose a motion or other matter in the trial or appellate court	Yes	191.4(c)(2), (c)(3)

✦

---

§4.5 Notice of oral deposition. See *O'Connor's Texas Forms*, FORM 6F:1.

1. Contents of notice. The notice of intent to take a deposition must be in writing. *See* TRCP 199.2(a).

(1) Service. The notice of deposition must be served on the deponent and the other parties in the lawsuit. TRCP 199.2(a).

(2) Identity of deponent. The notice of deposition must identify the witness to be deposed. TRCP 199.2(b)(1).

(a) Party witness. When the deponent is a party or is retained by, employed by, or subject to the control of a party, the notice of deposition served on the party's attorney has the same effect as a subpoena served on the deponent. TRCP 199.3.

(b) Nonparty witness. When the deponent is not a party, the notice should include the deponent's address so the officer or court reporter who issues the subpoena can locate the witness. *See* TRCP 176.5. See "Subpoenas," ch. 1-L, p. 84; "Challenging nonparty discovery subpoena," ch. 6-I, §5.5, p. 571.

(c) Unknown corporate witness. When the deposition notice is sent to a corporation or other entity and the identity of a person in the organization with knowledge of a certain subject is unknown, the notice can require the organization to identify a witness to be deposed. TRCP 199.2(b)(1); *Allstate Tex. Lloyds v. Johnson*, 784 S.W.2d 100, 104 (Tex.App.—Waco 1989, orig. proceeding). The notice must describe the subjects about which testimony is requested and direct the organization to designate the person who will testify on its behalf. TRCP 199.2(b)(1); *Lindsey v. O'Neill*, 689 S.W.2d 400, 402 (Tex.1985). This procedure does not limit a party's right to depose other employees of the entity. *Hospital Corp. v. Farrar*, 733 S.W.2d 393, 395 (Tex.App.—Fort Worth 1987, orig. proceeding).

2. Date for oral deposition. The notice of deposition must state the day and time for the oral deposition. TRCP 199.2(b)(2); *cf. St. Luke's Episcopal Hosp. v. Garcia*, 928 S.W.2d 307, 312 (Tex.App.—Houston [14th Dist.] 1996, orig. proceeding) (because subpoena did not identify date for deposition on written questions, nonparty did not waive its objections). After stating the date, the notice should include the phrase, "and continuing from day to day until the deposition is completed." The date for the deposition depends on how much notice a party must give the other party and the deponent, which in turn depends on whether the deponent is a party or nonparty and whether the deponent is required to bring documents or other things to the deposition. See "Deadlines to Serve Notice & Subpoena," chart 6-9, p. 530.

(1) For deposition with documents.

(a) Party deposition with documents.

[1] Initial setting. For a deposition of a party when production of documents or tangible things is requested, the notice of deposition must be served on the witness at least 30 days before the deposition. *See* TRCP 199 cmt. 1. TRCP 199.2(b)(5) incorporates into deposition procedures the requirements for requests for production under TRCP 196, including the 30-day deadline for responses. TRCP 199 cmt. 1; *see* TRCP 196.2(a) (response to request for production must be served within 30 days). See "Deadline to respond," ch. 6-I, §3.3.2, p. 567. The date for the deposition should probably be set at least 40 days after the date the notice is served, so the party noticing the deposition can reschedule it if the witness files a response on the last day refusing to produce.

[2] Rescheduled setting. When rescheduling the deposition of a party with documents or tangible things, the party noticing the deposition is not required to provide an additional 30 days' notice as long as no additional documents or things are requested. Because it is the request for documents that triggers the 30 days' notice requirement, the purpose of the 30 days' notice—to provide the deponent time to file a response to the request for documents—is satisfied by the first notice. *See* TRCP 199.2(b)(5).

(b) Nonparty deposition with documents. For a deposition of a nonparty when production of documents or tangible things is requested, the notice of deposition must be served on the nonparty a reasonable

✦

time before the date for compliance. TRCP 199.2(a); Pemberton, *The First Year*, §II(D). The party must also serve a subpoena to appear and produce with or after the notice of deposition. TRCP 205.2. Although a document request to a party requires a 30-day response period, there is no similar requirement for a document request to a nonparty. Pemberton, *The First Year*, §II(D).

(2) For deposition without documents.

(a) Party deposition without documents. To take a deposition of a party without a request for production of documents or tangible things, the notice of deposition must be served a reasonable time before the date of the deposition. TRCP 199.2(a), (b)(2). Neither TRCP 199.2(a) nor 199.2(b)(2) states how much notice is reasonable. As a general rule, ten days' notice should be reasonable, but depending on the circumstances, a shorter time might also be reasonable. *Compare **Gutierrez v. Walsh**,* 748 S.W.2d 27, 28 (Tex.App.—Corpus Christi 1988, no writ) (six days was reasonable), *and **Bohmfalk v. Linwood**,* 742 S.W.2d 518, 520 (Tex.App.—Dallas 1987, no writ) (four days was reasonable), *with **Hycarbex, Inc. v. Anglo-Suisse, Inc.**,* 927 S.W.2d 103, 111 (Tex.App.—Houston [14th Dist.] 1996, no writ) (four days was unreasonable), ***Bloyed v. General Motors Corp.**,* 881 S.W.2d 422, 437 (Tex.App.—Texarkana 1994) (Thursday notice of Monday deposition was unreasonable), *aff'd*, 916 S.W.2d 949 (Tex.1996), *and **Hogan v. Beckel**,* 783 S.W.2d 307, 309 (Tex.App.—San Antonio 1989, writ denied) (same).

(b) Nonparty deposition without documents. To take a deposition of a nonparty without a request for documents or tangible things, the party must serve the notice and the subpoena a reasonable time before the date for the deposition. TRCP 199.2(a), 205.2. However, the notice must be served before or at the same time as the subpoena; the subpoena cannot be served before the notice. TRCP 205.2.

3. Place for deposition. The notice of deposition must identify a reasonable location for the deposition. TRCP 199.2(b)(2). Where the deposition may be taken depends on a number of factors. *Id.*

(1) Deposition of most witnesses. The deposition of most witnesses may be taken in the following places: (1) the county of the witness's residence, (2) the county where the witness is employed or regularly transacts business in person, or (3) any convenient place, as directed by the court in which the case is pending. TRCP 199.2(b)(2)(A), (b)(2)(B), (b)(2)(E); ***Grass v. Golden**,* 153 S.W.3d 659, 662 (Tex.App.—Tyler 2004, orig. proceeding); *see **First State Bank v. Chappell & Handy, P.C.**,* 729 S.W.2d 917, 922 (Tex.App.—Corpus Christi 1987, writ ref'd n.r.e.) (court can order deposition in county other than one provided for in rule when deponent is being difficult about scheduling deposition); *see, e.g., **In re Rogers**,* 43 S.W.3d 20, 29 (Tex.App.—Amarillo 2001, orig. proceeding) (court could not order depositions in Dallas when nothing in record showed Dallas to be reasonable or convenient for any of the witnesses).

(2) Deposition of party & representative. The deposition of a party, or a person designated by a party under TRCP 199.2(b)(1), may also be taken in the county of suit. TRCP 199.2(b)(2)(C); ***Grass**,* 153 S.W.3d at 662; ***Davis v. Ruffino**,* 881 S.W.2d 186, 187 (Tex.App.—Houston [1st Dist.] 1994, orig. proceeding); *see also **Wal-Mart Stores v. Street**,* 754 S.W.2d 153, 155 (Tex.1988) (when deponent was associated with party but was not designated representative, his deposition could not be taken in county of suit over his objection); ***Borden, Inc. v. Valdez**,* 773 S.W.2d 718, 721 (Tex.App.—Corpus Christi 1989, orig. proceeding) (same).

(3) Deposition of nonresident or transient. The deposition of a person who is either a nonresident of Texas or a transient may be taken (1) in the county where the witness was served with the subpoena, (2) within 150 miles of the place of service, or (3) in any convenient place, as directed by the court in which the case is pending. TRCP 199.2(b)(2)(D), (b)(2)(E); ***Grass**,* 153 S.W.3d at 662; *see, e.g., **Street**,* 754 S.W.2d at 155 (chairman of the board, who was not a designated witness, had to be deposed in the county for Bentonville, Arkansas, his county of residence); ***Butan Valley, N.V. v. Smith**,* 921 S.W.2d 822, 829 (Tex.App.—Houston [14th Dist.] 1996, no writ) (corporate director, who was not a designated witness, had to be deposed in his country of residence, Saudi Arabia). "Convenience" is determined from the perspective of the witness. *Grass*, 153 S.W.3d at 662.

───────────────── ✦ ─────────────────

4. Alternative means for conducting deposition. If the deposition is to be taken by telephone, other remote electronic means, or by a nonstenographic recording (audio or video recording), the notice must identify the means for conducting the deposition. TRCP 199.2(b)(3). To take a deposition by alternative means, the party must observe additional notice requirements.

(1) For telephonic deposition. For a deposition by telephone, the notice must be served a reasonable time before the deposition. TRCP 199.1(b). See "Deposition by Telephone," §14, p. 541.

(2) For electronically recorded deposition. For a deposition by nonstenographic means, the notice must be served at least five days before the deposition. TRCP 199.1(c). See "Deposition by Nonstenographic Recording Device," §13, p. 540.

5. Additional attendee. The notice of deposition, or a separate notice, must identify any person who will attend the deposition who is not listed in TRCP 199.5(a)(3)—that is, any person who is not the deponent, one of the parties, the spouse of one of the parties, an attorney, an employee of one of the attorneys, or the officer taking the deposition. TRCP 199.2(b)(4), 199.5(a)(3); *see, e.g.*, *Burrhus v. M&S Sup.*, 933 S.W.2d 635, 640-41 (Tex. App.—San Antonio 1996, writ denied) (party attending deposition required to give notice before bringing an expert to deposition of other party's expert). If a party other than the party who set the deposition intends to bring to the deposition a person not listed in TRCP 199.5(a)(3), that party must give the other parties reasonable notice. TRCP 199.5(a)(3); *Burrhus*, 933 S.W.2d at 641. To exclude a person from the deposition, a party must secure a protective order. *Burrhus*, 933 S.W.2d at 641.

6. Request for documents. The notice of deposition may include a request that the witness produce at the deposition documents or tangible things within the scope of discovery and within the witness's possession, custody, or control. TRCP 199.2(b)(5).

(1) Documents from parties. A notice of deposition to a party or its agents that includes a request for documents or tangible things has the same effect as a subpoena. TRCP 199.3.

(2) Documents from nonparties. To be compelled to bring documents or tangible things to a deposition, a nonparty must be served with the notice of deposition and a subpoena. TRCP 199.2(b)(5). The subpoena and the notice of deposition must include the list of documents or things to be produced at the deposition. *See* TRCP 176.2(b) (subpoena must command person to produce "designated" documents), TRCP 199.2(b)(5) (list of materials to be produced by nonparty that are identified in subpoena must be attached to or included in deposition notice), TRCP 200.1(b) (same).

7. Signed. The notice of deposition must be signed by the attorney (or party when pro se). TRCP 191.3(a). See "Certification by signature," ch. 6-A, §4.1, p. 427.

PRACTICE TIP

Before the adoption of the 1999 discovery rules, court reporters issued subpoenas and notices of depositions with their own signatures. Now, because discovery must be signed by the attorney, court reporters are sending subpoenas and notices to the attorneys for their signatures, which is burdensome. To simplify this process, the attorneys can agree that all deposition subpoenas and notices may be signed by the court reporter as the attorney's agent. See "Modifying discovery by agreement," ch. 6-A, §6.1, p. 429.

---

8. Certificate of service. The notice of deposition must contain a certificate of service stating that it was served on all parties. *See* TRCP 21, 199.2(a). If it is not served on all parties, the deposition cannot be used at trial. *Shenandoah Assocs. v. J&K Props., Inc.*, 741 S.W.2d 470, 492-93 (Tex.App.—Dallas 1987, writ denied). See "Certificate of service," ch. 1-B, §3.2.12, p. 10.

✦

6-9. DEADLINES TO SERVE NOTICE & SUBPOENA						
Purpose of discovery	Type of discovery		Party or nonparty	Time for notice	Time for subpoena	Cross-reference
To secure testimony	Oral deposition	1	Party	Reasonable time. TRCP 199.2(a).		§4.5.2(2)(a), p. 528
		2	Nonparty	Reasonable time. TRCP 199.2(a).	With or after notice. TRCP 205.2.	§4.5.2(2)(b), p. 528
	Deposition on written questions	3	Party	20 days. TRCP 200.1(a).		§15.3.3, p. 541
		4	Nonparty	20 days. TRCP 200.1(a).	With or after notice. TRCP 205.2.	§15.3.3, p. 541
To secure testimony and tangible things	Oral deposition and request for documents	5	Party	30 days. TRCP 196.2(a), 199.2(b)(5) & cmt. 1.		§4.5.2(1)(a), p. 527
		6	Nonparty	Reasonable time. TRCP 199.2(b)(5), 205.2.	With or after notice. TRCP 205.2.	§4.5.2(1)(b), p. 527
	Deposition on written questions and request for documents	7	Party	30 days. TRCP 196.2(a), 199.2(b)(5), 200.1(b).		§15.3.3, p. 541
		8	Nonparty	20 days. TRCP 199.2(b)(5), 200.1(a).	With or after notice. TRCP 205.2.	§15.3.3, p. 541
To secure tangible things (not testimony)	Request for production	9	Party	30 days. ❶ TRCP 196.2(a).		ch. 6-I, §3.1.2, p. 565
	Subpoena for production	10	Nonparty	Reasonable time. TRCP 205.3(a).	10 days after notice. TRCP 205.2.	ch. 6-I, §5.3.1, p. 570

❶ When request is served before answer is due, defendant has 50 days after service to respond to request.

§4.6 Responding to notice of deposition.

1. When no documents requested. When no documents are requested, no response is necessary unless the party objects to the time, place, or other conditions of the deposition. See "Objecting Before Oral Deposition," §7, p. 533.

2. When documents requested. For the procedure to object to production of documents, see "Making objections," ch. 6-A, §18.1, p. 443. For the procedure to assert privileges, see "Asserting privileges," ch. 6-A, §18.2, p. 443. To object to the time, place, or other conditions of the deposition, see "Objecting Before Oral Deposition," §7, p. 533.

(1) **Party's response.** When a party, or a witness subject to its control, is served with a deposition notice that requests the production of documents or tangible things, the party's response, objections, and privilege claims are governed by the request-for-production rule (TRCP 196), as well as the procedures and duties imposed by TRCP 193. TRCP 199.2(b)(5) & cmt. 1. When a party is requested to produce documents at a deposition, it must file a response to the request, just as if it had been served with a request for production of documents. For parties and witnesses subject to the party's control, TRCP 199.2(b)(5) incorporates the procedures for responding to requests for production under TRCP 196. TRCP 199 cmt. 1. See "Procedure to respond," ch. 6-I, §3.3, p. 567.

(2) **Nonparty's response.** When a nonparty is served with a notice and subpoena to appear at a deposition and produce documents or tangible things, the nonparty's response, objections, motion for protective order,

———————————— ✦ ————————————

and privilege claims are governed by TRCP 176 (subpoena rule), as well as TRCP 205 (rule governing discovery from nonparties). TRCP 199.2(b)(5); *see also* TRCP 176.6(c) (production of documents), TRCP 193.3 (asserting a privilege). See "Subpoenas," ch. 1-L, p. 84; "Challenging nonparty discovery subpoena," ch. 6-I, §5.5, p. 571. When a nonparty objects to a subpoena to produce documents at a deposition, it must make its objections and assertions of privilege in writing before the time specified for compliance in the subpoena. TRCP 176.6(d). If the nonparty contends that the subpoenaed documents are privileged, it must comply with TRCP 193.3 and file a withholding statement. See "Making objections," ch. 6-A, §18.1, p. 443; "Asserting privileges," ch. 6-A, §18.2, p. 443. The nonparty must comply with the subpoena to the extent that it does not object or assert privileges to the documents. TRCP 176.6(d).

3. When organization deposed. When a deposition notice directs a corporation or other entity to identify a person with knowledge of a certain subject, the organization must (1) designate the persons who will testify on behalf of the organization, and (2) identify the matters each person will testify about. TRCP 199.2(b)(1); *see also* TRCP 176.6(b) (when subpoena directed to an organization). The organization's response must be served on the other party a "reasonable time before the deposition." TRCP 199.2(b)(1).

§4.7 Oath. Before beginning the deposition, the deponent must be sworn. TRCP 199.5(b); TRE 603. The oath must be administered by the deposition officer. TRCP 203.2(a). See "Deposition Officer," §3, p. 525. When a deposition is taken outside Texas, the person administering the oath must have the power to administer an oath in that jurisdiction. TRCP 201.1(b); *see also* CPRC §20.001(b) and (c) (persons who may take deposition).

§4.8 Interrogation. The scope of the examination is governed by TRCP 192. See "Scope of Discovery," ch. 6-B, p. 460; "To cancel or limit because of privilege," §7.2, p. 533.

1. First question. No matter who noticed the deponent to appear, the attorney who asks the first question at the deposition is the attorney who (1) will get the deposition from the court reporter, and (2) is personally responsible, along with her firm, for the cost of taking the deposition. TRCP 203.3(a)(1) (get deposition); Gov't Code §52.059(a), (d)(2)(C) (personally responsible). See "Paying for deposition," §4.13, p. 532.

2. Oral examination. The attorney who noticed the deponent to appear will most often begin the interrogation. If the deponent was called as an adverse witness, the deposition will begin with cross-examination. That attorney should finish all questions before any other attorney attempts to question the deponent. After the examination by the attorney who noticed the deposition, the other attorneys, one at a time, have the opportunity to examine the deponent.

3. Written questions. A party may, instead of participating in the examination, serve written questions in a sealed envelope on the party noticing the oral deposition. The noticing party must then deliver them to the deposition officer, who must open the envelope and propound the questions to the witness at the deposition. TRCP 199.5(b).

4. Documents. When required to bring documents, the deponent may provide copies of the documents if the originals are made available for inspection. TRCP 203.4. If the deponent brings the originals, the court reporter will make copies, attach them to the deposition, and return the originals to the deponent. *Id.* The originals must be available for production for a hearing or for the trial on seven days' notice from any party. *Id.*

PRACTICE TIP

When a witness provides documents as part of a deposition, and the witness is not going to appear in person at trial, you must "prove up" the documents during the deposition. Documents are not admissible simply because they were produced during a deposition. See **James v. Hudgins***, 876 S.W.2d 418, 422 (Tex.App.—El Paso 1994, writ denied).*

---

§4.9 Signing deposition. Once the deposition is prepared, the deponent must review it and sign it under oath, unless the parties and the deponent agree to waive the signature. TRCP 203.1. The court reporter usually handles the signature in one of the following ways:

———————— ✦ ————————

1. Represented deponent. If the deponent is represented by an attorney at the deposition, the court reporter will send the original deposition to the attorney, along with a sheet to note corrections. TRCP 203.1(a). The attorney will arrange for the deponent to review the deposition, sign the signature page under oath, and return the deposition to the court reporter. TRCP 203.1(b).

2. Unrepresented deponent. If the deponent is not represented by an attorney at the deposition, the court reporter will send the deposition (usually a copy) and a correction sheet directly to the deponent to be reviewed, signed, notarized, and returned. *See* TRCP 203.1.

§4.10 Changing answers. The deponent may submit changes to the deposition and the reasons for the changes—in writing and under oath—to the court reporter within 20 days after the submission of the deposition to the deponent or counsel. TRCP 203.1(b). If the deponent does not return the deposition to the court reporter within 20 days after receiving it, the deponent waives the right to make changes. *Id.* The changes should be noted on a form provided for changes; they are not made in the deposition itself. *See id.* The court reporter will attach the deponent's changes to the deposition; the original transcription is not retyped.

§4.11 Refusing to sign deposition. When a party files a motion to suppress the deposition under TRCP 203.5 because the deponent refused to sign the deposition, the court must determine whether the reason the witness refused to sign impugns the reliability of the deposition. *Hill v. Rich*, 522 S.W.2d 597, 600 (Tex.App.—Austin 1975, writ ref'd n.r.e.). Suppression is not justified by the mere lack of a signature. *Smith v. Smith*, 720 S.W.2d 586, 599 (Tex. App.—Houston [1st Dist.] 1986, no writ). Unless the deposition is suppressed, it may be used at trial. *See* TRCP 203.5, 203.6.

§4.12 Not filed. Depositions are not filed with the court; they are kept by the custodial attorney. *See* TRCP 203.3(a). After the court reporter receives the signed deposition, the court reporter must (1) attach any corrections, (2) send the deposition to the attorney who asked the first question (unless the parties agreed otherwise) with notice to the other attorneys, and (3) file with the trial court a sworn certificate that meets the requirements of TRCP 203.2. TRCP 203.1(b), 203.2, 203.3. If the deposition is taken by nonstenographic means, the original record of the deposition is sent to the party who requested the nonstenographic recording, not the party who asked the first question. *See* TRCP 203.3(a).

§4.13 Paying for deposition.

1. Cost of original. The attorney who takes the deposition and that attorney's firm are jointly and severally liable for the court reporter's charges for reporting the deposition, for transcribing it, and for providing the copies of it requested by that attorney. Gov't Code §52.059(a). An attorney "takes" a deposition if the attorney secures the deponent's appearance through formal or informal means or asks the first question. Gov't Code §52.059(d)(2); *see* TRCP 203.3(a) (original deposition transcript is delivered to the attorney "who asked the first question"). The attorney (and the attorney's firm) who asks for a copy of the deposition is personally responsible for the court reporter's charges for that copy. Gov't Code §52.059(b); *cf.* CPRC §7.011 (attorney who is not a party is not liable for the costs of the proceedings). If the attorney refuses to be bound by the provisions of Gov't Code §52.059(a) and (b), the attorney must state on the record who will pay the cost of the deposition. Gov't Code §52.059(c).

2. Cost of copy. The custodial attorney must make the original deposition available to other parties for copying. TRCP 203.3(c). It is not necessary for the parties to pay the court reporter for more than the original transcript of the deposition; the court reporter's charge for a copy of a deposition is much higher than the photocopy cost. The parties can agree to split the cost of the original deposition and the cost of the photocopy.

§5. SUBPOENAS FOR DEPOSITION

See "Subpoenas," ch. 1-L, p. 84; "Securing Things from a Nonparty," ch. 6-I, §5, p. 569.

§6. TIME LIMITS ON ORAL DEPOSITIONS

§6.1 Limits under discovery-control plans. A party's or side's total deposition time depends on the discovery limitations for the case. For the definition of "side," see "Side," ch. 6-A, §2.7, p. 426. For discovery limitations for the case, see "Proposed TRCP Changes," ch. 6-A, §7.2, p. 431; "Discovery limitations," ch. 6-A, §7.2.3, p. 431; "Discovery limitations," ch. 6-A, §7.3.2, p. 432; "Discovery limitations," ch. 6-A, §7.4.2, p. 433.

★

§6.2 Limits on witness deposition. No side may examine or cross-examine a witness for more than six hours, excluding breaks. TRCP 199.5(c). For purposes of this rule, each person designated by an organization under TRCP 199.2(b)(1) is a separate witness. TRCP 199 cmt. 2. The time credited to a party includes ordinary pauses by the interrogator or the witness, but not off-the-record discussion or protracted lapses (e.g., when a witness is reviewing a stack of documents). *Uniform Format Manual*, §3.4 cmt., ¶3.

PRACTICE TIP
Because each side can depose a witness for only six hours, a party should prepare for depositions by conducting its written discovery first. The party should not waste valuable deposition time by covering subjects that can be asked about in written discovery.

---

§6.3 Breaks. Breaks do not count against the time limits. TRCP 199.5(c). Even though private conferences between the witness and the witness's attorney during the actual taking of the deposition are improper (except for determining whether a privilege should be asserted), during agreed recesses and adjournments, the witness may confer privately with the witness's attorney. TRCP 199.5(d).

§6.4 Timekeeper. The deposition officer, generally the court reporter, is the timekeeper for purposes of the time limits on discovery. *See* TRCP 203.2(e). When a deposition is recorded without a court reporter, the person administering the oath to the witness, generally a notary public, must act as the timekeeper. *See* TRCP 199.1(c), 203.2(e); *see also* Gov't Code §602.002(4) (notary public may administer oaths). The deposition officer can use a time-stamping machine, a stopwatch, or another time-keeping device. *Uniform Format Manual*, §3.4 cmt., ¶3. The sworn certificate filed with the court must state the amount of time used by each party at the deposition. TRCP 203.2(e).

§7. OBJECTING BEFORE ORAL DEPOSITION

To object to the time, place, manner of proceeding, or scope of a deposition, the party should file one of the following: (1) a written objection to the deposition, (2) a motion to quash the deposition, or (3) a motion for protective order. TRCP 192.6, 199.4. See "Objecting to Trial & Discovery Subpoenas," ch. 1-L, §4, p. 87; "Motion for Protective Order," ch. 6-A, §20, p. 449; *O'Connor's Texas Forms*, FORMS 6A:13, 6F:2. The objection or motion should be filed as soon as possible—certainly before the date of the deposition, unless filing the motion earlier is not feasible. *Bohmfalk v. Linwood*, 742 S.W.2d 518, 520 (Tex.App.—Dallas 1987, no writ); *see, e.g.*, *Siegel v. Smith*, 836 S.W.2d 193, 194 (Tex.App.—San Antonio 1992, writ denied) (P filed motion on day of deposition with evidence of medical reason for inability to attend).

§7.1 To object to time or place. To object to the time or place designated for an oral deposition, the party or witness must file a motion for protective order or a motion to quash the notice of deposition. TRCP 192.6(a), 199.4; *see, e.g.*, *Bohmfalk v. Linwood*, 742 S.W.2d 518, 520 (Tex.App.—Dallas 1987, no writ) (party waived inadequate notice of deposition because it did not file motion for protective order to reschedule it). The motion must identify a reasonable time and place for the deposition with which the party or witness will comply. TRCP 192.6(a); *Grass v. Golden*, 153 S.W.3d 659, 662 (Tex.App.—Tyler 2004, orig. proceeding). See "Date for oral deposition," §4.5.2, p. 527; "Place for deposition," §4.5.3, p. 528. If the motion is filed within three business days after service of the notice of deposition, the deposition is automatically stayed until the motion can be determined. TRCP 199.4. A TRCP 199.4 objection does not delay the time for compliance with a document request served with a deposition notice; it only delays the time of the deposition itself.

§7.2 To cancel or limit because of privilege. To prevent a deposition or limit the scope of the interrogation because of a particular privilege, the objecting party should file either a motion for protective order or a motion to quash the subpoena, with affidavits that prove it is entitled to the privilege. See "What Is Not Discoverable?," ch. 6-B, §3, p. 471. For example, if a consulting-only expert is noticed for deposition, the party seeking to prevent the deposition should file a motion for protective order or a motion to quash the subpoena and attach an affidavit swearing that the expert was hired in anticipation of litigation, the expert will not testify, and the expert's work has not been reviewed by a testifying expert. *See* *Essex Crane Rental Corp. v. Kitzman*, 723 S.W.2d 241, 242-43 (Tex.App.—Houston [1st Dist.] 1986, orig. proceeding).

—————————————— ✦ ——————————————

§7.3 To cancel apex deposition. To cancel the deposition of a corporate president or other high-level corporate official (an "apex deposition"), the corporation must file a motion for protective order or a motion to quash accompanied by the official's affidavit denying any personal knowledge of relevant facts. *In re Alcatel USA, Inc.*, 11 S.W.3d 173, 175 (Tex.2000); *Crown Cent. Pet. Corp. v. Garcia*, 904 S.W.2d 125, 128 (Tex.1995); *In re Continental Airlines, Inc.*, 305 S.W.3d 849, 852 (Tex.App.—Houston [14th Dist.] 2010, orig. proceeding). Once the motion is filed, the trial court must determine whether the party seeking the deposition has shown the official to have any unique or superior personal knowledge of discoverable information. *In re Alcatel*, 11 S.W.3d at 175-76; *Crown Cent.*, 904 S.W.2d at 128; *see In re BP Prods. N. Am., Inc.*, 244 S.W.3d 840, 842 n.2 (Tex.2008). If the party cannot establish that the official has such knowledge, the trial court should grant the motion and require the party to attempt to obtain the discovery through less-intrusive methods. *In re Alcatel*, 11 S.W.3d at 176; *Crown Cent.*, 904 S.W.2d at 128; *see, e.g., AMR Corp. v. Enlow*, 926 S.W.2d 640, 644 (Tex.App.—Fort Worth 1996, orig. proceeding) (highest-ranking officer could not be deposed simply because he had ultimate responsibility). After making a good-faith effort at less-intrusive discovery, the party seeking the apex deposition may attempt to show that (1) there is a reasonable indication the official's deposition will lead to the discovery of admissible evidence, and (2) the less-intrusive discovery was unsatisfactory, insufficient, or inadequate. *In re BP Prods.*, 244 S.W.3d at 842 n.2; *In re Alcatel*, 11 S.W.3d at 176; *Crown Cent.*, 904 S.W.2d at 128; *see In re Daisy Mfg. Co.*, 17 S.W.3d 654, 658 (Tex.2000) (merely completing some less-intrusive discovery does not trigger automatic right to depose apex official). The apex doctrine does not protect from deposition a corporate officer who is a named party in the suit. *Simon v. Bridewell*, 950 S.W.2d 439, 443 (Tex.App.—Waco 1997, orig. proceeding).

§7.4 To exclude extra person. To object to an extra person attending the deposition who was identified under TRCP 199.5(a)(3), the party should file an objection before the deposition and ask the court to exclude that person.

§7.5 To object to overbroad request. To object to a notice of a deposition that is overbroad or unlikely to produce relevant information, the party or witness should file a motion for protective order or a motion to quash the notice of deposition. *See In re Univar USA, Inc.*, 311 S.W.3d 186, 189 (Tex.App.—Beaumont 2010, orig. proceeding).

§7.6 To compel attendance.

1. Party witness. If a party (or a person retained by, employed by, or subject to the control of the party) refused to appear for a deposition, the party who noticed the deposition should file a motion to compel the party to attend the deposition and a motion for sanctions. The motions should be served on the party's attorney. *See* TRCP 199.3. See "Refusal to attend deposition," §10.1.1, p. 537.

2. Nonparty witness. If a nonparty witness refused to appear for a deposition, the party who subpoenaed the witness for deposition should file a motion to compel the witness to appear for the deposition and a motion to hold the witness in contempt of court. *See* TRCP 176.8(a). A witness who refuses to comply with a subpoena without an adequate excuse may be deemed in contempt of court. *Id.* See "Discovery abuse," ch. 5-K, §5.1, p. 380; "By nonparty witness-deponent," §10.1.1(3), p. 537.

§7.7 Other objections. See "Valid objections to discovery requests," ch. 6-A, §19.1, p. 448.

§8. CONDUCT DURING ORAL DEPOSITION

If the attorneys and witnesses do not comply with TRCP 199.5(d), the court may allow into evidence at trial the statements, objections, discussions, and other occurrences during the oral deposition that reflect on the credibility of the witness or the testimony. TRCP 199.5(d).

§8.1 Conduct of attorneys. Attorneys should cooperate with and be courteous to each other and the witness. TRCP 199.5(d). The oral deposition must be conducted in the same manner as if the testimony were being elicited in open court. *Id.* An attorney must not ask a question at an oral deposition solely to harass or mislead the witness, for any other improper purpose, or without a good-faith legal basis. TRCP 199.5(h). An attorney must not object to a question at an oral deposition, instruct the witness not to answer a question, or suspend the deposition unless there is a good-faith factual and legal basis to do so. *Id.*

———————————— ✦ ————————————

§8.2 Conduct of witness. The witness should not be evasive and should not unduly delay the examination. TRCP 199.5(d).

§8.3 Conferring with witness. Private conferences between the witness and the witness's attorney during the actual taking of the deposition are improper except for determining whether a privilege should be asserted. TRCP 199.5(d). Private conferences may be held during agreed recesses and adjournments. *Id.*

§8.4 Conduct of court reporter. The court reporter or other officer taking the oral deposition does not rule on objections, but records them for a ruling by the court. TRCP 199.5(e). The officer taking the oral deposition cannot stop recording the testimony when an objection has been made. *Id.*

§9. OBJECTING DURING ORAL DEPOSITION

§9.1 Procedure to object. Objections are made and recorded in the deposition and reserved for a ruling by the trial court. *See* TRCP 199.5(e).

1. Permissible objections. TRCP 199.5(e) governs the types of objections and limits the exact words that may be used in an objection. The only objections the parties can make during the deposition are (1) "Objection, leading," (2) "Objection, form," and (3) "Objection, nonresponsive." TRCP 199.5(e). If these objections are not stated as phrased in TRCP 199.5(e), they are waived. *Id.* All other objections should be made at trial, unless the parties agree to another method. *Id.*; *see* TRCP 191.1. The parties can agree to a running objection to repeated offers of the same evidence. See "Running objection," ch. 8-D, §6.4, p. 712. The parties can also agree to reserve all objections, including those stated in TRCP 199.5(e), until the time of trial. TRCP 191.1.

PRACTICE TIP
If the witness's testimony is to be presented at trial by deposition, the parties should agree to make all objections on the record during the deposition.

---

(1) Objection to leading question. Leading questions are those that suggest the desired answer. *GAB Bus. Servs. v. Moore*, 829 S.W.2d 345, 351 (Tex.App.—Texarkana 1992, no writ). See Brown & Rondon, *Evidence Handbook*, p. 618.

(2) Objection to form of question. Objections to the form of the question include the following: (1) the question assumes facts that are in dispute or are not in evidence, (2) the question is argumentative, (3) the question misquotes the deponent, (4) the question calls for speculation, (5) the question is vague, ambiguous, or confusing, (6) the question is compound, (7) the question is too general, (8) the question calls for a narrative answer, (9) the question has been asked and answered, (10) the question is harassing and oppressive, and (11) the question is an incomplete hypothetical. *See* TRCP 199 cmt. 4; *St. Luke's Episcopal Hosp. v. Garcia*, 928 S.W.2d 307, 309 (Tex.App.—Houston [14th Dist.] 1996, orig. proceeding).

(3) Objection to nonresponsiveness of answer. If the deponent's response addresses issues not raised by the question or states more than is strictly required to answer the question, the attorney must object or else any complaint is waived. *See* TRCP 199.5(e).

2. Request for explanation of objections. If requested by the party interrogating the deponent, the objecting party must give a clear and concise explanation of its objection, or the objection is waived. TRCP 199.5(e).

3. Sanctionable objections. Argumentative or suggestive objections or explanations waive the objection and may be grounds for terminating the oral deposition or assessing costs or other sanctions. TRCP 199.5(e).

§9.2 Instructions not to answer. There are very few instances when it is proper for an attorney to instruct the deponent not to answer. When requested by the opposing party, the attorney who instructed the witness not to answer must give a concise, nonargumentative, and nonsuggestive explanation of the grounds for the instruction. TRCP 199.5(f). After giving the requested explanation, if the attorney who asked the question insists that it is a proper line of inquiry, the objecting attorney may suspend the deposition to get a court ruling. See "Suspending deposition,"

———————————— ✦ ————————————

§9.3, this page. If the objecting attorney does not suspend the deposition but refuses to permit the deponent to answer, the attorney who asked the question may suspend the deposition and file a motion to compel the deponent to answer (referred to as "certifying the question"). *See generally Huie v. DeShazo*, 922 S.W.2d 920, 922 (Tex.1996) (Supreme Court stayed deposition while considering writ of mandamus on motion to compel testimony over assertion of attorney-client privilege). See "Motion to compel answer," §9.4, this page. An attorney may object and instruct a witness not to answer a question during an oral deposition only for one of the following reasons:

1. Preserve privileges. To prevent the discovery of privileged information, the attorney may object and instruct the witness not to answer. TRCP 199.5(f). If the witness answers and discloses privileged information, the privilege may be waived. *See Delaporte v. Preston Square, Inc.*, 680 S.W.2d 561, 564 (Tex.App.—Dallas 1984, writ ref'd n.r.e.) (party who answered question about privileged matter in deposition waived privilege; however, trial court excluded answer at trial). If necessary for an in camera review, the deposition questions can be answered in front of the court reporter in the absence of the party seeking discovery and then be submitted to the court in camera. TRCP 199.6.

2. Comply with court order or rules. An attorney may instruct a witness not to answer a question if answering would violate a court order or the TRCPs. TRCP 199.5(f); *In re Lowe's Cos.*, 134 S.W.3d 876, 878 (Tex. App.—Houston [14th Dist.] 2004, orig. proceeding). For example, if a deponent is asked for net-worth information in a suit that involves only actual damages, the deponent should be instructed not to answer because the information is not relevant under the TRCPs. If the deponent is asked for information the court has already ruled is not discoverable, the deponent should be instructed not to answer. *See* TRCP 199.5(f).

3. Protect a witness. An attorney may instruct a witness not to answer if one of the parties asks the deponent questions that are abusive or for which any answer would be misleading. TRCP 199.5(f). For example, an attorney could instruct a witness not to answer when the question incorporates such unfair assumptions or is so worded that any answer would necessarily be misleading—the "when did you stop beating your spouse" sort of question. TRCP 199 cmt. 4. Abusive questions include questions that inquire into matters clearly beyond the scope of discovery or that are argumentative, repetitious, or harassing. *Id.*

4. Stopwatch objection. When a party exceeds the deposition time limits, the other party should object and suspend the deposition to obtain a court ruling. TRCP 199.5(g).

§9.3 Suspending deposition. A party or witness may suspend the deposition for the time necessary to obtain a court ruling if the time limitations for the deposition have expired or the deposition is being conducted or defended in violation of the rules. TRCP 199.5(g).

§9.4 Motion to compel answer. When a witness refuses to answer a question at a deposition, the party asking the question may file a motion to compel along with a copy of the deposition (or the certified question) and request a hearing. TRCP 199.6, 215.1(b)(2)(B); *see, e.g., Huie v. DeShazo*, 922 S.W.2d 920, 922 (Tex.1996) (after witness refused to answer questions based on privilege, P filed motion to compel with certified questions); *Koepp v. Utica Mut. Ins.*, 833 S.W.2d 514, 514 (Tex.1992) (after P refused to answer questions about drug use, D filed motion to compel). The certified question is an excerpt from the deposition prepared by the court reporter to be used when a party intends to ask for an immediate court ruling. See "Motion to Compel Discovery," ch. 6-A, §22, p. 451.

§9.5 Motion to suppress. To object to errors or irregularities in the taking of a deposition—how the deposition was prepared, transcribed, signed, certified, sealed, endorsed, or delivered—the party must file a written motion to suppress and serve it on all other parties. TRCP 203.5; *see* TRCP 202.3(b)(2). The motion to suppress must be served before the trial commences if the deposition officer delivered the deposition at least one entire day before the day of trial. TRCP 203.5; *SAVA gumarska v. Advanced Polymer Sci., Inc.*, 128 S.W.3d 304, 316 (Tex.App.—Dallas 2004, no pet.); *Klorer v. Block*, 717 S.W.2d 754, 759 (Tex.App.—San Antonio 1986, writ ref'd n.r.e.). See *O'Connor's Texas Forms*, FORM 6F:3.

⭐

§10. DEPOSITION SANCTIONS

§10.1 Grounds for sanctions. A party or a deponent can be sanctioned for violating deposition procedures. For the standards for imposing sanctions, see "Motion for Sanctions," ch. 5-K, p. 377.

1. Refusal to attend deposition.

(1) By party-deponent. If the party to be deposed does not attend a noticed or court-ordered deposition, the trial court can impose sanctions, including the ultimate sanction of dismissal or default. TRCP 215.2(b); *see, e.g., Greater Houston Transp. Co. v. Wilson*, 725 S.W.2d 427, 431 (Tex.App.—Houston [14th Dist.] 1987, writ ref'd n.r.e.) (D did not attend deposition; default judgment entered); *Petitt v. Laware*, 715 S.W.2d 688, 691-92 (Tex. App.—Houston [1st Dist.] 1986, writ ref'd n.r.e.) (P refused to attend court-ordered deposition; case dismissed). *But see Hogan v. Beckel*, 783 S.W.2d 307, 308 (Tex.App.—San Antonio 1989, writ denied) (dismissal was improper when P did not appear for one noticed deposition). In addition to or instead of a sanctions order, the court can hold the party in contempt. TRCP 215.2(a), (b)(6). There is no requirement that the failure to attend be willful. *Meek v. Bishop, Peterson & Sharp*, 919 S.W.2d 805, 809 (Tex.App.—Houston [14th Dist.] 1996, writ denied); *see* TRCP 215.1(b)(2)(A).

(2) By party who noticed deposition. If the party giving notice of the deposition does not attend the deposition, and if another party or that party's attorney does attend, the court may award the attending party reasonable expenses, including attorney fees. TRCP 215.5(a); *Hlavinka v. Griffin*, 721 S.W.2d 521, 523-24 (Tex.App.—Corpus Christi 1986, no writ).

(3) By nonparty witness-deponent.

(a) If the witness does not attend a deposition, and the fault lies with the party giving notice, the court may order that party to pay reasonable expenses, including attorney fees, to any party that does attend. TRCP 215.5(b).

(b) If a nonparty witness refuses to attend a deposition after being subpoenaed by a party or ordered by the trial court, the court may hold the nonparty witness in contempt. TRCP 176.8(a), 215.2(a).

2. Refusal to answer questions.

If a deponent refuses to answer a proper question asked in a deposition, the trial court can impose sanctions. TRCP 215.1(b)(2)(B). A deponent's evasive or incomplete answer can be treated as a refusal to answer a question. TRCP 215.1(c). When a trial court orders a deponent to answer a question and the deponent refuses, the court can impose sanctions.

(1) Contempt. The court can hold the deponent (party or nonparty) in contempt and punish the deponent with a fine or confinement. TRCP 176.8(a), 215.2(a), (b)(2).

(2) Strike pleadings. The court can strike a party's pleadings. *See, e.g., First State Bank v. Chappell & Handy, P.C.*, 729 S.W.2d 917, 921 (Tex.App.—Corpus Christi 1987, writ ref'd n.r.e.) (court struck D-corporation's counterclaim and defensive pleadings because D's officer refused to answer questions after being ordered to answer).

(3) Award expenses. The court can require a party whose conduct necessitated the motion for sanctions, the attorney advising such conduct, or both to pay the moving party's reasonable expenses, including attorney fees. TRCP 215.2(b)(8); *see also* TRCP 215.3 (sanctions may be imposed for abusing discovery process). The court cannot order a nonparty deponent whose conduct necessitated the motion to pay the moving party's expenses. *In re White*, 227 S.W.3d 234, 237 (Tex.App.—San Antonio 2007, orig. proceeding); *City of Houston v. Chambers*, 899 S.W.2d 306, 309 (Tex.App.—Houston [14th Dist.] 1995, orig. proceeding).

3. Lying during deposition.

If a party-deponent lies (i.e., perjures herself) during a deposition, the trial court can impose sanctions ranging from the payment of expenses and attorney fees to a default judgment. *See* TRCP 215.2(b); *In re Reece*, 341 S.W.3d 360, 368 (Tex.2011). The court cannot, however, hold the party in contempt for lying during a deposition unless, by lying, the party has obstructed the court in the performance of its duties. *In re Reece*, 341 S.W.3d at 367.

—————————————— ✦ ——————————————

§10.2 Appropriate court to hear objections & motions. TRCP 215.1(a) determines the appropriate court to hear and determine objections and motions about a deposition.

1. Party deponent. The court where the suit is filed should hear and determine objections made about a deposition of a party. TRCP 215.1(a). Any district court in the district where a party's deposition is being taken may also hear a motion relating to the taking of a deposition. *Id.*

2. Nonparty deponent. A district court in the district where the deposition is being taken should hear and determine the objections made about the deposition of a nonparty. ***Latham v. Thornton***, 806 S.W.2d 347, 349 (Tex.App.—Fort Worth 1991, orig. proceeding).

§11. SUPPLEMENTING DEPOSITION TESTIMONY

§11.1 Deposition of fact witnesses. A party does not have a general duty to supplement the deposition testimony of fact witnesses who change their minds about facts disclosed in a deposition. TRCP 193 cmt. 5; ***Titus Cty. Hosp. Dist. v. Lucas***, 988 S.W.2d 740, 740 (Tex.1998); *see **Collins v. Collins***, 923 S.W.2d 569, 569 (Tex.1996).

—————————————————————————————

PRACTICE TIP
To avoid the surprise at trial that the other party's witnesses have changed their minds about the facts of the case, the parties can enter into a Rule 11 agreement to supplement the deposition testimony of fact witnesses who are aligned with each party.

—————————————————————————————

§11.2 Deposition testimony of retained expert. See "Supplementing discovery of retained testifying expert," ch. 6-D, §5.1, p. 511.

§11.3 Deposition testimony of nonretained expert. See "Supplementing discovery of nonretained testifying expert," ch. 6-D, §5.2, p. 512.

§12. USING DEPOSITION AT TRIAL

§12.1 Admissibility. A deposition is admissible at trial according to the rules of evidence. TRCP 203.6(b), (c); *see **Jones v. Colley***, 820 S.W.2d 863, 866 (Tex.App.—Texarkana 1991, writ denied) (party is entitled to offer deposition testimony into evidence in most effective manner, provided it does not convey false impression).

1. Deposition taken in same proceeding. A deposition taken in the same proceeding as the trial is not hearsay, and the deponent does not need to be unavailable for the deposition to be used as evidence. TRCP 203.6(b)(1); TRE 801(e)(3). The deposition can be used instead of or in addition to live testimony. "Same proceeding" includes any other suit involving the same subject matter between the same parties or their representatives or successors in interest. TRCP 203.6(b).

(1) Party not present at deposition. Depositions taken in the absence of a party may be used at trial if the party received notice but chose not to attend. ***Bohmfalk v. Linwood***, 742 S.W.2d 518, 520 (Tex.App.—Dallas 1987, no writ).

(2) Not party at time of deposition. A deposition may not be used against a party that was joined after the deposition was taken unless the late party had a reasonable opportunity to redepose the deponent after being joined and did not exercise that opportunity. TRCP 203.6(b)(2); ***Stevenson v. Koutzarov***, 795 S.W.2d 313, 317 (Tex.App.—Houston [1st Dist.] 1990, writ denied). See "Restricted use," §16.8.2, p. 546. If a deposition was taken before a party was joined, it can be used at trial if the late party has an interest similar to any party already in the suit when the deposition was taken.

★

PRACTICE TIP

*If you took a deposition before a party was added, and if the late party does not have similar interests with any other party, you should redepose the witness to give the late party the opportunity for cross-examination. See **Elizondo v. Tavarez**, 596 S.W.2d 667, 671 (Tex.App.—Corpus Christi 1980, writ ref'd n.r.e.). You can satisfy the requirement to redepose the witness by deposing the witness with written questions. If you represent a late party, and one of the parties sends a deposition on written questions to a witness who was deposed before your client was added, you should file objections to the deposition on written questions, and notice the witness to appear for an oral deposition. See **Stevenson**, 795 S.W.2d at 316 n.1.*

---

2. Deposition from other proceeding. Depositions from other proceedings can be used if they are admissible under the rules of evidence. TRCP 203.6(c); *see, e.g.*, **Dillee v. Sisters of Charity**, 912 S.W.2d 307, 310 n.6 (Tex.App.—Houston [14th Dist.] 1995, no writ) (deposition from another case was admissible under TRE 801 as admission by a party-opponent).

(1) Party deposition. The deposition of a party taken in another proceeding is admissible as a party-admission or as former testimony. *See* TRE 801(e)(2); *see, e.g.*, **Worley v. Butler**, 809 S.W.2d 242, 245 (Tex.App.—Corpus Christi 1990, no writ) (client's testimony at first trial about employment contract with his attorney was admissible against him in later lawsuit over attorney fees); *see also* TRE 801(e)(1) (prior statement by witness).

(2) Nonparty deposition. The deposition of a nonparty taken in another proceeding is admissible as former testimony if the deponent is unavailable to testify. TRE 804(b)(1); **Smith v. Smith**, 720 S.W.2d 586, 599 (Tex.App.—Houston [1st Dist.] 1986, no writ); *see* TRCP 203.6(c); *see, e.g.*, **Celotex Corp. v. Tate**, 797 S.W.2d 197, 205 (Tex.App.—Corpus Christi 1990, writ dism'd) (deposition of claimant in workers' compensation case, who died, was admissible in another case). Unavailability of a witness is defined as (1) a claim of privilege, (2) a refusal to testify, (3) a lack of memory, (4) a death or physical or mental illness or infirmity, or (5) an absence from the hearing and inability of the proponent to procure attendance or testimony. TRE 804(a); Brown & Rondon, *Evidence Handbook*, p. 908; *see, e.g.*, **Keene Corp. v. Rogers**, 863 S.W.2d 168, 177-78 (Tex.App.—Texarkana 1993, writ filed, bankruptcy stay granted 3-30-94) (because party did not prove unavailability, court should have excluded expert's deposition from another case). The party against whom the deposition is offered, or a person with a similar interest, must have had an opportunity and similar motive to develop the former testimony by direct examination, cross-examination, or redirect examination. TRE 804(b)(1).

§12.2 Procedure. Deposition testimony is introduced at trial as follows:

1. Read into evidence. The party offering deposition testimony must read a transcribed deposition (or play a videotape deposition) before the jury. *See* TRCP 203.6(b). When introducing a written deposition, one attorney reads the questions and another attorney, sitting in the witness stand, reads the answers given by the deponent.

CAUTION

*When you read a deposition into evidence or play a videotape deposition, insist that the court reporter transcribe the testimony as the jury hears it. If the court reporter does not transcribe the deposition testimony as it is presented at trial, the appellate record will not contain the deposition testimony of the witness. If you do not object on the record during the trial, you will waive the issue of an incomplete record on appeal. E.g., **Lascurain v. Crowley**, 917 S.W.2d 341, 344-45 (Tex.App.—El Paso 1996, no writ) (court reporter left courtroom during deposition testimony with permission of parties). If the court reporter appeared to be transcribing the testimony but was not, you may be able to reconstruct the record. **State Farm Fire & Cas. Ins. v. Vandiver**, 941 S.W.2d 343, 347-48 (Tex.App.—Waco 1997, no writ).*

———————————————— ✦ ————————————————

2. Submit deposition as offer of proof. If the court rules a deposition inadmissible, the party may submit the deposition as an offer of proof, have it marked as an exhibit, identify the portions offered by line and page number, and file it with the court reporter. *See* TRE 103(a)(2); *Soefje v. Stewart*, 847 S.W.2d 311, 313 (Tex. App.—San Antonio 1992, writ denied). The offer of proof should be made before the charge is read to the jury. If, for some reason, the deposition is not immediately offered as an offer of proof, it may be filed as a formal bill of exception after the trial. TRAP 33.2. See "Offer of Proof & Bill of Exception," ch. 8-E, p. 717.

§12.3 Trial objections to deposition testimony. At trial, unless the parties made a different agreement on objections, a party may urge (1) those objections to leading, form, and nonresponsiveness that were made during the deposition and (2) all other objections. TRCP 199.5(e). See "Procedure to object," §9.1, p. 535.

§12.4 Objection to trial testimony. A party may object to the trial testimony of a witness if it is materially different from the witness's deposition testimony. See "Impeaching by earlier inconsistent statement," ch. 8-C, §6.2, p. 702.

§12.5 Use in summary-judgment cases. When a deposition is used as summary-judgment evidence, it is not necessary for the deposition to be authenticated by an affidavit that certifies the truthfulness and correctness of the copied material. *See* TRCP 166a(d); TRE 901(a); *McConathy v. McConathy*, 869 S.W.2d 341, 342 (Tex.1994).

§13. DEPOSITION BY NONSTENOGRAPHIC RECORDING DEVICE

A party may take a deposition by videotape or other recording device. TRCP 199.1(c). A video deposition has a more powerful effect on the jury than a deposition that is read to the jury. *Ochs v. Martinez*, 789 S.W.2d 949, 956 (Tex. App.—San Antonio 1990, writ denied).

§13.1 Deposition officer. When a deposition is to be recorded by video or audio recording without a simultaneous stenographic recording by a court reporter, the party noticing the deposition is responsible for obtaining a person authorized by law to act as the deposition officer and administer the oath. TRCP 199.1(c), 203.2; *see Uniform Format Manual*, §3.7 cmt.

§13.2 Notice. To take a videotape deposition, the party must give the witness and the other parties at least five days' notice in writing. TRCP 199.1(c). The notice must state that the deposition (1) will be recorded by nonstenographic means, (2) will be recorded by videotape or audiotape (or by some other means), and (3) will or will not also be recorded stenographically. *Id.* The notice may be included in the deposition notice or served separately. *Id.* See "Notice of oral deposition," §4.5, p. 527; *O'Connor's Texas Forms*, FORM 6F:1, ¶3.

§13.3 Response. After a party gives notice of its intent to take a nonstenographic deposition, any other party may serve written notice designating an additional method of recording (usually stenographic) at its own expense. TRCP 199.1(c); *see also* TRCP 203.6(a) (court may require nonstenographic recording be reduced to writing by certified court reporter). TRCP 199.1(c) is a significant improvement over its predecessor because it eliminates the requirement that a videotaped deposition be accompanied by a stenographic transcript. Unless one of the parties elects to pay for a court reporter to transcribe the testimony, or the court orders that the deposition be transcribed for trial, no stenographic transcript is necessary. TRCP 199.1(c), 203.6(a).

§13.4 Recording. The party taking the deposition is responsible for ensuring that the recording is intelligible, accurate, and trustworthy. TRCP 199.1(c).

§13.5 Copies. The original video recording must be available for inspection. TRCP 203.3(c). All parties must have reasonable access to the video deposition and may obtain a duplicate copy at their own expense. *Id.*

§13.6 Use at trial. A party may play a recording of a nonstenographic deposition at trial instead of reading the deposition. TRCP 203.6(a). A party may use a written transcription of a nonstenographic deposition to the same extent as one taken by stenographic means. *Id.*; *Wrenn v. G.A.T.X. Logistics, Inc.*, 73 S.W.3d 489, 499 (Tex.App.— Fort Worth 2002, no pet.). The court, on a motion showing good cause, may order the party to provide a transcript of the deposition. TRCP 203.6(a).

★

---

§14. DEPOSITION BY TELEPHONE

A deposition by telephone is useful when the deponent is far away and the parties need only limited information.

§14.1 Notice. A written notice to take a deposition by telephone or other remote electronic means must be served on the witness and all parties a reasonable time before the deposition is to be taken. TRCP 199.1(b). See "Notice of oral deposition," §4.5, p. 527. To take a telephone deposition without a request for documents, see "For deposition without documents," §4.5.2(2), p. 528. To take a telephone deposition that requests the production of documents, see "For deposition with documents," §4.5.2(1), p. 527. See *O'Connor's Texas Forms*, FORM 6F:1, ¶5.

§14.2 Location of witness. A deposition by telephone is considered to have been taken "in the district and at the place where the witness is located when answering the questions." TRCP 199.1(b). The person administering the oath to the witness must have the power to administer an oath in the jurisdiction where the witness is located. *Id.*; *see* CPRC §20.001(b), (c).

§14.3 Location of deposition officer. The deposition officer may be located with the party who noticed the deposition or with the witness. TRCP 199.1(b); *see Clone Component Distribs. v. State*, 819 S.W.2d 593, 598 (Tex. App.—Dallas 1991, no writ).

§14.4 Exhibits. If it is necessary to question the witness about exhibits and the deposition officer is not physically in the same room as the witness, the parties should send premarked exhibits to the witness before the deposition. Another option is to use a fax machine to transfer copies of exhibits during the deposition. *See Clone Component Distribs. v. State*, 819 S.W.2d 593, 599-600 (Tex.App.—Dallas 1991, no writ).

§15. DEPOSITION ON WRITTEN QUESTIONS

Depositions on written questions are useful for securing testimony from a deponent with limited relevant information—for example, a custodian of business records. A deposition on written questions is relatively inexpensive compared to an oral deposition. Depositions on written questions are similar to interrogatories in that the questions are drafted in advance. They are unlike interrogatories in other ways—depositions on written questions can be served on nonparties (interrogatories can be served only on parties), and depositions on written questions are not limited in number (interrogatories are limited). Depositions on written questions cannot be used to circumvent the limits on interrogatories. TRCP 190 cmt. 5.

§15.1 Procedure. A deposition on written questions proceeds much like the standard oral deposition that is transcribed by a court reporter. For most of the requirements, see "Procedure for Standard Oral Deposition," §4, p. 526. This section will focus on the differences between the two procedures.

§15.2 Deposition officer. The only persons who can take a deposition on written questions are (1) a clerk of the district court, (2) a judge or clerk of the county court, (3) a court reporter, or (4) a notary public. CPRC §20.001(a) (persons 1, 2, and 4).

§15.3 Notice of deposition on written questions. The notice to take a deposition on written questions must comply with the following rules on oral depositions: TRCP 199.1(b), 199.2(b), and 199.5(a)(3). TRCP 200.1(b).

1. Name of deponent. The notice must state the deponent's name (if known) and the deponent's address for service. *See* TRCP 199.2(b)(1) (contents of notice), TRCP 200.1(a) (notice must be served on witness). The name of the deponent might not be known if the deponent is a custodian of records or if the party has asked an organization to provide a deponent to give testimony about a certain subject. *See* TRCP 199.2(b)(1), 200.1(b). The notice of a deposition on written questions to a nonparty business association or business entity can require the nonparty to designate a deponent to testify on a particular subject. *See* TRCP 199.2(b)(1), 200.1(b).

2. Place for deposition. The notice must state the place for the deposition, which must be reasonable. TRCP 199.2(b)(2), TRCP 200.1(b). See "Place for deposition," §4.5.3, p. 528.

3. Date for deposition. The notice must state the time for the deposition, which must be reasonable. TRCP 199.2(b)(2), TRCP 200.1(b). The notice must be served on the witness and all parties at least 20 days before

★

the deposition is to be taken. TRCP 200.1(a). When a notice requests that a party (not a nonparty) produce documents, the notice must be served at least 30 days before the deposition. See "Party deposition with documents," §4.5.2(1)(a), p. 527; "Deadlines to Serve Notice & Subpoena," chart 6-9, p. 530; *O'Connor's Texas Forms*, FORM 6F:4.

4. Designation of documents. The notice must identify the documents and other items the deponent is required to produce. *See* TRCP 200.1(b).

5. Extra persons in attendance. The notice must identify any person not listed in TRCP 199.5(a)(3) who will attend the deposition. TRCP 200.1(b). See "Additional attendee," §4.5.5, p. 529.

6. Signed. The notice must be signed by the attorney (or party when pro se). TRCP 191.3(a). See "Certification by signature," ch. 6-A, §4.1, p. 427.

7. Subpoena. When the deponent is a nonparty, a subpoena must be issued. TRCP 200.2, 205.1(b); *St. Luke's Episcopal Hosp. v. Garcia*, 928 S.W.2d 307, 311 (Tex.App.—Houston [14th Dist.] 1996, orig. proceeding). If the nonparty deponent is required to produce documents, the subpoena must meet the requirements of TRCP 176. TRCP 176, 199.2(b)(5), 200.1(b). See "Subpoenas," ch. 1-L, p. 84; "Securing Things from a Nonparty," ch. 6-I, §5, p. 569.

8. Direct questions. The questions the deponent is required to answer must be attached to the notice. TRCP 200.3(a). See *O'Connor's Texas Forms*, FORM 6F:5 (deposition on written questions for custodian of records).

9. Provide to deposition officer. The party that noticed the deposition must send a copy of the notice and copies of all questions to the officer designated to take the deposition, generally the court reporter. TRCP 200.1(a). If the deponent is a nonparty, the court reporter will issue a subpoena.

§15.4 Cross-questions. Any other party in the suit may serve cross-questions within ten days after the notice and the direct questions are served. TRCP 200.3(b). See *O'Connor's Texas Forms*, FORM 6F:6.

§15.5 Redirect questions. The propounder of the direct questions may serve redirect questions within five days after being served cross-questions. TRCP 200.3(b).

§15.6 Recross questions. The other parties may serve recross questions within three days after being served redirect questions. TRCP 200.3(b).

§15.7 Objections to form of question. Objections to the form of questions must be served on the party propounding them within the time allowed for serving the succeeding cross-questions or other questions and within five days after service of the last authorized questions. TRCP 200.3(b); *see St. Luke's Episcopal Hosp. v. Garcia*, 928 S.W.2d 307, 310 (Tex.App.—Houston [14th Dist.] 1996, orig. proceeding). The deadline for objections applies only to objections to form, not objections to substantive issues or privileges. *St. Luke's*, 928 S.W.2d at 310. Objections to the form of the question are waived unless asserted in accordance with TRCP 200.3(b). TRCP 200.3(c). See *O'Connor's Texas Forms*, FORM 6F:6.

§15.8 Objections to assertions of privileges. To lodge objections to assertions of privilege, the deponent or a party should file a motion to quash or a motion for protective order. If the deponent is a nonparty, the movant should press for a hearing before the date of the deposition. See "Objecting Before Oral Deposition," §7, p. 533.

§15.9 Taking deposition. At the time of the deposition, the deposition officer administers the oath, asks the questions, receives any documents produced, and transcribes the deponent's testimony. *See* TRCP 200.4; *see also In re Toyota Motor Corp.*, 191 S.W.3d 498, 503 (Tex.App.—Waco 2006, orig. proceeding) (attorneys are not permitted to answer written deposition questions for clients). The officer then prepares the questions and answers and certifies and delivers them to the deponent for examination and signature. TRCP 200.4. When necessary, the officer has authority to summon and administer an oath to an interpreter. *Id.*

§15.10 Filing deposition. Nonparty deposition notices and subpoenas must be filed with the court. TRCP 191.4(b)(1). No other deposition documents should be filed. TRCP 191.4(a)(1). For exceptions to the do-not-file rule, see "Exceptions," ch. 6-A, §12.1.3, p. 436.

——————————————— ✦ ———————————————

§16. DEPOSITION BEFORE SUIT

A deposition before suit or to investigate a claim is an examination by oral or written questions taken by court order before a lawsuit is filed. TRCP 202.1. The proceeding is not, in itself, a separate lawsuit but is incident to and in anticipation of a suit. *Office Empls. Int'l Un. v. Southwestern Drug Corp.*, 391 S.W.2d 404, 406 (Tex.1965) (applying former TRCP 187); *Valley Baptist Med. Ctr. v. Gonzalez*, 18 S.W.3d 673, 675 (Tex.App.—Corpus Christi 1999), *vacated as moot*, 33 S.W.3d 821 (Tex.2000). It is an ancillary proceeding. *In re Jorden*, 249 S.W.3d 416, 419 (Tex. 2008); *Valley Baptist*, 18 S.W.3d at 676. TRCP 202 applies to all discovery before suit covered by the former rules governing depositions to perpetuate testimony (former TRCP 187) and bills of discovery (former TRCP 737). TRCP 202 cmt. 1.

NOTE

*Courts must strictly limit and carefully supervise presuit discovery to prevent abuse of TRCP 202. **In re Wolfe**, 341 S.W.3d 932, 933 (Tex.2011). A party cannot obtain relief through a TRCP 202 proceeding that would be denied in the anticipated action or potential claim. **In re Wolfe**, 341 S.W.3d at 933. Thus, to prevent a party from circumventing discovery limitations that would govern the anticipated suit or potential claim, the scope of discovery in presuit depositions is the same as if the anticipated suit or potential claim had already been filed. Id.; see TRCP 202.5.*

---

§16.1 Petition. The requirements for the petition are stated in TRCP 202.2.

1. Form. The petition must be in the name of the petitioner and must be verified. TRCP 202.2(a), (c). See *O'Connor's Texas Forms*, FORM 6F:8.

2. Grounds. The petition must state one of two possible grounds for a deposition before suit. TRCP 202.2(d)(1), (d)(2); *In re Southwest Secs., Inc.*, No. 05-99-01836-CV (Tex.App.—Dallas 2000, orig. proceeding) (no pub.; 6-14-00).

(1) Anticipation of another suit. A petition for a TRCP 202 deposition may be filed in anticipation of another suit. TRCP 202.2(d)(1). Such a petition must include the statement: "The petitioner anticipates the institution of a suit in which the petitioner may be a party." *Id.* In addition, the petition must do the following:

(a) Identify subject. The petition must identify the subject matter of the anticipated action and the petitioner's interest in it. TRCP 202.2(e). The petitioner is not required to plead a specific cause of action. *City of Houston v. U.S. Filter Wastewater Grp.*, 190 S.W.3d 242, 245 n.2 (Tex.App.—Houston [1st Dist.] 2006, no pet.).

(b) Identify adverse persons. The petition must either (1) include the names, addresses, and telephone numbers of the persons whom the petitioner expects to have interests adverse to the petitioner's in the anticipated suit, or (2) state that the information cannot be ascertained through diligent inquiry and describe those persons. TRCP 202.2(f); *see U.S. Gov't v. Marks*, 949 S.W.2d 320, 322 (Tex.1997) (former TRCP 187).

(2) Investigate claim. A petition for a TRCP 202 deposition may be filed to investigate a claim. TRCP 202.2(d)(2). Such a petition must include the statement: "The petitioner seeks to investigate a potential claim by or against the petitioner." *Id.* Under TRCP 202.2(d)(2), there is no expectation of another suit. This ground can help plaintiffs comply with TRCP 13 and CPRC §9.011, which require plaintiffs to make a good-faith inquiry before deciding whether to file suit. *See also* CPRC §10.001 (certificate by signature).

(a) Adverse persons. When investigating a claim, unlike in a deposition in anticipation of suit, the petitioner is not required to identify those who may have an adverse interest. *See* TRCP 202.2(f); Fineberg & Shore, *Discovery Update*, at 3.

(b) Improper use.

[1] Health-care claim. A presuit deposition under TRCP 202 cannot be taken to investigate a potential claim against a health-care provider until after an expert report is served. *In re Jorden*, 249 S.W.3d 416, 418 (Tex.2008); *see* CPRC §74.351(s).

★

[2] **Trade secret.** A presuit deposition under TRCP 202 cannot be taken to discover trade-secret information to determine if the petitioner has a potential claim. *In re Rockafellow*, ___ S.W.3d ___ (Tex. App.—Amarillo 2011, orig. proceeding) (No. 07-11-00066-CV; 7-19-11).

3. Deponent information. The petition must identify (1) the persons to be deposed by name, address, and telephone number, (2) the substance of the testimony the petitioner expects to elicit from each, and (3) the petitioner's reasons for desiring to obtain the testimony of each. TRCP 202.2(g). If documents need to be produced at the deposition, the petition should also identify the documents the persons will be requested to bring. See "Request for documents," §4.5.6, p. 529; "Taking deposition," §16.7, p. 546. The person sought to be deposed does not need to be a potentially liable defendant in the claim under investigation. *U.S. Filter*, 190 S.W.3d at 245.

4. Prayer. The petition must request an order authorizing the petitioner to take the depositions of the persons named in the petition. TRCP 202.2(h).

§16.2 Where to file. A petition under TRCP 202 must be filed where venue of the anticipated suit may lie, if suit is anticipated, or where the witness resides, if no suit is anticipated. TRCP 202.2(b); *In re Akzo Nobel Chem., Inc.*, 24 S.W.3d 919, 920 (Tex.App.—Beaumont 2000, orig. proceeding).

§16.3 Notice & service.

1. Persons named in petition. At least 15 days before the hearing, the petition and the notice of the hearing must be served on the deponent and any potential adverse party named in the petition. TRCP 202.3(a); *U.S. Gov't v. Marks*, 949 S.W.2d 320, 322 (Tex.1997). See *O'Connor's Texas Forms*, FORMS 6F:10-11. The petitioner may request a shorter period of notice if "justice or necessity" requires that the deposition be taken on shorter notice. TRCP 202.3(d). TRCP 202.3(a) provides that service can be accomplished under TRCP 21a. However, to secure the attendance of the witness at the hearing, the witness must be served with a subpoena.

NOTE

The procedures and limitations set forth in the discovery rules may be modified in any suit by agreement of the parties. TRCP 191.1. See "Modifying Discovery Procedures," ch. 6-A, §6, p. 429. Although parties can modify discovery procedures by agreement, some parties cannot agree to modifications of TRCP 202 procedures at the expense of other parties. See, e.g., In re Does 1&2, 337 S.W.3d 862, 864-65 (Tex.2011) (P and D-1 could not agree that D-1 would produce documents under subpoena duces tecum, rather than through TRCP 202 deposition, without also agreeing with D-2 and D-3, who were potentially adverse parties). Thus, parties who want to agree to modifications of discovery procedures that may affect a party's rights under TRCP 202 should make sure to include all potentially adverse parties in the agreement to avoid circumventing TRCP 202's procedural protections.

---

2. Persons not named in petition. Unnamed persons who are described in the petition and who the petitioner expects will have interests adverse to the petitioner may be served by publication. The notice must state the place for the hearing and the time it will be held, which must be more than 14 days after the first publication of the notice. TRCP 202.3(b)(1). The petition and notice must be published once each week for two consecutive weeks in the newspaper of broadest circulation in the county in which the petition is filed, or if no such newspaper exists, in the newspaper of broadest circulation in the nearest county where a newspaper is published. *Id.* Any interested party may move, in the proceeding or by bill of review, to suppress any deposition, in whole or in part, taken on notice by publication, and may also attack or oppose the deposition by any other means available. TRCP 202.3(b)(2).

3. In probate cases. A petition to take a deposition in anticipation of an application for probate of a will, and a notice of the hearing on the petition, may be served by posting as prescribed by Probate Code §33(f)(2). TRCP 202.3(c). The notice and petition must be directed to all parties interested in the testator's estate and must comply with the requirements of Probate Code §33(c), to the extent that it applies. TRCP 202.3(c).

§16.4 Response.

1. Objecting to deposition. If the deponent or any potential adverse party objects to the taking of the deposition, it should file a motion to vacate the order for the deposition and ask for a hearing. *See U.S. Gov't v. Marks*, 949 S.W.2d 320, 322 (Tex.1997) (former TRCP 187). If a potential adverse party did not receive notice and wants to object to the deposition, that party should file a motion to intervene as an interested party. *See id.* at 322-23.

2. Not removable to federal court. A TRCP 202 proceeding is not removable to federal court. *See Texas v. Real Parties in Interest*, 259 F.3d 387, 394 (5th Cir.2001) (when TRCP 202 is used as investigatory tool for potential claims, claim is not subject to removal); *McCrary v. Kansas City S. R.R.*, 121 F.Supp.2d 566, 569 (E.D.Tex.2000) (TRCP 202 proceeding is not a "civil action" under 28 U.S.C. §1441(b) because it does not assert a claim on which relief can be granted); *Mayfield-George v. Texas Rehab. Comm'n*, 197 F.R.D. 280, 283 (N.D.Tex.2000) (same). The All Writs Act, 28 U.S.C. §1651(a), does not provide an independent ground to remove a TRCP 202 claim from state court. *Real Parties*, 259 F.3d at 392. For a TRCP 202 proceeding to be enjoined under the All Writs Act, it must develop into a claim that threatens an earlier federal-court judgment. *Real Parties*, 259 F.3d at 395. For a detailed discussion of the use of the All Writs Act to support removal, see Hoffman, *Removal Jurisdiction & the All Writs Act*, 148 U.Pa.L.Rev. 401 (1999).

§16.5 Hearing.

1. Subpoena witness. The petitioner should issue and serve a subpoena on the witness to appear at the hearing.

2. Proof. The petitioner should show (1) that allowing the deposition may prevent a failure or delay of justice in an anticipated suit, or (2) that the likely benefits of allowing the deposition to investigate a potential claim outweigh the burden or expense of the procedure. TRCP 202.4(a); *see, e.g.*, *In re Hewlett Packard*, 212 S.W.3d 356, 363 (Tex.App.—Austin 2006, orig. proceeding) (petitioner did not show that benefit of potentially avoiding lawsuit outweighed burden of disclosure of trade secrets).

§16.6 Order. See *O'Connor's Texas Forms*, FORM 6F:11.

1. Required findings. The order must contain one of the following findings: (1) allowing the deposition may prevent a failure or delay of justice in an anticipated suit, or (2) the likely benefits of allowing the deposition to investigate a potential claim outweigh the burden or expense of the procedure. TRCP 202.4(a); *In re Emergency Consultants, Inc.*, 292 S.W.3d 78, 79 (Tex.App.—Houston [14th Dist.] 2007, orig. proceeding). The required findings cannot be implied from support in the record. *In re Does 1&2*, 337 S.W.3d 862, 865 (Tex.2011).

2. Discovery permitted.

(1) Deposition. The order must state the type of deposition (oral or written) to be conducted and may also state the time and place for the deposition. TRCP 202.4(b). The time and place may be stated in the notice of deposition instead of in the order. *Id.* Depositions are the only form of discovery that may be ordered under TRCP 202. *In re Akzo Nobel Chem., Inc.*, 24 S.W.3d 919, 921 (Tex.App.—Beaumont 2000, orig. proceeding).

(2) Subpoena for documents. As part of the deposition, the court may permit the issuance of a subpoena to produce documents at the deposition. *See* TRCP 199.2(b)(5), 200.1(b); Fineberg & Shore, *Discovery Update*, at 4.

3. Protection for others. The order must also contain any provisions the court deems necessary to protect the witness or any other person who might be affected by the deposition. TRCP 202.4(b); *e.g.*, *Valley Baptist Med. Ctr. v. Gonzalez*, 18 S.W.3d 673, 678 (Tex.App.—Corpus Christi 1999) (suggested court could order bond to protect D from costs), *vacated as moot*, 33 S.W.3d 821 (Tex.2000); *In re Fernandez*, No. 04-99-00841-CV (Tex.App.—San Antonio 1999, orig. proceeding) (no pub.; 12-30-99) (ordered counsel to consult doctor before deposing ill party).

———————————— ✦ ————————————

§16.7   Taking deposition. The same rules apply in taking presuit depositions as in other depositions. TRCP 202.5. See "Procedure for Standard Oral Deposition," §4, p. 526.

§16.8   Use at trial.

1. Impeachment. Testimony from a presuit deposition is admissible to impeach a witness, even if the other parties were not notified of the deposition. Fineberg & Shore, *Discovery Update*, §I.A.4, at 4.

2. Restricted use. The court may restrict or prohibit the use of a deposition taken under TRCP 202 in a later lawsuit to protect from unfair prejudice a person who was not served with notice of the deposition. TRCP 202.5. If a party objects to the use of a TRCP 202 deposition, the party must show that it (1) did not receive notice of the deposition and (2) will be unfairly prejudiced by the use of the deposition. To show unfair prejudice, the party would probably have to prove the deponent gave false testimony. *See* Fineberg & Shore, *New Investigative Discovery*, Tab A, §2-C.

§16.9   Appellate review.

1. Appeal. A TRCP 202 order allowing or denying presuit discovery from a third party against whom suit is not contemplated is a final, appealable order. *Ross Stores v. Redken Labs.*, 810 S.W.2d 741, 742 (Tex.1991); *IFS Sec. Grp. v. American Equity Ins.*, 175 S.W.3d 560, 563 (Tex.App.—Dallas 2005, no pet.); *Thomas v. Fitzgerald*, 166 S.W.3d 746, 747 (Tex.App.—Waco 2005, no pet.).

2. Mandamus. A TRCP 202 order allowing or denying presuit discovery from a party against whom suit is contemplated is not a final, appealable order. *In re Hewlett Packard*, 212 S.W.3d 356, 360 (Tex.App.—Austin 2006, orig. proceeding); *IFS Sec. Grp.*, 175 S.W.3d at 563; *see Thomas*, 166 S.W.3d at 747. Thus, a party should challenge such a TRCP 202 order by filing a petition for mandamus. *See In re Wolfe*, 341 S.W.3d 932, 933 (Tex.2011). See "Review by mandamus," ch. 6-A, §26.2, p. 458.

§17.   DEPOSITION IN ANOTHER STATE

§17.1   Deposition officer. A deposition may be taken before a person authorized by state law to administer oaths in the place where the deposition is being taken. TRCP 201.1(b).

§17.2   Procedure. A deposition in another state may be taken by notice, letter rogatory, letter of request, agreement of the parties, or court order. TRCP 201.1(a). Parties may also take the deposition of a witness in another state by telephone or video conference while the parties and their attorneys are in Texas. TRCP 199.1(b), 201.1(g); *see Clone Component Distribs. v. State*, 819 S.W.2d 593, 598 (Tex.App.—Dallas 1991, no writ). See "Deposition by Telephone," §14, p. 541.

———————————————————————————
PRACTICE TIP
The easiest way to arrange for a deposition in another state is to contact an attorney or court reporter in the other state and make arrangements through that person.
———————————————————————————

§18.   DEPOSITION IN FOREIGN COUNTRY

Obtaining discovery in foreign countries is extremely complicated. Most foreign countries are hostile to the American form of pretrial discovery.

———————————————————————————
PRACTICE TIP
Before taking a deposition in a foreign country, refer to the website of the Department of State, Bureau of Consular Affairs, at www.travel.state.gov/law/judicial/judicial_2514.html.
———————————————————————————

§18.1   Procedure. The procedure for foreign discovery is outlined in TRCP 201. *Smith v. Smith*, 720 S.W.2d 586, 598-99 (Tex.App.—Houston [1st Dist.] 1986, no writ) (substantial compliance with former TRCP 188, now TRCP 201, is sufficient). A deposition in a foreign jurisdiction may be taken by notice, letter rogatory, letter of request, agreement of the parties, or court order. TRCP 201.1(a). A deposition may also be taken by any other means under the terms

———————————————— ✫ ————————————————

of any applicable treaty or convention. TRCP 201.1(d). The Hague Evidence Convention is the most well-known treaty for obtaining evidence abroad. *See* Martikan, Note, *The Boundaries of the Hague Evidence Convention: Lower Court Interest Balancing After the Aerospatiale Decision*, 68 Tex.L.Rev. 1003, 1004 (1990).

1. Notice. Parties may take by notice the deposition of a witness in a foreign jurisdiction before a person authorized to administer oaths, either under the law of the place where the examination is held or under Texas law. TRCP 201.1(b). There are two serious drawbacks to taking depositions by notice in foreign countries: (1) the parties have no power to compel the attendance of a witness, and (2) taking testimony in some countries violates local laws and, in some cases, results in criminal penalties. Bishop, *International Litigation in Texas*, 19 Hous.L.Rev. at 364-65.

2. Letter of request. Generally, if the foreign country subscribes to the Hague Evidence Convention, the method to obtain discovery is by letter of request under the Convention. Bishop, *International Litigation in Texas*, 19 Hous.L.Rev. at 371. The Hague Evidence Convention supplements, but does not replace, other means of obtaining evidence located abroad. ***Societe Nationale Industrielle Aerospatiale v. U.S. Dist. Ct.***, 482 U.S. 522, 534-39 (1987); ***Sandsend Fin. Consultants v. Wood***, 743 S.W.2d 364, 365-66 (Tex.App.—Houston [1st Dist.] 1988, orig. proceeding). The procedure for discovery under the Hague Evidence Convention can be found in 28 U.S.C. chapter 117.

3. Letter rogatory. If a country does not subscribe to the Hague Evidence Convention, a party must use a letter rogatory to take the deposition in a foreign country. *See* Bureau of Consular Affairs, *Preparation of Letters Rogatory*, www.travel.state.gov/law/judicial/judicial_683.html. A letter rogatory is a judicial request addressed to a foreign authority asking it to use its coercive powers to require a person within its territory to provide evidence. Bishop, *International Litigation in Texas*, 19 Hous.L.Rev. at 383. In some countries, only the judicial officer can ask the witness questions, not the attorneys. *Id.* at 384. The letter rogatory must be addressed to the appropriate authority in the jurisdiction. TRCP 201.1(c)(1).

§18.2 Officer to conduct deposition. A deposition may be taken in a foreign country by one of the following:

1. A U.S. minister, commissioner, or charge d'affaires who is a resident of and is accredited in the country where the deposition is taken. CPRC §20.001(c)(1).

2. A U.S. consul general, consul, vice-consul, commercial agent, vice-commercial agent, deputy consul, or consular agent who is a resident of and is accredited in the country where the deposition is taken. *Id.* §20.001(c)(2).

3. Any notary public. *Id.* §20.001(c)(3); *e.g.*, ***Kugle v. DaimlerChrysler Corp.***, 88 S.W.3d 355, 362 (Tex. App.—San Antonio 2002, pet. denied) (deponent in Mexico permitted to be sworn by Texas notary); *see also* TRCP 201.1(b) (deposition officer may be a person authorized to administer oaths in place where deposition taken).

4. If the deponent is a witness who is a member of the U.S. Armed Forces or Auxiliary or a civilian employed by such forces or auxiliary outside the United States, the deposition may be taken by a commissioned officer in the Armed Forces or Auxiliary or Reserve. CPRC §20.001(d).

§18.3 Depositions in Texas for use in foreign jurisdictions. If a court of record of any other state or foreign jurisdiction issues an order that requires a witness's oral or written deposition testimony in Texas, the witness may be compelled to appear and testify in the same manner and by the same process used for taking testimony in a proceeding pending in Texas. TRCP 201.2.

―――――――――――――――― ✦ ――――――――――――――――

G. INTERROGATORIES

§1. GENERAL

§1.1 Rules. TRCP 197.

§1.2 Purpose. Interrogatories are written questions served on a party that require the party to file written answers, generally under oath. Interrogatories are used to narrow the issues.

§1.3 Forms. See *O'Connor's Texas Civil Forms* (2012), FORMS 6G.

§1.4 Other references. Downing et al., *"Be Careful What You Ask For, You May Get It": Common Sense Discovery Requests & Responses*, Advanced Family Law Course, State Bar of Texas CLE, ch. 15, §III.B (2006); Griesel, *The "New" Texas Discovery Rules: Three Years Later*, Advanced Evidence & Discovery Course, State Bar of Texas CLE, ch. 2, §XI, p. 24 (2002).

§2. SCOPE

The scope of discovery for interrogatories is governed by TRCP 192 and 197. See "Scope of Discovery," ch. 6-B, p. 460. Interrogatories are used to find out the specific legal and factual contentions supporting the other party's claims or defenses.

§2.1 Party contentions. An interrogatory may ask whether the party makes specific legal or factual contentions and may ask the party to state its legal theories and to describe, in general, the factual bases for the party's claims or defenses. TRCP 197.1. See "Party contentions," §3.2.5, p. 550.

§2.2 Trial witnesses. An interrogatory may ask the other party to provide a list of its trial witnesses. See "Trial witnesses," §3.2.3, p. 550. Formerly, a party could secure a list of trial witnesses only by court order.

§2.3 Limits of interrogatories.

1. Not for testifying-expert information. An interrogatory cannot be used to request information about another party's testifying expert witnesses. *See* TRCP 195.1 (party may request information about testifying expert witnesses only through request for disclosure or depositions and reports allowed under TRCP 195); TRCP 197.1 (interrogatories cannot be used to secure information covered by TRCP 195).

2. No fishing. An interrogatory cannot be used to fish for information or to require the responding party to provide a statement of all its available proof. TRCP 197.1 & cmt. 1; *K Mart Corp. v. Sanderson*, 937 S.W.2d 429, 431 (Tex.1996).

§3. SERVING INTERROGATORIES

§3.1 Procedure. The interrogatories must be in writing. TRCP 197.1. See *O'Connor's Texas Forms*, FORMS 6G:1-2.

―――――――――――――――――――――――――――――――――

PRACTICE TIP
Ask the other party to agree to e-mail a copy of any request for written discovery. It will make responding to interrogatories and other discovery much simpler.

―――――――――――――――――――――――――――――――――

1. Serve on party. Interrogatories can be served only on another party. TRCP 197.1. They cannot be served on nonparty witnesses. TRCP 205.1.

2. Time to serve interrogatories. Interrogatories can be served anytime after suit is filed. *See* TRCP 190.2(c)(1), 190.3(b)(1). The discovery rules permit the plaintiff to serve the initial set of discovery with its original petition. The deadline to serve interrogatories is 30 days before the end of the discovery period. TRCP 197.1. See "Discovery Periods," ch. 6-A, §8, p. 433. When served by mail or fax, interrogatories should be served at least 34 days before the end of the discovery period. See "Deadline to Respond to Discovery," ch. 6-A, §14, p. 437.

★

---

3. Number of interrogatories.

(1) Limited interrogatories. The number of interrogatories each party is permitted to serve (other than those about documents) is governed by the discovery-control plan in effect. See "Discovery-Control Plans," ch. 6-A, §7, p. 430. Parties in all three levels are limited to 25 interrogatories, unless expressly changed by court order. TRCP 190.2(c)(3), 190.3(b)(3), 190.4(b). Each discrete subpart of an interrogatory is considered a separate interrogatory. TRCP 190.2(c)(3), 190.3(b)(3). A discrete subpart asks for information not logically or factually related to the primary interrogatory. TRCP 190 cmt. 3; *In re SWEPI L.P.*, 103 S.W.3d 578, 589 (Tex.App.—San Antonio 2003, orig. proceeding). Not every separate factual inquiry is a discrete subpart. TRCP 190 cmt. 3. If a party needs more than the allotted number of interrogatories, it must get an agreement with the other party or file a motion to modify the discovery-control plan and ask for a court order. TRCP 190.5, 191.1. See "Modifying discovery by agreement," ch. 6-A, §6.1, p. 429.

(13)

PROPOSED TRCP CHANGES

In response to Gov't Code §22.004(h), the Supreme Court has proposed TRCP 169 to establish a process for the prompt, efficient, and cost-effective resolution of civil actions (expedited actions) in which only monetary relief is sought and the amount in controversy is no more than $100,000. See Tex.Sup.Ct. Order, Misc. Docket No. 12-9191 (eff. Mar. 1, 2013). The Supreme Court has proposed corresponding amendments to TRCP 190.2 that would (1) change the Level 1 discovery-control plan to apply to these expedited actions under TRCP 169 and (2) change the limits on the number of interrogatories that can be served in Level 1 discovery. See Tex.Sup.Ct. Order, Misc. Docket No. 12-9191 (eff. Mar. 1, 2013). The public-comment period for the proposed amendments ends on February 1, 2013, and the rules are to take effect March 1, 2013. For the proposed version of the rules, see the appendix after this book's index. For the final version, go to the Supreme Court website at www.supreme.courts.state.tx.us. When the new and amended rules take effect, a supplement to this book—with updated rules and commentaries that reflect the changes—will be available at www.JonesMcClure.com/TRCPamendments.

(2) Unlimited interrogatories. There is no limit to the number of interrogatories a party may serve asking for the identification or authentication of specific documents. TRCP 190.2(c)(3), 190.3(b)(3).

(3) Unlimited sets. Although the number of interrogatories is limited, the number of sets of interrogatories that can be sent is unlimited. *See* TRCP 190 cmt. 3.

4. Specify time to answer. The interrogatories must specify when the answers are due, but the date must be at least 30 days after service of the interrogatories. *See* TRCP 197.2(a). In most cases, a party asks the other party to answer interrogatories within the shortest time permitted by TRCP 197.2(a)—that is, "within 30 days after service." When the plaintiff serves interrogatories on the defendant before the defendant's answer is due, the interrogatories should state the answers are due "within 50 days after service of these interrogatories." *Id.* See "Served before answer date – 50 days," ch. 6-A, §14.1.2, p. 437.

5. Combine with request for production. The discovery rules permit a party to combine different forms of discovery requests in the same document. TRCP 192.2. Thus, if an interrogatory asks for the identification of documents, it can be followed by a request to produce those documents.

✦

---

§3.2 Standard interrogatories. The following are interrogatories that seek information not subject to a request for disclosure under TRCP 194. See *O'Connor's Texas Forms*, FORM 6G:2.

1. Documents.

(1) Existence & location. An interrogatory may ask about the existence, description, nature, custody, condition, location, and contents of documents that are relevant or will lead to relevant evidence. TRCP 192.3(b). See "Possession," ch. 6-A, §2.5, p. 425; *O'Connor's Texas Forms*, FORM 6G:2. An interrogatory that asks for information about documents can be followed by a request to produce those documents. TRCP 192.2.

(2) Authentication. An interrogatory may ask for the authentication of specific documents. TRCP 190.2(c)(3), 190.3(b)(3).

2. Person answering.
An interrogatory may ask the other party to identify the persons answering the interrogatories, supplying information, or in any way assisting with the preparation of the answers. A party may want to depose anyone who provided information for the answers. See *O'Connor's Texas Forms*, FORM 6G:2.

3. Trial witnesses.
An interrogatory may ask the other party to identify its trial witnesses (fact and expert). TRCP 192.3(d). Because the only information that is authorized by TRCP 192.3(d) is the identity of trial witnesses, it should not conflict with the limitations in TRCP 195.1 and 197.1, which limit the discovery tools a party can use to seek information about the testifying experts. See "Trial witnesses," ch. 6-B, §2.9, p. 462; *O'Connor's Texas Forms*, FORM 6G:2.

4. Discoverable consulting experts.
An interrogatory may ask for information about discoverable consulting expert witnesses.

(1) Consultant's work reviewed. When the consulting expert's opinions, mental impressions, or work product were reviewed by a testifying expert, a party is entitled to discover the same information about the consulting expert as about the testifying expert. TRCP 192.3(e). See "Discovery about consulting expert + work reviewed," ch. 6-D, §3.2.2, p. 506; *O'Connor's Texas Forms*, FORM 6G:2.

(2) Consultant with facts. When a consulting expert has firsthand knowledge about the case or secondhand knowledge gained outside the consultation, a party is entitled to discover the same information about the consulting expert as about other fact witnesses. See "Discovery about consulting expert + obtained facts," ch. 6-D, §3.2.3, p. 506; *O'Connor's Texas Forms*, FORM 6G:2.

5. Party contentions.
An interrogatory may ask whether the party makes specific legal or factual contentions and may ask the party to state its legal theories and to describe, in general, the factual bases for the party's claims or defenses. TRCP 197.1; *see also* TRCP 194.2(c) (disclosure request). For example, an interrogatory may ask whether the party claims a breach of implied warranty, or when the party contends that limitations began to run. TRCP 197 cmt. 1. However, an interrogatory cannot ask the party to state all its legal and factual assertions or to marshal all its proof or the proof the party intends to offer at trial. TRCP 197.1 & cmt. 1. See *O'Connor's Texas Forms*, FORM 6G:2.

6. Impeachment & rebuttal evidence.
The party should consider asking for the other party's rebuttal and impeachment evidence and witnesses. TRCP 192.3(d); *see* TRCP 166(h). Rebuttal and impeachment evidence is discoverable only if the party responding to the request has enough information to anticipate its use at trial. TRCP 192.3(d). Unless specifically asked, a party is not required to anticipate the other party's case and identify witnesses to be used for impeachment or rebuttal. *See* TRCP 192.3(d) (party cannot obtain discovery of rebuttal or impeaching witnesses whose testimony cannot reasonably be anticipated before trial). See "Impeachment & rebuttal evidence not produced in discovery," ch. 8-C, §5.3, p. 700; *O'Connor's Texas Forms*, FORM 6G:2.

7. Elements of claim or defense.
An interrogatory may ask for information based on the elements of the claim or defense. See *O'Connor's Texas Forms*, FORMS 6G for interrogatories in the following types of lawsuits: breach of contract (FORMS 6G:4-5), suit on a sworn account (FORMS 6G:6-7), automobile accident (FORMS 6G:8-9), slip-and-fall (FORMS 6G:10-11), and suit under the DTPA (FORMS 6G:12-13).

§4. RESPONDING TO INTERROGATORIES

§4.1 Procedure.

1. Form of answers. The answers to interrogatories must be made in the form required by TRCP 197.2. See *O'Connor's Texas Forms*, FORM 6G:3.

(1) In writing. The party must respond to interrogatories in writing. TRCP 197.2(a). Oral information is not a substitute for written answers. *See, e.g.*, *Sharp v. Broadway Nat'l Bank*, 784 S.W.2d 669, 671 (Tex.1990) (oral identification of witness was not sufficient). Each answer, objection, or other response must follow the question it applies to. TRCP 193.1.

(2) Separate answers. Each interrogatory must be answered separately. *Orkin Exterminating Co. v. Williamson*, 785 S.W.2d 905, 910 (Tex.App.—Austin 1990, writ denied). If an interrogatory asks a question already answered in response to another interrogatory, the answer to the later interrogatory may refer to the earlier answer.

(3) Separate answer set. In most cases, a party should file a separate set of answers for each set of interrogatories. In a multiparty case, a party responding to the same interrogatories from different opposing parties may file one response that is sufficient to answer all sets. *See, e.g.*, *Ward v. O'Connor*, 816 S.W.2d 446, 447 (Tex.App.—San Antonio 1991, no writ) (Ps filed one list of fact and expert witnesses in response to requests from two Ds). *But see Clark Equip. Co. v. Pitner*, 923 S.W.2d 117, 121-22 (Tex.App.—Houston [14th Dist.] 1996, writ denied) (dicta; even though P provided complete information to D-1, because incomplete information was provided to D-2, D-1 could have asked to limit testimony).

(4) Signed & verified by party. The party must sign most answers to interrogatories under oath. TRCP 197.2(d). An affidavit verifying the answers to interrogatories must be unqualified and cannot be made "to the best of my knowledge." *See Ebeling v. Gawlik*, 487 S.W.2d 187, 189 (Tex.App.—Houston [1st Dist.] 1972, no writ). There are two exceptions to the rule that requires a party to sign and verify its answers under oath: (1) a party is not required to verify its answer when the answer states that it is based on information obtained from other persons, and (2) a party is not required to sign or verify its answer to an interrogatory that asks about persons with knowledge of relevant facts, trial witnesses, and legal contentions. TRCP 197.2(d).

(5) Signed by attorney. The party's attorney must sign the answers to interrogatories. TRCP 191.3(a)(1); TRCP 197 cmt. 2. An attorney is not required to verify the answers. TRCP 197.2(d).

2. Time to respond. Generally, a party has 30 days after the date of service of the interrogatories to respond, depending on the type of service. TRCP 21, 21a, 197.2(a). When interrogatories are served on a defendant before the defendant's answer is due, the defendant has 50 days after service to respond. TRCP 197.2(a). See "Served before answer date – 50 days," ch. 6-A, §14.1.2, p. 437. To extend the time, see "Extending Time to Respond to Discovery," ch. 6-A, §15, p. 438.

3. Not filed. The answers to interrogatories are not filed with the court. TRCP 191.4(a). See "Exceptions," ch. 6-A, §12.1.3, p. 436.

§4.2 Answers.
Each interrogatory must be answered fully. The party must make a complete response, based on all information reasonably available to the responding party or its attorney when the response is made. TRCP 193.1. The sufficiency of the answers to any set of interrogatories must be decided on a case-by-case basis. *Alexander v. Barlow*, 671 S.W.2d 531, 533 (Tex.App.—Houston [1st Dist.] 1983, writ ref'd n.r.e.). The court will treat an evasive or incomplete answer as a failure to answer. TRCP 215.1(c). When the interrogatory asks for information permitted by the rules of discovery, the information must be disclosed. When the interrogatory asks for more information than the rules permit, the party must file an objection.

1. Existence & location of documents. When asked in an interrogatory, a party is required to supply information about the existence, description, nature, custody, condition, location, and contents of documents that are relevant or will lead to relevant evidence. TRCP 192.3(b). See "Possession," ch. 6-A, §2.5, p. 425.

★

2. Evidence equally available. When an interrogatory asks for information that is available from public records, from the business records of the responding party, or from a compilation, abstract, or summary of the responding party's business records, the responding party is not obligated to give a narrative answer to the interrogatory if the burden of ascertaining the answer is substantially the same for both parties. TRCP 197.2(c). In such a case, the responding party may answer the interrogatory by specifying and, when applicable, producing the records or a compilation, abstract, or summary of the records. *Id.*; *see Clear Lake City Water Auth. v. Winograd*, 695 S.W.2d 632, 641 (Tex.App.—Houston [1st Dist.] 1985, writ ref'd n.r.e.). The records must be specified in sufficient detail to permit the requesting party to locate and identify them as readily as the responding party can. TRCP 197.2(c). If the responding party has specified business records, it must state a reasonable time and place for examination of the documents. *Id.* The responding party must produce the documents at the time and place stated and must provide the requesting party a reasonable opportunity to inspect them. *Id.* The rule requires a balancing test of the relative burden imposed on the two parties. *See, e.g.*, *State Farm Mut. Auto. Ins. v. Engelke*, 824 S.W.2d 747, 752 (Tex.App.—Houston [1st Dist.] 1992, orig. proceeding) (because responding party's witness testified information was available from its computer, it was less burdensome for responding party to produce information).

3. Witnesses. When asked in an interrogatory, a party is required to identify the following witnesses:

(1) Person answering. The party must identify any person answering the interrogatories, supplying information, or assisting with the preparation of the answers.

(2) Trial witnesses. The party must list all persons the party plans to call as witnesses at trial, no matter what they will testify about. *See* TRCP 192.3(d); *see, e.g.*, *Jamail v. Anchor Mortg. Servs.*, 809 S.W.2d 221, 223 (Tex.1991) (witness who was called to testify about lending regulations of mortgage company should have been listed as fact witness, even though witness did not know facts of case). The response should list the following persons as trial witnesses:

(a) Fact witnesses. The party must list all persons who have knowledge of relevant facts that it might call as witnesses at trial. See "Fact witnesses," ch. 6-B, §2.8, p. 462. Along with its own witnesses, the party should consider including the following: (1) any person who was deposed, (2) the other party, (3) the other party's fact witnesses, (4) the other party's consulting expert with knowledge of facts, and (5) character witnesses. *See Clayton v. First State Bank*, 777 S.W.2d 577, 580 (Tex.App.—Fort Worth 1989, writ denied) (character witnesses). Parties should err on the side of inclusion. At trial, the court will not permit a party to call a witness that the party did not specifically identify.

PRACTICE TIP
If a named party is not listed in response to an interrogatory asking for trial witnesses, the unlisted party can still testify. See TRCP 193.6(a).

(b) Expert witnesses. The party should list all experts that it intends to call to testify, which could include the following: (1) retained testifying experts, (2) nonretained testifying experts, (3) the party (if the party intends to testify as an expert), (4) the party's attorney (for attorney fees), (5) the opposing party's testifying experts (if the party intends to call them), and (6) the opposing party's consulting experts who lost their consulting-only status. *See, e.g.*, *Baylor Med. Plaza Servs. v. Kidd*, 834 S.W.2d 69, 73 (Tex.App.—Texarkana 1992, writ denied) (party could not call witness it did not designate but who was designated by another party). The party should compare this list to the list of testifying experts it produced in response to a request for disclosures. If any of the experts listed in response to an interrogatory asking for trial witnesses is not listed in response to a request for experts under TRCP 194.2(f), the party should amend its response to the request.

(c) Impeachment & rebuttal witnesses. When an interrogatory asks for impeachment and rebuttal information, and the responding party knows it will impeach or rebut the other party's witness or evidence, the responding party must list that evidence. See "Impeachment & rebuttal evidence," §3.2.6, p. 550; "Impeachment & rebuttal evidence not produced in discovery," ch. 8-C, §5.3, p. 700.

★

---

4. Discoverable consulting experts. When asked in an interrogatory, a party is required to identify the following expert witnesses:

(1) Consultant's work reviewed. If any opinions, mental impressions, or work product of an informally consulted expert were reviewed by a testifying expert, the other party is entitled to obtain the same information about the consulting expert as about the testifying expert. TRCP 192.3(e). See "Discovery about consulting expert + work reviewed," ch. 6-D, §3.2.2, p. 506; "Information Discoverable from Experts," ch. 6-D, §4, p. 506.

(2) Consultant with facts. A consulting expert who obtained knowledge about the case either firsthand or in some way other than in consultation about the case is discoverable as a fact witness. TRCP 192.3(c). When a consulting expert has firsthand knowledge of facts or secondhand knowledge acquired in some way other than in consultation about the case, the other party is entitled to obtain the same information about the expert as about other fact witnesses. See "Discovery about consulting expert + obtained facts," ch. 6-D, §3.2.3, p. 506.

5. Contentions. When asked in an interrogatory, a party is required to provide information about specific factual or legal assertions. *See* TRCP 197.1 & cmt. 1. See "Party contentions," §3.2.5, p. 550. The use of the answers to these "contention interrogatories" is limited, just like the use of similar disclosures under TRCP 194.6. TRCP 197 cmt. 1.

§5. SUPPLEMENTING OR AMENDING ANSWERS TO INTERROGATORIES

§5.1 What to supplement. When a party discovers additional information after responding to discovery, the party must supplement or amend its response. TRCP 193.5(a) (duty to supplement), TRCP 193.6 (effect of failure to supplement). For the substance of what additional information to provide, see "Supplementing Discovery Responses," ch. 6-A, §17, p. 440.

§5.2 Deadline to supplement. A party must serve supplemental or amended answers to interrogatories reasonably promptly after the party discovers the need for such a response, but no later than 30 days before trial. TRCP 193.5(b). See "Deadline to supplement responses," ch. 6-A, §17.4, p. 441.

§5.3 Form of supplement. Supplemental or amended answers to interrogatories must be made in the same form as the original answers. TRCP 193.5(b). See "Form of supplemental discovery," ch. 6-A, §17.6, p. 442. For the exceptions, see "Information provided by other means," ch. 6-A, §17.3.2, p. 441.

§5.4 No continuing duty to supplement. If the party that served the interrogatory is dismissed from the suit, the party that answered the interrogatory no longer has a duty to supplement its answers to the dismissed party's interrogatories. *Austin Ranch Enters. v. Wells*, 760 S.W.2d 703, 710 (Tex.App.—Fort Worth 1988, writ denied). Thus, the remaining parties cannot object to the responding party's failure to supplement answers to interrogatories propounded by the dismissed party. *Id.*

§6. OBJECTING TO QUESTIONS

§6.1 Procedure to object. See "Making objections," ch. 6-A, §18.1, p. 443.

1. When to serve. Objections to interrogatories must be served on the other party on or before the date the answers to the interrogatories are due. TRCP 193.2(a). See "Timely objection," ch. 6-A, §18.1.1, p. 443.

2. Objection defers answer. When a party objects to an interrogatory, the answer to that interrogatory is deferred until the court rules on the objection. TRCP 193.2(b). The party must answer all other interrogatories by the answer deadline. *Id.*

3. Form of objections. In the response or in a separate document, the party should state the specific objection to the interrogatory. TRCP 193.2(a).

4. Partial compliance. The party must comply with each part of the request to which the party has not objected or has not asserted a privilege. See "Burden to partially comply," ch. 6-A, §18.10, p. 447. Any material subject to an objection or assertion of privilege should be withheld from the information the party produces. TRCP 192.3(a), 193.3(a).

━━━━━━━━━━━━━━━━━━━━━━━ ☆ ━━━━━━━━━━━━━━━━━━━━━━━

5. Not filed. The objections to interrogatories are not filed with the court. TRCP 191.4(a). See "Filing discovery," ch. 6-A, §12.1, p. 436.

§6.2 Valid objections. For a list of objections, see "Types of Objections to Discovery," ch. 6-A, §19, p. 448. See *O'Connor's Texas Forms*, FORM 6G:3. The following are some additional objections that are specific to interrogatories:

1. Number of questions. "The interrogatories ask more than 25 questions." *See* TRCP 190.2(c)(3), 190.3(b)(3). See "Number of interrogatories," §3.1.3, p. 549. When a party asks more than 25 questions, the responding party cannot merely object and refuse to answer any of them. The party's options are (1) to answer the first 25 and object to the rest of them, or (2) to file objections and a motion for protective order to stay the deadline to answer until the set of interrogatories is redrafted to comply with the rules. *See Childs v. Argenbright*, 927 S.W.2d 647, 652 (Tex.App.—Tyler 1996, no writ); *Owens v. Wallace*, 821 S.W.2d 746, 749 (Tex.App.—Tyler 1992, orig. proceeding) (citing former TRCP 168, which allowed 30 questions).

---

⑬   **PROPOSED TRCP CHANGES**

In response to Gov't Code §22.004(h), the Supreme Court has proposed TRCP 169 to establish a process for the prompt, efficient, and cost-effective resolution of civil actions (expedited actions) in which only monetary relief is sought and the amount in controversy is no more than $100,000. See Tex.Sup.Ct. Order, Misc. Docket No. 12-9191 (eff. Mar. 1, 2013). The Supreme Court has proposed corresponding amendments to TRCP 190.2 that would (1) change the Level 1 discovery-control plan to apply to these expedited actions under TRCP 169 and (2) change the limits on the number of interrogatories that can be served in Level 1 discovery. See Tex.Sup.Ct. Order, Misc. Docket No. 12-9191 (eff. Mar. 1, 2013). The public-comment period for the proposed amendments ends on February 1, 2013, and the rules are to take effect March 1, 2013. For the proposed version of the rules, see the appendix after this book's index. For the final version, go to the Supreme Court website at www.supreme.courts.state.tx.us. When the new and amended rules take effect, a supplement to this book—with updated rules and commentaries that reflect the changes—will be available at www.JonesMcClure.com/TRCPamendments.

---

2. Improper request. "The interrogatory requests information about testifying experts, which is obtainable only through requests for disclosure under TRCP 194 or through depositions." *See* TRCP 197.1. See "Requests for Disclosure," ch. 6-E, p. 515.

3. Premature request. "The interrogatory is premature because it requests information that will not be known until after additional discovery is completed. This interrogatory will be answered promptly once additional discovery is completed." *See* TRCP 193.1 (responding party must make complete response based on information available).

4. Duplicative. "The interrogatory duplicates matters already produced in response to a request for disclosure under TRCP 194.2. See Response to Discovery Request number ____."

§6.3 Invalid objections. See "Invalid objections to discovery requests," ch. 6-A, §19.2, p. 449.

§6.4 Waiver of objections. A party waives any error in the form or substance of the interrogatories if it does not object within the time provided to answer. TRCP 193.2(e). When a party answers an interrogatory without making an objection, the party must answer fully, even if the interrogatory is objectionable. *In re Striegler*, 915 S.W.2d 629, 641 (Tex.App.—Amarillo 1996, writ denied).

§7. ASSERTING A PRIVILEGE

A party cannot object to an interrogatory on the grounds that it calls for privileged information. Instead, the party must assert a privilege under TRCP 193.3. See "Asserting privileges," ch. 6-A, §18.2, p. 443.

★

§8. OBJECTING TO ANSWERS

§8.1 Move to compel answers. A party may file a motion to compel answers when the interrogatories are not answered, when they are not answered properly, or when objections are served. TRCP 215.1(b), 215.2(b), 215.3. See "Motion to Compel Discovery," ch. 6-A, §22, p. 451.

§8.2 Object to formal defects. A party must object to formal (i.e., technical) defects in the answer so that the responding party has the opportunity to correct them before trial. *See State Farm Fire & Cas. Co. v. Morua*, 979 S.W.2d 616, 620 (Tex.1998) (court should not exclude witness based on technical defect in answer when no objection was made before trial); *$23,900 v. State*, 899 S.W.2d 314, 317 (Tex.App.—Houston [14th Dist.] 1995, no writ) (party should file pretrial objections or motion to compel compliance with rules). Formal defects do not impair the integrity of the answers unless the party refuses to cure the defect after it is identified by the other party. *See* TRCP 197 cmt. 2; *see also* TRCP 193.5(b) (failure to properly supplement discovery does not make response untimely unless party refuses to correct defect).

§8.3 Challenge privileges after withholding statement. After receiving a withholding statement indicating that information is being withheld on grounds of privilege, the party seeking discovery should ask the withholding party to provide a privilege log. TRCP 193.3(b). See "Request privilege log," ch. 6-A, §18.2.2, p. 444.

§8.4 Move for sanctions. See "Motion for Discovery Sanctions," ch. 6-A, §24, p. 455.

1. Late or inadequate answer. When an answer to an interrogatory is inadequate, the party seeking discovery can ask the court to impose reasonable sanctions. *See, e.g.*, *Hamill v. Level*, 917 S.W.2d 15, 16 (Tex.1996) (even though P was repeatedly late in answering interrogatories, dismissal was not warranted because no less-severe sanction had been imposed); *Clark Equip. Co. v. Pitner*, 923 S.W.2d 117, 121-22 (Tex.App.—Houston [14th Dist.] 1996, writ denied) (because P's answer to D-1's interrogatory provided everything but substance of expert's testimony, D-2 could have asked to limit testimony, not exclude expert); *Orkin Exterminating Co. v. Williamson*, 785 S.W.2d 905, 910-11 (Tex.App.—Austin 1990, writ denied) (because D's answer was not sufficient to identify witness, witness not permitted to testify). If an answer is evasive or incomplete, the court will treat it as a failure to answer. TRCP 215.1(c).

2. No answers. When a party refuses to file answers to interrogatories, the party seeking discovery may ask the court to dismiss the suit, render a default judgment, exclude evidence, or impose other sanctions. *See* TRCP 215.1(b)(3)(A) (failure to serve response), TRCP 215.1(b)(3)(B) (failure to answer particular interrogatory); *see, e.g.*, *Swain v. Southwestern Bell Yellow Pages, Inc.*, 998 S.W.2d 731, 732-33 (Tex.App.—Fort Worth 1999, no pet.) (P not permitted to testify about damages because he refused to respond to interrogatory about damages); *Fears v. Mechanical & Indus. Technicians, Inc.*, 654 S.W.2d 524, 529 (Tex.App.—Tyler 1983, writ ref'd n.r.e.) (default rendered because D did not file answers to interrogatories). When a party completely fails to answer, the party seeking discovery is not required to file a motion to compel before filing a motion for sanctions. *Swain*, 998 S.W.2d at 733.

§8.5 Request hearing. The party seeking discovery must request a hearing on the objection or on the motion to compel, or it will waive its objections to the answers to the interrogatories. TRCP 193.4; *McKinney v. National Un. Fire Ins.*, 772 S.W.2d 72, 75 (Tex.1989). See "Burden to secure hearing & ruling," ch. 6-A, §18.6, p. 445.

§9. USING INTERROGATORIES AS EVIDENCE

§9.1 By whom, against whom.

1. Against answering party. Generally, the answers to interrogatories cannot be used as evidence by the party that answered them. TRCP 197.3; *Morgan v. Anthony*, 27 S.W.3d 928, 929 (Tex.2000); *Yates v. Fisher*, 988 S.W.2d 730, 731 (Tex.1998). However, when a party is questioned under oath about an answer, is subject to cross-examination, and affirms that everything contained in the answer is true, the interrogatory answer becomes competent evidence. *Morgan*, 27 S.W.3d at 929; *see Price Pfister, Inc. v. Moore & Kimmey, Inc.*, 48 S.W.3d 341, 348-49 (Tex.App.—Houston [14th Dist.] 2001, pet. denied).

✦

2. By any other party. Even if the parties in a multiparty case do not have common causes of action, all parties can rely on the answers to interrogatories by any other party. *E.g.*, *Ticor Title Ins. v. Lacy*, 803 S.W.2d 265, 265-66 (Tex.1991) (in case predating request for disclosures, nonsettling D was entitled to rely on P's failure to designate witnesses in response to settling D's interrogatories).

§9.2 Using answers in trial. Interrogatories are considered evidence once they are admitted into evidence by a ruling of the court. *See Cornell v. Cornell*, 570 S.W.2d 22, 23 (Tex.App.—San Antonio 1978, no writ). A party's answers to interrogatories are not hearsay. *See* TRE 801(e)(1)(A) (inconsistent with trial testimony), TRE 801(e)(2) (admission by party-opponent). There are three steps to introducing the answers to interrogatories.

1. Identify. The interrogatories and answers must be identified. The best procedure is to mark the interrogatories with an exhibit number.

2. Offer. The interrogatories and answers must be formally offered into evidence.

3. Admit. The court must admit them into evidence. Once the answers are read into evidence, they become testimonial evidence. *Eubanks v. Eubanks*, 892 S.W.2d 181, 181-82 (Tex.App.—Houston [14th Dist.] 1994, no writ). Interrogatories that are not admitted into evidence cannot be considered in support of the judgment. *Sammons Enters. v. Manley*, 540 S.W.2d 751, 757 (Tex.App.—Texarkana 1976, writ ref'd n.r.e.); *see Cornell*, 570 S.W.2d at 23.

§9.3 Using supplanted answers. Supplanted answers to interrogatories are not valid answers and cannot be used as evidence. They can, in some cases, be used to impeach the new answers. *See Thomas v. International Ins.*, 527 S.W.2d 813, 820 (Tex.App.—Waco 1975, writ ref'd n.r.e.). However, supplanted answers that inquire about either a party's legal theories or damages cannot be used for impeachment. TRCP 197.3.

§9.4 Using answers in summary judgment. Interrogatory answers can be used in a summary-judgment proceeding. *Judwin Props., Inc. v. Griggs & Harrison*, 911 S.W.2d 498, 503-04 (Tex.App.—Houston [1st Dist.] 1995, no writ). Because answers can be used only against the party answering them, a party cannot rely on its own answers to raise a fact issue. *See* TRCP 197.3; *Yates v. Fisher*, 988 S.W.2d 730, 731 (Tex.1998); *see also Buck v. Blum*, 130 S.W.3d 285, 290 (Tex.App.—Houston [14th Dist.] 2004, no pet.) (answers cannot be used against another party, even a codefendant); *Garcia v. National Eligibility Express, Inc.*, 4 S.W.3d 887, 890 (Tex.App.—Houston [1st Dist.] 1999, no pet.) (answers cannot be used in favor of answering party even if other party puts them in evidence and does not timely challenge them on appeal).

§10. OBJECTING TO UNIDENTIFIED TRIAL WITNESS

See "Objecting to Unidentified Witness," ch. 6-E, §10, p. 522.

§11. REVIEW

For the rules and forms for prosecuting or responding to an appeal or original proceeding, see *O'Connor's Texas Civil Appeals* (2012).

✦

H. REQUESTS FOR ADMISSIONS

§1. GENERAL

§1.1 Rule. TRCP 198.

§1.2 Purpose. Requests for admissions are narrowly drawn questions that call for the responding party to either admit or deny a specific fact. They seldom lead to the discovery of additional evidence. Their primary function is to simplify trials by eliminating matters that there is no real controversy about but that may be difficult or expensive to prove. *Stelly v. Papania*, 927 S.W.2d 620, 622 (Tex.1996); *Boulet v. State*, 189 S.W.3d 833, 838 (Tex.App.—Houston [1st Dist.] 2006, no pet.); *Natural Gas Pipeline Co. v. Pool*, 30 S.W.3d 639, 652 (Tex.App.—Amarillo 2000), *rev'd on other grounds*, 124 S.W.3d 188 (Tex.2003).

§1.3 Forms. See *O'Connor's Texas Civil Forms* (2012), FORMS 6H.

§1.4 Other references. Griesel, *The "New" Texas Discovery Rules: Three Years Later*, Advanced Evidence & Discovery Course, State Bar of Texas CLE, ch. 2, §XII, p. 25 (2002).

§2. SCOPE

The scope of discovery by requests for admissions is governed principally by TRCP 192. See "Scope of Discovery," ch. 6-B, p. 460. Requests for admissions are often used to prove the genuineness of documents and may be used to ask a party to admit an opinion or fact or the application of law to facts. TRCP 198.1. However, requests for admissions cannot be used to ask a party to admit a conclusion of law. *Boulet v. State*, 189 S.W.3d 833, 838 (Tex.App.—Houston [1st Dist.] 2006, no pet.).

§3. REQUESTS FOR ADMISSIONS

Before drafting requests for admissions, the attorney should examine the live pleadings of both parties. The requests for admissions should be used to affirm evidence of incidental but important issues in the pleadings (e.g., the identity of the property owner, the validity of the signatures on the contract, that notice was timely).

§3.1 Procedure. Requests for admissions must be in writing. TRCP 198.1. See *O'Connor's Texas Forms*, FORMS 6H:1-2.

1. Serve on party. Requests for admissions may be served only on other parties. TRCP 198.1. A party's duty to respond to requests for admissions depends on receipt of the requests. *Approximately $14,980.00 v. State*, 261 S.W.3d 182, 186 (Tex.App.—Houston [14th Dist.] 2008, no pet.); *Payton v. Ashton*, 29 S.W.3d 896, 898 (Tex. App.—Amarillo 2000, no pet.); *see* TRCP 21a.

2. Time to serve requests for admissions. Requests for admissions may be served anytime after suit is filed. TRCP 190.2(c)(1), 190.3(b)(1). The discovery rules permit the plaintiff to serve the initial set of discovery with its original petition. See "Serving discovery with original pleadings," ch. 6-A, §13.2, p. 437. The deadline to serve requests for admissions is 30 days before the end of the discovery period. TRCP 198.1. See "Discovery Periods," ch. 6-A, §8, p. 433. When served by mail or fax, the requests should be served at least 34 days before the end of the discovery period. See "Deadline to Respond to Discovery," ch. 6-A, §14, p. 437.

3. Number of requests. There is no limit on the number of requests for admissions or the number of sets of requests a party may serve.

---

⑬ *PROPOSED TRCP CHANGES*

In response to Gov't Code §22.004(h), the Supreme Court has proposed TRCP 169 to establish a process for the prompt, efficient, and cost-effective resolution of civil actions (expedited actions) in which only monetary relief is sought and the amount in controversy is no more than $100,000. See Tex.Sup.Ct. Order, Misc. Docket No. 12-9191 (eff. Mar. 1, 2013). The Supreme Court has proposed corresponding amendments to TRCP 190.2 that would (1) change the Level 1 discovery-control plan to apply to these expedited actions under TRCP 169 and (2) include limits on the number of requests for admissions that can be served in Level 1 discovery. See

⭐

Tex.Sup.Ct. Order, Misc. Docket No. 12-9191 (eff. Mar. 1, 2013). The public-comment period for the proposed amendments ends on February 1, 2013, and the rules are to take effect March 1, 2013. For the proposed version of the rules, see the appendix after this book's index. For the final version, go to the Supreme Court website at www.supreme.courts.state.tx.us. When the new and amended rules take effect, a supplement to this book—with updated rules and commentaries that reflect the changes—will be available at www.JonesMcClure.com/TRCPamendments.

4. Specify time to answer. The request must specify the time to answer, generally 30 days after the service of the request. TRCP 198.2(a). If the request is to be served on a defendant before its answer is due, the request must state that the defendant has 50 days after service of the request to respond. *Id.* See "Deadline to Respond to Discovery," ch. 6-A, §14, p. 437.

§3.2 Typical requests. The requests for admissions should begin with a request that the party "admit the truth of the following statements." TRCP 198.1. The requests should be made in short, simple, declarative sentences. For example, "Admit or deny the following: The promissory note, a copy of which is attached to this request and marked Exhibit A, is a genuine copy of the note that is the subject of this litigation." A party should not pair a request with its mirror opposite; if both admissions are deemed admitted, the admissions establish both the positive and negative of the proposition, thus creating a fact issue. *E.g.*, *CEBI Metal v. Garcia*, 108 S.W.3d 464, 466-67 (Tex.App.—Houston [14th Dist.] 2003, no pet.) (deemed admissions of requests paired with exact opposites could not support summary judgment); *Noons v. Arabghani*, No. 13-03-628-CV (Tex.App.—Corpus Christi 2005, pet. denied) (memo op.; 8-25-05) (same). See *O'Connor's Texas Forms*, FORMS 6H for requests for admissions in the following types of lawsuits: breach of contract (FORMS 6H:4-5), suit on a sworn account (FORMS 6H:6-7), automobile accident (FORMS 6H:8-9), slip-and-fall (FORMS 6H:10-11), and suit under the DTPA (FORMS 6H:12-13).

§4. RESPONDING TO REQUESTS FOR ADMISSIONS

§4.1 Procedure.

1. Form of answers. The answers to requests for admissions must be made in the form required by TRCP 198.2. See *O'Connor's Texas Forms*, FORM 6H:3.

(1) In writing. The party must respond to requests for admissions in writing. TRCP 198.2(a). Each answer, objection, or other response must be preceded by the request it applies to. TRCP 193.1.

(2) Signed. The response to the requests for admissions must be signed by the attorney (or party when pro se). TRCP 191.3(a); *see In re Estate of Herring*, 970 S.W.2d 583, 588-89 (Tex.App.—Corpus Christi 1998, no pet.) (unsigned responses were deemed admitted). *But see* TRCP 191.3(d) (failure to sign can be corrected).

(3) Not verified. The answers to the requests for admissions do not need to be verified. *Guzman v. Carnevale*, 964 S.W.2d 311, 313-14 (Tex.App.—Corpus Christi 1998, no pet.).

2. Time to respond. Generally, a party has 30 days after the date of service of the requests for admissions to serve a response, depending on the type of service. TRCP 198.2(a). When requests for admissions are served on a defendant before the defendant's answer is due, the defendant has 50 days after service to respond. *Id.* See "Deadline to Respond to Discovery," ch. 6-A, §14, p. 437.

3. Extending time to respond.

(1) By Rule 11 agreement. A party may ask opposing counsel for a Rule 11 agreement extending the time to respond to requests for admissions. See "Agreements Between Attorneys – Rule 11," ch. 1-H, §9, p. 61.

(2) By motion. A party may ask the court to extend the time to respond to requests for admissions only if the motion is made before the date to answer. See "Extending Time to Respond to Discovery," ch. 6-A, §15, p. 438. Once the time to respond expires, it is too late to ask the court for more time to serve answers to requests for admissions. *Cherry v. North Am. Lloyds*, 770 S.W.2d 4, 5 (Tex.App.—Houston [1st Dist.] 1989, writ denied).

———————————— ✦ ————————————

The answers are automatically deemed admitted against the defaulting party the day after the answers are due. *Id.* To avoid the effect of the deemed answers, the defaulting party must file a motion to strike, withdraw, or amend the deemed admissions. *Id.* See "Avoiding Deemed Admissions," §7, p. 561.

§4.2 Response. The response to a request for admissions must (1) admit, (2) specifically deny, (3) set forth in detail the reasons why the answering party cannot truthfully admit or deny the matter, (4) object, (5) assert a privilege, or (6) move for a protective order. TRCP 198.2(b) (responses 1-5); *Reynolds v. Murphy*, 188 S.W.3d 252, 261 (Tex.App.—Fort Worth 2006, pet. denied) (response 6). If the court determines that a response does not comply with the requirements of TRCP 198, it may (1) deem the matter admitted or (2) require an amended answer. TRCP 215.4(a).

1. Admissions. To admit, the party simply states that it admits the request. TRCP 198.2(b). Evasive or incomplete answers are treated as a failure to answer, and the request is deemed admitted. TRCP 215.4(a).

2. Denials. To deny, the party simply states that it denies the request. TRCP 198.2(b). A denial must "fairly meet the substance of the request." *Id.* A party may qualify an answer or deny part of a request only when good faith requires. *Id.*

3. Cannot admit or deny. If the party claims it cannot admit or deny the request, it must explain in detail the reasons why it cannot admit or deny. TRCP 198.2(b).

4. Lack of information. A party can refuse to admit or deny the request on the ground that it lacks information or knowledge to admit or deny only if the party states (1) it made a reasonable inquiry, and (2) the information known or easily obtained by the party is insufficient to enable the party to admit or deny. TRCP 198.2(b); *see Montes v. Lazzara Shipyard*, 657 S.W.2d 886, 888-89 (Tex.App.—Corpus Christi 1983, no writ). Once the party acquires information responsive to the answer, it must supplement its answer.

5. Objections & privileges. The party must make its objections and assert its privileges before the time to serve the answers expires. TRCP 193.2, 193.3, 198.2. Objections and privileges served after the deadline are waived, and the requests are deemed admitted. See "Answer deemed admitted," §6.1, p. 561.

(1) Objections. Objections must be specific. To object to only part of the matter in a request, the party must identify the specific part and admit or deny the remainder. TRCP 193.2, 198.2(b).

(a) Valid objections. Examples of valid objections to requests for admissions include the following: • The request asks the party to admit a proposition of law. *Cedyco Corp. v. Whitehead*, 253 S.W.3d 877, 880-81 (Tex.App.—Beaumont 2008, pet. denied); *Esparza v. Diaz*, 802 S.W.2d 772, 775 (Tex.App.—Houston [14th Dist.] 1990, no writ). Answers that constitute admissions of law are not binding on a court and do not prevent a party from proving fact issues. *Esparza*, 802 S.W.2d at 775. • The request asks the party to admit matters that are hearsay. *E.g.*, *Gaynier v. Ginsberg*, 715 S.W.2d 749, 759 (Tex.App.—Dallas 1986, writ ref'd n.r.e.) (improper to ask whether certain documents were those of treating doctor, now deceased). • The request is premature because the party will not know the answer until discovery is completed. *See* TRCP 193.1. • The party cannot admit or deny the genuineness of the document attached to the request because the copy is illegible. The party must be able to inspect the original before responding. *See* TRCP 198.2(b). • When the State is a party, it may object before trial that the requests for admissions will prejudice the rights of the State under the provisions of Gov't Code §402.004. *See Lowe v. Texas Tech Univ.*, 540 S.W.2d 297, 300-01 (Tex.1976); *Carrasco v. Texas Transp.*, 908 S.W.2d 575, 578-79 (Tex.App.—Waco 1995, no writ); *see also Employees Ret. Sys. v. Bass*, 840 S.W.2d 710, 713-14 (Tex.App.—Eastland 1992, no writ) (Gov't Code §402.004 prevents deemed admissions against State).

(b) Invalid objections. Examples of invalid objections to requests for admissions include the following: • The request relates to statements of opinion or of fact. TRCP 198.1. • The request relates to the application of law to fact, or to mixed questions of law and fact. *Id.*; *Laycox v. Jaroma, Inc.*, 709 S.W.2d 2, 4 (Tex.App.—Corpus Christi 1986, writ ref'd n.r.e.). • The request relates to a document that will not be admissible at trial. TRCP 192.3(a). The general rule is that as long as information appears reasonably calculated to lead to the discovery of admissible evidence, it is discoverable. *Id.* • The request presents a genuine issue for trial. TRCP 198.2(b).

✦

(2) Privileges. A party must assert its privileges in a withholding statement. TRCP 193.3(a). See "Asserting privileges," ch. 6-A, §18.2, p. 443.

6. Protective order. A party may file a motion for protective order within the time period for answering requests for admissions. *See* TRCP 192.6(a). See "Motion for Protective Order," ch. 6-A, §20, p. 449. If a party objects that a set of requests for admissions is unduly burdensome and harassing, the party does not need to file a more specific objection to each request to prevent the requests from being deemed. *E.g.*, *Reynolds*, 188 S.W.2d at 260 (Ds' motion objecting that P's 996 requests for admissions were unduly burdensome and harassing prevented deemed admissions). Even if the trial court does not rule on the motion for a protective order, a timely motion prevents the requests from being deemed admitted. *Id.* at 261.

§4.3 Amending or withdrawing answers. The court has the authority to permit a party to amend or withdraw its admissions. *Marshall v. Vise*, 767 S.W.2d 699, 700 (Tex.1989). The court may permit amendment or withdrawal when the moving party shows (1) good cause, (2) that the party relying on the responses will not be unduly prejudiced, and (3) that the withdrawal will serve the purpose of legitimate discovery and the merits of the case. TRCP 198.3; *Stelly v. Papania*, 927 S.W.2d 620, 622 (Tex.1996); *e.g.*, *Texas Capital Secs. v. Sandefer*, 58 S.W.3d 760, 770-71 (Tex.App.—Houston [1st Dist.] 2001, pet. denied) (motion to withdraw did not show good cause).

§5. CHALLENGING THE RESPONSE

§5.1 Challenging response to requests. The requesting party can move to determine the sufficiency of the responding party's answers or objections. TRCP 215.4(a).

1. Challenging answers. If the court decides an answer does not comply with TRCP 198, the court may deem the request admitted or order that an amended answer be served. TRCP 215.4(a); *Taylor v. Taylor*, 747 S.W.2d 940, 945 (Tex.App.—Amarillo 1988, writ denied). See *O'Connor's Texas Forms*, FORM 6H:16.

(1) Evasive answer. The party who served the requests should challenge answers that do not specifically deny or affirm the requests. *See* TRCP 198.2(b). The court may treat an evasive answer as a failure to answer and deem the request admitted. TRCP 215.4(a); *State v. Carrillo*, 885 S.W.2d 212, 216 (Tex.App.—San Antonio 1994, no writ).

(2) Quibbling. The party who served the requests should challenge answers that quibble over the meaning of simple words. If an answer quibbles over the meaning of a word, the court may hold that the answer is evasive and deem the request admitted. *See McPeak v. Texas DPS*, 346 S.W.2d 138, 140 (Tex.App.—Dallas 1961, no writ).

(3) Refusal to answer. The party who served the requests should challenge a refusal to answer made on the ground that the responding party did not have sufficient information. The refusal to answer is not valid unless the party also states that it made a reasonable effort to ascertain the requested matters. *U.S. Fire Ins. v. Maness*, 775 S.W.2d 748, 749 (Tex.App.—Houston [1st Dist.] 1989, writ ref'd); *Stewart v. Vaughn*, 504 S.W.2d 600, 602 (Tex.App.—Houston [14th Dist.] 1974, no writ).

2. Challenging objections. If the court determines that an objection is not justified, it may order the request to be answered or deem it admitted. For example, a party should challenge an objection made on the ground that the request was confusing if it was not. *See, e.g., Gray v. Armstrong*, 364 S.W.2d 485, 488 (Tex.App.—Dallas 1962, no writ) (because request was not confusing, court deemed it admitted).

3. Challenging privileges. After receiving a withholding statement in response to a request for admission indicating that information has been withheld on grounds of privilege, the party seeking the discovery may ask the withholding party to provide a privilege log. TRCP 193.3(b). See "Request privilege log," ch. 6-A, §18.2.2, p. 444.

§5.2 Expenses for failure to admit. If the responding party refuses to admit the truth of a matter asked or the genuineness of a document, and the party who served the request later proves the matter to be true or the document genuine, the requesting party may be entitled to reasonable expenses incurred in making that proof, including reasonable attorney fees. TRCP 215.4(b); *Peralta v. Durham*, 133 S.W.3d 339, 341 (Tex.App.—Dallas 2004, no

✦

pet.); *see also* ***Tharp v. Blackwell***, 570 S.W.2d 154, 158 (Tex.App.—Texarkana 1978, no writ) (attorney fees available for failure to comply with predecessor to TRCP 198.2). The award of costs is mandatory unless the court finds one of the following: (1) the request was objectionable, (2) the admission sought was of no substantial importance, (3) the responding party had a reasonable ground to believe that it would prevail on the matter, or (4) there was another good reason for the refusal to admit. TRCP 215.4(b); ***Peralta***, 133 S.W.3d at 341.

§6. DEEMED ADMISSIONS

§6.1 Answer deemed admitted. Requests are automatically deemed admitted as a matter of law on the day after the answers are due if no answers, objections, or assertions of privilege are served. TRCP 198.2(c); *see **Marino v. King***, 355 S.W.3d 629, 633 (Tex.2011); ***Marshall v. Vise***, 767 S.W.2d 699, 700 (Tex.1989); ***Payton v. Ashton***, 29 S.W.3d 896, 897-98 (Tex.App.—Amarillo 2000, no pet.). The trial court does not have the discretion to refuse to deem the requests admitted. ***Barker v. Harrison***, 752 S.W.2d 154, 155 (Tex.App.—Houston [1st Dist.] 1988, writ dism'd).

§6.2 Motion to deem.

1. Not necessary. Once the answers are overdue and no response has been served, it is not necessary for the requesting party to file a motion to ask the court to deem unanswered requests for admissions admitted. TRCP 198.2(c); *see **Marshall v. Vise***, 767 S.W.2d 699, 700 (Tex.1989).

2. Necessary. When a party responding to requests for admissions serves timely but evasive answers or invalid objections, the party who sent the requests should file a motion asking the court to deem the requests admitted. TRCP 215.4(a); *see **State v. Carrillo***, 885 S.W.2d 212, 216 (Tex.App.—San Antonio 1994, no writ); ***Taylor v. Taylor***, 747 S.W.2d 940, 945 (Tex.App.—Amarillo 1988, writ denied). See *O'Connor's Texas Forms*, FORM 6H:14.

§6.3 Response to motion to deem. When a party files a motion to deem answers admitted, the other party should file a response that challenges the grounds in the motion or asks the court for permission to amend its answers. *See* TRCP 215.4(a). See *O'Connor's Texas Forms*, FORM 6H:15.

§7. AVOIDING DEEMED ADMISSIONS

§7.1 Take a nonsuit. If the statute of limitations has not run, a plaintiff can avoid the effect of deemed admissions by taking a nonsuit and refiling the case. Deemed admissions in one suit are not effective in another. TRCP 198.3; ***Osteen v. Glynn Dodson, Inc.***, 875 S.W.2d 429, 431 (Tex.App.—Waco 1994, writ denied). See *O'Connor's Texas Forms*, FORM 7F:1.

§7.2 Strike deemed admissions. A party may move to withdraw or amend the admissions deemed against it. In many cases, a party first realizes the requests for admissions were deemed admitted when the propounding party files a motion for summary judgment based on deemed admissions. *See **Wheeler v. Green***, 157 S.W.3d 439, 441-42 (Tex.2005); ***Cherry v. North Am. Lloyds***, 770 S.W.2d 4, 5-6 (Tex.App.—Houston [1st Dist.] 1989, writ denied). When this occurs, the party should follow the procedure outlined here:

1. Motion for continuance. If a motion for summary judgment (or any other motion that depends on the deemed admissions) is pending, the party against whom the admissions were deemed should file a motion to continue the summary-judgment hearing. The party attempting to challenge the deemed findings will need more time than permitted under TRCP 166a to respond to the motion for summary judgment. See "Motion for Continuance," ch. 5-D, p. 336; *O'Connor's Texas Forms*, FORMS 5D:1-2, 7B:4. If the party does not realize the admissions were deemed until the hearing and the motion for summary judgment is granted, the party can file a motion for new trial. *See **Wheeler***, 157 S.W.3d at 441-42. See "No opportunity to file response," ch. 10-B, §11.1.2(2), p. 801.

2. Motion to strike deemed admissions. The party against whom the admissions were deemed should file a motion to strike the deemed admissions. See *O'Connor's Texas Forms*, FORM 6H:17. TRCP 198.3 permits the trial court to allow a party to withdraw or amend its admissions. The motion must include the following:

(1) Good cause. The party must state good cause, explaining why it did not timely serve its answers to the requests for admissions. TRCP 198.3(a); ***Wheeler***, 157 S.W.3d at 442; ***Wal-Mart Stores v. Deggs***, 968 S.W.2d

---

✯

354, 356 (Tex.1998). Good cause can be an accident or mistake, as long as it was not intentional or the result of conscious indifference. *E.g.*, *Marino v. King*, 355 S.W.3d 629, 633 (Tex.2011) (mistake in calculating time to serve response to requested admissions); *Wheeler*, 157 S.W.3d at 442 (same); *Boulet v. State*, 189 S.W.3d 833, 837 (Tex. App.—Houston [1st Dist.] 2006, no pet.) (mistake in calendar entry).

(2) **No prejudice.** The party must state that the other party will not be unduly prejudiced by the striking of the deemed admissions. TRCP 198.3(b); *Wheeler*, 157 S.W.3d at 442. Undue prejudice depends on whether withdrawing admissions will delay the trial or significantly hamper the other party's ability to prepare for it. *E.g.*, *Marino*, 355 S.W.3d at 633 (trial court should have permitted withdrawal of deemed admissions; P's filing of responses to admissions one day late but several months before summary-judgment hearing would not hamper D in preparing for trial); *Wheeler*, 157 S.W.3d at 443 (trial court should have permitted withdrawal of deemed admissions; P's filing of responses to admissions two days late but six months before summary judgment hearing did not hamper D in preparing for trial); *Deggs*, 968 S.W.2d at 357 (trial court should have permitted withdrawal of deemed admissions; P did not depend on admissions to develop case); *Morgan v. Timmers Chevrolet, Inc.*, 1 S.W.3d 803, 806-07 (Tex. App.—Houston [1st Dist.] 1999, pet. denied) (trial court should not have permitted withdrawal of deemed admissions in middle of trial; Ps were unduly prejudiced because they had relied on admissions to limit discovery).

(3) **Presentation of merits will suffer.** The party against whom the admissions were deemed should state that if the admissions are not struck, presentation of the merits will suffer because the case would be decided on deemed—but possibly untrue—facts. *Wheeler*, 157 S.W.3d at 443 n.2; *see* TRCP 198.3(b) ("presentation of the merits of the action will be subserved"); *Boulet*, 189 S.W.3d at 838 (allowing deemed admissions that may preclude presentation of merits raises due-process issues); *see, e.g.*, *In re Kellogg-Brown & Root, Inc.*, 45 S.W.3d 772, 777 (Tex.App.—Tyler 2001, orig. proceeding) (trial court's denial of motion to withdraw deemed admissions precluded D from presenting any viable defense at trial).

3. Attachments to motion to strike. The party against whom the admissions were deemed should attach the following to the motion to strike:

(1) **Affidavits.** In affidavits, the party should state detailed facts that support the excuses and explanations for all three elements: good cause, no prejudice, and presentation of merits. *See, e.g.*, *Ramsey v. Criswell*, 850 S.W.2d 258, 259-60 (Tex.App.—Texarkana 1993, no writ) (court denied motion because it was unverified and party had not attached or offered affidavits or other proof).

(2) **Answers.** The party should attach the answers it would have served in response to the requests for admissions if it had not missed the deadline.

4. Response to motion to strike. When a party files a motion to strike the deemed admissions, the party requesting the admissions should file a response that challenges the grounds in the motion. See *O'Connor's Texas Forms*, FORM 6H:18.

5. Hearing.

(1) **Request hearing.** The party who filed the motion to strike the deemed admissions should request a hearing on the motion.

(2) **Present evidence.** The party who filed the motion to strike the deemed admissions should present the testimony of as many witnesses as are necessary to convince the trial court to permit withdrawal of the admissions. The hearing should be treated as a full trial on the issues of good cause and no prejudice.

(3) **Record hearing.** The party should make sure the court reporter transcribes the hearing. Without a record of the hearing, it is impossible to prove good cause and lack of prejudice on appeal. *See Ruiz v. Nicolas Trevino Forwarding Agency, Inc.*, 888 S.W.2d 86, 89 (Tex.App.—San Antonio 1994, no writ).

6. Secure ruling. The party attempting to set aside the deemed admissions must make sure the court rules on its motion to strike. *Laycox v. Jaroma, Inc.*, 709 S.W.2d 2, 3 (Tex.App.—Corpus Christi 1986, writ ref'd n.r.e.).

✦

(1) Deemed admissions set aside. The courts have set aside deemed admissions in the following instances: • When the party rebuts the presumption of service. *See, e.g.*, *Approximately $14,980.00 v. State*, 261 S.W.3d 182, 189 (Tex.App.—Houston [14th Dist.] 2008, no pet.) (notice sent by certified mail was returned "unclaimed," and return receipt showed two unsuccessful delivery attempts). • When the requests were not answered because of some confusion caused by the party serving the request. *See, e.g.*, *City of Houston v. Riner*, 896 S.W.2d 317, 319-20 (Tex.App.—Houston [1st Dist.] 1995, writ denied) (P left requests with building guard, who was not a representative of D, and D never received them); *Birdo v. Holbrook*, 775 S.W.2d 411, 413 (Tex.App.—Fort Worth 1989, writ denied) (pro se P sent multiple requests for same information). • When the party shows diligence in attempting to resolve the problem as soon as it was discovered. *See, e.g.*, *In re Kellogg-Brown & Root, Inc.*, 45 S.W.3d at 776 (attorney immediately prepared and delivered responses after she realized she never received requests and could not find them in her office); *Esparza v. Diaz*, 802 S.W.2d 772, 776 (Tex.App.—Houston [14th Dist.] 1990, no writ) (D filed answers six months before trial, P was not injured, and trial was not delayed); *Employers Ins. of Wausau v. Hilton*, 792 S.W.2d 462, 467 (Tex.App.—Dallas 1990, writ denied) (attorney drafted answers immediately after receiving requests for admissions, but they were not typed and served; attorney filed motion to set aside deemed answers as soon as he discovered the problem); *Boone v. Texas Employers' Ins.*, 790 S.W.2d 683, 688-89 (Tex. App.—Tyler 1990, no writ) (attorney immediately filed motion to withdraw deemed admissions). • When the error is clerical. *See, e.g.*, *Burden v. John Watson Landscape Illumination*, 896 S.W.2d 253, 255-56 (Tex.App.—Eastland 1995, writ denied) (attorney did not see letter from court shortening time to respond to 14 days); *Cudd v. Hydrostatic Transmission, Inc.*, 867 S.W.2d 101, 104 (Tex.App.—Corpus Christi 1993, no writ) (mistake in counting days to answer); *North River Ins. v. Greene*, 824 S.W.2d 697, 701 (Tex.App.—El Paso 1992, writ denied) (incorrect diary entry for date answers were due).

(2) Deemed admissions not set aside. The courts have refused to set aside deemed admissions in the following instances: • The party's failure to respond to requests for admissions was the result of a disputed oral agreement to extend time. *Hoffman v. Texas Commerce Bank Nat'l Ass'n*, 846 S.W.2d 336, 339-40 (Tex. App.—Houston [14th Dist.] 1992, writ denied). • The party did not attach affidavits to unverified motion to withdraw deemed admissions or offer other evidence to support its allegations that he was sick and his attorney was out of town on the day of filing. *Ramsey*, 850 S.W.2d at 259-60.

§8. ADMISSIONS AS EVIDENCE

§8.1 Admissions as evidence. Admissions may be used by all parties in the lawsuit, including parties joined after the admissions were made. *See Grimes v. Jalco, Inc.*, 630 S.W.2d 282, 284 (Tex.App.—Houston [1st Dist.] 1981, writ ref'd n.r.e), *overruled on other grounds*, *Medina v. Herrera*, 927 S.W.2d 597 (Tex.1996).

1. Only in same suit. Answers to requests for admissions are admissible only in the same suit. TRCP 198.3; *Osteen v. Glynn Dodson, Inc.*, 875 S.W.2d 429, 431 (Tex.App.—Waco 1994, writ denied).

2. Only against party addressed. Answers to requests for admissions and deemed admissions are admissible only against the party to whom the requests for admissions were addressed. TRCP 198.3; *Thalman v. Martin*, 635 S.W.2d 411, 414 (Tex.1982); *Hartman v. Trio Transp.*, 937 S.W.2d 575, 578 (Tex.App.—Texarkana 1996, writ denied). An admission by an agent or servant is admissible against the principal only if (1) the statement concerns a matter within the scope of the agency or employment, and (2) it was made during the existence of that relationship. TRE 801(e)(2)(D); *Hartman*, 937 S.W.2d at 579-80.

3. Not against other parties. Admissions of a party are not admissible against a third party and do not bind coparties. *Wal-Mart Stores v. Deggs*, 968 S.W.2d 354, 357 (Tex.1998) (allowing party to fall into trap produced by another party's failure to respond is contrary to intent of rules); *see Bleeker v. Villarreal*, 941 S.W.2d 163, 168-69 (Tex.App.—Corpus Christi 1996, writ dism'd); *USX Corp. v. Salinas*, 818 S.W.2d 473, 479 (Tex.App.—San Antonio 1991, writ denied).

4. Not by addressed party. The party to whom the requests were addressed cannot use its own self-serving answers. *Sympson v. Mor-Win Prods.*, 501 S.W.2d 362, 364 (Tex.App.—Fort Worth 1973, no writ); *see also* TRE 801(e)(2) (admission by party-opponent).

✦

5. Not the denial. A party cannot introduce into evidence a party's denial or refusal to admit a fact. *See Americana Motel, Inc. v. Johnson*, 610 S.W.2d 143, 143 (Tex.1980) (denial of request for admission cannot be used as summary-judgment evidence). When a party denies or refuses to make an admission of fact, it is nothing more than a refusal to admit a fact; it is not evidence of any fact except the fact of refusal. *Newman v. Utica Nat'l Ins.*, 868 S.W.2d 5, 8 (Tex.App.—Houston [1st Dist.] 1993, writ denied).

§8.2 Using admissions at trial. When a party intends to use the other party's response to requests for admissions at trial, that party should file them with the clerk. *See* TRCP 191.4(c)(2). Admissions made by parties in response to requests for admissions that are on file with the court do not need to be introduced into evidence to be properly before the trial and appellate courts. *Red Ball Motor Freight, Inc. v. Dean*, 549 S.W.2d 41, 43 (Tex.App.—Tyler 1977, writ dism'd). If the trier of fact returns findings that contradict a judicial admission, the admission must be accepted as controlling. *Beutel v. Dallas Cty. Flood Control Dist.*, 916 S.W.2d 685, 694 (Tex.App.—Waco 1996, writ denied).

PRACTICE TIP

*For dramatic effect, a party may introduce the admissions into evidence by formally reading the specific admissions to the jury. See **Wal-Mart Stores v. Deggs**, 968 S.W.2d 354, 356 (Tex.1998); **Parkway Hosp., Inc. v. Lee**, 946 S.W.2d 580, 587 (Tex.App.—Houston [14th Dist.] 1997, writ denied), disapproved on other grounds, **Roberts v. Williamson**, 111 S.W.3d 113 (Tex.2003).*

---

1. No contradictory proof. A request for admission, once admitted or deemed, is a judicial admission, and a party cannot introduce conflicting testimony over an objection. *Marshall v. Vise*, 767 S.W.2d 699, 700 (Tex. 1989); *Beutel*, 916 S.W.2d at 694; *Bay Area Thoracic & Cardiovascular Surgical Ass'n v. Nathanson*, 908 S.W.2d 10, 11 (Tex.App.—Houston [1st Dist.] 1995, no writ).

2. Waiver of admissions. A party can waive its right to rely on the other party's admissions. When the admitting party attempts to offer evidence that contradicts the admissions, the party relying on the admissions must object, or it will waive its right to rely on the binding effect of the admissions. *Marshall*, 767 S.W.2d at 700; *see, e.g.*, *Acevedo v. Commission for Lawyer Discipline*, 131 S.W.3d 99, 104-05 (Tex.App.—San Antonio 2004, pet. denied) (no obligation to object because no controverting evidence offered). If controverting evidence is introduced without objection, the admissions are no longer conclusive, but they are still evidence. *Parkway Hosp.*, 946 S.W.2d at 587-88.

§8.3 Using admissions in summary judgment. The same rules apply when relying on admissions in a summary-judgment procedure as at trial—answers to requests for admissions and deemed admissions are admissible only against the party to whom the requests for admissions were addressed. *See Americana Motel, Inc. v. Johnson*, 610 S.W.2d 143, 143 (Tex.1980) (cannot use denials to request for admissions); *Schulz v. State Farm Mut. Auto. Ins.*, 930 S.W.2d 872, 876 (Tex.App.—Houston [1st Dist.] 1996, no writ) (cannot use own answers to admissions). The trial court cannot consider affidavits to contradict deemed admissions. *Beasley v. Burns*, 7 S.W.3d 768, 770-71 (Tex.App.—Texarkana 1999, pet. denied). See "Using admissions at trial," §8.2, this page.

§9. REVIEW

For the rules and forms for prosecuting or responding to an appeal or original proceeding, see *O'Connor's Texas Civil Appeals* (2012).

§9.1 Standard on appeal. The trial court has broad discretion to grant or refuse a party leave to withdraw deemed admissions. *Stelly v. Papania*, 927 S.W.2d 620, 622 (Tex.1996); *Approximately $14,980.00 v. State*, 261 S.W.3d 182, 185 (Tex.App.—Houston [14th Dist.] 2008, no pet.); *In re Kellogg-Brown & Root, Inc.*, 45 S.W.3d 772, 775 (Tex.App.—Tyler 2001, orig. proceeding). The trial court's decision will be set aside on appeal only on a showing of a clear abuse of discretion. *Stelly*, 927 S.W.2d at 622.

§9.2 Appeal or mandamus. Generally, mandamus relief is not available to review a trial court's action relating to deemed admissions. *See Sutherland v. Moore*, 716 S.W.2d 119, 121 (Tex.App.—El Paso 1986, orig. proceeding) (mandamus not available to review trial court's withdrawal of deemed admissions). See "Review of Discovery Orders," ch. 6-A, §26, p. 458.

★

I. SECURING DOCUMENTS & TANGIBLE THINGS

§1. GENERAL

§1.1 Rules. TRCP 176, 196, 205.

§1.2 Purpose. TRCP 196 provides the discovery procedure for obtaining documents and other tangible things from a party, and TRCP 176 provides the procedure for obtaining documents and other tangible things from a nonparty.

§1.3 Forms. See *O'Connor's Texas Civil Forms* (2012), FORMS 6I.

§1.4 Other references. Griesel, *The "New" Texas Discovery Rules: Three Years Later*, Advanced Evidence & Discovery Course, State Bar of Texas CLE, ch. 2, §X, p. 22 (2002).

§2. SCOPE

A party may secure the production of any document, tangible item, or information in electronic or magnetic form that is not privileged and is relevant or reasonably calculated to lead to the discovery of admissible evidence. TRCP 192.3(a). See "Documents & tangible things," ch. 6-B, §2.11, p. 463. A party may also request the production of an item for inspection, sampling, testing, photographing, and copying. TRCP 196.1(a); *see, e.g., General Motors Corp. v. Tanner*, 892 S.W.2d 862, 863 (Tex.1995) (party wanted to examine item under microscope); *General Elec. Co. v. Salinas*, 861 S.W.2d 20, 23 (Tex.App.—Corpus Christi 1993, orig. proceeding) (party wanted to test materials involved in residential fire).

§3. SECURING THINGS FROM A PARTY

To obtain documents and other tangible things from another party, a party serves a request for production. TRCP 196.1(a). No motion is necessary.

§3.1 Procedure.

1. Form of request. The request for production must be in writing. TRCP 192.7(a); *see City of San Antonio v. Vela*, 762 S.W.2d 314, 319 (Tex.App.—San Antonio 1988, writ denied). See *O'Connor's Texas Forms*, FORMS 6I:1-2.

2. Specify place & time to respond. The request must state the place and date for production. TRCP 196.1(b), 196.2(a). The date to respond to the request is generally 30 days after the date the request was served. TRCP 196.2(a). When a request is served on a defendant before the defendant's answer is due, the defendant has 50 days after service to respond to the request, counting from the day the request was served. *Id.* See "Served before answer date – 50 days," ch. 6-A, §14.1.2, p. 437.

3. Deadline to serve. A request for production may be served anytime after the suit is filed. TRCP 190.2(c)(1), 190.3(b)(1). The deadline for serving a request is 30 days before the end of the discovery period. TRCP 196.1(a). See "Discovery Periods," ch. 6-A, §8, p. 433. When served by mail or fax, the request should be served at least 34 days before the end of the discovery period. See "Deadline to Respond to Discovery," ch. 6-A, §14, p. 437.

4. Number of requests. There is no limit in TRCP 196 to the number of items a party can ask to have produced or the number of sets of requests it can serve.

⓫ *PROPOSED TRCP CHANGES*

In response to Gov't Code §22.004(h), the Supreme Court has proposed TRCP 169 to establish a process for the prompt, efficient, and cost-effective resolution of civil actions (expedited actions) in which only monetary relief is sought and the amount in controversy is no more than $100,000. See Tex.Sup.Ct. Order, Misc. Docket No. 12-9191 (eff. Mar. 1, 2013). The Supreme Court has proposed corresponding amendments to TRCP 190.2 that would (1) change the Level 1

───────────────────────────── ✦ ─────────────────────────────

> *discovery-control plan to apply to these expedited actions under TRCP 169 and (2) include limits on the number of requests for production that can be served in Level 1 discovery. See Tex.Sup.Ct. Order, Misc. Docket No. 12-9191 (eff. Mar. 1, 2013). The public-comment period for the proposed amendments ends on February 1, 2013, and the rules are to take effect March 1, 2013. For the proposed version of the rules, see the appendix after this book's index. For the final version, go to the Supreme Court website at www.supreme.courts.state.tx.us. When the new and amended rules take effect, a supplement to this book—with updated rules and commentaries that reflect the changes—will be available at www.JonesMcClure.com/TRCPamendments.*

5. Not filed. The request for production is not filed with the court. TRCP 191.4(a)(1). See "Exceptions," ch. 6-A, §12.1.3, p. 436.

§3.2 Request. A request for documents or things must be reasonably tailored to request only matters relevant to the case. *Texaco, Inc. v. Sanderson*, 898 S.W.2d 813, 815 (Tex.1995).

1. Items to produce. The request for production must identify items, either individually or by category, and describe each item and category with reasonable particularity. TRCP 196.1(b); *see, e.g., Texaco*, 898 S.W.2d at 815 (request for all documents generally too broad); *County of Dallas v. Harrison*, 759 S.W.2d 530, 531 (Tex. App.—Dallas 1988, no writ) (request for photographs did not include videotape). A request for production cannot be used as a fishing expedition for information. *In re American Optical Corp.*, 988 S.W.2d 711, 713 (Tex.1998); *Dillard Dept. Stores v. Hall*, 909 S.W.2d 491, 492 (Tex.1995). See "Overbroad," ch. 6-A, §20.1.3, p. 450.

(1) Electronic information. To obtain discovery of magnetic or electronic information, the requesting party must (1) specifically request the data, (2) specify the form in which the data should be produced, and (3) specify any extraordinary steps necessary for retrieval and translation. TRCP 196.4 & cmt. 3. See "Requests for production," ch. 6-C, §8.1.5, p. 498.

(2) Other things. The request for production should ask for documents and other things based on the elements of the claim or defense. See *O'Connor's Texas Forms*, FORMS 6I for suggested requests for production in the following types of lawsuits: breach of contract (FORM 6I:4), suit on a sworn account (FORM 6I:5), automobile accident (FORMS 6I:6-7), slip-and-fall (FORMS 6I:8-9), and suit under the DTPA (FORMS 6I:10-11).

2. Items to be tested. If the requesting party intends to test or sample the requested item, the party must describe with specificity the means, manner, and procedure for testing or sampling. TRCP 196.1(b). The requesting party should identify to what extent, if any, the testing or sampling will destroy or alter the item. If the testing will destroy or materially alter the item, the requesting party must secure a court order before conducting the test. *See* TRCP 196.5.

3. Particulars for compliance. The request for production should state the particulars for compliance: the deadline (generally 30 days after service of the request), the place to produce documents (generally the office of the attorney), and the way to produce the documents (organized as they are kept in the ordinary course of business or organized and labeled to correspond with each particular request). TRCP 196.1(b), 196.3(c). See "Deadline to serve response," ch. 6-A, §14.1, p. 437.

4. Appropriate requests. The following requests were held proper: • Request for all documents relating to incident in which plaintiff was injured, excluding work product. *K Mart Corp. v. Sanderson*, 937 S.W.2d 429, 430-31 (Tex.1996). • Request for personnel file. *Tri-State Wholesale Associated Grocers, Inc. v. Barrera*, 917 S.W.2d 391, 399 (Tex.App.—El Paso 1996, writ dism'd). See "Personnel files," ch. 6-B, §2.11.9, p. 464. • Request for "any and all" lease agreements between the parties since 1974. *Chamberlain v. Cherry*, 818 S.W.2d 201, 204 (Tex. App.—Amarillo 1991, orig. proceeding).

─── ✦ ───

PRACTICE TIP

If you believe the other party is going to hide documents, skip the request for production. Instead, as early as possible in the lawsuit, subpoena for an oral deposition the lowest-level employee of the party who keeps the documents and request a list of documents as part of the deposition notice. You have a better chance of getting the documents if a layperson (not an attorney) is subpoenaed (not noticed) for deposition and swears under oath (not just states in response to a request for production) that the documents produced are all the documents that were requested.

---

5. Inappropriate requests.

(1) Trial exhibits. A party should not ask for copies of the other party's trial exhibits in a request for production. *Texas Tech Univ. Health Sci. Ctr. v. Schild*, 828 S.W.2d 502, 504 (Tex.App.—El Paso 1992, orig. proceeding). Trial exhibits may be secured before trial if a pretrial or discovery-control order requires their production. TRCP 166(*l*), 190.4. See "Exhibits," ch. 5-A, §3.9.3, p. 317.

(2) To create a document. A party should not ask the other party to create a document. *In re Colonial Pipeline Co.*, 968 S.W.2d 938, 942 (Tex.1998); *McKinney v. National Un. Fire Ins.*, 772 S.W.2d 72, 73 n.2 (Tex.1989); *see also In re Guzman*, 19 S.W.3d 522, 525 (Tex.App.—Corpus Christi 2000, orig. proceeding) (court cannot require nonparty to create document). To be subject to discovery, the thing or document must be in the custody, control, or possession of a party on whom the request is served. *In re Colonial*, 968 S.W.2d at 942; *Smith v. O'Neal*, 850 S.W.2d 797, 799 (Tex.App.—Houston [14th Dist.] 1993, no writ).

§3.3 Procedure to respond.

1. Form of response. See *O'Connor's Texas Forms*, FORM 6I:3.

(1) In writing. The party responding to a request for production must serve a written response on the requesting party. TRCP 196.2(a); *see Cellular Mktg., Inc. v. Houston Cellular Tel. Co.*, 838 S.W.2d 331, 333 n.2 (Tex.App.—Houston [14th Dist.] 1992, writ denied). Each answer, objection, or other response must be preceded by the request it applies to. TRCP 193.1.

(2) Not verified. The response does not need to be verified. *See* TRCP 191.3(a).

(3) Signed. The response must be signed by the attorney (or party when pro se). TRCP 191.3(a).

2. Deadline to respond. Generally, a party has 30 days after the date of service of the request for documents to respond, depending on the type of service. TRCP 196.2(a); *see Schein v. American Rest. Grp.*, 852 S.W.2d 496, 497 n.2 (Tex.1993). However, a defendant that is served with a request before the defendant's answer is due has 50 days to respond. TRCP 196.2(a). See "Deadline to Respond to Discovery," ch. 6-A, §14, p. 437. The party must file its answers and objections and assert its privileges by this deadline; if not, the party waives its objections and privileges. See "Waiver of objections & privileges," ch. 6-A, §25.3, p. 456. Once a party's objections and privileges are waived, the party must produce the requested documents. To extend the time, see "Extending Time to Respond to Discovery," ch. 6-A, §15, p. 438.

3. Not filed. The written response and the documents produced in response to the request are not filed with the court. TRCP 191.4(a). The documents should be kept by the party that requested their production. Other parties should be provided with copies of the documents.

4. Costs. The cost of producing materials is the responsibility of the responding party. TRCP 196.6. The cost of inspecting, sampling, testing, photographing, or copying materials is the responsibility of the requesting party. *Id.*; *Limas v. De Delgado*, 770 S.W.2d 953, 954 (Tex.App.—El Paso 1989, no writ). For good cause, the court can order that costs be apportioned differently than provided for in TRCP 196.6. TRCP 196.6.

———————————————— ✦ ————————————————

§3.4 Contents of response. See *O'Connor's Texas Forms*, FORM 6I:3. For each item or category of items, the responding party must make one of the following responses:

1. Party will comply. When complying with the request, the party should state that the production, inspection, or other requested action will be permitted as requested. TRCP 196.2(b)(1).

(1) Production of things. A party must produce all the documents and things that are requested, discoverable, in its possession (actual or constructive), and not subject to an objection. TRCP 196.3(a). See "Possession," ch. 6-A, §2.5, p. 425.

(2) Organization of documents. Documents must be produced either (1) organized as they are kept in the ordinary course of business, or (2) organized and labeled to correspond to each particular request. TRCP 196.3(c); *e.g.*, *Steenbergen v. Ford Motor Co.*, 814 S.W.2d 755, 758-59 (Tex.App.—Dallas 1991, writ denied) (D could produce documents as kept in course of business because P's request did not seek to organize or label according to categories). A party producing documents cannot collect the requested documents and shuffle them before turning them over to the requesting party.

(3) Electronic or magnetic data. When a request for production asks for electronic or magnetic information, the responding party must produce the data responsive to the request. TRCP 196.4. If the responding party cannot reasonably retrieve the requested information or produce it in the form requested, the responding party must object to the request. TRCP 196.4; *see* TRCP 193.2(b).

2. Party objects to procedure to respond. When a party intends to comply with the request but objects to the time, place, or method identified in the request for compliance, the response should state both the objection and the solution.

(1) Objection to time & place. When a party objects to the time or place of production or inspection, the response should state that it would be more reasonable to produce or inspect the documents at a different time or place and describe the suggested terms (e.g., at the corporate office instead of the attorney's office, or produce all copies instead of permitting inspection first). TRCP 193.2(b), 196.2(b). The responding party must then comply with that time and place without further request or order. TRCP 193.2(b).

(2) Objection to method of compliance. When a party objects to a request for production because it asks the party to produce a large number of documents, the responding party may notify the requesting party in its response that the documents are available in its office for inspection and copying. *See Overall v. Southwestern Bell Yellow Pages, Inc.*, 869 S.W.2d 629, 631 (Tex.App.—Houston [14th Dist.] 1994, no writ). When a request for production asks for a manageable number of documents, the responding party should attach them to the response. *See, e.g., id.* (documents excluded from trial for failure to provide copies with response).

3. Party objects to production. When objecting to the production of documents and things, the objection must be in writing, must be contained either in the response or in a separate document, and must provide specific reasons why the discovery should not be permitted. TRCP 193.2(a). A party's objections must be supported by a good-faith factual or legal basis. TRCP 193.2(c). A party must comply with the requests to which it does not object. TRCP 193.2(b) & cmt. 2. See "Burden to partially comply," ch. 6-A, §18.10, p. 447.

(1) Overbroad. A party can object when a request asks for "all documents" without limiting the request in time, place, or subject matter, can refuse to comply with it entirely, or can file a motion for a protective order. *See* TRCP 192.6(a), 193 cmt. 2. See "Overbroad," ch. 6-A, §20.1.3, p. 450; *O'Connor's Texas Forms* FORMS 6A:8-9.

(2) Destruction by testing. A party can object when testing or sampling the thing to be produced will destroy or materially alter the condition of it. *See* TRCP 196.5; *General Motors Corp. v. Tanner*, 892 S.W.2d 862, 863-64 (Tex.1995) (applying former TRCP 167(1)(g); must support objection with evidence).

(3) Other objections. For other objections, see "Valid objections to discovery requests," ch. 6-A, §19.1, p. 448; "Grounds to limit scope of discovery," ch. 6-A, §20.1, p. 449.

———————————— ✦ ————————————

4. Party asserts privileges. When asserting privileges in response to the request, the party must file a withholding statement to comply with TRCP 193.3. TRCP 193.2(f); *see* 196.2(b). See "Asserting privileges," ch. 6-A, §18.2, p. 443. A party must comply with the requests to which it does not assert a privilege. TRCP 193.2(b) & cmt. 2. See "Burden to partially comply," ch. 6-A, §18.10, p. 447.

5. Party unable to locate things. If a party is unable to locate documents or things responsive to the request, it must state that after a diligent search no items were identified that are responsive to the request. TRCP 196.2(b)(4).

§3.5 Hearing on objections & privileges. Generally, the burden to secure a hearing, to present evidence, and to secure a ruling on objections or assertions of privileges is on the party seeking discovery. See "Burden to secure hearing & ruling," ch. 6-A, §18.6, p. 445; "Burden to provide evidence," ch. 6-A, §18.7, p. 446.

§3.6 Supplementing or amending responses. When a party discovers additional information after responding to discovery, the party must supplement or amend its response. TRCP 193.5 (duty to supplement), TRCP 193.6 (sanctions for failure to supplement). For the substance of what additional information to provide, see "Supplementing Discovery Responses," ch. 6-A, §17, p. 440.

1. Time to serve supplemental or amended response. A party should serve a supplemental or amended response to requests for production reasonably promptly after the party discovers the need for such a response. TRCP 193.5(b).

2. Form of response. Supplemental or amended responses must be made in the same form as the original responses. TRCP 193.5(b).

§4. SECURING THINGS FROM A PARTY ABOUT A NONPARTY

§4.1 Nonparty information. When a party seeks information from another party about a nonparty, the production can affect the privacy interests of the nonparty. *In re Temple-Inland, Inc.*, 8 S.W.3d 459, 462-63 (Tex. App.—Beaumont 2000, orig. proceeding). The court can restrict the dissemination of discoverable information about nonparties, even when no privilege is involved. *See, e.g., id.* (court limited dissemination of list of former employees that ascribed criminal and other embarrassing conduct to them). For a nonparty's medical records in the possession of a party, see "Request to Party for Nonparty's Medical Records," ch. 6-J, §4, p. 577.

§4.2 Who can object. Any person affected by the discovery request can object to it—including other parties and nonparties. TRCP 192.6(a).

§5. SECURING THINGS FROM A NONPARTY

To secure documents and other tangible things from a nonparty, the party serves a notice to produce or appear and a discovery subpoena. TRCP 205.3(a); *see* TRCP 196 cmt. 6. A party is not required to file a motion for production to obtain documents from a nonparty in an ongoing suit. TRCP 205 cmt. By comparison, a party is required to file a motion and secure a court order to depose a nonparty before suit under TRCP 202, to secure a physical or mental examination of a nonparty under TRCP 204, and to secure entry on a nonparty's land under TRCP 196.7. TRCP 205.1.

§5.1 Notice.

1. Contents of notice.

(1) For documents only. When a nonparty is required to produce documents or things without appearing for a deposition, the notice of production must provide: (1) the name of the person from whom production is sought, (2) a reasonable time and place for production, (3) a description of the items to be produced, and (4) if testing or sampling is requested, information about the means, manner, and procedure. TRCP 205.3(b).

(2) For documents at deposition. When a nonparty is required to produce documents at an oral deposition, the notice for the deposition must comply with TRCP 199.2. TRCP 205.1(c). See "Contents of notice," ch. 6-F, §4.5.1, p. 527.

2. Filing. Discovery notices served on nonparties must be filed with the clerk. TRCP 191.4(b)(1).

COMMENTARIES
CHAPTER 6. DISCOVERY
I. SECURING DOCUMENTS & TANGIBLE THINGS

§5.2 The discovery subpoena. The subpoena is the instrument that compels a nonparty to comply with a notice for discovery. *See St. Luke's Episcopal Hosp. v. Garcia*, 928 S.W.2d 307, 312 (Tex.App.—Houston [14th Dist.] 1996, orig. proceeding). For general information about subpoenas, see "Subpoenas," ch. 1-L, p. 84. The scope of production of a discovery subpoena is governed by TRCP 192.3. *See Martin v. Khoury*, 843 S.W.2d 163, 166 (Tex.App.—Texarkana 1992, orig. proceeding). A subpoena cannot be used to secure information that is not discoverable by other forms of discovery requests. *See* TRCP 176.3(b) (prohibits use of subpoena to circumvent discovery rules); *Prestige Ford Co. v. Gilmore*, 56 S.W.3d 73, 80 (Tex.App.—Houston [14th Dist.] 2001, pet. denied) (same).

1. Types of discovery subpoenas. There are three types of discovery subpoenas.

(1) To produce. A nonparty may be subpoenaed to produce documents or things, without requiring the nonparty to appear for a deposition. TRCP 176.6(c), 205.3(a). When the subpoena commands a witness to produce documents or other things but not to give testimony, the witness does not need to appear in person at the time and place of production. TRCP 176.6(c).

(2) To appear. A nonparty may be subpoenaed to appear for a deposition without producing any documents. TRCP 205.1(a), (b). The discovery subpoena should direct the witness to appear for deposition at the time and place stated in the notice of deposition. TRCP 176.1(e), 176.2.

(3) To appear & produce. A nonparty may be subpoenaed to appear for a deposition and produce documents or other things. TRCP 205.1(c); *see In re Amaya*, 34 S.W.3d 354, 356-57 (Tex.App.—Waco 2001, orig. proceeding) (nonparty could not refuse to appear and produce documents); *see also* TRCP 205.3(a) (production of documents and things without deposition). See "Documents from nonparties," ch. 6-F, §4.5.6(2), p. 529.

2. Filing. Subpoenas required to be served on nonparties must be filed with the clerk. TRCP 191.4(b)(1).

§5.3 Time to serve notice & subpoena. The notice (of either intent to take the nonparty's deposition or intent to compel the nonparty to produce documents and things, or both) and the subpoena compelling the nonparty to comply must be served on the nonparty and the other parties. TRCP 205.2. See "Deadlines to Serve Notice & Subpoena," chart 6-9, p. 530.

1. Nonparty documents without deposition. To compel the production of documents from a nonparty without requiring the nonparty to appear for an oral deposition, the notice to produce and the subpoena must be served a reasonable time before the response is due. TRCP 205.3(a). The notice to produce must be served at least ten days before service of the subpoena. TRCP 205.2. The ten-day gap between service of the notice and the subpoena gives anyone (party or nonparty) who objects to the production of the documents time to move for a protective order before the nonparty produces the documents.

2. Nonparty deposition with documents. To compel the production of documents from a nonparty at a deposition, the notice of deposition and the subpoena must be served a reasonable time before the deposition. See "Nonparty deposition with documents," ch. 6-F, §4.5.2(1)(b), p. 527.

3. Nonparty deposition without documents. To compel the appearance of a nonparty at a deposition without requiring the production of documents, the notice of deposition and the subpoena must be served a reasonable time before the deposition; the subpoena cannot be served before the notice. See "Nonparty deposition without documents," ch. 6-F, §4.5.2(2)(b), p. 528.

§5.4 Nonparty's response to discovery subpoena. A nonparty must respond to the discovery subpoena and notice as required by TRCP 176.6. TRCP 205.3(d). The rules governing a nonparty's response to a notice and subpoena to produce documents are similar to the rules governing a party's response to a request for production. See "Procedure to respond," §3.3, p. 567.

1. No appearance necessary. A nonparty requested to produce documents or other things is not required to appear in person at the time and place of production unless the person is also subpoenaed to attend and give testimony. TRCP 176.6(c).

─────────────── ✦ ───────────────

2. Organization of documents. A nonparty must produce the documents either (1) as they are kept in the ordinary course of business, or (2) organized and labeled to correspond to each request. TRCP 176.6(c). See "Organization of documents," §3.4.1(2), p. 568.

§5.5 Challenging nonparty discovery subpoena. See "Objecting to Trial & Discovery Subpoenas," ch. 1-L, §4, p. 87; *O'Connor's Texas Forms*, FORMS 6A:11-12.

1. Who can challenge. The subpoena can be challenged by the person subpoenaed, by a party to the suit, or by any person affected by the subpoena. *See* TRCP 176.6(d), (e).

2. Deadline to challenge. Any challenge to the subpoena must be made before the time specified for compliance in the subpoena. TRCP 176.6(d), (e).

3. How to challenge subpoena.

(1) Objections & privileges. A person who has been subpoenaed may make written objections to production or assert privileges by withholding documents under TRCP 193.3. *See* TRCP 176.6(c), (d). See "Types of challenges," ch. 1-L, §4.3, p. 87; "Asserting privileges," ch. 6-A, §18.2, p. 443.

(2) Motion for protective order. A person who has been subpoenaed, a party, or any person affected by the discovery subpoena may file a motion for protective order under TRCP 192.6. TRCP 176.6(e). See "Motion for Protective Order," ch. 6-A, §20, p. 449.

4. Effect of challenge to discovery.

(1) Objection to time & place. When a nonparty or party objects to the time or place of a nonparty's oral deposition by filing a motion for protection or a motion to quash within three business days after service of the notice of deposition, the motion stays the deposition until the motion can be decided by the court. TRCP 199.4.

(2) Other objections by nonparty. When the nonparty challenges the subpoena by filing objections, assertions of privileges, or a motion for protection, the nonparty should produce all requested information not subject to its challenges. *See* TRCP 192.6(a), (b).

(3) Other objections by parties & third persons. When a party or a third person affected by the discovery challenges the discovery sought from a nonparty by filing a motion for protection or a motion to quash, the motion does not prevent the nonparty from producing the discovery. *See* TRCP 176.6(e) (although subpoenaed witness "need not" produce documents for which protection is sought, rule does not prohibit production). The party or affected person must secure a court order staying production of the discovery, or the nonparty may produce it. See "On objections by other persons," §5.5.5(2), this page.

5. Burden to get ruling.

(1) On objection by nonparty. The burden to get a ruling on a nonparty's objections is on the party that issued the subpoena. Although TRCP 176.6(d) and (e) require the subpoenaed person to object to a discovery subpoena or seek a protective order before the time specified for compliance, they do not require the witness to get a ruling before the time for compliance. *See Olinger v. Curry*, 926 S.W.2d 832, 835 (Tex.App.—Fort Worth 1996, orig. proceeding). The party who issued the subpoena may move for an order anytime after an objection is made or a motion for protection is filed. TRCP 176.6(d), (e).

(2) On objections by other persons. The burden to get a ruling on objections filed by a party or third person affected by the subpoena is on the party or third person that filed the motion objecting to production. The reason the burden is on the party or third person is that, unless prevented by a court order, a nonparty may produce documents even when a motion for protection was filed. *See* TRCP 176.6(e) (rule does not prohibit subpoenaed witness from producing after objection filed).

6. Ruling on objections. The court may sustain objections, grant a protective order, or impose reasonable conditions on compliance with a subpoena, including compensation to the nonparty for undue hardship. *See* TRCP 176.7.

─────────────────── ✦ ───────────────────

§5.6 Cost of document production. The party who issues the subpoena requiring production of documents or other things must reimburse the nonparty for the reasonable costs of production. TRCP 205.3(f).

§5.7 Copies for other parties. The party who issued the subpoena must make the produced materials available to the other parties for inspection on reasonable notice. TRCP 205.3(e). At their own expense, the other parties may obtain copies of the documents from the party who issued the subpoena. *Id.*

§6. COMPELLING PRODUCTION & SANCTIONS

§6.1 Motion to compel & for sanctions. If the party or nonparty responding to the request for or notice of production refuses to produce documents, the party requesting documents can move to compel production and move for sanctions or an order of contempt. *See* TRCP 215.2. See "Motion to Compel Discovery," ch. 6-A, §22, p. 451; "Motion for Discovery Sanctions," ch. 6-A, §24, p. 455.

1. Sanctions against party. When a party refuses to produce a properly requested document, the trial court can exclude the document, limit the testimony about the document or the issue, or impose any other sanction listed in TRCP 215.2(b). See "Sanctions for discovery abuse," ch. 5-K, §7.1, p. 384.

2. Sanctions against nonparty. Contempt is the only sanction the court may impose on a nonparty for not complying with an order under TRCP 205.3. TRCP 176.8(a), 215.2(a), (c). See "Discovery abuse," ch. 5-K, §4.4.1, p. 380.

§6.2 Other remedies. When the party requesting documents believes the responding party has overlooked or ignored relevant documents in responding to the request, the requesting party can (1) ask the court to appoint a master, (2) take depositions, or (3) send written interrogatories. *Texaco, Inc. v. Dominguez*, 812 S.W.2d 451, 456 (Tex. App.—San Antonio 1991, orig. proceeding). The party cannot ask the court for permission to go through the other party's files. *Id.* at 455-56.

§7. SECURING DOCUMENTS FROM A FINANCIAL INSTITUTION

§7.1 Exclusive discovery procedure. To secure a customer's records from a bank or other financial institution, a party must comply with Finance Code §59.006, which is the exclusive method to compel discovery of a customer's records. Fin. Code §59.006(a); *see* CPRC §30.007; *Enviro Prot., Inc. v. National Bank*, 989 S.W.2d 454, 455 (Tex.App.—El Paso 1999, no pet.) (applying provisions from former CPRC §30.007).

§7.2 Definitions under Finance Code §59.001.

1. Financial institution. A "financial institution" is defined as any of the following, but does not include an entity organized under the laws of another state or under federal law that has its main office in another state and does not maintain a branch or other office in Texas. Fin. Code §59.001(5).

(1) A bank, whether chartered under the laws of Texas, another state, the United States, or another country. *Id.* §201.101(1)(A).

(2) A savings-and-loan association chartered under Finance Code chapter 62 or similar laws of another state. *Id.* §201.101(1)(B).

(3) A federal savings-and-loan association, federal savings bank, federal credit union, or credit union chartered under Finance Code chapter 122 or similar laws of another state. *Id.* §201.101(1)(C), (1)(D).

(4) A trust company chartered under the laws of Texas or another state. *Id.* §201.101(1)(E).

2. Record. "Record" means financial or other customer information maintained by a financial institution. Fin. Code §59.001(7).

3. Record request. "Record request" means a valid and enforceable subpoena, request for production, or other instrument issued under authority of a tribunal that compels production of a customer record. Fin. Code §59.001(8).

———————————— ✦ ————————————

4. Tribunal. "Tribunal" means a court or other adjudicatory tribunal with jurisdiction to issue a request for records, including a government agency exercising adjudicatory functions and an alternative-dispute-resolution mechanism, voluntary or required, under which a party may compel the production of records. Fin. Code §59.001(10).

§7.3 Procedure to secure party-customer records.

1. Requesting records. The party requesting records from a financial institution about one of its customers who is a party to the suit must do the following:

(1) Serve the bank with a record request that gives the financial institution at least 24 days to comply with the request. Fin. Code §59.006(b)(1); *see, e.g.*, ***Enviro Prot., Inc. v. National Bank***, 989 S.W.2d 454, 456 (Tex.App.—El Paso 1999, no pet.) (subpoena to produce records from bank not valid because it was not issued with 24 days' notice).

(2) Pay the financial institution's reasonable costs of complying with the record request or post a cost bond in an amount estimated by the financial institution to cover the costs before the financial institution complies with the record request. Fin. Code §59.006(b)(2). Costs include costs of reproduction, postage, research, delivery, and attorney fees. *Id.*

2. Objecting to request. The bank's customer has the burden of preventing or limiting the financial institution's compliance with a record request by seeking an appropriate remedy, including filing a motion to quash the record request or a motion for a protective order. Fin. Code §59.006(e); *see, e.g.*, ***In re Estate of Gaines***, 262 S.W.3d 50, 54 (Tex.App.—Houston [14th Dist.] 2008, no pet.) (bank-account holder filed motion to quash subpoena). Any motion must be served on the financial institution and the requesting party before the date that compliance with the request is required. Fin. Code §59.006(e).

§7.4 Procedure to secure nonparty-customer records.

1. Requesting records. When the financial institution's customer is not a party to the proceeding in which the request was issued, the requesting party must do the following:

(1) Serve the financial institution with a record request. See "Requesting records," §7.3.1, this page.

(2) Pay the financial institution's reasonable costs. See "Requesting records," §7.3.1, this page.

(3) Give notice to the nonparty-customer stating the customer's rights under Finance Code §59.006(e), and serve a copy of the request on the customer under TRCP 21a. Fin. Code §59.006(c)(1).

(4) File with the tribunal and the financial institution a certificate of service indicating that the nonparty-customer was mailed or served with the notice and a copy of the record request. *Id.* §59.006(c)(2).

(5) Request the nonparty-customer's written consent authorizing the financial institution to comply with the request. *Id.* §59.006(c)(3).

2. Objecting to request. The nonparty-customer's procedure to object is to withhold written consent authorizing the financial institution to comply with the request. *See* Fin. Code §59.006(d) (sole means of obtaining access to records of nonparty is to file motion seeking in camera inspection).

3. Procedure to compel disclosure for nonparty-customer records.

(1) **File motion for in camera review.** When a nonparty-customer refuses to give consent or does not respond to the request under Finance Code §59.006(c)(3) by the date for compliance, the sole means of obtaining access to the requested record is for the requesting party to file a written motion seeking an in camera inspection of the requested record by the court. Fin. Code §59.006(d).

(2) **Court inspection.** In response to a motion for in camera inspection, the court may inspect the requested record to determine its relevance to the matter before the tribunal. Fin. Code §59.006(d). The tribunal may order redaction of parts of the record that it determines should not be produced. *Id.* The court must sign a protective

★

order preventing the record from being disclosed to a person who is not a party to the proceeding and from being used for any purpose other than resolving the dispute before the court. *Id.*

§7.5 Deadline to produce.

1. Party-customer. The financial institution must produce the records of a party within 24 days after receiving the record request, as provided by Finance Code §59.006(b). Fin. Code §59.006(f)(1).

2. Nonparty-customer. The financial institution must produce the records of a nonparty before the later of the following:

(1) The 15th day after receiving a customer consent to disclose a record. Fin. Code §59.006(f)(2).

(2) If the nonparty-customer did not sign a consent, the 15th day after the date a court ordered production of the records. *Id.* §59.006(f)(3).

§7.6 No interlocutory appeal.
By statute, an order to quash or for protection or other remedy granted or denied by the tribunal under Finance Code §59.006(d) or (e) is not a final order and is not subject to an interlocutory appeal. Fin. Code §59.006(g).

§7.7 Exemptions.
Finance Code §59.006 does not create a right of privacy in a customer record. Fin. Code §59.006(a); *Martin v. Darnell*, 960 S.W.2d 838, 843 (Tex.App.—Amarillo 1997, orig. proceeding) (citing statutory language from former CPRC §30.007(b)). Section 59.006 does not apply to and does not require or authorize a financial institution to give a customer notice of the following:

1. A demand or inquiry from a state or federal government agency authorized by law to conduct an examination of the financial institution. Fin. Code §59.006(a)(1).

2. A record request from a state or federal government agency or instrumentality under statutory or administrative authority that provides for, or is accompanied by, a specific mechanism for discovery and protection of a financial institution's customer record, including a record request from a federal agency subject to the Right to Financial Privacy Act of 1978, 12 U.S.C. §3401 et seq., as amended, or from the IRS under §1205, Internal Revenue Code of 1986. Fin. Code §59.006(a)(2).

3. A record request from or report to a government agency arising from the investigation or prosecution of a criminal offense or the investigation of alleged abuse, neglect, or exploitation of an elderly or disabled person in accordance with Human Resources Code ch. 48. Fin. Code §59.006(a)(3).

4. A record request in connection with a garnishment proceeding in which the financial institution is the garnishee and the customer is the debtor. Fin. Code §59.006(a)(4).

5. A record request by a duly appointed receiver for the customer. *Id.* §59.006(a)(5).

6. An investigative demand or inquiry from a state legislative investigating committee. *Id.* §59.006(a)(6).

7. An investigative demand or inquiry from the Texas Attorney General as authorized by law other than the procedural law governing discovery in civil cases. *Id.* §59.006(a)(7).

8. The voluntary use or disclosure of a record by a financial institution subject to other applicable state or federal law. *Id.* §59.006(a)(8).

§8. USING REQUESTED DOCUMENTS

§8.1 Offering documents.
To use a document produced in response to a request for or notice of production, the party offering the document must prove its authenticity and its admissibility.

1. Self-authenticating. A party's production of a document in response to written discovery authenticates the document for use against that party in any pretrial proceeding or at trial, unless the producing party timely objects to the document's authenticity. TRCP 193.7. See "Objection to authenticity," §8.3.1, p. 575. Authentication, however, does not establish admissibility. TRCP 193 cmt. 7; *see* TRE 901(a).

———————————— ✦ ————————————

    2. Admissibility. To use a document produced in response to a request for or notice of production, the party offering the document must prove it is admissible, lay the proper predicate for its admission, offer it into evidence, and get the court to rule on its admissibility. *See* TRE 104, 105, 402. See "Introducing Evidence," ch. 8-C, p. 698. Just because a document was produced by the other party in discovery does not mean the document is admissible. For example, although an insurance policy is discoverable, it is generally not admissible. TRE 411.

    §8.2 Using the response. When relevant to the suit, a party may read into evidence the other party's response to the request for documents. *See, e.g.*, ***Wal-Mart Stores v. Cordova***, 856 S.W.2d 768, 772 (Tex.App.—El Paso 1993, writ denied) (on rebuttal, P read into evidence D's response that D had no safety manual at the time of the accident).

    §8.3 Objections to documents.

    1. Objection to authenticity. A party may object, either in writing or on the record, to the authenticity of all or part of a document it produced in discovery. TRCP 193.7. The objection must be made within ten days after the party had actual notice the document would be used. *Id.* In appropriate circumstances, the court can alter the ten-day period. TRCP 193 cmt. 7. The objection to authenticity must specify the basis for the objection and must have a good-faith factual and legal basis. TRCP 193.7. An objection made to the authenticity of part of a document does not affect the authenticity of the remainder. *Id.* Once an objection is made, the court must permit the party attempting to use the document a reasonable opportunity to establish its authenticity. *Id.*

PRACTICE TIP

To avoid complications about authenticity at trial, a party should ask the court to require in its pretrial order that the parties identify all the documents they intend to offer at trial. This will trigger the obligation to object to authenticity and the ability to "snap back" an inadvertently produced privileged document. TRCP 193 cmt. 7; see TRCP 193.3(d). See "Exhibits," ch. 5-A, §3.9.3, p. 317.

---

    2. Other objections to documents. To object to a document produced in response to a request for or notice of production, see "Objecting to Evidence," ch. 8-D, p. 708.

§9. REVIEW

For the rules and forms for prosecuting or responding to an appeal or original proceeding, see *O'Connor's Texas Civil Appeals* (2012).

    §9.1 Record. If the court rules that documents presented for an in camera inspection under seal are not discoverable, the party that was denied discovery of the documents must make sure the documents are transferred under seal to the appellate court to permit the appellate court to evaluate them. ***Pope v. Stephenson***, 787 S.W.2d 953, 954 (Tex.1990).

    §9.2 Appeal or mandamus? See "Review of Discovery Orders," ch. 6-A, §26, p. 458.

★

J. MEDICAL RECORDS

§1. GENERAL

§1.1 Rules. TRCP 194.2(j), (k), 204; TRE 509(e)(4), 510(d)(5). See Occ. Code §159.002(b); Health & Safety Code §§241.151(2), 241.152.

§1.2 Purpose. The discovery rules provide two procedures specific to the discovery of medical records: a written request for disclosure and a motion to examine the person. The parties may also use all the other traditional methods of discovery: a request for production, a notice of deposition with a notice to the party to bring the medical records, and a deposition on written questions of a records custodian.

§1.3 Forms. See *O'Connor's Texas Civil Forms* (2012), FORMS 6J.

§1.4 Other references. Fineberg & Shore, *Discovery Update*, Advanced Civil Trial Course, State Bar of Texas CLE, ch. 1, §IV.A.2, p. 24 (2001); Griesel, *The "New" Texas Discovery Rules: Three Years Later*, Advanced Evidence & Discovery Course, State Bar of Texas CLE, ch. 2, §XVIII, p. 31 (2002).

§2. SCOPE

A party may discover the medical records of any person who is claiming physical or mental injury arising from the event that is the subject of the suit. TRCP 194.2(j). See "Certain physician-patient information," ch. 6-B, §2.18, p. 468; "Certain mental-health information," ch. 6-B, §2.19, p. 469; "Certain medical matters under TRCP 204," ch. 6-B, §2.20, p. 469; "Certain medical requests under Family Code," ch. 6-B, §2.21, p. 469.

§3. REQUEST FOR PARTY'S MEDICAL RECORDS OR AUTHORIZATION

§3.1 Request for disclosure of medical records or for authorization. In a suit alleging physical or mental injury and damages, a party may request that the injured party either produce all relevant medical records and bills or furnish an authorization permitting the disclosure of those medical records. TRCP 194.2(j). The request should be made as part of a TRCP 194 request for disclosure. TRCP 194.1. See "Medical records," ch. 6-E, §3.2.1(9), p. 517.

§3.2 Medical authorization.

1. Disclosure from hospital. A party may serve a written request for the injured party to sign a medical authorization permitting a hospital to disclose the party's medical records. *See* Health & Safety Code §241.152. A medical authorization is valid for 180 days after the date it is signed, unless it provides otherwise or is revoked. *Id.* §241.152(c), (d).

(1) Requirements. An authorization must (1) be in writing, (2) be dated and signed by the patient or legal representative, (3) identify the information to be disclosed, (4) describe the purpose of the requested disclosure, (5) identify the person or entity authorized to make the requested disclosure, (6) identify the person or entity to whom the information is to be disclosed, (7) include the expiration date or expiration event of the authorization, and (8) be contained in a separate document from the one that contains the consent to medical treatment obtained from the patient. *See* 45 C.F.R. §164.508(b) (authorizations generally); Health & Safety Code §241.152(b) (authorization for hospital to disclose information).

NOTE

Federal law requires that all medical authorizations contain statements that place the patient or legal representative on notice of (1) her right to revoke the authorization in writing, (2) the ability or inability to condition treatment, payment, enrollment, or eligibility for benefits on the authorization, and (3) the potential for the disclosed information to be redisclosed and no longer protected. 45 C.F.R. §164.508(b). These notice statements are designed to cover authorizations requested for a variety of reasons, not just for the disclosure of medical records. Although they are not applicable to every situation, they should be included in all authorizations nonetheless.

— ★ —

(2) Providing records. The hospital or its agent must provide copies of the medical records within 15 days after the request and payment for reasonable fees are received. Health & Safety Code §241.154(a). The hospital or its agent is permitted to charge fees as set out in Health & Safety Code §241.154(b).

2. Disclosure from other health-care provider or entity. A party may serve a written request for the injured party to sign a medical authorization permitting a health-care provider or entity other than a hospital to disclose the party's medical records. *See* 45 C.F.R. §164.508(a). The authorization must (1) be dated and signed by the patient or legal representative, and if signed by a representative, describe the representative's authority to act for the patient, (2) identify the information to be disclosed, (3) describe the purpose of the requested disclosure, (4) identify the person or entity authorized to make the requested disclosure, (5) identify the person or entity to whom the information is to be disclosed, and (6) include the expiration date or expiration event of the authorization. *Id.* §164.508(b). The authorization must also contain certain notice statements. See "Note," §3.2.1(1), p. 576.

3. No ex parte discovery. A party should consider adding to a medical authorization a statement that the patient does not authorize any health-care professional to discuss the patient's treatment with anyone outside the presence of the patient's attorney. *In re Trostel*, No. 05-00-02059-CV (Tex.App.—Dallas 2001, orig. proceeding) (no pub.; 6-15-01). See "Discovery from treating doctors," ch. 6-D, §3.1.2(3), p. 505.

§3.3 Health-care-liability claim. In a suit asserting a health-care-liability claim, the parties are entitled to obtain copies of the claimant's medical records from any other party in possession of the records within 45 days after receiving a written request for the records. CPRC §74.051(d).

§3.4 Order compelling production. An order compelling the release of medical records must be restricted to maintain the confidentiality of records not relevant to the underlying suit. *Groves v. Gabriel*, 874 S.W.2d 660, 661 (Tex.1994); *see* TRCP 196.1(c)(3). The order must meet the standard set out in *Mutter v. Wood*, 744 S.W.2d 600, 601 (Tex.1988). Depending on the circumstances, *Mutter* may require a time limitation on disclosure. *Groves*, 874 S.W.2d at 661.

§4. REQUEST TO PARTY FOR NONPARTY'S MEDICAL RECORDS

§4.1 Service on nonparty. When a party requests that another party produce a nonparty's medical records, the requesting party must serve the nonparty with the request for production under TRCP 21a unless (1) the nonparty signed a release that is effective for the requesting party, (2) the identity of the nonparty will not be disclosed, either directly or indirectly, by production of the records, or (3) the court orders that service is not required based on good cause. TRCP 196.1(c)(1), (c)(2), 205.3(c); *see also In re Columbia Valley Reg'l Med. Ctr.*, 41 S.W.3d 797, 800-02 (Tex.App.—Corpus Christi 2001, orig. proceeding) (redaction of information does not defeat medical privilege).

§4.2 Confidentiality. Production of a nonparty's medical records under TRCP 196.1(c) is subject to the laws concerning confidentiality of medical and mental-health records. TRCP 196.1(c)(3); *In re Columbia Valley Reg'l Med. Ctr.*, 41 S.W.3d 797, 800 (Tex.App.—Corpus Christi 2001, orig. proceeding). See "Certain medical records under HIPAA," ch. 6-B, §2.22, p. 470. TRCP 196.1(c) does not expand the scope of discovery of a nonparty's medical records. TRCP 196 cmt. 8; *In re Columbia Valley*, 41 S.W.3d at 800. See "Certain physician-patient information," ch. 6-B, §2.18, p. 468; "Physician-patient privilege," ch. 6-B, §3.10, p. 476.

§5. MOTION TO EXAMINE THE PERSON

§5.1 Motion. To request a mental or physical examination under TRCP 204.1, the movant must file a motion for an order compelling the examination of the person. See *O'Connor's Texas Forms*, FORM 6J:2. The examination under TRCP 204.1 is limited to a party or a person in the custody or conservatorship or under the legal control of a party. TRCP 204.1(a).

1. Elements. The court may issue an order for examination only when (1) the movant shows good cause, and (2) either (a) the mental or physical condition of a party, or of a person under the legal control of a party, is in controversy, or (b) the party responding to the motion designated a psychologist as a testifying expert or disclosed a psychologist's records for possible use at trial. TRCP 204.1(c); *In re Transwestern Publ'g Co.*, 96 S.W.3d 501, 504-05 (Tex.App.—Fort Worth 2002, orig. proceeding).

★

(1) Good cause. There must be good cause for the examination. TRCP 204.1(c); *Coates v. Whittington*, 758 S.W.2d 749, 753 (Tex.1988). "Good cause" requires a showing of each of the following components:

(a) The examination is relevant to the genuine issues. *Coates*, 758 S.W.2d at 753. The movant must show that the examination will produce or is likely to lead to evidence relevant to the case. *Id.*; *see, e.g.*, *In re Caballero*, 36 S.W.3d 143, 145 (Tex.App.—Corpus Christi 2000, orig. proceeding) (mandamus to compel physical examination denied because Ds were unable to articulate why examination would shed any light on P's condition before hysterectomy).

(b) There is a reasonable connection between the condition in controversy and the examination sought. *Coates*, 758 S.W.2d at 753.

(c) It is not possible to obtain the information sought through some other, less-intrusive means. *Id.*; *e.g.*, *In re Caballero*, 36 S.W.3d at 145 (mandamus denied because Ds did not show information was not available through less-intrusive means).

(2) In controversy. The movant may show that the mental or physical condition (including the blood type) of a party, or of a person in the custody or conservatorship or under the legal control of a party, is in controversy. TRCP 204.1(c)(1); *In re Transwestern*, 96 S.W.3d at 504-05; *see In re M.A.C.*, 49 S.W.3d 923, 924 (Tex.App.—Beaumont 2001, pet. granted, judgm't vacated w.r.m.); *Coates*, 758 S.W.2d at 750-51. The requirement for showing a condition is "in controversy" may be satisfied by a party's pleadings or by proof.

(a) Pleading "in controversy."

[1] Objecting party's pleadings. A condition may be in controversy if the party objecting to the examination made it an issue by pleading the condition in support of or in defense of its position. *See, e.g.*, *Laub v. Millard*, 925 S.W.2d 363, 364-65 (Tex.App.—Houston [1st Dist.] 1996, orig. proceeding) (in suit to set aside gifts, P pleaded statute of limitations was tolled because she was incompetent); *Crouch v. Gleason*, 875 S.W.2d 738, 740 (Tex.App.—Amarillo 1994, orig. proceeding) (in contract dispute, P alleged D exploited P's mental weakness); *Beamon v. O'Neill*, 865 S.W.2d 583, 586 (Tex.App.—Houston [14th Dist.] 1993, orig. proceeding) (in PI suit, P put physical condition in controversy); *Exxon Corp. v. Starr*, 790 S.W.2d 883, 887 (Tex.App.—Tyler 1990, orig. proceeding) (P claimed severe mental injury and designated psychological experts). A party's mental condition is not in controversy just because the party makes a routine request for damages for mental anguish or emotional distress. *Coates*, 758 S.W.2d at 753; *see, e.g.*, *In re Doe*, 22 S.W.3d 601, 607-08 (Tex.App.—Austin 2000, orig. proceeding) (court abused discretion in ordering mental examination in PI suit alleging sexual assault). A party's state of mind is not equivalent to a mental condition. *E.g.*, *Amis v. Ashworth*, 802 S.W.2d 374, 378 (Tex.App.—Tyler 1990, orig. proceeding) (mental-health professional not permitted to examine party based on pleadings of self-defense).

[2] Movant's pleadings. The condition may be in controversy if the movant put it in controversy by pleading the condition in support of or in defense of its position. *See, e.g.*, *Coates*, 758 S.W.2d at 752 (D's allegations of contributory negligence did not justify examination of P); *Spear v. Gayle*, 857 S.W.2d 122, 125 (Tex. App.—Houston [1st Dist.] 1993, orig. proceeding) (P's allegations that D was negligent in failing to seek help to cure psychosexual disorder did not put D's mental health in controversy).

(b) Proof of "in controversy." If the parties' pleadings did not put a party's mental or physical condition in controversy, the movant must provide evidence showing it is in controversy. *E.g.*, *Walsh v. Ferguson*, 712 S.W.2d 885, 887 (Tex.App.—Austin 1986, orig. proceeding) (examination not permitted in divorce because husband did not assert his mental or physical condition in support or in defense of his position, and wife did not offer any proof at hearing).

(3) Other party's psychologist. Instead of showing the condition is "in controversy," a movant may show the other party identified a psychologist as a testifying expert or disclosed a psychologist's records for possible use at trial. TRCP 204.1(c)(2). The movant must still demonstrate good cause. TRCP 204.1(c); *In re Transwestern*, 96 S.W.3d at 504-05. This provision does not apply in cases under Family Code title 2 or 5. TRCP 204.1(c)(2). See "In Family Code matters," §5.4.1(2), p. 579.

―――――――――――――――――― ✦ ――――――――――――――――――

2. Physician. The motion should suggest a physician or psychologist who will conduct the examination. *See* TRCP 204.1(d) (order must identify person to perform examination); ***Employers Mut. Cas. Co. v. Street***, 702 S.W.2d 779, 780-81 (Tex.App.—Fort Worth 1986, orig. proceeding) (moving party does not have absolute right to choose examining physician; trial court has discretion to choose neutral physician to conduct examination).

3. Time to serve motion for examination. A motion requesting a physical or mental examination may be served anytime after suit is filed. TRCP 190.2(c)(1), 190.3(b)(1). The deadline to serve the motion is 30 days before the end of the discovery period. TRCP 204.1(a). See "Discovery Periods," ch. 6-A, §8, p. 433. When served by mail or fax, the motion should be served at least 34 days before the end of the discovery period. See "Deadline to Respond to Discovery," ch. 6-A, §14, p. 437.

4. Notice. The party seeking the examination must give notice to all parties and to the person to be examined. TRCP 204.1(b).

5. Hearing request. The party seeking discovery must ask for and secure a hearing on the motion. TRCP 204.1 (requires motion, notice, showing of good cause, and order). If there is no hearing, the request for examination is waived.

§5.2 Hearing. The court must conduct a hearing on a motion made under TRCP 204. At the hearing, the movant must present evidence. ***Walsh v. Ferguson***, 712 S.W.2d 885, 887 (Tex.App.—Austin 1986, orig. proceeding). If the court grants the motion without receiving evidence at the hearing, the appellate court will find that the trial court abused its discretion and will reverse. *See id.*

§5.3 Order. The order must (1) be in writing, (2) identify the person to be examined, (3) specify the time, place, manner, conditions, and scope of the examination, and (4) identify the person or persons to make the examination. TRCP 204.1(d). See *O'Connor's Texas Forms*, FORM 6J:4.

§5.4 Examination.

1. Medical professional.

(1) In most cases. A qualified physician may conduct a mental or physical examination. TRCP 204.1(a)(1). A psychologist may conduct a mental examination if the party responding to the motion identified a psychologist as a testifying expert or disclosed a psychologist's records for possible use at trial. TRCP 204.1(c)(2). A vocational rehabilitation specialist is not a physician or a psychologist and cannot conduct an examination. *See* TRCP 204.5; ***Moore v. Wood***, 809 S.W.2d 621, 624 (Tex.App.—Houston [1st Dist.] 1991, orig. proceeding) (construing former TRCP 167a(a)). *But see* TRCP 191 cmt. 1 (trial court may order, or parties may agree to, discovery methods other than those prescribed in the rules).

(2) In Family Code matters. In cases arising under title 2 or 5 of the Family Code, TRCP 204.4 provides that the court on a party's motion or on its own initiative may appoint the following:

(a) A psychiatrist or psychologist to make mental examinations of any children who are the subject of the suit, or of any other parties. TRCP 204.4(a).

(b) A nonphysician expert qualified in paternity testing to take blood and other bodily fluids to conduct tests in paternity disputes. TRCP 204.4(b); *see also* Fam. Code §§160.501-160.511 (genetic testing).

2. Attendance of attorney. The trial court has the discretion to permit or prohibit a party's attorney from attending the person's examination. ***Simmons v. Thompson***, 900 S.W.2d 403, 404 (Tex.App.—Texarkana 1995, orig. proceeding) (physical examination). Because the medical professional conducting the examination is chosen by the adverse party, the party's attorney should probably be permitted to attend. *See id.* (Grant, J., dissenting).

§6. USING MEDICAL RECORDS

§6.1 Medical records. Medical records may be introduced into evidence by a custodian who testifies by affidavit or in person that the records are kept in the course of regularly conducted business activity. TRE 803(6), (7), 902(10). See "Business record by witness," ch. 8-C, §8.4.3(8), p. 706; "Business record by affidavit," ch. 8-C, §8.4.4(1), p. 707.

★

§6.2 Physical or mental examination. If a physical or mental examination was ordered under TRCP 204, the parties may introduce the testimony of the doctor or medical professional who conducted the examination, either by deposition or as a live witness. *See* TRCP 204.2(b). Mental-health information is discoverable if it was disclosed by a patient during a court-ordered examination, and the judge finds that the patient was told the communication would not be privileged. TRE 510(d)(4).

§6.3 Refusal to make a report. If a physician or psychologist does not make a report required by court order, the court may exclude the testimony if offered at trial. TRCP 204.2(a).

§6.4 Effect of no examination. If no examination is sought under TRCP 204, the party whose condition is in controversy cannot comment to the fact-finder that she was willing to submit to an examination or that the other party did not seek an examination. TRCP 204.3. The primary purpose of TRCP 204.3 is to ensure that the defendant is not penalized for not seeking a physical examination. *Parkway Hosp., Inc. v. Lee*, 946 S.W.2d 580, 585 (Tex. App.—Houston [14th Dist.] 1997, writ denied) (interpreting former TRCP 167a(c)), *disapproved on other grounds*, *Roberts v. Williamson*, 111 S.W.3d 113 (Tex.2003).

§7. REVIEW

See "Review of Discovery Orders," ch. 6-A, §26, p. 458. For the rules and forms for prosecuting or responding to an appeal or original proceeding, see *O'Connor's Texas Civil Appeals* (2012).

K. ENTRY ON LAND

§1. GENERAL

§1.1 Rules. TRCP 196.7.

§1.2 Purpose. A request or motion for entry on land allows a party to gain entry to land to inspect, measure, survey, photograph, test, and sample the property or any designated object or operation on the property. TRCP 196.7(a).

§1.3 Forms. See *O'Connor's Texas Civil Forms* (2012), FORMS 6K.

§1.4 Other references. Griesel, *The "New" Texas Discovery Rules: Three Years Later*, Advanced Evidence & Discovery Course, State Bar of Texas CLE, ch. 2, §X, p. 22 (2002).

§2. SCOPE

The scope of discovery for entry on land is governed by TRCP 196.7. The rules of discovery do not entitle a party to gain entry to another's property to reenact an event that is the basis of the suit. *Amis v. Ashworth*, 802 S.W.2d 374, 377 (Tex.App.—Tyler 1990, orig. proceeding). See "Scope of Discovery," ch. 6-B, p. 460.

§3. REQUEST TO ENTER LAND OF A PARTY

A party may gain entry on the land of another party by serving a request on all parties; a motion to the court is not required. TRCP 196.7(a)(1). A party is not entitled to trespass on another party's property to conduct an investigation or inspection without first serving a request under TRCP 196.7(a). *Schenck v. Ebby Halliday Real Estate, Inc.*, 803 S.W.2d 361, 372 (Tex.App.—Fort Worth 1990, no writ).

§3.1 The request. To gain entry on land of another party, the party must serve a request, which should include the following: (1) the identification of the land or other property in the possession or control of the party, (2) the particulars about the inspection—the time, place, manner, condition, and scope of the inspection, (3) a specific description of the desired means, manner, and procedure for testing or sampling (i.e., to inspect, measure, survey, photograph, test, or sample property), and (4) the identity of the person or persons who are to conduct the inspection, testing, or sampling. TRCP 196.7(a), (b). The test cannot materially alter or destroy the thing to be examined. TRCP 196.5; *General Motors Corp. v. Tanner*, 892 S.W.2d 862, 863-64 (Tex.1995). See *O'Connor's Texas Forms*, FORM 6K:1.

✯

---

§3.2 Deadline. A request for entry on land may be served anytime after suit is filed. TRCP 190.2(c)(1), 190.3(b)(1). The deadline to serve the request is 30 days before the end of the discovery period. TRCP 196.7(a). See "Discovery Periods," ch. 6-A, §8, p. 433. When served by mail or fax, the request should be served at least 34 days before the end of the discovery period. TRCP 196.7(a).

§3.3 Response.

1. Time to respond. Generally, a party has 30 days after the date of service of a request to enter land to respond to the request, depending on the type of service. TRCP 196.7(c)(1). When a request is served on a defendant before the defendant's answer is due, the defendant has 50 days after service of the request to respond. *Id.* See "Deadline to Respond to Discovery," ch. 6-A, §14, p. 437. To extend the time, see "Extending Time to Respond to Discovery," ch. 6-A, §15, p. 438.

2. Contents of response. In response to a request for entry on land, a party must assert its objections and claims of privilege and then state one of the following: (1) entry will be permitted as requested, (2) entry will be permitted with certain conditions or limitations, (3) entry will be permitted at a different time or place, as specified in the response, or (4) entry will not be permitted. TRCP 196.7(c)(2). If entry will not be permitted, the party must state its reasons in the response. TRCP 196.7(c)(2)(C). See *O'Connor's Texas Forms*, FORM 6K:2.

§4. MOTION TO ENTER LAND OF A NONPARTY

A party may gain entry on the land of a nonparty by filing a motion, requesting a hearing, and obtaining an order. TRCP 196.7(a)(2), (b).

§4.1 Motion. To gain entry on the land of a nonparty, the party must file a motion. The motion should include the following: (1) good cause, (2) the relevance of entry to the lawsuit, (3) the scope of the inspection, (4) the desired means, manner, and procedure for testing or sampling, (5) who will conduct the inspection, testing, or sampling, and (6) a request for a hearing. TRCP 196.7(a)(2), (b), (d); *see In re SWEPI L.P.*, 103 S.W.3d 578, 583 (Tex. App.—San Antonio 2003, orig. proceeding) (good cause, relevance). See *O'Connor's Texas Forms*, FORM 6K:3.

§4.2 Deadline. The deadline to serve a motion for entry on the land of a nonparty is 30 days before the end of the discovery period. TRCP 196.7(a); *see In re SWEPI L.P.*, 103 S.W.3d 578, 583 (Tex.App.—San Antonio 2003, orig. proceeding). See "Discovery Periods," ch. 6-A, §8, p. 433. When served by mail or fax, the request should be served at least 34 days before the end of the discovery period. *See* TRCP 21a, 196.7(a).

§4.3 Notice & hearing. The party seeking entry on the land of a nonparty must give notice to the nonparty and all the parties and request a hearing. TRCP 196.7(a)(2).

§4.4 Response. The nonparty has the following options:

1. Comply. The nonparty may inform the party requesting entry that it has no objection to the motion.

2. Object. The nonparty may inform the party requesting entry that it objects to the motion requesting entry. See *O'Connor's Texas Forms*, FORM 6K:4. Once the requesting party learns that the nonparty will not permit entry, the party must request a hearing.

3. Move for protective order. The nonparty may file a motion for protective order under TRCP 192.6 to protect itself from undue burden, unnecessary expense, harassment, annoyance, or invasion of personal, constitutional, or property rights. See "Motion for Protective Order," ch. 6-A, §20, p. 449.

§4.5 Hearing. The court cannot sign an order requiring inspection of the property of a nonparty without a hearing. TRCP 196.7(a)(2). At the hearing, the parties and the nonparty may assert objections. *See* TRCP 176.6(d).

§4.6 Order. The order for entry on a nonparty's property should include the following: (1) identification of the property and its owner, (2) good cause, (3) a statement that the land or property or an object on it is relevant to the subject matter of the action, (4) the time, place, manner, conditions, and scope of the inspection, (5) a description

★

of any desired means, manner, and procedure for testing or sampling, and (6) a list of the persons performing the inspection, testing, or sampling. TRCP 196.7(b), (d). See *O'Connor's Texas Forms*, FORM 6K:5.

§5. USING EVIDENCE AT TRIAL

To introduce the inspection, measurement, survey, photograph, results of a test, or samples of the land, the party offering the evidence must prove that it is admissible, lay the proper predicate for its admission, offer it into evidence, and get the court to rule on its admissibility. *See* TRE 104, 105, 402. Just because information was gained in response to a request or motion for entry on land does not mean it is admissible.

NOTE

If a party attempts to introduce evidence about property gained by trespass, the court should exclude it. **Schenck v. Ebby Halliday Real Estate, Inc.***, 803 S.W.2d 361, 372-73 (Tex.App.— Fort Worth 1990, no writ) (testimony of appraiser);* **Day & Zimmermann, Inc. v. Strickland***, 483 S.W.2d 541, 546-47 (Tex.App.—Texarkana 1972, writ ref'd n.r.e.) (testimony of architect).*

---

§6. REVIEW

See "Review of Discovery Orders," ch. 6-A, §26, p. 458. For the rules and forms for prosecuting or responding to an appeal or original proceeding, see *O'Connor's Texas Civil Appeals* (2012).

✦

---

7. DISPOSITION WITHOUT TRIAL

A. DEFAULT JUDGMENT

§1. GENERAL

§1.1 Rules. TRCP 99, 106, 107, 124, 239-241, 243, 245, 252, 306, 320, 321, 329. See TRAP 26.1, 30.

§1.2 Purpose. A default judgment permits the trial court to render judgment for the plaintiff without a traditional trial. Only a plaintiff is entitled to a default judgment; a default judgment cannot be rendered for a defendant on the merits of its answer. *Freeman v. Freeman*, 327 S.W.2d 428, 431 (Tex.1959), *disapproved on other grounds*, *Mapco, Inc. v. Forrest*, 795 S.W.2d 700 (Tex.1990); *State v. Herrera*, 25 S.W.3d 326, 327-28 (Tex.App.—Austin 2000, no pet.). When a plaintiff does not appear at trial, the proper remedy is dismissal of the suit for want of prosecution, not a default judgment. *Smock v. Fischel*, 207 S.W.2d 891, 892 (Tex.1948); *Leeper v. Haynsworth*, 179 S.W.3d 742, 745 (Tex.App.—El Paso 2005, no pet.). See "Involuntary Dismissal," ch. 7-G, p. 658.

§1.3 Timetables & forms. Timetable, Pretrial Motions, p. 1216; Timetable, No-Answer Default Judgment, p. 1225; *O'Connor's Texas Civil Forms* (2012), FORMS 7A, 9C:2, 9C:3.

§1.4 Other references. Dyer, *A Practical Guide to the Equitable Bill of Review*, 10 J. Consumer & Commercial L. 104 (2007); Hodges, *Collateral Attacks on Judgments*, 41 Tex.L.Rev. 163 (1962); Miller, *Misnomers: Default Judgments & Strict Compliance with Service of Process Rules*, 46 Baylor L.Rev. 633 (1994); Pendery et al., *Dealing with Default Judgments*, 35 St. Mary's L.J. 1 (2003); *O'Connor's Texas Causes of Action* (2013) (*O'Connor's Texas COA*); *O'Connor's Texas Civil Appeals* (2012) (*O'Connor's Texas Appeals*).

§2. TYPES OF DEFAULT JUDGMENTS

Default judgments can be conveniently divided into two types—those rendered before the defendant files an answer to the lawsuit (no-answer default) and those rendered after the defendant files an answer (post-answer default). The major distinction is that in a no-answer default case, the defendant admits all of the plaintiff's allegations except unliquidated damages. In contrast, in a post-answer default case, the defendant denies the allegations in the plaintiff's petition and the plaintiff must prove all the elements of its claims. See "No-Answer Default," §3, p. 588; "Post-Answer Default," §4, p. 596.

7-1. COMPARISON OF DEFAULT JUDGMENTS		
	No-answer default	**Post-answer default**
1	Court can grant default judgment without a hearing, except for unliquidated damages.	Court cannot grant default judgment without a hearing.
2	Default constitutes admission by D of allegations in P's pleadings, except for unliquidated damages.	Default does not constitute admission by D of P's claims or abandonment of D's defenses.
3	P must prove unliquidated damages and causal nexus.	P must prove all elements of cause of action and damages, as in a trial on the merits.
4	D does not waive pleading defects.	D waives pleading defects unless D filed special exceptions.
5	D has no right to notice of hearing unless D files answer before final judgment rendered.	D has right to notice of hearing or trial.
6	D has no right to participate unless D files answer or makes appearance before hearing on unliquidated damages.	D has right to participate if D makes appearance.
7	If D files answer requesting jury after default judgment rendered but before hearing on damages, D is entitled to jury trial on damages alone; if D does not make appearance, D waives right to jury.	If jury trial was requested before default, D has right to jury if D makes appearance; if D does not make appearance, D waives right to jury.

★

7-1. COMPARISON OF DEFAULT JUDGMENTS (CONTINUED)		
	No-answer default	Post-answer default
8	P must file certificate of last known address and servicemembers' affidavit.	P is not required to file certificate of last known address or servicemembers' affidavit.
9	Sufficiency of service of process on D is an issue; default judgment will be set aside if service defective.	Sufficiency of service is not an issue because D has answered.

§3. NO-ANSWER DEFAULT

A no-answer default judgment can be rendered when the defendant does not file an answer. Before taking a default judgment, the plaintiff should confirm that the petition, the citation, the service, and the return are adequate to support a default judgment. If the plaintiff amends, it may need to re-serve the defendant before taking a default.

§3.1 Effect of defendant's failure to answer. The court may render a default judgment on the pleadings against a defendant that has not filed an answer. TRCP 239. When a defendant does not file an answer, all allegations of facts—including those establishing liability—in the plaintiff's petition are deemed admitted except for the amount of unliquidated damages. *Paradigm Oil, Inc. v. Retamco Oper., Inc.*, 372 S.W.3d 177, 183 (Tex.2012); *Jackson v. Biotectronics, Inc.*, 937 S.W.2d 38, 41 (Tex.App.—Houston [14th Dist.] 1996, no writ); *see Dolgencorp v. Lerma*, 288 S.W.3d 922, 930 (Tex.2009); *Argyle Mech., Inc. v. Unigus Steel, Inc.*, 156 S.W.3d 685, 687 (Tex.App.—Dallas 2005, no pet.). After a no-answer default, the only claim the plaintiff is required to prove is its claim for unliquidated damages. *Dolgencorp*, 288 S.W.3d at 930; *see* TRCP 243; *Paradigm Oil*, 372 S.W.3d at 183.

§3.2 Sufficiency of plaintiff's petition. The plaintiff's petition will support a default judgment if the petition (1) states a cause of action within the court's jurisdiction, (2) gives fair notice to the defendant of the claim asserted, and (3) does not affirmatively disclose the invalidity of the claim on its face. *Jackson v. Biotectronics, Inc.*, 937 S.W.2d 38, 42 (Tex.App.—Houston [14th Dist.] 1996, no writ); *see Paramount Pipe & Sup. Co. v. Muhr*, 749 S.W.2d 491, 494 (Tex.1988).

13

PROPOSED TRCP CHANGES

In response to Gov't Code §22.004(h), the Supreme Court has proposed TRCP 169 to establish a process for the prompt, efficient, and cost-effective resolution of civil actions (expedited actions) in which only monetary relief is sought and the amount in controversy is no more than $100,000. See Tex.Sup.Ct. Order, Misc. Docket No. 12-9191 (eff. Mar. 1, 2013). The Supreme Court has proposed corresponding amendments to TRCP 47 that would require a party, in an original pleading, to make a more specific statement of the relief sought; that is, the party would have to plead into or out of the expedited-actions process under TRCP 169. See Tex.Sup.Ct. Order, Misc. Docket No. 12-9191 (eff. Mar. 1, 2013). The public-comment period for the proposed amendments ends on February 1, 2013, and the rules are to take effect March 1, 2013. For the proposed version of the rules, see the appendix after this book's index. For the final version, go to the Supreme Court website at www.supreme.courts.state.tx.us. When the new and amended rules take effect, a supplement to this book—with updated rules and commentaries that reflect the changes—will be available at www.JonesMcClure.com/TRCPamendments.

1. Amending the petition.

(1) Adding claims or damages – service required. When, after service of the original petition, the plaintiff amends to ask for a more onerous judgment by adding claims or increasing damages, the plaintiff must serve the defendant with the amended petition before taking a default judgment. *In re E.A.*, 287 S.W.3d 1, 6 (Tex. 2009). The plaintiff does not need to serve the defendant with a new citation. *Id.*

★

NOTE

Service of a new citation is not required when serving a more onerous amended petition on a nonanswering defendant. **In re E.A.**, *287 S.W.3d at 6. The Supreme Court held that TRCP 21a, which applies to all pleadings required to be served under TRCP 21 other than the original petition, does not require the plaintiff to serve a new citation for amended petitions. Id. at 4.*

---

(2) **No additional claims or damages – no service required.** If the amended petition does not add claims or increase damages, it does not need to be re-served. *E.g.,* ***Palomin v. Zarsky Lumber Co.***, 26 S.W.3d 690, 694 (Tex.App.—Corpus Christi 2000, pet. denied) (amended petition made minor change in D's name); ***Halligan v. First Heights, F.S.A.***, 850 S.W.2d 801, 802-03 (Tex.App.—Houston [14th Dist.] 1993, no writ) (amended petition in intervention did not assert new claims or seek additional damages). When the plaintiff amends its petition to delete the TRCP 47(b) allegation (damages are within the jurisdictional limits of the court) and replace it with a specific amount of damages, the amended petition does not increase damages; thus, the plaintiff does not need to serve the defendant with a new citation or the amended petition. ***Henry S. Miller Co. v. Hamilton***, 813 S.W.2d 631, 636 (Tex.App.—Houston [1st Dist.] 1991, no writ).

2. **Variance between pleadings & judgment.** A default judgment must be based on the pleadings. The judgment, therefore, cannot rely on causes of action that are not adequately pleaded or award damages in excess of the damages specifically pleaded. *See* ***Capitol Brick, Inc. v. Fleming Mfg. Co.***, 722 S.W.2d 399, 401 (Tex.1986); ***Gulf States Pet. Corp. v. General Elec. Capital Auto Lease***, 134 S.W.3d 504, 511 (Tex.App.—Eastland 2004, no pet.); ***Simon v. BancTexas Quorum***, 754 S.W.2d 283, 286 (Tex.App.—Dallas 1988, writ denied). There is no variance between the pleadings and the judgment when the court awards damages based on a TRCP 47(b) allegation (damages are within the jurisdictional limits of the court). *See* ***Continental Sav. Ass'n v. Gutheinz***, 718 S.W.2d 377, 383-84 (Tex.App.—Amarillo 1986, writ ref'd n.r.e.).

§3.3 Sufficiency of citation. The citation must strictly comply with TRCP 99. See "Requirements for the Citation," ch. 2-H, §2, p. 158.

§3.4 Sufficiency of service. The face of the record must show strict compliance with the type of service used, but the court is not required to review the entire record to determine proper service. ***All Commercial Floors, Inc. v. Barton & Rasor***, 97 S.W.3d 723, 726 (Tex.App.—Fort Worth 2003, no pet.). See "Serving the Defendant with Suit," ch. 2-H, p. 157. A default judgment cannot withstand a direct attack by a defendant who was not served in strict compliance with the appropriate service rules. ***Wood v. Brown***, 819 S.W.2d 799, 800 (Tex.1991); *see* ***Uvalde Country Club v. Martin Linen Sup. Co.***, 690 S.W.2d 884, 885 (Tex.1985). See "Direct attacks on default judgment," §7.1, p. 598. Actual notice of suit is not a substitute for proper service. ***Wilson v. Dunn***, 800 S.W.2d 833, 836 (Tex. 1990). A default judgment is void unless the defendant (1) was served with process in strict compliance with the law, (2) accepted or waived service, or (3) made an appearance. TRCP 124; ***Min v. Avila***, 991 S.W.2d 495, 500 (Tex. App.—Houston [1st Dist.] 1999, no pet.); *see, e.g.,* ***All Commercial Floors***, 97 S.W.3d at 727 (return not signed by person designated to receive service for corporation; default J void); ***Ackerly v. Ackerly***, 13 S.W.3d 454, 457-58 (Tex.App.—Corpus Christi 2000, no pet.) (docket sheet did not show issue, service, or return of citation; default J void).

§3.5 Sufficiency of return. For the requirements for the return, see "Proof of Service – The Return," ch. 2-H, §9, p. 168.

§3.6 Amending citation & return. The court can permit an amendment to the citation and the return. TRCP 118. See "Amending citation & return," ch. 2-H, §10.2, p. 171.

§3.7 Sufficiency of defendant's answer. An answer, even if defective, places the merits of the plaintiff's case at issue and will prevent a no-answer default judgment if it is filed before the rendition (i.e., the announcement) of

---

✯

---

judgment. When an answer is defective, the plaintiff's remedy is to file special exceptions. See "Special Exceptions—Challenging the Pleadings," ch. 3-G, p. 248.

1. Filing constituted answer. In the following cases, the court found the defendant's filing sufficient to constitute an answer: • Pauper's affidavit. *Hughes v. Habitat Apts.*, 860 S.W.2d 872, 873 (Tex.1993). • Letter from pro se defendant to district clerk in which defendant confirmed he received the citation and provided his current address. *Smith v. Lippmann*, 826 S.W.2d 137, 138 (Tex.1992). • Letter to court acknowledging acceptance of citation and responding to P's allegations. *Guadalupe Econ. Servs. v. DeHoyos*, 183 S.W.3d 712, 716-17 (Tex.App.—Austin 2005, no pet.). • Answer for corporation signed by a nonattorney. *Custom-Crete, Inc. v. K-Bar Servs.*, 82 S.W.3d 655, 657-58 (Tex.App.—San Antonio 2002, no pet.); *Handy Andy, Inc. v. Ruiz*, 900 S.W.2d 739, 741 (Tex. App.—Corpus Christi 1994, writ denied). • Plea in abatement. *Alcala v. Williams*, 908 S.W.2d 54, 56 (Tex. App.—San Antonio 1995, no writ); *Schulz v. Schulz*, 726 S.W.2d 256, 258 (Tex.App.—Austin 1987, no writ). • Letter to court from secretary-treasurer of corporation that contained defendant's address, admitted debt, and made counterclaim. *Santex Roofing & Sheet Metal, Inc. v. Venture Steel, Inc.*, 737 S.W.2d 55, 56-57 (Tex.App.—San Antonio 1987, no writ). • Answer not signed by either the party or the attorney. *Frank v. Corbett*, 682 S.W.2d 587, 588 (Tex.App.—Waco 1984, no writ).

2. Filing did not constitute an answer. In the following cases, the court did not find the defendant's filing sufficient to constitute an answer: • Letter from pro se defendant to plaintiff's attorney that did not have a case heading or certificate of service. *Cotton v. Cotton*, 57 S.W.3d 506, 511-12 (Tex.App.—Waco 2001, no pet.). • Motion for new trial. *First State Bldg. & Loan Ass'n v. B.L. Nelson & Assocs.*, 735 S.W.2d 287, 289 (Tex.App.—Dallas 1987, no writ); *Gonzalez v. Regalado*, 542 S.W.2d 689, 691 (Tex.App.—Waco 1976, writ ref'd n.r.e.). • Motion to transfer venue. *Duplantis v. Noble Toyota, Inc.*, 720 S.W.2d 863, 866 (Tex.App.—Beaumont 1986, no writ).

§3.8 Timeliness of defendant's answer.

1. Before deadline. If the defendant filed an answer before the deadline to answer, the plaintiff cannot obtain a default judgment. *See* TRCP 239. The deadline to file an answer is 10:00 a.m. on the first Monday after 20 days have passed from the date the defendant was served with citation. TRCP 99(b). See "Deadline to Answer," ch. 3-E, §2, p. 227.

2. After deadline. If the defendant filed an answer after the deadline but before the court rendered a default judgment, the court cannot render a default judgment. *E.g.*, *Davis v. Jefferies*, 764 S.W.2d 559, 560 (Tex.1989) (answer filed one day after deadline, but more than two hours before default J was rendered); *Dowell Schlumberger, Inc. v. Jackson*, 730 S.W.2d 818, 819-20 (Tex.App.—El Paso 1987, writ ref'd n.r.e.) (answer filed during default hearing but before court rendered J); *see* TRCP 239. See "Rendition," ch. 9-C, §3.1, p. 765. If an answer is mailed to the clerk before a default judgment is announced, it is considered filed before the judgment is rendered, even if it is not received until after the judgment is signed. *Milam v. Miller*, 891 S.W.2d 1, 2 (Tex.App.—Amarillo 1994, writ ref'd); *Thomas v. Gelber Grp.*, 905 S.W.2d 786, 788-89 (Tex.App.—Houston [14th Dist.] 1995, no writ). See "Mail," ch. 1-C, §4.1, p. 22.

§3.9 Moving for no-answer default judgment.

1. When to move for default.

(1) In most cases. The plaintiff may move for a default judgment when the defendant's deadline to file an answer has expired and the citation and proof of service have been on file with the clerk at least ten days, not counting the day of filing and the day of the judgment. TRCP 107(h); *Union Pac. Corp. v. Legg*, 49 S.W.3d 72, 78 (Tex.App.—Austin 2001, no pet.). See "Filing date," ch. 2-H, §9.4.9, p. 170; "Deadline to Answer," ch. 3-E, §2, p. 227. The plaintiff should move for default as soon as it can because the defendant can prevent a default judgment by filing an answer even if the deadline has passed. See "After deadline," §3.8.2, this page.

★

CAUTION

*If a plaintiff obtains a no-answer default judgment against a defendant who is covered by insurance but the defendant has not notified its carrier according to the notice-of-suit provision in the insurance policy, the carrier may not be liable for the judgment against the defendant. See **Liberty Mut. Ins. v. Cruz**, 883 S.W.2d 164, 165-66 (Tex.1993). Compliance with the notice provision is a condition precedent to the carrier's liability. **Harwell v. State Farm Mut. Auto. Ins.**, 896 S.W.2d 170, 173-74 (Tex.1995); see also **Liberty Mut. Ins.**, 883 S.W.2d at 166 (if insurer knows of suit, it might choose to answer for insured-D and litigate merits of suit). If the carrier is not notified about the suit until after a judgment becomes final and nonappealable, the carrier is prejudiced as a matter of law and is not bound by the judgment against the insured. **Harwell**, 896 S.W.2d at 174-75.*

---

(2) After motion to quash granted. If the court grants a motion to quash service or citation, the plaintiff may move for a default judgment if the defendant does not file an answer by 10:00 a.m. on the first Monday after 20 days from the date the service or citation was quashed. TRCP 122; *Wells v. Southern States Lumber & Sup.*, 720 S.W.2d 227, 228 (Tex.App.—Houston [14th Dist.] 1986, no writ). See "Motion to Quash—Challenging the Service," ch. 3-J, p. 264.

(3) After Secretary of State served. If the Secretary of State was served as the defendant's agent, the period for filing the answer runs from the date the Secretary of State was served, not from the date the Secretary of State forwarded the process to the defendant. *Bonewitz v. Bonewitz*, 726 S.W.2d 227, 230 (Tex.App.—Austin 1987, writ ref'd n.r.e.). The Secretary of State is considered the agent of the defendant for service of process, and service on the Secretary of State is constructive service on the defendant. *Id.* Before taking a default, the plaintiff must obtain a certificate (referred to as a "*Whitney* Certificate") from the Secretary of State certifying compliance with the statute that authorizes substituted service—that is, certifying that process was forwarded to the defendant by certified mail, return receipt requested. *See Whitney v. L&L Rlty. Corp.*, 500 S.W.2d 94, 96 (Tex.1973). The defendant is considered served even if the process is returned to the Secretary of State with a notation that it was refused or unclaimed. See "Proof of service," ch. 2-H, §5.2, p. 164.

(4) After notice to Attorney General. In some suits against the State, the plaintiff must send a notice of intent to take a default to the Attorney General by certified mail, return receipt requested, at least ten days before the entry of the default judgment. CPRC §§30.004(b), 39.001. Before taking a default judgment against the State, any state agency, or any state official or employee, the plaintiff should check the list of persons and entities in CPRC chapter 104 that must be represented by the Attorney General. If the plaintiff does not give the Attorney General notice, the default judgment will be set aside without costs. *Id.* §§30.004(d), 39.002. Whether a plaintiff must give the Attorney General ten days' notice before taking a post-answer default judgment against the State has not been decided. *See Director, State Empls. Workers' Comp. Div. v. Evans*, 889 S.W.2d 266, 267 n.1 (Tex.1994).

(5) No default after service by publication. There is no procedure in Texas for a default judgment when service is by publication. *McCarthy v. Jesperson*, 527 S.W.2d 825, 826 (Tex.App.—El Paso 1975, no writ). Instead, the plaintiff must follow the unique trial procedure outlined in TRCP 244. See "Trial," ch. 10-B, §10.1, p. 800.

2. Required documents to file.

(1) Proposed default judgment. The plaintiff should always file a proposed default judgment, either final or partial. For a form for the judgment, see *O'Connor's Texas Forms*, FORM 9C:2.

(a) Liquidated damages. If damages are liquidated and proved by a written instrument attached to the petition, the plaintiff can file a proposed final default judgment. See "Liquidated damages – hearing not required," §3.13.1, p. 593.

———————————— ✦ ————————————

(b) Unliquidated damages. If damages are unliquidated, the plaintiff can file a proposed partial default judgment on liability and ask for a hearing to determine the amount of unliquidated damages. See "Unliquidated damages – hearing required," §3.13.2, p. 593. The advantage of getting the court to sign a partial default judgment as soon as possible is that if the defendant files an answer after the court renders a judgment on liability but before the hearing on damages, the judgment on liability will not be set aside. See "Hearing on liability for no-answer default," §3.11, p. 593. If the plaintiff can prove the unliquidated-damages claim before the court renders the default judgment on liability, the plaintiff should file a final default judgment.

(2) Certificate of last known address. At the time or immediately before a default judgment is rendered, the plaintiff must certify to the clerk in writing the last known mailing address of the defendant. TRCP 239a; *Xu v. Davis*, 884 S.W.2d 916, 917 (Tex.App.—Waco 1994, orig. proceeding). See *O'Connor's Texas Forms*, FORM 7A:2. The certificate must be filed in the papers of the court. TRCP 239a. The clerk must mail written notice to the defaulting party at the address given. *Id.*; *John v. State*, 826 S.W.2d 138, 139 n.1 (Tex.1992). The notice must contain the style and the number of the case. TRCP 239a. The plaintiff's failure to comply with this requirement does not affect the finality of the judgment. *Id.* However, failure to comply with TRCP 239a can be grounds for reversal in a bill-of-review proceeding, but not in a restricted appeal. *Jordan v. Jordan*, 36 S.W.3d 259, 264 (Tex.App.—Beaumont 2001, pet. denied). See "Bill of review," §7.1.3, p. 600.

(3) Affidavit to prove notice. If the defendant made an appearance but did not file an answer, notice of the default hearing is required, and the plaintiff must prove it gave the defendant notice of the hearing. As a general rule, the plaintiff can prove notice by filing an affidavit with the certificate of service from the notice of hearing sent to the defendant. See "Notice required," §3.11.1(1), p. 593.

(4) Instrument to prove damages. The court can award damages based on affidavits, live testimony, or documents; however, the court can only award liquidated damages proved by a written instrument attached to the petition. *Aavid Thermal Techs. v. Irving ISD*, 68 S.W.3d 707, 711-12 (Tex.App.—Dallas 2001, no pet.). See "Hearing on damages for no-answer default," §3.13, p. 593. If the plaintiff relies solely on affidavit evidence to prove unliquidated damages, the affidavit must establish a causal nexus. See "Establish causal nexus," §3.13.2(3), p. 594; *O'Connor's Texas Forms*, FORM 7A:4.

(5) Servicemembers' affidavit. If the defendant is a member of the armed services, the plaintiff must file an affidavit setting forth facts that show that (1) the defendant is not currently in the military, (2) the defendant is currently in the military, or (3) the plaintiff is unable to determine whether the defendant is in the military. 50 U.S.C. app. §521(b)(1); *Hawkins v. Hawkins*, 999 S.W.2d 171, 174 (Tex.App.—Austin 1999, no pet.). If the defendant is not in the military, the court can render a default judgment. If the defendant is in the military, the court must appoint an attorney to represent the defendant. 50 U.S.C. app. §521(b)(2). If the court is unable to determine whether the defendant is in the military, the plaintiff may be required to file a bond. *Id.* §521(b)(3). See *O'Connor's Texas Forms*, FORM 7A:3.

3. Optional documents to file.

(1) Motion for default judgment. Most default judgments are granted on a motion. However, it is not necessary to file a motion for default judgment to obtain a default judgment. The plaintiff is entitled to have the judge or clerk call the case for default judgment on appearance day. TRCP 238, 239; *Maldonado v. Puente*, 694 S.W.2d 86, 90 (Tex.App.—San Antonio 1985, no writ); *see Texas Prop. & Cas. Ins. Guar. Ass'n v. Johnson*, 4 S.W.3d 328, 332 n.2 (Tex.App.—Austin 1999, pet. denied). When the case is called for default, the court can grant a default judgment if no answer is on file and the citation has been on file with the clerk for at least ten days, not counting the day the citation was filed and the day of the default judgment. TRCP 107(h); *see* TRCP 238, 239. See "Filing date," ch. 2-H, §9.4.9, p. 170; "Deadline to Answer," ch. 3-E, §2, p. 227; *O'Connor's Texas Forms*, FORM 7A:1.

(2) Motion for severance. If a plaintiff is taking a default judgment against one defendant in a case with multiple defendants, the plaintiff should consider filing a motion to sever its claims against that defendant so the default judgment can become final and the judgment can be executed. *Castano v. Foremost Cty. Mut. Ins.*, 31 S.W.3d 387, 388 (Tex.App.—San Antonio 2000, no pet.). See "Final judgment," §5.3, p. 597.

———————— ✦ ————————

§3.10 Response to motion for default – the answer. If the defendant gets notice that a motion for no-answer default is pending, it should immediately file an answer. The clerk should note on the answer the date and the exact minute it was filed. If the answer is filed after the deadline to answer but before the trial court renders judgment, the court cannot render a default judgment. See "After deadline," §3.8.2, p. 590.

§3.11 Hearing on liability for no-answer default.

1. Right to notice. Whether a defendant that did not file an answer is entitled to notice of the hearing on liability depends on whether it made an appearance in the case.

(1) Notice required. If the defendant appeared in the case but did not file an answer, the plaintiff must give the defendant notice, as a matter of due process, before the court can render the default judgment. *LBL Oil Co. v. International Power Servs.*, 777 S.W.2d 390, 390-91 (Tex.1989); *Coastal Banc SSB v. Helle*, 48 S.W.3d 796, 801 (Tex.App.—Corpus Christi 2001, pet. denied). *But see Wells v. Southern States Lumber & Sup.*, 720 S.W.2d 227, 228 (Tex.App.—Houston [14th Dist.] 1986, no writ) (when D filed motion to quash under TRCP 122 but did not file answer, notice of default-judgment hearing was not required). When the defendant makes an appearance in a case, it submits itself to the jurisdiction of the court in which it is sued. *Bass v. Duffey*, 620 S.W.2d 847, 850 (Tex. App.—Houston [14th Dist.] 1981, no writ). An appearance, as contemplated by TRCP 120 and 330(a), is entered by appearing in open court and having the appearance noted on the court's docket. *Freeman v. Freeman*, 327 S.W.2d 428, 430 (Tex.1959), *disapproved on other grounds*, *Mapco, Inc. v. Forrest*, 795 S.W.2d 700 (Tex.1990).

(2) Notice not required. If the defendant did not file an answer or make an appearance, the plaintiff is not required to give the defendant notice of the hearing before the court renders the default judgment. *Long v. McDermott*, 813 S.W.2d 622, 624 (Tex.App.—Houston [1st Dist.] 1991, no writ); *Olivares v. Cauthorn*, 717 S.W.2d 431, 434 (Tex.App.—San Antonio 1986, writ dism'd); *see Novosad v. Brian K. Cunningham, P.C.*, 38 S.W.3d 767, 772-73 (Tex.App.—Houston [14th Dist.] 2001, no pet.). The defendant received all the notice it is entitled to when it was served with process. *Continental Carbon Co. v. Sea-Land Serv.*, 27 S.W.3d 184, 189 (Tex.App.—Dallas 2000, pet. denied).

2. Right to answer. If the defendant appears at the hearing on liability, it should immediately file an answer, even if handwritten. A late answer will prevent a default judgment from being rendered as long as the court has not already rendered a judgment. See "After deadline," §3.8.2, p. 590.

§3.12 Rendition of default judgment. The court renders a no-answer default judgment either by announcing in open court that it renders judgment or by signing a judgment to that effect. See "Rendition," ch. 9-C, §3.1, p. 765.

§3.13 Hearing on damages for no-answer default. Once the court renders a no-answer default judgment, whether a hearing on damages is necessary depends on the type of damages the plaintiff requested in its petition.

1. Liquidated damages – hearing not required. "Liquidated damages" are damages that can be accurately calculated from (1) the factual (as opposed to conclusory) allegations in the petition and (2) a written instrument attached to the petition. TRCP 241; *Aavid Thermal Techs. v. Irving ISD*, 68 S.W.3d 707, 711 (Tex.App.—Dallas 2001, no pet.); *Novosad v. Brian K. Cunningham, P.C.*, 38 S.W.3d 767, 773 (Tex.App.—Houston [14th Dist.] 2001, no pet.); *Abcon Paving, Inc. v. Crissup*, 820 S.W.2d 951, 953 (Tex.App.—Fort Worth 1991, no writ). When damages are liquidated, it is not necessary to hold a hearing on damages, unless the defendant is entitled to and demands a jury trial. TRCP 241; *Aavid Thermal*, 68 S.W.3d at 711. The trial court can award liquidated damages that are proved by a written instrument. TRCP 241; *e.g.*, *Aavid Thermal*, 68 S.W.3d at 711 (amount of ad valorem taxes calculated from petition and attached documents); *Novosad*, 38 S.W.3d at 773 (amount for professional services and attorney fees proved by original invoices).

2. Unliquidated damages – hearing required. "Unliquidated damages" are damages that cannot be accurately calculated from (1) the factual allegations in the petition and (2) attached instruments. *Atwood v. B&R Sup. & Equip. Co.*, 52 S.W.3d 265, 268 (Tex.App.—Corpus Christi 2001, no pet.). Unliquidated damages are disputed

—————————————— ✦ ——————————————

or uncertain. *See Paradigm Oil, Inc. v. Retamco Oper., Inc.*, 372 S.W.3d 177, 186 (Tex.2012) (unliquidated damages cannot be calculated exactly and involve range of possible answers); *see, e.g., Fogel v. White*, 745 S.W.2d 444, 446 (Tex.App.—Houston [14th Dist.] 1988, orig. proceeding) (because outcome of tort claim is uncertain, damages are unliquidated). If a claim for liquidated damages is inadequately described in the plaintiff's petition, or if the claim is not supported by a written instrument attached to the petition, the damages are considered unliquidated. *See, e.g., Atwood*, 52 S.W.3d at 268 (because written instrument was not submitted, claim was unliquidated); *Kelley v. Southwestern Bell Media, Inc.*, 745 S.W.2d 447, 448-49 (Tex.App.—Houston [1st Dist.] 1988, no writ) (because petition did not allege date of default, claim was unliquidated). When damages are unliquidated, the court must hold a hearing and receive evidence on damages before it can render a final default judgment. TRCP 243; *Holt Atherton Indus. v. Heine*, 835 S.W.2d 80, 83 (Tex.1992); *Argyle Mech., Inc. v. Unigus Steel, Inc.*, 156 S.W.3d 685, 688 (Tex.App.—Dallas 2005, no pet.). If the defendant appears at the hearing on damages, it has the right to participate at the hearing. *Paradigm Oil*, 372 S.W.3d at 183. See "Right to participate," §3.13.3(3), p. 595. On appeal, if the appellate court finds the plaintiff did not present legally sufficient evidence at the hearing, the court will remand for a new trial on the damages issue. *Dolgencorp v. Lerma*, 288 S.W.3d 922, 929 (Tex.2009); *Holt Atherton*, 835 S.W.2d at 86.

   (1) Ask for court reporter. When the defendant is not present for the no-answer default hearing on damages and evidence is introduced, the plaintiff should make sure the court reporter transcribes the hearing. Generally, when a defendant, through no fault of its own, is unable to procure a record of the evidence presented, it may be entitled to a new trial. *Smith v. Smith*, 544 S.W.2d 121, 123 (Tex.1976); *Alvarado v. Reif*, 783 S.W.2d 303, 305 (Tex.App.—Eastland 1989, no writ).

   (2) Offer proof of damages. At the hearing, the plaintiff must present evidence of its damages. For example, in a personal-injury case, the plaintiff must present evidence of pain, suffering, lost wages, medical expenses, and the reasonableness and necessity of the medical expenses. *Transport Concepts, Inc. v. Reeves*, 748 S.W.2d 302, 305 (Tex.App.—Dallas 1988, no writ). TRCP 243 does not specify either the type of hearing or the type of evidence required. *Arenivar v. Providian Nat'l Bank*, 23 S.W.3d 496, 498 (Tex.App.—Amarillo 2000, no pet.). Thus, the court can award unliquidated damages based on affidavits or live testimony. *E.g., Ingram Indus. v. U.S. Bolt Mfg.*, 121 S.W.3d 31, 37 (Tex.App.—Houston [1st Dist.] 2003, no pet.) (affidavit testimony satisfied TRCP 243's requirement without need for evidentiary hearing); *Pentes Design, Inc. v. Perez*, 840 S.W.2d 75, 80 (Tex.App.—Corpus Christi 1992, writ denied) (witness testimony at default hearing supported claims for unliquidated damages). Unobjected-to hearsay evidence in an affidavit can support an award of damages. *Texas Commerce Bank v. New*, 3 S.W.3d 515, 517 (Tex.1999).

   (3) Establish causal nexus. When damages are unliquidated, the plaintiff must present evidence of the "causal nexus" between the event sued on and the plaintiff's injuries. *Morgan v. Compugraphic Corp.*, 675 S.W.2d 729, 732 (Tex.1984). By its default, the defendant admits only that it caused the event that led to the suit, not that there is a connection between the event and the damages. *Id.* Thus, the plaintiff must offer proof of its damages and connect the damages to the defendant's conduct. *Id.* Types of suits in which courts have required plaintiffs to prove a causal nexus include the following: • Breach of warranty and violation of the DTPA. *Capitol Brick, Inc. v. Fleming Mfg. Co.*, 722 S.W.2d 399, 402 (Tex.1986). • Personal injury. *Morgan*, 675 S.W.2d at 731-32; *Transport Concepts*, 748 S.W.2d at 304-05. • Breach of warranty of title to real estate. *Gibraltar Sav. Ass'n v. Kilpatrick*, 770 S.W.2d 14, 18 (Tex.App.—Texarkana 1989, writ denied).

   (4) Prove attorney fees.

      (a) Evidence. A demand for reasonable attorney fees is a claim for unliquidated damages, and the award must be based on evidence. *Higgins v. Smith*, 722 S.W.2d 825, 827-28 (Tex.App.—Houston [14th Dist.] 1987, no writ); *Nettles v. Del Lingco*, 638 S.W.2d 633, 636 (Tex.App.—El Paso 1982, no writ). Attorney fees can be proved by affidavit. See "Proof of attorney fees," ch. 1-H, §10.4, p. 66; *O'Connor's Texas COA*, "Proving Attorney Fees," ch. 45-A, §4, p. 1359. The court should not consider the unsworn testimony of the plaintiff's attorney to support attorney fees. *Bloom v. Bloom*, 767 S.W.2d 463, 471 (Tex.App.—San Antonio 1989, writ denied). However, if the court awards attorney fees based on unsworn testimony at a hearing at which the defendant was present but did not object, the defendant waives that issue on appeal. See "Attorney's appearance before court," ch. 1-H, §5.2, p. 55.

———————————— ✦ ————————————

(b) No judicial notice. Attorney fees in a default-judgment case cannot be established by the judicial-notice provision in CPRC §38.004. That provision permits judicial notice of attorney fees only when a case is tried on the merits. See "Judicial notice," ch. 1-H, §10.2.2, p. 63.

3. Defendant's rights in a no-answer default.

(1) Right to notice. Ordinarily, a defendant against whom a no-answer default judgment was rendered does not have a right to notice of a hearing on unliquidated damages. *Long v. McDermott*, 813 S.W.2d 622, 624 (Tex.App.—Houston [1st Dist.] 1991, no writ). But when a defendant makes an appearance or files an answer after default judgment was rendered but before the hearing on damages, the defendant is entitled to notice of all later hearings. *See Bradford v. Bradford*, 971 S.W.2d 595, 597 (Tex.App.—Dallas 1998, no pet.).

(2) Right to jury. If the defendant filed an answer requesting a jury after the court rendered a default judgment on liability but before the hearing on damages, the defendant is entitled to a jury trial on damages. TRCP 241, 243. TRCP 243 calls this limited jury trial on damages a "writ of inquiry." *Marr v. Marr*, 905 S.W.2d 331, 334 (Tex.App.—Waco 1995, no writ); *Maywald Trailer Co. v. Perry*, 238 S.W.2d 826, 827 (Tex.App.—Galveston 1951, writ ref'd n.r.e.).

(3) Right to participate. If the defendant appears at the hearing on damages, it has the right to cross-examine witnesses and to present evidence on unliquidated damages only. *Northeast Wholesale Lumber, Inc. v. Leader Lumber, Inc.*, 785 S.W.2d 402, 407 (Tex.App.—Dallas 1989, no writ); *Bass v. Duffey*, 620 S.W.2d 847, 849-50 (Tex.App.—Houston [14th Dist.] 1981, no writ); *Maywald Trailer*, 238 S.W.2d at 827. See "Unliquidated damages – hearing required," §3.13.2, p. 593. The defendant may introduce evidence to mitigate the plaintiff's unliquidated damages and evidence to negate the causal nexus. *See Morgan*, 675 S.W.2d at 732; *Fiduciary Mortg. Co. v. City Nat'l Bank*, 762 S.W.2d 196, 199 (Tex.App.—Dallas 1988, writ denied); *Maywald Trailer*, 238 S.W.2d at 827. Once the court renders a default judgment on liability, the defendant cannot offer evidence to support its defenses or call witnesses to disprove liability. *See, e.g., Downer v. Aquamarine Operators, Inc.*, 701 S.W.2d 238, 243 (Tex. 1985) (once its answer was struck and default J rendered on liability, D was not entitled to introduce evidence of contributory negligence).

NOTE

When a trial court strikes a defendant's answer as a discovery sanction, the resulting default—which is technically post-answer but is similar to a no-answer default judgment—must be evaluated under both the general rules for default judgments and those for discovery abuse. Paradigm Oil, 372 S.W.3d at 184. Thus, even though a sanctions order striking an answer may prevent the defendant from contesting liability, the order generally cannot prevent the defendant from participating at a post-default hearing for unliquidated damages. E.g., id. at 187 (sanction of default judgment rendered against D on liability was appropriate, but sanction preventing D from participating in post-default trial on damages and attorney fees, both of which were unliquidated, was excessive). A sanction barring a defendant from participating at the hearing on unliquidated damages might be justified, however, if the defendant was responsible for destruction of evidence (i.e., spoliation) that directly and significantly impaired a party's ability to prove damages. Id. at 186; see In re Dynamic Health, Inc., 32 S.W.3d 876, 885 (Tex.App.—Texarkana 2000, orig. proceeding).

---

§3.14 Findings of fact. When the trial court awards unliquidated damages after a default, the defendant should ask the court to file findings of fact and conclusions of law. *See IKB Indus. v. Pro-Line Corp.*, 938 S.W.2d 440, 443 (Tex.1997). See "Requesting Findings of Fact," ch. 10-E, §3, p. 820. A request for findings of fact and conclusions of law accomplishes two things. First, it extends the time for the trial court to consider the basis for its judgment. *IKB Indus.*, 938 S.W.2d at 442-43. Second, it extends the time for perfecting the appeal. TRAP 26.1(a)(4). See "Effect on appellate timetable," ch. 10-E, §6.1, p. 823. Findings of fact and conclusions of law are not appropriate for a default judgment based on liquidated damages. *IKB Indus.*, 938 S.W.2d at 443.

—————————— ✯ ——————————

§3.15 Waiver. The plaintiff waives the right to default if it proceeds to trial as though the defendant had filed an answer. *Artripe v. Hughes*, 857 S.W.2d 82, 87 (Tex.App.—Corpus Christi 1993, writ denied). Once the parties announce ready for trial and the jury has been selected, it is too late to ask for a default judgment. *Dodson v. Citizens State Bank*, 701 S.W.2d 89, 94 (Tex.App.—Amarillo 1986, writ ref'd n.r.e.).

§4. POST-ANSWER DEFAULT

A post-answer default occurs when a defendant who filed an answer does not appear at trial or a dispositive hearing. *Dolgencorp v. Lerma*, 288 S.W.3d 922, 925 (Tex.2009); *Stoner v. Thompson*, 578 S.W.2d 679, 682 (Tex.1979).

§4.1 Effect of defendant's answer. By filing an answer, the defendant prevents the court from rendering a default judgment without a hearing. *See Dolgencorp v. Lerma*, 288 S.W.3d 922, 930 (Tex.2009). Even if the defendant does not appear at trial, a filed answer serves as a denial of the plaintiff's allegations. *Frymire Eng'g Co. v. Grantham*, 524 S.W.2d 680, 681 (Tex.1975); *Flores v. Brimex L.P.*, 5 S.W.3d 816, 820 (Tex.App.—San Antonio 1999, no pet.). Thus, the plaintiff must offer evidence and prove its case as in a trial on the merits. *Dolgencorp*, 288 S.W.3d at 930. See "The trial," §4.5, p. 597.

§4.2 Sufficiency of plaintiff's pleadings. A post-answer default, like a no-answer default, must be supported by the plaintiff's petition. *See Stoner v. Thompson*, 578 S.W.2d 679, 684 (Tex.1979). See "Sufficiency of plaintiff's petition," §3.2, p. 588.

§4.3 Notice of the trial or dispositive hearing. A post-answer default is valid only if the defendant received notice of the setting for trial or other dispositive hearing at which the default was rendered. *$429.30 v. State*, 896 S.W.2d 363, 366 (Tex.App.—Houston [1st Dist.] 1995, no writ); *Matsushita Elec. Corp. v. McAllen Copy Data, Inc.*, 815 S.W.2d 850, 853 (Tex.App.—Corpus Christi 1991, writ denied); *see* TRCP 21a, 245. A court can render a default judgment for failure to appear only if the hearing is a dispositive hearing. *See Masterson v. Cox*, 886 S.W.2d 436, 437-38 (Tex.App.—Houston [1st Dist.] 1994, no writ). Before rendering a default judgment against a defendant that answered but did not appear for trial or a dispositive hearing, the trial court should determine whether the defendant received notice. *See, e.g.*, *Cliff v. Huggins*, 724 S.W.2d 778, 779 (Tex.1987) (reversed; D did not receive notice of trial setting); *Murphree v. Ziegelmair*, 937 S.W.2d 493, 495 (Tex.App.—Houston [1st Dist.] 1995, no writ) (reversed; Ds did not have notice that failure to attend pretrial conference could result in immediate disposition).

  1. Due process. A defendant that appeared in the case or filed an answer has a constitutional right to notice of all hearings. *E.g.*, *LBL Oil Co. v. International Power Servs.*, 777 S.W.2d 390, 390-91 (Tex.1989) (appeared); *Smith v. Holmes*, 53 S.W.3d 815, 817 (Tex.App.—Austin 2001, no pet.) (filed answer). A party's right to be heard in a contested case is fundamental. *See LBL Oil*, 777 S.W.2d at 390-91; *Bloom v. Bloom*, 767 S.W.2d 463, 472 (Tex.App.—San Antonio 1989, writ denied).

  2. TRCP 245. A defendant that appeared in the case or filed an answer must be given 45 days' notice of a setting that results in a post-answer default judgment. *See* TRCP 245; *Pessel v. Jenkins*, 125 S.W.3d 807, 808-09 (Tex.App.—Texarkana 2004, no pet.); *Burress v. Richardson*, 97 S.W.3d 806, 807 (Tex.App.—Dallas 2003, no pet.); *Custom-Crete, Inc. v. K-Bar Servs.*, 82 S.W.3d 655, 659 (Tex.App.—San Antonio 2002, no pet.). The defendant is entitled to 45 days' notice of the first trial setting; if the trial date is reset, the defendant is entitled to "reasonable" notice of the second or later setting. TRCP 245. Because the notice is mandatory and involves constitutional rights, a post-answer default must be set aside when the court's notice is returned as undeliverable. *Burress*, 97 S.W.3d at 807 (appeal, no motion for new trial); *Transoceanic Shipping Co. v. General Univ'l Sys.*, 961 S.W.2d 418, 419-20 (Tex.App.—Houston [1st Dist.] 1997, no writ) (appeal by writ of error). *Contra Withrow v. Schou*, 13 S.W.3d 37, 41-42 (Tex.App.—Houston [14th Dist.] 1999, pet. denied) (disagreeing with *Transoceanic*; trial court is not required to find D's attorney and send another notice of trial setting after first notice was returned as undeliverable).

§4.4 The motion. A motion for post-answer default is not always necessary. Generally, when a defendant does not appear for trial or a dispositive hearing, the court decides to go forward with a post-answer default hearing on its own initiative. For the form for a motion for post-answer default, see *O'Connor's Texas Forms*, FORM 7A:7.

✦

---

§4.5 The trial. If the defendant does not appear at a scheduled trial, the trial court can conduct the trial without the defendant and grant a default judgment if the plaintiff proves all aspects of its case with evidence. *Bradley Motors, Inc. v. Mackey*, 878 S.W.2d 140, 141 (Tex.1994).

1. Right to jury. When the defendant does not appear for a scheduled trial, the case can be tried by the court, even if the defendant requested a jury. When the defendant does not appear at trial, it waives its right to a jury trial. *Bradley Motors*, 878 S.W.2d at 141; *Hanners v. State Bar*, 860 S.W.2d 903, 911 (Tex.App.—Dallas 1993, no writ). If the defendant requested a jury trial before its answer was struck, and if the defendant appears for trial, it is entitled to a jury trial. *See, e.g., Brantley v. Etter*, 662 S.W.2d 752, 756 (Tex.App.—San Antonio 1983) (D was still entitled to jury trial on damages after D's answer was struck as a sanction), *writ ref'd n.r.e.*, 677 S.W.2d 503 (Tex.1984); *see also Otis Elevator Co. v. Parmelee*, 850 S.W.2d 179, 181 (Tex.1993) (trial court could not award unliquidated damages without a hearing after imposing sanction equivalent to default J).

2. Ask for court reporter. The plaintiff should ask the court reporter to record the hearing. If the defendant is unable to get the court reporter to prepare a record because the reporter did not transcribe the hearing, the defendant is entitled to a new trial in most cases. *Smith v. Smith*, 544 S.W.2d 121, 123 (Tex.1976); *Carstar Collision, Inc. v. Mercury Fin. Co.*, 23 S.W.3d 368, 370 (Tex.App.—Houston [1st Dist.] 1999, pet. denied); *see, e.g., Sharif v. Par Tech, Inc.*, 135 S.W.3d 869, 873 (Tex.App.—Houston [1st Dist.] 2004, no pet.) (default J reversed because there was no reporter's record). See *O'Connor's Texas Appeals*, "Default judgment – post-answer," ch. 6-C, §4.1.6, p. 228.

3. Prove liability & damages. At trial, the plaintiff must carry its burden to prove all the elements of its cause of action; the defendant has admitted nothing by its default. *Stoner v. Thompson*, 578 S.W.2d 679, 682 (Tex. 1979); *Flores v. Brimex L.P.*, 5 S.W.3d 816, 820 (Tex.App.—San Antonio 1999, no pet.); *Onwuteaka v. Gill*, 908 S.W.2d 276, 281 (Tex.App.—Houston [1st Dist.] 1995, no writ); *Holberg v. Short*, 731 S.W.2d 584, 587 (Tex.App.—Houston [14th Dist.] 1987, no writ). The plaintiff's evidence must be sufficient to support both the liability finding and the damages award. *See Stone Res. v. Barnett*, 661 S.W.2d 148, 151 (Tex.App.—Houston [1st Dist.] 1983, no writ). On appeal, if the appellate court finds the plaintiff did not present legally sufficient evidence to support the post-answer default, the court will remand for a new trial. *Dolgencorp v. Lerma*, 288 S.W.3d 922, 930 (Tex.2009).

§5. DRAFTING THE DEFAULT JUDGMENT

For a no-answer default judgment, see *O'Connor's Texas Forms*, FORM 9C:2; for a post-answer default judgment, see FORM 9C:3.

§5.1 General terms. The default judgment, like any judgment, should identify the parties and the relief granted. See "The Judgment," ch. 9-C, p. 764.

§5.2 Service & jurisdiction. The no-answer default judgment should recite all the jurisdictional requisites: (1) the citation was duly served with process, (2) the return of service was on file for ten days before the default was rendered, and (3) the defendant failed to answer and appear. For documents that may need to be attached to the judgment, see "Required documents to file," §3.9.2, p. 591.

§5.3 Final judgment.

1. No-answer default. To be final and appealable, a no-answer default judgment must dispose of all issues and parties in the plaintiff's petition. *Houston Health Clubs, Inc. v. First Ct. of Appeals*, 722 S.W.2d 692, 693 (Tex.1986); *see Castano v. Foremost Cty. Mut. Ins.*, 31 S.W.3d 387, 388 (Tex.App.—San Antonio 2000, no pet.) (default J against one D was not final because order to sever other Ds not signed). There is no presumed disposition of issues in a no-answer default-judgment case. *Houston Health Clubs*, 722 S.W.2d at 693. See "Summary disposition," ch. 9-C, §6.3.2(2), p. 773.

─────────────── ★ ───────────────

PRACTICE TIP

*If you are suing multiple defendants, some of whom have answered and some of whom have not, and you are seeking a default judgment against only one, do not draft the default judgment to say that the judgment disposes of all parties and all claims and is therefore final. See **In re Daredia**, 317 S.W.3d 247, 248-49 (Tex.2010). Otherwise, you may lose your right to obtain a judgment against the remaining defendants because they have been unequivocally, even though inadvertently, dismissed from the case. See id. See "Statement of finality," ch. 9-C, §4.3, p. 767.*

---

    2. Post-answer default. Because a post-answer default judgment can be rendered only after notice to the defendant (see "Notice of the trial or dispositive hearing," §4.3, p. 596) and a trial of the issues (see "The trial," §4.5, p. 597), a post-answer default judgment is presumed to dispose of all issues. *See **Strut Cam Dimensions, Inc. v. Sutton**, 896 S.W.2d 799, 801-02 (Tex.App.—Corpus Christi 1994, writ denied) (post-answer default J disposes of all claims by implication); **Thomas v. DuBovy-Longo**, 786 S.W.2d 506, 507 (Tex.App.—Dallas 1990, writ denied) (post-answer default J is presumed to be final). Unlike a no-answer default, a post-answer default is not a summary disposition of the claims.

§6. NOTICE OF DEFAULT JUDGMENT

    §6.1 Notice after no-answer default. The clerk of the trial court is required to send to the defendant, at the mailing address certified by the plaintiff, written notice that a no-answer default judgment has been rendered against it. TRCP 239a. The clerk must note on the docket that it mailed the notice to the defendant immediately after the default judgment was signed. *Id.* The purpose of TRCP 239a is to give the defendant an opportunity to file a motion for new trial after a no-answer default judgment. ***Bloom v. Bloom***, 767 S.W.2d 463, 468 (Tex.App.—San Antonio 1989, writ denied). Because TRCP 239a does not specify the type of notice, the notice must be sent as required by TRCP 21a—either by personal delivery, receipted delivery, or certified or registered mail. *See **Continental Cas. Co. v. Davilla**, 139 S.W.3d 374, 383 (Tex.App.—Fort Worth 2004, pet. denied) (Gardner, J., concurring). Once notice is properly sent, a rebuttable presumption arises that the defendant received the notice. *Id.* The clerk's failure to give notice does not affect the finality of the judgment. TRCP 239a; ***Garza v. Attorney Gen.***, 166 S.W.3d 799, 815 (Tex. App.—Corpus Christi 2005, no pet.); *see **Campbell v. Fincher***, 72 S.W.3d 723, 724-25 (Tex.App.—Waco 2002, no pet.) (failure to give notice not reversible error).

    §6.2 Notice after post-answer default. Notice of a post-answer default judgment is governed by the rule that governs notice of judgments. See "TRCP 306a," ch. 9-C, §5.2.1, p. 771.

§7. ATTACKING THE DEFAULT JUDGMENT

The procedure to use to attack a default judgment depends on (1) the date the defendant received notice of the default judgment, (2) whether the defendant took any action at the time, and (3) the reason for the default. Pendery et al., *Dealing with Default Judgments*, 35 St. Mary's L.J. at 11. Default judgments may be attacked either directly or collaterally. A direct attack seeks to set aside the judgment and must be brought within a set period of time. *See **PNS Stores v. Rivera**, 379 S.W.3d 267, 271 (Tex.2012). A collateral attack seeks to avoid the effect of the judgment, not to set it aside, and can be brought at any time. *See id.* See "Collateral attacks on default judgment," §7.2, p. 602.

    §7.1 Direct attacks on default judgment. Direct attacks at the trial-court level include a motion for new trial and a bill of review; direct attacks at the appellate-court level include a restricted appeal, an appeal of a denial of a bill of review, and an ordinary appeal after the denial of a motion for new trial. *See, e.g., **Primate Constr., Inc. v. Silver**, 884 S.W.2d 151, 152 (Tex.1994) (restricted appeal); **Min v. Avila**, 991 S.W.2d 495, 499-500 (Tex.App.— Houston [1st Dist.] 1999, no pet.) (bill of review); **Webb v. Oberkampf Sup.**, 831 S.W.2d 61, 63-64 (Tex.App.— Amarillo 1992, no writ) (appeal after denial of motion for new trial). When a no-answer default judgment is challenged by a direct attack, the judgment's recitals regarding service do not raise a presumption of proper service; every

★

step of the proceeding from service of process to final judgment is open to examination. *Primate Constr.*, 884 S.W.2d at 152; *Min*, 991 S.W.2d at 499; *Webb*, 831 S.W.2d at 64. If the record does not show strict compliance with the manner and mode of service, the service is invalid and the default judgment is void. *Insurance Co. of Pa. v. Lejeune*, 297 S.W.3d 254, 256 (Tex.2009); *Primate Constr.*, 884 S.W.2d at 152; *Min*, 991 S.W.2d at 500; *Webb*, 831 S.W.2d at 64; *see, e.g., In re Discount Rental, Inc.*, 216 S.W.3d 831, 832 (Tex.2007) (because default J was taken without proper service, it was void).

1. Motion for new trial. A defendant that suffered a default judgment may ask the trial court to overturn the default by granting a motion for new trial. *See* TRCP 320. A motion for new trial must be filed within 30 days after the judgment was signed. See "Deadlines for MNT," ch. 10-B, §5, p. 791. A defendant can file a motion for new trial if (1) the defendant was not properly served with notice of the suit, the trial, or the hearing, or (2) after receiving proper notice, the defendant did not appear because of a mistake or accident. See "MNT After Default Judgment," ch. 10-B, §9, p. 795. If the trial court denies relief, the defendant can obtain review in the court of appeals. See "Review," ch. 10-B, §17, p. 809.

2. Restricted appeal. A defendant who did not participate in the trial of a cause of action may obtain review of the judgment by a restricted appeal. TRAP 30; *Quaestor Invs. v. State of Chiapas*, 997 S.W.2d 226, 227 & n.1 (Tex.1999); *Norman Comms. v. Texas Eastman Co.*, 955 S.W.2d 269, 270 (Tex.1997).

(1) Deadline. A restricted appeal must be filed within six months after the judgment was signed. TRAP 26.1(c); *Hubicki v. Festina*, 226 S.W.3d 405, 407 (Tex.2007); *Quaestor Invs.*, 997 S.W.2d at 227. Some statutes and older cases refer to the restricted appeal by its old name, "writ of error." *E.g.*, CPRC §51.013; *Primate Constr.*, 884 S.W.2d at 152.

(2) Allegations. To obtain review by restricted appeal, the defendant must show the following:

(a) The restricted appeal was filed within six months after the judgment. CPRC §51.013; TRAP 26.1(c); *Norman Comms.*, 955 S.W.2d at 270; *see also Quaestor Invs.*, 997 S.W.2d at 229 (removal suspends six-month timetable; time clock restarts when federal court executes remand order and mails certified copy to state court).

(b) The defendant was a party in the suit being challenged. *Norman Comms.*, 955 S.W.2d at 270. A restricted appeal is also available to (1) a person whose privity of estate, title, or interest is apparent from the record in the trial court, or (2) a person who is a party under the doctrine of virtual representation. *Gunn v. Cavanaugh*, 391 S.W.2d 723, 725 (Tex.1965). See "Virtual party," ch. 2-B, §3.1.2, p. 96.

(c) The defendant did not participate, either in person or through counsel, in the actual trial of the case. TRAP 30; *Norman Comms.*, 955 S.W.2d at 270; *Stubbs v. Stubbs*, 685 S.W.2d 643, 644 (Tex.1985); *see Texaco, Inc. v. Central Power & Light Co.*, 925 S.W.2d 586, 588 (Tex.1996) (discussing former TRAP 45, now TRAP 30). If the record shows the defendant participated in the "decision-making event" that produced the final judgment adjudicating the defendant's rights, the defendant cannot proceed by restricted appeal. *Texaco, Inc.*, 925 S.W.2d at 589. "Participation" means taking part in a hearing in open court that leads to the rendition of judgment on questions of law (if the case was disposed of on the questions of law) or on questions of fact (if the final judgment was rendered on the facts). *Withem v. Underwood*, 922 S.W.2d 956, 957 (Tex.1996); *see also Stubbs*, 685 S.W.2d at 645 (party who signed waiver of citation could still appeal by writ of error). The policy behind the nonparticipation requirement is to deny restricted appeal to those who should have pursued a quicker, ordinary appeal. *Texaco, Inc.*, 925 S.W.2d at 590.

(d) The defendant did not file a postjudgment motion, a request for findings of fact, or a notice of appeal within the time permitted by TRAP 26.1(a). TRAP 30; *Aviation Composite Techs. v. CLB Corp.*, 131 S.W.3d 181, 184 (Tex.App.—Fort Worth 2004, no pet.).

(e) The trial court erred, and the error is apparent from the face of the record. *Norman Comms.*, 955 S.W.2d at 270; *General Elec. Co. v. Falcon Ridge Apts., Jt.V.*, 811 S.W.2d 942, 943 (Tex.1991); *Stubbs*, 685 S.W.2d at 644. A restricted appeal requires error to be apparent from the face of the record, not inferred from the record.

✯

Gold v. Gold, 145 S.W.3d 212, 213 (Tex.2004); *e.g.*, *Ginn v. Forrester*, 282 S.W.3d 430, 431 (Tex.2009) (no reversible error when record was silent on whether notice was sent); *Alexander v. Lynda's Boutique*, 134 S.W.3d 845, 849-50 (Tex.2004) (same). The "face of the record" includes the reporter's record, if any, and the clerk's record. *See Norman Comms.*, 955 S.W.2d at 270. Only documents on file with the court at the time of the judgment determine the face of the record. *Laas v. Williamson*, 156 S.W.3d 854, 857 (Tex.App.—Beaumont 2005, no pet.). The appellate court cannot consider evidence outside the record. *General Elec.*, 811 S.W.2d at 944; *see Ginn*, 282 S.W.3d at 432. If the petition, citation, or return of service is inadequate on its face to support a no-answer default judgment, the court of appeals will reverse the default judgment. *See Hubicki*, 226 S.W.3d at 407-08; *see, e.g.*, *Autozone, Inc. v. Duenes*, 108 S.W.3d 917, 920-21 (Tex.App.—Corpus Christi 2003, no pet.) (invalid service on foreign corporation); *Dolly v. Aethos Comms. Sys.*, 10 S.W.3d 384, 388-89 (Tex.App.—Dallas 2000, no pet.) (return of service did not follow requirements of trial court's order of substituted service).

3. Bill of review. A defendant may attack a default judgment by a bill of review after it is too late either to appeal or to file a motion for new trial. *Mabon Ltd. v. Afri-Carib Enters.*, 369 S.W.3d 809, 812 (Tex.2012); *Caldwell v. Barnes*, 154 S.W.3d 93, 96 (Tex.2004) (*Caldwell II*); *King Ranch, Inc. v. Chapman*, 118 S.W.3d 742, 751 (Tex.2003); *Wembley Inv. v. Herrera*, 11 S.W.3d 924, 926-27 (Tex.1999); *Caldwell v. Barnes*, 975 S.W.2d 535, 537 (Tex.1998) (*Caldwell I*); *State v. 1985 Chevrolet Pickup Truck*, 778 S.W.2d 463, 464 (Tex.1989); *see* TRCP 329b(f). Although a bill of review attacks a default judgment from a particular case, the bill of review is an independent suit filed under a different cause number. *In re J.J.*, ___ S.W.3d ___ (Tex.App.—El Paso 2012, n.p.h.) (No. 08-11-00187-CV; 7-18-12). The bill of review must, however, be brought in the court that rendered the original judgment. *Frost Nat'l Bank v. Fernandez*, 315 S.W.3d 494, 504 (Tex.2010); *see also In re J.J.*, ___ S.W.3d at ___ (once jurisdiction attaches to proper court, bill of review may be transferred to different court).

NOTE

In this bill-of-review section, the defendant in the earlier suit (now the petitioner for the bill of review) is referred to as the defendant-petitioner; the plaintiff in the earlier suit (now the respondent for the bill of review) is referred to as the plaintiff-respondent.

---

(1) Deadline.

(a) Generally. A petition for bill of review must be filed after the trial court's plenary power expires, but within the residual four-year statute of limitations. *See* CPRC §16.051 (residual limitations period); TRCP 329b(f) (plenary power); *PNS Stores v. Rivera*, 379 S.W.3d 267, 275 (Tex.2012) (within four years after rendition of judgment); *Caldwell I*, 975 S.W.2d at 538 (residual four-year limitations period applies to bill of review).

(b) Exception. The only exception to the four-year statute is when the defendant-petitioner can show extrinsic fraud. *PNS Stores*, 379 S.W.3d at 275; *Temple v. Archambo*, 161 S.W.3d 217, 223-24 (Tex.App.—Corpus Christi 2005, no pet.); *Law v. Law*, 792 S.W.2d 150, 153 (Tex.App.—Houston [1st Dist.] 1990, writ denied). Extrinsic fraud is wrongful conduct outside the trial—such as keeping a party away from court or making false promises of compromise—that prevents a losing party from fully litigating rights or defenses and prevents a real trial on the issues involved. *Temple*, 161 S.W.3d at 224; *see, e.g.*, *PNS Stores*, 379 S.W.3d at 275-76 (some evidence of extrinsic fraud shown when P's attorney did not comply with TRCP 239a; he provided clerk with address of D's registered agent rather than D's last known address, which he knew); *see also Alexander v. Hagedorn*, 226 S.W.2d 996, 1002 (Tex.1950) (bill of review not proper because false testimony on element of cause of action was intrinsic fraud). Although evidence of extrinsic fraud tolls the four-year statute of limitations, it does not do so indefinitely—the limitations period begins to run when the defendant-petitioner knew or should have known about the default judgment. *PNS Stores*, 379 S.W.3d at 277 n.16.

(2) Grounds. The defendant-petitioner must file a sworn pleading that states the grounds for the bill of review. *Baker v. Goldsmith*, 582 S.W.2d 404, 408 (Tex.1979); *see Beck v. Beck*, 771 S.W.2d 141, 141 (Tex.1989). For a defendant-petitioner to be entitled to a hearing, it must make a prima facie showing of sufficient cause, which

★

is not defined by TRCP 329b(f). *See 1985 Chevrolet*, 778 S.W.2d at 464. The grounds for sufficient cause depend on whether the defendant-petitioner claims a due-process violation (i.e., no service of process, no notice of trial setting or dispositive hearing) in the bill of review.

(a) No due-process violation. To establish sufficient cause when there is no due-process violation claimed, a defendant-petitioner must demonstrate the following:

[1] Meritorious defense. The defendant-petitioner must present a prima facie meritorious defense to the action and show that it did not have an opportunity to present the defense. *Caldwell II*, 154 S.W.3d at 96; *1985 Chevrolet*, 778 S.W.2d at 464-65; *Beck*, 771 S.W.2d at 142; *see Mabon, Ltd.*, 369 S.W.3d at 812. A defendant establishes a meritorious defense when it proves that (1) its defense is not barred as a matter of law, and (2) it will be entitled to judgment on retrial if no contrary evidence is offered. *Baker*, 582 S.W.2d at 408-09; *Ortmann v. Ortmann*, 999 S.W.2d 85, 88 (Tex.App.—Houston [14th Dist.] 1999, pet. denied).

[2] Justification for failure to assert defense. The defendant-petitioner must justify its failure to present a defense by alleging fraud, accident, wrongful act by the plaintiff, or official mistake. *Mabon, Ltd.*, 369 S.W.3d at 812; *Caldwell II*, 154 S.W.3d at 96; *Wembley Inv.*, 11 S.W.3d at 927; *Caldwell I*, 975 S.W.2d at 537; *1985 Chevrolet*, 778 S.W.2d at 464; *see, e.g., Baker*, 582 S.W.2d at 407 (letter that constituted answer was misplaced at courthouse).

[3] No fault or negligence. The defendant-petitioner must show the default judgment was not rendered as a result of its own fault or negligence. *Mabon, Ltd.*, 369 S.W.3d at 812; *Caldwell II*, 154 S.W.3d at 96; *Caldwell I*, 975 S.W.2d at 537; *Texas Mach. & Equip. Co. v. Gordon Knox Oil & Expl. Co.*, 442 S.W.2d 315, 317-18 (Tex.1969); *see King Ranch*, 118 S.W.3d at 752 (allegations of fraud or negligence by party's own attorney insufficient to support bill of review); *see, e.g., Campus Invs. v. Cullever*, 144 S.W.3d 464, 466 (Tex.2004) (bill of review denied for D who was negligent in not updating addresses with Secretary of State for registered agent and registered office). To establish a lack of fault or negligence, the defendant-petitioner must also show that it diligently pursued all legal remedies as to any motions (e.g., motion for new trial, motion to reinstate) that could have been filed in the underlying proceeding. *Mabon, Ltd.*, 369 S.W.3d at 813; *Gold*, 145 S.W.3d at 214. But the defendant-petitioner is not required to show that it diligently monitored the case status. *Mabon, Ltd.*, 369 S.W.3d at 813.

(b) Due-process violation. To establish sufficient cause when there is a due-process violation claimed, a defendant-petitioner is not required to prove the first two elements set out above in "No due-process violation," §7.1.3(2)(a). *Mabon, Ltd.*, 369 S.W.3d at 812; *Caldwell II*, 154 S.W.3d at 96-97; *see Peralta v. Heights Med. Ctr., Inc.*, 485 U.S. 80, 86 (1988) (J rendered without service violates due process); *see also Lopez v. Lopez*, 757 S.W.2d 721, 723 (Tex.1988) (because D had no notice of trial setting, D was not required to prove meritorious defense). Thus, when a defendant-petitioner claims it was not served with process or it did not receive notice of the trial or default judgment, it must prove only the third element (i.e., no fault or negligence in allowing a default judgment to be rendered). *Mabon, Ltd.*, 369 S.W.3d at 812; *see Caldwell II*, 154 S.W.3d at 97. This element is conclusively established if the defendant-petitioner proves it was not served or it did not receive notice. *See Mabon, Ltd.*, 369 S.W.3d at 812; *Ross v. National Ctr. for the Empl. of the Disabled*, 197 S.W.3d 795, 797 (Tex.2006); *Caldwell II*, 154 S.W.3d at 97. A defendant who was not served with process or who did not receive notice cannot be at fault or negligent in allowing a default judgment to be rendered. *See Caldwell II*, 154 S.W.3d at 97; *Cash v. Beaumont Dealers Auto Auction, Inc.*, 275 S.W.3d 915, 919 (Tex.App.—Beaumont 2009, no pet.).

(3) Defenses. The plaintiff-respondent can raise a number of defenses to the petition for bill of review.

(a) Untimeliness. The defendant-petitioner is generally not entitled to relief by bill of review unless it files the petition within the residual four-year statute of limitations. See "Deadline," §7.1.3(1), p. 600.

(b) Failure to exhaust other remedies. The defendant-petitioner is not entitled to relief by bill of review unless it exhausted all other remedies available under Texas law at the time it filed the bill of review. *Wembley Inv.*, 11 S.W.3d at 927; *Caldwell I*, 975 S.W.2d at 537-38. For example, a defendant-petitioner is not entitled to relief by way of bill of review if it could have, but did not, file a motion to reinstate, a motion for new trial, or

DEFAULT JUDGMENT

★

a direct appeal. *See Gold*, 145 S.W.3d at 214. By comparison, a defendant-petitioner is not required to file a restricted appeal in order to have "exhausted all other remedies." *Id.* (restricted appeal not prerequisite to bill of review). See "Restricted appeal," §7.1.2, p. 599.

(c) Laches. Because a bill of review is an equitable remedy, laches may be raised as a defense. *Caldwell I*, 975 S.W.2d at 538. The two elements of laches are (1) unreasonable delay by one with legal or equitable rights in asserting them, and (2) a good-faith change of position by another to its own detriment because of the delay. *Id.*; *Rogers v. Ricane Enters.*, 772 S.W.2d 76, 80 (Tex.1989). Generally, laches will not bar a suit before the limitations period expires unless some extraordinary circumstance rendered it inequitable to permit the defendant-petitioner to assert its rights. *E.g.*, *Caldwell I*, 975 S.W.2d at 538-39 (laches did not bar bill of review filed almost two years after petitioner first learned of J). See *O'Connor's Texas COA*, "Laches," ch. 52, §3.2, p. 1497.

(4) Trial. After the defendant-petitioner meets the standards of prima facie proof, the court will hold a separate trial (a jury trial if one was requested) in which (1) the defendant-petitioner must prove the elements of the bill of review by a preponderance of the evidence, and (2) if the defendant-petitioner is successful, the court will permit the parties to revert to their original status as plaintiff and defendant with the burden on the original plaintiff to prove the underlying cause of action. *Caldwell II*, 154 S.W.3d at 97-98; *1985 Chevrolet*, 778 S.W.2d at 464-65; *see Beck*, 771 S.W.2d at 142 (after pretrial hearing determining that prima facie proof of meritorious defense is presented, court should proceed with discovery and trial on merits of bill of review); *see, e.g.*, *Boateng v. Trailblazer Health Enters.*, 171 S.W.3d 481, 492 (Tex.App.—Houston [14th Dist.] 2005, pet. denied) (court erred when it signed final J at pretrial hearing granting Ps relief on the merits without notice of separate trial). Once the trial is finished, the court will render a new final judgment. *1985 Chevrolet*, 778 S.W.2d at 465.

§7.2 Collateral attacks on default judgment. If a defendant is unable to attack a default judgment directly by one of the above methods, it may be able to attack the judgment collaterally to avoid the effect of the judgment. *See PNS Stores v. Rivera*, 379 S.W.3d 267, 272-73 (Tex.2012).

1. When to use. A defendant can collaterally attack only a void judgment. *See PNS Stores*, 379 S.W.3d at 272-73 (void judgment can be attacked directly or collaterally, but voidable judgment can only be attacked directly). If a judgment of a court of general jurisdiction is void, it can be collaterally attacked in another court of equal jurisdiction. *Browning v. Placke*, 698 S.W.2d 362, 363 (Tex.1985); *Armentor v. Kern*, 178 S.W.3d 147, 149 (Tex. App.—Houston [1st Dist.] 2005, no pet.). Certain jurisdictional defects render a judgment void; all other defects render the judgment voidable, and those judgments can only be attacked directly. *Placke*, 698 S.W.2d at 363; *see PNS Stores*, 379 S.W.3d at 272-73. See "Direct attacks on default judgment," §7.1, p. 598.

(1) Defects in jurisdiction – generally. A judgment is void and can be collaterally attacked if the court rendering the judgment had no jurisdiction over the parties or property, no jurisdiction over the subject matter, no jurisdiction to enter that particular judgment, or no capacity to act as a court. *PNS Stores*, 379 S.W.3d at 272; *Placke*, 698 S.W.2d at 363; *cf. Browning v. Prostok*, 165 S.W.3d 336, 346 (Tex.2005) (attack on bankruptcy order).

(2) Defects in personal jurisdiction – no due process. A judgment is void and can be collaterally attacked when the record identifies substantial defects in personal jurisdiction that violate due process. *PNS Stores*, 379 S.W.3d at 273; *see In re E.R.*, ___ S.W.3d ___ (Tex.2012) (No. 11-0282; 7-6-12). For defects in personal jurisdiction to violate due process, there must be a complete failure or lack of service rather than merely technical defects in service. *PNS Stores*, 379 S.W.3d at 274.

2. Review of record. In a collateral attack, the judgment is presumed to be valid. *PNS Stores*, 379 S.W.3d at 273; *Stewart v. USA Custom Paint & Body Shop, Inc.*, 870 S.W.2d 18, 20 (Tex.1994). Although the judgment is presumed valid, the court may look beyond the face of the judgment to determine whether the record demonstrates that the court lacked jurisdiction. *PNS Stores*, 379 S.W.3d at 273. The presumption disappears if the record establishes a jurisdictional defect sufficient to void the judgment. *Id.*; *see Alfonso v. Skadden*, 251 S.W.3d 52, 55 (Tex. 2008); *Wagner v. D'Lorm*, 315 S.W.3d 188, 194 n.2 (Tex.App.—Austin 2010, no pet.). *But see Toles v. Toles*, 113 S.W.3d 899, 914 (Tex.App.—Dallas 2003, no pet.) (collateral attack will be unsuccessful if judgment contains jurisdictional recitals, even if other parts of record show lack of jurisdiction).

★

§7.3 Mandamus. Mandamus is not an appropriate means of reviewing a final default judgment if the trial court had jurisdiction when it rendered the default judgment. *In re Barber*, 982 S.W.2d 364, 368 (Tex.1998); *see Thursby v. Stovall*, 647 S.W.2d 953, 954 (Tex.1983). In certain unique circumstances, however, mandamus relief may be appropriate. *See, e.g., In re Barber*, 982 S.W.2d at 368 (mandamus appropriate when trial court did not acknowledge validity of its own order setting aside default).

B. MOTION FOR SUMMARY JUDGMENT—GENERAL RULES

§1. GENERAL

§1.1 Rule. TRCP 166a.

§1.2 Purpose. The purpose of summary-judgment procedure is to allow courts to summarily end a case when only a question of law is involved and there is no genuine issue of fact. *G&H Towing Co. v. Magee*, 347 S.W.3d 293, 296-97 (Tex.2011); *see City of Houston v. Clear Creek Basin Auth.*, 589 S.W.2d 671, 678 n.5 (Tex.1979) (SJ procedure allows trial court to promptly dispose of cases that involve unmeritorious claims or untenable defenses). Summary-judgment procedure should not deprive litigants of their right to a trial by jury or to try a case by affidavit and deposition testimony. *See Clear Creek*, 589 S.W.2d at 678 n.5; *Collins v. County of El Paso*, 954 S.W.2d 137, 145 (Tex.App.—El Paso 1997, pet. denied).

§1.3 Timetable & forms. Timetable, Motion for Summary Judgment, p. 1226; *O'Connor's Texas Civil Forms* (2012), FORMS 7B, 7C, 9C:4, 10B:6.

§1.4 Other references. Brown & Rondon, *Texas Rules of Evidence Handbook* (2013) (referred to as Brown & Rondon, *Evidence Handbook*); 3 McDonald & Carlson, *Texas Civil Practice* §18.19[f] (2d ed. 2000 & Supp.2011-12); Patton, *Summary Judgments in Texas: Practice, Procedure & Review* ch. 6 (3d ed. 2002 & Supp.2012) (referred to as Patton, *Summary Judgments in Texas*); *O'Connor's Texas Causes of Action* (2013) (*O'Connor's Texas COA*); *O'Connor's Texas Civil Appeals* (2012) (*O'Connor's Texas Appeals*).

§2. TYPES OF MOTIONS FOR SUMMARY JUDGMENT

There are two types of motions for summary judgment. The first type of motion is the traditional motion, which depends on summary-judgment evidence. TRCP 166a(c). See "Traditional Motion for Summary Judgment," ch. 7-C, p. 628. The second type of motion is a no-evidence summary judgment, which is usually made without summary-judgment evidence. TRCP 166a(i). See "No-Evidence Motion for Summary Judgment," ch. 7-D, p. 640. A party may, in a single motion, present grounds appropriate for a traditional summary judgment and grounds appropriate for a no-evidence summary judgment. *Binur v. Jacobo*, 135 S.W.3d 646, 650-51 (Tex.2004). This motion is sometimes called a hybrid motion for summary judgment. *See Buck v. Palmer*, ___ S.W.3d ___ n.2 (Tex.2012) (No. 11-0057; 8-31-12); *Young Ref. Corp. v. Pennzoil Co.*, 46 S.W.3d 380, 385 (Tex.App.—Houston [1st Dist.] 2001, pet. denied). The party should specify the standard on which the summary judgment is sought. *See, e.g., Waite v. Woodard, Hall & Primm, P.C.*, 137 S.W.3d 277, 281 (Tex.App.—Houston [1st Dist.] 2004, no pet.) (hybrid motion that did not cite to or make argument under TRCP 166a(c) did not give "fair notice" of attempt to obtain traditional SJ).

7-2. COMPARISON OF SUMMARY-JUDGMENT PROCEDURES		
	Regular MSJ—TRCP 166a(a), (b)	No-evidence MSJ—TRCP 166a(i)
1	Initial assumption	Nonmovant has a supportable claim or defense.	Nonmovant does not have a supportable claim or defense.
2	Movant's burden	Movant must prove its claim or defense or disprove an element of nonmovant's claim or defense as a matter of law.	Movant must allege there is no evidence to prove a specific element of nonmovant's claim or defense.

★

7-2. COMPARISON OF SUMMARY-JUDGMENT PROCEDURES (CONTINUED)		
	Regular MSJ—TRCP 166a(a), (b)	No-evidence MSJ—TRCP 166a(i)
3	Nonmovant's burden	Nonmovant does not have burden until movant offers proof it is entitled to SJ as a matter of law.	Nonmovant has the burden to raise fact issue on its claim or defense.
4	Shifting of burden to nonmovant	Burden shifts to nonmovant when movant produces SJ evidence proving that it is entitled to SJ.	Burden shifts to nonmovant when movant alleges nonmovant has no evidence.
5	Earliest time to file MSJ	Anytime after lawsuit is filed.	After adequate time for discovery.

§3. SUMMARY JUDGMENT *OR* SPECIAL EXCEPTIONS

Defects in the other party's petition, counterclaim, or cross-claim can be challenged by special exceptions (which can lead to an order of dismissal or the striking of the claim) or by a motion for summary judgment (which can lead to a judgment). To determine whether a party should challenge defects in the other party's pleadings by special exceptions rather than by a motion for summary judgment, see "Special Exceptions & Summary Judgments," ch. 3-G, §10, p. 255.

§4. MOTION FOR SUMMARY JUDGMENT

For the requirements of and burden of proof for a motion for summary judgment, see "Traditional Motion for Summary Judgment," ch. 7-C, p. 628, and "No-Evidence Motion for Summary Judgment," ch. 7-D, p. 640.

§5. SPECIAL EXCEPTIONS IN SUMMARY-JUDGMENT PROCEDURE

The purpose of special exceptions in the summary-judgment procedure is to ensure that the parties and the trial court are focused on the same grounds. *McConnell v. Southside ISD*, 858 S.W.2d 337, 342-43 (Tex.1993); *see Harwell v. State Farm Mut. Auto. Ins.*, 896 S.W.2d 170, 175 (Tex.1995). See *O'Connor's Texas Forms*, FORM 7B:1.

§5.1 **When necessary.** If the motion or response states grounds that are unclear or ambiguous, it is "prudent trial practice" to file special exceptions. *McConnell v. Southside ISD*, 858 S.W.2d 337, 342-43 (Tex.1993); *see Pettitte v. SCI Corp.*, 893 S.W.2d 746, 748 (Tex.App.—Houston [1st Dist.] 1995, no writ).

§5.2 **When not necessary.** It is not necessary to file special exceptions in the following situations: (1) when the grounds for the motion or response are stated only in a brief or other document but not in the motion or response, (2) when the motion or response presents no grounds, or (3) when the motion or response clearly presents some grounds but not others. *McConnell v. Southside ISD*, 858 S.W.2d 337, 340-42 (Tex.1993).

§5.3 **In writing.** The special exceptions must be in writing. *McConnell v. Southside ISD*, 858 S.W.2d 337, 343 n.7 (Tex.1993).

§5.4 **Ruling.** The party who files special exceptions in a summary-judgment proceeding should ask the trial court to sign a written order overruling or sustaining the special exceptions at or before the hearing on the motion for summary judgment. *See McConnell v. Southside ISD*, 858 S.W.2d 337, 343 n.7 (Tex.1993). Only if the trial court abuses its discretion will its ruling on the special exceptions be disturbed. *Alejandro v. Bell*, 84 S.W.3d 383, 389 (Tex. App.—Corpus Christi 2002, no pet.). See "Standard of review," ch. 3-G, §12.1.2, p. 256. The ruling on the special exceptions can be included in the summary judgment. The courts disagree on the effect of a trial court's failure or refusal to rule on the nonmovant's special exceptions.

1. **Express ruling required.** Some courts require the nonmovant to secure an express ruling on its special exceptions to avoid waiving them as a ground for error on appeal. These courts hold that the failure or refusal to rule on special exceptions, coupled with the granting of a summary judgment, does not amount to a ruling on the special exceptions. *See Franco v. Slavonic Mut. Fire Ins.*, 154 S.W.3d 777, 785 (Tex.App.—Houston [14th Dist.]

★

2004, no pet.) (appellate court cannot infer from granting of D's SJ motion that trial court overruled P's special exceptions); **Rosas v. Hatz**, 147 S.W.3d 560, 563 (Tex.App.—Waco 2004, no pet.) (same). These courts maintain the requirement for an express ruling even if the nonmovant requested a ruling and the court refused to rule. *See, e.g.*, **Franco**, 154 S.W.3d at 784 (appellant presented order for overruling special exceptions but court refused to sign it). See "Express ruling required," §10.2.2, p. 622.

2. Implicit ruling sufficient. Some courts hold that a court's failure or refusal to rule on the nonmovant's special exceptions, coupled with the granting of a summary judgment, implicitly overrules the special exceptions and preserves error for the appeal. *See **Alejandro**, 84 S.W.3d at 389. Because special exceptions are a type of objection, the same rules should apply to their overruling as are applied to objections. See "Implicit ruling sufficient," §10.2.1, p. 621.

§5.5 Deadlines for special exceptions. See "For special exceptions," §6.7, p. 607.

§6. SUMMARY-JUDGMENT DEADLINES

§6.1 By rule – 21 days before hearing.

1. Filing & serving motion & notice. The nonmovant is entitled to at least 21 days' notice of the date set for the hearing or submission of the motion. TRCP 166a(c); **Lewis v. Blake**, 876 S.W.2d 314, 316 (Tex.1994). That is, the movant must file and serve the motion and notice of hearing at least 21 days before the hearing. TRCP 166a(c); *see also* **Jones v. Illinois Employers Ins.**, 136 S.W.3d 728, 734-35 (Tex.App.—Texarkana 2004, no pet.) (cross-motion for SJ embodied in response to motion for SJ not timely when filed seven days before hearing; 21 days' notice required). The nonmovant is entitled to 21 days' notice of each motion. TRCP 166a(c); *see **Luna v. Estate of Rodriguez***, 906 S.W.2d 576, 582 (Tex.App.—Austin 1995, no writ). However, reconsideration of the court's ruling on the motion does not require another 21 days' notice. **Winn v. Martin Homebuilders, Inc.**, 153 S.W.3d 553, 556 (Tex. App.—Amarillo 2004, pet. denied).

(1) Deadlines affected by type of service. Depending on the type of service, the movant may be required to serve the motion and notice of hearing at least 24 days (rather than 21 days) before the hearing.

(a) By delivery – 21 days. When the motion and notice of hearing are served by delivery, they must be served at least 21 days before the hearing. *See* TRCP 166a(c); *Lewis*, 876 S.W.2d at 316.

(b) By mail – 24 days. When the motion and notice of hearing are served by mail, they must be mailed at least 24 days before the hearing because TRCP 21a extends the minimum notice by three days. *Lewis*, 876 S.W.2d at 315; **Chadderdon v. Blaschke**, 988 S.W.2d 387, 388 (Tex.App.—Houston [1st Dist.] 1999, no pet.); *see* TRCP 21a, 166a(c).

(c) By fax – 24 days. When the motion and notice of hearing are served by fax, they generally must be faxed at least 24 days before the hearing because TRCP 21a extends the minimum notice by three days. *See* TRCP 21a, 166a(c).

CAUTION

A party serving the motion and notice of hearing by fax must be aware of the exact time the documents are faxed because if the fax is received after 5:00 p.m. local time of the recipient, the documents are deemed served on the next day rather than the day they are faxed. See TRCP 21a. See "Fax," ch. 1-D, §6.3, p. 37. In this situation, the day the motion and notice of hearing are faxed must be at least 25 days before the hearing. See "Computing Response Deadlines," chart 1-2, p. 37; "Computing days," §6.1.1(2), p. 606.

(d) By e-service.

[1] County & district court – 24 days. When the motion and notice of hearing are served electronically in a county or district court, they generally must be served at least 24 days before the hearing. *See* Loc. E-filing Rules Template, rules 5.2, 5.3, www.courts.state.tx.us/jcit/efiling/EfilingHome.asp.

⭐

[2] Justice court – 21 days. When the motion and notice of hearing are served electronically in a justice court, they generally must be served at least 21 days before the hearing. *See* JP E-Filing & E-Service Rules, rule 5.2, Tex.Sup.Ct. Order, Misc. Docket No. 07-9200 (eff. Jan. 1, 2008).

CAUTION

A party serving the motion and notice of hearing by e-service must be aware of the exact time the documents are e-served because if e-service is completed after 5:00 p.m. local time of the recipient, the documents are deemed served on the next day rather than the day they are e-served. See Loc. E-filing Rules Template, rules 5.2(c), 5.3, www.courts.state.tx.us/jcit/efiling/ EfilingHome.asp; JP E-Filing & E-Service Rules, rule 5.2(c), Tex.Sup.Ct. Order, Misc. Docket No. 07-9200 (eff. Jan. 1, 2008). See "E-service," ch. 1-D, §6.4, p. 37. In this situation, the day the motion and notice of hearing are e-served must be at least 25 days before the hearing in a county or district court and 22 days before the hearing in a justice court. See "Computing Response Deadlines," chart 1-2, p. 37; "Computing days," §6.1.1(2), this page.

---

(2) Computing days. The 21 (or 24) days' notice of the hearing must be calculated from the date of service of the motion and notice of hearing. *See Lewis*, 876 S.W.2d at 316. In computing the number of days, the day the motion and notice of hearing are served is not counted (it is "day 0"), but the day of the hearing is counted (it is "day 21" or "day 24"). *Id.*; *see* TRCP 4, 166a(c). If the motion is filed and served before the hearing date is set and the notice of the hearing is filed and served later, the 21 (or 24) days' notice of the hearing must be calculated from the date of service of the notice, not the motion. *Chadderdon*, 988 S.W.2d at 388. For a detailed discussion of computing deadlines, see "Computing time limits – days," ch. 1-C, §7.1, p. 26; "Computing Response Deadlines," ch. 1-D, §6, p. 36; "Computing Response Deadlines," chart 1-2, p. 37.

2. Form for notice of hearing. If the date for the hearing is known before the motion for summary judgment is served, the notice of the hearing can be included in the motion itself or served as a separate document from the motion with its own certificate of service. If the date for the hearing is not known at the time the motion for summary judgment is served, the notice of the hearing must be served as a separate document with its own certificate of service. See "Included in SJ motion," §7.3, p. 609; "Separate notice," §7.4, p. 610.

§6.2 By agreement. The parties may change the deadlines by agreement. If the agreement meets the requirements of TRCP 11, the court should enforce it. *See, e.g., EZ Pawn Corp. v. Mancias*, 934 S.W.2d 87, 91 (Tex.1996) (because parties made Rule 11 agreement to permit nonmovant to file response a week before the hearing, trial court should have disregarded response filed after that deadline). See "Agreements Between Attorneys – Rule 11," ch. 1-H, §9, p. 61.

§6.3 By court order. The court may permit the hearing to be set with less than 21 days' notice, with advance notice to the parties. TRCP 166a(c); *see, e.g., Hall v. Stephenson*, 919 S.W.2d 454, 461 (Tex.App.—Fort Worth 1996, writ denied) (with advance notice, court reduced 21 days' notice to 17 days). *But see Stephens v. Turtle Creek Apts., Ltd.*, 875 S.W.2d 25, 26-27 (Tex.App.—Houston [14th Dist.] 1994, no writ) (even with advance notice, court cannot reduce 21 days' notice to six days). A court cannot grant leave for a shorter hearing period to excuse the movant's inadequate notice after the nonmovant complains of the inadequate notice. *See* TRCP 166a(c).

§6.4 For response – 7 days before hearing. The nonmovant must file and serve its response and affidavits at least seven days before the hearing. TRCP 166a(c); *Carpenter v. Cimarron Hydrocarbons Corp.*, 98 S.W.3d 682, 686 (Tex.2002); *K-Six TV, Inc. v. Santiago*, 75 S.W.3d 91, 96 (Tex.App.—San Antonio 2002, no pet.); *see also Alford v. Thornburg*, 113 S.W.3d 575, 586 (Tex.App.—Texarkana 2003, no pet.) (affidavit that was timely filed but served late was not considered by court because P did not ask to serve late affidavit or request continuance); *Hammonds v. Thomas*, 770 S.W.2d 1, 2 (Tex.App.—Texarkana 1989, no writ) (court should have considered nonmovant's affidavits filed six days before hearing because seventh day before hearing was July 4, a national holiday). See "Computing time limits – days," ch. 1-C, §7.1, p. 26. The response may be filed by mailing it on the day it is due, and it is timely filed even if it reaches the court less than seven days before the hearing, as long as it is received by the clerk no more than ten days after the due date. TRCP 5; *Geiselman v. Cramer Fin. Grp.*, 965 S.W.2d 532, 535 (Tex. App.—Houston [14th Dist.] 1997, no writ). The three-day rule for mailing in TRCP 21a does not require the non-movant to mail the response ten days before the hearing. *Holmes v. Ottawa Truck, Inc.*, 960 S.W.2d 866, 869 (Tex. App.—El Paso 1997, pet. denied). The seven-day deadline gives the nonmovant at least 14 days to obtain and file summary-judgment evidence. *Extended Servs. Program, Inc. v. First Extended Serv.*, 601 S.W.2d 469, 470 (Tex. App.—Dallas 1980, writ ref'd n.r.e.) (21 days' notice of hearing minus the seven-day deadline to file response before the hearing = 14 days to file response and SJ evidence).

§6.5 For SJ evidence. The deadline to file affidavits, unfiled discovery, and other summary-judgment evidence is the same deadline that applies to the motion or response. TRCP 166a(c), (d). No evidence can be filed after the court rules on the motion, even if the motion was a partial motion. *See* TRCP 166a(c); *Valores Corporativos, S.A. de C.V. v. McLane Co.*, 945 S.W.2d 160, 162 (Tex.App.—San Antonio 1997, writ denied). See "Filing late evidence," §6.9.4, p. 608.

§6.6 For movant's reply to response. If the nonmovant filed a response to the motion for summary judgment, the movant may want to reply to the response. There is no deadline in TRCP 166a for a movant's reply to a response. *Callaghan Ranch, Ltd. v. Killam*, 53 S.W.3d 1, 4 (Tex.App.—San Antonio 2000, pet. denied); *Knapp v. Eppright*, 783 S.W.2d 293, 296 (Tex.App.—Houston [14th Dist.] 1989, no writ); *see, e.g.*, *Reynolds v. Murphy*, 188 S.W.3d 252, 259 (Tex.App.—Fort Worth 2006, pet. denied) (movant's objections to nonmovant's response filed the day of hearing were not untimely). However, the local rules of some courts set time limits for responsive pleadings. *See, e.g.*, Harris Cty. Loc. R. 3.3.3 (in county courts at law, replies must be filed at least three working days before submission). If the movant needs time to cure defects in its motion, pleadings, or summary-judgment evidence, it should request a continuance of the hearing.

§6.7 For special exceptions.

1. For nonmovant. If the nonmovant challenges the motion for summary judgment by special exceptions, it must file and serve them at least seven days before the hearing. *McConnell v. Southside ISD*, 858 S.W.2d 337, 343 n.7 (Tex.1993).

2. For movant. If the movant challenges the response to the motion for summary judgment by special exceptions, it must file and serve them at least three days before the hearing. *McConnell*, 858 S.W.2d at 343 n.7.

§6.8 For filing an amendment to pleadings. The filing deadlines for amendments to the pleadings (petition and answer) are different from the filing deadlines for amendments to the summary-judgment motion and response. See "Procedure to amend," §8.1, p. 610.

§6.9 Late filing.

1. Filing a late motion. To file a motion for summary judgment with less than 21 days' notice, the movant must obtain leave of court. TRCP 166a(c). However, if the nonmovant does not object to the late motion, the error is waived. *Ajibade v. Edinburg Gen. Hosp.*, 22 S.W.3d 37, 40 (Tex.App.—Corpus Christi 2000, no pet.); *Luna v. Estate of Rodriguez*, 906 S.W.2d 576, 582 (Tex.App.—Austin 1995, no writ).

2. Filing an amended motion after the hearing. To file an amendment or supplement to add an additional ground to the motion for summary judgment after the hearing, the movant must give the nonmovant another 21 days to respond. *See, e.g.*, *Sams v. N.L. Indus.*, 735 S.W.2d 486, 488 (Tex.App.—Houston [1st Dist.] 1987, no writ) (movant's post-hearing "reply" that added new grounds for SJ required 21 days' notice).

3. Filing a late response. To file a response (or an amendment to a response) less than seven days before the summary-judgment hearing, the nonmovant must obtain leave of court. TRCP 166a(c). To secure permission to file the response less than seven days before the hearing, the nonmovant must file a motion for leave to file a late summary-judgment response that establishes (1) good cause and (2) no undue prejudice. *Wheeler v. Green*, 157 S.W.3d 439, 442 (Tex.2005). Good cause is established by sworn proof that the nonmovant's failure to timely respond was not intentional or the result of conscious indifference, but was the result of an accident or mistake. *Id.*

★

The lack of undue prejudice is established by showing the late response will not unduly delay or otherwise injure the movant. *Id.* at 443. This standard for allowing a late summary-judgment response is the same as for withdrawing a deemed admission. ***Carpenter v. Cimarron Hydrocarbons Corp.***, 98 S.W.3d 682, 687-88 (Tex.2002). For a discussion of good cause and no undue prejudice, see "Motion to strike deemed admissions," ch. 6-H, §7.2.2, p. 561. If the record does not contain some indication that the trial court granted the nonmovant leave to file a late response, the nonmovant waives the issues raised in the late response. *See **INA v. Bryant***, 686 S.W.2d 614, 615 (Tex.1985); ***K-Six TV, Inc. v. Santiago***, 75 S.W.3d 91, 96 (Tex.App.—San Antonio 2002, no pet.). In its motion for leave to file a late response, the nonmovant can ask the court to continue the hearing to a later date as an alternative. See "Motion to continue hearing," §6.10.1, this page.

    4. Filing late evidence. To file late summary-judgment evidence, the party (movant or nonmovant) must obtain leave of court. TRCP 166a(c); ***Benchmark Bank v. Crowder***, 919 S.W.2d 657, 663 (Tex.1996). The party must obtain a written ruling on its motion for leave to file late summary-judgment evidence, or the evidence will not be considered on appeal. *See **Mathis v. RKL Design/Build***, 189 S.W.3d 839, 842-43 (Tex.App.—Houston [1st Dist.] 2006, no pet.). If a party files late summary-judgment evidence or a late amendment to the evidence and no ruling appears in the record, the evidence will not be considered as being before the trial court when it ruled on the motion for summary judgment. ***Benchmark Bank***, 919 S.W.2d at 663; ***Mathis***, 189 S.W.3d at 843; *see, e.g.*, ***Mello v. A.M.F., Inc.***, 7 S.W.3d 329, 332 (Tex.App.—Beaumont 1999, pet. denied) (no ruling permitting filing of supplemental evidence by nonmovants on day of SJ hearing); ***Basin Credit Consultants, Inc. v. Obregon***, 2 S.W.3d 372, 374 (Tex. App.—San Antonio 1999, pet. denied) (same, for affidavits filed by nonmovant after SJ hearing); ***Luna***, 906 S.W.2d at 582 & n.6 (same, for evidence filed by both parties on day of hearing); ***Texas Airfinance Corp. v. Lesikar***, 777 S.W.2d 559, 561 (Tex.App.—Houston [14th Dist.] 1989, no writ) (same, for affidavit filed by movant 12 days before hearing).

§6.10 Motions for more time.

    1. Motion to continue hearing. When a nonmovant needs additional time to secure affidavits or discovery or to amend its pleading, it should file a motion for continuance. *See* TRCP 166a(g). See "Motion to continue SJ hearing," ch. 5-D, §9.3, p. 340; *O'Connor's Texas Forms*, FORM 7B:5. The trial court has the discretion to deny a motion for continuance under TRCP 251. A motion for continuance is not the correct motion to file when the nonmovant did not get the required 21 days' notice. See "Motion to reset SJ hearing," §6.10.2, this page.

    2. Motion to reset SJ hearing. When a nonmovant did not get 21 days' notice of the hearing, it should file a motion to reset the hearing date. The trial court does not have the discretion to deny a motion to reset the hearing when the nonmovant was not given the full 21 days' notice required by TRCP 166a(c). See "Motion to reset SJ hearing for lack of 21 days' notice," ch. 5-D, §9.2, p. 340; *O'Connor's Texas Forms*, FORM 7B:2.

§6.11 Summary chart for SJ deadlines. Chart 7-3, below, summarizes the filing deadlines in summary-judgment cases, including whether leave is required for a late filing, whether an objection to a late filing is necessary, and whether error is waived if no objection is made.

7-3. FILING DEADLINES IN SUMMARY-JUDGMENT CASES				
Document	Deadline to file before hearing*	Ask for leave to file late	Objection necessary if late	If no objection, is complaint waived?
Movant				
1 Motion for SJ	21 days	Yes	Yes	Yes
2 SJ evidence to support motion	21 days	Yes	No	No
3 Amended motion with new ground	21 days	Yes	Yes	Yes

★

7-3. FILING DEADLINES IN SUMMARY-JUDGMENT CASES (CONTINUED)				
Document	Deadline to file before hearing*	Ask for leave to file late	Objection necessary if late	If no objection, is complaint waived?
Movant (continued)				
4 Amended pleading (e.g., answer)	7 days	No	Yes	Yes
5 Special exceptions to the response	3 days	Yes	?	?
Nonmovant				
6 Response to motion for SJ	7 days	Yes	No	No
7 SJ evidence to support response	7 days	Yes	No	No
8 Amended response	7 days	Yes	No	No
9 Amended pleading (e.g., petition)	7 days	No	Yes	Yes
10 Special exceptions to the motion	7 days	Yes	?	?

*Service deadlines may vary if service is accomplished by a method other than personal delivery. See ch. 1-D, §6, p. 36.

§7. NOTICE

§7.1 Notice of SJ hearing. The nonmovant is entitled to receive sufficient notice of the hearing or submission (collectively "the hearing") date on the summary-judgment motion so that it knows when its response is due. *Martin v. Martin, Martin & Richards, Inc.*, 989 S.W.2d 357, 359 (Tex.1998); *Rorie v. Goodwin*, 171 S.W.3d 579, 583 (Tex.App.—Tyler 2005, no pet.); *Aguirre v. Phillips Props., Inc.*, 111 S.W.3d 328, 332 (Tex.App.—Corpus Christi 2003, pet. denied).

PRACTICE TIP
The movant's attorney should contact the attorneys for the other parties and discuss mutually agreeable dates before calling the court clerk to set the summary-judgment hearing.

---

1. First setting. The movant is required to give the nonmovant 21 days' notice of the hearing on a summary-judgment motion. TRCP 166a(c); *Lewis v. Blake*, 876 S.W.2d 314, 316 (Tex.1994). To compute the 21 days, see "By rule – 21 days before hearing," §6.1, p. 605.

2. Resetting the hearing. Once a nonmovant is given 21 days' notice of the hearing, if the hearing date is reset, the nonmovant is not entitled to another 21 days' notice of the new date. *Birdwell v. Texins Credit Un.*, 843 S.W.2d 246, 250 (Tex.App.—Texarkana 1992, no writ).

§7.2 In writing. The movant must give the nonmovant written notice of the hearing on the motion for summary judgment. *See* TRCP 21a ("[e]very notice required by these rules … may be served by delivering…."), TRCP 166a(c) (does not specify written notice). The notice must include the fact that a hearing has been set, and it must give the date and time for the hearing. *Mosser v. Plano Three Venture*, 893 S.W.2d 8, 11 (Tex.App.—Dallas 1994, no writ). If the movant does not provide timely notice, the summary judgment will be reversed. *Etheredge v. Hidden Valley Airpark Ass'n*, 169 S.W.3d 378, 383 (Tex.App.—Fort Worth 2005, pet. denied); *Guinn v. Zarsky*, 893 S.W.2d 13, 17 (Tex.App.—Corpus Christi 1994, no writ).

§7.3 Included in SJ motion. The notice of the date and time for the hearing may be attached to the motion for summary judgment. The notice must state the actual date and time for the hearing; a movant's written request for a certain date for a hearing is not notice of the date of the hearing. *Veal v. Veterans Life Ins.*, 767 S.W.2d 892, 895 (Tex.App.—Texarkana 1989, no writ).

⭐

---

§7.4 Separate notice. If the notice of the hearing is a separate document from the motion for summary judgment, the notice must contain its own certificate of service. *Tanksley v. CitiCapital Commercial Corp.*, 145 S.W.3d 760, 763 (Tex.App.—Dallas 2004, pet. denied); *see* TRCP 21a; *see, e.g., Guinn v. Zarsky*, 893 S.W.2d 13, 17 (Tex. App.—Corpus Christi 1994, no writ) (notice of hearing, which was on a separate sheet in same envelope as SJ motion, was not sufficient because it was not certified). If the motion is filed and served before the hearing date is set and the notice of the hearing is filed and served later, the movant must give the nonmovant 21 days' notice of the hearing, counting from the date of service of the notice, not the motion. *Chadderdon v. Blaschke*, 988 S.W.2d 387, 388 (Tex.App.—Houston [1st Dist.] 1999, no pet.). Regardless of how long the motion is on file, the movant must give the nonmovant 21 days' notice of the hearing date when it sets the motion for a hearing. *Id.* See "Filing & serving motion & notice," §6.1.1, p. 605.

§8. AMENDING THE PETITION OR ANSWER

The filing requirements and deadlines for amending the pleadings (petition and answer) are different from the filing requirements and deadlines for amending the motion for summary judgment and response. By understanding the differences, a nonmovant may be able to avoid a final summary judgment.

§8.1 Procedure to amend. The trial court must render a summary judgment on the pleadings on file at the time of the hearing. TRCP 166a(c). A party may file an amended pleading after it files its motion or response. *See, e.g., Cluett v. Medical Prot. Co.*, 829 S.W.2d 822, 825-26 (Tex.App.—Dallas 1992, writ denied) (movant filed amended petition after SJ motion but four months before hearing).

1. Amending pleadings before hearing. A party should file an amended petition or answer as soon as it becomes aware it is necessary, but no later than seven days before the hearing. TRCP 63; *Sosa v. Central Power & Light*, 909 S.W.2d 893, 895 (Tex.1995). In computing the seven-day period, the day the party files the amended pleading is not counted, but the day of the hearing on the motion for summary judgment is counted. *Sosa*, 909 S.W.2d at 895. If the party decides to amend after the seven-day deadline (e.g., six days before the hearing), it should file its amended pleading before the hearing even if a motion for leave to amend has not been filed. *See Goswami v. Metropolitan S&L Ass'n*, 751 S.W.2d 487, 490 (Tex.1988) (nonmovant filed amended petition four days before hearing). Unless the record shows that the court denied leave to file, the appellate courts will assume the trial court considered the amended pleading. *See Goswami*, 751 S.W.2d at 490-91. *But see Honea v. Morgan Drive Away, Inc.*, 997 S.W.2d 705, 707 (Tex.App.—Eastland 1999, no pet.) (when order said it considered all "timely" pleadings, court presumably did not consider late-amended pleadings). Leave to file within seven days before the hearing is presumed granted when (1) the summary judgment states that all pleadings were considered, (2) the record does not show that an amended pleading was not considered, and (3) the opposing party does not show surprise. *Continental Airlines, Inc. v. Kiefer*, 920 S.W.2d 274, 276 (Tex.1996) (amended pleading filed five days before hearing); *see Goswami*, 751 S.W.2d at 490. If the late amendment creates a fact issue, the appellate courts will reverse the summary judgment. *See Goswami*, 751 S.W.2d at 490-91.

2. Amending pleadings after hearing. Once the hearing date for the motion for summary judgment has passed, a party may file an amended pleading before the court signs a judgment if the party secures a written order granting leave to file. *See* TRCP 166a(c); *see, e.g., Cherry v. McCall*, 138 S.W.3d 35, 42-43 (Tex.App.—San Antonio 2004, pet. denied) (nonmovant did not obtain leave to file amended petition almost three weeks after hearing); *Hussong v. Schwan's Sales Enters.*, 896 S.W.2d 320, 323 (Tex.App.—Houston [1st Dist.] 1995, no writ) (nonmovant did not get permission to file amended petition one month after hearing and before court granted SJ). Unless the record shows that the court granted leave to file, the appellate courts will assume leave was denied. *Leinen v. Buffington's Bayou City Serv.*, 824 S.W.2d 682, 685 (Tex.App.—Houston [14th Dist.] 1992, no writ).

§8.2 Objecting to amendment.

1. Amendment filed before hearing. Under TRCP 63, the party opposing the amendment has the burden to show surprise. If a party objects to a late amendment, it should make sure the record reflects its objection and the court's ruling. Unless the record shows that the court denied leave to file the late amendment, the appellate courts will assume it was granted. *Goswami v. Metropolitan S&L Ass'n*, 751 S.W.2d 487, 490 (Tex.1988).

———————————————— ✦ ————————————————

2. Amendment filed after hearing. The party opposing an amendment filed after the hearing has no burden to object unless the party filing the amendment asks for leave to file.

§9. SUMMARY-JUDGMENT EVIDENCE

Summary-judgment evidence must be admissible under the rules of evidence. *United Blood Servs. v. Longoria*, 938 S.W.2d 29, 30 (Tex.1997); *see* TRCP 166a(f) (affidavits must set forth facts that would be admissible in evidence). That is, facts must be proved by the same type of evidence that would be admissible at trial, except that facts are proved by affidavits, depositions, interrogatories, and other discovery, rather than by oral testimony. *See* TRCP 166a(c); *Jensen Constr. Co. v. Dallas Cty.*, 920 S.W.2d 761, 768 (Tex.App.—Dallas 1996, writ denied), *disapproved on other grounds*, *Travis Cty. v. Pelzel & Assocs.*, 77 S.W.3d 246 (Tex.2002). Evidentiary exclusions also apply to summary-judgment proceedings as they would at trial. *Fort Brown Villas III Condo. Ass'n v. Gillenwater*, 285 S.W.3d 879, 882 (Tex.2009); *see* TRCP 193.6 (party cannot introduce into evidence information not timely disclosed or offer testimony of witness not timely identified). See "Timely," ch. 6-A, §16.3, p. 439.

§9.1 Pleadings as proof.

1. General rule. As a general rule, pleadings are not summary-judgment evidence. *Laidlaw Waste Sys. v. City of Wilmer*, 904 S.W.2d 656, 660 (Tex.1995); *Hidalgo v. Surety S&L Ass'n*, 462 S.W.2d 540, 545 (Tex.1971).

(1) Petition or answer. A party cannot rely on factual statements contained in its own petition or answer as summary-judgment proof. *Hidalgo*, 462 S.W.2d at 545; *Flameout Design & Fabrication, Inc. v. Pennzoil Caspian Corp.*, 994 S.W.2d 830, 838 (Tex.App.—Houston [1st Dist.] 1999, no pet.).

(2) Motion or response. A party cannot rely on factual statements contained in its own motion for summary judgment or response as summary-judgment proof, even if the motion or response is verified. *Quanaim v. Frasco Rest. & Catering*, 17 S.W.3d 30, 42 (Tex.App.—Houston [14th Dist.] 2000, pet. denied) (response); *Barrow v. Jack's Catfish Inn*, 641 S.W.2d 624, 625 (Tex.App.—Corpus Christi 1982, no writ) (motion).

(3) Pleadings as exhibits. A party cannot rely on other pleadings attached as exhibits to its own motion or response as summary-judgment evidence, even if the pleadings are verified. *See, e.g.*, *Laidlaw Waste*, 904 S.W.2d at 660-61 (P could not rely on its own verified petition attached as an exhibit to its response).

2. Exceptions.

(1) Other party's pleadings. When a party's pleadings contain statements admitting facts or conclusions that directly contradict the party's own theory of recovery or defense, the pleadings may constitute summary-judgment proof for the other party. *See Lyons v. Lindsey Morden Claims Mgmt.*, 985 S.W.2d 86, 92 (Tex.App.—El Paso 1998, no pet.) (SJ may be granted on other party's pleadings that contain judicial admissions); *see also Perry v. Houston ISD*, 902 S.W.2d 544, 547-48 (Tex.App.—Houston [1st Dist.] 1995, writ dism'd) (nonmovant can use movant's exhibit against movant to create fact issues). Although pleadings are not "evidence," when the motion for summary judgment is based on the nonmovant's pleadings, the court assumes the facts in the nonmovant's pleadings are true. See "Moving on the pleadings," ch. 7-C, §2.5.2, p. 629.

(2) Suit on sworn account. When the underlying claim is a suit on a sworn account, the plaintiff's pleadings establish a prima facie case if the defendant does not file a verified denial. *Powers v. Adams*, 2 S.W.3d 496, 498 (Tex.App.—Houston [14th Dist.] 1999, no pet.).

§9.2 Organizing the evidence.
If a party intends to rely on a few affidavits or other documents, it can attach them to the motion or the response. The motion or response should contain a section called "Summary-Judgment Evidence," identifying the attached documents. The motion or response must specifically identify the portions of the evidence that the party wants the court to consider. *Gonzales v. Shing Wai Brass & Metal Wares Factory, Ltd.*, 190 S.W.3d 742, 746 (Tex.App.—San Antonio 2005, no pet.). When an entire document is attached to a motion or response (e.g., a deposition) and the motion or response refers to it only generally, that reference does not satisfy the requirement for specificity. *West v. Hamilton*, ___ S.W.3d ___ (Tex.App.—Amarillo 2008, no pet.) (No.

✯

07-07-0235-CV; 10-9-08) (undesignated op.); **Gonzales**, 190 S.W.3d at 746; *see, e.g.*, **Upchurch v. Albear**, 5 S.W.3d 274, 284-85 (Tex.App.—Amarillo 1999, pet. denied) (3,000 pages attached to motion was not proper SJ evidence because it was not indexed, and motion did not cite to specific parts of it). There is an exception: when a no-evidence motion for summary judgment alleges a complete absence of evidence, specific references to the record are not necessary. **City of Arlington v. State Farm Lloyds**, 145 S.W.3d 165, 167-68 (Tex.2004). If the party is going to rely on an assortment of evidence, it should organize the evidence in an appendix. *See* TRCP 166a(d). If all the summary-judgment proof is presented in an appendix, the following items should be included:

1. Table of contents. Include a table of contents with references to the tabs where the different items are located.

2. Incorporation by reference. Include a statement that all the summary-judgment proof in the appendix is incorporated by reference into the motion or response. The same statement should be included in the motion or response.

3. Verification of proof. Include a verification for all evidence that is required to be verified. See "Verification," ch. 1-B, §3.2.15, p. 11; "Affidavits," ch. 1-B, §3.2.16, p. 11. For the requirements for using an unsworn declaration in place of a verification or an affidavit, see "Unsworn declaration," ch. 1-B, §3.2.14, p. 10. It is not necessary to separately authenticate each piece of documentary evidence. **Llopa, Inc. v. Nagel**, 956 S.W.2d 82, 87 (Tex. App.—San Antonio 1997, pet. denied).

§9.3 Types of witnesses.

1. Disinterested witness. The best summary-judgment proof may be the uncontradicted testimony of a disinterested witness. *See, e.g.*, **Hunsucker v. Omega Indus.**, 659 S.W.2d 692, 696 (Tex.App.—Dallas 1983, no writ) (testimony of disinterested witnesses, who identified truck that left accident scene as belonging to defendant, raised fact issue of whether driver was within scope of employment).

2. Interested witness. To establish facts through an interested witness, the testimony must be clear, positive, direct, credible, free from contradiction, and uncontroverted even though it could have been readily controverted. TRCP 166a(c); **McIntyre v. Ramirez**, 109 S.W.3d 741, 749 (Tex.2003); **Trico Techs. v. Montiel**, 949 S.W.2d 308, 310 (Tex.1997). If the testimony does not meet these requirements, it will not support a summary judgment. *See* **Casso v. Brand**, 776 S.W.2d 551, 558 (Tex.1989). The phrase "could have been readily controverted" in TRCP 166a(c) does not simply mean the party's summary-judgment proof could have been easily and conveniently rebutted; instead, it means the testimony is of a nature that can be effectively countered by opposing evidence. **Trico Techs.**, 949 S.W.2d at 310; **Casso**, 776 S.W.2d at 558. If the credibility of the affiant is likely to be a dispositive factor in the resolution of the case, summary judgment is not appropriate. **Casso**, 776 S.W.2d at 558; **CEBI Metal v. Garcia**, 108 S.W.3d 464, 465 (Tex.App.—Houston [14th Dist.] 2003, no pet.).

3. Expert witness. An expert's opinion testimony can establish or defeat a claim as a matter of law. *See* **Burrow v. Arce**, 997 S.W.2d 229, 235 (Tex.1999). For purposes of summary-judgment proof, experts are considered interested witnesses. *See* TRCP 166a(c) (last sentence). An expert's testimony (fact or opinion) must be clear, positive, direct, credible, free from contradiction, and uncontroverted even though it could have been readily controverted by another expert. TRCP 166a(c); **Wadewitz v. Montgomery**, 951 S.W.2d 464, 466 (Tex.1997); **Anderson v. Snider**, 808 S.W.2d 54, 55 (Tex.1991). The expert's opinion must meet the test for expert testimony. See "*Daubert-Robinson* Test for Expert Testimony," ch. 5-N, §2, p. 410. The testimony of an expert should include (1) the expert's qualifications, (2) the opinion, (3) the facts on which the opinion is based, and (4) the reasoning on which the opinion is based. *See* **United Blood Servs. v. Longoria**, 938 S.W.2d 29, 30 (Tex.1997) (qualifications of expert); **Anderson**, 808 S.W.2d at 55 (expert's reasoning). Expert testimony that merely states unsubstantiated legal conclusions is not proper summary-judgment evidence. **Burrow**, 997 S.W.2d at 235; **Wadewitz**, 951 S.W.2d at 466; **Anderson**, 808 S.W.2d at 55; **Barraza v. Eureka Co.**, 25 S.W.3d 225, 230 (Tex.App.—El Paso 2000, pet. denied). See "Not legal conclusions," §9.4.5, p. 614. If an expert's testimony meets the test under TRE 702 and the requirements of TRCP 166a(c) and (f), it will support a summary judgment even when the expert is a party to the suit. *See* **Anderson**, 808 S.W.2d at 55;

★

Shook v. Herman, 759 S.W.2d 743, 746 (Tex.App.—Dallas 1988, writ denied). If the expert's opinion is based on records, the records should be attached to the affidavit or included in the other summary-judgment evidence. *See* TRCP 166a(f); *Ceballos v. El Paso Health Care Sys.*, 881 S.W.2d 439, 445 (Tex.App.—El Paso 1994, writ denied). See "Failure to attach exhibit," §10.1.1(1)(b), p. 619.

CAUTION

If you use an expert's affidavit in a summary-judgment hearing, you cannot later claim consulting-only status for that expert. **Hardesty v. Douglas**, *894 S.W.2d 548, 551 (Tex.App.— Waco 1995, orig. proceeding). That expert's opinion will be subject to discovery. See "Consulting expert + work reviewed = testifying expert," ch. 6-D, §2.2.2, p. 503.*

---

(1) Attorney expert. If unchallenged, the movant's affidavit by an attorney as an expert on attorney fees is sufficient to support a summary judgment for fees. See "Proof of attorney fees," ch. 1-H, §10.4, p. 66. If the nonmovant believes the amount of attorney fees the movant claims is unreasonable, the nonmovant should challenge the attorney fees in the response and file a controverting affidavit by an attorney as an expert on attorney fees. *See Guity v. C.C.I. Enter.*, 54 S.W.3d 526, 528 (Tex.App.—Houston [1st Dist.] 2001, no pet.). If the movant's affidavit is controverted, the court cannot award attorney fees without holding a hearing. *See id.* See *O'Connor's Texas COA*, "Attorney Fees," ch. 45, p. 1349.

(2) Medical expert. CPRC chapter 74 limits the persons who can testify as experts in a medical-malpractice case against doctors and other health-care providers. *See* CPRC §§74.401-74.403. See *O'Connor's Texas COA*, "Expert's qualifications," ch. 20-A, §8.3, p. 635.

§9.4 Affidavits. The most common form of summary-judgment evidence is the affidavit. Because a defective affidavit cannot support a summary judgment, the affidavit must meet certain requirements. See "Objections to Summary-Judgment Evidence," §10, p. 617.

1. Sworn. The minimum requirement for an affidavit is that it must be sworn; however, a jurat is not specifically required. *See Mansions in the Forest, L.P. v. Montgomery Cty.*, 365 S.W.3d 314, 316-17 (Tex.2012). See "Affidavits," ch. 1-B, §3.2.16, p. 11. An unsworn statement that purports to be an affidavit will not support a summary judgment. *See Mansions in the Forest*, 365 S.W.3d at 316; *Perkins v. Crittenden*, 462 S.W.2d 565, 568 (Tex. 1970).

2. Admissible evidence. The affidavit must contain facts that would be admissible in evidence at a conventional trial on the merits. TRCP 166a(f); *United Blood Servs. v. Longoria*, 938 S.W.2d 29, 30 (Tex.1997); *see, e.g.*, *Rabe v. Dillard's, Inc.*, 214 S.W.3d 767, 769 (Tex.App.—Dallas 2007, no pet.) (confidential ADR communications described in SJ affidavit were inadmissible and should have been excluded); *Powell v. Vavro, McDonald & Assocs.*, 136 S.W.3d 762, 765 (Tex.App.—Dallas 2004, no pet.) (hearsay statements in SJ affidavits were inadmissible and should have been excluded); *Beasley v. Burns*, 7 S.W.3d 768, 770 (Tex.App.—Texarkana 1999, pet. denied) (party cannot offer affidavit that contradicts deemed admissions).

3. Competent witness. The affidavit must affirmatively show that the witness is competent to testify about the matters in the affidavit. TRCP 166a(f). See "Competency of witness," ch. 1-B, §3.2.16(2), p. 12; "Lack of competence," §10.1.1(2), p. 619.

NOTE

*The courts often treat a witness's competence and personal knowledge as the same issue, but they are not. Competence, a TRE 601 issue, is whether the witness has the ability to testify—is the witness too young, too old, or too mentally unstable to testify?—and it is evaluated under TRE 104(a) without considering the admissibility of specific testimony. See Brown & Rondon, *Evidence Handbook*, pp. 537-38. Personal knowledge, a TRE 602 issue, is whether the witness knows enough about the subject to testify, and it is evaluated under TRE 104(b). See Brown & Rondon, *Evidence Handbook*, p. 549.*

★

4. Personal knowledge. A summary-judgment affidavit must state that it is based on the affiant's personal knowledge and that the facts in it are true. TRCP 166a(f); *Ryland Grp. v. Hood*, 924 S.W.2d 120, 122 (Tex. 1996); *Garner v. Long*, 106 S.W.3d 260, 267 (Tex.App.—Fort Worth 2003, no pet.); *e.g.*, *Spradlin v. State*, 100 S.W.3d 372, 381 (Tex.App.—Houston [1st Dist.] 2002, no pet.) (affidavit not proper SJ evidence because affiant's personal knowledge was explained only by her status). *But see Closs v. Goose Creek Consol. ISD*, 874 S.W.2d 859, 868 (Tex. App.—Texarkana 1994, no writ) (because affiant was custodian of school-district records, affidavit satisfied TRCP 166a(f) even though there was no specific recitation that affidavit was based on personal knowledge). Statements based merely on the affiant's "best knowledge" are not sufficient to raise a fact issue and are improper summary-judgment evidence. *Price v. American Nat'l Ins.*, 113 S.W.3d 424, 429-30 (Tex.App.—Houston [1st Dist.] 2003, no pet.); *Geiselman v. Cramer Fin. Grp.*, 965 S.W.2d 532, 537 (Tex.App.—Houston [14th Dist.] 1997, no writ); *see Flanagan v. Martin*, 880 S.W.2d 863, 866 (Tex.App.—Waco 1994, writ dism'd) (best knowledge and belief). See "Personal knowledge," ch. 1-B, §3.2.16(3)(a), p. 12; "Lack of personal knowledge," §10.1.1(3), p. 619.

5. Not legal conclusions. The affidavit must state facts and cannot merely recite legal conclusions. *Brownlee v. Brownlee*, 665 S.W.2d 111, 112 (Tex.1984). Legal conclusions not supported by facts will not support a summary judgment. *See Anderson v. Snider*, 808 S.W.2d 54, 55 (Tex.1991). Legal conclusions in affidavits have no probative force. *801 Nolana, Inc. v. RTC Mortg. Trust*, 944 S.W.2d 751, 754 (Tex.App.—Corpus Christi 1997, writ denied); *see Life Ins. Co. of Va. v. Gar-Dal, Inc.*, 570 S.W.2d 378, 381-82 (Tex.1978). The following are examples of legal conclusions for which no underlying facts were stated: • The assault had nothing to do with work; it occurred for reasons personal to the physician. *Walls Reg'l Hosp. v. Bomar*, 9 S.W.3d 805, 807 (Tex.1999). • The defendant did not commit legal malpractice, was not negligent, and did not breach the contract. *Anderson*, 808 S.W.2d at 55. • The indebtedness was renewed and extended. *Mercer v. Daoran Corp.*, 676 S.W.2d 580, 583 (Tex.1984). • The parties modified the contractual obligations. *Brownlee*, 665 S.W.2d at 112. • The party held adverse possession to the property. *Ellis v. Jansing*, 620 S.W.2d 569, 571 (Tex.1981). • Not all offsets and payments were credited. *Gar-Dal*, 570 S.W.2d at 381-82. • The note was purchased for valuable consideration, in good faith, and without notice of default or dishonor. *Hidalgo v. Surety S&L Ass'n*, 487 S.W.2d 702, 703 (Tex.1972).

6. Not factual conclusions. The affidavit must be based on facts and cannot merely recite factual conclusions. Conclusory statements that are not supported by facts are not proper summary-judgment proof. *See McIntyre v. Ramirez*, 109 S.W.3d 741, 749-50 (Tex.2003); *Purcell v. Bellinger*, 940 S.W.2d 599, 601-02 (Tex.1997); *Ryland Grp.*, 924 S.W.2d at 122. Unsupported conclusory statements are not credible and are not susceptible to being readily controverted. *Ryland Grp.*, 924 S.W.2d at 122; *see* TRCP 166a(c).

(1) By expert witness. Unsupported conclusory statements by an expert witness will not support a summary judgment. *IHS Cedars Treatment Ctr. v. Mason*, 143 S.W.3d 794, 803 (Tex.2004); *McIntyre*, 109 S.W.3d at 749-50; *see, e.g.*, *Ryland Grp.*, 924 S.W.2d at 122 (statement that D's failure to notify anyone of use of untreated wood on P's deck violated industry practice was conclusory); *Karen Corp. v. Burlington N. & Santa Fe Ry.*, 107 S.W.3d 118, 126 (Tex.App.—Fort Worth 2003, pet. denied) (statement that attorney fees were excessive was conclusory); *Griffin v. Methodist Hosp.*, 948 S.W.2d 72, 75 (Tex.App.—Houston [14th Dist.] 1997, no writ) (statement that nurses properly assessed patient's condition was conclusory). Opinion testimony cannot be based on the assumption of an unproven fact. *Sipes v. General Motors Corp.*, 946 S.W.2d 143, 148 (Tex.App.—Texarkana 1997, writ denied). Opinion testimony can rise no higher than the facts it is based on. *Id.*

(2) By lay witness. Unsupported conclusory statements by a lay witness will not support a summary judgment. *See, e.g.*, *Purcell*, 940 S.W.2d at 601-02 (mother's statement about child's interest in pursuing paternity suit was conclusory); *Laidlaw Waste Sys. v. City of Wilmer*, 904 S.W.2d 656, 661 (Tex.1995) (statements that area exceeded statutory minimum size and that boundary did not close were conclusory); *Continental Casing Corp. v. Samedan Oil Corp.*, 751 S.W.2d 499, 501 (Tex.1988) (statement about offset was conclusory because it did not expressly state whether it was taken before or after bankruptcy).

★

7. Exhibits to affidavits. The affidavit must show that any exhibits attached to the affidavit are authentic and admissible. See "Exhibits," ch. 1-B, §3.2.13, p. 10; "Party's own discovery responses," §9.5.3(1)(b), p. 616.

8. Filing the affidavits.

(1) Attach to motion or response. The affidavits should be incorporated by reference in and filed with the motion or response. Affidavits attached to the original petition or the answer but not included as part of the motion or response are not competent summary-judgment proof. *E.g.*, *Speck v. First Evangelical Lutheran Ch.*, 235 S.W.3d 811, 816 (Tex.App.—Houston [1st Dist.] 2007, no pet.) (affidavit attached to pleadings but not to SJ response was not competent SJ proof); *Boeker v. Syptak*, 916 S.W.2d 59, 61-62 (Tex.App.—Houston [1st Dist.] 1996, no writ) (copy of petition and its affidavits attached to SJ motion was competent SJ proof); *Sugarland Bus. Ctr., Ltd. v. Norman*, 624 S.W.2d 639, 642 (Tex.App.—Houston [14th Dist.] 1981, no writ) (affidavit attached to pleadings but not to SJ motion was not competent SJ proof).

(2) Affidavit & amended motion or response. An amended motion or response should expressly incorporate by reference the affidavits attached to the earlier motion or response, but failure to do so is not fatal. *Vaughn v. Burroughs Corp.*, 705 S.W.2d 246, 248 (Tex.App.—Houston [14th Dist.] 1986, no writ); *see R.I.O. Sys. v. Union Carbide Corp.*, 780 S.W.2d 489, 492 (Tex.App.—Corpus Christi 1989, writ denied) (SJ proof attached to earlier motion was proper proof for later motion). *But see Corpus Christi Mun. Gas Corp. v. Tuloso-Midway ISD*, 595 S.W.2d 203, 204 (Tex.App.—Eastland 1980, writ ref'd n.r.e.) (evidence attached to earlier motion could not support SJ).

9. Affidavits made in bad faith. If a party relies on an affidavit made in bad faith or solely for the purpose of delay, the court must award the other party reasonable expenses caused by the affidavit, including reasonable attorney fees. TRCP 166a(h); *Ramirez v. Encore Wire Corp.*, 196 S.W.3d 469, 476 (Tex.App.—Dallas 2006, no pet.). Any offending party or attorney may be found guilty of contempt. TRCP 166a(h); *Ramirez*, 196 S.W.3d at 476.

10. "Sham" affidavit. A "sham" affidavit contradicts an affiant's earlier deposition testimony for the purpose of creating a fact issue to avoid summary judgment. *Farroux v. Denny's Rests., Inc.*, 962 S.W.2d 108, 111 (Tex.App.—Houston [1st Dist.] 1997, no pet.). Under the sham-affidavit doctrine, the contradictory affidavit should be disregarded and thus cannot raise a fact issue when (1) the affidavit is made after the deposition and (2) there is a clear contradiction on a material point without any explanation. *Pando v. Southwest Convenience Stores*, 242 S.W.3d 76, 79 (Tex.App.—Eastland 2007, no pet.); *see Trostle v. Trostle*, 77 S.W.3d 908, 915 (Tex.App.—Amarillo 2002, no pet.); *Eslon Thermoplastics v. Dynamic Sys.*, 49 S.W.3d 891, 901 (Tex.App.—Austin 2001, no pet.); *Farroux*, 962 S.W.2d at 111. If the affiant was confused at the deposition or discovered additional relevant materials after the deposition, the sham-affidavit doctrine does not apply. *See Farroux*, 962 S.W.2d at 111 n.1. Some courts have held that when conflicting inferences can be drawn between a party's summary-judgment affidavit and earlier deposition testimony on a material issue, a fact issue is created that can defeat a summary-judgment motion. *E.g.*, *Randall v. Dallas Power & Light Co.*, 752 S.W.2d 4, 5 (Tex.1988); *Davis v. City of Grapevine*, 188 S.W.3d 748, 756 (Tex.App.—Fort Worth 2006, pet. denied); *cf. Pierce v. Washington Mut. Bank*, 226 S.W.3d 711, 716-17 (Tex. App.—Tyler 2007, pet. denied) (fact issue raised when conflicting inferences can be drawn from interrogatory answer and affidavit). One court has explained the discrepancy in case law as a matter of degree based on the level of details and contradiction between the affidavit and the deposition testimony. *See Cantu v. Peacher*, 53 S.W.3d 5, 10-11 (Tex.App.—San Antonio 2001, pet. denied) (if allegations in deposition and affidavit are generally consistent but vary in detail, affidavit is not a sham, but if affidavit clearly contradicts deposition testimony on material issues, without explanation, affidavit is a sham and cannot defeat SJ). For more information on the sham-affidavit rule, see Wilson, *The Sham Affidavit Doctrine in Texas*, 66 Tex.B.J. 962 (2003).

§9.5 Discovery products. Discovery products used to support a summary-judgment motion or a response can be filed separately or attached to the motion or response. *See Enterprise Leasing Co. v. Barrios*, 156 S.W.3d 547, 549 (Tex.2004); *McConathy v. McConathy*, 869 S.W.2d 341, 342 n.2 (Tex.1994).

✦

NOTE

Two types of discovery products cannot be used as summary-judgment evidence: a party's own answers to interrogatories and a party's own denials in response to requests for admissions. See "Using answers in summary judgment," ch. 6-G, §9.4, p. 556; "Using admissions in summary judgment," ch. 6-H, §8.3, p. 564.

---

1. Discovery on file. To rely on discovery on file with the court, the motion or response must refer to it. TRCP 166a(c); *see, e.g., Steinkamp v. Caremark*, 3 S.W.3d 191, 194-95 (Tex.App.—El Paso 1999, pet. denied) (party made court aware of the particular evidence she was relying on by referring to portions of it and stating that it was already before the court).

2. Unfiled discovery. TRCP 166a(d) permits discovery not on file with the court to be used as summary-judgment evidence as long as the party files and serves the following on all parties:

(1) Statement of intent. Within the motion or response, the party should include a statement of intent to use unfiled discovery products as summary-judgment proof. TRCP 166a(d); *McConathy*, 869 S.W.2d at 342 n.2. The statement of intent can be included in or attached to the motion or response. *See, e.g., Garcia v. Andrews*, 867 S.W.2d 409, 411-12 (Tex.App.—Corpus Christi 1993, no writ) (statement of intent in motion for SJ satisfied requirement). Even if no specific "statement of intent" is made, the requirement in TRCP 166a(d) is satisfied if the party clearly relies on evidence attached to its motion or response. *McConathy*, 869 S.W.2d at 342 n.2; *see, e.g., Mathis v. RKL Design/Build*, 189 S.W.3d 839, 842 (Tex.App.—Houston [1st Dist.] 2006, no pet.) (response listing exhibits and identifying deposition excerpts by page number served as statement of intent).

(2) Unfiled discovery products. The party should attach one of the following to the motion or response: (1) copies of the unfiled discovery, (2) appendixes containing the unfiled discovery, or (3) a notice containing specific references to and quotes from the unfiled discovery. TRCP 166a(d); *e.g., Barraza v. Eureka Co.*, 25 S.W.3d 225, 228-29 (Tex.App.—El Paso 2000, pet. denied) (attaching unfiled discovery and making specific reference to some of it in SJ response was sufficient); *Guthrie v. Suiter*, 934 S.W.2d 820, 826 (Tex.App.—Houston [1st Dist.] 1996, no writ) (attaching deposition to motion was not sufficient; party should have identified what evidence in the deposition it relied on); *E.B. Smith Co. v. U.S. Fid. & Guar. Co.*, 850 S.W.2d 621, 623-24 (Tex.App.—Corpus Christi 1993, writ denied) (broad statements about unfiled discovery were not sufficient; quotes from unfiled discovery were necessary). *But see Gomez v. Tri City Cmty. Hosp., Ltd.*, 4 S.W.3d 281, 283-84 (Tex.App.—San Antonio 1999, no pet.) (court of appeals refused to consider deposition testimony not on file with trial court before entry of SJ). Objections to unfiled discovery are waived if they are not made before the court rules on the motion for summary judgment. *Grainger v. Western Cas. Life Ins.*, 930 S.W.2d 609, 613-14 (Tex.App.—Houston [1st Dist.] 1996, writ denied).

3. Unverified discovery. It is not necessary to verify by affidavit the authenticity of most discovery products.

(1) Discovery responses.

(a) Other party's discovery responses. When relying on another party's discovery responses (e.g., documents that are not self-authenticating, answers to interrogatories), a party does not need to authenticate them unless the producing party filed timely objections to their authenticity. TRCP 193.7; *Blanche v. First Nationwide Mortg. Corp.*, 74 S.W.3d 444, 451 (Tex.App.—Dallas 2002, no pet.).

(b) Party's own discovery responses. A party relying on its own discovery responses must authenticate them. *Blanche*, 74 S.W.3d at 451-52; *see, e.g., Banowsky v. State Farm Mut. Auto. Ins.*, 876 S.W.2d 509, 513 (Tex.App.—Amarillo 1994, no writ) (D should have authenticated release from its file). The affidavit authenticating a party's own documents must be made by a person with knowledge of the document's authenticity. *See In re G.F.O.*, 874 S.W.2d 729, 731 (Tex.App.—Houston [1st Dist.] 1994, no writ). See "Authenticity," ch. 8-C, §8.4, p. 704.

✯

(2) **Deposition excerpts.** When relying on deposition excerpts, it is not necessary to authenticate them. *McConathy*, 869 S.W.2d at 341. To prevent any objections to verification, the party should include in the photocopied excerpts a copy of the verification page signed by the court reporter.

§9.6 Stipulations. A party may rely on the parties' stipulations in a summary-judgment motion or response. TRCP 166a(c)(ii). The stipulations should be in writing, signed by both parties, and filed with the court. TRCP 11. See "Agreements Between Attorneys – Rule 11," ch. 1-H, §9, p. 61. Typical stipulations in summary-judgment proceedings include the terms of a contract in dispute, the agreed facts, and the legal issues in dispute. *See Francis v. International Serv. Ins.*, 546 S.W.2d 57, 58-59 (Tex.1976).

§9.7 Reporter's record.

1. From another hearing in same suit. If the trial court conducts another hearing in the same case before the hearing on the motion for summary judgment, the reporter's record from that hearing may be used as summary-judgment proof. On appeal, the record must reflect that the reporter's record was considered at the summary-judgment hearing. *Munoz v. Gulf Oil Co.*, 693 S.W.2d 372, 373 (Tex.1984) (reporter's record from hearing, which did not bear a file mark, could not be considered on appeal); *Munoz v. Gulf Oil Co.*, 732 S.W.2d 62, 64 (Tex.App.—Houston [14th Dist.] 1987, writ ref'd n.r.e.) (reporter's record from hearing, which bore a file mark, was proper SJ proof).

2. From another case. Sworn testimony from another case between the same parties may be used as summary-judgment proof. *Austin Bldg. Co. v. National Un. Fire Ins.*, 432 S.W.2d 697, 698-99 (Tex.1968); *see also Murillo v. Valley Coca-Cola Bottling Co.*, 895 S.W.2d 758, 761-62 (Tex.App.—Corpus Christi 1995, no writ) (reporter's record from another trial was admissible because D was sued for same incident by another P). See "Deposition from other proceeding," ch. 6-F, §12.1.2, p. 539.

§9.8 Public records. A party may rely on authenticated or certified public records as summary-judgment evidence. The document must be properly authenticated. TRE 902 lists documents that are self-authenticating. See "Authenticity," ch. 8-C, §8.4, p. 704.

§9.9 Conflicts in SJ proof. Conflicting statements in summary-judgment evidence made by the same witness may raise a fact issue. *Randall v. Dallas Power & Light Co.*, 752 S.W.2d 4, 5 (Tex.1988) (conflict between affidavit and deposition); *Gaines v. Hamman*, 358 S.W.2d 557, 562 (Tex.1962) (same); *Waldmiller v. Continental Express, Inc.*, 74 S.W.3d 116, 125 (Tex.App.—Texarkana 2002, no pet.) (conflict between affidavits); *see* TRCP 166a(c) ("free from contradictions"). Courts disagree about whether a fact issue is created when a party submits an affidavit that conflicts with earlier deposition testimony. See "'Sham' affidavit," §9.4.10, p. 615. When the first statement is confusing, a later, more specific statement does not conflict with the first statement. *See Gold v. City of Coll. Station*, 40 S.W.3d 637, 647 n.6 (Tex.App.—Houston [1st Dist.] 2001, pet. granted, judgm't vacated w.r.m.). A court cannot strike a party's affidavit because it is inconsistent with an earlier affidavit from the same party. *See Thompson v. City of Corsicana Hous. Auth.*, 57 S.W.3d 547, 556-57 (Tex.App.—Waco 2001, no pet.). Instead, after the trial on the merits, the court may impose sanctions for filing an affidavit in bad faith. *See* 3 McDonald & Carlson, *Texas Civil Practice*, §18.19[f]. See "Affidavits made in bad faith," §9.4.9, p. 615.

§9.10 No oral testimony. No oral testimony may be considered in support of a motion for summary judgment or response. TRCP 166a(c). See "Hearing on submission," §11.2, p. 622.

§10. OBJECTIONS TO SUMMARY-JUDGMENT EVIDENCE

§10.1 Generally. If a party's affidavits (or other summary-judgment proof) contain evidence that would not be admissible at trial, the opposing party should object and move to strike the inadmissible evidence. *See* TRCP 166a(f) ("affidavits … shall set forth such facts as would be admissible in evidence"). The general rule is that a party must object in writing (in a response, a reply, special exceptions, separate objections, or a motion to strike) to formal deficiencies in the summary-judgment proof, or it waives the objection. *See City of Houston v. Clear Creek Basin*

★

Auth., 589 S.W.2d 671, 677 (Tex.1979). The exception to that rule is that if the defect is one of substance, no objection is necessary to preserve the error and the defect may be raised for the first time on appeal. *Brown v. Brown*, 145 S.W.3d 745, 751 (Tex.App.—Dallas 2004, pet. denied); *see Clear Creek*, 589 S.W.2d at 677; *Rizkallah v. Conner*, 952 S.W.2d 580, 584-85 (Tex.App.—Houston [1st Dist.] 1997, no writ). A defect is formal (and the objection to it is waivable) if the summary-judgment proof is competent but inadmissible; a defect is substantive (and the objection to it is not waivable) if the summary-judgment proof is incompetent. *Mathis v. Bocell*, 982 S.W.2d 52, 60 (Tex. App.—Houston [1st Dist.] 1998, no pet.). While objections to formal defects in the evidence are objections to its admissibility that can be cured before judgment, objections to substantive defects in the evidence are never waived because incompetent evidence cannot support a judgment under any circumstances. *Id.*

CAUTION

*Courts of appeals often disagree about whether a particular defect is one of form or one of substance. See, e.g., **Brown**, 145 S.W.3d at 752 & n.1 (split of authority on failure to attach referenced document to affidavit or motion); **Dailey v. Albertson's, Inc.**, 83 S.W.3d 222, 226 (Tex.App.—El Paso 2002, no pet.) (whether lack of personal knowledge is defect of form or substance is subject of some confusion); see also **Trusty v. Strayhorn**, 87 S.W.3d 756, 762-63 (Tex.App.—Texarkana 2002, no pet.) (courts disagree about whether objections to defects in form under TRCP 166a(f) must be made by parties seeking reversal or affirmance on appeal or only when reversal is sought). See generally Patton, Summary Judgments in Texas, §6.10[1][b] (contrasting substantive and formal defects in SJ proof). See "Failure to attach exhibit," §10.1.1(1)(b), p. 619; "Lack of personal knowledge," §10.1.1(3), p. 619; "Failure to attach exhibit," §10.1.2(1), p. 620; "Lack of personal knowledge," §10.1.2(6), p. 621. Thus, to avoid waiver, parties should always object in writing to all defects in the evidence and obtain rulings on the objections. See **O'Connor's Texas Forms**, FORMS 7C:3-6, 7C:9, 7C:11.*

---

1. Waivable objections to evidence. TRCP 166a(f) requires a party to object to formal defects in the affidavits or their attachments (i.e., other evidence). Formal defects are not grounds for reversal unless the objecting party specifically objected and the other party was given the opportunity to amend but refused. TRCP 166a(f); *Bauer v. Jasso*, 946 S.W.2d 552, 556-57 (Tex.App.—Corpus Christi 1997, no writ). Most courts of appeals have held that both movants and nonmovants must object to formal defects in order to preserve error for appeal—the appellee cannot assert a formal defect to justify affirmance of a summary judgment in its favor unless it made the objection in writing. *See Trusty*, 87 S.W.3d at 762-63 (TRCP 166a(f) applies to defects in form asserted as grounds for affirmance); *Martin v. Durden*, 965 S.W.2d 562, 565 (Tex.App.—Houston [14th Dist.] 1997, pet. denied) (same). *But see Ceballos v. El Paso Health Care Sys.*, 881 S.W.2d 439, 444 (Tex.App.—El Paso 1994, writ denied) (stating in dicta that Rule 166a(f) requires objection to formal defect only when defect is urged as grounds for reversal, and not for affirmance, of SJ). The following are some of the objections to evidence that a party must specifically make to avoid waiver:

(1) Formal defects in affidavit.

(a) Defective content of affidavit. If the movant's affidavit meets the minimum requirements for a valid affidavit, formal defects in the affidavit are not grounds for reversal unless the nonmovant specifically objected and the movant was given the opportunity to amend but did not. TRCP 166a(f). For defects of substance, see "Nonwaivable objections to evidence," §10.1.2, p. 620. The party objecting to the content of an affidavit must identify the specific statements in the affidavit that are objectionable and state why they are objectionable. *See, e.g., Haynes v. Haynes*, 178 S.W.3d 350, 355 (Tex.App.—Houston [14th Dist.] 2005, pet. denied) (court of appeals overruled challenge to SJ because P did not identify the part of affidavit that contained hearsay). An entire affidavit cannot be excluded if only part of it is inadmissible. *See, e.g., Spradlin v. State*, 100 S.W.3d 372, 381 (Tex.App.—Houston [1st Dist.] 2002, no pet.) (specific statements in affidavit not based on personal knowledge excluded from

★

SJ evidence). When the trial court sustains an objection to an entire affidavit, the party offering the affidavit should either ask to amend it or ask that only the objectionable part be struck. See "Request for limited admissibility," ch. 8-D, §7.1.3(1), p. 715.

(b) Failure to attach exhibit. Some courts of appeals have held that the failure to attach a document referenced in an affidavit is a defect of form and thus will be waived if no objection is made. *See, e.g.,* **Sunsinger v. Perez**, 16 S.W.3d 496, 500-01 (Tex.App.—Beaumont 2000, pet. denied); **Martin**, 965 S.W.2d at 565; **Jones v. WKB Value Partners**, No. 04-07-00865-CV (Tex.App.—San Antonio 2008, no pet.) (memo op.; 6-4-08). Some courts determine whether the failure to attach documents is a defect of form or substance by analyzing whether the failure goes to the admissibility of the evidence or to its competence. *See, e.g.,* **Mathis**, 982 S.W.2d at 60 (lack of exhibits made affidavit inadmissible, not incompetent); *see also* **Brown**, 145 S.W.3d at 752 (lack of exhibits made affidavit conclusory). If an affidavit relies on facts contained in a missing exhibit but the same information is supplied elsewhere in the summary-judgment evidence, the missing exhibit is merely a formal defect and the error is waivable. *See* **Watts v. Hermann Hosp.**, 962 S.W.2d 102, 105 (Tex.App.—Houston [1st Dist.] 1997, no pet.). For a discussion of cases holding that the failure to attach an exhibit is a defect of substance, see "Failure to attach exhibit," §10.1.2(1), p. 620.

(c) Absence of jurat. When a purported affidavit lacks a jurat and the offering party does not provide extrinsic evidence to show that it was sworn to before an authorized officer, the opposing party must object, or the objection is waived. **Mansions in the Forest, L.P. v. Montgomery Cty.**, 365 S.W.3d 314, 317 (Tex.2012). See "Sworn," §9.4.1, p. 613.

NOTE

This defect may be raised for the first time on appeal in limited circumstances when a sworn or certified copy of a document must be attached to a petition. See **Mansions in the Forest**, *365 S.W.3d at 317; see, e.g.,* **Perkins v. Crittenden**, *462 S.W.2d 565, 567-68 (Tex.1970) (unsworn statement and unverified copy of promissory note could not support SJ in suit to recover on note; objection preserved when raised for first time on appeal).*

(d) Defect in jurat. The objection that a jurat is defective must be made, or else it is waived. *See* **Ford Motor Co. v. Leggat**, 904 S.W.2d 643, 645-46 (Tex.1995); *see, e.g.,* **Wasserberg v. 84 Lumber Co.**, No. 14-10-00136-CV (Tex.App.—Houston [14th Dist.] 2011, no pet.) (memo op.; 8-9-11) (error in date of jurat was defect in form).

(2) Lack of competence. The objection that an affidavit is made by an incompetent witness must be made, or else it is waived. **Rizkallah**, 952 S.W.2d at 586; *see* **Woods Expl. & Prod'g Co. v. Arkla Equip. Co.**, 528 S.W.2d 568, 570-71 (Tex.1975). TRCP 166a(f) states that the affidavit must show affirmatively that the witness is competent. See "Competency of witness," ch. 1-B, §3.2.16(2), p. 12.

NOTE

The courts often treat a witness's competence and personal knowledge as the same issue, but they are not. See "Competent witness," §9.4.3, p. 613; "Personal knowledge," §9.4.4, p. 614.

---

(3) Lack of personal knowledge. The Supreme Court has issued inconsistent opinions on whether the objection that an affidavit is not based on personal knowledge is a defect of form or of substance. *Compare* **Grand Prairie ISD v. Vaughan**, 792 S.W.2d 944, 945 (Tex.1990) (lack of personal knowledge is defect of form), *with* **Laidlaw Waste Sys. v. City of Wilmer**, 904 S.W.2d 656, 661 (Tex.1995) (reaching the opposite result without specifically affirming lower court's statement that lack of personal knowledge is defect of substance). Relying on **Vaughan**, some courts of appeals have held that an affidavit not based on personal knowledge is a defect of form and thus will be waived if no objection is made. **Rizkallah**, 952 S.W.2d at 585; *see* **Stewart v. Sanmina Tex. L.P.**, 156 S.W.3d 198,

━━━━━━━━━━━━━━━━━━━ ✦ ━━━━━━━━━━━━━━━━━━━

207 (Tex.App.—Dallas 2005, no pet.); *Youngblood v. U.S. Silica Co.*, 130 S.W.3d 461, 468-69 (Tex.App.—Texarkana 2004, pet. denied). For a discussion of cases holding that lack of personal knowledge is a defect of substance that can be raised for the first time on appeal, see "Lack of personal knowledge," §10.1.2(6), p. 621. See also "Personal knowledge," ch. 1-B, §3.2.16(3)(a), p. 12.

(4) Not readily controvertible. The objection that an affidavit contains declarations that are not easily controverted must be made, or else it is waived. *See Patterson v. Mobiloil Fed. Credit Un.*, 890 S.W.2d 551, 554 (Tex.App.—Beaumont 1994, no writ). See "Interested witness," §9.3.2, p. 612.

(5) Hearsay evidence. The objection that testimony contains hearsay must be made, or else it is waived. *Harrell v. Patel*, 225 S.W.3d 1, 6 (Tex.App.—El Paso 2005, pet. denied). Unless a party objects to hearsay evidence, the evidence will support a summary judgment. TRE 103(a)(1), 802; *see Harrell*, 225 S.W.3d at 6; *see, e.g.*, *Southland Corp. v. Lewis*, 940 S.W.2d 83, 85 (Tex.1997) (hearsay excluded because party objected); *Fortis Benefits v. Cantu*, 170 S.W.3d 755, 759 (Tex.App.—Waco 2005) (unobjected-to hearsay considered in support of SJ), *rev'd in part on other grounds*, 234 S.W.3d 642 (Tex.2007); *Columbia Rio Grande Reg'l Hosp. v. Stover*, 17 S.W.3d 387, 396 (Tex.App.—Corpus Christi 2000, no pet.) (hearsay objections waived because not specific enough).

(6) Failure to lay predicate. The objection that an affidavit does not lay the proper predicate for admissibility must be made, or else it is waived. *Life Ins. Co. of Va. v. Gar-Dal, Inc.*, 570 S.W.2d 378, 380-81 (Tex. 1978); *Seidner v. Citibank*, 201 S.W.3d 332, 334-35 (Tex.App.—Houston [14th Dist.] 2006, pet. denied); *Cottrell v. Carrillon Assocs.*, 646 S.W.2d 491, 494 (Tex.App.—Houston [1st Dist.] 1982, writ ref'd n.r.e.).

(7) Not "best evidence." The objection that the copy of a document offered is not the "best evidence" of the contents of the document must be made, or else it is waived. *See* TRE 1002 (an original writing is required to prove its contents unless admissible under another TRE or by law). A copy of a document is not admissible if the original document is not produced, its content is disputed, and its absence is not explained. *See Mercer v. Daoran Corp.*, 676 S.W.2d 580, 584 (Tex.1984) (court should have sustained objection to unsigned copy of note). The best-evidence rule applies only when a party seeks to prove the contents of a disputed document not in evidence. *See Osuna v. Quintana*, 993 S.W.2d 201, 206 (Tex.App.—Corpus Christi 1999, no pet.); *White v. Bath*, 825 S.W.2d 227, 231 (Tex.App.—Houston [14th Dist.] 1992, writ denied).

(8) Underlying methodology to expert opinion. The objection that expert testimony is not admissible under TRE 702 (testimony by experts) or TRCP 193.6(a) (exclusion of evidence for not timely responding to discovery) must be made, or else it is waived. *See, e.g.*, *Harris Cty. Appraisal Dist. v. Riverway Holdings, L.P.*, No. 14-09-00786-CV (Tex.App.—Houston [14th Dist.] 2011, pet. denied) (memo op.; 2-15-11) (challenge to expert's methodology, raised for first time in motion for new trial, could not be considered on appeal); *see also Pink v. Goodyear Tire & Rubber Co.*, 324 S.W.3d 290, 301 (Tex.App.—Beaumont 2010, pet. dism'd) (express ruling required to preserve objection to methodology, technique, or foundational data on which expert opinion is based). See "*Daubert-Robinson* Test for Expert Testimony," ch. 5-N, §2, p. 410; "Underlying methodology," ch. 5-N, §6.2.1, p. 418.

2. Nonwaivable objections to evidence. Substantive errors in the summary-judgment evidence are not waivable. See "Generally," §10.1, p. 617. A party should object to all errors in the summary-judgment evidence, however, even to nonwaivable errors. If a party did not object in the summary-judgment proceeding, the following are objections to defects of substance that can be made for the first time on appeal:

(1) Failure to attach exhibit. Several courts of appeals have held that the failure to attach a document referenced in an affidavit is a defect of substance, and no objection is necessary to preserve error. *See, e.g., Galindo v. Dean*, 69 S.W.3d 623, 627 (Tex.App.—Eastland 2002, no pet.) (medical records); *Natural Gas Clearinghouse v. Midgard Energy Co.*, 23 S.W.3d 372, 378-79 (Tex.App.—Amarillo 1999, pet. denied) (consultant's records supporting opinion on damages); *Mincron SBC Corp. v. Worldcom, Inc.*, 994 S.W.2d 785, 795-96 (Tex.App.—Houston [1st Dist.] 1999, no pet.) (invoices supporting disputed damages); *Gorrell v. Texas Utils. Elec. Co.*, 915 S.W.2d 55, 60 (Tex.App.—Fort Worth 1995, writ denied) (sworn or certified copies of exhibits); *Ceballos*, 881 S.W.2d at 445 (medical records supporting nontreating doctor's and nurse's opinions); *see also Sorrells v. Giberson*, 780

★

S.W.2d 936, 938 (Tex.App.—Austin 1989, writ denied) (in suit on a note, failure to attach note was reversible error because affidavit did not prove elements of suit). For a discussion of cases holding that failure to attach documents is merely a defect of form, see "Failure to attach exhibit," §10.1.1(1)(b), p. 619.

(2) Unsubstantiated legal conclusion. Legal conclusions unsupported by evidence are defects of substance, and no objection is necessary to preserve error. *Hou-Tex, Inc. v. Landmark Graphics*, 26 S.W.3d 103, 112 (Tex.App.—Houston [14th Dist.] 2000, no pet.); *Rizkallah*, 952 S.W.2d at 587. See "Not legal conclusions," §9.4.5, p. 614.

(3) Unsubstantiated factual conclusion. Factual conclusions, opinions, and subjective beliefs unsupported by evidence are defects of substance, and no objection is necessary to preserve error. *Harley-Davidson Motor Co. v. Young*, 720 S.W.2d 211, 213 (Tex.App.—Houston [14th Dist.] 1986, no writ). Bare conclusions are not evidence and are not probative of any facts. *See Bavishi v. Sterling Air Conditioning, Inc.*, No. 01-10-00610-CV (Tex.App.—Houston [1st Dist.] 2011, no pet.) (memo op.; 8-11-11). See "Not factual conclusions," §9.4.6, p. 614.

(4) Conflict in movant's SJ proof. If the movant's affidavit testimony or other evidence contains conflicting statements that raise a fact issue, the evidence will not support a summary judgment even if no objection is made. *See* TRCP 166a(c); *Dillard v. NCNB Tex. Nat'l Bank*, 815 S.W.2d 356, 360-61 (Tex.App.—Austin 1991, no writ), *disapproved on other grounds*, *Amberboy v. Societe de Banque Privee*, 831 S.W.2d 793 (Tex.1992).

(5) Conclusory expert opinion. If an expert's opinion is speculative or conclusory, no objection is necessary to preserve error. See "Conclusory evidence," ch. 5-N, §6.2.2, p. 418.

(6) Lack of personal knowledge. Some courts have held that if an affiant's testimony reflects a lack of personal knowledge, the defect is one of substance, and no objection is necessary to preserve error. *E.g.*, *Stone v. Midland Multifamily Equity REIT*, 334 S.W.3d 371, 375 (Tex.App.—Dallas 2011, no pet.); *Dailey*, 83 S.W.3d at 226; *Fernandez v. Peters*, No. 03-09-00687-CV (Tex.App.—Austin 2010, no pet.) (memo op.; 10-19-10); *see* Patton, *Summary Judgments in Texas*, §6.10[1][c][iii]. For a discussion of cases holding that lack of personal knowledge is merely a defect of form, see "Lack of personal knowledge," §10.1.1(3), p. 619.

§10.2 Secure ruling on objections. The nonmovant should ask the court to make written rulings on its objections to the summary-judgment evidence. *Jones v. Ray Ins. Agency*, 59 S.W.3d 739, 753 (Tex.App.—Corpus Christi 2001), *pet. denied*, 92 S.W.3d 530 (Tex.2002). Although the trial court has a duty to make written rulings on objections to summary-judgment evidence, some courts—perhaps to ensure their judgment is affirmed on appeal—refuse to do so. There is a split in authority in the courts of appeals—sometimes even within the same court—on whether error is preserved when the court fails or refuses to rule on the nonmovant's objections.

NOTE
Not securing a written ruling on an objection will cause problems only when the objection is waivable. If no objection is required to preserve error, then no ruling is required. For the summary-judgment objections that are preserved without the need for an objection, see "Non-waivable objections to evidence," §10.1.2, p. 620.

---

1. Implicit ruling sufficient. Some courts of appeals have held that if the trial court does not explicitly rule on the nonmovant's objections to the motion for summary judgment, the granting of the summary judgment implicitly overrules the objections. *E.g.*, *Slagle v. Prickett*, 345 S.W.3d 693, 702 (Tex.App.—El Paso 2011, no pet.); *Clement v. City of Plano*, 26 S.W.3d 544, 550 n.5 (Tex.App.—Dallas 2000, no pet.), *disapproved on other grounds*, *Telthorster v. Tennell*, 92 S.W.3d 457 (Tex.2002); *Dagley v. Haag Eng'g*, 18 S.W.3d 787, 795 n.9 (Tex.App.—Houston [14th Dist.] 2000, no pet.); *Columbia Rio Grande Reg'l Hosp. v. Stover*, 17 S.W.3d 387, 395-96 (Tex.App.—Corpus Christi 2000, no pet.); *Williams v. Bank One*, 15 S.W.3d 110, 114-15 (Tex.App.—Waco 1999, no pet.); *Frazier v. Yu*, 987 S.W.2d 607, 610 (Tex.App.—Fort Worth 1999, pet. denied). TRAP 33.1 relaxed the requirement in former TRAP 52(a) for an express ruling. *Frazier*, 987 S.W.2d at 610. Some courts hold that for there to be an implicit ruling, the trial court must do more than merely grant summary judgment; the record must affirmatively indicate that the trial court ruled on the objections in granting the summary judgment, or the order granting summary

——————————————————— ✦ ———————————————————

judgment must necessarily imply a ruling on the objections. *See* ***Trusty v. Strayhorn***, 87 S.W.3d 756, 760 (Tex. App.—Texarkana 2002, no pet.); ***Jones***, 59 S.W.3d at 752-53; *see, e.g.*, ***Mowbray v. Avery***, 76 S.W.3d 663, 689 n.45 (Tex.App.—Corpus Christi 2002, pet. denied) (because SJ order said court considered response, it implicitly overruled objections in response). For implicit rulings that preserve error in other contexts, see "Implicit ruling," ch. 1-G, §2.2.2, p. 47.

NOTE

A party cannot force the trial court to make a favorable ruling on an objection, but it should be able to force the court to make a ruling. See "Refusal to rule + objection," ch. 1-G, §2.2.3, p. 48. When a trial court refuses to rule on an objection, it is gaming the system to ensure its summary-judgment order cannot be challenged on appeal. The appellate courts that require the trial court to have ruled on an objection are encouraging this behavior.

---

2. **Express ruling required.** Some courts of appeals (including a few of the same ones listed above) have held that the nonmovant must secure a ruling on its objections or waive them. *E.g.*, ***Delfino v. Perry Homes, Jt.V.***, 223 S.W.3d 32, 35 (Tex.App.—Houston [1st Dist.] 2006, no pet.); ***Seidner v. Citibank***, 201 S.W.3d 332, 335 & n.2 (Tex.App.—Houston [14th Dist.] 2006, pet. denied); ***Stewart v. Sanmina Tex. L.P.***, 156 S.W.3d 198, 206-07 (Tex.App.—Dallas 2005, no pet.); ***Sunshine Mining & Ref. Co. v. Ernst & Young, L.L.P.***, 114 S.W.3d 48, 51 (Tex. App.—Eastland 2003, no pet.); ***Allen v. Albin***, 97 S.W.3d 655, 663 (Tex.App.—Waco 2002, no pet.); ***Montemayor v. Chapa***, 61 S.W.3d 758, 763 (Tex.App.—Corpus Christi 2001, no pet.), *disapproved on other grounds*, ***Coco v. Port of Corpus Christi Auth.***, 132 S.W.3d 689 (Tex.App.—Corpus Christi 2004, no pet.); ***Rodriguez v. Wal-Mart Stores***, 52 S.W.3d 814, 823 (Tex.App.—San Antonio 2001), *rev'd in part on other grounds*, 92 S.W.3d 502 (Tex.2002).

PRACTICE TIP

*To preserve error when a court refuses to overrule your objections to the motion for summary judgment, file a motion for new trial within 30 days after the judgment, reurge the objections, and include an objection to the court's refusal to rule. See **Alejandro v. Bell**, 84 S.W.3d 383, 388 (Tex.App.—Corpus Christi 2002, no pet.). When the motion for new trial is overruled, either by order or by operation of law, your objections are preserved for appeal. See "Refusal to rule + objection," ch. 1-G, §2.2.3, p. 48.*

---

§11. SUMMARY-JUDGMENT HEARING

§11.1 Notice. The nonmovant is entitled to receive sufficient notice of a hearing date on the motion so that it knows when its response is due. See "Notice," §7, p. 609.

§11.2 Hearing on submission. The hearing for summary judgment is for argument only; no oral testimony may be presented. TRCP 166a(c); ***Jack B. Anglin Co. v. Tipps***, 842 S.W.2d 266, 269 n.4 (Tex.1992); ***Martin v. Cohen***, 804 S.W.2d 201, 203 (Tex.App.—Houston [14th Dist.] 1991, no writ). A party is not entitled to a hearing to present argument for a motion for summary judgment. ***In re American Media Consol.***, 121 S.W.3d 70, 74 (Tex.App.—San Antonio 2003, orig. proceeding). The court can decide the motion for summary judgment on submission, without an appearance by the attorneys before the court. *See* ***Martin v. Martin, Martin & Richards, Inc.***, 989 S.W.2d 357, 359 (Tex.1998).

§11.3 Hearing on expert. If a movant files a motion for summary judgment that includes objections to the nonmovant's expert, the court should hold a ***Daubert-Robinson*** hearing separate from the hearing on the motion for summary judgment. *Cf.* ***Heller v. Shaw Indus.***, 167 F.3d 146, 151 (3d Cir.1999) (before considering motion for SJ, court held a ***Daubert*** hearing to determine admissibility of expert's opinion). *But see* ***Rayon v. Energy Special-***

★

ties, Inc., 121 S.W.3d 7, 19-20 (Tex.App.—Fort Worth 2002, no pet.) (trial court not required to hold *Daubert-Robinson* hearing separate from SJ hearing); *Weiss v. Mechanical Associated Servs.*, 989 S.W.2d 120, 124 & n.6 (Tex.App.—San Antonio 1999, pet. denied) (when trial court granted motion for SJ that included objection to nonmovant's expert, appellate court assumed trial court found expert's opinion inadmissible). The *Daubert-Robinson* ("DR") and summary-judgment ("SJ") hearings should be held separately for the following reasons: (1) the purposes of the hearings are different (DR – for testimony; SJ – for argument), (2) the trial burdens are different (DR – preponderance of the evidence; SJ – as a matter of law), (3) the appellate standards are different (DR – abuse of discretion; SJ – de novo), and (4) the appellate records are different (DR – reporter's record required; SJ – no reporter's record required). See "Hearing on submission," §11.2, p. 622; "Appellate record," §14.1, p. 625; "Motion to Exclude Expert," ch. 5-N, p. 410; "When both parties move for SJ," ch. 7-C, §4.8, p. 640.

§12. THE SUMMARY JUDGMENT

§12.1 Not sua sponte. The trial court does not have the authority to grant summary judgment on its own initiative. *Daniels v. Daniels*, 45 S.W.3d 278, 282 (Tex.App.—Corpus Christi 2001, no pet.). When granting a summary judgment, the court is limited to the grounds stated in the motion for summary judgment. See "Stated in motion," ch. 7-C, §2.4.1, p. 628.

§12.2 Judgment or order?

PRACTICE TIP

Whether the proposed order or judgment should be attached to the motion or brought to the hearing depends on a court's local rules. A party should attempt to reach an agreement on the wording of the order or judgment ("approved as to form") with opposing counsel before submitting it to the court. Some judges, however, prefer to draft their own orders and judgments.

---

1. Judgment. If the trial court grants the motion for summary judgment and no other issues remain, the court should sign a final judgment.

2. Order. See *O'Connor's Texas Forms*, FORM 7C:12.

(1) Denies SJ. If the trial court denies the motion for summary judgment, the court should sign an order denying the motion.

(2) Grants partial SJ. If the trial court grants the motion for summary judgment but other issues remain pending, the court should sign an order granting the partial summary judgment.

(a) Nonsuit or severance. If the case is not fully adjudicated on the motion, the court may nonsuit or sever the unadjudicated part of the case, in which case the order granting the summary judgment becomes final. If, after granting a partial summary judgment, the court signs an order of nonsuit or severance that disposes of or severs all remaining claims, the appellate deadlines for the summary judgment begin to run on the date the court signs the order of nonsuit or severance. *See Park Place Hosp. v. Estate of Milo*, 909 S.W.2d 508, 510 (Tex. 1995). See "Motion for Severance," ch. 5-I, §3, p. 364; "Voluntary Dismissal—Nonsuit," ch. 7-F, p. 650.

(b) Unadjudicated issues. Claims not adjudicated by the motion for summary judgment are preserved for disposition by the trial court after resolution of the motion. TRCP 166a(e); *see McNally v. Guevara*, 52 S.W.3d 195, 196 (Tex.2001) (no presumption that SJ motion addresses all of movant's claims).

§12.3 Drafting the SJ. See *O'Connor's Texas Forms*, FORM 9C:4.

1. Identify grounds. Although it is helpful on appeal for the summary judgment to include the grounds on which it was granted, it is not necessary. On appeal, the court will consider all grounds for summary judgment in-

✦

cluded in the motion for summary judgment. See "Grounds for review," §14.3.1, p. 625. The appellate court will not affirm a summary judgment on a ground not presented to the trial court in the motion. See "Stated in motion," ch. 7-C, §2.4.1, p. 628.

2. State whether final or partial. The judgment should state whether it is intended to be a final or partial summary judgment.

(1) Final SJ. If the parties intend the summary judgment to be a final, appealable judgment, the judgment should (1) actually dispose of all claims and parties, or (2) state with unmistakable clarity that it is a final judgment for all claims and all parties. *Lehmann v. Har-Con Corp.*, 39 S.W.3d 191, 192-93 (Tex.2001). A "Mother Hubbard" clause stating that "all relief not expressly granted herein is denied" is ambiguous and does not by itself indicate that a summary judgment is final for purposes of appeal. *See id.* See "Statement of finality," ch. 9-C, §4.3, p. 767; "What judgments are final," ch. 9-C, §6.3, p. 772.

NOTE

An order granting a motion for partial summary judgment that contains an unequivocal statement of finality is considered final for purposes of appeal, even if the party moving for summary judgment did not move for summary judgment on all claims and did not intend the summary judgment to be final. See **Lehmann**, *39 S.W.3d at 204. See "Final SJ," §14.2, p. 625; "Finality for appeal," ch. 9-C, §6.4.1, p. 774.*

---

(2) Partial SJ. If the parties intend the summary judgment to be a partial judgment, the judgment should say so. A summary judgment is a partial, interlocutory order if it does not dispose of all claims and all parties. *Lehmann*, 39 S.W.3d at 205. The following orders are not final orders:

(a) An order that adjudicates the plaintiff's claims but not a counterclaim, cross-claim, or third-party claim. *Id.* Or the converse, an order that adjudicates a counterclaim, cross-claim, or third-party claim but not the plaintiff's claims. *Id.*

(b) An order that disposes of the claims by only one of multiple plaintiffs. *Id.*; *Liu v. Yang*, 69 S.W.3d 225, 228 (Tex.App.—Corpus Christi 2001, no pet.). Or the converse, an order that disposes of the claims against only one of multiple defendants. *Lehmann*, 39 S.W.3d at 205.

(c) An order that resolves the issue of liability in favor of the movant but leaves the issue of damages for a later hearing. *See* TRCP 166a(a) (SJ may be rendered on issue of liability alone, although there is a genuine issue as to amount of damages). See "Unliquidated damages," ch. 2-B, §8.2, p. 107.

3. Resolve issues on the merits. A summary judgment should not state that the case is dismissed. *Martinez v. Southern Pac. Transp.*, 951 S.W.2d 824, 830 (Tex.App.—San Antonio 1997, no writ); *Heibel v. Bermann*, 407 S.W.2d 945, 947 (Tex.App.—Houston 1966, no writ). A summary judgment should dispose of claims on the merits, not by dismissal. *See, e.g.*, *Martinez*, 951 S.W.2d at 830 (appellate court reformed judgment to delete "dismissal with prejudice" language, leaving "take nothing" language).

4. Overrule objections. The nonmovant should make sure the summary judgment includes a statement that all of its objections and any special exceptions were overruled. See "Ruling," §5.4, p. 604; "Secure ruling on objections," §10.2, p. 621. If the court refuses to rule, the nonmovant should object to the refusal in writing. By objecting to the court's refusal to rule, the nonmovant will preserve error on the objection. TRAP 33.1(a)(2)(B). See "Refusal to rule + objection," ch. 1-G, §2.2.3, p. 48.

§12.4 To make partial SJ final. To convert a partial summary judgment into a final one, the unadjudicated claims can be resolved on the merits by another summary judgment or at trial, or resolved procedurally by a nonsuit or a severance. See "What judgments are final," ch. 9-C, §6.3, p. 772.

───────────────── ✦ ─────────────────

PRACTICE TIP

If you discover on appeal that what you thought was a final summary judgment is really a partial judgment, you may be able to convert it to a final judgment by asking the trial court to sever it from the rest of the suit, allowing you to continue with the appeal. See TRAP 27.2, 27.3; **State Farm Mut. Auto. Ins. v. Leeds***, 981 S.W.2d 693, 693 (Tex.App.—Houston [1st Dist.] 1998, order).*

§13. MOTION FOR RECONSIDERATION

A party may file a motion to reconsider the court's summary-judgment ruling. When a party files a motion requesting a reconsideration of a motion for summary judgment that was granted, the motion is effectively a motion for new trial. See "MNT After Summary Judgment," ch. 10-B, §11, p. 801; *O'Connor's Texas Forms*, FORM 10B:6. When a party files a motion requesting a reconsideration of a motion for summary judgment that was denied, the party should reurge all the grounds raised in the original motion for summary judgment and summarize any objections to the other party's motion or response. *See, e.g.,* **State Farm Lloyds v. Page***, 315 S.W.3d 525, 531-32 (Tex.2010) (because motion for reconsideration was limited to grounds in traditional MSJ and did not reurge no-evidence MSJ grounds, D's no-evidence MSJ arguments were not preserved). A party may also refile the motion for summary judgment.

§14. REVIEW

§14.1   Appellate record. The appellate record for summary judgment is limited to the clerk's record. As a rule, no reporter's record is necessary because no oral testimony can be received at the hearing. *See* TRCP 166a(c); *Mc-Connell v. Southside ISD*, 858 S.W.2d 337, 343 n.7 (Tex.1993). However, a reporter's record may be necessary if the court made rulings about the summary judgment that are reflected only in the reporter's record. *Aguilar v. LVDVD, L.C.*, 70 S.W.3d 915, 917 (Tex.App.—El Paso 2002, pet. denied) (hearing preserved ruling on written objections). See *O'Connor's Texas Appeals*, "Summary judgment," ch. 6-C, §4.2.1, p. 229.

§14.2   Final SJ. As a general rule, only final summary judgments can be appealed. See "Final Judgment," ch. 9-C, §6, p. 771. If a summary judgment leaves some claims unresolved, it is an interlocutory order and cannot be appealed until after the rendition of a final judgment. *See* **Lehmann v. Har-Con Corp.***, 39 S.W.3d 191, 205 (Tex. 2001). If the summary judgment grants more relief than requested in the motion but contains unequivocal language that it disposes of all claims and parties, the summary judgment is final for purposes of appeal. *See* **G&H Towing Co. v. Magee***, 347 S.W.3d 293, 298 (Tex.2011); *Ritzell v. Espeche*, 87 S.W.3d 536, 538 (Tex.2002); *Lehmann*, 39 S.W.3d at 205-06. See "Finality for purposes of appeal," ch. 9-C, §6.4, p. 774.

§14.3   Appeal when SJ granted. A summary judgment becomes final and appealable when the trial court disposes of all the parties and issues in the lawsuit. *Park Place Hosp. v. Estate of Milo*, 909 S.W.2d 508, 510 (Tex. 1995). Once the trial court grants a final summary judgment, the nonmovant may appeal.

   1.   Grounds for review. The appellate court may review and affirm on any ground the movant presented to the court in its motion for summary judgment, regardless of whether the trial court identified the ground relied on to grant the summary judgment. *Cincinnati Life Ins. v. Cates*, 927 S.W.2d 623, 625 (Tex.1996). When the summary judgment does not state the grounds on which it was granted, the nonmovant must show that each ground alleged in the motion is insufficient to support the judgment. *Jones v. Hyman*, 107 S.W.3d 830, 832 (Tex.App.—Dallas 2003, no pet.). Otherwise, the summary judgment may be affirmed on any one meritorious ground alleged. *Dow Chem. Co. v. Francis*, 46 S.W.3d 237, 242 (Tex.2001); *Carr v. Brasher*, 776 S.W.2d 567, 569 (Tex.1989); *Woodside v. Woodside*, 154 S.W.3d 688, 692 (Tex.App.—El Paso 2004, no pet.). The appellate court may even review grounds in earlier summary-judgment motions, even though they were denied. *Baker Hughes, Inc. v. Keco R. & D., Inc.*, 12 S.W.3d 1, 5 (Tex.1999).

   2.   SJ grants more relief than requested. A summary judgment on a claim not addressed in the motion is generally reversible error. *G&H Towing Co. v. Magee*, 347 S.W.3d 293, 297 (Tex.2011). When a summary judg-

✦

ment disposes of more claims than the motion requested, the appellate court should affirm the grounds on which the judgment was properly granted and reverse only those portions that are erroneous. *Id.* at 298; *Page v. Geller*, 941 S.W.2d 101, 102 (Tex.1997); *e.g., Bandera Elec. Coop. v. Gilchrist*, 946 S.W.2d 336, 337 (Tex.1997) (P's motion for SJ did not address counterclaim). The appellate court should not reverse the entire case. *See Bandera Elec.*, 946 S.W.2d at 337; *Page*, 941 S.W.2d at 102.

3. SJ erroneously granted. When a trial court erroneously grants a summary judgment, the appellate court should affirm the summary judgment if later events in the trial court made the erroneous decision harmless. *Progressive Cty. Mut. Ins. v. Boyd*, 177 S.W.3d 919, 921 (Tex.2005); *see, e.g., Martin v. Martin, Martin & Richards, Inc.*, 989 S.W.2d 357, 359 (Tex.1998) (harmless error to grant D's motion for SJ without notice to P because trial court considered P's response after SJ and reconfirmed its ruling).

4. Interlocutory appeal. Some interlocutory orders granting a summary judgment may be appealable if certain conditions are met.

(1) Before 9-1-11. For an action commenced before September 1, 2011, a trial court can allow an interlocutory appeal from an order that is not otherwise appealable only if the parties agree to the order granting an interlocutory appeal and the following conditions are met: (1) the order to be appealed involves a controlling question of law about which there is a substantial ground for difference of opinion and (2) an immediate appeal from the order may materially advance the ultimate termination of the litigation. See *O'Connor's Texas Appeals*, "Interlocutory appeal by agreement – before 9-1-11," ch. 3-P, §2.2, p. 152.

(2) On or after 9-1-11. For an action commenced on or after September 1, 2011, a trial court, on its own initiative or on a party's motion, can allow an appeal from an order that is not otherwise appealable if the following conditions are met: (1) the order to be appealed involves a controlling question of law about which there is a substantial ground for difference of opinion and (2) an immediate appeal from the order may materially advance the ultimate termination of the litigation. CPRC §51.014(d); TRCP 168. Permission must be stated in the order being appealed rather than in a separate order. TRCP 168 & cmt. Although the trial court can grant permission to appeal, the court of appeals has discretion to accept or refuse to hear the appeal. *See* CPRC §51.014(f). See *O'Connor's Texas Appeals*, "Interlocutory appeal by permission – on or after 9-1-11," ch. 3-P, §2.1, p. 149.

§14.4 Appeal when SJ denied. In most cases, an order denying a motion for summary judgment is not a final judgment and thus is not appealable. *See Ackermann v. Vordenbaum*, 403 S.W.2d 362, 365 (Tex.1966). There are exceptions:

1. Both parties move for SJ. When both parties move for a final summary judgment and the trial court grants one motion but denies the other, the party that did not prevail may appeal both on the summary judgment granted against it and on its motion for summary judgment that was denied. *Holmes v. Morales*, 924 S.W.2d 920, 922 (Tex.1996); *see Gilbert Tex. Constr., L.P. v. Underwriters at Lloyd's London*, 327 S.W.3d 118, 124 (Tex.2010); *Commissioners Ct. v. Agan*, 940 S.W.2d 77, 81 (Tex.1997); *Jones v. Strauss*, 745 S.W.2d 898, 900 (Tex.1988). If the appellate court finds that the summary judgment was erroneously granted, the court will review the ruling on the opposing motion and grant summary judgment based on that motion if it finds that the trial court should have granted it. *See Valence Oper. Co. v. Dorsett*, 164 S.W.3d 656, 661 (Tex.2005); *Texas Workers' Comp. Comm'n v. Patient Advocates*, 136 S.W.3d 643, 648 (Tex.2004); *FM Props. Oper. Co. v. City of Austin*, 22 S.W.3d 868, 872 (Tex.2000). The reviewing court should review the summary-judgment evidence presented by both sides and determine all questions presented. *Mid-Continent Cas. Co. v. Global Enercom Mgmt.*, 323 S.W.3d 151, 153-54 (Tex.2010); *Valence Oper.*, 164 S.W.3d at 661; *Agan*, 940 S.W.2d at 81. For the appellate court to reverse and render for the other party, that party must be entitled to a final—not partial—summary judgment as a matter of law. *CU Lloyd's v. Feldman*, 977 S.W.2d 568, 569 (Tex.1998); *Bowman v. Lumberton ISD*, 801 S.W.2d 883, 889 (Tex.1990); *see Strauss*, 745 S.W.2d at 900. See "When both parties move for SJ," ch. 7-C, §4.8, p. 640.

2. Denial of earlier SJ. In the appeal of a summary judgment, the appellate court may review grounds in earlier summary-judgment motions that the trial court denied. *Baker Hughes, Inc. v. Keco R. & D., Inc.*, 12 S.W.3d 1, 5 (Tex.1999).

★

3. Denial of official-immunity SJ.

(1) Appeal. Under CPRC §51.014(a)(5), an officer or employee of a state or political subdivision who asserts a qualified immunity may appeal the denial of a motion for summary judgment to the court of appeals before the entry of a final judgment. See *O'Connor's Texas Appeals*, "Denial of official-immunity summary judgment," ch. 1-B, §2.3.1(4), p. 12; *O'Connor's Texas COA*, "Summary judgment," ch. 24-A, §4.1.1(2), p. 843.

(2) Stay. The interlocutory appeal of an order denying a summary judgment based on an assertion of immunity does not automatically stay the commencement of trial during the appeal. CPRC §51.014(c). To determine whether a defendant is entitled to a stay after the denial of a summary judgment based on an assertion of immunity, see *O'Connor's Texas Appeals*, "Orders resulting in automatic stay after motion denied & deadlines met," ch. 3-P, §3.1.2, p. 154. An interlocutory appeal under CPRC §51.014(a)(5), however, does stay all other proceedings in the trial court pending resolution of that appeal. CPRC §51.014(b).

4. Denial of free-speech SJ.
Under CPRC §51.014(a)(6), a defendant in a defamation case may appeal the denial of a motion for summary judgment to the court of appeals if (1) the defendant is a member of the electronic or print media or a person whose communication was published by the electronic or print media, and (2) the defendant asserted a claim or defense involving free speech or free press under the First Amendment to the U.S. Constitution, Texas Constitution article 1, §8, or CPRC chapter 73 (libel). See *O'Connor's Texas Appeals*, "Denial of free-speech summary judgment," ch. 1-B, §2.3.1(5), p. 13; *O'Connor's Texas COA*, "Interlocutory appeal," ch. 18-A, §6.6, p. 541. An interlocutory appeal of an order denying a motion for summary judgment under CPRC §51.014(a)(6) automatically stays the commencement of trial during the appeal. CPRC §51.014(b).

§14.5 Mandamus.

1. Refusal to rule. Mandamus is appropriate when the trial court refuses to rule on a timely submitted motion for summary judgment, thereby preventing the movant from perfecting a statutory interlocutory appeal. *See In re American Media Consol.*, 121 S.W.3d 70, 73 (Tex.App.—San Antonio 2003, orig. proceeding) (mandamus denied); *Grant v. Wood*, 916 S.W.2d 42, 45 (Tex.App.—Houston [1st Dist.] 1995, orig. proceeding) (mandamus granted). If the record does not reflect a refusal to rule but shows only a failure to rule, mandamus is not appropriate. *See In re American Media*, 121 S.W.3d at 73.

2. Denial of SJ. Mandamus is generally not available when the trial court denies a motion for summary judgment, no matter how meritorious the motion. *In re United Servs. Auto. Ass'n*, 307 S.W.3d 299, 314 (Tex. 2010). But in certain extraordinary situations, mandamus relief may be granted. *E.g.*, *id.* (court granted mandamus because D had already been through one trial in forum that lacked jurisdiction, had subsequently appealed to both the court of appeals and the Supreme Court, and was facing another trial on claim that had since been barred by limitations).

✦

C. TRADITIONAL MOTION FOR SUMMARY JUDGMENT

§1. GENERAL

§1.1 Rule. TRCP 166a(c).

§1.2 Purpose. The purpose of the summary-judgment procedure is to permit the trial court to promptly dispose of cases that involve unmeritorious claims or untenable defenses. *City of Houston v. Clear Creek Basin Auth.*, 589 S.W.2d 671, 678 n.5 (Tex.1979).

§1.3 Timetable & forms. Timetable, Motion for Summary Judgment, p. 1226; *O'Connor's Texas Civil Forms* (2012), FORMS 7B, 7C.

§1.4 Other references. Patton, *Summary Judgments in Texas: Practice, Procedure & Review* ch. 3 (3d ed. 2002 & Supp.2012) (referred to as Patton, *Summary Judgments in Texas*); *O'Connor's CPRC Plus* (2012-13) (*O'Connor's CPRC*); *O'Connor's Texas Causes of Action* (2013) (*O'Connor's Texas COA*).

§2. TRADITIONAL MOTION FOR SUMMARY JUDGMENT

§2.1 When to file. A plaintiff may move for a traditional summary judgment anytime after the defendant answers the lawsuit. TRCP 166a(a). A defendant may move for a traditional summary judgment at any time. TRCP 166a(b).

§2.2 In writing. The motion for summary judgment must be in writing. *City of Houston v. Clear Creek Basin Auth.*, 589 S.W.2d 671, 677 (Tex.1979).

§2.3 Unverified. The motion for summary judgment should not be verified. A factual statement in a verified motion for summary judgment is not summary-judgment proof. *Hidalgo v. Surety S&L Ass'n*, 462 S.W.2d 540, 545 (Tex.1971). If a party needs sworn evidence to support its motion for summary judgment, it must attach affidavits or other sworn evidence.

§2.4 Grounds.

1. Stated in motion. The motion for summary judgment must state the grounds on which it is made. TRCP 166a(c); *McConnell v. Southside ISD*, 858 S.W.2d 337, 341 (Tex.1993); *Travis v. City of Mesquite*, 830 S.W.2d 94, 99-100 (Tex.1992). The trial court cannot grant a summary judgment on grounds not presented in the motion; doing so is generally reversible error. *G&H Towing Co. v. Magee*, 347 S.W.3d 293, 297 (Tex.2011); *see Johnson v. Brewer & Pritchard, P.C.*, 73 S.W.3d 193, 204 (Tex.2002); *Stiles v. Resolution Trust Corp.*, 867 S.W.2d 24, 26 (Tex. 1993); *see, e.g., Science Spectrum, Inc. v. Martinez*, 941 S.W.2d 910, 912 (Tex.1997) (D's motion for SJ did not raise issue that D had created dangerous condition); *Sysco Food Servs. v. Trapnell*, 890 S.W.2d 796, 805 (Tex.1994) (D waived issue of collateral estoppel because it raised issue only in its brief); *see also Teer v. Duddlesten*, 664 S.W.2d 702, 703-04 (Tex.1984) (court could not grant SJ for party that did not file motion for SJ). There is, however, a limited exception to this rule. The error is harmless if the ground not presented in the motion is precluded as a matter of law by other grounds raised in the case. *E.g., G&H Towing*, 347 S.W.3d at 297-98 (in case involving D's vicarious liability for agent's negligent entrustment, D's SJ motion was granted even though vicarious-liability issue was omitted; error was harmless because court determined agent had not negligently entrusted vehicle and thus D could not be vicariously liable). If a ground that may support a summary judgment is not stated in the motion, the ground cannot be supplied by a prayer for general relief. *Golden Triangle Energy v. Wickes Lumber*, 725 S.W.2d 439, 441 (Tex.App.—Beaumont 1987, no writ).

PRACTICE TIP

First, never file a trial brief to support a motion for summary judgment; instead, include in the motion all arguments supporting the grounds. See **McConnell**, *858 S.W.2d at 339-40. Second, begin each ground for summary judgment by incorporating by reference all the facts from other parts of the motion that are necessary to that ground. See* **Johnson**, *73 S.W.3d at 204.*

✯

2. Specificity = fair notice. The grounds in the motion are sufficiently specific if they give "fair notice" to the nonmovant. *Seaway Prods. Pipeline Co. v. Hanley*, 153 S.W.3d 643, 649 (Tex.App.—Fort Worth 2004, no pet.); *Thomas v. Cisneros*, 596 S.W.2d 313, 316 (Tex.App.—Austin 1980, writ ref'd n.r.e.); *see, e.g., Upchurch v. Albear*, 5 S.W.3d 274, 284-85 (Tex.App.—Amarillo 1999, pet. denied) (general reference to voluminous record, which did not direct attention to evidence relied on, did not satisfy fair-notice requirement). If the grounds are vague, the nonmovant should file special exceptions. See "Special Exceptions in Summary-Judgment Procedure," ch. 7-B, §5, p. 604; *O'Connor's Texas Forms*, FORM 7B:1.

3. Contained in pleadings. The grounds presented in the motion for summary judgment should be contained in the movant's pleadings. The movant should amend its pleadings if the grounds are not contained in the pleadings. See "Amending the Petition or Answer," ch. 7-B, §8, p. 610. If a party asserts a ground for summary judgment that is not contained in its pleadings (e.g., an affirmative defense), the nonmovant can defeat the motion for summary judgment by objecting to the lack of pleadings. See "Challenge movant's pleadings," §3.6.2, p. 632.

§2.5 SJ based on facts or pleadings.

1. Moving on the facts. When a movant files a motion for summary judgment based on the summary-judgment evidence, the court can grant the motion only when the movant's evidence, as a matter of law, either proves all the elements of the movant's claim or defense or disproves the facts of at least one element of the nonmovant's claim or defense. *See, e.g., Park Place Hosp. v. Estate of Milo*, 909 S.W.2d 508, 511 (Tex.1995) (causation disproved as a matter of law); *Lear Siegler, Inc. v. Perez*, 819 S.W.2d 470, 471-72 (Tex.1991) (same). When evaluating a motion for summary judgment based on summary-judgment proof, the trial court must do the following:

(1) Assume all the nonmovant's proof is true. *Limestone Prods. Distrib. v. McNamara*, 71 S.W.3d 308, 311 (Tex.2002); *Shah v. Moss*, 67 S.W.3d 836, 842 (Tex.2001); *M.D. Anderson Hosp. & Tumor Inst. v. Willrich*, 28 S.W.3d 22, 23 (Tex.2000); *Nixon v. Mr. Prop. Mgmt. Co.*, 690 S.W.2d 546, 548-49 (Tex.1985).

(2) Make every reasonable inference in favor of the nonmovant. *Provident Life & Acc. Ins. v. Knott*, 128 S.W.3d 211, 215 (Tex.2003); *M.D. Anderson*, 28 S.W.3d at 23; *Science Spectrum, Inc. v. Martinez*, 941 S.W.2d 910, 911 (Tex.1997); *Nixon*, 690 S.W.2d at 548-49.

(3) Resolve all doubts about the existence of a genuine issue of a material fact against the movant. *M.D. Anderson*, 28 S.W.3d at 23; *Johnson Cty. Sheriff's Posse, Inc. v. Endsley*, 926 S.W.2d 284, 285 (Tex.1996); *Nixon*, 690 S.W.2d at 548-49.

2. Moving on the pleadings. The movant may file a motion for summary judgment that shows the nonmovant has no viable cause of action or defense based on the nonmovant's pleadings. *See, e.g., National Un. Fire Ins. v. Merchants Fast Motor Lines, Inc.*, 939 S.W.2d 139, 141 (Tex.1997) (no duty to defend insurance claim based on allegations in pleadings and terms of policy); *Trinity River Auth. v. URS Consultants, Inc.*, 889 S.W.2d 259, 261 (Tex.1994) (petition showed statute of repose had run); *Helena Labs. v. Snyder*, 886 S.W.2d 767, 768-69 (Tex.1994) (no cause of action for negligent interference with family relationship); *City of Houston v. Clear Creek Basin Auth.*, 589 S.W.2d 671, 680 (Tex.1979) (under the Water Code, P-city had no cause of action against D for discharging polluted waste outside P's boundaries). In some cases when the motion is based on the pleadings, the parties may include summary-judgment proof. *See, e.g., St. John v. Pope*, 901 S.W.2d 420, 424 (Tex.1995) (facts in affidavit proved no doctor-patient relationship, and thus there was no duty). When evaluating a motion for summary judgment based on the nonmovant's pleadings, the trial court must do the following:

(1) Assume all allegations and facts in the nonmovant's pleading are true. *Natividad v. Alexsis, Inc.*, 875 S.W.2d 695, 699 (Tex.1994); *Valles v. Texas Comm'n on Jail Standards*, 845 S.W.2d 284, 286 (Tex.App.—Austin 1992, writ denied); *see also American Tobacco Co. v. Grinnell*, 951 S.W.2d 420, 434 (Tex.1997) (not incumbent on nonmovant-P to produce evidence supporting allegations made in her pleadings).

(2) Make all inferences in the nonmovant's pleadings in the light most favorable to the nonmovant. *Medina v. Herrera*, 927 S.W.2d 597, 602 (Tex.1996); *Natividad*, 875 S.W.2d at 699; *Valles*, 845 S.W.2d at 286.

★

(3)   Ensure that any defects in the pleadings cannot be cured by amendment. *In re B.I.V.*, 870 S.W.2d 12, 13 (Tex.1994).

PRACTICE TIP

*Before the court grants a "no cause of action" summary judgment, it must give the nonmovant adequate opportunity to amend to plead a viable cause of action. See **Perry v. S.N.**, 973 S.W.2d 301, 303 (Tex.1998). Thus, the movant should first file special exceptions to the pleading. See "No viable cause of action," ch. 3-G, §10.1, p. 255; "Defective pleading," ch. 3-G, §10.2, p. 255. If the nonmovant refused to cure defects in its pleadings after the defects were identified by special exceptions, a summary judgment for the movant is proper. **Natividad**, 875 S.W.2d at 699; see **Texas Dept. of Corr. v. Herring**, 513 S.W.2d 6, 10 (Tex.1974); Patton, Summary Judgments in Texas, §3.07[2].*

---

§2.6 Request for final SJ. If the movant intends for the summary judgment to be final, it must ask the court to dispose of all issues and all parties. *Continental Airlines, Inc. v. Kiefer*, 920 S.W.2d 274, 276-77 (Tex.1996); *Teer v. Duddlesten*, 664 S.W.2d 702, 703 (Tex.1984). If the motion does not dispose of everything, the judgment will not be final.

1. All parties. The motion should ask for relief for and against all parties in the suit and name all the parties. *See Continental Airlines*, 920 S.W.2d at 276-77.

2. All issues. The motion should ask the court to dispose of all the issues (claims, counterclaims, cross-claims, third-party claims), all theories of damages (actual, exemplary), and all other claims (attorney fees, costs, interest). The motion should identify all the issues on which it seeks summary judgment. *See Continental Airlines*, 920 S.W.2d at 276 (motion "on all claims" did not encompass issues outside motion). If the movant accidentally does not include one of its claims in its motion for summary judgment, it cannot contend on appeal that it intended to abandon that claim; the unadjudicated claim makes what was intended to be a final judgment interlocutory. *See, e.g., McNally v. Guevara*, 52 S.W.3d 195, 196 (Tex.2001) (when Ds' motion for SJ did not include their claim for attorney fees, judgment was not appealable because it did not appear final on its face and did not dispose of Ds' attorney-fees claim).

3. Request for final SJ. The motion should ask the court to render a final, appealable judgment. See "Statement of finality," ch. 9-C, §4.3, p. 767.

4. Sever or dismiss other claims. A summary judgment on some of the claims can be transformed into a final judgment by severing or dismissing the remaining claims.

§2.7 Request for partial SJ. A party may file a motion for partial summary judgment asking the court to dispose of some but not all of the issues or parties in the case.

1. Parties & claims. The motion should identify the parties against whom, and the claims on which, the movant seeks a partial summary judgment. *See* TRCP 166a(a), (b).

2. Request partial judgment. The motion should ask the court to grant a partial summary judgment. The order granting a partial summary judgment is interlocutory and cannot be appealed until a final judgment is rendered. To convert a partial summary judgment into a final judgment, see "To make partial SJ final," ch. 7-B, §12.4, p. 624.

§2.8 Supporting evidence. Most motions for summary judgment require supporting evidence. The summary-judgment proof should be incorporated by reference in and attached to the motion or the response. See "Summary-Judgment Evidence," ch. 7-B, §9, p. 611. Attaching evidence to a traditional motion for summary judgment does not preclude a party from asserting that there is no evidence on a particular element of a claim or defense. *Binur v. Jacobo*, 135 S.W.3d 646, 651 (Tex.2004). See "No-Evidence Motion for Summary Judgment," ch. 7-D, §2, p. 641.

★

---

§2.9 Attorney fees. If the movant is entitled to attorney fees, it should include a request for attorney fees in its original pleading and in the motion for summary judgment.

1. Proof of attorney fees. The movant should support the request for attorney fees with an affidavit by an attorney proving the amount, the necessity, and the reasonableness of the fees. *See Roberts v. Roper*, 373 S.W.3d 227, 233 (Tex.App.—Dallas 2012, n.p.h.). See "Attorney Fees from Adverse Party," ch. 1-H, §10, p. 62; *O'Connor's Texas Forms*, FORMS 1H:14, 7C:1; *O'Connor's Texas COA*, "Attorney Fees," ch. 45, p. 1349.

2. No judicial notice. Attorney fees in a summary-judgment case cannot be established using the judicial-notice provision in CPRC §38.004. That provision permits judicial notice of attorney fees only when a case is tried on the merits. See "Judicial notice," ch. 1-H, §10.2.2, p. 63.

§2.10 Successive motions. TRCP 166a does not place a limit on the number of motions for summary judgment that may be filed. *Cameron Cty. v. Carrillo*, 7 S.W.3d 706, 709 (Tex.App.—Corpus Christi 1999, no pet.).

§3. NONMOVANT'S RESPONSE TO TRADITIONAL MOTION FOR SUMMARY JUDGMENT

The response to the motion for summary judgment serves two functions: (1) it identifies defects in the motion, and (2) it presents reasons the summary judgment should not be granted. The only defect that does not need to be specifically raised in the response is an attack on the legal sufficiency of the grounds for the judgment. See "Objections to SJ motion," §3.6, p. 632. All other defects must be raised in the response.

§3.1 In writing. The response to the motion for summary judgment must be in writing. *City of Houston v. Clear Creek Basin Auth.*, 589 S.W.2d 671, 677 (Tex.1979).

§3.2 Unverified. The response should not be verified; a verified response does not present summary-judgment evidence. *See Quanaim v. Frasco Rest. & Catering*, 17 S.W.3d 30, 42 (Tex.App.—Houston [14th Dist.] 2000, pet. denied); *Webster v. Allstate Ins.*, 833 S.W.2d 747, 749 (Tex.App.—Houston [1st Dist.] 1992, no writ).

§3.3 Deadline. The response must be filed and served at least seven days before the hearing. See "For response – 7 days before hearing," ch. 7-B, §6.4, p. 606.

§3.4 Grounds to defeat SJ.

1. Defeating SJ on facts. To defeat a motion for summary judgment on the facts, the nonmovant can show any of the following:

(1) Movant's SJ burden not met. The movant did not prove as a matter of law all the elements of its cause of action or defense. *See City of Houston v. Clear Creek Basin Auth.*, 589 S.W.2d 671, 678 (Tex.1979); *Rizkallah v. Conner*, 952 S.W.2d 580, 582 (Tex.App.—Houston [1st Dist.] 1997, no writ).

(2) Fact issue. The summary-judgment evidence raises a genuine issue of material fact. *See, e.g., Dillard's, Inc. v. Newman*, 299 S.W.3d 144, 148 (Tex.App.—Amarillo 2008, pet. denied) (fact issue raised about D-movant's affirmative defense). The evidence that raises a fact issue can be either the movant's summary-judgment evidence or evidence produced by the nonmovant in response to the motion. See "Nonmovant's SJ evidence," §3.5, p. 632.

(3) Court barred. The court is barred by rules of law or evidence from giving weight to the movant's evidence offered to prove a vital fact. See "Objections to Summary-Judgment Evidence," ch. 7-B, §10, p. 617.

(4) Nonmovant's affirmative defense. The nonmovant has an affirmative defense to the movant's cause of action or defense. *See Ingersoll-Rand Co. v. Valero Energy Corp.*, 997 S.W.2d 203, 210-11 (Tex.1999). For the nonmovant to assert an affirmative defense to defeat a motion for summary judgment, it must assert the defense in its response and provide sufficient summary-judgment evidence to create a fact issue on each element of the defense. *See Via Net v. TIG Ins.*, 211 S.W.3d 310, 313 (Tex.2006); *Bassett v. American Nat'l Bank*, 145 S.W.3d 692, 696 (Tex.App.—Fort Worth 2004, no pet.); *see, e.g., Keenan v. Gibraltar Sav. Ass'n*, 754 S.W.2d 392, 393-94 (Tex. App.—Houston [14th Dist.] 1988, no writ) (nonmovant's defense that movant did not credit offsets did not preclude

SJ because nonmovant did not present proof). If the defense relied on is not also asserted in the nonmovant's pleadings, the nonmovant should amend its pleadings. *See Via Net*, 211 S.W.3d at 313 (when nonmovant raises unpleaded defense for first time in SJ response, movant can object that defense has not been properly pleaded). The nonmovant is not required to prove the affirmative defense by a preponderance of the evidence or as a matter of law; raising a fact issue is enough to defeat the summary judgment. *See American Petrofina, Inc. v. Allen*, 887 S.W.2d 829, 830 (Tex.1994); *Brownlee v. Brownlee*, 665 S.W.2d 111, 112 (Tex.1984). See "Burden of Proof," §4, p. 633.

2. Defeating SJ on pleadings. To defeat a motion for summary judgment on the pleadings, the nonmovant can show that the facts are undisputed and the motion for summary judgment presents a question of law that must be resolved in the nonmovant's favor. *See, e.g.*, *Zurich Am. Ins. v. McVey*, 339 S.W.3d 724, 734 (Tex.App.—Austin 2011, pet. denied) (undisputed facts established application of legal issue). When material facts are undisputed, a nonmovant may defeat a motion for summary judgment by establishing that the movant's legal position is unsound. *Pagosa Oil & Gas, L.L.C. v. Marrs & Smith Prtshp.*, 323 S.W.3d 203, 215 (Tex.App.—El Paso 2010, pet. denied).

§3.5 Nonmovant's SJ evidence. In most cases, the nonmovant should file summary-judgment evidence to raise a fact issue. See "Summary-Judgment Evidence," ch. 7-B, §9, p. 611. If the movant's summary-judgment evidence includes affidavits, the nonmovant should file counteraffidavits to raise fact issues. For example, if a movant files an affidavit alleging the reasonableness of attorney fees, the nonmovant must file a controverting affidavit if it wants to raise a fact issue. *See American 10-Minute Oil Change, Inc. v. Metropolitan Nat'l Bank-Farmers Branch*, 783 S.W.2d 598, 602 (Tex.App.—Dallas 1989, no pet.). See "Moving on the facts," §2.5.1, p. 629.

§3.6 Objections to SJ motion. In the response to the motion for summary judgment, the nonmovant must object to any defect in the form or substance of the motion, pleadings, or evidence. If the nonmovant does not make any objections in its response, its objections are waived, and on appeal it can argue only that the grounds for summary judgment presented to the trial court are insufficient as a matter of law. *City of Houston v. Clear Creek Basin Auth.*, 589 S.W.2d 671, 678 (Tex.1979); *see Scown v. Neie*, 225 S.W.3d 303, 307 (Tex.App.—El Paso 2006, pet. denied); *French v. Gill*, 206 S.W.3d 737, 743 (Tex.App.—Texarkana 2006, no pet.); *Roadside Stations, Inc. v. 7HBF, Ltd.*, 904 S.W.2d 927, 932 (Tex.App.—Fort Worth 1995, no writ).

1. Challenge movant's SJ evidence. The nonmovant should object to any defects in the movant's affidavits or other summary-judgment evidence. See "Objections to Summary-Judgment Evidence," ch. 7-B, §10, p. 617.

2. Challenge movant's pleadings. If the movant's pleadings do not support the motion for summary judgment, the nonmovant must object, or it waives the error.

(1) Defective pleadings. A motion for summary judgment should not be based on a pleading deficiency that could be cured by an amendment. *In re B.I.V.*, 870 S.W.2d 12, 13 (Tex.1994). See "Defective pleading," ch. 3-G, §10.2, p. 255. Thus, the nonmovant can object to the movant's motion for summary judgment on the ground that the motion is an attempt to circumvent the special-exceptions practice and request additional time to amend. *See Kassen v. Hatley*, 887 S.W.2d 4, 13 n.10 (Tex.1994); *Texas Dept. of Corr. v. Herring*, 513 S.W.2d 6, 10 (Tex. 1974).

(2) Inadequate pleadings. An unpleaded claim or defense included in the motion for summary judgment is tried by consent if the nonmovant does not object in its response. *See D.R. Horton-Tex., Ltd. v. Markel Int'l Ins. Co.*, 300 S.W.3d 740, 743 (Tex.2009); *see, e.g.*, *Roark v. Stallworth Oil & Gas, Inc.*, 813 S.W.2d 492, 495 (Tex. 1991) (P-nonmovant waived objection to Ds' unpleaded defense raised in Ds' motion but not in their answer); *Roadside Stations*, 904 S.W.2d at 930 (D-nonmovant waived objection to P's unpleaded claim raised in P's motion but not in its petition). When a nonmovant objects to the variance between the movant's motion for summary judgment and the movant's pleadings, the movant should immediately file an amended pleading that conforms the pleadings to the motion. See "Rules Regarding Amending Pleadings Before Trial," ch. 5-F, §3, p. 350; "Motion for Leave to Amend," ch. 8-F, §2, p. 721.

✯

---

3. Challenge movant's motion. The nonmovant should challenge all legal and procedural shortcomings in the motion for summary judgment. See "Motion for Summary Judgment—General Rules," ch. 7-B, p. 603. For example, if the movant sought summary judgment on a theory not included in its pleadings, the nonmovant should object that the pleadings do not support the motion.

4. Challenge movant's notice. If the movant did not timely file and serve the motion, the evidence, and the notice of hearing, the nonmovant must object to the lack of 21 days' notice in writing. *See* TRCP 166a(c). The 21-day notice requirement for the motion is waived if the nonmovant does not object in writing and under oath before or at the hearing. *Nguyen v. Short, How, Frels & Heitz, P.C.*, 108 S.W.3d 558, 560 (Tex.App.—Dallas 2003, pet. denied); *Veal v. Veterans Life Ins.*, 767 S.W.2d 892, 895 (Tex.App.—Texarkana 1989, no writ). The nonmovant should file a motion to reset the date of the hearing, along with an affidavit that identifies the date it received the motion and notice of hearing and a request that the hearing on the motion be reset to allow the full 21 days' notice. See "Summary-Judgment Deadlines," ch. 7-B, §6, p. 605; "Motion to reset SJ hearing," ch. 7-B, §6.10.2, p. 608; *O'Connor's Texas Forms*, FORM 7B:2.

5. File special exceptions. If the motion is unclear or ambiguous, the nonmovant should challenge it by special exceptions. See "Special Exceptions in Summary-Judgment Procedure," ch. 7-B, §5, p. 604.

§3.7 Waiver. The nonmovant should assert all of its challenges to the summary judgment in its response. On appeal, the appellate courts will not consider any issues as grounds for reversal that were not presented to the trial court by written response. TRCP 166a(c); *Lopez v. Muñoz, Hockema & Reed, L.L.P.*, 22 S.W.3d 857, 862 (Tex.2000); *City of Houston v. Clear Creek Basin Auth.*, 589 S.W.2d 671, 679 (Tex.1979).

§3.8 Consider amending pleadings. Amending the pleadings to add new issues or to delete factual admissions can sometimes be the easiest and most effective way to avoid a final summary judgment. *See Strather v. Dolgencorp, Inc.*, 96 S.W.3d 420, 423 (Tex.App.—Texarkana 2002, no pet.). See "Amending the Petition or Answer," ch. 7-B, §8, p. 610. Once the pleadings are amended to add or delete issues, the movant may respond by amending its motion for summary judgment. *Smith v. Atlantic Richfield Co.*, 927 S.W.2d 85, 88 (Tex.App.—Houston [1st Dist.] 1996, writ denied). If the movant does not amend its motion for summary judgment to address an amended petition adding new claims, only a partial summary judgment can be granted. See "Partial SJ," ch. 7-B, §12.3.2(2), p. 624.

§3.9 Consider nonsuit. If the statute of limitations has not run, a plaintiff may avoid a summary judgment by taking a nonsuit. The plaintiff can take a nonsuit after the defendant files a motion for summary judgment, but the nonsuit must be filed before the court rules on the motion for summary judgment. See "Deadlines for Nonsuit," ch. 7-F, §3, p. 652.

§4. BURDEN OF PROOF

§4.1 Burden on movant. The movant for summary judgment must show (1) there is no genuine issue of material fact and (2) the movant is entitled to judgment as a matter of law. TRCP 166a(c); *Provident Life & Acc. Ins. v. Knott*, 128 S.W.3d 211, 215-16 (Tex.2003); *M.D. Anderson Hosp. & Tumor Inst. v. Willrich*, 28 S.W.3d 22, 23 (Tex.2000); *Lear Siegler, Inc. v. Perez*, 819 S.W.2d 470, 471 (Tex.1991). Even if the nonmovant does not file a response and the motion for summary judgment is uncontroverted, the movant must still carry the burden of proof. *City of Houston v. Clear Creek Basin Auth.*, 589 S.W.2d 671, 678 (Tex.1979).

§4.2 Burden on nonmovant. When the movant does not meet its burden of proof, the burden does not shift to the nonmovant. *M.D. Anderson Hosp. & Tumor Inst. v. Willrich*, 28 S.W.3d 22, 23 (Tex.2000); *City of Houston v. Clear Creek Basin Auth.*, 589 S.W.2d 671, 678 (Tex.1979). The burden shifts to the nonmovant only after the movant has established that it is entitled to summary judgment as a matter of law. *Casso v. Brand*, 776 S.W.2d 551, 556 (Tex.1989). At that point, the nonmovant must produce summary-judgment evidence to raise a fact issue.

★

§4.3 When plaintiff moves for SJ on its cause of action.

7-4. P MOVES FOR SUMMARY JUDGMENT ON ITS CAUSE OF ACTION

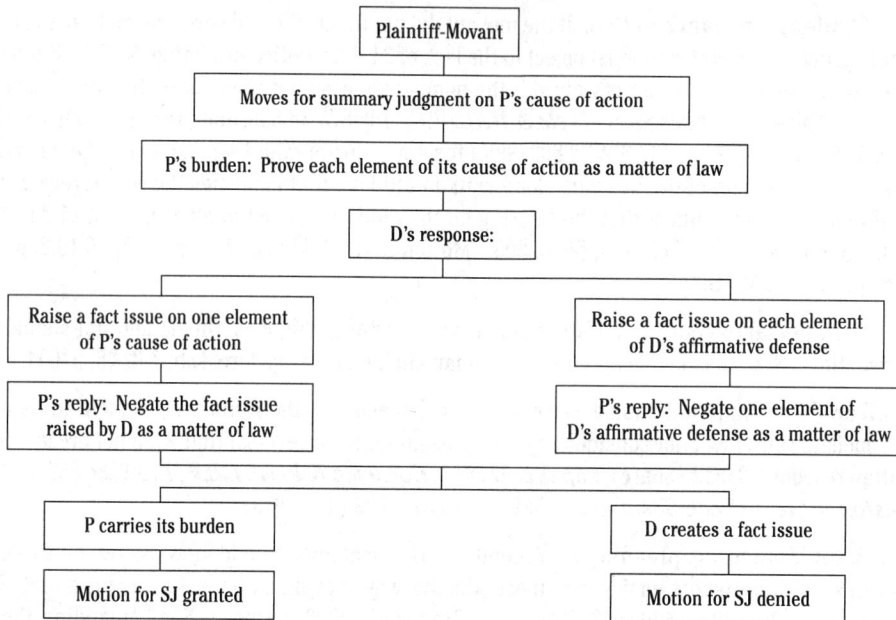

Plaintiff-Movant

Moves for summary judgment on P's cause of action

P's burden: Prove each element of its cause of action as a matter of law

D's response:

Raise a fact issue on one element of P's cause of action	Raise a fact issue on each element of D's affirmative defense
P's reply: Negate the fact issue raised by D as a matter of law	P's reply: Negate one element of D's affirmative defense as a matter of law
P carries its burden	D creates a fact issue
Motion for SJ granted	Motion for SJ denied

1. **Plaintiff's motion.** See *O'Connor's Texas Forms*, FORM 7C:1.

(1) **Prove plaintiff's cause of action.** When the plaintiff moves for summary judgment on its own cause of action, the plaintiff must prove it is entitled to summary judgment by establishing each element of its claim as a matter of law. *MMP, Ltd. v. Jones*, 710 S.W.2d 59, 60 (Tex.1986); *Fry v. Commission for Lawyer Discipline*, 979 S.W.2d 331, 334 (Tex.App.—Houston [14th Dist.] 1998, pet. denied). If the plaintiff does not conclusively establish all the elements necessary to its cause of action, summary judgment is improper. *See, e.g.*, *Wesson v. Jefferson S&L Ass'n*, 641 S.W.2d 903, 906 (Tex.1982) (because P did not prove it was D's duty to procure insurance, an essential element, SJ was improper).

(a) **Liquidated damages.** The plaintiff must prove its liquidated damages as a matter of law. See "Damages," ch. 2-B, §8, p. 107; *O'Connor's Texas COA*, "General Concepts," ch. 41-A, p. 1241.

(b) **Unliquidated damages.** When the damages are unliquidated, the court may grant an interlocutory summary judgment on liability and hold a hearing on damages. TRCP 166a(a); *see Pinnacle Anesthesia Consultants, P.A. v. Fisher*, 309 S.W.3d 93, 100 (Tex.App.—Dallas 2009, pet. denied); *Beck v. West Houston Airport Corp.*, No. 14-09-00471-CV (Tex.App.—Houston [14th Dist.] 2010, no pet.) (memo op.; 8-12-10).

(2) **Ignore defendant's affirmative defense.** When a defendant pleads an affirmative defense in its original answer, the plaintiff may ignore it in the motion for summary judgment. *See Bauer v. Jasso*, 946 S.W.2d 552, 555-56 (Tex.App.—Corpus Christi 1997, no writ). The defendant's affirmative defense will not, without summary-judgment evidence, defeat the plaintiff's motion for summary judgment. *Brownlee v. Brownlee*, 665 S.W.2d 111, 112 (Tex.1984); *Brown v. Aztec Rig Equip., Inc.*, 921 S.W.2d 835, 845 (Tex.App.—Houston [14th Dist.] 1996, writ denied). If the plaintiff wants to force the defendant to prove its affirmative defense, the plaintiff may move for a no-evidence summary judgment under TRCP 166a(i). See "No-Evidence Motion for Summary Judgment," ch. 7-D, p. 640.

⭐

NOTE

The distinction between an affirmative defense and a counterclaim is important in summary-judgment practice because the two place different burdens on the movant and provide different protections to the nonmovant. The distinction is that an affirmative defense is merely an assertion of a defense and does not seek damages; a counterclaim seeks damages. See "Affirmative defense vs. counterclaim," ch. 3-E, §5.1, p. 230.

---

2. Defendant's response to plaintiff's motion. See *O'Connor's Texas Forms*, FORM 7C:3. To prevent the trial court from granting the plaintiff's motion for summary judgment, the defendant can do the following:

(1) Create fact issue about plaintiff's cause of action. The defendant can defeat the plaintiff's motion for summary judgment by creating a fact issue about one element of the plaintiff's cause of action. To do that, the defendant must file a response that either identifies a fact issue in the summary-judgment evidence already in the record or includes summary-judgment evidence that creates a fact issue. *See, e.g.*, *Geiselman v. Cramer Fin. Grp.*, 965 S.W.2d 532, 537 (Tex.App.—Houston [14th Dist.] 1997, no writ) (D's response identified substantive defects in P's affidavits, preventing P from establishing ownership of promissory note as a matter of law).

(2) Create fact issue about affirmative defense. To avoid the plaintiff's motion for summary judgment, the defendant can create fact issues about its own affirmative defense. To do that, the defendant must file a response that identifies its affirmative defense and provides summary-judgment evidence that raises a fact issue on each element. *Brownlee*, 665 S.W.2d at 112; *Brown*, 921 S.W.2d at 845. The defendant is not required to prove its affirmative defense as a matter of law; it is required only to raise a fact issue about each element of its affirmative defense. *See Brownlee*, 665 S.W.2d at 112. If the defendant did not plead an affirmative defense in its answer, it can still assert one in its response if the plaintiff does not object. See "Challenge movant's pleadings," §3.6.2, p. 632. If the plaintiff moved for summary judgment under TRCP 166a(i) on the defendant's affirmative defense, the defendant is required to produce evidence to support its defense. See "Nonmovant's Response to No-Evidence Motion for Summary Judgment," ch. 7-D, §3, p. 642.

3. Plaintiff's reply to defendant's response. If the defendant, by its response and summary-judgment evidence, challenges the plaintiff's right to summary judgment, the plaintiff should file a reply to assure the court that summary judgment in its favor is still warranted.

(1) Negate fact issues about plaintiff's cause of action. If the defendant identifies or raises fact issues about the plaintiff's right to a summary judgment on its cause of action, the plaintiff may salvage its right to a summary judgment by showing as a matter of law that there are no fact issues.

(2) Negate fact issues about affirmative defenses. If the defendant raises fact issues to support its affirmative defense, the plaintiff may salvage its right to a summary judgment by negating as a matter of law the existence of at least one element of the affirmative defense.

★

§4.4 When plaintiff moves for SJ on defendant's counterclaim.

7-5. P MOVES FOR SUMMARY JUDGMENT ON D'S COUNTERCLAIM

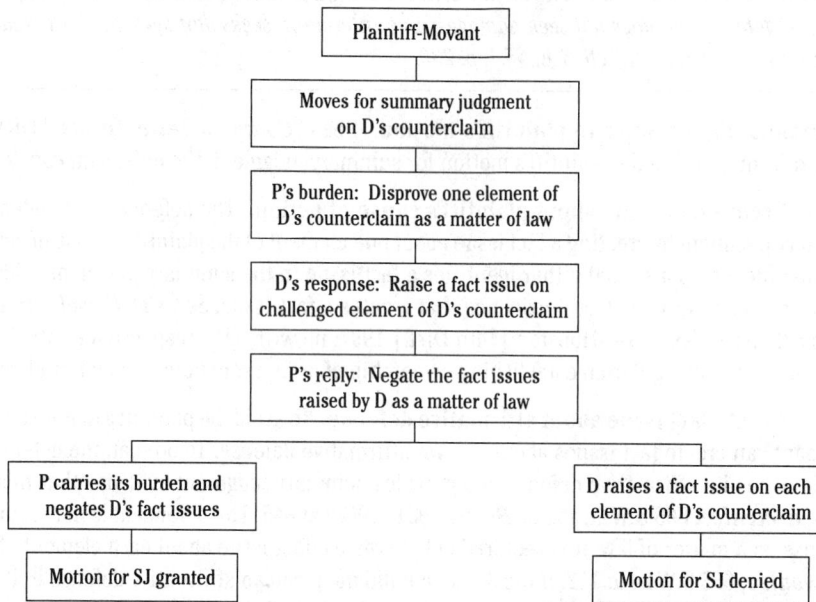

Plaintiff-Movant

Moves for summary judgment
on D's counterclaim

P's burden: Disprove one element of
D's counterclaim as a matter of law

D's response: Raise a fact issue on
challenged element of D's counterclaim

P's reply: Negate the fact issues
raised by D as a matter of law

P carries its burden and
negates D's fact issues

D raises a fact issue on each
element of D's counterclaim

Motion for SJ granted

Motion for SJ denied

1. Plaintiff's motion. When the defendant asserts a counterclaim in its original answer, for the plaintiff to be entitled to a final summary judgment under TRCP 166a(c), the plaintiff must prove as a matter of law all the elements of the plaintiff's cause of action and must negate as a matter of law at least one element of the defendant's counterclaim. *See Taylor v. GWR Oper. Co.*, 820 S.W.2d 908, 910 (Tex.App.—Houston [1st Dist.] 1991, writ denied). The plaintiff can also seek a no-evidence summary judgment on the counterclaim under TRCP 166a(i). See "No-Evidence Motion for Summary Judgment," ch. 7-D, §2, p. 641. The two motions can be combined in one motion for summary judgment, but they should each be argued separately in the motion.

2. Defendant's response to plaintiff's motion. If the plaintiff disproves as a matter of law one or more essential elements of the defendant's counterclaim, the plaintiff is entitled to a summary judgment unless the defendant can either (1) *identify* a fact issue in the elements the plaintiff negated or (2) *create* a fact issue by producing controverting evidence that raises a fact issue on one of the elements the plaintiff negated.

3. Plaintiff's reply to defendant's response. If the defendant produces controverting evidence that raises a fact issue on the elements of its counterclaim negated by the plaintiff, the plaintiff must eliminate the fact issue, or the summary judgment will be denied.

§4.5 When defendant moves for SJ on plaintiff's cause of action. The defendant can move for a traditional summary judgment on the plaintiff's cause of action under TRCP 166a(b)—that is, by proving conclusively that the plaintiff has no cause of action. *See Randall's Food Mkts., Inc. v. Johnson*, 891 S.W.2d 640, 644 (Tex.1995). See *O'Connor's Texas Forms*, FORM 7C:2. The defendant can also force the plaintiff to provide evidence supporting its cause of action under TRCP 166a(i). See "No-Evidence Motion for Summary Judgment," ch. 7-D, p. 640.

★

┌───┐
│   7-6. D MOVES FOR SUMMARY JUDGMENT ON P'S CAUSE OF ACTION   │
└───┘

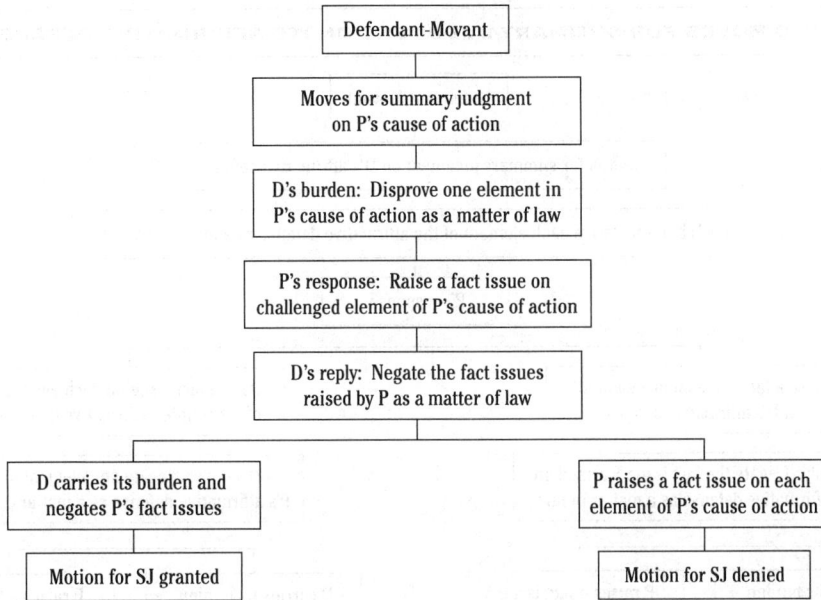

```
                        Defendant-Movant

                    Moves for summary judgment
                      on P's cause of action

                    D's burden:  Disprove one element in
                    P's cause of action as a matter of law

                    P's response:  Raise a fact issue on
                    challenged element of P's cause of action

                    D's reply:  Negate the fact issues
                    raised by P as a matter of law

       D carries its burden and          P raises a fact issue on each
         negates P's fact issues          element of P's cause of action

         Motion for SJ granted              Motion for SJ denied
```

1. Defendant's motion. A defendant moving for summary judgment on the plaintiff's cause of action assumes the burden of showing as a matter of law that the plaintiff has no cause of action. *See **Lear Siegler, Inc. v. Perez**, 819 S.W.2d 470, 471 (Tex.1991); **Griffin v. Rowden**, 654 S.W.2d 435, 436 (Tex.1983).* The defendant does not need to disprove all the elements of the plaintiff's cause of action; it must disprove only one. *See, e.g., **Walker v. Harris**, 924 S.W.2d 375, 378 (Tex.1996)* (D negated duty); ***Doe v. Boys Clubs of Greater Dallas, Inc.**, 907 S.W.2d 472, 481-82 (Tex.1995)* (D disproved causation); ***Lear Siegler**, 819 S.W.2d at 471* (same). The defendant must disprove the plaintiff's cause of action as pleaded. ***GNG Gas Sys. v. Dean**, 921 S.W.2d 421, 426 (Tex.App.—Amarillo 1996, writ denied).* If the defendant cannot meet that burden, the defendant is not entitled to a summary judgment. *See **Griffin**, 654 S.W.2d at 436.*

2. Plaintiff's response to defendant's motion. If the defendant disproves as a matter of law one or more essential elements of the plaintiff's cause of action, the defendant is entitled to a summary judgment unless the plaintiff can either (1) *identify* a fact issue in the elements the defendant negated or (2) *create* a fact issue by producing controverting evidence that raises a fact issue on one of the elements the defendant negated. *See **Centeq Rlty., Inc. v. Siegler**, 899 S.W.2d 195, 197 (Tex.1995)* (raise fact issue); ***Prescott v. CSPH, Inc.**, 878 S.W.2d 692, 693-94 (Tex.App.—Amarillo 1994, writ denied)* (create fact question); *see also **Gammill v. Jack Williams Chevrolet, Inc.**, 875 S.W.2d 27, 28-29 (Tex.App.—Fort Worth 1994, writ denied)* (Ps filed affidavits stating that tests showed vehicle was defective after Ds filed affidavits stating that it was not).

3. Defendant's reply to plaintiff's response. If the plaintiff produces controverting evidence that raises a fact issue on the elements of its cause of action negated by the defendant, the defendant must eliminate the fact issue or the summary judgment will be denied.

TRADITIONAL
SUMMARY JUDGMENT

§4.6 When defendant moves for SJ on its affirmative defense.

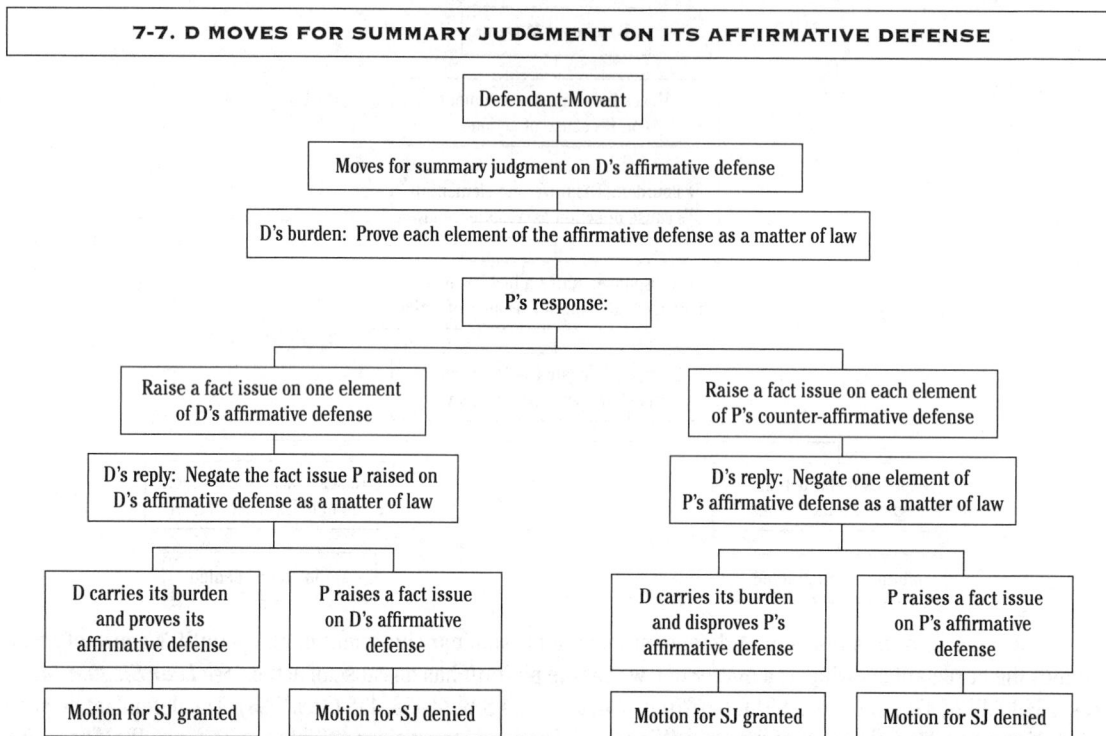

7-7. D MOVES FOR SUMMARY JUDGMENT ON ITS AFFIRMATIVE DEFENSE

Defendant-Movant

Moves for summary judgment on D's affirmative defense

D's burden: Prove each element of the affirmative defense as a matter of law

P's response:

| Raise a fact issue on one element of D's affirmative defense | Raise a fact issue on each element of P's counter-affirmative defense |

| D's reply: Negate the fact issue P raised on D's affirmative defense as a matter of law | D's reply: Negate one element of P's affirmative defense as a matter of law |

| D carries its burden and proves its affirmative defense | P raises a fact issue on D's affirmative defense | D carries its burden and disproves P's affirmative defense | P raises a fact issue on P's affirmative defense |

| Motion for SJ granted | Motion for SJ denied | Motion for SJ granted | Motion for SJ denied |

1. Defendant's motion. The defendant can move for summary judgment on its affirmative defense. *See Randall's Food Mkts., Inc. v. Johnson*, 891 S.W.2d 640, 644 (Tex.1995). A defendant that relies on an affirmative defense must plead the defense either in its answer to the suit or in a motion for summary judgment. *See Roark v. Stallworth Oil & Gas, Inc.*, 813 S.W.2d 492, 494 (Tex.1991) (unpleaded affirmative defense may serve as basis for SJ when it is raised in motion for SJ and nonmovant does not object). When a defendant moves for summary judgment on its affirmative defense, it must prove each element of its defense as a matter of law, leaving no issues of material fact. *Johnson & Johnson Med., Inc. v. Sanchez*, 924 S.W.2d 925, 927 (Tex.1996); *see FDIC v. Lenk*, 361 S.W.3d 602, 609 (Tex.2012); *McIntyre v. Ramirez*, 109 S.W.3d 741, 748 (Tex.2003). For example, when a defendant moves for summary judgment on a statute-of-limitations defense, the defendant must (1) conclusively prove when the cause of action accrued, and (2) if the plaintiff pleaded a tolling provision, conclusively negate its application as a matter of law. *See Rhône-Poulenc, Inc. v. Steel*, 997 S.W.2d 217, 224 (Tex.1999); *Velsicol Chem. Corp. v. Winograd*, 956 S.W.2d 529, 530 (Tex.1997); *Jennings v. Burgess*, 917 S.W.2d 790, 793 (Tex.1996); *see, e.g., In re Estate of Matejek*, 960 S.W.2d 650, 651 (Tex.1997) (when P does not raise discovery rule in pleadings, D is not required to negate it in motion for SJ). See *O'Connor's CPRC*, "Statutes of Limitations Chart," p. 896; *O'Connor's Texas Forms*, FORM 7C:3.

2. Plaintiff's response. The plaintiff, as the nonmovant, does not have any burden of proof unless the defendant conclusively proves all the elements of its affirmative defense. See *O'Connor's Texas Forms*, FORM 7C:7. If the defendant establishes its right to an affirmative defense as a matter of law, the defendant is entitled to summary judgment unless the plaintiff can do one of the following:

(1) Create fact issue. The plaintiff can create a fact issue by producing controverting evidence on one of the elements of the defendant's affirmative defense. *See, e.g., McFadden v. American United Life Ins.*, 658

S.W.2d 147, 148 (Tex.1983) (P created fact issue about insurance company's defense that medical procedure was not covered by policy); *Woodbine Elec. Serv. v. McReynolds*, 837 S.W.2d 258, 261-62 (Tex.App.—Eastland 1992, no writ) (P created fact issue about statute of limitations).

   (2) **Create fact issue about counter-affirmative defense.** The plaintiff can create a fact issue on each element of its own affirmative defense that counters the defendant's affirmative defense. *See, e.g., Ryland Grp. v. Hood*, 924 S.W.2d 120, 121 (Tex.1996) (to defeat SJ based on statute of repose, P who asserts fraudulent concealment has burden to create fact issue); *American Petrofina, Inc. v. Allen*, 887 S.W.2d 829, 830 (Tex.1994) (to defeat SJ based on statute of limitations, P who asserts fraudulent concealment has burden to create fact issue); *Williams v. Glash*, 789 S.W.2d 261, 264 (Tex.1990) (to defeat SJ based on release, P produced evidence to create fact issue about mutual mistake).

   (3) **Challenge the pleadings.** If the defendant moves for summary judgment on an affirmative defense that it did not plead in its original answer, the plaintiff can challenge the motion for summary judgment on that ground. In response, the defendant can then move to amend its pleadings. See "Challenge movant's pleadings," §3.6.2, p. 632.

§4.7 When defendant moves for SJ on its own counterclaim.

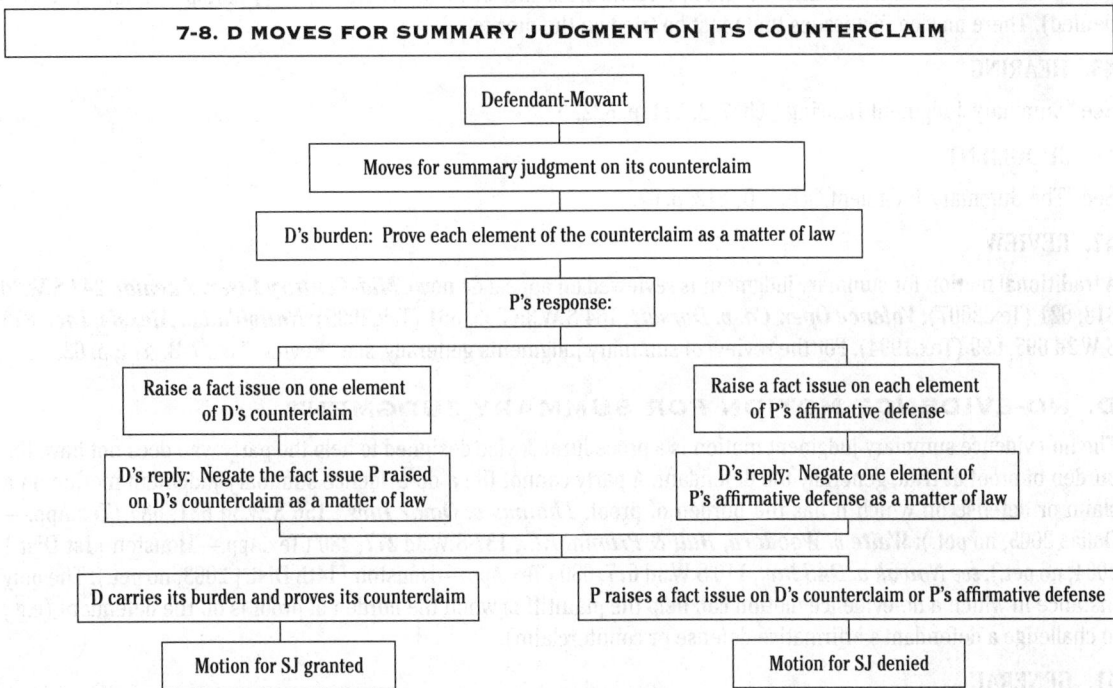

7-8. D MOVES FOR SUMMARY JUDGMENT ON ITS COUNTERCLAIM

   1. **Defendant's motion.** When the defendant moves for summary judgment on its counterclaim, the defendant's burden is the same as for a plaintiff moving for summary judgment on its cause of action—the defendant must prove each element of its counterclaim as a matter of law. *Texas Commerce Bank v. Correa*, 28 S.W.3d 723, 726 (Tex.App.—Corpus Christi 2000, pet. denied). See "Plaintiff's motion," §4.3.1, p. 634; *O'Connor's Texas Forms*, FORM 7C:2.

✯

2. Plaintiff's response. If the defendant establishes its right to summary judgment on its counterclaim as a matter of law, to defeat the summary judgment, the plaintiff must either (1) create a fact issue about at least one element of the counterclaim or (2) create a fact issue on each element of the plaintiff's own affirmative defense to the defendant's counterclaim. See "Defendant's response to plaintiff's motion," §4.3.2, p. 635; *O'Connor's Texas Forms*, FORM 7C:4.

§4.8 When both parties move for SJ.

1. Burdens. When both parties move for summary judgment, each party must carry its own burden as the movant and, in response to the other party's motion, as the nonmovant. See *Martin v. Harris Cty. Appr. Dist.*, 44 S.W.3d 190, 193 (Tex.App.—Houston [14th Dist.] 2001, pet. denied); *James v. Hitchcock ISD*, 742 S.W.2d 701, 703 (Tex.App.—Houston [1st Dist.] 1987, writ denied).

2. Evidence. When both motions are before the court, the court may consider all the summary-judgment evidence in deciding whether to grant either motion. *Martin*, 44 S.W.3d at 193; *Rose v. Baker & Botts*, 816 S.W.2d 805, 810 (Tex.App.—Houston [1st Dist.] 1991, writ denied). The court can rely on one party's evidence to supply missing evidence in the other party's motion. *Seaman v. Seaman*, 686 S.W.2d 206, 210 (Tex.App.—Houston [1st Dist.] 1984, writ ref'd n.r.e.).

3. SJ not automatic. Simply because both parties move for summary judgment does not mean the litigation can be resolved as a matter of law. See *Calhoun v. Killian*, 888 S.W.2d 51, 54 (Tex.App.—Tyler 1994, writ denied). There may be fact issues that must be tried on the merits.

§5. HEARING

See "Summary-Judgment Hearing," ch. 7-B, §11, p. 622.

§6. JUDGMENT

See "The Summary Judgment," ch. 7-B, §12, p. 623.

§7. REVIEW

A traditional motion for summary judgment is reviewed on appeal de novo. *Mid-Century Ins. v. Ademaj*, 243 S.W.3d 618, 621 (Tex.2007); *Valence Oper. Co. v. Dorsett*, 164 S.W.3d 656, 661 (Tex.2005); *Natividad v. Alexsis, Inc.*, 875 S.W.2d 695, 699 (Tex.1994). For the review of summary judgments generally, see "Review," ch. 7-B, §14, p. 625.

D. NO-EVIDENCE MOTION FOR SUMMARY JUDGMENT

The no-evidence summary-judgment motion is a procedural device designed to help the party who does not have the burden of proof at trial, generally the defendant. A party cannot file a no-evidence summary-judgment motion on a claim or defense on which it has the burden of proof. *Thomas v. Omar Invs.*, 156 S.W.3d 681, 684 (Tex.App.—Dallas 2005, no pet.); *Waite v. Woodard, Hall & Primm, P.C.*, 137 S.W.3d 277, 280 (Tex.App.—Houston [1st Dist.] 2004, no pet.); see *Nowak v. DAS Inv.*, 110 S.W.3d 677, 680 (Tex.App.—Houston [14th Dist.] 2003, no pet.). The only instance in which a no-evidence motion can help the plaintiff is when the burden of proof is on the defendant (e.g., to challenge a defendant's affirmative defense or counterclaim).

§1. GENERAL

§1.1 Rule. TRCP 166a(i).

§1.2 Purpose. The purpose of the no-evidence summary-judgment procedure, which is modeled after federal summary-judgment practice, is to "pierce the pleadings" and evaluate the evidence to see if a trial is necessary. *Benitz v. Gould Grp.*, 27 S.W.3d 109, 112 (Tex.App.—San Antonio 2000, no pet.). To accomplish this, the no-evidence summary-judgment procedure is designed to isolate and dispose of claims or defenses not supported by facts. Cf. *Celotex Corp. v. Catrett*, 477 U.S. 317, 323-24 (1986) (purpose of FRCP 56(e) is to dispose of unsupported claims). A no-evidence summary judgment does not violate the right to a jury trial. *Springer v. American Zurich Ins.*, 115 S.W.3d 582, 585 (Tex.App.—Waco 2003, pet. denied).

———————————— ✮ ————————————

§1.3 Timetable & forms. Timetable, Motion for Summary Judgment, p. 1226; *O'Connor's Texas Civil Forms* (2012), FORMS 7B, 7C.

§1.4 Other references. Patton, *Summary Judgments in Texas: Practice, Procedure & Review* ch. 5 (3d ed. 2002 & Supp.2012).

§2. NO-EVIDENCE MOTION FOR SUMMARY JUDGMENT

§2.1 When to file. The no-evidence motion for summary judgment cannot be filed until after the nonmovant has had "an adequate time for discovery." TRCP 166a(i); *Fort Brown Villas III Condo. Ass'n v. Gillenwater*, 285 S.W.3d 879, 882 (Tex.2009); *Moorehouse v. Chase Manhattan Bank*, 76 S.W.3d 608, 612 (Tex.App.—San Antonio 2002, no pet.). The rule does not require that discovery be completed. *Dishner v. Huitt-Zollars, Inc.*, 162 S.W.3d 370, 376 (Tex.App.—Dallas 2005, no pet.); *Specialty Retailers, Inc. v. Fuqua*, 29 S.W.3d 140, 145 (Tex.App.— Houston [14th Dist.] 2000, pet. denied).

1. After discovery period. When a no-evidence motion for summary judgment is filed after the discovery period for the case, the motion is presumed timely. *See* Notes & Comments to TRCP 166a(i) (discovery period set by pretrial order should be adequate opportunity for discovery unless there is a contrary showing).

2. During discovery period. When a no-evidence motion for summary judgment is filed before the end of the discovery period, it is considered timely as long as the nonmovant had adequate time for discovery. *See* TRCP 166a(i); *McInnis v. Mallia*, 261 S.W.3d 197, 200 (Tex.App.—Houston [14th Dist.] 2008, no pet.). Although a trial court has broad discretion to deny a request for continuance, a no-evidence summary judgment can be reversed on the ground that the nonmovant did not have adequate time for discovery. *See Brewer & Pritchard, P.C. v. Johnson*, 167 S.W.3d 460, 468 (Tex.App.—Houston [14th Dist.] 2005, pet. denied); *TemPay, Inc. v. TNT Concrete & Constr., Inc.*, 37 S.W.3d 517, 522-23 (Tex.App.—Austin 2001, pet. denied). See "Challenge timing of motion," §3.2.2, p. 643.

(1) Adequate time – factors. The amount of time necessary to be considered "adequate time" depends on the facts and circumstances of each case. *See McInnis*, 261 S.W.3d at 201. The courts examine the following factors when determining whether the nonmovant had adequate time for discovery: (1) the nature of the claim, (2) the evidence necessary to controvert the motion, (3) the length of time the case was on file, (4) the length of time the no-evidence motion was on file, (5) whether the movant requested stricter deadlines for discovery, (6) the amount of discovery already conducted, and (7) whether the discovery deadlines in place were specific or vague. *Community Initiatives, Inc. v. Chase Bank*, 153 S.W.3d 270, 278 (Tex.App.—El Paso 2004, no pet.); *McInnis*, 261 S.W.3d at 201. On appeal, the factors showing inadequate time for discovery must be specifically addressed in the appellant's brief, or the brief presents nothing for review. *See Robertson v. Southwestern Bell Yellow Pages, Inc.*, 190 S.W.3d 899, 903 (Tex.App.—Dallas 2006, no pet.).

(2) Adequate time – examples. The following are examples of when time for discovery was considered adequate: • Three-year-old case in which discovery had been pursued for a year and a half and the most important witness had been deposed. *Community Initiatives*, 153 S.W.3d at 278-79. • Twenty-eight-month-old case in which the plaintiff had had one year to develop case outside of bankruptcy stay and had already received continuance. *McMahan v. Greenwood*, 108 S.W.3d 467, 498 (Tex.App.—Houston [14th Dist.] 2003, pet. denied). • Seven-month-old case in which the plaintiff, who needed minimal evidence to controvert the defendant's motion, did not initiate or respond to discovery requests. *Restaurant Teams Int'l v. MG Secs. Corp.*, 95 S.W.3d 336, 339-41 (Tex.App.—Dallas 2002, no pet.). • Five-year-old case in which the plaintiff did not comply with the scheduling order it requested. *Martinez v. City of San Antonio*, 40 S.W.3d 587, 591-92 (Tex.App.—San Antonio 2001, pet. denied).

§2.2 Form of motion. The motion for no-evidence summary judgment must follow the general summary-judgment rules. That is, it must be in writing and should not be verified. See "In writing," ch. 7-C, §2.2, p. 628; "Unverified," ch. 7-C, §2.3, p. 628; *O'Connor's Texas Forms*, FORMS 7C:1, 2.

§2.3 Allegations. The no-evidence motion for summary judgment should be organized as follows:

1. Discovery statement. The motion should include the statement that an adequate time for discovery has passed. See "When to file," §2.1, this page. The movant should identify the date the suit was filed and describe the discovery completed and any pending discovery.

———————————————————— ✦ ————————————————————

2. Nonmovant's claim. The motion should identify and list the elements of the nonmovant's claims or defenses on which the movant requests a no-evidence summary judgment. *See Holloway v. Texas Elec. Util. Constr., Ltd.*, 282 S.W.3d 207, 213 (Tex.App.—Tyler 2009, no pet.).

3. Specific element challenged. The motion must state that there is no evidence to support one or more specific elements of a claim or defense on which the nonmovant has the burden of proof at trial. TRCP 166a(i); *Timpte Indus. v. Gish*, 286 S.W.3d 306, 310 (Tex.2009); *Thomas v. Omar Invs.*, 156 S.W.3d 681, 684 (Tex.App.—Dallas 2005, no pet.); *Trilogy Software, Inc. v. Callidus Software, Inc.*, 143 S.W.3d 452, 459 (Tex.App.—Austin 2004, pet. denied). The motion cannot be conclusory or generally allege that there is no evidence to support the non-movant's claim or defense. *Timpte Indus.*, 286 S.W.3d at 310; *Holloway*, 282 S.W.3d at 213; *Ortiz v. Collins*, 203 S.W.3d 414, 425 (Tex.App.—Houston [14th Dist.] 2006, pet. denied); Notes & Comments to TRCP 166a(i). The purpose of this specificity requirement is to provide the other parties with fair notice (i.e., provide adequate information for opposing the motion and define the issues). *Timpte Indus.*, 286 S.W.3d at 311. When a no-evidence motion for summary judgment does not challenge specific elements, it should be treated as a traditional motion for summary judgment under TRCP 166a(c), which imposes the burden of proof on the movant, not as a motion under TRCP 166a(i), which imposes the burden on the nonmovant. *See Michael v. Dyke*, 41 S.W.3d 746, 751-52 (Tex.App.—Corpus Christi 2001, no pet.); *Amouri v. Southwest Toyota, Inc.*, 20 S.W.3d 165, 168 (Tex.App.—Texarkana 2000, pet. denied); *Weaver v. Highlands Ins.*, 4 S.W.3d 826, 829 n.2 (Tex.App.—Houston [1st Dist.] 1999, no pet.); *see also Hamlett v. Holcomb*, 69 S.W.3d 816, 819 (Tex.App.—Corpus Christi 2002, no pet.) (when motion was ambiguous about whether it was no-evidence or traditional motion, court presumed it was filed as traditional motion under TRCP 166a(c)).

§2.4 Relief. The motion should include a prayer for relief requesting either final or partial summary judgment. See "Request for final SJ," ch. 7-C, §2.6, p. 630; "Request for partial SJ," ch. 7-C, §2.7, p. 630.

§2.5 No supporting evidence. A no-evidence motion for summary judgment does not require supporting evidence. *Williams v. Bank One*, 15 S.W.3d 110, 116 (Tex.App.—Waco 1999, no pet.); *see McClure v. Attebury*, 20 S.W.3d 722, 727 (Tex.App.—Amarillo 1999, no pet.); *Moore v. K Mart Corp.*, 981 S.W.2d 266, 269 (Tex.App.—San Antonio 1998, pet. denied). But the fact that evidence is attached to a no-evidence motion does not mean the court can disregard the motion or treat it as a traditional summary-judgment motion. *Binur v. Jacobo*, 135 S.W.3d 646, 651 (Tex.2004). See "Traditional Motion for Summary Judgment," ch. 7-C, §2, p. 628.

§2.6 Attorney fees. If the movant is entitled to attorney fees, the movant should include a request for attorney fees in the motion. Because the movant has the burden of proof on its attorney fees, the movant must support its claim for attorney fees with summary-judgment evidence. See "Attorney fees," ch. 7-C, §2.9, p. 631.

§2.7 Notice. The movant must give the nonmovant written notice of the hearing on the motion. See "Notice," ch. 7-B, §7, p. 609.

§3. NONMOVANT'S RESPONSE TO NO-EVIDENCE MOTION FOR SUMMARY JUDGMENT

The nonmovant's response to a no-evidence motion for summary judgment serves three functions: (1) it supplies evidence to raise a fact issue on the challenged element, (2) it identifies any procedural defect in the motion, and (3) it presents any other reasons why the summary judgment should not be granted. Because TRCP 166a(i) requires the trial court to grant the no-evidence motion for summary judgment if the nonmovant does not produce evidence that raises a genuine issue of material fact, the court may grant a no-evidence summary judgment by default if the nonmovant does not file a response and the motion states sufficient grounds for a final summary judgment. *Roventini v. Ocular Sci., Inc.*, 111 S.W.3d 719, 722 (Tex.App.—Houston [1st Dist.] 2003, no pet.). See "Mandatory," §7.1, p. 646.

§3.1 Form of response. The response to the no-evidence motion for summary judgment must follow the general summary-judgment rules. That is, it must be in writing and should not be verified. See "In writing," ch. 7-C, §3.1, p. 631; "Unverified," ch. 7-C, §3.2, p. 631.

─────────────────────────── ✯ ───────────────────────────

§3.2 Objections. In the response to the motion for summary judgment, the nonmovant should object to any defect in the form or substance of the motion or pleadings. The nonmovant will waive most objections to the summary judgment not included in its response. *See Fletcher v. Edwards*, 26 S.W.3d 66, 72 n.5 (Tex.App.—Waco 2000, pet. denied). See "Waiver," ch. 7-C, §3.7, p. 633. To preserve error on appeal, the nonmovant should ensure that the record includes written rulings on the objections. See "Secure ruling on objections," ch. 7-B, §10.2, p. 621; *O'Connor's Texas Forms*, FORMS 7C:3-6, 7C:9, 7C:11.

1. Challenge the notice. If the movant did not file and serve the motion, the notice of hearing, and the evidence at least 21 days before the hearing, the nonmovant must object. *See* TRCP 166a(d). See "Summary-Judgment Deadlines," ch. 7-B, §6, p. 605; "Challenge movant's notice," ch. 7-C, §3.6.4, p. 633; *O'Connor's Texas Forms*, FORM 7B:2.

2. Challenge timing of motion. If the no-evidence motion was filed before the end of the discovery period, the nonmovant may allege that the motion was premature because the nonmovant did not have adequate time for discovery. See "Adequate time – factors," §2.1.2(1), p. 641. The nonmovant must file either an affidavit explaining the need for further discovery or a verified motion for continuance. *Tenneco Inc. v. Enterprise Prods.*, 925 S.W.2d 640, 647 (Tex.1996); *Brown v. Brown*, 145 S.W.3d 745, 749 (Tex.App.—Dallas 2004, pet. denied). See "Motion to continue SJ hearing," ch. 5-D, §9.3, p. 340.

3. Challenge the motion. The nonmovant should challenge all legal and procedural shortcomings in the motion.

    (1) Lacks specificity. When a no-evidence motion globally challenges the nonmovant's claim or defense, the nonmovant should object. *See* Notes & Comments to TRCP 166a(i) ("paragraph (i) does not authorize conclusory motions or general no-evidence challenges"). However, the failure to object does not waive the error. *Bean v. Reynolds Rlty. Grp.*, 192 S.W.3d 856, 859 (Tex.App.—Texarkana 2006, no pet.); *In re Estate of Swanson*, 130 S.W.3d 144, 147 (Tex.App.—El Paso 2003, no pet.); *Crocker v. Paulyne's Nursing Home, Inc.*, 95 S.W.3d 416, 419 (Tex.App.—Dallas 2002, no pet.); *Cuyler v. Minns*, 60 S.W.3d 209, 213 (Tex.App.—Houston [14th Dist.] 2001, pet. denied); *Callaghan Ranch, Ltd. v. Killam*, 53 S.W.3d 1, 3 (Tex.App.—San Antonio 2000, pet. denied). *But see Williams v. Bank One*, 15 S.W.3d 110, 117 (Tex.App.—Waco 1999, no pet.) (failure to object to lack of specificity did not preserve error); *Roth v. FFP Oper. Partners*, 994 S.W.2d 190, 195 (Tex.App.—Amarillo 1999, pet. denied) (Ps could not challenge sufficiency of no-evidence motion on appeal because no objection presented to trial court). When a no-evidence motion for summary judgment does not challenge specific elements, it should be treated as a traditional motion for summary judgment under TRCP 166a(c), which imposes the burden of proof on the movant. See "Specific element challenged," §2.3.3, p. 642.

    (2) Movant's burden. When a no-evidence motion challenges the evidence to support an element on which the movant—not the nonmovant—has the burden of proof at trial, the nonmovant should object. *Texas Mut. Ins. v. Sara Care Child Care Ctr., Inc.*, 324 S.W.3d 305, 318 (Tex.App.—El Paso 2010, pet. denied).

    (3) Other challenges. See "Objections to SJ motion," ch. 7-C, §3.6, p. 632.

4. Challenge use of SJ. If the motion for summary judgment is based on a pleading defect in the nonmovant's petition or answer, the nonmovant should (1) object on the ground that the movant is required to challenge pleadings by special exceptions and (2) move to correct the defect. See "Special Exceptions & Summary Judgments," ch. 3-G, §10, p. 255; "Defective pleadings," ch. 7-C, §3.6.2(1), p. 632.

5. Challenge SJ evidence. If the movant has included evidence with its no-evidence motion or has filed a hybrid motion supported by evidence, the nonmovant should challenge the evidence. See "Objections to Summary-Judgment Evidence," ch. 7-B, §10, p. 617.

§3.3 Burden of proof. The nonmovant has the entire burden of proof once the movant files a no-evidence motion. TRCP 166a(i). The burden of proof in a summary-judgment proceeding is on the same party who would have the burden of proof at trial. *Marsaglia v. UTEP*, 22 S.W.3d 1, 3 (Tex.App.—El Paso 1999, pet. denied); *Esco Oil &*

Gas, Inc. v. Sooner Pipe & Sup., 962 S.W.2d 193, 197 n.3 (Tex.App.—Houston [1st Dist.] 1998, pet. denied). The burden on the nonmovant is to raise a genuine issue of material fact about the element challenged by the motion for summary judgment. TRCP 166a(i); *Dow Chem. Co. v. Francis*, 46 S.W.3d 237, 242 (Tex.2001); *Praytor v. Ford Motor Co.*, 97 S.W.3d 237, 241 (Tex.App.—Houston [14th Dist.] 2002, no pet.). The trial court must resolve all reasonable doubts about the facts in favor of the nonmovant. *Lehrer v. Zwernemann*, 14 S.W.3d 775, 777 (Tex.App.—Houston [1st Dist.] 2000, pet. denied).

7-9. NO-EVIDENCE MOTION FOR SUMMARY JUDGMENT UNDER TRCP 166a(i)

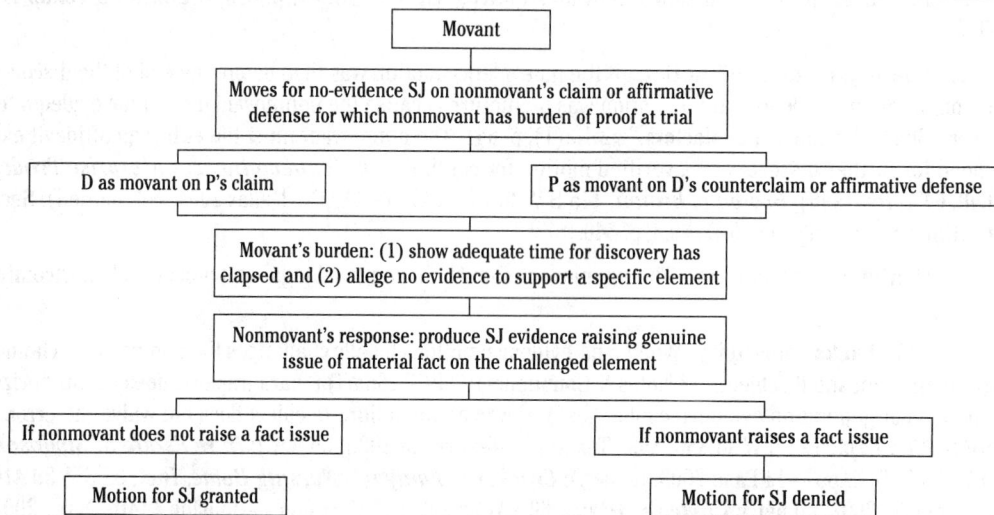

§3.4 Grounds for response. To defeat a no-evidence motion for summary judgment, the nonmovant must prove there is a genuine issue of material fact on the elements challenged by the movant. *See* TRCP 166a(i). The response should include a heading for each challenged element and under that heading a discussion of the evidence that creates a fact issue for that element. If the nonmovant discusses all the facts under one general heading called "Facts," the nonmovant may forget to address one of the elements. *Cf. Johnson v. Brewer & Pritchard, P.C.*, 73 S.W.3d 193, 204 (Tex.2002) (although movant addressed issue of fiduciary relationship, it did not address issue of breach).

PRACTICE TIP
*When a no-evidence motion challenges all the elements of the cause of action, the nonmovant should remember to support its damages with evidence. The court will grant a no-evidence motion for summary judgment when a nonmovant does not support a challenged damages element with evidence. **Dow Chem. Co. v. Francis**, 46 S.W.3d 237, 242 (Tex.2001).*

---

§3.5 Presenting SJ evidence under TRCP 166a(i). The Notes & Comments to TRCP 166a(i) state that to defeat a no-evidence motion, the nonmovant "is not required to marshal its proof; its response need only point out evidence that raises a fact issue on the challenged elements." *Saenz v. Southern Un. Gas Co.*, 999 S.W.2d 490, 493 (Tex.App.—El Paso 1999, pet. denied). The nonmovant should present summary-judgment evidence in the same form that would be admissible at trial. See "Summary-Judgment Evidence," ch. 7-B, §9, p. 611.

§3.6 Sufficiency of evidence. TRCP 166a(i) states that the court must grant the motion unless the nonmovant presents summary-judgment evidence that raises a genuine issue of material fact on each element challenged. *In re Mohawk Rubber Co.*, 982 S.W.2d 494, 498 (Tex.App.—Texarkana 1998, orig. proceeding). A no-evidence motion is essentially a motion for a pretrial directed verdict. *Thomas v. Omar Invs.*, 156 S.W.3d 681, 684 (Tex.App.—Dallas

⋆

2005, no pet.); *Ridgway v. Ford Motor Co.*, 82 S.W.3d 26, 29 (Tex.App.—San Antonio 2002), *rev'd on other grounds*, 135 S.W.3d 598 (Tex.2004). To defeat a no-evidence motion for summary judgment, the nonmovant must produce more than a scintilla of evidence to raise a genuine issue of material fact on the challenged elements. TRCP 166a(i); *Forbes, Inc. v. Granada Biosciences, Inc.*, 124 S.W.3d 167, 172 (Tex.2003); *Boales v. Brighton Builders, Inc.*, 29 S.W.3d 159, 164 (Tex.App.—Houston [14th Dist.] 2000, pet. denied). If the nonmovant presents more than a scintilla of evidence on the challenged elements, it is entitled to a trial on the merits. *Ridgway*, 82 S.W.3d at 29. A nonmovant produces more than a scintilla when the evidence "rises to a level that would enable reasonable and fair-minded people to differ in their conclusions." *Ford Motor Co. v. Ridgway*, 135 S.W.3d 598, 601 (Tex.2004); *Marsaglia v. UTEP*, 22 S.W.3d 1, 4 (Tex.App.—El Paso 1999, pet. denied); *cf. Merrell Dow Pharms. v. Havner*, 953 S.W.2d 706, 711 (Tex.1997) (jury trial). A nonmovant produces no more than a scintilla when the evidence is "so weak as to do no more than create a mere surmise or suspicion" of a fact. *Forbes, Inc.*, 124 S.W.3d at 172; *Marsaglia*, 22 S.W.3d at 4; *cf. Kindred v. Con/Chem, Inc.*, 650 S.W.2d 61, 63 (Tex.1983) (jury trial).

§3.7 Expert testimony. If expert testimony is required to defeat a no-evidence motion for summary judgment, the nonmovant must produce evidence that meets the test for expert testimony. *See Praytor v. Ford Motor Co.*, 97 S.W.3d 237, 242-43 (Tex.App.—Houston [14th Dist.] 2002, no pet.) (nonmovant did not produce TRE 702 proof for expert's opinion about causation). See "*Daubert-Robinson* Test for Expert Testimony," ch. 5-N, §2, p. 410.

§3.8 File motion for continuance. When a nonmovant needs additional time to secure affidavits or discovery, it should file a motion for continuance. See "Motion to continue SJ hearing," ch. 5-D, §9.3, p. 340; *O'Connor's Texas Forms*, FORM 7B:5.

§3.9 File motion for sanctions. A motion under TRCP 166a(i) is subject to sanctions provided by existing law. Notes & Comments to TRCP 166a(i). See "Groundless or frivolous pleadings," ch. 1-B, §3.3, p. 14.

§3.10 Other responsive pleadings. When appropriate, the nonmovant may file any of the following:

1. An amended petition or answer. See "Amending the Petition or Answer," ch. 7-B, §8, p. 610.

2. A cross-motion for summary judgment. See "When both parties move for SJ," ch. 7-C, §4.8, p. 640.

3. A nonsuit. See "Consider nonsuit," ch. 7-C, §3.9, p. 633.

§4. MOVANT'S REPLY TO NONMOVANT'S RESPONSE

§4.1 Deadline. There is no deadline in TRCP 166a for a movant to file a reply to the nonmovant's response. *Callaghan Ranch, Ltd. v. Killam*, 53 S.W.3d 1, 4 (Tex.App.—San Antonio 2000, pet. denied). See "For movant's reply to response," ch. 7-B, §6.6, p. 607.

§4.2 Negate nonmovant's evidence. In the reply, the movant can attempt to negate the nonmovant's claim that there is evidence of a triable fact regarding its claims or defenses. *Cf. Irby v. Bittick*, 44 F.3d 949, 953 (11th Cir. 1995) (under FRCP 56(e), nonmovant must do more than assert there is some doubt about the material facts).

§4.3 Object to nonmovant's SJ evidence. The movant should object to any of the nonmovant's summary-judgment evidence that would not be admissible at trial. *See* TRCP 166a(f). See "Objections to Summary-Judgment Evidence," ch. 7-B, §10, p. 617.

§4.4 Produce SJ evidence. When a nonmovant produces summary-judgment evidence supporting the challenged element of its claim or defense, the movant can produce summary-judgment evidence to attempt to disprove or discredit the nonmovant's evidence. See "Summary-Judgment Evidence," ch. 7-B, §9, p. 611.

§4.5 Respond to motion for continuance. See "Response to motion," ch. 5-D, §9.3.4, p. 342.

§4.6 File special exceptions. If the claims in the response are vague, unintelligible, unclear, or ambiguous, the movant can challenge them by special exceptions. See "Special Exceptions & Summary Judgments," ch. 3-G, §10, p. 255; "Special Exceptions in Summary-Judgment Procedure," ch. 7-B, §5, p. 604.

✦

§4.7 No additional grounds. In its reply, the movant cannot add new challenges to the nonmovant's claims or defenses. *See Community Initiatives, Inc. v. Chase Bank*, 153 S.W.3d 270, 280 (Tex.App.—El Paso 2004, no pet.) (movant may not use reply to meet specificity requirements of TRCP 166a(i) or to assert new grounds for SJ); *see, e.g.*, *Specialty Retailers, Inc. v. Fuqua*, 29 S.W.3d 140, 148 (Tex.App.—Houston [14th Dist.] 2000, pet. denied) (nonmovant had no burden to present evidence to support claims challenged for the first time in reply).

§5. NONMOVANT'S TIME TO CURE

The court should give the nonmovant the opportunity to cure any defects in its summary-judgment evidence identified by the movant in its reply. *See* TRCP 166a(f) (party should be given opportunity to cure defects in form of affidavits and attachments); *see also* TRCP 166a(g) (court may deny SJ or grant continuance to allow nonmovant to obtain affidavit or deposition testimony necessary to support its claims).

§5.1 Deadline to cure. Nothing in TRCP 166a provides a deadline to cure defects in a party's evidence once objections have been filed. Under the TRCP 166a(a)-(b) summary-judgment procedure, the time to cure is built in because an adverse ruling is not fatal to the party with the summary-judgment burden of proof. Under TRCP 166a(a)-(b), if the trial court rules adversely to the movant (the party with the summary-judgment burden of proof) based on defects in its evidence, the court merely denies the motion, which is in effect an opportunity to cure because the movant can file another motion. By comparison, in a no-evidence summary judgment under TRCP 166a(i), if the trial court rules adversely to the nonmovant (the party with the burden of proof) based on defects in the response or the evidence, the court grants the motion for summary judgment, which is fatal to the nonmovant's case. The opportunity to cure in TRCP 166a(f) should apply to both the movant and nonmovant in both types of summary judgments. *See, e.g.*, *Webster v. Allstate Ins.*, 833 S.W.2d 747, 750 (Tex.App.—Houston [1st Dist.] 1992, no writ) (trial court should not have sustained objections to party's evidence on day of hearing without giving party chance to amend).

§5.2 Motion for continuance. If the movant identified defects in the nonmovant's pleading, response, or evidence, the nonmovant should file a motion for continuance asking the court for time to cure the defects. *See Peerenboom v. HSP Foods, Inc.*, 910 S.W.2d 156, 160 (Tex.App.—Waco 1995, no writ); *Webster v. Allstate Ins.*, 833 S.W.2d 747, 750 (Tex.App.—Houston [1st Dist.] 1992, no writ). See "Motion to continue SJ hearing," ch. 5-D, §9.3, p. 340. The nonmovant will need additional time because the movant's reply, if filed by the three-day deadline recommended for the movant's special exceptions in *McConnell v. Southside ISD*, 858 S.W.2d 337, 343 n.7 (Tex. 1993), will not provide the nonmovant with sufficient time to cure the defect. The nonmovant should ask the court to state a deadline to cure the defects and a date for the hearing. *See, e.g.*, *Peerenboom*, 910 S.W.2d at 160 (appellate court did not consider evidence because party did not file it at least seven days before new hearing date).

§6. HEARING

See "Summary-Judgment Hearing," ch. 7-B, §11, p. 622.

§7. TRIAL COURT'S RULING UNDER TRCP 166a(i)

§7.1 Mandatory. TRCP 166a(i) requires the trial court to grant the motion for no-evidence summary judgment if the nonmovant does not produce summary-judgment evidence that raises a genuine issue of material fact. *Dolcefino v. Randolph*, 19 S.W.3d 906, 917 (Tex.App.—Houston [14th Dist.] 2000, pet. denied); *Saenz v. Southern Un. Gas Co.*, 999 S.W.2d 490, 493 (Tex.App.—El Paso 1999, pet. denied).

§7.2 Judgment. See "The Summary Judgment," ch. 7-B, §12, p. 623.

§8. REVIEW

In reviewing a no-evidence summary judgment, the appellate court must consider all the evidence in the light most favorable to the party against whom the summary judgment was rendered, crediting evidence favorable to that party if reasonable jurors could and disregarding contrary evidence unless reasonable jurors could not. *Timpte Indus. v. Gish*, 286 S.W.3d 306, 310 (Tex.2009); *see City of Keller v. Wilson*, 168 S.W.3d 802, 827 (Tex.2005). The appellate court will affirm a no-evidence summary judgment if the record shows one of the following: (1) there is no evidence on the challenged element, (2) the evidence offered to prove the challenged element is no more than a scintilla, (3) the evidence establishes the opposite of the challenged element, or (4) the court is barred by law or the rules of evidence from considering the only evidence offered to prove the challenged element. *City of Keller*, 168 S.W.3d at 810; *Patel v. City of Everman*, 179 S.W.3d 1, 17 (Tex.App.—Tyler 2004, pet. denied); *Taylor-Made Hose, Inc. v. Wilkerson*, 21 S.W.3d 484, 488 (Tex.App.—San Antonio 2000, pet. denied). Generally, the review of judgments granted under TRCP 166a(i) is the same as under TRCP 166a(a), (b). See "Review," ch. 7-B, §14, p. 625.

E. MOTION FOR JUDGMENT ON AGREED STATEMENT OF FACTS

§1. GENERAL

§1.1 Rules. TRCP 263. See TRCP 11.

§1.2 Purpose. The purpose of a motion for judgment on an agreed statement of facts under TRCP 263 is to ask the trial court to render a decision on the law when the facts are not in controversy. *State Bar v. Faubion*, 821 S.W.2d 203, 205 (Tex.App.—Houston [14th Dist.] 1991, writ denied). TRCP 263 requires the parties to agree on all facts essential for the determination of the lawsuit, leaving to the court the function of deciding questions of law.

§1.3 Forms. *O'Connor's Texas Civil Forms* (2012), FORMS 7E, 9C:5.

§2. DISTINCTION BETWEEN AGREED STATEMENT & STIPULATIONS

§2.1 Differences. An agreed case under TRCP 263 is not the same thing as a case tried on stipulated facts. *See Perry v. Aetna Life Ins.*, 380 S.W.2d 868, 875 (Tex.App.—Tyler 1964, writ ref'd n.r.e.). Parties may stipulate to some undisputed facts without submitting the case as an agreed case. *See id.* The ordinary stipulation permits the trial court to make any findings and inferences supported by the evidence. *Farah v. First Nat'l Bank*, 624 S.W.2d 341, 345 (Tex.App.—Fort Worth 1981, writ ref'd n.r.e.); *Parsons v. Watley*, 492 S.W.2d 61, 63 (Tex.App.—Eastland 1973, no writ); *Perry*, 380 S.W.2d at 874. Submitting a case on an agreed statement of facts does not permit the court to make inferences from the facts, unless the parties so stipulate. *Alma Grp. v. Palmer*, 143 S.W.3d 840, 843 (Tex. App.—Corpus Christi 2004, pet. denied); *Cummins & Walker Oil Co. v. Smith*, 814 S.W.2d 884, 886 (Tex. App.—San Antonio 1991, no writ); *Perry*, 380 S.W.2d at 874.

§2.2 Test for agreed case. To determine whether a stipulation of facts is an agreed statement of facts under TRCP 263, answer the following questions. If the answers are mostly "yes," the case probably falls under TRCP 263. • Does the instrument denote itself as an agreed statement of facts and refer to TRCP 263? *See Abbott v. Blue Cross & Blue Shield*, 113 S.W.3d 753, 759 (Tex.App.—Austin 2003, pet. denied). • Does it purport to contain all the facts necessary to decide the case? If it is clear from the record that the trial court considered other facts outside the stipulation, the case was not an agreed case under TRCP 263. *Peterson v. NCNB Tex. Nat'l Bank*, 838 S.W.2d 263, 265 (Tex.App.—Dallas 1992, no writ); *Farah v. First Nat'l Bank*, 624 S.W.2d 341, 345 (Tex.App.—Fort Worth 1981, writ ref'd n.r.e.); *see Parsons v. Watley*, 492 S.W.2d 61, 63 (Tex.App.—Eastland 1973, no writ). • Did the judge certify and approve the agreed statement of facts? *See* TRCP 263; *Peterson*, 838 S.W.2d at 265; *Parsons*, 492 S.W.2d at 63. • Does the instrument place the ultimate facts that are essential to determination of the case beyond the need for adjudication? *See Texas Farm Bur. Mut. Ins. v. Sturrock*, 146 S.W.3d 123, 125 n.2 (Tex.2004). • Does the judgment show the case was tried as an agreed case? *See Tarrant Appr. Dist. v. Gateway Ctr. Assocs.*, 34 S.W.3d 712, 713 (Tex.App.—Fort Worth 2000, no pet.).

§3. MOTION

§3.1 In writing. The motion for judgment on an agreed statement of facts must be in writing. *See* TRCP 11; *Beddall v. Reader's Wholesale Distribs.*, 408 S.W.2d 237, 238 (Tex.App.—Houston 1966, no writ) (oral stipulation in open court was not an agreed statement of facts under TRCP 263). *But see Lambda Constr. Co. v. Chamberlin Waterproofing & Roofing Sys.*, 784 S.W.2d 122, 125 (Tex.App.—Austin 1990, writ denied) (telephone conference was considered an agreed statement of facts under TRCP 263). See *O'Connor's Texas Forms*, FORM 7E:1.

✦

§3.2 Identify all necessary facts. The motion for judgment must state specific facts that the parties agree on and seek a judgment on. *See Cummins & Walker Oil Co. v. Smith*, 814 S.W.2d 884, 886 (Tex.App.—San Antonio 1991, no writ) (presumption that all facts are included in the agreed statement). The motion should expressly state that the case is to be tried on the agreed facts and that those are all the facts of the case. *See id.* Parties can agree only to the facts and cannot stipulate the law. See *O'Connor's Texas Forms*, FORM 7E:2.

§3.3 Request for judgment. The agreed statement should ask the court to resolve the controversy on the agreed statement of facts.

§3.4 Signatures of parties. The parties or their attorneys must sign the agreed statement of facts. *See* TRCP 11, 263.

§3.5 Certificate for judge. The agreed statement should contain a certificate for the court to sign, certifying and approving the agreed facts. TRCP 263; *Davis v. State*, 904 S.W.2d 946, 949 n.3 (Tex.App.—Austin 1995, no writ). The certification shows the appellate court the facts on which the trial court based its judgment. *State Farm Lloyds v. Kessler*, 932 S.W.2d 732, 735 (Tex.App.—Fort Worth 1996, writ denied). See *O'Connor's Texas Forms*, FORM 7E:2.

§3.6 Proposed judgment. The parties should submit a proposed judgment for the court to sign, and they should file it with the agreed statement. The judgment can be a simple, one-sentence judgment: "On the agreed statement of facts, judgment is rendered for...."

§3.7 Filed with court. The agreed statement must be filed with the court. TRCP 263.

§3.8 Strict compliance not required. When parties stipulate to all the facts in a case, the stipulation may be treated as a submission of an agreed statement even if it does not strictly comply with TRCP 263. *City of Galveston v. Giles*, 902 S.W.2d 167, 169 n.1 (Tex.App.—Houston [1st Dist.] 1995, no writ); *Reed v. Valley Fed. S&L Co.*, 655 S.W.2d 259, 264 (Tex.App.—Corpus Christi 1983, writ ref'd n.r.e.). Even if the parties did not meet the technical requirements of TRCP 263, if the final judgment appears to be the product of a TRCP 263 agreed case, the appellate court will treat it as one. *E.g.*, *Giles*, 902 S.W.2d at 169 n.1 (court did not sign or certify agreed statement); *Jim Sowell Constr. Co. v. Dallas Cent. Appr. Dist.*, 900 S.W.2d 82, 84 (Tex.App.—Dallas 1995, writ denied) (same); *City of Harlingen v. Alvarez*, 204 S.W.3d 452, 471 n.9 (Tex.App.—Corpus Christi 2005, pet. granted, judgm't vacated w.r.m.) (Castillo, J., concurring) (same).

§4. HEARING

§4.1 Argument only. The hearing under TRCP 263 is not for evidence; all material evidence must be included in the agreed statement. If the court holds a hearing, it is for argument only.

§4.2 Presumption of all facts. All facts necessary to the presentation of the case are conclusively presumed to have been brought before the court. *Jim Sowell Constr. Co. v. Dallas Cent. Appr. Dist.*, 900 S.W.2d 82, 84 (Tex. App.—Dallas 1995, writ denied). The court cannot draw any inference or find any facts not included in the agreement. *See Diamond Shamrock Ref. & Mktg. Co. v. Nueces Cty. Appr. Dist.*, 876 S.W.2d 298, 301 n.2 (Tex.1994); *Lawler v. Lomas & Nettleton Mortg. Investors*, 691 S.W.2d 593, 595 (Tex.1985); *Jim Sowell Constr.*, 900 S.W.2d at 84. But an inference of facts beyond the agreed statement of facts may be compelled by the facts as a matter of law. *Lawler*, 691 S.W.2d at 595; *Davis v. State*, 904 S.W.2d 946, 950 (Tex.App.—Austin 1995, no writ).

§4.3 Binding effect. The court is bound by the agreed statement of facts. *Tarrant Appr. Rev. Bd. v. Martinez Bros. Invs.*, 946 S.W.2d 914, 917 (Tex.App.—Fort Worth 1997, no writ); *Crow-Southland Jt.V. v. North Fort Worth Bank*, 838 S.W.2d 720, 723 (Tex.App.—Dallas 1992, writ denied).

§5. JUDGMENT

§5.1 Court certification. Once a case is submitted on an agreed statement, the court must sign and certify the statement as correct. TRCP 263; *Perry v. Aetna Life Ins.*, 380 S.W.2d 868, 874 (Tex.App.—Tyler 1964, writ ref'd n.r.e.). If the court does not sign or certify the statement as required by TRCP 263, the appellate court will consider it as a TRCP 263 case only if it is clear that the case was tried on agreed facts. *Crow-Southland Jt.V. v. North Fort*

⭐

Worth Bank, 838 S.W.2d 720, 723 (Tex.App.—Dallas 1992, writ denied); *see Abbott v. Blue Cross & Blue Shield*, 113 S.W.3d 753, 758-59 (Tex.App.—Austin 2003, pet. denied) (court refused to certify stipulations and considered evidence outside stipulations).

§5.2 The judgment. The court should sign a judgment declaring its interpretation of the law that applies to the agreed statement of facts. TRCP 263. The court's judgment must declare only the law necessarily arising from the agreed facts. *Harris Cty. Appr. Dist. v. Transamerica Container Leasing Inc.*, 920 S.W.2d 678, 680 (Tex. App.—Houston [1st Dist.] 1995, writ denied); *State Bar v. Faubion*, 821 S.W.2d 203, 205 (Tex.App.—Houston [14th Dist.] 1991, writ denied). See *O'Connor's Texas Forms*, FORM 9C:5.

§5.3 No findings of fact. The court cannot make findings of fact besides those agreed to by the parties. *Crow-Southland Jt.V. v. North Fort Worth Bank*, 838 S.W.2d 720, 725 (Tex.App.—Dallas 1992, writ denied). Findings of fact are not appropriate in the trial of an agreed case. *International Un. v. General Motors Corp.*, 104 S.W.3d 126, 129 (Tex.App.—Fort Worth 2003, no pet.); *Port Arthur ISD v. Port Arthur Teachers Ass'n*, 990 S.W.2d 955, 957 (Tex.App.—Beaumont 1999, pet. denied); *City of Galveston v. Giles*, 902 S.W.2d 167, 170 n.2 (Tex.App.—Houston [1st Dist.] 1995, no writ).

§5.4 Object to judgment. If the trial court interprets a statement by the parties as an agreement to submit the issue on agreed facts, a party not intending such an agreement must object to preserve error. *Lambda Constr. Co. v. Chamberlin Waterproofing & Roofing Sys.*, 784 S.W.2d 122, 125 (Tex.App.—Austin 1990, writ denied).

§6. REVIEW

§6.1 Record. The agreed statement signed and certified by the court, along with the court's judgment, is the record of the case for the appeal. TRCP 263; *Texas Farm Bur. Mut. Ins. v. Sturrock*, 146 S.W.3d 123, 125 n.2 (Tex. 2004).

§6.2 No presumptions. On appeal, the courts make no presumed findings in favor of the judgment. *Patterson-UTI Drilling Co. v. Webb Cty. Appr. Dist.*, 182 S.W.3d 14, 17 (Tex.App.—San Antonio 2005, no pet.); *State Farm Lloyds v. Kessler*, 932 S.W.2d 732, 735 (Tex.App.—Fort Worth 1996, writ denied).

§6.3 Limited scope. The appeal is limited to the single issue of whether the law as applied to the agreed facts is correct. *TPCIGA v. Morrison*, 212 S.W.3d 349, 353 (Tex.App.—Austin 2006, pet. denied); *Roberts v. Squyres*, 4 S.W.3d 485, 488 (Tex.App.—Beaumont 1999, pet. denied); *Tarrant Appr. Rev. Bd. v. Martinez Bros. Invs.*, 946 S.W.2d 914, 917 (Tex.App.—Fort Worth 1997, no writ); *Crow-Southland Jt.V. v. North Fort Worth Bank*, 838 S.W.2d 720, 723 (Tex.App.—Dallas 1992, writ denied). The review is de novo. *Patterson-UTI Drilling Co. v. Webb Cty. Appr. Dist.*, 182 S.W.3d 14, 17 (Tex.App.—San Antonio 2005, no pet.); *Orange Cty. Appr. Dist. v. Agape Neighborhood Imprv., Inc.*, 57 S.W.3d 597, 601 (Tex.App.—Beaumont 2001, pet. denied). The appellate court does not review the legal or factual sufficiency of the evidence. *City of Harlingen v. Avila*, 942 S.W.2d 49, 51 (Tex.App.—Corpus Christi 1997, writ denied); *Crow-Southland*, 838 S.W.2d at 723.

§6.4 Render or remand. If the appellate court determines that the trial court erred, in most cases it should render the judgment the trial court should have rendered. If, however, the appellate court decides there are factual issues unresolved by the agreed statement that prevent a judgment, the court should remand the case to the trial court. *See, e.g., Cameron Cty. Appr. Rev. Bd. v. Creditbanc Sav. Ass'n*, 763 S.W.2d 577, 580-81 (Tex.App.—Corpus Christi 1988, writ denied) (valuation of property improvements unresolved by agreed statement).

★

F. VOLUNTARY DISMISSAL—NONSUIT

§1. GENERAL

§1.1 Rules. TRCP 96, 162, 163.

§1.2 Purpose. A nonsuit is a voluntary dismissal of the party's claims.

§1.3 Forms. *O'Connor's Texas Civil Forms* (2012), FORMS 7F.

§1.4 Other references. *O'Connor's Texas Causes of Action* (2013) (*O'Connor's Texas COA*).

§2. MOTION

A plaintiff has a right to a nonsuit the moment it makes a timely oral or written request for nonsuit. *Travelers Ins. v. Joachim*, 315 S.W.3d 860, 862 (Tex.2010); *In re Greater Houston Orthopaedic Specialists, Inc.*, 295 S.W.3d 323, 325 (Tex.2009); *BHP Pet. Co. v. Millard*, 800 S.W.2d 838, 840 (Tex.1990); *Greenberg v. Brookshire*, 640 S.W.2d 870, 872 (Tex.1982). A nonsuit nullifies the controversy and renders certain interlocutory orders in the case moot. *In re Bennett*, 960 S.W.2d 35, 38 (Tex.1997); *see City of Dallas v. Albert*, 354 S.W.3d 368, 375 (Tex.2011). However, the plaintiff's nonsuit will not affect any pending claims for relief made by the defendant. See "Effect on defendant's claims," §6.3, p. 654. Once the plaintiff requests a nonsuit, she cannot withdraw the request. *Trigg v. Moore*, 335 S.W.3d 243, 245 (Tex.App.—Amarillo 2010, pet. denied).

§2.1 Oral or written. To take a nonsuit, the party can either file a written motion for nonsuit (sometimes called a notice of nonsuit) or make an oral announcement of the nonsuit in open court. *Greenberg v. Brookshire*, 640 S.W.2d 870, 872 (Tex.1982). In this section, "motion for nonsuit" refers to both an oral request and a written motion for nonsuit.

§2.2 Grounds. There are no formal requirements for the motion for nonsuit. *Greenberg v. Brookshire*, 640 S.W.2d 870, 872 (Tex.1982). The motion does not need to state a reason for taking the nonsuit. *See id.* See *O'Connor's Texas Forms*, FORM 7F:1.

§2.3 With or without prejudice. The motion should state whether the party requests a dismissal with or without prejudice. If the case is dismissed with prejudice, the order is a final adjudication on the merits and the lawsuit cannot be refiled. See "With prejudice," §5.4, p. 653. If the case is dismissed without prejudice, the order is not a final adjudication on the merits and the parties are merely placed in the positions they would have been if the suit had not been brought. See "Without prejudice," §5.3, p. 653.

§2.4 Movant.

1. Plaintiff. In most cases, the party taking a nonsuit is the plaintiff.

2. Defendant. A defendant may nonsuit its counterclaims. *See City of Dallas v. Albert*, 354 S.W.3d 368, 375 (Tex.2011); *Mackie v. McKenzie*, 890 S.W.2d 807, 808 (Tex.1994); *Mossler v. Shields*, 818 S.W.2d 752, 753 (Tex. 1991).

§2.5 Partial nonsuit.

1. Parties. The plaintiff can nonsuit some parties without nonsuiting others, as long as doing so will not prejudice another party. *See* TRCP 162, 163; *C/S Solutions, Inc. v. Energy Maint. Servs. Grp.*, 274 S.W.3d 299, 306 (Tex.App.—Houston [1st Dist.] 2008, no pet.).

2. Claims. The plaintiff cannot nonsuit only some of the claims against a party, but instead must nonsuit the entire case. *See* TRCP 162, 163; *C/S Solutions*, 274 S.W.3d at 306.

★

NOTE

Although a plaintiff cannot nonsuit only some of her claims, she can voluntarily dismiss certain claims either by filing an amended pleading that omits a claim under TRCP 63 or by abandoning a claim under TRCP 165. C/S Solutions, 274 S.W.3d at 306. See "Alternatives to nonsuit," §2.8, this page. If a plaintiff files a written "nonsuit" that abandons certain claims, it is actually an amended pleading voluntarily dismissing the claims, and will be treated as such, despite the fact that the word "nonsuit" appears. C/S Solutions, 274 S.W.3d at 306-07. The distinction between a nonsuit under TRCP 162 and an amended pleading that voluntarily dismisses some claims has no practical effect unless the "nonsuit" violates the timing requirements of TRCP 63. C/S Solutions, 274 S.W.3d at 306 & n.6.

---

§2.6 Service of notice. TRCP 162 requires the movant to serve notice of the nonsuit in accordance with TRCP 21a on any party that has answered or has been served with process. *Novosad v. Brian K. Cunningham, P.C.*, 38 S.W.3d 767, 772 (Tex.App.—Houston [14th Dist.] 2001, no pet.). A certificate of service creates a presumption that the nonsuit was received; the presumption vanishes when opposing evidence is introduced. *Wembley Inv. v. Herrera*, 11 S.W.3d 924, 927 (Tex.1999). But the lack of a certificate of service on a motion for nonsuit does not affect the finality of the judgment. *McGrew v. Heard*, 779 S.W.2d 455, 458 (Tex.App.—Houston [1st Dist.] 1989, orig. proceeding).

§2.7 Costs. The clerk must tax the court costs of the nonsuit against the party moving for dismissal, unless the court orders otherwise. TRCP 162; *Leon Springs Gas Co. v. Restaurant Equip. Leasing Co.*, 961 S.W.2d 574, 579 (Tex.App.—San Antonio 1997, no pet.).

§2.8 Alternatives to nonsuit. There are other ways to eliminate parties or claims from the suit.

1. Nonsuit by amendment. Because an amended pleading supersedes and supplants all previous pleadings, an amendment of the pleading can work as a nonsuit of parties and claims. *Randolph v. Jackson Walker L.L.P.*, 29 S.W.3d 271, 274 (Tex.App.—Houston [14th Dist.] 2000, pet. denied); *see* TRCP 65 (substituted instrument is no longer regarded as part of the pleadings). See "Amended pleadings," ch. 1-B, §3.6.1(1), p. 17.

(1) Omitted parties. As a general rule, omitting a party from an amended petition indicates an intent to nonsuit that party. *American Petrofina, Inc. v. Allen*, 887 S.W.2d 829, 831 (Tex.1994) (omitted Ps); *Webb v. Jorns*, 488 S.W.2d 407, 409 (Tex.1972) (omitted D); *Randolph*, 29 S.W.3d at 274 (omitted Ds); *see also Green v. Vidlak*, 76 S.W.3d 117, 119-20 (Tex.App.—Amarillo 2002, no pet.) (even though D listed in style of amended petition, omission of D's name from text of amended petition was nonsuit). If a petition omits a party by mistake but the party is renamed in a later petition, the omission does not operate as a nonsuit. *American Petrofina*, 887 S.W.2d at 831; *Woodruff v. Wright*, 51 S.W.3d 727, 733 (Tex.App.—Texarkana 2001, pet. denied). In such a case, the party seeking to exclude the temporarily dismissed party has the burden to show that it was prejudiced when the omitted party was later renamed. *American Petrofina*, 887 S.W.2d at 831. When a defendant is omitted from the preamble of the petition but is named in the body of the petition, the omission is not a nonsuit. *Cox v. Union Oil Co.*, 917 S.W.2d 524, 527 (Tex.App.—Beaumont 1996, no writ). By including the generic term "et al." in the style of the case of an amended petition, a party negates the intent to nonsuit any of the parties named in the earlier petition. *See American Petrofina*, 887 S.W.2d at 831; *Abramcik v. U.S. Home Corp.*, 792 S.W.2d 822, 824 (Tex.App.—Houston [14th Dist.] 1990, writ denied).

(2) Omitted claims. Omitting a claim from an amended petition indicates an intent to nonsuit that claim. *See, e.g., Dolenz v. All Saints Episcopal Hosp.*, 638 S.W.2d 141, 142 (Tex.App.—Fort Worth 1982, writ ref'd n.r.e.) (P abandoned claim because he went to trial on amended petition that did not contain the claim).

2. TRCP 165 – abandonment. A party may abandon any part of its claim and have that fact noted on the record. TRCP 165; *see also Jones v. Nightingale*, 900 S.W.2d 87, 90 (Tex.App.—San Antonio 1995, writ ref'd) (claims abandoned under TRCP 165 barred from relitigation by compulsory-counterclaim rule).

★

§3. DEADLINES FOR NONSUIT

§3.1 Before resting. A nonsuit in a trial must be taken before the plaintiff introduces all of its evidence other than rebuttal (i.e., before it rests). TRCP 162; *Epps v. Fowler*, 351 S.W.3d 862, 868 (Tex.2011); *In re Team Rocket, L.P.*, 256 S.W.3d 257, 259 (Tex.2008); *Villafani v. Trejo*, 251 S.W.3d 466, 468-69 (Tex.2008); *e.g.*, *UTMB v. Estate of Blackmon*, 195 S.W.3d 98, 100 (Tex.2006) (P had right to nonsuit during interlocutory appeal to court of appeals).

§3.2 Before SJ. A nonsuit in a summary-judgment proceeding must be taken before the court grants ("renders") a summary judgment. *Pace Concerts, Ltd v. Resendez*, 72 S.W.3d 700, 702 (Tex.App.—San Antonio 2002, pet. denied); *Taliaferro v. Smith*, 804 S.W.2d 548, 550 (Tex.App.—Houston [14th Dist.] 1991, no writ). See "Rendition," ch. 9-C, §3.1, p. 765.

§4. OBJECTIONS TO NONSUIT

There are not many legitimate objections to a nonsuit. See *O'Connor's Texas Forms*, FORM 7F:2. The following are some objections a party can make.

§4.1 Request too late. A defendant should object when the request for nonsuit is too late—that is, when (1) the plaintiff asks for a nonsuit after it introduced all of its evidence other than rebuttal (see "Before resting," §3.1, this page), or (2) the plaintiff asks for a nonsuit on a claim already resolved by summary judgment. *See Hyundai Motor Co. v. Alvarado*, 892 S.W.2d 853, 855 (Tex.1995) (once SJ is granted, P cannot take nonsuit on any claim resolved by SJ).

§4.2 Order too inclusive. A party must object when the order of nonsuit dismisses more claims or parties than requested in the nonsuit. *See Shadowbrook Apts. v. Abu-Ahmad*, 783 S.W.2d 210, 211 (Tex.1990).

§5. ORDER OF NONSUIT

§5.1 Court's authority. A trial court cannot nonsuit parties without a motion for nonsuit of those parties by the plaintiff. *Shadowbrook Apts. v. Abu-Ahmad*, 783 S.W.2d 210, 211 (Tex.1990). When properly requested, the court does not have the authority to deny a nonsuit. *Travelers Ins. v. Joachim*, 315 S.W.3d 860, 862 (Tex.2010); *Zimmerman v. Ottis*, 941 S.W.2d 259, 261 (Tex.App.—Corpus Christi 1996, orig. proceeding); *Baldwin v. Klanke*, 877 S.W.2d 879, 881 (Tex.App.—Houston [1st Dist.] 1994, no writ). *But see Oryx Capital Int'l v. Sage Apts., L.L.C.*, 167 S.W.3d 432, 438 (Tex.App.—San Antonio 2005, no pet.) (trial court cannot sign nonsuit when court of appeals has issued order staying proceedings in trial court).

§5.2 Written order. A written order is not required. TRCP 162; *Epps v. Fowler*, 351 S.W.3d 862, 868 (Tex.2011). When the court signs an order granting a nonsuit, it is simply a ministerial act. *Klein v. Hernandez*, 315 S.W.3d 1, 4 (Tex.2010); *Greenberg v. Brookshire*, 640 S.W.2d 870, 872 (Tex.1982). A written order, however, is important for establishing finality for appeal. See "Effect on finality of judgment," §6.8, p. 656.

   1. Most cases. Once a nonsuit is requested in open court or in writing, the court should sign an order granting the dismissal. The signing of the order of dismissal—not the filing of the nonsuit—triggers the appellate deadlines. *In re Bennett*, 960 S.W.2d 35, 38 (Tex.1997); *Park Place Hosp. v. Estate of Milo*, 909 S.W.2d 508, 510 (Tex.1995); *Farmer v. Ben E. Keith Co.*, 907 S.W.2d 495, 496 (Tex.1995); *see, e.g.*, *Coastal Banc SSB v. Helle*, 48 S.W.3d 796, 800 (Tex.App.—Corpus Christi 2001, pet. denied) (oral rendition of nonsuit did not begin appellate timetable); *Iacono v. Lyons*, 6 S.W.3d 715, 716 (Tex.App.—Houston [1st Dist.] 1999, no pet.) (docket notation that nonsuit was "entered" did not begin appellate timetable).

   2. After conventional trial on merits. A separate order on the nonsuit is not necessary when the nonsuit is filed before the court signs a judgment after a conventional trial on the merits (i.e., a jury or nonjury trial). After a conventional trial on the merits, the judgment is presumed to be final and dispositive. See "Judgment after conventional trial," ch. 9-C, §6.3.1(2), p. 772. A default judgment, summary judgment, or judgment of dismissal is not a conventional trial on the merits for purposes of transforming a nonsuit into a final judgment. *See In re Bro*

─────────────────────── ✦ ───────────────────────

Bro Props., Inc., 50 S.W.3d 528, 530 (Tex.App.—San Antonio 2000, orig. proceeding) (nonsuit announced before default J did not become effective by rendition of default J).

PRACTICE TIP

To avoid problems about the finality of the judgment, insist that the court sign an order of non-suit or memorialize the nonsuit in the final judgment.

---

§5.3 Without prejudice. In most cases, the court should sign an order dismissing the nonsuited claims without prejudice to their refiling. *See* TRCP 162.

    1. To plaintiff. The dismissal after a nonsuit is not an adjudication of the plaintiff's rights; the nonsuit merely places the plaintiff in the position it was in before filing the lawsuit. *McGowen v. Huang*, 120 S.W.3d 452, 462 (Tex.App.—Texarkana 2003, pet. denied); *KT Bolt Mfg. v. Texas Elec. Cooperatives*, 837 S.W.2d 273, 275 (Tex.App.—Beaumont 1992, writ denied).

    2. To defendant. If, at the time the plaintiff files a nonsuit, the defendant has already filed a counterclaim, motion for sanctions, or any other request for affirmative relief, the nonsuit does not prevent the court from considering the defendant's request. TRCP 96, 162. See "Effect on defendant's claims," §6.3, p. 654.

§5.4 With prejudice. A dismissal with prejudice is an adjudication on the merits. *Mossler v. Shields*, 818 S.W.2d 752, 754 (Tex.1991). Generally, if the court signs an order dismissing the suit with prejudice, res judicata applies and the plaintiff cannot relitigate the same claims against the same defendant. *Epps v. Fowler*, 351 S.W.3d 862, 868-69 (Tex.2011); *Travelers Ins. v. Joachim*, 315 S.W.3d 860, 862 (Tex.2010); *see, e.g.*, *Galvan v. America's Favorite Chicken Co.*, 934 S.W.2d 409, 410 (Tex.App.—San Antonio 1996, writ denied) (when party mistakenly filed for nonsuit with prejudice, res judicata barred later suit). See "Res Judicata – Claim Preclusion," ch. 9-D, §3, p. 781.

CAUTION

Check the order before the time expires to challenge it. If the order states that the dismissal is with prejudice when it should be without prejudice, you must attack the order directly—through a timely motion for new trial or a bill of review—or the order will be final and the underlying claim will be barred by res judicata. See **Travelers Ins.***, 315 S.W.3d at 866.*

---

§6. EFFECT OF NONSUIT

§6.1 Effect on plaintiff's suit. The nonsuit is effective as soon as the plaintiff files a motion for nonsuit or asks for one in open court. *Epps v. Fowler*, 351 S.W.3d 862, 868 (Tex.2011); *Travelers Ins. v. Joachim*, 315 S.W.3d 860, 862 (Tex.2010); *Greenberg v. Brookshire*, 640 S.W.2d 870, 872 (Tex.1982). However, the trial court may defer signing an order of dismissal to hear matters that are collateral to the merits of the underlying case (i.e., costs, attorney fees, sanctions). *Travelers Ins.*, 315 S.W.3d at 863; *UTMB v. Estate of Blackmon*, 195 S.W.3d 98, 100-01 (Tex. 2006); *see* TRCP 162; *In re Bennett*, 960 S.W.2d 35, 38 (Tex.1997). Although the court may hold a hearing on these matters, the nonsuit still renders the merits of the case moot. *E.g.*, *Estate of Blackmon*, 195 S.W.3d at 101 (court could sign order on costs requested by D in plea to jurisdiction, but P's nonsuit deprived court of jurisdiction over D's appeal); *see* *City of Dallas v. Albert*, 354 S.W.3d 368, 375 (Tex.2011); *Travelers Ins.*, 315 S.W.3d at 862. Pleadings filed by the defendant after the nonsuit will not continue the suit. *See Ault v. Mulanax*, 724 S.W.2d 824, 828 (Tex.App.—Texarkana 1986, orig. proceeding).

    §6.2 Effect on refiling suit.

    1. Rule. In most cases, when the court signs an order on the plaintiff's nonsuit dismissing the suit without prejudice, the plaintiff can refile the same suit. *In re Team Rocket, L.P.*, 256 S.W.3d 257, 259 (Tex.2008); *Aetna Cas. & Sur. Co. v. Specia*, 849 S.W.2d 805, 806 (Tex.1993); *see Epps v. Fowler*, 351 S.W.3d 862, 868 (Tex.2011).

NONSUIT

★

2. Exceptions.

(1) After statute of limitations. An attempt to litigate a claim that was earlier dismissed on a nonsuit (or a compulsory counterclaim to the nonsuited claim) is barred if the statute of limitations has run on the claim by the time the second suit is filed. *See Weiman v. Addicks-Fairbanks Rd. Sand Co.*, 846 S.W.2d 414, 421 (Tex. App.—Houston [14th Dist.] 1992, writ denied) (compulsory counterclaim); *Guaranty Cty. Mut. Ins. v. Reyna*, 700 S.W.2d 325, 327 (Tex.App.—San Antonio 1985) (nonsuit), *writ ref'd n.r.e.*, 709 S.W.2d 647 (Tex.1986); *see, e.g., Bailey v. Gardner*, 154 S.W.3d 917, 920 (Tex.App.—Dallas 2005, no pet.) (statute of limitations not tolled when P made tactical decision to nonsuit claim because expert was unavailable; refiling of suit barred by statute of limitations).

(2) After summary judgment. A plaintiff cannot escape the effect of a summary judgment on a claim by taking a nonsuit. *Hyundai Motor Co. v. Alvarado*, 892 S.W.2d 853, 854-55 (Tex.1995). When a plaintiff takes a nonsuit on a claim that was resolved by a partial summary judgment, the claim is considered dismissed with prejudice. *Id.* at 855. After the court grants a partial summary judgment, the plaintiff may take a nonsuit only on the unadjudicated claims. *See id.*

§6.3 Effect on defendant's claims. When the court signs an order on the plaintiff's nonsuit, the dismissal does not prevent the defendant or intervenor from being heard on its own claims for affirmative relief. TRCP 96, 162; *Epps v. Fowler*, 351 S.W.3d 862, 868 (Tex.2011); *In re Greater Houston Orthopaedic Specialists, Inc.*, 295 S.W.3d 323, 324 (Tex.2009); *Villafani v. Trejo*, 251 S.W.3d 466, 469 (Tex.2008); *BHP Pet. Co. v. Millard*, 800 S.W.2d 838, 840-41 (Tex.1990); *see City of Dallas v. Albert*, 354 S.W.3d 368, 375 (Tex.2011); *see also Klein v. Dooley*, 949 S.W.2d 307, 308 (Tex.1997) (nonsuit does not affect D's derivative DTPA claim for costs and attorney fees). Not all claims are claims for affirmative relief under TRCP 162.

1. Independent of P's claim. For a claim to qualify as a claim for affirmative relief under TRCP 162, it must allege the defendant has a cause of action on which it can recover independent of the plaintiff's claim, even if the plaintiff abandons or is unable to establish its claims. *UTMB v. Estate of Blackmon*, 195 S.W.3d 98, 101 (Tex. 2006); *General Land Office v. OXY U.S.A., Inc.*, 789 S.W.2d 569, 570 (Tex.1990); *see, e.g., Ulloa v. Davila*, 860 S.W.2d 202, 204 (Tex.App.—San Antonio 1993, no writ) (counterclaim did more than resist Ps' suit). The following are examples of independent claims: • An intervening insurance carrier's subrogation claim. *Texas Mut. Ins. v. Ledbetter*, 251 S.W.3d 31, 38 (Tex.2008). • A defendant's request for a declaratory judgment if it seeks resolution of continuing issues. *BHP Pet.*, 800 S.W.2d at 842. • A request for attorney fees if the defendant pleads a claim for which damages and attorney fees are recoverable. *See Leon Springs Gas Co. v. Restaurant Equip. Leasing Co.*, 961 S.W.2d 574, 578 (Tex.App.—San Antonio 1997, no pet.). • A request to compel arbitration. *Quanto Int'l Co. v. Lloyd*, 897 S.W.2d 482, 487 (Tex.App.—Houston [1st Dist.] 1995, orig. proceeding). *Contra In re Riggs*, 315 S.W.3d 613, 615 & n.2 (Tex.App.—Fort Worth 2010, orig. proceeding).

2. Derivative of P's claim. A claim that mirrors the controlling issues in a case is not an independent claim for affirmative relief. *In re Estate of Kidd*, 812 S.W.2d 356, 359 (Tex.App.—Amarillo 1991, writ denied). The following are examples of derivative claims: • A defendant's request for a declaratory judgment that seeks a finding of no liability. *BHP Pet.*, 800 S.W.2d at 841. • A request for attorney fees when a defendant claims them for defense of the plaintiff's suit. *Smith v. Texas Farmers Ins.*, 82 S.W.3d 580, 588-89 (Tex.App.—San Antonio 2002, pet. denied). *Contra In re C.A.S.*, 128 S.W.3d 681, 686 (Tex.App.—Dallas 2003, no pet.) (claim for attorney fees for defense is independent claim); *In re Frost Nat'l Bank*, 103 S.W.3d 647, 650 (Tex.App.—Corpus Christi 2003, orig. proceeding) (same). • A counterclaim that asks for indemnity, contribution, or costs. *Pleasants v. Emmons*, 871 S.W.2d 296, 298 (Tex.App.—Eastland 1994, no writ).

§6.4 Effect on venue. Whether a motion to transfer venue fixes venue in the county of the defendant's choice when the plaintiff's case is dismissed on a nonsuit depends on the state of the record at the time the nonsuit was filed. *GeoChem Tech v. Verseckes*, 962 S.W.2d 541, 543 (Tex.1998). The venue facts in the plaintiff's petition, the motion to transfer venue, and any response must be examined to determine whether the defendant established a prima facie case of venue. *See id.*

─────────────────────────── ✮ ───────────────────────────

1. Before D files venue motion. If the plaintiff takes a nonsuit before the defendant files a motion to transfer venue, the dismissal does not fix venue in the county where the plaintiff first filed suit unless the plaintiff's petition alleged facts invoking a mandatory-venue provision. *See Peysen v. Dawson*, 974 S.W.2d 377, 380 (Tex. App.—San Antonio 1998, no pet.) (because only venue fact in P's petition was that one of Ds lived in Bexar County, it was a county of permissive venue, not mandatory venue). Venue is not fixed merely by filing suit. *Hyman Farm Serv. v. Earth Oil & Gas Co.*, 920 S.W.2d 452, 456 (Tex.App.—Amarillo 1996, no writ).

2. Before court rules on D's motion. If the plaintiff takes a nonsuit after the defendant files a motion to transfer venue but before the court rules on the motion, the motion to transfer fixes venue in the county of the defendant's choice if the uncontradicted venue facts compel venue in that county. *See GeoChem Tech*, 962 S.W.2d at 543-44 (venue facts in Ds' motions permitted P to refile in either of two counties of mandatory venue).

3. After court rules on D's motion. If the plaintiff takes a nonsuit after the trial court grants the defendant's motion to transfer venue, the ruling fixes venue if the suit is later refiled. *In re Team Rocket, L.P.*, 256 S.W.3d 257, 260 (Tex.2008); *Le v. Kilpatrick*, 112 S.W.3d 631, 633 (Tex.App.—Tyler 2003, no pet.); *Hendrick Med. Ctr. v. Howell*, 690 S.W.2d 42, 44 (Tex.App.—Dallas 1985, orig. proceeding).

§6.5 Effect on injunction. When the underlying suit is dismissed by a nonsuit, any temporary injunction is automatically dissolved and any appeal becomes moot. *General Land Office v. OXY U.S.A., Inc.*, 789 S.W.2d 569, 571 (Tex.1990).

§6.6 Effect on attorney fees. When the plaintiff takes a nonsuit, the defendant, as a prevailing party, may be entitled to attorney fees as provided by an attorney-fees provision in a written contract. *See Epps v. Fowler*, 351 S.W.3d 862, 865 (Tex.2011). See *O'Connor's Texas COA*, "Attorney Fees Under Written Contract," ch. 45-C, p. 1377. If the contract does not define who is a prevailing party, the defendant's right to recover attorney fees is determined by whether the nonsuit was ordered with or without prejudice.

1. With prejudice. When the plaintiff takes a nonsuit with prejudice, the defendant is the prevailing party and is entitled to attorney fees. *Epps*, 351 S.W.3d at 868. Under res judicata, a nonsuit with prejudice makes a permanent and inalterable change in the parties' legal relationship because the plaintiff cannot sue the defendant again for a claim arising from the same subject matter. *Id.* at 868-69.

2. Without prejudice.

(1) Generally. When the plaintiff takes a nonsuit without prejudice, the defendant is generally not a prevailing party because the parties' legal relationship has not changed; the plaintiff can seek the same relief by refiling the same claims. *Epps*, 351 S.W.3d at 869.

───

NOTE

The mere possibility that limitations would bar future suits does not make a defendant a prevailing party. Epps, 351 S.W.3d at 869. There is no material change in the parties' legal relationship unless the defendant has secured a favorable ruling on a res judicata defense. Id.

───

(2) Plaintiff avoided unfavorable ruling. When the plaintiff takes a nonsuit without prejudice, a defendant is a prevailing party and is entitled to attorney fees if the court finds that the plaintiff took the nonsuit to avoid an unfavorable ruling on the merits. *Epps*, 351 S.W.3d at 870.

(a) Defendant's motion. The defendant must ask the court to find that the plaintiff took the nonsuit to avoid an unfavorable ruling on the merits. *Epps*, 351 S.W.3d at 870. Factors that may support the defendant's motion include the following:

[1] The plaintiff nonsuited after a motion for summary judgment was filed. *Id.* at 871.

[2] The plaintiff's failure to respond to requests for admissions or other discovery that could support entry of an adverse judgment was unexcused. *Id.* The defendant's motion will not be successful, however, if the plaintiff shows that later discovery revealed flaws in the plaintiff's claims that were not present when the claims were filed. *Id.*

─────────────────────── ✪ ───────────────────────

[3] The plaintiff did not timely identify experts or other critical witnesses. *Id.*

[4] There are procedural obstacles to receiving a favorable ruling, such as the plaintiff's inability to join necessary parties. *Id.*

(b) Evidence. To determine if the plaintiff took the nonsuit to avoid an unfavorable ruling, the court should rely on the record and affidavits as much as possible and should take live testimony only in rare instances. *Epps*, 351 S.W.3d at 870.

§6.7 Effect on sanctions.

1. Timing of motion. A party can bring a motion for sanctions before or after the nonsuit, as long as the motion is filed while the court retains plenary power. *Crites v. Collins*, 284 S.W.3d 839, 843 (Tex.2009); *see In re Bennett*, 960 S.W.2d 35, 38 (Tex.1997); *Scott & White Mem'l Hosp. v. Schexnider*, 940 S.W.2d 594, 596 (Tex. 1996). Once the court's plenary power expires, the court can no longer impose sanctions. *Crites*, 284 S.W.3d at 843; *Schexnider*, 940 S.W.2d at 596.

2. Order for sanctions. Whether a particular order for sanctions survives a nonsuit and can later be enforced or appealed depends on the purpose of the sanction. *Villafani v. Trejo*, 251 S.W.3d 466, 470 (Tex.2008).

(1) Sanction does not survive nonsuit. If a sanction serves no purpose beyond the specific proceeding, the sanctions order does not survive the nonsuit. *Villafani*, 251 S.W.3d at 470. For example, an order excluding a witness as a discovery sanction does not survive a nonsuit because the reason for the sanction—to ensure a party is afforded a fair trial—no longer matters. *Id.* Similarly, an order excluding evidence as a discovery sanction usually does not survive the dismissal and refiling of the same suit. *See, e.g.*, *Schein v. American Rest. Grp.*, 852 S.W.2d 496, 497 (Tex.1993) (sanction for failure to respond to interrogatories and request for production); *Aetna Cas. & Sur. Co. v. Specia*, 849 S.W.2d 805, 807 (Tex.1993) (sanction for failure to supplement discovery).

(2) Sanction survives nonsuit. If the sanction may serve a purpose beyond the specific proceeding, the sanctions order survives the nonsuit. *Villafani*, 251 S.W.3d at 470; *see Crites*, 284 S.W.3d at 842. For example, monetary sanctions survive a nonsuit because they may serve compensatory and punitive purposes. *Villafani*, 251 S.W.3d at 470.

§6.8 Effect on finality of judgment.
If the nonsuit specifically disposes of the last remaining claim in the suit, the order on the nonsuit is a final, appealable judgment. *See Unifund CCR Partners v. Villa*, 299 S.W.3d 92, 96-97 (Tex.2009); *Crites v. Collins*, 284 S.W.3d 839, 840-41 (Tex.2009); *Coastal Banc SSB v. Helle*, 48 S.W.3d 796, 799-800 (Tex.App.—Corpus Christi 2001, pet. denied). See "Judgment resolves all claims," ch. 9-C, §6.3.1(1), p. 772. If the nonsuit disposes of some claims but other, unadjudicated claims remain, the order on the nonsuit is interlocutory. *See Crites*, 284 S.W.3d at 840 (order of nonsuit does not necessarily dispose of any cross-actions unless they are specifically disposed of in the order); *see, e.g.*, *Law Offices of Windle Turley, P.C. v. French*, 109 S.W.3d 599, 601 (Tex.App.—Dallas 2003, no pet.) (nonsuit order that did not specifically state it was a final judgment or dispose of all claims was interlocutory); *In re Romero*, 956 S.W.2d 659, 662 (Tex.App.—San Antonio 1997, orig. proceeding) (because nonsuit order dismissing P's claim against D did not dispose of the insurer's subrogation claim, it was interlocutory). See "Interlocutory judgment – merger or severance," ch. 9-C, §6.3.1(3), p. 772.

§7. REINSTATEMENT OF NONSUITED CASE

At any time while the trial court has plenary power over its judgment, a party may ask the court to set aside the nonsuit and reinstate the case. *Missouri Pac. R.R. v. Whitaker*, 815 S.W.2d 348, 349 n.2 (Tex.App.—Tyler 1991, orig. proceeding). The nonsuit does not divest the trial court of jurisdiction. *Quanto Int'l Co. v. Lloyd*, 897 S.W.2d 482, 485 (Tex.App.—Houston [1st Dist.] 1995, orig. proceeding); *Missouri Pac. R.R.*, 815 S.W.2d at 349 n.2. A motion to reinstate a nonsuited case is not a motion to reinstate under TRCP 165a, which governs reinstatement of cases dismissed for want of prosecution. *See In re Simon Prop. Grp.*, 985 S.W.2d 212, 214 (Tex.App.—Corpus Christi 1999, orig. proceeding). The motion to set aside a nonsuited case can be labeled a motion to reinstate after nonsuit, a motion to set aside the nonsuit, a motion to withdraw the nonsuit, or even a motion for new trial. *See, e.g.*, *Osborne v.*

———————————————— ✦ ————————————————

St. Luke's Episcopal Hosp., 915 S.W.2d 906, 909 (Tex.App.—Houston [1st Dist.] 1996, writ denied) (motion to set aside nonsuit); *Quanto Int'l*, 897 S.W.2d at 484 (motion to reinstate); *Golodetz Trading Corp. v. Curland*, 886 S.W.2d 503, 504 (Tex.App.—Houston [1st Dist.] 1994, no writ) (motion to withdraw nonsuit). The parties may file an agreed motion to reinstate the case. *See McClendon v. State Farm Mut. Auto. Ins.*, 796 S.W.2d 229, 233 (Tex. App.—El Paso 1990, writ denied). See *O'Connor's Texas Forms*, FORM 7F:3.

§8. REVIEW

§8.1 Appeal.

1. Plaintiff's right to appeal. Taking a nonsuit does not prevent the plaintiff from challenging any action of the trial court before the nonsuit was taken. *E.g.*, *Felderhoff v. Knauf*, 819 S.W.2d 110, 111 (Tex.1991) (after nonsuit, P appealed sanctions imposed by trial court before nonsuit).

2. Defendant's right to appeal.

(1) No claim for affirmative relief. If a plaintiff takes a nonsuit against a defendant that has no outstanding claims for affirmative relief, the defendant is no longer a party to the suit with standing to appeal. *See, e.g.*, *United Oil & Minerals, Inc. v. Costilla Energy, Inc.*, 1 S.W.3d 840, 844 (Tex.App.—Corpus Christi 1999, pet. dism'd) (party nonsuited by amended petition had no standing to appeal final judgment); *Preston v. American Eagle Ins.*, 948 S.W.2d 18, 21 (Tex.App.—Dallas 1997, no writ) (persons nonsuited before SJ had no standing to appeal judgment). When the plaintiff nonsuits its claims, there is no longer a case or controversy and the court of appeals has no jurisdiction over the suit. *See, e.g.*, *UTMB v. Estate of Blackmon*, 195 S.W.3d 98, 101 (Tex.2006) (after P nonsuited case, court had no jurisdiction to issue order on D's interlocutory appeal from its plea to jurisdiction).

(2) Claim for affirmative relief. If the plaintiff takes a nonsuit against a defendant that has an affirmative claim for relief, the nonsuit does not prevent the defendant from appealing the trial court's ruling on that claim even if the ruling occurred before the nonsuit. *Villafani v. Trejo*, 251 S.W.3d 466, 470 (Tex.2008); *see Hernandez v. Ebrom*, 289 S.W.3d 316, 317 (Tex.2009).

3. Appellate deadlines. The appellate timetable runs from the signing date of whatever order makes a judgment final and appealable—that is, the order that disposes of any parties or issues remaining in the case after the nonsuit. *Martinez v. Humble Sand & Gravel, Inc.*, 875 S.W.2d 311, 313 (Tex.1994). If no other claims remain in the case after a nonsuit, the appellate deadlines run from the date the court signed the order of nonsuit. *In re Bennett*, 960 S.W.2d 35, 38 (Tex.1997); *Farmer v. Ben E. Keith Co.*, 907 S.W.2d 495, 496 (Tex.1995). If other claims remain in the case after a nonsuit, the appellate deadlines run from the date the court signed the final judgment or the date the court severed the claim from the rest of the case. See "What judgments are final," ch. 9-C, §6.3, p. 772. The period within which a party must perfect an appeal is calculated from the date the order or judgment was signed, not from the filing of the notice of nonsuit. *Farmer*, 907 S.W.2d at 496.

4. Plenary power. The court retains plenary power over an order of dismissal for 30 days after the date it signs the order. *America's Favorite Chicken Co. v. Galvan*, 897 S.W.2d 874, 876 (Tex.App.—San Antonio 1995, writ denied); *Harris Cty. Appr. Dist. v. Wittig*, 881 S.W.2d 193, 194 (Tex.App.—Houston [1st Dist.] 1994, orig. proceeding). If certain post-trial motions are filed, the court retains plenary power for as long as 105 days after the judgment is signed. See "Effect of PPE motions," ch. 9-C, §6.5.2, p. 776.

§8.2 Mandamus.

If a trial court refuses to grant a plaintiff's timely motion for nonsuit and there are no other pending claims, the plaintiff may seek mandamus relief. *In re Greater Houston Orthopaedic Specialists, Inc.*, 295 S.W.3d 323, 326 (Tex.2009); *Hooks v. Fourth Ct. of Appeals*, 808 S.W.2d 56, 59 (Tex.1991); *see Greenberg v. Brookshire*, 640 S.W.2d 870, 872 (Tex.1982). If a trial court reinstates a nonsuited case over the plaintiff's objection, the plaintiff may seek mandamus relief. *Johnson v. Harless*, 651 S.W.2d 259, 260 (Tex.1983); *Quanto Int'l Co. v. Lloyd*, 897 S.W.2d 482, 485 (Tex.App.—Houston [1st Dist.] 1995, orig. proceeding).

✯

G. INVOLUNTARY DISMISSAL

§1. GENERAL

§1.1 Rules. TRCP 165a.

§1.2 Purpose. The purpose of a dismissal is to dispose of the case without a trial.

§1.3 Timetables & forms. *O'Connor's Texas Civil Appeals* (2012), Timetables, Appeal After Late Notice of Judgment, p. 1127, Appeal of Dismissal for Want of Prosecution, p. 1135; *O'Connor's Texas Civil Forms* (2012), FORM 7G:1.

§1.4 Other references. Merritt & Merritt, *Rule 165a: Dismissal for Want of Prosecution*, 60 Tex.B.J. 555 (1997); *O'Connor's Texas Causes of Action* (2013) (*O'Connor's Texas COA*).

§2. GROUNDS FOR DISMISSAL

To be entitled to a dismissal in a Texas court, the defendant must make some complaint about the plaintiff's lawsuit or conduct that, if not cured, entitles the defendant to move for a dismissal. By comparison, in federal court a defendant can ask the court to dismiss the plaintiff's suit because the plaintiff's pleadings do not state a cause of action. *Fort Bend Cty. v. Wilson*, 825 S.W.2d 251, 253 (Tex.App.—Houston [14th Dist.] 1992, no writ) (discussing FRCP 12(b)(6), which permits federal courts to dismiss for failure to state a claim). In Texas, such a complaint is considered a general demurrer and is prohibited by TRCP 90. *Wilson*, 825 S.W.2d at 253.

§2.1 Bar to suit. Most requests to dismiss are made as part of another motion alleging that the plaintiff cannot maintain the suit as filed. The defendant must prove there is a bar to the plaintiff's suit or a defect in the pleadings, the court, the parties, or the claim for liability that cannot be cured by amendment. The following are some of the grounds that bar a suit:

1. The case is moot. See "Mootness," ch. 3-F, §3.4, p. 241.

2. The trial court does not have jurisdiction over the defendant or its property. See "Special Appearance—Challenging Personal Jurisdiction," ch. 3-B, p. 189.

3. The trial court does not have subject-matter jurisdiction. See "Plea to the Jurisdiction—Challenging the Court," ch. 3-F, p. 239.

4. The plaintiff's petition does not state a cause of action against the defendant. See "Special Exceptions—Challenging the Pleadings," ch. 3-G, p. 248; "Motion to Abate—Challenging the Suit," ch. 3-I, p. 257.

5. A Texas court is not the appropriate forum for the lawsuit. See "Forum Non Conveniens—Challenging the Texas Forum," ch. 3-D, p. 216. If the court sustains a motion to dismiss on the ground of forum non conveniens, it may either dismiss or stay the suit.

§2.2 Failure to prosecute. The trial court's authority to dismiss for want of prosecution comes from two sources: TRCP 165a and the court's inherent power. *Villarreal v. San Antonio Truck & Equip.*, 994 S.W.2d 628, 630 (Tex.1999).

1. TRCP 165a. A trial court may dismiss a suit under TRCP 165a for failure of a party to (1) appear at trial or a hearing after receiving notice or (2) dispose of the case within the time standards. *Villarreal*, 994 S.W.2d at 630. See *O'Connor's Texas Forms*, FORM 7G:1.

(1) Failure to appear. The court has the authority under TRCP 165a(1) to dismiss a suit when a party seeking affirmative relief (generally the plaintiff) does not appear at trial or another hearing after receiving notice of the setting. TRCP 165a(1); *Alexander v. Lynda's Boutique*, 134 S.W.3d 845, 851 (Tex.2004); *see, e.g., Degen v. General Coatings, Inc.*, 705 S.W.2d 734, 735 (Tex.App.—Houston [14th Dist.] 1986, no writ) (docket call was not hearing or trial; court could not dismiss suit under TRCP 165a for failure to appear at docket call). Before dismissing the suit, the court must give the plaintiff notice of its intent to dismiss and a date and time for the dismissal

✪

hearing. TRCP 165a(1). See "Notice of Intent to Dismiss," §3, p. 660. A separate notice of intent to dismiss is not required, however, if the court specifies in the notice of trial or hearing that a party's failure to appear may result in dismissal. *E.g.*, *Alexander*, 134 S.W.3d at 851-52 (pretrial-conference order stated failure to appear could result in dismissal); *see, e.g.*, *Bridwell v. Mulder*, 315 S.W.3d 657, 659 (Tex.App.—Dallas 2010, no pet.) (notice of trial setting stated failure to appear would result in dismissal). See "Dismissal for failure to appear," ch. 10-F, §3.4.1, p. 827.

⑫   **(2) Failure to comply with time standards.** The court has the authority under TRCP 165a(2) to dismiss a suit that was not disposed of within the time limits in the Rules of Judicial Administration. *Polk v. Southwest Crossing Homeowners Ass'n*, 165 S.W.3d 89, 96 (Tex.App.—Houston [14th Dist.] 2005, pet. denied); *Johnson-Snodgrass v. KTAO, Inc.*, 75 S.W.3d 84, 87 (Tex.App.—Fort Worth 2002, pet. dism'd). Rule 6 of the Rules of Judicial Administration provides that civil jury cases (other than family-law cases) should be brought to trial or final disposition within 18 months after the appearance date, and civil nonjury cases within 12 months after the appearance date. TRJA 6.1(b). Contested family-law cases should be disposed of within six months, and uncontested family-law cases within three months. TRJA 6.1(c). See "Failure to comply with time standards," ch. 10-F, §3.4.2(2), p. 827.

    2. Inherent power. Under the common law, the trial court has the inherent power to dismiss—independent of its authority under TRCP 165a—when a plaintiff does not prosecute its case with diligence. *Villarreal*, 994 S.W.2d at 630; *Binner v. Limestone Cty.*, 129 S.W.3d 710, 712 (Tex.App.—Waco 2004, pet. denied); *see Rizk v. Mayad*, 603 S.W.2d 773, 776 (Tex.1980); *Veterans' Land Bd. v. Williams*, 543 S.W.2d 89, 90 (Tex.1976). Factors the court may consider when deciding whether to dismiss under its inherent power include (1) the length of time the case was on file, (2) the extent of activity in the case, (3) whether a trial setting was requested, and (4) whether there were any reasonable excuses for the delay. *Texas Mut. Ins. v. Olivas*, 323 S.W.3d 266, 274 (Tex.App.—El Paso 2010, no pet.); *Maida v. Fire Ins. Exch.*, 990 S.W.2d 836, 842 (Tex.App.—Fort Worth 1999, no pet.). See "Inherent power," ch. 10-F, §3.4.2(3), p. 828.

    §2.3 Sanctions. Some rules and code provisions permit the trial court to strike pleadings or dismiss a suit as a sanction. *See, e.g.*, CPRC §9.012(e) (groundless suit); TRCP 13 (frivolous pleadings), TRCP 215.2(b)(5) (discovery abuse). See "Groundless or frivolous pleadings," ch. 1-B, §3.3, p. 14; "Conduct that Justifies Sanctions," ch. 5-K, §5, p. 380; "Motion for Discovery Sanctions," ch. 6-A, §24, p. 455.

    §2.4 Frivolous indigent suit. The trial court has the authority to dismiss a suit filed by an indigent if the trial court finds that (1) the allegation of poverty in the affidavit is false or (2) the action is frivolous or malicious. See "Suit by Indigent," ch. 2-I, p. 173.

    §2.5 Objections to medical-malpractice suit. When a plaintiff in a medical-malpractice suit does not comply with the provisions for filing an expert report under CPRC §74.351(a), the defendant may move to dismiss under CPRC §74.351(b)(2). See *O'Connor's Texas Forms*, FORM 7G:1; *O'Connor's Texas COA*, "Expert report," ch. 20-A, §7.2, p. 626.

    §2.6 Improper grounds for dismissal.

    1. Conflict in trial settings. The trial court cannot dismiss a suit if the party informs the court that its attorney is in another trial. *E.g.*, *Dancy v. Daggett*, 815 S.W.2d 548, 549 (Tex.1991) (attorney in criminal trial in federal court); *Seigle v. Hollech*, 892 S.W.2d 201, 203-04 (Tex.App.—Houston [14th Dist.] 1994, no writ) (attorney in criminal trial in state court). *But see Burton v. Hoffman*, 959 S.W.2d 351, 352-53 (Tex.App.—Austin 1998, no pet.) (dismissal upheld when attorney knew of conflicting trial settings but waited until Friday before Monday setting to seek continuance, sent associate to argue motion when case was called, and refused to put on evidence when given opportunity).

    2. Special exceptions. A court cannot dismiss a party's suit after sustaining special exceptions without giving the party the opportunity to amend its pleadings to cure the defect. See "Court sustains special exceptions," ch. 3-G, §9.2.2, p. 252; *O'Connor's Texas Forms*, FORM 7G:1.

━━━━━━━━━━━━━━━━━━━━━━━━ ✦ ━━━━━━━━━━━━━━━━━━━━━━━━

3. Summary judgment. A summary judgment should not state that the case is dismissed. See "Resolve issues on the merits," ch. 7-B, §12.3.3, p. 624.

§3. NOTICE OF INTENT TO DISMISS

A trial court cannot dismiss a suit without giving the plaintiff notice of its intent to dismiss. *Alexander v. Lynda's Boutique*, 134 S.W.3d 845, 852 (Tex.2004); *Villarreal v. San Antonio Truck & Equip.*, 994 S.W.2d 628, 630 (Tex. 1999); *Creel v. District Atty.*, 818 S.W.2d 45, 46 (Tex.1991). A dismissal without notice violates the party's due-process rights and must be reversed. *Villarreal*, 994 S.W.2d at 630; *Smith v. McKee*, 145 S.W.3d 299, 302 (Tex.App.—Fort Worth 2004, no pet.); *Hubert v. Illinois State Assistance Comm'n*, 867 S.W.2d 160, 163 (Tex.App.—Houston [14th Dist.] 1993, no writ). For the exception, see "Dismissal without notice," §3.2, this page.

§3.1 Requirements.

1. Identify grounds for dismissal. The notice to dismiss must state whether the dismissal is (a) under TRCP 165a(1) for failure to appear, (b) under TRCP 165a(2) for failure to comply with the Supreme Court's time standards, or (c) under the court's inherent power for failure to diligently prosecute the suit. *See Alexander v. Lynda's Boutique*, 134 S.W.3d 845, 850 (Tex.2004); *Villarreal v. San Antonio Truck & Equip.*, 994 S.W.2d 628, 630-31 & n.4 (Tex.1999). *But see Steward v. Colonial Cas. Ins.*, 143 S.W.3d 161, 164 (Tex.App.—Waco 2004, no pet.) (notice sufficient even without specific reference to TRCP 165a or inherent power). The trial court cannot dismiss on a ground that is not stated in the notice of dismissal. *See Villarreal*, 994 S.W.2d at 631-32 (notice under TRCP 165a(1) does not support dismissal under TRCP 165a(2) or inherent power); *Johnson-Snodgrass v. KTAO, Inc.*, 75 S.W.3d 84, 88 (Tex.App.—Fort Worth 2002, pet. dism'd) (notice under TRCP 165a does not support dismissal under inherent power); *Lopez v. Harding*, 68 S.W.3d 78, 80-81 (Tex.App.—Dallas 2001, no pet.) (same).

2. Sent to party or attorney. TRCP 165a(1) requires the clerk of the trial court to mail a notice of the court's intention to dismiss the suit to either the attorneys of record or the parties (if pro se). See "Sent to attorney or party," ch. 1-H, §6.2, p. 55.

(1) Notice to attorneys. TRCP 165a(1) requires the clerk to send a notice of the court's intent to dismiss to "each attorney of record." *Ginn v. Forrester*, 282 S.W.3d 430, 432 (Tex.2009); *Alexander*, 134 S.W.3d at 851; *e.g., Cannon v. ICO Tubular Servs.*, 905 S.W.2d 380, 388 (Tex.App.—Houston [1st Dist.] 1995, no writ) (dismissal reversed because notices not sent to all attorneys of record); *see also Kenley v. Quintana Pet. Corp.*, 931 S.W.2d 318, 320-21 (Tex.App.—San Antonio 1996, writ denied) (dismissal reversed because notice sent to attorney of record but not attorney in charge).

(2) Notice to pro se party. When a party is not represented by counsel, the notice must be sent to the party. TRCP 165a(1); *General Elec. Co. v. Falcon Ridge Apts., Jt.V.*, 811 S.W.2d 942, 943 (Tex.1991).

3. State when & where. The notice of intent to dismiss must identify the date and place of the dismissal hearing. TRCP 165a(1); *Ginn*, 282 S.W.3d at 433; *Alexander*, 134 S.W.3d at 851; *Brown v. Brookshires Grocery Store*, 10 S.W.3d 351, 353 (Tex.App.—Dallas 1999, pet. denied); *Rohus v. Licona*, 942 S.W.2d 111, 112 (Tex.App.—Houston [1st Dist.] 1997, no writ). The notice cannot merely state that the case will be dismissed if a timely motion to retain is not filed. *Cannon*, 905 S.W.2d at 388.

§3.2 Dismissal without notice. When an indigent's claim has "no arguable basis in law," some courts of appeals have held that the trial court can dismiss without giving notice of its intent to dismiss. See "Suit by Indigent," ch. 2-I, p. 173.

§4. RESPONSE TO THREAT OF DISMISSAL

§4.1 Motion to retain. When a case is set on the court's dismissal docket for want of prosecution, the plaintiff should file a verified motion to retain. *See* TRCP 165a(1). See *O'Connor's Texas Forms*, FORM 7G:2. The motion to retain informs the court why the case should not be dismissed.

★

1. Grounds. The motion should show good cause for keeping the case on the docket and comply with any requirements stated in the notice of dismissal. *See* TRCP 165a(1); *see, e.g.*, *Villarreal v. San Antonio Truck & Equip.*, 994 S.W.2d 628, 632 (Tex.1999) (notice of dismissal only required D to appear and announce ready for trial; D did not have to show good cause); *Douglas v. American Title Co.*, No. 14-08-00676-CV (Tex.App.—Houston [14th Dist.] 2009, no pet.) (memo op.; 11-19-09) (dismissal without hearing was proper because P did not comply with requirements in notice that he file a verified motion to retain showing of good cause); *Nabelek v. Aldrich*, No. 14-04-00886-CV (Tex.App.—Houston [14th Dist.] 2006, no pet.) (memo op.; 6-22-06) (if court wanted D to argue good cause in motion to retain, court needed to state so in notice of dismissal).

2. Ruling. If the court retains the case, it must assign a trial date, and any continuances must be by court order. TRCP 165a(1). If the court dismisses the case, the plaintiff should file a motion to reinstate to inform the court why the dismissal was wrong. See "Motion to Reinstate After Dismissal for Want of Prosecution," ch. 10-F, p. 826; *O'Connor's Texas Forms*, FORM 10F:1.

§4.2 Response to motion to dismiss. When the dismissal is based on the defendant's motion to dismiss, the plaintiff should file a response to the motion challenging the grounds for dismissal; if the defendant's motion was verified and included affidavits, so should the plaintiff's response.

§5. HEARING

If the trial court dismisses a lawsuit without a hearing, the lack of a hearing raises due-process concerns. *See Creel v. District Atty.*, 818 S.W.2d 45, 46 (Tex.1991) (no notice or hearing). In a few situations, however, a motion to dismiss may be submitted for the trial court's ruling without a hearing.

§5.1 Bar to suit. If the trial court sustains a challenge to the continuation of the suit by a motion to abate, special exceptions, or some other motion, and the plaintiff fails to correct the problem, the case is ripe for dismissal. See "Options for defendant," ch. 3-G, §9.4, p. 253. In some cases, the hearing on the initial motion satisfies the requirements of due process (e.g., the hearing on a motion to abate). In other cases, another hearing is necessary to determine whether the plaintiff's attempt to correct the problem was sufficient to satisfy the court's order (e.g., if the plaintiff amends after special exceptions).

§5.2 DWOP. Before dismissing a case for want of prosecution, the court should conduct an oral hearing and give the plaintiff the opportunity to present evidence. *See* TRCP 165a(1) (court must send notice of intention to dismiss and date and place of dismissal); *Alexander v. Lynda's Boutique*, 134 S.W.3d 845, 852 (Tex.2004) (court must give party opportunity to be heard before dismissing); *Villarreal v. San Antonio Truck & Equip.*, 994 S.W.2d 628, 630 (Tex.1999) (same). If the court provided notice that failure to attend a hearing might result in dismissal for want of prosecution, the court may decide at that hearing to dismiss the case if the party seeking relief does not attend. *Alexander*, 134 S.W.3d at 852. The court is not required to hold a separate dismissal hearing to allow the party to explain its reasons for not appearing. *See id.*

§5.3 Sanctions. The court must hold a hearing before dismissing a case as a sanction. See "Motion for Sanctions," ch. 5-K, p. 377.

§5.4 Frivolous indigent suit. The courts of appeals disagree about whether a hearing is necessary before the court can dismiss a suit filed by an indigent under TRCP 145. See "Hearing," ch. 2-I, §5.1, p. 175.

§6. ORDER OF DISMISSAL

§6.1 Language of dismissal. When a court dismisses a case, the order should be drafted to dismiss the suit and nothing else. If the order purports to make any decision on the merits, it is reversible error. *Garcia-Marroquin v. Nueces Cty. Bail Bond Bd.*, 1 S.W.3d 366, 379 n.8 (Tex.App.—Corpus Christi 1999, no pet.); *Alvarado v. Magic Valley Elec. Co-op, Inc.*, 784 S.W.2d 729, 733 (Tex.App.—San Antonio 1990, writ denied). For example, the statement "plaintiff take nothing" constitutes a decision on the merits. *Garcia-Marroquin*, 1 S.W.3d at 379 n.8; *De La Garza v. Express-News Corp.*, 722 S.W.2d 251, 253 (Tex.App.—San Antonio 1986, no writ). It is unclear, however,

⭐

whether the statement "all other relief is expressly denied" constitutes a decision on the merits. *Compare Alvarado*, 784 S.W.2d at 733 (statement is decision on merits), *with Christensen v. Chase Bank USA*, 304 S.W.3d 548, 553-54 (Tex.App.—Dallas 2009, pet. denied) (statement is not decision on merits).

§6.2 Type of dismissal. There are two types of dismissals: with and without prejudice. If the order of dismissal does not state that the case is dismissed with prejudice, the case is presumed to be dismissed without prejudice. *Greenwood v. Tillamook Country Smoker, Inc.*, 857 S.W.2d 654, 656 (Tex.App.—Houston [1st Dist.] 1993, no writ). See "Effect of dismissal," §6.3, this page.

1. Without prejudice. In most cases, the trial court can dismiss only without prejudice.

(1) Failure to prosecute. The trial court should dismiss without prejudice for a failure to appear or prosecute under TRCP 165a or under the court's inherent power. *See Attorney Gen. v. Rideaux*, 838 S.W.2d 340, 342 (Tex.App.—Houston [1st Dist.] 1992, no writ) (failure to prosecute or to appear does not support dismissal with prejudice). Because a dismissal for want of prosecution is not a trial on the merits, a take-nothing judgment, which is the equivalent of a dismissal with prejudice, is inappropriate. *Attorney Gen. v. Abbs*, 812 S.W.2d 605, 608 (Tex.App.—Dallas 1991, no writ); *see Dick Poe Motors, Inc. v. DaimlerChrysler Corp.*, 169 S.W.3d 478, 484-85 (Tex.App.—El Paso 2005, no pet.); *Maldonado v. Puente*, 694 S.W.2d 86, 92 (Tex.App.—San Antonio 1985, no writ).

(2) No jurisdiction. The trial court should dismiss without prejudice after it sustains a plea to the jurisdiction. See "Without prejudice – most pleas," ch. 3-F, §6.1.2(1), p. 245.

(3) Special exceptions. In most cases, if a party refuses to amend after the court sustains special exceptions, the court should dismiss the objectionable claims without prejudice. See "Without prejudice," ch. 3-G, §9.5.3(2)(a), p. 254.

(4) Case moot. A dismissal for mootness is not a ruling on the merits; thus, a case dismissed for mootness should be dismissed without prejudice. *Ritchey v. Vasquez*, 986 S.W.2d 611, 612 (Tex.1999).

2. With prejudice. In some cases, the trial court may dismiss all or part of a plaintiff's suit with prejudice. See "Dismissal with prejudice," §6.3.1, this page.

(1) Sanctions. For groundless pleadings, the TRCPs permit a court to dismiss a suit or strike pleadings as a sanction. *See* TRCP 13, 215.2(b)(5); *see also* CPRC §9.012(e) (permits court to dismiss a party or strike pleadings for groundless suit). For frivolous pleadings, CPRC §10.004 does not list dismissal as one of the sanctions available. When a case is dismissed as a sanction, the sanction is referred to as a "death-penalty" sanction. See "Motion for Sanctions," ch. 5-K, p. 377.

(2) Special exceptions. In a few cases, if a party refuses to amend after the court sustains special exceptions, the court can dismiss with prejudice. See "With prejudice," ch. 3-G, §9.5.3(2)(b), p. 254.

§6.3 Effect of dismissal.

1. Dismissal with prejudice. A dismissal with prejudice to refiling is a final determination on the merits. *Mossler v. Shields*, 818 S.W.2d 752, 754 (Tex.1991); *see Garcia-Marroquin v. Nueces Cty. Bail Bond Bd.*, 1 S.W.3d 366, 379 n.8 (Tex.App.—Corpus Christi 1999, no pet.) (take-nothing judgment is equivalent to decision on merits). Such a dismissal has full res judicata and collateral-estoppel effect, barring relitigation of the same cause of action or issues between the same parties. *Williams v. TDCJ-Inst. Div.*, 176 S.W.3d 590, 594 (Tex.App.—Tyler 2005, pet. denied); *see Barr v. Resolution Trust Corp.*, 837 S.W.2d 627, 630-31 (Tex.1992); *see, e.g., Hammonds v. Holmes*, 559 S.W.2d 345, 346-47 (Tex.1977) (P argued that 2nd suit was brought in different capacity). The plaintiff can appeal the dismissal but cannot refile the lawsuit unless the dismissal is reversed on appeal. *See Mossler*, 818 S.W.2d at 754.

★

INVOLUNTARY DISMISSAL

NOTE

The notation "with prejudice to refiling" is not appropriate when the trial court dismisses a motion, as opposed to a lawsuit. **Republic Royalty Co. v. Evins**, *931 S.W.2d 338, 344 (Tex.App.—Corpus Christi 1996, orig. proceeding). Such a notation does not prevent the party from refiling the motion. Id. At most, it is an indication that the trial court will not look favorably on another motion asking for the same relief. Id.*

---

2. Dismissal without prejudice. A dismissal without prejudice to refiling is not a final determination on the merits. Thus, if the statute of limitations has not run, the case may be refiled without appealing the order of dismissal. *See* **Webb v. Jorns**, 488 S.W.2d 407, 409 (Tex.1972); **Denton v. Texas DPS Officers Ass'n**, 862 S.W.2d 785, 787 (Tex.App.—Austin 1993), *aff'd*, 897 S.W.2d 757 (Tex.1995); **Palmer v. Cantrell**, 747 S.W.2d 39, 40 (Tex. App.—Houston [1st Dist.] 1988, no writ).

§6.4 Preservation of error. If the trial court's order dismissed a suit with prejudice when only a dismissal without prejudice was appropriate, the notation "with prejudice" must be challenged in some postjudgment motion (e.g., a motion for new trial, motion to modify the judgment, or as part of a motion to reinstate); otherwise, the error is waived and the suit cannot be refiled. **El Paso Pipe & Sup. v. Mountain States Leasing, Inc.**, 617 S.W.2d 189, 190 (Tex.1981). See "MNT After Dismissal," ch. 10-B, §12, p. 802.

§7. REQUEST FOR FINDINGS OF FACT

If the trial court holds a hearing and receives evidence before dismissing the case, the plaintiff should ask the court to file findings of fact and conclusions of law. To determine when findings should be requested, see "After dismissal hearings," ch. 10-E, §2.2.2, p. 818.

§8. NOTICE OF DISMISSAL ORDER

§8.1 Notice of order. The clerk must send notice that the court signed an order of dismissal by first-class mail; certified mail is not required. TRCP 165a(1), 306a(3). However, the clerk is not required to affirmatively show in the record that such notice was mailed. **Ginn v. Forrester**, 282 S.W.3d 430, 433 (Tex.2009); **Alexander v. Lynda's Boutique**, 134 S.W.3d 845, 849 (Tex.2004); **General Elec. Co. v. Falcon Ridge Apts., Jt.V.**, 811 S.W.2d 942, 943 (Tex. 1991). The clerk is not required to send a copy of the dismissal order; a postcard notice of the dismissal is sufficient. See "Notice of Judgment," ch. 9-C, §5, p. 770. If the clerk does not send the notice, the postjudgment periods listed in TRCP 306a(1) are not affected, except as provided by TRCP 306a(4). TRCP 165a(1). If a party receives late notice of the judgment, TRCP 306a(4) permits the party to file a motion that effectively extends the time for post-trial motions. See "Motion to Extend Postjudgment Deadlines," ch. 10-G, p. 831.

§8.2 Notice to attorneys. The clerk must send notice of the dismissal to the "attorneys of record," which includes all attorneys of record for the parties. TRCP 165a(1), 306a(3); **Cannon v. ICO Tubular Servs.**, 905 S.W.2d 380, 388 (Tex.App.—Houston [1st Dist.] 1995, no writ); *cf.* TRCP 8 ("attorney in charge" includes only one attorney for each party). See "Attorney," ch. 1-H, §6.2.1, p. 55.

§8.3 Notice to pro se party. The clerk must send notice of the dismissal to any party who is not represented by counsel. TRCP 165a(1), 306a(3); **General Elec. Co. v. Falcon Ridge Apts., Jt.V.**, 811 S.W.2d 942, 943 (Tex.1991).

§9. REINSTATEMENT

§9.1 Appealing DWOP. See "Motion to Reinstate After Dismissal for Want of Prosecution," ch. 10-F, p. 826.

§9.2 Appealing other dismissals. See "Motion for New Trial," ch. 10-B, p. 789.

§9.3 Appealing late notice of dismissal order. See "Motion to Extend Postjudgment Deadlines," ch. 10-G, p. 831.

★

---

§10. REVIEW

The order dismissing a case is a final, appealable order. *See Stewart v. USA Custom Paint & Body Shop, Inc.*, 870 S.W.2d 18, 20 (Tex.1994) (properly executed order of dismissal is a judgment).

H. OFFER OF SETTLEMENT

§1. GENERAL

§1.1 Rule. TRCP 167. See CPRC ch. 42.

§1.2 Purpose. The purpose of the offer-of-settlement procedure is to encourage early settlements by shifting litigation costs to the party that rejected a fair settlement offer.

§1.3 Timetable & forms. Timetable, Offer of Settlement, p. 1228; *O'Connor's Texas Civil Forms* (2012), FORMS 7H.

§1.4 Other references. Carlson, *Offers of Settlement: Understanding the New Rules*, Law Practice After HB4: What Every Practitioner Needs to Know, Univ. of Texas CLE, Tab 3 (2003) (referred to as Carlson, *Offers of Settlement*); Harrison, *Texas Hold 'Em: Offer of Settlement Under Rule 167*, 70 Tex.B.J. 936 (Dec.2007) (referred to as Harrison, *Texas Hold 'Em*); *O'Connor's Texas Causes of Action* (2013) (*O'Connor's Texas COA*).

§1.5 Similar provisions in other jurisdictions. Other jurisdictions have cost-shifting procedures; of those, TRCP 167 most closely resembles Florida's procedure. Carlson, *Offers of Settlement*, at 2; *see* Fla. Stat. Ann. §768.79 (2005 & Supp.2008). FRCP 68 contains a somewhat different procedure, which can shift post-offer costs (but not attorney fees) to a party who rejects a settlement offer.

§2. AVAILABILITY & ELECTION OF SETTLEMENT PROCEDURE

§2.1 Availability.

1. Available. The offer-of-settlement procedure can be used only for claims seeking monetary damages in cases filed on or after January 1, 2004. *See* CPRC §42.002(a); TRCP 167.1, 167.2(d); *see also* CPRC §42.001(1) (definition of claim).

2. Not available. The offer-of-settlement procedure cannot be used in the following cases:

(1) Class actions. CPRC §42.002(b)(1); TRCP 167.1(a).

NOTE

Neither CPRC chapter 42 nor TRCP 167 makes it clear whether "class action" includes all cases filed as class actions, or only those cases certified as class actions.

---

(2) Shareholder derivative actions. CPRC §42.002(b)(2); TRCP 167.1(b).

(3) Actions by or against a governmental unit. CPRC §42.002(b)(3); TRCP 167.1(c); *see also* CPRC §42.001(4) (definition of governmental unit).

(4) Family Code actions. CPRC §42.002(b)(4); TRCP 167.1(d).

(5) Workers' compensation actions. CPRC §42.002(b)(5); TRCP 167.1(e).

(6) Actions filed in a justice-of-the-peace court or small-claims court. CPRC §42.002(b)(6); TRCP 167.1(f).

(7) Mediation, arbitration, or other ADR proceedings. TRCP 167.7.

⎯⎯⎯⎯⎯⎯⎯⎯⎯⎯⎯ ★ ⎯⎯⎯⎯⎯⎯⎯⎯⎯⎯⎯

(8)   Suits seeking equitable relief only. *See* CPRC §42.001(1) ("claim" is limited to suit for monetary relief); TRCP 167.1 (same).

(9)   Cases filed before January 1, 2004. Acts 2003, 78th Leg., R.S., ch. 204, §2.02, eff. Sept. 1, 2003.

§2.2 Other settlement offers. Neither TRCP 167 nor CPRC chapter 42 affects other settlement offers.

1. Under TRCP 167. Parties can make settlement offers in cases to which TRCP 167 does not apply, in cases in which TRCP 167 has not been invoked, and in cases that do not comply with TRCP 167's requirements. TRCP 167.7. A settlement offer made outside of TRCP 167 cannot be the basis for awarding litigation costs under TRCP 167 to any party. TRCP 167.7.

2. Under CPRC chapter 42. Parties can make settlement offers in cases to which CPRC chapter 42 does not apply and in cases that do not comply with CPRC §42.003's requirements. CPRC §42.002(d). A settlement offer made outside of CPRC chapter 42 cannot be the basis for awarding litigation costs under CPRC chapter 42 to any party. CPRC §42.002(e).

§3. DEFENDANT'S DECLARATION

The offer-of-settlement procedure is not automatically available. Before either party (plaintiff or defendant) can make a settlement offer under TRCP 167, the defendant must file a declaration invoking the rule. CPRC §42.002(c); TRCP 167.2(a). Only a defendant can invoke the offer-of-settlement procedure. CPRC §42.002(c); TRCP 167.2(a).

⎯⎯⎯⎯⎯⎯⎯⎯⎯⎯⎯⎯⎯⎯⎯⎯⎯⎯⎯⎯⎯⎯⎯⎯⎯⎯⎯⎯⎯⎯⎯⎯⎯⎯⎯⎯
CAUTION
When filing a counterclaim or a TRCP 167 declaration, the defendant may end up paying the plaintiff's litigation costs. Therefore, a defendant should carefully consider whether to file a counterclaim or declaration.
⎯⎯⎯⎯⎯⎯⎯⎯⎯⎯⎯⎯⎯⎯⎯⎯⎯⎯⎯⎯⎯⎯⎯⎯⎯⎯⎯⎯⎯⎯⎯⎯⎯⎯⎯⎯

§3.1 Definition of defendant. A defendant is a person from whom a party seeks monetary damages, including a counterdefendant (i.e., a plaintiff subject to monetary damages in a counterclaim), cross-defendant, or third-party defendant. CPRC §42.001(3); *see* TRCP 167.1, 167.2(a).

§3.2 Multiple defendants. In a case with multiple defendants, the procedure applies only to the defendant filing the declaration. *See* CPRC §42.002(c); TRCP 167.2(a).

§3.3 Deadline. The defendant must file a TRCP 167 declaration at least 45 days before trial. TRCP 167.2(a). On a motion based on good cause, the court may sign a pretrial order modifying this time limit. TRCP 167.5(a). See Timetable, Offer of Settlement, p. 1228.

§3.4 No withdrawal. TRCP 167 does not provide for the withdrawal or revocation of a declaration once it has been filed. Harrison, *Texas Hold 'Em*, 70 Tex.B.J. at 937.

§4. SETTLEMENT OFFER

Once the defendant has invoked TRCP 167 by filing a declaration, either party may make a settlement offer under the offer-of-settlement procedure.

§4.1 In writing. A settlement offer must be in writing and must state that it is made under CPRC chapter 42 and TRCP 167. CPRC §42.003(a)(1), (a)(2); TRCP 167.2(b)(1), (b)(2); *see* CPRC §42.001(6).

§4.2 Parties. A settlement offer must identify the party or parties making the offer and the party or parties to whom the offer is made. TRCP 167.2(b)(3).

§4.3 Terms.

1. Monetary claims. A settlement offer must state the amount for which the monetary claims—including attorney fees, interest, and costs—between the parties may be settled. TRCP 167.2(b)(4); *see* CPRC §42.003(a)(3).

★

2. No nonmonetary claims. A settlement offer must not include nonmonetary claims or other claims that fall outside TRCP 167. TRCP 167.2(d); *see also* TRCP 167.1 (listing claims that fall outside TRCP 167).

3. Other conditions. A settlement offer may require the offeree to meet other reasonable conditions, including executing releases, indemnities, or other documents. TRCP 167.2(c). A condition is presumed reasonable unless an offeree objects in writing to the condition before the deadline for acceptance. *Id.* If an offeree objects to an offer's condition, that offer cannot be the basis for cost-shifting unless the trial court determines that the condition was reasonable. *Id.*

§4.4 Deadlines.

1. Making the offer. A settlement offer must be made as follows:

(1) After the defendant files a TRCP 167 declaration. TRCP 167.2(e)(1). See "Defendant's Declaration," §3, p. 665.

(2) More than 60 days after both the plaintiff and defendant have appeared in the case. TRCP 167.2(e)(2).

(3) More than 14 days before the case is set for a conventional trial on the merits (not summary judgment), unless the settlement offer answers an earlier offer and is made within seven days after the earlier offer. TRCP 167.2(e)(3).

2. Accepting the offer. The settlement offer must state an acceptance deadline. CPRC §42.003(a)(4); TRCP 167.2(b)(5). The acceptance deadline must be at least 14 days after the offer is served. TRCP 167.2(b)(5).

3. Modifying the deadlines. On a motion based on good cause, the court may sign a pretrial order modifying the time limits for making an offer. TRCP 167.5(a).

§4.5 Service.
A settlement offer must be served on all parties to whom it is made. CPRC §42.003(a)(5); TRCP 167.2(b)(6); *see* TRCP 21a.

§4.6 Filing.
A settlement offer does not need to be filed with the court. CPRC §42.003(b).

§4.7 Designating or joining additional party.
An offeror may designate a responsible third party or join another party after making a TRCP 167 offer. *See* TRCP 167.3(d). See "Third-party petitions," ch. 3-E, §7.3, p. 235; "RTP," ch. 3-E, §7.4, p. 235. The offer cannot be the basis for awarding litigation costs if the offeree files a timely objection after service of the pleading or designation. See "To additional parties," §5.2.2, this page.

§5. WITHDRAWAL, ACCEPTANCE, OBJECTIONS & REJECTION

§5.1 Withdrawing the offer.
Before a settlement offer is accepted, an offeror may withdraw it by serving written notice of the withdrawal on the offeree. TRCP 167.3(a). The withdrawal takes effect when the notice is served. *Id.*; *see* TRCP 21a. Once the offer is withdrawn, it cannot be accepted and cannot be the basis for cost-shifting. TRCP 167.3(a).

§5.2 Objecting to the offer.

1. To the conditions. An offeree may object to a settlement offer's conditions by serving written notice on the offeror before the acceptance deadline. TRCP 167.2(c). If the offeree objects to the offer on this ground, the offer cannot be the basis for cost-shifting unless the court finds that the conditions were reasonable. *Id.*

2. To additional parties. If an offeror joins another party or designates a responsible third party after making an offer, the offeree may file an objection to the offer within 15 days after service of the pleading or designation. TRCP 167.3(d). If the offeree objects to the offer on this ground, the offer cannot be the basis for cost-shifting. *Id.*

§5.3 Accepting the offer.
An offeree may accept a settlement offer by serving written notice on the offeror on or before the offer's acceptance deadline and before the offer is withdrawn. TRCP 167.3(b). When the offer is accepted, either party may file the offer and acceptance and ask the court to enforce the settlement. *Id.* See "Consent judgment," ch. 7-I, §4.2.1, p. 673.

✯

§5.4 Rejecting the offer. An offeree may reject a settlement offer by serving written notice on the offeror on or before the acceptance deadline. TRCP 167.3(c). An offer that is not withdrawn or accepted on or before the acceptance deadline is deemed rejected. *Id.*

§5.5 Making successive offers. A party may make another offer after having made or rejected an earlier offer. TRCP 167.2(f). Rejection of a later offer can be the basis for cost-shifting only if the offer was more favorable to the offeree than any other offer. *Id.*

§6. LITIGATION COSTS

Litigation costs are defined as the money spent and the obligations incurred that directly relate to the action in a settlement offer. CPRC §42.001(5); TRCP 167.4(c). Litigation costs include (1) court costs, (2) reasonable deposition costs, (3) reasonable fees for no more than two testifying expert witnesses, and (4) reasonable attorney fees. CPRC §42.001(5); TRCP 167.4(c). See *O'Connor's Texas COA*, "Court Costs," ch. 44, p. 1341; "Attorney Fees," ch. 45, p. 1349. An offeror can recover litigation costs from a rejecting offeree if the judgment to be rendered on the claim is significantly less favorable to the offeree than the rejected offer. CPRC §42.004(a); TRCP 167.4(a). For a discussion of the practical effects of and strategies for making or rejecting a settlement offer, see Harrison, *Texas Hold 'Em*, 70 Tex.B.J. at 938-40.

NOTE

Reasonable deposition costs are recoverable litigation costs only for cases filed on or after September 1, 2011. TRCP 167.4(c)(2); see Acts 2011, 82nd Leg., R.S., ch. 203, §§4.01, 6.01, 6.02, eff. Sept. 1, 2011.

---

§6.1 Significantly less favorable. A judgment is significantly less favorable in either of the following situations:

1. Plaintiff rejected offer. The judgment is significantly less favorable to the plaintiff if the plaintiff rejected the defendant's offer and the award is less than 80% of the rejected offer. CPRC §42.004(b)(1); TRCP 167.4(b)(1).

2. Defendant rejected offer. The judgment is significantly less favorable to the defendant if the defendant rejected the plaintiff's offer and the award is more than 120% of the rejected offer. CPRC §42.004(b)(2); TRCP 167.4(b)(2).

EXAMPLE

Assume that the jury awards the plaintiff $120,000 in damages. If the plaintiff rejected a settlement offer from the defendant that was over $150,000 (80% of $150,000 = $120,000), the verdict is "significantly less favorable" to the plaintiff than the defendant's settlement offer, and the plaintiff must pay the defendant's litigation costs. On the other hand, if the defendant rejected a settlement offer from the plaintiff that was under $100,000 (120% of $100,000 = $120,000), the verdict is "significantly less favorable" to the defendant than the plaintiff's settlement offer, and the defendant must pay the plaintiff's litigation costs.

---

§6.2 Calculating costs.

1. After rejection. The offeror may recover only those litigation costs it incurred between the date of rejection and the date of judgment. CPRC §42.004(c); TRCP 167.4(a).

2. Cap on costs. The judgment damages limit the recoverable litigation costs.

(1) Cases filed before 9-1-11. For an action commenced before September 1, 2011, the recoverable litigation costs cannot exceed the total of 50% of the plaintiff's economic damages, plus 100% of the plaintiff's

⎯⎯⎯⎯⎯⎯⎯⎯⎯⎯ ★ ⎯⎯⎯⎯⎯⎯⎯⎯⎯⎯

noneconomic, exemplary, and additional damages, minus any statutory or contractual liens connected to the occurrences or incidents giving rise to the claim. TRCP 167.4(d)(1); *see* Acts 2011, 82nd Leg., R.S., ch. 203, §§4.04, 6.01, 6.02, eff. Sept. 1, 2011.

EXAMPLE

Assume the defendant makes a $200,000 settlement offer, which the plaintiff rejects. The plaintiff then receives a verdict for $100,000 in economic damages and $20,000 in noneconomic damages. This verdict is significantly less favorable to the plaintiff than the settlement offer ($120,000 is less than $160,000, which is 80% of $200,000). The defendant may therefore recover up to $70,000 in litigation costs (50% of $100,000 = $50,000, plus 100% of $20,000). If the defendant had at least $70,000 in litigation costs, the plaintiff's total recovery would be $50,000 ($120,000 less a $70,000 offset). See "Defendant's costs awarded as offset," §6.2.3, this page.

---

(2) Cases filed on or after 9-1-11. For an action commenced on or after September 1, 2011, the recoverable litigation costs cannot exceed the total amount the plaintiff recovers or would recover before (1) adding an award of litigation costs under CPRC chapter 42 or TRCP 167 in favor of the plaintiff or (2) subtracting as an offset an award of litigation costs under CPRC chapter 42 or TRCP 167 in favor of the defendant. CPRC §42.004(d); TRCP 167.4(d)(2). Thus, the plaintiff could have to pay its entire award as recoverable litigation costs to the defendant; similarly, the defendant could have to pay litigation costs up to the amount of the plaintiff's verdict.

EXAMPLE

Assume the defendant makes a $200,000 settlement offer, which the plaintiff rejects. The plaintiff then receives a verdict for $120,000 in damages. This verdict is significantly less favorable to the plaintiff than the settlement offer ($120,000 is less than $160,000, which is 80% of $200,000). The defendant may therefore recover up to $120,000 in litigation costs. If the defendant had at least $120,000 in litigation costs, the plaintiff's total recovery would be $0 ($120,000 less a $120,000 offset). See "Defendant's costs awarded as offset," §6.2.3, this page.

---

3. Defendant's costs awarded as offset. If the defendant recovers litigation costs, those costs are awarded in the judgment as an offset against the plaintiff's recovery. CPRC §42.004(g); TRCP 167.4(g).

4. No double recovery. An offeror that recovers litigation costs under another law (e.g., CPRC chapter 38) cannot recover the same litigation costs under TRCP 167. CPRC §42.004(e); TRCP 167.4(e).

5. No costs to rejecting party. If a party is entitled to litigation costs under another law (e.g., CPRC chapter 38) but that party rejects a TRCP 167 settlement offer and litigation costs are imposed against it, the party cannot recover under the other law the litigation costs it incurred after rejecting the offer. CPRC §42.004(f); TRCP 167.4(f). In other words, a party that rejects a fair settlement offer may lose some of its own litigation costs as well as having to pay those of the other side.

§6.3 Awarding costs. The court will award TRCP 167 litigation costs by incorporating them with the jury's verdict into the final judgment. *See* TRCP 167.4(a).

1. Post-trial hearing. The court should hold a post-trial hearing on the amount and reasonableness of the litigation costs and on the reasonableness of any conditions in the rejected offer.

(1) Amount & reasonableness of litigation costs. On request, the court must hold a post-trial hearing for evidence before awarding litigation costs. TRCP 167.5(c). The court should determine the amount of litigation costs to be awarded and should consider any challenge to their reasonableness. *See* TRCP 167.4, 167.5. The court should determine reasonableness using the factors in ***Arthur Andersen & Co. v. Perry Equip. Corp.***, 945

⎯⎯⎯⎯⎯⎯⎯⎯⎯ ✦ ⎯⎯⎯⎯⎯⎯⎯⎯⎯

S.W.2d 812, 818 (Tex.1997), and Rule 1.04 of the Texas Disciplinary Rules of Professional Conduct. See "Attorney Fees from Adverse Party," ch. 1-H, §10, p. 62. If the reasonableness of the litigation costs is challenged and the court finds the costs to be reasonable, the court must award an additional amount to cover any attorney fees and expenses incurred in responding to post-trial discovery on reasonableness. TRCP 167.5(b).

(2) **Reasonableness of conditions.** When an offeree properly objected to an offer's condition (e.g., that the offeree execute a release, indemnity, or other document as part of the settlement), no award of litigation costs can be based on that offer unless the court determines that the condition was reasonable. TRCP 167.2(c). Thus, before the court awards litigation costs based on an offer with conditions that the offeree properly objected to, the court must conduct a hearing for evidence to determine the reasonableness of the conditions. *See id.* See "To the conditions," §5.2.1, p. 666.

2. Post-trial discovery. On a motion based on good cause, the rejecting party may conduct post-trial discovery on the reasonableness of the offeror's costs. TRCP 167.5(b).

3. Admissibility of evidence. Evidence relating to a settlement offer is admissible only as needed to enforce the settlement agreement or to obtain litigation costs. TRCP 167.6; *see* TRE 408. The provisions of TRCP 167 cannot be made known to the jury. TRCP 167.6.

4. Award mandatory. Normally, to recover attorney fees, a party must plead for their recovery in a petition or answer. *See Swate v. Medina Cmty. Hosp.*, 966 S.W.2d 693, 701 (Tex.App.—San Antonio 1998, pet. denied) (unless mandatory statute says otherwise, court's jurisdiction to render judgment for attorney fees must be invoked by pleadings). But TRCP 167's award of attorney fees (and other litigation costs) is mandatory once TRCP 167 is properly invoked. Thus, even when a party's petition or answer does not ask for attorney fees or other litigation costs, the court must award litigation costs against the party that rejected a TRCP 167 offer. *See* TRCP 167.4(a).

I. SETTLEMENT OF THE SUIT

§1. GENERAL

§1.1 Rules. TRCP 11, 76a, 97(a). See CPRC §§32.001-32.003.

§1.2 Purpose. When parties settle a lawsuit, they resolve the dispute according to the terms of a private contract. *See Montanaro v. Montanaro*, 946 S.W.2d 428, 431 (Tex.App.—Corpus Christi 1997, no writ). The settlement brings the lawsuit to a conclusion, preventing the expense and uncertainty of litigation. Public policy favors the amicable settlement of controversies. *Transport Ins. v. Faircloth*, 898 S.W.2d 269, 280 (Tex.1995).

§1.3 Forms. *O'Connor's Texas Civil Forms* (2012), FORMS 7H, 7I:1.

§1.4 Other references. Holman & Hogan, *Contribution, Indemnity, Joint & Several Liability, & Pitfalls of Multi-Party Settlements*, State Bar of Texas CLE, Advanced Personal Injury Law Course, Tab GG (1998); Shanahan, *The High-Low Agreement*, 33 For the Defense 25 (July 1991); Quinley & Khin, *We Love Settlements: An Insurer's Perspective*, For the Defense 26 (Jan.1991); Rubendall, *I Hate Settlements: A Defense Lawyer's Lament*, 32 For the Defense 11 (Feb.1990); Williams, *Fear of Fairness: A Comment on Williams v. Glash*, 24 Trial Lawyers Forum 27 (Nov.1990); *O'Connor's Texas Causes of Action* (2013) (*O'Connor's Texas COA*).

§2. ADVANTAGES OF SETTLEMENT VS. TRIAL

Some of the advantages of settlement over trial are the following: a trial will involve the public airing of the dispute and will delay its resolution; all trials are expensive, even short ones; a trial leaves the outcome of the dispute in the hands of the judge and jury; a trial affords limited types of relief—money damages and injunctive relief; by settlement, the parties may be able to construct remedies that give both parties something and permit both parties to avoid the possibility of a total loss. *See Transport Ins. v. Faircloth*, 898 S.W.2d 269, 280 (Tex.1995). For contrasting views, compare the two articles *We Love Settlements* and *I Hate Settlements*, cited in "Other references," §1.4, this page.

⎯⎯⎯⎯⎯⎯⎯⎯⎯⎯⎯⎯⎯⎯⎯ ✰ ⎯⎯⎯⎯⎯⎯⎯⎯⎯⎯⎯⎯⎯⎯⎯

§3. PROVISIONS IN SETTLEMENT AGREEMENT

Settlement agreements are governed by the law of contracts. *Schlumberger Tech. v. Swanson*, 959 S.W.2d 171, 178 (Tex.1997); *Williams v. Glash*, 789 S.W.2d 261, 264 (Tex.1990). See *O'Connor's Texas Forms*, FORM 7I:1.

§3.1 Release. A release is a contractual surrender by one party of its cause of action against the other party. *Lloyd v. Ray*, 606 S.W.2d 545, 547 (Tex.App.—San Antonio 1980, writ ref'd n.r.e.). A release extinguishes a claim or cause of action, the same way a judgment would. *Dresser Indus. v. Page Pet., Inc.*, 853 S.W.2d 505, 508 (Tex.1993); *Derr Constr. Co. v. City of Houston*, 846 S.W.2d 854, 858 (Tex.App.—Houston [14th Dist.] 1992, no writ). A release must meet the fair-notice requirements—it must be conspicuous and specific. *Dresser Indus.*, 853 S.W.2d at 509.

1. Identity of parties. To be effective, a release must identify the parties to the release.

(1) Releasing party. A release binds only the person or entity specifically identified or named in the release as the releasing party. Both parties and nonparties may release claims by settlement agreements. For example, spouses and other family members may relinquish possible causes of action that have not been asserted. When a minor releases rights, if there is a conflict of interest on the part of the child's parents or guardians, the minor must be represented by a guardian ad litem, who determines and advises the court whether the settlement is in the best interests of the minor. See "Appointing a Guardian Ad Litem Under TRCP 173," ch. 1-I, §3, p. 69.

PRACTICE TIP

The settlement agreement should always provide that both parties release each other, instead of just providing that the plaintiff releases the defendant. See TRCP 97(a) (agreed judgment between some parties before final disposition on the merits of other claims does not bar the claims of any other party if there is no written consent that the judgment will act as a bar).

---

(2) Released party. A release discharges only the person or entity specifically identified or named in the release. *E.g., Angus Chem. Co. v. IMC Fertilizer, Inc.*, 939 S.W.2d 138, 139 (Tex.1997) (release of tortfeasor did not release tortfeasor's insurer); *McMillen v. Klingensmith*, 467 S.W.2d 193, 196 (Tex.1971) (release of one doctor did not release other doctors); *see also Knutson v. Morton Foods, Inc.*, 603 S.W.2d 805, 806 (Tex.1980) (release of employee did not release principal under doctrine of respondeat superior). A person is specifically identified when the language is sufficiently particular so that a stranger to the release could readily identify the released party even though the party's name is missing. *E.g., Duncan v. Cessna Aircraft Co.*, 665 S.W.2d 414, 419-20 (Tex.1984) (release of "any other corporations ... responsible" in settlement with pilot did not release manufacturer of aircraft); *Frazer v. Texas Farm Bur. Mut. Ins.*, 4 S.W.3d 819, 823-24 (Tex.App.—Houston [1st Dist.] 1999, no pet.) (release of insurer "and its affiliated companies" sufficiently identified insurer's underwriters); *Lloyd*, 606 S.W.2d at 546-47 & n.1 (release of one doctor and "all other persons, firms and corporations" did not release a second, unnamed doctor). In a few situations, a release also releases entities not specifically named. *See, e.g., Winkler v. Kirkwood Atrium Office Park*, 816 S.W.2d 111, 113-14 (Tex.App.—Houston [14th Dist.] 1991, writ denied) (release of health club from any injuries suffered while participating in its programs released all individuals and entities involved in its operation, maintenance, and administration).

(3) Attorneys. Attorneys representing parties in a consent judgment are bound by that judgment. *Newman v. Link*, 889 S.W.2d 288, 289 (Tex.1994). If the attorneys have complaints about attorney fees and ad litem costs, they must object before the judgment becomes final. *See id.*

(4) Insurer. If the parties intend to release the defendant's insurer, the insurer should be named as a released party in the settlement papers. In Texas, if the injured party cannot sue the tortfeasor, it cannot sue the tortfeasor's insurer. *Angus Chem.*, 939 S.W.2d at 138. Thus, when an injured party releases the tortfeasor, it can no longer sue the tortfeasor's insurer in Texas. *Id.* However, the release of the tortfeasor does not prevent the injured party from suing the tortfeasor's insurer in another jurisdiction. *E.g., id.* at 138-39 (Louisiana law permits direct suits against insurers).

★

2. Dispute & released claim. The settlement agreement should describe the dispute and the extent to which the release is intended to settle it. A release discharges only the claims specifically mentioned in the release. *Keck, Mahin & Cate v. National Un. Fire Ins.*, 20 S.W.3d 692, 698 (Tex.2000); *Memorial Med. Ctr. v. Keszler*, 943 S.W.2d 433, 434-35 (Tex.1997); *Victoria Bank & Trust Co. v. Brady*, 811 S.W.2d 931, 938 (Tex.1991); *see Baty v. Protech Ins. Agency, Inc.*, 63 S.W.3d 841, 854-55 (Tex.App.—Houston [14th Dist.] 2001, pet. denied) (release that does not list one of the claims "strongly suggests" parties did not intend to release that claim). If the claim is not clearly within the subject matter of the release, it is not discharged. *Brady*, 811 S.W.2d at 938. The release does not have to specifically describe each potential cause of action to be released. *Keck, Mahin & Cate*, 20 S.W.3d at 698; *Kalyanaram v. Burck*, 225 S.W.3d 291, 299 (Tex.App.—El Paso 2006, no pet.); *see Memorial Med. Ctr.*, 943 S.W.2d at 434-35. The release may be broad (releasing all claims, known or unknown) or narrow (releasing only the particular claims asserted in the lawsuit). *See, e.g., Keck, Mahin & Cate*, 20 S.W.3d at 698 (all claims for malpractice attributable to legal services); *Memorial Med. Ctr.*, 943 S.W.2d at 435 (all present and future claims relating to doctor's relationship with hospital); *Brady*, 811 S.W.2d at 938 (claims attributable to specific loan transaction between bank and customer); *Kalyanaram*, 225 S.W.3d at 299-300 (all known and unknown claims arising from employment relationship).

PRACTICE TIP

*If the release is a separate instrument from the settlement agreement, make sure the description of the released claims is stated in identical language in both the release and the settlement agreement. In **Memorial Med. Ctr.**, 943 S.W.2d at 434, the terms were much broader in the release than in the settlement agreement, and the court held that the defendant was released according to the terms stated in the release, not in the settlement agreement.*

---

3. Consideration. The settlement agreement should state the consideration for the release. *See Torchia v. Aetna Cas. & Sur. Co.*, 804 S.W.2d 219, 223 (Tex.App.—El Paso 1991, writ denied) (release stated consideration and identified claims released). The financial inadequacy of the compensation is not a sufficient reason to set aside a release. *Id.* Although in most cases the consideration is the payment of money damages, the settlement of a contested lawsuit may itself be sufficient consideration to support a settlement agreement. *Schuh v. Schuh*, 453 S.W.2d 203, 204 (Tex.App.—Dallas 1970, no writ); *see also Adams v. Petrade Int'l*, 754 S.W.2d 696, 723 (Tex.App.—Houston [1st Dist.] 1988, writ denied) (release is surrender of cause of action, which may be given for inadequate or no consideration).

§3.2 Other provisions.

1. Assignment of causes of action. If the identity of persons to be released is unknown, the plaintiff may assign any unreleased claims to the released parties. Such an assignment prevents the plaintiff from later suing any other persons without authority from the owner of the claim. *Duke v. Brookshire Grocery Co.*, 568 S.W.2d 470, 472 (Tex.App.—Texarkana 1978, no writ). A settling defendant that is jointly responsible for the plaintiff's personal injuries cannot preserve contribution rights against codefendants by purchasing the plaintiff's claim. *Beech Aircraft Corp. v. Jinkins*, 739 S.W.2d 19, 22 (Tex.1987); *see International Proteins Corp. v. Ralston-Purina Co.*, 744 S.W.2d 932, 934 (Tex.1988); *Filter Fab, Inc. v. Delauder*, 2 S.W.3d 614, 617 (Tex.App.—Houston [14th Dist.] 1999, no pet.).

2. Indemnity. Settlement agreements may contain provisions by which the plaintiff agrees to indemnify the defendant. An indemnity agreement is a promise by the indemnitor to safeguard or hold the indemnitee harmless against existing or future loss or liability, or both. *Dresser Indus. v. Page Pet., Inc.*, 853 S.W.2d 505, 508 (Tex. 1993); *Wallerstein v. Spirt*, 8 S.W.3d 774, 779 (Tex.App.—Austin 1999, no pet.). Unlike a release, which bars a cause of action, an indemnity provision creates a potential cause of action between the indemnitee and the indemnitor. *Wallerstein*, 8 S.W.3d at 779. By the agreement, the plaintiff accepts liability for any claims that third parties may assert against the settling defendant arising from the matter being settled. Thus, the indemnity protects that defendant against liability on cross-claims and other claims. The agreement creates a circular pattern of indemnity that

---

★

---

extinguishes the plaintiff's cause of action. For example, in *Bonniwell v. Beech Aircraft Corp.*, 663 S.W.2d 816, 819 (Tex.1984), the plaintiffs settled with defendant-operator and agreed to indemnify it from any further liability. As the court explained, any judgment the plaintiffs obtained against the defendant-manufacturer would be collected from defendant-operator, which would be reimbursed by the plaintiffs. *Bonniwell*, 663 S.W.2d at 819; *see also Phillips Pipe Line Co. v. McKown*, 580 S.W.2d 435, 440 (Tex.App.—Tyler 1979, writ ref'd n.r.e.) (when landowner released contractor, he also released pipeline owner because contractor had a duty to indemnify pipeline owner). A defendant who is a party to a settlement agreement cannot then seek indemnity from its codefendants. *Trussway, Inc. v. Wetzel*, 928 S.W.2d 174, 176 (Tex.App.—Beaumont 1996, writ denied).

3. Covenants not to execute. Settlement agreements may contain covenants not to execute on the judgment against the settling defendant. Covenants not to execute are often made between a plaintiff and a defendant when the defendant's insurer has refused to provide a defense. These covenants are usually given in exchange for an assignment to the plaintiff of the defendant's rights against its insurer. Covenants not to execute are invalid if (1) they are made before the plaintiff's claim is adjudicated in a full adversarial trial, (2) the defendant's insurer tendered a defense, and (3) the insurer has either accepted coverage or made a good-faith effort to adjudicate coverage issues before adjudication of the plaintiff's claim. *State Farm Fire & Cas. Co. v. Gandy*, 925 S.W.2d 696, 714 (Tex.1996).

4. Confidentiality. Settlement agreements may contain confidentiality provisions. These agreements, however, are subject to the restrictions in TRCP 76a(2)(b). Under TRCP 76a(2)(b), the parties cannot by their settlement agreements, without notice and hearing, seal information that relates to matters that may adversely affect the general public health or safety, the administration of public office, or the operation of government. See "Motion to Seal Court Records," ch. 5-L, p. 394.

5. Structured payment. Settlement agreements may contain a provision for structured payment of damages by which the plaintiff receives deferred payments rather than one lump sum. The benefit to the plaintiff is the assurance of support for a number of years; the benefit to the defendant is the reduced cost of settlement because of delayed payments. CPRC chapter 139 covers structured settlements in personal-injury cases.

(1) Offer must be in writing. If a plaintiff is either incapacitated, as defined by Probate Code §601(14), or substantially disabled as a result of the personal injury, an offer of structured settlement must be in writing and presented to the plaintiff's attorney. *See* CPRC §§139.002, 139.101.

(2) Offer must be explained. Before the offer expires, the plaintiff's attorney must explain to the plaintiff or the plaintiff's representative the terms, conditions, and other attributes of the settlement agreement and the appropriateness of the settlement under the circumstances. CPRC §139.102(b).

6. Agreement to vacate judgment. Settlement agreements may contain an agreement to vacate the judgments of the trial court and the court of appeals in the case. *Houston Cable TV, Inc. v. Inwood W. Civic Ass'n*, 860 S.W.2d 72, 73 (Tex.1993). A settlement agreement does not require an appellate court to vacate its opinion. *Crown Life Ins. v. Casteel*, 22 S.W.3d 378, 392 (Tex.2000). In most cases, the opinion will not be vacated, just the judgment. *Houston Cable*, 860 S.W.2d at 73. A private agreement between litigants does not operate to vacate a court's writing on matters of public importance. *Id.*

7. Reservation of right to appeal. Settlement agreements may contain a reservation of the right to appeal some issues. *See Coble v. City of Mansfield*, 134 S.W.3d 449, 453 (Tex.App.—Fort Worth 2004, no pet.). An opinion issued in an appeal from a judgment rendered on a settlement agreement does not constitute an advisory opinion.

8. Reservation of other claims. Settlement agreements may contain a reservation of the right to pursue other claims. *See, e.g., Transportation Ins. v. Moriel*, 879 S.W.2d 10, 15-16 (Tex.1994) (settlement release preserved right to sue for bad faith and punitive damages); *Indiana Lumbermen's Mut. Ins. v. State*, 1 S.W.3d 264, 268 (Tex.App.—Fort Worth 1999, pet. denied) (party reserved its right to defend against another lawsuit by the State).

✭

---

9. Agreed judgment or dismissal order. The settlement agreement can state that the parties will ask the court to render an agreed judgment or dismiss the case. *See* CPRC §154.071; *Compania Financiara Libano, S.A. v. Simmons*, 53 S.W.3d 365, 368 (Tex.2001). If the parties agree to memorialize the settlement by an agreed judgment, the judgment should accurately state the terms of the settlement. *Vickrey v. American Youth Camps, Inc.*, 532 S.W.2d 292, 292 (Tex.1976). However, it is not necessary for the judgment to incorporate all the terms of the settlement agreement; even unincorporated terms can be enforced. *Compania Financiara*, 53 S.W.3d at 368.

§3.3 Relationships between settling parties. Once a settlement agreement is executed, it extinguishes any duty of good faith and fair dealing that existed between the parties before settlement. *See, e.g., Stewart Title Guar. Co. v. Aiello*, 941 S.W.2d 68, 71-72 (Tex.1997) (insurer no longer had duties to insured after settlement). The parties become judgment-creditor and judgment-debtor, with all the remedies for enforcing the judgment. *See id.*

§4. ENFORCEABLE SETTLEMENT AGREEMENTS

§4.1 Agreement to settle.

1. Presuit settlement agreement. An oral agreement to settle a dispute before a lawsuit is filed is not governed by TRCP 11. *See Estate of Pollack v. McMurrey*, 858 S.W.2d 388, 393 (Tex.1993) (TRCP 11 applies only to agreements in pending suits). An oral agreement to settle before suit is filed is governed by the law of contracts and by Business & Commerce Code §26.01, the statute of frauds. *See Carter v. Allstate Ins.*, 962 S.W.2d 268, 270-71 (Tex.App.—Houston [1st Dist.] 1998, pet. denied) (agreement by insurer to settle before suit was enforceable); *see also Banda v. Garcia*, 955 S.W.2d 270, 272 (Tex.1997) (court assumed without discussion that oral pretrial settlement agreement was enforceable).

2. Settlement agreement after suit filed. To be enforceable, a settlement agreement must comply with TRCP 11. *Padilla v. LaFrance*, 907 S.W.2d 454, 460 (Tex.1995); *Roeglin v. Daves*, 83 S.W.3d 326, 330 (Tex. App.—Austin 2002, pet. denied). The agreement must be in writing, signed, and filed with the papers as part of the record, or it must be made in open court and entered of record. *Padilla*, 907 S.W.2d at 459; *Neasbitt v. Warren*, 105 S.W.3d 113, 116 (Tex.App.—Fort Worth 2003, no pet.); *Ronin v. Lerner*, 7 S.W.3d 883, 886 (Tex.App.—Houston [1st Dist.] 1999, no pet.). The Supreme Court does not, however, require "slavish adherence" to the literal requirements of TRCP 11. *Kennedy v. Hyde*, 682 S.W.2d 525, 529 (Tex.1984). See "Agreements Between Attorneys – Rule 11," ch. 1-H, §9, p. 61.

(1) In writing, signed & filed. A written settlement agreement must contain all the essential terms of the settlement, be signed by the parties, and be filed with the papers as part of the record of the case. *See Padilla*, 907 S.W.2d at 461. It is not necessary for the entire agreement to be contained in one document. *Id.* at 460 (series of faxes). The agreement may be filed with the court even after one of the parties withdraws consent to the settlement; however, it must be filed before one of the parties attempts to enforce it. *Id.* at 461.

(2) In open court. An oral settlement agreement is enforceable if it is made in open court and entered of record, satisfying the requirements of TRCP 11. *Padilla*, 907 S.W.2d at 459; *Neasbitt*, 105 S.W.3d at 116; *Ronin*, 7 S.W.3d at 886. The TRCP 11 requirement "entered of record" is satisfied if the agreement is noted in the judgment or in an order of the court. *City of Houston v. Clear Creek Basin Auth.*, 589 S.W.2d 671, 677 (Tex.1979).

§4.2 Enforcing settlement agreement. A binding settlement agreement may be enforced by the entry of a consent judgment or by a lawsuit.

1. Consent judgment. When the parties reach a settlement agreement in pending litigation, the court may render a judgment based on the agreement as long as no party has withdrawn consent. *Padilla v. LaFrance*, 907 S.W.2d 454, 461 (Tex.1995); *Staley v. Herblin*, 188 S.W.3d 334, 337 (Tex.App.—Dallas 2006, pet. denied); *e.g., S&A Rest. Corp. v. Leal*, 892 S.W.2d 855, 857-58 (Tex.1995) (party withdrew consent to settlement agreement dictated into record before court rendered judgment; judgment reversed); *Kelley v. Pirtle*, 826 S.W.2d 653, 654 (Tex. App.—Texarkana 1992, writ denied) (court orally rendered judgment in open court before party withdrew consent; judgment affirmed); *see also Chisholm v. Chisholm*, 209 S.W.2d 96, 98 (Tex.2006) (party never gave consent because

---

✦

---

she said she did not understand agreement before judgment was signed). A court's approval of a settlement agreement in open court is not a rendition of judgment. *S&A Rest.*, 892 S.W.2d at 858. See "Rendering, Signing & Entering Judgment," ch. 9-C, §3, p. 765.

PRACTICE TIP
Once you reach a settlement, immediately ask the court to render judgment on the settlement agreement to prevent the other party from revoking the agreement. If the agreement is dictated into the record, ask the trial judge to state on the record, "I now render judgment on the agreement." **Galerie D'Tile, Inc. v. Shinn**, *792 S.W.2d 792, 794 (Tex.App.—Houston [14th Dist.] 1990, no writ). Make sure the judge uses the present tense and not the future. See, e.g.,* **Tinney v. Willingham**, *897 S.W.2d 543, 545 n.2 (Tex.App.—Fort Worth 1995, no writ) (because court said "I will" approve, it did not render judgment). The judge can sign the written judgment later.*

---

2. Suit to enforce as contract. If the court cannot render judgment on a settlement agreement because a party withdrew consent, the settlement agreement may be enforced as a contract if the agreement complies with TRCP 11. **Ford Motor Co. v. Castillo**, 279 S.W.3d 656, 663 (Tex.2009); **Padilla**, 907 S.W.2d at 461; **City of Roanoke v. Town of Westlake**, 111 S.W.3d 617, 626 (Tex.App.—Fort Worth 2003, pet. denied). A settlement agreement is enforceable as a contract even if its terms are not incorporated into a judgment. **Compania Financiara Libano, S.A. v. Simmons**, 53 S.W.3d 365, 368 (Tex.2001); **Padilla**, 907 S.W.2d at 461; *see also* CPRC §154.071(a) (settlement agreements reached in ADR are enforceable like other contracts). If the suit that gave rise to the settlement agreement is still pending in the trial court, a party seeking to enforce the agreement may amend its pleadings in the suit to add a claim for breach of contract. **Mantas v. Fifth Ct. of Appeals**, 925 S.W.2d 656, 658 (Tex.1996); *e.g.*, **Neasbitt v. Warren**, 105 S.W.3d 113, 117-18 (Tex.App.—Fort Worth 2003, no pet.) (motion to enforce settlement was sufficient as amended pleading); *see also* **Ford Motor**, 279 S.W.3d at 663 (party withdrawing consent can conduct discovery to prepare defense against breach-of-contract claim). If the suit is not pending in the trial court, a party seeking to enforce the settlement agreement must file a separate breach-of-contract suit under a new cause number. **Mantas**, 925 S.W.2d at 658-59; *see* **Ford Motor**, 279 S.W.3d at 663.

§5. SETTLEMENT CREDITS UNDER PROPORTIONATE RESPONSIBILITY

The Texas proportionate-responsibility statute provides rules for apportioning liability for damages among the plaintiff and multiple defendants. *See* CPRC ch. 33. In 2003, CPRC chapter 33 was substantially revised by the Legislature. For a detailed discussion of the 2003 amendments to proportionate responsibility and contribution, see *O'Connor's Texas COA*, "Proportionate Responsibility & Contribution," ch. 51, p. 1461.

§5.1 Settlement credits. The proportionate-responsibility statute provides rules for applying a settlement "credit" (or a reduction of damages) based on a plaintiff's settlement with one of the defendants in a lawsuit. That is, if the plaintiff settled with a defendant, the court must reduce the amount the plaintiff can recover from a non-settling defendant. For a detailed discussion of settlement credits, see *O'Connor's Texas COA*, "Settlement credit," ch. 51, §5.2, p. 1471.

§5.2 One-satisfaction rule. The one-satisfaction rule provides that a party is entitled to recover damages only once for a single injury. **Crown Life Ins. v. Casteel**, 22 S.W.3d 378, 390 (Tex.2000); **Buccaneer Homes v. Pelis**, 43 S.W.3d 586, 589 (Tex.App.—Houston [1st Dist.] 2001, no pet.). The rule prevents a party from recovering more than the amount required for the full satisfaction of its damages. **First Title Co. v. Garrett**, 860 S.W.2d 74, 78 (Tex.1993). The one-satisfaction rule applies whether the defendants committed joint or separate acts that resulted in the injury. **Crown Life**, 22 S.W.3d at 390. See *O'Connor's Texas COA*, "One-Satisfaction Rule," ch. 41-A, §4, p. 1247.

⭐

─────────────── ★ ───────────────

★

★

8. THE TRIAL

A. JURY SELECTION

§1. GENERAL

§1.1 Rules. TRCP 221-236, 281, 284. See Gov't Code §§62.001-62.501 (petit juries).

§1.2 Purpose. The purpose of jury selection is to seat a fair and impartial jury. *Hallett v. Houston Nw. Med. Ctr.*, 689 S.W.2d 888, 889 (Tex.1985). The right to a fair and impartial trial is codified in Gov't Code §62.105. *Babcock v. Northwest Mem'l Hosp.*, 767 S.W.2d 705, 708 (Tex.1989).

§1.3 Forms. *O'Connor's Texas Civil Forms* (2012), FORMS 8A.

§1.4 Other references. Babcock & Gilman, *Use of Social Media in Voir Dire*, 60 The Advocate: State Bar Litigation Section Report 44 (Fall 2012); Ballesteros, Comment, *Don't Mess with Texas Voir Dire*, 39 Hous.L.Rev. 201 (2002); Enoch & Johnson, *Narrowing the Ability to Strike Jurors: The Texas Supreme Court Addresses Important Voir Dire Issues*, 39 Tex. Tech L.Rev. 229 (2006-07); Godfrey, *Civil Voir Dire in Texas*, 31 S.Tex.L.Rev. 409 (1990); Hart & Cawyer, *Batson & its Progeny Prohibit the Use of Peremptory Challenges Based Upon Disability & Religion: A Practitioner's Guide for Requesting a Civil Batson Hearing*, 26 Tex. Tech L.Rev. 109 (1995); Sheehan & Hollingsworth, *Allocation of Peremptory Challenges Among Multiple Parties*, 10 St. Mary's L.J. 511 (1979); Wright, Article, *Challenges for Cause Due to Bias or Prejudice: The Blind Leading the Blind Down the Road of Disqualification*, 46 Baylor L.Rev. 825 (1994); *O'Connor's CPRC Plus* (2012-13) (*O'Connor's CPRC*).

§2. NUMBER OF JURORS

§2.1 District court. A jury in district court is composed of 12 persons. Tex. Const. art. 5, §13; Gov't Code §62.201; *McDaniel v. Yarbrough*, 898 S.W.2d 251, 252 (Tex.1995); *see also* TRCP 292 (where as many as three jurors die or become disabled from sitting, the remaining jurors may render and return a verdict). However, the parties may agree to try a case with fewer than 12 jurors. Gov't Code §62.201. See "Verdict by Fewer than 12 Jurors," ch. 8-K, §3, p. 753.

§2.2 Constitutional county court, county court at law, or justice court. A jury in county court or justice court is composed of six persons. Gov't Code §62.301; *see* Tex. Const. art. 5, §17.

§2.3 Statutory probate court. Generally, a jury in statutory probate court is composed of six persons. *See* Gov't Code §§25.0027, 62.301. In cases involving matters in which the statutory probate court has concurrent jurisdiction with the district court, however, the jury is composed of 12 persons. *See id.* §§25.0027, 62.201.

§2.4 Alternate jurors.

    1. **District court.** In district court, up to four alternate jurors may be impaneled. Gov't Code §62.020(a).

    2. **County court.** In county court, up to two alternate jurors may be impaneled. Gov't Code §62.020(b).

§3. QUALIFICATIONS & EXEMPTIONS OF JURORS

§3.1 General qualifications. All individuals are considered competent jurors unless disqualified by statute. Gov't Code §62.101. To be qualified to serve as a juror, a person must:

    1. Be at least 18 years of age. *Id.* §62.102(1).

    2. Be a citizen of Texas and the county where she is to serve. *Id.* §62.102(2).

    3. Be qualified to vote in the county where she is to serve. *Id.* §62.102(3). A person who is not registered to vote is not disqualified from serving as a juror. *Id.* §62.1031.

    4. Be of sound mind and good moral character. *Id.* §62.102(4).

───────────────────────────── ✦ ─────────────────────────────

5. **Be able to read and write.** *Id.* §62.102(5); ***Jenkins v. Chapman***, 636 S.W.2d 238, 240 (Tex.App.—Texarkana 1982, writ dism'd). The trial court may suspend this requirement if there are not enough jurors in the county who can read and write. Gov't Code §62.103(a).

6. **Have not served as a juror** for six or more days during the preceding three months in the county court or during the preceding six months in the district court. *Id.* §62.102(6). The court may suspend this restriction if the county's sparse population makes it seriously inconvenient to enforce. *Id.* §62.103(b).

7. **Have not been convicted of misdemeanor theft or a felony.** *Id.* §62.102(7); *see also **Volkswagen v. Ramirez***, 79 S.W.3d 113, 119-21 (Tex.App.—Corpus Christi 2002) (dismissal of felony conviction after community supervision restored felon's right to serve on jury), *rev'd on other grounds*, 159 S.W.3d 897 (Tex.2004).

NOTE

Even though a person convicted of a felony cannot serve on a jury, TRCP 230 prohibits asking a panelist if she was convicted of one of the disqualifying offenses or if she has been charged with theft or any felony.

---

8. **Not be under indictment** or other legal accusation for misdemeanor theft or a felony. Gov't Code §62.102(8); *see **Palmer Well Servs. v. Mack Trucks, Inc.***, 776 S.W.2d 575, 576 (Tex.1989). The parties may waive the error by agreeing to continue with a juror who is under indictment. ***Mendoza v. Varon***, 563 S.W.2d 646, 648 (Tex.App.—Dallas 1978, writ ref'd n.r.e.). If a juror's indictment is discovered after the verdict is rendered and that juror's vote is required for a verdict of ten jurors, the judgment must be reversed. ***Palmer Well Servs.***, 776 S.W.2d at 577.

§3.2 Physical qualifications. A blind or deaf person is not disqualified solely because of the disability, unless the disability renders the person unfit in that particular case. Gov't Code §62.104(b) (blindness), §62.1041(b) (deafness); *cf. **Galloway v. Superior Court***, 816 F.Supp. 12, 18-19 (D.D.C.1993) (Americans with Disabilities Act prevented court from automatically excluding blind persons from juries). The court is required to provide an interpreter for a deaf juror during the trial and the deliberations. CPRC §§21.002(a), 21.009; *cf. **Saunders v. State***, 49 S.W.3d 536, 539-40 (Tex.App.—Eastland 2001, pet. ref'd) (criminal case; juror entitled to interpreter during deliberations).

§3.3 Statutory disqualifications. If a person is disqualified by statute, the court must excuse that person from service. *Compton v. Henrie*, 364 S.W.2d 179, 182 (Tex.1963). Under Gov't Code §62.105, a panelist is disqualified from serving as a juror on a particular case in the following instances:

1. **Witness.** The person is a witness in the case. Gov't Code §62.105(1).

2. **Interest.** The person has a direct or indirect interest in the case. Gov't Code §62.105(2). The trial court must make a factual determination whether a panelist is connected with or interested in the case. ***Pharo v. Chambers Cty.***, 922 S.W.2d 945, 949 (Tex.1996).

   (1) **Examples of disqualifying interests.** • The employee of a party. ***Galveston H.&S.A. Ry. v. Thornsberry***, 17 S.W. 521, 522 (Tex.1891); ***Preston v. Ohio Oil Co.***, 121 S.W.2d 1039, 1041-42 (Tex.App.—Eastland 1938, writ ref'd). *But see **Pharo***, 922 S.W.2d at 949 & n.4 (employee of governmental unit-party was not automatically disqualified). • Stockholders of a party corporation. ***Texas Power & Light Co. v. Adams***, 404 S.W.2d 930, 943 (Tex.App.—Tyler 1966, no writ). • Insureds of a party insurer. ***Texas Employers' Ins. v. Lane***, 251 S.W.2d 181, 182 (Tex.App.—Fort Worth 1952, writ ref'd n.r.e.). • A close friend of one of the parties. *E.g.,* ***Texas Cent. R.R. v. Blanton***, 81 S.W. 537, 538 (Tex.App.—Fort Worth 1904, no writ) (P, an attorney, had represented panelist and won lawsuit for him; panelist had named child after attorney).

   (2) **Examples of interests too remote to disqualify.** • Social relationship with employee of governmental unit-party. *E.g., Pharo*, 922 S.W.2d at 947-49 (juror dating a deputy sheriff in suit against county for negligence of sheriff). • Members of a cooperative buying club that is a party. *E.g.,* ***Guerra v. Wal-Mart Stores***, 943

★

S.W.2d 56, 59 (Tex.App.—San Antonio 1997, writ denied) (panelists were members of "Sam's Club," and its parent company was sued in negligence case). • Taxpayer residents of a city-party. *City of Hawkins v. E.B. Germany & Sons*, 425 S.W.2d 23, 26 (Tex.App.—Tyler 1968, writ ref'd n.r.e.). • A casual friend who had former business relationship with one of the parties. *E.g.*, *Gant v. Dumas Glass & Mirror, Inc.*, 935 S.W.2d 202, 208-09 (Tex.App.—Amarillo 1996, no writ) (panelist rented property from D eight years earlier and became friendly with him).

3. Relative. The person is related by consanguinity or affinity within the third degree to a party in the case. Gov't Code §§62.105(3), 573.022-573.025. Degrees of relationship are determined according to the civil-law system. See the charts in *O'Connor's CPRC*, p. 946, showing which relatives are within the third degree.

4. Same case. The person has served as a juror in an earlier trial of the same case or in another case involving the same questions of fact. Gov't Code §62.105(5).

5. Bias or prejudice. The person has a bias or prejudice in favor of or against a party in the case. Gov't Code §62.105(4). A bias is an inclination toward one side of an issue over the other. *Hyundai Motor Co. v. Vasquez*, 189 S.W.3d 743, 751 (Tex.2006); *Goode v. Shoukfeh*, 943 S.W.2d 441, 453 (Tex.1997); *Compton*, 364 S.W.2d at 182. Prejudice is the prejudgment of an issue. *Hyundai Motor*, 189 S.W.3d at 751; *Compton*, 364 S.W.2d at 182. Prejudice includes bias. *Hyundai Motor*, 189 S.W.3d at 751; *Goode*, 943 S.W.2d at 453; *Compton*, 364 S.W.2d at 182. A panelist who is biased or prejudiced in favor of or against a party or the type of lawsuit should be disqualified. *Murff v. Pass*, 249 S.W.3d 407, 411 (Tex.2008). For a panelist to be disqualified on the basis of bias, the panelist's state of mind must lead to the inference that she cannot or will not act with impartiality. *Cortez v. HCCI-San Antonio, Inc.*, 159 S.W.3d 87, 94 (Tex.2005); *Compton*, 364 S.W.2d at 182. A panelist does not have a disqualifying bias if she states that she has a "better understanding" of or an initial "leaning" toward one party if the statement is based on skepticism or an opinion about the evidence rather than an ultimate conclusion. *Cortez*, 159 S.W.3d at 93-94; *see El Hafi v. Baker*, 164 S.W.3d 383, 385 (Tex.2005) (perspective based on knowledge and experience does not make panelist biased). A statement that is more of a preview of a panelist's opinion rather than an expression of actual bias is not a ground for disqualification. *Cortez*, 159 S.W.3d at 94. Disqualification for bias or prejudice does not depend on a few "magic words" but on the record as a whole. *Id.* at 93. If bias or prejudice is established as a matter of law, the prospective juror is automatically disqualified. *Goode*, 943 S.W.2d at 452-53; *Compton*, 364 S.W.2d at 182. If bias or prejudice is not established as a matter of law, the trial court must make a factual determination whether the panelist's bias or prejudice merits disqualification. *Malone v. Foster*, 977 S.W.2d 562, 564 (Tex.1998); *Swap Shop v. Fortune*, 365 S.W.2d 151, 154 (Tex.1963); *see Cortez*, 159 S.W.3d at 93.

(1) Rehabilitation. When a panelist makes a statement that appears to show bias or prejudice, additional questioning may help clarify the statement and "rehabilitate" the panelist. *Cortez*, 159 S.W.3d at 92-93. Voir dire does not stop the moment a panelist gives an answer that might be disqualifying. *Id.* at 91-92. Because the appearance of partiality may result from inappropriate leading questions, confusion, misunderstanding, or ignorance of the law, the trial court should allow examination to continue to inquire into the panelist's apparent bias. *E.g.*, *id.* at 92-93 (insurance adjuster who initially said "I would feel bias" was permitted to explain that he was biased against lawsuit abuse, not P's case); *McMillin v. State Farm Lloyds*, 180 S.W.3d 183, 196-97 (Tex.App.—Austin 2005, pet. denied) (panelists who admitted they were initially biased were not disqualified because they later stated they could award the full amount of damages if proved). The trial court also has the discretion to stop the line of questioning to clarify the panelist's response. *Murff*, 249 S.W.3d at 411.

(2) No recantation. When the record as a whole shows a panelist is materially biased or prejudiced, the panelist's ultimate recantation or denial of bias will not prevent disqualification. *Cortez*, 159 S.W.3d at 92. For example, a panelist's statement that she can be "fair and impartial" does not rehabilitate the panelist if the record as a whole shows she is biased. *Id.* at 93.

(3) Examples of bias or prejudice. • Panelist stated he could not be fair to defendant because of results of his father's medical treatment. *Shepherd v. Ledford*, 962 S.W.2d 28, 34 (Tex.1998). • Panelists stated they would award damages to plaintiff even if he did not prove his case. *Silsbee Hosp., Inc. v. George*, 163 S.W.3d 284,

———————————————— ✦ ————————————————

295 (Tex.App.—Beaumont 2005, pet. denied). • Juror placed higher burden on juvenile than required by law. *W.D.A. v. State*, 835 S.W.2d 227, 229 (Tex.App.—Waco 1992, no writ). • Juror was prejudiced against drinking and said it would affect her judgment. *Flowers v. Flowers*, 397 S.W.2d 121, 123-24 (Tex.App.—Amarillo 1965, no writ).

(4) **Examples of no bias or prejudice.** • Panelist, confused about the definition of "preponderance of the evidence," stated he would hold plaintiff to a clear-and-convincing standard of proof but later agreed he would follow instructions given by the court. *Murff*, 249 S.W.3d at 411. • Panelist admitted that being a personal-injury defense attorney would influence how he viewed the evidence. *El Hafi*, 164 S.W.3d at 385. • Panelist admitted he had preconceived notions about the case because he worked as an insurance adjuster, but on further questioning stated he would listen to the evidence. *Cortez*, 159 S.W.3d at 93. • Panelist stated he did not know if he could award plaintiffs loss-of-consortium damages. *Malone*, 977 S.W.2d at 564.

§3.4 Exemptions from jury service. A person qualified to be a juror may claim an exemption from jury service by filing a statement of exemption before the date on which she is required to appear. Gov't Code §62.107(a). After that date, the person must present sworn evidence before the court.

1. Statutorily defined exemptions.

(1) **Specific exemptions.** Gov't Code §62.106 allows the following persons to claim exemptions from jury service: (1) a person over 70, (2) a person with legal custody of a child younger than 12, if jury service would require leaving the child without adequate supervision, (3) a student in secondary school or an institution of higher education, (4) an officer or employee of the legislative branch of state government, (5) the primary caretaker of an invalid, (6) in a county with a population over 200,000, a person who has served as a juror during the preceding 24-month period, (7) in a county with a population over 250,000, a person who has served as a juror during the preceding 36-month period, if the county's jury wheel has not been reconstituted since the person served as a juror, or (8) a member of the U.S. military serving on active duty and deployed to a location away from her home station and outside her county of residence.

(2) **Reasonable excuse.** For exemptions not listed in Gov't Code §62.106, the court may grant an exemption for any "reasonable sworn excuse" and release the person from jury service. Gov't Code §62.110(a). The commissioners court may approve a plan permitting the court's designee to hear any reasonable excuse and release the person from jury service if (1) the excuse is considered sufficient and (2) the juror provides the court's designee with a statement of the grounds for the exception, lack of qualification, or other excuse. *Id.* §62.110(b). Neither the court nor the court's designee may release a person from service for economic reasons under §62.110(a) or (b) unless each party of record is present and approves the release. *Id.* §62.110(c).

2. Permanent exemptions. A person who is older than 70, has a physical or mental impairment, or is unable to comprehend or communicate in English may establish a permanent exemption from jury service. Gov't Code §§62.108, 62.109.

§4. ASSEMBLING PROSPECTIVE JURORS

§4.1 Jury source. The Secretary of State compiles a list of prospective jurors by combining the lists of licensed drivers and registered voters. Gov't Code §62.001(a). The Secretary of State sends each county its list of prospective jurors before the end of each year. *Id.* §62.001(g).

§4.2 Counties with interchangeable jury panels. The laws for interchangeable jury panels govern (1) counties with at least three district courts and (2) counties with a single district court and a single county court at law that has concurrent jurisdiction with the district court on any matter. *See* Gov't Code §§62.016, 62.0175. In addition, district judges in counties with two district courts can elect to be governed by the laws for interchangeable jury panels. *Id.* §62.017(j) (the adoption of this method is discretionary). The judges of the county are required to determine the approximate number of prospective jurors necessary for each week of the year for the general panel. *Id.* §§62.016(a), 62.0175(a). The names are drawn from the jury wheel or compiled by a mechanical device. *See id.* §§62.016(b), 62.0175(b). When impaneled, the prospective jurors constitute a general panel for service in all courts of the county.

———————————————— ✦ ————————————————

Id. §§62.016(e), 62.0175(e). The district judge who impanels the jury for the week inquires into the prospective jurors' general qualifications for jury duty. *See Benavides v. Soto*, 893 S.W.2d 69, 70-71 (Tex.App.—Corpus Christi 1994, no writ). When one of the courts in the county needs a jury, the presiding judge, acting through the clerk, sends about 32 prospective jurors to a district court or 18 to a county court. If the attorneys in the case believe additional prospective jurors will be necessary because they anticipate the case will result in a number of challenges for cause, they can ask the trial judge to request a larger panel.

§4.3 Other counties. In counties not governed by the laws providing for interchangeable jury panels, the clerk assembles a panel for a particular court by randomly drawing slips of paper with names on them from a container and listing them in the order selected. TRCP 224. In those counties, the clerk is authorized to select 24 panelists for the district court and 12 for the county court. *Id.*

§4.4 Objection to prospective jurors. There are two ways to object to the selection of prospective jurors.

1. Challenge the array. A party may challenge the array, which is an objection that challenges the procedure for selecting and summoning prospective jurors or asserts a violation of the jury-wheel statute. *Martinez v. City of Austin*, 852 S.W.2d 71, 73 (Tex.App.—Austin 1993, writ denied); *see* Gov't Code §§62.001-62.021. The challenge must be by written motion, supported by affidavit and filed with the particular judge in charge of the local jury system. TRCP 221; *State v. Smith*, 671 S.W.2d 32, 36 (Tex.1984); *Texas Employers Ins. v. Burge*, 610 S.W.2d 524, 525 (Tex.App.—Beaumont 1980, writ ref'd n.r.e.). Noncompliance with TRCP 221 waives any objection to the array, unless there was fundamental error. *See Mann v. Ramirez*, 905 S.W.2d 275, 278 (Tex.App.—San Antonio 1995, writ denied) (procedural errors do not rise to level of fundamental error). An objection to the array may be made to the trial judge only if the party had no opportunity to object at the time the impaneling judge assembled the array. *E.g., Mendoza v. Ranger Ins.*, 753 S.W.2d 779, 780-81 (Tex.App.—Fort Worth 1988, writ denied) (lack of randomness of panel did not become apparent until voir dire). If the movant successfully challenges the array, the entire array is dismissed, and a new one is summoned. *Martinez*, 852 S.W.2d at 73.

2. Request jury shuffle. After the panel is assigned to a court and before voir dire, a party may request a jury shuffle. TRCP 223; *Martinez*, 852 S.W.2d at 73. When a detailed, case-specific juror questionnaire is used, the phrase "before voir dire" means before the responses to the questionnaire are examined by the parties. *E.g., Carr v. Smith*, 22 S.W.3d 128, 133-34 (Tex.App.—Fort Worth 2000, pet. denied) (distinguishing between standard juror questionnaire and 13-page form with 63 specially tailored questions). The order in which the panelists are listed on the jury list is important because the first 12 (or six in county court) unchallenged panelists will sit on the jury. When requested, the names of the members of the panel must be placed in a receptacle, shuffled, drawn, and transcribed on the jury list in the order drawn. TRCP 223; *see Whiteside v. Watson*, 12 S.W.3d 614, 617-18 (Tex.App.—Eastland 2000, pet. granted, judgm't vacated w.r.m.) (shuffle of jury cards did not comply with rule). It is not necessary for the judge to draw the names from the receptacle; the bailiff can perform that task. *Whiteside*, 12 S.W.3d at 618-19 n.1. Only one jury shuffle is allowed in each case. TRCP 223; *Martinez*, 852 S.W.2d at 73. *But see Whiteside*, 12 S.W.3d at 618-19 (second shuffle was harmless error because first shuffle did not comply with rule).

§5. VOIR DIRE EXAMINATION

§5.1 Purpose. During voir dire, each party has the opportunity to examine the members of the panel to determine whether any of them are disqualified or should not serve on the case. *See Implement Dealers Mut. Ins. v. Castleberry*, 368 S.W.2d 249, 254 (Tex.App.—Beaumont 1963, writ ref'd n.r.e.). The right to conduct a proper voir dire is linked to the constitutional right to a fair trial. *Babcock v. Northwest Mem'l Hosp.*, 767 S.W.2d 705, 709 (Tex. 1989). Voir dire protects the right to an impartial jury by exposing possible juror biases. *Hyundai Motor Co. v. Vasquez*, 189 S.W.3d 743, 749 (Tex.2006); *see also In re Commitment of Hill*, 334 S.W.3d 226, 228 (Tex.2011) (parties have right to question panelists to discover biases and to properly use peremptory challenges).

§5.2 Right to initiate voir dire. Except for good cause shown on the record, the party with the burden of proof on the whole case should be allowed to initiate voir dire. *See* TRCP 265, 266; *Ocean Transp. v. Greycas, Inc.*, 878 S.W.2d 256, 268-69 (Tex.App.—Corpus Christi 1994, writ denied).

★
---

§5.3 Control of voir dire. The trial court has broad discretion in conducting voir dire. *Cortez v. HCCI-San Antonio, Inc.*, 159 S.W.3d 87, 92 (Tex.2005). This discretion includes whether to permit questions about the weight a panelist would give (or not give) to a particular fact or set of facts. *Hyundai Motor Co. v. Vasquez*, 189 S.W.3d 743, 753 (Tex.2006).

1. Scope of examination. A party is entitled to inquire into matters reasonably related to the kinds of issues presented by the case. *See Babcock v. Northwest Mem'l Hosp.*, 767 S.W.2d 705, 709 (Tex.1989); *Texas Employers Ins. v. Loesch*, 538 S.W.2d 435, 440 (Tex.App.—Waco 1976, writ ref'd n.r.e.). The trial court is more likely to be reversed on appeal if it prevents a party from asking a question that may reveal an external bias or prejudice than if it allows the question. *See Babcock*, 767 S.W.2d at 708-09. The court should give the attorneys broad latitude during the examination of the jury panel. *Id.*; *Loesch*, 538 S.W.2d at 440. The examination must probe for a panelist's bias or prejudice against a party or claim. However, after the recitation of facts, the examination cannot be used to gauge the potential impact of evidence on the panelist's verdict. *Hyundai Motor*, 189 S.W.3d at 756-57. Thus, if the question is directed at finding out the weight a panelist would place on certain evidence, the trial court has the discretion to prohibit the question. *Id.* at 758; *In re Commitment of Barbee*, 192 S.W.3d 835, 846 (Tex.App.—Beaumont 2006, no pet.). The substance of a question, not its form, determines whether it probes for prejudices or previews a potential verdict. *Hyundai Motor*, 189 S.W.3d at 757-58. If the trial court prohibits a question, the attorney should propose a different question or specify the area of inquiry to preserve error. *Id.* at 758.

(1) Proper questions & comments. The following matters have been found to be proper on voir dire: • The panelist's ability to have a party prove both required elements of a statute before deciding the verdict. *In re Commitment of Hill*, 334 S.W.3d 226, 229-30 (Tex.2011). • The panelist's relationship to a party. *See* Gov't Code §§62.105(3), 573.022-573.025. • The panelist's interest in the "lawsuit crisis" or the "insurance crisis." *Babcock*, 767 S.W.2d at 708-09; *see National Cty. Mut. Fire Ins. v. Howard*, 749 S.W.2d 618, 621 (Tex.App.—Fort Worth 1988, writ denied). • The panelist's bias or prejudice against the type of lawsuit. *Compton v. Henrie*, 364 S.W.2d 179, 182 (Tex.1963). • The panelist's bias in favor of or against a party because of nationality, wealth, or status. *Haryanto v. Saeed*, 860 S.W.2d 913, 918 (Tex.App.—Houston [14th Dist.] 1993, writ denied). • Informing the panel of the party's own insurance coverage. *University of Tex. v. Hinton*, 822 S.W.2d 197, 201 (Tex.App.—Austin 1991, no writ). • The panelist's bias or prejudice in favor of or against a party in the case. *American Cyanamid Co. v. Frankson*, 732 S.W.2d 648, 653 (Tex.App.—Corpus Christi 1987, writ ref'd n.r.e.); *see* Gov't Code §62.105(4). • The panelist's ability to award a certain sum of money if warranted by the evidence. *Cavnar v. Quality Control Parking, Inc.*, 678 S.W.2d 548, 555 (Tex.App.—Houston [14th Dist.] 1984), *rev'd in part on other grounds*, 696 S.W.2d 549 (Tex.1985). • The panelist's acquaintance with potential witnesses. *Employers Mut. Liab. Ins. v. Butler*, 511 S.W.2d 323, 325-26 (Tex.App.—Texarkana 1974, writ ref'd n.r.e.). • The panelist's relationship with an organization that the other attorney belongs to. *Lopez v. Allee*, 493 S.W.2d 330, 335 (Tex.App.—San Antonio 1973, writ ref'd n.r.e.). • The panelist's bias against the use of intoxicants. *Flowers v. Flowers*, 397 S.W.2d 121, 122-23 (Tex.App.—Amarillo 1965, no writ). • The panelist's representation by one of the attorneys. *Implement Dealers Mut. Ins. v. Castleberry*, 368 S.W.2d 249, 254 (Tex.App.—Beaumont 1963, writ ref'd n.r.e.). • The panelist's financial interest in the litigation. *Carey v. Planters' State Bank*, 280 S.W. 251, 252 (Tex.App.—San Antonio 1926, writ dism'd); *see* Gov't Code §62.105(2). • The panelist's relationship with the other attorney. *Anderson v. Owen*, 269 S.W. 454, 455 (Tex.App.—Galveston 1924, no writ).

PRACTICE TIP

In exemplary-damages cases, attorneys cannot question panelists about exemplary damages based on a preponderance of the evidence because the burden for exemplary damages is clear and convincing evidence. See CPRC §41.003(a). See "Motion to Bifurcate Exemplary Damages," ch. 5-I, §5, p. 369.

---

(2) Improper questions & comments. The following matters have been found to be improper on voir dire: • Isolating one specific fact of the case and asking whether the panelist could be fair, regardless of the other

★

evidence, based on that specific fact. *Hyundai Motor*, 189 S.W.3d at 756-57; *see, e.g.*, *In re Commitment of Barbee*, 192 S.W.3d at 846 (improper to ask if panelist could be fair to party who was previously convicted for crimes against children). • Asking the panelist if one party is starting out ahead after the panelist heard a summary of the facts of the case. *Cortez*, 159 S.W.3d at 94. • For a plaintiff, telling the panel that the defendant has insurance or the plaintiff has no insurance; for a defendant, telling the panel that the plaintiff has insurance. *Ford v. Carpenter*, 216 S.W.2d 558, 559 (Tex.1949). • Asking a question for which the prejudicial effect outweighs the probative value. *Gulf States Utils. Co. v. Reed*, 659 S.W.2d 849, 855-56 (Tex.App.—Houston [14th Dist.] 1983, writ ref'd n.r.e.); *see Loesch*, 538 S.W.2d at 440. • Advising the panel of the effect of their answers. *Loesch*, 538 S.W.2d at 442; *Robinson v. Lovell*, 238 S.W.2d 294, 298 (Tex.App.—Galveston 1951, writ ref'd n.r.e.). • Discussing evidence that will be inadmissible at trial. *See, e.g.*, *Travelers Ins. v. DeLeon*, 456 S.W.2d 544, 545 (Tex.App.—Amarillo 1970, writ ref'd n.r.e.) (in workers' compensation case, weekly compensation benefits); *Christie v. Brewer*, 374 S.W.2d 908, 911-12 (Tex. App.—Austin 1964, writ ref'd n.r.e.) (in suit on a contract, that the other party was indicted for matters relating to same transaction).

2. Time for examination. The trial court has the right to reasonably limit the time for questioning the panelists. *Greer v. Seales*, No. 09-05-00001-CV (Tex.App.—Beaumont 2006, no pet.) (memo op.; 2-23-06); *see McCoy v. Wal-Mart Stores*, 59 S.W.3d 793, 797 (Tex.App.—Texarkana 2001, no pet.); *McCarter v. State*, 837 S.W.2d 117, 119 (Tex.Crim.App.1992). To preserve error when the trial court limits the time for voir dire, the objecting party must show all of the following: (1) the party did not attempt to prolong voir dire, (2) the party was prevented from asking proper and relevant voir dire questions because the court imposed unreasonable time limitations, and (3) the party was not permitted to examine prospective jurors who actually served on the jury. *McCoy*, 59 S.W.3d at 797; *Greer*, No. 09-05-00001-CV (memo op.). The party must identify the specific questions it was not permitted to ask. *See, e.g.*, *Clemments v. State*, 940 S.W.2d 207, 209-10 (Tex.App.—San Antonio 1996, pet. ref'd) (identifying specific questions preserved error); *Greer*, No. 09-05-00001-CV (memo op.) (identifying general topics for questions did not preserve error). The specific questions must be identified to the court before the jury is selected. *See S.D.G. v. State*, 936 S.W.2d 371, 380-81 (Tex.App.—Houston [14th Dist.] 1996, writ denied).

3. Objections to judge's bias. A party may object to improper comments made by a trial judge during voir dire that showed the judge's bias to the jury. *See In re Commitment of Barbee*, 192 S.W.3d at 847; *see also Metzger v. Sebek*, 892 S.W.2d 20, 37-38 (Tex.App.—Houston [1st Dist.] 1994, writ denied) (objection to comments made by judge during trial). Generally, the court does not show bias when it (1) discusses how to phrase a particular question, (2) speculates on reasons for an attorney's question, or (3) criticizes the attorney. *See Dow Chem. Co. v. Francis*, 46 S.W.3d 237, 240 (Tex.2001) (judicial remarks during trial that are critical of, disapproving of, or hostile to counsel, parties, or their cases ordinarily do not constitute bias); *see, e.g.*, *In re Commitment of Barbee*, 192 S.W.3d at 847-48 (judge's remark that counsel was trying to "bust" entire panel and that he wanted counsel to be honest did not constitute bias). Although the judge can have these discussions with the attorney in the panel's presence, she should avoid doing so. *See In re Commitment of Barbee*, 192 S.W.3d at 847-48. To preserve error, the attorney must object to the judge's comments at the time they are made and request an instruction to cure any error. *Dow Chem.*, 46 S.W.3d at 241; *In re Commitment of Barbee*, 192 S.W.3d at 847.

§5.4 Error.

1. Types of errors. The following are types of errors that can be made during voir dire examination.

(1) By court – refusal to allow questions. The trial court refuses to allow a permissible line of questioning. *In re Commitment of Hill*, 334 S.W.3d 226, 228-29 (Tex.2011); *Babcock v. Northwest Mem'l Hosp.*, 767 S.W.2d 705, 708-09 (Tex.1989). This type of error may be a ground for a new trial. *See In re Commitment of Hill*, 334 S.W.3d at 230; *Babcock*, 767 S.W.2d at 709. See "Abuse of discretion," §11.2, p. 695; "Motion for New Trial," ch. 10-B, p. 789.

(2) By attorney – improper question or statement. An attorney asks an improper question or makes an improper statement. *See, e.g.*, *Texas Employers Ins. v. Loesch*, 538 S.W.2d 435, 440-41 (Tex.App.—Waco

———————————————— ✦ ————————————————

1976, writ ref'd n.r.e.) (P's attorney attacked D and its attorneys by indicating that D did not want to comply with provisions of its insurance policy, was attempting to avoid liability by deception, and engaged in conspiracy by concealing P's true condition). If the question or statement is curable, the other attorney must object and, if the objection is sustained, ask for an instruction to disregard the question or statement. See "Object to improper question or statement & pursue adverse ruling," §5.4.2(3), p. 687.

(3) By panelist.

(a) Erroneous answer. A panelist makes an erroneous or incorrect material answer to a question. TRCP 327(a). This type of error may be a ground for a new trial. See "Erroneous juror answer on voir dire," ch. 10-B, §14.1.4, p. 806.

(b) Prejudicial statement. A panelist makes a spontaneous, prejudicial statement. *See Brentwood Fin. Corp. v. Lamprecht*, 736 S.W.2d 836, 840 (Tex.App.—San Antonio 1987, writ ref'd n.r.e.). If the statement is curable, the party must object and, if the objection is sustained, ask for an instruction to disregard the statement. See "Object to improper question or statement & pursue adverse ruling," §5.4.2(3), p. 687. If the statement poisons the panel, the party should move to strike the entire panel. *See, e.g., Reviea v. Marine Drilling Co.*, 800 S.W.2d 252, 256 (Tex.App.—Corpus Christi 1990, writ denied) (panelist's spontaneous remark about excessive insurance rates did not require trial court to strike panel). In most cases, the party moving to strike the entire panel must ask the panel follow-up questions to establish that the panel was affected by the statement. *See Brentwood Fin.*, 736 S.W.2d at 840.

(c) No response. A panelist does not respond to a question. The courts, however, generally find the lack of a response not to be juror misconduct and hold that there is no harm to the complainant. *See Kiefer v. Continental Airlines, Inc.*, 10 S.W.3d 34, 40 (Tex.App.—Houston [14th Dist.] 1999, pet. denied); *Durbin v. Dal-Briar Corp.*, 871 S.W.2d 263, 272-73 (Tex.App.—El Paso 1994, writ denied), *disapproved on other grounds*, *Golden Eagle Archery Inc. v. Jackson*, 24 S.W.3d 362 (Tex.2000); *Missouri Pac. R.R. v. Cunningham*, 515 S.W.2d 678, 685 (Tex.App.—San Antonio 1974, writ dism'd).

2. Preserving error. To preserve error during voir dire, the attorney should take the following steps:

(1) Make a record. The attorney should always ask the court reporter to record the complete voir dire, including bench conferences. *See* TRAP 13.1(a) (duties of court reporter include making a full record of all proceedings); *see, e.g., Soto v. Texas Indus.*, 820 S.W.2d 217, 219 (Tex.App.—Fort Worth 1991, no writ) (court of appeals could not consider a *Batson* objection because no record was made of voir dire); *Loesch*, 538 S.W.2d at 441 (D could not complain of error in P's voir dire because record did not include its own voir dire). *But see McCoy v. Wal-Mart Stores*, 59 S.W.3d 793, 796 (Tex.App.—Texarkana 2001, no pet.) (court of appeals permitted case to be abated for hearing on what transpired at unrecorded bench conferences during voir dire). See "Duties of Court Reporter," ch. 1-E, §3, p. 40. The record must contain the question the party wanted to ask and the court's ruling that prevented the question. *See In re Commitment of Hill*, 334 S.W.3d at 229; *Babcock*, 767 S.W.2d at 708. If the nature of the question is apparent from the context, it is not necessary to state the specific question on the record. *E.g., Babcock*, 767 S.W.2d at 708 (language in motion in limine and recorded voir dire made it obvious what questions P wanted to ask).

(2) Conduct complete voir dire. The attorney must conduct a complete voir dire. Without a complete voir dire, the party waives the right to complain of prejudice. *City of San Antonio v. Willinger*, 345 S.W.2d 577, 578 (Tex.App.—San Antonio 1961, no writ). A complete voir dire includes the following:

(a) An inquiry about the subject on voir dire. *Id.* at 578-79.

(b) Specific rather than general questions. *Id.* Because individual panelists are often reluctant to respond to general questions, general questions are not a good predicate for complaints of concealment of information, incorrect answers, or a failure to answer. *See, e.g., Durbin*, 871 S.W.2d at 273 (question whether anyone had a problem with large jury verdicts did not preserve error); *Soliz v. Saenz*, 779 S.W.2d 929, 933 (Tex.App.—Corpus

---

✦

Christi 1989, writ denied) (question whether panelists could follow the law did not preserve error); *Barron v. State*, 378 S.W.2d 144, 145-46 (Tex.App.—San Antonio 1964, no writ) (question whether any person knew the State's witnesses did not preserve error).

(c) Questions that are clear and unambiguous. *Willinger*, 345 S.W.2d at 578-79. The attorney must ensure that the members of the jury panel hear the questions and understand them. *E.g.*, *Barron*, 378 S.W.2d at 145-46 (panelist did not pay attention to questions); *see, e.g.*, *Burton v. R.E. Hable Co.*, 852 S.W.2d 745, 746 (Tex. App.—Tyler 1993, no writ) (panelist did not understand question).

(d) The pursuit of inquiries suggested by the answers of the panelists. *Willinger*, 345 S.W.2d at 578-79.

(3) Object to improper question or statement & pursue adverse ruling. When an attorney asks an objectionable question or makes an objectionable statement that is curable or a panelist makes a prejudicial statement that is curable, the attorney opposing the question or statement must object; if the objection is sustained, the attorney must request an instruction to disregard the question or statement. *See, e.g.*, *Brentwood Fin.*, 736 S.W.2d at 840 (instruction was sufficient to cure adverse effect of panelist's statement); *Loesch*, 538 S.W.2d at 441 (D's attorney objected but did not ask for instruction to disregard P's attorney's improper statements). If the court sustains the objection and instructs the jury to disregard, the attorney must then ask for a mistrial to preserve error for appeal. This is called "pursuing an adverse ruling." If the attorney does not pursue the objection to an adverse ruling, the error is waived. See "When jury hears inadmissible evidence," ch. 8-D, §6.6, p. 713; "Motion for mistrial," ch. 8-D, §6.6.4, p. 714.

§6. CHALLENGES FOR CAUSE

§6.1 Purpose. A challenge for cause is an objection to a panelist, alleging some fact that by law disqualifies the person from serving as a juror or renders the person unfit to sit on the jury. TRCP 228; *Wooten v. Southern Pac. Transp.*, 928 S.W.2d 76, 80 (Tex.App.—Houston [14th Dist.] 1995, no writ). The challenge for cause permits the parties to eliminate panelists who are disqualified from serving on the jury (e.g., for bias or prejudice). As soon as it becomes apparent that a panelist may be disqualified, the attorney should ask the panelist to approach the bench for questioning outside the hearing of the rest of the panel.

§6.2 Grounds for challenges for cause.

1. **General qualifications.** See "General qualifications," §3.1, p. 679.

2. **Statutory disqualification.** See "Statutory disqualifications," §3.3, p. 680.

3. **Other grounds for disqualification.** The court may exercise its discretion and excuse a panelist for cause even when there is no statutory ground for disqualification. *See* TRCP 228 ("or which in the opinion of the court, renders him an unfit person to sit on the jury").

§6.3 Preserving error. To complain about error when the trial court refuses to permit a challenge for cause, the attorney must follow the procedure set out in *Cortez v. HCCI-San Antonio, Inc.*, 159 S.W.3d 87 (Tex.2005) and *Hallett v. Houston Nw. Med. Ctr.*, 689 S.W.2d 888 (Tex.1985). To preserve error, the attorney must take the following steps:

1. **Challenge for cause.** During voir dire, the attorney must challenge a panelist for cause (the "for-cause panelist"). The record must reflect that the court overruled the challenge for cause. If there is a discussion with the for-cause panelist at the bench, the attorney must make sure the court reporter records it.

2. **Object to exhaustion.** The timing of the objection to the exhaustion of the peremptory strikes is critical. The record must show that the attorney objected to the exhaustion of peremptory strikes before or at the same time the attorney submitted its peremptory-strike list to the clerk. See "Turn in strike list," §6.3.3, p. 688. To properly object, the party must do all of the following:

★

(1) **Notice of exhaustion.** Inform the court that, as a result of the court's refusal to strike the for-cause panelist, the party will exhaust its peremptory challenges before it can strike an objectionable panelist on the list. *See Cortez*, 159 S.W.3d at 90-91; *Hallett*, 689 S.W.2d at 890. The latest this notice can be given is before the party learns of the other party's peremptory strikes and of the composition of the jury. *See Cortez*, 159 S.W.3d at 91. Once a jury is chosen, it is too late to notify the court that an objectionable panelist is on the jury. *See id.*

(2) **Identification of objectionable panelist.** Identify an objectionable panelist who will remain on the jury list once the party uses its last peremptory strike. *Cortez*, 159 S.W.3d at 90-91; *see Hallett*, 689 S.W.2d at 890.

(a) The objectionable panelist may be either the panelist who should have been struck for cause or another objectionable panelist. *See, e.g., Cortez*, 159 S.W.3d at 90 (panelist other than for-cause panelist left on list); *Shepherd v. Ledford*, 962 S.W.2d 28, 34 (Tex.1998) (for-cause panelist left on list); *Hallett*, 689 S.W.2d at 889-90 (same); *Pharo v. Chambers Cty.*, 893 S.W.2d 264, 268 (Tex.App.—Houston [1st Dist.] 1995) (panelist other than for-cause panelist left on list), *aff'd*, 922 S.W.2d 945 (Tex.1996). In most appeals, the error is waived because the party did not identify the objectionable panelist who remained on the panel. *See, e.g., Pharo*, 893 S.W.2d at 268 (statement that "I object to this juror" did not identify panelist). The party does not need to state why the panelist is objectionable. *Cortez*, 159 S.W.3d at 91.

(b) The objectionable panelist must actually serve on the jury. To determine if a panelist will probably remain on the panel, the attorney should count 12 panelists, skipping the party's own peremptory strikes and any strikes the attorney believes the other party will make. The attorney should identify someone within those 12 panelists as the objectionable panelist. The rationale for identifying someone who could remain on the panel is the harmless-error rule—the objectionable panelist might be struck by the other party or might be so far down the list that the panelist could not have been picked for the jury. *See Carpenter v. Wyatt Constr. Co.*, 501 S.W.2d 748, 750-51 (Tex.App.—Houston [14th Dist.] 1973, writ ref'd n.r.e.), *disapproved on other grounds, Cortez v. HCCI-San Antonio, Inc.*, 159 S.W.3d 87 (Tex.2005).

PRACTICE TIP

It is probably not necessary to take the additional step of specifying the relief you want—either a reversal of the for-cause ruling or an additional peremptory strike. See Sullemon v. U.S. Fid. & Guar. Co., 734 S.W.2d 10, 13-14 (Tex.App.—Dallas 1987, no writ). However, until the Supreme Court specifically addresses the issue, a party should always identify the relief it wants.

---

3. Turn in strike list. After notifying the court that an objectionable juror will remain on the jury list, the attorney should turn in the strike list. *See Cortez*, 159 S.W.3d at 90-91.

PRACTICE TIP

To preserve error, the attorney should state on the record, "Because the court refused to remove Mr. Smith for cause, the {party} will have no peremptory strikes left to challenge an objectionable panelist, {identify either Mr. Smith or another objectionable panelist on the jury list}. To cure the error, the {party} asks the court to strike Mr. Smith for cause or, in the alternative, grant the {party} an additional peremptory strike." If the request is denied, the attorney should state, "Having stated my objection on the record, I now hand my list of peremptory challenges to the clerk." After the jury is selected, the attorney should ask the court reporter to take possession of the juror information sheets and the strike lists so they can be included in the record.

---

§7. PEREMPTORY CHALLENGES

Peremptory challenges, commonly referred to as "peremptory strikes," are made after the panel has been interviewed by both sides and all challenges for cause have been resolved.

—— ★ ——

§7.1 Purpose. A peremptory strike is a challenge to a panelist without assigning a reason. TRCP 232; *Hyundai Motor Co. v. Vasquez*, 189 S.W.3d 743, 749-50 (Tex.2006); *Patterson Dental Co. v. Dunn*, 592 S.W.2d 914, 917 (Tex.1979). Peremptory strikes permit the parties to reject certain panelists who may be unsympathetic to their position; the strikes do not permit the parties to select the members for the jury. *Hyundai Motor*, 189 S.W.3d at 750; *Patterson Dental*, 592 S.W.2d at 919.

§7.2 Allocation of strikes.

1. Two-party case. In a two-party case, each side is entitled to six peremptory strikes in district court or three in county court. TRCP 233; *Perkins v. Freeman*, 518 S.W.2d 532, 533 (Tex.1974).

2. Multiparty case. In a case in which there are multiple parties on the same side, the number of peremptory strikes allocated to each party depends on (1) how the parties are aligned and (2) whether the parties aligned on the same side are antagonistic to each other. *See* TRCP 233; *Scurlock Oil Co. v. Smithwick*, 724 S.W.2d 1, 5 (Tex.1986); *Garcia v. Central Power & Light Co.*, 704 S.W.2d 734, 736 (Tex.1986).

(1) Are parties properly aligned? In most multiparty cases, the alignment of the parties is not at issue. When there are multiple parties, all plaintiffs and all defendants are aligned as if they were simply one plaintiff and one defendant. *See Patterson Dental Co. v. Dunn*, 592 S.W.2d 914, 917 (Tex.1979) (litigants on same side of docket are deemed to be one "party" under TRCP 233). This alignment presumes that the designation of each party as a "plaintiff" or "defendant" correctly identifies which side of the docket the party belongs on. But this presumption may not be true in all cases. The term "side" is defined as litigants with a common interest in an issue to be submitted to the jury, and thus is not synonymous with terms such as "party," "litigant," or "person." TRCP 233; *"Y" Propane Serv. v. Garcia*, 61 S.W.3d 559, 569 (Tex.App.—San Antonio 2001, no pet.). If there is an issue on which a party has a common interest with an opposing party such that they may no longer be considered adversaries, the two may be considered on the same side. *See, e.g., Moore v. Altra Energy Techs.*, 321 S.W.3d 727, 747 (Tex.App.—Houston [14th Dist.] 2010, pet. denied) (trial court should have aligned co-D with P and given each side same number of strikes); *American Cyanamid Co. v. Frankson*, 732 S.W.2d 648, 651 (Tex.App.—Corpus Christi 1987, writ ref'd n.r.e.) (co-Ds expected to settle with P were aligned with P and received no jury strikes). To overcome the presumption of sides, a party must make a motion to realign the parties before the exercise of peremptory strikes and show which parties share a common interest on the jury issues. *See* TRCP 233; *Pojar v. Cifre*, 199 S.W.3d 317, 326 (Tex.App.—Corpus Christi 2006, pet. denied).

(2) Are aligned parties antagonistic to each other? When there are multiple parties, the trial court must determine whether the parties on the same side of the suit—not opposing parties—are antagonistic to each other before the court can allocate peremptory strikes. *Central Power*, 704 S.W.2d at 736; *Patterson Dental*, 592 S.W.2d at 918. The antagonism must relate to an issue of fact that the jury will decide, not a matter that constitutes a pure question of law. *Patterson Dental*, 592 S.W.2d at 918; *see, e.g., "Y" Propane*, 61 S.W.3d at 570 (antagonism in future contribution suit did not establish antagonism in primary suit). For example, defendants are considered antagonistic to each other when each contends the other is solely responsible for the plaintiff's injuries. *Patterson Dental*, 592 S.W.2d at 918. When determining whether parties are antagonistic to each other, the court can consider the pleadings, pretrial discovery, statements made during voir dire examination, and any other information brought to its attention. *Scurlock Oil*, 724 S.W.2d at 5; *Central Power*, 704 S.W.2d at 737. The court's finding must be made after voir dire but before the parties exercise their peremptory strikes. *E.g., Central Power*, 704 S.W.2d at 737 (statements made during voir dire established there was no antagonism); *see* TRCP 233; *Patterson Dental*, 592 S.W.2d at 919.

(3) How should strikes be allocated?

(a) No antagonism. If the court decides the parties on the same side are not antagonistic to each other, each side must receive the same number of strikes—that is, six strikes for district court or three strikes for county court. *See* TRCP 233; *Central Power*, 704 S.W.2d at 736.

★

(b) Antagonism. If the court decides the parties on the same side are antagonistic to each other, each party gets its own set of strikes. *See Patterson Dental*, 592 S.W.2d at 918 (it is error to require antagonistic parties on same side to share six strikes); *see, e.g.*, *Van Allen v. Blackledge*, 35 S.W.3d 61, 64 (Tex.App.—Houston [14th Dist.] 2000, pet. denied) (antagonistic Ds each received 6 strikes for total of 12 strikes on their side). If antagonistic parties are given additional strikes, they should not be permitted to coordinate their strikes. *See In re M.N.G.*, 147 S.W.3d 521, 532 (Tex.App.—Fort Worth 2004, pet. denied); *Van Allen*, 35 S.W.3d at 65.

(c) Motion to equalize. If the allocation of strikes would result in one party or side gaining an unfair advantage, a party can—before the exercise of strikes—make a motion to equalize the peremptory strikes. TRCP 233; *see, e.g.*, *Patterson Dental*, 592 S.W.2d at 920 (four-to-one ratio of strikes between sides was erroneous; generally, two-to-one ratio is maximum disparity allowed). The motion should be made orally after voir dire. *See, e.g.*, *Patterson Dental*, 592 S.W.2d at 917 (party objected to court's allocation of strikes and made oral motion to equalize); *Texas Commerce Bank Reagan v. Lebco Constructors, Inc.*, 865 S.W.2d 68, 77-78 (Tex.App.—Corpus Christi 1993, writ denied) (pretrial motion to equalize did not preserve error when no objection to court's allocation of strikes was made after voir dire); *Diamond Shamrock Corp. v. Wendt*, 718 S.W.2d 766, 768 (Tex.App.—Corpus Christi 1986, writ ref'd n.r.e.) (party objected to court's allocation of strikes and made oral motion to equalize). Equalization, for purposes of allocating strikes, does not mean that each side or party gets the same number of peremptory strikes. *E.g.*, *Patterson Dental*, 592 S.W.2d at 920 (two-to-one ratio of strikes between sides is generally not considered abuse of discretion); *Pojar*, 199 S.W.3d at 330 (when P received six strikes, co-Ds were not entitled to six strikes each just because they were antagonistic to each other). When the court equalizes strikes, it can do so by increasing the strikes allocated to a single party on one side, decreasing the strikes allocated to multiple parties on the other side, or both. *Patterson Dental*, 592 S.W.2d at 920; *see, e.g.*, *Diamond Shamrock*, 718 S.W.2d at 770 (error to give two antagonistic Ds each 6 strikes and increase P's strikes to 12 when one D's interests were closely identified with those of P); *Williams v. Texas City Ref., Inc.*, 617 S.W.2d 823, 826-27 (Tex.App.—Houston [14th Dist.] 1981, writ ref'd n.r.e.) (because of antagonism to D and settlement agreement with P, third-party D was given one strike).

3. Objections. When the court errs in allocating peremptory strikes, to preserve error, the party must object to the allocation of strikes after voir dire and before the exercise of the strikes. *In re T.E.T.*, 603 S.W.2d 793, 798 (Tex.1980); *In re M.N.G.*, 147 S.W.3d at 532; *Van Allen*, 35 S.W.3d at 65. The party must be specific about whether it is objecting to the allocation of the strikes or the alignment of the parties. *See, e.g.*, *Pojar*, 199 S.W.3d at 327-28 (error not preserved on allocation-of-strikes issue because D only argued for realignment of sides at trial).

4. Alternate jurors. When the trial court impanels alternate jurors under Gov't Code §62.020, the sides must be given additional peremptory strikes. *Temple EasTex, Inc. v. Old Orchard Creek Partners*, 848 S.W.2d 724, 738 (Tex.App.—Dallas 1992, writ denied). If the trial court impanels one or two alternate jurors, the sides are each entitled to one additional peremptory strike. Gov't Code §62.020(e). If the trial court impanels three or four alternate jurors, the sides are each entitled to two additional peremptory strikes. *Id.*

§7.3 *Batson* limitations on peremptory strikes. The objection that a panelist was excluded because of some protected classification is called a *Batson* challenge, after the first criminal case that held racially based challenges were unconstitutional. *Batson v. Kentucky*, 476 U.S. 79, 96 (1986). *But see Goode v. Shoukfeh*, 943 S.W.2d 441, 450 (Tex.1997) (calls it *Edmonson* challenge). A party in a civil case has standing to assert the equal-protection rights of a panelist who was excluded from the jury because of a protected classification. *Edmonson v. Leesville Concrete Co.*, 500 U.S. 614, 630 (1991); *see Powers v. Palacios*, 813 S.W.2d 489, 490-91 (Tex.1991). It is not necessary for the struck panelist and the party challenging the strike to be members of the same cognizable group. *Powers v. Ohio*, 499 U.S. 400, 402 (1991); *Davis v. Fisk Elec. Co.*, 268 S.W.3d 508, 516 n.5 (Tex.2008). A party may challenge any peremptory strike that violates a panelist's equal-protection rights. *Ohio*, 499 U.S. at 415-16. The TRCPs have not been amended to incorporate the *Batson* holding. *Goode*, 943 S.W.2d at 450. Therefore, the courts often look to criminal cases for guidance. *Id.*

1. Protected classifications. Litigants cannot exercise peremptory strikes to exclude panelists solely for the following characteristics: • Race. *Batson*, 476 U.S. at 96; *Davis*, 268 S.W.3d at 510; *e.g.*, *Palacios*, 813 S.W.2d

★

at 490 & n.1 (only black panelist struck and race "figured into" strike). • **Ethnicity.** *Hernandez v. New York*, 500 U.S. 352, 362 (1991) (Hispanic); *Benavides v. American Chrome & Chems., Inc.*, 893 S.W.2d 624, 626-27 (Tex. App.—Corpus Christi 1994) (same), *writ denied*, 907 S.W.2d 516 (Tex.1995). • **Gender.** *J.E.B. v. Alabama*, 511 U.S. 127, 143 (1994); *Davis*, 268 S.W.3d at 510. Strikes based on characteristics that are disproportionately associated with one gender are not necessarily prohibited. *See, e.g., J.E.B.*, 511 U.S. at 143 n.16 (challenge to all nurses is not gender-based even though it would disproportionately affect women).

   2. Others may be protected. Other "cognizable" groups under *Batson* may include the following: • Native Americans. *See U.S. v. Childs*, 5 F.3d 1328, 1337 (9th Cir.1993); *U.S. v. Iron Moccasin*, 878 F.2d 226, 229 (8th Cir.1989); *U.S. v. Chalan*, 812 F.2d 1302, 1313-14 (10th Cir.1987). • Italian-Americans. *See U.S. v. Biaggi*, 853 F.2d 89, 95-96 (2d Cir.1988). *But see U.S. v. Bucci*, 839 F.2d 825, 832-33 (1st Cir.1988) (whether Italian-Americans are a cognizable group is a question of fact). A list of cases involving *Batson* challenges to Italian-Americans can be found in *U.S. v. Campione*, 942 F.2d 429, 432-33 (7th Cir.1991). • Asian-Americans. *See U.S. v. Sneed*, 34 F.3d 1570, 1578-79 (10th Cir.1994). • Disabled persons. Protections similar to *Batson* may prevent litigants from striking disabled persons from the jury panel solely because of their disability. The Americans with Disabilities Act (ADA) and the Texas Government Code prohibit the automatic exclusion of a person on the grounds of disability. *See* 42 U.S.C. §12132 (any disability); Gov't Code §62.104(a) (blindness), §62.1041(a) (deafness). The ADA applies to everything the State does, including acts of the judiciary. *E.g., Galloway v. Superior Court*, 816 F.Supp. 12, 18-19 (D.D.C.1993) (ADA prevented federal court from automatically excluding blind persons from juries). • Religious affiliation. No civil court has addressed this issue. The Court of Criminal Appeals has held that *Batson* does not prohibit strikes based on religion. *Casarez v. State*, 913 S.W.2d 468, 495-96 (Tex.Crim.App.1995). The Fifth Circuit has stated that no current precedent clearly dictates that *Batson* should be extended to religion. *Fisher v. Texas*, 169 F.3d 295, 305 (5th Cir. 1999). *But see Davis v. Minnesota*, 511 U.S. 1115, 1117 (1994) (Thomas, J., dissenting from denial of certiorari) ("*J.E.B.* would seem to have extended *Batson's* equal protection analysis to all strikes based on … religion"); *U.S. v. Stafford*, 136 F.3d 1109, 1114 (7th Cir.1998) (improper to strike a juror because he is a Jew, Catholic, or Muslim), *modified on other grounds*, 136 F.3d 1115 (7th Cir.1998).

   3. Unprotected classifications. Litigants may exercise peremptory strikes to exclude panelists based on the following: • Appearance. *Purkett v. Elem*, 514 U.S. 765, 769 (1995) (long, unkempt hair, mustache, and beard); *Mayr v. Lott*, 943 S.W.2d 553, 556-57 (Tex.App.—Waco 1997, no writ) (large, flamboyant hat). • Age or employment status. *Brumfield v. Exxon Corp.*, 63 S.W.3d 912, 916 (Tex.App.—Houston [14th Dist.] 2002, pet. denied); *Dominguez v. State Farm Ins.*, 905 S.W.2d 713, 716-17 (Tex.App.—El Paso 1995, writ dism'd). • Medical treatment received by panelist. *Mayr*, 943 S.W.2d at 556.

   4. Procedure for *Batson* challenge. After voir dire, if one party (*Batson* movant) believes the other party (*Batson* respondent) used its peremptory strikes in a discriminatory manner, the *Batson* movant should follow the three-step procedure adopted in *Goode*, 943 S.W.2d at 445-46.

   (1) Step 1 – Movant makes prima facie case. The *Batson* movant must make a prima facie case of discriminatory use of peremptory strikes by the *Batson* respondent. *Goode*, 943 S.W.2d at 445. A prima facie case is established by a suspect pattern of strikes against members of a protected class. *Dominguez*, 905 S.W.2d at 715. A reasonable inference is sufficient to establish a prima facie case. *Johnson v. California*, 545 U.S. 162, 167-68 & n.3 (2005). To make a *Batson* challenge, the movant must show (1) the *Batson* respondent exercised a peremptory strike to remove a panelist of a protected class, and (2) that peremptory strike, along with other circumstances, raises an inference that the *Batson* respondent excluded the panelist because of her status. *See Lott v. City of Fort Worth*, 840 S.W.2d 146, 150 (Tex.App.—Fort Worth 1992, no writ). A prima facie case requires a party to come forward with facts, not just numbers. *See, e.g., Brown v. Kinney Shoe Corp.*, 237 F.3d 556, 562-63 (5th Cir.2001) (standing alone, fact that P used four peremptory strikes to remove white jurors did not make a prima facie case). If the *Batson* movant makes a prima facie case, it creates a rebuttable presumption of discriminatory use of strikes by the *Batson* respondent. *Lott*, 840 S.W.2d at 150.

★

(2) Step 2 – Respondent offers neutral explanation. After the *Batson* movant makes a prima facie case, the burden shifts to the *Batson* respondent to offer a neutral explanation for the strike. *Goode*, 943 S.W.2d at 445. The issue at this stage is the facial validity of the explanation. *Id.*

(a) Neutral explanation. To rebut the movant's prima facie case, the *Batson* respondent should offer a neutral explanation for each strike challenged by the *Batson* movant. *In re A.D.E.*, 880 S.W.2d 241, 243 (Tex.App.—Corpus Christi 1994, no writ), *disapproved on other grounds*, *In re J.F.C.*, 96 S.W.3d 256 (Tex.2002). A neutral explanation is one based on something other than the race, gender, or other discriminatory characteristic of the panelist. *Goode*, 943 S.W.2d at 445. A neutral explanation may be the attorney's hunch, the panelist's failure to make eye contact, inattentiveness, appearance, or employment status. *See, e.g., TXI Transp. Co. v. Hughes*, 224 S.W.3d 870, 892-93 (Tex.App.—Fort Worth 2007) (occupation and length of residence in community sufficient reasons to strike panelist), *rev'd on other grounds*, 306 S.W.3d 230 (Tex.2010); *Mayr*, 943 S.W.2d at 556-57 (large, flamboyant hat sufficient reason to strike panelist). The explanation does not need to be plausible. *Purkett*, 514 U.S. at 768; *Molina v. Pigott*, 929 S.W.2d 538, 545 (Tex.App.—Corpus Christi 1996, writ denied). When a peremptory strike is based on a panelist's nonverbal conduct, the *Batson* respondent must specifically describe that conduct. *Davis*, 268 S.W.3d at 518; *Price v. Short*, 931 S.W.2d 677, 682 (Tex.App.—Dallas 1996, no writ). The *Batson* respondent must do more than just assert that the nonverbal conduct happened; the conduct must be proved and reflected in the record. *Davis*, 268 S.W.3d at 518.

(b) Interpretation of explanation. At step two, the court will consider the reason offered as neutral unless a discriminatory intent is inherent in the explanation. *Goode*, 943 S.W.2d at 445. Even if the respondent offers a "silly or superstitious" explanation for the strike, the trial court must assume that the reasons given are true. *Id.* The persuasiveness of the explanation becomes an issue only at step three. *Id.* If the *Batson* respondent admits the discriminatory characteristic played any role in making its strike, the peremptory strike is constitutionally defective. *Benavides*, 893 S.W.2d at 626-27.

(3) Step 3 – Court analyzes arguments. The *Batson* movant has the right to rebut the respondent's explanations and cross-examine the respondent's attorney regarding the motivation for the strikes. *Goode*, 943 S.W.2d at 451-52; *see Davis*, 268 S.W.3d at 514-15. After both parties present their positions, the court must determine whether the *Batson* respondent's explanations were neutral or if they were merely a pretext for purposeful discrimination. *Purkett*, 514 U.S. at 768; *Lott*, 840 S.W.2d at 150; *see Goode*, 943 S.W.2d at 446 (step three is stage in which court makes its determination). The courts must look at "all relevant circumstances" when considering a *Batson* challenge. *Davis*, 268 S.W.3d at 511-12; *see Miller-El v. Dretke*, 545 U.S. 231, 240 (2005). Courts have identified several factors that can be used in making a determination on a *Batson* challenge, including:

(a) Whether an analysis of the statistical data on the peremptory strikes indicates a disparity too great to be mere happenstance. *Miller-El*, 545 U.S. at 240-41; *e.g., Davis*, 268 S.W.3d at 516 (D struck 83% of black panelists and 5.5% of nonblack panelists; court called the statistics "remarkable").

(b) Whether there was any questioning directed to the challenged juror and whether the questions asked were meaningful. *Lott*, 840 S.W.2d at 151; *see Short*, 931 S.W.2d at 685 (unless panelist was questioned, court may assume the attorney's explanation for a strike is a pretext for a racially discriminatory strike).

(c) Whether there was disparate treatment (i.e., the *Batson* respondent did not strike persons with characteristics the same as or similar to the challenged juror). *Lott*, 840 S.W.2d at 151; *see Davis*, 268 S.W.3d at 512 (referred to as "comparative juror analysis").

(d) Whether there was a disparate examination of panelists (i.e., the *Batson* respondent questioned the challenged juror to elicit a certain response without asking the same question of other panelists). *Lott*, 840 S.W.2d at 151; *see Davis*, 268 S.W.3d at 513-14; *see, e.g., Miller-El*, 545 U.S. at 255 (prosecutors gave black panelists a graphic account of the death penalty and nonblacks a bland description before asking about panelist's feelings on the subject).

(e) Whether the *Batson* respondent offered an explanation based on a group bias when the group trait was not shown to apply to the challenged juror. *Lott*, 840 S.W.2d at 151.

★

(f) Whether the reasons the *Batson* respondent gave for the peremptory strike were related to the facts of the case. *Lott*, 840 S.W.2d at 151; *see, e.g.*, *Mayr*, 943 S.W.2d at 556 (in PI case, striking a juror because she had undergone chiropractic treatment was related to case).

(g) Whether the use of the jury shuffle indicates the respondent's decisions were probably based on race. *See, e.g.*, *Miller-El*, 545 U.S. at 253 (prosecution sought jury shuffle when predominant number of black panelists were seated in the front of the panel and delayed making formal objection to D's shuffle until after racial composition was revealed, raising suspicion that prosecution sought to exclude black panelists from jury).

(h) Whether there is a history of systematically excluding members of a protected classification from juries. *See, e.g.*, *Miller-El*, 545 U.S. at 263-64 (D.A.'s office had adopted formal policy to exclude minorities from jury service).

5. Deadline for *Batson* challenge. A *Batson* movant must make a *Batson* challenge before the court impanels the jury and dismisses the excluded panelists. Code Crim. Proc. art. 35.261(a); *see In re K.M.B.*, 91 S.W.3d 18, 27 (Tex.App.—Fort Worth 2002, no pet.); *Pierson v. Noon*, 814 S.W.2d 506, 508 (Tex.App.—Houston [14th Dist.] 1991, writ denied). If the *Batson* movant makes an objection for the first time in a motion for new trial, it is too late. *See Jones v. Martin K. Eby Constr. Co.*, 841 S.W.2d 426, 430 (Tex.App.—Dallas 1992, writ denied).

6. *Batson* record. The *Batson* movant must make a record to illustrate on appeal that the trial court abused its discretion. *See Goode*, 943 S.W.2d at 446; *In re A.D.E.*, 880 S.W.2d at 245. There are two parts of the record for a *Batson* objection. First, the *Batson* movant should introduce into evidence the information cards provided by the panelists. *See Goode*, 943 S.W.2d at 451; *In re A.D.E.*, 880 S.W.2d at 245. Although the cards do not contain information about the races of the panelists, they can be used to show the pretext of the strike. Second, the *Batson* movant should (1) ask the court to take judicial notice of the racial composition of the panel, (2) state the composition on the record, and (3) identify the panelists who were excluded by name, race, or other status, and their position on the panel. For example, the *Batson* movant should state the panel was composed of 24 persons, including 16 white, 5 African-American, and 3 Mexican-American; identify the panel number of each minority member; and list those who were excluded—panelist number three, Mrs. Smith, who is an African-American, etc.

7. *Batson* hearing. A *Batson* hearing must be held in open court. *Goode*, 943 S.W.2d at 451. The *Batson* respondent's attorney does not need to be put under oath; unsworn statements may be offered to explain peremptory strikes. *Id.* The *Batson* movant has the right to cross-examine the *Batson* respondent's attorney. *Id.* at 452. For making a *Batson* record, see "*Batson* record," §7.3.6, this page. For introducing other evidence, the TRCPs and TREs apply. *Goode*, 943 S.W.2d at 451.

PRACTICE TIP

*If the **Batson** respondent's attorney uses voir dire notes to refresh her recollection while giving testimony during the hearing, the **Batson** movant's attorney is entitled to examine the notes. **Goode**, 943 S.W.2d at 449; see TRE 612(1). But see **Brooks v. Armco, Inc.**, 194 S.W.3d 661, 666 (Tex.App.—Texarkana 2006, pet. denied) (in dicta, court said D's attorney cited to notes only to confirm truth of testimony, not to refresh memory; P's attorney not entitled to review notes). If the **Batson** respondent's attorney uses voir dire notes only before the hearing, the issue of whether to require the production of the notes is within the trial court's discretion. **Goode**, 943 S.W.2d at 449; see TRE 612(2).*

---

8. Court's ruling. If the court determines the explanation was merely pretext, the misused strikes will not be restored to the party because doing so would reward the party for attempting discriminatory strikes. *Peetz v. State*, 180 S.W.3d 755, 760-61 (Tex.App.—Houston [14th Dist.] 2005, no pet.).

9. Trial remedies. The civil courts often look to criminal cases to determine remedies for a *Batson* violation. *Texas Tech Univ. Health Sci. Ctr. v. Apodaca*, 876 S.W.2d 402, 406 (Tex.App.—El Paso 1994, writ denied).

———————————————————— ✮ ————————————————————

If the trial court decides a panelist was improperly excluded, the court may reinstate the challenged panelist to the panel or may dismiss the panel and call a new one. *Batson*, 476 U.S. at 99 n.24; *see, e.g.*, *Short*, 931 S.W.2d at 681 (trial court reinstated four panelists).

§8. JURY PANEL

§8.1 After challenges for cause. In a two-party case, after the parties make their challenges for cause, at least 24 persons must remain on the panel in district court (12 in county court). If the jury panel has fewer than those numbers, the trial court must direct the clerk to call other panelists to complete the jury. TRCP 231, 235; *Thomas v. City of O'Donnell*, 811 S.W.2d 757, 759 (Tex.App.—Amarillo 1991, no writ). *But see McRae v. Echols*, 8 S.W.3d 797, 798-99 (Tex.App.—Waco 2000, pet. denied) (harmless error to begin voir dire with 23 jurors). The burden is on the trial court, not the parties, to summon additional panelists. TRCP 231, 235; *Thomas*, 811 S.W.2d at 759.

§8.2 After peremptory strikes. After the parties deliver their peremptory strikes to the clerk, the clerk calls the names of the panelists who have not been struck by either party, and those persons make up the jury panel. Once the jury is called, the court cannot add or subtract jurors. *Dunlap v. Excel Corp.*, 30 S.W.3d 427, 433 (Tex.App.—Amarillo 2000, no pet.).

    1. District court. In a district court, the first 12 persons not struck make up the jury panel. TRCP 234; *Dunlap*, 30 S.W.3d at 433; *see* Tex. Const. art. 5, §13; Gov't Code §62.201.

    2. County court. In a county court, the first six persons not struck make up the jury panel. TRCP 234; *see* Tex. Const. art. 5, §17; Gov't Code §62.301.

§9. JUROR COMMUNICATION

Immediately after jurors are selected for a case, the court must instruct them about limitations on their outside communication during the case. *See* TRCP 226a, §II, 284.

§9.1 No electronic devices. Jurors must turn off their phones and other electronic devices and may not communicate with anyone through any electronic device while in the courtroom or while deliberating. TRCP 226a, §II(1), 284.

§9.2 No posting or searching for information about case. Jurors cannot post any information about the case on the Internet or search for information about the case on the Internet or elsewhere. TRCP 284; *see* TRCP 226a, §II(1).

§9.3 No communication about case. When jurors are allowed to separate, either during trial or after the case is submitted to them, they may not communicate with, or permit themselves to be addressed by, anyone about anything related to the case. TRCP 284. Jurors cannot communicate about the case either in person or by electronic means (e.g., by phone, text message, e-mail, chat room, blog, or social-networking site). TRCP 226a, §II(4).

§9.4 No communication with person in case. Jurors should not talk to lawyers, witnesses, parties, or anyone else involved in the case other than to exchange casual greetings like "hello" and "good morning." TRCP 226a, §II(2). If a juror has a question or needs to communicate with the court, the presiding juror will tell the officer in charge of the jury, who will inform the court. TRCP 285. See "Jury's questions to trial court," ch. 8-I, §8.1, p. 744.

§10. JUROR NOTE-TAKING

The vast majority of states and most of the federal circuits permit jurors to take notes. Annotation, *Taking & Use of Trial Notes by Jury*, 36 ALR 5th 255, 275 (1996). The Texas Supreme Court recently amended the Texas Rules of Civil Procedure to allow jurors to take notes in civil cases. *See* TRCP 226a, §II(10), 281; *cf. Price v. State*, 887 S.W.2d 949, 954 (Tex.Crim.App.1994) (juror note-taking approved in criminal cases). Jurors may take notes during a civil trial if it will help focus their attention on the evidence; the notes themselves, however, are not evidence. TRCP 226a, §II(10). Jurors must use only the materials provided by the court and cannot use a personal electronic device. *Id.* Jurors are admonished not to take notes if it will distract them from the evidence. *Id.*

★

§10.1 **Consulting notes.** The court can permit jurors to consult their notes during deliberations. TRCP 226a, §II(10), 281. Jurors cannot share their notes with anyone, however, including with other jurors. TRCP 226a, §II(10).

§10.2 **Location of notes.** Jurors must leave their notes in the jury room or with the bailiff during trial. TRCP 226a, §II(10). If the court allows the jurors to consult their notes during deliberations the bailiff will collect the notes and give them to the court when the jurors are not deliberating. *Id.* After deliberations, the bailiff will collect the notes and will destroy them when the jurors are released. *Id.*

§11. REVIEW

§11.1 **Appellate record.** To create a record for challenging most errors in selecting the jury (e.g., *Batson* challenge, strike for cause), the party should ask the court reporter to take possession of the juror information sheets and the strike lists and request that they be included in the appellate record.

§11.2 **Abuse of discretion.** The test for abuse of discretion is whether the trial court acted without reference to any guiding rules and principles or whether the act was arbitrary and unreasonable. Abuse of discretion is the standard used to review the following types of error:

1. Error in voir dire. *In re Commitment of Hill*, 334 S.W.3d 226, 229 (Tex.2011); *see, e.g.*, *Hyundai Motor Co. v. Vasquez*, 189 S.W.3d 743, 760 (Tex.2006) (trial court did not abuse discretion in denying line of questions); *Babcock v. Northwest Mem'l Hosp.*, 767 S.W.2d 705, 709 (Tex.1989) (trial court abused discretion by denying line of questions). For example, a court abuses its discretion when it denies a party's right to ask a proper question and that denial prevents the determination of whether there are grounds to challenge for cause or denies intelligent use of peremptory challenges. *Babcock*, 767 S.W.2d at 709.

2. Erroneous ruling on challenge for cause. *Cortez v. HCCI-San Antonio, Inc.*, 159 S.W.3d 87, 93 (Tex. 2005).

3. Erroneous *Batson* ruling. *Davis v. Fisk Elec. Co.*, 268 S.W.3d 508, 515 (Tex.2008); *Goode v. Shoukfeh*, 943 S.W.2d 441, 446 (Tex.1997). But in federal courts and in Texas criminal courts, the standard is "clearly erroneous." *Whitsey v. State*, 796 S.W.2d 707, 726 (Tex.Crim.App.1990); *see Hernandez v. New York*, 500 U.S. 352, 365-66 (1991).

§11.3 **Harmless error.** The test for harmless error is whether the error probably caused the rendition of an improper judgment or probably prevented the appellant from properly presenting its case to the appellate court. TRAP 44.1(a). The harmless-error standard is used to review procedural errors in impaneling a jury, such as the following:

1. Court's refusal to shuffle. *E.g.*, *Rivas v. Liberty Mut. Ins.*, 480 S.W.2d 610, 612 (Tex.1972) (court refused to shuffle jury panel after proper request; no improper judgment).

2. Clerk's mistake in calling jurors. *E.g.*, *Wells v. Barrow*, 153 S.W.3d 514, 517-18 (Tex.App.—Amarillo 2004, no pet.) (clerk omitted panelist's name when calling names for jury, and unselected panelist served instead; no improper judgment because unselected panelist was qualified).

§11.4 **Relaxed harmless error.** The test for the "relaxed" harmless-error rule is whether the trial was materially unfair. *Lopez v. Foremost Paving, Inc.*, 709 S.W.2d 643, 644 (Tex.1986). The party challenging the error does not need to show injury. *See Patterson Dental Co. v. Dunn*, 592 S.W.2d 914, 921 (Tex.1979); *cf. Compton v. Henrie*, 364 S.W.2d 179, 182 (Tex.1963) (no need to establish probable injury in juror-disqualification cases; decided before adoption of relaxed harmless-error rule). To show the trial was materially unfair, the movant must show the evidence was conflicting and hotly contested. *Lopez*, 709 S.W.2d at 644. The existence of antagonism between the parties is a question of law reviewable de novo. *Pojar v. Cifre*, 199 S.W.3d 317, 324 (Tex.App.—Corpus Christi 2006, pet. denied); *see Garcia v. Central Power & Light Co.*, 704 S.W.2d 734, 736 (Tex.1986); *Patterson Dental*, 592 S.W.2d at 919. The relaxed harmless-error standard has been used to review the following types of error:

1. Allocation of strikes. *E.g.*, *Lopez*, 709 S.W.2d at 644 (error in awarding twice as many strikes to Ds as to Ps). *But see Torrington Co. v. Stutzman*, 46 S.W.3d 829, 851 (Tex.2000) (dicta; party must show erroneous allocation probably caused rendition of improper judgment).

✪

2. Error in selecting jury. *E.g.*, *Carr v. Smith*, 22 S.W.3d 128, 135 (Tex.App.—Fort Worth 2000, pet. denied) (error in granting shuffle after voir dire began); *Mann v. Ramirez*, 905 S.W.2d 275, 281 (Tex.App.—San Antonio 1995, writ denied) (error in excusing panelist for nonstatutory reasons).

B. OPENING STATEMENT

§1. GENERAL

§1.1 Rules. TRCP 265(a), 266. See TRCP 269 (closing argument).

§1.2 Purpose. Immediately after the jury is impaneled, the parties make opening statements in which they briefly tell the jury the nature of their claims or defenses, the relief sought, and what they expect to prove. TRCP 265(a). Assertions made during opening argument are not evidence and are not judicial admissions. *Weslaco Fed'n of Teachers v. Texas Educ. Agency*, 27 S.W.3d 258, 263 (Tex.App.—Austin 2000, no pet.) (not judicial admissions); *Carrasco v. Texas Transp.*, 908 S.W.2d 575, 580 (Tex.App.—Waco 1995, no writ) (not evidence).

§1.3 Forms. *O'Connor's Texas Civil Forms* (2012), FORMS 8B.

§2. RIGHT TO MAKE FIRST OPENING STATEMENT

The right to make the first opening statement is an important advantage—the party that makes the first opening statement gets to summarize its case to the jury before its opponent. *See* TRCP 265(a). The right to make the first opening statement is related to the right to initiate voir dire, the right to open and close the evidence, and the right to open and close the final argument. See "Right to initiate voir dire," ch. 8-A, §5.2, p. 683; "Right to Open Evidence," ch. 8-C, §2, p. 698; "Right to Open & Close Final Argument," ch. 8-J, §2, p. 748.

§2.1 The rule – P goes first. The party with the burden of proof on the whole case has the right to make the first opening statement to the jury (and introduce evidence first). TRCP 265(a)-(b). Most often, that party is the plaintiff.

§2.2 The exceptions – D goes first. There are exceptions to the rule that the plaintiff has the right to make the first opening statement.

1. **Burden of proof.** A defendant has the right to make the first opening statement and introduce evidence first if it has the burden of proof for the entire case under the pleadings. TRCP 265(a)-(b). To determine who has the burden of proof on the whole case, ask which party would lose the case if no evidence were introduced. If the defendant would lose, then the defendant has the burden of proof. *Union City Transfer v. Adams*, 248 S.W.2d 256, 260 (Tex.App.—Fort Worth 1952, writ ref'd n.r.e.); *see, e.g.*, *Ocean Transp. v. Greycas, Inc.*, 878 S.W.2d 256, 269 (Tex.App.—Corpus Christi 1994, writ denied) (in suit on a note, D did not have right to make first opening statement because P had burden to prove deficiency and attorney fees).

2. **Admission under TRCP 266.** A defendant has the right to make the first opening statement (and introduce evidence first) if, before the trial begins, the defendant admits the plaintiff is entitled to recover, subject to proof of defensive allegations in the answer. TRCP 266; *cf. First State Bank v. Fatheree*, 847 S.W.2d 391, 397 (Tex. App.—Amarillo 1993, writ denied) (D stipulated to liability on promissory notes subject to findings on her affirmative defenses; D had right to open and close final argument). The admission must relieve the plaintiff from the necessity of offering any evidence to support its case. *E.g.*, *Trice v. Stamford Builders Sup.*, 248 S.W.2d 213, 215 (Tex.App.—Eastland 1952, no writ) (D stipulated P held title to property unless D could prove title through plea of limitation; D had right to open and close final argument). A defendant cannot secure the right to open merely by voluntarily assuming the burden of proof; the defendant must unequivocally admit liability and damages or establish them as a matter of law and remove them as issues from the case. *See, e.g.*, *Seigler v. Seigler*, 391 S.W.2d 403, 404 (Tex.1965) (contestants of will could not voluntarily assume burden; they had to remove issue of testamentary capacity from case); *4M Linen & Unif. Sup. v. W.P. Ballard & Co.*, 793 S.W.2d 320, 324-25 (Tex.App.—Houston [1st Dist.] 1990, writ denied) (even though D stipulated liability, P had burden on attorney fees; P had right to open and close final argument).

⭐

§3. ORDER OF OPENING STATEMENTS

§3.1 First opening statement. The party who the court decided has the right to make the first opening statement will make its statement after the jury is impaneled and before any evidence is introduced. *See* TRCP 265(a).

§3.2 Other opening statements.

1. Two-party case. The party adverse to the party who made the first statement may make a statement of the case either (1) after the other party's opening statement and before any evidence is introduced or (2) before the adverse party introduces its own evidence. *See* TRCP 265(a), (c).

2. Multiparty case. In a multiparty case, the court will determine the order for other parties to make their statements. TRCP 265(a). The trial court may require all the parties on one side to make their opening statements together, either after the first opening statement or before introducing their own evidence. *E.g.*, *Fibreboard Corp. v. Pool*, 813 S.W.2d 658, 691 (Tex.App.—Texarkana 1991, writ denied) (all Ds must make opening statements at same time).

§4. LIMITS OF OPENING STATEMENT

The trial court has broad discretion to limit opening statements. *Tacon Mech. Contractors v. Grant Sheet Metal Inc.*, 889 S.W.2d 666, 675 (Tex.App.—Houston [14th Dist.] 1994, writ denied).

§4.1 Rules for opening statements. The opening statements must observe the following rules:

1. Brief. The parties must briefly state to the jury the nature of their claims or defenses, what they expect to prove, and the relief they seek. TRCP 265(a).

2. No details. The parties may not detail the evidence by naming witnesses they intend to call and outlining the substance of their expected testimony. *Guerrero v. Smith*, 864 S.W.2d 797, 799 (Tex.App.—Houston [14th Dist.] 1993, no writ); *e.g.*, *Ranger Ins. v. Rogers*, 530 S.W.2d 162, 170 (Tex.App.—Austin 1975, writ ref'd n.r.e.) (party improperly identified witnesses and summarized expected testimony).

3. No display. The parties may not read from, describe, or display documents or photographs to the jury. *Ranger Ins.*, 530 S.W.2d at 170 (documents); *e.g.*, *Guerrero*, 864 S.W.2d at 799-800 (party displayed photograph during opening statement).

§4.2 Improper argument by both parties. If both parties make improper comments in their opening statements, the error in one cancels the other and on appeal will be considered harmless error. *See Wells v. HCA Health Servs.*, 806 S.W.2d 850, 855 (Tex.App.—Fort Worth 1990, writ denied); *Ranger Ins. v. Rogers*, 530 S.W.2d 162, 170-71 (Tex.App.—Austin 1975, writ ref'd n.r.e.). If one party discusses a particular issue, that party cannot object if the other party also discusses it. *See, e.g.*, *Smith v. Smith*, 720 S.W.2d 586, 593 (Tex.App.—Houston [1st Dist.] 1986, no writ) (P's attorney referred to criminal proceedings after D's attorney referred to them).

§5. OBJECTING & PRESERVING ERROR

§5.1 Timely. A complaint about an improper comment during the opening statement is waived unless an objection is timely made, which means the objection must be made at the earliest practical moment. *City of Corsicana v. Herod*, 768 S.W.2d 805, 816 (Tex.App.—Waco 1989, no writ). If the party does not object to the first reference, it waives any error. *Id.* To preserve error, the party must distinctly point out the error and state the grounds of the objection. *Id.*

§5.2 Incurable error. Although the rule is that a party must object to improper opening statements, if the cumulative effect of the improper statements is so prejudicial that an instruction to disregard would not remove the prejudice produced, the error is not waived. *Mapco, Inc. v. Jenkins*, 476 S.W.2d 55, 61-62 (Tex.App.—Amarillo 1971, writ ref'd n.r.e.). The same rules regarding incurable error in the final argument apply to the opening statement. See "Incurable argument," ch. 8-J, §5.2, p. 751.

———————————————— ★ ————————————————

C. INTRODUCING EVIDENCE

§1. GENERAL

§1.1 Rules. TRCP 265-267; TRE 103, 403, 614, 701-705, 1008; TRAP 33.1.

§1.2 Purpose. The parties prove their case for the jury (or the judge in a nonjury trial) by introducing evidence. Most evidence is introduced in the form of the testimony of witnesses, who, under oath, relate facts within their knowledge. *Goudeau v. Marquez*, 830 S.W.2d 681, 683 (Tex.App.—Houston [1st Dist.] 1992, no writ); *Bloom v. Bloom*, 767 S.W.2d 463, 470 (Tex.App.—San Antonio 1989, writ denied). The decision to admit evidence—as opposed to the task of evaluating it—is within the exclusive authority of the trial court. *City of Brownsville v. Alvarado*, 897 S.W.2d 750, 753 (Tex.1995).

§1.3 Timetable & forms. Timetable, Offer of Proof & Bill of Exception, p. 1230; *O'Connor's Texas Civil Forms* (2012), FORMS 8C.

§1.4 Other references. Brown & Rondon, *Texas Rules of Evidence Handbook* (2013) (referred to as Brown & Rondon, *Evidence Handbook*); Morales, *Social Media Evidence: "What You Post or Tweet Can & Will Be Used Against You in a Court of Law,"* 60 The Advocate: State Bar Litigation Section Report 32 (Fall 2012); Wilson, *Admissibility of Web-Based Data*, 52 The Advocate: State Bar Litigation Section Report 31 (Fall 2010); *O'Connor's Texas Causes of Action* (2013) (*O'Connor's Texas COA*).

§2. RIGHT TO OPEN EVIDENCE

The party with the burden of proof on the entire case has the right to present its evidence first. TRCP 265(b), 266; *Amis v. Ashworth*, 802 S.W.2d 379, 384 (Tex.App.—Tyler 1990, orig. proceeding). In most cases, the opening party is the plaintiff, not because the plaintiff filed the suit, but because the plaintiff is usually the party asking for relief. *Pace Corp. v. Jackson*, 284 S.W.2d 340, 350 (Tex.1955). See "Right to Make First Opening Statement," ch. 8-B, §2, p. 696.

§3. INVOKING "THE RULE"

To exclude witnesses from the courtroom during the trial, a party should invoke "the Rule" at the beginning of the trial. TRCP 267(a) and TRE 614 require the trial court, at the request of either party, to administer the oath to the witnesses and remove them from the courtroom so they cannot hear the testimony given by other witnesses. *Drilex Sys. v. Flores*, 1 S.W.3d 112, 117 (Tex.1999). Neither TRCP 267 nor TRE 614 can prevent a witness from talking about the case before trial. *Kennedy v. Eden*, 837 S.W.2d 98, 98 (Tex.1992) (TRE 614).

§3.1 Court's instructions. The court must instruct the witnesses that they are not to converse about the case with each other or with any person other than the attorneys in the case (except by permission of the court) and that they are not to read any reports of or comments on the testimony in the case while under the Rule. TRCP 267(d); *see* TRE 614; *Drilex Sys. v. Flores*, 1 S.W.3d 112, 117 (Tex.1999). The parties are obligated to ensure that their witnesses comply with the Rule unless they are exempted from it. *Drilex*, 1 S.W.3d at 120.

§3.2 Persons not excluded. The following persons should not be excluded from the courtroom during trial: (1) a party who is a natural person or spouse, (2) an officer or employee of a party that is not a natural person and who is designated as its representative by its attorney, or (3) a person whose presence is shown by a party to be essential to the presentation of the case. TRCP 267(b); TRE 614; *Drilex Sys. v. Flores*, 1 S.W.3d 112, 116-17 (Tex.1999); *see also Century 21 Real Estate Corp. v. Hometown Real Estate Co.*, 890 S.W.2d 118, 129 (Tex.App.—Texarkana 1994, writ denied) (trial court should have required corporation to name representative and excluded other officers); *Fazzino v. Guido*, 836 S.W.2d 271, 277 (Tex.App.—Houston [1st Dist.] 1992, writ denied) (parties could remain in courtroom).

§3.3 Exemption. Once the Rule is invoked, the parties should ask the court to exempt any witnesses whose presence in the courtroom is essential to the presentation of the case. TRCP 267(b)(3); TRE 614(3); *Drilex Sys. v. Flores*, 1 S.W.3d 112, 120 (Tex.1999). Witnesses whom the trial court exempts are not placed under the Rule. *Drilex*,

─────────────── ✦ ───────────────

1 S.W.3d at 117. To exempt an expert from the Rule, the party must show that the expert needs to be present in the courtroom to form an opinion based on more accurate factual assumptions. TRE 703; *see Drilex*, 1 S.W.3d at 119.

§3.4 Violation of the Rule. A nonexempt witness violates the Rule by remaining in the courtroom during the testimony of another witness, by learning about another's trial testimony through discussions with persons other than the attorneys, or by reading comments about the testimony. *Drilex Sys. v. Flores*, 1 S.W.3d 112, 117 (Tex.1999). When a witness who was placed under the Rule violates the Rule, the trial court can allow or exclude all or part of the witness's testimony or hold the witness in contempt. TRCP 267(e); *Drilex*, 1 S.W.3d at 117; *In re K.M.B.*, 91 S.W.3d 18, 28 (Tex.App.—Fort Worth 2002, no pet.). When a witness who was not placed under the Rule violates the restrictions of the Rule, the court can exclude the witness's testimony but cannot hold the witness in contempt. *See Drilex*, 1 S.W.3d at 120.

§4. SCOPE OF EXAMINATION

§4.1 Direct examination. The scope of direct examination is limited by the pleadings. When evidence is not relevant under the pleadings, it should not be admitted. TRE 402. The court should admit all relevant evidence unless some rule or principle requires its exclusion. *Stokes v. Puckett*, 972 S.W.2d 921, 926 (Tex.App.—Beaumont 1998, pet. denied). See Brown & Rondon, *Evidence Handbook*, p. 173. When evidence is relevant but its probative value is substantially outweighed by its prejudicial effect, the evidence should be excluded. TRE 403. See Brown & Rondon, *Evidence Handbook*, p. 190. Rules that exclude relevant evidence bearing on the truth sought must be supported by good cause and solid policy reasons. *See Davis v. Davis*, 521 S.W.2d 603, 607 (Tex.1975).

§4.2 Cross-examination. A witness may be cross-examined on any matter relevant to any issue in the case, including credibility. TRE 611(b); *see* TRE 405(a) (cross-examination allowed on relevant specific instances of conduct); *Continental Cas. Co. v. Thomas*, 463 S.W.2d 501, 506-07 (Tex.App.—Beaumont 1971, no writ) (cross-examination allowed in all phases of case). See Brown & Rondon, *Evidence Handbook*, p. 616. Due process requires that a party be given the opportunity to confront and cross-examine adverse witnesses. *Davidson v. Great Nat'l Life Ins.*, 737 S.W.2d 312, 314 (Tex.1987); *State Office of Risk Mgmt. v. Escalante*, 162 S.W.3d 619, 628 (Tex.App.—El Paso 2005, pet. dism'd). Texas does not limit a litigant's cross-examination to the matters covered by direct examination. *CPS Int'l v. Harris & Westmoreland*, 784 S.W.2d 538, 543 (Tex.App.—Texarkana 1990, no writ). A party's cross-examination may be limited by its response to a contention in a request for disclosure. See "Contentions," ch. 6-E, §4.2.3, p. 519.

§4.3 Redirect examination. On redirect examination, the party may ask the witness to explain answers given on cross-examination, including material elicited for the first time. *Sims v. Brackett*, 885 S.W.2d 450, 455 (Tex. App.—Corpus Christi 1994, writ denied). The purpose of redirect is to prevent the jury from being left with a false and incomplete picture created by cross-examination. *Sims*, 885 S.W.2d at 455. The TREs do not address the scope of redirect examination. Brown & Rondon, *Evidence Handbook*, p. 617. A trial court cannot deny the parties the right to conduct redirect examination. *Sims*, 885 S.W.2d at 455.

§4.4 Recross examination. On recross examination, the party may ask the witness to explain answers given on redirect examination and to amplify new material elicited for the first time. *See* TRE 611(b).

§4.5 Rebuttal evidence. Once the plaintiff or the defendant rests, the other party may introduce evidence to rebut the last round of evidence. On rebuttal, a party is limited to evidence that directly answers or disproves the last round of the other party's evidence. *In re Bledsoe*, 41 S.W.3d 807, 813 (Tex.App.—Fort Worth 2001, orig. proceeding); *Gendke v. Travelers Ins.*, 368 S.W.2d 3, 5 (Tex.App.—Waco 1963, no writ).

§4.6 Questions by jurors. It is not clear whether the trial court in a civil case should permit jurors to ask questions. The courts that have addressed this question have held that if it is error to permit questions by jurors, the error must be preserved by an objection. *E.g., Hudson v. Markum*, 948 S.W.2d 1, 3 (Tex.App.—Dallas 1997, writ denied); *Fazzino v. Guido*, 836 S.W.2d 271, 275-76 (Tex.App.—Houston [1st Dist.] 1992, writ denied). The Court of Criminal Appeals has held that questions by jurors compromise a fair trial by modifying the jury's role as a neutral

★

fact-finder. *Morrison v. State*, 845 S.W.2d 882, 889 (Tex.Crim.App.1992). For an article that recommends permitting jurors to ask questions and outlines the procedures currently used in civil courts, see Curry & Krugler, *The Sound of Silence: Are Silent Juries the Best Juries?*, 62 Tex.B.J. 441 (1999).

§5. INTRODUCING TESTIMONY

§5.1 Discovery products. See "Using Disclosures as Evidence," ch. 6-E, §8, p. 522; "Using Deposition at Trial," ch. 6-F, §12, p. 538; "Using Interrogatories as Evidence," ch. 6-G, §9, p. 555; "Admissions as Evidence," ch. 6-H, §8, p. 563; "Using Requested Documents," ch. 6-I, §8, p. 574; "Using Medical Records," ch. 6-J, §6, p. 579; "Using Evidence at Trial," ch. 6-K, §5, p. 582.

§5.2 Over closed-circuit TV. If a witness was deposed before trial, the parties may file an agreed motion asking the court to permit the witness to be examined over closed-circuit television or other two-way electronic communication that is capable of visually and audibly recording the proceedings. CPRC §30.012(a), (b).

§5.3 Impeachment & rebuttal evidence not produced in discovery. A party may introduce rebuttal or impeachment evidence, even though it was not produced in discovery, if (1) the evidence is solely for impeachment or rebuttal, (2) its use could not have been anticipated, and (3) the evidence is not responsive to a direct discovery request. *See, e.g.*, *Aluminum Co. of Am. v. Bullock*, 870 S.W.2d 2, 4 (Tex.1994) (party should have been permitted to use undesignated expert to rebut unexpected change in material testimony of the other party's expert); *Emery v. Rollins*, 880 S.W.2d 237, 239-40 (Tex.App.—Houston [14th Dist.] 1994, writ denied) (documents could be used as rebuttal evidence because their need was unanticipated); *Dennis v. Haden*, 867 S.W.2d 48, 51-52 (Tex.App.—Texarkana 1993, writ denied) (when D did not supply expert's report as required, P should have been permitted to use deposition of undesignated witness on rebuttal); *Munoz v. Missouri Pac. R.R.*, 823 S.W.2d 766, 769 (Tex.App.—Corpus Christi 1992, no writ) (D's rebuttal testimony was admitted when D did not learn of impeachment witness until trial-time deposition of another witness); *Tinkle v. Henderson*, 777 S.W.2d 537, 540 (Tex.App.—Tyler 1989, writ denied) (fact witness offered to rebut matter that arose during trial); *Ellsworth v. Bishop Jewelry & Loan Co.*, 742 S.W.2d 533, 534 (Tex.App.—Dallas 1987, writ denied) (party had good cause to use undisclosed medical expert to rebut the testimony of a medical expert who testified beyond the subject matter identified in the interrogatory); *see also* TRCP 166(h) (exchange of list of fact witnesses at pretrial conference does not include rebuttal or impeaching witnesses the necessity of whose testimony cannot be anticipated before trial).

§5.4 Testimony of a fact witness. The testimony of a fact witness is limited to the facts within the witness's personal knowledge. *United Way v. Helping Hands Lifeline Found.*, 949 S.W.2d 707, 713 (Tex.App.—San Antonio 1997, writ denied). A lay witness (i.e., nonexpert witness) may testify in the form of opinion or inference only if the opinion or inference is (1) rationally based on the perception of the witness and (2) helpful to a clear understanding of the witness's testimony or the determination of a fact in issue. TRE 701. See Brown & Rondon, *Evidence Handbook*, p. 659.

PRACTICE TIP
*If a witness refers to notes while on the stand, TRE 612(1) grants the adverse party access to the notes; if a witness uses notes to refresh her recollection before taking the stand, TRE 612(2) gives the trial court discretion to allow the adverse party access to the notes. **Goode v. Shoukfeh**, 943 S.W.2d 441, 449 (Tex.1997). See Brown & Rondon, **Evidence Handbook**, p. 621.*

---

§5.5 Testimony from expert. If specialized knowledge will help the fact-finder understand the evidence or decide a fact issue, a witness who qualifies as an expert may testify in the form of an opinion. TRE 702; *Broders v. Heise*, 924 S.W.2d 148, 152-53 (Tex.1996). See "*Daubert-Robinson* Test for Expert Testimony," ch. 5-N, §2, p. 410; Brown & Rondon, *Evidence Handbook*, p. 675. Opinion testimony from an expert "can rise no higher than the facts upon which it is based." *Sipes v. General Motors Corp.*, 946 S.W.2d 143, 148 (Tex.App.—Texarkana 1997, writ denied). Once an expert is challenged, the party offering the expert has the burden to respond to each objection and

✦

show the testimony is admissible by a preponderance of the evidence. *E.I. du Pont de Nemours & Co. v. Robinson*, 923 S.W.2d 549, 557 (Tex.1995). That party must prove the reliability of the underlying tests on which the expert's opinion is based. *Merrell Dow Pharms. v. Havner*, 953 S.W.2d 706, 712-14 (Tex.1997). To prove admissibility, see "Sponsor's response to objection," ch. 5-N, §3.3, p. 415. For the qualifications of and objections to an expert who testifies in a medical-liability suit against a physician or other health-care provider, see *O'Connor's Texas COA*, "Expert Testimony," ch. 20-A, §8, p. 634.

§5.6 Testimony from expert about learned treatise. To use a "learned treatise" on direct examination, a party must take the following steps: (1) prove the treatise was published, (2) prove the expert relied on it as authority (by admission or judicial notice) before trial to corroborate her opinion, and then (3) read the statement in the treatise to the jury. *See* TRE 803(18). To use a "learned treatise" on cross-examination, a party must take the following steps: (1) prove the treatise was published, (2) prove the treatise is authoritative, and (3) read the statement in the treatise to the jury. *See id.* Statements from a learned treatise are admissible only when used in the direct or cross-examination of an expert. *Owens-Corning Fiberglas Corp. v. Malone*, 916 S.W.2d 551, 559 (Tex.App.—Houston [1st Dist.] 1996), *aff'd*, 972 S.W.2d 35 (Tex.1998). The treatise itself cannot be introduced into evidence as an exhibit or taken by the jury to the jury room. TRE 803(18); *e.g.*, *Kahanek v. Rogers*, 12 S.W.3d 501, 504 (Tex. App.—San Antonio 1999, pet. denied) (because physician's desk reference was learned treatise, it could not be taken into jury room). See Brown & Rondon, *Evidence Handbook*, p. 889.

§5.7 Proving a dying declaration. To introduce a dying declaration, a party must prove the following: (1) the declarant made a statement when she believed death was imminent, (2) the statement was about the cause or circumstances of what the declarant believed to be her impending death, (3) the declarant was physically and mentally able to recollect and accurately narrate the cause or circumstances, and (4) the declarant is unavailable at the time of trial. *See* TRE 804(b)(2). See Brown & Rondon, *Evidence Handbook*, p. 916.

§5.8 Audio or video recording. If a recording is a fair representation of a transaction, conversation, or occurrence, it is admissible. *Seymour v. Gillespie*, 608 S.W.2d 897, 898 (Tex.1980). To introduce a recording, a party must establish the following: (1) the recording machine can accurately record and reproduce sounds or images, (2) the operator was experienced and qualified to operate the recording machine, (3) the recording is authentic or correct—the witness heard (or saw) what was being recorded, (4) no changes, additions, or deletions were made to the recording, (5) the recording was preserved in a proper manner, (6) the witness recognizes and can identify the voices heard (and the locations and persons seen) on the recording, and (7) if the subject of the recording is a conversation, the testimony elicited was made voluntarily without any kind of inducement. *Id.* Some of these elements may be inferred from the evidence and are not required to be proved. *Id.*

PRACTICE TIP

*When introducing orally recorded testimony (video, tape, or digitally recorded), make sure the court reporter stays in the courtroom and transcribes the testimony as it is heard by the jury. Court reporters often take a coffee break while taped testimony is played and simply type into the record, "The tape was played for the jury." Thus, that part of the evidence is not included in the appellate record. If you do not object to the court reporter's absence, you will waive the issue of an incomplete record. E.g., **Lascurain v. Crowley**, 917 S.W.2d 341, 344-45 (Tex.App.—El Paso 1996, no writ) (court reporter left courtroom during deposition testimony with permission of parties). If the court reporter appeared to be transcribing the testimony but was not, you may be able to reconstruct the record. **State Farm Fire & Cas. Ins. v. Vandiver**, 941 S.W.2d 343, 347-49 (Tex.App.—Waco 1997, no writ).*

---

§5.9 Results of experiment. To introduce the results of an experiment that the other party was not invited to attend, the offering party must prove the following: (1) the party conducted an out-of-court experiment, and (2) the circumstances surrounding the experiment were substantially similar to the conditions that gave rise to the litigation.

✦

Fort Worth & Denver Ry. v. Williams, 375 S.W.2d 279, 281-82 (Tex.1964); *Horn v. Hefner*, 115 S.W.3d 255, 256 (Tex.App.—Texarkana 2003, no pet.); *see, e.g.*, *Ford Motor Co. v. Miles*, 967 S.W.2d 377, 388-89 (Tex.1998) (because party never contended tests were conducted under similar conditions, videotapes of tests should have been excluded); *Alice Leasing Corp. v. Castillo*, 53 S.W.3d 433, 446 (Tex.App.—San Antonio 2001, pet. denied) (because videotaped demonstration was substantially similar to conditions of accident, it was admissible). It is not necessary that the conditions be identical. *Williams*, 375 S.W.2d at 282; *Horn*, 115 S.W.3d at 256; *see Mottu v. Navistar Int'l Transp.*, 804 S.W.2d 144, 148 (Tex.App.—Houston [14th Dist.] 1990, writ denied) (if major dissimilarities in conditions are present, videotapes of tests are excluded).

§5.10 Similar accidents. To introduce evidence of earlier, similar accidents, the party must show with specificity that the earlier accidents occurred in a similar manner and could be attributed to a similar cause. *Huckaby v. A.G. Perry & Son, Inc.*, 20 S.W.3d 194, 202 (Tex.App.—Texarkana 2000, pet. denied). If the party does not establish the factors listed below, evidence of similar accidents is neither relevant nor material and is prejudicial. *Id.*

    1. The conditions surrounding the earlier accidents were reasonably similar. *Id.*; *Fredericksburg Indus. v. Franklin Int'l*, 911 S.W.2d 518, 521-22 (Tex.App.—San Antonio 1995, writ denied); *Henry v. Mrs. Baird's Bakeries, Inc.*, 475 S.W.2d 288, 294 (Tex.App.—Fort Worth 1971, writ ref'd n.r.e.).

    2. The conditions of the earlier accidents and the party's accident were connected in some special way. *Huckaby*, 20 S.W.3d at 202; *Henry*, 475 S.W.2d at 294; *see, e.g.*, *Dallas Ry. & Terminal Co. v. Farnsworth*, 227 S.W.2d 1017, 1019-20 (Tex.1950) (evidence street-car operator started car too quickly at each of three stops before P got off was closely related to issue of whether operator gave P enough time to get off car before starting it).

    3. The earlier accidents were attributable to the same condition that caused the party's accident. *See Huckaby*, 20 S.W.3d at 202; *Henry*, 475 S.W.2d at 294; *see, e.g.*, *Bell v. Buddies Super-Mkt.*, 516 S.W.2d 447, 450-51 (Tex.App.—Tyler 1974, writ ref'd n.r.e.) (earlier "near-falls" were caused by ramp's rough concrete and were not attributable to ramp's steep slope, which caused P's fall).

§6. IMPEACHING A WITNESS

The credibility of a witness may be attacked by any party, including the party calling the witness. TRE 607; *e.g.*, *Owens-Corning Fiberglas Corp. v. Malone*, 916 S.W.2d 551, 567 (Tex.App.—Houston [1st Dist.] 1996) (court permitted Ps to call D's expert in their case-in-chief and impeach him), *aff'd*, 972 S.W.2d 35 (Tex.1998). See Brown & Rondon, *Evidence Handbook*, p. 573.

§6.1 Impeaching by reputation for truthfulness. There are two questions to ask a witness about the reputation of another witness: (1) Does the witness know the general character or reputation for truthfulness of the witness intended to be impeached? (2) If so, what is the character of the witness, good or bad? *International Sec. Life Ins. v. Melancon*, 463 S.W.2d 762, 767 (Tex.App.—Beaumont 1971, writ ref'd n.r.e.); *see* TRE 404(a)(3), 608. Once the court determines the impeaching witness is qualified to speak on the general reputation of the other witness, the other party has the right to cross-examine the impeaching witness about her means of knowledge before she answers the question about the other witness's reputation for truthfulness. *See Melancon*, 463 S.W.2d at 767. See Brown & Rondon, *Evidence Handbook*, p. 579.

§6.2 Impeaching by earlier inconsistent statement. To impeach a witness with an earlier statement (whether oral or written) that is inconsistent with the witness's trial statement, the attorney must (1) tell the witness about the contents of the earlier statement and when, where, and to whom it was made and (2) give the witness an opportunity to explain or deny it. TRE 613(a). If the statement is in writing, it does not need to be shown to the witness, but, on request, it must be shown to opposing counsel. *Id.* If the witness unequivocally admits to having made the statement, extrinsic evidence of the earlier statement is not admissible. *Id.*; *Downen v. Texas Gulf Shrimp Co.*, 846 S.W.2d 506, 512 (Tex.App.—Corpus Christi 1993, writ denied). Extrinsic evidence is admissible only if the witness denies the statement. *See* TRE 613(a). This provision does not apply to admissions of a party-opponent as defined in TRE 801(e)(2). TRE 613(a). See Brown & Rondon, *Evidence Handbook*, p. 628.

──────────────── ✦ ────────────────

§6.3 Impeaching by bias. To impeach a witness by proof of circumstances or statements showing bias or interest, the attorney must (1) tell the witness about the circumstances supporting the claim of bias or the details of the statement, including the contents and when, where, and to whom it was made and (2) give the witness an opportunity to explain or deny the circumstances or statement. TRE 613(b). If the statement is in writing, it does not need to be shown to the witness, but it must be shown to opposing counsel on request. *Id.* If the witness unequivocally admits to the bias or interest, extrinsic evidence of the earlier statement is not admissible. *Id.*; *Walker v. Packer*, 827 S.W.2d 833, 839 n.5 (Tex.1992). Extrinsic evidence is admissible only if the witness denies bias or interest. *See* TRE 613(b). See Brown & Rondon, *Evidence Handbook*, p. 636.

§6.4 Impeaching by conviction. Before attempting to attack the credibility of a witness by proving a conviction, the party must give the other party advance written notice (if the other party timely requested it) of the intent to use the conviction. TRE 609(f). The credibility of a witness may be attacked on the ground that the witness was convicted of a crime if (1) the witness admits the conviction on the stand or the conviction is of public record, (2) the crime was a felony or involved moral turpitude, and (3) the court determines the probative value of admitting the evidence outweighs its prejudicial effect. TRE 609(a); *see Porter v. Nemir*, 900 S.W.2d 376, 382 (Tex.App.—Austin 1995, no writ). To impeach by conviction, a party must prove the following: (1) the witness was convicted of a felony or a crime that involved moral turpitude, (2) the conviction is not over ten years old, (3) the witness has not been pardoned, the conviction has not been annulled, and a certificate of rehabilitation has not been issued, (4) the conviction was not the result of a juvenile adjudication, and (5) no appeal is pending on the conviction. TRE 609; *see In re G.M.P.*, 909 S.W.2d 198, 209 (Tex.App.—Houston [14th Dist.] 1995, no writ); *see, e.g., Reviea v. Marine Drilling Co.*, 800 S.W.2d 252, 258 (Tex.App.—Corpus Christi 1990, writ denied) (20-year-old conviction too remote to impeach). See Brown & Rondon, *Evidence Handbook*, p. 591.

§7. REHABILITATING A WITNESS

§7.1 Proving truthfulness. In most civil cases, supporting evidence of a party's good character is not admissible. *Commonwealth Lloyd's Ins. v. Thomas*, 678 S.W.2d 278, 294 (Tex.App.—Fort Worth 1984, writ ref'd n.r.e.); *see* TRE 608(a)(2); *Rose v. Intercontinental Bank*, 705 S.W.2d 752, 757 (Tex.App.—Houston [1st Dist.] 1986, writ ref'd n.r.e.). Testimony of a witness's good character for truth or honesty, however, is admissible when the character of the witness is directly at issue, after a witness is impeached, or when one party (in its pleadings or by the evidence) charges the other party with a crime of moral turpitude. *Thomas*, 678 S.W.2d at 294; *see, e.g., State Bar v. Evans*, 774 S.W.2d 656, 658 (Tex.1989) (attorney charged with conduct involving moral turpitude was permitted to offer evidence of pertinent character trait). To rehabilitate a witness's character for truth, the party must introduce evidence through another witness as follows: (1) prove the rehabilitating witness has knowledge of the character of the witness who was attacked (i.e., establish facts that show how the witness knows of the character of the person), (2) prove the witness has an opinion about that person's character for truthfulness, and (3) have the witness state her opinion regarding that person's character for truthfulness. *See* TRE 404(a)(3), 608(a). See Brown & Rondon, *Evidence Handbook*, p. 583.

§7.2 Rebutting charge of recent fabrication or improper influence. When a witness who testified at a trial or hearing is accused of recent fabrication or improper influence during cross-examination, a party may introduce an earlier consistent statement to prove through a second witness that (1) the first witness made an out-of-court statement consistent with testimony before testifying, and (2) the statement was made before a reason to fabricate arose. TRE 801(e)(1)(B); *Skillern & Sons, Inc. v. Rosen*, 359 S.W.2d 298, 301-02 (Tex.1962); *Reviea v. Marine Drilling Co.*, 800 S.W.2d 252, 257 (Tex.App.—Corpus Christi 1990, writ denied); *cf. Tome v. U.S.*, 513 U.S. 150, 156-58 (1995) (criminal case interpreting FRE 801(d)). See Brown & Rondon, *Evidence Handbook*, p. 807.

§8. INTRODUCING DOCUMENTS

Every exhibit must meet certain threshold requirements before it can be admitted into evidence: (1) the qualifying witness must be competent, (2) the witness must have personal knowledge sufficient to authenticate the exhibit, (3) the exhibit must be relevant to the trial, and (4) the exhibit must be authenticated. *See* TRE 401 (relevance);

★

TRE 601 (competence); TRE 602 (personal knowledge); TRE 901(a) (authentication). However, just because an exhibit is relevant and authentic does not mean it is admissible; the exhibit may be excluded on other grounds (e.g., hearsay). *Director, State Empls. Worker's Comp. Div. v. Lara*, 901 S.W.2d 635, 638 (Tex.App.—El Paso 1995, writ denied).

§8.1 Competence. The witness must be competent to testify, which means the witness must be able to accurately perceive, recall, and recount. *See* TRE 601. See "Competency of witness," ch. 1-B, §3.2.16(2), p. 12. Courts often confuse competence with personal knowledge.

§8.2 Personal knowledge. The witness must have personal knowledge on which to base the authentication. TRE 602; *see, e.g.*, *City of Dallas v. GTE Sw., Inc.*, 980 S.W.2d 928, 935 (Tex.App.—Fort Worth 1998, pet. denied) (witness did not have personal knowledge about exhibit); *Savage v. Psychiatric Inst.*, 965 S.W.2d 745, 753-54 (Tex. App.—Fort Worth 1998, pet. denied) (attorney's affidavit did not establish his personal knowledge about documents); *see also Davidson v. Great Nat'l Life Ins.*, 737 S.W.2d 312, 314-15 (Tex.1987) (although court said witness was competent to authenticate photographs, court discussed personal knowledge). See "Personal knowledge," ch. 1-B, §3.2.16(3)(a), p. 12; Brown & Rondon, *Evidence Handbook*, p. 547.

§8.3 Relevance. To be relevant, the exhibit must tend to make the existence of a material fact more or less probable than it would otherwise have been. TRE 401; *Edwards v. TEC*, 936 S.W.2d 462, 466-67 (Tex.App.—Fort Worth 1996, no writ); *see, e.g.*, *Prestige Ford Co. v. Gilmore*, 56 S.W.3d 73, 80 (Tex.App.—Houston [14th Dist.] 2001, pet. denied) (report made existence of material fact less probable). See Brown & Rondon, *Evidence Handbook*, p. 180.

§8.4 Authenticity. Authentication is a prerequisite to admissibility. TRE 901(a); *In re G.F.O.*, 874 S.W.2d 729, 731 (Tex.App.—Houston [1st Dist.] 1994, no writ). See Brown & Rondon, *Evidence Handbook*, p. 928.

1. Proof of authenticity. Authentication is established by evidence that the matter in question is what its proponent claims it to be. TRE 901(b)(1); *In re G.F.O.*, 874 S.W.2d at 731. A document is considered authentic if (1) the document is being used against the party or nonparty who produced it in response to written discovery, (2) a sponsoring witness vouches for the document's authenticity, or (3) the document meets the requirements for self-authentication. *See* TRCP 176.6(c), 193.7; TRE 901(b)(10), 902; *In re G.F.O.*, 874 S.W.2d at 731.

2. Presumption of authenticity. Documents produced in response to written discovery are presumed authentic and may be used in a pretrial proceeding or at trial against the producing party or nonparty. TRCP 176.6(c), 193.7; *see also* TRE 901(b)(10) (any method of authentication provided by rule meets requirements of TRE 901(a)). See "Using Requested Documents," ch. 6-I, §8, p. 574; "Other party's discovery responses," ch. 7-B, §9.5.3(1)(a), p. 616. To use a discovery document against someone other than the producing party, a witness must vouch for the document's authenticity, or the document must satisfy the requirements for self-authentication. *See In re G.F.O.*, 874 S.W.2d at 731. *But see Lection v. Dyll*, 65 S.W.3d 696, 702-03 (Tex.App.—Dallas 2001, pet. denied) (in case involving bylaws produced by D-hospital, it was not necessary to authenticate them for use against D-doctor). See §8.4.3, below; "Documents that are self-authenticating," §8.4.4, p. 706.

3. Documents authenticated by witness.

(1) Signed instrument. To introduce a signed document, a party must do one of the following: (1) call the signing person (as an adverse witness, if necessary) to identify the signature as her own, (2) call a witness who saw the person sign the document, (3) call a witness who is familiar with the person's signature and can identify it, or (4) call a handwriting expert who can testify that, based on handwriting comparisons, the signature was made by the person. *See* TRE 901(b). See Brown & Rondon, *Evidence Handbook*, p. 931.

(2) Copy of document. A duplicate is admissible as an original unless a question is raised about the authenticity of the original or it would be unfair to introduce the duplicate. TRE 1003; *ESIS, Inc. v. Johnson*, 908 S.W.2d 554, 561 (Tex.App.—Fort Worth 1995, writ denied); *see also Owens-Corning Fiberglas Corp. v. Malone*, 916 S.W.2d 551, 558 (Tex.App.—Houston [1st Dist.] 1996) (copy admissible despite extraneous markings), *aff'd*, 972

———————————— ✦ ————————————

S.W.2d 35 (Tex.1998). See Brown & Rondon, *Evidence Handbook*, p. 999. If a question is raised regarding the authenticity of the original, to introduce a copy, the party must prove the following: (1) the original was lost or destroyed, is not obtainable, is outside Texas, or is in the possession of the opponent, (2) a copy of the original was made, and (3) the offered document is a true and accurate copy of the original. TRE 1003, 1004.

PRACTICE TIP

*Do not object to a witness discussing the contents of a document in evidence with the "best-evidence" objection. The best-evidence rule comes into play only when a witness is asked to discuss the contents of a disputed document that is not in evidence. **White v. Bath**, 825 S.W.2d 227, 231 (Tex.App.—Houston [14th Dist.] 1992, writ denied). Once the document is introduced, a witness may discuss it or read from it.*

---

(3) Summary. To introduce a summary, a party must prove the following: (1) the chart, summary, or calculation is a summary of other records, (2) the other records are voluminous writings, recordings, or photographs that are admissible, (3) the other records cannot be conveniently examined in court, and (4) the other records were made available to the other party for inspection and copying. TRE 1006; *see, e.g.*, *Aquamarine Assocs. v. Burton Shipyard, Inc.*, 659 S.W.2d 820, 821-22 (Tex.1983) (because underlying business records were not shown to be admissible, summary was not admissible); *Duncan Dev. v. Haney*, 634 S.W.2d 811, 812-13 (Tex.1982) (summary of invoices received from subcontractors was admissible as summary of business records of contractor). The court may order that the other records be produced in court. TRE 1006. See Brown & Rondon, *Evidence Handbook*, p. 1021.

(4) Computer printout. To introduce a computer record, a party must prove the following: (1) the witness is a qualified computer operator, (2) the computer used is accepted as standard and efficient equipment, (3) appropriate procedures were followed regarding data entry and checks for accuracy, (4) the computer was operated and programmed properly, (5) a reliable software program was used, and (6) the record is properly identified as the output in question. Brown & Rondon, *Evidence Handbook*, p. 1005. For data stored in a computer, any printout or other output readable by sight and shown to accurately reflect the data is an "original." TRE 1001(c).

(5) Websites. To introduce a printout from a website, a party must prove that the printout accurately reflects the content of the website and the image of the page on the computer from which the printout was made. Wilson, *Admissibility of Web-Based Data*, at 32. Authentication of the printout of a website is generally proved through affidavit testimony. *Id.*; *see* TRE 901(b)(1). Courts disagree on whether an affidavit can simply state that the printout is a true and correct copy of a web page. *Compare* **Burnett Ranches, Ltd. v. Cano Pet., Inc.**, 289 S.W.3d 862, 871 (Tex.App.—Amarillo 2009, pet. denied) (P's attorney's affidavit stating document was true and correct copy of "Environmental Overview" printed from D's website was not properly authenticated because affidavit did not establish that website from which he obtained the document was D's), *with* **Daimler-Benz A.G. v. Olson**, 21 S.W.3d 707, 717 (Tex.App.—Austin 2000, pet. dism'd) (P's attorney's affidavit that attachments containing information from D's websites were within his personal knowledge and were accurate copies of original was proper to authenticate attachments). To avoid these problems with the sufficiency of affidavit testimony, a party should consider using discovery methods such as requests for admissions (e.g., ask the party to admit that Exhibit A came from its website) or deposition testimony (e.g., ask the witness if a specific web address is the employer's website). Wilson, *Admissibility of Web-Based Data*, at 32. The printout of a website may also be authenticated by its appearance, contents, substance, internal patterns, or other distinctive characteristics. *See* TRE 901(b)(4). For a more detailed discussion of the authenticity of electronic information such as websites, e-mail, and instant messages, see Brown & Rondon, *Evidence Handbook*, pp. 936-38, 947-51.

(6) Photograph. To introduce a photograph, a party must prove the following: (1) the witness saw the subject of the photograph at or near the time of the event in issue, (2) the witness recognizes the exhibit as a representation of the subject seen, and (3) the exhibit is a true and accurate representation of the subject as it appeared at the relevant time. *State v. City of Greenville*, 726 S.W.2d 162, 168 (Tex.App.—Dallas 1986, writ ref'd n.r.e.).

———————————————— ✦ ————————————————

An original of a photograph includes the negative or any print made from it. TRE 1001(c). If a verbal description of the matter is admissible, a photograph of it is generally also admissible. *City of Greenville*, 726 S.W.2d at 168. A court should exclude a photograph if its probative value is substantially outweighed by the danger of unfair prejudice. TRE 403; *Castro v. Sebesta*, 808 S.W.2d 189, 193 (Tex.App.—Houston [1st Dist.] 1991, no writ). *But see Fibreboard Corp. v. Pool*, 813 S.W.2d 658, 671 (Tex.App.—Texarkana 1991, writ denied) (if relevant, a photograph is admissible, even if gruesome). See Brown & Rondon, *Evidence Handbook*, p. 1011.

(7) Public records by witness. To introduce public records, reports, statements, or data compilations of public offices or agencies, the records must show on their face (or it must be proved by a witness) that they contain reports of (1) the activities of the office or agency, (2) matters observed under a duty imposed by law and for which there was a duty to report, or (3) factual findings resulting from an investigation made under authority granted by law. TRE 803(8); *see State v. Foltin*, 930 S.W.2d 270, 272 (Tex.App.—Houston [14th Dist.] 1996, writ denied). The court should admit records that meet these requirements unless the circumstances indicate a lack of trustworthiness. TRE 803(8). Conclusions and opinions contained in an investigatory report admissible under TRE 803(8)(C) are admissible if they are based on the factual investigation and satisfy TRE 803's requirement of trustworthiness. *See Ter-Vartanyan v. R&R Freight, Inc.*, 111 S.W.3d 779, 784 (Tex.App.—Dallas 2003, pet. denied) (police accident report admissible); *McRae v. Echols*, 8 S.W.3d 797, 800 (Tex.App.—Waco 2000, pet. denied) (same). Not everything in an official record is exempt from the hearsay rule. For example, a statement of an eyewitness included in a police report is not admissible under TRE 803(8). *Kratz v. Exxon Corp.*, 890 S.W.2d 899, 905 (Tex. App.—El Paso 1994, no writ). See Brown & Rondon, *Evidence Handbook*, p. 877.

(8) Business record by witness. To introduce a business record through a witness, a party must prove the following: (1) the record is a memorandum, report, record, or other compilation of data, (2) the witness is the custodian or another qualified witness, (3) the record was made from information transmitted by a person with knowledge of the facts, (4) the record was made at or near the time of the acts, events, conditions, opinions, or diagnoses appearing on it, (5) the record was made as part of the regular practice of that business activity, and (6) the record was kept in the course of a regularly conducted business activity. TRE 803(6); *see Brooks v. Housing Auth.*, 926 S.W.2d 316, 322 (Tex.App.—El Paso 1996, no writ) (records of security guard admissible as business records); *Connor v. Wright*, 737 S.W.2d 42, 44-45 (Tex.App.—San Antonio 1987, no writ) (business records of attorney admissible to prove attorney fees); *see, e.g., Freeman v. American Motorists Ins.*, 53 S.W.3d 710, 715 (Tex.App.—Houston [1st Dist.] 2001, no pet.) (letter from doctor to P's attorney about P's condition was inadmissible as business record because it did not qualify as a routine entry). The business records of one company can contain business records received from another company. *See GT&MC, Inc. v. Texas City Ref., Inc.*, 822 S.W.2d 252, 257-58 (Tex. App.—Houston [1st Dist.] 1991, writ denied); *see, e.g., Duncan Dev.*, 634 S.W.2d at 813-14. See Brown & Rondon, *Evidence Handbook*, p. 865.

PRACTICE TIP

Avoid relying on a live witness to prove business records. A witness may stumble over her answers to the questions, and the answers of another party's employee cannot be predicted. An affidavit should always be filed to authenticate a business record. See "Business record by affidavit," §8.4.4(1), p. 707.

---

4. Documents that are self-authenticating. If a document can overcome the hearsay objection, it can be admitted into evidence without a sponsoring witness as long as it is self-authenticating. TRE 902; *see Larson v. Family Violence & Sexual Assault Prevention Ctr.*, 64 S.W.3d 506, 511 (Tex.App.—Corpus Christi 2001, pet. denied). A self-authenticating document under TRE 902 must satisfy the requirements of TRE 901. Brown & Rondon, *Evidence Handbook*, p. 973. A party can object to a self-authenticating document on grounds other than authentication, such as relevancy, hearsay, or unfair prejudice. *Id.*

———————————— ✦ ————————————

⓭

PROPOSED TRE CHANGES

The Supreme Court has proposed TRE 902(10)(c) to provide a self-authenticating form affidavit to prove medical expenses. See Tex.Sup.Ct. Order, Misc. Docket No. 12-9191 (eff. Mar. 1, 2013). The public-comment period for the proposed rule ends on February 1, 2013, and the rule is to take effect March 1, 2013. For the proposed version of the rule, see the appendix after this book's index. For the final version, go to the Supreme Court website at www.supreme.courts .state.tx.us. When the new rule takes effect, a supplement to this book—with updated rules and commentaries that reflect the changes—will be available at www.JonesMcClure.com/ TRCPamendments.

(1) Business record by affidavit. To introduce a business record by affidavit of a custodian or other qualified witness, a party must show the following: (1) the record is admissible under TRE 803(6) or 803(7), (2) the affidavit required by TRE 902(10)(b) is attached to the record, (3) the record and the affidavit were filed with the clerk at least 14 days before trial, (4) the other parties were given prompt notice of the filing of the affidavit, and (5) the notice includes the name and employer of the person making the affidavit and a statement that the record was available for inspection and copying. TRE 902(10); *see, e.g.*, *Fullick v. City of Baytown*, 820 S.W.2d 943, 945-46 (Tex.App.—Houston [1st Dist.] 1991, no writ) (tax statements from school districts were self-authenticated); *March v. Victoria Lloyds Ins.*, 773 S.W.2d 785, 789 (Tex.App.—Fort Worth 1989, writ denied) (test of alcohol level in blood was admissible as business record with affidavit); *National Stand. Ins. v. Gayton*, 773 S.W.2d 75, 76 (Tex. App.—Amarillo 1989, no writ) (doctor's records, with factual observations and diagnosis, were admissible as business record with affidavit). If the affidavit is the same as or substantially complies with the sample provided in TRE 902(10)(b), it will satisfy the requirement of authentication. *March*, 773 S.W.2d at 789. The 14-day requirement applies only if the party offering the record relies on the affidavit to prove it; if, instead, the party relies on a qualified witness to prove the record, the other party cannot object that the record was not on file in the court 14 days before trial. *Chemical Bank v. Commercial Indus.*, 668 S.W.2d 336, 337 (Tex.1984). See Brown & Rondon, *Evidence Handbook*, p. 989; *O'Connor's Texas Forms*, FORM 8C:2.

(2) Affidavit for past expenses. CPRC §18.001 permits a party to prove the reasonableness and necessity of past expenses with an affidavit from either the person who provided the service or the person in charge of records, showing the service provided and the charge made. CPRC §18.001(b), (c); *see id.* §18.002 (form of affidavit); *Beauchamp v. Hambrick*, 901 S.W.2d 747, 749 (Tex.App.—Eastland 1995, no writ) (CPRC §18.001 allows for admissibility by affidavit of reasonableness and necessity of charges that would otherwise be inadmissible hearsay). The affidavit must be served on each party at least 30 days before the first day evidence is presented at trial. CPRC §18.001(d). The affidavit must (1) be made by the person who provided the service or the person in charge of records, (2) state that the services were necessary and were provided at a cost reasonable at the time and place of service, and (3) include an itemized statement of the services and charges. CPRC §18.001(b), (c); *see id.* §18.002; *Walker v. Ricks*, 101 S.W.2d 740, 747-48 (Tex.App.—Corpus Christi 2003, no pet.). If an opposing party wants to controvert the affidavit on the cost and necessity of services, it must serve its counteraffidavit on each party or each party's attorney. CPRC §18.001(e). The counteraffidavit must show (1) the affiant is qualified as an expert to contravene the particular service and charge involved and (2) the specific reason why the service was not necessary or the charge was unreasonable. *Turner v. Peril*, 50 S.W.3d 742, 747 (Tex.App.—Dallas 2001, pet. denied); *see* CPRC §18.001(f). See *O'Connor's Texas Forms*, FORMS 8C:4-6; *O'Connor's Texas COA*, "Affidavit for past expenses," ch. 41-B, §6.3.1(1)(b), p. 1263.

(3) Domestic public record under seal. To introduce a domestic record under seal, a party must show the following: (1) the document bears a seal of the United States, a state, or any other political subdivision listed in TRE 902(1), and (2) the document bears a signature purporting to be an attestation or execution. TRE 902(1), 1005. The document must also meet the requirements of TRE 803(8)(A), (8)(B), or (8)(C). See "Public records by witness," §8.4.3(7), p. 706.

★

(4) Domestic public record not under seal. To introduce a public record that is not under seal, a party must show the following: (1) the document bears the signature in the official capacity of an officer or employee of an entity listed in TRE 902(1), and (2) a public officer having a seal and having official duties in the district or political subdivision of the officer or employee certifies that the signer of the document has the official capacity and that the person's signature is genuine. TRE 902(2), 1005; *see Al-Nayem Int'l Trading, Inc. v. Irving ISD*, 159 S.W.3d 762, 764 (Tex.App.—Dallas 2005, no pet.) (tax statements, not certified); *Shaw v. Kennedy, Ltd.*, 879 S.W.2d 240, 246 (Tex.App.—Amarillo 1994, no writ) (copies of application for and order accepting the closing of bankruptcy proceedings, certified by bankruptcy court).

(5) Foreign public documents. To introduce public documents from other countries, see TRE 902(3) and Brown & Rondon, *Evidence Handbook*, p. 978.

(6) Excerpt from commercial publication. To introduce an excerpt from a commercial publication, a party must show the following: (1) the document is the original or a photocopy of a market quotation, tabulation, list, directory, or other published compilation, and (2) the publication is generally used and relied on by the public or by persons in particular occupations. TRE 803(17) (market reports and commercial publications), TRE 902(6) (newspapers and periodicals); *Lewis v. Southmore Sav. Ass'n*, 480 S.W.2d 180, 186 (Tex.1972) (market reports); *see, e.g.*, *Curran v. Unis*, 711 S.W.2d 290, 296-97 (Tex.App.—Dallas 1986, no writ) (photocopies of pages from business-reporting service regarding ownership of a partnership were admissible).

D. OBJECTING TO EVIDENCE

§1. GENERAL

§1.1 Rules. TRCP 166(m), 267; TRE 103-106, 403, 614; TRAP 33.1, 44.1.

§1.2 Purpose. The primary reason to object to evidence is to prevent it from being introduced in the trial and heard by the jury. A secondary reason to object is to preserve the issue for appellate review. *See* TRE 103(a); TRAP 33.1(a).

§1.3 Forms. *O'Connor's Texas Civil Forms* (2012), FORMS 5E.

§1.4 Other references. Brown & Rondon, *Texas Rules of Evidence Handbook* (2013) (referred to as Brown & Rondon, *Evidence Handbook*); 1 *McCormick on Evidence* §52 (6th ed. 2006); 1 Wigmore, *Evidence* §18 (Tillers rev. 1983 & Supp.2012-13); *O'Connor's Texas Civil Appeals* (2012) (*O'Connor's Texas Appeals*).

§2. TIME TO MAKE OBJECTIONS

§2.1 Pretrial objections.

1. Motion in limine. A party can object to evidence before trial in a motion in limine. A ruling on a motion in limine is not a ruling on the admissibility of the evidence and does not preserve error on appeal; it merely prevents the attorneys from referring to the subject matter of the motion in front of a jury without first obtaining a ruling. When the evidence is offered at trial, the party must object to preserve error. See "Motion in Limine," ch. 5-E, p. 347.

2. Motion to exclude. A party can object to evidence before trial in a motion to exclude. *See Owens-Corning Fiberglas Corp. v. Malone*, 916 S.W.2d 551, 557 (Tex.App.—Houston [1st Dist.] 1996), *aff'd*, 972 S.W.2d 35 (Tex.1998). At trial, the court may reconsider its pretrial rulings on the admissibility of evidence. *Reveal v. West*, 764 S.W.2d 8, 11 (Tex.App.—Houston [1st Dist.] 1988, orig. proceeding). Unlike rulings on motions in limine, rulings on motions to exclude evidence preserve error on appeal. *See Owens-Corning*, 916 S.W.2d at 557. However, despite a pretrial ruling, if a party affirmatively states at trial that it has no objection to the admission of evidence, the party waives any error in the admission of the evidence. *Pojar v. Cifre*, 199 S.W.3d 317, 341 (Tex.App.—Corpus Christi 2006, pet. denied).

✦

3. Objections to exhibits. A trial court may require parties to submit written pretrial objections to tendered exhibits. TRCP 166(m); *see* TRCP 193 cmt. 7.

§2.2 Trial objections. When objectionable evidence is offered at trial, the party that believes the evidence is not admissible must object. *Clark v. Trailways, Inc.*, 774 S.W.2d 644, 647 (Tex.1989). If a party does not object to the evidence, it waives any error in its admission. TRE 103(a)(1); TRAP 33.1(a); *see Service Corp. v. Guerra*, 348 S.W.3d 221, 234 (Tex.2011). To preserve error, the party must state the substance of the objection on the record. TRAP 33.1(a)(1)(A). If the objection is apparent from the context, however, the objection alone will preserve error. *Id.*; *Ramirez v. Volkswagen*, 788 S.W.2d 700, 705 (Tex.App.—Corpus Christi 1990, writ denied).

NOTE

If a party timely objects to evidence offered at trial and that same evidence was addressed by the opposing attorney during voir dire of the jury panel without objection, the objection at trial is not waived. Service Corp., 348 S.W.3d at 234. Error is not waived because statements made by attorneys during the jury-selection process are not evidence. Id. See "Voir Dire Examination," ch. 8-A, §5, p. 683; "Waiver," §6.7, p. 714.

---

§2.3 Timing of objections. An objection to evidence during trial must be made as soon as the reason for the objection becomes apparent. TRE 103(a)(1); *Wolfe v. East Tex. Seed Co.*, 583 S.W.2d 481, 482 (Tex.App.—Houston [1st Dist.] 1979, writ dism'd).

1. Too early. If an objection is premature, it does not preserve error. *See Correa v. General Motors Corp.*, 948 S.W.2d 515, 518 (Tex.App.—Corpus Christi 1997, no writ) (general objection to anticipated evidence does not preserve error); *see, e.g.*, *Bushell v. Dean*, 803 S.W.2d 711, 711-12 (Tex.1991) (error not preserved because D objected before witness testified and did not reurge objection during testimony).

2. On time. Generally, the objection must be made at the time the evidence is offered. *MBank Dallas v. Sunbelt Mfg.*, 710 S.W.2d 633, 638 (Tex.App.—Dallas 1986, writ ref'd n.r.e.). For testimonial evidence, the objection must be made after the question is asked and before the witness answers. An objection made after the witness answers is timely in some situations, such as when the witness makes an objectionable answer to a proper question, the witness answers an objectionable question too quickly for the objection to be made, or the witness volunteers an objectionable statement. *See* Brown & Rondon, *Evidence Handbook*, pp. 55-56; *see, e.g.*, *Beall v. Ditmore*, 867 S.W.2d 791, 794 (Tex.App.—El Paso 1993, writ denied) (in response to D's question, P mentioned insurance). In these instances, the party must also make other objections. See "When jury hears inadmissible evidence," §6.6, p. 713.

3. Too late. An objection is not timely if it is not made as soon as the question is asked or shortly thereafter. *E.g.*, *Miles v. Ford Motor Co.*, 922 S.W.2d 572, 591 (Tex.App.—Texarkana 1996) (objection to expert's testimony regarding previously undisclosed theory of recovery was untimely when made after theory was completely introduced), *rev'd in part on other grounds*, 967 S.W.2d 377 (Tex.1998); *Seneca Res. v. Marsh & McLennan, Inc.*, 911 S.W.2d 144, 152 (Tex.App.—Houston [1st Dist.] 1995, no writ) (objection made after lengthy testimony in violation of motion in limine was untimely). *But see Beall*, 867 S.W.2d at 795 (when P mentioned insurance in response to D's question, objection was lodged after next question and answer was timely). An objection is not timely if it is made the second time the evidence is offered. *In re A.V.*, 849 S.W.2d 393, 396 (Tex.App.—Fort Worth 1993, writ denied).

§3. SPECIFIC VS. GENERAL OBJECTIONS

§3.1 Specific objections. An objection must be specific. TRE 103(a)(1); TRAP 33.1(a)(1)(A); *Service Corp. v. Guerra*, 348 S.W.3d 221, 234 (Tex.2011). There are at least three reasons the courts require a specific objection. A specific objection (1) enables the court to understand the challenge, (2) permits the court to make an informed ruling, and (3) gives the party offering the evidence the opportunity to remedy the defect and offer it again in admissible form. *McKinney v. National Un. Fire Ins.*, 772 S.W.2d 72, 74 (Tex.1989).

✦

1. How to make specific objections. There are two parts to an objection. First, the objection must identify the exact part of the question or the evidence that is objectionable. *Speier v. Webster Coll.*, 616 S.W.2d 617, 619 (Tex.1981). Second, the objection must identify the legal principle the court will violate if it admits the evidence (if it is not apparent from the context). TRE 103(a)(1); *United Cab Co. v. Mason*, 775 S.W.2d 783, 785 (Tex.App.—Houston [1st Dist.] 1989, writ denied).

2. Rulings on specific objections on appeal.

(1) Untenable specific objection sustained. If the trial court sustains an untenable specific objection and excludes the evidence, the appellate court should uphold the ruling if there was any valid ground for excluding the evidence. *State Bar v. Evans*, 774 S.W.2d 656, 658 n.5 (Tex.1989). Thus, if a party made the wrong objection and the court sustained it, on appeal, the ruling is not reversible error if it is supported by the record. *See* Brown & Rondon, *Evidence Handbook*, pp. 50-51.

(2) Untenable specific objection overruled. If the trial court overrules an untenable specific objection and admits the evidence, the appellate court will uphold the ruling even if the party could have made valid objections to the evidence. *Wilkerson v. PIC Rlty. Corp.*, 590 S.W.2d 780, 782 (Tex.App.—Houston [14th Dist.] 1979, no writ); *see, e.g.*, *Smith v. Levine*, 911 S.W.2d 427, 436 (Tex.App.—San Antonio 1995, writ denied) (overruling of relevance objection to photos upheld even though party could have objected that photos were not produced in discovery); *Richard Gill Co. v. Jackson's Landing Owners' Ass'n*, 758 S.W.2d 921, 927-28 (Tex.App.—Corpus Christi 1988, writ denied) (overruling of objection to designation of expert upheld even though party could have objected to subject matter of testimony).

§3.2 General objections. A general objection is one that merely challenges the admissibility of the evidence or objects to evidence for vague or inexact reasons. *See Sciarrilla v. Osborne*, 946 S.W.2d 919, 924 (Tex.App.—Beaumont 1997, pet. denied); *Mayfield v. Employers Reinsurance Corp.*, 539 S.W.2d 398, 400 (Tex.App.—Tyler 1976, writ ref'd n.r.e.); *see, e.g.*, *Lege v. Jones*, 919 S.W.2d 870, 874 (Tex.App.—Houston [14th Dist.] 1996, no writ) (objection that evidence is "immaterial and irrelevant" is a general objection); *Ramirez v. Johnson*, 601 S.W.2d 149, 151 (Tex.App.—San Antonio 1980, writ ref'd n.r.e.) ("note our exception" does not preserve objection).

1. Reason to avoid general objections. A general objection is no objection at all. *Murphy v. Waldrip*, 692 S.W.2d 584, 591 (Tex.App.—Fort Worth 1985, writ ref'd n.r.e.).

2. Rulings on general objections on appeal.

(1) General objection sustained. When the trial court sustains a general objection and excludes the evidence, the appellate court will uphold the objection if there was a valid ground for excluding the evidence and the proponent of the evidence did not request a more specific objection. 1 *McCormick on Evidence* §52, at 98; 1 Wigmore, *Evidence* §18, at 827. The appellate court will assume the valid ground for the objection was apparent to the trial court when neither the trial court nor the proponent of the evidence asked for a more specific objection. *General Acc. Fire & Life Assur. Corp. v. Camp*, 348 S.W.2d 782, 784 (Tex.App.—Houston [1st Dist.] 1961, no writ); *see, e.g.*, *Hannum v. General Life & Acc. Ins.*, 745 S.W.2d 500, 502 (Tex.App.—Corpus Christi 1988, no writ) (because document was not properly authenticated, no error to exclude it on a general objection).

(2) General objection overruled. When the trial court overrules a general objection and admits the evidence, the appellate court will hold that the general objection did not preserve error. *Speier v. Webster Coll.*, 616 S.W.2d 617, 619 (Tex.1981); *Lege*, 919 S.W.2d at 874. Normally, a party cannot complain on appeal that the trial court erred in overruling a general objection by raising a ground it did not raise with the trial court. *See Pfeffer v. Southern Tex. Laborers' Pension Trust Fund*, 679 S.W.2d 691, 693 (Tex.App.—Houston [1st Dist.] 1984, writ ref'd n.r.e.) (appellant may not enlarge ground for error with objection not asserted at trial). There are two exceptions: (1) if the ground for exclusion is so obvious that it is indicated by a general phrase and (2) if the evidence was not admissible for any purpose. *Ramirez*, 601 S.W.2d at 151 (#1); *Mueller v. Central Power & Light Co.*, 403 S.W.2d 901, 904 (Tex.App.—Corpus Christi 1966, no writ) (#2); *see* TRE 103(a)(1) (#1).

───────────── ✦ ─────────────

§4. OBJECTING TO A WITNESS

§4.1 Taking witness on voir dire. If a party believes a witness is not qualified to testify because of lack of knowledge, the party should object; if the objection is overruled, the party should ask to take the witness on voir dire before the witness testifies. *See Marling v. Maillard*, 826 S.W.2d 735, 739 (Tex.App.—Houston [14th Dist.] 1992, no writ). This technique is essentially a cross-examination of the witness on the limited issue of knowledge before the proponent's direct examination.

1. No right to voir dire. The party does not have an absolute right to conduct a voir dire examination. TRE 705(b). The court has the discretion to permit or deny voir dire. *In re Estate of Trawick*, 170 S.W.3d 871, 875 (Tex.App.—Texarkana 2005, no pet.); *see* TRE 705(b). If the court permits voir dire, it must be conducted outside the presence of the jury. TRE 705(b); *see Exxon Corp. v. Makofski*, 116 S.W.3d 176, 192-93 (Tex.App.—Houston [14th Dist.] 2003, pet. denied). See Brown & Rondon, *Evidence Handbook*, p. 739.

2. Repeat objection after voir dire. After completing the voir dire of the witness, the party should repeat its objection to the testimony. When the party does not object after voir dire, the court will assume the party decided not to challenge the witness. *Marling*, 826 S.W.2d at 739.

3. Scope of examination. The purpose of a voir dire examination is to test the personal knowledge of a witness. *See Celotex Corp. v. Tate*, 797 S.W.2d 197, 206 (Tex.App.—Corpus Christi 1990, writ dism'd) (either cross-examination or voir dire can be used to challenge knowledge of witness).

§4.2 Objection to opinion of expert. To object to the opinion of an expert, the party should object that the expert is not qualified, the opinion is not relevant or reliable, or the probative value of the opinion is substantially outweighed by the danger of unfair prejudice, confusion, or delay. TRE 104(a), 401-403, 702, 703, 705; *E.I. du Pont de Nemours & Co. v. Robinson*, 923 S.W.2d 549, 556-57 (Tex.1995). See "Motion to Exclude Expert," ch. 5-N, p. 410.

§4.3 Objection to witness who violated "the Rule." If a witness violates "the Rule," the trial court must determine whether it will permit the witness to testify. *See, e.g., Drilex Sys. v. Flores*, 1 S.W.3d 112, 117-18 (Tex.1999) (court struck expert for violating the Rule); *In re D.T.C.*, 30 S.W.3d 43, 49-50 (Tex.App.—Houston [14th Dist.] 2000, no pet.) (court struck three witnesses for violating the Rule); *Guerrero v. Smith*, 864 S.W.2d 797, 800-01 (Tex. App.—Houston [14th Dist.] 1993, no writ) (witness who heard D's testimony was permitted to testify). See "Invoking 'the Rule'," ch. 8-C, §3, p. 698.

§4.4 Failing to supplement discovery. If a party attempts to introduce evidence that was not disclosed even though a pretrial order or a discovery request required disclosure, the other party should object. *See* TRCP 193.6(a). See "Pretrial Conference," ch. 5-A, p. 315; "Objecting to Unidentified Witness," ch. 6-E, §10, p. 522.

§4.5 Preserving error. When evidence is excluded, the party must make an offer of proof (or, after trial, a bill of exception) to preserve the testimony of the witness so the appellate courts can determine whether the erroneous exclusion was harmful. See "Offer of Proof & Bill of Exception," ch. 8-E, p. 717.

§5. OBJECTING TO A QUESTION

Generally, an improper question that is not answered by the witness does not constitute reversible error. *See Luna v. North Star Dodge Sales*, 667 S.W.2d 115, 119-20 (Tex.1984). In most cases, the error in asking a prejudicial question can be cured by an instruction to the jury to disregard the question. When the trial court sustains the objection, to preserve error, the party should "pursue an adverse ruling." See "When jury hears inadmissible evidence," §6.6, p. 713. Whether the error is reversible is judged by the same standard as for improper jury argument, set out in *Standard Fire Ins. v. Reese*, 584 S.W.2d 835, 839-40 (Tex.1979). *Luna*, 667 S.W.2d at 120. See "Test for reversible jury argument," ch. 8-J, §6.2, p. 752.

§6. OBJECTING TO THE EVIDENCE

§6.1 Outside presence of jury. Objections to evidence made during the trial but outside the presence of the jury do not need to be repeated in front of the jury to preserve error. TRE 103(a)(1); *Clark v. Trailways, Inc.*, 774 S.W.2d 644, 647 n.2 (Tex.1989); *Austin v. Weems*, 337 S.W.3d 415, 421 (Tex.App.—Houston [1st Dist.] 2011, no pet.);

✦

Huckaby v. A.G. Perry & Son, Inc., 20 S.W.3d 194, 204 (Tex.App.—Texarkana 2000, pet. denied); *see also* TRAP 33.1(c) (no formal exception or separate order is required to preserve complaint for appeal).

§6.2 Multiple parties. In a multiparty case, each party has the obligation and the right to make its own objections to the admission and exclusion of evidence. *Bohls v. Oakes*, 75 S.W.3d 473, 477 (Tex.App.—San Antonio 2002, pet. denied); *Wolfe v. East Tex. Seed Co.*, 583 S.W.2d 481, 482 (Tex.App.—Houston [1st Dist.] 1979, writ dism'd). One party's objection does not preserve error for any other party. *E.g.*, *Beutel v. Dallas Cty. Flood Control Dist.*, 916 S.W.2d 685, 694 (Tex.App.—Waco 1996, writ denied) (offer of proof by one D did not preserve error for other D); *HOW Ins. v. Patriot Fin. Servs.*, 786 S.W.2d 533, 544 (Tex.App.—Austin 1990, writ denied) (objection to evidence by one D did not preserve error for other Ds), *overruled on other grounds, Hines v. Hash*, 843 S.W.2d 464 (Tex.1992); *Howard v. Phillips*, 728 S.W.2d 448, 451 (Tex.App.—Fort Worth 1987, no writ) (offer of proof by one D did not preserve error for other D); *Wolfe*, 583 S.W.2d at 482 (objection to evidence by one D did not preserve error for other D). There is an exception to this rule—one party's objection may preserve error for another party if the trial court has ruled that objections made by one party preserve error for the other parties on the same side. *Owens-Corning Fiberglas Corp. v. Malone*, 916 S.W.2d 551, 556-57 (Tex.App.—Houston [1st Dist.] 1996), *aff'd*, 972 S.W.2d 35 (Tex.1998); *Celotex Corp. v. Tate*, 797 S.W.2d 197, 201-02 (Tex.App.—Corpus Christi 1990, writ dism'd).

§6.3 Repeating the objection. A party should object every time inadmissible evidence is offered. If a party objects to certain evidence but later does not object when the same evidence is introduced, the party waives its objection. *Richardson v. Green*, 677 S.W.2d 497, 501 (Tex.1984); *Marling v. Maillard*, 826 S.W.2d 735, 739 (Tex.App.—Houston [14th Dist.] 1992, no writ). For a limited exception to this rule, see §6.4, below.

§6.4 Running objection. A party can preserve error for repeated offers of the same evidence through a running objection. *Volkswagen v. Ramirez*, 159 S.W.3d 897, 907 (Tex.2004). By making a running objection, a party avoids annoying the jury by repeatedly making the same objection. However, a running objection must be specific and unambiguous. *Id.*; *see Low v. Henry*, 221 S.W.3d 609, 619 (Tex.2007). Unless a party has explicitly obtained a running objection from the trial court, a party could waive its objection on appeal by not continuing to object to the same or similar evidence each time it is mentioned. Brown & Rondon, *Evidence Handbook*, p. 57. In a jury trial, the safest procedure is to object each time objectionable evidence is offered. *See id.* Some of the types of waiver that can result from a running objection include:

    1. Different evidence. A running objection does not preserve error against evidence that is similar to but slightly different from the evidence subject to the running objection. *See, e.g.*, *Pojar v. Cifre*, 199 S.W.3d 317, 339 & n.8 (Tex.App.—Corpus Christi 2006, pet. denied) (dicta; running objection to any mention of D's marijuana use may not have applied to testimony about bumper stickers on D's car that advocated legalizing marijuana); *cf. Richardson v. Green*, 677 S.W.2d 497, 501 (Tex.1984) (party's objection to testimony about first interview of child did not apply to videotaped recording of second interview of child because, despite being on same topic, interviews were distinct).

    2. Different witness. In a jury trial, a running objection does not apply to similar evidence from other witnesses. *Davis v. Fisk Elec. Co.*, 187 S.W.3d 570, 587 (Tex.App.—Houston [14th Dist.] 2006), *rev'd in part on other grounds*, 268 S.W.3d 508 (Tex.2008). However, if the trial court grants a specific request that a running objection apply to similar evidence from all witnesses, the objection will be effective for all. *Huckaby v. A.G. Perry & Son, Inc.*, 20 S.W.3d 194, 203 (Tex.App.—Texarkana 2000, pet. denied). In a nonjury trial, a clearly made running objection is effective for all evidence from all witnesses. *Commerce, Crowdus & Canton, Ltd. v. DKS Constr., Inc.*, 776 S.W.2d 615, 620 (Tex.App.—Dallas 1989, no writ).

    3. Other waivers. The following are examples of other ways a party may waive error despite a running objection: • Running objection was waived when objecting party introduced same evidence. *Halim v. Ramchandani*, 203 S.W.3d 482, 492 (Tex.App.—Houston [14th Dist.] 2006, no pet.). • Running objection to the questioning of a witness did not apply to jury argument. *Davis v. Stallones*, 750 S.W.2d 235, 238 (Tex.App.—Houston [1st Dist.] 1987, no writ).

⎯⎯⎯⎯⎯⎯⎯⎯⎯⎯ ✦ ⎯⎯⎯⎯⎯⎯⎯⎯⎯⎯

§6.5 Rule of optional completeness. A party may object on the ground of optional completeness when the other party attempts to introduce part of a document or written statement. *See* TRE 106, 107; *Jones v. Colley*, 820 S.W.2d 863, 866 (Tex.App.—Texarkana 1991, writ denied). To rely on TRE 106 or 107 to introduce omitted parts of a document, the party offering the remainder of the document must show that (1) the other party introduced only part of a document or written statement, and (2) the remainder of the document or written statement should be admitted so that in fairness it can be considered contemporaneously with the original part introduced. *See* TRE 106, 107. TRE 106 and 107 also apply to depositions. *See Jones*, 820 S.W.2d at 866.

§6.6 When jury hears inadmissible evidence. Occasionally, evidence is presented to a jury before the party can object; for example, when a witness blurts out an answer or gives an answer that is not responsive to the question. To preserve error after the jury hears inadmissible evidence (or an improper statement from an attorney), the party must make a number of objections in the proper order until the court makes an adverse ruling. *One Call Sys. v. Houston Lighting & Power*, 936 S.W.2d 673, 677 (Tex.App.—Houston [14th Dist.] 1996, writ denied); *Hur v. City of Mesquite*, 893 S.W.2d 227, 231 (Tex.App.—Amarillo 1995, writ denied). This procedure is called "pursuing an adverse ruling." The order of making the objections is as follows:

1. **Make objection.** The party must make a proper and specific objection.

   • **Objection overruled – error preserved.** If the court overrules the objection, the error is preserved. *See Lone Star Ford, Inc. v. Carter*, 848 S.W.2d 850, 854 (Tex.App.—Houston [14th Dist.] 1993, no writ) (improper jury argument). When a court overrules an objection, the party has secured an adverse ruling, and it is not necessary to request an instruction to disregard or move for a mistrial.

   • **Objection sustained – pursue adverse ruling.** If the court sustains the objection, to preserve error the party must pursue an adverse ruling by making the objections listed below in §§6.6.2-6.6.4. *One Call*, 936 S.W.2d at 677. If the party stops before receiving an adverse ruling, the error is not preserved. *Hur*, 893 S.W.2d at 231; *Ortiz v. Ford Motor Credit Co.*, 859 S.W.2d 73, 77-78 (Tex.App.—Corpus Christi 1993, writ denied). A party cannot complain on appeal after it received all the relief it requested from the trial court. *Cook v. Caterpillar, Inc.*, 849 S.W.2d 434, 442 (Tex.App.—Amarillo 1993, writ denied). Therefore, to preserve error once the objection is sustained, the party must continue with the following steps:

2. **Request instruction.** The party must ask the court to instruct the jury to disregard the evidence. *State Bar v. Evans*, 774 S.W.2d 656, 658 n.6 (Tex.1989); *Peshak v. Greer*, 13 S.W.3d 421, 424-25 (Tex.App.—Corpus Christi 2000, no pet.); *Chavis v. Director, State Workers' Comp. Div.*, 924 S.W.2d 439, 447 (Tex.App.—Beaumont 1996, no writ). If the party makes no other objection or skips the request for an instruction to disregard and asks for a mistrial, the party waives any objection to curable error. *Evans*, 774 S.W.2d at 658 n.6; *Peshak*, 13 S.W.3d at 424-25. The party must press the court to instruct the jury to disregard or to deny the request. If the court instructs the jury, the party must continue with the steps described in §§6.6.3-6.6.4, below, to preserve error.

PRACTICE TIP
If the error is incurable by an instruction to disregard, it is not necessary to request an instruction. See Evans, 774 S.W.2d at 658 n.6. However, do not assume the error is incurable. Ask for an instruction even if you think the error is incurable.

---

3. **Motion to strike.** It is not certain whether a motion to strike the evidence must be made along with the other objections. TRE 103(a)(1), entitled "Objection," refers to an objection or a motion to strike. *See Ortiz*, 859 S.W.2d at 77 (opinion did not list motion to strike as one of necessary objections). Most courts use the two terms interchangeably. *See Smith Motor Sales v. Texas Motor Vehicle Comm'n*, 809 S.W.2d 268, 272 (Tex.App.—Austin 1991, writ denied) (to challenge evidence on appeal, party must make timely objection or motion to strike). However, two courts have said a motion to strike is necessary along with the other objections. *See Parallax Corp. v. City of El Paso*, 910 S.W.2d 86, 90 (Tex.App.—El Paso 1995, writ denied) (party waived error because it did not make motion to strike); *Hur*, 893 S.W.2d at 231 (mentions motion to strike as one of the necessary objections). If the court

⭐

grants a motion to strike, the ruling purports to, but does not, strike the information from the court reporter's record. If the court grants the motion, the party must continue with the step described in §6.6.4, below, to preserve error.

4. Motion for mistrial. If the court sustains the objections and instructs the jury to disregard, the party must make a motion for mistrial to preserve error. ***Hur***, 893 S.W.2d at 231-32; ***Ortiz***, 859 S.W.2d at 77. *But see **Condra Funeral Home v. Rollin***, 314 S.W.2d 277, 279-80 (Tex.1958) (not necessary for P to move for mistrial after trial court sustained objection and instructed jury to disregard); ***Hur v. City of Mesquite***, 916 S.W.2d 510, 511-12 (Tex. App.—Amarillo 1995, no writ) (on motion for rehearing, court reviewed evidence of error, seeming to shift from position that motion for mistrial is necessary to preserve error).

8-1. PURSUING AN ADVERSE RULING

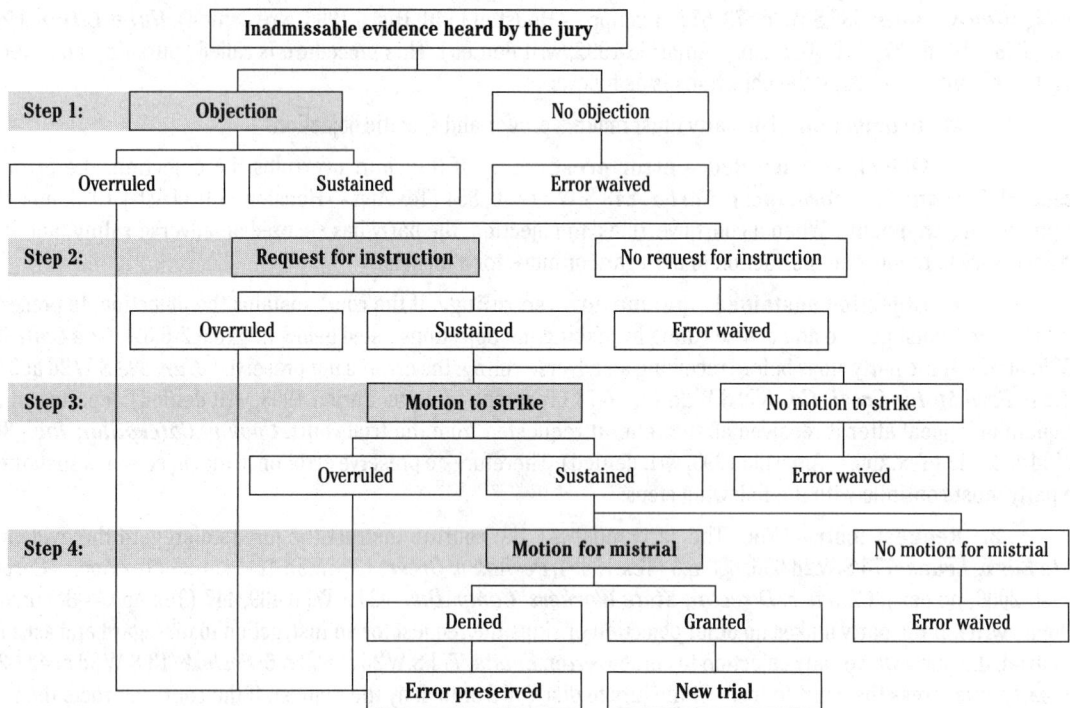

§6.7 Waiver.

1. Different forms of same evidence. An objection to evidence is waived if the same evidence was previously admitted without objection, even though the evidence is in a different form. ***Sauceda v. Kerlin***, 164 S.W.3d 892, 919 (Tex.App.—Corpus Christi 2005), *rev'd on other grounds*, 263 S.W.3d 920 (Tex.2008); *see, e.g.*, ***Texaco, Inc. v. Pennzoil Co.***, 729 S.W.2d 768, 842 (Tex.App.—Houston [1st Dist.] 1987, writ ref'd n.r.e.) (no error in admitting magazine article over objection because same evidence was admitted through author's testimony).

2. Withdrawn objection. If an objection is withdrawn, it does not preserve error. ***Beken v. Elstner***, 503 S.W.2d 408, 410 (Tex.App.—Houston [14th Dist.] 1973, no writ).

3. No adverse ruling. If the jury hears objectionable evidence, the error is waived if the party does not pursue an adverse ruling through an objection, a motion to instruct the jury to disregard, a motion to strike, and a motion for mistrial. *See **Hur v. City of Mesquite***, 893 S.W.2d 227, 231 (Tex.App.—Amarillo 1995, writ denied). See "When jury hears inadmissible evidence," §6.6, p. 713.

4. After conditional admissibility. When a proponent's evidence is subject to the objection of relevance (and therefore admissibility), the trial court may admit the evidence subject to the condition that the proponent later

★

"prove up" the relevance. If the proponent does not prove up the relevance before it closes, the opposing party must repeat the objection and pursue an adverse ruling (objection, instruction, request to strike, and motion for mistrial). *See Owens-Corning Fiberglas Corp. v. Keeton*, 922 S.W.2d 658, 661-62 (Tex.App.—Austin 1996, writ denied) (opposing party waived error because it made only a motion for mistrial).

§7. RULING ON OBJECTION

The trial court has the discretion to admit or exclude evidence; the appellate courts will reverse only for an abuse of discretion. *See National Liab. & Fire Ins. v. Allen*, 15 S.W.3d 525, 527-28 (Tex.2000); *City of Brownsville v. Alvarado*, 897 S.W.2d 750, 753 (Tex.1995).

§7.1 Ruling.

1. Sustains objection. If the trial court sustains the objection, it will not admit the evidence. The party who offered the evidence still has other options that it must exercise, or it waives the error. See §7.1.3, below.

2. Overrules objection. If the trial court overrules the objection, it will admit the evidence. The party whose objection was overruled still has other options that it must exercise, or it waives the error. See §7.1.3, below.

3. Next objection & request.

(1) Request for limited admissibility. After the trial court rules on the admissibility of evidence, whichever party received an adverse ruling—either the party offering it or the party objecting to it—may ask the court to limit the admissibility of the evidence by instructing the jury to consider it only for a certain purpose. *See Larson v. Cactus Util. Co.*, 730 S.W.2d 640, 642 (Tex.1987). If the court ruled the evidence was inadmissible, the party that offered it should offer the evidence again by asking the court to admit it for limited purposes. *See* TRE 105(b); *Bean v. Baxter Healthcare Corp.*, 965 S.W.2d 656, 660 (Tex.App.—Houston [14th Dist.] 1998, no pet.). If the court ruled the evidence was admissible, the party that objected to it should ask the court to limit the purpose for which the evidence may be considered. *See* TRE 105(a); *Horizon/CMS Healthcare Corp. v. Auld*, 34 S.W.3d 887, 906 (Tex.2000); *In re K.S.*, 76 S.W.3d 36, 40 (Tex.App.—Amarillo 2002, no pet.); *City of Austin v. Houston Lighting & Power Co.*, 844 S.W.2d 773, 793 (Tex.App.—Dallas 1992, writ denied). Unless a party requests that the court instruct the jury to consider the evidence only for a limited purpose, the party waives a complaint on the general admission of the evidence. *Horizon*, 34 S.W.3d at 906; *Birchfield v. Texarkana Mem'l Hosp.*, 747 S.W.2d 361, 365 (Tex. 1987); *In re K.S.*, 76 S.W.3d at 40.

(2) Request for partial admission of evidence. If the trial court ruled the evidence was inadmissible, the party offering it can offer the evidence again with the objectionable part excised. The party that offers the evidence that is admitted subject to the deletion of specifically identified information has a duty to redact or sanitize the document before submitting the evidence to the jury. *American Gen. Fire & Cas. Co. v. McInnis Book Store*, 860 S.W.2d 484, 488 (Tex.App.—Corpus Christi 1993, no writ); *see also Olson v. Bayland Publ'g*, 781 S.W.2d 659, 665 (Tex.App.—Houston [1st Dist.] 1989, writ denied) (court did not abuse discretion by excluding evidence that offering party did not attempt to redact), *overruled on other grounds*, *Sage St. Assocs. v. Northdale Constr.*, 863 S.W.2d 438 (Tex.1993).

§7.2 Types of rulings.
Under TRAP 33.1(a)(2), error is preserved by an express ruling, an implicit ruling, or a refusal to rule when a proper objection is made. See "Types of rulings," ch. 1-G, §2.2, p. 47.

PRACTICE TIP
When a court avoids making a ruling by saying "move on" or "handle that on cross," it is not an implicit ruling and does not preserve error. To preserve error, you must ask the court for an actual ruling; if the court refuses, then you have preserved error. Do not count on preserving error by an implicit ruling.

---

§8. REVIEW

§8.1 Admissibility. In making the preliminary decision on the admissibility of evidence, the trial court is not bound by the TREs, except those relating to privileges. TRE 104(a). Thus, the review of an erroneous decision on privilege is probably a review of a legal error, not abuse of discretion. Other decisions on admissibility are reviewed for abuse of discretion. *See, e.g.*, ***Crescendo Invs. v. Brice***, 61 S.W.3d 465, 477-78 (Tex.App.—San Antonio 2001, pet. denied) (compensation information); ***Southwestern Bell Tel. Co. v. Sims***, 615 S.W.2d 858, 862 (Tex.App.—Houston [1st Dist.] 1981, no writ) (qualifications of expert).

§8.2 Record on appeal. To successfully challenge a ruling on the admissibility of evidence, the appellant must request the court reporter's record. See *O'Connor's Texas Appeals*, "Rulings on evidence," ch. 6-C, §4.1.3, p. 226; "Requesting Reporter's Record," ch. 6-C, §7, p. 232. If evidence was excluded, the record must contain an offer of proof or a bill of exception. See "Offer of Proof & Bill of Exception," ch. 8-E, p. 717.

§8.3 Evidence rulings & harmless-error rule. If evidence is erroneously admitted or excluded, the appellate courts will apply the harmless-error review in TRAP 44.1(a) to determine whether the error is reversible. *See* ***Owens-Corning Fiberglas Corp. v. Malone***, 972 S.W.2d 35, 43 (Tex.1998); *see also* ***Dow Chem. Co. v. Francis***, 46 S.W.3d 237, 241 (Tex.2001) (remanded because court of appeals did not conduct harm analysis under TRAP 44.1(a)). There is no specific test for harmless-error review; it is a matter of judgment based on the appellate court's evaluation of the entire case, considering the state of the evidence, the strength and weakness of the case, and the verdict. ***Reliance Steel & Aluminum Co. v. Sevcik***, 267 S.W.3d 867, 871 (Tex.2008); *see* ***State v. Central Expressway Sign Assocs.***, 302 S.W.3d 866, 870 (Tex.2009).

1. Types of error regarding evidence.

(1) Error in admitting evidence. To obtain a reversal based on the erroneous admission of evidence, the appellant should show three elements: (1) the trial court erroneously admitted evidence, (2) the admitted evidence was crucial to a key issue and was not cumulative of other evidence, and (3) the error probably caused the rendition of an improper judgment. TRAP 44.1(a)(1) (element 3); ***Reliance Steel***, 267 S.W.3d at 871, 873 (elements 2 & 3); ***Nissan Motor Co. v. Armstrong***, 145 S.W.3d 131, 144 (Tex.2004) (elements 2 & 3); ***Texas Dept. of Human Servs. v. White***, 817 S.W.2d 62, 63 (Tex.1991) (elements 1 & 3); *see* ***Central Expressway Sign***, 302 S.W.3d at 870. The court can also consider (1) the amount of emphasis placed on the erroneous evidence and (2) whether the admission of the erroneous evidence was calculated or inadvertent. ***Reliance Steel***, 267 S.W.3d at 873-74; ***Nissan Motor***, 145 S.W.3d at 144.

(2) Error in excluding evidence. To obtain a reversal based on the erroneous exclusion of evidence, the appellant—after showing the evidence that was excluded (generally in an offer of proof)—must establish three elements: (1) the trial court erroneously excluded the evidence, (2) the excluded evidence was controlling on a material issue and was not cumulative of other evidence, and (3) the error probably caused the rendition of an improper judgment. TRAP 44.1(a)(1) (element 3); ***Reliance Steel***, 267 S.W.3d at 873 (element 2); ***Texas DOT v. Able***, 35 S.W.3d 608, 617 (Tex.2000) (elements 2 & 3); ***Williams Distrib. Co. v. Franklin***, 898 S.W.2d 816, 817 (Tex.1995) (element 2); ***McCraw v. Maris***, 828 S.W.2d 756, 757 (Tex.1992) (elements 1 & 3). To show that the evidence is controlling does not require a showing that it was the only evidence of its kind. *See* ***Williams Distrib.***, 898 S.W.2d at 817. The court can also consider whether the rest of the evidence was so one-sided that the error likely made no difference in the judgment. ***Central Expressway Sign***, 302 S.W.3d at 870.

2. Not the "but for" test.
Over the years, the Supreme Court has developed two conflicting lines of authority on the appellant's burden when challenging an erroneous ruling admitting or excluding evidence. The Supreme Court has vacillated between the heavy burden of requiring the appellant to show that "but for" the court's ruling a different judgment would have resulted, and the less onerous burden of requiring the appellant to show that the error "probably" resulted in an improper judgment. In the 1992 *McCraw* opinion, the Supreme Court seemed to settle the issue when it held the appellant is not required to show that but for the erroneous ruling on evidence a different judgment would have resulted; rather, the Court held the appellant is required to show only that the exclusion of evidence probably resulted in the rendition of an improper judgment. *McCraw*, 828 S.W.2d at 758. However,

✦

three years later the Supreme Court confused the issue again by stating that a successful challenge to a ruling on evidence usually requires the appellant to show that the judgment "turns on" the evidence excluded or admitted. *City of Brownsville v. Alvarado*, 897 S.W.2d 750, 753-54 (Tex.1995). The "turns on" test from *Alvarado* appears to conflict with the "probably" test in *McCraw*. *See $18,000 in U.S. Currency v. State*, 961 S.W.2d 257, 266 & n.3 (Tex. App.—Houston [1st Dist.] 1997, no writ) ("turns on" test is just another name for "but for" test). To the extent that there is a conflict between the *McCraw* and *Alvarado* lines of authority, the issue is resolved in favor of *McCraw* because TRAP 44.1(a), adopted after the two cases were issued, requires the appellant to show the error probably caused the rendition of an improper judgment. Because *McCraw* is consistent with TRAP 44.1(a) and both are inconsistent with *Alvarado*, the "turns on" test in *Alvarado* should be dismissed as a mistake.

CAUTION

Because of the conflicting lines of authority in the Supreme Court opinions, you can find the courts of appeals making the same error. On appeal, when error is alleged in the admission or exclusion of evidence, make sure your opponent, and ultimately the court, uses the correct standard of review stated in TRAP 44.1(a).

---

§8.4 Reversing judgment. If the appellate court sets aside a verdict because of an erroneous ruling excluding evidence, the court cannot render a judgment contrary to the verdict. *Transport Ins. v. Faircloth*, 898 S.W.2d 269, 275 (Tex.1995); *see Hyundai Motor Co. v. Chandler*, 882 S.W.2d 606, 620 (Tex.App.—Corpus Christi 1994, writ denied). Instead, the court must remand for a new trial to give the opposing party an opportunity to impeach the evidence or to respond with rebuttal evidence. *Transport Ins.*, 898 S.W.2d at 275. If, however, the court can exclude the improperly admitted evidence, the record may be sufficient to support a rendition. *See, e.g.*, *McElroy v. Fitts*, 876 S.W.2d 190, 199 (Tex.App.—El Paso 1994, writ dism'd) (court subtracted amounts attributable to evidence that should have been excluded and, as modified, affirmed that part of the judgment).

E. OFFER OF PROOF & BILL OF EXCEPTION

§1. GENERAL

§1.1 Rules. TRE 103(a)(2) (offer of proof); TRAP 33.2 (bill of exception). See TRCP 75a (exhibits tendered on bill of exception).

§1.2 Purpose. The primary purpose of an offer of proof and a bill of exception is to include excluded evidence in the record so the appellate court can determine whether the trial court erred in excluding it. *Mack Trucks, Inc. v. Tamez*, 206 S.W.3d 572, 577 (Tex.2006); *Ludlow v. DeBerry*, 959 S.W.2d 265, 269-70 (Tex.App.—Houston [14th Dist.] 1997, no writ); *Sullivan v. Bickel & Brewer*, 943 S.W.2d 477, 484 (Tex.App.—Dallas 1995, writ denied); *see* TRE 103(a)(2), (b); TRAP 33.1, 33.2. Another purpose is to permit the trial court to reconsider its ruling in light of the actual evidence. *Ludlow*, 959 S.W.2d at 270.

§1.3 Timetable & forms. Timetable, Offer of Proof & Bill of Exception, p. 1230; *O'Connor's Texas Civil Forms* (2012), FORMS 8E.

§1.4 Other references. Brown & Rondon, *Texas Rules of Evidence Handbook* (2013) (referred to as Brown & Rondon, *Evidence Handbook*).

§2. DIFFERENCE BETWEEN OFFER & BILL

To preserve error when the trial court excludes evidence, a party must comply with TRE 103(a)(2), which states that error cannot be predicated on the exclusion of evidence unless the substance of the evidence was made known to the court by an offer. *Ludlow v. DeBerry*, 959 S.W.2d 265, 269-70 (Tex.App.—Houston [14th Dist.] 1997, no writ). There are two types of offers, one made during trial (an offer of proof) and one made after trial (a formal bill of exception). *Clone Component Distribs. v. State*, 819 S.W.2d 593, 596 (Tex.App.—Dallas 1991, no writ).

———————————— ✦ ————————————

§2.1 Offer of proof. An offer of proof (formerly called an informal bill of exception) is a trial-time offer of evidence the court excluded. *See* TRE 103(a)(2); TRAP 33.1(a)(1)(B). A party makes an offer of proof by presenting the excluded evidence in the form of a summary or in question-and-answer form, outside the presence of the jury.

§2.2 Formal bill of exception. A formal bill of exception is a post-trial offer of evidence in written form. *See* TRAP 33.2; *Clone Component Distribs. v. State*, 819 S.W.2d 593, 596-97 (Tex.App.—Dallas 1991, no writ). A formal bill is necessary only when the complaint or evidence is not preserved in an offer of proof. *See* TRAP 33.2.

§3. OFFER OF PROOF

When the trial court rules evidence is not admissible and excludes it, the party who offered the evidence should make an offer of proof to get the evidence into the record for the appeal. TRE 103(a)(2); *Akin v. Santa Clara Land Co.*, 34 S.W.3d 334, 339 (Tex.App.—San Antonio 2000, pet. denied); *Wade v. Commission for Lawyer Discipline*, 961 S.W.2d 366, 374 (Tex.App.—Houston [1st Dist.] 1997, no writ); *see E.I. du Pont de Nemours & Co. v. Robinson*, 923 S.W.2d 549, 552 (Tex.1995). See Brown & Rondon, *Evidence Handbook*, p. 63. If the substance of the evidence is apparent from the record, an offer of proof is not necessary. TRE 103(a)(2); *Marathon Corp. v. Pitzner*, 55 S.W.3d 114, 143 (Tex.App.—Corpus Christi 2001), *rev'd on other grounds*, 106 S.W.3d 724 (Tex.2003); *see Chance v. Chance*, 911 S.W.2d 40, 52 (Tex.App.—Beaumont 1995, writ denied). A party should preserve excluded evidence in an offer of proof instead of a formal bill of exception. An offer of proof is easier to make than a formal bill.

§3.1 Offer evidence. Before a party is entitled to make an offer of proof, it must offer the evidence at trial. *Ulogo v. Villanueva*, 177 S.W.3d 496, 501 (Tex.App.—Houston [1st Dist.] 2005, no pet.); *Estate of Veale v. Teledyne Indus.*, 899 S.W.2d 239, 242 (Tex.App.—Houston [14th Dist.] 1995, writ denied). The party cannot rely on a motion-in-limine ruling. *Ulogo*, 177 S.W.3d at 500-01. *But see Durbin v. Dal-Briar Corp.*, 871 S.W.2d 263, 270 (Tex. App.—El Paso 1994, writ denied) (formal offer was not necessary because D stipulated that P could submit depositions as bill of exception), *disapproved on other grounds*, *Golden Eagle Archery, Inc. v. Jackson*, 24 S.W.3d 362 (Tex.2000).

§3.2 Specify purpose of evidence. When an objection is lodged, the party offering the evidence should specify the purpose for which the evidence is offered and the reason it is admissible. *Ulogo v. Villanueva*, 177 S.W.3d 496, 501-02 (Tex.App.—Houston [1st Dist.] 2005, no pet.); *Estate of Veale v. Teledyne Indus.*, 899 S.W.2d 239, 242 (Tex.App.—Houston [14th Dist.] 1995, writ denied).

§3.3 Get a ruling excluding evidence. Before a party is entitled to make an offer of proof, the court must make a ruling that the evidence is inadmissible. TRAP 33.1(a)(2); *Ulogo v. Villanueva*, 177 S.W.3d 496, 502 (Tex. App.—Houston [1st Dist.] 2005, no pet.); *see Estate of Veale v. Teledyne Indus.*, 899 S.W.2d 239, 242 (Tex.App.— Houston [14th Dist.] 1995, writ denied).

§3.4 Make an offer. Once the court rules the evidence is inadmissible, the party must make an offer of proof. *See Estate of Veale v. Teledyne Indus.*, 899 S.W.2d 239, 242-43 (Tex.App.—Houston [14th Dist.] 1995, writ denied). To preserve error, the offer of proof must show the nature of the excluded evidence with sufficient specificity to allow the reviewing court to determine its admissibility. *In re N.R.C.*, 94 S.W.3d 799, 806 (Tex.App.—Houston [14th Dist.] 2002, pet. denied); *e.g.*, *Chapman v. Olbrich*, 217 S.W.3d 482, 494-95 (Tex.App.—Houston [14th Dist.] 2006, no pet.) (error not preserved because offer of proof did not include excluded exhibit). Formal proof is not required, and courts prefer a concise statement over a lengthy presentation. *In re N.R.C.*, 94 S.W.3d at 806.

1. Oral testimony. To preserve testimonial evidence, the party offering it must make an offer of proof in the presence of the judge, the court reporter, and opposing counsel, but outside the presence of the jury. The offer of proof is conducted out of the hearing of the jury to prevent the jury from hearing inadmissible evidence. TRE 103(c). When making an offer of proof, the attorney should make a concise statement of what testimony would be elicited from the witness. *In re N.R.C.*, 94 S.W.3d at 806. At the request of either party, the trial court should permit the offer to be made in question-and-answer form. TRE 103(b). *But see Chance v. Chance*, 911 S.W.2d 40, 51-52 (Tex.App.— Beaumont 1995, writ denied) (no error to refuse question-and-answer form of offer). The trial court may add a comment to the offer to show the character of the evidence, the form in which it was offered, the objection, and the ruling. TRE 103(b).

——————————————— ✦ ———————————————

2. Documents & things. To preserve documentary evidence, the party should, at the time the document is excluded, say, "I make an offer of proof of this document and ask that it be filed with the record." An offer of proof to preserve an excluded document may be made in the presence of the jury because the jury is not prejudiced by evidence in an excluded document that it cannot see. The court reporter should mark the document as an offer of proof and identify it with an exhibit number. The document will be filed with the court clerk so it will be included with the exhibits in the reporter's record. TRCP 75a; *see Owens-Illinois, Inc. v. Chatham*, 899 S.W.2d 722, 731 (Tex.App.—Houston [14th Dist.] 1995, writ dism'd).

(1) Filed discovery. Even when a document is already on file with the court—for example, a deposition—if the court refuses to permit it to be introduced into evidence, the party should submit it as an offer of proof and get the court to rule on the offer. *See, e.g., McInnes v. Yamaha Motor Corp.*, 673 S.W.2d 185, 187 (Tex. 1984) (excluded deposition that was not offered as bill did not preserve error); *Malone v. Foster*, 956 S.W.2d 573, 577 (Tex.App.—Dallas 1997) (same), *aff'd*, 977 S.W.2d 562 (Tex.1998).

(2) Taped evidence. To preserve tape-recorded evidence ruled inadmissible by the trial court, the party should, at the time the tape is excluded, say, "I make an offer of proof of this tape and ask that it be filed with the record." As part of the offer, the party must describe the excluded evidence on the tape and specify the purpose of the evidence. *See, e.g., Chubb Lloyds Ins. v. Kizer*, 943 S.W.2d 946, 949 (Tex.App.—Fort Worth 1997, writ denied) (error waived because party did not make bill to preserve audio portion of tape when court permitted only the video portion). If a transcript of the tape is available, the party should file it as part of the offer; if not, the party should ask permission to file a transcript as part of the offer of proof as soon as one can be made.

§3.5 Obtain a ruling. Error is preserved by the court's explicit ruling that the evidence in the offer of proof is not admissible during trial. *See, e.g., Greenstein, Logan & Co. v. Burgess Mktg., Inc.*, 744 S.W.2d 170, 181 (Tex. App.—Waco 1987, writ denied) (error was not preserved because reporter's record did not show what was refused). However, under TRAP 33, error can also be preserved if the trial court implicitly overrules the offer or if the court refuses to rule on the offer and the complaining party objects to the refusal. TRAP 33.1(a)(B)(2). See "Types of rulings," ch. 1-G, §2.2, p. 47.

§3.6 Deadline. An offer of proof must be made before the court reads the charge to the jury. *See* TRE 103(b) (offer of proof shall be made "as soon as practicable, but before the court's charge is read to the jury"). Although nothing in TRAP 33 states a deadline for making an offer of proof, under TRAP 33.1(a)(1)(B), the record must show that the parties complied with the TREs. Making the offer before the charge is read to the jury gives the trial court the opportunity to correct the error.

§4. FORMAL BILL OF EXCEPTION

The formal bill of exception is a procedure to preserve error about matters outside the record. *See* TRAP 33.2. The formal bill is an archaic leftover from a different era of trial practice. Because the requirements for a formal bill are so strict, it can be a trap. On the other hand, a formal bill may be the last chance, and sometimes the only chance, to preserve some kinds of error.

§4.1 In writing. The formal bill of exception must be in writing. *See* TRAP 33.2(a). It should state the party's objection and the trial court's ruling or action, together with the circumstances or evidence needed to explain the situation. *See* TRAP 33.2. All factual statements contained in the bill must be verified by affidavit.

§4.2 Presented to judge. The formal bill must be presented to the trial judge for a ruling. TRAP 33.2(c)(1).

1. Parties agree. If the parties agree on the contents of the bill, the judge must sign the bill and file it with the clerk. TRAP 33.2(c)(2). The bill is then complete.

2. Parties do not agree. If the parties do not agree on the contents of the bill, the judge, after providing notice and a hearing, must do one of the following:

(1) Judge signs bill. If the judge finds that the bill is correct, she should sign the bill and file it with the clerk. TRAP 33.2(c)(2)(A). The bill is then complete.

★

(2) Judge suggests corrections. If the judge finds that the bill is incorrect, the judge may suggest a correction or amendment to accurately reflect the trial-court proceedings. TRAP 33.2(c)(2)(B). If the complaining party agrees with the suggested corrections, the changes can be made, and the judge will sign the amended bill and file it with the trial-court clerk. *Id.* The bill is then complete.

(3) Judge refuses to sign bill. If the judge finds that the bill is incorrect and the complaining party rejects the suggested corrections, the judge should endorse the bill "refused" and return it to the party. TRAP 33.2(c)(2)(C).

(a) Judge's bill. The judge should prepare and sign a bill that, in the judge's opinion, correctly reflects what was said or what happened in the trial court. TRAP 33.2(c)(2)(C); *Houston Lighting & Power Co. v. Russo Props., Inc.*, 710 S.W.2d 711, 717 (Tex.App.—Houston [1st Dist.] 1986, no writ). In most instances, the other party in the case will prepare a proposed judge's bill for the judge's signature.

(b) Party files refused bill. If the complaining party disagrees with the judge's bill, the party can file the refused bill with the trial-court clerk. TRAP 33.2(c)(3).

NOTE

When the judge disagrees with the party's bill, TRAP 33.2(c)(2)(C) contemplates that two bills will be filed, one by the party and one by the judge. See **Houston Lighting & Power**, *710 S.W.2d at 717.*

(c) Bystanders' bill. The party filing the refused bill must also file a "bystanders' bill," in which at least three bystanders, who are not interested in the outcome of the case, state they were present and observed the matter that the bill addresses. TRAP 33.2(c)(3); *see also* **Smith v. United Gas Pipe Line Co.**, 228 S.W.2d 139, 143 (Tex.1950) (attorneys in the case cannot submit bystanders' affidavits); **Circle Y v. Blevins**, 826 S.W.2d 753, 755 (Tex.App.—Texarkana 1992, writ denied) (same). Filing the bystanders' affidavits without the bill of exception does not preserve error. **Citizens Law Inst. v. State**, 559 S.W.2d 381, 383 (Tex.App.—Dallas 1977, no writ). Filing the refused bill without the bystanders' affidavits does not preserve error. **Boddy v. Canteau**, 441 S.W.2d 906, 914 (Tex. App.—San Antonio 1969, writ ref'd n.r.e.).

§4.3 Additional affidavits. Any party may file affidavits to controvert or maintain the judge's or party's bill of exception within ten days after the bill was filed. TRAP 33.2(c)(3).

§4.4 Objections to bill. The other parties in the case must be given the opportunity to review the bill, make objections, and file controverting affidavits. *See* TRAP 33.2(c)(3). Additional affidavits must be filed within ten days. *Id.*

§4.5 Deadline. The deadline for filing the complete formal bill of exception is 30 days after the party's notice of appeal is filed. TRAP 33.2(e)(1). The court of appeals may extend the time to file a formal bill if, within 15 days after the date the bill is due, the party files a motion to extend time that complies with TRAP 10.5(b). TRAP 33.2(e)(3).

§5. REFUSAL TO PERMIT OFFER OR BILL

It is reversible error for the trial court to refuse to permit a party to make a timely offer of proof or bill of exception. **State v. Biggers**, 360 S.W.2d 516, 517 (Tex.1962); **In re Goodwin**, 562 S.W.2d 532, 533 (Tex.App.—Texarkana 1978, no writ). However, if the appellate court can determine from the record what evidence would have been preserved, the trial court's refusal to permit a party to make a bill is not reversible error. **Pennington v. Brock**, 841 S.W.2d 127, 131 (Tex.App.—Houston [14th Dist.] 1992, no writ); *see* **Ledisco Fin. Servs. v. Viracola**, 533 S.W.2d 951, 959 (Tex. App.—Texarkana 1976, no writ). If the evidence the party attempted to preserve in a bill was immaterial to the outcome of the suit, the court's refusal to permit the party to make a bill is not reversible error. **4M Linen & Unif. Sup. v. W.P. Ballard & Co.**, 793 S.W.2d 320, 328 (Tex.App.—Houston [1st Dist.] 1990, writ denied); **Dorn v. Cartwright**, 392 S.W.2d 181, 186 (Tex.App.—Dallas 1965, writ ref'd n.r.e.).

─────────────────── ✦ ───────────────────

§6. REVIEW

An appellate court cannot reach the question of whether evidence was erroneously excluded unless the excluded evidence is included in the record for its review. *McInnes v. Yamaha Motor Corp.*, 673 S.W.2d 185, 187 (Tex.1984); *Hartford Ins. v. Jiminez*, 814 S.W.2d 551, 552-53 (Tex.App.—Houston [1st Dist.] 1991, no writ).

§6.1 Record. Testimonial and documentary evidence in an offer of proof will be included in the reporter's record. *Owens-Illinois, Inc. v. Chatham*, 899 S.W.2d 722, 729 (Tex.App.—Houston [14th Dist.] 1995, writ dism'd). Testimonial and documentary evidence included in a formal bill of exception will be included in the clerk's record. TRAP 33.2(f).

§6.2 Standard of review. To challenge evidence erroneously excluded, see "Evidence rulings & harmless-error rule," ch. 8-D, §8.3, p. 716.

§6.3 Conflict between record & bill. On appeal, if the appellate court finds a conflict between the provisions of a bill of exception and the reporter's record, the bill will control. TRAP 33.2(d); *Mea v. Mea*, 464 S.W.2d 201, 204 (Tex.App.—Tyler 1971, no writ).

§6.4 Another party's bill. A party cannot rely on another party's bill of exception unless the party specifically adopts the other party's bill or joins in making it. *Howard v. Phillips*, 728 S.W.2d 448, 451 (Tex.App.—Fort Worth 1987, no writ).

F. MOTION TO AMEND PLEADINGS—TRIAL & POST-TRIAL

Three sections in this book discuss amending pleadings. See "Amending or supplementing pleadings," ch. 1-B, §3.6, p. 16; "Motion to Amend Pleadings—Pretrial," ch. 5-F, p. 350; and this subchapter.

§1. GENERAL

§1.1 Rules. TRCP 62-67.

§1.2 Purpose. A trial or post-trial amendment allows a party to amend its pleadings to (1) correct errors and defects, (2) add or delete claims or defenses, or (3) conform the pleadings to the evidence. TRCP 66, 67.

§1.3 Forms. *O'Connor's Texas Civil Forms* (2012), FORMS 8F.

§2. MOTION FOR LEAVE TO AMEND

A party may amend its pleadings during trial or after the verdict but before the court renders judgment. *See* TRCP 63, 66; *Greenhalgh v. Service Lloyds Ins.*, 787 S.W.2d 938, 940 (Tex.1990).

§2.1 When motion required.

1. During trial. A party should seek leave to amend its pleadings during trial whenever it introduces evidence that is unsupported by its pleadings or is notified—usually by an opposing party's objection—of a defect, fault, or omission in its pleadings. *See* TRCP 63, 66; *see, e.g.*, *Ritchie v. Rupe*, 339 S.W.3d 275, 306 (Tex.App.—Dallas 2011, pet. granted 10-26-12) (after Ds moved for directed verdict asserting they were not liable in their individual capacities, P sought leave to amend); *THI of Tex. v. Perea*, 329 S.W.3d 548, 570-71 (Tex.App.—Amarillo 2010, pet. denied) (Ps sought leave to amend to add claim after introducing evidence during their case-in-chief); *Deutsch v. Hoover, Bax & Slovacek, L.L.P.*, 97 S.W.3d 179, 185 (Tex.App.—Houston [14th Dist.] 2002, no pet.) (counter-D moved for directed verdict asserting statute of limitations and sought leave to amend after counter-P objected that limitations had not been pleaded).

2. Before submission of jury charge. A party should seek leave to amend its pleadings before the charge is submitted to the jury to conform the pleadings to the evidence. *See* TRCP 63, 66, 67; *State Bar v. Kilpatrick*, 874 S.W.2d 656, 657-58 (Tex.1994); *Matthews v. General Acc. Fire & Life Assur. Corp.*, 343 S.W.2d 251, 254-55

━━━━━━━━━━━━━━━━━━━━━━━━━ ★ ━━━━━━━━━━━━━━━━━━━━━━━━━

(Tex.1961); *see, e.g., Texas Indus. v. Vaughan*, 919 S.W.2d 798, 803-04 (Tex.App.—Houston [14th Dist.] 1996, writ denied) (court should have allowed amendment to add claim for mental anguish offered after objection at jury-charge conference).

3. Post-trial. A party should seek leave to amend its pleadings after the verdict has been returned to conform the pleadings to the verdict and the evidence when it recognizes or is notified—usually by an opposing party's objection—that the verdict is unsupported by the pleadings. *See* TRCP 63, 66; *Greenhalgh v. Service Lloyds Ins.*, 787 S.W.2d 938, 939-40 (Tex.1990); *see, e.g., Allstate Prop. & Cas. Ins. v. Gutierrez*, 281 S.W.3d 535, 538-39 (Tex. App.—El Paso 2008, no pet.) (D sought leave to amend to add affirmative defense after verdict); *Weidner v. Sanchez*, 14 S.W.3d 353, 377 (Tex.App.—Houston [14th Dist.] 2000, no pet.) (P sought leave to amend to conform damages to verdict); *see also* TRCP 301 (judgment must conform to pleadings, evidence, and verdict); *Hampden Corp. v. Remark, Inc.*, 331 S.W.2d 489, 495 (Tex.App.—Dallas 2010, pet. denied) (nonjury trial; post-trial amendment made after closing argument but before court rendered judgment). See "Amendments After Judgment," §4, p. 725.

§2.2 When motion not required. When an unpleaded issue is tried by consent, the issue is treated as if it had been raised by the pleadings. TRCP 67; *Roark v. Stallworth Oil & Gas, Inc.*, 813 S.W.2d 492, 495 (Tex.1991). Thus, the proponent of an issue tried by consent is not required to seek leave to amend its pleadings. *See* TRCP 66, 67; *Hartford Fire Ins. v. C. Springs 300, Ltd.*, 287 S.W.3d 771, 779-80 (Tex.App.—Houston [1st Dist.] 2009, pet. denied); *Ranger Ins. v. Robertson*, 707 S.W.2d 135, 142 (Tex.App.—Austin 1986, writ ref'd n.r.e.). However, if the party can make a motion to amend its pleadings before judgment is rendered, it should probably do so. *See, e.g., Bell v. Meeks*, 725 S.W.2d 179, 179-80 (Tex.1987) (Ps permitted to add DTPA misrepresentation claim after verdict); *Campbell v. Salazar*, 960 S.W.2d 719, 731 (Tex.App.—El Paso 1997, pet. denied) (in addition to TRCP 63 and 66, TRCP 67 supported trial amendment to conform pleadings to evidence submitted to jury without objection); *Centroplex Ford, Inc. v. Kirby*, 736 S.W.2d 261, 265 (Tex.App.—Austin 1987, no writ) (no error in permitting post-verdict amendment when motion to amend was intended to conform pleadings to verdict). See "TRCP 67," §2.4.2, p. 723.

§2.3 Procedure.

1. Seek leave. A party must seek leave from the court to amend its pleadings. TRCP 63, 67; *see* TRCP 66. The motion for leave to amend may be made orally or in writing. *See Smith Detective Agency & Nightwatch Serv. v. Stanley Smith Sec., Inc.*, 938 S.W.2d 743, 746 (Tex.App.—Dallas 1996, writ denied).

2. Offer written amendment. A party must offer its proposed amendment to the pleadings. *See Hunt v. Baldwin*, 68 S.W.3d 117, 134-35 (Tex.App.—Houston [14th Dist.] 2001, no pet.); *Smith Detective Agency*, 938 S.W.2d at 748. The amended pleadings must be in writing or orally dictated into the record. *See City of Fort Worth v. Zimlich*, 29 S.W.3d 62, 73 (Tex.2000) (must be in writing); *Hunt*, 68 S.W.3d at 134-35 (record must reflect that written trial amendment was offered); *Pennington v. Gurkoff*, 899 S.W.2d 767, 771 (Tex.App.—Fort Worth 1995, writ denied) (in limited instances, oral trial amendment is allowed if dictated into record); *see, e.g., McDuffee v. Miller*, 327 S.W.3d 808, 813 (Tex.App.—Beaumont 2010, no pet.) (court allowed attorneys to orally dictate trial amendments into record). The amended pleadings should be signed by the attorney or the party and tendered to the court for filing. *See* TRCP 45(d), 63; *Smith Detective Agency*, 938 S.W.2d at 748.

§2.4 Grounds. A party's right to amend its pleadings is subject only to the opposing party's right to show surprise or prejudice. *Greenhalgh v. Service Lloyds Ins.*, 787 S.W.2d 938, 939-40 (Tex.1990); *see* TRCP 63, 66. See "Prove surprise or prejudice," §3.2, p. 724. But when making the motion for leave to amend, the party should state why the amendment is appropriate and necessary.

1. TRCP 63 & 66. A party may amend its pleadings to correct errors and defects, to add or delete claims or defenses, or to conform the pleadings to the evidence or the verdict. TRCP 63, 66. See "When motion required," §2.1, p. 721. If the opposing party does not show surprise or prejudice, amendments must be freely permitted when they serve the presentation of the merits of the case. *See* TRCP 63, 66. Amendments that correct formal, procedural defects and do not change the substantive issues should almost always be granted. *See Chapin & Chapin, Inc. v. Texas Sand & Gravel Co.*, 844 S.W.2d 664, 665 (Tex.1992); *Francis v. Coastal Oil & Gas Corp.*, 130 S.W.3d 76, 91 (Tex.App.—Houston [1st Dist.] 2003, no pet.).

✦

2. TRCP 67. Although no amendment of the pleadings is necessary when an issue is tried by consent, a party may amend its pleadings when an unpleaded issue was fully developed at trial without objection. *See* TRCP 67; *Allstate Prop. & Cas. Ins. v. Gutierrez*, 281 S.W.3d 535, 540 (Tex.App.—El Paso 2008, no pet.). See "When motion not required," §2.2, p. 722. If an issue is tried by consent, an amendment would merely conform the pleadings to the evidence and should be granted unless the opposing party shows surprise or prejudice. *See Chapin & Chapin*, 844 S.W.2d at 665; *Allstate Prop. & Cas.*, 281 S.W.3d at 539-40.

(1) Issue tried by consent. An issue is tried by consent when (1) a party introduces evidence to support an unpleaded issue and (2) the opposing party does not object to the admission of that evidence or to the submission of a jury question on that issue. *See* TRCP 66, 67; *Ingram v. Deere*, 288 S.W.3d 886, 893 (Tex.2009); *Pine Trail Shores Owners' Ass'n v. Aiken*, 160 S.W.3d 139, 146 (Tex.App.—Tyler 2005, no pet.). This rule applies only in exceptional cases in which the record clearly shows the parties tried an unpleaded issue by consent. *Mastin v. Mastin*, 70 S.W.3d 148, 154 (Tex.App.—San Antonio 2001, no pet.); *In re Walters*, 39 S.W.3d 280, 289 (Tex.App.—Texarkana 2001, no pet.). A party who allows an issue to be tried by consent and then does not challenge the lack of a pleading before submission of the case to the jury cannot assert the pleading deficiency for the first time on appeal. *Roark v. Stallworth Oil & Gas, Inc.*, 813 S.W.2d 492, 495 (Tex.1991); *National Convenience Stores v. Erevia*, 73 S.W.3d 518, 522 (Tex.App.—Houston [1st Dist.] 2002, pet. denied).

(2) Issue not tried by consent.

(a) Opposing party objects. When the opposing party objects to either the introduction of evidence or the submission of a jury question on the ground that the evidence or question is not supported by the pleadings, the issue is not tried by consent. *Hirsch v. Hirsch*, 770 S.W.2d 924, 926 (Tex.App.—El Paso 1989, no writ) (objection to jury question); *see Bedgood v. Madalin*, 600 S.W.2d 773, 775-76 (Tex.1980) (objection to evidence and jury question); *Texas Indus. v. Vaughan*, 919 S.W.2d 798, 803 (Tex.App.—Houston [14th Dist.] 1996, writ denied) (objection to jury question).

(b) Issue not developed. When a party introduces some evidence on an unpleaded issue but does not develop it, the issue is not tried by consent. *Whatley v. City of Dallas*, 758 S.W.2d 301, 306-07 (Tex.App.—Dallas 1988, writ denied); *Realtex Corp. v. Tyler*, 627 S.W.2d 441, 443-44 (Tex.App.—Houston [1st Dist.] 1981, no writ).

(c) Evidence relevant to pleaded issue. When a party introduces evidence that is relevant to both pleaded and unpleaded issues, the unpleaded issue is not tried by consent. *See Boyles v. Kerr*, 855 S.W.2d 593, 601 (Tex.1993); *Marrs & Smith Prtshp. v. D.K. Boyd Oil & Gas Co.*, 223 S.W.3d 1, 18-19 (Tex.App.—El Paso 2005, pet. denied); *Harrison v. City of San Antonio*, 695 S.W.2d 271, 278 (Tex.App.—San Antonio 1985, no writ).

§3. RESPONSE TO MOTION FOR LEAVE TO AMEND

§3.1 Object. The party opposing the amendment must object to the motion for leave to amend.

1. To form.

(1) No leave sought. The opposing party must object if the amending party did not seek leave to amend its pleadings. If the opposing party does not object and the court and the parties act as if leave had been granted, on appeal, the court will presume leave was granted. *Diesel Fuel Injection Serv. v. Gabourel*, 893 S.W.2d 610, 611 (Tex.App.—Corpus Christi 1994, no writ). See "Seek leave," §2.3.1, p. 722.

(2) No written amendment filed. The opposing party must object if the amending party did not file written amended pleadings. If the court accepts an oral amendment and the opposing party does not object, the error is waived. *See* TRAP 33.1; *City of Fort Worth v. Zimlich*, 29 S.W.3d 62, 73 (Tex.2000); *Kreighbaum v. Lester*, No. 05-06-01333-CV (Tex.App.—Dallas 2007, no pet.) (memo op.; 6-27-07). See "Offer written amendment," §2.3.2, p. 722.

2. To substance. The opposing party must object to the amendment on the ground that it either causes surprise or prejudice or asserts a new cause of action or defense and thus is prejudicial on its face. TRCP 63, 66; *Greenhalgh v. Service Lloyds Ins.*, 787 S.W.2d 938, 939 (Tex.1990); *Smith Detective Agency & Nightwatch Serv.*

✦

v. Stanley Smith Sec., Inc., 938 S.W.2d 743, 748-49 (Tex.App.—Dallas 1996, writ denied). If the party does not object, the court must grant the trial amendment. *Greenhalgh*, 787 S.W.2d at 939-40; *e.g.*, *Varel Mfg. v. Acetylene Oxygen Co.*, 990 S.W.2d 486, 493 (Tex.App.—Corpus Christi 1999, no pet.) (D did not object to motion for leave to amend, so court had no basis to deny motion).

§3.2 **Prove surprise or prejudice.** The party opposing the amendment on substantive grounds must prove the amendment either (1) causes surprise or prejudice or (2) asserts a new cause of action or defense and thus is prejudicial on its face.

1. **Show surprise or prejudice.** The opposing party must present evidence of surprise or prejudice. TRCP 63 (surprise), TRCP 66 (prejudice); *Greenhalgh v. Service Lloyds Ins.*, 787 S.W.2d 938, 939 (Tex.1990). For example, the party may show that its pretrial preparation was made in reliance on the pleadings on file, or that it decided not to pursue other avenues of pretrial investigation that it would have pursued under the proposed amended pleading. *Whole Foods Mkt., L.P. v. Tijerina*, 979 S.W.2d 768, 777 (Tex.App.—Houston [14th Dist.] 1998, pet. denied); *see, e.g.*, *Krishnan v. Ramirez*, 42 S.W.3d 205, 225 (Tex.App.—Corpus Christi 2001, pet. denied) (no surprise or prejudice when opposing party did not make any showing that her settlement strategy or trial posture would have changed); *Miller v. Wal-Mart Stores*, 918 S.W.2d 658, 666 (Tex.App.—Amarillo 1996, writ denied) (D proved surprise or prejudice by showing that trial strategy would have been different because amendment would have introduced new substantive matter reshaping P's theory of recovery). The party must show more than bare allegations of surprise or prejudice. *See Parkway Hosp., Inc. v. Lee*, 946 S.W.2d 580, 590 (Tex.App.—Houston [14th Dist.] 1997, writ denied), *disapproved on other grounds*, *Roberts v. Williamson*, 111 S.W.3d 113 (Tex.2003). If the party does not show surprise or prejudice, the court must grant the amendment. TRCP 63, 66; *Greenhalgh*, 787 S.W.2d at 939; *e.g.*, *Texas Indus. v. Vaughan*, 919 S.W.2d 798, 803-04 (Tex.App.—Houston [14th Dist.] 1996, writ denied) (trial court erred by not allowing trial amendment when opposing party did not present evidence of surprise or prejudice).

(1) **Amendments conforming pleadings to damages award.** An amendment seeking to conform the pleadings to a higher damages award does not automatically constitute surprise to the opposing party. *Greenhalgh*, 787 S.W.2d at 940. The opposing party must be able to show the increase resulted in surprise. *Id.*; *see, e.g.*, *Minnesota Life Ins. v. Vasquez*, 133 S.W.3d 320, 331 (Tex.App.—Corpus Christi 2004) (no evidence of surprise or prejudice because opposing party acknowledged that amount in dispute was greater than what was pleaded for and because increase was not enough to require different trial strategy), *rev'd on other grounds*, 192 S.W.3d 774 (Tex.2006); *Weidner v. Sanchez*, 14 S.W.3d 353, 376-77 (Tex.App.—Houston [14th Dist.] 2000, no pet.) (P pleaded for $210,000 in actual damages and was awarded $275,000; opposing party should not have been surprised or prejudiced by increase because total amount of damages sought in pleadings was $360,000); *Benefit Trust Life Ins. v. Littles*, 869 S.W.2d 453, 478 (Tex.App.—San Antonio 1993) (court found surprise and denied post-trial amendment when verdict increased punitive damages by 8,000%), *writ granted w.r.m.*, 873 S.W.2d 704 (Tex.1994).

(2) **Amendments adding prejudgment interest.** An amendment seeking to add a claim for prejudgment interest cannot cause surprise or prejudice to the opposing party because prejudgment interest requires no evidentiary proof at trial. *Benavidez v. Isles Constr. Co.*, 726 S.W.2d 23, 26 (Tex.1987); *Firefighters' & Police Officers' Civil Serv. Comm'n v. Herrera*, 981 S.W.2d 728, 734-35 (Tex.App.—Houston [1st Dist.] 1998, pet. denied).

2. **Show prejudice on its face.** The opposing party must show the amendment asserts a new cause of action or defense and thus is prejudicial on its face. *Greenhalgh*, 787 S.W.2d at 939; *see* TRCP 66; *Dallas City Limits Prop. Co. v. Austin Jockey Club, Ltd.*, 376 S.W.3d 792, 797 (Tex.App.—Dallas 2012, n.p.h.). However, not all amendments that add a new cause of action are prejudicial as a matter of law. *Hampden Corp. v. Remark, Inc.*, 331 S.W.3d 489, 498 (Tex.App.—Dallas 2010, pet. denied); *Stephenson v. LeBoeuf*, 16 S.W.3d 829, 839 (Tex.App.—Houston [14th Dist.] 2000, pet. denied); *e.g.*, *Allstate Prop. & Cas. Ins. v. Gutierrez*, 281 S.W.3d 535, 539-40 (Tex.App.—El Paso 2008, no pet.) (D amended pleading to include affirmative defense already tried by consent); *see State Bar v. Kilpatrick*, 874 S.W.2d 656, 658 (Tex.1994). A pleading that asserts a new claim or defense is prejudicial on its face if all of the following are met:

(1) **Reshapes lawsuit.** The pleading asserts a new substantive matter that reshapes the nature of the lawsuit. *Dallas City Limits*, 376 S.W.3d at 797; *Apodaca v. Rios*, 163 S.W.3d 297, 301 (Tex.App.—El Paso 2005,

★

no pet.); *see also Chapin & Chapin, Inc. v. Texas Sand & Gravel Co.*, 844 S.W.2d 664, 665 (Tex.1992) (whether trial court should deny leave to amend depends on whether amendment is substantive or merely procedural).

(2) Not anticipated. The new matter could not have been anticipated by the opposing party in light of the development of the case. *Dallas City Limits*, 376 S.W.3d at 797; *Apodaca*, 163 S.W.3d at 301.

(3) Detrimental. If the amendment is permitted, the opposing party's presentation of the case will be adversely affected. *Dallas City Limits*, 376 S.W.3d at 797; *Apodaca*, 163 S.W.3d at 301.

§3.3 Show issue not tried by consent. The opposing party should argue that the issue was not tried by consent. *See, e.g., Hampden Corp. v. Remark, Inc.*, 331 S.W.3d 489, 495 (Tex.App.—Dallas 2010, pet. denied) (Ds argued that issue was not tried by consent, in addition to arguing surprise or prejudice). See "TRCP 67," §2.4.2, p. 723.

§3.4 Motion for continuance. If the court grants the motion for leave to amend, the opposing party may ask for a continuance. *See* TRCP 66 (court may grant postponement to enable opposing party to make trial amendment); *Deutsch v. Hoover, Bax & Slovacek, L.L.P.*, 97 S.W.3d 179, 185 (Tex.App.—Houston [14th Dist.] 2002, no pet.) (postponement may cure prejudice resulting from trial amendment). See "Motion for Continuance," ch. 5-D, p. 336.

§3.5 Motion for additional discovery. If the court grants the motion for leave to amend, the opposing party may be entitled to ask for additional discovery on the unpleaded issue. *See* TRCP 66.

§3.6 Sworn proof. In most cases, the response to an oral motion to amend is also made orally. *See Smith Detective Agency & Nightwatch Serv. v. Stanley Smith Sec., Inc.*, 938 S.W.2d 743, 748 (Tex.App.—Dallas 1996, writ denied). If the response is oral and the attorney states facts outside the record, the attorney should ask to be sworn; if the response is written and includes facts outside the record, it should be verified by affidavit. See "Attorney's appearance before court," ch. 1-H, §5.2, p. 55.

§4. AMENDMENTS AFTER JUDGMENT

§4.1 No new claims. After the trial court renders judgment, it is too late to seek leave to amend the pleadings to add new parties or claims. *Mitchell v. LaFlamme*, 60 S.W.3d 123, 132 (Tex.App.—Houston [14th Dist.] 2000, no pet.); *Cantu v. Martin*, 934 S.W.2d 859, 860-61 (Tex.App.—Corpus Christi 1996, no writ). See "Rendering, Signing & Entering Judgment," ch. 9-C, §3, p. 765.

§4.2 Conform pleadings to evidence. After the court renders judgment, it may be possible to amend the pleadings to conform them to the evidence as long as the court still has plenary power. *See Cantu v. Martin*, 934 S.W.2d 859, 861 (Tex.App.—Corpus Christi 1996, no writ) (dicta). To determine whether the court has plenary power, see "Plenary-Power Deadlines," chart 9-1, p. 778.

§5. REVIEW

See "Appellate review of amended pleadings," ch. 1-B, §3.6.3, p. 17.

G. MOTION FOR DIRECTED VERDICT

§1. GENERAL

§1.1 Rules. TRCP 268; TRAP 33.1.

§1.2 Purpose. The motion for directed verdict is a procedural device to ask the court to render judgment without submitting the charge to the jury because there is nothing for the jury to decide. *HMC Hotel Props. II L.P. v. Keystone-Tex. Prop. Holding Corp.*, No. 04-10-00620-CV (Tex.App.—San Antonio 2011, pet. filed 5-16-12) (memo op.; 11-23-11). A directed verdict is also called an instructed verdict. Compare the title to TRCP 268, which calls it a motion for instructed verdict, with the body of the rule, which calls it a motion for directed verdict. A motion for directed verdict may be made in a nonjury trial, even though the name of the motion is technically incorrect because

✦

there is no jury to "direct." ***Carrasco v. Texas Transp.***, 908 S.W.2d 575, 576 (Tex.App.—Waco 1995, no writ). In a nonjury trial, the correct procedure is to make a "motion for judgment." *See **McKinley Iron Works v. TEC***, 917 S.W.2d 468, 469-70 (Tex.App.—Fort Worth 1996, no writ).

§1.3 Forms. *O'Connor's Texas Civil Forms* (2012), FORMS 8G.

§1.4 Other references. *O'Connor's Federal Rules * Civil Trials* (2013) (*O'Connor's Federal Rules*).

§2. WHO CAN MAKE THE MOTION & WHEN

There are several times during a trial when the parties can move for a directed verdict.

§2.1 After plaintiff rests. After the plaintiff rests (i.e., completes the presentation of its evidence), the defendant may make a motion for directed verdict. *See **Wedgeworth v. Kirskey***, 985 S.W.2d 115, 116 (Tex.App.—San Antonio 1998, pet. denied) (court cannot render directed verdict before P rests); ***Nassar v. Hughes***, 882 S.W.2d 36, 38 (Tex.App.—Houston [1st Dist.] 1994, writ denied) (same); ***Buckner v. Buckner***, 815 S.W.2d 877, 878 (Tex. App.—Tyler 1991, no writ) (directed verdict before trial is premature). *But see **Tana Oil & Gas Corp. v. McCall***, 104 S.W.3d 80, 82 (Tex.2003) (no error for court to grant directed verdict before Ps rested because directed verdict was not based on lack of evidence, but rather on fact that Ps limited their claim to damages they could not recover as a matter of law). If the court grants a motion before the plaintiff rests, on appeal the appellant must show it was harmed because it was not able to present its evidence. *See **Tana Oil***, 104 S.W.3d at 82.

§2.2 After defendant rests. After the defendant rests, either party may make a motion for directed verdict. *See, e.g.*, ***Cecil Pond Constr. Co. v. Ed Bell Invs.***, 864 S.W.2d 211, 214 (Tex.App.—Tyler 1993, no writ) (P's motion for directed verdict, made before D presented evidence, was premature).

§2.3 After both sides close. After both sides close (i.e., offer their rebuttal testimony), either party may make a motion for directed verdict. To preserve error in the overruling of an earlier motion for directed verdict, the party must reurge the motion at the close of the evidence. See "Reurging Motion at End of Evidence," §6, p. 728.

§2.4 If jury unable to reach verdict. If the trial court discharges the jury because it is unable to reach a verdict but does not grant a mistrial, the court may reconsider one of the party's motions for directed verdict. ***Encina Prtshp. v. Corenergy, L.L.C.***, 50 S.W.3d 66, 69 (Tex.App.—Corpus Christi 2001, pet. denied); ***Nelson v. Data Terminal Sys.***, 762 S.W.2d 744, 748-49 (Tex.App.—San Antonio 1988, writ denied).

§2.5 On court's motion. The court may grant a motion for directed verdict on its own initiative. ***Adams v. Houston Nat'l Bank***, 1 S.W.2d 878, 879 (Tex.Comm'n App.1928, holding approved); ***Valero Eastex Pipeline Co. v. Jarvis***, 926 S.W.2d 789, 792 (Tex.App.—Tyler 1996, writ denied). Before granting a motion on its own initiative, the court must give the parties notice that it intends to consider granting a directed verdict sua sponte. The party against whom the motion may be granted should be given the opportunity to amend its pleadings or introduce additional evidence before the court grants a motion sua sponte. See "Motion to Amend Pleadings—Trial & Post-trial," ch. 8-F, p. 721; "Motion to Reopen for Additional Evidence," ch. 8-H, p. 729.

§3. MOTION

§3.1 Oral or written. A motion for directed verdict may be in writing or may be made orally. ***Dillard v. Broyles***, 633 S.W.2d 636, 645 (Tex.App.—Corpus Christi 1982, writ ref'd n.r.e.); *see also* TRCP 268 ("shall state the specific grounds"). If the motion is made orally, it must be recorded by the court reporter and included in the reporter's record to preserve the grounds.

§3.2 Partial directed verdict. Although a partial directed verdict is not expressly contemplated by TRCP 268, the device can be used to remove certain parts of a case from the fact-finder. *E.g.*, ***Johnson v. Swain***, 787 S.W.2d 36, 36 & n.1 (Tex.1989) (court granted partial directed verdict, holding D liable for damages caused by vicious animal).

§3.3 Specific reasons. The motion for directed verdict should state the specific reasons for the motion. TRCP 268. If, however, the court grants a directed verdict on a ground that is not specified in the motion, and there are no fact issues for the jury to resolve, it is not reversible error. ***Texas Employers Ins. v. Page***, 553 S.W.2d 98, 102 (Tex.

✪

1977); *Deutsch v. Hoover, Bax & Slovacek, L.L.P.*, 97 S.W.3d 179, 195 (Tex.App.—Houston [14th Dist.] 2002, no pet.); *Crescendo Invs. v. Brice*, 61 S.W.3d 465, 472 (Tex.App.—San Antonio 2001, pet. denied).

§4. GROUNDS FOR DIRECTED VERDICT

A party is entitled to a directed verdict in the following instances:

§4.1 No evidence. When the evidence does not raise a fact issue on a material issue in the suit. *Prudential Ins. v. Financial Rev. Servs.*, 29 S.W.3d 74, 77 (Tex.2000); *Double Ace, Inc. v. Pope*, 190 S.W.3d 18, 26 (Tex. App.—Amarillo 2005, no pet.); *Cherqui v. Westheimer St. Festival Corp.*, 116 S.W.3d 337, 343 (Tex.App.—Houston [14th Dist.] 2003, no pet.). The evidence must be evaluated in the light most favorable to the nonmovant. *Prudential Ins.*, 29 S.W.3d at 82.

PRACTICE TIP

To avoid a directed verdict based on failure to prove part of the cause of action or defense, the party should prepare a draft of the charge before trial. During the trial, the party should use the draft of the charge as a checklist of the elements that must be supported with evidence.

---

§4.2 Conclusive evidence. When the evidence conclusively proves a fact that establishes the movant's right to judgment or that negates the nonmovant's right. *Westchester Fire Ins. v. Admiral Ins.*, 152 S.W.3d 172, 191 (Tex.App.—Fort Worth 2004, pet. denied); *Rowland v. City of Corpus Christi*, 620 S.W.2d 930, 932 (Tex.App.—Corpus Christi 1981, writ ref'd n.r.e.); *see Prudential Ins. v. Financial Rev. Servs.*, 29 S.W.3d 74, 77 (Tex.2000); *Cortez v. HCCI-San Antonio, Inc.*, 131 S.W.3d 113, 120 (Tex.App.—San Antonio 2004), *aff'd*, 159 S.W.3d 87 (Tex.2005). That is, the court should direct a verdict when reasonable minds can draw only one conclusion from the evidence. *Vance v. My Apt. Steak House*, 677 S.W.2d 480, 483 (Tex.1984); *Collora v. Navarro*, 574 S.W.2d 65, 68 (Tex.1978); *see, e.g., Shelton v. Swift Motors, Inc.*, 674 S.W.2d 337, 341 (Tex.App.—San Antonio 1984, writ ref'd n.r.e.) (evidence showed P sued wrong party; D was not liable to P). If there is any conflicting probative evidence, the trial court must submit the issue to the jury. *Air Conditioning, Inc. v. Harrison-Wilson-Pearson*, 253 S.W.2d 422, 425 (Tex.1952); *Facciolla v. Linbeck Constr. Corp.*, 968 S.W.2d 435, 440 (Tex.App.—Texarkana 1998, no pet.); *Nelson v. American Nat'l Bank*, 921 S.W.2d 411, 415 (Tex.App.—Corpus Christi 1996, no writ).

§4.3 Defect in pleadings. When the nonmovant's pleadings contain a specific defect that makes them incapable of supporting a judgment for the nonmovant. *Double Ace, Inc. v. Pope*, 190 S.W.3d 18, 26 (Tex.App.—Amarillo 2005, no pet.); *Sherman v. Elkowitz*, 130 S.W.3d 316, 319 (Tex.App.—Houston [14th Dist.] 2004, no pet.). For example, a motion for directed verdict should be granted when the substantive law does not permit the plaintiff to recover on its cause of action or does not permit the defendant to assert its defense. *See, e.g., Dietrich v. Goodman*, 123 S.W.3d 413, 419 (Tex.App.—Houston [14th Dist.] 2003, no pet.) (court directed verdict because, under Water Code, flood water did not qualify as "surface water"); *Arguelles v. UT Fam. Med. Ctr.*, 941 S.W.2d 255, 258 (Tex. App.—Corpus Christi 1996, no writ) (court directed verdict because Texas does not recognize the "lost chance of survival" doctrine in medical-malpractice suits); *Anderson v. Vinson Expl., Inc.*, 832 S.W.2d 657, 665 (Tex. App.—El Paso 1992, writ denied) (court directed verdict because under DTPA, an investor is not a "consumer"); *see also Southwestern Bell Tel. Co. v. DeLanney*, 809 S.W.2d 493, 494-95 (Tex.1991) (court could have directed verdict on negligence claim because P was limited to breach of contract).

§5. RESPONSE

§5.1 Objections. Generally, the party opposing the motion should respond to the motion and state the converse of the movant's allegations: (1) a fact issue was raised on all material issues in the case, (2) the evidence does not conclusively prove anything, and (3) no legal theory precludes a judgment. The party should argue that all the issues should be submitted to the jury.

§5.2 Leave to amend. If the motion for directed verdict is based on a defect in the pleadings that is curable by amendment, the nonmovant should ask for permission to amend the pleadings. See "Motion to Amend Pleadings—Trial & Post-trial," ch. 8-F, p. 721.

———————————————— ✦ ————————————————

§5.3 Motion to reopen. If the motion for directed verdict is based on a lack of evidence of an essential element, the nonmovant should ask to reopen the evidence. *See MCI Telecomm. v. Tarrant Cty. Appr. Dist.*, 723 S.W.2d 350, 353 (Tex.App.—Fort Worth 1987, no writ). See "Motion to Reopen for Additional Evidence," ch. 8-H, p. 729.

§6. REURGING MOTION AT END OF EVIDENCE

§6.1 Rule. If the court overrules a motion for directed verdict during the trial, the movant has two options: (1) stand on the motion and test the ruling on appeal or (2) introduce additional evidence. If the movant chooses to introduce more evidence, the movant must make a second motion at the close of all the evidence; if it does not, it waives the grounds stated in the first motion. *1986 Dodge Pickup v. State*, 129 S.W.3d 180, 183 (Tex.App.—Texarkana 2004, no pet.); *Horton v. Horton*, 965 S.W.2d 78, 86 (Tex.App.—Fort Worth 1998, no pet.); *Cliffs Drilling Co. v. Burrows*, 930 S.W.2d 709, 712 (Tex.App.—Houston [1st Dist.] 1996, no writ). This rule applies in both jury and nonjury trials. *See Horton*, 965 S.W.2d at 86 (jury); *Wenk v. City Nat'l Bank*, 613 S.W.2d 345, 348 (Tex. App.—Tyler 1981, no writ) (nonjury). In deciding the second motion, the trial court must consider the evidence introduced before the first motion and the evidence introduced before the second motion. To preserve error, all grounds in the first motion must be restated in the second motion, along with any additional grounds.

§6.2 Criticism & exceptions. The application of the rule requiring the motion to be reurged after the introduction of additional evidence has been criticized. *Sipco Servs. Mar., Inc. v. Wyatt Field Serv.*, 857 S.W.2d 602, 609-10 (Tex.App.—Houston [1st Dist.] 1993, writ dism'd) (Cohen, J., concurring). Before FRCP 50 was amended in 2006, federal courts operated under the same rule requiring the motion to be reurged at the close of the evidence. Now a party is only required to reurge the motion after a verdict has been reached. See *O'Connor's Federal Rules*, "Renewing Motion," ch. 8-G, §6, p. 717.

§7. ORDER

The order sustaining or overruling the motion for directed verdict can be made in writing and filed with the clerk or made orally on the record. *See* TRAP 33.1(c) (signed order not required to preserve complaint for appeal).

§8. REVIEW

§8.1 Record on appeal. To successfully challenge the granting or denial of a directed verdict, the appellant must file a complete reporter's record in the appellate court. *McDonald v. State*, 936 S.W.2d 734, 737 (Tex.App.—Waco 1997, no writ).

§8.2 Directed verdict denied. In reviewing the denial of a directed verdict, the appellate court is limited to the specific grounds stated in the motion. *Cooper v. Lyon Fin. Servs.*, 65 S.W.3d 197, 207 (Tex.App.—Houston [14th Dist.] 2001, no pet.); *American Petrofina Co. v. Panhandle Pet. Prod.*, 646 S.W.2d 590, 593 (Tex.App.—Amarillo 1983, no writ). An appeal from the denial of a directed verdict is a challenge to the legal sufficiency of the evidence. *Haynes & Boone, L.L.P. v. Chason*, 81 S.W.3d 307, 309 (Tex.App.—Tyler 2001, pet. denied); *Lochinvar Corp. v. Meyers*, 930 S.W.2d 182, 187-88 (Tex.App.—Dallas 1996, no writ); *see City of Keller v. Wilson*, 168 S.W.3d 802, 827-28 (Tex.2005). The denial of a motion for directed verdict lays the foundation for challenging the evidence on appeal by issues or points of error contending there was "no evidence" of a certain fact or that a fact was established "as a matter of law." *See Weidner v. Sanchez*, 14 S.W.3d 353, 366 (Tex.App.—Houston [14th Dist.] 2000, no pet.) (no evidence); *White v. Liberty Eylau ISD*, 920 S.W.2d 809, 813 (Tex.App.—Texarkana 1996, writ denied) (as a matter of law).

§8.3 Directed verdict granted. In reviewing the granting of a directed verdict, the appellate court can consider any reason the directed verdict should have been granted, even one that is not stated in the court's order or the party's motion. *Reyna v. First Nat'l Bank*, 55 S.W.3d 58, 69 (Tex.App.—Corpus Christi 2001, no pet.); *Gonzales v. Willis*, 995 S.W.2d 729, 740 (Tex.App.—San Antonio 1999, no pet.); *see Double Ace, Inc. v. Pope*, 190 S.W.3d 18, 26 (Tex.App.—Amarillo 2005, no pet.). The appellate court must consider all the evidence in the light most favorable to the party against whom the verdict was directed, crediting favorable evidence if reasonable jurors could and disregarding contrary evidence if reasonable jurors could not. *Robertson v. Odom*, 296 S.W.3d 151, 155 (Tex.App.—

★

Houston [14th Dist.] 2009, no pet.); *see City of Keller v. Wilson*, 168 S.W.3d 802, 827 (Tex.2005). The appellate court must determine whether there is any probative evidence to raise a fact issue. *Porterfield v. Brinegar*, 719 S.W.2d 558, 559 (Tex.1986). If the record contains any probative and conflicting evidence on a material issue, the issue should have been resolved by the jury, and the appellate court must reverse. *See White v. Southwestern Bell Tel. Co.*, 651 S.W.2d 260, 262 (Tex.1983); *Rente Co. v. Truckers Express, Inc.*, 116 S.W.3d 326, 330 (Tex.App.—Houston [14th Dist.] 2003, no pet.); *Mills v. Angel*, 995 S.W.2d 262, 267 (Tex.App.—Texarkana 1999, no pet.).

§8.4 Nonjury trial. In reviewing the trial court's granting of a motion for judgment in a nonjury case, the appellate court examines the record as if the trial court had granted a motion for judgment based on all the facts and does not just rule on whether there was no evidence or whether a proposition was established as a matter of law. *Qantel Bus. v. Custom Controls Co.*, 761 S.W.2d 302, 303-04 (Tex.1988).

H. MOTION TO REOPEN FOR ADDITIONAL EVIDENCE

§1. GENERAL

§1.1 Rule. TRCP 270.

§1.2 Purpose. A party should move to reopen the evidence when it is necessary to include additional evidence in the record. When a party finishes presenting its evidence, it announces that it "rests." When all parties have rested, the parties proceed to offer their rebuttal evidence. After a party offers its rebuttal testimony, the party announces that it "closes." When all parties have closed, the evidence part of the trial is over, unless the court reopens the case for more evidence.

§1.3 Forms. *O'Connor's Texas Civil Forms* (2012), FORM 8H:1.

§2. MOTION TO REOPEN

Reopening is particularly important when the trial court excluded evidence the party attempted to introduce, and after the party closed, the other party introduced evidence making the excluded evidence relevant. Reopening is also important when the trial court announces it intends to grant a directed verdict for lack of evidence. *See MCI Telecomm. v. Tarrant Cty. Appr. Dist.*, 723 S.W.2d 350, 353 (Tex.App.—Fort Worth 1987, no writ).

§2.1 Form. An oral motion to reopen is sufficient, but if the party has the opportunity, it should file a written motion. *See* TRCP 270. Most of the time, however, motions to reopen are made orally in open court when the party suddenly realizes it should offer additional testimony.

§2.2 Grounds. When asking the court to reopen, the party should show all of the following:

1. Diligence. The party was diligent in obtaining evidence. *Moore v. Jet Stream Invs.*, 315 S.W.3d 195, 201 (Tex.App.—Texarkana 2010, pet. denied); *Hernandez v. Lautensack*, 201 S.W.3d 771, 779 (Tex.App.—Fort Worth 2006, pet. denied); *Lopez v. Lopez*, 55 S.W.3d 194, 201 (Tex.App.—Corpus Christi 2001, no pet.); *In re A.F.*, 895 S.W.2d 481, 484 (Tex.App.—Austin 1995, no writ).

2. Decisive evidence. The additional evidence is decisive. *Moore*, 315 S.W.3d at 201; *Hernandez*, 201 S.W.3d at 779; *Lopez*, 55 S.W.3d at 201; *In re A.F.*, 895 S.W.2d at 484.

3. No undue delay. The receipt of additional evidence will not cause undue delay. *Moore*, 315 S.W.3d at 201; *Hernandez*, 201 S.W.3d at 779; *Lopez*, 55 S.W.3d at 201; *In re A.F.*, 895 S.W.2d at 484.

4. No injustice. The receipt of additional evidence will not cause an injustice. *Moore*, 315 S.W.3d at 201; *Hernandez*, 201 S.W.3d at 779; *Lopez*, 55 S.W.3d at 201; *In re A.F.*, 895 S.W.2d at 484.

§2.3 Verification. Although the motion to reopen is not required by TRCP 270 to be in writing, when the motion is in writing, it should be verified if it contains factual allegations outside the record.

✦

§3. RESPONSE

A party must object to the other party's motion to reopen, or it waives error in the reopening. *MCI Telecomm. v. Tarrant Cty. Appr. Dist.*, 723 S.W.2d 350, 353 (Tex.App.—Fort Worth 1987, no writ).

§4. STANDARD

§4.1 Sound discretion. A trial court should permit a party to reopen the evidence when it clearly appears necessary to the administration of justice. TRCP 270. The decision to reopen is within the trial court's sound discretion. *Poag v. Flories*, 317 S.W.3d 820, 828 (Tex.App.—Fort Worth 2010, pet. denied); *Lopez v. Lopez*, 55 S.W.3d 194, 201 (Tex.App.—Corpus Christi 2001, no pet.); *In re Hawk*, 5 S.W.3d 874, 876-77 (Tex.App.—Houston [14th Dist.] 1999, no pet.). The trial court should liberally exercise its discretion to permit both sides to fully develop the case. *Lopez*, 55 S.W.3d at 201.

§4.2 Duty to reopen. The court may have the duty to reopen the evidence when the party moving to reopen has been diligent, the receipt of additional evidence would not cause undue delay or injustice, and the evidence would be decisive. *In re H.W.*, 85 S.W.3d 348, 357-58 (Tex.App.—Tyler 2002, no pet.); *Word of Faith World Outreach Ctr. Ch., Inc. v. Oechsner*, 669 S.W.2d 364, 367 (Tex.App.—Dallas 1984, no writ); *see Alkas v. United Sav. Ass'n*, 672 S.W.2d 852, 860 (Tex.App.—Corpus Christi 1984, writ ref'd n.r.e.); *see also Hill v. Melton*, 311 S.W.2d 496, 500 (Tex. App.—Dallas 1958, writ dism'd) (because party had right to reopen, abuse of discretion was not the correct standard of review).

§5. DEADLINE

The court can allow a party to offer additional evidence at any time. TRCP 270. But in a jury trial, the court cannot admit evidence on a controversial matter after the jury returns the verdict. *Id.*

§5.1 Party permitted to reopen. In the following cases, the trial court permitted or should have permitted the party to reopen: • Before the trial court rendered judgment more than two years after the trial (delay caused by an appeal), trial court should have permitted the party to reopen. *Greater Fort Worth & Tarrant Cty. Cmty. Action Agency v. Mims*, 627 S.W.2d 149, 151 (Tex.1982). • After case was submitted to the jury, court permitted party to reopen to establish standing. *Krishnan v. Ramirez*, 42 S.W.3d 205, 223 (Tex.App.—Corpus Christi 2001, pet. denied). • Before judgment, court should have permitted party to reopen to test the correctness of a plat prepared after trial that the court wanted attached to the judgment. *Templeton v. Dreiss*, 961 S.W.2d 645, 663-65 (Tex. App.—San Antonio 1998, pet. denied). • After the jury began considering the evidence, the trial court permitted the introduction of an invoice that was part of a series of invoices introduced during the trial. *Turner v. Lone Star Indus.*, 733 S.W.2d 242, 244-45 (Tex.App.—Houston [1st Dist.] 1987, writ ref'd n.r.e.). • After the defendant's motion for directed verdict. *MCI Telecomm. v. Tarrant Cty. Appr. Dist.*, 723 S.W.2d 350, 353 (Tex.App.—Fort Worth 1987, no writ). • After argument but before judgment. *Word of Faith World Outreach Ctr. Ch., Inc. v. Oechsner*, 669 S.W.2d 364, 368 (Tex.App.—Dallas 1984, no writ) (case was submitted on stipulated evidence). • After the plaintiff had rested, court permitted the plaintiff to reopen to introduce testimony on damages to her mobile home that her attorney had inadvertently omitted during direct examination. *Lifestyle Mobile Homes v. Ricks*, 653 S.W.2d 602, 604 (Tex.App.—Beaumont 1983, writ ref'd n.r.e.). • Court should have reopened evidence when, just after the close of evidence, the plaintiffs realized they had not proved damages. *Hill v. Melton*, 311 S.W.2d 496, 499-500 (Tex. App.—Dallas 1958, writ dism'd).

§5.2 Party not permitted to reopen. In the following cases, the trial court did not permit the party to reopen: • After the trial court granted other party's motion for summary judgment. *Poag v. Flories*, 317 S.W.3d 820, 824, 828 (Tex.App.—Fort Worth 2010, pet. denied) (movant did not show diligence in timely presenting additional evidence). • After resting, the plaintiff was not permitted to reopen to prove notice, which the defendant had denied by verified plea. *Apresa v. Montfort Ins.*, 932 S.W.2d 246, 250 (Tex.App.—El Paso 1996, no writ). • To ask for attorney fees under the Open Records Act after close of hearing. *McNamara v. Fulks*, 855 S.W.2d 782, 784 (Tex.App.—El Paso 1993, no writ). • Several months after closing and after the trial court announced its judgment. *Fisher v. Kerr Cty.*, 739

S.W.2d 434, 437 (Tex.App.—San Antonio 1987, no writ) (movant did not show diligence in presenting evidence at trial). • After the jury sent out a question about the evidence. *Walton Neon Co. v. Travel-Tex Corp.*, 482 S.W.2d 934, 936-37 (Tex.App.—Corpus Christi 1972, writ ref'd n.r.e.).

§6. REVIEW

§6.1 Record. When a party is prevented from reopening, the party should make an offer of proof setting out the evidence the party tried to introduce. *See Word of Faith World Outreach Ctr. Ch., Inc. v. Oechsner*, 669 S.W.2d 364, 366 (Tex.App.—Dallas 1984, no writ) (error preserved by bill of exception); *Walton Neon Co. v. Travel-Tex Corp.*, 482 S.W.2d 934, 937 (Tex.App.—Corpus Christi 1972, writ ref'd n.r.e.) (error not preserved because no bill of exception). See "Offer of Proof & Bill of Exception," ch. 8-E, p. 717.

§6.2 Standard of review. The trial court's action in ruling on a motion to reopen the evidence should not be disturbed unless it clearly appears that the court abused its discretion. *In re H.W.*, 85 S.W.3d 348, 358 (Tex.App.—Tyler 2002, no pet.); *In re T.V.*, 27 S.W.3d 622, 624 (Tex.App.—Waco 2000, no pet.); *Word of Faith World Outreach Ctr. Ch., Inc. v. Oechsner*, 669 S.W.2d 364, 366 (Tex.App.—Dallas 1984, no writ). The error is reversible only if it probably caused the rendition of an improper judgment—that is, if the evidence could have produced a different result than that reached by the trial court in its judgment. *See* TRAP 44.1(a)(1); *Word of Faith*, 669 S.W.2d at 368.

I. THE CHARGE

§1. GENERAL

§1.1 Rules. TRCP 271-279, 285-289.

§1.2 Purpose. The charge is the collection of questions, instructions, and definitions the court submits to the jury to resolve the factual disputes in the case. It is the trial court's responsibility to submit a proper charge. *Spencer v. Eagle Star Ins.*, 876 S.W.2d 154, 158 (Tex.1994).

§1.3 Forms. *O'Connor's Texas Civil Forms* (2012), FORMS 8I.

§1.4 Other references. Texas Pattern Jury Charges—General Negligence & Intentional Personal Torts (2010), Malpractice, Premises & Products (2010), Business, Consumer, Insurance & Employment (2010), Family (2012); *Benchbook for the Texas Judiciary* (2001); Arnot & Johnson, *Current Trends in Texas Charge Practice: Preservation of Error and Broad-Form Use*, 38 St. Mary's L.J. 371 (2007); Muldrow & Underwood, *Application of the Harmless Error Standard to Errors in the Charge*, 48 Baylor L.Rev. 815 (1996).

§2. PREPARING A DRAFT OF THE CHARGE

Each party should have prepared a complete version of the charge—including its opponent's jury questions, instructions, and definitions—before engaging in discovery. The charge is each party's road map to the evidence it needs to develop or rebut. Just before trial, each party should review and revise the proposed charge. After the introduction of evidence is completed and before the informal charge conference, the parties should again review and revise their proposed charge.

§2.1 Broad-form questions.

1. Broad form required. The trial court must use broad-form submissions whenever feasible. TRCP 277; *Thota v. Young*, 366 S.W.3d 678, 689 (Tex.2012); *Columbia Rio Grande Healthcare, L.P. v. Hawley*, 284 S.W.3d 851, 855 (Tex.2009); *Hyundai Motor Co. v. Rodriguez*, 995 S.W.2d 661, 663-64 (Tex.1999). A broad-form submission should include all elements of proof within a single question with accompanying instructions. *See Diamond Offshore Mgmt. v. Guidry*, 171 S.W.3d 840, 844 (Tex.2005); *Keetch v. Kroger Co.*, 845 S.W.2d 262, 268 (Tex.1992) (Hecht, J., concurring).

2. Broad form not required. A broad-form submission is not always feasible when the governing law is unsettled or when there is doubt about the legal sufficiency of the evidence. *E.g., Harris Cty. v. Smith*, 96 S.W.3d 230, 235-36 (Tex.2002) (charge mixed valid and invalid elements of damages in single broad-form question); *see*

—————————————— ✦ ——————————————

Texas Comm'n on Human Rights v. Morrison, ___ S.W.3d ___ (Tex.2012) (No. 11-0644; 8-31-12); *Romero v. KPH Consol., Inc.*, 166 S.W.3d 212, 215 (Tex.2005); *Crown Life Ins. v. Casteel*, 22 S.W.3d 378, 390 (Tex.2000).

3. Preserve error. When there is doubt about the governing law or the legal sufficiency of the evidence, the party should object and ask the court to either (1) eliminate the doubtful element or (2) submit the doubtful element as a separate question. *See Smith*, 96 S.W.3d at 236. When a specific element of damages should not be included in a broad-form submission because there is no evidence to support its submission, the party must object to preserve error. *In re A.V.*, 113 S.W.3d 355, 362 (Tex.2003); *Smith*, 96 S.W.3d at 236; *see Thota*, 366 S.W.3d at 691; *In re B.L.D.*, 113 S.W.3d 340, 349 (Tex.2003). See "Review," §9, p. 745.

§2.2 Proper tender of requests. Each party should reexamine the live pleadings and the evidence before preparing the draft charge.

1. Controlling & disputed fact issues. The litigants are entitled to have controlling and disputed fact issues submitted to the jury. *Bel-Ton Elec. Serv. v. Pickle*, 915 S.W.2d 480, 481 (Tex.1996); *Aero Energy v. Circle C Drilling Co.*, 699 S.W.2d 821, 823 (Tex.1985). A controlling issue is one that requires a factual determination to render judgment in the case. *Lehmann v. Wieghat*, 917 S.W.2d 379, 382 (Tex.App.—Houston [14th Dist.] 1996, writ denied). A fact issue that is established with uncontroverted evidence and is not in dispute should not be submitted to the jury. *T.O. Stanley Boot Co. v. Bank of El Paso*, 847 S.W.2d 218, 223 (Tex.1992).

2. Supported by pleadings & evidence. The litigants are entitled to have controlling issues submitted to the jury if they are properly pleaded and supported by the evidence. TRCP 278; *Union Pac. R.R. v. Williams*, 85 S.W.3d 162, 166 (Tex.2002); *Triplex Comms. v. Riley*, 900 S.W.2d 716, 718 (Tex.1995); *Samedan Oil Corp. v. Intrastate Gas Gathering, Inc.*, 78 S.W.3d 425, 446 (Tex.App.—Tyler 2001, pet. granted, judgm't vacated w.r.m.). For evidence to support the submission, see "Questions," §6.1, p. 741.

3. Form of requests. The draft of the charge must be in writing. TRCP 272; *Woods v. Crane Carrier Co.*, 693 S.W.2d 377, 379 (Tex.1985). The written request must be separate from the oral objections. TRCP 273; *Alaniz v. Jones & Neuse, Inc.*, 907 S.W.2d 450, 451 (Tex.1995).

§2.3 Cluster of related requests. The parties should submit the proposed charge in "clusters" of related requests. *See, e.g.*, *Lester v. Logan*, 907 S.W.2d 452, 453 (Tex.1995) (disapproving of court of appeals' opinion that held request on one piece of paper that included five related matters—one question, two instructions, and two definitions—was improper); *Aetna Cas. & Sur. Co. v. Moore*, 361 S.W.2d 183, 187 (Tex.1962) (request for question as part of series of nine related questions was proper and did not mislead or confuse trial court). Each cluster should include the name of the party submitting the request and a space for the judge's ruling and signature and the date. A single request with a large number of questions, instructions, and definitions is as weak as its most vulnerable part; when a request includes an objectionable question, instruction, or definition, the court can deny the entire request. *See, e.g.*, *Tempo Tamers, Inc. v. Crow-Houston Four, Ltd.*, 715 S.W.2d 658, 666-67 (Tex.App.—Dallas 1986, writ ref'd n.r.e.) (20 questions in a single request); *Hoover v. Barker*, 507 S.W.2d 299, 305 (Tex.App.—Austin 1974, writ ref'd n.r.e.) (54 questions in a single request). By organizing the requests in clusters of related questions, instructions, and definitions, the party will not necessarily preserve error if the trial court does not submit all or part of the request to the jury; the party must specifically object to the omission and obtain a ruling. *See Cruz v. Andrews Restoration, Inc.*, 364 S.W.3d 817, 830-31 (Tex.2012). See "Formal Charge Conference," §4, p. 734.

1. Each cluster must be complete. All the elements—questions, instructions, and definitions—necessary for each cluster must be included in that cluster. *See, e.g.*, *Owens-Corning Fiberglas Corp. v. Keeton*, 922 S.W.2d 658, 662 (Tex.App.—Austin 1996, writ denied) (failure to submit proper instructions with broad-form question waived error); *see also* TRCP 279 (omissions from the charge). When a request contains a word or phrase that requires an instruction or definition, the appropriate instruction or definition must be included as part of the request. *See, e.g.*, *Select Ins. v. Boucher*, 561 S.W.2d 474, 479-80 (Tex.1978) (requested instruction on partial incapacity did not include definition of earning capacity); *Griffin v. Eakin*, 656 S.W.2d 187, 189-90 (Tex.App.—Austin

✦

1983, writ ref'd n.r.e.) (request contained reference to "negligence, as that term is defined herein," but did not include definition of negligence). A party cannot complain on appeal if the trial court did not submit an instruction or definition with one cluster when it was not requested as part of that cluster but only as part of another cluster. *See Universal Servs. v. Ung*, 904 S.W.2d 638, 640 (Tex.1995).

2. Each request in cluster must be correct. The party must tender the requests in "substantially correct wording." TRCP 278; *Willis v. Maverick*, 760 S.W.2d 642, 647 (Tex.1988); *Harris Cty. Flood Control Dist. v. Glenbrook Patiohome Owners Ass'n*, 933 S.W.2d 570, 580 (Tex.App.—Houston [1st Dist.] 1996, writ denied). If any part of the cluster is defective, the entire request is not substantially correct. The trial court may refuse the whole request if it finds any part of the request defective. *See Willis*, 760 S.W.2d at 647 (question was not substantially correct because phrase "should have discovered" was omitted); *Greenstein, Logan & Co. v. Burgess Mktg., Inc.*, 744 S.W.2d 170, 182 (Tex.App.—Waco 1987, writ denied) (request did not place burden of proof). There is no clear-cut rule to determine when a request meets the "substantially correct" standard. As long as a request falls somewhere between absolutely correct and not affirmatively incorrect, it should be sufficient. *See, e.g., Southwestern Bell Tel. Co. v. John Carlo Tex., Inc.*, 843 S.W.2d 470, 472 (Tex.1992) (although definition was not exactly correct, it was substantially correct); *Exxon Corp. v. Perez*, 842 S.W.2d 629, 630 n.1 (Tex.1992) (question was not affirmatively incorrect); *Placencio v. Allied Indus.*, 724 S.W.2d 20, 22 (Tex.1987) (question was affirmatively incorrect because it was not conditioned on the affirmative answer to another question).

§2.4 Proper burden of persuasion. The party must tender each question with the proper placement of the burden of persuasion. *Texas Employers' Ins. v. Olivarez*, 694 S.W.2d 92, 93-94 (Tex.App.—San Antonio 1985, no writ). Generally, to place the burden of persuasion properly, the question should be asked so the party with the burden will benefit from an affirmative answer. *Turk v. Robles*, 810 S.W.2d 755, 759 (Tex.App.—Houston [1st Dist.] 1991, writ denied). In cases in which a party must prove a negative, it is sometimes difficult to determine who has the burden of persuasion and how to word the question so as not to confuse the jury. *See id.* (instruction on testamentary capacity to revoke will). If there is doubt about who has the burden of persuasion on a question, the instruction should ask the jury to answer the question with a complete statement, not just a yes or no. *See Walker v. Eason*, 643 S.W.2d 390, 391 (Tex.1982). For example, when a jury is required to fill in the blank with either "She did have sufficient mental capacity" or "She did not have sufficient mental capacity," any error in misplacing the burden is harmless. *See id.* In cases submitted with broad-form questions, it is sometimes impossible to determine which party has the burden for each part of the charge. *State Dept. of Hwys. & Pub. Transp. v. Payne*, 838 S.W.2d 235, 240 (Tex.1992).

§2.5 Proper condition. When the answer to a follow-up question is conditioned on the jury's answer to an earlier question, the follow-up question must be preceded by an instruction telling the jury to answer the next question only if it responds in a certain way to the earlier question (e.g., "If you have answered 'Yes' to Question 3, then answer Question 4; otherwise, do not answer Question 4."). A request for a jury question is not correct if it conditions a question on the wrong question. If a party does not object to an erroneous conditional submission, the party waives the error. *Wilgus v. Bond*, 730 S.W.2d 670, 672 (Tex.1987); *Matthews v. Candlewood Builders, Inc.*, 685 S.W.2d 649, 650 (Tex.1985). If an erroneous conditional submission deprives a party of the submission of an issue raised by the pleadings and evidence, it constitutes reversible error. *Varme v. Gordon*, 881 S.W.2d 877, 881 (Tex.App.—Houston [14th Dist.] 1994, writ denied); *see, e.g., Washington v. Reliable Life Ins.*, 581 S.W.2d 153, 160 (Tex.1979) (remanded for new trial because conditioned question was not reached); *Byrne v. Harris Adacom Network Servs.*, 11 S.W.3d 244, 248-49 (Tex.App.—Texarkana 1999, pet. denied) (improper conditioning was harmless error); *Owens-Corning Fiberglas Corp. v. Martin*, 942 S.W.2d 712, 723 (Tex.App.—Dallas 1997, no writ) (same). The submission of a conditional damages question is expressly permitted by TRCP 277, even though it incidentally informs the jury of the legal effect of its answers. *H.E. Butt Grocery Co. v. Bilotto*, 985 S.W.2d 22, 24 (Tex.1998).

§2.6 Proper damages questions. The damages questions must be submitted so they reflect the following:

1. Proper measure. The party must tender a damages question that asks the jury to consider the correct legal measure of damages. *Jackson v. Fontaine's Clinics, Inc.*, 499 S.W.2d 87, 90 (Tex.1973). A jury question that does not guide the jury to a finding on any proper legal measure of damages is fatally defective. *Id.*; *Samedan*

THE CHARGE

✦

Oil Corp. v. Intrastate Gas Gathering, Inc., 78 S.W.3d 425, 452 (Tex.App.—Tyler 2001, pet. granted, judgm't vacated w.r.m.); *Browning Oil Co. v. Luecke*, 38 S.W.3d 625, 643 (Tex.App.—Austin 2000, pet. denied).

2. Proper segregation. The party must tender damages questions that properly segregate the damages due to each plaintiff, due from each defendant, and due on each individual claim. *See, e.g.*, *Minnesota Mining & Mfg. v. Nishika Ltd.*, 953 S.W.2d 733, 739 (Tex.1997) (damages were not segregated between Ps); *Green Int'l v. Solis*, 951 S.W.2d 384, 389-90 (Tex.1997) (attorney fees were not segregated according to claims); *Wingate v. Hajdik*, 795 S.W.2d 717, 719-20 (Tex.1990) (damages were not segregated between those due to corporation and those due to stockholder). However, the party does not have to tender damages questions that segregate the damages between multiple parties if the injury is indivisible. *See Stewart & Stevenson Servs. v. Serv-Tech, Inc.*, 879 S.W.2d 89, 101 (Tex.App.—Houston [14th Dist.] 1994, writ denied).

3. Proper condition. The party must tender the damages question that properly conditions it to an affirmative answer to the corresponding liability question. *See Wilgus v. Bond*, 730 S.W.2d 670, 672 (Tex.1987).

4. Alternative theories of damages. A party is entitled to seek damages on alternative theories of liability. *Waite Hill Servs. v. World Class Metal Works, Inc.*, 959 S.W.2d 182, 184 (Tex.1998). Once the jury's verdict is in, the plaintiff should elect its remedy to avoid application of the "one satisfaction" rule. *Id.* at 184-85; *see Birchfield v. Texarkana Mem'l Hosp.*, 747 S.W.2d 361, 367 (Tex.1987); *Household Credit Servs. v. Driscol*, 989 S.W.2d 72, 82 (Tex.App.—El Paso 1998, pet. denied).

§3. INFORMAL CHARGE CONFERENCE

The informal charge conference is held whenever the local rules provide or the judge prefers. Normally, the judge calls a recess after both sides close, and the attorneys meet with the judge in chambers to assemble the charge.

§3.1 Deadline for requests. Each party must submit its requested questions, instructions, and definitions to the court by whatever deadline the court imposes. Under TRCP 166(k), the court can require the parties to submit the requests at or before the pretrial conference. Local rules often require the attorneys to submit their requests before trial.

§3.2 Proposed charge. The court compiles the proposed charge during the informal charge conference by assembling questions, instructions, and definitions from those the attorneys provide and making any changes it believes necessary. The court then gives the proposed charge to the attorneys to examine.

§3.3 Time to examine. The trial court must allow the parties a reasonable amount of time to examine the proposed charge. TRCP 272. The court has the discretion to determine how much time to give the parties to examine the charge. *E.g.*, *Bekins Moving & Storage Co. v. Williams*, 947 S.W.2d 568, 575 (Tex.App.—Texarkana 1997, no writ) (32 minutes to review 51-page charge was reasonable; charge was largely in same form as before charge conference). If the trial court refuses to allow reasonable time to examine the charge, a party must make an objection on the record to preserve error. The objection must state the following: (1) that the party was not given adequate time to examine the charge, (2) how much time was given, (3) how much time was necessary, (4) that the charge was too complex and lengthy to examine in the amount of time given, and (5) that the lack of adequate time to examine the charge caused harm because the party was not able to make a proper record for appeal. *See, e.g.*, *Dillard v. Dillard*, 341 S.W.2d 668, 675 (Tex.App.—Austin 1960, writ ref'd n.r.e.) (although 15 minutes was not enough time to examine the charge, appellant did not show harm). The evidence of the harm can be included in a bill of exception if any error is discovered later, after a closer examination of the charge. See "Offer of Proof & Bill of Exception," ch. 8-E, p. 717.

§4. FORMAL CHARGE CONFERENCE

After the informal charge conference, the trial court will hold a formal charge conference with a court reporter present to record the parties' comments on the charge. The parties must make all their objections to the charge, present any requests for additional questions and instructions, and get rulings on all objections and requests.

★

CAUTION

At the formal charge conference, you must make a record of all the objections and requests for questions, instructions, and definitions that you have for the proposed charge, even if you discussed the same requests at the informal charge conference. See **Cruz v. Andrews Restoration, Inc.,** *364 S.W.3d 817, 830-31 (Tex.2012). To ensure that the objections and requests you made during the informal charge conference are preserved, restate the objections on the record, have the court overrule them orally, and ask the court to mark your written requests "refused" and sign them. See id.;* **Alaniz v. Jones & Neuse, Inc.,** *907 S.W.2d 450, 451 (Tex.1995). See "Written rulings," §5.2.2, p. 741.*

---

§4.1 Challenging charge. To preserve error in the charge, the party must make objections to defective submissions in the court's charge or submit written requests for additional questions, instructions, or definitions that are omitted from the charge. *See* TRCP 273. Under the rules relating to the charge, objections and requests are not interchangeable. *See id.* An objection to the charge can be made orally or in writing and must be specific. A request is a written question, instruction, or definition, submitted in substantially correct form.

For years, the Supreme Court strictly applied the rules for challenging the charge. However, in *State Dept. of Hwys. & Pub. Transp. v. Payne*, 838 S.W.2d 235, 241 (Tex.1992), the Court liberalized the procedure for objecting to the charge. The Court said there should be only one test to determine whether a party has preserved error in the jury charge: Did the party make the trial court "aware of the complaint, timely and plainly," and obtain a ruling? *Payne*, 838 S.W.2d at 241; *e.g.*, *Thota v. Young*, 366 S.W.3d 678, 689-91 (Tex.2012) (error preserved when party made specific and timely no-evidence objection to charge and submitted proposed charge that omitted the objected-to instructions); *Cruz v. Andrews Restoration, Inc.*, 364 S.W.3d 817, 829 (Tex.2012) (error not preserved because party did not timely or plainly make trial court aware of its charge complaint or obtain a ruling); *see also* *Galveston Cty. Fair & Rodeo, Inc. v. Glover*, 940 S.W.2d 585, 586-87 (Tex.1996) (complaint preserved even though party did not separately request in writing any definitions or instructions); *Alaniz v. Jones & Neuse, Inc.*, 907 S.W.2d 450, 451 (Tex. 1995) (complaint preserved even though request was not separate from completed charge).

PRACTICE TIP

When you are making your objections and requests, follow the rules set out below. On appeal, if you are worried you did not preserve error for appeal, cite **Payne** *and show that you timely made the trial court aware of your complaint and got a ruling.*

---

1. When to object – defect in charge. Object, no matter who has the burden of proof, when the court submits an erroneous or defective question, instruction, or definition. *See Equistar Chems., L.P. v. Dresser-Rand Co.*, 240 S.W.3d 864, 868 (Tex.2007) (erroneous instruction); *St. Joseph Hosp. v. Wolff*, 94 S.W.3d 513, 525 (Tex. 2002) (erroneous definition); *Spencer v. Eagle Star Ins.*, 876 S.W.2d 154, 157 (Tex.1994) (defective instruction); *Religious of the Sacred Heart v. City of Houston*, 836 S.W.2d 606, 613-14 (Tex.1992) (defective question). *But see Payne*, 838 S.W.2d at 241 (request for a question preserved error in defective instruction); *Matthiessen v. Schaefer*, 900 S.W.2d 792, 797 (Tex.App.—San Antonio 1995, writ denied) (request for a question preserved error in defective question).

2. When to request – omission in charge.

(1) Question omitted. A party must submit a request when it has the burden of proof and the court omits a question. *W.O. Bankston Nissan, Inc. v. Walters*, 754 S.W.2d 127, 128 (Tex.1988); *Wright Way Constr. Co. v. Harlingen Mall Co.*, 799 S.W.2d 415, 419 (Tex.App.—Corpus Christi 1990, writ denied). When a party submits a written request before trial, if the court omits part of it from the charge but was aware of the request and refused it, the party can preserve error by objecting and identifying the portion of its written request that the court

★

omitted. *See Cruz*, 364 S.W.3d at 830-31; *Alaniz*, 907 S.W.2d at 451. The party should probably locate its copy of the written request and ask the court to include it in the charge or write "refused" on it. See "Written rulings," §5.2.2, p. 741.

(2) Definition or instruction omitted. A party must make a written request, no matter who has the burden of proof, when the court omits an instruction or definition. TRCP 274, 278; *Gerdes v. Kennamer*, 155 S.W.3d 523, 534 (Tex.App.—Corpus Christi 2004, pet. denied); *Jarrin v. Sam White Oldsmobile Co.*, 929 S.W.2d 21, 25 (Tex.App.—Houston [1st Dist.] 1996, writ denied). A party cannot dictate a requested instruction into the record. *Fairfield Estates L.P. v. Griffin*, 986 S.W.2d 719, 724 (Tex.App.—Eastland 1999, no pet.); *Jarrin*, 929 S.W.2d at 25; *Hartnett v. Hampton Inns, Inc.*, 870 S.W.2d 162, 165 (Tex.App.—San Antonio 1993, writ denied).

3. When to either object or request.

(1) Opponent's question omitted. A party may object or submit a request when its opponent has the burden of proof and the court omits part of the opponent's cause or defense. *See, e.g.*, *Payne*, 838 S.W.2d at 239 (State preserved error by submitting the missing element of a question, even though it did not have the burden of proof); *Religious of the Sacred Heart*, 836 S.W.2d at 613-14 (city preserved error by objecting to the omission of a proper damages question on which P had burden); *Ramos v. Frito-Lay, Inc.*, 784 S.W.2d 667, 668 (Tex.1990) (D should have objected when court did not submit element of P's cause of action).

PRACTICE TIP

It may seem odd to object to errors made by the other party in its jury questions, but if you do not, you may be bound by adverse express or deemed findings. See "Incomplete claim or defense submitted," §7.2, p. 743.

---

(2) Erroneous burden of persuasion. A party may object to a question or submit a request when the court improperly places the burden of persuasion. *See Morris v. Holt*, 714 S.W.2d 311, 312-13 (Tex.1986) (preserved by request); *Turk v. Robles*, 810 S.W.2d 755, 759 (Tex.App.—Houston [1st Dist.] 1991, writ denied) (preserved by objection).

4. Rule to challenge charge. Challenging the charge can be confusing. When there is doubt about whether to object or request, a party should always object. If a party has the burden of proof on a question, it should also (not instead) submit a request. If a definition or instruction is omitted, the party should object and make a request, no matter who has the burden. Finally, the party should analyze its objections and requests in light of *Payne*: Did the party make the trial court "aware of the complaint, timely and plainly," and obtain a ruling? *Payne*, 838 S.W.2d at 241.

§4.2 Deadline to object & request.

1. The charge.

(1) General rule. The parties must make all objections and requests to amend the language of the charge before the court reads the charge to the jury. TRCP 272; *Cruz v. Andrews Restoration, Inc.*, 364 S.W.3d 817, 830 (Tex.2012); *Missouri Pac. R.R. v. Cross*, 501 S.W.2d 868, 873 (Tex.1973). The parties will waive any objections to errors in the charge that are made after the jury retires. TRCP 272; *Cross*, 501 S.W.2d at 873; *see, e.g.*, *Mitchell v. Bank of Am.*, 156 S.W.3d 622, 627-28 (Tex.App.—Dallas 2004, pet. denied) (objections to charge in motion for new trial were untimely). A party cannot preserve error by a late objection, even if the trial court permits it and the other party agrees. *Cross*, 501 S.W.2d at 873; *Sudderth v. Howard*, 560 S.W.2d 511, 516 (Tex.App.—Amarillo 1977, writ ref'd n.r.e.).

(2) Exceptions. There are two exceptions to this rule. First, it is not necessary to challenge the legal sufficiency of the evidence before the charge is submitted to the jury. A legal-sufficiency challenge can be made for the first time in a motion for JNOV or in a motion for new trial. See "Preserving legal-sufficiency point," ch. 10-B,

§13.1.3, p. 803. Second, it is not necessary to object that a certain legal theory precludes recovery. *See, e.g.*, *Holland v. Wal-Mart Stores*, 1 S.W.3d 91, 94 (Tex.1999) (statute did not permit attorney fees).

2. Supplemental instructions. If, after the jury retires to deliberate, the trial court decides to give the jury additional instructions, the parties must make any objections or requests before the court reads the supplemental charge to the jury. See "Supplemental instructions to jury," §8.2, p. 744.

3. Presumption of timeliness. On appeal, the court will presume the parties timely objected unless the record shows otherwise. TRCP 272; *Accord v. General Motors Corp.*, 669 S.W.2d 111, 114 (Tex.1984) (court's statement of "overruled" following objections of both parties was held to be a timely ruling on P's objections). If the record shows that a party did not object timely, the party waives the error. *Morales v. Morales*, 98 S.W.3d 343, 346 (Tex. App.—Corpus Christi 2003, pet. denied); *Ruff v. Christian Servs.*, 627 S.W.2d 799, 801 (Tex.App.—Tyler 1982, no writ).

§4.3 Making formal objections.

1. Orally or in writing. A party may object to the charge either orally, by dictating objections to the court reporter, or in writing. TRCP 272. At the formal charge conference, the parties will probably dictate the objections to the court reporter. The objections must be made in the presence of the trial judge, opposing counsel, and the court reporter. *Brantley v. Sprague*, 636 S.W.2d 224, 225 (Tex.App.—Texarkana 1982, writ ref'd n.r.e.). If the trial judge is not present, the objections are waived. *Id.*

2. Specific. A party must make timely and specific objections to the charge. *See* TRCP 274; TRAP 33.1(a)(1)(A). The objection must clearly identify the error and explain the grounds for the complaint. TRCP 274; *Texas Comm'n on Human Rights v. Morrison*, ___ S.W.3d ___ (Tex.2012) (No. 11-0644; 8-31-12); *Castleberry v. Branscum*, 721 S.W.2d 270, 276 (Tex.1986); *Brown v. American Transfer & Storage Co.*, 601 S.W.2d 931, 938 (Tex. 1980). If the objection does not meet both of these requirements, it will not preserve error. *Castleberry*, 721 S.W.2d at 276; *see Texas Comm'n*, ___ S.W.3d at ___. A specific objection enables the trial court to understand the precise grounds and make an informed ruling. *Castleberry*, 721 S.W.2d at 276. It also affords the trial court an opportunity to remedy the defect. *Id.*; *Osteen v. Crumpton*, 519 S.W.2d 263, 264 (Tex.App.—Dallas 1975, writ ref'd). If a general objection is paired with a written request that clearly reflects the error, the objection will be preserved. *Universal Underwriters Ins. v. Pierce*, 795 S.W.2d 771, 773 (Tex.App.—Houston [1st Dist.] 1990, writ denied).

PRACTICE TIP
When you object, (1) identify the defect, (2) specify how the question, instruction, or definition is defective, (3) state why it is defective, and (4) state the exact correction you want the court to make.

---

3. Not obscured by other objections. A party should not obscure a correct objection among voluminous, unfounded, and "stock" objections. TRCP 274; *Monsanto Co. v. Milam*, 494 S.W.2d 534, 536 (Tex.1973). See "Bad objections," §4.3.5(2), p. 739 (objection (a)). There is no rule of thumb for when an objection has been "obscured." Generally, it is not the number of objections, but the use of repetitious or stock objections, that obscures a valid complaint. *See, e.g.*, *Monsanto Co.*, 494 S.W.2d at 536-37 (42 pages of stock objections on grounds of "no pleadings" and "insufficient pleadings" concealed valid objection); *Hinote v. Oil, Chem. & Atomic Workers Int'l Un.*, 777 S.W.2d 134, 143-45 (Tex.App.—Houston [14th Dist.] 1989, writ denied) (30 pages of invalid and stock objections on grounds of "factual insufficiency" and "against the great weight and preponderance of the evidence" concealed valid objection); *Baker Material Handling Corp. v. Cummings*, 692 S.W.2d 142, 145-46 (Tex.App.—Dallas 1985) (17 objections did not obscure valid objection because there were no stock objections), *writ dism'd*, 713 S.W.2d 96 (Tex.1986).

4. No adoption by reference. A party cannot adopt an objection from one question or instruction and apply it by reference to other questions or objections. TRCP 274; *C.T.W. v. B.C.G.*, 809 S.W.2d 788, 793 (Tex.App.—Beaumont 1991, no writ); *Washburn v. Krenek*, 684 S.W.2d 187, 190 (Tex.App.—Houston [14th Dist.] 1984, writ

⋆

ref'd n.r.e.). A party cannot adopt another party's objections; each party must state its own objections to the charge. *C.M. Asfahl Agency v. Tensor, Inc.*, 135 S.W.3d 768, 795-96 (Tex.App.—Houston [1st Dist.] 2004, no pet.); *Wright Way Constr. Co. v. Harlingen Mall Co.*, 799 S.W.2d 415, 420-21 (Tex.App.—Corpus Christi 1990, writ denied). However, the trial court at its discretion may permit joint objections to save time. *See Owens-Corning Fiberglas Corp. v. Malone*, 916 S.W.2d 551, 556 (Tex.App.—Houston [1st Dist.] 1996), *aff'd*, 972 S.W.2d 35 (Tex.1998).

5. Examples.

(1) Good objections. A valid objection is one that is appropriate to the charge in the case. The following are some good objections, if relevant to the case. Each of the statements below should be preceded with the statement "the party objects because."

(a) The charge submits an issue established as a matter of law. It is not necessary to submit *{identify issue}* to the jury because it was judicially admitted in the other party's pleadings. Once a fact is conclusively established by judicial admission, a jury question concerning the fact should not be submitted. *Horizon/CMS Healthcare Corp. v. Auld*, 34 S.W.3d 887, 905 (Tex.2000).

(b) The charge omits an element from the *{cause of action/defense}*, in that the element of *{identify the missing element}* is required to be submitted. *{Submit a written request for the missing element.}*

(c) There is no evidence to support the submission of question number ___, and that question should not be submitted to the jury.

(d) There is no evidence to support the submission of *{identify element in broad-form submission that has no support}*; the court should either submit individual questions for each element in the broad-form question or delete that element from the broad-form question. See "Broad form not required," §2.1.2, p. 731.

(e) The only evidence to support the submission of question number ___ is circumstantial evidence, and because the evidence is equally consistent with either of two facts, neither fact can be inferred and the issue cannot be submitted to the jury. See "Circumstantial evidence," §6.1.2, p. 741.

(f) Question number ___, which inquires about *{identify cause of action}*, is improper because there are no pleadings to support its submission, and the issue was not tried by consent. *See Recognition Comm. v. American Auto. Ass'n*, 154 S.W.3d 878, 885-86 (Tex.App.—Dallas 2005, pet. denied). *{Identify the variance between the pleadings and the proof.}* See "Issue not tried by consent," ch. 8-F, §2.4.2(2), p. 723.

(g) Question number ___ *{is not conditioned/is improperly conditioned}* on an affirmative answer to question number ___.

(h) Question number ___ should not be submitted to the jury because it is not a controlling question. *{State reason.}*

(i) Question number ___ is immaterial to the outcome of the case. *See Oliver v. Oliver*, 889 S.W.2d 271, 273-74 (Tex.1994) (because court disregarded immaterial question without proper objection, uncertain if objection was necessary to preserve error).

(j) The charge does not contain an *{instruction/definition}* necessary to the submission of the question of ___, which is *{state the instruction or definition}*. *{Submit a written request for the omitted instruction or definition.}*

(k) Question number ___ duplicates question number ___.

(l) Question number ___ does not properly place the burden of persuasion because *{state the reason}*.

(m) The following language in *{question/instruction/definition number ___}*, *{quote the language}*, is a comment on the weight of the evidence because it suggests the trial court's opinion that *{state exactly why it is a comment on the evidence}*. TRCP 277; *Alvarez v. Missouri, K.T. R.R.*, 683 S.W.2d 375, 377 (Tex.1984); *Garza v. Southland Corp.*, 836 S.W.2d 214, 220 (Tex.App.—Houston [14th Dist.] 1992, no writ).

✦

(n) Question number ___ presents an inferential-rebuttal defense. TRCP 277. An inferential-rebuttal issue is permitted only as an instruction. *Id. {Submit the inferential-rebuttal instruction.}*

(o) The instruction regarding ___ should not be included because (1) the other party did not plead it, (2) the case was not tried on that theory, and (3) the jury questions do not rely on it. *See Texas Workers' Comp. Ins. Fund v. Mandlbauer*, 34 S.W.3d 909, 912 (Tex.2000).

(p) The instruction regarding ___ is defective because *{state why}*.

(q) Definition number ___ is an improper statement of the law in that *{state why}*. *See St. Joseph Hosp. v. Wolff*, 94 S.W.3d 513, 529 (Tex.2002).

(r) The instruction regarding ___ is unnecessary, and even though it is a correct statement of the law, it amounts to a comment on the weight of the evidence that tilts or nudges the jury by *{state exactly how it nudges the jury}*. *Wal-Mart Stores v. Johnson*, 106 S.W.3d 718, 723-24 (Tex.2003); *Lone Star Gas Co. v. Lemond*, 897 S.W.2d 755, 756 (Tex.1995); *Lemos v. Montez*, 680 S.W.2d 798, 801 (Tex.1984). The more closely contested the case, the greater the chance that a superfluous instruction is error. *Johnson*, 106 S.W.3d at 724; *see Timberwalk Apts., Partners v. Cain*, 972 S.W.2d 749, 756 n.25 (Tex.1998); *Ford Motor Co. v. Miles*, 967 S.W.2d 377, 387 (Tex. 1998).

(s) The charge, which is based on a statutory cause of action, does not track the language of the statute. *See Borneman v. Steak & Ale*, 22 S.W.3d 411, 413 (Tex.2000).

(t) The damages question is not properly related to the cause of action on which it must be conditioned. Question number ___ must be conditioned on an affirmative answer to question number ___. See "Proper condition," §2.6.3, p. 734.

(u) *{The causes of action have different types of damages/The damages are owed to different plaintiffs}*, and the damages must be segregated. Question number ___ must be conditioned on an affirmative answer to question number ___, and question number ___ must be conditioned on an affirmative answer to question number ___.

(v) The instruction on the exemplary-damages question does not limit the jury's consideration to the harm caused to the plaintiff because it seeks to punish the defendant for harm caused to nonparties. *See Philip Morris USA v. Williams*, 549 U.S. 346, 354-55 (2007).

(w) Question number ___ on attorney fees does not segregate the reasonable and necessary attorney fees incurred for prosecuting the causes of action on which attorney fees are recoverable from the causes of action on which no attorney fees may be recovered. Or, the question does not segregate the reasonable and necessary attorney fees incurred for prosecuting the cause of action against this party from the other parties. See "Proper segregation," §2.6.2, p. 734.

(2) **Bad objections.** The following objections should not be made in any case.

(a) There is factually insufficient evidence to support the submission of question number ___; or, question number ___ is against the great weight of the evidence. An attorney should never object that the question should not be submitted because the evidence is "factually insufficient" or "against the great weight and preponderance" of the evidence. Such complaints are without merit at the charge conference. *Long Island Owner's Ass'n v. Davidson*, 965 S.W.2d 674, 680 (Tex.App.—Corpus Christi 1998, pet. denied); *Hinote*, 777 S.W.2d at 143. The trial court determines whether to submit a question to the jury on legal-sufficiency grounds, not on factual-sufficiency grounds. The court has a duty to submit the question if there is any probative evidence to support it. *American Home Assur. Co. v. Brandt*, 778 S.W.2d 141, 144 (Tex.App.—Texarkana 1989, writ denied). When a party makes factual-sufficiency objections to the charge, it undermines the party's valid objections to the charge and the attorney's credibility with the court. *See Hinote*, 777 S.W.2d at 143.

(b) With regard to question number ___, there is a variance between the pleadings and the proof. This statement alone is not sufficient. If there is a variance between the pleadings and the proof, the party must identify the specific variance or defect in its objection. *Brown*, 601 S.W.2d at 938; *Ron Craft Chevrolet, Inc. v. Davis*, 836 S.W.2d 672, 675 (Tex.App.—El Paso 1992, writ denied).

─────────────── ✪ ───────────────

(c) Question number ___ "should read" a particular way. This objection alone is improper because it does not identify the error. *Garza*, 836 S.W.2d at 218.

(d) Question number ___ could not form "a basis of liability" or "the basis of any judgment." To be proper, such objections must be more specific and must call the court's attention to the failure of the charge to submit a proper question. *Anderson v. Broome*, 233 S.W.2d 901, 904 (Tex.App.—El Paso 1950, writ ref'd n.r.e.).

(e) The instruction on ___ may "confuse the jury" or "prejudice the defendant." Such complaints are too general because they do not explain how the instruction would confuse the jury or how it would prejudice the defendant. *Castleberry*, 721 S.W.2d at 277.

(f) The charge contains two (or more) theories of damages and will give the plaintiff a double recovery. Because a party is entitled to seek damages on alternative theories, this is not a valid objection. See "Alternative theories of damages," §2.6.4, p. 734.

§4.4 Making formal request for additions to charge.

1. In writing. Once the court submits the proposed charge to the parties at the formal charge conference, if either party wants the court to include any additional questions, instructions, or definitions the party must tender the additional request in writing or object to the omission of a written request that was made at the informal charge conference. *See* TRCP 273; *see, e.g.*, *Alaniz v. Jones & Neuse, Inc.*, 907 S.W.2d 450, 451 (Tex.1995) (objection at formal charge conference to exclusion of request offered before informal charge conference preserved error).

2. Separate from objections. A party must tender the request separately from any objections. TRCP 273, 278; *Woods v. Crane Carrier Co.*, 693 S.W.2d 377, 379 (Tex.1985); *Texas Employers' Ins. v. Eskue*, 574 S.W.2d 814, 818 (Tex.App.—El Paso 1978, no writ).

§5. COURT'S RULINGS ON REQUESTS & OBJECTIONS

§5.1 Deadline for rulings. The court should announce its ruling on the requests and objections before it reads the charge to the jury. TRCP 272. The trial court's rulings on the objections should appear in the record. *See Reliance Ins. v. Dahlstrom Corp.*, 568 S.W.2d 733, 734 (Tex.App.—Eastland 1978, writ ref'd n.r.e.). However, if the court submits proposed questions or instructions over objections without a ruling, the court implicitly overrules the objections. *Acord v. General Motors Corp.*, 669 S.W.2d 111, 114 (Tex.1984); *see also* TRAP 33.1(a)(2)(A) (trial court can make ruling on request or objection either expressly or implicitly). For the rule in *Acord* to apply, the record must show that the court in some manner acknowledged receiving the requested questions. *Anderson v. Vinson Expl., Inc.*, 832 S.W.2d 657, 668 (Tex.App.—El Paso 1992, writ denied).

PRACTICE TIP

If the court overruled your requested questions, instructions, or definitions at the charge conference, but the record from the charge conference does not clearly show it, while the trial court still has plenary power, you should ask the court to sign an order reflecting its rulings and stating they were made before the charge was submitted to the jury. It is critical that the record reflect the court's ruling.

---

§5.2 Method of ruling.

1. Oral rulings. If the objections are dictated into the record, the court should state its ruling on the objections immediately after each party makes its objections. TRCP 272, 276. On appeal, the trial court's ruling can be inferred from the record. For example, if a party makes an objection and the trial court makes no change in the charge, the objection is overruled. *Acord v. General Motors Corp.*, 669 S.W.2d 111, 114 (Tex.1984); *see* TRAP 33.1(a)(2)(A). If a commonsense interpretation of the objection and the court's ruling shows that the trial court necessarily overruled the objection, the appellate courts will hold that the objection was overruled. *Betty Leavell Rlty. Co. v. Raggio*, 669 S.W.2d 102, 104 (Tex.1984).

✦

2. Written rulings. When the court refuses or modifies a request, it should endorse the request as either "refused" or "modified" and sign it. TRCP 272, 276. When the court endorses "modified" on a request, the court should also state how the request has been modified. TRCP 276. If the court does not indicate its ruling by endorsing the request, the request does not preserve error. *Anderson v. Vinson Expl., Inc.*, 832 S.W.2d 657, 667-68 (Tex.App.—El Paso 1992, writ denied); *see Munoz v. Berne Grp.*, 919 S.W.2d 470, 472 (Tex.App.—San Antonio 1996, no writ). If, however, the record clearly shows that the trial court was aware of the request and refused it, even if the trial court did not sign the refused instruction as required by TRCP 276, the error is preserved. *See* TRAP 33.1(a)(2)(A); *Cruz v. Andrews Restoration, Inc.*, 364 S.W.3d 817, 830 (Tex.2012); *Dallas Mkt. Ctr. Dev. Co. v. Liedeker*, 958 S.W.2d 382, 386 (Tex.1997), *overruled on other grounds*, *Torrington Co. v. Stutzman*, 46 S.W.3d 829 (Tex.2000); *Chemical Express Carriers, Inc. v. Pina*, 819 S.W.2d 585, 589 (Tex.App.—El Paso 1991, writ denied). When there are several pages of requests, the record must show that the court endorsed and signed the requests, either separately or as a group; otherwise, the requests will not preserve error. *Greenstein, Logan & Co. v. Burgess Mktg., Inc.*, 744 S.W.2d 170, 181 (Tex.App.—Waco 1987, writ denied).

§6. CHARGE SUBMITTED TO JURY

The trial court is required to read the charge to the jury before the attorneys make their final arguments. TRCP 275.

§6.1 Questions. TRCP 278 requires the trial court to submit a requested question to the jury if the pleadings and any evidence support it. *Elbaor v. Smith*, 845 S.W.2d 240, 243 (Tex.1992); *Komet v. Graves*, 40 S.W.3d 596, 603 (Tex.App.—San Antonio 2001, no pet.). The trial court has broad discretion in submitting questions to the jury as long as the questions submitted control the disposition of the case and properly present the disputed issues for the jury's determination. *Moore v. Kitsmiller*, 201 S.W.3d 147, 153 (Tex.App.—Tyler 2006, pet. denied). The court can refuse to submit a question if (1) there is no evidence to support it, (2) there are no pleadings to support it and the issue was not tried by consent, or (3) the issue is uncontroverted. *See Alaniz v. Jones & Neuse, Inc.*, 907 S.W.2d 450, 452 (Tex.1995) (no pleadings or evidence for lost future profits); *T.O. Stanley Boot Co. v. Bank of El Paso*, 847 S.W.2d 218, 222-23 (Tex.1992) (no evidence of intention not to perform; uncontroverted evidence on amount of notes).

1. Direct evidence. When a material fact is supported by direct evidence, the issue must be submitted to the jury. *See Farley v. M M Cattle Co.*, 529 S.W.2d 751, 753-54 (Tex.1975).

2. Circumstantial evidence. When a material fact is supported by circumstantial evidence, the issue may be submitted to the jury if the material fact can reasonably be inferred from the facts proved. *Russell v. Russell*, 865 S.W.2d 929, 933 (Tex.1993). When circumstantial evidence supports more than one reasonable inference, the jury must decide which inference is more reasonable, subject to judicial review only to ensure the evidence is factually sufficient. *Lozano v. Lozano*, 52 S.W.3d 141, 148 (Tex.2001). The jury has the power to choose between competing reasonable inferences. *Id.* at 149. Properly applied, the equal-inference rule is a type of "no-evidence" rule; when circumstantial evidence is so slight that any plausible inference is purely a guess, it is in effect no evidence. *Id.* at 148.

§6.2 Instructions. The instructions to the jury include the general instructions given in all jury trials and the instructions that are specific to the case.

1. General. The trial court must give the jury the general instructions prescribed by Section III of TRCP 226a.

2. Specific. The trial court must give the jury the special instructions for the case. The court must submit any explanatory instructions necessary to enable the jury to reach a verdict. TRCP 277; *Wichita Cty. v. Hart*, 917 S.W.2d 779, 783-84 (Tex.1996). For an instruction to be proper, it must (1) assist the jury in its deliberations, (2) accurately state the law, and (3) be supported by the pleadings and evidence. *Thota v. Young*, 366 S.W.3d 678,

———————————————— ✦ ————————————————

687 (Tex.2012); *Columbia Rio Grande Healthcare, L.P. v. Hawley*, 284 S.W.3d 851, 855 (Tex.2009); *Texas Workers' Comp. Ins. Fund v. Mandlbauer*, 34 S.W.3d 909, 912 (Tex.2000). The court has considerable discretion in deciding what instructions are necessary. *Thota*, 366 S.W.3d at 687; *Columbia Rio Grande Healthcare*, 284 S.W.3d at 856; *State Farm Lloyds v. Nicolau*, 951 S.W.2d 444, 451 (Tex.1997); *Mobil Chem. Co. v. Bell*, 517 S.W.2d 245, 256 (Tex.1974).

(1) **Inferential-rebuttal instructions.** If the defendant introduced evidence that raised an inferential rebuttal, the inferential-rebuttal issue is submitted to the jury as an instruction, not as a question. TRCP 277; *Bed, Bath & Beyond, Inc. v. Urista*, 211 S.W.3d 753, 757 (Tex.2006). The purpose of the instruction is to tell the jury it is not required to find the defendant responsible for the accident if the true cause was something else. *Dew v. Crown Derrick Erectors, Inc.*, 208 S.W.3d 448, 450 (Tex.2006) (plurality op.). Jurors do not need to agree on who or what caused the accident, only that it was not the defendant. *Dillard v. Texas Elec. Coop.*, 157 S.W.3d 429, 434 (Tex.2005). *See generally* Texas Pattern Jury Charges—General Negligence & Intentional Personal Torts (2010), PJC ch. 3 (inferential-rebuttal instructions). See "Good objections," §4.3.5(1), p. 738 (objection (n)).

(2) **Exemplary-damages instructions.** For cases involving exemplary damages, the court—before closing arguments—must provide a written charge that informs the jury that its answer to the question regarding the amount of exemplary damages must be unanimous. CPRC §41.003(e); *see* TRCP 226a, §III. See "Exemplary-damages cases," ch. 8-K, §4.2, p. 754.

3. Erroneous.

(1) **Misstatement of law.** An instruction that misstates the law as applied to the facts of the case is reversible error. *Wakefield v. Bevly*, 704 S.W.2d 339, 350 (Tex.App.—Corpus Christi 1985, no writ).

(2) **Improper burden of proof.** An instruction that imposes a greater burden than the law requires is reversible error. *American Home Assur. Co. v. Brandt*, 778 S.W.2d 141, 143 (Tex.App.—Texarkana 1989, writ denied); *see, e.g., Marathon Oil Co. v. Salazar*, 682 S.W.2d 624, 628-29 (Tex.App.—Houston [1st Dist.] 1984, writ ref'd n.r.e.) (misstatement of probable cause).

§6.3 Definitions. A definition defines a term used in the charge. The purpose of a definition is to enable jurors to understand legal words or phrases so that they can properly answer the jury questions. *Oadra v. Stegall*, 871 S.W.2d 882, 890 (Tex.App.—Houston [14th Dist.] 1994, no writ). The trial court must submit any definitions necessary to enable the jury to reach a verdict. TRCP 277; *St. James Transp. v. Porter*, 840 S.W.2d 658, 664 (Tex.App.—Houston [1st Dist.] 1992, writ denied); *Lumbermens Mut. Cas. Co. v. Garcia*, 758 S.W.2d 893, 894 (Tex.App.—Corpus Christi 1988, writ denied). The sufficiency of the definitions is left to the discretion of the trial court. *Porter*, 840 S.W.2d at 664. Only legal or technical terms need to be defined. *E.g., Whiteside v. Watson*, 12 S.W.3d 614, 624 (Tex.App.—Eastland 2000, pet. granted, judgm't vacated w.r.m.) ("earning capacity" and "physical impairment" have specific legal definitions); *Allen v. Allen*, 966 S.W.2d 658, 660 (Tex.App.—San Antonio 1998, pet. denied) ("cohabitation" did not need to be defined); *Turner v. Roadway Express, Inc.*, 911 S.W.2d 224, 227 (Tex.App.—Fort Worth 1995, writ denied) ("recklessly" did not need to be defined). If a term is used more than once in the charge and the term requires a definition, the definition should follow the general instructions. *Woods v. Crane Carrier Co.*, 693 S.W.2d 377, 379 (Tex.1985).

§7. WAIVER OF GROUNDS & OMITTED ELEMENTS

§7.1 Entire claim or defense omitted. A party waives an entire theory of recovery or defense by not objecting to its omission from the charge. TRCP 279; *Gulf States Utils. Co. v. Low*, 79 S.W.3d 561, 565 (Tex.2002); *Harmes v. Arklatex Corp.*, 615 S.W.2d 177, 179 (Tex.1981); *see, e.g., American Physicians Ins. Exch. v. Garcia*, 876 S.W.2d 842, 848 n.12 (Tex.1994) (D waived estoppel defense); *Southwestern Bell Tel. Co. v. DeLanney*, 809 S.W.2d 493, 495 (Tex.1991) (P waived breach-of-contract claim). If, however, the complete theory of recovery or defense was proved as a matter of law, there is no waiver because a jury question is not required. *See Brown v. Bank of Galveston*, 963 S.W.2d 511, 515 (Tex.1998).

★

§7.2 Incomplete claim or defense submitted. TRCP 279 describes the procedure when an element of a ground of recovery or defense is omitted from the jury charge. *See Service Corp. v. Guerra*, 348 S.W.3d 221, 228-29 (Tex.2011); *Chon Tri v. J.T.T.*, 162 S.W.3d 552, 557 (Tex.2005); *In re J.F.C.*, 96 S.W.3d 256, 262-63 (Tex.2002).

    1. Neither party objected. The trial court may make an express finding in support of the judgment when the charge was submitted with an element missing from a claim or defense and (1) the party with the burden of proof on the incomplete claim or defense did not request the missing element, (2) the opposing party did not object to the missing element, (3) the claim or defense consisted of more than one element, (4) the missing element is "necessarily referable" to the claim or defense, and (5) there is factually sufficient evidence to support a finding on the missing element. TRCP 279; *see Gulf States Utils. Co. v. Low*, 79 S.W.3d 561, 564 (Tex.2002); *Clayton W. Williams, Jr., Inc. v. Olivo*, 952 S.W.2d 523, 529 (Tex.1997); *Ramos v. Frito-Lay, Inc.*, 784 S.W.2d 667, 668 (Tex.1990); *Wal-Mart Stores v. Renteria*, 52 S.W.3d 848, 850 (Tex.App.—San Antonio 2001, pet. denied). By not objecting, the parties waive a jury trial on the omitted element and agree to submit the issue to the trial court. *Gulf States*, 79 S.W.3d at 565. If the trial court does not make an express finding on the omitted element before rendering judgment, the appellate court will deem a finding on the omitted element that supports the trial court's judgment. TRCP 279; *Service Corp.*, 348 S.W.3d at 228-29; *Chon Tri*, 162 S.W.3d at 557-58; *see, e.g.*, *Ramos*, 784 S.W.2d at 668 (Supreme Court deemed findings in support of trial court's judgment); *Cielo Dorado Dev., Inc. v. Certainteed Corp.*, 744 S.W.2d 10, 11 (Tex.1988) (same). The deemed finding must be supported by legally sufficient evidence from the trial. *See Service Corp.*, 348 S.W.3d at 229.

    2. Opposing party objected. The trial court must render judgment against the party who had the burden of proof on a missing element when (1) the opposing party objected to the missing element, (2) an affirmative finding on the missing element is essential to the claim or defense, and (3) the missing element is not established as a matter of law in favor of the party with the burden of proof. *McKinley v. Stripling*, 763 S.W.2d 407, 410 (Tex. 1989); *Physicians & Surgeons Gen. Hosp. v. Koblizek*, 752 S.W.2d 657, 660 (Tex.App.—Corpus Christi 1988, writ denied). When the opposing party objects to a missing element, a court cannot deem the missing element in favor of the party with the burden of proof on that element. *See Physicians & Surgeons*, 752 S.W.2d at 660. In such a case, the party with the burden of proof did not secure a finding on the omitted element, which forecloses that claim or defense. *Olivo*, 952 S.W.2d at 529; *Dallas Cty. Med. Soc'y v. Ubiñas-Brache*, 68 S.W.3d 31, 40 (Tex.App.—Dallas 2001, pet. denied).

§7.3 How trial court makes express findings. The trial court may make an express finding anytime before it renders the judgment. *See* TRCP 279.

    1. The party who will benefit from an express finding should ask the court to make an express, written finding. The trial court cannot make an express finding without a request from one of the parties. *Id.*

    2. The other parties must be given notice of the request. *Id.*

    3. The court must conduct a hearing on the request. *Id.*

    4. The court must make an express finding in writing before rendering judgment. *Id.* When the court makes an express finding, it will render a judgment on the complete verdict. For example, assume that in a simple-negligence case no proximate-cause question was submitted, and the jury found the defendant negligent. If the court makes an express finding that the negligence was a proximate cause of the plaintiff's injury, the court will render judgment for the plaintiff. However, if the court makes an express finding that the negligence was not a proximate cause of the plaintiff's injury, the court will render judgment for the defendant.

§7.4 How appellate courts make deemed findings. The appellate courts may make a deemed finding only in the following circumstances:

    1. The trial court did not make an express finding in writing before rendering judgment. TRCP 279; *In re J.F.C.*, 96 S.W.3d 256, 262-63 (Tex.2002).

    2. The appellate court makes a finding to support the trial court's judgment. TRCP 279; *Gulf States Utils. Co. v. Low*, 79 S.W.3d 561, 564 (Tex.2002); *see In re J.F.C.*, 96 S.W.3d at 262-63. The appellate court cannot deem a

─────────────────── ✦ ───────────────────

finding that requires a different judgment than the one rendered by the trial court. *Gulf States*, 79 S.W.3d at 564; *see also **Logan v. Mullis***, 686 S.W.2d 605, 609 (Tex.1985) (court of appeals erred by deeming a finding in support of verdict instead of final judgment).

§8. SUPPLEMENTAL INSTRUCTIONS TO JURY

§8.1 Jury's questions to trial court. If the jury has a question or needs to communicate with the court, the presiding juror will tell the officer in charge of the jury, who will inform the trial court. TRCP 285; *Ross v. Texas Employers' Ins.*, 267 S.W.2d 541, 542 (Tex.1954). The trial court should assemble the jury and the attorneys in the courtroom, where the presiding juror will communicate with the court, either orally or in writing. TRCP 285, 286; *Mid-South Bottling Co. v. Cigainero*, 799 S.W.2d 385, 387 n.1 (Tex.App.—Texarkana 1990, writ denied). If the jury asks for additional instructions on the law, its request must be in writing. TRCP 286.

§8.2 Supplemental instructions to jury. After the jury retires, the trial court may give the jury additional instructions on any matters of law, either at the request of the jury, on the court's own initiative, or on the motion of a party. *See, e.g.*, *Lochinvar Corp. v. Meyers*, 930 S.W.2d 182, 187 (Tex.App.—Dallas 1996, no writ) (party made late objection to error in charge, which court corrected by supplemental instruction). When the jury is assembled for a supplemental charge, the court must give the instruction in writing. TRCP 286. The court must give the attorneys an opportunity to object to the supplemental instructions before it reads them to the jury. *Scroggs v. Morgan*, 130 S.W.2d 283, 285 (Tex.1939). The trial court may allow additional argument at its discretion. *See **Geesbreght v. Geesbreght***, 570 S.W.2d 427, 433 (Tex.App.—Fort Worth 1978, writ dism'd).

§8.3 Verdict-urging instructions. TRCP 289 permits the trial court to discharge a jury without a verdict when (1) the jurors cannot agree and the parties consent to their discharge, (2) the jurors have been kept together for such time as to render it altogether improbable that they can agree, or (3) a calamity or accident occurs that, in the opinion of the court, requires discharge. *Shaw v. Greater Houston Transp.*, 791 S.W.2d 204, 205 (Tex.App.—Corpus Christi 1990, no writ). To determine whether the jurors will be able to reach a verdict, the trial court can ask them and in some circumstances can instruct them, to resume deliberations and attempt to reach a verdict. The supplemental charge is sometimes called an "*Allen*" charge, after *Allen v. U.S.*, 164 U.S. 492 (1896), or the "dynamite charge," because it is used to "blast" a jury out of deadlock to reach a verdict. *Stevens v. Travelers Ins.*, 563 S.W.2d 223, 226 (Tex.1978). The trial court cannot keep the jurors captive once they have announced they cannot reach a verdict. *See **Shaw***, 791 S.W.2d at 210 (court's refusal to release jury was coercive and reversible).

1. Propriety of supplemental charge. There are two questions to consider when a jury has been unable to reach a verdict: (1) what kind of supplemental charge is permissible, and (2) how long should the jury be held?

(1) Supplemental charge. A supplemental charge should not be coercive. To determine whether a particular charge is coercive, it must be broken down into its parts and analyzed for possible coercive statements. *Stevens*, 563 S.W.2d at 229; *see **Firestone Tire & Rubber Co. v. Battle***, 745 S.W.2d 909, 916-17 (Tex.App.—Houston [1st Dist.] 1988, writ denied). A potentially coercive statement will not invalidate the charge unless it retains its coercive nature as a whole when all of the circumstances surrounding its rendition are considered. *Stevens*, 563 S.W.2d at 229; *see **Golden v. First City Nat'l Bank***, 751 S.W.2d 639, 642 (Tex.App.—Dallas 1988, no writ); *see, e.g.*, *Souris v. Robinson*, 725 S.W.2d 339, 343 (Tex.App.—Houston [14th Dist.] 1987, no writ) (supplemental charge that asked jury to return a verdict "today" was not coercive). The supplemental charge should not be addressed to the jurors who do not agree with the majority. *Stevens*, 563 S.W.2d at 228. It must not suggest that the court will confine the jury until it reaches a verdict. *Id.* at 232; *Shaw*, 791 S.W.2d at 209. It must not tell the jury that it breached its responsibility by not reaching a verdict. *Shaw*, 791 S.W.2d at 209.

(2) Length of deliberation. The length of time the jury is held in an effort to secure a verdict is left to the discretion of the trial court. *Conrey v. McGehee*, 473 S.W.2d 617, 620 (Tex.App.—Houston [14th Dist.] 1971, writ ref'd n.r.e.). Once it becomes clear the jury is deadlocked, either by their notes or by the passage of time, the trial court must release them. For example, the trial judge in *Shaw* should have released the jury after three days of deliberation when the jury repeatedly said it was deadlocked and even said it was unable to abide by the instruction. *Shaw*, 791 S.W.2d at 209-10; *see also Conrey*, 473 S.W.2d at 620 (holding jury for seven hours was not error).

2. Preserve error. To preserve error in the supplemental charge, the party must object.

(1) To supplemental charge. The party must object to the supplemental charge and identify each statement in the supplemental charge that is coercive and state why. The objection must be made before the court submits the supplemental charge to the jury. *E.g.*, *Golden*, 751 S.W.2d at 642 (D waived error by not objecting at the time the court submitted verdict-urging instruction to jury).

(2) To continuation of deliberations. The party should also object to the continued confinement of the jury by making a motion for mistrial. *See Shaw*, 791 S.W.2d at 206-07.

§9. REVIEW

§9.1 Standard of review.

1. Show error caused harm. For the appellate court to reverse on a jury-charge error, the appellant must show harmful error. *Boatland, Inc. v. Bailey*, 609 S.W.2d 743, 749-50 (Tex.1980). Error in the jury charge is reversible only if it probably caused the rendition of an improper judgment or probably prevented the appellant from properly presenting the case on appeal. TRAP 44.1(a); *Thota v. Young*, 366 S.W.3d 678, 687 (Tex.2012); *Columbia Rio Grande Healthcare, L.P. v. Hawley*, 284 S.W.3d 851, 856 (Tex.2009); *see Wal-Mart Stores v. Johnson*, 106 S.W.3d 718, 723 (Tex.2003); *Timberwalk Apts., Partners v. Cain*, 972 S.W.2d 749, 756 (Tex.1998); *Reinhart v. Young*, 906 S.W.2d 471, 473 (Tex.1995). A misunderstanding of the court's charge by the jury is not grounds for reversible error. *Stephens Cty. Museum, Inc. v. Swenson*, 517 S.W.2d 257, 260 (Tex.1974); *Holiday Inns v. State*, 931 S.W.2d 614, 621 (Tex.App.—Amarillo 1996, writ denied). Jury-charge error is generally considered harmful if it relates to a contested, critical issue. *Thota*, 366 S.W.3d at 687; *Columbia Rio Grande Healthcare*, 284 S.W.3d at 856. To determine harm, the appellate court must consider the entire record—the pleadings, the evidence, and the charge. *Timberwalk Apts.*, 972 S.W.2d at 756; *Reinhart*, 906 S.W.2d at 473; *Island Recreational Dev. Corp. v. Republic of Tex. Sav. Ass'n*, 710 S.W.2d 551, 555 (Tex.1986).

(1) Submitted question, instruction, or definition. The submission of an erroneous jury question, instruction, or definition is generally reversible error if it relates to a contested issue in the case. *E.g.*, *Transcontinental Ins. v. Crump*, 330 S.W.3d 211, 224-25 (Tex.2010) (in workers' compensation case, omission of but-for component of producing-cause definition was reversible error); *Johnson*, 106 S.W.3d at 724 (in negligence case, unnecessary spoliation instruction was reversible error); *Quantum Chem. Corp. v. Toennies*, 47 S.W.3d 473, 480 (Tex. 2001) (in age-discrimination case, erroneous instruction on causation was reversible error); *see, e.g.*, *Timberwalk Apts.*, 972 S.W.2d at 755-56 (in premises case, unnecessary instruction on tenant's requirement to give written request for repairs was reversible error). But the submission of an erroneous question, instruction, or definition is generally harmless if the jury's findings on other issues support the judgment. *Boatland, Inc.*, 609 S.W.2d at 750; *see, e.g.*, *Reinhart*, 906 S.W.2d at 474 (in negligence case, erroneous submission of unavoidable-accident instruction was harmless because P did not object to similar sudden-emergency instruction); *City of Brownsville v. Alvarado*, 897 S.W.2d 750, 752 (Tex.1995) (submission of contributory-negligence question was harmless because jury's answer to first question finding no negligence rendered it immaterial); *see also Grohman v. Kahlig*, 318 S.W.3d 882, 889 (Tex.2010) (submission of question of law was harmless error because jury answered question as trial court should have). Even if other jury findings support the judgment, the submission of an erroneous question, instruction, or definition can be reversible error if the erroneously submitted issue confused or misled the jury. *Boatland, Inc.*, 609 S.W.2d at 750.

(2) Refused question, instruction, or definition. The refusal to submit a jury question, instruction, or definition is reversible error if it was reasonably necessary to enable the jury to render a proper verdict. *See* TRCP 277, 278; *Texas Workers' Comp. Ins. Fund v. Mandlbauer*, 34 S.W.3d 909, 912 (Tex.2000); *see, e.g.*, *Columbia Rio Grande Healthcare*, 284 S.W.3d at 862 (failure to include instructions on independent-contractor status of

─────────────────── ✦ ───────────────────

doctor and lost chance of survival was reversible error); *Southwestern Bell Tel. Co. v. John Carlo Tex., Inc.*, 843 S.W.2d 470, 472 (Tex.1992) (failure to define "justification," a defensive issue, was reversible error); *Wilen v. Falkenstein*, 191 S.W.3d 791, 804 (Tex.App.—Fort Worth 2006, pet. denied) (failure to include "knowingly" in definition of trespass was not error); *Vinson & Elkins v. Moran*, 946 S.W.2d 381, 405-06 (Tex.App.—Houston [14th Dist.] 1997, writ dism'd) (failure to define "agreed" in contract case was not reversible error).

(3) **Broad-form questions – challenging evidence.** On appeal, broad-form questions reduce the chances of successfully challenging the evidence to support a jury question. To successfully challenge a finding on a broad-form question containing multiple theories of liability, the appellant must show there was inadequate evidence to support at least one element of each cause of action. *See Prudential Ins. v. Jefferson Assocs.*, 896 S.W.2d 156, 160 (Tex.1995). To successfully challenge a broad-form question on damages containing multiple elements, the appellant must show there was inadequate evidence to support the entire damages award considering all of the elements. *Price v. Short*, 931 S.W.2d 677, 688 (Tex.App.—Dallas 1996, no writ); *Greater Houston Transp. v. Zrubeck*, 850 S.W.2d 579, 589 (Tex.App.—Corpus Christi 1993, writ denied).

2. Presumed harm.

(1) Multiple theories of liability.

(a) Valid & invalid theories – applicable. When a trial court submits a broad-form question with multiple theories of liability, some of which are invalid, the error is presumed to be harmful, and a new trial may be required if the appellate court cannot determine whether the improperly submitted theories formed the sole basis for the jury's finding. *Crown Life Ins. v. Casteel*, 22 S.W.3d 378, 388 (Tex.2000); *e.g.*, *Texas Comm'n on Human Rights v. Morrison*, ___ S.W.3d ___ (Tex.2012) (No. 11-0644; 8-31-12) (applied *Casteel*'s presumed-harm analysis to broad-form question that allowed jury to find liability based on legal theory that was jurisdictionally barred); *see, e.g.*, *Romero v. KPH Consol., Inc.*, 166 S.W.3d 212, 227-28 (Tex.2005) (applied *Casteel*'s presumed-harm analysis to broad-form proportionate-responsibility question that included factually unsupported claim); *see also* TRAP 44.1(a)(2) (reversal if error probably prevented appellant from presenting case to appellate court). This type of error is often referred to as *Casteel* error. *See Thota*, 366 S.W.3d at 691. If the appellate court is reasonably certain that the jury was not significantly influenced by the improperly submitted theory, however, error is not necessarily reversible. *Romero*, 166 S.W.3d at 227-28.

───

NOTE

*A party does not have to specifically cite or reference **Casteel** to preserve an appellate court's right to apply the presumed-harm analysis, if applicable, to the disputed charge issues. **Thota**, 366 S.W.3d at 691. Instead, error is preserved by making timely and specific objections to the charge. Id. See "Specific," §4.3.2, p. 737.*

───

(b) Defenses & inferential-rebuttal instructions – not applicable. Defenses and inferential-rebuttal instructions are not theories of liability; thus, *Casteel* does not apply to cases involving a single theory of liability in which improper defenses or inferential-rebuttal instructions have also been submitted. *See Thota*, 366 S.W.3d at 692-93; *Bed, Bath & Beyond, Inc. v. Urista*, 211 S.W.3d 753, 756-57 (Tex.2006). Instead, the court must apply a traditional harm analysis. *Thota*, 366 S.W.3d at 693; *Urista*, 211 S.W.3d at 757. See "Show error caused harm," §9.1.1, p. 745.

(2) Multiple elements of damages. *Casteel*'s presumed-harm analysis when multiple theories of liability are submitted applies equally when a trial court submits a broad-form question that commingles valid elements of damages and invalid elements of damages for which there was no evidence. *See Harris Cty. v. Smith*, 96 S.W.3d 230, 234 (Tex.2002). In such a case, the error is presumed to be harmful, and a new trial may be required if the appellate court cannot determine whether the improperly submitted elements of damages formed the sole basis for the jury's finding. *Id.*

✦

---

§9.2 Challenge findings on omitted elements. A party should treat the court's findings on omitted elements—either the trial court's express findings or the court of appeals' deemed findings—as jury findings. The findings, express or deemed, should be challenged with factual-sufficiency and legal-sufficiency points of error in both the motion for new trial and the brief on appeal. The court of appeals will review deemed findings by the factual-sufficiency test and the legal-sufficiency test. *Crosbyton Seed Co. v. Mechura Farms*, 875 S.W.2d 353, 364 (Tex. App.—Corpus Christi 1994, no writ). The Supreme Court can review deemed findings only by the legal-sufficiency test. *American Nat'l Pet. Co. v. Transcontinental Gas Pipe Line Corp.*, 798 S.W.2d 274, 278-79 (Tex.1990); *Crosbyton Seed*, 875 S.W.2d at 364 n.9.

§9.3 Jury notations. On appeal, the courts will not consider the jury's margin notations on the verdict regarding its findings. *Thomas v. Oldham*, 895 S.W.2d 352, 359 (Tex.1995). The jury's notes are not the jury's verdict. *Id.* at 360; *Wal-Mart Stores v. Alexander*, 868 S.W.2d 322, 328 (Tex.1993).

§9.4 Remedy for error. Depending on the error in the submission of the jury charge, if the party complaining of the judgment objected to the erroneous submission, the appropriate remedy for harmful charge error is remand for a new trial or rendition of judgment. If neither party objected to the erroneous submission, the party in whose favor the court rendered judgment is entitled to an affirmance; the other party has waived the opportunity to have the case submitted under the correct substantive law. *See State Farm Life Ins. v. Beaston*, 907 S.W.2d 430, 436-37 (Tex.1995); *Allen v. American Nat'l Ins.*, 380 S.W.2d 604, 609 (Tex.1964); *see, e.g.*, *Green Int'l v. Solis*, 951 S.W.2d 384, 389-90 (Tex.1997) (party did not object that attorney-fee question did not segregate attorney fees). See "Neither party objected," §7.2.1, p. 743.

1. Defective submission.

(1) Objection – remand. If a defective question, instruction, or definition was submitted over the objection of the party without the burden of proof and the jury returns a verdict in favor of the party with the burden of proof, the party who objected is entitled to a new trial (not rendition of judgment) if there is any evidence supporting the defective question. *See Transcontinental Ins. v. Crump*, 330 S.W.3d 211, 226-27 (Tex.2010) (remanding because of defective definition); *Ford Motor Co. v. Ledesma*, 242 S.W.3d 32, 44 (Tex.2007) (same); *Borneman v. Steak & Ale*, 22 S.W.3d 411, 413 (Tex.2000) (remanding because of defective question); *Minnesota Mining & Mfg. v. Nishika Ltd.*, 953 S.W.2d 733, 739 (Tex.1997) (remanding because damages issue did not segregate between Ps); *Spencer v. Eagle Star Ins.*, 876 S.W.2d 154, 157 (Tex.1994) (remanding because of defective instruction). In some cases, the court does not mention whether the party objected to the defective charge. *Arthur Andersen & Co. v. Perry Equip. Corp.*, 945 S.W.2d 812, 817 (Tex.1997) (remanding because of defective instruction); *Jackson v. Fontaine's Clinics, Inc.*, 499 S.W.2d 87, 90 (Tex.1973) (remanding because of defective damages question).

NOTE

*The Texas Pattern Jury Charge is not always correct. See, e.g., **Ledesma**, 242 S.W.3d at 41 (erroneous definitions of "manufacturing defect" and "producing cause"); **State v. Williams**, 940 S.W.2d 583, 584 (Tex.1996) (erroneous premises-liability charge). When a case is submitted on an erroneous charge from the PJC, the appellate court should reverse and remand, not render judgment. **Ledesma**, 242 S.W.3d at 45; **City of San Antonio v. Rodriguez**, 931 S.W.2d 535, 536 (Tex.1996).*

---

(2) No objection – affirm. If neither party objected to the submission of a defective question, the party in whose favor the verdict was returned is entitled to an affirmance. The other party waived the opportunity to have the case submitted under the correct substantive law. *Green Int'l*, 951 S.W.2d at 389-90 (party failed to object that attorney-fee question did not segregate attorney fees); *Allen*, 380 S.W.2d at 609 (jury found against P under erroneous submission); *Casteel-Diebolt v. Diebolt*, 912 S.W.2d 302, 304 (Tex.App.—Houston [14th Dist.] 1995, no writ) (when party agrees to charge as submitted, it cannot complain about contents of charge on appeal).

——————————————— ✦ ———————————————

2. Incomplete submission.

(1) Objection – render. If an incomplete question was submitted over the objection of the party without the burden of proof and the jury returned a verdict for the party with the burden of proof, the party who objected is entitled to a rendition. *See State Dept. of Hwys. & Pub. Transp. v. Payne*, 838 S.W.2d 235, 241 (Tex.1992); *Cosgrove v. Grimes*, 774 S.W.2d 662, 666 (Tex.1989).

(2) No objection – affirm. If an incomplete question was submitted and neither party objected, the party in whose favor the court rendered judgment is entitled to an affirmance. *See State Farm*, 907 S.W.2d at 436-37; *Ramos v. Frito-Lay, Inc.*, 784 S.W.2d 667, 668 (Tex.1990).

J. FINAL ARGUMENT

§1. GENERAL

§1.1 Rules. TRCP 266, 269.

§1.2 Purpose. After all the evidence is introduced, the attorneys summarize their case to the jury and argue the effect of the evidence.

§1.3 Forms. *O'Connor's Texas Civil Forms* (2012), FORMS 8J.

§1.4 Other references. Brown & Rondon, *Texas Rules of Evidence Handbook* (2013) (referred to as Brown & Rondon, *Evidence Handbook*); Townsend, *Improper Jury Argument and Professionalism: Rethinking Standard Fire v. Reese*, 67 Tex.B.J. 448 (2004).

§2. RIGHT TO OPEN & CLOSE FINAL ARGUMENT

§2.1 Plaintiff opens & closes. As a general rule, the plaintiff has the right to open and close the final argument. TRCP 266.

§2.2 Defendant opens & closes. There are two exceptions to the general rule that the plaintiff has the right to open and close the final argument.

1. Burden of proof. A defendant has the right to open and close the final argument if it had the burden of proof for the whole case. TRCP 269(a). To determine who has the burden of proof, see "Burden of proof," ch. 8-B, §2.2.1, p. 696.

2. Burden in the charge. A defendant has the right to open and close the final argument if it has the burden on all matters submitted to the jury in the court's charge. TRCP 269(a); *see First State Bank v. Fatheree*, 847 S.W.2d 391, 397 (Tex.App.—Amarillo 1993, writ denied); *Horton v. Dental Capital Leasing Corp.*, 649 S.W.2d 655, 657 (Tex.App.—Texarkana 1983, no writ). Because TRCP 269 does not become applicable until after the evidence is closed and the charge is read to the jury, it does not affect the right to make the opening statement or introduce evidence. *See Amis v. Ashworth*, 802 S.W.2d 379, 383 (Tex.App.—Tyler 1990, orig. proceeding).

§2.3 Other considerations. When there are several parties that have separate claims or defenses, the court must determine the order of the argument. TRCP 269(a). The court must assign an intervenor a position in the argument according to the nature of its claim. TRCP 269(c).

§3. MANAGEMENT OF ARGUMENT

§3.1 Court's authority. The trial court has the duty to supervise the scope of jury argument and to limit arguments of the evidence. *City of Dallas v. Andrews*, 236 S.W.2d 609, 611 (Tex.1951); *see National Un. Fire Ins. v. Soto*, 819 S.W.2d 619, 623-24 (Tex.App.—El Paso 1991, writ denied). The court should control the argument, even without an objection by opposing counsel. TRCP 269(g); *Texas Employers' Ins. v. Guerrero*, 800 S.W.2d 859, 867-68 (Tex.App.—San Antonio 1990, writ denied).

✦

§3.2 Time to argue. The court has discretion in allotting time for the arguments. *Aultman v. Dallas Ry. & Terminal Co.*, 260 S.W.2d 596, 600 (Tex.1953). To complain on appeal that the court did not permit sufficient time for argument, the party must show the following: (1) it objected, (2) it requested additional time, (3) the court denied the request, and (4) the error probably caused the rendition of an improper judgment. *See* TRAP 44.1(a)(1); *Aetna Cas. & Sur. Co. v. Shiflett*, 593 S.W.2d 768, 772 (Tex.App.—Texarkana 1979, writ ref'd n.r.e.).

§3.3 Nonjury trial. In a nonjury trial, the court has discretion in deciding whether it will hear oral arguments. *City of Corpus Christi v. Krause*, 584 S.W.2d 325, 330 (Tex.App.—Corpus Christi 1979, no writ).

§4. LIMITS OF FINAL ARGUMENT

§4.1 Order of argument. See "Right to Make First Opening Statement," ch. 8-B, §2, p. 696.

1. Concluding argument. The party with the burden on the case or on all matters submitted to the jury (generally the plaintiff) is entitled to make the concluding argument. TRCP 269(a). The plaintiff should present its entire case in the concluding argument. TRCP 269(b).

2. Responsive argument. The other party (generally the defendant) is entitled to present its case to the jury.

3. Rebuttal argument. The plaintiff's rebuttal is limited to matters in reply to the defendant's argument. TRCP 269(b).

§4.2 What attorneys may argue. Attorneys have great latitude to indulge in "flights of oratory." *Southwestern Greyhound Lines, Inc. v. Dickson*, 236 S.W.2d 115, 119 (Tex.1951).

1. Questions of fact. Attorneys should argue the facts to the jury. TRCP 269(e); *see Circle Y v. Blevins*, 826 S.W.2d 753, 758 (Tex.App.—Texarkana 1992, writ denied). Attorneys should discuss the reasonableness of the evidence and its probative effect or lack of probative effect. *Texas Sand Co. v. Shield*, 381 S.W.2d 48, 57-58 (Tex. 1964). Based on the evidence, attorneys may suggest the correct answer to the jury questions.

2. Inferences from facts. Attorneys may argue reasonable deductions and inferences from the facts. *Anderson v. Vinson Expl., Inc.*, 832 S.W.2d 657, 667 (Tex.App.—El Paso 1992, writ denied). The argument that the jury should "send a message" is permissible when it is based on the facts. *Schindler Elevator Corp. v. Anderson*, 78 S.W.3d 392, 405 (Tex.App.—Houston [14th Dist.] 2001, pet. granted, judgm't vacated w.r.m.), *disapproved on other grounds*, *Roberts v. Williamson*, 111 S.W.3d 113 (Tex.2003).

3. Fair criticism. Attorneys may make fair and reasonable criticism of a witness's testimony, may comment on bias or interest of parties and witnesses, and may discuss the reasonableness or unreasonableness of the evidence. *Dyer v. Hardin*, 323 S.W.2d 119, 127 (Tex.App.—Amarillo 1959, writ ref'd n.r.e.).

4. Effect of answer under evidence. Attorneys may argue the legal effect of the jury's answer only if the attorney qualifies it with a request to make the finding "under the evidence." *Cavnar v. Quality Control Parking, Inc.*, 678 S.W.2d 548, 554-55 (Tex.App.—Houston [14th Dist.] 1984), *rev'd in part on other grounds*, 696 S.W.2d 549 (Tex.1985). But see "Legal effect of answer," §4.3.2, this page.

5. Concluding argument. In the concluding argument, attorneys are permitted to reply only to the argument of the opposing party. TRCP 269(b).

§4.3 What attorneys may not argue. There are limits to an attorney's jury arguments. *Southwestern Greyhound Lines, Inc. v. Dickson*, 236 S.W.2d 115, 119 (Tex.1951).

1. Questions of law. Attorneys cannot argue questions of law to the jury. The attorneys must address arguments on the law to the court. TRCP 269(d). An attorney cannot embellish or mischaracterize the charge given by the court. *Timberwalk Apts., Partners v. Cain*, 972 S.W.2d 749, 755 (Tex.1998).

2. Legal effect of answer. Attorneys should not tell the jury the legal effect of its answers. *Magic Chef, Inc. v. Sibley*, 546 S.W.2d 851, 857 (Tex.App.—San Antonio 1977, writ ref'd n.r.e.). *But see Louisiana & Ark. Ry. v. Capps*, 766 S.W.2d 291, 295-96 (Tex.App.—Texarkana 1989, writ denied) (it was not reversible error because same information was in the jury questions). For an exception, see "Effect of answer under evidence," §4.2.4, this page.

✦

3. Outside the record. Attorneys must stay within the evidence presented at trial. TRCP 269(e); *e.g.*, *Texas Sand Co. v. Shield*, 381 S.W.2d 48, 57-58 (Tex.1964) (D's attorney should not have argued that P's attorney also represented the infamous Billy Sol Estes, not a party in the suit); *Lone Star Ford, Inc. v. Carter*, 848 S.W.2d 850, 853 (Tex.App.—Houston [14th Dist.] 1993, no writ) (in a suit for contract damages, attorney should not have argued about persons killed in the Ford Pinto).

4. Matters covered by order in limine. Attorneys should not comment on matters in violation of a court's order in limine. *National Un. Fire Ins. v. Kwiatkowski*, 915 S.W.2d 662, 664 (Tex.App.—Houston [14th Dist.] 1996, no writ). See "Motion in Limine," ch. 5-E, p. 347.

5. Improper viewpoint. Even though attorneys may argue the "Golden Rule," they cannot ask the jury to consider the case from an improper viewpoint. *E.g.*, *World Wide Tire Co. v. Brown*, 644 S.W.2d 144, 145-46 (Tex. App.—Houston [14th Dist.] 1982, writ ref'd n.r.e.) (argument asked jury to award what would satisfy them as Ps, instead of basing award on the evidence).

6. Sidebar remarks. Attorneys cannot engage in sidebar remarks while the other attorney is making jury argument (or examining a witness). *See Davis v. Southern Pac. Transp.*, 585 S.W.2d 801, 803-04 (Tex.App.—Houston [1st Dist.] 1979, no writ). TRCP 269(f) requires the trial court to repress sidebar remarks. *Wal-Mart Stores v. Reece*, 32 S.W.3d 339, 347 (Tex.App.—Waco 2000), *rev'd on other grounds*, 81 S.W.3d 812 (Tex.2002).

7. Personal criticism. Attorneys should not criticize each other during jury argument. TRCP 269(e); *Living Ctrs. v. Peñalver*, 256 S.W.2d 678, 681 (Tex.2008); *see, e.g.*, *Circle Y v. Blevins*, 826 S.W.2d 753, 758-59 (Tex. App.—Texarkana 1992, writ denied) (improper to argue attorney manufactured evidence); *Beavers v. Northrop Worldwide Aircraft Servs.*, 821 S.W.2d 669, 680 (Tex.App.—Amarillo 1991, writ denied) (improper to argue attorney misrepresented facts); *American Petrofina, Inc. v. PPG Indus.*, 679 S.W.2d 740, 755 (Tex.App.—Fort Worth 1984, writ dism'd) (improper to attack attorney's integrity); *see also Amelia's Auto., Inc. v. Rodriguez*, 921 S.W.2d 767, 772-73 (Tex.App.—San Antonio 1996, no writ) (reversible error for P's attorney to mention during examination of witness that D's trial attorney had been disbarred for five years for filing frivolous lawsuit); *Byas v. State*, 906 S.W.2d 86, 87-88 (Tex.App.—Fort Worth 1995, pet. ref'd) (reversible error in criminal case for prosecutor to refer to defense counsel as "very slick attorney").

8. Passion or prejudice. Attorneys cannot make arguments that appeal to the jury's racial, religious, or other passions or prejudices. *Dickson*, 236 S.W.2d at 119; *see, e.g.*, *Living Ctrs.*, 256 S.W.3d at 679 (reversed because P compared D's attorney's attempts to limit damages in suit against nursing home to Germany's WWII T-Four project, in which the elderly and infirm were experimented on and killed); *Texas Employers' Ins. v. Haywood*, 266 S.W.2d 856, 858 (Tex.1954) (reversed because D argued that P's witnesses were not as believable as white people); *Texas Employers' Ins. v. Jones*, 361 S.W.2d 725, 726-27 (Tex.App.—Waco 1962, writ ref'd n.r.e.) (reversed because, among other things, P referred to religion of D's witness in derogatory fashion).

9. Credibility of witness. Attorneys cannot argue that, in their opinion, a witness is credible or not. Tex. Disciplinary R. Prof'l Conduct 3.04(c)(3); *cf. Menefee v. State*, 614 S.W.2d 167, 168 (Tex.Crim.App.1981) (criminal case reversed because attorney argued "I don't believe I have ever seen anybody that I thought was any more honest than she is.").

10. Invocation of privilege. Generally, attorneys cannot comment on the other party's invocation of a privilege. TRE 513(a). For exceptions, see TRE 504(b)(2), 513(c). See Brown & Rondon, *Evidence Handbook*, p. 528.

11. Failure to seek medical exam. When the defendant does not seek a medical examination of the plaintiff under TRCP 204, the plaintiff's attorney cannot comment that (1) the plaintiff was willing to submit to a medical examination, (2) the defendant had the right to such an examination, or (3) the defendant did not seek an examination. TRCP 204.3. See "Effect of no examination," ch. 6-J, §6.4, p. 580.

§5. TYPES OF ERROR IN ARGUMENT

There are two types of error in jury argument, curable and incurable. *Otis Elevator Co. v. Wood*, 436 S.W.2d 324, 333 (Tex.1968); *Gannett Outdoor Co. v. Kubeczka*, 710 S.W.2d 79, 86 (Tex.App.—Houston [14th Dist.] 1986, no writ).

✦

---

§5.1 Curable argument. Most improper jury arguments can be cured of their harmful effects by an objection and the court's instruction to the jury to disregard what it has just heard. *Otis Elevator Co. v. Wood*, 436 S.W.2d 324, 333 (Tex.1968).

   1. Preserving error. If an improper argument is curable, the party must object promptly. *Otis Elevator*, 436 S.W.2d at 333; *see Standard Fire Ins. v. Reese*, 584 S.W.2d 835, 840-41 (Tex.1979); *Isern v. Watson*, 942 S.W.2d 186, 198 (Tex.App.—Beaumont 1997, pet. denied). The party must make sure the trial court rules on the objection, either sustaining or overruling it. TRAP 33.1(a)(2). Without a ruling on the objection, no error is preserved. *Marling v. Maillard*, 826 S.W.2d 735, 740-41 (Tex.App.—Houston [14th Dist.] 1992, no writ); *see, e.g.*, *Phillips v. Bramlett*, 288 S.W.3d 876, 883 (Tex.2009) (error waived because party did not request or obtain ruling on objection). When the trial court sustains the objection, to preserve error, the party should pursue an adverse ruling through a request to instruct the jury to disregard, a motion to strike, and a motion for mistrial. See "When jury hears inadmissible evidence," ch. 8-D, §6.6, p. 713.

   2. Examples of curable jury argument. The errors in the following arguments were not so egregious that they were preserved without an objection: • Suggesting fraud by arguing a close connection between the plaintiff's attorney and the doctor who treated the plaintiff. *Standard Fire*, 584 S.W.2d at 840-41. • Going outside the record to tell the jury that the other party's attorney represented a reprehensible party in another suit. *Texas Sand Co. v. Shield*, 381 S.W.2d 48, 57-58 (Tex.1964). • In medical-malpractice case, suggesting the jury needed to "send a message" to doctors in the county where the court was located by awarding a large sum of money. *Phillips*, 288 S.W.3d at 882-83. • Remarking that opposing counsel had been suspended. *Double Ace, Inc. v. Pope*, 190 S.W.3d 18, 30 (Tex.App.—Amarillo 2005, no pet.). • In a products-liability case, referencing previous litigation such as Ford Pintos, asbestos, and Dalkon shields. *Schindler Elevator Corp. v. Anderson*, 78 S.W.3d 392, 406 (Tex.App.—Houston [14th Dist.] 2001, pet. granted, judgm't vacated w.r.m.), *disapproved on other grounds*, *Roberts v. Williamson*, 111 S.W.3d 113 (Tex.2003). • Mentioning insurance. *Isern*, 942 S.W.2d at 198. • Mentioning collateral benefits in personal-injury action. *Macias v. Ramos*, 917 S.W.2d 371, 375 (Tex.App.—San Antonio 1996, no writ). • Asking the jury to place itself in the shoes of the party. *Goswami v. Thetford*, 829 S.W.2d 317, 320-21 (Tex.App.—El Paso 1992, writ denied).

§5.2 Incurable argument. An incurable argument is an argument so prejudicial or inflammatory that an instruction to the jury to disregard it cannot eliminate its harm. *Otis Elevator Co. v. Wood*, 436 S.W.2d 324, 333 (Tex.1968); *Melendez v. Exxon Corp.*, 998 S.W.2d 266, 280 (Tex.App.—Houston [14th Dist.] 1999, no pet.); *see Phillips v. Bramlett*, 288 S.W.3d 876, 883 (Tex.2009) (argument must be so extreme that it could have persuaded a juror of ordinary intelligence to agree to a verdict contrary to what she otherwise would have agreed); *Living Ctrs. v. Peñalver*, 256 S.W.3d 678, 680-81 (Tex.2008) (argument by its nature, degree, and extent must be such error that instruction from court or retraction of argument could not remove its effects).

   1. Preserving error. When the harmful effects of an incurable jury argument cannot be cured by an instruction to disregard, the failure to object at trial does not waive the error for appeal. *Otis Elevator*, 436 S.W.2d at 333; *Texas Employers' Ins. v. Guerrero*, 800 S.W.2d 859, 863 (Tex.App.—San Antonio 1990, writ denied); *Mapco, Inc. v. Jenkins*, 476 S.W.2d 55, 61-62 (Tex.App.—Amarillo 1971, writ ref'd n.r.e.). If the attorney did not object to the argument during trial, to preserve error the attorney must complain about the argument in a motion for new trial. TRCP 324(b)(5); *Phillips*, 288 S.W.3d at 883; *Clark v. Bres*, 217 S.W.3d 501, 509 & n.1 (Tex.App.—Houston [14th Dist.] 2006, pet. denied); *Austin v. Shampine*, 948 S.W.2d 900, 906 (Tex.App.—Texarkana 1997, no writ).

PRACTICE TIP

Always object to an improper jury argument. Never assume a jury argument is so prejudicial that no objection is necessary. If you do not object and the appellate court decides the error was curable, you will have waived the error.

---

   2. Examples of incurable jury argument. The errors in the following arguments were so egregious that no objection was necessary to preserve them, and even when an objection was made and the court instructed

———————————————— ✦ ————————————————

the jury to disregard, the error was not cured: • In wrongful-death suit against nursing home, argument by plaintiff's attorney comparing defendant's attempts to limit damages to Germany's World War II T-Four project, in which the elderly and infirm were experimented on and killed. *Living Ctrs.*, 256 S.W.3d at 679. • Personal address by party to jury, without court's permission, thanking them in Spanish. *General Motors Corp. v. Iracheta*, 161 S.W.3d 462, 472 (Tex.2005) (D's attorney objected after argument). • Appeals to racial prejudice. *E.g.*, *Texas Employers' Ins. v. Haywood*, 266 S.W.2d 856, 858 (Tex.1954) (D argued that P's witnesses were not as believable as white people). • Argument by plaintiff's attorney that defendant's counsel had characterized plaintiff as a liar, fraud, cheat, and impostor. *Southwestern Greyhound Lines, Inc. v. Dickson*, 236 S.W.2d 115, 118-19 (Tex.1951). *But see Clark*, 217 S.W.3d at 510-11 (characterization of P as liar, fraud, thief, and cheat was not incurable argument when supported by facts or invited by P). • Charges that opposing counsel manufactured evidence. *Circle Y v. Blevins*, 826 S.W.2d 753, 758-59 (Tex.App.—Texarkana 1992, writ denied) (there was an objection). *But see Checker Bag Co. v. Washington*, 27 S.W.3d 625, 643-44 (Tex.App.—Waco 2000, pet. denied) (no error when P's attorney commented that D's attorney tampered with evidence; comment was quickly withdrawn and D's attorney should have asked for instruction to disregard). • Appeals to ethnic solidarity. *Guerrero*, 800 S.W.2d at 866. • Personal attacks on opposing counsel. *American Petrofina, Inc. v. PPG Indus.*, 679 S.W.2d 740, 754-55 (Tex.App.—Fort Worth 1984, writ dism'd) (there was an objection). • Appeals to religious prejudice. *Texas Employers' Ins. v. Jones*, 361 S.W.2d 725, 727 (Tex. App.—Waco 1962, writ ref'd n.r.e.).

§6. REVIEW

§6.1 Record of argument. To show error in improper argument, the appellant must prove the improper argument was not invited or provoked. *Living Ctrs. v. Peñalver*, 256 S.W.3d 678, 680 (Tex.2008); *Standard Fire Ins. v. Reese*, 584 S.W.2d 835, 839 (Tex.1979). To establish this, the appellant must provide the appellate court with the entire record—the jury's voir dire, the opening statements, the evidence, and the final argument. *See Phillips v. Bramlett*, 258 S.W.3d 158, 170 (Tex.App.—Amarillo 2007), *rev'd on other grounds*, 288 S.W.3d 876 (Tex.2009); *Central Nat'l Gulfbank v. Comdata Network, Inc.*, 773 S.W.2d 626, 628 (Tex.App.—Corpus Christi 1989, no writ); *see also General Motors Corp. v. Iracheta*, 90 S.W.3d 725, 744 (Tex.App.—San Antonio 2002) (although P's statement to jury in Spanish during closing argument was not transcribed, judge noted content of statement on record, and copy of interpretation was filed with court; court could review impropriety of statement), *rev'd on other grounds*, 161 S.W.3d 462 (Tex.2005).

§6.2 Test for reversible jury argument. In *Standard Fire Ins. v. Reese*, 584 S.W.2d 835, 839 (Tex.1979), the Supreme Court outlined the elements of improper, reversible jury argument.

    1. The attorney made an improper argument. *Standard Fire*, 584 S.W.2d at 839.

    2. The improper argument was not invited or provoked. *Id.*

    3. The error was preserved by proper trial predicate (objection, motion to instruct, motion to strike, motion for mistrial). *Id.*

    4. The error was not curable by instruction, prompt withdrawal of the statement, or reprimand by the court. *Id.* An appellant is required to show the error was incurable only if the trial court gave a curative instruction or the appellant did not ask for one. An appellant is not required to show the error was incurable if the appellant's objection to the argument was overruled or its request for a curative instruction was denied. *See Lone Star Ford, Inc. v. Carter*, 848 S.W.2d 850, 854 (Tex.App.—Houston [14th Dist.] 1993, no writ).

    5. The argument, by its nature, degree, and extent, constituted reversible error. *Standard Fire*, 584 S.W.2d at 839. Relevant factors include the duration of the argument, whether it was repeated or abandoned, and whether such errors were cumulative. *Id.* at 839-40; *see, e.g.*, *Clark Equip. Co. v. Pitner*, 923 S.W.2d 117, 125 (Tex.App.—Houston [14th Dist.] 1996, writ denied) (counsel's comment about other lawsuits was not harmful error because it was a single sentence and was not repeated); *Brown v. Hopkins*, 921 S.W.2d 306, 319 (Tex.App.—Corpus Christi 1996, no writ) (improper comments were isolated and were later corrected); *National Un. Fire Ins. v. Kwiatkowski*, 915 S.W.2d 662, 665 (Tex.App.—Houston [14th Dist.] 1996, no writ) (based on the trial's short duration and the number of prejudicial remarks, error was harmful).

★

6.   The court must review the entire record to determine whether the argument had a probable effect on a material finding. *Standard Fire*, 584 S.W.2d at 840. The court reviews the evidence to determine whether the verdict was based on the evidence or the improper argument. *Texas Sand Co. v. Shield*, 381 S.W.2d 48, 58-59 (Tex. 1964); *Wooten v. Southern Pac. Transp.*, 928 S.W.2d 76, 80 (Tex.App.—Houston [14th Dist.] 1995, no writ). If a juror of ordinary intelligence could have been persuaded by the improper argument to agree to a verdict contrary to what she would have agreed to without the argument, the error was harmful. *Wells v. HCA Health Servs.*, 806 S.W.2d 850, 854 (Tex.App.—Fort Worth 1990, writ denied); *Gannett Outdoor Co. v. Kubeczka*, 710 S.W.2d 79, 86-87 (Tex. App.—Houston [14th Dist.] 1986, no writ). To obtain a reversal for abuse of discretion, a complaining party must make an affirmative showing of injury. *Aetna Cas. & Sur. Co. v. Shiflett*, 593 S.W.2d 768, 772 (Tex.App.— Texarkana 1979, writ ref'd n.r.e.).

K. THE VERDICT

§1. GENERAL

§1.1 Rules. TRCP 290-295.

§1.2 Forms. None.

§1.3 Other references. *O'Connor's Texas Causes of Action* (2013) (*O'Connor's Texas COA*).

§2. JURY DELIBERATIONS

§2.1 Kept together. When the jury retires for deliberation, the jurors must be kept together under the charge of an officer until they agree on a verdict or are discharged by the court. TRCP 282. The court may permit the jurors to separate for the night, for meals, and for other proper purposes. *Id.*

§2.2 No recording. No person may use a device to produce or make any recording (audio, visual, still photograph) of a jury while it is deliberating. CPRC §24.001 (civil jury); Code of Crim. Proc. art. 36.215 (criminal jury).

§3. VERDICT BY FEWER THAN 12 JURORS

In district court, a jury consists of 12 persons. TRCP 234. See "Jury Panel," ch. 8-A, §8, p. 694. A trial cannot proceed with fewer than 12 jurors unless a juror dies, a juror is constitutionally "disabled," or the parties agree. *E.g., Dempsey v. Beaumont Hosp., Inc.*, 38 S.W.3d 287, 289 (Tex.App.—Beaumont 2001, pet. dism'd) (midtrial discovery that juror was ineligible to serve because of felony conviction required a mistrial).

§3.1 Juror disabled.

1. Definition of disabled. The term "disabled," as used in Texas Constitution article 5, §13, encompasses physical or mental incapacity, and any other condition or circumstance rendering a person incapable of fulfilling the function of a juror. *McDaniel v. Yarbrough*, 898 S.W.2d 251, 252-53 (Tex.1995). The juror must become mentally incompetent or sick or suffer some other physical or mental incapacity to be considered disabled. *Id.*; *see Fiore v. Fiore*, 946 S.W.2d 436, 438 (Tex.App.—Fort Worth 1997, writ denied) (juror's prejudice against a party is not a disqualification, even if prejudice results in physical manifestations); *City of Jersey Village v. Campbell*, 920 S.W.2d 694, 698 (Tex.App.—Houston [1st Dist.] 1996, writ denied) (juror's bias or prejudice is not the same as loss of mental faculties). If the death or serious illness of a family member renders a juror unable to discharge her responsibilities, the trial may proceed with fewer than 12 jurors. *Yanes v. Sowards*, 996 S.W.2d 849, 852 (Tex.1999); *Summit Mach. Tool Mfg. v. Great N. Ins.*, 997 S.W.2d 840, 852 (Tex.App.—Austin 1999, no pet.). Temporary detention by flooding does not rise to the level of constitutional disability. *McDaniel*, 898 S.W.2d at 253.

2. Effect of disability. A 12-person jury may continue to deliberate even if as many as three jurors die or become disabled. Tex. Const. art. 5, §13; *see* TRCP 292(a); *Yanes*, 996 S.W.2d at 850; *Palmer Well Servs. v. Mack Trucks, Inc.*, 776 S.W.2d 575, 576 n.2 (Tex.1989). If only nine of the original 12 remain, those remaining must render a unanimous verdict. *See* Tex. Const. art. 5, §13; TRCP 292(a). If four or more persons die or become disabled, the court must declare a mistrial unless the parties agree to continue.

§3.2 Agreement. The parties may agree to proceed with a jury composed of fewer than 12 jurors. Gov't Code §62.201.

★

§4. JURY VERDICT

§4.1 Most trials. A verdict may be rendered by the concurrence, on each answer made, of the same 10 or more members of a 12-person jury (or five or more members of a six-person jury). TRCP 292(a); *see* TRCP 226a, §III; *Palmer Well Servs. v. Mack Trucks, Inc.*, 776 S.W.2d 575, 576 n.2 (Tex.1989); *Dunlap v. Excel Corp.*, 30 S.W.3d 427, 432 (Tex.App.—Amarillo 2000, no pet.). If the same ten jurors do not agree on all the answers, the court may require the jury to continue its deliberations. *See Gonzalez v. Gutierrez*, 694 S.W.2d 384, 390 (Tex.App.—San Antonio 1985, no writ). The plaintiff must prove most issues by a preponderance of the evidence, which means the greater weight and degree of credible evidence. *Upjohn Co. v. Freeman*, 847 S.W.2d 589, 591 (Tex.App.—Dallas 1992, no writ).

§4.2 Exemplary-damages cases. For exemplary-damages cases, all 12 jurors must agree on both Phase 1 issues (liability and actual damages) and Phase 2 issues (amount of exemplary damages). *See* CPRC §41.003(d); TRCP 292(b). Thus, all jurors must unanimously find the following: (1) liability on at least one claim for actual damages that will support an award of exemplary damages, (2) any additional conduct, such as fraud, malice, or gross negligence, required for an award of exemplary damages, and (3) the amount of exemplary damages. TRCP 226a, §III; *see* CPRC §41.003(a); TRCP 292(b). The jury is not required to be unanimous in finding the amount of actual damages. TRCP 226a, §III. For the burden of proof for the Phase 1 and Phase 2 issues, see "Plaintiff's burden," ch. 5-I, §5.4, p. 369; *O'Connor's Texas COA*, "Trial procedure," ch. 42-B, §9.2, p. 1332.

§5. REQUEST TO POLL JURY

§5.1 Request. As soon as the verdict is returned, the parties should examine it for clerical and other errors and promptly ask the court to poll the jury before it is discharged. *Pate v. Texline Feed Mills, Inc.*, 689 S.W.2d 238, 243 (Tex.App.—Amarillo 1985, writ ref'd n.r.e.). The parties should always ask for a poll when the jury returns less than a unanimous verdict to determine whether the same jurors agreed on their answers to each question. *See Gonzalez v. Gutierrez*, 694 S.W.2d 384, 390-91 (Tex.App.—San Antonio 1985, no writ). The right to poll the jury can be waived and must be requested to be invoked. *Suggs v. Fitch*, 64 S.W.3d 658, 660 (Tex.App.—Texarkana 2001, no pet.). To preserve error, the party must secure a ruling refusing to poll. *E.g.*, *Greater Houston Transp. v. Zrubeck*, 850 S.W.2d 579, 585 (Tex.App.—Corpus Christi 1993, writ denied) (court never ruled it would not poll).

§5.2 Procedure. To poll the jury, the court should read each question and the corresponding answer, call the name of each juror, and ask if that is the verdict of that juror. TRCP 294. *But see J.D. Abrams, Inc. v. McIver*, 966 S.W.2d 87, 95 (Tex.App.—Houston [1st Dist.] 1998, pet. denied) (judge did not read the questions and answers, only asked "whether this was his/her answer to the questions").

§6. DISCHARGING JURY

§6.1 Objections to verdict. If there is a conflict, inconsistency, or unanswered question in the jury's verdict, the parties must object before the court discharges the jury; if not, the error is waived. *Fleet v. Fleet*, 711 S.W.2d 1, 2-3 (Tex.1986) (unanswered question); *Columbia Med. Ctr. v. Bush*, 122 S.W.3d 835, 861 (Tex.App.—Fort Worth 2003, pet. denied) (conflict or inconsistency); *Norwest Mortg., Inc. v. Salinas*, 999 S.W.2d 846, 865 (Tex.App.—Corpus Christi 1999, pet. denied) (same); *see, e.g.*, *Rice Food Mkts. v. Ramirez*, 59 S.W.3d 726, 730 (Tex.App.—Amarillo 2001, no pet.) (D did not object to jury's breakdown of damages in separate components, as opposed to lump sum).

§6.2 No recall. Once the court receives the jury verdict, the court will discharge the jury. Once it discharges the jury, it cannot recall the jury for additional deliberations. *Archer Daniels Midland Co. v. Bohall*, 114 S.W.3d 42, 46-47 (Tex.App.—Eastland 2003, no pet.); *Branham v. Brown*, 925 S.W.2d 365, 368 (Tex.App.—Houston [1st Dist.] 1996, no writ).

§6.3 Juror notes. After the court discharges the jury, the bailiff will promptly destroy all juror notes. TRCP 226a, §II(10).

✦

§7. POSTVERDICT CONTACT WITH JURORS

Communication between parties, counsel, and discharged jurors can be a valuable experience for all concerned. ***Commission for Lawyer Discipline v. Benton***, 980 S.W.2d 425, 433 (Tex.1998). In particular, an attorney who has lost the case may ask the jurors why they were not persuaded and thus learn something that will help her in the future. *Id.* Federal courts generally disfavor postverdict interviewing of jurors, even when leave is sought to educate counsel and not to impeach the verdict. ***Haeberle v. Texas Int'l Airlines***, 739 F.2d 1019, 1021 (5th Cir.1984). In state court, an attorney's postverdict contact with jurors is limited by the Texas Disciplinary Rules of Professional Conduct. Rule 3.06(d) prohibits attorneys connected with the case from asking "questions of or mak[ing] comments to a member of that jury that are calculated merely to harass or embarrass the juror or to influence his actions in future jury service." Tex. Disciplinary R. Prof'l Conduct 3.06(d). The Supreme Court has limited Rule 3.06(d) by striking the term "embarrass" and narrowing the term "harass" by defining it to include four elements: "(1) a course of conduct, (2) directed at a specific person or persons, (3) causing or tending to cause substantial distress, and (4) having no legitimate purpose." ***Benton***, 980 S.W.2d at 439-40.

§8. REVIEW

§8.1 Disregard jury findings. To ask the court to disregard some or all of the jury findings, see "Motion for JNOV," ch. 9-B, p. 761.

§8.2 Juror misconduct. To ask the court for a new trial based on jury misconduct, see "MNT Based on Jury or Bailiff Misconduct," ch. 10-B, §14, p. 804.

§8.3 Fatal conflict in jury answers. A party can argue on appeal that the jury's answers fatally conflict and thus that the verdict should be reversed. *See **Arvizu v. Estate of Puckett***, 364 S.W.3d 273, 275 (Tex.2012). In reviewing the jury's answers for fatal conflict, the court must determine whether the jury's findings create a conflict about the same material fact, and if so, whether the conflict is fatal to the entry of judgment. *Id.* at 275-76. To determine if the conflict is fatal, the court must consider the jury's answers by disregarding each conflicting answer one at a time while taking into consideration the rest of the verdict. *Id.* at 276. If, when considered in this way, one of the conflicting findings requires entry of a judgment that is different from that which the court has entered (e.g., one of conflicting answers would require judgment for the plaintiff and the other would require judgment for the defendant), then the answers fatally conflict. *E.g., id.* at 276-77 (conflict was not fatal because D would lose no matter which conflicting answer was disregarded).

★

★

9. THE JUDGMENT

A. MOTION FOR JUDGMENT

§1. GENERAL

§1.1 Rules. TRCP 300-316.

§1.2 Purpose. The motion for judgment is a request for the court to sign the draft of the judgment prepared by the movant.

§1.3 Forms. *O'Connor's Texas Civil Forms* (2012), FORMS 9A.

§1.4 Other references. *O'Connor's Texas Causes of Action* (2013) (*O'Connor's Texas COA*).

§2. MOTION

§2.1 Motion for judgment on the verdict. A motion for judgment should include a proposed judgment for the court to sign.

    1. Winner. A party who won the case and wants a judgment on the jury's verdict (or in a nonjury trial, on the decision announced by the court) should file a motion for judgment. *O'Connor's Texas Forms*, FORM 9A:1. If the party files a motion for judgment and the court enters the judgment, the party cannot later attack the judgment unless it has reserved the right to do so. *Casu v. Marathon Ref. Co.*, 896 S.W.2d 388, 391-92 (Tex.App.—Houston [1st Dist.] 1995, writ denied). See "On the verdict," §2.1.2(1), this page.

    (1) Damages & interest. If the fact-finder found that one of the parties is entitled to damages, the motion should request damages and interest (prejudgment and postjudgment). See "Damages," ch. 9-C, §4.4, p. 767; "Prejudgment interest," ch. 9-C, §4.5, p. 768; "Postjudgment interest," ch. 9-C, §4.6, p. 769.

    (2) Attorney fees. The motion should request attorney fees when appropriate. See "Attorney Fees from Adverse Party," ch. 1-H, §10, p. 62.

    (3) Costs. The motion should make a general request for costs. Itemization is not necessary. The court clerk will prepare a bill of costs. See "Costs," ch. 9-C, §4.9, p. 769.

    (4) Other relief. The motion should request any other relief appropriate to the case.

    2. Loser. A party who lost the case often wants the court to sign a judgment so it can begin the appeal process. *O'Connor's Texas Forms*, FORM 9A:2.

    (1) On the verdict. The losing party can ask the court to render a judgment on the verdict without losing the right to challenge the judgment on appeal. To preserve the right to appeal, the motion for judgment should state that the party (1) disagrees with the content and result of the proposed judgment, (2) agrees only to the form of the proposed judgment, and (3) plans to challenge the judgment on appeal. *See First Nat'l Bank v. Fojtik*, 775 S.W.2d 632, 633 (Tex.1989). If the losing party asks the court to render a judgment without reserving the right to appeal, the party cannot complain about the judgment on appeal. *Casu*, 896 S.W.2d at 389-90; *see Green v. Texas Workers' Comp. Ins. Facility*, 993 S.W.2d 839, 843 (Tex.App.—Austin 1999, pet. denied) (party cannot, after moving for rendition of J, take position on appeal inconsistent with that J); *see also Hardy v. Mann Frankfort Stein & Lipp Advisors, Inc.*, 263 S.W.3d 232, 252 (Tex.App.—Houston [1st Dist.] 2007) (presenting draft J requesting that trial court enter written J that conforms to its earlier oral decision does not waive right to complain about judgment on appeal), *rev'd on other grounds sub nom. Mann Frankfort Stein & Lipp Advisors, Inc. v. Fielding*, 289 S.W.3d 844 (Tex.2009). *But see Harry v. University of Tex. Sys.*, 878 S.W.2d 342, 344 (Tex.App.—El Paso 1994, no writ) (party moving for J on the verdict only waives its right to complain about sufficiency of the evidence on appeal). To be effective, the reservation of the right to appeal should be contained in the motion for judgment. *See, e.g.*, *Fojtik*, 775 S.W.2d at 633 (motion for J contained reservation of right to appeal); *Litton Indus. Prods. v. Gammage*, 668 S.W.2d 319, 322 (Tex.1984) (reservation of right to appeal in brief accompanying motion for J was disapproved). *But see*

─────────────────────────────── ✦ ───────────────────────────────

Chappell Hill Bank v. Lane Bank Equip. Co., 38 S.W.3d 237, 247 (Tex.App.—Texarkana 2001, pet. denied) (objection in oral argument made before motion for J was filed preserved error).

(2) To limit damages. If the defendant is entitled to limit damages, the motion should so state. Damages are limited under a number of statutes: • In suits seeking exemplary damages. See *O'Connor's Texas COA*, "Damages Act cap," ch. 42-B, §7.1, p. 1326. • In DTPA suits, the plaintiff is limited to economic damages unless the defendant committed the act knowingly or intentionally. See *O'Connor's Texas COA*, "Remedies," ch. 8, §3, p. 227.

(3) To force election of remedies. When a plaintiff prevails on two theories of recovery for the same injury, the defendant should ask the trial court to require the plaintiff to elect damages, because the plaintiff is not entitled to a double recovery. *E.g.*, *Waite Hill Servs. v. World Class Metal Works, Inc.*, 959 S.W.2d 182, 184 (Tex.1998) (before rendition of J, D requested that trial court require P to elect its remedy).

§2.2 Motion for judgment contrary to verdict. A party who seeks a judgment contrary to the jury's verdict should prepare a motion for judgment notwithstanding the verdict. See "Motion for JNOV," ch. 9-B, p. 761.

§2.3 Motion for judgment on agreement. A party who wants the court to sign a judgment on a settlement agreement should file a motion for judgment on the agreement and attach a verified copy of the settlement agreement. See "Agreements Between Attorneys – Rule 11," ch. 1-H, §9, p. 61. A judgment rendered on the parties' agreement cures all nonjurisdictional defects. *Mailhot v. Mailhot*, 124 S.W.3d 775, 777 (Tex.App.—Houston [1st Dist.] 2003, no pet.).

§3. DRAFT OF JUDGMENT

The trial court will often ask the attorneys to prepare the judgment to reflect its decision, and it will sign the judgment at a later date. In most cases, the prevailing party will prepare a draft of the judgment for the trial court's signature and send copies to the other parties. Any party, however, may prepare a draft of the judgment. TRCP 305.

§4. MOTION TO SEVER, DISMISS, OR NONSUIT

If the court renders a judgment on only part of the lawsuit, a party may file a motion to sever, dismiss, or nonsuit the remaining claims, making the judgment final and appealable. See "What judgments are final," ch. 9-C, §6.3, p. 772.

§5. RESPONSE

Filing a response to a motion for judgment is generally not necessary. However, if the motion asks for relief to which the party is not entitled, the other party should file a response objecting to the relief. *See, e.g.*, *Wal-Mart Stores v. McKenzie*, 997 S.W.2d 278, 280 (Tex.1999) (D preserved error by objecting in its response to damages sought in motion for J). See *O'Connor's Texas Forms*, FORM 9A:3.

§6. HEARING

A hearing on the motion for judgment is not necessary. If a party wants a hearing, it should request one in writing.

§7. PRESERVATION OF ERROR

The motion for judgment preserves error in case the trial court modifies or rejects the proposed judgment. *See, e.g.*, *Emerson v. Tunnell*, 793 S.W.2d 947, 947-48 (Tex.1990) (P's motion for J on verdict for $238,000 preserved error when trial court signed J for only $208,284); *Texas Commerce Bank Reagan v. Lebco Constructors, Inc.*, 865 S.W.2d 68, 81 (Tex.App.—Corpus Christi 1993, writ denied) (Ps' proposed final J that included another party as jointly entitled to J preserved error when trial court did not include that party in J). The trial court does not need to overrule a motion for judgment; the motion is overruled if the trial court enters a judgment different from the one proposed by the motion. *See, e.g.*, *Salinas v. Rafati*, 948 S.W.2d 286, 288 (Tex.1997) (when court granted motion to disregard jury findings, it automatically overruled motion for J on findings, thus preserving error); *see also* TRAP 33.1(a)(2)(A) (trial court may rule on motion expressly or implicitly).

B. MOTION FOR JNOV

§1. GENERAL

§1.1 Rule. TRCP 301.

§1.2 Purpose. A motion for judgment notwithstanding the verdict (JNOV) and a motion to disregard a jury answer both ask the trial court to disregard all or some of the jury's answers to the jury questions and to render judgment for the movant. The only distinction between the two motions is that the motion for JNOV asks the trial court to disregard all the jury findings and sign a judgment contrary to those findings; the motion to disregard asks the trial court to disregard only some of the jury answers and sign a judgment on the remaining ones. *See **Teston v. Miller**,* 349 S.W.2d 296, 299 (Tex.App.—Beaumont 1961, writ ref'd n.r.e.). Motions for JNOV and motions to disregard preserve the "no evidence" and "as a matter of law" points for appeal. Here, both motions will be referred to as a motion for JNOV.

§1.3 Forms. *O'Connor's Texas Civil Forms* (2012), FORMS 9B.

§1.4 Other references. *O'Connor's Texas Civil Appeals* (2012) (*O'Connor's Texas Appeals*).

§2. MOTION

§2.1 Written motion. The trial court cannot disregard a material jury finding on its own initiative—it can do so only on written motion. TRCP 301; *Law Offices of Windle Turley, P.C. v. French*, 140 S.W.3d 407, 414 (Tex. App.—Fort Worth 2004, no pet.); *Rush v. Barrios*, 56 S.W.3d 88, 93 (Tex.App.—Houston [14th Dist.] 2001, pet. denied); *Lamb v. Franklin*, 976 S.W.2d 339, 343 (Tex.App.—Amarillo 1998, no pet.).

§2.2 Specific reasons. The motion must specifically identify the findings to be disregarded, present the reasons and authority for disregarding them, and request that the court sign either a judgment on the remaining findings or, if all the findings are to be disregarded, a judgment contrary to all the findings. *Dupree v. Piggly Wiggly Shop Rite Foods, Inc.*, 542 S.W.2d 882, 892 (Tex.App.—Corpus Christi 1976, writ ref'd n.r.e.), *disapproved on other grounds*, *Fifth Club, Inc. v. Ramirez*, 196 S.W.3d 788 (Tex.2006). One court has held that once a party files a motion for JNOV, the court can grant a JNOV on a ground not included in the motion. *E.g.*, *McDade v. Texas Commerce Bank*, 822 S.W.2d 713, 717-18 (Tex.App.—Houston [1st Dist.] 1991, writ denied) (D's motion asserted there was no evidence to support two jury answers; court granted JNOV on statute of limitations).

§2.3 Attach proposed judgment. The party should attach a draft of the proposed judgment to the motion for JNOV. See *O'Connor's Texas Forms*, FORMS 9B:1, 9B:3.

§2.4 Effect of motion on plenary power & appellate deadlines. See "Motion for JNOV," ch. 9-C, §6.5.1(1)(c)[3], p. 776; "Changing judgment during plenary power," ch. 9-C, §7.1, p. 778.

§3. GROUNDS FOR JNOV

A JNOV is proper only when a directed verdict would have been proper. TRCP 301; *Fort Bend Cty. Drainage Dist. v. Sbrusch*, 818 S.W.2d 392, 394 (Tex.1991); *Wal-Mart Stores v. Bolado*, 54 S.W.3d 837, 841 (Tex.App.—Corpus Christi 2001, no pet.). See "Grounds for Directed Verdict," ch. 8-G, §4, p. 727. A motion for JNOV is proper in the following situations:

§3.1 No evidence. The court should grant a motion for JNOV if there is no evidence to support the jury finding. *Tiller v. McLure*, 121 S.W.3d 709, 713 (Tex.2003); *Wal-Mart Stores v. Miller*, 102 S.W.3d 706, 709 (Tex.2003); *Brown v. Bank of Galveston*, 963 S.W.2d 511, 513 (Tex.1998). When the evidence is no more than a scintilla, it is no evidence. *Tabrizi v. Daz-Rez Corp.*, 153 S.W.3d 63, 66 (Tex.App.—San Antonio 2004, no pet.); *Rush v. Barrios*, 56 S.W.3d 88, 94-95 (Tex.App.—Houston [14th Dist.] 2001, pet. denied).

§3.2 Conclusive evidence. The court should grant a JNOV if an issue contrary to the jury finding was established as a matter of law. *E.g.*, *Gallas v. Car Biz, Inc.*, 914 S.W.2d 592, 593 (Tex.App.—Dallas 1995, writ denied) (JNOV was proper because sale was void); *John Masek Corp. v. Davis*, 848 S.W.2d 170, 173-74 (Tex.App.—Houston [1st

✯

Dist.] 1992, writ denied) (JNOV was proper because D had right to unilaterally liquidate business and Ps could not sue for liquidation); *see, e.g., TRT Dev. Co. v. Meyers*, 15 S.W.3d 281, 285 (Tex.App.—Corpus Christi 2000, no pet.) (JNOV was proper when statements were protected by qualified privilege).

PRACTICE TIP

In a motion for JNOV, never argue that the evidence was factually insufficient. A motion for JNOV will not preserve a complaint that the evidence was factually insufficient. Kratz v. Exxon Corp., 890 S.W.2d 899, 902 (Tex.App.—El Paso 1994, no writ). To preserve a complaint that the evidence was factually insufficient, the party must file a motion for new trial. See "MNT to Challenge the Evidence," ch. 10-B, §13, p. 802.

---

§3.3 Legal bar. The court should grant a motion for JNOV when a legal principle prevents a party from prevailing on its claim or defense even if that party proves all the allegations in its pleadings. *United Parcel Serv. v. Tasdemiroglu*, 25 S.W.3d 914, 916 n.4 (Tex.App.—Houston [14th Dist.] 2000, pet. denied); *John Masek Corp. v. Davis*, 848 S.W.2d 170, 173 (Tex.App.—Houston [1st Dist.] 1992, writ denied); *see, e.g., Rush v. Barrios*, 56 S.W.3d 88, 94 (Tex.App.—Houston [14th Dist.] 2001, pet. denied) (JNOV was proper, based on equity, to reduce fee of discharged attorney); *Farias v. Laredo Nat'l Bank*, 985 S.W.2d 465, 473-74 (Tex.App.—San Antonio 1997, pet. denied) (JNOV should have been granted because limitations expired); *Franklin Nat'l Bank v. Boser*, 972 S.W.2d 98, 106 (Tex.App.—Texarkana 1998, pet. denied) (JNOV should have been granted because D had a perfected security interest).

§3.4 Immaterial jury finding. The trial court may, without a motion, disregard the finding on an immaterial jury question. *See Hall v. Hubco, Inc.*, 292 S.W.3d 22, 27 (Tex.App.—Houston [14th Dist.] 2006, pet. denied); *Farias v. Laredo Nat'l Bank*, 985 S.W.2d 465, 470 (Tex.App.—San Antonio 1997, pet. denied). A jury finding is immaterial if (1) the question should not have been submitted, (2) the question was properly submitted but was made immaterial by other findings, or (3) the finding cannot change the verdict's effect. *Salinas v. Rafati*, 948 S.W.2d 286, 288 (Tex.1997) (#1, 2); *City of Brownsville v. Alvarado*, 897 S.W.2d 750, 752 (Tex.1995) (#3); *Spencer v. Eagle Star Ins.*, 876 S.W.2d 154, 157 (Tex.1994) (#1, 2); *see Quick v. City of Austin*, 7 S.W.3d 109, 116 (Tex.1999) (court may disregard as immaterial a jury's finding on a question of law). Although a party is not required to challenge an immaterial jury finding, it should bring the error to the court's attention in some postverdict motion—a motion for JNOV, a motion to disregard immaterial finding, or a motion for new trial. *See, e.g., City of Dallas v. Moreau*, 718 S.W.2d 776, 779 (Tex.App.—Corpus Christi 1986, writ ref'd n.r.e.) (court should have granted motion for JNOV because governmental immunity made jury's answers immaterial). If the court disregards an immaterial jury finding and signs a judgment based on the remaining findings, the judgment is not a JNOV. *Anderson, Greenwood & Co. v. Martin*, 44 S.W.3d 200, 216 (Tex.App.—Houston [14th Dist.] 2001, pet. denied).

§4. DEADLINES

§4.1 To file motion. TRCP 301 does not identify a filing deadline for a motion for JNOV. *Kirschberg v. Lowe*, 974 S.W.2d 844, 846 (Tex.App.—San Antonio 1998, no pet.). For years, courts have disagreed about the deadline for a motion for JNOV. *Compare BCY Water Sup. v. Residential Invs.*, 170 S.W.3d 596, 604-05 (Tex.App.—Tyler 2005, pet. denied) (motion for JNOV can be filed as long as trial court has jurisdiction over case), *and Needville ISD v. S.P.J.S.T. Rest Home*, 566 S.W.2d 40, 42 (Tex.App.—Beaumont 1978, no writ) (motion for JNOV can be filed after J entered until J is final), *with Commonwealth Lloyd's Ins. v. Thomas*, 825 S.W.2d 135, 141 (Tex.App.—Dallas 1992) (motion for JNOV must be filed within 30 days after signing of J), *writ granted w.r.m.*, 843 S.W.2d 486 (Tex.1993). Despite the courts' disagreement, the motion for JNOV must be filed within the same deadline as a motion for new trial—30 days after the date the court signed the judgment—to extend the appellate deadlines and the court's plenary power. See "Motion for JNOV," ch. 9-C, §6.5.1(1)(c)[3], p. 776; "Deadlines for MNT," ch. 10-B, §5, p. 791.

★

PRACTICE TIP
Until the Supreme Court settles the disagreement, always file your motion for JNOV within the deadline for a motion for new trial and ask the trial court to rule on the motion no later than 75 days after the trial court signed the judgment.

---

§4.2 For ruling. TRCP 301 does not identify a deadline for the trial court to sign an order on the motion for JNOV. The best practice is for the movant to request that the court sign a written order on the motion for JNOV before the deadline for overruling the motion for new trial—75 days after the court signed the judgment. Some courts have held that a motion for JNOV does not preserve error unless the court overrules it within the time limit for ruling on a motion for new trial. *E.g.*, *Spiller v. Lyons*, 737 S.W.2d 29, 29 (Tex.App.—Houston [14th Dist.] 1987, no writ); *Commercial Std. Ins. v. Southern Farm Bur. Cas. Ins.*, 509 S.W.2d 387, 392 (Tex.App.—Corpus Christi 1974, writ ref'd n.r.e.). Other courts have held that the motion for JNOV will preserve error if it is overruled before the judgment becomes final—105 days after the court signed the judgment. *E.g.*, *Eddings v. Black*, 602 S.W.2d 353, 357 (Tex.App.—El Paso 1980), *writ ref'd n.r.e.*, 615 S.W.2d 168 (Tex.1981); *Needville ISD v. S.P.J.S.T. Rest Home*, 566 S.W.2d 40, 42 (Tex.App.—Beaumont 1978, no writ).

§5. RESPONSE

If there is any chance the trial court might seriously consider the movant's motion for JNOV, the nonmovant should file a response explaining why a JNOV would be improper. See *O'Connor's Texas Forms*, FORMS 9B:2, 9B:4.

§6. ORDER

§6.1 Hearing. The hearing on a motion for JNOV is for argument only; no oral testimony may be presented. The court can decide the motion on submission, without an appearance by the attorneys before the court. See "Hearing on Motion," ch. 1-E, §4, p. 41.

§6.2 Written order. The order granting or denying the motion for JNOV should be in writing. However, an oral ruling made on the record or an implicit ruling will also preserve error. See "Types of rulings," ch. 1-G, §2.2, p. 47.

§6.3 Order or judgment. If the trial court grants the motion for JNOV, it should sign a final judgment. If the trial court denies the motion for JNOV, it should sign an order denying the motion. For the form of the judgment, see *O'Connor's Texas Forms*, FORMS 9C.

§7. REVIEW

§7.1 Standard of review. To determine whether the trial court erred in granting or denying a motion for JNOV based on the legal insufficiency of the evidence ("no evidence" or "conclusive evidence"), the appellate court must credit favorable evidence if reasonable jurors could do so and disregard contrary evidence unless reasonable jurors could not. *See Tanner v. Nationwide Mut. Fire Ins.*, 289 S.W.3d 828, 830 (Tex.2009); *Ingram v. Deere*, 288 S.W.3d 886, 893 (Tex.2009); *City of Keller v. Wilson*, 168 S.W.3d 802, 827 (Tex.2005). See "Challenging sufficiency of evidence," ch. 10-B, §13.1, p. 802.

§7.2 Challenging a JNOV.

1. Parties' arguments. On appeal, the parties should take the following positions:

(1) **Appellant.** The appellant's arguments on appeal are the standard ones: the trial court erred in its ruling on the motion for JNOV when it either granted or denied the motion.

(2) **Appellee.** The appellee's argument as the successful movant for JNOV (i.e., appellee received an adverse jury verdict but the trial court granted a JNOV in appellee's favor) is that the trial court correctly granted its motion for JNOV. If there are additional reasons the court should affirm the judgment, the appellee must raise those issues as cross-points, or it will waive those arguments. *See* TRAP 38.2(b)(1); TRCP 324(c). Issues that must be raised by cross-point include (1) insufficient evidence to support the verdict, (2) improper jury argument, and

★

(3) any other reason that would vitiate the verdict or prevent reinstating the verdict. TRAP 38.2(b)(1); TRCP 324(c). The cross-points can include grounds not raised in the motion for JNOV. *Ingram v. Deere*, 288 S.W.3d 886, 893 (Tex. 2009). For a more detailed discussion of the appellee's cross-points, see *O'Connor's Texas Appeals*, "Appeal in JNOV case," ch. 7-C, §6.7.3(1), p. 263.

2. Relief.

(1) No error in JNOV ruling. If the appellate court agrees with the appellee that the trial court correctly overruled or granted the motion for JNOV, it will affirm the judgment.

(2) Error in denying JNOV. If the appellate court agrees with the appellant that the trial court erred in denying the motion for JNOV, it will generally reverse and render a judgment for the appellant, unless it is necessary to remand for further proceedings or for a new trial in the interest of justice. TRAP 43.3; *see, e.g.*, *Jones & Gonzalez, P.C. v. Trinh*, 340 S.W.3d 830, 838 (Tex.App.—San Antonio 2011, no pet.) (appellate court reversed and rendered on liability issues and entitlement to attorney fees, but remanded solely to determine amount of attorney fees); *Prestige Ford Garland L.P. v. Morales*, 336 S.W.3d 833, 839 (Tex.App.—Dallas 2011, no pet.) (appellate court reversed and rendered judgment that appellee take nothing because suit was barred by statute of limitations); *cf. Scott v. Liebman*, 404 S.W.2d 288, 294 (Tex.1966) (court found error in granting JNOV and remanded in interest of justice because law on which case was originally tried had changed between time of trial and time of appeal). An appellate court may only remand for a new trial in the interest of justice under unusual circumstances, and the record must reflect that the court had a sufficient reason for doing so. *Cf. Jackson v. Ewton*, 411 S.W.2d 715, 718 (Tex.1967) (error in granting JNOV).

(3) Error in granting JNOV. If the appellate court agrees with the appellant that the trial court erred in granting the motion for JNOV, it should reverse the judgment and render judgment in harmony with the verdict, unless (1) the appellee raises viable cross-points, including factual-sufficiency challenges, that would either vitiate the verdict or preclude affirming a judgment if the trial court had rendered judgment on the verdict, (2) a remand is necessary for further proceedings, or (3) the interest of justice requires that the case be remanded for a new trial. *See* TRAP 38.2(b), 43.3, 44.1(b); TRCP 324(c); *Miller v. Bock Laundry Mach. Co.*, 568 S.W.2d 648, 652 (Tex.1977); *Jackson*, 411 S.W.2d at 717; *Downing v. Burns*, 348 S.W.3d 415, 427-28 (Tex.App.—Houston [14th Dist.] 2011, no pet.); *see, e.g.*, *Scott*, 404 S.W.2d at 294 (remanded for new trial in interest of justice because law on which case was originally tried had changed between time of trial and time of appeal).

C. THE JUDGMENT

§1. GENERAL

§1.1 Rules. TRCP 300-316.

§1.2 Purpose. The judgment is the official announcement of the resolution of the issues in the lawsuit. *Comet Aluminum Co. v. Dibrell*, 450 S.W.2d 56, 58-59 (Tex.1970). The judgment grants the prevailing party the relief it earned by its victory. *Jones v. Springs Ranch Co.*, 642 S.W.2d 551, 553 (Tex.App.—Amarillo 1982, no writ). The purpose of a signed judgment under TRCP 306a is to fix a certain date from which appellate deadlines can be determined. *Burrell v. Cornelius*, 570 S.W.2d 382, 383 (Tex.1978).

§1.3 Timetables & forms. Timetable, Motion to Extend Postjudgment Deadlines, p. 1234; Timetable, Appeal to the Court of Appeals, p. 1235; *O'Connor's Texas Civil Forms* (2012), FORMS 9C.

§1.4 Other references. Carlson & Dunn, *Navigating Procedural Minefields: Nuances in Determining Finality of Judgments, Plenary Power, & Appealability*, 41 S.Tex.L.Rev. 953 (2000); *O'Connor's Texas Causes of Action* (2013) (*O'Connor's Texas COA*); *O'Connor's Texas Civil Appeals* (2012) (*O'Connor's Texas Appeals*).

§2. ESSENTIALS OF VALID JUDGMENT

§2.1 Conforms to pleadings or agreement. The judgment must conform to the pleadings or a settlement agreement.

───────────────────── ✦ ─────────────────────

1. Pleadings & proof. When a case is resolved by a fact-finder, the judgment must conform to the pleadings and proof. TRCP 301; *Latch v. Gratty, Inc.*, 107 S.W.3d 543, 546 (Tex.2003); *Mapco, Inc. v. Carter*, 817 S.W.2d 686, 688 (Tex.1991). See *O'Connor's Texas Forms*, FORM 9C:1.

2. Agreement. When a case is resolved by a settlement agreement, the judgment must strictly conform to the terms of the agreement. *Vickrey v. American Youth Camps, Inc.*, 532 S.W.2d 292, 292 (Tex.1976).

§2.2 Definite & certain. The judgment must be sufficiently definite and certain to define and protect the rights of the litigants. *Stewart v. USA Custom Paint & Body Shop, Inc.*, 870 S.W.2d 18, 20 (Tex.1994). If a judgment is not definite, it must provide a means of determining rights so the ministerial officers can execute on the judgment. *Id.*; *Olympia Marble & Granite v. Mayes*, 17 S.W.3d 437, 440 (Tex.App.—Houston [1st Dist.] 2000, no pet.). If a judgment is not definite and its meaning cannot be determined, it is not a final judgment. *See, e.g., Hatton v. Burgess*, 167 S.W.2d 260, 262-63 (Tex.App.—Beaumont 1942, writ ref'd w.o.m.) (J was void because it did not provide sufficient information to identify land awarded to prevailing party).

§2.3 Jurisdiction. The judgment is void unless the court has jurisdiction.

1. Parties. The trial court must have jurisdiction over the parties. *State v. Owens*, 907 S.W.2d 484, 485 (Tex.1995); *Browning v. Placke*, 698 S.W.2d 362, 363 (Tex.1985).

2. Subject matter. The trial court must have jurisdiction over the subject matter of the suit. *Owens*, 907 S.W.2d at 485; *Browning*, 698 S.W.2d at 363; *see Carroll v. Carroll*, 304 S.W.3d 366, 368 (Tex.2010); *Dubai Pet. Co. v. Kazi*, 12 S.W.3d 71, 74-75 (Tex.2000).

3. Case. The trial court must have jurisdiction to render a judgment in the case. *Owens*, 907 S.W.2d at 485; *see, e.g., Texas Prop. & Cas. Ins. Guar. Ass'n v. De Los Santos*, 47 S.W.3d 584, 588 (Tex.App.—Corpus Christi 2001, no pet.) (court did not have jurisdiction to sign second J 54 days after signing first J when no MNT was filed).

4. Judge. The trial judge must be qualified by law to sit in the court. *See Tesco Am., Inc. v. Strong Indus.*, 221 S.W.3d 550, 555 (Tex.2006) (any orders or judgments rendered by constitutionally disqualified trial judge are void); *Owens*, 907 S.W.2d at 485 (court must have capacity to act as a court).

§3. RENDERING, SIGNING & ENTERING JUDGMENT

A judgment routinely goes through three stages: rendition, signing, and entry. *General Elec. Capital Auto Fin. Leasing Servs. v. Stanfield*, 71 S.W.3d 351, 354 (Tex.App.—Tyler 2001, pet. denied); *Oak Creek Homes, Inc. v. Jones*, 758 S.W.2d 288, 290 (Tex.App.—Waco 1988, no writ). The judgment becomes effective once it is "rendered." *General Elec. Capital*, 71 S.W.3d at 354. The timetables for the appeal begin to run once the judgment is signed by the court. *Id.* When the judgment is "entered," it is noted in the court's records by the court clerk. The entry of the judgment has no legal significance for the parties or for the appellate timetable. *Id.*

§3.1 Rendition. Rendition is a present act that resolves the issues on which the ruling is made. *Reese v. Piperi*, 534 S.W.2d 329, 330 (Tex.1976); *see Becker v. Becker*, 997 S.W.2d 394, 395 (Tex.App.—Beaumont 1999, no pet.). A judgment is rendered when the court makes an official announcement—either orally in open court or by written memorandum filed with the clerk—of its decision on the matter submitted for adjudication. *S&A Rest. Corp. v. Leal*, 892 S.W.2d 855, 857 (Tex.1995); *In re Guerra & Moore, L.L.P.*, 35 S.W.3d 210, 217 (Tex.App.—Corpus Christi 2000, orig. proceeding). The rendition of a judgment is the critical moment when the judgment becomes effective. *See Verret v. Verret*, 570 S.W.2d 138, 140 (Tex.App.—Houston [1st Dist.] 1978, no writ).

1. Methods of rendition.

(1) Written. A written judgment is the preferred method of announcing or rendering a judgment. Some letters from the trial court announcing the ruling can be the equivalent of a rendition of judgment. See "Letters," ch. 1-G, §3.4, p. 50. If possible, the parties should prepare a written judgment before the hearing at which the judgment will be announced. For example, the party filing a motion for summary judgment should prepare a summary judgment to submit along with its motion.

───────────────────── ★ ─────────────────────

(2) Oral. When it is not possible to prepare a written judgment before the hearing, the alternative method of rendering the judgment is to have the court announce the judgment in open court on the record. The judge must announce the rendition as a present act, not as an intention to perform a future act. *S&A Rest.*, 892 S.W.2d at 858; *Reese*, 534 S.W.2d at 330; *e.g.*, *Able Cabling Servs. v. Aaron-Carter Elec., Inc.*, 16 S.W.3d 98, 100-01 (Tex. App.—Houston [1st Dist.] 2000, pet. denied) (court's statement that "judgment *will be* rendered in accordance with the terms dictated into the record" did not indicate a present intent to render J).

─────────────────────────────────────
PRACTICE TIP
The prevailing party should make sure the trial judge makes an effective oral rendition of the judgment on the record. On the record, the judge should say "I now render the following judgment: (state the result)." Listen carefully. If the judge uses the future tense ("I plan to sign a judgment that will provide...."), ask the judge to restate the rendition as a present act, not a future one.
─────────────────────────────────────

2. Not rendition.

(1) Docket entry. Docket-sheet entries are inherently unreliable and are seldom specific enough to satisfy the requirements for a rendition. See "Docket entries," ch. 1-G, §3.3, p. 49.

(2) Approval of settlement. A statement by the trial court that it understands the parties have agreed to settle and will prepare an order for a ruling is not the rendition of a judgment. *S&A Rest.*, 892 S.W.2d at 857-58; *Formby's KOA v. BHP Water Sup.*, 730 S.W.2d 428, 430 (Tex.App.—Dallas 1987, no writ); *see In re Kasschau*, 11 S.W.3d 305, 311 (Tex.App.—Houston [14th Dist.] 1999, orig. proceeding).

(3) Order granting motion for judgment. An order that merely grants a motion for judgment is not a rendition of judgment; it adjudicates nothing. *E.g.*, *Naaman v. Grider*, 126 S.W.3d 73, 74 (Tex.2003) (appellate deadlines began when final J was signed, not one month later when motion for J was granted).

§3.2 Signing. When the trial judge signs a judgment without first making an oral announcement in open court, the act of signing the judgment is the official act of rendering the judgment. *Wittau v. Storie*, 145 S.W.3d 732, 735 (Tex.App.—Fort Worth 2004, no pet.). When the trial judge makes an oral announcement of the judgment in open court, the act of signing the judgment is only a ministerial act. *Dunn v. Dunn*, 439 S.W.2d 830, 832 (Tex.1969); *In re Bland*, 960 S.W.2d 123, 124 (Tex.App.—Houston [1st Dist.] 1997, orig. proceeding) (O'Connor, J., dissenting). The signature may be made by the judge personally or by someone authorized by the judge. See "Signature," ch. 1-G, §3.1.2, p. 49. The signing of the judgment is significant because the deadlines for filing postjudgment motions and for perfecting an appeal start on the date the trial court signs the judgment or final order disposing of the case. *See* TRCP 306a(1); *In re Bennett*, 960 S.W.2d 35, 38 (Tex.1997); *Farmer v. Ben E. Keith Co.*, 907 S.W.2d 495, 496 (Tex. 1995); *Martinez v. Humble Sand & Gravel, Inc.*, 875 S.W.2d 311, 313 (Tex.1994); *see also* TRCP 329b(a), (b), (g) (time for filing motions); *Newsom v. Ballinger ISD*, 213 S.W.3d 375, 379 (Tex.App.—Austin 2006, no pet.) (deadlines start on date trial court signs J, even if J is void). The appellate deadlines begin when the judgment is signed, even if it is merely a ministerial act. *Harris Cty. Appr. Dist. v. Wittig*, 881 S.W.2d 193, 194 (Tex.App.—Houston [1st Dist.] 1994, orig. proceeding). The period of the court's plenary power to change the judgment is calculated from the date the final judgment is signed. *See* TRCP 329b(d).

§3.3 Entry. A judgment is entered when the court clerk performs the ministerial act of entering the judgment in the minutes of the court. *Oak Creek Homes, Inc. v. Jones*, 758 S.W.2d 288, 290 (Tex.App.—Waco 1988, no writ); *see Dunn v. Dunn*, 439 S.W.2d 830, 832 (Tex.1969); *see also Keim v. Anderson*, 943 S.W.2d 938, 942 (Tex.App.—El Paso 1997, no writ) (distinguishing entry of J from rendition of J). Once the judgment is signed by the trial court, it should be given to the clerk to file with the other documents of the case, and the clerk should make an entry in the minutes of the court. A signed judgment is valid whether or not it is filed or entered in the record. *See In re Barber*, 982 S.W.2d 364, 367 (Tex.1998) (date of signing controls, not date of entry); *see, e.g., Prinz v. Dutschmann*, 678 S.W.2d 256, 258 (Tex.App.—Corpus Christi 1984, no writ) (divorce decree was rendered when signed, not when entered in the record).

✯

§4. FORM OF JUDGMENT

§4.1 Parties. The judgment must contain the full names of the parties as stated in the pleadings. TRCP 306; *City of Austin v. Castillo*, 25 S.W.3d 309, 314 (Tex.App.—Austin 2000, pet. denied); *Crystal City ISD v. Wagner*, 605 S.W.2d 743, 747 (Tex.App.—San Antonio 1980, writ ref'd n.r.e.). The judgment must identify the parties in their correct capacities, that is, the same capacities in which the plaintiff brought suit and the defendant was sued. *See, e.g., Werner v. Colwell*, 909 S.W.2d 866, 869-70 (Tex.1995) (court could not render J against D as trustee when D was sued only as individual).

§4.2 Declaration of legal effects of facts. The judgment should determine the rights of all the parties and dispose of all the issues. The judgment must state for whom and against whom it is rendered. TRCP 306.

§4.3 Statement of finality.

1. Final. The judgment should state whether it is intended to be a final or partial judgment. See "What judgments are final," §6.3, p. 772. A statement that the plaintiff takes nothing or that the case is dismissed makes the judgment final as long as there are no other claims by other parties. *Lehmann v. Har-Con Corp.*, 39 S.W.3d 191, 205 (Tex.2001). But language about dismissal should not be used in a proceeding that resolves the case on the merits (e.g., a summary judgment); it should be used only in cases in which dismissal is appropriate. See "Resolve issues on the merits," ch. 7-B, §12.3.3, p. 624; "Grounds for Dismissal," ch. 7-G, §2, p. 658. The following statements will indicate that the judgment is intended to be final:

(1) "This judgment finally disposes of all parties and all claims and is appealable." *In re Daredia*, 317 S.W.3d 247, 248 (Tex.2010); *Lehmann*, 39 S.W.3d at 206. This is the preferred statement to include in any judgment intended to be final. *See In re Daredia*, 317 S.W.3d at 248.

(2) "This judgment disposes of all parties and all claims in this cause of action and is therefore final." *E.g., id.* at 248-49 (although use of the word "final" is slightly less clear than "appealable," court held it was clear enough to constitute statement of finality).

PRACTICE TIP

*In a conventional trial on the merits, the judgment does not need to include a statement of finality because such judgments are presumed to be final. **Moritz v. Preiss**, 121 S.W.3d 715, 718-19 (Tex.2003); **John v. Marshall Health Servs.**, 58 S.W.3d 738, 740 (Tex.2001); **North E. ISD v. Aldridge**, 400 S.W.2d 893, 897-98 (Tex.1966). See "Judgment after conventional trial," §6.3.1(2), p. 772. However, if any of the claims were disposed of outside a conventional trial on the merits (e.g., by summary judgment, default judgment, or dismissal), the inclusion of a statement of finality will ensure that the judgment is final and appealable.*

---

2. Not final. A judgment is not final just because it is captioned a "final judgment," because the word "final" appears somewhere in the order, because it awards costs, or because it says it is appealable. *Lehmann*, 39 S.W.3d at 205.

§4.4 Damages. A money judgment should either state with certainty the amount to be recovered or furnish a means for determining the amount. *Beam v. Southwestern Bell Tel. Co.*, 164 S.W.3d 412, 416 (Tex.App.—Waco 1942, writ ref'd w.o.m.). If the amount of money awarded is uncertain, the judgment will be considered interlocutory. *E.g., Olympia Marble & Granite v. Mayes*, 17 S.W.3d 437, 440 (Tex.App.—Houston [1st Dist.] 2000, no pet.) (J was not final because questions remained about date when prejudgment interest would begin to accrue); *H.E. Butt Grocery Co. v. Bay, Inc.*, 808 S.W.2d 678, 680-81 (Tex.App.—Corpus Christi 1991, writ denied) (default J was not final because it did not specify which interest rate applied for prejudgment interest); *Jones v. Liberty Mut. Ins.*, 733 S.W.2d 240, 242 (Tex.App.—El Paso 1987, no writ) (subrogation J was not final because medical payments for which insurance company was to be reimbursed had no termination date). See *O'Connor's Texas COA*, "General Concepts," ch. 41-A, p. 1241.

─────────────────────────────── ★ ───────────────────────────────

1. Proportionate responsibility. In tort cases, the percentage of damages each party to a lawsuit must pay is determined using the proportionate-responsibility method. *See* CPRC ch. 33. If a plaintiff is partially responsible for its own damages, the plaintiff's recovery is reduced or barred by the percentage of those damages attributed to the plaintiff. See *O'Connor's Texas COA*, "Proportionate Responsibility & Contribution," ch. 51, p. 1461.

2. Alternative theories of recovery & defense.

(1) Alternative recoveries. When a plaintiff's petition contains alternative theories for recovery, the court cannot render a judgment awarding relief on all the theories. *Waite Hill Servs. v. World Class Metal Works, Inc.*, 959 S.W.2d 182, 184 (Tex.1998); *Southern Cty. Mut. Ins. v. First Bank & Trust*, 750 S.W.2d 170, 173-74 (Tex.1988). A judgment on multiple theories would result in an impermissible double recovery for the same injury. *See Waite Hill*, 959 S.W.2d at 184; *Southern Cty.*, 750 S.W.2d at 173-74. See *O'Connor's Texas COA*, "Applied to theories of liability," ch. 41-A, §4.2.1, p. 1247. When the jury returns favorable findings on alternative theories, the plaintiff is entitled to recover on the theory that results in the largest or most favorable recovery. *Parkway Co. v. Woodruff*, 901 S.W.2d 434, 441 (Tex.1995); *Boyce Iron Works, Inc. v. Southwestern Bell Tel. Co.*, 747 S.W.2d 785, 787 (Tex.1988); *Woodlands Land Dev. Co. v. Jenkins*, 48 S.W.3d 415, 419 (Tex.App.—Beaumont 2001, no pet.). If the plaintiff does not make an election, the trial court should render a judgment allowing the greatest recovery. *Birchfield v. Texarkana Mem'l Hosp.*, 747 S.W.2d 361, 367 (Tex.1987); *Hill v. Heritage Res.*, 964 S.W.2d 89, 128 (Tex. App.—El Paso 1997, pet. denied).

(2) Alternative defenses. A court can render a judgment sustaining all the defendant's alternative defenses. By rendering a judgment for the defendant on all its defensive theories, the trial court can avoid a remand if one of the grounds is reversed on appeal. *See Oak Park Townhouses v. Brazosport Bank*, 851 S.W.2d 189, 190 (Tex.1993).

§4.5 Prejudgment interest. When prejudgment interest is allowed, the judgment should include the exact amount of prejudgment interest due. If the calculation is not available, the judgment must include the appropriate interest rate and the date of accrual. See *O'Connor's Texas COA*, "Prejudgment Interest," ch. 43, §2, p. 1335.

1. Accrual. Prejudgment interest begins to accrue either (1) 180 days after the date the defendant received written notice of the claim or (2) on the date the suit in which judgment is rendered was filed, whichever is earlier. Fin. Code §304.104; *Johnson & Higgins v. Kenneco Energy, Inc.*, 962 S.W.2d 507, 531 (Tex.1998); *Town of Flower Mound v. Teague*, 111 S.W.3d 742, 763 (Tex.App.—Fort Worth 2003, pet. denied). Prejudgment interest stops accruing the day before the judgment is "rendered." Fin. Code §304.104. "Rendered" in §304.104 is interpreted as the date the judgment is signed. *See Chapman v. Coker Equip. Sales, Inc.*, No. 07-04-0333-CV (Tex.App.—Amarillo 2006, pet. denied) (memo op.; 1-26-06). If a settlement offer was extended, the interest is calculated by different rules. *See* Fin. Code §§304.104, 304.105. See *O'Connor's Texas COA*, "Time of accrual," ch. 43, §2.3.3, p. 1338.

2. Rate. Prejudgment interest is computed as simple interest—that is, it does not compound. Fin. Code §304.104; *Johnson & Higgins*, 962 S.W.2d at 532.

(1) Most cases. The rate for prejudgment interest is the same as for postjudgment interest. Fin. Code §304.103; *Johnson & Higgins*, 962 S.W.2d at 532. See "Most cases," §4.6.2(1), p. 769. Although Finance Code §304.103 sets the rate for prejudgment interest only for cases involving wrongful death, personal injury, and property damage, the Supreme Court has adopted the same rules for calculating prejudgment interest in all other cases. *Johnson & Higgins*, 962 S.W.2d at 530-31.

(2) Some contract cases. In breach-of-contract cases in which no rate of interest is specified and damages can be ascertained from the contract, prejudgment interest accrues at a rate of 6%. *See* Fin. Code §302.002; *Aquila Sw. Pipeline, Inc. v. Harmony Expl., Inc.*, 48 S.W.3d 225, 242 (Tex.App.—San Antonio 2001, pet. denied).

3. Prejudgment interest not permitted. A party is not entitled to prejudgment interest on the following: • Future damages. Fin. Code §304.1045. • Exemplary damages. CPRC §41.007; *Ellis Cty. State Bank v. Keever*, 888 S.W.2d 790, 797 (Tex.1994). • Attorney fees and costs. *Ellis Cty.*, 888 S.W.2d at 797 n.13. • Prejudgment interest itself. *Id.* • DTPA treble damages. Bus. & Com. Code §17.50(e), (f)(2); *Vail v. Texas Farm Bur. Mut. Ins.*, 754 S.W.2d

✦

129, 137 (Tex.1988). • Interpleaded funds. *See State Farm Life Ins. v. Martinez*, 216 S.W.3d 799, 808 (Tex.2007). See *O'Connor's Texas COA*, "When not recoverable," ch. 43, §2.1.2, p. 1336.

§4.6 Postjudgment interest. Since all money judgments accrue postjudgment interest, a judgment must specify the applicable postjudgment-interest rate. Fin. Code §304.001. See *O'Connor's Texas COA*, "Postjudgment Interest," ch. 43, §3, p. 1339.

    1. Accrual. Postjudgment interest on a money judgment begins to accrue on the date the judgment is rendered and stops accruing on the date the judgment is satisfied. Fin. Code §304.005(a).

    2. Rate. Postjudgment interest is compounded annually. Fin. Code §304.006.

        (1) Most cases. Finance Code §304.003 controls the postjudgment-interest rate in most cases. The postjudgment-interest rate is the prime rate as published by the Board of Governors of the Federal Reserve System on the date of computation. Fin. Code §304.003(c)(1). If the prime rate is less than 5%, the postjudgment-interest rate is 5%; if the prime rate is more than 15%, the postjudgment-interest rate is 15%. *Id.* §304.003(c)(2), (c)(3). The rate is published each month and can be checked either online at www.occc.state.tx.us (by selecting "interest rates") or by calling the Office of Consumer Credit Commissioner at (512) 936-7600.

        (2) Some contract cases. If a contract provides for interest or a time-price differential fee, the judgment earns postjudgment interest at a rate equal to the lesser of (1) the rate specified in the contract, which may be a variable rate, or (2) 18% a year. Fin. Code §304.002; *see, e.g., AU Pharm. v. Boston*, 986 S.W.2d 331, 336 (Tex. App.—Texarkana 1999, no pet.) (because contract provided for a zero post-J interest rate, no post-J interest could be awarded).

§4.7 Attorney fees. When appropriate, the judgment should include a provision awarding attorney fees. See "Attorney Fees from Adverse Party," ch. 1-H, §10, p. 62; *O'Connor's Texas COA*, "Attorney Fees," ch. 45, p. 1349. A claim for additional attorney fees incurred for enforcement and collection of the judgment does not make the judgment interlocutory. *Pillitteri v. Brown*, 165 S.W.3d 715, 718 (Tex.App.—Dallas 2004, no pet.). See *O'Connor's Texas Appeals*, "Is the language of the judgment definite?," ch. 1-B, §2.1.4, p. 7.

§4.8 Guardian ad litem fees. See "Taxed as costs," ch. 1-I, §6.4, p. 75.

§4.9 Costs. The judgment should state that costs are awarded against a certain party, not the amount of the costs awarded. After the judgment is signed, the clerk will send a cost bill to the party taxed with the costs. A trial court, however, is not required to assess costs for its judgment to be final. *City of Marshall v. Gonzales*, 107 S.W.3d 799, 803 (Tex.App.—Texarkana 2003, no pet.); *Thompson v. Beyer*, 91 S.W.3d 902, 904-05 (Tex.App.—Dallas 2002, no pet.). See "What judgments are final," §6.3, p. 772; *O'Connor's Texas COA*, "Court Costs," ch. 44, p. 1341.

    1. Who is entitled to costs.

        (1) Successful party. The successful party to a suit is entitled to recover from the other party all taxable court costs it incurred. TRCP 131; *Roberts v. Williamson*, 111 S.W.3d 113, 124 (Tex.2003); *Furr's Supermkts., Inc. v. Bethune*, 53 S.W.3d 375, 378 (Tex.2001); *Rogers v. Walmart Stores*, 686 S.W.2d 599, 601 (Tex. 1985). Taxing costs against the successful party is contrary to TRCP 131. *Martinez v. Pierce*, 759 S.W.2d 114, 114 (Tex.1988). A "successful party" is one who obtains a judgment of a competent court vindicating a civil claim of right. See *O'Connor's Texas COA*, "Successful party," ch. 44, §2.2.1(1), p. 1342. Whether a party is successful must be based on success on the merits, not on whether damages were awarded. *Mag Instr., Inc. v. G.T. Sales, Inc.*, 294 S.W.3d 800, 808 (Tex.App.—Dallas 2009, pet. denied); *Nicholson v. Tashiro*, 140 S.W.3d 445, 447 (Tex.App.—Corpus Christi 2004, no pet.). When both parties are successful, the trial court may tax costs against both. *Niemeyer v. Tana Oil & Gas Corp.*, 39 S.W.3d 380, 389-90 (Tex.App.—Austin 2001, pet. denied); *Building Concepts, Inc. v. Duncan*, 667 S.W.2d 897, 905-06 (Tex.App.—Houston [14th Dist.] 1984, writ ref'd n.r.e.).

        (2) Unsuccessful party. For the court to award costs to the unsuccessful party, the court must find good cause and state the reasons on the record. TRCP 141; *Roberts*, 111 S.W.3d at 124; *Furr's*, 53 S.W.3d at 378; *Rogers*, 686 S.W.2d at 601; *see Marshall Investigation & Sec. Agency v. Whitaker*, 962 S.W.2d 62, 63 (Tex.App.— Houston [1st Dist.] 1997, no pet.) (case remanded for trial court to state good cause). See *O'Connor's Texas COA*,

─────────────── ✦ ───────────────

"'Good cause' exception," ch. 44, §2.2.2, p. 1344. As a matter of law, potential harm to the unsuccessful party's emotional state is not good cause to tax costs against the successful party. *Furr's*, 53 S.W.3d at 378.

2. Taxable court costs. Each party to a suit is responsible for accurately recording all costs and fees incurred during the lawsuit if the judgment provides for adjudication of such costs. CPRC §31.007(a). For a list of costs taxable as court costs, see *O'Connor's Texas COA*, "Taxable costs," ch. 44, §2.3.1, p. 1345. For a list of costs not taxable as court costs, see *O'Connor's Texas COA*, "Nontaxable costs," ch. 44, §2.3.2, p. 1347.

§4.10 No findings of fact. The judgment in a nonjury case should not contain findings of fact. The findings of fact must be filed separately and should not be recited in the judgment. TRCP 299a. See "Not in judgment," ch. 10-E, §3.4.1, p. 821.

§4.11 Date signed. The judgment should have a line, immediately above the trial judge's signature line, that reads: "Signed on _____, 201__." *Burrell v. Cornelius*, 570 S.W.2d 382, 384 (Tex.1978). The date the judgment is signed is important because it starts the appellate timetable. *Farmer v. Ben E. Keith Co.*, 907 S.W.2d 495, 496 (Tex.1995); *Reese v. Piperi*, 534 S.W.2d 329, 331 (Tex.1976); *see Coinmach, Inc. v. Aspenwood Apt. Corp.*, 98 S.W.3d 377, 382 (Tex.App.—Houston [1st Dist.] 2003, no pet.) (signature date of judgment, not filing date, is relevant for determining appellate deadlines). The absence of a date on the judgment does not invalidate the judgment. TRCP 306a(2); *Hammett v. Lee*, 730 S.W.2d 350, 351 (Tex.App.—Dallas 1987, writ dism'd). If the date is omitted and it is an issue on appeal, the appellate court can ask the trial court to certify the date the judgment was signed. *See Hammett*, 730 S.W.2d at 351.

§4.12 Signature line for judge. The judgment must contain a signature line for the trial judge.

§4.13 Signature line for attorneys. Traditionally, the judgment contains signature lines for the attorneys to approve the form of the judgment. To ensure the judgment is not construed as a consent judgment, the attorneys representing the losing party should sign under the statement "approved as to form only," not "approved as to form and substance." *See Transmission Exch. Inc. v. Long*, 821 S.W.2d 265, 275 (Tex.App.—Houston [1st Dist.] 1991, writ denied). However, even when an attorney signs under the statement "approved as to form and substance," the appellate courts will look to the circumstances surrounding the judgment to determine whether the parties intended to enter into a consent judgment. *Chang v. Linh Nguyen*, 81 S.W.3d 314, 316 n.1 (Tex.App.—Houston [14th Dist.] 2001, no pet.); *First Am. Title Ins. v. Adams*, 829 S.W.2d 356, 364 (Tex.App.—Corpus Christi 1992, writ denied); *Hill v. Bellville Gen. Hosp.*, 735 S.W.2d 675, 678 (Tex.App.—Houston [1st Dist.] 1987, no writ).

§5. NOTICE OF JUDGMENT

§5.1 Clerk's duty to give notice. The clerk must give the parties immediate notice, by first-class mail, that the court signed a judgment or an appealable order. TRCP 306a(3); *see Board of Trs. of Bastrop ISD v. Toungate*, 958 S.W.2d 365, 367 (Tex.1997); *Hubert v. Illinois State Assistance Comm'n*, 867 S.W.2d 160, 163 (Tex.App.—Houston [14th Dist.] 1993, no writ). The clerk must provide notice of the signing of the judgment and the date it was signed. *Winkins v. Frank Winther Invs.*, 881 S.W.2d 557, 558 (Tex.App.—Houston [1st Dist.] 1994, no writ). If the clerk does not give notice of the judgment, the party's right to due process—not merely a rule of procedure—is violated because the party is deprived of its right to be heard by the court. *Hubert*, 867 S.W.2d at 163. However, the lack of notice does not affect the beginning of the time periods listed in TRCP 306a(1) (except as provided by TRCP 306a(4) and TRAP 4.2) and does not constitute reversible error. *See* TRCP 306a(3); *Campbell v. Fincher*, 72 S.W.3d 723, 724 (Tex.App.—Waco 2002, no pet.) (notice of default judgment).

───────────────────────────────

NOTE

*In **Lehmann v. Har-Con Corp.**, 39 S.W.3d 191, 206 (Tex.2001), the Supreme Court seemed to suggest that the court clerk is required to send the parties a copy of the judgment, citing TRCP 306a(3). However, by its very language, TRCP 306a(3) only requires the clerk to give notice that a judgment or an appealable order was signed. See TRCP 306a(3); see also TRCP 165a(1) (notice of signing, not copy of order), TRCP 239a (notice of judgment, not copy of judgment).*

───────────────────────────────

★

---

§5.2 Rules requiring notice. There are three rules requiring the clerk to notify the parties that the court signed a judgment or appealable order: TRCP 165a(1), 239a, and 306a(3). These rules are for the administrative convenience of the parties. *See Campbell v. Fincher*, 72 S.W.3d 723, 724 (Tex.App.—Waco 2002, no pet.) (TRCP 239a).

    1. TRCP 306a. Under TRCP 306a(3), the clerk of the trial court must give the parties or their attorneys of record immediate notice by first-class mail that the court signed a judgment or an appealable order. *John v. Marshall Health Servs.*, 58 S.W.3d 738, 739 n.3 (Tex.2001). The notice must be sent to all attorneys of record, not just to lead counsel. TRCP 306a(3); *Cannon v. ICO Tubular Servs.*, 905 S.W.2d 380, 388 (Tex.App.—Houston [1st Dist.] 1995, no writ).

    2. TRCP 165a. Under TRCP 165a(1), the clerk must give the parties notice that the court signed an order of dismissal. See "Notice of Dismissal Order," ch. 7-G, §8, p. 663.

    3. TRCP 239a. Under TRCP 239a, the clerk must give the defendant notice that the court signed a no-answer default judgment. See "Notice after no-answer default," ch. 7-A, §6.1, p. 598.

§5.3 Late notice. The time periods for the court's plenary power and for filing postjudgment motions are calculated from the date the judgment is signed. See "Signing," §3.2, p. 766. When a party receives late notice of the judgment and files a motion to extend postjudgment deadlines, the time periods are calculated from the date of actual notice. *See* TRCP 306a(4), (5). See "Motion to Extend Postjudgment Deadlines," ch. 10-G, p. 831.

§6. FINAL JUDGMENT

Whether a judgment is final has important implications for both parties. An appeal can be prosecuted only from a final judgment (with certain statutory exceptions). *See* CPRC §§51.012, 51.014. The date the judgment or final order disposing of the case is signed starts the deadlines for filing postjudgment motions and for perfecting an appeal. TRCP 306a(1); *In re Bennett*, 960 S.W.2d 35, 38 (Tex.1997); *Farmer v. Ben E. Keith Co.*, 907 S.W.2d 495, 496 (Tex.1995); *Martinez v. Humble Sand & Gravel, Inc.*, 875 S.W.2d 311, 313 (Tex.1994); *see* TRCP 329b(a), (b), (g). The period of the court's plenary power to change the judgment is also calculated from the date the final judgment is signed. *See* TRCP 329b(e). See "Changing judgment during plenary power," §7.1, p. 778. Even a void judgment can be final and can start the period for calculating deadlines. *See Newsom v. Ballinger ISD*, 213 S.W.3d 375, 379 (Tex.App.—Austin 2006, no pet.) (trial court's plenary power is not contingent on validity of J). *But see Metropolitan Transit Auth. v. Jackson*, 212 S.W.3d 797, 802-03 (Tex.App.—Houston [1st Dist.] 2006, pet. denied) (void J does not cause trial court's plenary power to expire). Only a final judgment is given preclusive effect in later suits. Most importantly, only a final judgment can be enforced. *See* TRCP 622; *In re Burlington Coat Factory Whs.*, 167 S.W.3d 827, 831 (Tex. 2005). For more extensive treatment of issues relating to finality of judgments, see *O'Connor's Texas Appeals*, "Types of Appeals," ch. 1-B, §2, p. 5.

§6.1 One-final-judgment rule.

    1. Rule. As a general rule, only one final judgment may be signed in a lawsuit. TRCP 301; *Logan v. Mullis*, 686 S.W.2d 605, 609 (Tex.1985); *Quanaim v. Frasco Rest. & Catering*, 17 S.W.3d 30, 35 (Tex.App.—Houston [14th Dist.] 2000, pet. denied); *Tindall v. Bishop, Peterson & Sharp, P.C.*, 961 S.W.2d 248, 252 (Tex.App.—Houston [1st Dist.] 1997, no writ). By limiting the number of judgments to one per case, the one-final-judgment rule also limits the number of appeals to one per case.

    2. Exceptions. There are a number of exceptions to the rule that only one final, appealable judgment can be signed in each case. The most common types of proceedings that have multiple final judgments are probate, receivership, and partition cases. See *O'Connor's Texas Appeals*, "Appeals from 'multiple final judgment' cases," ch. 1-B, §2.2, p. 8.

§6.2 Replacement judgment. When the court signs a judgment within its plenary power that is intended to replace an earlier judgment, it should specifically state that the first judgment is vacated. *See Mullins v. Thomas*, 150 S.W.2d 83, 84 (Tex.1941); *Hammett v. Lee*, 730 S.W.2d 350, 351 (Tex.App.—Dallas 1987, writ dism'd). If the second judgment does not expressly vacate the first judgment, however, many courts will presume that the first judgment is vacated unless the record indicates a contrary intent. *See, e.g.*, *SLT Dealer Grp. v. Americredit Fin. Servs.*,

★

336 S.W.3d 822, 832 (Tex.App.—Houston [1st Dist.] 2011, no pet.); *Lavender v. Lavender*, 291 S.W.3d 19, 22 (Tex. App.—Texarkana 2009, no pet.); *Abercia v. Kingvision Pay-Per-View, Ltd.*, 217 S.W.3d 688, 706 (Tex.App.—El Paso 2007, pet. denied); *Price Constr., Inc. v. Castillo*, 147 S.W.3d 431, 441 (Tex.App.—San Antonio 2004, pet. denied); *Quanaim v. Frasco Rest. & Catering*, 17 S.W.3d 30, 39-40 (Tex.App.—Houston [14th Dist.] 2000, pet. denied); *Owens-Corning Fiberglas Corp. v. Wasiak*, 883 S.W.2d 402, 411 (Tex.App.—Austin 1994, order). See "Second-judgment problems," ch. 10-B, §5.6, p. 792; *O'Connor's Texas Appeals*, "'Second judgment' problems," ch. 5-A, §8.1, p. 205.

§6.3 What judgments are final.

1. Judgments that are final.

(1) Judgment resolves all claims. A judgment is final if it disposes of all parties and claims in the lawsuit. *Ford v. Exxon Mobil Chem. Co.*, 235 S.W.3d 615, 617 (Tex.2007); *Childers v. Advanced Found. Repair, L.P.*, 193 S.W.3d 897, 898 (Tex.2006); *Lehmann v. Har-Con Corp.*, 39 S.W.3d 191, 200 (Tex.2001); *Park Place Hosp. v. Estate of Milo*, 909 S.W.2d 508, 510 (Tex.1995). If the judgment resolves all claims, it is final even if it says it is not final. *Lehmann*, 39 S.W.3d at 200; *see In re Burlington Coat Factory Whs.*, 167 S.W.3d 827, 830 (Tex.2005); *see also Newsom v. Ballinger ISD*, 213 S.W.3d 375, 379 (Tex.App.—Austin 2006, no pet.) (if judgment resolves all claims, it is final even if it is void). The judgment must either sufficiently define and protect the rights of all litigants or provide a definite means of determining those rights. *Hinde v. Hinde*, 701 S.W.2d 637, 639 (Tex.1985).

(2) Judgment after conventional trial. There is a presumption that a judgment signed following a conventional trial on the merits disposes of all parties and claims and is final. *Vaughn v. Drennon*, 324 S.W.3d 560, 562-63 (Tex.2010); *Moritz v. Preiss*, 121 S.W.3d 715, 718-19 (Tex.2003); *North E. ISD v. Aldridge*, 400 S.W.2d 893, 897-98 (Tex.1966). A judgment after a conventional trial on the merits does not need to expressly dispose of all parties and claims to be final. *Vaughn*, 324 S.W.3d at 562; *see, e.g., John v. Marshall Health Servs.*, 58 S.W.3d 738, 740 (Tex.2001) (even though J did not expressly dispose of P's claims against Ds with whom P was negotiating settlement, finality presumption was appropriate). If a judgment signed after a conventional trial contains a "Mother Hubbard" provision ("all relief not granted is denied"), it indicates the trial court intended to render a final judgment. *See Lehmann*, 39 S.W.3d at 203-04.

(3) Interlocutory judgment – merger or severance. Generally, an interlocutory judgment is not final and appealable. See *O'Connor's Texas Appeals*, "Appeals from interlocutory orders," ch. 1-B, §2.3, p. 9. An interlocutory judgment can be converted into a final judgment by merger or severance. *See City of Beaumont v. Guillory*, 751 S.W.2d 491, 492 (Tex.1988); *Teer v. Duddlesten*, 664 S.W.2d 702, 704 (Tex.1984). A judgment becomes final on the date the judgment or order disposing of the last claim is signed, or on the date the last unadjudicated claim is severed from the adjudicated claims.

(a) Last claim resolved = merger. An interlocutory judgment is merged into a final judgment when all the remaining claims are resolved, either on the merits or by dismissal. *See, e.g., Parking Co. v. Wilson*, 58 S.W.3d 742, 742 (Tex.2001) (J signed after trial of last claim made earlier partial SJ final); *John*, 58 S.W.3d at 740 (J signed after directed verdict made earlier nonsuit and partial SJ final); *Clark v. Pimienta*, 47 S.W.3d 485, 486 (Tex. 2001) (last partial SJ made earlier partial SJs final); *Wembley Inv. v. Herrera*, 11 S.W.3d 924, 926 (Tex.1999) (order nonsuiting last Ds made earlier default J as to other Ds final); *Webb v. Jorns*, 488 S.W.2d 407, 408-09 (Tex.1972) (order dismissing hospital became final when it was merged into final J); *Texas Sting, Ltd. v. R.B. Foods, Inc.*, 82 S.W.3d 644, 648 n.4 (Tex.App.—San Antonio 2002, pet. denied) (postanswer default made earlier dismissal final); *Campbell v. Kosarek*, 44 S.W.3d 647, 649 (Tex.App.—Dallas 2001, pet. denied) (J disposing of remaining Ds made earlier dismissal order against other Ds final). Under the merger doctrine, interlocutory judgments and orders are merged into the final judgment, even when they are not recorded in the judgment. *Webb*, 488 S.W.2d at 408-09; *Radelow-Gittens Real Prop. Mgmt. v. Pamex Foods*, 735 S.W.2d 558, 560 (Tex.App.—Dallas 1987, writ ref'd n.r.e.).

(b) Unresolved claim severed. An interlocutory judgment becomes final when the trial court severs the interlocutory judgment from the unadjudicated claims. *See* TRCP 41; *see, e.g., Harris Cty. Flood Control Dist. v. Adam*, 66 S.W.3d 265, 266 (Tex.2001) (when order of severance was signed, SJ for two Ds became final);

★

Cherokee Water Co. v. Ross, 698 S.W.2d 363, 365-66 (Tex.1985) (when order severing P's SJ from D's counterclaim was signed, SJ became final); *Castano v. Foremost Cty. Mut. Ins.*, 31 S.W.3d 387, 388 (Tex.App.—San Antonio 2000, no pet.) (because no-answer default J against one D was not severed, it was not final). Courts sometimes condition the severance on a future act or event, but conditional language in a severance order should be avoided because it may cause confusion about when the severance becomes effective and when the severed interlocutory judgment becomes final. *See, e.g., **Doe v. Pilgrim Rest Baptist Ch.***, 218 S.W.3d 81, 82 (Tex.2007) (severance order conditioned on compliance with procedure did not become final until P paid filing fee); ***Diversified Fin. Sys. v. Hill, Heard, O'Neal, Gilstrap & Goetz, P.C.***, 63 S.W.3d 795, 795 (Tex.2001) (partial SJ was not final at severance because order said partial SJ was to "proceed as such to final judgment"); ***Martinez v. Humble Sand & Gravel, Inc.***, 875 S.W.2d 311, 313-14 (Tex.1994) (partial SJ was not final at severance because order allowed for other Ds to be added). The severance order is effective immediately, and the judgment is final and appealable even if there is no separate physical file created or different cause number assigned to the order. ***McRoberts v. Ryals***, 863 S.W.2d 450, 452-53 & n.4 (Tex.1993); ***McWherter v. Agua Frio Ranch***, 224 S.W.3d 285, 290 (Tex.App.—El Paso 2005, no pet.). To be severable, a cause must be capable of becoming a separate suit with a separate, final judgment. ***Martinez***, 875 S.W.2d at 312. See "Motion for Severance," ch. 5-I, §3, p. 364.

(4) **Summary disposition + statement of finality.** When a trial court resolves some claims by summary disposition, leaving other claims unresolved, the judgment is final if it unequivocally states that it finally disposes of all claims. *See In re Burlington Coat Factory*, 167 S.W.3d at 830; *Ritzell v. Espeche*, 87 S.W.3d 536, 538 (Tex.2002); *Jacobs v. Satterwhite*, 65 S.W.3d 653, 655 (Tex.2001); *Lehmann*, 39 S.W.3d at 200; *see also **M.O. Dental Lab v. Rape***, 139 S.W.3d 671, 674-75 (Tex.2004) (SJ was final even though it did not dispose of claims against unserved D); *In re Miranda*, 142 S.W.3d 354, 357 (Tex.App.—El Paso 2004, orig. proceeding) (same). For example, if a defendant moves for summary judgment on only one of the plaintiff's claims but the trial court signs a judgment that the plaintiff take nothing, the judgment is erroneous but final, as long as there are no other claims by other parties. *Jacobs*, 65 S.W.3d at 655; *Lehmann*, 39 S.W.3d at 200; *see Ritzell*, 87 S.W.3d at 538; *see also Ford*, 235 S.W.3d at 617 (order disposing of all claims that does not itemize each element of damages pleaded may be erroneous, but is final). A judgment granting more relief than a party is entitled to is not, for that reason alone, interlocutory. *Lehmann*, 39 S.W.3d at 200. When a judgment says it is final even though it does not resolve all claims, the issue of finality must be resolved on appeal. A "Mother Hubbard" provision ("all relief not granted is denied") in a summary-disposition case does not indicate that the judgment is final. *Lehmann*, 39 S.W.3d at 192. See "Finality for review," §6.4.2, p. 774.

NOTE

*The Supreme Court has approved the statement "[t]his judgment finally disposes of all parties and all claims and is appealable" as an unequivocal expression of the trial court's intent to render a final judgment for purposes of appeal. **In re Daredia**, 317 S.W.3d 247, 248-49 (Tex.2010); In re Burlington Coat Factory, 167 S.W.3d at 830; Lehmann, 39 S.W.3d at 206.*

---

(5) **Some partial judgments = final judgments.** There are some proceedings in which more than one "final" judgment can be signed in the same case. See "Exceptions," §6.1.2, p. 771. In those cases, the resolution of certain discrete claims is considered a final judgment.

2. Judgments that are not final.

(1) **Conventional trial + separate claims.** When a trial court separates (but does not sever) an issue for later disposition, the judgment or order signed after the first trial is not a final judgment. *Hall v. City of Austin*, 450 S.W.2d 836, 838 (Tex.1970).

(2) **Summary disposition.** There is no presumption that a judgment signed after a summary disposition (e.g., summary judgment, no-answer default judgment) resolves all claims and is final. *See Crites v. Collins*, 284 S.W.3d 839, 840 (Tex.2009); *Ford*, 235 S.W.3d at 617; *In re Burlington Coat Factory*, 167 S.W.3d at 829;

✩

Lehmann, 39 S.W.3d at 199-200; *see, e.g.*, *McNally v. Guevara*, 52 S.W.3d 195, 196 (Tex.2001) (SJ was not final because there was no presumption Ds abandoned claims not included in their SJ motion). When a trial court resolves some claims by summary disposition but leaves other claims unresolved, the judgment is not final. *See Lehmann*, 39 S.W.3d at 199-200; *see, e.g.*, *In re Burlington Coat Factory*, 167 S.W.3d at 831 (default judgment was interlocutory because it did not dispose of all claims); *Nash v. Harris Cty.*, 63 S.W.3d 415, 416 (Tex.2001) (SJ was interlocutory because it did not dispose of all Ds); *Parking Co.*, 58 S.W.3d at 742 (SJ was interlocutory because it did not dispose of all claims); *Bobbitt v. Stran*, 52 S.W.3d 734, 735 (Tex.2001) (SJ was interlocutory because it did not dispose of all parties and claims); *McNally*, 52 S.W.3d at 196 (SJ was interlocutory because it did not dispose of claim for attorney fees); *Guajardo v. Conwell*, 46 S.W.3d 862, 864 (Tex.2001) (SJ was interlocutory because it did not dispose of claims by and against intervenor). However, an otherwise interlocutory judgment is final for purposes of appeal if it clearly and unequivocally states that it finally disposes of all claims, even if it does not actually resolve all claims. See "Summary disposition + statement of finality," §6.3.1(4), p. 773.

PRACTICE TIP

*If a party discovers on appeal that the judgment being appealed is actually an interlocutory judgment, the party can ask the appellate court to abate the appeal so the trial court can sign an order of severance from the rest of the suit. See TRAP 27.2, 27.3; **State Farm Mut. Auto. Ins. v. Leeds**, 981 S.W.2d 693, 693 (Tex.App.—Houston [1st Dist.] 1998, order). If an appellate court is unsure whether the trial court intended the order to be final or interlocutory, it can abate the appeal to allow the trial court to clarify the finality of the order. **Lehmann**, 39 S.W.3d at 206.*

---

(3) Bill of review. A bill of review that does not dispose of all the issues in the underlying case on the merits is interlocutory and not a final, appealable order. *Kiefer v. Touris*, 197 S.W.3d 300, 302 (Tex.2006); *Tesoro Pet. v. Smith*, 796 S.W.2d 705, 705 (Tex.1990); *In re S.D.E.*, 170 S.W.3d 642, 643 (Tex.App.—El Paso 2005, no pet.); *In re J.B.A.*, 127 S.W.3d 850, 851 (Tex.App.—Fort Worth 2004, no pet.); *Shahbaz v. Feizy Imp. & Exp. Co.*, 827 S.W.2d 63, 64-65 (Tex.App.—Houston [1st Dist.] 1992, no writ). To be a final judgment, the bill of review should either (1) deny any relief to the petitioner or (2) set aside the former judgment and substitute a new judgment that properly adjudicates all the issues of the case on the merits. *In re S.D.E.*, 170 S.W.3d at 643; *In re J.B.A.*, 127 S.W.3d at 851; *Shahbaz*, 827 S.W.2d at 64; *see, e.g.*, *Kiefer*, 197 S.W.3d at 302 (bill of review that set aside former parentage adjudication but did not substitute a new one was not final and appealable). See "Judgment resolves all claims," §6.3.1(1), p. 772.

§6.4 Finality for purposes of appeal.

1. Finality for appeal. If a judgment actually disposes of all claims and parties, or if it expressly states that it disposes of all claims and parties even if it does not, it is a final judgment for purposes of filing the notice of appeal. *Lehmann v. Har-Con Corp.*, 39 S.W.3d 191, 192-93 (Tex.2001). Even if the parties do not intend for the judgment to dispose of all parties and issues but the judgment erroneously says it does, the judgment begins the appellate deadlines. *Id.* at 204. For example, if a defendant moves for summary judgment on one of the plaintiff's four claims, but the trial court signs a judgment that clearly and unequivocally states that it disposes of all claims and parties, the judgment is final—erroneous, but final. *Id.* at 200. To determine whether a judgment purporting to be final is actually final, the appellate court may need to review the record. *See id.* at 205-06; *see, e.g.*, *Jacobs v. Satterwhite*, 65 S.W.3d 653, 655 (Tex.2001) (when there were no other claims by other parties, SJ stating P "take nothing" was final for purposes of appeal); *Taub v. Dedman*, 56 S.W.3d 83, 87 (Tex.App.—Houston [14th Dist.] 2001, pet. denied) (specific enumeration of some of the Ds in SJ order indicated court did not intend to dispose of all parties).

2. Finality for review. If an appellant timely files a notice of appeal to challenge a judgment that purports to be final but is not, the appellate court will review the appellate record to determine whether the judgment was final. *Lehmann*, 39 S.W.3d at 205-06; *see M.O. Dental Lab v. Rape*, 139 S.W.3d 671, 674 (Tex.2004); *see, e.g.*,

———————————— ✯ ————————————

Jacobs, 65 S.W.3d at 655 (because motion asked for SJ on only one of two claims, SJ was not final on review). If a judgment did not resolve all claims, the appellate court should state why in its opinion the judgment was not final and either dismiss the appeal or abate and remand to the trial court to decide whether to sign a final judgment. *See, e.g.*, *McNally v. Guevara*, 52 S.W.3d 195, 196 (Tex.2001) (Supreme Court remanded to court of appeals to determine whether to abate appeal to allow trial court to sign final judgment or whether to dismiss appeal for want of jurisdiction); *see also* TRAP 27.2 (appellate court may permit interlocutory order to be modified to make it final).

§6.5 Finality for purposes of changing the judgment. A judgment becomes final for purposes of changing it when the trial court loses plenary power. *See* TRCP 306a(1). See "Power to Change Judgment," §7, p. 778. The date the court loses plenary power depends on the date the judgment was signed, whether one of the postjudgment motions extending the court's plenary power was filed, and if filed, whether the motion was overruled or granted. If no postjudgment motions are filed, the trial court loses plenary power and the judgment becomes final 30 days after it was signed. *Lane Bank Equip. Co. v. Smith S. Equip., Inc.*, 10 S.W.3d 308, 310 (Tex.2000).

1. Postjudgment motions & finality. Any postjudgment motion—no matter what it is called—will extend plenary power if it (1) seeks a substantive change in the judgment and (2) is filed within the time limits for a motion for new trial. *See Lane Bank*, 10 S.W.3d at 313-14; *In re Gillespie*, 124 S.W.3d 699, 703 (Tex.App.—Houston [14th Dist.] 2003, orig. proceeding).

NOTE

For a comparison of the effect of these motions on the court's plenary power and the appellate deadlines, see O'Connor's Texas Appeals, *"Comparing Effect of Postjudgment Motions on Plenary Power & Appellate Timetable," chart 5-2, p. 202.*

---

(1) Motions that extend plenary power. The following motions extend the court's plenary power over the judgment:

(a) MNT. A motion for new trial. TRCP 329b(a), (e); *Lane Bank*, 10 S.W.3d at 310. See "Motion for New Trial," ch. 10-B, p. 789.

(b) Motion to reinstate. A verified motion to reinstate after dismissal for want of prosecution. TRCP 165a(3); *see Silguero v. State*, 287 S.W.3d 146, 149-50 (Tex.App.—Corpus Christi 2009, orig. proceeding) (affidavit or other sufficient evidence in record can substitute for verification and extend court's plenary power); *see, e.g.*, *3V, Inc. v. JTS Enters.*, 40 S.W.3d 533, 538-39 (Tex.App.—Houston [14th Dist.] 2000, no pet.) (affidavits were sufficient to verify motion to reinstate). See "Motion to Reinstate After Dismissal for Want of Prosecution," ch. 10-F, p. 826.

(c) Motion to modify judgment. A motion to modify, correct, or reform the judgment. *See* TRCP 329b(g); *Lane Bank*, 10 S.W.3d at 310; *Padilla v. LaFrance*, 907 S.W.2d 454, 458 (Tex.1995). See "Motion to Modify the Judgment," ch. 10-D, p. 814. For example:

[1] Motion for sanctions. A motion for sanctions to be incorporated in the judgment. *Lane Bank*, 10 S.W.3d at 309-10; *Alpert v. Crain, Caton & James, P.C.*, 178 S.W.3d 398, 410 (Tex.App.—Houston [1st Dist.] 2005, pet. denied); *In re Estate of Davis v. Cook*, 9 S.W.3d 288, 296 (Tex.App.—San Antonio 1999, no pet.). See "Motion for Sanctions," ch. 5-K, p. 377.

[2] Motion for remittitur. No court has considered whether a motion for remittitur filed separately from a motion for new trial extends the court's plenary power, but it should, under *Lane Bank*, because it seeks a substantive change in the judgment. A request for remittitur can be made in a motion for new trial, but it should extend the court's plenary power when filed separately. *Cf. Arkoma Basin Expl. Co. v. FMF Assocs. 1990-A, Ltd.*, 249 S.W.3d 380, 391 (Tex.2008) (signed order suggesting remittitur restarts appellate deadlines). See "Motion for Remittitur," ch. 10-C, p. 811.

───────────────────────────── ✦ ─────────────────────────────

[3] Motion for JNOV. No court has considered whether a motion for JNOV extends the court's plenary power, but it should, under *Lane Bank*, because it seeks a substantive change in the judgment. By comparison, a motion for JNOV will extend the appellate deadlines if it is filed within the time limit for a motion for new trial and if it "assails" the trial court's judgment. *See Ryland Enter. v. Weatherspoon*, 355 S.W.3d 664, 666 (Tex. 2011); *Kirschberg v. Lowe*, 974 S.W.2d 844, 847-48 (Tex.App.—San Antonio 1998, no pet.). See "Deadlines," ch. 9-B, §4, p. 762; *O'Connor's Texas Appeals*, "Postjudgment Motions that Extend the Appellate Timetable," ch. 5-A, §6, p. 199.

(2) Motions that do not extend plenary power. The following postjudgment motions do not extend the court's plenary power.

(a) Request for findings of fact. A proper request for findings of fact does not extend the court's plenary power. *In re Gillespie*, 124 S.W.3d at 703; *Pursley v. Ussery*, 982 S.W.2d 596, 599 (Tex.App.—San Antonio 1998, pet. denied). A request for findings of fact does not seek a substantive change in the judgment. *In re Gillespie*, 124 S.W.3d at 703. By comparison, TRAP 26.1(a)(4) specifically states that a request for findings of fact extends appellate deadlines. See "Effect on appellate timetable," ch. 10-E, §6.1, p. 823.

(b) Unverified motion to reinstate. Generally, an unverified motion to reinstate does not extend the court's plenary power. *Silguero*, 287 S.W.3d at 149; *3V, Inc.*, 40 S.W.3d at 538. But courts are generous in allowing alternative methods of verification. *See Silguero*, 287 S.W.3d at 149-50 (affidavit or other sufficient evidence in record can substitute for verification and extend court's plenary power); *see, e.g., In re Dobbins*, 247 S.W.3d 394, 396-97 (Tex.App.—Dallas 2008, orig. proceeding) (evidentiary hearing and court master's recommendation of approval, made within 30 days, was sufficient substitute for verification and extended court's plenary power).

(c) Motion to enforce judgment. A motion for sanctions for failure to comply with the judgment does not extend the court's plenary power. *Guajardo v. Conwell*, 30 S.W.3d 15, 16 (Tex.App.—Houston [14th Dist.] 2000), *aff'd*, 46 S.W.3d 862 (Tex.2001).

(d) Other motions for nonsubstantive change in judgment. Generally, any other postjudgment motion asking for a nonsubstantive change in the judgment does not affect the trial court's plenary power over its judgment. *E.g., Lane Bank*, 10 S.W.3d at 313-14 & n.4 (motion for judgment nunc pro tunc filed after court loses plenary power does not extend trial court's plenary power). However, if the trial court modifies the judgment while it still has plenary power, even if the change is nonsubstantive, the court's plenary power is extended. *See id.* at 313. See "Restarts appellate timetable," ch. 10-D, §6.2.1, p. 816.

2. Effect of PPE motions. The effect of a plenary-power-extending motion (PPE motion) on the court's power to change the judgment is as follows:

(1) No PPE motion filed. If no PPE motion was filed, the trial court has plenary power to change its judgment for 30 days after it signs the judgment. TRCP 329b(d); *Lane Bank*, 10 S.W.3d at 310; *Board of Trs. of Bastrop ISD v. Toungate*, 958 S.W.2d 365, 367 (Tex.1997); *Sadeghian v. Shaw*, 76 S.W.3d 229, 231 (Tex.App.—Texarkana 2002, no pet.).

(2) PPE motion overruled. When a party timely files a PPE motion, the trial court's plenary power over its judgment is extended until 30 days after the motion is overruled, either by written order or by operation of law, whichever occurs first. TRCP 329b(e), (g); TRAP 4.3(a); *Lane Bank*, 10 S.W.3d at 310; *Faulkner v. Culver*, 851 S.W.2d 187, 188 (Tex.1993). Such motions are overruled by operation of law on the 76th day after the judgment is signed, if not overruled earlier by a written order. TRCP 329b(c) ("on expiration of" 75 days); *see In re Hidalgo*, 279 S.W.3d 456, 460 (Tex.App.—Dallas 2009), *rev'd on other grounds sub nom. Hidalgo v. Hidalgo*, 310 S.W.3d 887 (Tex.2010). When a PPE motion is overruled by operation of law on the 76th day after judgment, the trial court has plenary power over the judgment for 105 days, counting from the date it signed the judgment. *See L.M. Healthcare, Inc. v. Childs*, 929 S.W.2d 442, 444 (Tex.1996); *In re Hidalgo*, 279 S.W.3d at 460; *see, e.g., Coinmach, Inc. v. Aspenwood Apt. Corp.*, 98 S.W.3d 377, 378 & n.1 (Tex.App.—Houston [1st Dist.] 2003, no pet.) (after MNT was overruled by operation of law, court granted MNT during its additional 30 days of plenary power). If the trial court overrules a motion for new trial, an amended motion for the new trial does not extend plenary power; the court has only

THE JUDGMENT

———————————— ✯ ————————————

30 days from the date the first motion for new trial was overruled to rule on the amended motion. *In re Brookshire Grocery Co.*, 250 S.W.3d 66, 69-70 (Tex.2008). If, however, a party timely files a PPE motion other than an amended motion for new trial (e.g., motion to modify the judgment) after the trial court overrules a motion for new trial, that PPE motion will extend the trial court's plenary power over its judgment. *Id.* at 72; *see* TRCP 329b(e), (g); *L.M. Healthcare, Inc.*, 929 S.W.2d at 444.

(3) PPE motion granted.

(a) MNT.

[1] MNT granted + new-trial judgment. When a trial court grants a motion for new trial, the original judgment is set aside and the case is reinstated on the trial court's docket. *Wilkins v. Methodist Health Care Sys.*, 160 S.W.3d 559, 563 (Tex.2005). The trial court retains ongoing plenary power until it signs another final judgment. *See In re Baylor Med. Ctr.*, 280 S.W.3d 227, 230-31 (Tex.2008). The trial court's plenary power is extended until 30 days after the new judgment is signed, unless one of the parties files a new PPE motion based on that judgment. *See* TRCP 329b(d). If a new PPE motion is filed, the date the trial court loses plenary power depends on whether the motion is overruled, granted, or withdrawn. See "Finality for purposes of changing the judgment," §6.5, p. 775.

[2] MNT granted + order "ungranted." When a trial court grants a motion for new trial, it retains ongoing plenary power over the case and can set aside the new trial order any time before it signs another final judgment. *Hidalgo v. Hidalgo*, 310 S.W.3d 887, 889 (Tex.2010); *In re Baylor Med.*, 280 S.W.3d at 230-31. If the trial court "ungrants" the new-trial order and reinstates the original judgment, the trial court's plenary power is extended until 30 days after the date the judgment was reinstated, unless one of the parties files a new PPE motion. *Cf. In re Baylor Med.*, 280 S.W.3d at 231 (trial court's withdrawal of modification of judgment is itself a modification that restarts appellate timetable). The order ungranting a new trial does not automatically reinstate the original judgment; the trial court must enter a new judgment. *In re Department of Family & Prot. Servs.*, 273 S.W.3d 637, 644 (Tex.2009). If a new PPE motion is filed, the date the trial court loses plenary power depends on whether the motion is overruled, granted, or withdrawn. See "Finality for purposes of changing the judgment," §6.5, p. 775.

(b) Other PPE motions. When a trial court grants a PPE motion (other than a motion for new trial) and modifies the judgment or signs a new judgment, the trial court's plenary power is extended until 30 days after the modified or new judgment is signed, unless one of the parties files a new PPE motion based on that modified or new judgment. *See* TRCP 329b(d). If a new PPE motion is filed, the date the trial court loses plenary power depends on whether the motion is overruled, granted, or withdrawn. See "Finality for purposes of changing the judgment," §6.5, p. 775.

(4) PPE motion withdrawn. If the party who filed a PPE motion withdraws it, the limit of the trial court's plenary power reverts to 30 days after the judgment was signed. *Rogers v. Clinton*, 794 S.W.2d 9, 11 (Tex. 1990); *In re Dilley ISD*, 23 S.W.3d 189, 191 (Tex.App.—San Antonio 2000, orig. proceeding). The withdrawal of a PPE motion is treated like a notice of nonsuit—it is effective immediately. *Rogers*, 794 S.W.2d at 11. If the party withdraws the motion more than 30 days after the judgment is signed, the trial court no longer has jurisdiction to change the judgment because its plenary power has already expired. *In re Dilley ISD*, 23 S.W.3d at 191-92.

PRACTICE TIP

To ensure appellate review, every party should file a motion for new trial even when another party has already filed a PPE motion. Without filing its own motion for new trial, the party could miss the appellate deadlines if the other party withdraws its PPE motion.

★

		9-1. PLENARY-POWER DEADLINES	
	Situation	**Last day trial court has plenary power**	**Cross-reference**
1	No PPE motion filed	Date judgment signed + 30 days	§6.5.2(1), p. 776
2	PPE motion overruled by court order	Date order signed overruling PPE motion + 30 days, but no later than 105 days after date judgment signed	§6.5.2(2), p. 776
3	PPE motion overruled by operation of law	Date judgment signed + 75 days + 30 days = 105 days	§6.5.2(2), p. 776
4	PPE motion granted by court order	Date new or modified judgment signed + 30 days, unless new PPE motion filed	§6.5.2(3), p. 777
5	PPE motion withdrawn by party	Date judgment signed + 30 days	§6.5.2(4), p. 777

§7. POWER TO CHANGE JUDGMENT

§7.1 Changing judgment during plenary power. The trial court has the power to change its judgment as long as it has plenary power over the judgment. See "Plenary-Power Deadlines," chart 9-1, this page. If the trial court changes the judgment by signing a modified judgment while it still has plenary power over the judgment, the time-tables for postjudgment motions and appellate documents start over. TRCP 329b(h); TRAP 4.3(a); *see* TRAP 27.3. See "Modified judgment & postjudgment deadlines," ch. 10-D, §6.2, p. 816.

§7.2 Changing judgment after plenary power. The court generally cannot change its judgment once it loses plenary power. There are two exceptions:

1. Correcting clerical errors. The trial court can correct clerical errors in the judgment. Only in a few cases are the appellate timetables extended if the court changes the judgment after it loses plenary power. See "Correction made after losing plenary power – judgment nunc pro tunc," ch. 10-H, §7.1.2, p. 839.

2. Retaxing costs. The trial court can retax costs (i.e., correct errors in the clerk's tabulation of costs) after it loses plenary power. *Operation Rescue-Nat'l v. Planned Parenthood*, 937 S.W.2d 60, 87 (Tex.App.—Houston [14th Dist.] 1996), *aff'd as modified*, 975 S.W.2d 546 (Tex.1998). Taxing costs, as distinguished from adjudicating costs, is merely a ministerial duty of the clerk. *Wood v. Wood*, 320 S.W.2d 807, 813 (Tex.1959); *Operation Rescue*, 937 S.W.2d at 87; *see* TRCP 149, 622. The court must retax costs before the mandate in the case is issued and costs are paid. *Operation Rescue*, 937 S.W.2d at 87; *see Hartzell Propeller, Inc. v. Alexander*, 517 S.W.2d 455, 456 (Tex.App.—Texarkana 1974, no writ). *But see County of El Paso v. Dorado*, 180 S.W.3d 854, 873 (Tex.App.—El Paso 2005, pet. denied) (party can file motion to retax costs if it believes the bill of costs attached to the mandate is erroneous).

§8. POWER TO ENFORCE JUDGMENT

The trial court has the power to enforce its orders after its plenary power expires. *Allen v. Allen*, 717 S.W.2d 311, 312 (Tex.1986); *Kenseth v. Dallas Cty.*, 126 S.W.3d 584, 600 (Tex.App.—Dallas 2004, pet. denied); *see Katz v. Bianchi*, 848 S.W.2d 372, 374 (Tex.App.—Houston [14th Dist.] 1993, orig. proceeding). Enforcement orders cannot be inconsistent with the original judgment and cannot materially change a part of the judgment that was substantially adjudicated. *Cook v. Stallcup*, 170 S.W.3d 916, 920 (Tex.App.—Dallas 2005, no pet.); *Matz v. Bennion*, 961 S.W.2d 445, 452 (Tex.App.—Houston [1st Dist.] 1997, pet. denied).

§9. REVIEW

§9.1 Calculating appellate deadlines. Appellate deadlines are calculated from the date the court signs a final judgment or appealable order and depend on whether either party filed a motion extending the appellate deadlines. Motions extending the appellate deadlines include (1) a motion for new trial, (2) a motion to modify the judgment,

---

★

---

(3) a motion to reinstate under TRCP 165a, (4) a request for findings of fact when findings either are required by the TRCPs or could properly be considered by the appellate court, and (5) any motion that seeks a substantive change in the judgment. TRAP 26.1(a) (#1-4); *Lane Bank Equip. Co. v. Smith S. Equip., Inc.*, 10 S.W.3d 308, 314 (Tex. 2000) (#5). See *O'Connor's Texas Appeals*, "Postjudgment Motions that Extend the Appellate Timetable," ch. 5-A, §6, p. 199.

9-2. APPELLATE DEADLINES				
	Appeal from final judgment		**Appeal from interlocutory order**	
	Notice of appeal	Appellate record	Notice of appeal	Appellate record
1	When no ADE motion* filed	30 days from judgment. TRAP 26.1.	60 days from judgment. TRAP 35.1.	20 days from order. *See* TRAP 26.1(b), 28.1(a).	10 days from notice of appeal. TRAP 35.1(b).
2	When ADE motion* filed	90 days from judgment. TRAP 26.1(a).	120 days from judgment. TRAP 35.1(a).	20 days from order. *See* TRAP 26.1(b), 28.1(a).	10 days from notice of appeal. TRAP 35.1(b).
* ADE motion = a timely filed appellate-deadline-extending motion.				

§9.2 Accepting judgment. A party cannot treat a judgment as both right and wrong. *Texas State Bank v. Amaro*, 87 S.W.3d 538, 544 (Tex.2002); *Carle v. Carle*, 234 S.W.2d 1002, 1004 (Tex.1950); *L.P.D. v. R.C.*, 959 S.W.2d 728, 731 (Tex.App.—Austin 1998, pet. denied).

1. Plaintiff.

(1) Acceptance of payment.

(a) Generally. The general rule for a plaintiff (the judgment creditor) is that if it accepts the benefits of a judgment, it is estopped from challenging the judgment by appeal. *Carle*, 234 S.W.2d at 1004; *Williams v. LifeCare Hosps.*, 207 S.W.3d 828, 830 (Tex.App.—Fort Worth 2006, no pet.); *Rapp v. Mandell & Wright, P.C.*, 123 S.W.3d 431, 433-34 (Tex.App.—Houston [14th Dist.] 2003, pet. denied); *Bloom v. Bloom*, 935 S.W.2d 942, 945 (Tex.App.—San Antonio 1996, no writ). In other words, the appeal becomes moot.

(b) Exceptions. There are two narrow exceptions to the rule that acceptance of payment makes the case moot.

[1] No effect of reversal. If the reversal of the judgment could not possibly affect the judgment creditor's right to the benefits it accepted under the judgment, the judgment creditor may appeal even though it accepted those benefits. *Amaro*, 87 S.W.3d at 544; *Carle*, 234 S.W.2d at 1004; *Williams*, 207 S.W.3d at 830; *e.g.*, *Molina v. Moore*, 33 S.W.3d 323, 326-27 (Tex.App.—Amarillo 2000, no pet.) (appeal was not moot because P requested only reversal of JNOV and rendition of judgment on jury verdict for damages; because remand was not requested, P could not receive amount of damages less than those awarded by trial court); *Briargrove Park Prop. Owners, Inc. v. Riner*, 867 S.W.2d 58, 60-61 (Tex.App.—Texarkana 1993, writ denied) (acceptance of past-due amounts awarded in judgment did not estop appeal on attorney fees).

[2] Involuntary acceptance of payment. If a judgment creditor accepts benefits because of financial duress or other similar economic circumstances, there is no voluntary acceptance of payment, and the judgment creditor may appeal even though it accepted the benefits. *Williams*, 207 S.W.3d at 830; *e.g.*, *Cooper v. Bushong*, 10 S.W.3d 20, 23-24 (Tex.App.—Austin 1999, pet. denied) (no voluntary acceptance for P who filed bankruptcy and used benefits to pay for family necessities); *Smith v. Texas Commerce Bank*, 822 S.W.2d 812, 814 (Tex. App.—Corpus Christi 1992, writ denied) (acceptance of benefits to pay property taxes was not evidence of financial duress).

✦

(2) Release of judgment. A judgment creditor who signs a release of judgment is estopped from challenging the judgment by appeal. *Rapp*, 123 S.W.3d at 434. A release of judgment is itself a complete relinquishment by the judgment creditor of all its rights in the judgment. *Id.* When a judgment creditor accepts money in complete satisfaction and release of judgment, the judgment has no further force or authority. *Id.*; *see Reames v. Logue*, 712 S.W.2d 802, 804-05 (Tex.App.—Dallas 1986, writ ref'd n.r.e.).

2. Defendant.

(1) Generally. The general rule for a defendant (the judgment debtor) is that the appeal becomes moot if the defendant voluntarily pays the judgment. *Marshall v. Housing Auth.*, 198 S.W.3d 782, 787 (Tex.2006); *Continental Cas. Co. v. Huizar*, 740 S.W.2d 429, 430 (Tex.1987).

(2) Exceptions. The general rule has diminished in scope, and significant exceptions apply. *See Miga v. Jensen*, 299 S.W.3d 98, 103-04 (Tex.2009) (voluntary-payment rule has been affirmatively applied only twice in last 40 years).

(a) Express intent. Payment of a judgment will not make the appeal moot if the judgment is appealable and the judgment debtor clearly expresses an intent to appeal. *Marshall*, 198 S.W.3d at 787; *see, e.g.*, *Miga*, 299 S.W.3d at 105 (appeal not moot when party made clear its intent to appeal and seek restitution if appeal was successful).

(b) Involuntary payment. Payment of a judgment will not make the appeal moot if it is the result of fraud, duress, or compulsion. *See Miga*, 299 S.W.3d at 103; *see, e.g.*, *Riner v. Briargrove Park Prop. Owners, Inc.*, 858 S.W.2d 370, 370-71 (Tex.1993) (judgment debtor did not waive appeal when it paid to avoid execution); *Highland Ch. of Christ v. Powell*, 640 S.W.2d 235, 236-37 (Tex.1982) (same).

D. RES JUDICATA & COLLATERAL ESTOPPEL

§1. GENERAL

§1.1 Rules. None.

§1.2 Purpose. Res judicata is sometimes used as a generic term for a group of related concepts about the conclusive effects of final judgments. *Barr v. Resolution Trust Corp.*, 837 S.W.2d 627, 628 (Tex.1992). Res judicata is designed to promote judicial efficiency and protect litigants from multiple lawsuits. *Citizens Ins. v. Daccach*, 217 S.W.3d 430, 449 (Tex.2007).

§1.3 Forms. See *O'Connor's Texas Civil Forms* (2012), FORM 3E:11 (affirmative defenses), FORM 7C:2 (defendant's motion for summary judgment based on counterclaim or affirmative defense).

§1.4 Other references. Restatement (2d) of Judgments (1982); Ratliff, *Offensive Collateral Estoppel & the Option Effect*, 67 Tex.L.Rev. 63 (1988).

§2. RES JUDICATA & COLLATERAL ESTOPPEL

§2.1 Comparison. Within the general doctrine of res judicata, there are two principal categories: (1) claim preclusion (also known as res judicata) and (2) issue preclusion (also known as collateral estoppel). *Barr v. Resolution Trust Corp.*, 837 S.W.2d 627, 628 (Tex.1992). In this book, res judicata refers only to claim preclusion and is not used as the generic term covering both categories.

1. Res judicata – claim preclusion. Res judicata bars the litigation of claims actually litigated as well as those arising from the same transaction that could have been litigated. *Igal v. Brightstar Info. Tech.*, 250 S.W.3d 78, 86 (Tex.2008); *Compania Financiara Libano, S.A. v. Simmons*, 53 S.W.3d 365, 367 (Tex.2001); *Barr*, 837 S.W.2d at 630. Thus, res judicata focuses on what could have been litigated. *Van Dyke v. Boswell, O'Toole, Davis & Pickering*, 697 S.W.2d 381, 384 (Tex.1985). Res judicata requires mutuality of interests—the party invoking it and the party to be bound must have been parties in the earlier suit. See "Same parties," §3.2.2, p. 782. Res judicata is broader than collateral estoppel. *Van Dyke*, 697 S.W.2d at 384.

✦

2. Collateral estoppel – issue preclusion. Collateral estoppel bars the litigation of specific issues already decided in an earlier case; it does not bar an entire cause of action or defense. Thus, collateral estoppel focuses on what was actually litigated and essential to the judgment. *Van Dyke*, 697 S.W.2d at 384. Collateral estoppel does not require mutuality of interests—only the party against whom it is asserted or a person in privity with that party must have been a party in the earlier suit. See "Cast as adversaries," §4.2.3, p. 784.

§2.2 Preclusive effect. The policies behind res judicata and collateral estoppel reflect the need to bring litigation to an end, prevent vexatious litigation, maintain the stability of court decisions, promote judicial economy, and prevent double recovery. *Barr v. Resolution Trust Corp.*, 837 S.W.2d 627, 629 (Tex.1992). When a lawsuit is divided into separate parts, neither res judicata nor collateral estoppel prevents the litigation of the second part of the lawsuit after the first part is litigated. *E.g.*, *Van Dyke v. Boswell, O'Toole, Davis & Pickering*, 697 S.W.2d 381, 384 (Tex.1985) (favorable resolution of claim for attorney fees did not preclude claim for legal malpractice because trial court severed the issues); *see also Finger v. Southern Refrigeration Servs.*, 881 S.W.2d 890, 895-96 (Tex.App.—Houston [1st Dist.] 1994, writ denied) (after directed verdict against P1 was reversed on appeal, the unfavorable resolution of the rest of the suit did not preclude retrial by P2 who had been directed out of suit); *Chandler v. Hendrick Mem'l Hosp.*, 317 S.W.2d 248, 251 (Tex.App.—Eastland 1958, writ ref'd n.r.e.) (judgment stated it did not resolve issue of hospital fees). An interlocutory order on matters incidental to the main suit does not operate as res judicata or collateral estoppel. *E.g.*, *Texacadian Energy, Inc. v. Lone Star Energy Storage, Inc.*, 829 S.W.2d 369, 373 (Tex.App.—Corpus Christi 1992, writ denied) (denial of motion to perpetuate testimony did not resolve merits of fraud claim).

NOTE

Under CPRC §31.004(a), if a plaintiff brings suit in a district court after filing suit in a lower trial court (i.e., small-claims court, justice-of-the-peace court, county court, statutory county court), only those claims that were actually litigated in the lower trial court are barred by res judicata or collateral estoppel. C/S Solutions, Inc. v. Energy Maint. Servs. Grp., 274 S.W.3d 299, 310 & n.11 (Tex.App.—Houston [1st Dist.] 2008, no pet.); see, e.g., Kizer v. Meyer, Lytton, Alen & Whitaker, Inc., 228 S.W.3d 384, 391-92 (Tex.App.—Austin 2007, no pet.) (although breach-of-warranty claim in county court at law and breach-of-contract claim in district court were based on same conduct and likely sought same damages, claims were different and required proof of different elements; thus, breach-of-contract claim was not litigated in county court at law and could be brought in district court); see also CPRC §31.004(c) (defining "lower trial court"). Thus, if a claim could have been litigated in the lower trial court, but was not, it is not barred. C/S Solutions, 274 S.W.3d at 310; Kizer, 228 S.W.3d at 391. Similarly, under CPRC §31.005, if a plaintiff brings suit in a county court or statutory county court after filing suit in a small-claims court or justice-of-the-peace court, only the claims that were actually litigated are barred. Wren v. Gusnowski, 919 S.W.2d 847, 848-49 (Tex.App.—Austin 1996, no writ).

---

§2.3 Which jurisdiction's law. The preclusive effect of a judgment must be determined according to the law of the jurisdiction that issued the initial judgment. *See, e.g.*, *Geary v. Texas Commerce Bank*, 967 S.W.2d 836, 839 (Tex.1998) (court applied federal res judicata to determine preclusive effect of bankruptcy judgment); *Purcell v. Bellinger*, 940 S.W.2d 599, 601 (Tex.1997) (court applied NY res judicata to determine preclusive effect of NY judgment).

§3. RES JUDICATA – CLAIM PRECLUSION

§3.1 Purpose. Res judicata, or claim preclusion, prevents the relitigation of a claim or cause of action that was adjudicated and resolved by a final judgment, as well as related matters that with the use of diligence should have been litigated in the earlier suit. *Citizens Ins. v. Daccach*, 217 S.W.3d 430, 449 (Tex.2007); *Hallco Tex., Inc. v. McMullen Cty.*, 221 S.W.3d 50, 58 (Tex.2006); *State & Cty. Mut. Fire Ins. v. Miller*, 52 S.W.3d 693, 696 (Tex.2001); *Amstadt v. U.S. Brass Corp.*, 919 S.W.2d 644, 652 (Tex.1996). Claim preclusion prevents splitting a cause of action.

⭐

Barr v. Resolution Trust Corp., 837 S.W.2d 627, 629 (Tex.1992); *Jeanes v. Henderson*, 688 S.W.2d 100, 103 (Tex. 1985); *see Ingersoll-Rand Co. v. Valero Energy Corp.*, 997 S.W.2d 203, 206-07 (Tex.1999). Texas courts apply the transactional test from the Restatement (2d) of Judgments to determine whether two claims involve the same cause of action for res judicata purposes. *Barr*, 837 S.W.2d at 631; *see Citizens Ins.*, 217 S.W.3d at 449; Restatement (2d) of Judgments §24. Under that test, the critical issue is whether the two claims arise from the same transaction and are based on the same "nucleus of operative facts." *Musgrave v. Owen*, 67 S.W.3d 513, 519 (Tex.App.—Texarkana 2002, no pet.). A transaction is determined pragmatically, "giving weight to such considerations as whether the facts are related in time, space, origin, or motivation, whether they form a convenient trial unit, and whether their treatment as a trial unit conforms with the parties' expectations or business understanding or usage." *Citizens Ins.*, 217 S.W.3d at 449; Restatement (2d) of Judgments §24(2); *e.g.*, *Barr*, 837 S.W.2d at 631 (partnership note and guarantee were part of single transaction); *see, e.g.*, *Southern Cty. Mut. Ins. v. Ochoa*, 19 S.W.3d 452, 466-67 (Tex.App.— Corpus Christi 2000, no pet.) (claim for breach of insurance contract should have been brought in *Stowers* suit).

§3.2 Elements of res judicata. A claim of res judicata requires proof of the following elements:

1. Final judgment. A court of competent jurisdiction signed a final judgment on the merits in the first suit. *Citizens Ins. v. Daccach*, 217 S.W.3d 430, 449 (Tex.2007); *Amstadt v. U.S. Brass Corp.*, 919 S.W.2d 644, 652 (Tex.1996); *see, e.g.*, *Travelers Ins. v. Joachim*, 315 S.W.3d 860, 866 (Tex.2010) (order of dismissal with prejudice after nonsuit, although erroneous, was merely voidable and thus was final determination on the merits because P did not directly attack order; P's refiling of same cause of action was barred by res judicata); *Igal v. Brightstar Info. Tech.*, 250 S.W.3d 78, 86 (Tex.2008) (administrative agency's final judgment on P's claims barred P's later-filed common-law action on same claims); *Martin v. Martin, Martin & Richards, Inc.*, 989 S.W.2d 357, 358-59 (Tex. 1998) (dismissal with prejudice of declaratory-judgment action did not resolve issue of validity of contract); *see also Glazer's Wholesale Distribs. v. Heineken USA, Inc.*, 95 S.W.3d 286, 301-02 (Tex.App.—Dallas 2001, pet. dism'd) (res judicata applies to arbitration awards reduced to final judgment).

2. Same parties. The parties in the first suit are the same as those in the second suit or are in privity with them. *Igal*, 250 S.W.3d at 86; *Citizens Ins.*, 217 S.W.3d at 449; *Amstadt*, 919 S.W.2d at 652-53; *e.g.*, *State Farm Lloyds v. C.M.W.*, 53 S.W.3d 877, 886 (Tex.App.—Dallas 2001, pet. denied) (doctrine did not apply; insurer and insured were not in privity in underlying liability suit in which insurer reserved its rights to contest coverage); *Southwest Guar. Trust Co. v. Providence Trust Co.*, 970 S.W.2d 777, 784 (Tex.App.—Austin 1998, pet. denied) (doctrine did not apply because parties were not the same). Due process requires that res judicata operate only against persons who have already had their day in court, either as a party in the earlier suit or as a person in privity with a party. *Benson v. Wanda Pet. Co.*, 468 S.W.2d 361, 363 (Tex.1971). A party is in privity with another party when the party is a successor in interest to the other party and derives its claims through the other party. *Montgomery First Corp. v. Caprock Inv.*, 89 S.W.3d 179, 186 (Tex.App.—Eastland 2002, no pet.); *see also Mayes v. Stewart*, 11 S.W.3d 440, 449 (Tex.App.—Houston [14th Dist.] 2000, pet. denied) (privity is not established by mere fact that persons happen to be interested in same question or in proving same facts). When the parties are coparties rather than opposing parties, res judicata acts as a bar to a coparty's claim in a later suit only if one coparty filed a cross-action against another coparty in the earlier suit. *Getty Oil Co. v. Insurance Co. of N. Am.*, 845 S.W.2d 794, 800 (Tex.1992); *Smith v. Baker*, 380 S.W.2d 725, 726 (Tex.App.—Waco 1964), *writ ref'd n.r.e.*, 383 S.W.2d 570 (Tex.1964).

3. Same or related claims. The second suit is based on the same claims that were raised or that could have been raised in the first suit. *Igal*, 250 S.W.3d at 86; *Citizens Ins.*, 217 S.W.3d at 449; *Compania Financiara Libano, S.A. v. Simmons*, 53 S.W.3d 365, 367 (Tex.2001); *e.g.*, *Robinson v. Garcia*, 5 S.W.3d 348, 351-52 (Tex. App.—Corpus Christi 1999, pet. denied) (P's claims, in both tax suit and fee suit, arose from attorney's representation of him in earlier lawsuit; tax suit was barred by fee suit). The claim must have existed at the time the original suit was filed; res judicata does not bar a claim that accrued after the original judgment. *Hernandez v. Del Ray Chem. Int'l*, 56 S.W.3d 112, 116 (Tex.App.—Houston [14th Dist.] 2001, no pet.); *see, e.g.*, *Compania Financiara*, 53 S.W.3d at 367 (res judicata did not bar P's suit to compel performance of settlement agreement after D breached agreement). When there is a legal relationship (e.g., under a lease, contract, or marriage) all claims resulting from the relationship will arise from the same subject matter and will be subject to res judicata. *Genecov Grp. v. Roosth Prod.*, 144

———————————— ✦ ————————————

S.W.3d 546, 552 (Tex.App.—Tyler 2003, pet. denied); *Pinebrook Props., Ltd. v. Brookhaven Lake Prop. Owners Ass'n*, 77 S.W.3d 487, 497 (Tex.App.—Texarkana 2002, pet. denied). The same principles apply to compulsory counterclaims—a defendant must bring as a counterclaim any claim arising from the transaction that is the subject of the plaintiff's suit. *State & Cty. Mut. Fire Ins. v. Miller*, 52 S.W.3d 693, 696 (Tex.2001); *Barr v. Resolution Trust Corp.*, 837 S.W.2d 627, 630 (Tex.1992). Res judicata applies to (1) the cause of action filed by the plaintiff, (2) any counterclaims actually filed by the defendant, and (3) all compulsory counterclaims the defendant should have filed but did not. *See Musgrave v. Owen*, 67 S.W.3d 513, 519 (Tex.App.—Texarkana 2002, no pet.); Restatement (2d) of Judgments §§18, 21-23. See "Compulsory-counterclaim rule," ch. 2-E, §6.1, p. 131.

§4. COLLATERAL ESTOPPEL – ISSUE PRECLUSION

§4.1 Purpose. Collateral estoppel, or issue preclusion, prevents a party from relitigating a particular fact issue that the party already litigated and lost in an earlier suit. *State & Cty. Mut. Fire Ins. v. Miller*, 52 S.W.3d 693, 696 (Tex.2001); *Quinney Elec., Inc. v. Kondos Entm't, Inc.*, 988 S.W.2d 212, 213 (Tex.1999); *Barr v. Resolution Trust Corp.*, 837 S.W.2d 627, 628 (Tex.1992); *Spera v. Fleming, Hovenkamp & Grayson, P.C.*, 25 S.W.3d 863, 869 (Tex. App.—Houston [14th Dist.] 2000, no pet.). To invoke collateral estoppel, a party must establish (1) the same facts sought to be litigated in the second suit were fully litigated in the first suit, (2) those facts were essential to the judgment in the first suit, and (3) the parties were cast as adversaries in the first suit. *Sysco Food Servs. v. Trapnell*, 890 S.W.2d 796, 801 (Tex.1994); *Eagle Props. Ltd. v. Scharbauer*, 807 S.W.2d 714, 721 (Tex.1990).

§4.2 Elements of collateral estoppel. The claim of collateral estoppel requires proof of the following elements:

1. Issues litigated.

(1) Same issue actually litigated. Collateral estoppel applies only if the issue was actually litigated in an earlier proceeding. *E.g.*, *Texas DPS v. Petta*, 44 S.W.3d 575, 579 (Tex.2001) (issue of whether P reasonably believed she faced imminent harm was litigated in P's criminal trial); *Johnson & Higgins v. Kenneco Energy, Inc.*, 962 S.W.2d 507, 521 (Tex.1998) (issue of contingency insurance was not litigated in federal court); *Housing Auth. v. Massey*, 878 S.W.2d 624, 626-27 (Tex.App.—Corpus Christi 1994, no writ) (collateral estoppel did not bar litigation of issues arising after first suit). "Actually litigated" means that an issue was raised by the pleadings or otherwise submitted for determination and was determined by the fact-finder. *Rexrode v. Bazar*, 937 S.W.2d 614, 617 (Tex.App.—Amarillo 1997, no writ). The issue decided in the first suit must be identical to the issue in the pending suit. *State & Cty. Mut. Fire Ins. v. Miller*, 52 S.W.3d 693, 696 (Tex.2001); *Petta*, 44 S.W.3d at 579. Collateral estoppel may bar relitigation of issues even if the later suit is based on a different cause of action. *Johnson & Higgins*, 962 S.W.2d at 521.

(2) Issue fully & fairly litigated. Collateral estoppel applies only if the issue was fully and fairly litigated in the first suit. *Miller*, 52 S.W.3d at 696; *Petta*, 44 S.W.3d at 579; *Sysco Food Servs. v. Trapnell*, 890 S.W.2d 796, 801 (Tex.1994); *e.g.*, *Rexrode*, 937 S.W.2d at 617 (P who sued D and D's insurer nonsuited D during trial; insurer granted directed verdict; P could not sue D again); *Phillips v. Allums*, 882 S.W.2d 71, 74-75 (Tex.App.—Houston [14th Dist.] 1994, writ denied) (D did not have full and fair opportunity to litigate issue of wrongful foreclosure in summary-judgment action); *Robbins v. HNG Oil Co.*, 878 S.W.2d 351, 357-58 (Tex.App.—Beaumont 1994, writ dism'd) (in first suit, 200 heirs sued Ds in federal court based on interpretation of deed, which was resolved against heirs; second suit, in which another heir sued based on same deed, was precluded by collateral estoppel).

2. Essential to judgment. Collateral estoppel applies only if the factual issues were essential to the first judgment. *Miller*, 52 S.W.3d at 696; *Sysco Food*, 890 S.W.2d at 801. To determine whether the same facts were essential to the first judgment, an attorney should remove those facts from the first judgment to see whether their absence changes the judgment. If it does, the facts were essential; if it does not, the facts were not essential. If the first judgment is based on the determination of two issues, either of which is sufficient to support the judgment, the judgment is not conclusive on either issue standing alone. *Eagle Props. Ltd. v. Scharbauer*, 807 S.W.2d 714, 722 (Tex. 1990); Restatement (2d) of Judgments §27 cmt. i; *see Parker v. State Farm Mut. Auto. Ins.*, 83 S.W.3d 179, 182

✫

(Tex.App.—San Antonio 2002, no pet.) (when jury refuses to find D negligent, its damages findings are not essential to the outcome of the lawsuit; thus, collateral estoppel does not bar relitigation of same damages in another suit). In other words, there generally cannot be collateral estoppel by alternative holdings in a trial court's judgment. *Johnson & Higgins*, 962 S.W.2d at 522. The rationale is that when a judgment is based on alternative findings, each finding may not have been as rigorously considered as it would have been if only one had been necessary for the result, and the losing party might have been dissuaded from appealing one issue because the other one might uphold the judgment. *Eagle Props.*, 807 S.W.2d at 722. There is an exception to this rule: if the judgment based on alternative holdings was appealed and affirmed on both grounds, the judgment is conclusive on both. *Johnson & Higgins*, 962 S.W.2d at 522; Restatement (2d) of Judgments §27 cmt. o.

3. Cast as adversaries. Collateral estoppel bars a party from relitigating an issue resolved in an earlier suit against the same party, someone in privity with that party, or someone whose interest was actually and adequately represented in the earlier trial. *Benson v. Wanda Pet. Co.*, 468 S.W.2d 361, 363 (Tex.1971); *see Sysco Food*, 890 S.W.2d at 802-03. Strict mutuality of parties is not required. *Petta*, 44 S.W.3d at 579; *Sysco Food*, 890 S.W.2d at 801. The party asserting collateral estoppel does not need to have been a party or in privity with a party to the earlier litigation; only the party against whom the plea is being asserted must have been a party or in privity with a party. *Eagle Props.*, 807 S.W.2d at 721; *Logan v. McDaniel*, 21 S.W.3d 683, 687-88 (Tex.App.—Austin 2000, pet. denied).

(1) Defensive collateral estoppel. A defendant uses defensive collateral estoppel to prevent a plaintiff from relitigating issues the plaintiff lost against another defendant. *Johnson & Higgins*, 962 S.W.2d at 519; *Texas Gen. Indem. Co. v. Texas Workers' Comp. Comm'n*, 36 S.W.3d 635, 638 (Tex.App.—Austin 2000, no pet.); *see, e.g., Hardy v. Fleming*, 553 S.W.2d 790, 791-92 (Tex.App.—El Paso 1977, writ ref'd n.r.e.) (in first suit, P sued employer under workers' compensation for an on-the-job heart attack, but jury found he did not have heart attack; in second suit, P sued doctor for malpractice for advising him he could return to work just before alleged heart attack; doctor used defense of collateral estoppel to prevent relitigation of whether P had heart attack). If the party defending the claim prevailed in the first suit, the judgment bars the relitigation of issues actually litigated and essential to the first suit. *Eagle Props.*, 807 S.W.2d at 721-22.

(2) Offensive collateral estoppel. A plaintiff uses offensive collateral estoppel to assert liability against a party who previously litigated and lost a fact issue. *Logan*, 21 S.W.3d at 687; *Trapnell v. Sysco Food Servs.*, 850 S.W.2d 529, 536 (Tex.App.—Corpus Christi 1992), *aff'd*, 890 S.W.2d 796 (Tex.1994).

§4.3 Exceptions to collateral estoppel.

1. Unfairness. The trial court has discretion to refuse to apply collateral estoppel when it is unfair to do so. *See Sysco Food Servs. v. Trapnell*, 890 S.W.2d 796, 804 (Tex.1994); *Scurlock Oil Co. v. Smithwick*, 724 S.W.2d 1, 7 (Tex.1986); *Tankersley v. Durish*, 855 S.W.2d 241, 245 (Tex.App.—Austin 1993, writ denied). In exercising its discretion, the trial court should consider the fairness factors discussed by the U.S. Supreme Court in *Parklane Hosiery Co. v. Shore*, 439 U.S. 322, 330-31 (1979). *Scurlock Oil*, 724 S.W.2d at 7; *Goldstein v. Commission for Lawyer Discipline*, 109 S.W.3d 810, 813 (Tex.App.—Dallas 2003, pet. denied).

2. Restatement exceptions. The exceptions to the general rule of collateral estoppel listed in Restatement (2d) of Judgments §28 are the following:

(1) The party against whom preclusion is sought could not, as a matter of law, have obtained review of the judgment in the initial action.

(2) The issue is one of law, and either (1) the two actions involve substantially unrelated claims, or (2) a new determination is warranted to take account of an intervening change in the applicable legal context or otherwise to avoid inequitable administration of the laws. *See, e.g., Sysco Food*, 890 S.W.2d at 804 (P was prevented by law from suing all Ds in federal court; collateral estoppel did not apply, giving P opportunity to bring claims against those Ds in state court); *see also Marino v. State Farm Fire & Cas. Ins.*, 787 S.W.2d 948, 949-50 (Tex.1990) (cause of action for bad faith was not barred by res judicata because it was based on rights acquired after first lawsuit and was not part of that cause of action).

RES JUDICATA & COLLATERAL ESTOPPEL

✦

(3)   A new determination of the issue is warranted by differences in the quality or extensiveness of the procedures followed in the two courts or by factors relating to the allocation of jurisdiction between them.

(4)   The party against whom preclusion is sought had a significantly heavier burden of persuasion on the issue in the first action than it had in the second action, the burden has shifted to its adversary, or the adversary has a significantly heavier burden than it had in the first action.

(5)   There is a clear and convincing need for a new determination of the issue because of one of the following: (1) the determination could have an adverse impact on the public interest or the interests of persons who were not parties in the initial action, (2) it was not sufficiently foreseeable at the time of the first action that the issue would arise in the context of another action, or (3) the party against whom preclusion is sought, as a result of the conduct of its adversary or other special circumstances, did not have an adequate opportunity or incentive to obtain a full and fair adjudication in the initial action. *See, e.g.*, ***Finger v. Southern Refrigeration Servs.***, 881 S.W.2d 890, 895-96 (Tex.App.—Houston [1st Dist.] 1994, writ denied) (suit was not barred because P, whom D sought to preclude, was improperly excluded from trial by D's motion for directed verdict on grounds that P had no damages; D argued to jury not to consider any damages to P who was excluded).

§5.   EFFECT OF PENDING APPEAL

A trial court's judgment is final for purposes of the preclusive effect of res judicata or collateral estoppel, even while the case is on appeal. ***Scurlock Oil Co. v. Smithwick***, 724 S.W.2d 1, 6 (Tex.1986); *see* Restatement (2d) of Judgments §13 cmt. b. This rule does not apply if the appeal is a trial de novo. ***Scurlock Oil***, 724 S.W.2d at 6.

✦

★

CHAPTER 10

★

---

10. POSTJUDGMENT MOTIONS

A. INTRODUCTION

To preserve a complaint for appeal, a party must make an objection or present a motion to the trial court and obtain a ruling. TRAP 33 requires that most appellate complaints be presented first to the trial court. See "Preserving Error," ch. 1-F, §4, p. 45. Immediately after trial, the attorney should mentally review the record and ask: Did the trial court do anything or refuse to do anything that the party wants to complain about on appeal? The attorney should make a list and check it against the record to see if, on each matter, there was a request, an objection, or a motion and either a ruling or a refusal to rule. If the attorney did not make a request, make an objection, make a motion, or get a ruling, the attorney may be able to preserve the complaint in a post-trial motion. As long as the trial court has plenary power over the case, a party may ask the trial court to make a written ruling on an issue raised during the trial.

Some complaints can be made for the first time only in a post-trial motion. Postjudgment motions are thus the absolute last chance to preserve error for appeal.

B. MOTION FOR NEW TRIAL

§1. GENERAL

§1.1 Rules. TRCP 306c, 320-329b; TRAP 33.1. See Gov't Code §51.317(b)(2) ($15 filing fee).

§1.2 Purpose. In a motion for new trial, a party asks the trial court to reconsider and rectify trial error—the court's rulings or the jury's findings—by granting a new trial. *Smith v. Brock*, 514 S.W.2d 140, 142 (Tex.App.—Texarkana 1974, no writ); *see Barry v. Barry*, 193 S.W.3d 72, 74 (Tex.App.—Houston [1st Dist.] 2006, no pet.) (MNT must, by its very nature, seek to set aside existing judgment and request relitigation of issues). There are at least three reasons to file a motion for new trial: (1) to give the trial court one last chance to correct what the appellant will claim on appeal is reversible error, (2) to preserve that error for appeal, and (3) to extend the appellate deadlines. A party has the right to file a motion for new trial merely to extend the timetables for the appeal, even if there are no reasonable grounds for a new trial. *Old Republic Ins. v. Scott*, 846 S.W.2d 832, 833 (Tex.1993).

§1.3 Timetable & forms. Timetable, Appeal to the Court of Appeals, p. 1235; *O'Connor's Texas Civil Forms* (2012), FORMS 10B.

§1.4 Other references. Brown & Rondon, *Texas Rules of Evidence Handbook* (2013) (referred to as Brown & Rondon, *Evidence Handbook*); Copeland, Comment, *Room Without a View: Inquiries Into Jury Misconduct After the Adoption of Texas Rule of Evidence 606(b)*, 38 Baylor L.Rev. 965 (1986); O'Connor, *Appealing Jury Findings*, 12 Hous.L.Rev. 65 (1974); *O'Connor's Texas Civil Appeals* (2012) (*O'Connor's Texas Appeals*).

§2. MOTION

§2.1 When MNT necessary. TRCP 324(b) lists most of the complaints that must be urged in a motion for new trial to preserve error for appeal. In the appeal of a jury trial, the party must file a motion for new trial in the following instances.

NOTE

A motion for new trial is not necessary to preserve most errors in a nonjury trial. See "MNT After Nonjury Trial," §15, p. 808.

---

1. To preserve post-trial complaints on which evidence must be heard—for example: • Jury misconduct. TRCP 324(b)(1). • Newly discovered evidence. *Id.* • Failure to set aside a default judgment. *Id.* • Lack of consent to an agreed judgment. *Sohocki v. Sohocki*, 897 S.W.2d 422, 424 (Tex.App.—Corpus Christi 1995, no writ). • Challenge to an award of fees to a guardian ad litem. *Navistar Int'l v. Valles*, 740 S.W.2d 4, 6 (Tex.App.—El Paso 1987, no writ).

✦

2. To preserve the complaint that the evidence is factually insufficient to support a jury finding or, conversely, that the jury finding is against the overwhelming weight of the evidence. TRCP 324(b)(2), (b)(3); *Fredonia State Bank v. General Am. Life Ins.*, 881 S.W.2d 279, 281 (Tex.1994); *Cecil v. Smith*, 804 S.W.2d 509, 512 (Tex. 1991). See "MNT to Challenge the Evidence," §13, p. 802.

3. To preserve the complaint that the jury's damages are inadequate or excessive. TRCP 324(b)(4); *Hawthorne v. Guenther*, 917 S.W.2d 924, 937 (Tex.App.—Beaumont 1996, writ denied).

4. To preserve the complaint of incurable jury argument if the trial court did not already rule on it. TRCP 324(b)(5); *Warrantech Corp. v. Computer Adapters Servs.*, 134 S.W.3d 516, 531 n.10 (Tex.App.—Fort Worth 2004, no pet.).

5. To preserve complaints not brought to the trial court's attention during the trial or included in some other post-trial motion. *See* TRCP 324(a), (b) (listing complaints that require MNT to preserve error); TRAP 33.1(a)(1) (complaint is preserved for appellate review by presenting it to trial court and obtaining a ruling); *see, e.g.*, *Luna v. Southern Pac. Transp.*, 724 S.W.2d 383, 384 (Tex.1987) (complaint about apportionment of damages was waived because it was not preserved in MNT or earlier).

§2.2 In writing. The motion for new trial must be in writing and signed by the attorney or the party. TRCP 320.

§2.3 Points of error. The motion for new trial must list the complaints in the points of error. TRCP 321. The complaints in the points must be specific. TRCP 322. The party should state what happened and why it was error. The points should cover the "who," "what," and "why" of the complaint. For example:

> *The trial court (who) erred in overruling the defendant's objections that jury question number 4 contained a comment on the evidence (what) because the question assumed as true that the defendant was negligent (why).*

On appeal, these points can be used as the statement of the issues presented in the brief. *See* TRAP 38.1(f) (in appellate briefs, parties must "state concisely all issues or points presented for review"); *Gerdes v. Kennamer*, 155 S.W.3d 523, 532 (Tex.App.—Corpus Christi 2004, pet. denied) (issues raised on appeal must correspond with motion made to trial court).

§2.4 Prayer. The motion for new trial must include a request to relitigate the case. *Barry v. Barry*, 193 S.W.3d 72, 74 (Tex.App.—Houston [1st Dist.] 2006, no pet.); *Mercer v. Band*, 454 S.W.2d 833, 836 (Tex.App.—Houston [14th Dist.] 1970, no writ); *see, e.g.*, *Finley v. J.C. Pace Ltd.*, 4 S.W.3d 319, 320 (Tex.App.—Houston [1st Dist.] 1999, order) (although motion requested rehearing, it was MNT because it sought to set aside judgment for the purpose of litigating the issues). If the motion asks for other relief (e.g., to enter a different judgment), it is not a motion for new trial. *Mercer*, 454 S.W.2d at 836.

§2.5 Effect of MNT.

1. On plenary power. The timely filing of a motion for new trial extends the trial court's plenary power over the judgment. The exact date to which the plenary power is extended depends on whether the motion is denied or granted and on what date it is denied or granted. If the motion is denied, plenary power is extended until 30 days after the motion is denied, either by written order or by operation of law, whichever occurs first; but it cannot be extended more than 105 days after the date the judgment was signed. *Lane Bank Equip. Co. v. Smith S. Equip., Inc.*, 10 S.W.3d 308, 310 (Tex.2000). If the motion is granted, plenary power is extended no more than 75 days after the date the judgment was signed. See "Finality for purposes of changing the judgment," ch. 9-C, §6.5, p. 775; "Plenary-Power Deadlines," chart 9-1, p. 778.

2. On appellate deadlines. See "Calculating appellate deadlines," ch. 9-C, §9.1, p. 778.

§3. VERIFICATION & AFFIDAVITS

It is usually not necessary to verify most motions for new trial or to attach affidavits. For example, sworn proof is not necessary to challenge the sufficiency of the evidence.

—————————————— ✪ ——————————————

§3.1 When verification required. It is necessary to verify a motion for new trial and include affidavits when the motion is based on the grounds listed in TRCP 324(b)(1) (jury misconduct, newly discovered evidence, failure to set aside a default judgment) or on any other ground that requires the presentation of evidence at a hearing. *See Zuniga v. Zuniga*, 13 S.W.3d 798, 803 n.4 (Tex.App.—San Antonio 1999, no pet.), *disapproved on other grounds*, *In re Z.L.T.*, 124 S.W.3d 163 (Tex.2003). See "Verification," ch. 1-B, §3.2.15, p. 11; "Affidavits," ch. 1-B, §3.2.16, p. 11; *O'Connor's Texas Forms*, FORMS 1B:6, 7. When in doubt, parties should verify the motion. For the requirements for using an unsworn declaration instead of a verification or an affidavit, see "Unsworn declaration," ch. 1-B, §3.2.14, p. 10; *O'Connor's Texas Forms*, FORM 1B:8.

§3.2 Controverting affidavits. When the movant files a motion with affidavits, the nonmovant should consider filing controverting affidavits. On appeal, if there is no recorded hearing and no controverting affidavits, the appellate court will assume the movant's affidavit is true. *Director, State Empls. Workers' Comp. Div. v. Evans*, 889 S.W.2d 266, 268-69 (Tex.1994); *Onyeanu v. Rivertree Apts. & Guar. Builders, Inc.*, 920 S.W.2d 397, 398 (Tex. App.—Houston [1st Dist.] 1996, no writ).

§4. FILING FEE FOR MNT

§4.1 Amount & timing of fee. A $15 filing fee must be paid at the time a motion for new trial is filed. Gov't Code §51.317(b)(2). Before filing, the attorney should check with the court clerk to see if the county has other fees. For example, the filing fee for a motion for new trial in Harris County is $36, and Bexar County has two fees for civil cases—$20 for family-law cases and $25 for other civil cases. There will be an additional fee, not more than $5, for court-records archiving. Gov't Code §51.317(b)(5).

§4.2 MNT timely but fee late. If a motion for new trial is filed without payment of the fee, the document is considered "conditionally filed" on the date it was tendered to the clerk. *Jamar v. Patterson*, 868 S.W.2d 318, 319 (Tex.1993). When the filing fee is paid, the document is deemed filed on the date it was originally tendered. *Id.* Case law distinguishes between the effect of late payment on appellate deadlines and on the preservation of error of the issues in the motion for new trial.

1. Late fee & appellate deadlines. The payment of the filing fee has no effect on the appellate deadlines; the appellate deadlines are extended even when the filing fee for a motion for new trial is never paid. *Garza v. Garcia*, 137 S.W.3d 36, 37-38 (Tex.2004) (fee not paid); *Tate v. E.I. DuPont de Nemours & Co.*, 934 S.W.2d 83, 84 (Tex.1996) (fee paid late).

2. Late fee & preservation of error.

(1) Paid before loss of plenary power.

(a) Before MNT overruled. When the filing fee for a motion for new trial is paid before the trial court loses plenary power and before the motion is overruled, the motion probably preserves error for appeal. *See Jamar*, 868 S.W.2d at 319 n.3 (trial court should not consider MNT before fee is paid).

(b) After MNT overruled. When the filing fee for a motion for new trial is paid before the trial court loses plenary power but after the motion is overruled, it is uncertain whether the motion preserves error for appeal. *See Tate*, 934 S.W.2d at 84 n.1 (Supreme Court refused to resolve issue).

(2) Paid after loss of plenary power. When the filing fee for a motion for new trial is paid after the trial court loses plenary power, the motion does not preserve error for those issues that must be preserved in a motion for new trial. *See, e.g.*, *Garza*, 137 S.W.3d at 38 (trial court was not required to review factual-sufficiency complaint in MNT because fee was never paid); *Marathon Corp. v. Pitzner*, 55 S.W.3d 114, 123-25 (Tex.App.—Corpus Christi 2001) (appellate court refused to consider D's factual-sufficiency points), *rev'd on other grounds*, 106 S.W.3d 724 (Tex.2003).

§5. DEADLINES FOR MNT

§5.1 Original MNT. A motion for new trial must be filed within 30 days after the date the judgment was signed. TRCP 329b(a); *Padilla v. LaFrance*, 907 S.W.2d 454, 458 (Tex.1995); *Jamar v. Patterson*, 868 S.W.2d 318, 319 (Tex.

✦

1993); *see, e.g.*, ***Williams v. Flores***, 88 S.W.3d 631, 632 (Tex.2002) (MNT timely filed on 32nd day after judgment because 30th day was Sunday and 31st day was legal holiday). A motion for new trial filed more than 30 days after the judgment was signed is void and cannot be considered by the appellate courts. *See **Equinox Enters. v. Associated Media Inc.***, 730 S.W.2d 872, 875 (Tex.App.—Dallas 1987, no writ).

§5.2 No extensions. TRCP 5 prohibits the trial court from extending the time period "for taking any action under the rules relating to new trials." ***Moritz v. Preiss***, 121 S.W.3d 715, 720 (Tex.2003); ***Lind v. Gresham***, 672 S.W.2d 20, 22 (Tex.App.—Houston [14th Dist.] 1984, no writ). Thus, the trial court cannot grant an extension of time to file the motion for new trial. ***Moritz***, 121 S.W.3d at 720; ***Lind***, 672 S.W.2d at 22. If the court signs a modified judgment within its plenary power and changes the date, however, the modified judgment acts as a new judgment that gives the parties another 30 days to file a motion for new trial. ***Check v. Mitchell***, 758 S.W.2d 755, 756 (Tex.1988); *see* TRCP 329b(h) (if judgment is modified "in any respect, the time for appeal shall run" from date of modified judgment). See "Motion to Modify the Judgment," ch. 10-D, p. 814.

§5.3 Late MNT + plenary power. Even though the trial court cannot extend the time to file the motion for new trial, it can grant a new trial on the grounds stated in a late motion if the motion is filed before the court loses plenary power. ***Moritz v. Preiss***, 121 S.W.3d 715, 720 (Tex.2003); *see* TRCP 320. The court is not actually granting the late motion; it is granting a new trial on its own initiative. The late motion is meaningless for preserving error for appeal, but the grounds stated in the motion may convince the trial court that a new trial is necessary. *See **Moritz***, 121 S.W.3d at 720; ***Kalteyer v. Sneed***, 837 S.W.2d 848, 851 (Tex.App.—Austin 1992, no writ).

§5.4 Premature MNT. A premature motion for new trial, filed before the judgment is signed, is deemed filed on the day of, but immediately after, the signing of the judgment. TRCP 306c; ***Ryland Enter. v. Weatherspoon***, 355 S.W.3d 664, 666 (Tex.2011); ***Padilla v. LaFrance***, 907 S.W.2d 454, 458 (Tex.1995).

§5.5 Amended MNT. An amended or supplemental motion for new trial is timely and may be filed without leave of court if it is filed within 30 days of the judgment and the trial court has not overruled the earlier motion for new trial. ***In re Brookshire Grocery Co.***, 250 S.W.3d 66, 69-70 (Tex.2008). Even if filed with leave of court, an amended motion for new trial is not timely for purposes of extending plenary power if it is filed after an earlier motion for new trial was overruled. *Id.* at 71. A timely amended or supplemental motion for new trial preserves complaints for appeal. *See **Moritz v. Preiss***, 121 S.W.3d 715, 721 (Tex.2003) (untimely amended MNT does not preserve issues for appellate review, even if they arose after court overruled earlier MNT).

NOTE

A trial court has discretion to consider an untimely amended motion for new trial as long as it has plenary power. ***In re Brookshire Grocery***, *250 S.W.3d at 71-72 & n.8. But an untimely amended motion for new trial can only provide the court with guidance in the exercise of its inherent authority.* ***Moritz***, *121 S.W.3d at 720. Because an untimely amended motion for new trial does not preserve complaints for appeal, a party should wait as long as possible to file an original motion for new trial to reduce the risk that it will waive issues on appeal.* ***In re Brookshire Grocery***, *250 S.W.3d at 75 (Hecht, J., dissenting).*

---

§5.6 Second-judgment problems.

1. Preservation of error. When the trial court corrects the judgment by signing a second judgment, a motion for new trial filed to challenge the first judgment is effective for the second judgment if the substance of the motion challenges the second judgment. ***Fredonia State Bank v. General Am. Life Ins.***, 881 S.W.2d 279, 281 (Tex. 1994); *see* TRAP 27.3.

2. Extending appellate deadlines. A motion for new trial filed after the first judgment, but not granted, is a prematurely filed motion as to a second judgment, and it extends the appellate timetable from the signing of the second judgment if the grounds in the motion "assail" the second judgment. TRCP 306c; ***Wilkins v. Methodist Health***

✯

Care Sys., 160 S.W.3d 559, 562 (Tex.2005); *see* TRAP 27.2; *see also Padilla v. LaFrance*, 907 S.W.2d 454, 458 (Tex. 1995) (motion for reconsideration of first judgment, filed before second judgment, extended appellate deadlines). However, a motion for new trial that is granted after the first judgment does not assail the second judgment for purposes of determining the appellate timetable. *Wilkins*, 160 S.W.3d at 564. In such a case, the motion for new trial is not prematurely filed as to the second judgment, and thus the appellate deadlines are not extended. *E.g., id.* (because MNT was granted before second judgment, notice of appeal was due 30 days after second judgment, not 90 days after).

§5.7 Late notice of judgment. If a party receives notice of the judgment 21 to 90 days after the judgment was signed, the deadline for filing a motion for new trial is counted from the date the party actually learned of or received notice of the judgment, rather than the date the judgment was signed. TRCP 306a(4), (5). See "Motion to Extend Postjudgment Deadlines," ch. 10-G, p. 831.

§5.8 MNT after citation by publication. The defendant may file a motion for new trial within two years after the court signs a judgment after citation by publication. TRCP 329(a); *Montgomery v. R.E.C. Interests, Inc.*, 130 S.W.3d 444, 445 n.1 (Tex.App.—Texarkana 2004, no pet.). The same is true if a judgment was signed after the citation was posted on the courthouse door. *Gray v. PHI Res.*, 710 S.W.2d 566, 568 (Tex.1986). See "MNT After Service by Publication," §10, p. 799.

§5.9 After domesticated foreign judgment. Under the Uniform Enforcement of Foreign Judgments Act (UEFJA), CPRC §35.003, a plaintiff's filing of an authenticated copy of a foreign judgment in a Texas court constitutes both the plaintiff's original petition and a final Texas judgment. *Walnut Equip. Leasing Co. v. Wu*, 920 S.W.2d 285, 286 (Tex.1996). The defendant must file a motion for new trial within 30 days after the petition is filed. *Moncrief v. Harvey*, 805 S.W.2d 20, 23 (Tex.App.—Dallas 1991, no writ); *see Walnut Equip.*, 920 S.W.2d at 286. Any motion to contest the enforcement of a foreign judgment under the UEFJA operates as a motion for new trial. *Moncrief*, 805 S.W.2d at 23; *e.g., Wolf v. Andreas*, 276 S.W.3d 23, 26 (Tex.App.—El Paso 2008, no pet.) (counterclaim for declaratory judgment and injunctive relief was considered postjudgment motion).

§6. RESPONSE

When the movant files an unsworn motion for new trial, the nonmovant probably does not need to file a response. However, because some local rules infer acquiescence when the nonmovant does not file a response, the nonmovant's attorney should always check the local rules. *See, e.g.*, Harris Cty. Loc. R. 3.3.2 (district courts; not filing response can be considered representation of no opposition). When the movant files a sworn motion for new trial, the nonmovant should file a sworn response. See *O'Connor's Texas Forms*, FORM 10B:7.

§7. HEARING

§7.1 Unsworn MNT – no hearing. Most motions for new trial do not require a hearing. The hearing on an unsworn motion is for argument only, and no evidence may be presented.

§7.2 Sworn MNT – hearing. If a motion for new trial requires sworn evidence to support it, it also requires a hearing to receive evidence. The types of motions for new trial that require a hearing include jury misconduct, newly discovered evidence, failure to set aside a default judgment, and any other motion that must be supported by evidence. *See, e.g., Hensley v. Salinas*, 583 S.W.2d 617, 618 (Tex.1979) (hearing required for MNT challenging agreed judgment); *Navistar Int'l v. Valles*, 740 S.W.2d 4, 6 (Tex.App.—El Paso 1987, no writ) (hearing required for MNT challenging attorney ad litem fees). A party is not entitled to a hearing unless it has filed a sworn motion with specific allegations. *See, e.g., Hatton v. Highlands Ins.*, 631 S.W.2d 787, 789 (Tex.App.—Tyler 1982, no writ) (affidavit attached to MNT based on jury misconduct specified acts of misconduct and names of jurors who committed misconduct).

1. Setting. When a motion for new trial requires a hearing, the movant must ask the court for a setting and not allow its motion to be overruled by operation of law. *See Shamrock Roofing Sup. v. Mercantile Nat'l Bank*, 703 S.W.2d 356, 357-58 (Tex.App.—Dallas 1985, no writ). *But see Limestone Constr., Inc. v. Summit Commercial*

———————————————— ✫ ————————————————

Indus. Props., Inc., 143 S.W.3d 538, 546 (Tex.App.—Austin 2004, no pet.) (because movant's affidavit established right to MNT, nonmovant had burden to request hearing).

2. Affidavits. When affidavits are filed as part of a motion for new trial, the proponent of the affidavits is not required to introduce them into evidence at the hearing on the motion. *Director, State Empls. Workers' Comp. Div. v. Evans*, 889 S.W.2d 266, 268 (Tex.1994). It is sufficient that the affidavits are attached to the motion for new trial and made part of the record. *Id.*

§8. ORDER

§8.1 In writing. The trial court's order on a motion for new trial must be in writing and signed by the trial court. TRCP 329b(c); *In re Lovito-Nelson*, 278 S.W.3d 773, 775 (Tex.2009); *In re Barber*, 982 S.W.2d 364, 366 (Tex.1998). See "In writing," ch. 1-G, §3.1, p. 49; *O'Connor's Texas Forms*, FORM 10B:8. The trial court's oral pronouncement and docket entry are not substitutes for a written order. *In re Lovito-Nelson*, 278 S.W.3d at 775; *Faulkner v. Culver*, 851 S.W.2d 187, 188 (Tex.1993); *see also Estate of Townes v. Wood*, 934 S.W.2d 806, 807 (Tex.App.—Houston [1st Dist.] 1996, orig. proceeding) (written, signed order setting case for trial is not substitute for written, signed order granting MNT). See "Not an order," ch. 1-G, §3.3.1, p. 49.

§8.2 Grounds. The trial court has broad discretion in granting a new trial. *In re Columbia Med. Ctr.*, 290 S.W.3d 204, 210 (Tex.2009). A new trial may be granted "for good cause, on motion or on the court's own motion." TRCP 320; *In re Columbia Med. Ctr.*, 290 S.W.3d at 210. The court must clearly identify its specific reasons for granting a new trial. *In re Columbia Med. Ctr.*, 290 S.W.3d at 212.

CAUTION

Broad statements like "in the interest of justice" are no longer adequate for granting a new trial. In re Columbia Med. Ctr., 290 S.W.3d at 215. The Supreme Court has disapproved of prior cases granting a new trial in the interest of justice and held that an order must clearly specify the reasons for granting the new trial. Id. at 213.

---

§8.3 Partial new trial. TRCP 320 permits the trial court to grant a new trial on part of the case under the following conditions:

1. Separable. The matter is clearly separable. TRCP 320; *State Dept. of Hwys. & Pub. Transp. v. Cotner*, 845 S.W.2d 818, 819 (Tex.1993); *see also Satellite Earth Stations E., Inc. v. Davis*, 756 S.W.2d 385, 387 (Tex. App.—Eastland 1988, writ denied) (when attorney fees are mandatory, they are clearly separable). To determine what is separable, consult TRCP 41 and 174(b). A partial new trial may be ordered despite the prohibition in TRCP 41 against postsubmission severances; thus, TRCP 320 is an exception to TRCP 41. *Cotner*, 845 S.W.2d at 819.

2. Not unfair. The matter is separable without unfairness to the parties. TRCP 320; *see, e.g., Cotner*, 845 S.W.2d at 819 (in PI suit, court could not grant partial new trial to one P and affirm for other P).

3. Liquidated damages. The damages are liquidated, or the damages are unliquidated and liability is not contested. The court cannot grant a partial new trial on unliquidated damages if liability is contested. TRCP 320; *see Redman Homes, Inc. v. Ivy*, 920 S.W.2d 664, 669 (Tex.1996).

§8.4 Deadline to sign order on MNT. The court should sign an order granting or denying the motion within 75 days after the date the judgment was signed; if not, the motion is overruled by operation of law on the 76th day after the date the judgment was signed. TRCP 329b(c) ("overruled by operation of law on expiration of" 75 days); *Thomas v. Oldham*, 895 S.W.2d 352, 356 (Tex.1995) (court may grant MNT within 75 days after judgment was signed); *see In re Dickason*, 987 S.W.2d 570, 571 (Tex.1998) (trial court has plenary power for 75 days). On two separate occasions, the Supreme Court has mistakenly said that a motion for new trial is overruled by operation of law on the 75th day, instead of "on expiration of" 75 days. *See Faulkner v. Culver*, 851 S.W.2d 187, 188 (Tex.1993) (MNT

———————————————— ✪ ————————————————

was overruled by operation of law 75 days after judgment was signed); ***Clark & Co. v. Giles***, 639 S.W.2d 449, 450 (Tex.1982) (MNT was overruled by operation of law on 75th day).

§8.5 Deadline to change order on MNT. The court can change its order on the motion for new trial as long as it has plenary power over the judgment. To determine when plenary power expires, see "Plenary-Power Deadlines," chart 9-1, p. 778.

1. When MNT granted. When a trial court grants a motion for new trial, it retains ongoing plenary power over the case and can set aside the new trial order anytime before it signs another final judgment. See "MNT granted + order 'ungranted'," ch. 9-C, §6.5.2(3)(a)[2], p. 777.

2. When MNT overruled. When the motion for new trial is overruled (either by written order or by operation of law), the court has the power to grant a new trial as long as it has plenary power over the judgment—that is, 30 days after the date the motion was overruled, but not later than 105 days after the date the judgment was signed. TRCP 329b(c), (e); ***L.M. Healthcare, Inc. v. Childs***, 929 S.W.2d 442, 444 (Tex.1996). See "PPE motion overruled," ch. 9-C, §6.5.2(2), p. 776.

§9. MNT AFTER DEFAULT JUDGMENT

Most default judgments are granted because a defendant does not file an answer (no-answer default) or does not appear for trial or another dispositive hearing (post-answer default).

§9.1 Sworn motion. Before filing a motion for new trial to challenge a default judgment, the party should determine how and when the default judgment was rendered. Was the judgment rendered before or after the defendant answered? Was service on the defendant defective? Did the defendant have notice of the trial? How much time has passed since the judgment was rendered? A motion for new trial is not the only way to challenge a default judgment. For other ways, see "Attacking the Default Judgment," ch. 7-A, §7, p. 598.

1. Improper service + no-answer default.

(1) Defects in service of process & plaintiff's petition. To challenge a no-answer default judgment rendered after improper service of process, the motion for new trial should object to any deficiencies in the service documents and the plaintiff's petition.

(a) Deficiencies in citation. The defendant should challenge defects in the citation. The citation must meet all the requirements of TRCP 15 and 99. See "Requirements for the Citation," ch. 2-H, §2, p. 158; *O'Connor's Texas Forms*, FORM 10B:3, §A.

(b) Deficiencies in service. The defendant should challenge defects in the service of the process. See "Sufficiency of service," ch. 7-A, §3.4, p. 589; *O'Connor's Texas Forms*, FORM 10B:3, §B.

(c) Deficiencies in return. The defendant should challenge defects in the return of the service. The return must meet all the requirements of TRCP 107. See "Proof of Service – The Return," ch. 2-H, §9, p. 168; *O'Connor's Texas Forms*, FORM 10B:3; §F.

(d) Deficiencies in plaintiff's petition. The defendant should challenge defects in the plaintiff's petition. A plaintiff's petition will support a default judgment if it (1) attempts to state a cause of action within the court's jurisdiction against a defendant who is amenable to process, (2) gives fair notice to the defendant of its claim, and (3) does not affirmatively disclose the invalidity of its claim. ***Paramount Pipe & Sup. Co. v. Muhr***, 749 S.W.2d 491, 494 (Tex.1988); ***Stoner v. Thompson***, 578 S.W.2d 679, 684-85 (Tex.1979). For cases on the sufficiency of the plaintiff's petition, see "Plaintiff's Original Petition," ch. 2-B, p. 95; "Sufficiency of plaintiff's petition," ch. 7-A, §3.2, p. 588; *O'Connor's Texas Forms*, FORM 10B:3, §H.

(2) *Craddock* factors. If the defendant asserts that it did not file an answer because of improper service and proves that service was improper, the defendant does not need to establish the factors from ***Craddock v. Sunshine Bus Lines, Inc.***, 133 S.W.2d 124, 126 (Tex.1939), to be entitled to a new trial. *See **Sutherland v. Spencer***, 376 S.W.3d 752, 755 (Tex.2012); ***Fidelity & Guar. Ins. v. Drewery Constr. Co.***, 186 S.W.3d 571, 574 (Tex.2006);

───────────────── ✦ ─────────────────

Kaminetzky v. Newman, No. 01-10-01113-CV (Tex.App.—Houston [1st Dist.] 2011, no pet.) (memo op.; 12-29-11); *cf. Peralta v. Heights Med. Ctr., Inc.*, 485 U.S. 80, 86 (1988) (bill of review; when no-answer default is rendered against D after improper service and D had no notice of judgment, D is not required to prove meritorious defense to be entitled to new trial). Even if the defendant has actual notice of the lawsuit, without proper service, the defendant has no duty to act; thus, the court cannot render a default judgment. *Wilson v. Dunn*, 800 S.W.2d 833, 837 (Tex. 1990); *see Fidelity & Guar. Ins.*, 186 S.W.3d at 574 n.1 (receiving suit papers or actual notice through procedure not authorized for service is treated the same as never receiving them). If the defendant is uncertain whether the court will sustain its argument that it did not receive proper service or notice, the defendant should allege and prove the three *Craddock* factors as an alternative ground for reversal. See "Failure to answer or appear after proper notice," §9.1.3, this page.

2. No notice of trial + post-answer default.

(1) Allege no notice. When a post-answer default is rendered without proper notice, the motion should allege and prove that the defendant did not receive notice of the trial or dispositive hearing. See "Notice of the trial or dispositive hearing," ch. 7-A, §4.3, p. 596. Proof of lack of notice satisfies the first prong from *Craddock* because, without notice, a defendant cannot intentionally or with conscious indifference fail to appear. *Texas Sting, Ltd. v. R.B. Foods, Inc.*, 82 S.W.3d 644, 651-52 (Tex.App.—San Antonio 2002, pet. denied). See "Failure to answer or appear after proper notice," §9.1.3, this page; *O'Connor's Texas Forms*, FORM 10B:4, §A.

(2) Other *Craddock* factors unnecessary. If a defendant is able to prove lack of notice of the trial or dispositive hearing, the defendant does not need to establish the remaining *Craddock* factors to be entitled to a new trial. *See Mathis v. Lockwood*, 166 S.W.3d 743, 744 (Tex.2005) (if first *Craddock* factor is established, D does not have to prove meritorious defense); *Lopez v. Lopez*, 757 S.W.2d 721, 723 (Tex.1988) (same); *Mahand v. Delaney*, 60 S.W.3d 371, 375 (Tex.App.—Houston [1st Dist.] 2001, no pet.) (if first *Craddock* factor is established, D does not have to prove meritorious defense or no delay or injury to P). See "Failure to answer or appear after proper notice," §9.1.3, this page. Once a defendant makes an appearance, it is entitled to notice of the trial setting as a matter of due process under the 14th Amendment to the U.S. Constitution. *LBL Oil Co. v. International Power Servs.*, 777 S.W.2d 390, 390-91 (Tex.1989).

(3) Allege *Craddock* factors in alternative. If the defendant is uncertain whether the court will sustain its argument that it did not receive proper notice, the defendant should allege and prove the three *Craddock* factors as an alternative ground for reversal. See "Failure to answer or appear after proper notice," §9.1.3, this page; *O'Connor's Texas Forms*, FORM 10B:4, §B.

3. Failure to answer or appear after proper notice.

When a default judgment is rendered against a defendant who had notice of the suit, trial, or hearing but did not file an answer to the suit or did not appear at a trial or hearing, the motion for new trial should allege the three elements listed below from *Craddock*. *Sutherland*, 376 S.W.3d at 755; *see Fidelity & Guar. Ins.*, 186 S.W.3d at 574; *Director, State Empls. Workers' Comp. Div. v. Evans*, 889 S.W.2d 266, 268 (Tex.1994); *Old Republic Ins. v. Scott*, 873 S.W.2d 381, 382 (Tex.1994). When the defendant has notice of the trial and its attorney appears but the defendant does not, the defendant is not entitled to argue the *Craddock* factors. *In re K.C.*, 88 S.W.3d 277, 279 (Tex.App.—San Antonio 2002, pet. denied). When a defendant establishes the *Craddock* factors, the trial court must set aside the default judgment. *Evans*, 889 S.W.2d at 268. See *O'Connor's Texas Forms*, FORMS 10B:3, §I, 10B:4, §B.

(1) Not intentional, but accidental. The defendant must show that its failure to file an answer or appear at a hearing was not intentional or the result of conscious indifference but was due to a mistake or accident. *Sutherland*, 376 S.W.3d at 754; *Dolgencorp v. Lerma*, 288 S.W.3d 922, 925 (Tex.2009); *In re R.R.*, 209 S.W.3d 112, 114 (Tex.2006); *Craddock*, 133 S.W.2d at 126. A mistake of law may satisfy this requirement. *Bank One v. Moody*, 830 S.W.2d 81, 85 (Tex.1992). However, not every mistake of law is sufficient. *Id.* at 84. "Not intentional" and "mistake or accident" are only one element, not two. *Id.* at 82-83. If the factual allegations in the defendant's motion and affidavits negate conscious indifference and the plaintiff does not controvert these allegations, the court must find

✦

that the defendant's failure to answer was the result of a mistake or accident. *Milestone Oper., Inc. v. Exxon-Mobil Corp.*, ___ S.W.3d ___ (Tex.2012) (No. 11-0647; 10-26-12); *Sutherland*, 376 S.W.3d at 755; *see Fidelity & Guar. Ins.*, 186 S.W.3d at 575-76; *Scott*, 873 S.W.2d at 382. See "Uncontroverted motion," §9.5.2, p. 799. The *Craddock* standard is that the defendant knew it was sued but did not care. *Sutherland*, 376 S.W.3d at 755; *Fidelity & Guar. Ins.*, 186 S.W.3d at 575-76; *e.g.*, *Levine v. Shackelford, Melton & McKinley, L.L.P*, 248 S.W.3d 166, 168-69 (Tex.2008) (pattern of ignoring deadlines and warnings from opposing party amounted to conscious indifference). Even a bad excuse can be sufficient to disprove conscious indifference. *Milestone Oper.*, ___ S.W.3d at ___; *Sutherland*, 376 S.W.3d at 755; *In re R.R.*, 209 S.W.3d at 115; *Fidelity & Guar. Ins.*, 186 S.W.3d at 576.

(a) **Failure to answer or appear = accident.** Default judgments in the following cases were reversed because the defendant pleaded and proved its failure to answer or appear was accidental. • Defendant's agent testified that he did not remember being served and had not turned over any suit papers to defendant's attorney, which was his normal procedure for responding to service of suit papers; plaintiff did not controvert the testimony. *Milestone Oper.*, ___ S.W.3d at ___. • The citation was left in a stack of papers on a desk and forgotten because the defendants spent limited time at the office due to weather conditions over a nearly three-week period during the Christmas holiday season. *Sutherland*, 376 S.W.3d at 755. • Attorney informed court of conflicting preferential trial setting in another county before trial and reasonably believed court would delay the trial. *Dolgencorp*, 288 S.W.3d at 927. • Defendant's registered agent received the petition and citation but could not verify that the documents were ever forwarded to the defendant; affidavits detailing procedures for handling service documents negated conscious indifference. *Fidelity & Guar. Ins.*, 186 S.W.3d at 575-76. • Because the executors were unaware of the suit when the Secretary of State was served on their behalf, their failure to answer was not intentional. *Estate of Pollack v. McMurrey*, 858 S.W.2d 388, 391 (Tex.1993). • In a writ-of-garnishment proceeding, the bank president testified the bank did not file an answer because he thought the bank had complied with procedures. *Bank One*, 830 S.W.2d at 84-85. • Defendant's office staff misplaced the citation it was supposed to send to attorney. *Strackbein v. Prewitt*, 671 S.W.2d 37, 39 (Tex.1984); *see also In re A.P.P.*, 74 S.W.3d 570, 574 (Tex.App.—Corpus Christi 2002, no pet.) (D's coworker delivered notice and petition to attorney's office, where notice was inadvertently misfiled). • Defendant searched his house after receiving an inquiry about the lawsuit, found the citation, and took it to the insurance company the next day. *Ward v. Nava*, 488 S.W.2d 736, 737-38 (Tex.1972). • Defendant's attorney thought only one suit was filed and assumed additional petitions e-mailed to him were duplicates of original. *Titan Indem. Co. v. Old S. Ins. Grp.*, 221 S.W.3d 703, 711 (Tex.App.—San Antonio 2006, no pet.). • Attorney did not inform defendant that, because of a conflict of interest, he could no longer represent him. *Hahn v. Whiting Pet. Corp.*, 171 S.W.3d 307, 310 (Tex.App.—Corpus Christi 2005, no pet.). • Husband's letter to the court administrator requesting clarification of the trial setting on his belief that he would get 45 days' notice negated conscious indifference. *In re Parker*, 20 S.W.3d 812, 819 (Tex.App.—Texarkana 2000, no pet.). • The citation was lost in the mail when it was sent by the defendant's office in Michigan to a claims office in Texas for handling. *K-Mart Corp. v. Armstrong*, 944 S.W.2d 59, 60 (Tex.App.—Amarillo 1997, writ denied). • Attorney's secretary made a mistake in getting a new trial setting, and the attorney was in another trial. *Aero Mayflower Transit Co. v. Spoljaric*, 669 S.W.2d 158, 160 (Tex.App.—Fort Worth 1984, writ dism'd). • Party changed attorneys; the new attorney believed a bankruptcy stay was in effect. *Martin v. Allman*, 668 S.W.2d 795, 799 (Tex.App.—Dallas 1984, no writ). • Corporate officer was served with two citations, one for each corporation; the officer thought the citations were copies, and only one corporation filed an answer. *National Rigging, Inc. v. City of San Antonio*, 657 S.W.2d 171, 172-73 (Tex.App.—San Antonio 1983, writ ref'd n.r.e.).

(b) **Failure to answer or appear = conscious indifference.** Default judgments in the following cases were affirmed because the defendant did not plead and prove it was not consciously indifferent. • Reliance on an agent, such as an insurance carrier, to file an answer did not satisfy the test because there was no proof the agent was not guilty of conscious indifference. *Holt Atherton Indus. v. Heine*, 835 S.W.2d 80, 83 (Tex.1992); *Memorial Hosp. Sys. v. Fisher Ins. Agency, Inc.*, 835 S.W.2d 645, 652 (Tex.App.—Houston [14th Dist.] 1992, no writ), *disapproved on other grounds*, *Michiana Easy Livin' Country, Inc. v. Holten*, 168 S.W.3d 777 (Tex.2005). • Pro se defendant's refusal to retrieve certified letter after notice by post office. *Osborn v. Osborn*, 961 S.W.2d 408,

✦

412-13 (Tex.App.—Houston [1st Dist.] 1997, pet. denied). • Defendant's affidavit containing only general statements without dates and other verifying information did not disprove its conscious indifference. *Liberty Mut. Fire Ins. v. Ybarra*, 751 S.W.2d 615, 617-18 (Tex.App.—El Paso 1988, no writ); *see also Sheraton Homes, Inc. v. Shipley*, 137 S.W.3d 379, 382 (Tex.App.—Dallas 2004, no pet.) (affidavits contained conclusory allegations that P's failure to answer was because P intended to retain attorney who was no longer in private practice; no explanations of mistake were provided). • Mistaken belief about bankruptcy was not a reason to reverse a default judgment. *Novosad v. Brian K. Cunningham, P.C.*, 38 S.W.3d 767, 771 (Tex.App.—Houston [14th Dist.] 2001, no pet.); *Dupnik v. Aransas Cty. Nav. Dist.*, 732 S.W.2d 780, 782 (Tex.App.—Corpus Christi 1987, no writ). • Defendant misunderstood the citation and thought he would get a notice of trial, but did not ask or seek advice about the papers he had received. *Johnson v. Edmonds*, 712 S.W.2d 651, 652-53 (Tex.App.—Fort Worth 1986, no writ).

    (2) Meritorious defense. The defendant must "set up" a meritorious defense. *Dolgencorp*, 288 S.W.3d at 927; *In re R.R.*, 209 S.W.3d at 114; *Ivy v. Carrell*, 407 S.W.2d 212, 214 (Tex.1966); *Craddock*, 133 S.W.2d at 126. The defendant is not, however, required to prove the meritorious defense. *Titan Indem.*, 221 S.W.3d at 711; *In re A.P.P.*, 74 S.W.3d at 575; *see Evans*, 889 S.W.2d at 270. A meritorious defense is one that, if proved, would cause a different result on retrial, although not necessarily the opposite result. *Liepelt v. Oliveira*, 818 S.W.2d 75, 77 (Tex. App.—Corpus Christi 1991, no writ). To set up a meritorious defense, the defendant must allege facts, supported by affidavits or other evidence, that would constitute a defense to the plaintiff's cause of action. *Dolgencorp*, 288 S.W.3d at 928; *Estate of Pollack*, 858 S.W.2d at 392; *Ivy*, 407 S.W.2d at 214; *e.g., Lara v. Rosales*, 159 S.W.3d 121, 124 (Tex. App.—Corpus Christi 2004, pet. denied) (in PI case, Ds' allegation that P's own negligence caused auto accident because P stopped suddenly in intersection set up meritorious defense); *see, e.g., Angelo v. Champion Rest. Equip. Co.*, 713 S.W.2d 96, 97 (Tex.1986) (in suit on open account, allegation that payment had been made, supported by canceled checks and affidavit, set up meritorious defense); *Continental Carbon Co. v. Sea-Land Serv.*, 27 S.W.3d 184, 191 (Tex.App.—Dallas 2000, pet. denied) (in suit on sworn account, D's allegation that it did not owe debt was insufficient to set up meritorious defense). The trial court cannot consider controverting affidavits on the issue of a meritorious defense. *Dolgencorp*, 288 S.W.3d at 928; *Estate of Pollack*, 858 S.W.2d at 392; *see Gotcher v. Barnett*, 757 S.W.2d 398, 403 (Tex.App.—Houston [14th Dist.] 1988, no writ) (P can establish lack of legal sufficiency of D's defenses but cannot controvert or negate those defenses).

    (3) No delay or injury. The defendant must state that a new trial will not cause the plaintiff any delay or injury. *Dolgencorp*, 288 S.W.3d at 925; *In re R.R.*, 209 S.W.3d at 114-15; *Craddock*, 133 S.W.2d at 126. The defendant should state it is ready for trial and willing to reimburse the plaintiff for all reasonable expenses incurred in getting the default. *Evans*, 889 S.W.2d at 270 n.3; *Titan Indem.*, 221 S.W.3d at 712; *Tanknology/NDE Corp. v. Bowyer*, 80 S.W.3d 97, 103 (Tex.App.—Eastland 2002, pet. denied); *In re A.P.P.*, 74 S.W.3d at 575. Failure to offer reimbursement does not necessarily prevent a new trial. *Angelo*, 713 S.W.2d at 98; *General Elec. Capital Auto Fin. Leasing Servs. v. Stanfield*, 71 S.W.3d 351, 356 (Tex.App.—Tyler 2001, pet. denied). Once the defendant alleges that granting the motion will not cause delay or prejudice, the burden shifts to the plaintiff to prove injury. *Dolgencorp*, 288 S.W.3d at 929; *In re R.R.*, 209 S.W.3d at 116; *Evans*, 889 S.W.2d at 270; *Estate of Pollack*, 858 S.W.2d at 393. The purpose of this element is to protect the plaintiff against the sort of delay that would cause it to be disadvantaged in the trial of its case (e.g., the loss of witnesses or other valuable evidence). *Dolgencorp*, 288 S.W.3d at 929; *Evans*, 889 S.W.2d at 270.

    §9.2 Verification. The defaulting party must attach affidavits to support the factual allegations in the motion. See "Affidavits," ch. 1-B, §3.2.16, p. 11. For the requirements for using an unsworn declaration instead of a verification or an affidavit, see "Unsworn declaration," ch. 1-B, §3.2.14, p. 10. If the factual allegations in the affidavits are not controverted, the trial court must accept them as true. *Director, State Empls. Workers' Comp. Div. v. Evans*, 889 S.W.2d 266, 269 (Tex.1994); *Old Republic Ins. v. Scott*, 873 S.W.2d 381, 382 (Tex.1994); *Litchfield v. Litchfield*, 794 S.W.2d 105, 106 (Tex.App.—Houston [1st Dist.] 1990, no writ). Not all of the allegations in the motion for new trial must be supported by affidavits. The defendant is not required to file sworn proof to support its allegations of a meritorious defense or of no delay or injury. See "Meritorious defense," §9.1.3(2), this page; "No delay or injury," §9.1.3(3), this page.

✦

---

1. No-answer default. The factual allegations that must be supported by affidavits when challenging a no-answer default judgment include (1) facts regarding any defects in the service, citation, or return of service, or (2) facts supporting the defendant's allegation that its failure to file an answer was not intentional or the result of conscious indifference but was due to a mistake or accident.

2. Post-answer default. The factual allegations that must be supported by affidavits when challenging a post-answer default judgment include (1) facts regarding lack of notice of the hearing or trial, or (2) facts supporting the defendant's allegations that its failure to appear was not intentional or the result of conscious indifference but was due to a mistake or accident.

§9.3 Request hearing. In its motion for new trial, the defendant should request a hearing and attach sworn affidavits to support the allegations in the motion. See "When verification required," §3.1, p. 791. If the defendant requests a hearing but does not get one, the trial court must accept all statements in the sworn pleadings and affidavits as true. *Thermex Energy Corp. v. Rantec Corp.*, 766 S.W.2d 402, 406 (Tex.App.—Dallas 1989, writ denied); *Van Der Veken v. Joffrion*, 740 S.W.2d 28, 31 (Tex.App.—Texarkana 1987, no writ); *see, e.g.*, *Ward v. Nava*, 488 S.W.2d 736, 737 (Tex.1972) (in reversing denial of MNT, court relied solely on affidavit of movant when no evidentiary hearing was held).

§9.4 Sworn response. In most cases, the plaintiff should file a response and object to the motion for new trial. When appropriate, the plaintiff should also file a controverting affidavit to prevent the court from assuming the facts stated in the defendant's motion are true. If the defendant's sworn facts support the *Craddock* factors, and if those facts are not controverted by the plaintiff, the defendant will prevail. *McClure v. Landis*, 959 S.W.2d 679, 681 (Tex. App.—Austin 1997, pet. denied). See "Uncontroverted motion," §9.5.2, this page.

§9.5 Hearing. When the court holds a hearing on the motion for new trial and controverting evidence is introduced, the issues in the affidavits become fact questions for the court to resolve. *Jackson v. Mares*, 802 S.W.2d 48, 50 (Tex.App.—Corpus Christi 1990, writ denied); *see Young v. Kirsch*, 814 S.W.2d 77, 80 (Tex.App.—San Antonio 1991, no writ). At the hearing, it is not necessary to introduce the affidavits into evidence; it is sufficient that the affidavits are attached to the motion and are part of the record. *Director, State Empls. Workers' Comp. Div. v. Evans*, 889 S.W.2d 266, 268 (Tex.1994). The affidavits are considered for purposes of the *Craddock* test even if they are not introduced into evidence. *Evans*, 889 S.W.2d at 268; *McClure v. Landis*, 959 S.W.2d 679, 681 (Tex.App.—Austin 1997, pet. denied).

1. Controverted motion. A hearing is necessary if any of the facts in the motion that support the *Craddock* factors are controverted. *Estate of Pollack v. McMurrey*, 858 S.W.2d 388, 392 (Tex.1993); *Puri v. Mansukhani*, 973 S.W.2d 701, 715 (Tex.App.—Houston [14th Dist.] 1998, no pet.). Thus, if the plaintiff controverts the facts in the motion, the defendant must request an evidentiary hearing; otherwise, the motion may be overruled and the defendant will not be able to show an abuse of discretion on appeal. *Puri*, 973 S.W.2d at 715; *see Evans*, 889 S.W.2d at 268; *Cocke v. Saks*, 776 S.W.2d 788, 789-90 (Tex.App.—Corpus Christi 1989, writ denied); *see, e.g.*, *Liberty Mut. Fire Ins. v. Ybarra*, 751 S.W.2d 615, 617-18 (Tex.App.—El Paso 1988, no writ) (trial court overruled MNT based on P's controverting affidavit).

2. Uncontroverted motion. A hearing is not necessary on an uncontroverted motion. The trial court must accept as true the defendant's uncontroverted affidavits. *Averitt v. Bruton Paint & Floor Co.*, 773 S.W.2d 574, 576 (Tex.App.—Dallas 1989, no writ). If the factual allegations in the defendant's affidavit support the *Craddock* factors, the court should grant a new trial. *See Holt Atherton Indus. v. Heine*, 835 S.W.2d 80, 82 (Tex.1992); *Strackbein v. Prewitt*, 671 S.W.2d 37, 38-39 (Tex.1984).

§10. MNT AFTER SERVICE BY PUBLICATION

Service by publication is the method of notice that is least likely to bring the defendant's attention to the lawsuit. *Mullane v. Central Hanover Bank & Trust Co.*, 339 U.S. 306, 315 (1950); *see Gray v. PHI Res.*, 710 S.W.2d 566, 567-68 (Tex.1986) (posting petition on courthouse door is analogous to citation by publication). When the plaintiff serves the defendant by publication, special rules control the trial and the motion for new trial.

✦

§10.1 Trial. When the plaintiff moves for judgment against a defendant who was served by publication and has not answered or appeared, the trial court must appoint an attorney ad litem to defend the case. TRCP 244; *Cahill v. Lyda*, 826 S.W.2d 932, 933 (Tex.1992); *Isaac v. Westheimer Colony Ass'n*, 933 S.W.2d 588, 590-91 (Tex. App.—Houston [1st Dist.] 1996, writ denied). The attorney must be paid a reasonable fee, which is taxed as part of the costs, for the attorney's services for the trial and appeal. *J.D. Abrams, Inc. v. McIver*, 966 S.W.2d 87, 97 (Tex. App.—Houston [1st Dist.] 1998, pet. denied). After judgment is rendered, the court must approve and sign a statement of the evidence. TRCP 244. A signed and approved statement of the evidence is separate from the court reporter's record. *Montgomery v. R.E.C. Interests, Inc.*, 130 S.W.3d 444, 446 (Tex.App.—Texarkana 2004, no pet.).

§10.2 Sworn MNT. A motion for new trial after service by publication is equivalent to an equitable bill of review. *Stock v. Stock*, 702 S.W.2d 713, 714 (Tex.App.—San Antonio 1985, no writ); *see Hunsinger v. Boyd*, 26 S.W.2d 905, 907 (Tex.1930). The motion must be verified by an affidavit and, if based on a ground other than invalid service, must show good cause for granting a new trial. TRCP 329(a). If the motion is based on invalid service, the party does not have to show good cause. *In re E.R.*, ___ S.W.3d ___ (Tex.2012) (No. 11-0282; 7-6-12); *Velasco v. Ayala*, 312 S.W.3d 783, 792 (Tex.App.—Houston [1st Dist.] 2009, no pet.); *see Wiebusch v. Wiebusch*, 636 S.W.2d 540, 542 (Tex. App.—San Antonio 1982, no writ). See *O'Connor's Texas Forms*, FORM 10B:5.

1. Service valid. The following are some of the allegations the defendant can make in a motion for new trial even if service was valid.

(1) The trial court did not appoint an attorney as required by TRCP 244. *Isaac v. Westheimer Colony Ass'n*, 933 S.W.2d 588, 591 (Tex.App.—Houston [1st Dist.] 1996, writ denied).

(2) The trial court did not approve and sign the statement of evidence as required by TRCP 244.

(3) There was insufficient evidence presented at the hearing to support the trial court's judgment.

(4) The court made an error in applying the law to the facts.

2. Service invalid. The following are some of the allegations the defendant can make in a motion for new trial to indicate that service was invalid.

(1) The plaintiff served citation by publication without conducting a diligent search for the defendant. *In re E.R.*, ___ S.W.3d at ___. See "Diligent search," ch. 2-H, §4.4.1(2), p. 162.

(2) The citation by publication was defective. For example, the citation did not contain a brief statement of the nature of the suit as required by TRCP 114. *Wiebusch*, 636 S.W.2d at 542.

(3) The plaintiff procured the service by fraud. *See, e.g., Morris v. Morris*, 759 S.W.2d 707, 709 (Tex. App.—San Antonio 1988, writ denied) (wife committed fraud in procuring divorce after citation by publication because she knew where husband was and could have served him with citation).

§10.3 Notice. The defendant must give notice of the motion for new trial to all parties to the trial court's judgment. *See* TRCP 329(a).

§10.4 Deadline. A defendant who was served by publication has two years after a judgment is rendered and signed to file a motion for new trial. TRCP 329(a); *In re E.R.*, ___ S.W.3d ___ (Tex.2012) (No. 11-0282; 7-6-12); *Montgomery v. R.E.C. Interests, Inc.*, 130 S.W.3d 444, 445 n.1 (Tex.App.—Texarkana 2004, no pet.). If the motion for new trial is filed more than 30 days after the judgment was rendered and signed, the time period for the trial court's plenary power will be computed as if the judgment had been signed on the date the motion was filed. TRCP 306a(7), 329(d); *see Montgomery*, 130 S.W.3d at 446.

§10.5 Execution. The defendant can suspend the execution of the judgment during the pendency of the motion for new trial by filing a bond. TRCP 329(b). The amount for the bond is determined the same way supersedeas

———————————————— ✦ ————————————————

bonds are determined. *Id.*; *see also* TRAP 24.2 (supersedeas bonds). See *O'Connor's Texas Appeals*, "Superseding the Judgment," ch. 4-B, p. 162.

§10.6 Property sold. If property is sold under execution of the judgment before the defendant posts the bond, the defendant will not be able to recover the property. If the court grants a new trial, the defendant will be able to get a judgment equal to the proceeds of the sale. TRCP 329(c).

§10.7 Hearing. A hearing on the motion for new trial does not seem to be necessary. *See* TRCP 329(a) (court may grant a new trial upon petition supported by affidavits). If the plaintiff controverts any of the defendant's facts by filing an affidavit, the defendant should ask for a hearing. At the hearing, the defendant should introduce evidence to support all the facts in its motion for new trial.

§11. MNT AFTER SUMMARY JUDGMENT

§11.1 Not generally necessary. An appellant does not need to file a motion for new trial to preserve most errors in a summary judgment. *See* TRCP 324(a); TRAP 33.1(a). The appellant can file a motion for new trial just to extend the appellate deadlines. ***Thomley v. Southwood-Driftwood Apts., Ltd.***, 961 S.W.2d 6, 8 (Tex.App.—Amarillo 1996, order). See *O'Connor's Texas Forms*, FORM 10B:6.

1. Not required. As a general rule, a motion for new trial is not necessary to preserve error about the merits of the summary judgment. ***Lee v. Braeburn Valley W. Civic Ass'n***, 786 S.W.2d 262, 263 (Tex.1990). In most cases, the objections to the motion for summary judgment are made in the response to the motion, in a motion requesting more time for discovery, or in a motion to file a late response. As long as the objections to the motion for summary judgment are preserved for appeal in some prejudgment motion or objection, a motion for new trial is not necessary. For example, if the nonmovant filed a motion for permission to file a late response and the court overruled the motion, the nonmovant is not required to file a motion for new trial; its motion to file a late response preserved the error. See "Secure ruling on objections," ch. 7-B, §10.2, p. 621.

2. Required.

(1) Newly discovered evidence. A party should file a motion for new trial to assert newly discovered evidence or any other matter on which evidence must be heard. TRCP 324(b)(1). See "When MNT necessary," §2.1, p. 789.

(2) No opportunity to file response. When the nonmovant did not have an opportunity to file a summary-judgment response or to seek a continuance or permission to file a late response before summary judgment was rendered, the nonmovant should file a sworn motion for new trial, probably relying on the factors from ***Craddock v. Sunshine Bus Lines, Inc.***, 133 S.W.2d 124, 126 (Tex.1939). In rare situations when, after summary judgment is rendered, a nonmovant discovers a procedural mistake that should have been included in a response, the nonmovant can raise the issue in a motion for new trial. *See, e.g.*, ***Marino v. King***, 355 S.W.3d 629, 633-34 (Tex.2011) (pro se party could request in MNT to withdraw deemed admissions because she did not know that her responses to requests for admissions had been served untimely, that she should have moved to withdraw deemed admissions, or that she needed to file response to summary-judgment motion); ***Wheeler v. Green***, 157 S.W.3d 439, 442 (Tex.2005) (same); ***Petree v. Southern Farm Bur. Cas. Ins.***, 315 S.W.3d 254, 258 (Tex.App.—Corpus Christi 2010, no pet.) (pro se party could request in MNT to file motion to withdraw deemed admissions or to have Ds re-serve requests for admissions because she did not know that she needed to move to withdraw deemed admissions or that she needed to file response to summary-judgment motion arguing lack of service); *see also* ***Imkie v. Methodist Hosp.***, 326 S.W.3d 339, 345 (Tex.App.—Houston [1st Dist.] 2010, no pet.) (***Wheeler*** extended ***Craddock*** to summary judgments in rare circumstances when pro se party appeared at summary-judgment hearing but mistakenly did not file response to summary-judgment motion). The motion for new trial should include the grounds the nonmovant would have included in a timely response. For a discussion of the ***Craddock*** factors, see "Failure to answer or appear after proper notice," §9.1.3, p. 796.

★

CAUTION

Do not confuse (1) a motion for new trial filed after the nonmovant did not have an opportunity to file a response with (2) a motion for new trial filed after the nonmovant had an opportunity to file a motion for leave to file a late response or a motion to continue the summary-judgment hearing. In **Carpenter v. Cimarron Hydrocarbons Corp.**, *98 S.W.3d 682, 686 (Tex. 2002), the Supreme Court held that a motion for new trial establishing the* **Craddock** *factors is not appropriate to challenge the trial court's denial of permission to file a late response to a motion for summary judgment. Instead, the nonmovant must base its appeal on the trial court's abuse of discretion in denying the motion for permission to file a late response. See* **Carpenter**, *98 S.W.3d at 686. See "Filing a late response," ch. 7-B, §6.9.3, p. 607.*

---

(3) Other matters. A party should file a motion for new trial to complain about any matter to which the party has not already objected or on which the court has not ruled. For example, if the trial court refused to rule on the nonmovant's objections to a motion for summary judgment, the nonmovant should file a motion for new trial reurging those objections and objecting to the court's earlier refusal to rule. When the motion for new trial is overruled, either by order or by operation of law, the objections will be preserved for appeal. See "Refusal to rule + objection," ch. 1-G, §2.2.3, p. 48.

§11.2 Verification. See "When verification required," §3.1, p. 791.

§12. MNT AFTER DISMISSAL

The type of motion (verified vs. unverified) and the grounds to challenge a dismissal order depend on the underlying reason for the dismissal.

§12.1 Dismissal for failure to prosecute. If the trial court dismissed the suit for failure to prosecute or failure to appear at trial, the party should follow the procedures for a verified motion outlined in "Motion to Reinstate After Dismissal for Want of Prosecution," ch. 10-F, p. 826.

§12.2 Other dismissals. To determine the grounds for a motion for new trial following other dismissals, check the grounds on which the dismissal was based (e.g., for a motion for new trial following special exceptions, see "Special Exceptions—Challenging the Pleadings," ch. 3-G, p. 248).

1. Verified vs. unverified motion. As a general rule, if both the dismissal order and the motion for new trial are based on the pleadings, verification of the motion is not necessary; if either the dismissal order or the motion for new trial is based on evidence, verification is necessary. See "When verification required," §3.1, p. 791.

2. Inappropriate order of dismissal. If the trial court's order dismissed the suit with prejudice when the order should have dismissed without prejudice, the dismissal "with prejudice" must be challenged in a motion for new trial or a motion to reinstate; otherwise, the error is waived for appeal and the suit cannot be refiled. *See* **El Paso Pipe & Sup. v. Mountain States Leasing, Inc.**, 617 S.W.2d 189, 190 (Tex.1981).

§13. MNT TO CHALLENGE THE EVIDENCE

§13.1 Challenging sufficiency of evidence. Most motions for new trial following a jury trial are filed to challenge the sufficiency of the evidence. Because challenges to jury findings are some of the most important challenges a party can assert on appeal, it is important to preserve them in the motion for new trial. For a more detailed analysis on appealing jury findings and for additional flowcharts about the process, see O'Connor, *Appealing Jury Findings*, 12 Hous.L.Rev. 65 (1974).

1. Legal & factual sufficiency. Each jury finding is susceptible to two challenges—legal sufficiency and factual sufficiency. Chart 10-1, below, shows how each adverse jury finding may be challenged.

★

10-1. GROUNDS FOR CHALLENGING ADVERSE JURY FINDINGS

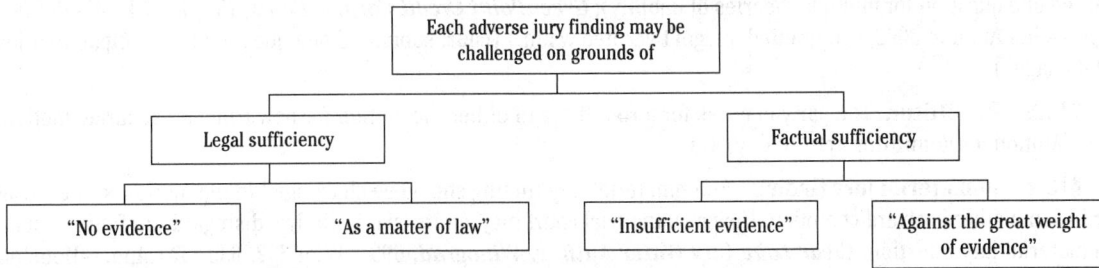

```
                    Each adverse jury finding may be
                       challenged on grounds of

          Legal sufficiency                    Factual sufficiency

  "No evidence"   "As a matter of law"   "Insufficient evidence"   "Against the great weight
                                                                        of evidence"
```

Choosing the proper terms for challenging a jury finding depends on who had the burden of proof on the issue at trial. If the movant had the burden of proof and the jury returned an adverse finding, the movant challenges the jury finding by saying that (1) the movant proved its issue as a matter of law, or (2) the jury's answer is against the great weight and preponderance of the evidence. If the movant did not have the burden of proof, it challenges an adverse finding by saying that (1) there is no evidence to support the jury answer, or (2) there is insufficient evidence to support the jury answer.

2. Preserving factual-sufficiency point. The only way to preserve factual-sufficiency challenges after a jury trial is in a motion for new trial. TRCP 324(b)(2); *Cecil v. Smith*, 804 S.W.2d 509, 510 (Tex.1991).

3. Preserving legal-sufficiency point. There are four ways to preserve legal-sufficiency challenges: (1) in a motion for directed verdict, (2) in an objection to the submission of a jury question, (3) in a motion for JNOV (or motion to disregard), and (4) in a motion for new trial. *Cecil*, 804 S.W.2d at 510-11; *Steves Sash & Door Co. v. Ceco Corp.*, 751 S.W.2d 473, 477 (Tex.1988). If the party properly preserves error in a motion for directed verdict, an objection to the charge, or a motion for JNOV, and if the appellate court sustains the challenge, the party may be entitled to rendition of judgment. However, if a party makes a legal-sufficiency challenge for the first and only time in a motion for new trial, the party will not be entitled to rendition on appeal, only remand. *Horrocks v. Texas DOT*, 852 S.W.2d 498, 499 (Tex.1993); *Cecil*, 804 S.W.2d at 512; *Ana, Inc. v. Lowry*, 31 S.W.3d 765, 772 (Tex.App.— Houston [1st Dist.] 2000, no pet.); *see* O'Connor, *Appealing Jury Findings*, 12 Hous.L.Rev. at 76 n.57 (challenges to adverse jury findings).

4. Standard challenges. The following are models for challenging jury findings on the evidence:

(1) When party has burden of proof on jury question.

• The evidence proves conclusively as a matter of law that [*state what the evidence proves*]. The jury's answer to question number ___ is wrong, and the court erred in overruling [*the objections to the charge, the motion for directed verdict, or the motion for JNOV*].

• The jury's answer to question number ___ is against the great weight and preponderance of the evidence and is manifestly unjust.

(2) When party does not have burden of proof.

• There is no evidence to support the jury's answer to question number ___, and the court erred in overruling [*the objections to the charge, the motion for directed verdict, or the motion for JNOV*].

• The evidence is insufficient to support the jury's answer to question number ___.

§13.2 Challenging broad-form jury question. The Supreme Court insists that trial courts submit jury questions in broad form. *Texas Dept. of Human Servs. v. E.B.*, 802 S.W.2d 647, 649 (Tex.1990). The submission of a broad-form jury question makes it more difficult for the losing party to successfully challenge the evidence on appeal. To challenge a verdict when the charge asked separate questions for each element of a cause of action, the appellant can focus on each adverse finding. To challenge a verdict when the charge asked only a broad-form question,

★

the appellant must assume the jury found against it on all the elements of the cause of action and thus must challenge all the elements. *See, e.g.*, *Prudential Ins. v. Jefferson Assocs.*, 896 S.W.2d 156, 160 (Tex.1995) (court submitted one question for multiple theories of liability); *GreenPoint Credit Corp. v. Perez*, 75 S.W.3d 40, 45-46 (Tex. App.—San Antonio 2002, pet. granted, judgm't vacated w.r.m.) (court submitted one question for multiple theories of damages).

§13.3　Remittitur. The party may ask for a remittitur in either the motion for new trial or a separate motion. See "Motion for Remittitur," ch. 10-C, p. 811.

§13.4　Immaterial jury finding. An immaterial jury finding should be challenged in the motion for new trial or in some other postverdict motion. However, the trial court may, on its own initiative, disregard the finding on an immaterial jury question. *Clear Lake City Water Auth. v. Winograd*, 695 S.W.2d 632, 639 (Tex.App.—Houston [1st Dist.] 1985, writ ref'd n.r.e.). A jury finding is immaterial if the question was one that should not have been submitted or, even though properly submitted, was rendered immaterial by other findings. *Spencer v. Eagle Star Ins.*, 876 S.W.2d 154, 157 (Tex.1994). A jury's findings on a question of law may be deemed immaterial. *Quick v. City of Austin*, 7 S.W.3d 109, 116 (Tex.1999); *Spencer*, 876 S.W.2d at 157.

§14.　MNT BASED ON JURY OR BAILIFF MISCONDUCT

A new trial based on misconduct by the jury or the officer in charge of the jury (the bailiff) is controlled by TRCP 327 and TRE 606(b). *See also* TRCP 226a (general instructions to jury), TRCP 283 (instructions to bailiff), TRCP 285 (communications between jury and bailiff). See Brown & Rondon, *Evidence Handbook*, p. 560. Because of the restrictions on a juror's testimony in TRCP 327(b) and TRE 606(b), it is very difficult to prove jury misconduct. *See Golden Eagle Archery, Inc. v. Jackson*, 24 S.W.3d 362, 375 (Tex.2000) (restrictions on juror testimony in TRCP 327(b) and TRE 606(b) are constitutional).

§14.1　Misconduct. TRCP 327(a) lists four types of misconduct: jury misconduct, bailiff misconduct, an unauthorized communication to the jury, or an incorrect, material juror answer on voir dire.

1.　Jury misconduct during deliberations. A juror cannot testify about statements made or matters that occurred during the jury's deliberations. TRCP 327(b); TRE 606(b); *Golden Eagle Archery, Inc. v. Jackson*, 24 S.W.3d 362, 370 (Tex.2000). This includes anything that affected a juror's mental processes and influenced that juror in joining or dissenting from the verdict. TRCP 327(b); TRE 606(b); *Golden Eagle*, 24 S.W.3d at 368. Generally, the only thing a juror may testify about is whether an outside influence was improperly brought to bear. TRCP 327(b); TRE 606(b); *Soliz v. Saenz*, 779 S.W.2d 929, 931 (Tex.App.—Corpus Christi 1989, writ denied); *see Ford Motor Co. v. Castillo*, 279 S.W.3d 656, 666 (Tex.2009); *Golden Eagle*, 24 S.W.3d at 370.

(1)　Outside influence. To constitute outside influence, the information must have come from a source outside the jury (i.e., a nonjuror who introduces information affecting the verdict). *Golden Eagle*, 24 S.W.3d at 370; *Editorial Caballero, S.A. de C.V. v. Playboy Enters.*, 359 S.W.3d 318, 324 (Tex.App.—Corpus Christi 2012, pet. denied); *Hutton v. AER Mfg. II, Inc.*, 224 S.W.3d 459, 463 (Tex.App.—Dallas 2007, pet. denied). Examples of outside influence include tampering with evidence, conversations between the judge and a juror, and threats to a juror. *Clancy v. Zale Corp.*, 705 S.W.2d 820, 829 (Tex.App.—Dallas 1986, writ ref'd n.r.e.).

(2)　Not outside influence. Broadly speaking, anything occurring during jury deliberations is not an outside influence. *See Golden Eagle*, 24 S.W.3d at 370. Comments and statements made by a juror to the other jurors during deliberations are not outside influences. *Kendall v. Whataburger, Inc.*, 759 S.W.2d 751, 756 (Tex. App.—Houston [1st Dist.] 1988, no writ); *see* TRCP 327(b); *Golden Eagle*, 24 S.W.3d at 370; *Editorial Caballero*, 359 S.W.3d at 324. The following are some matters that were not considered outside influences.

(a)　Jury charge & instructions. • The jurors' trading votes on two issues, in violation of court instructions. *Golden Eagle*, 24 S.W.3d at 370. • The jurors' misunderstanding or misinterpretation of the court's charge. *Compton v. Henrie*, 364 S.W.2d 179, 184 (Tex.1963); *Cortez v. Medical Prot. Co.*, 560 S.W.2d 132, 137 (Tex.App.—Corpus Christi 1977, writ ref'd n.r.e.). • The jury's response to a verdict-urging "dynamite" charge (i.e.,

✦

"Allen" charge). *Shaw v. Greater Houston Transp.*, 791 S.W.2d 204, 210 (Tex.App.—Corpus Christi 1990, no writ); *Golden v. First City Nat'l Bank*, 751 S.W.2d 639, 644 (Tex.App.—Dallas 1988, no writ); *see also Rosell v. Central W. Motor Stages, Inc.*, 89 S.W.3d 643, 661 (Tex.App.—Dallas 2002, pet. denied) (bailiff told jury that court would require them to deliberate another day after reaching deadlock, which motivated jury to trade votes to reach verdict). • The jurors' discussion about their impressions of the scene, in violation of court instructions. *Soliz*, 779 S.W.2d at 932.

(b) Evidence not in record. • The jurors' speculation that the plaintiff had used alcohol and had received a settlement. *Golden Eagle*, 24 S.W.3d at 370. • A juror's belief that the plaintiff had filed a workers' compensation claim to get someone to pay his medical bills. *Weaver v. Westchester Fire Ins.*, 739 S.W.2d 23, 24 (Tex.1987). • A juror who conducted Internet research and read the appellate decision on the first trial of the case. *Editorial Caballero*, 359 S.W.3d at 325-26. • A juror who used a dictionary to look up the word "negligence" and shared the definition with her fellow jurors. *Cooper Tire & Rubber Co. v. Mendez*, 155 S.W.3d 382, 413 (Tex. App.—El Paso 2004), *rev'd on other grounds*, 204 S.W.3d 797 (Tex.2006). • A juror who had worked in the construction industry and gave his opinion on the cost of home repairs. *Dietrich v. Goodman*, 123 S.W.3d 413, 422 (Tex. App.—Houston [14th Dist.] 2003, no pet.). • The jury's use of a discount formula from a juror's college textbook. *Crowson v. Kansas City S. Ry.*, 11 S.W.3d 300, 304-05 (Tex.App.—Eastland 1999, no pet.). • The jurors' discussion about the effect the plaintiff's victory would have on the talc mine and their fear that similar suits might close it down, leaving many without jobs. *Durbin v. Dal-Briar Corp.*, 871 S.W.2d 263, 272 (Tex.App.—El Paso 1994, writ denied), *disapproved on other grounds*, *Golden Eagle Archery, Inc. v. Jackson*, 24 S.W.3d 362 (Tex.2000). • A juror's discussion of personal experiences, insurance-liability questions, and a newspaper article not in evidence. *King v. Bauer*, 767 S.W.2d 197, 198 (Tex.App.—Corpus Christi 1989, writ denied); *Moon v. Firestone Tire & Rubber Co.*, 742 S.W.2d 792, 792-93 (Tex.App.—Houston [14th Dist.] 1987, writ denied). • A juror's statement that the plaintiff would still recover if the jury answered "no" to the negligence and proximate-cause questions. *Kendall*, 759 S.W.2d at 755-56.

2. Bailiff misconduct. TRCP 283 prohibits the bailiff from communicating with the jury except to inquire if they have agreed on a verdict and to make other communications as ordered by the court. *Pharo v. Chambers Cty.*, 922 S.W.2d 945, 950 (Tex.1996); *see, e.g.*, *Logan v. Grady*, 482 S.W.2d 313, 322 (Tex.App.—Fort Worth 1972, no writ) (reversible error for bailiff to tell jury, when it asked to rehear evidence, that it already had all it needed to answer jury question). To show probable injury, there must be some indication that the bailiff's misconduct probably caused a juror to vote differently on one or more issues vital to the judgment. See "Most cases," §14.4.1, p. 807.

3. Improper contact with jury. A juror is not permitted to accept any favors from any of the attorneys, parties, witnesses, or anyone who might be connected with or interested in the case, or to converse with them about the case. TRCP 226a, §II(2), (3). See "Juror Communication," ch. 8-A, §9, p. 694. A juror can testify about improper contacts with individuals outside the jury. *Golden Eagle*, 24 S.W.3d at 370. When a party's contact with a juror is held to be improper, a judgment in favor of the party responsible for the improper contact will be reversed. *See, e.g.*, *Texas Employers' Ins. v. McCaslin*, 317 S.W.2d 916, 921 (Tex.1958) (party went to juror's office and asked her to do all she could for her); *Texas Milk Prods. v. Birtcher*, 157 S.W.2d 633, 634 (Tex.1941) (party purchased soft drink for juror); *Campbell v. Struve*, 30 S.W.2d 344, 346-47 (Tex.App.—San Antonio 1930, writ ref'd) (attorney drove juror home); *Texas Employers' Ins. v. Brooks*, 414 S.W.2d 945, 945-46 (Tex.App.—Beaumont 1967, no writ) (juror requested and received rides from P and P's brother-in-law); *Occidental Life Ins. v. Duncan*, 404 S.W.2d 52, 53-54 (Tex.App.—San Antonio 1966, writ ref'd n.r.e.) (party asked juror for an aspirin); *see also Texas Employers' Ins. v. Moore*, 549 S.W.2d 37, 39 (Tex.App.—El Paso 1977, no writ) (if jurors had drunk coffee supplied by one of the attorneys, it would have been reversible error). *But see Mercado v. Warner-Lambert Co.*, 106 S.W.3d 393, 396-97 (Tex. App.—Houston [1st Dist.] 2003, pet. denied) (no reversible error when D's shadow juror requested cigarette and quarter from actual juror). If the contact was improper, the juror's disavowal of influence is irrelevant. *McCaslin*, 317 S.W.2d at 920.

✦

4. Erroneous juror answer on voir dire. When a juror responds to a question during voir dire with an answer that is untruthful, erroneous, or incomplete, it constitutes juror misconduct. *See* TRCP 327(a); *see, e.g., Doucet v. Owens-Corning Fiberglas Corp.*, 966 S.W.2d 161, 163-64 (Tex.App.—Beaumont 1998, pet. denied) (withheld information was material but did not cause injury); *Missouri Pac. R.R. v. Cunningham*, 515 S.W.2d 678, 685 (Tex. App.—San Antonio 1974, writ dism'd) (withheld information was immaterial); *see also* TRAP 44.1(a) (standard for reversible error). A false answer on voir dire entitles a party to a new trial only if the juror's concealment was in response to a specific and direct question calling for disclosure. *Wooten v. Southern Pac. Transp.*, 928 S.W.2d 76, 79 (Tex.App.—Houston [14th Dist.] 1995, no writ). Jurors and nonjurors may testify about voir dire. *Golden Eagle*, 24 S.W.3d at 369; *see, e.g., Kiefer v. Continental Airlines, Inc.*, 10 S.W.3d 34, 40 (Tex.App.—Houston [14th Dist.] 1999, pet. denied) (at MNT hearing, juror testified she may have seen in public one of the witnesses introduced by P's attorney at voir dire); *Burton v. R.E. Hable Co.*, 852 S.W.2d 745, 746 (Tex.App.—Tyler 1993, no writ) (juror testified he misunderstood voir dire question). However, a juror cannot testify that another juror's voir dire response was untruthful if the juror learned of the untruthfulness during jury deliberations. *See Golden Eagle*, 24 S.W.3d at 372.

§14.2 Testimony.

1. Juror testimony.

(1) Misconduct during deliberations. A juror can testify about an outside influence improperly brought to bear on a juror during deliberations. TRCP 327(b); TRE 606(b); *Golden Eagle Archery, Inc. v. Jackson*, 24 S.W.3d 362, 370 (Tex.2000); *Weaver v. Westchester Fire Ins.*, 739 S.W.2d 23, 24 (Tex.1987). Deliberations begin when the jury retires to deliberate on the jury charge and end when the jury is discharged from its duties. *See Golden Eagle*, 24 S.W.3d at 371 (deliberations begin when jury retires to weigh evidence); *Archer Daniels Midland Co. v. Bohall*, 114 S.W.3d 42, 46 (Tex.App.—Eastland 2003, no pet.) (deliberations cannot continue when jury is discharged); *Durkay v. Madco Oil Co.*, 862 S.W.2d 14, 23 n.2 (Tex.App.—Corpus Christi 1993, writ denied) (same). A juror cannot testify about any matter or statement that occurred during the jury's deliberations or about the effect of anything on a juror's mental processes. TRCP 327(b); TRE 606(b); *Golden Eagle*, 24 S.W.3d at 368; *Weaver*, 739 S.W.2d at 24; *see Chavarria v. Valley Transit Co.*, 75 S.W.3d 107, 111 (Tex.App.—San Antonio 2002, no pet.) (jurors' discussion of case during breaks in deliberation is the same as deliberation itself). See "Jury misconduct during deliberations," §14.1.1, p. 804.

(2) Misconduct outside of deliberations. A juror can testify about any misconduct (her own, another juror's, or a nonjuror's) if it occurred outside of deliberations—that is, between voir dire and the beginning of deliberations. *See, e.g., Golden Eagle*, 24 S.W.3d at 370 (incidental conversation between jurors during a trial break was not part of deliberations). A juror's testimony about conduct that occurred outside of deliberations is restricted by the general rules of evidence, but not by TRCP 327(b) or TRE 606(b). *Golden Eagle*, 24 S.W.3d at 370. Some of the matters a juror can testify about include the following: improper contacts with nonjurors; a conversation with another juror during a trial break; that another juror improperly viewed the scene of the event involved in the suit; and information showing that another juror is disqualified as a juror, if the information was not acquired during deliberations. *Id.*

2. Nonjuror testimony. A nonjuror can testify about any misconduct (her own, another nonjuror's, or a juror's), whether it occurred during or outside of deliberations. *Golden Eagle*, 24 S.W.3d at 369. A nonjuror's testimony is restricted by the general rules of evidence, but not by TRCP 327(b) or TRE 606(b). *Golden Eagle*, 24 S.W.3d at 369. For example, although a nonjuror can testify about what she saw happen at trial, she cannot testify about the jury's deliberations because the information would be hearsay. *See id.*; *see, e.g., Mitchell v. Southern Pac. Transp.*, 955 S.W.2d 300, 323 (Tex.App.—San Antonio 1997, no writ) (conversation with daughter-in-law of alternate juror about what happened in jury's deliberation was hearsay), *disapproved on other grounds*, *Golden Eagle Archery, Inc. v. Jackson*, 24 S.W.3d 362 (Tex.2000).

§14.3 Sworn motion.
TRCP 324(b) and 327 govern the procedure for preserving error based on jury or bailiff misconduct.

✦

---

1. Allegations in MNT. The movant should allege (1) there was jury or bailiff misconduct, (2) the misconduct was material, and (3) based on the entire record, the misconduct probably resulted in injury to the movant. TRCP 327(a); *Golden Eagle Archery, Inc. v. Jackson*, 24 S.W.3d 362, 372 (Tex.2000); *Redinger v. Living, Inc.*, 689 S.W.2d 415, 419 (Tex.1985). The allegations in the motion for new trial must be based on knowledge of misconduct, not just suspicion. *American Home Assur. Co. v. Guevara*, 717 S.W.2d 381, 384-85 (Tex.App.—San Antonio 1986, no writ). The motion must describe the misconduct.

2. Affidavits. The motion must be supported by affidavits confirming the claim of misconduct. TRCP 327(a); *Weaver v. Westchester Fire Ins.*, 739 S.W.2d 23, 24 (Tex.1987). See "Affidavits," ch. 1-B, §3.2.16, p. 11. The movant must attach one of the following types of affidavits:

(1) An affidavit by a juror describing the misconduct that occurred. See "Juror testimony," §14.2.1, p. 806. If the misconduct occurred during deliberations, it must amount to an "outside influence" on the jury. TRE 606(b); *Golden Eagle*, 24 S.W.3d at 369. See "Misconduct," §14.1, p. 804.

(2) An affidavit by a nonjuror describing misconduct. See "Nonjuror testimony," §14.2.2, p. 806.

(3) An affidavit by an attorney or other person explaining why affidavits are not available and describing the diligence used in attempting to procure affidavits. *Roy Jones Lumber Co. v. Murphy*, 163 S.W.2d 644, 646 (Tex.1942); *see, e.g., Ramsey v. Lucky Stores*, 853 S.W.2d 623, 636 (Tex.App.—Houston [1st Dist.] 1993, writ denied) (statement describing improper contacts with jurors did not explain lack of affidavit by juror); *American Home*, 717 S.W.2d at 384-85 (statement that jurors refused to sign affidavits was not enough to show diligence).

NOTE
Although TRCP 327(a) requires the motion to be supported by an affidavit, CPRC §132.001 was amended in 2011 to allow for the use of an unsworn declaration instead of an affidavit. See CPRC §132.001(a). For the procedure for using an unsworn declaration, see "Unsworn declaration," ch. 1-B, §3.2.14, p. 10.

---

3. Request evidentiary hearing. In the motion for new trial, the movant should request a hearing to introduce evidence. The attorney should check the provisions of the local rules on securing a hearing for the receipt of evidence.

§14.4 Burden.

1. Most cases. To obtain a new trial based on misconduct, the movant must prove (1) there was jury or bailiff misconduct, (2) the misconduct was material, and (3) based on the entire record, the misconduct probably resulted in injury to the movant. TRCP 327(a); *Golden Eagle Archery, Inc. v. Jackson*, 24 S.W.3d 362, 372 (Tex. 2000); *Redinger v. Living, Inc.*, 689 S.W.2d 415, 419 (Tex.1985); *Strauss v. Continental Airlines, Inc.*, 67 S.W.3d 428, 446 (Tex.App.—Houston [14th Dist.] 2002, no pet.). To show probable injury, the record must indicate the misconduct "most likely" caused a juror to vote differently on one or more issues vital to the judgment. *Redinger*, 689 S.W.2d at 419; *e.g., Pharo v. Chambers Cty.*, 922 S.W.2d 945, 950 (Tex.1996) (in damages suit against county, no probable injury when bailiff made reference to "raising taxes" because comment was made casually and was perceived as joke by jury). Determining whether misconduct occurred and caused injury is a question of fact. *Golden Eagle*, 24 S.W.3d at 372. Proof of misconduct only establishes error; it is not proof of injury.

2. Direct contact with juror. Some acts are so prejudicial to fairness that injury is proved simply by showing the improper act occurred. *Texas Employers' Ins. v. McCaslin*, 317 S.W.2d 916, 921 (Tex.1958); *Mercado v. Warner-Lambert Co.*, 106 S.W.3d 393, 396 (Tex.App.—Houston [1st Dist.] 2003, pet. denied). A favor requested by a party or given to a juror is considered reversible error even without proof that it influenced the juror. For example, a party's request to a juror for favorable treatment is reversible error. *McCaslin*, 317 S.W.2d at 921. For other examples, see "Improper contact with jury," §14.1.3, p. 805.

⭐

§14.5 Hearing. The trial court must conduct a hearing if the movant attached affidavits to the motion that either (1) described the misconduct or (2) stated a reasonable excuse for not filing affidavits alleging misconduct. *See* TRCP 327(a); *Golden Eagle Archery, Inc. v. Jackson*, 24 S.W.3d 362, 369 (Tex.2000); *Roy Jones Lumber Co. v. Murphy*, 163 S.W.2d 644, 646 (Tex.1942); *Ramsey v. Lucky Stores*, 853 S.W.2d 623, 635-36 (Tex.App.—Houston [1st Dist.] 1993, writ denied); *American Home Assur. Co. v. Guevara*, 717 S.W.2d 381, 384-85 (Tex.App.—San Antonio 1986, no writ). If the movant does not attach affidavits alleging misconduct and does not state in affidavits why it could not attach affidavits alleging misconduct, the court has discretion to grant a hearing. *Roy Jones Lumber*, 163 S.W.2d at 646; *see American Home*, 717 S.W.2d at 384-85. The movant should ask for a court reporter to transcribe the hearing.

§15. MNT AFTER NONJURY TRIAL

§15.1 Not generally necessary. A party does not need to file a motion for new trial to preserve most errors in a nonjury trial. TRCP 324(a); *Park v. Essa Tex. Corp.*, 311 S.W.2d 228, 229 (Tex.1958); *see* TRAP 33.1(a). Parties often file a motion for new trial in a nonjury case just to extend the appellate deadlines.

1. Not required. In a nonjury trial, there is no need to complain in a motion for new trial about factual insufficiency of the evidence ("insufficient evidence" or "against the great weight"), about legal insufficiency of the evidence ("no evidence" or "as a matter of law"), or that damages are too large or too small. *See* TRCP 324(b)(2), (b)(4); *In re Parker*, 20 S.W.3d 812, 816 (Tex.App.—Texarkana 2000, no pet.); *Strickland v. Coleman*, 824 S.W.2d 188, 191 (Tex.App.—Houston [1st Dist.] 1991, no writ). These issues can be raised for the first time on appeal without a motion for new trial. *See* TRAP 33.1(d).

2. Required. If the complaint was not presented to the trial court during trial or in some other postjudgment motion, or if the complaint is one on which evidence must be presented, the complaining party must file a motion for new trial to preserve error. TRCP 324(b); *see* TRAP 33.1(a). Thus, the party must file a motion for new trial to complain about newly discovered evidence and any other matter on which evidence must be heard or about which the party has not already objected. TRCP 324(b)(1). See "When MNT necessary," §2.1, p. 789.

§15.2 Verification. See "When verification required," §3.1, p. 791.

§16. MNT BASED ON NEWLY DISCOVERED EVIDENCE

Whether the court grants a motion for new trial based on newly discovered evidence is a matter within its discretion. *Jackson v. Van Winkle*, 660 S.W.2d 807, 809 (Tex.1983), *overruled on other grounds*, *Moritz v. Preiss*, 121 S.W.3d 715 (Tex.2003); *In re A.G.C.*, 279 S.W.3d 441, 454 (Tex.App.—Houston [14th Dist.] 2009, no pet.); *Hooper v. Smallwood*, 270 S.W.3d 234, 245 (Tex.App.—Texarkana 2008, pet. denied).

§16.1 Motion. To make a claim for a new trial because of newly discovered evidence, the movant must allege the following:

1. The movant discovered admissible and competent evidence after the trial. *Jackson v. Van Winkle*, 660 S.W.2d 807, 809 (Tex.1983), *overruled on other grounds*, *Moritz v. Preiss*, 121 S.W.3d 715 (Tex.2003); *see, e.g.*, *Waffle House, Inc. v. Williams*, 313 S.W.3d 796, 813 (Tex.2010) (movant did not establish that evidence would have been admissible). The knowledge of both the party and the attorney is relevant. *See, e.g.*, *Dankowski v. Dankowski*, 922 S.W.2d 298, 305 (Tex.App.—Fort Worth 1996, writ denied) (evidence was not new).

2. The late discovery of the new evidence was not due to a lack of diligence. *Waffle House*, 313 S.W.3d at 813; *Jackson*, 660 S.W.2d at 809; *Dankowski*, 922 S.W.2d at 305. To establish this element, the movant generally must show the evidence could not have been discovered sooner because (1) the movant had no notice before trial that the evidence existed, and (2) the movant used due diligence before trial to discover all available evidence. *See, e.g.*, *Alvarez v. Anesthesiology Assocs.*, 967 S.W.2d 871, 882-83 (Tex.App.—Corpus Christi 1998, no pet.) (even though Ds requested documents, Ds did not file a motion to compel when P refused; MNT denied).

★

3. The evidence is not merely cumulative of other evidence. *Waffle House*, 313 S.W.3d at 813; *Jackson*, 660 S.W.2d at 809. Evidence is cumulative when it is of the same kind and tends to prove the same point as other evidence. *New Amsterdam Cas. Co. v. Jordan*, 359 S.W.2d 864, 866 (Tex.1962); *In re Yarbrough*, 719 S.W.2d 412, 415 (Tex.App.—Amarillo 1986, no writ); *see, e.g.*, *Mitchell v. Bank of Am.*, 156 S.W.3d 622, 629 (Tex.App.—Dallas 2004, pet. denied) (documents from bank showing new address were cumulative of bank statement showing new address).

4. The evidence is not merely for impeachment. *New Amsterdam*, 359 S.W.2d at 866. When the only purpose of the new evidence is to impeach a witness, a new trial should not be granted. *Eckert v. Smith*, 589 S.W.2d 533, 538 (Tex.App.—Amarillo 1979, writ ref'd n.r.e.).

5. The evidence is so material that it would probably produce a different result at a new trial. *Waffle House*, 313 S.W.3d at 813; *Jackson*, 660 S.W.2d at 809. The new evidence must bring to light a new and independent truth so decisive that it demonstrates justice was not obtained. *New Amsterdam*, 359 S.W.2d at 867-68; *see, e.g.*, *State Farm Lloyds v. Nicolau*, 951 S.W.2d 444, 452 (Tex.1997) (new evidence would not have resulted in different verdict).

§16.2 Sworn motion. The motion must be verified and should include affidavits supporting each element listed above. *See Brown v. Hopkins*, 921 S.W.2d 306, 310-11 (Tex.App.—Corpus Christi 1996, no writ) (elements must be established by affidavit). *See generally Jackson v. Van Winkle*, 660 S.W.2d 807, 809 (Tex.1983) (requirements for seeking a new trial on grounds of newly discovered evidence), *overruled on other grounds*, *Moritz v. Preiss*, 121 S.W.3d 715 (Tex.2003). See "Verification & Affidavits," §3, p. 790.

§16.3 Hearing. The movant should request an evidentiary hearing and ask for a court reporter to transcribe it. *See National Med. Fin. Servs. v. Irving ISD*, 150 S.W.3d 901, 905 (Tex.App.—Dallas 2004, no pet.) (section labeled "Notice of Hearing" at end of MNT was not a request to the court for a hearing). If the motion and affidavits are in proper form and timely filed, the movant is entitled to a hearing. *Hensley v. Salinas*, 583 S.W.2d 617, 618 (Tex. 1979). *But see State Farm Lloyds v. Nicolau*, 951 S.W.2d 444, 452 (Tex.1997) (D was not entitled to MNT hearing because there was no showing that new evidence would likely result in different verdict). At the hearing, the movant must introduce evidence to prove each allegation in the motion. *Bell v. Showa Denko K.K.*, 899 S.W.2d 749, 757 (Tex.App.—Amarillo 1995, writ denied).

§17. REVIEW

§17.1 Appellate deadlines. A timely motion for new trial extends the appellate deadlines. TRAP 26.1(a)(1). See "Calculating appellate deadlines," ch. 9-C, §9.1, p. 778.

§17.2 Standard of review. The standard of review for the trial court's ruling on a motion for new trial is abuse of discretion. *Director, State Empls. Workers' Comp. Div. v. Evans*, 889 S.W.2d 266, 268 (Tex.1994); *Cliff v. Huggins*, 724 S.W.2d 778, 778-79 (Tex.1987).

§17.3 Appellate record. If the movant filed a verified motion for new trial and the trial court conducted a hearing and received evidence, to appeal the court's denial of the motion, the movant must ask the court reporter to transcribe the hearing and include it in the reporter's record. *See American Paging v. El Paso Paging, Inc.*, 9 S.W.3d 237, 240 (Tex.App.—El Paso 1999, pet. denied). If no hearing was conducted on the motion, the appellate court can review a ruling based on the affidavits attached to a verified motion for new trial following a default judgment. *Ward v. Nava*, 488 S.W.2d 736, 737 (Tex.1972).

§17.4 Order denying new trial. The order denying a new trial is appealable as part of the appeal from the final judgment. However, an order denying an untimely motion for new trial does not preserve issues for appellate review, even if the trial court acts within its plenary-power period. *Moritz v. Preiss*, 121 S.W.3d 715, 720 (Tex.2003).

§17.5 Order granting new trial. The order granting a new trial is an interlocutory order that is generally not reviewable by mandamus or on appeal following a final judgment. *See Wilkins v. Methodist Health Care Sys.*, 160 S.W.3d 559, 563 (Tex.2005); *Cummins v. Paisan Constr. Co.*, 682 S.W.2d 235, 236 (Tex.1984). But the order can be subject to appellate review in the following situations:

──────── ✦ ────────

1. Void order. The trial court's order is reviewable by mandamus or on appeal when it is wholly void. *See In re Columbia Med. Ctr.*, 290 S.W.3d 204, 209 (Tex.2009); *Johnson v. 7th Ct. of Appeals*, 350 S.W.2d 330, 331 (Tex.1961); *see, e.g., In re Dickason*, 987 S.W.2d 570, 571 (Tex.1998) (mandamus was granted to set aside void order granting MNT, which was signed after court lost plenary power); *In re Dilley ISD*, 23 S.W.3d 189, 191 (Tex. App.—San Antonio 2000, orig. proceeding) (same; once counsel withdrew timely filed MNT, court lost its plenary power to consider new MNT not filed within 30-day time limit).

2. Jury answers not in conflict. The trial court's order is reviewable by mandamus or on appeal when it states that the answers to jury questions are in fatal conflict, but they are not. *See In re Columbia Med. Ctr.*, 290 S.W.3d at 209; *Johnson*, 350 S.W.2d at 331.

3. Reasons stated in order not valid or specific. The trial court's order is reviewable by mandamus when the court's stated reasons for granting the new trial are not legally valid or reasonably specific. *In re United Scaffolding, Inc.*, 377 S.W.3d 685, 688-89 (Tex.2012).

(1) Reason not valid. The trial court's order is reviewable by mandamus if the court's stated reason for granting a new trial, whether specific or not, is one for which a new trial is not legally valid. *In re United Scaffolding*, 377 S.W.3d at 689. Examples of when the court's reason is not legally valid include the following: (1) the court's reasons plainly state that the trial court merely substituted its own judgment for the jury's, (2) the trial court disliked one party's lawyer, or (3) the court's reason was based on invidious discrimination. *Id.*

(2) Reason not specific. The trial court's order is reviewable by mandamus if the court did not specifically state its reasons for granting the new trial; that is, the order provides little or no insight into the judge's reasoning. *See In re United Scaffolding*, 377 S.W.3d at 689; *In re Columbia Med. Ctr.*, 290 S.W.3d at 209, 215. The court must provide a cogent and reasonably specific explanation of its reasoning for granting a new trial—simply restating a pro forma template is not sufficient. *In re United Scaffolding*, 377 S.W.3d at 689; *see In re Columbia Med. Ctr.*, 290 S.W.3d at 213 (must be more than a vague explanation); *see also In re Cook*, 356 S.W.3d 493, 495 (Tex. 2011) (successor judge's order stating that original order granting MNT should remain unchanged was not sufficient under *In re Columbia Med. Ctr.*; successor judge must issue her own statement of specific reasons for granting MNT). The order must indicate that the court considered the specific facts and circumstances of the case and must explain how the evidence, or lack of evidence, undermines the jury's findings; in doing so, however, the trial court does not need to provide a detailed catalog of the evidence. *In re United Scaffolding*, 377 S.W.3d at 689. A broad statement like "in the interest of justice" is not a sufficiently specific reason for granting a new trial. *In re Columbia Med. Ctr.*, 290 S.W.3d at 213; *e.g., In re United Scaffolding*, 377 S.W.3d at 689-90 (mandamus appropriate because although court stated several reasons for granting new trial, its last reason was "in the interest of justice and fairness," and court used "and/or" between its reasons in the order, which left open the possibility that "in the interest of justice and fairness" was its sole reason). Nor is the mere recitation of a legal standard a sufficiently specific reason for granting a new trial. *E.g., In re United Scaffolding*, 377 S.W.3d at 689 (mere statement that finding is against great weight and preponderance of evidence is not sufficient).

───────────── ✦ ─────────────

C. MOTION FOR REMITTITUR

§1. GENERAL

§1.1 Rules. TRCP 315, 320; TRAP 46.

§1.2 Purpose. A request for remittitur asks the court to reduce the damages because they are excessive. Remittitur procedure is designed to discourage the expense and delay of appeals. Both trial courts and courts of appeals may suggest remittitur. TRAP 46.1, 46.3. The trial court's power to suggest a remittitur is derived from its power to grant a new trial. *See* TRCP 320. The court does not have the power to increase the amount by additur. *See* ***Ponce v. Sandoval***, 68 S.W.3d 799, 805 (Tex.App.—Amarillo 2001, no pet.) (TRCPs do not provide for "additur" by the courts).

§1.3 Forms. *O'Connor's Texas Civil Forms* (2012), FORMS 10C.

§1.4 Other references. *O'Connor's Texas Causes of Action* (2013) (*O'Connor's Texas COA*).

§2. REQUEST

§2.1 Form. The request for remittitur is usually included in the motion for new trial, although it may be made in a separate motion. *See* ***C.M. Asfahl Agency v. Tensor, Inc.***, 135 S.W.3d 768, 797 (Tex.App.—Houston [1st Dist.] 2004, no pet.); *see, e.g.*, ***Landmark Am. Ins. v. Pulse Ambulance Serv.***, 813 S.W.2d 497, 498 (Tex.1991) (party filed "motion for new trial, or in the alternative, for remittitur"); ***Brookshire Bros. v. Wagnon***, 979 S.W.2d 343, 354 (Tex.App.—Tyler 1998, pet. denied) (party filed "motion for remittitur"). See "Motion for New Trial," ch. 10-B, p. 789; *O'Connor's Texas Forms*, FORM 10C:1. If a party does not ask for a remittitur in a postjudgment motion, it waives the complaint. *See* ***Hawthorne v. Guenther***, 917 S.W.2d 924, 937 (Tex.App.—Beaumont 1996, writ denied).

§2.2 Suggest amount. In the motion, the movant should suggest the amount by which the judgment should be reduced. ***Tidy Didy Wash, Inc. v. Barnett***, 246 S.W.2d 303, 306 (Tex.App.—Galveston 1952, writ ref'd n.r.e.); *see also* ***Marathon Oil Co. v. Sterner***, 777 S.W.2d 128, 132 (Tex.App.—Houston [14th Dist.] 1989, no writ) (because D proposed reduction by $5,000 at trial, it could not argue on appeal for reduction by $10,000).

§3. DEADLINE

Whether the request for remittitur is filed as part of the motion for new trial or separately, it must be filed within the time limits for a motion for new trial. *See* TRCP 320. See "Deadlines for MNT," ch. 10-B, §5, p. 791. If filed as a separate document, the request must be filed before the motion for new trial is overruled and within 30 days after the date the judgment was signed. *See* TRCP 329b(b).

§4. RESPONSE TO REQUEST

A party may respond to a request for remittitur and explain why there is sufficient evidence to support the damages award in the judgment. See *O'Connor's Texas Forms*, FORM 10C:2.

§5. ORDER

§5.1 Standard. The standard the trial court applies to a request for remittitur is the factual sufficiency of the evidence. ***Rose v. Doctors Hosp.***, 801 S.W.2d 841, 847 (Tex.1990); ***Larson v. Cactus Util. Co.***, 730 S.W.2d 640, 641 (Tex.1987). The court must examine all the evidence to determine whether there is sufficient evidence to support the damages award, remitting only the portion that is so factually insufficient (or against the great weight and preponderance of the evidence) as to be manifestly unjust. ***Pope v. Moore***, 711 S.W.2d 622, 624 (Tex.1986); ***Gray v. Allen***, 41 S.W.3d 330, 332 (Tex.App.—Fort Worth 2001, no pet.); ***Gainsco Cty. Mut. Ins. v. Martinez***, 27 S.W.3d 97, 108 (Tex.App.—San Antonio 2000, pet. granted, judgm't vacated w.r.m.).

───────────────────────────

NOTE

When damages are challenged on appeal with a no-evidence point and the court of appeals finds no evidence to support them, the court should render a take-nothing judgment, not suggest a remittitur. ***Larson***, *730 S.W.2d at 641.*

───────────────────────────

✯

§5.2 Must condition on new trial. The trial court cannot "order" a remittitur; it can only "suggest" a remittitur as an alternative to a new trial. *Arkoma Basin Expl. Co. v. FMF Assocs. 1990-A, Ltd.*, 249 S.W.3d 380, 390 (Tex.2008). The trial court cannot reduce the damages unless it gives the plaintiff the choice between remitting part of the damages or trying the case again. See *O'Connor's Texas Forms*, FORM 10C:3.

§6. RESPONSE TO SUGGESTION OF REMITTITUR

§6.1 Acceptance. A party who is awarded damages, generally the plaintiff, may remit any part of the judgment in open court or may execute and file with the court clerk a written remittitur signed and acknowledged by the party or the party's attorney. TRCP 315. See *O'Connor's Texas Forms*, FORM 10C:4. If the party files a remittitur, the court will reform the judgment and affirm it in accordance with the remittitur. *Rose v. Doctors Hosp.*, 801 S.W.2d 841, 847 (Tex.1990).

§6.2 Rejection. If the party rejects the suggestion of remittitur, the court will grant a new trial. *See Rose v. Doctors Hosp.*, 801 S.W.2d 841, 847 (Tex.1990). The party cannot appeal the order granting a new trial. *Kolfeldt v. Thoma*, 822 S.W.2d 366, 368-69 (Tex.App.—Houston [14th Dist.] 1992, orig. proceeding).

§7. REVIEW

§7.1 Appellate timetable begins. The appellate timetable begins to run on the date the trial court signs the order suggesting the remittitur. *Arkoma Basin Expl. Co. v. FMF Assocs. 1990-A, Ltd.*, 249 S.W.3d 380, 391 (Tex. 2008). The order suggesting the remittitur acts as a modified judgment for purposes of the appellate timetable. *Id.* If the court later withdraws its order suggesting the remittitur, the judgment is considered to have been modified again. *See id.* (trial court that modifies judgment and then withdraws modification has modified judgment twice rather than never).

§7.2 Right to appeal. If the defendant ("the party benefiting from the remittitur") files an appeal, the plaintiff ("the remitting party") may perfect its own appeal to challenge the propriety of the remittitur. TRAP 46.2; *see J. Wigglesworth Co. v. Peeples*, 985 S.W.2d 659, 665 (Tex.App.—Fort Worth 1999, pet. denied).

§7.3 Exemplary-damages award. When an exemplary-damages award is challenged on appeal, the court of appeals must describe in detail the evidence supporting the award. *Transportation Ins. v. Moriel*, 879 S.W.2d 10, 31 (Tex.1994); *see Leonard & Harral Packing Co. v. Ward*, 937 S.W.2d 425, 425 (Tex.1996); *Gray v. Allen*, 41 S.W.3d 330, 332 (Tex.App.—Fort Worth 2001, no pet.). Whether an award of exemplary damages is impermissibly excessive involves a Fourteenth Amendment due-process analysis. *BMW v. Gore*, 517 U.S. 559, 568 (1996). See *O'Connor's Texas COA*, "Due-process cap," ch. 42-B, §7.2, p. 1328.

§7.4 Remittitur in court of appeals.

1. Standards.

(1) To review damages. The standard the court of appeals applies to review an issue of remittitur is the factual sufficiency of the evidence. *Transportation Ins. v. Moriel*, 879 S.W.2d 10, 30 (Tex.1994); *Pope v. Moore*, 711 S.W.2d 622, 624 (Tex.1986); *Gray v. Allen*, 41 S.W.3d 330, 332 (Tex.App.—Fort Worth 2001, no pet.). The court of appeals applies the same standard when it reviews a trial court's suggestion of remittitur as when it reviews a request for remittitur made on appeal. *Moriel*, 879 S.W.2d at 30; *see, e.g.*, *Pope*, 711 S.W.2d at 623 (review of suggestion of remittitur by court of appeals); *Gray*, 41 S.W.3d at 332 (review of suggestion of remittitur by trial court). A court of appeals will uphold the trial court's order suggesting remittitur (or make its own suggestion of remittitur) only if the evidence supporting the damages is so factually insufficient or so against the great weight and preponderance of the evidence as to be manifestly unjust. *Moriel*, 879 S.W.2d at 30; *Gray*, 41 S.W.3d at 332; *see, e.g.*, *Durham Transp. v. Beettner*, 201 S.W.3d 859, 876 (Tex.App.—Waco 2006, pet. denied) (court suggested remittitur to reduce damages for past medical expenses by $5,604); *Johnson v. J. Hiram Moore, Ltd.*, 763 S.W.2d 496, 502-03 (Tex. App.—Austin 1988, writ denied) (court suggested reduction of exemplary damages from $463,202 to $134,649). Abuse of discretion is not the correct standard. *Larson v. Cactus Util. Co.*, 730 S.W.2d 640, 641 (Tex.1987).

———————————— ✭ ————————————

(2) To review attorney fees. If the court of appeals suggests a remittitur for damages on a claim for which the jury also awarded attorney fees (e.g., DTPA), the court can remand the case for a new trial on attorney fees if it believes the jury was influenced by the damages it awarded. *Bossier Chrysler-Dodge II, Inc. v. Rauschenberg*, 238 S.W.3d 376, 376 (Tex.2007); *Young v. Qualls*, 223 S.W.3d 312, 314 (Tex.2007); *Barker v. Eckman*, 213 S.W.3d 306, 314-15 (Tex.2006). The proper standard of review for this issue is whether the court is "reasonably certain" the jury was "significantly influenced" by the erroneous amount of damages it awarded. *Barker*, 213 S.W.3d at 313-14.

2. Review of trial-court remittitur. If the court of appeals sustains the plaintiff's contention on appeal that the trial court should not have suggested remittitur, the court of appeals must render the judgment that the trial court should have rendered. TRAP 46.2.

3. Suggestion of remittitur by CA. If the court of appeals suggests a remittitur, the court will affirm the trial court's judgment on the condition that the plaintiff accepts the court of appeals' suggestion.

(1) P accepts. If the plaintiff files a remittitur in compliance with the court of appeals' suggestion, the court will reform the trial court's judgment and affirm it. *Rose v. Doctors Hosp.*, 801 S.W.2d 841, 847 (Tex.1990). After the court of appeals renders its opinion, the plaintiff may appeal the remittitur issue to the Supreme Court. *See id.* at 847-48. Remittitur is not a "take-it-or-leave-it" offer that bars an appeal to the Supreme Court. *See id.*

(2) P rejects. If the plaintiff refuses to file or does not timely file a remittitur, the court of appeals will reverse the trial court's judgment and remand for a new trial. TRAP 46.3; *Rose*, 801 S.W.2d at 847; *see Missouri Pac. R.R. v. Alderete*, 945 S.W.2d 148, 153 (Tex.App.—San Antonio 1996, no writ).

§7.5 Voluntary remittitur. If the court of appeals reverses the trial court's judgment because of a legal error affecting only a portion of the damages awarded, the affected party may, within 15 days after the court of appeals' judgment, voluntarily remit the amount it believes will cure the error. TRAP 46.5. If the court of appeals determines that remittitur is appropriate but that the voluntary remittitur is not sufficient to cure the error, the court must suggest an appropriate remittitur. See "Standards," §7.4.1, p. 812. If the court of appeals determines that the voluntary remittitur cures the reversible error, the court of appeals must accept the remittitur and reform and affirm the trial court's judgment in accordance with the remittitur. TRAP 46.5.

§7.6 Review by Supreme Court.

1. Permissible.

(1) Standard of review. The Supreme Court can review the standard the court of appeals applied in its review of a remittitur point. *Redman Homes, Inc. v. Ivy*, 920 S.W.2d 664, 669 (Tex.1996); *Pope v. Moore*, 711 S.W.2d 622, 623 (Tex.1986).

(2) Constitutionality of damages. The Supreme Court can remand cases for a determination of an appropriate remittitur if the damages awarded are unconstitutional. *Tony Gullo Motors I, L.P. v. Chapa*, 212 S.W.3d 299, 310 (Tex.2006).

2. Impermissible.

(1) Challenges to remittitur. Because the Supreme Court has no authority to review challenges to the factual sufficiency of the evidence, it cannot review challenges to remittitur. *Maritime Overseas Corp. v. Ellis*, 971 S.W.2d 402, 407 (Tex.1998); *Redman Homes*, 920 S.W.2d at 669; *see Tony Gullo Motors*, 212 S.W.3d at 310.

(2) Accepting remittitur. TRAP 46 does not authorize the Supreme Court to accept remittiturs. *Tony Gullo Motors*, 212 S.W.3d at 310 & n.59; *Formosa Plastics Corp. v. Presidio Eng'rs & Contractors, Inc.*, 960 S.W.2d 41, 51 (Tex.1998); *Redman Homes*, 920 S.W.2d at 669. However, in the past, the Court has accepted remittiturs when the remittiturs cured an error in a portion of the jury's verdict that was (1) tainted by misconduct or impropriety and (2) clearly and definitely ascertainable. *Moore v. Grantham*, 599 S.W.2d 287, 292 (Tex.1980); *Texas Employers' Ins. v. Lightfoot*, 162 S.W.2d 929, 931 (Tex.1942).

─────────────────── ★ ───────────────────

D. MOTION TO MODIFY THE JUDGMENT

§1. GENERAL

§1.1 Rules. TRCP 329b; TRAP 26.1(a)(2).

§1.2 Purpose. A motion to modify the judgment is the procedure for asking the trial court to change the judgment.

§1.3 Form. *O'Connor's Texas Civil Forms* (2012), FORM 10D:1.

§1.4 Other references. *O'Connor's Texas Causes of Action* (2013) (*O'Connor's Texas COA*).

§2. MOTION

§2.1 Grounds. If the judgment did not award a party all the relief it was entitled to, or awarded the other party more relief than it was entitled to, the complaint must be brought to the trial court's attention in a written motion. *See* TRCP 329b(g). The following are some examples of when a party should file a motion to modify the judgment.

1. Prejudgment interest. A party should file a motion to modify the judgment when the court does not award the correct amount of prejudgment interest. If a party does not bring the issue to the trial court's attention in a motion to modify the judgment or make some other objection on the record, the party cannot raise the issue on appeal. *Larrumbide v. Doctors Health Facilities*, 734 S.W.2d 685, 693 (Tex.App.—Dallas 1987, writ denied); *Bulgerin v. Bulgerin*, 724 S.W.2d 943, 946 (Tex.App.—San Antonio 1987, no writ), *overruled on other grounds*, *Trinity Univ'l Ins. v. Cowan*, 945 S.W.2d 819 (Tex.1997); *see Allright, Inc. v. Pearson*, 735 S.W.2d 240, 240 (Tex.1987). But in one case, without addressing the issue of waiver, the Supreme Court reversed the court of appeals and modified the date from which prejudgment interest was to accrue, even though no motion to modify the judgment had been filed. *C&H Nationwide, Inc. v. Thompson*, 903 S.W.2d 315, 327-28 (Tex.1994), *overruled on other grounds*, *Carl J. Battaglia, M.D., P.A. v. Alexander*, 177 S.W.3d 893 (Tex.2005). The court of appeals had held that the plaintiffs waived error in the calculation of interest because they did not file a motion to modify the judgment. *See C&H Nationwide, Inc. v. Thompson*, 810 S.W.2d 259, 276 (Tex.App.—Houston [1st Dist.] 1991), *rev'd*, 903 S.W.2d 315 (Tex.1994). See *O'Connor's Texas COA*, "Prejudgment Interest," ch. 43, §2, p. 1335.

2. Attorney fees. A party should file a motion to modify the judgment when the court does not award attorney fees or does not award the correct amount of fees. *See Texas Educ. Agency v. Maxwell*, 937 S.W.2d 621, 623 (Tex.App.—Eastland 1997, writ denied); *American Bank v. Waco Airmotive, Inc.*, 818 S.W.2d 163, 178 (Tex.App.—Waco 1991, writ denied). See *O'Connor's Texas COA*, "Attorney Fees," ch. 45, p. 1349.

3. Costs. A party should file a motion to modify the judgment when the court does not award costs, awards costs to the wrong party, or does not award the correct amount of costs. *See Portland S&L Ass'n v. Bernstein*, 716 S.W.2d 532, 541 (Tex.App.—Corpus Christi 1985, writ ref'd n.r.e.), *overruled on other grounds*, *Dawson-Austin v. Austin*, 968 S.W.2d 319 (Tex.1998). To challenge the clerk's tabulation of the costs, the party should file a motion to retax costs. See "Retaxing costs," ch. 9-C, §7.2.2, p. 778; *O'Connor's Texas COA*, "Court Costs," ch. 44, p. 1341.

4. Any other error or omission in judgment. A party should file a motion to modify the judgment when there is any other error in the judgment. *See, e.g.*, *L.M. Healthcare, Inc. v. Childs*, 929 S.W.2d 442, 443 (Tex.1996) (to change dismissal from "with prejudice" to "without prejudice"); *Heard v. Houston Post Co.*, 684 S.W.2d 210, 214 (Tex.App.—Houston [1st Dist.] 1984, writ ref'd n.r.e.) (after court ordered sheriff to turn over all information about a criminal investigation except the victim's name, Houston Post filed motion to modify the J to ask for the name).

§2.2 Not verified. A motion to modify the judgment should not be verified or supported with affidavits unless it presents facts not in the record.

§3. DEADLINES

The same rules apply to motions to modify judgments as to motions for new trial. See "Deadlines for MNT," ch. 10-B, §5, p. 791.

━━━━━━━━━━━━━━━━━━━━━━━ ✦ ━━━━━━━━━━━━━━━━━━━━━━━

§3.1 Original or amended motion. The deadline to file a motion to modify, correct, or reform an error in the judgment is the same as for a motion for new trial—within 30 days after the date the judgment was signed. TRCP 329b(a), (g); *L.M. Healthcare, Inc. v. Childs*, 929 S.W.2d 442, 443 (Tex.1996); *Padilla v. LaFrance*, 907 S.W.2d 454, 458 (Tex.1995). An amended motion to modify may be filed within 30 days after the date the judgment was signed as long as the original motion to modify has not been overruled by order of the trial court.

§3.2 After MNT overruled but within 30 days. A party can file a motion to modify the judgment even after the court has overruled a motion for new trial, as long as the motion to modify is filed within 30 days after the date the judgment was signed. *In re Brookshire Grocery Co.*, 250 S.W.3d 66, 72 (Tex.2008); *L.M. Healthcare, Inc. v. Childs*, 929 S.W.2d 442, 443 (Tex.1996); *Dal-Chrome Co. v. Brenntag Sw., Inc.*, 183 S.W.3d 133, 146 (Tex.App.—Dallas 2006, no pet.).

§3.3 Premature motion. A premature motion to modify the judgment, filed before the judgment is signed, is deemed filed on the day of, but immediately after, the signing of the judgment. *Padilla v. LaFrance*, 907 S.W.2d 454, 458 (Tex.1995) (motion to reconsider); *see* TRCP 306c, 329b(g); *see also* TRAP 27.2 (premature proceeding relating to an appeal is not ineffective); *Ryland Enter. v. Weatherspoon*, 355 S.W.3d 664, 666 (Tex.2011) (premature-filing rules apply equally to motion for new trial and motion to modify judgment).

§3.4 Late motion. If a party discovers an error in the judgment more than 30 days after the judgment was signed, it should still file a motion to modify the judgment. Although a late motion to modify will not preserve error or extend appellate deadlines, the court has the authority to correct the error on its own initiative if it still has plenary power over the judgment, even without a motion. See "Power to Change Judgment," ch. 9-C, §7, p. 778. If the court has lost plenary power, the party should title the motion as a "Motion for Judgment Nunc Pro Tunc" and argue that the error is clerical and can be corrected even after the court loses plenary power. See "Motion for Judgment Nunc Pro Tunc," ch. 10-H, p. 837.

§4. HEARING

The hearing on a motion to modify the judgment is for argument only, not evidence. However, if a party files a motion to modify that for some reason must be supported by evidence, the party should ask for a court reporter and present evidence at the hearing.

§5. ORDER

§5.1 In writing. The court's order granting a motion to modify the judgment must be in writing and signed by the trial court—just like a motion for new trial. TRCP 329b(c). See "In writing," ch. 10-B, §8.1, p. 794.

§5.2 Deadlines. The deadlines to grant or overrule a motion to modify the judgment are the same as for an order on a motion for new trial. See "Deadline to sign order on MNT," ch. 10-B, §8.4, p. 794.

1. Grant motion. The trial court must sign an order granting a motion to modify within 75 days after the date the judgment was signed. TRCP 329b(c); *see, e.g., L.M. Healthcare, Inc. v. Childs*, 929 S.W.2d 442, 443-44 (Tex.1996) (motion to modify granted on 75th day after J was signed).

2. Overrule motion. The trial court may overrule a motion to modify by written order; if it does not, the motion is overruled by operation of law on the 76th day after the judgment was signed—just like a motion for new trial. *See* TRCP 329b(c); *cf. Health Care Ctrs. v. Nolen*, 62 S.W.3d 813, 816 (Tex.App.—Waco 2001, no pet.) (MNT).

§6. REVIEW

§6.1 Motion to modify & postjudgment deadlines.

1. Finality of judgment. A motion to modify the judgment delays the date the judgment becomes final—just like a motion for new trial. TRCP 329b(g); *Home Owners Funding Corp. v. Scheppler*, 815 S.W.2d 884, 887 (Tex.App.—Corpus Christi 1991, no writ); *see Lane Bank Equip. Co. v. Smith S. Equip., Inc.*, 10 S.W.3d 308, 313 (Tex.2000); *Mackie v. McKenzie*, 890 S.W.2d 807, 808 (Tex.1994). See "Finality for purposes of changing the judgment," ch. 9-C, §6.5, p. 775.

✦

2. Appellate deadlines. The filing of a timely motion to substantively modify the judgment extends appellate deadlines in the same way as a motion for new trial. TRCP 329b(g); *Ryland Enter. v. Weatherspoon*, 355 S.W.3d 664, 666 (Tex.2011); *Lane Bank*, 10 S.W.3d at 310; *see L.M. Healthcare, Inc. v. Childs*, 929 S.W.2d 442, 444 (Tex.1996). A motion to modify the judgment extends appellate deadlines even if the motion is denied. See "Calculating appellate deadlines," ch. 9-C, §9.1, p. 778.

§6.2 Modified judgment & postjudgment deadlines.

1. Restarts appellate timetable. Any modification of the judgment, whether material or not, made while the trial court has plenary power restarts the appellate timetable. TRCP 329b(h); TRAP 4.3(a), 27.3; *Lane Bank Equip. Co. v. Smith S. Equip., Inc.*, 10 S.W.3d 308, 313 (Tex.2000). Even clerical changes to the judgment made while the court has plenary power will restart the appellate timetable. *Lane Bank*, 10 S.W.3d at 313.

(1) Substantive & clerical changes. Some examples of changes to the judgment that restarted the appellate timetable include: • Revising docket number to reflect severance, correcting attorney's misspelled name, and stating that court and jury made findings required for termination. *In re J.L.*, 163 S.W.3d 79, 82-83 (Tex.2005). • Adding "Mother Hubbard" clause ("all relief not granted is denied"). *Mackie v. McKenzie*, 890 S.W.2d 807, 808 (Tex.1994). • An order reinstating a default judgment. *Old Republic Ins. v. Scott*, 846 S.W.2d 832, 833 (Tex.1993). • An order reducing damages. *Abercia v. Kingvision Pay-Per-View, Ltd.*, 217 S.W.3d 688, 706 (Tex.App.—El Paso 2007, pet. denied). • An order identifying different grounds for summary judgment. *Quanaim v. Frasco Rest. & Catering*, 17 S.W.3d 30, 39-40 (Tex.App.—Houston [14th Dist.] 2000, pet. denied). • A change to the signature date. *Owens-Corning Fiberglas Corp. v. Wasiak*, 883 S.W.2d 402, 405 (Tex.App.—Austin 1994, order).

(2) Exception. The only exception to the rule that any modification of the judgment—even an immaterial one—restarts the appellate deadlines is if the face of the record shows that the trial court signed the modified judgment for the sole purpose of restarting the deadlines. *Mackie*, 890 S.W.2d at 808; *Abercia*, 217 S.W.3d at 706; *e.g.*, *Wang v. Hsu*, 899 S.W.2d 409, 411-12 (Tex.App.—Houston [14th Dist.] 1995, writ denied) (no evidence on face of record indicating court used second J to extend appellate deadlines; plenary power extended by second J that had different date from first J).

NOTE

Any change—whether substantive or clerical—the court makes to its judgment while it has plenary power will restart the appellate timetable under TRCP 329b(h). By comparison, only a motion that seeks a substantive change to the judgment will extend the appellate deadlines and the court's plenary power under TRCP 329b(g). Lane Bank, 10 S.W.3d at 313. See "Finality for purposes of changing the judgment," ch. 9-C, §6.5, p. 775.

---

2. Extending appellate deadlines for second judgment. When the trial court modifies the judgment by signing a second judgment, the appellate deadlines can be extended in two ways.

(1) Motion to modify after first judgment. Generally, a motion to modify a judgment filed after the first judgment does not extend appellate deadlines for the second judgment. *See Trans-Continental Props., Ltd. v. Taylor*, 717 S.W.2d 890, 890-91 (Tex.1986). However, if the complaint in the motion filed after the first judgment was not corrected by the second judgment and the substance of the motion is still a viable complaint about the second judgment, the motion extends the appellate deadlines for the second judgment. *Maddox v. Cosper*, 25 S.W.3d 767, 770 n.3 (Tex.App.—Waco 2000, no pet.); *Clark v. McFerrin*, 760 S.W.2d 822, 825 (Tex.App.—Corpus Christi 1988, writ denied). See "Second-judgment problems," ch. 10-B, §5.6, p. 792.

(2) Motion to modify after second judgment. If the party files a motion to modify or another plenary-power-extending motion after the second judgment is signed, the motion extends the appellate deadlines for the second judgment. See "Motions that extend plenary power," ch. 9-C, §6.5.1(1), p. 775.

─────────── ✦ ───────────

E. REQUEST FOR FINDINGS OF FACT & CONCLUSIONS OF LAW

§1. GENERAL

§1.1 Rules. TRCP 296-299a, 306c; TRAP 26.1(a)(4).

§1.2 Purpose. Findings of fact in a nonjury trial serve the same function as the jury's answers to jury questions—they resolve the factual disputes in the case. Conclusions of law are the court's statements of the legal principles it applied to the facts to resolve the case. Findings of fact are more important on appeal than conclusions of law because appellate courts review findings of fact for sufficiency of the evidence but review conclusions of law de novo. See "Review of conclusions of law," §6.3, p. 825.

§1.3 Timetables & forms. Timetable, Request for Findings of Fact & Conclusions of Law, p. 1232; Timetable, Appeal to the Court of Appeals, p. 1235; *O'Connor's Texas Civil Forms* (2012), FORMS 10E.

NOTE

Throughout §§2-4, findings of fact and conclusions of law will be referred to collectively as findings of fact.

---

§1.4 Other references. *O'Connor's Texas Civil Appeals* (2012) (*O'Connor's Texas Appeals*); *O'Connor's Texas Family Law Handbook* (2013) (*O'Connor's Fam. Law Handbook*).

§2. AVAILABILITY OF FINDINGS OF FACT

§2.1 Findings of fact are necessary. In the following instances, parties should always ask the court to file findings of fact.

1. After nonjury trial of facts. Findings of fact may be requested in "any case tried in the district or county court without a jury." TRCP 296. A case is "tried" when there is a hearing before the court on conflicting evidence. *Besing v. Moffitt*, 882 S.W.2d 79, 81 (Tex.App.—Amarillo 1994, no writ). Litigants are entitled to findings of fact only on the merits of the case. See "Only on controlling issues," §5.1.3, p. 823.

2. After motion for judgment in nonjury trial. Findings of fact should be requested in a nonjury case resolved by a judgment after the plaintiff rests. *Qantel Bus. v. Custom Controls Co.*, 761 S.W.2d 302, 304 (Tex. 1988).

3. After mandamus initiated in trial court. Findings of fact should be requested in an original mandamus proceeding in the trial court, which is considered a civil action subject to the TRCPs. *Anderson v. City of Seven Points*, 806 S.W.2d 791, 792 n.1 (Tex.1991); *see City of Beaumont v. Spivey*, 1 S.W.3d 385, 389 (Tex.App.—Beaumont 1999, pet. denied).

4. To supply omitted elements of an issue. When only some elements of an issue are submitted to a jury, the party should request findings of fact on the omitted elements. *See* TRCP 299; *see also Insurance Co. of St. Louis v. Bellah*, 373 S.W.2d 691, 692 (Tex.App.—Fort Worth 1963, no writ) (court was required to file findings of fact when certain issues were omitted from jury charge). See "Incomplete claim or defense submitted," ch. 8-I, §7.2, p. 743.

5. When part of case is decided by court. When part of a case is tried to a jury and part is decided by the court, findings of fact should be requested on the court-decided issues. *IKB Indus. v. Pro-Line Corp.*, 938 S.W.2d 440, 443 (Tex.1997); *Toles v. Toles*, 45 S.W.3d 252, 264 n.5 (Tex.App.—Dallas 2001, pet. denied); *see, e.g., Awde v. Dabeit*, 938 S.W.2d 31, 33 (Tex.1997) (after dismissal and award of sanctions, hearing on attorney fees); *Schwartz v. Pinnacle Comms.*, 944 S.W.2d 427, 431 (Tex.App.—Houston [14th Dist.] 1997, no writ) (after no-answer default judgment rendered, hearing on damages); *Heafner & Assocs. v. Koecher*, 851 S.W.2d 309, 313 (Tex.App.—Houston [1st Dist.] 1992, no writ) (issue of attorney fees was tried to court).

✦

---

6. To supply specific damages findings in nonjury trial. Findings of fact should be requested when the trial court makes a broad-form finding of actual damages and one of the damages elements is not supported by the evidence. *See Tagle v. Galvan*, 155 S.W.3d 510, 516 (Tex.App.—San Antonio 2004, no pet.).

§2.2 Findings of fact are helpful. Findings of fact are appropriate when (1) the trial court conducts an evidentiary hearing and (2) the findings could properly be considered by the appellate court. *See IKB Indus. v. Pro-Line Corp.*, 938 S.W.2d 440, 442-43 (Tex.1997). Findings in these instances are not given the same weight on appeal as findings made under TRCP 296 and 297. *IKB Indus.*, 938 S.W.2d at 442. See "Review of findings of fact," §6.2, p. 823.

1. After hearing on sanctions under TRCP 215. When a judgment is rendered as a sanction for discovery abuse, findings of fact supporting the sanctions are helpful. *IKB Indus.*, 938 S.W.2d at 442; *Chrysler Corp. v. Blackmon*, 841 S.W.2d 844, 852 (Tex.1992); *TransAmerican Nat. Gas Corp. v. Powell*, 811 S.W.2d 913, 919 n.9 (Tex. 1991). The findings should be specifically tied to the appropriate legal standard. *Chrysler Corp.*, 841 S.W.2d at 853.

2. After dismissal hearings.

(1) Failure to prosecute. Findings of fact after a hearing on a motion to dismiss for failure to prosecute can help the appellate court understand the reasons why the trial court refused to reinstate. See "Motion to Reinstate After Dismissal for Want of Prosecution," ch. 10-F, p. 826.

PRACTICE TIP

If you decide to file a request for findings of fact after a case is dismissed for want of prosecution, remember that the request is due before the motion to reinstate. Compare TRCP 296 (20 days) with TRCP 165a(3) (30 days).

---

(2) Jurisdictional challenge. Findings of fact can be helpful when the court rules on jurisdictional challenges after receiving evidence (e.g., when the trial court rules on a special appearance challenging personal jurisdiction or on a plea to the jurisdiction challenging subject-matter jurisdiction). *See Goodenbour v. Goodenbour*, 64 S.W.3d 69, 75 (Tex.App.—Austin 2001, pet. denied) (special appearance); *Hernandez v. Texas Dept. of Ins.*, 923 S.W.2d 192, 194 (Tex.App.—Austin 1996, no writ) (plea to the jurisdiction).

(3) Groundless pleadings. It is not necessary to ask for separate findings of fact when sanctions are imposed under TRCP 13 and CPRC §10.001; the court is required to include findings in the sanctions order. For sanctions under CPRC §9.012, separately filed findings of fact are helpful.

(4) Late report. In a medical-malpractice case, findings of fact are helpful when the court dismisses a plaintiff's suit for filing a late report. *See Mocega v. Urquhart*, 79 S.W.3d 61, 63-64 (Tex.App.—Houston [14th Dist.] 2002, pet. denied) (former TRCS art. 4590i, §13.01, now CPRC §74.351).

3. After hearing on venue. Findings of fact can be helpful to review a venue ruling. *See Coke v. Coke*, 802 S.W.2d 270, 278 (Tex.App.—Dallas 1990, writ denied); *Gaston v. Chaney*, 734 S.W.2d 735, 737 (Tex.App.—Eastland 1987, no writ).

4. After judgment with exemplary damages. When the trial court awards exemplary damages, findings of fact stating the court's reasons for refusing to disturb the jury's exemplary-damages award will "facilitate meaningful post-verdict review." *Transportation Ins. v. Moriel*, 879 S.W.2d 10, 33 (Tex.1994). Although it is optional for the trial court to make these findings, the courts of appeals are required to make them, whether they uphold, reduce, or eliminate the award. *See* CPRC §41.013(a).

5. After hearing on remittitur. Findings of fact stating the trial court's reasons for suggesting remittitur are helpful for appellate courts. *Landon v. Jean-Paul Budinger, Inc.*, 724 S.W.2d 931, 940 (Tex.App.—Austin 1987, no writ).

─────────────────────────── ★ ───────────────────────────

6. After hearing to reinstate. Findings of fact are helpful after a hearing on a motion to reinstate a case that was dismissed for want of prosecution. *Cf. Phillips v. Beavers*, 938 S.W.2d 446, 446-47 (Tex.1997) (after dismissal for want of prosecution). See "Motion to Reinstate After Dismissal for Want of Prosecution," ch. 10-F, p. 826.

7. After hearing on MNT. Findings of fact are helpful after a hearing on a motion for new trial at which evidence was received. *See, e.g., Higginbotham v. General Life & Acc. Ins.*, 796 S.W.2d 695, 695 (Tex.1990) (MNT after no-answer default judgment).

8. After default judgment on unliquidated damages. Findings of fact are helpful when the court renders a default judgment on unliquidated damages. *IKB Indus.*, 938 S.W.2d at 443.

§2.3 Findings of fact are permitted after appealable orders. Specific rules permit the trial court to file findings of fact in the appeal of interlocutory orders. The request for findings of fact in an appeal of an interlocutory order does not extend the time to perfect the appeal. TRAP 28.1(b). See *O'Connor's Texas Appeals*, "Motion for Interlocutory Appeal & Stay Pending Appeal," ch. 3-P, p. 148.

1. After TRO or temporary injunction. TRCP 683 requires each order granting a TRO or temporary injunction to include the reasons for its issuance in the order. *Transport Co. v. Robertson Transps.*, 261 S.W.2d 549, 553 (Tex.1953). The trial court can, but is not required to, file separate findings of fact. *See Transport Co.*, 261 S.W.2d at 553; *Operation Rescue-Nat'l v. Planned Parenthood*, 937 S.W.2d 60, 82 (Tex.App.—Houston [14th Dist.] 1996), *aff'd as modified*, 975 S.W.2d 546 (Tex.1998).

2. After class-action certification. Implicit in TRCP 42(b)(3) is the requirement that the trial court make findings about the application of TRCP 42 to the facts of the case. TRCP 42 does not state whether the findings should be incorporated into the certification order or filed separately as findings of fact. *See, e.g., General Motors Corp. v. Bloyed*, 916 S.W.2d 949, 955-56 (Tex.1996) (trial court filed findings of fact); *Texas Dept. of MHMR v. Petty*, 778 S.W.2d 156, 160 (Tex.App.—Austin 1989, writ dism'd) (trial court's findings were part of order certifying class). To award attorney fees in a class-action certification, the trial court must state its findings in writing or orally on the record. TRCP 42(h)(3).

3. After other appealable orders. TRAP 28.1(c) permits, but does not require, the trial court to file findings of fact after rendering an interlocutory order. *See Mueller v. Beamalloy, Inc.*, 994 S.W.2d 855, 858 (Tex. App.—Houston [1st Dist.] 1999, no pet.) (appointment of receiver).

4. To review supersedeas bonds. TRAP 24.4(d) permits the appellate court to remand the issue of the sufficiency of a supersedeas bond to the trial court to take evidence and file findings of fact. *TransAmerican Nat. Gas Corp. v. Finkelstein*, 911 S.W.2d 153, 155 (Tex.App.—San Antonio 1995, order). See *O'Connor's Texas Appeals*, "Superseding the Judgment," ch. 4-B, p. 162.

§2.4 Findings of fact are not appropriate. Findings of fact are not appropriate when they have no purpose. *IKB Indus. v. Pro-Line Corp.*, 938 S.W.2d 440, 443 (Tex.1997). In such cases, findings should not be requested, made, or considered on appeal. *Id.* When findings of fact are not appropriate, a request for findings does not extend the time to perfect an appeal, as it does when they are appropriate. *Id.*; *Linwood v. NCNB Tex.*, 885 S.W.2d 102, 103 (Tex. 1994).

1. After jury trial. Findings of fact are not appropriate on issues tried to a jury. *Favaloro v. Commission for Lawyer Discipline*, 13 S.W.3d 831, 840 (Tex.App.—Dallas 2000, no pet.).

2. After summary judgment. Findings of fact are not appropriate after the court renders a summary judgment. *IKB Indus.*, 938 S.W.2d at 441-42; *Linwood*, 885 S.W.2d at 103; *Willms v. Americas Tire Co.*, 190 S.W.3d 796, 810 (Tex.App.—Dallas 2006, pet. denied).

3. After directed verdict. Findings of fact are not appropriate in a case resolved by a directed verdict. *IKB Indus.*, 938 S.W.2d at 443; *Ditto v. Ditto Inv.*, 309 S.W.2d 219, 220 (Tex.1958).

⎯⎯⎯⎯⎯⎯⎯⎯ ★ ⎯⎯⎯⎯⎯⎯⎯⎯

4. After JNOV. Findings of fact are not appropriate after the court renders a judgment notwithstanding the verdict. *IKB Indus.*, 938 S.W.2d at 443; *Fancher v. Cadwell*, 314 S.W.2d 820, 822 (Tex.1958).

5. After trial of agreed case. Findings of fact are not appropriate after the court renders a judgment on an agreed statement of facts under TRCP 263. See "No findings of fact," ch. 7-E, §5.3, p. 649.

6. After default judgment on liquidated damages. Findings of fact are not appropriate after the court renders a default judgment based on liquidated damages. *IKB Indus.*, 938 S.W.2d at 443.

7. After dismissal on pleadings without evidence. Findings of fact are not appropriate after the court (1) dismisses a case for want of prosecution without a hearing to receive evidence, (2) dismisses for lack of subject-matter jurisdiction without sworn proof, (3) dismisses after refusal to amend following an order on special exceptions, or (4) renders any judgment without an evidentiary hearing. *See IKB Indus.*, 938 S.W.2d at 443 (listing inappropriate cases for findings of fact); *see, e.g., Awde v. Dabeit*, 938 S.W.2d 31, 33 (Tex.1997) (based on pleadings, suit dismissed for lack of subject-matter jurisdiction); *F-Star Socorro, L.P. v. El Paso Cent. Appr. Dist.*, 324 S.W.3d 172, 174-75 (Tex.App.—El Paso 2010, no pet.) (after hearing parties' legal arguments, court dismissed suit for lack of subject-matter jurisdiction); *CMS Partners v. Plumrose USA, Inc.*, 101 S.W.3d 730, 736-37 (Tex.App.—Texarkana 2003, no pet.) (suit dismissed under forum-selection clause).

8. On undisputed issues. See "Only on controlling issues," §5.1.3, p. 823.

§3. REQUESTING FINDINGS OF FACT

Either party may request that the court file findings of fact under TRCP 296. In cases governed by TRCP 296, the party who loses should always request findings of fact; otherwise, all findings are deemed in favor of the judgment. *Worford v. Stamper*, 801 S.W.2d 108, 109 (Tex.1990); *Roberson v. Robinson*, 768 S.W.2d 280, 281 (Tex.1989). Although the prevailing party probably does not want to ask for findings of fact, once the losing party makes a proper request for findings, the prevailing party should make sure they are filed. The rules provide for three requests for findings of fact.

§3.1 First request. TRCP 296 states that the original request must be entitled "Request for Findings of Fact and Conclusions of Law." See *O'Connor's Texas Forms*, FORM 10E:1.

1. Deadline. The first request must be filed within 20 days after the date the judgment was signed. TRCP 296; *Willms v. Americas Tire Co.*, 190 S.W.3d 796, 801 (Tex.App.—Dallas 2006, pet. denied); *Ohio Cas. Grp. v. Risinger*, 960 S.W.2d 708, 712 (Tex.App.—Tyler 1997, writ denied); *Lopez v. Hansen*, 947 S.W.2d 587, 589 (Tex. App.—Houston [1st Dist.] 1997, no writ). If the request for findings is filed before the judgment is signed, it is considered a premature request and is deemed filed on the day of, but immediately after, the signing of the judgment. TRCP 306c; *Pursley v. Ussery*, 982 S.W.2d 596, 599 (Tex.App.—San Antonio 1998, pet. denied); *Vargas v. TDPRS*, 973 S.W.2d 423, 426 (Tex.App.—Austin 1998, pet. granted, judgm't vacated w.r.m.); *see* TRAP 27.2. The party requesting findings of fact must send a copy of the request to the other party. TRCP 21a.

2. Clerk's duty. The court clerk must immediately call the request to the attention of the judge who tried the case. TRCP 296.

§3.2 Court's deadline to file findings. The trial court should file findings of fact within 20 days after the date the party requested findings. TRCP 297. The court must mail a copy of the findings of fact to all the parties. *Id.* Therefore, the party requesting findings should receive a copy in the mail. If it does not receive the findings, the party should file a second request. See "Second request," §3.3, this page.

§3.3 Second request. If the trial court does not file findings of fact within 20 days after the first request is filed, the party who asked for findings has 30 days after the date it filed its original request to file a "Notice of Past Due Findings of Fact and Conclusions of Law." TRCP 297. A party that does not file a notice of past-due findings of fact waives the right to complain that the trial court did not file findings. *Sonnier v. Sonnier*, 331 S.W.3d 211, 214 (Tex.App.—Beaumont 2011, no pet.); *Gnerer v. Johnson*, 227 S.W.3d 385, 389 (Tex.App.—Texarkana 2007, no pet.).

★

In the notice of past-due findings of fact, the party must state the date the original request was filed and the date the findings of fact were due. TRCP 297; *Curtis v. Commission for Lawyer Discipline*, 20 S.W.3d 227, 232 (Tex. App.—Houston [14th Dist.] 2000, no pet.). See *O'Connor's Texas Forms*, FORM 10E:3.

PRACTICE TIP

Although all courts agree a premature first request for findings is considered timely, at least two courts have held that a premature notice of past-due findings is not timely. E.g., **Estate of Gorski v. Welch**, *993 S.W.2d 298, 301 (Tex.App.—San Antonio 1999, pet. denied);* **Echols v. Echols**, *900 S.W.2d 160, 161-62 (Tex.App.—Beaumont 1995, writ denied). These courts held that TRCP 306c ("No ... request for findings of fact ... shall be held ineffective because prematurely filed....") does not apply to notices of past-due findings.* **Estate of Gorski**, *993 S.W.2d at 301;* **Echols**, *900 S.W.2d at 161.*

---

§3.4 Court files findings. Once a second request is filed, the trial court has 40 days after the date the first request was filed to file findings of fact. TRCP 297.

1. Not in judgment. The requirement for filing findings under TRCP 296-298 cannot be satisfied by findings of fact in the judgment. TRCP 299a prohibits the trial court from reciting findings of fact in the judgment. *Frommer v. Frommer*, 981 S.W.2d 811, 814 (Tex.App.—Houston [1st Dist.] 1998, pet. dism'd). *But see In re Estate of Jones*, 197 S.W.3d 894, 900 n.4 (Tex.App.—Beaumont 2006, pet. denied) (if findings are recited in the judgment, if no one complains, and if there is no conflict with separately filed findings, the findings in the judgment should not be ignored on appeal).

2. Send findings to parties. Once the court makes findings of fact, it must mail a copy of the findings to each party. TRCP 297. This gives the parties time to meet the deadline in TRCP 298 for requesting additional or amended findings within ten days after the original findings are filed.

§3.5 Third request – for additional or amended findings. Once the trial court files findings of fact, either party may ask the trial court to make additional or amended findings.

1. Deadline to request. The request for additional or amended findings of fact must be filed within ten days after the trial court's initial findings. TRCP 298; *SMI/USA, Inc. v. Profile Techs.*, 38 S.W.3d 205, 209 (Tex. App.—Waco 2001, no pet.). If the request for additional findings is made before the trial court makes any findings, one court has said the premature request is ineffective. *See Mohnke v. Greenwood*, 915 S.W.2d 585, 590 (Tex. App.—Houston [14th Dist.] 1996, no writ). *But see* TRCP 306c (no premature request for findings shall be ineffective).

2. Proposed findings. The party must submit specific proposed findings of fact; a broad request for additional or amended findings is not sufficient. *Alvarez v. Espinoza*, 844 S.W.2d 238, 242 (Tex.App.—San Antonio 1992, writ dism'd). If the court omitted a finding on a material element, the party should ask the court to make the omitted finding; if the court made an error in a finding, the party should ask the court to amend the finding. See *O'Connor's Texas Forms*, FORM 10E:4.

(1) By prevailing party. The prevailing party should request additional or amended findings of fact that support the judgment in its favor.

(2) By losing party. The losing party's request for additional or amended findings of fact is difficult to make because a request for findings inconsistent with the judgment will be denied, and a request for findings consistent with the judgment might be considered a waiver. *See In re Marriage of Grossnickle*, 115 S.W.3d 238, 254 (Tex.App.—Texarkana 2003, no pet.) (trial court is not required to make additional or amended findings contrary to other findings); *ASAI v. Vanco Insulation Abatement, Inc.*, 932 S.W.2d 118, 122 (Tex.App.—El Paso 1996, no writ) (same). In its request for additional findings, the losing party should (1) inform the trial court that a

---

★

---

material issue disputed during the trial was not addressed in any of the findings, (2) request specific, additional findings on that issue that are consistent with the judgment, (3) inform the trial court that the party does not agree with the additional findings it requests, and (4) state that the findings are necessary so that, on appeal, the party may challenge either the findings or, if the additional findings are not entered, the lack of those findings. *See, e.g.*, *Vickery v. Commission for Lawyer Discipline*, 5 S.W.3d 241, 254 (Tex.App.—Houston [14th Dist.] 1999, pet. denied) (appellant's request did not inform trial court that it had omitted two essential elements in its original findings).

§3.6 Court's deadline to file additional findings. The trial court must file any additional or amended findings of fact no later than ten days after the date the request for additional findings is filed. TRCP 298. If the court refuses to make additional findings of fact requested by the losing party, the prevailing party cannot argue on appeal that findings should be deemed in support of the judgment. TRCP 299; *Boy Scouts v. Responsive Terminal Sys.*, 790 S.W.2d 738, 742-43 (Tex.App.—Dallas 1990, writ denied). Thus, the prevailing party should encourage the court to make additional findings when they are necessary.

§3.7 Findings in child-support cases. In a contested child-support case, Family Code §154.130 requires the court to file findings of fact when properly requested, "without regard to rules 296 through 299." The request for findings of fact under Family Code §154.130(a) may be made either orally during the hearing or in writing, filed within ten days after the hearing. If the request is oral, it must be made on the record. *See* Fam. Code §154.130(a)(2). Family Code §154.130(b) lists the specific findings the court must make. The trial court must make and enter these findings within 15 days after the request is made. Fam. Code §154.130(a-1). See *O'Connor's Fam. Law Handbook*, "Findings," ch. 4-F, §18.3.8, p. 514.

§4. RESPONSE

The prevailing party should draft findings of fact when it receives notice that the other party has requested findings of fact. See *O'Connor's Texas Forms*, FORM 10E:2. In drafting the findings of fact, the party should include a finding on each element of the cause of action and each defense. See generally *O'Connor's Texas Causes of Action* (2013).

§5. COURT'S FINDINGS OF FACT & CONCLUSIONS OF LAW

§5.1 Form & content. The findings of fact and conclusions of law are generally prepared by the prevailing party. *Vickery v. Commission for Lawyer Discipline*, 5 S.W.3d 241, 253 (Tex.App.—Houston [14th Dist.] 1999, pet. denied); *Grossnickle v. Grossnickle*, 935 S.W.2d 830, 837 n.1 (Tex.App.—Texarkana 1996, writ denied). The findings must be made in writing, not orally. *See Larry F. Smith, Inc. v. Weber Co.*, 110 S.W.3d 611, 615 (Tex.App.—Dallas 2003, pet. denied).

1. Same document, separate headings. The findings and conclusions should be in the same document, but they should be stated under separate headings. When a finding of fact is mislabeled as a conclusion of law, the appellate court can treat it as a finding of fact. *Ray v. Farmers' State Bank*, 576 S.W.2d 607, 608 n.1 (Tex.1979); *see Posner v. Dallas Cty. Child Welfare Unit*, 784 S.W.2d 585, 586-87 (Tex.App.—Eastland 1990, writ denied).

2. Not in the judgment. TRCP 299a requires the trial court to file findings of fact in a document separate from the judgment. TRCP 299a; *Guridi v. Waller*, 98 S.W.3d 315, 316-17 (Tex.App.—Houston [1st Dist.] 2003, no pet.); *Salinas v. Beaudrie*, 960 S.W.2d 314, 317 (Tex.App.—Corpus Christi 1997, no pet.). When factual findings in the judgment conflict with those in the findings of fact, the separately filed findings of fact will control. TRCP 299a. The courts of appeals are split on whether to review findings that are included in the judgment. *Compare Casino Magic Corp. v. King*, 43 S.W.3d 14, 19 n.6 (Tex.App.—Dallas 2001, pet. denied) (findings in judgment were not considered to be findings of fact for review), *Salinas*, 960 S.W.2d at 317 (on appeal, court cannot consider findings contained in judgment), *and Sutherland v. Cobern*, 843 S.W.2d 127, 131 n.7 (Tex.App.—Texarkana 1992, writ denied) (same), *with In re C.A.B.*, 289 S.W.3d 874, 880-81 (Tex.App.—Houston [14th Dist.] 2009, no pet.) (on appeal, court can consider findings contained in judgment unless they conflict with separately filed findings), *In re Sigmar*, 270 S.W.3d 289, 295 n.2 (Tex.App.—Waco 2008, orig. proceeding) (same), *In re Estate of Jones*, 197 S.W.3d 894, 899-900

────────────── ✦ ──────────────

& n.4 (Tex.App.—Beaumont 2006, pet. denied) (same), *Tate v. Tate*, 55 S.W.3d 1, 8 n.4 (Tex.App.—El Paso 2000, no pet.) (same), *and Hill v. Hill*, 971 S.W.2d 153, 157 (Tex.App.—Amarillo 1998, no pet.) (same). When no findings are requested and no separate findings are filed, findings included in the judgment should not be considered. *See Guridi*, 98 S.W.3d at 317.

3. Only on controlling issues. The trial court is required to make findings of fact and conclusions of law only on controlling factual issues. *ASAI v. Vanco Insulation Abatement, Inc.*, 932 S.W.2d 118, 122 (Tex. App.—El Paso 1996, no writ); *Rafferty v. Finstad*, 903 S.W.2d 374, 376 (Tex.App.—Houston [1st Dist.] 1995, writ denied). An issue is controlling when it will support a judgment for one of the parties. *Taylor v. Texas DPS*, 754 S.W.2d 464, 468 (Tex.App.—Fort Worth 1988, writ denied). The trial court is not required to make findings on undisputed issues. *Barker v. Eckman*, 213 S.W.3d 306, 310 (Tex.2006).

§5.2 Late findings of fact & conclusions of law. The trial court can file findings of fact and conclusions of law after the deadline to file them has expired. *Robles v. Robles*, 965 S.W.2d 605, 610 (Tex.App.—Houston [1st Dist.] 1998, pet. denied); *Morrison v. Morrison*, 713 S.W.2d 377, 380 (Tex.App.—Dallas 1986, writ dism'd). The trial court can file late findings and conclusions even after it loses plenary power. *In re Gillespie*, 124 S.W.3d 699, 703 (Tex.App.—Houston [14th Dist.] 2003, orig. proceeding); *see Morrison*, 713 S.W.2d at 380. *But see Sonnier v. Sonnier*, 331 S.W.3d 211, 214-15 (Tex.App.—Beaumont 2011, no pet.) (trial court cannot make findings and conclusions after it loses plenary power because appellate court has exclusive jurisdiction). Because findings of fact and conclusions of law do not change the judgment, the court's loss of plenary power does not matter. *In re Gillespie*, 124 S.W.3d at 703.

§6. REVIEW

§6.1 Effect on appellate timetable. A timely request for findings of fact and conclusions of law extends the time to perfect the appeal when (1) the findings and conclusions are required by TRCP 296 or (2) the trial court conducts an evidentiary hearing and the findings and conclusions can properly be considered by the appellate court. TRAP 26.1(a)(4); *IKB Indus. v. Pro-Line Corp.*, 938 S.W.2d 440, 443 (Tex.1997); *Awde v. Dabeit*, 938 S.W.2d 31, 33 (Tex. 1997). See *O'Connor's Texas Appeals*, "Filing deadlines extended," ch. 5-A, §6.1.4, p. 200.

1. Time extended. When a timely request for findings of fact is made in a case in which findings are required (see "Findings of fact are necessary," §2.1, p. 817) or findings are helpful but not required (see "Findings of fact are helpful," §2.2, p. 818), the request extends the time to perfect an appeal. *IKB Indus.*, 938 S.W.2d at 443; *see Gene Duke Builders, Inc. v. Abilene Hous. Auth.*, 138 S.W.3d 907, 908 (Tex.2004).

2. Time not extended. A request for findings of fact does not extend the time to perfect an appeal in the appeal of interlocutory orders (see "Findings of fact are permitted after appealable orders," §2.3, p. 819) or when findings are not appropriate (see "Findings of fact are not appropriate," §2.4, p. 819). See *O'Connor's Texas Appeals*, "Generally," ch. 5-A, §5.2.2(1), p. 196; "Filing deadlines not extended," ch. 5-A, §6.2.3, p. 201.

§6.2 Review of findings of fact.

1. When all necessary findings filed. An appellant should treat the findings of fact as if they were jury findings and challenge all findings for legal and factual sufficiency. *Catalina v. Blasdel*, 881 S.W.2d 295, 297 (Tex. 1994); *Las Colinas Obstetrics-Gynecology-Infertility Ass'n v. Villalba*, 324 S.W.3d 634, 638 (Tex.App.—Dallas 2010, no pet.). When a reporter's record is part of the appellate record, findings of fact are not conclusive on appeal, even if unchallenged. *Zac Smith & Co. v. Otis Elevator Co.*, 734 S.W.2d 662, 666 (Tex.1987); *see Las Colinas*, 324 S.W.3d at 638; *City of Beaumont v. Spivey*, 1 S.W.3d 385, 392 (Tex.App.—Beaumont 1999, pet. denied). Before reversing on a factual-sufficiency point of error, the court of appeals must clearly state why the finding of fact is not supported by the evidence. *Ortiz v. Jones*, 917 S.W.2d 770, 772 (Tex.1996).

2. When some findings omitted. When a party requests findings of fact and the court files them, the court of appeals can presume that omitted findings support the judgment only when (1) an element of the ground of recovery was included in the findings of fact, (2) the omitted element was not properly requested, and (3) the omitted finding is supported by the evidence. TRCP 299; *American Nat'l Ins. v. Paul*, 927 S.W.2d 239, 245 (Tex.App.—

✫

Austin 1996, writ denied); *Warehouse Partners v. Gardner*, 910 S.W.2d 19, 23 (Tex.App.—Dallas 1995, writ denied); *see, e.g.*, *Tarrant Cty. Water Control & Imprv. Dist. v. Haupt, Inc.*, 854 S.W.2d 909, 913 (Tex.1993) (because record contained some evidence of reasonableness, issue was deemed to support trial court's judgment). When a party does not request (and the trial court does not make) findings on an entire ground of recovery or defense, the appellate court cannot presume that specific ground of recovery or defense supports the judgment. TRCP 299; *see F.R. Hernandez Constr. & Sup. v. National Bank of Commerce*, 578 S.W.2d 675, 678-79 (Tex.1979). When findings are not requested or made on an entire claim or defense, the party waives its claim or defense just as if, in a jury trial, the party did not request a jury question on a claim or defense.

3. When findings in conflict. If the trial court issues amended or additional findings of fact that conflict with the original findings, the later findings control. *Jefferson Cty. Drainage Dist. v. Lower Neches Valley Auth.*, 876 S.W.2d 940, 960 (Tex.App.—Beaumont 1994, writ denied).

4. When findings filed late. If the trial court files late findings of fact, the only issue is whether the appellant was harmed. *In re E.A.C.*, 162 S.W.3d 438, 443 (Tex.App.—Dallas 2005, no pet.); *Robles v. Robles*, 965 S.W.2d 605, 610 (Tex.App.—Houston [1st Dist.] 1998, pet. denied). *But see Sonnier v. Sonnier*, 331 S.W.3d 211, 214-16 (Tex.App.—Beaumont 2011, no pet.) (trial court's jurisdiction is also an issue; if appellate court has exclusive jurisdiction, trial court's late findings and conclusions are a nullity). The appellant may be harmed because she (1) was unable to request additional findings or (2) was prevented from properly presenting her appeal. *In re E.A.C.*, 162 S.W.3d at 443; *Robles*, 965 S.W.2d at 610. If harm is shown, the appellate court may abate the appeal to give the appellant an opportunity to request additional or amended findings. *Robles*, 965 S.W.2d at 610; *Jefferson Cty. Drainage Dist.*, 876 S.W.2d at 960; *Morrison v. Morrison*, 713 S.W.2d 377, 381 (Tex.App.—Dallas 1986, writ dism'd).

5. When no additional findings requested. If the appellant did not ask for additional findings, it cannot challenge the lack of findings on appeal. *Smith v. Smith*, 22 S.W.3d 140, 149 (Tex.App.—Houston [14th Dist.] 2000, no pet.); *Robles*, 965 S.W.2d at 611.

6. When findings not required but helpful.

(1) General rule. When findings of fact are not required by TRCP 296 or some other rule or statute but are helpful to the appellate court, they are not reviewed for legal and factual sufficiency of the evidence as are findings made under TRCP 296. *See Chrysler Corp. v. Blackmon*, 841 S.W.2d 844, 852 (Tex.1992). When findings of fact are not required but are helpful, they do not have the same weight on appeal as findings made under TRCP 296 and are not binding on the appellate court. *IKB Indus. v. Pro-Line Corp.*, 938 S.W.2d 440, 442 (Tex.1997).

(2) Exception – special appearance. Even though findings of fact are not required by TRCP 296 or any other rule after a special appearance, when the trial court files findings after it denies a special appearance, those findings are reviewed for legal and factual sufficiency of the evidence. *BMC Software Belgium, N.V. v. Marchand*, 83 S.W.3d 789, 794 (Tex.2002).

7. When findings requested but not filed. When properly requested, the trial court has a mandatory duty to file findings of fact. *Cherne Indus. v. Magallanes*, 763 S.W.2d 768, 772 (Tex.1989); *In re Davis*, 30 S.W.3d 609, 613 (Tex.App.—Texarkana 2000, no pet.). See "Findings of fact are necessary," §2.1, p. 817.

(1) Harmful error. If the trial court does not file findings of fact, it is presumed harmful error unless the record affirmatively shows the appellant suffered no harm. *Tenery v. Tenery*, 932 S.W.2d 29, 30 (Tex.1996); *Cherne Indus.*, 763 S.W.2d at 772; *Willms v. Americas Tire Co.*, 190 S.W.3d 796, 801 (Tex.App.—Dallas 2006, pet. denied). Error is harmful if it prevents a party from properly presenting its case to the appellate court. TRAP 44.1(a)(2); *Tenery*, 932 S.W.2d at 30. Generally, an appellant is harmed if the circumstances of the particular case require the appellant to guess at the reasons for the trial court's decision. *Liberty Mut. Fire Ins. v. Laca*, 243 S.W.3d 791, 794 (Tex.App.—El Paso 2007, no pet.); *Willms*, 190 S.W.3d at 801-02; *Goggins v. Leo*, 849 S.W.2d 373, 379 (Tex.App.—Houston [14th Dist.] 1993, no writ). In a complicated case with disputed facts or two or more grounds for recovery or defenses, the inference of harm cannot be overcome. *Randall v. Jennings*, 788 S.W.2d 931, 932 (Tex.

———————————— ★ ————————————

App.—Houston [14th Dist.] 1990, no writ); *see Liberty Mut.*, 243 S.W.3d at 794. Oral findings made on the record are not a substitute for written findings. *Larry F. Smith, Inc. v. Weber Co.*, 110 S.W.3d 611, 615 (Tex.App.—Dallas 2003, pet. denied). *But see Sagemont Plaza Shopping v. Harris Cty. Appr. Dist.*, 30 S.W.3d 425, 427 (Tex.App.—Corpus Christi 2000, pet. denied) (ruling announced in open court gave parties the reason for the ruling; no harm in court not filing findings); *Texas Workers' Comp. Ins. Fund v. Ashy*, 972 S.W.2d 208, 212 (Tex.App.—Beaumont 1998, pet. denied) (same); *Elizondo v. Gomez*, 957 S.W.2d 862, 865 (Tex.App.—San Antonio 1997, pet. denied) (same).

(a) **Curable.** If the error is curable, the appellate court may abate the appeal and remand the case to the trial court to make findings of fact. *See* TRAP 44.4(a)(2) (no reversal if trial court can correct failure to act); *see, e.g.*, TRCP 18 (successor judge can make findings of fact if judge who handled case dies, resigns, or is disabled during her term); *Cherne Indus.*, 763 S.W.2d at 773 (trial judge was still on bench and could correct error); *Brooks v. Housing Auth.*, 926 S.W.2d 316, 319 (Tex.App.—El Paso 1996, no writ) (appeal was abated and trial judge was given 30 days to file findings).

(b) **Not curable.** If the error is not curable, the appellate court may reverse and remand the case for a new trial. *See, e.g.*, *Liberty Mut.*, 243 S.W.3d at 796 (reversed and remanded because judge who handled case was replaced as result of election); *Weber Co.*, 110 S.W.3d at 616 (same).

(2) **Harmless error.** If the trial court does not file findings of fact, and the lack of findings is harmless error, the appellate court will affirm. TRAP 44.1(a). The lack of findings is harmless if the record affirmatively shows the complaining party suffered no injury. *Cherne Indus.*, 763 S.W.2d at 772; *Gnerer v. Johnson*, 227 S.W.3d 385, 389 (Tex.App.—Texarkana 2007, no pet.). For example, when the facts are undisputed and the only matters presented on appeal are legal issues to be reviewed de novo, the lack of findings of fact is harmless error. *Rollins v. American Express Travel Related Servs. Co.*, 219 S.W.3d 1, 5 (Tex.App.—Houston [1st Dist.] 2006, no pet.).

8. When findings not requested or filed. When no findings of fact are requested or filed, the trial court's judgment implies all findings of fact necessary to support it. *Sixth RMA Partners v. Sibley*, 111 S.W.3d 46, 52 (Tex.2003); *BMC Software*, 83 S.W.3d at 795; *Worford v. Stamper*, 801 S.W.2d 108, 109 (Tex.1990). When a reporter's record is filed, the implied findings are not conclusive, and an appellant may challenge them for both legal and factual sufficiency. *Sibley*, 111 S.W.3d at 52; *BMC Software*, 83 S.W.3d at 795; *Roberson v. Robinson*, 768 S.W.2d 280, 281 (Tex.1989).

§6.3 Review of conclusions of law. The legal conclusions of the trial court are not binding on an appellate court; appellate courts are free to draw their own legal conclusions. *See Pegasus Energy Grp. v. Cheyenne Pet. Co.*, 3 S.W.3d 112, 121 (Tex.App.—Corpus Christi 1999, pet. denied); *Austin Hardwoods, Inc. v. Vanden Berghe*, 917 S.W.2d 320, 322 (Tex.App.—El Paso 1995, writ denied). An appellate court may uphold the trial court's conclusions of law if the judgment is supported by the evidence under any correct legal theory. *City of Houston v. Cotton*, 171 S.W.3d 541, 546 (Tex.App.—Houston [14th Dist.] 2005, pet. denied). The standard the court of appeals applies to review conclusions of law is de novo. *Hydrocarbon Mgmt. v. Tracker Expl., Inc.*, 861 S.W.2d 427, 431 (Tex.App.—Amarillo 1993, no writ).

──────────────────── ✦ ────────────────────

F. MOTION TO REINSTATE AFTER DISMISSAL FOR WANT OF PROSECUTION

§1. GENERAL

§1.1 Rules. TRCP 165a; TRAP 26.1(a)(3).

§1.2 Purpose. TRCP 165a permits a plaintiff to ask the court to reinstate a case after it was dismissed for want of prosecution (DWOP).

§1.3 Timetable & forms. Timetable, Motion to Reinstate After Dismissal for Want of Prosecution, p. 1233; *O'Connor's Texas Civil Forms* (2012), FORMS 10F.

§2. BEFORE DISMISSAL

The trial court's authority to dismiss for want of prosecution comes from two sources: TRCP 165a and the court's inherent power. See "Failure to prosecute," ch. 7-G, §2.2, p. 658.

§2.1 Notice case is on dismissal docket. See "Notice of Intent to Dismiss," ch. 7-G, §3, p. 660.

§2.2 Motion to retain. A plaintiff should file a motion to retain after it receives notice of the court's intent to dismiss and before the actual dismissal. See "Motion to retain," ch. 7-G, §4.1, p. 660.

§3. MOTION TO REINSTATE

§3.1 Court's initiative. A trial court can reinstate the case on its own initiative without a motion within 30 days after dismissal. *Neese v. Wray*, 893 S.W.2d 169, 170 (Tex.App.—Houston [1st Dist.] 1995, no writ); *see Texas DPS v. Deck*, 954 S.W.2d 108, 111-12 (Tex.App.—San Antonio 1997, no writ).

§3.2 Plaintiff's motion. A motion to reinstate is not a prerequisite to appeal a DWOP. *Maida v. Fire Ins. Exch.*, 990 S.W.2d 836, 838 n.1 (Tex.App.—Fort Worth 1999, no pet.); *Hosey v. County of Victoria*, 832 S.W.2d 701, 703 (Tex.App.—Corpus Christi 1992, no writ). However, the motion to reinstate gives the plaintiff one last chance to convince the trial court to restore the case to the docket, permits the plaintiff to make a record for appeal, and extends the court's plenary power and the appellate deadlines. *See* TRCP 165a(3) (timely filed motion to reinstate extends court's plenary power to reinstate case until 30 days after motion is overruled).

§3.3 Verified. The plaintiff or its attorney must verify the motion to reinstate and, when necessary, attach affidavits. *See* TRCP 165a(3); *McConnell v. May*, 800 S.W.2d 194, 194 (Tex.1990); *Kenley v. Quintana Pet. Corp.*, 931 S.W.2d 318, 321 (Tex.App.—San Antonio 1996, writ denied). See "Verification," ch. 1-B, §3.2.15, p. 11; "Affidavits," ch. 1-B, §3.2.16, p. 11. An affidavit by the plaintiff's attorney can act as a substitute for verification. *Andrews v. Stanton*, 198 S.W.3d 4, 8-9 (Tex.App.—El Paso 2006, no pet.); *3V, Inc. v. JTS Enters.*, 40 S.W.3d 533, 538-39 (Tex. App.—Houston [14th Dist.] 2000, no pet.); *see, e.g., Guest v. Dixon*, 195 S.W.3d 687, 689 (Tex.2006) (affidavit of P's former attorney who had represented P for majority of time that case was pending was sufficient verification). In addition, the plaintiff can use an unsworn declaration instead of the verification. See "Unsworn declaration," ch. 1-B, §3.2.14, p. 10. An unverified motion does not extend the trial court's plenary power or the deadlines for perfecting an appeal. *Guest*, 195 S.W.3d at 688; *McConnell*, 800 S.W.2d at 194. The trial court can grant an unverified motion to reinstate, however, if it signs a written order within 30 days after the order of dismissal. *Dardari v. Texas Commerce Bank*, 961 S.W.2d 466, 469 (Tex.App.—Houston [1st Dist.] 1997, no pet.). The court cannot grant an unverified motion to reinstate more than 30 days after the order of dismissal because it no longer has plenary power. *In re Garcia*, 94 S.W.3d 832, 833-34 (Tex.App.—Corpus Christi 2002, orig. proceeding).

§3.4 Grounds to reinstate. The motion to reinstate must address the grounds for dismissal stated in the trial court's order. *Shook v. Gilmore & Tatge Mfg.*, 951 S.W.2d 294, 296 (Tex.App.—Waco 1997, pet. denied). When the dismissal order does not identify the grounds for dismissal, the motion must address and negate all possible grounds. *Nichols v. Sedalco Constr. Servs.*, 228 S.W.3d 341, 342-43 (Tex.App.—Waco 2007, pet. denied); *Manning v. North*, 82 S.W.3d 706, 713 (Tex.App.—Amarillo 2002, no pet.). See *O'Connor's Texas Forms*, FORM 10F:1.

✦

1. Dismissal for failure to appear. When a court dismisses a suit for the plaintiff's failure to appear at the trial or other dispositive hearing under TRCP 165a(1), the plaintiff must establish by a verified motion that (1) it had no notice of the trial or hearing, (2) it had no notice of the court's intent to dismiss, or (3) although it had notice, its failure to appear was due to a mistake or accident.

(1) No notice of trial or hearing. If the plaintiff had no notice of the trial or hearing, the verified motion to reinstate should state that the plaintiff did not appear at the trial or hearing because it had no notice. The trial court cannot dismiss a suit for failure to appear unless the plaintiff was given proper notice of a trial or hearing. TRCP 165a(1). See "Notice of Intent to Dismiss," ch. 7-G, §3, p. 660.

(2) No notice of intent to dismiss. If the plaintiff had no notice of the court's intent to dismiss the suit or of the date and place of the dismissal hearing, the motion should state that the court could not dismiss the suit due to this lack of notice. The trial court cannot dismiss a suit for failure to appear without giving notice and an opportunity to be heard. See "Failure to appear," ch. 7-G, §2.2.1(1), p. 658.

(3) Mistake or accident. If the plaintiff received notice of the trial or hearing and notice that failure to appear could result in dismissal, the verified motion should state that the plaintiff's failure to appear was not intentional or the result of conscious indifference, but was the result of a mistake or accident or is otherwise reasonably explained. *See* TRCP 165a(3); ***Smith v. Babcock & Wilcox Constr. Co.***, 913 S.W.2d 467, 468 (Tex.1995). When the plaintiff received notice of the trial or hearing but did not appear, the standard of review is essentially the same as the ***Craddock*** standard for setting aside a default judgment. ***Smith***, 913 S.W.2d at 468; *see* ***Craddock v. Sunshine Bus Lines, Inc.***, 133 S.W.2d 124, 126 (Tex.1939). See "Failure to answer or appear after proper notice," ch. 10-B, §9.1.3, p. 796. The failure to appear is not intentional or due to conscious indifference within the meaning of TRCP 165a(3) merely because it is deliberate; it must also be without adequate justification. ***Smith***, 913 S.W.2d at 468. Conscious indifference means more than just negligence. *See, e.g., id.* (attorney, in trial in one county, mistakenly thought a continuance would be granted in case in another county; no conscious indifference); ***Quita, Inc. v. Haney***, 810 S.W.2d 469, 470 (Tex.App.—Eastland 1991, no writ) (attorney, in trial in one county, thought trial in other county would not be reached; no conscious indifference). Proof of justification (i.e., accident, mistake, or other reasonable explanation) negates intent or conscious indifference. ***Smith***, 913 S.W.2d at 468. A mistake of law may satisfy this requirement. ***Bank One v. Moody***, 830 S.W.2d 81, 85 (Tex.1992).

2. Dismissal for failure to prosecute. A motion to reinstate a case dismissed for failure to diligently prosecute gives the plaintiff the opportunity to ask the court to reconsider the dismissal. ***Ellmossallamy v. Huntsman***, 830 S.W.2d 299, 302 (Tex.App.—Houston [14th Dist.] 1992, no writ).

(1) No notice of intent to dismiss. If the court dismissed the suit for failure to diligently prosecute without giving the plaintiff notice of its intent to dismiss, the plaintiff should file a verified motion to reinstate (1) proving lack of proper notice and (2) refuting the grounds for failure to prosecute. See "Notice of Intent to Dismiss," ch. 7-G, §3, p. 660. The court can overrule the motion if the plaintiff merely proves lack of notice and does not address the failure to prosecute. *See* ***Texas Sting, Ltd. v. R.B. Foods, Inc.***, 82 S.W.3d 644, 649 (Tex.App.—San Antonio 2002, pet. denied).

(2) Failure to comply with time standards. When a court dismisses a suit under TRCP 165a(2) for failure to comply with the Supreme Court's time standards, the plaintiff should file a verified motion to reinstate showing one of the following: (1) the suit was dismissed before the expiration of the appropriate time standard, (2) the plaintiff has a reasonable excuse for failing to prosecute the case within the time limits, or (3) there is good cause to maintain the case on the docket. *See, e.g.,* ***Polk v. Southwest Crossing Homeowners Ass'n***, 165 S.W.3d 89, 96 (Tex.App.—Houston [14th Dist.] 2005, pet. denied) (dismissal affirmed; P did not bring case to trial or disposition for almost five years after D's appearance dates); ***Steward v. Colonial Cas. Ins.***, 143 S.W.3d 161, 164 (Tex.App.—Waco 2004, no pet.) (dismissal affirmed; dismissal notice sent more than two years after appearance date was well outside TRCP 165a(2) time standards); ***Johnson-Snodgrass v. KTAO, Inc.***, 75 S.W.3d 84, 87 (Tex.App.—Fort Worth 2002, pet. dism'd) (dismissal reversed; case was dismissed before it was 18 months old). See "Failure to comply with time standards," ch. 7-G, §2.2.1(2), p. 659.

───────────────────── ✦ ─────────────────────

(3) Inherent power. When a court dismisses a suit under its inherent power for failure to prosecute, the plaintiff should file a verified motion to reinstate addressing the following issues: (1) the length of time the case was on file, (2) the extent of activity in the case (i.e., showing plaintiff's diligence), (3) whether a trial setting was requested, and (4) a reasonable explanation for the delay. *See Maida v. Fire Ins. Exch.*, 990 S.W.2d 836, 842 (Tex.App.—Fort Worth 1999, no pet.); *Bard v. Frank B. Hall & Co.*, 767 S.W.2d 839, 843 (Tex.App.—San Antonio 1989, writ denied). The purpose of the motion is to show that the plaintiff was "reasonably diligent" in prosecuting the suit. *See MacGregor v. Rich*, 941 S.W.2d 74, 75 (Tex.1997); *see also Veterans' Land Bd. v. Williams*, 543 S.W.2d 89, 90 (Tex.1976) ("due diligence"). A plaintiff is "reasonably diligent" if it acted as an ordinary, prudent person would have under the same or similar circumstances. *Manning*, 82 S.W.3d at 713. The motion must prove the plaintiff took the steps necessary to prepare for trial. *See, e.g., Ellmossallamy*, 830 S.W.2d at 302 (P diligently pursued discovery, complied with D's requests, and was ready to proceed to trial).

CAUTION

*The courts are split on whether the conscious-indifference standard of TRCP 165a(3) applies only to dismissal for failure to appear or whether it also applies when the case is dismissed for noncompliance with the Supreme Court's time standards or when the court exercises its inherent power to dismiss for lack of diligence. Compare **Zarychta v. Montgomery Cty. D.A.**, ___ S.W.3d ___ (Tex.App.—Corpus Christi 2011, pet. dism'd) (No. 13-10-00558-CV; 8-18-11) (conscious-indifference standard applies to all three grounds), and **Cappetta v. Hermes**, 222 S.W.3d 160, 167 (Tex.App.—San Antonio 2006, no pet.) (same), with **Steward**, 143 S.W.3d at 164-65 (conscious-indifference standard applies only to cases dismissed for failure to appear), and **Maida**, 990 S.W.2d at 840-41 (same).*

---

§3.5 Challenging language of dismissal order. If the trial court's order mistakenly dismissed the suit "with prejudice" or stated that the plaintiff "take nothing," that statement must be challenged in the motion to reinstate or in a motion for new trial; otherwise, the error is waived and the suit cannot be refiled. *See El Paso Pipe & Sup. v. Mountain States Leasing, Inc.*, 617 S.W.2d 189, 190 (Tex.1981). See "Order of Dismissal," ch. 7-G, §6, p. 661. The wrong notation regarding dismissal does not require reinstatement of the case, just a correction of the order.

§3.6 Requesting hearing. Even though the court is required to hold a hearing on a proper motion to reinstate and a request for a hearing is not necessary, the plaintiff should ask for a hearing. See *O'Connor's Texas Forms*, FORM 10F:1. Even when a plaintiff does not ask for a hearing, the trial court must conduct one unless the plaintiff actually waives it. *See Thordson v. City of Houston*, 815 S.W.2d 550, 550 (Tex.1991); *Andrews v. Stanton*, 198 S.W.3d 4, 9 (Tex.App.—El Paso 2006, no pet.). *But see Johnson v. Sepulveda*, 178 S.W.3d 117, 119 (Tex.App.—Houston [14th Dist.] 2005, no pet.) (relying on *Cabrera*, court held P was required to alert court of need for hearing); *Rainbow Home Health, Inc. v. Schmidt*, 76 S.W.3d 53, 57 (Tex.App.—San Antonio 2002, pet. denied) (same); *Cabrera v. Cedarapids Inc.*, 834 S.W.2d 615, 618 (Tex.App.—Houston [14th Dist.] 1992, writ denied) (relying on cases predating 1983 version of TRCP 165a, court held P was required to ask for hearing).

PRACTICE TIP

Always ask for a hearing for the motion to reinstate, attempt to get a setting for a hearing, and complain in writing if you do not get one.

---

§3.7 Amending the motion. The plaintiff must file an amended motion to reinstate within 30 days after the date the dismissal order was signed. *See, e.g., Mandujano v. Oliva*, 755 S.W.2d 512, 514 (Tex.App.—San Antonio 1988, writ denied) (P amended its petition to add verification before 30 days expired). If the court has already overruled the original motion, the plaintiff must seek leave of court to file an amended motion. TRCP 329b(b); *see also Mandujano*, 755 S.W.2d at 513 (amended motion was filed before trial court signed order overruling original motion).

✦

§4. DEADLINE

The deadline for filing a motion to reinstate depends on whether the plaintiff received timely notice of the dismissal. See "Notice of Dismissal Order," ch. 7-G, §8, p. 663; "Notice of Judgment," ch. 9-C, §5, p. 770.

§4.1 Timely notice of dismissal. If the plaintiff received timely notice of the dismissal of the suit, the plaintiff must file a motion to reinstate within 30 days after the trial court signed the order of dismissal. *Memorial Hosp. v. Gillis*, 741 S.W.2d 364, 365 (Tex.1987); *In re Montemayor*, 2 S.W.3d 542, 545 (Tex.App.—San Antonio 1999, orig. proceeding). Timely notice of dismissal is notice within 20 days after the dismissal. *Danforth Mem'l Hosp. v. Harris*, 573 S.W.2d 762, 763 (Tex.1978); *see* TRCP 306a(4); *In re Montemayor*, 2 S.W.3d at 545.

§4.2 Late notice of dismissal. If the plaintiff received notice of the dismissal of the suit 21 to 90 days after the date the judgment was signed, the plaintiff must file a motion to reinstate within 30 days after receiving notice of the dismissal and must include the allegations required for a motion to extend postjudgment deadlines. TRCP 306a(4), (5); TRAP 4.2(a)(1); *see Danforth Mem'l Hosp. v. Harris*, 573 S.W.2d 762, 763 (Tex.1978). See "Motion to Extend Postjudgment Deadlines," ch. 10-G, p. 831.

§4.3 Premature motion. If a plaintiff filed a motion to reinstate after dismissal but before the judgment was signed, the premature motion should be treated as timely. *In re Bokeloh*, 21 S.W.3d 784, 787-88 (Tex.App.—Houston [14th Dist.] 2000, orig. proceeding); *see* TRAP 27.2 (premature motion is considered effective); *Perez v. Texas Employers' Ins.*, 926 S.W.2d 425, 427 (Tex.App.—Austin 1996, order) (premature motion extends appellate timetable). *But see Brim Laundry Mach. Co. v. Washex Mach. Corp.*, 854 S.W.2d 297, 301 (Tex.App.—Fort Worth 1993, writ denied) (court ignored former TRAP 58, now TRAP 27, and applied TRCP 306c, which lists items that premature-filing rule applies to; prematurely filed motion to reinstate was ineffective). A motion to retain cannot be treated as a prematurely filed motion to reinstate. *In re Bokeloh*, 21 S.W.3d at 790-91.

§5. DUTY OF COURT

§5.1 Clerk. The court clerk must deliver a copy of the motion to reinstate to the trial court. TRCP 165a(3); *Bush v. Ward*, 747 S.W.2d 43, 45 (Tex.App.—Beaumont 1988, no writ).

§5.2 Setting for hearing. When a timely motion to reinstate is filed, the trial court must set it for a hearing. See "Hearing mandatory," §7.1, this page. The hearing must be held as soon as possible. TRCP 165a(3).

§5.3 Notice of hearing. The court must notify all parties of the date, time, and place of the hearing. TRCP 165a(3).

§6. RESPONSE

The defendant should file a response to a motion to reinstate and challenge the grounds in the motion, verifying any factual allegations in the response with affidavits. See *O'Connor's Texas Forms*, FORM 10F:2.

§7. HEARING

The hearing on the motion to reinstate remedies any violations of the plaintiff's due-process rights (e.g., lack of notice of the hearing or the dismissal) that occurred before the dismissal. *Manning v. North*, 82 S.W.3d 706, 715 (Tex. App.—Amarillo 2002, no pet.); *Texas Sting, Ltd. v. R.B. Foods, Inc.*, 82 S.W.3d 644, 648-49 (Tex.App.—San Antonio 2002, pet. denied). See "Notice of Intent to Dismiss," ch. 7-G, §3, p. 660.

§7.1 Hearing mandatory. An oral hearing to receive evidence on a timely motion to reinstate is mandatory. *Thordson v. City of Houston*, 815 S.W.2d 550, 550 (Tex.1991); *Gulf Coast Inv. v. NASA 1 Bus. Ctr.*, 754 S.W.2d 152, 153 (Tex.1988); *Matheson v. American Carbonics*, 867 S.W.2d 146, 148 (Tex.App.—Texarkana 1993, no writ). Whether the plaintiff requests a hearing on a motion to reinstate is irrelevant; a hearing is required unless it is affirmatively waived. *Matheson*, 867 S.W.2d at 147-48 & n.2; *see, e.g., Kelly v. Cunningham*, 848 S.W.2d 370, 371 (Tex.App.—Houston [1st Dist.] 1993, no writ) (Ps waived right to oral hearing by setting motion to reinstate on court's submission docket). If the trial court denies the motion to reinstate without first conducting a hearing, it is

★

reversible error. ***Bush v. Ward***, 747 S.W.2d 43, 45 (Tex.App.—Beaumont 1988, no writ). However, if the court reinstates the case without a hearing, the order is valid. ***Eagle Signal Corp. v. Wittig***, 766 S.W.2d 390, 392-93 (Tex. App.—Houston [1st Dist.] 1989, orig. proceeding).

CAUTION

Although the 1983 amendment to TRCP 165a requires the trial court to hold a hearing, some opinions issued after 1983 have erroneously relied on pre-1983 cases to hold that the hearing can be waived. See "Requesting hearing," §3.6, p. 828.

---

§7.2 Evidence. The plaintiff must present all necessary evidence at the hearing in support of each element of the grounds to reinstate. *See **Bard v. Frank B. Hall & Co.**,* 767 S.W.2d 839, 845 (Tex.App.—San Antonio 1989, writ denied). See "Grounds to reinstate," §3.4, p. 826. Both the plaintiff and its attorney should be sworn and should formally present testimony about the reason for the dismissal, good cause to reinstate, and when necessary, the late notice of the dismissal. If no evidence is presented at the hearing, the dismissal will be affirmed on appeal. *See **MacGregor v. Rich**,* 941 S.W.2d 74, 76 (Tex.1997); ***Balla v. Northeast Lincoln Mercury***, 717 S.W.2d 183, 185 (Tex. App.—Fort Worth 1986, no writ). The plaintiff should offer into evidence the affidavits attached to the motion, but it is not required to do so. *Cf. **Director, State Empls. Workers' Comp. Div. v. Evans**,* 889 S.W.2d 266, 268 (Tex.1994) (motion for new trial challenging post-answer default judgment).

§8. REQUEST FOR FINDINGS OF FACT

If the trial court denied the motion to reinstate after receiving evidence, the plaintiff should ask the court to file findings of fact and conclusions of law. *See **Burns v. Drew Woods, Inc.**,* 900 S.W.2d 128, 129-30 (Tex.App.—Waco 1995, writ denied) (in appeal from denial of motion to reinstate, court focuses on trial court's role in fact-finding process); *cf. **Phillips v. Beavers**,* 938 S.W.2d 446, 447 (Tex.1997) (findings are appropriate after hearing on motion to dismiss for want of prosecution).

§9. ORDER

§9.1 In writing. An order granting a motion to reinstate must be in writing and signed by the trial court. ***Emerald Oaks Hotel/Conf. Ctr., Inc. v. Zardenetta***, 776 S.W.2d 577, 578 (Tex.1989); ***Walker v. Harrison***, 597 S.W.2d 913, 915 (Tex.1980); ***In re Wal-Mart Stores***, 20 S.W.3d 734, 740 (Tex.App.—El Paso 2000, orig. proceeding). An oral order and docket entry are ineffective to reinstate, and the motion will be deemed overruled by operation of law. ***Emerald Oaks***, 776 S.W.2d at 578; ***In re Wal-Mart***, 20 S.W.3d at 740.

§9.2 Deadline to reinstate.

    1. Timely notice of dismissal. If the plaintiff filed a proper, timely, and verified motion to reinstate, the court must sign an order on the motion to reinstate within 75 days after the date the judgment was signed, or the motion will be overruled by operation of law on the 76th day. TRCP 165a(3); ***Emerald Oaks Hotel/Conf. Ctr., Inc. v. Zardenetta***, 776 S.W.2d 577, 578 (Tex.1989). Once the motion is overruled, the trial court retains plenary power to change its ruling for 30 more days. TRCP 165a(3); ***Nealy v. Home Indem. Co.***, 770 S.W.2d 592, 594 (Tex.App.— Houston [14th Dist.] 1989, no writ). See "Plenary-Power Deadlines," chart 9-1, p. 778.

    2. Late notice of dismissal. If the plaintiff received late notice that the case was dismissed, the provisions of TRCP 306a(4)-(5) apply to determine when the motion to reinstate must be filed and when the trial court must sign the order on the motion. If the trial court determines the plaintiff received notice of the dismissal within the 21- to 90-day window in TRCP 306a(4) and TRAP 4.2(a)(1), the reinstatement order must be signed no later than 75 days after the date of actual notice, or the motion will be overruled by operation of law. See "Motion to Extend Postjudgment Deadlines," ch. 10-G, p. 831.

§10. REVIEW

§10.1 Effect of motion to reinstate. Filing a proper motion to reinstate has the same effect on appellate deadlines and the court's plenary power as the filing of a motion for new trial. ***Butts v. Capitol City Nursing Home, Inc.***, 705 S.W.2d 696, 697 (Tex.1986). See "Effect of MNT," ch. 10-B, §2.5, p. 790. If a motion is not verified or is not timely,

─────────────────── ✦ ───────────────────

it does not extend the deadlines or the court's plenary power. *McConnell v. May*, 800 S.W.2d 194, 194 (Tex.1990); *Butts*, 705 S.W.2d at 697. If a motion to reinstate seeks more than reinstatement (e.g., it challenges the order that the case was dismissed "with prejudice"), it can be classified as a motion for new trial, and even an unverified motion will extend the appellate deadlines. *State v. Martini*, 902 S.W.2d 138, 140-41 (Tex.App.—Houston [1st Dist.] 1995, no writ). If the plaintiff files a motion for new trial after dismissal for want of prosecution, the motion will be treated as a motion to reinstate, and it must be verified to extend the appellate deadlines. *City of McAllen v. Ramirez*, 875 S.W.2d 702, 704-705 (Tex.App.—Corpus Christi 1994, orig. proceeding). See "Verified," §3.3, p. 826.

§10.2 Grounds for review. On appeal, the plaintiff may make either or both of the following arguments: (1) the trial court erred when it dismissed the case, and (2) the trial court erred when it refused to reinstate the case. *Maida v. Fire Ins. Exch.*, 990 S.W.2d 836, 838 (Tex.App.—Fort Worth 1999, no pet.).

§10.3 Reporter's record. To appeal an order denying reinstatement, the plaintiff must file the reporter's record with the evidence from the hearing.

§10.4 Standard of review. To reverse a judgment of dismissal, the appellant must prove the trial court abused its discretion. *See MacGregor v. Rich*, 941 S.W.2d 74, 75 (Tex.1997) (dismissal for failure to prosecute); *State v. Rotello*, 671 S.W.2d 507, 509 (Tex.1984) (dismissal under local rule and court's inherent power for failure to prosecute); *Johnson-Snodgrass v. KTAO, Inc.*, 75 S.W.3d 84, 87 (Tex.App.—Fort Worth 2002, pet. dism'd) (dismissal under TRCP 165a). The standard of review for a motion to reinstate after failure to appear is conscious indifference—essentially the same standard used for setting aside a default judgment. *Smith v. Babcock & Wilcox Constr. Co.*, 913 S.W.2d 467, 468 (Tex.1995).

§10.5 Mandamus. If the trial court erroneously reinstated a case after it lost plenary power, the reinstatement order can be challenged by mandamus. *Estate of Howley v. Haberman*, 878 S.W.2d 139, 140 (Tex.1994); *In re Garcia*, 94 S.W.3d 832, 833 (Tex.App.—Corpus Christi 2002, orig. proceeding); *In re Bokeloh*, 21 S.W.3d 784, 793 (Tex. App.—Houston [14th Dist.] 2000, orig. proceeding); *e.g.*, *City of McAllen v. Ramirez*, 875 S.W.2d 702, 704-05 (Tex. App.—Corpus Christi 1994, orig. proceeding) (trial court erroneously granted unverified motion for reinstatement and new trial).

G. MOTION TO EXTEND POSTJUDGMENT DEADLINES

This is a motion in search of a name. TRCP 306a(4), TRCP 306a(5), and TRAP 4.2 describe the procedure for this motion without assigning it a name. Since the first edition of this book, this subchapter has been renamed four times. Beginning in 1991, it was called a "motion to amend date of judgment"; then, a "motion to extend the effective date of judgment"; then, a "motion to reopen the time for appeal"; then, a "motion for additional time to file documents," the name suggested in TRAP 4.2(a). In 2001, we adopted the name used by the Supreme Court in *John v. Marshall Health Servs.*, 58 S.W.3d 738, 739 (Tex.2001)—"motion to extend postjudgment deadlines."

§1. GENERAL

§1.1 Rules. TRCP 306a(4), (5); TRAP 4.2.

§1.2 Purpose. A motion to extend postjudgment deadlines is the procedure used to ask the court to designate a new date for making motions on the judgment because the party did not receive timely notice of the judgment. A motion under TRCP 306a(5) extends the trial court's plenary power to consider postjudgment motions.

§1.3 Timetable & forms. Timetable, Motion to Extend Postjudgment Deadlines, p. 1234; *O'Connor's Texas Civil Forms* (2012), FORMS 10G.

§1.4 Other references. *O'Connor's Texas Civil Appeals* (2012) (*O'Connor's Texas Appeals*).

§2. NOTICE OF JUDGMENT

There are three rules requiring the court clerk to notify the parties about the judgment: TRCP 165a(1) (notice of signing order of dismissal for failure to prosecute), TRCP 239a (notice of no-answer default judgment), and TRCP 306a(3)

———————————————— ✯ ————————————————

(notice of judgment). See "Notice after no-answer default," ch. 7-A, §6.1, p. 598; "Notice of Intent to Dismiss," ch. 7-G, §3, p. 660; "Notice of Judgment," ch. 9-C, §5, p. 770. The clerk's failure to give the parties notice of the judgment as required by the rules does not affect the beginning of the time periods listed in TRCP 306a(1), except as provided by TRCP 306a(4). TRCP 306a(3).

§3. MOTION

When a party does not receive any notice of a judgment (official or actual) within 20 days after the judgment is signed, TRCP 306a(4) provides a limited time to request an extension before the judgment becomes final and the trial court loses plenary power. TRAP 4.2(a)(1); *John v. State*, 826 S.W.2d 138, 140 n.2 (Tex.1992).

§3.1 Form. A motion to extend postjudgment deadlines (MEPD) may be made as part of a motion for new trial or a motion to reinstate, or it may be filed as a separate motion. See "Motion for New Trial," ch. 10-B, p. 789; "Motion to Reinstate After Dismissal for Want of Prosecution," ch. 10-F, p. 826. An MEPD, however it is made, will extend the time to file post-trial motions, the trial court's plenary power, and the appellate deadlines. *See, e.g.*, *In re Wal-Mart Stores*, 20 S.W.3d 734, 739 n.6 (Tex.App.—El Paso 2000, orig. proceeding) (court's plenary power could have been extended by either motion to reinstate or MEPD); *University of Tex. v. Joki*, 735 S.W.2d 505, 506-07 (Tex.App.—Austin 1987, writ denied) (MNT extended time to perfect appeal); *see also* *Butts v. Capitol City Nursing Home, Inc.*, 705 S.W.2d 696, 697 (Tex.1986) (motion to reinstate extends time to perfect appeal, just like MNT).

§3.2 Allegations. See *O'Connor's Texas Forms*, FORM 10G:1. The MEPD should cover the following issues:

1. Date of first notice. The motion must state that (1) the movant or its attorney received the first notice of the judgment on a specific date, and (2) the date was more than 20 days after the judgment was signed but not more than 90 days after the judgment was signed ("date of actual notice"). TRCP 306a(4), (5); TRAP 4.2(a)(1); *see Levit v. Adams*, 850 S.W.2d 469, 469-70 (Tex.1993); *see, e.g.*, *Gem Vending, Inc. v. Walker*, 918 S.W.2d 656, 657-58 (Tex.App.—Fort Worth 1996, orig. proceeding) (because notice was received within 20 days after judgment, tolling provisions of TRCP 306a(4) did not apply). Notice to the party's attorney is notice to the party. *Gem Vending*, 918 S.W.2d at 658. Notice to the law firm is notice to the attorney. *See A. Copeland Enters. v. Tindall*, 683 S.W.2d 596, 599 (Tex.App.—Fort Worth 1985, writ ref'd n.r.e.).

2. Description of first notice. The motion must describe the notice and include who gave it, who received it and when, the type of notice, and any other relevant information. *See* TRCP 306a(4), (5). The motion must identify the specific date the notice was received. *See, e.g.*, *Nathan A. Watson Co. v. Employers Mut. Cas. Co.*, 218 S.W.3d 797, 801-02 (Tex.App.—Fort Worth 2007, no pet.) (attorney's affidavit identifying date he first received notice was sufficient); *Womack-Humphreys Architects, Inc. v. Barrasso*, 886 S.W.2d 809, 814 (Tex.App.—Dallas 1994, writ denied) ("after Dec. 25" was not sufficient), *disapproved on other grounds*, *John v. Marshall Health Servs.*, 58 S.W.3d 738 (Tex.2001). If the movant knows, it should state why the notice was late.

3. No earlier actual notice. The motion must state that neither the movant nor its attorney had actual knowledge of the judgment before the date of the first notice. TRCP 306a(5); *Nathan A. Watson Co.*, 218 S.W.3d at 801-02; *Womack-Humphreys*, 886 S.W.2d at 815; *see, e.g.*, *St. Louis Fed. S&L Ass'n v. Summerhouse Jt.V.*, 739 S.W.2d 441, 442 (Tex.App.—Corpus Christi 1987, no writ) (oral notice to attorney within 20 days after judgment was actual notice of judgment).

4. No earlier notice from clerk. The motion must state that neither the movant nor its attorney received from the clerk any notice of the judgment before the date of the first notice. TRCP 306a(5); *Womack-Humphreys*, 886 S.W.2d at 815. TRCP 306a(4) requires the movant to negate timely receipt of the clerk's notice. *Womack-Humphreys*, 886 S.W.2d at 814-15.

§3.3 Request hearing. The movant should request a hearing on the motion and comply with the requirements of the local rules for securing a hearing. *Xu v. Davis*, 884 S.W.2d 916, 917-18 (Tex.App.—Waco 1994, orig. proceeding). The trial court must hold a hearing before ruling on the motion. See "Hearing required," §6.1, p. 835.

★

---

§3.4 Sworn motion. TRCP 306a(5) requires the movant to file a "sworn motion." The sworn motion establishes a prima facie case that the party did not receive timely notice and extends the court's plenary power to conduct a hearing to determine the exact date of notice. *In re Lynd Co.*, 195 S.W.3d 682, 685 (Tex.2006). See "Plenary-power limits," §4.1, this page. An unverified motion with attached affidavits satisfies TRCP 306a(5) if the affidavits verify the facts in the motion. *City of Laredo v. Schuble*, 943 S.W.2d 124, 126 (Tex.App.—San Antonio 1997, orig. proceeding); *see Womack-Humphreys Architects, Inc. v. Barrasso*, 886 S.W.2d 809, 814 n.4 (Tex.App.—Dallas 1994, writ denied), *disapproved on other grounds*, *John v. Marshall Health Servs.*, 58 S.W.3d 738 (Tex.2001). To be safe, the motion should be verified separately from the affidavits.

NOTE

In 2011, CPRC §132.001 was amended to allow for the use of an unsworn declaration instead of a verification or an affidavit. See CPRC §132.001(a). For the procedure for using an unsworn declaration, see "Unsworn declaration," ch. 1-B, §3.2.14, p. 10.

---

1. Verification. The verification (or affidavit) should directly and unequivocally state that the facts in the motion are true and within the affiant's personal knowledge. *Schuble*, 943 S.W.2d at 126 n.2. See "Verification," ch. 1-B, §3.2.15, p. 11.

2. Affidavits. The motion should include the affidavits of the people who should have learned about the judgment but did not—the attorney and the party. *See, e.g.*, *Grondona v. Sutton*, 991 S.W.2d 90, 92 (Tex.App.—Austin 1998, pet. denied) (MEPD was overruled because attorney did not timely file affidavit, even though party's affidavit was timely filed). The affidavits must be based on personal knowledge. See "Affidavits," ch. 1-B, §3.2.16, p. 11.

(1) Attorney. The attorney should (1) swear she did not receive timely notice of the judgment, (2) state the exact date the notice was received, (3) describe the type of notice received (notice from the clerk or actual knowledge elsewhere), and (4) state that no earlier notice was received from the clerk. *See Nathan A. Watson Co. v. Employers Mut. Cas. Co.*, 218 S.W.3d 797, 801 (Tex.App.—Fort Worth 2007, no pet.); *Womack-Humphreys*, 886 S.W.2d at 814-15. The attorney might also describe the office procedure for processing notices from the court and state that a review of the procedure revealed that no notice was received before that date. See *O'Connor's Texas Forms*, FORM 10G:3.

(2) Party. The party should (1) swear it did not receive timely notice of the judgment, (2) state the exact date the notice was received, and (3) describe the type of notice received. *See, e.g.*, *In re Simpson*, 932 S.W.2d 674, 678 (Tex.App.—Amarillo 1996, no writ) (motion did not negate possibility that party received notice within 20 days). When the party is a corporation or other legal entity, an employee or agent may file the affidavit on behalf of the entity. *See, e.g.*, *Federal Ins. v. Ticor Title Ins. Co.*, 774 S.W.2d 103, 104-05 (Tex.App.—Beaumont 1989, no writ) (affidavit filed by party's bond-claim attorney was sufficient). See *O'Connor's Texas Forms*, FORM 10G:2.

(3) Clerk. If the court clerk has information about the late notice, the attorney should prepare an affidavit for the clerk to execute. *See In re Simpson*, 932 S.W.2d at 676-77.

§3.5 File notice of appeal. The party should file the notice of appeal with the trial court as soon as possible after learning of the judgment. Even if the notice of appeal is early, it will perfect the appeal. *See* TRAP 27.1(a) (premature notice of appeal). See *O'Connor's Texas Appeals*, "Notice of Appeal," ch. 5-A, p. 189.

PRACTICE TIP

File a notice of appeal promptly to ensure that the notice is timely whether the MEPD is granted or overruled.

---

§4. DEADLINES FOR MOVANT

§4.1 Plenary-power limits. A motion to extend the time to file postjudgment motions under TRCP 306a(5) can be filed only while the trial court has plenary power. *John v. Marshall Health Servs.*, 58 S.W.3d 738, 741 (Tex. 2001). The regular plenary-power timetable begins when the trial court signs the judgment (or order disposing of

★

the case) and ends 30 days later if no motion for new trial or other plenary-power-extending (PPE) motion is filed. TRCP 306a(1) (beginning), TRCP 329b(d) (end). The extended plenary-power timetable, invoked by a proper MEPD, begins on the date of notice of the judgment (not the date the judgment was signed) and ends 30 days later if no motion for new trial or other PPE motion is filed. *See John*, 58 S.W.3d at 740-41; *Grondona v. Sutton*, 991 S.W.2d 90, 92 (Tex.App.—Austin 1998, pet. denied). For a list of PPE motions, see "Motions that extend plenary power," ch. 9-C, §6.5.1(1), p. 775. For the effect of PPE motions on the deadline to file an MEPD, see "Plenary-Power Deadlines," chart 9-1, p. 778.

§4.2 TRCP 306a(4) limits.

1. Notice of judgment. A party that receives notice of the judgment between 21 and 90 days after the judgment is signed may file an MEPD. *See* TRCP 306a(4); TRAP 4.2(a)(1).

(1) Earliest notice. Notice received 21 days after the judgment is signed is the earliest notice that entitles a party to file an MEPD. *See* TRCP 306a(4); TRAP 4.2(a)(1). When a party receives notice of a judgment within 20 days after the date the judgment is signed, the party cannot file an MEPD. *E.g.*, *In re Parker*, 117 S.W.3d 484, 487 (Tex.App.—Texarkana 2003, orig. proceeding) (party received notice 11 days after judgment); *In re Montemayor*, 2 S.W.3d 542, 545 (Tex.App.—San Antonio 1999, orig. proceeding) (party received notice 14 days after judgment). Notice of intent to enter judgment is not notice of the signing of the judgment. *See Western Imp. Motors, Inc. v. Mechinus*, 739 S.W.2d 125, 126 (Tex.App.—San Antonio 1987, writ denied).

(2) Latest notice. TRCP 306a does not address the deadline for receiving late notice of the judgment. The courts have interpreted the statement in TRCP 306a(4), that "in no event shall such periods [in TRCP 306a(1)] begin more than 90 days after" the judgment, as preventing an MEPD when the notice of judgment is received more than 90 days after the judgment is signed. *See, e.g.*, *Estate of Howley v. Haberman*, 878 S.W.2d 139, 140 (Tex.1994) (too late to file MEPD because P learned of DWOP more than 90 days after dismissal); *Levit v. Adams*, 850 S.W.2d 469, 470 (Tex.1993) (same, because P learned of DWOP 91 days after dismissal).

2. Deadline for motion. TRCP 306a does not address the deadline for filing an MEPD. *John v. Marshall Health Servs.*, 58 S.W.3d 738, 741 (Tex.2001). A party may file an MEPD anytime within the trial court's plenary power, measured from the date determined under TRCP 306a(4). *E.g.*, *John*, 58 S.W.3d at 741 (MEPD filed 71 days after notice, which was 93 days after J signed). See "Plenary-Power Deadlines," chart 9-1, p. 778; Timetable, Motion to Extend Postjudgment Deadlines, p. 1234.

(1) Short plenary-power period. When no PPE motions (e.g., motion for new trial) are filed, the court's plenary power expires 30 days after the party received late notice of the judgment. In these cases, the deadline to file an MEPD is 30 days after the date of the notice. *John*, 58 S.W.3d at 741; *e.g.*, *Green v. Guidry*, 34 S.W.3d 669, 670 (Tex.App.—Waco 2000, no pet.) (because no PPE motion was filed, deadline to file MEPD was 30 days after notice of judgment).

(2) Long plenary-power period. When a PPE motion (e.g., motion for new trial) is filed within 30 days after the late notice of judgment, the court's plenary power expires 30 days after that motion is overruled by written order or by operation of law, but no more than 105 days after the notice of judgment. *Green*, 34 S.W.3d at 670. A PPE motion is one that seeks a substantive change in the judgment. *Lane Bank Equip. Co. v. Smith S. Equip., Inc.*, 10 S.W.3d 308, 313 (Tex.2000). For a list of PPE motions, see "Motions that extend plenary power," ch. 9-C, §6.5.1(1), p. 775. When a PPE motion is filed within 30 days after the late notice of judgment, that motion extends the time to file an MEPD, which can be filed as long as the court has plenary power. *See, e.g.*, *John*, 58 S.W.3d at 741 (MNT filed 13 days after notice of judgment; MEPD filed 71 days after notice, within plenary power); *Grondona v. Sutton*, 991 S.W.2d 90, 92 (Tex.App.—Austin 1998, pet. denied) (MNT filed two days after notice of judgment; MEPD filed 84 days after notice of judgment, within plenary power); *Vineyard Bay Dev. Co. v. Vineyard on Lake Travis*, 864 S.W.2d 170, 172 (Tex.App.—Austin 1993, writ denied) (joint MNT and MEPD filed 24 days after notice of judgment, within plenary power). When a PPE motion is overruled by operation of law, the absolute last day to file an MEPD is 105 days after the party received notice of the judgment. *Green*, 34 S.W.3d at 670 n.1.

★

EXAMPLE

Assume the judgment was signed on day 0, P received notice of the judgment on day 50, and P filed an MNT on day 60. The MNT will extend the time P has to file an MEPD because it was filed within 30 days after the notice of judgment. The time to file the MEPD is 30 days after the date the MNT is overruled, either by written order or by operation of law. Thus, the deadline to file an MEPD depends on whether the MNT is overruled by written order or by operation of law. If the court overrules the MNT by written order on day 70, P has until the end of day 100 to file the MEPD (70 + 30 = 100). If the court does not sign an order overruling the MNT, the MNT is overruled by operation of law on the expiration of day 125 (50 + 75 = 125); P has until the end of day 155 to file an MEPD (125 + 30 = 155). If no MNT is filed, P has until the end of day 80 to file an MEPD (50 + 30 = 80).

---

§5. RESPONSE

If the nonmovant objects to the allegations in the MEPD, the nonmovant should file a response challenging the motion. If the response contains factual recitations, it should be supported by affidavits. See *O'Connor's Texas Forms*, FORM 10G:4.

§6. HEARING

§6.1 Hearing required. The trial court is required to hold a hearing on an MEPD. *Cantu v. Longoria*, 878 S.W.2d 131, 132 (Tex.1994); *In re Bokeloh*, 21 S.W.3d 784, 792 (Tex.App.—Houston [14th Dist.] 2000, orig. proceeding); *Xu v. Davis*, 884 S.W.2d 916, 918 (Tex.App.—Waco 1994, orig. proceeding); *see* TRCP 306a(5); TRAP 4.2(c). As a result of the Supreme Court's holding in *John v. Marshall Health Servs.*, 58 S.W.3d 738 (Tex.2001), an MEPD could conceivably be filed on the last day of the trial court's plenary power, which might preclude a hearing.

    1. No hearing.

        (1) Effect on evidence. If the trial court does not hold a hearing, it must accept the movant's affidavits as true. *Womack-Humphreys Architects, Inc. v. Barrasso*, 886 S.W.2d 809, 816 n.9 (Tex.App.—Dallas 1994, writ denied), *disapproved on other grounds*, *John v. Marshall Health Servs.*, 58 S.W.3d 738 (Tex.2001); *cf. Limestone Constr., Inc. v. Summit Commercial Indus. Props., Inc.*, 143 S.W.3d 538, 546 (Tex.App.—Austin 2004, no pet.) (no hearing after MNT).

        (2) Effect on appeal. If the trial court does not hold a hearing, the movant may file an original mandamus proceeding in the appellate court to require the trial court to conduct a hearing. *Cantu*, 878 S.W.2d at 132; *see In re Bokeloh*, 21 S.W.3d at 792.

    2. Hearing. If the trial court holds a hearing, the court can consider evidence controverting the movant's proof. *See, e.g., Xu*, 884 S.W.2d at 917 (nonmovant's contentions that movant received timely notice of judgment should be considered at a hearing).

    §6.2 Burden. At the hearing, the movant must prove (1) the date it received the official notice of the judgment or actual knowledge of the signing of the judgment, (2) that the date was more than 20 days after the judgment was signed, and (3) that the date was within 90 days after the judgment was signed. TRCP 306a(5) (elements 1 and 2); TRAP 4.2(b) (elements 1 and 2); *In re Lynd Co.*, 195 S.W.3d 682, 686 (Tex.2006) (elements 1-3); *Estate of Howley v. Haberman*, 878 S.W.2d 139, 140 (Tex.1994) (element 3).

    §6.3 Deadline for hearing & ruling. TRCP 306a does not set a deadline for the court to conduct the hearing or make a ruling on the motion. The trial court should conduct a hearing and rule on the motion before its plenary power expires.

    §6.4 Record. The movant should make sure the court reporter records the hearing on the motion so the movant can challenge an adverse ruling on appeal. If the court reporter does not record the evidence received at the hearing, the movant cannot offer proof of the late notice of the judgment in the appellate court. *See Corro v. Southwestern Bell Media, Inc.*, 784 S.W.2d 471, 474 (Tex.App.—Corpus Christi 1989, no writ).

————————————————————— ★ —————————————————————

§7. ORDER

§7.1 Written finding. The appellate rule, TRAP 4.2(c), requires the trial court to sign an order and to make a finding of the date of actual notice or knowledge of the judgment. *In re Bokeloh*, 21 S.W.3d 784, 792 (Tex.App.—Houston [14th Dist.] 2000, orig. proceeding); *Sharm Inc. v. Martinez*, 885 S.W.2d 165, 166-67 (Tex.App.—Corpus Christi 1993, no writ) (former TRAP 5(b)(5)). By comparison, the trial rule, TRCP 306a, does not require the trial court to sign an order with such a finding. *In re Lynd Co.*, 195 S.W.3d 682, 686 (Tex.2006). If the trial court grants the motion but does not identify the date of actual notice, the date may be implied from the court's order granting the motion, unless there is no evidence to support the implied finding or the party establishes an alternate notice date as a matter of law. *Id.*

PRACTICE TIP
*Even though TRCP 306a does not require the trial court to issue a written finding designating the actual date the party received notice of the judgment, TRAP 4.2(c) does; thus, the party should request one. See **In re Lynd Co.**, 195 S.W.3d at 686. See **O'Connor's Texas Forms**, FORM 10G:5.*

---

§7.2 Court grants motion. If the trial court grants the MEPD, it must designate a new date for the judgment based on the date the movant received actual notice of the judgment. *See* TRCP 306a(4); TRAP 4.2(c); *In re Lynd Co.*, 195 S.W.3d 682, 686-87 (Tex.2006); *Levit v. Adams*, 850 S.W.2d 469, 469-70 (Tex.1993); *see, e.g.*, *Western Imp. Motors, Inc. v. Mechinus*, 739 S.W.2d 125, 126 (Tex.App.—San Antonio 1987, writ denied) (because movants learned of judgment on 59th day after it was signed, deadlines began to run on that date). Once the trial court establishes the new date for the judgment, the motion for new trial and notice of appeal will be considered timely if they are already filed. TRCP 306a(4) limits the reopening of the appellate time periods to the party who received late notice. The period cannot begin later than 90 days after the date the judgment or order was signed. TRCP 306a(4); TRAP 4.2(a)(1); *Levit*, 850 S.W.2d at 470.

§7.3 Court denies motion. If the trial court denies the MEPD, the date of the judgment will not change from the date it was signed. Even if the court denies the MEPD, it should make a written finding of the date of actual notice or knowledge of the judgment. TRAP 4.2(c).

§8. REVIEW

§8.1 Appeal. The issue of late notice of judgment cannot be raised for the first time on appeal. *See In re Estate of Padilla*, 103 S.W.3d 563, 567 (Tex.App.—San Antonio 2003, no pet.).

1. Court denied motion. If the trial court refused to designate a new date of the judgment within the 21- to 90-day period provided in TRCP 306a(4), the movant may challenge the ruling by appeal. *See Hot Shot Messenger Serv. v. State*, 798 S.W.2d 413, 414-15 (Tex.App.—Austin 1990, writ denied); *Jimmy Swaggart Ministries v. City of Arlington*, 718 S.W.2d 83, 84-85 (Tex.App.—Fort Worth 1986, no writ).

2. Standard of review. The trial court's ruling is reviewed on appeal for legal and factual sufficiency of the evidence. *Nathan A. Watson Co. v. Employers Mut. Cas. Co.*, 218 S.W.3d 797, 800-01 (Tex.App.—Fort Worth 2007, no pet.); *Hot Shot*, 798 S.W.2d at 414.

3. When MEPD not available. When a party received notice of judgment too late for an MEPD, the party may be able to challenge the judgment by a restricted appeal or a bill of review. *See Levit v. Adams*, 850 S.W.2d 469, 470 (Tex.1993). See "Attacking the Default Judgment," ch. 7-A, §7, p. 598.

§8.2 Mandamus.

1. Available.

(1) Court refuses hearing. If the trial court refuses to hold a hearing on the MEPD, the refusal can be challenged by mandamus. *Cantu v. Longoria*, 878 S.W.2d 131, 132 (Tex.1994); *see In re Bokeloh*, 21 S.W.3d 784, 792 (Tex.App.—Houston [14th Dist.] 2000, orig. proceeding).

⭐

(2) **Court grants late motion.** If the trial court grants a motion filed after 90 days, the order can be challenged by mandamus. *Estate of Howley v. Haberman*, 878 S.W.2d 139, 140 (Tex.1994).

2. Not available. When the party received notice of the judgment after the 90-day period, it is too late to file an MEPD, and the party cannot challenge the judgment by mandamus.

H. MOTION FOR JUDGMENT NUNC PRO TUNC

§1. GENERAL

§1.1 Rules. TRCP 306a(6), 316, 329b; TRAP 4.3(b).

§1.2 Purpose. The purpose of a judgment nunc pro tunc is to correct a clerical error in the judgment after the court's plenary power has expired. *Jenkins v. Jenkins*, 16 S.W.3d 473, 482 (Tex.App.—El Paso 2000, no pet.); *Ferguson v. Naylor*, 860 S.W.2d 123, 126 (Tex.App.—Amarillo 1993, writ denied); *West Tex. State Bank v. General Res.*, 723 S.W.2d 304, 306 (Tex.App.—Austin 1987, writ ref'd n.r.e.).

§1.3 Forms. *O'Connor's Texas Civil Forms* (2012), FORMS 10H.

§2. MOTION

§2.1 Ground. The only ground for a motion for judgment nunc pro tunc is to correct a clerical error made in entering the judgment. *Escobar v. Escobar*, 711 S.W.2d 230, 231 (Tex.1986) (contrasted with judicial error made in rendering judgment). The inquiry in a proceeding for a judgment nunc pro tunc is what judgment was rendered, not what judgment should or might have been rendered. *Id.*; *Hernandez v. Lopez*, 288 S.W.3d 180, 185 (Tex.App.—Houston [1st Dist.] 2009, no pet.); *Jenkins v. Jenkins*, 16 S.W.3d 473, 482 (Tex.App.—El Paso 2000, no pet.). The court cannot correct a judicial error by signing a judgment nunc pro tunc after the expiration of its plenary power. See "Incorrect judgment nunc pro tunc," §6.2, p. 839. When the error is judicial, a party must file a timely motion to modify the judgment. See "Motion to Modify the Judgment," ch. 10-D, p. 814.

1. Test to determine type of error. To determine whether an error was clerical or judicial, the attorney should ask the following: Was the error the result of judicial reasoning and determination? *Gonzalez v. Doctors Hosp.*, 814 S.W.2d 536, 537 (Tex.App.—Houston [1st Dist.] 1991, no writ); *see Esse v. Empire Energy III, Ltd.*, 333 S.W.3d 166, 176 (Tex.App.—Houston [1st Dist.] 2010, pet. denied). If the answer is no, the error was clerical, and the trial court can correct the error, even though the judgment is final, by signing a judgment nunc pro tunc. If the answer is yes, the error was a judicial error, and it cannot be corrected by the trial court after the court loses plenary power. *Finlay v. Jones*, 435 S.W.2d 136, 138 (Tex.1968); *Esse*, 333 S.W.3d at 176. The decision whether an error is clerical or judicial is a question of law. *Escobar*, 711 S.W.2d at 232; *Esse*, 333 S.W.3d at 176.

2. Difference between clerical & judicial errors.

(1) **Clerical error.**

(a) **Defined.** A clerical error is a discrepancy between the entry of a judgment in the official record and the judgment as it was actually rendered. *Universal Underwriters Ins. v. Ferguson*, 471 S.W.2d 28, 29-30 (Tex.1971); *Hernandez*, 288 S.W.3d at 184. A clerical error does not result from judicial reasoning or determination. *Andrews v. Koch*, 702 S.W.2d 584, 585 (Tex.1986); *Hernandez*, 288 S.W.3d at 184; *Claxton v. (Upper) Lake Fork Water Control & Imprv. Dist.*, 220 S.W.2d 537, 543 (Tex.App.—Texarkana 2006, no pet.). It is an error in entering or recording the court's decision. *Escobar*, 711 S.W.2d at 231. Correction of a clerical error is not a substantive change in the judgment. *In re Marriage of Ward*, 137 S.W.3d 910, 913 (Tex.App.—Texarkana 2004, no pet.); *Dickens v. Willis*, 957 S.W.2d 657, 659 (Tex.App.—Austin 1997, no pet.).

(b) **Examples.** The following are examples of clerical errors (which can be corrected by a judgment nunc pro tunc): • A discrepancy in the acreage description of land. *See Escobar*, 711 S.W.2d at 232. • An unintended judgment of dismissal caused by the clerk. *Knox v. Long*, 257 S.W.2d 289, 292-93 (Tex.1953), *overruled on other grounds*, *Jackson v. Hernandez*, 285 S.W.2d 184 (Tex.1955). • An error in the date of signing of the judgment.

———————————————————————— ★ ————————————————————————

Claxton, 220 S.W.3d at 543. • A discrepancy between the judgment signed and the judgment the court intended to sign. *E.g.*, *Andrews*, 702 S.W.2d at 586 (probate order to sell was different from order confirming sale); *Delaup v. Delaup*, 917 S.W.2d 411, 413 (Tex.App.—Houston [14th Dist.] 1996, no writ) (judgment did not reflect settlement agreement made in open court). • A mathematical error in the amount of damages. *Travelers Cos. v. Wolfe*, 838 S.W.2d 708, 710 n.2 (Tex.App.—Amarillo 1992, no writ). • A mistake in the party designations. *See, e.g.*, *Dickens*, 957 S.W.2d at 659-60 ("respondent" should have been "petitioner"). • A mistake in a party's name in the judgment. *E.g.*, *Gonzalez*, 814 S.W.2d at 537 (changed P's name from John to Juan). • A discrepancy between the body of the judgment actually rendered and the title of the document. *See, e.g.*, *Butler v. Continental Airlines, Inc.*, 31 S.W.3d 642, 647 (Tex.App.—Houston [1st Dist.] 2000, pet. denied) (only reference to motion for sanctions was in title of order).

(2) Judicial error.

(a) Defined. A judicial error occurs when the court considers an issue and makes an erroneous decision. *See Comet Aluminum Co. v. Dibrell*, 450 S.W.2d 56, 58-59 (Tex.1970). It is an error in rendering the judgment. *In re Daredia*, 317 S.W.3d 247, 249 (Tex.2010); *Escobar*, 711 S.W.2d at 231; *Claxton*, 220 S.W.3d at 543.

(b) Examples. The following are examples of judicial errors (which cannot be corrected by a judgment nunc pro tunc): • Mistake in award of prejudgment interest. *Comet Aluminum*, 450 S.W.2d at 59. • Erroneous recital that supported default judgment. *E.g.*, *Lone Star Cement Corp. v. Fair*, 467 S.W.2d 402, 405-06 (Tex. 1971) (recital that D failed to appear and answer); *Finlay*, 435 S.W.2d at 138-39 (recital that D was served but did not answer). • An unintended judgment of dismissal. *In re Daredia*, 317 S.W.3d at 249-50; *Love v. State Bank & Trust Co.*, 90 S.W.2d 819, 820-21 (Tex.1936). • A judgment on arrears that incorrectly stated the date as a year later, creating another payment obligation. *Hernandez*, 288 S.W.3d at 188. • A judgment that granted a nonsuit with prejudice, instead of without prejudice. *In re Fuselier*, 56 S.W.3d 265, 268 (Tex.App.—Houston [1st Dist.] 2001, orig. proceeding) (drafting error made by attorney). *But see Thompson v. Texas Dept. of Human Res.*, 859 S.W.2d 482, 485 (Tex.App.—San Antonio 1993, no writ) (court permitted judgment nunc pro tunc 12 years after judgment to change dismissal from "with prejudice" to "without prejudice").

§2.2 Notice. The movant must give all interested parties notice of a motion for judgment nunc pro tunc. TRCP 316. If an interested party does not receive notice, the corrected judgment is a nullity. *West Tex. State Bank v. General Res.*, 723 S.W.2d 304, 307 (Tex.App.—Austin 1987, writ ref'd n.r.e.); *see* TRCP 316.

§3. DEADLINE

Attorneys often confuse the purpose, deadline, and effect of motions to modify the judgment with those of motions for judgment nunc pro tunc. The motion's purpose—whether it is to correct a judicial error or a clerical error—determines its deadline.

§3.1 For motion to modify the judgment. The deadline to file a motion to modify, correct, or reform an error in the judgment is the same as for a motion for new trial—30 days after the trial court signs the judgment. TRCP 329b(a), (g). See "Deadlines for MNT," ch. 10-B, §5, p. 791. The motion to modify the judgment can correct both types of error, judicial and clerical. *Riner v. Briargrove Park Prop. Owners, Inc.*, 976 S.W.2d 680, 682 n.1 (Tex.App.—Houston [1st Dist.] 1997, no writ); *see Lane Bank Equip. Co. v. Smith S. Equip., Inc.*, 10 S.W.3d 308, 313 (Tex. 2000).

§3.2 For a motion for judgment nunc pro tunc. There is no deadline for filing a motion for judgment nunc pro tunc. *See* TRCP 316. The earliest a motion for judgment nunc pro tunc can be filed is the day after the court loses plenary power over the judgment. *See Riner v. Briargrove Park Prop. Owners, Inc.*, 976 S.W.2d 680, 682 (Tex. App.—Houston [1st Dist.] 1997, no writ) (judgment nunc pro tunc can be rendered only after court loses plenary power).

§4. RESPONSE

The party opposing the motion for judgment nunc pro tunc is not required to file a response. If a party believes the error was a judicial error and not a clerical one, it should file a motion citing authority to support its allegation that the error in the judgment was not clerical and cannot be changed because the court no longer has plenary power.

✦

§5. HEARING

Because the decision whether the error was clerical or judicial is a legal decision, the hearing on a motion for judgment nunc pro tunc is merely for argument, not for the receipt of evidence. *See Finlay v. Jones*, 435 S.W.2d 136, 138 (Tex.1968). However, if it is necessary to introduce facts to prove the decision was clerical and not judicial, the movant should introduce sworn testimony and have the court reporter transcribe it.

§6. RULING

§6.1 Misnomer of judgment. If the court signs a corrected judgment while it still has plenary power, it is a modified judgment, not a judgment nunc pro tunc. *See Alford v. Whaley*, 794 S.W.2d 920, 922 (Tex.App.—Houston [1st Dist.] 1990, no writ). Even if the court mistakenly names the judgment a "judgment nunc pro tunc," the judgment is not a judgment nunc pro tunc. *Mathes v. Kelton*, 569 S.W.2d 876, 878 (Tex.1978); *Go Leasing, Inc. v. Groos Nat'l Bank*, 628 S.W.2d 143, 144-45 (Tex.App.—San Antonio 1982, no writ).

§6.2 Incorrect judgment nunc pro tunc. If the court attempts to correct a judicial error by signing a judgment nunc pro tunc after its plenary power expires, the judgment is void. *See Dikeman v. Snell*, 490 S.W.2d 183, 186 (Tex.1973); *Barton v. Gillespie*, 178 S.W.3d 121, 126 (Tex.App.—Houston [1st Dist.] 2005, no pet.); *In re Rollins Leasing, Inc.*, 987 S.W.2d 633, 638 (Tex.App.—Houston [14th Dist.] 1999, orig. proceeding); *Wood v. Griffin & Brand*, 671 S.W.2d 125, 132 (Tex.App.—Corpus Christi 1984, no writ). After the court's plenary power expires, the court cannot change the judgment by calling the correction of a judicial error a "judgment nunc pro tunc." *See Dikeman*, 490 S.W.2d at 186.

NOTE

As long as the trial court has plenary power over the judgment, it can correct any error, clerical or judicial, and a motion to correct the judgment should be titled "Motion to Modify (or Correct or Reform) the Judgment Under TRCP 329b." A TRCP 329b motion eliminates the argument whether the error in the judgment was clerical or judicial. After the court loses plenary power over the judgment, a motion to correct a clerical mistake in the judgment should be titled "Motion for Judgment Nunc Pro Tunc Under TRCP 316."

---

§7. REVIEW

§7.1 Appeal from granting motion. If the trial court corrects a clerical error in the judgment, the time to appeal depends on whether the court still had plenary power over the judgment.

1. Correction made before losing plenary power – modified judgment. Any change made to the judgment before the trial court loses plenary power, even a clerical change, will restart the deadlines for the appeal. *Lane Bank Equip. Co. v. Smith S. Equip., Inc.*, 10 S.W.3d 308, 313 (Tex.2000). See "Modified judgment & postjudgment deadlines," ch. 10-D, §6.2, p. 816.

2. Correction made after losing plenary power – judgment nunc pro tunc. If, after it has lost plenary power, the court signs a judgment nunc pro tunc that corrects a clerical error, the deadline to challenge the correction begins when the trial court signs the judgment nunc pro tunc. *See* TRCP 306a(6); TRAP 4.3(b).

(1) Does not extend appellate deadlines. A judgment nunc pro tunc does not extend the appellate timetable for any complaint about the original judgment. TRCP 306a(6); *e.g., Gonzalez v. Doctors Hosp.*, 814 S.W.2d 536, 537 (Tex.App.—Houston [1st Dist.] 1991, no writ) (correction of P's name from John to Juan six months after judgment was signed did not extend appellate timetable); *Cavalier Corp. v. Store Enters.*, 742 S.W.2d 785, 787 (Tex.App.—Dallas 1987, writ denied) (correction of corporate P's name after plenary power expired did not extend appellate deadlines).

(2) Does extend appellate deadlines. A judgment nunc pro tunc extends the appellate deadlines for any complaint about a matter not in the original judgment. TRAP 4.3(b) states that if the trial court corrects or

★

reforms a judgment under TRCP 316 after the court's plenary power expires, all periods run from the date of the corrected judgment, but only for complaints that would not apply to the original judgment. TRCP 329b(h) states that if the trial court signs a corrected judgment after it loses plenary power over the judgment, no complaint will be heard on appeal that could have been presented in an appeal from the original judgment. Thus, if the trial court corrected a clerical error after it lost plenary power over the judgment, and that clerical correction requires some complaint not available before the trial court signed the judgment nunc pro tunc, the deadlines to complain about that issue are extended.

§7.2 No appeal from denial of motion. The movant cannot appeal from the order denying a motion for judgment nunc pro tunc because the order is not a final, appealable judgment. *Shadowbrook Apts. v. Abu-Ahmad*, 783 S.W.2d 210, 211 (Tex.1990).

§7.3 Mandamus. If the trial court denies a motion for judgment nunc pro tunc, the denial may be reviewable by mandamus. *See In re Bridges*, 28 S.W.3d 191, 195-96 (Tex.App.—Fort Worth 2000, orig. proceeding) (court reasoned that, because Supreme Court held in *Shadowbrook Apts.* that a party cannot appeal denial of a motion for judgment nunc pro tunc, P lacked an adequate remedy at law; thus, mandamus relief was appropriate).

─────────────── ★ ───────────────

TEXAS RULES OF CIVIL PROCEDURE

ANNOTATED RULES
TABLE OF CONTENTS

⭐

TRCP

★

TRCP

⭐

★

TRCP

———————————— ★ ————————————

TRCP

⭐

Editor's note: All new and amended TRCPs are marked with ⑫, and all proposed TRCP amendments are marked with ⑬, to highlight the change and alert you to check the effective date. The new rule language is underlined.

PART I. GENERAL RULES

TRCP 1. OBJECTIVE OF RULES

The proper objective of rules of civil procedure is to obtain a just, fair, equitable and impartial adjudication of the rights of litigants under established principles of substantive law. To the end that this objective may be attained with as great expedition and dispatch and at the least expense both to the litigants and to the state as may be practicable, these rules shall be given a liberal construction.

History of TRCP 1: Adopted eff. Sept. 1, 1941, by order of Oct. 29, 1940 (3 Tex.B.J. 525 [1940]). Source: New rule.

See *Commentaries*, "Introduction to the Texas Rules," ch. 1-A, p. 5.

TRCP 2. SCOPE OF RULES

These rules shall govern the procedure in the justice, county, and district courts of the State of Texas in all actions of a civil nature, with such exceptions as may be hereinafter stated. Where any statute in effect immediately prior to September 1, 1941, prescribed a rule of procedure in lunacy, guardianship, or estates of decedents, or any other probate proceedings in the county court differing from these Rules, and not included in the "List of Repealed Statutes," such statute shall apply; and where any statute in effect immediately prior to September 1, 1941, and not included in the "List of Repealed Statutes," prescribed a rule of procedure in any special statutory proceeding differing from these rules, such statute shall apply. All statutes in effect immediately prior to September 1, 1941, prescribing rules of procedure in bond or recognizance forfeitures in criminal cases are hereby continued in effect as rules of procedure governing such cases, but where such statutes prescribed no rules of procedure in such cases, these rules shall apply. All statutes in effect immediately prior to September 1, 1941, prescribing rules of procedure in tax suits are hereby continued in effect as rules of procedure governing such cases, but where such statutes prescribed no rules of procedure in such cases, these rules shall apply; provided, however, that Rule 117a shall control with respect to citation in tax suits.

History of TRCP 2: Amended eff. Sept. 1, 1986, by order of Apr. 10, 1986 (705-06 S.W.2d [Tex.Cases] xxxii): Deleted reference to appellate procedure. Amended eff. Dec. 31, 1947, by order of Aug. 18, 1947 (10 Tex.B.J. 389 [1947]).

Amended eff. Dec. 31, 1943, by order of June 16, 1943 (6 Tex.B.J. 327 [1943]). Amended eff. Dec. 31, 1941, by order of Sept. 20, 1941 (4 Tex.B.J. 489 [1941]). Adopted eff. Sept. 1, 1941, by order of Oct. 29, 1940 (3 Tex.B.J. 525 [1940]). Source: FRCP 1 (adapted).

See *Commentaries*, "Introduction to the Texas Rules," ch. 1-A, p. 5.

TRCP 3. CONSTRUCTION OF RULES

Unless otherwise expressly provided, the past, present or future tense shall each include the other; the masculine, feminine, or neuter gender shall each include the other; and the singular and plural number shall each include the other.

History of TRCP 3: Adopted eff. Sept. 1, 1941, by order of Oct. 29, 1940 (3 Tex.B.J. 525 [1940]). Source: TRCS art. 10(2)-(4) (repealed, now Gov't Code §312.003).

See Gov't Code §312.003.

TRCP 3a. LOCAL RULES

Each administrative judicial region, district court, county court, county court at law, and probate court may make and amend local rules governing practice before such courts, provided:

(1) that any proposed rule or amendment shall not be inconsistent with these rules or with any rule of the administrative judicial region in which the court is located;

(2) no time period provided by these rules may be altered by local rules;

(3) any proposed local rule or amendment shall not become effective until it is submitted and approved by the Supreme Court of Texas;

(4) any proposed local rule or amendment shall not become effective until at least thirty days after its publication in a manner reasonably calculated to bring it to the attention of attorneys practicing before the court or courts for which it is made;

(5) all local rules or amendments adopted and approved in accordance herewith are made available upon request to the members of the bar;

(6) no local rule, order, or practice of any court, other than local rules and amendments which fully comply with all requirements of this Rule 3a, shall ever be applied to determine the merits of any matter.

History of TRCP 3a: Amended eff. Sept. 1, 1990, by order of Apr. 24, 1990 (785-86 S.W.2d [Tex.Cases] xxxiii): To make TRCP timetables mandatory and to preclude use of unpublished local rules or other "standing" orders or local practices to determine issues of substantive merit; title changed; added (2) and (6); sections renumbered; and changed "rules" to "local rules." Amended eff. Jan. 1, 1988, by order of July 15, 1987 (733-34 S.W.2d [Tex.Cases] xxxvi). Amended eff. Sept. 1, 1986, by order of Apr. 10, 1986 (705-06 S.W.2d [Tex.Cases] xxxii): Deleted reference to appellate procedure and words "Court of Appeals, each." Amended eff. Apr. 1, 1984, by order of Dec. 5, 1983 (661-62 S.W.2d [Tex.Cases] xxxv): To emphasize the superiority of the general rules over local rules of procedure, amendment moved TRCP 817 to TRCP 3a; and to achieve uniformity, local rules require Supreme Court approval.

★

See Gov't Code §51.807 (local rules for fax filing); TRJA 10; *Commentaries*, "Local Rules," ch. 1-A, §4, p. 6.

Approximately $1,589.00 v. State, 230 S.W.3d 871, 874 (Tex.App.—Houston [14th Dist.] 2007, no pet.). "Rule 3a(2) absolutely prohibits application of a local rule that alters a time period set forth in the [TRCPs]. Rule 3a(2) does not distinguish a local rule that shortens a time period from a local rule that lengthens a time period."

TRCP 4. COMPUTATION OF TIME

In computing any period of time prescribed or allowed by these rules, by order of court, or by any applicable statute, the day of the act, event, or default after which the designated period of time begins to run is not to be included. The last day of the period so computed is to be included, underline unless it is a Saturday, Sunday or legal holiday underline, in which event the period runs until the end of the next day which is not a Saturday, Sunday or legal holiday. Saturdays, Sundays and legal holidays shall not be counted for any purpose in any time period of five days or less in these rules, except that Saturdays, Sundays and legal holidays shall be counted for purpose of the three-day periods in Rules 21 and 21a, extending other periods by three days when service is made by registered or certified mail or by telephonic document transfer, and for purposes of the five-day periods provided for under Rules 748, 749, 749a, 749b, and 749c.

History of TRCP 4: Amended eff. Sept. 1, 1990, by order of Apr. 24, 1990 (785-86 S.W.2d [Tex.Cases] xxxiv): Changed title; added last sentence; and omits counting of Saturdays, Sundays, and legal holidays in all periods of less than five days with certain exceptions. Amended eff. Jan. 1, 1961, by order of July 26, 1960 (23 Tex.B.J. 619 [Oct. 1960]): Added word "Saturday" in second sentence. Adopted eff. Sept. 1, 1941, by order of Oct. 29, 1940 (3 Tex.B.J. 525 [1940]). Source: FRCP 6(a), with changes: Omitted federal provision excluding intermediate Sundays or holidays when period of time is less than seven days, and federal reference to half-holidays.

See Gov't Code §311.014; *Commentaries*, "Rules for Filing Documents," ch. 1-C, p. 21; "Rules for Serving Documents," ch. 1-D, p. 34; "Motion for Summary Judgment—General Rules," ch. 7-B, p. 603.

Sosa v. Central Power & Light, 909 S.W.2d 893, 895 (Tex.1995). Ps filed their amended petition seven days before the hearing on the motion for summary judgment. "When Rule 4 is applied, the day on which [Ps] filed their amendment is not counted but the seventh day after it was filed is counted. … As we held in *Lewis*, the last day counted from the date of the filing may be the date of the hearing. Therefore, [Ps] timely filed their second amended original petition."

Lewis v. Blake, 876 S.W.2d 314, 316 (Tex.1994). TRCP 4 "applies to *any* period of time prescribed by the rules of procedure…. Applying Rule 4 to [TRCP] 166a(c), the … hearing on a motion for summary judgment may be set as early as the 21st day after the motion is served, or the 24th day if the motion is served by mail."

Peacock v. Humble, 933 S.W.2d 341, 342-43 (Tex. App.—Austin 1996, orig. proceeding). "The Code Construction Act and Rule 4 … are not consistent in the manner in which they address Saturdays, Sundays, and legal holidays when computing time periods of five days or less. [¶] When a rule of procedure conflicts with a statute, the rule yields to the legislative enactment. … Because the three-day filing period in the present case is statutory, the Code Construction Act's method for computing time applies rather than the method contained in Rule 4."

TRCP 5. ENLARGEMENT OF TIME

When by these rules or by a notice given thereunder or by order of court an act is required or allowed to be done at or within a specified time, the court for cause shown may, at any time in its discretion (a) with or without motion or notice, order the period enlarged if application therefor is made before the expiration of the period originally prescribed or as extended by a previous order; or (b) upon motion permit the act to be done after the expiration of the specified period where good cause is shown for the failure to act. The court may not enlarge the period for taking any action under the rules relating to new trials except as stated in these rules.

If any document is sent to the proper clerk by first-class United States mail in an envelope or wrapper properly addressed and stamped and is deposited in the mail on or before the last day for filing same, the same, if received by the clerk not more than ten days tardily, shall be filed by the clerk and be deemed filed in time. A legible postmark affixed by the United States Postal Service shall be prima facie evidence of the date of mailing.

History of TRCP 5: Amended eff. Sept. 1, 1990, by order of Apr. 24, 1990 (785-86 S.W.2d [Tex.Cases] xxxiv): Amended to make last date for mailing under TRCP 5 coincide with last date for filing. Amended eff. Sept. 1, 1986, by order of Apr. 10, 1986 (705-06 S.W.2d [Tex.Cases] xxxiii): Deleted reference to appellate procedure and deleted phrases "or motions for rehearing or the period for taking an appeal … or the period for application for writ of error in the Supreme Court" and "motion for rehearing, any matter relating to taking an appeal … or application for writ of error." Amended eff. Jan. 1, 1976, by order of July 22, 1975 (525-26 S.W.2d [Tex.Cases] xliv): A legible postmark shall be prima facie, not conclusive, evidence of date of mailing. Amended eff. Feb. 1,

---

★

1973, by order of Oct. 3, 1972 (483-484 S.W.2d [Tex.Cases] xxi): Inserted words "affixed by the United States Postal Service" in the final proviso. Amended eff. Jan. 1, 1971, by order of July 21, 1970 (455-56 S.W.2d [Tex.Cases] xxiv): Changed to eliminate requirement that date of mailing be shown by postmark on envelope and added additional proviso to make a legible postmark conclusive as to date of mailing. Amended eff. Mar. 1, 1950, by order of Oct. 12, 1949 (12 Tex.B.J. 529 [1949]): Added the first proviso at the end of the rule. Adopted eff. Sept. 1, 1941, by order of Oct. 29, 1940 (3 Tex.B.J. 525 [1940]). Source: FRCP 6(b), with changes: Second clause in federal rule requires a showing that failure to act "was the result of excusable neglect." Also, specific reference is made in this rule to time limitations relating to motions for new trial and for re-hearings and to appeals and writs of error, while in the federal rule, cross-reference to such subjects is by rule number.

See TRAP 4; *Commentaries*, "Rules for Filing Documents," ch. 1-C, p. 21; "Motion for Continuance," ch. 5-D, p. 336; "General Rules for Discovery," ch. 6-A, p. 425; "Motion for New Trial," ch. 10-B, p. 789.

ANNOTATIONS

In re Brookshire Grocery Co., 250 S.W.3d 66, 73 (Tex.2008). "Rule 5 provides that a trial court 'may not enlarge the period for taking any action under the rules relating to new trial except as stated in these rules.' The [TRCPs] place no such limitation on motions relating to modifying, correcting, or reforming the judgment; treating such a motion as a motion for new trial—thereby extending the trial court's otherwise expired plenary power—would permit an end run around Rule 5's prohibition."

Ramos v. Richardson, 228 S.W.3d 671, 673 (Tex. 2007). "The respondents argue that, for purposes of [TRCP 5,] the 'mailbox rule,' placing the notices of appeal into the outgoing prison mailbox is not the equivalent of placing them into the U.S. mail. But ... an inmate who does everything necessary to satisfy timeliness requirements must not be penalized if the document is ultimately filed tardily because of an error on the part of officials over whom the inmate has no control." *See also Arnold v. Shuck*, 24 S.W.3d 470, 472 (Tex.App.—Texarkana 2000, pet. denied) (a legible U.S. Postal Service postmark is prima facie evidence of date of mailing).

Warner v. Glass, 135 S.W.3d 681, 684 (Tex.2004). "'[A]n instrument is deemed ... filed at the time it is left with the clerk, regardless of whether or not a file mark is placed on the instrument and regardless of whether the file mark gives some other date of filing.' Once a party has satisfied his duty to put a legal instrument in the custody and the control of the court clerk, he should not be penalized for errors made by the court clerk."

Stokes v. Aberdeen Ins., 917 S.W.2d 267, 268 (Tex. 1996). "[W]e hold that mailing the document to the proper court address is *conditionally effective* as mailing it to the proper court clerk's address. [¶] The clerk still must receive the document within ten days to perfect the filing."

Lofton v. Allstate Ins., 895 S.W.2d 693, 693-94 (Tex.1995). "While a postmark is *prima facie* evidence of mailing, no postmark is available in this case. In the absence of a proper postmark or certificate of mailing, an attorney's uncontroverted affidavit may be evidence of the date of mailing." *See also Landers v. State Farm Lloyds*, 257 S.W.3d 740, 745 (Tex.App.—Houston [1st Dist.] 2008, no pet.).

Miller Brewing Co. v. Villarreal, 829 S.W.2d 770, 771-72 (Tex.1992). "[A] party who finds the courthouse closed on the last day that a document must be filed ... may mail the document that day, and if it is received by the clerk not more than ten days later it is timely filed. He may also locate the clerk or judge of the court and file the document with them. In some circumstances a party may also move for an enlargement of time." *See also Garcia v. State Farm Lloyds*, 287 S.W.3d 809, 815 (Tex.App.—Corpus Christi 2009, pet. denied) ("not more than ten days tardily" requirement in Rule 5 refers to ten days past the filing deadline).

Pediatrix Med. Servs. v. De La O, 368 S.W.3d 34, 38-39 (Tex.App.—El Paso 2012, no pet.). "Rule 5 does not enlarge the time in which to file a pleading, but instead defines when it is 'deemed filed in time.' Therefore, the U.S. Post Office acts as a branch of the court clerk's office for purposes of filing pleadings only when the provisions of Rule 5 are satisfied. The rule applies to filings that contemplate a filing deadline. Indeed, if the language of Rule 5 is construed under its plain meaning, it requires a pleading to be considered filed when it is deposited in the mail only if the pleading has to be filed on or before the last day for filing. [¶] [The] second amended petition was mailed on December 30, 2009 and it was received and filed by the court clerk on January 4, 2010. Because there was no preset deadline to file the second amended petition, the provisions of Rule 5 do not apply. Therefore, [the] second amended petition was filed on January 4, 2010, the date the court clerk actually received and filed it...."

TRCP 6. SUITS COMMENCED ON SUNDAY

No civil suit shall be commenced nor process issued or served on Sunday, except in cases of injunction, attachment, garnishment, sequestration, or distress proceedings; provided that citation by publication published on Sunday shall be valid.

History of TRCP 6: Amended eff. Feb. 1, 1973, by order of Oct. 3, 1972 (483-84 S.W.2d [Tex.Cases] xxii): Added provision about publication of citation on Sunday. Adopted eff. Sept. 1, 1941, by order of Oct. 29, 1940 (3 Tex.B.J. 525 [1940]). Source: TRCS art. 1974 (repealed).

See *Commentaries*, "Serving the Defendant with Suit," ch. 2-H, p. 157.

TRCP 7. MAY APPEAR BY ATTORNEY

Any party to a suit may appear and prosecute or defend his rights therein, either in person or by an attorney of the court.

History of TRCP 7: Adopted eff. Sept. 1, 1941, by order of Oct. 29, 1940 (3 Tex.B.J. 525 [1940]). Source: TRCS art. 1993 (repealed).

See *Commentaries*, "Rules for Serving Documents," ch. 1-D, p. 34; "The Attorney," ch. 1-H, p. 52; *O'Connor's Texas Forms*, FORM 1H:1.

ANNOTATIONS

Kunstoplast v. Formosa Plastics Corp., 937 S.W.2d 455, 456 (Tex.1996). "Generally a corporation may be represented only by a licensed attorney.... We hold, however, that ... a nonlawyer [is not precluded] from performing the specific ministerial task of depositing cash with a clerk in lieu of a cost bond."

Ayres v. Canales, 790 S.W.2d 554, 557 (Tex.1990). "Ordering a party to be represented by an attorney violates Rule 7."

Kaminetzky v. Newman, No. 01-10-01113-CV (Tex.App.—Houston [1st Dist.] 2011, no pet.) (memo op.; 12-29-11). The right to represent oneself pro se "only applies ... when the person is litigating his rights on his own behalf, instead of litigating certain rights in a representative capacity."

In re A.H.L., III, 214 S.W.3d 45, 52 (Tex.App.—El Paso 2006, pet. denied). "The right to self-representation ... is not absolute. [A]n inmate does not have an absolute right to appear in person in every court proceeding. The inmate's right of access to the courts must be weighed against the protection of the correctional system's integrity."

TRCP 8. ATTORNEY IN CHARGE

On the occasion of a party's first appearance through counsel, the attorney whose signature first appears on the initial pleadings for any party shall be the attorney in charge, unless another attorney is specifically designated therein. Thereafter, until such designation is changed by written notice to the court and all other parties in accordance with Rule 21a, said attorney in charge shall be responsible for the suit as to such party.

All communications from the court or other counsel with respect to a suit shall be sent to the attorney in charge.

History of TRCP 8: Amended eff. Jan. 1, 1988, by order of July 15, 1987 (733-34 S.W.2d [Tex.Cases] xxxvi). Adopted eff. Sept. 1, 1941, by order of Oct. 29, 1940 (3 Tex.B.J. 525 [1940]). Source: Tex. Rules for Dist. & Cty. Cts. 45.

See *Commentaries*, "The Attorney," ch. 1-H, p. 52; *O'Connor's Texas Forms*, FORM 1H:1.

ANNOTATIONS

City of Tyler v. Beck, 196 S.W.3d 784, 787 (Tex. 2006). "[N]othing in [TRCP 8] indicates that a motion filed by an attorney other than the designated attorney in charge is void or that other attorneys are not authorized to act on behalf of the party." *See also Sunbeam Env'tl Servs. v. Texas Workers' Comp. Ins. Facility*, 71 S.W.3d 846, 851 (Tex.App.—Austin 2002, no pet.).

Gem Vending, Inc. v. Walker, 918 S.W.2d 656, 658 (Tex.App.—Fort Worth 1996, orig. proceeding). "Notice to an attorney is notice to a party. [O]nce an attorney has entered an appearance in a case, all communications *must* be sent to that attorney."

Palmer v. Cantrell, 747 S.W.2d 39, 41 (Tex.App.—Houston [1st Dist.] 1988, no writ). "Where a single adverse party is represented by two attorneys who are not associated in a firm, we believe that it is sufficient to serve the attorney who is designated as lead counsel because he has 'control in the management of the cause....'"

TRCP 9. NUMBER OF COUNSEL HEARD

Not more than two counsel on each side shall be heard on any question or on the trial, except in important cases, and upon special leave of the court.

History of TRCP 9: Adopted eff. Sept. 1, 1941, by order of Oct. 29, 1940 (3 Tex.B.J. 525 [1940]). Source: Tex. Rules for Dist. & Cty. Cts. 44.

See *Commentaries*, "The Attorney," ch. 1-H, p. 52.

TRCP 10. WITHDRAWAL OF ATTORNEY

An attorney may withdraw from representing a party only upon written motion for good cause shown. If another attorney is to be substituted as attorney for the party, the motion shall state: the name, address, telephone number, telecopier number, if any, and State Bar of Texas identification number of the substitute attorney; that the party approves the substitution; and that the withdrawal is not sought for delay only. If another attorney is not to be substituted as attorney for the party, the motion shall state: that a copy of the motion has been delivered to the party; that the party has been notified in writing of his right to object to the motion; whether the party consents to the motion; the party's last known address and all pending settings and dead-

★

lines. If the motion is granted, the withdrawing attorney shall immediately notify the party in writing of any additional settings or deadlines of which the attorney has knowledge at the time of the withdrawal and has not already notified the party. The Court may impose further conditions upon granting leave to withdraw. Notice or delivery to a party shall be either made to the party in person or mailed to the party's last known address by both certified and regular first class mail. If the attorney in charge withdraws and another attorney remains or becomes substituted, another attorney in charge must be designated of record with notice to all other parties in accordance with Rule 21a.

History of TRCP 10: Amended eff. Sept. 1, 1990, by order of Apr. 24, 1990 (785-86 S.W.2d [Tex.Cases] xxxv): Rewrote rule; repealed present rule; and clarified requirements for withdrawal. Amended eff. Jan. 1, 1988, by order of July 15, 1987 (733-34 S.W.2d [Tex.Cases] xxxvii): Repealed present rule; set forth requirements for withdrawal of counsel and withdrawal with substitution of counsel; and carried forward requirements of amended TRCP 8 regarding designation of attorney in charge. Adopted eff. Sept. 1, 1941, by order of Oct. 29, 1940 (3 Tex.B.J. 525 [1940]). Source: Tex. Rules for Dist. & Cty. Cts. 46.

See *Commentaries*, "The Attorney," ch. 1-H, p. 52; *O'Connor's Texas Forms*, FORMS 1H:6, 7.

ANNOTATIONS

Rogers v. Clinton, 794 S.W.2d 9, 10 n.1 (Tex.1990). "Although a client may discharge his attorney at any time even without cause, an attorney may withdraw from representation of a client only if he satisfies the requirements of [TRCP] 10."

Harrison v. Harrison, 367 S.W.3d 822, 827 (Tex. App.—Houston [14th Dist.] 2012, pet. filed 7-11-12). TRCP 10 "does not define 'good cause.' However, the Texas Disciplinary Rules of Professional Conduct articulate considerations relevant to the consideration of Rule 10 motions. [¶] [The Disciplinary Rules] provide[], among other things, that a lawyer shall not withdraw from representing a client 'unless withdrawal can be accomplished without material adverse effect on the interests of the client'; the client 'fails substantially to fulfill an obligation to the lawyer regarding the lawyer's services, including an obligation to pay the lawyer's fee as agreed, and has been given reasonable warning that the lawyer will withdraw unless the obligation is fulfilled'; and the representation 'will result in an unreasonable financial burden on the lawyer or has been rendered unreasonably difficult by the client.'"

Sims v. Fitzpatrick, 288 S.W.3d 93, 100 (Tex. App.—Houston [1st Dist.] 2009, no pet.). "A court abuses its discretion when it grants a motion to withdraw that does not comply with the mandatory requirements of rule 10. However, 'such error may be harmless

if the court allows the party time to secure new counsel and time for the new counsel to investigate the case and prepare for trial.'" *See also* **Gillie v. Boulas**, 65 S.W.3d 219, 221 (Tex.App.—Dallas 2001, pet. denied).

TRCP 11. AGREEMENTS TO BE IN WRITING

Unless otherwise provided in these rules, no agreement between attorneys or parties touching any suit pending will be enforced unless it be in writing, signed and filed with the papers as part of the record, or unless it be made in open court and entered of record.

History of TRCP 11: Amended eff. Jan. 1, 1988, by order of July 15, 1987 (733-34 S.W.2d [Tex.Cases] xxxvii): Amendment clarified that TRCP 11 is subject to modification by any other rule of Civil Procedure. Adopted eff. Sept. 1, 1941, by order of Oct. 29, 1940 (3 Tex.B.J. 526 [1940]). Source: Tex. Rules for Dist. & Cty. Cts. 47.

See TRCP 191.1 (agreements in discovery matters); *Commentaries*, "Agreements Between Attorneys – Rule 11," ch. 1-H, §9, p. 61; "Settlement of the Suit," ch. 7-I, p. 669; *O'Connor's Texas Forms*, FORM 1H:13.

ANNOTATIONS

Fortis Benefits v. Cantu, 234 S.W.3d 642, 651 (Tex. 2007). "Rule 11 aims to remove misunderstandings and controversies that accompany verbal assurances, and the written agreements 'speak for themselves.'"

Exito Elecs. Co. v. Trejo, 142 S.W.3d 302, 305 (Tex. 2004). "A Rule 11 Agreement between the parties, in and of itself, is not a plea, pleading, or motion. *At 306:* [W]hile filing a Rule 11 Agreement with the trial court is a requirement for enforcement, it is not in and of itself a request for enforcement or any other affirmative action by the trial court."

Compania Financiara Libano, S.A. v. Simmons, 53 S.W.3d 365, 368 (Tex.2001). A settlement agreement is enforceable as a contract even if its terms are not incorporated into the judgment.

Padilla v. LaFrance, 907 S.W.2d 454, 461 (Tex. 1995). "The ... filing requirement [in TRCP 11] is satisfied so long as the agreement is filed before it is sought to be enforced."

Coale v. Scott, 331 S.W.3d 829, 831-32 (Tex.App.— Amarillo 2011, no pet.). "[T]he trial court's authority to approve a Rule 11 agreement does not depend upon whether it has [plenary] jurisdiction. It may enforce a Rule 11 agreement touching upon the suit executed after the cause was tried and finally resolved via judgment. [A] settlement agreement ... executed while the parties were attempting to sway the trial court to enforce its judgment logically falls within the scope of 'any suit pending' for purposes of Rule 11. [¶] [Party

---

argued] that the Rule 11 agreement was unenforceable because they allegedly withdrew their consent to it before the trial court ordered its enforcement. We disagree. [¶] Rule 11 requires that the agreement be filed of record before the court may enforce it. If the accord is in writing, signed by the parties or their attorneys, and filed of record, it does not matter whether a party no longer agrees to it when the trial court is finally asked to enforce it. This is so because the agreement becomes a contract when executed, not when the trial court attempts to enforce it."

ExxonMobil Corp. v. Valence Oper. Co., 174 S.W.3d 303, 309 (Tex.App.—Houston [1st Dist.] 2005, pet. denied). "[I]t is not sufficient that a party's consent to a Rule 11 agreement may have been given at one time; consent must exist at the time that judgment is rendered." *See also Baylor Coll. of Med. v. Camberg*, 247 S.W.3d 342, 346-47 (Tex.App.—Houston [14th Dist.] 2008, pet. denied).

TRCP 12. ATTORNEY TO SHOW AUTHORITY

A party in a suit or proceeding pending in a court of this state may, by sworn written motion stating that he believes the suit or proceeding is being prosecuted or defended without authority, cause the attorney to be cited to appear before the court and show his authority to act. The notice of the motion shall be served upon the challenged attorney at least ten days before the hearing on the motion. At the hearing on the motion, the burden of proof shall be upon the challenged attorney to show sufficient authority to prosecute or defend the suit on behalf of the other party. Upon his failure to show such authority, the court shall refuse to permit the attorney to appear in the cause, and shall strike the pleadings if no person who is authorized to prosecute or defend appears. The motion may be heard and determined at any time before the parties have announced ready for trial, but the trial shall not be unnecessarily continued or delayed for the hearing.

History of TRCP 12: Amended eff. Jan. 1, 1981, by order of June 10, 1980 (599-600 S.W.2d [Tex.Cases] xxxiv): Changed rule to permit challenge to plaintiff's attorney, so that all attorneys are subject to a challenge that they are in court without authority. Adopted eff. Sept. 1, 1941, by order of Oct. 29, 1940 (3 Tex.B.J. 526 [1940]). Source: TRCS art. 320 (repealed), minor textual changes and added requirement that notice be served at least ten days before hearing on the motion.

See *Commentaries*, "The Attorney," ch. 1-H, p. 52; *O'Connor's Texas Forms*, FORMS 1H:8-10.

ANNOTATIONS

In re Users Sys. Servs., 22 S.W.3d 331, 335 (Tex. 1999). "[T]he procedure prescribed by Rule 12 for requiring an attorney to show his authority to act for a party presupposes the possibility that an attorney can be counsel of record for a party he is not authorized to represent. The [TRCPs] contemplate that authorization may not have existed or may cease before the attorney has withdrawn from the case."

Air Park-Dallas Zoning Cmte. v. Crow-Billingsley Airpark, Ltd., 109 S.W.3d 900, 906 (Tex.App.— Dallas 2003, no pet.). "[A] Rule 12 motion may be properly brought when a new and different attorney attempts to appear as attorney of record purporting to advance a motion for new trial after the trial has concluded."

TRCP 13. EFFECT OF SIGNING OF PLEADINGS, MOTIONS & OTHER PAPERS; SANCTIONS

The signatures of attorneys or parties constitute a certificate by them that they have read the pleading, motion, or other paper; that to the best of their knowledge, information, and belief formed after reasonable inquiry the instrument is not groundless and brought in bad faith or groundless and brought for the purpose of harassment. Attorneys or parties who shall bring a fictitious suit as an experiment to get an opinion of the court, or who shall file any fictitious pleading in a cause for such a purpose, or shall make statements in pleading which they know to be groundless and false, for the purpose of securing a delay of the trial of the cause, shall be held guilty of a contempt. If a pleading, motion or other paper is signed in violation of this rule, the court, upon motion or upon its own initiative, after notice and hearing, shall impose an appropriate sanction available under Rule 215-2b,[1] upon the person who signed it, a represented party, or both.

Courts shall presume that pleadings, motions, and other papers are filed in good faith. No sanctions under this rule may be imposed except for good cause, the particulars of which must be stated in the sanction order. "Groundless" for purposes of this rule means no basis in law or fact and not warranted by good faith argument for the extension, modification, or reversal of existing law. A general denial does not constitute a violation of this rule. The amount requested for damages does not constitute a violation of this rule.

1. **Editor's note:** Now TRCP 215.2(b).

History of TRCP 13: Amended eff. Sept. 1, 1990, by order of Apr. 24, 1990 (785-86 S.W.2d [Tex.Cases] xxxvi): Requires notice and hearing before a court determines to impose sanctions; specifies that any sanction imposed be appropriate; eliminates 90-day grace period provided in former version of rule; and deleted last par. in the comment to the 1988 change. Amended eff. Jan. 1, 1988, by order of July 15, 1987 (733-34 S.W.2d [Tex.Cases] xxxvii): TRCP 13 contained

———————————————————— ✦ ————————————————————

the following as the last par. in the rule: "SB No. 5, art. 2. Trial; Judgment, Section 2.01. Subtitle A, Title 2, CPRC, Chapter 9 'Frivolous Pleadings and Claims' otherwise to be effective Sept. 2, 1987, insofar as it conflicts with this rule, is repealed pursuant to Tex. Const. art. 5, §31, and Tex. Gov't Code §22.004(c)." Adopted eff. Sept. 1, 1941, by order of Oct. 29, 1940 (3 Tex.B.J. 526 [1940]). Source: Tex. Rules for Dist. & Cty. Cts. 51.

See CPRC chs. 9, 10; *Commentaries*, "Groundless or frivolous pleadings," ch. 1-B, §3.3, p. 14; "Motion for Sanctions," ch. 5-K, p. 377; *O'Connor's Texas Forms*, FORMS 5J:1, 2, 5.

ANNOTATIONS

GTE Comms. Sys. v. Tanner, 856 S.W.2d 725, 731 (Tex.1993). TRCP 13 "prescribes that courts presume that papers are filed in good faith. Thus, the burden is on the party moving for sanctions to overcome this presumption. [¶] Rule 13 requires that sanctions imposed be 'appropriate,' which is the equivalent of 'just' under [TRCP] 215." *See also Olibas v. Gomez*, 242 S.W.3d 527, 534 (Tex.App.—El Paso 2007, pet. denied).

Parker v. Walton, 233 S.W.3d 535, 539-40 (Tex. App.—Houston [14th Dist.] 2007, no pet.). "When determining whether Rule 13 sanctions are proper, the trial court must examine the facts available to the litigant and the circumstances existing when the litigant filed the pleading. Rule 13 requires sanctions based on the acts or omissions of the represented party or counsel and not merely on the legal merit of the pleading. The trial court must provide notice and hold an evidentiary hearing 'to make the necessary factual determinations about the motives and credibility of the person signing the groundless petition.' ... Bad faith is not simply bad judgment or negligence; rather, it is the conscious doing of a wrong for dishonest, discriminatory, or malicious purposes. Improper motive is an essential element of bad faith. Harassment means that the pleading was intended to annoy, alarm, and abuse another person." *See also Thielemann v. Kethan*, 371 S.W.3d 286, 294 (Tex.App.—Houston [1st Dist.] 2012, pet. denied) (party moving for sanctions must prove pleading party's subjective state of mind); *Lake Travis ISD v. Lovelace*, 243 S.W.3d 244, 254 (Tex.App.—Austin 2007, no pet.) (merely filing motion or pleading that trial court denies does not entitle opposing party to TRCP 13 sanctions).

Loeffler v. Lytle ISD, 211 S.W.3d 331, 349-50 (Tex. App.—San Antonio 2006, pet. denied). "At the time these pleadings and motions were filed, [P] at the most provided the factual basis for these claims. The decision of what legal claims, objections, and motions to file was part and parcel of [P's] legal representation and was entrusted to ... her attorney. Because a party should not be punished for their attorney's conduct unless the party is implicated apart from having entrusted its legal representation, we conclude the trial court abused its discretion in imposing sanctions against [P] under ... Rule 13." *See also Metzger v. Sebek*, 892 S.W.2d 20, 52-53 (Tex.App.—Houston [1st Dist.] 1994, writ denied) (party should be fined smaller amount because he was responsible only for affidavit with false information, not for pleadings).

TRCP 14. AFFIDAVIT BY AGENT

Whenever it may be necessary or proper for any party to a civil suit or proceeding to make an affidavit, it may be made by either the party or his agent or his attorney.

History of TRCP 14: Adopted eff. Sept. 1, 1941, by order of Oct. 29, 1940 (3 Tex.B.J. 526 [1940]). Source: TRCS art. 24 (repealed).

See TRCP 197.2(d); *Commentaries*, "Affidavits," ch. 1-B, §3.2.16, p. 11; *O'Connor's Texas Forms*, FORM 1B:7.

ANNOTATIONS

Cantu v. Holiday Inns, Inc., 910 S.W.2d 113, 116 (Tex.App.—Corpus Christi 1995, writ denied). "A party's attorney may verify the pleading where he has knowledge of the facts, but does not have authority to verify based merely on his status as counsel. Here, counsel does not show any basis in the pleading or in her affidavit for her personal knowledge of relevant facts."

TRCP 14a. REPEALED

Repealed eff. Sept. 1, 1986, by order of Apr. 10, 1986 (705-06 S.W.2d [Tex.Cases] xxxiii).

TRCP 14b. RETURN OR OTHER DISPOSITION OF EXHIBITS

The clerk of the court in which the exhibits are filed shall retain and dispose of the same as directed by the Supreme Court.

History of TRCP 14b: Amended eff. Jan. 1, 1988, by order of July 15, 1987 (733-34 S.W.2d [Tex.Cases] xxxviii). Adopted eff. Jan. 1, 1967, by order of July 20, 1966 (401-02 S.W.2d [Tex.Cases] xxxi). Source: New rule.

See TRCP 75b.

ORDER RELATING TO RETENTION & DISPOSITION OF EXHIBITS IN CIVIL CASES

In compliance with the provisions of Texas Rule of Civil Procedure 14b, the Supreme Court hereby directs that exhibits offered or admitted into evidence shall be retained and disposed of by the clerk of the court in which the exhibits are filed upon the following basis.

The order shall apply only to: (1) those cases in which judgment has been rendered on service of pro-

---
⭐
---

cess by publication and in which no motion for new trial was filed within two years after judgment was signed; and (2) all other cases in which judgment has been signed for one year and in which no appeal was perfected or in which a perfected appeal was dismissed or concluded by a final judgment as to all parties and the issuance of the appellate court's mandate such that the case is no longer pending on appeal or in the trial court.

The party who offered an exhibit may withdraw it from the clerk's office within thirty days of the later of (1) a case becoming subject to this order, or (2) the effective date of this order. The clerk, unless otherwise directed by the court, may dispose of any exhibits remaining after such time period.

History of TRCP 14b, Order on Exhibits: Amended eff. June 1, 2005, by order of Jan. 27, 2005 (Tex.Sup.Ct. Order, Misc. Docket No. 05-9026). Adopted eff. Jan. 1, 1988, by order of July 15, 1987 (733-34 S.W.2d [Tex.Cases] xxxviii).

TRCP 14c. DEPOSIT IN LIEU OF SURETY BOND

Wherever these rules provide for the filing of a surety bond, the party may in lieu of filing the bond deposit cash or other negotiable obligation of the government of the United States of America or any agency thereof, or with leave of court, deposit a negotiable obligation of any bank or savings and loan association chartered by the government of the United States of America or any state thereof that is insured by the government of the United States of America or any agency thereof, in the amount fixed for the surety bond, conditioned in the same manner as would be a surety bond for the protection of other parties. Any interest thereon shall constitute a part of the deposit.

History of TRCP 14c: Adopted eff. Jan. 1, 1981, by order of June 10, 1980 (599-600 S.W.2d [Tex.Cases] xxxiv): New rule authorizes various deposits in lieu of a surety bond. Source: New rule.

PART II. RULES OF PRACTICE IN DISTRICT & COUNTY COURTS

SECTION 1. GENERAL RULES

TRCP 15. WRITS & PROCESS

The style of all writs and process shall be "The State of Texas"; and unless otherwise specially provided by law or these rules every such writ and process shall be directed to any sheriff or any constable within the State of Texas, shall be made returnable on the Monday next after expiration of twenty days from the date of service thereof, and shall be dated and attested by the clerk with the seal of the court impressed thereon; and the date of issuance shall be noted thereon.

History of TRCP 15: Adopted eff. Sept. 1, 1941, by order of Oct. 29, 1940 (3 Tex.B.J. 526 [1940]). Source: TRCS art. 2286 (repealed). Eliminated requirement that writ be addressed to sheriff or any constable of a specific county and that writ be returnable to a term of court. Compare to TRCP 101.

See Loc. Gov't Code §86.021; *Commentaries*, "Serving the Defendant with Suit," ch. 2-H, p. 157; "Default Judgment," ch. 7-A, p. 587; *O'Connor's Texas Forms*, FORMS 2H:2, 3.

ANNOTATIONS

Williams v. Williams, 150 S.W.3d 436, 445 (Tex. App.—Austin 2004, pet. denied). "[W]e ... hold that citations *must* be expressly directed to the defendant under [TRCP] 99 and *may* also be addressed to the sheriff or constable under [TRCP] 15, but failure to include the sheriff or constable on the form of the citation will not render it void." *See also* ***Barker CATV Constr., Inc. v. Ampro, Inc.***, 989 S.W.2d 789, 792 (Tex.App.—Houston [1st Dist.] 1999, no pet.).

TRCP 16. SHALL ENDORSE ALL PROCESS

Every officer or authorized person shall endorse on all process and precepts coming to his hand the day and hour on which he received them, the manner in which he executed them, and the time and place the process was served and shall sign the returns officially.

History of TRCP 16: Amended eff. Jan. 1, 1988, by order of July 15, 1987 (733-34 S.W.2d [Tex.Cases] xxxix): To conform with TRCS art. 3926a (eff. Sept. 1, 1981; repealed, now Local Gov't Code §118.131), which authorized commissioners court of each county to set "reasonable" fee for service of process; mileage no longer authorized as an expense. Adopted eff. Sept. 1, 1941, by order of Oct. 29, 1940 (3 Tex.B.J. 526 [1940]). Source: TRCS art. 6875 (repealed).

See Loc. Gov't Code §§85.021, 86.021; TRCP 107; *Commentaries*, "Serving the Defendant with Suit," ch. 2-H, p. 157; "Default Judgment," ch. 7-A, p. 587.

TRCP 17. OFFICER TO EXECUTE PROCESS

Except where otherwise expressly provided by law or these rules, the officer receiving any process to be executed shall not be entitled in any case to demand his fee for executing the same in advance of such execution, but his fee shall be taxed and collected as other costs in the case.

History of TRCP 17: Adopted eff. Sept. 1, 1941, by order of Oct. 29, 1940 (3 Tex.B.J. 526 [1940]). Source: TRCS art. 3911 (repealed).

See *Commentaries*, "Serving the Defendant with Suit," ch. 2-H, p. 157; "Default Judgment," ch. 7-A, p. 587.

TRCP 18. WHEN JUDGE DIES DURING TERM, RESIGNS OR IS DISABLED

If the judge dies, resigns, or becomes unable to hold court during the session of court duly convened for the term, and the time provided by law for the holding of said court has not expired, such death, resignation, or inability on the part of the judge shall not operate to ad-

───────────────────── ★ ─────────────────────

journ said court for the term, but such court shall be deemed to continue in session. If a successor to such judge shall qualify and assume office during the term, or if a judge be transferred to said district from some other judicial district, he may continue to hold said court for the term provided, and all motions undisposed of shall be heard and determined by him, and statements of facts and bills of exception shall be approved by him. If the time for holding such court expires before a successor shall qualify, and before a judge can be transferred to said district from some other judicial district, then all motions pending, including those for new trial, shall stand as continued in force until such successor has qualified and assumed office, or a judge has been transferred to said district who can hold said court, and thereupon such judge shall have power to act thereon at the succeeding term, or on an earlier day in vacation, on notice to all parties to the motion, and such orders shall have the same effect as if rendered in term time. The time for allowing statement of facts and bills of exception from such orders shall date from the time the motion was decided.

History of TRCP 18: Amended eff. Dec. 31, 1943, by order of June 16, 1943 (6 Tex.B.J. 329 [1943]). Adopted eff. Sept. 1, 1941, by order of Oct. 29, 1940 (3 Tex.B.J. 527 [1940]). Source: TRCS art. 2288 (repealed).

See Gov't Code §74.053.

ANNOTATIONS

2900 Smith, Ltd. v. Constellation NewEnergy, Inc., 301 S.W.3d 741, 744 n.6 (Tex.App.—Houston [14th Dist.] 2009, no pet.). TRCP 18 "'allows successor judges to dispose of unresolved matters and enter various orders so long as the successor judge does not render judgment without hearing evidence.'" *See also **W.C. Banks, Inc. v. Team, Inc.***, 783 S.W.2d 783, 786 (Tex. App.—Houston [1st Dist.] 1990, no writ).

TRCP 18a. RECUSAL & DISQUALIFICATION OF JUDGES

(a) *Motion; Form and Contents.* A party in a case in any trial court other than a statutory probate court or justice court may seek to recuse or disqualify a judge who is sitting in the case by filing a motion with the clerk of the court in which the case is pending. The motion:

(1) must be verified;

(2) must assert one or more of the grounds listed in Rule 18b;

(3) must not be based solely on the judge's rulings in the case; and

(4) must state with detail and particularity facts that:

(A) are within the affiant's personal knowledge, except that facts may be stated on information and belief if the basis for that belief is specifically stated;

(B) would be admissible in evidence; and

(C) if proven, would be sufficient to justify recusal or disqualification.

(b) *Time for Filing Motion.*

(1) *Motion to recuse.* A motion to recuse:

(A) must be filed as soon as practicable after the movant knows of the ground stated in the motion; and

(B) must not be filed after the tenth day before the date set for trial or other hearing unless, before that day, the movant neither knew nor reasonably should have known:

(i) that the judge whose recusal is sought would preside at the trial or hearing; or

(ii) that the ground stated in the motion existed.

(2) *Motion to disqualify.* A motion to disqualify should be filed as soon as practicable after the movant knows of the ground stated in the motion.

(c) *Response to Motion.*

(1) *By another party.* Any other party in the case may, but need not, file a response to the motion. Any response must be filed before the motion is heard.

(2) *By the respondent judge.* The judge whose recusal or disqualification is sought should not file a response to the motion.

(d) *Service of Motion or Response.* A party who files a motion or response must serve a copy on every other party. The method of service must be the same as the method of filing, if possible.

(e) *Duty of the Clerk.*

(1) *Delivery of a motion or response.* When a motion or response is filed, the clerk of the court must immediately deliver a copy to the respondent judge and to the presiding judge of the administrative judicial region in which the court is located ("the regional presiding judge").

(2) *Delivery of order of recusal or referral.* When a respondent judge signs and files an order of recusal or referral, the clerk of the court must immediately deliver a copy to the regional presiding judge.

(f) Duties of the Respondent Judge; Failure to Comply.

(1) *Responding to the motion.* Regardless of whether the motion complies with this rule, the respondent judge, within three business days after the motion is filed, must either:

(A) sign and file with the clerk an order of recusal or disqualification; or

(B) sign and file with the clerk an order referring the motion to the regional presiding judge.

(2) *Restrictions on further action.*

(A) *Motion filed before evidence offered at trial.* If a motion is filed before evidence has been offered at trial, the respondent judge must take no further action in the case until the motion has been decided, except for good cause stated in writing or on the record.

(B) *Motion filed after evidence offered at trial.* If a motion is filed after evidence has been offered at trial, the respondent judge may proceed, subject to stay by the regional presiding judge.

(3) *Failure to comply.* If the respondent judge fails to comply with a duty imposed by this rule, the movant may notify the regional presiding judge.

(g) Duties of Regional Presiding Judge.

(1) *Motion.* The regional presiding judge must rule on a referred motion or assign a judge to rule. If a party files a motion to recuse or disqualify the regional presiding judge, the regional presiding judge may still assign a judge to rule on the original, referred motion. Alternatively, the regional presiding judge may sign and file with the clerk an order referring the second motion to the Chief Justice for consideration.

(2) *Order.* The ruling must be by written order.

(3) *Summary denial for noncompliance.*

(A) *Motion to recuse.* A motion to recuse that does not comply with this rule may be denied without an oral hearing. The order must state the nature of the noncompliance. Even if the motion is amended to correct the stated noncompliance, the motion will count for purposes of determining whether a tertiary recusal motion has been filed under the Civil Practice and Remedies Code.

(B) *Motion to disqualify.* A motion to disqualify may not be denied on the ground that it was not filed or served in compliance with this rule.

(4) *Interim orders.* The regional presiding judge or judge assigned to decide the motion may issue interim or ancillary orders in the pending case as justice may require.

(5) *Discovery.* Except by order of the regional presiding judge or the judge assigned to decide the motion, a subpoena or discovery request may not issue to the respondent judge and may be disregarded unless accompanied by the order.

(6) *Hearing.*

(A) *Time.* The motion must be heard as soon as practicable and may be heard immediately after it is referred to the regional presiding judge or an assigned judge.

(B) *Notice.* Notice of the hearing must be given to all parties in the case.

(C) *By telephone.* The hearing may be conducted by telephone on the record. Documents submitted by facsimile or email, otherwise admissible under the rules of evidence, may be considered.

(7) *Reassignment of case if motion granted.* If the motion is granted, the regional presiding judge must transfer the case to another court or assign another judge to the case.

(h) Sanctions. After notice and hearing, the judge who hears the motion may order the party or attorney who filed the motion, or both, to pay the reasonable attorney fees and expenses incurred by other parties if the judge determines that the motion was:

(1) groundless and filed in bad faith or for the purpose of harassment, or

(2) clearly brought for unnecessary delay and without sufficient cause.

(i) Chief Justice. The Chief Justice of the Supreme Court of Texas may assign judges and issue any orders permitted by this rule or pursuant to statute.

(j) Appellate Review.

(1) *Order on motion to recuse.*

(A) *Denying motion.* An order denying a motion to recuse may be reviewed only for abuse of discretion on appeal from the final judgment.

(B) *Granting motion.* An order granting a motion to recuse is final and cannot be reviewed by appeal, mandamus, or otherwise.

(2) *Order on motion to disqualify.* An order granting or denying a motion to disqualify may be reviewed by mandamus and may be appealed in accordance with other law.

★

Comment to 2011 change: Rule 18a governs the procedure for recusing or disqualifying a judge sitting in any trial court other than a statutory probate court, justice court, or municipal court. Chapter 25 of the Government Code governs statutory probate courts, Rule 528 governs justice courts, and Chapter 29 of the Government Code governs municipal courts. Under Rule 18a, a judge's rulings may not be the sole basis for a motion to recuse or disqualify the judge. But when one or more sufficient other bases are raised, the judge hearing the motion may consider evidence of rulings when considering whether to grant the motion. For purposes of this rule, the term "rulings" is not meant to encompass a judge's statements or remarks about a case.

History of TRCP 18a: Amended eff. Aug. 1, 2011, by order of July 22, 2011 (Tex.Sup.Ct. Order, Misc. Docket No. 11-9141). Amended eff. Aug. 1, 2011, by order of July 5, 2011 (Tex.Sup.Ct. Order, Misc. Docket No. 11-9126). Amended eff. Sept. 1, 1990, by order of Apr. 24, 1990 (785-86 S.W.2d [Tex.Cases] xxxvi): "Court Administration Act" in (g) changed to "statute." Amended eff. Jan. 1, 1988, by order of July 15, 1987 (733-34 S.W.2d [Tex.Cases] xxxix): Amended pars. (a), (g), (h). Amended eff. Sept. 1, 1986, by order of Apr. 10, 1986 (705-06 S.W.2d [Tex.Cases] xxxiii): Added words "the Court of Criminal Appeals" to (a); and subsec. (1) to (g). Amended eff. Apr. 1, 1984, by order of Dec. 5, 1983 (661-62 S.W.2d [Tex.Cases] xxxvi): Changed (a) textually. Adopted eff. Jan. 1, 1981, by order of June 10, 1980 (599-600 S.W.2d [Tex.Cases] xxxiv). Source: New rule.

See Gov't Code §§74.053, 74.059(c)(3); TRAP 16; *Commentaries*, "Motion to Challenge the Judge," ch. 5-C, p. 325; *O'Connor's Texas Forms*, FORMS 5C.

ANNOTATIONS

In re Perritt, 992 S.W.2d 444, 445 (Tex.1999). "[A] judge designated by the presiding judge of the administrative judicial district to hear a recusal motion under [TRCP] 18a is also an assigned judge subject to objection and mandatory disqualification under [Gov't Code] §74.053(b)...."

In re Union Pac. Res., 969 S.W.2d 427, 428 (Tex. 1998). Mandamus is not available to review the denial of a motion to recuse made under the TRCPs. TRCP 18a(f), now 18a(j)(1)(A), "expressly provide[s] for appellate review from a final judgment after denial of a recusal motion. If the appellate court determines ... the trial judge should have been recused, the appellate court can reverse the trial court's judgment and remand for a new trial before a different judge."

In re D.C., No. 07-09-00320-CV (Tex.App.—Amarillo 2010, no pet.) (memo op.; 9-23-10). "[T]he law is clear that, unlike statutory recusal, disqualification cannot be waived, and may be raised at any time. Appellant may raise the issue of the trial judge's disqualification for the first time on appeal."

Brosseau v. Ranzau, 28 S.W.3d 235, 238 (Tex. App.—Beaumont 2000, no pet.). "[T]he judge named in the motion [to recuse is] not ... permitted to act in *any* way other than the two options provided for in [TRCP 18a(f)(1)]. [I]f a trial court fails to comply with the strictures provided in Rule 18a, all actions taken by the judge subsequent to such violation are void." *See also In re A.R.*, 236 S.W.3d 460, 477 (Tex.App.—Dallas 2007, no pet.).

TRCP 18b. GROUNDS FOR RECUSAL & DISQUALIFICATION OF JUDGES

(a) *Grounds for Disqualification.* A judge must disqualify in any proceeding in which:

(1) the judge has served as a lawyer in the matter in controversy, or a lawyer with whom the judge previously practiced law served during such association as a lawyer concerning the matter;

(2) the judge knows that, individually or as a fiduciary, the judge has an interest in the subject matter in controversy; or

(3) either of the parties may be related to the judge by affinity or consanguinity within the third degree.

(b) *Grounds for Recusal.* A judge must recuse in any proceeding in which:

(1) the judge's impartiality might reasonably be questioned;

(2) the judge has a personal bias or prejudice concerning the subject matter or a party;

(3) the judge has personal knowledge of disputed evidentiary facts concerning the proceeding;

(4) the judge or a lawyer with whom the judge previously practiced law has been a material witness concerning the proceeding;

(5) the judge participated as counsel, adviser or material witness in the matter in controversy, or expressed an opinion concerning the merits of it, while acting as an attorney in government service;

(6) the judge knows that the judge, individually or as a fiduciary, or the judge's spouse or minor child residing in the judge's household, has a financial interest in the subject matter in controversy or in a party to the proceeding, or any other interest that could be substantially affected by the outcome of the proceeding;

(7) the judge or the judge's spouse, or a person within the third degree of relationship to either of them, or the spouse of such a person:

(A) is a party to the proceeding or an officer, director, or trustee of a party;

(B) is known by the judge to have an interest that could be substantially affected by the outcome of the proceeding; or

(C) is to the judge's knowledge likely to be a material witness in the proceeding.

(8) the judge or the judge's spouse, or a person within the first degree of relationship to either of them, or the spouse of such a person, is acting as a lawyer in the proceeding.

★

(c) *Financial Interests.* A judge should inform himself or herself about personal and fiduciary financial interests, and make a reasonable effort to inform himself or herself about the personal financial interests of his or her spouse and minor children residing in the household.

(d) *Terminology and Standards.* In this rule:

(1) "proceeding" includes pretrial, trial, or other stages of litigation;

(2) the degree of relationship is calculated according to the civil law system;

(3) "fiduciary" includes such relationships as executor, administrator, trustee, and guardian;

(4) "financial interest" means ownership of a legal or equitable interest, however small, or a relationship as director, adviser, or other active participant in the affairs of a party, except that:

(A) ownership in a mutual or common investment fund that holds securities is not a "financial interest" in such securities unless the judge participates in the management of the fund;

(B) an office in an educational, religious, charitable, fraternal, or civic organization is not a "financial interest" in securities held by the organization;

(C) the proprietary interest of a policyholder in a mutual insurance company, of a depositor in a mutual savings association, or a similar proprietary interest, is a "financial interest" in the organization only if the outcome of the proceeding could substantially affect the value of the interest;

(D) ownership of government securities is a "financial interest" in the issuer only if the outcome of the proceeding could substantially affect the value of the securities;

(E) an interest as a taxpayer or utility ratepayer, or any similar interest, is not a "financial interest" unless the outcome of the proceeding could substantially affect the liability of the judge or a person related to him within the third degree more than other judges.

(e) *Waiving a Ground for Recusal.* The parties to a proceeding may waive any ground for recusal after it is fully disclosed on the record.

(f) *Discovery and Divestiture.* If a judge does not discover that the judge is recused under subparagraphs (b)(6) or (b)(7)(B) until after the judge has devoted substantial time to the matter, the judge is not required to recuse himself or herself if the judge or the person

related to the judge divests himself or herself of the interest that would otherwise require recusal.

Comment to 2011 change: The amendments to Rule 18b are not intended to be substantive.

History of TRCP 18b: Amended eff. Aug. 1, 2011, by order of July 22, 2011 (Tex.Sup.Ct. Order, Misc. Docket No. 11-9141). Amended eff. Aug. 1, 2011, by order of July 5, 2011 (Tex.Sup.Ct. Order, Misc. Docket No. 11-9126). Amended eff. Sept. 1, 1990, by order of Apr. 24, 1990 (785-86 S.W.2d [Tex.Cases] xxxvii): Rule entirely rewritten; expanded grounds for judge's mandatory recusal from those in earlier TRCP 18b(2). Adopted eff. Jan. 1, 1988, by order of July 15, 1987 (733-34 S.W.2d [Tex.Cases] xl). Source: New rule. Former TRCP 18b repealed eff. Sept. 1, 1986, by order of Apr. 10, 1986 (705-06 S.W.2d [Tex.Cases] xxxiv).

See Tex. Const. art. 5, §11; Gov't Code §§21.005, 74.053, 74.059(c)(3), 573.022-573.025; TRAP 16; *Commentaries*, "Motion to Challenge the Judge," ch. 5-C, p. 325; *O'Connor's Texas Forms*, FORMS 5C.

ANNOTATIONS

In re O'Connor, 92 S.W.3d 446, 449 (Tex.2002). Rule 18b(1)(a), now 18b(a)(1), "recognizes that a judge is vicariously disqualified under the [Texas] Constitution as having 'been counsel in the case' if a lawyer with whom the judge previously practiced law served as counsel to a party concerning the matter during their association." *See also Tesco Am., Inc. v. Strong Indus.*, 221 S.W.3d 550, 553 (Tex.2006) (disqualification of appellate judges); *Pena v. Pena*, 986 S.W.2d 696, 700 (Tex.App.—Corpus Christi 1998), *pet. denied*, 8 S.W.3d 639 (Tex.1999) (trial judge's attorney-client relationship with opposing counsel did not amount to constitutional disqualification).

In re C.J.O., 325 S.W.3d 261, 267 (Tex.App.—Eastland 2010, pet. denied). "The movant bears the burden of proving that a recusal is warranted and satisfies that burden only if he shows bias or partiality to such an extent as to deprive him of a fair trial. Bias sufficient to warrant a recusal commonly stems from an extrajudicial source. But, when recusal is based on in-court proceedings, the alleged biased rulings or remarks must display a deep-seated favoritism or antagonism that would make a fair judgment impossible."

Kennedy v. Wortham, 314 S.W.3d 34, 36 (Tex.App.—Texarkana 2010, pet. denied). "The interest that disqualifies a judge is an interest, however small, which rests on a direct pecuniary or personal interest in the result of the case. *At 37:* [P's] petition did not seek money damages; therefore, [trial judge] has no pecuniary interest in this case. Instead, [P] sought injunctive relief prohibiting 'all judges from discriminating.' [¶] Even if [P] obtained a judgment prohibiting all judges ... from discriminating, it would not add one additional burden or duty that [trial judge] does not already have imposed by law. [¶] [Trial judge] did not

---

✦

---

have a direct interest in the case that would require her disqualification."

Ludlow v. DeBerry, 959 S.W.2d 265, 271 (Tex. App.—Houston [14th Dist.] 1997, no writ). "[J]udicial remarks during the course of a trial that are critical or disapproving or even hostile to counsel, parties, or their cases, ordinarily do not support recusal. Such remarks *may* do so if they reveal an opinion deriving from an extrajudicial source and such remarks *will* do so if they reveal such a high degree of favoritism or antagonism as to make fair judgment impossible." *See also* ***Hansen v. JP Morgan Chase Bank***, 346 S.W.3d 769, 776 (Tex. App.—Dallas 2011, no pet.).

TRCP 18c. RECORDING & BROADCASTING OF COURT PROCEEDINGS

A trial court may permit broadcasting, televising, recording, or photographing of proceedings in the courtroom only in the following circumstances:

(a) in accordance with guidelines promulgated by the Supreme Court for civil cases, or

(b) when broadcasting, televising, recording, or photographing will not unduly distract participants or impair the dignity of the proceedings and the parties have consented, and consent to being depicted or recorded is obtained from each witness whose testimony will be broadcast, televised, or photographed, or

(c) the broadcasting, televising, recording, or photographing of investiture, or ceremonial proceedings.

History of TRCP 18c: Adopted eff. Sept. 1, 1990, by order of Apr. 24, 1990 (785-86 S.W.2d [Tex.Cases] xxxix): New rule to provide guidelines for broadcasting, televising, recording, and photographing court proceedings. Source: New rule.

TRCP 19. NON-ADJOURNMENT OF TERM

Every term of court shall commence and convene by operation of law at the time fixed by statute without any act, order, or formal opening by a judge or other official thereof, and shall continue to be open at all times until and including the last day of the term unless sooner adjourned by the judge thereof.

History of TRCP 19: Amended eff. Dec. 31, 1943, by order of June 16, 1943 (6 Tex.B.J. 330 [1943]). Adopted eff. Sept. 1, 1941, by order of Oct. 29, 1940 (3 Tex.B.J. 527 [1940]). Source: TRCS art. 1922 (repealed).

TRCP 20. MINUTES READ & SIGNED

On the last day of the session, the minutes shall be read, corrected and signed in open court by the judge. Each special judge shall sign the minutes of such proceedings as were had by him.

History of TRCP 20: Adopted eff. Sept. 1, 1941, by order of Oct. 29, 1940 (3 Tex.B.J. 527 [1940]): Eliminated former requirement that minutes be signed daily; and extension of the rule to judges of both district and county courts. Source: TRCS art. 1918 (repealed).

TRCP 21. FILING & SERVING PLEADINGS & MOTIONS

Every pleading, plea, motion or application to the court for an order, whether in the form of a motion, plea or other form of request, unless presented during a hearing or trial, shall be filed with the clerk of the court in writing, shall state the grounds therefor, shall set forth the relief or order sought, and at the same time a true copy shall be served on all other parties, and shall be noted on the docket.

An application to the court for an order and notice of any hearing thereon, not presented during a hearing or trial, shall be served upon all other parties not less than three days before the time specified for the hearing unless otherwise provided by these rules or shortened by the court.

If there is more than one other party represented by different attorneys, one copy of such pleading shall be delivered or mailed to each attorney in charge.

The party or attorney of record, shall certify to the court compliance with this rule in writing over signature on the filed pleading, plea, motion or application.

After one copy is served on a party that party may obtain another copy of the same pleading upon tendering reasonable payment for copying and delivering.

History of TRCP 21: Amended eff. Sept. 1, 1990, by order of Apr. 24, 1990 (785-86 S.W.2d [Tex.Cases] xxxix): Rule entirely rewritten to require filing and service of all pleadings and motions on all parties and to consolidate notice and service TRCP 21, 72, and 73. Amended eff. Jan. 1, 1981, by order of June 10, 1980 (599-600 S.W.2d [Tex.Cases] xxxv): Rule broadened to encompass matters other than motions and to require three-day notice unless period is shortened. Amended eff. Jan. 1, 1978, by order of July 11, 1977 (553-54 S.W.2d [Tex.Cases] xlii): Deleted phrase "if it relates to a pending suit" from end of first sentence and phrase "If the motion does not relate to a pending suit" from beginning of second sentence. Amended eff. Dec. 31, 1947, by order of Aug. 18, 1947 (10 Tex.B.J. 390 [1947]). Amended eff. Dec. 31, 1941, by order of Sept. 20, 1941 (4 Tex.B.J. 491 [1941]). Adopted eff. Sept. 1, 1941, by order of Oct. 29, 1940 (3 Tex.B.J. 527 [1940]). Source: TRCS art. 2291 (repealed).

See *Commentaries*, "Rules of Pleading," ch. 1-B, p. 6; "Rules for Filing Documents," ch. 1-C, p. 21; "Rules for Serving Documents," ch. 1-D, p. 34; "Pretrial Motions," ch. 5, p. 311.

ANNOTATIONS

Jamar v. Patterson, 868 S.W.2d 318, 319 (Tex. 1993). "[T]he date of filing is when the document is first tendered to the clerk [even if no filing fee is paid]. The filing [of the motion for new trial] was completed ... when [D] paid the filing fee. *At 319 n.3:* The filing is not completed until the fee is paid, and absent emergency or other rare circumstances, the court should not

---

⭐

---

consider it before then." *See also* **Tate v. E.I. DuPont de Nemours & Co.**, 934 S.W.2d 83, 84 (Tex.1996).

Perkins v. City of San Antonio, 293 S.W.3d 650, 654-55 (Tex.App.—San Antonio 2009, no pet.). TRCP 21 "is inapplicable to a trial setting. [When] the trial court's hearing [is] dispositive of the merits of [the] underlying case, the hearing [is] effectively a trial setting [and should be governed by TRCP 245]."

Approximately $1,589.00 v. State, 230 S.W.3d 871, 873-74 (Tex.App.—Houston [14th Dist.] 2007, no pet.). "Rule 21 does not expressly require that a motion and notice of hearing be *filed* at least three days before hearing. However, Rule 21 expressly requires that a motion and notice of hearing be *served* on opposing parties at the time of filing. Therefore, Rule 21 effectively requires that a motion and notice of hearing be *filed* at least three days before hearing, unless otherwise provided by the [TRCPs] or shortened by the court."

TRCP 21a. METHODS OF SERVICE

Every notice required by these rules, and every pleading, plea, motion, or other form of request required to be served under Rule 21, other than the citation to be served upon the filing of a cause of action and except as otherwise expressly provided in these rules, may be served by delivering a copy to the party to be served, or the party's duly authorized agent or attorney of record, as the case may be, either in person or by agent or by courier receipted delivery or by certified or registered mail, to the party's last known address, or by telephonic document transfer to the recipient's current telecopier number, or by such other manner as the court in its discretion may direct. Service by mail shall be complete upon deposit of the paper, enclosed in a postpaid, properly addressed wrapper, in a post office or official depository under the care and custody of the United States Postal Service. Service by telephonic document transfer after 5:00 p.m. local time of the recipient shall be deemed served on the following day. Whenever a party has the right or is required to do some act within a prescribed period after the service of a notice or other paper upon him and the notice or paper is served upon by mail or by telephonic document transfer, three days shall be added to the prescribed period. Notice may be served by a party to the suit, an attorney of record, a sheriff or constable, or by any other person competent to testify. The party or attorney of record shall certify to the court compliance with this rule in writing over signature and on the filed instrument. A certificate by a party or an attorney of record, or the return of an officer, or the affidavit of any person showing service of a notice shall be prima facie evidence of the fact of service. Nothing herein shall preclude any party from offering proof that the notice or instrument was not received, or, if service was by mail, that it was not received within three days from the date of deposit in a post office or official depository under the care and custody of the United States Postal Service, and, upon so finding, the court may extend the time for taking the action required of such party or grant such other relief as it deems just. The provisions hereof relating to the method of service of notice are cumulative of all other methods of service prescribed by these rules.

History of TRCP 21a: Amended eff. Sept. 1, 1990, by order of Apr. 24, 1990 (785-86 S.W.2d [Tex.Cases] xl): To allow for service by current delivery means and technologies; title changed; expanded to include not just notice but "every pleading, plea, motion, or other form of request required to be served under Rule 21"; and allows service by telephonic document transfer. Amended eff. Apr. 1, 1984, by order of Dec. 5, 1983 (661-62 S.W.2d [Tex.Cases] xxxvii): This rule consolidates TRCP 21a and TRCP 21b. Amended eff. Jan. 1, 1981, by order of June 10, 1980 (599-600 S.W.2d [Tex.Cases] xxxvi): Next-to-last sentence from end of former rule requiring three-day notice is deleted because TRCP 21 was concurrently amended to require that notice. Amended eff. Jan. 1, 1978, by order of July 11, 1977 (553-54 S.W.2d [Tex.Cases] xlii): Deleted phrase "not relating to a pending suit" in next-to-last sentence. Amended eff. Feb. 1, 1973, by order of Oct. 3, 1972 (483-84 S.W.2d [Tex.Cases] xxiii): Substituted words "Postal Service" for "Post Office Department"; inserted sentence authorizing court to grant extension of time or other relief upon finding that notice or document was not received or, if service was by mail, was not received within three days from date of deposit in the mail. Amended eff. Jan. 1, 1971, by order of July 21, 1970 (455-56 S.W.2d [Tex.Cases] xxv): Second and third sentences added to make service by mail complete upon proper deposit in the mail and to enlarge time for acting after service by mail; eliminated sentence which provided for notice of a motion by filing and entry on the motion docket. Adopted eff. Dec. 31, 1947, by order of Aug. 18, 1947 (10 Tex.B.J. 390 [1947]). Source: New rule.

See *Commentaries*, "Rules of Pleading," ch. 1-B, p. 6; "Rules for Filing Documents," ch. 1-C, p. 21; "Rules for Serving Documents," ch. 1-D, p. 34; *O'Connor's Texas Forms*, FORMS 1B:11, 12.

In re E.A., 287 S.W.3d 1, 4 (Tex.2009). "Nothing in the rules requires a plaintiff to serve a nonanswering defendant with new citation for a more onerous amended petition. While a nonanswering defendant must be served with a more onerous amended petition in order for a default judgment to stand, ... Rule 21a service satisfies that requirement. *At 6*: Service of new citation is no longer required."

Mathis v. Lockwood, 166 S.W.3d 743, 745 (Tex. 2005). "[N]otice properly sent pursuant to Rule 21a raises a presumption that notice was received. But we cannot presume that notice was properly sent; when that is challenged, it must be proved according to the rule. [¶] [T]he record contains no certificate of service, no return receipt from certified or registered mail, and no affidavit certifying service. Instead, the only evidence of service in the record was the oral assurance of counsel. As the rule's requirements are neither vague nor onerous, we decline to expand them this far." *See also* **Thomas v. Ray**, 889 S.W.2d 237, 238-39 (Tex. 1994); **Dixon v. Sanders**, No. 01-10-00814-CV (Tex. App.—Houston [1st Dist.] 2011, no pet.) (memo op.; 5-19-11).

Wembley Inv. v. Herrera, 11 S.W.3d 924, 928 (Tex. 1999). "[W]hen the sender of a document relies on office routine or custom to support an inference that the document was mailed, the sender must provide corroborating evidence that the practice was actually carried out. ... At best, [witness's] affidavit is only an 'opinion[]' that the notice w[as] *probably* sent,' and does not controvert [D's] attorneys' affidavits attesting that the nonsuit motion was not received."

Lewis v. Blake, 876 S.W.2d 314, 315 (Tex.1994). TRCP 21a "extends that minimum notice by three days when the motion is served by mail. *At 316:* [The] hearing on a motion for summary judgment may be set as early as the 21st day after the motion is served, or the 24th day if the motion is served by mail."

Polinard v. Medina, No. 13-11-00403-CV (Tex. App.—Corpus Christi 2012, n.p.h.) (memo op.; 7-19-12). See annotation under TRCP 165a, p. 925.

Brown v. Ogbolu, 331 S.W.3d 530, 534 (Tex.App.—Dallas 2011, no pet.). "[P] argues the record shows the counterclaim was not served on him because [D] did not complete the blank for the day on the certificate of service. We disagree. [¶] [D] served the counterclaim under rule 21a and included a certificate of service. While it is normal—and better practice—to include the date and manner of service in the certificate of service, the text of the rule does not require either. We conclude the certificate of service on [D's] counterclaim sufficiently complied with the certification requirement to raise the presumption of service." *See also* **Approximately $14,980.00 v. State**, 261 S.W.3d 182, 187 (Tex. App.—Houston [14th Dist.] 2008, no pet.).

Goforth v. Bradshaw, 296 S.W.3d 849, 853 (Tex. App.—Texarkana 2009, no pet.). "[T]he pivotal issue is whether [Ps'] actual and direct delivery of the documents to [Ds] by regular mail, and [Ds'] acknowledged receipt of those documents before the statutory deadline, accomplished ... 'service' under Rule 21a. *At 854:* Though a certificate of service is required by Rule 21a

and is recognized as presumptively establishing service, here we have acknowledged, actual delivery. We believe that is the key...." *See also* **Spiegel v. Strother**, 262 S.W.3d 481, 482-84 (Tex.App.—Beaumont 2008, no pet.) (delivery by priority mail meets Rule 21a requirements).

Amaya v. Enriquez, 296 S.W.3d 781, 784-85 (Tex. App.—El Paso 2009, pet. denied). "The critical issue is whether [D] is entitled to have the 21-day period [provided by CPRC §74.351(a)] extended by three days because [P] served him by *both* fax and personal delivery. ... The [TRCPs] do not address whether the additional three-day period applies when a party is served on the same day by two methods of service[,] only one of which allows for the addition of three days to the time to respond. ... The apparent purpose of Rule 21a's provision adding three days to a time period when a party is served by fax or mail is to ensure that the party has roughly the same time to respond as if the party had been served by personal delivery. But when a party is served by both fax and hand-delivery on the same day, there is no logical reason to give the party an additional three days."

Etheredge v. Hidden Valley Airpark Ass'n, 169 S.W.3d 378, 382 (Tex.App.—Fort Worth 2005, pet. denied). "[W]hen a party does not receive actual notice, if the serving party has complied with the requirements of Rule 21a, 'constructive notice' may be established if the serving party presents evidence that the intended recipient engaged in instances of selective acceptance or refusal of certified mail relating to the case, ... or that the intended recipient refused all deliveries of certified mail."

TRCP 21b. SANCTIONS FOR FAILURE TO SERVE OR DELIVER COPY OF PLEADINGS & MOTIONS

If any party fails to serve on or deliver to the other parties a copy of any pleading, plea, motion, or other application to the court for an order in accordance with Rules 21 and 21a, the court may in its discretion, after notice and hearing, impose an appropriate sanction available under Rule 215-2b.[1]

1. **Editor's note:** Now TRCP 215.2(b).

History of TRCP 21b: Adopted eff. Sept. 1, 1990, by order of Apr. 24, 1990 (785-86 S.W.2d [Tex.Cases] xl): Repealed provisions of TRCP 73, to the extent same are to remain operative, were moved to new TRCP 21b to provide sanctions for failure to serve any filed documents on all parties. Former TRCP 21b repealed eff. Apr. 1, 1984, by order of Dec. 5, 1983 (661-62 S.W.2d [Tex.Cases] xxxvii). Source: New rule.

✦

See *Commentaries*, "Rules of Pleading," ch. 1-B, p. 6; "Rules for Filing Documents," ch. 1-C, p. 21; "Rules for Serving Documents," ch. 1-D, p. 34; "Motion for Sanctions," ch. 5-K, p. 377; *O'Connor's Texas Forms*, FORMS 5J:3-5.

Union City Body Co. v. Ramirez, 911 S.W.2d 196, 201 (Tex.App.—San Antonio 1995, orig. proceeding). "[A] complaint of inadequate notice under [TRCPs] 21 or 21a is waived absent a timely and specific objection."

TRCP 21c. REPEALED

Repealed eff. Sept. 1, 1986, by order of Apr. 10, 1986 (705-06 S.W.2d [Tex.Cases] xxxiv).

SECTION 2. INSTITUTION OF SUIT

TRCP 22. COMMENCED BY PETITION

A civil suit in the district or county court shall be commenced by a petition filed in the office of the clerk.

History of TRCP 22: Adopted eff. Sept. 1, 1941, by order of Oct. 29, 1940 (3 Tex.B.J. 527 [1940]). Source: TRCS art. 1971 (repealed).

See *Commentaries*, "Rules for Filing Documents," ch. 1-C, p. 21; "Plaintiff's Original Petition," ch. 2-B, p. 95; "Serving the Defendant with Suit," ch. 2-H, p. 157; *O'Connor's Texas Forms*, FORMS 2B.

TRCP 23. SUITS TO BE NUMBERED CONSECUTIVELY

It shall be the duty of the clerk to designate the suits by regular consecutive numbers, called file numbers, and he shall mark on each paper in every case the file number of the cause.

History of TRCP 23: Adopted eff. Sept. 1, 1941, by order of Oct. 29, 1940 (3 Tex.B.J. 527 [1940]). Source: Tex. Rules for Dist. & Cty. Cts. 82.

See *Commentaries*, "Rules for Filing Documents," ch. 1-C, p. 21.

TRCP 24. DUTY OF CLERK

When a petition is filed with the clerk he shall indorse thereon the file number, the day on which it was filed and the time of filing, and sign his name officially thereto.

History of TRCP 24: Adopted eff. Sept. 1, 1941, by order of Oct. 29, 1940 (3 Tex.B.J. 527 [1940]). Source: TRCS art. 1972 (repealed).

See TRCP 74; *Commentaries*, "Rules for Filing Documents," ch. 1-C, p. 21.

Biffle v. Morton Rubber Indus., 785 S.W.2d 143, 144 (Tex.1990). "An instrument is deemed in law filed at the time it is delivered to the clerk, regardless of whether the instrument is filemarked."

TRCP 25. CLERK'S FILE DOCKET

Each clerk shall keep a file docket which shall show in convenient form the number of the suit, the names of the attorneys, the names of the parties to the suit, and the nature thereof, and, in brief form, the officer's return on the process, and all subsequent proceedings had in the case with the dates thereof.

History of TRCP 25: Adopted eff. Sept. 1, 1941, by order of Oct. 29, 1940 (3 Tex.B.J. 527 [1940]). Source: TRCS art. 1973 (repealed).

See *Commentaries*, "Rules for Filing Documents," ch. 1-C, p. 21.

TRCP 26. CLERK'S COURT DOCKET

Each clerk shall also keep a court docket in a permanent record that shall include the number of the case and the names of parties, the names of the attorneys, the nature of the action, the pleas, the motions, and the ruling of the court as made.

History of TRCP 26: Amended eff. Sept. 1, 1990, by order of Apr. 24, 1990 (785-86 S.W.2d [Tex.Cases] xli): Changed "well-bound book" to "permanent record." Adopted eff. Sept. 1, 1941, by order of Oct. 29, 1940 (3 Tex.B.J. 528 [1940]). Source: Tex. Rules for Dist. & Cty. Cts. 79.

See *Commentaries*, "Rules for Filing Documents," ch. 1-C, p. 21.

TRCP 27. ORDER OF CASES

The cases shall be placed on the docket as they are filed.

History of TRCP 27: Adopted eff. Sept. 1, 1941, by order of Oct. 29, 1940 (3 Tex.B.J. 528 [1940]). Source: Tex. Rules for Dist. & Cty. Cts. 80.

See *Commentaries*, "Rules for Filing Documents," ch. 1-C, p. 21.

SECTION 3. PARTIES TO SUITS

TRCP 28. SUITS IN ASSUMED NAME

Any partnership, unincorporated association, private corporation, or individual doing business under an assumed name may sue or be sued in its partnership, assumed or common name for the purpose of enforcing for or against it a substantive right, but on a motion by any party or on the court's own motion the true name may be substituted.[1]

1. **Editor's note:** Unincorporated nonprofit associations are legal entities liable for their contracts and torts, and their members are relieved from individual liability. Bus. Orgs. Code §252.006(a), (b).

History of TRCP 28: Amended eff. Jan. 1, 1971, by order of July 21, 1970 (455-56 S.W.2d [Tex.Cases] xxv): Added "an individual doing business under an assumed name," and partnership or common name to make the rule applicable to a private corporation and authorize the true name of the party to be substituted on motion. Adopted eff. Sept. 1, 1941, by order of Oct. 29, 1940 (3 Tex.B.J. 528 [1940]). Source: Part of FRCP 17(b).

See *Commentaries*, "Parties," ch. 2-B, §3, p. 96; *O'Connor's Texas Forms*, FORMS 2B:9-18.

Sixth RMA Partners v. Sibley, 111 S.W.3d 46, 53 (Tex.2003). "Rule 28 requires that the correct legal name be substituted, but it does not mandate the procedural method by which substitution may be accomplished. … Under Rule 28, the 'true name' may be substituted 'on a motion by any party or on the court's own motion.' Therefore, the correct legal name may be substituted by filing either a motion requesting substitution or a pleading that substitutes the correct legal name for the assumed name." *See also CA Partners v. Spears*, 274 S.W.3d 51, 69 (Tex.App.—Houston [14th

---

⭐

Dist.] 2008, pet. denied); *Holberg & Co. v. Citizens Nat'l Assur. Co.*, 856 S.W.2d 515, 518 (Tex.App.—Houston [1st Dist.] 1993, no writ).

Chilkewitz v. Hyson, 22 S.W.3d 825, 830 (Tex. 1999). "Rule 28 is not a tolling provision when a party is sued in the name under which it conducts business and that party has actual notice of the suit. Rule 28 allows suit directly against the correct party in its assumed name. To the extent that [earlier opinions] indicate that Rule 28 is a tolling provision, we disapprove of them." *See also University of Tex. Health Sci. Ctr. v. Bailey*, 332 S.W.3d 395, 399-400 (Tex.2011); *Ibrahim v. Young*, 253 S.W.3d 790, 799-800 (Tex.App.—Eastland 2008, pet. denied).

KM-Timbercreek, LLC v. Harris Cty. Appr. Dist., 312 S.W.3d 722, 730 (Tex.App.—Houston [1st Dist.] 2009, no pet.). "For a party to take advantage of Rule 28 and sue in its common name, 'there must be a showing that the named entity is in fact *doing business under* that common name.' For example, although others may commonly and informally use the name of the premises location to refer to a particular entity, this does not mean that the entity is 'doing business under' the premises name as an assumed or common name. Whether an entity does business under an assumed or common name is a question of fact for the trial court." *See also Seidler v. Morgan*, 277 S.W.3d 549, 553 (Tex. App.—Texarkana 2009, pet. denied).

TRCP 29. SUIT ON CLAIM AGAINST DISSOLVED CORPORATION

When no receiver has been appointed for a corporation which has dissolved, suit may be instituted on any claim against said corporation as though the same had not been dissolved, and service of process may be obtained on the president, directors, general manager, trustee, assignee, or other person in charge of the affairs of the corporation at the time it was dissolved, and judgment may be rendered as though the corporation had not been dissolved.

History of TRCP 29: Adopted eff. Sept. 1, 1941, by order of Oct. 29, 1940 (3 Tex.B.J. 528 [1940]). Source: TRCS art. 1391 (repealed).

See Bus. Orgs. Code §11.356; TRCP 160.

TRCP 30. PARTIES TO SUITS

Assignors, endorsers and other parties not primarily liable upon any instruments named in the chapter of the Business and Commerce Code, dealing with commercial paper, may be jointly sued with their principal obligors, or may be sued alone in the cases provided for by statute.

History of TRCP 30: Amended eff. Jan. 1, 1988, by order of July 15, 1987 (733-34 S.W.2d [Tex.Cases] xl). Adopted eff. Sept. 1, 1941, by order of Oct. 29, 1940 (3 Tex.B.J. 528 [1940]). Source: TRCS art. 572 (repealed).

See *Commentaries*, "Parties," ch. 2-B, §3, p. 96; *O'Connor's Texas Forms*, FORMS 2B:10-18.

ANNOTATIONS

Reed v. Buck, 370 S.W.2d 867, 872 (Tex.1963). "We hold that when a party signs a note in the capacity of a maker, the payee (or one standing in the shoes of a payee) may sue such maker singly and proceed to judgment upon the note without joining in the suit another or others who may also appear upon the note as co-makers."

TRCP 31. SURETY NOT TO BE SUED ALONE

No surety shall be sued unless his principal is joined with him, or unless a judgment has previously been rendered against his principal, except in cases otherwise provided for in the law and these rules.

History of TRCP 31: Adopted eff. Sept. 1, 1941, by order of Oct. 29, 1940 (3 Tex.B.J. 528 [1940]). Source: TRCS art. 6251 (repealed).

See CPRC §17.001; *Commentaries*, "Secondary parties," ch. 2-E, §6.2.1(2), p. 133.

ANNOTATIONS

McGrath v. Bank of the W., 786 S.W.2d 754, 757 (Tex.App.—Houston [1st Dist.] 1990, no writ). Surety "acquired and perfected a valid and enforceable security interest in the certificate of deposit as security for [principal] debt. As such, [surety] was not required, under [TRCP] 31, to join [principal] and attempt collection prior to exercising its rights in the collateral."

Hart v. First Fed. S&L Ass'n, 727 S.W.2d 723, 726 (Tex.App.—Austin 1987, no writ). "[T]he necessity of joining the principal debtor in the creditor's suit against the guarantor is subject to an exception for cases where the debtor is 'hopelessly insolvent.' *At 726 n.1:* [TRCP] 31 incorporates, in effect, the provisions of [CPRC] §17.001."

TRCP 32. MAY HAVE QUESTION OF SURETYSHIP TRIED

When any suit is brought against two or more defendants upon any contract, any one or more of the defendants being surety for the other, the surety may cause the question of suretyship to be tried and determined upon the issue made for the parties defendant at the trial of the cause, or at any time before or after the trial or at a subsequent term. Such proceedings shall not delay the suit of the plaintiff.

History of TRCP 32: Adopted eff. Sept. 1, 1941, by order of Oct. 29, 1940 (3 Tex.B.J. 528 [1940]). Source: TRCS art. 6246 (repealed).

TRCP 28

───────────────── ✦ ─────────────────

TRCP 33. SUITS BY OR AGAINST COUNTIES

Suits by or against a county or incorporated city, town or village shall be in its corporate name.

History of TRCP 33: Adopted eff. Sept. 1, 1941, by order of Oct. 29, 1940 (3 Tex.B.J. 528 [1940]). Source: TRCS art. 1980 (repealed).

See *Commentaries*, "Parties," ch. 2-B, §3, p. 96; *O'Connor's Texas Forms*, FORM 2B:19.

ANNOTATIONS

Scott v. Graham, 292 S.W.2d 324, 327 (Tex.1956). "A county is not made a party to a suit by joining the commissioners and other officials of the county as parties."

TRCP 34. AGAINST SHERIFF, ETC.

Whenever a sheriff, constable, or a deputy or either has been sued for damages for any act done in his official character, and has taken an indemnifying bond for the acts upon which the suit is based, he may make the principal and surety on such bond parties defendant in such suit, and the cause may be continued to obtain service on such parties.

History of TRCP 34: Adopted eff. Sept. 1, 1941, by order of Oct. 29, 1940 (3 Tex.B.J. 528 [1940]). Source: TRCS art. 1988 (repealed).

TRCP 35. ON OFFICIAL BONDS

In suits brought by the State or any county, city, independent school district, irrigation district, or other political subdivision of the State, against any officer who has held an office for more than one term, or against any depository which has been such depository for more than one term, or has given more than one official bond, the sureties on each and all such bonds may be joined as defendants in the same suit whenever it is difficult to determine when the default sued for occurred and which set of sureties on such bonds is liable therefor.

History of TRCP 35: Amended eff. Dec. 31, 1943, by order of June 16, 1943 (6 Tex.B.J. 331 [1943]): Interpolated phrase "irrigation district, or other political subdivision of the State"; omitted second "or"; added comma after "city." Adopted eff. Sept. 1, 1941, by order of Oct. 29, 1940 (3 Tex.B.J. 528 [1940]). Source: TRCS art. 1989 (repealed).

TRCP 36. DIFFERENT OFFICIALS & BONDSMEN

In suits by the State upon the official bond of a State officer, any subordinate officer who has given bond, payable either to the State or such superior officer, to cover all or part of the default sued for, together with the sureties on his official bond, may be joined as defendants with such superior officer and his bondsmen whenever it is alleged in the petition that both of such officers are liable for the money sued for.

History of TRCP 36: Adopted eff. Sept. 1, 1941, by order of Oct. 29, 1940 (3 Tex.B.J. 529 [1940]). Source: TRCS art. 1990 (repealed).

TRCP 37. ADDITIONAL PARTIES

Before a case is called for trial, additional parties, necessary or proper parties to the suit, may be brought in, either by the plaintiff or the defendant, upon such terms as the court may prescribe; but not at a time nor in a manner to unreasonably delay the trial of the case.

History of TRCP 37: Adopted eff. Sept. 1, 1941, by order of Oct. 29, 1940 (3 Tex.B.J. 529 [1940]). Source: TRCS art. 1992 (repealed).

See *Commentaries*, "Parties & Claims," ch. 2-E, p. 129.

ANNOTATIONS

Gomez v. Kestermeier, 924 S.W.2d 210, 212 (Tex. App.—Eastland 1996, writ denied). Ds urge "that the trial court erred by rendering judgment without the joinder of … grantors. … Even though they did raise the issue at trial, [Ds] did not preserve the issue for review because … they made no effort themselves to join [grantors] as parties."

TRCP 38. THIRD-PARTY PRACTICE

(a) **When defendant may bring in third party.** At any time after commencement of the action a defending party, as a third-party plaintiff, may cause a citation and petition to be served upon a person not a party to the action who is or may be liable to him or to the plaintiff for all or part of the plaintiff's claim against him. The third-party plaintiff need not obtain leave to make the service if he files the third-party petition not later than thirty (30) days after he serves his original answer. Otherwise, he must obtain leave on motion upon notice to all parties to the action. The person served, hereinafter called the third-party defendant, shall make his defenses to the third-party plaintiff's claim under the rules applicable to the defendant, and his counterclaims against the third-party plaintiff and cross-claims against other third-party defendants as provided in Rule 97. The third-party defendant may assert against the plaintiff any defenses which the third-party plaintiff has to the plaintiff's claim. The third-party defendant may also assert any claim against the plaintiff arising out of the transaction or occurrence that is the subject matter of the plaintiff's claim against the third-party plaintiff. The plaintiff may assert any claim against the third-party defendant arising out of the transaction or occurrence that is the subject matter of the plaintiff's claim against the third-party plaintiff, and the third-party defendant thereupon shall assert his defenses and his counterclaims and cross-claims.

TRCP 38

Any party may move to strike the third-party claim, or for its severance or separate trial. A third-party defendant may proceed under this rule against any person not a party to the action who is or who may be liable to him or to the third-party plaintiff for all or part of the claim made in the action against the third-party defendant.

(b) When plaintiff may bring in third party. When a counterclaim is asserted against a plaintiff, he may cause a third party to be brought in under circumstances which under this rule would entitle a defendant to do so.

(c) This rule shall not be applied, in tort cases, so as to permit the joinder of a liability or indemnity insurance company, unless such company is by statute or contract liable to the person injured or damaged.

(d) This rule shall not be applied so as to violate any venue statute, as venue would exist absent this rule.

History of TRCP 38: Amended eff. Apr. 1, 1984, by order of Dec. 5, 1983 (661-62 S.W.2d [Tex.Cases] xxxvii): Removed need to secure leave of court to begin third-party action; made textual changes to clarify terminology. Amended eff. Sept. 1, 1941, by order of Mar. 31, 1941 (4 Tex.B.J. 169 [1941]): Added pars. (c) and (d). Adopted eff. Sept. 1, 1941, by order of Oct. 29, 1940 (3 Tex.B.J. 529 [1940]). Source: FRCP 14.

See CPRC §33.004 (responsible third parties); *Commentaries*, "Parties & Claims," ch. 2-E, p. 129; "The Answer—Denying Liability," ch. 3-E, p. 227.

ANNOTATIONS

Goose Creek Consol. ISD v. Jarrar's Plumbing, Inc., 74 S.W.3d 486, 492 (Tex.App.—Texarkana 2002, pet. denied). "A third-party action is not an independent cause of action, but is derivative of the plaintiff's claim against the responsible third party. As such, an action for indemnification or contribution does not accrue for limitations purposes until a plaintiff recovers damages or settles its suit against a defendant."

TRCP 39. JOINDER OF PERSONS NEEDED FOR JUST ADJUDICATION

(a) Persons to be Joined if Feasible. A person who is subject to service of process shall be joined as a party in the action if (1) in his absence complete relief cannot be accorded among those already parties, or (2) he claims an interest relating to the subject of the action and is so situated that the disposition of the action in his absence may (i) as a practical matter impair or impede his ability to protect that interest or (ii) leave any of the persons already parties subject to a substantial risk of incurring double, multiple, or otherwise inconsistent obligations by reason of his claimed interest. If he has not been so joined, the court shall order that he

be made a party. If he should join as a plaintiff but refuses to do so, he may be made a defendant, or, in a proper case, an involuntary plaintiff.

(b) Determination by Court Whenever Joinder Not Feasible. If a person as described in subdivision (a)(1)-(2) hereof cannot be made a party, the court shall determine whether in equity and good conscience the action should proceed among the parties before it, or should be dismissed, the absent person being thus regarded as indispensable. The factors to be considered by the court include: first, to what extent a judgment rendered in the person's absence might be prejudicial to him or those already parties; second, the extent to which, by protective provisions in the judgment, by the shaping of relief, or other measures, the prejudice can be lessened or avoided; third, whether a judgment rendered in the person's absence will be adequate; fourth, whether the plaintiff will have an adequate remedy if the action is dismissed for non-joinder.

(c) Pleading Reasons for Nonjoinder. A pleading asserting a claim for relief shall state the names, if known to the pleader, of any persons as described in subdivision (a)(1)-(2) hereof who are not joined, and the reasons why they are not joined.

(d) Exception of Class Actions. This rule is subject to the provisions of Rule 42.

History of TRCP 39: Amended eff. Jan. 1, 1971, by order of July 21, 1970 (455-56 S.W.2d [Tex.Cases] xxxv): Rule completely rewritten to adopt, with minor changes, provisions of FRCP 19 as amended. Adopted eff. Sept. 1, 1941, by order of Oct. 29, 1940 (3 Tex.B.J. 529 [1940]). Source: FRCP 19.

See TRCP 40, 41, 51, 174; *Commentaries*, "Plaintiff's Original Petition," ch. 2-B, p. 95; "Parties & Claims," ch. 2-E, p. 129; "The Answer—Denying Liability," ch. 3-E, p. 227; "Motion to Abate—Challenging the Suit," ch. 3-I, p. 257; "Motions for Severance & Separate Trials," ch. 5-I, p. 364.

ANNOTATIONS

Brooks v. Northglen Ass'n, 141 S.W.3d 158, 162 (Tex.2004). "Rule 39 determines whether a trial court has authority to proceed without joining a person whose presence in the litigation is made mandatory by the Declaratory Judgment Act. [¶] [N]othing in the rule precluded the trial court from rendering complete relief among [parties] who had sued for a declaration of rights. Although the parties continue to litigate its correctness, the trial court's judgment represents a final and complete adjudication of the dispute for the parties who were before the court." *See also* ***Indian Beach Prop. Owners' Ass'n v. Linden***, 222 S.W.3d 682, 697 (Tex.App.—Houston [1st Dist.] 2007, no pet.).

───────────────── ✦ ─────────────────

Cooper v. Texas Gulf Indus., 513 S.W.2d 200, 204 (Tex.1974). "Under the provisions of our present Rule 39 it would be rare indeed if there were a person whose presence was so indispensable in the sense that his absence deprives the court of jurisdiction to adjudicate between the parties already joined." *See also State Office of Risk Mgmt. v. Herrera*, 288 S.W.3d 543, 549 (Tex.App.—Amarillo 2009, no pet.) (City was indispensable).

Longoria v. Exxon Mobil Corp., 255 S.W.3d 174, 180 (Tex.App.—San Antonio 2008, pet. denied). "Although [TRCP 39] provides for joinder in mandatory terms, 'there is no arbitrary standard or precise formula for determining whether a particular person falls within its provision.' If the trial court determines an absent person falls within the provisions of the rule, the court has a duty to effect the person's joinder. If a person required to be joined under Rule 39(a) cannot be joined, the trial court must decide 'whether in equity and in good conscience the action should proceed among the parties before it, or should be dismissed' by considering the factors listed in Rule 39(b). [¶] The joinder provisions of Rule 39 apply to both trespass to try title and declaratory judgment claims."

Gilmer ISD v. Dorfman, 156 S.W.3d 586, 588 (Tex.App.—Tyler 2003, no pet.). "A state official primarily responsible for enforcement of a statute must be joined in any suit affecting the constitutionality of that statute. Failure to add a necessary and indispensable party to the constitutional challenge of a statute leaves the trial court without jurisdiction."

TRCP 40. PERMISSIVE JOINDER OF PARTIES

(a) Permissive Joinder. All persons may join in one action as plaintiffs if they assert any right to relief jointly, severally, or in the alternative in respect of or arising out of the same transaction, occurrence, or series of transactions or occurrences and if any question of law or fact common to all of them will arise in the action. All persons may be joined in one action as defendants if there is asserted against them jointly, severally, or in the alternative any right to relief in respect of or arising out of the same transaction, occurrence, or series of transactions or occurrences and if any question of law or fact common to all of them will arise in the action. A plaintiff or defendant need not be interested in obtaining or defending against all the relief demanded. Judgment may be given for one or more of the plaintiffs

according to their respective rights to relief, and against one or more defendants according to their respective liabilities.

(b) Separate Trials. The court may make such orders as will prevent a party from being embarrassed, delayed, or put to expense by the inclusion of a party against whom he asserts no claim and who asserts no claim against him, and may order separate trials or make other orders to prevent delay or prejudice.

History of TRCP 40: Adopted eff. Sept. 1, 1941, by order of Oct. 29, 1940 (3 Tex.B.J. 530 [1940]). Source: FRCP 20.

See TRCP 39, 41, 51, 174; *Commentaries*, "Plaintiff's Original Petition," ch. 2-B, p. 95; "Parties & Claims," ch. 2-E, p. 129; "The Answer—Denying Liability," ch. 3-E, p. 227; "Motion to Abate—Challenging the Suit," ch. 3-I, p. 257; "Motions for Severance & Separate Trials," ch. 5-I, p. 364.

ANNOTATIONS

Landers v. East Tex. Salt Water Disposal Co., 248 S.W.2d 731, 734 (Tex.1952). "Where the tortious acts of two or more wrongdoers join to produce an indivisible injury, … all of the wrongdoers will be held jointly and severally liable for the entire damages and the injured party may proceed to judgment against any one separately or against all in one suit. If fewer than the whole number of wrongdoers are joined as defendants …, those joined may by proper cross action … bring in those omitted."

TRCP 41. MISJOINDER & NON-JOINDER OF PARTIES

Misjoinder of parties is not ground for dismissal of an action. Parties may be dropped or added, or suits filed separately may be consolidated, or actions which have been improperly joined may be severed and each ground of recovery improperly joined may be docketed as a separate suit between the same parties, by order of the court on motion of any party or on its own initiative at any stage of the action, before the time of submission to the jury or to the court if trial is without a jury, on such terms as are just. Any claim against a party may be severed and proceeded with separately.

History of TRCP 41: Amended eff. Sept. 1, 1941, by order of Mar. 31, 1941 (4 Tex.B.J. 169 [1941]): Eliminated the procedure "after judgment." Adopted eff. Sept. 1, 1941, by order of Oct. 29, 1940 (3 Tex.B.J. 530 [1940]): Added provision for adding and dropping parties, for consolidating suits, and for severing actions in case of misjoinder of parties or causes. Source: FRCP 21.

See TRCP 39, 40, 51, 174; *Commentaries*, "Parties & Claims," ch. 2-E, p. 129; "The Answer—Denying Liability," ch. 3-E, p. 227.

ANNOTATIONS

F.F.P. Oper. Partners v. Duenez, 237 S.W.3d 680, 693 (Tex.2007). "'A claim is properly severable if (1) the controversy involves more than one cause of ac-

---⋆---

tion, (2) the severed claim is one that would be the proper subject of a lawsuit if independently asserted, and (3) the severed claim is not so interwoven with the remaining action that they involve the same facts and issues.' [A]voiding prejudice, doing justice, and increasing convenience are the controlling reasons to allow a severance." *See also Guaranty Fed. Sav. Bank v. Horseshoe Oper. Co.*, 793 S.W.2d 652, 658 (Tex.1990).

Liberty Nat'l Fire Ins. v. Akin, 927 S.W.2d 627, 630 (Tex.1996). "A severance may ... be necessary in some bad faith [and contract] cases. A trial court will ... confront instances in which evidence admissible only on the bad faith claim would prejudice the insurer to such an extent that a fair trial on the contract claim would become unlikely. One example would be when the insurer has made a settlement offer on the disputed contract claim."

State Dept. of Hwys. & Pub. Transp. v. Cotner, 845 S.W.2d 818, 819 (Tex.1993). TRCP 41 "does not 'permit a trial court to sever a case after it has been submitted to the trier of fact.' [¶] A partial new trial may be ordered notwithstanding the prohibition in Rule 41 against post-submission severances. [TRCP] 320 is thus an exception to Rule 41."

Nichols v. Nichols, 331 S.W.3d 800, 804 (Tex. App.—Fort Worth 2010, no pet.). "In contrast to [TRCP] 329b, [TRCP] 41 [does not require] that a severance be determined 'by *written* order.' Furthermore, unlike Rule 329b, which requires a motion for new trial to be granted in writing before the relevant time period expires, nothing in Rule 41 requires a severance order to be in writing and signed before the remaining case is submitted to the trier of fact. [¶] [S]ubmission of the remaining cause to the trier of fact does not prevent a severance because a properly severable cause of action, if not tried, may still be tried separately. There is no justification for treating a properly severable cause of action differently. [T]he controlling reason for severance is to do justice, avoid prejudice, and promote convenience, not to prevent the trial of potentially viable claims."

TRCP 42. CLASS ACTIONS

(a) Prerequisites to a Class Action. One or more members of a class may sue or be sued as representative parties on behalf of all only if (1) the class is so numerous that joinder of all members is impracticable, (2) there are questions of law or fact common to the class, (3) the claims or defenses of the representa-

tive parties are typical of the claims or defenses of the class, and (4) the representative parties will fairly and adequately protect the interests of the class.

(b) Class Actions Maintainable. An action may be maintained as a class action if the prerequisites of subdivision (a) are satisfied, and in addition:

(1) the prosecution of separate actions by or against individual members of the class would create a risk of

(A) inconsistent or varying adjudications with respect to individual members of the class which would establish incompatible standards of conduct for the party opposing the class, or

(B) adjudications with respect to individual members of the class which would as a practical matter be dispositive of the interests of the other members not parties to the adjudications or substantially impair or impede their ability to protect their interests; or

(2) the party opposing the class has acted or refused to act on grounds generally applicable to the class, thereby making appropriate final injunctive relief or corresponding declaratory relief with respect to the class as a whole; or

(3) the questions of law or fact common to the members of the class predominate over any questions affecting only individual members, and a class action is superior to other available methods for the fair and efficient adjudication of the controversy. The matters pertinent to these issues include:

(A) the interest of members of the class in individually controlling the prosecution or defense of separate actions;

(B) the extent and nature of any litigation concerning the controversy already commenced by or against members of the class;

(C) the desirability or undesirability of concentrating the litigation of the claims in the particular forum; and

(D) the difficulties likely to be encountered in the management of a class action.

(c) Determining by Order Whether to Certify a Class Action; Notice and Membership in Class.

(1)(A) When a person sues or is sued as a representative of a class, the court must—at an early practicable time—determine by order whether to certify the action as a class action.

(B) An order certifying a class action must define the class and the class claims, issues, or defenses, and must appoint class counsel under Rule 42(g).

(C) An order under Rule 42(c)(1) may be altered or amended before final judgment. The court may order the naming of additional parties in order to insure the adequacy of representation.

(D) An order granting or denying certification under Rule 42(b)(3) must state:

(i) the elements of each claim or defense asserted in the pleadings;

(ii) any issues of law or fact common to the class members;

(iii) any issues of law or fact affecting only individual class members;

(iv) the issues that will be the object of most of the efforts of the litigants and the court;

(v) other available methods of adjudication that exist for the controversy;

(vi) why the issues common to the members of the class do or do not predominate over individual issues;

(vii) why a class action is or is not superior to other available methods for the fair and efficient adjudication of the controversy; and

(viii) if a class is certified, how the class claims and any issues affecting only individual members, raised by the claims or defenses asserted in the pleadings, will be tried in a manageable, time efficient manner.

(2)(A) For any class certified under Rule 42(b)(1) or (2), the court may direct appropriate notice to the class.

(B) For any class certified under Rule 42(b)(3), the court must direct to class members the best notice practicable under the circumstances, including individual notice to all members who can be identified through reasonable effort. The notice must concisely and clearly state in plain, easily understood language:

(i) the nature of the action;

(ii) the definition of the class certified;

(iii) the class claims, issues, or defenses;

(iv) that a class member may enter an appearance through counsel if the member so desires;

(v) that the court will exclude from the class any member who requests exclusion, stating when and how members may elect to be excluded; and

(vi) the binding effect of a class judgment on class members under Rule 42(c)(3).

(3) The judgment in an action maintained as a class action under subdivision (b)(1), or (b)(2), whether or not favorable to the class, shall include and describe those whom the court finds to be members of the class. The judgment in an action maintained as a class action under subdivision (b)(3), whether or not favorable to the class, shall include and specify or describe those to whom the notice provided in subdivision (c)(2) was directed, and who have not requested exclusion, and whom the court finds to be members of the class.

(d) Actions Conducted Partially as Class Actions; Multiple Classes and Subclasses. When appropriate (1) an action may be brought or maintained as a class action with respect to particular issues, or (2) a class may be divided into subclasses and each subclass treated as a class, and the provisions of this rule shall then be construed and applied accordingly.

(e) Settlement, Dismissal, or Compromise.

(1)(A) The court must approve any settlement, dismissal, or compromise of the claims, issues, or defenses of a certified class.

(B) Notice of the material terms of the proposed settlement, dismissal or compromise, together with an explanation of when and how the members may elect to be excluded from the class, shall be given to all members in such manner as the court directs.

(C) The court may approve a settlement, dismissal, or compromise that would bind class members only after a hearing and on finding that the settlement, dismissal, or compromise is fair, reasonable, and adequate.

(2) The parties seeking approval of a settlement, dismissal, or compromise under Rule 42(e)(1) must file a statement identifying any agreement made in connection with the proposed settlement, dismissal, or compromise.

(3) In an action previously certified as a class action under Rule 42(b)(3), the court may not approve a settlement unless it affords a new opportunity to request exclusion to individual class members who had an earlier opportunity to request exclusion but did not do so.

(4)(A) Any class member may object to a proposed settlement, dismissal, or compromise that requires court approval under Rule 42(e)(1)(A).

TRCP 42

(B) An objection made under Rule 42(e)(4)(A) may be withdrawn only with the court's approval.

(f) Discovery. Unnamed members of a class action are not to be considered as parties for purposes of discovery.

(g) Class Counsel.

(1) *Appointing Class Counsel.*

(A) Unless a statute provides otherwise, a court that certifies a class must appoint class counsel.

(B) An attorney appointed to serve as class counsel must fairly and adequately represent the interests of the class.

(C) In appointing class counsel, the court

(i) must consider:

• the work counsel has done in identifying or investigating potential claims in the action;

• counsel's experience in handling class actions, other complex litigation, and claims of the type asserted in the action;

• counsel's knowledge of the applicable law; and

• the resources counsel will commit to representing the class;

(ii) may consider any other matter pertinent to counsel's ability to fairly and adequately represent the interests of the class;

(iii) may direct potential class counsel to provide information on any subject pertinent to the appointment and to propose terms for attorney fees and nontaxable costs; and

(iv) may make further orders in connection with the appointment.

(2) *Appointment Procedure.*

(A) The court may designate interim counsel to act on behalf of the putative class before determining whether to certify the action as a class action.

(B) When there is one applicant for appointment as class counsel, the court may appoint that applicant only if the applicant is adequate under Rule 42(g)(1)(B) and (C). If more than one adequate applicant seeks appointment as class counsel, the court must appoint the applicant or applicants best able to represent the interests of the class.

(C) The order appointing class counsel may include provisions about the award of attorney fees or nontaxable costs under Rule 42(h) and (i).

(h) Procedure for Determining Attorney Fees Award. In an action certified as a class action, the court may award attorney fees in accordance with subdivision (i) and nontaxable costs authorized by law or by agreement of the parties as follows:

(1) *Motion for Award of Attorney Fees.* A claim for an award of attorney fees and nontaxable costs must be made by motion, subject to the provisions of this subdivision, at a time set by the court. Notice of the motion must be served on all parties and, for motions by class counsel, directed to class members in a reasonable manner.

(2) *Objections to Motion.* A class member, or a party from whom payment is sought, may object to the motion.

(3) *Hearing and Findings.* The court must hold a hearing in open court and must find the facts and state its conclusions of law on the motion. The court must state its findings and conclusions in writing or orally on the record.

(i) Attorney's Fees Award.

(1) In awarding attorney fees, the court must first determine a lodestar figure by multiplying the number of hours reasonably worked times a reasonable hourly rate. The attorney fees award must be in the range of 25% to 400% of the lodestar figure. In making these determinations, the court must consider the factors specified in Rule 1.04(b), Tex. Disciplinary R. Prof. Conduct.

(2) If any portion of the benefits recovered for the class are in the form of coupons or other noncash common benefits, the attorney fees awarded in the action must be in cash and noncash amounts in the same proportion as the recovery for the class.

(j) Effective Date. Rule 42(i) applies only in actions filed after September 1, 2003.

Comments to 2003 amendments:

1. The second paragraph of subdivision (a) regarding derivative suits has been deleted because it is redundant of art. 5.14 of the Business Corporation Act, which sets forth detailed procedures for derivative suits.

2. Subparagraph (b)(3) is omitted as unnecessary.

3. The requirement that certification be decided "at an early practicable time" is a change from the previous Texas rule 42(c)(1) and federal rule 23(c)(1), which required the trial court to decide the certification issue "as soon as practicable after the commencement of [the suit]." The amended language is not intended to permit undue delay or permit excessive discovery unrelated to certification, but is designed to encourage good practices in making certification decisions only after receiving the information necessary to decide whether certification should be granted or denied and how to define the class if certification is granted.

History of TRCP 42: Amended eff. Jan. 1, 2004, by order of Oct. 9, 2003 (Tex.Sup.Ct. Order, Misc. Docket No. 03-9160). Amended eff. Apr. 1, 1984, by order of Dec. 5, 1983 (661-62 S.W.2d [Tex.Cases] xxxviii): Par. concerning derivative suit added to (a). Amended eff. Sept. 1, 1977, by order of May 9, 1977 (553-54 S.W.2d [Tex.Cases] xxxvi): Rewrote TRCP 42; copied (a) from revised FRCP 23(a), (b)(1) from revised FRCP 23(b)(2), and (b)(2) from revised FRCP 23(b)(2); added (b)(3) from present TRCP 42(a)(3), omitting reference to the

⭐

character of the right as "several"; adopted (b)(4) from revised FRCP 23(b)(3); adopted (c)(1) from revised FRCP (c)(1) with little change except in the choice of words; second sentence in (c)(1) is not found in the FRCP although the idea is implicit in it; copied (d) from revised FRCP 23(c)(4), and (e) from revised FRCP 23(e). Amended eff. Dec. 31, 1941, by order of Sept. 20, 1941 (4 Tex.B.J. 494 [1941]). Adopted eff. Sept. 1, 1941, by order of Oct. 29, 1940 (3 Tex.B.J. 530 [1940]). Source: FRCP 23, with change: In (b) deleted requirement that the action is not collusive.

See CPRC §51.014(a)(3); *O'Connor's Texas Civil Appeals* (2012), "Class certification," ch. 1-B, §2.3.1(2), p. 11.

ANNOTATIONS

Generally

Citizens Ins. v. Daccach, 217 S.W.3d 430, 449 (Tex. 2007). TRCP 42 "is a form of joinder, a procedural mechanism established to increase judicial economy and efficiency for suits with parties too numerous for conventional joinder. *At 450:* Basic principles of res judicata apply to class actions just as they do to any other form of litigation. *At 455:* [W]hile we agree that Rule 42(d) allows a trial court to consider certifying a class whose representative has abandoned or split claims, we decline to take the further step of excepting a final judgment in such a class action from the principles of res judicata. *At 457:* We hold, therefore, that [TRCP] 42 requires the trial court ... to consider the risk that a judgment in the class action may preclude subsequent litigation of claims not alleged, abandoned, or split from the class action. The trial court abuses its discretion if it fails to consider the preclusive effect of a judgment on abandoned claims, as res judicata could undermine the adequacy of representation requirement." *See also* **Bowden v. Phillips Pet. Co.**, 247 S.W.3d 690, 697-98 (Tex.2008).

State Farm Mut. Auto. Ins. v. Lopez, 156 S.W.3d 550, 556 (Tex.2004). "[A] trial plan is required in every certification order to allow reviewing courts to assure that *all* requirements for certification under Rule 42 have been satisfied. The formulation of a trial plan assures that a trial court has fulfilled its obligation to rigorously analyze all certification prerequisites, and understands the claims, defenses, relevant facts, and applicable substantive law in order to make a meaningful determination of the certification issues." (Internal quotes omitted.) *See also* **BMG Direct Mktg., Inc. v. Peake**, 178 S.W.3d 763, 778 (Tex.2005); **North Am. Mortg. Co. v. O'Hara**, 153 S.W.3d 43, 44-45 (Tex.2004).

Intratex Gas Co. v. Beeson, 22 S.W.3d 398, 403-04 (Tex.2000). "For a class to be sufficiently defined, it must be precise: the class members must be presently ascertainable by reference to objective criteria. This means that the class should not be defined by criteria that are subjective or that require an analysis of the merits of the case. [H]owever, ... a class definition will not fail merely because every potential class member cannot be identified at the suit's commencement."

Standing

Heckman v. Williamson Cty., 369 S.W.3d 137, 151 (Tex.2012). "A plaintiff who brings a class action, rather than just suing on his own behalf, must still prove that he individually had standing to sue. The court must consider this threshold question even before reaching the separate issue of whether it can certify the putative class. Just as it must dismiss a case where the plaintiff lacks standing to bring any of his claims, a court must dismiss a class action for want of jurisdiction if the named plaintiff entirely lacked *individual* standing at the time he sued. [¶] We see no reason why a plaintiff who seeks to represent a class, but lacks standing on some of the purported class's claims, completely lacks standing to bring *any* claims. *At 152-53:* Whether considering the standing of one plaintiff or many, the court must analyze the standing of each individual plaintiff to bring each individual claim he or she alleges when that issue is before the court. ... Thus, ... the court must assess standing plaintiff by plaintiff, claim by claim. *At 154:* [W]here plaintiffs seek to represent a class, a plaintiff need not have standing on each and every one of the class's claims in order to satisfy the standing requirement. So long as an individual plaintiff has standing on *some* claim, he has standing to pursue class certification as to that claim."

Southwestern Bell Tel. Co. v. Marketing on Hold Inc., 308 S.W.3d 909, 918-19 (Tex.2010). "[T]he valid assignment of claims to a party is not invalidated by the party's designation as the representative in a class suit. Nothing unique to the class action context or to this case dictates that we take the extraordinary step of invalidating otherwise contractually valid assignments on ... public policy grounds. [¶] [Assignee] is a member of the class that the trial court certified. [¶] If we were to hold, as [D] contends we should, that [assignee's] assignments are void on public policy grounds, we would abrogate [assignee's] individual standing to bring its claims as either a member of the putative class as defined by the trial court or in an individual lawsuit. [Assignee's] individual standing does not change based on whether it asserts that standing as a class member, in support of its bid to serve as the class representative, or as an individual litigant. The standing requirements remain the same because each class member and the class representative is an individual claimant seeking a personal recovery."

DaimlerChrysler Corp. v. Inman, 252 S.W.3d 299, 304-05 (Tex.2008). "For standing, a plaintiff must be personally aggrieved; his alleged injury must be concrete and particularized, actual or imminent, not hypothetical. A plaintiff does not lack standing simply because he cannot prevail on the merits of his claim; he lacks standing because his claim of injury is too slight for a court to afford redress. *At 307:* The dissent argues that standing requires only, one, a real controversy that, two, will be determined. Those are requirements for standing, but so is concrete injury, because if injury is only hypothetical, there is no real controversy. [¶] [W]hen a claim of injury is extremely remote, the jurisdictional inquiry cannot be laid aside in an expectation that the claimant will also lose on the merits. [¶] If the named plaintiffs in a putative class action do not have standing to assert their own individual claims, the entire actions must be dismissed." *See also M.D. Anderson Cancer Ctr. v. Novak*, 52 S.W.3d 704, 711 (Tex. 2001) (if named P lacks individual standing, court should dismiss entire suit for want of jurisdiction).

Mootness Exception

Heckman v. Williamson Cty., 369 S.W.3d 137, 162 (Tex.2012). "In a typical civil action, where a solo plaintiff brings a claim on his own behalf, the mootness analysis is usually straightforward: If the plaintiff's individual interest becomes moot, the entire suit ordinarily becomes moot. In a class action, however, the plaintiff brings a claim not just on his own behalf, but on behalf of an entire class of similarly-injured individuals. There, the named plaintiff's individual interest can become moot without necessarily affecting the class's interest in how the suit turns out. *At 163:* Should a class action lawsuit survive when the individual claim of the named plaintiff becomes moot? [¶] Where, as here, the individual claims of the named plaintiffs become moot before the trial court decides whether to certify the class, the class action may still survive so long as it fits [some] limited exception[]. [¶] One such exception applies to 'inherently transitory' claims. This exception is premised on the idea that some claims, by their nature, are so short-lived that it may be impossible for the trial court to decide on certification before the named plaintiff's individual claims become

moot. At the same time, ... there continues to exist a population of individuals who suffer from the same alleged harms and therefore have the same inherently transitory claims against the same defendant. Such a claim, therefore, would apply to many people, yet simultaneously would never be subject to judicial review because it would continuously become moot before a judge could certify the putative class. *At 164-65:* [T]o qualify for the exception for 'inherently transitory' claims, the named plaintiff must show ... that the claim is one of short duration, and ... that there likely exists a continuing class of persons suffering the same alleged harm as the named plaintiff."

Typicality

Southwestern Bell Tel. Co. v. Marketing on Hold Inc., 308 S.W.3d 909, 920 (Tex.2010). "We have not previously had an opportunity to address the typicality of an assignee-class representative's claims. Other courts considering this issue have focused on the legal theories behind the claims asserted, not the characteristics of the assignee, unless a defense unique to the assignee will 'skew the focus of the litigation and create a danger that absent class members will suffer if their representative is preoccupied with defenses unique to it.' [¶] Because [assignee] is the assignee of the customer-assignors, [assignee] steps into the customers' shoes and may assert a claim for the injury shared by the assignor and all members of the class. By definition, [assignee's] claims against [D] are the same as the class members. ... We therefore conclude that [assignee] has satisfied the typicality requirement."

Predominance

Stonebridge Life Ins. v. Pitts, 236 S.W.3d 201, 206-07 (Tex.2007). "Equitable defenses raise important substantive issues that may have a significant effect on class-action litigation. [¶] In *Bernal*, we rejected the 'certify now and worry later' approach, holding it is improper to certify a class when it cannot be determined from the outset that individual issues can be considered in a manageable, time-efficient, and fair manner. [¶] Just as fairness and manageability concerns made *Bernal* inappropriate for class certification, the important and diverse individual issues involved in evaluating the class members' money-had-and-received claim compel the same result. [¶] At least one court has concluded that equitable claims for 'money had and received' are uncertifiable for this very reason: In order to prevail on money had and received, the plaintiffs will

───────────────────── ✦ ─────────────────────

have to establish that they paid money to the defendants, either by mistake or fraud, that, in equity or good conscience, should be returned to the plaintiffs. This theory of recovery, therefore, requires individualized inquiry into the state of mind of each plaintiff. [¶] [T]he class representatives in this case failed to prove at the outset that individual issues can be considered in a fair, manageable, and time-efficient manner on a class-wide basis. Accordingly, Rule 42(b)(3)'s predominance requirement is not satisfied...." (Internal quotes omitted.) *See also Best Buy Co. v. Barrera*, 248 S.W.3d 160, 162 (Tex.2007).

Southwestern Ref. Co. v. Bernal, 22 S.W.3d 425, 434 (Tex.2000). "Courts determine if common issues predominate by identifying the substantive issues of the case that will control the outcome of the litigation, assessing which issues will predominate, and determining if the predominating issues are, in fact, those common to the class. The test for predominance is not whether common issues outnumber uncommon issues but ... 'whether common or individual issues will be the object of most of the efforts of the litigants and the court.' If, after common issues are resolved, presenting and resolving individual issues is likely to be an overwhelming or unmanageable task for a single jury, then common issues do not predominate." *See also Southwestern Bell Tel. Co. v. Marketing on Hold Inc.*, 308 S.W.3d 909, 920-21 (Tex.2010); *Snyder Comms. v. Magaña*, 142 S.W.3d 295, 299-300 (Tex.2004); *Henry Schein, Inc. v. Stromboe*, 102 S.W.3d 675, 688 (Tex. 2002).

Adequacy

Southwestern Bell Tel. Co. v. Marketing on Hold Inc., 308 S.W.3d 909, 925 (Tex.2010). "An assignee's interests are not 'necessarily antagonistic' solely because it is an assignee, but the perils of permitting an assignee to represent the class raise important concerns under rule 42. We believe courts should scrutinize carefully the motivating interests and incentives of parties that agree at an apparent financial loss to obtain the right to serve as the class representative. Rule 42's adequacy requirement raises these considerations, which include but are not limited to: (1) the assignee's connection to the classwide injury; (2) the benefits the assignee receives under the assignments; and (3) the assignee's motivation in asserting claims on behalf of the assignor(s). These considerations, in addition to other concerns that may be raised by the facts of each case,

aim to ensure that the assignee's interests are aligned with the interests of the unnamed class members. *At 927:* [Assignee's] lack of any claim of its own makes it unique among the members of the class. Its only knowledge of the claims it holds must be obtained from its assignors. ... While we recognize that class counsel's control over class litigation is often greater than it is in non-class litigation, the class action rule contemplates that the class representative is 'not simply lending [its] name[] to a suit controlled entirely by the class attorney.' In this case, [assignee's] interest in the litigation by assignment removes it and its counsel one step further from the class members, enhancing the risk of conflicts."

Enron Oil & Gas Co. v. Joffrion, 116 S.W.3d 215, 219 (Tex.App.—Tyler 2003, no pet.). The "factors to consider in determining if the adequacy of representation element is satisfied [include]: (1) adequacy of counsel; (2) potential for conflicts of interest; (3) personal integrity of the plaintiffs; (4) whether the class is unmanageable because of geographic limitations; (5) whether the representative plaintiffs can afford to finance the class action; and (6) the representative plaintiffs' familiarity with the litigation and his or her belief in the legitimacy of the action." *See also Supportkids, Inc. v. Morris*, 167 S.W.3d 422, 425-26 (Tex. App.—Houston [14th Dist.] 2005, pet. dism'd).

Discovery

In re SCI Tex. Funeral Servs., 236 S.W.3d 759, 760 (Tex.2007). The Supreme Court has "rejected a blanket rule that all class-wide discovery should be abated until after certification. But we also rejected the opposite rule (full class-wide discovery before certification), noting the special risk in class actions that one party might seek to improve its bargaining position by heaping massive discovery on the other. Instead, ... trial courts [should] limit pre-certification discovery to the particular issues governing certification in each case, considering factors such as the importance, benefit, burden, expense, and time needed to produce the proposed discovery. *At 761:* The discovery orders here do not comply with this rule. ... While [Ps] could have made a strong case for discovery related to the size of the class and representative samples of how [D] did business (necessary to establish numerosity, typicality, and so on), these issues did not justify the burden and expense of producing every [Ps'] contract and every ... invoice [of D's]—discovery perhaps necessary to prove the ultimate issues but not tailored to the certification question before the court. [T]he trial court abused its discretion by compelling discovery that was not narrowly tailored to the relevant dispute."

Appellate Review

Exxon Mobil Corp. v. Gill, 299 S.W.3d 124, 129 (Tex.2009). "When a class has been certified based on a significant misunderstanding of the law, we have concluded that 'remand to the trial court is appropriate so that it may determine the effect ... on the requirements for class certification.'"

Stonebridge Life Ins. v. Pitts, 236 S.W.3d 201, 204-05 (Tex.2007). The Supreme Court "reviews a trial court's decision to certify a class under an abuse of discretion standard, but does so without indulging every presumption in favor of the trial court's decision. Actual conformance with Rule 42 is indispensable, and compliance with the rule must be demonstrated, not presumed." *See also* ***National W. Life Ins. v. Rowe***, 164 S.W.3d 389, 392 (Tex.2005).

Ford Motor Co. v. Sheldon, 22 S.W.3d 444, 449 (Tex.2000). Unless the Supreme Court has specific statutory authority, it cannot review most interlocutory orders on class certification.

Deloitte & Touche LLP v. 14th Ct. of Appeals, 951 S.W.2d 394, 396 (Tex.1997). The Supreme Court has mandamus jurisdiction to review an interlocutory class certification order over which it has no appellate jurisdiction.

De Los Santos v. Occidental Chem. Corp., 933 S.W.2d 493, 495 (Tex.1996). CPRC §51.014(a)(3) permits an interlocutory appeal to the court of appeals from an order that changes a class from opt-out to mandatory because "it alters the fundamental nature of the class."

Phillips Pet. Co. v. Yarbrough, No. 14-11-00944-CV (Tex.App.—Houston [14th Dist.] 2012, pet. granted 9-21-12) (memo op.; 1-24-12). "[A] trial court's exercise of its continuing power to alter or amend the nature of an existing certified class by an order increasing its size does not 'certify or refuse to certify a class' so as to permit an interlocutory appeal. Similarly, an order modifying the class definition is not subject to interlocutory appeal under [CPRC] §51.014(a)(3). In other words, an order that merely alters attributes of a class and does not affect the underlying certification of the action as a class action is not appealable under [CPRC §]51.014(a)(3)."

Settlement

McAllen Med. Ctr., Inc. v. Cortez, 66 S.W.3d 227, 233 (Tex.2001). "Rule 42's typicality and adequacy-of-representation criteria ... demand heightened scrutiny when a settlement occurs. ... And when a settlement occurs, the potential for class representatives and counsel to ignore differences among class members, or even collude with defendants at absent class members' expense, mandates that the trial court rigorously scrutinize Rule 42's typicality and adequacy-of-representation criteria."

TRCP 43. INTERPLEADER

Persons having claims against the plaintiff may be joined as defendants and required to interplead when their claims are such that the plaintiff is or may be exposed to double or multiple liability. It is not ground for objection to the joinder that the claims of the several claimants or the titles on which their claims depend do not have a common origin or are not identical but are adverse to and independent of one another, or that the plaintiff avers that he is not liable in whole or in part to any or all of the claimants. A defendant exposed to similar liability may obtain such interpleader by way of cross-claim or counterclaim. The provisions of this rule supplement and do not in any way limit the joinder of parties permitted in any other rules.

History of TRCP 43: Adopted eff. Sept. 1, 1941, by order of Oct. 29, 1940 (3 Tex.B.J. 531 [1940]). Source: FRCP 22(1).

See ***Commentaries***, "Joining Parties or Claims," ch. 5-J, p. 371; *O'Connor's Texas Forms*, FORMS 5I:4-6.

ANNOTATIONS

State Farm Life Ins. v. Martinez, 216 S.W.3d 799, 807 (Tex.2007). "[I]nterpleader is not improper merely because it is delayed; while some courts have listed prompt filing as an interpleader requirement, the rules of procedure require only conflicting claims. When rival claims exist, courts must decide who gets the proceeds no matter how tardy the deposit; we cannot simply 'toss the money back out the clerk's window,' or return it to a stakeholder who makes no claim to it. Thus ... delay may bar recovery of attorney's fees and incur [any applicable] statutory penalties...."

Great Am. Reserve Ins. v. Sanders, 525 S.W.2d 956, 958 (Tex.1975). Insurance company "was entitled to maintain an interpleader suit if there existed a reasonable doubt, either of fact or law, as to which of the rival claimants was entitled to the proceeds of the policy."

★

Clayton v. MONY Life Ins., 284 S.W.3d 398, 404 (Tex.App.—Beaumont 2009, no pet.). "Rule 43 requires only conflicting claims. [I]nterpleader is not precluded merely because one of the rival claimants alleges the stakeholder is also independently liable to that claimant, and the stakeholder denies that independent liability, but makes no claim to the stake. *At 405:* While independent liability does not necessarily and automatically preclude interpleader under Rule 43, liability for the independent pre-interpleader claims is not necessarily and automatically discharged by the tender."

TRCP 44. MAY APPEAR BY NEXT FRIEND

Minors, lunatics, idiots, or persons non compos mentis who have no legal guardian may sue and be represented by "next friend" under the following rules:

(1) Such next friend shall have the same rights concerning such suits as guardians have, but shall give security for costs, or affidavits in lieu thereof, when required.

(2) Such next friend or his attorney of record may with the approval of the court compromise suits and agree to judgments, and such judgments, agreements and compromises, when approved by the court, shall be forever binding and conclusive upon the party plaintiff in such suit.

History of TRCP 44: Adopted eff. Sept. 1, 1941, by order of Oct. 29, 1940 (3 Tex.B.J. 531 [1940]). Source: TRCS art. 1994, now Prop. Code §142.002.

See TRCP 173; *Commentaries*, "Guardian Ad Litem Under TRCP 173," ch. 1-I, p. 67; *O'Connor's Texas Forms*, FORMS 1I:1-3.

ANNOTATIONS

American Gen. Fire & Cas. Co. v. Vandewater, 907 S.W.2d 491, 492-93 (Tex.1995). "[A]n appellate court should evaluate whether the minor's interests have been properly protected and whether a deficiency in notice or due process has been shown to determine whether a trial court has obtained personal jurisdiction over a minor. In this case, the answer of [mother] in her capacity as [minor's] next friend was sufficient indication that [minor's] legal representative knew about the proceedings and could therefore defend against them." *See also* *Doe v. Texas Ass'n of Sch. Bds., Inc.*, 283 S.W.3d 451, 463 (Tex.App.—Fort Worth 2009, pet. denied).

Urbish v. 127th Judicial Dist. Ct., 708 S.W.2d 429, 432 (Tex.1986). "[T]rial courts are authorized to replace next friends and attorneys when it appears to the court that either has an interest adverse to the minor."

Gracia v. RC Cola-7-Up Bottling Co., 667 S.W.2d 517, 519 (Tex.1984). "In a suit by a 'next friend,' the real party plaintiff is the child and not the next friend."

In re KC Greenhouse Patio Apts., LP, ___ S.W.3d ___ (Tex.App.—Houston [1st Dist.] 2012, orig. proceeding) (No. 01-12-00226-CV; 8-16-12). TRCP 44 "does not authorize a trial court to transfer [the right to represent a minor] from a minor's parent to a third party by unilaterally replacing the parent as the minor's 'next friend' when a conflict of interest arises. [¶] [TRCP] 173—not rule 44—is the rule that grants a trial court authority to address conflicts of interest, and it does so through the appointment of a guardian ad litem, not the replacement of the next friend. Neither rule 44 nor rule 173 permits another person to sue as next friend for a minor who has a legal guardian or permits a court to replace a legal guardian with another person to act as next friend for purposes of pursuing a lawsuit on behalf of a minor."

SECTION 4. PLEADING

A. GENERAL

TRCP 45. DEFINITION & SYSTEM

Pleadings in the district and county courts shall

(a) be by petition and answer;

(b) consist of a statement in plain and concise language of the plaintiff's cause of action or the defendant's grounds of defense. That an allegation be evidentiary or be of legal conclusion shall not be grounds for objection when fair notice to the opponent is given by the allegations as a whole;

(c) contain any other matter which may be required by any law or rule authorizing or regulating any particular action or defense;

(d) be in writing, on paper measuring approximately 8½ inches by 11 inches, and signed by the party or his attorney, and either the signed original together with any verification or a copy of said original and copy of any such verification shall be filed with the court. The use of recycled paper is strongly encouraged.

When a copy of the signed original is tendered for filing, the party or his attorney filing such copy is required to maintain the signed original for inspection by the court or any party incident to the suit, should a question be raised as to its authenticity.

All pleadings shall be construed so as to do substantial justice.

⭐

History of TRCP 45: Amended eff. Sept. 1, 1990 (retroactive), by order of Sept. 4, 1990 (793-94 S.W.2d [Tex.Cases] xxxii): To amend the Sept. 1, 1990 amendment by adding sentence regarding use of recycled paper to (d). Amended eff. Sept. 1, 1990, by order of Apr. 24, 1990 (785-86 S.W.2d [Tex.Cases] xli): Par. under (d) added and (d) changed to provide for filing of pleadings having either original or copies of signatures and verifications including documents telephonically transferred. Amended eff. Jan. 1, 1988, by order of July 15, 1987 (733-34 S.W.2d [Tex.Cases] xl). Adopted eff. Sept. 1, 1941, by order of Oct. 29, 1940 (3 Tex.B.J. 531 [1940]). Source: Part of TRCS art. 1997 (repealed); Tex. Rules for Dist. & Cty. Cts. 1 & 32; and FRCP 8(f).

See *Commentaries*, "Rules of Pleading," ch. 1-B, p. 6; "Rules for Filing Documents," ch. 1-C, p. 21; "Plaintiff's Original Petition," ch. 2-B, p. 95; "Special Exceptions—Challenging the Pleadings," ch. 3-G, p. 248; "Default Judgment," ch. 7-A, p. 587.

ANNOTATIONS

Paramount Pipe & Sup. Co. v. Muhr, 749 S.W.2d 491, 494-95 (Tex.1988). "The purpose of the fair notice requirement is to provide the opposing party with sufficient information to enable him to prepare a defense. [¶] Rule 45 does not require that the plaintiff set out in his pleadings the evidence upon which he relies to establish his asserted cause of action." *See also **Perez v. Briercroft Serv.***, 809 S.W.2d 216, 218 (Tex.1991); ***Roark v. Allen***, 633 S.W.2d 804, 810 (Tex.1982).

Coffey v. Johnson, 142 S.W.3d 414, 417 (Tex. App.—Eastland 2004, no pet.). TRCP 45 "requires that a petition give fair notice of the plaintiff's claims. The test of fair notice is whether an opposing attorney of reasonable competence, with the pleadings before him, can determine the nature of the controversy and the testimony that would probably be relevant. A court must be able, from an examination of the plaintiff's pleadings alone, to ascertain with reasonable certainty the elements of a cause of action and the relief sought with sufficient particularity…." *See also **Taylor v. Taylor***, 337 S.W.3d 398, 401 (Tex.App.—Fort Worth 2011, no pet.).

TRCP 46. PETITION & ANSWER; EACH ONE INSTRUMENT OF WRITING

The original petition, first supplemental petition, second supplemental petition, and every other, shall each be contained in one instrument of writing, and so with the original answer and each of the supplemental answers.

History of TRCP 46: Adopted eff. Sept. 1, 1941, by order of Oct. 29, 1940 (3 Tex.B.J. 531 [1940]). Source: Tex. Rules for Dist. & Cty. Cts. 9.

⑬ TRCP 47. CLAIMS FOR RELIEF*

An original pleading which sets forth a claim for relief, whether an original petition, counterclaim, crossclaim, or third party claim, shall contain

(a) a short statement of the cause of action sufficient to give fair notice of the claim involved,

(b) in all claims for unliquidated damages only the statement that the damages sought are within the jurisdictional limits of the court, and

(c) a demand for judgment for all the other relief to which the party deems himself entitled.

Relief in the alternative or of several different types may be demanded; provided, further, that upon special exception the court shall require the pleader to amend so as to specify the maximum amount claimed.

* Editor's note: The Supreme Court has proposed amendments to TRCP 47 that would require a party, in an original pleading, to make a more specific statement of the relief sought; that is, the party would have to plead into or out of the expedited-actions process under proposed TRCP 169. *See* Tex.Sup.Ct. Order, Misc. Docket No. 12-9191 (eff. Mar. 1, 2013). In response to Gov't Code §22.004(h), the Supreme Court proposed TRCP 169 to establish a process for the prompt, efficient, and cost-effective resolution of civil actions (expedited actions) in which only monetary relief is sought and the amount in controversy is no more than $100,000. *See* Tex.Sup.Ct. Order, Misc. Docket No. 12-9191 (eff. Mar. 1, 2013). The public-comment period for the proposed amendments ends on February 1, 2013, and the rules are to take effect March 1, 2013. For the proposed version of the rules, see the appendix after this book's index. For the final version, go to the Supreme Court website at www.supreme.courts.state.tx.us. When the new and amended rules take effect, a supplement to this book—with updated rules and commentaries that reflect the changes—will be available at www.JonesMcClure.com/TRCPamendments.

History of TRCP 47: Amended eff. Sept. 1, 1990, by order of Apr. 24, 1990 (785-86 S.W.2d [Tex.Cases] xli): Changed (b) to require damages to be within court's jurisdictional limits. Amended eff. Jan. 1, 1978, by order of July 11, 1977 (553-54 S.W.2d [Tex.Cases] xliii): Changed first sentence; revised all of (b); changed first sentence of and added proviso in (c). Adopted eff. Sept. 1, 1941, by order of Oct. 29, 1940 (3 Tex.B.J. 531 [1940]). Source: FRCP 8(a).

See *Commentaries*, "Rules of Pleading," ch. 1-B, p. 6; "Plaintiff's Original Petition," ch. 2-B, p. 95; "Special Exceptions—Challenging the Pleadings," ch. 3-G, p. 248; "Default Judgment," ch. 7-A, p. 587; *O'Connor's Texas Forms*, FORMS 2B:1-8.

ANNOTATIONS

Boyles v. Kerr, 855 S.W.2d 593, 601 (Tex.1993). "A court should uphold the petition as to a cause of action that may be reasonably inferred from what is specifically stated, even if an element of the cause of action is not specifically alleged." *See also **In re P.D.D.***, 256 S.W.3d 834, 839 (Tex.App.—Texarkana 2008, no pet.).

Maswoswe v. Nelson, 327 S.W.3d 889, 894 (Tex. App.—Beaumont 2010, no pet.). "A reviewing court should liberally construe the plaintiff's petition to assert any claim that could reasonably be inferred from the specific language in the petition. However, 'a reviewing court cannot use a liberal construction of the petition as a license to read into the petition a claim that it does not contain.'"

TRCP 48. ALTERNATIVE CLAIMS FOR RELIEF

A party may set forth two or more statements of a claim or defense alternatively or hypothetically, either in one count or defense or in separate counts or de-

★

fenses. When two or more statements are made in the alternative and one of them if made independently would be sufficient, the pleading is not made insufficient by the insufficiency of one or more of the alternative statements. A party may also state as many separate claims or defenses as he has regardless of consistency and whether based upon legal or equitable grounds or both.

History of TRCP 48: Adopted eff. Sept. 1, 1941, by order of Oct. 29, 1940 (3 Tex.B.J. 531 [1940]). Source: FRCP 8(e), in part.

See *Commentaries*, "Alternative claims or defenses," ch. 1-B, §3.2.8, p. 8.

ANNOTATIONS

Birchfield v. Texarkana Mem'l Hosp., 747 S.W.2d 361, 367 (Tex.1987). "[W]here the prevailing party fails to elect between alternative measures of damages, the court should utilize the findings affording the greater recovery and render judgment accordingly."

Horizon Offshore Contractors, Inc. v. Aon Risk Servs., 283 S.W.3d 53, 59-60 (Tex.App.—Houston [14th Dist.] 2009, pet. denied). "[A] party may assert inconsistent facts or remedies simultaneously against different defendants, settle with one defendant, and still recover judgment against the other defendant even though the facts or remedies alleged against the second defendant are inconsistent with the facts or remedies alleged against the settling defendant. However, if a party successfully pursues one remedy against one defendant based on one set of alleged facts and then files a subsequent action against another defendant, the election of remedies will bar the second suit if the alleged facts or remedies in that suit are sufficiently inconsistent with the alleged facts or remedy sought in the first suit."

Household Credit Servs. v. Driscol, 989 S.W.2d 72, 80 (Tex.App.—El Paso 1998, pet. denied). "If a plaintiff pleads alternate theories of liability under Rule 48, a judgment that awards damages based upon more than one theory does not amount to a double recovery if the theories of liability arise from two separate and distinct injuries, and there has been a separate and distinct finding of damages on both theories of liability."

TRCP 49. WHERE SEVERAL COUNTS

Where there are several counts in the petition, and entire damages are given, the verdict or judgment, as the case may be, shall be good, notwithstanding one or more of such counts may be defective.

History of TRCP 49: Adopted eff. Sept. 1, 1941, by order of Oct. 29, 1940 (3 Tex.B.J. 532 [1940]). Source: TRCS art. 2213 (repealed).

TRCP 50. PARAGRAPHS, SEPARATE STATEMENTS

All averments of claim or defense shall be made in numbered paragraphs, the contents of each of which shall be limited as far as practicable to a statement of a single set of circumstances; and a paragraph may be referred to by number in all succeeding pleadings, so long as the pleading containing such paragraph has not been superseded by an amendment as provided by Rule 65. Each claim founded upon a separate transaction or occurrence and each defense other than denials shall be stated in a separate count or defense whenever a separation facilitates the clear presentation of the matters set forth.

History of TRCP 50: Adopted eff. Sept. 1, 1941, by order of Oct. 29, 1940 (3 Tex.B.J. 532 [1940]). Source: FRCP 10(b).

See *Commentaries*, "Rules of Pleading," ch. 1-B, p. 6; "Plaintiff's Original Petition," ch. 2-B, p. 95.

TRCP 51. JOINDER OF CLAIMS & REMEDIES

(a) **Joinder of Claims.** The plaintiff in his petition or in a reply setting forth a counterclaim and the defendant in an answer setting forth a counterclaim may join either as independent or as alternate claims as many claims either legal or equitable or both as he may have against an opposing party. There may be a like joinder of claims when there are multiple parties if the requirements of Rules 39, 40, and 43 are satisfied. There may be a like joinder of cross claims or third-party claims if the requirements of Rules 38 and 97, respectively, are satisfied.

(b) **Joinder of Remedies.** Whenever a claim is one heretofore cognizable only after another claim has been prosecuted to a conclusion, the two claims may be joined in a single action; but the court shall grant relief in that action only in accordance with the relative substantive rights of the parties. This rule shall not be applied in tort cases so as to permit the joinder of a liability or indemnity insurance company, unless such company is by statute or contract directly liable to the person injured or damaged.

History of TRCP 51: Amended eff. Jan. 1, 1961, by order of July 26, 1960 (23 Tex.B.J. 619 [Oct. 1960]): Word "statute" substituted for word "law" in last sentence of (b). Amended eff. Dec. 31, 1941, by order of Sept. 20, 1941 (4 Tex.B.J. 496 [1941]): Added last sentence. Adopted eff. Sept. 1, 1941, by order of Oct. 29, 1940 (3 Tex.B.J. 532 [1940]). Source: FRCP 18. Omitted reference to the right of plaintiff to join an action upon a claim for money and an action to set aside a fraudulent conveyance as unnecessary.

See TRCP 39, 40, 41, 174.

TRCP 51

TRCP 52. ALLEGING A CORPORATION

An allegation that a corporation is incorporated shall be taken as true, unless denied by the affidavit of the adverse party, his agent or attorney, whether such corporation is a public or private corporation and however created.

History of TRCP 52: Adopted eff. Sept. 1, 1941, by order of Oct. 29, 1940 (3 Tex.B.J. 532 [1940]). Source: TRCS art. 1999 (repealed).

See TRCP 93(6); *Commentaries*, "The Answer—Denying Liability," ch. 3-E, p. 227; "Motion to Abate—Challenging the Suit," ch. 3-I, p. 257.

TRCP 53. SPECIAL ACT OR LAW

A pleading founded wholly or in part on any private or special act or law of this State or of the Republic of Texas need only recite the title thereof, the date of its approval, and set out in substance so much of such act or laws as may be pertinent to the cause of action or defense.

History of TRCP 53: Adopted eff. Sept. 1, 1941, by order of Oct. 29, 1940 (3 Tex.B.J. 532 [1940]). Source: TRCS art. 2000 (repealed).

TRCP 54. CONDITIONS PRECEDENT

In pleading the performance or occurrence of conditions precedent, it shall be sufficient to aver generally that all conditions precedent have been performed or have occurred. When such performances or occurrences have been so plead, the party so pleading same shall be required to prove only such of them as are specifically denied by the opposite party.

History of TRCP 54: Amended eff. Sept. 1, 1941, by order of Mar. 31, 1941 (4 Tex.B.J. 496 [1941]): Changed wording of last sentence for clarity. Adopted eff. Sept. 1, 1941, by order of Oct. 29, 1940 (3 Tex.B.J. 532 [1940]). Source: FRCP 9(c).

See *Commentaries*, "Conditions Precedent," ch. 2-B, §11, p. 109; "Denial of conditions precedent," ch. 3-E, §6.1, p. 234; *O'Connor's Texas Forms*, FORMS 2B:1-8, 3E:1-11.

ANNOTATIONS

Associated Indem. Corp. v. CAT Contracting, Inc., 964 S.W.2d 276, 283 n.6 (Tex.1998). "Where a party avers generally that all conditions precedent have been performed or have occurred, he or she need only prove those that are specifically denied by the opposite party. This pleading rule, however, does not shift the burden of proof on those conditions which the opposite party denies." *See also Greathouse v. Charter Nat'l Bank*, 851 S.W.2d 173, 177 (Tex.1992).

TRCP 55. JUDGMENT

In pleading a judgment or decision of a domestic or foreign court, judicial or quasi-judicial tribunal, or of a board or officer, it shall be sufficient to aver the judgment or decision without setting forth matter showing jurisdiction to render it.

History of TRCP 55: Adopted eff. Sept. 1, 1941, by order of Oct. 29, 1940 (3 Tex.B.J. 532 [1940]). Source: FRCP 9(e).

See CPRC ch. 36.

TRCP 56. SPECIAL DAMAGE

When items of special damage are claimed, they shall be specifically stated.

History of TRCP 56: Adopted eff. Sept. 1, 1941, by order of Oct. 29, 1940 (3 Tex.B.J. 532 [1940]). Source: FRCP 9(g).

See *Commentaries*, "Special damages," ch. 2-B, §8.3.1(2), p. 108.

ANNOTATIONS

Arthur Andersen & Co. v. Perry Equip. Corp., 945 S.W.2d 812, 816 (Tex.1997). "Consequential damages [also known as special damages] result naturally, but not necessarily, from the defendant's wrongful acts." *See also Naegeli Transp. v. Gulf Electroquip, Inc.*, 853 S.W.2d 737, 739 (Tex.App.—Houston [14th Dist.] 1993, writ denied).

TRCP 57. SIGNING OF PLEADINGS

Every pleading of a party represented by an attorney shall be signed by at least one attorney of record in his individual name, with his State Bar of Texas identification number, address, telephone number, and, if available, telecopier number. A party not represented by an attorney shall sign his pleadings, state his address, telephone number, and, if available, telecopier number.

History of TRCP 57: Amended eff. Sept. 1, 1990, by order of Apr. 24, 1990 (785-86 S.W.2d [Tex.Cases] xlii): To supply attorney telecopier information with other identifying information on pleadings; documents telephonically transferred are permitted to be filed under changes to TRCP 45. Amended eff. Jan. 1, 1981, by order of June 10, 1980 (599-600 S.W.2d [Tex.Cases] xxxvi): Rule changed to require statement on pleadings of attorney's State Bar of Texas identification number, telephone number, and telephone number of a party not represented by an attorney. Adopted eff. Sept. 1, 1941, by order of Oct. 29, 1940 (3 Tex.B.J. 533 [1940]). Source: FRCP 11, first two sentences.

See TRCP 191.3; *Commentaries*, "Rules of Pleading," ch. 1-B, p. 6; "Plaintiff's Original Petition," ch. 2-B, p. 95; *O'Connor's Texas Forms*, FORM 1B:3.

ANNOTATIONS

W.C. Turnbow Pet. Co. v. Fulton, 194 S.W.2d 256, 257 (Tex.1946). "Counsel should sign their names to motions and pleadings 'to make themselves responsible for what is stated in them, and so as to leave no doubt as to the parties for whom they appear.' But ... the signature to a pleading is a formal requisite and ... failure to comply with the requirement is not fatal to the pleading."

TRCP 58. ADOPTION BY REFERENCE

Statements in a pleading may be adopted by reference in a different part of the same pleading or in another pleading or in any motion, so long as the pleading containing such statements has not been superseded by an amendment as provided by Rule 65.

⭐

History of TRCP 58: Adopted eff. Sept. 1, 1941, by order of Oct. 29, 1940 (3 Tex.B.J. 533 [1940]). Source: FRCP 10(c), first sentence.

See *Commentaries*, "Rules of Pleading," ch. 1-B, p. 6.

ANNOTATIONS

Texas Gas Utils. Co. v. Barrett, 460 S.W.2d 409, 416 (Tex.1970). Because "[t]he original petition had been superseded by [the] First Amended Original Petition[,] statements in the former were not subject to adoption by reference in the supplemental petitions."

TRCP 59. EXHIBITS & PLEADING

Notes, accounts, bonds, mortgages, records, and all other written instruments, constituting, in whole or in part, the claim sued on, or the matter set up in defense, may be made a part of the pleadings by copies thereof, or the originals, being attached or filed and referred to as such, or by copying the same in the body of the pleading in aid and explanation of the allegations in the petition or answer made in reference to said instruments and shall be deemed a part thereof for all purposes. Such pleadings shall not be deemed defective because of the lack of any allegations which can be supplied from said exhibit. No other instrument of writing shall be made an exhibit in the pleading.

History of TRCP 59: Adopted eff. Sept. 1, 1941, by order of Oct. 29, 1940 (3 Tex.B.J. 533 [1940]). Source: Tex. Rules for Dist. & Cty. Cts. 19.

TRCP 60. INTERVENOR'S PLEADINGS

Any party may intervene by filing a pleading, subject to being stricken out by the court for sufficient cause on the motion of any party.

Comment to 1990 change: Rules 21 and 21a control notice and service of pleadings of intervenors.

History of TRCP 60: Amended eff. Sept. 1, 1990, by order of Apr. 24, 1990 (785-86 S.W.2d [Tex.Cases] xlii): Title changed; rule rewritten. Adopted eff. Sept. 1, 1941, by order of Oct. 29, 1940 (3 Tex.B.J. 533 [1940]). Source: TRCS art. 1998 (repealed).

See *Commentaries*, "Joining Parties or Claims," ch. 5-J, p. 371; *O'Connor's Texas Forms*, FORMS 5I:1-3.

ANNOTATIONS

In re Union Carbide Corp., 273 S.W.3d 152, 154-55 (Tex.2008). "Because intervention is allowed as a matter of right, the 'justiciable interest' requirement is of paramount importance: it defines the category of nonparties who may, without consultation with or permission from the original parties or the court, interject their interests into a pending suit to which the intervenors have not been invited. ... If any party to the pending suit moves to strike the intervention, the intervenors have the burden to show a justiciable interest in the pending suit. [¶] To constitute a justiciable interest, '[t]he intervenor's interest must be such that if the original action had never been commenced, and he had first brought it as the sole plaintiff, he would have been entitled to recover in his own name to the extent at least of a part of the relief sought' in the original suit."

Texas Mut. Ins. v. Ledbetter, 251 S.W.3d 31, 36 (Tex.2008). "There is no deadline for intervention in the [TRCPs]. Generally one cannot intervene after final judgment. But when a subrogee's interest has been adequately represented and then suddenly abandoned by someone else, it can intervene even after judgment or on appeal so long as there is neither unnecessary delay nor prejudice to the existing parties." *See also Allen Parker Co. v. Trustmark Nat'l Bank*, No. 14-11-00027-CV (Tex.App.—Houston [14th Dist.] 2012, no pet.) (memo op.; 2-16-12) (petition for intervention filed after judgment may not be considered until judgment is set aside).

Baker v. Monsanto Co., 111 S.W.3d 158, 160 (Tex. 2003). "Typically, an intervention involves a claim against persons who have already appeared. Under these circumstances, the plea in intervention is properly served by any of the methods provided in [TRCP] 21a. However, absent a subsequent appearance, service of citation is necessary against an original defendant when the intervenor seeks affirmative relief against a defendant who has not appeared at the time the intervention was filed. [¶] [I]ntervenors are required to serve citation on a defendant when that defendant fails to appear and answer the plaintiff's petition. [A]n intervenor must serve citation on any third-party defendant it seeks to bring into the suit. And if the intervenor's claim is against the plaintiff, it must serve citation on the plaintiff, if the plaintiff does not make any further appearance in the case after the intervention."

Guaranty Fed. Sav. Bank v. Horseshoe Oper. Co., 793 S.W.2d 652, 657 (Tex.1990). "An intervenor is not required to secure the court's permission to intervene; the party who opposed the intervention has the burden to challenge it by a motion to strike. [¶] [I]t is an abuse of discretion to strike a plea in intervention if (1) the intervenor [could have brought some or all of the same action in its own name, or, if the action had been brought against it, it could defeat some or all of the recovery], (2) the intervention will not complicate the case by an excessive multiplication of the issues, and (3) the intervention is almost essential to effectively protect the intervenor's interest." *See also In re*

───────────────────────── ★ ─────────────────────────

Marriage of J.B. & H.B., 326 S.W.3d 654, 660 (Tex. App.—Dallas 2010, pet. filed 2-17-11).

TRCP 61. TRIAL: INTERVENORS: RULES APPLY TO ALL PARTIES

These rules of pleading shall apply equally, so far as it may be practicable to intervenors and to parties, when more than one, who may plead separately.

History of TRCP 61: Adopted eff. Sept. 1, 1941, by order of Oct. 29, 1940 (3 Tex.B.J. 533 [1940]). Source: TRCS art. 1998 (repealed); Tex. Rules for Dist. & Cty. Cts. 30.

TRCP 62. AMENDMENT DEFINED

The object of an amendment, as contra-distinguished from a supplemental petition or answer, is to add something to, or withdraw something from, that which has been previously pleaded so as to perfect that which is or may be deficient, or to correct that which has been incorrectly stated by the party making the amendment, or to plead new matter, additional to that formerly pleaded by the amending party, which constitutes an additional claim or defense permissible to the suit.

History of TRCP 62: Adopted eff. Sept. 1, 1941, by order of Oct. 29, 1940 (3 Tex.B.J. 533 [1940]). Source: Tex. Rules for Dist. & Cty. Cts. 12, 15.

TRCP 63. AMENDMENTS & RESPONSIVE PLEADINGS

Parties may amend their pleadings, respond to pleadings on file of other parties, file suggestions of death and make representative parties, and file such other pleas as they may desire by filing such pleas with the clerk at such time as not to operate as a surprise to the opposite party; provided, that any pleadings, responses or pleas offered for filing within seven days of the date of trial or thereafter, or after such time as may be ordered by the judge under Rule 166, shall be filed only after leave of the judge is obtained, which leave shall be granted by the judge unless there is a showing that such filing will operate as a surprise to the opposite party.

History of TRCP 63: Amended eff. Sept. 1, 1990, by order of Apr. 24, 1990 (785-86 S.W.2d [Tex.Cases] xlii): Changed title; added "respond to pleadings on file of other parties"; requires that all trial pleadings of all parties, except those permitted by TRCP 66, be on file at least seven days before trial unless leave of court permits later filing. Amended eff. Jan. 1, 1961, by order of July 26, 1960 (23 Tex.B.J. 620 [Oct. 1960]): Added language "or after such time as may be ordered by the judge under TRCP 166." Adopted eff. Sept. 1, 1941, by order of Oct. 29, 1940 (3 Tex.B.J. 533 [1940]). Source: TRCS art. 2001(1), (2) (repealed), with changes: Authorizes amendment without leave of court when filed seven days or more before the date of trial; requires leave to amend thereafter, which may be granted by the judge instead of by the court. Art. 2001(3) was superseded by TRCPs 66 and 67.

See *Commentaries*, "Motion to Amend Pleadings—Pretrial," ch. 5-F, p. 350; "Motion to Amend Pleadings—Trial & Post-trial," ch. 8-F, p. 721; *O'Connor's Texas Forms*, FORMS 5F, 8F.

Kelly v. General Interior Constr., Inc., 301 S.W.3d 653, 659 (Tex.2010). "When the pleading is wholly devoid of jurisdictional facts, the plaintiff should amend the pleading to include the necessary factual allegations, ... allowing jurisdiction to be decided based on evidence rather than allegations, as it should be."

Chapin & Chapin, Inc. v. Texas Sand & Gravel Co., 844 S.W.2d 664, 665 (Tex.1992). Under TRCPs 63 and 66, "'a trial court has no discretion to refuse an amendment unless: (1) the opposing party presents evidence of surprise or prejudice ...; or (2) the amendment asserts a new cause of action or defense, and thus is prejudicial on its face....' [¶] [W]e conclude that the trial court's refusal to allow [D] to verify its denial [less than seven days before trial] was an abuse of discretion." *See also* *Greenhalgh v. Service Lloyds Ins.*, 787 S.W.2d 938, 940 (Tex.1990).

Goswami v. Metropolitan S&L Ass'n, 751 S.W.2d 487, 490 (Tex.1988). "[I]n the absence of a sufficient showing of surprise by the opposing party, the failure to obtain leave of court when filing a late pleading may be cured by the trial court's action in considering the amended pleading. [¶] A summary judgment proceeding is a trial within the meaning of Rule 63." *See also* *Halmos v. Bombardier Aerospace Corp.*, 314 S.W.3d 606, 622 (Tex.App.—Dallas 2010, no pet.).

Halmos v. Bombardier Aerospace Corp., 314 S.W.3d 606, 623 (Tex.App.—Dallas 2010, no pet.). "An amendment that is prejudicial on its face has three defining characteristics: (1) it asserts a new substantive matter that reshapes the nature of trial itself; (2) the opposing party could not have anticipated the new matter in light of the development of the case up to the time the amendment was requested; and (3) the amendment would detrimentally affect the opposing party's presentation of its case."

TRCP 64. AMENDED INSTRUMENT

The party amending shall point out the instrument amended, as "original petition," or "plaintiff's first supplemental petition," or as "original answer," or "defendant's first supplemental answer" or other instrument filed by the party and shall amend by filing a substitute therefor, entire and complete in itself, indorsed "amended original petition," or "amended first supple-

———————————— ⭐ ————————————

mental petition," or "amended original answer," or "amended first supplemental answer," accordingly as said instruments of pleading are designated.

History of TRCP 64: Adopted eff. Sept. 1, 1941, by order of Oct. 29, 1940 (3 Tex.B.J. 533 [1940]). Source: Tex. Rules for Dist. & Cty. Cts. 13.

TRCP 65. SUBSTITUTED INSTRUMENT TAKES PLACE OF ORIGINAL

Unless the substituted instrument shall be set aside on exceptions, the instrument for which it is substituted shall no longer be regarded as a part of the pleading in the record of the cause, unless some error of the court in deciding upon the necessity of the amendment, or otherwise in superseding it, be complained of, and exception be taken to the action of the court, or unless it be necessary to look to the superseded pleading upon a question of limitation.

History of TRCP 65: Adopted eff. Sept. 1, 1941, by order of Oct. 29, 1940 (3 Tex.B.J. 534 [1940]). Source: Tex. Rules for Dist. & Cty. Cts. 14.

See *Commentaries*, "Amended pleadings," ch. 1-B, §3.6.1(1), p. 17; "Non-suit by amendment," ch. 7-F, §2.8.1, p. 651.

ANNOTATIONS

FKM Prtshp. v. Board of Regents of the Univ. of Houston Sys., 255 S.W.3d 619, 633 (Tex.2008). "[A]mended pleadings and their contents take the place of prior pleadings. So, causes of action not contained in amended pleadings are effectively dismissed at the time the amended pleading is filed...." *See also Deadmon v. DART*, 347 S.W.3d 442, 444 (Tex.App.—Dallas 2011, no pet.) (omitting parties' names from an amended pleading dismisses them as effectively as entry of a formal order of dismissal); *Kothmann v. F. Vosburg Hall & Marylou Hall Children's Crisis Found.*, No. 03-09-00081-CV (Tex.App.—Austin 2010, no pet.) (memo op.; 7-15-10) (footnote 3) (omitted claims are withdrawn even if summary judgment already granted on those claims).

Bennett v. Wood Cty., 200 S.W.3d 239, 241 (Tex. App.—Tyler 2006, no pet.). "A new citation is necessary for a party who has not appeared when the plaintiff, by amended petition, seeks a more onerous judgment than that prayed for in the original pleading. 'More onerous' is anything that exposes the defendant to additional liability."

TRCP 66. TRIAL AMENDMENT

If evidence is objected to at the trial on the ground that it is not within the issues made by the pleading, or if during the trial any defect, fault or omission in a pleading, either of form or substance, is called to the attention of the court, the court may allow the pleadings to be amended and shall do so freely when the presentation of the merits of the action will be subserved thereby and the objecting party fails to satisfy the court that the allowance of such amendment would prejudice him in maintaining his action or defense upon the merits. The court may grant a postponement to enable the objecting party to meet such evidence.

History of TRCP 66: Amended eff. Sept. 1, 1941, by order of Mar. 31, 1941 (4 Tex.B.J. 498 [1941]). Adopted eff. Sept. 1, 1941, by order of Oct. 29, 1940 (3 Tex.B.J. 534 [1940]). Source: FRCP 15(b), last two sentences.

See *Commentaries*, "Motion to Amend Pleadings—Trial & Post-trial," ch. 8-F, p. 721; *O'Connor's Texas Forms*, FORMS 8F.

ANNOTATIONS

City of Fort Worth v. Zimlich, 29 S.W.3d 62, 73 (Tex.2000). "A trial amendment must be filed as a written pleading; an oral statement at trial is insufficient to modify the pleadings. However, a party waives its complaint of any defect, omission, or fault in the pleadings if the party fails to specifically object before the submission of the charge to the jury."

State Bar v. Kilpatrick, 874 S.W.2d 656, 658 (Tex. 1994). "A court may not refuse a trial amendment unless (1) the opposing party presents evidence of surprise or prejudice, or (2) the amendment asserts a new cause of action or defense, and thus is prejudicial on its face. The burden of showing surprise or prejudice rests on the party resisting the amendment." *See also Greenhalgh v. Service Lloyds Ins.*, 787 S.W.2d 938, 941 (Tex. 1990); *CA Partners v. Spears*, 274 S.W.3d 51, 70 (Tex. App.—Houston [14th Dist.] 2008, pet. denied).

Deutsch v. Hoover, Bax & Slovacek, L.L.P., 97 S.W.3d 179, 185-86 (Tex.App.—Houston [14th Dist.] 2002, no pet.). TRCP 66 "suggests a postponement may cure any prejudice from a trial amendment. [N]othing in the rule [suggests] an offer of a mistrial does so, especially when the trial is virtually completed. A party seeking leave to amend its pleadings after the trial has commenced should not be rewarded by forcing the judge, jury, and opposing party to either acquiesce in the tardy amendment or start over. [T]he mistrial was the trial court's suggestion.... [D's] decision to refuse the trial court's offer ... did not amount to a relinquishment of his objection [to the trial amendment]."

TRCP 67. AMENDMENTS TO CONFORM TO ISSUES TRIED WITHOUT OBJECTION

When issues not raised by the pleadings are tried by express or implied consent of the parties, they shall be

---

★

---

treated in all respects as if they had been raised in the pleadings. In such case such amendment of the pleadings as may be necessary to cause them to conform to the evidence and to raise these issues may be made by leave of court upon motion of any party at any time up to the submission of the case to the Court or jury, but failure so to amend shall not affect the result of the trial of these issues; provided that written pleadings, before the time of submission, shall be necessary to the submission of questions, as is provided in Rules 277 and 279.

History of TRCP 67: Amended eff. Sept. 1, 1990, by order of Apr. 24, 1990 (785-86 S.W.2d [Tex.Cases] xlii): Changed "special issues" to "questions." Amended eff. Sept. 1, 1941, by order of Mar. 31, 1941 (4 Tex.B.J. 498 [1941]). Adopted eff. Sept. 1, 1941, by order of Oct. 29, 1940 (3 Tex.B.J. 534 [1940]). Source: FRCP 15(b).

See *Commentaries*, "TRCP 67," ch. 8-F, §2.4.2, p. 723.

ANNOTATIONS

Bedgood v. Madalin, 600 S.W.2d 773, 775-76 (Tex. 1980). "Rule 67 ... requires that written pleadings, before the time of submission, shall be necessary to the submission of special issues even where issues are tried by implied consent. Since there were no proper pleadings, the trial court erred in overruling [Ds'] objections to the introduction of evidence and the submission of special issues...."

Oil Field Haulers Ass'n v. Railroad Comm'n, 381 S.W.2d 183, 191 (Tex.1964). "[A] plaintiff may not sustain a favorable judgment on an unpleaded cause of action[] in the absence of trial by consent...."

Johnson v. Oliver, 250 S.W.3d 182, 186 (Tex. App.—Dallas 2008, no pet.). "A party's unpleaded issue may be deemed tried by consent when evidence on the issue is developed under circumstances indicating that the parties understood that the issue was in the case, and the other party fails to make an appropriate complaint. To determine whether an issue was tried by consent, the reviewing court must examine the record, not for evidence of the issue, but rather for evidence of trial of the issue." *See also Gamboa v. Gamboa*, ___ S.W.3d ___ (Tex.App.—San Antonio 2012, no pet.) (No. 04-10-00861-CV; 8-31-12); *In re A.B.H.*, 266 S.W.3d 596, 600 (Tex.App.—Fort Worth 2008, no pet.).

UMLIC VP LLC v. T&M Sales & Env'tl Sys., 176 S.W.3d 595, 605 (Tex.App.—Corpus Christi 2005, pet. denied). "An objection to the submission of a jury question on an unpleaded issue prevents the trial of that issue by implied consent."

TRCP 68. COURT MAY ORDER REPLEADER

The court, when deemed necessary in any case, may order a repleader on the part of one or both of the parties, in order to make their pleadings substantially conform to the rules.

History of TRCP 68: Adopted eff. Sept. 1, 1941, by order of Oct. 29, 1940 (3 Tex.B.J. 534 [1940]). Source: Tex. Rules for Dist. & Cty. Cts. 29.

ANNOTATIONS

Miller v. Kossey, 802 S.W.2d 873, 877 (Tex.App.—Amarillo 1991, writ denied). "[W]hen [P] failed to comply with the court's ... order to send a new notice establishing a necessary element of her cause of action, the court was authorized to dismiss her DTPA action. Consequently, the court did not err in dismissing the action."

TRCP 69. SUPPLEMENTAL PETITION OR ANSWER

Each supplemental petition or answer, made by either party, shall be a response to the last preceding pleading by the other party, and shall not repeat allegations formerly pleaded further than is necessary as an introduction to that which is stated in the pleading then being drawn up. These instruments, to wit, the original petition and its several supplements, and the original answer and its several supplements, shall respectively, constitute separate and distinct parts of the pleadings of each party; and the position and identity, by number and name, with the indorsement of each instrument, shall be preserved throughout the pleadings of either party.

History of TRCP 69: Adopted eff. Sept. 1, 1941, by order of Oct. 29, 1940 (3 Tex.B.J. 534 [1940]). Source: Tex. Rules for Dist. & Cty. Cts. 10.

ANNOTATIONS

Sixth RMA Partners v. Sibley, 111 S.W.3d 46, 53 (Tex.2003). "Rule 28 requires that the correct legal name be substituted, but it does not mandate the procedural method by which substitution may be accomplished." The correct name may be substituted by motion of a party or the court, by amended pleading, and if there is no objection, by supplemental pleading.

TRCP 70. PLEADING: SURPRISE: COST

When either a supplemental or amended pleading is of such character and is presented at such time as to take the opposite party by surprise, the court may charge the continuance of the cause, if granted, to the

———————————————— ✦ ————————————————

party causing the surprise if the other party satisfactorily shows that he is not ready for trial because of the allowance of the filing of such supplemental or amended pleading, and the court may, in such event, in its discretion require the party filing such pleading to pay to the surprised party the amount of reasonable costs and expenses incurred by the other party as a result of the continuance, including attorney fees, or make such other order with respect thereto as may be just.

History of TRCP 70: Amended eff. Jan. 1, 1981, by order of June 10, 1980 (599-600 S.W.2d [Tex.Cases] xxxvii): Enlarges sanctions that may be applied in the discretion of trial court for filing of a pleading that takes opposite party by surprise. Adopted eff. Sept. 1, 1941, by order of Oct. 29, 1940 (3 Tex.B.J. 534 [1940]). Source: Tex. Rules for Dist. & Cty. Cts. 16.

See *Commentaries*, "Motion for Continuance," ch. 5-D, p. 336; "Motion to Amend Pleadings—Pretrial," ch. 5-F, p. 350; "Motion to Amend Pleadings—Trial & Post-trial," ch. 8-F, p. 721; *O'Connor's Texas Forms*, FORMS 5F, 8F.

TRCP 71. MISNOMER OF PLEADING

When a party has mistakenly designated any plea or pleading, the court, if justice so requires, shall treat the plea or pleading as if it had been properly designated. Pleadings shall be docketed as originally designated and shall remain identified as designated, unless the court orders redesignation. Upon court order filed with the clerk, the clerk shall modify the docket and all other clerk records to reflect redesignation.

History of TRCP 71: Amended eff. Jan. 1, 1988, by order of July 15, 1987 (733-34 S.W.2d [Tex.Cases] xli). Adopted eff. Sept. 1, 1941, by order of Oct. 29, 1940 (3 Tex.B.J. 534 [1940]). Source: FRCP 8(c), last sentence. See TRCP 94 for rest of FRCP 8.

See *Commentaries*, "Misnomer," ch. 2-B, §3.3.1(2)(a), p. 98.

ANNOTATIONS

State Bar v. Heard, 603 S.W.2d 829, 833 (Tex. 1980). "We look to the substance of a plea for relief to determine the nature of the pleading, not merely at the form of title given to it." *See also Johnson v. State Farm Lloyds*, 204 S.W.3d 897, 899 n.1 (Tex.App.— Dallas 2006), *aff'd*, 290 S.W.3d 886 (Tex.2009).

TRCP 72, 73. REPEALED

TRCP 72 repealed eff. Sept. 1, 1990, by order of Apr. 24, 1990 (785-86 S.W.2d [Tex.Cases] xliii): Surviving provisions moved to TRCP 21. TRCP 73 repealed eff. Sept. 1, 1990, by order of Apr. 24, 1990 (785-86 S.W.2d [Tex.Cases] xliii): Surviving provisions moved to TRCP 21b.

TRCP 74. FILING WITH THE COURT DEFINED

The filing of pleadings, other papers and exhibits as required by these rules shall be made by filing them with the clerk of the court, except that the judge may permit the papers to be filed with him, in which event he shall note thereon the filing date and time and forthwith transmit them to the office of the clerk.

History of TRCP 74: Amended eff. Jan. 1, 1967, by order of July 20, 1966 (401-02 S.W.2d [Tex.Cases] xxxii): Scope of rule expanded to include exhibits. Adopted eff. Sept. 1, 1941, by order of Oct. 29, 1940 (3 Tex.B.J. 535 [1940]). Source: FRCP 5(e), with changes: Permits the judge to accept instruments for filing and directs him, when he does so, to note thereon the date and time.

See TRCP 24; *Commentaries*, "Rules for Filing Documents," ch. 1-C, p. 21.

ANNOTATIONS

Miller Brewing Co. v. Villarreal, 829 S.W.2d 770, 771 (Tex.1992). "Under our current rules, a party who finds the courthouse closed on the last day that a document must be filed … may also locate the clerk or judge of the court and file the document with them."

Standard Fire Ins. v. LaCoke, 585 S.W.2d 678, 680 (Tex.1979). "The rule is traditionally stated to be that an instrument is deemed in law filed at the time it is left with the clerk, regardless of whether or not a file mark is placed on the instrument and regardless of whether the file mark gives some other date of filing." *See also Pipkin v. Kroger Tex., L.P.*, ___ S.W.3d ___ (Tex.App.—Houston [14th Dist.] 2012, n.p.h.) (No. 14-11-00755-CV; 9-6-12) (despite court order making e-filing mandatory, hard copy of affidavit was filed when left with clerk because court cannot contradict Texas law on when document is deemed filed).

TRCP 75. FILED PLEADINGS; WITHDRAWAL

All filed pleadings shall remain at all times in the clerk's office or in the court or in custody of the clerk, except that the court may by order entered on the minutes allow a filed pleading to be withdrawn for a limited time whenever necessary, on leaving a certified copy on file. The party withdrawing such pleading shall pay the costs of such order and certified copy.

History of TRCP 75: Adopted eff. Sept. 1, 1941, by order of Oct. 29, 1940 (3 Tex.B.J. 535 [1940]). Source: TRCS art. 2002a, second and third sentences (repealed).

ANNOTATIONS

Trinity Indus. v. Rivera, 745 S.W.2d 525, 526 (Tex. App.—Corpus Christi 1988, no writ). A party cannot terminate a suit by withdrawing its pleadings. "Under [the TRCPs], a final order terminating a lawsuit may be accomplished by a judgment on the merits, a dismissal or a non-suit."

TRCP 75a. FILING EXHIBITS: COURT REPORTER TO FILE WITH CLERK

The court reporter or stenographer shall file with the clerk of the court all exhibits which were admitted

───────────────────── ✦ ─────────────────────

in evidence or tendered on bill of exception during the course of any hearing, proceeding, or trial.

History of TRCP 75a: Adopted eff. Jan. 1, 1967, by order of July 20, 1966 (401-02 S.W.2d [Tex.Cases] xxxii). Source: New rule.

See TRAP 13.1(b), (c).

TRCP 75b. FILED EXHIBITS: WITHDRAWAL

All filed exhibits admitted in evidence or tendered on bill of exception shall, until returned or otherwise disposed of as authorized by Rule 14b, remain at all times in the clerk's office or in the court or in the custody of the clerk except as follows:

(a) The court may by order entered on the minutes allow a filed exhibit to be withdrawn by any party only upon such party's leaving on file a certified, photo, or other reproduced copy of such exhibit. The party withdrawing such exhibit shall pay the costs of such order and copy.

(b) The court reporter or stenographer of the court conducting the hearing, proceedings, or trial in which exhibits are admitted or offered in evidence, shall have the right to withdraw filed exhibits, upon giving the clerk proper receipt therefor, whenever necessary for the court reporter or stenographer to transmit such original exhibits to an appellate court under the provisions of Rule 379 or to otherwise discharge the duties imposed by law upon said court reporter or stenographer.

History of TRCP 75b: Adopted eff. Jan. 1, 1967, by order of July 20, 1966 (401-02 S.W.2d [Tex.Cases] xxxii). Source: New rule.

ANNOTATIONS

Perez v. Bagous, 833 S.W.2d 671, 674 (Tex.App.—Corpus Christi 1992, no writ). "Once a party has admitted an exhibit into evidence at trial, the exhibit may not be retrieved and used to create another during a jury recess without notifying opposing counsel or the court. It is wholly outside the scope of the rule to then enter this newly created exhibit into evidence without informing opposing counsel of the use of the entered exhibit."

TRCP 76. MAY INSPECT PAPERS

Each attorney at law practicing in any court shall be allowed at all reasonable times to inspect the papers and records relating to any suit or other matter in which he may be interested.

History of TRCP 76: Adopted eff. Sept. 1, 1941, by order of Oct. 29, 1940 (3 Tex.B.J. 535 [1940]). Source: TRCS art. 318 (repealed).

ANNOTATIONS

U.S. Gov't v. Marks, 949 S.W.2d 320, 326 (Tex. 1997). "[T]here are exceptions [to TRCP 76], such as documents submitted *in camera* under a claim of privilege, documents subject to a protective order, or materials sealed under [TRCP] 76a. Rule 76 does not give [P] an absolute right to the transcript of the *in camera* hearing. *At 327:* However, the district court's order was overly broad in sealing the entire record rather than those portions that pertained to the grand jury proceeding."

Davenport v. Garcia, 834 S.W.2d 4, 24 (Tex.1992). "[A]ccess to [court records] is separately guaranteed to '[e]ach attorney at law practicing in any court....' A court may not escape the strict obligations of [TRCPs 76 and 76a] by tacitly closing the record through an unwritten order."

TRCP 76a. SEALING COURT RECORDS

1. Standard for Sealing Court Records. Court records may not be removed from court files except as permitted by statute or rule. No court order or opinion issued in the adjudication of a case may be sealed. Other court records, as defined in this rule, are presumed to be open to the general public and may be sealed only upon a showing of all of the following:

(a) a specific, serious and substantial interest which clearly outweighs:

(1) this presumption of openness;

(2) any probable adverse effect that sealing will have upon the general public health or safety;

(b) no less restrictive means than sealing records will adequately and effectively protect the specific interest asserted.

2. Court Records. For purposes of this rule, court records means:

(a) all documents of any nature filed in connection with any matter before any civil court, except:

(1) documents filed with a court in camera, solely for the purpose of obtaining a ruling on the discoverability of such documents;

(2) documents in court files to which access is otherwise restricted by law;

(3) documents filed in an action originally arising under the Family Code.

(b) settlement agreements not filed of record, excluding all reference to any monetary consideration,

---- ★ ----

that seek to restrict disclosure of information concerning matters that have a probable adverse effect upon the general public health or safety, or the administration of public office, or the operation of government.

(c) discovery, not filed of record, concerning matters that have a probable adverse effect upon the general public health or safety, or the administration of public office, or the operation of government, except discovery in cases originally initiated to preserve bona fide trade secrets or other intangible property rights.

3. Notice. Court records may be sealed only upon a party's written motion, which shall be open to public inspection. The movant shall post a public notice at the place where notices for meetings of county governmental bodies are required to be posted, stating: that a hearing will be held in open court on a motion to seal court records in the specific case; that any person may intervene and be heard concerning the sealing of court records; the specific time and place of the hearing; the style and number of the case; a brief but specific description of both the nature of the case and the records which are sought to be sealed; and the identity of the movant. Immediately after posting such notice, the movant shall file a verified copy of the posted notice with the clerk of the court in which the case is pending and with the Clerk of the Supreme Court of Texas.

4. Hearing. A hearing, open to the public, on a motion to seal court records shall be held in open court as soon as practicable, but not less than fourteen days after the motion is filed and notice is posted. Any party may participate in the hearing. Non-parties may intervene as a matter of right for the limited purpose of participating in the proceedings, upon payment of the fee required for filing a plea in intervention. The court may inspect records in camera when necessary. The court may determine a motion relating to sealing or unsealing court records in accordance with the procedures prescribed by Rule 120a.

5. Temporary Sealing Order. A temporary sealing order may issue upon motion and notice to any parties who have answered in the case pursuant to Rules 21 and 21a upon a showing of compelling need from specific facts shown by affidavit or by verified petition that immediate and irreparable injury will result to a specific interest of the applicant before notice can be posted and a hearing held as otherwise provided herein. The temporary order shall set the time for the hearing required by paragraph 4 and shall direct that the movant immediately give the public notice required by paragraph 3. The court may modify or withdraw any temporary order upon motion by any party or intervenor, notice to the parties, and hearing conducted as soon as practicable. Issuance of a temporary order shall not reduce in any way the burden of proof of a party requesting sealing at the hearing required by paragraph 4.

6. Order on Motion to Seal Court Records. A motion relating to sealing or unsealing court records shall be decided by written order, open to the public, which shall state: the style and number of the case; the specific reasons for finding and concluding whether the showing required by paragraph 1 has been made; the specific portions of court records which are to be sealed; and the time period for which the sealed portions of the court records are to be sealed. The order shall not be included in any judgment or other order but shall be a separate document in the case; however, the failure to comply with this requirement shall not affect its appealability.

7. Continuing Jurisdiction. Any person may intervene as a matter of right at any time before or after judgment to seal or unseal court records. A court that issues a sealing order retains continuing jurisdiction to enforce, alter, or vacate that order. An order sealing or unsealing court records shall not be reconsidered on motion of any party or intervenor who had actual notice of the hearing preceding issuance of the order, without first showing changed circumstances materially affecting the order. Such circumstances need not be related to the case in which the order was issued. However, the burden of making the showing required by paragraph 1 shall always be on the party seeking to seal records.

8. Appeal. Any order (or portion of an order or judgment) relating to sealing or unsealing court records shall be deemed to be severed from the case and a final judgment which may be appealed by any party or intervenor who participated in the hearing preceding issuance of such order. The appellate court may abate the appeal and order the trial court to direct that further public notice be given, or to hold further hearings, or to make additional findings.

9. Application. Access to documents in court files not defined as court records by this rule remains governed by existing law. This rule does not apply to any court records sealed in an action in which a final judgment has been entered before its effective date.

───────────────────────── ★ ─────────────────────────

This rule applies to cases already pending on its effective date only with regard to:

(a) all court records filed or exchanged after the effective date;

(b) any motion to alter or vacate an order restricting access to court records, issued before the effective date.

History of TRCP 76a: Adopted eff. Sept. 1, 1990, by order of Apr. 24, 1990 (785-86 S.W.2d [Tex.Cases] xliv): To establish guidelines for sealing certain court records in compliance with Gov't Code §22.010. Source: New rule.

See Pen. Code §31.05(a)(4) (definition of "trade secret"); *Commentaries*, "Motion to Seal Court Records," ch. 5-L, p. 394; "Scope of Discovery," ch. 6-B, p. 460; *O'Connor's Texas Forms*, FORMS 5K:1-8.

In re Continental Gen. Tire, Inc., 979 S.W.2d 609, 614 (Tex.1998). "[E]ven if a trade secret produced under a protective order is later determined to be a court record, this does not necessarily mean that the information must be made public. Rule 76a allows the information to remain sealed upon a showing that it meets the criteria specified in Rule 76a(1). That a document contains trade secret information is a factor to be considered in applying this sealing standard."

General Tire, Inc. v. Kepple, 970 S.W.2d 520, 525 (Tex.1998). "[W]e hold that when a party seeks a protective order under [TRCP] 166b(5)(c) [now TRCP 192.6] to restrict the dissemination of unfiled discovery, and no party or intervenor contends that the discovery is a 'court record,' a trial court need not conduct a hearing or render any findings on that issue. If a party or intervenor opposing a protective order claims that the discovery is a 'court record,' the court must make a threshold determination on that issue. However, public notice and a [TRCP] 76a hearing are mandated only if the court finds that the documents are court records."

In re Coastal Bend Coll., 276 S.W.3d 83, 86 (Tex. App.—San Antonio 2008, no pet.). "'It is the burden of the party claiming the documents are open to the public to prove by a preponderance of the evidence that the documents are court records as defined by Rule 76a'.... *At 87:* [A] party must be allowed to tender a document in camera when necessary without converting the document to a 'court record.' 'Were it otherwise, trial courts could not review the documents themselves in determining how to apply Rule 76a without requiring [the party] to relinquish the very relief sought under the rule.' [¶] [In addition, inclusion of the words 'court records' in the title of the] pleading, absent a clear, deliberate and unequivocal statement within the pleading

itself that the documents were 'court records' as defined by Rule 76a(2), is not a judicial admission."

Compaq Computer Corp. v. Lapray, 75 S.W.3d 669, 673 (Tex.App.—Beaumont 2002, no pet.). "Rule 76a contains no requirement that the trial court determine the discoverability of **court records** prior to determining whether to seal or unseal those records. Only under the 76a(2)(a)(1) exception—for documents filed in camera 'solely for the purpose of obtaining a ruling on the discoverability of such documents'—must the issue of discoverability be decided before the documents may become court records."

TRCP 77. LOST RECORDS & PAPERS

When any papers or records are lost or destroyed during the pendency of a suit, the parties may, with the approval of the judge, agree in writing on a brief statement of the matters contained therein; or either party may supply such lost records or papers as follows:

a. After three days' notice to the adverse party or his attorney, make written sworn motion before the court stating the loss or destruction of such record or papers, accompanied by certified copies of the originals if obtainable, or by substantial copies thereof.

b. If, upon hearing, the court be satisfied that they are substantial copies of the original, an order shall be made substituting such copies or brief statement for the originals.

c. Such substituted copies or brief statement shall be filed with the clerk, constitute a part of the cause, and have the force and effect of the originals.

History of TRCP 77: Amended eff. Dec. 31, 1943, by order of June 16, 1943 (3 Tex.B.J. 338 [1943]): Reworded b. Adopted eff. Sept. 1, 1941, by order of Oct. 29, 1940 (3 Tex.B.J. 535 [1940]). Source: TRCS art. 2289 (repealed).

See TRAP 34.5(e), 34.6(f); TRE 1003, 1004; *Commentaries*, "Lost pleadings," ch. 1-C, §11.4, p. 32.

Coke v. Coke, 802 S.W.2d 270, 275 (Tex.App.— Dallas 1990, writ denied). The court overruled the party's objection to the trial court's reconstruction of the lost file from the other party's documents. The party "testified that as far as he could tell, the copies were true duplicates of the originals."

B. PLEADINGS OF PLAINTIFF

TRCP 78. PETITION; ORIGINAL & SUPPLEMENTAL; INDORSEMENT

The pleading of plaintiff shall consist of an original petition, and such supplemental petitions as may be necessary in the course of pleading by the parties to the

✦

suit. The original petition and the supplemental petitions shall be indorsed, so as to show their respective positions in the process of pleading, as "original petition," "plaintiff's first supplemental petition," "plaintiff's second supplemental petition," and so on, to be successively numbered, named, and indorsed.

History of TRCP 78: Adopted eff. Sept. 1, 1941, by order of Oct. 29, 1940 (3 Tex.B.J. 536 [1940]). Source: Tex. Rules for Dist. & Cty. Cts. 3.

TRCP 78a. CASE INFORMATION SHEET

(a) *Requirement.* A civil case information sheet, in the form promulgated by the Supreme Court of Texas, must accompany the filing of:

(1) an original petition or application; and

(2) a post-judgment petition for modification or motion for enforcement in a case arising under the Family Code.

(b) *Signature.* The civil case information sheet must be signed by the attorney for the party filing the pleading or by the party.

(c) *Enforcement.* The court and clerk must take appropriate measures to enforce this rule. But the clerk may not reject a pleading because the pleading is not accompanied by a civil case information sheet.

(d) *Limitation on Use.* The civil case information sheet is for data collection for statistical and administrative purposes and does not affect any substantive right.

(e) *Applicability.* The civil case information sheet is not required in cases filed in justice courts or small-claims courts, or in cases arising under Title 3 of the Family Code.

Editor's note: *Instructions for Completing the Texas Civil Case Information Sheet* and a printable form of the Civil Case Information Sheet can be found on our website at www.jonesmcclure.com/productsupport.aspx.

Comment to 2010 change:

Rule 78a is added to require the submission of a civil case information sheet to collect data for statistical and administrative purposes, *see, e.g.*, Tex. Gov't Code §71.035. A civil case information sheet is not a pleading. Rule 78a is placed with other rules regarding pleadings because civil case information sheets must accompany pleadings.

History of TRCP 78a: Adopted eff. Sept. 1, 2010, by order of Aug. 16, 2010 (73 Tex.B.J. 686 [2010]).

See *Commentaries*, "Case-information sheet," ch. 1-B, §3.2.19, p. 14; *O'Connor's Texas Forms*, FORM 1B:16.

TRCP 79. THE PETITION

The petition shall state the names of the parties and their residences, if known, together with the contents prescribed in Rule 47 above.

History of TRCP 79: Adopted eff. Sept. 1, 1941, by order of Oct. 29, 1940 (3 Tex.B.J. 536 [1940]). Source: New rule.

See *Commentaries*, "Plaintiff's Original Petition," ch. 2-B, p. 95; *O'Connor's Texas Forms*, FORMS 2B.

ANNOTATIONS

Enserch Corp. v. Parker, 794 S.W.2d 2, 4-5 (Tex. 1990). "If the plaintiff merely misnames the correct defendant (misnomer), limitations is tolled and a subsequent amendment ... relates back to the date of the original petition. If, however, the plaintiff is mistaken as to which of two defendants is the correct one and there is ... a corporation with the name of the erroneously named defendant (misidentification), then the plaintiff has sued the wrong party and limitations is not tolled."

TRCP 80. PLAINTIFF'S SUPPLEMENTAL PETITION

The plaintiff's supplemental petitions may contain special exceptions, general denials, and the allegations of new matter not before alleged by him, in reply to those which have been alleged by the defendant.

History of TRCP 80: Adopted eff. Sept. 1, 1941, by order of Oct. 29, 1940 (3 Tex.B.J. 536 [1940]). Source: Tex. Rules for Dist. & Cty. Cts. 5.

ANNOTATIONS

Moody-Rambin Interests v. Moore, 722 S.W.2d 790, 792 (Tex.App.—Houston [14th Dist.] 1987, no writ). "'The proper way to bring new parties into a suit is by an amended pleading, and not by a supplemental pleading.' An exception to this rule exists if the necessity for adding a new party arises from facts pled in the defendant's answer."

TRCP 81. DEFENSIVE MATTERS

When the defendant sets up a counter claim, the plaintiff may plead thereto under rules prescribed for pleadings of defensive matter by the defendant, so far as applicable. Whenever the defendant is required to plead any matter of defense under oath, the plaintiff shall be required to plead such matters under oath when relied on by him.

History of TRCP 81: Adopted eff. Sept. 1, 1941, by order of Oct. 29, 1940 (3 Tex.B.J. 536 [1940]). Source: TRCS art. 2004 (repealed).

ANNOTATIONS

Greater Fort Worth & Tarrant Cty. Cmty. Action Agency v. Mims, 627 S.W.2d 149, 152 (Tex.1982). "If the plaintiff contesting the counterclaim does not intend to urge any defensive theory which must be verified or any affirmative defense under [TRCP] 94, he is not required to answer the defendant's counterclaim."

TRCP 81

✦

TRCP 82. SPECIAL DEFENSES

The plaintiff need not deny any special matter of defense pleaded by the defendant, but the same shall be regarded as denied unless expressly admitted.

History of TRCP 82: Adopted eff. Sept. 1, 1941, by order of Oct. 29, 1940 (3 Tex.B.J. 536 [1940]). Source: TRCS art. 2005 (repealed).

C. PLEADINGS OF DEFENDANT

TRCP 83. ANSWER; ORIGINAL & SUPPLEMENTAL; INDORSEMENT

The answer of defendant shall consist of an original answer, and such supplemental answers as may be necessary, in the course of pleading by the parties to the suit. The original answer and the supplemental answers shall be indorsed, so as to show their respective positions in the process of pleading, as "original answer," "defendant's first supplemental answer," "defendant's second supplemental answer," and so on, to be successively numbered, named and indorsed.

History of TRCP 83: Adopted eff. Sept. 1, 1941, by order of Oct. 29, 1940 (3 Tex.B.J. 536 [1940]). Source: Tex. Rules for Dist. & Cty. Cts. 6.

See *Commentaries*, "Defendant's Pleadings," ch. 3-A, p. 183.

ANNOTATIONS

Smith v. Lippmann, 826 S.W.2d 137, 138 (Tex. 1992). "[A] defendant, who timely files a pro se answer by a signed letter that identifies the parties, the case, and the defendant's current address, has sufficiently appeared by answer and deserves notice of any subsequent proceedings in the case."

TRCP 84. ANSWER MAY INCLUDE SEVERAL MATTERS

The defendant in his answer may plead as many several matters, whether of law or fact, as he may think necessary for his defense, and which may be pertinent to the cause, and such matters shall be heard in such order as may be directed by the court, special appearance and motion to transfer venue, and the practice thereunder being excepted herefrom.

History of TRCP 84: Amended eff. Sept. 1, 1983, by order of June 15, 1983 (651-52 S.W.2d [Tex.Cases] xxxi): To conform to S.B. 898, 68th Leg., 1983. Amended eff. Sept. 1, 1962, by order of Apr. 12, 1962 (25 Tex.B.J. 371 [1962]): Words "special appearance and" inserted before "plea of privilege." Amended eff. Mar. 1, 1950, by order of Oct. 12, 1949 (2 Tex.B.J. 529 [1949]): Eliminated requirement that defensive matters must be filed at the same time and in due order of pleading; and provisions of last clause changed to allow pleas to be heard in such order as the court may direct, excepting a plea of privilege. Adopted eff. Sept. 1, 1941, by order of Oct. 29, 1940 (3 Tex.B.J. 536 [1940]). Source: TRCS arts. 2006 and 2012 (repealed). See TRCP 92 for rest of art. 2006.

See *Commentaries*, "Defendant's Pleadings," ch. 3-A, p. 183.

ANNOTATIONS

Glover v. Moser, 930 S.W.2d 940, 944 (Tex.App.—Beaumont 1996, writ denied). "We believe the clear intent of Rule 84 was to prevent exactly what occurred in [this] case, i.e., the trial court proceeding on meritorious matters prior to its determination of whether venue is properly before it."

TRCP 85. ORIGINAL ANSWER; CONTENTS

The original answer may consist of motions to transfer venue, pleas to the jurisdiction, in abatement, or any other dilatory pleas; of special exceptions, of general denial, and any defense by way of avoidance or estoppel, and it may present a cross-action, which to that extent will place defendant in the attitude of a plaintiff. Matters in avoidance and estoppel may be stated together, or in several special pleas, each presenting a distinct defense, and numbered so as to admit of separate issues to be formed on them.

History of TRCP 85: Amended eff. Sept. 1, 1983, by order of June 15, 1983 (651-52 S.W.2d [Tex.Cases] xxxii): To conform to S.B. 898, 68th Leg., 1983. Adopted eff. Sept. 1, 1941, by order of Oct. 29, 1940 (3 Tex.B.J. 536 [1940]). Source: Tex. Rules for Dist. & Cty. Cts. 7.

See *Commentaries*, "Defendant's Response & Pleadings," ch. 3, p. 179; *O'Connor's Texas Forms*, FORMS 3E.

ANNOTATIONS

Hines v. Hash, 843 S.W.2d 464, 469 (Tex.1992). "To be timely, the request for an abatement [under the DTPA] must be made while the purpose of notice—settlement and avoidance of litigation expense—remains viable. Thus, [a] defendant must request an abatement with the filing of an answer or very soon thereafter. If the trial court determines that [the] plaintiff has failed to give notice as required by the [DTPA] statute, the action must be abated."

TRCP 86. MOTION TO TRANSFER VENUE

1. Time to File. An objection to improper venue is waived if not made by written motion filed prior to or concurrently with any other plea, pleading or motion except a special appearance motion provided for in Rule 120a. A written consent of the parties to transfer the case to another county may be filed with the clerk of the court at any time. A motion to transfer venue because an impartial trial cannot be had in the county where the action is pending is governed by the provisions of Rule 257.

2. How to File. The motion objecting to improper venue may be contained in a separate instrument filed

✦

concurrently with or prior to the filing of the movant's first responsive pleading or the motion may be combined with other objections and defenses and included in the movant's first responsive pleading.

3. Requisites of Motion. The motion, and any amendments to it, shall state that the action should be transferred to another specified county of proper venue because:

(a) The county where the action is pending is not a proper county; or

(b) Mandatory venue of the action in another county is prescribed by one or more specific statutory provisions which shall be clearly designated or indicated.

The motion shall state the legal and factual basis for the transfer of the action and request transfer of the action to a specific county of mandatory or proper venue. Verification of the motion is not required. The motion may be accompanied by supporting affidavits as provided in Rule 87.

4. Response and Reply. Except as provided in paragraph 3(a) of Rule 87, a response to the motion to transfer is not required. Verification of a response is not required.

5. Service. A copy of any instrument filed pursuant to Rule 86 shall be served in accordance with Rule 21a.

History of TRCP 86: Amended eff. Sept. 1, 1983, by order of June 15, 1983 (651-52 S.W.2d [Tex.Cases] xxxii): To conform to S.B. 898, 68th Leg., 1983. Amended eff. Sept. 1, 1962, by order of Apr. 12, 1962 (25 Tex.B.J. 371 [1962]): Requisites of plea of privilege to be sued in county other than county of one's residence prescribed, and note regarding 1943 amendment rewritten. Amended eff. Jan. 1, 1955, by order of July 20, 1954 (17 Tex.B.J. 566 [1954]): Copy of plea of privilege required to be served on adverse party or his attorney by delivery to him in person or by registered mail, and requiring filing of controverting affidavit within ten days after receipt thereof. Amended eff. Dec. 31, 1943, by order of June 16, 1943 (6 Tex.B.J. 339 [1943]): Controverting affidavit required to be filed within ten days after appearance day if plea of privilege is filed in vacation, otherwise within ten days after appearance day or after filing of plea of privilege, whichever is the later date. Amended eff. Sept. 1, 1941, by order of Mar. 31, 1941 (4 Tex.B.J. 500 [1941]): Changed "or" to read "of" between "service" and "process." Adopted eff. Sept. 1, 1941, by order of Oct. 29, 1940 (3 Tex.B.J. 537 [1940]). Source: TRCS art. 2007 (repealed). Changes: Requires the plea of privilege to state post-office address of defendant or attorney; increased time for filing a controverting affidavit to ten days.

See CPRC ch. 15; *Commentaries*, "Motion to Transfer—Challenging Venue," ch. 3-C, p. 203; *O'Connor's Texas Forms*, FORMS 3C.

ANNOTATIONS

Wichita Cty. v. Hart, 917 S.W.2d 779, 781 (Tex. 1996). "A defendant raises the question of proper venue by objecting to a plaintiff's venue choice through a motion to transfer venue. The fact that mandatory venue lies in another county provides one ground for a motion to transfer venue. If the plaintiff's chosen venue rests on a permissive venue statute and the defendant

files a meritorious motion to transfer based on a mandatory venue provision, the trial court must grant the motion. A trial court's erroneous denial of a motion to transfer venue requires reversal of the judgment and remand for a new trial."

Toliver v. Dallas Fort Worth Hosp. Council, 198 S.W.3d 444, 446-47 (Tex.App.—Dallas 2006, no pet.). "A party may expressly waive venue rights by clear, overt acts evidencing an intent to waive, or impliedly, by taking some action inconsistent with an intent to pursue the venue motion. ... But filing a notice of removal to federal court before filing a motion to transfer in state court does not waive the motion." *See also **Duran v. Entrust, Inc.***, No. 01-08-00589-CV (Tex.App.—Houston [1st Dist.] 2010, pet. denied) (memo op.; 3-25-10) (D waived motion to transfer venue by waiting four years to seek setting on the venue motion and by filing two summary-judgment motions during that time).

TRCP 87. DETERMINATION OF MOTION TO TRANSFER

1. Consideration of Motion. The determination of a motion to transfer venue shall be made promptly by the court and such determination must be made in a reasonable time prior to commencement of the trial on the merits. The movant has the duty to request a setting on the motion to transfer. Except on leave of court each party is entitled to at least 45 days notice of a hearing on the motion to transfer.

Except on leave of court, any response or opposing affidavits shall be filed at least 30 days prior to the hearing of the motion to transfer. The movant is not required to file a reply to the response but any reply and any additional affidavits supporting the motion to transfer must, except on leave of court, be filed not later than 7 days prior to the hearing date.

2. Burden of Establishing Venue.

(a) *In General.* A party who seeks to maintain venue of the action in a particular county in reliance upon Section 15.001[1] (General Rule), Sections 15.011-15.017 (Mandatory Venue), Sections 15.031-15.040 (Permissive Venue), or Sections 15.061 and 15.062 (Multiple Claims), Civil Practice and Remedies Code, has the burden to make proof, as provided in paragraph 3 of this rule, that venue is maintainable in the county of suit. A party who seeks to transfer venue of the action to another specified county under Section 15.001[1] (General Rule), Sections 15.011-15.017 (Mandatory Venue), Sections 15.031-15.040 (Permissive Venue), or

---

★

Sections 15.061 and 15.062 (Multiple Claims), Civil Practice and Remedies Code, has the burden to make proof, as provided in paragraph 3 of this rule, that venue is maintainable in the county to which transfer is sought. A party who seeks to transfer venue of the action to another specified county under Sections 15.011-15.017, Civil Practice and Remedies Code on the basis that a mandatory venue provision is applicable and controlling has the burden to make proof, as provided in paragraph 3 of this rule, that venue is maintainable in the county to which transfer is sought by virtue of one or more mandatory venue exceptions.

(b) *Cause of Action.* It shall not be necessary for a claimant to prove the merits of a cause of action, but the existence of a cause of action, when pleaded properly, shall be taken as established as alleged by the pleadings. When the defendant specifically denies the venue allegations, the claimant is required, by prima facie proof as provided in paragraph 3 of this rule, to support such pleading that the cause of action taken as established by the pleadings, or a part of such cause of action, accrued in the county of suit. If a defendant seeks transfer to a county where the cause of action or a part thereof accrued, it shall be sufficient for the defendant to plead that if a cause of action exists, then the cause of action or part thereof accrued in the specific county to which transfer is sought, and such allegation shall not constitute an admission that a cause of action in fact exists. But the defendant shall be required to support his pleading by prima facie proof as provided in paragraph 3 of this rule, that, if a cause of action exists, it or a part thereof accrued in the county to which transfer is sought.

(c) *Other Rules.* A motion to transfer venue based on the written consent of the parties shall be determined in accordance with Rule 255. A motion to transfer venue on the basis that an impartial trial cannot be had in the county where the action is pending shall be determined in accordance with Rules 258 and 259.

3. Proof.

(a) *Affidavit and Attachments.* All venue facts, when properly pleaded, shall be taken as true unless specifically denied by the adverse party. When a venue fact is specifically denied, the party pleading the venue fact must make prima facie proof of that venue fact; provided, however, that no party shall ever be required for venue purposes to support by prima facie proof the existence of a cause of action or part thereof, and at the hearing the pleadings of the parties shall be taken as conclusive on the issues of existence of a cause of action. Prima facie proof is made when the venue facts are properly pleaded and an affidavit, and any duly proved attachments to the affidavit, are filed fully and specifically setting forth the facts supporting such pleading. Affidavits shall be made on personal knowledge, shall set forth specific facts as would be admissible in evidence, and shall show affirmatively that the affiant is competent to testify.

(b) *The Hearing.* The court shall determine the motion to transfer venue on the basis of the pleadings, any stipulations made by and between the parties and such affidavits and attachments as may be filed by the parties in accordance with the preceding subdivision of this paragraph 3 or of Rule 88.

(c) If a claimant has adequately pleaded and made prima facie proof that venue is proper in the county of suit as provided in subdivision (a) of paragraph 3, then the cause shall not be transferred but shall be retained in the county of suit, unless the motion to transfer is based on the grounds that an impartial trial cannot be had in the county where the action is pending as provided in Rules 257-259 or on an established ground of mandatory venue. A ground of mandatory venue is established when the party relying upon a mandatory exception to the general rule makes prima facie proof as provided in subdivision (a) of paragraph 3 of this rule.

(d) In the event that the parties shall fail to make prima facie proof that the county of suit or the specific county to which transfer is sought is a county of proper venue, then the court may direct the parties to make further proof.

4. No Jury. All venue challenges shall be determined by the court without the aid of a jury.

5. Motion for Rehearing. If venue has been sustained as against a motion to transfer, or if an action has been transferred to a proper county in response to a motion to transfer, then no further motions to transfer shall be considered regardless of whether the movant was a party to the prior proceedings or was added as a party subsequent to the venue proceedings, unless the motion to transfer is based on the grounds that an impartial trial cannot be had under Rules 257-259 or on the ground of mandatory venue, provided that such claim was not available to the other movant or movants.

Parties who are added subsequently to an action and are precluded by this rule from having a motion to

✦

transfer considered may raise the propriety of venue on appeal, provided that the party has timely filed a motion to transfer.

6. There shall be no interlocutory appeals from such determination.

1. **Editor's note:** Now CPRC §15.002.

History of TRCP 87: Amended eff. Sept. 1, 1990, by order of Apr. 24, 1990 (785-86 S.W.2d [Tex.Cases] xlvi): Added last phrase of 2(b) and phrase in second sentence of 3(b) beginning "provided, however"; title to 5 changed; clarifies that no proof of any kind is required of any party to establish any element of a cause of action or part thereof; proof is restricted to place, if any, and the pleadings establish all other elements and may not be controverted for venue purposes as to the existence of a cause of action or part thereof. Amended eff. Jan. 1, 1988, by order of July 15, 1987 (733-34 S.W.2d [Tex.Cases] xli): Changes to 2(a). Amended eff. Sept. 1, 1983, by order of June 15, 1983 (651-52 S.W.2d [Tex.Cases] xxxiii): Rule completely rewritten to conform to S.B. 898, 68th Leg., 1983. Amended eff. Dec. 31, 1947, by order of Aug. 18, 1947 (10 Tex.B.J. 390 [1947]): Added sentence beginning "If the defendant" and ending "at the same time." Amended eff. Dec. 31, 1943, by order of June 16, 1943 (6 Tex.B.J. 340 [1943]): Interpolated words "or shall have been delivered to defendant or his attorney" between the words "privilege" and "at." Amended eff. Dec. 31, 1941, by order of Sept. 20, 1941 (4 Tex.B.J. 501 [1941]): Added second sentence. Adopted eff. Sept. 1, 1941, by order of Oct. 29, 1940 (3 Tex.B.J. 537 [1940]). Source: TRCS art. 2008 (repealed in part by TRCPs). Change: Substituted service of notice of the controverting affidavit by registered mail for service by officer. Provisions for interlocutory appeals from orders sustaining or overruling pleas of privilege are included in art. 2008, which is deemed jurisdictional.

See CPRC ch. 15; *Commentaries*, "Choosing the Court—Venue," ch. 2-G, p. 150; "Motion to Transfer—Challenging Venue," ch. 3-C, p. 203; *O'Connor's Texas Forms*, FORMS 3C.

ANNOTATIONS

In re Team Rocket, L.P., 256 S.W.3d 257, 259-60 (Tex.2008). "[O]nly one venue determination may be made in a proceeding and [TRCP] 87 specifically prohibits changes in venue after the initial venue ruling. ... Although a trial court's ruling transferring venue is interlocutory for the parties, and thus not subject to immediate appeal, the order is final for the transferring court as long as it is not altered within the court's 30-day plenary jurisdiction. ... Just as a decision on the merits cannot be circumvented by nonsuiting and refiling the case, a final determination fixing venue in a particular county must likewise be protected from relitigation. [¶] Reading [CPRC] §15.064 ... and Rule 87 together, we conclude that once a venue determination has been made, that determination is conclusive as to those parties and claims. Because venue is then fixed in any suit involving the same parties and claims, it cannot be overcome by a nonsuit and subsequent refiling in another county. [¶] To interpret the provisions otherwise would allow forum shopping, a practice we have repeatedly prohibited." *See also In re Reynolds*, 369 S.W.3d 638, 647 (Tex.App.—Tyler 2012, orig. proceeding); *Gilcrease v. Garlock, Inc.*, 211 S.W.3d 448, 460 (Tex.App.—El Paso 2006, no pet.).

HCA Health Servs. v. Salinas, 838 S.W.2d 246, 247-48 (Tex.1992). "[I]t is an abuse of discretion, correctable by mandamus, for a trial court to rule on a motion to transfer venue without giving the parties the notice required by [TRCP 87(1)]."

Rodriguez v. Printone Color Corp., 982 S.W.2d 69, 71 (Tex.App.—Houston [1st Dist.] 1998, pet. denied). "[S]tatements such as 'Defendant specifically denies those venue facts pleaded in Plaintiff's Petition' do not constitute a 'specific denial' as required by [TRCP] 87."

TRCP 88. DISCOVERY & VENUE

Discovery shall not be abated or otherwise affected by pendency of a motion to transfer venue. Issuing process for witnesses and taking depositions shall not constitute a waiver of a motion to transfer venue, but depositions taken in such case may be read in evidence in any subsequent suit between the same parties concerning the same subject matter in like manner as if taken in such subsequent suit. Deposition transcripts, responses to requests for admission, answers to interrogatories and other discovery products containing information relevant to a determination of proper venue may be considered by the court in making the venue determination when they are attached to, or incorporated by reference in, an affidavit of a party, a witness or an attorney who has knowledge of such discovery.

History of TRCP 88: Amended eff. Jan. 1, 1988, by order of July 15, 1987 (733-34 S.W.2d [Tex.Cases] xlii). Amended eff. Sept. 1, 1983, by order of June 15, 1983 (651-52 S.W.2d [Tex.Cases] xxxv): To conform to S.B. 898, 68th Leg., 1983. Adopted eff. Sept. 1, 1941, by order of Oct. 29, 1940 (3 Tex.B.J. 537 [1940]). Source: TRCS art. 2018 (repealed).

See *Commentaries*, "Motion to Transfer—Challenging Venue," ch. 3-C, p. 203.

ANNOTATIONS

Montalvo v. 4th Ct. of Appeals, 917 S.W.2d 1, 2 (Tex.1995). "[T]he trial court set a shortened schedule for completing discovery related to venue, filing [Ps'] response to the motions to transfer, and the hearing. [Ps] offered no argument or evidence that the limitation on discovery or the abbreviated schedule deprived them of any ability to develop evidence pertinent to the venue issue. Without a showing of such harm, the record is wholly insufficient to establish that [Ps] lacked an adequate remedy by appeal."

TRCP 89. TRANSFERRED IF MOTION IS SUSTAINED

If a motion to transfer venue is sustained, the cause shall not be dismissed, but the court shall transfer said cause to the proper court; and the costs incurred prior to the time such suit is filed in the court to which said cause is transferred shall be taxed against the plaintiff. The clerk shall make up a transcript of all the orders made in said cause, certifying thereto officially under the seal of the court, and send it with the original papers in the cause to the clerk of the court to which the venue has been changed. Provided, however, if the cause be severable as to parties defendant and shall be ordered transferred as to one or more defendants but not as to all, the clerk, instead of sending the original papers, shall make certified copies of such filed papers as directed by the court and forward the same to the clerk of the court to which the venue has been changed. After the cause has been transferred, as above provided for the clerk of the court to which the cause has been transferred shall mail notification to the plaintiff or his attorney that transfer of the cause has been completed, that the filing fee in the proper court is due and payable within thirty days from the mailing of such notification, and that the case may be dismissed if the filing fee is not timely paid; and if such filing fee is timely paid, the cause will be subject to trial at the expiration of thirty days after the mailing of notification to the parties or their attorneys by the clerk that the papers have been filed in the court to which the cause has been transferred; and if the filing fee is not timely paid, any court of the transferee county to which the case might have been assigned, upon its own motion or the motion of a party, may dismiss the cause without prejudice to the refiling of same.

History of TRCP 89: Amended eff. Sept. 1, 1983, by order of June 15, 1983 (651-52 S.W.2d [Tex.Cases] xxxv): To conform to S.B. 898, 68th Leg., 1983. Amended eff. Dec. 31, 1943, by order of June 16, 1943 (6 Tex.B.J. 340 [1943]). Adopted eff. Sept. 1, 1941, by order of Oct. 29, 1940 (3 Tex.B.J. 537 [1940]). Source: TRCS arts. 2019, 2020 (repealed).

See *Commentaries*, "Motion to Transfer—Challenging Venue," ch. 3-C, p. 203.

ANNOTATIONS

WTFO, Inc. v. Braithwaite, 899 S.W.2d 709, 718 (Tex.App.—Dallas 1995, no writ). "Where a cause of action is against several defendants jointly and severally, the trial court shall transfer the action as to those defendants whose motions are sustained. Comakers on a note are jointly and severally liable. Accordingly, because venue was proper in Dallas County, the trial court did not abuse its discretion in severing [D's] cause of action and transferring it to Dallas County."

TRCP 90. WAIVER OF DEFECTS IN PLEADING

General demurrers shall not be used. Every defect, omission or fault in a pleading either of form or of substance, which is not specifically pointed out by exception in writing and brought to the attention of the judge in the trial court before the instruction or charge to the jury or, in a non-jury case, before the judgment is signed, shall be deemed to have been waived by the party seeking reversal on such account; provided that this rule shall not apply as to any party against whom default judgment is rendered.

History of TRCP 90: Amended eff. Jan. 1, 1981, by order of June 10, 1980 (599-600 S.W.2d [Tex.Cases] xxxvii): Deleted words "motion or" before "exception," and changed "rendition of judgment" to "judgment is signed." Adopted eff. Sept. 1, 1941, by order of Oct. 29, 1940 (3 Tex.B.J. 537 [1940]). Source: New rule.

See *Commentaries*, "Special Exceptions—Challenging the Pleadings," ch. 3-G, p. 248.

ANNOTATIONS

Friesenhahn v. Ryan, 960 S.W.2d 656, 658 (Tex. 1998). "Special exceptions may be used to challenge the sufficiency of a pleading. When the trial court sustains special exceptions, it must give the pleader an opportunity to amend the pleading. If a party refuses to amend, or the amended pleading fails to state a cause of action, then summary judgment may be granted. Summary judgment may also be proper if a pleading deficiency is of the type that could not be cured by an amendment."

Shoemake v. Fogel, Ltd., 826 S.W.2d 933, 937 (Tex. 1992). "[D] filed no special exceptions to clarify [P's] claim. Thus, [D] cannot now complain that [P's] pleading was insufficiently specific." *See also Steves Sash & Door Co. v. Ceco Corp.*, 751 S.W.2d 473, 476 (Tex. 1988).

TRCP 91. SPECIAL EXCEPTIONS

A special exception shall not only point out the particular pleading excepted to, but it shall also point out intelligibly and with particularity the defect, omission, obscurity, duplicity, generality, or other insufficiency in the allegations in the pleading excepted to.

History of TRCP 91: Amended eff. Sept. 1, 1941, by order of Mar. 31, 1941 (4 Tex.B.J. 501 [1941]). Adopted eff. Sept. 1, 1941, by order of Oct. 29, 1940 (3 Tex.B.J. 538 [1940]). Source: Tex. Rules for Dist. & Cty. Cts. 18.

See *Commentaries*, "Special Exceptions—Challenging the Pleadings," ch. 3-G, p. 248; *O'Connor's Texas Forms*, FORMS 3G.

ANNOTATIONS

Parker v. Barefield, 206 S.W.3d 119, 120 (Tex. 2006). If the trial court does not allow the party an opportunity to amend its pleadings, "the aggrieved party must prove that the opportunity to replead was requested and denied to preserve the error for review."

Friesenhahn v. Ryan, 960 S.W.2d 656, 658 (Tex. 1998). "Special exceptions may be used to challenge the sufficiency of a pleading. When the trial court sustains special exceptions, it must give the pleader an opportunity to amend the pleading. If a party refuses to amend, or the amended pleading fails to state a cause of action, then summary judgment may be granted. Summary judgment may also be proper if a pleading deficiency is of the type that could not be cured by an amendment."

Peek v. Equipment Serv., 779 S.W.2d 802, 805 (Tex.1989). "[T]he omission of any allegation regarding the amount in controversy from [P's] petition did not deprive the court of jurisdiction, but was instead a defect in pleading subject to special exception and amendment."

Gallien v. Washington Mut. Home Loans, Inc., 209 S.W.3d 856, 862-63 (Tex.App.—Texarkana 2006, no pet.). "[A]s a general rule, the trial court cannot dismiss a suit with prejudice when the plaintiff does not cure the objections made by special exceptions. More specifically, a trial court cannot dismiss a plaintiff's entire case with prejudice if the pleadings state a valid cause of action, but are vague, overbroad, or otherwise susceptible to valid special exceptions."

⓭ **TRCP 91a. DISMISSAL OF BASELESS CAUSES OF ACTION***

* Editor's note: In response to Gov't Code §22.004(g), the Supreme Court has proposed TRCP 91a to allow a party to file a motion to dismiss a cause of action that has no basis in law or fact. *See* Tex.Sup.Ct. Order, Misc. Docket No. 12-9191 (eff. Mar. 1, 2013). The public-comment period for the proposed rule ends on February 1, 2013, and the rule is to take effect March 1, 2013. For the proposed version of the rule, see the appendix after this book's index. For the final version, go to the Supreme Court website at www.supreme.courts.state.tx.us. When the new rule takes effect, a supplement to this book—with updated rules and commentaries that reflect the changes—will be available at www.JonesMcClure.com/TRCPamendments.

TRCP 92. GENERAL DENIAL

A general denial of matters pleaded by the adverse party which are not required to be denied under oath, shall be sufficient to put the same in issue. When the defendant has pleaded a general denial, and the plaintiff shall afterward amend his pleading, such original denial shall be presumed to extend to all matters subsequently set up by the plaintiff.

When a counterclaim or cross-claim is served upon a party who has made an appearance in the action, the party so served, in the absence of a responsive pleading, shall be deemed to have pleaded a general denial of the counterclaim or cross-claim, but the party shall not be deemed to have waived any special appearance or motion to transfer venue. In all other respects the rules prescribed for pleadings of defensive matter are applicable to answers to counterclaims and cross-claims.

History of TRCP 92: Amended eff. Apr. 1, 1985, by order of Dec. 19, 1984 (683-84 S.W.2d [Tex.Cases] xxxiv): The phrase "plea of privilege" was corrected to "motion to transfer venue." Amended eff. Apr. 1, 1984, by order of Dec. 5, 1983 (661-62 S.W.2d [Tex.Cases] xxxix): Added second paragraph to clarify ambiguity in the law and to codify the law. Adopted eff. Sept. 1, 1941, by order of Oct. 29, 1940 (3 Tex.B.J. 538 [1940]). Source: TRCS arts. 2006, 2012 (repealed). See TRCP 84 for rest of art. 2006.

See *Commentaries*, "The Answer—Denying Liability," ch. 3-E, p. 227.

ANNOTATIONS

Shell Chem. Co. v. Lamb, 493 S.W.2d 742, 744 (Tex.1973). "[A] general denial puts [P] on proof of every fact essential to his case and issue is joined on all material facts asserted by [P] except those which are required to be denied under oath."

TRCP 93. CERTAIN PLEAS TO BE VERIFIED

A pleading setting up any of the following matters, unless the truth of such matters appear of record, shall be verified by affidavit.

1. That the plaintiff has not legal capacity to sue or that the defendant has not legal capacity to be sued.

2. That the plaintiff is not entitled to recover in the capacity in which he sues, or that the defendant is not liable in the capacity in which he is sued.

3. That there is another suit pending in this State between the same parties involving the same claim.

4. That there is a defect of parties, plaintiff or defendant.

5. A denial of partnership as alleged in any pleading as to any party to the suit.

6. That any party alleged in any pleading to be a corporation is not incorporated as alleged.

7. Denial of the execution by himself or by his authority of any instrument in writing, upon which any pleading is founded, in whole or in part and charged to have been executed by him or by his authority, and not alleged to be lost or destroyed. Where such instrument in writing is charged to have been executed by a person then deceased, the affidavit shall be sufficient if it states that the affiant has reason to believe and does believe that such instrument was not executed by the decedent or by his authority. In the absence of such a

---

★

---

sworn plea, the instrument shall be received in evidence as fully proved.

8. A denial of the genuineness of the indorsement or assignment of a written instrument upon which suit is brought by an indorsee or assignee and in the absence of such a sworn plea, the indorsement or assignment thereof shall be held as fully proved. The denial required by this subdivision of the rule may be made upon information and belief.

9. That a written instrument upon which a pleading is founded is without consideration, or that the consideration of the same has failed in whole or in part.

10. A denial of an account which is the foundation of the plaintiff's action, and supported by affidavit.

11. That a contract sued upon is usurious. Unless such plea is filed, no evidence of usurious interest as a defense shall be received.

12. That notice and proof of loss or claim for damage has not been given as alleged. Unless such plea is filed such notice and proof shall be presumed and no evidence to the contrary shall be admitted. A denial of such notice or such proof shall be made specifically and with particularity.

13. In the trial of any case appealed to the court from the Industrial Accident Board[1] the following, if pleaded, shall be presumed to be true as pleaded and have been done and filed in legal time and manner, unless denied by verified pleadings:

(a) Notice of injury.

(b) Claim for compensation.

(c) Award of the Board.

(d) Notice of intention not to abide by the award of the Board.

(e) Filing of suit to set aside the award.

(f) That the insurance company alleged to have been the carrier of the workers' compensation insurance at the time of the alleged injury was in fact the carrier thereof.

(g) That there was good cause for not filing claim with the Industrial Accident Board within the one year period provided by statute.

(h) Wage rate.

A denial of any of the matters set forth in subdivisions (a) or (g) of paragraph 13 may be made on information and belief.

Any such denial may be made in original or amended pleadings; but if in amended pleadings the same must be filed not less than seven days before the case proceeds to trial. In case of such denial the things so denied shall not be presumed to be true, and if essential to the case of the party alleging them, must be proved.

14. That a party plaintiff or defendant is not doing business under an assumed name or trade name as alleged.

15. In the trial of any case brought against an automobile insurance company by an insured under the provisions of an insurance policy in force providing protection against uninsured motorists, an allegation that the insured has complied with all the terms of the policy as a condition precedent to bringing the suit shall be presumed to be true unless denied by verified pleadings which may be upon information and belief.

16. Any other matter required by statute to be pleaded under oath.

1. **Editor's note:** In 1989, the name of the Industrial Accident Board was changed to the Texas Workers' Compensation Commission. Acts 1989, 71st Leg., 2d C.S., ch. 1, §17.01, eff. Apr. 1, 1990. In 2005, the Commission was abolished, and most of its functions were transferred to the newly created Division of Workers' Compensation, Texas Department of Insurance. Acts 2005, 79th Leg., ch. 265, §1.003, eff. Sept. 1, 2005.

History of TRCP 93: Amended eff. Apr. 1, 1984, by order of Dec. 5, 1983 (661-62 S.W.2d [Tex.Cases] xl): Sec. 10 was changed to conform to amended TRCP 185. Amended eff. Sept. 1, 1983, by order of June 15, 1983 (651-52 S.W.2d [Tex.Cases] xxxvi): To conform to S.B. 291 and 898, 68th Leg., 1983. Amended eff. Jan. 1, 1976, by order of July 22, 1975 (525-26 S.W.2d [Tex.Cases] xlv): Subdiv. (p) was adopted to simplify issues in uninsured motorist cases. Amended eff. Jan. 1, 1971, by order of July 21, 1970 (455-56 S.W.2d [Tex.Cases] xxxvi): Final clause of subdiv. (k) was changed to harmonize with TRCP 185 as amended; sec. (8) was added to subdiv. (n). Amended eff. Mar. 1, 1950, by order of Oct. 12, 1949 (12 Tex.B.J. 530 [1949]): A new subdiv. (o) was added and the subdiv. formerly lettered (o) was designated as (p). Amended eff. Dec. 31, 1943 June 16, 1943 (6 Tex.B.J. 341 [1943]): Section (7) and the new sentence concerning secs. (1) and (7) were added to subdiv. (n) and minor textual changes were made in this par. Amended eff. Dec. 31, 1941, by order of Sept. 20, 1941 (4 Tex.B.J. 501 [1941]): Sec. (6) was added to subdiv. (n). Amended eff. Sept. 1, 1941, by order of Mar. 31, 1941 (4 Tex.B.J. 501 [1941]): Subdivs. (m) and (n) added from TRCS art. 5546 (repealed eff. Sept. 1, 1985; now CPRC §16.071); subdiv. (o) added. Adopted eff. Sept. 1, 1941, by order of Oct. 29, 1940 (3 Tex.B.J. 538 [1940]). Source: TRCS arts. 573, 1999, 2010, 3734, 5074 (repealed), with changes: Basic statute relating to sworn pleadings, art. 2010, was combined with provisions from a number of other statutes which required sworn pleas. No change of meaning was intended by the combination. The scope of sworn denials, however, was broadened. Subdiv. (b) includes the plea that "the defendant has not legal capacity to be sued." Subdiv. (c) was extended to include a denial of defendant's liability in the capacity in which he is sued. In subdiv. (d) the term "cause of action" was replaced by the word "claim." Subdivs. (f) and (g) apply to allegations in any pleading, not merely to the petition as formerly stated in art. 2010.

See *Commentaries*, "Verified Pleas," ch. 3-E, §4, p. 228; *O'Connor's Texas Forms*, FORM 3E:10.

ANNOTATIONS

Sixth RMA Partners v. Sibley, 111 S.W.3d 46, 56 (Tex.2003). "When capacity is contested, [TRCP 93(1)] requires that a verified plea be filed unless the truth of the matter appears of record. [¶] An argument that an

⬥

opposing party does not have the capacity to participate in a suit can be waived by [the] failure to properly raise the issue in the trial court. [D] never raised [P's] failure to file an assumed name certificate ... in the trial court. Therefore, [D] waived the complaint." *See also Nootsie, Ltd. v. Williamson Cty. Appr. Dist.*, 925 S.W.2d 659, 662 (Tex.1996); *Werner v. Colwell*, 909 S.W.2d 866, 870 (Tex.1995).

Pledger v. Schoellkopf, 762 S.W.2d 145, 146 (Tex. 1988). "When capacity [to sue] is contested, Rule 93(2) requires that a verified plea be filed anytime the record does not affirmatively demonstrate the plaintiff's or defendant's right to bring suit or be sued in *whatever* capacity he is suing."

TRCP 94. AFFIRMATIVE DEFENSES

In pleading to a preceding pleading, a party shall set forth affirmatively accord and satisfaction, arbitration and award, assumption of risk, contributory negligence, discharge in bankruptcy, duress, estoppel, failure of consideration, fraud, illegality, injury by fellow servant, laches, license, payment, release, res judicata, statute of frauds, statute of limitations, waiver, and any other matter constituting an avoidance or affirmative defense. Where the suit is on an insurance contract which insures against certain general hazards, but contains other provisions limiting such general liability, the party suing on such contract shall never be required to allege that the loss was not due to a risk or cause coming within any of the exceptions specified in the contract, nor shall the insurer be allowed to raise such issue unless it shall specifically allege that the loss was due to a risk or cause coming within a particular exception to the general liability; provided that nothing herein shall be construed to change the burden of proof on such issue as it now exists.

History of TRCP 94: Amended eff. Sept. 1, 1941, by order of Mar. 31, 1941 (4 Tex.B.J. 502 [1941]): Added second sentence. Adopted eff. Sept. 1, 1941, by order of Oct. 29, 1940 (3 Tex.B.J. 538 [1940]). Source: Part of FRCP 8(c).

See *Commentaries*, "Affirmative Defenses," ch. 3-E, §5, p. 230; *O'Connor's Texas Forms*, FORM 3E:11.

ANNOTATIONS

FDIC v. Lenk, 361 S.W.3d 602, 609 (Tex.2012). "[D] failed to raise the statute of repose as an affirmative defense in the trial court, and, in this Court, [D] expressly disclaims reliance on the statutes of repose and limitations as independent grounds for summary judgment. It is settled that '[a] court cannot grant summary judgment on grounds that were not presented.' [A]s an affirmative defense, the statute of repose is only available to parties that properly raise it in the trial court."

State v. Lueck, 290 S.W.3d 876, 880 (Tex.2009). "[A]n affirmative defense ... cannot be raised by a plea to the jurisdiction."

Quantum Chem. Corp. v. Toennies, 47 S.W.3d 473, 481 (Tex.2001). "It is the defendant's burden to plead and request instructions on an affirmative defense." *See also Rio Grande Reg'l Hosp., Inc. v. Villarreal*, 329 S.W.3d 594, 621 (Tex.App.—Corpus Christi 2010, pet. argued 2-9-12).

Kinnear v. Texas Comm'n on Human Rights, 14 S.W.3d 299, 300 (Tex.2000). "Because the [Texas Commission on Human Rights] never pleaded sovereign immunity from liability as an affirmative defense to the requested attorney fees, it waived the defense, and the court of appeals erred in overturning the attorney fees award on sovereign immunity grounds." *See also Land Title Co. v. F.M. Stigler, Inc.*, 609 S.W.2d 754, 756 (Tex.1980) (ratification is affirmative defense that is waived unless affirmatively pleaded).

Texas Beef Cattle Co. v. Green, 921 S.W.2d 203, 212 (Tex.1996). "[A]n affirmative defense ... is one of confession and avoidance. An affirmative defense does not seek to defend by merely denying the plaintiff's claims, but rather seeks to establish 'an independent reason why the plaintiff should not recover.'" *See also Moncrief Oil Int'l v. OAO Gazprom*, 332 S.W.3d 1, 15 (Tex.App.—Fort Worth 2010, pet. filed 4-20-11); *In re P.D.D.*, 256 S.W.3d 834, 839 (Tex.App.—Texarkana 2008, no pet.).

Shoemake v. Fogel, Ltd., 826 S.W.2d 933, 937 (Tex. 1992). "Rule 94's requirement of pleading is not absolute. [¶] [T]he defense of [parental] immunity ... is not waived by the failure to specifically plead it if it is apparent on the face of the petition and established as a matter of law." *See also Lewkowicz v. El Paso Apparel Corp.*, 625 S.W.2d 301, 303 (Tex.1981) (same for defense of illegality).

SecurityComm Grp. v. Brocail, No. 14-09-00295-CV (Tex.App.—Houston [14th Dist.] 2010, pet. denied) (memo op.; 12-28-10). "Although, typically, affirmative defenses are pleaded by a party opposing a claim for recovery or relief, the language of Rule 94 clearly requires the pleading of any 'matter constituting an avoidance' of any other matter—claim for relief or defense—asserted in another pleading, regardless of the alignment of the parties. [I]n order for a plaintiff to rely on an af-

✦

firmative defense, or 'matter in avoidance,' to defeat a defendant's affirmative defense, the plaintiff must allege it in a petition or supplemental petition."

Texas Workers' Comp. Comm'n v. Horton, 187 S.W.3d 282, 291 (Tex.App.—Beaumont 2006, no pet.). "A claim that a statute is unconstitutional as applied to a particular plaintiff is a plea in confession or avoidance and must be pleaded under the [TRCPs]."

TRCP 95. PLEAS OF PAYMENT

When a defendant shall desire to prove payment, he shall file with his plea an account stating distinctly the nature of such payment, and the several items thereof; failing to do so, he shall not be allowed to prove the same, unless it be so plainly and particularly described in the plea as to give the plaintiff full notice of the character thereof.

History of TRCP 95: Adopted eff. Sept. 1, 1941, by order of Oct. 29, 1940 (3 Tex.B.J. 539 [1940]). Source: TRCS art. 2014 (repealed).

See *Commentaries*, "The Answer—Denying Liability," ch. 3-E, p. 227.

ANNOTATIONS

Texas Mut. Ins. v. Ledbetter, 251 S.W.3d 31, 37 (Tex.2008). "Rule 95 … governs payment as an affirmative *defense*, not payment as an affirmative *claim*."

Southwestern Fire & Cas. Co. v. Larue, 367 S.W.2d 162, 163 (Tex.1963). Under TRCPs 94 and 95, payment is "an affirmative defense on which the defendant has the burden of proof, which must be specially pleaded, and may not be shown under a general denial." *See also* ***Sage St. Assocs. v. Northdale Constr. Co.***, 863 S.W.2d 438, 443 (Tex.1993).

Imperial Lofts, Ltd. v. Imperial Woodworks, Inc., 245 S.W.3d 1, 5 (Tex.App.—Waco 2007, pet. denied). "Payment is an affirmative defense to a claim on a debt, such as a promissory note, where typically the defendant alleges that it has paid the alleged debt. But the Rule 95 cases cited by [P] concern alleged payments made by the defendant to the plaintiff, not by third parties such as insurers. We thus reject [P's] application of Rule 95 to [D's] pleading of settlement payments, credits, and offsets [paid to P by insurance companies]. Accordingly, [D] was not barred by Rule 95 from presenting evidence of those payments, credits, and offsets."

TRCP 96. NO DISCONTINUANCE

Where the defendant has filed a counterclaim seeking affirmative relief, the plaintiff shall not be permit-

ted by a discontinuance of his suit, to prejudice the right of the defendant to be heard on such counterclaim.

History of TRCP 96: Adopted eff. Sept. 1, 1941, by order of Oct. 29, 1940 (3 Tex.B.J. 539 [1940]). Source: TRCS art. 2016 (repealed).

See TRCP 162; *Commentaries*, "Effect on defendant's claims," ch. 7-F, §6.3, p. 654.

ANNOTATIONS

BHP Pet. Co. v. Millard, 800 S.W.2d 838, 840 (Tex. 1990). "The plaintiff's right to take a nonsuit is *unqualified and absolute* as long as the defendant has not made a claim for affirmative relief."

TRCP 97. COUNTERCLAIM & CROSS-CLAIM

(a) Compulsory Counterclaims. A pleading shall state as a counterclaim any claim within the jurisdiction of the court, not the subject of a pending action, which at the time of filing the pleading the pleader has against any opposing party, if it arises out of the transaction or occurrence that is the subject matter of the opposing party's claim and does not require for its adjudication the presence of third parties of whom the court cannot acquire jurisdiction; provided, however, that a judgment based upon a settlement or compromise of a claim of one party to the transaction or occurrence prior to a disposition on the merits shall not operate as a bar to the continuation or assertion of the claims of any other party to the transaction or occurrence unless the latter has consented in writing that said judgment shall operate as a bar.

(b) Permissive Counterclaims. A pleading may state as a counterclaim any claim against an opposing party whether or not arising out of the transaction or occurrence that is the subject matter of the opposing party's claim.

(c) Counterclaim Exceeding Opposing Claim. A counterclaim may or may not diminish or defeat the recovery sought by the opposing party. It may claim relief exceeding in amount or different in kind from that sought in the pleading of the opposing party, so long as the subject matter is within the jurisdiction of the court.

(d) Counterclaim Maturing or Acquired After Pleading. A claim which either matured or was acquired by the pleader after filing his pleading may be presented as a counterclaim by amended pleading.

(e) Cross-Claim Against Co-Party. A pleading may state as a cross-claim any claim by one party

———————————————————— ✦ ————————————————————

against a co-party arising out of the transaction or occurrence that is the subject matter either of the original action or of a counterclaim therein. Such cross-claim may include a claim that the party against whom it is asserted is or may be liable to the cross-claimant for all or part of a claim asserted in the action against the cross-claimant.

(f) Additional Parties. Persons other than those made parties to the original action may be made parties to a third party action, counterclaim or cross-claim in accordance with the provisions of Rules 38, 39 and 40.

(g) Tort shall not be the subject of set-off or counterclaim against a contractual demand nor a contractual demand against tort unless it arises out of or is incident to or is connected with same.

(h) Separate Trials; Separate Judgments. If the court orders separate trials as provided in Rule 174, judgment on a counterclaim or cross-claim may be rendered when the court has jurisdiction so to do, even if the claims of the opposing party have been dismissed or otherwise disposed of.

History of TRCP 97: Amended eff. Apr. 1, 1984, by order of Dec. 5, 1983 (661-62 S.W.2d [Tex.Cases] xl): Rewrote sec. (f). Amended eff. Jan. 1, 1971, by order of July 21, 1970 (455-56 S.W.2d [Tex.Cases] xxix): Added proviso concerning effect of judgment based upon settlement or compromise of claim of one party to a transaction to sec. (a). Amended eff. Sept. 1, 1941, by order of Mar. 31, 1941 (4 Tex.B.J. 503 [1941]): Proviso in sec. (f) takes the place of the last sentence of sec. (f) in original TRCP 97, and sec. (g) in original TRCP 97 was changed to (h). Adopted eff. Sept. 1, 1941, by order of Oct. 29, 1940 (3 Tex.B.J. 539 [1940]). Secs. (d), (e), (f), and (g) correspond to secs. (e), (g), (h), and (I) of FRCP 13. Limited the compulsory counterclaim to a claim within the jurisdiction of the court in TRCP 97(a) and (c). Added sentence in (f) to prevent any construction that would authorize the joinder of a liability or indemnity insurer in the original action to establish the obligation of the assured. Source: FRCP 13, with changes.

See CPRC §33.004 (responsible third parties); *Commentaries*, "Parties & Claims," ch. 2-E, p. 129; "The Answer—Denying Liability," ch. 3-E, p. 227; *O'Connor's Texas Forms*, FORMS 3E.

ANNOTATIONS

State & Cty. Mut. Fire Ins. v. Miller, 52 S.W.3d 693, 696 (Tex.2001). "[W]hen the parties are co-parties rather than opposing parties, the compulsory counterclaim rule and res judicata only act as a bar to a co-party's claim in a subsequent action if the co-parties had 'issues drawn between them' in the first action. For the purposes of res judicata, co-parties have issues drawn between them and become adverse when one co-party files a cross-action against a second co-party." *See also Getty Oil Co. v. Insurance Co. of N. Am.*, 845 S.W.2d 794, 800 (Tex.1992).

Ingersoll-Rand Co. v. Valero Energy Corp., 997 S.W.2d 203, 207 (Tex.1999). "[A] counterclaim is compulsory only if: (1) it is within the jurisdiction of the court; (2) it is not at the time of filing the answer the subject of a pending action; (3) the claim is mature and owned by the defendant at the time of filing the answer; (4) it arose out of the same transaction or occurrence that is the subject matter of the opposing party's claim; (5) it is against an opposing party in the same capacity; and (6) it does not require the presence of third parties over whom the court cannot acquire jurisdiction. A claim having all of these elements must be asserted in the initial action and cannot be asserted in later actions." *See also Wyatt v. Shaw Plumbing Co.*, 760 S.W.2d 245, 247 (Tex.1988).

Commint Tech. Servs. v. Quickel, 314 S.W.3d 646, 652 (Tex.App.—Houston [14th Dist.] 2010, no pet.). "[T]he test adopted by the Texas Supreme Court [in *Wyatt v. Shaw Plumbing Co.*, 760 S.W.2d 245 (Tex.1988), for determining whether a counterclaim is compulsory rather than permissive,] results in a different outcome than a direct application of Rule 97(a). ... Rule 97(a) provides that the claim not be 'the subject of a pending action which at the time of filing *the pleading* the pleader has against any opposing party,' while the Court stated the claim must not be 'at the time of filing *the answer* the subject of a pending action.' [Counterclaimant] argues that according to the Texas Supreme Court's wording of the compulsory counterclaim test, their claims are not compulsory because at the time they were required to file *an answer* in Collin County, an action was already pending in Harris County—the action they filed two days after being served. However, under Rule 97(a), their Harris County claims would be barred because at the time of filing their pleading in Harris County, there was already an action pending in Collin County. [¶] Following [counterclaimant's] argument, parties could easily escape the application of the compulsory counterclaim rule by following the course of action taken by [counterclaimant]. After being served with notice of the lawsuit, a party could then race to the courthouse and file a similar action against the opposing party before his answer was due in the original suit, without triggering the compulsory counterclaim rule. We conclude the Texas Supreme Court did not intend through an application of its compulsory counterclaim test, that it would create such an easy path of avoidance and thereby increase the number of lawsuits filed. Therefore, we will apply the language from Rule 97(a), regarding this component of the Supreme Court's test."

⸺ ★ ⸺

Musgrave v. Owen, 67 S.W.3d 513, 519 (Tex. App.—Texarkana 2002, no pet.). "[W]here a defendant [interposes] a claim as a counterclaim and a valid and final judgment is rendered against him on the counterclaim, the defendant becomes a counter-defendant for res judicata purposes and is required to assert all claims against the plaintiff arising from the subject matter of the original claim."

TRCP 98. SUPPLEMENTAL ANSWERS

The defendant's supplemental answers may contain special exceptions, general denial, and the allegations of new matter not before alleged by him, in reply to that which has been alleged by the plaintiff.

History of TRCP 98: Amended eff. Sept. 1, 1941, by order of Mar. 31, 1941 (4 Tex.B.J. 504 [1941]). Adopted eff. Sept. 1, 1941, by order of Oct. 29, 1940 (3 Tex.B.J. 539 [1940]). Source: Tex. Rules for Dist. & Cty. Cts. 8.

ANNOTATIONS

State v. Texas Mun. Power Agency, 565 S.W.2d 258, 277 (Tex.App.—Houston [1st Dist.] 1978, writ dism'd). "A supplemental answer is properly filed in response to any pleading of the plaintiff, regardless of whether it is an amended petition or a supplemental petition."

SECTION 5. CITATION

⑫ ### TRCP 99. ISSUANCE & FORM OF CITATION

a. **Issuance.** Upon the filing of the petition, the clerk, when requested, shall forthwith issue a citation and deliver the citation as directed by the requesting party. The party requesting citation shall be responsible for obtaining service of the citation and a copy of the petition. Upon request, separate or additional citations shall be issued by the clerk. The clerk must retain a copy of the citation in the court's file.

b. **Form.** The citation shall (1) be styled "The State of Texas," (2) be signed by the clerk under seal of court, (3) contain name and location of the court, (4) show date of filing of the petition, (5) show date of issuance of citation, (6) show file number, (7) show names of parties, (8) be directed to the defendant, (9) show the name and address of attorney for plaintiff, otherwise the address of plaintiff, (10) contain the time within which these rules require the defendant to file a written answer with the clerk who issued citation, (11) contain address of the clerk, and (12) shall notify the defendant that in case of failure of defendant to file an answer, judgment by default may be rendered for the relief demanded in the petition. The citation shall direct the defendant to file a written answer to the plaintiff's petition on or before 10:00 a.m. on the Monday next after the expiration of twenty days after the date of service thereof. The requirement of subsections 10 and 12 of this section shall be in the form set forth in section c of this rule.

c. **Notice.** The citation shall include the following notice to the defendant: "You have been sued. You may employ an attorney. If you or your attorney do not file a written answer with the clerk who issued this citation by 10:00 a.m. on the Monday next following the expiration of twenty days after you were served this citation and petition, a default judgment may be taken against you."

d. **Copies.** The party filing any pleading upon which citation is to be issued and served shall furnish the clerk with a sufficient number of copies thereof for use in serving the parties to be served, and when copies are so furnished the clerk shall make no charge for the copies.

History of TRCP 99: Amended eff. Jan. 1, 2012, by order of Dec. 12, 2011 (Tex.Sup.Ct. Order, Misc. Docket No. 11-9250): Added last sentence in (a). Amended eff. Jan. 1, 1988, by order of July 15, 1987 (733-34 S.W.2d [Tex.Cases] xlii). Amended eff. Feb. 1, 1946, by order of Oct. 10, 1945 (8 Tex.B.J. 532 [1945]). Adopted eff. Sept. 1, 1941, by order of Oct. 29, 1940 (3 Tex.B.J. 540 [1940]). Source: TRCS art. 2021 (repealed).

See *Commentaries*, "Serving the Defendant with Suit," ch. 2-H, p. 157; "Default Judgment," ch. 7-A, p. 587; *O'Connor's Texas Forms*, FORMS 2H.

ANNOTATIONS

Primate Constr., Inc. v. Silver, 884 S.W.2d 151, 153 (Tex.1994). "It is the responsibility of the one requesting service, not the process server, to see that service is properly accomplished. This responsibility extends to seeing that service is properly reflected in the record." *See also In re Buggs*, 166 S.W.3d 506, 508 (Tex.App.—Texarkana 2005, orig. proceeding).

Williams v. Williams, 150 S.W.3d 436, 445 (Tex. App.—Austin 2004, pet. denied). See annotation under TRCP 15, p. 855.

Roberts v. Padre Island Brewing Co., 28 S.W.3d 618, 621-22 (Tex.App.—Corpus Christi 2000, pet. denied). "Reliance on the process server does not constitute due diligence in attempting service of process. A reasonable person ... would have employed an alternate process server, a constable, or would have attempted service through other alternative court approved methods such as service through a court appointed third party. ... Although the existence of diligence is usually a question of fact, a lack of diligence

———————— ✦ ————————

exists as a matter of law because it is clear that [P] did not exhaust all of the alternatives available to achieve proper service." *See also* **Holmes v. Texas Mut. Ins.**, 335 S.W.3d 738, 742 (Tex.App.—El Paso 2011, pet. abated 4-8-11); **Boyattia v. Hinojosa**, 18 S.W.3d 729, 734 (Tex.App.—Dallas 2000, pet. denied).

TRCP 100 TO 102. REPEALED

Repealed eff. Jan. 1, 1988, by order of July 15, 1987 (733-34 S.W.2d [Tex.Cases] xliii).

TRCP 103. WHO MAY SERVE

Process—including citation and other notices, writs, orders, and other papers issued by the court—may be served anywhere by (1) any sheriff or constable or other person authorized by law, (2) any person authorized by law or by written order of the court who is not less than eighteen years of age, or (3) any person certified under order of the Supreme Court. Service by registered or certified mail and citation by publication must, if requested, be made by the clerk of the court in which the case is pending. But no person who is a party to or interested in the outcome of a suit may serve any process in that suit, and, unless otherwise authorized by a written court order, only a sheriff or constable may serve a citation in an action of forcible entry and detainer, a writ that requires the actual taking of possession of a person, property or thing, or process requiring that an enforcement action be physically enforced by the person delivering the process. The order authorizing a person to serve process may be made without written motion and no fee may be imposed for issuance of such order.

Comment to 2005 change: The rule is amended to include among the persons authorized to effect service those who meet certification requirements promulgated by the Supreme Court and to prohibit private individuals from serving certain types of process unless, in rare circumstances, a court authorizes an individual to do so.

History of TRCP 103: Amended eff. July 1, 2005, by order of June 29, 2005 (173-74 S.W.3d [Tex.Cases] xvii). Amended eff. Jan. 1, 1988, by order of July 15, 1987 (733-34 S.W.2d [Tex.Cases] xliii): Amendment makes clear that courts may authorize persons other than sheriffs or constables to serve citation. Further, sheriffs or constables are not restricted to service in their county. Added last sentence to avoid the necessity of motions and fees. Amended eff. Jan. 1, 1981, by order of June 10, 1980 (599-600 S.W.2d [Tex.Cases] xxxviii): Rule amended to permit service by mail by an officer of the county in which the case is pending or the party is found, and also service by the court clerk. Adopted eff. Sept. 1, 1941, by order of Oct. 29, 1940 (3 Tex.B.J. 540 [1940]). Source: New rule.

See *Commentaries*, "Serving the Defendant with Suit," ch. 2-H, p. 157; "Default Judgment," ch. 7-A, p. 587.

ANNOTATIONS

Mayfield v. Dean Witter Fin. Servs., 894 S.W.2d 502, 505 (Tex.App.—Austin 1995, writ denied). "[S]ervice of process by a private process server in Texas …

requires authorization by law or a written order of the court. *At 506:* The parties do not dispute that pursuant to [TRCP] 103, a standing court order authorized … the private process server[ ] to serve citation and other notices in any lawsuit filed in the district court of Travis County in which he was not an interested party."

TRCP 104. REPEALED

Repealed eff. Jan. 1, 1988, by order of July 15, 1987 (733-34 S.W.2d [Tex.Cases] xliv): TRCP 104 was rendered unnecessary because of amendments to TRCP 103.

TRCP 105. DUTY OF OFFICER OR PERSON RECEIVING

The officer or authorized person to whom process is delivered shall endorse thereon the day and hour on which he received it, and shall execute and return the same without delay.

History of TRCP 105: Amended eff. Jan. 1, 1988, by order of July 15, 1987 (733-34 S.W.2d [Tex.Cases] xliv). Amended eff. Jan. 1, 1978, by order of July 11, 1977 (553-54 S.W.2d [Tex.Cases] xliv): Corrected spelling of word "indorse" to "endorse." Adopted eff. Sept. 1, 1941, by order of Oct. 29, 1940 (3 Tex.B.J. 540 [1940]). Source: TRCS art. 2025 (repealed).

See *Commentaries*, "Serving the Defendant with Suit," ch. 2-H, p. 157; "Default Judgment," ch. 7-A, p. 587.

ANNOTATIONS

Insurance Co. of Pa. v. Lejeune, 297 S.W.3d 254, 256 (Tex.2009). "Strict compliance with the rules governing service of citation is mandatory if a default judgment is to withstand an attack on appeal. Failure to comply with these rules constitutes error on the face of the record. Here, although [P] served [D] by certified mail, the record shows that the return of citation lacks the required notation showing the hour of receipt of citation. [P's] default judgment, therefore, cannot stand." *See also* **Business Staffing, Inc. v. Gonzalez**, 331 S.W.3d 791, 792 (Tex.App.—Eastland 2010, no pet.).

TRCP 106. METHOD OF SERVICE

(a) Unless the citation or an order of the court otherwise directs, the citation shall be served by any person authorized by Rule 103 by

(1) delivering to the defendant, in person, a true copy of the citation with the date of delivery endorsed thereon with a copy of the petition attached thereto, or

(2) mailing to the defendant by registered or certified mail, return receipt requested, a true copy of the citation with a copy of the petition attached thereto.

(b) Upon motion supported by affidavit stating the location of the defendant's usual place of business or usual place of abode or other place where the defendant can probably be found and stating specifically the facts showing that service has been attempted under either (a)(1) or (a)(2) at the location named in such affidavit but has not been successful, the court may authorize service

⚸ **(1)** by leaving a true copy of the citation, with a copy of the petition attached, with anyone over sixteen years of age at the location specified in such affidavit, or

(2) in any other manner that the affidavit or other evidence before the court shows will be reasonably effective to give the defendant notice of the suit.

History of TRCP 106: Amended eff. Sept. 1, 1990, by order of Apr. 24, 1990 (785-86 S.W.2d [Tex.Cases] xlvii). Subsec. (b) changed by deleting "or" and substituting "of" before "abode or other." Amended eff. Jan. 1, 1988, by order of July 15, 1987 (733-34 S.W.2d [Tex.Cases] xliv): Conforms to amended TRCP 103. Amended eff. Jan. 1, 1981, by order of June 10, 1980 (599-600 S.W.2d [Tex. Cases] xxxviii): Rule reorganized to clarify meaning. Alternate methods of service are authorized if either (a)(1) or (a)(2) are tried without success. Both methods are not required. Amended eff. Jan. 1, 1978, by order of July 11, 1977 (553-54 S.W.2d [Tex.Cases] xliv): Rewrote rule; added subsecs. (b) and (e). Amended eff. Jan. 1, 1976, by order of July 22, 1975 (525-26 S.W.2d [Tex.Cases] xlv): Service "by registered or certified mail" is authorized in certain instances. Amended eff. Dec. 31, 1947, by orders of Aug. 18, 1947 (10 Tex.B.J. 391 [1947]). Adopted eff. Sept. 1, 1941, by order of Oct. 29, 1940 (3 Tex.B.J. 540 [1940]). Source: TRCS art. 2026 (repealed).

See *Commentaries*, "Serving the Defendant with Suit," ch. 2-H, p. 157; "Default Judgment," ch. 7-A, p. 587.

ANNOTATIONS

State Farm Fire & Cas. Co. v. Costley, 868 S.W.2d 298, 298-99 (Tex.1993). "Under Rule 106(b) a court may authorize substituted service only after a plaintiff has unsuccessfully tried to effect personal service or service by certified mail, return receipt requested, as required by Rule 106(a). ... Thus, to require proof of actual notice upon substituted service would frustrate Rule 106(b)'s purpose of providing alternate methods [of service]."

Wilson v. Dunn, 800 S.W.2d 833, 836 (Tex.1990). "[S]ubstitute service is not authorized under Rule 106(b) without an affidavit which meets the requirements of the rule demonstrating the necessity for other than personal service."

Uvalde Country Club v. Martin Linen Sup. Co., 690 S.W.2d 884, 885 (Tex.1985). "There are no presumptions in favor of valid issuance, service, and return of citation in the face of a writ of error [now a restricted appeal] attack on a default judgment. Moreover, failure to affirmatively show strict compliance with the [TRCPs] renders the attempted service of process invalid and of no effect."

In re M.C.B., ___ S.W.3d ___ (Tex.App.—Dallas 2012, n.p.h.) (No. 05-10-00158-CV; 2-28-12). "When a trial court orders substituted service under rule 106,

the only authority for the substituted service is the order itself. Therefore, the requirements set forth in the order must be strictly followed. Any deviation from the trial court's order authorizing substituted service necessitates a reversal of the default judgment based on service. A default judgment is improper against a defendant who has not been served in strict compliance with law, even if he has actual knowledge of the lawsuit." *See also Steinke v. Mann*, 276 S.W.3d 608, 609-10 (Tex.App.—Waco 2008, no pet.) (court must expressly authorize service in accordance with either Rule 106(b)(1) or (b)(2)).

James v. Commission for Lawyer Discipline, 310 S.W.3d 586, 591 (Tex.App.—Dallas 2010, no pet.). "Rule 106 does not require that personal service be attempted at multiple locations before the trial court may authorize substituted service...."

Coronado v. Norman, 111 S.W.3d 838, 842 (Tex. App.—Eastland 2003, pet. denied). The process server's "affidavit does not contain sufficient facts to satisfy Rule 106(b). While the ... inclusion of the dates and times of attempted service [is not specifically required,] the specific dates and times of attempted service are important to establish sufficient facts to uphold a default judgment under Rule 106(b). Every attempt at personal service in this case may have been while [D] was at work. When told that [D] 'was not there,' the process server apparently did not try to find out where [D] could be located or when he would return."

⑫ TRCP 107. RETURN OF SERVICE

(a) The officer or authorized person executing the citation must complete a return of service. The return may, but need not, be endorsed on or attached to the citation.

(b) The return, together with any document to which it is attached, must include the following information:

(1) the cause number and case name;

(2) the court in which the case is filed;

(3) a description of what was served;

(4) the date and time the process was received for service;

(5) the person or entity served;

(6) the address served;

(7) the date of service or attempted service;

(8) the manner of delivery of service or attempted service;

⎯⎯⎯⎯⎯⎯⎯⎯⎯⎯⎯ ✦ ⎯⎯⎯⎯⎯⎯⎯⎯⎯⎯⎯

(9) the name of the person who served or attempted to serve the process;

(10) if the person named in (9) is a process server certified under order of the Supreme Court, his or her identification number and the expiration date of his or her certification; and

(11) any other information required by rule or law.

(c) When the citation was served by registered or certified mail as authorized by Rule 106, the return by the officer or authorized person must also contain the return receipt with the addressee's signature.

(d) When the officer or authorized person has not served the citation, the return shall show the diligence used by the officer or authorized person to execute the same and the cause of failure to execute it, and where the defendant is to be found, if ascertainable.

(e) The officer or authorized person who serves or attempts to serve a citation must sign the return. If the return is signed by a person other than a sheriff, constable, or the clerk of the court, the return must either be verified or be signed under penalty of perjury. A return signed under penalty of perjury must contain the statement below in substantially the following form:

"My name is _____ (First) _____ (Middle) _____ (Last), my date of birth is _____, and my address is _____, (Street) _____, (City) _____, (State) _____ (Zip Code), and _____ (Country). I declare under penalty of perjury that the foregoing is true and correct.

Executed in _____ County, State of _____, on the _____ day of _____ (Month), _____ (Year).

⎯⎯⎯⎯⎯⎯⎯⎯⎯⎯

Declarant"

(f) Where citation is executed by an alternative method as authorized by Rule 106, proof of service shall be made in the manner ordered by the court.

(g) The return and any document to which it is attached must be filed with the court and may be filed electronically or by facsimile, if those methods of filing are available.

(h) No default judgment shall be granted in any cause until proof of service as provided by this rule or by Rules 108 or 108a, or as ordered by the court in the event citation is executed by an alternative method under Rule 106, shall have been on file with the clerk of the court ten days, exclusive of the day of filing and the day of judgment.

History of TRCP 107: Amended eff. Jan. 1, 2012, by order of Dec. 12, 2011 (Tex.Sup.Ct. Order, Misc. Docket No. 11-9250). Amended eff. Sept. 1, 1990, by order of Apr. 24, 1990 (785-86 S.W.2d [Tex.Cases] xlviii): Added references to TRCPs 108 and 108a in last par.; states more directly that default judgment can be obtained when defendant has been served with process in a foreign country pursuant to those provisions. Amended eff. Jan. 1, 1988, by order of July 15, 1987 (733-34 S.W.2d [Tex.Cases] xlv): Amended to conform to changes in TRCP 103. Amended eff. Jan. 1, 1981, by order of June 10, 1980 (599-600 S.W.2d [Tex.Cases] xxxix): Changed references to TRCP 106. Amended eff. Jan. 1, 1978, by order of July 11, 1977 (553-54 S.W.2d [Tex.Cases] xlv): Changed to provide manner of return when service by mail or by an alternative method. Adopted eff. Sept. 1, 1941, by order of Oct. 29, 1940 (3 Tex.B.J. 540 [1940]). Source: TRCS arts. 2034, 2036 (repealed).

See TRCP 16; *Commentaries*, "Proof of Service – The Return," ch. 2-H, §9, p. 168; "Default Judgment," ch. 7-A, p. 587; *O'Connor's Texas Forms*, FORMS 2H:4-6.

ANNOTATIONS

Campus Invs. v. Cullever, 144 S.W.3d 464, 466 (Tex.2004). "When substituted service on a statutory agent is allowed, the designee is not an agent for *serving* but for *receiving* process on the defendant's behalf. A certificate … from the Secretary of State *conclusively* establishes that process was served. As the purpose of Rule 107 is to establish whether there has been proper citation and service, the Secretary's certificate fulfills that purpose."

Primate Constr., Inc. v. Silver, 884 S.W.2d 151, 152-53 (Tex.1994). "The return of service is not a trivial, formulaic document. It has long been considered prima facie evidence of the facts recited therein. [¶] The officer's return does not cease to be prima facie evidence of the facts of service simply because the facts are recited in a form rather than filled in by the officer. … If the facts as recited in the sheriff's return, pre-printed or otherwise, are incorrect and do not show proper service, the one requesting service must amend the return prior to judgment."

James v. Commission for Lawyer Discipline, 310 S.W.3d 586, 591 (Tex.App.—Dallas 2010, no pet.). "The trial court's order for substituted service did not prescribe a manner for the proof of service, and [D] argues that omission rendered the order for substituted service void. We disagree. '[I]n the absence of a specification in the trial court's [TRCP] 106 order of a *different* manner of proving service, proof of service in the normal manner authorized by [TRCP] 107 is sufficient.'"

Silver B & Laviolette, LLC v. GH Contracting, Inc., No. 03-10-00091-CV (Tex.App.—Austin 2010, no pet.) (memo op.; 10-12-10). "If any of the requirements of Rule 107 are not met, the return is fatally defective and will not support a default judgment under direct at-

---

✦

---

tack. Strict compliance, however, does not require obei-sance to the minutest detail. As long as the record as a whole shows that the citation was served on the defen-dant, service of process will not be invalidated." (Inter-nal quotes omitted.)

Myan Mgmt. Grp. v. Adam Sparks Family Revo-cable Trust, 292 S.W.3d 750, 753-54 (Tex.App.—Dallas 2009, no pet.). "Service is invalid if the name on the re-turn alters the identity of the defendant, but a minor change in the name does not render the return defec-tive. [¶] Examples of name differences held not to in-validate service include the removal of a middle initial on the return, the omission of the corporate designa-tion 'Inc.,' the lack of an accent mark on a corporate name, and the substitution of '@' for 'at.' [¶] [Here, r]emoving periods from 'L.L.C.' is a variation as minor as the lack of an accent mark on a corporate name.... Similarly, dropping 'Group, L.L.C.' from the entity name is like dropping 'Inc.' from the entity name.... Neither omission suggests that a different entity was served than the one listed in the petition."

Redwood Grp. v. Louiseau, 113 S.W.3d 866, 869 (Tex.App.—Austin 2003, no pet.). "While a return is prima facie evidence of the facts recited *therein*, this does not mean that the return is prima facie evidence of anything about which it is silent. For example, the two returns in question here contain nothing about the contents of the two lost citations; we cannot presume they conformed to the requirements of [TRCP 99] specifying the contents of a valid citation."

All Commercial Floors, Inc. v. Barton & Rasor, 97 S.W.3d 723, 727 (Tex.App.—Fort Worth 2003, no pet.). "[A] corporation is not a person capable of ac-cepting process, and it must be served through its agents. Therefore, because the record shows on its face that the return was not signed by the addressee or reg-istered agent and [D] is not capable of receiving ser-vice, [P] has failed to strictly comply with Rule 107."

Union Pac. Corp. v. Legg, 49 S.W.3d 72, 78 (Tex. App.—Austin 2001, no pet.). "The clerk's return of the citation directed to [D] and the accompanying certi-fied-mail receipt do not bear a file mark or other indica-tion that they were in fact filed with the clerk on a par-ticular day, or that they were, indeed, filed at all. Consequently, they do not show they were 'on file' for the requisite ten days before default judgment was granted. We hold this violates the strict-compliance re-quirement."

⑫ ## TRCP 108. SERVICE IN ANOTHER STATE

Where the defendant is absent from the State, or is a nonresident of the State, the form of notice to such defendant of the institution of the suit shall be the same as prescribed for citation to a resident defendant; and such notice may be served by any disinterested per-son who is not less than eighteen years of age, in the same manner as provided in Rule 106 hereof. The re-turn of service in such cases shall be completed in ac-cordance with Rule 107. A defendant served with such notice shall be required to appear and answer in the same manner and time and under the same penalties as if he had been personally served with a citation within this State to the full extent that he may be re-quired to appear and answer under the Constitution of the United States in an action either in rem or in per-sonam.

History of TRCP 108: Amended eff. Jan. 1, 2012, by order of Dec. 12, 2011 (Tex.Sup.Ct. Order, Misc. Docket No. 11-9250). Amended eff. Jan. 1, 1976, by or-der of July 22, 1975 (525-26 S.W.2d [Tex.Cases] xlv): Added words after "State" in last sentence to permit acquisition of in personam jurisdiction to the consti-tutional limits. Adopted eff. Sept. 1, 1941, by order of Oct. 29, 1940 (3 Tex.B.J. 541 [1940]). Source: TRCS arts. 2037, 2038 (repealed).

See *Commentaries*, "Serving the Defendant with Suit," ch. 2-H, p. 157.

ANNOTATIONS

Paramount Pipe & Sup. Co. v. Muhr, 749 S.W.2d 491, 495-96 (Tex.1988). TRCP 108 "is a valid procedural alternative to service under the long-arm statute. ... So long as the allegations confronting [D] were sufficient to satisfy due process requirements, the trial court had jurisdiction to render judgment by default against him. The only question ... is whether the jurisdictional alle-gations in the petitions were sufficient, under the [U.S.] Constitution ..., to require [D] to answer."

World Distribs., Inc. v. Knox, 968 S.W.2d 474, 479 (Tex.App.—El Paso 1998, no pet.). "We have ... found no authority for the Secretary of State to serve process. [N]umerous statutes require the Secretary of State to act as agent for service, but no statute authorizes him to serve process. [¶] We fail to perceive how the Secre-tary of State may act as [D's] agent for service and at the same time still qualify as a 'disinterested person.'"

TRCP 108a. SERVICE OF PROCESS IN FOREIGN COUNTRIES

(1) Manner. Service of process may be effected upon a party in a foreign country if service of the cita-tion and petition is made: (a) in the manner prescribed by the law of the foreign country for service in that country in an action in any of its courts of general juris-

---

✦

---

diction; or (b) as directed by the foreign authority in response to a letter rogatory or a letter of request; or (c) in the manner provided by Rule 106; or (d) pursuant to the terms and provisions of any applicable treaty or convention; or (e) by diplomatic or consular officials when authorized by the United States Department of State; or (f) by any other means directed by the court that is not prohibited by the law of the country where service is to be made. The method for service of process in a foreign country must be reasonably calculated, under all of the circumstances, to give actual notice of the proceedings to the defendant in time to answer and defend. A defendant served with process under this rule shall be required to appear and answer in the same manner and time and under the same penalties as if he had been personally served with citation within this state to the full extent that he may be required to appear and answer under the Constitution of the United States or under any applicable convention or treaty in an action either in rem or in personam.

(2) Return. Proof of service may be made as prescribed by the law of the foreign country, by order of the court, by Rule 107, or by a method provided in any applicable treaty or convention.

History of TRCP 108a: Adopted eff. Apr. 1, 1984, by order of Dec. 5, 1983 (661-62 S.W.2d [Tex.Cases] xli). Source: New rule.

See CPRC §§17.044, 17.045; *Commentaries*, "Service Outside the United States," ch. 2-H, §11, p. 172.

ANNOTATIONS

Commission of Contracts v. Arriba, Ltd., 882 S.W.2d 576, 584 (Tex.App.—Houston [1st Dist.] 1994, no writ). "[Ps] argue that service on a resident of a foreign country under the long-arm statute is improper, and that a resident of a foreign country can only be served according to the methods of service prescribed in [TRCP] 108a. *At 585:* We find a party in a foreign country may be served under the long-arm statute."

TRCP 109. CITATION BY PUBLICATION

When a party to a suit, his agent or attorney, shall make oath that the residence of any party defendant is unknown to affiant, and to such party when the affidavit is made by his agent or attorney, or that such defendant is a transient person, and that after due diligence such party and the affiant have been unable to locate the whereabouts of such defendant, or that such defendant is absent from or is a nonresident of the State, and that the party applying for the citation has attempted to obtain personal service of nonresident notice as provided for in Rule 108, but has been unable to do so, the clerk shall issue citation for such defendant for service by publication. In such cases it shall be the duty of the court trying the case to inquire into the sufficiency of the diligence exercised in attempting to ascertain the residence or whereabouts of the defendant or to obtain service of nonresident notice, as the case may be, before granting any judgment on such service.

History of TRCP 109: Amended eff. Apr. 1, 1984, by order of Dec. 5, 1983 (661-62 S.W.2d [Tex.Cases] xli): Deleted last sentence of former rule. Amended eff. Jan. 1, 1976, by order of July 22, 1975 (525-26 S.W.2d [Tex.Cases] xlvi): Deleted the word "continental" before "United States" in last sentence. Amended eff. Feb. 1, 1946, by order of Oct. 10, 1945 (8 Tex.B.J. 532 [1945]). Adopted eff. Sept. 1, 1941, by order of Oct. 29, 1940 (3 Tex.B.J. 541 [1940]). Source: TRCS art. 2039 (repealed), first sentence.

See *Commentaries*, "Serving the Defendant with Suit," ch. 2-H, p. 157; "Default Judgment," ch. 7-A, p. 587; "MNT After Service by Publication," ch. 10-B, §10, p. 799.

ANNOTATIONS

Wood v. Brown, 819 S.W.2d 799, 800 (Tex.1991). "In his affidavit, [P's] counsel stated that [D] had moved from his last known address in Oklahoma and that neighbors thought that [D] had moved to Florida. The affidavit, however, does not state that [D's] residence was unknown to [P's] attorney, that [D] was a transient person, that [D] was absent from Texas or that [D] did not reside in Texas. Therefore, the affidavit ... did not meet any of the requirements for service by publication under Rule 109."

TRCP 109a. OTHER SUBSTITUTED SERVICE

Whenever citation by publication is authorized, the court may, on motion, prescribe a different method of substituted service, if the court finds, and so recites in its order, that the method so prescribed would be as likely as publication to give defendant actual notice. When such method of substituted service is authorized, the return of the officer executing the citation shall state particularly the manner in which service is accomplished, and shall attach any return receipt, returned mail, or other evidence showing the result of such service. Failure of defendant to respond to such citation shall not render the service invalid. When such substituted service has been obtained and the defendant has not appeared, the provisions of Rules 244 and 329 shall apply as if citation had been served by publication.

History of TRCP 109a: Adopted eff. Jan. 1, 1976, by order of July 22, 1975 (525-26 S.W.2d [Tex.Cases] xlvi). Source: New rule.

See *Commentaries*, "Serving the Defendant with Suit," ch. 2-H, p. 157; *O'Connor's Texas Forms*, FORMS 2H:4-6.

TRCP 109a

───────────────── ✦ ─────────────────

TRCP 110. EFFECT OF RULES ON OTHER STATUTES

Where by statute or these rules citation by publication is authorized and the statute or rules do not specify the requisites of such citation or the method of service thereof, or where they direct that such citation be issued or served as in other civil actions, the provisions of these rules shall govern. Where, however, the statute authorizing citation by publication provides expressly for requisites of such citation or service thereof, or both, differing from the provisions of Rules 114, 115, and 116, these rules shall not govern, but the special statutory procedure shall continue in force; provided, however, that Rule 117a shall control with respect to citation in tax suits.

History of TRCP 110: Amended eff. Dec. 31, 1947, by order of Aug. 18, 1947 (10 Tex.B.J. 391 [1947]). Adopted eff. Sept. 1, 1941, by order of Oct. 29, 1940 (3 Tex.B.J. 541 [1940]). Source: New rule.

TRCP 111. CITATION BY PUBLICATION IN ACTION AGAINST UNKNOWN HEIRS OR STOCKHOLDERS OF DEFUNCT CORPORATIONS

If the plaintiff, his agent, or attorney, shall make oath that the names of the heirs or stockholders against whom an action is authorized by Section 17.004, Civil Practice and Remedies Code, are unknown to the affiant, the clerk shall issue a citation for service by publication. Such citation shall be addressed to the defendants by a concise description of their classification, as "the Unknown Heirs of A.B., deceased," or "Unknown Stockholders of _____ Corporation," as the case may be, and shall contain the other requisites prescribed in Rules 114 and 115 and shall be served as provided by Rule 116.

History of TRCP 111: Amended eff. Jan. 1, 1988, by order of July 15, 1987 (733-34 S.W.2d [Tex.Cases] xlv). Adopted eff. Sept. 1, 1941, by order of Oct. 29, 1940 (3 Tex.B.J. 541 [1940]). Source: TRCS art. 2040 (repealed).

See *Commentaries*, "Serving the Defendant with Suit," ch. 2-H, p. 157; "MNT After Service by Publication," ch. 10-B, §10, p. 799.

TRCP 112. PARTIES TO ACTIONS AGAINST UNKNOWN OWNERS OR CLAIMANTS OF INTEREST IN LAND

In suits authorized by Section 17.005, Civil Practice and Remedies Code, all persons claiming under such conveyance whose names are known to plaintiff shall be made parties by name and cited to appear, in the manner now provided by law as in other suits; all other persons claiming any interest in such land under such conveyance may be made parties to the suit and cited by publication under the designation "all persons claiming any title or interest in land under deed heretofore given to _____ of _____ as grantee" (inserting in the blanks the name and residence of grantee as given in such conveyance). It shall be permissible to join in one suit all persons claiming under two or more conveyances affecting title to the same tract of land.

History of TRCP 112: Amended eff. Jan. 1, 1988, by order of July 15, 1987 (733-34 S.W.2d [Tex.Cases] xlvi). Adopted eff. Sept. 1, 1941, by order of Oct. 29, 1940 (3 Tex.B.J. 542 [1940]). Source: TRCS art. 2040 (repealed).

See CPRC §17.005; TRCP 113; *Commentaries*, "Serving the Defendant with Suit," ch. 2-H, p. 157; "MNT After Service by Publication," ch. 10-B, §10, p. 799.

TRCP 113. CITATION BY PUBLICATION IN ACTIONS AGAINST UNKNOWN OWNERS OR CLAIMANTS OF INTEREST IN LAND

In suits authorized by Section 17.005, Civil Practice and Remedies Code, plaintiff, his agent or attorney shall make and file with the clerk of the court an affidavit, stating

(a) the name of the grantee as set out in the conveyance constituting source of title of defendants, and

(b) stating that affiant does not know the names of any persons claiming title or interest under such conveyance other than as stated in plaintiff's petition and

(c) if the conveyance is to a company or association name as grantee, further stating whether grantee is incorporated or unincorporated, if such fact is known, and if such fact is unknown, so stating.

Said clerk shall thereupon issue a citation for service upon all persons claiming any title or interest in such land under such conveyance. The citation in such cases shall contain the requisites and be served in the manner provided by Rules 114, 115 and 116.

History of TRCP 113: Amended eff. Sept. 1, 1990, by order of Apr. 24, 1990 (785-86 S.W.2d [Tex.Cases] xlviii): Changed letters "T.R.C.P." in last sentence to "Rules." Amended eff. Jan. 1, 1988, by order of July 15, 1987 (733-34 S.W.2d [Tex.Cases] xlvi): Changed letters "T.R.S." in last sentence to "T.R.C.P." Amended eff. Jan. 1, 1955, by order of July 20, 1954 (17 Tex.B.J. 567 [1954]). Adopted eff. Sept. 1, 1941, by order of Oct. 29, 1940 (3 Tex.B.J. 542 [1940]). Source: TRCS art. 2041a (repealed).

See CPRC §17.005; TRCP 112; *Commentaries*, "Serving the Defendant with Suit," ch. 2-H, p. 157; "MNT After Service by Publication," ch. 10-B, §10, p. 799.

ANNOTATIONS

Quarles v. Champion Int'l, 760 S.W.2d 792, 794 (Tex.App.—Beaumont 1988, writ denied). Service of citation by publication on a known party is improper, and "this notice requirement to a known party is of due process dimension."

TRCP 114. CITATION BY PUBLICATION; REQUISITES

Where citation by publication is authorized by these rules, the citation shall contain the requisites prescribed by Rules 15 and 99, in so far as they are not inconsistent herewith, provided that no copy of the plaintiff's petition shall accompany this citation, and the citation shall be styled "The State of Texas" and shall be directed to the defendant or defendants by name, if their names are known, or to the defendant or defendants as designated in the petition, if unknown, or such other classification as may be fixed by any statute or by these rules. Where there are two or more defendants or classes of defendants to be served by publication, the citation may be directed to all of them by name and classification, so that service may be completed by publication of the one citation for the required number of times. The citation shall contain the names of the parties, a brief statement of the nature of the suit (which need not contain the details and particulars of the claim) a description of any property involved and of the interest of the named or unknown defendant or defendants, and, where the suit involves land, the requisites of Rule 115. If issued from the district or county court, the citation shall command such parties to appear and answer at or before 10 o'clock a.m. of the first Monday after the expiration of 42 days from the date of issuance thereof, specifying the day of the week, the day of the month, and the time of day the defendant is required to answer. If issued from the justice of the peace court, such citation shall command such parties to appear and answer on or before the first day of the first term of court which convenes after the expiration of 42 days from the date of issue thereof, specifying the day of the week, and the day of the month, that such term will meet.

History of TRCP 114: Amended eff. Jan. 1, 1988, by order of July 15, 1987 (733-34 S.W.2d [Tex.Cases] xlvi). Amended eff. Dec. 31, 1941, by order of Sept. 20, 1941 (6 Tex.B.J. 506 [1941]). Adopted eff. Sept. 1, 1941, by order of Oct. 29, 1940 (3 Tex.B.J. 543 [1940]). Source: TRCS arts. 2041, 2092(6) (repealed).

TRCP 115. FORM OF PUBLISHED CITATION IN ACTIONS INVOLVING LAND

In citations by publication involving land, it shall be sufficient in making the brief statement of the claim in such citation to state the kind of suit, the number of acres of land involved in the suit, or the number of the lot and block, or any other plat description that may be

of record if the land is situated in a city or town, the survey on which and the county in which the land is situated, and any special pleas which are relied upon in such suit.

History of TRCP 115: Adopted eff. Sept. 1, 1941, by order of Oct. 29, 1940 (3 Tex.B.J. 543 [1940]). Source: TRCS art. 2041 (repealed).

TRCP 116. SERVICE OF CITATION BY PUBLICATION

The citation, when issued, shall be served by the sheriff or any constable of any county of the State of Texas or by the clerk of the court in which the case is pending, by having the same published once each week for four (4) consecutive weeks, the first publication to be at least twenty-eight (28) days before the return day of the citation. In all suits which do not involve the title to land or the partition of real estate, such publication shall be made in the county where the suit is pending, if there be a newspaper published in said county, but if not, then in an adjoining county where a newspaper is published. In all suits which involve the title to land or partition of real estate, such publication shall be made in the county where the land, or a portion thereof, is situated, if there be a newspaper in such county, but if not, then in an adjoining county to the county where the land or a part thereof is situated, where a newspaper is published.

History of TRCP 116: Amended eff. Apr. 1, 1984, by order of Dec. 5, 1983 (661-62 S.W.2d [Tex.Cases] xli): TRCP 116 was not amended when TRCP 103 was changed eff. Jan. 1, 1981; it was therefore inconsistent with TRCP 103. Adopted eff. Sept. 1, 1941, by order of Oct. 29, 1940 (3 Tex.B.J. 543 [1940]). Source: TRCS arts. 2042, 2092(6) (repealed).

See *Commentaries*, "Service by publication," ch. 2-H, §4.4, p. 162.

12 TRCP 117. RETURN OF CITATION BY PUBLICATION

The return of the officer executing such citation shall show how and when the citation was executed, specifying the dates of such publication, be signed by him officially and shall be accompanied by a printed copy of such publication.

History of TRCP 117: Amended eff. Jan. 1, 2012, by order of Dec. 12, 2011 (Tex.Sup.Ct. Order, Misc. Docket No. 11-9250): Deleted the words "be indorsed or attached to the same, and" after the words "citation shall." Adopted eff. Sept. 1, 1941, by order of Oct. 29, 1940 (3 Tex.B.J. 543 [1940]). Source: TRCS art. 2043, unchanged (repealed).

TRCP 117a. CITATION IN SUITS FOR DELINQUENT AD VALOREM TAXES

In all suits for collection of delinquent ad valorem taxes, the rules of civil procedure governing issuance and service of citation shall control the issuance and service of citation therein, except as herein otherwise specially provided.

★

---

1. Personal Service: Owner and Residence Known, Within State: Where any defendant in a tax suit is a resident of the State of Texas and is not subject to citation by publication under subdivision 3 below, the process shall conform substantially to the form hereinafter set out for personal service and shall contain the essential elements and be served and returned and otherwise regulated by the provisions of Rules 99 to 107, inclusive.

2. Personal Service: Owner and Residence Known, Out of State: Where any such defendant is absent from the State or is a nonresident of the State and is not subject to citation by publication under subdivision 3 below, the process shall conform substantially to the form hereinafter set out for personal service and shall contain the essential elements and be served and returned and otherwise regulated by the provisions of Rule 108.

3. Service by Publication: Nonresident, Absent from State, Transient, Name Unknown, Residence Unknown, Owner Unknown, Heirs Unknown, Corporate Officers, Trustees, Receivers or Stockholders Unknown, Any Other Unknown Persons Owing or Claiming or Having an Interest: Where any defendant in a tax suit is a nonresident of the State, or is absent from the State, or is a transient person, or the name or the residence of any owner of any interest in any property upon which a tax lien is sought to be foreclosed, is unknown to the attorney requesting the issuance of process or filing the suit for the taxing unit, and such attorney shall make affidavit that such defendant is a nonresident of the State, or is absent from the State, or is a transient person, or that the name or residence of such owner is unknown and cannot be ascertained after diligent inquiry, each such person in every such class above mentioned, together with any and all other persons, including adverse claimants, owning or claiming or having any legal or equitable interest in or lien upon such property, may be cited by publication. All unknown owners of any interest in any property upon which any taxing unit seeks to foreclose a lien for taxes, including stockholders of corporations—defunct or otherwise—their successors, heirs, and assigns, may be joined in such suit under the designation of "unknown owners" and citation be had upon them as such; provided, however, that record owners of such property or of any apparent interest therein, including, without limitation, record lien holders, shall not be included in the designation of "unknown owners"; and provided further that where any record owner has rendered the property involved within five years before the tax suit is filed, citation on such record owner may not be had by publication or posting unless citation for personal service has been issued as to such record owner, with a notation thereon setting forth the same address as is contained on the rendition sheet made within such five years, and the sheriff or other person to whom citation has been delivered makes his return thereon that he is unable to locate the defendant. Where any attorney filing a tax suit for a taxing unit, or requesting the issuance of process in such suit, shall make affidavit that a corporation is the record owner of any interest in any property upon which a tax lien is sought to be foreclosed, and that he does not know, and after diligent inquiry has been unable to ascertain, the location of the place of business, if any, of such corporation, or the name or place of residence of any officer of such corporation upon whom personal service may be had, such corporation may be cited by publication as herein provided. All defendants of the classes enumerated above may be joined in the same citation by publication.

An affidavit which complies with the foregoing requirements therefor shall be sufficient basis for the citation above mentioned in connection with it but shall be held to be made upon the criminal responsibility of affiant.

Such citation by publication shall be directed to the defendants by names or by designation as hereinabove provided, and shall be issued and signed by the clerk of the court in which such tax suit is pending. It shall be sufficient if it states the file number and style of the case, the date of the filing of the petition, the names of all parties by name or by designation as hereinabove provided, and the court in which the suit is pending; shall command such parties to appear and defend such suit at or before 10 o'clock a.m. of the first Monday after the expiration of forty-two days from the date of the issuance thereof, specifying such date when such parties are required to answer; shall state the place of holding the court, the nature of the suit, and the date of the issuance of the citation; and shall be signed and sealed by the clerk.

The citation shall be published in the English language one time a week for two weeks in some newspaper published in the county in which the property is lo-

⋆

cated, which newspaper must have been in general circulation for at least one year immediately prior to the first publication and shall in every respect answer the requirements of the law applicable to newspapers which are employed for such a purpose, the first publication to be not less than twenty-eight days prior to the return day fixed in the citation; and the affidavit of the editor or publisher of the newspaper giving the date of publication, together with a printed copy of the citation as published, shall constitute sufficient proof of due publication when returned and filed in court. If there is no newspaper published in the county, then the publication may be made in a newspaper in an adjoining county, which newspaper shall in every respect answer the requirements of the law applicable to newspapers which are employed for such a purpose. The maximum fee for publishing the citation shall be the lowest published word or line rate of that newspaper for classified advertising. If the publication of the citation cannot be had for this fee, chargeable as costs and payable upon sale of the property, as provided by law, and this fact is supported by the affidavit of the attorney for the plaintiff or the attorney requesting the issuance of the process, then service of the citation may be made by posting a copy at the courthouse door of the county in which the suit is pending, the citation to be posted at least twenty-eight days prior to the return day fixed in the citation. Proof of the posting of the citation shall be made by affidavit of the attorney for the plaintiff, or of the person posting it. When citation is served as here provided it shall be sufficient, and no other form of citation or notice to the named defendants therein shall be necessary.

4. Citation in Tax Suits: General Provisions: Any process authorized by this rule may issue jointly in behalf of all taxing units who are plaintiffs or intervenors in any tax suit. The statement of the nature of the suit, to be set out in the citation, shall be sufficient if it contains a brief general description of the property upon which the taxes are due and the amount of such taxes, exclusive of interest, penalties, and costs, and shall state, in substance, that in such suit the plaintiff and all other taxing units who may set up their claims therein seek recovery of the delinquent ad valorem taxes due on said property, and the (establishment and foreclosure) of liens, if any, securing the payment of same, as provided by law; that in addition to the taxes all interest, penalties, and costs allowed by law up to

and including the day of judgment are included in the suit; and that all parties to the suit, including plaintiff, defendants, and intervenors, shall take notice that claims for any taxes on said property becoming delinquent subsequent to the filing of the suit and up to the day of judgment, together with all interest, penalties, and costs allowed by law thereon, may, upon request therefor, be recovered therein without further citation or notice to any parties thereto. Such citation need not be accompanied by a copy of plaintiff's petition and no such copy need be served. Such citation shall also show the names of all taxing units which assess and collect taxes on said property not made parties to such suit, and shall contain, in substance, a recitation that each party to such suit shall take notice of, and plead and answer to, all claims and pleadings then on file or thereafter filed in said cause by all other parties therein, or who may intervene therein and set up their respective tax claims against said property. After citation or notice has been given on behalf of any plaintiff or intervenor taxing unit, the court shall have jurisdiction to hear and determine the tax claims of all taxing units who are parties plaintiff, intervenor or defendant at the time such process is issued and of all taxing units intervening after such process is issued, not only for the taxes, interest, penalties, and costs which may be due on said property at the time the suit is filed, but those becoming delinquent thereon at any time thereafter up to and including the day of judgment, without the necessity of further citation or notice to any party to said suit; and any taxing unit having a tax claim against said property may, by answer or intervention, set up and have determined its tax claim without the necessity of further citation or notice to any parties to such suit.

5. Form of Citation by Publication or Posting: The form of citation by publication or posting shall be sufficient if it is in substantially the following form, with proper changes to make the same applicable to personal property, where necessary, and if the suit includes or is for the recovery of taxes assessed on personal property, a general description of such personal property shall be sufficient:

THE STATE OF TEXAS   §

COUNTY OF _____   §

In the name and by the authority of the State of Texas

Notice is hereby given as follows:

To _____

_____

───────────────── ✯ ─────────────────

and any and all other persons, including adverse claimants, owning or having or claiming any legal or equitable interest in or lien upon the following described property delinquent to Plaintiff herein, for taxes, to-wit:

_____

_____

Which said property is delinquent to Plaintiff for taxes in the following amounts:

$_____, exclusive of interest, penalties, and costs, and there is included in this suit in addition to the taxes all said interest, penalties, and costs thereon, allowed by law up to and including the day of judgment herein.

You are hereby notified that suit has been brought by _____ as Plaintiffs, against _____ as Defendants, by petition filed on the ___ day of ____, 20__, in a certain suit styled _____ v. _____ for collection of the taxes on said property and that said suit is now pending in the District Court of _____ County, Texas, _____ Judicial District, and the file number of said suit is ____, that the names of all taxing units which assess and collect taxes on the property hereinabove described, not made parties to this suit, are _____.

Plaintiff and all other taxing units who may set up their tax claims herein seek recovery of delinquent ad valorem taxes on the property hereinabove described, and in addition to the taxes all interest, penalties, and costs allowed by law thereon up to and including the day of judgment herein, and the establishment and foreclosure of liens, if any, securing the payment of same, as provided by law.

All parties to this suit, including plaintiff, defendants, and intervenors, shall take notice that claims not only for any taxes which were delinquent on said property at the time this suit was filed but all taxes becoming delinquent thereon at any time thereafter up to the day of judgment, including all interest, penalties, and costs allowed by law thereon, may, upon request therefor, be recovered herein without further citation or notice to any parties herein, and all said parties shall take notice of and plead and answer to all claims and pleadings now on file and which may hereafter be filed in said cause by all other parties herein, and all of those taxing units above named who may intervene herein and set up their respective tax claims against said property.

You are hereby commanded to appear and defend such suit on the first Monday after the expiration of forty-two (42) days from and after the date of issuance hereof, the same being the ___ day of _____, A.D., 20___ (which is the return day of such citation), before the honorable District Court of _____ County, Texas, to be held at the courthouse thereof, then and there to show cause why judgment shall not be rendered for such taxes, penalties, interest, and costs, and condemning said property and ordering foreclosure of the constitutional and statutory tax liens thereon for taxes due the plaintiff and the taxing units parties hereto, and those who may intervene herein, together with all interest, penalties, and costs allowed by law up to and including the day of judgment herein, and all costs of this suit.

Issued and given under my hand and seal of said court in the City of _____, _____ County, Texas, this ___ day of _____, A.D., 20__.

_____

Clerk of the District Court

_____ County, Texas,

_____ Judicial District.

6. Form of Citation by Personal Service in or out of State: The form of citation for personal service shall be sufficient if it is in substantially the following form, with proper changes to make the same applicable to personal property, where necessary, and if the suit includes or is for the recovery of taxes assessed on personal property, a general description of such personal property shall be sufficient:

THE STATE OF TEXAS

To _____, Defendant,

GREETING:

YOU ARE HEREBY COMMANDED to appear and answer before the Honorable District Court, _____ Judicial District, County, Texas, at the Courthouse of said county in , Texas, at or before 10 o'clock a.m. of the Monday next after the expiration of 20 days from the date of service of this citation, then and there to answer the petition of _____, Plaintiff, filed in said Court on the ___ day of _____, A.D., 20__, against _____, Defendant, said suit being number _____ on the docket of said Court, the nature of which demand is a suit to collect delinquent ad valorem taxes on the property hereinafter described.

The amount of taxes due Plaintiff, exclusive of interest, penalties, and costs, is the sum of $_____, said property being described as follows, to-wit:

✦

The names of all taxing units which assess and collect taxes on said property, not made parties to this suit, are:

Plaintiff and all other taxing units who may set up their tax claims herein seek recovery of delinquent ad valorem taxes on the property hereinabove described, and in addition to the taxes all interest, penalties, and costs allowed by law thereon up to and including the day of judgment herein, and the establishment and foreclosure of liens securing the payment of same, as provided by law.

All parties to this suit, including plaintiff, defendants, and intervenors, shall take notice that claims not only for any taxes which were delinquent on said property at the time this suit was filed but all taxes becoming delinquent thereon at any time thereafter up to the day of judgment, including all interest, penalties, and costs allowed by law thereon, may, upon request therefor, be recovered herein without further citation or notice to any parties herein, and all said parties shall take notice of and plead and answer to all claims and pleadings now on file and which may hereafter be filed in this cause by all other parties hereto, and by all of those taxing units above named, who may intervene herein and set up their respective tax claims against said property.

If this citation is not served within 90 days after the date of its issuance, it shall be returned unserved.

The officer executing this return shall promptly serve the same according to the requirements of law and the mandates hereof and make due return as the law directs.

Issued and given under my hand and seal of said Court at ____, Texas, this the ___ day of _____, A.D., 20__.

Clerk of the District Court
_____ County, Texas,
By _____, Deputy

History of TRCP 117a: Amended eff. Jan. 1, 1988, by order of July 15, 1987 (733-34 S.W.2d [Tex.Cases] xlvii): Sec. 3 amended to update fee schedule for service of citation of publications to an acceptable fee level for both litigants and publications. Amended eff. Dec. 1, 1950, by order of July 17, 1950 (13 Tex.B.J. 423 [1950]). Amended eff. Oct. 1, 1948, by order of May 4, 1948 (11 Tex.B.J. 337 [1948]). Adopted eff. Dec. 31, 1947, by order of Aug. 18, 1947 (10 Tex.B.J. 391 [1947]). Source: New rule.

See *Commentaries*, "Serving the Defendant with Suit," ch. 2-H, p. 157.

ANNOTATIONS

Conseco Fin. Servicing Corp. v. Klein ISD, 78 S.W.3d 666, 675 (Tex.App.—Houston [14th Dist.] 2002, no pet.). "The permissive language in Rule 117a(4) indicates an intent to give all other taxing units the discretion to join the suit, rather than giving the taxing unit instituting the suit discretion to exclude other taxing units, or cause them to have to obtain issuance of their own citations. ... Rule 117a does not require other taxing units to join a tax suit, but it clearly permits them to intervene without further service."

TRCP 118. AMENDMENT

At any time in its discretion and upon such notice and on such terms as it deems just, the court may allow any process or proof of service thereof to be amended, unless it clearly appears that material prejudice would result to the substantial rights of the party against whom the process issued.

History of TRCP 118: Adopted eff. Sept. 1, 1941, by order of Oct. 29, 1940 (3 Tex.B.J. 543 [1940]). Source: TRCS art. 2044 (repealed), FRCP 4(h).

See *Commentaries*, "Serving the Defendant with Suit," ch. 2-H, p. 157.

ANNOTATIONS

Higginbotham v. General Life & Acc. Ins., 796 S.W.2d 695, 697 (Tex.1990). Because a trial court's order holding that service was proper was "tantamount to formal amendment of the return of citation, the record was sufficient to show valid service."

Gonzalez v. Tapia, 287 S.W.3d 805, 808 (Tex. App.—Corpus Christi 2009, pet. denied). A trial court can "amend the process server's proof of service after its plenary power has expired. ... Rule 118 allows a trial court to grant an amendment to a process server's proof of service ... after the default judgment [has] become final [and the] amendment relate[s] back to the original service date."

Dawson v. Briggs, 107 S.W.3d 739, 745 (Tex. App.—Fort Worth 2003, no pet.). "[T]he filing of a notice of appeal by [D] did not deprive the trial court of jurisdiction to sign an order during its plenary power granting [P's] motion to amend the citation."

TRCP 119. ACCEPTANCE OF SERVICE

The defendant may accept service of process, or waive the issuance or service thereof by a written memorandum signed by him, or by his duly authorized agent or attorney, after suit is brought, sworn to before a proper officer other than an attorney in the case, and

TRCP 119

★

---

filed among the papers of the cause, and such waiver or acceptance shall have the same force and effect as if the citation had been issued and served as provided by law. The party signing such memorandum shall be delivered a copy of plaintiff's petition, and the receipt of the same shall be acknowledged in such memorandum. In every divorce action such memorandum shall also include the defendant's mailing address.

History of TRCP 119: Amended eff. Jan. 1, 1961, by order of July 26, 1960 (23 Tex.B.J. 620 [Oct. 1960]): Added requirement that written memorandum constituting acceptance of process or waiver of issuance and service thereof be signed "after suit is brought." Amended eff. Jan. 1, 1955, by order of July 20, 1954 (17 Tex.B.J. 567 [1954]): Added last sentence. Amended eff. Dec. 31, 1941, by order of Sept. 20, 1941 (4 Tex.B.J. 507 [1941]): Provided that the officer shall be "other than an attorney in the case," and added last sentence. Adopted eff. Sept. 1, 1941, by order of Oct. 29, 1940 (3 Tex.B.J. 543 [1940]). Source: TRCS art. 2045 (repealed). Added requirement that the waiver of service be sworn to before an officer authorized to administer oaths.

See CPRC §30.001; *Commentaries*, "Serving the Defendant with Suit," ch. 2-H, p. 157; *O'Connor's Texas Forms*, FORM 2H:1.

ANNOTATIONS

Deen v. Kirk, 508 S.W.2d 70, 71 (Tex.1974). "Under the provisions of [TRCP 119], a defendant may waive the issuance and service of citation by filing among the papers of the cause a verified written memorandum 'signed by him, or by his duly authorized agent or attorney, after suit is brought.' [TRCS] art. 2224 [now CPRC §30.001] prohibits the waiver of process by an instrument executed prior to institution of suit." *See also **Tidwell v. Tidwell***, 604 S.W.2d 540, 541 (Tex.App.—Texarkana 1980, no writ).

Approximately $58,641.00 v. State, 331 S.W.3d 579, 583 (Tex.App.—Houston [14th Dist.] 2011, no pet.). "A written recitation that the acceptance of service meets all requirements of Rule 119 satisfies the requirement of a written memorandum."

TRCP 119a. COPY OF DECREE

The district clerk shall forthwith mail a certified copy of the final divorce decree or order of dismissal to the party signing a memorandum waiving issuance or service of process. Such divorce decree or order of dismissal shall be mailed to the signer of the memorandum at the address stated in such memorandum or to the office of his attorney of record.

History of TRCP 119a: Adopted eff. Jan. 1, 1955, by order of July 20, 1954 (17 Tex.B.J. 567 [1954]). Source: New rule.

TRCP 120. ENTERING APPEARANCE

The defendant may, in person, or by attorney, or by his duly authorized agent, enter an appearance in open court. Such appearance shall be noted by the judge upon his docket and entered in the minutes, and shall have the same force and effect as if the citation had been duly issued and served as provided by law.

History of TRCP 120: Adopted eff. Sept. 1, 1941, by order of Oct. 29, 1940 (3 Tex.B.J. 543 [1940]). Source: TRCS art. 2046 (repealed).

See *Commentaries*, "The Attorney," ch. 1-H, p. 52; "Special Appearance—Challenging Personal Jurisdiction," ch. 3-B, p. 189.

ANNOTATIONS

Mays v. Perkins, 927 S.W.2d 222, 225 (Tex.App.—Houston [1st Dist.] 1996, no writ). "A defendant's appearance before a court generally indicates a submission to the court's jurisdiction. However, the mere presence in court by an attorney, retained as counsel by a person formerly a party to the lawsuit, does not constitute a general appearance, unless the attorney seeks a judgment or an adjudication on some question."

TRCP 120a. SPECIAL APPEARANCE

1. Notwithstanding the provisions of Rules 121, 122 and 123, a special appearance may be made by any party either in person or by attorney for the purpose of objecting to the jurisdiction of the court over the person or property of the defendant on the ground that such party or property is not amenable to process issued by the courts of this State. A special appearance may be made as to an entire proceeding or as to any severable claim involved therein. Such special appearance shall be made by sworn motion filed prior to motion to transfer venue or any other plea, pleading or motion; provided however, that a motion to transfer venue and any other plea, pleading, or motion may be contained in the same instrument or filed subsequent thereto without waiver of such special appearance; and may be amended to cure defects. The issuance of process for witnesses, the taking of depositions, the serving of requests for admissions, and the use of discovery processes, shall not constitute a waiver of such special appearance. Every appearance, prior to judgment, not in compliance with this rule is a general appearance.

2. Any motion to challenge the jurisdiction provided for herein shall be heard and determined before a motion to transfer venue or any other plea or pleading may be heard. No determination of any issue of fact in connection with the objection to jurisdiction is a determination of the merits of the case or any aspect thereof.

3. The court shall determine the special appearance on the basis of the pleadings, any stipulations made by and between the parties, such affidavits and attachments as may be filed by the parties, the results of discovery processes, and any oral testimony. The affidavits, if any, shall be served at least seven days before the hearing, shall be made on personal knowledge, shall set forth specific facts as would be admissible in evidence, and shall show affirmatively that the affiant is competent to testify.

Should it appear from the affidavits of a party opposing the motion that he cannot for reasons stated present by affidavit facts essential to justify his opposition, the court may order a continuance to permit affidavits to be obtained or depositions to be taken or discovery to be had or may make such other order as is just.

Should it appear to the satisfaction of the court at any time that any of such affidavits are presented in violation of Rule 13, the court shall impose sanctions in accordance with that rule.

4. If the court sustains the objection to jurisdiction, an appropriate order shall be entered. If the objection to jurisdiction is overruled, the objecting party may thereafter appear generally for any purpose. Any such special appearance or such general appearance shall not be deemed a waiver of the objection to jurisdiction when the objecting party or subject matter is not amenable to process issued by the courts of this State.

History of TRCP 120a: Amended eff. Sept. 1, 1990, by order of Apr. 24, 1990 (785-86 S.W.2d [Tex.Cases] xlviii): Sec. 3 added and former sec. 3 renumbered to sec. 4; provides for proof by affidavit at special appearance hearings, with safeguards to responding parties; and preserves Texas's prior practice to place burden of proof on party contesting jurisdiction. Amended eff. Sept. 1, 1983, by order of June 15, 1983 (651-52 S.W.2d [Tex.Cases] xxxviii): To conform to S.B. 898, 68th Leg., 1983. Amended eff. Jan. 1, 1976, by order of July 22, 1975 (525-26 S.W.2d [Tex.Cases] xlvii): Added words in third sentence of sec. 1 to permit amendments to special appearance motion. Adopted eff. Sept. 1, 1962, by order of Apr. 12, 1962 (25 Tex.B.J. 372 [1962]). Source: New rule.

See CPRC §§17.041, 17.042, 51.014(a)(7); *Commentaries*, "Special Appearance—Challenging Personal Jurisdiction," ch. 3-B, p. 189; *O'Connor's Texas Forms*, FORMS 3B.

ANNOTATIONS

Generally

PHC-Minden, L.P. v. Kimberly-Clark Corp., 235 S.W.3d 163, 169-70 (Tex.2007). "We first determine the appropriate time period for assessing contacts for purposes of general jurisdiction, an issue on which our courts of appeals are in conflict. [¶] We conclude that the relevant period ends at the time suit is filed. [G]eneral jurisdiction is dispute-blind; accordingly, and in contrast to specific jurisdiction, the incident made the basis of the suit should not be the focus in assessing continuous and systematic contacts—contacts on

which jurisdiction over any claim may be based. We also agree that 'a mere one-time snapshot of the defendant's in-state activities' may not be sufficient, ... and contacts should be assessed over a reasonable number of years, up to the date suit is filed.... This includes contacts at the time the cause of action arose...."

Michiana Easy Livin' Country, Inc. v. Holten, 168 S.W.3d 777, 785 (Tex.2005). There are "[t]hree aspects of [the purposeful-availment requirement that] are relevant.... First, it is only the defendant's contacts with the forum that count.... [¶] Second, the acts relied on must be 'purposeful' rather than fortuitous. [¶] Third, a defendant must seek some benefit, advantage, or profit by 'availing' itself of the jurisdiction. [A] nonresident may purposefully avoid a particular jurisdiction by structuring its transactions so as neither to profit from the forum's laws nor be subject to its jurisdiction." *See also Zinc Nacional, S.A. v. Bouché Trucking, Inc.*, 308 S.W.3d 395, 397 (Tex.2010); *Moki Mac River Expeditions v. Drugg*, 221 S.W.3d 569, 575 (Tex.2007).

American Type Culture Collection, Inc. v. Coleman, 83 S.W.3d 801, 809-10 (Tex.2002). "Although the quantity of [D's] contacts may suggest that [D] had a significant relationship with Texas, we are not concerned with the quantity of contacts. Instead, we must look to the quality of those contacts. [D] does not advertise in Texas, has no physical presence in Texas, performs all its business services outside Texas, and carefully constructs its contracts to ensure it does not benefit from Texas laws. Under these circumstances, we must conclude that [D's] contacts with Texas were not continuous and systematic."

BMC Software Belgium, N.V. v. Marchand, 83 S.W.3d 789, 794 (Tex.2002). The "courts of appeals [should] review the trial court's factual findings for legal and factual sufficiency and review the trial court's legal conclusions *de novo*. [¶] Whether a court has personal jurisdiction over a defendant is a question of law. However, the trial court frequently must resolve questions of fact before deciding the jurisdiction question." *See also Zinc Nacional, S.A. v. Bouché Trucking, Inc.*, 308 S.W.3d 395, 397 (Tex.2010); *Moki Mac River Expeditions v. Drugg*, 221 S.W.3d 569, 574 (Tex.2007).

CMMC v. Salinas, 929 S.W.2d 435, 439 (Tex.1996). "[D's] mere knowledge that its winepress was to be sold and used in Texas and its wiring the machine for use in the U.S. were not sufficient to subject [D] to the jurisdiction of Texas courts. *At 440:* A manufacturer cannot fairly be expected to litigate in every part of the world where its products may end up; its contacts with the forum must be more purposeful ... before it can constitutionally be subjected to personal jurisdiction." *See also CSR Ltd. v. Link*, 925 S.W.2d 591, 595-96 (Tex. 1996).

Schlobohm v. Schapiro, 784 S.W.2d 355, 358 (Tex. 1990). The Texas standard for jurisdiction over a nonresident defendant requires that: "(1) The nonresident defendant or foreign corporation must purposefully do some act or consummate some transaction in the forum state; (2) The cause of action must arise from, or be connected with, such act or transaction; and (3) The assumption of jurisdiction by the forum state must not offend traditional notions of fair play and substantial justice.... [¶] [However], we modify the second part ... to state that jurisdiction may also arise from the continuing and systematic contacts of the defendant with Texas, even if the cause of action does not arise from a specific contact." *See also Guardian Royal Exch. Assur., Ltd. v. English China Clays, P.L.C.*, 815 S.W.2d 223, 226 (Tex.1991).

Waterman S.S. Corp. v. Ruiz, 355 S.W.3d 387, 401 (Tex.App.—Houston [1st Dist.] 2011, pet. denied). "A corporate officer may testify that information concerning the company's contacts with the forum state is within his personal knowledge 'without showing with particularity how he acquired that knowledge.' Even if an affiant later states that his affidavit testimony was based on his review of corporate business records, the affiant's 'acknowledgement of the sources from which he gathered his knowledge does not violate the personal knowledge requirement.' *At 402 n.6:* Even if [corporate officer] lacked personal knowledge and his affidavit was, therefore, defective, [D] still presented evidence supporting its special appearance. Rule 120a(3) does not require a party to file affidavits supporting a special appearance...."

Pleadings

Exito Elecs. Co. v. Trejo, 142 S.W.3d 302, 305 (Tex. 2004). TRCP 120a "requires only that a special appearance be filed before any other 'plea, pleading or motion.' A [TRCP] 11 Agreement between the parties, in and of itself, is not a plea, pleading, or motion. *At 306:* [W]hile filing a Rule 11 Agreement with the trial court is a requirement for enforcement, it is not in and of itself a request for enforcement or any other affirmative action by the trial court. [A] Rule 11 Agreement that extends a defendant's time to file an initial responsive pleading and is filed in the trial court before the defendant files a special appearance, even if the agreement is not expressly made subject to the special appearance, does not violate Rule 120a's 'due-order-of-pleading' requirement and ... does not constitute a general appearance."

Dawson-Austin v. Austin, 968 S.W.2d 319, 322-23 (Tex.1998). The Supreme Court held: (1) an unverified special appearance may be amended to cure the defect, even after the trial court has overruled it, as long as the amendment is filed before the defendant enters a general appearance; and (2) it is not necessary for the answer and other motions filed in the same instrument with the special appearance to contain "subject to" language. *See also Horowitz v. Berger*, 377 S.W.3d 115, ___ (Tex.App.—Houston [14th Dist.] 2012, no pet.) (amended special appearance relates back, curing and replacing the original special appearance).

Casino Magic Corp. v. King, 43 S.W.3d 14, 18 (Tex. App.—Dallas 2001, pet. denied). TRCP 120a "requires special appearances to be made by 'sworn motion.' Strict compliance with the rule is required. [¶] In this case, the special appearance was not sworn or verified. Although [D] attached an affidavit to the special appearance which set out various 'jurisdictional facts,' in that affidavit [D's] general counsel stated only that the allegations in the *affidavit* were true and correct, not that the facts set out in the *special appearance* were true and correct. [W]e conclude the affidavit did not strictly comply with rule 120a and it, therefore, could not serve to verify the special appearance."

Discovery

In re Stern, 321 S.W.3d 828, 839-40 (Tex.App.—Houston [1st Dist.] 2010, orig. proceeding). "The trial court may permit a continuance so that the opposing party may obtain [any] necessary jurisdictional discovery. However, Rule 120a(3) does not authorize postponement of a special appearance hearing to allow a party to obtain discovery prior to the court's ruling on the special appearance that is unnecessary or irrelevant to the establishment of jurisdictional facts. [¶] We ... conclude that those cases holding that 'nothing in Rule 120a specifically limits discovery to matters relating to the special appearance' are limited to those situations in which the issue is whether a defendant waives a special appearance by participating in discov-

⬥

ery and that they do not apply when the issue is ... whether a trial court abuses its discretion by ordering or failing to order discovery at the request of a party opposing a special appearance. Those cases are controlled by the plain language of Rule 120a(3) and by *Dawson-Austin v. Austin*[, 968 S.W.2d 319 (Tex.1998),] and its progeny."

Waiver

Exito Elecs. Co. v. Trejo, 142 S.W.3d 302, 307 (Tex. 2004). "It is simply illogical to allow the parties to engage in relevant discovery, which can be a vital part of resolving a special appearance, but prohibit the nonresident defendant from seeking the trial court's ruling on disputes that may affect the evidence presented at the special appearance hearing. [A] trial court's resolution of discovery matters related to the special appearance does not amount to a general appearance by the party contesting personal jurisdiction." *See also Minucci v. Sogevalor, S.A.*, 14 S.W.3d 790, 801 (Tex. App.—Houston [1st Dist.] 2000, no pet.).

GFTA Trendanalysen v. Varme, 991 S.W.2d 785, 786 (Tex.1999). "[A] party [does not waive] a due process challenge for want of minimum contacts by challenging the method of service in the special appearance." *See also Moore v. Pulmosan Safety Equip. Corp.*, 278 S.W.3d 27, 33 (Tex.App.—Houston [14th Dist.] 2008, pet. denied).

Milacron Inc. v. Performance Rail Tie, L.P., 262 S.W.3d 872, 875-76 (Tex.App.—Texarkana 2008, no pet.). "Rule 120a requires that the specially appearing defendant timely request a hearing, specifically bring that request to the trial court's attention, and secure a ruling on the preliminary question of personal jurisdiction. [¶] A defendant waives his special appearance by not timely pressing for a hearing. It is inappropriate, especially when considering judicial economy, to litigate the special appearance in connection with the trial of the matter."

TRCP 121. ANSWER IS APPEARANCE

An answer shall constitute an appearance of the defendant so as to dispense with the necessity for the issuance or service of citation upon him.

History of TRCP 121: Adopted eff. Sept. 1, 1941, by order of Oct. 29, 1940 (3 Tex.B.J. 543 [1940]). Source: TRCS art. 2047 (repealed).

ANNOTATIONS

Torres v. Johnson, 91 S.W.3d 905, 910 (Tex.App.— Fort Worth 2002, no pet.). "[N]o new service was re-

quired because [D] entered an appearance in the suit by moving for summary judgment after [P] amended his pleadings."

Moody Nat'l Bank v. Riebschlager, 946 S.W.2d 521, 524 (Tex.App.—Houston [14th Dist.] 1997, writ denied). "In order for an act of the garnishee to constitute an appearance, it must seek a judgment or adjudication by the court on some issue. ... When a garnishee appears for the purpose of filing a motion to quash the garnishment, such an appearance does not confer jurisdiction on the court for all purposes, and does not operate as a waiver of an objection as to jurisdiction."

TRCP 122. CONSTRUCTIVE APPEARANCE

If the citation or service thereof is quashed on motion of the defendant, such defendant shall be deemed to have entered his appearance at ten o'clock a.m. on the Monday next after the expiration of twenty (20) days after the day on which the citation or service is quashed, and such defendant shall be deemed to have been duly served so as to require him to appear and answer at that time, and if he fails to do so, judgment by default may be rendered against him.

History of TRCP 122: Adopted eff. Sept. 1, 1941, by order of Oct. 29, 1940 (3 Tex.B.J. 543 [1940]). Source: TRCS arts. 2048, 2092(8) (repealed).

See *Commentaries*, "Motion to Quash—Challenging the Service," ch. 3-J, p. 264.

ANNOTATIONS

Kawasaki Steel Corp. v. Middleton, 699 S.W.2d 199, 202 (Tex.1985). "[A] non-resident defendant, like any other defendant, may move to quash the citation for defects in the process, but his only relief is additional time to answer rather than dismissal of the cause."

Ramirez v. Consolidated HGM Corp., 124 S.W.3d 914, 917 (Tex.App.—Amarillo 2004, no pet.). The trial court does not have to "resolve a motion to quash as a condition to preserving a complaint about service."

TRCP 123. REVERSAL OF JUDGMENT

Where the judgment is reversed on appeal or writ of error for the want of service, or because of defective service of process, no new citation shall be issued or served, but the defendant shall be presumed to have entered his appearance to the term of the court at which the mandate shall be filed.

History of TRCP 123: Adopted eff. Sept. 1, 1941, by order of Oct. 29, 1940 (3 Tex.B.J. 544 [1940]). Source: TRCS art. 2049 (repealed).

⭐

See *Commentaries*, "Motion to Quash—Challenging the Service," ch. 3-J, p. 264.

Boyd v. Kobierowski, 283 S.W.3d 19, 23 (Tex. App.—San Antonio 2009, no pet.). TRCP 123 "presumes the non-resident defendant's general appearance after reversal of a judgment based on defective or no service. *At 24:* [D] could have escaped Rule 123's presumption of a general appearance using [TRCP] 120a's special appearance."

TRCP 124. NO JUDGMENT WITHOUT SERVICE

In no case shall judgment be rendered against any defendant unless upon service, or acceptance or waiver of process, or upon an appearance by the defendant, as prescribed in these rules, except where otherwise expressly provided by law or these rules.

When a party asserts a counterclaim or a cross-claim against another party who has entered an appearance, the claim may be served in any manner prescribed for service of citation or as provided in Rule 21(a).[1]

1. **Editor's note:** This is TRCP 21a.

History of TRCP 124: Amended eff. Apr. 1, 1984, by order of Dec. 5, 1983 (661-62 S.W.2d [Tex.Cases] xlii): Last sentence clarifies that service of a counterclaim may be done in any manner prescribed for service of citation, and pursuant to Rule 21(a). Removes uncertainty as to whether service of counterclaim must be made by citation. Adopted eff. Sept. 1, 1941, by order of Oct. 29, 1940 (3 Tex.B.J. 544 [1940]). Source: TRCS art. 2050 (repealed).

See *Commentaries*, "Serving the Defendant with Suit," ch. 2-H, p. 157; "Default Judgment," ch. 7-A, p. 587.

Werner v. Colwell, 909 S.W.2d 866, 870 (Tex.1995). "[M]erely appearing as a witness in a cause [does not serve] as a general appearance, subjecting one to the jurisdiction of the court."

Strawder v. Thomas, 846 S.W.2d 51, 62 (Tex. App.—Corpus Christi 1992, no writ). "Rules relating to service of process are mandatory, and a failure to comply therewith, if a judgment be rendered against a party who was not served in accordance with those rules (and who did not waive service of citation or appear voluntarily) renders the judgment void." *See also* **Exito Elecs. Co. v. Trejo**, 166 S.W.3d 839, 852 (Tex.App.—Corpus Christi 2005, no pet.).

SECTION 6. COSTS & SECURITY THEREFOR

TRCP 125. PARTIES RESPONSIBLE

Each party to a suit shall be liable to the officers of the court for all costs incurred by himself.

History of TRCP 125: Adopted eff. Sept. 1, 1941, by order of Oct. 29, 1940 (3 Tex.B.J. 544 [1940]). Source: TRCS art. 2051, first sentence (repealed).

Borg-Warner Prot. Servs. v. Flores, 955 S.W.2d 861, 870 (Tex.App.—Corpus Christi 1997, no pet.). "[T]he right to costs is based entirely on statutes or procedural rules, and therefore the trial court is the proper authority to determine and award costs."

TRCP 126. FEE FOR EXECUTION OF PROCESS, DEMAND

No sheriff or constable shall be compelled to execute any process in civil cases coming from any county other than the one in which he is an officer, unless the fees allowed him by law for the service of such process shall be paid in advance; except when affidavit is filed, as provided by law or these rules. The clerk issuing the process shall indorse thereon the words "pauper oath filed," and sign his name officially below them; and the officer in whose hands such process is placed for service shall serve the same.

History of TRCP 126: Adopted eff. Sept. 1, 1941, by order of Oct. 29, 1940 (3 Tex.B.J. 544 [1940]). Source: TRCS art. 2051, second sentence (repealed).

TRCP 127. PARTIES LIABLE FOR OTHER COSTS

Each party to a suit shall be liable for all costs incurred by him. If the costs cannot be collected from the party against whom they have been adjudged, execution may issue against any party in such suit for the amount of costs incurred by such party, but no more.

History of TRCP 127: Adopted eff. Sept. 1, 1941, by order of Oct. 29, 1940 (3 Tex.B.J. 544 [1940]). Source: TRCS art. 2052 (repealed).

TRCP 128. REPEALED

Repealed eff. Apr. 1, 1984, by order of Dec. 5, 1983 (661-62 S.W.2d [Tex.Cases] xlii): Rule was obsolete.

TRCP 129. HOW COSTS COLLECTED

If any party responsible for costs fails or refuses to pay the same within ten days after demand for payment, the clerk or justice of the peace may make certified copy of the bill of costs then due, and place the same in the hands of the sheriff or constable for collection. All taxes imposed on law proceedings shall be included in the bill of costs. Such certified bill of costs shall have the force and effect of an execution. The removal of a case by appeal shall not prevent the issuance of an execution for costs.

History of TRCP 129: Amended eff. Apr. 1, 1984, by order of Dec. 5, 1983 (661-62 S.W.2d [Tex.Cases] xlii): The words "at the end of the term" are dropped from the last sentence. Adopted eff. Sept. 1, 1941, by order of Oct. 29, 1940 (3 Tex.B.J. 544 [1940]). Source: TRCS art. 2054 (repealed).

★

TRCP 130. OFFICER TO LEVY

The sheriff or constable upon demand and failure to pay said bill of costs, may levy upon a sufficient amount of property of the person from whom said costs are due to satisfy the same, and sell such property as under execution. Where such party is not a resident of the county where such suit is pending, the payment of such costs may be demanded of his attorney of record; and neither the clerk nor justice of the peace shall be allowed to charge any fee for making out such certified bill of costs, unless he is compelled to make a levy.

History of TRCP 130: Adopted eff. Sept. 1, 1941, by order of Oct. 29, 1940 (3 Tex.B.J. 544 [1940]). Source: TRCS art. 2055 (repealed).

TRCP 131. SUCCESSFUL PARTY TO RECOVER

The successful party to a suit shall recover of his adversary all costs incurred therein, except where otherwise provided.

History of TRCP 131: Adopted eff. Sept. 1, 1941, by order of Oct. 29, 1940 (3 Tex.B.J. 544 [1940]). Source: TRCS art. 2056 (repealed).

See CPRC §31.007; *Commentaries*, "The Judgment," ch. 9-C, p. 764.

ANNOTATIONS

Furr's Supermkts., Inc. v. Bethune, 53 S.W.3d 375, 376 (Tex.2001). "Taxing costs against a successful party in the trial court … generally contravenes [TRCP] 131. Yet the trial court's ruling on costs under [TRCP] 141 is permitted within its sound discretion, although that discretion is not unlimited. *At 378:* Rule 131's underlying purpose is to ensure that the prevailing party is freed of the burden of court costs and that the losing party pays those costs." *See also Martinez v. Pierce*, 759 S.W.2d 114, 114 (Tex.1988).

Headington Oil Co. v. White, 287 S.W.3d 204, 212 (Tex.App.—Houston [14th Dist.] 2009, no pet.). "[R]ecoverable costs do not generally include expert-witness fees."

Bayer Corp. v. DX Terminals, Ltd., 214 S.W.3d 586, 611-12 (Tex.App.—Houston [14th Dist.] 2006, pet. denied). "A 'successful party' under the rules is one that obtains a judgment vindicating a civil right. [¶] Texas appellate courts have not been entirely consistent in reviewing trial courts' splitting of costs between opposing parties, particularly when claims and counterclaims are involved. Some courts have held that the party receiving the larger recovery is entitled to costs. Other courts have held that when both sides successfully prosecute their claims, a trial court can in its discretion split costs between the parties." *See also*

Mag Instr., Inc. v. G.T. Sales, Inc., 294 S.W.3d 800, 808 (Tex.App.—Dallas 2009, pet. denied) (whether party is successful is based on merits, not on award of damages); *Imperial Lofts, Ltd. v. Imperial Woodworks, Inc.*, 245 S.W.3d 1, 8 (Tex.App.—Waco 2007, pet. denied) (D who obtains take-nothing judgment is successful party).

TRCP 132. REPEALED

Repealed eff. Apr. 1, 1984, by order of Dec. 5, 1983 (661-62 S.W.2d [Tex.Cases] xlii): Rule was obsolete.

TRCP 133. COSTS OF MOTION

The court may give or refuse costs on motions at its discretion, except where otherwise provided by law or these rules.

History of TRCP 133: Adopted eff. Sept. 1, 1941, by order of Oct. 29, 1940 (3 Tex.B.J. 544 [1940]). Source: TRCS art. 2058 (repealed).

TRCP 134, 135. REPEALED

Repealed eff. Apr. 1, 1984, by order of Dec. 5, 1983 (661-62 S.W.2d [Tex.Cases] xlii-xliii): Rules were obsolete.

TRCP 136. DEMAND REDUCED BY PAYMENTS

Where the plaintiff's demand is reduced by payment to an amount which would not have been within the jurisdiction of the court, the defendant shall recover his costs.

History of TRCP 136: Adopted eff. Sept. 1, 1941, by order of Oct. 29, 1940 (3 Tex.B.J. 545 [1940]). Source: TRCS art. 2061 (repealed).

TRCP 137. IN ASSAULT & BATTERY, ETC.

In civil actions for assault and battery, slander and defamation of character, if the verdict or judgment shall be for the plaintiff, but for less than twenty dollars, the plaintiff shall not recover his costs, but each party shall be taxed with the costs incurred by him in such suit.

History of TRCP 137: Adopted eff. Sept. 1, 1941, by order of Oct. 29, 1940 (3 Tex.B.J. 545 [1940]). Source: TRCS art. 2062 (repealed).

TRCP 138. COST OF NEW TRIALS

The costs of new trials may either abide the result of the suit or may be taxed against the party to whom the new trial is granted, as the court may adjudge when he grants such new trial.

History of TRCP 138: Adopted eff. Sept. 1, 1941, by order of Oct. 29, 1940 (3 Tex.B.J. 545 [1940]). Source: TRCS art. 2063 (repealed).

TRCP 139. ON APPEAL & CERTIORARI

When a case is appealed, if the judgment of the higher court be against the appellant, but for less amount than the original judgment, such party shall recover the costs of the higher court but shall be adjudged to pay the costs of the court below; if the judgment be against him for the same or a greater amount than in the court below, the adverse party shall recover the costs of both courts. If the judgment of the court above be in favor of the party appealing and for more than the original judgment, such party shall recover the costs of both courts; if the judgment be in his favor, but for the same or a less amount than in the court below, he shall recover the costs of the court below, and pay the costs of the court above.

History of TRCP 139: Adopted eff. Sept. 1, 1941, by order of Oct. 29, 1940 (3 Tex.B.J. 545 [1940]). Source: TRCS art. 2065 (repealed).

ANNOTATIONS

Keene Corp. v. Gardner, 837 S.W.2d 224, 232 (Tex. App.—Dallas 1992, writ denied). "Because the appellate relief given [D] is *de minimis* compared to [Ps'] overall award affirmed on appeal, we assess all costs of this appeal against [D]."

TRCP 140. NO FEE FOR COPY

No fee for a copy of a paper not required by law or these rules to be copied shall be taxed in the bill of costs.

History of TRCP 140: Adopted eff. Sept. 1, 1941, by order of Oct. 29, 1940 (3 Tex.B.J. 545 [1940]). Source: TRCS art. 3906 (repealed).

ANNOTATIONS

Crescendo Invs. v. Brice, 61 S.W.3d 465, 481 (Tex. App.—San Antonio 2001, pet. denied). "Transcripts 'necessarily obtained for use in the suit' seems to obviously include depositions and trial testimony used to question witnesses and prepare for argument at trial. [Ds] are not recovering for 'making copies' as prohibited by Rule 140. The expense of depositions has long been recognized as a chargeable item of court costs. Awarding costs for certified copies of depositions which may be admitted at trial does not violate Rule 140." *But see* **Gumpert v. ABF Freight Sys.**, 312 S.W.3d 237, 241 (Tex.App.—Dallas 2010, no pet.) (costs to videotape depositions and obtain copies of deposition transcripts are not recoverable as taxable costs).

TRCP 141. COURT MAY OTHERWISE ADJUDGE COSTS

The court may, for good cause, to be stated on the record, adjudge the costs otherwise than as provided by law or these rules.

History of TRCP 141: Adopted eff. Sept. 1, 1941, by order of Oct. 29, 1940 (3 Tex.B.J. 545 [1940]). Source: TRCS art. 2066 (repealed).

ANNOTATIONS

Roberts v. Williamson, 111 S.W.3d 113, 124 (Tex. 2003). The trial court "observed that because an ad litem is there for the benefit of all parties, it is 'fair' to split costs between the losing and prevailing parties. ... Certainly, fairness can be good cause, but the record must substantiate the connection. [¶] [T]he trial court's finding of good cause is premised on the perception that the prevailing party incidentally [benefited] from the guardian ad litem's services. ... Rule 141 still requires that the trial court state its reasons 'on the record' and with more specificity than the court's general notion of fairness here. Grounds of perceived fairness, without more, are insufficient to constitute good cause."

Furr's Supermkts., Inc. v. Bethune, 53 S.W.3d 375, 376-77 (Tex.2001). "Rule 141 has two requirements—that there be good cause and that it be stated on the record. 'Good cause' is an elusive concept that varies from case to case. Typically though, 'good cause' has meant that the prevailing party unnecessarily prolonged the proceedings, unreasonably increased costs, or otherwise did something that should be penalized." *See also* **Diaz v. Diaz**, 350 S.W.3d 251, 256 (Tex. App.—San Antonio 2011, pet. denied) (trial courts in family-law context are not bound by good-cause requirement); **Rankin v. FPL Energy LLC**, 266 S.W.3d 506, 515 (Tex.App.—Eastland 2008, pet. denied) (party's emotional distress at having to pay costs, inability to pay, and trial court's perceived fairness do not constitute good cause).

Hatfield v. Solomon, 316 S.W.3d 50, 67 (Tex. App.—Houston [14th Dist.] 2010, no pet.). The "power to allocate costs in a manner different from the norm does not encompass the power to tax as costs items that are not normally allowed as taxable court costs."

TRCP 142. SECURITY FOR COSTS

The clerk shall require from the plaintiff fees for services rendered before issuing any process unless filing is requested pursuant to Rule 145 of these rules.

History of TRCP 142: Amended eff. Jan. 1, 1988, by order of July 15, 1987 (733-34 S.W.2d [Tex.Cases] xlviii). Amended eff. Sept. 1, 1941, by order of Mar. 31, 1941 (4 Tex.B.J. 509 [1941]): Added second sentence (deleted in 1988). Adopted eff. Sept. 1, 1941, by order of Oct. 29, 1940 (3 Tex.B.J. 545 [1940]). Source: TRCS art. 2067 (repealed).

TRCP 143. RULE FOR COSTS

A party seeking affirmative relief may be ruled to give security for costs at any time before final judg-

★

ment, upon motion of any party, or any officer of the court interested in the costs accruing in such suit, or by the court upon its own motion. If such rule be entered against any party and he failed to comply therewith on or before twenty (20) days after notice that such rule has been entered, the claim for affirmative relief of such party shall be dismissed.

History of TRCP 143: Amended eff. Jan. 1, 1971, by order of July 21, 1970 (455-56 S.W.2d [Tex.Cases] xxx): Changed language to provide that any party seeking affirmative relief may be ruled for costs upon motion of any party or by the court on its own motion, and deleted words "knowledge or" which appeared before word "notice" in last sentence. Adopted eff. Sept. 1, 1941, by order of Oct. 29, 1940 (3 Tex.B.J. 545 [1940]). Source: TRCS art. 2068 (repealed). Change: Substituted 20-day period for reference to next term of court.

ANNOTATIONS

Clanton v. Clark, 639 S.W.2d 929, 931 (Tex.1982). Held: Under TRCP 143, the trial court may order a party to give security to cover accrued costs of the trial. If the party does not file the security, or files it late, the trial court may dismiss the suit.

TransAmerican Nat. Gas Corp. v. Mancias, 877 S.W.2d 840, 844 (Tex.App.—Corpus Christi 1994, orig. proceeding). TRCP 143 "generally allows the trial court to require a party to post security for costs that have already accrued, but not to fix a specific amount for anticipated costs which a party is required to pay or post security for prematurely." *See also Hager v. Apollo Paper Corp.*, 856 S.W.2d 512, 515 (Tex.App.—Houston [1st Dist.] 1993, no writ).

TRCP 143a. COSTS ON APPEAL TO COUNTY COURT

If the appellant fails to pay the costs on appeal from a judgment of a justice of the peace or small claims court within twenty (20) days after being notified to do so by the county clerk, the appeal shall be deemed not perfected and the county clerk shall return all papers in said cause to the justice of the peace having original jurisdiction and the justice of the peace shall proceed as though no appeal had been attempted.

History of TRCP 143a: Adopted eff. Jan. 1, 1976, by order of July 22, 1975 (525-26 S.W.2d [Tex.Cases] xlvii). Rule requires appellant to pay costs on appeal. Source: New rule.

ANNOTATIONS

Farmer v. McGee Servs., 704 S.W.2d 927, 929 (Tex. App.—Tyler 1986, no writ). "Since no notice [of costs] had been given, the trial court erred in applying Rule 143a to dismiss [D's] appeal."

TRCP 144. JUDGMENT ON COST BOND

All bonds given as security for costs shall authorize judgment against all the obligors in such bond for the said costs, to be entered in the final judgment of the cause.

History of TRCP 144: Adopted eff. Sept. 1, 1941, by order of Oct. 29, 1940 (3 Tex.B.J. 545 [1940]). Source: TRCS art. 2069 (repealed).

ANNOTATIONS

Mosher v. Tunnell, 400 S.W.2d 402, 404 (Tex. App.—Houston [1st Dist.] 1966, writ ref'd n.r.e.). TRCP 144 "provides the bond shall authorize judgment against the obligors for said costs. This means such costs as shall be adjudged against the principal whatever be the amount."

TRCP 145. AFFIDAVIT ON INDIGENCY

(a) *Affidavit.* In lieu of paying or giving security for costs of an original action, a party who is unable to afford costs must file an affidavit as herein described. A "party who is unable to afford costs" is defined as a person who is presently receiving a governmental entitlement based on indigency or any other person who has no ability to pay costs.

Upon the filing of the affidavit, the clerk must docket the action, issue citation and provide such other customary services as are provided any party.

(b) *Contents of Affidavit.* The affidavit must contain complete information as to the party's identity, nature and amount of governmental entitlement income, nature and amount of employment income, other income, (interest, dividends, etc.), spouse's income if available to the party, property owned (other than homestead), cash or checking account, dependents, debts, and monthly expenses. The affidavit shall contain the following statements: "I am unable to pay the court costs. I verify that the statements made in this affidavit are true and correct." The affidavit shall be sworn before a notary public or other officer authorized to administer oaths. If the party is represented by an attorney on a contingent fee basis, due to the party's indigency, the attorney may file a statement to that effect to assist the court in understanding the financial condition of the party.

(c) *IOLTA Certificate.* If the party is represented by an attorney who is providing free legal services, without contingency, because of the party's indigency and the attorney is providing services either directly or by referral from a program funded by the Interest on Lawyers Trust Accounts (IOLTA) program, the attorney may file an IOLTA certificate confirming that the IOLTA-funded program screened the party for income eligibility under the IOLTA income guidelines. A party's affidavit of inability accompanied by an attorney's IOLTA certificate may not be contested.

(d) Contest. The defendant or the clerk may contest an affidavit that is not accompanied by an IOLTA certificate by filing a written contest giving notice to all parties and, in an appeal under Texas Government Code, section 28.052, notice to both the small claims court and the county clerk. A party's affidavit of inability that attests to receipt of government entitlement based on indigency may be contested only with respect to the veracity of the attestation. Temporary hearings will not be continued pending the filing of the contest. If the court finds at the first regular hearing in the course of the action that the party (other than a party receiving a governmental entitlement based on indigency) is able to afford costs, the party must pay the costs of the action. Reasons for such a finding must be contained in an order. Except with leave of court, no further steps in the action will be taken by a party who is found able to afford costs until payment is made. If the party's action results in monetary award, and the court finds sufficient monetary award to reimburse costs, the party must pay the costs of the action. If the court finds that another party to the suit can pay the costs of the action, the other party must pay the costs of the action.

(e) Attorney's Fees and Costs. Nothing herein will preclude any existing right to recover attorney's fees, expenses or costs from any other party.

Comment to 2005 change: The Rule is amended to prohibit the contest of an affidavit that is accompanied by an attorney's IOLTA certificate.

History of TRCP 145: Amended eff. Dec. 1, 2005, by order of Sept. 19, 2005 (173-74 S.W.3d [Tex.Cases] xxii). Amended eff. Jan. 1, 1988, by order of July 15, 1987 (733-34 S.W.2d [Tex.Cases] xlviii): Purpose of rule is to allow indigents to file suit and have citation issued based solely on an affidavit of indigency filed with the suit. Amended eff. Apr. 1, 1984, by order of Dec. 5, 1983 (661-62 S.W.2d [Tex.Cases] xliii): Deleted requirement that the contest be tried at the term of court at which the affidavit is filed. Adopted eff. Sept. 1, 1941, by order of Oct. 29, 1940 (3 Tex.B.J. 545 [1940]). Source: TRCS art. 2070 (repealed).

See CPRC chs. 13, 14; *Commentaries*, "Suit by Indigent," ch. 2-I, p. 173; *O'Connor's Texas Forms*, FORMS 2I.

ANNOTATIONS

Griffin Indus. v. 13th Ct. of Appeals, 934 S.W.2d 349, 354 (Tex.1996). When a contingent-fee agreement "provides that the attorney is to pay or advance costs, and the [party] makes no further showing [at a hearing to determine indigency status], the agreement

would be some evidence that the [party] has a source of funds from which to pay costs. But, when the facts establish that the attorney will not or cannot pay those costs, … we cannot erect a legal fiction that an indigent has the ability to pay [costs]."

Equitable Gen. Ins. v. Yates, 684 S.W.2d 669, 671 (Tex.1984). "An uncontested affidavit of inability to pay is conclusive as a matter of law."

In re Villanueva, 292 S.W.3d 236, 243-44 (Tex. App.—Texarkana 2009, orig. proceeding). "[A] new trial conditioned on a party's payment of attorney's fees [is] improper when that party [has] filed an uncontested affidavit of inability to pay costs pursuant to Rule 145…. The Texas Supreme Court [has] addressed, and ultimately ignored, the distinction between 'costs' and 'fees' as it relates to Rule 145…. [T]he proper focus is not directed at the distinct characterization of the 'fees' or 'costs' to be paid. Rather, the focus is on Rule 145's intended effect of guaranteeing a forum for indigent litigants."

TRCP 146. DEPOSIT FOR COSTS

In lieu of a bond for costs, the party required to give the same may deposit with the clerk of court or the justice of the peace such sum as the court or justice from time to time may designate as sufficient to pay the accrued costs.

History of TRCP 146: Adopted eff. Sept. 1, 1941, by order of Oct. 29, 1940 (3 Tex.B.J. 546 [1940]). Source: TRCS art. 2071 (repealed).

TRCP 147. APPLIES TO ANY PARTY

The foregoing rules as to security and rule for costs shall apply to any party who seeks a judgment against any other party.

History of TRCP 147: Amended eff. Apr. 1, 1984, by order of Dec. 5, 1983 (661-62 S.W.2d [Tex.Cases] xliii): Rules for security and rule for costs are made applicable to any party. Adopted eff. Sept. 1, 1941, by order of Oct. 29, 1940 (3 Tex.B.J. 546 [1940]). Source: TRCS art. 2073 (repealed).

ANNOTATIONS

Ex parte Shaffer, 649 S.W.2d 300, 302 (Tex.1983). "[O]ne who involuntarily comes into court and does not seek any affirmative relief cannot be required to post a cost bond."

TRCP 148. SECURED BY OTHER BOND

No further security shall be required if the costs are secured by the provisions of an attachment or other bond filed by the party required to give security for costs.

History of TRCP 148: Adopted eff. Sept. 1, 1941, by order of Oct. 29, 1940 (3 Tex.B.J. 546 [1940]). Source: TRCS art. 2074 (repealed).

TRCP 149. EXECUTION FOR COSTS

When costs have been adjudged against a party and are not paid, the clerk or justice of the court in which the suit was determined may issue execution, accompanied by an itemized bill of costs, against such party to be levied and collected as in other cases; and said officer, on demand of any party to whom any such costs are due, shall issue execution for costs at once. This rule shall not apply to executors, administrators or guardians in cases where costs are adjudged against the estate of a deceased person or of a ward. No execution shall issue in any case for costs until after judgment rendered therefor by the court.

History of TRCP 149: Adopted eff. Sept. 1, 1941, by order of Oct. 29, 1940 (3 Tex.B.J. 546 [1940]). Source: TRCS art. 2077 (repealed).

SECTION 7. ABATEMENT & DISCONTINUANCE OF SUIT

TRCP 150. DEATH OF PARTY

Where the cause of action is one which survives, no suit shall abate because of the death of any party thereto before the verdict or decision of the court is rendered, but such suit may proceed to judgment as hereinafter provided.

History of TRCP 150: Adopted eff. Sept. 1, 1941, by order of Oct. 29, 1940 (3 Tex.B.J. 546 [1940]). Source: TRCS art. 2078 (repealed).

See *Commentaries*, "Plea to the Jurisdiction—Challenging the Court," ch. 3-F, p. 239; "Motion to Abate—Challenging the Suit," ch. 3-I, p. 257.

ANNOTATIONS

Palomino v. Palomino, 960 S.W.2d 899, 900-01 (Tex.App.—El Paso 1997, pet. denied). "The general rule in Texas is that a cause of action for divorce ... becomes moot and abates upon the death of either spouse. ... However, when a trial court has rendered judgment on the merits in a divorce case, the cause does not abate when a party dies, and the cause cannot be dismissed." *See also Pollard v. Pollard*, 316 S.W.3d 246, 250-51 (Tex.App.—Dallas 2010, no pet.).

TRCP 151. DEATH OF PLAINTIFF

If the plaintiff dies, the heirs, or the administrator or executor of such decedent may appear and upon suggestion of such death being entered of record in open court, may be made plaintiff, and the suit shall proceed in his or their name. If no such appearance and suggestion be made within a reasonable time after the death of the plaintiff, the clerk upon the application of defendant, his agent or attorney, shall issue a scire facias for the heirs or the administrator or executor of such decedent, requiring him to appear and prosecute such suit.

After service of such scire facias, should such heir or administrator or executor fail to enter appearance within the time provided, the defendant may have the suit dismissed.

History of TRCP 151: Amended eff. Apr. 1, 1984, by order of Dec. 5, 1983 (661-62 S.W.2d [Tex.Cases] xliii). Adopted eff. Sept. 1, 1941, by order of Oct. 29, 1940 (3 Tex.B.J. 546 [1940]). Source: TRCS art. 2078, 2079 (repealed).

See *Commentaries*, "Plaintiff's Original Petition," ch. 2-B, p. 95; "Motion to Abate—Challenging the Suit," ch. 3-I, p. 257.

ANNOTATIONS

Mayhew v. Dealey, 143 S.W.3d 356, 370-71 (Tex. App.—Dallas 2004, pet. denied). "Ordinarily, only the executor or administrator may bring suit to recover property belonging to the estate, such as in a survival action. There are exceptions to this general rule. The first exception is that heirs at law may bring a survival action on behalf of the estate when no administration is pending and none is necessary. [¶] The second exception provides that heirs may bring suit when the personal representative cannot, or will not, bring the suit or when the personal representative's interests are antagonistic to those of the estate."

TRCP 152. DEATH OF DEFENDANT

Where the defendant shall die, upon the suggestion of death being entered of record in open court, or upon petition of the plaintiff, the clerk shall issue a scire facias for the administrator or executor or heir requiring him to appear and defend the suit and upon the return of such service, the suit shall proceed against such administrator or executor or heir.

History of TRCP 152: Adopted eff. Sept. 1, 1941, by order of Oct. 29, 1940 (3 Tex.B.J. 547 [1940]). Source: TRCS art. 2080 (repealed).

See *Commentaries*, "Motion to Abate—Challenging the Suit," ch. 3-I, p. 257.

ANNOTATIONS

Estate of Pollack v. McMurrey, 858 S.W.2d 388, 390 n.2 (Tex.1993). "*Scire facias* ... provides for substitution of any person or persons succeeding to the rights of the original party, whether executor, administrator, heir, or person holding the same practical relation."

Henson v. Estate of Crow, 734 S.W.2d 648, 649 (Tex.1987). After D died, P amended its petition naming D's estate as D. Even though an answer was filed on behalf of the estate, court rendered take-nothing judgment because the estate was not a legal entity. The suit should have proceeded against personal representative of the estate.

TRCP 153. WHEN EXECUTOR, ETC., DIES

When an executor or administrator shall be a party to any suit, whether as plaintiff or as defendant, and shall die or cease to be such executor or administrator, the suit may be continued by or against the person succeeding him in the administration, or by or against the heirs, upon like proceedings being had as provided in the two preceding rules, or the suit may be dismissed, as provided in Rule 151.

History of TRCP 153: Amended eff. Apr. 1, 1984, by order of Dec. 5, 1983 (661-62 S.W.2d [Tex.Cases] xliii). Adopted eff. Sept. 1, 1941, by order of Oct. 29, 1940 (3 Tex.B.J. 547 [1940]). Source: TRCS art. 2081 (repealed).

TRCP 154. REQUISITES OF SCIRE FACIAS

The scire facias and returns thereon, provided for in this section, shall conform to the requisites of citations and the returns thereon, under the provisions of these rules.

History of TRCP 154: Adopted eff. Sept. 1, 1941, by order of Oct. 29, 1940 (3 Tex.B.J. 547 [1940]). Source: TRCS art. 2091 (repealed).

TRCP 155. SURVIVING PARTIES

Where there are two or more plaintiffs or defendants, and one or more of them die, upon suggestion of such death being entered upon the record, the suit shall at the instance of either party proceed in the name of the surviving plaintiffs or against the surviving defendants, as the case may be.

History of TRCP 155: Adopted eff. Sept. 1, 1941, by order of Oct. 29, 1940 (3 Tex.B.J. 547 [1940]). Source: TRCS art. 2082 (repealed).

ANNOTATIONS

First Nat'l Bank v. Hawn, 392 S.W.2d 377, 379 (Tex.App.—Dallas 1965, writ ref'd n.r.e.). "Having elected to proceed under Rule 155 against the surviving [D], approving a judgment against that [D] and that judgment having become final …, [P] had no right to … suggest [other D's] death and endeavor to reinstate the suit as to his legal representative."

TRCP 156. DEATH AFTER VERDICT OR CLOSE OF EVIDENCE

When a party in a jury case dies between verdict and judgment, or a party in a non-jury case dies after the evidence is closed and before judgment is pronounced, judgment shall be rendered and entered as if all parties were living.

History of TRCP 156: Amended eff. Jan. 1, 1978, by order of July 11, 1977 (553-54 S.W.2d [Tex.Cases] xlv): Rule applies to non-jury as well as jury cases. Adopted eff. Sept. 1, 1941, by order of Oct. 29, 1940 (3 Tex.B.J. 547 [1940]). Source: TRCS art. 2083 (repealed).

TRCP 157. REPEALED

Repealed eff. Jan. 1, 1988, by order of July 15, 1987 (733-34 S.W.2d [Tex.Cases] xlix).

TRCP 158. SUIT FOR THE USE OF ANOTHER

When a plaintiff suing for the use of another shall die before verdict, the person for whose use such suit was brought, upon such death being suggested on the record in open court, may prosecute the suit in his own name, and shall be as responsible for costs as if he brought the suit.

History of TRCP 158: Adopted eff. Sept. 1, 1941, by order of Oct. 29, 1940 (3 Tex.B.J. 547 [1940]). Source: TRCS art. 2085 (repealed).

TRCP 159. SUIT FOR INJURIES RESULTING IN DEATH

In cases arising under the provisions of the title relating to injuries resulting in death, the suit shall not abate by the death of either party pending the suit, but in such case, if the plaintiff dies, where there is only one plaintiff, some one or more of the parties entitled to the money recovered may be substituted and the suit prosecuted to judgment in the name of such party or parties, for the benefit of the person entitled; if the defendant dies, his executor, administrator or heir may be made a party, and the suit prosecuted to judgment.

History of TRCP 159: Adopted eff. Sept. 1, 1941, by order of Oct. 29, 1940 (3 Tex.B.J. 547 [1940]). Source: TRCS art. 2086 (repealed).

TRCP 160. DISSOLUTION OF CORPORATION

The dissolution of a corporation shall not operate to abate any pending suit in which such corporation is a defendant, but such suit shall continue against such corporation and judgment shall be rendered as though the same were not dissolved.

History of TRCP 160: Adopted eff. Sept. 1, 1941, by order of Oct. 29, 1940 (3 Tex.B.J. 547 [1940]). Source: TRCS art. 1390 (repealed).
See Bus. Orgs. Code §11.356; TRCP 29.

TRCP 161. WHERE SOME DEFENDANTS NOT SERVED

When some of the several defendants in a suit are served with process in due time and others are not so served, the plaintiff may either dismiss as to those not so served and proceed against those who are, or he may take new process against those not served, or may obtain severance of the case as between those served and those not served, but no dismissal shall be allowed as to a principal obligor without also dismissing the parties secondarily liable except in cases provided by statute. No defendant against whom any suit may be so dis-

⭐

missed shall be thereby exonerated from any liability, but may at any time be proceeded against as if no such suit had been brought and no such dismissal ordered.

History of TRCP 161: Amended eff. Jan. 1, 1988, by order of July 15, 1987 (733-34 S.W.2d [Tex.Cases] xlix). Amended eff. Oct. 1, 1984, by order of Apr. 24, 1984 (667-68 S.W.2d [Tex.Cases] xl). Amended eff. Apr. 1, 1984, by order of Dec. 5, 1983 (661-62 S.W.2d [Tex.Cases] xliv). Adopted eff. Sept. 1, 1941, by order of Oct. 29, 1940 (3 Tex.B.J. 547 [1940]). Source: TRCS art. 2087 (repealed).

See TRCP 240.

ANNOTATIONS

Young v. Hunderup, 763 S.W.2d 611, 612-13 (Tex. App.—Austin 1989, no writ). "Where the judgment disposes of all named parties except those which have not been served and have not appeared, ... the judgment is considered final for purposes of appeal and the case stands as if there had been a discontinuance as to those parties not served." *See also Osborne v. St. Luke's Episcopal Hosp.*, 915 S.W.2d 906, 908 (Tex. App.—Houston [1st Dist.] 1996, writ denied). *Contra Reed v. Gum Keepsake Diamond Ctr.*, 657 S.W.2d 524, 525 (Tex.App.—Corpus Christi 1983, no writ) (judgment was not final because co-D was not served, did not waive service, did not make appearance, and was not dismissed).

TRCP 162. DISMISSAL OR NON-SUIT

At any time before the plaintiff has introduced all of his evidence other than rebuttal evidence, the plaintiff may dismiss a case, or take a non-suit, which shall be entered in the minutes. Notice of the dismissal or nonsuit shall be served in accordance with Rule 21a on any party who has answered or has been served with process without necessity of court order.

Any dismissal pursuant to this rule shall not prejudice the right of an adverse party to be heard on a pending claim for affirmative relief or excuse the payment of all costs taxed by the clerk. A dismissal under this rule shall have no effect on any motion for sanctions, attorney's fees or other costs, pending at the time of dismissal, as determined by the court. Any dismissal pursuant to this rule which terminates the case shall authorize the clerk to tax court costs against dismissing party unless otherwise ordered by the court.

History of TRCP 162: Amended eff. Jan. 1, 1988, by order of July 15, 1987 (733-34 S.W.2d [Tex.Cases] xlix): Purpose of rule is to fix a definite time after which a party may not voluntarily dismiss or nonsuit the cause of action. In addition, these amendments will not disturb any pending motions for sanctions or attorney fees filed before the motion for nonsuit or dismissal. Amended eff. Apr. 1, 1984, by order of Dec. 5, 1983 (661-62 S.W.2d [Tex.Cases] xliv): Rewrote rule. Adopted eff. Sept. 1, 1941, by order of Oct. 29, 1940 (3 Tex.B.J. 548 [1940]). Source: TRCS art. 2089 (repealed).

See TRCP 96; *Commentaries*, "Voluntary Dismissal—Nonsuit," ch. 7-F, p. 650; *O'Connor's Texas Forms*, FORMS 7F.

ANNOTATIONS

Epps v. Fowler, 351 S.W.3d 862, 868-69 (Tex.2011). "[W]e have no doubt that a defendant who is the beneficiary of a nonsuit with prejudice would be a prevailing party [and would be entitled to attorney fees]. ... The res judicata effect of a nonsuit with prejudice works a permanent, inalterable change in the parties' legal relationship to the defendant's benefit: the defendant can never again be sued by the plaintiff or its privies for claims arising out of the same subject matter. [¶] In contrast, a nonsuit without prejudice works no such change in the parties' legal relationship; typically, the plaintiff remains free to re-file the same claims seeking the same relief. *At 870:* [But] a defendant may be a prevailing party when a plaintiff nonsuits without prejudice if the trial court determines, on the defendant's motion, that the nonsuit was taken to avoid an unfavorable ruling on the merits."

In re Greater Houston Orthopaedic Specialists, Inc., 295 S.W.3d 323, 325 (Tex.2009). "Granting a nonsuit is a ministerial act, and a plaintiff's right to a nonsuit exists from the moment a written motion is filed or an oral motion is made in open court, unless the defendant has, prior to that time, sought affirmative relief." *See also Indian Beach Prop. Owners' Ass'n v. Linden*, 222 S.W.3d 682, 701 (Tex.App.—Houston [1st Dist.] 2007, no pet.).

Villafani v. Trejo, 251 S.W.3d 466, 469 (Tex.2008). "A nonsuit under Rule 162 ... has 'no effect on any motion for sanctions, attorney's fees or other costs, pending at the time of dismissal.' [P] argues that since the trial court denied [D's] motion [for sanctions] before [P] filed the nonsuit, the motion was not a *pending* claim for affirmative relief[, and therefore,] Rule 162 does not protect [D's] motion from the nullifying effect of the nonsuit. [¶] We disagree.... Rule 162 protects a party's 'pending claim for affirmative relief' from the general rule that a party is required to get a ruling (or a refusal to rule) from a trial court to preserve a right to appeal. 'Rule 162 merely acknowledges that a nonsuit does not affect ... a pending sanctions motion; it does not purport to limit the trial court's power to act.' *At 470:* [W]e do not read Rule 162 to mean that a nonsuit prevents a non-moving party from appealing a trial court's ruling on claims for affirmative relief merely because the ruling occurred prior to the nonsuit." *See also Uni-*

⭐

fund *CCR Partners v. Villa*, 299 S.W.3d 92, 96 (Tex. 2009); *Crites v. Collins*, 284 S.W.3d 839, 843 (Tex. 2009).

Texas Mut. Ins. v. Ledbetter, 251 S.W.3d 31, 37 (Tex.2008). "Parties have an absolute right to nonsuit *their own* claims, but not *someone else's* claims they are trying to avoid. *At 38:* Rule 162 ... provides that '[a]ny dismissal pursuant to this rule shall not prejudice the right of an adverse party to be heard on a pending claim for affirmative relief.' A claim for affirmative relief is one 'on which the claimant could recover compensation or relief even if the plaintiff abandons his cause of action.' A carrier's subrogation claim is just such a claim, as it can be prosecuted by a carrier even if an injured worker never does. [T]he carrier here sought no affirmative relief *from* [Ps], seeking instead reimbursement from the funds [Ds] were about to pay them. But Rule 162 is not limited to affirmative claims *against the nonsuiter*; it prohibits dismissal if the effect would be to prejudice any pending claim for affirmative relief, period. [¶] [T]he dismissal here prejudiced the carrier's pending claim for affirmative relief. ... While [Ps] were entitled to nonsuit their own affirmative claims, they were not entitled to dismissal from the case." *See also General Land Office v. OXY U.S.A., Inc.*, 789 S.W.2d 569, 570 (Tex.1990).

UTMB v. Estate of Blackmon, 195 S.W.3d 98, 101 (Tex.2006). "Rule 162 permits the trial court to hold hearings and enter orders affecting costs, attorney's fees, and sanctions, even after notice of nonsuit is filed, while the court retains plenary power. Thus, the trial court has discretion to defer signing an order of dismissal so that it can 'allow a reasonable amount of time' for holding hearings on these matters which are 'collateral to the merits of the underlying case.' Although the Rule permits motions for costs, attorney's fees, and sanctions to remain viable in the trial court, it does not forestall the nonsuit's effect of rendering the merits of the case moot." *See also Travelers Ins. v. Joachim*, 315 S.W.3d 860, 862-63 (Tex.2010).

In re Bennett, 960 S.W.2d 35, 38 (Tex.1997). "[P]laintiffs have the right under [TRCP] 162 to take a nonsuit at any time until they have introduced all evidence other than rebuttal evidence. Such a nonsuit may have the effect of vitiating earlier interlocutory orders and of precluding further action by the trial court.... [¶] Appellate timetables do not run from the date a nonsuit is filed, but rather from the date the trial court

signs an order of dismissal." *See also Klein v. Hernandez*, 315 S.W.3d 1, 3 (Tex.2010); *Farmer v. Ben E. Keith Co.*, 907 S.W.2d 495, 496 (Tex.1995); *Hyundai Motor Co. v. Alvarado*, 892 S.W.2d 853, 854-55 (Tex. 1995).

In re Tecore, Inc., 371 S.W.3d 603, 604-05 (Tex. App.—Dallas 2012, orig. proceeding). "[D]'s argument is that a non-suit cannot be taken while the case has been stayed by the trial court. We disagree. Relators' right to take a non-suit was 'unqualified and absolute' and could not be prevented by a stay order entered by the trial court."

Energy Transfer Fuel, L.P. v. Trammell, No. 12-09-00059-CV (Tex.App.—Tyler 2010, no pet.) (memo op.; 8-31-10). "A nonsuit may be taken after a temporary restraining order has been obtained but before the hearing on the temporary injunction. But the nonsuit does not defeat the right of a restrained party who is damaged by the temporary restraining order to sue for wrongful injunction."

C/S Solutions, Inc. v. Energy Maint. Servs. Grp., 274 S.W.3d 299, 306-07 (Tex.App.—Houston [1st Dist.] 2008, no pet.). "[T]reatises have drawn a distinction between a pure [TRCP] 162 nonsuit, which voluntarily dismisses the entire case, and a voluntary dismissal that abandons the case as to certain parties and/or claims. This distinction has no practical effect when a plaintiff files a written 'nonsuit' that abandons the case as to certain claims so long as the written 'nonsuit' does not run afoul of the time restrictions in [TRCP] 63. Under our liberal pleading rules, the document is in substance an amended pleading voluntarily dismissing the claims, notwithstanding the fact that the word 'nonsuit' appears. Similarly, the distinction between a pure Rule 162 nonsuit and a voluntary dismissal that abandons the case as to certain parties has no practical effect unless a plaintiff 'nonsuits' those parties in a situation in which another party is prejudiced under [TRCP] 163."

Reynolds v. Murphy, 266 S.W.3d 141, 145-46 (Tex. App.—Fort Worth 2008, pet. denied). "Although a nonsuit may have the effect of vitiating a trial court's earlier interlocutory orders, a nonsuit does not vitiate a trial court's previously-made decisions on the merits, such as a summary judgment, or even a partial summary judgment, which becomes final upon disposition of the other issues in the case. [¶] The parties disagree as to whether the trial court's rulings striking

★

[P's] amended petition are equivalent to a decision on the merits as to the new claims in the amended petition. [D] contends that the rulings were merely incidental interlocutory rulings because they did not involve any judgments on the merits of those claims.... [¶] [B]y striking [P's] new causes of action in [the amended] petition, and by refusing to allow discovery on those causes of action, the trial court effected a dismissal of those causes of action with prejudice without affording [P] an opportunity to replead. In essence, ... the trial court effected the same type of disposition as a dismissal or a partial summary judgment precluding consideration of those claims. [W]e conclude [P's] nonsuit of its sole remaining claim did not vitiate the trial court's rulings effectively barring him from pursuing his new claims...." *See also* **Waterman S.S. Corp. v. Ruiz**, 355 S.W.3d 387, 400 (Tex.App.—Houston [1st Dist.] 2011, pet. denied).

Bailey v. Gardner, 154 S.W.3d 917, 920 (Tex. App.—Dallas 2005, no pet.). "[P] made a tactical decision to nonsuit his case rather than face trial without expert testimony to support his claim. Taking a voluntary nonsuit for tactical advantage will not support an equitable extension of the limitations period. [E]quitable tolling does not apply to give [P] an extension on the limitations period [to refile his suit]."

TRCP 163. DISMISSAL AS TO PARTIES SERVED, ETC.

When it will not prejudice another party, the plaintiff may dismiss his suit as to one or more of several parties who were served with process, or who have answered, but no such dismissal shall in any case, be allowed as to a principal obligor, except in the cases provided for by statute.

History of TRCP 163: Amended eff. Jan. 1, 1988, by order of July 15, 1987 (733-34 S.W.2d [Tex.Cases] I). Amended eff. Apr. 1, 1984, by order of Dec. 5, 1983 (661-62 S.W.2d [Tex.Cases] xliv). Adopted eff. Sept. 1, 1941, by order of Oct. 29, 1940 (3 Tex.B.J. 548 [1940]). Source: TRCS art. 2090 (repealed).

See *Commentaries*, "Voluntary Dismissal—Nonsuit," ch. 7-F, p. 650.

ANNOTATIONS

Texas Cab Co. v. Giles, 783 S.W.2d 695, 697 (Tex. App.—El Paso 1989, no writ). "Unless the settlement with the deleted [D] was properly presented to the trial court, there generally could have been no dismissal to that [D] under [TRCP] 162 or 163, as the dismissal would have prejudiced [co-D]."

TRCP 164. REPEALED

Repealed eff. Jan. 1, 1988, by order of July 15, 1987 (733-34 S.W.2d [Tex.Cases] I).

TRCP 165. ABANDONMENT

A party who abandons any part of his claim or defense, as contained in the pleadings, may have that fact entered of record, so as to show that the matters therein were not tried.

History of TRCP 165: Adopted eff. Sept. 1, 1941, by order of Oct. 29, 1940 (3 Tex.B.J. 548 [1940]). Source: Tex. Rules for Dist. & Cty. Cts. 33.

See *Commentaries*, "Voluntary Dismissal—Nonsuit," ch. 7-F, p. 650.

ANNOTATIONS

Alan Reuber Chevrolet, Inc. v. Grady Chevrolet, Ltd., 287 S.W.3d 877, 887 (Tex.App.—Dallas 2009, no pet.). "Rule 165 permits an abandonment of a part of a claim or defense before, but not after, trial of the cause and entry of the judgment. This is the same requirement as for a nonsuit."

In re Shaw, 966 S.W.2d 174, 177 (Tex.App.—El Paso 1998, no pet.). "Whether a pleading has been abandoned is a question of law which we review de novo. Formal amendment of the pleadings is not required in order to show abandonment. Indeed, a stipulation may form the basis for abandonment."

TRCP 165a. DISMISSAL FOR WANT OF PROSECUTION

1. Failure to Appear. A case may be dismissed for want of prosecution on failure of any party seeking affirmative relief to appear for any hearing or trial of which the party had notice. Notice of the court's intention to dismiss and the date and place of the dismissal hearing shall be sent by the clerk to each attorney of record, and to each party not represented by an attorney and whose address is shown on the docket or in the papers on file, by posting same in the United States Postal Service. At the dismissal hearing, the court shall dismiss for want of prosecution unless there is good cause for the case to be maintained on the docket. If the court determines to maintain the case on the docket, it shall render a pretrial order assigning a trial date for the case and setting deadlines for the joining of new parties, all discovery, filing of all pleadings, the making of a response or supplemental responses to discovery and other pretrial matters. The case may be continued thereafter only for valid and compelling reasons specifically determined by court order. Notice of the signing of the order of dismissal shall be given as provided in Rule 306a. Failure to mail notices as required by this rule shall not affect any of the periods mentioned in Rule 306a except as provided in that rule.

✦
---

2. Non-Compliance With Time Standards. Any case not disposed of within time standards promulgated by the Supreme Court under its Administrative Rules may be placed on a dismissal docket.

3. Reinstatement. A motion to reinstate shall set forth the grounds therefor and be verified by the movant or his attorney. It shall be filed with the clerk within 30 days after the order of dismissal is signed or within the period provided by Rule 306a. A copy of the motion to reinstate shall be served on each attorney of record and each party not represented by an attorney whose address is shown on the docket or in the papers on file. The clerk shall deliver a copy of the motion to the judge, who shall set a hearing on the motion as soon as practicable. The court shall notify all parties or their attorneys of record of the date, time and place of the hearing.

The court shall reinstate the case upon finding after a hearing that the failure of the party or his attorney was not intentional or the result of conscious indifference but was due to an accident or mistake or that the failure has been otherwise reasonably explained.

In the event for any reason a motion for reinstatement is not decided by signed written order within seventy-five days after the judgment is signed, or, within such other time as may be allowed by Rule 306a, the motion shall be deemed overruled by operation of law. If a motion to reinstate is timely filed by any party, the trial court, regardless of whether an appeal has been perfected, has plenary power to reinstate the case until 30 days after all such timely filed motions are overruled, either by a written and signed order or by operation of law, whichever occurs first.

4. Cumulative Remedies. This dismissal and reinstatement procedure shall be cumulative of the rules and laws governing any other procedures available to the parties in such cases. The same reinstatement procedures and timetable are applicable to all dismissals for want of prosecution including cases which are dismissed pursuant to the court's inherent power, whether or not a motion to dismiss has been filed.

History of TRCP 165a: Amended eff. Jan. 1, 1988, by order of July 15, 1987 (733-34 S.W.2d [Tex.Cases] I). Amended eff. Apr. 1, 1984, by order of Dec. 5, 1983 (661-62 S.W.2d [Tex.Cases] xliv): Rewrote to provide a statewide rule for dismissal and reinstatement of cases. Amended eff. Jan. 1, 1976, by order of July 22, 1975 (525-26 S.W.2d [Tex.Cases] xlviii): Deleted words "or docket call" after word "trial" in first sentence. Adopted eff. Feb. 1, 1973, by order of Oct. 3, 1972 (483-84 S.W.2d [Tex.Cases] xxiv). Source: New rule.

See *Commentaries*, "Involuntary Dismissal," ch. 7-G, p. 658; "Motion to Reinstate After Dismissal for Want of Prosecution," ch. 10-F, p. 826; *O'Connor's Texas Forms*, FORMS 7G.

ANNOTATIONS

Alexander v. Lynda's Boutique, 134 S.W.3d 845, 849-50 (Tex.2004). "[T]he clerk has an affirmative duty under Rule 165a to give notice, but no duty to affirmatively show in the record that such notice was given…. [¶] [T]he fact that the record is silent about the sending of notices under Rule 165a does not establish error on the face of the record. [M]ere silence as to whether notice was sent does not establish that notice was not sent or that it was sent to the wrong address. *At 852:* Rule 165a(1) does not preclude a trial court from scheduling a pre-trial hearing, giving notice that failure to attend that hearing may result in dismissal for want of prosecution, and also deciding at that hearing whether the case should be dismissed for want of prosecution if a party seeking relief fails to attend. All Rule 165a(1) requires is notice of intent to dismiss and of a date, time, and place for the hearing."

Villarreal v. San Antonio Truck & Equip., 994 S.W.2d 628, 630 (Tex.1999). "The trial court's authority to dismiss for want of prosecution stems from two sources: (1) Rule 165a … and (2) the court's inherent power. [¶] The failure to provide adequate notice of the trial court's intent to dismiss for want of prosecution requires reversal." *See also Ringer v. Kimball*, 274 S.W.3d 865, 867 (Tex.App.—Fort Worth 2008, no pet.).

Smith v. Babcock & Wilcox Constr. Co., 913 S.W.2d 467, 468 (Tex.1995). "A failure to appear is not intentional or due to conscious indifference within the meaning of [TRCP 165a] merely because it is deliberate; it must also be without adequate justification. Proof of such justification—accident, mistake or other reasonable explanation—negates the intent or conscious indifference for which reinstatement can be denied. Also, conscious indifference means more than mere negligence." *See also Johnson v. Hawkins*, 255 S.W.3d 394, 398 (Tex.App.—Dallas 2008, pet. denied) (whether failure to appear was not intentional or result of conscious indifference is fact-finding within trial court's discretion).

United Residential Props., L.P. v. Theis, ___ S.W.3d ___ (Tex.App.—Houston [14th Dist.] 2012, no pet.) (No. 14-11-00330-CV; 8-21-12). The 30-day deadline to file a motion to reinstate "is jurisdictional, and a trial court loses jurisdiction to reinstate a dismissed case after the deadline."

✦

Polinard v. Medina, No. 13-11-00403-CV (Tex. App.—Corpus Christi 2012, n.p.h.) (memo op.; 7-19-12). "[P] claims that [TRCP] 165a, when read together with [TRCP] 21a, requires that notice of potential dismissal for want of prosecution be sent by 'certified or registered mail.' We disagree. ... Rule 21a is a permissive provision; it allows service of notices to be effectuated by certain methods but does not proscribe others. Rule 165a(1) expressly authorizes service by the U.S. Postal Service and does not make reference to certified or registered mail. The two rules do not conflict. When read together, they authorize service by regular U.S. Postal Service mail."

Davis v. Friedson, No. 14-08-01098-CV (Tex. App.—Houston [14th Dist.] 2010, no pet.) (memo op.; 3-16-10) (footnote 16). "[P] contends [D] cannot request that only his counterclaims be reinstated because [TRCP] 165a speaks to 'cases' being reinstated and not 'claims.' [P] does not cite any authority construing Rule 165a in this manner. [P] also claims [D's] remaining counterclaims depended entirely on a contract for which no money had changed hands, and which [D] had successfully attacked as unenforceable. Rule 165a does not require that the party seeking to reinstate the case establish a 'meritorious' claim or defense."

Cappetta v. Hermes, 222 S.W.3d 160, 167 (Tex. App.—San Antonio 2006, no pet.). "Several courts of appeals have concluded that Rule 165a(3)'s reinstatement standard should not apply to cases dismissed under the trial court's inherent power, but fail to explain what alternative reinstatement standard should then apply. Because a case may be dismissed for lack of diligence under either Rule 165a(2) or the court's inherent power, no purpose is served in creating two separate standards for review. The standard should be the same regardless of whether a case is dismissed pursuant to Rule 165a or the court's inherent power. [¶] We ... hold the Rule 165a(3) standard applies to all dismissals for want of prosecution, whether rule-based or inherent power-based." *Contra Maida v. Fire Ins. Exch.*, this page.

In re Wal-Mart Stores, 20 S.W.3d 734, 740 (Tex. App.—El Paso 2000, orig. proceeding). "Rule 165a(3) requires that a case be reinstated by signed written order.... An oral pronouncement by the court reinstating the case, even when accompanied by a docket entry, is ordinarily inadequate to reinstate the case."

Maida v. Fire Ins. Exch., 990 S.W.2d 836, 840-41 (Tex.App.—Fort Worth 1999, no pet.). We agree with our sister courts that "have held [TRCP] 165a(3)'s standard for reinstatement only applies to cases dismissed for failure to appear. [¶] The standard set out in [TRCP] 165a(3) is essentially the same standard as that for setting aside a default judgment. Such a standard is well suited for analyzing specific instances of conduct. On the other hand, it does not easily lend itself to determining whether a party diligently prosecuted a case or whether the disposition of the case complies with the supreme court's time standards for disposition. [¶] Furthermore, [TRCP] 165a(4) is consistent with application of [TRCP 165a(3)] to only instances of dismissal based on a failure to appear. [TRCP] 165a(4) requires that the *procedures* and *timetable*, be applied to all dismissals for want of prosecution. Therefore, we hold that [TRCP] 165a(3)'s reinstatement standard, 'conscious indifference,' only applies to cases dismissed for failure to appear." *Contra Cappetta v. Hermes*, this page.

SECTION 8. PRETRIAL PROCEDURE

TRCP 166. PRETRIAL CONFERENCE

In an appropriate action, to assist in the disposition of the case without undue expense or burden to the parties, the court may in its discretion direct the attorneys for the parties and the parties or their duly authorized agents to appear before it for a conference to consider:

(a) All pending dilatory pleas, motions and exceptions;

(b) The necessity or desirability of amendments to the pleadings;

(c) A discovery schedule;

(d) Requiring written statements of the parties' contentions;

(e) Contested issues of fact and simplification of the issues;

(f) The possibility of obtaining stipulations of fact;

(g) The identification of legal matters to be ruled on or decided by the court;

(h) The exchange of a list of direct fact witnesses, other than rebuttal or impeaching witnesses the necessity of whose testimony cannot reasonably be anticipated before the time of trial, who will be called to testify at trial, stating their address and telephone number, and the subject of the testimony of each such witness;

✦

(i) The exchange of a list of expert witnesses who will be called to testify at trial, stating their address and telephone number, and the subject of the testimony and opinions that will be proffered by each expert witness;

(j) Agreed applicable propositions of law and contested issues of law;

(k) Proposed jury charge questions, instructions, and definitions for a jury case or proposed findings of fact and conclusions of law for a nonjury case;

(l) The marking and exchanging of all exhibits that any party may use at trial and stipulation to the authenticity and admissibility of exhibits to be used at trial;

(m) Written trial objections to the opposite party's exhibits, stating the basis for each objection;

(n) The advisability of a preliminary reference of issues to a master or auditor for findings to be used as evidence when the trial is to be by jury;

(o) The settlement of the case, and to aid such consideration, the court may encourage settlement;

(p) Such other matters as may aid in the disposition of the action.

The court shall make an order that recites the action taken at the pretrial conference, the amendments allowed to the pleadings, the time within which same may be filed, and the agreements made by the parties as to any of the matters considered, and which limits the issues for trial to those not disposed of by admissions, agreements of counsel, or rulings of the court; and such order when issued shall control the subsequent course of the action, unless modified at the trial to prevent manifest injustice. The court in its discretion may establish by rule a pretrial calendar on which actions may be placed for consideration as above provided and may either confine the calendar to jury actions or extend it to all actions.

Pretrial proceedings in multidistrict litigation may also be governed by Rules 11 and 13 of the Rules of Judicial Administration.

History of TRCP 166: Amended eff. Sept. 1, 2003, by order of Aug. 29, 2003 (114-15 S.W.3d [Tex.Cases] xx): Added par. on multidistrict litigation. Amended eff. Sept. 1, 1990, by order of Apr. 24, 1990 (785-86 S.W.2d [Tex.Cases] xlix): First sentence amended to add word "appropriate" and phrase "to assist in the disposition of the case without undue expense or burden to the parties"; (a) amended to add "pending" and to change phrase "all motions and exceptions relating to a suit pending" to "motions and exceptions"; (c) changed to (b); new (c) and (d) added; former (b) changed to (e) and phrase "Contested issues of fact and" added; former (d) changed to (f), word "admissions" changed to "stipulations" and deleted phrase "and of documents which will avoid unnecessary proof"; (g)-(m) added; former (f) changed to (n); (o) added; former (g) changed to (p); added words "or rulings of the court" and changed "entered" to "issued" in last par.; to broaden the scope of the rule and to confirm the ability of the trial courts at pretrial hearings to encourage settlement. Amended eff. Jan. 1, 1961, by order of July 26, 1960 (23 Tex.B.J. 620 [1961]): Added requirement that court's order at pretrial conference allowing amendments show "the time within which same may be filed." Adopted eff. Sept. 1, 1941, by order of Oct. 29, 1940 (3 Tex.B.J. 548 [1940]). Source: FRCP 16. Rule gives court the power to compel appearance of parties or their agents, as well as the attorneys; case may be referred to an auditor.

See Gov't Code §21.001(a); TRCP 248; TRJA 11, 13; *Commentaries*, "Pretrial Conference," ch. 5-A, p. 315; "Motion to Transfer to Multidistrict Litigation Pretrial Court," ch. 5-G, p. 355; *O'Connor's Texas Forms*, FORM 5A:1.

ANNOTATIONS

Koslow's v. Mackie, 796 S.W.2d 700, 703 (Tex. 1990). TRCP 166 "includes the power to order the parties through their attorneys (or through themselves if appearing pro se) to confer to narrow the issues for the written pretrial conference report."

Provident Life & Acc. Ins. v. Hazlitt, 216 S.W.2d 805, 807 (Tex.1949). "The purpose of [TRCP 166] is to simplify and shorten the trial…. [N]o controverted issues of fact could be adjudicated at [the pretrial] conference, but orders could be entered disposing of issues which are founded upon admitted or undisputed facts."

In re Estate of Henry, 250 S.W.3d 518, 526 (Tex. App.—Dallas 2008, no pet.). "Rule 166 … provides that an order made at a pretrial conference hearing 'shall control the subsequent course of the action.' However, the trial court retains authority under rule 166 to modify an order to prevent manifest injustice. 'Rule 166 recognizes the fundamental rule that a trial court has the inherent right to change or modify any interlocutory order or judgment until the time the judgment on the merits in the case becomes final.'"

In re Bledsoe, 41 S.W.3d 807, 812 (Tex.App.—Fort Worth 2001, orig. proceeding). "The trial court has power, implicit under rule 166, to sanction a party for failing to obey its pretrial orders." *See also* ***Taylor v. Taylor***, 254 S.W.3d 527, 532 (Tex.App.—Houston [1st Dist.] 2008, no pet.).

Lindley v. Johnson, 936 S.W.2d 53, 55 (Tex.App.—Tyler 1996, writ denied). "When a trial court's pretrial scheduling order changes the deadlines set forth in a procedural rule, the trial court's order prevails."

TRCP 166a. SUMMARY JUDGMENT

(a) For Claimant. A party seeking to recover upon a claim, counterclaim, or cross-claim or to obtain a declaratory judgment may, at any time after the adverse party has appeared or answered, move with or without supporting affidavits for a summary judgment in his favor upon all or any part thereof. A summary judgment,

———————————— ★ ————————————

interlocutory in character, may be rendered on the issue of liability alone although there is a genuine issue as to amount of damages.

(b) For Defending Party. A party against whom a claim, counterclaim, or cross-claim is asserted or a declaratory judgment is sought may, at any time, move with or without supporting affidavits for a summary judgment in his favor as to all or any part thereof.

(c) Motion and Proceedings Thereon. The motion for summary judgment shall state the specific grounds therefor. Except on leave of court, with notice to opposing counsel, the motion and any supporting affidavits shall be filed and served at least twenty-one days before the time specified for hearing. Except on leave of court, the adverse party, not later than seven days prior to the day of hearing may file and serve opposing affidavits or other written response. No oral testimony shall be received at the hearing. The judgment sought shall be rendered forthwith if (i) the deposition transcripts, interrogatory answers, and other discovery responses referenced or set forth in the motion or response, and (ii) the pleadings, admissions, affidavits, stipulations of the parties, and authenticated or certified public records, if any, on file at the time of the hearing, or filed thereafter and before judgment with permission of the court, show that, except as to the amount of damages, there is no genuine issue as to any material fact and the moving party is entitled to judgment as a matter of law on the issues expressly set out in the motion or in an answer or any other response. Issues not expressly presented to the trial court by written motion, answer or other response shall not be considered on appeal as grounds for reversal. A summary judgment may be based on uncontroverted testimonial evidence of an interested witness, or of an expert witness as to subject matter concerning which the trier of fact must be guided solely by the opinion testimony of experts, if the evidence is clear, positive and direct, otherwise credible and free from contradictions and inconsistencies, and could have been readily controverted.

(d) Appendices, References and Other Use of Discovery Not Otherwise on File. Discovery products not on file with the clerk may be used as summary judgment evidence if copies of the material, appendices containing the evidence, or a notice containing specific references to the discovery or specific references to other instruments, are filed and served on all parties together with a statement of intent to use the specified discovery as summary judgment proofs: (i) at least twenty-one days before the hearing if such proofs are to be used to support the summary judgment; or (ii) at least seven days before the hearing if such proofs are to be used to oppose the summary judgment.

(e) Case Not Fully Adjudicated on Motion. If summary judgment is not rendered upon the whole case or for all the relief asked and a trial is necessary, the judge may at the hearing examine the pleadings and the evidence on file, interrogate counsel, ascertain what material fact issues exist and make an order specifying the facts that are established as a matter of law, and directing such further proceedings in the action as are just.

(f) Form of Affidavits; Further Testimony. Supporting and opposing affidavits shall be made on personal knowledge, shall set forth such facts as would be admissible in evidence, and shall show affirmatively that the affiant is competent to testify to the matters stated therein. Sworn or certified copies of all papers or parts thereof referred to in an affidavit shall be attached thereto or served therewith. The court may permit affidavits to be supplemented or opposed by depositions or by further affidavits. Defects in the form of affidavits or attachments will not be grounds for reversal unless specifically pointed out by objection by an opposing party with opportunity, but refusal, to amend.

(g) When Affidavits Are Unavailable. Should it appear from the affidavits of a party opposing the motion that he cannot for reasons stated present by affidavit facts essential to justify his opposition, the court may refuse the application for judgment or may order a continuance to permit affidavits to be obtained or depositions to be taken or discovery to be had or may make such other order as is just.

(h) Affidavits Made in Bad Faith. Should it appear to the satisfaction of the court at any time that any of the affidavits presented pursuant to this rule are presented in bad faith or solely for the purpose of delay, the court shall forthwith order the party employing them to pay to the other party the amount of the reasonable expenses which the filing of the affidavits caused him to incur, including reasonable attorney's fees, and any offending party or attorney may be adjudged guilty of contempt.

(i) No-Evidence Motion. After adequate time for discovery, a party without presenting summary judgment evidence may move for summary judgment on the

★

ground that there is no evidence of one or more essential elements of a claim or defense on which an adverse party would have the burden of proof at trial. The motion must state the elements as to which there is no evidence. The court must grant the motion unless the respondent produces summary judgment evidence raising a genuine issue of material fact.

Notes & Comments to TRCP 166a(i): This comment is intended to inform the construction and application of the rule. Paragraph (i) authorizes a motion for summary judgment based on the assertion that, after adequate opportunity for discovery, there is no evidence to support one or more specified elements of an adverse party's claim or defense. A discovery period set by pretrial order should be adequate opportunity for discovery unless there is a showing to the contrary, and ordinarily a motion under paragraph (i) would be permitted after the period but not before. The motion must be specific in challenging the evidentiary support for an element of a claim or defense; paragraph (i) does not authorize conclusory motions or general no-evidence challenges to an opponent's case. Paragraph (i) does not apply to ordinary motions for summary judgment under paragraphs (a) or (b), in which the movant must prove it is entitled to judgment by establishing each element of its own claim or defense as a matter of law. To defeat a motion made under paragraph (i), the respondent is not required to marshal its proof; its response need only point out evidence that raises a fact issue on the challenged elements. The existing rules continue to govern the general requirements of summary judgment practice. A motion under paragraph (i) is subject to sanctions provided by existing law (CPRC §§9.001-10.006) and rules (TRCP 13). The denial of a motion under paragraph (i) is no more reviewable by appeal or mandamus than the denial of a motion under paragraph (c).

History of TRCP 166a: Amended eff. Sept. 1, 1997, by order of Aug. 15, 1997 (60 Tex.B.J. 872 (Oct. 1997)): Amended (e) and added (i); see comment above. Amended eff. Sept. 1, 1990, by order of Apr. 24, 1990 (785-86 S.W.2d [Tex.Cases] l): Added (d); Amendment provides a mechanism for using previously unfiled discovery in summary judgment practice; such proofs must be filed in advance of the hearing in accordance with TRCP 166a; renumbered (d)-(g) to (e)-(h). Amended eff. Jan. 1, 1988, by order of July 15, 1987 (733-34 S.W.2d [Tex.Cases] li): Amended (c). Amended eff. Apr. 1, 1984, by order of Dec. 5, 1983 (661-62 S.W.2d [Tex.Cases] xlv): Amended (c) to include stipulations and authenticated and certified public records as matters in support of a summary judgment. Amended eff. Jan. 1, 1981, by order of June 10, 1980 (599-600 S.W.2d [Tex.Cases] xxxix): Added to second sentence the words "with notice to opposing counsel," "and any supporting affidavits," and "filed and"; added "file and" in third sentence. Amended eff. Jan. 1, 1978, by order of July 11, 1977 (553-54 S.W.2d [Tex.Cases] xlvi): Changed time requirements in (c); added third, fourth, and fifth sentences of (c), and last sentence of (e). Amended eff. Jan. 1, 1971, by order of July 21, 1970 (455-56 S.W.2d [Tex.Cases] xxxi): Added first sentence of (c); inserted words "answers to interrogatories" in fifth sentence of (c). Amended eff. Jan. 1, 1967, by order of July 20, 1966 (401-02 S.W.2d [Tex.Cases] xxxiii): Added third sentence of (c). Amended eff. Mar. 1, 1952, by order of Oct. 1, 1951 (14 Tex.B.J. 533 [1951]): Added last sentence to (a). Adopted eff. Mar. 1, 1950, by order of Oct. 12, 1949 (12 Tex.B.J. 531 [1949]). Source: FRCP 56, with changes: Substituted phrase "adverse party has appeared or answered" for the phrase "pleading in answer thereto was served" in (a).

See *Commentaries*, "Motion for Summary Judgment—General Rules," ch. 7-B, p. 603; "Traditional Motion for Summary Judgment," ch. 7-C, p. 628; "No-Evidence Motion for Summary Judgment," ch. 7-D, p. 640; *O'Connor's Texas Forms*, FORMS 7B, 7C.

ANNOTATIONS

Traditional SJ

Frost Nat'l Bank v. Fernandez, 315 S.W.3d 494, 508 (Tex.2010). "A defendant who conclusively negates at least one of the essential elements of a cause of action or conclusively establishes an affirmative defense is entitled to summary judgment." *See also **Cathey v. Booth***, 900 S.W.2d 339, 341 (Tex.1995).

Proulx v. Wells, 235 S.W.3d 213, 215 (Tex.2007). "Our jurisprudence has at times been less than clear in explaining the summary-judgment burden that inheres when the diligent-service question is presented. *At 216:* [O]nce a defendant has affirmatively pled the limitations defense and shown that service was effected after limitations expired, the burden shifts to the plaintiff 'to explain the delay.' Thus, it is the plaintiff's burden to present evidence regarding the efforts that were made to serve the defendant, and to explain every lapse in effort or period of delay. In some instances, the plaintiff's explanation may be *legally* improper to raise the diligence issue and the defendant will bear no burden at all. In others, the plaintiff's explanation of its service efforts may demonstrate a lack of due diligence as a matter of law, as when one or more lapses between service efforts are unexplained or patently unreasonable. But if the plaintiff's explanation for the delay raises a material fact issue concerning the diligence of service efforts, the burden shifts back to the defendant to conclusively show why, as a matter of law, the explanation is insufficient." *See also **Farmers Ins. Exch. v. Rodriguez***, 366 S.W.3d 216, 221 (Tex.App.—Houston [14th Dist.] 2012, pet. filed 8-1-12).

Valence Oper. Co. v. Dorsett, 164 S.W.3d 656, 661 (Tex.2005). "When both parties move for partial summary judgment on the same issues and the trial court grants one motion and denies the other ..., the reviewing court considers the summary judgment evidence presented by both sides, determines all questions presented, and if the reviewing court determines that the trial court erred, renders the judgment the trial court should have rendered."

Park Place Hosp. v. Estate of Milo, 909 S.W.2d 508, 510 (Tex.1995). For Ds "to prevail, they were required to prove that there was no genuine issue as to any material fact and that they were entitled to judgment as a matter of law. In reviewing a summary judgment, we must accept as true evidence favoring [P], indulging every reasonable inference and resolving all doubts in [P's] favor." *See also **Western Invs. v. Urena***, 162 S.W.3d 547, 550 (Tex.2005); ***Huckabee v. Time Warner Entm't Co.***, 19 S.W.3d 413, 422 (Tex.2000).

McConnell v. Southside ISD, 858 S.W.2d 337, 341 (Tex.1993). "In determining whether grounds are expressly presented, reliance may not be placed on briefs or summary judgment evidence."

✦

Tello v. Bank One, 218 S.W.3d 109, 118-19 (Tex. App.—Houston [14th Dist.] 2007, no pet.). "[S]ummary judgments must stand or fall on their own merits, and the non-movant's failure to answer or respond cannot supply by default the summary judgment proof necessary to establish the movant's right. If a non-movant fails to present any issues in its response or answer, the movant's right is not established and the movant must still establish its entitlement to summary judgment. 'The effect of such a failure is that the non-movant is limited on appeal to arguing the legal sufficiency of the grounds presented by the movant.'" *See also Medlock v. Commission for Lawyer Discipline*, 24 S.W.3d 865, 870 (Tex.App.—Texarkana 2000, no pet.).

Rush v. Barrios, 56 S.W.3d 88, 98 (Tex.App.—Houston [14th Dist.] 2001, pet. denied). "A trial court may ... properly grant summary judgment after having previously denied [it] without a motion by or prior notice to the parties, as long as the court retains jurisdiction over the case."

Michael v. Dyke, 41 S.W.3d 746, 751 (Tex.App.—Corpus Christi 2001, no pet.). "When it is not readily apparent to the trial court that summary judgment is sought under rule 166a(i), the court should presume that it is filed under the traditional summary judgment rule and analyze it according to those well-recognized standards. [The] order granting summary judgment should clarify whether the motion is granted on no-evidence grounds or traditional grounds. When an order fails to so clarify, a motion requesting such clarification should be filed with the trial court."

No-Evidence SJ

Mack Trucks, Inc. v. Tamez, 206 S.W.3d 572, 581-82 (Tex.2006). A no-evidence motion for "summary judgment ... is essentially a motion for a pretrial directed verdict. Once such a motion is filed, the burden shifts to the nonmoving party to present evidence raising an issue of material fact as to the elements specified in the motion. We review the evidence presented by the motion and response in the light most favorable to the party against whom the summary judgment was rendered, crediting evidence favorable to that party if reasonable jurors could, and disregarding contrary evidence unless reasonable jurors could not." *See also Timpte Indus. v. Gish*, 286 S.W.3d 306, 310 (Tex.2009).

King Ranch, Inc. v. Chapman, 118 S.W.3d 742, 751 (Tex.2003). "'A no evidence point will be sustained when (a) there is a complete absence of evidence of a vital fact, (b) the court is barred by rules of law or of evidence from giving weight to the only evidence offered to prove a vital fact, (c) the evidence offered to prove a vital fact is no more than a mere scintilla, or (d) the evidence conclusively establishes the opposite of the vital fact.' ... More than a scintilla of evidence exists when the evidence, 'rises to a level that would enable reasonable and fair-minded people to differ in their conclusions.'" *See also Ford Motor Co. v. Ridgway*, 135 S.W.3d 598, 601 (Tex.2004) (evidence that does no more than create mere suspicion of existence of a fact is, in legal effect, no evidence).

Dyer v. Accredited Home Lenders, Inc., No. 02-11-00046-CV (Tex.App.—Fort Worth 2012, pet. denied) (memo op.; 2-2-12). "When filing a no-evidence motion ... the movant's burden is to produce a legally sufficient motion—the movant has no burden to produce evidence. ... If the movant for some reason attaches evidence to its motion, the trial court may not consider the evidence except in the limited circumstance when the evidence raises a fact issue. But under normal circumstances, no evidence is attached, and none is required for the trial court to grant the motion."

Madison v. Williamson, 241 S.W.3d 145, 155 (Tex. App.—Houston [1st Dist.] 2007, pet. denied). "To determine whether adequate time for discovery [under TRCP 166a(i)] has elapsed, we examine such factors as: (1) the nature of the case; (2) the nature of evidence necessary to controvert the no-evidence motion; (3) the length of time the case was active; (4) the amount of time the no-evidence motion was on file; (5) whether the movant had requested stricter deadlines for discovery; (6) the amount of discovery already completed; and (7) whether the discovery deadlines in place were specific or vague." *See also McInnis v. Mallia*, 261 S.W.3d 197, 202-03 (Tex.App.—Houston [14th Dist.] 2008, no pet.) (time allocated for discovery in docket control order is strong indicator of adequate time).

Flores v. Flores, 225 S.W.3d 651, 654-55 (Tex. App.—El Paso 2006, pet. denied). "Ordinarily, a no-evidence motion for summary judgment would not be permitted during the discovery period. When a party contends that it has not had an adequate opportunity for discovery before a summary judgment hearing, it

★

must file either an affidavit explaining the need for further discovery or a verified motion for continuance. [Ps] did not file [either one]. [Ps] have waived their argument regarding an adequate time for discovery." *See also Davis v. West*, 317 S.W.3d 301, 313-14 (Tex. App.—Houston [1st Dist.] 2009, no pet.).

Hybrid Motion

Binur v. Jacobo, 135 S.W.3d 646, 650-51 (Tex. 2004). TRCP 166a "does not prohibit a party from combining in a single motion a request for summary judgment that utilizes the procedures under either subsection (a) or (b), with a request for summary judgment that utilizes subsection (i)…. The fact that evidence may be attached to a motion … under subsection (a) or (b) does not foreclose a party from also asserting that there is no evidence with regard to a particular element. Similarly, if a motion brought solely under subsection (i) attaches evidence, that evidence should not be considered unless it creates a fact question, but such a motion should not be disregarded or treated as a motion under subsection (a) or (b). [¶] [U]sing headings to clearly delineate the basis for summary judgment under subsection (a) or (b) from the basis for summary judgment under subsection (i) would be helpful …, but the rule does not require it."

East Hill Mar., Inc. v. Rinker Boat Co., 229 S.W.3d 813, 816 (Tex.App.—Fort Worth 2007, pet. denied). "When a party moves for summary judgment under both [TRCPs] 166a(c) and 166a(i), we will first review the trial court's judgment under the standards of rule 166a(i). If the nonmovant failed to produce more than a scintilla of evidence under that burden, then there is no need to analyze whether the movant's summary judgment proof satisfied the less stringent rule 166a(c) burden." *See also Ford Motor Co. v. Ridgway*, 135 S.W.3d 598, 600 (Tex.2004).

Waite v. Woodard, Hall & Primm, P.C., 137 S.W.3d 277, 281 (Tex.App.—Houston [1st Dist.] 2004, no pet.). "Although [TRCP] 166a does not prohibit a hybrid motion, the motion must give fair notice to the non-movant of the basis on which the summary judgment is sought. [P's] motion did not give fair notice that it was attempting to establish its entitlement to judgment as a matter of law…."

SJ Evidence

Morgan v. Anthony, 27 S.W.3d 928, 929 (Tex. 2000). "Generally, a party cannot rely on its own answer to an interrogatory as summary judgment evidence.

However, [P] was questioned in one of her depositions about her seven-page interrogatory answer …, and the interrogatory answer was attached to her deposition as an exhibit. … The interrogatory answer became competent summary judgment evidence when it became a deposition exhibit, [P] affirmed in her deposition that it was correct, and she was subject to cross-examination about the assertions in her interrogatory answer." *See also Watson v. Henderson*, No. 05-08-01158-CV (Tex.App.—Dallas 2010, pet. denied) (memo op.; 1-20-10).

Wadewitz v. Montgomery, 951 S.W.2d 464, 466 (Tex.1997). "Conclusory statements by an expert are insufficient to support or defeat summary judgment." *See also United Blood Servs. v. Longoria*, 938 S.W.2d 29, 30 (Tex.1997).

Trico Techs. v. Montiel, 949 S.W.2d 308, 310 (Tex. 1997). "The mere fact that the affidavit is self-serving does not necessarily make the evidence an improper basis for summary judgment. Summary judgment based on the uncontroverted affidavit of an interested witness is proper if the evidence is clear, positive, direct, otherwise credible, free from contradictions and inconsistencies, and could have been readily controverted. 'Could have been readily controverted' does not mean that the summary judgment evidence could have been easily and conveniently rebutted, but rather indicates that the testimony could have been effectively countered by opposing evidence." *See also Davis v. City of Grapevine*, 188 S.W.3d 748, 754 (Tex.App.—Fort Worth 2006, pet. denied).

Wilson v. Burford, 904 S.W.2d 628, 629 (Tex.1995). "Rule 166a(c) plainly includes in the record evidence attached either to the motion or to a response." *See also Johnson v. Driver*, 198 S.W.3d 359, 363 (Tex.App.—Tyler 2006, no pet.).

McConathy v. McConathy, 869 S.W.2d 341, 341 (Tex.1994). "[D]eposition excerpts [and other discovery] submitted as summary judgment evidence need not be authenticated. *At 342:* All parties have ready access to depositions taken in a cause, and thus deposition excerpts submitted with a motion for summary judgment may be easily verified as to their accuracy."

Casso v. Brand, 776 S.W.2d 551, 558 (Tex.1989). "If the credibility of the affiant … is likely to be a dispositive factor in the resolution of the case, then summary judgment is inappropriate. On the other hand, if the non-movant must, in all likelihood, come forth with in-

⭐

dependent evidence to prevail, then summary judgment may well be proper in the absence of such controverting proof."

Rad v. Calbeck, No. 03-10-00429-CV (Tex.App.—Austin 2011, no pet.) (memo op.; 12-30-11). "[D]iscovery documents from the same case do not need to be authenticated to serve as summary judgment proof. However, unless ... this discovery documents exception [applies], documents submitted as summary judgment evidence must be sworn or certified. Therefore, although court records from other cases are acceptable summary judgment evidence, they must be certified or attested to under oath as authentic."

Rockwall Commons Assocs. v. MRC Mortg. Grantor Trust I, 331 S.W.3d 500, 507 (Tex.App.—El Paso 2010, no pet.). "Substantive defects include affidavits that include legal or factual conclusions. Among the objections that may be raised at trial regarding the form of an affidavit are: (1) lack of personal knowledge; (2) hearsay; (3) statement of an interested witness that is not clear, positive, direct, or free from contradiction; and (4) competence."

Kastner v. Jenkens & Gilchrist, P.C., 231 S.W.3d 571, 581 (Tex.App.—Dallas 2007, no pet.). "The [TRCPs] do not require that summary judgment evidence be physically attached to the motion. Instead, the rules embody an infinitely more practical requirement that evidence be 'filed and served' with the motion."

Rabe v. Dillard's, Inc., 214 S.W.3d 767, 769 (Tex.App.—Dallas 2007, no pet.). "[P's] only summary judgment evidence consisted of statements she made in an affidavit. One of these statements describes the alleged threat made by the attorney for [D] during the mediation. This statement is not competent summary judgment evidence. The [TRCPs] require that affidavits submitted as summary judgment evidence set forth facts that would be admissible in evidence. Communications made during an alternative dispute resolution procedure are confidential, and may not be used as evidence."

Chau v. Riddle, 212 S.W.3d 699, 704 (Tex.App.—Houston [1st Dist.] 2006), *rev'd on other grounds*, 254 S.W.3d 453 (Tex.2008). "The affidavit of an expert who is not properly designated may not be used as evidence in a summary judgment context. Where the expert's testimony will be excluded at trial on the merits, it will be excluded from a summary judgment proceeding."

Brown v. Brown, 145 S.W.3d 745, 751 (Tex.App.—Dallas 2004, pet. denied). "Defects in the form of an affidavit must be objected to, and the opposing party must have the opportunity to amend the affidavit. The failure to obtain a ruling on an objection to the form of the affidavit waives the objection. Defects in the substance of an affidavit are not waived by the failure to obtain a ruling from the trial court on the objection, and they may be raised for the first time on appeal." *See also* ***Watts v. Hermann Hosp.***, 962 S.W.2d 102, 105 (Tex.App.—Houston [1st Dist.] 1997, no pet.) (without objection, defects in authentication of attachments supporting SJ motion or response are waived).

Goss v. Bobby D. Assocs., 94 S.W.3d 65, 71 (Tex. App.—Tyler 2002, no pet.). "The trial court cannot consider affidavits offered by the non-movant to contradict deemed admissions in cases involving summary judgment."

Final vs. Partial SJ

M.O. Dental Lab v. Rape, 139 S.W.3d 671, 674 (Tex. 2004). "The court of appeals ... held that the trial court's order granting summary judgment was final for purposes of this appeal [even though it did not dispose of one D] because [that D] was never served and the record contains no pleadings or motions filed by [that D]. ... We [previously] held [in a similar circumstance that] 'the case stands as if there had been a discontinuance as to [unserved party], and the judgment is to be regarded as final for the purposes of appeal.' [¶] [Here, P] stated '[t]he location for service of [unserved D] is unknown at this time, so no citation is requested.' [B]oth [P] and [served Ds] agreed ... that [unserved D] was never served with process....*At 675:* [W]e conclude that the trial court's order granting summary judgment is final for the purposes of this appeal." *See also* ***In re Miranda***, 142 S.W.3d 354, 356-57 (Tex.App.—El Paso 2004, orig. proceeding).

Jacobs v. Satterwhite, 65 S.W.3d 653, 655 (Tex. 2001). "'[I]f a defendant moves for summary judgment on only one of [multiple] claims asserted by the plaintiff, but the trial court renders judgment that the plaintiff take nothing on all claims asserted, the judgment is final—erroneous, but final.'"

McNally v. Guevara, 52 S.W.3d 195, 196 (Tex. 2001). "[A] party's omission of one of his claims from a motion for summary judgment does not waive the claim because a party can always move for partial summary judgment, and thus there can be no presumption that a

⭐

motion for summary judgment addresses all of the movant's claims. Nothing in the trial court's judgment, other than its award of costs to [Ds], suggests that it intended to deny [Ds'] claim for attorney fees. The award of costs, by itself, does not make the judgment final."

Lehmann v. Har-Con Corp., 39 S.W.3d 191, 192-93 (Tex.2001). "We no longer believe that a Mother Hubbard clause in an order or in a judgment issued without a full trial can be taken to indicate finality. We therefore hold that in cases in which only one final and appealable judgment can be rendered, a judgment issued without a conventional trial is final for purposes of appeal if and only if either it actually disposes of all claims and parties then before the court, regardless of its language, or it states with unmistakable clarity that it is a final judgment as to all claims and all parties." *See also* ***Page v. Geller***, 941 S.W.2d 101, 102 (Tex.1997).

Pleadings in SJ Cases

Sosa v. Central Power & Light, 909 S.W.2d 893, 895 (Tex.1995). "Because [Ps] timely filed their second amended original petition, it superseded their first amended original petition containing the statements on which [Ds] based their motion for summary judgment. Contrary to statements in live pleadings, those contained in superseded pleadings are not conclusive and indisputable judicial admissions. Therefore, the basis for [Ds'] motion no longer existed and summary judgment was improper."

Laidlaw Waste Sys. v. City of Wilmer, 904 S.W.2d 656, 660 (Tex.1995). "Generally, pleadings are not competent evidence, even if sworn or verified."

Natividad v. Alexsis, Inc., 875 S.W.2d 695, 699 (Tex.1994). "A review of the pleadings [when an SJ is based on the pleadings] is de novo, with the reviewing court taking all allegations, facts, and inferences in the pleadings as true and viewing them in a light most favorable to the pleader. The reviewing court will affirm the summary judgment only if the pleadings are legally insufficient."

In re B.I.V., 870 S.W.2d 12, 13 (Tex.1994). "A summary judgment should not be based on a pleading deficiency that could be cured by amendment."

Burt v. Harwell, 369 S.W.3d 623, 625 (Tex.App.—Dallas 2012, no pet.). "Although summary judgment generally may not be granted on a claim not addressed in the summary judgment proceeding, it may be granted on later pleaded causes of action if the grounds asserted in the motion show that the plaintiff could not recover from the defendant on the later pleaded causes of action."

Austin v. Countrywide Homes Loans, 261 S.W.3d 68, 75 (Tex.App.—Houston [1st Dist.] 2008, pet. denied). "Once the hearing date for a motion for summary judgment has passed, the movant must secure a written order granting leave in order to file an amended pleading."

Motion for Continuance

Carpenter v. Cimarron Hydrocarbons Corp., 98 S.W.3d 682, 688 (Tex.2002). "[A] motion for leave to file a late summary-judgment response should be granted when a litigant establishes good cause for failing to timely respond by showing that (1) the failure to respond was not intentional or the result of conscious indifference, but the result of accident or mistake, and (2) allowing the late response will occasion no undue delay or otherwise injure the party seeking summary judgment."

Tenneco Inc. v. Enterprise Prods., 925 S.W.2d 640, 647 (Tex.1996). "When a party contends that it has not had an adequate opportunity for discovery before a summary judgment hearing, it must file either an affidavit explaining the need for further discovery or a verified motion for continuance." *See also* ***Poynor v. BMW of N. Am., LLC***, ___ S.W.3d ___ (Tex.App.—Dallas 2012, n.p.h.) (No. 05-10-00724-CV; 7-31-12); ***Carter v. MacFadyen***, 93 S.W.3d 307, 310 (Tex.App.—Houston [14th Dist.] 2002, pet. denied).

Tri-Steel Structures, Inc. v. Baptist Found., 166 S.W.3d 443, 448 (Tex.App.—Fort Worth 2005, pet. denied). "[I]f additional evidence is requested to be submitted through the initiation of discovery for 'want of testimony,' (1) the summary judgment hearing must be continued to allow the new evidence to be presented to the court, and (2) a motion for continuance consistent with [TRCP] 252 is required. [¶] On the other hand, if an amended affidavit is requested to be substituted for the affidavit already admitted[,] then the court may allow through a timely 'request,' as opposed through a motion for continuance, a corrected affidavit to be substituted for the previous affidavit already considered."

Notice

Rorie v. Goodwin, 171 S.W.3d 579, 583 (Tex. App.—Tyler 2005, no pet.). "A trial court must give notice of the submission date for a motion for summary

---

★

---

judgment because this date determines the date the nonmovant's response is due. The date of submission has the same meaning as the day of hearing under [TRCP] 166a(c). *At 584:* Failure to give proper notice violates the most rudimentary demands of due process of law."

TRCP 166b, 166c. REPEALED

Repealed eff. Jan. 1, 1999, by order of Nov. 9, 1998 (977-78 S.W.2d [Tex. Cases] xxxiii). For subject matter of former TRCP 166b, see TRCP 192. For subject matter of former TRCP 166c, see TRCP 191.1.

TRCP 167. OFFER OF SETTLEMENT; AWARD OF LITIGATION COSTS

167.1 **Generally.** Certain litigation costs may be awarded against a party who rejects an offer made substantially in accordance with this rule to settle a claim for monetary damages—including a counterclaim, crossclaim, or third-party claim—except in:

(a) a class action;

(b) a shareholder's derivative action;

(c) an action by or against the State, a unit of state government, or a political subdivision of the State;

(d) an action brought under the Family Code;

(e) an action to collect workers' compensation benefits under title 5, subtitle A of the Labor Code; or

(f) an action filed in a justice of the peace court or small claims court.

167.2 **Settlement Offer.**

(a) *Defendant's declaration a prerequisite; deadline.* A settlement offer under this rule may not be made until a defendant—a party against whom a claim for monetary damages is made—files a declaration invoking this rule. When a defendant files such a declaration, an offer or offers may be made under this rule to settle only those claims by and against that defendant. The declaration must be filed no later than 45 days before the case is set for conventional trial on the merits.

(b) *Requirements of an offer.* A settlement offer must:

(1) be in writing;

(2) state that it is made under Rule 167 and Chapter 42 of the Texas Civil Practice and Remedies Code;

(3) identify the party or parties making the offer and the party or parties to whom the offer is made;

(4) state the terms by which all monetary claims—including any attorney fees, interest, and costs that would be recoverable up to the time of the offer—

between the offeror or offerors on the one hand and the offeree or offerees on the other may be settled;

(5) state a deadline—no sooner than 14 days after the offer is served—by which the offer must be accepted;

(6) be served on all parties to whom the offer is made.

(c) *Conditions of offer.* An offer may be made subject to reasonable conditions, including the execution of appropriate releases, indemnities, and other documents. An offeree may object to a condition by written notice served on the offeror before the deadline stated in the offer. A condition to which no such objection is made is presumed to have been reasonable. Rejection of an offer made subject to a condition determined by the trial court to have been unreasonable cannot be the basis for an award of litigation costs under this rule.

(d) *Non-monetary and excepted claims not included.* An offer must not include non-monetary claims and other claims to which this rule does not apply.

(e) *Time limitations.* An offer may not be made:

(1) before a defendant's declaration is filed;

(2) within 60 days after the appearance in the case of the offeror or offeree, whichever is later;

(3) within 14 days before the date the case is set for a conventional trial on the merits, except that an offer may be made within that period if it is in response to, and within seven days of, a prior offer.

(f) *Successive offers.* A party may make an offer after having made or rejected a prior offer. A rejection of an offer is subject to imposition of litigation costs under this rule only if the offer is more favorable to the offeree than any prior offer.

167.3 Withdrawal, Acceptance, and Rejection of Offer.

(a) *Withdrawal of offer.* An offer can be withdrawn before it is accepted. Withdrawal is effective when written notice of the withdrawal is served on the offeree. Once an unaccepted offer has been withdrawn, it cannot be accepted or be the basis for awarding litigation costs under this rule.

(b) *Acceptance of offer.* An offer that has not been withdrawn can be accepted only by written notice served on the offeror by the deadline stated in the offer. When an offer is accepted, the offeror or offeree may

TRCP 167

★

file the offer and acceptance and may move the court to enforce the settlement.

(c) *Rejection of offer.* An offer that is not withdrawn or accepted is rejected. An offer may also be rejected by written notice served on the offeror by the deadline stated in the offer.

(d) *Objection to offer made before an offeror's joinder or designation of responsible third party.* An offer made before an offeror joins another party or designates a responsible third party may not be the basis for awarding litigation costs under this rule against an offeree who files an objection to the offer within 15 days after service of the offeror's pleading or designation.

167.4 Awarding Litigation Costs.

(a) *Generally.* If a settlement offer made under this rule is rejected, and the judgment to be awarded on the monetary claims covered by the offer is significantly less favorable to the offeree than was the offer, the court must award the offeror litigation costs against the offeree from the time the offer was rejected to the time of judgment.

(b) *"Significantly less favorable" defined.* A judgment award on monetary claims is significantly less favorable than an offer to settle those claims if:

(1) the offeree is a claimant and the judgment would be less than 80% of the offer; or

(2) the offeree is a defendant and the judgment would be more than 120% of the offer.

(c) *Litigation costs.* Litigation costs are the expenditures actually made and the obligations actually incurred—directly in relation to the claims covered by a settlement offer under this rule—for the following:

(1) court costs;

(2) reasonable deposition costs, in cases filed on or after September 1, 2011;

(3) reasonable fees for not more than two testifying expert witnesses; and

(4) reasonable attorney fees.

(d) *Limits on litigation costs.*

(1) In cases filed before September 1, 2011, the litigation costs that may be awarded under this rule must not exceed the following amount:

(A) the sum of the noneconomic damages, the exemplary or additional damages, and one-half of the economic damages to be awarded to the claimant in the judgment; minus

(B) the amount of any statutory or contractual liens in connection with the occurrences or incidents giving rise to the claim.

(2) In cases filed on or after September 1, 2011, the litigation costs that may be awarded to any party under this rule must not exceed the total amount that the claimant recovers or would recover before adding an award of litigation costs under this rule in favor of the claimant or subtracting as an offset an award of litigation costs under this rule in favor of the defendant.

(e) *No double recovery permitted.* A party who is entitled to recover attorney fees and costs under another law may not recover those same attorney fees and costs as litigation costs under this rule.

(f) *Limitation on attorney fees and costs recovered by a party against whom litigation costs are awarded.* A party against whom litigation costs are awarded may not recover attorney fees and costs under another law incurred after the date the party rejected the settlement offer made the basis of the award.

(g) *Litigation costs to be awarded to defendant as a setoff.* Litigation costs awarded to a defendant must be made a setoff to the claimant's judgment against the defendant.

167.5 Procedures.

(a) *Modification of time limits.* On motion, and for good cause shown, the court may—by written order made before commencement of trial on the merits—modify the time limits for filing a declaration under Rule 167.2(a) or for making an offer.

(b) *Discovery permitted.* On motion, and for good cause shown, a party against whom litigation costs are to be awarded may conduct discovery to ascertain the reasonableness of the costs requested. If the court determines the costs to be reasonable, it must order the party requesting discovery to pay all attorney fees and expenses incurred by other parties in responding to such discovery.

(c) *Hearing required.* The court must, upon request, conduct a hearing on a request for an award of litigation costs, at which the affected parties may present evidence.

167.6 Evidence Not Admissible. Evidence relating to an offer made under this rule is not admissible except for purposes of enforcing a settlement agree-

---

✦

---

ment or obtaining litigation costs. The provisions of this rule may not be made known to the jury by any means.

167.7 Other Settlement Offers Not Affected. This rule does not apply to any offer made in a mediation or arbitration proceeding. A settlement offer not made in compliance with this rule, or a settlement offer not made under this rule, or made in an action to which this rule does not apply, cannot be the basis for awarding litigation costs under this rule as to any party. This rule does not limit or affect a party's right to make a settlement offer that does not comply with this rule, or in an action to which this rule does not apply.

History of TRCP 167: Amended eff. Sept. 1, 2011, by order of Sept. 9, 2011 (Tex.Sup.Ct. Order, Misc. Docket No. 11-9182). Adopted eff. Jan. 1, 2004, by order of Oct. 9, 2003 (Tex.Sup.Ct. Order, Misc. Docket No. 03-9160). Source: New rule. Former TRCP 167 repealed eff. Jan. 1, 1999, by order of Nov. 9, 1998 (977-78 S.W.2d [Tex.Cases] xxxiii). For subject matter of former TRCP 167, see TRCP 196.

See *Commentaries*, "Offer of Settlement," ch. 7-H, p. 664.

TRCP 167a. REPEALED

Repealed eff. Jan. 1, 1999, by order of Nov. 9, 1998 (977-78 S.W.2d [Tex.Cases] xxxiii). For subject matter of former TRCP 167a, see TRCP 204.

TRCP 168. PERMISSION TO APPEAL

On a party's motion or on its own initiative, a trial court may permit an appeal from an interlocutory order that is not otherwise appealable, as provided by statute. Permission must be stated in the order to be appealed. An order previously issued may be amended to include such permission. The permission must identify the controlling question of law as to which there is a substantial ground for difference of opinion, and must state why an immediate appeal may materially advance the ultimate termination of the litigation.

Comment to 2011 change: Rule 168 is a new rule, added to implement amendments to section 51.014(d)-(f) of the Texas Civil Practice and Remedies Code. Rule 168 applies only to cases filed on or after Sept. 1, 2011. Rule 168 clarifies that the trial court's permission to appeal should be included in the order to be appealed rather than in a separate order. Rule of Appellate Procedure 28.3 sets out the corollary requirements for permissive appeals in the courts of appeals.

History of TRCP 168: Adopted eff. Sept. 1, 2011, by order of Sept. 9, 2011 (Tex.Sup.Ct. Order, Misc. Docket No. 11-9183). Source: New rule. Former TRCP 168 repealed eff. Jan. 1, 1999, by order of Nov. 9, 1998 (977-78 S.W.2d [Tex.Cases] xxxiii). For subject matter of former TRCP 168, see TRCP 197.

⓭ TRCP 169. EXPEDITED ACTIONS*

* **Editor's note:** In response to Gov't Code §22.004(h), the Supreme Court has proposed TRCP 169 to establish a process for the prompt, efficient, and cost-effective resolution of civil actions (expedited actions) in which only monetary relief is sought and the amount in controversy is no more than $100,000. *See* Tex.Sup.Ct. Order, Misc. Docket No. 12-9191 (eff. Mar. 1, 2013). The public-comment period for the proposed rule ends on February 1, 2013, and the rule is to take effect March 1, 2013. For the proposed version of the rule, see the appendix after this book's index. For the final version, go to the Supreme Court web-

site at www.supreme.courts.state.tx.us. When the new rule takes effect, a supplement to this book—with updated rules and commentaries that reflect the changes—will be available at www.JonesMcClure.com/TRCPamendments.

History of TRCP 169: Source: New rule. Former TRCP 169 repealed eff. Jan. 1, 1999, by order of Nov. 9, 1998 (977-78 S.W.2d [Tex.Cases] xxxiii). For subject matter of former TRCP 169, see TRCP 198.

TRCP 170. REPEALED

Repealed eff. Apr. 1, 1984, by order of Dec. 5, 1983 (661-62 S.W.2d [Tex.Cases] lvi): See TRCP 215.

TRCP 171. MASTER IN CHANCERY

The court may, in exceptional cases, for good cause appoint a master in chancery, who shall be a citizen of this State, and not an attorney for either party to the action, nor related to either party, who shall perform all of the duties required of him by the court, and shall be under orders of the court, and have such power as the master of chancery has in a court of equity.

The order of reference to the master may specify or limit his powers, and may direct him to report only upon particular issues, or to do or perform particular acts, or to receive and report evidence only and may fix the time and place for beginning and closing the hearings, and for the filing of the master's report. Subject to the limitations and specifications stated in the order, the master has and shall exercise the power to regulate all proceedings in every hearing before him and to do all acts and take all measures necessary or proper for the efficient performance of his duties under the order. He may require the production before him of evidence upon all matters embraced in the reference, including the production of books, papers, vouchers, documents and other writings applicable thereto. He may rule upon the admissibility of evidence, unless otherwise directed by the order of reference and has the authority to put witnesses on oath, and may, himself, examine them, and may call the parties to the action and examine them upon oath. When a party so requests, the master shall make a record of the evidence offered and excluded in the same manner as provided for a court sitting in the trial of a case.

The clerk of the court shall forthwith furnish the master with a copy of the order of reference.

The parties may procure the attendance of witnesses before the master by the issuance and service of process as provided by law and these rules.

The court may confirm, modify, correct, reject, reverse or recommit the report, after it is filed, as the court may deem proper and necessary in the particular circumstances of the case. The court shall award reasonable compensation to such master to be taxed as costs of suit.

History of TRCP 171: Amended eff. Dec. 31, 1941, by order of Sept. 20, 1941 (4 Tex.B.J. 513 [1941]). Adopted eff. Sept. 1, 1941, by order of Oct. 29, 1940 (3 Tex.B.J. 550 [1940]). Source: TRCS art. 2320 (repealed), FRCP 53.

See *Commentaries*, "Master in Chancery," ch. 1-K, p. 80.

ANNOTATIONS

Academy of Model Aeronautics, Inc. v. Packer, 860 S.W.2d 419, 419 (Tex.1993). "[T]he trial court abused its discretion in entering an order referring all pending and future discovery matters to a master."

Simpson v. Canales, 806 S.W.2d 802, 811 (Tex. 1991). "Rule 171 permits appointment of a master only 'in exceptional cases, for good cause.' [T]his requirement cannot be met merely by showing that a case is complicated or time-consuming, or that the court is busy." *See also* ***Hourani v. Katzen***, 305 S.W.3d 239, 247 (Tex.App.—Houston [1st Dist.] 2009, pet. denied).

In re Harris, 315 S.W.3d 685, 705 (Tex.App.—Houston [1st Dist.] 2010, orig. proceeding). "[C]ourts have found sufficient justification for the appointment of a master to supervise 'discovery questions which require extensive examination of highly technical and complex documents by a person having both a technical and a legal background.' [¶] Here, the case is not of a 'highly technical nature.' The fact that production of some of the discovery sought by [P] might require expert forensic examination of electronic media is not sufficient to show that this is an 'exceptional case' requiring expertise in computer forensics. Electronic discovery is a common component of modern litigation, and its mere presence alone does not constitute a showing of good cause for appointing a special master."

AIU Ins. v. Mehaffy, 942 S.W.2d 796, 803 (Tex. App.—Beaumont 1997, orig. proceeding). "The cases construing Rule 171 provide that if a party timely and formally objects to a master's ruling, that party is entitled to a de novo hearing before a judge or jury. We conclude this right is automatic and is not subject to a harmless error analysis."

TRCP 172. AUDIT

When an investigation of accounts or examination of vouchers appears necessary for the purpose of justice between the parties to any suit, the court shall appoint an auditor or auditors to state the accounts between the parties and to make report thereof to the court as soon as possible. The auditor shall verify his report by his affidavit stating that he has carefully examined the state of the account between the parties, and that his report contains a true statement thereof, so far as the same has come within his knowledge. Exceptions to such report or of any item thereof must be filed within 30 days of the filing of such report. The court shall award reasonable compensation to such auditor to be taxed as costs of suit.

History of TRCP 172: Amended eff. Jan. 1, 1988, by order of July 15, 1987 (733-34 S.W.2d [Tex.Cases] lvi). Adopted eff. Sept. 1, 1941, by order of Oct. 29, 1940 (3 Tex.B.J. 550 [1940]). Source: TRCS art. 2292 (repealed).

See TRE 706.

TRCP 173. GUARDIAN AD LITEM

173.1 Appointment Governed by Statute or Other Rules.

This rule does not apply to an appointment of a guardian ad litem governed by statute or other rules.

173.2 Appointment of Guardian ad Litem.

(a) *When Appointment Required or Prohibited.* The court must appoint a guardian ad litem for a party represented by a next friend or guardian only if:

(1) the next friend or guardian appears to the court to have an interest adverse to the party, or

(2) the parties agree.

(b) *Appointment of the Same Person for Different Parties.* The court must appoint the same guardian ad litem for similarly situated parties unless the court finds that the appointment of different guardians ad litem is necessary.

173.3 Procedure.

(a) *Motion Permitted But Not Required.* The court may appoint a guardian ad litem on the motion of any party or on its own initiative.

(b) *Written Order Required.* An appointment must be made by written order.

(c) *Objection.* Any party may object to the appointment of a guardian ad litem.

173.4 Role of Guardian ad Litem.

(a) *Court Officer and Advisor.* A guardian ad litem acts as an officer and advisor to the court.

(b) *Determination of Adverse Interest.* A guardian ad litem must determine and advise the court whether a party's next friend or guardian has an interest adverse to the party.

(c) *When Settlement Proposed.* When an offer has been made to settle the claim of a party represented

───────────────── ✦ ─────────────────

by a next friend or guardian, a guardian ad litem has the limited duty to determine and advise the court whether the settlement is in the party's best interest.

(d) *Participation in Litigation Limited.* A guardian ad litem:

(1) may participate in mediation or a similar proceeding to attempt to reach a settlement;

(2) must participate in any proceeding before the court whose purpose is to determine whether a party's next friend or guardian has an interest adverse to the party, or whether a settlement of the party's claim is in the party's best interest;

(3) must not participate in discovery, trial, or any other part of the litigation unless:

(A) further participation is necessary to protect the party's interest that is adverse to the next friend's or guardian's, and

(B) the participation is directed by the court in a written order stating sufficient reasons.

173.5 Communications Privileged.

Communications between the guardian ad litem and the party, the next friend or guardian, or their attorney are privileged as if the guardian ad litem were the attorney for the party.

173.6 Compensation.

(a) *Amount.* If a guardian ad litem requests compensation, he or she may be reimbursed for reasonable and necessary expenses incurred and may be paid a reasonable hourly fee for necessary services performed.

(b) *Procedure.* At the conclusion of the appointment, a guardian ad litem may file an application for compensation. The application must be verified and must detail the basis for the compensation requested. Unless all parties agree to the application, the court must conduct an evidentiary hearing to determine the total amount of fees and expenses that are reasonable and necessary. In making this determination, the court must not consider compensation as a percentage of any judgment or settlement.

(c) *Taxation as Costs.* The court may tax a guardian ad litem's compensation as costs of court.

(d) *Other Benefit Prohibited.* A guardian ad litem may not receive, directly or indirectly, anything of value in consideration of the appointment other than as provided by this rule.

173.7 Review.

(a) *Right of Appeal.* Any party may seek mandamus review of an order appointing a guardian ad litem or directing a guardian ad litem's participation in the litigation. Any party and a guardian ad litem may appeal an order awarding the guardian ad litem compensation.

(b) *Severance.* On motion of the guardian ad litem or any party, the court must sever any order awarding a guardian ad litem compensation to create a final, appealable order.

(c) *No Effect on Finality of Settlement or Judgment.* Appellate proceedings to review an order pertaining to a guardian ad litem do not affect the finality of a settlement or judgment.

Comments to 2005 change:

1. The rule is completely revised.

2. This rule does not apply when the procedures and purposes for appointment of guardians ad litem (as well as attorneys ad litem) are prescribed by statutes, such as the Family Code and the Probate Code, or by other rules, such as the Parental Notification Rules.

3. The rule contemplates that a guardian ad litem will be appointed when a party's next friend or guardian appears to have an interest adverse to the party because of the division of settlement proceeds. In those situations, the responsibility of the guardian ad litem as prescribed by the rule is very limited, and no reason exists for the guardian ad litem to participate in the conduct of the litigation in any other way or to review the discovery or the litigation file except to the limited extent that it may bear on the division of settlement proceeds. See *Jocson v. Crabb*, 133 S.W.3d 268 (Tex.2004) (per curiam). A guardian ad litem may, of course, choose to review the file or attend proceedings when it is unnecessary, but the guardian ad litem may not be compensated for unnecessary expenses or services.

4. Only in extraordinary circumstances does the rule contemplate that a guardian ad litem will have a broader role. Even then, the role is limited to determining whether a party's next friend or guardian has an interest adverse to the party that should be considered by the court under Rule 44. In no event may a guardian ad litem supervise or supplant the next friend or undertake to represent the party while serving as guardian ad litem.

5. As an officer and advisor to the court, a guardian ad litem should have derived judicial immunity.

6. Though an officer and adviser to the court, a guardian ad litem must not have *ex parte* communications with the court. See Tex. Code Jud. Conduct, Canon 3.

7. Because the role of guardian ad litem is limited in all but extraordinary situations, and any risk that might result from services performed is also limited, compensation, if any is made, should ordinarily be limited.

8. A violation of this rule is subject to appropriate sanction.

History of TRCP 173: Amended eff. Feb. 1, 2005, by order of Jan. 27, 2005 (Tex.Sup.Ct. Order, Misc. Docket No. 05-9021). Adopted eff. Sept. 1, 1941, by order of Oct. 29, 1940 (3 Tex.B.J. 550 [1940]). Source: TRCS art. 2159 (repealed).

See *Commentaries*, "Guardian Ad Litem Under TRCP 173," ch. 1-I, p. 67; *O'Connor's Texas Forms*, FORMS 1I.

ANNOTATIONS

Ford Motor Co. v. Chacon, 370 S.W.3d 359, 362 (Tex.2012). "A guardian ad litem has the burden to ensure that his services do not exceed the scope of the role assigned by the trial court. In the context of that appointment, a guardian ad litem 'may be reimbursed for reasonable and necessary expenses incurred and

⭐

may be paid a reasonable hourly fee for necessary services performed.' The amount of the award is within the trial court's discretion. [¶] [I]n determining the nature and duties of an appointment, we look to the context of the appointment and the duties assigned to the ad litem. [¶] The context of [ad litem's] appointment as guardian ad litem clearly indicates that [ad litem] was appointed for the limited purpose of determining and advising the court whether the ... settlement [with D1] was in [minor's] best interest. ... After the ... settlement [with D1] was finalized and judgment was entered, [ad litem] filed an application for compensation for guardian ad litem services he provided in connection with the [D1] settlement, which the court awarded in full. There was no subsequent motion or request for appointment of a guardian ad litem in connection with the [D2] settlement, nor did the trial court enter an order appointing one. In light of the requirements of Rule 173, we conclude that [ad litem's] work regarding the [D2] settlement was beyond the scope of his original appointment."

Ford Motor Co. v. Garcia, 363 S.W.3d 573, 580 (Tex.2012). "Rule 173.6 does not preclude awarding compensation for persons other than the person designated in the trial court's order as guardian ad litem if the evidence shows particular, unusual circumstances making services of other persons necessary for the ad litem's duties to be fulfilled. Such circumstances might exist, for example, if paralegals or other staff under the supervision of the appointed guardian ad litem could perform tasks necessary for the ad litem to properly fulfill his or her appointed role, but at a lesser hourly rate than the ad litem, or an unexpected emergency requires the guardian ad litem to miss a mandatory hearing and an associated attorney familiar with the matter appears instead. *At 580 n.5:* [A] Rule 173 guardian ad litem might need to incur unusual expenses in order to properly advise the court. For example, expenses for an actuary or accountant to evaluate the economics of a structured settlement may be necessary."

Land Rover U.K., Ltd. v. Hinojosa, 210 S.W.3d 604, 607 (Tex.2006). "A guardian ad litem is not an attorney for the child but an officer appointed by the court to assist in protecting the child's interests when a conflict of interest arises between the child and the child's guardian or next friend. As the personal representative of a minor, a guardian ad litem is required to participate in the case only to the extent necessary to protect the mi-

nor's interest and should not duplicate the work performed by the plaintiff's attorney. If a guardian ad litem performs work beyond the scope of this role, such work is non-compensable. [¶] An appointed guardian ad litem may request a reasonable fee for services performed. ... To determine a reasonable fee for a guardian ad litem's services, a trial court applies the factors used to determine the reasonableness of attorney's fees." *See also Brownsville-Valley Reg'l Med. Ctr., Inc. v. Gamez*, 894 S.W.2d 753, 755 (Tex.1995) (when conflict of interest no longer exists, trial court should remove guardian ad litem); *Owens v. Perez*, 158 S.W.3d 96, 111 (Tex.App.—Corpus Christi 2005, no pet.) (potential conflict sufficient for appointment; actual conflict not required).

Jocson v. Crabb, 133 S.W.3d 268, 270 (Tex.2004). "[O]bjections to ad litem fees are timely if raised at the post-trial fee hearing.... [¶] While the parties would be wise to seek direction ... when they disagree about an ad litem's role, it could be expensive and disruptive ... to pursue every disagreement to a hearing throughout the pretrial process. The final fee hearing is an appropriate forum to assert any objections to the fee request and obtain a ruling."

In re KC Greenhouse Patio Apts., LP, ___ S.W.3d ___ (Tex.App.—Houston [1st Dist.] 2012, orig. proceeding) (No. 01-12-00226-CV; 8-16-12). See annotation under TRCP 44, p. 875.

Jocson v. Crabb, 196 S.W.3d 302, 306 (Tex.App.—Houston [1st Dist.] 2006, no pet.). "[A]n ad litem will not be compensated for unnecessary work and *no reason* exists for the guardian ad litem to participate in the conduct of the litigation or to review the discovery or the litigation file except to the limited extent that it may bear on the division of settlement proceeds."

TRCP 174. CONSOLIDATION; SEPARATE TRIALS

(a) Consolidation. When actions involving a common question of law or fact are pending before the court, it may order a joint hearing or trial of any or all the matters in issue in the actions; it may order all the actions consolidated; and it may make such orders concerning proceedings therein as may tend to avoid unnecessary costs or delay.

(b) Separate Trials. The court in furtherance of convenience or to avoid prejudice may order a separate trial of any claim, cross-claim, counterclaim, or third-

★

party claim, or of any separate issue or of any number of claims, cross-claims, counterclaims, third-party claims, or issues.

History of TRCP 174: Adopted eff. Sept. 1, 1941, by order of Oct. 29, 1940 (3 Tex.B.J. 551 [1940]). Source: FRCP 42. Supersedes TRCS art. 2160 (repealed).

See TRCP 39-41, 51; *Commentaries*, "Motions for Severance & Separate Trials," ch. 5-I, p. 364; "Joining Parties or Claims," ch. 5-J, p. 371; *O'Connor's Texas Forms*, FORMS 5H, 5I:7-9.

ANNOTATIONS

Tarrant Reg'l Water Dist. v. Gragg, 151 S.W.3d 546, 556 (Tex.2004). TRCP 174(b) "allows a trial court to order a separate trial on any issue in the interest of convenience or to avoid prejudice. *At 557:* [S]eparate trials would have resulted in considerable and unnecessary evidentiary repetition. [I]t is likely that many, if not most, of the same witnesses would have been called to testify in both the liability and compensation trials had the trial court bifurcated the proceedings. '[T]here were several weeks of common questions of law and of fact involved in the matters that would have been considered in the first phase and the second phase of a bifurcated trial.' ... Under these circumstances, we cannot say that the trial court abused its discretion in refusing to bifurcate the proceedings."

In re Ethyl Corp., 975 S.W.2d 606, 611-12 (Tex. 1998). "The maximum number of claims that can be aggregated is not an absolute, and the particular circumstances determine the outer limits beyond which trial courts cannot go. [¶] While considerations of judicial economy are a factor, '[c]onsiderations of convenience and economy must yield to a paramount concern for a fair and impartial trial.'" *See also In re Shell Oil Co.*, 202 S.W.3d 286, 290-91 (Tex.App.—Beaumont 2006, orig. proceeding).

Liberty Nat'l Fire Ins. v. Akin, 927 S.W.2d 627, 630 (Tex.1996). "A severance may ... be necessary in some bad faith [and contract] cases. A trial court will ... confront instances in which evidence admissible only on the bad faith claim would prejudice the insurer to such an extent that a fair trial on the contract claim would become unlikely. One example would be when the insurer has made a settlement offer on the disputed contract claim."

In re Travelers Lloyds of Tex. Ins., 273 S.W.3d 368, 374 (Tex.App.—San Antonio 2008, orig. proceeding). "Several Texas courts of appeals have ... reviewed orders employing bifurcation as an alternative to sever

ance and abatement of extra-contractual claims. Some of our sister courts have held the trial court did not abuse its discretion in employing bifurcation in lieu of severance and abatement. Others have concluded bifurcation was not an acceptable alternative to severance. We decline to follow the cases rejecting bifurcation. [¶] Bifurcation has been embraced by the Texas Supreme Court to address evidence of a defendant's net worth, which has the potential to prejudice the jury's determination of disputed issues in a tort case. We see no reason why bifurcation cannot be similarly employed to address evidence of a settlement offer, which has the potential to prejudice the jury's determination of disputed issues in a breach of contract case."

In re Gulf Coast Bus. Dev. Corp., 247 S.W.3d 787, 794-95 (Tex.App.—Dallas 2008, orig. proceeding). "Rule 174 give[s] the trial court broad discretion to consolidate cases with common issues of law or fact. [¶] The trial court may consolidate actions that relate to substantially the same transaction, occurrence, subject matter, or question. The actions should be so related that the evidence presented will be material, relevant, and admissible in each case. [¶] Even if the cases share common questions of law and fact, an abuse of discretion may be found if the consolidation results in prejudice to the complaining party. However, we may not presume prejudice; it must be demonstrated. Where the cases do share common questions of law and fact, and the record does not reveal actual prejudice, the consolidation does not provide a basis for reversal." *See also Vafaiyan v. State*, No. 02-09-00098-CV (Tex.App.—Fort Worth 2010, pet. denied) (memo op.; 8-31-10) (in deciding whether to consolidate, court must balance judicial economy gained by consolidation against risk of unfair outcome because of prejudice or jury confusion).

TRCP 175. ISSUE OF LAW & DILATORY PLEAS

When a case is called for trial in which there has been no pretrial hearing as provided by Rule 166, the issues of law arising on the pleadings, all pleas in abatement and other dilatory pleas remaining undisposed of shall be determined; and it shall be no cause for postponement of a trial of the issues of law that a party is not prepared to try the issues of fact.

History of TRCP 175: Adopted eff. Sept. 1, 1941, by order of Oct. 29, 1940 (3 Tex.B.J. 551 [1940]). Source: TRCS art. 2166 (repealed).

TRCP 175

⭐

Garcia v. Texas Employers' Ins., 622 S.W.2d 626, 630 n.3 (Tex.App.—Amarillo 1981, writ ref'd n.r.e.). "The language of Rule 175 imposes on the party relying upon a dilatory plea a duty to demand action by the court thereon at the time the rule requires action by the court, and his failure to do so is a waiver of the plea."

SECTION 9. EVIDENCE & DISCOVERY

Explanatory Statement Accompanying the 1999 Amendments to the Rules of Civil Procedure Governing Discovery[1]

The rules pertaining to discovery have been substantively revised and reorganized to clarify and streamline discovery procedures and to reduce costs and delays associated with discovery practice. The notes and comments appended to the rules, unlike most other notes and comments in the Rules of Civil Procedure, are intended to inform their construction and application by both courts and practitioners.

Discovery in civil cases is founded on the principle that justice is best served when litigants may obtain information not in their possession to prosecute and defend claims. Discovery provides access to that information, but at a price. Recent years' experience has shown that discovery may be misused to deny justice to parties by driving up the costs of litigation until it is unaffordable and stalling resolution of cases. As any litigant on a budget knows, the benefits to be gained by discovery in a particular case must be weighed against its costs. The rules of procedure must provide both adequate access to information and effective means of curbing discovery when appropriate to preserve litigation as a viable, affordable, and expeditious dispute resolution mechanism.

These revisions recognize the importance of discovery as well as the necessity for reasonable limits. The scope of discovery, always broad, is unchanged. All the forms of discovery under the prior rules are retained, and a new one—disclosure—is added. Disclosure is not required unless requested and thus does not burden cases in which it is not sought. When requested, it provides ready access to basic information without objection. At the same time, the necessity of a discovery control plan in each case, whether by rule or by order, is intended to focus courts and parties on both the need for discovery and its costs in each case. The Level 1 plan allows a party seeking recovery of no more than $50,000

to insist that discovery be minimal. The Level 2 plan will provide adequate discovery in most cases, and Level 3 is available for cases needing special attention. No single set of rules can address so diverse and changing a practice as discovery, and thus the rules maintain the ability of parties by agreement and courts by order to tailor discovery to individual cases.

Presentation of objections and assertions of privilege are streamlined under these rules. A party who objects to only part of a discovery request must usually comply with the rest of the request. Assertions of privilege are not to be made prophylactically against the threat of waiver, but only when information is actually withheld. Documents produced in discovery are now presumed to be authentic for use against the party producing them, thus avoiding the cost of proving authentication when there is no dispute. Procedures for oral depositions are revised to encourage focused examination by imposing time limits and to discourage colloquy between counsel.

An important aspect of these revisions has been the regrouping of provisions in a more logical sequence and the elimination of archaic and confusing language.

1. **Editor's note:** Adopted eff. Jan. 1, 1999, by order of Nov. 9, 1998 (977-78 S.W.3d [Tex.Cases] xxxv).

A. EVIDENCE

TRCP 176. SUBPOENAS

176.1 Form. Every subpoena must be issued in the name of "The State of Texas" and must:

(a) state the style of the suit and its cause number;

(b) state the court in which the suit is pending;

(c) state the date on which the subpoena is issued;

(d) identify the person to whom the subpoena is directed;

(e) state the time, place, and nature of the action required by the person to whom the subpoena is directed, as provided in Rule 176.2;

(f) identify the party at whose instance the subpoena is issued, and the party's attorney of record, if any;

(g) state the text of Rule 176.8(a); and

(h) be signed by the person issuing the subpoena.

176.2 Required Actions. A subpoena must command the person to whom it is directed to do either or both of the following:

(a) attend and give testimony at a deposition, hearing, or trial;

(b) produce and permit inspection and copying of designated documents or tangible things in the possession, custody, or control of that person.

176.3 Limitations.

(a) *Range.* A person may not be required by subpoena to appear or produce documents or other things in a county that is more than 150 miles from where the person resides or is served. However, a person whose appearance or production at a deposition may be compelled by notice alone under Rules 199.3 or 200.2 may be required to appear and produce documents or other things at any location permitted under Rules 199.2(b)(2).

(b) *Use for discovery.* A subpoena may not be used for discovery to an extent, in a manner, or at a time other than as provided by the rules governing discovery.

176.4 Who May Issue. A subpoena may be issued by:

(a) the clerk of the appropriate district, county, or justice court, who must provide the party requesting the subpoena with an original and a copy for each witness to be completed by the party;

(b) an attorney authorized to practice in the State of Texas, as an officer of the court; or

(c) an officer authorized to take depositions in this State, who must issue the subpoena immediately on a request accompanied by a notice to take a deposition under Rules 199 or 200, or a notice under Rule 205.3, and who may also serve the notice with the subpoena.

176.5 Service.

(a) *Manner of service.* A subpoena may be served at any place within the State of Texas by any sheriff or constable of the State of Texas, or any person who is not a party and is 18 years of age or older. A subpoena must be served by delivering a copy to the witness and tendering to that person any fees required by law. If the witness is a party and is represented by an attorney of record in the proceeding, the subpoena may be served on the witness's attorney of record.

(b) *Proof of service.* Proof of service must be made by filing either:

(1) the witness's signed written memorandum attached to the subpoena showing that the witness accepted the subpoena; or

(2) a statement by the person who made the service stating the date, time, and manner of service, and the name of the person served.

176.6 Response.

(a) *Compliance required.* Except as provided in this subdivision, a person served with a subpoena must comply with the command stated therein unless discharged by the court or by the party summoning such witness. A person commanded to appear and give testimony must remain at the place of deposition, hearing, or trial from day to day until discharged by the court or by the party summoning the witness.

(b) *Organizations.* If a subpoena commanding testimony is directed to a corporation, partnership, association, governmental agency, or other organization, and the matters on which examination is requested are described with reasonable particularity, the organization must designate one or more persons to testify on its behalf as to matters known or reasonably available to the organization.

(c) *Production of documents or tangible things.* A person commanded to produce documents or tangible things need not appear in person at the time and place of production unless the person is also commanded to attend and give testimony, either in the same subpoena or a separate one. A person must produce documents as they are kept in the usual course of business or must organize and label them to correspond with the categories in the demand. A person may withhold material or information claimed to be privileged but must comply with Rule 193.3. A nonparty's production of a document authenticates the document for use against the nonparty to the same extent as a party's production of a document is authenticated for use against the party under Rule 193.7.

(d) *Objections.* A person commanded to produce and permit inspection or copying of designated documents and things may serve on the party requesting issuance of the subpoena—before the time specified for compliance—written objections to producing any or all of the designated materials. A person need not comply with the part of a subpoena to which objection is made as provided in this paragraph unless ordered to do so by the court. The party requesting the subpoena may move for such an order at any time after an objection is made.

(e) *Protective orders.* A person commanded to appear at a deposition, hearing, or trial, or to produce and permit inspection and copying of designated docu-

---

★

---

ments and things, and any other person affected by the subpoena, may move for a protective order under Rule 192.6(b)—before the time specified for compliance—either in the court in which the action is pending or in a district court in the county where the subpoena was served. The person must serve the motion on all parties in accordance with Rule 21a. A person need not comply with the part of a subpoena from which protection is sought under this paragraph unless ordered to do so by the court. The party requesting the subpoena may seek such an order at any time after the motion for protection is filed.

(f) *Trial subpoenas.* A person commanded to attend and give testimony, or to produce documents or things, at a hearing or trial, may object or move for protective order before the court at the time and place specified for compliance, rather than under paragraphs (d) and (e).

176.7 **Protection of Person from Undue Burden and Expense.** A party causing a subpoena to issue must take reasonable steps to avoid imposing undue burden or expense on the person served. In ruling on objections or motions for protection, the court must provide a person served with a subpoena an adequate time for compliance, protection from disclosure of privileged material or information, and protection from undue burden or expense. The court may impose reasonable conditions on compliance with a subpoena, including compensating the witness for undue hardship.

176.8 **Enforcement of Subpoena.**

(a) *Contempt.* Failure by any person without adequate excuse to obey a subpoena served upon that person may be deemed a contempt of the court from which the subpoena is issued or a district court in the county in which the subpoena is served, and may be punished by fine or confinement, or both.

(b) *Proof of payment of fees required for fine or attachment.* A fine may not be imposed, nor a person served with a subpoena attached, for failure to comply with a subpoena without proof by affidavit of the party requesting the subpoena or the party's attorney of record that all fees due the witness by law were paid or tendered.

Comments to 1999 change:

1. This rule combines the former rules governing subpoenas for trial and discovery. When a subpoena is used for discovery, the protections from undue burden and expense apply, just as with any discovery.

2. Rule 176.3(b) prohibits the use of a subpoena to circumvent the discovery rules. Thus, for example, a deposition subpoena to a party is subject to the procedures of Rules 196, 199, and 200, and a deposition subpoena to a nonparty is subject to the procedures of Rule 205.

History of TRCP 176: Adopted eff. Jan. 1, 1999, by order of Nov. 9, 1998 (977-78 S.W.2d [Tex.Cases] xxxvi): Repealed former TRCP 176. Source: New rule.

See CPRC §22.001; *Commentaries*, "Subpoenas," ch. 1-L, p. 84; "Depositions," ch. 6-F, p. 525; *O'Connor's Texas Forms*, FORMS 1L, 6F:1-11.

ANNOTATIONS

Automatic Drilling Machs., Inc. v. Miller, 515 S.W.2d 256, 259 (Tex.1974). "On motion ... the court is authorized by [TRCP] 177a [now TRCP 176.7] to quash or modify the subpoena if it is unreasonable or oppressive or condition denial of the motion on advancement of reasonable costs by the party in whose behalf the subpoena was issued."

St. Luke's Episcopal Hosp. v. Garcia, 928 S.W.2d 307, 310 (Tex.App.—Houston [14th Dist.] 1996, orig. proceeding). "In determining whether a deposition notice or subpoena duces tecum is unreasonable and oppressive, the following factors are relevant: '(1) the quantity of materials subpoenaed, (2) the ease or difficulty of collecting and transporting the materials, (3) the length of time before the deposition, (4) the availability of the information from other sources, and (5) the relevance of the materials.'"

TRCP 177 TO 179. REPEALED

Repealed eff. Jan. 1, 1999, by order of Nov. 9, 1998 (977-78 S.W.2d [Tex.Cases] xxxiii). For subject matter of former TRCPs 177-179, see TRCP 176.

TRCP 180. REFUSAL TO TESTIFY

Any witness refusing to give evidence may be committed to jail, there to remain without bail until such witness shall consent to give evidence.

History of TRCP 180: Adopted eff. Sept. 1, 1941, by order of Oct. 29, 1940 (3 Tex.B.J. 552 [1940]). Source: TRCS art. 3709 (repealed).

See TRCP 176; *Commentaries*, "Subpoenas," ch. 1-L, p. 84; "Depositions," ch. 6-F, p. 525.

TRCP 181. PARTY AS WITNESS

Either party to a suit may examine the opposing party as a witness, and shall have the same process to compel his attendance as in the case of any other witness.

History of TRCP 181: Adopted eff. Sept. 1, 1941, by order of Oct. 29, 1940 (3 Tex.B.J. 552 [1940]). Source: TRCS art. 3711 (repealed). Note: Same as TRCP 176.

See TRCP 176, 199-201; *Commentaries*, "Subpoenas," ch. 1-L, p. 84; "Depositions," ch. 6-F, p. 525.

TRCP 182, 182a. REPEALED

TRCP 182 repealed eff. Jan. 1, 1988, by order of July 15, 1987 (733-34 S.W.2d [Tex.Cases] lvii.): TRE 607 and TRE 610(c) fully satisfy the needs served by TRCP 182. TRCP 182a repealed eff. Jan. 1, 1988, by order of July 15, 1987 (733-34 S.W.2d [Tex.Cases] lvii): TRCP 182a, which was added to TRE 601(b), is no longer necessary.

⭐

TRCP 183. INTERPRETERS

The court may appoint an interpreter of its own selection and may fix the interpreter's reasonable compensation. The compensation shall be paid out of funds provided by law or by one or more of the parties as the court may direct, and may be taxed ultimately as costs, in the discretion of the court.

History of TRCP 183: Amended eff. Sept. 1, 1990, by order of Apr. 24, 1990 (785-86 S.W.2d [Tex.Cases] lix): Rewrote to adopt procedures for the appointment and compensation of interpreters; source for amendment, FRCP 43(f); deleted provision regarding summoning interpreters and their conduct because it is covered by TRE 604. Adopted eff. Sept. 1, 1941, by order of Oct. 29, 1940 (3 Tex.B.J. 552 [1940]). Source: TRCS art. 3712 (repealed).

See TRCP 200.4; TRE 604; *Commentaries*, "Depositions," ch. 6-F, p. 525.

TRCP 184, 184a. REPEALED

Repealed eff. Sept. 1, 1990, by order of Apr. 24, 1990 (785-86 S.W.2d [Tex.Cases] lx): TRCP 184 is covered by TRE 202, and TRCP 184a is covered by TRE 203.

TRCP 185. SUIT ON ACCOUNT

When any action or defense is founded upon an open account or other claim for goods, wares and merchandise, including any claim for a liquidated money demand based upon written contract or founded on business dealings between the parties, or is for personal service rendered, or labor done or labor or materials furnished, on which a systematic record has been kept, and is supported by the affidavit of the party, his agent or attorney taken before some officer authorized to administer oaths, to the effect that such claim is, within the knowledge of affiant, just and true, that it is due, and that all just and lawful offsets, payments and credits have been allowed, the same shall be taken as prima facie evidence thereof, unless the party resisting such claim shall file a written denial, under oath. A party resisting such a sworn claim shall comply with the rules of pleading as are required in any other kind of suit, provided, however, that if he does not timely file a written denial, under oath, he shall not be permitted to deny the claim, or any item therein, as the case may be. No particularization or description of the nature of the component parts of the account or claim is necessary unless the trial court sustains special exceptions to the pleadings.

History of TRCP 185: Amended eff. Apr. 1, 1984, by order of Dec. 5, 1983 (661-62 S.W.2d [Tex.Cases] lvii): Rule rewritten so that suits on accounts are subject to ordinary rules of pleading and practice. Amended eff. Jan. 1, 1971, by order of July 21, 1970 (455-56 S.W.2d [Tex.Cases] xxxiii): Changed phrase "stating that such claim is not just or true, in whole or in part, and if in part only, stating the items and particulars which are unjust" to the phrase "stating that each and every item is not just or true, or that some specified item or items are not just and true." Amended eff. Mar. 1, 1950, by order of Oct. 12, 1949 (12 Tex.B.J. 532 [1949]): Rule extended to include claim for "labor done or labor or materials furnished"; and the provision that when a counter-affidavit is filed on the day of trial, party asserting the claim shall have the right to con-

tinue the cause until the next term of court was changed to the following: "the party asserting such verified claim shall have the right to postpone such cause for a reasonable time." Several textual changes not affecting substance of rule also made. Adopted eff. Sept. 1, 1941, by order of Oct. 29, 1940 (3 Tex.B.J. 552 [1940]). Source: TRCS art. 3736 (repealed).

See *O'Connor's Texas Causes of Action* (2013), "Suit on Sworn Account," ch. 5-E, p. 121; *O'Connor's Texas Forms*, FORMS 2B:3, 4, 3E:3, 4, 10.

ANNOTATIONS

Vance v. Holloway, 689 S.W.2d 403, 403-04 (Tex. 1985). "The petition and affidavit filed by [P] clearly met the requirements of [TRCP] 185. [D] answered by way of an unverified general denial only. He failed to meet the requirements of [TRCPs] 185 and 93(10) which state that a written denial of the plaintiff's action must be verified. [¶] [D], therefore, waived his right to dispute the amount and ownership of the account." *See also Rizk v. Financial Guardian Ins. Agency*, 584 S.W.2d 860, 862 (Tex.1979); *Day Cruises Maritime, L.L.C. v. Christus Spohn Health Sys.*, 267 S.W.3d 42, 53 (Tex.App.—Corpus Christi 2008, pet. denied).

Williams v. Unifund CCR Partners Assignee of Citibank, 264 S.W.3d 231, 234 (Tex.App.—Houston [1st Dist.] 2008, no pet.). "Rule 185 is a procedural tool that limits the evidence necessary to establish a prima facie right to recovery on certain types of accounts. Rule 185 applies only 'to transactions between persons, in which there is a sale upon one side and a purchase upon the other, whereby title to *personal* property passes from one to the other, and the relation of debtor and creditor is thereby created by general course of dealing....'" *See also Meaders v. Biskamp*, 316 S.W.2d 75, 78 (Tex.1958).

Powers v. Adams, 2 S.W.3d 496, 498 (Tex.App.—Houston [14th Dist.] 1999, no pet.). "Under [TRCP] 185], [P's] petition on sworn account must contain a systematic, itemized statement of the goods or services sold, reveal offsets made to the account, and be supported by an affidavit stating the claim is within the affiant's knowledge, and that it is 'just and true.'" *See also Dibco Underground, Inc. v. JCF Bridge & Concrete, Inc.*, No. 03-09-00255-CV (Tex.App.—Austin 2010, no pet.) (memo op.; 4-8-10) (account must include specifics about how the figures were established).

Worley v. Butler, 809 S.W.2d 242, 245 (Tex.App.—Corpus Christi 1990, no writ). "To prevail in a cause of action on sworn account, a party must show: (1) that there was a sale and delivery of the merchandise or performance of the services; (2) that the amount of the account is just, that is, that the prices were charged in accordance with an agreement or in the absence of an

---

⭐

---

agreement, they are the usual, customary and reasonable prices for that merchandise or services; and (3) that the amount is unpaid."

TRCP 186 TO 186b. REPEALED

Repealed eff. Apr. 1, 1984, by order of Dec. 5, 1983 (661-62 S.W.2d [Tex.Cases] lvii). For subject matter of former TRCP 186, see TRCPs 199, 200, 202, and 252. For subject matter of former TRCPs 186a and 186b, see TRCPs 192 and 193.

TRCP 187, 188. REPEALED

Repealed eff. Jan. 1, 1999, by order of Nov. 9, 1998 (977-78 S.W.2d [Tex.Cases] xxxiii). For subject matter of former TRCP 187, see TRCPs 199 and 203. For subject matter of former TRCP 188, see TRCPs 176 and 199.

TRCP 189. REPEALED

Repealed eff. Apr. 1, 1984, by order of Dec. 5, 1983 (661-62 S.W.2d [Tex.Cases] lix). For subject matter of former TRCP 189, see TRCP 200.

B. DISCOVERY

TRCP 190. DISCOVERY LIMITATIONS*

190.1 **Discovery Control Plan Required.** Every case must be governed by a discovery control plan as provided in this Rule. A plaintiff must allege in the first numbered paragraph of the original petition whether discovery is intended to be conducted under Level 1, 2, or 3 of this Rule.

190.2 **Discovery Control Plan—Suits Involving $50,000 or Less (Level 1).**

(a) *Application.* This subdivision applies to:

(1) any suit in which all plaintiffs affirmatively plead that they seek only monetary relief aggregating $50,000 or less, excluding costs, pre-judgment interest and attorneys' fees, and

(2) any suit for divorce not involving children in which a party pleads that the value of the marital estate is more than zero but not more than $50,000.

(b) *Exceptions.* This subdivision does not apply if:

(1) the parties agree that Rule 190.3 should apply;

(2) the court orders a discovery control plan under Rule 190.4; or

(3) any party files a pleading or an amended or supplemental pleading that seeks relief other than that to which this subdivision applies.

A pleading, amended pleading (including trial amendment), or supplemental pleading that renders this subdivision no longer applicable may not be filed without leave of court less than 45 days before the date set for trial. Leave may be granted only if good cause for filing the pleading outweighs any prejudice to an opposing party.

(c) *Limitations.* Discovery is subject to the limitations provided elsewhere in these rules and to the following additional limitations:

(1) *Discovery period.* All discovery must be conducted during the discovery period, which begins when the suit is filed and continues until 30 days before the date set for trial.

(2) *Total time for oral depositions.* Each party may have no more than six hours in total to examine and cross-examine all witnesses in oral depositions. The parties may agree to expand this limit up to ten hours in total, but not more except by court order. The court may modify the deposition hours so that no party is given unfair advantage.

(3) *Interrogatories.* Any party may serve on any other party no more than 25 written interrogatories, excluding interrogatories asking a party only to identify or authenticate specific documents. Each discrete subpart of an interrogatory is considered a separate interrogatory.

(d) *Reopening discovery.* When the filing of a pleading or an amended or supplemental pleading renders this subdivision no longer applicable, the discovery period reopens, and discovery must be completed within the limitations provided in Rules 190.3 or 190.4, whichever is applicable. Any person previously deposed may be redeposed. On motion of any party, the court should continue the trial date if necessary to permit completion of discovery.

190.3 **Discovery Control Plan—By Rule (Level 2).**

(a) *Application.* Unless a suit is governed by a discovery control plan under Rules 190.2 or 190.4, discovery must be conducted in accordance with this subdivision.

(b) *Limitations.* Discovery is subject to the limitations provided elsewhere in these rules and to the following additional limitations:

(1) *Discovery period.* All discovery must be conducted during the discovery period, which begins when suit is filed and continues until:

(A) 30 days before the date set for trial, in cases under the Family Code; or

(B) in other cases, the earlier of

(i) 30 days before the date set for trial, or

(ii) nine months after the earlier of the date of the first oral deposition or the due date of the first response to written discovery.

(2) *Total time for oral depositions.* Each side may have no more than 50 hours in oral depositions to examine and cross-examine parties on the opposing side, experts designated by those parties, and persons who are subject to those parties' control. "Side" refers to all the litigants with generally common interests in the litigation. If one side designates more than two experts, the opposing side may have an additional six hours of total deposition time for each additional expert designated. The court may modify the deposition hours and must do so when a side or party would be given unfair advantage.

(3) *Interrogatories.* Any party may serve on any other party no more than 25 written interrogatories, excluding interrogatories asking a party only to identify or authenticate specific documents. Each discrete subpart of an interrogatory is considered a separate interrogatory.

190.4 Discovery Control Plan—By Order (Level 3).

(a) *Application.* The court must, on a party's motion, and may, on its own initiative, order that discovery be conducted in accordance with a discovery control plan tailored to the circumstances of the specific suit. The parties may submit an agreed order to the court for its consideration. The court should act on a party's motion or agreed order under this subdivision as promptly as reasonably possible.

(b) *Limitations.* The discovery control plan ordered by the court may address any issue concerning discovery or the matters listed in Rule 166, and may change any limitation on the time for or amount of discovery set forth in these rules. The discovery limitations of Rule 190.2, if applicable, or otherwise of Rule 190.3 apply unless specifically changed in the discovery control plan ordered by the court. The plan must include:

(1) a date for trial or for a conference to determine a trial setting;

(2) a discovery period during which either all discovery must be conducted or all discovery requests must be sent, for the entire case or an appropriate phase of it;

(3) appropriate limits on the amount of discovery; and

(4) deadlines for joining additional parties, amending or supplementing pleadings, and designating expert witnesses.

190.5 Modification of Discovery Control Plan. The court may modify a discovery control plan at any time and must do so when the interest of justice requires. The court must allow additional discovery:

(a) related to new, amended or supplemental pleadings, or new information disclosed in a discovery response or in an amended or supplemental response, if:

(1) the pleadings or responses were made after the deadline for completion of discovery or so nearly before that deadline that an adverse party does not have an adequate opportunity to conduct discovery related to the new matters, and

(2) the adverse party would be unfairly prejudiced without such additional discovery;

(b) regarding matters that have changed materially after the discovery cutoff if trial is set or postponed so that the trial date is more than three months after the discovery period ends.

190.6 Certain Types of Discovery Excepted. This rule's limitations on discovery do not apply to or include discovery conducted under Rule 202 ("Depositions Before Suit or to Investigate Claims"), or Rule 621a ("Discovery and Enforcement of Judgment"). But Rule 202 cannot be used to circumvent the limitations of this rule.

Comments to 1999 change:

1. This rule establishes three tiers of discovery plans and requires that every case be in one at all times. A case is in Level 1 if it is pleaded by the plaintiff so as to invoke application of Level 1, as provided by Rule 190.2(a). If a plaintiff does not or cannot plead the case in compliance with Rule 190.2(a) so as to invoke the application of Level 1, the case is automatically in Level 2. A case remains in Level 1 or Level 2, as determined by the pleadings, unless and until it is moved to Level 3. To be in Level 3, the court must order a specific plan for the case, either on a party's motion or on the court's own initiative. The plan may be one agreed to by the parties and submitted as an agreed order. A Level 3 plan may simply adopt Level 1 or Level 2 restrictions. Separate Level 3 plans for phases of the case may be appropriate. The initial pleading required by Rule 190.1 is merely to notify the court and other parties of the plaintiff's intention; it does not determine the applicable discovery level or bind the court or other parties. Thus, a plaintiff's failure to state in the initial pleading that the case should be in Level 1, as provided in Rule 190.1, does not alone make the case subject to Level 2 because the discovery level is determined by Rule 190.2. Likewise, a plaintiff's statement in the initial paragraph of the petition that the case is to be governed by Level 3 does not make Level 3 applicable, as a case can be in Level 3 only by court order. A plaintiff's failure to plead as required by Rule 190.1 is subject to special exception.

2. Rule 190.2 does not apply to suits for injunctive relief or divorces involving children. The requirement of an affirmative pleading of limited relief (*e.g.*: "Plaintiff affirmatively pleads that he seeks only monetary relief aggregating $50,000 or less, excluding costs, pre-judgment interest and attorneys' fees") does not conflict with other pleading requirements, such as Rule 47 and Tex. Rev. Civ. Stat. Ann. art. 4590i, §5.01. In a suit to which Rule 190.2 applies, the relief awarded cannot exceed the limitations of Level 1 because the purpose of the rule, unlike Rule 47, is to bind the pleader to a maximum claim. To this extent, the rule in *Greenhalgh v. Service Lloyds Ins. Co.*, 787 S.W.2d 938 (Tex. 1990), does not apply.

TRCP 190

⭐

---

3. "Discrete subparts" of interrogatories are counted as single interrogatories, but not every separate factual inquiry is a discrete subpart. See FRCP 33(a). While not susceptible of precise definition, see *Braden v. Downey*, 811 S.W.2d 922, 927-928 (Tex.1991), a "discrete subpart" is, in general, one that calls for information that is not logically or factually related to the primary interrogatory. The number of sets of interrogatories is no longer limited to two.

4. As other rules make clear, unless otherwise ordered or agreed, parties seeking discovery must serve requests sufficiently far in advance of the end of the discovery period that the deadline for responding will be within the discovery period. The court may order a deadline for sending discovery requests in lieu of or in addition to a deadline for completing discovery.

5. Use of forms of discovery other than depositions and interrogatories, such as requests for disclosure, admissions, or production of documents, are not restricted in Levels 1 and 2. But depositions on written questions cannot be used to circumvent the limits on interrogatories.

6. The concept of "side" in Rule 190.3(b)(2) borrows from Rule 233, which governs the allocation of peremptory strikes, and from FRCP 30(a)(2). In most cases there are only two sides—plaintiffs and defendants. In complex cases, however, there may be more than two sides, such as when defendants have sued third parties not named by plaintiffs, or when defendants have sued each other. As an example, if P1 and P2 sue D1, D2, and D3, and D1 sues D2 and D3, Ps would together be entitled to depose Ds and others permitted by the rule (*i.e.*, Ds' experts and persons subject to Ds' control) for 50 hours, and Ds would together be entitled to depose Ps and others for 50 hours. D1 would also be entitled to depose D2 and D3 and others for 50 hours on matters in controversy among them, and D2 and D3 would together be entitled to depose D1 and others for 50 hours.

7. Any matter listed in Rule 166 may be addressed in an order issued under Rule 190.4. A pretrial order under Rule 166 may be used in individual cases regardless of the discovery level.

8. For purposes of defining discovery periods, "trial" does not include summary judgment.

* **Editor's note:** The Supreme Court has proposed amendments to TRCP 190.2 and 190.5 that would (1) change the Level 1 discovery-control plan to apply to expedited actions under proposed TRCP 169, (2) modify the length of the discovery period in Level 1 cases, and (3) limit the modification of a discovery-control plan when a suit is governed by TRCP 169. *See* Tex.Sup.Ct. Order, Misc. Docket No. 12-9191 (eff. Mar. 1, 2013). In response to Gov't Code §22.004(h), the Supreme Court proposed TRCP 169 to establish a process for the prompt, efficient, and cost-effective resolution of civil actions (expedited actions) in which only monetary relief is sought and the amount in controversy is no more than $100,000. *See* Tex.Sup.Ct. Order, Misc. Docket No. 12-9191 (eff. Mar. 1, 2013). The public-comment period for the proposed amendments ends on February 1, 2013, and the rules are to take effect March 1, 2013. For the proposed version of the rules, see the appendix after this book's index. For the final version, go to the Supreme Court website at www.supreme.courts.state.tx.us. When the new and amended rules take effect, a supplement to this book—with updated rules and commentaries that reflect the changes—will be available at www.JonesMcClure.com/TRCPamendments.

History of TRCP 190: Amended eff. Jan. 1, 1999, by order of Dec. 31, 1998 (981-82 S.W.2d [Tex.Cases] xxxviii). Adopted eff. Jan. 1, 1999, by order of Nov. 9, 1998 (977-78 S.W.2d [Tex.Cases] xxxix). Applies to cases filed on or after Jan. 1, 1999. Source: New rule.

See *Commentaries*, "General Rules for Discovery," ch. 6-A, p. 425; *O'Connor's Texas Forms*, FORMS 6A:5-7.

ANNOTATIONS

In re Alford Chevrolet-Geo, 997 S.W.2d 173, 181 (Tex.1999). "[C]ourts may limit discovery pending resolution of threshold issues like venue, jurisdiction, forum non conveniens, and official immunity."

Brescia v. Slack & Davis, L.L.P., No. 03-08-00042-CV (Tex.App.—Austin 2010, pet. denied) (memo op.; 11-19-10). "Rule 190.4 does not require that the court's order provide deadlines different from those under a Level-2 case. Rather, the decision to provide different

deadlines is left to the court's discretion. [¶] Depending on the discovery plan level, the discovery rules establish a date certain for the completion of discovery. Under the discovery rules, no longer is there a concern that discovery will be incomplete at the summary judgment phase. The specific deadline established by the pretrial discovery rules ensures that the evidence presented at the summary judgment stage and at the trial stage remains the same."

In re SWEPI L.P., 103 S.W.3d 578, 589 (Tex. App.—San Antonio 2003, orig. proceeding). "A review of the interrogatories reveals none that have multiple 'discrete subparts.' Each question relates to a particular claim and asks [P] to provide certain details about the facts underlying that claim. The 'subparts' objected to by [P] simply identify the types of facts [D] would like to have disclosed so that it can understand the parameters of the claims and prepare its defenses. [T]he interrogatories do not exceed the number allowed by Rule 190.3(b)(3)...."

TRCP 191. MODIFYING DISCOVERY PROCEDURES & LIMITATIONS; CONFERENCE REQUIREMENT; SIGNING DISCLOSURES, DISCOVERY REQUESTS, RESPONSES, & OBJECTIONS; FILING REQUIREMENTS

191.1 **Modification of Procedures.** Except where specifically prohibited, the procedures and limitations set forth in the rules pertaining to discovery may be modified in any suit by the agreement of the parties or by court order for good cause. An agreement of the parties is enforceable if it complies with Rule 11 or, as it affects an oral deposition, if it is made a part of the record of the deposition.

191.2 **Conference.** Parties and their attorneys are expected to cooperate in discovery and to make any agreements reasonably necessary for the efficient disposition of the case. All discovery motions or requests for hearings relating to discovery must contain a certificate by the party filing the motion or request that a reasonable effort has been made to resolve the dispute without the necessity of court intervention and the effort failed.

191.3 **Signing of Disclosures, Discovery Requests, Notices, Responses, and Objections.**

(a) *Signature required.* Every disclosure, discovery request, notice, response, and objection must be signed:

─────────── ✦ ───────────

(1) by an attorney, if the party is represented by an attorney, and must show the attorney's State Bar of Texas identification number, address, telephone number, and fax number, if any; or

(2) by the party, if the party is not represented by an attorney, and must show the party's address, telephone number, and fax number, if any.

(b) *Effect of signature on disclosure.* The signature of an attorney or party on a disclosure constitutes a certification that to the best of the signer's knowledge, information, and belief, formed after a reasonable inquiry, the disclosure is complete and correct as of the time it is made.

(c) *Effect of signature on discovery request, notice, response, or objection.* The signature of an attorney or party on a discovery request, notice, response, or objection constitutes a certification that to the best of the signer's knowledge, information, and belief, formed after a reasonable inquiry, the request, notice, response, or objection:

(1) is consistent with the rules of civil procedure and these discovery rules and warranted by existing law or a good faith argument for the extension, modification, or reversal of existing law;

(2) has a good faith factual basis;

(3) is not interposed for any improper purpose, such as to harass or to cause unnecessary delay or needless increase in the cost of litigation; and

(4) is not unreasonable or unduly burdensome or expensive, given the needs of the case, the discovery already had in the case, the amount in controversy, and the importance of the issues at stake in the litigation.

(d) *Effect of failure to sign.* If a request, notice, response, or objection is not signed, it must be stricken unless it is signed promptly after the omission is called to the attention of the party making the request, notice, response, or objection. A party is not required to take any action with respect to a request or notice that is not signed.

(e) *Sanctions.* If the certification is false without substantial justification, the court may, upon motion or its own initiative, impose on the person who made the certification, or the party on whose behalf the request, notice, response, or objection was made, or both, an appropriate sanction as for a frivolous pleading or motion under Chapter 10 of the Civil Practice and Remedies Code.

191.4 **Filing of Discovery Materials.**

(a) *Discovery materials not to be filed.* The following discovery materials must not be filed:

(1) discovery requests, deposition notices, and subpoenas required to be served only on parties;

(2) responses and objections to discovery requests and deposition notices, regardless on whom the requests or notices were served;

(3) documents and tangible things produced in discovery; and

(4) statements prepared in compliance with Rule 193.3(b) or (d).

(b) *Discovery materials to be filed.* The following discovery materials must be filed:

(1) discovery requests, deposition notices, and subpoenas required to be served on nonparties;

(2) motions and responses to motions pertaining to discovery matters; and

(3) agreements concerning discovery matters, to the extent necessary to comply with Rule 11.

(c) *Exceptions.* Notwithstanding paragraph (a)—

(1) the court may order discovery materials to be filed;

(2) a person may file discovery materials in support of or in opposition to a motion or for other use in a court proceeding; and

(3) a person may file discovery materials necessary for a proceeding in an appellate court.

(d) *Retention requirement for persons.* Any person required to serve discovery materials not required to be filed must retain the original or exact copy of the materials during the pendency of the case and any related appellate proceedings begun within six months after judgment is signed, unless otherwise provided by the trial court.

(e) *Retention requirement for courts.* The clerk of the court shall retain and dispose of deposition transcripts and depositions upon written questions as directed by the Supreme Court.

191.5 **Service of Discovery Materials.** Every disclosure, discovery request, notice, response, and objection required to be served on a party or person must be served on all parties of record.

Comments to 1999 change:

1. Rule 191.1 preserves the ability of parties by agreement and trial courts by order to adapt discovery to different circumstances. That ability is broad but

---

⭐

---

not unbounded. Parties cannot merely by agreement modify a court order without the court's concurrence. Trial courts cannot simply "opt out" of these rules by form orders or approve or order a discovery control plan that does not contain the matters specified in Rule 190.4, but trial courts may use standard or form orders for providing discovery plans, scheduling, and other pretrial matters. In individual instances, courts may order, or parties may agree, to use discovery methods other than those prescribed in these rules if appropriate. Because the general rule is stated here, it is not repeated in each context in which it applies. Thus, for example, parties can agree to enlarge or shorten the time permitted for a deposition and to change the manner in which a deposition is conducted, notwithstanding Rule 199.5, although parties could not agree to be abusive toward a witness.

2. Rule 191.2 expressly states the obligation of parties and their attorneys to cooperate in conducting discovery.

3. The requirement that discovery requests, notices, responses, and objections be signed also applies to documents used to satisfy the purposes of such instruments. An example is a statement that privileged material or information has been withheld, which may be separate from a response to the discovery request but is nevertheless part of the response.

History of TRCP 191: Adopted eff. Jan. 1, 1999, by order of Nov. 9, 1998 (977-78 S.W.2d [Tex.Cases] xliii). TRCPs 191.3 and 191.4 apply only to discovery conducted after Jan. 1, 1999. Source: New rule.

See CPRC §10.001; TRCP 11, 13, 57; *Commentaries*, "General Rules for Discovery," ch. 6-A, p. 425.

ANNOTATIONS

In re BP Prods. N. Am., Inc., 244 S.W.3d 840, 846 (Tex.2008). "This Court has not previously addressed the scope of a trial court's power to set aside an otherwise enforceable Rule 191.1 agreement. Consistent with its powers over discovery, a trial court may modify discovery procedures and limitations for 'good cause.' This power, however, is not 'unbounded.' Wherever possible, a trial court should give effect to agreements between the parties. [¶] A court should be particularly reluctant to set aside a Rule 191.1 agreement after one party has acted in reliance on the agreed procedure and performed its obligations under the agreement. *At 847:* In the absence of a motion for sanctions, proper notice and opportunity to be heard, or the trial court's invocation of the court's power to sanction, the order striking the discovery agreement is not supportable as a sanctions order."

In re Alford Chevrolet-Geo, 997 S.W.2d 173, 184 (Tex.1999). "[W]e expect class-action litigants to cooperate on discovery plans and make any agreements reasonably necessary for the efficient disposition of the case."

Groves v. Gabriel, 874 S.W.2d 660, 661 n.3 (Tex. 1994). "[P] complains that [D's] motion to compel discovery did not contain the certificate of conference required under [TRCP 166b(7), now 191.2]. Because this rule is for the benefit of the trial court, the court's failure to require a certificate of conference does not justify mandamus relief."

TRCP 192. PERMISSIBLE DISCOVERY: FORMS & SCOPE; WORK PRODUCT; PROTECTIVE ORDERS; DEFINITIONS

192.1 **Forms of Discovery.** Permissible forms of discovery are:

(a) requests for disclosure;

(b) requests for production and inspection of documents and tangible things;

(c) requests and motions for entry upon and examination of real property;

(d) interrogatories to a party;

(e) requests for admission;

(f) oral or written depositions; and

(g) motions for mental or physical examinations.

192.2 **Sequence of Discovery.** The permissible forms of discovery may be combined in the same document and may be taken in any order or sequence.

192.3 **Scope of Discovery.**

(a) *Generally.* In general, a party may obtain discovery regarding any matter that is not privileged and is relevant to the subject matter of the pending action, whether it relates to the claim or defense of the party seeking discovery or the claim or defense of any other party. It is not a ground for objection that the information sought will be inadmissible at trial if the information sought appears reasonably calculated to lead to the discovery of admissible evidence.

(b) *Documents and tangible things.* A party may obtain discovery of the existence, description, nature, custody, condition, location, and contents of documents and tangible things (including papers, books, accounts, drawings, graphs, charts, photographs, electronic or videotape recordings, data, and data compilations) that constitute or contain matters relevant to the subject matter of the action. A person is required to produce a document or tangible thing that is within the person's possession, custody, or control.

(c) *Persons with knowledge of relevant facts.* A party may obtain discovery of the name, address, and telephone number of persons having knowledge of relevant facts, and a brief statement of each identified person's connection with the case. A person has knowledge of relevant facts when that person has or may have knowledge of any discoverable matter. The person need not have admissible information or personal knowledge of the facts. An expert is "a person with

───────────────────────────────── ✦ ─────────────────────────────────

knowledge of relevant facts" only if that knowledge was obtained first-hand or if it was not obtained in preparation for trial or in anticipation of litigation.

(d) *Trial witnesses.* A party may obtain discovery of the name, address, and telephone number of any person who is expected to be called to testify at trial. This paragraph does not apply to rebuttal or impeaching witnesses the necessity of whose testimony cannot reasonably be anticipated before trial.

(e) *Testifying and consulting experts.* The identity, mental impressions, and opinions of a consulting expert whose mental impressions and opinions have not been reviewed by a testifying expert are not discoverable. A party may discover the following information regarding a testifying expert or regarding a consulting expert whose mental impressions or opinions have been reviewed by a testifying expert:

(1) the expert's name, address, and telephone number;

(2) the subject matter on which a testifying expert will testify;

(3) the facts known by the expert that relate to or form the basis of the expert's mental impressions and opinions formed or made in connection with the case in which the discovery is sought, regardless of when and how the factual information was acquired;

(4) the expert's mental impressions and opinions formed or made in connection with the case in which discovery is sought, and any methods used to derive them;

(5) any bias of the witness;

(6) all documents, tangible things, reports, models, or data compilations that have been provided to, reviewed by, or prepared by or for the expert in anticipation of a testifying expert's testimony;

(7) the expert's current resume and bibliography.

(f) *Indemnity and insuring agreements.* Except as otherwise provided by law, a party may obtain discovery of the existence and contents of any indemnity or insurance agreement under which any person may be liable to satisfy part or all of a judgment rendered in the action or to indemnify or reimburse for payments made to satisfy the judgment. Information concerning the indemnity or insurance agreement is not by reason of disclosure admissible in evidence at trial.

(g) *Settlement agreements.* A party may obtain discovery of the existence and contents of any relevant portions of a settlement agreement. Information concerning a settlement agreement is not by reason of disclosure admissible in evidence at trial.

(h) *Statements of persons with knowledge of relevant facts.* A party may obtain discovery of the statement of any person with knowledge of relevant facts—a "witness statement"—regardless of when the statement was made. A witness statement is (1) a written statement signed or otherwise adopted or approved in writing by the person making it, or (2) a stenographic, mechanical, electrical, or other type of recording of a witness's oral statement, or any substantially verbatim transcription of such a recording. Notes taken during a conversation or interview with a witness are not a witness statement. Any person may obtain, upon written request, his or her own statement concerning the lawsuit, which is in the possession, custody or control of any party.

(i) *Potential parties.* A party may obtain discovery of the name, address, and telephone number of any potential party.

(j) *Contentions.* A party may obtain discovery of any other party's legal contentions and the factual bases for those contentions.

192.4 Limitations on Scope of Discovery. The discovery methods permitted by these rules should be limited by the court if it determines, on motion or on its own initiative and on reasonable notice, that:

(a) the discovery sought is unreasonably cumulative or duplicative, or is obtainable from some other source that is more convenient, less burdensome, or less expensive; or

(b) the burden or expense of the proposed discovery outweighs its likely benefit, taking into account the needs of the case, the amount in controversy, the parties' resources, the importance of the issues at stake in the litigation, and the importance of the proposed discovery in resolving the issues.

192.5 Work Product.

(a) *Work product defined.* Work product comprises:

(1) material prepared or mental impressions developed in anticipation of litigation or for trial by or for a party or a party's representatives, including the party's attorneys, consultants, sureties, indemnitors, insurers, employees, or agents; or

---

✪

---

(2) a communication made in anticipation of litigation or for trial between a party and the party's representatives or among a party's representatives, including the party's attorneys, consultants, sureties, indemnitors, insurers, employees, or agents.

(b) *Protection of work product.*

(1) *Protection of core work product—attorney mental processes.* Core work product—the work product of an attorney or an attorney's representative that contains the attorney's or the attorney's representative's mental impressions, opinions, conclusions, or legal theories—is not discoverable.

(2) *Protection of other work product.* Any other work product is discoverable only upon a showing that the party seeking discovery has substantial need of the materials in the preparation of the party's case and that the party is unable without undue hardship to obtain the substantial equivalent of the material by other means.

(3) *Incidental disclosure of attorney mental processes.* It is not a violation of subparagraph (1) if disclosure ordered pursuant to subparagraph (2) incidentally discloses by inference attorney mental processes otherwise protected under subparagraph (1).

(4) *Limiting disclosure of mental processes.* If a court orders discovery of work product pursuant to subparagraph (2), the court must—insofar as possible—protect against disclosure of the mental impressions, opinions, conclusions, or legal theories not otherwise discoverable.

(c) *Exceptions.* Even if made or prepared in anticipation of litigation or for trial, the following is not work product protected from discovery:

(1) information discoverable under Rule 192.3 concerning experts, trial witnesses, witness statements, and contentions;

(2) trial exhibits ordered disclosed under Rule 166 or Rule 190.4;

(3) the name, address, and telephone number of any potential party or any person with knowledge of relevant facts;

(4) any photograph or electronic image of underlying facts (*e.g.*, a photograph of the accident scene) or a photograph or electronic image of any sort that a party intends to offer into evidence; and

(5) any work product created under circumstances within an exception to the attorney-client privilege in Rule 503(d) of the Rules of Evidence.

(d) *Privilege.* For purposes of these rules, an assertion that material or information is work product is an assertion of privilege.

192.6 **Protective Orders.**

(a) *Motion.* A person from whom discovery is sought, and any other person affected by the discovery request, may move within the time permitted for response to the discovery request for an order protecting that person from the discovery sought. A person should not move for protection when an objection to written discovery or an assertion of privilege is appropriate, but a motion does not waive the objection or assertion of privilege. If a person seeks protection regarding the time or place of discovery, the person must state a reasonable time and place for discovery with which the person will comply. A person must comply with a request to the extent protection is not sought unless it is unreasonable under the circumstances to do so before obtaining a ruling on the motion.

(b) *Order.* To protect the movant from undue burden, unnecessary expense, harassment, annoyance, or invasion of personal, constitutional, or property rights, the court may make any order in the interest of justice and may—among other things—order that:

(1) the requested discovery not be sought in whole or in part;

(2) the extent or subject matter of discovery be limited;

(3) the discovery not be undertaken at the time or place specified;

(4) the discovery be undertaken only by such method or upon such terms and conditions or at the time and place directed by the court;

(5) the results of discovery be sealed or otherwise protected, subject to the provisions of Rule 76a.

192.7 **Definitions.** As used in these rules—

(a) *Written discovery* means requests for disclosure, requests for production and inspection of documents and tangible things, requests for entry onto property, interrogatories, and requests for admission.

(b) *Possession, custody, or control* of an item means that the person either has physical possession of the item or has a right to possession of the item that is equal or superior to the person who has physical possession of the item.

(c) A *testifying expert* is an expert who may be called to testify as an expert witness at trial.

—★—

(d) A *consulting expert* is an expert who has been consulted, retained, or specially employed by a party in anticipation of litigation or in preparation for trial, but who is not a testifying expert.

Comments to 1999 change:

1. While the scope of discovery is quite broad, it is nevertheless confined by the subject matter of the case and reasonable expectations of obtaining information that will aid resolution of the dispute. The rule must be read and applied in that context. See *In re American Optical Corp.*, 988 S.W.2d 711 (Tex.1998) (per curiam); *K-Mart v. Sanderson*, 937 S.W.2d 429 (Tex.1996) (per curiam); *Dillard Dept. Stores v. Hall*, 909 S.W.2d 491 (Tex.1995) (per curiam); *Texaco, Inc. v. Sanderson*, 898 S.W.2d 813 (Tex.1995) (per curiam); *Loftin v. Martin*, 776 S.W.2d 145, 148 (Tex.1989).

2. The definition of documents and tangible things has been revised to clarify that things relevant to the subject matter of the action are within the scope of discovery regardless of their form.

3. Rule 192.3(c) makes discoverable a "brief statement of each identified person's connection with the case." This provision does not contemplate a narrative statement of the facts the person knows, but at most a few words describing the person's identity as relevant to the lawsuit. For instance: "treating physician," "eyewitness," "chief financial officer," "director," "plaintiff's mother and eyewitness to accident." The rule is intended to be consistent with *Axelson v. McIlhany*, 798 S.W.2d 550 (Tex.1990).

4. Rule 192.3(g) does not suggest that settlement agreements in other cases are relevant or irrelevant.

5. Rule 192.3(j) makes a party's legal and factual contentions discoverable but does not require more than a basic statement of those contentions and does not require a marshaling of evidence.

6. The sections in former Rule 166b concerning land and medical records are not included in this rule. They remain within the scope of discovery and are discussed in other rules.

7. The court's power to limit discovery based on the needs and circumstances of the case is expressly stated in Rule 192.4. The provision is taken from Rule 26(b)(2) of the Federal Rules of Civil Procedure. Courts should limit discovery under this rule only to prevent unwarranted delay and expense as stated more fully in the rule. A court abuses its discretion in unreasonably restricting a party's access to information through discovery.

8. Work product is defined for the first time, and its exceptions stated. Work product replaces the "attorney work product" and "party communication" discovery exemptions from former Rule 166b.

9. Elimination of the "witness statement" exemption does not render all witness statements automatically discoverable but subjects them to the same rules concerning the scope of discovery and privileges applicable to other documents or tangible things.

History of TRCP 192: Amended eff. Jan. 1, 1999, by order of Dec. 31, 1998 (981-82 S.W.2d [Tex.Cases] xxxviii). Adopted eff. Jan. 1, 1999, by order of Nov. 9, 1998 (977-78 S.W.2d [Tex.Cases] xlvi). This is former TRCP 166b, with modification. Source: New rule.

See *Commentaries*, "General Rules for Discovery," ch. 6-A, p. 425; "Scope of Discovery," ch. 6-B, p. 460; "Electronic Discovery," ch. 6-C, p. 485; *O'Connor's Texas Forms*, FORMS 6A:10-14.

ANNOTATIONS

Definition

In re Kuntz, 124 S.W.3d 179, 183 (Tex.2003). "[D] argues that he 'should not be ordered to produce documents in the physical possession of his corporate employer in this suit brought against him individually.' *At 184:* [D's] access is strictly limited to use of the [documents] in furtherance of his employer's services.... [¶] [M]ere access to the [documents] does not constitute 'physical possession' of the documents

under the definition of 'possession, custody, or control' set forth in [TRCP] 192.7(b)."

GTE Comms. Sys. v. Tanner, 856 S.W.2d 725, 729 (Tex.1993). "The phrase, 'possession, custody or control,' within the meaning of [TRCP 192.7(b)], includes not only actual physical possession, but constructive possession, and the right to obtain possession from a third party, such as an agent or representative." *See also Hallum v. Hallum*, No. 01-09-00095-CV (Tex. App.—Houston [1st Dist.] 2010, no pet.) (memo op.; 12-2-10).

Scope of Discovery

In re Weekley Homes, L.P., 295 S.W.3d 309, 313-14 (Tex.2009). TRCP 192.3(b) "provides for discovery of documents, [including] electronic information that is relevant to the subject matter of the action." *See also In re Honza*, 242 S.W.3d 578, 581 (Tex.App.—Waco 2008, orig. proceeding).

In re Dana Corp., 138 S.W.3d 298, 302 (Tex.2004). "Rule 192.3(f) does not foreclose discovery of insurance information beyond that identified in the rule; however, we also conclude that the plain language of Rule 192.3(f), by itself, does not provide a sufficient basis to order discovery beyond the production of the 'existence and contents' of the policies. [A] party may discover information beyond an insurance agreement's existence and contents only if the information is otherwise discoverable under our scope-of-discovery rule."

K Mart Corp. v. Sanderson, 937 S.W.2d 429, 431 (Tex.1996). No "discovery device can be used to 'fish.'"

Irving Healthcare Sys. v. Brooks, 927 S.W.2d 12, 18 (Tex.1996). "[R]outine business records of a health-care entity such as a patient's medical records do not become privileged and are not shielded from discovery simply because a medical peer review committee has reviewed or considered them."

Ford Motor Co. v. Leggat, 904 S.W.2d 643, 649 (Tex.1995). "Settlement agreements are discoverable, to the extent they are relevant. Settlement agreements themselves, of course, are not admissible at trial to prove liability." *See also In re Univar USA, Inc.*, 311 S.W.3d 175, 180 (Tex.App.—Beaumont 2010, orig. proceeding).

Monsanto Co. v. May, 889 S.W.2d 274, 276 (Tex. 1994). "A party is entitled to discovery that is relevant to the subject matter of the claim, and which appears reasonably calculated to lead to the discovery of admis-

⭐

sible evidence." *See also **Ford Motor Co. v. Castillo**,* 279 S.W.3d 656, 664 (Tex.2009); ***Volkswagen, A.G. v. Valdez***, 909 S.W.2d 900, 902 (Tex.1995).

Experts

In re Christus Spohn Hosp. Kleberg, 222 S.W.3d 434, 440 (Tex.2007). See annotation under TRCP 193.3—*Privileges*, p. 956.

In re City of Georgetown, 53 S.W.3d 328, 334 (Tex. 2001). "The [TRCPs] expressly provide that a party is not required to disclose the identity, mental impressions, and opinions of consulting experts. *At 337:* [I]f documents are privileged or confidential under the [TRCPs] or [TREs], they are within a 'category of information [that] is expressly made confidential under other law' within the meaning of [Gov't Code] §552.022...."

General Motors Corp. v. Gayle, 951 S.W.2d 469, 474 (Tex.1997). "'The policy behind the consulting expert privilege is to encourage parties to seek expert advice in evaluating their case and to prevent a party from receiving undue benefit from an adversary's efforts and diligence.' [¶] Without the consulting-expert privilege, parties would be reluctant to test an uncertain theory, for fear that it would provide evidence for the other side. *At 476:* [W]e conclude that the trial court's crash-test order constitutes an abuse of discretion by infringing on [D's] consulting-expert privilege."

In re Makris, 217 S.W.3d 521, 524 (Tex.App.—San Antonio 2006, orig. proceeding). "[P]ersonal financial records of a nonparty witness are not discoverable for the sole purpose of showing bias. [U]nder Rule 192.3(e)(5), in order to obtain discovery of personal documents from a nonparty expert solely for impeachment purposes, the party seeking the documents must first present evidence 'raising the possibility that the expert is biased.'"

Work Product

In re Bexar Cty. Crim. Dist. Atty's Office, 224 S.W.3d 182, 187-88 (Tex.2007). "Rule 192.5(b)(1) distinguishes everyday work product from 'core work product' and makes clear that the latter ... is inviolate and flatly 'not discoverable[ ]'.... Core work product is sacrosanct and its protection impermeable."

Occidental Chem. Corp. v. Banales, 907 S.W.2d 488, 490 (Tex.1995). "The attorney work product privilege protects two related but different concepts. First,

the privilege protects the attorney's thought process, which includes strategy decisions and issue formulation, and notes or writings evincing those mental processes. Second, the privilege protects the mechanical compilation of information to the extent such compilation reveals the attorney's thought processes. The work product exemption is of continuing duration." *See also **National Tank Co. v. Brotherton***, 851 S.W.2d 193, 200 (Tex.1993).

National Un. Fire Ins. v. Valdez, 863 S.W.2d 458, 461 (Tex.1993). "[N]o legitimate purpose is served by allowing a party to discover an opponent's litigation file. Our decision today does not prevent a party from requesting specific documents or categories of documents relevant to issues in a pending case, even though some or all of the documents may be contained in an attorney's files."

In re Energy XXI Gulf Coast, Inc., No. 01-10-00371-CV (Tex.App.—Houston [1st Dist.] 2010, orig. proceeding) (memo op.; 12-23-10). "The 'anticipation of litigation' test is met when a reasonable person would have concluded from the totality of the circumstances that there was a substantial chance that litigation would ensue and the party asserting the work product privilege subjectively believed in good faith that there was a substantial chance that litigation would ensue. A 'substantial chance of litigation' does not 'refer to any particular statistical probability that litigation will occur' but 'simply means that litigation is more than merely an abstract possibility or unwarranted fear.' Common sense dictates that a party may reasonably anticipate suit being filed, and conduct an investigation to prepare for anticipated litigation, before a party manifests an intent to sue by filing suit."

Protective Orders

General Tire, Inc. v. Kepple, 970 S.W.2d 520, 525 (Tex.1998). "[W]e hold that when a party seeks a protective order under [TRCP 166b(5), now TRCP 192.6,] to restrict the dissemination of unfiled discovery, and no party or intervenor contends that the discovery is a 'court record,' a trial court need not conduct a hearing or render any findings on that issue. If a party or intervenor opposing a protective order claims that the discovery is a 'court record,' the court must make a threshold determination on that issue. However, public notice and a [TRCP] 76a hearing are mandated only if the court finds that the documents are court records."

⭐

Crown Cent. Pet. Corp. v. Garcia, 904 S.W.2d 125, 128 (Tex.1995). "When a party seeks to depose a ... high level corporate official [i.e., an apex deposition] and that official (or the corporation) files a motion for protective order ... denying any knowledge of relevant facts, the trial court should first determine whether the party seeking the deposition has arguably shown that the official has any unique or superior personal knowledge of discoverable information. If the party seeking the deposition cannot [so] show ..., the trial court should grant the motion for protective order and first require the party seeking the deposition to attempt to obtain the discovery through less intrusive methods."

In re Shell E&P, Inc., 179 S.W.3d 125, 130 (Tex. App.—San Antonio 2005, orig. proceeding). "[T]he non-party owner of [a] document[ ] ha[s] the right under Rule 192.6(a) to seek protection from disclosure of its documents in the trial court, whether through an objection, assertion of privilege, motion for a protective order, or motion for enforcement of an existing protective order. The trial court's ... order holding that [non-party] lacks standing to object to the disclosure of its documents conflicts with Rule 192.6(a) ...; therefore, ... the trial court clearly abused its discretion."

TRCP 193. WRITTEN DISCOVERY: RESPONSE; OBJECTION; ASSERTION OF PRIVILEGE; SUPPLEMENTATION & AMENDMENT; FAILURE TO TIMELY RESPOND; PRESUMPTION OF AUTHENTICITY

193.1 Responding to Written Discovery; Duty to Make Complete Response. A party must respond to written discovery in writing within the time provided by court order or these rules. When responding to written discovery, a party must make a complete response, based on all information reasonably available to the responding party or its attorney at the time the response is made. The responding party's answers, objections, and other responses must be preceded by the request to which they apply.

193.2 Objecting to Written Discovery.

(a) *Form and time for objections.* A party must make any objection to written discovery in writing—either in the response or in a separate document—within the time for response. The party must state specifically the legal or factual basis for the objection and the extent to which the party is refusing to comply with the request.

(b) *Duty to respond when partially objecting; objection to time or place of production.* A party must comply with as much of the request to which the party has made no objection unless it is unreasonable under the circumstances to do so before obtaining a ruling on the objection. If the responding party objects to the requested time or place of production, the responding party must state a reasonable time and place for complying with the request and must comply at that time and place without further request or order.

(c) *Good faith basis for objection.* A party may object to written discovery only if a good faith factual and legal basis for the objection exists at the time the objection is made.

(d) *Amendment.* An objection or response to written discovery may be amended or supplemented to state an objection or basis that, at the time the objection or response initially was made, either was inapplicable or was unknown after reasonable inquiry.

(e) *Waiver of objection.* An objection that is not made within the time required, or that is obscured by numerous unfounded objections, is waived unless the court excuses the waiver for good cause shown.

(f) *No objection to preserve privilege.* A party should not object to a request for written discovery on the grounds that it calls for production of material or information that is privileged but should instead comply with Rule 193.3. A party who objects to production of privileged material or information does not waive the privilege but must comply with Rule 193.3 when the error is pointed out.

193.3 Asserting a Privilege. A party may preserve a privilege from written discovery in accordance with this subdivision.

(a) *Withholding privileged material or information.* A party who claims that material or information responsive to written discovery is privileged may withhold the privileged material or information from the response. The party must state—in the response (or an amended or supplemental response) or in a separate document—that:

(1) information or material responsive to the request has been withheld,

(2) the request to which the information or material relates, and

(3) the privilege or privileges asserted.

(b) *Description of withheld material or information.* After receiving a response indicating that ma-

★

terial or information has been withheld from production, the party seeking discovery may serve a written request that the withholding party identify the information and material withheld. Within 15 days of service of that request, the withholding party must serve a response that:

(1) describes the information or materials withheld that, without revealing the privileged information itself or otherwise waiving the privilege, enables other parties to assess the applicability of the privilege, and

(2) asserts a specific privilege for each item or group of items withheld.

(c) *Exemption.* Without complying with paragraphs (a) and (b), a party may withhold a privileged communication to or from a lawyer or lawyer's representative or a privileged document of a lawyer or lawyer's representative—

(1) created or made from the point at which a party consults a lawyer with a view to obtaining professional legal services from the lawyer in the prosecution or defense of a specific claim in the litigation in which discovery is requested, and

(2) concerning the litigation in which the discovery is requested.

(d) *Privilege not waived by production.* A party who produces material or information without intending to waive a claim of privilege does not waive that claim under these rules or the Rules of Evidence if—within ten days or a shorter time ordered by the court, after the producing party actually discovers that such production was made—the producing party amends the response, identifying the material or information produced and stating the privilege asserted. If the producing party thus amends the response to assert a privilege, the requesting party must promptly return the specified material or information and any copies pending any ruling by the court denying the privilege.

193.4 **Hearing and Ruling on Objections and Assertions of Privilege.**

(a) *Hearing.* Any party may at any reasonable time request a hearing on an objection or claim of privilege asserted under this rule. The party making the objection or asserting the privilege must present any evidence necessary to support the objection or privilege. The evidence may be testimony presented at the hearing or affidavits served at least seven days before the hearing or at such other reasonable time as the court

permits. If the court determines that an *in camera* review of some or all of the requested discovery is necessary, that material or information must be segregated and produced to the court in a sealed wrapper within a reasonable time following the hearing.

(b) *Ruling.* To the extent the court sustains the objection or claim of privilege, the responding party has no further duty to respond to that request. To the extent the court overrules the objection or claim of privilege, the responding party must produce the requested material or information within 30 days after the court's ruling or at such time as the court orders. A party need not request a ruling on that party's own objection or assertion of privilege to preserve the objection or privilege.

(c) *Use of material or information withheld under claim of privilege.* A party may not use—at any hearing or trial—material or information withheld from discovery under a claim of privilege, including a claim sustained by the court, without timely amending or supplementing the party's response to that discovery.

193.5 **Amending or Supplementing Responses to Written Discovery.**

(a) *Duty to amend or supplement.* If a party learns that the party's response to written discovery was incomplete or incorrect when made, or, although complete and correct when made, is no longer complete and correct, the party must amend or supplement the response:

(1) to the extent that the written discovery sought the identification of persons with knowledge of relevant facts, trial witnesses, or expert witnesses, and

(2) to the extent that the written discovery sought other information, unless the additional or corrective information has been made known to the other parties in writing, on the record at a deposition, or through other discovery responses.

(b) *Time and form of amended or supplemental response.* An amended or supplemental response must be made reasonably promptly after the party discovers the necessity for such a response. Except as otherwise provided by these rules, it is presumed that an amended or supplemental response made less than 30 days before trial was not made reasonably promptly. An amended or supplemental response must be in the same form as the initial response and must be verified by the party if the original response was required to be verified by the party, but the failure to comply with this requirement does not make the amended or supplemental response

---

✦

---

untimely unless the party making the response refuses to correct the defect within a reasonable time after it is pointed out.

193.6 Failing to Timely Respond—Effect on Trial.

(a) *Exclusion of evidence and exceptions.* A party who fails to make, amend, or supplement a discovery response in a timely manner may not introduce in evidence the material or information that was not timely disclosed, or offer the testimony of a witness (other than a named party) who was not timely identified, unless the court finds that:

(1) there was good cause for the failure to timely make, amend, or supplement the discovery response; or

(2) the failure to timely make, amend, or supplement the discovery response will not unfairly surprise or unfairly prejudice the other parties.

(b) *Burden of establishing exception.* The burden of establishing good cause or the lack of unfair surprise or unfair prejudice is on the party seeking to introduce the evidence or call the witness. A finding of good cause or of the lack of unfair surprise or unfair prejudice must be supported by the record.

(c) *Continuance.* Even if the party seeking to introduce the evidence or call the witness fails to carry the burden under paragraph (b), the court may grant a continuance or temporarily postpone the trial to allow a response to be made, amended, or supplemented, and to allow opposing parties to conduct discovery regarding any new information presented by that response.

193.7 Production of Documents Self-Authenticating. A party's production of a document in response to written discovery authenticates the document for use against that party in any pretrial proceeding or at trial unless—within ten days or a longer or shorter time ordered by the court, after the producing party has actual notice that the document will be used—the party objects to the authenticity of the document, or any part of it, stating the specific basis for objection. An objection must be either on the record or in writing and must have a good faith factual and legal basis. An objection made to the authenticity of only part of a document does not affect the authenticity of the remainder. If objection is made, the party attempting to use the document should be given a reasonable opportunity to establish its authenticity.

Comments to 1999 change:

1. This rule imposes a duty upon parties to make a complete response to written discovery based upon all information reasonably available, subject to objections and privileges.

2. An objection to written discovery does not excuse the responding party from complying with the request to the extent no objection is made. But a party may object to a request for "all documents relevant to the lawsuit" as overly broad and not in compliance with the rule requiring specific requests for documents and refuse to comply with it entirely. See *Loftin v. Martin*, 776 S.W.2d 145 (Tex.1989). A party may also object to a request for a litigation file on the ground that it is overly broad and may assert that on its face the request seeks only materials protected by privilege. See *National Union Fire Ins. Co. v. Valdez*, 863 S.W.2d 458 (Tex.1993). A party who objects to production of documents from a remote time period should produce documents from a more recent period unless that production would be burdensome and duplicative should the objection be overruled.

3. This rule governs the presentation of all privileges including work product. It dispenses with objections to written discovery requests on the basis that responsive information or materials are protected by a specific privilege from discovery. Instead, the rule requires parties to state that information or materials have been withheld and to identify the privilege upon which the party relies. The statement should not be made prophylactically, but only when specific information and materials have been withheld. The party must amend or supplement the statement if additional privileged information or material is found subsequent to the initial response. Thus, when large numbers of documents are being produced, a party may amend the initial response when documents are found as to which the party claims privilege. A party need not state that material created by or for lawyers for the litigation has been withheld as it can be assumed that such material will be withheld from virtually any request on the grounds of attorney-client privilege or work product. However, the rule does not prohibit a party from specifically requesting the material or information if the party has a good faith basis for asserting that it is discoverable. An example would be material or information described by Rule 503(d)(1) of the Rules of Evidence.

4. Rule 193.3(d) is a new provision that allows a party to assert a claim of privilege to material or information produced inadvertently without intending to waive the privilege. The provision is commonly used in complex cases to reduce costs and risks in large document productions. The focus is on the intent to waive the privilege, not the intent to produce the material or information. A party who fails to diligently screen documents before producing them does not waive a claim of privilege. This rule is thus broader than TRE 511 and overturns *Granada Corp. v. First Court of Appeals*, 844 S.W.2d 223 (Tex.1992), to the extent the two conflict. The ten-day period (which may be shortened by the court) allowed for an amended response does not run from the production of the material or information but from the party's first awareness of the mistake. To avoid complications at trial, a party may identify prior to trial the documents intended to be offered, thereby triggering the obligation to assert any overlooked privilege under this rule. A trial court may also order this procedure.

5. This rule imposes no duty to supplement or amend deposition testimony. The only duty to supplement deposition testimony is provided in Rule 195.6.

6. Any party can request a hearing in which the court will resolve issues brought up in objections or withholding statements. The party seeking to avoid discovery has the burden of proving the objection or privilege.

7. The self-authenticating provision is new. Authentication is, of course, but a condition precedent to admissibility and does not establish admissibility. See TRE 901(a). The ten-day period allowed for objection to authenticity (which period may be altered by the court in appropriate circumstances) does not run from the production of the material or information but from the party's actual awareness that the document will be used. To avoid complications at trial, a party may identify prior to trial the documents intended to be offered, thereby triggering the obligation to object to authenticity. A trial court may also order this procedure. An objection to authenticity must be made in good faith.

History of TRCP 193: Amended eff. Jan. 1, 1999, by order of Dec. 31, 1998 (981-82 S.W.2d [Tex.Cases] xxxviii-ix). Adopted eff. Jan. 1, 1999, by order of Nov. 9, 1998 (977-78 S.W.2d [Tex.Cases] li): This is former TRCP 166b, with modification. Discovery responses, objections, amendments, assertions of privilege, and supplementations made prior to Jan. 1, 1999, are not subject to TRCP 193. Source: New rule.

———————————————— ⭐ ————————————————

See *Commentaries*, "General Rules for Discovery," ch. 6-A, p. 425; "Scope of Discovery," ch. 6-B, p. 460; *O'Connor's Texas Forms*, FORMS 6A:9, 15-16, 19, 22.

TRCP 193.1—Duty

Lucas v. Clark, 347 S.W.3d 800, 805 (Tex.App.—Austin 2011, pet. denied). "[T]ypically any challenge to a request for admission must be in compliance with Rule 193.1, [but the] question of a deemed admission's overbreadth only arises when a request for admission has been deemed admitted, which, by definition, occurs after a party has failed to timely respond or object to the request. No request for admission would be deemed admitted if the responding party had objected in writing within the parameters of Rule 193.1. Therefore, were we to require a party to object in writing to a request for admission's overbreadth in order to preserve the issue on appeal, no appellate court would ever face the issue. [¶] [N]o objection was necessary to reach the merits of the issue in this Court. This is true because the question before us is one of evidentiary sufficiency rather than procedural error. In viewing the effect of an overly broad request for admission, our analysis centers on whether a trial court is permitted to find that the request for admission irrefutably established the facts therein such that no additional evidence is required."

TRCP 193.2—Objections

General Motors Corp. v. Tanner, 892 S.W.2d 862, 863 (Tex.1995). "As the party objecting to the request, [P] was required to provide evidence in support of his objection."

TRCP 193.3—Privileges

In re Christus Spohn Hosp. Kleberg, 222 S.W.3d 434, 439 (Tex.2007). "The snap-back provision [in TRCP 193.3(d)] has typically been applied when a party inadvertently produces privileged documents to an opposing party. In this case, however, the privileged material was produced by a party to its own testifying expert, invoking [TRCP] 192.3(e)(6)'s overlapping directive that all materials provided to a testifying expert must be produced. *At 440-41:* [TRCPs] 192.3(e)(6) and 192.5(c)(1) prevail over Rule 193.3(d)'s snap-back provision so long as the expert intends to testify at trial despite the inadvertent document production. That is, once privileged documents are disclosed to a testifying expert, and the party who designated the expert continues to rely upon that designation for trial, the documents may not be retrieved even if they were inadvertently produced. Of course, inadvertently produced material that could not by its nature have influenced the expert's opinion does not evoke the concerns the expert-disclosure rule was designed to prevent and the policy concerns underlying the rule's disclosure requirement would presumably never arise. In that event, there would be nothing to prevent the snap-back rule's application, although we note that a party seeking snap-back under such circumstances would bear a heavy burden in light of the disclosure rule's underlying purpose. *At 445:* An attorney who discovers that privileged documents have been inadvertently provided to a testifying expert may presumably withdraw the expert's designation and name another."

In re E.I. DuPont de Nemours & Co., 136 S.W.3d 218, 223 (Tex.2004). "[A]n affidavit, even if it addresses groups of documents rather than each document individually, has been held to be sufficient to make a prima facie showing of attorney-client and/or work product privilege. *At 224:* However, an affidavit is of no probative value if it merely presents global allegations that documents come within the asserted privilege. [D's affidavit] sets forth the factual basis for the applicability of the attorney-client and/or work product privileges to the documents at issue. [T]he specificity of [D's] affidavit and the log taken together are reasonably adequate to establish a prima facie case of privilege...." *See also* ***In re BP Prods.***, 263 S.W.3d 106, 113-14 (Tex.App.—Houston [1st Dist.] 2006, orig. proceeding).

In re Union Pac. Res., 22 S.W.3d 338, 340 (Tex. 1999). "'Any party who seeks to deny the production of evidence must claim a specific privilege against such production. The burden is on the party asserting a privilege from discovery to produce evidence *concerning the applicability of a particular privilege.*'" *See also* ***In re Monsanto Co.***, 998 S.W.2d 917, 926 (Tex.App.—Waco 1999, orig. proceeding).

In re Certain Underwriters, 294 S.W.3d 891, 902 (Tex.App.—Beaumont 2009, orig. proceeding). "Because the rules do not expressly define the term 'party who produces,' it is not clear that Rule 193.3(d) is confined to reach only parties to a suit. *At 903:* Because the law allows privileged information to be shared for certain purposes with specific others, privilege rules are necessarily designed to apply to persons other than the privilege's holder. Should the 'snap-back' provision ap-

★

ply only to the parties to the suit, that interpretation would effectively negate the privilege holder's enforcement rights when nonparties to the suit produce privileged information. Thus, we conclude that an interpretation of Rule 193.3(d) to read 'party who produces' as meaning 'party to the lawsuit who produces' would allow, rather than discourage, efforts to obtain privileged information from nonparties."

Warrantech Corp. v. Computer Adapters Servs., 134 S.W.3d 516, 524-25 (Tex.App.—Fort Worth 2004, no pet.). "The focus of [TRCP] 193.3(d) is on the intent to waive the privilege, not the intent to produce the material or information. [A] party who fails to diligently screen documents before producing them does not waive a claim of privilege, and the ten-day period runs from the party's first awareness of the mistake, not from the date of production. [A] party may identify before trial the documents intended to be offered, thereby triggering the obligation to assert any overlooked privilege under this rule." *See also **In re Certain Underwriters***, 294 S.W.3d 891, 904 (Tex.App.—Beaumont 2009, orig. proceeding).

TRCP 193.4—Hearing

In re CI Host, Inc., 92 S.W.3d 514, 517 (Tex.2002). "Our discovery rules do not require notice to third parties so that they might have an opportunity to be heard on their own objections."

TRCP 193.5—Supplementing Discovery

Titus Cty. Hosp. Dist. v. Lucas, 988 S.W.2d 740, 740 (Tex.1998). TRCP 166b(6), now 193.5, "requires supplementation of a 'response' to a 'request for discovery.' An interrogatory answer is a response to a request for discovery, but testimony in a deposition is not. A general duty to supplement deposition testimony (as opposed to a narrow duty for certain expert testimony, for example) would impose too great a burden on litigants. We therefore disapprove the court of appeals' holding that deposition testimony must be supplemented."

Exxon Corp. v. West Tex. Gathering Co., 868 S.W.2d 299, 304 (Tex.1993). "Our rules do not prevent experts from refining calculations and perfecting reports through the time of trial. The testimony of an expert should not be barred because a change in some minor detail of the person's work has not been disclosed a month before trial. The additional supplementation requirement of [TRCP 166b(6), now 193.5,] does require that opposing parties have sufficient information about

an expert's opinion to prepare a rebuttal with their own experts and cross-examination, and that they be promptly and fully advised when further developments have rendered past information incorrect or misleading."

Snider v. Stanley, 44 S.W.3d 713, 715 (Tex.App.—Beaumont 2001, pet. denied). "'An amended or supplemental response must be made reasonably promptly after the party discovers the necessity for such a response.' It is presumed that response made within 30 days of trial is not reasonably promptly made. [D's] response, made 30 days before trial, is not subject to the presumption. [Ps] argue that the opposite presumption applies, that is, the supplementation was made reasonably promptly. We disagree. Had such a presumption been intended, it would have been incorporated into the rules."

TRCP 193.6—Effect of Failing to Respond

Hooper v. Chittaluru, 222 S.W.3d 103, 110 (Tex. App.—Houston [14th Dist.] 2006, pet. denied). "[P's] cross-designations were reasonably prompt and included the information that was available to him at the time. He could not possibly have disclosed [D's expert's] name before [D] disclosed it to him or detailed [D's expert's] favorable opinions before he learned of them during the deposition. [T]o the extent [P] could have provided any of his cross-designation supplements earlier, … exclusion [of evidence is not justified] because he had no information to disclose beyond that which he … had already received…."

TRCP 193.6—Good Cause

Alvarado v. Farah Mfg., 830 S.W.2d 911, 914 (Tex. 1992). The salutary purpose of TRCP 193.6 "is to require complete responses to discovery so as to promote responsible assessment of settlement and prevent trial by ambush. The rule is mandatory, and its sole sanction—exclusion of evidence—is automatic, unless there is good cause to excuse its imposition. The good cause exception permits a trial court to excuse a failure to comply with discovery in difficult or impossible circumstances. The trial court has discretion to determine whether the offering party has met his burden of showing good cause to admit the testimony; but the trial court has no discretion to admit testimony excluded by the rule without a showing of good cause." *See also **Good v. Smith Cty. Judge, Baker***, 339 S.W.3d 260, 271 (Tex.App.—Texarkana 2011, pet. denied); ***Reservoir***

⭐

Sys. v. TGS-NOPRC Geophysical Co., 335 S.W.3d 297, 310-11 (Tex.App.—Houston [14th Dist.] 2010, pet. denied).

TRCP 193.7—Self-Authenticating

Blanche v. First Nationwide Mortg. Corp., 74 S.W.3d 444, 451-52 (Tex.App.—Dallas 2002, no pet.). TRCP 193.7 "alleviate[s] the burden on a party receiving documents through discovery from proving the authenticity of those documents when they are used against the party who produced them. Rule 193.7 does not help [Ps] here because the documents attached to their summary judgment response were not produced to them by [D], the party against whom the documents were used. ... A party cannot authenticate a document for use in its own favor by merely producing it in response to a discovery request."

TRCP 194. REQUESTS FOR DISCLOSURE

194.1 **Request.** A party may obtain disclosure from another party of the information or material listed in Rule 194.2 by serving the other party—no later than 30 days before the end of any applicable discovery period—the following request: "Pursuant to Rule 194, you are requested to disclose, within 30 days of service of this request, the information or material described in Rule [state rule, e.g., 194.2, or 194.2(a), (c), and (f), or 194.2(d)-(g)]."

194.2 **Content.** A party may request disclosure of any or all of the following:

(a) the correct names of the parties to the lawsuit;

(b) the name, address, and telephone number of any potential parties;

(c) the legal theories and, in general, the factual bases of the responding party's claims or defenses (the responding party need not marshal all evidence that may be offered at trial);

(d) the amount and any method of calculating economic damages;

(e) the name, address, and telephone number of persons having knowledge of relevant facts, and a brief statement of each identified person's connection with the case;

(f) for any testifying expert:

(1) the expert's name, address, and telephone number;

(2) the subject matter on which the expert will testify;

(3) the general substance of the expert's mental impressions and opinions and a brief summary of the basis for them, or if the expert is not retained by, employed by, or otherwise subject to the control of the responding party, documents reflecting such information;

(4) if the expert is retained by, employed by, or otherwise subject to the control of the responding party:

(A) all documents, tangible things, reports, models, or data compilations that have been provided to, reviewed by, or prepared by or for the expert in anticipation of the expert's testimony; and

(B) the expert's current resume and bibliography;

(g) any indemnity and insuring agreements described in Rule 192.3(f);

(h) any settlement agreements described in Rule 192.3(g);

(i) any witness statements described in Rule 192.3(h);

(j) in a suit alleging physical or mental injury and damages from the occurrence that is the subject of the case, all medical records and bills that are reasonably related to the injuries or damages asserted or, in lieu thereof, an authorization permitting the disclosure of such medical records and bills;

(k) in a suit alleging physical or mental injury and damages from the occurrence that is the subject of the case, all medical records and bills obtained by the responding party by virtue of an authorization furnished by the requesting party;

(*l*) the name, address, and telephone number of any person who may be designated as a responsible third party.

194.3 **Response.** The responding party must serve a written response on the requesting party within 30 days after service of the request, except that:

(a) a defendant served with a request before the defendant's answer is due need not respond until 50 days after service of the request, and

(b) a response to a request under Rule 194.2(f) is governed by Rule 195.

194.4 **Production.** Copies of documents and other tangible items ordinarily must be served with the response. But if the responsive documents are voluminous, the response must state a reasonable time and place for the production of documents. The responding party must produce the documents at the time and

TRCP 193

place stated, unless otherwise agreed by the parties or ordered by the court, and must provide the requesting party a reasonable opportunity to inspect them.

194.5 **No Objection or Assertion of Work Product.** No objection or assertion of work product is permitted to a request under this rule.

194.6 **Certain Responses Not Admissible.** A response to requests under Rule 194.2(c) and (d) that has been changed by an amended or supplemental response is not admissible and may not be used for impeachment.

Comments to 1999 change:

1. Disclosure is designed to afford parties basic discovery of specific categories of information, not automatically in every case, but upon request, without preparation of a lengthy inquiry, and without objection or assertion of work product. In those extremely rare cases when information ordinarily discoverable should be protected, such as when revealing a person's residence might result in harm to the person, a party may move for protection. A party may assert any applicable privileges other than work product using the procedures of Rule 193.3 applicable to other written discovery. Otherwise, to fail to respond fully to a request for disclosure would be an abuse of the discovery process.

2. Rule 194.2(c) and (d) permit a party further inquiry into another's legal theories and factual claims than is often provided in notice pleadings. So-called "contention interrogatories" are used for the same purpose. Such interrogatories are not properly used to require a party to marshal evidence or brief legal issues. Paragraphs (c) and (d) are intended to require disclosure of a party's basic assertions, whether in prosecution of claims or in defense. Thus, for example, a plaintiff would be required to disclose that he or she claimed damages suffered in a car wreck caused by defendant's negligence in speeding, and would be required to state how loss of past earnings and future earning capacity was calculated, but would not be required to state the speed at which defendant was allegedly driving. Paragraph (d) does not require a party, either a plaintiff or a defendant, to state a method of calculating non-economic damages, such as for mental anguish. In the same example, defendant would be required to disclose his or her denial of the speeding allegation and any basis for contesting the damage calculations.

3. Responses under Rule 194.2(c) and (d) that have been amended or supplemented are inadmissible and cannot be used for impeachment, but other evidence of changes in position is not likewise barred.

History of TRCP 194: Amended eff. Mar. 3, 2004, by order of Mar. 3, 2004 (130 S.W.3d [Tex.Cases] xvii): TRCP 194.2(*l*) added as required by changes in CPRC ch. 33; the amendment applies in all cases filed on or after July 1, 2003, in which a request under TRCP 194.1 is made after May 1, 2004. Amended eff. Jan. 1, 1999, by order of Dec. 31, 1998 (981-82 S.W.2d [Tex.Cases] xxxix). Adopted eff. Jan. 1, 1999, by order of Nov. 9, 1998 (977-78 S.W.2d [Tex.Cases] lvi). Source: New rule.

See *Commentaries*, "General Rules for Discovery," ch. 6-A, p. 425; "Securing Discovery from Experts," ch. 6-D, p. 502; "Requests for Disclosure," ch. 6-E, p. 515; *O'Connor's Texas Forms*, FORMS 6D, 6E.

ANNOTATIONS

$27,877.00 Current Money v. State, 331 S.W.3d 110, 120 (Tex.App.—Fort Worth 2010, pet. denied). "[F]ailure to respond to a request for the mental impressions and opinions of the expert [under TRCP 194.2(f)] is a complete failure to respond, triggering the automatic exclusion under [TRCP] 193.6, … not just an incomplete answer, which the Texas Supreme Court has held requires a pretrial objection or a pretrial motion to compel or for sanctions…."

Moore v. Memorial Hermann Hosp. Sys., 140 S.W.3d 870, 875 (Tex.App.—Houston [14th Dist.] 2004, no pet.). "[P] claims that she was not required to disclose the information required under [TRCP] 194.2(f) because [P's expert] was a rebuttal witness and not a designated or retained expert. However, once [D] disclosed the opinions of … its testifying expert, [P] could reasonably have anticipated the need to rebut the testimony of [D's expert] at trial. Therefore, [P's expert] was simply an ordinary rebuttal witness whose use reasonably could have been anticipated; rebuttal witnesses as such are not exempt from the scope of the written discovery rules."

Castellanos v. Littlejohn, 945 S.W.2d 236, 239 (Tex.App.—San Antonio 1997, orig. proceeding). "The issue presented … is whether a party who has inadvertently listed a consulting-only expert as a testifying expert may 'de-designate' him to reflect his proper status. We believe the party can do so, so long as the 'de-designation' does not constitute 'an offensive and unacceptable use of discovery mechanisms' or 'violate[] the clear purpose and policy underlying the rules of discovery.'"

TRCP 195. DISCOVERY REGARDING TESTIFYING EXPERT WITNESSES

195.1 **Permissible Discovery Tools.** A party may request another party to designate and disclose information concerning testifying expert witnesses only through a request for disclosure under Rule 194 and through depositions and reports as permitted by this rule.

195.2 **Schedule for Designating Experts.** Unless otherwise ordered by the court, a party must designate experts—that is, furnish information requested under Rule 194.2(f)—by the later of the following two dates: 30 days after the request is served, or—

(a) with regard to all experts testifying for a party seeking affirmative relief, 90 days before the end of the discovery period;

(b) with regard to all other experts, 60 days before the end of the discovery period.

195.3 **Scheduling Depositions.**

(a) *Experts for party seeking affirmative relief.* A party seeking affirmative relief must make an expert retained by, employed by, or otherwise in the control of the party available for deposition as follows:

---

(1) *If no report furnished.* If a report of the expert's factual observations, tests, supporting data, calculations, photographs, and opinions is not produced when the expert is designated, then the party must make the expert available for deposition reasonably promptly after the expert is designated. If the deposition cannot—due to the actions of the tendering party—reasonably be concluded more than 15 days before the deadline for designating other experts, that deadline must be extended for other experts testifying on the same subject.

(2) *If report furnished.* If a report of the expert's factual observations, tests, supporting data, calculations, photographs, and opinions is produced when the expert is designated, then the party need not make the expert available for deposition until reasonably promptly after all other experts have been designated.

(b) *Other experts.* A party not seeking affirmative relief must make an expert retained by, employed by, or otherwise in the control of the party available for deposition reasonably promptly after the expert is designated and the experts testifying on the same subject for the party seeking affirmative relief have been deposed.

195.4 Oral Deposition. In addition to disclosure under Rule 194, a party may obtain discovery concerning the subject matter on which the expert is expected to testify, the expert's mental impressions and opinions, the facts known to the expert (regardless of when the factual information was acquired) that relate to or form the basis of the testifying expert's mental impressions and opinions, and other discoverable matters, including documents not produced in disclosure, only by oral deposition of the expert and by a report prepared by the expert under this rule.

195.5 Court-Ordered Reports. If the discoverable factual observations, tests, supporting data, calculations, photographs, or opinions of an expert have not been recorded and reduced to tangible form, the court may order these matters reduced to tangible form and produced in addition to the deposition.

195.6 Amendment and Supplementation. A party's duty to amend and supplement written discovery regarding a testifying expert is governed by Rule 193.5. If an expert witness is retained by, employed by, or otherwise under the control of a party, that party must also amend or supplement any deposition testimony or written report by the expert, but only with regard to the expert's mental impressions or opinions and the basis for them.

195.7 Cost of Expert Witnesses. When a party takes the oral deposition of an expert witness retained by the opposing party, all reasonable fees charged by the expert for time spent in preparing for, giving, reviewing, and correcting the deposition must be paid by the party that retained the expert.

Comments to 1999 change:

1. This rule does not limit the permissible methods of discovery concerning consulting experts whose mental impressions or opinions have been reviewed by a testifying expert. See Rule 192.3(e). Information concerning purely consulting experts, of course, is not discoverable.

2. This rule and Rule 194 do not address depositions of testifying experts who are not retained by, employed by, or otherwise subject to the control of the responding party, nor the production of the materials identified in Rule 192.3(e)(5) and (6) relating to such experts. Parties may obtain this discovery, however, through Rules 176 and 205.

3. In scheduling the designations and depositions of expert witnesses, the rule attempts to minimize unfair surprise and undue expense. A party seeking affirmative relief must either produce an expert's report or tender the expert for deposition before an opposing party is required to designate experts. A party who does not wish to incur the expense of a report may simply tender the expert for deposition, but a party who wishes an expert to have the benefit of an opposing party's expert's opinions before being deposed may trigger designation by providing a report. Rule 191.1 permits a trial court, for good cause, to modify the order or deadlines for designating and deposing experts and the allocation of fees and expenses.

History of TRCP 195: Amended eff. Jan. 1, 1999, by order of Dec. 31, 1998 (981-82 S.W.2d [Tex.Cases] xxxix). Adopted eff. Jan. 1, 1999, by order of Nov. 9, 1998 (977-78 S.W.2d [Tex.Cases] lviii): New rule combines all provisions regarding discovery of expert witnesses by incorporating former TRCP 166b(e). Source: New rule.

See *Commentaries*, "General Rules for Discovery," ch. 6-A, p. 425; "Securing Discovery from Experts," ch. 6-D, p. 502; "Requests for Disclosure," ch. 6-E, p. 515; "Depositions," ch. 6-F, p. 525; *O'Connor's Texas Forms*, FORMS 6D, 6E, 6F:1-3.

ANNOTATIONS

Snider v. Stanley, 44 S.W.3d 713, 716 (Tex.App.—Beaumont 2001, pet. denied). "[Ds] did not designate [their expert] as soon as he was retained, employed, or otherwise in their control. Instead, they waited until 30 days before trial. We hold the trial court did not abuse its discretion in finding [Ds] did not supplement their discovery responses 'reasonably promptly.'"

TRCP 196. REQUESTS FOR PRODUCTION & INSPECTION TO PARTIES; REQUESTS & MOTIONS FOR ENTRY UPON PROPERTY

196.1 Request for Production and Inspection to Parties.

(a) *Request.* A party may serve on another party—no later than 30 days before the end of the discovery period—a request for production or for inspection, to inspect, sample, test, photograph and copy documents or tangible things within the scope of discovery.

(b) *Contents of request.* The request must specify the items to be produced or inspected, either by individual item or by category, and describe with reasonable particularity each item and category. The request must specify a reasonable time (on or after the date on which the response is due) and place for production. If the requesting party will sample or test the requested items, the means, manner and procedure for testing or sampling must be described with sufficient specificity to inform the producing party of the means, manner, and procedure for testing or sampling.

(c) *Requests for production of medical or mental health records regarding nonparties.*

(1) *Service of request on nonparty.* If a party requests another party to produce medical or mental health records regarding a nonparty, the requesting party must serve the nonparty with the request for production under Rule 21a.

(2) *Exceptions.* A party is not required to serve the request for production on a nonparty whose medical records are sought if:

(A) the nonparty signs a release of the records that is effective as to the requesting party;

(B) the identity of the nonparty whose records are sought will not directly or indirectly be disclosed by production of the records; or

(C) the court, upon a showing of good cause by the party seeking the records, orders that service is not required.

(3) *Confidentiality.* Nothing in this rule excuses compliance with laws concerning the confidentiality of medical or mental health records.

196.2 **Response to Request for Production and Inspection.**

(a) *Time for response.* The responding party must serve a written response on the requesting party within 30 days after service of the request, except that a defendant served with a request before the defendant's answer is due need not respond until 50 days after service of the request.

(b) *Content of response.* With respect to each item or category of items, the responding party must state objections and assert privileges as required by these rules, and state, as appropriate, that:

(1) production, inspection, or other requested action will be permitted as requested;

(2) the requested items are being served on the requesting party with the response;

(3) production, inspection, or other requested action will take place at a specified time and place, if the responding party is objecting to the time and place of production; or

(4) no items have been identified—after a diligent search—that are responsive to the request.

196.3 **Production.**

(a) *Time and place of production.* Subject to any objections stated in the response, the responding party must produce the requested documents or tangible things within the person's possession, custody or control at either the time and place requested or the time and place stated in the response, unless otherwise agreed by the parties or ordered by the court, and must provide the requesting party a reasonable opportunity to inspect them.

(b) *Copies.* The responding party may produce copies in lieu of originals unless a question is raised as to the authenticity of the original or in the circumstances it would be unfair to produce copies in lieu of originals. If originals are produced, the responding party is entitled to retain the originals while the requesting party inspects and copies them.

(c) *Organization.* The responding party must either produce documents and tangible things as they are kept in the usual course of business or organize and label them to correspond with the categories in the request.

196.4 **Electronic or Magnetic Data.** To obtain discovery of data or information that exists in electronic or magnetic form, the requesting party must specifically request production of electronic or magnetic data and specify the form in which the requesting party wants it produced. The responding party must produce the electronic or magnetic data that is responsive to the request and is reasonably available to the responding party in its ordinary course of business. If the responding party cannot—through reasonable efforts—retrieve the data or information requested or produce it in the form requested, the responding party must state an objection complying with these rules. If the court orders the responding party to comply with the request, the court must also order that the requesting party pay the reasonable expenses of any extraordinary steps required to retrieve and produce the information.

★

196.5 Destruction or Alteration. Testing, sampling or examination of an item may not destroy or materially alter an item unless previously authorized by the court.

196.6 Expenses of Production. Unless otherwise ordered by the court for good cause, the expense of producing items will be borne by the responding party and the expense of inspecting, sampling, testing, photographing, and copying items produced will be borne by the requesting party.

196.7 Request or Motion for Entry Upon Property.

(a) *Request or motion.* A party may gain entry on designated land or other property to inspect, measure, survey, photograph, test, or sample the property or any designated object or operation thereon by serving—no later than 30 days before the end of any applicable discovery period—

(1) a request on all parties if the land or property belongs to a party, or

(2) a motion and notice of hearing on all parties and the nonparty if the land or property belongs to a nonparty. If the identity or address of the nonparty is unknown and cannot be obtained through reasonable diligence, the court must permit service by means other than those specified in Rule 21a that are reasonably calculated to give the nonparty notice of the motion and hearing.

(b) *Time, place, and other conditions.* The request for entry upon a party's property, or the order for entry upon a nonparty's property, must state the time, place, manner, conditions, and scope of the inspection, and must specifically describe any desired means, manner, and procedure for testing or sampling, and the person or persons by whom the inspection, testing, or sampling is to be made.

(c) *Response to request for entry.*

(1) *Time to respond.* The responding party must serve a written response on the requesting party within 30 days after service of the request, except that a defendant served with a request before the defendant's answer is due need not respond until 50 days after service of the request.

(2) *Content of response.* The responding party must state objections and assert privileges as required by these rules, and state, as appropriate, that:

(A) entry or other requested action will be permitted as requested;

(B) entry or other requested action will take place at a specified time and place, if the responding party is objecting to the time and place of production; or

(C) entry or other requested action cannot be permitted for reasons stated in the response.

(d) *Requirements for order for entry on nonparty's property.* An order for entry on a nonparty's property may issue only for good cause shown and only if the land, property, or object thereon as to which discovery is sought is relevant to the subject matter of the action.

Comments to 1999 change:

1. "Document and tangible things" are defined in Rule 192.3(b).

2. A party requesting sampling or testing must describe the procedure with sufficient specificity to enable the responding party to make any appropriate objections.

3. A party requesting production of magnetic or electronic data must specifically request the data, specify the form in which it wants the data produced, and specify any extraordinary steps for retrieval and translation. Unless ordered otherwise, the responding party need only produce the data reasonably available in the ordinary course of business in reasonably usable form.

4. The rule clarifies how the expenses of production are to be allocated absent a court order to the contrary.

5. The obligation of parties to produce documents within their possession, custody or control is explained in Rule 192.3(b).

6. Parties may request production and inspection of documents and tangible things from nonparties under Rule 205.3.

7. Rule 196.3(b) is based on TRE 1003.

8. Rule 196.1(c) is merely a notice requirement and does not expand the scope of discovery of a nonparty's medical records.

History of TRCP 196: Amended eff. Jan. 1, 1999, by order of Dec. 31, 1998 (981-82 S.W.2d [Tex.Cases] xxxix). Adopted eff. Jan. 1, 1999, by order of Nov. 9, 1998 (977-78 S.W.2d [Tex.Cases] lx): New rule combines former TRCPs 167(1)(b) and 166(2)(c). Source: New rule.

See *Commentaries*, "General Rules for Discovery," ch. 6-A, p. 425; "Scope of Discovery," ch. 6-B, p. 460; "Electronic Discovery," ch. 6-C, p. 485; "Depositions," ch. 6-F, p. 525; "Securing Documents & Tangible Things," ch. 6-I, p. 565; "Medical Records," ch. 6-J, p. 576; "Entry on Land," ch. 6-K, p. 580; *O'Connor's Texas Forms*, FORMS 6I-6K.

ANNOTATIONS

In re Weekley Homes, L.P., 295 S.W.3d 309, 314-15 (Tex.2009). "[E]mail communications constitute 'electronic data,' and their characterization as such does not change when they are deleted from a party's inbox. Thus, deleted emails are within Rule 196.4's purview.... [I]t is a simple matter to request emails that have been deleted; knowledge as to the particular method or means of retrieving them is not necessary at the requesting stage of discovery. Once a specific request is made the parties can, and should, communicate as to the particularities of a party's computer storage system and potential methods of retrieval to assess the feasibility of their recovery. But even though it was not stated in [P's] written request that deleted emails

★

were included within its scope, that [P] thought they were and was seeking this form of electronic information became abundantly clear in the course of discovery and before the hearing on the motion to compel. The purpose of Rule 196.4's specificity requirement is to ensure that requests for electronic information are clearly understood and disputes avoided. Because the scope of [P's] requests was understood before trial court intervention, [D] was not prejudiced by [P's] failure to follow the rule and the trial court did not abuse its discretion by ordering production of the deleted emails. To ensure compliance with the rules and avoid confusion, however, parties seeking production of deleted emails should expressly request them." *See also In re Harris*, 315 S.W.3d 685, 700-01 (Tex.App.—Houston [1st Dist.] 2010, orig. proceeding).

In re Colonial Pipeline Co., 968 S.W.2d 938, 942 (Tex.1998). "While [Ps] may be entitled to production of any relevant discovery from the related cases 'as they are kept in the usual course of business,' [Ds] cannot be forced to prepare an inventory of the documents for [Ps]."

General Motors Corp. v. Gayle, 951 S.W.2d 469, 475-76 (Tex.1997). "[Ps] rely on [TRCP] 167(1)(b) [now TRCP 196.7(a)] to support their claim to attend [D's crash] testing. ... The rule allowing entry upon land does not render discoverable items which are privileged under [TRCP 193.3]. [TRCP 196.7(a)] does not authorize [Ps] to enter into testing facilities under [D's] control to view privileged tests."

Dillard Dept. Stores v. Hall, 909 S.W.2d 491, 492 (Tex.1995). "[P] admits that he wants the document production to explore whether he can in good faith allege racial discrimination. This is the very kind of 'fishing expedition' that is not allowable under [TRCP 196.1]."

Sears, Roebuck & Co. v. Ramirez, 824 S.W.2d 558, 559 (Tex.1992). The trial court ordered D to produce its annual reports *and* its federal income-tax statements. The Supreme Court held there was "no justification for requiring [D] to produce the same information in different form."

Texas Gen. Land Office v. Porretto, 369 S.W.3d 276, 290 (Tex.App.—Houston [1st Dist.] 2011, pet. filed 7-9-12). "Much as a trial court cannot compel a party to create indices or reduce information to tangible form in response to a request for production, a trial court cannot sanction a party for failing to orga-nize responsive materials according to the method its opponent prefers when the discovery response complies with an alternate method permitted under the rules."

In re Family Dollar Stores, No. 09-11-00432-CV (Tex.App.—Beaumont 2011, orig. proceeding) (memo op.; 11-3-11). "Rule 196.4 ... requires a specific request for production of electronic or magnetic data, and the request is required to specify the form in which the data is to be produced. [¶] [R]equiring a party to reduce raw data from an electronic database to a paper report or to a list in an electronic form requires [D] to make a list that does not currently exist. Because Rule 196.1 does not allow one party to require that others make lists, the trial court's amended discovery order is broader than the scope of discovery permitted by the [TRCPs]."

In re SWEPI L.P., 103 S.W.3d 578, 584 (Tex. App.—San Antonio 2003, orig. proceeding). "It does not appear any Texas court has directly addressed what constitutes 'good cause' for a discovery order allowing entry onto land. Generally, 'good cause' for a discovery order is shown where ... (1) the discovery sought is relevant and material, that is, the information will in some way aid the movant in the preparation or defense of the case; and (2) the substantial equivalent of the material cannot be obtained through other means."

In re Lincoln Elec. Co., 91 S.W.3d 432, 437 (Tex. App.—Beaumont 2002, orig. proceeding). "In keeping with the overall spirit of non-waiver apparent in the ... discovery rules ..., we believe [TRCP 196.2(b)] permits a responding party ... to make 'objections' to such things as vagueness, overbreadth, [and] relevance ..., have these 'objections' ruled upon, and then make any assertions of privilege ... at a later time."

TRCP 197. INTERROGATORIES TO PARTIES

197.1 **Interrogatories.** A party may serve on another party—no later than 30 days before the end of the discovery period—written interrogatories to inquire about any matter within the scope of discovery except matters covered by Rule 195. An interrogatory may inquire whether a party makes a specific legal or factual contention and may ask the responding party to state the legal theories and to describe in general the factual bases for the party's claims or defenses, but interrogatories may not be used to require the responding party

★

to marshal all of its available proof or the proof the party intends to offer at trial.

197.2 Response to Interrogatories.

(a) *Time for response.* The responding party must serve a written response on the requesting party within 30 days after service of the interrogatories, except that a defendant served with interrogatories before the defendant's answer is due need not respond until 50 days after service of the interrogatories.

(b) *Content of response.* A response must include the party's answers to the interrogatories and may include objections and assertions of privilege as required under these rules.

(c) *Option to produce records.* If the answer to an interrogatory may be derived or ascertained from public records, from the responding party's business records, or from a compilation, abstract or summary of the responding party's business records, and the burden of deriving or ascertaining the answer is substantially the same for the requesting party as for the responding party, the responding party may answer the interrogatory by specifying and, if applicable, producing the records or compilation, abstract or summary of the records. The records from which the answer may be derived or ascertained must be specified in sufficient detail to permit the requesting party to locate and identify them as readily as can the responding party. If the responding party has specified business records, the responding party must state a reasonable time and place for examination of the documents. The responding party must produce the documents at the time and place stated, unless otherwise agreed by the parties or ordered by the court, and must provide the requesting party a reasonable opportunity to inspect them.

(d) *Verification required; exceptions.* A responding party—not an agent or attorney as otherwise permitted by Rule 14—must sign the answers under oath except that:

(1) when answers are based on information obtained from other persons, the party may so state, and

(2) a party need not sign answers to interrogatories about persons with knowledge of relevant facts, trial witnesses, and legal contentions.

197.3 Use. Answers to interrogatories may be used only against the responding party. An answer to an interrogatory inquiring about matters described in Rule 194.2(c) and (d) that has been amended or supplemented is not admissible and may not be used for impeachment.

Comments to 1999 change:

1. Interrogatories about specific legal or factual assertions—such as, whether a party claims a breach of implied warranty, or when a party contends that limitations began to run—are proper, but interrogatories that ask a party to state all legal and factual assertions are improper. As with requests for disclosure, interrogatories may be used to ascertain basic legal and factual claims and defenses but may not be used to force a party to marshal evidence. Use of the answers to such interrogatories is limited, just as the use of similar disclosures under Rule 194.6 is.

2. Rule 191's requirement that a party's attorney sign all discovery responses and objections applies to interrogatory responses and objections. In addition, the responding party must sign some interrogatory answers under oath, as specified by the rule. Answers in amended and supplemental responses must be signed by the party under oath only if the original answers were required to be signed under oath. The failure to sign or verify answers is only a formal defect that does not otherwise impair the answers unless the party refuses to sign or verify the answers after the defect is pointed out.

History of TRCP 197: Amended eff. Jan. 1, 1999, by order of Dec. 31, 1998 (981-82 S.W.2d [Tex.Cases] xxxix). Adopted eff. Jan. 1, 1999, by order of Nov. 9, 1998 (977-78 S.W.2d [Tex.Cases] lxiv): This is former TRCP 168, with modification. Source: New rule.

See *Commentaries*, "General Rules for Discovery," ch. 6-A, p. 425; "Interrogatories," ch. 6-G, p. 548; *O'Connor's Texas Forms*, FORMS 6G.

ANNOTATIONS

Morgan v. Anthony, 27 S.W.3d 928, 929 (Tex. 2000). See annotation under TRCP 166a—*SJ Evidence*, p. 930.

Ticor Title Ins. v. Lacy, 803 S.W.2d 265, 266 (Tex. 1991). "'A party must be able to rely on the interrogatories and answers of other parties in the same suit. Otherwise, a multiparty case would require redundant interrogatories with identical questions and answers.'"

Palmer v. Espey Huston & Assocs., 84 S.W.3d 345, 356 (Tex.App.—Corpus Christi 2002, pet. denied). "[I]nterrogatories may be used only against the responding party. [D] settled prior to trial and was not a party at the time [Ps] attempted to offer his answers to interrogatories. Therefore, [D's] answers were not admissible against the remaining [Ds]."

TRCP 198. REQUESTS FOR ADMISSIONS

198.1 Request for Admissions. A party may serve on another party—no later than 30 days before the end of the discovery period—written requests that the other party admit the truth of any matter within the scope of discovery, including statements of opinion or of fact or of the application of law to fact, or the genuineness of any documents served with the request or otherwise made available for inspection and copying. Each matter for which an admission is requested must be stated separately.

⭐

198.2 Response to Requests for Admissions.

(a) *Time for response.* The responding party must serve a written response on the requesting party within 30 days after service of the request, except that a defendant served with a request before the defendant's answer is due need not respond until 50 days after service of the request.

(b) *Content of response.* Unless the responding party states an objection or asserts a privilege, the responding party must specifically admit or deny the request or explain in detail the reasons that the responding party cannot admit or deny the request. A response must fairly meet the substance of the request. The responding party may qualify an answer, or deny a request in part, only when good faith requires. Lack of information or knowledge is not a proper response unless the responding party states that a reasonable inquiry was made but that the information known or easily obtainable is insufficient to enable the responding party to admit or deny. An assertion that the request presents an issue for trial is not a proper response.

(c) *Effect of failure to respond.* If a response is not timely served, the request is considered admitted without the necessity of a court order.

198.3 Effect of Admissions; Withdrawal or Amendment. Any admission made by a party under this rule may be used solely in the pending action and not in any other proceeding. A matter admitted under this rule is conclusively established as to the party making the admission unless the court permits the party to withdraw or amend the admission. The court may permit the party to withdraw or amend the admission if:

(a) the party shows good cause for the withdrawal or amendment; and

(b) the court finds that the parties relying upon the responses and deemed admissions will not be unduly prejudiced and that the presentation of the merits of the action will be subserved by permitting the party to amend or withdraw the admission.

History of TRCP 198: Adopted eff. Jan. 1, 1999, by order of Nov. 9, 1998 (977-78 S.W.2d [Tex.Cases] lxv): This is former TRCP 169, with modification. Source: New rule.

See *Commentaries*, "General Rules for Discovery," ch. 6-A, p. 425; "Requests for Admissions," ch. 6-H, p. 557; *O'Connor's Texas Forms*, FORMS 6H.

U.S. Fid. & Guar. Co. v. Goudeau, 272 S.W.3d 603, 610 (Tex.2008). "[A] party appearing in one capacity cannot be bound by an admission sent to it in another, because admissions are binding only against 'the party making the admission.'" Held: P could not use admissions from insurance carrier in its capacity as intervenor against same insurance company in its capacity as D.

Wheeler v. Green, 157 S.W.3d 439, 442 (Tex.2005). "[W]ithdrawing deemed admissions ... is proper upon a showing of (1) good cause, and (2) no undue prejudice. Good cause is established by showing the failure [to respond] was an accident or mistake, not intentional or the result of conscious indifference. *At 443:* Undue prejudice depends on whether withdrawing an admission ... will delay trial or significantly hamper the opposing party's ability to prepare for [trial]." *See also Marino v. King*, 355 S.W.3d 629, 633 (Tex.2011); *Wal-Mart Stores v. Deggs*, 968 S.W.2d 354, 356 (Tex. 1998).

Duff v. Spearman, 322 S.W.3d 869, 884 (Tex. App.—Beaumont 2010, pet. denied). "A party that, without objection, allows the trial court to admit evidence controverting a matter deemed admitted may waive his right to rely upon the matter."

TRCP 199. DEPOSITIONS UPON ORAL EXAMINATION

199.1 Oral Examination; Alternative Methods of Conducting or Recording.

(a) *Generally.* A party may take the testimony of any person or entity by deposition on oral examination before any officer authorized by law to take depositions. The testimony, objections, and any other statements during the deposition must be recorded at the time they are given or made.

(b) *Depositions by telephone or other remote electronic means.* A party may take an oral deposition by telephone or other remote electronic means if the party gives reasonable prior written notice of intent to do so. For the purposes of these rules, an oral deposition taken by telephone or other remote electronic means is considered as having been taken in the district and at the place where the witness is located when answering the questions. The officer taking the deposition may be located with the party noticing the deposition instead of with the witness if the witness is

TRCP 199

⭐

placed under oath by a person who is present with the witness and authorized to administer oaths in that jurisdiction.

(c) *Nonstenographic recording.* Any party may cause a deposition upon oral examination to be recorded by other than stenographic means, including videotape recording. The party requesting the nonstenographic recording will be responsible for obtaining a person authorized by law to administer the oath and for assuring that the recording will be intelligible, accurate, and trustworthy. At least five days prior to the deposition, the party must serve on the witness and all parties a notice, either in the notice of deposition or separately, that the deposition will be recorded by other than stenographic means. This notice must state the method of nonstenographic recording to be used and whether the deposition will also be recorded stenographically. Any other party may then serve written notice designating another method of recording in addition to the method specified, at the expense of such other party unless the court orders otherwise.

199.2 **Procedure for Noticing Oral Deposition.**

(a) *Time to notice deposition.* A notice of intent to take an oral deposition must be served on the witness and all parties a reasonable time before the deposition is taken. An oral deposition may be taken outside the discovery period only by agreement of the parties or with leave of court.

(b) *Content of notice.*

(1) *Identity of witness; organizations.* The notice must state the name of the witness, which may be either an individual or a public or private corporation, partnership, association, governmental agency, or other organization. If an organization is named as the witness, the notice must describe with reasonable particularity the matters on which examination is requested. In response, the organization named in the notice must—a reasonable time before the deposition—designate one or more individuals to testify on its behalf and set forth, for each individual designated, the matters on which the individual will testify. Each individual designated must testify as to matters that are known or reasonably available to the organization. This subdivision does not preclude taking a deposition by any other procedure authorized by these rules.

(2) *Time and place.* The notice must state a reasonable time and place for the oral deposition. The place may be in:

(A) the county of the witness's residence;

(B) the county where the witness is employed or regularly transacts business in person;

(C) the county of suit, if the witness is a party or a person designated by a party under Rule 199.2(b)(1);

(D) the county where the witness was served with the subpoena, or within 150 miles of the place of service, if the witness is not a resident of Texas or is a transient person; or

(E) subject to the foregoing, at any other convenient place directed by the court in which the cause is pending.

(3) *Alternative means of conducting and recording.* The notice must state whether the deposition is to be taken by telephone or other remote electronic means and identify the means. If the deposition is to be recorded by nonstenographic means, the notice may include the notice required by Rule 199.1(c).

(4) *Additional attendees.* The notice may include the notice concerning additional attendees required by Rule 199.5(a)(3).

(5) *Request for production of documents.* A notice may include a request that the witness produce at the deposition documents or tangible things within the scope of discovery and within the witness's possession, custody, or control. If the witness is a nonparty, the request must comply with Rule 205 and the designation of materials required to be identified in the subpoena must be attached to, or included in, the notice. The nonparty's response to the request is governed by Rules 176 and 205. When the witness is a party or subject to the control of a party, document requests under this subdivision are governed by Rules 193 and 196.

199.3 **Compelling Witness to Attend.** A party may compel the witness to attend the oral deposition by serving the witness with a subpoena under Rule 176. If the witness is a party or is retained by, employed by, or otherwise subject to the control of a party, however, service of the notice of oral deposition upon the party's attorney has the same effect as a subpoena served on the witness.

199.4 **Objections to Time and Place of Oral Deposition.** A party or witness may object to the time and place designated for an oral deposition by motion for protective order or by motion to quash the notice of deposition. If the motion is filed by the third business day after service of the notice of deposition, an objection to the time and place of a deposition stays the oral deposition until the motion can be determined.

199.5 Examination, Objection, and Conduct During Oral Depositions.

(a) *Attendance.*

(1) *Witness.* The witness must remain in attendance from day to day until the deposition is begun and completed.

(2) *Attendance by party.* A party may attend an oral deposition in person, even if the deposition is taken by telephone or other remote electronic means. If a deposition is taken by telephone or other remote electronic means, the party noticing the deposition must make arrangements for all persons to attend by the same means. If the party noticing the deposition appears in person, any other party may appear by telephone or other remote electronic means if that party makes the necessary arrangements with the deposition officer and the party noticing the deposition.

(3) *Other attendees.* If any party intends to have in attendance any persons other than the witness, parties, spouses of parties, counsel, employees of counsel, and the officer taking the oral deposition, that party must give reasonable notice to all parties, either in the notice of deposition or separately, of the identity of the other persons.

(b) *Oath; examination.* Every person whose deposition is taken by oral examination must first be placed under oath. The parties may examine and cross-examine the witness. Any party, in lieu of participating in the examination, may serve written questions in a sealed envelope on the party noticing the oral deposition, who must deliver them to the deposition officer, who must open the envelope and propound them to the witness.

(c) *Time limitation.* No side may examine or cross-examine an individual witness for more than six hours. Breaks during depositions do not count against this limitation.

(d) *Conduct during the oral deposition; conferences.* The oral deposition must be conducted in the same manner as if the testimony were being obtained in court during trial. Counsel should cooperate with and be courteous to each other and to the witness. The witness should not be evasive and should not unduly delay the examination. Private conferences between the witness and the witness's attorney during the ac-

tual taking of the deposition are improper except for the purpose of determining whether a privilege should be asserted. Private conferences may be held, however, during agreed recesses and adjournments. If the lawyers and witnesses do not comply with this rule, the court may allow in evidence at trial statements, objections, discussions, and other occurrences during the oral deposition that reflect upon the credibility of the witness or the testimony.

(e) *Objections.* Objections to questions during the oral deposition are limited to "Objection, leading" and "Objection, form." Objections to testimony during the oral deposition are limited to "Objection, nonresponsive." These objections are waived if not stated as phrased during the oral deposition. All other objections need not be made or recorded during the oral deposition to be later raised with the court. The objecting party must give a clear and concise explanation of an objection if requested by the party taking the oral deposition, or the objection is waived. Argumentative or suggestive objections or explanations waive objection and may be grounds for terminating the oral deposition or assessing costs or other sanctions. The officer taking the oral deposition will not rule on objections but must record them for ruling by the court. The officer taking the oral deposition must not fail to record testimony because an objection has been made.

(f) *Instructions not to answer.* An attorney may instruct a witness not to answer a question during an oral deposition only if necessary to preserve a privilege, comply with a court order or these rules, protect a witness from an abusive question or one for which any answer would be misleading, or secure a ruling pursuant to paragraph (g). The attorney instructing the witness not to answer must give a concise, nonargumentative, nonsuggestive explanation of the grounds for the instruction if requested by the party who asked the question.

(g) *Suspending the deposition.* If the time limitations for the deposition have expired or the deposition is being conducted or defended in violation of these rules, a party or witness may suspend the oral deposition for the time necessary to obtain a ruling.

(h) *Good faith required.* An attorney must not ask a question at an oral deposition solely to harass or mislead the witness, for any other improper purpose, or without a good faith legal basis at the time. An attorney must not object to a question at an oral deposition, in-

⭐

struct the witness not to answer a question, or suspend the deposition unless there is a good faith factual and legal basis for doing so at the time.

199.6 **Hearing on Objections.** Any party may, at any reasonable time, request a hearing on an objection or privilege asserted by an instruction not to answer or suspension of the deposition; provided the failure of a party to obtain a ruling prior to trial does not waive any objection or privilege. The party seeking to avoid discovery must present any evidence necessary to support the objection or privilege either by testimony at the hearing or by affidavits served on opposing parties at least seven days before the hearing. If the court determines that an *in camera* review of some or all of the requested discovery is necessary to rule, answers to the deposition questions may be made in camera, to be transcribed and sealed in the event the privilege is sustained, or made in an affidavit produced to the court in a sealed wrapper.

Comments to 1999 change:

1. Rule 199.2(b)(5) incorporates the procedures and limitations applicable to requests for production or inspection under Rule 196, including the 30-day deadline for responses, as well as the procedures and duties imposed by Rule 193.

2. For purposes of Rule 199.5(c), each person designated by an organization under Rule 199.2(b)(1) is a separate witness.

3. The requirement of Rule 199.5(d) that depositions be conducted in the same manner as if the testimony were being obtained in court is a limit on the conduct of the lawyers and witnesses in the deposition, not on the scope of the interrogation permitted by Rule 192.

4. An objection to the form of a question includes objections that the question calls for speculation, calls for a narrative answer, is vague, is confusing, or is ambiguous. Ordinarily, a witness must answer a question at a deposition subject to the objection. An objection may therefore be inadequate if a question incorporates such unfair assumptions or is worded so that any answer would necessarily be misleading. A witness should not be required to answer whether he has yet ceased conduct he denies ever doing, subject to an objection to form (*i.e.*, that the question is confusing or assumes facts not in evidence) because any answer would necessarily be misleading on account of the way in which the question is put. The witness may be instructed not to answer. Abusive questions include questions that inquire into matters clearly beyond the scope of discovery or that are argumentative, repetitious, or harassing.

History of TRCP 199: Adopted eff. Jan. 1, 1999, by order of Nov. 9, 1998 (977-78 S.W.2d [Tex.Cases] lxvi): This is former TRCP 200 and 201, with modification. Source: New rule.

See CPRC §20.001; Gov't Code §§52.021, 52.031, 52.059 (imposes joint and several liability for cost of deposition on attorney who asks first question and attorney's firm); TRE 603; *Commentaries*, "General Rules for Discovery," ch. 6-A, p. 425; "Depositions," ch. 6-F, p. 525; *O'Connor's Texas Forms*, FORMS 6F:1-3. For important information about the deposition procedure, see Court Reporters Certification Board, *Uniform Format Manual for Texas Reporters' Records* (2010), §§3.4 cmt., 3.7 cmt., www.crcb.state.tx.us/ufm.asp.

ANNOTATIONS

In re Reaud, 286 S.W.3d 574, 580 (Tex.App.— Beaumont 2009, orig. proceeding). "The third category of nonparty witnesses [in TRCP 199.3] are those ...

'otherwise controlled,' [a term that] is not defined by the procedural rules. [The term is limited] to include only control of the same kind, class, or nature as the types of control parties would have over employees or retained experts. ... While [TRCPs 199.3 and 205.1] contain language that allow them to reach beyond retained experts and employees, it is now clear that these two rules do not extend to nonparties over whom the party does not have the type of control as it has over an employee or a retained expert."

In re Turner, 243 S.W.3d 843, 846 (Tex.App.— Eastland 2008, orig. proceeding). "When a deposition takes place outside one of the counties specifically identified by [TRCP] 199.2(b)(2), it must be at a *convenient place*. This imposes an additional requirement and may, therefore, alter the analysis. But because it is clearly easier for an international traveler to travel to Dallas than Stephenville, if the trial court was authorized to order [relator] to come to Stephenville for a deposition, it did not abuse its discretion by moving the deposition to Dallas." See also *In re Alamex, NV*, No. 01-12-00037-CV (Tex.App.—Houston [1st Dist.] 2012, orig. proceeding) (memo op.; 5-3-12) (convenience is determined from witness's viewpoint).

TRCP 200. DEPOSITIONS UPON WRITTEN QUESTIONS

200.1 **Procedure for Noticing Deposition Upon Written Questions.**

(a) *Who may be noticed; when.* A party may take the testimony of any person or entity by deposition on written questions before any person authorized by law to take depositions on written questions. A notice of intent to take the deposition must be served on the witness and all parties at least 20 days before the deposition is taken. A deposition on written questions may be taken outside the discovery period only by agreement of the parties or with leave of court. The party noticing the deposition must also deliver to the deposition officer a copy of the notice and of all written questions to be asked during the deposition.

(b) *Content of notice.* The notice must comply with Rules 199.1(b), 199.2(b), and 199.5(a)(3). If the witness is an organization, the organization must comply with the requirements of that provision. The notice also may include a request for production of documents as permitted by Rule 199.2(b)(5), the provisions of which will govern the request, service, and response.

───────────────────── ✦ ─────────────────────

200.2 Compelling Witness to Attend. A party may compel the witness to attend the deposition on written questions by serving the witness with a subpoena under Rule 176. If the witness is a party or is retained by, employed by, or otherwise subject to the control of a party, however, service of the deposition notice upon the party's attorney has the same effect as a subpoena served on the witness.

200.3 Questions and Objections.

(a) Direct questions. The direct questions to be propounded to the witness must be attached to the notice.

(b) Objections and additional questions. Within ten days after the notice and direct questions are served, any party may object to the direct questions and serve cross-questions on all other parties. Within five days after cross-questions are served, any party may object to the cross-questions and serve redirect questions on all other parties. Within three days after redirect questions are served, any party may object to the redirect questions and serve recross questions on all other parties. Objections to recross questions must be served within five days after the earlier of when recross questions are served or the time of the deposition on written questions.

(c) Objections to form of questions. Objections to the form of a question are waived unless asserted in accordance with this subdivision.

200.4 Conducting the Deposition Upon Written Questions. The deposition officer must: take the deposition on written questions at the time and place designated; record the testimony of the witness under oath in response to the questions; and prepare, certify, and deliver the deposition transcript in accordance with Rule 203. The deposition officer has authority when necessary to summon and swear an interpreter to facilitate the taking of the deposition.

Comments to 1999 change:

1. The procedures for asserting objections during oral depositions under Rule 199.5(e) do not apply to depositions on written questions.

2. Section 20.001 of the CPRC provides that a deposition on written questions of a witness who is alleged to reside or to be in this state may be taken by a clerk of a district court, a judge or clerk of a county court, or a notary public of this state.

History of TRCP 200: Amended eff. Jan. 1, 1999, by order of Dec. 31, 1998 (981-82 S.W.2d [Tex.Cases] xxxix). Adopted eff. Jan. 1, 1999, by order of Nov. 9, 1998 (977-78 S.W.2d [Tex.Cases] lxxi): Repealed former TRCP 200. For subject matter of former TRCP 200, see TRCP 199. Source: New rule.

See CPRC §20.001; Gov't Code §§52.021, 52.031; *Commentaries*, "General Rules for Discovery," ch. 6-A, p. 425; "Depositions," ch. 6-F, p. 525; *O'Connor's Texas Forms*, FORMS 6F:4-6.

In re Toyota Motor Corp., 191 S.W.3d 498, 503 (Tex.App.—Waco 2006, orig. proceeding). "[D's] counsel [was ordered not to] be present when the depositions on written questions are conducted. [D] objects to being forced to rely on 'canned interrogatory answers prepared by [P's] counsel.' However, attorneys are not to answer written depositions for their clients. Thus, a deposition officer, not [Ps'] counsel, will record [the] answers to [D's] deposition questions."

St. Luke's Episcopal Hosp. v. Garcia, 928 S.W.2d 307, 310 (Tex.App.—Houston [14th Dist.] 1996, orig. proceeding). "Because relator has no objection to the form of [the] written questions, relator claims the provision in [TRCP 200] regarding timeliness of objections is inapplicable. We agree. In its objections to the deposition notice and subpoena duces tecum, relator's primary objections are substantive objections relating to privilege. We hold that the ten-day limitation in [TRCP 200] is inapplicable to substantive objections."

TRCP 201. DEPOSITIONS IN FOREIGN JURISDICTIONS FOR USE IN TEXAS PROCEEDINGS; DEPOSITIONS IN TEXAS FOR USE IN FOREIGN PROCEEDINGS

201.1 Depositions in Foreign Jurisdictions for Use in Texas Proceedings.

(a) Generally. A party may take a deposition on oral examination or written questions of any person or entity located in another state or a foreign country for use in proceedings in this State. The deposition may be taken by:

(1) notice;

(2) letter rogatory, letter of request, or other such device;

(3) agreement of the parties; or

(4) court order.

(b) By notice. A party may take the deposition by notice in accordance with these rules as if the deposition were taken in this State, except that the deposition officer may be a person authorized to administer oaths in the place where the deposition is taken.

(c) By letter rogatory. On motion by a party, the court in which an action is pending must issue a letter rogatory on terms that are just and appropriate, regardless of whether any other manner of obtaining the deposition is impractical or inconvenient. The letter must:

✦

---

(1) be addressed to the appropriate authority in the jurisdiction in which the deposition is to be taken;

(2) request and authorize that authority to summon the witness before the authority at a time and place stated in the letter for examination on oral or written questions; and

(3) request and authorize that authority to cause the witness's testimony to be reduced to writing and returned, together with any items marked as exhibits, to the party requesting the letter rogatory.

(d) *By letter of request or other such device.* On motion by a party, the court in which an action is pending, or the clerk of that court, must issue a letter of request or other such device in accordance with an applicable treaty or international convention on terms that are just and appropriate. The letter or other device must be issued regardless of whether any other manner of obtaining the deposition is impractical or inconvenient. The letter or other device must:

(1) be in the form prescribed by the treaty or convention under which it is issued, as presented by the movant to the court or clerk; and

(2) must state the time, place, and manner of the examination of the witness.

(e) *Objections to form of letter rogatory, letter of request, or other such device.* In issuing a letter rogatory, letter of request, or other such device, the court must set a time for objecting to the form of the device. A party must make any objection to the form of the device in writing and serve it on all other parties by the time set by the court, or the objection is waived.

(f) *Admissibility of evidence.* Evidence obtained in response to a letter rogatory, letter of request, or other such device is not inadmissible merely because it is not a verbatim transcript, or the testimony was not taken under oath, or for any similar departure from the requirements for depositions taken within this State under these rules.

(g) *Deposition by electronic means.* A deposition in another jurisdiction may be taken by telephone, videoconference, teleconference, or other electronic means under the provisions of Rule 199.

201.2 Depositions in Texas for Use in Proceedings in Foreign Jurisdictions. If a court of record of any other state or foreign jurisdiction issues a mandate, writ, or commission that requires a witness's oral or written deposition testimony in this State, the wit-

ness may be compelled to appear and testify in the same manner and by the same process used for taking testimony in a proceeding pending in this State.

Comments to 1999 change:

1. Rule 201.1 sets forth procedures for obtaining deposition testimony of a witness in another state or foreign jurisdiction for use in Texas court proceedings. It does not, however, address whether any of the procedures listed are, in fact, permitted or recognized by the law of the state or foreign jurisdiction where the witness is located. A party must first determine what procedures are permitted by the jurisdiction where the witness is located before using this rule.

2. Section 20.001 of the CPRC provides a nonexclusive list of persons who are qualified to take a written deposition in Texas and who may take depositions (oral or written) in another state or outside the United States.

3. Rule 201.2 is based on Section 20.002 of the CPRC.

History of TRCP 201: Adopted eff. Jan. 1, 1999, by order of Nov. 9, 1998 (977-78 S.W.2d [Tex.Cases] lxxii): Repealed former TRCP 201. For subject matter of former TRCP 201, see TRCP 199. Source: New rule.

See CPRC §§20.001, 20.002; *Commentaries*, "General Rules for Discovery," ch. 6-A, p. 425; "Depositions," ch. 6-F, p. 525; *O'Connor's Texas Forms*, FORMS 6F:1-6.

ANNOTATIONS

Kugle v. DaimlerChrysler Corp., 88 S.W.3d 355, 362 (Tex.App.—San Antonio 2002, pet. denied). "[Ps] contend that the trial court erred in admitting the deposition testimony of [three deponents] because the depositions were taken in Mexico but the witnesses were only sworn in by a Texas notary public. However, a foreign deposition may be taken by any notary public. [T]he trial court did not abuse its discretion in admitting the depositions."

TRCP 202. DEPOSITIONS BEFORE SUIT OR TO INVESTIGATE CLAIMS

202.1 Generally. A person may petition the court for an order authorizing the taking of a deposition on oral examination or written questions either:

(a) to perpetuate or obtain the person's own testimony or that of any other person for use in an anticipated suit; or

(b) to investigate a potential claim or suit.

202.2 Petition. The petition must:

(a) be verified;

(b) be filed in a proper court of any county:

(1) where venue of the anticipated suit may lie, if suit is anticipated; or

(2) where the witness resides, if no suit is yet anticipated;

(c) be in the name of the petitioner;

(d) state either:

(1) that the petitioner anticipates the institution of a suit in which the petitioner may be a party; or

---

★

---

(2) that the petitioner seeks to investigate a potential claim by or against petitioner;

(e) state the subject matter of the anticipated action, if any, and the petitioner's interest therein;

(f) if suit is anticipated, either:

(1) state the names of the persons petitioner expects to have interests adverse to petitioner's in the anticipated suit, and the addresses and telephone numbers for such persons; or

(2) state that the names, addresses, and telephone numbers of persons petitioner expects to have interests adverse to petitioner's in the anticipated suit cannot be ascertained through diligent inquiry, and describe those persons;

(g) state the names, addresses and telephone numbers of the persons to be deposed, the substance of the testimony that the petitioner expects to elicit from each, and the petitioner's reasons for desiring to obtain the testimony of each; and

(h) request an order authorizing the petitioner to take the depositions of the persons named in the petition.

202.3 **Notice and Service.**

(a) *Personal service on witnesses and persons named.* At least 15 days before the date of the hearing on the petition, the petitioner must serve the petition and a notice of the hearing—in accordance with Rule 21a—on all persons petitioner seeks to depose and, if suit is anticipated, on all persons petitioner expects to have interests adverse to petitioner's in the anticipated suit.

(b) *Service by publication on persons not named.*

(1) *Manner.* Unnamed persons described in the petition whom the petitioner expects to have interests adverse to petitioner's in the anticipated suit, if any, may be served by publication with the petition and notice of the hearing. The notice must state the place for the hearing and the time it will be held, which must be more than 14 days after the first publication of the notice. The petition and notice must be published once each week for two consecutive weeks in the newspaper of broadest circulation in the county in which the petition is filed, or if no such newspaper exists, in the newspaper of broadest circulation in the nearest county where a newspaper is published.

(2) *Objection to depositions taken on notice by publication.* Any interested party may move, in the proceeding or by bill of review, to suppress any deposition, in whole or in part, taken on notice by publication, and may also attack or oppose the deposition by any other means available.

(c) *Service in probate cases.* A petition to take a deposition in anticipation of an application for probate of a will, and notice of the hearing on the petition, may be served by posting as prescribed by Section 33(f)(2) of the Probate Code. The notice and petition must be directed to all parties interested in the testator's estate and must comply with the requirements of Section 33(c) of the Probate Code insofar as they may be applicable.

(d) *Modification by order.* As justice or necessity may require, the court may shorten or lengthen the notice periods under this rule and may extend the notice period to permit service on any expected adverse party.

202.4 **Order.**

(a) *Required findings.* The court must order a deposition to be taken if, but only if, it finds that:

(1) allowing the petitioner to take the requested deposition may prevent a failure or delay of justice in an anticipated suit; or

(2) the likely benefit of allowing the petitioner to take the requested deposition to investigate a potential claim outweighs the burden or expense of the procedure.

(b) *Contents.* The order must state whether a deposition will be taken on oral examination or written questions. The order may also state the time and place at which a deposition will be taken. If the order does not state the time and place at which a deposition will be taken, the petitioner must notice the deposition as required by Rules 199 or 200. The order must contain any protections the court finds necessary or appropriate to protect the witness or any person who may be affected by the procedure.

202.5 **Manner of Taking and Use.** Except as otherwise provided in this rule, depositions authorized by this rule are governed by the rules applicable to depositions of nonparties in a pending suit. The scope of discovery in depositions authorized by this rule is the same as if the anticipated suit or potential claim had been filed. A court may restrict or prohibit the use of a deposition taken under this rule in a subsequent suit to

TRCP 202

⭐

protect a person who was not served with notice of the deposition from any unfair prejudice or to prevent abuse of this rule.

Comments to 1999 change:

1. This rule applies to all discovery before suit covered by former rules governing depositions to perpetuate testimony and bills of discovery.

2. A deposition taken under this rule may be used in a subsequent suit as permitted by the rules of evidence, except that a court may restrict or prohibit its use to prevent taking unfair advantage of a witness or others. The bill of discovery procedure, which Rule 202 incorporates, is equitable in nature, and a court must not permit it to be used inequitably.

History of TRCP 202: Adopted eff. Jan. 1, 1999, by order of Nov. 9, 1998 (977-78 S.W.2d [Tex.Cases] lxxiv): Repealed former TRCP 202. For subject matter of former TRCP 202, see TRCP 199. Source: New rule.

See CPRC §20.001; *Commentaries*, "General Rules for Discovery," ch. 6-A, p. 425; "Depositions," ch. 6-F, p. 525; *O'Connor's Texas Forms*, FORMS 6F:8-11.

ANNOTATIONS

Generally

In re Wolfe, 341 S.W.3d 932, 933 (Tex.2011). "[P]re-suit discovery 'is not an end within itself'; rather, it 'is in aid of a suit which is anticipated' and 'ancillary to the anticipated suit.' To prevent an end-run around discovery limitations that would govern the anticipated suit, Rule 202 restricts discovery in depositions to 'the same as if the anticipated suit or potential claim had been filed.' [A potential party] cannot obtain by Rule 202 what it would be denied in the anticipated action. [¶] Rule 202 is not a license for forced interrogations. Courts must strictly limit and carefully supervise pre-suit discovery to prevent abuse of the rule."

In re Does 1&2, 337 S.W.3d 862, 863 (Tex.2011). "[A] court may not order pre-suit discovery by agreement of the witness over the objections of other interested parties without making the findings required by Rule 202.4(a).... *At 865:* [P] argues that compliance with Rule 202 was excused because of its agreement with [D]. ... But [P] and [D] were not the only parties to the proceeding. Rule 202.3(a) requires that 'all persons petitioner expects to have interests adverse to petitioner's in the anticipated suit' be served with the petition and given notice of hearing. [P] asserted that relators would be defendants in the anticipated lawsuit, and by their motions to quash, relators made an appearance in the proceeding. [P] and [D] could not modify the procedures prescribed by Rule 202 by an agreement that did not include relators. [¶] ... Rule 202 expressly requires that discovery may be ordered 'only if' the required findings are made. The rule does not permit the findings to be implied from support in the record. [¶] The trial court clearly abused its discretion in failing to follow Rule 202."

In re Jorden, 249 S.W.3d 416, 418 (Tex.2008). CPRC §74.351(s) "limits discovery in health-care lawsuits until the plaintiff serves an expert report summarizing how each defendant violated standards of care and caused the plaintiff injury. The issue here is whether that statute applies to presuit depositions authorized by [TRCP] 202.... Because the statute prohibits 'all discovery' other than three exceptions—and Rule 202 depositions are not listed among them—we hold the statute prohibits such depositions until after an expert report is served."

In re Akzo Nobel Chem., Inc., 24 S.W.3d 919, 921 (Tex.App.—Beaumont 2000, orig. proceeding). "Neither by its language nor by implication can we construe Rule 202 to authorize a trial court, before suit is filed, to order any form of discovery but deposition."

Removal

Texas v. Real Parties in Interest, 259 F.3d 387, 394-95 (5th Cir.2001). When Rule 202 is used as an investigatory tool for potential claims, the proceeding is not subject to removal. *See also Mayfield-George v. Texas Rehab. Comm'n*, 197 F.R.D. 280, 283 (N.D.Tex. 2000).

TRCP 203. SIGNING, CERTIFICATION & USE OF ORAL & WRITTEN DEPOSITIONS

203.1 Signature and Changes.

(a) *Deposition transcript to be provided to witness.* The deposition officer must provide the original deposition transcript to the witness for examination and signature. If the witness is represented by an attorney at the deposition, the deposition officer must provide the transcript to the attorney instead of the witness.

(b) *Changes by witness; signature.* The witness may change responses as reflected in the deposition transcript by indicating the desired changes, in writing, on a separate sheet of paper, together with a statement of the reasons for making the changes. No erasures or obliterations of any kind may be made to the original deposition transcript. The witness must then sign the transcript under oath and return it to the deposition officer. If the witness does not return the transcript to the deposition officer within 20 days of the date the transcript was provided to the witness or the witness's attorney, the witness may be deemed to have waived the right to make the changes.

TRCP 202

(c) *Exceptions.* The requirements of presentation and signature under this subdivision do not apply:

(1) if the witness and all parties waive the signature requirement;

(2) to depositions on written questions; or

(3) to nonstenographic recordings of oral depositions.

203.2 **Certification.** The deposition officer must file with the court, serve on all parties, and attach as part of the deposition transcript or nonstenographic recording of an oral deposition a certificate duly sworn by the officer stating:

(a) that the witness was duly sworn by the officer and that the transcript or nonstenographic recording of the oral deposition is a true record of the testimony given by the witness;

(b) that the deposition transcript, if any, was submitted to the witness or to the attorney for the witness for examination and signature, the date on which the transcript was submitted, whether the witness returned the transcript, and if so, the date on which it was returned.

(c) that changes, if any, made by the witness are attached to the deposition transcript;

(d) that the deposition officer delivered the deposition transcript or nonstenographic recording of an oral deposition in accordance with Rule 203.3;

(e) the amount of time used by each party at the deposition;

(f) the amount of the deposition officer's charges for preparing the original deposition transcript, which the clerk of the court must tax as costs; and

(g) that a copy of the certificate was served on all parties and the date of service.

203.3 **Delivery.**

(a) *Endorsement; to whom delivered.* The deposition officer must endorse the title of the action and "Deposition of (name of witness)" on the original deposition transcript (or a copy, if the original was not returned) or the original nonstenographic recording of an oral deposition, and must return:

(1) the transcript to the party who asked the first question appearing in the transcript, or

(2) the recording to the party who requested it.

(b) *Notice.* The deposition officer must serve notice of delivery on all other parties.

(c) *Inspection and copying; copies.* The party receiving the original deposition transcript or nonstenographic recording must make it available upon reasonable request for inspection and copying by any other party. Any party or the witness is entitled to obtain a copy of the deposition transcript or nonstenographic recording from the deposition officer upon payment of a reasonable fee.

203.4 **Exhibits.** At the request of a party, the original documents and things produced for inspection during the examination of the witness must be marked for identification by the deposition officer and annexed to the deposition transcript or nonstenographic recording. The person producing the materials may produce copies instead of originals if the party gives all other parties fair opportunity at the deposition to compare the copies with the originals. If the person offers originals rather than copies, the deposition officer must, after the conclusion of the deposition, make copies to be attached to the original deposition transcript or nonstenographic recording, and then return the originals to the person who produced them. The person who produced the originals must preserve them for hearing or trial and make them available for inspection or copying by any other party upon seven days' notice. Copies annexed to the original deposition transcript or nonstenographic recording may be used for all purposes.

203.5 **Motion to Suppress.** A party may object to any errors and irregularities in the manner in which the testimony is transcribed, signed, delivered, or otherwise dealt with by the deposition officer by filing a motion to suppress all or part of the deposition. If the deposition officer complies with Rule 203.3 at least one day before the case is called to trial, with regard to a deposition transcript, or 30 days before the case is called to trial, with regard to a nonstenographic recording, the party must file and serve a motion to suppress before trial commences to preserve the objections.

203.6 **Use.**

(a) *Nonstenographic recording; transcription.* A nonstenographic recording of an oral deposition, or a written transcription of all or part of such a recording, may be used to the same extent as a deposition taken by stenographic means. However, the court, for good cause shown, may require that the party seeking to use a nonstenographic recording or written transcription first obtain a complete transcript of the deposition recording from a certified court reporter. The court reporter's transcription must be made from the original or a certified copy of the deposition recording. The court reporter must, to the extent applicable, comply with the provisions of this rule, except that the court reporter must deliver the original transcript to the attorney requesting the transcript, and the court reporter's certificate must include a statement that the transcript is a true record of the nonstenographic recording. The party to whom the court reporter delivers the original transcript must make the transcript available, upon reasonable request, for inspection and copying by the witness or any party.

(b) *Same proceeding.* All or part of a deposition may be used for any purpose in the same proceeding in which it was taken. If the original is not filed, a certified copy may be used. "Same proceeding" includes a proceeding in a different court but involving the same subject matter and the same parties or their representatives or successors in interest. A deposition is admissible against a party joined after the deposition was taken if:

(1) the deposition is admissible pursuant to Rule 804(b)(1) of the Rules of Evidence, or

(2) that party has had a reasonable opportunity to redepose the witness and has failed to do so.

(c) *Different proceeding.* Depositions taken in different proceedings may be used as permitted by the Rules of Evidence.

History of TRCP 203: Adopted eff. Jan. 1, 1999, by order of Nov. 9, 1998 (977-78 S.W.2d [Tex.Cases] lxxvi): Repealed former TRCP 203. For subject matter of former TRCP 203, see TRCP 176. New rule is former TRCPs 206 and 207, with modification. Source: New rule.

See Gov't Code §52.021; *Commentaries*, "General Rules for Discovery," ch. 6-A, p. 425; "Depositions," ch. 6-F, p. 525; . For important information about the deposition procedure, see Court Reporters Certification Board, *Uniform Format Manual for Texas Reporters' Records* (2010), §§3.4 cmt., 3.7 cmt., www.crcb.state.tx.us/ufm.asp.

ANNOTATIONS

Jones v. Colley, 820 S.W.2d 863, 866 (Tex.App.—Texarkana 1991, writ denied). "No rule requires that a deposition be read into the record or played before the jury in chronological order. A party, as a matter of trial strategy, is entitled to present his evidence in the order he believes constitutes the most effective presentation of his case, provided that it does not convey a *distinctly false* impression."

Klorer v. Block, 717 S.W.2d 754, 759 (Tex. App.—San Antonio 1986, writ ref'd n.r.e.). "The statement … that a deposition shall have been filed at least

one entire day before the day of trial is a condition precedent to the filing of a *written* motion to suppress. This rule does not require that *all* depositions must be filed at least one entire day before the day of trial."

TRCP 204. PHYSICAL & MENTAL EXAMINATIONS

204.1 **Motion and Order Required.**

(a) *Motion.* A party may—no later than 30 days before the end of any applicable discovery period—move for an order compelling another party to:

(1) submit to a physical or mental examination by a qualified physician or a mental examination by a qualified psychologist; or

(2) produce for such examination a person in the other party's custody, conservatorship or legal control.

(b) *Service.* The motion and notice of hearing must be served on the person to be examined and all parties.

(c) *Requirements for obtaining order.* The court may issue an order for examination only for good cause shown and only in the following circumstances:

(1) when the mental or physical condition (including the blood group) of a party, or of a person in the custody, conservatorship or under the legal control of a party, is in controversy; or

(2) except as provided in Rule 204.4, an examination by a psychologist may be ordered when the party responding to the motion has designated a psychologist as a testifying expert or has disclosed a psychologist's records for possible use at trial.

(d) *Requirements of order.* The order must be in writing and must specify the time, place, manner, conditions, and scope of the examination and the person or persons by whom it is to be made.

204.2 **Report of Examining Physician or Psychologist.**

(a) *Right to report.* Upon request of the person ordered to be examined, the party causing the examination to be made must deliver to the person a copy of a detailed written report of the examining physician or psychologist setting out the findings, including results of all tests made, diagnoses and conclusions, together with like reports of all earlier examinations of the same condition. After delivery of the report, upon request of the party causing the examination, the party against whom the order is made must produce a like report of

---

★

---

any examination made before or after the ordered examination of the same condition, unless the person examined is not a party and the party shows that the party is unable to obtain it. The court on motion may limit delivery of a report on such terms as are just. If a physician or psychologist fails or refuses to make a report the court may exclude the testimony if offered at the trial.

(b) *Agreements; relationship to other rules.* This subdivision applies to examinations made by agreement of the parties, unless the agreement expressly provides otherwise. This subdivision does not preclude discovery of a report of an examining physician or psychologist or the taking of a deposition of the physician or psychologist in accordance with the provisions of any other rule.

204.3 **Effect of No Examination.** If no examination is sought either by agreement or under this subdivision, the party whose physical or mental condition is in controversy must not comment to the court or jury concerning the party's willingness to submit to an examination, or on the right or failure of any other party to seek an examination.

204.4 **Cases Arising Under Titles II or V, Family Code.** In cases arising under Family Code Titles II or V, the court may—on its own initiative or on motion of a party—appoint:

(a) one or more psychologists or psychiatrists to make any and all appropriate mental examinations of the children who are the subject of the suit or of any other parties, and may make such appointment irrespective of whether a psychologist or psychiatrist has been designated by any party as a testifying expert;

(b) one or more experts who are qualified in paternity testing to take blood, body fluid, or tissue samples to conduct paternity tests as ordered by the court.

204.5 **Definition.** For the purpose of this rule, a psychologist is a person licensed or certified by a state or the District of Columbia as a psychologist.

History of TRCP 204: Adopted eff. Jan. 1, 1999, by order of Nov. 9, 1998 (977-78 S.W.2d [Tex.Cases] lxxix): Repealed former TRCP 204. For subject matter of former TRCP 204, see TRCP 199. New rule is former TRCP 167a, with modification. Source: New rule.

See TRE 510(d)(5); *Commentaries,* "General Rules for Discovery," ch. 6-A, p. 425; "Medical Records," ch. 6-J, p. 576; *O'Connor's Texas Forms*, FORMS 6J.

ANNOTATIONS

In re Transwestern Publ'g Co., 96 S.W.3d 501, 506 (Tex.App.—Fort Worth 2002, orig. proceeding). "Rule

204.1 … requires a showing of good cause *and* either proof of the 'in controversy' element *or* proof that the party to be examined has designated a psychologist to testify or has disclosed a psychologist's records for possible use at trial. Thus, … even if the person to be examined has designated a psychologist to testify regarding her mental condition, the party seeking the examination must still demonstrate 'good cause' for the examination. 'Good cause' is not assumed merely because a psychologist has been appointed to testify as an expert regarding the subject's mental condition." *See also* **Coates v. Whittington**, 758 S.W.2d 749, 751 (Tex.1988) (applying former TRCP 167a, now TRCP 204.1).

In re Caballero, 36 S.W.3d 143, 145 (Tex.App.— Corpus Christi 2000, orig. proceeding). Good cause "requires an affirmative showing of three components: (1) that an examination is relevant to issues that are genuinely in controversy in the case; (2) that a reasonable nexus exists between the condition in controversy and the examination sought; and (3) that it is not possible to obtain the desired information through means that are less intrusive than a compelled examination."

TRCP 205. DISCOVERY FROM NONPARTIES

205.1 **Forms of Discovery; Subpoena Requirement.** A party may compel discovery from a nonparty—that is, a person who is not a party or subject to a party's control—only by obtaining a court order under Rules 196.7, 202, or 204, or by serving a subpoena compelling:

(a) an oral deposition;

(b) a deposition on written questions;

(c) a request for production of documents or tangible things, pursuant to Rule 199.2(b)(5) or Rule 200.1(b), served with a notice of deposition on oral examination or written questions; and

(d) a request for production of documents and tangible things under this rule.

205.2 **Notice.** A party seeking discovery by subpoena from a nonparty must serve, on the nonparty and all parties, a copy of the form of notice required under the rules governing the applicable form of discovery. A notice of oral or written deposition must be served before or at the same time that a subpoena compelling attendance or production under the notice is served. A notice to produce documents or tangible things under

---

★

Rule 205.3 must be served at least 10 days before the subpoena compelling production is served.

205.3 **Production of Documents and Tangible Things Without Deposition.**

(a) *Notice; subpoena.* A party may compel production of documents and tangible things from a nonparty by serving—a reasonable time before the response is due but no later than 30 days before the end of any applicable discovery period—the notice required in Rule 205.2 and a subpoena compelling production or inspection of documents or tangible things.

(b) *Contents of notice.* The notice must state:

(1) the name of the person from whom production or inspection is sought to be compelled;

(2) a reasonable time and place for the production or inspection; and

(3) the items to be produced or inspected, either by individual item or by category, describing each item and category with reasonable particularity, and, if applicable, describing the desired testing and sampling with sufficient specificity to inform the nonparty of the means, manner, and procedure for testing or sampling.

(c) *Requests for production of medical or mental health records of other nonparties.* If a party requests a nonparty to produce medical or mental health records of another nonparty, the requesting party must serve the nonparty whose records are sought with the notice required under this rule. This requirement does not apply under the circumstances set forth in Rule 196.1(c)(2).

(d) *Response.* The nonparty must respond to the notice and subpoena in accordance with Rule 176.6.

(e) *Custody, inspection and copying.* The party obtaining the production must make all materials produced available for inspection by any other party on reasonable notice, and must furnish copies to any party who requests at that party's expense.

(f) *Cost of production.* A party requiring production of documents by a nonparty must reimburse the nonparty's reasonable costs of production.

Comment to 1999 change: Under this rule, a party may subpoena production of documents and tangible things from nonparties without need for a motion or oral or written deposition.

History of TRCP 205: Amended eff. Jan. 1, 1999, by order of Dec. 31, 1998 (981-82 S.W.2d [Tex.Cases] xxxix-xl). Adopted eff. Jan. 1, 1999, by order of Nov. 9, 1998 (977-78 S.W.2d [Tex.Cases] lxxx): Repealed former TRCP 205. For subject matter of former TRCP 205, see TRCP 203. Source: New rule.

See *Commentaries,* "Securing discovery from nonparties," ch. 6-A, §9.2, p. 435; "Depositions," ch. 6-F, p. 525; "Securing Documents & Tangible Things," ch. 6-I, p. 565; *O'Connor's Texas Forms,* FORM 6I:12.

Automatic Drilling Machs., Inc. v. Miller, 515 S.W.2d 256, 259 (Tex.1974). "[A] subpoena may be issued in a proper case to require a witness to produce, at the time and place of giving his deposition, documents and other tangible things which constitute or contain evidence relating to any of the matters within the scope of [discovery]."

In re University of Tex. Health Ctr., 198 S.W.3d 392, 397 (Tex.App.—Texarkana 2006, orig. proceeding). "By requiring notice of proposed testing and the manner and means of the proposed testing, the [TRCPs] clearly indicate production is available to test tangible objects beyond simple inspection. [¶] The rules expressly provide for production of a tangible item for testing, and one contemplated method by which that production may be accomplished is physically delivering possession of the item to the requesting party or that party's agent."

In re Diversicare Gen. Partner, 41 S.W.3d 788, 794 (Tex.App.—Corpus Christi 2001, orig. proceeding), *overruled on other grounds*, *In re Arriola*, 159 S.W.3d 670 (Tex.App.—Corpus Christi 2004, orig. proceeding). "[P]ersonal and clinical records do not have to be in the nonparty's possession to be described as nonparty records, they only have to be personal and clinical records *regarding* the nonparty."

TRCP 206 TO 208. REPEALED

Repealed eff. Jan. 1, 1999, by order of Nov. 9, 1998 (977-78 S.W.2d [Tex.Cases] xxxiii). For subject matter of former TRCPs 206 and 207, see TRCP 203. For subject matter of former TRCP 208, see TRCP 200.

TRCP 208a. REPEALED

Repealed eff. Apr. 1, 1984, by order of Dec. 5, 1983 (661-62 S.W.2d [Tex.Cases] lxvii). For subject matter of former TRCP 208a, see TRCP 203.

TRCP 209. REPEALED

Repealed eff. Jan. 1, 1999, by order of Nov. 9, 1998 (977-78 S.W.2d [Tex.Cases] xxxiii).

TRCP 210 TO 214. REPEALED

Repealed eff. Apr. 1, 1984, by order of Dec. 5, 1983 (661-62 S.W.2d [Tex.Cases] lxviii): For subject matter of former TRCP 210, see TRCP 203. For subject matter of former TRCPs 211-213, see TRCP 203.

TRCP 215. ABUSE OF DISCOVERY; SANCTIONS

215.1 Motion for Sanctions or Order Compelling Discovery. A party, upon reasonable notice to other parties and all other persons affected thereby, may apply for sanctions or an order compelling discovery as follows:

★

(a) *Appropriate court.* On matters relating to a deposition, an application for an order to a party may be made to the court in which the action is pending, or to any district court in the district where the deposition is being taken. An application for an order to a deponent who is not a party shall be made to the court in the district where the deposition is being taken. As to all other discovery matters, an application for an order will be made to the court in which the action is pending.

(b) *Motion.*

(1) If a party or other deponent which is a corporation or other entity fails to make a designation under Rules 199.2(b)(1) or 200.1(b); or

(2) If a party, or other deponent, or a person designated to testify on behalf of a party or other deponent fails:

(A) to appear before the officer who is to take his deposition, after being served with a proper notice; or

(B) to answer a question propounded or submitted upon oral examination or upon written questions; or

(3) if a party fails:

(A) to serve answers or objections to interrogatories submitted under Rule 197, after proper service of the interrogatories; or

(B) to answer an interrogatory submitted under Rule 197; or

(C) to serve a written response to a request for inspection submitted under Rule 196, after proper service of the request; or

(D) to respond that discovery will be permitted as requested or fails to permit discovery as requested in response to a request for inspection submitted under Rule 196;

the discovering party may move for an order compelling a designation, an appearance, an answer or answers, or inspection or production in accordance with the request, or apply to the court in which the action is pending for the imposition of any sanction authorized by Rule 215.2(b) without the necessity of first having obtained a court order compelling such discovery.

When taking a deposition on oral examination, the proponent of the question may complete or adjourn the examination before he applies for an order.

If the court denies the motion in whole or in part, it may make such protective order as it would have been empowered to make on a motion pursuant to Rule 192.6.

(c) *Evasive or incomplete answer.* For purposes of this subdivision an evasive or incomplete answer is to be treated as a failure to answer.

(d) *Disposition of motion to compel: award of expenses.* If the motion is granted, the court shall, after opportunity for hearing, require a party or deponent whose conduct necessitated the motion or the party or attorney advising such conduct or both of them to pay, at such time as ordered by the court, the moving party the reasonable expenses incurred in obtaining the order, including attorney fees, unless the court finds that the opposition to the motion was substantially justified or that other circumstances make an award of expenses unjust. Such an order shall be subject to review on appeal from the final judgment.

If the motion is denied, the court may, after opportunity for hearing, require the moving party or attorney advising such motion to pay to the party or deponent who opposed the motion the reasonable expenses incurred in opposing the motion, including attorney fees, unless the court finds that the making of the motion was substantially justified or that other circumstances make an award of expenses unjust.

If the motion is granted in part and denied in part, the court may apportion the reasonable expenses incurred in relation to the motion among the parties and persons in a just manner.

In determining the amount of reasonable expenses, including attorney fees, to be awarded in connection with a motion, the trial court shall award expenses which are reasonable in relation to the amount of work reasonably expended in obtaining an order compelling compliance or in opposing a motion which is denied.

(e) *Providing person's own statement.* If a party fails to comply with any person's written request for the person's own statement as provided in Rule 192.3(h), the person who made the request may move for an order compelling compliance. If the motion is granted, the movant may recover the expenses incurred in obtaining the order, including attorney fees, which are reasonable in relation to the amount of work reasonably expended in obtaining the order.

215.2 **Failure to Comply with Order or with Discovery Request.**

(a) *Sanctions by court in district where deposition is taken.* If a deponent fails to appear or to be sworn or to answer a question after being directed to do so by a district court in the district in which the deposition is being taken, the failure may be considered a contempt of that court.

(b) *Sanctions by court in which action is pending.* If a party or an officer, director, or managing agent of a party or a person designated under Rules 199.2(b)(1) or 200.1(b) to testify on behalf of a party fails to comply with proper discovery requests or to obey an order to provide or permit discovery, including an order made under Rules 204 or 215.1, the court in which the action is pending may, after notice and hearing, make such orders in regard to the failure as are just, and among others the following:

(1) an order disallowing any further discovery of any kind or of a particular kind by the disobedient party;

(2) an order charging all or any portion of the expenses of discovery or taxable court costs or both against the disobedient party or the attorney advising him;

(3) an order that the matters regarding which the order was made or any other designated facts shall be taken to be established for the purposes of the action in accordance with the claim of the party obtaining the order;

(4) an order refusing to allow the disobedient party to support or oppose designated claims or defenses, or prohibiting him from introducing designated matters in evidence;

(5) an order striking out pleadings or parts thereof, or staying further proceedings until the order is obeyed, or dismissing with or without prejudice the action or proceedings or any part thereof, or rendering a judgment by default against the disobedient party;

(6) in lieu of any of the foregoing orders or in addition thereto, an order treating as a contempt of court the failure to obey any orders except an order to submit to a physical or mental examination;

(7) when a party has failed to comply with an order under Rule 204 requiring him to appear or produce another for examination, such orders as are listed in paragraphs (1), (2), (3), (4) or (5) of this subdivision, unless the person failing to comply shows that he is unable to appear or to produce such person for examination.

(8) In lieu of any of the foregoing orders or in addition thereto, the court shall require the party failing to obey the order or the attorney advising him, or both, to pay, at such time as ordered by the court, the reasonable expenses, including attorney fees, caused by the failure, unless the court finds that the failure was substantially justified or that other circumstances make an award of expenses unjust. Such an order shall be subject to review on appeal from the final judgment.

(c) *Sanction against nonparty for violation of Rules 196.7 or 205.3.* If a nonparty fails to comply with an order under Rules 196.7 or 205.3, the court which made the order may treat the failure to obey as contempt of court.

215.3 **Abuse of Discovery Process in Seeking, Making, or Resisting Discovery.** If the court finds a party is abusing the discovery process in seeking, making or resisting discovery or if the court finds that any interrogatory or request for inspection or production is unreasonably frivolous, oppressive, or harassing, or that a response or answer is unreasonably frivolous or made for purposes of delay, then the court in which the action is pending may, after notice and hearing, impose any appropriate sanction authorized by paragraphs (1), (2), (3), (4), (5), and (8) of Rule 215.2(b). Such order of sanction shall be subject to review on appeal from the final judgment.

215.4 **Failure to Comply with Rule 198.**

(a) *Motion.* A party who has requested an admission under Rule 198 may move to determine the sufficiency of the answer or objection. For purposes of this subdivision an evasive or incomplete answer may be treated as a failure to answer. Unless the court determines that an objection is justified, it shall order that an answer be served. If the court determines that an answer does not comply with the requirements of Rule 198, it may order either that the matter is admitted or that an amended answer be served. The provisions of Rule 215.1(d) apply to the award of expenses incurred in relation to the motion.

(b) *Expenses on failure to admit.* If a party fails to admit the genuineness of any document or the truth of any matter as requested under Rule 198 and if the party requesting the admissions thereafter proves the genuineness of the document or the truth of the matter, he may apply to the court for an order requiring the other party to pay him the reasonable expenses incurred in making that proof, including reasonable attorney fees. The court shall make the order unless it finds that (1) the request was held objectionable pursuant to Rule 193, or (2) the admission sought was of no substantial importance, or (3) the party failing to admit

---

had a reasonable ground to believe that he might prevail on the matter, or (4) there was other good reason for the failure to admit.

215.5 Failure of Party or Witness to Attend or to Serve Subpoena; Expenses.

(a) *Failure of party giving notice to attend.* If the party giving the notice of the taking of an oral deposition fails to attend and proceed therewith and another party attends in person or by attorney pursuant to the notice, the court may order the party giving the notice to pay such other party the reasonable expenses incurred by him and his attorney in attending, including reasonable attorney fees.

(b) *Failure of witness to attend.* If a party gives notice of the taking of an oral deposition of a witness and the witness does not attend because of the fault of the party giving the notice, if another party attends in person or by attorney because he expects the deposition of that witness to be taken, the court may order the party giving the notice to pay such other party the reasonable expenses incurred by him and his attorney in attending, including reasonable attorney fees.

215.6 Exhibits to Motions and Responses. Motions or responses made under this rule may have exhibits attached including affidavits, discovery pleadings, or any other documents.

Comment to 1999 change: The references in this rule to other discovery rules are changed to reflect the revisions in those rules, and former Rule 203 is added as Rule 215.5 in place of the former provision, which is superseded by Rule 193.6.

History of TRCP 215: Amended eff. Jan. 1, 1999, by order of Dec. 31, 1998 (981-82 S.W.2d [Tex.Cases] xl). Amended eff. Jan. 1, 1999, by order of Nov. 9, 1998 (977-78 S.W.2d [Tex.Cases] lxxxii). Amended eff. Sept. 1, 1990, by order of Apr. 24, 1990 (785-86 S.W.2d [Tex.Cases] lxiii): Requires notice and hearing before an imposition of sanctions in TRCP 215.3; adds "appropriate" before "sanction" in same par. Amended eff. Jan. 1, 1988, by order of July 15, 1987 (733-34 S.W.2d [Tex.Cases] lxiv): Changed TRCPs 215.5 and 215.6; amendment states that the party offering the evidence has burden of establishing good cause for any failure to supplement discovery before trial and provides manner for making record for discovery hearings. Added new rule eff. Apr. 1, 1984, by order of Dec. 5, 1983 (661-62 S.W.2d [Tex.Cases] lxviii): TRCP 170 deleted because TRCP 215 covers conduct in violation of TRCP 167; purpose of revisions to TRCP 168, deletion of TRCP 170, and provisions of new TRCP 215 is to clarify when the most severe sanctions are authorized; TRCP 215 retains conclusion reached in *Lewis v. Illinois Employers Ins. Co.*, 590 S.W.2d 119 (Tex.1979), and extends such rule to cover all discovery requests, except requests for admissions; TRCP 215 leaves to the discretion of the court whether to impose sanctions with or without an order compelling discovery, so that the court will be free to apply proper sanction or order based upon degree of discovery abuse involved; rule rewritten to gather all discovery sanctions into single rule; includes specific provisions concerning consequences of failing to comply with TRCP 169, and spells out penalties imposable upon a party who fails to supplement discovery responses; provides for sanctions for those who seek to make discovery in an abusive manner. Adopted eff. Sept. 1, 1941, by order of Oct. 29, 1940 (3 Tex.B.J. 557 [1940]). Source: TRCS art. 3768 (repealed). Original TRCP 215 related to deposition of party.

See CPRC ch. 10; *Commentaries*, "Motion for Sanctions," ch. 5-K, p. 377; "General Rules for Discovery," ch. 6-A, p. 425; "Depositions," ch. 6-F, p. 525; "Interrogatories," ch. 6-G, p. 548; "Requests for Admissions," ch. 6-H, p. 557; "Securing Documents & Tangible Things," ch. 6-I, p. 565; *O'Connor's Texas Forms*, FORMS 6A:23-28.

ANNOTATIONS

American Flood Research, Inc. v. Jones, 192 S.W.3d 581, 584 (Tex.2006). "While there is no direct evidence that the employees knew of the depositions and deliberately failed to attend, in the context of an enduring attorney-client relationship, knowledge acquired by the attorney is imputed to the client. [Ds' attorney] was present when the trial judge ordered [the depositions] in open court …, yet neither [attorney] nor the employees appeared. Thus, a Rule 215.2 prerequisite to imposing sanctions—a party's failure to comply with an order to permit discovery—was satisfied."

Meyer v. Cathey, 167 S.W.3d 327, 333 (Tex.2005). "[W]aiver bars a trial court from awarding posttrial sanctions based on pretrial conduct of which a party 'was aware' before trial; lack of 'conclusive evidence' is not an excuse." *See also* ***Remington Arms Co. v. Caldwell***, 850 S.W.2d 167, 170 (Tex.1993).

Cire v. Cummings, 134 S.W.3d 835, 842 (Tex.2004). "Nothing … requires that a trial court test the effectiveness of lesser sanctions by actually implementing and ordering each and every sanction that could possibly be imposed before striking the pleadings of a disobedient party. [A] trial court [is not required] to list each possible lesser sanction in its order and then explain why each would be ineffective. [T]he record [must] reflect that the court 'consider' the availability of appropriate lesser sanctions, and cautions that in all but the most exceptional cases, the trial court must actually test the lesser sanctions before striking the pleadings. [I]n cases of exceptional misconduct …, the trial court is not required to test lesser sanctions before striking pleadings … so long as the record reflects that the trial court considered lesser sanctions before striking pleadings and the party's conduct justifies the presumption that its claims lack merit. [A] trial court must analyze the available sanctions and offer a reasoned explanation as to the appropriateness of the sanction imposed." *See also* ***Low v. Henry***, 221 S.W.3d 609, 620 (Tex.2007); ***Chrysler Corp. v. Blackmon***, 841 S.W.2d 844, 849 (Tex.1992).

Spohn Hosp. v. Mayer, 104 S.W.3d 878, 882 (Tex. 2003). For sanctions to be just, "there must be a direct nexus among the offensive conduct, the offender, and the sanction imposed. A just sanction must be directed against the abuse and toward remedying the prejudice caused to the innocent party, and the sanction should be visited upon the offender. The trial court must attempt to determine whether the offensive conduct is attributable to counsel only, to the party only, or to both."

Occidental Chem. Corp. v. Banales, 907 S.W.2d 488, 490 (Tex.1995). "The sanction imposed for discovery abuse should be no more severe than necessary to satisfy the legitimate purposes of the discovery process offended. The work product privilege is essential to the attorney-client relationship. Requiring the production of the attorney's notes from interviews of witnesses is a severe sanction and should receive an appropriately strict review. Piercing the work product privilege, like the 'death penalty' sanction, should apply only when lesser sanctions are inadequate to correct the discovery abuse that has occurred, i.e., when it is the only appropriate sanction. Here the record does not reflect why lesser traditional sanctions might not cure the discovery abuse."

TransAmerican Nat. Gas Corp. v. Powell, 811 S.W.2d 913, 917 (Tex.1991). The punishment for discovery abuse "should fit the crime. *At 918:* Discovery sanctions cannot be used to adjudicate the merits of a party's claims or defenses unless a party's hindrance of the discovery process justifies a presumption that its claims or defenses lack merit." *See also Paradigm Oil, Inc. v. Retamco Oper., Inc.*, 372 S.W.3d 177, 184 (Tex. 2012); *Hernandez v. Mid-Loop, Inc.*, 170 S.W.3d 138, 143 (Tex.App.—San Antonio 2005, no pet.).

In re Vossdale Townhouse Ass'n, 302 S.W.3d 890, 893-94 (Tex.App.—Houston [14th Dist.] 2009, orig. proceeding). "An order directing that counsel may no longer represent his clients in the subject litigation is not among those sanctions enumerated in Rule 215.2(b). While Rule 215.2(b) does not limit the types of discovery sanctions the trial court may impose to those enumerated in the rule, the imposition of a sanction that is not specifically authorized in derogation of a clearly established legal right cannot be just. The trial court's order … was imposed in derogation of the clearly established right to counsel of choice."

In re White, 227 S.W.3d 234, 236 (Tex.App.—San Antonio 2007, orig. proceeding). "Rule 215.2(b) does not authorize the trial court to impose sanctions on nonparty deponents. *At 237:* [P] argues the cost of conducting [nonparty's] deposition after obtaining the or-

der compelling [nonparty] to answer questions can reasonably be considered part of the 'expenses incurred in obtaining the order.' We disagree. [T]he Texas Supreme Court has expressly authorized trial courts to charge the costs and expenses of discovery against a *party* that fails to comply with discovery requests. We find no such authority with respect to nonparties."

TRCP 215a TO 215c. REPEALED

Repealed eff. Apr. 1, 1984, by order of Dec. 5, 1983 (661-62 S.W.2d [Tex.Cases] lxviii): For subject matter of former TRCP 215a, see TRCP 215. For subject matter of former TRCP 215b, see TRCP 203. For subject matter of former TRCP 215c, see TRCP 202.

SECTION 10. THE JURY IN COURT

TRCP 216. REQUEST & FEE FOR JURY TRIAL

a. Request. No jury trial shall be had in any civil suit, unless a written request for a jury trial is filed with the clerk of the court a reasonable time before the date set for trial of the cause on the non-jury docket, but not less than thirty days in advance.

b. Jury Fee. Unless otherwise provided by law, a fee of ten dollars if in the district court and five dollars if in the county court must be deposited with the clerk of the court within the time for making a written request for a jury trial. The clerk shall promptly enter a notation of the payment of such fee upon the court's docket sheet.

History of TRCP 216: Amended eff. Sept. 1, 1990, by order of Apr. 24, 1990 (785-86 S.W.2d [Tex.Cases] lxiv): Secs. (1) and (2) renumbered as a. and b.; "Unless otherwise provided by law" added to beginning of b.; additional fees for jury trials may be required by other law, e.g., Gov't Code §51.604. Amended eff. Jan. 1, 1988, by order of July 15, 1987 (733-34 S.W.2d [Tex.Cases] lxv). Amended eff. Mar. 1, 1950, by order of Oct. 12, 1949 (12 Tex.B.J. 534 [1949]). Amended eff. Dec. 31, 1941, by order of Sept. 20, 1941 (4 Tex.B.J. 520 [1941]). Amended eff. Sept. 1, 1941, by order of Mar. 31, 1941 (4 Tex.B.J. 172 [1941]). Adopted eff. Sept. 1, 1941, by order of Oct. 29, 1940 (3 Tex.B.J. 558 [1940]). Source: TRCS arts. 2124, 2125 (repealed).

See U.S. Const. amend. 7; Tex. Const. art. 1, §15; Gov't Code §51.604; *Commentaries*, "Request for Jury Trial," ch. 5-B, p. 320; *O'Connor's Texas Forms*, FORMS 5B:1-4.

ANNOTATIONS

General Motors Corp. v. Gayle, 951 S.W.2d 469, 476 (Tex.1997). "Even where a party does not timely pay the jury fee, … a trial court should accord the right to jury trial if it can be done without interfering with the court's docket, delaying the trial, or injuring the opposing party. *At 477:* [D] established that a 30-day continuance to perfect [D's] jury trial demand would not cause [Ps] any injury or delay. [T]he trial court's seriatim trial schedule seems only a sham to hold [D] to its mistake in not paying the jury fee without penalizing the other side." *See also* ***Crittenden v. Crittenden***, 52 S.W.3d 768, 769 (Tex.App.—San Antonio 2001, pet. denied).

Ricardo N., Inc. v. Turcios de Argueta, 907 S.W.2d 423, 429 (Tex.1995). "Assuming [D's] request for a jury in advance of the first trial setting was not timely made, that request had certainly become timely when the case was remanded from federal court four years later."

Halsell v. Dehoyos, 810 S.W.2d 371, 371 (Tex. 1991). "A [jury] request in advance of the 30-day deadline [of TRCP 216] is presumed to have been made a reasonable time before trial." *See also* ***Sims v. Fitzpatrick***, 288 S.W.3d 93, 102 (Tex.App.—Houston [1st Dist.] 2009, no pet.) (party may rebut presumption by showing that granting jury trial would injure adverse party, disrupt court's docket, or impede handling of court's business); ***Brockie v. Webb***, 244 S.W.3d 905, 908 (Tex.App.—Dallas 2008, pet. denied) (party may waive its right to jury if request is made after case is certified for trial and less than 30 days before trial).

In re K.M.H., 181 S.W.3d 1, 8 (Tex.App.—Houston [14th Dist.] 2005, no pet.). "When a party has perfected its right to a jury trial … but the trial court proceeds to trial without a jury, the party must, to preserve error, either object on the record to the trial court's action or indicate affirmatively in the record it intends to stand on its perfected right to a jury trial." *See also* ***Stallworth v. Stallworth***, 201 S.W.3d 338, 346 (Tex.App.—Dallas 2006, no pet.).

TRCP 217. OATH OF INABILITY

The deposit for a jury fee shall not be required when the party shall within the time for making such deposit, file with the clerk his affidavit to the effect that he is unable to make such deposit, and that he cannot, by the pledge of property or otherwise, obtain the money necessary for that purpose; and the court shall then order the clerk to enter the suit on the jury docket.

History of TRCP 217: Adopted eff. Sept. 1, 1941, by order of Oct. 29, 1940 (3 Tex.B.J. 558 [1940]). Source: TRCS art. 2127 (repealed).

See *Commentaries*, "Request for Jury Trial," ch. 5-B, p. 320.

TRCP 218. JURY DOCKET

The clerks of the district and county courts shall each keep a docket, styled, "The Jury Docket," in which shall be entered in their order the cases in which jury fees have been paid or affidavit in lieu thereof has been filed as provided in the two preceding rules.

History of TRCP 218: Adopted eff. Sept. 1, 1941, by order of Oct. 29, 1940 (3 Tex.B.J. 558 [1940]). Source: TRCS art. 2128 (repealed).

TRCP 219. JURY TRIAL DAY

The court shall designate the days for taking up the jury docket and the trial of jury cases. Such order may be revoked or changed in the court's discretion.

History of TRCP 219: Amended eff. Apr. 1, 1984, by order of Dec. 5, 1983 (661-62 S.W.2d [Tex.Cases] lxxiii). Adopted eff. Sept. 1, 1941, by order of Oct. 29, 1940 (3 Tex.B.J. 558 [1940]). Source: TRCS art. 2129 (repealed).

TRCP 220. WITHDRAWING CAUSE FROM JURY DOCKET

When any party has paid the fee for a jury trial, he shall not be permitted to withdraw the cause from the jury docket over the objection of the parties adversely interested. If so permitted, the court in its discretion may by an order permit him to withdraw also his jury fee deposit. Failure of a party to appear for trial shall be deemed a waiver by him of the right to trial by jury.

History of TRCP 220: Amended eff. Jan. 1, 1971, by order of July 21, 1970 (455-56 S.W.2d [Tex.Cases] xliii): Sentence added to provide that failure of party to appear for trial is deemed waiver of jury trial. Amended eff. Dec. 31, 1947, by order of Aug. 18, 1947 (8 Tex.B.J. 395 [1947]): Substituted words "any party" for "one party"; "the cause" for "such cause"; and "over the objection" for "without the consent." Adopted eff. Sept. 1, 1941, by order of Oct. 29, 1940 (3 Tex.B.J. 558 [1940]). Source: TRCS art. 2130 (repealed).

See *Commentaries*, "Request for Jury Trial," ch. 5-B, p. 320; *O'Connor's Texas Forms*, FORMS 5B:4, 5.

ANNOTATIONS

Mercedes-Benz Credit Corp. v. Rhyne, 925 S.W.2d 664, 666 (Tex.1996). "Only when a party demands a jury *and* pays the fee can the opposing party rely on those actions. In such a case, the trial court may not remove the case from the jury docket over the objections of the opposing party." *See also* ***Green v. W.E. Grace Mfg.***, 422 S.W.2d 723, 726 (Tex.1968).

In re T.K., No. 09-09-00472-CV (Tex.App.—Beaumont 2010, no pet.) (memo op.; 3-11-10). "[F]or Rule 220 purposes, a party, although not personally present, appears for trial when his attorney is present. If counsel refuses to go forward with the trial, however, that refusal constitutes a jury waiver. Likewise, late arrival by both counsel and the litigant waives the right to trial by jury." (Internal quotes omitted.)

In re J.N.F., 116 S.W.3d 426, 434-35 (Tex.App.—Houston [14th Dist.] 2003, no pet.). "'[U]nless an objection is made to the withdrawal of a case from the jury docket, the non-requesting party has no right to a jury trial.' If a party who has requested a jury trial in an initial pleading could effectively withdraw the request simply by omitting it in subsequent pleadings, the non-requesting party would be forced to scrutinize all such pleadings in order to avoid waiving a jury trial by failing to object to the withdrawal. [¶] [O]mitting a jury request from subsequent pleadings does not rise to the level of inaction that has been held to constitute the requesting party's waiver of a jury trial."

TRCP 221. CHALLENGE TO THE ARRAY

When the jurors summoned have not been selected by jury commissioners or by drawing the names from a jury wheel, any party to a suit which is to be tried by a jury may, before the jury is drawn challenge the array upon the ground that the officer summoning the jury has acted corruptly, and has wilfully summoned jurors known to be prejudiced against the party challenging or biased in favor of the adverse party. All such challenges must be in writing setting forth distinctly the grounds of such challenge and supported by the affidavit of the party or some other credible person. When such challenge is made, the court shall hear evidence and decide without delay whether or not the challenge shall be sustained.

History of TRCP 221: Adopted eff. Sept. 1, 1941, by order of Oct. 29, 1940 (3 Tex.B.J. 558 [1940]). Source: TRCS art. 2131 (repealed).

See Gov't Code §62.001; *Commentaries*, "Jury Selection," ch. 8-A, p. 679.

TRCP 222. WHEN CHALLENGE IS SUSTAINED

If the challenge be sustained, the array of jurors summoned shall be discharged, and the court shall order other jurors summoned in their stead, and shall direct that the officer who summoned the persons so discharged, and on account of whose misconduct the challenge has been sustained, shall not summon any other jurors in the case.

History of TRCP 222: Adopted eff. Sept. 1, 1941, by order of Oct. 29, 1940 (3 Tex.B.J. 558 [1940]). Source: TRCS art. 2132 (repealed).

See Gov't Code §§62.101-62.110.

ANNOTATIONS

Martinez v. City of Austin, 852 S.W.2d 71, 73 (Tex. App.—Austin 1993, writ denied). A challenge to the array "alleges a defect in the juror selection and summons procedure or a violation of the jury-wheel statute. If the movant is successful, the entire array is dismissed and a new array summoned. The challenge [to the array] must be presented in a written motion supported by affidavit to the particular judge in charge of the local jury system."

TRCP 223. JURY LIST IN CERTAIN COUNTIES

In counties governed as to juries by the laws providing for interchangeable juries, the names of the jurors shall be placed upon the general panel in the order in which they are randomly selected, and jurors shall be assigned for service from the top thereof, in the order in which they shall be needed, and jurors returned to the general panel after service in any of such courts shall be enrolled at the bottom of the list in the order of their respective return; provided, however, after such assignment to a particular court, the trial judge of such court, upon the demand prior to voir dire examination by any party or attorney in the case reached for trial in such court, shall cause the names of all members of such assigned jury panel in such case to be placed in a receptacle, shuffled, and drawn, and such names shall be transcribed in the order drawn on the jury list from which the jury is to be selected to try such case. There shall be only one shuffle and drawing by the trial judge in each case.

History of TRCP 223: Amended eff. Sept. 1, 1990, by order of Apr. 24, 1990 (785-86 S.W.2d [Tex.Cases] lxiv): "Drawn from the wheel" changed to "randomly selected"; everything after "provided, however," completely rewritten to provide uniformity in jury shuffles. Adopted eff. Sept. 1, 1941, by order of Oct. 29, 1940 (3 Tex.B.J. 558 [1940]). Source: TRCS art. 2138 (repealed).

See Gov't Code §§62.016, 62.017 (interchangeable juries in certain counties); *Commentaries*, "Jury Selection," ch. 8-A, p. 679.

ANNOTATIONS

Rivas v. Liberty Mut. Ins., 480 S.W.2d 610, 612 (Tex.1972). "The court of civil appeals recognized the listing and reshuffle provisions of Rule 223 are designed to insure a random selection of jurors. While the method used here did not conform to the method prescribed by the rule, it did insure a degree of randomness in the listing of the jurors."

Carr v. Smith, 22 S.W.3d 128, 134 (Tex.App.—Fort Worth 2000, pet. denied). "After the venire panel has been sworn and once substantive inquiry begins and responses have been observed or made available to the parties or their counsel, whether verbally or in writing, voir dire has begun."

TRCP 224. PREPARING JURY LIST

In counties not governed as to juries by the laws providing for interchangeable juries, when the parties have announced ready for trial the clerk shall write the name of each regular juror entered of record for that week on separate slips of paper, as near the same size and appearance as may be, and shall place the slips in a box and mix them well. The clerk shall draw from the box, in the presence of the court, the names of twenty-four jurors, if in the district court, or so many as there may be, if there be a less number in the box; and the names of twelve jurors if in the county court, or so

---

many as there may be, and write the names as drawn upon two slips of paper and deliver one slip to each party to the suit or his attorney.

History of TRCP 224: Adopted eff. Sept. 1, 1941, by order of Oct. 29, 1940 (3 Tex.B.J. 559 [1940]). Source: TRCS arts. 2139, 2140 (repealed).

See *Commentaries*, "Jury Selection," ch. 8-A, p. 679.

ANNOTATIONS

Southwestern Pub. Serv. v. Morris, 380 S.W.2d 648, 649 (Tex.App.—Amarillo 1964, no writ). "[E]rror was committed by the court in refusing condemnor's request that the jury panel be drawn before the selection of the jury." Such error may be harmless.

TRCP 225. SUMMONING TALESMAN

When there are not as many as twenty-four names drawn from the box, if in the district court, or as many as twelve, if in the county court, the court shall direct the sheriff to summon such number of qualified persons as the court deems necessary to complete the panel. The names of those thus summoned shall be placed in the box and drawn and entered upon the slips as provided in the preceding rules.

History of TRCP 225: Adopted eff. Sept. 1, 1941, by order of Oct. 29, 1940 (3 Tex.B.J. 559 [1940]). Source: TRCS art. 2141 (repealed).

TRCP 226. OATH TO JURY PANEL

Before the parties or their attorneys begin the examination of the jurors whose names have thus been listed, the jurors shall be sworn by the court or under its direction, as follows: "You, and each of you, do solemnly swear that you will true answers give to all questions propounded to you concerning your qualifications as a juror, so help you God."

History of TRCP 226: Adopted eff. Sept. 1, 1941, by order of Oct. 29, 1940 (3 Tex.B.J. 559 [1940]). Source: New rule.

See *Commentaries*, "Jury Selection," ch. 8-A, p. 679.

ANNOTATIONS

Barron v. State, 378 S.W.2d 144, 147 (Tex. App.—San Antonio 1964, no writ). "[F]ailure to swear the jury panel prior to the voir dire examination as required by Rule 226 ... was waived by [the] failure to timely complain of same."

TRCP 226a. INSTRUCTIONS TO JURY PANEL & JURY

The court must give instructions to the jury panel and the jury as prescribed by order of the Supreme Court under this rule.

History of TRCP 226a: Amended eff. Feb. 1, 2005, by order of Jan. 27, 2005 (Tex.Sup.Ct. Order, Misc. Docket No. 05-9021): Rule is clarified; with these amendments, the Supreme Court has ordered changes in the prescribed jury instructions consistent with Act of June 2, 2003, 78th Leg., R.S., ch. 204, §13.04, 2003 Tex. Gen. Laws 847, 888, codified as CPRC §41.003. Adopted eff. Jan. 1, 1967, by order of July 20, 1966 (401-02 S.W.2d [Tex.Cases] xxxvi). Source: New rule.

APPROVED INSTRUCTIONS

I.

That the following oral instructions, with such modifications as the circumstances of the particular case may require, shall be given by the court to the members of the jury panel after they have been sworn in as provided in Rule 226 and before the voir dire examination:

Members of the Jury Panel [or Ladies and Gentlemen of the Jury Panel]:

Thank you for being here. We are here to select a jury. Twelve [six] of you will be chosen for the jury. Even if you are not chosen for the jury, you are performing a valuable service that is your right and duty as a citizen of a free country.

Before we begin: Turn off all phones and other electronic devices. While you are in the courtroom, do not communicate with anyone through any electronic device. [For example, do not communicate by phone, text message, email message, chat room, blog, or social networking websites such as Facebook, Twitter, or Myspace.] [I will give you a number where others may contact you in case of an emergency.] Do not record or photograph any part of these court proceedings, because it is prohibited by law.

If you are chosen for the jury, your role as jurors will be to decide the disputed facts in this case. My role will be to ensure that this case is tried in accordance with the rules of law.

Here is some background about this case. This is a civil case. It is a lawsuit that is not a criminal case. The parties are as follows: The plaintiff is _____, and the defendant is _____. Representing the plaintiff is _____, and representing the defendant is _____. They will ask you some questions during jury selection. But before their questions begin, I must give you some instructions for jury selection.

Every juror must obey these instructions. You may be called into court to testify about any violations of these instructions. If you do not follow these instructions, you will be guilty of juror misconduct, and I might have to order a new trial and start this process over again. This would waste your time and the parties' money, and would require the taxpayers of this county to pay for another trial.

---⭐---

These are the instructions.

1. To avoid looking like you are friendly with one side of the case, do not mingle or talk with the lawyers, witnesses, parties, or anyone else involved in the case. You may exchange casual greetings like "hello" and "good morning." Other than that, do not talk with them at all. They have to follow these instructions too, so you should not be offended when they follow the instructions.

2. Do not accept any favors from the lawyers, witnesses, parties, or anyone else involved in the case, and do not do any favors for them. This includes favors such as giving rides and food.

3. Do not discuss this case with anyone, even your spouse or a friend, either in person or by any other means [including by phone, text message, email message, chat room, blog, or social networking websites such as Facebook, Twitter, or Myspace]. Do not allow anyone to discuss the case with you or in your hearing. If anyone tries to discuss the case with you or in your hearing, tell me immediately. We do not want you to be influenced by something other than the evidence admitted in court.

4. The parties, through their attorneys, have the right to ask you questions about your background, experiences, and attitudes. They are not trying to meddle in your affairs. They are just being thorough and trying to choose fair jurors who do not have any bias or prejudice in this particular case.

5. Remember that you took an oath that you will tell the truth, so be truthful when the lawyers ask you questions, and always give complete answers. If you do not answer a question that applies to you, that violates your oath. Sometimes a lawyer will ask a question of the whole panel instead of just one person. If the question applies to you, raise your hand and keep it raised until you are called on.

Do you understand these instructions? If you do not, please tell me now.

The lawyers will now begin to ask their questions.

II.

That the following oral and written instructions, with such modifications as the circumstances of the particular case may require, shall be given by the court to the jury immediately after the jurors are selected for the case:

Members of the Jury [or Ladies and Gentlemen]:

You have been chosen to serve on this jury. Because of the oath you have taken and your selection for the jury, you become officials of this court and active participants in our justice system.

[Hand out the written instructions.]

You have each received a set of written instructions. I am going to read them with you now. Some of them you have heard before and some are new.

1. Turn off all phones and other electronic devices. While you are in the courtroom and while you are deliberating, do not communicate with anyone through any electronic device. [For example, do not communicate by phone, text message, email message, chat room, blog, or social networking websites such as Facebook, Twitter, or Myspace.] [I will give you a number where others may contact you in case of an emergency.] Do not post information about the case on the Internet before these court proceedings end and you are released from jury duty. Do not record or photograph any part of these court proceedings, because it is prohibited by law.

2. To avoid looking like you are friendly with one side of the case, do not mingle or talk with the lawyers, witnesses, parties, or anyone else involved in the case. You may exchange casual greetings like "hello" and "good morning." Other than that, do not talk with them at all. They have to follow these instructions too, so you should not be offended when they follow the instructions.

3. Do not accept any favors from the lawyers, witnesses, parties, or anyone else involved in the case, and do not do any favors for them. This includes favors such as giving rides and food.

4. Do not discuss this case with anyone, even your spouse or a friend, either in person or by any other means [including by phone, text message, email message, chat room, blog, or social networking websites such as Facebook, Twitter, or Myspace]. Do not allow anyone to discuss the case with you or in your hearing. If anyone tries to discuss the case with you or in your hearing, tell me immediately. We do not want you to be influenced by something other than the evidence admitted in court.

5. Do not discuss this case with anyone during the trial, not even with the other jurors, until the end of the trial. You should not discuss the case with your fellow

★

jurors until the end of the trial so that you do not form opinions about the case before you have heard everything.

After you have heard all the evidence, received all of my instructions, and heard all of the lawyers' arguments, you will then go to the jury room to discuss the case with the other jurors and reach a verdict.

6. Do not investigate this case on your own. For example, do not:

a. try to get information about the case, lawyers, witnesses, or issues from outside this courtroom;

b. go to places mentioned in the case to inspect the places;

c. inspect items mentioned in this case unless they are presented as evidence in court;

d. look anything up in a law book, dictionary, or public record to try to learn more about the case;

e. look anything up on the Internet to try to learn more about the case; or

f. let anyone else do any of these things for you.

This rule is very important because we want a trial based only on evidence admitted in open court. Your conclusions about this case must be based only on what you see and hear in this courtroom because the law does not permit you to base your conclusions on information that has not been presented to you in open court. All the information must be presented in open court so the parties and their lawyers can test it and object to it. Information from other sources, like the Internet, will not go through this important process in the courtroom. In addition, information from other sources could be completely unreliable. As a result, if you investigate this case on your own, you could compromise the fairness to all parties in this case and jeopardize the results of this trial.

7. Do not tell other jurors about your own experiences or other people's experiences. For example, you may have special knowledge of something in the case, such as business, technical, or professional information. You may even have expert knowledge or opinions, or you may know what happened in this case or another similar case. Do not tell the other jurors about it. Telling other jurors about it is wrong because it means the jury will be considering things that were not admitted in court.

8. Do not consider attorneys' fees unless I tell you to. Do not guess about attorneys' fees.

9. Do not consider or guess whether any party is covered by insurance unless I tell you to.

10. During the trial, if taking notes will help focus your attention on the evidence, you may take notes using the materials the court has provided. Do not use any personal electronic devices to take notes. If taking notes will distract your attention from the evidence, you should not take notes. Your notes are for your own personal use. They are not evidence. Do not show or read your notes to anyone, including other jurors.

You must leave your notes in the jury room or with the bailiff. The bailiff is instructed not to read your notes and to give your notes to me promptly after collecting them from you. I will make sure your notes are kept in a safe, secure location and not disclosed to anyone.

[You may take your notes back into the jury room and consult them during deliberations. But keep in mind that your notes are not evidence. When you deliberate, each of you should rely on your independent recollection of the evidence and not be influenced by the fact that another juror has or has not taken notes. After you complete your deliberations, the bailiff will collect your notes.]

When you are released from jury duty, the bailiff will promptly destroy your notes so that nobody can read what you wrote.

11. I will decide matters of law in this case. It is your duty to listen to and consider the evidence and to determine fact issues that I may submit to you at the end of the trial. After you have heard all the evidence, I will give you instructions to follow as you make your decision. The instructions also will have questions for you to answer. You will not be asked and you should not consider which side will win. Instead, you will need to answer the specific questions I give you.

Every juror must obey my instructions. If you do not follow these instructions, you will be guilty of juror misconduct, and I may have to order a new trial and start this process over again. This would waste your time and the parties' money, and would require the taxpayers of this county to pay for another trial.

Do you understand these instructions? If you do not, please tell me now.

Please keep these instructions and review them as we go through this case. If anyone does not follow these instructions, tell me.

★

III.

COURT'S CHARGE

Before closing arguments begin, the court must give to each member of the jury a copy of the charge, which must include the following written instructions, with such modifications as the circumstances of the particular case may require:

Members of the Jury [or Ladies & Gentlemen of the Jury]:

After the closing arguments, you will go to the jury room to decide the case, answer the questions that are attached, and reach a verdict. You may discuss the case with other jurors only when you are all together in the jury room.

Remember my previous instructions: Do not discuss the case with anyone else, either in person or by any other means. Do not do any independent investigation about the case or conduct any research. Do not look up any words in dictionaries or on the Internet. Do not post information about the case on the Internet. Do not share any special knowledge or experiences with the other jurors. Do not use your phone or any other electronic device during your deliberations for any reason. [I will give you a number where others may contact you in case of an emergency.]

[Any notes you have taken are for your own personal use. You may take your notes back into the jury room and consult them during deliberations, but do not show or read your notes to your fellow jurors during your deliberations. Your notes are not evidence. Each of you should rely on your independent recollection of the evidence and not be influenced by the fact that another juror has or has not taken notes.]

[You must leave your notes with the bailiff when you are not deliberating. The bailiff will give your notes to me promptly after collecting them from you. I will make sure your notes are kept in a safe, secure location and not disclosed to anyone. After you complete your deliberations, the bailiff will collect your notes. When you are released from jury duty, the bailiff will promptly destroy your notes so that nobody can read what you wrote.]

Here are the instructions for answering the questions.

1. Do not let bias, prejudice, or sympathy play any part in your decision.

2. Base your answers only on the evidence admitted in court and on the law that is in these instructions and questions. Do not consider or discuss any evidence that was not admitted in the courtroom.

3. You are to make up your own minds about the facts. You are the sole judges of the credibility of the witnesses and the weight to give their testimony. But on matters of law, you must follow all of my instructions.

4. If my instructions use a word in a way that is different from its ordinary meaning, use the meaning I give you, which will be a proper legal definition.

5. All the questions and answers are important. No one should say that any question or answer is not important.

6. Answer "yes" or "no" to all questions unless you are told otherwise. A "yes" answer must be based on a preponderance of the evidence [unless you are told otherwise]. Whenever a question requires an answer other than "yes" or "no," your answer must be based on a preponderance of the evidence [unless you are told otherwise].

The term "preponderance of the evidence" means the greater weight of credible evidence presented in this case. If you do not find that a preponderance of the evidence supports a "yes" answer, then answer "no." A preponderance of the evidence is not measured by the number of witnesses or by the number of documents admitted in evidence. For a fact to be proved by a preponderance of the evidence, you must find that the fact is more likely true than not true.

7. Do not decide who you think should win before you answer the questions and then just answer the questions to match your decision. Answer each question carefully without considering who will win. Do not discuss or consider the effect your answers will have.

8. Do not answer questions by drawing straws or by any method of chance.

9. Some questions might ask you for a dollar amount. Do not agree in advance to decide on a dollar amount by adding up each juror's amount and then figuring the average.

10. Do not trade your answers. For example, do not say, "I will answer this question your way if you answer another question my way."

11. [Unless otherwise instructed] The answers to the questions must be based on the decision of at least 10 of the 12 [5 of the 6] jurors. The same 10 [5] jurors must agree on every answer. Do not agree to be bound by a vote of anything less than 10 [5] jurors, even if it would be a majority.

★

As I have said before, if you do not follow these instructions, you will be guilty of juror misconduct, and I might have to order a new trial and start this process over again. This would waste your time and the parties' money, and would require the taxpayers of this county to pay for another trial. If a juror breaks any of these rules, tell that person to stop and report it to me immediately.

[Definitions, questions, and special instructions given to the jury will be transcribed here. If exemplary damages are sought against a defendant, the jury must unanimously find, with respect to that defendant, (i) liability on at least one claim for actual damages that will support an award of exemplary damages, (ii) any additional conduct, such as malice or gross negligence, required for an award of exemplary damages, and (iii) the amount of exemplary damages to be awarded. The jury's answers to questions regarding (ii) and (iii) must be conditioned on a unanimous finding regarding (i), except in an extraordinary circumstance when the conditioning instruction would be erroneous. The jury need not be unanimous in finding the amount of actual damages. Thus, if questions regarding (ii) and (iii) are submitted to the jury for defendants D1 and D2, instructions in substantially the following form must immediately precede such questions:

Preceding question (ii):

Answer Question (ii) for D1 only if you unanimously answered "Yes" to Question[s] (i) regarding D1. Otherwise, do not answer Question (ii) for D1. [Repeat for D2.]

You are instructed that in order to answer "Yes" to [any part of] Question (ii), your answer must be unanimous. You may answer "No" to [any part of] Question (ii) only upon a vote of 10 [5] or more jurors. Otherwise, you must not answer [that part of] Question (ii).

Preceding question (iii):

Answer Question (iii) for D1 only if you answered "Yes" to Question (ii) for D1. Otherwise, do not answer Question (iii) for D1. [Repeat for D2.]

You are instructed that you must unanimously agree on the amount of any award of exemplary damages.

These examples are given by way of illustration.]

Presiding Juror:

1. When you go into the jury room to answer the questions, the first thing you will need to do is choose a presiding juror.

2. The presiding juror has these duties:

a. have the complete charge read aloud if it will be helpful to your deliberations;

b. preside over your deliberations, meaning manage the discussions, and see that you follow these instructions;

c. give written questions or comments to the bailiff who will give them to the judge;

d. write down the answers you agree on;

e. get the signatures for the verdict certificate; and

f. notify the bailiff that you have reached a verdict.

Do you understand the duties of the presiding juror? If you do not, please tell me now.

Instructions for Signing the Verdict Certificate:

1. [Unless otherwise instructed] You may answer the questions on a vote of 10 [5] jurors. The same 10 [5] jurors must agree on every answer in the charge. This means you may not have one group of 10 [5] jurors agree on one answer and a different group of 10 [5] jurors agree on another answer.

2. If 10 [5] jurors agree on every answer, those 10 [5] jurors sign the verdict.

If 11 jurors agree on every answer, those 11 jurors sign the verdict.

If all 12 [6] of you agree on every answer, you are unanimous and only the presiding juror signs the verdict.

3. All jurors should deliberate on every question. You may end up with all 12 [6] of you agreeing on some answers, while only 10 [5] or 11 of you agree on other answers. But when you sign the verdict, only those 10 [5] who agree on every answer will sign the verdict.

4. [Added if the charge requires some unanimity] There are some special instructions before Questions ____ explaining how to answer those questions. Please follow the instructions. If all 12 [6] of you answer those questions, you will need to complete a second verdict certificate for those questions.

Do you understand these instructions? If you do not, please tell me now.

_____

Judge Presiding

VERDICT CERTIFICATE

Check one:

____ Our verdict is unanimous. All 12 [6] of us have agreed to each and every answer. The presiding juror has signed the certificate for all 12 [6] of us.

⭐

Signature of Presiding Juror

Printed Name of Presiding Juror

____ _Our verdict is not unanimous. Eleven of us have agreed to each and every answer and have signed the certificate below._

____ _Our verdict is not unanimous. Ten [Five] of us have agreed to each and every answer and have signed the certificate below._

SIGNATURE	NAME PRINTED
1. _____	_____
2. _____	_____
3. _____	_____
4. _____	_____
5. _____	_____
6. _____	_____
7. _____	_____
8. _____	_____
9. _____	_____
10. _____	_____
11. _____	_____

_If you have answered Question No. ____ [the exemplary damages amount], then you must sign this certificate also._

ADDITIONAL CERTIFICATE
[Used when some questions require unanimous answers]

I certify that the jury was unanimous in answering the following questions. All 12 [6] of us agreed to each of the answers. The presiding juror has signed the certificate for all 12 [6] of us.

[Judge to list questions that require a unanimous answer, including the predicate liability question.]

Signature of Presiding Juror

Printed Name of Presiding Juror

IV.

That the following oral instructions shall be given by the court to the jury after the verdict has been accepted by the court and before the jurors are released from jury duty:

Thank you for your verdict.

I have told you that the only time you may discuss the case is with the other jurors in the jury room. I now release you from jury duty. Now you may discuss the case with anyone. But you may also choose not to discuss the case; that is your right.

After you are released from jury duty, the lawyers and others may ask you questions to see if the jury followed the instructions, and they may ask you to give a sworn statement. You are free to discuss the case with them and to give a sworn statement. But you may choose not to discuss the case and not to give a sworn statement; that is your right.

History of instructions to TRCP 226a: Amended eff. Apr. 13, 2011, by order of Apr. 13, 2011 (Tex.Sup.Ct. Order, Misc. Docket No. 11-9047a). Amended eff. Apr. 1, 2011, by order of Mar. 15, 2011 (Tex.Sup.Ct. Order, Misc. Docket No. 11-9047). Amended eff. Feb. 1, 2005, by order of Jan. 27, 2005 (Tex.Sup.Ct. Order, Misc. Docket No. 05-9022): Changed instructions from III, par. 6 to end. Amended eff. Jan. 1, 1988, by order of Jan. 28, 1988 (741-42 S.W.2d [Tex.Cases] xlv): Changed instructions from III, par. 6 to end; corrected order of Dec. 16, 1987. Amended eff. Jan. 1, 1988, by order of Dec. 16, 1987 (741-42 S.W.2d [Tex.Cases] xliv): Instructions from III, par. 6 to end changed to correct amendment of July 15, 1987, which had unintentionally included the last par. "The presiding juror ... the juror not to do so again"; that par. deleted by this correction. Amended eff. Jan. 1, 1988, by order of July 15, 1987 (733-34 S.W.2d [Tex.Cases] lxv): Changed instructions from II, par. 10 to III, par. 6. Amended eff. Apr. 1, 1984, by orders of Dec. 5, 1983 (661-62 S.W.2d [Tex.Cases] lxxiii): Changed word "foreman" to "presiding juror." Amended eff. Feb. 1, 1973, by order of Oct. 3, 1972 (483-84 S.W.2d [Tex.Cases] xlvii): Changed instructions from III, par. 6. Amended eff. Jan. 1, 1971, by order of July 21, 1970 (455-56 S.W.2d [Tex.Cases] xxii): Changed instructions from II, par. 9. Adopted eff. Jan. 1, 1967, by order of July 20, 1966 (401-02 S.W.2d [Tex.Cases] xxxvii). Source: New rule.

See **Commentaries**, "Jury Selection," ch. 8-A, p. 679; "The Charge," ch. 8-I, p. 731; **O'Connor's Texas Forms**, FORM 8I:1.

ANNOTATIONS

Woods v. Crane Carrier Co., 693 S.W.2d 377, 379 (Tex.1985). "[W]hen terms requiring definitions are used more than once in a charge, it is preferable that the definition or instruction occur immediately after the general instructions required by [TRCP] 226a...."

TRCP 227. CHALLENGE TO JUROR

A challenge to a particular juror is either a challenge for cause or a peremptory challenge. The court shall decide without delay any such challenge, and if sustained, the juror shall be discharged from the particular case. Either such challenge may be made orally on the formation of a jury to try the case.

History of TRCP 227: Adopted eff. Sept. 1, 1941, by order of Oct. 29, 1940 (3 Tex.B.J. 559 [1940]). Source: TRCS art. 2142 (repealed).

See Gov't Code §§62.101-62.110; **Commentaries**, "Jury Selection," ch. 8-A, p. 679.

ANNOTATIONS

Lopez v. Southern Pac. Transp., 847 S.W.2d 330, 333 (Tex.App.—El Paso 1993, no writ). "A party exercises its peremptory challenges by delivering its list of peremptory challenges to the court."

★

TRCP 228. "CHALLENGE FOR CAUSE" DEFINED

A challenge for cause is an objection made to a juror, alleging some fact which by law disqualifies him to serve as a juror in the case or in any case, or which in the opinion of the court, renders him an unfit person to sit on the jury. Upon such challenge the examination is not confined to the answers of the juror, but other evidence may be heard for or against the challenge.

History of TRCP 228: Adopted eff. Sept. 1, 1941, by order of Oct. 29, 1940 (3 Tex.B.J. 559 [1940]). Source: TRCS art. 2144 (repealed).

See *Commentaries*, "Challenges for Cause," ch. 8-A, §6, p. 687.

ANNOTATIONS

Compton v. Henrie, 364 S.W.2d 179, 182 (Tex. 1963). "[T]he statutory disqualification of bias or prejudice extends not only to the litigant personally, but to the subject matter of the litigation as well."

TRCP 229. CHALLENGE FOR CAUSE

When twenty-four or more jurors, if in the district court, or twelve or more, if in the county court, are drawn, and the lists of their names delivered to the parties, if either party desires to challenge any juror for cause, the challenge shall then be made. The name of a juror challenged and set aside for cause shall be erased from such lists.

History of TRCP 229: Adopted eff. Sept. 1, 1941, by order of Oct. 29, 1940 (3 Tex.B.J. 559 [1940]). Source: TRCS art. 2143 (repealed).

See Gov't Code §§62.101-62.110; *Commentaries*, "Challenges for Cause," ch. 8-A, §6, p. 687.

ANNOTATIONS

Cortez v. HCCI-San Antonio, Inc., 159 S.W.3d 87, 90-91 (Tex.2005). "[T]o preserve error when a challenge for cause is denied, a party must use a peremptory challenge against the veniremember involved, exhaust its remaining challenges, and notify the trial court that a specific objectionable veniremember will remain on the jury list. [¶] While it is unclear whether [P] gave his notice to the trial court before or after he delivered his strike list, it does appear that the two events were roughly contemporaneous. More importantly, notice was given before the jury was seated…. We therefore hold that error was preserved. [¶] The fact that [P] prevailed at trial is not relevant [to whether any error was harmless] because … 'harm occurs' when 'the party uses all of his peremptory challenges and is thus prevented from striking other objectionable jurors from the list because he has no additional peremptory challenges.' … Here, … we presume harm." *See also* **Hallett v. Houston Nw. Med. Ctr.**, 689 S.W.2d 888, 890 (Tex.1985).

TRCP 230. CERTAIN QUESTIONS NOT TO BE ASKED

In examining a juror, he shall not be asked a question the answer to which may show that he has been convicted of an offense which disqualifies him, or that he stands charged by some legal accusation with theft or any felony.

History of TRCP 230: Adopted eff. Sept. 1, 1941, by order of Oct. 29, 1940 (3 Tex.B.J. 559 [1940]). Source: TRCS art. 2145 (repealed).

See *Commentaries*, "Jury Selection," ch. 8-A, p. 679.

ANNOTATIONS

Palmer Well Servs. v. Mack Trucks, Inc., 776 S.W.2d 575, 576 (Tex.1989). Gov't Code §62.102 "disqualifies a person to serve as a petit juror if he is 'under indictment or other legal accusation of misdemeanor or felony theft, or any other felony.'"

TRCP 231. NUMBER REDUCED BY CHALLENGES

If the challenges reduce the number of jurors to less than twenty-four, if in the district court, or to less than twelve, if in the county court, the court shall order other jurors to be drawn from the wheel or from the central jury panel or summoned, as the practice may be in the particular county, and their names written upon the list instead of those set aside for cause. Such jurors so summoned may likewise be challenged for cause.

History of TRCP 231: Adopted eff. Sept. 1, 1941, by order of Oct. 29, 1940 (3 Tex.B.J. 559 [1940]). Source: TRCS art. 2146 (repealed).

ANNOTATIONS

Williams v. State, 631 S.W.2d 955, 957 (Tex.App.—Austin 1982, no writ). TRCP 231 "authorizes the calling of additional individuals to supplement a jury panel rendered insufficient (by disqualifications or peremptory strikes) to supply a jury of 12."

TRCP 232. MAKING PEREMPTORY CHALLENGES

If there remain on such lists not subject to challenge for cause, twenty-four names, if in the district court, or twelve names, if in the county court, the parties shall proceed to make their peremptory challenges. A peremptory challenge is made to a juror without assigning any reason therefor.

History of TRCP 232: Adopted eff. Sept. 1, 1941, by order of Oct. 29, 1940 (3 Tex.B.J. 560 [1940]). Source: TRCS art. 2147 (repealed).

See *Commentaries*, "Peremptory Challenges," ch. 8-A, §7, p. 688.

⭐

ANNOTATIONS

Davis v. Fisk Elec. Co., 268 S.W.3d 508, 518-19 (Tex.2008). "Nonverbal conduct or demeanor, often elusive and always subject to interpretation, may well mask a race-based strike. For that reason, trial courts must carefully examine such rationales. ... *Batson* requires a 'clear and reasonably specific explanation' of the legitimate reasons for a strike ... and merely stating that a juror nonverbally 'reacted' is insufficient. *At 525:* [C]ourts must consider 'all relevant circumstances' when reviewing *Batson* challenges. And here, the relevant circumstances include many [factors], including a statistical disparity and unequal treatment of comparable jurors."

Goode v. Shoukfeh, 943 S.W.2d 441, 445-46 (Tex. 1997). "At the first step of the [*Batson*] process, the opponent of the peremptory challenge must establish a prima facie case of racial discrimination. [¶] During the second step of the process, the burden shifts to the party who has exercised the strike to come forward with a race-neutral explanation. ... The issue ... at this juncture is the facial validity of the explanation. ... It is not until the third step that the persuasiveness of the justification for the challenge becomes relevant. At the third step of the process, the trial court must determine if the party challenging the strike has proven purposeful racial discrimination, and the trial court may believe or not believe the explanation offered by the party who exercised the peremptory challenge. It is at this stage that implausible justifications for striking potential jurors 'may (and probably will) be found [by the trial court] to be pretexts for purposeful discrimination.'"

Powers v. Palacios, 813 S.W.2d 489, 491 (Tex. 1991). "We hold that equal protection is denied when race is a factor in counsel's exercise of a peremptory challenge to a prospective juror."

TRCP 233. NUMBER OF PEREMPTORY CHALLENGES

Except as provided below, each party to a civil action is entitled to six peremptory challenges in a case tried in the district court, and to three in the county court.

Alignment of the Parties. In multiple party cases, it shall be the duty of the trial judge to decide whether any of the litigants aligned on the same side of the docket are antagonistic with respect to any issue to be submitted to the jury, before the exercise of peremptory challenges.

Definition of Side. The term "side" as used in this rule is not synonymous with "party," "litigant," or "person." Rather, "side" means one or more litigants who have common interests on the matters with which the jury is concerned.

Motion to Equalize. In multiple party cases, upon motion of any litigant made prior to the exercise of peremptory challenges, it shall be the duty of the trial judge to equalize the number of peremptory challenges so that no litigant or side is given unfair advantage as a result of the alignment of the litigants and the award of peremptory challenges to each litigant or side. In determining how the challenges should be allocated the court shall consider any matter brought to the attention of the trial judge concerning the ends of justice and the elimination of an unfair advantage.

History of TRCP 233: Amended eff. Apr. 1, 1984, by order of Dec. 5, 1983 (661-62 S.W.2d [Tex.Cases] lxxiv): Rule was adopted to conform with *Patterson Dental Co. v. Dunn*, 592 S.W.2d 914 (Tex.1979), and other Supreme Court decisions. Adopted eff. Sept. 1, 1941, by order of Oct. 29, 1940 (3 Tex.B.J. 560 [1940]). Source: TRCS art. 2148 (repealed).

See *Commentaries*, "Peremptory Challenges," ch. 8-A, §7, p. 688; *O'Connor's Texas Forms*, FORMS 8A:1, 2.

ANNOTATIONS

Garcia v. Central Power & Light Co., 704 S.W.2d 734, 736 (Tex.1986). "The existence of antagonism [between litigants on the same side of a lawsuit] is a question of law. If no antagonism exists, each side must receive the same number of strikes. *At 737:* [I]n determining whether antagonism exists, the trial court must consider the pleadings, information disclosed by pretrial discovery, information and representations made during voir dire of the jury panel, and any other information brought to the attention of the trial court before the exercise of the strikes by the parties." *See also Moore v. Altra Energy Techs.*, 321 S.W.3d 727, 741 (Tex.App.—Houston [14th Dist.] 2010, pet. denied).

In re M.N.G., 147 S.W.3d 521, 532 (Tex.App.—Fort Worth 2004, pet. denied). "[W]hen defendants have collaborated on the exercise of their peremptory challenges so that no double strikes are made, this factor supports a finding that the defendants have used their ostensibly antagonistic positions unfairly."

TRCP 234. LISTS RETURNED TO THE CLERK

When the parties have made or declined to make their peremptory challenges, they shall deliver their lists to the clerk. The clerk shall, if the case be in the

---

⭐

---

district court, call off the first twelve names on the lists that have not been erased; and if the case be in the county court, he shall call off the first six names on the lists that have not been erased; those whose names are called shall be the jury.

History of TRCP 234: Adopted eff. Sept. 1, 1941, by order of Oct. 29, 1940 (3 Tex.B.J. 560 [1940]). Source: TRCS art. 2149 (repealed).

See *Commentaries*, "Jury Selection," ch. 8-A, p. 679.

Lopez v. Southern Pac. Transp., 847 S.W.2d 330, 333 (Tex.App.—El Paso 1993, no writ). To preserve error when the court refuses to strike a panelist for cause, the party must name the objectionable panelist before giving its peremptory strikes to the clerk.

TRCP 235. IF JURY IS INCOMPLETE

When by peremptory challenges the jury is left incomplete, the court shall direct other jurors to be drawn or summoned to complete the jury; and such other jurors shall be impaneled as in the first instance.

History of TRCP 235: Adopted eff. Sept. 1, 1941, by order of Oct. 29, 1940 (3 Tex.B.J. 560 [1940]). Source: TRCS art. 2150 (repealed).

See *Commentaries*, "Jury Selection," ch. 8-A, p. 679.

TRCP 236. OATH TO JURY

The jury shall be sworn by the court or under its direction, in substance as follows: "You, and each of you, do solemnly swear that in all cases between parties which shall be to you submitted, you will a true verdict render, according to the law, as it may be given you in charge by the court, and to the evidence submitted to you under the rulings of the court. So help you God."

History of TRCP 236: Adopted eff. Sept. 1, 1941, by order of Oct. 29, 1940 (3 Tex.B.J. 560 [1940]). Source: TRCS arts. 2151, 2179 (repealed).

SECTION 11. TRIAL OF CAUSES

A. APPEARANCE & PROCEDURE

TRCP 237. APPEARANCE DAY

If a defendant, who has been duly cited, is by the citation required to answer on a day which is in term time, such day is appearance day as to him. If he is so required to answer on a day in vacation, he shall plead or answer accordingly, and the first day of the next term is appearance day as to him.

History of TRCP 237: Amended eff. Jan. 1, 1955, by order of July 20, 1954 (17 Tex.B.J. 568 [1954]): Deleted second paragraph about removal to federal court. Amended eff. Sept. 1, 1941, by order of Mar. 31, 1941 (4 Tex.B.J. 172 [1941]): Added last paragraph. Adopted eff. Sept. 1, 1941, by order of Oct. 29, 1940 (3 Tex.B.J. 560 [1940]). Source: TRCS art. 2152 (repealed), with changes: Appearance day, where the answer is to be filed during the term, depends upon date of service rather than on terms of court.

See *Commentaries*, "Default Judgment," ch. 7-A, p. 587.

Texas Alcoholic Bev. Comm'n v. Wilson, 573 S.W.2d 832, 835 (Tex.App.—Beaumont 1978, writ ref'd n.r.e.). "[D] had no valid notice that a hearing would be held prior to appearance day.... Any judgment entered before the time at which a defendant is commanded by the citation to appear and answer is erroneous and must be set aside."

TRCP 237a. CASES REMANDED FROM FEDERAL COURT

When any cause is removed to the Federal Court and is afterwards remanded to the state court, the plaintiff shall file a certified copy of the order of remand with the clerk of the state court and shall forthwith give written notice of such filing to the attorneys of record for all adverse parties. All such adverse parties shall have fifteen days from the receipt of such notice within which to file an answer. No default judgment shall be rendered against a party in a removed action remanded from federal court if that party filed an answer in federal court during removal.

History of TRCP 237a: Amended eff. Sept. 1, 1990, by order of Apr. 24, 1990 (785-86 S.W.2d [Tex.Cases] lxv): Added last sentence to expressly provide, consistent with existing law, that a default judgment cannot be taken in a case remanded from federal court if an answer was filed in federal court during removal. Amended eff. Apr. 1, 1984, by order of Dec. 5, 1983 (661-62 S.W.2d [Tex.Cases] lxxiv). Amended eff. Jan. 1, 1988, by order July 15, 1987 (733-34 S.W.2d [Tex.Cases] lxvii). Adopted eff. Jan. 1, 1955, by order of July 20, 1954 (17 Tex.B.J. 568 [1954]). Source: New rule.

Quaestor Invs. v. State of Chiapas, 997 S.W.2d 226, 229 (Tex.1999). "[W]e hold that jurisdiction revests in the state court when the federal district court executes the remand order and mails a certified copy to the state court. [¶] We are ... persuaded that nothing more is required to recommence the appellate timetable than the state court's reacquiring jurisdiction over a case. ... The court of appeals erred when it inferred from ... rule 237a ... that any further affirmative action was needed." See also *Gonzalez v. Guilbot*, 315 S.W.3d 533, 538 (Tex.2010) (jurisdiction revests when remand order hand-delivered).

Toliver v. Dallas Fort Worth Hosp. Council, 198 S.W.3d 444, 449 (Tex.App.—Dallas 2006, no pet.). "[R]ule 237a did not establish a deadline to answer in this case because [Ds] filed an answer in federal court and did not have to also file an answer in state court to avoid a default. [¶] [T]he rules that establish deadlines by which a defendant must answer a lawsuit do

TRCP 237a

─────────────── ★ ───────────────

not provide that an answer or other pleading is waived if not filed by the deadline. Instead, the rules provide a date before which the plaintiff may not take a default judgment, even if no answer has been filed."

HBA E., Ltd. v. JEA Boxing Co., 796 S.W.2d 534, 538 (Tex.App.—Houston [1st Dist.] 1990, writ denied). "Reading [TRCPs] 237a and 239 together, we conclude that a default judgment cannot be granted against a defendant following remand of a case from federal to state court until 15 days have expired from the defendant's receipt of the remand notice from the plaintiff." *See also Kashan v. McLane Co.*, No. 03-11-00125-CV (Tex. App.—Austin 2012, no pet.) (memo op.; 6-7-12).

TRCP 238. CALL OF APPEARANCE DOCKET

On the appearance day of a particular defendant and at the hour named in the citation, or as soon thereafter as may be practicable, the court or clerk in open court shall call, in their order, all the cases on the docket in which such day is appearance day as to any defendant, or, the court or clerk failing therein, any such case shall be so called on request of the plaintiff's attorney.

History of TRCP 238: Adopted eff. Sept. 1, 1941, by order of Oct. 29, 1940 (3 Tex.B.J. 560 [1940]). Source: TRCS art. 2153 (repealed).

12   ### TRCP 239. JUDGMENT BY DEFAULT

Upon such call of the docket, or at any time after a defendant is required to answer, the plaintiff may in term time take judgment by default against such defendant if he has not previously filed an answer, and provided that the return of service shall have been on file with the clerk for the length of time required by Rule 107.

History of TRCP 239: Amended eff. Jan. 1, 2012, by order of Dec. 12, 2011 (Tex.Sup.Ct. Order, Misc. Docket No. 11-9250): Deleted the words "citation with the officer's return thereon," and replaced them with "return of service." Amended eff. Sept. 1, 1962, by order of Apr. 12, 1962 (25 Tex.B.J. 428 [1962]): Added final clause beginning with words "and provided that." Adopted eff. Sept. 1, 1941, by order of Oct. 29, 1940 (3 Tex.B.J. 560 [1940]). Source: TRCS art. 2154 (repealed): Added words "In term time."

See *Commentaries*, "Default Judgment," ch. 7-A, p. 587; "MNT After Default Judgment," ch. 10-B, §9, p. 795; *O'Connor's Texas Forms*, FORMS 7A.

ANNOTATIONS

Kao Holdings, L.P. v. Young, 261 S.W.3d 60, 61 (Tex.2008). "[P] sued [limited partnership] for damages…. [P] did not sue [general partner] individually but served the partnership by serving him. When [limited partnership] did not answer, [P] filed a motion for default judgment stating that '[D-general partner] was properly and personally served' and had not answered.

At 65: [TRCP] 239 … provides for default judgment only against 'a defendant.' [General partner] was not a defendant. [TRCP] 301 requires that '[t]he judgment of the court shall conform to the pleadings.' [P] pleaded no claim against [general partner]. [D]efault judgment against [general partner] was improper."

In re Burlington Coat Factory Whs., 167 S.W.3d 827, 830 (Tex.2005). "[A] default judgment that fails to dispose of all claims can be final only if 'intent to finally dispose of the case' is 'unequivocally expressed in the words of the order itself.'" *See also Lehmann v. Har-Con Corp.*, 39 S.W.3d 191, 200 (Tex.2001).

LeBlanc v. LeBlanc, 778 S.W.2d 865, 865 (Tex. 1989). "*Craddock* has general application to all judgments of default, both those 'entered on failure of a defendant to file an answer and those entered on failure to appear for trial.'"

Lopez v. Lopez, 757 S.W.2d 721, 723 (Tex.1988). "Because the record here establishes that [D] had no actual or constructive notice of the trial setting, the lower courts erred in requiring him to show that he had a meritorious defense as a condition to granting his motion for new trial."

Craddock v. Sunshine Bus Lines, Inc., 133 S.W.2d 124, 126 (Tex.1939). "A default judgment should be set aside and a new trial ordered in any case in which the failure of the defendant to answer before judgment was not intentional, or the result of conscious indifference on his part, but was due to a mistake or accident; provided the motion for a new trial sets up a meritorious defense and is filed at a time when the granting thereof will occasion no delay or otherwise work an injury to the plaintiff."

TRCP 239a. NOTICE OF DEFAULT JUDGMENT

At or immediately prior to the time an interlocutory or final default judgment is rendered, the party taking the same or his attorney shall certify to the clerk in writing the last known mailing address of the party against whom the judgment is taken, which certificate shall be filed among the papers in the cause. Immediately upon the signing of the judgment, the clerk shall mail written notice thereof to the party against whom the judgment was rendered at the address shown in the certificate, and note the fact of such mailing on the docket. The notice shall state the number and style of the case, the court in which the case is pending, the names of the parties in whose favor and against whom

───────────────── ✦ ─────────────────

the judgment was rendered, and the date of the signing of the judgment. Failure to comply with the provisions of this rule shall not affect the finality of the judgment.

History of TRCP 239a: Amended eff. Jan. 1, 1988, by order of July 15, 1987 (733-34 S.W.2d [Tex.Cases] lxvii). Adopted eff. Jan. 1, 1967, by order of July 20, 1966 (401-02 S.W.2d [Tex.Cases] xlii). Source: New rule.

See *Commentaries*, "Certificate of last known address," ch. 7-A, §3.9.2(2), p. 592; "Notice of Default Judgment," ch. 7-A, §6, p. 598.

ANNOTATIONS

Campbell v. Fincher, 72 S.W.3d 723, 724 (Tex. App.—Waco 2002, no pet.). "Rule 239a is designed as an administrative convenience for the parties, and failure to give notice of the entry of a default judgment does not constitute reversible error."

TRCP 240. WHERE ONLY SOME ANSWER

Where there are several defendants, some of whom have answered or have not been duly served and some of whom have been duly served and have made default, an interlocutory judgment by default may be entered against those who have made default, and the cause may proceed or be postponed as to the others.

History of TRCP 240: Adopted eff. Sept. 1, 1941, by order of Oct. 29, 1940 (3 Tex.B.J. 560 [1940]). Source: TRCS art. 2155 (repealed).

See TRCP 161; *Commentaries*, "Default Judgment," ch. 7-A, p. 587.

ANNOTATIONS

Castano v. Foremost Cty. Mut. Ins., 31 S.W.3d 387, 388 (Tex.App.—San Antonio 2000, no pet.). "Where the plaintiff's petition names multiple defendants …, and the plaintiff obtains a no-answer default judgment against one of the defendants, the default judgment is interlocutory and cannot be appealed until the trial court either renders a final judgment in the case, or signs an order of severance making the interlocutory default judgment final."

TRCP 241. ASSESSING DAMAGES ON LIQUIDATED DEMANDS

When a judgment by default is rendered against the defendant, or all of several defendants, if the claim is liquidated and proved by an instrument in writing, the damages shall be assessed by the court, or under its direction, and final judgment shall be rendered therefor, unless the defendant shall demand and be entitled to a trial by jury.

History of TRCP 241: Amended eff. Apr. 1, 1984, by order of Dec. 5, 1983 (661-62 S.W.2d [Tex.Cases] lxxv). Adopted eff. Sept. 1, 1941, by order of Oct. 29, 1940 (3 Tex.B.J. 560 [1940]). Source: TRCS art. 2156 (repealed).

See *Commentaries*, "Liquidated damages – hearing not required," ch. 7-A, §3.13.1, p. 593.

ANNOTATIONS

Sherman Acquisition II LP v. Garcia, 229 S.W.3d 802, 809 (Tex.App.—Waco 2007, no pet.). "A claim is liquidated if the amount of damages caused by the defendant can be accurately calculated from (1) the factual, as opposed to conclusory, allegations in the petition, and (2) an instrument in writing. Whether a claim is liquidated must be determined from the language of the petition, as a seemingly liquidated claim may be unliquidated because of pleading allegations which require proof for resolution." *See also Novosad v. Brian K. Cunningham, P.C.*, 38 S.W.3d 767, 773 (Tex.App.—Houston [14th Dist.] 2001, no pet.).

TRCP 242. REPEALED

Repealed eff. Dec. 31, 1941, by order of Sept. 20, 1941 (4 Tex.B.J. 523 [1941]).

TRCP 243. UNLIQUIDATED DEMANDS

If the cause of action is unliquidated or be not proved by an instrument in writing, the court shall hear evidence as to damages and shall render judgment therefor, unless the defendant shall demand and be entitled to a trial by jury in which case the judgment by default shall be noted, a writ of inquiry awarded, and the cause entered on the jury docket.

History of TRCP 243: Amended eff. Sept. 1, 1941, by order of Mar. 31, 1941 (4 Tex.B.J. 172 [1941]): Substituted words "cause of action" for "claim." Adopted eff. Sept. 1, 1941, by order of Oct. 29, 1940 (3 Tex.B.J. 561 [1940]). Source: TRCS art. 2157 (repealed).

See *Commentaries*, "Unliquidated damages – hearing required," ch. 7-A, §3.13.2, p. 593.

ANNOTATIONS

Paradigm Oil, Inc. v. Retamco Oper., Inc., 372 S.W.3d 177, 182 (Tex.2012). "[D] does not contest the trial court's decision to strike its answer as a discovery sanction or the default judgment rendered against it on liability. [D]'s appeal focuses instead on its exclusion from the trial on damages. [A] defaulted[] defendant has the right to participate in such a trial when, as here, the plaintiff's damages are unliquidated. *At 186:* So what kind of abuse would justify barring a defaulted defendant's participation at the hearing on unliquidated damages? [S]poliation [i]s one [possible] example[, b]ut [that] is not at issue in this case. *At 187:* Given … the … sanction that ended the liability litigation, the additional sanction … barring [D's] participation in the damages trial was [excessive]."

★

Texas Commerce Bank v. New, 3 S.W.3d 515, 516 (Tex.1999). "We conclude that because unobjected-to hearsay is, as a matter of law, probative evidence, affidavits can be evidence for purposes of an unliquidated-damages hearing pursuant to Rule 243."

Holt Atherton Indus. v. Heine, 835 S.W.2d 80, 86 (Tex.1992). "After a default judgment is granted, the trial court must hear evidence of unliquidated damages. ... Therefore, when an appellate court sustains a no evidence point after an *uncontested* hearing on unliquidated damages following a no-answer default judgment, the appropriate disposition is a remand for a new trial on the issue of unliquidated damages."

Ingram Indus. v. U.S. Bolt Mfg., 121 S.W.3d 31, 37 (Tex.App.—Houston [1st Dist.] 2003, no pet.). "A trial court may award unliquidated damages based on affidavit testimony. [T]he trial court based the award of damages on its consideration of 'the pleadings and evidence on file.' The evidence on file contained [the affidavit of P's general manager, which] set out [P's] damages. The trial court thus considered [the] affidavit to be proof of [P's] damages. Therefore, the trial court satisfied Rule 243's hearing requirement without the need of holding an evidentiary hearing."

TRCP 244. ON SERVICE BY PUBLICATION

Where service has been made by publication, and no answer has been filed nor appearance entered within the prescribed time, the court shall appoint an attorney to defend the suit in behalf of the defendant, and judgment shall be rendered as in other cases; but, in every such case a statement of the evidence, approved and signed by the judge, shall be filed with the papers of the cause as a part of the record thereof. The court shall allow such attorney a reasonable fee for his services, to be taxed as part of the costs.

History of TRCP 244: Adopted eff. Sept. 1, 1941, by order of Oct. 29, 1940 (3 Tex.B.J. 561 [1940]). Source: TRCS art. 2158 (repealed).

See *Commentaries*, "MNT After Service by Publication," ch. 10-B, §10, p. 799; *O'Connor's Texas Forms*, FORM 10B:5.

ANNOTATIONS

Cahill v. Lyda, 826 S.W.2d 932, 933 (Tex.1992). "Rule 244 ... requires that a trial court appoint an attorney ad litem to represent defendants served with citation by publication who fail to file an answer or appear before the court. Rule 244 also requires that the attorney ad litem be paid a reasonable fee for his services, which is to be taxed as part of the costs. The attorney ad

litem must exhaust all remedies available to his client and, if necessary, represent his client's interest on appeal." *See also Atlantic Shippers of Tex., Inc. v. Jefferson Cty.*, 363 S.W.3d 276, 286-87 (Tex.App.—Beaumont 2012, no pet.).

Barnes v. Domain, 875 S.W.2d 32, 33 (Tex.App.—Houston [14th Dist.] 1994, no writ). "Neither the case law nor the language of [TRCP 244] reveals any indication that the burden is on the attorney to move the court to make such appointment."

TRCP 245. ASSIGNMENT OF CASES FOR TRIAL

The Court may set contested cases on written request of any party, or on the court's own motion, with reasonable notice of not less than forty-five days to the parties of a first setting for trial, or by agreement of the parties; provided, however, that when a case previously has been set for trial, the Court may reset said contested case to a later date on any reasonable notice to the parties or by agreement of the parties. Noncontested cases may be tried or disposed of at any time whether set or not, and may be set at any time for any other time.

A request for trial setting constitutes a representation that the requesting party reasonably and in good faith expects to be ready for trial by the date requested, but no additional representation concerning the completion of pretrial proceedings or of current readiness for trial shall be required in order to obtain a trial setting in a contested case.

History of TRCP 245: Amended eff. Sept. 1, 1990, by order of Apr. 24, 1990 (785-86 S.W.2d [Tex.Cases] lxv): First par., to harmonize a first-time nonjury setting with the time for jury demand, and to set a more realistic notice for trial; second par., to standardize the readiness requirement to obtain a trial setting. Amended eff. Apr. 1, 1984, by order of Dec. 5, 1983 (661-62 S.W.2d [Tex.Cases] lxxv): Deleted last sentence of former TRCP 245 and moved it to TRCP 306a. Amended eff. Jan. 1, 1976, by order of July 22, 1975 (525-26 S.W.2d [Tex.Cases] xlix): Rewritten to require notice of settings in county and district courts. Adopted eff. Sept. 1, 1941, by order of Oct. 29, 1940 (3 Tex.B.J. 561 [1940]). Source: FRCP 40.

See Tex. Const. art. 1, §19; *Commentaries*, "Trial setting," ch. 5-A, §3.3, p. 315; "Notice of the trial or dispositive hearing," ch. 7-A, §4.3, p. 596; "Motion for New Trial," ch. 10-B, p. 789.

ANNOTATIONS

Custom-Crete, Inc. v. K-Bar Servs., 82 S.W.3d 655, 659 (Tex.App.—San Antonio 2002, no pet.). "A trial court's failure to comply with Rule 245 in a contested case deprives a party of its constitutional right to be present at the hearing, to voice its objections in an appropriate manner, and results in a violation of funda-

---

⭐

---

mental due process. Failure to give the required notice constitutes lack of due process and is grounds for reversal."

TRCP 246. CLERK TO GIVE NOTICE OF SETTINGS

The clerk shall keep a record in his office of all cases set for trial, and it shall be his duty to inform any non-resident attorney of the date of setting of any case upon request by mail from such attorney, accompanied by a return envelope properly addressed and stamped. Failure of the clerk to furnish such information on proper request shall be sufficient ground for continuance or for a new trial when it appears to the court that such failure has prevented the attorney from preparing or presenting his claim or defense.

History of TRCP 246: Adopted eff. Sept. 1, 1941, by order of Oct. 29, 1940 (3 Tex.B.J. 561 [1940]). Source: New rule.

ANNOTATIONS

Bruneio v. Bruneio, 890 S.W.2d 150, 156 n.2 (Tex. App.—Corpus Christi 1994, no writ). TRCP 246 "merely provides an additional vehicle for notice to any of the various attorneys who may be working on the case and want direct notification…. Accordingly, Rule 246 [expands] the requirements of notice to include non-resident attorneys who would not otherwise be entitled to direct notification of the setting under [TRCP] 245 as the attorney in charge."

TRCP 247. TRIED WHEN SET

Every suit shall be tried when it is called, unless continued or postponed to a future day or placed at the end of the docket to be called again for trial in its regular order. No cause which has been set upon the trial docket of the court shall be taken from the trial docket for the date set except by agreement of the parties or for good cause upon motion and notice to the opposing party.

History of TRCP 247: Amended eff. Apr. 1, 1984, by order of Dec. 5, 1983 (661-62 S.W.2d [Tex.Cases] lxxv). Adopted eff. Sept. 1, 1941, by order of Oct. 29, 1940 (3 Tex.B.J. 561 [1940]). Source: TRCS art. 2162 (repealed): Added last sentence.

See *Commentaries*, "Motion for Continuance," ch. 5-D, p. 336.

TRCP 248. JURY CASES

When a jury has been demanded, questions of law, motions, exceptions to pleadings, and other unresolved pending matters shall, as far as practicable, be heard and determined by the court before the trial commences, and jurors shall be summoned to appear on the day so designated.

History of TRCP 248: Amended eff. Sept. 1, 1990, by order of Apr. 24, 1990 (785-86 S.W.2d [Tex.Cases] lxv): Adds words "and other unresolved pending matters" after "pleadings" and changes phrase "before the day designated for the trial" to "before the trial commences" to encourage resolution of matters prior to trial. Amended eff. Apr. 1, 1984, by order of Dec. 5, 1983 (661-62 S.W.2d [Tex.Cases] lxxv). Adopted eff. Sept. 1, 1941, by order of Oct. 29, 1940 (3 Tex.B.J. 561 [1940]). Source: TRCS art. 2164 (repealed).

See TRCP 166.

TRCP 249. CALL OF NON-JURY DOCKET

The non-jury docket shall be taken up at such times as not unnecessarily to interfere with the dispatch of business on the jury docket.

History of TRCP 249: Adopted eff. Sept. 1, 1941, by order of Oct. 29, 1940 (3 Tex.B.J. 561 [1940]). Source: TRCS art. 2165 (repealed).

TRCP 250. REPEALED

Repealed eff. Dec. 31, 1941, by order of Sept. 20, 1941 (4 Tex.B.J. 524 [1941]).

B. CONTINUANCE & CHANGE OF VENUE

TRCP 251. CONTINUANCE

No application for a continuance shall be heard before the defendant files his defense, nor shall any continuance be granted except for sufficient cause supported by affidavit, or by consent of the parties, or by operation of law.

History of TRCP 251: Adopted eff. Sept. 1, 1941, by order of Oct. 29, 1940 (3 Tex.B.J. 562 [1940]). Source: TRCS art. 2167 (repealed).

See *Commentaries*, "Motion for Continuance," ch. 5-D, p. 336; *O'Connor's Texas Forms*, FORMS 5D.

ANNOTATIONS

Tenneco Inc. v. Enterprise Prods., 925 S.W.2d 640, 647 (Tex.1996). "When a party contends that it has not had an adequate opportunity for discovery before a summary judgment hearing, it must file either an affidavit explaining the need for further discovery or a verified motion for continuance."

Villegas v. Carter, 711 S.W.2d 624, 626 (Tex.1986). "Generally, when movants fail to comply with [TRCP] 251's requirement that the motion for continuance be 'supported by affidavit,' we presume that the trial court did not abuse its discretion in denying the motion." *See also Garner v. Fidelity Bank*, 244 S.W.3d 855, 858-59 (Tex.App.—Dallas 2008, no pet.) (Rule 251 does not require party opposing motion for continuance to object to lack of verification; failure to object does not preclude party from raising objection for first time on appeal).

In re Guardianship of Cantu de Villareal, 330 S.W.3d 11, 26-27 (Tex.App.—Corpus Christi 2010, no pet.). "[A] trial court is not required to grant a motion for continuance just because a party is unable to be present at trial. When a continuance is sought because of the unavailability of a party, we examine [TRCP] 252." *See also* **Murphree v. Cooper**, No. 14-11-00416-CV (Tex.App.—Houston [14th Dist.] 2012, no pet.) (memo op.; 6-19-12).

TRCP 252. APPLICATION FOR CONTINUANCE

If the ground of such application be the want of testimony, the party applying therefor shall make affidavit that such testimony is material, showing the materiality thereof, and that he has used due diligence to procure such testimony, stating such diligence, and the cause of failure, if known; that such testimony cannot be procured from any other source; and, if it be for the absence of a witness, he shall state the name and residence of the witness, and what he expects to prove by him; and also state that the continuance is not sought for delay only, but that justice may be done; provided that, on a first application for a continuance, it shall not be necessary to show that the absent testimony cannot be procured from any other source.

The failure to obtain the deposition of any witness residing within 100 miles of the courthouse of the county in which the suit is pending shall not be regarded as want of diligence when diligence has been used to secure the personal attendance of such witness under the rules of law, unless by reason of age, infirmity or sickness, or official duty, the witness will be unable to attend the court, or unless such witness is about to leave, or has left, the State or county in which the suit is pending and will not probably be present at the trial.

History of TRCP 252: Amended eff. Apr. 1, 1984, by order of Dec. 5, 1983 (661-62 S.W.2d [Tex.Cases] lxxv): Added second paragraph to former rule. Adopted eff. Sept. 1, 1941, by order of Oct. 29, 1940 (3 Tex.B.J. 562 [1940]). Source: TRCS art. 2168 (repealed).

See *Commentaries*, "Motion for Continuance," ch. 5-D, p. 336; *O'Connor's Texas Forms*, FORMS 5D.

ANNOTATIONS

State v. Wood Oil Distrib., 751 S.W.2d 863, 865 (Tex.1988). "[T]he failure of a litigant to diligently utilize the rules of civil procedure for discovery purposes will not authorize the granting of a continuance."

Ramirez v. State, 973 S.W.2d 388, 391 (Tex. App.—El Paso 1998, no pet.). D's continuance motion "failed to specify the information and testimony he sought or why it was material. [D] did not state the

names of the witnesses from whom he sought testimony, nor did he state what he expected to prove from said witnesses."

Verkin v. Southwest Ctr. One, Ltd., 784 S.W.2d 92, 94 (Tex.App.—Houston [1st Dist.] 1989, writ denied). When a motion for continuance is (1) in substantial compliance with the rule, (2) verified, and (3) uncontroverted, the court "must accept the statements in the motion as true."

TRCP 253. ABSENCE OF COUNSEL AS GROUND FOR CONTINUANCE

Except as provided elsewhere in these rules, absence of counsel will not be good cause for a continuance or postponement of the cause when called for trial, except it be allowed in the discretion of the court, upon cause shown or upon matters within the knowledge or information of the judge to be stated on the record.

History of TRCP 253: Adopted eff. Sept. 1, 1941, by order of Oct. 29, 1940 (3 Tex.B.J. 562 [1940]). Source: Tex. Rules for Dist. & Cty. Cts. 49.

See *Commentaries*, "Motion for Continuance," ch. 5-D, p. 336; *O'Connor's Texas Forms*, FORM 5D:2.

ANNOTATIONS

Villegas v. Carter, 711 S.W.2d 624, 626 (Tex.1986). "[T]he trial court abused its discretion because the evidence shows that [P] was not negligent or at fault in causing his attorney's withdrawal. The court granted [P's] attorney's motion to voluntarily withdraw two days before trial—too short a time for [P] to find a new attorney and for that new attorney to investigate the case and prepare for trial."

Rehabilitation Facility v. Cooper, 962 S.W.2d 151, 155 (Tex.App.—Austin 1998, no pet.). "In general, absence of counsel is not good cause for a continuance. The court does have the discretion, however, to allow a continuance if good cause is shown. *At 156:* [A]nother attorney from the same law firm … had signed pleadings and conducted discovery in this case before trial. Nothing in the record suggests that attorney was incapable of rendering adequate representation." *See also* **Murphree v. Cooper**, No. 14-11-00416-CV (Tex.App.—Houston [14th Dist.] 2012, no pet.) (memo op.; 6-19-12).

TRCP 254. ATTENDANCE ON LEGISLATURE

In all civil actions, including matters of probate, and in all matters ancillary to such suits which require action by or the attendance of an attorney, including ap-

⎯⎯⎯⎯⎯⎯⎯⎯ ✦ ⎯⎯⎯⎯⎯⎯⎯⎯

peals but excluding temporary restraining orders, at any time within thirty days of a date when the legislature is to be in session, or at any time the legislature is in session, or when the legislature sits as a Constitutional Convention, it shall be mandatory that the court continue the cause if it shall appear to the court, by affidavit, that any party applying for continuance, or any attorney for any party to the cause, is a member of either branch of the legislature, and will be or is in actual attendance on a session of the same. If the member of the legislature is an attorney for a party to the cause, his affidavit shall contain a declaration that it is his intention to participate actively in the preparation and/or presentation of the case. Where a party to any cause, or an attorney for any party to a cause, is a member of the legislature, his affidavit need not be corroborated. On the filing of such affidavit, the court shall continue the cause until thirty days after adjournment of the legislature and the affidavit shall be proof of the necessity for the continuance, and the continuance shall be deemed one of right and shall not be charged against the movant upon any subsequent application for continuance.

The right to a continuance shall be mandatory, except only where the attorney was employed within ten days of the date the suit is set for trial, the right to continuance shall be discretionary.

History of TRCP 254: Amended eff. Jan. 1, 1981, by order of June 10, 1980 (599-600 S.W.2d [Tex.Cases] xlvi): Rule amended to conform with TRCS art. 2168a. Adopted eff. Sept. 1, 1941, by order of Oct. 29, 1940 (3 Tex.B.J. 562 [1940]). Source: TRCS art. 2168a (repealed).

See CPRC §30.003 for other requirements of a legislative continuance; *Commentaries*, "Motion for Continuance," ch. 5-D, p. 336; *O'Connor's Texas Forms*, FORM 5D:2.

ANNOTATIONS

In re Ford Motor Co., 165 S.W.3d 315, 319 (Tex. 2005). "'[A] legislative continuance is mandatory except in those cases in which the party opposing the continuance alleges that a substantial existing right will be defeated or abridged by delay.' When a party opposes a legislative continuance in such circumstances, the trial court must conduct a hearing on the allegations and deny the motion if the allegations are shown to be meritorious." *See also* ***Waites v. Sondock***, 561 S.W.2d 772, 776 (Tex.1977).

TRCP 255. CHANGE OF VENUE BY CONSENT

Upon the written consent of the parties filed with the papers of the cause, the court, by an order entered on the minutes, may transfer the same for trial to the court of any other county having jurisdiction of the subject matter of such suit.

History of TRCP 255: Adopted eff. Sept. 1, 1941, by order of Oct. 29, 1940 (3 Tex.B.J. 562 [1940]). Source: TRCS art. 2169 (repealed).

See CPRC §15.020; *Commentaries*, "Consent of the Parties," ch. 3-C, §4, p. 213; *O'Connor's Texas Forms*, FORMS 3C:10, 11.

ANNOTATIONS

Farris v. Ray, 895 S.W.2d 351, 352 (Tex.1995). "[A] signed written agreement filed in the record of the *transferee* court meets all the requirements of [TRCP] 11. Such an agreement, enforceable against the signatories under the terms of the rule, operates as an express waiver of any error there may have been in the initial transfer."

TRCP 256. REPEALED

Repealed eff. Sept. 1, 1941, by order of Mar. 31, 1941 (4 Tex.B.J. 173 [1941]).

TRCP 257. GRANTED ON MOTION

A change of venue may be granted in civil causes upon motion of either party, supported by his own affidavit and the affidavit of at least three credible persons, residents of the county in which the suit is pending, for any following cause:

(a) That there exists in the county where the suit is pending so great a prejudice against him that he cannot obtain a fair and impartial trial.

(b) That there is a combination against him instigated by influential persons, by reason of which he cannot expect a fair and impartial trial.

(c) That an impartial trial cannot be had in the county where the action is pending.

(d) For other sufficient cause to be determined by the court.

History of TRCP 257: Amended eff. Sept. 1, 1983, by order of June 15, 1983 (651-52 S.W.2d [Tex.Cases] xxxviii): To conform to S.B. 898, 68th Leg., 1983. Adopted eff. Sept. 1, 1941, by order of Oct. 29, 1940 (3 Tex.B.J. 563 [1940]). Source: TRCS art. 2170 (repealed).

See *Commentaries*, "Motion to Transfer—Challenging Venue," ch. 3-C, p. 203; *O'Connor's Texas Forms*, FORMS 3C:4, 8.

ANNOTATIONS

Acker v. Denton Publ'g, 937 S.W.2d 111, 118 (Tex. App.—Fort Worth 1996, no writ). "The inability to obtain a fair and impartial trial of a civil case may be grounds for a change of venue. A motion on those grounds must be supported by competent affidavits of the party seeking the transfer and three credible residents of the county where the suit is pending." *See also* ***Dorchester Gas Prod'g Co. v. Harlow Corp.***, 743 S.W.2d 243, 253 n.6 (Tex.App.—Amarillo 1987, no writ);

★

Tenneco, Inc. v. Salyer, 739 S.W.2d 448, 449 (Tex. App.—Corpus Christi 1987, orig. proceeding).

TRCP 258. SHALL BE GRANTED

Where such motion to transfer venue is duly made, it shall be granted, unless the credibility of those making such application, or their means of knowledge or the truth of the facts set out in the said application are attacked by the affidavit of a credible person; when thus attacked, the issue thus formed shall be tried by the judge; and the application either granted or refused. Reasonable discovery in support of, or in opposition to, the application shall be permitted, and such discovery as is relevant, including deposition testimony on file, may be attached to, or incorporated by reference in, the affidavit of a party, a witness, or an attorney who has knowledge of such discovery.

History of TRCP 258: Amended eff. Sept. 1, 1983, by order of June 15, 1983 (651-52 S.W.2d [Tex.Cases] xxxix): To conform to S.B. 898, 68th Leg., 1983. Adopted eff. Sept. 1, 1941, by order of Oct. 29, 1940 (3 Tex.B.J. 563 [1940]). Source: TRCS art. 2171 (repealed).

See *Commentaries*, "Motion to Transfer—Challenging Venue," ch. 3-C, p. 203.

ANNOTATIONS

City of Abilene v. Downs, 367 S.W.2d 153, 155 (Tex.1963). "Rule 258 by its terms is mandatorily operative. It provides the only means by which issue can be joined."

In re East Tex. Med. Ctr. Athens, 154 S.W.3d 933, 935 (Tex.App.—Tyler 2005, orig. proceeding). "A trial court can deny the motion to transfer if the movant does not comply with [TRCP] 257. If the motion is challenged as permitted by [TRCP] 258, the judge must try the issue. If the motion is not challenged in the manner provided by Rule 258, transfer is mandatory."

TRCP 259. TO WHAT COUNTY

If the motion under Rule 257 is granted, the cause shall be removed:

(a) If from a district court, to any county of proper venue in the same or an adjoining district;

(b) If from a county court, to any adjoining county of proper venue;

(c) If (a) or (b) are not applicable, to any county of proper venue;

(d) If a county of proper venue (other than the county of suit) cannot be found, then if from

(1) A district court, to any county in the same or an adjoining district or to any district where an impartial trial can be had;

(2) A county court, to any adjoining county or to any district where an impartial trial can be had;

but the parties may agree that venue shall be changed to some other county, and the order of the court shall conform to such agreement.

History of TRCP 259: Amended eff. Sept. 1, 1983, by order of June 15, 1983 (651-52 S.W.2d [Tex.Cases] xxxix): To conform to S.B. 898, 68th Leg., 1983. Adopted eff. Sept. 1, 1941, by order of Oct. 29, 1940 (3 Tex.B.J. 563 [1940]). Source: TRCS art. 2172 (repealed).

See *Commentaries*, "Motion to Transfer—Challenging Venue," ch. 3-C, p. 203.

ANNOTATIONS

Dorchester Gas Prod'g Co. v. Harlow Corp., 743 S.W.2d 243, 253 (Tex.App.—Amarillo 1987, no writ). "[W]hen the trial court determined that [P] could not obtain a fair and impartial trial in that county, the court had two options under Rule 259(d)—either to remove the case to any county in the same or an adjoining district or to any district where an impartial trial could be had."

TRCP 260. REPEALED

Repealed eff. Sept. 1, 1990, by order of Apr. 24, 1990 (785-86 S.W.2d [Tex.Cases] lxvi): No longer needed.

TRCP 261. TRANSCRIPT ON CHANGE

When a change of venue has been granted, the clerk shall immediately make out a correct transcript of all the orders made in said cause, certifying thereto officially under the seal of the court, and send the same, with the original papers in the cause, to the clerk of the court to which the venue has been changed.

History of TRCP 261: Adopted eff. Sept. 1, 1941, by order of Oct. 29, 1940 (3 Tex.B.J. 563 [1940]). Source: TRCS art. 2174 (repealed).

C. THE TRIAL

TRCP 262. TRIAL BY THE COURT

The rules governing the trial of causes before a jury shall govern in trials by the court in so far as applicable.

History of TRCP 262: Adopted eff. Sept. 1, 1941, by order of Oct. 29, 1940 (3 Tex.B.J. 563 [1940]). Source: TRCS art. 2176 (repealed).

ANNOTATIONS

Qantel Bus. v. Custom Controls Co., 761 S.W.2d 302, 304-05 (Tex.1988). "When a plaintiff rests, he indicates that he does not desire to put on further evidence, except by rebuttal testimony, and that he has fully developed his case." In a nonjury case, the court is presumed to have ruled on the sufficiency of the evidence when it grants judgment for the defendant after the plaintiff rests.

★

TRCP 263. AGREED CASE

Parties may submit matters in controversy to the court upon an agreed statement of facts filed with the clerk, upon which judgment shall be rendered as in other cases; and such agreed statement signed and certified by the court to be correct and the judgment rendered thereon shall constitute the record of the cause.

History of TRCP 263: Adopted eff. Sept. 1, 1941, by order of Oct. 29, 1940 (3 Tex.B.J. 563 [1940]). Source: TRCS art. 2177 (repealed).

See *Commentaries*, "Motion for Judgment on Agreed Statement of Facts," ch. 7-E, p. 647; *O'Connor's Texas Forms*, FORMS 7E.

ANNOTATIONS

Taylor v. First Cmty. Credit Un., 316 S.W.3d 863, 866 (Tex.App.—Houston [14th Dist.] 2010, no pet.). "Strict compliance with [TRCP 263] is not required. When ... the record indicates that the trial court heard the case on stipulated facts, a reviewing court may treat the case as one involving an agreed statement of facts under Rule 263."

State Farm Lloyds v. Kessler, 932 S.W.2d 732, 735 (Tex.App.—Fort Worth 1996, writ denied). "An agreed statement of facts under rule 263 is similar to a special verdict; it is the parties' request for judgment under the applicable law. The only issue on appeal is whether the trial court properly applied the law to the agreed facts. The appellate court is limited to those facts unless other facts are necessarily implied from the express facts in the statement. In an appeal of an 'agreed' case, there are no presumed findings in favor of the judgment, and the pleadings are immaterial." *See also Ultrasound Tech. Servs. v. Dallas Cent. Appr. Dist.*, 357 S.W.3d 174, 176 (Tex.App.—Dallas 2011, pet. denied).

City of Galveston v. Giles, 902 S.W.2d 167, 170 n.2 (Tex.App.—Houston [1st Dist.] 1995, no writ). "Findings of fact have no place in the trial of an agreed case. Once the parties stipulate to all the facts, the court may not make additional fact findings."

TRCP 264. VIDEOTAPE TRIAL

By agreement of the parties, the trial court may allow that all testimony and such other evidence as may be appropriate be presented at trial by videotape. The expenses of such videotape recordings shall be taxed as costs. If any party withdraws agreement to a videotape trial, the videotape costs that have accrued will be taxed against the party withdrawing from the agreement.

History of TRCP 264: Adopted eff. Jan. 1, 1988, by order of July 15, 1987 (733-34 S.W.2d [Tex.Cases] lxvii). Former TRCP 264 repealed eff. Jan. 1, 1988, by order of July 15, 1987 (733-34 S.W.2d [Tex.Cases] lxvii). Source: New rule.

TRCP 265. ORDER OF PROCEEDINGS ON TRIAL BY JURY

The trial of cases before a jury shall proceed in the following order unless the court should, for good cause stated in the record, otherwise direct:

(a) The party upon whom rests the burden of proof on the whole case shall state to the jury briefly the nature of his claim or defense and what said party expects to prove and the relief sought. Immediately thereafter, the adverse party may make a similar statement, and intervenors and other parties will be accorded similar rights in the order determined by the court.

(b) The party upon whom rests the burden of proof on the whole case shall then introduce his evidence.

(c) The adverse party shall briefly state the nature of his claim or defense and what said party expects to prove and the relief sought unless he has already done so.

(d) He shall then introduce his evidence.

(e) The intervenor and other parties shall make their statement, unless they have already done so, and shall introduce their evidence.

(f) The parties shall then be confined to rebutting testimony on each side.

(g) But one counsel on each side shall examine and cross-examine the same witness, except on leave granted.

History of TRCP 265: Amended eff. Jan. 1, 1978, by order of July 11, 1977 (553-54 S.W.2d [Tex.Cases] xlviii): Eliminated provisions in (a), (c), and (e) about reading of pleadings. Amended eff. Jan. 1, 1967, by order of July 20, 1966 (401-02 S.W.2d [Tex.Cases] xlii): Rewrote rule to permit each party to either read his pleading or state the nature of his claim/defense to the jury, but not both. Amended eff. Sept. 1, 1941, by order of Mar. 31, 1941 (4 Tex.B.J. 173 [1941]): Added (j) from Tex. Rules for Dist. & Cty. Cts. 43. Adopted eff. Sept. 1, 1941, by order of Oct. 29, 1940 (3 Tex.B.J. 563 [1940]). Source: TRCS art. 2180 (repealed).

TRCP 266. OPEN & CLOSE— ADMISSION

Except as provided in Rule 269 the plaintiff shall have the right to open and conclude both in adducing his evidence and in the argument, unless the burden of proof on the whole case under the pleadings rests upon the defendant, or unless the defendant or all of the defendants, if there should be more than one, shall, after the issues of fact are settled and before the trial commences, admit that the plaintiff is entitled to recover as set forth in the petition, except so far as he may be defeated, in whole or in part, by the allegations of the answer constituting a good defense, which may be established on the trial; which admission shall be entered of record, whereupon the defendant, or the defendants, if more than one, shall have the right to open and conclude in adducing the evidence and in the argument of the cause. The admission shall not serve to admit any allegation which is inconsistent with such defense, which defense shall be one that defendant has the burden of establishing, as for example, and without excluding other defenses: accord and satisfaction, adverse possession, arbitration and award, contributory negligence, discharge in bankruptcy, duress, estoppel, failure of consideration, fraud, release, res judicata, statute of frauds, statute of limitations, waiver, and the like.

History of TRCP 266: Adopted eff. Sept. 1, 1941, by order of Oct. 29, 1940 (3 Tex.B.J. 564 [1940]). Source: Tex. Rules for Dist. & Cty. Cts. 31.

See *Commentaries*, "Opening Statement," ch. 8-B, p. 696; "Final Argument," ch. 8-J, p. 748; *O'Connor's Texas Forms*, FORMS 8B, 8J.

ANNOTATIONS

4M Linen & Unif. Sup. v. W.P. Ballard & Co., 793 S.W.2d 320, 324 (Tex.App.—Houston [1st Dist.] 1990, writ denied). "Rule 266 ... provides that the plaintiff has the right to open and close argument. There are two exceptions.... First, a defendant has the right to open and close if the burden of proof for the entire case under the pleadings is on defendant. Second, a defendant has the right to open and close if, before trial begins, defendant admits that plaintiff is entitled to recover, subject to proof of defensive allegations...."

TRCP 267. WITNESSES PLACED UNDER RULE

a. At the request of either party, in a civil case, the witnesses on both sides shall be sworn and removed out of the courtroom to some place where they cannot hear the testimony as delivered by any other witness in the cause. This is termed placing witnesses under the rule.

b. This rule does not authorize exclusion of (1) a party who is a natural person or the spouse of such natural person, or (2) an officer or employee of a party that is not a natural person and who is designated as its representative by its attorney, or (3) a person whose presence is shown by a party to be essential to the presentation of the cause.

c. If any party be absent, the court in its discretion may exempt from the rule a representative of such party.

d. Witnesses, when placed under Rule 614 of the Texas Rules of Civil Evidence, shall be instructed by the court that they are not to converse with each other or with any other person about the case other than the attorneys in the case, except by permission of the court, and that they are not to read any report of or comment upon the testimony in the case while under the rule.

e. Any witness or other person violating such instructions may be punished for contempt of court.

History of TRCP 267: Amended eff. Jan. 1, 1988, by order of July 15, 1987 (733-34 S.W.2d [Tex.Cases] lxvii). Adopted eff. Sept. 1, 1941, by order of Oct. 29, 1940 (3 Tex.B.J. 564 [1940]). Source: Code Crim. Proc. arts. 644, 647 (repealed, now Code Crim. Proc. arts. 36.03, 36.06).

See TRE 614; *Commentaries*, "Invoking 'the Rule'," ch. 8-C, §3, p. 698.

ANNOTATIONS

Drilex Sys. v. Flores, 1 S.W.3d 112, 118-19 (Tex. 1999). "Although an expert witness may *typically* be found exempt under the essential presence exception, experts are not *automatically* exempt. Instead, [TRE] 614 and [TRCP] 267 vest in trial judges broad discretion to determine whether a witness is essential. *At 120:* We acknowledge that the court never expressly placed [D's expert] under [TRE 614] and never instructed him not to discuss the case with others. However, a court may, in its discretion, exclude the testimony of a prospective witness who technically violates [TRE 614] even though the witness was never actually placed under [TRE 614]."

TRCP 268. MOTION FOR INSTRUCTED VERDICT

A motion for directed verdict shall state the specific grounds therefor.

History of TRCP 268: Adopted eff. Sept. 1, 1941, by order of Oct. 29, 1940 (3 Tex.B.J. 564 [1940]). Source: Last sentence of FRCP 50(a), unchanged.

See *Commentaries*, "Motion for Directed Verdict," ch. 8-G, p. 725; *O'Connor's Texas Forms*, FORMS 8G.

ANNOTATIONS

City of Keller v. Wilson, 168 S.W.3d 802, 827 (Tex. 2005). "As both the inclusive and exclusive standards for the scope of legal-sufficiency review have a long history in Texas, as both have been used in other contexts to review matter-of-law motions, as the federal courts have decided the differences between the two are more semantic than real, and as both—properly applied—must arrive at the same result, we see no compelling reason to choose among them. [¶] The key qualifier, of course, is 'properly applied.' The final test for legal sufficiency must always be whether the evidence at trial would enable reasonable and fair-minded people to reach the verdict under review. Whether a reviewing court begins by considering all the evidence or only the evidence supporting the verdict, legal-suffi-ciency review [of the denial of a directed verdict] must credit favorable evidence if reasonable jurors could, and disregard contrary evidence unless reasonable jurors could not." *See also* **Mauricio v. Castro**, 287 S.W.3d 476, 479 (Tex.App.—Dallas 2009, no pet.).

S.V. v. R.V., 933 S.W.2d 1, 8 (Tex.1996). "In reviewing a directed verdict, we examine the evidence in the light most favorable to the person suffering an adverse judgment."

Szczepanik v. First S. Trust Co., 883 S.W.2d 648, 649 (Tex.1994). "In reviewing ... an instructed verdict, we must determine whether there is any evidence of probative force to raise a fact issue on the material questions presented. ... If there is any conflicting evidence of probative value on any theory of recovery, an instructed verdict is improper...."

TRCP 269. ARGUMENT

(a) After the evidence is concluded and the charge is read, the parties may argue the case to the jury. The party having the burden of proof on the whole case, or on all matters which are submitted by the charge, shall be entitled to open and conclude the argument; where there are several parties having separate claims or defenses, the court shall prescribe the order of argument between them.

(b) In all arguments, and especially in arguments on the trial of the case, the counsel opening shall present his whole case as he relies on it, both of law and facts, and shall be heard in the concluding argument only in reply to the counsel on the other side.

(c) Counsel for an intervenor shall occupy the position in the argument assigned by the court according to the nature of the claim.

(d) Arguments on questions of law shall be addressed to the court, and counsel should state the substance of the authorities referred to without reading more from books than may be necessary to verify the statement. On a question on motions, exceptions to the evidence, and other incidental matters, the counsel will be allowed only such argument as may be necessary to present clearly the question raised, and refer to authorities on it, unless further discussion is invited by the court.

(e) Arguments on the facts should be addressed to the jury, when one is impaneled in a case that is being tried, under the supervision of the court. Counsel shall

be required to confine the argument strictly to the evidence and to the arguments of opposing counsel. Mere personal criticism by counsel upon each other shall be avoided, and when indulged in shall be promptly corrected as a contempt of court.

(f) Side-bar remarks, and remarks by counsel of one side, not addressed to the court, while the counsel on the other side is examining a witness or arguing any question to the court, or addressing the jury, will be rigidly repressed by the court.

(g) The court will not be required to wait for objections to be made when the rules as to arguments are violated; but should they not be noticed and corrected by the court, opposing counsel may ask leave of the court to rise and present his point of objection. But the court shall protect counsel from any unnecessary interruption made on frivolous and unimportant grounds.

(h) It shall be the duty of every counsel to address the court from his place at the bar, and in addressing the court to rise to his feet; and while engaged in the trial of a case, he shall remain at his place in the bar.

History of TRCP 269: Amended eff. Sept. 1, 1990, by order of Apr. 24, 1990 (785-86 S.W.2d [Tex.Cases] lxvi): Deleted words "whether upon special issues or otherwise" in (a). Amended eff. Sept. 1, 1941, by order of Mar. 31, 1941 (4 Tex.B.J. 173 [1941]): Added (b)-(h), from Tex. Rules for Dist. & Cty. Cts. 36-42. Adopted eff. Sept. 1, 1941, by order of Oct. 29, 1940 (3 Tex.B.J. 564 [1940]). Source of TRCP 269(a): TRCS art. 2183 (repealed).

See *Commentaries*, "Final Argument," ch. 8-J, p. 748; *O'Connor's Texas Forms*, FORMS 8J.

ANNOTATIONS

Living Ctrs. v. Peñalver, 256 S.W.3d 678, 680-81 (Tex.2008). "Error as to improper jury argument must ordinarily be preserved by a timely objection which is overruled. The complaining party must not have invited or provoked the improper argument. Typically, retraction of the argument or instruction from the court can cure any probable harm, but in rare instances the probable harm or prejudice cannot be cured. In such instances the argument is incurable and complaint about the argument may be made even though objection was not timely made. To prevail on a claim that improper argument was incurable, the complaining party generally must show that the argument by its nature, degree, and extent constituted such error that an instruction from the court or retraction of the argument could not remove its effects. [¶] [J]ury argument that strikes at the appearance of and the actual impartiality, equality, and fairness of justice rendered by courts is incurably harmful not only because of its harm to the litigants involved, but also because of its capacity to damage the

─────────────── ★ ───────────────

judicial system. Such argument is not subject to the general harmless error analysis." *See also Standard Fire Ins. v. Reese*, 584 S.W.2d 835, 839 (Tex. 1979); *Richmond Condos. v. Skipworth Commercial Plumbing, Inc.*, 245 S.W.3d 646, 667-68 (Tex.App.—Fort Worth 2008, pet. denied).

Jones v. Republic Waste Servs., 236 S.W.3d 390, 401 (Tex.App.—Houston [1st Dist.] 2007, pet. denied). "To obtain reversal, appellants must first prove 'an error' that was not 'invited or provoked.' Counsel must confine argument 'strictly to the evidence and to the arguments of opposing counsel.' Criticism, censure, or abuse of counsel is not permitted. Appeals to passion and prejudice are improper, as are calls to punish a litigant for the acts of counsel." *See also Popcap Games, Inc. v. MumboJumbo, LLC*, 350 S.W.3d 699, 721 (Tex. App.—Dallas 2011, pet. denied).

Sanchez v. Espinoza, 60 S.W.3d 392, 395 (Tex. App.—Amarillo 2001, pet. denied). In the argument, counsel "may discuss the 'environments' or circumstances of the case, the reasonableness or unreasonableness of the evidence, and the probative effect (or lack thereof) of the evidence. So too does he have the leeway to 'present his case as to make the law contained in the charge applicable to the facts of the case.' This leeway also includes the opportunity to encourage the jury to weigh, evaluate, and test the evidence before it."

TRCP 270. ADDITIONAL TESTIMONY

When it clearly appears to be necessary to the due administration of justice, the court may permit additional evidence to be offered at any time; provided that in a jury case no evidence on a controversial matter shall be received after the verdict of the jury.

History of TRCP 270: Amended eff. Apr. 1, 1984, by order of Dec. 5, 1983 (661-62 S.W.2d [Tex.Cases] lxxvi). Adopted eff. Sept. 1, 1941, by order of Oct. 29, 1940 (3 Tex.B.J. 564 [1940]). Source: TRCS art. 2181 (repealed).

See *Commentaries*, "Motion to Reopen for Additional Evidence," ch. 8-H, p. 729; *O'Connor's Texas Forms*, FORM 8H:1.

ANNOTATIONS

Moore v. Jet Stream Invs., 315 S.W.3d 195, 201 (Tex.App.—Texarkana 2010, pet. denied). "A trial court's discretion to permit additional evidence 'should be exercised liberally to allow both parties to fully present their case.' ... In deciding whether to permit additional evidence, a trial court may consider (1) whether the movant showed due diligence in obtaining the evidence; (2) whether the additional evi-

dence is decisive; (3) whether reopening the evidence will cause undue delay; and (4) whether reopening the evidence will cause injustice." *See also Naguib v. Naguib*, 137 S.W.3d 367, 372-73 (Tex.App.—Dallas 2004, pet. denied); *Lopez v. Lopez*, 55 S.W.3d 194, 201 (Tex.App.—Corpus Christi 2001, no pet.).

D. CHARGE TO THE JURY

TRCP 271. CHARGE TO THE JURY

Unless expressly waived by the parties, the trial court shall prepare and in open court deliver a written charge to the jury.

History of TRCP 271: Amended eff. Jan. 1, 1988, by order of July 15, 1987 (733-34 S.W.2d [Tex.Cases] lxviii). Amended eff. Sept. 1, 1973, by order of May 25, 1973 (493-94 S.W.2d [Tex.Cases] xxiii): Deleted last two sentences of original rule. Adopted eff. Sept. 1, 1941, by order of Oct. 29, 1940 (3 Tex.B.J. 565 [1940]). Source: TRCS art. 2184 (repealed).

See *Commentaries*, "The Charge," ch. 8-I, p. 731.

TRCP 272. REQUISITES

The charge shall be in writing, signed by the court, and filed with the clerk, and shall be a part of the record of the cause. It shall be submitted to the respective parties or their attorneys for their inspection, and a reasonable time given them in which to examine and present objections thereto outside the presence of the jury, which objections shall in every instance be presented to the court in writing, or be dictated to the court reporter in the presence of the court and opposing counsel, before the charge is read to the jury. All objections not so presented shall be considered as waived. The court shall announce its rulings thereon before reading the charge to the jury and shall endorse the rulings on the objections if written or dictate same to the court reporter in the presence of counsel. Objections to the charge and the court's rulings thereon may be included as a part of any transcript or statement of facts on appeal and, when so included in either, shall constitute a sufficient bill of exception to the rulings of the court thereon. It shall be presumed, unless otherwise noted in the record, that the party making such objections presented the same at the proper time and excepted to the ruling thereon.

History of TRCP 272: Amended eff. Jan. 1, 1988, by order of July 15, 1987 (733-34 S.W.2d [Tex.Cases] lxviii). Amended eff. Jan. 1, 1976, by order of July 22, 1975 (525-26 S.W.2d [Tex.Cases] xlix): Rule rewritten. Amended eff. Sept. 1, 1973, by order of May 25, 1973 (493-94 S.W.2d [Tex.Cases] xxiii): Deleted last sentence of original rule. Amended eff. Dec. 31, 1941, by order of Sept. 20, 1941 (4 Tex.B.J. 527 [1941]). Adopted eff. Sept. 1, 1941, by order of Oct. 29, 1940 (3 Tex.B.J. 565 [1940]). Source: TRCS art. 2185 (repealed).

See *Commentaries*, "The Charge," ch. 8-I, p. 731; *O'Connor's Texas Forms*, FORMS 8I.

⭐

Cruz v. Andrews Restoration, Inc., 364 S.W.3d 817, 829 (Tex.2012). "'There should be but one test for determining if a party has preserved error in the jury charge, and that is whether the party made the trial court aware of the complaint, timely and plainly, and obtained a ruling.' *At 830:* A proposed charge, whether drafted by a party or by the court, may misalign the parties; misstate the burden of proof; leave out essential elements; or omit a defense, cause of action, or (as here) a line for attorney's fees. Our procedural rules require the lawyers to tell the court about such errors before the charge is formally submitted to a jury. Failing to do so squanders judicial resources, decreases the accuracy of trial court judgments and wastes time the judge, jurors, lawyers, and parties have devoted to the case. *At 831:* Here, the parties had ample time to review the draft charge and point out discrepancies to the trial court. The charge that was ultimately submitted to the jury was 40 pages long and contained 32 questions, most of which had multiple subparts. [P] can complain on appeal only if it made the trial court aware, timely and plainly, of the purported problem and obtained a ruling. Filing a pretrial charge that includes a question containing [a] subpart [that was omitted by the court], when no other part of the record reflects a discussion of the issue or objection to the question ultimately submitted, does not sufficiently alert the trial court to the issue." *See also State Dept. of Hwys. & Pub. Transp. v. Payne*, 838 S.W.2d 235, 241 (Tex.1992).

State Farm Life Ins. v. Beaston, 907 S.W.2d 430, 440 (Tex.1995). "The failure to object to the conditional submission of the damages issue waives error as to form and substance of the submission."

City of Brownsville v. Alvarado, 897 S.W.2d 750, 752 (Tex.1995). "Submission of an improper jury question can be harmless error if the jury's answers to other questions render the improper question immaterial. A jury question is considered immaterial when its answer can be found elsewhere in the verdict or when its answer cannot alter the effect of the verdict."

TRCP 273. JURY SUBMISSIONS

Either party may present to the court and request written questions, definitions, and instructions to be given to the jury; and the court may give them or a part thereof, or may refuse to give them, as may be proper. Such requests shall be prepared and presented to the court and submitted to opposing counsel for examination and objection within a reasonable time after the charge is given to the parties or their attorneys for examination. A request by either party for any questions, definitions, or instructions shall be made separate and apart from such party's objections to the court's charge.

History of TRCP 273: Amended eff. Jan. 1, 1988, by order of July 15, 1987 (733-34 S.W.2d [Tex.Cases] lxviii). Amended eff. Mar. 1, 1950, by order of Oct. 12, 1949 (12 Tex.B.J. 534 [1950]). Adopted eff. Sept. 1, 1941, by order of Oct. 29, 1940 (3 Tex.B.J. 565 [1940]). Source: TRCS art. 2186 (repealed).

See *Commentaries*, "The Charge," ch. 8-I, p. 731; *O'Connor's Texas Forms*, FORMS 8I.

Cruz v. Andrews Restoration, Inc., 364 S.W.3d 817, 831 (Tex.2012). "A charge filed before trial begins rarely accounts fully for the inevitable developments during trial. For these reasons, [TRCP 273 requires] that requests be prepared and presented to the court 'within a reasonable time *after* the charge is given to the parties or their attorneys for examination.' Notwithstanding our rules, we have held that a party may rely on a pretrial charge as long as the record shows that the trial court knew of the written request and refused to submit it."

Galveston Cty. Fair & Rodeo, Inc. v. Glover, 940 S.W.2d 585, 586-87 (Tex.1996). "The court of appeals ... held that [D] 'did not separately request in writing any definitions or instructions on' 'what constitutes wrongful disqualification' as required by Rule 273.... We disagree. [D's] written request was separate from its oral objection. This request fully complied with Rule 273."

Lester v. Logan, 907 S.W.2d 452, 453 (Tex.1995). Disapproved of the court of appeals' opinion that held a request on one sheet of paper that included five related matters—one question, two instructions, and two definitions—was improper.

Alaniz v. Jones & Neuse, Inc., 907 S.W.2d 450, 451 (Tex.1995). TRCP 273 "does not prohibit including the request in a complete charge as long as it is not obscured."

TRCP 274. OBJECTIONS & REQUESTS

A party objecting to a charge must point out distinctly the objectionable matter and the grounds of the objection. Any complaint as to a question, definition, or instruction, on account of any defect, omission, or fault in pleading, is waived unless specifically included in the objections. When the complaining party's objection, or requested question, definition, or instruction is, in the opinion of the appellate court, obscured or concealed by voluminous unfounded objections, minute differentiations or numerous unnecessary requests, such objection or request shall be untenable. No objection to one part of the charge may be adopted and applied to any other part of the charge by reference only.

History of TRCP 274: Amended eff. Jan. 1, 1988, by order of July 15, 1987 (733-34 S.W.2d [Tex.Cases] lxix). Amended eff. Dec. 31, 1941, by order of Sept. 20, 1941 (4 Tex.B.J. 528 [1941]). Adopted eff. Sept. 1, 1941, by order of Oct. 29, 1940 (3 Tex.B.J. 566 [1940]). Source: New rule.

See *Commentaries*, "The Charge," ch. 8-I, p. 731.

ANNOTATIONS

Holubec v. Brandenberger, 111 S.W.3d 32, 39 (Tex. 2003). "[Ds] plainly sought the submission of their statutory defense. Because the question actually submitted was defective, however, [Ds] did not have to submit their own substantially correct question. [Ds'] objection was sufficient to preserve error." *See also Moss v. Waste Mgmt.*, 305 S.W.3d 76, 80 (Tex.App.—Houston [1st Dist.] 2009, pet. denied).

Harris Cty. v. Smith, 96 S.W.3d 230, 236 (Tex. 2002). If an element of damages in a broad-form submission is not supported by evidence, the party must object and ask the court to either (1) not include that element in the broad-form damages question or (2) submit the elements separately.

Universal Servs. v. Ung, 904 S.W.2d 638, 640 (Tex. 1995). A party cannot complain on appeal that the trial court did not submit an instruction or definition with the correct cluster if the party did not request it as part of that cluster.

General Chem. Corp. v. De La Lastra, 852 S.W.2d 916, 920 (Tex.1993). "[D] requested the very issues that it now seeks to avoid. Parties may not invite error by requesting an issue and then objecting to its submission."

Cleveland Reg'l Med. Ctr., L.P. v. Celtic Props., L.C., 323 S.W.3d 322, 339-40 (Tex.App.—Beaumont 2010, pet. denied). "To preserve error, the complaining party must specifically object, clearly identify the error, and explain the grounds for the objection. ... Where a party's objections are too general and too profuse it cannot be said that the trial court was fully cognizant of the grounds of the objection and deliberately chose to overrule it. Thus, where a party's objection is obscured or concealed among voluminous, general, unfounded objections, it will not preserve error. *At 342:* Generally, a request for a different instruction is not a substitute for an objection and does not preserve error." *See also Con-*

tinental Cas. Co. v. Baker, 355 S.W.3d 375, 383 (Tex. App.—Houston [1st Dist.] 2011, no pet.) (objection to wording of definition adequately preserved error); *Reliant Energy Servs. v. Cotton Valley Compression, L.L.C.*, 336 S.W.3d 764, 785 n.23 (Tex.App.—Houston [1st Dist.] 2011, no pet.) (general objection that instruction was "not raised by evidence" was not specific enough complaint).

C.M. Asfahl Agency v. Tensor, Inc., 135 S.W.3d 768, 795 (Tex.App.—Houston [1st Dist.] 2004, no pet.). "Rule 274's prohibition against adopting by reference has generally been interpreted as prohibiting one party from incorporating by reference its own objections to another portion of the charge. Yet, nothing in the rule limits its application to that context. *At 796:* [Ds] did not preserve any error premised on erroneously submitting question ... to the jury merely by 'joining' the six substantive objections lodged by [co-D]. Instead, [Ds] were required to present their own objections."

TRCP 275. CHARGE READ BEFORE ARGUMENT

Before the argument is begun, the trial court shall read the charge to the jury in the precise words in which it was written, including all questions, definitions, and instructions which the court may give.

History of TRCP 275: Amended eff. Jan. 1, 1988, by order of July 15, 1987 (733-34 S.W.2d [Tex.Cases] lxix). Adopted eff. Sept. 1, 1941, by order of Oct. 29, 1940 (3 Tex.B.J. 566 [1940]). Source: TRCS art. 2187 (repealed).

See *Commentaries*, "The Charge," ch. 8-I, p. 731.

ANNOTATIONS

Board of Regents v. S&G Constr. Co., 529 S.W.2d 90, 98 (Tex.App.—Austin 1975, writ ref'd n.r.e.), *overruled on other grounds, Federal Sign v. Texas S. Univ.*, 951 S.W.2d 401 (Tex.1997). A trial court does not violate TRCP 275 by amending the written charge to correct errors after oral argument.

TRCP 276. REFUSAL OR MODIFICATION

When an instruction, question, or definition is requested and the provisions of the law have been complied with and the trial judge refuses the same, the judge shall endorse thereon "Refused," and sign the same officially. If the trial judge modifies the same the judge shall endorse thereon "Modified as follows: (stating in what particular the judge has modified the same) and given, and exception allowed" and sign the same officially. Such refused or modified instruction, question, or definition, when so endorsed shall consti-

TRCP 274

tute a bill of exceptions, and it shall be conclusively presumed that the party asking the same presented it at the proper time, excepted to its refusal or modification, and that all the requirements of law have been observed, and such procedure shall entitle the party requesting the same to have the action of the trial judge thereon reviewed without preparing a formal bill of exceptions.

History of TRCP 276: Amended eff. Jan. 1, 1988, by order of July 15, 1987 (733-34 S.W.2d [Tex.Cases] lxix). Adopted eff. Sept. 1, 1941, by order of Oct. 29, 1940 (3 Tex.B.J. 566 [1940]). Source: TRCS art. 2188 (repealed).

See *Commentaries*, "The Charge," ch. 8-I, p. 731.

ANNOTATIONS

Dallas Mkt. Ctr. Dev. Co. v. Liedeker, 958 S.W.2d 382, 386-87 (Tex.1997), *overruled on other grounds*, ***Torrington Co. v. Stutzman***, 46 S.W.3d 829 (Tex. 2000). Although Rule 276 requires the trial court to endorse refused requests "Refused" and sign them officially, that is not the only way to preserve error. The court can state on the record that they are refused. *See also* ***City of Lufkin v. AKJ Props., Inc.***, No. 06-12-00005-CV (Tex.App.—Texarkana 2012, no pet.) (memo op.; 6-26-12).

TRCP 277. SUBMISSION TO THE JURY

In all jury cases the court shall, whenever feasible, submit the cause upon broad-form questions. The court shall submit such instructions and definitions as shall be proper to enable the jury to render a verdict.

Inferential rebuttal questions shall not be submitted in the charge. The placing of the burden of proof may be accomplished by instructions rather than by inclusion in the question.

In any cause in which the jury is required to apportion the loss among the parties the court shall submit a question or questions inquiring what percentage, if any, of the negligence or causation, as the case may be, that caused the occurrence or injury in question is attributable to each of the persons found to have been culpable. The court shall also instruct the jury to answer the damage question or questions without any reduction because of the percentage of negligence or causation, if any, of the person injured. The court may predicate the damage question or questions upon affirmative findings of liability.

The court may submit a question disjunctively when it is apparent from the evidence that one or the other of the conditions or facts inquired about necessarily exists.

The court shall not in its charge comment directly on the weight of the evidence or advise the jury of the effect of their answers, but the court's charge shall not be objectionable on the ground that it incidentally constitutes a comment on the weight of the evidence or advises the jury of the effect of their answers when it is properly a part of an instruction or definition.

History of TRCP 277: Amended eff. Jan. 1, 1988, by order July 15, 1987 (733-34 S.W.2d [Tex.Cases] lxx): Amendment to par. 1 will unify the practice of submitting broad-form questions to the jury in the form approved by *Lemos v. Montez*, 680 S.W.2d 798 (Tex.1984); amendment to par. 3 includes a textual change and recognizes that damage issues may be predicated on affirmative-liability findings. Amended eff. Apr. 1, 1984, by order Dec. 5, 1983 (661-62 S.W.2d [Tex.Cases] lxxvi). Amended eff. Sept. 1, 1973, by order of May 25, 1973 (493-94 S.W.2d [Tex.Cases] xxiv): Inserted words "controlling the disposition of the case that are" in par. 1; deleted provisions of the former rule requiring issues to be submitted distinctly and separately, in the affirmative, and in plain and simple language; rewrote provision concerning placing the burden of proof; added first three sentences of par. 2 and all of pars. 4, 5, and 7 were added; deleted last sentence of original rule; and a number of minor textual changes were made. Amended eff. Sept. 1, 1941, by order of Mar. 31, 1941 (4 Tex.B.J. 173 [1941]). Adopted eff. Sept. 1, 1941, by order of Oct. 29, 1940 (3 Tex.B.J. 566 [1940]). Source: TRCS art. 2189 (repealed).

See *Commentaries*, "The Charge," ch. 8-I, p. 731.

ANNOTATIONS

Bed, Bath & Beyond, Inc. v. Urista, 211 S.W.3d 753, 757 (Tex.2006). "When, as here, the broad-form questions submitted a single liability theory (negligence) to the jury, *Casteel*'s multiple-liability-theory analysis does not apply. Moreover, when a defensive theory is submitted through an inferential rebuttal instruction, *Casteel*'s solution of departing from broad-form submission and instead employing granulated submission cannot apply. Unlike alternate theories of liability and damage elements, inferential rebuttal issues cannot be submitted in the jury charge as separate questions and instead must be presented through jury instructions. Therefore, although harm can be presumed when meaningful appellate review is precluded because valid and invalid liability theories or damage elements are commingled, we are not persuaded that harm must likewise be presumed when proper jury questions are submitted along with improper inferential rebuttal instructions." *See also* ***Thota v. Young***, 366 S.W.3d 678, 692-93 (Tex.2012).

Diamond Offshore Mgmt. v. Guidry, 171 S.W.3d 840, 844 (Tex.2005). "Broad-form submission does not entail omitting elements of proof from the charge. While the trial court could certainly have inquired about the separate issues … in a single question with proper instructions, [D] was not obligated to request such a question. It was required only to object to the absence of any inquiry, which the trial court acknowledged [D] had done with its requested questions."

Harris Cty. v. Smith, 96 S.W.3d 230, 234 (Tex. 2002). "[T]he trial court erred in overruling [D's] timely and specific objection to the charge, which mixed valid and invalid elements of damages in a single broad-form submission, and that such error was harmful because it prevented the appellate court from determining 'whether the jury based its verdict on an improperly submitted invalid' element of damage. *At 236:* We hold that ***Casteel***'s reasoning [as to broad-form liability questions] applies equally to broad-form damage questions, and under its rationale we conclude that the charge error in this case was harmful."

Crown Life Ins. v. Casteel, 22 S.W.3d 378, 389 (Tex.2000). "When a single broad-form liability question erroneously commingles valid and invalid liability theories and the appellant's objection is timely and specific, the error is harmful when it cannot be determined whether the improperly submitted theories formed the sole basis for the jury's finding. *At 390:* Rule 277 is not absolute; rather, it mandates broad-form submission 'whenever feasible.' [Submitting] 'alternative liability standards when the governing law is unsettled might very well be a situation where broad-form submission is not feasible.' Similarly, when the trial court is unsure whether it should submit a particular theory of liability, separating liability theories best serves the policy of judicial economy underlying Rule 277 by avoiding the need for a new trial when the basis for liability cannot be determined. Furthermore, Rule 277 mandates that '[t]he court shall submit such instructions and definitions as shall be proper to enable the jury to render a verdict.' It is implicit in this mandate that the jury be able to base its verdict on legally valid questions and instructions. Thus, it may not be feasible to submit a single broad-form liability question that incorporates wholly separate theories of liability." *See also* ***Texas Comm'n on Human Rights v. Morrison***, ___ S.W.3d ___ (Tex.2012) (No. 11-0644; 8-31-12).

Hyundai Motor Co. v. Rodriguez, 995 S.W.2d 661, 664 (Tex.1999). "[S]ubmission of a single question relating to multiple theories may be necessary to avoid the risk that the jury will become confused and answer questions inconsistently. The goal of the charge is to submit to the jury the issues for decision logically, simply, clearly, fairly, correctly, and completely." *See also* ***Texas Dept. of Human Servs. v. E.B.***, 802 S.W.2d 647, 649 (Tex.1990).

H.E. Butt Grocery Co. v. Bilotto, 985 S.W.2d 22, 24 (Tex.1998). "[W]hen an instruction merely directs the jury to answer a damages question only if some condition or conditions have been met, it does not directly instruct the jury about the legal effect of its answers."

Texas Mut. Ins. v. Boetsch, 307 S.W.3d 874, 879-80 (Tex.App.—Dallas 2010, pet. denied). "An impermissible comment on the weight of the evidence occurs when, after examining the entire charge, it is determined that the judge assumed the truth of a material controverted fact or exaggerated, minimized, or withdrew some pertinent evidence from the jury's consideration. An instruction also will be held to be an improper comment on the weight of the evidence if it suggests to the jury the trial judge's opinion concerning the matter about which the jury is asked. Reversal is required if an improper comment on the weight of the evidence is one that was calculated to cause and probably did cause the rendition of an improper judgment." *See also* ***Flying J Inc. v. Meda, Inc.***, 373 S.W.3d 680, 687 (Tex.App.—San Antonio 2012, no pet.).

Valence Oper. Co. v. Anadarko Pet. Corp., 303 S.W.3d 435, 442 (Tex.App.—Texarkana 2010, no pet.). "A definition may properly be submitted to the jury if a term used in the charge has a distinct legal meaning, or if it differs in meaning from the usual and commonly accepted meaning. If the meaning that the parties intended to give to a term is a question of fact for the jury, and there is conflicting evidence before the jury as to the meaning of the term, it should not be defined, and the jury may decide the question based on its view of the evidence."

TRCP 278. SUBMISSION OF QUESTIONS, DEFINITIONS, & INSTRUCTIONS

The court shall submit the questions, instructions and definitions in the form provided by Rule 277, which are raised by the written pleadings and the evidence. Except in trespass to try title, statutory partition proceedings, and other special proceedings in which the pleadings are specially defined by statutes or procedural rules, a party shall not be entitled to any submission of any question raised only by a general denial and not raised by affirmative written pleading by that party. Nothing herein shall change the burden of proof from what it would have been under a general denial. A judgment shall not be reversed because of the failure to submit other and various phases or different shades of the same question. Failure to submit a question shall not be deemed a ground for reversal of the judgment, unless its submission, in substantially correct wording, has been requested in writing and tendered by the party complaining of the judgment; provided, however, that objection to such failure shall suffice in such respect if the question is one relied upon by the opposing party. Failure to submit a definition or instruction shall not be deemed a ground for reversal of the judgment unless a substantially correct definition or instruction has been requested in writing and tendered by the party complaining of the judgment.

History of TRCP 278: Adopted eff. Jan. 1, 1988, by order of July 15, 1987 (733-34 S.W.2d [Tex.Cases] lxxi). Former TRCP 278 repealed eff. Sept. 1941, by order of Mar. 31, 1941 (4 Tex.B.J. 174 [1941]). Source: New rule. See former TRCP 279, first par.

See *Commentaries*, "The Charge," ch. 8-I, p. 731; *O'Connor's Texas Forms*, FORM 8I:1.

ANNOTATIONS

Shupe v. Lingafelter, 192 S.W.3d 577, 579 (Tex. 2006). "When a trial court refuses to submit a requested instruction on an issue raised by the pleadings and evidence, the question on appeal is whether the request was reasonably necessary to enable the jury to render a proper verdict. The omission of an instruction is reversible error only if the omission probably caused the rendition of an improper judgment." *See also Grohman v. Kahlig*, 318 S.W.3d 882, 888 (Tex.2010); *Texas Workers' Comp. Ins. Fund v. Mandlbauer*, 34 S.W.3d 909, 912 (Tex.2000).

In re S.A.P., 156 S.W.3d 574, 577 (Tex.2005). "An unpleaded issue may be tried by consent, but it still must be submitted to the jury."

Union Pac. R.R. v. Williams, 85 S.W.3d 162, 166 (Tex.2002). "A party is entitled to a jury question, instruction, or definition if the pleadings and evidence raise an issue. An instruction is proper if it (1) assists the jury, (2) accurately states the law, and (3) finds support in the pleadings and evidence." *See also Transcontinental Ins. v. Crump*, 330 S.W.3d 211, 221 (Tex. 2010); *Faust v. BNSF Ry.*, 337 S.W.3d 325, 332 (Tex. App.—Fort Worth 2011, pet. denied).

Triplex Comms. v. Riley, 900 S.W.2d 716, 718 (Tex. 1995). "If an issue is properly pleaded and is supported by some evidence, a litigant is entitled to have controlling questions submitted to the jury." *See also Elbaor v. Smith*, 845 S.W.2d 240, 243 (Tex.1992).

Southwestern Bell Tel. Co. v. John Carlo Tex., Inc., 843 S.W.2d 470, 472 (Tex.1992). "The court of appeals ... held the error [of refusing to define justification] harmless. We disagree. Virtually the entire factual dispute between the parties has been over whether [D's] conduct was justified. To ask the jury to resolve this dispute without a proper legal definition to the essential legal issue was reversible error."

Lone Starr Multi-Theatres, Ltd. v. Max Interests, Ltd., 365 S.W.3d 688, 699 (Tex.App.—Houston [1st Dist.] 2011, no pet.). "A trial court has wide discretion in submitting jury questions as well as instructions and definitions. This discretion is subject only to the requirement that the questions submitted must: (1) control the disposition of the case; (2) be raised by the pleadings and the evidence; and (3) properly submit the disputed issues for the jury's determination." *See also Texas Disposal Sys. Landfill, Inc. v. Waste Mgmt. Holdings, Inc.*, 219 S.W.3d 563, 580 (Tex. App.—Austin 2007, pet. denied).

In re F.L.R., 293 S.W.3d 278, 281 (Tex.App.—Waco 2009, no pet.). An oral request for a jury instruction, even when dictated on the record, does not satisfy TRCP 278. *See also Yzaguirre v. University of Tex. Health Sci. Ctr.*, No. 04-09-00550-CV (Tex.App.—San Antonio 2010, no pet.) (memo op.; 4-7-10) (dictating a requested instruction will not support an appeal). *But see In re M.P.*, 126 S.W.3d 228, 230-31 (Tex.App.—San Antonio 2003, no pet.) (allowing attorney's oral request on record).

McCarthy v. Wani Venture, A.S., 251 S.W.3d 573, 585 (Tex.App.—Houston [1st Dist.] 2007, pet. denied). "A party is required to request and tender to the trial court a substantially correct instruction in writing when the trial court omits the instruction from the jury charge. If a party fails to do so, any error by the trial court in not submitting the instruction to the jury is waived." *See also Cullum v. White*, ___ S.W.3d ___ (Tex.App.—San Antonio 2011, pet. denied) (No. 04-09-00695-CV; 12-14-11).

TRCP 279. OMISSIONS FROM THE CHARGE

Upon appeal all independent grounds of recovery or of defense not conclusively established under the evidence and no element of which is submitted or requested are waived. When a ground of recovery or de-

★

fense consists of more than one element, if one or more of such elements necessary to sustain such ground of recovery or defense, and necessarily referable thereto, are submitted to and found by the jury, and one or more of such elements are omitted from the charge, without request or objection, and there is factually sufficient evidence to support a finding thereon, the trial court, at the request of either party, may after notice and hearing and at any time before the judgment is rendered, make and file written findings on such omitted element or elements in support of the judgment. If no such written findings are made, such omitted element or elements shall be deemed found by the court in such manner as to support the judgment. A claim that the evidence was legally or factually insufficient to warrant the submission of any question may be made for the first time after verdict, regardless of whether the submission of such question was requested by the complainant.

History of TRCP 279: Amended eff. Jan. 1, 1988, by order of July 15, 1987 (733-34 S.W.2d [Tex.Cases] lxxi): First par. transferred to TRCP 278. Amended eff. Sept. 1, 1941, by order of Mar. 31, 1941 (4 Tex.B.J. 174 [1941]). Adopted eff. Sept. 1, 1941, by order of Oct. 29, 1940 (3 Tex.B.J. 567 [1940]). Source: TRCS art. 2190 (repealed).

See *Commentaries*, "The Charge," ch. 8-I, p. 731.

ANNOTATIONS

DiGiuseppe v. Lawler, 269 S.W.3d 588, 599 (Tex. 2008). "The purpose of the 'necessarily referable' requirement in Rule 279 is to give parties, against whom issues are to be deemed, fair notice of a partial submission, so that they have an opportunity to object to the charge or request submission of the missing issues to the ground of recovery or defense. Once a party is on notice of the independent ground of recovery or defense due to the existence of an issue 'necessarily referable' thereto, if that party fails to object or request submission of the missing issues, he cannot be heard to complain on appeal, as he is said to have consented to the court's findings on the missing issues." (Internal quotes omitted.)

Chon Tri v. J.T.T., 162 S.W.3d 552, 558 (Tex.2005). "If one or more elements of that cause of action was omitted from the charge, and there was no request to include the omitted element or objection to its exclusion, and no written findings were made by the trial court on the omitted element, then the omitted element must be deemed found by the trial court in a manner that supports its judgment." *See also In re J.F.C.*, 96 S.W.3d 256, 262-63 (Tex.2002).

Gulf States Utils. Co. v. Low, 79 S.W.3d 561, 564 (Tex.2002). "Rule 279 may support a deemed finding only when it can be deemed found 'in such manner as to support the judgment.' ... The court of appeals misapplied Rule 279 to deem a finding, not to support the trial court's judgment, but to render a new judgment for actual damages in an amount nearly 15 times the trial court's award."

T.O. Stanley Boot Co. v. Bank of El Paso, 847 S.W.2d 218, 222-23 (Tex.1992). "[P] failed to submit or request any element of its affirmative claim to the jury. Unless [P's] affirmative claim is conclusively established under the evidence, the ground of recovery is waived upon appeal." *See also Bank of Tex. v. VR Elec., Inc.*, 276 S.W.3d 671, 676-77 (Tex.App.—Houston [1st Dist.] 2008, pet. denied); *Mangum v. Turner*, 255 S.W.3d 223, 227-28 (Tex.App.—Waco 2008, pet. denied).

E. CASE TO THE JURY

TRCP 280. PRESIDING JUROR OF JURY

Each jury shall appoint one of their body presiding juror.

History of TRCP 280: Amended eff. Apr. 1, 1984, by order of Dec. 5, 1983 (661-62 S.W.2d [Tex.Cases] lxxvii): Changed word "foreman" to "presiding juror." Adopted eff. Sept. 1, 1941, by order of Oct. 29, 1940 (3 Tex.B.J. 568 [1940]). Source: TRCS art. 2192 (repealed).

TRCP 281. PAPERS TAKEN TO JURY ROOM

With the court's permission, the jury may take with them to the jury room any notes they took during the trial. In addition, the jury may, and on request shall, take with them in their retirement the charges and instructions, general or special, which were given and read to them, and any written evidence, except the depositions of witnesses, but shall not take with them any special charges which have been refused. Where only part of a paper has been read in evidence, the jury shall not take the same with them, unless the part so read to them is detached from that which was excluded.

History of TRCP 281: Amended eff. Apr. 1, 2011, by order of Mar. 15, 2011 (Tex.Sup.Ct. Order, Misc. Docket No. 11-9047). Amended eff. Apr. 1, 1984, by order of Dec. 5, 1983 (661-62 S.W.2d [Tex.Cases] lxxvii). Adopted eff. Sept. 1, 1941, by order of Oct. 29, 1940 (3 Tex.B.J. 568 [1940]). Source: TRCS art. 2193 (repealed).

See *Commentaries*, "Juror Note-Taking," ch. 8-A, §10, p. 694.

ANNOTATIONS

First Employees Ins. v. Skinner, 646 S.W.2d 170, 172 (Tex.1983). "Rule 281 is mandatory and ... the trial court is required to send all exhibits admitted into evi-

✦

dence to the jury room during the deliberations of the jury. Furthermore, this rule is self-operative and requires no request from the jurors or counsel." *See also* ***Country Vill. Homes, Inc. v. Patterson***, 236 S.W.3d 413, 448 (Tex.App.—Houston [1st Dist.] 2007, pet. granted, judgm't vacated w.r.m.).

Formosa Plastics Corp. v. Kajima Int'l, 216 S.W.3d 436, 464 (Tex.App.—Corpus Christi 2006, pet. denied). "[A]ny error in failing to send exhibits to the jury room during deliberations does not call for reversal unless the error probably caused the rendition of an improper judgment."

TRCP 282. JURY KEPT TOGETHER

The jury may either decide a case in court or retire for deliberation. If they retire, they shall be kept together in some convenient place, under the charge of an officer, until they agree upon a verdict or are discharged by the court; but the court in its discretion may permit them to separate temporarily for the night and at their meals, and for other proper purposes.

History of TRCP 282: Adopted eff. Sept. 1, 1941, by order of Oct. 29, 1940 (3 Tex.B.J. 568 [1940]). Source: TRCS art. 2194 (repealed).

ANNOTATIONS

Union City Transfer v. Adams, 248 S.W.2d 256, 260 (Tex.App.—Fort Worth 1952, writ ref'd n.r.e.). "Permitting the jury to separate temporarily for their meal was within the discretion of the court."

TRCP 283. DUTY OF OFFICER ATTENDING JURY

The officer in charge of the jury shall not make nor permit any communication to be made to them, except to inquire if they have agreed upon a verdict, unless by order of the court; and he shall not before their verdict is rendered communicate to any person the state of their deliberations or the verdict agreed upon.

History of TRCP 283: Adopted eff. Sept. 1, 1941, by order of Oct. 29, 1940 (3 Tex.B.J. 568 [1940]). Source: TRCS art. 2195 (repealed).

ANNOTATIONS

Logan v. Grady, 482 S.W.2d 313, 322 (Tex.App.—Fort Worth 1972, no writ). "[T]he jury bailiff violated [TRCPs] 283 and 285 ... when he did not make the jury's wish as communicated to him known to the court and also when he instructed the jury that its members already had in the jury room all that it needed in order to answer Issue No. 14."

TRCP 284. JUDGE TO CAUTION JURY

Immediately after jurors are selected for a case, the court must instruct them to turn off their phones and other electronic devices and not to communicate with anyone through any electronic device while they are in the courtroom or while they are deliberating. The court must also instruct them that, while they are serving as jurors, they must not post any information about the case on the Internet or search for any information outside of the courtroom, including on the Internet, to try to learn more about the case.

If jurors are permitted to separate before they are released from jury duty, either during the trial or after the case is submitted to them, the court must instruct them that it is their duty not to communicate with, or permit themselves to be addressed by, any other person about any subject relating to the case.

History of TRCP 284: Amended eff. Apr. 1, 2011, by order of Mar. 15, 2011 (Tex.Sup.Ct. Order, Misc. Docket No. 11-9047). Adopted eff. Sept. 1, 1941, by order of Oct. 29, 1940 (3 Tex.B.J. 568 [1940]). Source: TRCS art. 2196 (repealed).

TRCP 285. JURY MAY COMMUNICATE WITH COURT

The jury may communicate with the court by making their wish known to the officer in charge, who shall inform the court, and they may then in open court, and through their presiding juror, communicate with the court, either verbally or in writing. If the communication is to request further instructions, Rule 286 shall be followed.

History of TRCP 285: Amended eff. Apr. 1, 1984, by order of Dec. 5, 1983 (661-62 S.W.2d [Tex.Cases] lxxvii): Changed word "foreman" to "presiding juror." Adopted eff. Sept. 1, 1941, by order of Oct. 29, 1940 (3 Tex.B.J. 569 [1940]). Source: TRCS art. 2197 (repealed). Added last sentence.

See ***Commentaries***, "Supplemental Instructions to Jury," ch. 8-I, §8, p. 744.

TRCP 286. JURY MAY RECEIVE FURTHER INSTRUCTIONS

After having retired, the jury may receive further instructions from the court touching any matter of law, either at their request or upon the court's own motion. For this purpose they shall appear before the judge in open court in a body, and if the instruction is being given at their request, they shall through their presiding juror state to the court, in writing, the particular question of law upon which they desire further instruction. The court shall give such instruction in writing, but no instruction shall be given except in conformity with the rules relating to the charge. Additional argument may be allowed in the discretion of the court.

TRCP 286

✦

History of TRCP 286: Amended eff. Jan. 1, 1988, by order of July 15, 1987 (733-34 S.W.2d [Tex.Cases] lxxi). Amended eff. Apr. 1, 1984, by order of Dec. 5, 1983 (661-62 S.W.2d [Tex.Cases] lxxviii): Changed word "foreman" to "presiding juror." Adopted eff. Sept. 1, 1941, by order of Oct. 29, 1940 (3 Tex.B.J. 569 [1940]). Source: TRCS art. 2198 (repealed).

See *Commentaries*, "Supplemental Instructions to Jury," ch. 8-I, §8, p. 744.

ANNOTATIONS

Stevens v. Travelers Ins., 563 S.W.2d 223, 229 (Tex.1978). "[E]ven though there is a latent danger of coercion, supplemental, verdict-urging instructions are not, in and of themselves, erroneous, so long as the particular charge given is not otherwise objectionable."

Lochinvar Corp. v. Meyers, 930 S.W.2d 182, 187 (Tex.App.—Dallas 1996, no writ). "[R]ule 286 allow[s] a court the opportunity to correct an error by modifying its charge. [¶] The instruction was given to the jury in writing[, but the trial court did not] reassemble the jury in the courtroom. [D waived the error because it] did not object to the court's failure to reassemble the jury and read the modified charge."

TRCP 287. DISAGREEMENT AS TO EVIDENCE

If the jury disagree as to the statement of any witness, they may, upon applying to the court, have read to them from the court reporter's notes that part of such witness' testimony on the point in dispute; but, if there be no such reporter, or if his notes cannot be read to the jury, the court may cause such witness to be again brought upon the stand and the judge shall direct him to repeat his testimony as to the point in dispute, and no other, as nearly as he can in the language used on the trial; and on their notifying the court that they disagree as to any portion of a deposition or other paper not permitted to be carried with them in their retirement, the court may, in like manner, permit such portion of said deposition or paper to be again read to the jury.

History of TRCP 287: Adopted eff. Sept. 1, 1941, by order of Oct. 29, 1940 (3 Tex.B.J. 569 [1940]). Source: TRCS art. 2199 (repealed), as amended.

ANNOTATIONS

Krishnan v. Ramirez, 42 S.W.3d 205, 225 (Tex. App.—Corpus Christi 2001, pet. denied). "The judge is given broad discretion in determining what portions of the testimony are relevant to the jury's request to have testimony re-read."

TRCP 288. COURT OPEN FOR JURY

The court, during the deliberations of the jury, may proceed with other business or recess from time to time, but shall be deemed open for all purposes connected with the case before the jury.

History of TRCP 288: Adopted eff. Sept. 1, 1941, by order of Oct. 29, 1940 (3 Tex.B.J. 569 [1940]). Source: TRCS art. 2201 (repealed).

TRCP 289. DISCHARGE OF JURY

The jury to whom a case has been submitted may be discharged by the court when they cannot agree and the parties consent to their discharge, or when they have been kept together for such time as to render it altogether improbable that they can agree, or when any calamity or accident may, in the opinion of the court, require it, or when by sickness or other cause their number is reduced below the number constituting the jury in such court.

The cause shall again be placed on the jury docket and shall again be set for trial as the court directs.

History of TRCP 289: Amended eff. Apr. 1, 1984, by order of Dec. 5, 1983 (661-62 S.W.2d [Tex.Cases] lxxviii). Adopted eff. Sept. 1, 1941, by order of Oct. 29, 1940 (3 Tex.B.J. 569 [1940]). Source: TRCS art. 2200 (repealed).

See *Commentaries*, "Verdict-urging instructions," ch. 8-I, §8.3, p. 744.

ANNOTATIONS

Shaw v. Greater Houston Transp., 791 S.W.2d 204, 209 (Tex.App.—Corpus Christi 1990, no writ). It was coercive for the trial court to refuse to release the jury after they stated three times that they were deadlocked.

F. VERDICT

TRCP 290. DEFINITION & SUBSTANCE

A verdict is a written declaration by a jury of its decision, comprehending the whole or all the issues submitted to the jury, and shall be either a general or special verdict, as directed, which shall be signed by the presiding juror of the jury.

A general verdict is one whereby the jury pronounces generally in favor of one or more parties to the suit upon all or any of the issues submitted to it. A special verdict is one wherein the jury finds the facts only on issues made up and submitted to them under the direction of the court.

A special verdict shall, as between the parties, be conclusive as to the facts found.

History of TRCP 290: Amended eff. Apr. 1, 1984, by order of Dec. 5, 1983 (661-62 S.W.2d [Tex.Cases] lxxviii): Changed word "foreman" to "presiding juror." Adopted eff. Sept. 1, 1941, by order of Oct. 29, 1940 (3 Tex.B.J. 569 [1940]). Source: TRCS art. 2202 (repealed).

ANNOTATIONS

Wal-Mart Stores v. Alexander, 868 S.W.2d 322, 328 (Tex.1993). "A jury's marginal notations generally

---

may not be considered on appeal. They reflect the jury's mental processes, but they are not part of its verdict."

Houston Fire & Cas. Ins. v. Gerhardt, 281 S.W.2d 176, 178 (Tex.App.—San Antonio 1955, orig. proceeding). "A verdict form reflecting answers to special issues but not signed by the foreman may or may not be a verdict, and presents a question which must be determined by the hearing of evidence."

TRCP 291. FORM OF VERDICT

No special form of verdict is required, and the judgment shall not be arrested or reversed for mere want of form therein if there has been substantial compliance with the requirements of the law in rendering a verdict.

History of TRCP 291: Amended eff. Feb. 1, 1973, by order of Oct. 3, 1972 (483-84 S.W.2d [Tex.Cases] xl): Deleted sentence requiring concurrence of all members of the jury in the verdict. Adopted eff. Sept. 1, 1941, by order of Oct. 29, 1940 (3 Tex.B.J. 570 [1940]). Source: TRCS art. 2203 (repealed).

TRCP 292. VERDICT BY PORTION OF ORIGINAL JURY

(a) Except as provided in subsection (b), a verdict may be rendered in any cause by the concurrence, as to each and all answers made, of the same ten or more members of an original jury of twelve or of the same five or more members of an original jury of six. However, where as many as three jurors die or be disabled from sitting and there are only nine of the jurors remaining of an original jury of twelve, those remaining may render and return a verdict. If less than the original twelve or six jurors render a verdict, the verdict must be signed by each juror concurring therein.

(b) A verdict may be rendered awarding exemplary damages only if the jury was unanimous in finding liability for and the amount of exemplary damages.

History of TRCP 292: Amended eff. Feb. 1, 2005, by order of Jan. 27, 2005 (Tex.Sup.Ct. Order, Misc. Docket No. 05-9021): Divided rule into two subsections; subsec. (a) is clarified; subsec. (b) is added to make rule consistent with Act of June 2, 2003, 78th Leg., R.S., ch. 204, §13.04, 2003, Tex. Gen. Laws 847, 888, codified as CPRC §41.003. Amended eff. Feb. 1, 1973, by order of Oct. 3, 1972 (483-84 S.W.2d [Tex.Cases] xl): Inserted first sentence, which provides for rendition of a verdict by ten members of an original jury of 12 and by 5 members of an original jury of 6; and rewrote third sentence to require that any verdict rendered by less than the original 12 or 6 jurors be signed by each juror concurring in it. Adopted eff. Sept. 1, 1941, by order of Oct. 29, 1940 (3 Tex.B.J. 570 [1940]). Source: TRCS art. 2204 (repealed).

See *Commentaries*, "The Verdict," ch. 8-K, p. 753.

ANNOTATIONS

Yanes v. Sowards, 996 S.W.2d 849, 850 (Tex.1999). "[T]rial courts have broad discretion in determining whether a juror is disabled from sitting when there is evidence of constitutional disqualification. But not just any inconvenience or delay is a disability. A constitu-

tional disability must be in the nature of an actual physical or mental incapacity." (Internal quotes omitted.) *See also* ***McDaniel v. Yarbrough***, 898 S.W.2d 251, 253 (Tex.1995).

Schlafly v. Schlafly, 33 S.W.3d 863, 870 (Tex. App.—Houston [14th Dist.] 2000, pet. denied). "There is no reason to treat a jury comprised of 12 members, one of whom is an alternate, any differently than a jury comprised of 12 regular members. ... We find 'original jurors' means all the jurors empaneled, both regular members and alternates."

TRCP 293. WHEN THE JURY AGREE

When the jury agree upon a verdict, they shall be brought into court by the proper officer, and they shall deliver their verdict to the clerk; and if they state that they have agreed, the verdict shall be read aloud by the clerk. If the verdict is in proper form, no juror objects to its accuracy, no juror represented as agreeing thereto dissents therefrom, and neither party requests a poll of the jury, the verdict shall be entered upon the minutes of the court.

History of TRCP 293: Amended eff. Feb. 1, 1973, by order of Oct. 3, 1972 (483-84 S.W.2d [Tex.Cases] xl): Inserted in second sentence words "objects to its accuracy, no juror represented as agreeing thereto," and made other minor changes. Adopted eff. Sept. 1, 1941, by order of Oct. 29, 1940 (3 Tex.B.J. 570 [1940]). Source: TRCS art. 2205 (repealed), with changes: Eliminated requirement that jurors' names be called by the clerk.

TRCP 294. POLLING THE JURY

Any party shall have the right to have the jury polled. A jury is polled by reading once to the jury collectively the general verdict, or the questions and answers thereto consecutively, and then calling the name of each juror separately and asking the juror if it is the juror's verdict. If any juror answers in the negative when the verdict is returned signed only by the presiding juror as a unanimous verdict, or if any juror shown by the juror's signature to agree to the verdict should answer in the negative, the jury shall be retired for further deliberation.

History of TRCP 294: Amended eff. Sept. 1, 1990, by order of Apr. 24, 1990 (785-86 S.W.2d [Tex.Cases] lxvii): Changed "his" to "the juror's," "him" to "the juror," "special issues" to "questions" and the first word from "Either" to "Any." Amended eff. Apr. 1, 1984, by order of Dec. 5, 1983 (661-62 S.W.2d [Tex.Cases] lxxviii): Changed word "foreman" to "presiding juror." Amended eff. Feb. 1, 1973, by order of Oct. 3, 1972 (483-84 S.W.2d [Tex.Cases] xli): Rewrote last sentence to provide that the jury shall be retired for further deliberation if any juror answers in the negative where the verdict is returned as a unanimous verdict or if any juror shown by his signature to agree to the verdict answers in the negative. Adopted eff. Sept. 1, 1941, by order of Oct. 29, 1940 (3 Tex.B.J. 570 [1940]). Source: TRCS art. 2206 (repealed), with changes: Eliminated words "which is done by" and added language of second sentence through words "and then."

See *Commentaries*, "Request to Poll Jury," ch. 8-K, §5, p. 754.

★

Suggs v. Fitch, 64 S.W.3d 658, 660 (Tex.App.—Texarkana 2001, no pet.). "The right to poll the jury pursuant to [TRCP] 294 is a waivable right and must be requested in order to be invoked."

Pate v. Texline Feed Mills, Inc., 689 S.W.2d 238, 243 (Tex.App.—Amarillo 1985, writ ref'd n.r.e.). "Once the request is promptly made before the jury is discharged, the trial court has no discretion but to poll the jury, and the requesting party's motive is immaterial."

TRCP 295. CORRECTION OF VERDICT

If the purported verdict is defective, the court may direct it to be reformed. If it is incomplete, or not responsive to the questions contained in the court's charge, or the answers to the questions are in conflict, the court shall in writing instruct the jury in open court of the nature of the incompleteness, unresponsiveness, or conflict, provide the jury such additional instructions as may be proper, and retire the jury for further deliberations.

History of TRCP 295: Amended eff. Jan. 1, 1988, by order of July 15, 1987 (733-34 S.W.2d [Tex.Cases] lxxii): Amendment clarified that the court may direct a complete yet defective verdict to be reformed. Amendment also clarified that in the event the verdict is incomplete or otherwise improper, court is limited to giving jury additional instructions in writing. Adopted eff. Sept. 1, 1941, by order of Oct. 29, 1940 (3 Tex.B.J. 570 [1940]). Source: TRCS art. 2207 (repealed).

Beltran v. Brookshire Grocery Co., 358 S.W.3d 263, 268 (Tex.App.—Dallas 2011, pet. filed 4-9-12). "Rule 295 provides a procedure for correcting conflicting jury answers. ... The court must be made aware of the conflict before the jury is discharged because, once the jury is discharged, 'a conflict in the jury's answers cannot be reformed.'"

Archer Daniels Midland Co. v. Bohall, 114 S.W.3d 42, 46 (Tex.App.—Eastland 2003, no pet.). TRCP 295 "applies only to defective verdicts, not defective charges. Before Rule 295 would authorize further instruction to the jury, the verdict must be incomplete, non-responsive to the questions contained in the court's charge, or contain answers which are in conflict." *See also* ***Fish v. Dallas ISD***, 170 S.W.3d 226, 229 (Tex.App.—Dallas 2005, pet. denied).

G. FINDINGS BY COURT
TRCP 296. REQUESTS FOR FINDINGS OF FACTS & CONCLUSIONS OF LAW

In any case tried in the district or county court without a jury, any party may request the court to state in writing its findings of fact and conclusions of law. Such request shall be entitled "Request for Findings of Fact and Conclusions of Law" and shall be filed within twenty days after judgment is signed with the clerk of the court, who shall immediately call such request to the attention of the judge who tried the case. The party making the request shall serve it on all other parties in accordance with Rule 21a.

History of TRCP 296: Amended eff. Sept. 1, 1990, by order of Apr. 24, 1990 (785-86 S.W.2d [Tex.Cases] lxvii): Rewrote rule and title to revise the practice and times for findings of fact and conclusions of law. [See TRCPs 297 and 298.] Amended eff. Apr. 1, 1984, by order of Dec. 5, 1983 (661-62 S.W.2d [Tex.Cases] lxxix): Changed time for filing request for findings and conclusions so that it must be made within ten days of the signing of final judgment. Amended eff. Jan. 1, 1981, by order of June 10, 1990 (599-600 S.W.2d [Tex.Cases] xlvii): Amended to commence the running of time for filing findings and conclusions to the date final judgment or order overruling a motion for new trial is signed or the motion is overruled by operation of law; last sentence of former TRCP 296 becomes second sentence of TRCP 297. Amended eff. Sept. 1, 1957, by order of Mar. 19, 1957 (20 Tex.B.J. 192 [1957]): Added provisions limiting time in which to request conclusions of fact and law and requiring notice to opposite party of filing of request. Adopted eff. Sept. 1, 1941, by order of Oct. 29, 1940 (3 Tex.B.J. 570 [1940]). Source: TRCS art. 2208 (repealed).

See *Commentaries*, "Request for Findings of Fact & Conclusions of Law," ch. 10-E, p. 817; *O'Connor's Texas Forms*, FORMS 10E:1, 2.

Black v. Dallas Cty. Child Welfare Unit, 835 S.W.2d 626, 630 n.10 (Tex.1992). "If no findings of fact or conclusions of law are filed, the reviewing court must imply all necessary fact findings in support of the trial court's judgment."

Liberty Mut. Fire Ins. v. Laca, 243 S.W.3d 791, 794 (Tex.App.—El Paso 2007, no pet.). A party "has been harmed if, under the circumstances of the case, he is forced to guess the reason(s) why the trial court ruled against him. If there is only a single ground of recovery or a single defense in the case, the record would show that the [party] has suffered no harm, because he is not forced to guess the reasons for the trial court's judgment. On the other hand, when there are multiple grounds for recovery or multiple defenses, [the party] is forced to guess what the trial court's findings were, unless they are provided to him. Putting the [party] in the position of having to guess the trial court's reasons for rendering judgment against him defeats the inherent purpose of [TRCPs] 296 and 297. The purpose of a request under the rules is to 'narrow the bases of the judgment to only a portion of [the multiple] claims and defenses, thereby reducing the number of contentions that ... must [be raised] on appeal.'"

Willms v. Americas Tire Co., 190 S.W.3d 796, 810 (Tex.App.—Dallas 2006, pet. denied). "When a trial court grants summary judgment relief, ... findings of fact are not appropriate because the summary judgment proceeding has not been 'tried' within the scope of rule 296. Findings of fact and conclusions of law have no place in a summary judgment proceeding. If summary judgment is proper, there are no facts to find, and the legal conclusions have already been stated in the motion and response." *See also* ***K2M3, LLC v. Cocoon Data Holding Pty. Ltd.***, No. 13-11-00194-CV (Tex. App.—Corpus Christi 2012, pet. denied) (memo op.; 6-28-12) (term "tried" includes trial court's disposition of a case rendered after evidentiary hearing on conflicting evidence; findings and conclusions have no purpose when judgment is rendered as a matter of law); ***In re Estate of Davis***, 216 S.W.3d 537, 542 (Tex.App.—Texarkana 2007, pet. denied) (no findings of fact and conclusions of law required for special appearance subject to interlocutory appeal).

TRCP 297. TIME TO FILE FINDINGS OF FACT & CONCLUSIONS OF LAW

The court shall file its findings of fact and conclusions of law within twenty days after a timely request is filed. The court shall cause a copy of its findings and conclusions to be mailed to each party in the suit.

If the court fails to file timely findings of fact and conclusions of law, the party making the request shall, within thirty days after filing the original request, file with the clerk and serve on all other parties in accordance with Rule 21a a "Notice of Past Due Findings of Fact and Conclusions of Law" which shall be immediately called to the attention of the court by the clerk. Such notice shall state the date the original request was filed and the date the findings and conclusions were due. Upon filing this notice, the time for the court to file findings of fact and conclusions of law is extended to forty days from the date the original request was filed.

History of TRCP 297: Amended eff. Sept. 1, 1990, by order of Apr. 24, 1990 (785-86 S.W.2d [Tex.Cases] lxvii): Rewrote rule and title to revise the practice and times for findings of fact and conclusion of law. [See TRCPs 296 and 298.] Amended eff. Apr. 1, 1984, by order of Dec. 5, 1983 (661-62 S.W.2d [Tex.Cases] lxxix): Changed time for filing findings and conclusions so that the judge shall prepare them within 30 days after judgment. Amended eff. Jan. 1, 1981, by order of June 10, 1980 (599-600 S.W.2d [Tex.Cases] xlvii): Amended rule to commence the running of time for filing findings and conclusions from the date final judgment or order overruling a motion for new trial is signed or the motion is overruled by operation of law. Adopted eff. Sept. 1, 1941, by order of Oct. 29, 1940 (3 Tex.B.J. 570 [1940]). Source: TRCS art. 2247 (repealed).

See *Commentaries*, "Request for Findings of Fact & Conclusions of Law," ch. 10-E, p. 817; *O'Connor's Texas Forms*, FORM 10E:3.

ANNOTATIONS

Tenery v. Tenery, 932 S.W.2d 29, 30 (Tex.1996). "[H]arm to the complaining party is presumed unless the contrary appears on the face of the record when the party makes a proper and timely request for findings and the trial court fails to comply. Error is harmful if it prevents an appellant from properly presenting a case to the appellate court." *See also* ***Cherne Indus. v. Magallanes***, 763 S.W.2d 768, 772 (Tex.1989); ***Granado v. Meza***, 360 S.W.3d 613, 616 (Tex.App.—San Antonio 2011, pet. filed 2-15-12).

Sonnier v. Sonnier, 331 S.W.3d 211, 214 (Tex. App.—Beaumont 2011, no pet.). "[T]he failure to file the required 'past due' notice is treated as a waiver of the right to complain of the trial court's failure to file findings. In that circumstance, when the record contains no findings of fact and conclusions of law, all necessary findings to support the judgment are implied." *See also* ***Curtis v. Commission for Lawyer Discipline***, 20 S.W.3d 227, 232 (Tex.App.—Houston [14th Dist.] 2000, no pet.).

Liberty Mut. Fire Ins. v. Laca, 243 S.W.3d 791, 794 (Tex.App.—El Paso 2007, no pet.). See annotation under TRCP 296, p. 1012.

In re E.A.C., 162 S.W.3d 438, 443 (Tex.App.—Dallas 2005, no pet.). "When a trial court files belated findings, the only issue that arises is whether the appellant was harmed, not whether the trial court had jurisdiction to make the findings. This harm may be in two forms: (1) the litigant is unable to request additional findings, or (2) the litigant was prevented from properly presenting his appeal."

TRCP 298. ADDITIONAL OR AMENDED FINDINGS OF FACT & CONCLUSIONS OF LAW

After the court files original findings of fact and conclusions of law, any party may file with the clerk of the court a request for specified additional or amended findings or conclusions. The request for these findings shall be made within ten days after the filing of the original findings and conclusions by the court. Each request made pursuant to this rule shall be served on each party to the suit in accordance with Rule 21a.

The court shall file any additional or amended findings and conclusions that are appropriate within ten days after such request is filed, and cause a copy to be mailed to each party to the suit. No findings or conclusions shall be deemed or presumed by any failure of the court to make any additional findings or conclusions.

History of TRCP 298: Amended eff. Sept. 1, 1990, by order of Apr. 24, 1990 (785-86 S.W.2d [Tex.Cases] lxviii): Rewrote rule and title to revise the practice and times for findings of fact and conclusions of law. [See TRCPs 296 and 297.]

⭐

Amended eff. Sept. 1, 1957, by order of Mar. 19, 1957 (20 Tex.B.J. 192 [1957]): Added provision requiring that notice of request be given to opposite party. Adopted eff. Sept. 1, 1941, by order of Oct. 29, 1940 (3 Tex.B.J. 570 [1940]). Source: TRCS art. 2247a (repealed).

See *Commentaries*, "Request for Findings of Fact & Conclusions of Law," ch. 10-E, p. 817; *O'Connor's Texas Forms*, FORM 10E:4.

ANNOTATIONS

Rich v. Olah, 274 S.W.3d 878, 886 (Tex.App.—Dallas 2008, no pet.). Under TRCP 298, "[a] trial court is not required to make additional findings of fact that are unsupported in the record, that are evidentiary, or that are contrary to other previous findings."

Pakdimounivong v. City of Arlington, 219 S.W.3d 401, 412 (Tex.App.—Fort Worth 2006, pet. denied). "Additional findings are not required if the original findings and conclusions properly and succinctly relate the ultimate findings of fact and law necessary to apprise the party of adequate information for the preparation of the party's appeal. An ultimate fact is one that would have a direct effect on the judgment. If the refusal to file additional findings does not prevent a party from adequately presenting an argument on appeal, there is no reversible error. If the requested findings will not result in a different judgment, the findings need not be made."

Gentry v. Squires Constr., Inc., 188 S.W.3d 396, 408 (Tex.App.—Dallas 2006, no pet.). "The failure of a party to request additional or amended findings or conclusions waives the party's right to complain on appeal about the presumed finding."

Vickery v. Commission for Lawyer Discipline, 5 S.W.3d 241, 254 (Tex.App.—Houston [14th Dist.] 1999, pet. denied). "[B]efore the failure to grant additional findings will impede an appellate court from presuming implied findings, the omission must be made manifest to the trial court. ... If the trial court is not specifically made aware of the missing element, the omission is presumed to be inadvertent."

TRCP 299. OMITTED FINDINGS

When findings of fact are filed by the trial court they shall form the basis of the judgment upon all grounds of recovery and of defense embraced therein. The judgment may not be supported upon appeal by a presumed finding upon any ground of recovery or defense, no element of which has been included in the findings of fact; but when one or more elements thereof have been found by the trial court, omitted unrequested elements, when supported by evidence, will be supplied by presumption in support of the judgment. Refusal of the court to make a finding requested shall be reviewable on appeal.

History of TRCP 299: Amended eff. Sept. 1, 1990, by order of Apr. 24, 1990 (785-86 S.W.2d [Tex.Cases] lxviii): Changed "where" to "when," "presumption of finding" to "presumed finding" and "which has been found by the trial court" to "which has been included in the findings of fact." Amended eff. Dec. 31, 1941, by order of Sept. 20, 1941 (4 Tex.B.J. 532 [1941]). Adopted eff. Sept. 1, 1941, by order of Oct. 29, 1940 (3 Tex.B.J. 570 [1940]). Source: New rule.

See *Commentaries*, "Request for Findings of Fact & Conclusions of Law," ch. 10-E, p. 817.

ANNOTATIONS

Worford v. Stamper, 801 S.W.2d 108, 109 (Tex. 1990). "In this case, no findings of fact or conclusions of law were requested or filed. It is therefore implied that the trial court made all the findings necessary to support its judgment. In determining whether some evidence supports the judgment and the implied findings of fact, 'it is proper to consider only that evidence most favorable to the issue and to disregard entirely that which is opposed to it or contradictory in its nature.'" *See also Black v. Dallas Cty. Child Welfare Unit*, 835 S.W.2d 626, 630 n.10 (Tex.1992).

O'Brien v. Daboval, ___ S.W.3d ___ (Tex.App.—Houston [1st Dist.] 2012, no pet.) (No. 01-11-00436-CV; 8-30-12). "If the findings of fact and the judgment are in conflict, the unchallenged findings control over the judgment."

Vickery v. Commission for Lawyer Discipline, 5 S.W.3d 241, 252 (Tex.App.—Houston [14th Dist.] 1999, pet. denied). "When a court makes findings of fact, but inadvertently omits an essential element of a ground of recovery or defense, the presumption of validity will supply the omitted element by implication. However, if the record demonstrates the trial judge deliberately omitted the element, the presumption is refuted and the element cannot logically be supplied by implication."

TRCP 299a. FINDINGS OF FACT TO BE SEPARATELY FILED & NOT RECITED IN A JUDGMENT

Findings of fact shall not be recited in a judgment. If there is a conflict between findings of fact recited in a judgment in violation of this rule and findings of fact made pursuant to Rules 297 and 298, the latter findings will control for appellate purposes. Findings of fact shall be filed with the clerk of the court as a document or documents separate and apart from the judgment.

History of TRCP 299a: Adopted eff. Sept. 1, 1990, by order of Apr. 24, 1990 (785-86 S.W.2d [Tex.Cases] lxix): To require that findings of fact be separate from the judgment and that such separate findings of fact are controlling on appeal. Source: New rule.

TRCP 298

See *Commentaries*, "The Judgment," ch. 9-C, p. 764; "Request for Findings of Fact & Conclusions of Law," ch. 10-E, p. 817.

ANNOTATIONS

Colbert v. DFPS, 227 S.W.3d 799, 809 (Tex.App.—Houston [1st Dist.] 2006), *pet. denied sub nom. In re D.N.C.*, 252 S.W.3d 317 (Tex.2008). "[A] trial court's recitation in the judgment of its ground for termination of parental rights is not a fact-finding that is prohibited under rule 299a...."

In re Estate of Jones, 197 S.W.3d 894, 900 n.4 (Tex.App.—Beaumont 2006, pet. denied). "[I]f findings are recited in the judgment, and no one complains or requests findings, and there is no conflict with separately filed findings of fact, the findings of fact in the judgment should not be ignored on appeal." *See also South Plains Lamesa R.R. v. Heinrich*, 280 S.W.3d 357, 364-65 (Tex.App.—Amarillo 2008, no pet.). *But see Sutherland v. Cobern*, this page. For a discussion of the split in the courts of appeals on this issue, see "Not in the judgment," ch. 10-E, §5.1.2, p. 822.

Sutherland v. Cobern, 843 S.W.2d 127, 131 n.7 (Tex.App.—Texarkana 1992, writ denied). "Findings of fact contained in the body of a judgment may not be considered on appeal. Therefore, for our purposes, we review this case as one in which no findings of fact were made." *See also Casino Magic Corp. v. King*, 43 S.W.3d 14, 19 n.6 (Tex.App.—Dallas 2001, pet. denied). *But see In re Estate of Jones*, this page. For a discussion of the split in the courts of appeals on this issue, see "Not in the judgment," ch. 10-E, §5.1.2, p. 822.

H. JUDGMENTS

TRCP 300. COURT TO RENDER JUDGMENT

Where a special verdict is rendered, or the conclusions of fact found by the judge are separately stated the court shall render judgment thereon unless set aside or a new trial is granted, or judgment is rendered notwithstanding verdict or jury finding under these rules.

History of TRCP 300: Adopted eff. Sept. 1, 1941, by order of Oct. 29, 1940 (3 Tex.B.J. 571 [1940]). Source: TRCS art. 2209 (repealed).

ANNOTATIONS

Astec Indus. v. Suarez, 921 S.W.2d 794, 798 (Tex.App.—Fort Worth 1996, no writ). "In order for a judge's ministerial duty to render judgment under rule 300 ... to arise, the jury must first return a sufficient verdict for the judge to receive."

TRCP 301. JUDGMENTS

The judgment of the court shall conform to the pleadings, the nature of the case proved and the verdict, if any, and shall be so framed as to give the party all the relief to which he may be entitled either in law or equity. Provided, that upon motion and reasonable notice the court may render judgment non obstante veredicto if a directed verdict would have been proper, and provided further that the court may, upon like motion and notice, disregard any jury finding on a question that has no support in the evidence. Only one final judgment shall be rendered in any cause except where it is otherwise specially provided by law. Judgment may, in a proper case, be given for or against one or more of several plaintiffs, and for or against one or more of several defendants or intervenors.

History of TRCP 301: Amended eff. Sept. 1, 1990, by order of Apr. 24, 1990 (785-86 S.W.2d [Tex.Cases] lxix): Added last two sentences. Amended eff. Jan. 1, 1988, by order of July 15, 1987 (733-34 S.W.2d [Tex.Cases] lxxii). Adopted eff. Sept. 1, 1941, by order of Oct. 29, 1940 (3 Tex.B.J. 571 [1940]). Source: TRCS art. 2211 (repealed).

See *Commentaries*, "Motion for JNOV," ch. 9-B, p. 761; "The Judgment," ch. 9-C, p. 764; *O'Connor's Texas Forms*, FORMS 9B, 9C:1.

ANNOTATIONS

Tanner v. Nationwide Mut. Fire Ins., 289 S.W.3d 828, 830 (Tex.2009). "We review a JNOV under a no-evidence standard, meaning we 'credit evidence favoring the jury verdict if reasonable jurors could, and disregard contrary evidence unless reasonable jurors could not.'"

Tiller v. McLure, 121 S.W.3d 709, 713 (Tex.2003). "A trial court may grant a [JNOV] if there is no evidence to support one or more of the jury findings on issues necessary to liability."

Spencer v. Eagle Star Ins., 876 S.W.2d 154, 157 (Tex.1994). "A trial court may disregard a jury finding only if it is unsupported by evidence ... or if the issue is immaterial. A question is immaterial when it should not have been submitted, or when it was properly submitted but has been rendered immaterial by other findings. A question which calls for a finding beyond the province of the jury, such as a question of law, may be deemed immaterial." *See also Wal-Mart Stores v. McKenzie*, 997 S.W.2d 278, 280 (Tex.1999).

Stewart v. USA Custom Paint & Body Shop, Inc., 870 S.W.2d 18, 20 (Tex.1994). "A judgment must be sufficiently definite and certain to define and protect the rights of all litigants, or it should provide a definite means of ascertaining such rights, to the end that min-

TRCP 301

isterial officers can carry the judgment into execution without ascertainment of facts not therein stated."

Pitts & Collard, L.L.P. v. Schechter, 369 S.W.3d 301, 320 (Tex.App.—Houston [1st Dist.] 2011, no pet.). "The motion [for JNOV] should be granted (1) when the evidence is conclusive, and one party is entitled to recover as a matter of law or (2) when a legal principle precludes recovery. A motion for [JNOV] based on a legal principle is appropriately granted when it is conclusively established that recovery is precluded even though all the allegations are proven."

Solomon v. Steitler, 312 S.W.3d 46, 55 (Tex.App.—Texarkana 2010, no pet.). "Generally, a judgment for damages in excess of the amount sought by the pleadings is error, even if a larger award might be warranted by the evidence. [A] trial court cannot render judgment for an amount in excess of what a plaintiff requested in the live pleadings."

James v. Commission for Lawyer Discipline, 310 S.W.3d 598, 612 (Tex.App.—Dallas 2010, no pet.). "'In determining whether [a] judgment conform[s] to the pleadings, an appellate court should view the pleadings as a whole. A prayer for general relief will support any relief raised by the evidence and consistent with the allegations in the petition.'"

Hartford Fire Ins. v. C. Springs 300, Ltd., 287 S.W.3d 771, 779-80 (Tex.App.—Houston [1st Dist.] 2009, pet. denied). "There are … exceptions to rule 301. Unpleaded claims or defenses that are tried by express or implied consent of the parties are treated as if they had been raised by the pleadings. The party who allows an issue to be tried by consent and who fails to raise the lack of a pleading before submission of the case cannot later raise the pleading deficiency for the first time on appeal."

TRCP 302. ON COUNTERCLAIM

If the defendant establishes a demand against the plaintiff upon a counterclaim exceeding that established against him by the plaintiff, the court shall render judgment for defendant for such excess.

History of TRCP 302: Amended eff. Apr. 1, 1984, by order of Dec. 5, 1983 (661-62 S.W.2d [Tex.Cases] lxxix). Adopted eff. Sept. 1, 1941, by order of Oct. 29, 1940 (3 Tex.B.J. 571 [1940]). Source: TRCS art. 2215 (repealed).

TRCP 303. ON COUNTERCLAIM FOR COSTS

When a counterclaim is pleaded, the party in whose favor final judgment is rendered shall also recover the costs, unless it be made to appear on the trial that the counterclaim of the defendant was acquired after the commencement of the suit, in which case, if the plaintiff establishes a claim existing at the commencement of the suit, he shall recover his costs.

History of TRCP 303: Amended eff. Apr. 1, 1984, by order of Dec. 5, 1983 (661-62 S.W.2d [Tex.Cases] lxxix). Adopted eff. Sept. 1, 1941, by order of Oct. 29, 1940 (3 Tex.B.J. 571 [1940]). Source: TRCS art. 2216 (repealed).
See TRCP 131, 141.

ANNOTATIONS

Reyna v. First Nat'l Bank, 55 S.W.3d 58, 74 (Tex. App.—Corpus Christi 2001, no pet.). "[O]n appeal, [P] asserts that since [D] did not prevail on its counterclaim, then some of the costs should be assessed against [D]. Given that the counterclaim was … acquired before the suit, and [P] did not prevail on any of his claims, we conclude … the trial court correctly assessed all costs against [P]."

TRCP 304. JUDGMENT UPON RECORD

Judgments rendered upon questions raised upon citations, pleadings, and all other proceedings, constituting the record proper as known at common law, must be entered at the date of each term when pronounced.

History of TRCP 304: Adopted eff. Sept. 1, 1941, by order of Oct. 29, 1940 (3 Tex.B.J. 571 [1940]). Source: Tex. Rules for Dist. & Cty. Cts. 65.

TRCP 305. PROPOSED JUDGMENT

Any party may prepare and submit a proposed judgment to the court for signature.

Each party who submits a proposed judgment for signature shall serve the proposed judgment on all other parties to the suit who have appeared and remain in the case, in accordance with Rule 21a.

Failure to comply with this rule shall not affect the time for perfecting an appeal.

History of TRCP 305: Amended eff. Sept. 1, 1990, by order of Apr. 24, 1990 (785-86 S.W.2d [Tex.Cases] lxix): Completely rewrote rule to clarify the practice for proposed judgments and notice to other parties. Adopted eff. Sept. 1, 1941, by order of Oct. 29, 1940 (3 Tex.B.J. 571 [1940]). Source: Tex. Rules for Dist. & Cty. Cts. 48.
See *Commentaries*, "The Judgment," ch. 9-C, p. 764; *O'Connor's Texas Forms*, FORM 9C:1.

ANNOTATIONS

First Nat'l Bank v. Fojtik, 775 S.W.2d 632, 633 (Tex.1989). A party's motion asking the trial court to sign a judgment does not waive the party's right to complain about that judgment. "There must be a method by which a party who desires to initiate the appellate process may move the trial court to render judgment without being bound by its terms."

✦

Dikeman v. Snell, 490 S.W.2d 183, 185-86 (Tex. 1973). Even when a judgment is prepared by a party, a mistake in the rendered judgment is a judicial error.

Vann v. Brown, 244 S.W.3d 612, 617 (Tex.App.—Dallas 2008, no pet.). "We recognize that rule 305 suggests a party 'may' offer the trial court a proposed judgment, but that is not a requirement. We cannot agree with [P's] assertion that Rule 305 suggests [D] should have supplied a proposed judgment to the trial court. The parties even acknowledge in oral argument that it is customary for the party in whose favor the verdict was returned to provide a proposed judgment to the trial judge."

⑫ TRCP 306. RECITATION OF JUDGMENT

The entry of the judgment shall contain the full names of the parties, as stated in the pleadings, for and against whom the judgment is rendered. In a suit for termination of the parent-child relationship or a suit affecting the parent-child relationship filed by a governmental entity for managing conservatorship, the judgment must state the specific grounds for termination or for appointment of the managing conservator.

History of TRCP 306: Amended eff. Mar. 1, 2012, by order of Feb. 13, 2012 (Tex.Sup.Ct. Order, Misc. Docket No. 12-9030). Amended eff. Jan. 1, 1971, by order of July 21, 1970 (455-56 S.W.2d [Tex.Cases] xliii): Eliminated language requiring judgment to recite findings of jury. Adopted eff. Sept. 1, 1941, by order of Oct. 29, 1940 (3 Tex.B.J. 571 [1940]). Source: Tex. Rules for Dist. & Cty. Cts. 63, 64.

See *Commentaries*, "The Judgment," ch. 9-C, p. 764.

ANNOTATIONS

Crystal City ISD v. Wagner, 605 S.W.2d 743, 747 (Tex.App.—San Antonio 1980, writ ref'd n.r.e.). "Undoubtedly, the better practice is to recite the names of all the parties in the judgment.... Nevertheless, when ... the names of all the parties and the relief each is entitled to is easily ascertainable from the record, it would be a useless thing to remand the entire cause for the purpose of amending the judgment to include the names of all the parties."

TRCP 306a. PERIODS TO RUN FROM SIGNING OF JUDGMENT

1. **Beginning of periods.** The date of judgment or order is signed as shown of record shall determine the beginning of the periods prescribed by these rules for the court's plenary power to grant a new trial or to vacate, modify, correct or reform a judgment or order and for filing in the trial court the various documents that these rules authorize a party to file within such periods including, but not limited to, motions for new trial, motions to modify judgment, motions to reinstate a case dismissed for want of prosecution, motions to vacate judgment and requests for findings of fact and conclusions of law; but this rule shall not determine what constitutes rendition of a judgment or order for any other purpose.

2. **Date to be shown.** Judges, attorneys and clerks are directed to use their best efforts to cause all judgments, decisions and orders of any kind to be reduced to writing and signed by the trial judge with the date of signing stated therein. If the date of signing is not recited in the judgment or order, it may be shown in the record by a certificate of the judge or otherwise; provided, however, that the absence of a showing of the date in the record shall not invalidate any judgment or order.

3. **Notice of judgment.** When the final judgment or other appealable order is signed, the clerk of the court shall immediately give notice to the parties or their attorneys of record by first-class mail advising that the judgment or order was signed. Failure to comply with the provisions of this rule shall not affect the periods mentioned in paragraph (1) of this rule, except as provided in paragraph (4).

4. **No notice of judgment.** If within twenty days after the judgment or other appealable order is signed, a party adversely affected by it or his attorney has neither received the notice required by paragraph (3) of this rule nor acquired actual knowledge of the order, then with respect to that party all the periods mentioned in paragraph (1) shall begin on the date that such party or his attorney received such notice or acquired actual knowledge of the signing, whichever occurred first, but in no event shall such periods begin more than ninety days after the original judgment or other appealable order was signed.

5. **Motion, notice and hearing.** In order to establish the application of paragraph (4) of this rule, the party adversely affected is required to prove in the trial court, on sworn motion and notice, the date on which the party or his attorney first either received a notice of the judgment or acquired actual knowledge of the signing and that this date was more than twenty days after the judgment was signed.

6. **Nunc pro tunc order.** When a corrected judgment has been signed after expiration of the court's plenary power pursuant to Rule 316, the periods men-

★

tioned in paragraph (1) of this rule shall run from the date of signing the corrected judgment with respect to any complaint that would not be applicable to the original document.

7. When process served by publication. With respect to a motion for new trial filed more than thirty days after the judgment was signed pursuant to Rule 329 when process has been served by publication, the periods provided by paragraph (1) shall be computed as if the judgment were signed on the date of filing the motion.

History of TRCP 306a: Amended eff. Jan. 1, 1988, by order of July 15, 1987 (733-34 S.W.2d [Tex.Cases] lxxii): Changed sec. 6; amended to reflect repeal of TRCP 317. Amended eff. Sept. 1, 1986, by order of Apr. 10, 1986 (705-06 S.W.2d [Tex.Cases] xxxiv): Deleted references to appellate procedure; deleted from sec. 1 words beginning with "in connection with an appeal, including but not limited to" and ending with "for filing in the appellate court of the transcript and statement of facts"; deleted from sec. 4 words "except the period for filing a petition for writ of error"; deleted from sec. 7 words "thirty days before." Amended eff. Apr. 1, 1984, by order of Dec. 5, 1983 (661-62 S.W.2d [Tex.Cases] lxxxix): Rule collects all provisions concerning beginning of post-judgment periods that ordinarily run from date judgment is signed; sec. 1 is second sec. of former TRCP 306a, with addition of period of court's plenary power as defined in TRCP 329b(d), (e); sec. 2 is the first sec. of former TRCP 306a; sec. 3 incorporates former TRCP 306d by requiring notice by mail; secs. 4 and 5 are new and apply when actual notice of the signing of the judgment is not received within 20 days after the judgment was signed; sec. 6, with respect to nunc pro tunc orders, comes from former TRCP 306b and clarifies that secs. 1 and 4 do not revive the court's expired plenary power with respect to complaints that could have been made to original judgment; sec. 7 conforms TRCP 329 to the 1981 amendments to the appellate rules, and eliminates the discrepancy created by those amendments in providing for appeals that may expire before the time for filing a motion for new trial in cases of citation by publication. Amended eff. Jan. 1, 1981, by order of June 10, 1980 (599-600 S.W.2d [Tex.Cases] xlviii): Rewrote rule to eliminate use of the term "rendition of judgment," and to make period begin with date judgment is signed; certificate by judge is permitted to establish date of signing; deleted reference to notice of appeal and filing statement of facts in trial court, in view of amendments which omit these requirements. Amended eff. Feb. 1, 1946, by order of Oct. 10, 1945 (8 Tex.B.J. 533 [1945]). Adopted eff. Dec. 31, 1943, by order of June 16, 1943 (6 Tex.B.J. 373 [1943]). Source: New rule.

See *Commentaries*, "Default Judgment," ch. 7-A, p. 587; "The Judgment," ch. 9-C, p. 764; "Motion for New Trial," ch. 10-B, p. 789; "Motion to Reinstate After Dismissal for Want of Prosecution," ch. 10-F, p. 826; "Motion to Extend Post-judgment Deadlines," ch. 10-G, p. 831; "Motion for Judgment Nunc Pro Tunc," ch. 10-H, p. 837.

ANNOTATIONS

Generally

Board of Trs. of Bastrop ISD v. Toungate, 958 S.W.2d 365, 367 (Tex.1997). "We note that the trial court should have submitted the modified judgment to the clerk immediately upon signing it to avoid the burden of a notification hearing."

Martinez v. Humble Sand & Gravel, Inc., 875 S.W.2d 311, 312 (Tex.1994). "When ... an otherwise final judgment fails to dispose of all parties, the court may make the judgment final for purposes of appeal by severing the causes and parties disposed of by the judgment into a different cause. *At 313:* When a severance

order takes effect, the appellate timetable runs from the signing date of the order that made the judgment severed 'final' and appealable."

Wells Fargo Bank v. Erickson, 267 S.W.3d 139, 149 (Tex.App.—Corpus Christi 2008, no pet.). "[P] argues that a trial court cannot reconsider its decision to deny a rule 306a motion. We find nothing in the [TRCPs] that precludes a trial court from reconsidering its prior ruling on such a motion within its plenary power or from entertaining a second motion filed for the same purpose."

Coinmach, Inc. v. Aspenwood Apt. Corp., 98 S.W.3d 377, 378 (Tex.App.—Houston [1st Dist.] 2003, no pet.). "The issue for this Court is whether the effective date of the order granting a new trial is (1) the date the trial court signs the order or (2) the date the trial court clerk file-stamps the signed order. ... We hold that the order granting a new trial became effective on the date signed by the trial court...."

Burns v. Bishop, 48 S.W.3d 459, 465 (Tex.App.—Houston [14th Dist.] 2001, no pet.). "Signing and rendition are not synonymous. Signing an order is not among the official steps that would fall within the common meaning of 'proceedings.' Drafting and signing the judgment [are] preparatory, *administrative* acts that ... authenticate the record of the court's rendition. Rendition occurs when the trial court officially announces its decision (1) in open court in a manner that objectively reflects its intention to render or (2) by written memorandum *filed with the clerk*."

No Notice of Judgment

Ginn v. Forrester, 282 S.W.3d 430, 433 (Tex.2009). TRCP 306a does "not impose upon the clerk an affirmative duty to record the mailing of the required notice[ ]; accordingly, the absence of proof in the record that notice was provided does not establish error on the face of the record. [¶] We ... see [no] distinction ... between a record that is silent and a record that contains a written notation that the record is silent; either way, proof of error is absent."

In re Lynd Co., 195 S.W.3d 682, 686 (Tex.2006). "Rule 306a does not require that the trial court issue a signed order with ... a finding [of actual notice of final judgment]. [W]hen the trial court fails to specifically find the date of notice, the finding may be implied from the trial court's judgment, unless there is no evidence

⋆

supporting the implied finding or the party challenging the judgment establishes as a matter of law an alternate notice date."

John v. Marshall Health Servs., 58 S.W.3d 738, 741 (Tex.2001). "Rule 306a(5) does not prohibit a motion from being filed at any time within the trial court's plenary jurisdiction measured from the date determined under Rule 306a(4). Rule 306a simply imposes no deadline, and none can be added by decision, other than the deadline of the expiration of the trial court's jurisdiction."

Estate of Howley v. Haberman, 878 S.W.2d 139, 140 (Tex.1994). "A party who does not have actual knowledge of an order of dismissal within 90 days of the date it is signed cannot move for reinstatement. Since [P] did not learn of the dismissal within this period, the order of dismissal for want of prosecution was final.... [P's] only possible recourse is a bill of review." *See also* ***Levit v. Adams***, 850 S.W.2d 469, 470 (Tex. 1993).

TRCP 306b. REPEALED

Repealed eff. Apr. 1, 1984, by order of Dec. 5, 1983 (661-62 S.W.2d [Tex.Cases] lxxxi): See TRCP 306a(6), which supersedes this rule.

TRCP 306c. PREMATURELY FILED DOCUMENTS

No motion for new trial or request for findings of fact and conclusions of law shall be held ineffective because prematurely filed; but every such motion shall be deemed to have been filed on the date of but subsequent to the time of signing of the judgment the motion assails, and every such request for findings of fact and conclusions of law shall be deemed to have been filed on the date of but subsequent to the time of signing of the judgment.

History of TRCP 306c: Amended eff. Sept. 1, 1990, by order of Apr. 24, 1990 (785-86 S.W.2d [Tex.Cases] lxx): Changed phrase "subsequent to the date of signing of the judgment" to "subsequent to the time of signing of the judgment." Amended eff. Sept. 1, 1986, by order of Apr. 10, 1986 (705-06 S.W.2d [Tex.Cases] xxxv): Deleted any reference to appellate procedure; deleted phrases "appeal bond or affidavit in lieu thereof, notice of appeal, or notice of limitation of appeal," "and every such appeal bond or affidavit or notice of appeal or notice of limitation of appeal," and "or the date of the overruling of motion for new trial, if such a motion is filed." Amended eff. Apr. 1, 1984, by order of Dec. 5, 1983 (661-62 S.W.2d [Tex.Cases] lxxxi): Broadened rule to include prematurely filed request for findings of fact and conclusions of law. Amended eff. Jan. 1, 1976, by order of July 22, 1975 (525-26 S.W.2d [Tex.Cases] l): Added words "or notice of limitation of appeal" in two places. Amended eff. Sept. 1, 1962, by order of Apr. 12, 1962 (25 Tex.B.J. 428 [1962]): Expanded scope of rule to include notice of appeal. Adopted eff. Feb. 1, 1946, by order of Oct. 10, 1945 (8 Tex.B.J. 534 [1945]). Source: New rule.

See TRAP 27; See ***Commentaries***, "Motion for New Trial," ch. 10-B, p. 789; "Requesting Findings of Fact," ch. 10-E, §3, p. 820.

Ryland Enter. v. Weatherspoon, 355 S.W.3d 664, 666 (Tex.2011). "[T]he premature filing rules in [TRCP] 306c and [TRAP] 27.2 apply equally to motions for new trial or to modify the judgment. [T]he filing of a motion for new trial or to modify the judgment, before the judgment is signed or within 30 days after, extends the deadline for filing a notice of appeal to 90 days."

Wilkins v. Methodist Health Care Sys., 160 S.W.3d 559, 563 (Tex.2005). "When a motion for new trial is granted, it becomes moot as to any effect it may have on a subsequent judgment. *At 564:* [A] motion for new trial that has been granted cannot 'assail' a subsequent judgment for purposes of determining the deadline for filing a notice of appeal."

Fredonia State Bank v. General Am. Life Ins., 881 S.W.2d 279, 281 (Tex.1994). "[A] motion for new trial relating to an earlier judgment may be considered applicable to a second judgment when the substance of the motion could properly be raised with respect to the corrected judgment."

TRCP 306d. REPEALED

Repealed eff. Apr. 1, 1984, by order of Dec. 5, 1983 (661-62 S.W.2d [Tex.Cases] lxxxi): See TRCP 306a(3).

TRCP 307. EXCEPTIONS, ETC., TRANSCRIPT

In non-jury cases, where findings of fact and conclusions of law are requested and filed, and in jury cases, where a special verdict is returned, any party claiming that the findings of the court or the jury, as the case may be, do not support the judgment, may have noted in the record an exception to said judgment and thereupon take an appeal or writ of error, where such writ is allowed, without a statement of facts or further exceptions in the transcript, but the transcript in such cases shall contain the conclusions of law and fact or the special verdict and the judgment rendered thereon.

History of TRCP 307: Adopted eff. Sept. 1, 1941, by order of Oct. 29, 1940 (3 Tex.B.J. 571 [1940]). Source: TRCS art. 2210 (repealed).

TRCP 308. COURT SHALL ENFORCE ITS DECREES

The court shall cause its judgments and decrees to be carried into execution; and where the judgment is for personal property, and it is shown by the pleadings and evidence and the verdict, if any, that such property has an especial value to the plaintiff, the court may

---

★

---

award a special writ for the seizure and delivery of such property to the plaintiff; and in such case may enforce its judgment by attachment, fine and imprisonment.

History of TRCP 308: Adopted eff. Sept. 1, 1941, by order of Oct. 29, 1940 (3 Tex.B.J. 571 [1940]). Source: TRCS art. 2217 (repealed).

ANNOTATIONS

Cook v. Stallcup, 170 S.W.3d 916, 920-21 (Tex. App.—Dallas 2005, no pet.). After the court's plenary power expired, "the trial court had power only to enforce its judgment, subject to the limitation that any enforcement may not be inconsistent with the original judgment and must not constitute a material change in substantial adjudicated portions of the judgment." *See also **Kennedy v. Hudnall**,* 249 S.W.3d 520, 523 (Tex. App.—Texarkana 2008, no pet.); ***Bridas Corp. v. Unocal Corp.***, 16 S.W.3d 887, 889 (Tex.App.—Houston [14th Dist.] 2000, pet. dism'd).

TRCP 308a. IN SUITS AFFECTING THE PARENT-CHILD RELATIONSHIP

When the court has ordered child support or possession of or access to a child and it is claimed that the order has been violated, the person claiming that a violation has occurred shall make this known to the court. The court may appoint a member of the bar to investigate the claim to determine whether there is reason to believe that the court order has been violated. If the attorney in good faith believes that the order has been violated, the attorney shall take the necessary action as provided under Chapter 14, Family Code.[1] On a finding of a violation, the court may enforce its order as provided in Chapter 14, Family Code.[1]

Except by order of the court, no fee shall be charged by or paid to the attorney representing the claimant. If the court determines that an attorney's fee should be paid, the fee shall be adjudged against the party who violated the court's order. The fee may be assessed as costs of court, or awarded by judgment, or both.

1. **Editor's note:** Now Fam. Code ch. 157. For current provisions of Family Code ch. 14, see *O'Connor's Family Code* (2011-12) Disposition Table—Former to Current, p. 1339.

History of TRCP 308a: Amended eff. Sept. 1, 1990, by order of Apr. 24, 1990 (785-86 S.W.2d [Tex.Cases] lxx): Completely rewrote rule to broaden its application to cover problems dealing with possession and access to a child as well as support. Amended eff. Jan. 1, 1988, by order of July 15, 1987 (733-34 S.W.2d [Tex.Cases] lxxiii). Amended eff. Mar. 1, 1952, by order of Oct. 10, 1951 (14 Tex.B.J. 634 [1951]). Added eff. Mar. 1, 1950, by order of Oct. 12, 1949 (12 Tex.B.J. 534 [1949]).

ANNOTATIONS

Ex parte Herring, 438 S.W.2d 801, 803 (Tex.1969). TRCP 308a "contemplates that service under any of the applicable portions of [TRCP] 21a including service upon the attorney would constitute a compliance with the [TRCPs]. [¶] [I]t is a denial of due process to commit a person to prison for contempt who is not shown to be avoiding deliberately the service of process, and who has had *no* personal notice or knowledge of the show-cause hearing...." Relator discharged.

TRCP 309. IN FORECLOSURE PROCEEDINGS

Judgments for the foreclosure of mortgages and other liens shall be that the plaintiff recover his debt, damages and costs, with a foreclosure of the plaintiff's lien on the property subject thereto, and, except in judgments against executors, administrators and guardians, that an order of sale shall issue to any sheriff or any constable within the State of Texas, directing him to seize and sell the same as under execution, in satisfaction of the judgment; and, if the property cannot be found, or if the proceeds of such sale be insufficient to satisfy the judgment, then to take the money or any balance thereof remaining unpaid, out of any other property of the defendant, as in case of ordinary executions.

History of TRCP 309: Amended eff. Jan. 1, 1967, by order of July 20, 1966 (401-02 S.W.2d [Tex.Cases] xliii): Changed phrase "of any county of the State" to "within the State of Texas." Adopted eff. Sept. 1, 1941, by order of Oct. 29, 1940 (3 Tex.B.J. 572 [1940]). Source: TRCS art. 2218 (repealed), except that the order of sale is to be directed to the sheriff or constable of any county of the State, in harmony with the rules relating to executions.

ANNOTATIONS

Brown v. EMC Mortg. Corp., 326 S.W.3d 648, 653-54 (Tex.App.—Dallas 2010, pet. denied). "[T]he judgment of foreclosure in this case was not against an executor, administrator, or guardian. Thus, [TRCP] 309 requires the order of sale 'issue to any sheriff or any constable.' Instead, the trial court's order authorizes [D] to sell the property at public auction.... [¶] [D] argues that the trial court's order of sale is consistent with Texas law because it meets the requirements of [Prop. Code ch. 51]. [D] asks us to ignore rule 309's requirement that the property be sold by a sheriff or constable because this requirement is not also present in ch. 51. We decline to do so. [¶] The requirement that the sale of the property in a judicial foreclosure be conducted by a sheriff or constable is clear, unambiguous, and does not conflict with any provision of ch. 51. Indeed, ch. 51 distinguishes between foreclosure sales conducted under the chapter and those conducted under a court judgment foreclosing the lien. Because

★

nothing in ch. 51 conflicts with rule 309, we must assume that the legislature intended for judicial foreclosures to continue to be conducted by sheriffs or constables even after the enactment of ch. 51. Accordingly, the order of sale in this case is not in compliance with Texas law."

TRCP 310. WRIT OF POSSESSION

When an order foreclosing a lien upon real estate is made in a suit having for its object the foreclosure of such lien, such order shall have all the force and effect of a writ of possession as between the parties to the foreclosure suit and any person claiming under the defendant to such suit by any right acquired pending such suit; and the court shall so direct in the judgment providing for the issuance of such order. The sheriff or other officer executing such order of sale shall proceed by virtue of such order of sale to place the purchaser of the property sold thereunder in possession thereof within thirty days after the day of sale.

History of TRCP 310: Adopted eff. Sept. 1, 1941, by order of Oct. 29, 1940 (3 Tex.B.J. 572 [1940]). Source: TRCS art. 2219 (repealed).

TRCP 311. ON APPEAL FROM PROBATE COURT

Judgment on appeal or certiorari from any county court sitting in probate shall be certified to such county court for observance.

History of TRCP 311: Adopted eff. Sept. 1, 1941, by order of Oct. 29, 1940 (3 Tex.B.J. 572 [1940]). Source: TRCS art. 2220 (repealed).

TRCP 312. ON APPEAL FROM JUSTICE COURT

Judgments on appeal or certiorari from a justice court shall be enforced by the county or district court rendering the judgment.

History of TRCP 312: Adopted eff. Sept. 1, 1941, by order of Oct. 29, 1940 (3 Tex.B.J. 572 [1940]). Source: TRCS art. 2221 (repealed).

TRCP 313. AGAINST EXECUTORS, ETC.

A judgment for the recovery of money against an executor, administrator or guardian, as such, shall state that it is to be paid in the due course of administration. No execution shall issue thereon, but it shall be certified to the county court, sitting in matters of probate, to be there enforced in accordance with law, but judgment against an executor appointed and acting under a will dispensing with the action of the county court in reference to such estate shall be enforced against the property of the testator in the hands of such executor, by execution, as in other cases.

History of TRCP 313: Adopted eff. Sept. 1, 1941, by order of Oct. 29, 1940 (3 Tex.B.J. 572 [1940]). Source: TRCS art. 2222 (repealed).

TRCP 314. CONFESSION OF JUDGMENT

Any person against whom a cause of action exists may, without process, appear in person or by attorney, and confess judgment therefor in open court as follows:

(a) A petition shall be filed and the justness of the debt or cause of action be sworn to by the person in whose favor the judgment is confessed.

(b) If the judgment is confessed by attorney, the power of attorney shall be filed and its contents be recited in the judgment.

(c) Every such judgment duly made shall operate as a release of all errors in the record thereof, but such judgment may be impeached for fraud or other equitable cause.

History of TRCP 314: Adopted eff. Sept. 1, 1941, by order of Oct. 29, 1940 (3 Tex.B.J. 572 [1940]). Source: TRCS art. 2225 (repealed).

I. REMITTITUR & CORRECTION

TRCP 315. REMITTITUR

Any party in whose favor a judgment has been rendered may remit any part thereof in open court, or by executing and filing with the clerk a written remittitur signed by the party or the party's attorney of record, and duly acknowledged by the party or the party's attorney. Such remittitur shall be a part of the record of the cause. Execution shall issue for the balance only of such judgment.

History of TRCP 315: Amended eff. Jan. 1, 1988, by order of July 15, 1987 (733-34 S.W.2d [Tex.Cases] lxxiii). Adopted eff. Sept. 1, 1941, by order of Oct. 29, 1940 (3 Tex.B.J. 573 [1940]). Source: TRCS art. 2227 (repealed).

See *Commentaries*, "Motion for Remittitur," ch. 10-C, p. 811; *O'Connor's Texas Forms*, FORMS 10C.

ANNOTATIONS

Larson v. Cactus Util. Co., 730 S.W.2d 640, 641 (Tex.1987). "A court of appeals should uphold a trial court remittitur only when the evidence is factually insufficient to support the verdict. [¶] If a court of appeals holds that there is no evidence to support a damages verdict, it should render a take nothing judgment as to that amount. If part of a damage verdict lacks sufficient evidentiary support, the proper course is to suggest a remittitur of that part of the verdict."

TRCP 316. CORRECTION OF CLERICAL MISTAKES IN JUDGMENT RECORD

Clerical mistakes in the record of any judgment may be corrected by the judge in open court according to the

TRCP 316

★

truth or justice of the case after notice of the motion therefor has been given to the parties interested in such judgment, as provided in Rule 21a, and thereafter the execution shall conform to the judgment as amended.

History of TRCP 316: Amended eff. Jan. 1, 1988, by order of July 15, 1987 (733-34 S.W.2d [Tex.Cases] lxxiv). Amended eff. Dec. 31, 1943, by order of June 16, 1943 (10 Tex.B.J. 375 [1943]): Added last sentence. Adopted eff. Sept. 1, 1941, by order of Oct. 29, 1940 (3 Tex.B.J. 573 [1940]). Source: TRCS art. 2228 (repealed).

See *Commentaries*, "Motion for Judgment Nunc Pro Tunc," ch. 10-H, p. 837; *O'Connor's Texas Forms*, FORMS 10H.

ANNOTATIONS

Escobar v. Escobar, 711 S.W.2d 230, 231 (Tex. 1986). "After the trial court loses its jurisdiction over a judgment, it can correct only clerical errors in the judgment by judgment nunc pro tunc. In this regard, the trial court has plenary power to correct a clerical error made in *entering* final judgment. [¶] A judicial error is an error which occurs in the *rendering* as opposed to the *entering* of a judgment." *See also In re Daredia*, 317 S.W.3d 247, 249-50 (Tex.2010); *Andrews v. Koch*, 702 S.W.2d 584, 585 (Tex.1986).

Holland v. Holland, 357 S.W.2d 192, 199 (Tex. App.—Dallas 2012, no pet.). "No party had moved for the nunc pro tunc order, and the trial court did not give the parties any notice before entering the nunc pro tunc order. ... A judgment nunc pro tunc entered without notice to the parties as required by rule 316 is a nullity."

In re Marriage of Snead, No. 13-11-00200-CV (Tex.App.—Corpus Christi 2012, no pet.) (memo op.; 8-16-12). "A judgment nunc pro tunc does not disturb the initial judgment rendered by the trial court; it merely brings the court records into conformity with it. Accordingly, a judgment nunc pro tunc, although signed later, relates back to the date of the original judgment and is effective as of the earlier date."

Key Fin. Corp. v. Priority Servs., No. 09-09-00531-CV (Tex.App.—Beaumont 2010, no pet.) (memo op.; 9-9-10). "Whether an error in a judgment is a judicial or clerical error is a question of law. A clerical error is a mistake preventing a judgment, as entered in the official record, from accurately reflecting the judgment that was rendered. Conceivably a judgment *nunc pro tunc* may be issued in appropriate circumstances to correct the date an order was signed if the original date is shown to have been incorrect. However, Rule 316 may not be used to simply backdate the signing of a written judgment that was not in fact signed earlier."

TRCP 317 TO 319. REPEALED

Repealed eff. Jan. 1, 1988, by order of July 15, 1987 (733-34 S.W.2d [Tex.Cases] lxxiv).

J. NEW TRIALS

TRCP 320. MOTION & ACTION OF COURT THEREON

New trials may be granted and judgment set aside for good cause, on motion or on the court's own motion on such terms as the court shall direct. New trials may be granted when the damages are manifestly too small or too large. When it appears to the court that a new trial should be granted on a point or points that affect only a part of the matters in controversy and that such part is clearly separable without unfairness to the parties, the court may grant a new trial as to that part only, provided that a separate trial on unliquidated damages alone shall not be ordered if liability issues are contested. Each motion for new trial shall be in writing and signed by the party or his attorney.

History of TRCP 320: Amended eff. Jan. 1, 1988, by order of July 15, 1987 (733-34 S.W.2d [Tex.Cases] lxxiv). Amended eff. Apr. 1, 1984, by order of Dec. 5, 1983 (661-62 S.W.2d [Tex.Cases] lxxxi): Rewrote rule to be consistent with TRCP 329b(d). Amended eff. Jan. 1, 1981, by order of June 10, 1980 (599-600 S.W.2d [Tex.Cases] xlviii): Substituted words "point or points" for "ground or grounds." [See TRCP 321 and former TRCP 418(d), 458, 469(e), and 515.] Amended eff. Jan. 1, 1978, by order of July 11, 1977 (553-54 S.W.2d [Tex.Cases] xlix): Deleted part requiring a specification of each ground from last sentence. Amended eff. Jan. 1, 1976, by order of July 22, 1975 (525-26 S.W.2d [Tex.Cases] l): Permits partial retrials in certain cases. Amended eff. Jan. 1, 1955, by order of July 20, 1954 (17 Tex.B.J. 568 [1954]): Eliminated (a) and (d) because they are covered in TRCP 329a and 329b. Adopted eff. Sept. 1, 1941, by order of Oct. 29, 1940 (3 Tex.B.J. 573 [1940]). Source: TRCS art. 2232 (repealed), with changes: Inserted exceptions to harmonize with provisions for special situations.

See *Commentaries*, "Motion for New Trial," ch. 10-B, p. 789; *O'Connor's Texas Forms*, FORMS 10B.

ANNOTATIONS

In re Columbia Med. Ctr., 290 S.W.3d 204, 206 (Tex.2009). "The issue before us is whether, after a jury has rendered its verdict, the trial court may disregard that verdict, grant a new trial, and explain its action only as being 'in the interests of justice and fairness.' We conclude that just as appellate courts that set aside jury verdicts are required to detail reasons for doing so, trial courts must give more explanation than 'in the interest of justice' for setting aside a jury verdict. *At 212-13:* We do not retreat from the position that trial courts have significant discretion in granting new trials. However, such discretion should not, and does not, permit a trial judge to substitute his or her own views for that of the jury without a valid basis. ... The trial court's action in failing to give its reasons for disre-

TRCP 316

⭐

---

garding the jury verdict as to [D] was arbitrary and an abuse of discretion."

Old Republic Ins. v. Scott, 846 S.W.2d 832, 833 (Tex.1993). "The **filing** of a motion for new trial in order to extend the appellate timetable is a matter of right, whether or not there is any sound or reasonable basis for the conclusion that a further motion is necessary."

State Dept. of Hwys. & Pub. Transp. v. Cotner, 845 S.W.2d 818, 819 (Tex.1993). "A partial new trial may be ordered notwithstanding the prohibition in [TRCP] 41 against post-submission severances. [TRCP] 320 is thus an exception to Rule 41."

TRCP 321. FORM

Each point relied upon in a motion for new trial or in arrest of judgment shall briefly refer to that part of the ruling of the court, charge given to the jury, or charge refused, admission or rejection of evidence, or other proceedings which are designated to be complained of, in such a way that the objection can be clearly identified and understood by the court.

History of TRCP 321: Amended eff. Jan. 1, 1981, by order of June 10, 1980 (599-600 S.W.2d [Tex.Cases] xlix): Substituted "point" for "ground." [See TRCP 320 and former TRCPs 418(d), 458, 469(e), and 515.] Adopted eff. Sept. 1, 1941, by order of Oct. 29, 1940 (3 Tex.B.J. 573 [1940]). Source: Tex. Rules for Dist. & Cty. Cts. 67.

See *Commentaries*, "Motion for New Trial," ch. 10-B, p. 789; *O'Connor's Texas Forms*, FORMS 10B.

TRCP 322. GENERALITY TO BE AVOIDED

Grounds of objections couched in general terms— as that the court erred in its charge, in sustaining or overruling exceptions to the pleadings, and in excluding or admitting evidence, the verdict of the jury is contrary to law, and the like—shall not be considered by the court.

History of TRCP 322: Adopted eff. Sept. 1, 1941, by order of Oct. 29, 1940 (3 Tex.B.J. 573 [1940]). Source: Tex. Rules for Dist. & Cty. Cts. 68.

See *Commentaries*, "Points of error," ch. 10-B, §2.3, p. 790.

ANNOTATIONS

Arkoma Basin Expl. Co. v. FMF Assocs. 1990-A, Ltd., 249 S.W.3d 380, 388 (Tex.2008). "If a single jury question involves many issues, it is possible that a general objection may not tell the trial court where to start. But post-trial objections will rarely be as detailed as an appellate brief because time is short, the record may not be ready, and the trial court is already familiar with the case. In that context, an objection is not necessarily inadequate because it does not specify every reason the

evidence was insufficient. Like all other procedural rules, those regarding the specificity of post-trial objections should be construed liberally so that the right to appeal is not lost unnecessarily."

TRCP 323. REPEALED

Repealed eff. Jan. 1, 1978, by order of July 11, 1977 (553-54 S.W.2d [Tex.Cases] xlix).

TRCP 324. PREREQUISITES OF APPEAL

(a) Motion for New Trial Not Required. A point in a motion for new trial is not a prerequisite to a complaint on appeal in either a jury or a nonjury case, except as provided in subdivision (b).

(b) Motion for New Trial Required. A point in a motion for new trial is a prerequisite to the following complaints on appeal:

(1) A complaint on which evidence must be heard such as one of jury misconduct or newly discovered evidence or failure to set aside a judgment by default;

(2) A complaint of factual insufficiency of the evidence to support a jury finding;

(3) A complaint that a jury finding is against the overwhelming weight of the evidence;

(4) A complaint of inadequacy or excessiveness of the damages found by the jury; or

(5) Incurable jury argument if not otherwise ruled on by the trial court.

(c) Judgment Notwithstanding Findings; Cross-Points. When judgment is rendered non obstante veredicto or notwithstanding the findings of a jury on one or more questions, the appellee may bring forward by cross-point contained in his brief filed in the Court of Appeals any ground which would have vitiated the verdict or would have prevented an affirmance of the judgment had one been rendered by the trial court in harmony with the verdict, including although not limited to the ground that one or more of the jury's findings have insufficient support in the evidence or are against the overwhelming preponderance of the evidence as a matter of fact, and the ground that the verdict and judgment based thereon should be set aside because of improper argument of counsel.

The failure to bring forward by cross-points such grounds as would vitiate the verdict shall be deemed a waiver thereof; provided, however, that if a cross-point is upon a ground which requires the taking of evidence in addition to that adduced upon the trial of the cause,

⭐

it is not necessary that the evidentiary hearing be held until after the appellate court determines that the cause be remanded to consider such a cross-point.

History of TRCP 324: Amended eff. Jan. 1, 1988, by order of July 15, 1987 (733-34 S.W.2d [Tex.Cases] lxxiv): Amended (c). Amended eff. Apr. 1, 1984, by order of Dec. 5, 1983 (661-62 S.W.2d [Tex.Cases] lxxxii): Added requirement for motion for new trial concerning factual complaints of jury findings, excessiveness and inadequacy of damages, and incurable jury argument. Amended eff. Jan. 1, 1981, by order of June 10, 1980 (599-600 S.W.2d [Tex.Cases] xlix): Rewrote third sentence; deleted fourth sentence. Amended eff. Jan. 1, 1978, by order of July 11, 1977 (553-54 S.W.2d [Tex.Cases] xlix): Eliminated requirement for a motion for new trial in jury cases in most (though not all) instances. Amended eff. Sept. 1, 1962, by order of Apr. 12, 1962 (25 Tex.B.J. 428 [1962]): Rewrote proviso in first sentence to clarify its effect as declared in *Wagner v. Foster*, 341 S.W.2d 887 (Tex.1960). Deleted words "in a case coming within the proviso of Rule 329-a" which formerly appeared after "non-jury case" in the first sentence; rewrote notes regarding original change and 1941 amendments. Amended eff. Sept. 1, 1957, by order of Mar. 19, 1957 (20 Tex.B.J. 192 [1957]): Expanded provisions dealing with cross-points of error of appellee when judgment is rendered JNOV to require cross-points as to any matter, not requiring the taking of evidence, which would vitiate the verdict; amendment is intended to modify holding in *De Winne v. Allen*, 277 S.W.2d 95, 99 (Tex.1955). Amended eff. Jan. 1, 1955, by order of July 20, 1954 (17 Tex.B.J. 568 [1954]): Rewrote and rearranged. Amended eff. Dec. 31, 1941, by order of Sept. 20, 1941 (4 Tex.B.J. 535 [1941]): Deleted reference to cross-assignments of error and motion for new trial from sentence regarding appellee's right to complain of errors committed against him in the trial; added sentence providing that a motion for new trial shall not be necessary on behalf of appellee, except where he complains of the judgment or a part thereof; expanded provisions of par. dealing with right to complain on appeal without an assignment in a motion for new trial to include action of court "in withdrawing the case from the jury and rendering judgment." Amended eff. Sept. 1, 1941, by order of Mar. 31, 1941 (4 Tex.B.J. 175 [1941]): Added par. providing that an assignment in a motion for new trial shall not be a prerequisite to the right to complain on appeal of the action of the court in giving an instructed verdict, rendering or refusing to render judgment non obstante veredicto, or overruling appellant's motion for judgment on the verdict. Adopted eff. Sept. 1, 1941, by order of Oct. 29, 1940 (3 Tex.B.J. 574 [1940]). Source: Tex. Rules for Dist. & Cty. Cts. 71a, with changes: Eliminated reference to fundamental error as an exceptional situation not requiring motion for new trial; added proviso authorizing appellee, when judgment is rendered JNOV, to complain of any prejudicial error committed against him over his objection on the trial by cross-assignments of error filed in the Court of Civil Appeals, without having first presented such complaint in a motion for new trial.

See *Commentaries*, "Making & Preserving Objections," ch. 1-F, p. 43; "Motion for JNOV," ch. 9-B, p. 761; "Motion for New Trial," ch. 10-B, p. 789.

ANNOTATIONS

Phillips v. Bramlett, 288 S.W.3d 876, 883 (Tex. 2009). "A complaint of incurable argument may be asserted and preserved in a motion for new trial, even without a complaint and ruling during the trial. Incurable jury argument is rare, however, because '[t]ypically, retraction of the argument or instruction from the court can cure any probable harm....' The party claiming incurable harm must persuade the court that, based on the record as a whole, the offensive argument was so extreme that a 'juror of ordinary intelligence could have been persuaded by that argument to agree to a verdict contrary to that to which he would have agreed but for such argument.'" *See also **Austin v. Weems***, 337 S.W.3d 415, 428 (Tex.App.—Houston [1st Dist.] 2011,

no pet.) (incurable argument is one that compromises the basic premise that a trial provides impartial, equal justice).

State Farm Lloyds v. Nicolau, 951 S.W.2d 444, 452 (Tex.1997). D was not entitled to a new trial based on newly discovered evidence because it had "not shown any likelihood that the new evidence, if introduced at trial, would have resulted in a different verdict on any of [Ps'] claims."

Lee v. Braeburn Valley W. Civic Ass'n, 786 S.W.2d 262, 263 (Tex.1990). "[A] motion for new trial is not a prerequisite for an appeal of a summary judgment proceeding."

TRCP 325. REPEALED

Repealed eff. Jan. 1, 1978, by order of July 11, 1977 (553-54 S.W.2d [Tex.Cases] l).

TRCP 326. NOT MORE THAN TWO

Not more than two new trials shall be granted either party in the same cause because of insufficiency or weight of the evidence.

History of TRCP 326: Adopted eff. Sept. 1, 1941, by order of Oct. 29, 1940 (3 Tex.B.J. 574 [1940]). Source: TRCS art. 2233 (repealed).

TRCP 327. FOR JURY MISCONDUCT

a. When the ground of a motion for new trial, supported by affidavit, is misconduct of the jury or of the officer in charge of them, or because of any communication made to the jury, or that a juror gave an erroneous or incorrect answer on voir dire examination, the court shall hear evidence thereof from the jury or others in open court, and may grant a new trial if such misconduct proved, or the communication made, or the erroneous or incorrect answer on voir dire examination, be material, and if it reasonably appears from the evidence both on the hearing of the motion and the trial of the case and from the record as a whole that injury probably resulted to the complaining party.

b. A juror may not testify as to any matter or statement occurring during the course of the jury's deliberations or to the effect of anything upon his or any other juror's mind or emotions as influencing him to assent to or dissent from the verdict concerning his mental processes in connection therewith, except that a juror may testify whether any outside influence was improperly brought to bear upon any juror. Nor may his affidavit or evidence of any statement by him concerning a matter about which he would be precluded from testifying be received for these purposes.

───────────── ★ ─────────────

History of TRCP 327: Amended eff. Apr. 1, 1984, by order of Dec. 5, 1983 (661-62 S.W.2d [Tex.Cases] lxxxiii): Codified existing law that there must be affidavits before the trial judge need have a hearing; incorporates the provisions of TRE 606(b). Amended eff. Jan. 1, 1955, by order of July 20, 1954 (17 Tex.B.J. 568 [1954]): Inserted phrase "or that a juror gave an erroneous or incorrect answer on voir dire examination." Adopted eff. Sept. 1, 1941, by order of Oct. 29, 1940 (3 Tex.B.J. 574 [1940]). Source: TRCS art. 2234 (repealed), except to impose burden on complaining party to show probability of injury.

See TRE 606(b); *Commentaries*, "MNT Based on Jury or Bailiff Misconduct," ch. 10-B, §14, p. 804; *O'Connor's Texas Forms*, FORM 10B:1.

ANNOTATIONS

Ford Motor Co. v. Castillo, 279 S.W.3d 656, 666 (Tex.2009). "[B]y their plain language, [TRCP 327(b) and TRE 606(b)] apply to motions for new trials, reasons jurors voted for or against verdicts, and inquiries into the validity of verdicts or indictments. Even when those types of issues are involved, the rules specifically allow jurors to testify about outside influence brought to bear on any of them."

Golden Eagle Archery, Inc. v. Jackson, 24 S.W.3d 362, 370 (Tex.2000). "A juror may testify about jury misconduct provided it does not require delving into deliberations. [¶] [TRCP 327(b) and TRE 606(b)] contemplate that an 'outside influence' originates from sources other than the jurors themselves. *At 371:* [An] alleged conversation between [jurors] during a trial break ... should not be considered 'deliberations' and therefore barred by [TRE] 606(b) and [TRCP] 327(b)." *See also Vargas de Damian v. Bell Helicopter Textron, Inc.*, 352 S.W.3d 124, 161 (Tex.App.—Fort Worth 2011, pet. denied) (juror testimony that they traded answers not evidence of outside influence).

Pharo v. Chambers Cty., 922 S.W.2d 945, 950 (Tex. 1996). The bailiff's misconduct "justifies a new trial only if it reasonably appears from the record that injury probably resulted to the complaining party. To show probable injury, there must be some indication in the record that the alleged misconduct most likely caused a juror to vote differently than he would otherwise have done on one or more issues vital to the judgment. Determining the existence of probable injury is a question of law." (Internal quotes omitted.) *See also Holland v. Lovelace*, 352 S.W.3d 777, 783 (Tex.App.—Dallas 2011, pet. denied) (juror misconduct).

Jefferson v. Fuller, No. 01-11-00199-CV (Tex. App.—Houston [1st Dist.] 2012, pet. filed 11-9-12) (memo op.; 6-21-12). "'A juror can commit misconduct if he lies in voir dire about a matter on which he was clearly biased or prejudiced.' For false answers to voir dire questions to entitle a party to a new trial, the concealment must be in response to a specific and direct question calling for disclosure. To establish jury misconduct on grounds that the juror concealed information during voir dire, a party must obtain proof of concealment from a source other than jury deliberations."

Hutton v. AER Mfg. II, Inc., 224 S.W.3d 459, 463 (Tex.App.—Dallas 2007, pet. denied). "[P] complains jury misconduct occurred as a result of the trial court's instruction after the jury said it was deadlocked. [A]s a matter of law, jury instructions are not an outside influence. Thus, to the extent [P] supports his misconduct claim solely with juror affidavits and testimony that they changed their votes or bargained away their positions as a result of the supplemental charge, such evidence was inadmissible under [TRCP] 327(b) and [TRE] 606(b) as evidence about deliberations."

Brandt v. Surber, 194 S.W.3d 108, 134 (Tex.App.—Corpus Christi 2006, pet. denied). "An outside influence does not include 'information not in evidence, unknown to the jurors prior to trial, acquired by a juror and communicated to one or more other jurors between the time the jurors received their instructions from the court and the rendition of the verdict[ ]'.... [¶] [One juror's] affidavit stating that other jurors discussed newspaper articles during deliberations was not evidence of any outside influence, but only described matters on the minds of other jurors during deliberations. The affidavit is, therefore, incompetent to serve as evidence of juror misconduct." *See also Editorial Caballero, S.A. de C.V. v. Playboy Enters.*, 359 S.W.3d 318, 326-27 (Tex.App.—Corpus Christi 2012, pet. denied) (Internet research was not outside influence).

TRCP 328. REPEALED

Repealed eff. Jan. 1, 1988, by order of July 15, 1987 (733-34 S.W.2d [Tex.Cases] lxxv).

TRCP 329. MOTION FOR NEW TRIAL ON JUDGMENT FOLLOWING CITATION BY PUBLICATION

In cases in which judgment has been rendered on service of process by publication, when the defendant has not appeared in person or by attorney of his own selection:

(a) The court may grant a new trial upon petition of the defendant showing good cause, supported by affidavit, filed within two years after such judgment was signed. The parties adversely interested in such judgment shall be cited as in other cases.

(b) Execution of such judgment shall not be suspended unless the party applying therefor shall give a

⭐

good and sufficient bond payable to the plaintiff in the judgment, in an amount fixed in accordance with Appellate Rule 47 relating to supersedeas bonds, to be approved by the clerk, and conditioned that the party will prosecute his petition for new trial to effect and will perform such judgment as may be rendered by the court should its decision be against him.

(c) If property has been sold under the judgment and execution before the process was suspended, the defendant shall not recover the property so sold, but shall have judgment against the plaintiff in the judgment for the proceeds of such sale.

(d) If the motion is filed more than thirty days after the judgment was signed, the time period shall be computed pursuant to Rule 306a(7).

History of TRCP 329: Amended eff. Jan. 1, 1988, by order of July 15, 1987 (733-34 S.W.2d [Tex.Cases] lxxv): Changed first par., (b), and (d). Amended eff. Apr. 1, 1984, by order of Dec. 5, 1983 (661-62 S.W.2d [Tex.Cases] lxxxiii): Conforms rule to 1981 amendments to TRCPs 329b, 356, 386, and other rules that make periods for appeal begin to run from the signing of judgment rather than from overruling motion for new trial. Amended eff. Jan. 1, 1981, by order of June 10, 1980 (599-600 S.W.2d [Tex.Cases] l): Changed word "rendered" in first sentence of (a) to "signed." Adopted eff. Sept. 1, 1941, by order of Oct. 29, 1940 (3 Tex.B.J. 574 [1940]). Source: TRCS art. 2236 (repealed).

See *Commentaries*, "MNT After Service by Publication," ch. 10-B, §10, p. 799; *O'Connor's Texas Forms*, FORM 10B:5.

ANNOTATIONS

In re E.R., ___ S.W.3d ___ (Tex.2012) (No. 11-0282; 7-6-12). "When judgment is rendered on service of process by publication, a party has two years to move for a new trial, which the trial court may grant for 'good cause.' But if the service was invalid, a party is entitled to a new trial without showing good cause."

In re Boshears, No. 09-10-00187-CV (Tex.App.—Beaumont 2010, orig. proceeding) (memo op.; 6-10-10). "A bill of review filed within the time for filing a Rule 329 motion may be treated as a motion for new trial."

TRCP 329a. COUNTY COURT CASES

If a case or other matter is on trial or in the process of hearing when the term of the county court expires, such trial, hearing or other matter may be proceeded with at the next or any subsequent term of court and no motion or plea shall be considered as waived or overruled, because not acted upon at the term of court at which it was filed, but may be acted upon at any time the judge may fix or at which it may have been postponed or continued by agreement of the parties with leave of the court. This subdivision is not applicable to original or amended motions for new trial which are governed by Rule 329b.

History of TRCP 329a: Amended eff. Jan. 1, 1961, by order of July 26, 1960 (23 Tex.B.J. 681 [1961]): Completely rewrote rule. Amended eff. Sept. 1, 1957, by order of Mar. 19, 1957 (20 Tex.B.J. 193 [1957]): Changed time for filing motion from two days to ten days. Adopted eff. Jan. 1, 1955, by order of July 20, 1954 (17 Tex.B.J. 569 [1954]). Source: New rule.

TRCP 329b. TIME FOR FILING MOTIONS

The following rules shall be applicable to motions for new trial and motions to modify, correct, or reform judgments (other than motions to correct the record under Rule 316) in all district and county courts:

(a) A motion for new trial, if filed, shall be filed prior to or within thirty days after the judgment or other order complained of is signed.

(b) One or more amended motions for new trial may be filed without leave of court before any preceding motion for new trial filed by the movant is overruled and within thirty days after the judgment or other order complained of is signed.

(c) In the event an original or amended motion for new trial or a motion to modify, correct or reform a judgment is not determined by written order signed within seventy-five days after the judgment was signed, it shall be considered overruled by operation of law on expiration of that period.

(d) The trial court, regardless of whether an appeal has been perfected, has plenary power to grant a new trial or to vacate, modify, correct, or reform the judgment within thirty days after the judgment is signed.

(e) If a motion for new trial is timely filed by any party, the trial court, regardless of whether an appeal has been perfected, has plenary power to grant a new trial or to vacate, modify, correct, or reform the judgment until thirty days after all such timely-filed motions are overruled, either by a written and signed order or by operation of law, whichever occurs first.

(f) On expiration of the time within which the trial court has plenary power, a judgment cannot be set aside by the trial court except by bill of review for sufficient cause, filed within the time allowed by law; provided that the court may at any time correct a clerical error in the record of a judgment and render judgment nunc pro tunc under Rule 316, and may also sign an order declaring a previous judgment or order to be void because signed after the court's plenary power had expired.

(g) A motion to modify, correct, or reform a judgment (as distinguished from motion to correct the record of a judgment under Rule 316), if filed, shall be

★

filed and determined within the time prescribed by this rule for a motion for new trial and shall extend the trial court's plenary power and the time for perfecting an appeal in the same manner as a motion for new trial. Each such motion shall be in writing and signed by the party or his attorney and shall specify the respects in which the judgment should be modified, corrected, or reformed. The overruling of such a motion shall not preclude the filing of a motion for new trial, nor shall the overruling of a motion for new trial preclude the filing of a motion to modify, correct, or reform.

(h) If a judgment is modified, corrected or reformed in any respect, the time for appeal shall run from the time the modified, corrected, or reformed judgment is signed, but if a correction is made pursuant to Rule 316 after expiration of the period of plenary power provided by this rule, no complaint shall be heard on appeal that could have been presented in an appeal from the original judgment.

History of TRCP 329b: Amended eff. Jan. 1, 1988, by order of July 15, 1987 (733-34 S.W.2d [Tex.Cases] lxxv): Amended to conform with repeal of TRCP 317. Amended eff. Apr. 1, 1984, by order of Dec. 5, 1983 (661-62 S.W.2d [Tex.Cases] lxxxiii): Changed (c) to include motion to modify, correct, or reform judgment; amended (h) to avoid opening case for general appeal after time for appeal expired by the device of a corrected judgment nunc pro tunc pursuant to TRCP 316 or 317. Amended eff. Jan. 1, 1981, by order of June 10, 1980 (599-600 S.W.2d [Tex.Cases] l): Completely rewrote rule so appellate steps run from date judgment or order is signed; motion for new trial may be filed and amended within 30 days from date judgment is signed, is overruled by operation of law 75 days after judgment is signed, and trial court has power over its judgment for 30 more days an amended motion for new trial gains no additional time; eliminated requirement of "presentment" and provision for an agreed postponement. Amended eff. Jan. 1, 1978, by order of July 11, 1977 (553-54 S.W.2d [Tex.Cases] l): Substituted words "if filed" for "when required" in (1). Amended eff. Feb. 1, 1973, by order of Oct. 3, 1972 (483-84 S.W.2d [Tex.Cases] xxi, xli): Added (8). Amended eff. Jan. 1, 1967, by order of July 20, 1966 (401-02 S.W.2d [Tex.Cases] xliii): Substituted word "without" for "by" in first sentence of (2). Amended eff. Jan. 1, 1961, by order of July 26, 1960 (23 Tex.B.J. 681 [1961]): Broadened rule to apply to county courts. Adopted eff. Jan. 1, 1955, by order of July 20, 1954 (17 Tex.B.J. 569 [1954]). Source: New rule. See TRCP 330(j)-(*l*), before Jan. 1, 1955 changes to TRCP 330.

See *Commentaries*, "Rules for Filing Documents," ch. 1-C, p. 21; "Motion for JNOV," ch. 9-B, p. 761; "The Judgment," ch. 9-C, p. 764; "Motion for New Trial," ch. 10-B, p. 789; "Motion to Modify the Judgment," ch. 10-D, p. 814; "Motion for Judgment Nunc Pro Tunc," ch. 10-H, p. 837.

ANNOTATIONS

Plenary Power

In re Baylor Med. Ctr., 280 S.W.3d 227, 230-31 (Tex.2008). Rule 329b "terminates the trial court's plenary power 30 days after all timely motions for new trial are *overruled*, but there is no provision limiting its plenary power if such motions are *granted*. Under the current rules, if no judgment is signed, no plenary-power clock is ticking. [¶] When a new trial is granted, the case stands on the trial court's docket 'the same as though no trial had been had.' Accordingly, the trial court should then have the power to set aside a new trial order 'any time before a final judgment is entered.' [¶] [W]e recently clarified that 'a trial judge who modifies a judgment and then withdraws the modification has modified the judgment *twice* rather than never.' Rule 329b(h) provides that if a judgment is modified '*in any respect*' the appellate timetables are restarted. Surely a judgment that is set aside by a new trial order has been modified in *some* respect, even if it is later reinstated. Thus, if a new trial is granted and later withdrawn, the appellate deadlines run from the later order granting reinstatement rather than the earlier order. *At 232:* 'There is no sound reason why the court may not reconsider its ruling [granting] a new trial' at any time."

In re Brookshire Grocery Co., 250 S.W.3d 66, 69 (Tex.2008). "[A]n amended motion [for new trial] may be filed without leave of court when: (1) no preceding motion for new trial has been overruled *and* (2) it is filed within 30 days of judgment. 'And' is conjunctive: an amended new-trial motion is timely filed only *before* the court overrules a prior one. An amended motion filed afterwards: (1) need not be considered by the trial court and (2) does not extend the trial court's plenary power. *At 72:* [T]he trial court retains plenary power for 30 days after overruling a motion for new trial; thus, the losing party may ask the trial court to reconsider its order denying a new trial—or the court may grant a new trial on its own initiative—so long as the court issues an order granting new trial within its period of plenary power. [¶] Additionally, under Rule 329b, a trial court's plenary power to grant a new trial expires 30 days after it overrules a motion for new trial, only provided no other *type* of 329b motion (such as a motion to modify, correct, or reform the judgment) is 'timely filed.' Thus, a party whose motion for new trial is overruled within 30 days of judgment may still file a motion to modify, correct, or reform the judgment—provided it is filed within 30 days of judgment—and thereby extend the trial court's plenary power."

Moritz v. Preiss, 121 S.W.3d 715, 720 (Tex.2003). "[A]n amended motion for new trial filed more than 30 days after the trial court signs a final judgment is untimely. [T]he trial court may, at its discretion, consider the grounds raised in an untimely motion and grant a new trial under its inherent authority before the court loses plenary power. [¶] 'If the trial court ignores the tardy motion, it is ineffectual for any purpose. [I]f the

★

court denies a new trial, the belated motion is a nullity and supplies no basis for consideration upon appeal of grounds which were required to be set forth in a timely motion.' *At 721:* [A]n untimely amended motion for new trial does not preserve issues for appellate review, even if the trial court considers and denies the untimely motion within its plenary power period."

Lane Bank Equip. Co. v. Smith S. Equip., Inc., 10 S.W.3d 308, 312 (Tex.2000). "[A] motion made after judgment to incorporate a sanction as a part of the final judgment does propose a change to that judgment. Such a motion is, on its face, a motion to modify, correct or reform the existing judgment within the meaning of Rule 329b(g). *At 314:* We ... hold that [such a motion] qualifies as a motion to modify under Rule 329b(g), thus extending the trial court's plenary jurisdiction and the appellate timetable." *See also Moore v. Kitsmiller*, 201 S.W.3d 147, 151 (Tex.App.—Tyler 2006, pet. denied).

Scott & White Mem'l Hosp. v. Schexnider, 940 S.W.2d 594, 596 (Tex.1996). "A trial court's power to decide a motion for sanctions pertaining to matters occurring before judgment is no different than its power to decide any other motion during its plenary jurisdiction. [T]he time during which the trial court has authority to impose sanctions on such a motion is limited to when it retains plenary jurisdiction...." *See also Law Offices of Robert D. Wilson v. Texas Univest-Frisco, Ltd.*, 291 S.W.3d 110, 113 (Tex.App.—Dallas 2009, no pet.).

L.M. Healthcare, Inc. v. Childs, 929 S.W.2d 442, 443 (Tex.1996). "That the trial court overruled [P's] motion for new trial does not shorten the trial court's plenary power to resolve a motion to modify the judgment. *At 444:* [TRCP 329b(e) and (g)] provide that a timely filed motion to modify judgment extends the trial court's plenary power, separate and apart from a motion for new trial." *See also Board of Trs. of Bastrop ISD v. Toungate*, 958 S.W.2d 365, 367 (Tex.1997).

PNS Stores v. Rivera, 335 S.W.3d 265, 279-80 (Tex. App.—San Antonio 2010), *rev'd on other grounds*, 379 S.W.3d 267 (Tex.2012). "Generally, only a timely filed bill of review is available to set aside a judgment when the trial court's plenary power has expired. However, in *Middleton* [*v. Murff*, 689 S.W.2d 212 (Tex.1985)], the supreme court recognized an exception to rule 329b(f). According to the supreme court, the rule's mandate that only a timely filed bill of review is available to set aside

a trial court's judgment after the court's plenary power has expired does not apply where the court had no jurisdictional power to render judgment. Importantly, however, the court specifically defined 'jurisdictional power' to mean 'jurisdiction over the subject matter, the power to hear and determine cases of the general class to which the particular one belongs.' Any other direct attack on a void judgment must comply with rule 329b(f), i.e., must be an attack by a timely filed bill of review. [¶] Accordingly, under *Middleton*, it appears that an untimely bill of review is proper only if there is an absence of subject matter jurisdiction."

Claxton v. (Upper) Lake Fork Water Control & Imprv. Dist., 220 S.W.3d 537, 541 (Tex.App.—Texarkana 2006, no pet.). "Even if both parties agreed that a different date actually existed, we are constrained by the rules to determine our jurisdiction by reference to the date on which the judgment was signed—a party cannot confer or waive jurisdiction by consent or agreement."

Written Order

In re Lovito-Nelson, 278 S.W.3d 773, 775 (Tex. 2009). "We have been clear that Rule 329b(c) requires a written order to grant a new trial. ... Although we have never had occasion to apply the rule to scheduling orders, the courts of appeals have, and have mostly held that such orders do not grant new trials." *See also Faulkner v. Culver*, 851 S.W.2d 187, 188 (Tex.1993) (trial judge's oral pronouncement cannot substitute for a written order).

Appellate Deadlines

Ryland Enter. v. Weatherspoon, 355 S.W.3d 664, 665-66 (Tex.2011). TRCP "329b states that a motion for new trial is timely if filed '*prior to* or within 30 days after the judgment ... complained of is signed.' This 'prior to' language is supplemented and clarified by [TRCP] 306c, which provides that '[n]o motion for new trial ... shall be held ineffective because prematurely filed; but every such motion shall be deemed to have been filed on the date of but subsequent to the time of signing of the judgment the motion assails.' [R]ule 329b(g) states that a 'motion to modify ... shall be filed and determined ... and shall extend ... the time for perfecting an appeal in the same manner as a motion for new trial.'"

Arkoma Basin Expl. Co. v. FMF Assocs. 1990-A, Ltd., 249 S.W.3d 380, 390-91 (Tex.2008). "'If a judgment is modified in any respect,' appellate deadlines do not run from the original judgment but 'from the date when the modified judgment is signed.' [¶] [T]he deadlines are restarted by '*any* change, whether or not material or substantial.' Thus, appellate deadlines are restarted by an order that does nothing more than change the docket number or deny all relief not expressly granted." *See also In re J.L.*, 163 S.W.3d 79, 82 (Tex.2005) (because trial court modified and corrected judgment while it retained plenary power, time for filing notice of appeal was calculated from date of new final judgment); *Abercia v. Kingvision Pay-Per-View, Ltd.*, 217 S.W.3d 688, 706 (Tex.App.—El Paso 2007, pet. denied) (even when later judgment differs from original judgment only by signature date, later judgment vacates former judgment).

Garza v. Garcia, 137 S.W.3d 36, 37-38 (Tex.2004). "A motion for new trial is 'conditionally filed' if tendered without the requisite fee, and appellate deadlines run from and are extended by that date: '[T]he failure to pay the fee before the motion is overruled by operation of law may forfeit altogether the movant's opportunity to have the trial court consider the motion; it does not, however, retroactively invalidate the conditional filing for purposes of the appellate timetable.' [¶] Although we have previously reserved ruling on a fee that was never paid, we now extend the ... rule.... [¶] This is not to say filing fees are irrelevant. '[A]bsent emergency or other rare circumstances' a motion for new trial should not be considered until the filing fee is paid." *See also Tate v. E.I. DuPont de Nemours & Co.*, 934 S.W.2d 83, 84 (Tex.1996).

Farmer v. Ben E. Keith Co., 907 S.W.2d 495, 496 (Tex.1995). "[T]he appellate timetable runs from the signing date of whatever order that makes a judgment final and appealable, i.e. whatever *order* disposes of any parties or issues remaining before the court. Further, the appellate timetable can begin yet again with the signing of an order or judgment where there is nothing on the face of the record to indicate it was signed for the sole purpose of *extending* the appellate timetable and the order is signed within the trial court's plenary power."

K. Certain District Courts

TRCP 330. RULES OF PRACTICE & PROCEDURE IN CERTAIN DISTRICT COURTS

The following rules of practice and procedure shall govern and be followed in all civil actions in district courts in counties where the only district court of said county vested with civil jurisdiction, or all the district courts thereof having civil jurisdiction, have successive terms in said county throughout the year, without more than two days intervening between any of such terms, whether or not any one or more of such district courts include one or more other counties within its jurisdiction.

(a) Appealed Cases. In cases appealed to said district courts from inferior courts, the appeal, including transcript, shall be filed in the district court within thirty (30) days after the rendition of the judgment or order appealed from, and the appellee shall enter his appearance on the docket or answer to said appeal on or before ten o'clock a.m. of the Monday next after the expiration of twenty (20) days from the date the appeal is filed in the district court.

(b) [Repealed by order of July 22, 1975, eff. Jan. 1, 1976 (525-26 S.W.2d (Tex.Cases) li).]

(c) Postponement or Continuance. Cases may be postponed or continued by agreement with the approval of the court, or upon the court's own motion or for cause. When a case is called for trial and only one party is ready, the court may for good cause either continue the case for the term or postpone and reset it for a later day in the same or succeeding term.

(d) Cases May Be Reset. A case that is set and reached for trial may be postponed for a later day in the term or continued and reset for a day certain in the succeeding term on the same grounds as an application for continuance would be granted in other district courts. After any case has been set and reached in its due order and called for trial two (2) or more times and not tried, the court may dismiss the same unless the parties agree to a postponement or continuance but the court shall respect written agreements of counsel for postponement and continuance if filed in the case when or before it is called for trial unless to do so will unreasonably delay or interfere with other business of the court.

(e) Exchange and Transfer. Where in such county there are two or more district courts having civil jurisdiction, the judges of such courts may, in their discretion, exchange benches or districts from time to time, and may transfer cases and other proceedings from one court to another, and any of them may in his own courtroom try and determine any case or proceeding pending in another court without having the case transferred, or may sit in any other of said courts and

TRCP 330

there hear and determine any case there pending, and every judgment and order shall be entered in the minutes of the court in which the case is pending and at the time the judgment or order is rendered, and two (2) or more judges may try different cases in the same court at the same time, and each may occupy his own courtroom or the room of any other court. The judge of any such court may issue restraining orders and injunctions returnable to any other judge or court, and any judge may transfer any case or proceeding pending in his court to any other of said courts, and the judge of any court to which a case or proceeding is transferred shall receive and try the same, and in turn shall have power in his discretion to transfer any such case to any other of said courts and any other judge may in his courtroom try any case pending in any other of such courts.

(f) Cases Transferred to Judges Not Occupied. Where in such counties there are two or more district courts having civil jurisdiction, when the judge of any such court shall become disengaged, he shall notify the presiding judge, and the presiding judge shall transfer to the court of the disengaged judge the next case which is ready for trial in any of said courts. Any judge not engaged in his own court may try any case in any other court.

(g) Judge May Hear Only Part of Case. Where in such counties there are two or more district courts having civil jurisdiction, any judge may hear any part of any case or proceeding pending in any of said courts and determine the same, or may hear and determine any question in any case, and any other judge may complete the hearing and render judgment in the case.

(h) Any Judge May Hear Dilatory Pleas. Where in such county there are two or more district courts having civil jurisdiction, any judge may hear and determine motions, petitions for injunction, applications for appointment of receivers, interventions, pleas of privilege, pleas in abatement, all dilatory pleas and special exceptions, motions for a new trial and all preliminary matters, questions and proceedings and may enter judgment or order thereon in the court in which the case is pending without having the case transferred to the court of the judge acting, and the judge in whose court the case is pending may thereafter proceed to hear, complete and determine the case or other matter, or any part thereof, and render final judgment therein.

Any judgment rendered or action taken by any judge in any of said courts in the county shall be valid and binding.

(i) Acts in Succeeding Terms. If a case or other matter is on trial, or in the process of hearing when the term of court expires, such trial, hearing or other matter may be proceeded with at the next or any subsequent term of court and no motion or plea shall be considered as waived or overruled, because not acted upon at the term of court at which it was filed, but may be acted upon at any time the judge may fix or at which it may have been postponed or continued by agreement of the parties with leave of the court. This subdivision is not applicable to original or amended motions for new trial which are governed by Rule 329b.

History of TRCP 330: Amended eff. Jan. 1, 1976, by order of July 22, 1975 (525-26 S.W.2d [Tex.Cases] li): Repealed TRCP 330(b), to avoid a conflict with amended TRCP 245. Amended eff. Feb. 1, 1973, by order of Oct. 3, 1972 (483-84 S.W.2d [Tex.Cases] li-lii): Deleted former par. (i), which provided for the selection of a presiding judge; relettered former (j) as (i). [See TRCS art. 200b (repealed).] Amended eff. Jan. 1, 1961, by order of July 26, 1960 (23 Tex.B.J. 683 [1961]): Authorized court to proceed with hearing at "any subsequent term" of court. Adopted eff. Jan. 1, 1955, by order of July 20, 1954 (17 Tex.B.J. 570 [1954]). TRCP 329b incorporated the provisions of former TRCP 330(j)-(*l*). Adopted eff. Sept. 1, 1941, by order of Oct. 29, 1940 (3 Tex.B.J. 575 [1940]). Source: TRCS art. 2092 (repealed).

See Gov't Code §24.003.

ANNOTATIONS

In re U.S. Silica Co., 157 S.W.3d 434, 438-39 (Tex. 2005). "We disagree that all orders signed by a transferring court after transfer are void; many are not. This is especially true here because the transfers involved district courts in a single county. [¶] Trial courts have broad discretion to exchange benches and enter orders on other cases in the same county, even without a formal order or transfer. Given the broad powers district courts have to act for one another, we do not agree that these [interim] orders were entered without jurisdiction."

Wilson v. Dunn, 800 S.W.2d 833, 835 n.6 (Tex. 1990). "The 236th District Court and the 67th District Court both sit in Tarrant County. They are permitted to, and do, hear each other's civil cases under Rule 330." *See also* **Pinnacle Gas Treating, Inc. v. Read**, 160 S.W.3d 564, 566 (Tex.2005) (87th District Court and 278th District Court are both in Leon County and have concurrent jurisdiction).

Hull v. South Coast Catamarans, L.P., 365 S.W.3d 35, 41 (Tex.App.—Houston [1st Dist.] 2011, pet. denied). "[R]ule 330(g) does not authorize a district judge who heard none of the case to render judgment in

─────────────── ★ ───────────────

a bench trial. *At 42:* But [this] exception to the free exchange of benches is a narrow one."

Polk v. Southwest Crossing Homeowners Ass'n, 165 S.W.3d 89, 93 (Tex.App.—Houston [14th Dist.] 2005, pet. denied). "[P] does not have a protected proprietary interest in having her case heard by a particular district judge. Counties may adopt local rules to further govern the transfer of cases from one district court to another if they are not inconsistent with Rule 330(e). *At 94:* [A] failure to comply with the local rule's *procedural* requirements does not deprive a court of its jurisdiction. While the transferring and receiving courts should have complied with their own local rules regarding the transfer of cases, their failure to do so did not deprive [the district court] of jurisdiction over [P's] case." *See also* ***In re Rio Grande Valley Gas Co.,*** 987 S.W.2d 167, 173 (Tex.App.—Corpus Christi 1999, orig. proceeding).

TRCP 331 TO 351. REPEALED
Editor's note: For a comprehensive history of the amendments and repealers to these rules, see *O'Connor's Texas Rules * Civil Trials* (2002), p. 809.

PART III. RULES OF PROCEDURE FOR THE COURTS OF APPEALS

TRCP 352 TO 473. REPEALED
Editor's note: For a comprehensive history of the amendments and repealers to these rules, see *O'Connor's Texas Rules * Civil Trials* (2002), p. 809.

PART IV. RULES OF PRACTICE FOR THE SUPREME COURT

TRCP 474 TO 522. REPEALED
Editor's note: For a comprehensive history of the amendments and repealers to these rules, see *O'Connor's Texas Rules * Civil Trials* (2002), p. 809.

PART V. RULES OF PRACTICE IN JUSTICE COURTS

SECTION 1. GENERAL

TRCP 523. DISTRICT COURT RULES GOVERN

All rules governing the district and county courts shall also govern the justice courts, insofar as they can be applied, except where otherwise specifically provided by law or these rules.

History of TRCP 523: Adopted eff. Sept. 1, 1941, by order of Oct. 29, 1940 (3 Tex.B.J. 606 [1940]). Source: TRCS arts. 2381, 2410 (repealed).

ANNOTATIONS

Searcy v. Sagullo, 915 S.W.2d 595, 597 (Tex. App.—Houston [14th Dist.] 1996, no writ). TRCPs 567 and 571 "specifically provide the procedures and time

constraints to be used by justice courts in motions for new trial and appeals. Thus, [TRCP] 523 does not allow the justice court to grant new trials beyond the period provided in rule 567."

SECTION 2. INSTITUTION OF SUIT

TRCP 524. DOCKET

Each justice shall keep a civil docket in which he shall enter:

(a) The title of all suits commenced before him.

(b) The time when the first process was issued against the defendant, when returnable, and the nature thereof.

(c) The time when the parties, or either of them, appeared before him, either with or without a citation.

(d) A brief statement of the nature of the plaintiff's demand or claim, and the amount claimed, and a brief statement of the nature of the defense made by the defendant, if any.

(e) Every adjournment, stating at whose request and to what time.

(f) The time when the trial was had, stating whether the same was by a jury or by the justice.

(g) The verdict of the jury, if any.

(h) The judgment signed by the justice and the time of signing same.

(i) All applications for setting aside judgments or granting new trials and the order of the justice thereon, with the date thereof.

(j) The time of issuing execution, to whom directed and delivered, and the amount of debt, damages and costs; and, when any execution is returned, he shall note such return on said docket, with the manner in which it was executed.

(k) All stays and appeals that may be taken, and the time when taken, the amount of the bond and the names of the sureties.

(*l*) He shall also keep such other dockets, books and records as may be required by law or these rules, and shall keep a fee book in which shall be taxed all costs accruing in every suit commenced before him.

History of TRCP 524: Amended eff. Jan. 1, 1981, by order of June 10, 1980 (599-600 S.W.2d [Tex.Cases] lxxiv): Changed the words "rendered" and "rendering" to "signed" and "signing." Adopted eff. Sept. 1, 1941, by order of Oct. 29, 1940 (3 Tex.B.J. 607 [1940]). Source: TRCS art. 2382 (repealed).

ANNOTATIONS

Kahn v. Marik, 286 S.W.2d 639, 641 (Tex.App.— Galveston 1956, writ ref'd n.r.e.). "[T]he civil docket,

---

★

---

which the law requires the justice of the peace to keep, is the proper place for the judgment to be entered and also serves as what we would call the execution docket in the county or district court."

TRCP 525. ORAL PLEADINGS

The pleadings shall be oral, except where otherwise specially provided; but a brief statement thereof may be noted on the docket; provided that after a case has been appealed and is docketed in the county (or district) court all pleadings shall be reduced to writing.

History of TRCP 525: Adopted eff. Sept. 1, 1941, by order of Oct. 29, 1940 (3 Tex.B.J. 607 [1940]). Source: TRCS art. 2388 (repealed).

TRCP 526. SWORN PLEADINGS

An answer or other pleading setting up any of the matters specified in Rule 93 shall be in writing and signed by the party or his attorney and verified by affidavit.

History of TRCP 526: Adopted eff. Sept. 1, 1941, by order of Oct. 29, 1940 (3 Tex.B.J. 607 [1940]). Source: TRCS art. 2389 (repealed).

TRCP 527. MOTION TO TRANSFER

A motion to transfer filed in the justice court shall contain the requisites prescribed in Rule 86; and in addition shall set forth the precinct to which transfer is sought.

History of TRCP 527: Amended eff. Sept. 1, 1983, by order of June 15, 1983 (651-52 S.W.2d [Tex.Cases] xl): To conform to S.B. 898, 68th Leg., 1983. Adopted eff. Sept. 1, 1941, by order of Oct. 29, 1940 (3 Tex.B.J. 607 [1940]). Source: TRCS art. 2389(1) (repealed).

TRCP 528. VENUE CHANGED ON AFFIDAVIT

If any party to a suit before any justice shall make an affidavit supported by the affidavit of two other credible persons, citizens of the county, that they have good reason to believe, and do believe, that such party cannot have a fair and impartial trial before such justice or in such justice's precinct, the justice shall transfer such suit to the court of the nearest justice within the county not subject to the same or some other disqualification.

History of TRCP 528: Adopted eff. Sept. 1, 1941, by order of Oct. 29, 1940 (3 Tex.B.J. 607 [1940]). Source: TRCS art. 2394 (repealed).
See CPRC §§15.081-15.100.

ANNOTATIONS

Merritt v. Davis, 331 S.W.3d 857, 861 (Tex.App.—Dallas 2011, pet. denied). TRCP "18a does not apply to justice courts. ... The justice-court rules include their own specific and simplified recusal provision, [TRCP] 528. We conclude that the drafters of the rules in-

tended rule 528 to be the sole recusal mechanism in justice court."

Crowder v. Franks, 870 S.W.2d 568, 571-72 (Tex. App.—Houston [1st Dist.] 1993, no writ). "Rule 528 incorporates in a single procedure the legislature's decision to give a civil litigant in a justice of the peace court an absolute right to the transfer of a case to avoid the alleged prejudice of a judge or potential jury. ... The affidavits required are sufficient even though they may be only conclusionary, albeit sworn, allegations of impartiality and residency. There is no provision in the rule for the allegations to be factually contested, nor for an eventual fact-finding made by the justice of the peace as to their accuracy."

TRCP 529. "NEAREST JUSTICE" DEFINED

By the term "nearest justice," as used in this section, is meant the justice whose place of holding his court is nearest to that of the justice before whom the proceeding is pending or should have been brought.

History of TRCP 529: Adopted eff. Sept. 1, 1941, by order of Oct. 29, 1940 (3 Tex.B.J. 607 [1940]). Source: TRCS art. 2395 (repealed).

TRCP 530. BY CONSENT

The venue may also be changed to the court of any other justice of the county, upon the written consent of the parties or their attorneys, filed with the papers of the cause.

History of TRCP 530: Adopted eff. Sept. 1, 1941, by order of Oct. 29, 1940 (3 Tex.B.J. 607 [1940]). Source: TRCS art. 2396 (repealed).

TRCP 531. ORDER OF TRANSFER

The order of transfer in such cases shall state the cause of the transfer, and the name of the court to which the transfer is made, and shall require the parties and witnesses to appear before such court at its next ensuing term.

History of TRCP 531: Adopted eff. Sept. 1, 1941, by order of Oct. 29, 1940 (3 Tex.B.J. 607 [1940]). Source: TRCS art. 2397 (repealed).

TRCP 532. TRANSCRIPT

When such order of transfer is made, the justice who made the order shall immediately make out a true and correct transcript of all the entries made on his docket in the cause, certify thereto officially, and send it, with a certified copy of the bill of costs taken from his fee book, and the original papers in the cause, to the justice of the precinct to which the same has been transferred.

History of TRCP 532: Adopted eff. Sept. 1, 1941, by order of Oct. 29, 1940 (3 Tex.B.J. 607 [1940]). Source: TRCS art. 2398 (repealed).

———————————— ✦ ————————————

TRCP 533. REQUISITES OF PROCESS

Every writ or process from the justice courts shall be issued by the justice, shall be in writing and signed by him officially. The style thereof shall be "The State of Texas." It shall, except where otherwise specially provided by law or these rules be directed to the person or party upon whom it is to be served, be made returnable to some regular term of court, and have noted thereon the date of its issuance.

History of TRCP 533: Adopted eff. Sept. 1, 1941, by order of Oct. 29, 1940 (3 Tex.B.J. 608 [1940]). Source: TRCS art. 2400 (repealed).

⑫ TRCP 534. ISSUANCE & FORM OF CITATION

a. Issuance. When a claim or demand is lodged with a justice for suit, the clerk when requested shall forthwith issue a citation and deliver the citation as directed by the requesting party. The party requesting citation shall be responsible for obtaining service of the citation and a copy of the petition if any is filed. Upon request, separate or additional citations shall be issued by the clerk. The clerk must retain a copy of the citation in the court's file.

b. Form. The citation shall (1) be styled "The State of Texas", (2) be signed by the clerk under seal of court or by the Justice of the Peace, (3) contain name and location of the court, (4) show date of filing of the petition if any is filed, (5) show date of issuance of citation, (6) show file number and names of parties, (7) state the nature of plaintiff's demand, (8) be directed to the defendant, (9) show name and address of attorney for plaintiff, otherwise the address of plaintiff, (10) contain the time within which these rules require defendant to file a written answer with the clerk who issued citation, (11) contain address of the clerk, and (12) shall notify defendant that in case of failure of defendant to file an answer, judgment by default may be rendered for the relief demanded in the petition. The citation shall direct defendant to file a written answer to plaintiff's petition on or before 10:00 a.m. on the Monday next after the expiration of ten days after the date of service thereof. The requirement of subsections 10 and 12 of this rule shall be in the form set forth in section c of this rule.

c. Notice. The citation shall include the following notice to defendant: "You have been sued. You may employ an attorney. If you or your attorney do not file a written answer with the clerk who issued this citation by 10:00 a.m. on the Monday next following the expira-tion of ten days after you were served this citation and petition, a default judgment may be taken against you."

d. Copies. The party filing any pleading upon which citation is to be issued and served shall furnish the clerk with a sufficient number of copies thereof for use in serving the parties to be served, and when copies are so furnished the clerk shall make no charge for the copies.

History of TRCP 534: Amended eff. Jan. 1, 2012, by order of Dec. 12, 2011 (Tex.Sup.Ct. Order, Misc. Docket No. 11-9250): Added last sentence in (a). Amended eff. Sept. 1, 1990, by order of Apr. 24, 1990 (785-86 S.W.2d [Tex.Cases] lxxi): Rule completely rewritten to conform justice court service of citation, to the extent practicable, to service of citation for other trial courts; secs. b-d added. Amended eff. Dec. 31, 1947, by order of Aug. 18, 1947 (10 Tex.B.J. 399 [1947]). Adopted eff. Sept. 1, 1941, by order of Oct. 29, 1940 (3 Tex.B.J. 608 [1940]). Source: TRCS art. 2401 (repealed).

TRCP 535. ANSWER FILED

Where citation has been personally served at least ten days before appearance day, exclusive of the day of service and of return, the answer of the defendant shall be filed at or before ten o'clock a.m. on such day. Where citation has been served by publication, and the first publication has been made at least twenty-eight days before appearance day, the answer of the defendant shall be filed at or before ten o'clock a.m. on the first day of the first term which shall convene after the expiration of forty-two days from the date of issuance of such citation.

History of TRCP 535: Adopted eff. Sept. 1, 1941, by order of Oct. 29, 1940 (3 Tex.B.J. 608 [1940]). Source: TRCS arts. 2009, 2404 (repealed).

TRCP 536. WHO MAY SERVE & METHOD OF SERVICE

(a) Process—including citation and other notices, writs, orders, and other papers issued by the court—may be served anywhere by (1) any sheriff or constable or other person authorized by law, (2) any person authorized by law or by written order of the court who is not less than eighteen years of age, or (3) any person certified under order of the Supreme Court. Service by registered or certified mail and citation by publication must, if requested, be made by the clerk of the court in which the case is pending. But no person who is a party to or interested in the outcome of a suit may serve any process, and, unless otherwise authorized by a written court order, only a sheriff or constable may serve a citation in an action of forcible entry and detainer, a writ that requires the actual taking of possession of a person, property or thing, or process requiring that an enforcement action be physically enforced by the person delivering the process. The order authorizing a person

★

to serve process may be made without written motion and no fee may be imposed for issuance of such order.

(b) Unless the citation or an order of the court otherwise directs, the citation shall be served by any person authorized by this rule by:

(1) delivering to the defendant, in person, a true copy of the citation with the date of delivery endorsed thereon with a copy of the petition attached thereto, or

(2) mailing to the defendant by registered or certified mail, return receipt requested, a true copy of the citation with a copy of the petition attached thereto if any is filed.

(c) Upon motion supported by affidavit stating the location of the defendant's usual place of business or usual place of abode or other place where the defendant can probably be found and stating specifically the facts showing that service has been attempted under either (a)(1) or (a)(2) at the location named in such affidavit but has not been successful, the court may authorize service:

(1) by leaving a true copy of the citation, with a copy of the petition attached, with anyone over sixteen years of age at the location specified in such affidavit, or

(2) in any other manner that the affidavit or other evidence before the court shows will be reasonably effective to give the defendant notice of the suit.

Comment to 2005 change: Subsection (a) is amended to include among the persons authorized to effect service those who meet certification requirements promulgated by the Supreme Court and to prohibit private individuals from serving certain types of process unless, in rare circumstances, a court authorizes an individual to do so.

History of TRCP 536: Amended eff. July 1, 2005, by order of June 29, 2005 (173-74 S.W.3d [Tex.Cases] xvii). Amended eff. Sept. 1, 1990, by order of Apr. 24, 1990 (785-86 S.W.2d [Tex.Cases] lxxii): Completely rewrote to conform justice court service of citation, to the extent practicable, to service of citation for other trial courts. Adopted eff. Sept. 1, 1941, by order of Oct. 29, 1940 (3 Tex.B.J. 608 [1940]). Source: TRCS art. 2402 (repealed).

⑫ TRCP 536a. DUTY OF OFFICER OR PERSON RECEIVING & RETURN OF CITATION

(a) The officer or authorized person to whom process is delivered shall endorse thereon the day and hour on which he received it, and shall execute and return the same without delay.

(b) The officer or authorized person executing the citation must complete a return of service. The return may, but need not, be endorsed on or attached to the citation.

(c) The return, together with any document to which it is attached, must include the following information:

(1) the cause number and case name;

(2) the court in which the case is filed;

(3) a description of what was served;

(4) the date and time the process was received for service;

(5) the person or entity served;

(6) the address served;

(7) the date of service or attempted service;

(8) the manner of delivery of service or attempted service;

(9) the name of the person who served or attempted to serve the process;

(10) if the person named in (9) is a process server certified under order of the Supreme Court, his or her identification number and the expiration date of his or her certification; and

(11) any other information required by rule or law.

(d) When the citation was served by registered or certified mail as authorized by Rule 536, the return by the officer or authorized person must also contain the receipt with the addressee's signature.

(e) When the officer or authorized person has not served the citation, the return shall show the diligence used by the officer or authorized person to execute the same and the cause of failure to execute it, and where the defendant is to be found, if ascertainable.

(f) The officer or authorized person who serves or attempts to serve a citation must sign the return. If the return is signed by a person other than a sheriff, constable, or the clerk of the court, the return must either be verified or be signed under penalty of perjury. A return signed under penalty of perjury must contain the statement below in substantially the following form:

"My name is _____ (First) _____ (Middle) _____ (Last), my date of birth is _____, and my address is _____, (Street) _____, (City) _____, (State) _____ (Zip Code), and _____ (Country). I declare under penalty of perjury that the foregoing is true and correct.

Executed in _____ County, State of _____, on the _____ day of _____ (Month), _____ (Year).

_____
Declarant"

(g) Where citation is executed by an alternative method as authorized by Rule 536, proof of service shall be made in the manner ordered by the court.

———————————— ✪ ————————————

(h) The return and any document to which it is attached must be filed with the court and may be filed electronically or by facsimile, if those methods of filing are available.

(i) No default judgment shall be granted in any cause until proof of service as provided by this rule, or as ordered by the court in the event citation is executed by an alternative method under Rule 536, shall have been on file with the clerk of the court three (3) days, exclusive of the day of filing and the day of judgment.

History of TRCP 536a: Amended eff. Jan. 1, 2012, by order of Dec. 12, 2011 (Tex.Sup.Ct. Order, Misc. Docket No. 11-9250). Adopted eff. Sept. 1, 1990, by order of Apr. 24, 1990 (785-86 S.W.2d [Tex.Cases] lxxiii): Conforms justice court service of citation, to the extent practicable, to service of citation for other trial courts. Source: New rule.

SECTION 3. APPEARANCE & TRIAL

TRCP 537. APPEARANCE DAY

If a defendant who has been duly cited is required by the citation to answer on a day which is in term time, such day is appearance day as to him. If he is so required to answer on a day in vacation, the first day of the next term is appearance day as to him. Where service of citation has been had by publication, the first day of the term of court which convenes after the expiration of 42 days from the date of issuance of the citation shall be appearance day.

History of TRCP 537: Amended eff. Dec. 31, 1947, by order of Aug. 18, 1947 (8 Tex.B.J. 399 [1947]). Adopted eff. Sept. 1, 1941, by order of Oct. 29, 1940 (3 Tex.B.J. 608 [1940]). Source: TRCS art. 2404 (repealed).

TRCP 538. IF DEFENDANT FAILS TO APPEAR

If the defendant who has been duly served with a citation shall fail to appear at, or before, ten o'clock a.m. on appearance day, the justice shall proceed in the following manner:

(a) If the plaintiff's claim be liquidated and proved by an instrument of writing purporting to have been executed by the defendant, or be upon an open account duly verified by affidavit, the justice shall, whether the plaintiff appear or not, render judgment in his favor against the defendant for the amount of such written obligation or sworn account, after deducting all credits indorsed thereon.

(b) If the plaintiff's claim is not so liquidated, and the plaintiff appears in person or by attorney, the justice shall proceed to hear the testimony; and, if it appears therefrom that the plaintiff is entitled to recover, judgment shall be rendered against the defendant for such amount as the testimony shows the plaintiff entitled to; otherwise, judgment shall be rendered for the defendant.

History of TRCP 538: Adopted eff. Sept. 1, 1941, by order of Oct. 29, 1940 (3 Tex.B.J. 608 [1940]). Source: TRCS art. 2405 (repealed).

TRCP 539. APPEARANCE NOTED

If the defendant appear, the same shall be noted on the docket, and the cause shall stand for trial in its order.

History of TRCP 539: Adopted eff. Sept. 1, 1941, by order of Oct. 29, 1940 (3 Tex.B.J. 609 [1940]). Source: TRCS art. 2406, unchanged (repealed).

TRCP 540. IF NO DEMAND FOR JURY

If neither party shall demand and be entitled to a jury, the justice shall try the cause without a jury.

History of TRCP 540: Adopted eff. Sept. 1, 1941, by order of Oct. 29, 1940 (3 Tex.B.J. 609 [1940]). Source: TRCS art. 2407 (repealed).

TRCP 541. CONTINUANCE

The justice for good cause shown, supported by affidavit, may continue any suit pending before him to the next regular term of his court, or postpone the same to some other day of the term.

History of TRCP 541: Adopted eff. Sept. 1, 1941, by order of Oct. 29, 1940 (3 Tex.B.J. 609 [1940]). Source: TRCS art. 2403 (repealed).

TRCP 542. CALL OF NON-JURY DOCKET

The docket of cases to be tried by the justice shall be called regularly, and the cases shall be tried when called unless continued or postponed.

History of TRCP 542: Adopted eff. Sept. 1, 1941, by order of Oct. 29, 1940 (3 Tex.B.J. 609 [1940]). Source: TRCS art. 2408 (repealed).

TRCP 543. DISMISSAL

If the plaintiff shall fail to appear when the cause is called in its order for trial, the justice, on motion of the defendant, may dismiss the suit.

History of TRCP 543: Adopted eff. Sept. 1, 1941, by order of Oct. 29, 1940 (3 Tex.B.J. 609 [1940]). Source: TRCS art. 2409 (repealed).

TRCP 544. JURY TRIAL DEMANDED

Either party shall be entitled to a trial by jury. Except in forcible entry and detainer cases, the party desiring a jury shall before the case is called for trial not less than one day in advance of the date set for trial of the cause make a demand for a jury, and also deposit a jury fee of five dollars, which shall be noted on the docket; and the case shall be set down as a jury case.

History of TRCP 544: Amended eff. Jan. 1, 1988, by order of July 15, 1987 (733-34 S.W.2d [Tex.Cases] lxxvii). Adopted eff. Sept. 1, 1941, by order of Oct. 29, 1940 (3 Tex.B.J. 609 [1940]). Source: TRCS art. 2411 (repealed).

TRCP 544

★

TRCP 545. JURY TRIAL DAY

The justice shall, on the first day of the term, fix a day for taking up the jury cases, if any, pending for trial at such term, and he may fix said first day of the term for that purpose.

History of TRCP 545: Adopted eff. Sept. 1, 1941, by order of Oct. 29, 1940 (3 Tex.B.J. 609 [1940]). Source: TRCS art. 2412 (repealed).

TRCP 546. CALL OF JURY DOCKET

When the required number of jurors is present, the jury cases set for trial shall be called.

History of TRCP 546: Adopted eff. Sept. 1, 1941, by order of Oct. 29, 1940 (3 Tex.B.J. 609 [1940]). Source: TRCS art. 2419 (repealed).

TRCP 547. CHALLENGE TO THE ARRAY

When the parties to a jury case have announced themselves for trial, either party may challenge the array of jurors. The cause and the manner of making such challenge, the decision thereof and the proceedings, when such challenge is sustained, shall be as provided for similar proceedings in the district and county courts.

History of TRCP 547: Adopted eff. Sept. 1, 1941, by order of Oct. 29, 1940 (3 Tex.B.J. 609 [1940]). Source: TRCS art. 2420 (repealed).

TRCP 548. DRAWING JURY

If no challenge to the array is made, the justice shall write the names of all the jurors present on separate slips of paper, as nearly alike as may be, and shall place them in a box and mix them well, and shall then draw the names one by one from the box, and write them down as they are drawn, upon several slips of paper, and deliver one slip to each of the parties, or their attorneys.

History of TRCP 548: Adopted eff. Sept. 1, 1941, by order of Oct. 29, 1940 (3 Tex.B.J. 610 [1940]). Source: TRCS art. 2421 (repealed).

TRCP 549. CHALLENGE FOR CAUSE

If either party desires to challenge any juror for cause, such challenge shall now be made. The causes of such challenge, and the manner of making it and the decision thereof, and the proceedings, when such challenge is sustained, shall be as provided for similar proceedings in the district and county courts.

History of TRCP 549: Adopted eff. Sept. 1, 1941, by order of Oct. 29, 1940 (3 Tex.B.J. 610 [1940]). Source: TRCS art. 2422 (repealed).

TRCP 550. PEREMPTORY CHALLENGE

When a juror has been challenged for cause, and the challenge has been sustained, his name shall be erased from the slips furnished to the parties; and, if as many

as twelve names remain on such slips, the parties may make their peremptory challenges governed by the rules prescribed for the district and county courts. Each party shall be entitled to three peremptory challenges.

History of TRCP 550: Adopted eff. Sept. 1, 1941, by order of Oct. 29, 1940 (3 Tex.B.J. 610 [1940]). Source: TRCS art. 2423 (repealed).
See *Commentaries*, "Jury Selection," ch. 8-A, p. 679.

TRCP 551. THE JURY

When the peremptory challenges are made, they shall deliver their slips to the justice, who shall call off the first six names on the slips that have not been erased, and these shall be the jury to try the case.

History of TRCP 551: Adopted eff. Sept. 1, 1941, by order of Oct. 29, 1940 (3 Tex.B.J. 610 [1940]). Source: TRCS art. 2424 (repealed).

TRCP 552. IF JURY IS INCOMPLETE

If the jury by peremptory challenges is left incomplete, the justice shall direct the sheriff or constable to summon others to complete the jury; and the same proceedings shall be had in selecting and impaneling such jurors as are had in the first instance.

History of TRCP 552: Adopted eff. Sept. 1, 1941, by order of Oct. 29, 1940 (3 Tex.B.J. 610 [1940]). Source: TRCS art. 2425 (repealed).

TRCP 553. JURY SWORN

When the jury has been selected, such of them as have not been previously sworn for the trial of civil cases shall be sworn by the justice. The form of the oath shall be in substance as follows: "You and each of you do solemnly swear that in all cases between parties which shall be to you submitted you will a true verdict render, according to the law and the evidence. So help you God."

History of TRCP 553: Adopted eff. Sept. 1, 1941, by order of Oct. 29, 1940 (3 Tex.B.J. 610 [1940]). Source: TRCS art. 2426 (repealed).

TRCP 554. JUSTICE SHALL NOT CHARGE JURY

The justice of the peace shall not charge the jury in any cause tried in his court before a jury.

History of TRCP 554: Adopted eff. Sept. 1, 1941, by order of Oct. 29, 1940 (3 Tex.B.J. 610 [1940]). Source: TRCS art. 2410, part (repealed).

TRCP 555. VERDICT

When the suit is for the recovery of specific articles, the jury shall, if they find for the plaintiff, assess the value of each of such articles separately, according to the proof.

History of TRCP 555: Adopted eff. Sept. 1, 1941, by order of Oct. 29, 1940 (3 Tex.B.J. 610 [1940]). Source: TRCS art. 2427 (repealed).
See *Commentaries*, "The Verdict," ch. 8-K, p. 753.

SECTION 4. JUDGMENT

TRCP 556. JUDGMENT UPON VERDICT

Where the case has been tried by a jury and a verdict has been returned by them, the justice shall announce the same in open court and note it in his docket, and shall proceed to render judgment thereon.

History of TRCP 556: Adopted eff. Sept. 1, 1941, by order of Oct. 29, 1940 (3 Tex.B.J. 610 [1940]). Source: TRCS art. 2429 (repealed).

ANNOTATIONS

Pullin v. Parrish, 306 S.W.2d 241, 242 (Tex. App.—San Antonio 1957, writ ref'd). "A judgment is a prerequisite to an appeal from the justice court. [¶] An appeal from a docketed verdict, but not the judgment, is void. [¶] We do not hold that a judgment is inadequate if it is informal or merely noted on the docket sheet; … the record must show that it is a judgment and not a verdict."

TRCP 557. CASE TRIED BY JUSTICE

When the case has been tried by the justice without a jury, he shall announce his decision in open court and note the same in his docket and render judgment thereon.

History of TRCP 557: Adopted eff. Sept. 1, 1941, by order of Oct. 29, 1940 (3 Tex.B.J. 610 [1940]). Source: TRCS art. 2430 (repealed).

TRCP 558. JUDGMENT

The judgment shall be recorded at length in the justice's docket, and shall be signed by the justice. It shall clearly state the determination of the rights of the parties in the subject matter in controversy and the party who shall pay the costs, and shall direct the issuance of such process as may be necessary to carry the judgment into execution.

History of TRCP 558: Adopted eff. Sept. 1, 1941, by order of Oct. 29, 1940 (3 Tex.B.J. 610 [1940]). Source: TRCS art. 2431 (repealed).
See *Commentaries*, "The Judgment," ch. 9-C, p. 764.

TRCP 559. COSTS

The successful party in the suit shall recover his costs, except in cases where it is otherwise expressly provided.

History of TRCP 559: Adopted eff. Sept. 1, 1941, by order of Oct. 29, 1940 (3 Tex.B.J. 611 [1940]). Source: TRCS art. 2432 (repealed).
See *Commentaries*, "Costs," ch. 9-C, §4.9, p. 769.

TRCP 560. JUDGMENT FOR SPECIFIC ARTICLES

Where the judgment is for the recovery of specific articles, their value shall be separately assessed, and the judgment shall be that the plaintiff recover such specific articles, if they can be found, and if not, then their value as assessed with interest thereon at the rate of six per cent from the date of judgment.

History of TRCP 560: Adopted eff. Sept. 1, 1941, by order of Oct. 29, 1940 (3 Tex.B.J. 611 [1940]). Source: TRCS art. 2433 (repealed).

ANNOTATIONS

National Sur. Co. v. Odle, 40 S.W.2d 876, 877 (Tex. App.—Waco 1931, no writ). Held: If the specific articles cannot be recovered under the judgment, the value to be given those articles is the value of the property at the date of judgment.

TRCP 561. TO ENFORCE JUDGMENT

The court shall cause its judgments to be carried into execution, and where the judgment is for personal property and the verdict, if any, is that such property has an especial value to the plaintiff the court may award a special writ for the seizure and delivery of such property to the plaintiff, and may, in addition to the other relief granted in such cases, enforce its judgment by attachment, fine and imprisonment.

History of TRCP 561: Adopted eff. Sept. 1, 1941, by order of Oct. 29, 1940 (3 Tex.B.J. 611 [1940]). Source: TRCS art. 2434 (repealed).

TRCP 562. NO JUDGMENT WITHOUT CITATION

No judgment, other than judgment by confession, shall be rendered by the justice of the peace against any party who has not entered an appearance or accepted service, unless such party has been duly cited.

History of TRCP 562: Adopted eff. Sept. 1, 1941, by order of Oct. 29, 1940 (3 Tex.B.J. 611 [1940]). Source: TRCS art. 2435 (repealed).

TRCP 563. CONFESSION OF JUDGMENT

Any party may appear in person, or by an agent or attorney, before any justice of the peace, without the issuance or service of process, and confess judgment for any amount within the jurisdiction of the justice court; and such judgment shall be entered on the justice's docket as in other cases; but, in such cases, the plaintiff, his agent or attorney shall make and file an affidavit signed by him, to the justness of his claim.

History of TRCP 563: Adopted eff. Sept. 1, 1941, by order of Oct. 29, 1940 (3 Tex.B.J. 611 [1940]). Source: TRCS art. 2436 (repealed).

TRCP 564. WARRANT OF ATTORNEY

Where such judgment is confessed by an agent or attorney, the warrant of attorney shall be in writing and filed with the justice and noted in the judgment.

History of TRCP 564: Adopted eff. Sept. 1, 1941, by order of Oct. 29, 1940 (3 Tex.B.J. 611 [1940]). Source: TRCS art. 2437 (repealed).

TRCP 564

★

TRCP 565. RULES GOVERNING

The rules governing the district and county courts in relation to judgment and confession thereof, shall also apply to justice courts, insofar as they do not conflict with some provision of the rules applicable to justice courts.

History of TRCP 565: Adopted eff. Sept. 1, 1941, by order of Oct. 29, 1940 (3 Tex.B.J. 611 [1940]). Source: TRCS art. 2438 (repealed).

ANNOTATIONS

Triple T Inns v. Roberts, 800 S.W.2d 681, 683 (Tex. App.—Amarillo 1990, writ denied). "[P]roper application of Rule 565 gives the justice [of the peace] the same right to instruct a verdict possessed by county and district judges."

SECTION 5. NEW TRIAL

TRCP 566. JUDGMENTS BY DEFAULT

A justice may within ten days after a judgment by default or of dismissal is signed, set aside such judgment, on motion in writing, for good cause shown, supported by affidavit. Notice of such motion shall be given to the opposite party at least one full day prior to the hearing thereof.

History of TRCP 566: Amended eff. Jan. 1, 1981, by order of June 10, 1980 (599-600 S.W.2d [Tex.Cases] lxxiv): Deleted from first sentence "the rendition of" following "after" and added "is signed" after "dismissal." Adopted eff. Sept. 1, 1941, by order of Oct. 29, 1940 (3 Tex.B.J. 611 [1940]). Source: TRCS art. 2439 (repealed).

TRCP 567. NEW TRIALS

The justice, within ten days after the rendition of a judgment in any suit tried before him, may grant a new trial therein on motion in writing showing that justice has not been done in the trial of the cause.

If the grounds of the motion be other than that the verdict or judgment is contrary to the law or the evidence, or that the justice erred in some matter of law, the motion shall be supported by affidavit.

History of TRCP 567: Amended eff. Jan. 1, 1988, by order of July 15, 1987 (733-34 S.W.2d [Tex.Cases] lxxvii). Adopted eff. Sept. 1, 1941, by order of Oct. 29, 1940 (3 Tex.B.J. 611 [1940]). Source: TRCS art. 2440 (repealed).

ANNOTATIONS

Searcy v. Sagullo, 915 S.W.2d 595, 596-97 (Tex. App.—Houston [14th Dist.] 1996, no writ). TRCP 567 "provides that a justice court may grant a new trial within ten days of rendering judgment. [F]iling a motion for new trial in justice court does not enlarge the time period for filing an appeal bond. Because the justice court did not act on [P's] motion for new trial, it was overruled by operation of law ... ten days after the justice court rendered judgment. [I]f a party files a motion for new trial in justice court, there is a **maximum** of 20 days to file an appeal bond. *At 596 n.2:* We note that rule 567 provides that the new trial time period begins when judgment is **rendered** rather than when the judgment is **signed** as is the case in district and county courts."

TRCP 568. REPEALED

Repealed eff. Jan. 1, 1988, by order of July 15, 1987 (733-34 S.W.2d [Tex.Cases] lxxvii): Former TRCP 568 merged with TRCP 567.

TRCP 569. NOTICE

All motions to set aside a judgment or to grant a new trial, under the two preceding rules, shall be made within five days after the rendition of judgment and one day's notice thereof shall be given the opposite party or his attorney.

History of TRCP 569: Adopted eff. Sept. 1, 1941, by order of Oct. 29, 1940 (3 Tex.B.J. 611 [1940]). Source: TRCS art. 2442 (repealed).

TRCP 570. BUT ONE NEW TRIAL

But one new trial may be granted to either party.

History of TRCP 570: Adopted eff. Sept. 1, 1941, by order of Oct. 29, 1940 (3 Tex.B.J. 611 [1940]). Source: TRCS art. 2444 (repealed).

SECTION 6. APPEAL

TRCP 571. APPEAL BOND

The party appealing, his agent or attorney, shall within ten days from the date a judgment or order overruling motion for new trial is signed, file with the justice a bond, with two or more good and sufficient sureties, to be approved by the justice, in double the amount of the judgment, payable to the appellee, conditioned that appellant shall prosecute his appeal to effect, and shall pay off and satisfy the judgment which may be rendered against him on appeal; or if the appeal is by the plaintiff by reason of judgment denying in whole or in part his claim, he shall file with the justice a bond in the same ten-day period, payable to the appellee, with two or more good and sufficient sureties, to be approved by the justice, in double the amount of the costs incurred in the justice court and estimated costs in the county court, less such sums as may have been paid by the plaintiff on the costs, conditioned that he shall prosecute his appeal to effect and shall pay off and satisfy such costs if judgment for costs be rendered against him on appeal. When such bond has been filed with the justice, the appeal shall be held to be thereby perfected and all parties to said suit or to any suit so appealed shall make their appearance at the next term of

TRCP 565

★

court to which said case has been appealed. Within five days following the filing of such appeal bond, the party appealing shall give notice as provided in Rule 21a of the filing of such bond to all parties to the suit who have not filed such bond. No judgment shall be taken by default against any party in the court to which the cause has been appealed without first showing that this rule has been complied with. The appeal shall not be dismissed for defects or irregularities in procedure, either of form or substance, without allowing appellant five days after notice within which to correct or amend same.

History of TRCP 571: Amended eff. Sept. 1, 1990, by order of Apr. 24, 1990 (785-86 S.W.2d [Tex.Cases] lxxiv): Deleted reference to TRCP 21b. Amended eff. Jan. 1, 1981, by order of June 10, 1980 (599-600 S.W.2d [Tex.Cases] lxxiv): Changed first sentence to read: "The party appealing, his agent or attorney, shall within ten days from the date a judgment or order overruling motion for new trial is signed, file with the justice a bond...." Amended eff. Jan. 1, 1967, by order of July 20, 1966 (401-02 S.W.2d [Tex.Cases] xlvii): Added provision requiring filing of an appeal bond by plaintiff whose claim is denied in whole or in part. Amended eff. Sept. 1, 1962, by order of Apr. 12, 1962 (25 Tex.B.J. 435 [1962]): Added provision requiring notice of filing of appeal bond. Adopted eff. Sept. 1, 1941, by order of Oct. 29, 1940 (3 Tex.B.J. 612 [1940]). Source: TRCS arts. 2456, 2457 (repealed), with changes: Allows ten days from order overruling motion for new trial during which appeal bond may be filed.

ANNOTATIONS

Rowe v. Watkins, 340 S.W.3d 860, 863 (Tex. App.—El Paso 2011, no pet.). "When the appeal bond contains defects or irregularities, either of form or substance, the case should not be dismissed without first allowing the appealing party five days, after notice of the defect, to correct or amend the defective appeal. Although the rules do not prescribe a specific type of notice, we have held that the notice must, in the very least, conform to due process which is met if the notice affords the party a fair opportunity to appear and defend her interests. As compliance with the appellate requirements of Rule 571 is jurisdictional, ... if the appealing party fails to meet any one of the rule's prerequisites, and also fails to correct the defect within five days of notice, the appellate court, i.e., the county court, lacks jurisdiction to hear the appeal and must dismiss the same."

TRCP 572. AFFIDAVIT OF INABILITY

Where appellant is unable to pay the costs of appeal, or give security therefor, he shall nevertheless be entitled to appeal by making strict proof of such inability within five days after the judgment or order overruling motion for new trial is signed, which shall consist of his affidavit filed with the justice of the peace stating his inability to pay such costs, or any part thereof, or to give

security, which may be contested within five days after the filing of such affidavit and notice thereof to the opposite party or his attorney of record by any officer of court or party to the suit, whereupon it shall be the duty of the justice of the peace in whose court the suit is pending to hear evidence and determine the right of the party to appeal, and he shall enter his finding on the docket as a part of the record. It will be presumed prima facie that the affidavit speaks the truth, and, unless contested within five days after the filing and notice thereof, the presumption shall be deemed conclusive; but if a contest is filed, the burden shall then be on the appellant to prove his alleged inability by competent evidence other than by the affidavit above referred to. If the justice of the peace denies the right of appeal, appellant may, within five days thereafter, bring the matter before the county judge of the county for final decision, and, on request, the justice shall certify to the county judge appellant's affidavit, the contest thereof, and all documents and papers pertaining thereto. The county judge shall set a day for hearing, not later than ten days, and shall hear the contest de novo, and if the appeal is granted, shall direct the justice to transmit to the clerk of the county court, the transcript, records and papers of the case, as provided in these rules.

History of TRCP 572: Amended eff. Jan. 1, 1981, by order of June 10, 1980 (599-600 S.W.2d [Tex.Cases] lxxiv): Added in first sentence the words "is signed" after "new trial." Adopted eff. Sept. 1, 1941, by order of Oct. 29, 1940 (3 Tex.B.J. 612 [1940]). Source: TRCS art. 2457 (repealed).

TRCP 573. APPEAL PERFECTED

When the bond, or the affidavit in lieu thereof, provided for in the rules applicable to justice courts, has been filed and the previous requirements have been complied with, the appeal shall be held to be perfected.

History of TRCP 573: Adopted eff. Sept. 1, 1941, by order of Oct. 29, 1940 (3 Tex.B.J. 612 [1940]). Source: TRCS art. 2458 (repealed).

ANNOTATIONS

Williams v. Schneiber, 148 S.W.3d 581, 583 (Tex. App.—Fort Worth 2004, no pet.). "'[I]t is well-settled that perfection of an appeal to county court from a justice court for trial de novo vacates and annuls the judgment of the justice court.' To perfect such an appeal, an appellant ... must file with the justice of the peace an appeal bond within 10 days from the date a judgment or order overruling a motion for new trial is signed. If the appeal bond is not timely filed, the county court is without jurisdiction to hear the appeal, and the appeal must be dismissed for lack of jurisdiction." *See also **Molina v. Negley**,* 425 S.W.2d 896, 898 (Tex.App.—San Antonio 1968, no writ).

TRCP 574. TRANSCRIPT

Whenever an appeal has been perfected from the justice court, the justice who made the order, or his successor, shall immediately make out a true and correct copy of all the entries made on his docket in the cause, and certify thereto officially, and immediately send it together with a certified copy of the bill of costs taken from his fee book, and the original papers in the cause, to the clerk of the county court of his county, or other court having jurisdiction.

History of TRCP 574: Adopted eff. Sept. 1, 1941, by order of Oct. 29, 1940 (3 Tex.B.J. 612 [1940]). Source: TRCS art. 2459 (repealed).

Advance Imps., Inc. v. Gibson Prods., 533 S.W.2d 168, 170 (Tex.App.—Dallas 1976, no writ). "[T]he duty of the justice to prepare a transcript of his docket entries and transmit it, along with the original papers, to the clerk of the county court, and the duty of the clerk to file the transcript and papers and collect the filing fee do not arise until the appeal 'has been perfected' by filing the bond or affidavit. Consequently, failure of the justice or clerk to perform any of these ministerial duties does not reinstate the judgment of the justice court. That judgment is vacated by filing the appeal bond."

TRCP 574a. NEW MATTER MAY BE PLEADED

Either party may plead any new matter in the county or district court which was not presented in the court below, but no new ground of recovery shall be set up by the plaintiff, nor shall any set-off or counterclaim be set up by the defendant which was not pleaded in the court below. The pleading thereof shall be in writing and filed in the cause before the parties have announced ready for trial.

History of TRCP 574a: Adopted eff. Jan. 1, 1988, by order of July 15, 1987 (733-34 S.W.2d [Tex.Cases] lxxvii). Source: New rule.

See CPRC §31.005 (judgment or determination of fact or law in justice-court proceeding not res judicata in county or statutory county court, except judgment rendered as to recovery or denial of recovery is binding on the parties).

Houtex Ready Mix Concrete & Materials v. Eagle Constr. & Env'tl Servs., 226 S.W.2d 514, 521 n.2 (Tex.App.—Houston [1st Dist.] 2006, no pet.). "Texas courts have noted that [TRCP] 574a has little practical effect in light of [CPRC] §§31.004 and 31.005. While Rule 574a prevents a party from bringing a 'new ground of recovery' in the de novo appeal of the justice court judgment, §§31.004 and 31.005 allow a party to circumvent Rule 574a by bringing the new claim in a separate action in county court or district court." *See also **Harrill v. A.J.'s Wrecker Serv.**,* 27 S.W.3d 191, 195 (Tex.App.—Dallas 2000, pet. dism'd).

Crumpton v. Stevens, 936 S.W.2d 473, 476 (Tex.App.—Fort Worth 1996, no writ). "[A] statutory claim for attorney's fees that is dependent on a cause of action that was originally pleaded in the justice court may be asserted for the first time in a de novo appeal to the county court at law."

TRCP 574b. TRIAL DE NOVO

The cause shall be tried de novo in the county or district court; and judgment shall be rendered.

History of TRCP 574b: Adopted eff. Jan. 1, 1988, by order of July 15, 1987 (733-34 S.W.2d [Tex.Cases] lxxviii). Source: New rule.

In re Garza, 990 S.W.2d 372, 374 (Tex.App.—Corpus Christi 1999, orig. proceeding). "When an appeal from a justice court judgment is perfected in a county court, the judgment of the justice court is annulled. Once this occurs, the burden is on the appellee to obtain a new judgment."

SECTION 7. CERTIORARI

TRCP 575. ORDER FOR WRIT

The writ of certiorari shall be issued by order of the county court or the judge thereof (or district court or judge thereof, if jurisdiction is transferred to the district court) as provided in these rules.

History of TRCP 575: Adopted eff. Sept. 1, 1941, by order of Oct. 29, 1940 (3 Tex.B.J. 613 [1940]). Source: TRCS art. 942 (repealed).

TRCP 576. REQUISITES OF WRIT

The writ shall command the justice to immediately make and certify a copy of the entries in the cause on his docket, and immediately transmit the same, with the papers in his possession and a certified copy of the bill of costs to the proper court.

History of TRCP 576: Adopted eff. Sept. 1, 1941, by order of Oct. 29, 1940 (3 Tex.B.J. 613 [1940]). Source: TRCS arts. 943 and 2460 (repealed).

TRCP 577. AFFIDAVIT OF SUFFICIENT CAUSE

The writ shall not be granted unless the applicant or some person for him having knowledge of the facts, shall make affidavit setting forth sufficient cause to entitle him thereto.

History of TRCP 577: Adopted eff. Sept. 1, 1941, by order of Oct. 29, 1940 (3 Tex.B.J. 613 [1940]). Source: TRCS art. 944 (repealed).

ANNOTATIONS

Centro Jurici De Instituto Tecnologico v. Inter-travel, Inc., 2 S.W.3d 446, 449 (Tex.App.—San Antonio 1999, no pet.). "'Sufficient cause' includes a lack of jurisdiction."

TRCP 578. APPLICATION FOR CERTIORARI

To constitute a sufficient cause, the facts stated must show that either the justice of the peace had not jurisdiction, or that injustice was done to the applicant by the final determination of the suit or proceeding, and that such injustice was not caused by his own inexcusable neglect.

History of TRCP 578: Adopted eff. Sept. 1, 1941, by order of Oct. 29, 1940 (3 Tex.B.J. 613 [1940]). Source: TRCS art. 945 (repealed).

TRCP 579. WITHIN WHAT TIME GRANTED

Such writ shall not be granted after ninety days from the time the final judgment is signed.

History of TRCP 579: Amended eff. Jan. 1, 1981, by order of June 10, 1980 (599-600 S.W.2d [Tex.Cases] lxxv): Time will run from the time the judgment is signed. Adopted eff. Sept. 1, 1941, by order of Oct. 29, 1940 (3 Tex.B.J. 613 [1940]). Source: TRCS art. 946 (repealed).

TRCP 580. BOND WITH SURETIES REQUIRED

The writ shall not be issued unless the applicant shall first cause to be filed a bond with two or more good and sufficient sureties, to be approved by the clerk, payable to the adverse party, in such sum as the judge shall direct, to the effect that the party applying therefor will perform the judgment of the county or district court, if the same shall be against him.

History of TRCP 580: Adopted eff. Sept. 1, 1941, by order of Oct. 29, 1940 (3 Tex.B.J. 613 [1940]). Source: TRCS art. 947 (repealed).

TRCP 581. BOND, AFFIDAVIT & ORDER

The bond and affidavit, with the order of the judge, when made in vacation, shall be filed with the clerk of the court to which the same is returnable.

History of TRCP 581: Adopted eff. Sept. 1, 1941, by order of Oct. 29, 1940 (3 Tex.B.J. 613 [1940]). Source: TRCS art. 948 (repealed).

TRCP 582. WRIT TO ISSUE INSTANTER

As soon as such affidavit, order of the judge, and bond, shall have been filed, the clerk shall issue a writ of certiorari.

History of TRCP 582: Adopted eff. Sept. 1, 1941, by order of Oct. 29, 1940 (3 Tex.B.J. 613 [1940]). Source: TRCS art. 949 (repealed).

TRCP 583. JUSTICE SHALL STAY PROCEEDINGS

Upon service of such writ of certiorari being made upon the justice of the peace, he shall stay further proceedings on the judgment and forthwith comply with said writ.

History of TRCP 583: Adopted eff. Sept. 1, 1941, by order of Oct. 29, 1940 (3 Tex.B.J. 613 [1940]). Source: TRCS art. 950 (repealed).

TRCP 584. CITATION AS IN OTHER CASES

Whenever a writ of certiorari has been issued, the clerk shall forthwith issue a citation for the party adversely interested.

History of TRCP 584: Adopted eff. Sept. 1, 1941, by order of Oct. 29, 1940 (3 Tex.B.J. 613 [1940]). Source: TRCS art. 951 (repealed).

TRCP 585. CAUSE DOCKETED

The action shall be docketed in the name of the original plaintiff, as plaintiff, and of the original defendant, as defendant.

History of TRCP 585: Adopted eff. Sept. 1, 1941, by order of Oct. 29, 1940 (3 Tex.B.J. 613 [1940]). Source: TRCS art. 952 (repealed).

TRCP 586. MOTION TO DISMISS

Within thirty days after the service of citation on the writ of certiorari, the adverse party may move to dismiss the certiorari for want of sufficient cause appearing in the affidavit, or for want of sufficient bond.

History of TRCP 586: Adopted eff. Sept. 1, 1941, by order of Oct. 29, 1940 (3 Tex.B.J. 613 [1940]). Source: TRCS art. 953 (repealed).

TRCP 587. AMENDMENT OF BOND OR OATH

The affidavit or bond may be amended in the discretion of the court in which it is filed.

History of TRCP 587: Adopted eff. Sept. 1, 1941, by order of Oct. 29, 1940 (3 Tex.B.J. 614 [1940]). Source: TRCS art. 954 (repealed).

TRCP 588. JUDGMENT OF DISMISSAL

If the certiorari be dismissed, the judgment shall direct the justice to proceed with the execution of the judgment below.

History of TRCP 588: Adopted eff. Sept. 1, 1941, by order of Oct. 29, 1940 (3 Tex.B.J. 614 [1940]). Source: TRCS art. 955 (repealed).

TRCP 589. PLEADING

After the transcript of the proceedings in the justice court, together with the original papers and a bill of costs, have been filed in the county (or district) court, all pleadings in the cause which are not already written shall be reduced to writing.

History of TRCP 589: Adopted eff. Sept. 1, 1941, by order of Oct. 29, 1940 (3 Tex.B.J. 614 [1940]). Source: TRCS arts. 956, 957 (repealed).

TRCP 590. NEW MATTER MAY BE PLEADED

Either party may plead any new matter in the county or district court which was not presented in the court below, but no new ground of recovery shall be set up by the plaintiff, nor shall any set-off or counterclaim be set up by the defendant which was not pleaded in the court below. The pleading thereof shall be in writing and filed in the cause before the parties have announced ready for trial.

History of TRCP 590: Adopted eff. Sept. 1, 1941, by order of Oct. 29, 1940 (3 Tex.B.J. 614 [1940]). Source: TRCS art. 958 (repealed).

ANNOTATIONS

Hamby Co. v. Palmer, 631 S.W.2d 589, 591 (Tex. App.—Amarillo 1982, no writ). "[A]lthough set out in a section of the [TRCPs] dealing with certiorari proceedings, [TRCP 590] also applies to appeals from justice court[s] to higher courts."

TRCP 591. TRIAL DE NOVO

The cause shall be tried de novo in the county or district court; and judgment shall be rendered as in cases appealed from justice courts.

History of TRCP 591: Adopted eff. Sept. 1, 1941, by order of Oct. 29, 1940 (3 Tex.B.J. 614 [1940]). Source: TRCS art. 959 (repealed).

PART VI. RULES RELATING TO ANCILLARY PROCEEDINGS

SECTION 1. ATTACHMENT

TRCP 592. APPLICATION FOR WRIT OF ATTACHMENT & ORDER

Either at the commencement of a suit or at any time during its progress the plaintiff may file an application for the issuance of a writ of attachment. Such application shall be supported by affidavits of the plaintiff, his agent, his attorney, or other persons having knowledge of relevant facts. The application shall comply with all statutory requirements and shall state the grounds for issuing the writ and the specific facts relied upon by the plaintiff to warrant the required findings by the court. The writ shall not be quashed because two or more grounds are stated conjunctively or disjunctively. The application and any affidavits shall be made on personal knowledge and shall set forth such facts as would be admissible in evidence; provided that facts may be stated based upon information and belief if the grounds of such belief are specifically stated.

No writ shall issue except upon written order of the court after a hearing, which may be ex parte. The court,

in its order granting the application, shall make specific findings of facts to support the statutory grounds found to exist, and shall specify the maximum value of property that may be attached, and the amount of bond required of plaintiff, and, further shall command that the attached property be kept safe and preserved subject to further orders of the court. Such bond shall be in an amount which, in the opinion of the court, will adequately compensate the defendant in the event plaintiff fails to prosecute his suit to effect, and to pay all damages and costs which may be adjudged against him for wrongfully suing out the writ of attachment. The court shall further find in its order the amount of bond required of defendant to replevy, which, unless the defendant chooses to exercise his option as provided in Rule 599, shall be the amount of plaintiff's claim, one year's accrual of interest if allowed by law on the claim, and the estimated costs of court. The order may direct the issuance of several writs at the same time, or in succession, to be sent to different counties.

History of TRCP 592: Adopted eff. Jan. 1, 1978, by order of July 11, 1977 (553-54 S.W.2d [Tex.Cases] lx): New rule added to meet constitutional demands of due process in prejudgment remedies. Former TRCP 592 repealed and renumbered as TRCP 592b, eff. Jan. 1, 1978, by order of July 11, 1977 (553-54 S.W.2d [Tex.Cases] lx). Source: New rule.

ANNOTATIONS

In re Argyll Equities, LLC, 227 S.W.3d 268, 271 (Tex.App.—San Antonio 2007, orig. proceeding). "The validity of a writ of attachment does not depend on the truthfulness of the allegations, but on compliance with the statute in making the affidavit. [¶] Generally, a writ of attachment is not available when the applicant's claims are for unliquidated damages. *At n.6:* When the defendant cannot be served in Texas, [however,] a writ of attachment may issue in a suit for an unliquidated claim."

TRCP 592a. BOND FOR ATTACHMENT

No writ of attachment shall issue until the party applying therefor has filed with the officer authorized to issue such writ a bond payable to the defendant in the amount fixed by the court's order, with sufficient surety or sureties as provided by statute to be approved by such officer, conditioned that the plaintiff will prosecute his suit to effect and pay to the extent of the penal amount of the bond all damages and costs as may be adjudged against him for wrongfully suing out such writ of attachment.

After notice to the opposite party, either before or after the issuance of the writ, the defendant or plaintiff may file a motion to increase or reduce the amount of such bond, or to question the sufficiency of the sureties thereon, in the court in which such suit is pending. Upon hearing, the court shall enter its order with respect to such bond and sufficiency of the sureties.

History of TRCP 592a: Adopted eff. Jan. 1, 1978, by order of July 11, 1977 (553-54 S.W.2d [Tex.Cases] lxi). Source: New rule.

TRCP 592b. FORM OF ATTACHMENT BOND

The following form of bond may be used:

"The State of Texas,

County of _____,

"We, the undersigned, _____ as principal, and _____ and _____ as sureties, acknowledge ourselves bound to pay to C.D. the sum of _____ dollars, conditioned that the above bound plaintiff in attachment against the said C.D., defendant, will prosecute his said suit to effect, and that he will pay all such damages and costs to the extent of the penal amount of this bond as shall be adjudged against him for wrongfully suing out such attachment. Witness our hands this ___ day of _____, 20___."

History of TRCP 592b: Adopted eff. Jan. 1, 1978, by order of July 11, 1977 (553-54 S.W.2d [Tex.Cases] lxi): Renumbered from TRCP 592; added words "to the extent of the penal amount of this bond." Source: New rule. See former TRCP 592, repealed eff. Jan. 1, 1978, by order of July 11, 1977 (553-54 S.W.2d [Tex.Cases] lx).

TRCP 593. REQUISITES FOR WRIT

A writ of attachment shall be directed to the sheriff or any constable within the State of Texas. It shall command him to attach and hold, unless replevied, subject to the further order of the court, so much of the property of the defendant, of a reasonable value in approximately the amount fixed by the court, as shall be found within his county.

History of TRCP 593: Amended eff. Jan. 1, 1978, by order of July 11, 1977 (553-54 S.W.2d [Tex.Cases] lxii): Writ must be directed to the officer "within" the State of Texas; writ recognizes the right to replevy, commands officer to hold property of a reasonable value fixed by the court, and attachment is subject to further orders of the court. Adopted eff. Sept. 1, 1941, by order of Oct. 29, 1940 (3 Tex.B.J. 615 [1940]). Source: TRCS art. 282 (repealed in part by TRCP).

TRCP 594. FORM OF WRIT

The following form of writ may be issued:

"The State of Texas.

"To the Sheriff or any Constable of any County of the State of Texas, greeting:

"We command you that you attach forthwith so much of the property of C.D., if it be found in your county, repleviable on security, as shall be of value sufficient to make the sum of _____ dollars, and the probable costs of suit, to satisfy the demand of A.B., and that you keep and secure in your hands the property so attached, unless replevied, that the same may be liable to further proceedings thereon to be had before our court in _____, County of _____. You will true return make of this writ on or before 10 a.m. of Monday, the _____ day of _____, 20___, showing how you have executed the same."

History of TRCP 594: Adopted eff. Sept. 1, 1941, by order of Oct. 29, 1940 (3 Tex.B.J. 615 [1940]). Source: TRCS art. 284 (repealed).

TRCP 595. SEVERAL WRITS

Several writs of attachment may, at the option of the plaintiff, be issued at the same time, or in succession, and sent to different counties, until sufficient property shall be attached to satisfy the writ.

History of TRCP 595: Adopted eff. Sept. 1, 1941, by order of Oct. 29, 1940 (3 Tex.B.J. 615 [1940]). Source: TRCS art. 283 (repealed).

TRCP 596. DELIVERY OF WRIT

The writ of attachment shall be dated and tested as other writs, and may be delivered to the sheriff or constable by the officer issuing it, or he may deliver it to the plaintiff, his agent or attorney, for that purpose.

History of TRCP 596: Adopted eff. Sept. 1, 1941, by order of Oct. 29, 1940 (3 Tex.B.J. 615 [1940]). Source: TRCS art. 285 (repealed).

TRCP 597. DUTY OF OFFICER

The sheriff or constable receiving the writ shall immediately proceed to execute the same by levying upon so much of the property of the defendant subject to the writ, and found within his county, as may be sufficient to satisfy the command of the writ.

History of TRCP 597: Adopted eff. Sept. 1, 1941, by order of Oct. 29, 1940 (3 Tex.B.J. 615 [1940]). Source: TRCS art. 286 (repealed).

TRCP 598. LEVY, HOW MADE

The writ of attachment shall be levied in the same manner as is, or may be, the writ of execution upon similar property.

History of TRCP 598: Adopted eff. Sept. 1, 1941, by order of Oct. 29, 1940 (3 Tex.B.J. 615 [1940]). Source: TRCS art. 289 (repealed).

TRCP 598a. SERVICE OF WRIT ON DEFENDANT

The defendant shall be served in any manner prescribed for service of citation, or as provided in Rule 21a, with a copy of the writ of attachment, the application, accompanying affidavits, and orders of the court as soon as practicable following the levy of the writ. There shall be prominently displayed on the face of the

---

✦

---

copy of the writ served on the defendant, in ten-point type and in a manner calculated to advise a reasonably attentive person of its contents, the following:

"To _____, Defendant:

You are hereby notified that certain properties alleged to be owned by you have been attached. If you claim any rights in such property, you are advised:

"YOU HAVE A RIGHT TO REGAIN POSSESSION OF THE PROPERTY BY FILING A REPLEVY BOND. YOU HAVE A RIGHT TO SEEK TO REGAIN POSSESSION OF THE PROPERTY BY FILING WITH THE COURT A MOTION TO DISSOLVE THIS WRIT."

History of TRCP 598a: Adopted eff. Jan. 1, 1978, by order of July 11, 1977 (553-54 S.W.2d [Tex.Cases] lxii): Rule affords defendant notice of the proceedings and informs him of some of his rights. Source: New rule.

TRCP 599. DEFENDANT MAY REPLEVY

At any time before judgment, should the attached property not have been previously claimed or sold, the defendant may replevy the same, or any part thereof, or the proceeds from the sale of the property if it has been sold under order of the court, by giving bond with sufficient surety or sureties as provided by statute, to be approved by the officer who levied the writ, payable to plaintiff, in the amount fixed by the court's order, or, at the defendant's option, for the value of the property sought to be replevied (to be estimated by the officer), plus one year's interest thereon at the legal rate from the date of the bond, conditioned that the defendant shall satisfy, to the extent of the penal amount of the bond, any judgment which may be rendered against him in such action.

On reasonable notice to the opposing party (which may be less than three days) either party shall have the right to prompt judicial review of the amount of bond required, denial of bond, sufficiency of sureties, and estimated value of the property, by the court which authorized issuance of the writ. The court's determination may be made upon the basis of affidavits, if uncontroverted, setting forth such facts as would be admissible in evidence; otherwise, the parties shall submit evidence. The court shall forthwith enter its order either approving or modifying the requirements of the officer or of the court's prior order, and such order of the court shall supersede and control with respect to such matters.

On reasonable notice to the opposing party (which may be less than three days) the defendant shall have the right to move the court for a substitution of prop-

erty, of equal value as that attached, for the property attached. Provided that there has been located sufficient property of the defendants to satisfy the order of attachment, the court may authorize substitution of one or more items of defendant's property for all or for part of the property attached. The court shall first make findings as to the value of the property to be substituted. If property is substituted, the property released from attachment shall be delivered to defendant, if such property is personal property, and all liens upon such property from the original order of attachment or modification thereof shall be terminated. Attachment of substituted property shall be deemed to have existed from the date of levy on the original property attached, and no property on which liens have become affixed since the date of levy on the original property may be substituted.

History of TRCP 599: Amended eff. Jan. 1, 1978, by order of July 11, 1977 (553-54 S.W.2d [Tex.Cases] lxii): Gives defendant right to replevy proceeds from sale of property; changes amount of bond from double the amount of plaintiff's debt to amount fixed by the court; more clearly fixes the conditions of the replevy bond; gives parties a hearing; authorizes substitution of property. Adopted eff. Sept. 1, 1941, by order of Oct. 29, 1940 (3 Tex.B.J. 616 [1940]). Source: TRCS art. 292 (repealed).

TRCP 600. SALE OF PERISHABLE PROPERTY

Whenever personal property which has been attached shall not have been claimed or replevied, the judge, or justice of the peace, out of whose court the writ was issued, may, either in term time or in vacation, order the same to be sold, when it shall be made to appear that such property is in danger of serious and immediate waste or decay, or that the keeping of the same until the trial will necessarily be attended with such expense or deterioration in value as greatly to lessen the amount likely to be realized therefrom.

History of TRCP 600: Adopted eff. Sept. 1, 1941, by order of Oct. 29, 1940 (3 Tex.B.J. 616 [1940]). Source: TRCS art. 293 (repealed).

TRCP 601. TO PROTECT INTERESTS

In determining whether the property attached is perishable, and the necessity or advantage of ordering a sale thereof, the judge or justice of the peace may act upon affidavits in writing or oral testimony, and may by a preliminary order entered of record, with or without notice to the parties as the urgency of the case in his opinion requires, direct the sheriff or constable to sell such property at public auction for cash, and thereupon the officer shall sell it accordingly.

History of TRCP 601: Adopted eff. Sept. 1, 1941, by order of Oct. 29, 1940 (3 Tex.B.J. 616 [1940]). Source: TRCS art. 294 (repealed).

★

TRCP 602. BOND OF APPLICANT FOR SALE

If the application for an order of sale be filed by any person or party other than the defendant from whose possession the property was taken by levy, the court shall not grant such order unless the applicant shall file with such court a bond payable to such defendant, with two or more good and sufficient sureties, to be approved by said court, conditioned that they will be responsible to the defendant for such damages as he may sustain in case such sale be illegally and unjustly applied for, or be illegally and unjustly made.

History of TRCP 602: Adopted eff. Sept. 1, 1941, by order of Oct. 29, 1940 (3 Tex.B.J. 616 [1940]). Source: New rule as applied to attachment proceedings. See TRCS art. 5233 (repealed).

TRCP 603. PROCEDURE FOR SALE

Such sale of attached perishable personal property shall be conducted in the same manner as sales of personal property under execution; provided, however, that the time of the sale, and at the time of advertisement thereof, may be fixed by the judge or justice of the peace at a time earlier than ten days, according to the exigency of the case, and in such event notice thereof shall be given in such manner as directed by the order.

History of TRCP 603: Adopted eff. Sept. 1, 1941, by order of Oct. 29, 1940 (3 Tex.B.J. 616 [1940]). Source: TRCS art. 295 (repealed).

TRCP 604. RETURN OF SALE

The officer making such sale of perishable property shall promptly pay the proceeds of such sale to the clerk of such court or justice of the peace, as the case may be, and shall make written return of the order of sale signed by him officially, stating the time and place of the sale, the name of the purchaser, and the amount of money received, with an itemized account of the expenses attending the sale. Such return shall be filed with the papers of the case.

History of TRCP 604: Adopted eff. Sept. 1, 1941, by order of Oct. 29, 1940 (3 Tex.B.J. 616 [1940]). Source: TRCS art. 296 (repealed).

TRCP 605. JUDGE MAY MAKE NECESSARY ORDERS

When the perishable personal property levied on under the attachment writ has not been claimed or replevied, the judge or justice of the peace may make such orders, either in term time or vacation, as may be necessary for its preservation or use.

History of TRCP 605: Adopted eff. Sept. 1, 1941, by order of Oct. 29, 1940 (3 Tex.B.J. 616 [1940]). Source: TRCS art. 297 (repealed).

TRCP 606. RETURN OF WRIT

The officer executing the writ of attachment shall return the writ, with his action endorsed thereon, or attached thereto, signed by him officially, to the court from which it issued, at or before 10 o'clock a.m. of the Monday next after the expiration of fifteen days from the date of issuance of the writ. Such return shall describe the property attached with sufficient certainty to identify it, and state when the same was attached, and whether any personal property attached remains still in his hands, and, if not, the disposition made of the same. When property has been replevied he shall deliver the replevy bond to the clerk or justice of the peace to be filed with the papers of the cause.

History of TRCP 606: Adopted eff. Sept. 1, 1941, by order of Oct. 29, 1940 (3 Tex.B.J. 617 [1940]). Source: TRCS art. 298 (repealed).

TRCP 607. REPORT OF DISPOSITION OF PROPERTY

When the property levied on is claimed, replevied or sold, or otherwise disposed of after the writ has been returned, the officer having the custody of the same shall immediately make a report in writing, signed by him officially, to the clerk, or justice of the peace, as the case may be, showing such disposition of the property. Such report shall be filed among the papers of the cause.

History of TRCP 607: Adopted eff. Sept. 1, 1941, by order of Oct. 29, 1940 (3 Tex.B.J. 617 [1940]). Source: TRCS art. 299 (repealed).

TRCP 608. DISSOLUTION OR MODIFICATION OF WRIT OF ATTACHMENT

A defendant whose property has been attached or any intervening party who claims an interest in such property, may by sworn written motion, seek to vacate, dissolve, or modify the writ, and the order directing its issuance, for any grounds or cause, extrinsic or intrinsic. Such motion shall admit or deny each finding of the order directing the issuance of the writ except where the movant is unable to admit or deny the finding, in which case movant shall set forth the reasons why he cannot admit or deny. Unless the parties agree to an extension of time, the motion shall be heard promptly, after reasonable notice to the plaintiff (which may be less than three days), and the issue shall be determined not later than ten days after the motion is filed. The filing of the motion shall stay any further proceedings under the writ, except for any orders concerning the care, preservation, or sale of perishable property, until a hearing is had and the issue is determined. The writ

⭐

shall be dissolved unless at such hearing, the plaintiff shall prove the grounds relied upon for its issuance, but the court may modify its previous order granting the writ and the writ issued pursuant thereto. The movant shall, however, have the burden to prove that the reasonable value of the property attached exceeds the amount necessary to secure the debt, interest for one year, and probable costs. He shall also have the burden to prove the facts to justify substitution of property.

The court's determination may be made upon the basis of affidavits, if uncontroverted, setting forth such facts as would be admissible in evidence; otherwise, the parties shall submit evidence. The court may make all such orders, including orders concerning the care, preservation, or disposition of the property (or the proceeds therefrom if the same has been sold), as justice may require. If the movant has given a replevy bond, an order to vacate or dissolve the writ shall vacate the replevy bond and discharge the sureties thereon, and if the court modifies its order or the writ issued pursuant thereto, it shall make such further orders with respect to the bond as may be consistent with its modification.

History of TRCP 608: Amended eff. Jan. 1, 1978, by order of July 11, 1977 (553-54 S.W.2d [Tex.Cases] lxiii): Rule affords a prompt hearing, provides for the procedures, burden of proof, and the kind of proof. Adopted eff. Sept. 1, 1941, by order of Oct. 29, 1940 (3 Tex.B.J. 617 [1940]). Source: TRCS art. 303 (repealed).

TRCP 609. AMENDMENT

Clerical errors in the affidavit, bond, or writ of attachment, or the officer's return thereof, may upon application in writing to the judge or justice of the court in which the suit is filed, and after notice to the opponent, be amended in such manner and on such terms as the judge or justice shall authorize by an order entered in the minutes of the court or noted on the docket of the justice of the peace, provided the amendment does not change or add to the grounds of such attachment as stated in the affidavit, and provided such amendment appears to the judge or justice to be in furtherance of justice.

History of TRCP 609: Adopted eff. Sept. 1, 1941, by order of Oct. 29, 1940 (3 Tex.B.J. 617 [1940]). Source: New rule.

SECTION 2. DISTRESS WARRANT

TRCP 610. APPLICATION FOR DISTRESS WARRANT & ORDER

Either at the commencement of a suit or at any time during its progress the plaintiff may file an application for the issuance of a distress warrant with the justice of the peace. Such application may be supported by affidavits of the plaintiff, his agent, his attorney, or other persons having knowledge of relevant facts, but shall include a statement that the amount sued for is rent, or advances described by statute, or shall produce a writing signed by the tenant to that effect, and shall further swear that such warrant is not sued out for the purpose of vexing and harassing the defendant. The application shall comply with all statutory requirements and shall state the grounds for issuing the warrant and the specific facts relied upon by the plaintiff to warrant the required findings by the justice of the peace. The warrant shall not be quashed because two or more grounds are stated conjunctively or disjunctively. The application and any affidavits shall be made on personal knowledge and shall set forth such facts as would be admissible in evidence provided that facts may be stated based upon information and belief if the grounds of such belief are specifically stated.

No warrant shall issue before final judgment except on written order of the justice of the peace after a hearing, which may be ex parte. Such warrant shall be made returnable to a court having jurisdiction of the amount in controversy. The justice of the peace in his order granting the application shall make specific findings of fact to support the statutory grounds found to exist, and shall specify the maximum value of property that may be seized, and the amount of bond required of plaintiff, and, further shall command that property be kept safe and preserved subject to further orders of the court having jurisdiction. Such bond shall be in an amount which, in the opinion of the court, shall adequately compensate defendant in the event plaintiff fails to prosecute his suit to effect, and pay all damages and costs as shall be adjudged against him for wrongfully suing out the warrant. The justice of the peace shall further find in his order the amount of bond required to replevy, which, unless the defendant chooses to exercise his option as provided in Rule 614, shall be the amount of plaintiff's claim, one year's accrual of interest if allowed by law on the claim, and the estimated costs of court. The order may direct the issuance of several warrants at the same time, or in succession, to be sent to different counties.

History of TRCP 610: Adopted eff. Jan. 1, 1981, by order of June 10, 1980 (599-600 S.W.2d [Tex.Cases] lxxv): Rule written to conform with due-process requirements of *Fuentes v. Shevin*, 407 U.S. 67 (1972), *Mitchell v. W.T. Grant Co.*, 416 U.S. 600 (1974), and *North Ga. Finishing, Inc. v. Di-Chem, Inc.*, 419 U.S. 601 (1975). Former TRCP 610 repealed eff. Jan. 1, 1981, by order of June 10, 1986 (599-600 S.W.2d [Tex.Cases] lxxvi). Source: New rule.

ANNOTATIONS

Lincoln Ten, Ltd. v. White, 706 S.W.2d 125, 128 (Tex.App.—Houston [14th Dist.] 1986, orig. proceeding). "According to Rule 610, no distress warrant will issue before final judgment except on written order of a justice of the peace. This complies with the requirement that the writ must be issued by a judicial officer."

TRCP 611. BOND FOR DISTRESS WARRANT

No distress warrant shall issue before final judgment until the party applying therefor has filed with the justice of the peace authorized to issue such warrant a bond payable to the defendant in an amount approved by the justice of the peace, with sufficient surety or sureties as provided by statute, conditioned that the plaintiff will prosecute his suit to effect and pay all damages and costs as may be adjudged against him for wrongfully suing out such warrant.

After notice to the opposite party, either before or after the issuance of the warrant, the defendant or plaintiff may file a motion to increase or reduce the amount of such bond, or to question the sufficiency of the sureties thereon, in a court having jurisdiction of the subject matter. Upon hearing, the court shall enter its order with respect to such bond and sufficiency of the sureties.

History of TRCP 611: Adopted eff. Jan. 1, 1981, by order of June 10, 1980 (599-600 S.W.2d [Tex.Cases] lxxvi): Rule written to conform with due-process requirements. See history note to TRCP 610. Former TRCP 611 repealed eff. Jan. 1, 1981, by order of June 10, 1980 (599-600 S.W.2d [Tex.Cases] lxxvi). Source: New rule.

TRCP 612. REQUISITES FOR WARRANT

A distress warrant shall be directed to the sheriff or any constable within the State of Texas. It shall command him to attach and hold, unless replevied, subject to the further orders of the court having jurisdiction, so much of the property of the defendant, not exempt by statute, of reasonable value in approximately the amount fixed by the justice of the peace, as shall be found within his county.

History of TRCP 612: Adopted eff. Jan. 1, 1981, by order of June 10, 1980 (599-600 S.W.2d [Tex.Cases] lxxvi): Rule written to conform with due-process requirements. See history note to TRCP 610. Former TRCP 612 repealed eff. Jan. 1, 1981, by order of June 10, 1980 (599-600 S.W.2d [Tex.Cases] lxxvi). Source: New rule.

TRCP 613. SERVICE OF WARRANT ON DEFENDANT

The defendant shall be served in any manner prescribed for service of citation, or as provided in Rule 21a, with a copy of the distress warrant, the application, accompanying affidavits, and orders of the justice of the peace as soon as practicable following the levy of the warrant. There shall be prominently displayed on the face of the copy of the warrant served on the defendant, in 10-point type and in a manner calculated to advise a reasonably attentive person of its contents, the following:

To _____, Defendant:

You are hereby notified that certain properties alleged to be owned by you have been seized. If you claim any rights in such property, you are advised:

"YOU HAVE A RIGHT TO REGAIN POSSESSION OF THE PROPERTY BY FILING A REPLEVY BOND. YOU HAVE A RIGHT TO SEEK TO REGAIN POSSESSION OF THE PROPERTY BY FILING WITH THE COURT A MOTION TO DISSOLVE THIS WARRANT."

History of TRCP 613: Adopted eff. Jan. 1, 1981, by order of June 10, 1980 (599-600 S.W.2d [Tex.Cases] lxxvii): Rule written to conform with due-process requirements. See history note to TRCP 610. Former TRCP 613 repealed eff. Jan. 1, 1981, by order of June 10, 1980 (599-600 S.W.2d [Tex.Cases] lxxvii). Source: New rule.

TRCP 614. DEFENDANT MAY REPLEVY

At any time before judgment, should the seized property not have been previously claimed or sold, the defendant may replevy the same, or any part thereof, or the proceeds from the sale of the property if it has been sold under order of the court, by giving bond with sufficient surety or sureties as provided by statute, to be approved by a court having jurisdiction of the amount in controversy payable to plaintiff in double the amount of the plaintiff's debt, or, at the defendant's option for not less than the value of the property sought to be replevied, plus one year's interest thereon at the legal rate from the date of the bond, conditioned that the defendant shall satisfy to the extent of the penal amount of the bond any judgment which may be rendered against him in such action.

On reasonable notice to the opposing party (which may be less than three days) either party shall have the right to prompt judicial review of the amount of bond required, denial of bond, sufficiency of sureties, and estimated value of the property, by a court having jurisdiction of the amount in controversy. The court's determination may be made upon the basis of affidavits if uncontroverted setting forth such facts as would be admissible in evidence, otherwise the parties shall submit evidence. The court shall forthwith enter its order either approving or modifying the requirements of the

---

★

---

order of the justice of the peace, and such order of the court shall supersede and control with respect to such matters.

On reasonable notice to the opposing party (which may be less than three days) the defendant shall have the right to move the court for a substitution of property, of equal value as that attached, for the property seized. Provided that there has been located sufficient property of the defendant's to satisfy the order of seizure, the court may authorize substitution of one or more items of defendant's property for all or part of the property seized. The court shall first make findings as to the value of the property to be substituted. If property is substituted, the property released from seizure shall be delivered to defendant, if such property is personal property, and all liens upon such property from the original order of seizure or modification thereof shall be terminated. Seizure of substituted property shall be deemed to have existed from the date of levy on the original property seized, and no property on which liens have become affixed since the date of levy on the original property may be substituted.

History of TRCP 614: Adopted eff. Jan. 1, 1981, by order of June 10, 1980 (599-600 S.W.2d [Tex.Cases] lxxvii): Rule written to conform with due-process requirements. See history note to TRCP 610. Former TRCP 614 repealed eff. Jan. 1, 1981, by order of June 10, 1980 (599-600 S.W.2d [Tex.Cases] lxxvii). Source: New rule.

TRCP 614a. DISSOLUTION OR MODIFICATION OF DISTRESS WARRANT

A defendant whose property has been seized or any intervening claimant who claims an interest in such property, may by sworn written motion, seek to vacate, dissolve, or modify the seizure, and the order directing its issuance, for any grounds or cause, extrinsic or intrinsic. Such motion shall admit or deny each finding of the order directing the issuance of the warrant except where the movant is unable to admit or deny the finding, in which case movant shall set forth the reasons why he cannot admit or deny. Unless the parties agree to an extension of time, the motion shall be heard promptly, after reasonable notice to the plaintiff (which may be less than three days), and the issue shall be determined not later than 10 days after the motion is filed. The filing of the motion shall stay any further proceedings under the warrant, except for any orders concerning the care, preservation, or sale of any perishable property, until a hearing is had, and the issue is determined. The warrant shall be dissolved unless, at such hearing, the plaintiff shall prove the specific facts al-

leged and the grounds relied upon for its issuance, but the court may modify the order of the justice of the peace granting the warrant and the warrant issued pursuant thereto. The movant shall however have the burden to prove that the reasonable value of the property seized exceeds the amount necessary to secure the debt, interest for one year, and probable costs. He shall also have the burden to prove the facts to justify substitution of property.

The court's determination may be made upon the basis of affidavits setting forth such facts as would be admissible in evidence, but additional evidence, if tendered by either party shall be received and considered. The court may make all such orders, including orders concerning the care, preservation, or disposition of the property (or the proceeds therefrom if the same has been sold), as justice may require. If the movant has given a replevy bond, an order to vacate or dissolve the warrant shall vacate the replevy bond and discharge the sureties thereon, and if the court modifies the order of the justice of the peace or the warrant issued pursuant thereto, it shall make such further orders with respect to the bond as may be consistent with its modification.

History of TRCP 614a: Adopted eff. Jan. 1, 1981, by order of June 10, 1980 (599-600 S.W.2d [Tex.Cases] lxxviii). Rule written to conform with due-process requirements. See history note to TRCP 610. Source: New rule.

TRCP 615. SALE OF PERISHABLE PROPERTY

Whenever personal property which has been levied on under a distress warrant shall not have been claimed or replevied, the judge, or justice of the peace, to whose court such writ is made returnable may, either in term time or in vacation, order the same to be sold, when it shall be made to appear that such property is in danger of serious and immediate waste or decay, or that the keeping of the same until the trial will necessarily be attended with such expense or deterioration in value as greatly to lessen the amount likely to be realized therefrom.

History of TRCP 615: Adopted eff. Sept. 1, 1941, by order of Oct. 29, 1940 (3 Tex.B.J. 619 [1940]). Source: TRCS art. 5233 (repealed).

TRCP 616. TO PROTECT INTERESTS

In determining whether the property levied upon is perishable, and the necessity or advantage of ordering a sale thereof, the judge or justice of the peace may act upon affidavits in writing or oral testimony, and may by a preliminary order entered of record with or without notice to the parties as the urgency of the case in his opinion requires, direct the sheriff or constable to sell

───────────── ✦ ─────────────

such property at public auction for cash, and thereupon the sheriff or constable shall sell it accordingly. If the application for an order of sale be filed by any person or party other than the defendant from whose possession the property was taken by levy, the court shall not grant such order, unless the applicant shall file with such court a bond payable to such defendant, with two or more good and sufficient sureties, to be approved by said court, conditioned that they will be responsible to the defendant for such damages as he may sustain in case such sale be illegally and unjustly applied for, or be illegally and unjustly made.

History of TRCP 616: Adopted eff. Sept. 1, 1941, by order of Oct. 29, 1940 (3 Tex.B.J. 619 [1940]). Source: TRCS arts. 294, 5233 (repealed).

TRCP 617. PROCEDURE FOR SALE

Such sale of perishable personal property shall be conducted in the same manner as sales of personal property under execution; provided, however, that the time of the sale, and the time of advertisement thereof, may be fixed by the judge or justice of the peace at a time earlier than ten days, according to the exigency of the case, and in such event notice thereof shall be given in such manner as directed by the order.

History of TRCP 617: Adopted eff. Sept. 1, 1941, by order of Oct. 29, 1940 (3 Tex.B.J. 619 [1940]). Source: TRCS art. 295 (repealed).

TRCP 618. RETURN OF SALE

The officer making such sale of perishable property shall promptly pay the proceeds of such sale to the clerk of such court or to the justice of the peace, as the case may be, and shall make written return of the order of sale, signed by him officially, stating the time and place of the sale, the name of the purchaser, and the amount of money received, with an itemized account of the expenses attending the sale. Such return shall be filed with the papers of the case.

History of TRCP 618: Adopted eff. Sept. 1, 1941, by order of Oct. 29, 1940 (3 Tex.B.J. 619 [1940]). Source: TRCS art. 296 (repealed).

TRCP 619. CITATION FOR DEFENDANT

The justice at the time he issues the warrant shall issue a citation to the defendant requiring him to answer before such justice at the first day of the next succeeding term of court, stating the time and place of holding the same, if he has jurisdiction to finally try the cause, and upon its being returned served, to proceed to judgment as in ordinary cases; and, if he has not such jurisdiction, the citation shall require the defendant to answer before the court to which the warrant was made returnable at or before ten o'clock a.m. of the Monday next after the expiration of twenty days from the date of service thereof, stating the place of holding the court, and shall be returned with the other papers to such court. If the defendant has removed from the county without service, the proper officer shall state this fact in his return on the citation; and the court shall proceed to try the case ex parte, and may enter judgment.

History of TRCP 619: Adopted eff. Sept. 1, 1941, by order of Oct. 29, 1940 (3 Tex.B.J. 619 [1940]). Source: TRCS art. 5234 (repealed).

TRCP 620. PETITION

When the warrant is made returnable to the district or county court, the plaintiff shall file his petition within ten days from the date of the issuance of the writ.

History of TRCP 620: Adopted eff. Sept. 1, 1941, by order of Oct. 29, 1940 (3 Tex.B.J. 619 [1940]). Source: TRCS art. 5235 (repealed).

SECTION 3. EXECUTIONS

TRCP 621. ENFORCEMENT OF JUDGMENT

The judgments of the district, county, and justice courts shall be enforced by execution or other appropriate process. Such execution or other process shall be returnable in thirty, sixty, or ninety days as requested by the plaintiff, his agent or attorney.

History of TRCP 621: Adopted eff. Sept. 1, 1941, by order of Oct. 29, 1940 (3 Tex.B.J. 619 [1940]). Source: TRCS arts. 2445, 3784 (repealed).

TRCP 621a. DISCOVERY & ENFORCEMENT OF JUDGMENT

At any time after rendition of judgment, and so long as said judgment has not been suspended by a supersedeas bond or by order of a proper court and has not become dormant as provided by Article 3773, V.A.T.S., the successful party may, for the purpose of obtaining information to aid in the enforcement of such judgment, initiate and maintain in the trial court in the same suit in which said judgment was rendered any discovery proceeding authorized by these rules for pretrial matters. Also, at any time after rendition of judgment, either party may, for the purpose of obtaining information relevant to motions allowed by Texas Rules of Appellate Procedure 47[1] and 49[1] initiate and maintain in the trial court in the same suit in which said judgment was rendered any discovery proceeding authorized by these rules for pre-trial matters. The rules governing and related to such pre-trial discovery proceedings shall apply in like manner to discovery proceedings after judgment. The rights herein granted to

⋆

the parties shall inure to their successors or assignees, in whole or in part. Judicial supervision of such discovery proceedings after judgment shall be the same as that provided by law or these rules for pre-trial discovery and proceedings insofar as applicable.

1. **Editor's note:** Now TRAP 24.

History of TRCP 621a: Amended eff. Jan. 1, 1988, by order of July 15, 1987 (733-34 S.W.2d [Tex.Cases] lxxviii). Adopted eff. Jan. 1, 1971, by order of July 21, 1970 (455-56 S.W.2d [Tex.Cases] xliv). Source: New rule.

ANNOTATIONS

In re Smith, 192 S.W.3d 564, 569 (Tex.2006). Judgment debtors "refused to answer much of the written post-judgment enforcement discovery.... Further, the parties had been engaged in post-judgment enforcement discovery for several months, and it was not until the eve of [one of their] deposition[s] that [judgment debtors] filed their cash deposits in lieu of bond and affidavits of net worth to supersede enforcement of the judgment. The trial court's conclusion that [judgment debtors] were attempting to avoid answering post-judgment enforcement discovery by filing the cash deposits in lieu of bond and affidavits of net worth was reasonable. [T]he trial court did not abuse its discretion by ordering [them] to respond to the discovery requests." *See also* ***Arndt v. Farris***, 633 S.W.2d 497, 499 (Tex. 1982).

In re Elmer, 158 S.W.3d 603, 605 (Tex.App.—San Antonio 2005, orig. proceeding). TRCP 621a "contemplates that the judgment to be enforced has at least two characteristics. First, the judgment must be of the type that it can be enforced. In order to enforce a judgment, the judgment must be final. [¶] Secondly, ... the judgment at issue must be susceptible to being 'suspended by a supersedeas bond.' In order to suspend a judgment by a supersedeas bond, the judgment must also be final and appealable. [¶] [T]he trial court abused its discretion in compelling answers to interrogatories in aid of judgment in the absence of a final, appealable judgment."

Fisher v. P.M. Clinton Int'l Investigations, 81 S.W.3d 484, 486 (Tex.App.—Houston [1st Dist.] 2002, no pet.). "Because a post-judgment discovery order does not resolve all the disputes between the parties, a rule 621a order is not a final and appealable order."

TRCP 622. EXECUTION

An execution is a process of the court from which it is issued. The clerk of the district or county court or the justice of the peace, as the case may be, shall tax the costs in every case in which a final judgment has been rendered and shall issue execution to enforce such judgment and collect such costs. The execution and subsequent executions shall not be addressed to a particular county, but shall be addressed to any sheriff or any constable within the State of Texas.

History of TRCP 622: Amended eff. Dec. 31, 1941, by order of Sept. 20, 1941 (4 Tex.B.J. 580 [1941]). Adopted eff. Sept. 1, 1941, by order of Oct. 29, 1940 (3 Tex.B.J. 620 [1940]). Source: TRCS arts. 2446, 2447, 3770, 3780-3782 (repealed).

ANNOTATIONS

In re Burlington Coat Factory Whs., 167 S.W.3d 827, 831 (Tex.2005). "[A]n interlocutory judgment may not be enforced through execution."

TRCP 623. ON DEATH OF EXECUTOR

When an executor, administrator, guardian or trustee of an express trust dies, or ceases to be such executor, administrator, guardian or trustee after judgment, execution shall issue on such judgment in the name of his successor, upon an affidavit of such death or termination being filed with the clerk of the court or the justice of the peace, as the case may be, together with the certificate of the appointment of such successor under the hand and seal of the clerk of the court wherein the appointment was made.

History of TRCP 623: Adopted eff. Sept. 1, 1941, by order of Oct. 29, 1940 (3 Tex.B.J. 620 [1940]). Source: TRCS art. 3776 (repealed).

TRCP 624. ON DEATH OF NOMINAL PLAINTIFF

When a person in whose favor a judgment is rendered for the use of another dies after judgment, execution shall issue in the name of the party for whose use the suit was brought upon an affidavit of such death being filed with the clerk of the court or the justice of the peace.

History of TRCP 624: Adopted eff. Sept. 1, 1941, by order of Oct. 29, 1940 (3 Tex.B.J. 620 [1940]). Source: TRCS art. 3777 (repealed).

TRCP 625. ON MONEY OF DECEASED

If a sole defendant dies after judgment for money against him, execution shall not issue thereon, but the judgment may be proved up and paid in due course of administration.

History of TRCP 625: Adopted eff. Sept. 1, 1941, by order of Oct. 29, 1940 (3 Tex.B.J. 620 [1940]). Source: TRCS art. 3778 (repealed).

TRCP 626. ON PROPERTY OF DECEASED

In any case of judgment other than a money judgment, where the sole defendant, or one or more of several joint defendants, shall die after judgment, upon an affidavit of such death being filed with the clerk, together with the certificate of the appointment of a representative of such decedent under the hand and seal of the clerk of the court wherein such appointment was made, the proper process on such judgment shall issue against such representative.

History of TRCP 626: Adopted eff. Sept. 1, 1941, by order of Oct. 29, 1940 (3 Tex.B.J. 620 [1940]). Source: TRCS art. 3779 (repealed).

TRCP 627. TIME FOR ISSUANCE

If no supersedeas bond or notice of appeal, as required of agencies exempt from filing bonds, has been filed and approved, the clerk of the court or justice of the peace shall issue the execution upon such judgment upon application of the successful party or his attorney after the expiration of thirty days from the time a final judgment is signed. If a timely motion for new trial or in arrest of judgment is filed, the clerk shall issue the execution upon the judgment on application of the party or his attorney after the expiration of thirty days from the time the order overruling the motion is signed or from the time the motion is overruled by operation of law.

History of TRCP 627: Amended eff. Apr. 1, 1984, by order of Dec. 5, 1983 (661-62 S.W.2d [Tex.Cases] cxv): Added words "from the time the motion" after "or" in second sentence. Amended eff. Jan. 1, 1981, by order of June 10, 1980 (599-600 S.W.2d [Tex.Cases] lxxix): Time will run from the time the judgment or order is signed or overruled by operation of law. Amended eff. Jan. 1, 1976, by order of July 22, 1975 (525-26 S.W.2d [Tex.Cases] lix): Changed "twenty" to "thirty." Adopted eff. Sept. 1, 1941, by order of Oct. 29, 1940 (3 Tex.B.J. 620 [1940]). Source: TRCS arts. 2448, 3771 (repealed).

See CPRC §§65.013, 65.014.

ANNOTATIONS

Akin, Gump, Strauss, Hauer & Feld, L.L.P. v. National Dev. & Research Corp., 299 S.W.3d 106, 113 (Tex.2009). "Depending on the particular case's circumstances ... the 30-day period [under TRCP 627] may be shortened or extended. Further, unless the judgment debtor properly supersedes the judgment, the judgment creditor is not precluded from immediately filing an abstract of judgment to aid in seeking satisfaction of its judgment."

Hood v. Amarillo Nat'l Bank, 815 S.W.2d 545, 548 (Tex.1991). "[A] writ of execution will not issue until after a final and appealable judgment is signed."

Mackey v. Great Lakes Invs., 255 S.W.3d 243, 254 (Tex.App.—San Antonio 2008, pet. denied). Under "'Rule 627, executions of final judgments from district courts may not issue until after 30 days have elapsed since the rendition of the final judgment or after the overruling of any motions for a new trial.' However, a prematurely issued execution of judgment is not void, only voidable." *See also Winkle v. Winkle*, 951 S.W.2d 80, 89 (Tex.App.—Corpus Christi 1997, pet. denied).

TRCP 628. EXECUTION WITHIN THIRTY DAYS

Such execution may be issued at any time before the thirtieth day upon the filing of an affidavit by the plaintiff in the judgment or his agent or attorney that the defendant is about to remove his personal property subject to execution by law out of the county, or is about to transfer or secrete such personal property for the purpose of defrauding his creditors.

History of TRCP 628: Amended eff. Jan. 1, 1976, by order of July 22, 1975 (525-26 S.W.2d [Tex.Cases] lix): Changed word "twentieth" to "thirtieth." Adopted eff. Sept. 1, 1941, by order of Oct. 29, 1940 (3 Tex.B.J. 620 [1940]). Source: TRCS arts. 2449, 3774 (repealed).

See CPRC §§65.013, 65.014.

ANNOTATIONS

Perfection Casting Corp. v. Aluminum Alloys, Inc., 733 S.W.2d 385, 386 (Tex.App.—San Antonio 1987, no writ). Held: It was proper for the trial court to allow immediate execution on a judgment, even though the affidavit did not allege sufficient facts to warrant immediate execution, when, after the affidavit was filed and execution was granted, the party received a hearing on the sufficiency of the affidavit.

TRCP 629. REQUISITES OF EXECUTION

The style of the execution shall be "The State of Texas." It shall be directed to any sheriff or any constable within the State of Texas. It shall be signed by the clerk or justice officially, and bear the seal of the court, if issued out of the district or county court, and shall require the officer to execute it according to its terms, and to make the costs which have been adjudged against the defendant in execution and the further costs of executing the writ. It shall describe the judgment, stating the court in which, and the time when, rendered, and the names of the parties in whose favor and against whom the judgment was rendered. A correct copy of the bill of costs taxed against the defendant in execution shall be attached to the writ. It shall require the officer to return it within thirty, sixty, or ninety days, as directed by the plaintiff or his attorney.

History of TRCP 629: Amended eff. Dec. 20, 1941, by order of Sept. 20, 1941 (4 Tex.B.J. 580 [1941]). Adopted eff. Sept. 1, 1941, by order of Oct. 29, 1940 (3 Tex.B.J. 621 [1940]). Source: TRCS arts. 2446, 3783, 3784 (repealed).

See CPRC §§65.013, 65.014.

★

TRCP 630. EXECUTION ON JUDGMENT FOR MONEY

When an execution is issued upon a judgment for a sum of money, or directing the payment simply of a sum of money, it must specify in the body thereof the sum recovered or directed to be paid and the sum actually due when it is issued and the rate of interest upon the sum due. It must require the officer to satisfy the judgment and costs out of the property of the judgment debtor subject to execution by law.

History of TRCP 630: Adopted eff. Sept. 1, 1941, by order of Oct. 29, 1940 (3 Tex.B.J. 621 [1940]). Source: TRCS art. 3783(2) (repealed).

See CPRC §§65.013, 65.014.

TRCP 631. EXECUTION FOR SALE OF PARTICULAR PROPERTY

An execution issued upon a judgment for the sale of particular chattels or personal property or real estate, must particularly describe the property, and shall direct the officer to make the sale by previously giving the public notice of the time and place of sale required by law and these rules.

History of TRCP 631: Adopted eff. Sept. 1, 1941, by order of Oct. 29, 1940 (3 Tex.B.J. 621 [1940]). Source: TRCS art. 3783(3) (repealed).

See CPRC §§65.013, 65.014.

TRCP 632. EXECUTION FOR DELIVERY OF CERTAIN PROPERTY

An execution issued upon a judgment for the delivery of the possession of a chattel or personal property, or for the delivery of the possession of real property, shall particularly describe the property, and designate the party to whom the judgment awards the possession. The writ shall require the officer to deliver the possession of the property to the party entitled thereto.

History of TRCP 632: Adopted eff. Sept. 1, 1941, by order of Oct. 29, 1940 (3 Tex.B.J. 621 [1940]). Source: TRCS art. 3783(4) (repealed).

See CPRC §§65.013, 65.014.

TRCP 633. EXECUTION FOR POSSESSION OR VALUE OF PERSONAL PROPERTY

If the judgment be for the recovery of personal property or its value, the writ shall command the officer, in case a delivery thereof cannot be had, to levy and collect the value thereof for which the judgment was recovered, to be specified therein, out of any property of the party against whom judgment was rendered, liable to execution.

History of TRCP 633: Adopted eff. Sept. 1, 1941, by order of Oct. 29, 1940 (3 Tex.B.J. 621 [1940]). Source: TRCS art. 3783(5) (repealed).

See CPRC §§65.013, 65.014.

TRCP 634. EXECUTION SUPERSEDED

The clerk or justice of the peace shall immediately issue a writ of supersedeas suspending all further proceedings under any execution previously issued when a supersedeas bond is afterward filed and approved within the time prescribed by law or these rules.

History of TRCP 634: Adopted eff. Sept. 1, 1941, by order of Oct. 29, 1940 (3 Tex.B.J. 621 [1940]). Source: TRCS art. 3772 (repealed).

See CPRC §§65.013, 65.014.

TRCP 635. STAY OF EXECUTION IN JUSTICE COURT

At any time within ten days after the rendition of any judgment in a justice court, the justice may grant a stay of execution thereof for three months from the date of such judgment, if the person against whom such judgment was rendered shall, with one or more good and sufficient sureties, to be approved by the justice, appear before him and acknowledge themselves and each of them bound to the successful party in such judgment for the full amount thereof, with interest and costs, which acknowledgment shall be entered in writing on the docket, and signed by the persons binding themselves as sureties; provided, no such stay of execution shall be granted unless the party applying therefor shall first file an affidavit with the justice that he has not the money with which to pay such judgment, and that the enforcement of same by execution prior to three months would be a hardship upon him and would cause a sacrifice of his property which would not likely be caused should said execution be stayed. Such acknowledgment shall be entered by the justice on his docket and shall constitute a judgment against the defendant and such sureties, upon which execution shall issue in case the same is not paid on or before the expiration of such day.

History of TRCP 635: Adopted eff. Sept. 1, 1941, by order of Oct. 29, 1940 (3 Tex.B.J. 621 [1940]). Source: TRCS art. 2453 (repealed).

See CPRC §§65.013, 65.014.

TRCP 636. INDORSEMENTS BY OFFICER

The officer receiving the execution shall indorse thereon the exact hour and day when he received it. If he receives more than one on the same day against the same person he shall number them as received.

History of TRCP 636: Adopted eff. Sept. 1, 1941, by order of Oct. 29, 1940 (3 Tex.B.J. 622 [1940]). Source: TRCS art. 3785, first sentence and first part of second sentence (repealed in part by TRCP).

TRCP 637. LEVY OF EXECUTION

When an execution is delivered to an officer he shall proceed without delay to levy the same upon the

---

property of the defendant found within his county not exempt from execution, unless otherwise directed by the plaintiff, his agent or attorney. The officer shall first call upon the defendant, if he can be found, or, if absent, upon his agent within the county, if known, to point out property to be levied upon, and the levy shall first be made upon the property designated by the defendant, or his agent. If in the opinion of the officer the property so designated will not sell for enough to satisfy the execution and costs of sale, he shall require an additional designation by the defendant. If no property be thus designated by the defendant, the officer shall levy the execution upon any property of the defendant subject to execution.

History of TRCP 637: Adopted eff. Sept. 1, 1941, by order of Oct. 29, 1940 (3 Tex.B.J. 622 [1940]). Source: TRCS arts. 3788-3790 (repealed).

ANNOTATIONS

Hickey v. Couchman, 797 S.W.2d 103, 109 (Tex. App.—Corpus Christi 1990, writ denied). "When the deputy learned that bankruptcy had not been filed [as alleged], he had a duty to execute immediately. We hold that where a sheriff is aware of the debtor's non-exempt assets and is able to seize them but does not, he willfully and intentionally violates [CPRC] §34.065."

Collum v. DeLoughter, 535 S.W.2d 390, 393 (Tex. App.—Texarkana 1976, writ ref'd n.r.e.). "[T]he failure of the officer to make any attempt to give [debtor] an opportunity to designate property, as required by [TRCP] 637, was an irregularity. [¶] [That irregularity,] together with an inadequate price paid for the property, and the trial court's presumed finding that these irregularities were calculated to ... contribute to such inadequacy of price, [is] sufficient to avoid the sale."

TRCP 638. PROPERTY NOT TO BE DESIGNATED

A defendant in execution shall not point out property which he has sold, mortgaged or conveyed in trust, or property exempt from forced sale.

History of TRCP 638: Adopted eff. Sept. 1, 1941, by order of Oct. 29, 1940 (3 Tex.B.J. 622 [1940]). Source: TRCS art. 3791 (repealed).

TRCP 639. LEVY

In order to make a levy on real estate, it shall not be necessary for the officer to go upon the ground but it shall be sufficient for him to indorse such levy on the writ. Levy upon personal property is made by taking possession thereof, when the defendant in execution is entitled to the possession. Where the defendant in execution has an interest in personal property, but is not entitled to the possession thereof, a levy is made thereon by giving notice thereof to the person who is entitled to the possession, or one of them where there are several.

History of TRCP 639: Adopted eff. Sept. 1, 1941, by order of Oct. 29, 1940 (3 Tex.B.J. 622 [1940]). Source: TRCS art. 3793 (repealed).

ANNOTATIONS

Beaurline v. Sinclair Ref. Co., 191 S.W.2d 774, 777 (Tex.App.—San Antonio 1945, writ ref'd n.r.e.). "[W]here a levy is made on property ... which is so cumbersome that it may not be moved except at large expense and effort, it is sufficient if the officer goes upon the premises, points out the property, asserts dominion over it and forbids its removal by the person against whom the writ has been issued. The officer in making a levy on such property must do some act which would constitute a trespass except for the immunity furnished him by the writ."

TRCP 640. LEVY ON STOCK RUNNING AT LARGE

A levy upon livestock running at large in a range, and which cannot be herded and penned without great inconvenience and expense, may be made by designating by reasonable estimate the number of animals and describing them by their marks and brands, or either; such levy shall be made in the presence of two or more credible persons, and notice thereof shall be given in writing to the owner or his herder or agent, if residing within the county and known to the officer.

History of TRCP 640: Adopted eff. Sept. 1, 1941, by order of Oct. 29, 1940 (3 Tex.B.J. 622 [1940]). Source: TRCS art. 3794 (repealed).

TRCP 641. LEVY ON SHARES OF STOCK

A levy upon shares of stock of any corporation or joint stock company for which a certificate is outstanding is made by the officer seizing and taking possession of such certificate. Provided, however, that nothing herein shall be construed as restricting any rights granted under Section 8.317[1] of the Texas Uniform Commercial Code.

1. **Editor's note:** Deleted by Acts 1995, 74th Leg., ch. 962, §1, eff. Sept. 1, 1995. See B&CC §8.112.

History of TRCP 641: Amended eff. Jan. 1, 1971, by order of July 21, 1970 (455-56 S.W.2d [Tex.Cases] xlv): Substituted words "Section 8.317 of the Texas Uniform Commercial Code" for references to TRCS arts. 1358-13, 1358-14 (repealed eff. Aug. 28, 1961). Amended eff. Dec. 31, 1947, by order of Aug. 18, 1947 (10 Tex.B.J. 399 [1947]): Materially altered wording and meaning of former rule. Adopted eff. Sept. 1, 1941, by order of Oct. 29, 1940 (3 Tex.B.J. 623 [1940]). Source: TRCS art. 3795 (repealed).

⭐

Benson v. Greenville Nat'l Exch. Bank, 253 S.W.2d 918, 928 (Tex.App.—Texarkana 1952, writ ref'd n.r.e.). "[W]hile the mere delivery of a stock certificate ... would not transfer title, yet the mere delivery of the stock would create a right in the bank as pledgee, by virtue of which it could resort to equity if its security was in any way threatened."

TRCP 642. REPEALED

Repealed eff. Jan. 1, 1976, by order of July 22, 1975 (525-26 S.W.2d [Tex.Cases] lix). Former TRCS art. 6132b, §§25(2)(c) and 28 superseded repealed rule.

TRCP 643. LEVY ON GOODS PLEDGED OR MORTGAGED

Goods and chattels pledged, assigned or mortgaged as security for any debt or contract, may be levied upon and sold on execution against the person making the pledge, assignment or mortgage subject thereto; and the purchaser shall be entitled to the possession when it is held by the pledgee, assignee or mortgagee, on complying with the conditions of the pledge, assignment or mortgage.

History of TRCP 643: Adopted eff. Sept. 1, 1941, by order of Oct. 29, 1940 (3 Tex.B.J. 623 [1940]). Source: TRCS art. 3797 (repealed).

Conseco Fin. Servicing Corp. v. J&J Mobile Homes, Inc., 120 S.W.3d 878, 886 (Tex.App.—Fort Worth 2003, pet. denied). "[P] reasons that under [TRCP] 643 a tax lien is the equivalent of a judicial lien created when an officer levies upon personal property under a writ of execution. [P] argues a tax lien is therefore subordinate to a security interest noted on the certificate of title. We disagree. [P] ignores the fact that tax liens are, by statute, given express priority status over security interests noted on certificates of title."

Grocers Sup. v. Intercity Inv. Props., 795 S.W.2d 225, 227 (Tex.App.—Houston [14th Dist.] 1990, no writ). "[T]he right of ... a prior secured creditor, to take possession of its collateral was superior to the right of ... a mere judgment creditor, and [the prior secured creditor] could regain possession of the collateral from the constable who had levied on the property."

TRCP 644. MAY GIVE DELIVERY BOND

Any personal property taken in execution may be returned to the defendant by the officer upon the delivery by the defendant to him of a bond, payable to the plaintiff, with two or more good and sufficient sureties, to be approved by the officer, conditioned that the property shall be delivered to the officer at the time and place named in the bond, to be sold according to law, or for the payment to the officer of a fair value thereof, which shall be stated in the bond.

History of TRCP 644: Adopted eff. Sept. 1, 1941, by order of Oct. 29, 1940 (3 Tex.B.J. 623 [1940]). Source: TRCS art. 3801 (repealed).

TRCP 645. PROPERTY MAY BE SOLD BY DEFENDANT

Where property has been replevied, as provided in the preceding rule, the defendant may sell or dispose of the same, paying the officer the stipulated value thereof.

History of TRCP 645: Adopted eff. Sept. 1, 1941, by order of Oct. 29, 1940 (3 Tex.B.J. 623 [1940]). Source: TRCS art. 3802 (repealed).

TRCP 646. FORFEITED DELIVERY BOND

In case of the non-delivery of the property according to the terms of the delivery bond, and non-payment of the value thereof, the officer shall forthwith indorse the bond "Forfeited" and return the same to the clerk of the court or the justice of the peace from which the execution issued; whereupon, if the judgment remain unsatisfied in whole or in part, the clerk or justice shall issue execution against the principal debtor and the sureties on the bond for the amount due, not exceeding the stipulated value of the property, upon which execution no delivery bond shall be taken, which instruction shall be indorsed by the clerk or justice on the execution.

History of TRCP 646: Adopted eff. Sept. 1, 1941, by order of Oct. 29, 1940 (3 Tex.B.J. 623 [1940]). Source: TRCS art. 3803 (repealed).

TRCP 646a. SALE OF REAL PROPERTY

Real property taken by virtue of any execution shall be sold at public auction, at the courthouse door of the county, unless the court orders that such sale be at the place where the real property is situated, on the first Tuesday of the month, between the hours of ten o'clock, a.m. and four o'clock, p.m.

History of TRCP 646a: Adopted eff. Jan. 1, 1961, by order of July 26, 1960 (23 Tex.B.J. 684 [1961]): Court may order sale at place where real property is situated. Source: TRCS art. 3804 (repealed).

TRCP 647. NOTICE OF SALE OF REAL ESTATE

The time and place of sale of real estate under execution, order of sale, or venditioni exponas, shall be advertised by the officer by having the notice thereof published in the English language once a week for

✦

three consecutive weeks preceding such sale, in some newspaper published in said county. The first of said publications shall appear not less than twenty days immediately preceding the day of sale. Said notice shall contain a statement of the authority by virtue of which the sale is to be made, the time of levy, and the time and place of sale; it shall also contain a brief description of the property to be sold, and shall give the number of acres, original survey, locality in the county, and the name by which the land is most generally known, but it shall not be necessary for it to contain field notes. Publishers of newspapers shall charge the legal rate of Two (2) Cents per word for the first insertion of such publication and One (1) Cent per word for such subsequent insertions, or such newspapers shall be entitled to charge for such publication at a rate equal to but not in excess of the published word or line rate of that newspaper for such class of advertising. If there be no newspaper published in the county, or none which will publish the notice of sale for the compensation herein fixed, the officer shall then post such notice in writing in three public places in the county, one of which shall be at the courthouse door of such county, for at least twenty days successively next before the day of sale. The officer making the levy shall give the defendant, or his attorney, written notice of such sale, either in person or by mail, which notice shall substantially conform to the foregoing requirements.

History of TRCP 647: Amended eff. Dec. 31, 1941, by order of Sept. 20, 1941 (4 Tex.B.J. 583 [1941]). Adopted eff. Sept. 1, 1941, by order of Oct. 29, 1940 (3 Tex.B.J. 624 [1940]). Source: TRCS art. 3808 (repealed).

ANNOTATIONS

Ray v. Castilian Vill. Townhouse Ass'n, No. 01-10-00937-CV (Tex.App.—Houston [1st Dist.] 2011, pet. denied) (memo op.; 3-24-11). "Although [TRCP] 647 speaks of regular mail, courts have noted that [TRCP] 21a, which applies to every notice required to be served by the [TRCPs], imposes the requirement of registered mail upon the general provisions for mail in rule 647." (Internal quotes omitted.) *See also Collum v. DeLoughter*, 535 S.W.2d 390, 392 (Tex.App.—Texarkana 1976, writ ref'd n.r.e.).

McCoy v. Rogers, 240 S.W.3d 267, 275 (Tex.App.—Houston [1st Dist.] 2007, pet. denied). "Compliance with the notice requirements for execution … is a prerequisite to the right of the trustee or sheriff to make the sale."

TRCP 648. "COURTHOUSE DOOR" DEFINED

By the term "courthouse door" of a county is meant either of the principal entrances to the house provided by the proper authority for the holding of the district court. If from any cause there is no such house, the door of the house where the district court was last held in that county shall be deemed to be the courthouse door. Where the courthouse, or house used by the court, has been destroyed by fire or other cause, and another has not been designated by the proper authority, the place where such house stood shall be deemed to be the courthouse door.

History of TRCP 648: Adopted eff. Sept. 1, 1941, by order of Oct. 29, 1940 (3 Tex.B.J. 624 [1940]). Source: TRCS art. 3809 (repealed).

ANNOTATIONS

Micrea, Inc. v. Eureka Life Ins., 534 S.W.2d 348, 358 (Tex.App.—Fort Worth 1976, writ ref'd n.r.e.). "In general the 'Courthouse Door' is either of the (several) entrances to the building provided for the holding of the district court."

TRCP 649. SALE OF PERSONAL PROPERTY

Personal property levied on under execution shall be offered for sale on the premises where it is taken in execution, or at the courthouse door of the county, or at some other place if, owing to the nature of the property, it is more convenient to exhibit it to purchasers at such place. Personal property susceptible of being exhibited shall not be sold unless the same be present and subject to the view of those attending the sale, except shares of stock in joint stock or incorporated companies, and in cases where the defendant in execution has merely an interest without right to the exclusive possession in which case the interest of defendant may be sold and conveyed without the presence or delivery of the property. When a levy is made upon livestock running at large on the range, it is not necessary that such stock, or any part thereof, be present at the place of sale, and the purchaser at such sale is authorized to gather and pen such stock and select therefrom the number purchased by him.

History of TRCP 649: Adopted eff. Sept. 1, 1941, by order of Oct. 29, 1940 (3 Tex.B.J. 624 [1940]). Source: TRCS arts. 3811, 3813, 3814 (repealed).

TRCP 650. NOTICE OF SALE OF PERSONAL PROPERTY

Previous notice of the time and place of the sale of any personal property levied on under execution shall be given by posting notice thereof for ten days successively immediately prior to the day of sale at the court-house door of any county and at the place where the sale is to be made.

History of TRCP 650: Adopted eff. Sept. 1, 1941, by order of Oct. 29, 1940 (3 Tex.B.J. 624 [1940]). Source: TRCS art. 3812 (repealed).

TRCP 651. WHEN EXECUTION NOT SATISFIED

When the property levied upon does not sell for enough to satisfy the execution, the officer shall proceed anew, as in the first instance, to make the residue.

History of TRCP 651: Adopted eff. Sept. 1, 1941, by order of Oct. 29, 1940 (3 Tex.B.J. 624 [1940]). Source: TRCS art. 3815 (repealed).

TRCP 652. PURCHASER FAILING TO COMPLY

If any person shall bid off property at any sale made by virtue of an execution, and shall fail to comply with the terms of the sale, he shall be liable to pay the plaintiff in execution twenty per cent on the value of the property thus bid off, besides costs, to be recovered on motion, five days notice of such motion being given to such purchaser; and should the property on a second sale bring less than on the former, he shall be liable to pay to the defendant in execution all loss which he sustains thereby, to be recovered on motion as above provided.

History of TRCP 652: Adopted eff. Sept. 1, 1941, by order of Oct. 29, 1940 (3 Tex.B.J. 625 [1940]). Source: TRCS art. 3821 (repealed).

ANNOTATIONS

Jackson v. Universal Life Ins., 582 S.W.2d 207, 209 (Tex.App.—Eastland 1979, writ ref'd n.r.e.). "[W]here a bidder fails to comply with the terms of an execution sale, he becomes liable under the express provisions of the rule, whether or not he acted in good faith."

TRCP 653. RESALE OF PROPERTY

When the terms of the sale shall not be complied with by the bidder the levying officer shall proceed to sell the same property again on the same day, if there be sufficient time; but if not, he shall readvertise and sell the same as in the first instance.

History of TRCP 653: Adopted eff. Sept. 1, 1941, by order of Oct. 29, 1940 (3 Tex.B.J. 625 [1940]). Source: TRCS art. 3822 (repealed).

TRCP 654. RETURN OF EXECUTION

The levying officer shall make due return of the execution, in writing and signed by him officially, stating concisely what such officer has done in pursuance of the requirements of the writ and of the law. The return shall be filed with the clerk of the court or the justice of the peace as the case may be. The execution shall be returned forthwith if satisfied by the collection of the money or if ordered by the plaintiff or his attorney indorsed thereon.

History of TRCP 654: Adopted eff. Sept. 1, 1941, by order of Oct. 29, 1940 (3 Tex.B.J. 625 [1940]). Source: TRCS art. 3828 (repealed).

ANNOTATIONS

Scott v. Wilson, 231 S.W.2d 912, 913 (Tex.App.—Amarillo 1950, no writ). "[A] sheriff's return upon an execution or order of sale may be amended."

TRCP 655. RETURN OF EXECUTION BY MAIL

When an execution is placed in the hands of an officer of a county other than the one in which the judgment is rendered, return may be made by mail; but money cannot be thus sent except by direction of the party entitled to receive the same or his attorney of record.

History of TRCP 655: Adopted eff. Sept. 1, 1941, by order of Oct. 29, 1940 (3 Tex.B.J. 625 [1940]). Source: TRCS art. 3823 (repealed).

TRCP 656. EXECUTION DOCKET

The clerk of each court shall keep an execution docket in which he shall enter a statement of all executions as they are issued by him, specifying the names of the parties, the amount of the judgment, the amount due thereon, the rate of interest when it exceeds six per cent, the costs, the date of issuing the execution, to whom delivered, and the return of the officer thereon, with the date of such return. Such docket entries shall be taken and deemed to be a record. The clerk shall keep an index and cross-index to the execution docket. When execution is in favor or against several persons, it shall be indexed in the name of each person. Any clerk who shall fail to keep said execution docket and index thereto, or shall neglect to make the entries therein, shall be liable upon his official bond to any person injured for the amount of damages sustained by such neglect.

History of TRCP 656: Adopted eff. Sept. 1, 1941, by order of Oct. 29, 1940 (3 Tex.B.J. 626 [1940]). Source: TRCS art. 3831 (repealed).

SECTION 4. GARNISHMENT

TRCP 657. JUDGMENT FINAL FOR GARNISHMENT

In the case mentioned in subsection 3, section 63.001, Civil Practice and Remedies Code, the judgment whether based upon a liquidated demand or an unliquidated demand, shall be deemed final and subsisting for the purpose of garnishment from and after the date it is

TRCP 650

✦

---

signed, unless a supersedeas bond shall have been approved and filed in accordance with Texas Rules of Appellate Procedure 47.[1]

1. **Editor's note:** Now TRAP 24.

History of TRCP 657: Amended eff. Jan. 1, 1988, by order of July 15, 1987 (733-34 S.W.2d [Tex.Cases] lxxviii). Amended eff. Jan. 1, 1981, by order of June 10, 1980 (599-600 S.W.2d [Tex.Cases] lxxx): Finality of judgment is counted from the time judgment is signed. Adopted eff. Sept. 1, 1941, by order of Oct. 29, 1940 (3 Tex.B.J. 626 [1940]). Source: New rule.

ANNOTATIONS

Bank One v. Sunbelt Sav., 824 S.W.2d 557, 558 (Tex.1992). "Garnishment is a statutory proceeding whereby the property, money, or credits of a debtor in the possession of another are applied to the payment of the debt."

Westerman v. Comerica Bank-Tex., 928 S.W.2d 679, 682 (Tex.App.—San Antonio 1996, writ denied). "[T]he record contains conclusive summary judgment proof showing that when the garnishment action was actually finalized, the judgment was still a 'valid subsisting judgment'…. The fact that the underlying judgment was reversed 14 months after the garnishment judgment was rendered does not subsequently render the garnishment proceedings wrongful."

TRCP 658. APPLICATION FOR WRIT OF GARNISHMENT & ORDER

Either at the commencement of a suit or at any time during its progress the plaintiff may file an application for a writ of garnishment. Such application shall be supported by affidavits of the plaintiff, his agent, his attorney, or other person having knowledge of relevant facts. The application shall comply with all statutory requirements and shall state the grounds for issuing the writ and the specific facts relied upon by the plaintiff to warrant the required findings by the court. The writ shall not be quashed because two or more grounds are stated conjunctively or disjunctively. The application and any affidavits shall be made on personal knowledge and shall set forth such facts as would be admissible in evidence; provided that facts may be stated based upon information and belief if the grounds of such belief are specifically stated.

No writ shall issue before final judgment except upon written order of the court after a hearing, which may be ex parte. The court in its order granting the application shall make specific findings of facts to support the statutory grounds found to exist, and shall specify the maximum value of property or indebtedness that may be garnished and the amount of bond required of

plaintiff. Such bond shall be in an amount which, in the opinion of the court, shall adequately compensate defendant in the event plaintiff fails to prosecute his suit to effect, and pay all damages and costs as shall be adjudged against him for wrongfully suing out the writ of garnishment. The court shall further find in its order the amount of bond required of defendant to replevy, which, unless defendant exercises his option as provided under Rule 664, shall be the amount of plaintiff's claim, one year's accrual of interest if allowed by law on the claim, and the estimated costs of court. The order may direct the issuance of several writs at the same time, or in succession, to be sent to different counties.

History of TRCP 658: Amended eff. Jan. 1, 1978, by order of July 11, 1977 (553-54 S.W.2d [Tex.Cases] lxiv): Amended to require reliable proof of grounds for issuance before judgment, findings, fixing value of property or indebtedness that may be garnished, fixing amount of bond as well as amount of replevy bond, and for issuance of several writs. Amended eff. Dec. 31, 1947, by order of Aug. 18, 1947 (10 Tex.B.J. 399 [1947]). Adopted eff. Sept. 1, 1941, by order of Oct. 29, 1940 (3 Tex.B.J. 626 [1940]). Source: TRCS art. 4078 (repealed).

ANNOTATIONS

El Periodico, Inc. v. Parks Oil Co., 917 S.W.2d 777, 779 (Tex.1996). Garnishor's "application did not meet the requirements of [TRCP] 658…. [¶] The allegation of [garnishee's] indebtedness to [judgment debtor] is made on belief of counsel, and the grounds of such belief are not specifically stated."

Simulis, L.L.C. v. G.E. Capital Corp., 276 S.W.3d 109, 115 (Tex.App.—Houston [1st Dist.] 2008, no pet.). "Although [TRCP 658's] first paragraph applies to both pre- and post-judgment garnishment proceedings, the … second paragraph applies only to pre-judgment proceedings. … Everything … within [the second] paragraph must be read in [the context of 'before final judgment,'] such as, for example, the requirements to obtain an order granting the application with findings of fact, to have the court determine the maximum value of property or indebtedness that may be garnished, and to set a bond for the plaintiff-creditor. … The reason for the bond is obviously to protect the defendant-debtor if the underlying suit for debt is not prosecuted…."

TRCP 658a. BOND FOR GARNISHMENT

No writ of garnishment shall issue before final judgment until the party applying therefor has filed with the officer authorized to issue such writ a bond payable to the defendant in the amount fixed by the court's order, with sufficient surety or sureties as provided by statute, conditioned that the plaintiff will prosecute his suit to

--- ★ ---

effect and pay to the extent of the penal amount of the bond all damages and costs as may be adjudged against him for wrongfully suing out such writ of garnishment.

After notice to the opposite party, either before or after the issuance of the writ, the defendant or plaintiff may file a motion to increase or reduce the amount of such bond, or to question the sufficiency of the sureties. Upon hearing, the court shall enter its order with respect to such bond and the sufficiency of the sureties.

Should it be determined from the garnishee's answer if such is not controverted that the garnishee is indebted to the defendant, or has in his hands effects belonging to the defendant, in an amount or value less than the amount of the debt claimed by the plaintiff, then after notice to the defendant the court in which such garnishment is pending upon hearing may reduce the required amount of such bond to double the sum of the garnishee's indebtedness to the defendant plus the value of the effects in his hands belonging to the defendant.

History of TRCP 658a: Amended eff. Jan. 1, 1978, by order of July 11, 1977 (553-54 S.W.2d [Tex.Cases] lxv): Rewrote par. 1; amount of bond is to be fixed by court order, amount will no longer be double the amount of debt claimed; either party after notice and hearing may increase or reduce the amount of the bond. Adopted eff. Jan. 1, 1961, by order of July 26, 1960 (23 Tex.B.J. 684 [1961]). Source: TRCS art. 4077 (repealed).

TRCP 659. CASE DOCKETED

When the foregoing requirements of these rules have been complied with, the judge, or clerk, or justice of the peace, as the case may be, shall docket the case in the name of the plaintiff as plaintiff and of the garnishee as defendant; and shall immediately issue a writ of garnishment directed to the garnishee, commanding him to appear before the court out of which the same is issued at or before 10 o'clock a.m. of the Monday next following the expiration of twenty days from the date the writ was served, if the writ is issued out of the district or county court; or the Monday next after the expiration of ten days from the date the writ was served, if the writ is issued out of the justice court. The writ shall command the garnishee to answer under oath upon such return date what, if anything, he is indebted to the defendant, and was when the writ was served, and what effects, if any, of the defendant he has in his possession, and had when such writ was served, and what other persons, if any, within his knowledge, are indebted to the defendant or have effects belonging to him in their possession.

History of TRCP 659: Amended eff. Jan. 1, 1978, by order of July 11, 1977 (553-54 S.W.2d [Tex.Cases] lxvi): Deleted provision for compliance with TRCS art. 4077, which was repealed. Amended eff. Dec. 31, 1947, by order of Aug. 18, 1947 (10 Tex.B.J. 399 [1947]). Amended eff. Dec. 31, 1941, by order of Sept. 20, 1941 (4 Tex.B.J. 586 [1941]). Adopted eff. Sept. 1, 1941, by order of Oct. 29, 1940 (3 Tex.B.J. 626 [1940]). Source: TRCS art. 4079 (repealed).

ANNOTATIONS

Cloughly v. NBC Bank-Seguin, 773 S.W.2d 652, 658 (Tex.App.—San Antonio 1989, writ denied). "Although the statute contemplates a separate docketing, we do not find harm in proceeding with a garnishment action in the same cause number. Although this was an irregularity in procedure, the validity of the judgment was not affected."

TRCP 660. REPEALED

Repealed eff. Dec. 31, 1947, by order of Aug. 18, 1947 (10 Tex.B.J. 400 [1947]).

TRCP 661. FORM OF WRIT

The following form of writ may be used:

"The State of Texas.

To E.F., Garnishee, greeting:

"Whereas, in the _____ Court of _____ County (if a justice court, state also the number of the precinct), in a certain cause wherein A.B. is plaintiff and C.D. is defendant, the plaintiff, claiming an indebtedness against the said C.D. of _____ dollars, besides interest and costs of suit, has applied for a writ of garnishment against you, E.F.; therefore you are hereby commanded to be and appear before said court at _____ in said county (if the writ is issued from the county or district court, here proceed: 'at 10 o'clock a.m. on the Monday next following the expiration of twenty days from the date of service hereof.' If the writ is issued from a justice of the peace court, here proceed: 'at or before 10 o'clock a.m. on the Monday next after the expiration of ten days from the date of service hereof.' In either event, proceed as follows:) then and there to answer upon oath what, if anything, you are indebted to the said C.D., and were when this writ was served upon you, and what effects, if any, of the said C.D. you have in your possession, and had when this writ was served, and what other persons, if any, within your knowledge, are indebted to the said C.D. or have effects belonging to him in their possession. You are further commanded NOT to pay to defendant any debt or to deliver to him any effects, pending further order of this court. Herein fail not, but make due answer as the law directs."

★

History of TRCP 661: Amended eff. Jan. 1, 1978, by order of July 11, 1977 (553-54 S.W.2d [Tex.Cases] lxvi): Added next-to-last sentence. Amended eff. Dec. 31, 1947, by order of Aug. 18, 1947 (10 Tex.B.J. 400 [1947]). Amended eff. Dec. 31, 1941, by order of Sept. 20, 1941 (4 Tex.B.J. 586 [1941]). Adopted eff. Sept. 1, 1941, by order of Oct. 29, 1940 (3 Tex.B.J. 627 [1940]). Source: TRCS art. 4081 (repealed).

ANNOTATIONS

Bank One v. Sunbelt Sav., 824 S.W.2d 557, 558 (Tex.1992). "When a creditor wants to challenge title to funds held by a third party, the creditor should seek a writ of garnishment naming the nominal owner not the true owner. The court is then responsible for determining true ownership."

TRCP 662. DELIVERY OF WRIT

The writ of garnishment shall be dated and tested as other writs, and may be delivered to the sheriff or constable by the officer who issued it, or he may deliver it to the plaintiff, his agent or attorney, for that purpose.

History of TRCP 662: Adopted eff. Sept. 1, 1941, by order of Oct. 29, 1940 (3 Tex.B.J. 627 [1940]). Source: TRCS art. 4082 (repealed).

ANNOTATIONS

Moody Nat'l Bank v. Riebschlager, 946 S.W.2d 521, 523 n.1 (Tex.App.—Houston [14th Dist.] 1997, writ denied). "Private process servers are prohibited from executing writs of garnishment as only a sheriff or constable may deliver the writs to a garnishee."

TRCP 663. EXECUTION & RETURN OF WRIT

The sheriff or constable receiving the writ of garnishment shall immediately proceed to execute the same by delivering a copy thereof to the garnishee, and shall make return thereof as of other citations.

History of TRCP 663: Adopted eff. Sept. 1, 1941, by order of Oct. 29, 1940 (3 Tex.B.J. 627 [1940]). Source: TRCS art. 4083 (repealed).

TRCP 663a. SERVICE OF WRIT ON DEFENDANT

The defendant shall be served in any manner prescribed for service of citation or as provided in Rule 21a with a copy of the writ of garnishment, the application, accompanying affidavits and orders of the court as soon as practicable following the service of the writ. There shall be prominently displayed on the face of the copy of the writ served on the defendant, in ten-point type and in a manner calculated to advise a reasonably attentive person of its contents, the following:

"To _____, Defendant:

"You are hereby notified that certain properties alleged to be owned by you have been garnished. If you claim any rights in such property, you are advised:

"YOU HAVE A RIGHT TO REGAIN POSSESSION OF THE PROPERTY BY FILING A REPLEVY BOND. YOU HAVE A RIGHT TO SEEK TO REGAIN POSSESSION OF THE PROPERTY BY FILING WITH THE COURT A MOTION TO DISSOLVE THIS WRIT."

History of TRCP 663a: Adopted eff. Jan. 1, 1978, by order of July 11, 1977 (553-54 S.W.2d [Tex.Cases] lxvii): Rule affords defendant notice of the proceedings and informs him of some of his rights. Source: New rule.

ANNOTATIONS

Lease Fin. Grp. v. Childers, 310 S.W.3d 120, 125 (Tex.App.—Fort Worth 2010, no pet.). "Actual knowledge or a voluntary appearance by the debtor is insufficient and does not waive rule 663a's requirement of service of the writ. Although rule 663a does not entitle a debtor to a minimum of 20 days' notice as with service of an original petition, ... the debtor does have the right to service of the writ of garnishment and related documents 'as soon as practicable following the service of the writ' on the garnishee. [¶] [P] contends there is sufficient evidence of service because the judgment recites [D] was served in compliance with rule 663a. ... In an attack upon a default judgment, a recitation of due service in the judgment does not lead to a presumption of due service. Instead, the plaintiff must 'prove that the defendant was served in the required manner.' *At 126:* We believe the rule applicable to default judgments should apply to judgments in garnishment and hold that a recitation of due service in a judgment in garnishment does not lead to a presumption of due service. [¶] [P] next contends rule 663a does not establish a prescribed period in which a garnishor must serve a writ of garnishment on the debtor. We disagree. ... 'As soon as practicable' is not susceptible to a definitive definition equally applicable in all cases, but we note that a 15-day delay before serving the debtor does not satisfy the strict requirements of rule 663a. *At 127:* [Here,] nothing in the record explains the 20-day delay in service. [W]e hold [P] failed to prove that it served [D] through its attorney 'as soon as practicable' as required by rule 663a."

Abdullah v. State, 211 S.W.3d 938, 943 (Tex. App.—Texarkana 2007, no pet.). "Rule 663a is unambiguous in its requirement that the debtor be given notice of the garnishment and of his rights to regain his property, and about the specific information that must be provided so that the writ may be contested. The rule makes no distinction between prejudgment and postjudgment notice to the debtor." *See also Zeecon Wireless Internet, LLC v. American Bank*, 305 S.W.3d 813,

★

817-18 (Tex.App.—Austin 2010, no pet.); *Simulis, L.L.C. v. G.E. Capital Corp.*, 276 S.W.3d 109, 115-16 (Tex.App.—Houston [1st Dist.] 2008, no pet.).

Mendoza v. Luke Fruia Invs., 962 S.W.2d 650, 652 (Tex.App.—Corpus Christi 1998, no pet.). "[R]ule 663a requires *strict compliance*. [W]hen a judgment debtor voluntarily answers and appears in a garnishment proceeding, the debtor waives only irregularities in the writ of garnishment, such as defects in the affidavit or bond. Voluntary appearance does not waive the requirements of the writ itself. [¶] Rights under a writ of garnishment are determined by priority in time, which itself is determined by service of the writ. Without proper service of the writ on the debtor, no control or custody of his property can be gained by his answer."

TRCP 664. DEFENDANT MAY REPLEVY

At any time before judgment, should the garnished property not have been previously claimed or sold, the defendant may replevy the same, or any part thereof, or the proceeds from the sale of the property if it has been sold under order of the court, by giving bond with sufficient surety or sureties as provided by statute, to be approved by the officer who levied the writ, payable to plaintiff, in the amount fixed by the court's order, or, at the defendant's option, for the value of the property or indebtedness sought to be replevied (to be estimated by the officer), plus one year's interest thereon at the legal rate from the date of the bond, conditioned that the defendant, garnishee, shall satisfy, to the extent of the penal amount of the bond, any judgment which may be rendered against him in such action.

On reasonable notice to the opposing party (which may be less than three days) either party shall have the right to prompt judicial review of the amount of bond required, denial of bond, sufficiency of sureties, and estimated value of the property, by the court which authorized issuance of the writ. The court's determination may be made upon the basis of affidavits, if uncontroverted, setting forth such facts as would be admissible in evidence; otherwise, the parties shall submit evidence. The court shall forthwith enter its order either approving or modifying the requirements of the officer or of the court's prior order, and such order of the court shall supersede and control with respect to such matters.

On reasonable notice to the opposing party (which may be less than three days) the defendant shall have

the right to move the court for a substitution of property, of equal value as that garnished, for the property garnished. Provided that there has been located sufficient property of the defendant's to satisfy the order of garnishment, the court may authorize substitution of one or more items of defendant's property for all or for part of the property garnished. The court shall first make findings as to the value of the property to be substituted. If property is substituted, the property released from garnishment shall be delivered to defendant, if such property is personal property, and all liens upon such property from the original order of garnishment or modification thereof shall be terminated. Garnishment of substituted property shall be deemed to have existed from date of garnishment on the original property garnished, and no property on which liens have become affixed since the date of garnishment of the original property may be substituted.

History of TRCP 664: Amended eff. Jan. 1, 1978, by order of July 11, 1977 (553-54 S.W.2d [Tex.Cases] lxvii): Rule rewritten to give defendant right to replevy, including proceeds from sale of property; changes amount of bond from double the amount of plaintiff's debt to amount fixed by the court; clearly fixes the conditions of the replevy bond; gives parties a hearing; authorizes substitution of property. Adopted eff. Sept. 1, 1941, by order of Oct. 29, 1940 (3 Tex.B.J. 627 [1940]). Source: TRCS art. 4084, second and third sentences (repealed in part by TRCP).

ANNOTATIONS

Woodall v. Clark, 802 S.W.2d 415, 418 (Tex.App.—Beaumont 1991, no writ). "[O]nce [D's] Replevy Bond was challenged by [P], a right provided to [P] by [TRCP] 664, the trial court was required to review, among other things, the sufficiency of the sureties."

TRCP 664a. DISSOLUTION OR MODIFICATION OF WRIT OF GARNISHMENT

A defendant whose property or account has been garnished or any intervening party who claims an interest in such property or account, may by sworn written motion, seek to vacate, dissolve or modify the writ of garnishment, and the order directing its issuance, for any grounds or cause, extrinsic or intrinsic. Such motion shall admit or deny each finding of the order directing the issuance of the writ except where the movant is unable to admit or deny the finding, in which case movant shall set forth the reasons why he cannot admit or deny. Unless the parties agree to an extension of time, the motion shall be heard promptly, after reasonable notice to the plaintiff (which may be less than three days), and the issue shall be determined not later than ten days after the motion is filed. The filing of the

★

motion shall stay any further proceedings under the writ, except for any orders concerning the care, preservation or sale of any perishable property, until a hearing is had, and the issue is determined. The writ shall be dissolved unless, at such hearing, the plaintiff shall prove the grounds relied upon for its issuance, but the court may modify its previous order granting the writ and the writ issued pursuant thereto. The movant shall, however, have the burden to prove that the reasonable value of the property garnished exceeds the amount necessary to secure the debt, interest for one year, and probable costs. He shall also have the burden to prove facts to justify substitution of property.

The court's determination may be made upon the basis of affidavits, if uncontroverted, setting forth such facts as would be admissible in evidence; otherwise, the parties shall submit evidence. The court may make all such orders including orders concerning the care, preservation or disposition of the property (or the proceeds therefrom if the same has been sold), as justice may require. If the movant has given a replevy bond, an order to vacate or dissolve the writ shall vacate the replevy bond and discharge the sureties thereon, and if the court modifies its order or the writ issued pursuant thereto, it shall make such further orders with respect to the bond as may be consistent with its modification.

History of TRCP 664a: Adopted eff. Jan. 1, 1978, by order of July 11, 1977 (553-54 S.W.2d [Tex.Cases] lxviii): Rule affords a prompt hearing, provides for the procedures, burden of proof and the kind of proof. Source: New rule.

ANNOTATIONS

Cadle Co. v. Davis, No. 04-09-00763-CV (Tex. App.—San Antonio 2010, pet. denied) (memo op.; 12-29-10). "Rule 664a provides a writ shall be dissolved unless at the hearing on the motion to dissolve the garnishor proves the grounds relied upon for its issuance. 'In the context of a post judgment garnishment proceeding, this means the garnishor must prove (a) it has a valid, subsisting judgment and (b) that within the garnishor's knowledge, the judgment debtor does not possess property in the state subject to execution sufficient to satisfy the judgment.'"

Simulis, L.L.C. v. G.E. Capital Corp., 276 S.W.3d 109, 115-16 (Tex.App.—Houston [1st Dist.] 2008, no pet.). The requirement in TRCP 664a to "'admit or deny each finding of the order directing the issuance of the writ' can apply only in a pre-judgment garnishment proceeding because such an order is required only at that stage."

Swiderski v. Victoria Bank & Trust Co., 706 S.W.2d 676, 678 (Tex.App.—Corpus Christi 1986, writ ref'd n.r.e.). "A Rule 664a hearing is a distinct proceeding from the writ of garnishment proceeding between the garnishor and garnishee. ... The issue to be determined in a Rule 664a hearing is that 'the plaintiff shall prove the grounds relied upon for its (the writ of garnishment's) issuance.' [¶] Therefore, at a Rule 664a hearing, the plaintiff does not have to prove that the garnishee is indebted to the defendant debtor...."

TRCP 665. ANSWER TO WRIT

The answer of the garnishee shall be under oath, in writing and signed by him, and shall make true answers to the several matters inquired of in the writ of garnishment.

History of TRCP 665: Adopted eff. Sept. 1, 1941, by order of Oct. 29, 1940 (3 Tex.B.J. 628 [1940]). Source: TRCS art. 4085 (repealed).

See *Commentaries*, "The Answer—Denying Liability," ch. 3-E, p. 227.

TRCP 666. GARNISHEE DISCHARGED

If it appears from the answer of the garnishee that he is not indebted to the defendant, and was not so indebted when the writ of garnishment was served upon him, and that he has not in his possession any effects of the defendant and had not when the writ was served, and if he has either denied that any other persons within his knowledge are indebted to the defendant or have in their possession effects belonging to the defendant, or else has named such persons, should the answer of the garnishee not be controverted as hereinafter provided, the court shall enter judgment discharging the garnishee.

History of TRCP 666: Amended eff. Dec. 31, 1947, by order of Aug. 18, 1947 (10 Tex.B.J. 400 [1947]). Adopted eff. Sept. 1, 1941, by order of Oct. 29, 1940 (3 Tex.B.J. 628 [1940]). Source: TRCS art. 4086 (repealed).

TRCP 667. JUDGMENT BY DEFAULT

If the garnishee fails to file an answer to the writ of garnishment at or before the time directed in the writ, it shall be lawful for the court, at any time after judgment shall have been rendered against the defendant, and on or after appearance day, to render judgment by default, as in other civil cases, against such garnishee for the full amount of such judgment against the defendant together with all interest and costs that may have accrued in the main case and also in the garnishment proceedings. The answer of the garnishee may be filed as in any other civil case at any time before such default judgment is rendered.

⭐

History of TRCP 667: Adopted eff. Sept. 1, 1941, by order of Oct. 29, 1940 (3 Tex.B.J. 628 [1940]). Source: TRCS art. 4087 (repealed).

See *Commentaries*, "Default Judgment," ch. 7-A, p. 587.

ANNOTATIONS

Invesco Inv. Servs. v. Fidelity Deposit & Disc. Bank, 355 S.W.3d 257, 259-60 (Tex.App.—Houston [1st Dist.] 2011, no pet.). "The assessment of the full amount of damages against the defaulting garnishee is premised on a presumption that the garnishee is indebted to the debtor in an amount sufficient to satisfy the claim of the garnishor."

Falderbaum v. Lowe, 964 S.W.2d 744, 747 (Tex. App.—Austin 1998, no pet.). Garnishee "cannot now claim that the district court lacks subject-matter jurisdiction *to enforce* the garnishment order when she failed to properly challenge the trial court's jurisdiction when the writ of garnishment was originally issued."

TRCP 668. JUDGMENT WHEN GARNISHEE IS INDEBTED

Should it appear from the answer of the garnishee or should it be otherwise made to appear and be found by the court that the garnishee is indebted to the defendant in any amount, or was so indebted when the writ of garnishment was served, the court shall render judgment for the plaintiff against the garnishee for the amount so admitted or found to be due to the defendant from the garnishee, unless such amount is in excess of the amount of the plaintiff's judgment against the defendant with interest and costs, in which case, judgment shall be rendered against the garnishee for the full amount of the judgment already rendered against the defendant, together with interest and costs of the suit in the original case and also in the garnishment proceedings. If the garnishee fail or refuse to pay such judgment rendered against him, execution shall issue thereon in the same manner and under the same conditions as is or may be provided for the issuance of execution in other cases.

History of TRCP 668: Adopted eff. Sept. 1, 1941, by order of Oct. 29, 1940 (3 Tex.B.J. 628 [1940]). Source: TRCS art. 4088 (repealed).

ANNOTATIONS

Wrigley v. First Nat'l Sec. Corp., 104 S.W.3d 259, 264 (Tex.App.—Beaumont 2003, no pet.). "The funds captured by the writ of garnishment are those held by the garnishee in the account of the judgment debtor on the date the writ is served, and any additional funds deposited through the date the garnishee is required to answer. [P's] right to recover those funds from the gar-

nishee is [not necessarily] fixed by whatever judgment [P] possesses on that date. The issuance and service of the writ of garnishment fixes the trial court's jurisdiction to determine whether the garnishee holds funds belonging to the judgment debtor, and necessarily that jurisdiction extends to a determination of title and ownership of the funds, regardless of how that ownership is placed in controversy. The garnishee may deposit the funds into the court, bring in all other claimants through interpleader, and the trial court may then adjudicate the conflicting claims of the parties."

TRCP 669. JUDGMENT FOR EFFECTS

Should it appear from the garnishee's answer, or otherwise, that the garnishee has in his possession, or had when the writ was served, any effects of the defendant liable to execution, including any certificates of stock in any corporation or joint stock company, the court shall render a decree ordering sale of such effects under execution in satisfaction of plaintiff's judgment and directing the garnishee to deliver them, or so much thereof as shall be necessary to satisfy plaintiff's judgment, to the proper officer for that purpose.

History of TRCP 669: Amended eff. Dec. 31, 1947, by order of Aug. 18, 1947 (10 Tex.B.J. 400 [1947]). Adopted eff. Sept. 1, 1941, by order of Oct. 29, 1940 (3 Tex.B.J. 628 [1940]). Source: TRCS art. 4089 (repealed).

TRCP 670. REFUSAL TO DELIVER EFFECTS

Should the garnishee adjudged to have effects of the defendant in his possession, as provided in the preceding rule, fail or refuse to deliver them to the sheriff or constable on such demand, the officer shall immediately make return of such failure or refusal, whereupon on motion of the plaintiff, the garnishee shall be cited to show cause upon a date to be fixed by the court why he should not be attached for contempt of court for such failure or refusal. If the garnishee fails to show some good and sufficient excuse for such failure or refusal, he shall be fined for such contempt and imprisoned until he shall deliver such effects.

History of TRCP 670: Adopted eff. Sept. 1, 1941, by order of Oct. 29, 1940 (3 Tex.B.J. 628 [1940]). Source: TRCS art. 4090 (repealed).

TRCP 671. REPEALED

Repealed eff. Dec. 31, 1947, by order of Aug. 18, 1947 (10 Tex.B.J. 400 [1947]).

TRCP 672. SALE OF EFFECTS

The sale so ordered shall be conducted in all respects as other sales of personal property under execution; and the officer making such sale shall execute a

TRCP 667

———————————— ✦ ————————————

transfer of such effects or interest to the purchaser, with a brief recital of the judgment of the court under which the same was sold.

History of TRCP 672: Amended eff. Dec. 31, 1947, by order of Aug. 18, 1947 (10 Tex.B.J. 400 [1947]). Adopted eff. Sept. 1, 1941, by order of Oct. 29, 1940 (3 Tex.B.J. 629 [1940]). Source: TRCS art. 4092 (repealed).

TRCP 673. MAY TRAVERSE ANSWER

If the plaintiff should not be satisfied with the answer of any garnishee, he may controvert the same by his affidavit stating that he has good reason to believe, and does believe, that the answer of the garnishee is incorrect, stating in what particular he believes the same to be incorrect. The defendant may also, in like manner, controvert the answer of the garnishee.

History of TRCP 673: Adopted eff. Sept. 1, 1941, by order of Oct. 29, 1940 (3 Tex.B.J. 629 [1940]). Source: TRCS art. 4094 (repealed).

TRCP 674. TRIAL OF ISSUE

If the garnishee whose answer is controverted, is a resident of the county in which the proceeding is pending, an issue shall be formed under the direction of the court and tried as in other cases.

History of TRCP 674: Adopted eff. Sept. 1, 1941, by order of Oct. 29, 1940 (3 Tex.B.J. 629 [1940]). Source: TRCS art. 4095 (repealed).

ANNOTATIONS

First Nat'l Bank v. Steves Sash & Door Co., 468 S.W.2d 133, 138 (Tex.App.—San Antonio 1971, writ ref'd n.r.e.). When garnishor filed an affidavit controverting the answer of nonresident garnishee, the court of the county in which garnishor resided "lost jurisdiction to proceed further, and any proceedings thereafter held were a nullity of no force and effect."

TRCP 675. DOCKET & NOTICE

The clerk of the court or the justice of the peace, on receiving certified copies filed in the county of the garnishee's residence under the provisions of the statutes, shall docket the case in the name of the plaintiff as plaintiff, and of the garnishee as defendant, and issue a notice to the garnishee, stating that his answer has been so controverted, and that such issue will stand for trial on the docket of such court. Such notice shall be directed to the garnishee, be dated and tested as other process from such court, and served by delivering a copy thereof to the garnishee. It shall be returnable, if issued from the district or county court, at ten o'clock a.m. of the Monday next after the expiration of twenty days from the date of its service; and if issued from the

justice court, to the next term of such court convening after the expiration of twenty days after the service of such notice.

History of TRCP 675: Amended eff. Dec. 31, 1941, by order of Sept. 20, 1941 (4 Tex.B.J. 588 [1941]). Adopted eff. Sept. 1, 1941, by order of Oct. 29, 1940 (3 Tex.B.J. 629 [1940]). Source: TRCS art. 4097 (repealed).

ANNOTATIONS

Atteberry, Inc. v. Standard Brass & Mfg., 270 S.W.2d 252, 255 (Tex.App.—Waco 1954, writ ref'd n.r.e.). "[T]he issuance of the writ of garnishment must come from the court where the judgment was rendered, but where the garnishee is the resident of another county and is not entitled to be discharged on its answer the cause must be docketed and tried in the court having jurisdiction of the subject matter in the county of the residence of the garnishee...."

TRCP 676. ISSUE TRIED AS IN OTHER CASES

Upon the return of such notice served, an issue shall be formed under the direction of the court and tried as in other cases.

History of TRCP 676: Adopted eff. Sept. 1, 1941, by order of Oct. 29, 1940 (3 Tex.B.J. 629 [1940]). Source: TRCS art. 4098 (repealed).

TRCP 677. COSTS

Where the garnishee is discharged upon his answer, the costs of the proceeding, including a reasonable compensation to the garnishee, shall be taxed against the plaintiff; where the answer of the garnishee has not been controverted and the garnishee is held thereon, such costs shall be taxed against the defendant and included in the execution provided for in this section; where the answer is contested, the costs shall abide the issue of such contest.

History of TRCP 677: Adopted eff. Sept. 1, 1941, by order of Oct. 29, 1940 (3 Tex.B.J. 629 [1940]). Source: TRCS art. 4100 (repealed).

ANNOTATIONS

General Elec. Capital Corp. v. ICO, Inc., 230 S.W.2d 702, 710 (Tex.App.—Houston [14th Dist.] 2007, pet. denied). "The term 'costs' in [TRCP 677] has repeatedly been interpreted as including attorney's fees. [¶] Rule 677 only [gives] a garnishee the right to recover attorney's fees, and nothing in the rule allows a garnishor to recover attorney's fees from a debtor. [¶] [H]ere it is the debtor who is seeking attorney's fees under Rule 677. The rule does not provide for a debtor to recover attorney's fees, any more than it provides for a garnishor's recovery of fees."

TRCP 677

⭐

TRCP 678. GARNISHEE DISCHARGED ON PROOF

It shall be a sufficient answer to any claim of the defendant against the garnishee founded on an indebtedness of such garnishee, or on the possession by him of any effects, for the garnishee to show that such indebtedness has been paid, or such effects, including any certificates of stock in any incorporated or joint stock company, have been delivered to any sheriff or constable as provided for in Rule 669.

History of TRCP 678: Amended eff. Dec. 31, 1947, by order of Aug. 18, 1947 (10 Tex.B.J. 401 [1947]). Adopted eff. Sept. 1, 1941, by order of Oct. 29, 1940 (3 Tex.B.J. 630 [1940]). Source: TRCS art. 4101 (repealed).

TRCP 679. AMENDMENT

Clerical errors in the affidavit, bond, or writ of garnishment or the officer's return thereof, may upon application in writing to the judge or justice of the court in which the suit is filed, and after notice to the opponent, be amended in such manner and on such terms as the judge or justice shall authorize by an order entered in the minutes of the court (or noted on the docket of the justice of the peace), provided such amendment appears to the judge or justice to be in furtherance of justice.

History of TRCP 679: Adopted eff. Sept. 1, 1941, by order of Oct. 29, 1940 (3 Tex.B.J. 630 [1940]). Source: New rule.

ANNOTATIONS

Metroplex Factors, Inc. v. First Nat'l Bank, 610 S.W.2d 862, 866 (Tex.App.—Fort Worth 1980, writ ref'd n.r.e.). "Rule 679 authorizes correction of clerical errors (such as the missing seal) but does not apply to substantive matters, such as the sufficiency of the required supporting affidavits or other deficiencies in the application for writ of garnishment."

SECTION 5. INJUNCTIONS

TRCP 680. TEMPORARY RESTRAINING ORDER

No temporary restraining order shall be granted without notice to the adverse party unless it clearly appears from specific facts shown by affidavit or by the verified complaint that immediate and irreparable injury, loss, or damage will result to the applicant before notice can be served and a hearing had thereon. Every temporary restraining order granted without notice shall be endorsed with the date and hour of issuance; shall be filed forthwith in the clerk's office and entered of record; shall define the injury and state why it is irreparable and why the order was granted without notice;

and shall expire by its terms within such time after signing, not to exceed fourteen days, as the court fixes, unless within the time so fixed the order, for good cause shown, is extended for a like period or unless the party against whom the order is directed consents that it may be extended for a longer period. The reasons for the extension shall be entered of record. No more than one extension may be granted unless subsequent extensions are unopposed. In case a temporary restraining order is granted without notice, the application for a temporary injunction shall be set down for hearing at the earliest possible date and takes precedence of all matters except older matters of the same character; and when the application comes on for hearing the party who obtained the temporary restraining order shall proceed with the application for a temporary injunction and, if he does not do so, the court shall dissolve the temporary restraining order. On two days' notice to the party who obtained the temporary restraining order without notice or on such shorter notice to that party as the court may prescribe, the adverse party may appear and move its dissolution or modification and in that event the court shall proceed to hear and determine such motion as expeditiously as the ends of justice require.

Every restraining order shall include an order setting a certain date for hearing on the temporary or permanent injunction sought.

History of TRCP 680: Amended eff. Jan. 1, 1988, by order of July 15, 1987 (733-34 S.W.2d [Tex.Cases] lxxviii): Extends length of initial temporary restraining order from 10 days to 14 days. Amended eff. Apr. 1, 1984, by order of Dec. 5, 1983 (661-62 S.W.2d [Tex.Cases] cxvi): Rule changed to avoid successive restraining orders and to require an order setting date for hearing on injunction. Adopted eff. Sept. 1, 1941, by order of Oct. 29, 1940 (3 Tex.B.J. 630 [1940]). Source: FRCP 65(b), superseding TRCS art. 4654.

See CPRC ch. 65; *Commentaries*, "Injunctive Relief," ch. 2-C, p. 111; *O'Connor's Texas Forms*, FORMS 2C:1-3.

ANNOTATIONS

In re Office of the Atty. Gen., 257 S.W.3d 695, 697 (Tex.2008). TRCPs 680 and 684 "require a trial court issuing a temporary restraining order to: (1) state why the order was granted without notice if it is granted *ex parte* …; (2) state the reasons for the issuance of the order by defining the injury and describing why it is irreparable …; (3) state the date the order expires and set a hearing on a temporary injunction …; and (4) set a bond…. Orders that fail to fulfill these requirements are void."

In re Texas Nat. Res. Conserv. Comm'n, 85 S.W.3d 201, 204-05 (Tex.2002). "[A]ll [TROs] are subject to Rule 680's limitations on duration. … Rule 680 provides the only method for extending a [TRO] beyond 14

TRCP 678

⭐

---

days. [¶] Rule 680 governs an extension of a [TRO], whether issued with or without notice, and permits but one extension for no longer than 14 days unless the restrained party agrees to a longer extension."

Ex parte Lesikar, 899 S.W.2d 654, 654 (Tex.1995). "An oral extension of a TRO is ineffective, and the contemnor must have notice of the actual written extension before he can be charged with contempt."

Davis v. Huey, 571 S.W.2d 859, 862 (Tex.1978). "At a hearing upon the request for a temporary injunction the only question before the trial court is whether the applicant is entitled to preservation of the status quo of the subject matter of the suit pending trial on the merits." *See also In re Newton*, 146 S.W.3d 648, 651 (Tex. 2004) (status quo is defined as the last, actual, peaceable, non-contested status which preceded the pending controversy).

TRCP 681. TEMPORARY INJUNCTIONS: NOTICE

No temporary injunction shall be issued without notice to the adverse party.

History of TRCP 681: Adopted eff. Sept. 1, 1941, by order of Oct. 29, 1940 (3 Tex.B.J. 631 [1940]). Source: FRCP 65(a).

See CPRC §51.014(a)(4) (interlocutory appeal of temporary injunction); *Commentaries*, "Injunctive Relief," ch. 2-C, p. 111.

ANNOTATIONS

State v. Cook United, Inc., 469 S.W.2d 709, 712 (Tex.1971). "In the absence of notice to or service of citation upon the Attorney General of the State of Texas, ... the temporary injunction is hereby modified to enjoin only the county and district attorneys of Tarrant and McLennan Counties [who had notice], and shall have no effect on the Attorney General ... or the other district and county attorneys in this State."

RRE VIP Borrower, LLC v. Leisure Life Senior Apt. Hous., Ltd., No. 14-09-00923-CV (Tex.App.— Houston [14th Dist.] 2011, no pet.) (memo op.; 5-3-11). "The notice requirements of Rule 681 impliedly require that the adverse party have the right to be heard. The opportunity to be heard and present evidence must amount to more than the mere opportunity to cross-examine the other party's witnesses."

TRCP 682. SWORN PETITION

No writ of injunction shall be granted unless the applicant therefor shall present his petition to the judge verified by his affidavit and containing a plain and intelligible statement of the grounds for such relief.

History of TRCP 682: Amended eff. Sept. 1, 1941, by order of Mar. 31, 1941 (4 Tex.B.J. 178 [1941]): Completely rewrote rule. Adopted eff. Sept. 1, 1941, by order of Oct. 29, 1940 (3 Tex.B.J. 632 [1940]). Source: New rule. See TRCS art. 4647 (repealed).

See *Commentaries*, "Injunctive Relief," ch. 2-C, p. 111; *O'Connor's Texas Forms*, FORMS 2C:1-4.

ANNOTATIONS

Butnaru v. Ford Motor Co., 84 S.W.3d 198, 204 (Tex.2002). "To obtain a temporary injunction, the applicant must plead and prove three specific elements: (1) a cause of action against the defendant; (2) a probable right to the relief sought; and (3) a probable, imminent, and irreparable injury in the interim."

Walling v. Metcalfe, 863 S.W.2d 56, 57 (Tex.1993). "A trial court may grant a temporary writ of injunction to preserve the status quo pending trial even though the applicant's prayer does not include a claim for equitable relief.... In such cases, however, a temporary injunction should only issue if the applicant establishes a probable right on final trial to the relief sought, and a probable injury in the interim."

Mattox v. Jackson, 336 S.W.3d 759, 763 (Tex. App.—Houston [1st Dist.] 2011, no pet.). "A verified petition for injunctive relief is not required to grant a temporary injunction ... when a full evidentiary hearing on evidence independent of the petition has been held."

Crystal Media, Inc. v. HCI Acquisition Corp., 773 S.W.2d 732, 734 (Tex.App.—San Antonio 1989, no writ). "If the insufficiency of the verification is not objected to prior to the introduction of evidence the defect [is] waived."

TRCP 683. FORM & SCOPE OF INJUNCTION OR RESTRAINING ORDER

Every order granting an injunction and every restraining order shall set forth the reasons for its issuance; shall be specific in terms; shall describe in reasonable detail and not by reference to the complaint or other document, the act or acts sought to be restrained; and is binding only upon the parties to the action, their officers, agents, servants, employees, and attorneys, and upon those persons in active concert or participation with them who receive actual notice of the order by personal service or otherwise.

Every order granting a temporary injunction shall include an order setting the cause for trial on the merits with respect to the ultimate relief sought. The ap-

---

★

---

peal of a temporary injunction shall constitute no cause for delay of the trial.

History of TRCP 683: Amended eff. Apr. 1, 1984, by order of Dec. 5, 1983 (661-62 S.W.2d [Tex.Cases] cxvi). Added last paragraph. Adopted eff. Sept. 1, 1941, by order of Oct. 29, 1940 (3 Tex.B.J. 631 [1940]). Source: FRCP 65(d).

See *Commentaries*, "Injunctive Relief," ch. 2-C, p. 111; "Request for Findings of Fact & Conclusions of Law," ch. 10-E, p. 817; *O'Connor's Texas Forms*, FORMS 2C:3, 4.

ANNOTATIONS

Qwest Comms. v. AT&T Corp., 24 S.W.3d 334, 337 (Tex.2000). The TRCPs "require that an order granting a temporary injunction set the cause for trial on the merits and fix the amount of security to be given by the applicant. These procedural requirements are mandatory, and an order granting a temporary injunction that does not meet them is subject to being declared void and dissolved." *See also InterFirst Bank San Felipe v. Paz Constr. Co.*, 715 S.W.2d 640, 641 (Tex.1986).

Ex parte Slavin, 412 S.W.2d 43, 44 (Tex.1967). An injunction decree "must spell out the details of compliance in clear, specific and unambiguous terms so that such person will readily know exactly what duties or obligations are imposed upon him." *See also RCI Entm't (San Antonio), Inc. v. City of San Antonio*, 373 S.W.3d 589, 603 (Tex.App.—San Antonio 2012, no pet.); *Murray v. Epic Energy Res.*, 300 S.W.3d 461, 470-71 (Tex.App.—Beaumont 2009, no pet.).

RCI Entm't (San Antonio), Inc. v. City of San Antonio, 373 S.W.3d 589, 603 (Tex.App.—San Antonio 2012, no pet.). "An injunction should be broad enough to prevent a repetition of the wrong sought to be corrected. But, it must not be so broad as to enjoin a defendant from activities that are a lawful and proper exercise of his rights. Where a party's acts are divisible, and some acts are permissible and some are not, an injunction should not issue to restrain actions that are legal or about which there is no asserted complaint. Thus, the entry of an injunction that enjoins lawful as well as unlawful acts may constitute an abuse of discretion." *See also Computek Computer & Office Sups. v. Walton*, 156 S.W.3d 217, 221 (Tex.App.—Dallas 2005, no pet.).

Senter Invs. v. Veerjee, 358 S.W.3d 841, 845-46 (Tex.App.—Dallas 2012, no pet.). Appellant "asserts the temporary injunction is void because it does not contain an order setting the case for trial on the merits. [TRCP] 683 requires every order granting a temporary injunction to include such an order. However, because this case involves a temporary injunction pending arbitration, we must also consider the application of the [Texas Arbitration Act (TAA)]. [¶] Once [appellant] decided to invoke the arbitration provision and the trial court compelled arbitration, the trial proceedings were governed by the TAA as well as the rules of civil procedure. Under the TAA, the trial court was required to stay the trial proceedings pending arbitration, subject to its jurisdiction to grant orders under [CPRC] §171.086, including an injunction. [¶] The specific provisions of the TAA in this circumstance control over the rules of civil procedure; therefore, the temporary injunction order properly abated the trial court proceedings."

Intercontinental Terminals Co. v. Vopak N. Am., Inc., 354 S.W.3d 887, 899 (Tex.App.—Houston [1st Dist.] 2011, no pet.). "Rule 683 mandates that a trial court granting a temporary injunction must explain in the order its reasons for believing that the applicant has shown that it will suffer injury if interlocutory relief is not granted but does not require the trial court to provide reasons for believing that the applicant has shown a probable right to final relief. An explanation of the pending harm to the temporary injunction applicant, along with a specific recitation of the conduct enjoined, is all that is necessary to achieve Rule 683's purpose: 'to inform a party just what he is enjoined from doing and the reasons why he is so enjoined.' For these reasons, we hold that Rule 683 does not mandate that the trial court's order expressly state that the trial court found a probable right of recovery." *See also Russell v. Waterwood Imprv. Ass'n*, No. 09-11-00413-CV (TexApp.—Beaumont 2011, no pet.) (memo op.; 11-17-11) (specificity requirement is not satisfied by mere recital of no adequate remedy at law and irreparable harm).

Emex Holdings, LLC v. Naim, No. 13-09-591-CV (Tex.App.—Corpus Christi 2010, no pet.) (memo op.; 5-27-10). "Requiring a trial date to be placed in every injunction order prevents a temporary injunction from effectively becoming permanent without a trial. [It] also places the onus upon the party requesting injunctive relief to renew the injunction if the trial is delayed beyond the trial date set forth in the order. [¶] [R]eference to an existing docket control order is not a substitute for stating a trial date in the order itself. Logically, if a pre-existing docket control order is insufficient to comply with rule 683, then a yet to be entered docket control order ... does not comply either." *See also In re Marriage of Grossnickle*, 115 S.W.3d 238, 244 (Tex.App.—Texarkana 2003, no pet.) (requirement

TRCP 683

that injunction order set cause for trial on the merits is effectively same as requiring specific trial date to be set in the order).

Qaddura v. Indo-European Foods, Inc., 141 S.W.3d 882, 891-92 (Tex.App.—Dallas 2004, pet. denied). "Rule 683 provides that an order granting an injunction 'shall set forth the reasons for its issuance.' This rule, however, applies only to temporary restraining orders and temporary injunctions, not permanent injunctions."

Fasken v. Darby, 901 S.W.2d 591, 593 (Tex. App.—El Paso 1995, no writ). "An injunction that fails to identify the harm that will be suffered if it does not issue must be declared void and be dissolved. This rule operates to invalidate an injunction even when the complaining party fails to bring the error to the trial court's attention." *See also Big D Props., Inc. v. Foster*, 2 S.W.3d 21, 23 (Tex.App.—Fort Worth 1999, no pet.) (Rule 683's requirements cannot be waived). *But see Texas Tech Univ. Health Sci. Ctr. v. Rao*, 105 S.W.3d 763, 768 (Tex.App.—Amarillo 2003, pet. dism'd) (error waived). For more cases dealing with waiver of TRCP 683's requirements, see "Dissolve," ch. 2-C, §8.2.2(2), p. 122.

TRCP 684. APPLICANT'S BOND

In the order granting any temporary restraining order or temporary injunction, the court shall fix the amount of security to be given by the applicant. Before the issuance of the temporary restraining order or temporary injunction the applicant shall execute and file with the clerk a bond to the adverse party, with two or more good and sufficient sureties, to be approved by the clerk, in the sum fixed by the judge, conditioned that the applicant will abide the decision which may be made in the cause, and that he will pay all sums of money and costs that may be adjudged against him if the restraining order or temporary injunction shall be dissolved in whole or in part.

Where the temporary restraining order or temporary injunction is against the State, a municipality, a State agency, or a subdivision of the State in its governmental capacity, and is such that the State, municipality, State agency, or subdivision of the State in its governmental capacity, has no pecuniary interest in the suit and no monetary damages can be shown, the bond shall be allowed in the sum fixed by the judge, and the liability of the applicant shall be for its face amount if the restraining order or temporary injunction shall be dissolved in whole or in part. The discretion of the trial court in fixing the amount of the bond shall be subject to review. Provided that under equitable circumstances and for good cause shown by affidavit or otherwise the court rendering judgment on the bond may allow recovery for less than its full face amount, the action of the court to be subject to review.

History of TRCP 684: Amended eff. Jan. 1, 1981, by order of June 10, 1980 (599-600 S.W.2d [Tex.Cases] lxxx): Rule changed so that amount of bond may be left to the discretion of the court. Amended eff. Mar. 1, 1950, by order of Oct. 12, 1949 (12 Tex.B.J. 538 [1949]). Amended eff. Dec. 31, 1943, by order of June 16, 1943 (6 Tex.B.J. 434 [1943]). Adopted eff. Sept. 1, 1941, by order of Oct. 29, 1940 (3 Tex.B.J. 631 [1940]). Source: TRCS art. 4649, harmonized with FRCP 65(d) by minor textual change (repealed).

ANNOTATIONS

In re Office of the Atty. Gen., 257 S.W.3d 695, 697 (Tex.2008). See annotation under TRCP 680, p. 1064.

DeSantis v. Wackenhut Corp., 793 S.W.2d 670, 685-86 (Tex.1990). To prevail in a suit on a bond, "the claimant must prove that the [TRO] or temporary injunction was issued or perpetuated when it should not have been, and that it was later dissolved. The claimant need not prove that the [TRO] or temporary injunction was obtained maliciously or without probable cause." *See also Goodin v. Jolliff*, 257 S.W.3d 341, 353 (Tex. App.—Fort Worth 2008, no pet.) (claimant must prove that issuance of injunction caused her damages).

Ex parte Jordan, 787 S.W.2d 367, 368 (Tex.1990). Respondent argues the order for temporary injunction "is void because it does not require a separate bond as required by [TRCP] 684. We agree." *See also Ex parte Lesher*, 651 S.W.2d 734, 736 (Tex.1983).

Bay Fin. Sav. Bank v. Brown, 142 S.W.3d 586, 590 (Tex.App.—Texarkana 2004, no pet.). "[A]n order granting a temporary injunction [must] fix the amount of security to be given by the applicant. *At 591:* A bond for a temporary restraining order does not continue on and act as security for a temporary injunction unless expressly authorized by the trial court."

TRCP 685. FILING & DOCKETING

Upon the grant of a temporary restraining order or an order fixing a time for hearing upon an application for a temporary injunction, the party to whom the same is granted shall file his petition therefor, together with the order of the judge, with the clerk of the proper court; and, if such orders do not pertain to a pending suit in said court, the cause shall be entered on the

———————————— ✦ ————————————

docket of the court in its regular order in the name of the party applying for the writ as plaintiff and of the opposite party as defendant.

History of TRCP 685: Adopted eff. Sept. 1, 1941, by order of Oct. 29, 1940 (3 Tex.B.J. 631 [1940]). Source: TRCS art. 4650, harmonized with FRCP 65(d) by minor textual change (repealed).

TRCP 686. CITATION

Upon the filing of such petition and order not pertaining to a suit pending in the court, the clerk of such court shall issue a citation to the defendant as in other civil cases, which shall be served and returned in like manner as ordinary citations issued from said court; provided, however, that when a temporary restraining order is issued and is accompanied with a true copy of plaintiff's petition, it shall not be necessary for the citation in the original suit to be accompanied with a copy of plaintiff's petition, nor contain a statement of the nature of plaintiff's demand, but it shall be sufficient for said citation to refer to plaintiff's claim as set forth in a true copy of plaintiff's petition which accompanies the temporary restraining order; and provided further that the court may have a hearing upon an application for a temporary restraining order or temporary injunction at such time and upon such reasonable notice given in such manner as the court may direct.

History of TRCP 686: Amended eff. Dec. 31, 1947, by order of Aug. 18, 1947 (10 Tex.B.J. 401 [1947]). Amended eff. Dec. 31, 1943, by order of June 16, 1943 (6 Tex.B.J. 434 [1943]). Adopted eff. Sept. 1, 1941, by order of Oct. 29, 1940 (3 Tex.B.J. 631 [1940]). Source: TRCS art. 4655 (repealed).

TRCP 687. REQUISITES OF WRIT

The writ of injunction shall be sufficient if it contains substantially the following requisites:

(**a**) Its style shall be, "The State of Texas."

(**b**) It shall be directed to the person or persons enjoined.

(**c**) It must state the names of the parties to the proceedings, plaintiff and defendant, and the nature of the plaintiff's application, with the action of the judge thereon.

(**d**) It must command the person or persons to whom it is directed to desist and refrain from the commission or continuance of the act enjoined, or to obey and execute such order as the judge has seen proper to make.

(**e**) If it is a temporary restraining order, it shall state the day and time set for hearing, which shall not exceed fourteen days from the date of the court's order granting such temporary restraining order; but if it is a temporary injunction, issued after notice, it shall be made returnable at or before ten o'clock a.m. of the Monday next after the expiration of twenty days from the date of service thereof, as in the case of ordinary citations.

(**f**) It shall be dated and signed by the clerk officially and attested with the seal of his office and the date of its issuance must be indorsed thereon.

History of TRCP 687: Amended eff. Sept. 1, 1990, by order of Apr. 24, 1990 (785-86 S.W.2d [Tex.Cases] lxxiv): Changed time limit in subsec. (e) from 10 days to 14 days. Adopted eff. Sept. 1, 1941, by order of Oct. 29, 1940 (3 Tex.B.J. 632 [1940]). Source: TRCS art. 4651 (repealed).

⑫ TRCP 688. CLERK TO ISSUE WRIT

When the petition, order of the judge and bond have been filed, the clerk shall issue the temporary restraining order or temporary injunction, as the case may be, in conformity with the terms of the order, and deliver the same to the sheriff or any constable of the county of the residence of the person enjoined, or to the applicant, as the latter shall direct. If several persons are enjoined, residing in different counties, the clerk shall issue such additional copies of the writ as shall be requested by the applicant. The clerk must retain a copy of the temporary restraining order or temporary injunction in the court's file.

History of TRCP 688: Amended eff. Jan. 1, 2012, by order of Dec. 12, 2011 (Tex.Sup.Ct. Order, Misc. Docket No. 11-9250): Added last sentence. Adopted eff. Sept. 1, 1941, by order of Oct. 29, 1940 (3 Tex.B.J. 632 [1940]). Source: TRCS art. 4652 (repealed).

ANNOTATIONS

Schliemann v. Garcia, 685 S.W.2d 690, 693 (Tex. App.—San Antonio 1984, orig. proceeding). The "order was improper [because the] injunction was not properly issued or served."

⑫ TRCP 689. SERVICE & RETURN

The officer receiving a writ of injunction shall indorse thereon the date of its receipt by him, and shall forthwith execute the same by delivering to the party enjoined a true copy thereof. The officer must complete and file a return in accordance with Rule 107.

History of TRCP 689: Amended eff. Jan. 1, 2012, by order of Dec. 12, 2011 (Tex.Sup.Ct. Order, Misc. Docket No. 11-9250). Adopted eff. Sept. 1, 1941, by order of Oct. 29, 1940 (3 Tex.B.J. 632 [1940]). Source: TRCS art. 4653 (repealed).

TRCP 690. THE ANSWER

The defendant to an injunction proceeding may answer as in other civil actions; but no injunction shall be dissolved before final hearing because of the denial of the material allegations of the plaintiff's petition, unless the answer denying the same is verified by the oath of the defendant.

⭐

History of TRCP 690: Adopted eff. Sept. 1, 1941, by order of Oct. 29, 1940 (3 Tex.B.J. 632 [1940]). Source: TRCS art. 4657 (repealed).

See *Commentaries*, "Verified Pleas," ch. 3-E, §4, p. 228.

Executive Tele-Comm. Sys. v. Buchbaum, 669 S.W.2d 400, 403 (Tex.App.—Dallas 1984, no writ). "The only prescribed response for a defendant to a temporary injunction proceeding is pronounced in Rule 690, and the failure to answer does not impair the defendant's right to a full hearing."

TRCP 691. BOND ON DISSOLUTION

Upon the dissolution of an injunction restraining the collection of money, by an interlocutory order of the court or judge, made in term time or vacation, if the petition be continued over for trial, the court or judge shall require of the defendant in such injunction proceedings a bond, with two or more good and sufficient sureties, to be approved by the clerk of the court, payable to the complainant in double the amount of the sum enjoined, and conditioned to refund to the complainant the amount of money, interest and costs which may be collected of him in the suit or proceeding enjoined if such injunction is made perpetual on final hearing. If such injunction is so perpetuated, the court, on motion of the complainant, may enter judgment against the principal and sureties in such bond for such amount as may be shown to have been collected from such defendant.

History of TRCP 691: Adopted eff. Sept. 1, 1941, by order of Oct. 29, 1940 (3 Tex.B.J. 632 [1940]). Source: TRCS art. 4659 (repealed).

TRCP 692. DISOBEDIENCE

Disobedience of an injunction may be punished by the court or judge, in term time or in vacation, as a contempt. In case of such disobedience, the complainant, his agent or attorney, may file in the court in which such injunction is pending or with the judge in vacation, his affidavit stating what person is guilty of such disobedience and describing the acts constituting the same; and thereupon the court or judge shall cause to be issued an attachment for such person, directed to the sheriff or any constable of any county, and requiring such officer to arrest the person therein named if found within his county and have him before the court or judge at the time and place named in such writ; or said court or judge may issue a show cause order, directing and requiring such person to appear on such date as may be designated and show cause why he should not be adjudged in contempt of court. On return of such attachment or show cause order, the judge shall proceed to hear proof; and if satisfied that such person has disobeyed the injunction, either directly or indirectly, may commit such person to jail without bail until he purges himself of such contempt, in such manner and form as the court or judge may direct.

History of TRCP 692: Amended eff. Dec. 31, 1943, by order of June 16, 1943 (6 Tex.B.J. 436 [1943]). Adopted eff. Sept. 1, 1941, by order of Oct. 29, 1940 (3 Tex.B.J. 633 [1940]). Source: TRCS art. 4661 (repealed).

City of San Antonio v. Singleton, 858 S.W.2d 411, 412 (Tex.1993). "A trial court generally retains jurisdiction to review, open, vacate or modify a permanent injunction upon a showing of changed conditions. The authority to exercise that jurisdiction, however, must be balanced against principles of res judicata. Whether right or wrong, an injunction 'is not subject to impeachment in its application to the conditions that existed at its making.'"

Ex parte Jackman, 663 S.W.2d 520, 524 (Tex. App.—Dallas 1983, orig. proceeding). "The injunction must be obeyed irrespective of the ultimate validity of the order, and a defendant cannot avoid compliance with the commands, or excuse his violation, of the injunction by simply moving to dissolve it...."

TRCP 693. PRINCIPLES OF EQUITY APPLICABLE

The principles, practice and procedure governing courts of equity shall govern proceedings in injunctions when the same are not in conflict with these rules or the provisions of the statutes.

History of TRCP 693: Adopted eff. Sept. 1, 1941, by order of Oct. 29, 1940 (3 Tex.B.J. 633 [1940]). Source: TRCS art. 4663 (repealed).

State v. Texas Pet Foods, Inc., 591 S.W.2d 800, 804 (Tex.1979). "[I]njunctive relief is proper when the trial court finds it justified under the rules of equity, notwithstanding a defendant's cessation of the activity or solemn promises to cease the activity. *At 805:* When it is determined that [a] statute is being violated, it is within the province of the district court to restrain it. The doctrine of balancing the equities has no application to ... statutorily authorized injunctive relief."

TRCP 693a. BOND IN DIVORCE CASE

In a divorce case the court in its discretion may dispense with the necessity of a bond in connection with an ancillary injunction in behalf of one spouse against the other.

TRCP 693a

★

History of TRCP 693a: Adopted eff. Dec. 31, 1943, by order of June 16, 1943 (6 Tex.B.J. 436 [1943]). Source: New rule.

SECTION 6. MANDAMUS

TRCP 694. NO MANDAMUS WITHOUT NOTICE

No mandamus shall be granted by the district or county court on ex parte hearing, and any peremptory mandamus granted without notice shall be abated on motion.

History of TRCP 694: Adopted eff. Sept. 1, 1941, by order of Oct. 29, 1940 (3 Tex.B.J. 633 [1940]). Source: TRCS art. 2328 (repealed).

SECTION 7. RECEIVERS

TRCP 695. NO RECEIVER OF IMMOVABLE PROPERTY APPOINTED WITHOUT NOTICE

Except where otherwise provided by statute, no receiver shall be appointed without notice to take charge of property which is fixed and immovable. When an application for appointment of a receiver to take possession of property of this type is filed, the judge or court shall set the same down for hearing and notice of such hearing shall be given to the adverse party by serving notice thereof not less than three days prior to such hearing. If the order finds that the defendant is a nonresident or that his whereabouts is unknown, the notice may be served by affixing the same in a conspicuous manner and place upon the property or if that is impracticable it may be served in such other manner as the court or judge may require.

History of TRCP 695: Amended eff. Dec. 31, 1943, by order of June 16, 1943 (6 Tex.B.J. 436 [1943]). Adopted eff. Sept. 1, 1941, by order of Oct. 29, 1940 (3 Tex.B.J. 633 [1940]). Source: New rule.

ANNOTATIONS

Krumnow v. Krumnow, 174 S.W.3d 820, 829 (Tex. App.—Waco 2005, pet. denied). "Real estate is 'fixed and immovable property' within the meaning of Rule 695. Appointment of a receiver without giving notice to adverse parties to be heard *on the application* is reversible error."

TRCP 695a. BOND, & BOND IN DIVORCE CASE

No receiver shall be appointed with authority to take charge of property until the party applying therefor has filed with the clerk of the court a good and sufficient bond, to be approved by such clerk, payable to the defendant in the amount fixed by the court, conditioned for the payment of all damages and costs in such suit, in case it should be decided that such receiver was wrongfully appointed to take charge of such property. The amount of such bond shall be fixed at a sum sufficient to cover all such probable damages and costs. In a divorce case the court or judge, as a matter of discretion, may dispense with the necessity of a bond.

History of TRCP 695a: Adopted eff. Dec. 31, 1943, by order of June 16, 1940 (6 Tex.B.J. 436 [1943]). Source: New rule.

ANNOTATIONS

Ahmad v. Ahmed, 199 S.W.3d 573, 575 (Tex.App.—Houston [1st Dist.] 2006, no pet.). "The applicant's bond is a prerequisite to the appointment of a receiver, and the trial court's failure to require the bond necessitates reversal of the order appointing the receiver. *At 576:* [T]he trial court's order does not require [P] to file a bond payable to [D]—nor does it indicate an appropriate amount for such a bond. ... Although the trial court properly required the receiver to post a bond [under CPRC §64.023], it did not incorporate the additional [TRCP] 695a bond requirement into its order. [T]he record does not indicate that [P] has posted the required Rule 695a bond. Therefore, ... the receivership must be dissolved."

In re Estate of Herring, 983 S.W.2d 61, 64 (Tex. App.—Corpus Christi 1998, no pet.). "[T]he bond requirements of Rule 695a do not apply to the appointment of a post-judgment receiver...."

SECTION 8. SEQUESTRATION

TRCP 696. APPLICATION FOR WRIT OF SEQUESTRATION & ORDER

Either at the commencement of a suit or at any time during its progress the plaintiff may file an application for a writ of sequestration. The application shall be supported by affidavits of the plaintiff, his agent, his attorney, or other persons having knowledge of relevant facts. The application shall comply with all statutory requirements and shall state the grounds for issuing the writ, including the description of the property to be sequestered with such certainty that it may be identified and distinguished from property of a like kind, giving the value of each article of the property and the county in which it is located, and the specific facts relied upon by the plaintiff to warrant the required findings by the court. The writ shall not be quashed because two or more grounds are stated conjunctively or disjunctively. The application and any affidavits shall be made on personal knowledge and shall set forth such facts as would

---

be admissible in evidence; provided that facts may be stated based upon information and belief if the grounds of such belief are specifically stated.

No writ shall issue except upon written order of the court after a hearing, which may be ex parte. The court, in its order granting the application, shall make specific findings of facts to support the statutory grounds found to exist, and shall describe the property to be sequestered with such certainty that it may be identified and distinguished from property of a like kind, giving the value of each article of the property and the county in which it is located. Such order shall further specify the amount of bond required of plaintiff which shall be in an amount which, in the opinion of the court, shall adequately compensate defendant in the event plaintiff fails to prosecute his suit to effect and pay all damages and costs as shall be adjudged against him for wrongfully suing out the writ of sequestration including the elements of damages stated in Sections 62.044 and 62.045, Civil Practice and Remedies Code. The court shall further find in its order the amount of bond required of defendant to replevy, which shall be in an amount equivalent to the value of the property sequestered or to the amount of plaintiff's claim and one year's accrual of interest if allowed by law on the claim, whichever is the lesser amount, and the estimated costs of court. The order may direct the issuance of several writs at the same time, or in succession, to be sent to different counties.

History of TRCP 696: Amended eff. Jan. 1, 1988, by order July 15, 1987 (733-34 S.W.2d [Tex.Cases] lxxix). Amended eff. Jan. 1, 1978, by order of July 11, 1977 (553-54 S.W.2d [Tex.Cases] lxix): Rewrote rule; application must be supported by proof; no writ shall issue until after hearing, court shall make findings, describe property, fix amount of bond, as well as amount of a replevy bond, and may provide for issuance of several writs. Adopted eff. Sept. 1, 1941, by order of Oct. 29, 1940 (3 Tex.B.J. 634 [1940]). Source: TRCS art. 6841 (repealed).

See CPRC §62.001.

ANNOTATIONS

Marrs v. South Tex. Nat'l Bank, 686 S.W.2d 675, 678 (Tex.App.—San Antonio 1985, writ ref'd n.r.e.). Held: A creditor may allege the value of the total inventory; it is not necessary to allege the value of each item.

Burnett Trailers, Inc. v. Polson, 387 S.W.2d 692, 695 (Tex.App.—San Antonio 1965, writ ref'd n.r.e.). To obtain exemplary damages, there must be "a finding that in bringing the suit and causing the writ of sequestration to issue[, the plaintiff] was activated by malice, or that [the plaintiff] caused the writ of sequestration to issue without probable cause."

TRCP 697. PETITION

If the suit be in the district or county court, no writ of sequestration shall issue, unless a petition shall have been first filed therein, as in other suits in said courts.

History of TRCP 697: Adopted eff. Sept. 1, 1941, by order of Oct. 29, 1940 (3 Tex.B.J. 634 [1940]). Source: TRCS art. 6842 (repealed).

TRCP 698. BOND FOR SEQUESTRATION

No writ of sequestration shall issue until the party applying therefor has filed with the officer authorized to issue such writ a bond payable to the defendant in the amount fixed by the court's order, with sufficient surety or sureties as provided by statute to be approved by such officer, conditioned that the plaintiff will prosecute his suit to effect and pay to the extent of the penal amount of the bond all damages and costs as may be adjudged against him for wrongfully suing out such writ of sequestration, and plaintiff may further condition the bond pursuant to the provisions of Rule 708, in which case he shall not be required to give additional bond to replevy unless so ordered by the court.

After notice to the opposite party, either before or after the issuance of the writ, the defendant or plaintiff may file a motion to increase or reduce the amount of such bond, or to question the sufficiency of the sureties thereon, in the court in which such suit is pending. Upon hearing, the court shall enter its order with respect to such bond and sufficiency of the sureties as justice may require.

History of TRCP 698: Amended eff. Jan. 1, 1978, by order of July 11, 1977 (553-54 S.W.2d [Tex.Cases] lxx): To fix amount of bond by court order; no longer will the amount be double the amount of value of property sequestered; either party, after notice and hearing, may ask to change amount of bond. Adopted eff. Sept. 1, 1941, by order of Oct. 29, 1940 (3 Tex.B.J. 634 [1940]). Source: TRCS art. 6843 (repealed).

ANNOTATIONS

Kelso v. Hanson, 388 S.W.2d 396, 399 (Tex.1965). "[T]he sequestration bond required by [TRCP] 698 and the replevy bond required by [TRCP] 708 serve two different purposes, and are conditioned against different contingencies. The sequestration bond guarantees the payment of damages and costs in case it is decided that the sequestration was wrongfully issued."

TRCP 699. REQUISITES OF WRIT

The writ of sequestration shall be directed "To the Sheriff or any Constable within the State of Texas" (not naming a specific county) and shall command him to take into his possession the property, describing the

---

★

---

same as it is described in the application or affidavits, if to be found in his county, and to keep the same subject to further orders of the court, unless the same is replevied. There shall be prominently displayed on the face of the writ, in ten-point type and in a manner calculated to advise a reasonably attentive person of its contents, the following:

"YOU HAVE A RIGHT TO REGAIN POSSESSION OF THE PROPERTY BY FILING A REPLEVY BOND. YOU HAVE A RIGHT TO SEEK TO REGAIN POSSESSION OF THE PROPERTY BY FILING WITH THE COURT A MOTION TO DISSOLVE THIS WRIT."

History of TRCP 699: Amended eff. Jan. 1, 1978, by order of July 11, 1977 (553-54 S.W.2d [Tex.Cases] lxxi): To require the writ be directed to officer "within" State of Texas; rule changes to conform to TRCS art. 6840 and informs party of some of his rights. Adopted eff. Sept. 1, 1941, by order of Oct. 29, 1940 (3 Tex.B.J. 634 [1940]). Source: TRCS art. 6845 (repealed).

See CPRC §§62.061-62.063.

Lindsey v. Williams, 228 S.W.2d 243, 248 (Tex. App.—Texarkana 1950, no writ). "The affidavit, the bond for sequestration, the writ, the seizure, and the officer's return are all to be read and considered together as parts of one proceeding. ... They constitute the 'face of the record' in the sequestration proceedings."

TRCP 700. AMENDMENT

Clerical errors in the affidavit, bond, or writ of sequestration or the officer's return thereof may upon application in writing to the judge of the court in which the suit is filed and after notice to the opponent, be amended in such manner and on such terms as the judge shall authorize by an order entered in the minutes of the court, provided the amendment does not change or add to the grounds of such sequestration as stated in the affidavit, and provided such amendment appears to the judge to be in furtherance of justice.

History of TRCP 700: Adopted eff. Sept. 1, 1941, by order of Oct. 29, 1940 (3 Tex.B.J. 634 [1940]). Source: New rule.

TRCP 700a. SERVICE OF WRIT ON DEFENDANT

The defendant shall be served in any manner provided for service of citation or as provided in Rule 21a, with a copy of the writ of sequestration, the application, accompanying affidavits, and orders of the court as soon as practicable following the levy of the writ. There shall also be prominently displayed on the face of the copy of the writ served on defendant, in ten-point type and in a manner calculated to advise a reasonably attentive person of its contents, the following:

"To _____, Defendant:

You are hereby notified that certain properties alleged to be claimed by you have been sequestered. If you claim any rights in such property, you are advised:

"YOU HAVE A RIGHT TO REGAIN POSSESSION OF THE PROPERTY BY FILING A REPLEVY BOND. YOU HAVE A RIGHT TO SEEK TO REGAIN POSSESSION OF THE PROPERTY BY FILING WITH THE COURT A MOTION TO DISSOLVE THIS WRIT."

History of TRCP 700a: Adopted eff. Jan. 1, 1978, by order of July 11, 1977 (553-54 S.W.2d [Tex.Cases] lxxi): Rule affords defendant notice of proceedings and informs him of some of his rights. Source: New rule.

TRCP 701. DEFENDANT MAY REPLEVY

At any time before judgment, should the sequestered property not have been previously claimed, replevied, or sold, the defendant may replevy the same, or any part thereof, or the proceeds from the sale of the property if it has been sold under order of the court, by giving bond, with sufficient surety or sureties as provided by statute, to be approved by the officer who levied the writ, payable to plaintiff in the amount fixed by the court's order, conditioned as provided in Rule 702 or Rule 703.

On reasonable notice to the opposing party (which may be less than three days) either party shall have the right to prompt judicial review of the amount of bond required, denial of bond, sufficiency of sureties, and estimated value of the property, by the court which authorized issuance of the writ. The court's determination may be made upon the basis of affidavits, if uncontroverted, setting forth such facts as would be admissible in evidence; otherwise, the parties shall submit evidence. The court shall forthwith enter its order either approving or modifying the requirements of the officer or of the court's prior order, and such order of the court shall supersede and control with respect to such matters.

History of TRCP 701: Amended eff. Jan. 1, 1978, by order of July 11, 1977 (553-54 S.W.2d [Tex.Cases] lxxii): Rewrote rule; changed amount of replevy bond from double the amount of value of property to amount fixed by the court, and conditioned as provided in TRCP 702 or 703; rule affords hearing to parties after notice about bond. Adopted eff. Sept. 1, 1941, by order of Oct. 29, 1940 (3 Tex.B.J. 635 [1940]). Source: TRCS art. 6849 (repealed).

Commercial Secs. Co. v. Thompson, 239 S.W.2d 911, 914 (Tex.App.—Fort Worth 1951, no writ). "[T]he purpose of a replevy bond is to insure that the property will be forthcoming after judgment in the same condition as when replevied."

TRCP 699

───────────────── ★ ─────────────────

TRCP 702. BOND FOR PERSONAL PROPERTY

If the property to be replevied be personal property, the condition of the bond shall be that the defendant will not remove the same out of the county, or that he will not waste, ill-treat, injure, destroy, or dispose of the same, according to the plaintiff's affidavit, and that he will have such property, in the same condition as when it is replevied, together with the value of the fruits, hire or revenue thereof, forthcoming to abide the decision of the court, or that he will pay the value thereof, or the difference between its value at the time of replevy and the time of judgment and of the fruits, hire or revenue of the same in case he shall be condemned to do so.

History of TRCP 702: Adopted eff. Sept. 1, 1941, by order of Oct. 29, 1940 (3 Tex.B.J. 635 [1940]). Source: TRCS art. 6850 (repealed).

ANNOTATIONS

Associates Inv. v. Soltes, 250 S.W.2d 593, 595 (Tex.App.—Dallas 1952, writ ref'd n.r.e.). "[T]he wording of Rule 702 that defendant 'will have such property, in the same condition as when it is replevied,' excludes any ordinary depreciation in market value…."

TRCP 703. BOND FOR REAL ESTATE

If the property be real estate, the condition of such bond shall be that the defendant will not injure the property, and that he will pay the value of the rents of the same in case he shall be condemned so to do.

History of TRCP 703: Adopted eff. Sept. 1, 1941, by order of Oct. 29, 1940 (3 Tex.B.J. 635 [1940]). Source: TRCS art. 6851 (repealed).

TRCP 704. RETURN OF BOND & ENTRY OF JUDGMENT

The bond provided for in the three preceding rules shall be returned with the writ to the court from whence the writ issued. In case the suit is decided against the defendant, final judgment shall be rendered against all the obligors in such bond, jointly and severally, for the value of the property replevied as of the date of the execution of the replevy bond, and the value of the fruits, hire, revenue, or rent thereof, as the case may be.

History of TRCP 704: Amended eff. Jan. 1, 1981, by order of June 10, 1980 (599-600 S.W.2d [Tex.Cases] lxxx): Changed word "entered" to "rendered." Adopted eff. Sept. 1, 1941, by order of Oct. 29, 1940 (3 Tex.B.J. 635 [1940]). Source: TRCS art. 6852 (repealed).

ANNOTATIONS

Transit Enters. v. Addicks Tire & Auto Sup., 725 S.W.2d 459, 463 (Tex.App.—Houston [1st Dist.] 1987, no writ). "The … cost of replacement is not evidence of the value of the fruits, hire, revenue, or rent of the property replevied, as required by Rule 704."

TRCP 705. DEFENDANT MAY RETURN SEQUESTERED PROPERTY

Within ten days after final judgment for personal property the defendant may deliver to the plaintiff, or to the officer who levied the sequestration or to his successor in office the personal property in question, and such officer shall deliver same to plaintiff upon his demand therefor; or such defendant shall deliver such property to the officer demanding same under execution issued therefor upon a judgment for the title or possession of the same; and such officer shall receipt the defendant for such property; provided, however, that such delivery to the plaintiff or to such officer shall be without prejudice to any rights of the plaintiff under the replevy bond given by the defendant. Where a mortgage or other lien of any kind is foreclosed upon personal property sequestered and replevied, the defendant shall deliver such property to the officer calling for same under order of sale issued upon a judgment foreclosing such mortgage or other lien, either in the county of defendant's residence or in the county where sequestered, as demanded by such officer; provided, however, that such delivery by the defendant shall be without prejudice to any rights of the plaintiff under the replevy bond given by the defendant.

History of TRCP 705: Amended eff. Dec. 31, 1941, by order of Sept. 20, 1941 (4 Tex.B.J. 594 [1941]). Adopted eff. Sept. 1, 1941, by order of Oct. 29, 1940 (3 Tex.B.J. 635 [1940]). Source: TRCS art. 6853 (repealed).

ANNOTATIONS

Shapiro v. Sampson Bros. & Cooper, Inc., 334 S.W.2d 200, 203 (Tex.App.—Eastland 1960, no writ). "The purpose of the finding of value at the time of the trial was to provide a basis for a credit on the judgment in the event the property was surrendered by the defendant in accordance with Rule 705…."

TRCP 706. DISPOSITION OF THE PROPERTY BY OFFICER

When the property is tendered back by the defendant to the officer who sequestered the same or to the officer calling for same under an order of sale, such officer shall receive said property and hold or dispose of the same as ordered by the court; provided, however, that such return to and receipt of same by the officer and any sale or disposition of said property by the officer under order or judgment of the court shall not affect or limit any rights of the plaintiff under the bond provided for in Rule 702.

History of TRCP 706: Amended eff. Dec. 31, 1941, by order of Sept. 20, 1941 (4 Tex.B.J. 594 [1941]). Adopted eff. Sept. 1, 1941, by order of Oct. 29, 1940 (3 Tex.B.J. 635 [1940]). Source: TRCS art. 6854 (repealed).

TRCP 706

★

TRCP 707. EXECUTION

If the property be not returned and received, as provided in the two preceding rules, execution shall issue upon said judgment for the amount due thereon, as in other cases.

History of TRCP 707: Adopted eff. Sept. 1, 1941, by order of Oct. 29, 1940 (3 Tex.B.J. 635 [1940]). Source: TRCS art. 6855 (repealed).

TRCP 708. PLAINTIFF MAY REPLEVY

When the defendant fails to replevy the property within ten days after the levy of the writ and service of notice on defendant, the officer having the property in possession shall at any time thereafter and before final judgment, deliver the same to the plaintiff upon his giving bond payable to defendant in a sum of money not less than the amount fixed by the court's order, with sufficient surety or sureties as provided by statute to be approved by such officer. If the property to be replevied be personal property, the condition of the bond shall be that he will have such property, in the same condition as when it is replevied, together with the value of the fruits, hire or revenue thereof, forthcoming to abide the decision of the court, or that he will pay the value thereof, or the difference between its value at the time of replevy and the time of judgment (regardless of the cause of such difference in value, and of the fruits, hire or revenue of the same in case he shall be condemned to do so). If the property be real estate, the condition of such bond shall be that the plaintiff will not injure the property, and that he will pay the value of the rents of the same in case he shall be condemned to do so.

On reasonable notice to the opposing party (which may be less than three days) either party shall have the right to prompt judicial review of the amount of bond required, denial of bond, sufficiency of sureties, and estimated value of the property, by the court which authorized issuance of the writ. The court's determination may be made upon the basis of affidavits, if uncontroverted, setting forth such facts as would be admissible in evidence; otherwise, the parties shall submit evidence. The court shall forthwith enter its order either approving or modifying the requirements of the officer or of the court's prior order, and such order of the court shall supersede and control with respect to such matters.

History of TRCP 708: Amended eff. Apr. 1, 1984, by order of Dec. 5, 1983 (661-62 S.W.2d [Tex.Cases] cxvii): To conform amount of bond with requirements of TRCP 698. Amended eff. Jan. 1, 1978, by order of July 11, 1977 (553-54 S.W.2d [Tex.Cases] lxxii): To afford notice and hearing for review of bond and

its terms; to provide for nature of hearing. Adopted eff. Sept. 1, 1941, by order of Oct. 29, 1940 (3 Tex.B.J. 636 [1940]). Source: TRCS art. 6856 (repealed).

ANNOTATIONS

Kelso v. Hanson, 388 S.W.2d 396, 399 (Tex.1965). See annotation under TRCP 698, p. 1071.

TRCP 709. WHEN BOND FORFEITED

The bond provided for in the preceding rule shall be returned by the officer to the court issuing the writ immediately after he has approved same, and in case the suit is decided against the plaintiff, final judgment shall be entered against all the obligors in such bond, jointly and severally for the value of the property replevied as of the date of the execution of the replevy bond, and the value of the fruits, hire, revenue or rent thereof as the case may be. The same rules which govern the discharge or enforcement of a judgment against the obligors in the defendant's replevy bond shall be applicable to and govern in case of a judgment against the obligors in the plaintiff's replevy bond.

History of TRCP 709: Adopted eff. Sept. 1, 1941, by order of Oct. 29, 1940 (3 Tex.B.J. 636 [1940]). Source: TRCS art. 6857, changed to harmonize with other rules (repealed).

ANNOTATIONS

Kelso v. Hanson, 388 S.W.2d 396, 399 (Tex.1965). "A plaintiff availing himself of the replevin proceeding, and those obligating themselves on the replevy bond guaranteeing the performance of its terms by the plaintiff, are bound to the conditions imposed by the rules governing the procedure."

TRCP 710. SALE OF PERISHABLE GOODS

If after the expiration of ten days from the levy of a writ of sequestration the defendant has failed to replevy the same, if the plaintiff or defendant shall make affidavit in writing that the property levied upon, or any portion thereof, is likely to be wasted or destroyed or greatly depreciated in value by keeping, and if the officer having possession of such property shall certify to the truth of such affidavit, it shall be the duty of the judge or justice of the peace to whose court the writ is returnable, upon the presentation of such affidavit and certificate, either in term time or vacation, to order the sale of said property or so much thereof as is likely to be so wasted, destroyed or depreciated in value by keeping, but either party may replevy the property at any time before such sale.

History of TRCP 710: Adopted eff. Sept. 1, 1941, by order of Oct. 29, 1940 (3 Tex.B.J. 636 [1940]). Source: TRCS art. 6859 (repealed).

⭐

TRCP 711. ORDER OF SALE FOR

The judge or justice granting the order provided for in the preceding rule shall issue an order directed to the officer having such property in possession, commanding such officer to sell such property in the same manner as under execution.

History of TRCP 711: Adopted eff. Sept. 1, 1941, by order of Oct. 29, 1940 (3 Tex.B.J. 636 [1940]). Source: TRCS art. 6860 (repealed).

TRCP 712. RETURN OF ORDER

The officer making such sale shall, within five days thereafter, return the order of sale to the court from whence the same issued, with his proceedings thereon, and shall, at the time of making such return, pay over to the clerk or justice of the peace the proceeds of such sale.

History of TRCP 712: Adopted eff. Sept. 1, 1941, by order of Oct. 29, 1940 (3 Tex.B.J. 636 [1940]). Source: TRCS art. 6861 (repealed).

TRCP 712a. DISSOLUTION OR MODIFICATION OF WRIT OF SEQUESTRATION

A defendant whose property has been sequestered or any intervening party who claims an interest in such property, may by sworn written motion, seek to vacate, dissolve, or modify the writ and the order directing its issuance, for any grounds or cause, extrinsic or intrinsic, including a motion to reduce the amount of property sequestered when the total amount described and authorized by such order exceeds the amount necessary to secure the plaintiff's claim, one year's interest if allowed by law on the claim, and costs. Such motion shall admit or deny each finding of the order directing the issuance of the writ except where the movant is unable to admit or deny the finding, in which case movant shall set forth the reasons why he cannot admit or deny. Unless the parties agree to an extension of time, the motion shall be heard promptly, after reasonable notice to the plaintiff (which may be less than three days), and the issue shall be determined not later than ten days after the motion is filed. The filing of the motion shall stay any further proceedings under the writ, except for any orders concerning the care, preservation, or sale of any perishable property, until a hearing is had, and the issue is determined. The writ shall be dissolved unless, at such hearing, the plaintiff shall prove the grounds relied upon for its issuance, but the court may modify its previous order granting the writ and the writ issued pursuant thereto. The movant shall, however, have the burden to prove that the reasonable value of the property sequestered exceeds the amount necessary to secure the debt, interest for one year, and probable costs.

The court's determination may be made upon the basis of affidavits, if uncontroverted, setting forth such facts as would be admissible in evidence; otherwise, the parties shall submit evidence. The court may make all such orders, including orders concerning the care, preservation, or disposition of the property (or the proceeds therefrom if the same has been sold) as justice may require. If the movant has given a replevy bond, an order to vacate or dissolve the writ shall vacate the replevy bond and discharge the sureties thereon, and if the court modifies its order or the writ issued pursuant thereto, it shall make such further orders with respect to the bond as may be consistent with its modification.

History of TRCP 712a: Adopted eff. Jan. 1, 1978, by order of July 11, 1977 (553-54 S.W.2d [Tex.Cases] lxxiii): Rule affords a prompt hearing, provides for the procedures, burden of proof and the kind of proof. Source: New rule.

See CPRC §62.045.

ANNOTATIONS

Monroe v. GMAC, 573 S.W.2d 591, 594 (Tex.App.—Waco 1978, no writ). "Attorney's fees and damages against [P] are authorized only if the writ is dissolved."

TRCP 713. SALE ON DEBT NOT DUE

If the suit in which the sequestration issued be for a debt or demand not yet due, and the property sequestered be likely to be wasted, destroyed or greatly depreciated in value by keeping, the judge or justice of the peace shall, under the regulations hereinbefore provided, order the same to be sold, giving credit on such sale until such debt or demand shall become due.

History of TRCP 713: Adopted eff. Sept. 1, 1941, by order of Oct. 29, 1940 (3 Tex.B.J. 636 [1940]). Source: TRCS art. 6862 (repealed).

See CPRC §62.003.

TRCP 714. PURCHASER'S BOND

In the case of a sale as provided for in the preceding rule, the purchaser of the property shall execute his bond, with two or more good and sufficient sureties, to be approved by the officer making the sale, and payable to such officer, in a sum not less than double the amount of the purchase money, conditioned that such purchaser shall pay such purchase money at the expiration of the time given.

History of TRCP 714: Adopted eff. Sept. 1, 1941, by order of Oct. 29, 1940 (3 Tex.B.J. 637 [1940]). Source: TRCS art. 6863 (repealed).

TRCP 714

★

TRCP 715. RETURN OF BOND

The bond provided for in the preceding rule shall be returned by the officer taking the same to the clerk or justice of the peace from whose court the order of sale issued, with such order, and shall be filed among the papers in the cause.

History of TRCP 715: Adopted eff. Sept. 1, 1941, by order of Oct. 29, 1940 (3 Tex.B.J. 637 [1940]). Source: TRCS art. 6864 (repealed).

TRCP 716. RECOVERY ON BOND

In case the purchaser does not pay the purchase money at the expiration of the time given, judgment shall be rendered against all the obligors in such bond for the amount of such purchase money, interest thereon and all costs incurred in the enforcement and collection of the same; and execution shall issue thereon in the name of the plaintiff in the suit, as in other cases, and the money when collected shall be paid to the clerk or justice of the peace to abide the final decision of the cause.

History of TRCP 716: Adopted eff. Sept. 1, 1941, by order of Oct. 29, 1940 (3 Tex.B.J. 637 [1940]). Source: TRCS art. 6864 (repealed).

SECTION 9. TRIAL OF RIGHT OF PROPERTY

TRCP 717. CLAIMANT MUST MAKE AFFIDAVIT

Whenever a distress warrant, writ of execution, sequestration, attachment, or other like writ is levied upon personal property, and such property, or any part thereof, shall be claimed by any claimant who is not a party to such writ, such claimant may make application that such claim is made in good faith, and file such application with the court in which such suit is pending. Such application may be supported by affidavits of the claimant, his agent, his attorney, or other persons having knowledge of relevant facts. The application shall comply with all statutory requirements and shall state the grounds for such claim and the specific facts relied upon by the claimant to warrant the required findings by the court.

The claim shall not be quashed because two or more grounds are stated conjunctively or disjunctively. The application and any affidavits shall be made on personal knowledge and shall set forth such facts as would be admissible in evidence; provided that facts may be stated based upon information and belief if the grounds of such belief are specifically stated.

No property shall be delivered to the claimant except on written order of the court after a hearing pursuant to Rule 718. The court in its order granting the application shall make specific findings of facts to support the statutory grounds found to exist and shall specify the amount of the bond required of the claimant.

History of TRCP 717: Adopted eff. Jan. 1, 1981, by order of June 10, 1980 (599-600 S.W.2d [Tex.Cases] lxxxi). TRCP 717 rewritten to conform with due-process requirements. See history note to TRCP 610. Former TRCP 717 repealed eff. Jan. 1, 1981, by order of June 10, 1980 (599-600 S.W.2d [Tex.Cases] lxxxi). Source: New rule.

TRCP 718. PROPERTY DELIVERED TO CLAIMANT

Any claimant who claims an interest in property on which a writ has been levied may, by sworn written motion, seek to obtain possession of such property. Such motion shall admit or deny each finding of the order directing the issuance of the writ except where the claimant is unable to admit or deny the finding, in which case claimant shall set forth the reasons why he cannot admit or deny. Such motion shall also contain the reasons why the claimant has superior right or title to the property claimed as against the plaintiff in the writ. Unless the parties agree to an extension of time, the motion shall be heard promptly, after reasonable notice to the plaintiff (which may be less than three days), and the issue shall be determined not later than 10 days after the motion is filed. The filing of the motion shall stay any further proceedings under the writ, except for any orders concerning the care, preservation, or sale of any perishable property, until a hearing is had, and the issue is determined. The claimant shall have the burden to show superior right or title to the property claimed as against the plaintiff and defendant in the writ.

The court's determination may be made upon the basis of affidavits, if uncontroverted, setting forth such facts as would be admissible in evidence, but additional evidence, if tendered by either party shall be received and considered. The court may make all such orders, including orders concerning the care, preservation, or disposition of the property, or the proceeds therefrom if the same has been sold, as justice may require, and if the court modifies its order or the writ issued pursuant thereto, it shall make such further orders with respect to the bond as may be consistent with its modification.

History of TRCP 718: Adopted eff. Jan. 1, 1981, by order of June 10, 1980 (599-600 S.W.2d [Tex.Cases] lxxxi): Rule written to conform with due-process requirements. See history note to TRCP 610. Former TRCP 718 repealed eff. Jan. 1, 1981, by order of June 10, 1980 (599-600 S.W.2d [Tex. Cases] lxxxi). Source: New rule.

★

TRCP 719. BOND

No property shall be put in the custody of the claimant until the claimant has filed with the officer who made the levy, a bond in an amount fixed by the court's order equal to double the value of the property so claimed, payable to the plaintiff in the writ, with sufficient surety or sureties as provided by statute to be approved by such officer, conditioned that the claimant will return the same to the officer making the levy, or his successor, in as good condition as he received it, and shall also pay the reasonable value of the use, hire, increase and fruits thereof from the date of said bond, or, in case he fails so to return said property and pay for the use of the same, that he shall pay the plaintiff the value of said property, with legal interest thereon from the date of the bond, and shall also pay all damages and costs that may be awarded against him for wrongfully suing out such claim.

The plaintiff or claimant may file a motion to increase or reduce the amount of such bond, or to question the sufficiency of the sureties thereon, in the court in which such suit is pending. Upon hearing, the court shall enter its order with respect to such bond and sufficiency of the sureties.

History of TRCP 719: Adopted eff. Jan. 1, 1981, by order of June 10, 1980 (599-600 S.W.2d [Tex.Cases] lxxxii): Rule written to conform with due-process requirements. See history note to TRCP 610. Former TRCP 719 repealed eff. Jan. 1, 1981, by order of June 10, 1980 (599-600 S.W.2d [Tex.Cases] lxxxii). Source: New rule.

TRCP 720. RETURN OF BOND

Whenever any person shall claim property and shall duly make the application and give the bond, if the writ under which the levy was made was issued by a justice of the peace or a court of the county where such levy was made, the officer receiving such application and bond shall endorse on the writ that such claim has been made and application and bond given, and by whom; and shall also endorse on such bond the value of the property as assessed by himself, and shall forthwith return such bond with a copy of the writ to the proper court having jurisdiction to try such claim.

History of TRCP 720: Adopted eff. Jan. 1, 1981, by order of June 10, 1980 (599-600 S.W.2d [Tex.Cases] lxxxiii): Rule written to conform with due-process requirements. See history note to TRCP 610. Former TRCP 720 repealed eff. Jan. 1, 1981, by order of June 10, 1980 (599-600 S.W.2d [Tex.Cases] lxxxiii). Source: New rule.

ANNOTATIONS

Sandler v. Bufkor, Inc., 658 S.W.2d 289, 292 (Tex. App.—Houston [1st Dist.] 1983, no writ). "Having waived the right to establish that the property was of lesser value than that estimated by the officer fixing the amount of the bond, [makers of the bond] became bound by the recitals of the assessed value appearing on the face of the bond they signed."

TRCP 721. OUT-COUNTY LEVY

Whenever any person shall claim property and shall make the application and give the bond as provided for herein, if the writ under which such levy was made was issued by a justice of the peace or a court of another county than that in which such levy was made, then the officer receiving such bond shall endorse on such bond the value of the property as assessed by himself, and shall forthwith return such bond with a copy of the writ, to the proper court having jurisdiction to try such claim.

History of TRCP 721: Adopted eff. Jan. 1, 1981, by order of June 10, 1980 (599-600 S.W.2d [Tex.Cases] lxxxiii): TRCP 722 renumbered as TRCP 721 and rewritten to conform with due-process requirements. See history note to TRCP 610. Former TRCP 721 repealed eff. Jan. 1, 1981, by order of June 10, 1980 (599-600 S.W.2d [Tex.Cases] lxxxiii). Source: New rule.

TRCP 722. RETURN OF ORIGINAL WRIT

The officer taking such bond shall also endorse on the original writ, if in his possession, that such claim has been made and application and bond given, stating by whom, the names of the surety or sureties, and to what justice or court the bond has been returned; and he shall forthwith return such original writ to the tribunal from which it issued.

History of TRCP 722: Adopted eff. Jan. 1, 1981, by order of June 10, 1980 (599-600 S.W.2d [Tex.Cases] lxxxiii): TRCP 723 renumbered as TRCP 722 and rewritten to conform with due-process requirements. See history note to TRCP 610. Former TRCP 722 repealed eff. Jan. 1, 1981, by order of June 10, 1980 (599-600 S.W.2d [Tex.Cases] lxxxiii). Source: New rule.

TRCP 723. DOCKETING CAUSE

Whenever any bond for the trial of the right of property shall be returned, the clerk of the court, or such justice of the peace, shall docket the same in the original writ proceeding in the name of the plaintiff in the writ as the plaintiff, and the claimant of the property as intervening claimant.

History of TRCP 723: Adopted eff. Jan. 1, 1981, by order of June 10, 1980 (599-600 S.W.2d [Tex.Cases] lxxxiv): Rule written to conform with due-process requirements. See history note to TRCP 610. Former TRCP 723 repealed eff. Jan. 1, 1981, by order of June 10, 1980 (599-600 S.W.2d [Tex.Cases] lxxxiv). Source: New rule. See former TRCP 725, adopted eff. Sept. 1, 1941, by order of Oct. 29, 1940 (3 Tex.B.J. 638 [1940]). See TRCS art. 7410 (repealed).

TRCP 724. ISSUE MADE UP

After the claim proceedings have been docketed, and on the hearing day set by the court, then the court, or the justice of the peace, as the case may be, shall enter an order directing the making and joinder of issues

───────────────────────────── ★ ─────────────────────────────

by the parties. Such issues shall be in writing and signed by each party or his attorney. The plaintiff shall make a brief statement of the authority and right by which he seeks to subject the property levied on to the process, and it shall be sufficient for the claimant and other parties to make brief statements of the nature of their claims thereto.

History of TRCP 724: Amended eff. Jan. 1, 1981, by order of June 10, 1980 (599-600 S.W.2d [Tex.Cases] lxxxiv): TRCP 726 renumbered as TRCP 724 and rewritten to conform with due-process requirements. See history note to TRCP 610. Source: See former TRCP 726, adopted eff. Sept. 1, 1941, by order of Oct. 29, 1940 (3 Tex.B.J. 638 [1940]). See TRCS arts. 7411, 7412 (repealed).

TRCP 725. JUDGMENT BY DEFAULT

If the plaintiff appears and the claimant fails to appear or neglects or refuses to join issue under the direction of the court or justice within the time prescribed for pleading, the plaintiff shall have judgment by default.

History of TRCP 725: Adopted new rule eff. Jan. 1, 1981, by order of June 10, 1980 (599-600 S.W.2d [Tex.Cases] lxxxiv): Rule is same as former TRCP 727 except word "defendant" in the first line changed to "claimant." Former TRCP 725 repealed eff. Jan. 1, 1981, by order of June 10, 1980 (599-600 S.W.2d [Tex.Cases] lxxxiv). Source: New rule. See former TRCP 727, adopted eff. Sept. 1, 1941, by order of Oct. 29, 1940 (3 Tex.B.J. 638 [1940]). See TRCS art. 7413 (repealed).

TRCP 726. JUDGMENT OF NON-SUIT

If the plaintiff does not appear, he shall be non-suited.

History of TRCP 726: Amended eff. Jan. 1, 1981, by order of June 10, 1980 (599-600 S.W.2d [Tex.Cases] lxxxv): Former TRCP 728 renumbered as TRCP 726 and rewritten to conform with due-process requirements. See history note to TRCP 610. Source: New rule. See former TRCP 728, adopted eff. Sept. 1, 1941, by order of Oct., 29, 1940 (3 Tex.B.J. 638 [1940]). See TRCS art. 7414 (repealed).

ANNOTATIONS

Union Bank & Trust Co. v. Mireles, 697 S.W.2d 745, 747 (Tex.App.—Corpus Christi 1985, no writ). "When [a plaintiff is nonsuited after failing to appear,] the claimant has possession of the property and this specialized proceeding is ended."

TRCP 727. PROCEEDINGS

The proceedings and practice on the trial shall be as nearly as may be the same as in other cases before such court or justice.

History of TRCP 727: Amended eff. Jan. 1, 1981, by order of June 10, 1980 (599-600 S.W.2d [Tex.Cases] lxxxv): Same as former TRCP 729. Source: See former TRCP 729, adopted eff. Sept. 1, 1941, by order of Oct. 29, 1940 (3 Tex.B.J. 638 [1940]). See TRCS art. 7415 (repealed).

TRCP 728. BURDEN OF PROOF

If the property was taken from the possession of the claimant pursuant to the original writ, the burden of proof shall be on the plaintiff in the writ. If it was taken from the possession of the defendant in such writ, or any other person than the claimant, the burden of proof shall be on the claimant.

History of TRCP 728: Amended eff. Jan. 1, 1981, by order of June 10, 1980 (599-600 S.W.2d [Tex.Cases] lxxxv): Former TRCP 730 renumbered as TRCP 728 and rewritten to conform with due-process requirements. See history note to TRCP 610. Source: New rule. See former TRCP 730, adopted eff. Sept. 1, 1941, by order of Oct. 29, 1940 (3 Tex.B.J. 638). See TRCS art. 7416 (repealed).

TRCP 729. COPY OF WRIT EVIDENCE

In all trials of the right of property, under the provisions of this section in any county other than that in which the writ issued under which the levy was made, the copy of the writ herein required to be returned by the officer making the levy shall be received in evidence in like manner as the original could be.

History of TRCP 729: Amended eff. Jan. 1, 1981, by order of June 10, 1980 (599-600 S.W.2d [Tex.Cases] lxxxv). Same as former TRCP 731. Source: See former TRCP 731, adopted eff. Sept. 1, 1941, by order of Oct. 29, 1940 (3 Tex.B.J. 638 [1940]). See TRCS art. 7419 (repealed).

TRCP 730. FAILURE TO ESTABLISH TITLE

Where any claimant has obtained possession of property, and shall ultimately fail to establish his right thereto, judgment may be rendered against him and his sureties for the value of the property, with legal interest thereon from the date of such bond. Such judgment shall be rendered in favor of the plaintiff or defendant in the writ, or of the several plaintiffs or defendants, if more than one, and shall fix the amount of the claim of each.

History of TRCP 730: Adopted eff. Jan. 1, 1981, by order of June 10, 1980 (599-600 S.W.2d [Tex.Cases] lxxxv): Rule written to conform with due-process requirements. See history note to TRCP 610. Former TRCP 730 repealed eff. Jan. 1, 1981, by order of June 20, 1980 (599-600 S.W.2d [Tex.Cases] lxxxv). Source: New rule. See former TRCP 732, adopted eff. Sept. 1, 1941, by order of Oct. 29, 1940 (3 Tex.B.J. 639 [1940]). See TRCS art. 7420 (repealed).

ANNOTATIONS

Sandler v. Bufkor, Inc., 658 S.W.2d 289, 292 (Tex. App.—Houston [1st Dist.] 1983, no writ). "Once [claimant] failed to establish its right to the property protected by the bond, [Ps] were entitled to judgment against [makers of the bond] and their surety for the value of the property."

TRCP 731. EXECUTION SHALL ISSUE

If such judgment should not be satisfied by a return of the property, then after the expiration of ten days from the date of the judgment, execution shall issue thereon in the name of the plaintiff or defendant for

───────────── ✦ ─────────────

the amount of the claim, or of all the plaintiffs or defendants for the sum of their several claims, provided the amount of such judgment shall inure to the benefit of any person who shall show superior right or title to the property claimed as against the claimant; but if such judgment be for a less amount than the sum of the several plaintiffs' or defendants' claims, then the respective rights and priorities of the several plaintiffs or defendants shall be fixed and adjusted in the judgment.

History of TRCP 731: Adopted eff. Jan. 1, 1981, by order of June 10, 1980 (599-600 S.W.2d [Tex.Cases] lxxxvi): Rule written to conform with due-process requirements. See history note to TRCP 610. Former TRCP 731 renumbered as TRCP 729, eff. Jan. 1, 1981, by order of June 10, 1980 (599-600 S.W.2d [Tex.Cases] lxxxvi). Source: New rule. See former TRCP 733, adopted eff. Sept. 1, 1941, by order of Oct. 29, 1940 (3 Tex.B.J. 639 [1940]). See TRCS arts. 7421, 7422 (repealed).

TRCP 732. RETURN OF PROPERTY BY CLAIMANT

If, within ten days from the rendition of said judgment, the claimant shall return such property in as good condition as he received it, and pay for the use of the same together with the damages and costs, such delivery and payment shall operate as a satisfaction of such judgment.

History of TRCP 732: Adopted eff. Jan. 1, 1981, by order of June 10, 1980 (599-600 S.W.2d [Tex.Cases] lxxxvi): Same as former TRCP 734. Former TRCP 732 repealed eff. Jan. 1, 1981, by order of June 10, 1980 (599-600 S.W.2d [Tex.Cases] lxxxvi). Source: See former TRCP 734, adopted eff. Sept. 1, 1941, by order of Oct. 29, 1940 (3 Tex.B.J. 639 [1940]). See TRCS art. 7423 (repealed).

ANNOTATIONS

Sandler v. Bufkor, Inc., 658 S.W.2d 289, 292-93 (Tex.App.—Houston [1st Dist.] 1983, no writ). "Although return of the property 'in as good condition as he received it' operates as a satisfaction of the judgment, partial tender and an offer to pay for missing property does not constitute such satisfaction. ... This is especially so where a 'substantial part' of the goods are missing."

TRCP 733. CLAIM IS A RELEASE OF DAMAGES

A claim made to the property, under the provisions of this section, shall operate as a release of all damages by the claimant against the officer who levied upon said property.

History of TRCP 733: Adopted eff. Jan. 1, 1981, by order of June 10, 1980 (599-600 S.W.2d [Tex.Cases] lxxxvi): Same as former TRCP 735. Former TRCP 733 repealed eff. Jan. 1, 1981, by order of June 10, 1980 (599-600 S.W.2d [Tex.Cases] lxxxvi). Source: See former TRCP 735, adopted eff. Sept. 1, 1941, by order of Oct. 29, 1940 (3 Tex.B.J. 639 [1940]). See TRCS art. 7424 (repealed).

TRCP 734. LEVY ON OTHER PROPERTY

Proceedings for the trial of right of property under these rules shall in no case prevent the plaintiff in the writ from having a levy made upon any other property of the defendant.

History of TRCP 734: Adopted eff. Jan. 1, 1981, by order of June 10, 1980 (599-600 S.W.2d [Tex.Cases] lxxxvii): Same as former TRCP 736. Source: See former TRCP 736, adopted eff. Sept. 1, 1941, by order of Oct. 29, 1940 (3 Tex.B.J. 639 [1940]). See TRCS art. 7425 (repealed).

PART VII. RULES RELATING TO SPECIAL PROCEEDINGS

SECTION 1. PROCEDURES RELATED TO FORECLOSURES OF CERTAIN LIENS

TRCP 735. FORECLOSURES REQUIRING A COURT ORDER

735.1 Liens Affected.

Rule 736 provides the procedure for obtaining a court order, when required, to allow foreclosure of a lien containing a power of sale in the security instrument, dedicatory instrument, or declaration creating the lien, including a lien securing any of the following:

(a) a home equity loan, reverse mortgage, or home equity line of credit under article XVI, sections 50(a)(6), 50(k), and 50(t) of the Texas Constitution;

(b) a tax lien transfer or property tax loan under sections 32.06 and 32.065 of the Tax Code; or

(c) a property owners' association assessment under section 209.0092 of the Property Code.

735.2 Other Statutory and Contractual Foreclosure Provisions Unaltered.

A Rule 736 order does not alter any foreclosure requirement or duty imposed under applicable law or the terms of the loan agreement, contract, or lien sought to be foreclosed. The only issue to be determined in a Rule 736 proceeding is whether a party may obtain an order under Rule 736 to proceed with foreclosure under applicable law and the terms of the loan agreement, contract, or lien sought to be foreclosed.

735.3 Judicial Foreclosure Unaffected.

A Rule 736 order is not a substitute for a judgment for judicial foreclosure, but any loan agreement, contract, or lien that may be foreclosed using Rule 736 procedures may also be foreclosed by judgment in an action for judicial foreclosure.

Comment to 2011 change: Rules 735 and 736 have been rewritten and expanded to cover property owners' associations' assessment liens, in accordance with amendments to chapter 209 of the Property Code. Rule 735.1 makes the expedited procedures of Rule 736 available only when the lienholder has a power of sale but a court order is nevertheless required by law to foreclose the lien. Rule 735.2 makes clear that Rule 736 is procedural only and does not affect other contractual or legal rights or duties. Any lien which can be foreclosed under Rule 736 may also be foreclosed in an action for judicial foreclosure, as Rule 735.3 states, but no lienholder is required to obtain both a Rule 736 order and a judgment for judicial foreclosure. The requirement of conspicuousness in Rule 736.1(d)(5) has reference to section 1.201(b)(10) of the Business and Commerce Code.

History of TRCP 735: Amended eff. Jan. 1, 2012, by order of Dec. 30, 2011 (Tex.Sup.Ct. Order, Misc. Docket No. 11-9260). Amended eff. Apr. 15, 2000, by order of Apr. 12, 2000 (15-16 S.W.3d [Tex.Cases] xxiii): Rules 735 and 736 do not change duties of a lender seeking foreclosure. These rules do not preclude a respondent from timely proceeding in district court to contest the right to foreclose or abate a Rule 736 proceeding. Adopted eff. May 15, 1998, by order of Jan. 27, 1998 (961-62 S.W.2d [Tex.Cases] xxxiv): Written to adopt procedures for foreclosure of home equity liens. Source: New rule.

See Tex. Const. art. 16, §50; Prop. Code §51.002.

⑫ TRCP 736. EXPEDITED ORDER PROCEEDING

736.1 Application.

(a) *Where Filed.* An application for an expedited order allowing the foreclosure of a lien listed in Rule 735 to proceed must be filed in a county where all or part of the real property encumbered by the loan agreement, contract, or lien sought to be foreclosed is located or in a probate court with jurisdiction over proceedings involving the property.

(b) *Style.* An application must be styled "In re: Order for Foreclosure Concerning [*state: property's mailing address*] under Tex. R. Civ. P. 736."

(c) *When Filed.* An application may not be filed until the opportunity to cure has expired under applicable law and the loan agreement, contract, or lien sought to be foreclosed.

(d) *Contents.* The application must:

(1) Identify by name and last known address each of the following parties:

(A) "Petitioner"—any person legally authorized to prosecute the foreclosure;

(B) "Respondent"—according to the records of the holder or servicer of the loan agreement, contract, or lien sought to be foreclosed:

(i) for a home equity loan, reverse mortgage, or home equity line of credit, each person obligated to pay the loan agreement, contract, or lien sought to be foreclosed and each mortgagor, if any, of the loan agreement, contract, or lien sought to be foreclosed;

(ii) for a tax lien transfer or property tax loan, each person obligated to pay the loan agreement, contract, or lien sought to be foreclosed, each mortgagor, if any, of the loan agreement, contract, or lien sought to be fore-

closed, each owner of the property, and the holder of any recorded preexisting first lien secured by the property;

(iii) for a property owners' association assessment, each person obligated to pay the loan agreement, contract, or lien sought to be foreclosed who has a current ownership interest in the property.

(2) Identify the property encumbered by the loan agreement, contract, or lien sought to be foreclosed by its commonly known street address and legal description.

(3) Describe or state:

(A) the type of lien listed in Rule 735 sought to be foreclosed and its constitutional or statutory reference;

(B) the authority of the party seeking foreclosure, whether as the servicer, beneficiary, lender, investor, property owners' association, or other person with authority to prosecute the foreclosure;

(C) each person obligated to pay the loan agreement, contract, or lien sought to be foreclosed;

(D) each mortgagor, if any, of the loan agreement, contract, or lien sought to be foreclosed who is not a maker or assumer of the underlying debt;

(E) as of a date that is not more than sixty days prior to the date the application is filed:

(i) if the default is monetary, the number of unpaid scheduled payments,

(ii) if the default is monetary, the amount required to cure the default,

(iii) if the default is non-monetary, the facts creating the default, and

(iv) if applicable, the total amount required to pay off the loan agreement, contract, or lien;

(F) that the requisite notice or notices to cure the default has or have been mailed to each person as required under applicable law and the loan agreement, contract, or lien sought to be foreclosed and that the opportunity to cure has expired; and

(G) that before the application was filed, any other action required under applicable law and the loan agreement, contract, or lien sought to be foreclosed was performed.

(4) For a tax lien transfer or property tax loan, state all allegations required to be contained in the application in accordance with section 32.06(c-1)(1) of the Tax Code.

(5) Conspicuously state:

(A) that legal action is not being sought against the occupant of the property unless the occupant is also named as a respondent in the application; and

(B) that if the petitioner obtains a court order, the petitioner will proceed with a foreclosure of the property in accordance with applicable law and the terms of the loan agreement, contract, or lien sought to be foreclosed.

(6) Include an affidavit of material facts in accordance with Rule 166a(f) signed by the petitioner or the servicer describing the basis for foreclosure and, depending on the type of lien sought to be foreclosed, attach a legible copy of:

(A) the note, original recorded lien, or pertinent part of a property owners' association declaration or dedicatory instrument establishing the lien, and current assignment of the lien, if assigned;

(B) each notice required to be mailed to any person under applicable law and the loan agreement, contract, or lien sought to be foreclosed before the application was filed and proof of mailing of each notice; and

(C) for a tax lien transfer or property tax loan:

(i) the property owner's sworn document required under section 32.06(a-1) of the Tax Code; and

(ii) the taxing authority's certified statement attesting to the transfer of the lien, required under section 32.06(b) of the Tax Code.

736.2 Costs.

All filing, citation, mailing, service, and other court costs and fees are costs of court and must be paid by petitioner at the time of filing an application with the clerk of the court.

736.3 Citation.

(a) *Issuance.*

(1) When the application is filed, the clerk must issue a separate citation for each respondent named in the application and one additional citation for the occupant of the property sought to be foreclosed.

(2) Each citation that is directed to a respondent must state that any response to the application is due the first Monday after the expiration of 38 days from the date the citation was placed in the custody of the U.S. Postal Service in accordance with the clerk's standard mailing procedures and state the date that the citation was placed in the custody of the U.S. Postal Service by the clerk.

(b) *Service and Return.*

(1) The clerk of the court must serve each citation, with a copy of the application attached, by both first class mail and certified mail. A citation directed to a respondent must be mailed to the respondent's last known address that is stated in the application. A citation directed to the occupant of the property sought to be foreclosed must be mailed to Occupant of [*state: property's mailing address*] at the address of the property sought to be foreclosed that is stated in the application.

(2) Concurrently with service, the clerk must complete a return of service in accordance with Rule 107, except that the return of service need not contain a return receipt. For a citation mailed by the clerk in accordance with (b)(1), the date of service is the date and time the citation was placed in the custody of the U.S. Postal Service in a properly addressed, postage prepaid envelope in accordance with the clerk's standard mailing procedures.

(3) The clerk must only charge one fee per respondent or occupant served under this rule.

736.4 Discovery.

No discovery is permitted in a Rule 736 proceeding.

736.5 Response.

(a) *Generally.* A respondent may file a response contesting the application.

(b) *Due Date.* Any response to the application is due the first Monday after the expiration of 38 days from the date the citation was placed in the custody of the U.S. Postal Service in accordance with the clerk's standard mailing procedures, as stated on the citation.

(c) *Form.* A response must be signed in accordance with Rule 57 and may be in the form of a general denial under Rule 92, except that a respondent must affirmatively plead:

(1) why the respondent believes a respondent did not sign a loan agreement document, if applicable, that is specifically identified by the respondent;

(2) why the respondent is not obligated for payment of the lien;

(3) why the number of months of alleged default or the reinstatement or pay off amounts are materially incorrect;

(4) why any document attached to the application is not a true and correct copy of the original; or

(5) proof of payment in accordance with Rule 95.

(d) *Other Claims.* A response may not state an independent claim for relief. The court must, without a hearing, strike and dismiss any counterclaim, cross claim, third party claim, intervention, or cause of action filed by any person in a Rule 736 proceeding.

736.6 Hearing Required When Response Filed.

The court must not conduct a hearing under this rule unless a response is filed. If a response is filed, the court must hold a hearing after reasonable notice to the parties. The hearing on the application must not be held earlier than 20 days or later than 30 days after a request for a hearing is made by any party. At the hearing, the petitioner has the burden to prove by affidavits on file or evidence presented the grounds for granting the order sought in the application.

736.7 Default When No Response Filed.

(a) If no response to the application is filed by the due date, the petitioner may file a motion and proposed order to obtain a default order. For the purposes of obtaining a default order, all facts alleged in the application and supported by the affidavit of material facts constitute prima facie evidence of the truth of the matters alleged.

(b) The court must grant the application by default order no later than 30 days after a motion is filed under (a) if the application complies with the requirements of Rule 736.1 and was properly served in accordance with Rule 736.3. The petitioner need not appear in court to obtain a default order.

(c) The return of service must be on file with the clerk of the court for at least 10 days before the court may grant the application by default.

736.8 Order.

(a) The court must issue an order granting the application if the petitioner establishes the basis for the foreclosure. Otherwise, the court must deny the application.

(b) An order granting the application must describe:

(1) the material facts establishing the basis for foreclosure;

(2) the property to be foreclosed by commonly known mailing address and legal description;

(3) the name and last known address of each respondent subject to the order; and

(4) the recording or indexing information of each lien to be foreclosed.

(c) An order granting or denying the application is not subject to a motion for rehearing, new trial, bill of review, or appeal. Any challenge to a Rule 736 order must be made in a suit filed in a separate, independent, original proceeding in a court of competent jurisdiction.

736.9 Effect of the Order.

An order is without prejudice and has no res judicata, collateral estoppel, estoppel by judgment, or other effect in any other judicial proceeding. After an order is obtained, a person may proceed with the foreclosure process under applicable law and the terms of the lien sought to be foreclosed.

736.10 Bankruptcy.

If a respondent provides proof to the clerk of the court that respondent filed bankruptcy before an order is signed, the proceeding under this rule must be abated so long as the automatic stay is effective.

736.11 Automatic Stay and Dismissal if Independent Suit Filed.

(a) A proceeding or order under this rule is automatically stayed if a respondent files a separate, original proceeding in a court of competent jurisdiction that puts in issue any matter related to the origination, servicing, or enforcement of the loan agreement, contract, or lien sought to be foreclosed prior to 5:00 p.m. on the Monday before the scheduled foreclosure sale.

(b) Respondent must give prompt notice of the filing of the suit to petitioner or petitioner's attorney and the foreclosure trustee or substitute trustee by any reasonable means necessary to stop the scheduled foreclosure sale.

(c) Within ten days of filing suit, the respondent must file a motion and proposed order to dismiss or vacate with the clerk of the court in which the application was filed giving notice that respondent has filed an original proceeding contesting the right to foreclose in a court of competent jurisdiction. If no order has been signed, the court must dismiss a pending proceeding. If an order has been signed, the court must vacate the Rule 736 order.

(d) If the automatic stay under this rule is in effect, any foreclosure sale of the property is void. Within 10 business days of notice that the foreclosure sale was void, the trustee or substitute trustee must return to the buyer of the foreclosed property the purchase price paid by the buyer.

———————————— ✦ ————————————

(e) The court may enforce the Rule 736 process under chapters 9 and 10 of the Civil Practices and Remedies Code.

736.12 Attachment of Order to Trustee's Deed.

A conformed copy of the order must be attached to the trustee or substitute trustee's foreclosure deed.

736.13 Promulgated Forms.

The Supreme Court of Texas may promulgate forms that conform to this rule.

Comment to 2011 change: Rules 735 and 736 have been rewritten and expanded to cover property owners' associations' assessment liens, in accordance with amendments to chapter 209 of the Property Code. Rule 735.1 makes the expedited procedures of Rule 736 available only when the lienholder has a power of sale but a court order is nevertheless required by law to foreclose the lien. Rule 735.2 makes clear that Rule 736 is procedural only and does not affect other contractual or legal rights or duties. Any lien which can be foreclosed under Rule 736 may also be foreclosed in an action for judicial foreclosure, as Rule 735.3 states, but no lienholder is required to obtain both a Rule 736 order and a judgment for judicial foreclosure. The requirement of conspicuousness in Rule 736.1(d)(5) has reference to section 1.201(b)(10) of the Business and Commerce Code.

History of TRCP 736: Amended eff. Jan. 1, 2012, by order of Dec. 30, 2011 (Tex.Sup.Ct. Order, Misc. Docket No. 11-9260). Amended eff. Apr. 15, 2000, by order of Apr. 12, 2000 (15-16 S.W.3d [Tex.Cases] xxiii): Rules 735 and 736 do not change duties of a lender seeking foreclosure. These rules do not preclude a respondent from timely proceeding in district court to contest the right to foreclose or abate a Rule 736 proceeding. Adopted eff. May 15, 1998, by order of Jan. 27, 1998 (961-62 S.W.2d [Tex.Cases] xxxiv): Written to adopt procedures for foreclosure of home equity liens. Source: New rule.

See Tex. Const. art. 16, §50; Prop. Code §51.002.

SECTION 2. JUSTICE COURT PROCEEDINGS TO ENFORCE LANDLORD'S DUTY TO REPAIR OR REMEDY RESIDENTIAL RENTAL PROPERTY

TRCP 737. [ENFORCING LANDLORD'S DUTY TO REPAIR OR REMEDY[1]]

737.1 Applicability of Rule. This rule applies to a suit filed in a justice court by a residential tenant under Chapter 92, Subchapter B of the Texas Property Code to enforce the landlord's duty to repair or remedy a condition materially affecting the physical health or safety of an ordinary tenant. Rules 523-574b also apply to the extent they are not inconsistent with this rule.

737.2 Contents of Petition; Copies; Forms and Amendments.

(a) *Contents of Petition.* The petition must be in writing and must include the following:

(1) the street address of the residential rental property;

(2) a statement indicating whether the tenant has received in writing the name and business street address of the landlord and landlord's management company;

(3) to the extent known and applicable, the name, business street address, and telephone number of the landlord and the landlord's management company, on-premises manager, and rent collector serving the residential rental property;

(4) for all notices the tenant gave to the landlord requesting that the condition be repaired or remedied:

(A) the date of the notice;

(B) the name of the person to whom the notice was given or the place where the notice was given;

(C) whether the tenant's lease is in writing and requires written notice;

(D) whether the notice was in writing or oral;

(E) whether any written notice was given by certified mail, return receipt requested, or by registered mail; and

(F) whether the rent was current or had been timely tendered at the time notice was given;

(5) a description of the property condition materially affecting the physical health or safety of an ordinary tenant that the tenant seeks to have repaired or remedied;

(6) a statement of the relief requested by the tenant, including an order to repair or remedy a condition, a reduction in rent, actual damages, civil penalties, attorney's fees, and court costs;

(7) if the petition includes a request to reduce the rent:

(A) the amount of rent paid by the tenant, the amount of rent paid by the government, if known, the rental period, and when the rent is due; and

(B) the amount of the requested rent reduction and the date it should begin;

(8) a statement that the total relief requested does not exceed $10,000, excluding interest and court costs but including attorney's fees; and

(9) the tenant's name, address, and telephone number.

(b) *Copies.* The tenant must provide the court with copies of the petition and any attachments to the petition for service on the landlord.

(c) *Forms and Amendments.* A petition substantially in the form promulgated by the Supreme Court is

✦

sufficient. A suit may not be dismissed for a defect in the petition unless the tenant is given an opportunity to correct the defect and does not promptly correct it.

737.3 **Citation: Issuance; Appearance Date.**

(a) *Issuance.* When the tenant files a written petition with a justice court, the justice must immediately issue citation directed to the landlord, commanding the landlord to appear before such justice at the time and place named in the citation.

(b) *Appearance Date.* The appearance date on the citation must not be earlier than the sixth day nor later than the tenth day after the date of service of the citation. For purposes of this rule, the appearance date on the citation is the trial date.

⑫ **737.4** **Service and Return of Citation; Alternative Service of Citation.**

(a) *Service and Return of Citation.* The sheriff, constable, or other person authorized by Rule 536 who receives the citation must serve the citation by delivering a copy of it, along with a copy of the petition and any attachments, to the landlord at least six days before the appearance date. At least one day before the appearance date, the person serving the citation must file a return of service with the court that issued the citation. The citation must be issued, served, and returned in like manner as ordinary citations issued from a justice court.

(b) *Alternative Service of Citation.*

(1) If the petition does not include the landlord's name and business street address, or if, after making diligent efforts on at least two occasions, the sheriff, constable, or other person authorized by Rule 536 is unsuccessful in serving the citation on the landlord under (a), the sheriff, constable, or other person authorized by Rule 536 must serve the citation by delivering a copy of the citation, petition, and any attachments to:

(A) the landlord's management company if the tenant has received written notice of the name and business street address of the landlord's management company; or

(B) if (b)(1)(A) does not apply and the tenant has not received the landlord's name and business street address in writing, the landlord's authorized agent for service of process, which may be the landlord's management company, on-premise manager, or rent collector serving the residential rental property.

(2) If the sheriff, constable, or other person authorized by Rule 536 is unsuccessful in serving citation under (b)(1) after making diligent efforts on at least two occasions at either the business street address of the landlord's management company, if (b)(1)(A) applies, or at each available business street address of the landlord's authorized agent for service of process, if (b)(1)(B) applies, the sheriff, constable, or other person authorized by Rule 536 must execute and file in the justice court a sworn statement that the sheriff, constable, or other person authorized by Rule 536 made diligent efforts to serve the citation on at least two occasions at all available business street addresses of the landlord and, to the extent applicable, the landlord's management company, on-premises manager, and rent collector serving the residential rental property, providing the times, dates, and places of each attempted service. The justice may then authorize the sheriff, constable, or other person authorized by Rule 536 to serve citation by:

(A) delivering a copy of the citation, petition, and any attachments to someone over the age of sixteen years, at any business street address listed in the petition, or, if nobody answers the door at a business street address, either placing the citation, petition, and any attachments through a door mail chute or slipping them under the front door, and if neither of these latter methods is practical, affixing the citation, petition, and any attachments to the front door or main entry to the business street address;

(B) within 24 hours of complying with (b)(2)(A), sending by first class mail a true copy of the citation, petition, and any attachments addressed to the landlord at the landlord's business street address provided in the petition; and

(C) noting on the return of the citation the date of delivery under (b)(2)(A) and the date of mailing under (b)(2)(B).

The delivery and mailing to the business street address under (b)(2)(A)-(B) must occur at least six days before the appearance date. At least one day before the appearance date, the citation, with the action written thereon, must be returned to the justice who issued the citation. It is not necessary for the tenant to request the alternative service authorized by this rule.

737.5 **Representation of Parties.** Parties may represent themselves. A party may also be represented by an authorized agent, but nothing in this rule autho-

★

rizes a person who is not an attorney licensed to practice law in this state to represent a party before the court if the party is present.

737.6 Docketing and Trial; Failure to Appear; Continuance.

(a) *Docketing and Trial.* The case shall be docketed and tried as other cases. The justice may develop the facts of the case in order to ensure justice.

(b) *Failure to Appear.*

(1) If the tenant appears at trial and the landlord has been duly served and fails to appear at trial, the justice may proceed to hear evidence. If the tenant establishes that the tenant is entitled to recover, the justice shall render judgment against the landlord in accordance with the evidence.

(2) If the tenant fails to appear for trial, the justice may dismiss the suit.

(c) *Continuance.* The justice may continue the trial for good cause shown. Continuances should be limited, and the case should be reset for trial on an expedited basis.

737.7 Discovery. Reasonable discovery may be permitted. Discovery is limited to that considered appropriate and permitted by the justice and must be expedited. In accordance with Rule 215, the justice may impose any appropriate sanction on any party who fails to respond to a court order for discovery.

737.8 Judgment: Amount; Form and Content; Issuance and Service; Failure to Comply.

(a) *Amount.* Judgment may be rendered against the landlord for failure to repair or remedy a condition at the residential rental property if the total judgment does not exceed $10,000, excluding interest and court costs but including attorney's fees. Any party who prevails in a suit brought under these rules may recover the party's court costs and reasonable attorney's fees as allowed by law.

(b) *Form and Content.*

(1) The judgment must be in writing, signed, and dated and must include the names of the parties to the proceeding and the street address of the residential rental property where the condition is to be repaired or remedied.

(2) In the judgment, the justice may:

(A) order the landlord to take reasonable action to repair or remedy the condition;

(B) order a reduction in the tenant's rent, from the date of the first repair notice, in proportion to the reduced rental value resulting from the condition until the condition is repaired or remedied;

(C) award a civil penalty of one month's rent plus $500;

(D) award the tenant's actual damages; and

(E) award court costs and attorney's fees, excluding any attorney's fees for a cause of action for damages relating to a personal injury.

(3) If the justice orders the landlord to repair or remedy a condition, the judgment must include in reasonable detail the actions the landlord must take to repair or remedy the condition and the date when the repair or remedy must be completed.

(4) If the justice orders a reduction in the tenant's rent, the judgment must state:

(A) the amount of the rent the tenant must pay, if any;

(B) the frequency with which the tenant must pay the rent;

(C) the condition justifying the reduction of rent;

(D) the effective date of the order reducing rent;

(E) that the order reducing rent will terminate on the date the condition is repaired or remedied; and

(F) that on the day the condition is repaired or remedied, the landlord must give the tenant written notice, served in accordance with Rule 21a, that the condition justifying the reduction of rent has been repaired or remedied and the rent will revert to the rent amount specified in the lease.

(c) *Issuance and Service.* The justice must issue the judgment. The judgment may be served on the landlord in open court or by any means provided in Rule 21a at an address listed in the citation, the address listed on any answer, or such other address the landlord furnishes to the court in writing. Unless the justice serves the landlord in open court or by other means provided in Rule 21a, the sheriff, constable, or other person authorized by Rule 536 who serves the landlord must promptly file a certificate of service in the justice court.

(d) *Failure to Comply.* If the landlord fails to comply with an order to repair or remedy a condition or reduce the tenant's rent, the failure is grounds for citing the landlord for contempt of court under Section 21.002 of the Government Code.

⋆

737.9 Counterclaims. Counterclaims and the joinder of suits against third parties are not permitted in suits under these rules. Compulsory counterclaims may be brought in a separate suit. Any potential causes of action, including a compulsory counterclaim, that are not asserted because of this rule are not precluded.

737.10 Post-Judgment Motions: Time and Manner; Disposition; Number.

(a) *Time and Manner.* A party may file a motion for new trial, a motion to amend the judgment, or a motion to set aside a default judgment or a dismissal for want of prosecution. The motion must be in writing and filed within ten days after the date the justice signs the judgment or dismissal order.

(b) *Disposition.*

(1) If the justice grants a motion for new trial or a motion to set aside a default judgment or a dismissal for want of prosecution, the resulting trial must occur within ten days after the date the justice signs the order granting the motion.

(2) If the justice grants a motion to amend the judgment, the justice must amend the judgment within fifteen days after the date the justice signs the original judgment.

(3) If the justice does not rule on a motion for new trial, a motion to amend the judgment, or a motion to set aside a default judgment or a dismissal for want of prosecution with a written, signed order within fifteen days after the justice signs the judgment or dismissal order, the motion is considered overruled by operation of law on expiration of that period.

(c) *Number.* A party may file only one motion for new trial, one motion to amend the judgment, and one motion to set aside a default judgment or a dismissal for want of prosecution.

737.11 Plenary Power. The justice court's plenary power expires when a party perfects an appeal. If a party does not perfect an appeal, the justice court has plenary power to grant a new trial, amend or vacate the judgment, or set aside a default judgment or a dismissal for want of prosecution within fifteen days after the date the justice signs the judgment or dismissal order.

737.12 Appeal: Time and Manner; Perfection; Effect; Costs; Trial on Appeal.

(a) *Time and Manner.* Either party may appeal the decision of the justice court to a statutory county court or, if there is no statutory county court with jurisdiction, a county court or district court with jurisdiction by filing a written notice of appeal with the justice court within twenty days after the date the justice signs the judgment. If the judgment is amended in any respect, any party has the right to appeal within twenty days after the date the justice signs the new judgment, in the same manner set out in this rule.

(b) *Perfection.* The posting of an appeal bond is not required for an appeal under these rules, and the appeal is considered perfected with the filing of a notice of appeal. Otherwise, the appeal is in the manner provided by law for appeal from a justice court.

(c) *Effect.* The timely filing of a notice of appeal stays the enforcement of any order to repair or remedy a condition or reduce the tenant's rent, as well as any other actions.

(d) *Costs.* The appellant must pay the costs on appeal to a county court in accordance with Rule 143a.

(e) *Trial on Appeal.* On appeal, the parties are entitled to a trial de novo. Either party is entitled to trial by jury on timely request and payment of a fee, if required. An appeal of a judgment of a justice court under these rules takes precedence in the county court and may be held at any time after the eighth day after the date the transcript is filed in the county court.

737.13 Effect of Writ of Possession. If a judgment for the landlord for possession of the residential rental property becomes final, any order to repair or remedy a condition is vacated and unenforceable.

1. **Editor's note:** The Texas Supreme Court order promulgating TRCP 737 does not specify a heading for the rule. The heading shown here was added by the editor. In addition to the rule, the Supreme Court promulgated a form petition that tenants can use in suits brought under Prop. Code §92.0563 and TRCP 737. This form, Appendix A, can be found on our website at www.jonesmcclure.com/productsupport.aspx.

Comment to 2010 change:

The heading of repealed Rule 737, regarding bills of discovery, is deleted. New Rule 737 is promulgated pursuant to Senate Bill 1448 to provide procedures for a tenant's request for relief in a justice court under Section 92.0563(a) of the Property Code. Except when otherwise specifically provided, the terms in Rule 737 are defined consistent with Section 92.001 of the Property Code. All suits must be filed in accordance with the venue provisions of Chapter 15 of the Civil Practice and Remedies Code.

History of TRCP 737: Amended eff. Jan. 1, 2012, by order of Dec. 12, 2011 (Tex.Sup.Ct. Order, Misc. Docket No. 11-9250). Amended eff. Jan. 1, 2010, by order of Dec. 14, 2009, (Tex.Sup.Ct. Order, Misc. Docket No. 09-9195). Former TRCP 737 was repealed eff. Jan. 1, 1999, by order of Nov. 9, 1998 (61 Tex.B.J. 1140 [1998]). For the subject matter of former TRCP 737, see TRCP 202.

SECTION 3. FORCIBLE ENTRY & DETAINER

TRCP 738. MAY SUE FOR RENT

A suit for rent may be joined with an action of forcible entry and detainer, wherever the suit for rent is

TRCP 737

within the jurisdiction of the justice court. In such case the court in rendering judgment in the action of forcible entry and detainer, may at the same time render judgment for any rent due the landlord by the renter; provided the amount thereof is within the jurisdiction of the justice court.

History of TRCP 738: Adopted eff. Sept. 1, 1941, by order of Oct. 29, 1940 (3 Tex.B.J. 640 [1940]). Source: TRCS art. 3976 (repealed).

See CPRC §15.084; Prop. Code §24.004.

TRCP 739. CITATION

When the party aggrieved or his authorized agent shall file his written sworn complaint with such justice, the justice shall immediately issue citation directed to the defendant or defendants commanding him to appear before such justice at a time and place named in such citation, such time being not more than ten days nor less than six days from the date of service of the citation.

The citation shall inform the parties that, upon timely request and payment of a jury fee no later than five days after the defendant is served with citation, the case shall be heard by a jury.

History of TRCP 739: Amended eff. Jan. 1, 1988, by order of July 15, 1987 (733-34 S.W.2d [Tex.Cases] lxxx). Adopted eff. Sept. 1, 1941, by order of Oct. 29, 1940 (3 Tex.B.J. 640 [1940]). Source: TRCS art. 3977 (repealed).

TRCP 740. COMPLAINANT MAY HAVE POSSESSION

The party aggrieved may, at the time of filing his complaint, or thereafter prior to final judgment in the justice court, execute and file a possession bond to be approved by the justice in such amount as the justice may fix as the probable amount of costs of suit and damages which may result to defendant in the event that the suit has been improperly instituted, and conditioned that the plaintiff will pay defendant all such costs and damages as shall be adjudged against plaintiff.

The defendant shall be notified by the justice court that plaintiff has filed a possession bond. Such notice shall be served in the same manner as service of citation and shall inform the defendant of all of the following rules and procedures:

(a) Defendant may remain in possession if defendant executes and files a counterbond prior to the expiration of six days from the date defendant is served with notice of the filing of plaintiff's bond. Said counterbond shall be approved by the justice and shall be in such amount as the justice may fix as the probable amount of costs of suit and damages which may result

to plaintiff in the event possession has been improperly withheld by defendant;

(b) Defendant is entitled to demand and he shall be granted a trial to be held prior to the expiration of six days from the date defendant is served with notice of the filing of plaintiff's possession bond;

(c) If defendant does not file a counterbond and if defendant does not demand that trial be held prior to the expiration of said six-day period, the constable of the precinct or the sheriff of the county where the property is situated, shall place the plaintiff in possession of the property promptly after the expiration of six days from the date defendant is served with notice of the filing of plaintiff's possession bond; and

(d) If, in lieu of a counterbond, defendant demands trial within said six-day period, and if the justice of the peace rules after trial that plaintiff is entitled to possession of the property, the constable or sheriff shall place the plaintiff in possession of the property five days after such determination by the justice of the peace.

History of TRCP 740: Amended eff. Sept. 1, 1977, by order of May 9, 1977 (553-54 S.W.2d [Tex.Cases] xxxviii): Substituted "five days" for "immediately" to avoid conflict with TRCP 748. Amended eff. Jan. 1, 1976, by order of July 22, 1975 (525-26 S.W.2d [Tex.Cases] lix): Eliminated requirement that defendant execute counterbond for double the amount of plaintiff's bond; rewritten to permit possession bond and counterbond in probable amount of costs and damages; new rule requires notice to defendant of rights and liabilities stated in secs. (a)-(d). Amended eff. Dec. 31, 1943, by order of June 16, 1943 (6 Tex.B.J. 443 [1943]): Regulations as to the bond of defendant were enlarged to include a case where an out-of-county officer effects service of citation and to make clear that six-days time will be allowed, before possession is given the aggrieved party, within which defendant may give such bond; other relevant changes made. Adopted eff. Sept. 1, 1941, by order of Oct. 29, 1940 (3 Tex.B.J. 640 [1940]). Source: TRCS art. 3978 (repealed).

TRCP 741. REQUISITES OF COMPLAINT

The complaint shall describe the lands, tenements or premises, the possession of which is claimed, with sufficient certainty to identify the same, and it shall also state the facts which entitled the complainant to the possession and authorize the action under Sections 24.001-24.004, Texas Property Code.

History of TRCP 741: Amended eff. Jan. 1, 1988, by order of July 15, 1987 (733-34 S.W.2d [Tex.Cases] lxxx). Amended eff. Apr. 1, 1984, by order of Dec. 5, 1983 (661-62 S.W.2d [Tex.Cases] cxvii): Adopted eff. Sept. 1, 1941, by order of Oct. 29, 1940 (3 Tex.B.J. 640 [1940]). Source: TRCS art. 3979 (repealed).

ANNOTATIONS

Family Inv. v. Paley, 356 S.W.2d 353, 355-56 (Tex. App.—Houston 1962, writ dism'd). "An insufficient description in the complaint in forcible entry and detainer is not such a defect as to deprive the court of jurisdiction. The complaint can be amended in the Justice of the Peace Court."

⭐

⑫ TRCP 742. SERVICE OF CITATION

The officer receiving such citation shall execute the same by delivering a copy of it to the defendant, or by leaving a copy thereof with some person over the age of sixteen years, at his usual place of abode, at least six days before the return day thereof; and on or before the day assigned for trial he must complete and file a return of service in accordance with Rule 536a with the court that issued the citation.

History of TRCP 742: Amended eff. Jan. 1, 2012, by order of Dec. 12, 2011 (Tex.Sup.Ct. Order, Misc. Docket No. 11-9250). Amended eff. Dec. 31, 1947, by order of Aug. 18, 1947 (10 Tex.B.J. 401 [1947]). Adopted eff. Sept. 1, 1941, by order of Oct. 29, 1940 (3 Tex.B.J. 640 [1940]). Source: TRCS art. 3980 (repealed).

ANNOTATIONS

American Spiritualist Ass'n v. Ravkind, 313 S.W.2d 121, 124 (Tex.App.—Dallas 1958, writ ref'd n.r.e.). "[T]he Justice Court judgment was fatally defective because of a lack of proper service of citation."

⑫ TRCP 742a. SERVICE BY DELIVERY TO PREMISES

If the sworn complaint lists all home and work addresses of the defendant which are known to the person filing the sworn complaint and if it states that such person knows of no other home or work addresses of the defendant in the county where the premises are located, service of citation may be by delivery to the premises in question as follows:

If the officer receiving such citation is unsuccessful in serving such citation under Rule 742, the officer shall no later than five days after receiving such citation execute a sworn statement that the officer has made diligent efforts to serve such citation on at least two occasions at all addresses of the defendant in the county where the premises are located as may be shown on the sworn complaint, stating the times and places of attempted service. Such sworn statement shall be filed by the officer with the justice who shall promptly consider the sworn statement of the officer. The justice may then authorize service according to the following:

(a) The officer shall place the citation inside the premises by placing it through a door mail chute or by slipping it under the front door; and if neither method is possible or practical, the officer shall securely affix the citation to the front door or main entry to the premises.

(b) The officer shall that same day or the next day deposit in the mail a true copy of such citation with a copy of the sworn complaint attached thereto, addressed to defendant at the premises in question and sent by first class mail;

(c) The officer shall note on the return of such citation the date of delivery under (a) above and the date of mailing under (b) above; and

(d) Such delivery and mailing to the premises shall occur at least six days before the return day of the citation; and on or before the day assigned for trial he must complete and file a return of service in accordance with Rule 536a with the court that issued the citation.

It shall not be necessary for the aggrieved party or his authorized agent to make request for or motion for alternative service pursuant to this rule.

History of TRCP 742a: Amended eff. Jan. 1, 2012, by order of Dec. 12, 2011 (Tex.Sup.Ct. Order, Misc. Docket No. 11-9250). Adopted eff. Aug. 15, 1982, by order of Apr. 15, 1982 (629-30 S.W.2d [Tex.Cases] xlii). Source: New rule.

ANNOTATIONS

Thomas v. Olympus/Nelson Prop. Mgmt., 148 S.W.3d 395, 400 (Tex.App.—Houston [14th Dist.] 2004, no pet.). "Rule 742a expressly contemplates that a defendant subject to service under its terms may have more than one 'home address.' *At 401:* [I]t is reasonable to require a plaintiff relying on Rule 742a to obtain service of citation to disclose … that it knows a defendant is currently living somewhere other than on the leased premises before that plaintiff can obtain constructive service by delivery to the leased premises."

TRCP 743. DOCKETED

The cause shall be docketed and tried as other cases. If the defendant shall fail to enter an appearance upon the docket in the justice court or file answer before the case is called for trial, the allegations of the complaint may be taken as admitted and judgment by default entered accordingly. The justice shall have authority to issue subpoenas for witnesses to enforce their attendance, and to punish for contempt.

History of TRCP 743: Amended eff. Dec. 31, 1947, by order of Aug. 18, 1947 (10 Tex.B.J. 401 [1947]). Adopted eff. Sept. 1, 1941, by order of Oct. 29, 1940 (3 Tex.B.J. 640 [1940]). Source: TRCS art. 3981 (repealed).

TRCP 744. DEMANDING JURY

Any party shall have the right of trial by jury, by making a request to the court on or before five days from the date the defendant is served with citation, and by paying a jury fee of five dollars. Upon such request, a jury shall be summoned as in other cases in justice court.

⭐

History of TRCP 744: Amended eff. Jan. 1, 1988, by order of July 15, 1987 (733-34 S.W.2d [Tex.Cases] lxxx). Adopted eff. Sept. 1, 1941, by order of Oct. 29, 1940 (3 Tex.B.J. 640 [1940]). Source: TRCS art. 3982 (repealed).

ANNOTATIONS

Collins v. Cleme Manor Apts., 37 S.W.3d 527, 531 (Tex.App.—Texarkana 2001, no pet.). "We find the best reading of Rule 744 to be that it applies strictly to justice court proceedings, with the last phrase clarifying that although there exists a different procedure for requesting a jury in justice court forcible detainer proceedings, the procedures for summoning such jury are those prescribed for ordinary justice court actions."

TRCP 745. TRIAL POSTPONED

For good cause shown, supported by affidavit of either party, the trial may be postponed not exceeding six days.

History of TRCP 745: Adopted eff. Sept. 1, 1941, by order of Oct. 29, 1940 (3 Tex.B.J. 640 [1940]). Source: TRCS art. 3983 (repealed).

TRCP 746. ONLY ISSUE

In case of forcible entry or of forcible detainer under Sections 24.001-24.008, Texas Property Code, the only issue shall be as to the right to actual possession; and the merits of the title shall not be adjudicated.

History of TRCP 746: Amended eff. Jan. 1, 1988, by order of July 15, 1987 (733-34 S.W.2d [Tex.Cases] lxxxi). Amended eff. Apr. 1, 1984, by order of Dec. 5, 1983 (661-62 S.W.2d [Tex.Cases] cxvii). Adopted eff. Sept. 1, 1941, by order of Oct. 29, 1940 (3 Tex.B.J. 641 [1940]). Source: TRCS art. 3984 (repealed).

ANNOTATIONS

Villalon v. Bank One, 176 S.W.3d 66, 70 (Tex. App.—Houston [1st Dist.] 2004, pet. denied). "To prevail in a forcible detainer action, a plaintiff is not required to prove title but is only required to show sufficient evidence of ownership to demonstrate a superior right to immediate possession. If the question of title is so intertwined with the issue of possession, then possession may not be adjudicated without first determining title." *See also Morris v. American Home Mortg. Servicing, Inc.*, 360 S.W.3d 32, 34 (Tex.App.— Houston [1st Dist.] 2011, no pet.).

Lopez v. Sulak, 76 S.W.3d 597, 605 (Tex.App.— Corpus Christi 2002, no pet.). "[W]here the right to immediate possession necessarily requires resolution of a title dispute, the justice court has no jurisdiction to enter a judgment and may be enjoined from doing so. Because a forcible detainer action is not exclusive, but is cumulative of any other remedy a party may have in the courts of this state, the displaced party is entitled to bring a separate suit in district court to determine the issue of title."

TRCP 747. TRIAL

If no jury is demanded by either party, the justice shall try the case. If a jury is demanded by either party, the jury shall be empaneled and sworn as in other cases; and after hearing the evidence it shall return its verdict in favor of the plaintiff or the defendant as it shall find.

History of TRCP 747: Amended eff. Jan. 1, 1981, by order of June 10, 1980 (599-600 S.W.2d [Tex.Cases] lxxxvii): Deleted last sentence of former rule because it is same provision as second sentence of TRCP 743. Amended eff. Dec. 31, 1943, by order of June 16, 1943 (6 Tex.B.J. 444 [1943]). Adopted eff. Sept. 1, 1941, by order of Oct. 29, 1940 (3 Tex.B.J. 641 [1940]). Source: TRCS art. 3985 (repealed).

TRCP 747a. REPRESENTATION BY AGENTS

In forcible entry and detainer cases for non-payment of rent or holding over beyond the rental term, the parties may represent themselves or be represented by their authorized agents in justice court.

History of TRCP 747a: Adopted eff. Aug. 15, 1982, by order of Apr. 15, 1982 (629-30 S.W.2d [Tex.Cases] xliii). Source: New rule.

TRCP 748. JUDGMENT & WRIT

If the judgment or verdict be in favor of the plaintiff, the justice shall give judgment for plaintiff for possession of the premises, costs, and damages; and he shall award his writ of possession. If the judgment or verdict be in favor of the defendant, the justice shall give judgment for defendant against the plaintiff for costs and any damages. No writ of possession shall issue until the expiration of five days from the time the judgment is signed.

History of TRCP 748: Amended eff. Jan. 1, 1988, by order of July 15, 1987 (733-34 S.W.2d [Tex.Cases] lxxxi). Amended eff. Jan. 1, 1981, by order of June 10, 1980 (599-600 S.W.2d [Tex.Cases] lxxxvii): Time runs from date judgment is signed. Amended eff. Jan. 1, 1976, by order of July 22, 1975 (525-26 S.W.2d [Tex.Cases] lx): Authorizes judgments for costs and damages, which TRCP 740 protects. Amended eff. Jan. 1, 1961, by order of July 26, 1960 (23 Tex.B.J. 685 [1961]): The time within which to issue writ of restitution changed from two days to five days. Adopted eff. Sept. 1, 1941, by order of Oct. 29, 1940 (3 Tex.B.J. 641 [1940]). Source: TRCS art. 3986, modified by eliminating verdict of "guilty" or "not guilty" (repealed).

ANNOTATIONS

Housing Auth. v. Sanders, 693 S.W.2d 2, 2-3 (Tex. App.—Tyler 1985, writ ref'd n.r.e.). "A justice court judgment is a prerequisite to an appeal to the county court."

TRCP 749. MAY APPEAL

In appeals in forcible entry and detainer cases, no motion for new trial shall be filed.

Either party may appeal from a final judgment in such case, to the county court of the county in which the

---

★

---

judgment is rendered by filing with the justice within five days after the judgment is signed, a bond to be approved by said justice, and payable to the adverse party, conditioned that he will prosecute his appeal with effect, or pay all costs and damages which may be adjudged against him.

The justice shall set the amount of the bond to include the items enumerated in Rule 752.

Within five days following the filing of such bond, the party appealing shall give notice as provided in Rule 21a of the filing of such bond to the adverse party. No judgment shall be taken by default against the adverse party in the court to which the cause has been appealed without first showing substantial compliance with this rule.

History of TRCP 749: Amended eff. Jan. 1, 1988, by order of July 15, 1987 (733-34 S.W.2d [Tex.Cases] lxxxi): To give notice to appellee that an appeal of case from justice court was perfected in county court. Amended eff. Jan. 1, 1981, by order of June 10, 1980 (599-600 S.W.2d [Tex.Cases] lxxxvii): Time runs from date judgment is signed. Amended eff. Jan. 1, 1976, by order of July 22, 1975 (525-26 S.W.2d [Tex.Cases] lxi): First sentence moved from within the rule. Amount of the appeal bond fixed by justice as prescribed by TRCP 752. Amended eff. Dec. 31, 1947, by order of Aug. 18, 1947 (10 Tex.B.J. 401 [1947]). Adopted eff. Sept. 1, 1941, by order of Oct. 29, 1940 (3 Tex.B.J. 641 [1940]). Source: TRCS art. 3987 (repealed).

ANNOTATIONS

RCJ Liquidating Co. v. Village, Ltd., 670 S.W.2d 643, 644 (Tex.1984). TRCP 749 makes no provision for delay in the appeal when a motion for new trial is filed.

Slay v. Nationstar Mortg., L.L.C., No. 02-11-00313-CV (Tex.App.—Fort Worth 2012, no pet.) (memo op.; 3-1-12). "[R]ule 749 [does not] state that any amount of bond will perfect an appeal as long as the amount is approved by the justice court. The judgment of possession set the bond at $10,000, and [D] only paid $1,950. [D's] bond was therefore defective. The justice court's approval of a bond does not affect its validity."

State v. Jones, 220 S.W.3d 604, 607 (Tex.App.—Texarkana 2007, no pet.). "The failure to file … an appeal bond in a timely manner is jurisdictional; absent such a timely filing, the county court is without jurisdiction to hear the case."

Mitchell v. Armstrong Capital Corp., 877 S.W.2d 480, 481 (Tex.App.—Houston [1st Dist.] 1994, no writ). "Rule 749 does not provide that giving notice of the filing of an appeal bond is jurisdictional."

TRCP 749a. PAUPER'S AFFIDAVIT

If appellant is unable to pay the costs of appeal, or file a bond as required by Rule 749, he shall neverthe-less be entitled to appeal by making strict proof of such inability within five days after the judgment is signed, which shall consist of his affidavit filed with the justice of the peace stating his inability to pay such costs, or any part thereof, or to give security, which may be contested within five days after the filing of such affidavit and notice thereof to the opposite party or his attorney of record by any officer of the court or party to the suit, whereupon it shall be the duty of the justice of the peace in whose court the suit is pending to hear evidence and determine the right of the party to appeal, and he shall enter his finding on the docket as part of the record. Upon the filing of a pauper's affidavit the justice of the peace or clerk of the court shall notice the opposing party of the filing of the affidavit of inability within one working day of its filing by written notification accomplished through first class mail. It will be presumed prima facie that the affidavit speaks the truth, and, unless contested within five days after the filing and notice thereof, the presumption shall be deemed conclusive; but if a contest is filed, the burden shall then be on the appellant to prove his alleged inability by competent evidence other than by the affidavit above referred to. When a pauper's affidavit is timely contested by the appellee, the justice shall hold a hearing and rule on the matter within five days.

If the justice of the peace disapproves the pauper's affidavit, appellant may, within five days thereafter bring the matter before the county judge for a final decision, and, on request, the justice shall certify to the county judge appellant's affidavit, the contest thereof, and all documents, and papers thereto. The county judge shall set a day for hearing, not later than five days, and shall hear the contest de novo. If the pauper's affidavit is approved by the county judge, he shall direct the justice to transmit to the clerk of the county court, the transcript, records and papers of the case.

A pauper's affidavit will be considered approved upon one of the following occurrences: (1) the pauper's affidavit is not contested by the other party; (2) the pauper's affidavit is contested by the other party and upon a hearing the justice determines that the pauper's affidavit is approved; or (3) upon a hearing by the justice disapproving of the pauper's affidavit the appellant appeals to the county judge who then, after a hearing, approves the pauper's affidavit.

No writ of possession may issue pending the hearing by the county judge of the appellant's right to appeal on a pauper's affidavit. If the county judge disapproves the pauper's affidavit, appellant may perfect his appeal by filing an appeal bond in the amount as required by Rule 749 within five days thereafter. If no appeal bond is filed within five days, a writ of possession may issue.

History of TRCP 749a: Amended eff. Sept. 1, 1990 (retroactive), by order of Sept. 4, 1990 (793-94 S.W.2d [Tex.Cases] xxxiii): Amended Sept. 1, 1990 amendment. Amended eff. Sept. 1, 1990, by order of Apr. 24, 1990 (785-86 S.W.2d [Tex.Cases] lxxv): Added second and last sentences to par. 1; added par. 3; county judge must now set hearing within five days rather than ten; changed "writ of restitution" to "writ of possession"; revised proceedings for pauper affidavits. Amended eff. Jan. 1, 1981, by order of June 10, 1980 (599-600 S.W.2d [Tex.Cases] lxxxviii): Time runs from date judgment is signed. Adopted eff. Sept. 1, 1977, by order of May 9, 1977 (553-54 S.W.2d [Tex.Cases] xxxviii). TRCP 749a tracks TRCP 572. Source: New rule.

ANNOTATIONS

Hughes v. Habitat Apts., 860 S.W.2d 872, 872 (Tex. 1993). "[D] orally answered [P's] allegations in a forcible entry and detainer action in the justice court. ... Pursuant to [D's] appeal in the county court, she filed a pauper's affidavit but failed to file a written answer as required by [TRCP] 753. *At 873:* [B]ecause the pauper's affidavit supplied the type of information we found adequate for a pro se answer in [*Smith v. Lippmann*, 826 S.W.2d 137 (Tex.1992)], we hold that [D] was entitled to notice of the hearing on [P's] motion for default judgment."

TRCP 749b. PAUPER'S AFFIDAVIT IN NONPAYMENT OF RENT APPEALS

In a nonpayment of rent forcible detainer case a tenant/appellant who has appealed by filing a pauper's affidavit under these rules shall be entitled to stay in possession of the premises during the pendency of the appeal, by complying with the following procedure:

(1) Within five days of the date that the tenant/appellant files his pauper's affidavit, he must pay into the justice court registry one rental period's rent under the terms of the rental agreement.

(2) During the appeal process as rent becomes due under the rental agreement, the tenant/appellant shall pay the rent into the county court registry within five days of the due date under the terms of the rental agreement.

(3) If the tenant/appellant fails to pay the rent into the court registry within the time limits prescribed by these rules, the appellee may file a notice of default in county court. Upon sworn motion by the appellee and a showing of default to the judge, the court shall issue a writ of restitution.

(4) Landlord/appellee may withdraw any or all rent in the county court registry upon a) sworn motion and hearing, prior to final determination of the case, showing just cause, b) dismissal of the appeal, or c) order of the court upon final hearing.

(5) All hearings and motions under this rule shall be entitled to precedence in the county court.

History of TRCP 749b: Adopted eff. Sept. 1, 1977, by order of May 9, 1977 (553-54 S.W.2d [Tex.Cases] xxxix). Source: New rule.

ANNOTATIONS

Frank v. Brittany Square Apts., No. 14-09-00423-CV (Tex.App.—Houston [14th Dist.] 2010, no pet.) (memo op.; 4-20-10). "The county court's determination that a tenant has not complied with Rule 749b is neither a final judgment nor an appealable interlocutory order. By its terms, Rule 749b addresses only entitlement to possess the premises 'during the pendency of the appeal' in the county court; it is not dispositive of that appeal itself. Consequently, a county court's order granting the landlord possession of the premises pursuant to Rule 749b is not a final order."

Ibarra v. Housing Auth., 791 S.W.2d 224, 226 (Tex. App.—Corpus Christi 1990, writ denied). "[R]ule 749b(3) does not provide for a hearing prior to a county court issuing a writ of restitution. The Due Process Clause requires only a single hearing before an impartial decision maker on the question of restitution. [D] had such a hearing.... [¶] [However,] before [P] could withdraw the ... rent from the court's registry, a hearing was required...." *See also Kennedy v. Highland Hills Apts.*, 905 S.W.2d 325, 327 (Tex.App.—Dallas 1995, no writ) (Rule 749b(3) does not expressly authorize county court to enter default judgment).

TRCP 749c. APPEAL PERFECTED

When an appeal bond has been timely filed in conformity with Rule 749 or a pauper's affidavit approved in conformity with Rule 749a, the appeal shall be perfected.

History of TRCP 749c: Amended eff. Sept. 1, 1990, by order of Apr. 24, 1990 (785-86 S.W.2d [Tex.Cases] lxxvi): Rewritten to dispense with the appellate requirement of payment of rent into the court registry. Amended eff. Aug. 15, 1982, by order of Apr. 15, 1982 (629-30 S.W.2d [Tex.Cases] xliii): Amended so that one month's rent need not be paid when an appeal bond is made. Adopted eff. Sept. 1, 1977, by order of May 9, 1977 (553-54 S.W.2d [Tex.Cases] xl). Source: New rule.

ANNOTATIONS

Walker v. Blue Water Garden Apts., 776 S.W.2d 578, 581-82 (Tex.1989). "The [TRCPs] prescribe no deadline for making the deposit of one month's rent re-

★

quired by Rule 749c. ... We choose not to imply a specific deadline in these rules where none exists expressly. Rather, we conclude that [D's] reasonably prompt efforts [50 days after judgment] to meet the requirements of Rule 749c were sufficient to perfect her appeal."

TRCP 750. FORM OF APPEAL BOND

The appeal bond authorized in the preceding article may be substantially as follows:

"The State of Texas,

"County of _____

"Whereas, upon a writ of forcible entry (or forcible detainer) in favor of A.B., and against C.D., tried before _____, a justice of the peace of _____ county, a judgment was rendered in favor of the said A.B. on the ___ day of _____, A.D. _____, and against the said C.D., from which the said C.D. has appealed to the county court; now, therefore, the said C.D. and _____ his sureties, covenant that he will prosecute his said appeal with effect and pay all costs and damages which may be adjudged against him, provided the sureties shall not be liable in an amount greater than $ _____, said amount being the amount of the bond herein.

"Given under our hands this _____ day of _____, A.D. _____."

History of TRCP 750: Amended eff. Jan. 1, 1976, by order of July 22, 1975 (525-26 S.W.2d [Tex.Cases] lxi): The form amended to state the limits of liability of the sureties. Adopted eff. Sept. 1, 1941, by order of Oct. 29, 1940 (3 Tex.B.J. 641 [1940]). Source: TRCS art. 3988 (repealed).

ANNOTATIONS

Pharis v. Culver, 677 S.W.2d 168, 170 (Tex.App.—Houston 1984, no writ). "While the form [of the forcible entry and detainer appeal bond in TRCP 750] is not mandatory, the bond must substantially comply with Rule 750."

Family Inv. v. Paley, 356 S.W.2d 353, 355 (Tex. App.—Houston 1962, writ dism'd). The trial court should have permitted amendment of the appeal bond because the defective bond was sufficient to confer jurisdiction over the appeal on the county court.

TRCP 751. TRANSCRIPT

When an appeal has been perfected, the justice shall stay all further proceedings on the judgment, and immediately make out a transcript of all the entries made on his docket of the proceedings had in the case; and he shall immediately file the same, together with the original papers and any money in the court registry, including sums tendered pursuant to Rule 749b(1), with the clerk of the county court of the county in which the trial was had, or other court having jurisdiction of such appeal. The clerk shall docket the cause, and the trial shall be de novo.

The clerk shall immediately notify both appellant and the adverse party of the date of receipt of the transcript and the docket number of the cause. Such notice shall advise the defendant of the necessity for filing a written answer in the county court when the defendant has pleaded orally in the justice court.

The trial, as well as all hearings and motions, shall be entitled to precedence in the county court.

History of TRCP 751: Amended eff. Sept. 1, 1990, by order of Apr. 24, 1990 (785-86 S.W.2d [Tex.Cases] lxxvi): Added phrase "including sums tendered pursuant to TRCP 749b(1)" after "any money in the court registry" in par. 1 to provide for transfer of subject funds. Amended eff. Jan. 1, 1988, by order of July 15, 1987 (733-34 S.W.2d [Tex.Cases] lxxxi): Provides due process to pro se defendants by advising them of the necessity of filing a written answer in the county court if they did not file one in the justice court. Amended eff. Sept. 1, 1977, by order of May 9, 1977 (553-54 S.W.2d [Tex.Cases] xl): Amended to require immediate filing of papers and money with clerk of county court; provided for precedence of trial, hearings, and motions. Adopted eff. Sept. 1, 1941, by order of Oct. 29, 1940 (3 Tex.B.J. 641 [1940]). Source: TRCS art. 3989 (repealed).

ANNOTATIONS

Polk v. Braddock, 864 S.W.2d 78, 80 (Tex.App.—Dallas 1992, no writ). TRCP 751 "makes it clear that the proper party for a mandamus proceeding concerning the failure to file appeal papers with the county court in an appeal from the justice court under rule 751 is the justice of the peace."

TRCP 752. DAMAGES

On the trial of the cause in the county court the appellant or appellee shall be permitted to plead, prove and recover his damages, if any, suffered for withholding or defending possession of the premises during the pendency of the appeal.

Damages may include but are not limited to loss of rentals during the pendency of the appeal and reasonable attorney fees in the justice and county courts provided, as to attorney fees, that the requirements of Section 24.006 of the Texas Property Code have been met. Only the party prevailing in the county court shall be entitled to recover damages against the adverse party. He shall also be entitled to recover court costs. He shall be entitled to recover against the sureties on the appeal bond in cases where the adverse party has executed such bond.

History of TRCP 752: Amended eff. Jan. 1, 1988, by order of July 15, 1987 (733-34 S.W.2d [Tex.Cases] lxxxii). Amended eff. Jan. 1, 1976, by order of July 22, 1975 (525-26 S.W.2d [Tex.Cases] lxi): Costs and damages are stated by this

TRCP 749c

rule rather than by other rules. Amended eff. Dec. 31, 1943, by order of June 16, 1943 (6 Tex.B.J. 445 [1943]): To extend, in a proper case, to appellant as well as to appellee; other relevant changes. Adopted eff. Sept. 1, 1941, by order of Oct. 29, 1940 (3 Tex.B.J. 641 [1940]). Source: TRCS art. 3990 (repealed).

ANNOTATIONS

Krull v. Somoza, 879 S.W.2d 320, 322 (Tex.App.—Houston [14th Dist.] 1994, writ denied). "Damage claims *related to* maintaining or obtaining possession of the premises may be joined with the detainer action and litigated in the county court. However, damages for other causes of action … are *not* recoverable in a forcible entry and detainer action."

Mastermark Homebuilders, Inc. v. Offenburger Constr., Inc., 857 S.W.2d 765, 768 (Tex.App.—Houston [14th Dist.] 1993, no writ). TRCP 752 "does not require that damages in the form of attorney's fees be plead in the justice court. The rule merely states that the requirements of [Prop. Code] §24.006 … be satisfied."

TRCP 753. JUDGMENT BY DEFAULT

Said cause shall be subject to trial at any time after the expiration of eight full days after the date the transcript is filed in the county court. If the defendant has filed a written answer in the justice court, the same shall be taken to constitute his appearance and answer in the county court, and such answer may be amended as in other cases. If the defendant made no answer in writing in the justice court, and if he fails to file a written answer within eight full days after the transcript is filed in the county court, the allegations of the complaint may be taken as admitted and judgment by default may be entered accordingly.

History of TRCP 753: Amended eff. Jan. 1, 1988, by order of July 15, 1987 (733-34 S.W.2d [Tex.Cases] lxxxii). Amended eff. Dec. 31, 1947, by order of Aug. 18, 1947 (10 Tex.B.J. 401 [1947]). Amended eff. Dec. 31, 1943, by order of June 16, 1943 (6 Tex.B.J. 445 [1943]). Adopted eff. Sept. 1, 1941, by order of Oct. 29, 1940 (3 Tex.B.J. 641 [1940]). Source: TRCS art. 3991 (repealed).

ANNOTATIONS

Okpala v. Coleman, 964 S.W.2d 698, 700 (Tex. App.—Houston [14th Dist.] 1998, no pet.). "An answer … must contain sufficient information to place in issue the claims made the basis of the suit. [¶] [W]e hold [D], while not filing a formal answer pursuant to rule 753, filed documents forming an answer sufficient to prevent the rendition of a default judgment."

TRCP 754. BLANK

TRCP 755. WRIT OF POSSESSION

The writ of possession, or execution, or both, shall be issued by the clerk of the county court according to the judgment rendered, and the same shall be executed by the sheriff or constable, as in other cases; and such writ of possession shall not be suspended or superseded in any case by appeal from such final judgment in the county court, unless the premises in question are being used as the principal residence of a party.

History of TRCP 755: Amended eff. Jan. 1, 1988, by order of July 15, 1987 (733-34 S.W.2d [Tex.Cases] lxxxiii). Adopted eff. Sept. 1, 1941, by order of Oct. 29, 1940 (3 Tex.B.J. 642 [1940]). Source: TRCS art. 3993 (repealed).

SECTION 4. PARTITION OF REAL ESTATE

TRCP 756. PETITION

The plaintiff's petition shall state:

(a) The names and residence, if known, of each of the other joint owners, or joint claimants, of such property.

(b) The share or interest which the plaintiff and the other joint owners, or joint claimants, of same own or claim so far as known to the plaintiff.

(c) The land sought to be partitioned shall be so described as that the same may be distinguished from any other and the estimated value thereof stated.

History of TRCP 756: Adopted eff. Sept. 1, 1941, by order of Oct. 29, 1940 (3 Tex.B.J. 642 [1940]). Source: TRCS art. 6083 (repealed in part by TRCP).
See Prop. Code §23.001.

ANNOTATIONS

Yoast v. Yoast, 649 S.W.2d 289, 292 (Tex.1983). "The court of appeals mischaracterized this case as a partition suit. [P's suit was for] trespass to try title. … Partition issues may be resolved in a trespass to try title suit once the controversy as to title or right to possession is settled. That, however, does not convert the cause of action to a partition suit. [¶] A partition suit is based on the theory of common title, rather than disputed ownership."

TRCP 757. CITATION & SERVICE

Upon the filing of a petition for partition, the clerk shall issue citation for each of the joint owners, or joint claimants, named therein, as in other cases, and such citations shall be served in the manner and for the time provided for the service of citations in other cases.

History of TRCP 757: Adopted eff. Sept. 1, 1941, by order of Oct. 29, 1940 (3 Tex.B.J. 642 [1940]). Source: TRCS art. 6084 (repealed).

ANNOTATIONS

Carper v. Halamicek, 610 S.W.2d 556, 557 (Tex. App.—Tyler 1980, writ ref'd n.r.e.). TRCP 757 "and past cases indicate that the joinder of all owners is mandatory and that no valid, binding decree of partition can be made in their absence."

TRCP 758. WHERE DEFENDANT IS UNKNOWN OR RESIDENCE IS UNKNOWN

If the plaintiff, his agent or attorney, at the commencement of any suit, or during the progress thereof, for the partition of land, shall make affidavit that an undivided portion of the land described in plaintiff's petition in said suit is owned by some person unknown to affiant, or that the place of residence of any known party owning an interest in land sought to be partitioned is unknown to affiant, the Clerk of the Court shall issue citation for publication, conforming to the requirements of Rules 114 and 115, and served in accordance with the directions of Rule 116. In case of unknown residence or party, the affidavit shall include a statement that after due diligence plaintiff and the affiant have been unable to ascertain the name or locate the residence of such party, as the case may be, and in such case it shall be the duty of the court trying the action to inquire into the sufficiency of the diligence so stated before granting any judgment.

History of TRCP 758: Amended eff. Apr. 1, 1985, by order of Dec. 19, 1984 (683-84 S.W.2d [Tex.Cases] xxxix): Deleted reference to deleted proviso in TRCP 109. Amended eff. Jan. 1, 1955, by order of July 20, 1954 (17 Tex.B.J. 572 [1954]): Inserted words "or that the place of residence of any known party owning an interest in the land sought to be partitioned is unknown to affiant" in first sentence, and added last sentence. Adopted eff. Sept. 1, 1941, by order of Oct. 29, 1940 (3 Tex.B.J. 642 [1940]). Source: TRCS art. 6085 (repealed), with changes: Eliminated specific declaration of requisites of citation by publication and service, and adopted (by reference) the general rules.

TRCP 759. JUDGMENT WHERE DEFENDANT CITED BY PUBLICATION

When the defendant has been duly cited by publication in accordance with the preceding rule, and no appearance is entered within the time prescribed for pleadings, the court shall appoint an attorney to defend in behalf of such owner or owners, and proceed as in other causes where service is made by publication. It shall be the special duty of the court in all cases to see that its decree protects the rights of the unknown parties thereto. The judge of the court shall fix the fee of the attorney so appointed, which shall be entered and collected as costs against said unknown owner or owners.

History of TRCP 759: Adopted eff. Sept. 1, 1941, by order of Oct. 29, 1940 (3 Tex.B.J. 642 [1940]). Caveat: [Article 6085] was amended in 1939, eff. date after the enactment of the Rule Making Statute. See *Garrett v. Mercantile Nat'l Bank*, 168 S.W.2d 636 (Tex.1943). Source: TRCS art. 6085, last two sentences (repealed).

TRCP 760. COURT SHALL DETERMINE, WHAT

Upon the hearing of the cause, the court shall determine the share or interest of each of the joint owners or claimants in the real estate sought to be divided, and all questions of law or equity affecting the title to such land which may arise.

History of TRCP 760: Adopted eff. Sept. 1, 1941, by order of Oct. 29, 1940 (3 Tex.B.J. 643 [1940]). Source: TRCS art. 6086 (repealed).

ANNOTATIONS

Johnson v. Johnson-McHenry, 978 S.W.2d 142, 144 (Tex.App.—Austin 1998, no pet.). "[I]n a partition suit, the trial court determines whether the partition will be by sale or in kind, the share or interest of the joint owners or claimants, and all questions of law or equity affecting title. The court then allocates to the parties their rightful shares or tracts. A trial court may also exercise equitable powers in a partition suit."

TRCP 761. APPOINTMENT OF COMMISSIONERS

The court shall determine before entering the decree of partition whether the property, or any part thereof, is susceptible of partition; and, if the court determines that the whole, or any part of such property is susceptible of partition, then the court for that part of such property held to be susceptible of partition shall enter a decree directing the partition of such real estate, describing the same, to be made in accordance with the respective shares or interests of each of such parties entitled thereto, specify in such decree the share or interest of each party, and shall appoint three or more competent and disinterested persons as commissioners to make such partition in accordance with such decree and the law, a majority of which commissioners may act.

History of TRCP 761: Adopted eff. Sept. 1, 1941, by order of Oct. 29, 1940 (3 Tex.B.J. 643 [1940]). Source: TRCS art. 6087 (repealed).

ANNOTATIONS

Benson v. Fox, 589 S.W.2d 823, 826 (Tex.App.—Tyler 1979, no writ). "Rule 761 employs the word 'partition' in a restricted sense as synonymous with the phrase 'partition in kind.'"

TRCP 762. WRIT OF PARTITION

The clerk shall issue a writ of partition, directed to the sheriff or any constable of the county, commanding such sheriff or constable to notify each of the commissioners of their appointment as such, and shall accompany such writ with a certified copy of the decree of the court directing the partition.

✦

History of TRCP 762: Adopted eff. Sept. 1, 1941, by order of Oct. 29, 1940 (3 Tex.B.J. 643 [1940]). Source: TRCS art. 6088 (repealed).

TRCP 763. SERVICE OF WRIT OF PARTITION

The writ of partition shall be served by reading the same to each of the persons named therein as commissioners, and by delivering to any one of them the accompanying certified copy of the decree of the court.

History of TRCP 763: Adopted eff. Sept. 1, 1941, by order of Oct. 29, 1940 (3 Tex.B.J. 643 [1940]). Source: TRCS art. 6089 (repealed).

TRCP 764. MAY APPOINT SURVEYOR

The court may, should it be deemed necessary, appoint a surveyor to assist the commissioners in making the partition, in which case the writ of partition shall name such surveyor, and shall be served upon him by reading the same to him.

History of TRCP 764: Adopted eff. Sept. 1, 1941, by order of Oct. 29, 1940 (3 Tex.B.J. 643 [1940]). Source: TRCS art. 6090 (repealed).

TRCP 765. RETURN OF WRIT

A writ of partition, unless otherwise directed by the court, shall be made returnable twenty days from date of service on the commissioner last served; and the officer serving it shall endorse thereon the time and manner of such service.

History of TRCP 765: Adopted eff. Sept. 1, 1941, by order of Oct. 29, 1940 (3 Tex.B.J. 643 [1940]). Source: TRCS art. 6091 (repealed).

TRCP 766. SHALL PROCEED TO PARTITION

The commissioners, or a majority of them, shall proceed to partition the real estate described in the decree of the court, in accordance with the directions contained in such decree and with the provisions of law and these rules.

History of TRCP 766: Adopted eff. Sept. 1, 1941, by order of Oct. 29, 1940 (3 Tex.B.J. 643 [1940]). Source: TRCS art. 6092 (repealed).

ANNOTATIONS

Mansfield v. Davenport, 362 S.W.2d 912, 913 (Tex. App.—San Antonio 1962, writ ref'd n.r.e.). "By its first order or judgment in a partition suit, a court may properly give such directions as may be necessary and appropriate."

TRCP 767. MAY CAUSE SURVEY

If the commissioners deem it necessary, they may cause to be surveyed the real estate to be partitioned into several tracts or parcels.

History of TRCP 767: Adopted eff. Sept. 1, 1941, by order of Oct. 29, 1940 (3 Tex.B.J. 643 [1940]). Source: TRCS art. 6093 (repealed).

TRCP 768. SHALL DIVIDE REAL ESTATE

The commissioners shall divide the real estate to be partitioned into as many shares as there are persons entitled thereto, as determined by the court, each share to contain one or more tracts or parcels, as the commissioners may think proper, having due regard in the division to the situation, quantity and advantages of each share, so that the shares may be equal in value, as nearly as may be, in proportion to the respective interests of the parties entitled. The commissioners shall then proceed by lot to set apart to each of the parties entitled one of said shares, as determined by the decrees of the court.

History of TRCP 768: Adopted eff. Sept. 1, 1941, by order of Oct. 29, 1940 (3 Tex.B.J. 643 [1940]). Source: TRCS art. 6094 (repealed).

ANNOTATIONS

Grimes v. Hall, 211 S.W.2d 956, 958 (Tex.App.— Eastland 1948, no writ). "Where the interests of the parties in the realty to be partitioned are unequal, selection of owners of shares by lot is not required."

TRCP 769. REPORT OF COMMISSIONERS

When the commissioners have completed the partition, they shall report the same in writing and under oath to the court, which report shall show:

(a) The property divided, describing the same.

(b) The several tracts or parcels into which the same was divided by them, describing each particularly.

(c) The number of shares and the land which constitutes each share, and the estimated value of each share.

(d) The allotment of each share.

(e) The report shall be accompanied by such field notes and maps as may be necessary to make the same intelligible.

The clerk shall immediately mail written notice of the filing of the report to all parties.

History of TRCP 769: Amended eff. Sept. 1, 1990, by order of Apr. 24, 1990 (785-86 S.W.2d [Tex.Cases] lxxvii): Added last paragraph to require clerk to notify parties of filing of report. Adopted eff. Sept. 1, 1941, by order of Oct. 29, 1940 (3 Tex.B.J. 644 [1940]). Source: TRCS art. 6095 (repealed).

ANNOTATIONS

Thomas v. McNair, 882 S.W.2d 870, 876 (Tex. App.—Corpus Christi 1994, no writ). The second decree in a partition suit "'approves the report of the commissioners and allocates to the respective parties their separate shares or tracts.'"

⭐

TRCP 770. PROPERTY INCAPABLE OF DIVISION

Should the court be of the opinion that a fair and equitable division of the real estate, or any part thereof, cannot be made, it shall order a sale of so much as is incapable of partition, which sale shall be for cash, or upon such other terms as the court may direct, and shall be made as under execution or by private or public sale through a receiver, if the court so order, and the proceeds thereof shall be returned into court and be partitioned among the persons entitled thereto, according to their respective interests.

History of TRCP 770: Amended eff. Mar. 1, 1950, by order of Oct. 12, 1949 (12 Tex.B.J. 538 [1949]). Adopted eff. Sept. 1, 1941, by order of Oct. 29, 1940 (3 Tex.B.J. 644 [1940]). Source: TRCS art. 6096 (repealed).

ANNOTATIONS

Cecola v. Ruley, 12 S.W.3d 848, 853 (Tex.App.—Texarkana 2000, no pet.). "Whether a piece of land can fairly be partitioned in kind is a question of fact for the court or jury to decide. The law favors partition in kind over partition by sale. Therefore, at trial the burden of proof falls on the party opposing partitioning in kind and seeking a partition by sale."

TRCP 771. OBJECTIONS TO REPORT

Either party to the suit may file objections to any report of the commissioners in partition within thirty days of the date the report is filed, and in such case a trial of the issues thereon shall be had as in other cases. If the report be found to be erroneous in any material respect, or unequal and unjust, the same shall be rejected, and other commissioners shall be appointed by the Court, and the same proceedings had as in the first instance.

History of TRCP 771: Amended eff. Sept. 1, 1990, by order of Apr. 24, 1990 (785-86 S.W.2d [Tex.Cases] lxxvii) (error showing Sup.Ct. order deleting phrase rather than adding it): Added phrase "within thirty days of the date the report is filed" to set a time within which objections to commissioners' report must be filed. Adopted eff. Sept. 1, 1941, by order of Oct. 29, 1940 (3 Tex.B.J. 644 [1940]). Source: TRCS art. 6097 (repealed).

ANNOTATIONS

Sand Point Ranch, Ltd. v. Smith, 363 S.W.3d 268, 272 (Tex.App.—Corpus Christi 2012, no pet.). "[A]ny complaint not made by a party in its rule 771 objection is waived on appeal."

Ellis v. First City Nat'l Bank, 864 S.W.2d 555, 557 (Tex.App.—Tyler 1993, no writ). "If the trial court finds the report of the commissioners is [erroneous or unequal,] it must reject the report and appoint other commissioners. The party objecting to the commissioners'

report had the burden of proving that it is materially erroneous or that it unequally and unjustly partitions the property."

SECTION 5. PARTITION OF PERSONAL PROPERTY

TRCP 772. PROCEDURE

An action seeking partition of personal property as authorized by Section 23.001, Texas Property Code, shall be commenced in the same manner as other civil suits, and the several owners or claimants of such property shall be cited as in other cases.

History of TRCP 772: Amended eff. Jan. 1, 1988, by order of July 15, 1987 (733-34 S.W.2d [Tex.Cases] lxxxiii). Adopted eff. Sept. 1, 1941, by order of Oct. 29, 1940 (3 Tex.B.J. 644 [1940]). Source: TRCS art. 6102, last clause (repealed in part by TRCP).

TRCP 773. VALUE ASCERTAINED

The separate value of each article of such personal property, and the allotment in kind to which each owner is entitled, shall be ascertained by the court, with or without a jury.

History of TRCP 773: Adopted eff. Sept. 1, 1941, by order of Oct. 29, 1940 (3 Tex.B.J. 644 [1940]). Source: TRCS art. 6103 (repealed).

ANNOTATIONS

Price v. Price, 394 S.W.2d 855, 858 (Tex.App.—Tyler 1965, writ ref'd n.r.e.). "The fact that the property has now been transformed into personal property in the form of money would not alter the application rule, but would only make the property more susceptible to a partition in kind."

TRCP 774. DECREE OF COURT EXECUTED

When partition in kind of personal property is ordered by the judgment of the court, a writ shall be issued in accordance with such judgment, commanding the sheriff or constable of the county where the property may be to put the parties forthwith in possession of the property allotted to each respectively.

History of TRCP 774: Adopted eff. Sept. 1, 1941, by order of Oct. 29, 1940 (3 Tex.B.J. 644 [1940]). Source: TRCS art. 6104 (repealed).

TRCP 775. PROPERTY SOLD

When personal property will not admit of a fair and equitable partition, the court shall ascertain the proportion to which each owner thereof is entitled, and order the property to be sold, and execution shall be issued to the sheriff or any constable of the county where the property may be describing such property and commanding such officer to sell the same as in other cases of execution, and pay over the proceeds of sale to the

---

parties entitled thereto, in the proportion ascertained by the judgment of the court.

History of TRCP 775: Adopted eff. Sept. 1, 1941, by order of Oct. 29, 1940 (3 Tex.B.J. 644 [1940]). Source: TRCS art. 6105 (repealed).

SECTION 6. PARTITION: MISCELLANEOUS PROVISIONS

TRCP 776. CONSTRUCTION

No provision of the statutes or rules relating to partition shall affect the mode of proceeding prescribed by law for the partition of estates of decedents among the heirs and legatees, nor preclude partition in any other manner authorized by the rules of equity, which rules shall govern in proceedings for partition in all respects not provided for by law or these rules.

History of TRCP 776: Adopted eff. Sept. 1, 1941, by order of Oct. 29, 1940 (3 Tex.B.J. 645 [1940]). Source: TRCS art. 6106 (repealed).

TRCP 777. PLEADING & PRACTICE

The same rules of pleading, practice and evidence which govern in other civil actions shall govern in suits for partition, when not in conflict with any provisions of the law or these rules relating to partition.

History of TRCP 777: Adopted eff. Sept. 1, 1941, by order of Oct. 29, 1940 (3 Tex.B.J. 645 [1940]). Source: TRCS art. 6107 (repealed).

ANNOTATIONS

Rayson v. Johns, 524 S.W.2d 380, 382 (Tex.App.—Texarkana 1975, writ ref'd n.r.e.). "[I]n whatever posture the question has arisen, the courts have treated disputed issues of fact in partition proceedings as being for the jury when one has been properly demanded. [¶] The law does not favor compelling an owner to sell his property against his will, but prefers a division in kind when such can be fairly and equitably made."

TRCP 778. COSTS

The court shall adjudge the costs in a partition suit to be paid by each party to whom a share has been allotted in proportion to the value of such share.

History of TRCP 778: Adopted eff. Sept. 1, 1941, by order of Oct. 29, 1940 (3 Tex.B.J. 645 [1940]). Source: TRCS art. 6109 (repealed).

SECTION 7. QUO WARRANTO

TRCP 779. JOINDER OF PARTIES

When it appears to the court or judge that the several rights of diverse parties to the same office or franchise may properly be determined on one information, the court or judge may give leave to join all such persons in the same information in order to try their respective rights to such office or franchise.

History of TRCP 779: Adopted eff. Sept. 1, 1941, by order of Oct. 29, 1940 (3 Tex.B.J. 645 [1940]). Source: TRCS art. 6254 (repealed).

ANNOTATIONS

Newsom v. State, 922 S.W.2d 274, 277 (Tex.App.—Austin 1996, writ denied). "[T]he State uses quo warranto actions to challenge the authority to engage in certain practices specifically enumerated by statute. A quo warranto proceeding may be instituted by the attorney general or by a district or county attorney. The State is the real plaintiff and controls the litigation, even though in some instances the actions may be at the behest of private parties."

Beach City v. State, 473 S.W.2d 656, 659 (Tex.App.—Houston [14th Dist.] 1971, writ dism'd). "[Q]uo warranto proceedings are governed by the same … rules of joinder of causes of action [as] apply … in other civil cases."

TRCP 780. CITATION TO ISSUE

When such information is filed, the clerk shall issue citation as in civil actions, commanding the defendant to appear and answer the relator in an information in the nature of a quo warranto.

History of TRCP 780: Adopted eff. Sept. 1, 1941, by order of Oct. 29, 1940 (3 Tex.B.J. 645 [1940]). Source: TRCS art. 6255 (repealed).

TRCP 781. PROCEEDINGS AS IN CIVIL CASES

Every person or corporation who shall be cited as hereinbefore provided shall be entitled to all the rights in the trial and investigation of the matters alleged against him, as in cases of trial in civil cases in this State. Either party may prosecute an appeal or writ of error from any judgment rendered, as in other civil cases, subject, however, to the provisions of Rule 42,[1] Texas Rules of Appellate Procedure, and the appellate court shall give preference to such case, and hear and determine the same as early as practicable.

1. **Editor's note:** Now TRAP 28.
History of TRCP 781: Amended eff. Sept. 1, 1990, by order of Apr. 24, 1990 (785-86 S.W.2d [Tex.Cases] lxxvii): Changed TRAP 384 reference to TRAP 42. Amended eff. Dec. 31, 1947, by order of Aug. 18, 1947 (10 Tex.B.J. 402 [1947]). Adopted eff. Sept. 1, 1941, by order of Oct. 29, 1940 (3 Tex.B.J. 645 [1940]). Source: TRCS art. 6256 (repealed).

ANNOTATIONS

State v. Wagner, 203 S.W.2d 795, 798 (Tex.App.—San Antonio 1947, writ ref'd). "[E]ither party in a quo warranto proceeding is entitled to prosecute an appeal as in other civil cases, provided the transcript is filed in the Court of … Appeals within 20 days after perfecting the appeal, and that the appellate court shall give preference to such cases and hear and determine them as early as practicable."

✦

TRCP 782. REMEDY CUMULATIVE

The remedy and mode of procedure hereby pre-scribed shall be construed to be cumulative of any now existing.

History of TRCP 782: Adopted eff. Sept. 1, 1941, by order of Oct. 29, 1940 (3 Tex.B.J. 645 [1940]). Source: TRCS art. 6258 (repealed).

SECTION 8. TRESPASS TO TRY TITLE

TRCP 783. REQUISITES OF PETITION

The petition shall state:

(a) The real names of the plaintiff and defendant and their residences, if known.

(b) A description of the premises by metes and bounds, or with sufficient certainty to identify the same, so that from such description possession thereof may be delivered, and state the county or counties in which the same are situated.

(c) The interest which the plaintiff claims in the premises, whether it be a fee simple or other estate; and, if he claims an undivided interest, the petition shall state the same and the amount thereof.

(d) That the plaintiff was in possession of the premises or entitled to such possession.

(e) That the defendant afterward unlawfully entered upon and dispossessed him of such premises, stating the date, and withholds from him the posses-sion thereof.

(f) If rents and profits or damages are claimed, such facts as show the plaintiff to be entitled thereto and the amount thereof.

(g) It shall conclude with a prayer for the relief sought.

History of TRCP 783: Adopted eff. Sept. 1, 1941, by order of Oct. 29, 1940 (3 Tex.B.J. 645 [1940]). Source: TRCS art. 7366 (repealed).

ANNOTATIONS

Yoast v. Yoast, 649 S.W.2d 289, 292 (Tex.1983). "A trespass to try title action is a procedure by which rival claims to title or right of possession may be adjudi-cated."

Smith v. Brooks, 825 S.W.2d 208, 210 (Tex.App.—Texarkana 1992, no writ). "In order to claim title by limitation based upon adverse possession, a party must plead it specifically."

TRCP 784. THE POSSESSOR SHALL BE DEFENDANT

The defendant in the action shall be the person in possession if the premises are occupied, or some per-son claiming title thereto in case they are unoccupied.

History of TRCP 784: Adopted eff. Sept. 1, 1941, by order of Oct. 29, 1940 (3 Tex.B.J. 646 [1940]). Source: TRCS art. 7370 (repealed).

TRCP 785. MAY JOIN AS DEFENDANTS, WHEN

The plaintiff may join as a defendant with the per-son in possession, any other person who, as landlord, remainderman, reversioner or otherwise, may claim title to the premises, or any part thereof, adversely to the plaintiff.

History of TRCP 785: Adopted eff. Sept. 1, 1941, by order of Oct. 29, 1940 (3 Tex.B.J. 646 [1940]). Source: TRCS art. 7371 (repealed).

TRCP 786. WARRANTOR, ETC., MAY BE MADE A PARTY

When a party is sued for lands, the real owner or warrantor may make himself, or may be made, a party defendant in the suit, and shall be entitled to make such defense as if he had been the original defendant in the action.

History of TRCP 786: Adopted eff. Sept. 1, 1941, by order of Oct. 29, 1940 (3 Tex.B.J. 646 [1940]). Source: TRCS art. 7368 (repealed).

ANNOTATIONS

Williams v. Ballard, 722 S.W.2d 9, 11 (Tex.App.—Dallas 1986, no writ). TRCP 786 allows the mortgagor to intervene as a matter of right.

TRCP 787. LANDLORD MAY BECOME DEFENDANT

When such action shall be commenced against a ten-ant in possession, the landlord may enter himself as the defendant, or he may be made a party on motion of such tenant; and he shall be entitled to make the same de-fense as if the suit had been originally commenced against him.

History of TRCP 787: Adopted eff. Sept. 1, 1941, by order of Oct. 29, 1940 (3 Tex.B.J. 646 [1940]). Source: TRCS art. 7369 (repealed).

TRCP 788. MAY FILE PLEA OF "NOT GUILTY" ONLY

The defendant in such action may file only the plea of "not guilty," which shall state in substance that he is not guilty of the injury complained of in the petition filed by the plaintiff against him, except that if he claims an allowance for improvements, he shall state the facts entitling him to the same.

History of TRCP 788: Adopted eff. Sept. 1, 1941, by order of Oct. 29, 1940 (3 Tex.B.J. 646 [1940]). Source: TRCS art. 7372 (repealed).

ANNOTATIONS

Cox v. Olivard, 482 S.W.2d 682, 685 (Tex.App.—Dallas 1972, writ ref'd n.r.e.). "[A] defendant in a tres-pass to try title action is not required to file a plea of

TRCP 782

'not guilty' but … a plea of general denial has the effect of putting the plaintiff upon proof of his right to recover the land in controversy."

TRCP 789. PROOF UNDER SUCH PLEA

Under such plea of "not guilty" the defendant may give in evidence any lawful defense to the action except the defense of limitations, which shall be specially pleaded.

History of TRCP 789: Adopted eff. Sept. 1, 1941, by order of Oct. 29, 1940 (3 Tex.B.J. 646 [1940]). Source: TRCS art. 7373 (repealed).

ANNOTATIONS

Walsh v. Austin, 590 S.W.2d 612, 616 (Tex.App.—Houston [1st Dist.] 1979, writ dism'd). "Where … the plaintiff has established a prima facie case, whether it be at a summary judgment hearing or upon a full trial, the defendant then has the burden of introducing some defensive evidence to raise an issue of material fact in order to prevent the rendition of a summary judgment or an instructed verdict."

TRCP 790. ANSWER TAKEN AS ADMITTING POSSESSION

Such plea or any other answer to the merits shall be an admission by the defendant, for the purpose of that action, that he was in possession of the premises sued for, or that he claimed title thereto at the time of commencing the action, unless he states distinctly in his answer the extent of his possession or claim, in which case it shall be an admission to such extent only.

History of TRCP 790: Adopted eff. Sept. 1, 1941, by order of Oct. 29, 1940 (3 Tex.B.J. 646 [1940]). Source: TRCS art. 7374 (repealed).

ANNOTATIONS

Brohlin v. McMinn, 341 S.W.2d 420, 422 (Tex. 1960). "In an action in trespass to try title, the answer of the defendant to the merits of the case by a plea of not guilty relieves the plaintiffs of the necessity of proving a trespass, since the plea constitutes an admission by the defendant for the purpose of the action that he was in possession of or claimed title to the premises sued for by the plaintiffs."

TRCP 791. MAY DEMAND ABSTRACT OF TITLE

After answer filed, either party may, by notice in writing, duly served on the opposite party or his attorney of record, not less than ten days before the trial of the cause, demand an abstract in writing of the claim or title to the premises in question upon which he relies.

History of TRCP 791: Adopted eff. Sept. 1, 1941, by order of Oct. 29, 1940 (3 Tex.B.J. 646 [1940]). Source: TRCS art. 7376 (repealed).

ANNOTATIONS

Ramsey v. Jones Enters., 810 S.W.2d 902, 904 (Tex.App.—Beaumont 1991, writ denied). "[T]he trial court erred in allowing [P] to prove up title … by nothing more than the oral expert testimony of an attorney. [¶] [TRCP] 791 provides for the demanding of an abstract of title by either party…. *At 905:* [I]n trespass to try title actions where documents pertaining to title exist, … testimony of an expert witness standing alone, constitutes no evidence of titles."

TRCP 792. TIME TO FILE ABSTRACT

Such abstract of title shall be filed with the papers of the cause that within thirty days after the service of the notice, or within such further time that the court on good cause shown may grant; and in default thereof, the court may, after notice and hearing prior to the beginning of trial, order that no written instruments which are evidence of the claim or title of such opposite party be given on trial.

History of TRCP 792: Amended eff. Sept. 1, 1990, by order of Apr. 24, 1990 (785-86 S.W.2d [Tex.Cases] lxxvii): Changed "order that no evidence of the claim" to "order that no written instruments which are evidence of the claim." Amended eff. Jan. 1, 1988, by order of July 15, 1987 (733-34 S.W.2d [Tex.Cases] lxxxiii). Adopted eff. Sept. 1, 1941, by order of Oct. 29, 1940 (3 Tex.B.J. 646 [1940]). Source: TRCS art. 7377 (repealed).

ANNOTATIONS

Hunt v. Heaton, 643 S.W.2d 677, 679 (Tex.1982). "[P] sought to prove his title by a chain of instruments beginning with a patent from the State…. Because of the failure to file an abstract of the chain of title, the trial court properly excluded any offer of proof by [P] relating to his claim or title. [P] failed to prove his superior title and therefore, the correct judgment is that he take nothing."

Corder v. Foster, 505 S.W.2d 645, 648 (Tex.App.—Houston [1st Dist.] 1973, writ ref'd n.r.e.). "[T]he time for filing an abstract in response to a demand will be extended where the grant of additional time will not prejudice the party making the demand and the refusal of an extension would result in injustice."

TRCP 793. ABSTRACT SHALL STATE, WHAT

The abstract mentioned in the two preceding rules shall state:

(a) The nature of each document or written instrument intended to be used as evidence and its date; or

TRCP 793

★

(b) If a contract or conveyance, its date, the parties thereto and the date of the proof of acknowledgment, and before what officer the same was made; and

(c) Where recorded, stating the book and page of the record.

(d) If not recorded in the county when the trial is had, copies of such instrument, with the names of the subscribing witnesses, shall be included. If such unrecorded instrument be lost or destroyed it shall be sufficient to state the nature of such instrument and its loss or destruction.

History of TRCP 793: Adopted eff. Sept. 1, 1941, by order of Oct. 29, 1940 (3 Tex.B.J. 647 [1940]). Source: TRCS art. 7378 (repealed).

ANNOTATIONS

Walker v. Barrow, 464 S.W.2d 480, 487 (Tex. App.—Houston [1st Dist.] 1971, writ ref'd n.r.e.). "[A]ny deficiency of the description contained in the abstract filed should have been called to the attention of [receiver] by motion before trial. There was no error in its admission."

TRCP 794. AMENDED ABSTRACT

The court may allow either party to file an amended abstract of title, under the same rules, which authorize the amendment of pleadings so far as they are applicable; but in all cases the documentary evidence of title shall at the trial be confined to the matters contained in the abstract of title.

History of TRCP 794: Adopted eff. Sept. 1, 1941, by order of Oct. 29, 1940 (3 Tex.B.J. 647 [1940]). Source: TRCS art. 7379 (repealed).

TRCP 795. RULES IN OTHER CASES OBSERVED

The trial shall be conducted according to the rules of pleading, practice and evidence in other cases in the district court and conformable to the principles of trial by ejectment, except as otherwise provided by these rules.

History of TRCP 795: Adopted eff. Sept. 1, 1941, by order of Oct. 29, 1940 (3 Tex.B.J. 647 [1940]). Source: TRCS art. 7365 (repealed).

ANNOTATIONS

Ramsey v. Jones Enters., 810 S.W.2d 902, 905 (Tex.App.—Beaumont 1991, writ denied). TREs 702, 703, and 704 do not "excuse the necessity for the production and admission of documentary evidence regarding title to real property. [TRE] 1002 ... requires that if documentary evidence exist as to title to ... real property, that such documentary evidence must be produced and admitted."

TRCP 796. SURVEYOR APPOINTED, ETC.

The judge of the court may, either in term time or in vacation, at his own discretion, or on motion of either party to the action appoint a surveyor, who shall survey the premises in controversy pursuant to the order of the court, and report his action under oath to such court. If said report be not rejected for good cause shown, the same shall be admitted as evidence on the trial.

History of TRCP 796: Adopted eff. Sept. 1, 1941, by order of Oct. 29, 1940 (3 Tex.B.J. 647 [1940]). Source: TRCS art. 7380 (repealed).

ANNOTATIONS

Mayflower Inv. v. Stephens, 345 S.W.2d 786, 796 (Tex.App.—Dallas 1960, writ ref'd n.r.e.). TRCP 796 "is applicable only in trespass to try title cases."

TRCP 797. SURVEY UNNECESSARY, WHEN

Where there is no dispute as to the lines or boundaries of the land in controversy, or where the defendant admits that he is in possession of the lands or tenements included in the plaintiff's claim, or title, an order of survey shall be unnecessary.

History of TRCP 797: Adopted eff. Sept. 1, 1941, by order of Oct. 29, 1940 (3 Tex.B.J. 647 [1940]). Source: TRCS art. 7381 (repealed).

TRCP 798. COMMON SOURCE OF TITLE

It shall not be necessary for the plaintiff to deraign title beyond a common source. Proof of a common source may be made by the plaintiff by certified copies of the deeds showing a chain of title to the defendant emanating from and under such common source. Before any such certified copies shall be read in evidence, they shall be filed with the papers of the suit three days before the trial, and the adverse party served with notice of such filing as in other cases. Such certified copies shall not be evidence of title in the defendant unless offered in evidence by him. The plaintiff may make any legal objection to such certified copies, or the originals thereof, when introduced by the defendant.

History of TRCP 798: Adopted eff. Sept. 1, 1941, by order of Oct. 29, 1940 (3 Tex.B.J. 647 [1940]). Source: TRCS art. 7382 (repealed).

ANNOTATIONS

Davis v. Gale, 330 S.W.2d 610, 612 (Tex.1960). "In a trespass to try title suit, where the parties agree as to a common source, it is incumbent upon the plaintiff to discharge the burden of proof resting upon him to establish a superior title from such source."

TRCP 793

★

Goggins v. Leo, 849 S.W.2d 373, 377 (Tex.App.—Houston [14th Dist.] 1993, no writ). TRCP 798 applies only to trespass-to-try-title suits, not to forcible-detainer cases.

TRCP 799. JUDGMENT BY DEFAULT

If the defendant, who has been personally served with citation according to law or these rules fails to appear and answer by himself or attorney within the time prescribed by law or these rules for other actions in the district court, then judgment by default may be entered against him and in favor of the plaintiff for the title to the premises, or the possession thereof, or for both, according to the petition, and for all costs, without any proof of title by the plaintiff.

History of TRCP 799: Adopted eff. Sept. 1, 1941, by order of Oct. 29, 1940 (3 Tex.B.J. 647 [1940]). Source: TRCS art. 7383 (repealed).

TRCP 800. PROOF EX PARTE

If the defendant has been cited only by publication, and fails to appear and answer by himself, or by attorney of his own selection, or if any defendant, having answered, fails to appear by himself or attorney when the case is called for trial on its merits, the plaintiff shall make such proof as will entitle him prima facie to recover, whereupon the proper judgment shall be entered.

History of TRCP 800: Adopted eff. Sept. 1, 1941, by order of Oct. 29, 1940 (3 Tex.B.J. 647 [1940]). Source: TRCS art. 7384 (repealed).

TRCP 801. WHEN DEFENDANT CLAIMS PART ONLY

Where the defendant claims part of the premises only, the answer shall be equivalent to a disclaimer of the balance.

History of TRCP 801: Adopted eff. Sept. 1, 1941, by order of Oct. 29, 1940 (3 Tex.B.J. 647 [1940]). Source: TRCS art. 7385 (repealed).

ANNOTATIONS

Salazar v. Garcia, 232 S.W.2d 685, 688 (Tex. App.—San Antonio 1950, writ ref'd). Because "[t]he answers filed by [Ds] in this cause do not claim title to [the real estate], but they limit their claim to an assertion of ownership of, or the right to fix a lien on the improvements[, t]he pleadings and evidence presented by [Ds] amount to a disclaimer by them of any title to the [real estate]."

TRCP 802. WHEN PLAINTIFF PROVES PART

Where the defendant claims the whole premises, and the plaintiff shows himself entitled to recover part, the plaintiff shall recover such part and costs.

History of TRCP 802: Adopted eff. Sept. 1, 1941, by order of Oct. 29, 1940 (3 Tex.B.J. 648 [1940]). Source: TRCS art. 7386 (repealed).

TRCP 803. MAY RECOVER A PART

When there are two or more plaintiffs or defendants any one or more of the plaintiffs may recover against one or more of the defendants the premises, or any part thereof, or any interest therein, or damages, according to the rights of the parties.

History of TRCP 803: Adopted eff. Sept. 1, 1941, by order of Oct. 29, 1940 (3 Tex.B.J. 648 [1940]). Source: TRCS art. 7387 (repealed).

TRCP 804. THE JUDGMENT

Upon the finding of the jury, or of the court where the case is tried by the court, in favor of the plaintiff for the whole or any part of the premises in controversy, the judgment shall be that the plaintiff recover of the defendant the title or possession, or both, as the case may be, of such premises, describing them, and where he recovers the possession, that he have his writ of possession.

History of TRCP 804: Adopted eff. Sept. 1, 1941, by order of Oct. 29, 1940 (3 Tex.B.J. 648 [1940]). Source: TRCS art. 7388 (repealed).

TRCP 805. DAMAGES

Where it is alleged and proved that one of the parties is in possession of the premises, the court or jury, if they find for the adverse party, shall assess the damages for the use and occupation of the premises. If special injury to the property be alleged and proved, the damages for such injury shall also be assessed, and the proper judgment shall be entered therefor, on which execution may issue.

History of TRCP 805: Adopted eff. Sept. 1, 1941, by order of Oct. 29, 1940 (3 Tex.B.J. 648 [1940]). Source: TRCS art. 7389 (repealed in part by TRCP).

TRCP 806. CLAIM FOR IMPROVEMENTS

When the defendant or person in possession has claimed an allowance for improvements in accordance with Sections 22.021-22.024, Texas Property Code, the claim for use and occupation and damages mentioned in the preceding rule shall be considered and acted on in connection with such claim by the defendant or person in possession.

History of TRCP 806: Amended eff. Jan. 1, 1988, by order of July 15, 1987 (733-34 S.W.2d [Tex.Cases] lxxxiii). Amended eff. Apr. 1, 1984, by order of Dec. 5, 1983 (661-62 S.W.2d [Tex.Cases] cxviii). Adopted eff. Sept. 1, 1941, by order of Oct. 29, 1940 (3 Tex.B.J. 648 [1940]). Source: TRCS art. 7390 (repealed).

TRCP 807. JUDGMENT WHEN CLAIM FOR IMPROVEMENTS IS MADE

When a claim for improvements is successfully made under Sections 22.021-22.024, Texas Property

---

⭐

Code, the judgment shall recite the estimated value of the premises without the improvements, and shall also include the conditions, stipulations and directions contained in Sections 22.021-22.024, Texas Property Code so far as applicable to the case before the court.

History of TRCP 807: Amended eff. Jan. 1, 1988, by order of July 15, 1987 (733-34 S.W.2d [Tex.Cases] lxxxiii). Amended eff. Apr. 1, 1984, by order of Dec. 5, 1983 (661-62 S.W.2d [Tex.Cases] cxviii). Adopted eff. Sept. 1, 1941, by order of Oct. 29, 1940 (3 Tex.B.J. 648 [1940]). Source: TRCS art. 7400 (repealed).

TRCP 808. THESE RULES SHALL NOT GOVERN, WHEN

Nothing in Sections 22.001-22.045, Texas Property Code, shall be so construed as to alter, impair or take away the rights of parties, as arising under the laws in force before the introduction of the common law, but the same shall be decided by the principles of the law under which the same accrued, or by which the same were regulated or in any manner affected.

History of TRCP 808: Amended eff. Jan. 1, 1988, by order of July 15, 1987 (733-34 S.W.2d [Tex.Cases] lxxxiii). Amended eff. Apr. 1, 1984, by order of Dec. 5, 1983 (661-62 S.W.2d [Tex.Cases] cxviii). Adopted eff. Sept. 1, 1941, by order of Oct. 29, 1940 (3 Tex.B.J. 648 [1940]). Source: TRCS art. 7392 (repealed eff. Jan. 1, 1984).

TRCP 809. THESE RULES SHALL NOT GOVERN, WHEN

Nothing in these rules relating to trespass to try title shall be so construed as to alter, impair or take away the rights of parties, as arising under the laws in force before the introduction of the common law, but the same shall be decided by the principles of the law under which the same accrued, or by which the same were regulated or in any manner affected.

History of TRCP 809: Adopted eff. Sept. 1, 1941, by order of Oct. 29, 1940 (3 Tex.B.J. 648 [1940]). Source: New rule.

SECTION 9. SUITS AGAINST NON-RESIDENTS

TRCP 810. REQUISITES OF PLEADINGS

The petition in actions authorized by Section 17.003, Civil Practice and Remedies Code, shall state the real names of the plaintiff and defendant, and shall describe the property involved with sufficient certainty to identify the same, the interest which the plaintiff claims, and such proceedings shall be had in such action as may be necessary to fully settle and determine the question of right or title in and to said property between the parties to said suit, and to decree the title or right of the party entitled thereto; and the court may issue the appropriate order to carry such decree, judgment or order into effect; and whenever such petition

has been duly filed and citation thereon has been duly served by publication as required by Rules 114-116, the plaintiff may, at any time prior to entering the decree by leave of court first had and obtained, file amended and supplemental pleadings that do not subject additional property to said suit without the necessity of reciting the defendants so cited as aforesaid.

History of TRCP 810: Amended eff. Jan. 1, 1988, by order of July 15, 1987 (733-34 S.W.2d [Tex.Cases] lxxxiv). Amended eff. Apr. 1, 1984, by order of Dec. 5, 1983 (661-62 S.W.2d [Tex.Cases] cxviii). Adopted eff. Sept. 1, 1941, by order of Oct. 29, 1940 (3 Tex.B.J. 649 [1940]). Source: TRCS art. 1977 (repealed).

TRCP 811. SERVICE BY PUBLICATION IN ACTIONS UNDER SECTION 17.003, CIVIL PRACTICE & REMEDIES CODE

In actions authorized by Section 17.003, Civil Practice and Remedies Code, service on the defendant or defendants may be made by publication as is provided by Rules 114-116 or by service of notice of the character and in the manner provided by Rule 108.

History of TRCP 811: Amended eff. Jan. 1, 1988, by order of July 15, 1987 (733-34 S.W.2d [Tex.Cases] lxxxiv). Amended eff. Apr. 1, 1984, by order of Dec. 5, 1983 (661-62 S.W.2d [Tex.Cases] cxviii). Adopted eff. Sept. 1, 1941, by order of Oct. 29, 1940 (3 Tex.B.J. 649 [1940]). Source: TRCS art. 1976 (repealed in part by TRCP).

TRCP 812. NO JUDGMENT BY DEFAULT

No judgment by default shall be taken in such case when service has been had by publication, but in such case the facts entitling the plaintiff to judgment shall be exhibited to the court on the trial; and a statement of facts shall be filed as provided by law and these rules in suits against nonresidents of this State served by publication, where no appearance has been made by them.

History of TRCP 812: Amended eff. Mar. 1, 1950, by order of Oct. 12, 1949 (12 Tex.B.J. 538 [1949]). Adopted eff. Sept. 1, 1941, by order of Oct. 29, 1940 (3 Tex.B.J. 649 [1940]). Source: TRCS art. 1978 (repealed).

TRCP 813. SUIT TO EXTINGUISH LIEN

If said suit shall be for the extinguishment of a lien or claim for money on said property that may be held by the defendant, the amount thereof, with interest, shall be ascertained by the court; and the same deposited in the registry of the court, subject to be drawn by the parties entitled thereto; but in such case no decree shall be entered until said sum is deposited; which fact shall be noted in said decree.

History of TRCP 813: Adopted eff. Sept. 1, 1941, by order of Oct. 29, 1940 (3 Tex.B.J. 649 [1940]). Source: TRCS art. 1979 (repealed).

PART VIII. CLOSING RULES

TRCP 814. EFFECTIVE DATE

These rules shall take effect on September 1st, 1941. They shall govern all proceedings in actions brought after they take effect, and also all further proceedings in actions then pending, except to the extent that in the opinion of the court their application in a particular action pending when the rules take effect would not be feasible or would work injustice, in which event the former procedure shall apply. All things properly done under any previously existing rule or statutes prior to the taking effect of these rules shall be treated as valid. Where citation or other process is issued and served in compliance with existing rules or laws prior to the taking effect of these rules, the party upon whom such citation or other process has been served shall have the time provided for under such previously existing rules or laws in which to comply therewith.

History of TRCP 814: Adopted eff. Sept. 1, 1941, by order of Oct. 29, 1940 (3 Tex.B.J. 649 [1940]). Source: FRCP 86.

TRCP 815. SUBSTANTIVE RIGHTS UNAFFECTED

These rules shall not be construed to enlarge or diminish any substantive rights or obligations of any parties to any civil action.

History of TRCP 815: Adopted eff. Sept. 1, 1941, by order of Oct. 29, 1940 (3 Tex.B.J. 649 [1940]). Source: TRCS art. 1731a (repealed, now Gov't Code §22.004(a)).

See Gov't Code §22.004(a).

TRCP 816. JURISDICTION & VENUE UNAFFECTED

These rules shall not be construed to extend or limit the jurisdiction of the courts of the State of Texas nor the venue of actions therein.

History of TRCP 816: Adopted eff. Sept. 1, 1941, by order of Oct. 29, 1940 (3 Tex.B.J. 649 [1940]). Source: FRCP 82.

TRCP 817. RENUMBERED

Repealed and renumbered as TRCP 3a, eff. Apr. 1, 1984, by order of Dec. 5, 1983 (661-62 S.W.2d [Tex.Cases] cxix).

TRCP 818. REFERENCE TO FORMER STATUTES

Wherever any statute or rule refers to any practice or procedure in any law, laws, statute or statutes, or to a title, chapter, section, or article of the statutes, or contains any reference of any such nature, and the matter referred to has been supplanted in whole or in part by these rules, every such reference shall be deemed to be to the pertinent part or parts of these rules.

History of TRCP 818: Adopted eff. Sept. 1, 1941, by order of Oct. 29, 1940 (3 Tex.B.J. 650 [1940]). Source: New rule.

TRCP 819. PROCEDURE CONTINUED

All procedure prescribed by statutes of the State of Texas not specifically listed in the accompanying enumeration of repealed articles shall, insofar as the same is not inconsistent with the provisions of these rules, continue in accordance with the provisions of such statutes as rules of court. In case of inconsistency between the provisions of these rules and any statutory procedure not specifically listed as repealed, these rules shall apply.

History of TRCP 819: Adopted eff. Sept. 1, 1941, by order of Oct. 29, 1940 (3 Tex.B.J. 650 [1940]). Source: New rule.

TRCP 820. WORKERS' COMPENSATION LAW

All portions of the Workers' Compensation Law, Articles 8306-8309-1, Revised Civil Statutes, and amendments thereto, which relate to matters of practice and procedure are hereby adopted and retained in force and effect as rules of court.

History of TRCP 820: Amended eff. Apr. 1, 1984, by order of Dec. 5, 1983 (661-62 S.W.2d [Tex.Cases] cxix). Adopted eff. Sept. 1, 1941, by order of Oct. 29, 1940 (3 Tex.B.J. 650 [1940]). Source: New rule.

TRCP 821. PRIOR COURT RULES REPEALED

These rules shall supersede all Court Rules heretofore promulgated for any court; and all of said prior Court Rules are hereby repealed; provided, however, any rules of procedure heretofore adopted by a particular county or district court or by any Court of Appeals which were not of general application but were solely to regulate procedure in the particular court promulgating such rules are to remain in force and effect insofar as they are not inconsistent with these rules.

History of TRCP 821: Amended eff. Apr. 1, 1984, by order of Dec. 5, 1983 (661-62 S.W.2d [Tex.Cases] cxix): Deleted "Civil" from "Court of Civil Appeals." Adopted eff. Sept. 1, 1941, by order of Oct. 29, 1940 (3 Tex.B.J. 650 [1940]). Source: New rule.

TRCP 822. TITLE

These rules may be known and cited as the Texas Rules of Civil Procedure.

History of TRCP 822: Adopted eff. Sept. 1, 1941, by order of Oct. 29, 1940 (3 Tex.B.J. 650 [1940]). Source: FRCP 85.

TEXAS RULES OF EVIDENCE
ANNOTATED RULES
TABLE OF CONTENTS

★

For an in-depth discussion of the Texas Rules of Evidence, see the current edition of *Texas Rules of Evidence Handbook*. To order, call 1-800-OCONNOR (1-800-626-6667) or visit www.JonesMcClure.com.

TRE

★

ARTICLE I. GENERAL PROVISIONS

TRE 101. TITLE & SCOPE

(a) Title. These rules shall be known and cited as the Texas Rules of Evidence.

(b) Scope. Except as otherwise provided by statute, these rules govern civil and criminal proceedings (including examining trials before magistrates) in all courts of Texas, except small claims courts.

(c) Hierarchical Governance in Criminal Proceedings. Hierarchical governance shall be in the following order: the Constitution of the United States, those federal statutes that control states under the supremacy clause, the Constitution of Texas, the Code of Criminal Procedure and the Penal Code, civil statutes, these rules, and the common law. Where possible, inconsistency is to be removed by reasonable construction.

(d) Special Rules of Applicability in Criminal Proceedings.

(1) *Rules not applicable in certain proceedings.* These rules, except with respect to privileges, do not apply in the following situations:

(A) the determination of questions of fact preliminary to admissibility of evidence when the issue is to be determined by the court under Rule 104;

(B) proceedings before grand juries;

(C) proceedings in an application for habeas corpus in extradition, rendition, or interstate detainer;

(D) a hearing under Code of Criminal Procedure article 46.02,[1] by the court out of the presence of a jury, to determine whether there is sufficient evidence of incompetency to require a jury determination of the question of incompetency;

(E) proceedings regarding bail except hearings to deny, revoke or increase bail;

(F) a hearing on justification for pretrial detention not involving bail;

(G) proceedings for the issuance of a search or arrest warrant; or

(H) proceedings in a direct contempt determination.

(2) *Applicability of privileges.* These rules with respect to privileges apply at all stages of all actions, cases, and proceedings.

(3) *Military justice hearings.* Evidence in hearings under the Texas Code of Military Justice, Tex. Gov't Code §432.001-432.195, shall be governed by that Code.

1. **Editor's note:** Now Code Crim. Proc. ch. 46B.

Comment to 1998 change: "Criminal proceedings" rather than "criminal cases" is used since that was the terminology used in the prior Rules of Criminal Evidence. In subpart (b), the reference to "trials before magistrates" comes from prior Criminal Rule 1101(a). In the prior Criminal Rules, both Rule 101 and Rule 1101 dealt with the same thing—the applicability of the rules. Thus, Rules 101(c) and (d) have been written to incorporate the provisions of former Criminal Rule 1101 and that rule is omitted.

History of TRE 101 (civil): Amended eff. Mar. 1, 1998, by order of Feb. 25, 1998 (960 S.W.2d [Tex.Cases] xxxi). Amended eff. Jan. 1, 1988, by order of Nov. 10, 1986 (733-34 S.W.2d [Tex.Cases] lxxxvi): Added "Civil" to title of rules in (a). Adopted eff. Sept. 1, 1983, by order of Nov. 23, 1982 (641-42 S.W.2d [Tex.Cases] xxxvi). Source: For TRE 101(a), see FRE 1103; for TRE 101(b), see FRE 101.

See Brown & Rondon, *Texas Rules of Evidence Handbook* (2013), p. 29.

TRE 102. PURPOSE & CONSTRUCTION

These rules shall be construed to secure fairness in administration, elimination of unjustifiable expense and delay, and promotion of growth and development of the law of evidence to the end that the truth may be ascertained and proceedings justly determined.

History of TRE 102 (civil): Amended eff. Mar. 1, 1998, by order of Feb. 25, 1998 (960 S.W.2d [Tex.Cases] xxxii). Adopted eff. Sept. 1, 1983, by order of Nov. 23, 1982 (641-42 S.W.2d [Tex.Cases] xxxvi). Source: FRE 102.

See Brown & Rondon, *Texas Rules of Evidence Handbook* (2013), p. 42.

TRE 103. RULINGS ON EVIDENCE

(a) Effect of Erroneous Ruling. Error may not be predicated upon a ruling which admits or excludes evidence unless a substantial right of the party is affected, and

(1) *Objection.* In case the ruling is one admitting evidence, a timely objection or motion to strike appears of record, stating the specific ground of objection, if the specific ground was not apparent from the context. When the court hears objections to offered evidence out of the presence of the jury and rules that such evidence be admitted, such objections shall be deemed to apply to such evidence when it is admitted before the jury without the necessity of repeating those objections.

(2) *Offer of proof.* In case the ruling is one excluding evidence, the substance of the evidence was made known to the court by offer, or was apparent from the context within which questions were asked.

(b) Record of Offer and Ruling. The offering party shall, as soon as practicable, but before the court's charge is read to the jury, be allowed to make, in the absence of the jury, its offer of proof. The court may add any other or further statement which shows the character of the evidence, the form in which it was offered, the objection made, and the ruling thereon. The court may, or at the request of a party shall, direct the making of an offer in question and answer form.

★

(c) Hearing of Jury. In jury cases, proceedings shall be conducted, to the extent practicable, so as to prevent inadmissible evidence from being suggested to the jury by any means, such as making statements or offers of proof or asking questions in the hearing of the jury.

(d) Fundamental Error in Criminal Cases. In a criminal case, nothing in these rules precludes taking notice of fundamental errors affecting substantial rights although they were not brought to the attention of the court.

Comment to 1998 change: The exception to the requirement of an offer of proof for matters that were apparent from the context within which questions were asked, found in paragraph (a)(2), is now applicable to civil as well as criminal cases.

History of TRE 103 (civil): Amended eff. Mar. 1, 1998, by order of Feb. 25, 1998 (960 S.W.2d [Tex.Cases] xxxii). Amended eff. Jan. 1, 1988, by order of July 15, 1987 (733-34 S.W.2d [Tex.Cases] xciv): Added second sentence to (a)(1), to conform to TRAP 52(b); deleted the phrase "or was apparent from the context within which questions were asked" from (a)(2); and added first sentence to (b), requiring party make offer before jury is charged. Amended eff. Nov. 1, 1984, by order of June 25, 1984 (669-70 S.W.2d [Tex.Cases] xxx): Substituted the words "a party" for "counsel" in the last sentence of (b). Adopted eff. Sept. 1, 1983, by order of Nov. 23, 1982 (641-42 S.W.2d [Tex.Cases] xxxvi). Source: FRE 103, with changes: Party entitled to make offer in question-and-answer form.

See TRAP 44.1; *Commentaries*, "Motion in Limine," ch. 5-E, p. 347; "Objecting to Evidence," ch. 8-D, p. 708; "Offer of Proof & Bill of Exception," ch. 8-E, p. 717; Brown & Rondon, *Texas Rules of Evidence Handbook* (2013), p. 44.

ANNOTATIONS

Bowman v. Patel, No. 01-10-00811-CV (Tex.App.—Houston [1st Dist.] 2012, no pet.) (memo op.; 2-16-12). "An offer of proof may be in the form of concise statement by counsel or in question-and-answer form. It is not required that the offer of proof show what specific facts the examination would reveal, but the appellant must clearly inform the trial court of the subject matter about which it wants to examine the witness."

Bobbora v. Unitrin Ins., 255 S.W.3d 331, 334-35 (Tex.App.—Dallas 2008, no pet.). "To preserve error concerning the exclusion of evidence, the complaining party must actually offer the evidence and secure an adverse ruling from the court. While the reviewing court may be able to discern from the record the nature of the evidence and the propriety of the trial court's ruling, without an offer of proof, we can never determine whether exclusion of the evidence was harmful. ... An offer of proof preserves error for appeal if: (1) it is made before the court, the court reporter, and opposing counsel, outside the presence of the jury; (2) it is preserved in the reporter's record; and (3) it is made before the charge is read to the jury. When no offer of proof is made before the trial court, the party must in-troduce the excluded testimony into the record by a formal bill of exception. A formal bill of exception must be presented to the trial court for its approval, and, if the parties agree to the contents of the bill, the trial court must sign the bill and file it with the trial court clerk. Failure to demonstrate the substance of the excluded evidence results in waiver." *See also Perez v. Lopez*, 74 S.W.3d 60, 66 (Tex.App.—El Paso 2002, no pet.).

Benavides v. Cushman, Inc., 189 S.W.3d 875, 885 (Tex.App.—Houston [1st Dist.] 2006, no pet.). "'[A]ny error in admitting evidence is cured where the same evidence comes in elsewhere without objection.'"

Greenberg Traurig of New York, P.C. v. Moody, 161 S.W.3d 56, 91 (Tex.App.—Houston [14th Dist.] 2004, no pet.). "Because a trial court's ruling on a motion in limine preserves nothing for review, a party must object at trial when the testimony is offered to preserve error for appellate review. However, not all pretrial motions are motions in limine. There is a distinction between a motion in limine and a pretrial ruling on admissibility. The trial court has the authority to make a pretrial ruling on the admissibility of evidence."

In re N.R.C., 94 S.W.3d 799, 806 (Tex.App.—Houston [14th Dist.] 2002, pet. denied). "To adequately and effectively preserve error, an offer of proof must show the nature of the evidence specifically enough so that the reviewing court can determine its admissibility. ... The offer of proof may be made by counsel, who should reasonably and specifically summarize the evidence offered and state its relevance unless already apparent. If counsel does make such an offer, he must describe the actual content of the testimony and not merely comment on the reasons for it." *See also PPC Transp. v. Metcalf*, 254 S.W.3d 636, 640-41 (Tex. App.—Tyler 2008, no pet.).

Bean v. Baxter Healthcare Corp., 965 S.W.2d 656, 660 (Tex.App.—Houston [14th Dist.] 1998, no pet.). "[P] preserved error after its initial offer of the videotape. If exclusion of evidence is based on the substance of the evidence, however, the offering party must reoffer it if it again becomes relevant. This may occur when the evidence is pertinent to rebuttal. Error is waived if the offering party fails to reoffer evidence for a limited purpose after it has been excluded pursuant to a general objection."

Hill v. Heritage Res., 964 S.W.2d 89, 136 (Tex. App.—El Paso 1997, pet. denied). "To obtain a reversal of judgment based upon a trial court's decision to admit

---

or exclude evidence, [D] must show: (1) that the trial court abused its discretion in making the decision; and (2) that the error was reasonably calculated to cause and probably did cause rendition of an improper judgment. [¶] It has been held that when evidence is sharply conflicting and the case is hotly contested, any error of law by the trial court will be reversible...."

Chance v. Chance, 911 S.W.2d 40, 52 (Tex.App.—Beaumont 1995, writ denied). "[T]he rule requiring that proffered evidence be incorporated in a bill of exception does not apply to cross examination of an adverse witness. When cross-examination testimony is excluded, [D] need not show the answer to be expected but only need show that the substance of the evidence was apparent from the context within which the question was asked."

TRE 104. PRELIMINARY QUESTIONS

(a) Questions of Admissibility Generally. Preliminary questions concerning the qualification of a person to be a witness, the existence of a privilege, or the admissibility of evidence shall be determined by the court, subject to the provisions of subdivision (b). In making its determination the court is not bound by the rules of evidence except those with respect to privileges.

(b) Relevancy Conditioned on Fact. When the relevancy of evidence depends upon the fulfillment of a condition of fact, the court shall admit it upon, or subject to, the introduction of evidence sufficient to support a finding of the fulfillment of the condition.

(c) Hearing of Jury. In a criminal case, a hearing on the admissibility of a confession shall be conducted out of the hearing of the jury. All other civil or criminal hearings on preliminary matters shall be conducted out of the hearing of the jury when the interests of justice so require or in a criminal case when an accused is a witness and so requests.

(d) Testimony by Accused Out of the Hearing of the Jury. The accused in a criminal case does not, by testifying upon a preliminary matter out of the hearing of the jury, become subject to cross-examination as to other issues in the case.

(e) Weight and Credibility. This rule does not limit the right of a party to introduce before the jury evidence relevant to weight or credibility.

History of TRE 104 (civil): Amended eff. Mar. 1, 1998, by order of Feb. 25, 1998 (960 S.W.2d [Tex.Cases] xxxiii). Adopted eff. Sept. 1, 1983, by order of Nov. 23, 1982 (641-42 S.W.2d [Tex.Cases] xxxvi). Source: FRE 104.

See *Commentaries*, "Motion in Limine," ch. 5-E, p. 347; "Objecting to Evidence," ch. 8-D, p. 708; Brown & Rondon, *Texas Rules of Evidence Handbook* (2013), p. 70.

Broders v. Heise, 924 S.W.2d 148, 151 (Tex.1996). "The qualification of a witness as an expert is within the trial court's discretion. [T]he party offering the expert's testimony bears the burden to prove that the witness is qualified under [TRE] 702."

E.I. du Pont de Nemours & Co. v. Robinson, 923 S.W.2d 549, 556 (Tex.1995). "The trial court is responsible for making the preliminary determination of whether the proffered testimony meets the standards set forth [for experts]."

Lofton v. Texas Brine Corp., 777 S.W.2d 384, 386 (Tex.1989). "Testimony by an interested witness may establish a fact as a matter of law only if the testimony could be readily contradicted if untrue, and is clear, direct and positive, and there are no circumstances tending to discredit or impeach it."

TRE 105. LIMITED ADMISSIBILITY

(a) Limiting Instruction. When evidence which is admissible as to one party or for one purpose but not admissible as to another party or for another purpose is admitted, the court, upon request, shall restrict the evidence to its proper scope and instruct the jury accordingly; but, in the absence of such request the court's action in admitting such evidence without limitation shall not be a ground for complaint on appeal.

(b) Offering Evidence for Limited Purpose. When evidence referred to in paragraph (a) is excluded, such exclusion shall not be a ground for complaint on appeal unless the proponent expressly offers the evidence for its limited, admissible purpose or limits its offer to the party against whom it is admissible.

History of TRE 105 (civil): Amended eff. Mar. 1, 1998, by order of Feb. 25, 1998 (960 S.W.2d [Tex.Cases] xxxiv). Adopted eff. Sept. 1, 1983, by order of Nov. 23, 1982 (641-42 S.W.2d [Tex.Cases] xxxvii). Source: FRE 105.

See *Commentaries*, "Request for limited admissibility," ch. 8-D, §7.1.3(1), p. 715; Brown & Rondon, *Texas Rules of Evidence Handbook* (2013), p. 80.

U-Haul Int'l v. Waldrip, ___ S.W.3d ___ (Tex. 2012) (No. 10-0781; 8-31-12). "Rule 105 does not apply when the evidence in question is not admissible against any party for any purpose."

Larson v. Cactus Util. Co., 730 S.W.2d 640, 642 (Tex.1987). "Where tendered evidence should be considered for only one purpose, it is the opponent's bur-

---

den to secure a limiting instruction. Absent a requested limiting instruction, [opponent of evidence] waived his grounds for complaint." *See also* **Horizon/CMS Healthcare Corp. v. Auld**, 34 S.W.3d 887, 906 (Tex. 2000).

TRE 106. REMAINDER OF OR RELATED WRITINGS OR RECORDED STATEMENTS

When a writing or recorded statement or part thereof is introduced by a party, an adverse party may at that time introduce any other part or any other writing or recorded statement which ought in fairness to be considered contemporaneously with it. "Writing or recorded statement" includes depositions.

History of TRE 106 (civil): Amended eff. Mar. 1, 1998, by order of Feb. 25, 1998 (960 S.W.2d [Tex.Cases] xxxiv). Amended eff. Nov. 1, 1984, by order of June 25, 1984 (669-70 S.W.2d [Tex.Cases] xxxi): The title was changed; the last sentence added to the rule; and references to Code Crim. Proc. art. 38.24 and to TRCE 610(a) were added to the comment. Adopted eff. Sept. 1, 1983, by order of Nov. 23, 1982 (641-42 S.W.2d [Tex.Cases] xxxvii). Source: FRE 106. This rule is the same as FRE 106, with one modification. Under FRE 106, a party may require its opponent to introduce evidence contrary to the latter's own case. The Committee believed it was better to permit the party to introduce such evidence contemporaneously with the introduction of the incomplete evidence. TRCE 106 does not in any way circumscribe the right of a party to develop fully the matter on cross-examination or as part of his own case. *Cf.* Code Crim. Proc. art. 38.24. Nor does it alter the common-law doctrine that the rule of optional completeness, as to writings, oral conversations, or other matters, may take precedence over exclusionary doctrines such as the hearsay or best-evidence rule or the firsthand knowledge requirement.

See Brown & Rondon, *Texas Rules of Evidence Handbook* (2013), p. 86.

ANNOTATIONS

Russell v. Beck, No. 06-11-00006-CV (Tex.App.—Texarkana 2011, no pet.) (memo op.; 6-7-11). "The rule of optional completeness only applies when one party introduces part of a statement or document, and in fairness, the opposing party is permitted to introduce as much of the balance as is necessary to explain the first part. It is permitted to correct any misleading impressions left when one party introduces only a portion of the evidence. A plain reading of [TRE] 106 and [TRE] 107 indicates their inapplicability when the same party seeks to offer an inadmissible omitted portion of a document it initially sought to introduce. [¶] Under the rule of optional completeness, additional material from a document or recording, part of which has been admitted into evidence, is admissible if that material 'ought in fairness to be considered contemporaneously.'"

Jones v. Colley, 820 S.W.2d 863, 866 (Tex.App.—Texarkana 1991, writ denied). "Rule 106 ... is not enforced by excluding the partial statement, but by allowing the opposing party to contemporaneously introduce any other part of the statement that should be considered with the portion introduced by the proponent."

TRE 107. RULE OF OPTIONAL COMPLETENESS

When part of an act, declaration, conversation, writing or recorded statement is given in evidence by one party, the whole on the same subject may be inquired into by the other, and any other act, declaration, writing or recorded statement which is necessary to make it fully understood or to explain the same may also be given in evidence, as when a letter is read, all letters on the same subject between the same parties may be given. "Writing or recorded statement" includes depositions.

Comment to 1998 change: This rule is the former Criminal Rule 107 except that the example regarding "when a letter is read" has been relocated in the rule so as to more accurately indicate the provision it explains. While this rule appeared only in the prior criminal rules, it is made applicable to civil cases because it accurately reflects the common law rule of optional completeness in civil cases.

History of TRE 107 (criminal): Amended eff. Mar. 1, 1998, by order of Feb. 25, 1998 (960 S.W.2d [Tex.Cases] xxxiv). Adopted eff. Sept. 1, 1986, by order of Dec. 18, 1985 (701-02 S.W.2d [Tex.Cases] xxxiv).

See Brown & Rondon, *Texas Rules of Evidence Handbook* (2013), p. 89.

ANNOTATIONS

Russell v. Beck, No. 06-11-00006-CV (Tex.App.—Texarkana 2011, no pet.) (memo op.; 6-7-11). See annotation under TRE 106, this page.

Crosby v. Minyard Food Stores, 122 S.W.3d 899, 903 (Tex.App.—Dallas 2003, no pet.). "Rule 107 is designed to guard against the possibility of confusion, distortion, or false impression that could be created when only a portion of evidence is introduced. There are two threshold requirements for the application of the rule. First, some portion of the matter sought to be 'completed' must have actually been introduced into evidence. Merely referring to a statement does not invoke the rule. Second, the party seeking to complete the matter must show that the remainder being offered under rule 107 is on the same subject and is necessary to fully understand or explain the matter."

ARTICLE II. JUDICIAL NOTICE

TRE 201. JUDICIAL NOTICE OF ADJUDICATIVE FACTS

(a) Scope of Rule. This rule governs only judicial notice of adjudicative facts.

(b) Kinds of Facts. A judicially noticed fact must be one not subject to reasonable dispute in that it is either (1) generally known within the territorial juris-

TRE 201

⭐

---

diction of the trial court or (2) capable of accurate and ready determination by resort to sources whose accuracy cannot reasonably be questioned.

(c) When Discretionary. A court may take judicial notice, whether requested or not.

(d) When Mandatory. A court shall take judicial notice if requested by a party and supplied with the necessary information.

(e) Opportunity to Be Heard. A party is entitled upon timely request to an opportunity to be heard as to the propriety of taking judicial notice and the tenor of the matter noticed. In the absence of prior notification, the request may be made after judicial notice has been taken.

(f) Time of Taking Notice. Judicial notice may be taken at any stage of the proceeding.

(g) Instructing Jury. In civil cases, the court shall instruct the jury to accept as conclusive any fact judicially noticed. In criminal cases, the court shall instruct the jury that it may, but is not required to, accept as conclusive any fact judicially noticed.

History of TRE 201 (civil): Amended eff. Mar. 1, 1998, by order of Feb. 25, 1998 (960 S.W.2d [Tex.Cases] xxxv). Adopted eff. Sept. 1, 1983, by order of Nov. 23, 1982 (641-42 S.W.2d [Tex.Cases] xxxvii). Source: FRE 201.

See CPRC §38.004; *Commentaries*, "Motion for Judicial Notice," ch. 5-M, p. 401; Brown & Rondon, *Texas Rules of Evidence Handbook* (2013), p. 96.

ANNOTATIONS

Freedom Comms. v. Coronado, 372 S.W.3d 621, 623 (Tex.2012). "[A] court will take judicial notice of another court's records if a party provides proof of the records."

In re J.L., 163 S.W.3d 79, 84 (Tex.2005). "If a fact is generally known, then obviously no expert is needed. [E]xpert testimony invariably concerns matters in dispute which are not capable of accurate resolution from outside, unquestioned sources. Because [expert's] testimony concerned disputed facts and opinions, it should not have been judicially noticed."

Office of Pub. Util. Counsel v. Public Util. Comm'n, 878 S.W.2d 598, 600 (Tex.1994). "A court of appeals has the power to take judicial notice for the first time on appeal."

Guyton v. Monteau, 332 S.W.3d 687, 692-93 (Tex. App.—Houston [14th Dist.] 2011, no pet.). "[T]he trial court's ruling was based on its judicial notice of all documents and testimony ever admitted in this case on any subject. [¶] Such sweeping judicial notice … was an abuse of discretion…. A judicially-noticed fact 'must

be one not subject to reasonable dispute in that it is either (1) generally known within the territorial jurisdiction of the trial court or (2) capable of accurate and ready determination by resort to sources whose accuracy cannot reasonably be questioned.' But '[p]ersonal knowledge is not judicial knowledge. The judge may personally know a fact of which he cannot take judicial notice.' Moreover, the trial court may not take judicial notice of the *truth* of factual statements and allegations contained in the pleadings, affidavits, or other documents in the file. [¶] It is inappropriate for a trial judge to take judicial notice of testimony even in a retrial of the same case." *See also 1.70 Acres v. State*, 935 S.W.2d 480, 489 (Tex.App.—Beaumont 1996, no writ) (variables such as vehicle's speed, road construction or repairs, weather, traffic, or accidents may be matters in someone's personal knowledge, but they are not necessarily matters subject to judicial review).

In re Sigmar, 270 S.W.3d 289, 302 (Tex.App.—Waco 2008, orig. proceeding). "[M]atters of legislative fact or of other non-adjudicative fact are subject to judicial notice but are not governed by Rule 201."

Barnard v. Barnard, 133 S.W.3d 782, 789 (Tex. App.—Fort Worth 2004, pet. denied). "A court may take judicial notice of its own files and the fact that a pleading has been filed in a case. 'A court may not … take judicial notice of the truth of allegations in its records.'"

Apostolic Ch. v. American Honda Motor Co., 833 S.W.2d 553, 555-56 (Tex.App.—Tyler 1992, writ denied). "Highway nomenclature and designations within the trial court's jurisdiction are matters of common knowledge and proper subjects for judicial notice. … In matters involving geographical knowledge, it is not necessary that a formal request for judicial notice be made by a party."

Marble Slab Creamery, Inc. v. Wesic, Inc., 823 S.W.2d 436, 439 (Tex.App.—Houston [14th Dist.] 1992, no writ). "The trial court is entitled to take judicial notice of its own records where the same subject matter between the same parties is involved. [W]e may presume that the trial court took such judicial notice of the record without any request being made and without any announcement that it has done so." *See also Sierad v. Barnett*, 164 S.W.3d 471, 481 (Tex.App.—Dallas 2005, no pet.) (trial court does not need to announce it is taking judicial notice). *But see In re C.L.*, 304 S.W.3d 512, 515-16 (Tex.App.—Waco 2009, no pet.) (appellate court held that trial court did not take judicial notice when

———————————— ✦ ————————————

party did not request it and trial court did not announce in open court it was taking judicial notice).

TRE 202. DETERMINATION OF LAW OF OTHER STATES

A court upon its own motion may, or upon the motion of a party shall, take judicial notice of the constitutions, public statutes, rules, regulations, ordinances, court decisions, and common law of every other state, territory, or jurisdiction of the United States. A party requesting that judicial notice be taken of such matter shall furnish the court sufficient information to enable it properly to comply with the request, and shall give all parties such notice, if any, as the court may deem necessary, to enable all parties fairly to prepare to meet the request. A party is entitled upon timely request to an opportunity to be heard as to the propriety of taking judicial notice and the tenor of the matter noticed. In the absence of prior notification, the request may be made after judicial notice has been taken. Judicial notice of such matters may be taken at any stage of the proceeding. The court's determination shall be subject to review as a ruling on a question of law.

History of TRE 202 (civil): Amended eff. Mar. 1, 1998, by order of Feb. 25, 1998 (960 S.W.2d [Tex.Cases] xxxv). Amended eff. Jan. 1, 1988, by order of Nov. 10, 1986 (733-34 S.W.2d [Tex.Cases] lxxxvi). Amended eff. Nov. 1, 1984, by order of June 25, 1984 (669-70 S.W.2d [Tex.Cases] xxxi): Language was added and deleted to make it clear that all parties are entitled to notice and hearing of the court's taking judicial notice of the law of other states; the last four sentences were added. Adopted eff. Sept. 1, 1983, by order of Nov. 23, 1982 (641-42 S.W.2d [Tex.Cases] xxxviii). Source: TRCP 184, 184a, TRCS art. 3731a (repealed). Former TRCP 184a, re judicial notice, was originally adopted eff. Feb. 1, 1946, by order of Oct. 10, 1945 (8 Tex.B.J. 533 [1945]).

See *Commentaries*, "Motion for Judicial Notice," ch. 5-M, p. 401; Brown & Rondon, *Texas Rules of Evidence Handbook* (2013), p. 127.

ANNOTATIONS

Daugherty v. Southern Pac. Transp., 772 S.W.2d 81, 83 (Tex.1989). "The failure to plead sister-state law does not preclude a court from judicially noticing that law. ... Rule 202 requires the moving party to furnish sufficient information to the trial court for it to determine the foreign law's applicability to the case and to furnish all parties any notice that the court finds necessary." *See also Colvin v. Colvin*, 291 S.W.3d 508, 514 (Tex.App.—Tyler 2009, no pet.) (preliminary motion required to assure application of laws from another jurisdiction).

Burlington N. & Santa Fe Ry. v. Gunderson, Inc., 235 S.W.3d 287, 292 (Tex.App.—Fort Worth 2007, no pet.). "Rule 202 simply provides a mechanism by which a party may compel the trial court to judicially notice

the law of another state; it does not force a party to make a definitive declaration as to which state's law applies."

TRE 203. DETERMINATION OF THE LAWS OF FOREIGN COUNTRIES

A party who intends to raise an issue concerning the law of a foreign country shall give notice in the pleadings or other reasonable written notice, and at least 30 days prior to the date of trial such party shall furnish all parties copies of any written materials or sources that the party intends to use as proof of the foreign law. If the materials or sources were originally written in a language other than English, the party intending to rely upon them shall furnish all parties both a copy of the foreign language text and an English translation. The court, in determining the law of a foreign nation, may consider any material or source, whether or not submitted by a party or admissible under the rules of evidence, including but not limited to affidavits, testimony, briefs, and treatises. If the court considers sources other than those submitted by a party, it shall give all parties notice and a reasonable opportunity to comment on the sources and to submit further materials for review by the court. The court, and not a jury, shall determine the laws of foreign countries. The court's determination shall be subject to review as a ruling on a question of law.

History of TRE 203 (civil): Amended eff. Mar. 1, 1998, by order of Feb. 25, 1998 (960 S.W.2d [Tex.Cases] xxxvi). Amended eff. Nov. 1, 1984, by order of June 25, 1984 (669-70 S.W.2d [Tex.Cases] xxxii): The words "all parties" were substituted for "to the opposing party or counsel" in the first and second sentences; in the fourth sentence, "all" was substituted for "the"; in the last sentence, "The court's" was substituted for "It's"; and the words "on appeal" were deleted. Adopted eff. Sept. 1, 1983, by order of Nov. 23, 1982 (641-42 S.W.2d [Tex.Cases] xxxviii). Source: TRCS art. 3718; FRCrP 26(1), 44(a)(1).

See *Commentaries*, "Motion for Judicial Notice," ch. 5-M, p. 401; Brown & Rondon, *Texas Rules of Evidence Handbook* (2013), p. 130.

ANNOTATIONS

Long Distance Int'l v. Telefonos de Mexico, S.A. de C.V., 49 S.W.3d 347, 351 (Tex.2001). "Rule 203 has been aptly characterized as a hybrid rule by which the presentation of the foreign law to the court resembles the presentment of evidence but which ultimately is decided as a question of law. Summary judgment is not precluded when experts disagree on the law's meaning if, as here, the parties do not dispute that all the pertinent foreign law was properly submitted in evidence. When experts disagree on how the foreign law applies to the facts, the court is presented with a question of law."

TRE 203

⭐

Pennwell Corp. v. Ken Assocs., 123 S.W.3d 756, 760-61 (Tex.App.—Houston [14th Dist.] 2003, pet. denied). "Although appearing under the subtitle 'Judicial Notice' in the [TREs], the procedure established under Rule 203 for presentment of foreign law is not considered a judicial notice procedure because that term refers only to adjudicative facts and not to matters of law. Thus, the specific procedures set forth in Rule 203 must be followed for the determination of foreign law. [A] party requesting judicial notice must furnish the court with sufficient information to enable it to properly comply with the request; otherwise, the failure to provide adequate proof results in a presumption that the law of the foreign jurisdiction is identical to that of Texas." *See also Gerdes v. Kennamer*, 155 S.W.3d 541, 548 (Tex.App.—Corpus Christi 2004, no pet.).

TRE 204. DETERMINATION OF TEXAS CITY & COUNTY ORDINANCES, THE CONTENTS OF THE TEXAS REGISTER, & THE RULES OF AGENCIES PUBLISHED IN THE ADMINISTRATIVE CODE

A court upon its own motion may, or upon the motion of a party shall, take judicial notice of the ordinances of municipalities and counties of Texas, of the contents of the Texas Register, and of the codified rules of the agencies published in the Administrative Code. Any party requesting that judicial notice be taken of such matter shall furnish the court sufficient information to enable it properly to comply with the request, and shall give all parties such notice, if any, as the court may deem necessary, to enable all parties fairly to prepare to meet the request. A party is entitled upon timely request to an opportunity to be heard as to the propriety of taking judicial notice and the tenor of the matter noticed. In the absence of prior notification, the request may be made after judicial notice has been taken. The court's determination shall be subject to review as a ruling on a question of law.

History of TRE 204 (civil): Amended eff. Mar. 1, 1998, by order of Feb. 25, 1998 (960 S.W.2d [Tex.Cases] xxxvi). Amended eff. Jan. 1, 1988, by order of Nov. 10, 1986 (733-34 S.W.2d [Tex.Cases] lxxxvii): Judicial notice upon motion of a party is made mandatory rather than discretionary. Adopted eff. Nov. 1, 1984, by order of June 25, 1984 (669-70 S.W.2d [Tex.Cases] xxxii). Source: New rule.

See *Commentaries*, "Motion for Judicial Notice," ch. 5-M, p. 401; Brown & Rondon, *Texas Rules of Evidence Handbook* (2013), p. 133.

ANNOTATIONS

Office of Pub. Util. Counsel v. Public Util. Comm'n, 878 S.W.2d 598, 600 (Tex.1994). "The court of appeals ... erred by refusing to take judicial notice of

the published order of [respondent]. ... The authenticity and contents of [respondent's] ratemaking order are capable of accurate and ready determination by resort to a published record whose accuracy cannot reasonably be questioned."

Eckmann v. Des Rosiers, 940 S.W.2d 394, 399 (Tex.App.—Austin 1997, no writ). "[T]he duty [to take judicial notice is] mandatory, even in the absence of a request under Rule 204, respecting administrative agency regulations published in the Texas Register and Texas Administrative Code. ... They are legislative facts, or a part of the body of law a court is required to apply in reasoning toward a decision."

ARTICLE III. PRESUMPTIONS
[No rules adopted at this time.]

ARTICLE IV. RELEVANCY & ITS LIMITS

TRE 401. DEFINITION OF "RELEVANT EVIDENCE"

"Relevant evidence" means evidence having any tendency to make the existence of any fact that is of consequence to the determination of the action more probable or less probable than it would be without the evidence.

History of TRE 401 (civil): Amended eff. Mar. 1, 1998, by order of Feb. 25, 1998 (960 S.W.2d [Tex.Cases] xxxvii). Amended eff. Nov. 1, 1984, by order of June 25, 1984 (669-70 S.W.2d [Tex.Cases] xxxiii): Title and entire rule were changed. Adopted eff. Sept. 1, 1983, by order of Nov. 23, 1982 (641-42 S.W.2d [Tex.Cases] xxxix). Source: FRE 401.

See Brown & Rondon, *Texas Rules of Evidence Handbook* (2013), p. 173.

ANNOTATIONS

Coastal Transp. Co. v. Crown Cent. Pet. Corp., 136 S.W.3d 227, 232 (Tex.2004). "Opinion testimony that is conclusory or speculative is not relevant evidence, because it does not tend to make the existence of a material fact 'more probable or less probable.'"

E.I. du Pont de Nemours & Co. v. Robinson, 923 S.W.2d 549, 556 (Tex.1995). "[T]o constitute scientific knowledge which will assist the trier of fact, the proposed [scientific] testimony must be relevant and reliable. [¶] The requirement that the proposed testimony be relevant incorporates traditional relevancy analysis under [TREs] 401 and 402.... To be relevant, the proposed testimony must be 'sufficiently tied to the facts of the case that it will aid the jury in resolving a factual dispute.'"

Transportation Ins. v. Moriel, 879 S.W.2d 10, 24-25 (Tex.1994). "Simply because a piece or pieces of evidence are *material* in the sense that they make a 'fact that is of consequence to the determination of the action more ... or less probable' does not render the evidence *legally sufficient*. As Professor McCormick succinctly put it, 'a brick is not a wall.'"

TRE 402. RELEVANT EVIDENCE GENERALLY ADMISSIBLE; IRRELEVANT EVIDENCE INADMISSIBLE

All relevant evidence is admissible, except as otherwise provided by Constitution, by statute, by these rules, or by other rules prescribed pursuant to statutory authority. Evidence which is not relevant is inadmissible.

History of TRE 402 (civil): Amended eff. Mar. 1, 1998, by order of Feb. 25, 1998 (960 S.W.2d [Tex.Cases] xxxvii). Adopted eff. Sept. 1, 1983, by order of Nov. 23, 1982 (641-42 S.W.2d [Tex.Cases] xxxix). Source: FRE 402.

See Brown & Rondon, *Texas Rules of Evidence Handbook* (2013), p. 173.

E.I. du Pont de Nemours & Co. v. Robinson, 923 S.W.2d 549, 556 (Tex.1995). "Evidence that has no relationship to any of the issues in the case is irrelevant and does not satisfy [TRE] 702's requirement that the testimony be of assistance to the jury. It is thus inadmissible under Rule 702 as well as under [TREs] 401 and 402."

Lunsford v. Morris, 746 S.W.2d 471, 473 (Tex. 1988), *disapproved on other grounds*, *Walker v. Packer*, 827 S.W.2d 833 (Tex.1992). The TREs do not "contemplate exclusion of otherwise relevant proof unless the evidence proffered is unfairly prejudicial, privileged, incompetent, or otherwise *legally* inadmissible."

Jampole v. Touchy, 673 S.W.2d 569, 573 (Tex. 1984), *disapproved on other grounds*, *Walker v. Packer*, 827 S.W.2d 833 (Tex.1992). "To increase the likelihood that all relevant evidence will be disclosed and brought before the trier of fact, the law circumscribes a significantly larger class of discoverable evidence [than admissible evidence] to include anything reasonably calculated to lead to the discovery of material evidence."

TRE 403. EXCLUSION OF RELEVANT EVIDENCE ON SPECIAL GROUNDS

Although relevant, evidence may be excluded if its probative value is substantially outweighed by the danger of unfair prejudice, confusion of the issues, or misleading the jury, or by considerations of undue delay, or needless presentation of cumulative evidence.

History of TRE 403 (civil): Amended eff. Mar. 1, 1998, by order of Feb. 25, 1998 (960 S.W.2d [Tex.Cases] xxxvii). Adopted eff. Sept. 1, 1983, by order of Nov. 23, 1982 (641-42 S.W.2d [Tex.Cases] xxxix). Source: FRE 403.

See *Commentaries*, "Objecting to Evidence," ch. 8-D, p. 708; Brown & Rondon, *Texas Rules of Evidence Handbook* (2013), p. 190.

Bay Area Healthcare Grp. v. McShane, 239 S.W.3d 231, 234 (Tex.2007). "[T]estimony is not inadmissible on the sole ground that it is 'prejudicial' because in our adversarial system, much of a proponent's evidence is legitimately intended to wound the opponent."

Owens-Corning Fiberglas Corp. v. Malone, 972 S.W.2d 35, 41 (Tex.1998). "Evidence that is not relevant, or is unduly prejudicial, and thus, not admissible to mitigate punitive damages, includes actual damage amounts paid by settlements or by judgments; the number of pending claims filed against a defendant for the same conduct; the number of anticipated claims for the same conduct; insurance coverage; unpaid punitive damages awards for the same course of conduct; and evidence of punitive damages that may be levied in the future."

Ford Motor Co. v. Miles, 967 S.W.2d 377, 389 (Tex. 1998). "[R]elevant photographic evidence is admissible unless it is merely calculated to arouse the sympathy, prejudice or passion [of] the jury where the photographs do not serve to illustrate disputed issues or aid the jury in understanding the case. The videos were calculated to arouse the sympathy and passions of the jury." (Internal quotes omitted.)

In re E.A.G., 373 S.W.3d 129, 147 (Tex.App.—San Antonio 2012, pet. denied). "The relevant criteria for determining whether the prejudice of admitting the evidence substantially outweighs the probative value include, but are not limited to, the following: (1) the probative value of the evidence; (2) the potential the evidence has to impress the jury in an irrational but nevertheless indelible way; (3) the time needed to develop the evidence; and (4) the proponent's need for the evidence to prove a fact of consequence."

Murray v. TDFPS, 294 S.W.3d 360, 368 (Tex.App.—Austin 2009, no pet.). "Rule 403 favors the admission of relevant evidence and carries a presumption that relevant evidence will be more probative than prejudicial. To exclude evidence under Rule 403 is an extraordinary remedy that must be used sparingly." (Internal quotes omitted.) *See also In re D.O.*, 338 S.W.3d 29, 37 (Tex. App.—Eastland 2011, no pet.).

✦

In re J.B.C., 233 S.W.3d 88, 94-95 (Tex.App.—Fort Worth 2007, pet. denied). "A court may consider the following factors in determining whether the probative value of photographs is substantially outweighed by the danger of unfair prejudice: (1) the number of exhibits offered, (2) their gruesomeness, (3) their detail, (4) their size, (5) whether they are offered in color or in black and white, (6) whether they are close-up, and (7) whether the body depicted is clothed or naked. Autopsy photographs are generally admissible unless they depict mutilation caused by the autopsy itself. However, photographs that depict the nature, location, and extent of a wound have been declared probative enough to outweigh any prejudicial effect. Changes rendered by the autopsy process are of minor significance if the disturbing nature of the photograph is primarily due to the injuries caused by the appellant." *See also In re K.Y.*, 273 S.W.3d 703, 710 (Tex.App.—Houston [14th Dist.] 2008, no pet.).

In re N.R.C., 94 S.W.3d 799, 807 (Tex.App.—Houston [14th Dist.] 2002, pet. denied). The TREs "discourage '*needless* presentation of cumulative evidence,' not cumulativeness in and of itself. The mere fact that another witness may have given the same or substantially the same testimony is not the decisive factor. Rather, we consider whether the excluded testimony would have added substantial weight to the complainant's case." *See also Benavides v. Cushman, Inc.*, 189 S.W.3d 875, 883-84 (Tex.App.—Houston [1st Dist.] 2006, no pet.).

TRE 404. CHARACTER EVIDENCE NOT ADMISSIBLE TO PROVE CONDUCT; EXCEPTIONS; OTHER CRIMES

(a) **Character Evidence Generally.** Evidence of a person's character or character trait is not admissible for the purpose of proving action in conformity therewith on a particular occasion, except:

(1) *Character of accused.* Evidence of a pertinent character trait offered:

(A) by an accused in a criminal case, or by the prosecution to rebut the same, or

(B) by a party accused in a civil case of conduct involving moral turpitude, or by the accusing party to rebut the same;

(2) *Character of victim.* In a criminal case and subject to Rule 412, evidence of a pertinent character trait of the victim of the crime offered by an accused, or by the prosecution to rebut the same, or evidence of peaceable character of the victim offered by the prosecution in a homicide case to rebut evidence that the victim was the first aggressor; or in a civil case, evidence of character for violence of the alleged victim of assaultive conduct offered on the issue of self-defense by a party accused of the assaultive conduct, or evidence of peaceable character to rebut the same;

(3) *Character of witness.* Evidence of the character of a witness, as provided in rules 607, 608 and 609.

(b) **Other Crimes, Wrongs or Acts.** Evidence of other crimes, wrongs or acts is not admissible to prove the character of a person in order to show action in conformity therewith. It may, however, be admissible for other purposes, such as proof of motive, opportunity, intent, preparation, plan, knowledge, identity, or absence of mistake or accident, provided that upon timely request by the accused in a criminal case, reasonable notice is given in advance of trial of intent to introduce in the State's case-in-chief such evidence other than that arising in the same transaction.

History of TRE 404 (civil): Amended eff. Mar. 1, 1998, by order of Feb. 25, 1998 (960 S.W.2d [Tex.Cases] xxxvii). Adopted eff. Sept. 1, 1983, by order of Nov. 23, 1982 (641-42 S.W.2d [Tex.Cases] xxxix). Source: FRE 404.

See Brown & Rondon, *Texas Rules of Evidence Handbook* (2013), p. 224.

ANNOTATIONS

Service Corp. v. Guerra, 348 S.W.3d 221, 235 (Tex. 2011). "Evidence of other wrongs or acts is not admissible to prove character in order to show 'action in conformity therewith.' But it is admissible to show a party's intent, if material, provided the prior acts are 'so connected with the transaction at issue that they may all be parts of a system, scheme or plan.' This can be shown through evidence of similar acts temporally relevant and of the same substantive basis."

State Bar v. Evans, 774 S.W.2d 656, 658 (Tex. 1989). "Since [attorney] was accused of conduct involving moral turpitude, he was allowed to offer evidence of a pertinent trait of his character, which he did; the State Bar was then allowed to offer rebuttal testimony, which it did."

In re V.V., 349 S.W.3d 548, 557 n.3 (Tex.App.—Houston [1st Dist.] 2010, pet. denied). "Rule 404(b) does not require a final conviction as a predicate to ad-

---

⭐

---

mission of extraneous offense evidence of other 'wrongs or acts,' if that evidence is otherwise relevant and admissible."

TRE 405. METHODS OF PROVING CHARACTER

(a) Reputation or Opinion. In all cases in which evidence of a person's character or character trait is admissible, proof may be made by testimony as to reputation or by testimony in the form of an opinion. In a criminal case, to be qualified to testify at the guilt stage of trial concerning the character or character trait of an accused, a witness must have been familiar with the reputation, or with the underlying facts or information upon which the opinion is based, prior to the day of the offense. In all cases where testimony is admitted under this rule, on cross-examination inquiry is allowable into relevant specific instances of conduct.

(b) Specific Instances of Conduct. In cases in which a person's character or character trait is an essential element of a charge, claim or defense, proof may also be made of specific instances of that person's conduct.

History of TRE 405 (civil): Amended eff. Mar. 1, 1998, by order of Feb. 25, 1998 (960 S.W.2d [Tex.Cases] xxxviii). Adopted eff. Sept. 1, 1983, by order of Nov. 23, 1982 (641-42 S.W.2d [Tex.Cases] xl). Source: FRE 405.

See Brown & Rondon, *Texas Rules of Evidence Handbook* (2013), p. 225.

ANNOTATIONS

In re G.M.P., 909 S.W.2d 198, 209 (Tex.App.—Houston [14th Dist.] 1995, no writ). "[W]hen a witness testifies as to the character of the accused, Rule 405(a) allows 'do you know' questions to be asked of the witness to test the basis for his personal opinion. Here, by making the statement 'My son wouldn't do that,' [D's father] became a character witness, espousing his opinion about [D's] propensity to commit the crime."

International Sec. Life Ins. v. Melancon, 463 S.W.2d 762, 767 (Tex.App.—Beaumont 1971, writ ref'd n.r.e.). In interrogating a witness on the subject of reputation, the only proper questions are "'[w]hether he knows the general character or reputation of the witness intended to be impeached in point of truth among his neighbors[.] If so, then what that character is, whether good or bad[.]' [¶] 'We think the proper practice should be, that, after the impeaching witness has, prima facie, thus first qualified himself to speak of the general reputation of the other witness, ... then, before he answers the question as to what that rep-

utation is, the opposite party, if he demands it, should have the right to cross-examine as to his means of knowledge....'"

TRE 406. HABIT; ROUTINE PRACTICE

Evidence of the habit of a person or of the routine practice of an organization, whether corroborated or not and regardless of the presence of eyewitnesses, is relevant to prove that the conduct of the person or organization on a particular occasion was in conformity with the habit or routine practice.

History of TRE 406 (civil): Amended eff. Mar. 1, 1998, by order of Feb. 25, 1998 (960 S.W.2d [Tex.Cases] xxxviii). Adopted eff. Sept. 1, 1983, by order of Nov. 23, 1982 (641-42 S.W.2d [Tex.Cases] xl). Source: FRE 406.

See Brown & Rondon, *Texas Rules of Evidence Handbook* (2013), p. 278; *O'Connor's Texas Forms*, FORM 5E:1.

ANNOTATIONS

Ortiz v. Glusman, 334 S.W.3d 812, 816 (Tex. App.—El Paso 2011, pet. denied). "To be admissible, the habit evidence must be 'a regular response to a repeated specific situation.' In other words, his response must be the same specific one to the same set of facts. One to two examples is insufficient to demonstrate a habit." *See also In re Astro Air, L.P.*, No. 12-10-00108-CV (Tex.App.—Tyler 2010, orig. proceeding) (memo op.; 9-15-10) (organization's routine practice does not conclusively establish fact to be proved).

TRE 407. SUBSEQUENT REMEDIAL MEASURES; NOTIFICATION OF DEFECT

(a) Subsequent Remedial Measures. When, after an injury or harm allegedly caused by an event, measures are taken that, if taken previously, would have made the injury or harm less likely to occur, evidence of the subsequent remedial measures is not admissible to prove negligence, culpable conduct, a defect in a product, a defect in a product's design, or a need for a warning or instruction. This rule does not require the exclusion of evidence of subsequent remedial measures when offered for another purpose, such as proving ownership, control, or feasibility of precautionary measures, if controverted, or impeachment.

(b) Notification of Defect. A written notification by a manufacturer of any defect in a product produced by such manufacturer to purchasers thereof is admissible against the manufacturer on the issue of existence of the defect to the extent that it is relevant.

TRE 407

---⭐---

History of TRE 407 (civil): Amended eff. July 1, 2003, by order of Aug. 29, 2003 (114-15 S.W.3d [Tex.Cases] xxii). Amended eff. Mar. 1, 1998, by order of Feb. 25, 1998 (960 S.W.2d [Tex.Cases] xxxix). Adopted eff. Sept. 1, 1983, by order of Nov. 23, 1982 (641-42 S.W.2d [Tex.Cases] xl). Source: FRE 407.

See Brown & Rondon, *Texas Rules of Evidence Handbook* (2013), p. 285; *O'Connor's Texas Forms*, FORM 5E:1.

ANNOTATIONS

Beavers v. Northrop Worldwide Aircraft Servs., 821 S.W.2d 669, 677 (Tex.App.—Amarillo 1991, writ denied). "[W]e hold the exclusion under Rule 407(a) does not apply to evidence of subsequent remedial measures taken by third parties when offered to show that a defendant was not the cause of plaintiff's injury."

E.V.R. II Assocs. v. Brundige, 813 S.W.2d 552, 556 (Tex.App.—Dallas 1991, no writ). "Evidence of subsequent remedial repair is inadmissible to establish negligence. The rule is one of policy and good sense to avoid discouraging safety measures. [T]he rule is inapplicable where the evidence would be valid as to other issues which also exist in the case."

TRE 408. COMPROMISE & OFFERS TO COMPROMISE

Evidence of (1) furnishing or offering or promising to furnish or (2) accepting or offering or promising to accept, a valuable consideration in compromising or attempting to compromise a claim which was disputed as to either validity or amount is not admissible to prove liability for or invalidity of the claim or its amount. Evidence of conduct or statements made in compromise negotiations is likewise not admissible. This rule does not require the exclusion of any evidence otherwise discoverable merely because it is presented in the course of compromise negotiations. This rule also does not require exclusion when the evidence is offered for another purpose, such as proving bias or prejudice or interest of a witness or a party, negativing a contention of undue delay, or proving an effort to obstruct a criminal investigation or prosecution.

History of TRE 408 (civil): Amended eff. Mar. 1, 1998, by order of Feb. 25, 1998 (960 S.W.2d [Tex.Cases] xxxix). Adopted eff. Sept. 1, 1983, by order of Nov. 23, 1982 (641-42 S.W.2d [Tex.Cases] xl). Source: FRE 408.

See Brown & Rondon, *Texas Rules of Evidence Handbook* (2013), p. 295.

ANNOTATIONS

Ford Motor Co. v. Leggat, 904 S.W.2d 643, 649 (Tex.1995). "Settlement agreements are discoverable to the extent they are relevant. Settlement agreements ... are not admissible at trial to prove liability." *See also Birchfield v. Texarkana Mem'l Hosp.*, 747 S.W.2d 361, 365 (Tex.1987).

Vinson Minerals, Ltd. v. XTO Energy, Inc., 335 S.W.3d 344, 351-52 (Tex.App.—Fort Worth 2010, pet. denied). "Offers of settlement are not admissible to prove liability or invalidity of a claim or its amount. In an offer of settlement or compromise, a party concedes some right to which he believes he is entitled in order to bring about a mutual settlement. But rule 408 does not bar the admission of settlement offers when offered for another relevant purpose. Thus, an offer or demand for settlement may be admissible for another purpose, such as to demonstrate bias or prejudice. [¶] The burden is on the party objecting to evidence under rule 408 to show that it was a part of settlement negotiations and not offered for another purpose."

Avary v. Bank of Am., 72 S.W.3d 779, 799 (Tex. App.—Dallas 2002, pet. denied). "[E]vidence of an offer to compromise is admissible to prove or disprove the extracontractual liability of an insurance company on a bad faith claim, even against the party making the offer.... [¶] Rule 408 does not prevent a party from proving a separate cause of action simply because some of the acts complained of took place during compromise negotiations."

TRE 409. PAYMENT OF MEDICAL & SIMILAR EXPENSES

Evidence of furnishing or offering or promising to pay medical, hospital, or similar expenses occasioned by an injury is not admissible to prove liability for the injury.

History of TRE 409 (civil): Amended eff. Mar. 1, 1998, by order of Feb. 25, 1998 (960 S.W.2d [Tex.Cases] xxxix). Adopted eff. Sept. 1, 1983, by order of Nov. 23, 1982 (641-42 S.W.2d [Tex.Cases] xli). Source: FRE 409.

See Brown & Rondon, *Texas Rules of Evidence Handbook* (2013), p. 314; *O'Connor's Texas Forms*, FORM 5E:1.

ANNOTATIONS

Port Neches ISD v. Soignier, 702 S.W.2d 756, 757 (Tex.App.—Beaumont 1986, writ ref'd n.r.e.). A letter from an insurance company authorizing medical expenses for a workers' compensation plaintiff and stating that all future medical bills should be sent to the insurance company goes beyond TRE 409 and actually admits coverage, and thus is admissible.

TRE 410. INADMISSIBILITY OF PLEAS, PLEA DISCUSSIONS & RELATED STATEMENTS

Except as otherwise provided in this rule, evidence of the following is not admissible against the defendant who made the plea or was a participant in the plea discussions:

TRE 407

⋆

(1) a plea of guilty that was later withdrawn;

(2) in civil cases, a plea of *nolo contendere*, and in criminal cases, a plea of *nolo contendere* that was later withdrawn;

(3) any statement made in the course of any proceedings under Rule 11 of the Federal Rules of Criminal Procedure or comparable state procedure regarding, in a civil case, either a plea of guilty that was later withdrawn or a plea of *nolo contendere*, or in a criminal case, either a plea of guilty that was later withdrawn or a plea of *nolo contendere* that was later withdrawn; or

(4) any statement made in the course of plea discussions with an attorney for the prosecuting authority, in a civil case, that do not result in a plea of guilty or that result in a plea of guilty later withdrawn, or in a criminal case, that do not result in a plea of guilty or a plea of *nolo contendere* or that results in a plea, later withdrawn, of guilty or *nolo contendere*.

However, such a statement is admissible in any proceeding wherein another statement made in the course of the same plea or plea discussions has been introduced and the statement ought in fairness be considered contemporaneously with it.

History of TRE 410 (civil): Amended eff. Mar. 1, 1998, by order of Feb. 25, 1998 (960 S.W.2d [Tex.Cases] xxxix). Adopted eff. Sept. 1, 1983, by order of Nov. 23, 1982 (641-42 S.W.2d [Tex.Cases] xli). Source: FRE 410.

See Brown & Rondon, *Texas Rules of Evidence Handbook* (2013), p. 318.

TRE 411. LIABILITY INSURANCE

Evidence that a person was or was not insured against liability is not admissible upon the issue whether the person acted negligently or otherwise wrongfully. This rule does not require the exclusion of evidence of insurance against liability when offered for another issue, such as proof of agency, ownership, or control, if disputed, or bias or prejudice of a witness.

History of TRE 411 (civil): Amended eff. Mar. 1, 1998, by order of Feb. 25, 1998 (960 S.W.2d [Tex.Cases] xl). Adopted eff. Sept. 1, 1983, by order of Nov. 23, 1982 (641-42 S.W.2d [Tex.Cases] xli). Source: FRE 411.

See Brown & Rondon, *Texas Rules of Evidence Handbook* (2013), p. 331; *O'Connor's Texas Forms*, FORM 5E:1.

ANNOTATIONS

Brownsville Pediatric Ass'n v. Reyes, 68 S.W.3d 184, 193 (Tex.App.—Corpus Christi 2002, no pet.). "[Ds] objected to the mention of insurance in the context of an insurance company issuing an annuity. The reference to insurance in this instance is not the type of injection of insurance into a case that is protected by

[TRE 411]. Thus, the harm the rule was designed to prevent does not come into play."

Beall v. Ditmore, 867 S.W.2d 791, 795 (Tex. App.—El Paso 1993, writ denied). "The mere mention of insurance during trial before a jury, though erroneous, does not result in an automatic mistrial or reversal."

TRE 412. EVIDENCE OF PREVIOUS SEXUAL CONDUCT IN CRIMINAL CASES

(a) Reputation or Opinion Evidence. In a prosecution for sexual assault or aggravated sexual assault, or attempt to commit sexual assault or aggravated sexual assault, reputation or opinion evidence of the past sexual behavior of an alleged victim of such crime is not admissible.

(b) Evidence of Specific Instances. In a prosecution for sexual assault or aggravated sexual assault, or attempt to commit sexual assault or aggravated sexual assault, evidence of specific instances of an alleged victim's past sexual behavior is also not admissible, unless:

(1) such evidence is admitted in accordance with paragraphs (c) and (d) of this rule;

(2) it is evidence:

(A) that is necessary to rebut or explain scientific or medical evidence offered by the State;

(B) of past sexual behavior with the accused and is offered by the accused upon the issue of whether the alleged victim consented to the sexual behavior which is the basis of the offense charged;

(C) that relates to the motive or bias of the alleged victim;

(D) is admissible under Rule 609; or

(E) that is constitutionally required to be admitted; and

(3) its probative value outweighs the danger of unfair prejudice.

(c) Procedure for Offering Evidence. If the defendant proposes to introduce any documentary evidence or to ask any question, either by direct examination or cross-examination of any witness, concerning specific instances of the alleged victim's past sexual behavior, the defendant must inform the court out of the hearing of the jury prior to introducing any such evidence or asking any such question. After this notice, the court shall conduct an in camera hearing, recorded

---

★

---

by the court reporter, to determine whether the proposed evidence is admissible under paragraph (b) of this rule. The court shall determine what evidence is admissible and shall accordingly limit the questioning. The defendant shall not go outside these limits or refer to any evidence ruled inadmissible in camera without prior approval of the court without the presence of the jury.

(d) Record Sealed. The court shall seal the record of the in camera hearing required in paragraph (c) of this rule for delivery to the appellate court in the event of an appeal.

History of TRE 412 (criminal): Amended eff. Jan. 1, 2007, by order of Dec. 13, 2006 (Tex.Crim.App. Order, Misc. Docket No. 06-101): Deleted TRE 412(e). Amended eff. Mar. 1, 1998, by order of Feb. 25, 1998 (960 S.W.2d [Tex.Cases] xl). Adopted eff. Sept. 1, 1986, by order of Dec. 18, 1985 (701-02 S.W.2d [Tex. Cases] xxxix).

See Brown & Rondon, *Texas Rules of Evidence Handbook* (2013), p. 339.

ANNOTATIONS

In re Doe, 22 S.W.3d 601, 611-12 (Tex.App.—Austin 2000, orig. proceeding). "[P] argues that the 'rape victims shield laws,' incorporated in [TRE] 412, should apply despite the fact that the Rule specifically applies only in criminal cases. [¶] At this early stage of the litigation and considering the fact that [P] pleads that this was a forcible assault and the grand jury indicted [D's employee] under the criminal statutes for the crime of sexual assault, we hold that until the record is more fully developed and these issues are clarified the rape shield laws ought to protect the victim ... at this time. We hold that the trial court abused its discretion by failing to issue a protective order preventing [D] from questioning [P] about her past and present sexual activity."

ARTICLE V. PRIVILEGES

TRE 501. PRIVILEGES RECOGNIZED ONLY AS PROVIDED

Except as otherwise provided by Constitution, by statute, by these rules, or by other rules prescribed pursuant to statutory authority, no person has a privilege to:

(1) refuse to be a witness;

(2) refuse to disclose any matter;

(3) refuse to produce any object or writing; or

(4) prevent another from being a witness or disclosing any matter or producing any object or writing.

History of TRE 501 (civil): Amended eff. Mar. 1, 1998, by order of Feb. 25, 1998 (960 S.W.2d [Tex.Cases] xli). Adopted eff. Sept. 1, 1983, by order of Nov. 23, 1982 (641-42 S.W.2d [Tex.Cases] xli). Source: Unif. R. Evid. 501

(1974). See TRCS arts. 41a-1, §26 (repealed); 3715 (repealed); 3715a (repealed); 4495b, §5.08 (repealed); 5561h (repealed). See also Code Crim. Proc. arts. 38.10, 38.11 (repealed).

See *Commentaries*, "Scope of Discovery," ch. 6-B, p. 460; Brown & Rondon, *Texas Rules of Evidence Handbook* (2013), p. 361.

ANNOTATIONS

Volkswagen, A.G. v. Valdez, 909 S.W.2d 900, 902-03 (Tex.1995). The trial court must weigh the following factors when evaluating a privilege of a foreign country: (1) the importance of the discovery request to the investigation or litigation; (2) the degree of specificity of the request; (3) whether the information originated in the U.S.; (4) the availability of alternative means of securing the information; and (5) the extent to which noncompliance with the request would undermine important interests of the U.S., or the extent to which compliance would undermine important interests of the foreign jurisdiction where the information is located.

State v. Lowry, 802 S.W.2d 669, 671 (Tex.1991). "Only in certain narrow circumstances is it appropriate to obstruct the search for truth by denying discovery. Very limited exceptions to the strongly preferred policy of openness are recognized in our state procedural rules and statutes."

Oyster Creek Fin. Corp. v. Richwood Invs., 957 S.W.2d 640, 646 (Tex.App.—Amarillo 1997, pet. denied). "[B]ecause evidence is presumed discoverable, the party resisting discovery ... bears the burden of establishing the privilege and, therefore, must plead it and present evidence which establishes that the document(s) in question qualify for the privilege as a matter of law."

TRE 502. REQUIRED REPORTS PRIVILEGED BY STATUTE

A person, corporation, association, or other organization or entity, either public or private, making a return or report required by law to be made has a privilege to refuse to disclose and to prevent any other person from disclosing the return or report, if the law requiring it to be made so provides. A public officer or agency to whom a return or report is required by law to be made has a privilege to refuse to disclose the return or report if the law requiring it to be made so provides. No privilege exists under this rule in actions involving perjury, false statements, fraud in the return or report, or other failure to comply with the law in question.

TRE 412

History of TRE 502 (civil): Amended eff. Mar. 1, 1998, by order of Feb. 25, 1998 (960 S.W.2d [Tex.Cases] xlii). Adopted eff. Sept. 1, 1983, by order of Nov. 23, 1982 (641-42 S.W.2d [Tex.Cases] xlii). Source: New rule. See proposed FRE 502 (1972).

See *Commentaries*, "Scope of Discovery," ch. 6-B, p. 460; Brown & Rondon, *Texas Rules of Evidence Handbook* (2013), p. 368.

TRE 503. LAWYER-CLIENT PRIVILEGE

(a) Definitions. As used in this rule:

(1) A "client" is a person, public officer, or corporation, association, or other organization or entity, either public or private, who is rendered professional legal services by a lawyer, or who consults a lawyer with a view to obtaining professional legal services from that lawyer.

(2) A "representative of the client" is:

(A) a person having authority to obtain professional legal services, or to act on advice thereby rendered, on behalf of the client, or

(B) any other person who, for the purpose of effectuating legal representation for the client, makes or receives a confidential communication while acting in the scope of employment for the client.

(3) A "lawyer" is a person authorized, or reasonably believed by the client to be authorized, to engage in the practice of law in any state or nation.

(4) A "representative of the lawyer" is:

(A) one employed by the lawyer to assist the lawyer in the rendition of professional legal services; or

(B) an accountant who is reasonably necessary for the lawyer's rendition of professional legal services.

(5) A communication is "confidential" if not intended to be disclosed to third persons other than those to whom disclosure is made in furtherance of the rendition of professional legal services to the client or those reasonably necessary for the transmission of the communication.

(b) Rules of Privilege.

(1) *General rule of privilege.* A client has a privilege to refuse to disclose and to prevent any other person from disclosing confidential communications made for the purpose of facilitating the rendition of professional legal services to the client:

(A) between the client or a representative of the client and the client's lawyer or a representative of the lawyer;

(B) between the lawyer and the lawyer's representative;

(C) by the client or a representative of the client, or the client's lawyer or a representative of the lawyer, to a lawyer or a representative of a lawyer representing another party in a pending action and concerning a matter of common interest therein;

(D) between representatives of the client or between the client and a representative of the client; or

(E) among lawyers and their representatives representing the same client.

(2) *Special rule of privilege in criminal cases.* In criminal cases, a client has a privilege to prevent the lawyer or lawyer's representative from disclosing any other fact which came to the knowledge of the lawyer or the lawyer's representative by reason of the attorney-client relationship.

(c) Who May Claim the Privilege. The privilege may be claimed by the client, the client's guardian or conservator, the personal representative of a deceased client, or the successor, trustee, or similar representative of a corporation, association, or other organization, whether or not in existence. The person who was the lawyer or the lawyer's representative at the time of the communication is presumed to have authority to claim the privilege but only on behalf of the client.

(d) Exceptions. There is no privilege under this rule:

(1) *Furtherance of crime or fraud.* If the services of the lawyer were sought or obtained to enable or aid anyone to commit or plan to commit what the client knew or reasonably should have known to be a crime or fraud;

(2) *Claimants through same deceased client.* As to a communication relevant to an issue between parties who claim through the same deceased client, regardless of whether the claims are by testate or intestate succession or by *inter vivos* transactions;

(3) *Breach of duty by a lawyer or client.* As to a communication relevant to an issue of breach of duty by a lawyer to the client or by a client to the lawyer;

(4) *Document attested by a lawyer.* As to a communication relevant to an issue concerning an attested document to which the lawyer is an attesting witness; or

(5) *Joint clients.* As to a communication relevant to a matter of common interest between or among two or more clients if the communication was made by any of them to a lawyer retained or consulted in common, when offered in an action between or among any of the clients.

Comment to 1998 change: The addition of subsection (a)(2)(B) adopts a subject matter test for the privilege of an entity, in place of the control group test previously used. See *National Tank Co. v. Brotherton*, 851 S.W.2d 193, 197-98 (Tex.1993).

History of TRE 503 (civil): Amended eff. Mar. 1, 1998, by order of Feb. 25, 1998 (960 S.W.2d [Tex.Cases] xlii). Amended eff. Nov. 1, 1984, by order of June 25, 1984 (669-70 S.W.2d [Tex.Cases] xxxiii): Changed (a)(4); deleted (d); relettered (e) as (d); the language of former par. (d) was deleted because it was deemed unnecessary; the deletion was not intended to change the common-law rule that communications privileged under this rule do not lose their privileged status by reason of the termination of the attorney-client relationship; this rule governs only the attorney-client privilege; it does not restrict the scope of the work-product doctrine. See former TRCP 166b. Adopted eff. Sept. 1, 1983, by order of Nov. 23, 1982 (641-42 S.W.2d [Tex.Cases] xlii). Source: Codification of common-law doctrine. See proposed FRE 503 (1972); Code Crim. Proc. art. 38.10 (repealed).

See *Commentaries*, "Asserting privileges," ch. 6-A, §18.2, p. 443; "Scope of Discovery," ch. 6-B, p. 460; Brown & Rondon, *Texas Rules of Evidence Handbook* (2013), p. 371; *O'Connor's Texas Forms*, FORM 5E:1.

ANNOTATIONS

Generally

In re XL Specialty Ins., 373 S.W.3d 46, 50 (Tex. 2012). "[T]he privilege defined in Rule 503(b)(1)(C) ... has been variously described as the 'joint client' privilege, the 'joint defense' privilege, and the 'common interest' privilege. Courts sometimes use these terms interchangeably, but they involve distinct doctrines that serve different purposes. [¶] The joint client ... doctrine applies '[w]hen the same attorney simultaneously represents two or more clients on the same matter.' *At 51-53:* The joint defense rule applies [only in the context of litigation and] when multiple parties to a lawsuit, each represented by different attorneys, communicate among themselves for the purpose of forming a common defense strategy. [¶] [Under t]he common interest rule[, t]he parties must share a mutual interest, but unlike the joint defense doctrine, the common interest rule applies to 'two or more separately represented persons whatever their denomination in pleadings and whether or not involved in litigation.' [¶] [Because] Texas requires that the communications be made in the context of a pending action[,] our privilege is not a 'common interest' privilege that extends beyond litigation. Nor is it a 'joint defense' privilege, as it applies not just to defendants but to any parties to a pending action. Rule 503(b)(1)(C)'s privilege is more appropriately termed an 'allied litigant' privilege. [¶] The allied litigant doctrine protects communications made between a client, or the client's lawyer, to another party's lawyer, not to the other party itself. This attor-

ney-sharing requirement makes clear that the privilege applies only when the parties have separate counsel." *See also In re JDN Real Estate-McKinney L.P.*, 211 S.W.3d 907, 922 (Tex.App.—Dallas 2006, orig. proceeding).

Duncan v. Board of Disciplinary Appeals, 898 S.W.2d 759, 762 (Tex.1995). "Our rules recognize that our system of justice relies on a client's privilege to speak frankly and candidly with his or her attorney." *See also In re XL Specialty Ins.*, 373 S.W.3d 46, 49 (Tex.2012).

Watson v. Kaminski, 51 S.W.3d 825, 827 (Tex. App.—Houston [1st Dist.] 2001, no pet.). "To be privileged, the communication must relate to pending or proposed litigation and must further the attorney's representation. [¶] The judge must consider the entire communication in its context and must extend the privilege to any statement that bears some relation to an existing or proposed judicial proceeding. All doubt should be resolved in favor of the communication's relation to the proceeding."

Boales v. Brighton Builders, Inc., 29 S.W.3d 159, 168 (Tex.App.—Houston [14th Dist.] 2000, pet. denied). "The [attorney-client] privilege extends to all matters concerning litigation or business transactions, regardless of whether the matters are pertinent to the matter for which the attorney was employed. The statements and advice of the attorney to the client are as protected as the communications of the client to the attorney." *See also In re Small*, 346 S.W.3d 657, 663 (Tex. App.—El Paso 2009, orig. proceeding).

Markowski v. City of Marlin, 940 S.W.2d 720, 726 (Tex.App.—Waco 1997, writ denied). "[A] governmental body has as much right as an individual to consult with its attorney without risking the disclosure of important confidential information."

Perez v. Kirk & Carrigan, 822 S.W.2d 261, 265 (Tex.App.—Corpus Christi 1991, writ denied). "An agreement to form an attorney-client relationship may be implied from the conduct of the parties. Moreover, the relationship does not depend upon the payment of a fee, but may exist as a result of rendering services gratuitously."

Exceptions to Privilege

Granada Corp. v. 1st Ct. of Appeals, 844 S.W.2d 223, 227 (Tex.1992). "The crime-fraud exception [to the attorney-client privilege in TRE 503(d)(1)] applies only if a prima facie case is made of contemplated fraud. Additionally, there must be a relationship between the document for which the privilege is challenged and the prima facie proof offered." *See also In re General Agents Ins. Co.*, 224 S.W.3d 806, 819 (Tex. App.—Houston [14th Dist.] 2007, orig. proceeding); *Warrantech Corp. v. Computer Adapters Servs.*, 134 S.W.3d 516, 527 (Tex.App.—Fort Worth 2004, no pet.).

In re Small, 346 S.W.3d 657, 666 (Tex.App.—El Paso 2009, orig. proceeding). "The *prima facie* requirement is met when the proponent offers evidence establishing the elements of fraud and that the fraud was ongoing, or about to be committed at the time the document was prepared. Mere allegations of fraud are not sufficient. [T]he fact that the plaintiff's cause of action involves fraudulent conduct is also insufficient. The fraud alleged to have occurred must have happened at or during the time the document was prepared, and the document must have been created as part of perpetrating the fraud. The trial court must make findings both that the *prima facie* case has been established and that a nexus exists between the document at issue and the alleged fraud." *See also In re General Agents Ins. Co.*, 224 S.W.3d 806, 819 (Tex.App.—Houston [14th Dist.] 2007, orig. proceeding); *Coats v. Ruiz*, 198 S.W.3d 863, 876-77 (Tex.App.—Dallas 2006, no pet.).

No Attorney-Client Privilege

Joe v. Two Thirty Nine Jt.V., 145 S.W.3d 150, 164 (Tex.2004). "Conducting legal research in preparation for a city council vote does not create an attorney-client relationship between [D] and the City, and sharing that information with fellow council members as part of deliberations does not change that conclusion. [D's] research … in preparation for a city council meeting [is] not part of legal services … and does not create an attorney-client relationship…." *See also In re Texas Farmers Ins. Exch.*, 990 S.W.2d 337, 340 (Tex.App.—Texarkana 1999, orig. proceeding).

Huie v. DeShazo, 922 S.W.2d 920, 921 (Tex.1996). "The issue … is whether the attorney-client privilege protects communications between a trustee and his or her attorney relating to trust administration from discovery by a trust beneficiary. We hold … only the trustee, not the trust beneficiary, is the client of the trustee's attorney. The beneficiary therefore may not discover communications between the trustee and attorney otherwise protected under [TRE] 503."

In re Monsanto Co., 998 S.W.2d 917, 930 (Tex. App.—Waco 1999, orig. proceeding). "We recognize that it might be argued [under TRE 503(a)(2)(B)] that all communications between corporate representatives could be claimed as privileged on the basis that 'the legal department can better represent us if we keep them informed.' We reject that assertion. We do not believe that it is necessary for the legal department to be advised of every development out in the field, no matter how minute."

Offensive Use

Republic Ins. v. Davis, 856 S.W.2d 158, 163 (Tex. 1993). "In an instance in which the privilege is being used as a sword rather than a shield, the privilege may be waived. [T]he following factors should guide the trial court in determining whether a waiver has occurred. [¶] First, … the party asserting the privilege must seek affirmative relief. Second, the privileged information sought must be such that, if believed by the fact finder, in all probability it would be outcome determinative of the cause of action asserted. Mere relevance is insufficient. A contradiction in position without more is insufficient. The confidential communication must go to the very heart of the affirmative relief sought. Third, disclosure of the confidential communication must be the only means by which the aggrieved party may obtain the evidence. If any one of these requirements is lacking, the trial court must uphold the privilege."

TRE 504. HUSBAND-WIFE PRIVILEGES

(a) Confidential Communication Privilege.

(1) *Definition.* A communication is confidential if it is made privately by any person to the person's spouse and it is not intended for disclosure to any other person.

(2) *Rule of privilege.* A person, whether or not a party, or the guardian or representative of an incompetent or deceased person, has a privilege during marriage and afterwards to refuse to disclose and to prevent another from disclosing a confidential communication made to the person's spouse while they were married.

(3) *Who may claim the privilege.* The confidential communication privilege may be claimed by the person or the person's guardian or representative, or by the spouse on the person's behalf. The authority of the spouse to do so is presumed.

TRE 504

★

(4) *Exceptions.* There is no confidential communication privilege:

(A) *Furtherance of crime or fraud.* If the communication was made, in whole or in part, to enable or aid anyone to commit or plan to commit a crime or fraud.

(B) *Proceeding between spouses in civil cases.* In (A)[1] a proceeding brought by or on behalf of one spouse against the other spouse, or (B)[2] a proceeding between a surviving spouse and a person who claims through the deceased spouse, regardless of whether the claim is by testate or intestate succession or by *inter vivos* transaction.

(C) *Crime against spouse or minor child.* In a proceeding in which the party is accused of conduct which, if proved, is a crime against the person of the spouse, any minor child, or any member of the household of either spouse, or, in a criminal proceeding, when the offense charged is under Section 25.01, Penal Code (Bigamy).

(D) *Commitment or similar proceeding.* In a proceeding to commit either spouse or otherwise to place that person or that person's property, or both, under the control of another because of an alleged mental or physical condition.

(E) *Proceeding to establish competence.* In a proceeding brought by or on behalf of either spouse to establish competence.

(b) Privilege not to Testify in Criminal Case.

(1) *Rule of privilege.* In a criminal case, the spouse of the accused has a privilege not to be called as a witness for the state. This rule does not prohibit the spouse from testifying voluntarily for the state, even over objection by the accused. A spouse who testifies on behalf of an accused is subject to cross-examination as provided in rule 611(b).

(2) *Failure to call as witness.* Failure by an accused to call the accused's spouse as a witness, where other evidence indicates that the spouse could testify to relevant matters, is a proper subject of comment by counsel.

(3) *Who may claim the privilege.* The privilege not to testify may be claimed by the person or the person's guardian or representative but not by that person's spouse.

(4) *Exceptions.* The privilege of a person's spouse not to be called as a witness for the state does not apply:

(A) *Certain criminal proceedings.* In any proceeding in which the person is charged with a crime against

the person's spouse, a member of the household of either spouse, or any minor, or in an offense charged under Section 25.01, Penal Code (Bigamy).

(B) *Matters occurring prior to marriage.* As to matters occurring prior to the marriage.

1. **Editor's note:** This should probably read "(i)."

2. **Editor's note:** This should probably read "(ii)."

Comment to 1998 change: The rule eliminates the spousal testimonial privilege for prosecutions in which the testifying spouse is the alleged victim of a crime by the accused. This is intended to be consistent with Code of Criminal Procedure art. 38.10, eff. September 1, 1995.

History of TRE 504 (civil): Amended eff. Jan. 1, 2007, by order of Dec. 13, 2006 (Tex.Crim.App. Order, Misc. Docket No. 06-101). Amended eff. Mar. 1, 1998, by order of Feb. 25, 1998 (960 S.W.2d [Tex.Cases] xliv). Adopted eff. Sept. 1, 1983, by order of Nov. 23, 1982 (641-42 S.W.2d [Tex.Cases] xliii). Source: TRCS art. 3715 (repealed); Code Crim. Proc. art. 38.11 (repealed).

See *Commentaries*, "Asserting privileges," ch. 6-A, §18.2, p. 443; "Scope of Discovery," ch. 6-B, p. 460; Brown & Rondon, *Texas Rules of Evidence Handbook* (2013), p. 418.

ANNOTATIONS

Marshall v. Ryder Sys., 928 S.W.2d 190, 195 (Tex. App.—Houston [14th Dist.] 1996, writ denied). In civil cases, "[t]he marital privilege is limited to *confidential* communications between spouses. Only in criminal cases is there a broad, general privilege protecting a person from being a witness against his or her spouse."

Earthman's, Inc. v. Earthman, 526 S.W.2d 192, 206 (Tex.App.—Houston [1st Dist.] 1975, no writ). "We do not regard as error the trial court's ruling which allowed evidence of communications between [parties] based on conversations prior to and after their divorce. This testimony insofar as relevant to the existing controversy between them was admissible notwithstanding the marital privilege."

TRE 505. COMMUNICATIONS TO MEMBERS OF THE CLERGY

(a) Definitions. As used in this rule:

(1) A "member of the clergy" is a minister, priest, rabbi, accredited Christian Science Practitioner, or other similar functionary of a religious organization or an individual reasonably believed so to be by the person consulting with such individual.

(2) A communication is "confidential" if made privately and not intended for further disclosure except to other persons present in furtherance of the purpose of the communication.

(b) General Rule of Privilege. A person has a privilege to refuse to disclose and to prevent another from disclosing a confidential communication by the person to a member of the clergy in the member's professional character as spiritual adviser.

✦

(c) Who May Claim the Privilege. The privilege may be claimed by the person, by the person's guardian or conservator, or by the personal representative of the person if the person is deceased. The member of the clergy to whom the communication was made is presumed to have authority to claim the privilege but only on behalf of the communicant.

History of TRE 505 (civil): Amended eff. Mar. 1, 1998, by order of Feb. 25, 1998 (960 S.W.2d [Tex.Cases] xlv). Adopted eff. Sept. 1, 1983, by order of Nov. 23, 1982 (641-42 S.W.2d [Tex.Cases] xliv). Source: TRCS art. 3715a (repealed). See Unif. R. Evid. 505 (1974).

See *Commentaries*, "Asserting privileges," ch. 6-A, §18.2, p. 443; "Scope of Discovery," ch. 6-B, p. 460; Brown & Rondon, *Texas Rules of Evidence Handbook* (2013), p. 442.

ANNOTATIONS

Nicholson v. Wittig, 832 S.W.2d 681, 685 (Tex. App.—Houston [1st Dist.] 1992, orig. proceeding). The clergy-communicant "privilege attaches when a person makes a communication with a reasonable expectation of confidentiality to a member of the clergy acting in his or her professional or spiritual capacity. [¶] An individual may invoke a privilege regardless of the nature of the underlying proceeding. *At 686:* Rule 505 makes no reference to the content of the communication; rather, the rule focuses on the counseling opportunity."

TRE 506. POLITICAL VOTE

Every person has a privilege to refuse to disclose the tenor of the person's vote at a political election conducted by secret ballot unless the vote was cast illegally.

History of TRE 506 (civil): Amended eff. Mar. 1, 1998, by order of Feb. 25, 1998 (960 S.W.2d [Tex.Cases] xlvi). Adopted eff. Sept. 1, 1983, by order of Nov. 23, 1982 (641-42 S.W.2d [Tex.Cases] xliv). Source: Elec. Code §221.009(a) (1986). See proposed FRE 507 (1972).

See *Commentaries*, "Asserting privileges," ch. 6-A, §18.2, p. 443; "Scope of Discovery," ch. 6-B, p. 460; Brown & Rondon, *Texas Rules of Evidence Handbook* (2013), p. 448.

ANNOTATIONS

Oliphint v. Christy, 299 S.W.2d 933, 939 (Tex. 1957). "The privilege of nondisclosure belongs only to the legal voter and the individual who votes illegally cannot be considered a 'voter' for any purpose." *See also Simmons v. Jones*, 838 S.W.2d 298, 300 (Tex.App.—El Paso 1992, no writ).

TRE 507. TRADE SECRETS

A person has a privilege, which may be claimed by the person or the person's agent or employee, to refuse to disclose and to prevent other persons from disclosing a trade secret owned by the person, if the allowance of the privilege will not tend to conceal fraud or otherwise work injustice. When disclosure is directed, the judge

shall take such protective measure as the interests of the holder of the privilege and of the parties and the furtherance of justice may require.

History of TRE 507 (civil): Amended eff. Mar. 1, 1998, by order of Feb. 25, 1998 (960 S.W.2d [Tex.Cases] xlvi). Adopted eff. Sept. 1, 1983, by order of Nov. 23, 1982 (641-42 S.W.2d [Tex.Cases] xliv). Source: Common law. See proposed FRE 508 (1972).

See Pen. Code §31.05(a)(4); *Commentaries*, "Asserting privileges," ch. 6-A, §18.2, p. 443; "Scope of Discovery," ch. 6-B, p. 460; Brown & Rondon, *Texas Rules of Evidence Handbook* (2013), p. 449.

ANNOTATIONS

In re Bass, 113 S.W.3d 735, 739-40 (Tex.2003). The following factors are used to "determine whether a trade secret exists …: '(1) the extent to which the information is known outside of his business; (2) the extent to which it is known by employees and others involved in his business; (3) the extent of the measures taken by him to guard the secrecy of the information; (4) the value of the information to him and to his competitors; (5) the amount of effort or money expended by him in developing the information; (6) the ease or difficulty with which the information could be properly acquired or duplicated by others.' [¶] Texas courts … are split on whether the six factors should be weighed as relevant criteria or whether a person claiming trade secret privilege must satisfy all six factors before trade secret status applies. [¶] We agree … that the party claiming a trade secret should not be required to satisfy all six factors because trade secrets do not fit neatly into each factor every time." *See also In re Union Pac. R.R.*, 294 S.W.2d 589, 592 (Tex.2009).

In re Bridgestone/Firestone, Inc., 106 S.W.3d 730, 732-33 (Tex.2003). "Just as a party who claims the trade secret privilege cannot do so generally but must provide detailed information in support of the claim, so a party seeking such information cannot merely assert unfairness but must demonstrate with specificity exactly how the lack of the information will impair the presentation of the case on the merits to the point that an unjust result is a real, rather than a merely possible, threat." *See also In re Continental Gen. Tire, Inc.*, 979 S.W.2d 609, 611 (Tex.1998).

Computer Assocs. Int'l v. Altai, Inc., 918 S.W.2d 453, 455 (Tex.1996). "A trade secret is any formula, pattern, device or compilation of information which is used in one's business and presents an opportunity to obtain an advantage over competitors who do not know or use it."

⭐

In re Cooper Tire & Rubber Co., 313 S.W.3d 910, 915 (Tex.App.—Houston [14th Dist.] 2010, orig. proceeding). "The party asserting the trade secret privilege has the burden of proving that the discovery information sought qualifies as a trade secret. If the resisting party meets its burden, the burden shifts to the party seeking the trade secret discovery to establish that the information is necessary for a fair adjudication of its claim. It is an abuse of discretion for the trial court to order production once trade secret status is proven if the party seeking production has not shown necessity for the requested materials." *See also In re Rockafellow*, ___ S.W.3d ___ (Tex.App.—Amarillo 2011, orig. proceeding) (No. 07-11-00066-CV; 7-19-11); *In re XTO Res. I, LP*, 248 S.W.3d 898, 901 (Tex.App.—Fort Worth 2008, orig. proceeding).

TRE 508. IDENTITY OF INFORMER

(a) Rule of Privilege. The United States or a state or subdivision thereof has a privilege to refuse to disclose the identity of a person who has furnished information relating to or assisting in an investigation of a possible violation of a law to a law enforcement officer or member of a legislative committee or its staff conducting an investigation.

(b) Who May Claim. The privilege may be claimed by an appropriate representative of the public entity to which the information was furnished, except the privilege shall not be allowed in criminal cases if the state objects.

(c) Exceptions.

(1) *Voluntary disclosure; informer a witness.* No privilege exists under this rule if the identity of the informer or the informer's interest in the subject matter of the communication has been disclosed to those who would have cause to resent the communication by a holder of the privilege or by the informer's own action, or if the informer appears as a witness for the public entity.

(2) *Testimony on merits.* If it appears from the evidence in the case or from other showing by a party that an informer may be able to give testimony necessary to a fair determination of a material issue on the merits in a civil case to which the public entity is a party, or on guilt or innocence in a criminal case, and the public entity invokes the privilege, the court shall give the public entity an opportunity to show in camera facts relevant to determining whether the informer can, in fact, supply that testimony. The showing will ordinarily be in the form of affidavits, but the court may direct that testimony be taken if it finds that the matter cannot be resolved satisfactorily upon affidavit. If the court finds that there is a reasonable probability that the informer can give the testimony, and the public entity elects not to disclose the informer's identity, the court in a civil case may make any order that justice requires, and in a criminal case shall, on motion of the defendant, and may, on the court's own motion, dismiss the charges as to which the testimony would relate. Evidence submitted to the court shall be sealed and preserved to be made available to the appellate court in the event of an appeal, and the contents shall not otherwise be revealed without consent of the public entity. All counsel and parties shall be permitted to be present at every stage of proceedings under this subdivision except a showing in camera, at which no counsel or party shall be permitted to be present.

(3) *Legality of obtaining evidence.* If information from an informer is relied upon to establish the legality of the means by which evidence was obtained and the court is not satisfied that the information was received from an informer reasonably believed to be reliable or credible, it may require the identity of the informer to be disclosed. The court shall, on request of the public entity, direct that the disclosure be made in camera. All counsel and parties concerned with the issue of legality shall be permitted to be present at every stage of proceedings under this subdivision except a disclosure in camera, at which no counsel or party shall be permitted to be present. If disclosure of the identity of the informer is made in camera, the record thereof shall be sealed and preserved to be made available to the appellate court in the event of an appeal, and the contents shall not otherwise be revealed without consent of the public entity.

History of TRE 508 (civil): Amended eff. Mar. 1, 1998, by order of Feb. 25, 1998 (960 S.W.2d [Tex.Cases] xlvi). Adopted eff. Sept. 1, 1983, by order of Nov. 23, 1982 (641-42 S.W.2d [Tex.Cases] xlv). Source: Proposed FRE 510 (1972) and Unif. R. Evid. 509 (1974).

See *Commentaries*, "Asserting privileges," ch. 6-A, §18.2, p. 443; "Scope of Discovery," ch. 6-B, p. 460; Brown & Rondon, *Texas Rules of Evidence Handbook* (2013), p. 452.

ANNOTATIONS

State v. Lowry, 802 S.W.2d 669, 673 (Tex.1991). "To establish the informant privilege, the State must initially show that the person has provided to a law enforcement officer information assisting in the investigation of a possible violation of the law."

TRE 507

In re Bates, 555 S.W.2d 420, 430 (Tex.1977). When the "role of the informer was very minor and occurred quite early in the [bribery] investigation; and absent other evidence concerning the relevance of the identity of the informer; the disclosure [of the informer's identity] is not required."

Warford v. Childers, 642 S.W.2d 63, 66-67 (Tex. App.—Amarillo 1982, no writ). The rule-blocking disclosure "is a recognition of the fact that most informants relay rumor, gossip and street talk of no evidentiary value and the exceptions [to the rule] are designed for the rare case where the informant can give eyewitness testimony about the alleged crime or arrest."

TRE 509. PHYSICIAN-PATIENT PRIVILEGE

(a) Definitions. As used in this rule:

(1) A "patient" means any person who consults or is seen by a physician to receive medical care.

(2) A "physician" means a person licensed to practice medicine in any state or nation, or reasonably believed by the patient so to be.

(3) A communication is "confidential" if not intended to be disclosed to third persons other than those present to further the interest of the patient in the consultation, examination, or interview, or those reasonably necessary for the transmission of the communication, or those who are participating in the diagnosis and treatment under the direction of the physician, including members of the patient's family.

(b) Limited Privilege in Criminal Proceedings. There is no physician-patient privilege in criminal proceedings. However, a communication to any person involved in the treatment or examination of alcohol or drug abuse by a person being treated voluntarily or being examined for admission to treatment for alcohol or drug abuse is not admissible in a criminal proceeding.

(c) General Rule of Privilege in Civil Proceedings. In a civil proceeding:

(1) Confidential communications between a physician and a patient, relative to or in connection with any professional services rendered by a physician to the patient are privileged and may not be disclosed.

(2) Records of the identity, diagnosis, evaluation, or treatment of a patient by a physician that are created or maintained by a physician are confidential and privileged and may not be disclosed.

(3) The provisions of this rule apply even if the patient received the services of a physician prior to the enactment of the Medical Liability and Insurance Improvement Act, Tex. Rev. Civ. Stat. art. 4590i.

(d) Who May Claim the Privilege in a Civil Proceeding. In a civil proceeding:

(1) The privilege of confidentiality may be claimed by the patient or by a representative of the patient acting on the patient's behalf.

(2) The physician may claim the privilege of confidentiality, but only on behalf of the patient. The authority to do so is presumed in the absence of evidence to the contrary.

(e) Exceptions in a Civil Proceeding. Exceptions to confidentiality or privilege in administrative proceedings or in civil proceedings in court exist:

(1) when the proceedings are brought by the patient against a physician, including but not limited to malpractice proceedings, and in any license revocation proceeding in which the patient is a complaining witness and in which disclosure is relevant to the claims or defense of a physician;

(2) when the patient or someone authorized to act on the patient's behalf submits a written consent to the release of any privileged information, as provided in paragraph (f);

(3) when the purpose of the proceedings is to substantiate and collect on a claim for medical services rendered to the patient;

(4) as to a communication or record relevant to an issue of the physical, mental or emotional condition of a patient in any proceeding in which any party relies upon the condition as a part of the party's claim or defense;

(5) in any disciplinary investigation or proceeding of a physician conducted under or pursuant to the Medical Practice Act, Tex. Rev. Civ. Stat. art. 4495b,[1] or of a registered nurse under or pursuant to Tex. Rev. Civ. Stat. arts. 4525,[2] 4527a,[2] 4527b,[2] and 4527c,[2] provided that the board shall protect the identity of any patient whose medical records are examined, except for those patients covered under subparagraph (e)(1) or those patients who have submitted written consent to the release of their medical records as provided by paragraph (f);

(6) in an involuntary civil commitment proceeding, proceeding for court-ordered treatment, or probable

⎯⎯⎯⎯⎯ ★ ⎯⎯⎯⎯⎯

cause hearing under Tex. Health & Safety Code ch. 462; tit. 7, subtit. C; and tit. 7, subtit. D;

(7) in any proceeding regarding the abuse or neglect, or the cause of any abuse or neglect, of the resident of an "institution" as defined in Tex. Health & Safety Code §242.002.

(f) Consent.

(1) Consent for the release of privileged information must be in writing and signed by the patient, or a parent or legal guardian if the patient is a minor, or a legal guardian if the patient has been adjudicated incompetent to manage personal affairs, or an attorney ad litem appointed for the patient, as authorized by Tex. Health & Safety Code tit. 7, subtits. C and D; Tex. Prob. Code ch. V; and Tex. Fam. Code §107.011; or a personal representative if the patient is deceased, provided that the written consent specifies the following:

(A) the information or medical records to be covered by the release;

(B) the reasons or purposes for the release; and

(C) the person to whom the information is to be released.

(2) The patient, or other person authorized to consent, has the right to withdraw consent to the release of any information. Withdrawal of consent does not affect any information disclosed prior to the written notice of the withdrawal.

(3) Any person who received information made privileged by this rule may disclose the information to others only to the extent consistent with the authorized purposes for which consent to release the information was obtained.

1. **Editor's note:** Now Occ. Code title 3, subtitles B, C.

2. **Editor's note:** Now Occ. Code ch. 301.

Comment to 1998 change: This comment is intended to inform the construction and application of this rule. Prior Criminal Rules of Evidence 509 and 510 are now in subparagraph (b) of this Rule. This rule governs disclosures of patient-physician communications only in judicial or administrative proceedings. Whether a physician may or must disclose such communications in other circumstances is governed by TRCS art. 4495b, §5.08 [now Occ. Code ch. 159]. Former subparagraph (d)(6) of the Civil Evidence Rules, regarding disclosures in a suit affecting the parent-child relationship, is omitted, not because there should be no exception to the privilege in suits affecting the parent-child relationship, but because the exception in such suits is properly considered under subparagraph (e)(4) of the new rule (formerly subparagraph (d)(4)), as construed in *R.K. v. Ramirez,* 887 S.W.2d 836 (Tex.1994). In determining the proper application of an exception in such suits, the trial court must ensure that the precise need for the information is not outweighed by legitimate privacy interests protected by the privilege. Subparagraph (e) of the new rule does not except from the privilege information relating to a nonparty patient who is or may be a consulting or testifying expert in the suit.

History of TRE 509 (civil): Amended eff. Mar. 1, 1998, by order of Feb. 25, 1998 (960 S.W.2d [Tex.Cases] xlvii). Amended eff. Jan. 1, 1988, by order of Nov. 10, 1986 (733-34 S.W.2d [Tex.Cases] lxxxvii): Rewrote (d)(4); added refer-ences to statutes relating to registered nurses in (d)(5). Amended eff. Nov. 1, 1984, by order of June 25, 1984 (669-70 S.W.2d [Tex.Cases] xxxiii): In (a)(2) added the words "in any state or nation, or reasonably believed by the patient so to be"; in (b)(3) substituted the word "provisions" for "prohibitions"; substituted the word "rule" for "section continue to," deleted the phrase "to confidential communications or records concerning any patient irrespective," substituted "even if" for "of when," added the phrase "prior to the enactment of the Medical Practice Act, TRCS art. 4590i (Vernon Supp.1984)"; in (c)(1) substituted the words "by a representative of the patient" for the word "physician"; and in (d)(7) deleted the words "when the disclosure is relevant to" and substituted the words "proceeding, proceeding for court-ordered treatment, or probable cause hearing" for "or hospitalization proceeding." Adopted eff. Sept. 1, 1983, by order of Nov. 23, 1982 (641-42 S.W.2d [Tex.Cases] xlvi). Source: TRCS art. 4495b, §5.08 (repealed).

See *Commentaries*, "Asserting privileges," ch. 6-A, §18.2, p. 443; "Scope of Discovery," ch. 6-B, p. 460; "Medical Records," ch. 6-J, p. 576; Brown & Ron-don, *Texas Rules of Evidence Handbook* (2013), p. 462; *O'Connor's Texas Forms*, FORM 5E:1.

ANNOTATIONS

R.K. v. Ramirez, 887 S.W.2d 836, 842 (Tex.1994). "[T]he patient-litigant exception to [TRE 509 and 510] privileges applies when a party's condition relates in a significant way to a party's claim or defense. *At 843 n.7:* Whether a condition is a part of a claim or defense should be determined on the face of the pleadings, without reference to the evidence that is allegedly privileged. *At 843:* [T]he exceptions to the medical and mental health privileges apply when (1) the records sought to be discovered are relevant to the condition at issue, and (2) the condition is relied upon as a part of a party's claim or defense, meaning that the condition itself is a fact that carries some legal significance."

Groves v. Gabriel, 874 S.W.2d 660, 661 (Tex.1994). "[A] trial court's order compelling release of medical records should be restrictively drawn so as to maintain the privilege with respect to records or communications not relevant to the underlying suit. The global release in this case does not meet the *Mutter* standard." *See also **In re Collins**,* 286 S.W.3d 911, 916 (Tex.2009).

Mutter v. Wood, 744 S.W.2d 600, 600 (Tex.1988). "There are … eight exceptions to the [physician-patient] privilege. *At 601:* In this case, the privilege was waived completely as to the defendant doctors and partially as to the treating doctors. To the extent, however, that the treating doctors had records or communications which were not relevant to the underlying suit, they remained privileged…."

In re Toyota Motor Corp., 191 S.W.3d 498, 502 (Tex.App.—Waco 2006, orig. proceeding). "A claim for mental anguish or emotional distress will not, standing alone, make a plaintiff's mental or emotional condition a part of the plaintiff's claim. [T]he allegation in [P's] petition that he suffered 'emotional shock' is not a suf-

TRE 509

ficient basis to make his mental or emotional condition an issue on which the jury will be required to make a factual determination. [¶] Therefore, [P's] communications ... are protected by the physician-patient privilege."

In re Arriola, 159 S.W.3d 670, 675-76 (Tex.App.—Corpus Christi 2004, orig. proceeding). "[Ds] contend the abuse-and-neglect exceptions [to TREs 509 and 510] apply only to proceedings brought by appropriate law enforcement agencies. [¶] However, the abuse-and-neglect exceptions ... contain no such limitation. [R]ules 509 and 510 state that the exceptions apply in administrative proceedings and civil proceedings in court. [¶] [Ds] contend numerous state statutes and administrative rules protect the records and medical information from disclosure.... [¶] However, each of the confidentiality and privilege provisions [Ds cite] contains an exception to nondisclosure where release of the information is required by law or ordered by the court. *At 677:* Here, the rules of evidence are the 'law' that requires release of the information."

In re Fort Worth Children's Hosp., 100 S.W.3d 582, 589 (Tex.App.—Fort Worth 2003, orig. proceeding). "[T]he record contains no proof that [patients' admittance papers] are completed and maintained by physicians rather than hospital employees. Because [D] did not present any evidence that [admittance papers] are records created or maintained by a physician, it failed to carry its burden to prove that the documents are subject to the physician-patient privilege under [TRE] 509.... [D] has no standing to assert the privilege on behalf of the nonparty patients."

In re Whiteley, 79 S.W.3d 729, 732-34 (Tex.App.—Corpus Christi 2002, orig. proceeding). D-doctor in medical-malpractice case triggered the TRE 509(e)(4) exception to physician-patient privilege when he testified in deposition that he successfully performed the same surgical procedure on nonparty patients; thus, nonparty patients' medical records became discoverable by P.

James v. Kloos, 75 S.W.3d 153, 160 (Tex.App.—Fort Worth 2002, no pet.). "[A] party can be prejudiced when his doctor meets with opposing counsel, but ... such prejudice may not be severe enough to disallow the doctor's testimony. [P]rejudice due to an improper meeting does not necessarily mean prejudice at trial, and, therefore, does not mean that an improper verdict necessarily results when a doctor is allowed to testify

after such a meeting. [T]here must be a showing that the ruling probably caused the rendition of an improper judgment." *See also* **Durst v. Hill Country Mem'l Hosp.**, 70 S.W.3d 233, 237 (Tex.App.—San Antonio 2001, no pet.).

TRE 510. CONFIDENTIALITY OF MENTAL HEALTH INFORMATION IN CIVIL CASES

(a) Definitions. As used in this rule:

(1) "Professional" means any person:

(A) authorized to practice medicine in any state or nation;

(B) licensed or certified by the State of Texas in the diagnosis, evaluation or treatment of any mental or emotional disorder;

(C) involved in the treatment or examination of drug abusers; or

(D) reasonably believed by the patient to be included in any of the preceding categories.

(2) "Patient" means any person who:

(A) consults, or is interviewed by, a professional for purposes of diagnosis, evaluation, or treatment of any mental or emotional condition or disorder, including alcoholism and drug addiction; or

(B) is being treated voluntarily or being examined for admission to voluntary treatment for drug abuse.

(3) A representative of the patient is:

(A) any person bearing the written consent of the patient;

(B) a parent if the patient is a minor;

(C) a guardian if the patient has been adjudicated incompetent to manage the patient's personal affairs; or

(D) the patient's personal representative if the patient is deceased.

(4) A communication is "confidential" if not intended to be disclosed to third persons other than those present to further the interest of the patient in the diagnosis, examination, evaluation, or treatment, or those reasonably necessary for the transmission of the communication, or those who are participating in the diagnosis, examination, evaluation, or treatment under the direction of the professional, including members of the patient's family.

(b) General Rule of Privilege.

(1) Communication between a patient and a professional is confidential and shall not be disclosed in civil cases.

TRE 510

✦

---

(2) Records of the identity, diagnosis, evaluation, or treatment of a patient which are created or maintained by a professional are confidential and shall not be disclosed in civil cases.

(3) Any person who received information from confidential communications or records as defined herein, other than a representative of the patient acting on the patient's behalf, shall not disclose in civil cases the information except to the extent that disclosure is consistent with the authorized purposes for which the information was first obtained.

(4) The provisions of this rule apply even if the patient received the services of a professional prior to the enactment of Tex. Rev. Civ. Stat. art. 5561h (Vernon Supp. 1984) (now codified as Tex. Health & Safety Code §§611.001-611.008).

(c) Who May Claim the Privilege.

(1) The privilege of confidentiality may be claimed by the patient or by a representative of the patient acting on the patient's behalf.

(2) The professional may claim the privilege of confidentiality but only on behalf of the patient. The authority to do so is presumed in the absence of evidence to the contrary.

(d) Exceptions. Exceptions to the privilege in court or administrative proceedings exist:

(1) when the proceedings are brought by the patient against a professional, including but not limited to malpractice proceedings, and in any license revocation proceedings in which the patient is a complaining witness and in which disclosure is relevant to the claim or defense of a professional;

(2) when the patient waives the right in writing to the privilege of confidentiality of any information, or when a representative of the patient acting on the patient's behalf submits a written waiver to the confidentiality privilege;

(3) when the purpose of the proceeding is to substantiate and collect on a claim for mental or emotional health services rendered to the patient;

(4) when the judge finds that the patient after having been previously informed that communications would not be privileged, has made communications to a professional in the course of a court-ordered examination relating to the patient's mental or emotional condition or disorder, providing that such communications shall not be privileged only with respect to issues in-volving the patient's mental or emotional health. On granting of the order, the court, in determining the extent to which any disclosure of all or any part of any communication is necessary, shall impose appropriate safeguards against unauthorized disclosure;

(5) as to a communication or record relevant to an issue of the physical, mental or emotional condition of a patient in any proceeding in which any party relies upon the condition as a part of the party's claim or defense;

(6) in any proceeding regarding the abuse or neglect, or the cause of any abuse or neglect, of the resident of an institution as defined in Tex. Health and Safety Code §242.002.

Comment to 1998 change: This comment is intended to inform the construction and application of this rule. This rule governs disclosures of patient-professional communications only in judicial or administrative proceedings. Whether a professional may or must disclose such communications in other circumstances is governed by Tex. Health & Safety Code §§611.001-611.008. Former subparagraph (d)(6) of the Civil Evidence Rules, regarding disclosures in a suit affecting the parent-child relationship, is omitted, not because there should be no exception to the privilege in suits affecting the parent-child relationship, but because the exception in such suits is properly considered under subparagraph (d)(5), as construed in *R.K. v. Ramirez*, 887 S.W.2d 836 (Tex.1994). In determining the proper application of an exception in such suits, the trial court must ensure that the precise need for the information is not outweighed by legitimate privacy interests protected by the privilege. Subparagraph (d) does not except from the privilege information relating to a nonparty patient who is or may be a consulting or testifying expert in the suit.

History of TRE 510 (civil): Amended eff. Mar. 1, 1998, by order of Feb. 25, 1998 (960 S.W.2d [Tex.Cases] I). Amended eff. Jan. 1, 1988, by order of Nov. 10, 1986 (733-34 S.W.2d [Tex.Cases] lxxxviii): Rewrote (d)(5). Amended eff. Nov. 1, 1984, by order of June 25, 1984 (669-70 S.W.2d [Tex.Cases] xxxiv): In the phrase "patient/client" the word "client" was deleted throughout rule; in (a)(2)(A) the word "other" was deleted; in (b)(4) the word "provisions" was substituted for "prohibitions" and the words "continue to" and "to confidential communications or records concerning any patient/client irrespective of when" were deleted; in (d)(5) the entire language has been substituted; in (d)(7) the words "TRCS art. 4442c, §2 (Vernon Supp. 1984)" were substituted for the "Sec. 1, ch. 684, Acts of the 67th Legislature, Regular Session 1981 (Art. 4442c, §2, Vernon's Texas Civil Statutes)." Adopted eff. Sept. 1, 1983, by order of Nov. 23, 1982 (641-42 S.W.2d [Tex.Cases] xlviii). Source: TRCS art. 5561h (repealed); Code Crim. Proc. art. 38.101.

See *Commentaries*, "Asserting privileges," ch. 6-A, §18.2, p. 443; "Scope of Discovery," ch. 6-B, p. 460; "Medical Records," ch. 6-J, p. 576; Brown & Rondon, *Texas Rules of Evidence Handbook* (2013), p. 483; *O'Connor's Texas Forms*, FORM 5E:1.

R.K. v. Ramirez, 887 S.W.2d 836, 843 (Tex.1994). "As a general rule, a mental condition will be a 'part' of a claim or defense if the pleadings indicate that the jury must make a factual determination concerning the condition itself."

Groves v. Gabriel, 874 S.W.2d 660, 661 (Tex.1994). "Because [P] alleges severe emotional damages, including 'post-traumatic stress disorder,' [she] waived the privilege as to any medical records relevant to her

TRE 510

claim for emotional damages." *See also* **Ginsberg v. 5th Ct. of Appeals**, 686 S.W.2d 105, 107 (Tex.1985).

In re Arriola, 159 S.W.3d 670, 675-76 (Tex.App.— Corpus Christi 2004, orig. proceeding). See annotation under TRE 509, p. 1127.

TRE 511. WAIVER OF PRIVILEGE BY VOLUNTARY DISCLOSURE

A person upon whom these rules confer a privilege against disclosure waives the privilege if:

(1) the person or a predecessor of the person while holder of the privilege voluntarily discloses or consents to disclosure of any significant part of the privileged matter unless such disclosure itself is privileged; or

(2) the person or a representative of the person calls a person to whom privileged communications have been made to testify as to the person's character or character trait insofar as such communications are relevant to such character or character trait.

History of TRE 511 (civil): Amended eff. Mar. 1, 1998, by order of Feb. 25, 1998 (960 S.W.2d [Tex.Cases] lii). Amended eff. Nov. 1, 1984, by order of June 25, 1984 (669-70 S.W.2d [Tex.Cases] xxxvii): Numbers (1) and (2) were added; the words "unless such disclosure itself is privileged, or (2) he or his representative calls a person to whom privileged communications have been made to testify as to his character or a trait of his character, insofar as such communications are relevant to such character or character trait" were added; the last sentence was deleted. Adopted eff. Sept. 1, 1983, by order of Nov. 23, 1982 (641-42 S.W.2d [Tex.Cases] l). Source: See Unif. R. Evid. 510 (1980).

See *Commentaries*, "Waiver of objections & privileges," ch. 6-A, §25.3, p. 456; Brown & Rondon, *Texas Rules of Evidence Handbook* (2013), p. 512.

ANNOTATIONS

In re Bexar Cty. Crim. Dist. Atty's Office, 224 S.W.3d 182, 189 (Tex.2007). "Although the DA's Office turned over its prosecution file without objection, which waived the work-product privilege as to the file's contents, the record is devoid of any indication that by doing so the DA likewise enlisted its current and former personnel to testify in [P's] suit regarding their case materials and related impressions and communications. The DA's waiver here is limited, not limitless, and agreeing to produce a prosecution file does not in itself require the DA to produce its personnel so that their mental processes and related case preparation may be further probed."

In re Ford Motor Co., 211 S.W.3d 295, 301 (Tex. 2006). "The privilege to maintain a document's confidentiality belongs to the document owner, not to the trial court. ... Mistaken document production by a court employee in violation of a court-signed protective order cannot constitute a party's voluntary waiver of confidentiality. ... No matter how many people eventually

[see] the materials, disclosures by a third-party, whether mistaken or malevolent, do not waive the privileged nature of the information. This principle should apply with particular force when documents are entrusted to a court."

Jordan v. 4th Ct. of Appeals, 701 S.W.2d 644, 649 (Tex.1985). "If the matter for which a privilege is sought has been disclosed to a third party, thus raising the question of waiver of the privilege, the party asserting the privilege has the burden of proving that no waiver has occurred."

In re Hicks, 252 S.W.3d 790, 794 (Tex.App.— Houston [14th Dist.] 2008, orig. proceeding). "An assignment of rights and claims does not automatically include a waiver of attorney-client privilege unless specifically stated in the language of the assignment." *See also* **In re General Agents Ins. Co.**, 224 S.W.3d 806, 814 (Tex.App.—Houston [14th Dist.] 2007, orig. proceeding).

TRE 512. PRIVILEGED MATTER DISCLOSED UNDER COMPULSION OR WITHOUT OPPORTUNITY TO CLAIM PRIVILEGE

A claim of privilege is not defeated by a disclosure which was (1) compelled erroneously or (2) made without opportunity to claim the privilege.

History of TRE 512 (civil): Amended eff. Mar. 1, 1998, by order of Feb. 25, 1998 (960 S.W.2d [Tex.Cases] lii). Adopted eff. Sept. 1, 1983, by order of Nov. 23, 1982 (641-42 S.W.2d [Tex.Cases] l). Source: Unif. R. Evid. 511 (1980).

See Brown & Rondon, *Texas Rules of Evidence Handbook* (2013), p. 523.

TRE 513. COMMENT UPON OR INFERENCE FROM CLAIM OF PRIVILEGE; INSTRUCTION

(a) Comment or Inference Not Permitted. Except as permitted in Rule 504(b)(2), the claim of a privilege, whether in the present proceeding or upon a prior occasion, is not a proper subject of comment by judge or counsel, and no inference may be drawn therefrom.

(b) Claiming Privilege Without Knowledge of Jury. In jury cases, proceedings shall be conducted, to the extent practicable, so as to facilitate the making of claims of privilege without the knowledge of the jury.

(c) Claim of Privilege Against Self-Incrimination in Civil Cases. Paragraphs (a) and (b) shall not apply with respect to a party's claim, in the present civil proceeding, of the privilege against self-incrimination.

(d) Jury Instruction. Except as provided in Rule 504(b)(2) and in paragraph (c) of this Rule, upon re-

---

★

---

quest any party against whom the jury might draw an adverse inference from a claim of privilege is entitled to an instruction that no inference may be drawn therefrom.

Comment to 1998 change: Subdivision (d) regarding a party's entitlement to a jury instruction about a claim of privilege is made applicable to civil cases.

History of TRE 513 (civil): Amended eff. Mar. 1, 1998, by order of Feb. 25, 1998 (960 S.W.2d [Tex.Cases] lii). Adopted eff. Sept. 1, 1983, by order of Nov. 23, 1982 (641-42 S.W.2d [Tex.Cases] l). Source: Unif. R. Evid. 512 (1980); proposed FRE 513.

See Brown & Rondon, *Texas Rules of Evidence Handbook* (2013), p. 527; *O'Connor's Texas Forms*, FORM 5E:1.

ANNOTATIONS

Texas DPS Officers Ass'n v. Denton, 897 S.W.2d 757, 760 (Tex.1995). "[J]uries in civil cases [may] make negative inferences based upon the assertion of the privilege [against self-incrimination]. Also, when a plaintiff invokes the privilege ..., the trial court can subsequently prohibit the plaintiff from introducing evidence on the subject, and such an act of judicial discretion does not constitute penalizing the plaintiff's use of the privilege."

Matbon, Inc. v. Gries, 288 S.W.3d 471, 489-90 (Tex.App.—Eastland 2009, no pet.). "[Ps] contend that the jury was free to draw negative inferences from [D's] repeated invocations of the Fifth Amendment. Although the jury was free to draw a negative inference, a 'claim of privilege is not a substitute for relevant evidence.' Without more, the negative inference that the jury may have drawn cannot rise beyond mere suspicion. Consequently, the inference could not be considered as evidence at all, particularly under a clear and convincing evidence standard." *See also In re Moore*, 153 S.W.3d 527, 534 (Tex.App.—Tyler 2004, orig. proceeding) (when two equally consistent inferences can be made from an assertion of the Fifth Amendment so that neither inference is more probable than the other, neither inference can be made).

In re Edge Capital Grp., 161 S.W.3d 764, 769-70 (Tex.App.—Beaumont 2005, orig. proceeding). "[W]hen a witness invokes the Fifth Amendment in response to inquiries, '[t]he judge is entitled to determine whether the refusal to answer appears to be based upon the good faith of the witness and is justifiable under all of the circumstances.' A motion for protection should not be filed solely to avoid the assertion of the Fifth Amendment privilege in a civil case."

Wil-Roye Inv. II v. Washington Mut. Bank, 142 S.W.3d 393, 404 (Tex.App.—El Paso 2004, no pet.). "Whether [TRE] 513(c) applies to a claim of privilege by a party's agent is one of first impression in Texas.

Rule 513(c) provides that Rule 513(a)'s prohibition against adverse inferences shall not apply with respect to a party's exercise of the privilege against self-incrimination, but it does not define what constitutes a party's claim ... of privilege. ... While it [appears] that Rule 513(c) would not apply to a non-party witness's assertion of the privilege, ... an analogy can be drawn between admissions by an agent under [TRE] 801(e)(2) and the silence of an agent or person in some other type of special relationship with a party. *At 406-07:* [W]e conclude that the rationale for allowing introduction of an agent's admissions against the principal under [TRE] 801(d)(2)(D) also justifies admission of evidence showing that the agent/witness has exercised his Fifth Amendment privilege at least where the questions substantially relate to a party's claim or defense." (Internal quotes omitted.)

In re L.S., 748 S.W.2d 571, 575 (Tex.App.—Amarillo 1988, writ denied). TRE 513(b) "reflects a desire to protect the parties from any adverse inference drawn by the jurors who witness the invocation of the privilege against self-incrimination. 'It is reasonable to anticipate that in most instances, planned reliance upon the privilege will be known in advance and the mandate of rule 513(b) can be implemented through the use of motions in limine.'"

ARTICLE VI. WITNESSES

TRE 601. COMPETENCY & INCOMPETENCY OF WITNESSES

(a) General Rule. Every person is competent to be a witness except as otherwise provided in these rules. The following witnesses shall be incompetent to testify in any proceeding subject to these rules:

(1) *Insane persons.* Insane persons who, in the opinion of the court, are in an insane condition of mind at the time when they are offered as a witness, or who, in the opinion of the court, were in that condition when the events happened of which they are called to testify.

(2) *Children.* Children or other persons who, after being examined by the court, appear not to possess sufficient intellect to relate transactions with respect to which they are interrogated.

(b) "Dead Man's Rule" in Civil Actions. In civil actions by or against executors, administrators, or guardians, in which judgment may be rendered for or against them as such, neither party shall be allowed to testify against the others as to any oral statement by

TRE 513

the testator, intestate or ward, unless that testimony to the oral statement is corroborated or unless the witness is called at the trial to testify thereto by the opposite party; and, the provisions of this article shall extend to and include all actions by or against the heirs or legal representatives of a decedent based in whole or in part on such oral statement. Except for the foregoing, a witness is not precluded from giving evidence of or concerning any transaction with, any conversations with, any admissions of, or statement by, a deceased or insane party or person merely because the witness is a party to the action or a person interested in the event thereof. The trial court shall, in a proper case, where this rule prohibits an interested party or witness from testifying, instruct the jury that such person is not permitted by the law to give evidence relating to any oral statement by the deceased or ward unless the oral statement is corroborated or unless the party or witness is called at the trial by the opposite party.

History of TRE 601 (civil): Amended eff. Mar. 1, 1998, by order of Feb. 25, 1998 (960 S.W.2d [Tex.Cases] liii). Amended eff. Jan. 1, 1988, by order of July 15, 1987 (733-34 S.W.2d [Tex.Cases] xcv): In (a)(2) deleted "or who do not understand the obligation of an oath"; in (b) added last sentence "The trial court shall ... opposite party." Amended eff. Nov. 1, 1984, by order of June 25, 1984 (669-70 S.W.2d [Tex.Cases] xxxvii): Added the words "at the trial" in the first sentence. Adopted eff. Sept. 1, 1983, by order of Nov. 23, 1982 (641-42 S.W.2d [Tex.Cases] li). Source: For (a), FRE 601; Code Crim. Proc. art. 38.06 (repealed); for (b), TRCS arts. 3714, 3716 (repealed).

See Brown & Rondon, *Texas Rules of Evidence Handbook* (2013), p. 535; *O'Connor's Texas Forms*, FORM 5E:1.

ANNOTATIONS

Pipkin v. Kroger Tex., L.P., ___ S.W.3d ___ (Tex. App.—Houston [14th Dist.] 2012, n.p.h.) (No. 14-11-00755-CV; 9-6-12). "[U]nder Rule 601, a child is considered competent to testify unless, after the child is examined by the court, it appears to the court that the child does not possess sufficient intellect to relate transactions about which he will testify. There is no age below which a child is automatically deemed incompetent to testify. When a trial court determines whether a child is competent to testify at trial, it considers (1) the competence of the child to observe intelligently the events in question at the time of the occurrence; (2) the child's capacity to recollect the events; and (3) the child's capacity to narrate the facts."

In re R.M.T., 352 S.W.3d 12, 25 (Tex.App.—Texarkana 2011, no pet.). "[T]o demonstrate incompetency under Rule 601, it must be shown that the witness lacked the ability to perceive the relevant events,

recall and narrate those events at the time of trial, or that the witness lacked the capacity to understand the obligation of the oath."

Fraga v. Drake, 276 S.W.3d 55, 61 (Tex.App.—El Paso 2008, no pet.). "[C]ourts construe the Dead Man's Rule narrowly. [TRE 601(b)] does not prohibit testimony concerning statements by the deceased that are properly corroborated. Corroborating evidence must tend to support some of the material allegations or issues that are raised by the pleadings and testified to by the witness whose evidence is sought to be corroborated. It may come from any other competent witness or other legal source, including documentary evidence. Corroborating evidence ... must tend to confirm and strengthen the testimony of the witness and show the probability of its truth. For example, it is sufficient if the corroborating evidence shows conduct by the deceased that is generally consistent with the testimony concerning the deceased's statements."

TRE 602. LACK OF PERSONAL KNOWLEDGE

A witness may not testify to a matter unless evidence is introduced sufficient to support a finding that the witness has personal knowledge of the matter. Evidence to prove personal knowledge may, but need not, consist of the testimony of the witness. This rule is subject to the provisions of Rule 703, relating to opinion testimony by expert witnesses.

History of TRE 602 (civil): Amended eff. Mar. 1, 1998, by order of Feb. 25, 1998 (960 S.W.2d [Tex.Cases] liv). Adopted eff. Sept. 1, 1983, by order of Nov. 23, 1982 (641-42 S.W.2d [Tex.Cases] li). Source: FRE 602.

See *Commentaries*, "Introducing Evidence," ch. 8-C, p. 698; "Objecting to Evidence," ch. 8-D, p. 708; Brown & Rondon, *Texas Rules of Evidence Handbook* (2013), p. 547.

ANNOTATIONS

Anderson Prod'g Inc. v. Koch Oil Co., 929 S.W.2d 416, 425 (Tex.1996). "[D] argues that the trial court erred [because P's attorney] failed to demonstrate personal knowledge supporting the testimony. The record reflects that [P's attorney's] testimony was based on his review of the documents executed by [D], and that [D] had ample opportunity to cross-examine [him] regarding the basis of his conclusion. Under these circumstances, the trial court did not abuse its discretion in failing to strike the testimony." *See also **Marks v. St. Luke's Episcopal Hosp.***, 319 S.W.3d 658, 666 (Tex. 2010) (affidavits based on supposition are legally insufficient).

⭐

TRE 603. OATH OR AFFIRMATION

Before testifying, every witness shall be required to declare that the witness will testify truthfully, by oath or affirmation administered in a form calculated to awaken the witness' conscience and impress the witness' mind with the duty to do so.

History of TRE 603 (civil): Amended eff. Mar. 1, 1998, by order of Feb. 25, 1998 (960 S.W.2d [Tex.Cases] liv). Adopted eff. Sept. 1, 1983, by order of Nov. 23, 1982 (641-42 S.W.2d [Tex.Cases] li). Source: FRE 603. See Tex. Const. art. I, §5.

See Brown & Rondon, *Texas Rules of Evidence Handbook* (2013), p. 550.

Glenn v. C&G Elec., Inc., 977 S.W.2d 686, 689 (Tex.App.—Fort Worth 1998, pet. denied). The "requirement [to testify truthfully under oath] applies not only to those who will testify in person in the courtroom, but also to those whose testimony at the trial will be presented by deposition."

TRE 604. INTERPRETERS

An interpreter is subject to the provisions of these rules relating to qualification as an expert and the administration of an oath or affirmation to make a true translation.

History of TRE 604 (civil): Amended eff. Mar. 1, 1998, by order of Feb. 25, 1998 (960 S.W.2d [Tex.Cases] liv). Amended eff. Sept. 1, 1990, by order of Apr. 24, 1990 (785-86 S.W.2d [Tex.Cases] cvi): Added comment with reference to TRCP 183, regarding appointment and compensation of interpreters. Adopted eff. Sept. 1, 1983, by order of Nov. 23, 1982 (641-42 S.W.2d [Tex.Cases] li). Source: FRE 604.

See TRCP 183, regarding appointment and compensation of interpreters; Brown & Rondon, *Texas Rules of Evidence Handbook* (2013), p. 553.

International Commercial Bank v. Hall-Fuston Corp., 767 S.W.2d 259, 261 (Tex.App.—Beaumont 1989, writ denied). When a foreign company attempts to introduce into evidence business records that are not written in English, one of its corporate representatives can orally interpret the documents under oath after being qualified as an expert.

TRE 605. COMPETENCY OF JUDGE AS A WITNESS

The judge presiding at the trial may not testify in that trial as a witness. No objection need be made in order to preserve the point.

History of TRE 605 (civil): Amended eff. Mar. 1, 1998, by order of Feb. 25, 1998 (960 S.W.2d [Tex.Cases] liv). Adopted eff. Sept. 1, 1983, by order of Nov. 23, 1982 (641-42 S.W.2d [Tex.Cases] lii). Source: FRE 605.

See Brown & Rondon, *Texas Rules of Evidence Handbook* (2013), p. 555.

In re M.S., 115 S.W.3d 534, 538 (Tex.2003). "A judge's findings of fact are not technically the same as testimony. ... In this case, the orders submitted into evidence, containing findings based on pretrial evidence by the very judge presiding over the termination proceeding, could be, like a judicial comment on the weight of the evidence, a form of judicial influence no less proscribed than judicial testimony. [T]he jury was permitted to see findings of fact made by the very judge presiding over the trial, and those facts were the very ones that the jury itself was being asked to find. The fact-finding present in the orders admitted as evidence comes far too close to 'indicat[ing] the opinion of the trial judge as to the verity or accuracy of the facts in inquiry'...." *See also In re A.T.K.*, No. 02-11-00520-CV (Tex.App.—Fort Worth 2012, n.p.h.) (memo op.; 9-27-12).

Triumph Trucking, Inc. v. Southern Corporate Ins. Managers, Inc., 226 S.W.3d 466, 472 (Tex.App.—Houston [1st Dist.] 2006, pet. denied). TRE 605 "prohibit[s] not only a judge's direct testimony, but also 'the functional equivalent of witness testimony.' [¶] [T]he documents to which [P] objected were [P's] application for turnover [of impleaded funds] and an unsigned order prepared by [P] for the judge's signature. [N]either of these documents was the functional equivalent of testimony by the judge...."

O'Quinn v. Hall, 77 S.W.3d 438, 448 (Tex.App.—Corpus Christi 2002, no pet.). "Rule 605 applies not only to members of the judiciary, 'but also to those performing judicial functions that conflict with a witness's role.' [¶] 'The judge is a neutral arbiter in the courtroom, and the rule seeks to preserve his posture of impartiality before the parties....'"

TRE 606. COMPETENCY OF JUROR AS A WITNESS

(a) At the Trial. A member of the jury may not testify as a witness before that jury in the trial of the case in which the juror is sitting as a juror. If the juror is called so to testify, the opposing party shall be afforded an opportunity to object out of the presence of the jury.

(b) Inquiry Into Validity of Verdict or Indictment. Upon an inquiry into the validity of a verdict or indictment, a juror may not testify as to any matter or statement occurring during the jury's deliberations, or

---

to the effect of anything on any juror's mind or emotions or mental processes, as influencing any juror's assent to or dissent from the verdict or indictment. Nor may a juror's affidavit or any statement by a juror concerning any matter about which the juror would be precluded from testifying be admitted in evidence for any of these purposes. However, a juror may testify: (1) whether any outside influence was improperly brought to bear upon any juror; or (2) to rebut a claim that the juror was not qualified to serve.

History of TRE 606 (civil): Amended eff. Mar. 1, 1998, by order of Feb. 25, 1998 (960 S.W.2d [Tex.Cases] liv). Adopted eff. Sept. 1, 1983, by order of Nov. 23, 1982 (641-42 S.W.2d [Tex.Cases] lii). Source: FRE 606.

See TRCP 327(b); *Commentaries*, "MNT Based on Jury or Bailiff Misconduct," ch. 10-B, §14, p. 804; Brown & Rondon, *Texas Rules of Evidence Handbook* (2013), p. 558.

Golden Eagle Archery, Inc. v. Jackson, 24 S.W.3d 362, 371 (Tex.2000). An "alleged conversation between [jurors] during a trial break ... should not be considered 'deliberations' and therefore barred by [TRE] 606(b) and [TRCP] 327(b). [The TRCPs] use the term 'deliberations' as meaning formal jury deliberations—when the jury weighs the evidence to arrive at a verdict." *See also Chavarria v. Valley Transit Co.*, 75 S.W.3d 107, 111 (Tex.App.—San Antonio 2002, no pet.) (jurors discussing case on breaks during deliberations same as deliberations themselves).

Rosell v. Central W. Motor Stages, Inc., 89 S.W.3d 643, 661 (Tex.App.—Dallas 2002, pet. denied). "The essence of the 'outside influence' rule is to prevent outside information that affects the merits of the case from reaching the jury. The only evidence here is that the jury was told that they probably would be required to deliberate another day. ... Thus, the bailiff informing the jury of the court's schedule was not misconduct. Further, the juror testimony that jurors traded answers on issues is testimony about deliberations and is not evidence of outside influences."

Perry v. Safeco Ins., 821 S.W.2d 279, 281 (Tex. App.—Houston [1st Dist.] 1991, writ denied). "Information gathered by a juror and introduced to other jurors by that juror—even if it were introduced to prejudice the vote—does not constitute outside influence. [¶] Further, the coercive influence of one juror upon the rest of the panel is not 'outside influence.' Proof of coercive statements and their effect on the jury is barred by the [TREs]."

TRE 607. WHO MAY IMPEACH

The credibility of a witness may be attacked by any party, including the party calling the witness.

History of TRE 607 (civil): Amended eff. Mar. 1, 1998, by order of Feb. 25, 1998 (960 S.W.2d [Tex.Cases] lv). Adopted eff. Sept. 1, 1983, by order of Nov. 23, 1982 (641-42 S.W.2d [Tex.Cases] lii). Source: FRE 607.

See *Commentaries*, "Impeaching a Witness," ch. 8-C, §6, p. 702; Brown & Rondon, *Texas Rules of Evidence Handbook* (2013), p. 573.

TRE 608. EVIDENCE OF CHARACTER & CONDUCT OF A WITNESS

(a) **Opinion and Reputation Evidence of Character.** The credibility of a witness may be attacked or supported by evidence in the form of opinion or reputation, but subject to these limitations:

(1) the evidence may refer only to character for truthfulness or untruthfulness; and

(2) evidence of truthful character is admissible only after the character of the witness for truthfulness has been attacked by opinion or reputation evidence or otherwise.

(b) **Specific Instances of Conduct.** Specific instances of the conduct of a witness, for the purpose of attacking or supporting the witness' credibility, other than conviction of crime as provided in Rule 609, may not be inquired into on cross-examination of the witness nor proved by extrinsic evidence.

History of TRE 608 (civil): Amended eff. Mar. 1, 1998, by order of Feb. 25, 1998 (960 S.W.2d [Tex.Cases] lv). Adopted eff. Sept. 1, 1983, by order of Nov. 23, 1982 (641-42 S.W.2d [Tex.Cases] lii). Source: FRE 608(a).

See *Commentaries*, "Rehabilitating a Witness," ch. 8-C, §7, p. 703; Brown & Rondon, *Texas Rules of Evidence Handbook* (2013), p. 579; *O'Connor's Texas Forms*, FORM 5E:1.

Commerce & Indus. Ins. v. Ferguson-Stewart, 339 S.W.3d 744, 747 (Tex.App.—Houston [1st Dist.] 2011, no pet.). "Texas courts have consistently upheld the exclusion of evidence of a witness's prior drug use for general impeachment purposes."

Rose v. Intercontinental Bank, 705 S.W.2d 752, 757 (Tex.App.—Houston [1st Dist.] 1986, writ ref'd n.r.e.). Under TRE 608(a), "the witness' reputation for truthfulness must first be attacked before [the party] can offer rehabilitating evidence."

TRE 609. IMPEACHMENT BY EVIDENCE OF CONVICTION OF CRIME

(a) **General Rule.** For the purpose of attacking the credibility of a witness, evidence that the witness has been convicted of a crime shall be admitted if elic-

TRE 609

⭐

---

ited from the witness or established by public record but only if the crime was a felony or involved moral turpitude, regardless of punishment, and the court determines that the probative value of admitting this evidence outweighs its prejudicial effect to a party.

(b) Time Limit. Evidence of a conviction under this rule is not admissible if a period of more than ten years has elapsed since the date of the conviction or of the release of the witness from the confinement imposed for that conviction, whichever is the later date, unless the court determines, in the interests of justice, that the probative value of the conviction supported by specific facts and circumstances substantially outweighs its prejudicial effect.

(c) Effect of Pardon, Annulment, or Certificate of Rehabilitation. Evidence of a conviction is not admissible under this rule if:

(1) based on the finding of the rehabilitation of the person convicted, the conviction has been the subject of a pardon, annulment, certificate of rehabilitation, or other equivalent procedure, and that person has not been convicted of a subsequent crime which was classified as a felony or involved moral turpitude, regardless of punishment;

(2) probation has been satisfactorily completed for the crime for which the person was convicted, and that person has not been convicted of a subsequent crime which was classified as a felony or involved moral turpitude, regardless of punishment; or

(3) based on a finding of innocence, the conviction has been the subject of a pardon, annulment, or other equivalent procedure.

(d) Juvenile Adjudications. Evidence of juvenile adjudications is not admissible, except for proceedings conducted pursuant to Title III, Family Code, in which the witness is a party, under this rule unless required to be admitted by the Constitution of the United States or Texas.

(e) Pendency of Appeal. Pendency of an appeal renders evidence of a conviction inadmissible.

(f) Notice. Evidence of a conviction is not admissible if after timely written request by the adverse party specifying the witness or witnesses, the proponent fails to give to the adverse party sufficient advance written notice of intent to use such evidence to provide the adverse party with a fair opportunity to contest the use of such evidence.

History of TRE 609 (civil): Amended eff. Mar. 1, 1998, by order of Feb. 25, 1998 (960 S.W.2d [Tex.Cases] lv). Adopted eff. Sept. 1, 1983, by order of Nov. 23, 1982 (641-42 S.W.2d [Tex.Cases] lii). Source: FRE 609.

See *Commentaries*, "Impeaching by conviction," ch. 8-C, §6.4, p. 703; Brown & Rondon, *Texas Rules of Evidence Handbook* (2013), p. 591; *O'Connor's Texas Forms*, FORM 5E:1.

ANNOTATIONS

Cortez v. Wyche, No. 02-11-00364-CV (Tex.App.—Fort Worth 2012, no pet.) (memo op.; 5-3-12). "In ***Theus*** [*v. State*, 845 S.W.2d 874, 880-81 (Tex.Crim. App.1992)], the court of criminal appeals set out a nonexclusive list of factors to be considered in weighing the probative value of a conviction against its prejudicial effect under rule 609(a), including: (1) the impeachment value of the prior crime; (2) the temporal proximity of the past crime relative to the charged offense and the witness's subsequent history; (3) the similarity between the past crime and the offense being prosecuted; (4) the importance of the defendant's testimony; and (5) the importance of the credibility issue. [¶] [As] to the first factor, if the crime involves deception, it has a higher impeachment value. The second weighs in favor of admission if the past crime is recent and the witness has shown a 'propensity for running afoul of the law.' With regard to the third factor, ... 'in a civil case, if conduct is in issue that is similar to a past crime, then the third factor should weigh against admission.' As to the intertwined last factors, 'in a civil case, as the importance of a particular witness's testimony and credibility increases, so does the need to allow impeachment of that witness with evidence of a criminal conviction.'" *See also* ***Porter v. Nemir***, 900 S.W.2d 376, 382 (Tex.App.—Austin 1995, no writ).

Taylor v. TDPRS, 160 S.W.3d 641, 653 (Tex.App.—Austin 2005, pet. denied). "[R]ule 609 is not a categorical limitation on the introduction of convictions for any purpose. Rather, it applies only to convictions offered for purposes of impeachment. Here, [P] offered [D's] convictions not solely to impeach her credibility but as relevant evidence going to the controlling issue in her case—the best interests of [child]."

U.S.A. Precision Mach. Co. v. Marshall, 95 S.W.3d 407, 410 (Tex.App.—Houston [1st Dist.] 2002, pet. denied). A conviction is not final for purposes of impeachment under TRE 609 if it was reversed, it is pending on appeal, or the case was dismissed after a new trial was granted.

★

In re M.R., 975 S.W.2d 51, 55 (Tex.App.—San Antonio 1998, pet. denied). TRE 609 "exists to establish when and within what parameters a prior conviction may be introduced. It does not *require* a conviction in order to admit some testimony."

TRE 610. RELIGIOUS BELIEFS OR OPINIONS

Evidence of the beliefs or opinions of a witness on matters of religion is not admissible for the purpose of showing that by reason of their nature the witness' credibility is impaired or enhanced.

Comment to 1998 change: This is prior Rule of Criminal Evidence 615.

History of TRE 610 (civil): Amended eff. Mar. 1, 1998, by order of Feb. 25, 1998 (960 S.W.2d [Tex.Cases] lvi). Adopted eff. Jan. 1, 1988, by order of Nov. 10, 1986 (733-34 S.W.2d [Tex.Cases] lxxxviii): While the rule forecloses inquiry into the religious beliefs or opinions of a witness for the purpose of showing that his character for truthfulness is affected by their nature, an inquiry for the purpose of showing interest or bias because of them is not within the prohibition; thus disclosure of affiliation with a church which is a party to the litigation is allowed under the rule. Former TRCE 610 renumbered TRCE 611. Source: New rule. See FRE 610.

See Brown & Rondon, *Texas Rules of Evidence Handbook* (2013), p. 611; *O'Connor's Texas Forms*, FORM 5E:1.

TRE 611. MODE & ORDER OF INTERROGATION & PRESENTATION

(a) Control by Court. The court shall exercise reasonable control over the mode and order of interrogating witnesses and presenting evidence so as to (1) make the interrogation and presentation effective for the ascertainment of the truth, (2) avoid needless consumption of time, and (3) protect witnesses from harassment or undue embarrassment.

(b) Scope of Cross-Examination. A witness may be cross-examined on any matter relevant to any issue in the case, including credibility.

(c) Leading Questions. Leading questions should not be used on the direct examination of a witness except as may be necessary to develop the testimony of the witness. Ordinarily leading questions should be permitted on cross-examination. When a party calls a hostile witness, an adverse party, or a witness identified with an adverse party, interrogation may be by leading questions.

History of TRE 611 (civil): Amended eff. Mar. 1, 1998, by order of Feb. 25, 1998 (960 S.W.2d [Tex.Cases] lvi). Amended eff. Jan. 1, 1988, by order of Nov. 10, 1986 (733-34 S.W.2d [Tex.Cases] lxxxix): This is former TRCE 610; the purpose of the amendment is to permit the court in its discretion the use of leading questions on preliminary or introductory matters, refreshing memory, questions to ignorant or illiterate persons or children; the rule also conforms to tradition in making the use of leading questions on cross-examination a matter of right; the purpose of the qualification "ordinarily" is to furnish a basis for denying the use of leading questions when the cross-examination is only in the form of cross-examination and not in fact, e.g., the "cross-examination" of a party by his own counsel after being called by the opponent or of an insured defendant who is friendly to the plaintiff. Adopted as TRCE 610 eff. Sept. 1, 1983, by order of Nov. 23, 1982 (641-42 S.W.2d [Tex.Cases] liv). Source: FRE 611.

See *Commentaries*, "Scope of Examination," ch. 8-C, §4, p. 699; Brown & Rondon, *Texas Rules of Evidence Handbook* (2013), p. 612.

ANNOTATIONS

State v. Gaylor Inv. Trust Prtshp., 322 S.W.3d 814, 819 (Tex.App.—Houston [14th Dist.] 2010, no pet.). "Every trial court has the inherent power to control the disposition of the cases on its docket with economy of time and effort for itself, for counsel, and for litigants. … The trial court's inherent power, together with applicable rules of procedure and evidence, accord trial courts broad, but not unfettered, discretion in handling trials." (Internal quotes omitted.)

Torres v. Danny's Serv. Co., 266 S.W.3d 485, 487 (Tex.App.—Eastland 2008, pet. denied). "[A] witness may be cross-examined on any issue that is probative of her credibility. [¶] Texas courts have not adopted hard and fast rules for determining whether a witness's mental health history is relevant to a credibility analysis, choosing instead to consider this evidence on an ad hoc basis. *At 488:* Because Texas follows an ad hoc approach, trial courts have broad discretion. If mental health evidence is admissible for impeachment, the trial court also has considerable discretion to limit the scope of any cross-examination. But the trial court's discretion is not limitless. The mere fact that the witness has suffered from, or received treatment for, a mental illness or disturbance is insufficient to justify its admission. The trial court must have some evidence that the illness is such that 'it might tend to reflect upon the witness's credibility.' This evidence can take many forms, but it must show that the witness's perception of events was affected or that the witness was otherwise impaired."

State Office of Risk Mgmt. v. Escalante, 162 S.W.3d 619, 628 (Tex.App.—El Paso 2005, pet. dism'd). "The right to cross examine a witness is a substantial one, and it is error to so restrict it as to prevent the cross-examining party from going fully into all matters connected with the examination in chief. Due process requires an opportunity to confront and cross-examine adverse witnesses."

Stam v. Mack, 984 S.W.2d 747, 752 (Tex.App.—Texarkana 1999, no pet.). "The trial court interrupted [P's] cross-examination because it felt that [P] was questioning the witness on immaterial issues and he was going into areas that were improper. The trial

★

court's interruption of the cross-examination was not improper, but was a proper action to maintain control and promote expedition."

TRE 612. WRITING USED TO REFRESH MEMORY

If a witness uses a writing to refresh memory for the purpose of testifying either

(1) while testifying;

(2) before testifying, in civil cases, if the court in its discretion determines it is necessary in the interests of justice; or

(3) before testifying, in criminal cases;

an adverse party is entitled to have the writing produced at the hearing, to inspect it, to cross-examine the witness thereon, and to introduce in evidence those portions which relate to the testimony of the witness. If it is claimed that the writing contains matters not related to the subject matter of the testimony the court shall examine the writing in camera, excise any portion not so related, and order delivery of the remainder to the party entitled thereto. Any portion withheld over objections shall be preserved and made available to the appellate court in the event of an appeal. If a writing is not produced or delivered pursuant to order under this rule, the court shall make any order justice requires, except that in criminal cases when the prosecution elects not to comply, the order shall be one striking the testimony or, if the court in its discretion determines that the interests of justice so require, declaring a mistrial.

History of TRE 612 (civil): Amended eff. Mar. 1, 1998, by order of Feb. 25, 1998 (960 S.W.2d [Tex.Cases] lvii). Amended eff. Jan. 1, 1988, by order of July 15, 1987 (733-34 S.W.2d [Tex.Cases] xcv): This is former TRCE 611; former TRCE 612 was amended and renumbered as TRCE 613. Adopted as TRCE 611 eff. Sept. 1, 1983, by order of Nov. 23, 1982 (641-42 S.W.2d [Tex.Cases] liv). Source: FRE 612.

See Brown & Rondon, *Texas Rules of Evidence Handbook* (2013), p. 621.

ANNOTATIONS

Goode v. Shoukfeh, 943 S.W.2d 441, 449 (Tex. 1997). "If a witness uses the writing while testifying the adverse party must be given access to it, but if the writing is used before the witness testifies, the court has the discretion to order the writing disclosed to the adverse party."

TRE 613. PRIOR STATEMENTS OF WITNESSES: IMPEACHMENT & SUPPORT

(a) **Examining Witness Concerning Prior Inconsistent Statement.** In examining a witness concerning a prior inconsistent statement made by the witness, whether oral or written, and before further cross-examination concerning, or extrinsic evidence of, such statement may be allowed, the witness must be told the contents of such statement and the time and place and the person to whom it was made, and must be afforded an opportunity to explain or deny such statement. If written, the writing need not be shown to the witness at that time, but on request the same shall be shown to opposing counsel. If the witness unequivocally admits having made such statement, extrinsic evidence of same shall not be admitted. This provision does not apply to admissions of a party-opponent as defined in Rule 801(e)(2).

(b) **Examining Witness Concerning Bias or Interest.** In impeaching a witness by proof of circumstances or statements showing bias or interest on the part of such witness, and before further cross-examination concerning, or extrinsic evidence of, such bias or interest may be allowed, the circumstances supporting such claim or the details of such statement, including the contents and where, when and to whom made, must be made known to the witness, and the witness must be given an opportunity to explain or to deny such circumstances or statement. If written, the writing need not be shown to the witness at that time, but on request the same shall be shown to opposing counsel. If the witness unequivocally admits such bias or interest, extrinsic evidence of same shall not be admitted. A party shall be permitted to present evidence rebutting any evidence impeaching one of said party's witnesses on grounds of bias or interest.

(c) **Prior Consistent Statements of Witnesses.** A prior statement of a witness which is consistent with the testimony of the witness is inadmissible except as provided in Rule 801(e)(1)(B).

History of TRE 613 (civil): Amended eff. Mar. 1, 1998, by order of Feb. 25, 1998 (960 S.W.2d [Tex.Cases] lvii). Amended eff. Jan. 1, 1988, by order of July 15, 1987 (733-34 S.W.2d [Tex.Cases] xcvi): This is former TRCE 612, with change; in first sentence of (b) deleted the comma after "interest"; former TRCE 613 was amended and renumbered as TRCE 614. Former TRCE 612 amended eff. Nov. 1, 1984, by order of June 25, 1984 (669-70 S.W.2d [Tex.Cases] xxxvii): Added "If written, the writing need not be shown to him at that time, but on request the same shall be shown to opposing counsel" to (a) and (b). Adopted as TRCE 612 eff. Sept. 1, 1983, by order of Nov. 23, 1982 (641-42 S.W.2d [Tex.Cases] liv). Source: FRE 613.

See *Commentaries*, "Impeaching a Witness," ch. 8-C, §6, p. 702; Brown & Rondon, *Texas Rules of Evidence Handbook* (2013), p. 627.

ANNOTATIONS

Walker v. Packer, 827 S.W.2d 833, 839 n.5 (Tex. 1992). "Evidence of bias is not admissible if the witness 'unequivocally admits such bias or interest' at

---

⭐

---

trial. [Because D's witness] flatly denied [bias], such evidence should be discoverable."

In re Weir, 166 S.W.3d 861, 864 (Tex.App.—Beaumont 2005, orig. proceeding). "Generally, an expert witness may be questioned regarding payment received for his work as an expert witness. However, pretrial discovery of all a witness's accounting and financial records, solely for the purpose of impeachment, may be denied. *At 865:* The parties' interests in obtaining discovery solely for impeachment must be weighed against the witness's legitimate interest in protecting unrelated financial information."

Downen v. Texas Gulf Shrimp Co., 846 S.W.2d 506, 512 (Tex.App.—Corpus Christi 1993, writ denied). "[T]o impeach a witness with a prior statement, a proper foundation must be established[, which] includes establishing where, when, and to whom the statement was made. Additionally, the party ... must allow the witness to admit or deny making the prior statement. If ... the witness admits unequivocally having made the statement the impeachment is complete and the prior statement is not admissible."

TRE 614. EXCLUSION OF WITNESSES

At the request of a party the court shall order witnesses excluded so that they cannot hear the testimony of other witnesses, and it may make the order of its own motion. This rule does not authorize exclusion of:

(1) a party who is a natural person or in civil cases the spouse of such natural person;

(2) an officer or employee of a party in a civil case or a defendant in a criminal case that is not a natural person designated as its representative by its attorney;

(3) a person whose presence is shown by a party to be essential to the presentation of the party's cause; or

(4) the victim in a criminal case, unless the victim is to testify and the court determines that the victim's testimony would be materially affected if the victim hears other testimony at the trial.

History of TRE 614 (civil): Amended eff. Mar. 1, 1998, by order of Feb. 25, 1998 (960 S.W.2d [Tex.Cases] lviii). Amended eff. Jan. 1, 1988, by order of July 15, 1987 (733-34 S.W.2d [Tex.Cases] xcvii): This is former TRCE 613. Adopted as TRCE 613 eff. Sept. 1, 1983, by order of Nov. 23, 1982 (641-42 S.W.2d [Tex.Cases] lv). Source: FRE 615.

See TRCP 267; *Commentaries*, "Invoking 'the Rule'", ch. 8-C, §3, p. 698; Brown & Rondon, *Texas Rules of Evidence Handbook* (2013), p. 642.

ANNOTATIONS

Drilex Sys. v. Flores, 1 S.W.3d 112, 118-19 (Tex. 1999). "Although an expert witness may *typically* be found exempt under the essential presence exception,

experts are not *automatically* exempt. Instead, [TRE] 614 and [TRCP] 267 vest in trial judges broad discretion to determine whether a witness is essential."

In re H.M.S., 349 S.W.3d 250, 253 (Tex.App.—Dallas 2011, pet. denied). "Rule 614 ..., commonly referred to as 'the rule,' requires the exclusion of witnesses from the courtroom upon the request of a party. Although there are four classes of witnesses that are exempt from the operation of the rule, 'officers of the court' are not among those exempted. Accordingly, [Judge] erred in refusing to exclude certain witnesses on the basis that they were court employees."

TRE 615. PRODUCTION OF STATEMENTS OF WITNESSES IN CRIMINAL CASES

(a) Motion for Production. After a witness other than the defendant has testified on direct examination, the court, on motion of a party who did not call the witness, shall order the attorney for the state or the defendant and defendant's attorney, as the case may be, to produce, for the examination and use of the moving party, any statement of the witness that is in their possession and that relates to the subject matter concerning which the witness has testified.

(b) Production of Entire Statement. If the entire contents of the statement relate to the subject matter concerning which the witness has testified, the court shall order that the statement be delivered to the moving party.

(c) Production of Excised Statement. If the other party claims that the statement contains matter that does not relate to the subject matter concerning which the witness has testified, the court shall order that it be delivered to the court in camera. Upon inspection, the court shall excise the portions of the statement that do not relate to the subject matter concerning which the witness has testified, and shall order that the statement, with such material excised, be delivered to the moving party. Any portion withheld over objection shall be preserved and made available to the appellate court in the event of appeal.

(d) Recess for Examination of Statement. Upon delivery of the statement to the moving party, the court, upon application of that party, shall recess proceedings in the trial for a reasonable examination of such statement and for preparation for its use in the trial.

TRE 615

(e) Sanction for Failure to Produce Statement. If the other party elects not to comply with an order to deliver a statement to the moving party, the court shall order that the testimony of the witness be stricken from the record and that the trial proceed, or, if it is the attorney for the state who elects not to comply, shall declare a mistrial if required by the interest of justice.

(f) Definition. As used in this rule, a "statement" of a witness means:

(1) a written statement made by the witness that is signed or otherwise adopted or approved by the witness;

(2) a substantially verbatim recital of an oral statement made by the witness that is recorded contemporaneously with the making of the oral statement and that is contained in a stenographic, mechanical, electrical, or other recording or a transcription thereof; or

(3) a statement, however taken or recorded, or a transcription thereof, made by the witness to a grand jury.

Comment to 1998 change: This is prior Rule of Criminal Evidence 614.

History of TRE 615 (criminal): Amended eff. Mar. 1, 1998, by order of Feb. 25, 1998 (960 S.W.2d [Tex.Cases] lviii). Adopted eff. Sept. 1, 1986, by order of Dec. 18, 1985 (701-02 S.W.2d [Tex.Cases] l).

See Brown & Rondon, *Texas Rules of Evidence Handbook* (2013), p. 649.

ARTICLE VII. OPINIONS & EXPERT TESTIMONY

TRE 701. OPINION TESTIMONY BY LAY WITNESSES

If the witness is not testifying as an expert, the witness' testimony in the form of opinions or inferences is limited to those opinions or inferences which are (a) rationally based on the perception of the witness and (b) helpful to a clear understanding of the witness' testimony or the determination of a fact in issue.

History of TRE 701 (civil): Amended eff. Mar. 1, 1998, by order of Feb. 25, 1998 (960 S.W.2d [Tex.Cases] lix). Adopted eff. Sept. 1, 1983, by order of Nov. 23, 1982 (641-42 S.W.2d [Tex.Cases] lv). Source: FRE 701.

See Brown & Rondon, *Texas Rules of Evidence Handbook* (2013), p. 659.

ANNOTATIONS

Natural Gas Pipeline Co. v. Justiss, ___ S.W.3d ___ (Tex.2012) (No. 10-0451; 12-14-12). "Based on the presumption that an owner is familiar with his property and its value, the Property Owner Rule is an exception to the requirement that a witness must otherwise establish his qualifications to express an opinion on land values. Under the Rule, an owner's valuation testimony fulfills the same role that expert testimony does.

At ___: Thus, as with expert testimony, property valuations may not be based solely on a property owner's *ipse dixit.* An owner may not simply echo the phrase 'market value' and state a number to substantiate his diminished value claim; he must provide the factual basis on which his opinion rests. [T]he owner's testimony may be challenged on cross-examination or refuted with independent evidence. But even if unchallenged, the testimony must support a verdict, and conclusory or speculative statements do not." *See also* ***Porras v. Craig***, 675 S.W.2d 503, 505 (Tex.1984).

Reid Rd. MUD v. Speedy Stop Food Stores, 337 S.W.3d 846, 851-52 (Tex.2011). "The line between who is a [TRE] 702 expert witness and who is a [TRE] 701 witness is not always bright. But when the main substance of the witness's testimony is based on application of the witness's specialized knowledge, skill, experience, training, or education to his familiarity with the property, then the testimony will generally be expert testimony within the scope of Rule 702. A witness giving such testimony must be properly disclosed and designated as an expert and the witness's testimony is subject to scrutiny under rules regarding experts and expert opinion. Any other principle would allow parties to conceal expert testimony by claiming the witness is one whose opinions are merely for the purpose of explaining the witness's perceptions and testimony. [¶] Accordingly, we do not categorically agree with [D's] contention that all persons with personal knowledge of real property can give opinion testimony as to the market value of that property without the testimony being considered and identified as expert testimony. Such a holding would allow circumvention of discovery and disclosure rules that allow parties to prepare for trial and protect themselves from trial by ambush. Instead, we hold that subject to the provisions of Rule 701, ... a witness who will be giving opinion evidence about a property's fair market value must be disclosed and designated as an expert pursuant to discovery and other applicable rules."

U.S. Fire Ins. v. Lynd Co., ___ S.W.3d ___ (Tex. App.—San Antonio 2012, pet. filed 11-26-12) (No. 04-11-00347-CV; 8-15-12). "[P] contends that lay testimony ... cannot controvert its scientific evidence, [and that] therefore, in the absence of any scientific evidence from [D], [P] was entitled to summary judgment. ... The question of whether hail fell on a particu-

⭐

lar location on a particular day, and whether it caused property damage, is not a matter solely within the scope of an expert's knowledge …; to the contrary, it is a matter of personal observation and common sense that is within the scope of lay testimony. [¶] In some areas such as medical malpractice, expert testimony is necessary to defeat a motion for summary judgment. [¶] Proof other than expert testimony will, however, constitute some evidence of causation when a layperson's general experience and common understanding would enable the layperson to determine from the evidence, with reasonable probability, the causal relationship between the event and the condition."

Kilgore Mech., LLC v. Shafiee, No. 14-10-00295-CV (Tex.App.—Houston [14th Dist.] 2011, no pet.) (memo op.; 5-12-11). "Some courts have concluded that an officer may offer a non-expert opinion as to causation where his or her testimony is rationally based on the officer's own perceptions at the scene of the accident and where the testimony aids the trier of fact in determining a fact in issue. Indeed, while police officers often qualify as expert witnesses in traffic collision cases, this qualification does not preclude them from also giving lay opinions where such opinions meet the requirements of Rule 701." *See also* ***Texas DPS v. Struve***, 79 S.W.3d 796, 803 (Tex.App.—Corpus Christi 2002, pet. denied) (police officer may express opinion on whether someone is intoxicated, but if based on training and experience, TRE 702 applies).

Sierad v. Barnett, 164 S.W.3d 471, 483-84 (Tex. App.—Dallas 2005, no pet.). TRE 701 "permits a lay-witness opinion if the witness bases his opinion on his perception and if his opinion helps in determining a fact in issue. Lay witnesses can give opinions on damages as long as they testify about matters within their knowledge. A lay witness can testify about value if he has personal knowledge of facts forming the opinion, a rational connection exists between the facts and opinion, and the opinion is helpful." *See also* ***Red Sea Gaming, Inc. v. Block Invs.***, 338 S.W.3d 562, 572-73 (Tex.App.—El Paso 2010, pet. denied); ***Whalen v. Condominium Consulting & Mgmt.***, 13 S.W.3d 444, 448 (Tex.App.—Corpus Christi 2000, pet. denied).

City of San Antonio v. Vela, 762 S.W.2d 314, 321 (Tex.App.—San Antonio 1988, writ denied). "'In general, a witness need not be an expert in medical matters to state an opinion as to his own physical health.'"

TRE 702. TESTIMONY BY EXPERTS

If scientific, technical, or other specialized knowledge will assist the trier of fact to understand the evidence or to determine a fact in issue, a witness qualified as an expert by knowledge, skill, experience, training, or education may testify thereto in the form of an opinion or otherwise.

History of TRE 702 (civil): Amended eff. Mar. 1, 1998, by order of Feb. 25, 1998 (960 S.W.2d [Tex.Cases] lix). Adopted eff. Sept. 1, 1983, by order of Nov. 23, 1982 (641-42 S.W.2d [Tex.Cases] lv). Source: FRE 702.

See *Commentaries*, "Motion to Exclude Expert," ch. 5-N, p. 410; "Testimony from expert," ch. 8-C, §5.5, p. 700; "Objection to opinion of expert," ch. 8-D, §4.2, p. 711; Brown & Rondon, *Texas Rules of Evidence Handbook* (2013), p. 675.

ANNOTATIONS

Generally

Reid Rd. MUD v. Speedy Stop Food Stores, 337 S.W.3d 846, 851-52 (Tex.2011). See annotation under TRE 701, p. 1138.

GTE Sw., Inc. v. Bruce, 998 S.W.2d 605, 620 (Tex. 1999). "Except in highly unusual circumstances, expert testimony concerning extreme and outrageous conduct would not meet [the standards of TRE 702]. Where … the issue involves only general knowledge and experience rather than expertise, it is within the province of the jury to decide…." *See also* ***K-Mart Corp. v. Honeycutt***, 24 S.W.3d 357, 360 (Tex.2000).

Marin v. IESI TX Corp., 317 S.W.3d 314, 320 (Tex. App.—Houston [1st Dist.] 2010, pet. denied). "A witness may qualify as both a fact witness and an expert witness."

Muhs v. Whataburger, Inc., No. 13-09-00434-CV (Tex.App.—Corpus Christi 2010, pet. denied) (memo op.; 11-18-10). "Accident reconstruction constitutes scientific evidence. … 'Texas has a long history of allowing qualified accident reconstruction experts to testify regarding the way in which an accident occurred.'"

In re G.M.P., 909 S.W.2d 198, 206 (Tex.App.—Houston [14th Dist.] 1995, no writ). "A determination of who is telling the truth is the sole province of the jury. [T]he trial court erred in allowing [expert] to testify that, in his expert opinion [witness] was telling the truth."

Qualification of Expert

In re Commitment of Bohannan, ___ S.W.3d ___ (Tex.2012) (No. 10-0605; 8-31-12). "That a witness has knowledge, skill, expertise, or training does not necessarily mean that the witness can assist the trier-of-fact.

—————————————— ★ ——————————————

Expert testimony assists the trier-of-fact when the expert's knowledge and experience on a relevant issue are beyond that of the average juror and the testimony helps the trier-of-fact understand the evidence or determine a fact issue. [¶] Credentials are important, but credentials alone do not qualify an expert to testify. [F]or example, ... a medical license does not automatically qualify the holder to testify as an expert on every medical question. Trial courts must ensure that those who purport to be experts truly have expertise concerning the actual subject about which they are offering an opinion. The test is whether the offering party has established that the expert has knowledge, skill, experience, training, or education regarding the specific issue before the court which would qualify the expert to give an opinion on that particular subject." (Internal quotes omitted.) *See also Broders v. Heise*, 924 S.W.2d 148, 152-53 (Tex.1996).

Havner v. E-Z Mart Stores, 825 S.W.2d 456, 460 n.4 (Tex.1992). "An investigating officer may properly testify as to causation." *See also Gainsco Cty. Mut. Ins. v. Martinez*, 27 S.W.3d 97, 104 (Tex.App.—San Antonio 2000, pet. granted, judgm't vacated w.r.m.).

Estorque v. Schafer, 302 S.W.3d 19, 26 (Tex. App.—Fort Worth 2009, no pet.). "Qualifications must appear in the expert report and cannot be inferred." *See also Philipp v. McCreedy*, 298 S.W.3d 682, 686 (Tex. App.—San Antonio 2009, no pet.).

Glasscock v. Income Prop. Servs., 888 S.W.2d 176, 180 (Tex.App.—Houston [1st Dist.] 1994, writ dism'd). A college degree is not required for a witness to qualify as an expert.

Reliability of Opinion

Transcontinental Ins. v. Crump, 330 S.W.3d 211, 215-16 (Tex.2010). "In determining whether expert testimony is reliable, a court should consider the [*Robinson*] factors ... as well as the expert's experience, knowledge, and training. '[I]n very few cases will the evidence be such that the trial court's reliability determination can properly be based only on the experience of a qualified expert to the exclusion of factors such as those set out in *Robinson*, or, on the other hand, properly be based only on factors such as those set out in *Robinson* to the exclusion of considerations based on a qualified expert's experience.'"

Whirlpool Corp. v. Camacho, 298 S.W.3d 631, 639-40 (Tex.2009). "The proponent [of expert testimony] must satisfy its burden regardless of the quality or quantity of the opposing party's evidence on the issue and regardless of whether the opposing party attempts to conclusively prove the expert testimony is wrong. [¶] Witnesses offered as experts in an area or subject will invariably have experience in that field. If courts merely accept 'experience' as a substitute for proof that an expert's opinions are reliable and then only examine the testimony for analytical gaps in the expert's logic and opinions, an expert can effectively insulate his or her conclusions from meaningful review by filling gaps in the testimony with almost any type of data or subjective opinions. We have recognized, and do recognize, that some subjects do not lend themselves to scientific testing and scientific methodology. But given the facts in this case, the analytical gap test was not the only factor that should have been considered. ... This is not one of the few cases in which appellate review of expert evidence should be limited to either an analysis focused solely on *Robinson*-like factors or solely on an analytical gap test. [P]roper appellate legal sufficiency review ... requires evaluating [expert's] testimony by considering both *Robinson*-type factors and examining for analytical gaps in his testimony." *See also TXI Transp. v. Hughes*, 306 S.W.3d 230, 235 (Tex.2010) (factors are difficult to apply for vehicular-accident-reconstruction testimony).

Mack Trucks, Inc. v. Tamez, 206 S.W.3d 572, 581 (Tex.2006). "The reliability inquiry as to expert testimony does not ask whether the expert's conclusions appear to be correct; it asks whether the methodology and analysis used to reach those conclusions is reliable." *See also Whirlpool Corp. v. Camacho*, 298 S.W.3d 631, 637 (Tex.2009) (each material part of expert's theory must be reliable).

Coastal Transp. Co. v. Crown Cent. Pet. Corp., 136 S.W.3d 227, 233 (Tex.2004). "When the expert's underlying methodology is challenged, the court 'necessarily looks beyond what the expert said' to evaluate the reliability of the expert's opinion. When the testimony is challenged as conclusory or speculative and therefore non-probative on its face, however, there is no need to go beyond the face of the record to test its reliability. [W]hen a reliability challenge requires the court to evaluate the underlying methodology, technique, or foundational data used by the expert, an objection must be timely made so that the trial court has the opportunity to conduct this analysis. However, when the challenge is restricted to the face of the

⭐

record … a party may challenge the legal sufficiency of the evidence even in the absence of any objection to its admissibility."

Gammill v. Jack Williams Chevrolet, Inc., 972 S.W.2d 713, 726 (Tex.1998). "Nothing in the language of [TRE 702] suggests that opinions based on scientific knowledge should be treated any differently than opinions based on technical or other specialized knowledge. It would be an odd rule of evidence that insisted that some expert opinions be reliable but not others. All expert testimony should be shown to be reliable before it is admitted." *See also **Helena Chem. Co. v. Wilkins**, 47 S.W.3d 486, 499 (Tex.2001).

Merrell Dow Pharms. v. Havner, 953 S.W.2d 706, 714 (Tex.1997). "If the foundational data underlying opinion testimony are unreliable, … any opinion drawn from that data is likewise unreliable. Further, an expert's testimony is unreliable even when the underlying data are sound if the expert draws conclusions from that data based on flawed methodology. A flaw in the expert's reasoning from the data may render reliance on a study unreasonable and render the inferences drawn therefrom dubious. Under that circumstance, the expert's scientific testimony is unreliable and, legally, no evidence." *See also **Cooper Tire & Rubber Co. v. Mendez***, 204 S.W.3d 797, 800-01 (Tex.2006).

E.I. du Pont de Nemours & Co. v. Robinson, 923 S.W.2d 549, 557 (Tex.1995). The factors to consider in determining the admissibility of scientific knowledge "include, but are not limited to: (1) the extent to which the theory has been or can be tested; (2) the extent to which the technique relies upon the subjective interpretation of the expert; (3) whether the theory has been subjected to peer review and/or publication; (4) the technique's potential rate of error; (5) whether the underlying theory or technique has been generally accepted as valid by the relevant scientific community; and (6) the non-judicial uses which have been made of the theory or technique."

Duncan-Hubert v. Mitchell, 310 S.W.3d 92, 102 (Tex.App.—Dallas 2010, pet. denied). "Scientific evidence that is not grounded in the methods and procedures of science is no more than subjective belief or unsupported speculation."

Taylor v. TDPRS, 160 S.W.3d 641, 650 (Tex.App.—Austin 2005, pet. denied). "[I]n fields other than the hard sciences, such as the social sciences, factors like an expert's education, training, and experience are more appropriate factors in testing reliability than the scientific method. Thus, when measuring the reliability of an expert's opinion in fields within the soft sciences, … courts should consider whether: (1) the field of expertise is a legitimate one; (2) the subject matter of the expert's testimony is within the scope of that field; and (3) the expert's testimony properly relies upon the principles involved in that field of study."

Deadline to Object

General Motors Corp. v. Iracheta, 161 S.W.3d 462, 471 (Tex.2005). "The unreliability of expert opinions may be apparent as early as the discovery process but also may not emerge until trial, during or after the expert's testimony, or even later. An objection must be timely, but it need not anticipate a deficiency before it is apparent. [W]e cannot say that [D's] objection following cross-examination came too late."

TRE 703. BASES OF OPINION TESTIMONY BY EXPERTS

The facts or data in the particular case upon which an expert bases an opinion or inference may be those perceived by, reviewed by, or made known to the expert at or before the hearing. If of a type reasonably relied upon by experts in the particular field in forming opinions or inferences upon the subject, the facts or data need not be admissible in evidence.

Comment to 1998 change: The former Civil Rule referred to facts or data "perceived by or reviewed by" the expert. The former Criminal Rule referred to facts or data "perceived by or made known to" the expert. The terminology is now conformed, but no change in meaning is intended.

History of TRE 703 (civil): Amended eff. Mar. 1, 1998, by order of Feb. 25, 1998 (960 S.W.2d [Tex.Cases] lx). Amended eff. Sept. 1, 1990, by order of Apr. 24, 1990 (785-86 S.W.2d [Tex.Cases] cvii): Changed the words "made known to him" to "reviewed by the expert"; this amendment conforms TRE 703 to the rules of discovery by using the term "reviewed by the expert." See former TRCP 166b. Adopted eff. Sept. 1, 1983, by order of Nov. 23, 1982 (641-42 S.W.2d [Tex.Cases] lv). Source: FRE 703.

See *Commentaries*, "Foundation test," ch. 5-N, §2.4, p. 414; Brown & Rondon, *Texas Rules of Evidence Handbook* (2013), p. 713.

ANNOTATIONS

In re Christus Spohn Hosp. Kleberg, 222 S.W.3d 434, 440 (Tex.2007). "[I]n many instances, experts may rely on inadmissible hearsay, privileged communications, and other information that the ordinary witness may not." *See also **Gannon v. Wyche***, 321 S.W.3d 881, 889 (Tex.App.—Houston [14th Dist.] 2010, pet. denied); ***Sosa v. Koshy***, 961 S.W.2d 420, 427 (Tex. App.—Houston [1st Dist.] 1997, pet. denied).

Merrell Dow Pharms. v. Havner, 953 S.W.2d 706, 711 (Tex.1997). "The substance of the [expert's] testimony must be considered. *At 712:* [A]n expert's bald

---

★

---

assurance of validity is not enough. *At 713:* The underlying data should be independently evaluated in determining if the opinion itself is reliable."

TRE 704. OPINION ON ULTIMATE ISSUE

Testimony in the form of an opinion or inference otherwise admissible is not objectionable because it embraces an ultimate issue to be decided by the trier of fact.

History of TRE 704 (civil): Amended eff. Mar. 1, 1998, by order of Feb. 25, 1998 (960 S.W.2d [Tex.Cases] lx). Adopted eff. Sept. 1, 1983, by order of Nov. 23, 1982 (641-42 S.W.2d [Tex.Cases] lv). Source: FRE 704.

See Brown & Rondon, *Texas Rules of Evidence Handbook* (2013), p. 726.

ANNOTATIONS

Birchfield v. Texarkana Mem'l Hosp., 747 S.W.2d 361, 365 (Tex.1987). "Fairness and efficiency dictate that an expert may state an opinion on a mixed question of law and fact as long as the opinion is confined to the relevant issues and is based on proper legal concepts." *See also* *Dickerson v. DeBarbieris*, 964 S.W.2d 680, 690 (Tex.App.—Houston [14th Dist.] 1998, no pet.) (expert cannot state opinion or conclusion on pure question of law).

TRE 705. DISCLOSURE OF FACTS OR DATA UNDERLYING EXPERT OPINION

(a) Disclosure of Facts or Data. The expert may testify in terms of opinion or inference and give the expert's reasons therefor without prior disclosure of the underlying facts or data, unless the court requires otherwise. The expert may in any event disclose on direct examination, or be required to disclose on cross-examination, the underlying facts or data.

(b) Voir dire. Prior to the expert giving the expert's opinion or disclosing the underlying facts or data, a party against whom the opinion is offered upon request in a criminal case shall, or in a civil case may, be permitted to conduct a *voir dire* examination directed to the underlying facts or data upon which the opinion is based. This examination shall be conducted out of the hearing of the jury.

(c) Admissibility of Opinion. If the court determines that the underlying facts or data do not provide a sufficient basis for the expert's opinion under Rule 702 or 703, the opinion is inadmissible.

(d) Balancing Test; Limiting Instructions. When the underlying facts or data would be inadmissible in evidence, the court shall exclude the underlying facts or data if the danger that they will be used for a purpose other than as explanation or support for the expert's opinion outweighs their value as explanation or support or are unfairly prejudicial. If otherwise inadmissible facts or data are disclosed before the jury, a limiting instruction by the court shall be given upon request.

Comment to 1998 change: Paragraphs (b), (c), and (d) are based on the former Criminal Rule and are made applicable to civil cases. This rule does not preclude a party in any case from conducting a *voir dire* examination into the qualifications of an expert.

History of TRE 705 (civil): Amended eff. Mar. 1, 1998, by order of Feb. 25, 1998 (960 S.W.2d [Tex.Cases] lx). Amended eff. Nov. 1, 1984, by order of June 25, 1984 (669-70 S.W.2d [Tex.Cases] xxxviii): Added "disclose on direct examination, or" and "on cross-examination" to last sentence. Adopted eff. Sept. 1, 1983, by order of Nov. 23, 1982 (641-42 S.W.2d [Tex.Cases] lv). Source: FRE 705.

See *Commentaries*, "Motion to Exclude Expert," ch. 5-N, p. 410; Brown & Rondon, *Texas Rules of Evidence Handbook* (2013), p. 732.

ANNOTATIONS

Arkoma Basin Expl. Co. v. FMF Assocs. 1990-A, Ltd., 249 S.W.3d 380, 389-90 (Tex.2008). "[E]xperts are not required to introduce … foundational data at trial unless the opposing party or the court insists."

Kerr-McGee Corp. v. Helton, 133 S.W.3d 245, 252 (Tex.2004). "[B]ecause Rule 705(a) contemplates that the party against whom the evidence is offered may elicit testimony regarding the underlying facts or data on cross-examination, a motion to strike the testimony after such cross-examination is timely."

Weiss v. Mechanical Associated Servs., 989 S.W.2d 120, 124-25 (Tex.App.—San Antonio 1999, pet. denied). "The non-exclusive list of factors the court may consider in deciding admissibility [under TRE 705(c)] includes the extent to which the theory has been or can be tested, the extent to which the technique relies upon the subjective interpretation of the expert, whether the theory has been subjected to peer review and/or publication, the technique's potential rate of error, whether the underlying theory or technique has been generally accepted as valid by the relevant scientific community, and the non-judicial uses that have been made of the theory or technique."

TRE 706. AUDIT IN CIVIL CASES

Despite any other evidence rule to the contrary, verified reports of auditors prepared pursuant to Rule of Civil Procedure 172, whether in the form of summaries, opinions, or otherwise, shall be admitted in evidence when offered by any party whether or not the facts or data in the reports are otherwise admissible

———————————— ✪ ————————————

and whether or not the reports embrace the ultimate issues to be decided by the trier of fact. Where exceptions to the reports have been filed, a party may contradict the reports by evidence supporting the exceptions.

History of TRE 706 (civil): Amended eff. Mar. 1, 1998, by order of Feb. 25, 1998 (960 S.W.2d [Tex.Cases] lxi). Adopted eff. Jan. 1, 1988, by order of July 15, 1987 (733-34 S.W.2d [Tex.Cases] xcvii): To conform to TRCP 172. Source: New rule.

See Brown & Rondon, *Texas Rules of Evidence Handbook* (2013), p. 748.

ANNOTATIONS

Lovelace v. Sabine Consol., Inc., 733 S.W.2d 648, 656 (Tex.App.—Houston [14th Dist.] 1987, writ denied). "The audit report ... contains no such affidavit as is required by [TRCP] 172. ... Further, six days before trial [P] filed an objection to the audit. Therefore, the trial court did not err in admitting evidence that contradicted and supplemented the auditor's report."

ARTICLE VIII. HEARSAY

TRE 801. DEFINITIONS

The following definitions apply under this article:

(a) Statement. A "statement" is (1) an oral or written verbal expression or (2) nonverbal conduct of a person, if it is intended by the person as a substitute for verbal expression.

(b) Declarant. A "declarant" is a person who makes a statement.

(c) Matter Asserted. "Matter asserted" includes any matter explicitly asserted, and any matter implied by a statement, if the probative value of the statement as offered flows from declarant's belief as to the matter.

(d) Hearsay. "Hearsay" is a statement, other than one made by the declarant while testifying at the trial or hearing, offered in evidence to prove the truth of the matter asserted.

(e) Statements Which Are Not Hearsay. A statement is not hearsay if:

(1) *Prior statement by witness.* The declarant testifies at the trial or hearing and is subject to cross-examination concerning the statement, and the statement is:

(A) inconsistent with the declarant's testimony, and was given under oath subject to the penalty of perjury at a trial, hearing, or other proceeding except a grand jury proceeding in a criminal case, or in a deposition;

(B) consistent with the declarant's testimony and is offered to rebut an express or implied charge against the declarant of recent fabrication or improper influence or motive;

(C) one of identification of a person made after perceiving the person; or

(D) taken and offered in a criminal case in accordance with Code of Criminal Procedure article 38.071.

(2) *Admission by party-opponent.* The statement is offered against a party and is:

(A) the party's own statement in either an individual or representative capacity;

(B) a statement of which the party has manifested an adoption or belief in its truth;

(C) a statement by a person authorized by the party to make a statement concerning the subject;

(D) a statement by the party's agent or servant concerning a matter within the scope of the agency or employment, made during the existence of the relationship; or

(E) a statement by a co-conspirator of a party during the course and in furtherance of the conspiracy.

(3) *Depositions.* In a civil case, it is a deposition taken in the same proceeding, as same proceeding is defined in Rule of Civil Procedure 203.6(b). Unavailability of deponent is not a requirement for admissibility.

History of TRE 801 (civil): Amended eff. Jan. 1, 1999, by order of Dec. 31, 1998 (981-82 S.W.2d [Tex.Cases] xxxviii). Amended eff. Mar. 1, 1998, by order of Feb. 25, 1998 (960 S.W.2d [Tex.Cases] lxi). Amended eff. Jan. 1, 1988, by order of Nov. 10, 1986 (733-34 S.W.2d [Tex.Cases] xc): Amended (c)(3). Adopted eff. Sept. 1, 1983, by order of Nov. 23, 1982 (641-42 S.W.2d [Tex.Cases] lvi): The definitions in TRE 801(a), (b), (c) and (d) combined bring within the hearsay rule four categories of conduct; these are described and illustrated below.

(1) A verbal (oral or written) explicit assertion. Illustration. Witness testifies that declarant said "A shot B." Declarant's conduct is a statement because it is an oral expression. Because it is an explicit assertion, the matter asserted is that A shot B. Finally, the statement is hearsay because it was not made while testifying at the trial and is offered to prove the truth of the matter asserted.

(2) A verbal (oral or written) explicit assertion, not offered to prove the matter explicitly asserted, but offered for the truth of a matter implied by the statement, the probative value of the statement flowing from declarant's belief as to the matter. Illustration. The only known remedy for X disease is medicine Y and the only known use of medicine Y is to cure X disease. To prove that Oglethorpe had X disease, witness testifies that declarant, a doctor, stated, "The best medicine for Oglethorpe is Y." The testimony is to a statement because it was a verbal expression. The matter asserted was that Oglethorpe had X disease because that matter is implied from the statement, the probative value of the statement as offered flowing from declarant's belief as to the matter. Finally, the statement is hearsay because it was not made while testifying at the trial and is offered to prove the truth of the matter asserted.

(3) Non-assertive verbal conduct offered for the truth of a matter implied by the statement, the probative value of the statement flowing from declarant's belief as to the matter. Illustration. In a rape prosecution to prove that Richard, the defendant, was in the room at the time of the rape, W testifies that declarant knocked on the door to the room and shouted, "Open the door, Richard." The testimony is to a statement because it was a verbal expression. The matter

★

asserted was that Richard was in the room because that matter is implied from the statement, the probative value of the statement as offered flowing from declarant's belief as to the matter. Finally, the statement is hearsay because it was not made while testifying at the trial and is offered to prove the truth of the matter asserted.

(4) Nonverbal assertive conduct intended as a substitute for verbal expression. Illustration. W testifies that A asked declarant "Which way did X go?" and declarant pointed north. This nonverbal conduct of declarant was intended by him as a substitute for verbal expression and so is a statement. The matter asserted is that X went north because that is implied from the statement and the probative value of the statement as offered flows from declarant's belief that X went north. Finally, the statement is hearsay because it was not made at trial and is offered to prove the truth of the matter asserted.

Source: FRE 801.

See *Commentaries*, "Admissibility," ch. 6-F, §12.1, p. 538; Brown & Rondon, *Texas Rules of Evidence Handbook* (2013), p. 782; *O'Connor's Texas Forms*, FORM 5E:1.

ANNOTATIONS

TRE 801(d)

In re M.S., 115 S.W.3d 534, 543 (Tex.2003). "[T]he Agreement [between D and Child Protective Services] was not offered as proof of [D's] inability to care for her children, or as proof that her parental rights should be terminated, or as proof that termination was in the children's best interest. Rather, the Agreement was offered to show that an agreement had been made and what its terms were. The Agreement was not hearsay."

Marten v. Silva, 200 S.W.3d 297, 303 (Tex.App.—Dallas 2006, no pet.). "[N]either the document showing [car's] serial number nor the note from [D] was offered to prove the truth of the matters asserted.... Instead, the documents merely evidence an ongoing series of communications and faxes between [D] and [P] concerning [P's] purchase of [car]. Under these circumstances, ... the documents were not hearsay...."

City of Austin v. Houston Lighting & Power Co., 844 S.W.2d 773, 791 (Tex.App.—Dallas 1992, writ denied). "Generally, Texas courts consider newspaper articles inadmissible hearsay. [N]ewspaper articles not offered for the truth of the matters asserted but used merely to show notice of those matters are not hearsay."

TRE 801(e)

Tome v. U.S., 513 U.S. 150, 156 (1995) (criminal case interpreting federal rule). If a witness was cross-examined about a statement, a party may introduce an earlier consistent statement to rebut the charge of recent fabrication or improper influence by proving, through another witness, that (1) before testifying, the testifying witness made an out-of-court statement consistent with the testimony, and (2) the statement was made before the testifying witness had reason to fabricate.

Reid Rd. MUD v. Speedy Stop Food Stores, 337 S.W.3d 846, 858 (Tex.2011). "[A]dmissions by a party opponent can occur outside a judicial proceeding and are not inadmissible simply because they occur in an administrative hearing...."

Bay Area Healthcare Grp. v. McShane, 239 S.W.3d 231, 235 (Tex.2007). "Rule 801(e)(2) is straightforward: subject to other [TREs] that may limit admissibility, *any* statement by a party-opponent is admissible against that party. [¶] Thus, the court of appeals erred in concluding that statements from the [superseded] pleadings would only be admissible if they contained 'some statement relevant to a material issue in the case' that is 'inconsistent with the position taken by the party against whom it is introduced.' [T]he [TREs] no longer require inconsistency when it comes to admissibility of superseded pleadings. ... We hold that there is no requirement that the statement be inconsistent with the party's position at trial...." *See also Quick v. Plastic Solutions*, 270 S.W.3d 173, 185 (Tex. App.—El Paso 2008, no pet.).

Trencor, Inc. v. Cornech Mach. Co., 115 S.W.3d 145, 151 (Tex.App.—Fort Worth 2003, pet. denied). "A statement by a party's agent or servant concerning a matter within the scope of his agency or employment and made during the existence of the relationship may be offered as an admission by the party itself. The fact of agency must, however, be established before the declaration can be admitted."

TRE 802. HEARSAY RULE

Hearsay is not admissible except as provided by statute or these rules or by other rules prescribed pursuant to statutory authority. Inadmissible hearsay admitted without objection shall not be denied probative value merely because it is hearsay.

History of TRE 802 (civil): Amended eff. Mar. 1, 1998, by order of Feb. 25, 1998 (960 S.W.2d [Tex.Cases] lxii). Adopted eff. Sept. 1, 1983, by order of Nov. 23, 1982 (641-42 S.W.2d [Tex.Cases] lvii). Source: FRE 802.

See Brown & Rondon, *Texas Rules of Evidence Handbook* (2013), p. 833; *O'Connor's Texas Forms*, FORM 5E:1.

ANNOTATIONS

Texas Commerce Bank v. New, 3 S.W.3d 515, 517 (Tex.1999). "Nothing in rule 802 limits its application to contested hearings. The rule is not ambiguous and requires no explication." Thus, an affidavit containing unobjected-to hearsay can establish facts in a default-judgment case. *See also* **Sherman Acquisition II LP v. Garcia**, 229 S.W.3d 802, 810-11 (Tex.App.—Waco 2007, no pet.).

Birchfield v. Texarkana Mem'l Hosp., 747 S.W.2d 361, 365 (Tex.1987). "Ordinarily an expert witness should not be permitted to recount a hearsay conversation with a third person, even if that conversation forms part of the basis of his opinion."

Lee v. Dykes, 312 S.W.3d 191, 198 (Tex.App.—Houston [14th Dist.] 2010, no pet.). "[I]nadmissible evidence is [not] necessarily probative if it is admitted without objection or is uncontroverted."

TRE 803. HEARSAY EXCEPTIONS; AVAILABILITY OF DECLARANT IMMATERIAL

The following are not excluded by the hearsay rule, even though the declarant is available as a witness:

(1) Present Sense Impression. A statement describing or explaining an event or condition made while the declarant was perceiving the event or condition, or immediately thereafter.

(2) Excited Utterance. A statement relating to a startling event or condition made while the declarant was under the stress of excitement caused by the event or condition.

(3) Then Existing Mental, Emotional, or Physical Condition. A statement of the declarant's then existing state of mind, emotion, sensation, or physical condition (such as intent, plan, motive, design, mental feeling, pain, or bodily health), but not including a statement of memory or belief to prove the fact remembered or believed unless it relates to the execution, revocation, identification, or terms of declarant's will.

(4) Statements for Purposes of Medical Diagnosis or Treatment. Statements made for purposes of medical diagnosis or treatment and describing medical history, or past or present symptoms, pain, or sensations, or the inception or general character of the cause or external source thereof insofar as reasonably pertinent to diagnosis or treatment.

(5) Recorded Recollection. A memorandum or record concerning a matter about which a witness once had personal knowledge but now has insufficient recollection to enable the witness to testify fully and accurately, shown to have been made or adopted by the witness when the matter was fresh in the witness'

memory and to reflect that knowledge correctly, unless the circumstances of preparation cast doubt on the document's trustworthiness. If admitted, the memorandum or record may be read into evidence but may not itself be received as an exhibit unless offered by an adverse party.

(6) Records of Regularly Conducted Activity. A memorandum, report, record, or data compilation, in any form, of acts, events, conditions, opinions, or diagnoses, made at or near the time by, or from information transmitted by, a person with knowledge, if kept in the course of a regularly conducted business activity, and if it was the regular practice of that business activity to make the memorandum, report, record, or data compilation, all as shown by the testimony of the custodian or other qualified witness, or by affidavit that complies with Rule 902(10), unless the source of information or the method or circumstances of preparation indicate lack of trustworthiness. "Business" as used in this paragraph includes any and every kind of regular organized activity whether conducted for profit or not.

(7) Absence of Entry in Records Kept in Accordance With the Provisions of Paragraph (6). Evidence that a matter is not included in the memoranda, reports, records, or data compilations, in any form, kept in accordance with the provisions of paragraph (6), to prove the nonoccurrence or nonexistence of the matter, if the matter was of a kind of which a memorandum, report, record, or data compilation was regularly made and preserved, unless the sources of information or other circumstances indicate lack of trustworthiness.

(8) Public Records and Reports. Records, reports, statements, or data compilations, in any form, of public offices or agencies setting forth:

(A) the activities of the office or agency;

(B) matters observed pursuant to duty imposed by law as to which matters there was a duty to report, excluding in criminal cases matters observed by police officers and other law enforcement personnel; or

(C) in civil cases as to any party and in criminal cases as against the state, factual findings resulting from an investigation made pursuant to authority granted by law;

unless the sources of information or other circumstances indicate lack of trustworthiness.

(9) Records of Vital Statistics. Records or data compilations, in any form, of births, fetal deaths, deaths,

---

✦

---

or marriages, if the report thereof was made to a public office pursuant to requirements of law.

(10) Absence of Public Record or Entry. To prove the absence of a record, report, statement, or data compilation, in any form, or the nonoccurrence or non-existence of a matter of which a record, report, statement, or data compilation, in any form, was regularly made and preserved by a public office or agency, evidence in the form of a certification in accordance with Rule 902, or testimony, that diligent search failed to disclose the record, report statement, or data compilation, or entry.

(11) Records of Religious Organizations. Statements of births, marriages, divorces, deaths, legitimacy, ancestry, relationship by blood or marriage, or other similar facts of personal or family history, contained in a regularly kept record of a religious organization.

(12) Marriage, Baptismal, and Similar Certificates. Statements of fact contained in a certificate that the maker performed a marriage or other ceremony or administered a sacrament, made by a member of the clergy, public official, or other person authorized by the rules or practices of a religious organization or by law to perform the act certified, and purporting to have been issued at the time of the act or within a reasonable time thereafter.

(13) Family Records. Statements of fact concerning personal or family history contained in family Bibles, genealogies, charts, engravings on rings, inscriptions on family portraits, engravings on urns, crypts, or tombstones, or the like.

(14) Records of Documents Affecting an Interest in Property. The record of a document purporting to establish or affect an interest in property, as proof of the content of the original recorded document and its execution and delivery by each person by whom it purports to have been executed, if the record is a record of a public office and an applicable statute authorizes the recording of documents of that kind in that office.

(15) Statements in Documents Affecting an Interest in Property. A statement contained in a document purporting to establish or affect an interest in property if the matter stated was relevant to the purpose of the document, unless dealings with the property

since the document was made have been inconsistent with the truth of the statement or the purport of the document.

(16) Statements in Ancient Documents. Statements in a document in existence twenty years or more the authenticity of which is established.

(17) Market Reports, Commercial Publications. Market quotations, tabulations, lists, directories, or other published compilations, generally used and relied upon by the public or by persons in particular occupations.

(18) Learned Treatises. To the extent called to the attention of an expert witness upon cross-examination or relied upon by the expert in direct examination, statements contained in published treatises, periodicals, or pamphlets on a subject of history, medicine, or other science or art established as a reliable authority by the testimony or admission of the witness or by other expert testimony or by judicial notice. If admitted, the statements may be read into evidence but may not be received as exhibits.

(19) Reputation Concerning Personal or Family History. Reputation among members of a person's family by blood, adoption, or marriage, or among a person's associates, or in the community, concerning a person's birth, adoption, marriage, divorce, death, legitimacy, relationship by blood, adoption, or marriage, ancestry, or other similar fact of personal or family history.

(20) Reputation Concerning Boundaries or General History. Reputation in a community, arising before the controversy, as to boundaries of or customs affecting lands in the community, and reputation as to events of general history important to the community or state or nation in which located.

(21) Reputation as to Character. Reputation of a person's character among associates or in the community.

(22) Judgment of Previous Conviction. In civil cases, evidence of a judgment, entered after a trial or upon a plea of guilty (but not upon a plea of *nolo contendere*), judging a person guilty of a felony, to prove any fact essential to sustain the judgment of conviction. In criminal cases, evidence of a judgment, entered after a trial or upon a plea of guilty or *nolo contendere*, adjudging a person guilty of a criminal offense, to prove any fact essential to sustain the judgment of conviction, but not including, when offered by the state for purposes other than impeachment, judgments against persons other than the accused. In all cases, the pendency of an appeal renders such evidence inadmissible.

(23) Judgment as to Personal, Family, or General History, or Boundaries. Judgments as proof of matters of personal, family or general history, or boundaries, essential to the judgment, if the same would be provable by evidence of reputation.

(24) Statement Against Interest. A statement which was at the time of its making so far contrary to the declarant's pecuniary or proprietary interest, or so far tended to subject the declarant to civil or criminal liability, or to render invalid a claim by the declarant against another, or to make the declarant an object of hatred, ridicule, or disgrace, that a reasonable person in declarant's position would not have made the statement unless believing it to be true. In criminal cases, a statement tending to expose the declarant to criminal liability is not admissible unless corroborating circumstances clearly indicate the trustworthiness of the statement.

History of TRE 803 (civil): Amended eff. Mar. 1, 1998, by order of Feb. 25, 1998 (960 S.W.2d [Tex.Cases] lxii). Amended eff. Jan. 1, 1988, by order of Nov. 10, 1986 (733-34 S.W.2d [Tex.Cases] xc): To (6), added "or by affidavit that complies with Rule 902(10)." Amended eff. Nov. 1, 1984, by order of June 25, 1984 (669-70 S.W.2d [Tex.Cases] xxxviii): Added the following comment: The provision in par. (6) rejects the doctrine of *Loper v. Andrews*, 404 S.W.2d 300, 305 (Tex.1966), which required that an entry of a medical opinion or diagnosis meet a test of "reasonable medical certainty." Adopted eff. Sept. 1, 1983, by order of Nov. 23, 1982 (641-42 S.W.2d [Tex.Cases] lvii). Source: FRE 803. See TRCS arts. 3718-3737e (repealed).

See Fam. Code §54.031 for statutory exceptions to hearsay rule for testimony of certain abuse victims in criminal proceedings; *Commentaries*, "Introducing Evidence," ch. 8-C, p. 698; Brown & Rondon, *Texas Rules of Evidence Handbook* (2013), p. 836.

ANNOTATIONS

Generally

Robinson v. Harkins & Co., 711 S.W.2d 619, 621 (Tex.1986). "All hearsay exceptions require a showing of trustworthiness."

Simien v. Unifund CCR Partners, 321 S.W.3d 235, 240 (Tex.App.—Houston [1st Dist.] 2010, no pet.). "The proponent of hearsay has the burden of showing that the testimony fits within an exception to the general rule prohibiting the admission of hearsay evidence."

TRE 803(1)

1.70 Acres v. State, 935 S.W.2d 480, 488 (Tex. App.—Beaumont 1996, no writ). "Present sense impressions are those comments made at the time the declarant is receiving the impression or immediately thereafter. They possess the following safeguards which render them reliable: (1) the report at the moment of the thing then seen, heard, etc. is safe from any error from defect of memory of the declarant; (2) there is little or no time for a calculated misstatement; (3) the statement will usually be made to another—the witness who reports it—who would have equal opportunity to observe and hence to check a misstatement."

TRE 803(2)

Volkswagen v. Ramirez, 159 S.W.3d 897, 908-09 (Tex.2004). "To be admissible as an excited utterance, a statement must be (1) a spontaneous reaction (2) to a personal observance of (3) a startling event (4) made while the declarant was still under the stress of excitement caused by the event. [¶] [The statement] must occur before the declarant has the opportunity to reflect on or ponder the shocking incident. Accordingly, we also consider the lapse in time between the startling event and the statement [as well as t]he declarant's tone and tenor of voice...."

Felix v. Gonzalez, 87 S.W.3d 574, 578-79 (Tex. App.—San Antonio 2002, pet. denied). "The core of [TRE 803(2)] is reliability—a statement made by an out-of-court declarant during a state of excitement is more reliable than a statement made after time for reflection upon a startling event. Once the timing of the state of excitement is demonstrated, so long as the statement made *relates to* the startling event, it falls within the purview of the excited utterance exception."

Almaraz v. Burke, 827 S.W.2d 80, 83 (Tex.App.— Fort Worth 1992, writ denied). "Although [*First Sw. Lloyds Ins. v. MacDowell*, below,] states that the witness's statement was a narrative account, given after he had returned to the scene of the fire, the opinion does not reflect whether the witness was still excited from the fire and the chase at the time the statement was given, nor does it state whether that mattered in reaching the result. If the witness in that case were still excited from the event at the time he told the fire marshal what had just happened, we would have held that the evidence qualified as an exception to the hearsay rule in accordance with rule 803(2). On the other hand, if there were no evidence that the witness was still under the excitement of the preceding events, we would agree with the opinion."

First Sw. Lloyds Ins. v. MacDowell, 769 S.W.2d 954, 959 (Tex.App.—Texarkana 1989, writ denied). "A statement that is simply a narrative of past acts or

TRE 803

⭐

events, as distinguished from a spontaneous utterance, does not qualify as an excited utterance regardless of how soon after the event that it is made. The circumstances must show that it was the event speaking through the person and not the person speaking about the event."

TRE 803(3)

Power v. Kelley, 70 S.W.3d 137, 141 (Tex. App.—San Antonio 2001, pet. denied). "'Statements admitted under [TRE 803(3)] are usually spontaneous remarks about pain or some other sensation, made by the declarant while the sensation, not readily observable by a third party, is being experienced.' 'The exception does not extend to statements of past external facts or conditions.'"

TRE 803(4)

In re L.S., 748 S.W.2d 571, 576 (Tex.App.—Amarillo 1988, writ denied). "The crucial issue under [TRE 803(4)] is whether the out-of-court statement was reasonably pertinent to diagnosis or treatment. [¶] [A] statement made by a victim of child abuse identifying the alleged perpetrator is pertinent to both physical and psychological diagnosis and treatment."

TRE 803(6)

Burroughs Wellcome Co. v. Crye, 907 S.W.2d 497, 500 (Tex.1995). "The diagnoses contained in [P's] medical and hospital records are admissible. However, to constitute evidence of causation, an expert opinion must rest in reasonable medical probability. [¶] The context of the opinions contained in the medical records ... indicates that these statements are merely recitations of medical history or opinion as to causation provided by other records, [P], or [her doctor]." Held: No evidence of causation.

Riddle v. Unifund CCR Partners, 298 S.W.3d 780, 782-83 (Tex.App.—El Paso 2009, no pet.). "Business records that have been created by one entity, but which have become another entity's primary record of the underlying transaction may be admissible pursuant to Rule 803(6). In addition, a document can comprise the records of another business if the second business determines the accuracy of the information generated by the first business. [¶] Although Rule 803(6) does not require the predicate witness to be the record's creator or have personal knowledge of the content of the record ..., the witness must have personal knowl-

edge of the manner in which the records were prepared. Documents received from another entity are not admissible under Rule 803(6) if the witness is not qualified to testify about the entity's record keeping." *See also Dodeka, L.L.C. v. Campos*, ___ S.W.3d ___ (Tex.App.—San Antonio 2012, no pet.) (No. 04-11-00339-CV; 5-2-12); *In re E.A.K.*, 192 S.W.3d 133, 142 (Tex.App.—Houston [14th Dist.] 2006, pet. denied). *But see Simien v. Unifund CCR Partners*, 321 S.W.3d 235, 244 (Tex.App.—Houston [1st Dist.] 2010, no pet.) (foundation witness's personal knowledge of record keeping by third party not necessary).

Trantham v. Isaacks, 218 S.W.3d 750, 755 (Tex. App.—Fort Worth 2007, pet. denied). "The foundation for admission of a business record may be established by testimony or by affidavit." *See also Benavides v. Cushman, Inc.*, 189 S.W.3d 875, 884 n.6 (Tex.App.—Houston [1st Dist.] 2006, no pet.).

Freeman v. American Motorists Ins., 53 S.W.3d 710, 715 (Tex.App.—Houston [1st Dist.] 2001, no pet.). The letter from P's physician "to [P's] attorney was dated ... over ten years after the cause of action accrued and a mere ten days before the summary judgment hearing. This time frame indicates a lack of trustworthiness. In the absence of [P's physician's] remaining records, it appears that he wrote the letter solely in response to a request from [P's] attorney. [The letter] does not qualify as a routine entry in [P's] medical history; therefore, it is inadmissible as a business record under rule 803(6)."

TRE 803(7)

Coleman v. United Sav. Ass'n, 846 S.W.2d 128, 131 (Tex.App.—Fort Worth 1993, no writ). "Testimony that is offered as evidence that a matter is not included in records to prove the nonoccurrence or nonexistence of the matter is inadmissible hearsay evidence unless rule 803(7) is satisfied. The initial foundational predicate of rule 803(7) is that the records that would include the matter, if it were not absent from those records, are kept in accordance with the provisions of rule 803(6). [D's] affidavit does not even attempt to satisfy the requirements of rule 803(6) and therefore cannot support the summary judgment."

TRE 803(8)

Texas DPS v. Caruana, 363 S.W.3d 558, 564 (Tex. 2012). "Law enforcement investigation reports are commonly admitted in civil cases—car wrecks, for ex-

TRE 803

---

ample. [¶] A report is no less admissible in a civil case merely because it is unsworn...."

F-Star Socorro, L.P. v. City of El Paso, 281 S.W.3d 103, 106 (Tex.App.—El Paso 2008, no pet.). "[D] argues that the certified tax statement is not a public record under Rule 803(8).... The findings in the certified tax statement appear to result from the tax assessor-collector's investigation of [D], as outlined in Rule 803(8)(C). Therefore, we find that the certified tax statement is a public record under the terms of Rule 803(8)."

Corrales v. TDFPS, 155 S.W.3d 478, 486 (Tex. App.—El Paso 2004, no pet.). "Generally speaking, the police reports were admissible as a public record. [¶] [T]he records also contained statements by witnesses which did not qualify as public records. Nevertheless, ... the reports are admissible unless the sources of information indicate a lack of trustworthiness. [T]here is a presumption of admissibility and the burden is placed on the party opposing the admission of a report to show its untrustworthiness." *See also* **Texas DPS v. Guajardo**, No. 13-09-00468-CV (Tex.App.—Corpus Christi 2010, no pet.) (memo op.; 7-29-10).

TRE 803(10)

Towne Square Assocs. v. Angelina Cty. Appr. Dist., 709 S.W.2d 776, 777 (Tex.App.—Beaumont 1986, no writ). "[Ds'] affidavits stated that, after a diligent search, [Ds] could find no notice of appeal filed in the records. [Ps] assert these affidavits are insufficient in that they contain hearsay and do not have some of the predicate language required for a business record in accordance with [TRE] 902. [Ps'] complete reliance on this rule is misplaced. The affidavits are controlled by [TRE] 803(10).... While it is true the affidavits do not meet the authentication requirements of Rule 902, they do contain testimony that a diligent search failed to disclose the notice of appeal."

TRE 803(14), (15)

Tri-Steel Structures, Inc. v. Baptist Found., 166 S.W.3d 443, 451 (Tex.App.—Fort Worth 2005, pet. denied). TRE 803(15) requires "that the document have some sort of official or formal nature, which an unsigned letter does not possess. [D]ealings with the property [must] not be inconsistent with the statement after it was made."

Compton v. WWV Enters., 679 S.W.2d 668, 671 (Tex.App.—Eastland 1984, no writ). "Hearsay exceptions [TRE 803(14) and (15)] must ... be construed to relate to recitals or statements made in deeds, leases, mortgages and other such 'documents affecting an interest in property' and not to affidavits of heirship which more properly fall within the hearsay exception stated under [TRE] 804(b)(3)."

TRE 803(16)

Guthrie v. Suiter, 934 S.W.2d 820, 825 (Tex.App.—Houston [1st Dist.] 1996, no writ). "Statements contained in documents 20 years old or older qualify as an exception to the hearsay rule, provided the documents are properly authenticated. To qualify for this exception, the document must be shown (1) in such condition as to create no suspicion concerning its authenticity; (2) that it was in a place where it would likely be if it were authentic; and (3) that it has been in existence 20 years or more at the time it is offered."

TRE 803(17)

New Braunfels Factory Outlet Ctr. v. IHOP Rlty. Corp., 872 S.W.2d 303, 310 (Tex.App.—Austin 1994, no writ). "The hearsay exception provided by [TRE] 803(17) permits the admission of certain objective data.... At common law, survey results were also admissible *provided* that the party opposing admission was given the opportunity to cross-examine the person who had conducted the survey."

TRE 803(18)

King v. Bauer, 767 S.W.2d 197, 199-200 (Tex. App.—Corpus Christi 1989, writ denied). Under TRE 803(18), P introduced a medical textbook that was published two years after P's therapy, but the earlier edition of which was recognized by D as a learned treatise. "The fact that the third edition [of the textbook] was not published until 1980 does not serve to disqualify the evidence which was aimed at illustrating an appropriate treatment plan for [P] in 1978. Treatises which directly refer to the standard of care in use at the time of the occurrence are material, relevant and therefore admissible."

TRE 803(19)

Akers v. Stevenson, 54 S.W.3d 880, 885 (Tex. App.—Beaumont 2001, pet. denied). The hearsay exception for evidence concerning personal or family history arises "from necessity and [is] founded on the

TRE 803

⭐

---

general reliability of statements by family members about family affairs when the statements by deceased persons regarding family history were made at a time when no pecuniary interest or other biased reason for the statements were present."

TRE 803(20)

Roberts v. Allison, 836 S.W.2d 185, 191 (Tex. App.—Tyler 1992, writ denied). "A reason for the exception [in TRE 803(20)] is '[t]he fact that a prolonged observation and discussion of certain matters of *general interest by a whole community will sift possible errors and bring the result down to us in a fairly trustworthy form furnishes a guarantee of correctness.*' [Ps'] proposed testimony pertains to an individual family's assertion of an easement; there is no contention of the ... community's knowledge of [Ps'] claim to access [D's] property. ... There was no proof of the recognized 'vehicles of reputation,' such as 'declarations of residents, old maps, surveys, deeds and leases' of the claimed easement. ... The trial court did not abuse its discretion in excluding [the] testimony of a claimed oral agreement granting an easement to [Ps] over the subject property."

TRE 803(22)

McCormick v. Texas Commerce Bank, 751 S.W.2d 887, 890 (Tex.App.—Houston [14th Dist.] 1988, writ denied). "Where (i) the issue at stake was identical to that in the criminal case, (ii) the issue had been actually litigated, and (iii) determination of the issue was a critical and necessary part of the prior judgment, the judgment is established by offensive collateral estoppel and is within the hearsay exception of [FRE] 803(22). [¶] Applying the standards of the federal judiciary to [TRE] 803(22), we hold that the trial court did not err in refusing to permit [D] to explain the circumstances of his criminal conviction."

TRE 803(24)

State v. Arnold, 778 S.W.2d 68, 69 (Tex.1989). Under TRE 803(24), a "statement may be self-serving in one respect but contrary to another interest. The court must balance these competing interests to determine their predominant nature and ultimately the level of trustworthiness to be accorded."

Green v. Reyes, 836 S.W.2d 203, 213 (Tex.App.—Houston [14th Dist.] 1992, no writ). "[A]ffidavits of persons who ... admit under oath an action which can subject them to criminal liability may be properly ad-

mitted at trial as an exception to the hearsay rule as statements against their interest."

TRE 804. HEARSAY EXCEPTIONS; DECLARANT UNAVAILABLE

(a) Definition of Unavailability. "Unavailability as a witness" includes situations in which the declarant:

(1) is exempted by ruling of the court on the ground of privilege from testifying concerning the subject matter of the declarant's statement;

(2) persists in refusing to testify concerning the subject matter of the declarant's statement despite an order of the court to do so;

(3) testifies to a lack of memory of the subject matter of the declarant's statement;

(4) is unable to be present or to testify at the hearing because of death or then existing physical or mental illness or infirmity; or

(5) is absent from the hearing and the proponent of the declarant's statement has been unable to procure the declarant's attendance or testimony by process or other reasonable means.

A declarant is not unavailable as a witness if the declarant's exemption, refusal, claim of lack of memory, inability, or absence is due to the procurement or wrong-doing of the proponent of the declarant's statement for the purpose of preventing the witness from attending or testifying.

(b) Hearsay Exceptions. The following are not excluded if the declarant is unavailable as a witness:

(1) *Former testimony.* In civil cases, testimony given as a witness at another hearing of the same or a different proceeding, or in a deposition taken in the course of another proceeding, if the party against whom the testimony is now offered, or a person with a similar interest, had an opportunity and similar motive to develop the testimony by direct, cross, or redirect examination. In criminal cases, testimony given as a witness at another hearing of the same or a different proceeding, if the party against whom the testimony is now offered had an opportunity and similar motive to develop the testimony by direct, cross, or redirect examination. In criminal cases the use of depositions is controlled by Chapter 39 of the Code of Criminal Procedure.

(2) *Dying declarations.* A statement made by a declarant while believing that the declarant's death was

---

imminent, concerning the cause or circumstances of what the declarant believed to be impending death.

(3) *Statement of personal or family history.*

(A) A statement concerning the declarant's own birth, adoption, marriage, divorce, legitimacy, relationship by blood, adoption, or marriage, ancestry, or other similar fact of personal or family history even though declarant had no means of acquiring personal knowledge of the matter stated; or

(B) A statement concerning the foregoing matters, and death also, of another person, if the declarant was related to the other by blood, adoption, or marriage or was so intimately associated with the other's family as to be likely to have accurate information concerning the matter declared.

History of TRE 804 (civil): Amended eff. Mar. 1, 1998, by order of Feb. 25, 1998 (960 S.W.2d [Tex.Cases] lxvi). Amended eff. Jan. 1, 1988, by order of Nov. 10, 1986 (733-34 S.W.2d [Tex.Cases] xc): To TRCE 804(b)(1), deleted "the same or" before "another proceeding"; in some circumstances, a deposition may be admissible without regard to unavailability of the deponent. See former TRCE 801(e)(3) and former TRCP 207. Adopted eff. Sept. 1, 1983, by order of Nov. 23, 1982 (641-42 S.W.2d [Tex.Cases] lx). Source: FRE 804.

See Brown & Rondon, *Texas Rules of Evidence Handbook* (2013), p. 906.

ANNOTATIONS

Fuller-Austin Insulation Co. v. Bilder, 960 S.W.2d 914, 921 (Tex.App.—Beaumont 1998, pet. granted, judgm't vacated w.r.m.). "[T]he fact that [witness] was uncooperative in attending trial did not mean he could not give his deposition.... Although [witness] may have been beyond the subpoena power of the court, [D] did not establish it was unable to take his deposition or otherwise procure his testimony in this cause."

Thompson v. Mayes, 707 S.W.2d 951, 957 (Tex. App.—Eastland 1986, writ ref'd n.r.e.). Under TRE 804(b)(2), "dying declarations which concern the cause or the circumstances of what the declarant believed to be his impending death are admissible as exceptions to the hearsay rule."

TRE 805. HEARSAY WITHIN HEARSAY

Hearsay included within hearsay is not excluded under the hearsay rule if each part of the combined statements conforms with an exception to the hearsay rule provided in these rules.

History of TRE 805 (civil): Amended eff. Mar. 1, 1998, by order of Feb. 25, 1998 (960 S.W.2d [Tex.Cases] lxvii). Adopted eff. Sept. 1, 1983, by order of Nov. 23, 1982 (641-42 S.W.2d [Tex.Cases] lxi). Source: FRE 805.

See Brown & Rondon, *Texas Rules of Evidence Handbook* (2013), p. 920.

ANNOTATIONS

Houston Lighting & Power Co. v. Klein ISD, 739 S.W.2d 508, 519 (Tex.App.—Houston [14th Dist.] 1987, writ denied). "[C]harts summarizing studies of power lines and health effects [were] objected to ... as hearsay because the underlying studies were hearsay. [T]he error [in admitting the charts did not] cause the rendition of an improper verdict."

TRE 806. ATTACKING & SUPPORTING CREDIBILITY OF DECLARANT

When a hearsay statement, or a statement defined in Rule 801(e)(2)(C), (D), or (E), or in civil cases a statement defined in Rule 801(e)(3), has been admitted in evidence, the credibility of the declarant may be attacked, and if attacked may be supported by any evidence which would be admissible for those purposes if declarant had testified as a witness. Evidence of a statement or conduct by the declarant at any time, offered to impeach the declarant, is not subject to any requirement that the declarant may have been afforded an opportunity to deny or explain. If the party against whom a hearsay statement has been admitted calls the declarant as a witness, the party is entitled to examine the declarant on the statement as if under cross-examination.

History of TRE 806 (civil): Amended eff. Mar. 1, 1998, by order of Feb. 25, 1998 (960 S.W.2d [Tex.Cases] lxvii). Adopted eff. Sept. 1, 1983, by order of Nov. 23, 1982 (641-42 S.W.2d [Tex.Cases] lxi). Source: FRE 806.

See Brown & Rondon, *Texas Rules of Evidence Handbook* (2013), p. 922.

ANNOTATIONS

Anthony Pools, Inc. v. Charles & David, Inc., 797 S.W.2d 666, 676 (Tex.App.—Houston [14th Dist.] 1990, writ denied). "Texas courts long have allowed the use of affidavits to impeach a witness. The jury could have been allowed to consider any inconsistencies between the affidavit and the deposition as damaging to the credibility of [witness's] deposition, but not as substantive evidence. [¶] Upon timely request and objection, ... the court was required to instruct the jury of the limited use to be made of the affidavit."

Victor M. Solis Underground Util. & Paving Co. v. City of Laredo, 751 S.W.2d 532, 537 (Tex.App.—San Antonio 1988, writ denied). "If a declarant is unavailable as a witness, [TRE] 806 ... provides that testimony by that person at a former hearing is not excluded as hearsay if the party against whom the testimony is

TRE 806

—★—

offered, 'or a person with similar interest, had an opportunity and similar motive to develop the testimony by direct, cross, or redirect examination.'"

Article IX. Authentication & Identification

TRE 901. Requirement of Authentication or Identification

(a) General Provision. The requirement of authentication or identification as a condition precedent to admissibility is satisfied by evidence sufficient to support a finding that the matter in question is what its proponent claims.

(b) Illustrations. By way of illustration only, and not by way of limitation, the following are examples of authentication or identification conforming with the requirements of this rule:

(1) *Testimony of witness with knowledge.* Testimony that a matter is what it is claimed to be.

(2) *Nonexpert opinion on handwriting.* Nonexpert opinion as to the genuineness of handwriting, based upon familiarity not acquired for purposes of the litigation.

(3) *Comparison by trier or expert witness.* Comparison by the trier of fact or by expert witness with specimens which have been found by the court to be genuine.

(4) *Distinctive characteristics and the like.* Appearance, contents, substance, internal patterns, or other distinctive characteristics, taken in conjunction with circumstances.

(5) *Voice identification.* Identification of a voice, whether heard firsthand or through mechanical or electronic transmission or recording, by opinion based upon hearing the voice at anytime under circumstances connecting it with the alleged speaker.

(6) *Telephone conversations.* Telephone conversations, by evidence that a call was made to the number assigned at the time by the telephone company to a particular person or business, if:

(A) in the case of a person, circumstances, including self-identification, show the person answering to be the one called; or

(B) in the case of a business, the call was made to a place of business and the conversation related to business reasonably transacted over the telephone.

(7) *Public records or reports.* Evidence that a writing authorized by law to be recorded or filed and in fact recorded or filed in a public office, or a purported public record, report, statement, or data compilation, in any form, is from the public office where items of this nature are kept.

(8) *Ancient documents or data compilation.* Evidence that a document or data compilation, in any form, (A) is in such condition as to create no suspicion concerning its authenticity, (B) was in a place where it, if authentic, would likely be, and (C) has been in existence twenty years or more at the time it is offered.

(9) *Process or system.* Evidence describing a process or system used to produce a result and showing that the process or system produces an accurate result.

(10) *Methods provided by statute or rule.* Any method of authentication or identification provided by statute or by other rule prescribed pursuant to statutory authority.

History of TRE 901 (civil): Amended eff. Mar. 1, 1998, by order of Feb. 25, 1998 (960 S.W.2d [Tex.Cases] lxvii). Adopted eff. Sept. 1, 1983, by order of Nov. 23, 1982 (641-42 S.W.2d [Tex.Cases] lxii). Source: FRE 901. See TRCS arts. 3725, 3737b (repealed).

See *Commentaries,* "Authenticity," ch. 8-C, §8.4, p. 704; Brown & Rondon, *Texas Rules of Evidence Handbook* (2013), p. 928.

ANNOTATIONS

General Motors Corp. v. Gayle, 951 S.W.2d 469, 475 (Tex.1997). "Any tests that a party ... offer[s] at trial will be admissible only if the trial court determines that there is a substantial similarity between the test conditions and the accident conditions."

Kirwan v. City of Waco, 249 S.W.3d 544, 549 (Tex. App.—Waco 2008), *rev'd on other grounds*, 298 S.W.3d 618 (Tex.2009). "'Admissibility of a photograph is conditioned upon its identification by a witness as an accurate portrayal of the facts, and on verification by that witness or a person with knowledge that the photograph is a correct representation of such facts.' [¶] It is not required that [witness] made the photographs, observed their making, or knew when they were taken. All that is necessary is testimony from a witness with personal knowledge that the photographs accurately depict what they are 'claimed to be.'"

Sanchez v. Texas State Bd. of Med. Exam'rs, 229 S.W.3d 498, 509 (Tex.App.—Austin 2007, no pet.). "[T]he predicate for admissibility under rule 901 may be proven by circumstantial evidence."

In re G.F.O., 874 S.W.2d 729, 731 (Tex.App.—Houston [1st Dist.] 1994, no writ). TRE 901(a) "requires the authentication or identification as a condi-

---

tion precedent to admissibility; the requirement is satisfied by evidence sufficient to support a finding that the matter in question is what its proponent claims. [¶] A document is considered authentic if a sponsoring witness vouches for its authenticity or if the document meets the requirements of self-authentication." *See also* **Baker v. City of Robinson**, 305 S.W.3d 783, 792 (Tex.App.—Waco 2009, pet. denied); **Durkay v. Madco Oil Co.**, 862 S.W.2d 14, 24 (Tex.App.—Corpus Christi 1993, writ denied).

⑬ TRE 902. SELF-AUTHENTICATION*

Extrinsic evidence of authenticity as a condition precedent to admissibility is not required with respect to the following:

(1) Domestic Public Documents Under Seal. A document bearing a seal purporting to be that of the United States, or of any State, district, Commonwealth, territory, or insular possession thereof, or the Panama Canal Zone, or the Trust Territory of the Pacific Islands, or of a political subdivision, department, officer, or agency thereof, and a signature purporting to be an attestation or execution.

(2) Domestic Public Documents Not Under Seal. A document purporting to bear the signature in the official capacity of an officer or employee of any entity included in paragraph (1) hereof, having no seal, if a public officer having a seal and having official duties in the district or political subdivision of the officer or employee certifies under seal that the signer has the official capacity and that the signature is genuine.

(3) Foreign Public Documents. A document purporting to be executed or attested in an official capacity by a person, authorized by the laws of a foreign country to make the execution or attestation, and accompanied by a final certification as to the genuineness of the signature and official position (A) of the executing or attesting person, or (B) of any foreign official whose certificate of genuineness of signature and official position relates to the execution or attestation or is in a chain of certificates of genuineness of signature and official position relating to the execution or attestation. A final certification may be made by a secretary of embassy or legation, consul general, consul, vice consul, or consular agent of the United States, or a diplomatic or consular official of the foreign country assigned or accredited to the United States. If reasonable opportunity has been given to all parties to investigate the authen-

ticity and accuracy of official documents, the court may, for good cause shown, order that they be treated as presumptively authentic without final certification or permit them to be evidenced by an attested summary with or without final certification. The final certification shall be dispensed with whenever both the United States and the foreign country in which the official record is located are parties to a treaty or convention that abolishes or displaces such requirement, in which case the record and the attestation shall be certified by the means provided in the treaty or convention.

(4) Certified Copies of Public Records. A copy of an official record or report or entry therein, or of a document authorized by law to be recorded or filed and actually recorded or filed in a public office, including data compilations in any form certified as correct by the custodian or other person authorized to make the certification, by certificate complying with paragraph (1), (2) or (3) of this rule or complying with any statute or other rule prescribed pursuant to statutory authority.

(5) Official Publications. Books, pamphlets, or other publications purporting to be issued by public authority.

(6) Newspapers and Periodicals. Printed materials purporting to be newspapers or periodicals.

(7) Trade Inscriptions and the Like. Inscriptions, signs, tags, or labels purporting to have been affixed in the course of business and indicating ownership, control, or origin.

(8) Acknowledged Documents. Documents accompanied by a certificate of acknowledgment executed in the manner provided by law by a notary public or other officer authorized by law to take acknowledgments.

(9) Commercial Paper and Related Documents. Commercial paper, signatures thereon, and documents relating thereto to the extent provided by general commercial law.

(10) Business Records Accompanied by Affidavit.

(a) *Records or photocopies; admissibility; affidavit; filing.* Any record or set of records or photographically reproduced copies of such records, which would be admissible under Rule 803(6) or (7) shall be admissible in evidence in any court in this state upon the affidavit of the person who would otherwise provide the prerequisites of Rule 803(6) or (7), that such records attached to such affidavit were in fact so kept as required

TRE 902

by Rule 803(6) or (7), provided further, that such record or records along with such affidavit are filed with the clerk of the court for inclusion with the papers in the cause in which the record or records are sought to be used as evidence at least fourteen days prior to the day upon which trial of said cause commences, and provided the other parties to said cause are given prompt notice by the party filing same of the filing of such record or records and affidavit, which notice shall identify the name and employer, if any, of the person making the affidavit and such records shall be made available to the counsel for other parties to the action or litigation for inspection and copying. The expense for copying shall be borne by the party, parties or persons who desire copies and not by the party or parties who file the records and serve notice of said filing, in compliance with this rule. Notice shall be deemed to have been promptly given if it is served in the manner contemplated by Rule of Civil Procedure 21a fourteen days prior to commencement of trial in said cause.

(b) *Form of affidavit.* A form for the affidavit of such person as shall make such affidavit as is permitted in paragraph (a) above shall be sufficient if it follows this form though this form shall not be exclusive, and an affidavit which substantially complies with the provisions of this rule shall suffice, to-wit:

No _____

John Doe	§	IN THE _____
(Name of Plaintiff)	§	COURT IN AND FOR
v.	§	
John Roe	§	_____ COUNTY
(Name of Defendant)	§	TEXAS

AFFIDAVIT

Before me, the undersigned authority, personally appeared _____, who, being by me duly sworn, deposed as follows:

My name is _____, I am of sound mind, capable of making this affidavit, and personally acquainted with the facts herein stated:

I am the custodian of the records of _____. Attached hereto are _____ pages of records from _____. These said _____ pages of records are kept by _____ in the regular course of business, and it was the regular course of business of _____ for an

employee or representative of _____, with knowledge of the act, event, condition, opinion, or diagnosis, recorded to make the record or to transmit information thereof to be included in such record; and the record was made at or near the time or reasonably soon thereafter. The records attached hereto are the original or exact duplicates of the original.

_____
Affiant

SWORN TO AND SUBSCRIBED before me on the _____ day of _____, 19 ____.

_____
Notary Public, State of Texas
Notary's printed name:

_____
My commission expires:

_____

(11) Presumptions Under Statutes or Other Rules. Any signature, document, or other matter declared by statute or by other rules prescribed pursuant to statutory authority to be presumptively or prima facie genuine or authentic.

* Editor's note: The Supreme Court has proposed TRE 902(10)(c) to provide a self-authenticating form affidavit to prove medical expenses. *See* Tex. Sup.Ct. Order, Misc. Docket No. 12-9191 (eff. Mar. 1, 2013). The public-comment period for the proposed rule ends on February 1, 2013, and the rule is to take effect March 1, 2013. For the proposed version of the rule, see the appendix after this book's index. For the final version, go to the Supreme Court website at www.supreme.courts.state.tx.us. When the new rule takes effect, a supplement to this book—with updated rules and commentaries that reflect the changes—will be available at www.JonesMcClure.com/TRCPamendments.

History of TRE 902 (civil): Amended eff. Mar. 1, 1998, by order of Feb. 25, 1998 (960 S.W.2d [Tex.Cases] lxix). Amended eff. Jan. 1, 1988, by order of Nov. 10, 1986 (733-34 S.W.2d [Tex.Cases] xci). Adopted eff. Sept. 1, 1983, by order of Nov. 23, 1982 (641-42 S.W.2d [Tex.Cases] lxiii). Source: FRE 902. See TRCS arts. 3718-3737e (repealed). TRCE 902(10) was based on portions of the affidavit authentication provisions of TRCS art. 3737e. It was intended that this method of authentication would be available for any kind of regularly kept record that satisfies the requirements of TRCE 803(6) and (7), including X-rays, hospital records, or any other kind of regularly kept medical record.

See *Commentaries*, "Documents that are self-authenticating," ch. 8-C, §8.4.4, p. 706; Brown & Rondon, *Texas Rules of Evidence Handbook* (2013), p. 970.

ANNOTATIONS

Kyle v. Countrywide Home Loans, Inc., 232 S.W.3d 355, 360-61 (Tex.App.—Dallas 2007, pet. denied). "[A]lthough [TRE] 902(10)(b) sets out a form of affidavit for use when business records are introduced under [TRE] 803(6), it also specifically states that the form is not exclusive, and that an affidavit must only 'substantially compl[y]' with the sample affidavit. Consequently, [affiant] was not required to recite the exact words that appear in Rule 902(10)(b).

⭐

She was also not required to state that all facts in the affidavit are 'true and correct.'" *See also Rockwall Commons Assocs. v. MRC Mortg. Grantor Trust I*, 331 S.W.3d 500, 509-10 (Tex.App.—El Paso 2010, no pet.); *March v. Victoria Lloyds Ins.*, 773 S.W.2d 785, 789 (Tex.App.—Fort Worth 1989, writ denied).

Murphy v. Countrywide Home Loans, Inc., 199 S.W.3d 441, 446 (Tex.App.—Houston [1st Dist.] 2006, pet. denied). "The deed of trust, substitute trustee's deed, and affidavit of mortgage in this case all contain file stamps which indicate that they have been filed in the [c]ounty real property records as official public records. Therefore, we hold these documents to be self-authenticated."

Al-Nayem Int'l Trading, Inc. v. Irving ISD, 159 S.W.3d 762, 764 (Tex.App.—Dallas 2005, no pet.). "Because the ... tax statements did not bear a seal or contain a certification under seal from a public officer, [they] were not self-authenticating as certified public records...."

In re N.C.M., 66 S.W.3d 417, 419 (Tex.App.—Tyler 2001, no pet.). "The plain language of Rule 902(10)(a) does not require that the affidavit be attached to a business record when the exhibit is offered into evidence."

Texas DPS v. Silva, 988 S.W.2d 873, 877 (Tex.App.—San Antonio 1999, pet. denied). "[D] cites no authority, nor have we found any requirement that the stamp state what the document is certifying or that the stamp be from the county where the documents were prepared."

TRE 903. SUBSCRIBING WITNESS' TESTIMONY UNNECESSARY

The testimony of a subscribing witness is not necessary to authenticate a writing unless required by the laws of the jurisdiction whose laws govern the validity of the writing.

History of TRE 903 (civil): Amended eff. Mar. 1, 1998, by order of Feb. 25, 1998 (960 S.W.2d [Tex.Cases] lxxi). Adopted eff. Sept. 1, 1983, by order of Nov. 23, 1982 (641-42 S.W.2d [Tex.Cases] lxvi). Source: FRE 903. See TRCS art. 3734a (repealed).

See Brown & Rondon, *Texas Rules of Evidence Handbook* (2013), p. 992.

ARTICLE X. CONTENTS OF WRITINGS, RECORDINGS, & PHOTOGRAPHS

TRE 1001. DEFINITIONS

For purposes of this article the following definitions are applicable:

(a) **Writings and Recordings.** "Writings" and "recordings" consist of letters, words, or numbers or their equivalent, set down by handwriting, typewriting, printing, photostating, photographing, magnetic impulse, mechanical or electronic recording, or other form of data compilation.

(b) **Photographs.** "Photographs" include still photographs, X-ray films, video tapes, and motion pictures.

(c) **Original.** An "original" of a writing or recording is the writing or recording itself or any counterpart intended to have the same effect by a person executing or issuing it. An "original" of a photograph includes the negative or any print therefrom. If data are stored in a computer or similar device, any printout or other output readable by sight, shown to reflect the data accurately, is an "original."

(d) **Duplicate.** A "duplicate" is a counterpart produced by the same impression as the original, or from the same matrix, or by means of photography, including enlargements and miniatures, or by mechanical or electronic re-recording, or by chemical reproduction, or by other equivalent techniques which accurately reproduce the original.

History of TRE 1001 (civil): Amended eff. Mar. 1, 1998, by order of Feb. 25, 1998 (960 S.W.2d [Tex.Cases] lxxii). Adopted eff. Sept. 1, 1983, by order of Nov. 23, 1982 (641-42 S.W.2d [Tex.Cases] lxvi). Source: FRE 1001.

See *Commentaries*, "Documents authenticated by witness," ch. 8-C, §8.4.3, p. 704; Brown & Rondon, *Texas Rules of Evidence Handbook* (2013), p. 998.

ANNOTATIONS

S.D.G. v. State, 936 S.W.2d 371, 381 (Tex.App.—Houston [14th Dist.] 1996, writ denied). "The predicate for introduction of a photograph and a videotape not accompanied by a sound recording requires proof of (1) its accuracy as a correct representation of the subject at a given time, and (2) its relevance to a material issue. ... Any witness who observed the object or the scene depicted in the photograph may lay the predicate."

TRE 1002. REQUIREMENT OF ORIGINALS

To prove the content of a writing, recording, or photograph, the original writing, recording, or photograph is required except as otherwise provided in these rules or by law.

History of TRE 1002 (civil): Amended eff. Mar. 1, 1998, by order of Feb. 25, 1998 (960 S.W.2d [Tex.Cases] lxxii). Adopted eff. Sept. 1, 1983, by order of Nov. 23, 1982 (641-42 S.W.2d [Tex.Cases] lxvi). Source: FRE 1002.

See Brown & Rondon, *Texas Rules of Evidence Handbook* (2013), p. 998.

TRE 1002

ANNOTATIONS

White v. Bath, 825 S.W.2d 227, 231 (Tex.App.—Houston [14th Dist.] 1992, writ denied). "[O]nly when one seeks to prove the contents of a document [does] the best evidence rule [apply]. When the document and its contents are only collaterally related to the issues in the case, the best evidence rule does not apply."

Ramsey v. Jones Enters., 810 S.W.2d 902, 905 (Tex.App.—Beaumont 1991, writ denied). "The best evidence of the content of documents is the documents themselves. The trial court erred in admitting hearsay testimony to prove up the content of documents without a proper showing that the subject documents were unavailable through no fault or failure on the part of the party offering same."

TRE 1003. ADMISSIBILITY OF DUPLICATES

A duplicate is admissible to the same extent as an original unless (1) a question is raised as to the authenticity of the original or (2) in the circumstances it would be unfair to admit the duplicate in lieu of the original.

History of TRE 1003 (civil): Amended eff. Mar. 1, 1998, by order of Feb. 25, 1998 (960 S.W.2d [Tex.Cases] lxxii). Adopted eff. Sept. 1, 1983, by order of Nov. 23, 1982 (641-42 S.W.2d [Tex.Cases] lxvi). Source: FRE 1003.

See *Commentaries*, "Copy of document," ch. 8-C, §8.4.3(2), p. 704; Brown & Rondon, *Texas Rules of Evidence Handbook* (2013), p. 999.

ANNOTATIONS

Ford Motor Co. v. Leggat, 904 S.W.2d 643, 646 (Tex.1995). "[I]n the absence of a challenge to the authenticity of the affidavit, submission of a copy is not grounds for rejecting it."

TRE 1004. ADMISSIBILITY OF OTHER EVIDENCE OF CONTENTS

The original is not required, and other evidence of the contents of a writing, recording, or photograph is admissible if:

(a) Originals Lost or Destroyed. All originals are lost or have been destroyed, unless the proponent lost or destroyed them in bad faith;

(b) Original Not Obtainable. No original can be obtained by any available judicial process or procedure;

(c) Original Outside the State. No original is located in Texas;

(d) Original in Possession of Opponent. At a time when an original was under the control of the party against whom offered, that party was put on notice, by the pleadings or otherwise, that the content would be a subject of proof at the hearing, and that party does not produce the original at the hearing; or

(e) Collateral Matters. The writing, recording or photograph is not closely related to a controlling issue.

History of TRE 1004 (civil): Amended eff. Mar. 1, 1998, by order of Feb. 25, 1998 (960 S.W.2d [Tex.Cases] lxxii). Adopted eff. Sept. 1, 1983, by order of Nov. 23, 1982 (641-42 S.W.2d [Tex.Cases] lxvii). Source: FRE 1004.

See TRCP 77; *Commentaries*, "Copy of document," ch. 8-C, §8.4.3(2), p. 704; Brown & Rondon, *Texas Rules of Evidence Handbook* (2013), p. 1013.

ANNOTATIONS

Coke v. Coke, 802 S.W.2d 270, 275 (Tex.App.—Dallas 1990, writ denied). "Under rule 1004, an original document is not required if the original is lost or destroyed without the fault of the proponent. Copies are admissible if 'there is a reasonable account for [the originals'] absence or if there is no question of their authenticity.'"

TRE 1005. PUBLIC RECORDS

The contents of an official record or of a document authorized to be recorded or filed and actually recorded or filed, including data compilations in any form, if otherwise admissible, may be proved by copy, certified as correct in accordance with Rule 902 or testified to be correct by a witness who has compared it with the original. If a copy which complies with the foregoing cannot be obtained by the exercise of reasonable diligence, then other evidence of the contents may be given.

History of TRE 1005 (civil): Amended eff. Mar. 1, 1998, by order of Feb. 25, 1998 (960 S.W.2d [Tex.Cases] lxxiii). Adopted eff. Sept. 1, 1983, by order of Nov. 23, 1982 (641-42 S.W.2d [Tex.Cases] lxvii). Source: FRE 1005.

See *Commentaries*, "Documents that are self-authenticating," ch. 8-C, §8.4.4, p. 706; Brown & Rondon, *Texas Rules of Evidence Handbook* (2013), p. 1018.

ANNOTATIONS

ESIS, Inc. v. Johnson, 908 S.W.2d 554, 561 (Tex. App.—Fort Worth 1995, writ denied). "A copy of a public record is considered authentic if a sponsoring witness vouches for its authenticity or if the document meets the certification requirements for self-authentication contained in [TRE] 902."

TRE 1006. SUMMARIES

The contents of voluminous writings, recordings, or photographs, otherwise admissible, which cannot conveniently be examined in court may be presented in the form of a chart, summary, or calculation. The originals, or duplicates, shall be made available for examination or copying, or both, by other parties at a reasonable time and place. The court may order that they be produced in court.

History of TRE 1006 (civil): Amended eff. Mar. 1, 1998, by order of Feb. 25, 1998 (960 S.W.2d [Tex.Cases] lxxiii). Adopted eff. Sept. 1, 1983, by order of Nov. 23, 1982 (641-42 S.W.2d [Tex.Cases] lxvii). Source: FRE 1006.

See Brown & Rondon, *Texas Rules of Evidence Handbook* (2013), p. 1021.

ANNOTATIONS

Aquamarine Assocs. v. Burton Shipyard, Inc., 659 S.W.2d 820, 821 (Tex.1983). "In cases involving voluminous records, the trial court has discretion to relax the best evidence rule and allow the admission of summaries.... The party sponsoring the summary must, however, lay the proper predicate for its admission." *See also* **Welder v. Welder**, 794 S.W.2d 420, 429 (Tex. App.—Corpus Christi 1990, no writ).

TRE 1007. TESTIMONY OR WRITTEN ADMISSION OF PARTY

Contents of writings, recordings, or photographs may be proved by the testimony or deposition of the party against whom offered or by that party's written admission, without accounting for the nonproduction of the original.

History of TRE 1007 (civil): Amended eff. Mar. 1, 1998, by order of Feb. 25, 1998 (960 S.W.2d [Tex.Cases] lxxiii). Amended eff. Jan. 1, 1988, by order of Nov. 10, 1986 (733-34 S.W.2d [Tex.Cases] xcii): In title, deleted "Permission" and added "Admission." Adopted eff. Sept. 1, 1983, by order of Nov. 23, 1982 (641-42 S.W.2d [Tex.Cases] lxvii). Source: FRE 1007.

See Brown & Rondon, *Texas Rules of Evidence Handbook* (2013), p. 1025.

TRE 1008. FUNCTIONS OF COURT & JURY

When the admissibility of other evidence of contents of writings, recordings, or photographs under these rules depends upon the fulfillment of a condition of fact, the question whether the condition has been fulfilled is ordinarily for the court to determine in accordance with the provisions of Rule 104. However, when an issue is raised (a) whether the asserted writing ever existed, or (b) whether another writing, recording, or photograph produced at the trial is the original, or (c) whether other evidence of contents correctly reflects the contents, the issue is for the trier of fact to determine as in the case of other issues of fact.

History of TRE 1008 (civil): Amended eff. Mar. 1, 1998, by order of Feb. 25, 1998 (960 S.W.2d [Tex.Cases] lxxiii). Adopted eff. Sept. 1, 1983, by order of Nov. 23, 1982 (641-42 S.W.2d [Tex.Cases] lxvii). Source: FRE 1008.

See Brown & Rondon, *Texas Rules of Evidence Handbook* (2013), p. 1027.

TRE 1009. TRANSLATION OF FOREIGN LANGUAGE DOCUMENTS

(a) Translations. A translation of foreign language documents shall be admissible upon the affidavit of a qualified translator setting forth the qualifications of the translator and certifying that the translation is fair and accurate. Such affidavit, along with the translation and the underlying foreign language documents, shall be served upon all parties at least 45 days prior to the date of trial.

(b) Objections. Any party may object to the accuracy of another party's translation by pointing out the specific inaccuracies of the translation and by stating with specificity what the objecting party contends is a fair and accurate translation. Such objection shall be served upon all parties at least 15 days prior to the date of trial.

(c) Effect of Failure to Object or Offer Conflicting Translation. If no conflicting translation or objection is timely served, the court shall admit a translation submitted under paragraph (a) without need of proof, provided however that the underlying foreign language documents are otherwise admissible under the Texas Rules of Evidence. Failure to serve a conflicting translation under paragraph (a) or failure to timely and properly object to the accuracy of a translation under paragraph (b) shall preclude a party from attacking or offering evidence contradicting the accuracy of such translation at trial.

(d) Effect of Objections or Conflicting Translations. In the event of conflicting translations under paragraph (a) or if objections to another party's translation are served under paragraph (b), the court shall determine whether there is a genuine issue as to the accuracy of a material part of the translation to be resolved by the trier of fact.

(e) Expert Testimony of Translator. Except as provided in paragraph (c), this Rule does not preclude the admission of a translation of foreign language documents at trial either by live testimony or by deposition testimony of a qualified expert translator.

(f) Varying of Time Limits. The court, upon motion of any party and for good cause shown, may enlarge or shorten the time limits set forth in this Rule.

(g) Court Appointment. The court, if necessary, may appoint a qualified translator, the reasonable value of whose services shall be taxed as court costs.

Comment to 1998 change: This is a new rule.

History of TRE 1009 (civil): Adopted eff. Mar. 1, 1998, by order of Feb. 25, 1998 (960 S.W.2d [Tex.Cases] lxxiv). Source: New rule.

See Brown & Rondon, *Texas Rules of Evidence Handbook* (2013), p. 1029.

ANNOTATIONS

In re DC, No. 01-11-00387-CV (Tex.App.—Houston [1st Dist.] 2012, pet. denied) (memo op.; 3-1-12). Father "complains that the initial return was in Spanish, and because it was not translated into English until after trial, it violated [TRE] 1009, which requires that all foreign documents to be admitted at trial must be translated 45 days before trial and be accompanied by an affidavit from a qualified translator. [¶] However, rule 1009 is a rule of evidence governing the admission of foreign documents of trial. [Father] has cited no cases in which rule 1009 requires the translation of foreign returns of service into English, or that such a translation could not be done in an amended return while the trial court still had plenary power. We have found no authority holding that rule 1009 trumps [TRCP] 118, which permits amended returns of service '[a]t any time.'"

Doncaster v. Hernaiz, 161 S.W.3d 594, 601 (Tex. App.—San Antonio 2005, no pet.). "[P] did file a copy of the [foreign-language document] with a translation with her initial summary judgment motion, but failed to attach the translator's affidavit. Later, [P] supplemented her motion with an affidavit from the translator.... Because of [P's] late supplementation, the trial court provided [D] a one-week continuance before conducting the summary judgment hearing. Rule 1009 provides the court with authority to lengthen or shorten the time limits set by the rule. [A]ny error in failing to initially provide the affidavit of the translator was cured by its inclusion in the supplement, and it was therefore within the court's discretion to admit [the document]."

⭐

To save space, we have eliminated the TRAPs relating to criminal appellate procedure and the TRAP history notes. For the complete TRAPs with annotations, see the current edition of *O'Connor's Texas Civil Appeals*. To order, call 1-800-OCONNOR (1-800-626-6667) or visit www.JonesMcClure.com.

TRAP

✦

Editor's note: All new TRAP amendments are marked with ⑫ to draw the reader's attention to the change and alert the reader to check the effective date of the change. New rule language is underlined.

SECTION ONE: GENERAL PROVISIONS

TRAP 1. SCOPE OF RULES; LOCAL RULES OF COURTS OF APPEALS

1.1 **Scope.** These rules govern procedure in appellate courts and before appellate judges and post-trial procedure in trial courts in criminal cases.

1.2 **Local Rules.**

(a) *Promulgation.* A court of appeals may promulgate rules governing its practice that are not inconsistent with these rules. Local rules governing civil cases must first be approved by the Supreme Court. Local rules governing criminal cases must first be approved by the Court of Criminal Appeals.

(b) *Copies.* The clerk must provide a copy of the court's local rules to anyone who requests it.

(c) *Party's noncompliance.* A court must not dismiss an appeal for noncompliance with a local rule without giving the noncomplying party notice and a reasonable opportunity to cure the noncompliance.

TRAP 2. SUSPENSION OF RULES

On a party's motion or on its own initiative an appellate court may—to expedite a decision or for other good cause—suspend a rule's operation in a particular case and order a different procedure; but a court must not construe this rule to suspend any provision in the Code of Criminal Procedure or to alter the time for perfecting an appeal in a civil case.

TRAP 3. DEFINITIONS; UNIFORM TERMINOLOGY

3.1 **Definitions.**

(a) *Appellant* means a party taking an appeal to an appellate court.

(b) *Appellate court* means the courts of appeals, the Court of Criminal Appeals, and the Supreme Court.

(c) *Appellee* means a party adverse to an appellant.

(d) *Applicant* means a person seeking relief by a habeas corpus in a criminal case.

(e) *Petitioner* means a party petitioning the Supreme Court or the Court of Criminal Appeals for review.

(f) *Relator* means a person seeking relief in an original proceeding in an appellate court other than by habeas corpus in a criminal case.

(g) *Reporter* or *court reporter* means the court reporter or court recorder.

(h) *Respondent* means:

(1) a party adverse to a petitioner in the Supreme Court or the Court of Criminal Appeals; or

(2) a party against whom relief is sought in an original proceeding in an appellate court.

3.2 **Uniform Terminology in Criminal Cases.**

TRAP 4. TIME & NOTICE PROVISIONS

4.1 **Computing Time.**

(a) *In general.* The day of an act, event, or default after which a designated period begins to run is not included when computing a period prescribed or allowed by these rules, by court order, or by statute. The last day of the period is included, but if that day is a Saturday, Sunday, or legal holiday, the period extends to the end of the next day that is not a Saturday, Sunday, or legal holiday.

(b) *Clerk's office closed or inaccessible.* If the act to be done is filing a document, and if the clerk's office where the document is to be filed is closed or inaccessible during regular hours on the last day for filing the document, the period for filing the document extends to the end of the next day when the clerk's office is open and accessible. The closing or inaccessibility of the clerk's office may be proved by a certificate of the clerk or counsel, by a party's affidavit, or by other satisfactory proof, and may be controverted in the same manner.

4.2 **No Notice of Trial Court's Judgment in Civil Case.**

(a) *Additional time to file documents.*

(1) *In general.* If a party affected by a judgment or other appealable order has not—within 20 days after the judgment or order was signed—either received the notice required by Texas Rule of Civil Procedure 306a.3 or acquired actual knowledge of the signing, then a period that, under these rules, runs from the signing will begin for that party on the earlier of the date when the party receives notice or acquires actual knowledge of the signing. But in no event may the period begin more than 90 days after the judgment or order was signed.

(2) *Exception for restricted appeal.* Subparagraph (1) does not extend the time for perfecting a restricted appeal.

(b) *Procedure to gain additional time.* The procedure to gain additional time is governed by Texas Rule of Civil Procedure 306a.5.

(c) *The court's order.* After hearing the motion, the trial court must sign a written order that finds the date when the party or the party's attorney first either received notice or acquired actual knowledge that the judgment or order was signed.

4.3 Periods Affected by Modified Judgment in Civil Case.

(a) *During plenary-power period.* If a judgment is modified in any respect while the trial court retains plenary power, a period that, under these rules, runs from the date when the judgment is signed will run from the date when the modified judgment is signed.

(b) *After plenary power expires.* If the trial court corrects or reforms the judgment under Texas Rule of Civil Procedure 316 after expiration of the trial court's plenary power, all periods provided in these rules that run from the date the judgment is signed run from the date the corrected judgment is signed for complaints that would not apply to the original judgment.

4.4 Periods Affected When Process Served by Publication. If process was served by publication and if a motion for new trial was filed under Texas Rule of Civil Procedure 329 more than 30 days after the judgment was signed, a period that, under these rules, runs from the date when the judgment is signed will be computed as if the judgment were signed on the date when the motion for new trial was filed.

4.5 No Notice of Judgment or Order of Appellate Court; Effect on Time to File Certain Documents.

(a) *Additional time to file documents.* A party may move for additional time to file a motion for rehearing or en banc reconsideration in the court of appeals, a petition for review, or a petition for discretionary review, if the party did not—until after the time expired for filing the document—either receive notice of the judgment or order from the clerk or acquire actual knowledge of the rendition of the judgment or order.

(b) *Procedure to gain additional time.* The motion must state the earliest date when the party or the party's attorney received notice or acquired actual knowledge that the judgment or order had been rendered. The motion must be filed within 15 days of that date but in no event more than 90 days after the date of the judgment or order.

(c) *Where to file.*

(1) A motion for additional time to file a motion for rehearing or en banc reconsideration in the court of appeals must be filed in and ruled on by the court of appeals in which the case is pending.

(2) A motion for additional time to file a petition for review must be filed in and ruled on by the Supreme Court.

(3) A motion for additional time to file a petition for discretionary review must be filed in and ruled on by the Court of Criminal Appeals.

(d) *Order of the court.* If the court finds that the motion for additional time was timely filed and the party did not—within the time for filing the motion for rehearing or en banc reconsideration, petition for review, or petition for discretionary review, as the case may be—receive the notice or have actual knowledge of the judgment or order, the court must grant the motion. The time for filing the document will begin to run on the date when the court grants the motion.

TRAP 5. FEES IN CIVIL CASES

A party who is not excused by statute or these rules from paying costs must pay—at the time an item is presented for filing—whatever fees are required by statute or Supreme Court order. The appellate court may enforce this rule by any order that is just.

TRAP 6. REPRESENTATION BY COUNSEL

6.1 Lead Counsel.

(a) *For appellant.* Unless another attorney is designated, lead counsel for an appellant is the attorney whose signature first appears on the notice of appeal.

(b) *For a party other than appellant.* Unless another attorney is designated, lead counsel for a party other than an appellant is the attorney whose signature first appears on the first document filed in the appellate court on that party's behalf.

(c) *How to designate.* The original or a new lead counsel may be designated by filing a notice stating that attorney's name, mailing address, telephone number, fax number, if any, and State Bar of Texas identifi-

TRAP 6

---

cation number. If a new lead counsel is being designated, both the new attorney and either the party or the former lead counsel must sign the notice.

6.2 Appearance of Other Attorneys. An attorney other than lead counsel may file a notice stating that the attorney represents a specified party to the proceeding and giving that attorney's name, mailing address, telephone number, fax number, if any, and State Bar of Texas identification number. The clerk will note on the docket the attorney's appearance. When a brief or motion is filed, the clerk will note on the docket the name of each attorney, if not already noted, who appears on the document.

6.3 To Whom Communications Sent. Any notice, copies of documents filed in an appellate court, or other communications must be sent to:

(a) each party's lead counsel on appeal;

(b) a party's lead counsel in the trial court if:

(1) that party was represented by counsel in the trial court;

(2) lead counsel on appeal has not yet been designated for that party; and

(3) lead counsel in the trial court has not filed a nonrepresentation notice or been allowed to withdraw;

(c) a party if the party is not represented by counsel.

6.4 Nonrepresentation Notice.

(a) *In general.* If, in accordance with paragraph 6.3(b), the lead counsel in the trial court is being sent notices, copies of documents, or other communications, that attorney may file a nonrepresentation notice in the appellate court. The notice must:

(1) state that the attorney is not representing the party on appeal;

(2) state that the court and other counsel should communicate directly with the party in the future;

(3) give the party's name and last known address and telephone number; and

(4) be signed by the party.

(b) *Appointed counsel.* In a criminal case, an attorney appointed by the trial court to represent an indigent party cannot file a nonrepresentation notice.

6.5 Withdrawal. An appellate court may, on appropriate terms and conditions, permit an attorney to withdraw from representing a party in the appellate court.

(a) *Contents of motion.* A motion for leave to withdraw must contain the following:

(1) a list of current deadlines and settings in the case;

(2) the party's name and last known address and telephone number;

(3) a statement that a copy of the motion was delivered to the party; and

(4) a statement that the party was notified in writing of the right to object to the motion.

(b) *Delivery to party.* The motion must be delivered to the party in person or mailed—both by certified and by first-class mail—to the party at the party's last known address.

(c) *If motion granted.* If the court grants the motion, the withdrawing attorney must immediately notify the party, in writing, of any deadlines or settings that the attorney knows about at the time of withdrawal but that were not previously disclosed to the party. The withdrawing attorney must file a copy of that notice with the court clerk.

(d) *Exception for substitution of counsel.* If an attorney substitutes for a withdrawing attorney, the motion to withdraw need not comply with (a) but must state only the substitute attorney's name, mailing address, telephone number, fax number, if any, and State Bar of Texas identification number. The withdrawing attorney must comply with (b) but not (c).

6.6 Agreements of Parties or Counsel. To be enforceable, an agreement of parties or their counsel concerning an appellate court proceeding must be in writing and signed by the parties or their counsel. Such an agreement is subject to any appellate court order necessary to ensure that the case is properly presented.

TRAP 7. SUBSTITUTING PARTIES

7.1 Parties Who Are Not Public Officers.

(a) *Death of a party.*

(1) *Civil cases.* If a party to a civil case dies after the trial court renders judgment but before the case has been finally disposed of on appeal, the appeal may be perfected, and the appellate court will proceed to adjudicate the appeal as if all parties were alive. The appellate court's judgment will have the same force and effect as if rendered when all parties were living. The decedent party's name may be used on all papers.

★

(2) *Criminal cases.*

(b) *Substitution for other reasons.* If substitution of a party in the appellate court is necessary for a reason other than death, the appellate court may order substitution on any party's motion at any time.

7.2 Public Officers.

(a) *Automatic substitution of officer.* When a public officer is a party in an official capacity to an appeal or original proceeding, and if that person ceases to hold office before the appeal or original proceeding is finally disposed of, the public officer's successor is automatically substituted as a party if appropriate. Proceedings following substitution are to be in the name of the substituted party, but any misnomer that does not affect the substantial rights of the parties may be disregarded. Substitution may be ordered at any time, but failure to order substitution of the successor does not affect the substitution.

(b) *Abatement.* If the case is an original proceeding under Rule 52, the court must abate the proceeding to allow the successor to reconsider the original party's decision. In all other cases, the suit will not abate, and the successor will be bound by the appellate court's judgment or order as if the successor were the original party.

TRAP 8. BANKRUPTCY IN CIVIL CASES

8.1 **Notice of Bankruptcy.** Any party may file a notice that a party is in bankruptcy. The notice must contain:

(a) the bankrupt party's name;

(b) the court in which the bankruptcy proceeding is pending;

(c) the bankruptcy proceeding's style and case number; and

(d) the date when the bankruptcy petition was filed.

8.2 **Effect of Bankruptcy.** A bankruptcy suspends the appeal and all periods in these rules from the date when the bankruptcy petition is filed until the appellate court reinstates or severs the appeal in accordance with federal law. A period that began to run and had not expired at the time the proceeding was suspended begins anew when the proceeding is reinstated or severed under 8.3. A document filed by a party while the proceeding is suspended will be deemed filed on the same day,

but after, the court reinstates or severs the appeal and will not be considered ineffective because it was filed while the proceeding was suspended.

8.3 **Motion to Reinstate or Sever Appeal Suspended by Bankruptcy.**

(a) *Motion to reinstate.* If a case has been suspended by a bankruptcy filing, a party may move that the appellate court reinstate the appeal if permitted by federal law or the bankruptcy court. If the bankruptcy court has lifted or terminated the stay, a certified copy of the order must be attached to the motion.

(b) *Motion to sever.* A party may move to sever the appeal with respect to the bankrupt party and to reinstate the appeal with respect to the other parties. The motion must show that the case is severable and must comply with applicable federal law regarding severance of a bankrupt party. The court may proceed under this paragraph on its own initiative.

TRAP 9. PAPERS GENERALLY

9.1 **Signing.**

(a) *Represented parties.* If a party is represented by counsel, a document filed on that party's behalf must be signed by at least one of the party's attorneys. For each attorney whose name appears on a document as representing that party, the document must contain that attorney's State Bar of Texas identification number, mailing address, telephone number, and fax number, if any.

(b) *Unrepresented parties.* A party not represented by counsel must sign any document that the party files and give the party's mailing address, telephone number, and fax number, if any.

9.2 **Filing.**

(a) *With whom.* A document is filed in an appellate court by delivering it to:

(1) the clerk of the court in which the document is to be filed; or

(2) a justice or judge of that court who is willing to accept delivery. A justice or judge who accepts delivery must note on the document the date and time of delivery, which will be considered the time of filing, and must promptly send it to the clerk.

(b) *Filing by mail.*

(1) *Timely filing.* A document received within ten days after the filing deadline is considered timely filed if:

TRAP 9

★

(A) it was sent to the proper clerk by United States Postal Service first-class, express, registered, or certified mail;

(B) it was placed in an envelope or wrapper properly addressed and stamped; and

(C) it was deposited in the mail on or before the last day for filing.

(2) *Proof of mailing.* Though it may consider other proof, the appellate court will accept the following as conclusive proof of the date of mailing:

(A) a legible postmark affixed by the United States Postal Service;

(B) a receipt for registered or certified mail if the receipt is endorsed by the United States Postal Service; or

(C) a certificate of mailing by the United States Postal Service.

(c) *Electronic filing.* Documents may be permitted or required to be filed, signed, or verified by electronic means by order of the Supreme Court or the Court of Criminal Appeals, or by local rule of a court of appeals. A technical failure that precludes a party's compliance with electronic-filing procedures cannot be a basis for disposing of any case.

9.3 Number of Copies; Electronic Copies.

(a) *Courts of appeals.*

(1) *Paper copies in general.* A party must file:

(A) the original and three copies of all documents in an original proceeding;

(B) the original and two copies of all motions in an appellate proceeding; and

(C) the original and five copies of all other documents.

(2) *Local rules.* A court of appeals may by local rule require:

(A) the filing of more or fewer paper copies of any document other than a petition for discretionary review; and

(B) an electronic copy of a document filed in paper form.

(b) *Supreme Court and Court of Criminal Appeals.*

(1) *Paper copies of document filed in paper form.* A party must file the original and 11 copies of any document addressed to either the Supreme Court or the Court of Criminal Appeals, except that in the Supreme Court, only an original and one copy must be filed of any motion, response to the motion, and reply in support of the motion, and in the Court of Criminal Appeals, only the original must be filed of a motion for extension of time or a response to the motion, or a pleading under Code of Criminal Procedure article 11.07.

(2) *Electronic copies of document filed in paper form.* An electronic copy of a document filed in paper form may be required by order of the Supreme Court or the Court of Criminal Appeals.

(3) *Paper copies of electronically filed document.* Copies of each document that is electronically filed with the Supreme Court or the Court of Criminal Appeals must be mailed or hand-delivered to the Supreme Court or the Court of Criminal Appeals, as appropriate, within one business day after the document is electronically filed. The number of paper copies required shall be determined, respectively, by order of the Supreme Court or the Court of Criminal Appeals.

(c) *Exception for record.* Only the original record need be filed in any proceeding.

12 **9.4** **Form.** Except for the record, a document filed with an appellate court must—unless the court accepts another form in the interest of justice—be in the following form:

(a) *Printing.* A document may be produced by standard typographic printing or by any duplicating process that produces a distinct black image. Printing may be on both sides of the paper.

(b) *Paper type and size.* The paper on which the document is produced must be white or nearly white, and opaque. Paper must be 8½ by 11 inches.

(c) *Margins.* Papers must have at least one-inch margins on both sides and at the top and bottom.

(d) *Spacing.* Text must be double-spaced, but footnotes, block quotations, short lists, and issues or points of error may be single-spaced.

(e) *Typeface.* A document produced on a computer must be printed in a conventional typeface no smaller than 14-point except for footnotes, which must be no smaller than 12-point. A typewritten document must be printed in standard 10-character-per-inch (cpi) monospaced typeface.

(f) *Binding and covering.* A document must be bound so as to ensure that it will not lose its cover or fall apart in regular use. A document should be stapled

TRAP 9

★

once in the top left-hand corner or be bound so that it will lie flat when open. A petition or brief should have durable front and back covers which must not be plastic or be red, black, or dark blue.

(g) *Contents of cover.* A document's front cover, if any, must contain the case style, the case number, the title of the document being filed, the name of the party filing the document, and the name, mailing address, telephone number, fax number, if any, and State Bar of Texas identification number of the lead counsel for the filing party. If a party requests oral argument in the court of appeals, the request must appear on the front cover of that party's first brief.

(h) *Appendix.* An appendix may be bound either with the document to which it is related or separately. If separately bound, the appendix must comply with paragraph (f). An appendix should be tabbed and indexed.

(i) *Length.*

(1) *Contents included and excluded.* In calculating the length of a document, every word and every part of the document, including headings, footnotes, and quotations, must be counted except the following: caption, identity of parties and counsel, statement regarding oral argument, table of contents, index of authorities, statement of the case, statement of issues presented, statement of jurisdiction, statement of procedural history, signature, proof of service, certification, certificate of compliance, and appendix.

(2) *Maximum length.* The documents listed below must not exceed the following limits:

(A) A brief and response in a direct appeal to the Court of Criminal Appeals in a case in which the death penalty has been assessed: 37,500 words if computer-generated, and 125 pages if not.

(B) A brief and response in an appellate court (other than a brief under subparagraph (A)) and a petition and response in an original proceeding in the court of appeals: 15,000 words if computer-generated, and 50 pages if not. In a civil case in the court of appeals, the aggregate of all briefs filed by a party must not exceed 27,000 words if computer-generated, and 90 pages if not.

(C) A reply brief in an appellate court and a reply to a response to a petition in an original proceeding in the court of appeals: 7,500 words if computer-generated, and 25 pages if not.

(D) A petition and response in an original proceeding in the Supreme Court, a petition for review and re-

sponse in the Supreme Court, a petition for discretionary review and response in the Court of Criminal Appeals, and a motion for rehearing and response in an appellate court: 4,500 words if computer-generated, and 15 pages if not.

(E) A reply to a response to a petition for review in the Supreme Court, a reply to a response to a petition in an original proceeding in the Supreme Court, and a reply to a response to a petition for discretionary review in the Court of Criminal Appeals: 2,400 words if computer-generated, and 8 pages if not.

(3) *Certificate of compliance.* A computer-generated document must include a certificate by counsel or an unrepresented party stating the number of words in the document. The person certifying may rely on the word count of the computer program used to prepare the document.

(4) *Extensions.* A court may, on motion, permit a document that exceeds the prescribed limit.

(j) *Nonconforming documents.* Unless every copy of a document conforms to these rules, the court may strike the document and return all nonconforming copies to the filing party. The court must identify the error to be corrected and state a deadline for the party to resubmit the document in a conforming format. If another nonconforming document is filed, the court may strike the document and prohibit the party from filing further documents of the same kind.

9.5 Service.

(a) *Service of all documents required.* At or before the time of a document's filing, the filing party must serve a copy on all parties to the proceeding. But a party need not serve a copy of the record.

(b) *Manner of service.* Service on a party represented by counsel must be made on that party's lead counsel. Service may be personal, by mail, by commercial delivery service, or by fax. Personal service includes delivery to any responsible person at the office of the lead counsel for the party served.

(c) *When complete.*

(1) Service by mail is complete on mailing.

(2) Service by commercial delivery service is complete when the document is placed in the control of the delivery service.

(3) Service by fax is complete on receipt.

(d) *Proof of service.* A document presented for filing must contain a proof of service in the form of either

---

✦

---

an acknowledgment of service by the person served or a certificate of service. Proof of service may appear on or be affixed to the filed document. The clerk may permit a document to be filed without proof of service, but will require the proof to be filed promptly.

(e) *Certificate requirements.* A certificate of service must be signed by the person who made the service and must state:

(1) the date and manner of service;

(2) the name and address of each person served; and

(3) if the person served is a party's attorney, the name of the party represented by that attorney.

9.6 Communications with the Court. Parties and counsel may communicate with the appellate court about a case only through the clerk.

9.7 Adoption by Reference. Any party may join in or adopt by reference all or any part of a brief, petition, response, motion, or other document filed in an appellate court by another party in the same case.

9.8 Protection of Minor's Identity in Parental-Rights Termination Cases and Juvenile Court Cases.

(a) *Alias defined.* For purposes of this rule, an alias means one or more of a person's initials or a fictitious name, used to refer to the person.

(b) *Parental-rights termination cases.* In an appeal or an original proceeding in an appellate court, arising out of a case in which the termination of parental rights was at issue:

(1) except for a docketing statement, in all papers submitted to the court, including all appendix items submitted with a brief, petition, or motion:

(A) a minor must be identified only by an alias unless the court orders otherwise;

(B) the court may order that a minor's parent or other family member be identified only by an alias if necessary to protect a minor's identity; and

(C) all documents must be redacted accordingly;

(2) the court must, in its opinion, use an alias to refer to a minor, and if necessary to protect the minor's identity, to the minor's parent or other family member.

(c) *Juvenile court cases.* In an appeal or an original proceeding in an appellate court, arising out of a case under Title 3 of the Family Code:

(1) except for a docketing statement, in all papers submitted to the court, including all appendix items submitted with a brief, petition, or motion:

(A) a minor must be identified only by an alias;

(B) a minor's parent or other family member must be identified only by an alias; and

(C) all documents must be redacted accordingly;

(2) the court must, in its opinion, use an alias to refer to a minor and to the minor's parent or other family member.

(d) *No alteration of appellate record.* Nothing in this rule permits alteration of the original appellate record except as specifically authorized by court order.

Comment to 2012 Change: Rule 9 is revised to consolidate all length limits and establish word limits for documents produced on a computer. All documents produced on a computer must comply with the word limits. Page limits are retained for documents that are typewritten or otherwise not produced on a computer.

2012 change: Amended eff. Dec. 1, 2012, by order of Nov. 13, 2012 (Tex. Sup.Ct. Order, Misc. Docket No. 12-9190).

TRAP 10. MOTIONS IN THE APPELLATE COURTS

10.1 Contents of Motions; Response.

(a) *Motion.* Unless these rules prescribe another form, a party must apply by motion for an order or other relief. The motion must:

(1) contain or be accompanied by any matter specifically required by a rule governing such a motion;

(2) state with particularity the grounds on which it is based;

(3) set forth the order or relief sought;

(4) be served and filed with any brief, affidavit, or other paper filed in support of the motion; and

(5) in civil cases, except for motions for rehearing and en banc reconsideration, contain or be accompanied by a certificate stating that the filing party conferred, or made a reasonable attempt to confer, with all other parties about the merits of the motion and whether those parties oppose the motion.

(b) *Response.* A party may file a response to a motion at any time before the court rules on the motion or by any deadline set by the court. The court may determine a motion before a response is filed.

10.2 Evidence on Motions. A motion need not be verified unless it depends on the following types of

---

★

---

facts, in which case the motion must be supported by affidavit or other satisfactory evidence. The types of facts requiring proof are those that are:

(a) not in the record;

(b) not within the court's knowledge in its official capacity; and

(c) not within the personal knowledge of the attorney signing the motion.

10.3 Determining Motions.

(a) *Time for determination.* A court should not hear or determine a motion until 10 days after the motion was filed, unless:

(1) the motion is to extend time to file a brief, a petition for review, or a petition for discretionary review;

(2) the motion states that the parties have conferred and that no party opposes the motion; or

(3) the motion is an emergency.

(b) *Reconsideration.* If a motion is determined prematurely, any party adversely affected may request the court to reconsider its order.

10.4 Power of Panel or Single Justice or Judge to Entertain Motions.

(a) *Single justice.* In addition to the authority expressly conferred by these rules or by law, a single justice or judge of an appellate court may grant or deny a request for relief that these rules allow to be sought by motion. But in a civil case, a single justice should not do the following:

(1) act on a petition for an extraordinary writ; or

(2) dismiss or otherwise determine an appeal or a motion for rehearing.

(b) *Panel.* An appellate court may provide, by order or rule, that a panel or the full court must act on any motion or class of motions.

10.5 Particular Motions.

(a) *Motions relating to informalities in the record.* A motion relating to informalities in the manner of bringing a case into court must be filed within 30 days after the record is filed in the court of appeals. The objection, if waivable, will otherwise be deemed waived.

(b) *Motions to extend time.*

(1) *Contents of motion in general.* All motions to extend time, except a motion to extend time for filing a notice of appeal, must state:

(A) the deadline for filing the item in question;

(B) the length of the extension sought;

(C) the facts relied on to reasonably explain the need for an extension; and

(D) the number of previous extensions granted regarding the item in question.

(2) *Contents of motion to extend time to file notice of appeal.* A motion to extend the time for filing a notice of appeal must:

(A) comply with (1)(A) and (C);

(B) identify the trial court;

(C) state the date of the trial court's judgment or appealable order; and

(D) state the case number and style of the case in the trial court.

(3) *Contents of motion to extend time to file petition for review or petition for discretionary review.* A motion to extend time to file a petition for review or petition for discretionary review must also specify:

(A) the court of appeals;

(B) the date of the court of appeals' judgment;

(C) the case number and style of the case in the court of appeals; and

(D) the date every motion for rehearing or en banc reconsideration was filed, and either the date and nature of the court of appeals' ruling on the motion, or that it remains pending.

(c) *Motions to postpone argument.* Unless all parties agree, or unless sufficient cause is apparent to the court, a motion to postpone argument of a case must be supported by sufficient cause.

TRAP 11. AMICUS CURIAE BRIEFS

An appellate clerk may receive, but not file, an amicus curiae brief. But the court for good cause may refuse to consider the brief and order that it be returned. An amicus curiae brief must:

(a) comply with the briefing rules for parties;

(b) identify the person or entity on whose behalf the brief is tendered;

(c) disclose the source of any fee paid or to be paid for preparing the brief; and

(d) certify that copies have been served on all parties.

TRAP 11

★

TRAP 12. DUTIES OF APPELLATE CLERK

12.1 **Docketing the Case.** On receiving a copy of the notice of appeal, the petition for review, the petition for discretionary review, the petition in an original proceeding, or a certified question, the appellate clerk must:

(a) endorse on the document the date of receipt;

(b) collect any filing fee;

(c) docket the case;

(d) notify all parties of the receipt of the document; and

(e) if the document filed is a petition for review filed in the Supreme Court, notify the court of appeals clerk of the filing of the petition.

12.2 **Docket Numbers.** The clerk must put the case's docket number on each item received in connection with the case and must put the docket number on the envelope in which the record is stored.

(a) *Numbering system.* Each case filed in a court of appeals must be assigned a docket number consisting of the following four parts, separated by hyphens:

(1) the number of the court of appeals district;

(2) the last two digits of the year in which the case is filed;

(3) the number assigned to the case; and

(4) the designation "CV" for a civil case or "CR" for a criminal case.

(b) *Numbering order.* Each case must be docketed in the order of its filing.

(c) *Multiple notices of appeal.* All notices of appeal filed in the same case must be given the same docket number.

(d) *Appeals not yet filed.* A motion relating to an appeal that has been perfected but not yet filed must be docketed and assigned a docket number that will also be assigned to the appeal when it is filed.

12.3 **Custody of Papers.** The clerk must safeguard the record and every other item filed in a case. If the record or any part of it or any other item is missing, the court will make an order for the replacement of the record or item that is just under the circumstances.

12.4 **Withdrawing Papers.** The clerk may permit the record or other filed item to be taken from the clerk's office at any time, on the following conditions:

(a) the clerk must have a receipt for the record or item;

(b) the clerk should make reasonable conditions to ensure that the withdrawn record or item is preserved and returned;

(c) the clerk may demand the return of the record or item at any time;

(d) after the case is submitted to the court and before the court's decision, the record cannot be withdrawn;

(e) after the court's decision, the losing party must be given priority in withdrawing the record;

(f) the clerk may not allow original documents filed under Rule 34.5(f) or original exhibits filed under Rule 34.6(g) to be taken from the clerk's office;

(g) if the court allows an original document or exhibit to be taken by a party and it is not returned, the court may accept the opposing party's statement concerning the document's or exhibit's nature and contents;

(h) withdrawn material must not be removed from the court's jurisdiction; and

(i) the court may, on the motion of any party or its own initiative, modify any of these conditions.

12.5 **Clerk's Duty to Account.** The clerk of an appellate court who receives money due another court must promptly pay the money to the court to whom it is due. This rule is enforceable by the Supreme Court.

12.6 **Notices of Court's Judgments and Orders.** In any proceeding, the clerk of an appellate court must promptly send a notice of any judgment, mandate, or other court order to all parties to the proceeding.

TRAP 13. COURT REPORTERS & COURT RECORDERS

13.1 **Duties of Court Reporters and Recorders.** The official court reporter or court recorder must:

(a) unless excused by agreement of the parties, attend court sessions and make a full record of the proceedings;

(b) take all exhibits offered in evidence during a proceeding and ensure that they are marked;

(c) file all exhibits with the trial court clerk after a proceeding ends;

(d) perform the duties prescribed by Rules 34.6 and 35; and

★

(e) perform other acts relating to the reporter's or recorder's official duties, as the trial court directs.

13.2 Additional Duties of Court Recorder. The official court recorder must also:

(a) ensure that the recording system functions properly throughout the proceeding and that a complete, clear, and transcribable recording is made;

(b) make a detailed, legible log of all proceedings being recorded, showing:

(1) the number and style of the case before the court;

(2) the name of each person speaking;

(3) the event being recorded such as the voir dire, the opening statement, direct and cross-examinations, and bench conferences;

(4) each exhibit offered, admitted, or excluded;

(5) the time of day of each event; and

(6) the index number on the recording device showing where each event is recorded;

(c) after a proceeding ends, file with the clerk the original log;

(d) have the original recording stored to ensure that it is preserved and is accessible; and

(e) ensure that no one gains access to the original recording without the court's written order.

13.3 Priorities of Reporters. The trial court must help ensure that the court reporter's work is timely accomplished by setting work priorities. The reporter's duties relating to proceedings before the court take preference over other work.

13.4 Report of Reporters. To aid the trial court in setting priorities under 13.3, each court reporter must give the trial court a monthly written report showing the amount and nature of the business pending in the reporter's office. A copy of this report must be filed with the appellate clerk of each district in which the court sits.

13.5 Appointing Deputy Reporter. When the official court reporter is unable to perform the duties in 13.1 or 13.2 because of illness, press of official work, or unavoidable absence or disability, the trial court may designate a deputy reporter. If the court appoints a deputy reporter, that person must file with the trial court clerk a document stating:

(a) the date the deputy worked;

(b) the court in which the deputy worked; and

(c) the number and style of the case on which the deputy worked.

13.6 Filing of Notes in a Criminal Case.

TRAP 14. RECORDING & BROADCASTING COURT PROCEEDINGS

14.1 Recording and Broadcasting Permitted. An appellate court may permit courtroom proceedings to be broadcast, televised, recorded, or photographed in accordance with this rule.

14.2 Procedure.

(a) *Request to cover court proceeding.*

(1) A person wishing to broadcast, televise, record, or photograph a court proceeding must file with the court clerk a request to cover the proceeding. The request must state:

(A) the case style and number;

(B) the date and time when the proceeding is to begin;

(C) the name of the requesting person or organization;

(D) the type of coverage requested (for example, televising or photographing); and

(E) the type and extent of equipment to be used.

(2) A request to cover argument of a case must be filed no later than five days before the date the case is set for argument and must be served on all parties to the case. A request to cover any other proceeding must be filed no later than two days before the date when the proceeding is to begin.

(b) *Response.* Any party may file a response to the request. If the request is to cover argument, the response must be filed no later than two days before the date set for argument. If a party objects to coverage of the argument, the response should state the injury that will allegedly result from coverage.

(c) *Court may shorten time.* The court may, in the interest of justice, shorten the time for filing a document under this rule if no party or interested person would be unduly prejudiced.

(d) *Decision of court.* In deciding whether to allow coverage, the court may consider information known *ex parte* to the court. The court may allow, deny, limit, or terminate coverage for any reason the court considers necessary or appropriate, such as protecting the parties' rights or the dignity of the court and ensuring the orderly conduct of the proceedings.

TRAP 14

⭐

14.3 Equipment and Personnel. The court may, among other things:

(a) require that a person seeking to cover a proceeding demonstrate or display the equipment that will be used;

(b) prohibit equipment that produces distracting sound or light;

(c) prohibit signal lights or devices showing when equipment is operating, or require their concealment;

(d) prohibit moving lights, flash attachments, or sudden lighting changes;

(e) require the use of the courtroom's existing video, audio, and lighting systems, if any;

(f) specify the placement of personnel and equipment;

(g) determine the number of cameras to be allowed in the courtroom; and

(h) require pooling of equipment if more than one person wishes to cover a proceeding.

14.4 Enforcement. The court may sanction a violation of this rule by measures that include barring a person or organization from access to future coverage of proceedings in that court for a defined period.

TRAP 15. ISSUANCE OF WRIT OR PROCESS BY APPELLATE COURT

15.1 In General.

(a) *Signature under seal.* A writ or process issuing from an appellate court must bear the court's seal and be signed by the clerk.

(b) *To whom directed; by whom served.* Unless a rule or statute provides otherwise, the writ or process must be directed to the person or court to be served. The writ or process may be served by the sheriff, constable, or other peace officer whose jurisdiction includes the county in which the person or court to be served may be found.

(c) *Return; lack of execution; simultaneous writs.* The writ or process must be returned to the issuing court according to the writ's direction. If the writ or process is not executed, the clerk may issue another writ or process if requested by the party who requested the former writ or process. At a party's request, the clerk may issue two or more writs simultaneously.

15.2 Appearance Without Service; Actual Knowledge. A party who appears in person or by attorney in an appellate court proceeding—or who has ac-

tual knowledge of the court's opinion, judgment, or order related to a writ or process—is bound by the opinion, judgment, or order to the same extent as if personally served under 15.1.

TRAP 16. DISQUALIFICATION OR RECUSAL OF APPELLATE JUDGES

16.1 Grounds for Disqualification. The grounds for disqualification of an appellate court justice or judge are determined by the Constitution and laws of Texas.

16.2 Grounds for Recusal. The grounds for recusal of an appellate court justice or judge are the same as those provided in the Rules of Civil Procedure. In addition, a justice or judge must recuse in a proceeding if it presents a material issue which the justice or judge participated in deciding while serving on another court in which the proceeding was pending.

16.3 Procedure for Recusal.

(a) *Motion.* A party may file a motion to recuse a justice or judge before whom the case is pending. The motion must be filed promptly after the party has reason to believe that the justice or judge should not participate in deciding the case.

(b) *Decision.* Before any further proceeding in the case, the challenged justice or judge must either remove himself or herself from all participation in the case or certify the matter to the entire court, which will decide the motion by a majority of the remaining judges sitting en banc. The challenged justice or judge must not sit with the remainder of the court to consider the motion as to him or her.

(c) *Appeal.* An order of recusal is not reviewable, but the denial of a recusal motion is reviewable.

TRAP 17. COURT OF APPEALS UNABLE TO TAKE IMMEDIATE ACTION

17.1 Inability to Act. A court of appeals is unable to take immediate action if it cannot—within the time when action must be taken—assemble a panel because members of the court are ill, absent, or unavailable. A justice who is disqualified or recused is unavailable. A court of appeals' inability to act immediately may be established by certificate of the clerk, a member of the court, or a party's counsel, or by affidavit of a party.

17.2 Nearest Available Court of Appeals. If a court of appeals is unable to take immediate action, the

TRAP 14

nearest court of appeals that is able to take immediate action may do so with the same effect as the other court. The nearest court of appeals is the one whose courthouse is nearest—measured by a straight line— the courthouse of the trial court.

17.3 Further Proceedings. After acting or refusing to act, the nearest court of appeals must promptly send a copy of its order, and the original or a copy of any document presented to it, to the other court, which will conduct any further proceedings in the matter.

TRAP 18. MANDATE

18.1 Issuance. The clerk of the appellate court that rendered the judgment must issue a mandate in accordance with the judgment and send it to the clerk of the court to which it is directed and to all parties to the proceeding when one of the following periods expires:

(a) *In the court of appeals.*

(1) Ten days after the time has expired for filing a motion to extend time to file a petition for review or a petition for discretionary review if:

(A) no timely petition for review or petition for discretionary review has been filed;

(B) no timely filed motion to extend time to file a petition for review or petition for discretionary review is pending; and

(C) in a criminal case, the Court of Criminal Appeals has not granted review on its own initiative.

(2) Ten days after the time has expired for filing a motion to extend time to file a motion for rehearing of a denial, refusal, or dismissal of a petition for review, or a refusal or dismissal of a petition for discretionary review, if no timely filed motion for rehearing or motion to extend time is pending.

(b) *In the Supreme Court and the Court of Criminal Appeals.* Ten days after the time has expired for filing a motion to extend time to file a motion for rehearing if no timely filed motion for rehearing or motion to extend time is pending.

(c) *Agreement to issue.* The mandate may be issued earlier if the parties so agree, or for good cause on the motion of a party.

18.2 Stay of Mandate. A party may move to stay issuance of the mandate pending the United States Supreme Court's disposition of a petition for writ of certiorari. The motion must state the grounds for the petition and the circumstances requiring the stay. The appellate court authorized to issue the mandate may grant a stay if it finds that the grounds are substantial and that the petitioner or others would incur serious hardship from the mandate's issuance if the United States Supreme Court were later to reverse the judgment. In a criminal case, the stay will last for no more than 90 days, to permit the timely filing of a petition for writ of certiorari. After that period and others mentioned in this rule expire, the mandate will issue.

18.3 Trial Court Case Number. The mandate must state the trial court case number.

18.4 Filing of Mandate. The clerk receiving the mandate will file it with the case's other papers and note it on the docket.

18.5 Costs. The mandate will be issued without waiting for costs to be paid. If the Supreme Court declines to grant review, Supreme Court costs must be included in the court of appeals' mandate.

18.6 Mandate in Accelerated Appeals. The appellate court's judgment on an appeal from an interlocutory order takes effect when the mandate is issued. The court may issue the mandate with its judgment or delay the mandate until the appeal is finally disposed of. If the mandate is issued, any further proceeding in the trial court must conform to the mandate.

18.7 Recall of Mandate. If an appellate court vacates or modifies its judgment or order after issuing its mandate, the appellate clerk must promptly notify the clerk of the court to which the mandate was directed and all parties. The mandate will have no effect and a new mandate may be issued.

TRAP 19. PLENARY POWER OF THE COURTS OF APPEALS & EXPIRATION OF TERM

19.1 Plenary Power of Courts of Appeals. A court of appeals' plenary power over its judgment expires:

(a) 60 days after judgment if no timely filed motion for rehearing or en banc reconsideration, or timely filed motion to extend time to file such a motion, is then pending; or

(b) 30 days after the court overrules all timely filed motions for rehearing or en banc reconsideration, and all timely filed motions to extend time to file such a motion.

★

19.2 Plenary Power Continues After Petition Filed. In a civil case, the court of appeals retains plenary power to vacate or modify its judgment during the periods prescribed in 19.1 even if a party has filed a petition for review in the Supreme Court.

19.3 Proceedings After Plenary Power Expires. After its plenary power expires, the court cannot vacate or modify its judgment. But the court may:

(a) correct a clerical error in its judgment or opinion;

(b) issue and recall its mandate as these rules provide;

(c) enforce or suspend enforcement of its judgment as these rules or applicable law provide;

(d) order or modify the amount and type of security required to suspend a judgment, and decide the sufficiency of the sureties, under Rule 24; and

(e) order its opinion published in accordance with Rule 47.

19.4 Expiration of Term. The expiration of the appellate court's term does not affect the court's plenary power or its jurisdiction over a case that is pending when the court's term expires.

TRAP 20. WHEN PARTY IS INDIGENT

20.1 Civil Cases.

(a) *Establishing indigence.*

(1) *By certificate.* If the appellant proceeded in the trial court without advance payment of costs pursuant to a certificate under Texas Rule of Civil Procedure 145(c) confirming that the appellant was screened for eligibility to receive free legal services under income guidelines used by a program funded by Interest on Lawyers Trust Accounts or the Texas Access to Justice Foundation, an additional certificate may be filed in the appellate court confirming that the appellant was re-screened after rendition of the trial court's judgment and again found eligible under program guidelines. A party's affidavit of inability accompanied by the certificate may not be contested.

(2) *By affidavit.* A party who cannot pay the costs in an appellate court may proceed without advance payment of costs if:

(A) the party files an affidavit of indigence in compliance with this rule;

(B) the claim of indigence is not contestable, is not contested, or, if contested, the contest is not sustained by written order; and

(C) the party timely files a notice of appeal.

(3) *By presumption of indigence.* In a suit filed by a governmental entity in which termination of the parent-child relationship or managing conservatorship is requested, a parent determined by the trial court to be indigent is presumed to remain indigent for the duration of the suit and any subsequent appeal, as provided by section 107.013 of the Family Code, and may proceed without advance payment of costs.

(b) *Contents of affidavit.* The affidavit of indigence must identify the party filing the affidavit and must state what amount of costs, if any, the party can pay. The affidavit must also contain complete information about:

(1) the nature and amount of the party's current employment income, government-entitlement income, and other income;

(2) the income of the party's spouse and whether that income is available to the party;

(3) real and personal property the party owns;

(4) cash the party holds and amounts on deposit that the party may withdraw;

(5) the party's other assets;

(6) the number and relationship to the party of any dependents;

(7) the nature and amount of the party's debts;

(8) the nature and amount of the party's monthly expenses;

(9) the party's ability to obtain a loan for court costs;

(10) whether an attorney is providing free legal services to the party without a contingent fee;

(11) whether an attorney has agreed to pay or advance court costs; and

(12) if applicable, the party's lack of the skill and access to equipment necessary to prepare the appendix, as required by Rule 38.5(d).

(c) *When and where affidavit filed.*

(1) *Appeals.* An appellant must file the affidavit of indigence in the trial court with or before the notice of appeal. The prior filing of an affidavit of indigence in the trial court pursuant to Texas Rule of Civil Procedure 145 does not meet the requirements of this rule, which requires a separate affidavit and proof of current indi-

gence, except in cases in which a presumption of indigence has been established as provided by Rule 20.1(a)(3). An appellee who is required to pay part of the cost of preparation of the record under Rule 34.5(b)(3) or 34.6(c)(3) must file an affidavit of indigence in the trial court within 15 days after the date when the appellee becomes responsible for paying that cost.

(2) Other proceedings. In any other appellate court proceeding, except in cases in which a presumption of indigence has been established as provided by Rule 20.1(a)(3), a petitioner must file the affidavit of indigence in the court in which the proceeding is filed, with or before the document seeking relief. A respondent who requests preparation of a record in connection with an appellate court proceeding must file an affidavit of indigence in the appellate court within 15 days after the date when the respondent requests preparation of the record, except in cases in which a presumption of indigence has been established as provided by Rule 20.1(a)(3).

(3) Extension of time. The appellate court may extend the time to file an affidavit of indigence if, within 15 days after the deadline for filing the affidavit, the party files in the appellate court a motion complying with Rule 10.5(b). But the court may not dismiss the appeal or affirm the trial court's judgment on the ground that the appellant has failed to file an affidavit or a sufficient affidavit of indigence unless the court has first provided the appellant notice of the deficiency and a reasonable time to remedy it.

(d) Duty of clerk.

(1) Trial court clerk. If the affidavit of indigence is filed with the trial court clerk under (c)(1), the clerk must promptly send a copy of the affidavit to the appropriate court reporter.

(2) Appellate court clerk. If the affidavit of indigence is filed with the appellate court clerk and if the filing party is requesting the preparation of a record, the appellate court clerk must:

(A) send a copy of the affidavit to the trial court clerk and the appropriate court reporter; and

(B) send to the trial court clerk, the court reporter, and all parties, a notice stating the deadline for filing a contest to the affidavit of indigence.

(e) Contest to indigence.

(1) If affidavit filed. The clerk, the court reporter, the court recorder, or any party may challenge an affidavit that is not accompanied by a TAJF certificate by filing—in the court in which the affidavit was filed—a contest to the affidavit. The contest must be filed on or before the date set by the clerk if the affidavit was filed in the appellate court, or within 10 days after the date when the affidavit was filed if the affidavit was filed in the trial court. The contest need not be sworn.

(2) If indigence presumed. The clerk, the court reporter, the court recorder, or any party may challenge a presumption of indigence that has been established as provided by Rule 20.1(a)(3) by filing a contest in the trial court. The contest must be filed within three days after a notice of appeal is filed. The contest must state specific facts demonstrating a good faith belief that the parent is no longer indigent due to a material and substantial change in the parent's financial circumstances. The contest need not be sworn.

(f) No contest filed. Unless a contest is timely filed, no hearing will be conducted, the affidavit's allegations will be deemed true, and the party will be allowed to proceed without advance payment of costs.

(g) Burden of proof.

(1) If affidavit filed. If a contest is filed, the party who filed the affidavit of indigence must prove the affidavit's allegations. If the indigent party is incarcerated at the time the hearing on a contest is held, the affidavit must be considered as evidence and is sufficient to meet the indigent party's burden to present evidence without the indigent party's attending the hearing.

(2) If indigence presumed. If a presumption of indigence has been established as provided by Rule 20.1(a)(3), the party filing the contest must prove that the parent is no longer indigent due to a material and substantial change in the parent's financial circumstances since the most recent determination of indigence.

(h) Decision in appellate court. If the affidavit of indigence is filed in an appellate court and a contest is filed, the court may:

(1) conduct a hearing and decide the contest;

(2) decide the contest based on the affidavit and any other timely filed documents;

(3) request the written submission of additional evidence and, without conducting a hearing, decide the contest based on the evidence; or

(4) refer the matter to the trial court with instructions to hear evidence and grant the appropriate relief.

★

(i) *Hearing and decision in the trial court.*

(1) *Notice required.* If the affidavit of indigence is filed in the trial court or a presumption of indigence has been established as provided by Rule 20.1(a)(3) and a contest is filed, or if the appellate court refers a contest to the trial court, the trial court must set a hearing and notify the parties and the appropriate court reporter of the setting.

(2) *Time for hearing.* The trial court must either conduct a hearing or sign an order extending the time to conduct a hearing:

(A) within 10 days after the contest was filed, if initially filed in the trial court; or

(B) within 10 days after the trial court received a contest referred from the appellate court.

(3) *Extension of time for hearing.* The time for conducting a hearing on the contest must not be extended for more than 20 days from the date the order is signed.

(4) *Time for written decision; effect.* Unless—within the period set for the hearing—the trial court signs an order sustaining the contest, the affidavit's allegations will be deemed true or the presumption of indigence will continue unabated, and the party will be allowed to proceed without advance payment of costs.

(j) *Review of trial court's decision.*

(1) *Motion.* If the trial court sustains a contest, the party claiming indigence may seek review of the court's order by filing a motion challenging the order with the appellate court without advance payment of costs.

(2) *Time for filing; extension.* The motion must be filed within 10 days after the order sustaining the contest is signed, or within 10 days after the notice of appeal is filed, whichever is later. The appellate court may extend the time for filing on motion complying with Rule 10.5(b).

(3) *Record.* Within three days after a motion is filed, the trial court clerk and court reporter, respectively, must prepare, certify, and file the clerk's record and reporter's record of the indigence hearing, if any, and the hearing on the contest. The record must be provided without advance payment of costs.

(4) *Ruling by operation of law.* If the appellate court does not deny the motion within 10 days after it is filed, the motion is granted by operation of law.

(5) *No review of order overruling contest.* An order overruling a contest is not subject to appellate review.

(k) *Record to be prepared without prepayment.* If a party establishes indigence, the trial court clerk and the court reporter must prepare the appellate record without prepayment.

(l) *Partial payment of costs.* If the party can pay or give security for some of the costs, the court must order the party, in writing, to pay or give security, or both, to the extent of the party's ability. The court will allocate the payment among the officials to whom payment is due.

(m) *Later ability to pay.* If a party who has proceeded in the appellate court without having to pay all the costs is later able to pay some or all of the costs, the appellate court may order the party to pay costs to the extent of the party's ability.

(n) *Costs defined.* As used in this rule, *costs* means:

(1) a filing fee relating to the case in which the affidavit of inability is filed; and

(2) the charges for preparing the appellate record in that case.

20.2 Criminal Cases.

2012 change: Amended eff. Mar. 1, 2012, by order of Feb. 13, 2012 (Tex. Sup.Ct. Order, Misc. Docket No. 12-9030).

SECTION TWO: APPEALS FROM TRIAL COURT JUDGMENTS & ORDERS

TRAP 21. NEW TRIALS IN CRIMINAL CASES

TRAP 22. ARREST OF JUDGMENT IN CRIMINAL CASES

TRAP 23. NUNC PRO TUNC PROCEEDINGS IN CRIMINAL CASES

TRAP 24. SUSPENSION OF ENFORCEMENT OF JUDGMENT PENDING APPEAL IN CIVIL CASES

24.1 Suspension of Enforcement.

(a) *Methods.* Unless the law or these rules provide otherwise, a judgment debtor may supersede the judgment by:

(1) filing with the trial court clerk a written agreement with the judgment creditor for suspending enforcement of the judgment;

(2) filing with the trial court clerk a good and sufficient bond;

★

(3) making a deposit with the trial court clerk in lieu of a bond; or

(4) providing alternate security ordered by the court.

(b) *Bonds.*

(1) A bond must be:

(A) in the amount required by 24.2;

(B) payable to the judgment creditor;

(C) signed by the judgment debtor or the debtor's agent;

(D) signed by a sufficient surety or sureties as obligors; and

(E) conditioned as required by (d).

(2) To be effective a bond must be approved by the trial court clerk. On motion of any party, the trial court will review the bond.

(c) *Deposit in lieu of bond.*

(1) *Types of deposits.* Instead of filing a surety bond, a party may deposit with the trial court clerk:

(A) cash;

(B) a cashier's check payable to the clerk, drawn on any federally insured and federally or state-chartered bank or savings-and-loan association; or

(C) with leave of court, a negotiable obligation of the federal government or of any federally insured and federally or state-chartered bank or savings-and-loan association.

(2) *Amount of deposit.* The deposit must be in the amount required by 24.2.

(3) *Clerk's duties.* The clerk must promptly deposit any cash or a cashier's check in accordance with law. The clerk must hold the deposit until the conditions of liability in (d) are extinguished. The clerk must then release any remaining funds in the deposit to the judgment debtor.

(d) *Conditions of liability.* The surety or sureties on a bond, any deposit in lieu of a bond, or any alternate security ordered by the court is subject to liability for all damages and costs that may be awarded against the debtor—up to the amount of the bond, deposit, or security—if:

(1) the debtor does not perfect an appeal or the debtor's appeal is dismissed, and the debtor does not perform the trial court's judgment;

(2) the debtor does not perform an adverse judgment final on appeal; or

(3) the judgment is for the recovery of an interest in real or personal property, and the debtor does not pay the creditor the value of the property interest's rent or revenue during the pendency of the appeal.

(e) *Orders of trial court.* The trial court may make any order necessary to adequately protect the judgment creditor against loss or damage that the appeal might cause.

(f) *Effect of supersedeas.* Enforcement of a judgment must be suspended if the judgment is superseded. Enforcement begun before the judgment is superseded must cease when the judgment is superseded. If execution has been issued, the clerk will promptly issue a writ of supersedeas.

24.2 Amount of Bond, Deposit, or Security.

(a) *Type of judgment.*

(1) *For recovery of money.* When the judgment is for money, the amount of the bond, deposit, or security must equal the sum of compensatory damages awarded in the judgment, interest for the estimated duration of the appeal, and costs awarded in the judgment. But the amount must not exceed the lesser of:

(A) 50 percent of the judgment debtor's current net worth; or

(B) 25 million dollars.

(2) *For recovery of property.* When the judgment is for the recovery of an interest in real or personal property, the trial court will determine the type of security that the judgment debtor must post. The amount of that security must be at least:

(A) the value of the property interest's rent or revenue, if the property interest is real; or

(B) the value of the property interest on the date when the court rendered judgment, if the property interest is personal.

(3) *Other judgment.* When the judgment is for something other than money or an interest in property, the trial court must set the amount and type of security that the judgment debtor must post. The security must adequately protect the judgment creditor against loss or damage that the appeal might cause. But the trial court may decline to permit the judgment to be superseded if the judgment creditor posts security ordered by the trial court in an amount and type that will secure the judgment debtor against any loss or damage caused by the relief granted the judgment creditor if an appellate court determines, on final disposition, that that relief was improper.

(4) *Conservatorship or custody.* When the judgment involves the conservatorship or custody of a minor or other person under legal disability, enforcement of the judgment will not be suspended, with or without security, unless ordered by the trial court. But upon a proper showing, the appellate court may suspend enforcement of the judgment with or without security.

(5) *For a governmental entity.* When a judgment in favor of a governmental entity in its governmental capacity is one in which the entity has no pecuniary interest, the trial court must determine whether to suspend enforcement, with or without security, taking into account the harm that is likely to result to the judgment debtor if enforcement is not suspended, and the harm that is likely to result to others if enforcement is suspended. The appellate court may review the trial court's determination and suspend enforcement of the judgment, with or without security, or refuse to suspend the judgment. If security is required, recovery is limited to the governmental entity's actual damages resulting from suspension of the judgment.

(b) *Lesser amount.* The trial court must lower the amount of security required by (a) to an amount that will not cause the judgment debtor substantial economic harm if, after notice to all parties and a hearing, the court finds that posting a bond, deposit, or security in the amount required by (a) is likely to cause the judgment debtor substantial economic harm.

(c) *Determination of net worth.*

(1) *Judgment debtor's affidavit required; contents; prima facie evidence.* A judgment debtor who provides a bond, deposit, or security under (a)(1)(A) in an amount based on the debtor's net worth must simultaneously file with the trial court clerk an affidavit that states the debtor's net worth and states complete, detailed information concerning the debtor's assets and liabilities from which net worth can be ascertained. An affidavit that meets these requirements is prima facie evidence of the debtor's net worth for the purpose of establishing the amount of the bond, deposit, or security required to suspend enforcement of the judgment. A trial court clerk must receive and file a net-worth affidavit tendered for filing by a judgment debtor.

(2) *Contest; discovery.* A judgment creditor may file a contest to the debtor's claimed net worth. The contest need not be sworn. The creditor may conduct reasonable discovery concerning the judgment debtor's net worth.

(3) *Hearing; burden of proof; findings; additional security.* The trial court must hear a judgment creditor's contest of the judgment debtor's claimed net worth promptly after any discovery has been completed. The judgment debtor has the burden of proving net worth. The trial court must issue an order that states the debtor's net worth and states with particularity the factual basis for that determination. If the trial court orders additional or other security to supersede the judgment, the enforcement of the judgment will be suspended for twenty days after the trial court's order. If the judgment debtor does not comply with the order within that period, the judgment may be enforced against the judgment debtor.

(d) *Injunction.* The trial court may enjoin the judgment debtor from dissipating or transferring assets to avoid satisfaction of the judgment, but the trial court may not make any order that interferes with the judgment debtor's use, transfer, conveyance, or dissipation of assets in the normal course of business.

24.3 **Continuing Trial Court Jurisdiction; Duties of Judgment Debtor.**

(a) *Continuing jurisdiction.* Even after the trial court's plenary power expires, the trial court has continuing jurisdiction to do the following:

(1) order the amount and type of security and decide the sufficiency of sureties; and

(2) if circumstances change, modify the amount or type of security required to continue the suspension of a judgment's execution.

(b) *Duties of judgment debtor.* If, after jurisdiction attaches in an appellate court, the trial court orders or modifies the security or decides the sufficiency of sureties, the judgment debtor must notify the appellate court of the trial court's action.

24.4 **Appellate Review.**

(a) *Motions; review.* A party may seek review of the trial court's ruling by motion filed in the court of appeals with jurisdiction or potential jurisdiction over the appeal from the judgment in the case. A party may seek review of the court of appeals' ruling on the motion by petition for writ of mandamus in the Supreme Court. The appellate court may review:

(1) the sufficiency or excessiveness of the amount of security, but when the judgment is for money, the appellate court must not modify the amount of security to exceed the limits imposed by Rule 24.2(a)(1);

(2) the sureties on any bond;

(3) the type of security;

(4) the determination whether to permit suspension of enforcement; and

(5) the trial court's exercise of discretion under Rule 24.3(a).

(b) *Grounds of review.* Review may be based both on conditions as they existed at the time the trial court signed an order and on changes in those conditions afterward.

(c) *Temporary orders.* The appellate court may issue any temporary orders necessary to preserve the parties' rights.

(d) *Action by appellate court.* The motion must be heard at the earliest practicable time. The appellate court may require that the amount of a bond, deposit, or other security be increased or decreased, and that another bond, deposit, or security be provided and approved by the trial court clerk. The appellate court may require other changes in the trial court order. The appellate court may remand to the trial court for entry of findings of fact or for the taking of evidence.

(e) *Effect of ruling.* If the appellate court orders additional or other security to supersede the judgment, enforcement will be suspended for 20 days after the appellate court's order. If the judgment debtor does not comply with the order within that period, the judgment may be enforced. When any additional bond, deposit, or security has been filed, the trial court clerk must notify the appellate court. The posting of additional security will not release the previously posted security or affect any alternative security arrangements that the judgment debtor previously made unless specifically ordered by the appellate court.

TRAP 25. PERFECTING APPEAL

12 **25.1** Civil Cases.

(a) *Notice of appeal.* An appeal is perfected when a written notice of appeal is filed with the trial court clerk. If a notice of appeal is mistakenly filed with the appellate court, the notice is deemed to have been filed the same day with the trial court clerk, and the appellate clerk must immediately send the trial court clerk a copy of the notice.

(b) *Jurisdiction of appellate court.* The filing of a notice of appeal by any party invokes the appellate court's jurisdiction over all parties to the trial court's judgment or order appealed from. Any party's failure to take any other step required by these rules, including the failure of another party to perfect an appeal under (c), does not deprive the appellate court of jurisdiction but is ground only for the appellate court to act appropriately, including dismissing the appeal.

(c) *Who must file notice.* A party who seeks to alter the trial court's judgment or other appealable order must file a notice of appeal. Parties whose interests are aligned may file a joint notice of appeal. The appellate court may not grant a party who does not file a notice of appeal more favorable relief than did the trial court except for just cause.

(d) *Contents of notice.* The notice of appeal must:

(1) identify the trial court and state the case's trial court number and style;

(2) state the date of the judgment or order appealed from;

(3) state that the party desires to appeal;

(4) state the court to which the appeal is taken unless the appeal is to either the First or Fourteenth Court of Appeals, in which case the notice must state that the appeal is to either of those courts;

(5) state the name of each party filing the notice;

(6) in an accelerated appeal, state that the appeal is accelerated and state whether it is a parental termination or child protection case, as defined in Rule 28.4;

(7) in a restricted appeal:

(A) state that the appellant is a party affected by the trial court's judgment but did not participate—either in person or through counsel—in the hearing that resulted in the judgment complained of;

(B) state that the appellant did not timely file either a postjudgment motion, request for findings of fact and conclusions of law, or notice of appeal; and

(C) be verified by the appellant if the appellant does not have counsel.

(8) state, if applicable, that the appellant is presumed indigent and may proceed without advance payment of costs as provided in Rule 20.1(a)(3).

(e) *Service of notice.* The notice of appeal must be served on all parties to the trial court's final judgment or, in an interlocutory appeal, on all parties to the trial court proceeding.

(f) *Clerk's duties.* The trial court clerk must immediately send a copy of the notice of appeal to the ap-

---

✫

---

pellate court clerk and to the court reporter or court reporters responsible for preparing the reporter's record.

(g) *Amending the notice.* An amended notice of appeal correcting a defect or omission in an earlier filed notice may be filed in the appellate court at any time before the appellant's brief is filed. The amended notice is subject to being struck for cause on the motion of any party affected by the amended notice. After the appellant's brief is filed, the notice may be amended only on leave of the appellate court and on such terms as the court may prescribe.

(h) *Enforcement of judgment not suspended by appeal.* The filing of a notice of appeal does not suspend enforcement of the judgment. Enforcement of the judgment may proceed unless:

(1) the judgment is superseded in accordance with Rule 24, or

(2) the appellant is entitled to supersede the judgment without security by filing a notice of appeal.

25.2 **Criminal Cases.**

2012 change: Amended eff. Mar. 1, 2012, by order of Feb. 13, 2012 (Tex. Sup.Ct. Order, Misc. Docket No. 12-9030).

TRAP 26. TIME TO PERFECT APPEAL

26.1 **Civil Cases.** The notice of appeal must be filed within 30 days after the judgment is signed, except as follows:

(a) the notice of appeal must be filed within 90 days after the judgment is signed if any party timely files:

(1) a motion for new trial;

(2) a motion to modify the judgment;

(3) a motion to reinstate under Texas Rule of Civil Procedure 165a; or

(4) a request for findings of fact and conclusions of law if findings and conclusions either are required by the Rules of Civil Procedure or, if not required, could properly be considered by the appellate court;

(b) in an accelerated appeal, the notice of appeal must be filed within 20 days after the judgment or order is signed;

(c) in a restricted appeal, the notice of appeal must be filed within six months after the judgment or order is signed; and

(d) if any party timely files a notice of appeal, another party may file a notice of appeal within the applicable period stated above or 14 days after the first filed notice of appeal, whichever is later.

26.2 **Criminal Cases.**

26.3 **Extension of Time.** The appellate court may extend the time to file the notice of appeal if, within 15 days after the deadline for filing the notice of appeal, the party:

(a) files in the trial court the notice of appeal; and

(b) files in the appellate court a motion complying with Rule 10.5(b).

TRAP 27. PREMATURE FILINGS

27.1 **Prematurely Filed Notice of Appeal.**

(a) *Civil cases.* In a civil case, a prematurely filed notice of appeal is effective and deemed filed on the day of, but after, the event that begins the period for perfecting the appeal.

(b) *Criminal cases.*

27.2 **Other Premature Actions.** The appellate court may treat actions taken before an appealable order is signed as relating to an appeal of that order and give them effect as if they had been taken after the order was signed. The appellate court may allow an appealed order that is not final to be modified so as to be made final and may allow the modified order and all proceedings relating to it to be included in a supplemental record.

27.3 **If Appealed Order Modified or Vacated.** After an order or judgment in a civil case has been appealed, if the trial court modifies the order or judgment, or if the trial court vacates the order or judgment and replaces it with another appealable order or judgment, the appellate court must treat the appeal as from the subsequent order or judgment and may treat actions relating to the appeal of the first order or judgment as relating to the appeal of the subsequent order or judgment. The subsequent order or judgment and actions relating to it may be included in the original or supplemental record. Any party may nonetheless appeal from the subsequent order or judgment.

TRAP 28. ACCELERATED, AGREED, & PERMISSIVE APPEALS IN CIVIL CASES

28.1 **Accelerated Appeals.**

(a) *Types of accelerated appeals.* Appeals from interlocutory orders (when allowed by statute), appeals in quo warranto proceedings, appeals required by statute to be accelerated or expedited, and appeals required

TRAP 25

by law to be filed or perfected within less than 30 days after the date of the order or judgment being appealed are accelerated appeals.

(b) *Perfection of accelerated appeal.* Unless otherwise provided by statute, an accelerated appeal is perfected by filing a notice of appeal in compliance with Rule 25.1 within the time allowed by Rule 26.1(b) or as extended by Rule 26.3. Filing a motion for new trial, any other post-trial motion, or a request for findings of fact will not extend the time to perfect an accelerated appeal.

(c) *Appeals of interlocutory orders.* The trial court need not file findings of fact and conclusions of law but may do so within 30 days after the order is signed.

(d) *Quo warranto appeals.* The trial court may grant a motion for new trial timely filed under Texas Rule of Civil Procedure 329b(a)-(b) until 50 days after the trial court's final judgment is signed. If not determined by signed written order within that period, the motion will be deemed overruled by operation of law on expiration of that period.

(e) *Record and briefs.* In lieu of the clerk's record, the appellate court may hear an accelerated appeal on the original papers forwarded by the trial court or on sworn and uncontroverted copies of those papers. The appellate court may allow the case to be submitted without briefs. The deadlines and procedures for filing the record and briefs in an accelerated appeal are provided in Rules 35.1 and 38.6.

28.2 **Agreed Interlocutory Appeals in Civil Cases.**

(a) *Perfecting appeal.* An agreed appeal of an interlocutory order permitted by statute must be perfected as provided in Rule 25.1. The notice of appeal must be filed no later than the 20th day after the date the trial court signs a written order granting permission to appeal, unless the court of appeals extends the time for filing pursuant to Rule 26.3.

(b) *Other requirements.* In addition to perfecting appeal, the appellant must file with the clerk of the appellate court a docketing statement as provided in Rule 32.1 and pay to the clerk of the appellate court all required fees authorized to be collected by the clerk.

(c) *Contents of notice.* The notice of accelerated appeal must contain, in addition to the items required by Rule 25.1(d), the following:

(1) a list of the names of all parties to the trial court proceeding and the names, addresses, and telefax numbers of all trial and appellate counsel;

(2) a copy of the trial court's order granting permission to appeal;

(3) a copy of the trial court order appealed from;

(4) a statement that all parties to the trial court proceeding agreed to the trial court's order granting permission to appeal;

(5) a statement that all parties to the trial court proceeding agreed that the order granting permission to appeal involves a controlling question of law as to which there is a substantial ground for difference of opinion;

(6) a brief statement of the issues or points presented; and

(7) a concise explanation of how an immediate appeal may materially advance the ultimate termination of the litigation.

(d) *Determination of jurisdiction.* If the court of appeals determines that a notice of appeal filed under this rule does not demonstrate the court's jurisdiction, it may order the appellant to file an amended notice of appeal. On a party's motion or its own initiative, the court of appeals may also order the appellant or any other party to file briefing addressing whether the appeal meets the statutory requirements, and may direct the parties to file supporting evidence. If, after providing an opportunity to file an amended notice of appeal or briefing addressing potential jurisdictional defects, the court of appeals concludes that a jurisdictional defect exists, it may dismiss the appeal for want of jurisdiction at any stage of the appeal.

(e) *Record; briefs.* The rules governing the filing of the appellate record and briefs in accelerated appeals apply. A party may address in its brief any issues related to the court of appeals' jurisdiction, including whether the appeal meets the statutory requirements.

(f) *No automatic stay of proceedings in trial court.* An agreed appeal of an interlocutory order permitted by statute does not stay proceedings in the trial court except as agreed by the parties and ordered by the trial court or the court of appeals.

28.3 **Permissive Appeals in Civil Cases.**

(a) *Petition required.* When a trial court has permitted an appeal from an interlocutory order that would not otherwise be appealable, a party seeking to appeal must petition the court of appeals for permission to appeal.

(b) *Where filed.* The petition must be filed with the clerk of the court of appeals having appellate jurisdiction over the action in which the order to be appealed is issued. The First and Fourteenth Courts of Appeals must determine in which of those two courts a petition will be filed.

(c) *When filed.* The petition must be filed within 15 days after the order to be appealed is signed. If the order is amended by the trial court, either on its own or in response to a party's motion, to include the court's permission to appeal, the time to petition the court of appeals runs from the date the amended order is signed.

(d) *Extension of time to file petition.* The court of appeals may extend the time to file the petition if the party:

(1) files the petition within 15 days after the deadline, and

(2) files a motion complying with Rule 10.5(b).

(e) *Contents.* The petition must:

(1) contain the information required by Rule 25.1 (d) to be included in a notice of appeal;

(2) attach a copy of the order from which appeal is sought;

(3) contain a table of contents, index of authorities, issues presented, and a statement of facts; and

(4) argue clearly and concisely why the order to be appealed involves a controlling question of law as to which there is a substantial ground for difference of opinion and how an immediate appeal from the order may materially advance the ultimate termination of the litigation.

(f) *Response; Reply; Cross-Petition; Time for filing.* If any party timely files a petition, any other party may file a response or a cross-petition within 10 days. A party may file a response to a cross-petition within 10 days of the date the cross-petition is filed. A petitioner or cross-petitioner may reply to any matter in a response within 7 days of the date the response is filed. The court of appeals may extend the time to file a response, reply, and cross-petition.

(g) *Length of petition, cross-petition, response, and reply.* A petition, cross-petition, response, and reply must comply with the page limitations in Rule 53.6.

(h) *Service.* A petition, cross-petition, response, and reply must be served on all parties to the trial court proceeding.

(i) *Docketing statement.* Upon filing the petition, the petitioner must file the docketing statement required by Rule 32.1.

(j) *Time for determination.* Unless the court of appeals orders otherwise, a petition, and any cross-petition, response, and reply, will be determined without oral argument, no earlier than 10 days after the petition is filed.

(k) *When petition granted.* If the petition is granted, a notice of appeal is deemed to have been filed under Rule 26.1(b) on that date, and the appeal is governed by the rules for accelerated appeals. A separate notice of appeal need not be filed. A copy of the order granting the petition must be filed with the trial court clerk.

⑫ 28.4 Accelerated Appeals in Parental Termination and Child Protection Cases.

(a) *Application and definitions.*

(1) Appeals in parental termination and child protection cases are governed by the rules of appellate procedure for accelerated appeals, except as otherwise provided in Rule 28.4.

(2) In Rule 28.4:

(A) a "parental termination case" means a suit in which termination of the parent-child relationship is at issue.

(B) a "child protection case" means a suit affecting the parent-child relationship filed by a governmental entity for managing conservatorship.

(b) *Appellate record.*

(1) *Responsibility for preparation of reporter's record.* In addition to the responsibility imposed on the trial court in Rule 35.3(c), when the reporter's responsibility to prepare, certify and timely file the reporter's record arises under Rule 35.3(b), the trial court must direct the official or deputy reporter to immediately commence the preparation of the reporter's record. The trial court must arrange for a substitute reporter, if necessary.

(2) *Extension of time.* The appellate court may grant an extension of time to file a record under Rule 35.3(c); however, the extension or extensions granted must not exceed 30 days cumulatively, absent extraordinary circumstances.

⎯⎯⎯⎯⎯⎯⎯ ✦ ⎯⎯⎯⎯⎯⎯⎯

(3) *Restriction on preparation inapplicable.* Section 13.003 of the Civil Practice & Remedies Code does not apply to an appeal from a parental termination or child protection case.

(c) *Remand for new trial.* If the judgment of the appellate court reverses and remands a parental termination or child protection case for a new trial, the judgment must instruct the trial court to commence the new trial no later than 180 days after the mandate is issued by the appellate court.

2012 change: Amended eff. Mar. 1, 2012, by order of Feb. 13, 2012 (Tex. Sup.Ct. Order, Misc. Docket No. 12-9030).

TRAP 29. ORDERS PENDING INTERLOCUTORY APPEAL IN CIVIL CASES

29.1 **Effect of Appeal.** Perfecting an appeal from an order granting interlocutory relief does not suspend the order appealed from unless:

(a) the order is superseded in accordance with 29.2; or

(b) the appellant is entitled to supersede the order without security by filing a notice of appeal.

29.2 **Security.** The trial court may permit an order granting interlocutory relief to be superseded pending an appeal from the order, in which event the appellant may supersede the order in accordance with Rule 24. If the trial court refuses to permit the appellant to supersede the order, the appellant may move the appellate court to review that decision for abuse of discretion.

29.3 **Temporary Orders of Appellate Court.** When an appeal from an interlocutory order is perfected, the appellate court may make any temporary orders necessary to preserve the parties' rights until disposition of the appeal and may require appropriate security. But the appellate court must not suspend the trial court's order if the appellant's rights would be adequately protected by supersedeas or another order made under Rule 24.

29.4 **Enforcement of Temporary Orders.** While an appeal from an interlocutory order is pending, only the appellate court in which the appeal is pending may enforce the order. But the appellate court may refer any enforcement proceeding to the trial court with instructions to:

(a) hear evidence and grant appropriate relief; or

(b) make findings and recommendations and report them to the appellate court.

29.5 **Further Proceedings in Trial Court.** While an appeal from an interlocutory order is pending, the trial court retains jurisdiction of the case and unless prohibited by statute may make further orders, including one dissolving the order complained of on appeal. If permitted by law, the trial court may proceed with a trial on the merits. But the court must not make an order that:

(a) is inconsistent with any appellate court temporary order; or

(b) interferes with or impairs the jurisdiction of the appellate court or effectiveness of any relief sought or that may be granted on appeal.

29.6 **Review of Further Orders.**

(a) *Motion to review further orders.* While an appeal from an interlocutory order is pending, on a party's motion or on the appellate court's own initiative, the appellate court may review the following:

(1) a further appealable interlocutory order concerning the same subject matter; and

(2) any interlocutory order that interferes with or impairs the effectiveness of the relief sought or that may be granted on appeal.

(b) *Record.* The party filing the motion may rely on the original record or may file a supplemental record with the motion.

TRAP 30. RESTRICTED APPEAL TO COURT OF APPEALS IN CIVIL CASES

A party who did not participate—either in person or through counsel—in the hearing that resulted in the judgment complained of and who did not timely file a postjudgment motion or request for findings of fact and conclusions of law, or a notice of appeal within the time permitted by Rule 26.1(a), may file a notice of appeal within the time permitted by Rule 26.1(c). Restricted appeals replace writ of error appeals to the court of appeals. Statutes pertaining to writ of error appeals to the court of appeals apply equally to restricted appeals.

TRAP 31. APPEALS IN HABEAS CORPUS, BAIL, & EXTRADITION PROCEEDINGS IN CRIMINAL CASES

TRAP 32. DOCKETING STATEMENT

12 **32.1** **Civil Cases.** Promptly upon filing the notice of appeal in a civil case, the appellant must file in the appellate court a docketing statement that includes the following information:

TRAP 32

★

(a)(1) if the appellant filing the statement has counsel, the name of that appellant and the name, address, telephone number, fax number, if any, and State Bar of Texas identification number of the appellant's lead counsel; or

(2) if the appellant filing the statement is not represented by an attorney, that party's name, address, telephone number, and fax number, if any;

(b) the date the notice of appeal was filed in the trial court and, if mailed to the trial court clerk, the date of mailing;

(c) the trial court's name and county, the name of the judge who tried the case, and the date the judgment or order appealed from was signed;

(d) the date of filing of any motion for new trial, motion to modify the judgment, request for findings of fact, motion to reinstate, or other filing that affects the time for perfecting the appeal;

(e) the names of all other parties to the trial court's judgment or the order appealed from, and:

(1) if represented by counsel, their lead counsel's names, addresses, telephone numbers, and fax numbers, if any; or

(2) if not represented by counsel, the name, address, and telephone number of the party, or a statement that the appellant diligently inquired but could not discover that information;

(f) the general nature of the case—for example, personal injury, breach of contract, or temporary injunction;

(g) whether the appeal's submission should be given priority, whether the appeal is an accelerated one under Rule 28 or another rule or statute, and whether it is a parental termination or child protection case, as defined in Rule 28.4;

(h) whether the appellant has requested or will request a reporter's record, and whether the trial was electronically recorded;

(i) the name of the court reporter;

(j) whether the appellant intends to seek temporary or ancillary relief while the appeal is pending;

(k)(1) the date of filing of any affidavit of indigence;

(2) the date of filing of any contest;

(3) the date of any order on the contest; and

(4) whether the contest was sustained or overruled;

(l) whether the appellant has filed or will file a supersedeas bond; and

(m) any other information the appellate court requires.

32.2 **Criminal Cases.**

32.3 **Supplemental Statements.** Any party may file a statement supplementing or correcting the docketing statement.

32.4 **Purpose of Statement.** The docketing statement is for administrative purposes and does not affect the appellate court's jurisdiction.

2012 change: Amended eff. Mar. 1, 2012, by order of Feb. 13, 2012 (Tex. Sup.Ct. Order, Misc. Docket No. 12-9030).

TRAP 33. PRESERVATION OF APPELLATE COMPLAINTS

33.1 **Preservation; How Shown.**

(a) *In general.* As a prerequisite to presenting a complaint for appellate review, the record must show that:

(1) the complaint was made to the trial court by a timely request, objection, or motion that:

(A) stated the grounds for the ruling that the complaining party sought from the trial court with sufficient specificity to make the trial court aware of the complaint, unless the specific grounds were apparent from the context; and

(B) complied with the requirements of the Texas Rules of Civil or Criminal Evidence or the Texas Rules of Civil or Appellate Procedure; and

(2) the trial court:

(A) ruled on the request, objection, or motion, either expressly or implicitly; or

(B) refused to rule on the request, objection, or motion, and the complaining party objected to the refusal.

(b) *Ruling by operation of law.* In a civil case, the overruling by operation of law of a motion for new trial or a motion to modify the judgment preserves for appellate review a complaint properly made in the motion, unless taking evidence was necessary to properly present the complaint in the trial court.

(c) *Formal exception and separate order not required.* Neither a formal exception to a trial court ruling or order nor a signed, separate order is required to preserve a complaint for appeal.

(d) *Sufficiency of evidence complaints in nonjury cases.* In a nonjury case, a complaint regarding

⭐

the legal or factual insufficiency of the evidence—including a complaint that the damages found by the court are excessive or inadequate, as distinguished from a complaint that the trial court erred in refusing to amend a fact finding or to make an additional finding of fact—may be made for the first time on appeal in the complaining party's brief.

33.2 Formal Bills of Exception. To complain on appeal about a matter that would not otherwise appear in the record, a party must file a formal bill of exception.

(a) *Form.* No particular form of words is required in a bill of exception. But the objection to the court's ruling or action, and the ruling complained of, must be stated with sufficient specificity to make the trial court aware of the complaint.

(b) *Evidence.* When the appellate record contains the evidence needed to explain a bill of exception, the bill itself need not repeat the evidence, and a party may attach and incorporate a transcription of the evidence certified by the court reporter.

(c) *Procedure.*

(1) The complaining party must first present a formal bill of exception to the trial court.

(2) If the parties agree on the contents of the bill of exception, the judge must sign the bill and file it with the trial court clerk. If the parties do not agree on the contents of the bill, the trial judge must—after notice and hearing—do one of the following things:

(A) sign the bill of exception and file it with the trial court clerk if the judge finds that it is correct;

(B) suggest to the complaining party those corrections to the bill that the judge believes are necessary to make it accurately reflect the proceedings in the trial court, and if the party agrees to the corrections, have the corrections made, sign the bill, and file it with the trial court clerk; or

(C) if the complaining party will not agree to the corrections suggested by the judge, return the bill to the complaining party with the judge's refusal written on it, and prepare, sign, and file with the trial court clerk such bill as will, in the judge's opinion, accurately reflect the proceedings in the trial court.

(3) If the complaining party is dissatisfied with the bill of exception filed by the judge under (2)(C), the party may file with the trial court clerk the bill that was rejected by the judge. That party must also file the affidavits of at least three people who observed the matter

to which the bill of exception is addressed. The affidavits must attest to the correctness of the bill as presented by the party. The matters contained in that bill of exception may be controverted and maintained by additional affidavits filed by any party within ten days after the filing of that bill. The truth of the bill of exception will be determined by the appellate court.

(d) *Conflict.* If a formal bill of exception conflicts with the reporter's record, the bill controls.

(e) *Time to file.*

(1) *Civil cases.* In a civil case, a formal bill of exception must be filed no later than 30 days after the filing party's notice of appeal is filed.

(2) *Criminal cases.*

(3) *Extension of time.* The appellate court may extend the time to file a formal bill of exception if, within 15 days after the deadline for filing the bill, the party files in the appellate court a motion complying with Rule 10.5(b).

(f) *Inclusion in clerk's record.* When filed, a formal bill of exception should be included in the appellate record.

TRAP 34. APPELLATE RECORD

34.1 Contents. The appellate record consists of the clerk's record and, if necessary to the appeal, the reporter's record. Even if more than one notice of appeal is filed, there should be only one appellate record in a case.

34.2 Agreed Record. By written stipulation filed with the trial court clerk, the parties may agree on the contents of the appellate record. An agreed record will be presumed to contain all evidence and filings relevant to the appeal. To request matter to be included in the agreed record, the parties must comply with the procedures in Rules 34.5 and 34.6.

34.3 Agreed Statement of the Case. In lieu of a reporter's record, the parties may agree on a brief statement of the case. The statement must be filed with the trial court clerk and included in the appellate record.

34.4 Form. The Supreme Court and Court of Criminal Appeals will prescribe the form of the appellate record.

34.5 Clerk's Record.

(a) *Contents.* Unless the parties designate the filings in the appellate record by agreement under Rule 34.2, the record must include copies of the following:

--- ⭐ ---

(1) in civil cases, all pleadings on which the trial was held;

(2) in criminal cases, the indictment or information, any special plea or defense motion that was presented to the court and overruled, any written waiver, any written stipulation, and, in cases in which a plea of guilty or nolo contendere has been entered, any documents executed for the plea;

(3) the court's docket sheet;

(4) the court's charge and the jury's verdict, or the court's findings of fact and conclusions of law;

(5) the court's judgment or other order that is being appealed;

(6) any request for findings of fact and conclusions of law, any post-judgment motion, and the court's order on the motion;

(7) the notice of appeal;

(8) any formal bill of exception;

(9) any request for a reporter's record, including any statement of points or issues under Rule 34.6(c);

(10) any request for preparation of the clerk's record;

(11) in civil cases, a certified bill of costs including the cost of preparing the clerk's record, showing credits for payments made;

(12) in criminal cases, the trial court's certification of the defendant's right of appeal under Rule 25.2; and

(13) subject to (b), any filing that a party designates to have included in the record.

(b) *Request for additional items.*

(1) *Time for request.* At any time before the clerk's record is prepared, any party may file with the trial court clerk a written designation specifying items to be included in the record.

(2) *Request must be specific.* A party requesting that an item be included in the clerk's record must specifically describe the item so that the clerk can readily identify it. The clerk will disregard a general designation, such as one for "all papers filed in the case."

(3) *Requesting unnecessary items.* In a civil case, if a party requests that more items than necessary be included in the clerk's record or any supplement, the appellate court may—regardless of the appeal's outcome—require that party to pay the costs for the preparation of the unnecessary portion.

(4) *Failure to timely request.* An appellate court must not refuse to file the clerk's record or a supple-mental clerk's record because of a failure to timely request items to be included in the clerk's record.

(c) *Supplementation.*

(1) If a relevant item has been omitted from the clerk's record, the trial court, the appellate court, or any party may by letter direct the trial court clerk to prepare, certify, and file in the appellate court a supplement containing the omitted item.

(2) If the appellate court in a criminal case orders the trial court to prepare and file findings of fact and conclusions of law as required by law or certification of the defendant's right of appeal as required by these rules, the trial court clerk must prepare, certify, and file in the appellate court a supplemental clerk's record containing those findings and conclusions.

(3) Any supplemental clerk's record will be part of the appellate record.

(d) *Defects or inaccuracies.* If the clerk's record is defective or inaccurate, the appellate clerk must inform the trial court clerk of the defect or inaccuracy and instruct the clerk to make the correction.

(e) *Clerk's record lost or destroyed.* If a filing designated for inclusion in the clerk's record has been lost or destroyed, the parties may, by written stipulation, deliver a copy of that item to the trial court clerk for inclusion in the clerk's record or a supplement. If the parties cannot agree, the trial court must—on any party's motion or at the appellate court's request—determine what constitutes an accurate copy of the missing item and order it to be included in the clerk's record or a supplement.

(f) *Original documents.* If the trial court determines that original documents filed with the trial court clerk should be inspected by the appellate court or sent to that court in lieu of copies, the trial court must make an order for the safekeeping, transportation, and return of those original documents. The order must list the original documents and briefly describe them. All the documents must be arranged in their listed sequence and bound firmly together. On any party's motion or its own initiative, the appellate court may direct the trial court clerk to send it any original document.

(g) *Additional copies of clerk's record in criminal cases.*

(h) *Clerk may consult with parties.* The clerk may consult with the parties concerning the contents of the clerk's record.

★

34.6 Reporter's Record.

(a) Contents.

(1) Stenographic recording. If the proceedings were stenographically recorded, the reporter's record consists of the court reporter's transcription of so much of the proceedings, and any of the exhibits, that the parties to the appeal designate.

(2) Electronic recording. If the proceedings were electronically recorded, the reporter's record consists of certified copies of all tapes or other audio-storage devices on which the proceedings were recorded, any of the exhibits that the parties to the appeal designate, and certified copies of the logs prepared by the court recorder under Rule 13.2.

(b) Request for preparation.

(1) Request to court reporter. At or before the time for perfecting the appeal, the appellant must request in writing that the official reporter prepare the reporter's record. The request must designate the exhibits to be included. A request to the court reporter— but not the court recorder—must also designate the portions of the proceedings to be included.

(2) Filing. The appellant must file a copy of the request with the trial court clerk.

(3) Failure to timely request. An appellate court must not refuse to file a reporter's record or a supplemental reporter's record because of a failure to timely request it.

(c) Partial reporter's record.

(1) Effect on appellate points or issues. If the appellant requests a partial reporter's record, the appellant must include in the request a statement of the points or issues to be presented on appeal and will then be limited to those points or issues.

(2) Other parties may designate additions. Any other party may designate additional exhibits and portions of the testimony to be included in the reporter's record.

(3) Costs; requesting unnecessary matter. Additions requested by another party must be included in the reporter's record at the appellant's cost. But if the trial court finds that all or part of the designated additions are unnecessary to the appeal, the trial court may order the other party to pay the costs for the preparation of the unnecessary additions. This paragraph does not affect the appellate court's power to tax costs differently.

(4) Presumptions. The appellate court must presume that the partial reporter's record designated by the parties constitutes the entire record for purposes of reviewing the stated points or issues. This presumption applies even if the statement includes a point or issue complaining of the legal or factual insufficiency of the evidence to support a specific factual finding identified in that point or issue.

(5) Criminal cases.

(d) Supplementation. If anything relevant is omitted from the reporter's record, the trial court, the appellate court, or any party may by letter direct the official court reporter to prepare, certify, and file in the appellate court a supplemental reporter's record containing the omitted items. Any supplemental reporter's record is part of the appellate record.

(e) Inaccuracies in the reporter's record.

(1) Correction of inaccuracies by agreement. The parties may agree to correct an inaccuracy in the reporter's record, including an exhibit, without the court reporter's recertification.

(2) Correction of inaccuracies by trial court. If the parties cannot agree on whether or how to correct the reporter's record so that the text accurately discloses what occurred in the trial court and the exhibits are accurate, the trial court must—after notice and hearing—settle the dispute. If the court finds any inaccuracy, it must order the court reporter to conform the reporter's record (including text and any exhibits) to what occurred in the trial court, and to file certified corrections in the appellate court.

(3) Correction after filing in appellate court. If the dispute arises after the reporter's record has been filed in the appellate court, that court may submit the dispute to the trial court for resolution. The trial court must then proceed as under subparagraph (e)(2).

(f) Reporter's record lost or destroyed. An appellant is entitled to a new trial under the following circumstances:

(1) if the appellant has timely requested a reporter's record;

(2) if, without the appellant's fault, a significant exhibit or a significant portion of the court reporter's notes and records has been lost or destroyed or—if the proceedings were electronically recorded—a significant portion of the recording has been lost or destroyed or is inaudible;

TRAP 34

⭐

(3) if the lost, destroyed, or inaudible portion of the reporter's record, or the lost or destroyed exhibit, is necessary to the appeal's resolution; and

(4) if the lost, destroyed or inaudible portion of the reporter's record cannot be replaced by agreement of the parties, or the lost or destroyed exhibit cannot be replaced either by agreement of the parties or with a copy determined by the trial court to accurately duplicate with reasonable certainty the original exhibit.

(g) *Original exhibits.*

(1) *Reporter may use in preparing reporter's record.* At the court reporter's request, the trial court clerk must give all original exhibits to the reporter for use in preparing the reporter's record. Unless ordered to include original exhibits in the reporter's record, the court reporter must return the original exhibits to the clerk after copying them for inclusion in the reporter's record. If someone other than the trial court clerk possesses an original exhibit, either the trial court or the appellate court may order that person to deliver the exhibit to the trial court clerk.

(2) *Use of original exhibits by appellate court.* If the trial court determines that original exhibits should be inspected by the appellate court or sent to that court in lieu of copies, the trial court must make an order for the safekeeping, transportation, and return of those exhibits. The order must list the exhibits and briefly describe them. To the extent practicable, all the exhibits must be arranged in their listed order and bound firmly together before being sent to the appellate clerk. On any party's motion or its own initiative, the appellate court may direct the trial court clerk to send it any original exhibit.

(h) *Additional copies of reporter's record in criminal cases.*

(i) *Supreme Court and Court of Criminal Appeals may set fee.* From time to time, the Supreme Court and the Court of Criminal Appeals may set the fee that the court reporters may charge for preparing the reporter's record.

TRAP 35. TIME TO FILE RECORD; RESPONSIBILITY FOR FILING RECORD

35.1 **Civil Cases.** The appellate record must be filed in the appellate court within 60 days after the judgment is signed, except as follows:

(a) if Rule 26.1(a) applies, within 120 days after the judgment is signed;

(b) if Rule 26.1(b) applies, within 10 days after the notice of appeal is filed; or

(c) if Rule 26.1(c) applies, within 30 days after the notice of appeal is filed.

35.2 **Criminal Cases.**

⑫ **35.3** **Responsibility for Filing Record.**

(a) *Clerk's record.* The trial court clerk is responsible for preparing, certifying, and timely filing the clerk's record if:

(1) a notice of appeal has been filed, and in criminal proceedings, the trial court has certified the defendant's right of appeal, as required by Rule 25.2(d); and

(2) the party responsible for paying for the preparation of the clerk's record has paid the clerk's fee, has made satisfactory arrangements with the clerk to pay the fee, or is entitled to appeal without paying the fee.

(b) *Reporter's record.* The official or deputy reporter is responsible for preparing, certifying, and timely filing the reporter's record if:

(1) a notice of appeal has been filed;

(2) the appellant has requested that the reporter's record be prepared; and

(3) the party responsible for paying for the preparation of the reporter's record has paid the reporter's fee, or has made satisfactory arrangements with the reporter to pay the fee, or is entitled to appeal without paying the fee.

(c) *Courts to ensure record timely filed.* The trial and appellate courts are jointly responsible for ensuring that the appellate record is timely filed. The appellate court may extend the deadline to file the record if requested by the clerk or reporter. Each extension must not exceed 30 days in an ordinary or restricted appeal, or 10 days in an accelerated appeal. The appellate court must allow the record to be filed late when the delay is not the appellant's fault, and may do so when the delay is the appellant's fault. The appellate court may enter any order necessary to ensure the timely filing of the appellate record.

2012 change: Amended eff. Mar. 1, 2012, by order of Feb. 13, 2012 (Tex. Sup.Ct. Order, Misc. Docket No. 12-9030).

TRAP 36. AGENCY RECORD IN ADMINISTRATIVE APPEALS

36.1 **Scope.** This rule applies only to cases involving judicial review of state agency decisions in contested cases under the Administrative Procedure Act.

TRAP 34

✦

36.2 Inclusion in Appellate Record. The record of an agency proceeding filed in the trial court may be included in either the clerk's record or the reporter's record.

36.3 Correcting the Record.

(a) *Correction by agreement.* At any stage of the proceeding, the parties may agree to correct an agency record filed under Section 2001.175(b) of the Government Code to ensure that the agency record accurately reflects the contested case proceedings before the agency. The court reporter need not recertify the agency record.

(b) *Correction by trial court.* If the parties cannot agree to a correction to the agency record, the appellate court must—on any party's motion or its own incentive—send the question to the trial court. After notice and hearing, the trial court must determine what constitutes an accurate copy of the agency record and order the agency to send an accurate copy to the clerk of the court in which the case is pending.

TRAP 37. DUTIES OF THE APPELLATE CLERK ON RECEIVING THE NOTICE OF APPEAL & RECORD

37.1 On Receiving the Notice of Appeal. If the appellate clerk determines that the notice of appeal or certification of defendant's right of appeal in a criminal case is defective, the clerk must notify the parties of the defect so that it can be remedied, if possible. If a proper notice of appeal or certification of a criminal defendant's right of appeal is not filed in the trial court within 30 days of the date of the clerk's notice, the clerk must refer the matter to the appellate court, which will make an appropriate order under this rule or Rule 34.5(c)(2).

37.2 On Receiving the Record. On receiving the clerk's record from the trial court clerk or the reporter's record from the reporter, the appellate clerk must determine whether each complies with the Supreme Court's and Court of Criminal Appeals' order on preparation of the record. If so, the clerk must endorse on each the date of receipt, file it, and notify the parties of the filing and the date. If not, the clerk must endorse on the clerk's record or reporter's record—whichever is defective—the date of receipt and return it to the official responsible for filing it. The appellate court clerk must specify the defects and instruct the official to correct the defects and return the record to the appellate court by a specified date.

37.3 If No Record Filed.

(a) *Notice of late record.*

(1) *Civil cases.* If the clerk's record or reporter's record has not been timely filed, the appellate clerk must send notice to the official responsible for filing it, stating that the record is late and requesting that the record be filed within 30 days if an ordinary or restricted appeal, or 10 days if an accelerated appeal. The appellate clerk must send a copy of this notice to the parties and the trial court. If the clerk does not receive the record within the stated period, the clerk must refer the matter to the appellate court. The court must make whatever order is appropriate to avoid further delay and to preserve the parties' rights.

(2) *Criminal cases.*

(b) *If no clerk's record filed due to appellant's fault.* If the trial court clerk failed to file the clerk's record because the appellant failed to pay or make arrangements to pay the clerk's fee for preparing the clerk's record, the appellate court may—on a party's motion or its own initiative—dismiss the appeal for want of prosecution unless the appellant was entitled to proceed without payment of costs. The court must give the appellant a reasonable opportunity to cure before dismissal.

(c) *If no reporter's record filed due to appellant's fault.* Under the following circumstances, and if the clerk's record has been filed, the appellate court may—after first giving the appellant notice and a reasonable opportunity to cure—consider and decide those issues or points that do not require a reporter's record for a decision. The court may do this if no reporter's record has been filed because:

(1) the appellant failed to request a reporter's record; or

(2)(A) appellant failed to pay or make arrangements to pay the reporter's fee to prepare the reporter's record; and

(B) the appellant is not entitled to proceed without payment of costs.

TRAP 38. REQUISITES OF BRIEFS

38.1 Appellant's Brief. The appellant's brief must, under appropriate headings and in the order here indicated, contain the following:

(a) *Identity of parties and counsel.* The brief must give a complete list of all parties to the trial court's

---

judgment or order appealed from, and the names and addresses of all trial and appellate counsel, except as otherwise provided in Rule 9.8.

(b) *Table of contents.* The brief must have a table of contents with references to the pages of the brief. The table of contents must indicate the subject matter of each issue or point, or group of issues or points.

(c) *Index of authorities.* The brief must have an index of authorities arranged alphabetically and indicating the pages of the brief where the authorities are cited.

(d) *Statement of the case.* The brief must state concisely the nature of the case (e.g., whether it is a suit for damages, on a note, or involving a murder prosecution), the course of proceedings, and the trial court's disposition of the case. The statement should be supported by record references, should seldom exceed one-half page, and should not discuss the facts.

(e) *Any statement regarding oral argument.* The brief may include a statement explaining why oral argument should or should not be permitted. Any such statement must not exceed one page and should address how the court's decisional process would, or would not, be aided by oral argument. As required by Rule 39.7, any party requesting oral argument must note that request on the front cover of the party's brief.

(f) *Issues presented.* The brief must state concisely all issues or points presented for review. The statement of an issue or point will be treated as covering every subsidiary question that is fairly included.

(g) *Statement of facts.* The brief must state concisely and without argument the facts pertinent to the issues or points presented. In a civil case, the court will accept as true the facts stated unless another party contradicts them. The statement must be supported by record references.

(h) *Summary of the argument.* The brief must contain a succinct, clear, and accurate statement of the arguments made in the body of the brief. This summary must not merely repeat the issues or points presented for review.

(i) *Argument.* The brief must contain a clear and concise argument for the contentions made, with appropriate citations to authorities and to the record.

(j) *Prayer.* The brief must contain a short conclusion that clearly states the nature of the relief sought.

(k) *Appendix in civil cases.*

(1) *Necessary contents.* Unless voluminous or impracticable, the appendix must contain a copy of:

(A) the trial court's judgment or other appealable order from which relief is sought;

(B) the jury charge and verdict, if any, or the trial court's findings of fact and conclusions of law, if any; and

(C) the text of any rule, regulation, ordinance, statute, constitutional provision, or other law (excluding case law) on which the argument is based, and the text of any contract or other document that is central to the argument.

(2) *Optional contents.* The appendix may contain any other item pertinent to the issues or points presented for review, including copies or excerpts of relevant court opinions, laws, documents on which the suit was based, pleadings, excerpts from the reporter's record, and similar material. Items should not be included in the appendix to attempt to avoid the page limits for the brief.

38.2 Appellee's Brief.

(a) *Form of brief.*

(1) An appellee's brief must conform to the requirements of Rule 38.1, except that:

(A) the list of parties and counsel is not required unless necessary to supplement or correct the appellant's list;

(B) the appellee's brief need not include a statement of the case, a statement of the issues presented, or a statement of facts, unless the appellee is dissatisfied with that portion of the appellant's brief; and

(C) the appendix to the appellee's brief need not contain any item already contained in an appendix filed by the appellant.

(2) When practicable, the appellee's brief should respond to the appellant's issues or points in the order the appellant presented those issues or points.

(b) *Cross-points.*

(1) *Judgment notwithstanding the verdict.* When the trial court renders judgment notwithstanding the verdict on one or more questions, the appellee must bring forward by cross-point any issue or point that would have vitiated the verdict or that would have prevented an affirmance of the judgment if the trial court had rendered judgment on the verdict. Failure to bring forward by cross-point an issue or point that would viti-

---

ate the verdict or prevent an affirmance of the judgment waives that complaint. Included in this requirement is a point that:

(A) the verdict or one or more jury findings have insufficient evidentiary support or are against the overwhelming preponderance of the evidence as a matter of fact; or

(B) the verdict should be set aside because of improper argument of counsel.

(2) *When evidentiary hearing needed.* The appellate court must remand a case to the trial court to take evidence if:

(A) the appellate court has sustained a point raised by the appellant; and

(B) the appellee raised a cross-point that requires the taking of additional evidence.

38.3 **Reply Brief.** The appellant may file a reply brief addressing any matter in the appellee's brief. However, the appellate court may consider and decide the case before a reply brief is filed.

⑫ **38.4** **DELETED.**

38.5 **Appendix for Cases Recorded Electronically.** In cases where the proceedings were electronically recorded, the following rules apply:

(a) *Appendix.*

(1) *In general.* At or before the time a party's brief is due, the party must file one copy of an appendix containing a transcription of all portions of the recording that the party considers relevant to the appellate issues or points. Unless another party objects, the transcription will be presumed accurate.

(2) *Repetition not required.* A party's appendix need not repeat evidence included in any previously filed appendix.

(3) *Form.* The form of the appendix and transcription must conform to any specifications of the Supreme Court and Court of Criminal Appeals concerning the form of the reporter's record except that it need not have the reporter's certificate.

(4) *Notice.* At the time the appendix is filed, the party must give written notice of the filing to all parties to the trial court's judgment or order. The notice must specify, by referring to the index numbers in the court recorder's logs, those parts of the recording that are included in the appendix. The filing party need not serve a copy of the appendix but must make a copy available to all parties for inspection and copying.

(b) *Presumptions.* The same presumptions that apply to a partial reporter's record under Rule 34.6(c)(4) apply to the parties' appendixes. The appellate court need not review any part of the electronic recording.

(c) *Supplemental appendix.* The appellate court may direct or allow a party to file a supplemental appendix containing a transcription of additional portions of the recording.

(d) *Inability to pay.* A party who cannot pay the cost of an appendix must file the affidavit provided for by Rule 20. The party must also state in the affidavit or a supplemental affidavit that the party has neither the access to the equipment necessary nor the skill necessary to prepare the appendix. If a contest to the affidavit is not sustained by written order, the court recorder must transcribe or have transcribed those portions of the recording that the party designates and must file the transcription as that party's appendix, along with all exhibits.

(e) *Inaccuracies.*

(1) *Correction by agreement.* The parties may agree to correct an inaccuracy in the transcription of the recording.

(2) *Correction by appellate or trial court.* If the parties dispute whether an electronic recording or transcription accurately discloses what occurred in the trial court but cannot agree on corrections, the appellate court may:

(A) settle the dispute by reviewing the recording; or

(B) submit the dispute to the trial court, which must—after notice and hearing—settle the dispute and ensure that the recording or transcription is made to conform to what occurred in the trial court.

(f) *Costs.* The actual expense of preparing the appendixes or the amount prescribed for official reporters, whichever is less, is taxed as costs. The appellate court may disallow the cost of any portion of the appendixes that it considers surplusage or that does not conform to any specifications prescribed by the Supreme Court or Court of Criminal Appeals.

38.6 **Time to File Briefs.**

(a) *Appellant's filing date.* Except in a habeas corpus or bail appeal, which is governed by Rule 31, an

★

appellant must file a brief within 30 days—20 days in an accelerated appeal—after the later of:

(1) the date the clerk's record was filed; or

(2) the date the reporter's record was filed.

(b) *Appellee's filing date.* The appellee's brief must be filed within 30 days—20 days in an accelerated appeal—after the date the appellant's brief was filed. In a civil case, if the appellant has not filed a brief as provided in this rule, an appellee may file a brief within 30 days—20 days in an accelerated appeal—after the date the appellant's brief was due.

(c) *Filing date for reply brief.* A reply brief, if any, must be filed within 20 days after the date the appellee's brief was filed.

(d) *Modifications of filing time.* On motion complying with Rule 10.5(b), the appellate court may extend the time for filing a brief and may postpone submission of the case. A motion to extend the time to file a brief may be filed before or after the date the brief is due. The court may also, in the interests of justice, shorten the time for filing briefs and for submission of the case.

38.7 Amendment or Supplementation. A brief may be amended or supplemented whenever justice requires, on whatever reasonable terms the court may prescribe.

38.8 Failure of Appellant to File Brief.

(a) *Civil cases.* If an appellant fails to timely file a brief, the appellate court may:

(1) dismiss the appeal for want of prosecution, unless the appellant reasonably explains the failure and the appellee is not significantly injured by the appellant's failure to timely file a brief;

(2) decline to dismiss the appeal and give further direction to the case as it considers proper; or

(3) if an appellee's brief is filed, the court may regard that brief as correctly presenting the case and may affirm the trial court's judgment upon that brief without examining the record.

(b) *Criminal cases.*

38.9 Briefing Rules to Be Construed Liberally. Because briefs are meant to acquaint the court with the issues in a case and to present argument that will en-

able the court to decide the case, substantial compliance with this rule is sufficient, subject to the following.

(a) *Formal defects.* If the court determines that this rule has been flagrantly violated, it may require a brief to be amended, supplemented, or redrawn. If another brief that does not comply with this rule is filed, the court may strike the brief, prohibit the party from filing another, and proceed as if the party had failed to file a brief.

(b) *Substantive defects.* If the court determines, either before or after submission, that the case has not been properly presented in the briefs, or that the law and authorities have not been properly cited in the briefs, the court may postpone submission, require additional briefing, and make any other order necessary for a satisfactory submission of the case.

2012 change: Amended eff. Dec. 1, 2012, by order of Nov. 13, 2012 (Tex. Sup.Ct. Order, Misc. Docket No. 12-9190): Deleted TRAP 38.4 to correspond to amendments to TRAP 9.4 consolidating length limits and establishing word limits for computer-generated documents.

TRAP 39. ORAL ARGUMENT; DECISION WITHOUT ARGUMENT

39.1 Right to Oral Argument. A party who has filed a brief and who has timely requested oral argument may argue the case to the court unless the court, after examining the briefs, decides that oral argument is unnecessary for any of the following reasons:

(a) the appeal is frivolous;

(b) the dispositive issue or issues have been authoritatively decided;

(c) the facts and legal arguments are adequately presented in the briefs and record; or

(d) the decisional process would not be significantly aided by oral argument.

39.2 Purpose of Argument. Oral argument should emphasize and clarify the written arguments in the briefs. Counsel should not merely read from prepared text. Counsel should assume that all members of the court have read the briefs before oral argument and counsel should be prepared to respond to questions. A party should not refer to or comment on matters not involved in or pertaining to what is in the record.

39.3 Time Allowed. The court will set the time that will be allowed for argument. Counsel must complete argument in the time allotted and may continue

TRAP 38

---

after the expiration of the allotted time only with permission of the court. Counsel is not required to use all the allotted time. The appellant must be allowed to conclude the argument.

39.4 Number of Counsel. Generally, only one counsel should argue for each side. Except on leave of court, no more than two counsel on each side may argue. Only one counsel may argue in rebuttal.

39.5 Argument by Amicus. With leave of court obtained before the argument and with a party's consent, an amicus curiae may share allotted time with that party. Otherwise, counsel for amicus may not argue.

39.6 When Only One Party Files a Brief. If counsel for only one party has filed a brief, the court may allow that party to argue.

39.7 Request and Waiver. A party desiring oral argument must note that request on the front cover of the party's brief. A party's failure to request oral argument waives the party's right to argue. But even if a party has waived oral argument, the court may direct the party to appear and argue.

39.8 Clerk's Notice. The clerk must send to the parties—at least 21 days before the date the case is set for argument or submission without argument—a notice telling the parties:

(a) whether the court will allow oral argument or will submit the case without argument;

(b) the date of argument or submission without argument;

(c) if argument is allowed, the time allotted for argument; and

(d) the names of the members of the panel to which the case will be argued or submitted, subject to change by the court.

A party's failure to receive the notice does not prevent a case's argument or submission on the scheduled date.

TRAP 40. ORDER OF DECISION

40.1 Civil Cases. The court of appeals may determine the order in which civil cases will be decided. But the following types of cases have precedence over all others:

(a) a case given precedence by law;

(b) an accelerated appeal; and

(c) a case that the court determines should be given precedence in the interest of justice.

40.2 Criminal Cases.

TRAP 41. PANEL & EN BANC DECISION

41.1 Decision by Panel.

(a) *Constitution of panel.* Unless a court of appeals with more than three justices votes to decide a case en banc, a case must be assigned for decision to a panel of the court consisting of three justices, although not every member of the panel must be present for argument. If the case is decided without argument, three justices must participate in the decision. A majority of the panel, which constitutes a quorum, must agree on the judgment. Except as otherwise provided in these rules, a panel's opinion constitutes the court's opinion, and the court must render a judgment in accordance with the panel opinion.

(b) *When panel cannot agree on judgment.* After argument, if for any reason a member of the panel cannot participate in deciding a case, the case may be decided by the two remaining justices. If they cannot agree on a judgment, the chief justice of the court of appeals must:

(1) designate another justice of the court to sit on the panel to consider the case;

(2) request the Chief Justice of the Supreme Court to temporarily assign an eligible justice or judge to sit on the panel to consider the case; or

(3) convene the court en banc to consider the case.

The reconstituted panel or the en banc court may order the case reargued.

(c) *When court cannot agree on judgment.* After argument, if for any reason a member of a court consisting of only three justices cannot participate in deciding a case, the case may be decided by the two remaining justices. If they cannot agree on a judgment, that fact must be certified to the Chief Justice of the Supreme Court. The Chief Justice may then temporarily assign an eligible justice or judge to sit with the court of appeals to consider the case. The reconstituted court may order the case reargued.

41.2 Decision by En Banc Court.

(a) *Constitution of en banc court.* An en banc court consists of all members of the court who are not disqualified or recused and—if the case was originally

★

argued before or decided by a panel—any members of the panel who are not members of the court but remain eligible for assignment to the court. A majority of the en banc court constitutes a quorum. A majority of the en banc court must agree on a judgment.

(b) *When en banc court cannot agree on judgment.* If a majority of an en banc court cannot agree on a judgment, that fact must be certified to the Chief Justice of the Supreme Court. The Chief Justice may then temporarily assign an eligible justice or judge to sit with the court of appeals to consider the case. The reconstituted court may order the case reargued.

(c) *En banc consideration disfavored.* En banc consideration of a case is not favored and should not be ordered unless necessary to secure or maintain uniformity of the court's decisions or unless extraordinary circumstances require en banc consideration. A vote to determine whether a case will be heard or reheard en banc need not be taken unless a justice of the court requests a vote. If a vote is requested and a majority of the court's members vote to hear or rehear the case en banc, the en banc court will hear or rehear the case. Otherwise, a panel of the court will consider the case.

41.3 **Precedent in Transferred Cases.** In cases transferred by the Supreme Court from one court of appeals to another, the court of appeals to which the case is transferred must decide the case in accordance with the precedent of the transferor court under principles of stare decisis if the transferee court's decision otherwise would have been inconsistent with the precedent of the transferor court. The court's opinion may state whether the outcome would have been different had the transferee court not been required to decide the case in accordance with the transferor court's precedent.

TRAP 42. DISMISSAL; SETTLEMENT

42.1 **Voluntary Dismissal and Settlement in Civil Cases.**

(a) *On motion or by agreement.* The appellate court may dispose of an appeal as follows:

(1) *On motion of appellant.* In accordance with a motion of appellant, the court may dismiss the appeal or affirm the appealed judgment or order unless such disposition would prevent a party from seeking relief to which it would otherwise be entitled.

(2) *By agreement.* In accordance with an agreement signed by the parties or their attorneys and filed with the clerk, the court may:

(A) render judgment effectuating the parties' agreement;

(B) set aside the trial court's judgment without regard to the merits and remand the case to the trial court for rendition of judgment in accordance with the agreement; or

(C) abate the appeal and permit proceedings in the trial court to effectuate the agreement.

(b) *Partial disposition.* A severable portion of the proceeding may be disposed of under (a) if it will not prejudice the remaining parties.

(c) *Effect on court's opinion.* In dismissing a proceeding, the appellate court will determine whether to withdraw any opinion it has already issued. An agreement or motion for dismissal cannot be conditioned on withdrawal of the opinion.

(d) *Costs.* Absent agreement of the parties, the court will tax costs against the appellant.

42.2 **Voluntary Dismissal in Criminal Cases.**

42.3 **Involuntary Dismissal in Civil Cases.** Under the following circumstances, on any party's motion—or on its own initiative after giving ten days' notice to all parties—the appellate court may dismiss the appeal or affirm the appealed judgment or order. Dismissal or affirmance may occur if the appeal is subject to dismissal:

(a) for want of jurisdiction;

(b) for want of prosecution; or

(c) because the appellant has failed to comply with a requirement of these rules, a court order, or a notice from the clerk requiring a response or other action within a specified time.

42.4 **Involuntary Dismissal in Criminal Cases.**

TRAP 43. JUDGMENT OF THE COURT OF APPEALS

43.1 **Time.** The court of appeals should render its judgment promptly after submission of a case.

43.2 **Types of Judgment.** The court of appeals may:

(a) affirm the trial court's judgment in whole or in part;

(b) modify the trial court's judgment and affirm it as modified;

───────────────── ★ ─────────────────

(c) reverse the trial court's judgment in whole or in part and render the judgment that the trial court should have rendered;

(d) reverse the trial court's judgment and remand the case for further proceedings;

(e) vacate the trial court's judgment and dismiss the case; or

(f) dismiss the appeal.

43.3 Rendition Appropriate Unless Remand Necessary. When reversing a trial court's judgment, the court must render the judgment that the trial court should have rendered, except when:

(a) a remand is necessary for further proceedings; or

(b) the interests of justice require a remand for another trial.

43.4 Judgment for Costs in Civil Cases. In a civil case, the court of appeal's judgment should award to the prevailing party the appellate costs—including preparation costs for the clerk's record and the reporter's record—that were incurred by that party. But the court of appeals may tax costs otherwise as required by law or for good cause.

43.5 Judgment Against Sureties in Civil Cases. When a court of appeals affirms the trial court judgment, or modifies that judgment and renders judgment against the appellant, the court of appeals must render judgment against the sureties on the appellant's supersedeas bond, if any, for the performance of the judgment and for any costs taxed against the appellant.

43.6 Other Orders. The court of appeals may make any other appropriate order that the law and the nature of the case require.

TRAP 44. REVERSIBLE ERROR

44.1 Reversible Error in Civil Cases.

(a) *Standard for reversible error.* No judgment may be reversed on appeal on the ground that the trial court made an error of law unless the court of appeals concludes that the error complained of:

(1) probably caused the rendition of an improper judgment; or

(2) probably prevented the appellant from properly presenting the case to the court of appeals.

(b) *Error affecting only part of case.* If the error affects part of, but not all, the matter in controversy and that part is separable without unfairness to the parties, the judgment must be reversed and a new trial ordered only as to the part affected by the error. The court may not order a separate trial solely on unliquidated damages if liability is contested.

44.2 Reversible Error in Criminal Cases.

44.3 Defects in Procedure. A court of appeals must not affirm or reverse a judgment or dismiss an appeal for formal defects or irregularities in appellate procedure without allowing a reasonable time to correct or amend the defects or irregularities.

44.4 Remediable Error of the Trial Court.

(a) *Generally.* A court of appeals must not affirm or reverse a judgment or dismiss an appeal if:

(1) the trial court's erroneous action or failure or refusal to act prevents the proper presentation of a case to the court of appeals; and

(2) the trial court can correct its action or failure to act.

(b) *Court of appeals direction if error remediable.* If the circumstances described in (a) exist, the court of appeals must direct the trial court to correct the error. The court of appeals will then proceed as if the erroneous action or failure to act had not occurred.

TRAP 45. DAMAGES FOR FRIVOLOUS APPEALS IN CIVIL CASES

If the court of appeals determines that an appeal is frivolous, it may—on motion of any party or on its own initiative, after notice and a reasonable opportunity for response—award each prevailing party just damages. In determining whether to award damages, the court must not consider any matter that does not appear in the record, briefs, or other papers filed in the court of appeals.

TRAP 46. REMITTITUR IN CIVIL CASES

46.1 Remittitur After Appeal Perfected. If the trial court suggests a remittitur but the case is appealed before the remittitur is filed, the party who would make the remittitur may do so in the court of appeals in the same manner as in the trial court. The court of appeals must then render the judgment that the trial court should have rendered if the remittitur had been made in the trial court.

TRAP 46

⭐

46.2 Appeal on Remittitur. If a party makes the remittitur at the trial judge's suggestion and the party benefiting from the remittitur appeals, the remitting party is not barred from contending in the court of appeals that all or part of the remittitur should not have been required, but the remitting party must perfect an appeal to raise that point. If the court of appeals sustains the remitting party's contention that remittitur should not have been required, the court must render the judgment that the trial court should have rendered.

46.3 Suggestion of Remittitur by Court of Appeals. The court of appeals may suggest a remittitur. If the remittitur is timely filed, the court must reform and affirm the trial court's judgment in accordance with the remittitur. If the remittitur is not timely filed, the court must reverse the trial court's judgment.

46.4 Refusal to Remit Must Not Be Mentioned in Later Trial. If the court of appeals suggests a remittitur but no remittitur is filed, evidence of the court's determination regarding remittitur is inadmissible in a later trial of the case.

46.5 Voluntary Remittitur. If a court of appeals reverses the trial court's judgment because of a legal error that affects only part of the damages awarded by the judgment, the affected party may—within 15 days after the court of appeals' judgment—voluntarily remit the amount that the affected party believes will cure the reversible error. A party may include in a motion for rehearing—without waiving any complaint that the court of appeals erred—a conditional request that the court accept the remittitur and affirm the trial court's judgment as reduced. If the court of appeals determines that the voluntary remittitur is not sufficient to cure the reversible error, but that remittitur is appropriate, the court must suggest a remittitur in accordance with Rule 46.3. If the remittitur is timely filed and the court of appeals determines that the voluntary remittitur cures the reversible error, then the court must accept the remittitur and reform and affirm the trial court judgment in accordance with the remittitur.

TRAP 47. OPINIONS, PUBLICATION & CITATION

47.1 Written Opinions. The court of appeals must hand down a written opinion that is as brief as practicable but that addresses every issue raised and necessary to final disposition of the appeal.

47.2 Designation and Signing of Opinions; Participating Justices.

(a) *Civil and criminal cases.* Each opinion of the court must be designated either an "Opinion" or a "Memorandum Opinion." A majority of the justices who participate in considering the case must determine whether the opinion will be signed by a justice or will be per curiam and whether it will be designated an opinion or memorandum opinion. The names of the participating justices must be noted on all written opinions or orders of the court or a panel of the court.

(b) *Criminal cases.*

(c) *Civil cases.* Opinions and memorandum opinions in civil cases issued on or after January 1, 2003 shall not be designated "do not publish."

47.3 Distribution of Opinions. All opinions of the courts of appeals are open to the public and must be made available to public reporting services, print or electronic.

47.4 Memorandum Opinions. If the issues are settled, the court should write a brief memorandum opinion no longer than necessary to advise the parties of the court's decision and the basic reasons for it. An opinion may not be designated a memorandum opinion if the author of a concurrence or dissent opposes that designation. An opinion must be designated a memorandum opinion unless it does any of the following:

(a) establishes a new rule of law, alters or modifies an existing rule, or applies an existing rule to a novel fact situation likely to recur in future cases;

(b) involves issues of constitutional law or other legal issues important to the jurisprudence of Texas;

(c) criticizes existing law; or

(d) resolves an apparent conflict of authority.

47.5 Concurring and Dissenting Opinions. Only a justice who participated in the decision of a case may file or join in an opinion concurring in or dissenting from the judgment of the court of appeals. Any justice on the court may file an opinion in connection with a denial of a hearing or rehearing en banc.

47.6 Change in Designation by En Banc Court. A court en banc may change a panel's designation of an opinion.

47.7 Citation of Unpublished Opinions.

(a) *Criminal cases.*

(b) *Civil cases.* Opinions and memorandum opinions designated "do not publish" under these rules by

TRAP 46

the courts of appeals prior to January 1, 2003 have no precedential value but may be cited with the notation, "(not designated for publication)." If an opinion or memorandum opinion issued on or after that date is erroneously designated "do not publish," the erroneous designation will not affect the precedential value of the decision.

TRAP 48. COPY OF OPINION & JUDGMENT TO INTERESTED PARTIES & OTHER COURTS

48.1 **Mailing Opinion and Judgment in All Cases.** On the date when an appellate court's opinion is handed down, the appellate clerk must mail or deliver copies of the opinion and judgment to the following persons:

(a) the trial judge;

(b) the trial court clerk;

(c) the regional administrative judge; and

(d) all parties to the appeal.

48.2 **Additional Recipients in Criminal Cases.**

48.3 **Filing Opinion and Judgment.** The trial court clerk must file a copy of the opinion and judgment among the papers of the case in that court.

48.4 **Opinion Sent to Criminal Defendant.**

TRAP 49. MOTION FOR REHEARING & EN BANC RECONSIDERATION

49.1 **Motion for Rehearing.** A motion for rehearing may be filed within 15 days after the court of appeals' judgment or order is rendered. The motion must clearly state the points relied on for the rehearing.

49.2 **Response.** No response to a motion for rehearing need be filed unless the court so requests. A motion will not be granted unless a response has been filed or requested by the court.

49.3 **Decision on Motion.** A motion for rehearing may be granted by a majority of the justices who participated in the decision of the case. Otherwise, it must be denied. If rehearing is granted, the court or panel may dispose of the case with or without rebriefing and oral argument.

49.4 **Accelerated Appeals.** In an accelerated appeal, the appellate court may deny the right to file a motion for rehearing or shorten the time to file such a motion.

49.5 **Further Motion for Rehearing.** After a motion for rehearing is decided, a further motion for rehearing may be filed within 15 days of the court's action if the court:

(a) modifies its judgment;

(b) vacates its judgment and renders a new judgment; or

(c) issues a different opinion.

49.6 **Amendments.** A motion for rehearing or en banc reconsideration may be amended as a matter of right anytime before the 15-day period allowed for filing the motion expires, and with leave of the court, anytime before the court of appeals decides the motion.

49.7 **En Banc Reconsideration.** A party may file a motion for en banc reconsideration as a separate motion, with or without filing a motion for rehearing. The motion must be filed within 15 days after the court of appeals' judgment or order, or when permitted, within 15 days after the court of appeals' denial of the party's last timely filed motion for rehearing or en banc reconsideration. While the court has plenary power, a majority of the en banc court may, with or without a motion, order en banc reconsideration of a panel's decision. If a majority orders reconsideration, the panel's judgment or order does not become final, and the case will be resubmitted to the court for en banc review and disposition.

49.8 **Extension of Time.** A court of appeals may extend the time for filing a motion for rehearing or en banc reconsideration if a party files a motion complying with Rule 10.5(b) no later than 15 days after the last date for filing the motion.

49.9 **Not Required for Review.** A motion for rehearing is not a prerequisite to filing a petition for review in the Supreme Court or a petition for discretionary review in the Court of Criminal Appeals nor is it required to preserve error.

⑫ **49.10** **DELETED.**

49.11 **Relationship to Petition for Review.** A party may not file a motion for rehearing or en banc reconsideration in the court of appeals after that party has filed a petition for review in the Supreme Court unless the court of appeals modifies its opinion or judgment after the petition for review is filed. The filing of a petition for review does not preclude another party from filing a motion for rehearing or en banc reconsid-

TRAP 49

eration or preclude the court of appeals from ruling on the motion. If a motion for rehearing or en banc reconsideration is timely filed after a petition for review is filed, the petitioner must immediately notify the Supreme Court clerk of the filing of the motion, and must notify the clerk when the last timely filed motion is overruled by the court of appeals.

49.12 Certificate of Conference Not Required. A certificate of conference is not required for a motion for rehearing or en banc reconsideration of a panel's decision.

2012 change: Amended eff. Dec. 1, 2012, by order of Nov. 13, 2012 (Tex. Sup.Ct. Order, Misc. Docket No. 12-9190): Deleted TRAP 49.10 to correspond to amendments to TRAP 9.4 consolidating length limits and establishing word limits for computer-generated documents.

TRAP 51. ENFORCEMENT OF JUDGMENTS AFTER MANDATE

51.1 Civil Cases.

(a) *Statement of costs.* The appellate clerk must prepare, and send to the trial court clerk with the mandate, a statement of costs showing:

(1) the preparation costs for the appellate record, and any court of appeals filing fees, with a notation of those items that have been paid and those that are owing; and

(2) the party or parties against whom costs have been adjudged.

(b) *Enforcement of judgment.* When the trial court clerk receives the mandate, the appellate court's judgment must be enforced. Appellate court costs must be included with the trial court costs in any process to enforce the judgment. If all or part of the costs are collected, the trial court clerk must immediately remit to the appellate court clerk any amount due to that clerk. The trial court need not make any further order in the case, and the appellate court's judgment may be enforced as in other cases, when the appellate judgment:

(1) affirms the trial court's judgment;

(2) modifies the trial court's judgment and, as so modified, affirms that judgment; or

(3) renders the judgment the trial court should have rendered.

51.2 Criminal Cases.

SECTION THREE: ORIGINAL PROCEEDINGS IN THE SUPREME COURT & THE COURTS OF APPEALS

TRAP 52. ORIGINAL PROCEEDINGS

52.1 Commencement. An original appellate proceeding seeking extraordinary relief—such as a writ of habeas corpus, mandamus, prohibition, injunction, or quo warranto—is commenced by filing a petition with the clerk of the appropriate appellate court. The petition must be captioned "*In re* [name of relator]."

52.2 Designation of Parties. The party seeking the relief is the relator. In original proceedings other than habeas corpus, the person against whom relief is sought—whether a judge, court, tribunal, officer, or other person—is the respondent. A person whose interest would be directly affected by the relief sought is a real party in interest and a party to the case.

52.3 Form and Contents of Petition. The petition must, under appropriate headings and in the order here indicated, contain the following:

(a) *Identity of parties and counsel.* The petition must give a complete list of all parties, and the names, and addresses of all counsel.

(b) *Table of contents.* The petition must include a table of contents with references to the pages of the petition. The table of contents must indicate the subject matter of each issue or point, or group of issues or points.

(c) *Index of authorities.* The petition must include an index of authorities arranged alphabetically and indicating the pages of the petition where the authorities are cited.

(d) *Statement of the case.* The petition must contain a statement of the case that should seldom exceed one page and should not discuss the facts. The statement must contain the following:

(1) a concise description of the nature of any underlying proceeding (e.g., a suit for damages, a contempt proceeding for failure to pay child support, or the certification of a candidate for inclusion on an election ballot);

(2) if the respondent is a judge, the name of the judge, the designation of the court in which the judge was sitting, and the county in which the court is located; and if the respondent is an official other than a judge, the designation and location of the office held by the respondent;

(3) a concise description of the respondent's action from which the relator seeks relief;

(4) if the relator seeks a writ of habeas corpus, a statement describing how and where the relator is being deprived of liberty;

★

(5) if the petition is filed in the Supreme Court after a petition requesting the same relief was filed in the court of appeals:

(A) the date the petition was filed in the court of appeals;

(B) the district of the court of appeals and the names of the justices who participated in the decision;

(C) the author of any opinion for the court of appeals and the author of any separate opinion;

(D) the citation of the court's opinion;

(E) the disposition of the case by the court of appeals, and the date of the court of appeals' order.

(e) *Statement of jurisdiction.* The petition must state, without argument, the basis of the court's jurisdiction. If the Supreme Court and the court of appeals have concurrent jurisdiction, the petition must be presented first to the court of appeals unless there is a compelling reason not to do so. If the petition is filed in the Supreme Court without first being presented to the court of appeals, the petition must state the compelling reason why the petition was not first presented to the court of appeals.

(f) *Issues presented.* The petition must state concisely all issues or points presented for relief. The statement of an issue or point will be treated as covering every subsidiary question that is fairly included.

(g) *Statement of facts.* The petition must state concisely and without argument the facts pertinent to the issues or points presented. Every statement of fact in the petition must be supported by citation to competent evidence included in the appendix or record.

(h) *Argument.* The petition must contain a clear and concise argument for the contentions made, with appropriate citations to authorities and to the appendix or record.

(i) *Prayer.* The petition must contain a short conclusion that clearly states the nature of the relief sought.

(j) *Certification.* The person filing the petition must certify that he or she has reviewed the petition and concluded that every factual statement in the petition is supported by competent evidence included in the appendix or record.

(k) *Appendix.*

(1) *Necessary contents.* The appendix must contain:

(A) a certified or sworn copy of any order complained of, or any other document showing the matter complained of;

(B) any order or opinion of the court of appeals, if the petition is filed in the Supreme Court;

(C) unless voluminous or impracticable, the text of any rule, regulation, ordinance, statute, constitutional provision, or other law (excluding case law) on which the argument is based; and

(D) if a writ of habeas corpus is sought, proof that the relator is being restrained.

(2) *Optional contents.* The appendix may contain any other item pertinent to the issues or points presented for review, including copies or excerpts of relevant court opinions, statutes, constitutional provisions, documents on which the suit was based, pleadings, and similar material. Items should not be included in the appendix to attempt to avoid the page limits for the petition. The appendix should not contain any evidence or other item that is not necessary for a decision.

52.4 **Response.** Any party may file a response to the petition, but it is not mandatory. The court must not grant relief—other than temporary relief—before a response has been filed or requested by the court. The response must conform to the requirements of 52.3, except that:

(a) the list of parties and counsel is not required unless necessary to supplement or correct the list contained in the petition;

(b) the response need not include a statement of the case, a statement of the issues presented, or a statement of the facts unless the responding party is dissatisfied with that portion of the petition;

(c) a statement of jurisdiction should be omitted unless the petition fails to assert valid grounds for jurisdiction, in which case the reasons why the court lacks jurisdiction must be concisely stated;

(d) the argument must be confined to the issues or points presented in the petition; and

(e) the appendix to the response need not contain any item already contained in an appendix filed by the relator.

52.5 **Relator's Reply to Response.** The relator may file a reply addressing any matter in the response. However, the court may consider and decide the case before a reply brief is filed.

TRAP 52

⑫ **52.6** DELETED.

52.7 Record.

(a) *Filing by relator required.* Relator must file with the petition:

(1) a certified or sworn copy of every document that is material to the relator's claim for relief and that was filed in any underlying proceeding; and

(2) a properly authenticated transcript of any relevant testimony from any underlying proceeding, including any exhibits offered in evidence, or a statement that no testimony was adduced in connection with the matter complained.

(b) *Supplementation permitted.* After the record is filed, relator or any other party to the proceeding may file additional materials for inclusion in the record.

(c) *Service of record on all parties.* Relator and any party who files materials for inclusion in the record must—at the same time—serve on each party:

(1) those materials not previously served on that party as part of the record in another original appellate proceeding in the same or another court; and

(2) an index listing the materials filed and describing them in sufficient detail to identify them.

52.8 Action on Petition.

(a) *Relief denied.* If the court determines from the petition and any response and reply that the relator is not entitled to the relief sought, the court must deny the petition. If the relator in a habeas corpus proceeding has been released on bond, the court must remand the relator to custody and issue an order of commitment. If the relator is not returned to custody, the court may declare the bond to be forfeited and render judgment against the surety.

(b) *Interim action.* If the court is of the tentative opinion that relator is entitled to the relief sought or that a serious question concerning the relief requires further consideration:

(1) the court must request a response if one has not been filed;

(2) the Supreme Court may request full briefing under Rule 55;

(3) in a habeas corpus proceeding, the court may order that relator be discharged on execution and filing of a bond in an amount set by the court; and

(4) the court may set the case for oral argument.

(c) *Relief granted.* If the court determines that relator is entitled to relief, it must make an appropriate order. The court may grant relief without hearing oral argument.

(d) *Opinion.* When denying relief, the court may hand down an opinion but is not required to do so. When granting relief, the court must hand down an opinion as in any other case. Rule 47 is applicable to an order or opinion by a court of appeals except that the court of appeals may not order an unpublished opinion published after the Supreme Court or Court of Criminal Appeals has acted on any party's petition for extraordinary relief addressing the same issues.

52.9 Motion for Rehearing. Any party may file a motion for rehearing within 15 days after the final order is rendered. The motion must clearly state the points relied on for the rehearing. No response to a motion for rehearing need be filed unless the court so requests. The court will not grant a motion for rehearing unless a response has been filed or requested. A motion or response must be no longer than 15 pages.

52.10 Temporary Relief.

(a) *Motion for temporary relief; certificate of compliance.* The relator may file a motion to stay any underlying proceedings or for any other temporary relief pending the court's action on the petition. The relator must notify or make a diligent effort to notify all parties by expedited means (such as by telephone or fax) that a motion for temporary relief has been or will be filed and must certify to the court that the relator has complied with this paragraph before temporary relief will be granted.

(b) *Grant of temporary relief.* The court—on motion of any party or on its own initiative—may without notice grant any just relief pending the court's action on the petition. As a condition of granting temporary relief, the court may require a bond to protect the parties who will be affected by the relief. Unless vacated or modified, an order granting temporary relief is effective until the case is finally decided.

(c) *Motion to reconsider.* Any party may move the court at any time to reconsider a grant of temporary relief.

52.11 Groundless Petition or Misleading Statement or Record. On motion of any party or on its own initiative, the court may—after notice and a reasonable opportunity to respond—impose just sanctions on a

---

⭐

---

party or attorney who is not acting in good faith as indicated by any of the following:

(a) filing a petition that is clearly groundless;

(b) bringing the petition solely for delay of an underlying proceeding;

(c) grossly misstating or omitting an obviously important and material fact in the petition or response; or

(d) filing an appendix or record that is clearly misleading because of the omission of obviously important and material evidence or documents.

2012 change: Amended eff. Dec. 1, 2012, by order of Nov. 13, 2012 (Tex. Sup.Ct. Order, Misc. Docket No. 12-9190): Deleted TRAP 52.6 to correspond to amendments to TRAP 9.4 consolidating length limits and establishing word limits for computer-generated documents.

SECTION FOUR: PROCEEDINGS IN THE SUPREME COURT

TRAP 53. PETITION FOR REVIEW

53.1 **Method of Review.** The Supreme Court may review a court of appeals' final judgment on a petition for review addressed to "The Supreme Court of Texas." A party who seeks to alter the court of appeals' judgment must file a petition for review. The petition for review procedure replaces the writ of error procedure. Statutes pertaining to the writ of error in the Supreme Court apply equally to the petition for review.

53.2 **Contents of Petition.** The petition for review must, under appropriate headings and in the order here indicated, contain the following items:

(a) *Identity of parties and counsel.* The petition must give a complete list of all parties to the trial court's final judgment, and the names and addresses of all trial and appellate counsel.

(b) *Table of contents.* The petition must have a table of contents with references to the pages of the petition. The table of contents must indicate the subject matter of each issue or point, or group of issues or points.

(c) *Index of authorities.* The petition must have an index of authorities arranged alphabetically and indicating the pages of the petition where the authorities are cited.

(d) *Statement of the case.* The petition must contain a statement of the case that should seldom exceed one page and should not discuss the facts. The statement must contain the following:

(1) a concise description of the nature of the case (e.g., whether it is a suit for damages, on a note, or in trespass to try title);

(2) the name of the judge who signed the order or judgment appealed from;

(3) the designation of the trial court and the county in which it is located;

(4) the disposition of the case by the trial court;

(5) the parties in the court of appeals;

(6) the district of the court of appeals;

(7) the names of the justices who participated in the decision in the court of appeals, the author of the opinion for the court, and the author of any separate opinion;

(8) the citation for the court of appeals' opinion; and

(9) the disposition of the case by the court of appeals, including the disposition of any motions for rehearing or en banc reconsideration, and whether any motions for rehearing or en banc reconsideration are pending in the court of appeals at the time the petition for review is filed.

(e) *Statement of jurisdiction.* The petition must state, without argument, the basis of the Court's jurisdiction.

(f) *Issues presented.* The petition must state concisely all issues or points presented for review. The statement of an issue or point will be treated as covering every subsidiary question that is fairly included. If the matter complained of originated in the trial court, it should have been preserved for appellate review in the trial court and assigned as error in the court of appeals.

(g) *Statement of facts.* The petition must affirm that the court of appeals correctly stated the nature of the case, except in any particulars pointed out. The petition must state concisely and without argument the facts and procedural background pertinent to the issues or points presented. The statement must be supported by record references.

(h) *Summary of the argument.* The petition must contain a succinct, clear, and accurate statement of the arguments made in the body of the petition. This summary must not merely repeat the issues or points presented for review.

(i) *Argument.* The petition must contain a clear and concise argument for the contentions made, with appropriate citations to authorities and to the record. The argument need not address every issue or point included in the statement of issues or points. Any issue or point not addressed may be addressed in the brief on

TRAP 53

✦

---

the merits if one is requested by the Court. The argument should state the reasons why the Supreme Court should exercise jurisdiction to hear the case with specific reference to the factors listed in Rule 56.1(a). The petition need not quote at length from a matter included in the appendix; a reference to the appendix is sufficient. The Court will consider the court of appeals' opinion along with the petition, so statements in that opinion need not be repeated.

(j) *Prayer.* The petition must contain a short conclusion that clearly states the nature of the relief sought.

(k) *Appendix.*

(1) *Necessary contents.* Unless voluminous or impracticable, the appendix must contain a copy of:

(A) the judgment or other appealable order of the trial court from which relief in the court of appeals was sought;

(B) the jury charge and verdict, if any, or the trial court's findings of fact and conclusions of law, if any;

(C) the opinion and judgment of the court of appeals; and

(D) the text of any rule, regulation, ordinance, statute, constitutional provision, or other law on which the argument is based (excluding case law), and the text of any contract or other document that is central to the argument.

(2) *Optional contents.* The appendix may contain any other item pertinent to the issues or points presented for review, including copies or excerpts of relevant court opinions, statutes, constitutional provisions, documents on which the suit was based, pleadings, and similar material. Items should not be included in the appendix to attempt to avoid the page limits for the petition.

53.3 **Response to Petition for Review.** Any other party to the appeal may file a response to the petition for review, but it is not mandatory. If no response is timely filed, or if a party files a waiver of response, the Court will consider the petition without a response. A petition will not be granted before a response has been filed or requested by the Court. The response must conform to the requirements of 53.2, except that:

(a) the list of parties and counsel is not required unless necessary to supplement or correct the list contained in the petition;

(b) a statement of the case and a statement of the facts need not be made unless the respondent is dissatisfied with that portion of the petition;

(c) a statement of the issues presented need not be made unless:

(1) the respondent is dissatisfied with the statement made in the petition;

(2) the respondent is asserting independent grounds for affirmance of the court of appeals' judgment; or

(3) the respondent is asserting grounds that establish the respondent's right to a judgment that is less favorable to the respondent than the judgment rendered by the court of appeals but more favorable to the respondent than the judgment that might be awarded to the petitioner (e.g., a remand for a new trial rather than a rendition of judgment in favor of the petitioner);

(d) a statement of jurisdiction should be omitted unless the petition fails to assert valid grounds for jurisdiction, in which case the reasons why the Supreme Court lacks jurisdiction must be concisely stated;

(e) the respondent's argument must be confined to the issues or points presented in the petition or asserted by the respondent in the respondent's statement of issues; and

(f) the appendix to the response need not contain any item already contained in an appendix filed by the petitioner.

53.4 **Points Not Considered in Court of Appeals.** To obtain a remand to the court of appeals for consideration of issues or points briefed in that court but not decided by that court, or to request that the Supreme Court consider such issues or points, a party may raise those issues or points in the petition, the response, the reply, any brief, or a motion for rehearing.

53.5 **Petitioner's Reply to Response.** The petitioner may file a reply addressing any matter in the response. However, the Court may consider and decide the case before a reply brief is filed.

12 **53.6** **DELETED.**

53.7 **Time and Place of Filing.**

(a) *Petition.* Unless the Supreme Court orders an earlier filing deadline, the petition must be filed with the Supreme Court clerk within 45 days after the following:

★

---

(1) the date the court of appeals rendered judgment, if no motion for rehearing or en banc reconsideration is timely filed; or

(2) the date of the court of appeals' last ruling on all timely filed motions for rehearing or en banc reconsideration.

(b) *Premature filing.* A petition filed before the last ruling on all timely filed motions for rehearing and en banc reconsideration is treated as having been filed on the date of, but after, the last ruling on any such motion. If a party files a petition for review while a motion for rehearing or en banc reconsideration is pending in the court of appeals, the party must include that information in its petition for review.

(c) *Petitions filed by other parties.* If a party files a petition for review within the time specified in 53.7(a)—or within the time specified by the Supreme Court in an order granting an extension of time to file a petition—any other party required to file a petition may do so within 45 days after the last timely motion for rehearing is overruled or within 30 days after any preceding petition is filed, whichever date is later.

(d) *Response.* Any response must be filed with the Supreme Court clerk within 30 days after the petition is filed.

(e) *Reply.* Any reply must be filed with the Supreme Court clerk within 15 days after the response is filed.

(f) *Extension of time.* The Supreme Court may extend the time to file a petition for review if a party files a motion complying with Rule 10.5(b) no later than 15 days after the last day for filing the petition. The Supreme Court may extend the time to file a response or reply if a party files a motion complying with Rule 10.5(b) either before or after the response or reply is due.

(g) *Petition filed in court of appeals.* If a petition is mistakenly filed in the court of appeals, the petition is deemed to have been filed the same day with the Supreme Court clerk, and the court of appeals clerk must immediately send the petition to the Supreme Court clerk.

53.8 Amendment. On motion showing good cause, the Court may allow the petition, response, or reply to be amended on such reasonable terms as the Court may prescribe.

53.9 Court May Require Revision. If a petition, response, or reply does not conform with these rules, the Supreme Court may require the document to be revised or may return the document to the party who filed it and consider the case without allowing the document to be revised.

2012 change: Amended eff. Dec. 1, 2012, by order of Nov. 13, 2012 (Tex. Sup.Ct. Order, Misc. Docket No. 12-9190): Deleted TRAP 53.6 to correspond to amendments to TRAP 9.4 consolidating length limits and establishing word limits for computer-generated documents.

TRAP 54. FILING THE RECORD

54.1 Request for Record. With or without granting the petition for review, the Supreme Court may request that the record from the court of appeals be filed with the clerk of the Supreme Court.

54.2 Duty of Court of Appeals Clerk.

(a) *Request for record.* The court of appeals clerk must not send the record to the Supreme Court unless it is requested. Upon receiving the Supreme Court clerk's request for the record, the court of appeals clerk must promptly send to the Supreme Court clerk all of the following:

(1) the original record;

(2) any motion filed in the court of appeals;

(3) copies of all orders of the court of appeals; and

(4) copies of all opinions and the judgment of the court of appeals.

(b) *Nondocumentary exhibits.* The clerk should not send any nondocumentary exhibits unless the Supreme Court specifically requests.

54.3 Expenses. The petitioner must pay to the court of appeals clerk a sum sufficient to pay the cost of mailing or shipping the record to and from the Supreme Court clerk.

54.4 Duty of Supreme Court Clerk. Upon receiving the record, the Supreme Court clerk must file it and enter the filing on the docket. The clerk may refuse the record if the charges for mailing or shipping have not been paid.

TRAP 55. BRIEFS ON THE MERITS

55.1 Request by Court. A brief on the merits must not be filed unless requested by the Court. With or without granting the petition for review, the Court may request the parties to file briefs on the merits. In appropriate cases, the Court may realign parties and direct that parties file consolidated briefs.

TRAP 55

55.2 Petitioner's Brief on the Merits. The petitioner's brief on the merits must be confined to the issues or points stated in the petition for review and must, under appropriate headings and in the order here indicated, contain the following items:

(a) *Identity of parties and counsel.* The brief must give a complete list of all parties to the trial court's final judgment, and the names and addresses of all trial and appellate counsel.

(b) *Table of contents.* The brief must have a table of contents with references to the pages of the brief. The table of contents must indicate the subject matter of each issue or point, or group of issues or points.

(c) *Index of authorities.* The brief must have an index of authorities arranged alphabetically and indicating the pages of the brief where the authorities are cited.

(d) *Statement of the case.* The brief must contain a statement of the case that should seldom exceed one page and should not discuss the facts. The statement must contain the following:

(1) a concise description of the nature of the case (e.g., whether it is a suit for damages, on a note, or in trespass to try title);

(2) the name of the judge who signed the order or judgment appealed from;

(3) the designation of the trial court and the county in which it is located;

(4) the disposition of the case by the trial court;

(5) the parties in the court of appeals;

(6) the district of the court of appeals;

(7) the names of the justices who participated in the decision in the court of appeals, the author of the opinion for the court, and the author of any separate opinion;

(8) the citation for the court of appeals' opinion, if available, or a statement that the opinion was unpublished; and

(9) the disposition of the case by the court of appeals.

(e) *Statement of jurisdiction.* The brief must state, without argument, the basis of the Court's jurisdiction.

(f) *Issues presented.* The brief must state concisely all issues or points presented for review. The statement of an issue or point will be treated as covering every subsidiary question that is fairly included. The phrasing of the issues or points need not be identical to the statement of issues or points in the petition for review, but the brief may not raise additional issues or points or change the substance of the issues or points presented in the petition.

(g) *Statement of facts.* The brief must affirm that the court of appeals correctly stated the nature of the case, except in any particulars pointed out. The brief must state concisely and without argument the facts and procedural background pertinent to the issues or points presented. The statement must be supported by record references.

(h) *Summary of the argument.* The brief must contain a succinct, clear, and accurate statement of the arguments made in the body of the brief. This summary must not merely repeat the issues or points presented for review.

(i) *Argument.* The brief must contain a clear and concise argument for the contentions made, with appropriate citations to authorities and to the record.

(j) *Prayer.* The brief must contain a short conclusion that clearly states the nature of the relief sought.

55.3 Respondent's Brief. If the petitioner files a brief on the merits, any other party to the appeal may file a brief in response, which must conform to 55.2, except that:

(a) the list of parties and counsel is not required unless necessary to supplement or correct the list contained in the petitioner's brief;

(b) a statement of the case and a statement of the facts need not be made unless the respondent is dissatisfied with that portion of the petitioner's brief; and

(c) a statement of the issues presented need not be made unless:

(1) the respondent is dissatisfied with the statement made in the petitioner's brief;

(2) the respondent is asserting independent grounds for affirmance of the court of appeals' judgment; or

(3) the respondent is asserting grounds that establish the respondent's right to a judgment that is less favorable to the respondent than the judgment rendered by the court of appeals but more favorable to the respondent than the judgment that might be awarded to the petitioner (e.g., a remand for a new trial rather than a rendition of judgment in favor of the petitioner);

───────────────────── ✦ ─────────────────────

(d) a statement of jurisdiction should be omitted unless the petition fails to assert valid grounds for jurisdiction; and

(e) the respondent's argument must be confined to the issues or points presented in the petitioner's brief or asserted by the respondent in the respondent's statement of issues.

55.4 **Petitioner's Brief in Reply.** The petitioner may file a reply brief addressing any matter in the brief in response. However, the Court may consider and decide the case before a reply brief is filed.

55.5 **Reliance on Prior Brief.** As a brief on the merits or a brief in response, a party may file the brief that the party filed in the court of appeals.

⑫ **55.6** **DELETED.**

55.7 **Time and Place of Filing; Extension of Time.** Briefs must be filed with the Supreme Court clerk in accordance with the schedule stated in the clerk's notice that the Court has requested briefs on the merits. If no schedule is stated in the notice, petitioner must file a brief on the merits within 30 days after the date of the notice, respondent must file a brief in response within 20 days after receiving petitioner's brief, and petitioner must file any reply brief within 15 days after receiving respondent's brief. On motion complying with Rule 10.5(b) either before or after the brief is due, the Supreme Court may extend the time to file a brief.

55.8 **Amendment.** On motion showing good cause, the Court may allow a party to amend a brief on such reasonable terms as the Court may prescribe.

55.9 **Court May Require Revision.** If a brief does not conform with these rules, the Supreme Court may require the brief to be revised or may return it to the party who filed it and consider the case without further briefing by that party.

2012 change: Amended eff. Dec. 1, 2012, by order of Nov. 13, 2012 (Tex. Sup.Ct. Order, Misc. Docket No. 12-9190): Deleted TRAP 55.6 to correspond to amendments to TRAP 9.4 consolidating length limits and establishing word limits for computer-generated documents.

TRAP 56. ORDERS ON PETITION FOR REVIEW

56.1 **Orders on Petition for Review.**

(a) *Considerations in granting review.* Whether to grant review is a matter of judicial discretion. Among the factors the Supreme Court considers in deciding whether to grant a petition for review are the following:

(1) whether the justices of the court of appeals disagree on an important point of law;

(2) whether there is a conflict between the courts of appeals on an important point of law;

(3) whether a case involves the construction or validity of a statute;

(4) whether a case involves constitutional issues;

(5) whether the court of appeals appears to have committed an error of law of such importance to the state's jurisprudence that it should be corrected; and

(6) whether the court of appeals has decided an important question of state law that should be, but has not been, resolved by the Supreme Court.

(b) *Petition denied or dismissed.* When the petition has been on file in the Supreme Court for 30 days, the Court may deny or dismiss the petition—whether or not a response has been filed—with one of the following notations:

(1) *"Denied."* If the Supreme Court is not satisfied that the opinion of the court of appeals has correctly declared the law in all respects, but determines that the petition presents no error that requires reversal or that is of such importance to the jurisprudence of the state as to require correction, the Court will deny the petition with the notation "Denied."

(2) *"Dismissed w.o.j."* If the Supreme Court lacks jurisdiction, the Court will dismiss the petition with the notation "Dismissed for Want of Jurisdiction."

(c) *Petition refused.* If the Supreme Court determines—after a response has been filed or requested— that the court of appeals' judgment is correct and that the legal principles announced in the opinion are likewise correct, the Court will refuse the petition with the notation "Refused." The court of appeals' opinion in the case has the same precedential value as an opinion of the Supreme Court.

(d) *Improvident grant.* If the Court has granted review but later decides that review should not have been granted, the Court may, without opinion, set aside the order granting review and dismiss the petition or deny or refuse review as though review had never been granted.

56.2 **Moot Cases.** If a case is moot, the Supreme Court may, after notice to the parties, grant the petition and, without hearing argument, dismiss the case or the appealable portion of it without addressing the merits of the appeal.

TRAP 56

---⭐---

56.3 Settled Cases. If a case is settled by agreement of the parties and the parties so move, the Supreme Court may grant the petition if it has not already been granted and, without hearing argument or considering the merits, render a judgment to effectuate the agreement. The Supreme Court's action may include setting aside the judgment of the court of appeals or the trial court without regard to the merits and remanding the case to the trial court for rendition of a judgment in accordance with the agreement. The Supreme Court may abate the case until the lower court's proceedings to effectuate the agreement are complete. A severable portion of the proceeding may be disposed of if it will not prejudice the remaining parties. In any event, the Supreme Court's order does not vacate the court of appeals' opinion unless the order specifically provides otherwise. An agreement or motion cannot be conditioned on vacating the court of appeals' opinion.

56.4 Notice to Parties. When the Supreme Court grants, denies, refuses, or dismisses a petition for review, the Supreme Court clerk must send a written notice of the disposition to the court of appeals, the trial court, and all parties to the appeal.

56.5 Return of Documents to Court of Appeals. When the Supreme Court denies, refuses, or dismisses a petition for review, the clerk will retain the petition, together with the record and accompanying papers, for 30 days after the order is rendered. If no motion for rehearing has been filed by the end of that period or when any motion for rehearing of the order has been overruled, the clerk must send a certified copy of its order to the court of appeals and return the record and all papers (except for documents filed in the Supreme Court) to the court of appeals clerk.

TRAP 57. DIRECT APPEALS TO THE SUPREME COURT

57.1 Application. This rule governs direct appeals to the Supreme Court that are authorized by the Constitution and by statute. Except when inconsistent with a statute or this rule, the rules governing appeals to courts of appeals also apply to direct appeals to the Supreme Court.

57.2 Jurisdiction. The Supreme Court may not take jurisdiction over a direct appeal from the decision of any court other than a district court or county court, or over any question of fact. The Supreme Court may decline to exercise jurisdiction over a direct appeal of an interlocutory order if the record is not adequately developed, or if its decision would be advisory, or if the case is not of such importance to the jurisprudence of the state that a direct appeal should be allowed.

57.3 Statement of Jurisdiction. Appellant must file with the record a statement fully but plainly setting out the basis asserted for exercise of the Supreme Court's jurisdiction. Appellee may file a response to appellant's statement of jurisdiction within ten days after the statement is filed.

57.4 Preliminary Ruling on Jurisdiction. If the Supreme Court notes probable jurisdiction over a direct appeal, the parties must file briefs under Rule 38 as in any other case. If the Supreme Court does not note probable jurisdiction over a direct appeal, the appeal will be dismissed.

57.5 Direct Appeal Exclusive While Pending. If a direct appeal to the Supreme Court is filed, the parties to the appeal must not, while that appeal is pending, pursue an appeal to the court of appeals. But if the direct appeal is dismissed, any party may pursue any other appeal available at the time when the direct appeal was filed. The other appeal must be perfected within ten days after dismissal of the direct appeal.

TRAP 58. CERTIFICATION OF QUESTIONS OF LAW BY UNITED STATES COURTS

58.1 Certification. The Supreme Court of Texas may answer questions of law certified to it by any federal appellate court if the certifying court is presented with determinative questions of Texas law having no controlling Supreme Court precedent. The Supreme Court may decline to answer the questions certified to it.

58.2 Contents of the Certification Order. An order from the certifying court must set forth:

(a) the questions of law to be answered; and

(b) a stipulated statement of all facts relevant to the questions certified, showing fully the nature of the controversy in which the questions arose.

58.3 Transmission of Certification Order. The clerk of the certifying court must send to the clerk of the Supreme Court of Texas the following:

(a) the certification order under the certifying court's official seal;

TRAP 56

★

(b) a list of the names of all parties to the pending case, giving the address and telephone number, if known, of any party not represented by counsel; and

(c) a list of the names, addresses, and telephone numbers of counsel for each party.

58.4 Transmission of Record. The certifying court should not send the Supreme Court of Texas the record in the pending case with the certification order. The Supreme Court may later require the original or copies of all or part of the record before the certifying court to be filed with the Supreme Court clerk.

58.5 Fees and Costs. Unless the certifying court orders otherwise in its certification order, the parties must bear equally the fees under Rule 5.

58.6 Notice. If the Supreme Court agrees to answer the questions certified to it, the Court will notify all parties and the certifying court. The Supreme Court clerk must also send a notice to the Attorney General of Texas if:

(a) the constitutionality of a Texas statute is the subject of a certified question that the Supreme Court has agreed to answer; and

(b) the State of Texas or an officer, agency, or employee of the state is not a party to the proceeding in the certifying court.

58.7 Briefs and Oral Argument.

(a) *Briefs.* The appealing party in the certifying court must file a brief with the Supreme Court clerk within 30 days after the date of the notice. Opposing parties must file an answering brief within 20 days after receiving the opening brief. Briefs must comply with Rule 55 to the extent its provisions apply. On motion complying with Rule 10.5(b), either before or after the brief is due, the Supreme Court may extend the time to file a brief.

(b) *Oral argument.* Oral argument may be granted either on a party's request or on the Court's own initiative. Argument is governed by Rule 59.

58.8 Intervention by the State. If the constitutionality of a Texas statute is the subject of a certified question that the Supreme Court has agreed to answer the State of Texas may intervene at any reasonable time for briefing and oral argument (if argument is allowed), on the question of constitutionality.

58.9 Opinion on Certified Questions. If the Supreme Court has agreed to answer a certified question, it will hand down an opinion as in any other case.

58.10 Answering Certified Questions. After all motions for rehearing have been overruled, the Supreme Court clerk must send to the certifying court the written opinion on the certified questions. The opinion must be under the Supreme Court's seal.

TRAP 59. SUBMISSION & ARGUMENT

59.1 Submission Without Argument. If at least six members of the Court so vote, a petition may be granted and an opinion handed down without oral argument.

59.2 Submission With Argument. If the Supreme Court decides that oral argument would aid the Court, the Court will set the case for argument. The clerk will notify all parties of the submission date.

59.3 Purpose of Argument. Oral argument should emphasize and clarify the written arguments in the briefs. Counsel should not merely read from a prepared text. Counsel should assume that all Justices have read the briefs before oral argument and should be prepared to respond to the Justices' questions.

59.4 Time for Argument. Each side is allowed only as much time as the Court orders. Counsel is not required to use all the allotted time. On motion filed before the day of argument, the Court may extend the time for argument. The Court may also align the parties for purposes of presenting argument.

59.5 Number of Counsel. Generally, only one counsel should argue for each side. Except on leave of court, no more than two counsel on each side may argue. Only one counsel may argue in rebuttal.

59.6 Argument by Amicus Curiae. With leave of court obtained before the argument and with a party's consent, an amicus may share allotted time with that party. Otherwise, counsel for amicus curiae may not argue.

TRAP 60. JUDGMENTS IN THE SUPREME COURT

60.1 Announcement of Judgments. The Court's judgments will be announced by the clerk.

60.2 Types of Judgment. The Supreme Court may:

TRAP 60

---- ★ ----

(a) affirm the lower court's judgment in whole or in part;

(b) modify the lower court's judgment and affirm it as modified;

(c) reverse the lower court's judgment in whole or in part and render the judgment that the lower court should have rendered;

(d) reverse the lower court's judgment and remand the case for further proceedings;

(e) vacate the judgments of the lower courts and dismiss the case; or

(f) vacate the lower court's judgment and remand the case for further proceedings in light of changes in the law.

60.3 **Remand in the Interest of Justice.** When reversing the court of appeals' judgment, the Supreme Court may, in the interest of justice, remand the case to the trial court even if a rendition of judgment is otherwise appropriate.

60.4 **Judgment for Costs.** The Supreme Court's judgment will award to the prevailing party the costs incurred by that party in the Supreme Court. If appropriate, the judgment may also award the prevailing party the costs—including preparation costs for the record—incurred by that party in the court of appeals and in the trial court. But the Court may tax costs otherwise as required by law or for good cause.

60.5 **Judgment Against Sureties.** When affirming, modifying, or rendering a judgment against the party who was the appellant in the court of appeals, the Supreme Court must render judgment against the sureties on that party's supersedeas bond, if any, for the performance of the judgment. If the Supreme Court taxes costs against the party who was the appellant in the court of appeals, the Court must render judgment for those costs against the sureties on that party's supersedeas bond, if any.

60.6 **Other Orders.** The Supreme Court may make any other appropriate order required by the law and the nature of the case.

TRAP 61. REVERSIBLE ERROR

61.1 **Standard for Reversible Error.** No judgment may be reversed on appeal on the ground that the

trial court made an error of law unless the Supreme Court concludes that the error complained of:

(a) probably caused the rendition of an improper judgment; or

(b) probably prevented the petitioner from properly presenting the case to the appellate courts.

61.2 **Error Affecting Only Part of the Case.** If the error affects a part, but not all, of the matter in controversy, and that part is separable without unfairness to the parties, the judgment must be reversed and a new trial ordered only as to the part affected by the error. The Court may not order a separate trial solely on unliquidated damages if liability is contested.

61.3 **Defects in Procedure.** The Supreme Court will not affirm or reverse a judgment or dismiss a petition for review for formal defects or irregularities in appellate procedure without allowing a reasonable time to correct or amend the defects or irregularities.

61.4 **Remediable Error of the Trial Court or Court of Appeals.**

(a) *Generally.* The Supreme Court will not affirm or reverse a judgment or dismiss a petition for review if:

(1) the trial court's or court of appeals' erroneous action or failure or refusal to act prevents the proper presentation of a case to the Supreme Court; and

(2) the trial court or court of appeals can correct its action or failure to act.

(b) *Supreme Court direction if error remediable.* If the circumstances described in (a) exist, the Supreme Court will direct the trial court or court of appeals to correct the error. The Supreme Court will then proceed as if the error had not occurred.

TRAP 62. DAMAGES FOR FRIVOLOUS APPEALS

If the Supreme Court determines that a direct appeal or a petition for review is frivolous, it may—on motion of any party or on its own initiative, after notice and a reasonable opportunity for response—award to each prevailing party just damages. In determining whether to award damages, the Court must not consider any matter that does not appear in the record, briefs, or other papers filed in the court of appeals or the Supreme Court.

TRAP 60

TRAP 63. OPINIONS; COPY OF OPINION & JUDGMENT TO INTERESTED PARTIES & OTHER COURTS

The Supreme Court will hand down a written opinion in all cases in which it renders a judgment. The clerk will send a copy of the opinion and judgment to the court of appeals clerk, the trial court clerk, the regional administrative judge, and all parties to the appeal.

TRAP 64. MOTION FOR REHEARING

64.1 Time for Filing. A motion for rehearing may be filed with the Supreme Court clerk within 15 days from the date when the Court renders judgment or makes an order disposing of a petition for review. In exceptional cases, if justice requires, the Court may shorten the time within which the motion may be filed or even deny the right to file it altogether.

64.2 Contents. The motion must specify the points relied on for the rehearing.

64.3 Response and Decision. No response to a motion for rehearing need be filed unless the Court so requests. A motion will not be granted unless a response has been filed or requested by the Court. But in exceptional cases, if justice so requires, the Court may deny the right to file a response and act on a motion any time after it is filed.

64.4 Second Motion. The Court will not consider a second motion for rehearing unless the Court modifies its judgment, vacates its judgment and renders a new judgment, or issues a different opinion.

64.5 Extensions of Time. The Court may extend the time to file a motion for rehearing in the Supreme Court, if a motion complying with Rule 10.5(b) is filed with the Court no later than 15 days after the last date for filing a motion for rehearing.

12 64.6 DELETED.

2012 change: Amended eff. Dec. 1, 2012, by order of Nov. 13, 2012 (Tex. Sup.Ct. Order, Misc. Docket No. 12-9190): Deleted TRAP 64.6 to correspond to amendments to TRAP 9.4 consolidating length limits and establishing word limits for computer-generated documents.

TRAP 65. ENFORCEMENT OF JUDGMENT AFTER MANDATE

65.1 Statement of Costs. The Supreme Court clerk will prepare, and send to the clerk to whom the mandate is directed, a statement of costs showing:

(a) the costs that were incurred in the Supreme Court, with a notation of those items that have been paid and those that are owing; and

(b) the party or parties against whom costs have been adjudged.

65.2 Enforcement of Judgment. If the Supreme Court renders judgment, the trial court need not make any further order. Upon receiving the Supreme Court's mandate, the trial court clerk must proceed to enforce the judgment of the Supreme Court's as in any other case. Appellate court costs must be included with the trial court costs in any process to enforce the judgment. If all or part of the costs are collected, the trial court clerk must immediately remit to the appellate court clerk any amount due to that clerk.

SECTION FIVE: PROCEEDINGS IN THE COURT OF CRIMINAL APPEALS

Section Five omitted by editor. For the full text, see O'Connor's Texas Civil Appeals (2012), p. 468.

TIMETABLES

TABLE OF CONTENTS

★

———————————————— ★ ————————————————

STEP	ACTION/FORM	RULE	DEADLINE	DUE	DONE
1	Plaintiff files suit; FORMS 2B-2D	TRCP 45-59, 78-82	Before limitations period expires		
2	Defendant is served; FORMS 2H	TRCP 99, 119	Before limitations period expires		
3	Deadline for defendant's answer	TRCP 99(b)	By 10:00 a.m. on the next Monday following 20 days after Step 2		
4	Defendant files special appearance; FORMS 3B:1, 2	TRCP 120a(1)	By Step 3 and before Step 5		
5	Defendant files answer—general denial; FORMS 3E	TRCP 85, 92	By Step 3, but after Step 4		
6	Plaintiff files response to special appearance; FORM 3B:3	TRCP 120a(3)	As soon as possible, at least 7 days before Step 10		
7	Plaintiff files sworn motion for continuance to secure affidavits or discovery; FORM 5D:1	TRCP 120a(3)	As necessary, but no later than Step 9		
8	File discovery and stipulations	TRCP 120a(3)	As necessary, but no later than Step 9		
9	File affidavits; FORM 1B:7	TRCP 120a(3)	At least 7 days before Step 10		
10	Hearing on special appearance, oral testimony permitted	TRCP 120a(2), (3)	Before Steps 13 and 14		
11	Order sustains special appearance; FORM 3B:4	TRCP 120a(4)	None, suit is dismissed		
12	Order overrules special appearance; FORM 3B:4	TRCP 120a(4)	None, suit continues		
13	Hearing on other pending motions (e.g., venue, TRCP 87)		After Step 12, but before Step 14		
14	Trial	TRCP 247, 262-265			

© 2013 McClure F.L.P.

Legend:

FORM	*O'Connor's Texas Civil Forms* (2012)
TRCP	Texas Rules of Civil Procedure

See **Commentaries**, "Special Appearance—Challenging Personal Jurisdiction," ch. 3-B, p. 189.

2. MOTION TO TRANSFER VENUE—WRONG OR INCONVENIENT COUNTY

--- ★ ---

STEP	ACTION/FORM	RULE	DEADLINE	DUE	DONE
1	Plaintiff files suit; FORMS 2B-2D	TRCP 45-59, 78-82	Before limitations period expires		
2	Defendant is served; FORMS 2H	TRCP 99, 119	Before limitations period expires		
3	Deadline for defendant's answer	TRCP 99(b)	By 10:00 a.m. on the next Monday following 20 days after Step 2		
4	Defendant files motion to transfer venue to another county; FORMS 3C:1-3	CPRC §15.063; TRCP 86(1)	By Step 3, but after filing special appearance and before or with Step 5		
5	Defendant files answer—general denial; FORMS 3E	TRCP 85, 92	By Step 3, but with or after Step 4		
6	Notice of hearing; FORM 1E:1	TRCP 87(1)	45 days before Step 10		
7	Plaintiff files response to motion to transfer; FORMS 3C:5-7	TRCP 87(1)	30 days before Step 10		
8	Plaintiff files affidavits with discovery attached; FORM 1B:7	TRCP 87(1), (3)(a), 88	30 days before Step 10		
9	Defendant files reply to plaintiff's response, with affidavits; FORMS 1B:7, 3C:9	TRCP 87(1)	7 days before Step 10		
10	Hearing on pending motions in due order: special appearance, then venue	TRCP 84, 87(1), 120a(2)	Promptly and a reasonable time before Step 13		
11	Order grants motion to transfer; FORM 3C:11	TRCP 89	None, suit transferred to other county		
12	Order denies motion to transfer; FORM 3C:11	TRCP 87(3)(c)	None, suit continues		
13	Trial	TRCP 247, 262-265			

© 2013 McClure F.L.P.

Legend:

CPRC	Texas Civil Practice & Remedies Code
FORM	*O'Connor's Texas Civil Forms* (2012)
TRCP	Texas Rules of Civil Procedure

See **Commentaries**, "Motion to Transfer—Challenging Venue," ch. 3-C, p. 203.

3. MOTION TO CHANGE VENUE—LOCAL PREJUDICE

— ★ —

STEP	ACTION/FORM	RULE	DEADLINE	DUE	DONE
1	Plaintiff files suit; FORMS 2B-2D	TRCP 45-59, 78-82	Before limitations period expires		
2	Defendant is served; FORMS 2H	TRCP 99, 119	Before limitations period expires		
3	Deadline for defendant's answer	TRCP 99(b)	By 10:00 a.m. on the next Monday following 20 days after Step 2		
4	Defendant files answer—general denial; FORMS 3E	TRCP 85, 92	By Step 3		
5	Movant (plaintiff/defendant) files motion to change venue because of local prejudice, with affidavits; FORMS 1B:7, 3C:4	TRCP 257	As soon as prejudice becomes known		
6	Nonmovant files response and controverting affidavit; FORMS 1B:7, 3C:8	TRCP 258			
7	Motion for continuance to secure discovery; FORM 5D:1	TRCP 251, 252	As necessary		
8	Hearing on motions in due order: special appearance, venue transfer, then venue change	TRCP 84, 87(1), 120a(2)	Promptly and a reasonable time before Step 9 or 10		
9	Order grants motion to change venue; FORM 3C:11	TRCP 257-259, 261	None, suit transferred to another county		
10	Order denies motion to change venue; FORM 3C:11	TRCP 258	None, suit continues		
11	Trial	TRCP 247, 262-265			

© 2013 McClure F.L.P.

Legend:
FORM   *O'Connor's Texas Civil Forms* (2012)
TRCP   Texas Rules of Civil Procedure

See **Commentaries**, "Local Prejudice," ch. 3-C, §3, p. 211.

★

STEP	ACTION/FORM	RULE	DEADLINE	DUE	DONE
1	Plaintiff files suit; FORMS 2B-2D	TRCP 45-59, 78-82	Before limitations period expires		
2	Defendant is served; FORMS 2H	TRCP 99, 119	Before limitations period expires		
3	Deadline for defendant's answer	TRCP 99(b)	By 10:00 a.m. on the next Monday following 20 days after Step 2		
4	Defendant files motion to dismiss on grounds of Code FNC; FORM 3D:1	CPRC §71.051(d)	Step 3 + 180 days		
5	Defendant files answer—general denial; FORMS 3E	TRCP 85, 92	By Step 3, but after filing special appearance or motion to transfer venue		
6	Plaintiff files response to motion to dismiss, with evidence to support pleadings; FORM 3D:3		A reasonable time before Step 9		
7	Motion for continuance, for good cause; FORMS 5D:1, 2	CPRC §71.051(g)	As necessary, but before Step 9		
8	Notice of hearing; FORM 1E:1	CPRC §71.051(d)	21 days before Step 9		
9	Hearing on pending motions in due order: special appearance, venue, then Code FNC	CPRC §71.051(d); TRCP 84, 87(1), 120a(2)	30 days before Step 12		
10	Order grants motion to dismiss or to stay; court has continuing jurisdiction if defendant violates court's order; FORM 3D:6	CPRC §71.051(c)	None, suit transferred to other forum		
11	Order denies motion to dismiss; FORM 3D:6	CPRC §71.051(e)	None, suit continues		
12	Trial	TRCP 247, 262-265			

© 2013 McClure F.L.P.

Legend:

CPRC	Texas Civil Practice & Remedies Code
FNC	Forum non conveniens
FORM	*O'Connor's Texas Civil Forms* (2012)
TRCP	Texas Rules of Civil Procedure

See *Commentaries*, "Code FNC Motion," ch. 3-D, §3, p. 216.

5. MOTION TO DISMISS—COMMON-LAW FORUM NON CONVENIENS

★

STEP	ACTION/FORM	RULE	DEADLINE	DUE	DONE
1	Plaintiff files suit; FORMS 2B-2D	TRCP 45-59, 78-82	Before limitations period expires		
2	Defendant is served; FORMS 2H	TRCP 99, 119	Before limitations period expires		
3	Deadline for defendant's answer	TRCP 99(b)	By 10:00 a.m. on the next Monday following 20 days after Step 2		
4	Defendant files answer—general denial; FORMS 3E	TRCP 85, 92	By Step 3		
5	Defendant files motion to dismiss on grounds of common-law FNC; FORM 3D:2		As soon as ground becomes apparent, but after filing special appearance or motion to transfer venue		
6	Defendant should file stipulation		At Step 5		
7	Plaintiff files response to motion to dismiss, with evidence to support pleadings; FORM 3D:4		Before Step 10		
8	Motion for continuance, for good cause; FORMS 5D:1, 2		Before Step 10		
9	Notice of hearing; FORM 1E:1	TRCP 21	At least 3 days before Step 10		
10	Hearing on pending motions in due order: special appearance, venue, then common-law FNC	TRCP 84, 87(1), 120a(2)	Before Step 13		
11	Order grants motion to dismiss or to stay; FORM 3D:6		None, suit transferred to other forum		
12	Order denies motion to dismiss or to stay; FORM 3D:6		None, suit continues		
13	Trial	TRCP 247, 262-265			

© 2013 McClure F.L.P.

Legend:

FNC	Forum non conveniens
FORM	*O'Connor's Texas Civil Forms* (2012)
TRCP	Texas Rules of Civil Procedure

See *Commentaries*, "Common-Law FNC Motion," ch. 3-D, §4, p. 221.

———————————————— ✪ ————————————————

STEP	ACTION/FORM	RULE	DEADLINE	DUE	DONE
1	Plaintiff files suit; FORMS 2B-2D	TRCP 45-59, 78-82	Before limitations period expires		
2	Defendant is served; FORMS 2H	TRCP 99, 119	Before limitations period expires		
3	Deadline for defendant's answer	TRCP 99(b)	By 10:00 a.m. on the next Monday following 20 days after Step 2		
4	Defendant files (as appropriate) special appearance, motion to transfer or change venue, and answer; FORMS 3B:1, 2, 3C:1-4, 3E	TRCP 85, 86, 92, 120a(1), 257	By Step 3		
5	Defendant files motion to abate; FORMS 3H:1, 2	TRCP 21, 85, 150-156, 158-160, 175	After Step 4, at least 3 days before Step 7, and while purpose of motion remains viable		
6	Plaintiff files response to motion to abate; FORM 3H:3		Before Step 7		
7	Hearing on pending motions in due order: special appearance, venue, then abate	TRCP 84, 87(1), 120a(2)	Before Step 12		
8	Order grants motion to abate		None, suit abated until obstacle to its prosecution is removed		
9	Order denies motion to abate		None, suit continues		
10	Plaintiff cures defect and files motion to revive suit		After Step 8, when obstacle to suit is removed		
11	Defendant files motion to dismiss suit; FORM 7G:1		After Step 8, if defect is not cured		
12	Trial	TRCP 247, 262-265			

© 2013 McClure F.L.P.

Legend:
FORM   *O'Connor's Texas Civil Forms* (2012)
TRCP   Texas Rules of Civil Procedure

See *Commentaries*, "Motion to Abate—Challenging the Suit," ch. 3-I, p. 257.

★

STEP	ACTION/FORM	RULE	DEADLINE	DUE	DONE
1	Plaintiff files suit; FORMS 2B-2D	TRCP 45-59, 78-82	Before limitations period expires		
2	Jury request by either party; FORM 5B:1	TRCP 216-220	At least 30 days before Step 31		
3	Hearing on TRO, if requested	TRCP 680	Immediately		
4	Court grants TRO; FORM 2C:3	TRCP 680			
5	TRO expires	TRCP 680	By its own terms or 14 days after Step 4		
6	Hearing on temporary injunction	TRCP 680, 681	As soon as possible; takes precedence		
7	Defendant is served; FORMS 2H	TRCP 99, 119	Before limitations period expires		
8	Return filed with court	TRCP 105, 107(g)	After Step 7		
9	Deadline for defendant's answer	TRCP 99(b)	By 10:00 a.m. on the next Monday following 20 days after Step 7		
10	Plaintiff files motion for no-answer default judgment; Timetable 10; FORM 7A:1	TRCP 107(h), 239	After Step 9 and at least 10 days after Step 8, but before defendant files answer		
11	Defendant files notice of removal to federal court; FEDFRM 4A:1	28 USC §1446(b)	30 days after Step 7 or receipt of a copy of the initial pleading ❶		
12	Plaintiff files motion to remand to state court; FEDFRM 4B:1	28 USC §1447(c)	Step 11 + 30 days		
13	Defendant files special appearance; Timetable 1; FORMS 3B:1, 2	TRCP 120a(1)	By Step 9 and before any other pleadings below		
14	Defendant files motion to transfer venue to another county; Timetable 2; FORMS 3C:1-3	TRCP 85, 86(1)	By Step 9, after Step 13, and before Steps 15-17		
15	Defendant files Code FNC motion to dismiss; Timetable 4; FORM 3D:1	CPRC §71.051(d)	Step 9 + 180 days		
16	Defendant files common-law FNC motion to dismiss; Timetable 5; FORM 3D:2		As soon as ground becomes apparent, but after Steps 13 and 14		
17	Defendant files motion to change venue because of local prejudice; Timetable 3; FORM 3C:4	TRCP 21, 257	As soon as prejudice becomes known, but at least 3 days before Step 26		

© 2013 McClure F.L.P.

❶ If a suit is removable at the time it is filed, the defendant must file the notice of removal within 30 days after receiving both the summons and a copy of the complaint. If a suit is not removable at the time it is initially filed, the suit must remain in state court unless a voluntary act by the plaintiff brings about a change that makes the suit removable. See *O'Connor's Federal Rules * Civil Trials* (2013), "Deadlines for Removal," ch. 4-A, §4, p. 242; Timetable, Removal & Remand, p. 1581.

⭐

STEP	ACTION/FORM	RULE	DEADLINE	DUE	DONE
18	Defendant files answer—general denial; FORMS 3E	TRCP 85, 92	By Step 9, but after Steps 13 and 14		
19	Plaintiff/Defendant files special exceptions; FORM 3G:1	TRCP 91	At or after Step 18, but must be ruled on before Step 31		
20	Plaintiff/Defendant files motion to abate; Timetable 6; FORMS 3H:1, 2	TRCP 21, 85	At or after Step 18 and at least 3 days before Step 26, but must be ruled on before Step 31		
21	Defendant files plea to the jurisdiction; FORM 3F:1	TRCP 85	As soon as ground becomes known		
22	Objection to assigned judge; FORM 5C:1	GOVT §74.053(c)	Before first hearing at which assigned judge is to preside or at least 7 days after receiving notice of assignment		
23	Motion to disqualify a judge; FORM 5C:3	Tex. Const. art. 5, §11; TRCP 18a(b)(2), 18b(a)	As soon as practicable after party learns of reason for disqualification		
24	Motion to recuse a judge; FORM 5C:5	TRCP 18a(b)(1), 18b(b)	At least 10 days before date set for hearing or trial ❷		
25	Plaintiff/Defendant serves MSJ; Timetable 11; FORMS 7C:1, 2	TRCP 166a(c), (i)	If traditional MSJ, after Step 7 and 21 days before SJ hearing If no-evidence MSJ, after adequate time for discovery and 21 days before SJ hearing		
26	Hearings on pending motions in due order: special appearance, venue, FNC, abate, etc.	CPRC §71.051(d); TRCP 84, 87(1), 120a(2)	30 days before Step 31		
27	Trial setting	TRCP 245	45 days before Step 31		
28	Motion in limine; FORM 5E:1		Before voir dire		
29	Plaintiff files nonsuit; FORM 7F:1	TRCP 162	Before plaintiff rests its case		
30	Offer of proof	TRE 103(b)	Before jury is charged		
31	Trial	TRCP 247, 262-265			

© 2013 McClure F.L.P.

❷ In limited circumstances, the party may file a motion to recuse after the tenth day before the date set for hearing or trial. See *Commentaries*, "Motion to recuse," ch. 5-C, §4.1.6(2), p. 331.

★

Legend:

CPRC	Texas Civil Practice & Remedies Code
FEDFRM	*O'Connor's Federal Civil Forms* (2012)
FNC	Forum non conveniens
FORM	*O'Connor's Texas Civil Forms* (2012)
GOVT	Texas Government Code
MSJ	Motion for summary judgment
SJ	Summary judgment
Tex. Const.	Texas Constitution
TRCP	Texas Rules of Civil Procedure
TRE	Texas Rules of Evidence
TRO	Temporary restraining order
USC	United States Code

Editor's note: In response to Gov't Code §22.004(g), the Supreme Court has proposed TRCP 91a to allow a party to file a motion to dismiss a cause of action that has no basis in law or fact. See Tex.Sup.Ct. Order, Misc. Docket No. 12-9191 (eff. Mar. 1, 2013). The motion to dismiss would have to be filed within 60 days after the first pleading that includes the baseless cause of action is served and would generally have to be ruled on within 45 days after the motion is filed. *See id.* The public-comment period for the proposed rule ends on February 1, 2013, and the rule is to take effect March 1, 2013. For the proposed version of the rule, see the appendix after this book's index. For the final version, go to the Supreme Court website at www.supreme.courts.state.tx.us. When the new rule takes effect, a supplement to this book—with updated rules and commentaries that reflect the changes—will be available at www.JonesMcClure.com/TRCPamendments.

─────────────────── ★ ───────────────────

STEP	ACTION/FORM	RULE	DEADLINE		DUE	DONE
1	Plaintiff files suit; FORMS 2B-2D	TRCP 45-59, 78-82	Before limitations period expires			
2	Discovery period begins	TRCP 190.2(c)(1)	At Step 1			
3	Defendant is served; FORMS 2H	TRCP 99, 119	Before limitations period expires			
4	Deadline for defendant's answer	TRCP 99(b)	By 10:00 a.m. on the next Monday following 20 days after Step 3			
5	Plaintiff serves discovery requests on defendant; FORMS 6E-6K	TRCP 194.1, 196.1(a), 196.7(a), 197.1, 198.1	No later than 30 days before Step 16	RFD		
				INT		
				RFP		
				RFA		
				RFE		
6	Defendant's deadline to respond or object to plaintiff's discovery requests; FORMS 6E-6K	TRCP 21a, 193.2(a), 194.3, 196.2(a), 196.7(c)(1), 197.2(a), 198.2(a)	If request is served before Step 4, Step 5 + 50-54 days, depending on type of service. If request is served after Step 4, Step 5 + 30-34 days, depending on type of service	RFD		
				INT		
				RFP		
				RFA		
				RFE		
7	Defendant serves discovery requests on plaintiff; FORMS 6E-6K	TRCP 194.1, 196.1(a), 196.7(a), 197.1, 198.1	No later than 30 days before Step 16	RFD		
				INT		
				RFP		
				RFA		
				RFE		
8	Plaintiff's deadline to respond or object to defendant's discovery requests; FORMS 6E-6K	TRCP 21a, 193.2(a), 194.3, 196.2(a), 196.7(c)(1), 197.2(a), 198.2(a)	Step 7 + 30-34 days, depending on type of service	RFD		
				INT		
				RFP		
				RFA		
				RFE		
9	Plaintiff designates its testifying experts	TRCP 194.2(f), 195.2	At Step 8, when plaintiff responds to RFD about experts, or 90 days before Step 16			
10	Plaintiff furnishes its retained testifying expert's report; FORM 6D:1	TRCP 194.2(f)(4), 195.5	At Step 9, or as ordered by the court			

© 2013 McClure F.L.P.

--- ⭐ ---

STEP	ACTION/FORM	RULE	DEADLINE	DUE	DONE
11	Plaintiff tenders its retained testifying expert for deposition	TRCP 195.3(a), 195.4	If plaintiff furnished expert report, reasonably promptly after Step 12 If plaintiff did not furnish expert report, reasonably promptly after Step 9		
12	Defendant designates its testifying experts	TRCP 194.2(f), 195.2	At Step 6, when defendant responds to RFD about experts, or 60 days before Step 16		
13	Defendant furnishes its retained testifying expert's report; FORM 6D:1	TRCP 194.2(f)(4), 195.5	At Step 12, or as ordered by the court		
14	Defendant tenders its retained testifying expert for deposition	TRCP 195.3(b), 195.4	Reasonably promptly after Step 12 and after plaintiff's experts testifying on the same subject have been deposed		
15	Deadline to supplement discovery responses; FORMS 6A:29, 30	TRCP 193.5(b)	Reasonably promptly after discovering need and no later than 30 days before Step 20		
16	Discovery period ends	TRCP ❶ 190.2(c)(1)	30 days before Step 20		
17	Deadline for MSJ; Timetable 11	TRCP 166a(c), (i)	If date not set by court: For traditional MSJ, after Step 4 but 21 days before Step 19 For no-evidence MSJ, after adequate time for discovery but 21 days before Step 19		
18	Pretrial conference	TRCP 166	Date set by court		
19	Hearing on MSJ	TRCP 166a(c)	At least 21 days after Step 17		
20	Trial	TRCP 247, 262-265	Date set by court		

© 2013 McClure F.L.P.

❶ In response to Gov't Code §22.004(h), the Supreme Court has proposed TRCP 169 to establish a process for the prompt, efficient, and cost-effective resolution of civil actions (expedited actions) in which only monetary relief is sought and the amount in controversy is no more than $100,000. *See* Tex.Sup.Ct. Order, Misc. Docket No. 12-9191 (eff. Mar. 1, 2013). The Supreme Court has proposed corresponding amendments to TRCP 190.2 that would (1) change the Level 1 discovery-control plan to apply to these expedited actions under TRCP 169 and (2) change the length of the discovery period in Level 1 cases. *See* Tex.Sup.Ct. Order, Misc. Docket No. 12-9191 (eff. Mar. 1, 2013). The public-comment period for the proposed amendments ends on February 1, 2013, and the rules are to take effect March 1, 2013. For the proposed version of the rules, see the appendix after this book's index. For the final version, go to the Supreme Court website at www.supreme.courts.state.tx.us. When the new and amended rules take effect, a supplement to this book—with updated rules and commentaries that reflect the changes—will be available at www.JonesMcClure.com/TRCPamendments.

⋆

Legend:

FORM	*O'Connor's Texas Civil Forms* (2012)
INT	Interrogatories
MSJ	Motion for summary judgment
RFA	Requests for admissions
RFD	Requests for disclosure
RFE	Request for entry on land
RFP	Requests for production of documents or things
TRCP	Texas Rules of Civil Procedure

See *Commentaries*, "Computing Response Deadlines," ch. 1-D, §6, p. 36; "Discovery," ch. 6, p. 419.

─────────── ✦ ───────────

STEP	ACTION/FORM	RULE	DEADLINE		DUE	DONE
1	Plaintiff files suit; FORMS 2B-2D	TRCP 45-59, 78-82	Before limitations period expires			
2	Discovery period begins	TRCP 190.3(b)(1)	At Step 1			
3	Defendant is served; FORMS 2H	TRCP 99, 119	Before statute of limitations expires			
4	Deadline for defendant's answer	TRCP 99(b)	By 10:00 a.m. on the next Monday following 20 days after Step 3			
5	Plaintiff serves discovery requests on defendant; FORMS 6E-6K	TRCP 190.3(b)(1)	No later than 30 days before Step 17	RFD		
				INT		
				RFP		
				RFA		
				RFE		
6	Defendant's deadline to respond or object to plaintiff's discovery requests; FORMS 6E-6K	TRCP 21a, 193.2(a), 194.3, 196.2(a), 196.7(c)(1), 197.2(a), 198.2(a)	If request is served before Step 4, Step 5 + 50-54 days, depending on type of service. If request is served after Step 4, Step 5 + 30-34 days, depending on type of service	RFD		
				INT		
				RFP		
				RFA		
				RFE		
7	Beginning of 9-month limitation for discovery in non-Family Code cases	TRCP 190.3(b)(1)(B)	Earlier of date of first oral deposition or due date for first response to written discovery			
8	Defendant serves discovery requests on plaintiff; FORMS 6E-6K	TRCP 190.3(b)(1)	No later than 30 days before Step 17	RFD		
				INT		
				RFP		
				RFA		
				RFE		
9	Plaintiff's deadline to respond or object to defendant's discovery requests; FORMS 6E-6K	TRCP 21a, 193.2(a), 194.3, 196.2(a), 196.7(c)(1), 197.2(a), 198.2(a)	Step 8 + 30-34 days, depending on type of service	RFD		
				INT		
				RFP		
				RFA		
				RFE		
10	Plaintiff designates its testifying experts	TRCP 194.2(f), 195.2	At Step 9, when plaintiff responds to RFD about experts, or 90 days before Step 17			

© 2013 McClure F.L.P.

9. Discovery Schedule for Level 2 (cont'd)

───────────────────── ★ ─────────────────────

STEP	ACTION/FORM	RULE	DEADLINE	DUE	DONE
11	Plaintiff furnishes its retained testifying expert's report; FORM 6D:1	TRCP 194.2(f)(4), 195.5	At Step 10, or as ordered by the court		
12	Plaintiff tenders its retained testifying expert for deposition	TRCP 195.3(a), 195.4	If plaintiff furnished expert report, reasonably promptly after Step 13 / If plaintiff did not furnish expert report, reasonably promptly after Step 10		
13	Defendant designates its testifying experts	TRCP 194.2(f), 195.2	At Step 6, when defendant responds to RFD about experts, or 60 days before Step 17		
14	Defendant furnishes its retained testifying expert's report; FORM 6D:1	TRCP 194.2(f)(4), 195.5	At Step 13, or as ordered by the court		
15	Defendant tenders its retained testifying expert for deposition	TRCP 195.3(b), 195.4	Reasonably promptly after Step 13 and after plaintiff's experts testifying on the same subject have been deposed		
16	Deadline to supplement discovery responses; FORMS 6A:29, 30	TRCP 193.5(b)	Reasonably promptly after discovering need and no later than 30 days before Step 21		
17	Discovery period ends	TRCP 190.3(b)(1)	Family Code cases: 30 days before Step 21 / Other cases: earlier of 30 days before Step 21, or Step 7 + 9 months		
18	Deadline for MSJ; Timetable 11	TRCP 166a(c), (i)	If date not set by court: For traditional MSJ, after Step 4 but 21 days before Step 20 / For no-evidence MSJ, after adequate time for discovery but 21 days before Step 20		
19	Pretrial conference	TRCP 166	Date set by court		
20	Hearing on MSJ	TRCP 166a(c)	At least 21 days after Step 18		
21	Trial	TRCP 247, 262-265	Date set by court		

───────────────── ★ ─────────────────

Legend:

FORM	*O'Connor's Texas Civil Forms* (2012)
INT	Interrogatories
MSJ	Motion for summary judgment
RFA	Requests for admissions
RFD	Requests for disclosure
RFE	Request for entry on land
RFP	Requests for production of documents or things
TRCP	Texas Rules of Civil Procedure

See *Commentaries*, "Computing Response Deadlines," ch. 1-D, §6, p. 36; "Discovery," ch. 6, p. 419.

★

STEP	ACTION/FORM	RULE	DEADLINE	DUE	DONE
1	Plaintiff files suit; FORMS 2B-2D	TRCP 45-59, 78-82	Before limitations period expires		
2	If suit is against the State, plaintiff must send copy of petition to Attorney General by certified mail	CPRC §30.004(b)	At Step 1		
3	Defendant is served; FORMS 2H	TRCP 99, 119	Before limitations period expires		
4	Return filed with the court	TRCP 105, 107(g)	After Step 3		
5	Deadline for defendant's answer	TRCP 99(b)	By 10:00 a.m. on the next Monday following 20 days after Step 3		
6	Plaintiff files motion for default judgment; FORM 7A:1	TRCP 107(h), 239	After Step 5 and at least 10 days after Step 4		
7	If suit is against the State, plaintiff must send notice of intent to take default to Attorney General	CPRC §39.001	No later than 10 days before entry of default judgment		
8	Plaintiff files certificate of last known address and/or military affidavit; FORMS 7A:2, 3	TRCP 239a; 50 USC app. §521(b)	By Step 10		
9	Hearing on motion for default judgment—unliquidated damages; FORM 7A:4	TRCP 243	At or before Step 10		
10	Default judgment signed; FORM 9C:2	TRCP 239a	At or after Step 9		
11	Clerk sends defendant notice of default judgment	TRCP 239a	After Step 10		

© 2013 McClure F.L.P.

Legend:

CPRC	Texas Civil Practice & Remedies Code
FORM	*O'Connor's Texas Civil Forms* (2012)
TRCP	Texas Rules of Civil Procedure
USC	United States Code

See *Commentaries*, "No-Answer Default," ch. 7-A, §3, p. 588.

━━━━━━━━━━━━━━━━━━━━━ ✦ ━━━━━━━━━━━━━━━━━━━━━

STEP	ACTION/FORM	RULE	DEADLINE	DUE	DONE
1	Plaintiff files suit; FORMS 2B-2D	TRCP 45-59, 78-82	Before limitations period expires		
2	Defendant is served; FORMS 2H	TRCP 99, 119	Before limitations period expires		
3	Deadline for defendant's answer	TRCP 99(b)	By 10:00 a.m. on the next Monday following 20 days after Step 2		
4	Defendant files answer; FORMS 3E	TRCP 83-98	At or before Step 3		
5	Movant (plaintiff/defendant) files MSJ; FORMS 7C:1, 2	TRCP 166a(a)-(c), (i)	At least 21 days before Step 15 and, if under TRCP 166a(i), after adequate time for discovery ❶		
6	Movant serves notice of date of SJ hearing	TRCP 166a(c)	At or after Step 5 and at least 21 days before Step 15 ❶		
7	If traditional SJ, movant files evidence to support MSJ	TRCP 166a(c), (d)	At Step 5 and at least 21 days before Step 15 ❶		
8	Nonmovant files response and objections to MSJ; FORMS 7C:3, 4, 11	TRCP 166a(c), (i)	7 days before Step 15		
9	Nonmovant files evidence to support response to MSJ	TRCP 166a(c), (d), (i)	7 days before Step 15		
10	Nonmovant files affidavit and motion for continuance; FORMS 7B:5, 6	TRCP 166a(g)	As soon as possible, but before Step 15		
11	Nonmovant files special exceptions to challenge vague or unclear MSJ; FORM 7B:1	TRCP 166a(c)	7 days before Step 15		
12	Nonmovant files amended pleading (petition or answer) adding new claims or defenses; FORMS 2B, 3E, 5F:1	TRCP 63	7 days before Step 15, unless leave of court obtained		
13	Movant files special exceptions to challenge vague or unclear response to MSJ; FORM 7B:1	TRCP 90, 91	3 days before Step 15 ❷		
14	Order on special exceptions signed; FORM 3G:2		At or before Step 15		
15	Hearing on MSJ	TRCP 166a(c), (i)	At least 21 days after Step 6 ❶		
16	SJ signed; FORM 7C:12	TRCP 166a	As soon as practical after Step 15		

© 2013 McClure F.L.P.

❶ Depending on the type of service, the movant may need to file and serve the motion and notice of hearing at least 24 days (rather than 21 days) before the hearing. *See* TRCP 21a. See *Commentaries*, "Filing & serving motion & notice," ch. 7-B, §6.1.1, p. 605.

❷ *See McConnell v. Southside ISD*, 858 S.W.2d 337, 343 n.7 (Tex.1993).

★

STEP	ACTION/FORM	RULE	DEADLINE	DUE	DONE
17	MNT filed; FORM 10B:6	TRCP 329b	Step 16 + 30 days		
18	MNT overruled; FORM 10B:8	TRCP 329b(c)	Step 16 + 75 days by operation of law, or earlier by written order		
19	Judgment becomes final and court loses plenary power	TRCP 329b(d), (e)	Step 16 or Step 18 + 30 days		

© 2013 McClure F.L.P.

Legend:

FORM	*O'Connor's Texas Civil Forms* (2012)
MNT	Motion for new trial
MSJ	Motion for summary judgment
SJ	Summary judgment
TRCP	Texas Rules of Civil Procedure

See *Commentaries*, "Motion for Summary Judgment—General Rules," ch. 7-B, p. 603; "MNT After Summary Judgment," ch. 10-B, §11, p. 801.

STEP	ACTION/FORM	RULE	DEADLINE	DUE	DONE
1	Plaintiff files suit; FORMS 2B-2D	TRCP 45-59, 78-82	Before limitations period expires		
2	Defendant is served; FORMS 2H	TRCP 99, 119	Before limitations period expires		
3	Deadline for defendant's answer	TRCP 99(b)	By 10:00 a.m. on the next Monday following 20 days after Step 2		
4	Defendant files answer; FORMS 3E	TRCP 83-98	At or before Step 3		
5	Defendant files TRCP 167 declaration with court; FORM 7H:1	TRCP 167.2(a)	45 days before Step 17		
6	Offeror (plaintiff/defendant) serves settlement offer on offeree; FORM 7H:2	TRCP 167.2(b)(6), (e)	At least 60 days after Step 4, after Step 5, and at least 14 days before Step 17		
7	Deadline for offeree to accept	TRCP 167.2(b)(5)	As stated in offer, but at least 14 days after Step 6		
8	Offeree serves objections to unreasonable conditions of offer; FORM 7H:3	TRCP 167.2(c)	By Step 7		
9	Offeror serves withdrawal of offer; FORM 7H:3	TRCP 167.3(a)	Before Step 10		
10	Offeree serves acceptance of offer; FORM 7H:3	TRCP 167.2(b)(5), 167.3(b)	Before Steps 7 and 9		
11	Offeree serves rejection of offer; FORM 7H:3	TRCP 167.3(c)	Before Steps 7 and 9		
12	Offeree serves counteroffer	TRCP 167.2(e)(3), (f)	Within 7 days after Step 6 or at least 14 days before Step 17, whichever is later		
13	Offeror joins third party or designates RTP	CPRC §33.004; TRCP 38, 40(a), 97(f)	As permitted by TRCP and CPRC ❶		
14	Offeree serves objections to offer based on joinder or designation	TRCP 167.3(d)	Within 15 days after Step 13		
15	Motion to modify deadlines for Steps 5 and 6	TRCP 167.5(a)	Before Step 16		
16	Order modifying deadlines for Steps 5 and 6	TRCP 167.5(a)	Before Step 18		

© 2013 McClure F.L.P.

❶ For the specific deadlines for joining a third party, see *Commentaries*, "Third-party petitions," ch. 3-E, §7.3, p. 235; "RTP," ch. 3-E, §7.4, p. 235.

★

STEP	ACTION/FORM	RULE	DEADLINE	DUE	DONE
17	Case set for trial on the merits	TRCP 167.2(a), 246			
18	Commencement of trial on the merits	TRCP 167.5(a), 247, 262-65			

© 2013 McClure F.L.P.

Legend:

CPRC	Texas Civil Practice & Remedies Code
FORM	*O'Connor's Texas Civil Forms* (2012)
RTP	Responsible third party
TRCP	Texas Rules of Civil Procedure

See *Commentaries*, "Offer of Settlement," ch. 7-H, p. 664.

─────────────── ★ ───────────────

STEP	ACTION/FORM	RULE	DEADLINE	DUE	DONE
1	Offer of proof	TRE 103(b)	Before Step 2		
2	Court reads charge to jury	TRCP 275	After close of evidence and before closing argument		
3	Jury returns verdict	TRCP 290-293			
4	Trial court signs judgment	TRCP 306a(1)	After Step 3		
5	Judgment becomes final and court loses plenary power	TRCP 329b(d), (e)	If no MNT, Step 4 + 30 days If MNT, Step 4 + 30 days after MNT is overruled by written order or by operation of law		
6	Movant (plaintiff/defendant) presents formal bill of exception to judge for signature; T-FORM 8E:1	TRAP 33.2(c)(1), (e)(1)	As soon as possible after Step 5, but no later than Step 16 + 30 days		
7	If parties agree to contents, judge signs and files bill with clerk	TRAP 33.2(c)(2), (e)(1)	Immediately after Step 6, but no later than Step 16 + 30 days		
8	If parties do not agree, judge notifies parties and holds hearing	TRAP 33.2(c)(2)	As soon as possible after Step 6		
9	If bill is approved, judge signs and files bill with clerk	TRAP 33.2(c)(2)(A), (e)(1)	Immediately after Step 8, but no later than Step 16 + 30 days		
10	If bill is disapproved, judge suggests changes	TRAP 33.2(c)(2)(B), (C)	Immediately after Step 8		
11	If movant agrees to judge's changes, bill is corrected and judge signs and files bill with clerk	TRAP 33.2(c)(2)(B), (e)(1)	Immediately after Step 10, but no later than Step 16 + 30 days		
12	If movant refuses to agree to changes, judge notes bill is refused and returns it to movant	TRAP 33.2(c)(2)(C)	Immediately after Step 10		
13	Judge prepares a bill of exception that accurately reflects court proceedings and files it with clerk	TRAP 33.2(c)(2)(C), (e)(1)	Immediately after Step 12, but no later than Step 16 + 30 days		
14	If movant disagrees with judge's bill, movant may file refused bill and affidavits of 3 bystanders with clerk; T-FORMS 8E:2, 3	TRAP 33.2(c)(3), (e)(1)	Immediately after Step 13, but no later than Step 16 + 30 days		
15	If nonmovant disagrees with movant's affidavits, nonmovant may file affidavits of bystanders with clerk; T-FORMS 8E:2, 3	TRAP 33.2(c)(3)	Step 14 + 10 days		

© 2013 McClure F.L.P.

13. OFFER OF PROOF & BILL OF EXCEPTION (CONT'D)

⭐

STEP	ACTION/FORM	RULE	DEADLINE	DUE	DONE
16	Movant (1) perfects appeal by filing notice of appeal in trial court and (2) files docketing statement in CA; A-FORM 5A:1	TRAP 25.1, 26.1, 32.1	If no MNT, Step 4 + 30 days If MNT, Step 4 + 90 days		
17	Movant files motion in CA for extension of time to file formal bill of exception	TRAP 10.5(b), 33.2(e)(3)	Last day for filing formal bill (Step 16 + 30 days) + 15 days		

© 2013 McClure F.L.P.

Legend:

CA	Court of appeals
FORMS	A-FORM – appeal form in *O'Connor's Texas Civil Appeals* (2012)
	T-FORM – trial form in *O'Connor's Texas Civil Forms* (2012)
MNT	Motion for new trial
TRAP	Texas Rules of Appellate Procedure
TRCP	Texas Rules of Civil Procedure
TRE	Texas Rules of Evidence

See *Commentaries*, "Offer of Proof & Bill of Exception," ch. 8-E, p. 717; *O'Connor's Texas Civil Appeals* (2012), "Notice of Appeal," ch. 5-A, p. 189.

14. REQUEST FOR FINDINGS OF FACT & CONCLUSIONS OF LAW

———————————— ✦ ————————————

STEP	ACTION/FORM	RULE	DEADLINE	DUE	DONE
1	Trial court signs judgment; T-FORMS 9C	TRCP 306a(1)			
2	Trial-court clerk sends notice that court signed judgment	TRCP 306a(3)	Immediately after Step 1		
3	Appellant files request for FoF	TRAP 26.1(a)(4); TRCP 296	Step 1 + 20 days		
4	Appellant files notice of past-due FoF	TRAP 26.1(a)(4); TRCP 297	Step 3 + 30 days		
5	Trial court files FoF	TRCP 297	Step 3 + 20 days, or Step 3 + 40 days, if Step 4		
6	Appellant files request for additional or amended FoF	TRCP 298	Step 5 + 10 days		
7	Trial court files additional or amended FoF	TRCP 298	Step 6 + 10 days		
8	Optional – appellant files MNT; T-FORMS 10B:1-6	TRCP 324, 329b(a)	Step 1 + 30 days		
9	MNT overruled	TRCP 329b(c)	Step 1 + 75 days by operation of law, or earlier by written order		
10	Appellant (1) perfects appeal by filing notice of appeal in trial court and (2) files docketing statement in CA; A-FORM 5A:1	TRAP 25.1, 26.1, 32.1	If no MNT or request for FoF, Step 1 + 30 days If MNT or request for FoF, Step 1 + 90 days		
11	Trial court loses plenary power over judgment	TRCP 329b(d), (e)	If no MNT, Step 1 + 30 days If MNT, Step 9 + 30 days		

For the deadlines for filing an appeal, see Timetable 17. From the timetable above, insert into Timetable 17 the dates that apply to the appeal: the date the trial court signed the judgment, the date the appeal was perfected, and the date the trial court lost plenary power.

© 2013 McClure F.L.P.

Legend:

CA	Court of appeals
FoF	Findings of fact and conclusions of law
FORMS	A-FORM – appeal form in *O'Connor's Texas Civil Appeals* (2012)
	T-FORM – trial form in *O'Connor's Texas Civil Forms* (2012)
MNT	Motion for new trial
TRAP	Texas Rules of Appellate Procedure
TRCP	Texas Rules of Civil Procedure

See *Commentaries*, "Request for Findings of Fact & Conclusions of Law," ch. 10-E, p. 817.

—————————————————————— ✦ ——————————————————————

STEP	ACTION/FORM	RULE	DEADLINE	DUE	DONE
1	Trial-court clerk sends notice of date case will be dismissed	TRCP 165a(1)			
2	Plaintiff files motion to retain on docket	TRCP 165a(1)	Before Step 4		
3	Date set for hearing on dismissal	TRCP 165a(1)	Set by trial court		
4	Trial court signs order dismissing case	TRCP 165a(1), 306a(1)			
5	Trial-court clerk sends notice of dismissal order	TRCP 165a(1), 306a(3)	Immediately after Step 4		
6	Plaintiff files VMR with affidavits; T-FORM 10F:1	TRCP 165a(3), 306a	Step 4 + 30 days		
7	Trial court sets date for hearing, with notice to parties	TRCP 165a(3)	As soon as possible and before Step 4 + 75 days		
8	Hearing on VMR	TRCP 165a(3)	When set by court		
9	VMR overruled	TRCP 165a(3), 306a	Step 4 + 75 days by operation of law, or earlier by written order		
10	Plaintiff (1) perfects appeal by filing notice of appeal in trial court and (2) files docketing statement in CA; A-FORM 5A:1	TRAP 25.1, 26.1, 32.1	If no VMR, Step 4 + 30 days. If VMR, Step 4 + 90 days		
11	Trial court loses plenary power over judgment	TRCP 165a(3), 329b(d), (e)	If no VMR, Step 4 + 30 days. If VMR, Step 9 + 30 days		

For the deadlines for filing an appeal, see Timetable 17. From the timetable above, insert into Timetable 17 the dates that apply to the appeal: the date of the order of dismissal, the date the appeal was perfected, and the date the trial court lost plenary power.

© 2013 McClure F.L.P.

Legend:
CA   Court of appeals
FORMS   A-FORM – appeal form in *O'Connor's Texas Civil Appeals* (2012)
            T-FORM – trial form in *O'Connor's Texas Civil Forms* (2012)
TRAP   Texas Rules of Appellate Procedure
TRCP   Texas Rules of Civil Procedure
VMR   Verified motion to reinstate the case

See **Commentaries**, "Motion to Reinstate After Dismissal for Want of Prosecution," ch. 10-F, p. 826.

⎯⎯⎯⎯⎯⎯⎯⎯⎯⎯ ★ ⎯⎯⎯⎯⎯⎯⎯⎯⎯⎯

STEP	ACTION/FORM	RULE	DEADLINE	DUE	DONE
1	Trial court signs judgment; T-FORMS 9C	TRCP 306a(1)			
2	Trial-court clerk sends notice that court signed judgment	TRCP 306a(3)	Immediately after Step 1		
3	Appellant receives late notice of judgment	TRAP 4.2; TRCP 306a(4)	Step 1 + 21 to 90 days		
4	Appellant (1) perfects appeal conditionally by filing notice of appeal in trial court and (2) files docketing statement in CA; A-FORM 5A:1	TRAP 25.1, 26.1, 32.1	As soon as possible, but no later than— Step 3 + 30 days if no MNT, or Step 3 + 90 days if MNT		
5	Appellant files MNT; T-FORMS 10B:1-6	TRCP 306a(4), 324, 329b(a)	Step 3 + 30 days		
6	MNT overruled	TRCP 306a(4), 329b(c)	Step 3 + 75 days by operation of law, or earlier by written order		
7	Appellant files MEPD with affidavits; T-FORMS 10G:1-3	TRCP 306a(4), (5), 329b(d)	Before Step 11		
8	Trial court conducts hearing on MEPD	TRCP 306a(4), (5)	As soon as possible, but before Step 11		
9	Court overrules MEPD; all appellate deadlines run from Step 1	TRCP 306a(1)	Enter date for judgment from Step 1		
10	Court grants MEPD and makes finding of date appellant received actual notice of judgment; all appellate deadlines run from Step 10	TRAP 4.2(c); TRCP 306a(5)	Enter new date for judgment (same as Step 3)		
11	Trial court loses plenary power over judgment	TRCP 306a(4), 329b(d), (e)	If no MNT, Step 3 + 30 days If MNT, Step 6 + 30 days		

For the deadlines for filing an appeal, see Timetable 17. From the timetable above, insert into Timetable 17 the dates that apply to the appeal: the new date for the judgment, the date the appeal was perfected, and the date the trial court lost plenary power.

© 2013 McClure F.L.P.

Legend:

CA	Court of appeals
FORMS	A-FORM – appeal form in *O'Connor's Texas Civil Appeals* (2012)
	T-FORM – trial form in *O'Connor's Texas Civil Forms* (2012)
MEPD	Motion to extend postjudgment deadlines
MNT	Motion for new trial
TRAP	Texas Rules of Appellate Procedure
TRCP	Texas Rules of Civil Procedure

See *Commentaries*, "Motion to Extend Postjudgment Deadlines," ch. 10-G, p. 831.

TIMETABLES

---- ★ ----

STEP	ACTION/FORM	RULE	DEADLINE	DUE	DONE
1	Trial court signs judgment; T-FORMS 9C	TRCP 306a(1)			
2	Appellant files MNT; T-FORMS 10B:1-6	TRCP 324, 329b(a)	Step 1 + 30 days		
3	MNT is overruled	TRCP 329b(c)	Step 1 + 75 days by operation of law, or earlier by written order		
4	Appellant (1) perfects appeal by filing notice of appeal in trial court and (2) files docketing statement in CA; A-FORM 5A:1	TRAP 25.1, 26.1, 32.1	If no MNT, Step 1 + 30 days If MNT, Step 1 + 90 days		
5	Optional – appellant files formal bill of exception; Timetable 13; T-FORM 8E:1	TRAP 33.2(e)(1)	Step 4 + 30 days		
6	Optional – appellant files motion to stay execution of judgment in trial court; A-FORMS 4B	TRAP 24.1, 24.2; TRCP 627	Before execution of judgment		
7	Appellant must arrange to pay trial-court clerk for clerk's record	TRAP 35.3(a)(2)	Before clerk's record is prepared		
8	Optional – appellant files request with trial-court clerk to include additional matters in clerk's record; A-FORM 6B:2	TRAP 34.5(b)	Before clerk's record is prepared		
9	Appellant must: (1) arrange to pay court reporter for reporter's record, (2) send written request to court reporter requesting record and list of exhibits, and (3) file copy of request in trial court; A-FORMS 6C	TRAP 34.6(b), 35.3(b)(3)	At or before Step 4		
10	Judgment becomes final and court loses plenary power	TRCP 329b(d), (e)	If no MNT, Step 1 + 30 days If MNT, Step 3 + 30 days		
11	Trial-court clerk files clerk's record in CA	TRAP 35.1, 35.3	If no MNT, Step 1 + 60 days If MNT, Step 1 + 120 days ❶		
12	Court reporter files reporter's record in CA				
13	CA clerk must notify parties of dates clerk's and reporter's records are filed	TRAP 37.2	At Steps 11 and 12		
14	Appellant files brief in CA; A-FORMS 7B	TRAP 38.1, 38.6(a), 39.7	30 days after later of Step 11 or 12; if accelerated appeal, 20 days after later of Step 11 or 12		

© 2013 McClure F.L.P.

❶ If a trial-court clerk or court reporter requests an extension of time to file the record, the appellate court may extend the deadline no more than 30 days in an ordinary or restricted appeal or 10 days in an accelerated appeal. TRAP 35.3(c).

★

STEP	ACTION/FORM	RULE	DEADLINE	DUE	DONE
15	Appellee files brief in CA; A-FORMS 7C	TRAP 38.2, 38.6(b), 39.7	Step 14 + 30 days; if accelerated appeal, Step 14 + 20 days		
16	Optional – appellant files reply brief in CA	TRAP 38.3, 38.6(c)	Step 15 + 20 days		
17	CA clerk sends notice regarding oral argument to parties	TRAP 39.8	21 days before Step 18		
18	Date for oral argument or written submission in CA	TRAP 39.8	As set by CA		
19	CA renders judgment and issues opinion	TRAP 43.1, 47.1	Promptly after Step 18		
20	Optional – movant (appellant/ appellee) files MReh in CA; A-FORMS 7H	TRAP 49.1, 49.5, 49.8	Step 19 + 15 days		
21	CA rules on MReh	TRAP 49.3			
22	CA may order en banc reconsideration with or without a motion	TRAP 49.7	Before Step 23		
23	CA loses plenary power over judgment	TRAP 19.1	If MReh or MET, Step 21 + 30 days If MEBR or MET, Step 22 + 30 days If no MReh, MEBR, or MET, Step 19 + 60 days		
24	For deadlines for filing a petition for review in the Texas Supreme Court, see *O'Connor's Texas Civil Appeals* (2012), Timetable, Petition for Review to Texas Supreme Court, p. 1143.				
25	Mandate issues	TRAP 18.1(a)	If no MReh or petition for review filed, 10 days after deadline to file motion to extend time to file MReh or petition for review		

© 2013 McClure F.L.P.

Legend:

CA   Court of appeals
FORMS   A-FORM – appeal form in *O'Connor's Texas Civil Appeals* (2012)
           T-FORM – trial form in *O'Connor's Texas Civil Forms* (2012)
MEBR   Motion for en banc reconsideration
MET   Motion to extend time
MNT   Motion for new trial
MReh   Motion for rehearing
TRAP   Texas Rules of Appellate Procedure
TRCP   Texas Rules of Civil Procedure

See *O'Connor's Texas Civil Appeals* (2012), "Perfecting Appeal," ch. 5, p. 187; "The Court of Appeals," ch. 7, p. 247; Timetable, Appeal of Jury Trial to Court of Appeals, p. 1110.

INDEX

ABANDONMENT
Claim or defense, TRCP 165

ABATE, MOTION TO
Generally, TRCP 150-165a; *257*
Affidavits, *257*
Answer, TRCP 85
Appeal, *263*
Burden of proof, *262*
Capacity, *258*
Corporations, dissolution, TRCP 160
Deadline, *257*
Death of party
    Generally, TRCP 150 et seq.
    After verdict, TRCP 156
    Continuance by surviving parties,
        TRCP 155
    Defendant, TRCP 152
    Executor or administrator, TRCP 153
    Plaintiff, TRCP 151
    Suit for injury resulting in death, TRCP 159
    Suit for use of another, TRCP 158
Determination, TRCP 175
Grounds
    Generally, *257, 258*
    Same dispute, administrative hearing, *260*
    Same dispute, another state's court, *261*
    Same dispute, another Texas court, *259*
    Same dispute, arbitration, *260*
    Same dispute, federal court, *261*
Hearing, TRCP 175; *262*
Mandamus, *263*
Misnomer, *258*
Order, trial court's, *262*
Pleadings defect, *258*
Pretrial conference, *316*
Response, *261*
Review, *263*
Scire facias, TRCP 151 et seq.
Stay, motion to, *see* Stay of Proceedings, Trial,
    this index
Types, *258*
Verification, *257*

ABSENCE
Attorneys, motion for continuance, TRCP 253,
    254
Court reporters, TRAP 13

ABSTRACT OF TITLE
See also Trespass to Try Title, this index
Generally, TRCP 791 et seq.

ABUSE OF DISCRETION
Generally, *45*
Amending pleadings, *17*
Evidence, motion to reopen, *730, 731*
Jury selection, *695*
Sanctions, *392*

ACCELERATED APPEALS
Generally, TRAP 28, 29
Agreed interlocutory appeals, TRAP 28.2
Deadlines, TRAP 28
Findings of fact, TRAP 28.1
Interlocutory orders, TRAP 28.1

ACCELERATED APPEALS (continued)
Motion for new trial, TRAP 28
Notice of appeal, TRAP 26.1(b)
Permissive interlocutory appeals, TRAP 28.3
Quo warranto, TRAP 28.1
Record, filing, TRAP 28.1
Rehearing, TRAP 49.4
Security, TRAP 29.2
Superseding the order, TRAP 29
Suspending execution, TRAP 29
Temporary orders, TRAP 29
Types, TRAP 28.1

ACCORD & SATISFACTION
Pleading, affirmative defense, TRCP 94

ACCOUNT
Audit before trial, TRCP 172
Filing with plea of payment, TRCP 95
Sworn account, suit on
    Generally, TRCP 185
    Denial, TRCP 93
Verification, TRCP 93

ACKNOWLEDGMENT
Stay of executions, justice court, TRCP 635

AD LITEM
Attorney, TRCP 244; *68, 800*
Comparison between guardian & attorney
    Generally, *67*
    Chart, *68*
Guardian, *see* Guardian Ad Litem, this index

ADDITIONAL RESOURCES
Generally, *359*
Applicability, *360*
Determination, *363*
Judicial Committee (JCAR), *359*
Motion, *360*
Necessary, determining when, *361*
Notice of action taken, *362*
Resources available, *360*
Review, *364*

ADJOURNMENT
Judge, death during term, TRCP 18
Justice court, enter on docket, TRCP 524(e)
New trial, motion for, TRCP 329a, 329b
Term, TRCP 19

ADMINISTRATIVE CODE
Judicial notice, TRE 204

ADMISSIBILITY, LIMITED
Generally, TRE 105; *715*

ADMISSIONS
Generally, TRCP 192, 198; *557*
Deemed
    Generally, *561*
    Answers, *561*
    Avoiding, *561*
    Good cause, *561*
    Hearing, *562*
    Motion to strike, *561*
Judicial admission, *see* this index
Pretrial conference, TRCP 166

ADMISSIONS (continued)
Requests
    Generally, *557*
    Compared to other discovery, *428*
    Serving, *557*
    Use, in summary judgment, *564*
    Use, in trial, *564*
Response to request
    Generally, *557*
    Amending, *560*
    Challenging, *560*
    Deadline, *558*
    Effect, *559*
    Form, *558*
    Objections, *559*
    Protective order, motion for, *560*
    Serving answers, *558*
    Unverified, *558*
Review, *564*
Special appearance, TRCP 120a
Trespass to try title, answers, TRCP 790
Use, *563*
Venue, motion to transfer, TRCP 88

ADOPTION
Hearsay exception for family history, TRE 804

ADOPTION BY REFERENCE
Pleadings, TRCP 58; *9*

ADR
See Alternative Dispute Resolution, this index

ADVERSE OR PECUNIARY INTEREST
Compromise & settlement, TRE 408
Statements against, TRE 803(24)
Witnesses, TRE 613

ADVERTISEMENTS
Executions
    Resale of property, TRCP 653
    Sale of real estate, TRCP 647
Sale of perishable property
    Attachment, TRCP 603
    Distress warrant, TRCP 617

AFFIDAVITS
Generally, *11*
Abate, motion to, *see* this index
Agents, *see* this index
Armed services, default judgment, *592*
Attorneys, *see* this index
Auditor's report, verification, TRCP 172
Bad-faith affidavits, TRCP 166a(h)
Citation by publication, unknown claimants of
    interest in land, TRCP 113
Continuance, *see* this index
Copy, *13*
Denying incorporation, TRCP 52
Discovery, resisting, *446*
Exhibits, attached, *13*
Forcible entry & detainer
    Generally, TRCP 749a
    Nonpayment-of-rent appeals, TRCP 749b
Form, *11*
Immediate action, appeal, TRAP 17

⎯⎯⎯⎯⎯⎯ ★ ⎯⎯⎯⎯⎯⎯

INDEX

★

INDEX

★

━━━━━━━━━━━━━━━━ ★ ━━━━━━━━━━━━━━━━

INDEX

INDEX

INDEX

★

INDEX

★

★

INDEX

——————⭐——————

★

INDEX

INDEX

─────────────────── ★ ───────────────────

INDEX

⎯⎯⎯⎯⎯⎯⎯⎯⎯⎯⎯⎯⎯⎯ ✪ ⎯⎯⎯⎯⎯⎯⎯⎯⎯⎯⎯⎯⎯⎯

INDEX

INDEX

⭐

INDEX

★

INDEX

⭐

INDEX

INDEX

※

⭐

INDEX

Page numbers in *boldface italic*

★

REMITTITUR
Generally, TRCP 315; TRAP 46; *811*
Appeal, *812*
Cross-point, appeal, TRAP 46
Deadline, *811*
Findings of fact, *818*
Judgment, TRCP 315
New trial, motion, *804*, *812*
Request, *811*
Response to request, *811*
Response to suggestion, *812*
Review, *812*
Suggestion by court of appeals, TRAP 46; *812*
Suggestion by trial court, TRCP 315; *811*
Supreme Court review, *813*
Voluntary, TRAP 46.5; *813*

REMOVAL FROM APPELLATE COURT
Books & papers, TRAP 12

RENDITION, APPEAL
Court of appeals, judgments, TRAP 43
Supreme Court, judgments, TRAP 65

REOPEN
See Evidence, this index

REPLEVIN
Attachment, report on disposition of property,
  TRCP 607
Executions, delivery bond, TRCP 644 et seq.
Garnishment
  Bond amount, TRCP 658a
  Defendant, TRCP 664
  Notice of rights, TRCP 663a
Justice-court judgment, TRCP 560
Sequestration
  Defendant, TRCP 701 et seq.
  Notice, writ, TRCP 699, 700a

REPLY BRIEFS, APPEAL
Habeas corpus, petitions, TRAP 52
Supreme Court, TRAP 55

REPLY POINTS OF ERROR, APPEAL
Court of appeals, TRAP 38.3
Supreme Court, TRAP 53

REPORTER'S RECORD
Generally, TRAP 34.6
Amending, TRAP 34.6
Contents, TRAP 34.6
Correcting, TRAP 34.6
Deadlines, TRAP 34.6, 35.3
Duty to file, TRAP 34.6, 35.3
Filing, TRAP 35.3
Free statement of facts, TRAP 20.1
Inaccuracies, TRAP 34.6
Partial statement of facts, TRAP 34.6
Receipt by court of appeals, TRAP 37
Reporter's fee, TRAP 34.6
Request for, TRAP 34.6
Supplementation, TRAP 34.6
Use of exhibits, TRAP 34.6

REPORTS
Court reporter, priorities, TRAP 13
Required by law, privilege, TRE 502; *482*

REPUTATION EVIDENCE
Boundaries, TRE 803(20)
Character, hearsay exception, TRE 803(21)
Family history, hearsay exception,
  TRE 803(19)
General history, TRE 803(20)
Personal history, hearsay exception,
  TRE 803(19)
Witness, TRE 608

REQUESTS
Admissions, *see* this index
Disclosures, *see* this index
Jury charge, *see* this index
Jury trial, *see* Jury, this index
Land, entry on, *see* this index
Production of documents & things,
  see this index
Res ipsa loquitur, *106*

RES JUDICATA
Generally, *781*
Claim preclusion, *781*
Elements, *782*
Pleading, TRCP 94

RESPONSE BRIEFS, APPEAL
Certified questions, federal, TRAP 58
Certified questions, state, TRAP 58
Court of appeals, rehearing, TRAP 49
Supreme Court, rehearing, TRAP 64

RESPONSIBLE THIRD PARTY
Generally, *235*
Designation, *236*
Identification, *235*
Joinder, *238*
Motion for leave to designate
  Deadline, *236*
  Grounds, *237*
Motion to strike designation, *238*
Objection to motion for leave, *237*

RESTRAINING ORDERS
See Injunctions, this index

RESTRICTED APPEALS
Allegations, *599*
Deadline, *599*
Default judgment, TRAP 30; *599*
Extension of time
  Generally, TRCP 5
  Exceptions, TRCP 307
  Quo warranto, TRCP 781
  Reversal for lack of service, TRCP 123
New trial, motion for, as prerequisite,
  TRCP 324

REVERSAL, APPEAL
Generally, TRAP 43, 44
Judgments & decrees, TRAP 51
Supreme Court, petition for review, TRAP 53,
  60, 61

REVIEW, BILL OF
See Bill of Review, this index

ROUTINE
Evidence of, TRE 406

RULE 11 AGREEMENTS
See Agreements, this index

RULING
Challenging, *51*
Deferred, *48*
Docket entry, *49*
Judgment, *see* this index
Letter, *50*
Oral, *47*
Record, *48*
Refusal to rule, *48*
Timing, *48*
Trial court, *see* this index
Types, *47*
Written, *49*

SALES
Foreclosure proceedings, TRCP 309
Garnished property, TRCP 672
Partition
  Personal property incapable of, TRCP 775
  Real property incapable of, TRCP 770
Perishable goods or property
  Attachment, TRCP 600 et seq.
  Distress warrant, TRCP 615 et seq.
Personal property, execution,
  TRCP 649 et seq.
Property pending execution, disposition of
  funds, TRCP 645

SANCTIONS
Generally, TRCP 13, 215; *377*
Appeal, TRAP 45, 62; *392*
Attorney fees, *391*, *392*
Burden of proof, *390*
Conduct justifying, *380*
Conduct not justifying, *383*
Contempt, *385*
Costs, *391*, *392*
Death penalty, *378*
Depositions
  Generally, *537*
  Failure to answer, *537*
  Failure to attend, *537*
Discovery
  Generally, TRCP 215; *380*
  Motion, *455*
  Waiver, *456*
Failure to serve documents, TRCP 21b; *39*
Findings of fact after, *459*, *818*
Frivolous appeals, TRAP 45
Groundless pleadings, *382*
Hearing, *389*
Improper, *387*
Interrogatories, failure to answer, *555*
Limine, violating motion in, *349*
Motion, *377*, *388*
Nonsuit, effect on pending, *656*
Notice, *390*

⭐

✦

INDEX

───────────── ★ ─────────────

INDEX

INDEX

★

INDEX

——————————— ★ ———————————

IN THE SUPREME COURT OF TEXAS
Misc. Docket No. 12-9191
ADOPTION OF RULES FOR DISMISSALS AND EXPEDITED ACTIONS

ORDERED that:

1. In accordance with the Act of May 25, 2011, 82nd Leg., R.S., ch. 203, §§1.01, 2.01 (HB 274), amending section 22.004 of the Texas Government Code, Rules 91a and 169 of the Texas Rules of Civil Procedure and Rule 902(c) of the Texas Rules of Evidence are adopted as follows, and Rules 47 and 190 of the Texas Rules of Civil Procedure are amended as follows, effective March 1, 2013.

2. The Clerk is directed to:

a. file a copy of this Order with the Secretary of State;

b. cause a copy of this Order to be mailed to each registered member of the State Bar of Texas by publication in the *Texas Bar Journal*;

c. send a copy of this Order to each elected member of the Legislature; and

d. submit a copy of the Order for publication in the *Texas Register*.

3. These amendments may be changed in response to comments received on or before February 1, 2013. Any interested party may submit written comments directed to Marisa Secco, Rules Attorney, at P.O. Box 12248, Austin, TX 78711, or marisa.secco@txcourts .gov.

Dated: November 13, 2012.

DISMISSAL RULE

New Rule 91a, Texas Rules of Civil Procedure:

91a. Dismissal of Baseless Causes of Action

91a.1 Motion and Grounds. Except in a case brought under the Family Code or a case governed by Chapter 14 of the Texas Civil Practice and Remedies Code, a party may move to dismiss a cause of action on the grounds that it has no basis in law or fact. A cause of action has no basis in law if the allegations, taken as true, together with inferences reasonably drawn from them, do not entitle the claimant to the relief sought. A cause of action has no basis in fact if no reasonable person could believe the facts pleaded.

91a.2 Contents of Motion. A motion to dismiss must state that it is made pursuant to this rule, must identify each cause of action to which it is addressed, and must state specifically the reasons the cause of action has no basis in law, no basis in fact, or both.

91a.3 Time for Motion and Ruling. A motion to dismiss must be:

(a) filed within 60 days after the first pleading containing the challenged cause of action is served on the movant;

(b) filed at least 21 days before the motion is heard; and

(c) granted or denied within 45 days after the motion is filed.

91a.4 Time for Response. Any response to the motion must be filed no later than 7 days before the date of the hearing.

91a.5 Effect of Nonsuit or Amendment; Withdrawal of Motion.

(a) The court may not rule on a motion to dismiss if, at least 7 days before the date of the hearing, the respondent files a nonsuit of the challenged cause of action, or the movant files a withdrawal of the motion.

(b) If the respondent amends the challenged cause of action at least 7 days before the date of the hearing, the movant may, before the date of the hearing, file a withdrawal of the motion or an amended motion directed to the amended cause of action.

(c) Except by agreement of the parties, the court must rule on a motion unless it has been withdrawn or the cause of action has been nonsuited in accordance with (a) or (b). In ruling on the motion, the court must not consider a nonsuit or amendment not filed as permitted by paragraphs (a) or (b).

(d) An amended motion filed in accordance with (b) restarts the time periods in this rule.

91a.6 Hearing; No Evidence Considered. Each party is entitled to at least 14 days notice of the hearing on the motion to dismiss. The court may, but is not required to, conduct an oral hearing on the motion. The court may not consider evidence in ruling on the motion and must decide the motion based solely on the pleading of the cause of action, together with any pleading exhibits permitted by Rule 59.

91a.7 Award of Costs and Attorney Fees Required. Except in an action by or against a governmental entity or a public official acting in his or her official capacity or under color of law, the court must award the prevailing party on the motion all costs and reasonable and necessary attorney fees incurred with respect to

---

⭐

---

the challenged cause of action in the trial court. The court must consider evidence regarding costs and fees in determining the award.

91a.8 Effect on Venue and Personal Jurisdiction. This rule is not an exception to the pleading requirements of Rules 86 and 120a, but a party does not, by filing a motion to dismiss pursuant to this rule or obtaining a ruling on it, waive a special appearance or a motion to transfer venue. By filing a motion to dismiss, a party submits to the court's jurisdiction in proceedings on the motion and is bound by the court's ruling, including an award of attorney fees and costs against the party.

91a.9 Dismissal Procedure Cumulative. This rule is in addition to, and does not supersede or affect, other procedures that authorize dismissal.

Comment to 2013 change: Rule 91a is a new rule implementing section 22.004(g) of the Texas Government Code, which was added in 2011 and calls for rules to provide for the dismissal of causes of action that have no basis in law or fact on motion and without evidence. A motion to dismiss filed under this rule must be ruled on by the court within 45 days unless the motion, pleading, or cause of action is withdrawn, amended, or nonsuited as specified in 91a.5. If an amended motion is filed in response to an amended cause of action in accordance with 91a.5(b), the court must rule on the motion within 45 days of the filing of the amended motion and the respondent must be given an opportunity to respond to the amended motion. The term "hearing" in the rule includes both submission and an oral hearing. Attorney fees awarded under 91a.7 are limited to those associated with challenged cause of action, including fees for preparing or responding to the motion to dismiss.

RULES FOR EXPEDITED ACTIONS

Amendments to Rule 47, Texas Rules of Civil Procedure:

Rule 47. Claims for Relief

An original pleading which sets forth a claim for relief, whether an original petition, counterclaim, cross-claim, or third party claim, shall contain:

(a) a short statement of the cause of action sufficient to give fair notice of the claim involved[,];

(b) [in all claims for unliquidated damages only the] a statement that the damages sought are within the jurisdictional limits of the court[,];

(c) a statement that the party seeks:

(1) only monetary relief of $100,000 or less, including damages of any kind, penalties, costs, expenses, pre-judgment interest, and attorney fees; or

(2) monetary relief of $100,000 or less and non-monetary relief; or

(3) monetary relief over $100,000 but not more than $500,000; or

(4) monetary relief over $500,000 but not more than $1,000,000; or

(5) monetary relief over $1,000,000; and

([e]d) a demand for judgment for all the other relief to which the party deems himself entitled.

Relief in the alternative or of several different types may be demanded; provided, further, that upon special exception the court shall require the pleader to amend so as to specify the maximum amount claimed. A party that fails to comply with (c) may not conduct discovery until the party's pleading is amended to comply.

Comment to 2013 change: Rule 47 is amended to require a more specific statement of the relief sought by a party. The amendment requires parties to plead into or out of the expedited actions process governed by Rule 169, added to implement section 22.004(h) of the Texas Government Code. A pleading other than a counterclaim that contains the statement in paragraph (c)(1) is governed by the expedited actions process. The further specificity in paragraphs (c)(2)-(5) is to provide information regarding the nature of cases filed and does not affect a party's substantive rights.

New Rule 169, Texas Rules of Civil Procedure:

Rule 169. Expedited Actions

(a) *Application.*

(1) The expedited actions process in this rule applies to a suit in which all claimants, other than counter-claimants, affirmatively plead that they seek only monetary relief aggregating $100,000 or less, including damages of any kind, penalties, costs, expenses, pre-judgment interest, and attorney fees.

(2) The expedited actions process does not apply to a suit in which a party has filed a claim governed by the Family Code, the Property Code, the Tax Code, or Chapter 74 of the Civil Practice & Remedies Code.

(b) *Recovery.* In no event may a party who prosecutes a suit under this rule recover a judgment in excess of $100,000, excluding post-judgment interest.

(c) *Removal from Process.*

(1) A court must remove a suit from the expedited actions process:

(A) on motion and a showing of good cause by any party; or

(B) if any claimant, other than a counter-claimant, files a pleading or an amended or supplemental pleading that seeks any relief other than the monetary relief allowed by (a)(1).

(2) A pleading, amended pleading, or supplemental pleading that removes a suit from the expedited actions process may not be filed without leave of court unless it is filed before the earlier of 30 days after the discovery

When the final version of these amendments takes effect, a supplement to this book will be available at www.JonesMcClure.com/TRCPamendments.

O'CONNOR'S TEXAS RULES A-2

━━━━━━━━━━━━━━━━━━━━━━━━ ★ ━━━━━━━━━━━━━━━━━━━━━━━━

period is closed or 30 days before the date set for trial. Leave to amend may be granted only if good cause for filing the pleading outweighs any prejudice to an opposing party.

(3) If a suit is removed from the expedited actions process, then the court must continue the trial date and reopen discovery under Rule 190.2(c).

(d) *Expedited Actions Process.*

(1) Discovery. Discovery is governed by Rule 190.2.

(2) Trial Setting. On any party's request, the court must set the case for a trial date that is within 90 days after the discovery period in Rule 190.2(b)(1) ends.

(3) Time Limits for Trial. Each side is allowed five hours to complete jury selection, opening statements, presentation of evidence, examination and cross-examination of witnesses, and closing arguments.

(A) The term "side" has the same definition set out in Rule 233.

(B) Time spent on objections, bench conferences, and challenges for cause to a juror under Rule 228 are not included in the time limit.

(4) Alternative Dispute Resolution. Unless the parties have agreed to engage in alternative dispute resolution or are required to do so by contract, the court must not—by order or local rule—require the parties to engage in alternative dispute resolution.

(5) Expert Testimony. Unless requested by the party sponsoring the expert, a party may only challenge the admissibility of expert testimony as an objection to summary judgment evidence under Rule 166a or during the trial on the merits. This paragraph does not apply to a motion to strike for late designation.

Comments to 2013 change:

1. Rule 169 is a new rule implementing section 22.004(h) of the Texas Government Code, which was added in 2011 and calls for rules to promote the prompt, efficient, and cost-effective resolution of civil actions when the amount in controversy does not exceed $100,000.

2. The expedited actions process created by Rule 169 is mandatory; any suit that falls within the definition of 169(a)(1) is subject to the provisions of the rule. If multiple claimants each seek the monetary relief allowed under 169(a)(1) against the same defendant, the defendant may move to remove the case from the rule pursuant to 169(c)(1)(a).

3. Rule 169(b) specifies that a party who prosecutes a suit under this rule cannot recover a judgment in excess of $100,000. Thus, the rule in *Greenhalgh v. Service Lloyds Ins. Co.*, 787 S.W.2d 938 (Tex. 1990), does not apply.

4. The discovery limitations for expedited actions are set out in Rule 190.2, which is also amended to implement section 22.004(h) of the Texas Government Code.

Amendments to Rule 190, Texas Rules of Civil Procedure:

Rule 190. Discovery Limitations

…

190.2. Discovery Control Plan—[Suits Involving $50,000 or Less] **Expedited Actions and Divorces Involving $50,000 or Less** (Level 1)

(a) *Application.* This subdivision applies to:

(1) [any suit in which all plaintiffs affirmatively plead that they seek only monetary relief aggregating $50,000 or less, excluding costs, pre-judgment interest and attorneys' fees] any suit that is governed by the expedited actions process in Rule 169, and

(2) any suit for divorce not involving children in which a party pleads that the value of the marital estate is more than zero but not more than $50,000.

[(b)] [Exceptions. This subdivision does not apply if:]

[(1)] [the parties agree that Rule 190.3 should apply;]

[(2)] [the court orders a discovery control plan under Rule 190.4; or]

[(3)] [any party files a pleading or an amended or supplemental pleading that seeks relief other than that to which this subdivision applies.]

[A pleading, amended pleading (including trial amendment), or supplemental pleading that renders this subdivision no longer applicable may not be filed without leave of court less than 45 days before the date set for trial. Leave may be granted only if good cause for filing the pleading outweighs any prejudice to an opposing party.]

([e]b) *Limitations.* Discovery is subject to the limitations provided elsewhere in these rules and to the following additional limitations:

(1) Discovery Period. All discovery must be conducted during the discovery period, which begins when the suit is filed and continues until [30 days before the date set for trial] 180 days after the date the first request for discovery of any kind is served on a party.

(2) Total Time for Oral Depositions. Each party may have no more than six hours in total to examine and cross-examine all witnesses in oral depositions. The parties may agree to expand this limit up to ten hours in total, but not more except by court order. The court may modify the deposition hours so that no party is given unfair advantage.

★

---

(3) Interrogatories. Any party may serve on any other party no more than [25] 15 written interrogatories, excluding interrogatories asking a party only to identify or authenticate specific documents. Each discrete subpart of an interrogatory is considered a separate interrogatory.

(4) Requests for Production. Any party may serve on any other party no more than 15 written requests for production. Each discrete subpart of a request for production is considered a separate request for production.

(5) Requests for Admissions. Any party may serve on any other party no more than 15 written requests for admissions. Each discrete subpart of a request for admission is considered a separate request for admission.

(6) Requests for Disclosure. In addition to the content subject to disclosure under Rule 194.2, a party may request disclosure of all documents, electronic information, and tangible items that the disclosing party has in its possession, custody, or control and may use to support its claims or defenses. A request for disclosure made pursuant to this paragraph is not considered a request for production.

([d]c) Reopening Discovery. [When the filing of a pleading or an amended or supplemental pleading renders this subdivision no longer applicable,] If a suit is removed from the expedited actions process in Rule 169 or, in a divorce, the filing of a pleading renders this subdivision no longer applicable, the discovery period reopens, and discovery must be completed within the limitations provided in Rules 190.3 or 190.4, whichever is applicable. Any person previously deposed may be redeposed. On motion of any party, the court should continue the trial date if necessary to permit completion of discovery.

...

190.5. Modification of Discovery Control Plan

The court may modify a discovery control plan at any time and must do so when the interest of justice requires. Unless a suit is governed by the expedited actions process in Rule 169, t[T]he court must allow additional discovery:

(a) related to new, amended or supplemental pleadings, or new information disclosed in a discovery response or in an amended or supplemental response, if:

(1) the pleadings or responses were made after the deadline for completion of discovery or so nearly before that deadline that an adverse party does not have an adequate opportunity to conduct discovery related to the new matters, and

(2) the adverse party would be unfairly prejudiced without such additional discovery;

(b) regarding matters that have changed materially after the discovery cutoff if trial is set or postponed so that the trial date is more than three months after the discovery period ends.

Comment to 2013 change: Rule 190 is amended to implement section 22.004(h) of the Texas Government Code, which calls for rules to promote the prompt, efficient, and cost-effective resolution of civil actions when the amount in controversy does not exceed $100,000. Rule 190.2 now applies to expedited actions, as defined by Rule 169. Rule 190.2 continues to apply to divorces not involving children in which the value of the marital estate is not more than $50,000, which are otherwise exempt from the expedited actions process. Amended Rule 190.2(b) ends the discovery period 180 days after the date the first discovery request is served; imposes a fifteen limit maximum on interrogatories, requests for production, and requests for admission; and allows for additional disclosures. Although expedited actions are not subject to mandatory additional discovery under amended Rule 190.5, the court may still allow additional discovery if the conditions of Rule 190.5(a) are met.

New Rule 902(c), Texas Rules of Evidence:

Rule 902. Self-Authentication

...

(c) *Medical expenses affidavit.* A party may make prima facie proof of medical expenses by affidavit that substantially complies with the following form:

Affidavit of Records Custodian of

_____

STATE OF TEXAS   §

                            §

COUNTY OF _____   §

Before me, the undersigned authority, personally appeared _____, who, being by me duly sworn, deposed as follows:

My name is _____. I am of sound mind and capable of making this affidavit, and personally acquainted with the facts herein stated.

I am a custodian of records for _____. Attached to this affidavit are records that provide an itemized statement of the service and the charge for the service that _____ provided to _____ on ___. The attached records are a part of this affidavit.

The attached records are kept by _____ in the regular course of business, and it was the regular

When the final version of these amendments takes effect, a supplement to this book will be available at www.JonesMcClure.com/TRCPamendments.

O'CONNOR'S TEXAS RULES   A-4

course of business of _____ for an employee or representative of _____, with knowledge of the service provided, to make the record or to transmit information to be included in the record. The records were made in the regular course of business at or near the time or reasonably soon after the time the service was provided. The records are the original or a duplicate of the original.

The services provided were necessary and the amount charged for the services was reasonable at the time and place that the services were provided.

The total amount paid for the services was $____ and the amount currently unpaid but which _____ has a right to be paid after any adjustments or credits is $____.

_____

Affiant

SWORN TO AND SUBSCRIBED before me on the ___ day of ____, ____.

_____

Notary Public, State of Texas

Notary's printed name: My commission expires:

_____   _____

    Comment to 2013 Change: Rule 902(c) is added to provide a form affidavit for proof of medical expenses. The affidavit is intended to comport with Section 41.0105 of the Civil Practice and Remedies Code, which allows evidence of only those medical expenses that have been paid or will be paid, after any required credits or adjustments. *See Haygood v. Escabedo*, 356 S.W.3d 390 (Tex. 2011).